THE STATESMAN'S YEAR-BOOK

1990–91

Man hat behauptet, die Welt werde durch Zahlen regiert: das aber weiss ich, dass die Zahlen uns belehren, ob sie gut oder schlecht regiert werde. GOETHE

Editors

Frederick Martin	1864–1883
Sir John Scott-Keltie	1883–1926
Mortimer Epstein	1911/27–1946
S. H. Steinberg	1946–1969
John Paxton	1963/69–1990

THE STATESMAN'S YEAR-BOOK

STATISTICAL AND HISTORICAL ANNUAL
OF THE STATES OF THE WORLD
FOR THE YEAR

1990–1991

EDITED BY

JOHN PAXTON

Published annually since 1864
127th edition first published 1990 by
THE MACMILLAN PRESS LTD
London and Basingstoke

Associated companies in Auckland, Delhi, Dublin, Gaborone, Hamburg, Harare, Hong Kong, Johannesburg, Kuala Lumpur, Lagos, Manzini, Melbourne, Mexico City, Nairobi, New York, Singapore, Tokyo.

British Library Cataloguing in Publication Data
Statesman's year-book.—1990-1991–
1. Social conditions—Serials
909.82'8'05 HN1

ISSN 0081–4601
ISBN 0–333–39154–3

Typeset in Great Britain by
A. J. LATHAM LIMITED
Dunstable, Bedfordshire

Printed in Great Britain by
Richard Clay (The Chaucer Press) Ltd, Bungay, Suffolk

FOREWORD

In its 127-year history John Paxton has acted as editor of THE STATESMAN'S YEAR-BOOK for the last 21 years. He is its fifth editor and has been responsible for taking what was a monument to Britain's imperial history into the modern age, this last year with the changes in Eastern Europe being its most dramatic. Although the basic rubrics for the compilation of the Year-Book were set out by the first editor in 1864, the publication has adapted to changing needs over the years and during John Paxton's editorship the main layout has been rethought to give quicker accessibility to facts and a three-part index introduced. With the change-over from hot metal to computer typesetting the opportunity was taken to change from its slightly imperialistic feel to a straight alphabetical listing of the countries of the world. The need for more details about cities and regions and for recent constitutional and political history led to the compilation by John Paxton of THE STATESMAN'S YEAR-BOOK WORLD GAZETTEER and THE STATESMAN'S YEAR-BOOK HISTORICAL COMPANION, both publications acting as supplements to the 1700-page main volume.

Many would be surprised to learn that each of the 21 editions edited by John Paxton have been compiled by him with only 3 or 4 assistants. It is a tribute not only to his wide knowledge but to his great stamina and tenacity of purpose that THE STATESMAN'S YEAR-BOOK remains to this day an example of the highest standard of reference book editing.

My late grandfather, Harold Macmillan, 1st Earl of Stockton, regarded the developments in THE STATESMAN'S YEAR-BOOK under John Paxton's editorship as having maintained the traditions of the work to the highest standards while modernising it to retain its pre-eminent position in the field; a view that I share and a tribute that I am happy to endorse.

Stockton

PREFACE

The 127th edition of THE STATESMAN'S YEAR-BOOK records momentous happenings, some were still in progress as we go to press. Such events as those leading to greater democracy in Eastern European countries, the releasing from prison of Nelson Mandela in the Republic of South Africa and independence of Namibia all bode well for a better world.

No changes in the order of contents have taken place. Namibia was placed in alphabetical sequence in the last edition when it was known that independence was near and I have not moved Burma to Myanmar for this edition.

Traditionally the preface of THE STATESMAN'S YEAR-BOOK is written in the third person but, as I am retiring from the editorship this summer writing in the third person is not a satisfactory way of thanking all those hundreds of people scattered all over the world who have helped me in my work over the last twenty-one years. Without their help THE STATESMAN'S YEAR-BOOK would not be found in most reference libraries of the world today and I am very grateful to them. In our 127-year history we have only had five editors and each has adapted SYB, as it is affectionately known, to changing needs, but all kept to the basic plan established by the first editor.

My successor, Brian Hunter, has served the publication for nearly as long as I have and I wish him well in the task which has given me tremendous satisfaction.

J.P.

THE STATESMAN'S YEAR-BOOK OFFICE,
THE MACMILLAN PRESS LTD,
LITTLE ESSEX STREET,
LONDON, WC2R 3LF

WEIGHTS AND MEASURES

On 1 Jan. 1960 following an agreement between the standards laboratories of Great Britain, Canada, Australia, New Zealand, South Africa and the USA, an international yard and an international pound (avoirdupois) came into existence. 1 yard = 91·44 centimetres; 1 lb. = 453·59237 grammes.

The abbreviation 'm' signifies 'million(s)' and tonnes implies metric tons.

Length

Centimetre	0·394 inch
Metre	1·094 yards
Kilometre	0·621 mile

Liquid Measure

Litre	1·75 pints
Hectolitre	22 gallons

Surface Measure

Square metre	10·76 sq. feet
Hectare	2·47 acres
Square kilometre	0·386 sq. mile

Dry Measure

Litre	0·91 quart
Hectolitre	2·75 bushels

Weight—Avoirdupois

Gramme	15·42 grains
Kilogramme	2·205 pounds
Quintal (= 100 kg)	220·46 pounds
Tonne (= 1,000 kg)	0·984 long ton; 1·102 short tons

Weight—Troy

Gramme	15·43 grains
Kilogramme	32·15 ounces; 2·68 pounds

BRITISH WEIGHTS AND MEASURES

Length

1 foot	0·305 metre
1 yard	0·914 metre
1 mile (= 1,760 yds)	1·609 kilometres

Surface Measure

1 sq. foot	9·290 sq. decimetres
1 sq. yard	0·836 sq. metre
1 acre	0·405 hectare
1 sq. mile	2·590 sq. kilometres

Weight

1 ounce (= 437·2 grains)	28·350 grammes
1 lb. (= 7,000 grains)	453·6 grammes
1 cwt. (= 112 lb.)	50·802 kilogrammes
1 long ton (= 2,240 lb.)	1·016 tonnes
1 short ton (= 2,000 lb.)	0·907 tonne

Liquid Measure

1 pint	0·568 litre
1 gallon	4·546 litres
1 quarter	2·909 hectolitres

CONTENTS

Comparative Statistical Tables

WHEAT	xv	MILLET	xxi
RYE	xvi	SORGHUM	xxii
BARLEY	xvii	SUGAR	xxiii
OATS	xviii	PETROLEUM	xxiv
MAIZE	xix	MARITIME LIMITS	xxvii
RICE	xx	CHRONOLOGY	xxxi

Part I: International Organizations

The United Nations

GENERAL ASSEMBLY 3
SECURITY COUNCIL 4
ECONOMIC AND SOCIAL COUNCIL 5
TRUSTEESHIP COUNCIL 6
INTERNATIONAL COURT OF JUSTICE 6
SECRETARIAT 7
BUDGET 7
MEMBER STATES OF THE UN 7
UNITED NATIONS SYSTEM

Specialized Agencies

International Atomic Energy Agency (IAEA) 12
International Labour Organisation (ILO) 13
Food and Agriculture Organization (FAO) 14
Educational, Scientific and Cultural Organization (UNESCO) 15
World Health Organization (WHO) 16
International Monetary Fund (IMF) 18
International Bank for Reconstruction and Development (IBRD) 20
International Development Association (IDA) 21
International Finance Corporation (IFC) 21
International Civil Aviation Organization (ICAO) 22
Universal Postal Union (UPU) 22
International Telecommunication Union (ITU) 23
World Meteorological Organization (WMO) 23
International Maritime Organization (IMO) 24
General Agreement on Tariffs and Trade (GATT) 25
World Intellectual Property Organization (WIPO) 27
International Fund for Agricultural Development (IFAD) 28

Other International Organizations

THE COMMONWEALTH 28
WORLD COUNCIL OF CHURCHES 32

INTERNATIONAL TRADE UNIONISM 33

EUROPEAN ORGANIZATIONS

- Organisation for Economic Co-operation and Development (OECD) 35
- North Atlantic Treaty Organization (NATO) 36
- Western European Union (WEU) 39
- Council of Europe 40
- European Communities 42
- European Free Trade Association (EFTA) 47
- The Warsaw Pact 48
- Council for Mutual Economic Assistance (COMECON) 48

COLOMBO PLAN 50

ASSOCIATION OF SOUTH EAST ASIAN NATIONS (ASEAN) 51

ORGANIZATION OF AMERICAN STATES (OAS) 52

LATIN AMERICAN ECONOMIC GROUPINGS 54

CARIBBEAN COMMUNITY (CARICOM) 55

SOUTH PACIFIC FORUM 56

ARAB LEAGUE 56

ORGANIZATION OF THE PETROLEUM EXPORTING COUNTRIES (OPEC) 57

ORGANIZATION OF AFRICAN UNITY (OAU) 58

DANUBE COMMISSION 58

Part II: Countries of the World A–Z

AFGHÁNISTÁN 63

ALBANIA 68

ALGERIA 74

ANDORRA 79

ANGOLA 81

ANGUILLA 85

ANTIGUA AND BARBUDA 87

ARGENTINA 90

AUSTRALIA 97

Territories

- Australian Capital Territory 119
- Northern Territory 120
- Australian External Territories 124

States

- New South Wales 128
- Queensland 137
- South Australia 142
- Tasmania 147
- Victoria 152
- Western Australia 159

AUSTRIA 168

BAHAMAS 174

BAHRAIN 179

BANGLADESH 184

BARBADOS 190

BELGIUM 194

BELIZE 204

BENIN 208

BERMUDA 212

BHUTÁN 215

BOLIVIA 218

BOTSWANA 224

BRAZIL 229

BRITISH ANTARCTIC TERRITORY 238

BRITISH INDIAN OCEAN TERRITORY 238

BRUNEI 239

BULGARIA 243

BURKINA FASO 250

BURMA 254

BURUNDI 258

CAMBODIA 261

CAMEROON 265

CANADA 270

Provinces 295

- Alberta 297
- British Columbia 300
- Manitoba 304
- New Brunswick 307
- Newfoundland and Labrador 311
- Nova Scotia 315
- Ontario 318

Prince Edward Island 322
Quebec 324
Saskatchewan 327
Territories
Northwest Territories 329
Yukon Territory 332
CAPE VERDE 336
CAYMAN ISLANDS 339
CENTRAL AFRICAN REPUBLIC 341
CHAD 345
CHILE 348
CHINA, PEOPLE'S REPUBLIC OF 354
TAIWAN 366
COLOMBIA 372
COMOROS 378
CONGO 381
COSTA RICA 385
CÔTE D'IVOIRE 390
CUBA 394
CYPRUS 400
'Turkish Republic of Northern Cyprus' 405
CZECHOSLOVAKIA 407
DENMARK 415
Faroe Islands 426
Greenland 427
DJIBOUTI 430
DOMINICA 433
DOMINICAN REPUBLIC 435
ECUADOR 440
EGYPT 446
EL SALVADOR 453
EQUATORIAL GUINEA 458
ETHIOPIA 461
FALKLAND ISLANDS 466
FIJI 469
FINLAND 473
FRANCE 483
Overseas Departments
Guadeloupe 498
Guiana 501
Martinique 503
Réunion 505
Territorial Collectivities
Mayotte 507
St Pierre and Miquelon 508
Overseas territories
Antarctic territories 510
New Caledonia 511
French Polynesia 513
Wallis and Futuna 516
GABON 518
GAMBIA 522
GERMANY 525
GERMAN DEMOCRATIC REPUBLIC (EAST) 526
GERMANY, FEDERAL REPUBLIC OF (WEST) 533
Baden-Württemberg 545
Bavaria 547
Berlin (West) 549
Bremen 550
Hamburg 551
Hessen 553
Lower Saxony 554
North Rhine-Westphalia 555
Rhineland-Palatinate 557
Saarland 559
Schleswig-Holstein 560
GHANA 563
GIBRALTAR 568
GREECE 571
GRENADA 578
GUATEMALA 581
GUINEA 586
GUINEA-BISSAU 589
GUYANA 592
HAITI 597
HONDURAS 602
HONG KONG 607
HUNGARY 614
ICELAND 623
INDIA 631
States and Territories 652
Andhra Pradesh 653
Arunachal Pradesh 655
Assam 656
Bihar 658
Goa 659
Gujarat 660
Haryana 662
Himachal Pradesh 663
Jammu and Kashmir 665
Karnataka 667
Kerala 669
Madhya Pradesh 670
Maharashtra 673
Manipur 675
Meghalaya 676
Mizoram 677

Nagaland 678
Orissa 679
Punjab 681
Rajasthan 683
Sikkim 684
Tamil Nadu 686
Tripura 689
Uttar Pradesh 690
West Bengal 692

Territories
Andaman and Nicobar Islands 694
Chandigarh 695
Dadra and Nagar Haveli 695
Daman and Diu 696
Delhi 696
Lakshadweep 697
Pondicherry 698

INDONESIA 700
IRAN 708
IRAQ 714
IRELAND 719
ISRAEL 734
ITALY 743
JAMAICA 754
JAPAN 759
JORDAN 768
KENYA 773
KIRIBATI 778
KOREA, REPUBLIC OF 781
North Korea 786
KUWAIT 791
LAOS 795
LEBANON 799
LESOTHO 804
LIBERIA 807
LIBYA 811
LIECHTENSTEIN 816
LUXEMBOURG 819
MADAGASCAR 823
MALAWI 827
MALAYSIA 831
Peninsular Malaysia 837
Sabah 839
Sarawak 842
MALDIVES, REPUBLIC OF 845
MALI 847
MALTA 850
MAURITANIA 856
MAURITIUS 859
MEXICO 863
MONACO 870
MONGOLIA 872
MONTSERRAT 877
MOROCCO 879
MOZAMBIQUE 885
NAMIBIA 889
NAURU 894
NEPÁL 896
NETHERLANDS 899
Aruba 911
Netherlands Antilles 913
NEW ZEALAND 916
Cook Islands 931
Niue 932
NICARAGUA 935
NIGER 940
NIGERIA 943
NORWAY 949
Dependencies 961
OMAN 965
PAKISTAN 970
PANAMA 980
PAPUA NEW GUINEA 986
PARAGUAY 992
PERU 998
PHILIPPINES 1004
PITCAIRN 1010
POLAND 1011
PORTUGAL 1020
Macao 1027
QATAR 1029
ROMANIA 1033
RWANDA 1041
ST CHRISTOPHER (KITTS) – NEVIS 1044
ST HELENA 1047
ST LUCIA 1049
ST VINCENT 1051
SAN MARINO 1054
SÃO TOMÉ 1056
SAUDI ARABIA 1058
SENEGAL 1064
SEYCHELLES 1068

SIERRA LEONE 1071
SINGAPORE 1075
SOLOMON ISLANDS 1082
SOMALIA 1085
SOUTH AFRICA, REPUBLIC OF 1088
Cape of Good Hope 1100
Natal 1101
Transvaal 1102
Orange Free State 1104
Bophuthatswana 1105
Transkei 1107
Venda 1108
Ciskei 1111
SOUTH GEORGIA AND THE SOUTH SANDWICH ISLANDS 1113
SPAIN 1114
Western Sahara 1126
SRI LANKA 1127
SUDAN 1135
SURINAME 1140
SWAZILAND 1144
SWEDEN 1148
SWITZERLAND 1164
SYRIA 1175
TANZANIA 1179
THAILAND 1184
TOGO 1190
TONGA 1195
TRINIDAD AND TOBAGO 1198
TUNISIA 1202
TURKEY 1207
TURKS AND CAICOS ISLANDS 1215
TUVALU 1217
UGANDA 1219
UNION OF SOVIET SOCIALIST REPUBLICS 1223
Russia 1253
Ukraine 1264
Belorussia 1266
Azerbaijan 1268
Georgia 1270
Armenia 1273
Moldavia 1275
Estonia 1276
Latvia 1278
Lithuania 1279
Central Asia 1281
Kazakhstan 1282
Turkmenistan 1284
Uzbekistan 1285
Tadzhikistan 1288
Kirghizia 1290
UNITED ARAB EMIRATES 1293
UNITED KINGDOM 1298
Great Britain 1298
Northern Ireland 1359
Isle of Man 1367
Channel Islands 1369
UNITED STATES OF AMERICA 1374
States 1427
Alabama 1427
Alaska 1429
Arizona 1433
Arkansas 1435
California 1437
Colorado 1440
Connecticut 1442
Delaware 1445
District of Columbia 1447
Florida 1449
Georgia 1451
Hawaii 1453
Idaho 1455
Illinois 1458
Indiana 1461
Iowa 1463
Kansas 1465
Kentucky 1467
Louisiana 1470
Maine 1472
Maryland 1475
Massachusetts 1478
Michigan 1480
Minnesota 1483
Mississippi 1486
Missouri 1488
Montana 1491
Nebraska 1493
Nevada 1495
New Hampshire 1498
New Jersey 1500
New Mexico 1503
New York 1505
North Carolina 1509
North Dakota 1511
Ohio 1513
Oklahoma 1516
Oregon 1519
Pennsylvania 1523
Rhode Island 1526
South Carolina 1528
South Dakota 1530
Tennessee 1532
Texas 1534
Utah 1537
Vermont 1539
Virginia 1541
Washington 1544
West Virginia 1546
Wisconsin 1549
Wyoming 1552

Outlying Territories 1555
Guam 1555
Republic of Palau 1557
Marshall Islands 1557
Micronesia 1558
Northern Marianas 1558
Samoa 1558
Other Pacific Territories 1561
Puerto Rico 1561
Virgin Islands 1563

URUGUAY 1567

VANUATU 1572

VATICAN CITY STATE 1575

VENEZUELA 1578

VIETNAM 1585

VIRGIN ISLANDS, BRITISH 1591

WESTERN SAMOA 1593

YEMEN ARAB REPUBLIC 1596

YEMEN, PEOPLE'S DEMOCRATIC REPUBLIC OF 1599

YUGOSLAVIA 1603
Bosnia and Herzegovina 1611
Croatia 1611
Macedonia 1612
Montenegro 1612
Serbia 1613
Kosovo 1614
Vojvodina 1614
Slovenia 1615

ZAÏRE 1616

ZAMBIA 1621

ZIMBABWE 1625

PLACE AND INTERNATIONAL ORGANIZATIONS INDEX 1633

PRODUCT INDEX 1667

NAME INDEX 1677

ADDENDA *xxxiv*

WHEAT

Countries	Area (1,000 hectares) Average 1979-81	1985	1986	1987	1988	Production (1,000 tonnes) Average 1979-81	1985	1986	1987	1988
Afghánistán	2,220	2,313	2,313	2,300	2,372	2,754	2,750	2,750	2,800	2,900
Algeria	1,943	1,668	1,520	1,510	1,495	1,270	1,478	1,229	1,175	1,150
Argentina	5,245	5,382	4,893	4,875	4,617*	8,060	8,700	8,700	9,000*	7,769*
Australia [1]	11,440	11,736	11,135	9,005	9,301	14,468	16,167	16,119	12,287	14,102
Bulgaria [1,2]	986	1,067	1,127	1,085	1,181	3,881	3,068	4,327	4,149	4,713
Canada	11,386	13,729	14,239	13,474	12,921	20,430	24,252	31,378	25,950	15,655
Chile [1]	513	506	569	677	577	882	1,165	1,626	1,874	1,734
China [1]	28,930	29,219	29,617	28,799	29,001	59,196	85,807	90,044	87,775	87,505
Czechoslovakia [2]	1,121	1,209	1,205	1,212	1,239	4,482	6,023	5,305	6,154	6,547
Egypt [1]	577	498	507	577	598	1,844	1,872	1,928	2,721	2,839
France	4,473	4,805	4,859	4,932	4,825	22,362	28,890	26,475	27,415	29,677
Germany, Fed. Rep. of [2]	1,642	1,624	1,648	1,671	1,761	8,177	9,866	10,406	9,932	12,044
Greece	1,022	881	905	886	875	2,770	1,791	2,839	2,213	2,550
Hungary [1,3]	1,187	1,358	1,318	1,315*	1,281*	4,800	6,578	5,793	5,748	6,962
India	22,364	23,565	22,997	23,131	22,604	34,550	44,069	47,052	44,323	45,096
Iran	5,824	5,978	6,405	6,725	6,900	6,215	6,626	7,577	7,960	8,200
Iraq	1,215	1,540	1,240	859	1,300	854	1,406	1,036	722	1,200*
Italy	3,373	3,034	3,136	3,087	2,895	8,989	8,461	9,102	9,381	7,945
Japan [1]	188	234	246	271	282*	571	874	876	864	1,021*
Mexico	723	1,224	1,201	988	900*	2,754	5,207	4,770	4,415	3,700*
Morocco	1,673	1,894	2,223	2,288	2,332	1,500	2,050	3,809	2,427	4,035
Pakistan [1]	6,865	7,259	7,403	7,706	7,307	10,760	11,703	13,923	12,016	12,675
Poland [1]	1,525	1,885	2,025	2,133	2,179	4,189	6,461	7,502	7,942	7,582
Romania [1]	2,154	2,366	2,360	2,400*	2,500*	5,471	5,666	7,320	9,672	9,000
S. Africa, Republic of	1,770	1,951	1,926	1,927	1,985*	1,965	1,680	2,321	3,135	3,400*
Spain [2]	2,628	2,043	2,114	2,221	2,332	4,510	5,329	4,392	5,791	6,514
Turkey [2]	9,208	9,275	9,356	9,331	9,341	17,058	17,032	19,032	18,932	20,500
USSR [1]	59,463	50,265	48,728	46.684	48,000*	89,859	78,078	92,306	83,312	84,500
UK	1,434	1,902	1,991	1.992	1,891	8,116	12,046	13,911	11,941	11,605
USA	28,898	26,197	24,574	22.646	21,519	66,229	65,999	56,926	57,357	49,295
Yugoslavia [2]	1,475	1,348	1,346	1.498	1,506	4,624	4,859	4,776	5,345	6,303
World total	235,073	230,319	228,319	221.609	220,406	443,618	505,729	536,709	517,152	509,952

RYE

Countries	Area (1,000 hectares) Average 1979–81	1985	1986	1987	1988	Production (1,000 tonnes) Average 1979–81	1985	1986	1987	1988
Argentina	199	115	65	96	55	169	105	60	88	41
Austria	105	88	83	85	80*	327	339	284	309	280*
Belgium	12	6	5	5*	3*	43	26	22	20	14*
Bulgaria [1]	21	32	30	32	32	29	49	52	49	58
Canada	362	353	315	313	245	636	569	609	493	257
China	733	600	550	650	650	1,167	1,000	900	1,000	1,000
Czechoslovakia [2]	192	179	155	142	143	534	620	547	496	534
Denmark	59	126	120	136*	80	221	565	546	513	366
Finland	44	31	27	38	26	88	72	71	74	49
France	121	87	81	82	79	368	297	229	299	276
German Demo. Rep.	671	690	680	655	606	1,848	2,505	2,406	2,283*	1,783
Germany, Fed. Rep. of	532	426	414	412	373	1,980	1,821	1,768	1,599	1,558
Hungary [1,2]	72	85	89	94	97*	117	166	172	186	245
Netherlands	10	5	4	6	7	39	19	19	25	27
Poland [1]	2,970	3,083	2,760	2,647	2,325	6,166	7,600	7,074	6,817	5,501
Portugal	166	123	124	128	124	128	97	100	108	73
Romania [1]	33	30*	35	37*	37	38	45*	66*	55	60*
Spain	219	211	221	222	222	239	273	220	318	357
Sweden	58	46	40	40	36	197	157	154	137	140
Turkey	439	232	221	240	222	558	360	350	380	293
USSR [1]	7,557	9,520	8,741	9,725	9,000	9,309	15,739	15,296	18,082	16,000*
USA	295	290	274	276	246	474	524	496	503	382
Yugoslavia	56	45	42	41	40	78	77	74	69	76
World total	15,076	16,592	15,283	16,272	14,903	24,980	33,282	31,794	34,145	29,617

* Unofficial figures. [1] Sown area. [2] Includes mixture of wheat and rye. [3] Field crops and other crops.

BARLEY

Countries	Area (1,000 hectares) Average 1979–81	1985	1986	Average 1987	1988	Production (1,000 tonnes) 1979–81	1985	1986	1987	1988
Australia [1]	2,539	3,284	2,274	2,346	2,272	3,278	4,868	3,548	3,417	3,270
Austria	370	334	333	291	277*	1,288	1,521	1,292	1,179	1,135
Belgium	173	131	146	139	131*	844	747	858	736	802*
Bulgaria [1]	425	260	318	295	345	1,439	800	1,144	1,091	1,306
Canada	4,631	4,750	4,829	5,005	4,132	11,199	12,387	14,569	13,957	10,125
China	1,295	1,020	1,100	990	990	3,133	2,700	2,520	2,800	3,000
Czechoslovakia	972	789	821	834	793	3,524	3,538	3,530	3,551	3,411
Denmark	1,580	1,094	1,078	943	1,154	6,250	5,251	5,134	4,292	5.419
Finland	579	646	589	583	682	1,421	1,854	1,714	1,306	1,612
France	2,670	2,255	2,090	1,992	1,916	10,997	11,440	10,063	10,489	10,086
German Demo. Rep.	959	882	895	891	874	3,592	4,366	4,293	4,198	3,798
Germany, Fed. Rep. of	2,011	1,949	1,947	1,850	1,841	8,566	9,690	9,377	8,571	9,609
Greece	344	316	266	241	261	838	588	681	573	695
Hungary [1,2]	265	279	253	208*	264*	848	1,046	857	794	1,161
India	1,802	1,253	1,369	1,225	1,148	2,020	1,556	1,962	1,669	1,593
Iran	1,336	2,084	2,200	2,200	2,200	1,397	2,298	2,500	2,500	2,500
Ireland	349	298	283	276	275	1,603	1,494	1,428	1,599	1,538
Italy	324	468	465	445	450	914	1,630	1,543	1,710	1,561
Japan [1]	120	113	107	105*	114*	392	378	344	353	399*
Korea, South [1]	386	237	190	204*	284	1,059	571	453	516	733*
Morocco	2,190	2,383	2,472	2,314	2,552	1,712	2,541	3,563	1,543	3,501
Poland [1]	1,362	1,242	1,335	1,286	1,250	3,563	4,086	4,412	4,335	3,804
Romania [1]	833	680	575*	560*	660	2,360	1,850	2,497	3,231	2,200*
Spain	3,520	4,246	4,340	4,401	4,175	6,571	10,698	7,431	9,836	12,070
Sweden	678	670	638	545	2,323	537	2,309	2,327	1,907	1,942
Syria	1,220	1,386	1,548	1,570	1,844	1,129	740	1,116	576	2,836
Turkey	2,846	3,336	3,343	3,298	3,300	5,480	6,500	7,000	6,900	7,500
USSR [1]	33,456	29,058	29,954	30,654	30,000	42,502	46,540	53,889	58,409	47,000
UK	2,333	1,966	1,917	1,831	1,895	10,058	9,740	10,014	9,226	8,765
USA	3,214	4,696	4,859	4,070	3,049	8,838	12,876	13,292	11,529	6,325
World total	81,044	79,189	79,448	78,088	75,961	156,844	176,582	182,387	181,699	168,423

* Unofficial figures. [1] Sown area. [2] Field crops and other crops.

OATS

Countries	Area (1,000 hectares) Average 1979–81	1985	1986	1987	1988	Production (1,000 tonnes) Average 1979-81	1985	1986	1987	1988
Argentina	353	333	312	476	446	431	400	495	718	620
Australia	1,201	1,068	1,140	1,275	1,439	1,386	1,330	1,584	1,698	1,815
Austria	93	75	73	69	70*	298	284	270	246	250*
Belgium	39	29*	23	22	21*	171	145	98	65	95*
Canada	1,501	1,263	1,287	1,263	1,418*	2,993	2,736	3,251	2,995	2,993
Chile	84	85	64	56	61	151	170	124	128	157
China	400	400	400	400	400	600	490	500	600	500
Czechoslovakia [2]	132	121	115	108	102	418	473	419	406	366
Denmark	40	42	27	23	44	166	168	111	95	202
Finland	444	411	403	368	388*	1,183	1,218	1,175	813*	857
France	525	433	312	281	273	1,850	1,770	1,066	1,122	1,074
German Demo. Rep.	154	178	163	149	148	571	746	666	637	508
Germany, Fed.Rep.of	700	584	506	459	474	2,777	2,806	2,276	2,008	2,036
Ireland	25	23	21	20	22	95	106	102	106	117
Italy	223	182	184	177	171	433	363	397	361	383
Netherlands	20	11	7	9	13	106	58	40	47	63
Norway	108	127	126	115	128	424	494	401	466	480
Poland [1]	1,082	995	924	856	850	2,387	2,682	2,486	2,429	2,222
Spain	453	459	393	353	335	527	680	433	502	537
Sweden	461	445	455	397	423	1,635	1,668	1,486	1,440	1,402
Turkey	199	167	158	178	158	350	314	300	325	276
USSR [1]	12,160	12,604	13,173	11,790	12,000	14,372	20,513	21,929	18,495	16,500
UK	142	134	97	99	121	587	614	503	451	557
USA	3,743	3,309	2,776	2,802	2,262	7,234	7,559	5,608	5,429	3,175
Yugoslavia	199	151	152	140	135	296	252	260	232	253
World total	25,691	25,156	24,847	23,489	23,549	42,582	49,376	47,417	43,223	38,848

* Unofficial figures. [1] Sown area. [2] Includes spelt. [3] Field crops and other crops.

MAIZE

Countries	Area (1,000 hectares) Average 1979–81	1985	1986	1987	1988	Production (1,000 tonnes) Average 1979–81	1985	1986	1987	1988
Argentina	2,895	3,340	3,231	2,900	2,438	9,333	11,900	12,100	9,250	9,200
Austria	190	208	217	207	202*	1,338	1,727	1,740	1,685	1,640*
Brazil	11,430	11,798	12,466	13,499	13,142	19,265	22,018	20,531	26,787	24,709
Bulgaria	605	435	574	497	494	2,626	1,350	2,848	1,858	1,625
Canada	1,039	1,123	994	999	981	5,904	6,970	5,912	7,015	5,369
China	19,986	17,756	19,199	20,291	19,792*	60,720	64,052	71,128	80,127	73,820
Egypt	800	804	623	761	900	3,159	3,699	2,918	3,367	4,088*
France	1,774	1,887	1,884	1,743	1,936	9,641	12,409	11,641	12,470	13,996
Greece	157	222	218	262	212	1,165	1,910	1,994	2,156	2,116
Hungary	1,270	1,082	1,146	1,170	1,122*	7,022	6,818	7,261	7,234	6,027
India	5,887	5,797	5,923	5,542	5,900*	6,486	6,644	7,593	5,629	7,500*
Indonesia	2,761	2,440	3,143	2,626	3,203	4,035	4,330	5,920	5,155	6,668
Italy	956	923	849	768	843	6,590	6,357	6,461	5,764	6,318
Kenya	1,273	1,790*	1,426	1,600*	1,800*	1,714	2,750*	2,898	2,250*	2,685
Malaŵi	1,120	1,210	1,193	1,153	1,216*	1,268	1,355	1,295	1,225	1,445*
Mexico	6,836	7,498	6,417	6,788	6,800	11,866	13,957	11,721	11,575	11,800
Nigeria	443	562	600	700	700	591	1,196	1,336	1,202	1,500
Philippines	3,267	3,511	3,595	3,683	3,745	3,174	3,863	4,091	4,278	4,428
Portugal	333	246	258	262	230	486	550	628	655	663
Romania	3,309	3,094	2,976	2,894	3,200	11,823	15,238	20,158	18,378	19,500
S. Africa, Republic of	4,900	3,887	4,044	4,014*	3,600*	11,207	7,658	8,077	7,372	6,900*
Spain	450	526	524	542	556	2,227	3,414	3,423	3,557	3,577
Tanzania	1,350	1,718*	1,626	1,650*	1,720*	1,762	2,093*	2,787	2,359	2,339*
Thailand	1,408	1,918	1,815	1,357	1,950	3,103	4,934	4,309	2,781	5,166
Turkey	583	567	560	570	560	1,263	1,900	2,300	2,400	2,100
USSR [1]	3,063	4,482	4,223	4,573	4,200*	9,076	14,406	12,479	14,808	16,000
USA	29,661	30,442	27,988	23,960	23,538	192,084	225,478	209,555	179,638	125,003
Yugoslavia	2,250	2,402	2,369	2,218	2,269	9,736	9,901	12,526	8,863	7,697
Zimbabwe	1,097	1,256	1,314	1,211	1,300	1,829	2,711	2,545	931	2,253
World total	126,060	129,235	128,337	125,983	126,613	421,873	487,367	485,066	458,028	405,460

* Unofficial figures. [1] For dry grain only.

RICE (Paddy)

Countries	Area (1,000 hectares) Average 1979–81	1985	1986	1987	1988	Production (1,000 tonnes) Average 1979–81	1985	1986	1987	1988
Bangladesh	10,310	10,399	10,610	10,322	10,000	20,125	22,562	23,110	23,120	21,900
Brazil	5,932	4,755	5,585	6,000	5,961	8,533	9,027	10,374	10,425	11,804
Burma	4,684	4,661	4,666	4,641	4,715	12,637	14,317	14,126	13,722	14,000
Cambodia	1,186	1,750	1,700	1,546	1,600	1,160	2,100	2,000	1,855	2,000
China	34,323	32,634	32,798	32,694	32,500	145,665	171,416	174,790	176,958	172,365
Colombia	428	386	325	385	389	1,831	1,798	1,521	1,865	1,775
Egypt	416	389	423	412	330*	2,376	2,311	2,445	2,279	1,900*
India	40,091	41,137	41,167	38,319	41,000	74,557	95,818	90,779	84,538	101,950
Indonesia	9,063	9,902	9,988	9,923	10,090	29,570	39,033	39,727	40,078	41,769
Iran	433	480	489	510	482	1,448	1,775	1,828	1,920	1,757*
Italy	176	186	192	190	198	989	1,123	1,137	1,064	1,094
Japan	2,384	2,342	2,303	2,146	2,132*	13,320	14,578	14,559	13,284	12,419
Korea, North	793	840	860	875	885	4,970	5,800	6,000	6,200	6,350
Korea, South	1,230	1,237	1,236	1,262	1,260	6,780	7,855	7,872	7,596	8,400*
Madagascar	1,182	1,181	1,188	1,214	1,200	2,055	2,178	2,230	2,296	2,100
Malaysia	658	656	628	641	630	2,053	1,953	1,745	1,697	1,669
Mexico	153	220	158	155	120*	528	809	545	591	420*
Nepál	1,275	1,391	1,333	1,423	1,400	2,361	2,804	2,372	2,982	2,787
Nigeria	517	700*	720*	730*	650	1,027	1,515*	1,416	1,450*	1,400
Pakistan	1,981	1,863	2,066	1,963	1,939	4,884	4,378	5,230	4,861	4,577
Philippines	3,513	3,306	3,464	3,256	3,293	7,893	8,806	9,247	8,540	8,971
Sri Lanka	819	867	836	679	811	2,093	2,661	2,588	2,128	2,466
Thailand	8,953	9,833	9,194	9,083	10,417	16,967	20,264	18,868	18,042	20,813
USSR	637	671	621	657	660	2,558	2,572	2,633	2,683	2,900
USA	1,345	1,009	955	944	1,172	6,968	6,120	6,049	5,879	7,237
Vietnam	5,558	5,704	5,689	5,594	5,600	11,663	15,875	16,003	15,103	15,200*
World total	145,602	144,493	145,157	141,497	145,602	396,290	472,714	472,482	464,514	483,466

* Unofficial figures.

MILLET

Countries	Area (1,000 hectares) Average 1979–81	1985	1986	1987	1988	Production (1,000 tonnes) Average 1979–81	1985	1986	1987	1988
Argentina	203	125	94	59	45	245	158	107	80	50
Australia	26	30	31	42	39	26	26	32	39	45
Burkina Faso	803	974	1,054	1,168	1,277	390	587	687	632	817
Cameroon	503	477	500	465	470	402	443	450	400	410
Chad	774	950*	1,078*	950	990*	409	526*	624*	518*	690*
China	3,981	3,319	2,981	2,689	2,701*	5,790	5,978	4,541	4,539	5,501
Egypt	172	143	156	133	155	641	547	606	551	578*
Ethiopia	226	230	230	230	230	203	190	188	180	200
Ghana	182	222	240	220	240	117	120	140	121*	140
India	17,845	16,207	16,645	13,886	16,000*	9,189	7,399	8,383	6,775	8,500
Kenya	80	56	60	60	60	84	60	65	60	60
Korea, North	418	435	440	445	448	447	535	545	560	575
Korea, South	3	4	3	2	2	4	5	3	3	3
Mali	1,077	1,582	1,634	1,540	1,624	801	1,249	1,301	1,207*	1,900*
Nepál	122	151	151	165	169	121	138	138	150	160
Niger	3,011	3,160	3,239	3,000	3,482	1,311	1,450	1,383	1,020	1,783
Nigeria	2,882	3,700*	3,900*	3,700	3,900	2,732	3,600*	4,111	3,905	4,000
Pakistan	509	561	509	293	270	255	258	233	135	125
Senegal	1,062	1,336	993	1,074	1,026	603	950	634	801	634
Sudan	1,094	1,725	1,543	1,091*	2,300*	458	428	285	153*	550*
Tanzania	450	341*	308	290*	300	370	300*	259	291*	280*
Togo	121	66	116	128	120*	44	74	82	71	50*
Uganda	297	312	342	295	300*	473	210	350	471	414
USSR	2,794	2,808	2,485	2,763	2,800	1,759	2,886	2,368	3,926	2,700
Zimbabwe [1]	353	250	295*	310	374	153	224*	141*	81	278
World total	40,101	40,256	40,419	36,284	40,641	27,784	29,269	28,711	27,679	31,536

* Unofficial figures. [1] On farms and estates.

SORGHUM

Countries	Area (1,000 hectares) Average 1979–81	1985	1986	1987	1988	Production (1,000 tonnes) Average 1979–81	1985	1986	1987	1988
Argentina	1,866	2,002	1,322	1,005	956	5,641	6,256	4,061	3,040	3,200
Australia	548	723	734	818	745	1,084	1,369	1,416	1,419	1,633
Burkina Faso	1,051	1,077	1,210	1,176	1,295	620	798	1,012	848	1,009
China	2,828	1,965	1,896	1,884	1,902*	7,034	5,696	5,481	5,531	6,115
Colombia	220	192	227	259	266	488	499	600	704	707
Ethiopia [1,2]	1,048	900	910	900	910	1,420	905	1,092	950	1,100
France	75	44	45	36	43	332	206	172	209	234
India	16,361	16,097	15,948	15,648	16,000*	11,380	10,197	9,185	11,847	11,000
Mexico	1,491	1,236	1,533	1,853	1,800	4,991	6,550	4,833	6,296	5,500
Niger	822	1,140	1,109	1,100	1,470	347	328	360	360	603
Nigeria	3,047	4,600	4,800	4,200	4,500	3,545	4,991	5,455	5,182	4,940
S. Africa, Republic of	377	315	307	314	313*	540	600	437	467	482*
Sudan	3,163	5,408	4,960	3,360	5,882*	2,361	3,542	3,282	1,300	4,640*
Thailand	220	292	184	160	184	237	404	211	192	215
Uganda	175	186	208	185	199*	312	148	280	286	289*
USA	5,273	6,792	5,609	4,291	3,663	19,157	28,456	23,829	18,778	14,670
Venezuela	227	250	381*	350*	350*	365	481	756	777	600*
Yemen Arab Republic	631	690	601	566	584	616	276	457	450	542
World total	44,143	48,747	46,200	42,684	45,590	64,522	76,465	67,265	62,843	61,787

* Unofficial figures. [1] Includes teff. [2] Unspecified millet and sorghum.

CENTRIFUGAL RAW SUGAR
(in 1,000 tonnes)

Countries	*Average 1979–81*	*1983*	*1984*	*1985*	*1986*	*1987*	*1988*
Argentina	1,584	1,625	1,545	1,174	1,120*	1,063	1,150*
Australia [1]	3,243	3,171	3,548	3,379	3,371	3,440	3,580*
Barbados [2]	113	85	100	100	111	83	83*
Brazil	7,991	9,576*	9,332*	8,274*	8,649*	8,458*	8,500*
Canada	118	132	113	54	122	147*	109*
China	3,809	4,910	5,352*	6,347*	6,340*	5,219*	5,925*
Colombia	1,192	1,379	1,178	1,367	1,297	1,390	1,415
Cuba	7,510	7,460	8,331*	8,101*	7,467	7,232	7,548*
Czechoslovakia	808	792	844*	939*	862	818	614
Dominican Rep.	1,142	1,219	1,156	921	895	866	800*
Egypt	666	782*	780	887*	959	1,007	1,029*
France	4,720	3,875	4,305	4,324	3,734*	3,973*	4,424*
Fiji [1]	446	276	480	341	502	401	420
German Demo.Rep.	675	692*	778*	798*	790*	760*	445*
Germany, Fed.Rep.of	3,261	2,725	3,151	3,454	3,479	2,963*	3,130
Guyana	294	248	238	265	249	234*	168*
India [3]	5,380	8,948	6,430	6,650	7,051	8,533	9,100
Indonesia [4]	1,286	1,643	1,500	1,767	2,013	2,073	1,800*
Italy	1,956	1,352	1,385*	1,352*	1,868*	1,867*	1,607*
Jamaica	238	198	193	225	206	189*	221*
Mauritius [4]	615	640	610	684	707	694	634
Mexico	2,796	3,108*	3,297*	3,489*	4,031*	3,986*	3,822*
Pakistan [3]	734	1,246	1,258	1,430	1,210	1,364	1,936
Peru	571	455*	620*	757*	599	560*	565*
Philippines	2,289	2,540	2,335	1,718	1,447	1,337	1,369
Poland	1,530	2,140	1,878	1,811	1,891	1,823	1,824*
Puerto Rico	156	90	87	98	87	87	93
S. Africa, Rep.of	2,011	1,495	2,560	2,280	2,248*	2,235*	2,260*
Spain	934	1,356	1,166	976	1,111	1,108	1,088*
Sweden	350	298	392	346	386	275	396*
Thailand	1,534	2,268*	2,350*	2,572	2,586	2,637	2,705
Trinidad	117	77	70	81	92	85	91*
Turkey	1,178	1,770*	1,655*	1,398*	1,414*	1,784*	1,595*
USSR	7,017	8,760*	8,685*	8,260*	8,700*	9,565*	9,240*
UK	1,215	1,185	1,400	1,317	1,433	1,335*	1,413*
USA [5]	5,345	5,107	5,363	5,473	6,075	6,651	6,260
World total	88,622	97,929	99,976	99,283	101,273	101,781	102,779

[1] 94° net titre.
[2] Includes the sugar equivalent of fancy molasses.
[3] Includes sugar (raw value) refined from gur.
[4] Tel quel.
[5] Includes Hawaii.
* Unofficial figures.

WORLD ESTIMATED CRUDE OIL PRODUCTION[1]

(in 1,000 tonnes)

	1960	*1970*	*1987*	*1988*
Africa				
Algeria	8,630	47,253	29,460	30,000
Angola	70	5,066	17,077	22,500
Congo	—	—	5,777	6,400
Côte d'Ivoire	—	—	1,200	800
Egypt	—	—	45,931	44,500
Gabon	850	5,460	7,980	8,750
Libya	—	159,201	46,790	48,500
Nigeria	880	53,420	63,670	70,000
Tunisia	—	4,151	5,000	4,800
Zaïre	—	—	1,530	1,400
Caribbean Area				
Colombia	8,100	11,071	19,418	17,380
Cuba	—	—	894	750
Trinidad	6,075	7,225	8,353	7,800
Venezuela	148,690	193,209	88,290	93,000
China	5,000	20,000	132,940	135,000
Far East				
Australia	—	8,292	25,785	24,500
Brunei	4,690	6,916	7,250	7,500
Burma	530	750	900	750
India	440	6,809	30,143	31,500
Indonesia	20,560	42,102	64,110	62,000
Japan	510	750	603	650
Malaysia	—	—	23,500	27,000
New Zealand	—	—	1,272	1,300
Pakistan	360	486	2,032	2,400
Thailand	—	—	1,600	1,900
Middle East				
Abu Dhabi	—	33,288	50,845	55,000
Bahrain	2,250	3,834	2,108	2,150
Dubai	—	—	18,140	17,000
Iran	52,065	191,663	113,370	113,000
Iraq	47,480	76,600	101,810	128,000
Kuwait	81,860	137,397	61,440	73,000
Oman	—	—	28,265	29,500
Qatar	8,210	17,257	15,050	15,200
Saudi Arabia	61,090	176,851	209,570	251,000
Sharjah	—	—	3,125	3,150
Syria	—	4,350	12,000	13,500
Turkey	350	3,461	2,643	2,500

[1] Excluding small scale production in Afghánistán, Bangladesh and Mongolia; including other small producers not specified here.

WORLD ESTIMATED CRUDE OIL PRODUCTION

(contd.)

(in 1,000 tonnes)

	1960	*1970*	*1987*	*1988*
North America				
Canada	27,480	69,954	88,560	93,000
USA	384,080	533,677	461,353	455,000
Latin America				
Argentina	9,160	19,969	21,630	23,000
Bolivia	990	1,128	915	900
Brazil	390	8,009	28,825	26,800
Chile		1,620	1,565	1,300
Ecuador	2,680	191	8,520	15,800
Mexico	14,125	21,877	142,960	143,000
Peru	450	3,450	8,071	700
USSR and Eastern Europe				
Albania	600	1,199	3,000	3,000
Bulgaria	200	334	280	280
Czechoslovakia	140	203	146	140
German Dem. Rep.	—	60	60	60
Hungary	1,215	1,937	1,916	1,900
Poland	195	424	145	140
Romania	11,500	13,377	10,500	10,000
USSR	148,000	352,667	624,000	624,000
Yugoslavia	1,040	2,854	3,868	3,700
Western Europe				
Austria	2,440	2,798	1,060	1,100
Denmark	—	—	4,599	4,800
France	2,260	2,308	3,235	3,500
Germany, Fed. Rep. of	5,560	7,536	3,728	3,900
Italy	1,990	1,408	3,632	4,500
Netherlands	1,920	1,919	4,681	4,300
Norway	—	49,500	56,000	
Spain	—	156	1,639	1,500
UK	90	84	123,306	115,000
World total	1,090,080	2,336,153	2,909,670	3,025,230

MARITIME LIMITS (IN MILES)

State	*Territorial Sea*	*Jurisdiction over fisheries (measured from the baseline of the territorial sea)*
Albania	15 (1976)	—
Algeria	12 (1963)	—
Angola	20 (1975)	200 (1975)
Antigua and Barbuda	12 (1982)	200 (1982) [1]
Argentina	200 (1967)	—
Australia	3 (1973)	200 (1979)
Bahamas	3 (1878)	200 (1977)
Bahrain	3	—
Bangladesh	12 (1974)	200 (1974) [1]
Barbados	12 (1977)	200 (1979) [1]
Belgium	3	up to median line (1978)
Belize	3 (1878)	—
Benin	200 (1976)	—
Brazil	200 (1970)	—
Brunei Darussalam	12 (1983)	200 (1983) (or median line)
Bulgaria	12 (1951)	200 (1987) [1]
Burma	12 (1968)	200 (1977) [1]
Cambodia	12(1969)	200 (1979) [1]
Cameroon	50 (1974)	—
Canada	12 (1970)	200 (1977)
Cape Verde	12 (1977)	200 (1977) [1]
Chile	12 (1986)	200 (1986) [1]
China	12 (1958)	—
Colombia	12 (1978)	200 (1978) [1]
Comoros	12 (1976)	200 (1982) [1]
Congo	200 (1977)	—
Costa Rica	12 (1982)	200 (1975) [1]
Côte d'Ivoire	12 (1977)	200 (1977) [1]
Cuba	12 (1977)	200 (1977) [1]
Cyprus	12 (1964)	—
Denmark (including Faroe Islands and Greenland)	3 (1966)	200 (1977)
Djibouti	12 (1979)	200 (1979) [1]
Dominica	12 (1981)	200 (1981) [1]
Dominican Republic	6 (1967)	200 (1977) [1]
Ecuador	200 (1966)	—
Egypt	12 (1958)	—
El Salvador	200 (1983)	—
Equatorial Guinea	12 (1984)	200 (1984) [1]
Ethiopia	12 (1953)	—
Fiji	12 (1978)	200 (1981) [1]
Finland	4 (1956)	12 (1975) (or agreed boundary)
France	12 (1971)	200 (1977) [1] (except Mediterranean)
Gabon	12 (1986)	200 (1986) [1]
Gambia	12 (1969)	200 (1978)
German Democratic Republic	12 (1985)	up to median line (1978)
Germany, Federal Republic of	3 [2]	200 (1977)
Ghana	12 (1986)	200 (1986) [1]
Greece	6 (1936)	—
Grenada	12 (1978)	200 (1978) [1]
Guatemala	12 (1976)	200 (1976) [1]
Guinea	12 (1980)	200 (1980) [1]
Guinea-Bissau	12 (1978)	200 (1978) [1]

[1] Economic zone. [2] 3–16 miles in North Sea (German Bight); area defined by coordinates.

MARITIME LIMITS (IN MILES)—*contd.*

State	*Territorial Sea*	*Jurisdiction over fisheries (measured from the baseline of the territorial sea)*
Guyana	12 (1977)	200 (1977) [9]
Haiti	12 (1972)	200 (1977) [1]
Honduras	12 (1965)	200 (1951) [1]
Iceland	12 (1979)	200 (1979) [1]
India	12 (1967)	200 (1977) [1]
Indonesia	12 (1957) [2]	200 (1980) [1,7]
Iran	12 (1959)	[8]
Iraq	12 (1958)	—
Ireland	3 (1959)	200 (1977)
Israel	6 (1956)	—
Italy	12 (1974)	—
Jamaica	12 (1971)	—
Japan	12 (1977)	200 (1977)
Jordan	3 (1943)	—
Kenya	12 (1971)	200 (1979) [1]
Kiribati	12 (1983)	200 (1983) [1]
Korea (North)	12 (1967) [2]	200 (1977) [1]
Korea (South)	12 (1978)	12
Kuwait	12 (1967)	—
Lebanon	12 (1983)	—
Liberia	200 (1976)	—
Libya	12 (1959)	—
Madagascar	12 (1985)	200 (1985) [1]
Malaysia	12 (1969)	200 (1984) [1]
Maldive, Republic of	12 (1975)	(1976) [1,3]
Malta	12 (1978)	25 (1978)
Mauritania	12 (1988)	200 (1988) [1]
Mauritius	12 (1977)	200 (1977) [1]
Mexico	12 (1972)	200 (1976) [1]
Monaco	12 (1973)	200 (1985)
Morocco	12 (1973) [4]	200 (1981) [1,4]
Mozambique	12 (1976)	200 (1976) [1]
Namibia	6 (1963)	12 (1963)
Nauru	12 (1971)	200 (1978)
Netherlands	12 (1985)	200 (1977)
New Zealand	12 (1977)	200 (1978) [1]
Nicaragua	(1979) [5]	200 (1979) [5]
Nigeria	30 (1971)	200 (1978) [1]
Norway	4 (1812)	200 (1977) [1]
Oman	12 (1977)	200 (1981) [1]
Pakistan	12 (1976)	200 (1976) [1]
Panama	200 (1967)	—
Papua New Guinea	12 (1978)	200 (1978) (offshore waters)
Peru	(1947) [5]	200 (1947) [5]
Philippines	[6]	200 (1978) [1]

[1] Economic zone.

[2] The territorial sea of Indonesia is measured by straight lines surrounding the archipelago.

[3] Territorial limits and economic zone defined by geographical co-ordinates.

[4] Limits with opposite or adjacent states to be fixed by agreement, failing which median line principle to apply.

[5] Sovereignty and jurisdiction over the sea, its soil and subsoil up to 200 miles (1947).

[6] The territorial sea of the Philippines is determined by straight base-lines joining appropriate points of the outermost islands forming the Philippine archipelago in accordance with Treaties of 1898, 1900 and 1930 (1961).

[7] 200 mile exclusive fisheries zone established 1985.

[8] Outer limits of the superjacent waters of the continental shelf. Median line in the Sea of Oman (1973).

[9] The Guyana Maritime Boundaries Act 1977 empowers the President to declare a 200 mile economic zone. In Jan. 1988 no such zone had been declared.

MARITIME LIMITS (IN MILES)—*contd.*

State	*Territorial Sea*	*Jurisdiction over fisheries (measured from the baseline of the territorial sea)*
Poland	12 (1978)	up to median line (1978)
Portugal	12 (1977)	200 (1977) [2]
Qatar	3	[1]
Romania	12 (1956)	200 (1986) [2]
St Christopher (St Kitts)–Nevis	12 (1984)	200 (1984) [2]
St Lucia	12 (1984)	200 (1984) [2]
St Vincent and the Grenadines	12 (1983)	200 (1983) [2]
São Tomé and Principe	12 (1978)	200 (1978) [2]
Saudi Arabia	12 (1958)	[6]
Senegal	12 (1985)	200 (1985) [2]
Seychelles	12 (1977)	200 (1977) [2]
Sierra Leone	200 (1971)	—
Singapore	3 (1878)	—
Solomon Islands	12 (1978)	200 (1986)
Somalia	200 (1972)	—
South Africa, Republic of	12 (1977)	200 (1977)
Spain	12 (1977)	200 (1978) [2] (except Mediterranean)
Sri Lanka	12 (1977)	200 (1977) [2]
Sudan	12 (1987)	—
Suriname	12 (1978)	200 (1978) [2]
Sweden	12 (1980)	200 (1978)
Syria	35 (1981)	—
Tanzania	12 (1989)	200 (1989) [1]
Thailand	12 (1966)	200 (1980) [2]
Togo	30 (1977)	200 (1977) [2]
Tonga	[3]	—
Trinidad and Tobago	12 (1969)	200 (1986) [2]
Tunisia	12 (1973)	—
Turkey	[7]	12 (1964) 200 (1986) [2] (Black Sea)
Tuvalu	12 (1984)	200 (1984) [2]
USSR	12 (1982)	200 (1984) [2]
United Arab Emirates	3 [4]	[5]
UK	12 (1987)	200 (1977)
USA	12 (1988)	200 (1983) [2]
Uruguay	200 (1969)	—
Vanuatu	12 (1978–82)	200 (1978–82) [2]
Venezuela	12 (1956)	200 (1978) [2]
Vietnam	12 (1977)	200 (1977) [2]
Western Samoa	12 (1971)	200 (1980) [2]
Yemen, People's Dem. Rep. of	12 (1970)	200 (1978) [2]
Yemen, Republic of	12 (1967)	—
Yugoslavia	12 (1979)	—
Zaïre	12 (1974)	—

[1] Limited by agreement by the outer limits of the superjacent waters of the continental shelf or by a median line (1974).
[2] Economic zone.
[3] Territorial limits defined by geographical co-ordinates (173–177° W. and 15–23° 30′ S.) (1887).
[4] Sharjah, 12 miles.
[5] Limits to be defined by agreement, failing which median line to apply (1980).
[6] Outer limits of the superjacent waters of the continental shelf.
[7] 6 Aegean (1964), 12 Black and Mediterranean.

The table above, reproduced from a survey prepared by the FAO of the UN shows: *(a)* the territorial sea limit, and *(b)* jurisdiction over fisheries.

Further Reading

Booth, K., *Law, Force and Diplomacy at Sea*. London, 1985
Buzan, B., *Seabed Politics*. New York, 1976
Janis, M. W., *Sea Power and the Law of the Sea*. Lexington, 1977
Luard, E., *The Control of the Sea-Bed*. London, 1974
Moore, G., *Coastal State Requirements for Foreign Fishing. FAO Legislative Study No. 21*. Rev. 2. Rome, 1985
Sangar, C., *Ordering the Oceans: The Making of the Law of the Sea*. Univ. of Toronto Press, 1987

CHRONOLOGY

1989

April 2 Tunisia. President Ben Ali, sole candidate in presidential elections, re-elected with 99% of votes cast.

5 Poland. Solidarity movement relegalized.

9 Namibia. Ceasefire agreement between Angola, Cuba and Republic of South Africa providing for surrender of arms by SWAPO guerrillas.

USSR. Mass pro-independence demonstrations in Georgian capital of Tbilisi suppressed by security forces.

12 Hungary. Resignation of 11-member politburo, re-election of Károly Grósz as party General Secretary.

13 Zimbabwe. Resignation of 3 ministers implicated in black market dealing.

15 China. Death of Hu Yaobang, former Communist Party General Secretary, inspired pro-democracy demands in Beijing.

25 USSR. Communist Party central committee retired 74 members as part of General Secretary Mikhail Gorbachev's reforming policies.

28 Bangladesh. 1,000 reported dead in tornado.

May 1 Czechoslovakia. Disruption of official May Day rally by opposition and human rights protestors.

4 China. Arrival of estimated 50,000 students in Tiananmen Square, Beijing.

13 China. Students in Tiananmen Square began hunger strike.

16 Lebanon. Assassination of Sheikh Hassan Khaled, Sunni Moslem religious leader.

17 Czechoslovakia. Release of dissident playwright Vaclav Havel.

20 Bulgaria. Ethnic Turkish protests violently suppressed.

China. Declaration of martial law in Beijing.

21 Morocco. Readmission of Egypt to Arab League.

June 1 El Salvador. Alfredo Cristiani sworn in as President.

3 Iran. Death of Ayatollah Khomeini.

4 China. Troops took control of central Beijing by force.

15–18 Europe. Elections to 518-seat European Parliament in 12 EC countries.

18 Poland. Solidarity won all but 1 available seat in new bicameral National Assembly elections.

19 Guinea-Bissau. Unopposed re-election of Gen. João Bernardo Vieira as President.

24 China. Zhao Ziyang dismissed as General Secretary of Chinese Communist Party, replaced by Jiang Zemin.

28 Sri Lanka. Tamil Tigers announced permanent ceasefire.

CHRONOLOGY—*contd.*

1989		
July	8	Argentina. Carlos Saul Menem sworn in as President.
	12	Ireland. Coalition government of Fianna Fáil and Progressive Democrats announced, with Charles Haughey as Prime Minister.
	17	Austria. Formal application for EC membership.
		Vatican. Restoration of full diplomatic relations with Poland.
	27	USSR. Supreme Soviet endorsed transition of Baltic republics to economic autonomy.
	29	Iran. Speaker Hashemi Rafsanjani elected Executive President.
Aug.	8	New Zealand. Geoffrey Palmer, former Deputy Prime Minister, elected Prime Minister.
	15	Republic of South Africa. Resignation of President P. W. Botha; F. W. de Klerk sworn in as acting President.
	20	Yugoslavia. Serbians staged nationalist protest against federal government.
	24	Poland. Formal ending of one-party rule.
Sept.	10	Hungary. Border with Austria opened allowing mass exodus of Germans from the Democratic Republic to West.
	14	Namibia. Sam Nujoma, president of SWAPO, returned after nearly 30 years' exile.
	18	Hungary. Ruling Communist Party and main opposition parties signed accord for new constitution and transition to western-style democracy.
		Sri Lanka. India suspended military operations against separatist Tamil Tigers.
	26	Cambodia. Official withdrawal of Vietnamese troops.
	27	Yugoslavia. Slovene parliament voted in constitutional amendment giving it the right to secede from Yugoslavia.
Oct.	3	German Democratic Republic. Border with Czechoslovakia closed in attempt to halt emigration to West.
		Panama. *Coup* attempt by junior officers put down by troops loyal to Gen. Manuel Noriega.
	8	USSR. Latvian Popular Front approved plan for independent statehood.
	10	Republic of South Africa. Release of Walter Sisulu, former Secretary General of African National Congress, and 7 other prominent political prisoners.
	18	German Democratic Republic. Erich Honecker retired as leader of ruling Communist Party in response to mass emigration and demonstrations; Egon Krenz named successor.
	19	Argentina. Formal cessation of hostilities with UK.
	24	USSR. Supreme Soviet voted to end quota system guaranteeing seats for Communist Party.
	29	Spain. Felipe González Márquez re-elected for third consecutive term.
	31	Turkey. Prime Minister Turgut Özal elected President.

CHRONOLOGY—*contd.*

1989

Nov. 9 German Democratic Republic. Hans Modrow became new chairman of Council of Ministers.

10 German Democratic Republic. Opening of Berlin Wall led to flood of visitors to West Berlin.

13 Liechtenstein. Death of Prince Francis Joseph II.

17 German Democratic Republic. New government under Hans Modrow endorsed by *Volkskammer*.

22 Lebanon. Assassination of President René Mouawad.

26 India. Defeat of Rajiv Gandhi's Congress (I) Party by National Front coalition in general election.

Uruguay. Luis Lacalle Herrera of National Party elected President.

27 Comoros. Assassination of President Ahmed Abdallah Abderemane.

28 Federal Republic of Germany. Chancellor Kohl presented plan for German confederation to *Bundestag*.

Dec. 10 Czechoslovakia. Formation of new federal government with non-communist majority.

12 Hong Kong. Start of involuntary repatriation of Vietnamese boat people.

13 Republic of South Africa. President F. W. de Klerk met imprisoned black nationalist leader Nelson Mandela.

20 Panama. US invasion and installation of Guillermo Endara Gallimany as head of state.

USSR. Lithuanian Communist Party declared its independence of Soviet Union Communist Party.

21 Romania. Deportation order served on Protestant pastor Fr Laszlo Tokes provoked start of revolution.

25 Romania. Fall and execution of President Nicolae Ceauşescu.

29 Czechoslovakia. Playwright Vaclav Havel elected President.

1990

Jan. 12 USSR. Mikhail Gorbachev proposes draft law allowing republics to secede from Soviet Union.

13 Romania. President Ion Iliescu outlaws Communist Party.

19 India. Government assumes direct political control of state of Jammu and Kashmir.

20 USSR. State of emergency in Baku, capital of Soviet Azerbaijan, enforced by troops.

23 Yugoslavia. Extraordinary congress of Communist Party votes to end Party's leading role and in favour of multi-party system.

26 Federal Republic of Germany. Netherlands and Belgium announce plans to withdraw troops.

29 Poland. Communist Party dissolved and reformed as Social Democracy of the Republic of Poland.

31 German Democratic Republic. Prime Minister Hans Modrow outlines proposals for creation of single neutral German state.

CHRONOLOGY—*contd.*

1989

Feb. 2 Republic of South Africa. Ban on African National Congress lifted.

4 Costa Rica. Rafael Angel Calderon of Social Christian Unity Party elected successor to President Oscar Arias.

6 USSR. Central committee of Communist Party approves constitutional amendment formally ending Party's leading role.

9 Hungary. Restoration of diplomatic relations with Vatican.

11 Republic of South Africa. Release of Nelson Mandela after 28 years in jail.

12 Australia. Carmen Lawrence takes office in Western Australia as first woman state premier.

Greece. Withdrawal of 3 main parties ends coalition government of Xenophon Zolotas.

15 Argentina. Restoration of diplomatic ties with UK.

China. Final draft published of proposed Hong Kong constitution under Chinese rule.

25 Pakistan. Prime Minister Benazir Bhutto dismissed Quaim Ali Shah, Chief Minister of Sind province.

26 Nicaragua. National Opposition Union (Uno) led by Violetta Chamorra defeats 10-year-old revolutionary government of President Daniel Ortega in general elections.

27 USSR. Supreme Soviet endorses creation of office of executive president.

March 4 Ciskei. President Lennox Sebe removed from power by bloodless military *coup*.

8 Afghánistán. Opposition leaders form Revolutionary Council in joint war effort against government of President Najib Najibullah.

11 Chile. President Patricio Aylwin assumes office.

Haiti. Resignation of military ruler General Prosper Avril.

USSR. Supreme Council of Lithuania passes unilateral act restoring independence from USSR.

13 Israel. Dismissal of Labour Deputy Prime Minister Shimon Peres leads to fall of Prime Minister Yitzhak Shamir's coalition government.

15 Brazil. Inauguration of President Fernando Collor de Mello.

20 Namibia. Sam Nujoma sworn in as President of new sovereign nation.

25 USSR. Communist Party of Estonia votes for independence from Moscow.

29 Australia. Andrew Peacock concedes defeat in general election and resigns as leader of opposition Liberal Party.

30 Lithuania. Soviet troops occupy government building in capital Vilnius.

31 Falkland Islands. 150-mile exclusion zone lifted by UK.

ADDENDA

ARAB LEAGUE. Headquarters will move from Tunis back to Cairo in Sept. 1990.

NAMIBIA. Joined Commonwealth 21 March 1990.

CHILE. Cabinet March 1990. *Foreign Affairs:* Enrique Silva Cimma. *Agriculture:* Juan Agustin Figueroa. *Interior:* Enrique Krauss. *Justice:* Francisco Cumplido. *Defence:* Patricio Rojas. *Finance:* Alejandro Foxley. *Labour:* Rene Cortázar. *Health:* Jorge Jiménez. *Mining:* Juan Hamilton. *National Planning:* Sergio Molina. *Presidential Secretary:* Edgardo Boeninger. *General Secretary of the Government:* Enrique Correa. *Economy:* Carlos Ominami. *Education:* Ricardo Lagos. *Transportation:* Germán Correa. *National Property:* Luis Alvarado. *Energy:* Jaime Toha. *Public Works:* Carlos Hurtado. *Corporation for Promotion of Production:* Rene Abeliuk. *Housing:* Alberto Etchegaray.

ZIMBABWE. Cabinet announced on 10 April 1990. *President:* Robert Mugabe. *Vice-President:* Simon Muzenda. *Senior Ministers:* Joshua Nkomo (*in President's Office*), Didymus Mutasa (*Political Affairs*), Bernard Chidzero (*Finance, Economic Planning and Development*). *Foreign Affairs:* Nathan Shamuyarira. *Justice and Parliamentary Affairs:* Emmerson Mnangagwa. *Defence:* Richard Hove. *Home Affairs:* Moven Mahachi. *Local Government, Development:* Joseph Msika. *Lands, Agriculture and Rural Resettlement:* Witness Mangwende. *Information, Posts and Telecommunications:* Victoria Chitepo. *Labour, Manpower Planning and Social Welfare:* John Nkomo. *Industry and Commerce:* Kumbirai Kangai. *Energy, Water Resources and Development:* Herbert Ushewokunze. *Mines:* Christian Andersen. *Transport and Supplies:* Dennis Norman. *Health:* Dr Timothy Stamps. *Community and Co-operative Development:* Joyce Mujuru. *Public Construction and Housing:* Enos Chikowore. *Environment and Tourism:* Herbert Murerwa. *Higher Education:* David Karimanzira. *Education and Culture:* Fay Chung. There are 8 Ministers of State.

GREECE. Cabinet Ministers appointed 11 April 1990. *Prime Minister:* Constantine Mitsotakis. *Deputy Prime Ministers:* Athanassios Kanellopoulos, Tzannis Tzannetakis. *Defence:* Ioannis Varvitsiotis. *Foreign Affairs:* Antonis Samaras. *Interior:* Sotiris Kouvelas.

ARGENTINA. *UK Ambassador:* The Hon. Humphrey Mand, CMG.

BRAZIL. *Ambassador to UK:* Paulo-Tarso Flecha de Lima.

PART I

INTERNATIONAL ORGANIZATIONS

THE UNITED NATIONS

The United Nations is an association of states which have pledged themselves, through signing the Charter, to maintain international peace and security and to co-operate in establishing political, economic and social conditions under which this task can be securely achieved. Nothing contained in the Charter authorizes the organization to intervene in matters which are essentially within the domestic jurisdiction of any state.

The United Nations Charter originated from proposals agreed upon at discussions held at Dumbarton Oaks (Washington, D.C.) between the USSR, US and UK from 21 Aug. to 28 Sept., and between US, UK and China from 29 Sept. to 7 Oct. 1944. These proposals were laid before the United Nations Conference on International Organization, held at San Francisco from 25 April to 26 June 1945, and (after amendments had been made to the original proposals) the Charter of the United Nations was signed on 26 June 1945 by the delegates of 50 countries. Ratification of all the signatures had been received by 31 Dec. 1945. (For the complete text of the Charter *see* THE STATESMAN'S YEAR-BOOK, 1946, pp. xxi–xxxii.)

The United Nations formally came into existence on 24 Oct. 1945, with the deposit of the requisite number of ratifications of the Charter with the US Department of State. The official languages of the United Nations are Arabic, Chinese, English, French, Russian and Spanish.

The headquarters of the United Nations is in New York City, USA.

Flag: UN emblem in white centred on a light blue ground.

Membership. Membership is open to all peace-loving states whose admission will be effected by the General Assembly upon recommendation of the Security Council. The table on pp. 7–8 shows the 159 member states of the United Nations.

The Principal Organs of the United Nations are: 1. The General Assembly. 2. The Security Council. 3. The Economic and Social Council. 4. The Trusteeship Council. 5. The International Court of Justice. 6. The Secretariat.

1. **The General Assembly** consists of all the members of the United Nations. Each member has only 1 vote. The General Assembly meets regularly once a year, commencing on the third Tuesday in Sept.; the session normally lasts until mid-December and is resumed for some weeks in the new year if this is required. Special sessions may be convoked by the Secretary-General if requested by the Security Council, by a majority of the members of the United Nations or by 1 member concurred with by the majority of the members. The Assembly also meets in emergency special session. The General Assembly elects its President for each session.

The first regular session was held in London from 10 Jan. to 14 Feb. and in New York from 23 Oct. to 16 Dec. 1946.

Special sessions have been held on Palestine (1947, 1948), Tunisia (1961), Financial Situation of UN (1963), South West Africa, Peace-Keeping, Postponement of Outer Space Conference (1967), Raw Materials and Development (1974), New International Economic Order (1975), Peace-keeping force in the Lebanon, Namibia, Disarmament (1978, 1982), Economic Issues (1980); Emergency Special sessions were held on Suez, Hungary (1956), Lebanon-Jordan-United Arab Republic dispute (1958), Congo (1960), Middle East (1967), Afghánistán, Palestine (1980, resumed 1982), Namibia (1981), Economic Situation in Africa (1986), Namibia (1986) and Third Special Session on Disarmament (1988).

The work of the General Assembly is divided between 7 Main Committees, on which every member state is represented. These are: First committee (disarmament and related international security matters); special political committee; second committee (economic and financial matters); third committee (social, humanitarian and cultural matters); fourth committee (decolonisation matters); fifth committee (administrative and budgetary matters); sixth committee (legal matters).

In addition there is a General Committee charged with the task of co-ordinating the proceedings of the Assembly and its Committees; and a Credentials Committee which verifies the credentials of the delegates. The General Committee consists of 29 members, comprising the President of the General Assembly, its 17 Vice-Presidents and the Chairmen of the 7 Main Committees. The Credentials Committee consists of 9 members, elected at the beginning of each session of the General Assembly. The Assembly has 2 standing committees—an Advisory Committee on Administrative and Budgetary Questions, and a Committee on Contributions. The General Assembly establishes subsidiary and *ad hoc* bodies when necessary to deal with specific matters. These include: Special Committee on Peace-keeping Operations (33 members), Commission on Human Rights (43 members), Committee on the peaceful uses of outer space (53 members), Conciliation Commission for Palestine (3 members), Conference on Disarmament (40 members), International Law Commission (34 members), Scientific Committee on the effects of atomic radiation (20 members), Special Committee on the implementation of the declaration on the granting of independence to colonial countries and peoples (24 members), Special Committee on the policies of Apartheid of the Government of the Republic of South Africa (18 members) and UN Commission on International Trade Law (36 members).

The General Assembly may discuss any matters within the scope of the Charter, and, with the exception of any situation or dispute on the agenda of the Security Council, may make recommendations on any such questions or matters. For decisions on important questions a two-thirds majority is required, on other questions a simple majority of members present and voting. In addition, the Assembly at its fifth session, in 1950, decided that if the Security Council, because of lack of unanimity of the permanent members, fails to exercise its primary responsibility for the maintenance of international peace and security in any case where there appears to be a threat to the peace, breach of the peace or act of aggression, the General Assembly shall consider the matter immediately with a view to making appropriate recommendations to members for collective measures, including in the case of a breach of the peace or act of aggression the use of armed force when necessary, to maintain or restore international peace and security.

The General Assembly receives and considers reports from the other organs of the United Nations, including the Security Council. The Secretary-General makes an annual report to it on the work of the Organization.

2. **The Security Council** consists of 15 members, each of which has 1 vote. There are 5 permanent and 10 non-permanent members elected for a 2-year term by a two-thirds majority of the General Assembly.

Retiring members are not eligible for immediate re-election. Any other member of the United Nations may be invited to participate without vote in the discussion of questions specially affecting its interests.

The Security Council bears the primary responsibility for the maintenance of peace and security. It is also responsible for the functions of the UN in trust territories classed as 'strategic areas'. Decisions on procedural questions are made by an affirmative vote of 9 members. On all other matters the affirmative vote of 9 members must include the concurring votes of all permanent members (in practice, however, an abstention by a permanent member is not considered a veto), subject to the provision that when the Security Council is considering methods for the peaceful settlement of a dispute, parties to the dispute abstain from voting.

For the maintenance of international peace and security the Security Council can, in accordance with special agreements to be concluded, call on armed forces, assistance and facilities of the member states. It is assisted by a Military Staff Committee consisting of the Chiefs of Staff of the permanent members of the Security Council or their representatives.

The Presidency of the Security Council is held for 1 month in rotation by the member states in the English alphabetical order of their names.

The Security Council functions continuously. Its members are permanently represented at the seat of the organization, but it may meet at any place that will best facilitate its work.

The Council has 2 standing committees of Experts and on the Admission of New Members. In addition, from time to time, it establishes *ad hoc* committees and commissions such as the Truce Supervision Organization in Palestine.

Permanent Members: China, France, USSR, UK, USA.

Non-Permanent Members: Cuba, Côte d'Ivoire, Democratic Republic of Yemen, Romania, Zaïre (until 31 Dec. 1991); Canada, Colombia, Ethiopia, Finland, Malaysia (until 31 Dec. 1990).

3. **The Economic and Social Council** is responsible under the General Assembly for carrying out the functions of the United Nations with regard to international economic, social, cultural, educational, health and related matters.

By Nov. 1977, 15 'specialized' inter-governmental agencies working in these fields had been brought into relationship with the United Nations. The Economic and Social Council may also make arrangements for consultation with international non-governmental organizations and, after consultation with the member concerned, with national organizations; by 1983 over 600 non-governmental organizations had been granted consultative status.

The Economic and Social Council consists of 54 Member States elected by a two-thirds majority of the General Assembly. Forty-two are elected each year for an 18-year term. Retiring members are eligible for immediate re-election. Each member has 1 vote. Decisions are made by a majority of the members present and voting.

The Council nominally holds 2 sessions a year, and special sessions may be held if required. The President is elected for 1 year and is eligible for immediate re-election.

The Economic and Social Council has the following commissions:

Regional Economic Commissions: ECE (Economic Commission for Europe. Geneva); ESCAP (Economic and Social Commission for Asia and the Pacific. Bangkok); ECLAC (Economic Commission for Latin America and the Caribbean. Santiago, Chile); ECA (Economic Commission for Africa. Addis Ababa). ESCWA (Economic Commission for Western Asia. Baghdad). These Commissions have been established to enable the nations of the major regions of the world to co-operate on common problems and also to produce economic information.

Six functional commissions, including: (1) a Statistical Commission with sub-commission on Statistical Sampling. (2) Commission on Human Rights; with sub-commission on Prevention of Discrimination and Protection of Minorities; (3) Social Development Commission; (4) Commission on the Status of Women; (5) Commission on Narcotic Drugs; (6) Population Commission.

The Economic and Social Council has the following standing committees: The Economic Committee, Social Committee, Co-ordination Committee, Committee on Non-Governmental Organizations, Interim Committee on Programme of Conferences, Committee for Industrial Development, Advisory Committee on the Application of Science and Technology to Development, Committee on Housing, Building and Planning.

Other special bodies are the International Narcotics Control Board, the Interim Co-ordinating Committee for International Commodity Arrangements and the Administrative Committee on Co-ordination to ensure (1) the most effective implementation of the agreements entered into between the United Nations and the specialized agencies and (2) co-ordination of activities.

Membership: Belize, Bolivia, Bulgaria, Canada, China, Denmark, Iran, Norway, Oman, Poland, Rwanda, Somalia, Sri Lanka, Sudan, USSR, United Kingdom, Uruguay, Zaïre (until 31 Dec. 1989). Colombia, Cuba, France, Federal Republic of Germany, Ghana, Greece, Guinea, India, Ireland, Japan, Lesotho, Liberia, Libya, Portugal, Saudi Arabia, Trinidad and Tobago, Venezuela, Yugoslavia (until 31 Dec.

1990); Bahamas, Brazil, Cameroon, Czechoslovakia, Indonesia, Iraq, Italy, Jordan, Kenya, Netherlands, New Zealand, Nicaragua, Niger, Thailand, Tunisia, Ukraine, USA, Zambia (until 31 Dec. 1991).

4. **The Trusteeship Council.** The Charter provides for an international trusteeship system to safeguard the interests of the inhabitants of territories which are not yet fully self-governing and which may be placed thereunder by individual trusteeship agreements. These are called trust territories.

All of the original 11 trust territories except one, the Pacific Islands (Micronesia), administered by the USA, have become independent or joined independent countries. The Trusteeship Council consists of the 1 member administering trust territories: USA; the permanent members of the Security Council that are not administering trust territories: China, France, USSR and UK. Decisions of the Council are made by a majority of the members present and voting, each member having 1 vote. The Council holds one regular session each year, and special sessions if required.

5. **The International Court of Justice** was created by an international treaty, the Statute of the Court, which forms an integral part of the United Nations Charter. All members of the United Nations are *ipso facto* parties to the Statute of the Court.

The Court is composed of independent judges, elected regardless of their nationality, who possess the qualifications required in their countries for appointment to the highest judicial offices, or are jurisconsults of recognized competence in international law. There are 15 judges, no 2 of whom may be nationals of the same state. They are elected by the Security Council and the General Assembly of the United Nations sitting independently. Candidates are chosen from a list of persons nominated by the national groups in the Permanent Court of Arbitration established by the Hague Conventions of 1899 and 1907. In the case of members of the United Nations not represented in the Permanent Court of Arbitration, candidates are nominated by national groups appointed for the purpose by their governments. The judges are elected for a 9-year term and are eligible for immediate re-election. When engaged on business of the Court, they enjoy diplomatic privileges and immunities.

The Court elects its own President and Vice-President for 3 years and remains permanently in session, except for judicial vacations. The full court of 15 judges normally sits, but a quorum of 9 judges is sufficient to constitute the Court. It may form chambers of 3 or more judges for dealing with a particular case or particular categories of cases. José Maria Ruda (Argentina) and Kéba Mbaye (Senegal) are, respectively, President and Vice-President of the Court until 1991.

Competence and Jurisdiction. Only states may be parties in cases before the Court, which is open to the states parties to its Statute. The conditions under which the Court will be open to other states are laid down by the Security Council. The Court exercises its jurisdiction in all cases which the parties refer to it and in all matters provided for in the Charter, or in treaties and conventions in force. Disputes concerning the jurisdiction of the Court are settled by the Court's own decision.

The Court may apply in its decision: *(a)* international conventions; *(b)* international custom; *(c)* the general principles of law recognized by civilized nations; and *(d)* as subsidiary means for the determination of the rules of law, judicial decisions and the teachings of highly qualified publicists. If the parties agree, the Court may decide a case *ex aequo et bono*. The Court may also give advisory opinions on legal questions to the General Assembly, the Security Council, certain other organs of the UN and a number of international organizations.

Procedure. The official languages of the Court are French and English. All questions are decided by a majority of the judges present. If the votes are equal, the President has a casting vote. The judgment is final and without appeal, but a revision may be applied for within 10 years from the date of the judgment on the ground of a new decisive factor. No court fees are paid by parties to the Statute.

Judges. The judges of the Court, elected by the Security Council and the General Assembly, are as follows: (1) To serve until 5 Feb. 1991: Raghunandan Swarup Pathak (India), José Maria Ruda (Argentina), Sir Robert Jennings (UK), Gilbert

Guillaume (France), Kéba Mbaye (Senegal). (2) To serve until 5 Feb. 1994: Taslim Olawale Elias (Nigeria), Manfred Lachs (Poland), Jens Evensen (Norway), Shigeru Oda (Japan), Ni Zhengyu (China). (3) To serve until 5 Feb. 1997: Roberto Ago (Italy), Mohamed Shahabuddeen (Guyana), Stephen Schwebel (USA), Mohammed Bedjaoui (Algeria), Nikolaï K. Tarasov (USSR).

If there is no judge on the bench of the nationality of a party to a case, that party has the right to choose a person to sit as judge for that case. Such judges take part in the decision on terms of complete equality with their colleagues.

The Court has its seat at The Hague, but may sit elsewhere whenever it considers this desirable. The expenses of the Court are borne by the UN.

Registrar: Eduardo Valencia-Ospina (Colombia).

6. **The Secretariat** is composed of the Secretary-General, who is the chief administrative officer of the organization, and an international staff appointed by him under regulations established by the General Assembly. However, the Secretary-General, the High Commissioner for Refugees and the Managing Director of the Fund are appointed by the General Assembly. The first Secretary-General was Trygve Lie (Norway), 1946–53; the second, Dag Hammarskjöld (Sweden), 1953–61; the third, U. Thant (Burma), 1961–71; the fourth, Kurt Waldheim (Austria), 1972–81.

The Secretary-General acts as chief administrative officer in all meetings of the General Assembly, the Security Council, the Economic and Social Council and the Trusteeship Council.

The financial year coincides with the calendar year; accountancy is in US$. Budget for 1988–89, $1,400m.

Secretary-General: Javier Perez de Cuellar (Peru), re-appointed 1 Jan. 1986 for a 5-year term.

The Secretary-General is assisted by Under-Secretaries-General and Assistant Secretaries-General.

MEMBER STATES OF THE UN

(as in 1989 with percentage scale of contribution)

Afghánistán	0·01	1946
Albania	0·01	1955
Algeria	0·14	1962
Angola	0·01	1976
Antigua and Barbuda	0·01	1981
Argentina [1]	0·62	1945
Australia [1]	1·66	1945
Austria	0·74	1955
Bahamas	0·01	1973
Bahrain	0·02	1971
Bangladesh	0·02	1974
Barbados	0·01	1966
Belgium [1]	1·18	1945
Belize	0·01	1981
Benin	0·01	1960
Bhután	0·01	1971
Bolivia [1]	0·01	1945
Botswana	0·01	1966
Brazil [1]	1·40	1945
Brunei Darussalam	0·04	1984
Bulgaria	0·16	1955
Burkina Faso	0·01	1960
Burma	0·01	1948
Burundi	0·01	1962
Byelorussia [1]	0·34	1945
Cambodia	0·01	1955
Cameroon	0·01	1960
Canada [1]	3·06	1945
Cape Verde	0·01	1975
Central African Rep.	0·01	1960
Chad	0·01	1960
Chile [1]	0·07	1945
China [1]	0·79	1945
Colombia [1]	0·13	1945
Comoros	0·01	1975
Congo	0·01	1960
Costa Rica [1]	0·02	1945
Côte d'Ivoire	0·02	1960
Cuba [1]	0·09	1945
Cyprus	0·02	1960
Czechoslovakia [1]	0·70	1945
Denmark [1]	0·72	1945
Djibouti	0·01	1977
Dominica	0·01	1978
Dominican Republic [1]	0·03	1945
Ecuador [1]	0·03	1945
Egypt [1]	0·07	1945
El Salvador [1]	0·01	1945

Equatorial Guinea	0·01	1968
Ethiopia [1]	0·01	1945
Fiji	0·01	1970
Finland	0·50	1955
France [1]	6·37	1945
Gabon	0·03	1960
Gambia	0·01	1965
German Democratic Rep.	1·33	1973
Germany, Federal Rep. of	8·26	1973
Ghana	0·01	1957
Greece [1]	0·44	1945
Grenada	0·01	1974
Guatemala [1]	0·02	1945
Guinea	0·01	1958
Guinea-Bissau	0·01	1974
Guyana	0·01	1966
Haiti [1]	0·01	1945
Honduras [1]	0·01	1945
Hungary	0·22	1955
Iceland	0·03	1946
India [1]	0·35	1945
Indonesia	0·14	1950
Iran [1]	0·63	1945
Iraq [1]	0·12	1945
Ireland	0·18	1955
Israel	0·22	1949
Italy	3·79	1955
Jamaica	0·02	1962
Japan	10·84	1956
Jordan	0·01	1955
Kenya	0·01	1963
Kuwait	0·29	1963
Laos People's Dem. Rep.	0·01	1955
Lebanon [1]	0·01	1945
Lesotho	0·01	1966
Liberia [1]	0·01	1945
Libyan Arab Jamahiriya	0·26	1955
Luxembourg [1]	0·05	1945
Madagascar	0·01	1960
Malawi	0·01	1964
Malaysia	0·10	1957
Maldives	0·01	1965
Mali	0·01	1960
Malta	0·01	1964
Mauritania	0·01	1961
Mauritius	0·01	1968
Mexico [1]	0·89	1945
Mongolia	0·01	1961
Morocco	0·05	1956
Mozambique	0·01	1975
Nepál	0·01	1955
Netherlands [1]	1·74	1945
New Zealand [1]	0·24	1945
Nicaragua [1]	0·01	1945
Niger	0·01	1960
Nigeria	0·19	1960
Norway [1]	0·54	1945

Oman	0·02	1971
Pakistan	0·06	1947
Panama [1]	0·02	1945
Papua New Guinea	0·01	1975
Paraguay [1]	0·02	1945
Peru [1]	0·07	1945
Philippines [1]	0·10	1945
Poland [1]	0·64	1945
Portugal	0·18	1955
Qatar	0·04	1971
Romania	0·19	1955
Rwanda	0·01	1962
St Christopher and Nevis	0·01	1983
St Lucia	0·01	1979
St Vincent and the Grenadines	0·01	1980
Samoa, Western	0·01	1976
São Tomé and Principe	0·01	1975
Saudi Arabia [1]	0·97	1945
Senegal	0·01	1960
Seychelles	0·01	1976
Sierra Leone	0·01	1961
Singapore	0·10	1965
Solomon Islands	0·01	1978
Somalia	0·01	1960
South Africa [1]	0·44	1945
Spain	2·03	1955
Sri Lanka	0·01	1955
Sudan	0·01	1956
Suriname	0·01	1975
Swaziland	0·01	1968
Sweden	1·25	1946
Syrian Arab Rep. [1]	0·04	1945
Tanzania	0·01	1961
Thailand	0·09	1946
Togo	0·01	1960
Trinidad and Tobago	0·04	1962
Tunisia	0·03	1956
Turkey [1]	0·34	1945
Uganda	0·01	1962
Ukrainian Soviet Socialist Rep. [1]	1·28	1945
USSR [1]	10·20	1945
United Arab Emirates	0·18	1971
UK [1]	4·86	1945
USA [1]	25·00	1945
Uruguay [1]	0·04	1945
Vanuatu	0·01	1981
Venezuela [1]	0·60	1945
Vietnam	0·01	1977
Yemen Arab Republic	0·01	1947
Yemen, P.D.R.	0·01	1967
Yugoslavia [1]	0·46	1945
Zaïre	0·01	1960
Zambia	0·01	1964
Zimbabwe	0·02	1980

[1] Original member.

Further Reading

Yearbook of the United Nations. New York, 1947 ff. Annual
United Nations Chronicle. Quarterly
Monthly Bulletin of Statistics
General Assembly: Official-Records: Resolutions
Reports of the Secretary-General of the United Nations on the Work of the Organization. 1946 ff.

Documents of the United Nations Conference on International Organization, San Francisco, 1945. 16 vols.
Charter of the United Nations and Statute of the International Court of Justice. Text in English, French, Chinese, Russian and Spanish.
Repertory of Practice of UN's Organs. 5 vols. New York, 1955
Official Records of the Security Council, the Economic and Social Council, Trusteeship Council and the Disarmament Commission
Demographic Yearbook, 1948 ff. New York, 1969
Everyone's United Nations. New York. 10th ed., 1986
Statistical Yearbook. New York, 1947 ff.
United Nations Handbook 1987. New Zealand Ministry of Foreign Affairs, Wellington, 1987
Yearbook of International Statistics. New York, 1950 ff.
World Economic Survey. New York, 1947 ff.
Economic Survey of Asia and the Far East. New York, 1946 ff.
Economic Survey of Latin America. New York, 1948 ff.
Economic Survey of Europe. New York, 1948 ff.
Economic Survey of Africa. New York, 1960 ff.
Foote, W., *Dag Hammarskjöld—Servant of Peace*. London, 1962
Forsythe, D., *United Nations Peacemaking: The Conciliation Commission for Palestine*. Johns Hopkins Univ. Press, 1973
Humana, C., *World Human Rights Guide*. 2nd ed. London, 1986
Lie, T., *In the Cause of Peace*. London, 1954
Luard, E., *A History of the United Nations*. Vol. 1. London, 1982
Osmanczyk, E., *Encyclopaedia of the United Nations*. London, 1985
Peterson, M. J., *The General Assembly in World Politics*. Winchester, Mass, 1986
Thant, U., *Towards World Peace*. New York, 1964
Walters, F. P., *A History of the League of Nations*. 2 vols. London, 1952
Williams, D., *The Specialised Agencies of the United Nations*. London, 1987
Witthauer, K., *Die Bevölkerung der Erde: Verteilung und Dynamik*. Gotha, 1958.—*Distribution and Dynamics Relating to World Population*. Gotha, 1969

United Nations Information Centre. 20 Buckingham Gate, London SW1E 6LB

UNITED NATIONS SYSTEM

The bulk of the work of the UN, measured in terms of money and personnel, is aimed at achieving the pledge made in Article 55 of the Charter to 'promote higher standards of living, full employment and conditions of economic and social progress and development'.

In addition to the 18 independent specialized agencies, there are some 14 major United Nations programmes and funds devoted to achieving economic and social progress in the developing countries.

Total contributions to the funds and programmes of the UN and specialized agencies for development activities amounted to $1,100m. (not including contributions to the World Bank group) in 1987. The highest total contributions in 1989 went to the UN Development Programme (UNDP – $1,200m.) the UN Children's Fund (UNICEF – $290m.) and the UN Fund for Population Activities (UNFPA – $167m.). The World Food Programme, which provides food aid to support development projects and emergency relief operations, provided aid worth $900m. in 1983, making it the largest single source of development assistance in the UN system, apart from the World Bank.

The *United Nations Development Programme* (UNDP) is the world's largest agency for multilateral technical and pre-investment co-operation. It is the funding source for most of the technical assistance provided by the United Nations system, and UNDP is active in 152 countries and territories and in virtually every economic and social sector. UNDP assistance is provided only at the request of Governments and in response to their priority needs, integrated into over-all national and regional plans.

There were (1988) 5,900 UNDP-supported projects currently in operation at the national, regional, inter-regional and global levels, all aimed at helping developing countries make better use of their assets, improve living standards and expand productivity. The volume of such work was $1,200m. in 1988.

UNICEF, established in 1946 to deliver post-war relief to children, now concentrates its assistance on development activities aimed at improving the quality of life for children and mothers in developing countries. During 1983, UNICEF was working in over 110 countries with a child population of some 1,300m., concentrating on basic services for children and maternal health care, nutrition, water supply and sanitation and education. *The State of the World's Children Report*, published annually by UNICEF, has helped to spread acceptance by local and national leaders of a strategy for child health and nutrition which UNICEF estimates could save the lives of 7m. children. UNICEF has focused on popularising four primary health care techniques which are low in cost and produce results in a relatively short time. These include: Oral rehydration therapy to fight the effects of diarrhoeal infections, which kill some 4m. children each year; expanded immunization against the 6 most common childhood diseases; child growth monitoring, and promotion of breast-feeding. The World Health Organization and UNICEF work closely together, providing training, equipment and the services of health care professionals. UNICEF is the world's largest supplier of vaccines and the 'cold chain' equipment needed to deliver them, as well as oral rehydration salts.

Executive Director: James P. Grant (USA).

The UN Population Fund (UNFPA) carries out programmes in over 130 countries and territories. The Fund's aims are to build up capacity to respond to needs in population and family planning; to promote awareness of population problems in both developed and developing countries and possible strategies to deal with them; to assist developing countries at their request in dealing with population problems. More than 25% of international population assistance to developing countries is channeled through UNFPA.

Executive Director: Dr Nafis Sadik (Philippines).

An International Conference on Population was convened by the United Nations in 1984 in Mexico City to review the World Population Plan of Action adopted by the 1974 population conference, and make recommendations for its future implementation.

Humanitarian relief to refugees and victims of natural and man-made disasters is also an important function of the UN system. Among the organizations involved in such relief activities are the Office of the UN Disaster Relief Co-ordinator (UNDRO), the Office of the UN High Commissioner for Refugees (UNHCR) and the UN Relief and Works Agency for Palestine Refugees in the Near East (UNRWA).

UNRWA was created by the General Assembly in 1949 as a temporary, non-political agency to provide relief to the nearly 750,000 people who became refugees as a result of the disturbances during and after the creation of the State of Israel in the former British Mandate territory of Palestine. 'Palestine refugees', as defined by UNRWA's mandate, are persons or descendants of persons whose normal residence was Palestine for at least 2 years prior to the 1948 conflict and who, as a result of the conflict, lost their homes and means of livelihood. UNRWA has also been called upon to assist persons displaced as a result of renewed hostilities in the Middle East in 1967. The situation of Palestine refugees in south Lebanon was of special concern to the Agency in 1984 which has carried out an emergency relief programme in that area for Palestine refugees affected in the aftermath of the Israeli invasion of Lebanon in 1982.

Over 2m. refugees are registered with the Agency which provides education, health care, supplementary feeding and relief services. Education and basic health care account for over 80% of the Agency's budget, which is financed by voluntary contributions from Governments. In 1986 its operating budget amounted to $230m., while cash contributions were expected to total only $194m.

Commissioner-General: Giorgio Giacomelli.

The *Office of the United Nations High Commissioner for Refugees* (UNHCR) was established by the UN General Assembly with effect from 1 Jan. 1951, originally for three years. Since 1954, its mandate has been renewed for successive five-year periods.

The work of UNHCR is of a purely humanitarian and non-political character. The main functions of the Office are to provide international protection for refugees and to seek permanent solutions to their problems through voluntary repatriation, local integration into the country of first asylum or resettlement in other countries. UNHCR may also be called upon to provide emergency relief and on-going material assistance where necessary.

UNHCR concerns itself with refugees who have been determined to come within its mandate under the Statute, and with persons in analogous circumstances whom it assists under the terms of the 'good offices' resolutions adopted by the General Assembly.

The High Commissioner is elected by the General Assembly and follows policy directives given by the General Assembly or the Economic and Social Council, mainly through the Geneva-based Executive Committee of the High Commissioner's Programme.

International protection is the primary function of UNHCR. Its main objective is to promote and safeguard the rights and interests of refugees. In so doing UNHCR devotes special attention to promoting a generous policy of asylum on the part of Governments and seeks to improve the status of refugees in their country of residence. It also helps them to cease being refugees through the acquisition of the nationality of their country of residence when voluntary repatriation is not possible. UNHCR pursues its objectives in the field of protection by encouraging the conclusion of intergovernmental legal instruments in favour of refugees, by supervising the implementation of their provisions and by encouraging Governments to adopt legislation and administrative procedures for the benefit of refugees.

UNHCR also provides material assistance to refugees, largely in camps and settlements, and seeks to promote their self-sufficiency leading to the attainment of durable solutions for their plight. Since 1951 UNHCR has assisted and found solutions for an estimated 30 million refugees and displaced persons.

In 1989 a number of major movements occurred in Africa and there were repatriations from the Sudan to Ethiopia and Uganda and of Ethiopians from Somalia and Djibouti. Afghans, estimated at 3m. in Pakistan and 2m. in Iran, remained the largest single refugee population in the world. Resettlement remained the main durable solution for South-East Asian refugees in camps in that region. An international Conference on Indo-Chinese refugees which took place in June 1984 adopted a comprehensive Plan of Action (CPA) which presents a package of inter-related measures covering such aspects of the problem as clandestine departures, regular departure programmes, reception of new arrivals, determination of the status of asylum-seekers and resettlement. The objective is to rechannel, to the extent possible, departures through legal means, while limiting entitlement to resettlement to recogized and *bona fide* refugees and encouraging voluntary return to countries of origin of rejected cases. Voluntary repatriation of 14,000 refugees in Central America (mainly Guatemalans, Nicaraguans and Salvadorans) took place.

In Oct. 1989 the Executive Committee of the High Commissioner's Programme approved a revised financial target of US$389·4m. for UNHCR general programmes in 1989. Projected requirements for 1990 put before the Committee for approval amounted to US$414m.

For its work on behalf of refugees around the world, UNHCR was awarded the Nobel Peace Prize in 1955 and again in 1981.

Headquarters: Palais des Nations, 1211, Geneva 10, Switzerland.
UK Office: 36 Westminster Palace Gardens, London, SW1P 1RR.

High Commissioner: Jean-Pierre Hocké (Swiss).

UN funds and programmes participating in the 1984 pledging conference for development activities:
UN Development Programme; Special Measures Fund for the Least Developed Countries; UN Development Programme Energy Account; UN Capital Development Fund; UN Special Fund for Land-Locked Developing Countries; UN

Revolving Fund for National Resources Exploration; Special Voluntary Fund for the UN Volunteers; UN Financing System for Science and Technology for Development; UN Trust Fund for Sudano-Sahelian Activities; UN Children's Fund; UN Fund for Population Activities; UN Industrial Development Fund; UN Trust Fund for African Development Activities; Voluntary Fund for the UN Decade for Women; UN Trust Fund for the International Research and Training Institute for the Advancement of Women; UN Centre for Human Settlements (Habitat): UN Habitat and Human Settlements Foundation; UN Trust Fund for the Transport and Communications Decade in Africa; Trust Fund for the UN Centre on Transnational Corporations; UN Institute for Training and Research; UN Fund for Drug Abuse Control; UN Trust Fund for Social Defence; UN Development Programme Study Programme; Fund of the UN Environment Programme.

SPECIALIZED AGENCIES OF THE UN

INTERNATIONAL ATOMIC ENERGY AGENCY (IAEA)

Origin. The International Atomic Energy Agency came into existence on 29 July 1957. Its statute had been approved on 26 Oct. 1956, at an international conference held at UN Headquarters, New York. A relationship agreement links it with the United Nations. The IAEA had 113 member states in 1986.

Functions. (1) To accelerate and enlarge the contribution of atomic energy to peace, health and prosperity throughout the world, and (2) to ensure that assistance provided by it or at its request or under its supervision or control is not used in such a way as to further any military purpose. In addition, under the terms of the Non-Proliferation Treaty, to verify states' obligation to prevent diversion of nuclear energy from peaceful uses to nuclear weapons or other nuclear explosive devices.

The IAEA gives advice and technical assistance to developing countries on nuclear power development, on nuclear safety, on radioactive waste management, on legal aspects of the use of atomic energy, and on prospecting for and exploiting nuclear raw materials; in addition it promotes the use of radiation and isotopes in agriculture, industry, medicine and hydrology through expert services, training courses and fellowships, grants of equipment and supplies, research contracts, scientific meetings and publications. During 1987, a total of 962 projects were operational and 64 training courses were held. These activities involved 1,808 expert assignments while 1,975 persons received training abroad. The IAEA has research laboratories in Austria and Monaco. At Trieste, the International Centre for Theoretical Physics was established in 1964 which is now operated jointly by UNESCO and IAEA.

In Dec. 1987, a total of 166 safeguards agreements were in force with 97 states. Safeguards are the technical means applied by the IAEA to verify that nuclear equipment or materials are used exclusively for peaceful purposes. IAEA safeguards cover more than 95% of the civilian nuclear installations outside the 5 nuclear-weapon states (China, France, UK, USA and USSR). All nuclear-weapon states have opened all (UK, USA) or some (China, France, USSR) of their civilian nuclear plants to IAEA safeguards inspection. Installations in non-nuclear weapon states under safeguards or containing safeguarded material at 31 Dec. 1987 were 185 power reactors, 172 research reactors and critical assemblies, 7 conversion plants, 40 fuel fabrication plants, 6 reprocessing plants, 6 enrichment plants, and 406 other installations.

Organization. The Statute provides for an annual General Conference, a Board of Governors of 35 members and a Secretariat headed by a Director-General.

Headquarters: Vienna International Centre, PO Box 100, A-1400 Vienna, Austria.

Director-General: Hans Blix (Sweden).

INTERNATIONAL LABOUR ORGANISATION (ILO)

Origin. The ILO, established in 1919 as an autonomous part of the League of Nations, is an intergovernmental agency with a tripartite structure, in which representatives of governments, employers and workers participate. It seeks through international action to improve labour conditions, raise living standards and promote productive employment. In 1946 the ILO was recognized by the United Nations as a specialized agency. In 1969 it was awarded the Nobel Peace Prize. In 1989 it numbered 150 members.

Functions. One of the ILO's principal functions is the formulation of international standards in the form of International Labour Conventions and Recommendations. Member countries are required to submit Conventions to their competent national authorities with a view to ratification. If a country ratifies a Convention it agrees to bring its laws into line with its terms and to report periodically how these regulations are being applied. More than 5,400 ratifications of 169 Conventions had been deposited by mid-1989. Machinery is available to ascertain whether Conventions thus ratified are effectively applied.

Recommendations do not require ratification, but member states are obliged to consider them with a view to giving effect to their provisions by legislation or other action. By the end of 1989 the International Labour Conference had adopted 176 recommendations.

Organization. The ILO consists of the International Labour Conference, the Governing Body and the International Labour Office.

The Conference is the supreme deliberative organ of the ILO; it meets annually at Geneva. National delegations are composed of 2 government delegates, 1 employers' delegate and 1 workers' delegate.

The Governing Body, elected by the Conference, is the executive council. It is composed of 28 government members, 14 workers' members and 14 employers' members.

Ten governments hold permanent seats on the Governing Body because of their industrial importance, namely, Brazil, China, Federal Republic of Germany, France, India, Italy, Japan, USA, USSR and UK. The remaining 18 government seats were, at the end of 1989, held by Algeria, Angola, Argentina, Burkina Faso, Canada, Ethiopia, Finland, Ghana, Hungary, Indonesia, Iraq, Jamaica, Mongolia, Nicaragua, Pakistan, Ukraine, Venezuela, Zimbabwe.

The Office serves as secretariat, operational headquarters, research centre and publishing house.

The ILO budget for 1990–91 amounted to US$330m.

Activities. In addition to its research and advisory activities, the ILO extends technical co-operation to governments under its regular budget and under the UN Development Programme and Funds-in-Trust in the fields of employment promotion, human resources development (including vocational and management training), development of social institutions, small-scale industries, rural development, social security, industrial safety and hygiene, productivity, etc. Technical co-operation also includes expert missions and a fellowship programme. Over $125m. was spent on technical co-operation in 1988. Projects were in progress in some 115 countries and about 900 experts involved.

Major emphasis is being given to the ILO's World Employment Programme, launched in 1969 with the purpose of stimulating national and international efforts to increase the volume of productive employment, and so to counter the problem of rising unemployment in developing countries. A World Employment Conference in 1976 linked employment generation to the satisfaction of over-all basic human needs. Employment strategy missions have provided policy guidance to numerous developing countries while practical assistance continues through regional teams of specialists in Africa, Asia and Latin America, backed by an intensive programme of world-wide research. The Programme is currently focusing on instructional efforts—in which the major financial institutions are involved—to mitigate the social consequences of economic structural adjustment.

The International Labour Conference (Geneva, June 1989) adopted a Convention concerning indigenous and tribal peoples in independent countries, and began the two-year process of setting new standards relating to safety in the use of chemicals at work, and night work.

In 1960 the ILO established in Geneva the International Institute for Labour Studies. The Institute specializes in advanced education and research on social and labour policy. It brings together for group study experienced persons from all parts of the world—government administrators, trade-union officials, industrial experts, management, university and other specialists.

A training institution was opened by the ILO in Turin, Italy, in 1965—the International Centre for Advanced Technical and Vocational Training. The Centre provides opportunities for technical, vocational and management training for individuals who have advanced beyond the facilities available in their own countries. Courses are geared particularly to the needs of developing countries.

Headquarters: International Labour Office, CH-1211 Geneva 22, Switzerland.
Director-General: Michel Hansenne (Belgium).
Chairman of the Governing Body: Douglas G. Poulter (Australia).
London Branch Office: 96/98 Marsham St., SW1P 4LY.

The ILO has regional offices in Abidjan (for Africa), Bangkok (for Asia and the Pacific), Lima (for Latin America and the Caribbean) and Geneva (for Arab States).

Further Reading

Publications: Regular periodicals in English, French and Spanish include the *International Labour Review, Legislative Series, Bulletin of Labour Statistics, Year Book of Labour Statistics, Official Bulletin* and *Labour Education. Women at Work* and the *Social and Labour Bulletin* are issued in English and French.

New volumes published in 1989 included: *Consumer Price Indices: An ILO Manual; Current Approaches to Collective Bargaining; From Pyramid to Pillar; Population Change and Social Security in Europe; International Migration in Africa: Legal and Administrative Aspects; Labour Relations in the Public Service: Developing Countries; Major Hazard Control: A Practical Manual; Market Liberalisation, Equity and Development; Training for Work in the Informal Sector; Urban Poverty and the Labour Market: Access to Jobs and Incomes in Asian and Latin American Cities; World Labour Report*, Vol. 4.

FOOD AND AGRICULTURE ORGANIZATION OF THE UNITED NATIONS (FAO)

Origin. The UN Conference on Food and Agriculture in May 1943, at Hot Springs, Virginia, set up an Interim Commission in Washington in July 1943 to plan the Organization, which came into being on 16 Oct. 1945.

Aims and Activities. The aims of FAO are to raise levels of nutrition and standards of living; to improve the production and distribution of all food and agricultural products from farms, forests and fisheries; to improve the living conditions of rural populations; and, by these means, to eliminate hunger.

In carrying out these aims, FAO promotes investment in agriculture, better soil and water management, improved yields of crops and livestock, and the transfer of technology to, and the development of agricultural research in, developing countries. FAO promotes the conservation of natural resources and the rational use of fertilizers and pesticides. The Organization combats animal diseases, promotes the development of marine and inland fisheries, and encourages the rational use of forest resources. Technical assistance is provided in all these fields and others such as nutrition, agricultural engineering, agrarian reform, development communications, remote sensing for natural resources, and the prevention of food losses.

Special FAO programmes help countries prepare for, and provide relief in the event of, emergency food situations, in particular through the setting up of food reserves. Since the early 1980s, Africa has needed special emphasis and FAO created a special task force for that continent. The Agricultural Rehabilitation Plan for Africa, begun in 1985, channelled some US$287m. to projects in 25 countries during its two years of operation. The Global Information and Early Warning System provides current information on the world food situation and identifies countries threatened by shortages to guide potential donors.

The Organization also has a major rôle in the collection, analysis and dissemination of information on natural resources and agricultural production.

FAO sponsors the World Food Programme (WFP) with the UN; WFP uses food commodities, cash and services contributed by member States of the UN to back programmes of social and economic development, as well as for relief in emergency situations.

Finance and Administration. The FAO Conference, composed of all member states, meets every other year to determine the policy and approve the budget and work programme of FAO. The Council, consisting of 49 member nations elected by the Conference, serves as FAO's governing body between Sessions of the Conference. At its 25th Session in Nov. 1989, the Conference approved a total working budget for the 1990-91 biennium, of US$568·8m. However outstanding contributions by member nations totalled US$175m., of which US$142m. were owed by the Organization's largest contributor, the United States. The working budget of FAO's Regular Programme, financed by contributions from member governments, covers the cost of the Organization's secretariat, its Technical Cooperation Programme (TCP) and part of the costs of several special programmes.

The technical assistance programme, however, is funded from extra-budgetary sources. The single largest contributor is the United Nations Development Programme (UNDP), which in 1989 accounted for US$130·6m., or 48·5% of field project expenditures. Equally important are the trust funds that come mainly from donor countries and international financing institutions, totalling US$120m., or 44·6% of technical assistance funds. FAO's contribution under its TCP was some US$18·6m., or 6·9%. FAO's total field programme expenditure for 1989 was an estimated US$363m., slightly more than the US$341m. spent in 1988. An estimated 50% of the expenditure was in Africa, 24% in Asia and the Pacific, 13% in the Near East, 8% in Latin America and the Caribbean, 1% in Europe, and 4% on interregional or global projects.

Headquarters: Via delle Terme di Caracalla, 00100 Rome, Italy.
Director-General: Dr Edouard Saouma (Lebanon).

Further Reading

FAO publications include: FAO Books in Print 1980–81: The State of Food and Agriculture (annual), 1947 ff.; *Animal Health Yearbook* (annual), 1957 ff.; *Production Yearbook* (annual), 1947 ff.; *Trade Yearbook* (annual), 1947 ff.; *FAO Commodity Review* (annual), 1961 ff.; *Yearbook of Forest Products Statistics* (annual), 1947 ff.; *Yearbook of Fishery Statistics* (in two volumes). *FAO Fertilizer Yearbook, FAO Plant Protection Bulletin* (quarterly).

UNITED NATIONS EDUCATIONAL, SCIENTIFIC AND CULTURAL ORGANIZATION (UNESCO)

Origin. A Conference for the establishment of an Educational, Scientific and Cultural Organization of the United Nations was convened by the Government of the UK in association with the Government of France, and met in London, 1–16 Nov. 1945. UNESCO came into being on 4 Nov. 1946.

Functions. The purpose of UNESCO is to contribute to peace and security by promoting collaboration among the nations through education, science and culture in order to further universal respect for justice, for the rule of law and for the human rights and fundamental freedoms which are affirmed for the peoples of the world, without distinction of race, sex, language or religion, by the Charter of the United Nations.

Activities. The education programme has four main objectives: The extension of education; the improvement of education; and life-long education for living in a world community.

To train teachers specialized in the techniques of fundamental education UNESCO is helping to establish regional and national training centres. A centre for Latin America was opened in Mexico in 1951, one for the Arab States was set up in

Egypt in 1953. UNESCO seeks to promote the progressive application of the right to free and compulsory education for all and to improve the quality of education everywhere.

In the natural sciences, UNESCO seeks to promote international scientific co-operation, such as the International Hydrological Programme which began in 1966. It encourages scientific research designed to improve the living conditions of mankind. Science co-operation offices have been set up in Montevideo, Cairo, New Delhi, Nairobi and Jakarta.

In the field of communication, UNESCO endeavours, by disseminating information, carrying out research and providing advice, to increase the scope and quality of press, film and radio services throughout the world.

In the cultural field, UNESCO assists member states in studying and preserving both the physical and the non-physical heritage of each society.

In the social sciences UNESCO helps in the development of research and teaching facilities and focuses on questions concerning Peace, Human Rights, Philosophy, Youth and Development Studies.

Organization. The organs of UNESCO are a General Conference (composed of representatives from each member state), an Executive Board (consisting of 51 government representatives elected by the General Conference) and a Secretariat. UNESCO had 158 members in 1988.

National commissions act as liaison groups between UNESCO and the educational, scientific and cultural life of their own countries.

Budget for 1988–89: $350,386,000.

Headquarters: UNESCO House, 7 Place de Fontenoy, Paris.
Director-General: Federico Mayor (Spain).

Further Reading

Periodicals. Museum (quarterly, English and French); *International Social Science Journal* (quarterly, English and French); *Impact of Science on Society* (quarterly, English and French); *Unesco Courier* (monthly, English, French and Spanish); *Prospects* (quarterly, English, French and Spanish); *Copyright Bulletin* (twice-yearly, English and French); *Unesco News* (English and French); *Nature and Resources* (quarterly, English, French and Spanish).

Hajnal, P. I., *Guide to UNESCO*. London and New York, 1983

WORLD HEALTH ORGANIZATION (WHO)

Origin. An International Conference, convened by the UN Economic and Social Council, to consider a single health organization resulted in the adoption on 22 July 1946 of the constitution of the World Health Organization. This constitution came into force on 7 April 1948.

Structure. The principal organs of WHO are the World Health Assembly, the Executive Board and the Secretariat. Each of the 166 member states and 1 Associate Member (1986) has the right to be represented at the Assembly, which meets annually usually in Geneva, Switzerland. The 31-member Executive Board is composed of technically qualified health experts designated by as many member states elected by the Assembly. The Secretariat consists of technical and administrative staff headed by a Director-General. Health activities in member countries are carried out through regional organizations which have been established in Africa (regional office, Brazzaville), South-East Asia (New Delhi), Europe (Copenhagen), Eastern Mediterranean (Alexandria) and Western Pacific (Manila). The Pan American Sanitary Bureau in Washington serves as the Regional Office of WHO for the Americas.

Functions. WHO's objective, as stated in the first article of the Constitution is 'the attainment by all peoples of the highest possible level of health'. As the directing and co-ordinating authority on international health it establishes and maintains collaboration with the UN, specialized agencies, government health administrations, professional and other groups concerned with health. The Constitution also directs

WHO to assist governments to strengthen their health services, to stimulate and advance work to eradicate diseases, to promote maternal and child health, mental health, medical research and the prevention of accidents; to improve standards of teaching and training in the health professions, and of nutrition, housing, sanitation, working conditions and other aspects of environment health. The Organization also is empowered to propose conventions, agreements and regulations and make recommendations about international health matters; to revise the international nomenclature of diseases, causes of death and public health practices; to develop, establish and promote international standards concerning foods, biological, pharmaceutical and similar substances.

Methods of work. Co-operation in country projects is undertaken only on the request of the government concerned, through the 6 regional offices of the Organization. Worldwide technical services are made available by headquarters. Expert committees whose members are chosen from the 54 advisory panels of experts meet to advise the Director-General on a given subject. Scientific groups and consultative meetings are called for similar purposes. To further the education of health personnel of all categories, seminars, technical conferences and training courses are organized and advisors, consultants and lecturers are provided. WHO awards fellowships for study to nationals of member countries.

Activities. The main thrust of WHO's activities in recent years has been towards promoting national, regional and global strategies for the attainment of the main social target of the Member States for the coming years: 'Health for All by the Year 2000', or the attainment by all citizens of the world of a level of health that will permit them to lead a socially and economically productive life.

Almost all countries indicated a high level of political commitment to this goal, and guiding principles for formulating corresponding strategies and plans of action were prepared.

The 42nd World Health Assembly which met in May 1989 approved a budget of US$653·74m. for 1990-91. Extrabudgetary funds amounting to approximately US$700m. in voluntary contributions are also expected for the biennium. The Assembly called on the international community to increase substantially co-operation particularly with countries in greatest need.

Health for All. 143 out of 166 Member States of WHO submitted reports on the progress of national health for all strategies. Delegates recognized the need to accelerate implementation of Health for All strategies.

The Assembly requested WHO to extend particular assistance to countries burdened by debt and other economic pressures, and to urge governments and non-governmental organizations to promote the role of women with a view to increasing their participation in the health sector and improving their educational and socio-economic status in society.

AIDS. The Assembly acknowledged the fact that non-governmental organizations could make a special impact on society regarding AIDS and the needs of AIDS patients and HIV-infected persons. WHO predicts a sharp rise in the number of people infected with HIV and the number of people with AIDS around the globe by the year 2000.

Tobacco or Health. While tobacco consumption is decreasing in industrialized countries as a result of effective health promotion supported by legislation and regulations, developing countries are registering increases. The Assembly recognized that tobacco use still causes more than 2m. premature deaths each year and that more active efforts must be made to resolve the economic problems involved in the reduction of tobacco production. It requested WHO to support national authorities in taking measures to disseminate information on the health risks of tobacco use, to promote tobacco-free life styles, and to control cigarette advertising.

Polio. A detailed plan to eradicate poliomyelitis before the year 2000 was examined and approved by the Assembly.

Palestine Issue. The Assembly recognized that the application of Palestine for full membership in WHO required further detailed study and requested the Director-General to report the outcome of his studies to the next World Health Assembly in 1990.

Trafficking of Human Organs. The Assembly called upon Member States to take appropriate measures to prevent the purchase and sale of human organs for transplantation.

Guinea Worm Disease. The Assembly declared possible the goal of eliminating dracunculiasis (Guinea Worm Disease) as a public health problem throughout the world during the 1990s.

Salmonellosis. The Assembly urged Member States to intensify their surveillance services in monitoring critical points of production, processing and marketing of animals and animal products with regard to salmonellosis and other zoonotic diseases.

Technical Discussions. The Assembly requested WHO to strengthen its programmes dealing with adolescents and youth and expressed concern at the high rate of unemployment among young people.

World Health Day. World Health Day, 7 April 1989, was devoted to the theme of communication for health. The theme chosen for 1990 is environmental health.

Further Reading

Basic Documents. 37th ed., 1988 (Arabic, Chinese, English, French, Russian, Spanish)
Handbook of Resolutions and Decisions. Vol. I, 1973, Vol. II, 1985 and Vol. III, 1 ed., 1987 (Arabic, English, French, Russian, Spanish)
World Health Forum (from 1980, quarterly: Arabic, Chinese, English, French, Russian and Spanish)
Bulletin of WHO (quarterly, 1947–51; 6 issues a year from 1978; bilingual English/French)
International Digest of Health Legislation (quarterly, from 1948; English and French)
World Health, the Magazine of WHO. 1957 ff. (10 issues a year; English, French, German, Portuguese, Russian and Spanish; and 4 issues a year. Arabic and Persian)
WHO Technical Report Series, 1950 ff. (Arabic, Chinese, English, French, Russian, Spanish)
Public Health Papers, 1959 ff. (Arabic, Chinese, English, French, Russian, Spanish)
World Health Statistics Annual (from 1952; English, French and Russian)
World Health Statistics Quarterly (monthly, 1947–76 then quarterly; bilingual English/ French)
Weekly Epidemiological Record (from 1926; bilingual English/French)
Publications of the WHO, 1947–57; catalogue: 1947–79 (1980); 1980–85 (1985), 1986
World Directories:
Medical Schools, 1987; Schools of Public Health and Postgraduate Training Programmes in Public Health (1985); *Schools for Medical Assistants, 1973* (1976); *Auxiliary Sanitarians 1973* (1978); *Dental Auxiliaries 1973* (1977); *Medical Lab. Technicians and Assistants, 1973* (1977)
The International Pharmacopoeia. 3rd. ed., 3 vols, 1979, 1981, 1987 (English, French and Spanish)
Manual of the International Statistical Classification of Diseases, Injuries and Causes of Death. 9th rev. (1977; English, French, Russian, Spanish)
IARC Monographs on the Evaluation of Carcinogenic Risk of Chemicals to Humans. 1967 *ff.* (English)
International Histological Classification of Tumours. Books and slides, from 1967, No. 25, 1980 (English, French, Russian and Spanish)
Report on the World Health Situation. 1959 ff. (Arabic, Chinese, English, French, Russian, Spanish); Seventh report (1987)
The Work of WHO, 1984–85: Biennial Report of the Director-General (1986) (Arabic, Chinese, English, French, Russian, Spanish)
International Health Regulations (1969). 3rd annotated ed., 1983 (Arabic, English, French, Russian, Spanish)

INTERNATIONAL MONETARY FUND (IMF)

The International Monetary Fund was established on 27 Dec. 1945 as an independent international organization and began operations on 1 March 1947; its relationship with the UN is defined in an agreement of mutual co-operation which came into force on 15 Nov. 1947. The first amendment to the Fund's articles creating the special drawing right (SDR) took effect on 28 July 1969 and the second amendment took effect on 1 April 1978.

The capital resources of the Fund comprise SDRs and currencies that the members pay under quotas calculated for them when they join the Fund. Members' quotas in the Fund, in 1989, amounted to SDR 89,987·6m. and are closely related to (*i*) subscription to the Fund, (*ii*) their drawing rights on the Fund under both regular and special facilities, (*iii*) their voting power, and (*iv*) their share of any allocations of SDRs. Every Fund member is required to subscribe to the Fund an amount equal to its quota. An amount not exceeding 25% of the quota has to be paid in reserve assets, the balance in the member's own currency.

The Fund is authorized under its Articles of Agreement to supplement its resources by borrowing. In Jan. 1962, a 4-year agreement was concluded with 10 industrial members (Belgium, Canada, France, Federal Republic of Germany, Italy, Japan, Netherlands, Sweden, UK, USA) who undertook to lend the Fund up to $6,000m. in their own currencies, if this should be needed to forestall or cope with an impairment of the international monetary system. Switzerland subsequently joined the group. These arrangements, known as the General Arrangements to Borrow (GAB), have been extended several times and the most recent 5-year renewal was to end in Dec. 1993. In early 1983 agreement was reached to increase the credit arrangements under the GAB to SDR 17,000m.; to permit use of GAB resources in transactions with Fund members that are not GAB participants; to authorize Swiss participation; and to permit borrowing arrangements with non-participating members to be associated with the GAB. Saudi Arabia and the Fund have entered into such an arrangement under which the Fund will be able to borrow up to SDR 1,500m. to assist in financing purchases by any member for the same purpose and under the same circumstances as in the GAB. The changes became effective by 26 Dec. 1983. The GAB have been used to finance drawings made by the UK in 1964, 1965, 1968, 1969, and 1977, by France in 1969 and 1970, and by the USA in 1978. The Fund has also borrowed from member countries and official institutions for two oil facilities and a supplementary financing facility. It has borrowed from the Saudi Arabian Monetary Agency (SAMA) and in 1986, concluded a 4-year SDR 3,000m. borrowing arrangement with Japan.

Purposes: To promote international monetary co-operation, the expansion of international trade and exchange rate stability; to assist in the removal of exchange restrictions and the establishment of a multilateral system of payments; and to alleviate any serious disequilibrium in members' international balance of payments by making the financial resources of the Fund available to them, usually subject to conditions to ensure the revolving nature of Fund resources.

Activities. Each member of the Fund undertakes a broad obligation to collaborate with the Fund and other members to ensure the existence of orderly exchange arrangements and to promote a system of stable exchange rates. In addition, members are subject to certain obligations relating to domestic and external policies that can affect the balance of payments and the exchange rate. The Fund makes its resources available, under proper safeguards, to its members to meet short-term or medium-term payments difficulties. The first allocation of special drawing rights was made on 1 Jan. 1970 with five SDR allocations since then. SDRs in existence now total SDR 21,400m. To further enhance its balance of payments assistance to its members the Fund established a compensatory financing facility on 27 Feb. 1963, temporary oil facilities in 1974 and 1975, a trust fund in 1976, and an extended facility for medium-term assistance to members with special balance of payments problems on 13 Sept. 1974 with additional financing now provided through a policy of enlarged access. In March 1986, it established the structural adjustment facility to provide assistance to low-income countries. In Dec. 1987, the Fund established the enhanced structural adjustment facility to provide further assistance to low-income countries facing high levels of indebtedness. In Aug. 1988, the compensatory and contingency financing facility was established, succeeding the compensatory financing facility; the new facility provides broader protection to members pursuing Fund-supported adjustment programmes.

The Committee on Reform of the International Monetary System and Related Issues, generally known as the Committee of Twenty, held its first session at the 1972 annual meeting, with the mandate to advise and report to the Board of Governors on all aspects of the international monetary system, including proposals for any amendments of the Articles of Agreement. The Committee of Twenty disbanded after submitting its final report in 1974. An Interim Committee of the Board of Governors on the International Monetary System and a Joint Ministerial Committee of the Boards of Governors of the World Bank and the Fund on the Transfer of Real Resources to Developing Countries (Development Committee) were established and held their initial meetings in Jan. 1975 and since then have met on a semi-annual basis. Details of the reform of the international monetary system were incorporated in the second amendment of the Fund's Articles of Agreement, effective April 1978. In order to oversee the compliance of members with their obligations under the Articles of Agreement, the Fund is required to exercise firm surveillance over their exchange rate policies.

Organization. The highest authority in the Fund is exercised by the Board of Governors on which each member government is represented. Normally the Governors meet once a year, although the Governors may take votes by mail or other means between annual meetings. The Board of Governors has delegated many of its powers to the executive directors in Washington, of whom there are 22, of which 6 are appointed by individual members and the other 16 elected by groups of countries. Each appointed director has voting power proportionate to the quota of the government he represents, while each elected director casts all the votes of the countries which elected him. The 6 appointed executive directors represent the US, UK, France, Federal Republic of Germany, Japan and Saudi Arabia.

The managing director is selected by the executive directors; he presides as chairman at their meetings, but may not vote except in case of a tie. His term is for 5 years, but may be extended or terminated at the discretion of the executive directors. He is responsible for the ordinary business of the Fund, under general control of the executive directors, and supervises a staff of about 1,700.

Headquarters: 700 19th St. NW, Washington, D.C., 20431. Offices in Paris and Geneva.

Managing Director: Michel Camdessus (France).

Further Reading

Publications. Summary Proceedings of Annual Meetings of the Board of Governors.— Annual Report of the Executive Board.—Selected Decisions of the International Monetary Fund and Selected Documents.—International Financial Statistics (monthly).—*IMF Survey* (bi-weekly).—*Balance of Payments Statistics.* Washington, monthly.—*IMF Staff Papers* (four times a year). Washington, from Feb. 1950.—*IMF Occasional Papers.—IMF Pamphlets.— Annual Report on Exchange Arrangements and Exchange Restrictions.* Washington, 1950 ff.—*Finance and Development.* Washington, from June 1964 (quarterly).—*Direction of Trade Statistics.* Washington (monthly). *IMF World Economic and Financial Surveys.* Washington. *Government Finance Statistics Yearbook. The International Monetary Fund, 1945–65: Twenty Years of International Monetary Co-operation.* 3 vols. Washington D.C. 1969

de Vries, M. G., *The International Monetary Fund, 1966–1971: The System Under Stress.* 2 vols. Washington D.C. 1976.—*The International Monetary Fund 1972–1978: Co-operation on Trial.* 3 vols. Washington D.C., 1985

INTERNATIONAL BANK FOR RECONSTRUCTION AND DEVELOPMENT (IBRD)

Conceived at the Bretton Woods Conference, July 1944, the 'World Bank' began operations in June 1946. Its purpose is to provide funds and technical assistance to facilitate economic development in its porer member countries.

The Bank obtains its funds from the following sources: Capital paid in by member countries; sales of its own securities; sales of parts of its loans; repayments; and net earnings. The subscribed capital of the Bank amounted to $115,668m. at 30 June 1989. On 27 April 1988, the Board of Governors adopted a resolution that increased the authorized capital stock of the Bank by $171,400m. This represented an increase of approximately $40,000m. The resolution provides that the paid-in portion of the shares authorized to be subscribed under it will be 3%. Outstanding medium- and long-term borrowings had reached $79,750m. by 30 June 1989. The Bank is self-supporting. Its net earnings for year ending 30 June 1989 amounted to $1,004m.

By 30 June 1989 the Bank had made 3,055 loans totalling $171,482m. in 103 of its 151 member countries. Lending was for the following purposes: Agriculture and rural development, $34,117m.; Development Finance Companies, $17,675m.; education, $6,052m.; energy, $37,738m.; industry (including tourism), $12,832m.; non-project, $13,334m.; population, health and nutrition, $1,251m.; small-scale enterprizes, $4,476m.; telecommunications, $2,596m.; transportation, $26,235m.; urban development, $7,148m.; water supply and sewerage, $7,698m., and technical assistance, $330m. In order to eliminate wasteful overlapping of development assistance and to ensure that the funds available are used to the best possible effect, the Bank has organized consortia or consultative groups of aidgiving nations for the following countries: Bangladesh, Bolivia, Burma, Colombia, Côte d'Ivoire, Egypt, Ethiopia, Ghana, Guinea, Guinea-Bissau, India, Kenya, Korea, Madagascar, Malaŵi, Mauritania, Mauritius, Morocco, Mozambique, Nepál, Nigeria, Pakistan, Papua New Guinea, Peru, the Philippines, Senegal, Somalia, Sri Lanka, Sudan, Tanzania, Thailand, Togo, Tunisia, Uganda, Zaïre, Zambia and the Caribbean Group for Co-operation in Economic Development. The Bank furnishes a wide variety of technical assistance. It acts as executing agency for a number of pre-investment surveys financed by the UN Development Programme. Resident missions have been established in 40 developing member countries as well as 3 regional missions in East and West Africa and Thailand primarily to assist in the preparation of projects. The Bank helps member countries to identify and prepare projects for the development of agriculture, education and water supply by drawing on the expertise of the FAO, WHO, UNIDO and UNESCO through its co-operative agreements with these organizations. The Bank maintains a staff college, the Economic Development Institute in Washington, D.C., for senior officials of the member countries.

Headquarters: 1818 H St., NW, Washington, D.C., 20433, USA. *European office:* 66 avenue d'Iéna, 75116 Paris, France. *London office:* New Zealand House, Haymarket, SW1Y 4TE, England. *Tokyo office:* Kokusai Building, 1–1, Marunouchi 3-chome, Chiyoda-ku, Tokyo 100, Japan.

President: Barber B. Conable, Jr., (USA).

Further Reading

Publications. Annual Reports. 1946 ff.—*Summary Proceedings of Annual Meetings.* 1947 ff.—*The World Bank & International Finance Company.* 1986.—*The World Bank Atlas.* 1967 ff.—*Catalog of Publications,* 1986 ff.—*World Development Report.* 1978 ff.

Payer, C., *The World Bank: A Critical Analysis.* London, 1982 .

INTERNATIONAL DEVELOPMENT ASSOCIATION (IDA)

A lending agency which came into existence on 24 Sept. 1960. Administered by the World Bank, IDA is open to all members of the Bank.

IDA concentrates its assistance on those countries with an annual *per capita* gross national product of less than $481 (1987 rate). Its resources consist mostly of subscriptions, general replenishments from its more industrialized and developed members, special contributions, and transfers from the net earnings of the Bank. IDA credits are made to Governments only. It had committed $52,700m. for 1,904 development projects in 84 countries, by 30 June 1989.

INTERNATIONAL FINANCE CORPORATION (IFC)

The Corporation, an affiliate of the World Bank, was established in July 1956. Paid-in capital at 30 June 1988 was $850·2m., subscribed by 133 member countries. In addition, it has accumulated earnings of $438·2m. IFC supplements the activities of the World Bank by encouraging the growth of productive private enterprises in less developed member countries. Chiefly, IFC makes investments in the form of subscriptions to the share capital of privately owned companies, or long-term loans, or both. The Corporation will help finance new ventures, and it will also assist established enterprises to expand, improve or diversify their operations.

At 30 June 1988 IFC had approved investments amounting to $10,500m., in over 90 countries.

President: Barber B. Conable, Jr., (USA).
Executive Vice-President: Sir William Ryrie (UK).

Publications. Annual Reports. 1956 ff.—*What IFC Does.* 1988

INTERNATIONAL CIVIL AVIATION ORGANIZATION (ICAO)

Origin. The Convention providing for the establishment of the International Civil Aviation Organization was drawn up by the International Civil Aviation Conference held in Chicago from 1 Nov. to 7 Dec. 1944. A Provisional International Civil Aviation Organization (PICAO) operated for 20 months until the formal establishment of ICAO on 4 April 1947.

The Convention on International Civil Aviation superseded the provisions of the Paris Convention of 1919, which established the International Commission for Air Navigation (ICAN), and the Pan American Convention on Air Navigation drawn up at Havana in 1928.

Functions. It assists international civil aviation by establishing technical standards for safety and efficiency of air navigation and promoting simpler procedures at borders; develops regional plans for ground facilities and services needed for international flying; disseminates air-transport statistics and prepares studies on aviation economics; fosters the development of air law conventions. As part of the UN Development Programme it provides technical assistance to States in developing civil aviation programmes.

Organization. The principal organs of ICAO are an Assembly, consisting of all members of the Organization, and a Council, which is composed of 33 states elected by the Assembly, for 3 years, and meets in virtually continuous session. In electing these states, the Assembly must give adequate representation to: (1) states of major importance in air transport; (2) states which make the largest contribution to the provision of facilities for the international civil air navigation; (3) those states not otherwise included whose election will ensure that all major geographical areas of the world are represented. The main subsidiary bodies are: The Air Navigation Commission, composed of 15 members appointed by the Council; Air Transport Committee, open to council members; and the Legal Committee, on which all members of ICAO may be represented. There are 162 members. Budget for 1989: US$31,640,000.

Headquarters: 1000 Sherbroke St. West, Montreal, Quebec, Canada H3A 2R2.
President: Dr Assad Kotaite (Lebanon).
Secretary-General: Dr Shivinder Singh Sidhu (India).

Annual Report of the Council. (English, French, Russian, Spanish)
ICAO Bulletin (Monthly)

UNIVERSAL POSTAL UNION (UPU)

Origin. The UPU was established on 1 July 1875, when the Universal Postal Convention adopted by the Postal Congress of Berne on 9 Oct. 1874 came into force. The UPU was known at first as the General Postal Union, its name being changed at the Congress of Paris in 1878. In 1989 there were 170 member countries.

Functions. The aim of the UPU is to assure the organization and perfection of the various postal services and to promote, in this field, the development of international collaboration. To this end, the members of UPU are united in a single postal territory for the reciprocal exchange of correspondence.

Organization. The UPU is composed of a Universal Postal Congress which usually meets every 5 years, a permanent Executive Council consisting of 40 members, a consultative Committee, which consists of 35 members elected on a geographical basis by each Congress, and an International Bureau, which functions as the permanent secretariat.

Since 1 July 1948 the Union has been governed by the Constitution of the UPU adopted at the 1964 Vienna Congress.

Budget for 1988: US$14m.

Headquarters: Weltpoststrasse 4, 3000, Berne 15, Switzerland.
Director-General: A. C. Botto de Barros (Brazil).

Further Reading

Publications. Documents of the Constitution of the UPU adopted at the 1964 Vienna Congress—Hamburg Congress 1984.—The Postal Union (monthly, Arabic, Chinese, English, French, German, Spanish, Russian).—*The UPU: Its Foundation and Development.* Bern, 1959.

INTERNATIONAL TELECOMMUNICATION UNION (ITU)

Origin. In 1932, at Madrid, the Union decided to merge the Telegraph Convention adopted in 1865 and the Radiotelegraph Convention adopted in 1906 into a single International Telecommunication Convention within annex, the Telephone, Telegraph and Radio Regulations. It also decided to change its name to International Telecommunication Union to better reflect all its new responsibilities. The ITU has been governed since 1 Jan. 1984 by the International Telecommunication Convention adopted in Nairobi in 1982.

Functions. (1) to maintain and extend international co-operation for the improvement and rational use of telecommunications of all kinds, as well as to promote and to offer technical assistance to developing countries in the field of telecommunications; (2) to promote the development of technical facilities and their most efficient operation with a view to improving the efficiency of telecommunication services, increasing their usefulness and making them, so far as possible, generally available to the public; (3) to harmonize the actions of nations in the attainment of those ends.

Organization. The ITU consists of the Plenipotentiary Conference, Administrative Conferences, the Administrative Council of 43 members, and of 5 permanent organs (the General Secretariat, the International Frequency Registration Board, and 2 international consultative committees, one for radio and one for telephone and telegraph and the Telecommunications Development Bureau).

Budget for 1989: Sw.Frs.132,000,000.

Headquarters: Place des Nations, Geneva, Switzerland.
Secretary-General: Dr Pekka Tarjanne (Finland).

WORLD METEOROLOGICAL ORGANIZATION (WMO)

Origin. A Conference of Directors of the International Meteorological Organization (set up in 1873), meeting in Washington in 1947, adopted a Convention creating the World Meteorological Organization. The WMO Convention became effective on 23 March 1950, and WMO was formally established on 19 March 1951, when the first session of its Congress was convened in Paris. An agreement to bring WMO into relationship with the United Nations was approved by this Congress and came into force on 21 Dec. 1951 with its approval by the General Assembly of the United Nations.

Functions. (1) To facilitate world-wide co-operation in the establishment of networks of stations for the making of meteorological observations as well as hydrological or other geophysical observations related to meteorology, and to promote the establishment and maintenance of meteorological centres charged with the provision of meteorological and related services; (2) to promote the establishment and maintenance of systems for the rapid exchange of meteorological and related information; (3) to promote standardization of meteorological and related observations and to ensure the uniform publication of observations and statistics; (4) to further the application of meteorology to aviation, shipping, water problems, agriculture and other human activities; (5) to promote activities in operational hydrology and to further close co-operation between meteorological and hydrological services; and (6) to encourage research and training in meteorology and, as appropriate, to assist in co-ordinating the international aspects of such research and training.

Organization. WMO is an inter-governmental organization of 155 member states and 5 member territories responsible for the operation of their own meteorological services. Constituent bodies of WMO are the World Meteorological Congress which meets every 4 years, the executive council composed of 36 members elected in their personal capacity and including the President and 3 Vice-Presidents of the Organization, 6 regional associations of members and 8 technical commissions established by the Congress. A permanent secretariat is maintained in Geneva.

Budget for 1988–91: Sw.Frs.170m.

Headquarters: Case postale No. 2300, CH-1211, Geneva 2, Switzerland.
Secretary-General: G. O. P. Obasi (Nigeria).

Publications. WMO Bulletin. 1952 ff.—*Meteorological Services of the World.* 1985. —*Publications of the World Meteorological Organization, 1951–1986.*

INTERNATIONAL MARITIME ORGANIZATION (IMO)

Origin. The International Maritime Organization, until 1982 known as Inter-Governmental Maritime Consultative Organization (IMCO), was established as a specialized agency of the UN by a convention drawn up at the UN Maritime Conference held at Geneva in Feb./March 1948. The Convention became effective on 17 March 1958 when it had been ratified by 21 countries, including 7 with at least 1m. gross tons of shipping each. The International Maritime Organization started operations in Jan. 1959.

Functions. To facilitate co-operation among governments on technical matters affecting merchant shipping, especially concerning safety at sea; to prevent and control marine pollution caused by ships; to facilitate international maritime traffic. The International Maritime Organization is responsible for convening international maritime conferences and for drafting international maritime conventions. It also provides technical assistance to countries wishing to develop their maritime activities.

Organization. The International Maritime Organization had 133 members (and 1 associate member) in 1990. The Assembly, composed of all member states, normally meets every 2 years. The Council of 32 member states acts as governing body between Assembly sessions. The Maritime Safety Committee deals with all technical questions relating to maritime safety. It has established several sub-committees to deal with specific problems and like the Marine Environment Protection Committee, Legal Committee, Facilitation Committee and Committee on Technical Co-operation is open to all International Maritime Organization members. The Secretariat is composed of international civil servants.

The International Maritime Organization is depositary authority for the International Convention for the Safety of Life at Sea, 1960, and the Regulations for Preventing Collisions at Sea, 1948 and 1960; the International Convention for the Prevention of Pollution of the Sea by Oil, 1954, as amended in 1962 and 1969; the Convention on Facilitation of International Maritime Traffic, 1965; the International Convention on Load Lines, 1966; the International Convention on Tonnage Measurement of Ships, 1969; the International Convention relating to Intervention on the High Seas in cases of Oil Pollution Casualties, 1969; the International Convention on Civil Liability for Oil Pollution Damage, 1969; Convention on International Compensation Fund for Oil Pollution Damage, 1971; Special Trade Passenger Ships Agreement, 1971; Convention on International Regulations for Preventing Collisions at Sea, 1972; the International Convention for Safe Containers, 1972; the International Convention on Prevention of Pollution from Ships, 1973 as modified by the Protocol of 1978; the International Convention for the Safety of Life at Sea, 1974; Athens Convention relating to the Carriage of Passengers and their Luggage by Sea, 1974; Convention on the International

Maritime Satellite Organization, 1976; Convention on Limitation of Maritime Claims, 1976; Torremolinos International Convention for the Safety of Fishing Vessels, 1977; International Convention on Standards of Training, Certification and Watchkeeping for Seafarers, 1978; International Convention on Maritime Search and Rescue, 1979; International Convention on Sabotage, 1979; Convention for the Suppression of Unlawful Acts Against the Safety of Maritime Navigation, 1988.

Headquarters: 4 Albert Embankment, London SE1 7SR.
Secretary-General: William O'Neil (Canada).
Assistant Secretary-General: T. A. Mensah (Ghana).

IMO News

GENERAL AGREEMENT ON TARIFFS AND TRADE (GATT)

Origin. The General Agreement on Tariffs and Trade was negotiated in 1947 and entered into force on 1 Jan. 1948. Its 23 original signatories were members of a Preparatory Committee appointed by the UN Economic and Social Council to draft the charter for a proposed International Trade Organization. Since this charter was never ratified, the General Agreement, intended as an interim arrangement, has instead remained as the only international instrument laying down trade rules accepted by countries responsible for nearly 90% of the world's trade. In Oct. 1988 there were 96 contracting parties, with one country acceding provisionally, and a further 28 countries applying GATT rules on a *de facto* basis.

Functions. GATT functions both as a multilateral treaty that lays down a common code of conduct in international trade and trade relations and as a forum for negotiation and consultation to overcome trade problems and reduce trade barriers. Key provisions of the Agreement guarantee most-favoured-nation treatment (exceptions being granted to customs unions and free trade areas, and for certain preferences in favour of developing countries); require that protection be given to domestic industry only through tariffs (apart from specified exceptions); provide for negotiations to reduce tariffs (which are then 'bound' against subsequent increase) and other trade distortions; and lay down principles (particularly in Part IV of the Agreement, added in 1965) to assist the trade of developing countries. The Agreement also provides for consultation on, and settlement of, disputes, for 'waivers' (the grant of authorization, when warranted, to derogate from specific GATT obligations) and for emergency action in defined circumstances.

Seven 'rounds' of multilateral trade negotiations, including the Kennedy Round of 1964–67, have been completed in GATT. The latest in this series, the Tokyo Round, although held in Geneva, was so called because it was launched at a Ministerial meeting in the Japanese capital in Sept. 1973.

Ninety-nine countries participated in the Tokyo Round. In Nov. 1979, the negotiations were concluded with agreements covering: An improved legal framework for the conduct of world trade (which includes recognition of tariff and nontariff treatment in favour of and among developing countries as a permanent legal feature of the world trading system); non-tariff measures (subsidies and countervailing duties; technical barriers to trade; government procurement; customs valuation; import licensing procedures; and a revision of the 1967 GATT anti-dumping code); bovine meat; dairy products; tropical products; and an agreement on free trade in civil aircraft. The agreements contain provisions for special and more favourable treatment for developing countries.

Participating countries also agreed to reduce tariffs on thousands of industrial and agricultural products, for the most part over a period of 7 years ending on 1 Jan. 1987. As a result of these concessions, industrialized countries reduced the average level of their import duties on manufactures by about 34%, a cut comparable to that achieved in the Kennedy Round.

The agreements providing an improved framework for the conduct of world trade took effect in Nov. 1979. The other agreements took effect on 1 Jan. 1980, except for those covering government procurement and customs valuation, which took effect on 1 Jan. 1981, and the concessions on tropical products which began as early as 1977. Committees were established to supervise implementation of each of the Tokyo Round agreements.

On 20 Sept. 1986, agreement was reached to launch the Uruguay Round of multilateral trade negotiations. In Oct. 1989, there were 105 states participating in the negotiations.

The Declaration is divided into two sections. The first covers negotiations on trade in goods. Its objectives are to bring about further liberalization and expansion of world trade; to strengthen the role of GATT and improve the multilateral trading system; to increase the responsiveness of GATT to the evolving international economic environment; and to encourage co-operation in strengthening the interrelationship between trade and other economic policies affecting growth and development.

In the area of trade in goods, Ministers committed themselves to a 'standstill' on new trade measures inconsistent with their GATT obligations and to a 'rollback' programme aimed at phasing out existing inconsistent measures. Negotiations are being undertaken in the following areas: Tariffs, non-tariff measures, tropical products, natural resource-based products, textiles and clothing, agriculture, subsidies, safeguards, trade-related aspects of intellectual property rights, including trade in counterfeit goods, and trade-related investment measures. Participants are reviewing certain GATT Articles, attempting to improve and strengthen the dispute settlement procedure, and negotiating to improve, clarify or expand the agreements reached during the Tokyo Round. One part of the negotiation is devoted to the functioning of the GATT system itself. The second part of the Declaration covers a negotiation on trade in services.

The first three years of the Uruguay Round were marked by intensive activity, both in Geneva, where the negotiations take place, and in the capitals of the participating countries. During this time the groups responsible for the negotiations held around 300 formal meetings and around 1,500 negotiating proposals and working papers were tabled.

In Dec. 1988, ministers met in Montreal for the Mid-term Review meeting of the Trade Negotiations Committee. Agreements on the future conduct of the Round were reached in 11 of the 15 negotiating areas. At the same time, ministers were able to agree a package of concessions on tropical products covering trade worth around US$20,000m.; a series of measures to streamline the disputes settlement system and a new trade policy review mechanism under which the trade policies of individual GATT contracting countries are subject to regular assessment. Each of these was implemented provisionally in 1989. In April 1989, a Trade Negotiations Committee meeting in Geneva succeeded in securing Mid-term agreements on the remaining 4 negotiating areas: Agriculture (covering both short-term commitments and long-term objectives), safeguards, textiles and clothing and intellectual property. In July 1989, the Trade Negotiations Committee agreed that the final meetings of the Round would be held in Dec. 1990, in Brussels.

To assist the trade of developing countries, GATT established in 1964 the International Trade Centre (since 1968 operated jointly with the UN, the latter acting through the UN Conference on Trade and Development) to provide information and training on export markets and marketing techniques. Other GATT action in favour of developing countries includes training courses on trade policy questions, organization of seminars and briefings, and technical assistance to delegations in the form of data and background documentation.

Budget for 1989: Sw. Frs. 64,861,000.

Headquarters: Centre William Rappard, 154 rue de Lausanne, 1211 Geneva 21, Switzerland.

Director-General: Arthur Dunkel (Switzerland).

Further Reading

Publications. Basic Instruments and Selected Documents. 4 vols. and 34 supplements 1952–87.—*International Trade* [i.e., annual review], 1952 ff. Annually from 1953.—*Review of Development in the Trading System.* Semi-annually from 1987.—*GATT, What It Is, What It*

Does.—GATT Activities, 1960 ff. Annually from 1972.—*GATT Focus.* From Feb. 1981 (10 issues a year).—*News of the Uruguay Round.* Monthly from March 1987.—*GATT Studies in International Trade.* 1971 ff. (irregular series).—*The Tokyo Round of Multilateral Trade Negotiations.* Report of the Director-General, 2 vols., 1979.—*Textile and Clothing in the World Economy,* 1984.—*The World Markets for Dairy Products.* Annually from 1981.—*The International Markets for Meat.* Annually from 1981.—*Trade in Natural Resource Products: Aluminium* (1987), *Lead* (1987), *Zinc* (1988).

Casadio, G. P., *Transatlantic Trade: USA–EEC Confrontation in the GATT Negotiations.* Farnborough, 1973

Dam, K. W., *The GATT: Law and International Economic Organization.* Chicago and London, 1970

Golt, S., *The GATT Negotiations, 1973–75: A Guide to the Issues.* London, 1974

Hudec, R. E., *The GATT Legal System and World Trade Diplomacy.* New York, 1975

Long, O., *Law and its Limitations in the GATT Multilateral Trade System.* Dordrecht, 1985

WORLD INTELLECTUAL PROPERTY ORGANIZATION (WIPO)

Origin. The Convention establishing WIPO was signed at Stockholm in 1967 by 51 countries, and entered into force in April 1970. In Dec. 1974 WIPO became a specialized agency of the UN. *Inter alia* it took over the functions of the United International Bureaux for the Protection of Intellectual Property, also known as BIRPI (the French acronym of that name), which were established in 1893 to administer the affairs of the two principal international intellectual property treaties – the Paris Convention for the Protection of Industrial Property of 1883 and the Berne Convention for the Protection of Literary and Artistic Works of 1886.

Functions. WIPO is responsible for the promotion of the protection of intellectual property throughout the world. Intellectual property comprises two main branches: Industrial property (patents and other rights in technological inventions, rights in trademarks, industrial designs, appellations of origin, etc.) and copyright and neighbouring rights (in literary, musical and artistic works, in films and performances of performing artists, phonograms, etc.). WIPO administers various international treaties, of which the most important are the Paris Convention for the Protection of Industrial Property and the Berne Convention for the Protection of Literary and Artistic Works. WIPO carries out a substantial programme of activities to promote creative intellectual activity, protection of intellectual property, international co-operation and the transfer of technology, especially to and among developing countries.

Membership of WIPO is open to any State which is a member of at least one of the Unions created by the Paris Convention and the Berne Convention and to other States which are members of the organizations of the United Nations system, are party to the Statute of the International Court of Justice, or are invited to join by the General Assembly of WIPO. Membership of the Unions is open to any State. The number of member states of WIPO was 126 on 1 Jan. 1990; in addition, 11 States are party to treaties administered by WIPO but have not yet become members of WIPO.

Organization. The bodies of WIPO are: The *General Assembly* consisting of all member states of WIPO which are members of any of the Unions. Among its other functions, the General Assembly appoints and gives instructions to the Director General, reviews and approves his reports and adopts the biennial budget of expenses common to the Unions. The *Conference,* consisting of all States members of WIPO whether or not they are members of any of the Unions. Among its functions, the Conference adopts its biennial budget and establishes the biennial programme of legal-technical assistance. The *Co-ordination Committee,* consisting of the States members of WIPO which are members of the Executive Committees of the Paris or Berne Unions.

In addition, the Paris and Berne Unions have Assemblies and Executive Committees, with functions similar to those of the WIPO bodies in respect of the biennial budgets and programmes of the Unions.

The *WIPO Permanent Committees for Development Co-operation Related to Industrial Property* and *Related to Copyright and Neighbouring Rights* plan and review activities in the said fields; the *WIPO Permanent Committee on Industrial Property Information* is responsible for intergovernmental co-operation in industrial property documentation and information matters such as the standardization and exchange of patent documents.

WIPO has an international staff of 325. The working languages of the Organization are: Arabic, English, French, Russian and Spanish.

Headquarters: 34, chemin des Colombettes, 1211 Geneva 20, Switzerland.
Director-General: Dr Arpad Bogsch (USA).

Further Reading

Periodicals. Industrial Property (monthly, in English and French).—*Copyright* (monthly, in English and French).—*Les Marques internationales* (monthly, in French).—*International Designs Bulletin* (monthly, in English and French)—*Newsletter* (irregular, in Arabic, English, French, Portuguese, Russian and Spanish)—*PCT Gazette* (fortnightly, in English and French)—*Les appellations d'origine* (irregular, in French)—*Intellectual Property in Asia and the Pacific* (quarterly, in English). The Organization also produces a large selection of publications related to intellectual property.

INTERNATIONAL FUND FOR AGRICULTURAL DEVELOPMENT (IFAD)

The establishment of IFAD was one of the major actions proposed by the 1974 World Food Conference. The agreement for IFAD entered into force on 30 Nov. 1977, and the agency began its operations the following month. By the end of 1989 the Fund had invested US$2·2m. in financing 245 projects in 91 developing countries. IFAD's purpose is to mobilise additional funds for agricultural and rural development in developing countries through projects and programmes directly benefiting the poorest rural populations while preserving their natural resource base. In line with the Fund's focus on the rural poor, its resources are being made available mainly in highly concessional loans as well as grants.

Organization. The Governing Council, consisting of the entire membership, directs the Fund's operations. The chief executive is the President, who is also the Chairman of the 18-member Executive Board.

President: Idriss Jazairy (Algeria).
Headquarters: 107 Via del Serafico, Rome, 00142, Italy.

THE COMMONWEALTH

The Commonwealth is a free association of sovereign independent states, numbering 48 at the beginning of 1989. There is no charter, treaty or constitution; the association is expressed in co-operation, consultation and mutual assistance for which the Commonwealth Secretariat is the central co-ordinating body.

The Commonwealth was first defined by the Imperial Conference of 1926 as a group of 'autonomous communities within the British Empire, equal in status, in no way subordinate one to another in any aspect of their domestic or foreign affairs, though united by a common allegiance to the Crown, and freely associated as members of the British Commonwealth of Nations'. The basis of the association changed from one owing allegiance to a common Crown, and the modern Commonwealth was born in 1949 when the member countries accepted India's intention of becoming a republic at the same time continuing 'her full membership of the Commonwealth of Nations and her acceptance of the King as the symbol of the free association of its independent member nations and as such the Head of the Commonwealth'. There were (1989) 17 Queen's realms, 26 republics, and 5 indigenous monarchies in the Commonwealth. All acknowledge the Queen symbolically as Head of the Commonwealth.

The Queen's legal title rests on the statute of 12 and 13 Will. III, c. 3, by which the succession to the Crown of Great Britain and Ireland was settled on the Princess Sophia of Hanover and the 'heirs of her body being Protestants'. By proclamation of 17 July 1917 the royal family became known as the House and Family of Windsor. On 8 Feb. 1960 the Queen issued a declaration varying her confirmatory declaration of 9 April 1952 to the effect that while the Queen and her children should continue to be known as the House of Windsor, her descendants, other than descendants entitled to the style of Royal Highness and the title of Prince or Princess, and female descendants who marry and their descendants should bear the name of Mountbatten-Windsor. The Royal Style and Titles of Queen Elizabeth are: In *Antigua and Barbuda* 'Elizabeth the Second, by the Grace of God, Queen of Antigua and Barbuda and of Her other Realms and Territories, Head of the Commonwealth'. In *Australia*: 'Elizabeth the Second, by the Grace of God Queen of Australia and Her other Realms and Territories, Head of the Commonwealth'. In the *Bahamas*: 'Elizabeth the Second, by the Grace of God, Queen of the Commonwealth of the Bahamas and of Her other Realms and Territories, Head of the Commonwealth'. In *Barbados*: 'Elizabeth the Second, by the Grace of God, Queen of Barbados and of Her other Realms and Territories, Head of the Commonwealth'. In *Belize*: 'Elizabeth the Second, by the Grace of God, Queen of Belize and of Her Other Realms and Territories, Head of the Commonwealth'. In *Canada*: 'Elizabeth the Second, by the Grace of God of the United Kingdom, Canada and Her other Realms and Territories Queen, Head of the Commonwealth, Defender of the Faith'. In *Grenada*: 'Elizabeth the Second, by the Grace of God, Queen of the United Kingdom of Great Britain and Northern Ireland and of Grenada and Her other Realms and Territories, Head of the Commonwealth'. In *Jamaica*: 'Elizabeth the Second, by the Grace of God of Jamaica and of Her other Realms and Territories Queen, Head of the Commonwealth'. In *Mauritius*: 'Elizabeth the Second, Queen of Mauritius and of Her other Realms and Territories, Head of the Commonwealth'. In *New Zealand*: 'Elizabeth the Second, by the Grace of God Queen of New Zealand and Her Other Realms and Territories, Head of the Commonwealth, Defender of the Faith'. In *Papua New Guinea*: 'Elizabeth the Second, Queen of Papua New Guinea and Her other Realms and Territories, Head of the Commonwealth'. In *Saint Christopher and Nevis:* 'Elizabeth the Second, by the Grace of God, Queen of Saint Christopher and Nevis and Her other Realms and Territories, Head of the Commonwealth'. In *Saint Lucia*: 'Elizabeth the Second, by the Grace of God, Queen of Saint Lucia and of Her other Realms and Territories, Head of Commonwealth'. In *Saint Vincent and the Grenadines*: 'Elizabeth the Second, by the Grace of God, Queen of Saint Vincent and the Grenadines and of Her other Realms and Territories, Head of the Commonwealth'. In *Solomon Islands*: 'Elizabeth the Second by the Grace of God Queen of Solomon Islands and of Her other Realms and Territories, Head of the Commonwealth'. In *Tuvalu*: 'Elizabeth the Second by the Grace of God Queen of Tuvalu and of Her other Realms and Territories, Head of the Commonwealth'. In the *United Kingdom*: 'Elizabeth the Second, by the Grace of God of the United Kingdom of Great Britain and Northern Ireland and of Her other Realms and Territories Queen, Head of the Commonwealth, Defender of the Faith'.

A number of territories, formerly under British jurisdiction or mandate did not join the Commonwealth: Egypt, Iraq, Transjordan, Burma, Palestine, Sudan, British Somaliland, South Cameroons, and Aden. Two countries, the Republic of South Africa in 1961 and Pakistan in 1972, have left the Commonwealth. Fiji's membership lapsed with the emergence of the Republic in 1987. Pakistan was re-admitted to the Commonwealth on 1 Oct. 1989.

Nauru and Tuvalu are special members, with the right to participate in all functional Commonwealth meetings and activities but not to attend meetings of Commonwealth Heads of Government.

Member States. The following are the member countries, with their dates of independence, and, where appropriate, the date on which they became republics: *United Kingdom*; *Canada* 1 July 1867[1]; *Australia* 1 Jan. 1901[1]; *New Zealand* 26 Sept. 1907[1]; *India* 15 Aug. 1947 (Republic on 26 Jan. 1950); *Sri Lanka* 4 Feb. 1948 (Republic on 22 May 1972); *Ghana* 6 March 1957 (Republic on 1 July 1960); *Malaysia* 31 Aug. 1957 as Federation of Malaya, 16 Sept. 1963 as Federation of Malaysia; *Cyprus* 16 Aug. 1960 (Republic on independence; joined Commonwealth on 13 March 1961); *Nigeria* 1 Oct. 1960 (Republic on 1 Oct. 1963); *Sierra Leone* 27 April 1961 (Republic on 19 April 1971); *Tanzania*–Tanganyika 9 Dec. 1961 (Republic on 9 Dec. 1962), Zanzibar 10 Dec. 1963 (Republic on 12 Jan. 1964), United Republic of Tanganyika and Zanzibar 26 April 1964; renamed United Republic of Tanzania 29 Oct. 1964; *Western Samoa* 1 Jan. 1962 (joined Commonwealth on 28 Aug. 1970); *Jamaica* 6 Aug. 1962; *Trinidad and Tobago* 31 Aug. 1962 (Republic on 1 Aug. 1976); *Uganda* 9 Oct. 1962 (Republic 8 Sept. 1967, second republic 25 Jan. 1971); *Kenya* 12 Dec. 1963 (Republic on 12 Dec. 1964); *Malaŵi* 6 July 1964 (Republic on 6 July 1966); *Malta* 21 Sept. 1964 (Republic on 13 Dec. 1974); *Zambia* 24 Oct. 1964 (Republic on independence); *The Gambia* 18 Feb. 1965 (Republic on 24 April 1970); *Maldives* 26 July 1965 (Republic on independence, joined Commonwealth on 9 July 1982); *Singapore* 16 Sept. 1963 as a state in the Federation of Malaysia, 9 Aug. 1965 as an independent state and republic not part of Malaysia; *Guyana* 26 May 1966 (Republic on 23 Feb. 1970); *Botswana* 30 Sept. 1966 (Republic on independence); *Lesotho* 4 Oct. 1966; *Barbados* 30 Nov. 1966; *Nauru* 31 Jan. 1968 (Republic on independence); *Mauritius* 12 March 1968; *Swaziland* 6 Sept. 1968; *Tonga* 4 June 1970; *Bangladesh* seceded from Pakistan as Republic 16 Dec. 1971, recognized by United Kingdom 4 Feb. 1972 (joined Commonwealth on 18 April 1972); *Bahamas* 10 July 1973; *Grenada* 7 Feb. 1974; *Papua New Guinea* 16 Sept. 1975; *Seychelles* 29 June 1976 (Republic on independence); *Solomon Islands* 7 July 1978; *Tuvalu* 1 Oct. 1978; *Dominica* 3 Nov. 1978 (Republic on independence); *Saint Lucia* 22 Feb. 1979; *Kiribati* 12 July 1979 (Republic on independence); *Saint Vincent and the Grenadines* 27 Oct. 1979; *Zimbabwe* 18 April 1980 (Republic on independence); *Vanuatu* 30 July 1980 (Republic on independence); *Belize* 21 Sept. 1981; *Antigua* and *Barbuda* 1 Nov. 1981; *Saint Christopher and Nevis* 19 Sept. 1983; *Brunei*[2] 1 Jan 1984; *Pakistan* re-admitted 1 Oct. 1989.

[1] These are the effective dates of independence, given legal effect by the Statute of Westminster 1931.

[2] Brunei was a sovereign state in treaty relationship with Britain, whereby Britain was responsible for the conduct of external affairs and had a consultative responsibility for defence. It had never been a dependent territory, and in 1971 had ceased to be a protected state. A Treaty of Friendship and Co-operation was signed on 7 Jan. 1979, becoming effective on 1 Jan. 1984 when Brunei assumed her full international responsibilities and Britain gave up her consultative commitment over defence matters.

Dependent Territories and Associated States. There are 15 British dependent territories, 7 Australian external territories, 2 New Zealand dependent territories and 2 New Zealand associated states. A dependent territory is a territory belonging by settlement, conquest or annexation to the British, Australian or New Zealand Crown.

United Kingdom dependent territories administered through the Foreign and Commonwealth Office comprise, in the Far East: Hong Kong; in the Indian Ocean: British Indian Ocean Territory; in the Mediterranean: Gibraltar; in the Atlantic Ocean: Bermuda, Falkland Islands, South Georgia and the South Sandwich Islands, British Antarctic Territory, St Helena, St Helena Dependencies (Ascension and Tristan da Cunha); in the Caribbean: Montserrat, British Virgin Islands, Cayman Islands, Turks and Caicos Islands, Anguilla; in the Western Pacific: Pitcairn Group of Islands. The Australian external territories are: Coral Sea Islands Territory, Cocos (Keeling) Islands, Christmas Island, Heard Island and McDonald Islands, Norfolk Island, Australian Antarctic Territory and the Territory of Ashmore and Cartier Islands. The New Zealand dependent territories are: Tokelau and Ross Dependency. The New Zealand associated states are: Cook Islands and Niue.

While constitutional responsibility to Parliament for the government of the British dependent territories rests with the Secretary of State for Foreign and Commonwealth Affairs, the administration of the territories is carried out by the Governments of the territories themselves.

British Government Department. With effect from 17 Oct. 1968, the Secretary of State for Foreign and Commonwealth Affairs is responsible for the conduct of relations with members of the Commonwealth as well as with foreign countries, and for the administration of British dependent territories.

Commonwealth Secretariat. The Commonwealth Secretariat is an international body at the service of all 48 member countries. It provides the central organization for joint consultation and co-operation in many fields. It was established in 1965 by Commonwealth Heads of Government and has observer status at the UN General Assembly.

The Secretariat disseminates information on matters of common concern, organizes and services meetings and conferences, co-ordinates many Commonwealth activities, and provides expert technical assistance for economic and social development through the multilateral Commonwealth Fund for Technical Cooperation. The Secretariat is organized in divisions and sections which correspond to its main areas of operation: International affairs, economic affairs, food production and rural development, youth, education, information, applied studies in government, science and technology, law and health. Within this structure the Secretariat organizes the biennial meetings of Commonwealth Heads of Government, annual meetings of Finance Ministers of member countries, and regular meetings of Ministers of Education, Law, Health, and others as appropriate.

To emphasize the multilateral nature of the association, meetings are held in different cities and regions within the Commonwealth. Heads of Government decided that the Secretariat should work from London as it has the widest range of communications of any Commonwealth city, as well as the largest assembly of diplomatic missions.

The Commonwealth Secretary-General, who has access to Heads of Government, is the head of the Secretariat which is staffed by officers from member countries and financed by contributions from member governments.

Commonwealth Day is observed throughout the Commonwealth on the second Monday in March.

Flag: Royal blue with the emblem of a globe surrounded by 49 rays, all in gold.

Headquarters: Marlborough House, Pall Mall, London, SW1Y 5HX.
Secretary-General: Emeka Anyaoku (Nigeria).

Further Reading

The Commonwealth Year-Book, HMSO, Annual
The Cambridge History of the British Empire. 8 vols. CUP, 1929 ff.
Austin, D., *The Commonwealth and Britain.* London, 1988
Burns, Sir Alan, *In Defence of Colonies.* London, 1957
Chadwick, J., *The Unofficial Commonwealth.* London, 1982
Dale, W., *The Modern Commonwealth.* London, 1983
Garner, J., *The Commonwealth Office, 1925–1968.* London, 1978
Hailey, Lord, *An African Survey.* Rev. ed. Oxford, 1957.—*Native Administration in the British African Territories.* 5 vols. HMSO, 1951 ff.
Hall, H. D., *Commonwealth: A History of the British Commonwealth.* London and New York, 1971
Judd, D. and Slinn, P., *The Evolution of the Modern Commonwealth.* London, 1982
Keeton, G. W. (ed.) *The British Commonwealth: Its Laws and Constitutions.* 9 vols. London, 1951 ff.
Mansergh, N., *The Commonwealth Experience.* 2 vols. London, 1982
Maxwell, W. H. and L. F., *A Legal Bibliography of the British Commonwealth of Nations.* 2nd ed. London, 1956
Moore, R. J., *Making the New Commonwealth.* Oxford, 1987
Papadopoulos, A. N., *Multilateral Diplomacy within the Commonwealth: A Decade of Expansion.* The Hague, 1982
Smith, A. and Sanger, C., *Stitches in Time: The Commonwealth in World Politics.* New York, 1983
Wade, E. C. S. and Phillips, G. G., *Constitutional Law: An Outline of the Law and Practice of the Constitution, Including Central and Local Government and the Constitutional Relations of the British Commonwealth and Empire.* 8th ed. London, 1970

WORLD COUNCIL OF CHURCHES

The World Council of Churches was formally constituted on 23 Aug. 1948, at Amsterdam, by an assembly representing 147 churches from 44 countries. By 1989 the member churches numbered over 300, from more than 100 countries.

The basis of membership (1975) states: 'The World Council of Churches is a fellowship of Churches which confess the Lord Jesus Christ as God and Saviour according to the Scriptures and therefore seek to fulfil together their common calling to the glory of the one God, Father, Son and Holy Spirit.' Membership is open to Churches which express their agreement with this basis and satisfy such criteria as the Assembly or Central Committee may prescribe. Today 307 Churches of Protestant, Anglican, Orthodox, Old Catholic and Pentecostal confessions belong to this fellowship.

The World Council was founded by the coming together of several diverse Christian movements. These included the overseas mission groups gathered from 1921 in the International Missionary Council, the Faith and Order Movement founded by American Episcopal Bishop Charles Brent, and the Life and Work Movement led by Swedish Lutheran Archbishop Nathan Söderblom.

On 13 May 1938 at Utrecht a provisional committee was appointed to prepare for the formation of a World Council of Churches. It was under the chairmanship of William Temple, then Archbishop of York.

Assembly. The governing body of the World Council, consisting of delegates specially appointed by the member Churches. It meets every 7 or 8 years to frame policy and to consider some main theme. The Assembly has no legislative powers and depends for the implementation of its decisions upon the action of the member Churches. Assemblies have been held in Amsterdam (1948), Evanston (1954), New Delhi (1961), Uppsala (1968), and Nairobi (1975) and most recently in Vancouver, Canada in 1983 under the theme 'Jesus Christ – the Life of the World'. In between assemblies, a 150-member Central Committee meets annually to carry out the assembly mandate, with a smaller 22-member Executive Committee meeting twice a year.

Presidents: Dame R. Nita Barrow (Barbados), Dr Marga Bührig (Switzerland), Metropolitan Paulos Mar Gregorios (India), Bishop Johannes Hempel (German Democratic Republic), Patriarch Ignatios IV (Syria), Most Rev. W. P. K. Makhulu (Botswana), Very Rev. Dr Lois Wilson (Canada).

WCC programmes are organized from headquarters in Geneva, Switzerland, by a staff of 307 and a range of supervisory committees drawn from member churches. The 3 programme units are:

(i) Faith and Witness includes the Commission on Faith and Order, World Mission and Evangelism, Church and Society and the sub-unit on Dialogue with People of Living Faiths.

(ii) Justice and Service which includes Inter-Church Aid, Refugee and World Service (channelling over $35m. from member churches to areas of need); the Commission on the Churches' Participation in Development; the Commission of the Churches on International Affairs, the Programme to Combat Racism and the Christian Medical Commission.

(iii) Education and Renewal includes sections dealing with renewal and congregational life, women, youth, church-related education, biblical studies, family ministry and the Programme on Theological Education.

A General Secretariat with a Communication Department, a Finance Department and a Library co-ordinates the work of the 3 Programme Units and supervises the work of Ecumenical Institute Céligny (Switzerland).

Since 1975 the WCC has held several major world conferences on such diverse themes as 'Faith, Science and the Future', 'Your Kingdom Come', 'Family Power and Social Change', 'Strategies for Churches Combating Racism in the 1980's', 'The Community of Women and Men in the Church', 'Giving an Account of the Hope that is in Us', 'Called to be Neighbours' and 'Your Will be Done—Mission in Christ's Way'.

Officers of the Central and Executive Committees: *Moderator:* Rev. Dr Heinz J. Held (Federal Republic of Germany). *Vice-moderators:* Dr Sylvia Ross Talbot (USA), Metropolitan Chrysostomos of Myra (Turkey). *General Secretary:* The Rev. Dr Emilio Castro.

Office: PO Box 2100, 150 route de Ferney, 1211 Geneva 2, Switzerland.

Further Reading

Official Reports: The First [*. . . etc.*] *Assembly* (London, 1948, 1955, 1962, Geneva, 1968, 1975, 1983)
Directory of Christian Councils. 1985
New Delhi to Uppsala 1961–68. Geneva, 1968
Uppsala to Nairobi 1968–75. Geneva, 1975
Nairobi to Vancouver. Geneva, 1983
Official Reports of the Faith and Order Conferences at Lausanne 1927, Edinburgh 1937, Lund 1952, Montreal 1963, Meeting of Faith and Order Commission, Louvain 1971, Accra 1974, Bangalore 1978, Vancouver 1983
Minutes of the Central Committee. Geneva, 1949 to date
Howell, L., *Acting in Faith: The World Council of Churches since 1975.* London, 1982
Potter, P., *Life in all its Fullness.* Geneva, 1981
van der Bent, A. J., *What in the World is the World Council of Churches?* Geneva, 1978.—*Handbook of Member Churches of the World Council of Churches.* Geneva, 1985
Vermaat, J. A. A., *The World Council of Churches and Politics.* New York, 1989
Visser 't Hooft, W. A., *The Genesis and Formation of the World Council of Churches.* Geneva, 1982

INTERNATIONAL TRADE UNIONISM

There are three main international trade union confederations *(i)* the International Confederation of Free Trade Unions (ICFTU) which has in membership most of the national trade union confederations in the Western industrialized countries as well as democratic organizations in Asia, Africa, and Latin America; *(ii)* the World Federation of Trade Unions (WFTU) which draws its support mainly from Eastern Europe, but which also has affiliates in France and in several developing countries; and *(iii)* the World Confederation of Labour (WCL) which has affiliates in Western Europe, Latin America and a small number of African and Asian countries. In addition, national trade unions are frequently members of international trade union federations, set up to protect the interests of working people in particular industries or trades, which are associated with the international confederations. The International Trade Secretariats (ITS) are associated with the ICFTU; Trade Union Internationals (TUI) with the WFTU; and the International Trade Federations (ITF) with the WCL.

Coldrick, A. P. and Jones, P., *International Directory of the Trade Union Movement.* London, 1979

History. The international trade union structure in 1988 was shaped mainly by developments since 1945. In that year the WFTU was set up with world-wide membership. Attempts by trade unions in Eastern Europe to turn the WFTU into an organization voicing unquestioning support for the policies of the USSR led most of the affiliates in the Western European countries to break away from the WFTU and to form the ICFTU in 1949.

EUROPEAN TRADE UNION CONFEDERATION. In Feb. 1973 the European Trade Union Confederation was formed by trade unionists in 15 Western European countries to deal with questions of interest to European working people arising inside and outside the EC. All the founding organizations were ICFTU affiliates but subsequently they accepted into membership European WCL affiliates, the Irish Congress of Trade Unions and the Italian Communist and Socialist trade union centre (CGIL) and other national organizations. The ETUC Congress meets every 3 years and the Executive Committee 5 times a year. The membership was (June 1988) about 44m. from 36 centres in 21 countries.

General Secretary: Mathias Hinterscheid.
Headquarters: Rue Montagne aux Herbes Potagères 37, 1000 Brussels.

INTERNATIONAL CONFEDERATION OF FREE TRADE UNIONS. The first congress of ICFTU was held in London in Dec. 1949. The constitution as amended provides for co-operation with the United Nations and the International Labour Organization and for regional organizations to promote free trade unionism, especially in less-developed countries.

Organization. The Congress meets every 4 years. It elects the Executive Board of 37 members nominated on an area basis for a 4-year period; 1 seat is reserved for a woman nominated by the Women's Committee; the Board meets at least twice a year. Various committees cover policy *vis-à-vis* such problems as those connected with nuclear energy and also the administration of the International Solidarity Fund. There are joint ICFTU–ITS committees for co-ordinating activities.

Headquarters: 37–41, rue Montagne aux Herbes Potagères, Brussels 1000, Belgium.

General Secretary: John Vanderveken.

Regional organizations exist in America, office in Mexico City; Asia, office in New Delhi; and Africa, office in Sierre Leone.

Membership. The ICFTU had Dec. 1989, 141 affiliated organizations in 98 countries, which together represent about 91m. workers. The 10 largest groups were the American Federation of Labor and Congress of Industrial Organizations (13·7m.), the British Trades Union Congress (9·1m.), Japanese Confederation of Labour, Rengo (8m.), the Federal German Deutscher Gewerkschaftsbund (7·1m.), the Confederazione Italiana Sindacati Lavoratori (3·1m.), the Swedish Landsorganisationen (2·1m.), the Indian National Trade Union Congress (4·7m.), Argentinian Confederacion General de Trabajo (6m.), Polish NSZZ Solidarnosc (5m.), Indian Hind Mazdoor Sabha (2·6m.).

Publications (in 4 languages). *Free Labour World* (fortnightly).

THE WORLD FEDERATION OF TRADE UNIONS. The WFTU formally came into existence on 3 Oct. 1945, representing trade-union organizations in more than 50 countries of the world, both Communist and non-Communist, excluding Federal Republic of Germany and Japan, as well as a number of lesser and colonial territories. Representation from the USA was limited to the Congress of Industrial Organizations, as the American Federation of Labor declined to participate.

In Jan. 1949 the British, USA and Netherlands trade unions withdrew from WFTU, which had come under complete Communist control; and by June 1951 all non-Communist trade-unions, and the Yugoslavian Federation, had left WFTU.

Organization. The Congress meets every 4 years. In between, the General Council, of 134 members (including deputies), is the governing body, meeting (in theory) at least once a year. The Bureau controls the activities of WFTU between meetings of the General Council; it consists of the President, the General Secretary and members from different continents, the total number being decided at each Congress. The Bureau is elected by the General Council.

General Secretary: I. Zakaria (Sudan).

Membership. A total membership of 206m. from 90 national centres is claimed. The biggest groups are the Soviet All-Union Central Council of Trade Unions (107m.), the German Democratic Republic Free German Trade Union Federation (8m.), the Czechoslovak Central Council of Trade Unions (6m.), the Romanian General Confederation of Labour (6·4m.), the Hungarian Central Council of Trade Unions (4·5m.) and the French Confederation of Labour (CGT, 1·5m.).

Publications. World Trade Union Movement (monthly, in 9 languages); *Trade Union Press* (fortnightly, in 6 languages).

WORLD CONFEDERATION OF LABOUR. The first congress of the

International Federation of Christian Trade Unions (IFCTU), as the WCL was then called, met in 1920; but a large proportion of its 3·4m. members were in Italy and Germany, where affiliated unions were suppressed by the Fascist and Nazi régimes, and in 1940 IFCTU went out of existence. It was reconstituted in 1945, and declined to merge with WFTU and, later, with ICFTU. The policy of IFCTU was based on the papal encyclicals *Rerum novarum* (1891) and *Quadragesimo anno* (1931), but in 1968, when the Federation became the WCL, it was broadened to include other concepts. The WCL now has Protestant, Buddhist and Moslem member confederations as well as its mainly Roman Catholic members.

Organization. The WCL is organized on a federative basis which leaves wide discretion to its autonomous constituent unions. Its governing body is the Congress, which meets every 4 years. The Congress appoints (or re-appoints) the Secretary-General at each 4-yearly meeting. The General Council which meets at least once a year, is composed of the members of the Confederal Board (at least 22 members, elected by the Congress) and representatives of national confederations, international trade federations, and trade union organizations where there is no confederation affiliated to the WCL. The Confederal Board is responsible for the general leadership of the WCL, in accordance with the decisions and directives of the Council and Congress. Headquarters: 71 rue Joseph II, Brussels 1040, Belgium.

Secretary-General: Jan Kulakowski.

There are regional organizations in Latin America (office in Caracas), Africa (office in Banjul, Gambia) and Asia (office in Manila) There is also a liaison centre in Montreal.

Membership. A total membership of 14m. in about 90 countries is claimed. The biggest group is the Confederation of Christian Trade Unions of Belgium (1·1m.).

Publication. Labour Press and Information (11 each year, in 5 languages).

ORGANISATION FOR ECONOMIC CO-OPERATION AND DEVELOPMENT (OECD)

History and Membership. On 30 Sept. 1961 the Organisation for European Economic Co-operation (OEEC), after a history of 13 years (*see* THE STATESMAN'S YEAR-BOOK , 1961, p. 32), was replaced by the Organisation for Economic Co-operation and Development. The change of title marks the Organisation's altered status and functions: With the accession of Canada and USA as full members it ceased to be a purely European body; while at the same time it added development aid to the list of its other activities. The member countries are now Australia, Austria, Belgium, Canada, Denmark, Federal Republic of Germany, Finland, France, Greece, Iceland, Ireland, Italy, Japan, Luxembourg, the Netherlands, New Zealand, Norway, Portugal, Spain, Sweden, Switzerland, Turkey, UK and USA. Yugoslavia participates in the Organisation's activities with a special status. The Commission of the European Communities generally takes part in OECD's work.

Objectives. To promote economic and social welfare throughout the OECD area by assisting its member governments in the formulation of policies designed to this end and by co-ordinating these policies; and to stimulate and harmonize its members' efforts in favour of developing countries.

Organs. The supreme body of the Organisation is the Council composed of one representative for each member country. It meets either at Heads of Delegations level (about once a week) under the Chairmanship of the Secretary-General, or at Ministerial level (usually once a year) under the Chairmanship of a Minister of a country elected annually to assume these functions. Decisions and Recommendations are adopted by mutual agreement of all members of the Council.

The Council is assisted by an Executive Committee composed of 14 members of the Council designated annually by the latter. The major part of the Organisation's work is, however, prepared and carried out in numerous specialized committees, working parties and sub-groups, of which there exist over 200. Thus, the Organisation comprises Committees for Economic Policy; Economic and Development Review; Development Assistance (DAC); North-South Economics Issues; Commodities; Trade; Capital Movements and Invisible Transactions; Financial Markets; Fiscal Affairs; Competition Law and Policy; Consumer Policy; Maritime Transport; International Investment and Multinational Enterprises; Tourism; Energy Policy; Industry; Steel; Scientific and Technological Policy; Information, Computer and Communications Policy; Road Transport Research; Education; Manpower and Social Affairs; Environment; Urban Affairs; Control of Chemicals; Agriculture; Fisheries, etc.

Four autonomous or semi-autonomous bodies also belong to the Organisation: The International Energy Agency (IEA); the Nuclear Energy Agency (NEA); the Development Centre and the Centre for Educational Research and Innovation (CERI). Each one of these bodies has its own governing committee.

The Council, the committees and the other bodies are serviced by an international Secretariat headed by the Secretary-General of the Organisation.

All member countries have established permanent Delegations to OECD, each headed by an Ambassador.

Chairman of the Council (ministerial): A minister from the country elected (annually) to assume this function.

Chairman of the Council (official level): The Secretary-General.

Secretary-General: Jean-Claude Paye (France).

Deputy Secretaries-General: R. A. Cornell (USA), Pierre Vinde (Sweden).

Executive Director of the International Energy Agency: Helga Steeg (Federal Republic of Germany).

Headquarters: 2, rue André Pascal, 75775 Paris Cedex 16, France.

Further Reading

OECD publishes numerous reports and statistical papers. Regular features include:
Activities of OECD. Annual
News from OECD. Monthly
Main Economic Indicators. Monthly
The OECD Observer. Bi-monthly
The OECD Economic Outlook. Semi-annual
OEEC/OECD Economic Surveys of Member Countries.
OECD Employment Outlook. Annual
Geographical Distribution of Financial Flows to Developing Countries. Annual
Development Co-operation Report. Annual
Tourism Policy and International Tourism in OECD Member Countries.
Maritime Transport. Annual
Energy Policies and Programmes of the IEA Member Countries.

NORTH ATLANTIC TREATY ORGANIZATION (NATO)

Western perceptions of the political situation in Europe following World War II gave rise, in 1947, to 2 major US initiatives – the Truman Doctrine and the Marshall Plan. These policies were designed to increase the ability of Western European countries to resist outside pressure and to assist them in bringing about their economic recovery. By 1948, on the initiative of the Foreign Secretary of the UK Ernest Bevin, 5 Western European nations had also entered into a treaty of mutual assistance in which they pledged themselves to come to each other's aid in the event of armed aggression against them (Brussels Treaty, 17 March 1948). The idea of a single mutual defence system involving North America as well as the European signatories of the Brussels Treaty was put forward by the Canadian Secretary of State for External Affairs in April 1948. It led, *via* the Vandenberg Resolution which enabled the US constitutionally to participate, to the creation of the Atlantic Alliance.

On 4 April 1949 the foreign ministers of Belgium, Canada, Denmark, France, Iceland, Italy, Luxembourg, the Netherlands, Norway, Portugal, the UK and the USA met in Washington and signed a treaty, the main clauses of which read as follows:

Article 1. The parties undertake, as set forth in the Charter of the United Nations, to settle any international disputes in which they may be involved by peaceful means in such a manner that international peace and security and justice are not endangered, and to refrain in their international relations from the threat or use of force in any manner inconsistent with the purposes of the United Nations.

Article 2. The parties will contribute toward the further development of peaceful and friendly international relations by strengthening their free institutions, by bringing about a better understanding of the principles upon which these institutions are founded, and by promoting conditions of stability and well-being. They will seek to eliminate conflict in their international economic policies and will encourage economic collaboration between any or all of them.

Article 3. In order more effectively to achieve the objectives of this treaty, the parties, separately and jointly by means of continuous and effective self-help and mutual aid, will maintain and develop their individual and collective capacity to resist armed attack.

Article 4. The parties will consult together whenever, in the opinion of any of them, the territorial integrity, political independence or security of any of the parties is threatened.

Article 5. The parties agree that an armed attack against one or more of them in Europe or North America shall be considered an attack against them all and consequently they agree that, if such an armed attack occurs, each of them, in exercise of the right of individual or collective self-defence recognized by article 51 of the Charter of the United Nations, will assist the party or parties so attacked by taking forthwith, individually and in concert with the other parties, such action as it deems necessary, including the use of armed force, to restore and maintain the security of the North Atlantic area. Any such armed attack and all measures taken as a result thereof shall immediately be reported to the Security Council. Such measures shall be terminated when the Security Council has taken the measures necessary to restore and maintain international peace and security.

Article 6. For the purpose of Article 5 an armed attack on one or more of the parties is deemed to include an armed attack *(i)* on the territory of any of the parties in Europe or North America, on the Algerian Departments of France, on the territory of Turkey or on the islands under the jurisdiction of any of the parties in the North Atlantic area north of the Tropic of Cancer; *(ii)* on the forces, vessels or aircraft of any of the parties, when in or over these territories or any other area in Europe in which occupation forces of any of the parties were stationed on the date when the treaty entered into force or the Mediterranean Sea or the North Atlantic area north of the Tropic of Cancer.

Article 8. Each party declares that none of the international engagements now in force between it and any other of the parties or any third state is in conflict with the provisions of this treaty, and undertakes not to enter into any international engagement in conflict with this treaty.

Article 10. The parties may, by unanimous agreement, invite any other European state in a position to further the principles of this treaty and to contribute to the security of the North Atlantic area to accede to this treaty. Any state so invited may become a party to the treaty by depositing its instrument of accession with the government of the United States of America. The government of the United States of America will inform each of the parties of the deposit of each such instrument of accession.

Article 12. After the treaty has been in force for 10 years, or at any time thereafter, the parties shall, if any of them so requests, consult together for the purpose of reviewing the treaty, having regard for the factors then affecting peace and security in the North Atlantic area, including the development of universal as well as regional arrangements under the Charter of the United Nations for the maintenance of international peace and security.

Article 13. After the treaty has been in force for 20 years, any party may cease to be a party one year after its notice of denunciation has been given to the government of the United States of America, which will inform the governments of the other parties of the deposit of each notice of denunciation.

The treaty came into force on 24 Aug. 1949. Greece and Turkey were admitted as parties to the treaty in 1952, the Federal Republic of Germany in 1955 and Spain in 1982.

NATO is an organization of sovereign states equal in status. Decisions taken are expressions of the collective will of member governments arrived at by common consent.

The North Atlantic Council is composed of representatives of the 16 member countries. At Ministerial Meetings of the Council, member nations are represented by Ministers of Foreign Affairs. These meetings are held twice a year. The Council also meets on occasion at the level of Heads of State and Government. In permanent session, at the level of Ambassadors, the Council meets at least once a week.

The Defence Planning Committee is composed of representatives of all member countries except France. Like the Council, it meets both in permanent session at the level of Ambassadors and twice a year at Ministerial level. At Ministerial Meetings member nations are represented by Defence Ministers.

The Council and Defence Planning Committee are chaired by the Secretary General of NATO at whatever level they meet. Opening sessions of Ministerial Meetings of the Council are presided over by the President, an honorary position held annually by the Foreign Minister of one of the member nations.

Nuclear matters are discussed by the Nuclear Planning Group in which 15 countries now participate. It meets regularly at the level of Permanent Representatives (Ambassadors) and twice a year at the level of Ministers of Defence.

The Permanent Representatives of member countries are supported by the National Delegations located at NATO Headquarters. The Delegations are composed of advisors and officials qualified to represent their countries on the various committees created by the Council. The Committees are supported by the International Staff responsible to the Secretary General.

Headquarters: 1110 Brussels, Belgium.
Secretary-General: Manfred Wörner (Federal Republic of Germany).
Flag: Dark blue with a white compass rose of 4 points in the centre.

The *Military Committee* is responsible for making recommendations to the Council and the Defence Planning Committee on military matters and for supplying guidance to the Allied Commanders. Composed of the Chiefs-of-Staff of all member countries except France and Iceland (which has no military forces), the Committee is assisted by an International Military Staff. It meets at Chiefs-of-Staff level at least twice a year but remains in permanent session at the level of national military representatives. Liaison between the Military Committee and the French High Command is effected through the French Mission to the Military Committee. The chairman of the Military Committee is elected by the Chiefs-of-Staff for a period of 2–3 years. The present chairman is Gen. Wolfgang Altenburg (Federal Republic of Germany), appointed Oct. 1986.

The area covered by the North Atlantic Treaty is divided among three commands: The Atlantic Ocean Command, the European Command and the Channel Command. Defence plans for the North American area are developed by the Canada–US Regional Planning Group.

The NATO commanders are responsible for the development of defence plans for their respective areas, for the determination of force requirements and for the deployment and exercise of the forces under their command.

The *Allied Command Europe* (ACE) covers the area extending from the North Cape to the Mediterranean and from the Atlantic to the eastern border of Turkey. Responsibilities relating to the defence of Portugal and the UK are included but these come within the purview of more than one NATO Command. The European area, which is subdivided into a number of subordinate commands, is under the Supreme Allied Commander Europe (SACEUR) whose Headquarters, near Mons in Belgium, are known as SHAPE (Supreme Headquarters Allied Powers Europe).

SACEUR has also under his orders the ACE Mobile Force, composed of both land and air force units from different member countries, which can be ready for action at very short notice in any threatened area. The present SACEUR is Gen. John R. Galvin (USA).

Under the Supreme Allied Commander Atlantic (SACLANT) the *Atlantic Command* extends from the North Pole to the Tropic of Cancer and from the coastal waters of North America to those of Europe and Africa, but excludes the Channel and the British Isles. SACLANT, who would have the primary task in wartime of ensuring the security of the sea lanes in the whole Atlantic area, is an operational rather than an administrative commander. Under his direct command is the

Standing Naval Force Atlantic (STANAVFORLANT) which is a permanent international squadron of ships drawn from NATO navies which normally operate in the Atlantic.

The present SACLANT, whose Headquarters are in Norfolk (USA), is Admiral Frank B. Kelso II (US), appointed Nov. 1988.

The *Channel Command* covers the English Channel and the southern North Sea. Under the Allied Commander-in-Chief Channel (CINCHAN) its mission is to control and protect merchant shipping in the area, co-operating with SACEUR in the air defence of the Channel. The forces earmarked to the Command in emergency are predominantly naval but include maritime air forces. CINCHAN also has under his command the NATO Standing Naval Force Channel (STANAVFORCHAN) which is a permanent force comprizing mine counter-measure ships of different NATO countries. The present CINCHAN, with Headquarters at Northwood (UK), is Admiral Sir Benjamin Bathurst, KCB (UK), appointed May 1987.

The *Canada–US Regional Planning Group*, which covers the North American area, develops and recommends to the Military Committee plans for the defence of this area. It meets alternately in Washington and Ottawa.

Further Reading

The NATO Information Service publishes documentation, reference material and information brochures including: *The NATO Handbook; NATO: Facts and Figures; The NATO Review* (periodical); economic and scientific publications.

Cook, D., *The Forging of an Alliance*. London, 1989
De Staercke, A., *Nato's Anxious Birth: The Prophetic Vision of the 1940's*. London, 1985
Godson, J., *Challenges to the Western Alliance*. London,1986
Goldstein, W., *Reagan's Leadership and the Atlantic Alliance*. New York, 1986
Hanning, H., *NATO–Our Guarantee for Peace*. London, 1986
Henderson, N., *The Birth of NATO*. London, 1982
Sloan, S. R., *NATO in the 1990s*. Washington, 1989
Williams, G. and Lee, A., *The European Defence Initiative*. London, 1986

WESTERN EUROPEAN UNION

On 17 March 1948 a 50-year treaty 'for collaboration in economic, social and cultural matters and for collective self-defence' was signed in Brussels by the Foreign Ministers of the UK, France, the Netherlands, Belgium and Luxembourg. (*See* THE STATESMAN'S YEAR-BOOK, 1954, pp. 32 f.)

On 20 Dec. 1950 the functions of the Western Union defence organization were transferred to the North Atlantic Treaty command, but it was decided that the reorganization of the military machinery should not affect the right of the Western Union Defence Ministers and the Chiefs of Staff to meet as they please to consider matters of mutual concern to the Brussels Treaty powers.

After the breakdown of the European Defence Community on 30 Aug. 1954 a conference was held in London from 28 Sept. to 3 Oct. 1954, attended by Belgium, Canada, France, the Federal Republic of Germany, Italy, Luxembourg, the Netherlands, the UK and the USA, at which it was decided to invite the Federal Republic of Germany and Italy to accede to the Brussels Treaty, to end the occupation of Western Germany and to invite the latter to accede to the North Atlantic Treaty; the Federal Republic agreed that it would voluntarily limit its arms production, and provision was made for the setting up of an agency to control the armaments of the 7 Brussels Treaty powers; the UK undertook not to withdraw from the Continent her 4 divisions and the Tactical Air Force assigned to the Supreme Allied Commander against the wishes of a majority, *i.e.*, 4 of the Brussels Treaty powers, except in the event of an acute overseas emergency.

At a Conference of Ministers held in Paris from 20 to 23 Oct. 1954 these decisions were embodied in 4 Protocols modifying the Brussels Treaty which were signed in Paris on 23 Oct. 1954 and came into force on 6 May 1955.

The *Council of WEU* consists of the Foreign Ministers of the 7 powers or their representatives; it is so organized as to be able to exercise its functions continuously. An *Assembly*, composed of representatives of the Brussels Treaty powers to the

Consultative Assembly of the Council of Europe, meets twice a year, usually in Paris. An *Agency for the Control of Armaments* and a *Standing Armaments Committee* have been set up in Paris. The social and cultural activities were transferred to the Council of Europe on 1 June 1960.

At a meeting of the Foreign, and Defence, Ministers of Western European Union held in Rome on 26–27 Oct. 1984, the Council adopted the 'Rome Declaration' and a document on the institutional reform of Western European Union. Member Governments support the reactivation of the Organization as a means of strengthening the European contribution to the North Atlantic Alliance and improving defence co-operation among the countries of Western Europe.

On 14 Nov. 1988, Spain and Portugal became members.

The Foreign Affairs and Defence Ministers meet twice a year. They met in Bonn, 22–23 April 1985, in Rome on 14 Nov. 1985, Venice on 29–30 April 1986, Luxembourg on 28 April 1987, The Hague on 26–27 Oct. 1987 and London on 14–15 Nov. 1988.

Secretariat-General: 9 Grosvenor Place, London, SW1X 7HL.
Secretary-General: Alfred Cahen.

COUNCIL OF EUROPE

In 1948 the 'Congress of Europe', bringing together at The Hague nearly 1,000 influential Europeans from 26 countries, called for the creation of a united Europe, including a European Assembly. This proposal, examined first by the Ministerial Council of the Brussels Treaty Organization, then by a conference of ambassadors, was at the origin of the Council of Europe, which is, with its 23 member States, the widest organization bringing together all European democracies. The Statute of the Council was signed at London on 5 May 1949 and came into force 2 months later. The founder members were Belgium, Denmark, France, Ireland, Italy, Luxembourg, the Netherlands, Norway, Sweden and the UK. Turkey and Greece joined in 1949, Iceland in 1950, the Federal Republic of Germany in 1951 (having been an associate since 1950), Austria in 1956, Cyprus in 1961, Switzerland in 1963, Malta in 1965, Portugal in 1976, Spain in 1977, Liechtenstein in 1978, San Marino in 1988 and Finland in 1989.

Membership is limited to European States which 'accept the principles of the rule of law and of the enjoyment by all persons within [their] jurisdiction of human rights and fundamental freedoms'. The Statute provides for both withdrawal (Art. 7) and suspension (Arts. 8 and 9). Greece withdrew from the Council in Dec. 1969 and rejoined in Nov. 1974.

Structure. Under the Statute two organs were set up: An inter-governmental *Committee of* [*Foreign*] *Ministers* with powers of decision and of recommendation to governments, and an inter-parliamentary deliberative body, the *Parliamentary Assembly* (referred to in the Statute as the *Consultative Assembly*)—both of which are served by the Secretariat. In addition, a large number of committees of experts have been established, two of them, the Council for Cultural Co-operation and the Committee on Legal Co-operation, having a measure of autonomy; on municipal matters the Committee of Ministers receives recommendations from the Standing Conference of Local and Regional Authorities of Europe.

The Committee of Ministers meets usually twice a year, their deputies 12 times a year.

The Parliamentary Assembly normally consists of 177 parliamentarians elected or appointed by their national parliaments (Austria 6, Belgium 7, Cyprus 3, Denmark 5, Finland 5, France 18, Federal Republic of Germany 18, Greece 7, Iceland 3, Ireland 4, Italy 18, Liechtenstein 2, Luxembourg 3, Malta 3, Netherlands 7, Norway 5, Portugal 7, San Marino 2, Spain 12, Sweden 6, Switzerland 6, Turkey 12, UK 18); it meets 3 times a year for approximately a week. The work of the Assembly is prepared by parliamentary committees.

The *Joint Committee* acts as an organ of co-ordination and liaison between representatives of the Committee of Ministers and members of the Parliamentary

Assembly and gives members an opportunity to exchange views on matters of important European interest.

The European Convention on Human Rights, signed in 1950, set up special machinery to guarantee internationally fundamental rights and freedoms. The *European Commission of Human Rights* investigates alleged violations of the Convention submitted to it either by States or, in most cases, by individuals. Its findings can then be examined by the *European Court on Human Rights* (set up in 1959), whose obligatory jurisdiction has been recognized by 20 States, or by the Committee of Ministers, empowered to take binding decisions by two-thirds majority vote.

The Social Development Fund, formerly the Resettlement Fund was created in 1956. The main purpose of the Fund is to give financial aid, particularly in the spheres of housing, vocational training, regional planning and development. Since 1956 the Fund has granted loans totalling ECU 7,000m.

In 1970 the Council set up a European Youth Centre at Strasbourg, where young people can discuss their own approach to international co-operation. More recently, a European Youth Foundation was created, and which provides money to subsidize activities by European Youth Organizations in their own countries.

Aims and Achievements. Art. 1 of the Statute states that the Council's aim is 'to achieve a greater unity between its members for the purpose of safeguarding and realising the ideals and principles which are their common heritage and facilitating their economic and social progress'; 'this aim shall be pursued. . . by discussion of questions of common concern and by agreements and common action'. The only limitation is provided by Art. 1 *(d)*, which excludes 'matters relating to national defence'.

Although without legislative powers, the Assembly acts as the power-house of the Council, initiating European action in key areas by making recommendations to the Committee of Ministers. As the widest parliamentary forum in Western Europe, the Assembly also acts as the conscience of the area by voicing its opinions on important current issues. These are embodied in resolutions. The Ministers' rôle is to translate the Assembly's recommendations into action, particularly as regards lowering the barriers between the European countries, harmonizing their legislation or introducing where possible common European laws, abolishing discrimination on grounds of nationality and undertaking certain tasks on a joint European basis.

In May 1976 the first plan of intergovernmental co-operation to be undertaken by the Council of Europe was adopted by the Committee of Ministers. The third one, adopted in Nov. 1986, will run until Dec. 1991. The plan takes account of political developments and progress achieved, and covers 9 key areas: Human rights, the media, social and socio-economic questions, education, culture and sport, youth, public health, heritage and environment, local and regional government, and legal co-operation.

Some 133 Conventions and Agreements have been concluded covering such matters as social security, cultural affairs, conservation of European wild life and natural habitats, protection of archaeological heritage, extradition, medical treatment, equivalence of degrees and diplomas, the protection of television broadcasts, adoption of children and transportation of animals. Treaties in the legal field include the adoption of the European Convention on the Suppression of Terrorism, the European Convention on the Legal Status of Migrant Workers and the Transfer of Sentenced Persons. The Committee of Ministers adopted a European Convention for the protection of individuals with regard to the automatic processing of personal data (1981), a Convention on the compensation of victims of violent crimes (1983), a Convention on spectator violence and misbehaviour at sport events and in particular at football matches (1985), the European Charter of Local Government (1985), and a Convention for the Prevention of Torture and Inhuman or Degrading Treatment or Punishment (1987). The European Social Charter of 1965 sets out the social and economic rights which all member governments agree to guarantee to their citizens.

The official languages are English and French.

Chairman of the Committee of Ministers: (held in rotation).
President of the Parliamentary Assembly: Anders Bjorck (Sweden).

President of the European Court on Human Rights: Rolv Ryssdal (Norway).
President of the European Commission of Human Rights: Carl Aage Nørgaard (Denmark).
Secretary-General: Catherine Lalumière.
Headquarters: Palais de l'Europe, 67006, Strasbourg, Cedex, France.
Flag: Blue with a ring of 12 gold stars in the centre.

Further Reading

The Information Department, Council of Europe, BP 431, R6-67006 Strasbourg-Cedex.
European Yearbook. The Hague, from 1955
Forum. Strasbourg, from 1978, 4 times a year
Yearbook on the Convention on Human Rights. Strasbourg, from 1958
Cook, C. and Paxton, J., *European Political Facts, 1918–84.* London, 1986

EUROPEAN COMMUNITIES

In May 1950 Belgium, France, the Federal Republic of Germany, Italy, Luxembourg and the Netherlands started negotiations with the aim of ensuring continual peace by a merging of their essential interests. The negotiations culminated in the signing in 1951 of the Treaty of Paris creating the European Coal and Steel Community (ECSC). Two more communities with the aims of gradually integrating the economies of the 6 nations and of moving towards closer political unity, the European Economic Community (EEC) and the European Atomic Energy Community (EAEC or Euratom) were created in 1957 by the signing of the Treaties of Rome.

On 30 June 1970 membership negotiations began between the Six and the UK, Denmark, Ireland and Norway. On 22 Jan. 1972 those 4 countries signed a Treaty of Accession, although this was rejected by Norway in a referendum in Nov. 1972. On 1 Jan. 1973 the UK, Denmark and Ireland became full members. Greece joined the Community on 1 Jan. 1981; Spain and Portugal on 1 Jan. 1986, although Community legislation will only apply to them entirely after a transitional period. In Dec. 1985 the Treaties were amended again by the Single Act of Luxembourg. Turkey applied for membership in April 1987.

The institutional arrangements of the Communities provide an independent executive with powers of proposal (the Commission), various consultative bodies, and a decision-making body drawn from the Governments (the Council). Until 1967 the 3 Communities were completely distinct, although they shared some nondecision-making bodies: From that date the executives were merged in the European Commission, and the decision-taking bodies in the Council. The institutions and organs of the Communities are as follows:

The *Commission* consists of 17 members appointed by the member states to serve for 4 years. The Commission acts independently of any country in the interests of the Community as a whole, with as its mandate the implementation and guardianship of the Treaties. In this it has the right of initiative (putting proposals to the Council for action); and execution (once the Council has decided); and can take the other institutions or individual countries before the Court of Justice (see below) should any of these renege upon its responsibilities.

Flag: Blue with a ring of 12 gold stars.
President: Jacques Delors.
Address: 200 rue de la Loi, 1049, Brussels, Belgium.

The *Council of Ministers* consists of foreign ministers from the 12 national governments and represents the national as opposed to the Community interests. It is the body which takes decisions under the Treaties. Since the adoption of the Single Act of Luxembourg, an increasing number of its decisions are taken by majority vote, though some areas (e.g. taxation) are still reserved to unanimity. Specialist Councils (e.g. the *Agriculture Council*) meet to discuss matters related to individual policies. The Single Act also formalizes the meetings of Heads of State and Government in the *European Council*, which meets 3 times a year; and of Foreign Ministers in *Political Co-operation*, to discuss co-operation outside the framework of the

Treaties. The Presidency of the Council is held for a 6-month term in the following order: Belgium, Denmark, Federal Republic of Germany, Greece, Spain, France, Ireland, Italy, Luxembourg, Netherlands, Portugal, UK.

Address: 170 rue de la Loi, 1048, Brussels.

The *European Parliament* consists of 518 members, directly elected from all Member States. France, the Federal Republic of Germany, Italy and the UK return 81 members each, Spain 60, the Netherlands 25, Belgium, Greece and Portugal 24, Denmark 16, Ireland 15 and Luxembourg 6. Party representation in Parliament was as follows: Socialists, 180; European People's Party (Christian Democratic Group), 121; European Democrats (formerly European Conservatives), 34; European United Left, 28; Greens, 30; Lelft unity, 14; Liberal, Democratic and Reform Group 49; European Democratic Alliance, 20; the 'Rainbow' group (a group of mixed tendencies), 13; the European Right, 17; Independents, 12. The Parliament has a right to be consulted on a wide range of legislative proposals, and forms one arm of the Community's Budgetary Authority. Since the Single Act it has an increased role in legislation, through the 'concertation' procedure, under which it can reject certain Council drafts in a second reading procedure. Elections were held in June 1989 for a 5-year mandate.

President: Lord Plumb.
Address: Centre européen du Kirchberg, Luxembourg.

The *Economic and Social Committee* has an advisory role and consists of 189 representatives, employers, trade unions, consumers, etc. The *Consultative Committee*, of 96 members, performs a similar role for the ECSC.

President: Alphonse Margot.
Address: 2, rue Ravenstein, 1000 Brussels.

The *European Court of Justice* is composed of 13 judges and 6 advocates-general, is responsible for the adjudication of disputes arising out of the application of the treaties, and its findings are enforceable in all member countries. A Chamber of First Instance was created under the Single Act in 1985.

President: Lord Mackenzie Stuart.
Address: Palais de la Cour de Justice, Kirchberg, Luxembourg.

The *Court of Auditors* was established by a Treaty signed on 22 July 1975 which took effect on 1 June 1977. It consists of 12 members, and replaced the former *Audit Board.* It audits all income and current and past expenditure of the European Communities.

President: Marcel Mart.
Address: 29 Rue Aldringen, Luxembourg.

Annual Report of the Court of Auditors, from 1977

The *European Investment Bank* (EIB) was created by the EEC Treaty to which its statute is annexed. Its governing body is the Board of Governors consisting of ministers designated by member states. Its main task is to contribute to the balanced development of the common market in the interest of the Community by financing projects: Developing less-developed regions; for modernizing or converting undertakings; or developing new activities.

Address: 100, Boulevard Konrad Adenauer, Plateau du Kirchberg, Luxembourg.

Annual Report of the European Investment Bank

Community Law. Provisions of the Treaties and secondary legislation may be either directly applicable in Member States or only applicable after Member States have enacted their own implementing legislation. Secondary legislation consists of: Regulations, which are of general application and binding in their entirety and directly applicable in all member states; directives which are binding upon each Member State as to the result to be achieved within a given time, but leave the national authority the choice of form and method of achieving this result; decisions, which are binding in their entirety on their addressees. In addition the Council and Commission can issue recommendations and opinions, which have no binding force.

The Community's Legislative Process starts with a proposal from the Commission (either at the suggestion of its services or in pursuit of its declared political aims) to the Council. The Council generally seeks the views of the European Parliament on the proposal, and the Parliament adopts a formal Opinion, after consideration of the matter by its specialist Committees. The Council may also (and in some cases is obliged to) consult the Economic and Social Committee, which similarly delivers an opinion. When these opinions have been received, the Council will decide. Most decisions are taken on a majority basis, but will take account of reserves expressed by individual member states. The text eventually approved may differ substantially from the original Commission proposal.

Community Finances. The general budget of the European Communities for 1988, in ECUm. (1 ECU at Nov. 1988 = UK£0·66 or US$1·20) was:

Receipts		*Expenditure*	
Agricultural levies and Import duties	11,146	Agriculture	30,021
VAT	24,149	Social	2,772
Miscellaneous	8,275	Regional and transport	4,424
		Industry, energy, research	1,187
	43,820	Development aid	870
		Administration and miscellaneous	4,546
			43,820

The resources of the Community (the levies and duties mentioned above, and up to a 1·4% VAT charge) have been surrendered to it by Treaty. The Budget is made by the Council and the Parliament acting jointly as the Budgetary Authority. The Parliament has control, within a certain margin, of non-obligatory expenditure (*i.e.*, expenditure where the amount to be spent is not set out in the legislation concerned), and can also reject the Budget. Otherwise, the Council decides. ECSC operations are partly funded by a turnover levy (1988: 0·31%) on the coal and steel industries of the Community, partly from the general budget. The ECSC operating budget for 1988 was ECU432m.

THE EUROPEAN COAL AND STEEL COMMUNITY. The ECSC was the first of the 3 Communities, coming into existence on 10 Aug. 1952 following the signature of the Treaty of Paris on 18 April 1951. Its aim was to contribute towards economic expansion, growth of employment and a rising standard of living in Member States, through common action in the coal and steel sector, in a Community open to other nations. Since 1957 it has had the same membership as the other Communities.

The Common Market for Coal and Steel. This was achieved for coal, iron ore and scrap in Feb. 1953, for steel in May 1953 and for special steels in Aug. 1954. The Common External Tariff on ECSC products is between 4-8%. Rules for fair competition within the Common Market, based on non-discrimination by nationality and the free movement of goods, have been established. The ECSC also gives readaptation and retraining grants to former workers in these industries, and makes capital grants for new industrial investment in former coal and steel areas.

The Commission has to approve take-overs and mergers of coal or steel undertakings, and has the power in the case of crisis (and with the approval of the Council) to set production quotas and minimum prices by product, with fines for non-observance.

THE EUROPEAN ECONOMIC COMMUNITY (EEC) or COMMON MARKET

Based on the Treaty of Rome of 25 March 1957 the EEC came into being on 1 Jan.

1958 with the same original members as the ECSC. The Treaty guarantees certain rights to the citizens of all Member States (*e.g.*, the outlawing of economic discrimination by nationality, and equal pay for equal work as between men and women) and sets out certain other areas where secondary legislation is to fill in the details. The most important policy areas are as follows:

Freedom of movement for persons, goods and capital. Under the Treaty individuals or companies from one Member State may establish themselves in another country (for the purposes of economic activity) or sell goods or services there on the same basis as nationals of that country. With a few exceptions, restrictions on the movement of capital have also been ended. Under the Single Act the Member States bound themselves to achieve the suppression of all barriers to free movement of persons, goods and services by 31 Dec. 1992.

Customs Union and External Trade Relations. Goods or Services originating in one Member State have free circulation within the EEC, which implies common arrangements for trade with the rest of the world. Member States can no longer make bilateral trade agreements with third countries: This power has been ceded to the Community. The Customs Union was achieved in July 1968, with the abolition of internal customs tariffs (or equivalents) and quantitative restrictions, and the establishment of the Common External Tariff. Denmark, Ireland and the UK adopted these from July 1977; Greece from Jan. 1986.

Following the 1973 accessions the Community made a series of agreements with the member states of EFTA to form an industrial free trade zone and to start the liberalization of agricultural trade. A new impetutus was given by the 1984 Luxembourg agreement, and the EFTA countries are now seeking to co-operate in the achievement of the Internal Market. Association agreements which could lead to accession or customs union have been made with Cyprus, Malta and Turkey; and commercial, industrial, technical and financial aid agreements with Algeria, Egypt, Israel, Jordan, Lebanon, Morocco, Syria, Tunisia and Yugoslavia. In 1976 Canada signed a framework agreement for co-operation in industrial trade, science and natural resources. Co-operation agreements also exist with a number of Latin American countries and groupings (e.g. the Andean Group) and with Arab and Asian countries; and an economic and commercial agreement has been signed with ASEAN.

In the *Development Aid* sector, the Community has an agreement (the Lomé Convention, originally signed in 1975 but renewed and enlarged in 1979 and 1984) with some 60 African, Caribbean and Pacific countries which removes customs duties without reciprocal arrangements for most of their imports to the Community, and under which ECU8,760m. of aid was granted between 1986–90. An economic and commercial agreement has also been signed with ASEAN.

The Common Agricultural Policy (CAP). The objectives set out in the Treaty are to increase agricultural productivity, to ensure a fair standard of living for the agricultural community, to stabilise markets, to assure supplies, and to ensure reasonable consumer prices. In Dec. 1960 the Council laid down the fundamental principles on which the CAP is based: A single market, which calls for common prices, stable currency parities and the harmonising of health and veterinary legislation; Community preference, which protects the single Community market from imports; common financing, through the European Agricultural Guidance and Guarantee Fund (EAGGF), which seeks to improve agriculture through its Guidance section, and to stabilise markets against world price fluctuations through market intervention, with levies and refunds on exports. At present common market organizations cover over 95% of EEC agricultural production. Greece is bringing its agricultural prices into line with the Community over a period of up to 7 years.

Following the disappearance of stable currency parities, artificial currency levels have been applied in the CAP. This factor, together with over-production due to high producer prices, means that the CAP consumes about two-thirds of the Communities' budget.

The European Monetary System (EMS), whose immediate objective is to create a zone of monetary stability in Europe by closer monetary co-operation, began operating in March 1979. All Member States (except Greece, the UK, Spain and

Portugal 1988) limit fluctuations in the exchange rates of their currencies against a central rate denominated in ECU.

Competition. The Competition (anti-trust) law of the Community is based on 2 principles: That businesses should not seek to nullify the creation of the common market by the erection of artificial national (or other) barriers to the free movement of goods; and against the abuse of dominant positions in any market. These two principles have led among other things to the outlawing of prohibitions on exports to other Member States, of price-fixing agreements and of refusal to supply; and to the refusal by the Commission to allow mergers or take-overs by dominant undertakings in specific cases. Increasingly heavy fines are imposed on offenders.

THE EUROPEAN ATOMIC ENERGY COMMUNITY (EURATOM)

Like the EEC, Euratom came into being on 1 Jan. 1958 following a Treaty signed in Rome on 25 March 1957, and it had the same Member States as the EEC. Its task is to promote common efforts between its members in the development of nuclear energy for peaceful purposes, and for this purpose it has monopoly powers of acquisition of fissile materials for civil purposes. It is in no way concerned with military uses of nuclear power.

The execution of the Treaty now rests with the European Commission, which is advised by the Scientific and Technical Committee (28 members). Major decisions rest with the Council. Euratom has 1 substantial research institute of its own, at Ispra, in Italy; it does other work in co-operation with research institutes in the Member States, or in joint and international undertakings.

A common market for nuclear materials and equipment came into force, and external tariffs were suspended, in Jan. 1959.

European Community Delegation to the US: 2111 M Street NW (Suite 707), Washington DC 20037.
Head of Delegation: Sir Roy Denman.
US Delegation to the European Community: 40 Boulevard du Régent, 1000 Brussels.
Head of Delegation: Alfred H. Kingon.
European Community Delegation to the United Nations: 1 Dag Hammarskjöld Plaza, 245 East 47th Street, New York NY 10017.
Head of Delegation: Jean-Pierre Derisbourg.

Further Reading

Official Journal of the European Communities.—General Report on the Activities of the European Communities (annual, from 1967).—*The Agricultural Situation in the Community.* (annual).—*The Social Situation in the Community.* (annual).—*Report on Competition Policy in the European Community.* (annual).—*Basic Statistics of the Community* (annual).— *Bulletin of the European Community* (monthly).—*Register of Current Community Legal Instruments.* 1983
Europe (monthly), obtainable from the Information Office of the European Commission, 8 Storey's Gate, London, SW1P 3AT
Arbuthnott, H. and Edwards, G. (eds.) *A Common Man's Guide to the Common Market.* London, 1979
Cook, C. and Francis, M., *The First European Elections.* London, 1979
Drew, J., *Doing Business with the European Community.* London, 1979
Fennell, R., *The Common Agricultural Policy of the European Community.* London, 1979
Fitzmaurice, J., *The European Parliament.* London, 1982
Hallstein, W., *Europe in the Making.* London, 1973
Lodge, J., *The European Community: Bibliographical Excursions.* London, 1983
Mayre, R., *Postwar Europe.* London, 1983
Morris, B. *and Boehm, K., The European Community: A Practical Directory and Guide for Business, Industry and Trade.* London, 2nd ed. 1986
Palmer, D. M., *Sources of Information on the European Communities.* London, 1979
Parry, A. and Dinnage, J., *EEC Law.* London, 1982
Paxton, J., *The Developing Common Market.* London, 1976.—*A Dictionary of the European Communities.* 2nd ed. London, 1982
Twitchett, C. C., *Harmonisation in the EEC.* London, 1981

Wallace, W. and Herreman, I. (eds.) *A Community of Twelve?* Bruges, 1978
Walsh, A. E. and Paxton, J., *Competition Policy*. London, 1975

EUROPEAN FREE TRADE ASSOCIATION (EFTA)

The European Free Trade Association has 6 member countries: Austria, Finland (an associate member from 1961–1985), Iceland, Norway, Sweden and Switzerland. The Stockholm Convention establishing the Association entered into force on 3 May 1960 and Finland became associated on 27 March 1961. Iceland joined EFTA on 1 March 1970 and was immediately granted duty-free entry for industrial goods exported to EFTA countries, while being given 10 years to abolish her own existing protective duties. The UK and Denmark, both founder members, left EFTA on 31 Dec. 1972 to join the EEC as did Portugal, also a founder member, on 31 Dec. 1985.

When the Association was created it had three objectives: To achieve free trade in industrial products between member countries, to assist in the creation of a single market embracing the countries of Western Europe, and to contribute to the expansion of world trade in general.

The first objective was achieved on 31 Dec. 1966, when virtually all inter-EFTA tariffs were removed. This was 3 years earlier than originally planned. Finland removed her remaining EFTA tariffs a year later on 31 Dec. 1967 and Iceland removed her tariffs on 31 Dec. 1979.

The fulfilment of the second aim was secured in 1972. On 22 Jan. 1972 the UK and Denmark signed the Treaty of Accession to the EEC whereby they became members of the enlarged Community from 1 Jan. 1973. On 22 July 1972, 5 other EFTA countries, Austria, Iceland, Portugal, Sweden and Switzerland signed Free Trade Agreements with the enlarged EEC. A similar agreement negotiated with Finland was signed on 5 Oct. 1973. Norway, whose intention of joining the EEC was reversed following a referendum, signed a similar agreement on 14 May 1973. The agreements now also apply to trade between the EFTA countries and the 3 countries which joined the EC at later dates: Greece (1 Jan. 1981) and Spain and Portugal (1 Jan. 1986). The Luxembourg Declaration of April 1984 which followed the final abolition of tariffs on EFTA-EC trade in industrial goods set out the guidelines for strengthening and developing EFTA-EC co-operation, with the aim of creating the European Economic Space comprising all the 18 countries in the European free trade system.

The third objective was to contribute to the expansion of world trade. In 1959 trade between the countries now in EFTA amounted to US$705·6m. and total exports from these countries were US$6,562m. In 1988 the respective figures were US$24,973m. and US$177,349m. More than half EFTA trade is with the EC.

EFTA tariff treatment applies to those industrial products which are of EFTA origin, and these are traded freely between member countries. Each EFTA country remains free, however, to impose its own rates of duty on products entering from outside either EFTA or the EC.

Generally, agricultural products do not come under the provisions for free trade, but bilateral agreements have been negotiated to increase trade in these products.

The operation of the Convention is the responsibility of a Council assisted by a small secretariat. Each EFTA country holds the chairmanship of the Council for 6 months.

Secretary-General: Georg Reisch (Austria).
Headquarters: 9–11 rue de Varembé, 1211 Geneva 20, Switzerland.

Convention Establishing the European Free Trade Association
EFTA Bulletin (Four issues a year)
EFTA What it is, What it does
The European Free Trade Association

THE WARSAW PACT

On 14 May 1955 the USSR, Albania, Bulgaria, Czechoslovakia, the German Democratic Republic, Hungary, Poland and Romania signed, in Warsaw, a 20-year treaty of friendship and collaboration, after the USSR annulled treaties of alliance with the UK and France. The treaty was extended for 10 years in July 1975 and renewed for 20 years in April 1985. Since 1985 the Pact's Political Consultative Committee has met annually in member countries in turn. It has established a Committee of Defence Ministers (1969), a Military Council (1969), a Technical Committee (1969) and a Committee of Foreign Ministers.

The main provisions of the treaty are as follows:

Article 4. In case of armed aggression in Europe against one or several States party to the pact by a State or group of States, each State member of the pact. . . will afford to the State or States which are the object of such aggression immediate assistance. . . with all means which appear necessary, including the use of armed force. . . These measures will cease as soon as the Security Council takes measures necessary for establishing and preserving international peace and security.

Article 5. The contracting Powers agree to set up a joint command of their armed forces to be allotted by agreement between the Powers, at the disposal of this command and used on the basis of jointly established principles. They will also take over agreed measures necessary to strengthen their defences.

Article 9. The present treaty is open to other States, irrespective of their social or Government regime, who declare their readiness to abide by the terms of the treaty in order to safeguard peace and security of the peoples.

Article 11. In the event of a system of collective security being set up in Europe and a pact to this effect being signed—to which each party to this treaty will direct its efforts—the present treaty will lapse from the day such a collective security treaty comes into force.

It is estimated (1988) that the armed forces of the Warsaw Pact countries total 3,090,000, compared with 2,213,593 NATO forces.

Gen. P. Lushev (appointed Feb. 1989) is C.-in-C. of the united Armed Forces, with headquarters in Moscow.

In 1968 Albania left the Warsaw Pact.

Two Soviet divisions are stationed in Poland, 19 in the German Democratic Republic, 4 in Hungary and 5 in Czechoslovakia.

Further Reading

Clawson, R. W. and Kaplan, L. S. (eds.) *The Warsaw Pact: Political Purpose and Military Means*. Wilmington, 1982

Holloway, D. and Sharp, J. M. O. (eds.) *The Warsaw Pact: Alliance in Transition*. London, 1984

Lewis, W. J., *The Warsaw Pact: Doctrine and Strategy*. Maidenhead, 1982

Nelson, D. N., *Alliance Behavior in the Warsaw Pact*. Boulder, 1986

COUNCIL FOR MUTUAL ECONOMIC ASSISTANCE[1]

Membership. Established in Jan. 1949; founder members were USSR, Bulgaria, Czechoslovakia, Hungary, Poland and Romania. Later admissions were Albania (1949; ceased participation 1961), German Democratic Republic (1950), Mongolia (1962), Cuba (1972), Vietnam (1978). Yugoslavia takes part in 19 CMEA activities, and Afghánistán, Angola, Ethiopia, Laos, Mozambique, Nicaragua and the People's Democratic Republic of Yemen send observers to some CMEA bodies.

External relations. The foreign trade of CMEA member countries was 316,000m. rubles in 1987 (with other CMEA members, 207,000m. rubles). A declaration of

[1] CMEA is the official abbreviation. Other unofficial abbreviations are COMECON and CEMA. The Russian form is *Sovet Ekonomicheskoi Vzaimopomoshchi* (SEV).

mutual recognition was signed with the EEC in June 1988. There are co-operation agreements with Afghánistán, Angola, Ethiopia, Finland, Iraq, Mexico, Mozambique, Nicaragua and the People's Democratic Republic of Yemen.

The Charter. The Charter (adopted in 1959) consists of a preamble and 18 articles. Extracts (in the language of the official English version) are as follows:

Article 1. Aims and Principles: 1 'The purpose of the Council is to promote, by uniting and co-ordinating the efforts of the member countries, the further extension and improvement of co-operation and the development of socialist economic integration, the planned development of their national economies, the acceleration of economic and technical progress in these countries, higher level of industrialization of the less industrialized countries, a continuous increase in labour productivity, a gradual approximation and equalization of economic development levels and a steady improvement in the wellbeing of the peoples. 2 The Council is based on the principles of the sovereign equality of all member countries.'

Article 2. Membership 'open to other countries which subscribe to the purposes and principles of the Council'.

Article 3. Functions and Powers to (a) 'organize all-round... co-operation of member countries in the most rational use of natural resources and acceleration of the development of their productive forces'; (b) 'foster the improvement of the international socialist division of labour by co-ordinating national economic development plans, and the specialization and co-operation of production in member countries'; (c) to assist in... carrying out joint measures for the development of industry and agriculture... transport... principal capital investments... [and] trade'.

Article 4. Recommendations and Decisions '... shall be adopted only with the consent of the interested member countries.'

The Structure. The supreme authority is the annual Council of all prime ministers held in members' capitals in rotation. Decisions must be unanimous.

There is an *Executive Committee* made up of 1 representative from each member state of deputy premier rank. It meets at least once every 3 months.

The administrative organ is the *Secretariat*.

Headquarters: Prospekt Kalinina, 56, Moscow, G-205.

Secretary: V. V. Sychev (appointed 1983).

In 1988 the Secretariat and its subordinate committees and permanent commissions were reduced in size and reorganized. Decision-making on trade matters has been delegated to enterprise level.

There are 6 *Committees: for Co-operation in Planning; for Scientific and Technical Co-operation; for Co-operation in Engineering; for Co-operation in the Agro-Industrial Complex; for Electronics; for Co-operation in Foreign Economic Relations.* There are also 11 *Permanent Commissions.*

The *Standing Conferences* of experts have been abolished.

There are 3 semi-autonomous bodies within CMEA: The Institute of Standardization, the Bureau for the Co-ordination of Ship Freighting and the International Institute of Economic Problems of the World Socialist System.

Also associated with CMEA are:

The **International Bank for Economic Co-operation** was founded in 1963 with a capital of 300m. transferable roubles (i.e., used for intra-CMEA clearing accounts only) and started operating on 1 Jan. 1964. It undertakes multilateral settlements and advances credits to finance trading and other operations.

The **International Investments Bank** was founded in 1970 and went into operation on 1 Jan. 1971 with a capital of 1,071m. transferable roubles.

Economic integration. Trading accounts between members have been settled in 'transferable roubles', but a decision to proceed towards currency convertibility was taken at the 1987 Council. At the 1988 Council all members except Romania agreed to the gradual creation of a common market.

Further Reading

Charter of the Council for Mutual Economic Assistance. Moscow, 1980
Comecon Foreign Trade Data. London, biennial, from 1979

Council for Mutual Economic Assistance: Thirty Years. Moscow, 1979
Comprehensive Programme for the Further Extension and Improvement of Co-operation and the Development of Socialist Economic Integration by the CMEA-member Countries. Moscow, 1971 (The official English-language version. This document also frequently referred to as the *Complex Programme*, etc.)
Ekonomicheskoe Sotrudnichestvo Stran-Chlenov SEV. Moscow, monthly
Multilateral Economic Co-operation of Socialist States: A Collection of Documents. Moscow, 1977
Statistical Year Book of CMEA Member Countries. Moscow, annual
Survey of CMEA Activities. Moscow, annual
Marrese, M. and Vanous, J., *Soviet Subsidization of Trade with Eastern Europe.* Berkeley, 1983
Nagy, L., *The Socialist Collective Agreement.* Budapest, 1984
Saunders, C. T. (ed.) *Regional Integration in East and West.* London, 1983
Schiavone, G., *The Institutions of Comecon.* London, 1981
Sobell, V., *The Red Market: Industrial Co-operation and Specialisation in Comecon.* Aldershot, 1984
Wallace, W. V. and Clarke, A. R., *Comecon, Trade and the West.* London, 1986

COLOMBO PLAN

History: Founded in 1950 to promote the development of newly independent Asian member countries, the Colombo Plan has grown from its modest beginning as a group of seven Commonwealth nations into an international organization of 26 countries.

Originally the Plan was conceived for a period of six years. Its life has since been extended from time to time, generally at five-year intervals. The Consultative Committee, the Plan's highest deliberative body, at its meeting in Jakarta in 1980, gave the Plan an indefinite span of life; its need and relevance will henceforth be examined only if considered necessary.

The Plan is multilateral in approach but bilateral in operation: Multilateral in that it takes cognizance of the problems of development of member countries in the Asia and Pacific region and endeavours to deal with them in a co-ordinated way; bilateral because negotiations for assistance are made direct between a donor and a recipient country.

Aims: The aims of the Colombo Plan are: *(a)* to promote interest in and support for the economic and social development in Asia and the Pacific; *(b)* to keep under review economic and social progress in the region and help accelerate development through co-operative effort; and *(c)* to facilitate development assistance to and within the region.

Member Countries: Afghánistán, Australia, Bangladesh, Bhután, Burma, Cambodia, Canada, Fiji, India, Indonesia, Iran, Japan, Republic of Korea, Lao People's Democratic Republic, Malaysia, Maldives, Nepál, New Zealand, Pakistan, Papua New Guinea, Philippines, Singapore, Sri Lanka, Thailand, UK and USA.

Development Assistance: Colombo Plan aid covers all fields of socio-economic development and amounted to US$6,729·3m. in 1988. It takes three principal forms:

(i) *Capital Aid* including grants and loans for national projects mainly from the six developed member countries of the Plan.
The total amount of capital aid and technical co-operation assistance provided by the developed donors under the plan in 1986 was as follows:

	US$1m.
Japan	4,404·1
USA	1,035·4
Australia	461·3
Canada	420·0
UK	399·0
New Zealand	9·5
Total	6,729·3

(ii) *Technical Co-operation:* Assistance is provided in the form of services of experts and volunteers, fellowships, and equipment for training and research. During 1988, 35,002 students and trainees received training, 8,226 experts and 1,615 volunteers were sent out. Total disbursements on technical co-operation by the developed member countries in 1988 amounted to $1,020·7m.

(iii) *Technical Co-operation Among Developing Countries (TCDC):* The promotion of TCDC is a major objective of the Plan. Under TCDC programmes in 1988, 2,356 students and trainees received training and 69 experts were sent out. TCDC expenditures during 1986 amounted to $9·8m.

Structure: There are four organs which give focus to the Plan:

Consultative Committee: The Committee is the highest deliberative body of the Plan and consists of Ministers of member Governments who meet once in two years. The Ministerial meeting is preceded by a meeting of senior officials who are directly concerned with the operation of the Plan in various countries.

Colombo Plan Council: The Council is also a deliberative body which meets several times a year in Colombo, where most member countries have resident diplomatic missions, to review the economic and social development of the Asia-Pacific region and promote co-operation among member countries.

Colombo Plan Bureau: Its functions include servicing the meetings of the Colombo Plan Council and the Consultative Committee, carrying out research, and dissemination of statistical and other information relating to activities under the Plan. Since 1973 the Bureau has been operating a Drug Advisory Programme to assist national and regional efforts to eliminate the causes and ameliorate the effects of drug abuse.

Colombo Plan Staff College: The Colombo Plan Staff College for Technician Education, established in 1975, transferred from Singapore to the Philippines in 1987. The College helps member countries in developing their systems of technician education, mainly through training courses, seminars and consultancies. It is separately financed by most Colombo Plan member countries and functions under the guidance of its own Governing Board consisting of the heads of member countries' diplomatic missions resident in Singapore.

Flag: Dark blue with a central white disc containing the Colombo Plan logo in black.

Headquarters: Colombo Plan Bureau, 12 Melbourne Avenue, PO Box 596, Colombo 4, Sri Lanka.

The Colombo Plan (Cmd. 8080). HMSO, 1950; reprinted 1952.—*Annual Report.* HMSO 1952 to 1971 followed by Colombo Plan Bureau, Sri Lanka, 1971–86

Reports of the Council for Technical Co-operation. HMSO annually until 1966–67 followed by the Colombo Plan Bureau, Sri Lanka, 1967–68 to date

ASSOCIATION OF SOUTH EAST ASIAN NATIONS (ASEAN)

History and Membership. The Association of South East Asian Nations is a regional organization formed by the governments of Indonesia, Malaysia, the Philippines, Singapore and Thailand through the Bangkok Declaration which was signed by the Foreign Ministers of ASEAN countries on 8 Aug. 1967. Brunei joined in 1984.

Objectives. The main objectives are to accelerate economic growth, social progress and cultural development, to promote active collaboration and mutual assistance in matters of common interest, to ensure the stability of the South East Asian region and to maintain close co-operation with existing international and regional organizations with similar aims. Principal projects concern economic co-operation and development, with the intensification of intra-ASEAN trade and trade between the region and the rest of the world; joint research and technological programmes; co-operation in transportation and communications; promotion of tourism and South

East Asian studies; including cultural, scientific, educational and administrative exchanges.

Organs. The highest authority in ASEAN are the Heads of Government of the Member Countries who meet as and when necessary to give directions to ASEAN. The highest policy-making body is the Meeting of Foreign Ministers, commonly known as the Annual Ministerial Meeting, which convenes in each of the ASEAN member countries on a rotational basis in alphabetical order. The Standing Committee, comprising the Foreign Minister of the country hosting the Ministerial Meeting in that particular year and the accredited ambassadors of the other member countries, carries out the work of the Association in between the Ministerial Meetings and handles the routine matters to ensure continuity and to make decisions based on the guidelines or policies set by the Ministerial Meetings and submit for the consideration of the Foreign Ministers all reports and recommendations of the various ASEAN committees. There are five economic committees under the ASEAN Economic Ministers and three non-economic committees that recommend and draw up programmes for ASEAN co-operation. These committees are responsible for the operation and implementation of ASEAN projects in their respective fields. Each ASEAN capital has an ASEAN National Secretariat. The central secretariat for ASEAN is located in Jakarta, Indonesia, and is headed by the Secretary General, a post that revolves among the member states in alphabetical order every 3 years. Bureau directors and other officers of the ASEAN Secretariat remain in office for 3 years.

Secretary-General: Roderick Yong (Brunei Darussalam).

Further Reading

Broinowski, A., *Understanding ASEAN*. London, 1982
Wawn, B., *The Economies of the ASEAN Countries*. London, 1982
Wong, J., *ASEAN Economics in Perspective*. London, 1979

ORGANIZATION OF AMERICAN STATES

On 14 April 1890 representatives of the American republics, meeting in Washington at the First International Conference of American States, established an 'International Union of American Republics' and, as its central office, a 'Commercial Bureau of American Republics', which later became the Pan American Union. This international organization's object was to foster mutual understanding and co-operation among the nations of the western hemisphere. Since that time, successive inter-American conferences have greatly broadened the scope of work of the organization.

This led to the adoption on 30 April 1948 by the Ninth International Conference of American States, at Bogotá, Colombia, of the Charter of the Organization of American States. This co-ordinated the work of all the former independent official entities in the inter-American system and defined their mutual relationships. The purposes of the OAS are to achieve an order of peace and justice, promote American solidarity, strengthen collaboration among the member states and defend their sovereignty, territorial integrity and independence. The OAS is a regional organization of the United Nations for the maintenance of peace and security.

Membership is on a basis of absolute equality. Each country has one vote in the Council of the Organization and its organs. The member countries were (1980): Antigua and Barbuda, Argentina, Bahamas, Barbados, Bolivia, Brazil, Chile, Colombia, Costa Rica, Cuba, Commonwealth of Dominica, Dominican Republic, Ecuador, El Salvador, Grenada, Guatemala, Haiti, Honduras, Jamaica, Mexico, Nicaragua, Panama, Paraguay, Peru, Saint Christopher (Kitts) and Nevis, Saint Lucia, Saint Vincent and the Grenadines, Suriname, Trinidad and Tobago, USA, Uruguay, Venezuela.

The OAS has been concerned increasingly in recent years with programmes to promote Latin American economic and social development. The OAS provides specialized training for thousands of Latin Americans each year in a wide variety of development-related fields. It also carries out several missions projects each year in response to requests from member governments.

Under the amended Charter, the OAS accomplishes its purposes by means of:

(a) The *General Assembly*, which meets annually in various countries of the member states.

(b) The *Meeting of Consultation of Ministers of Foreign Affairs*, held to consider problems of an urgent nature and of common interest.

(c) Three councils of equal rank: the *Permanent Council*, which replaces the old OAS Council; the *Inter-American Economic and Social Council*; and the *Inter-American Council for Education, Science and Culture*. Functions are to direct and co-ordinate work in the areas of their competence and render the governments such specialized services as they may request. Each council is composed of 1 representative from each member state, appointed by his government.

(d) The *Inter-American Juridical Committee* which acts as an advisory body to the OAS on juridical matters and promotes the development and codification of international law. Eleven jurists, elected every 4 years by the General Assembly, represent all the American States.

(e) The *Inter-American Commission on Human Rights* which oversees the observance and protection of human rights. Seven members represent all the OAS member states.

(f) The *General Secretariat* is the central and permanent organ of the OAS.

(g) The *Specialized Conferences*, meeting to deal with special technical matters or to develop specific aspects of inter-American co-operation.

(h) The *Specialized Organizations*, inter-governmental organizations established by multilateral agreements to discharge specific functions in their respective fields of action, such as women's affairs, agriculture, child welfare, Indian affairs, geography and history, and health.

Secretary-General: João Clemente Baena Soares (Brazil).
Assistant Secretary-General: Valerie T. McComie (Barbados).

The Secretary-General and the Assistant Secretary-General are elected by the General Assembly for 5-year terms. The General Assembly approves the annual budget for the Organization, which is financed by quotas contributed by the member governments.

General Secretariat: Washington, D.C., 20006, USA.
Flag: Light blue with the OAS seal in colour in the centre.

Further Reading

Publications of the OAS General Secretariat include:

Charter of the Organization of American States. 1948.—*As Amended by the Protocol of Buenos Aires in 1967*
Americas. Illustrated bi-monthly, from 1949 (Spanish and English edition)
Organization of American States, a Handbook. Rev. ed. 1977
Organization of American States. Directory. Quarterly, from 1951
Report on the Tenth Inter-American Conference, Caracas 1954. 1955
Inter-American Review of Bibliography. Quarterly, from 1951
Annual Report of the Secretary-General
Status of Inter-American Treaties and Conventions. Annual
The Alliance for Progress: The Charter of Punta del Este. 1962
The Americas in the 1980s: An Agenda for the Decade Ahead. 1982

Publications on Latin America (*see also* the bibliographical notes appended to each country):

Revenue, Expenditure and Public Debts of the Latin American Republics. Division of Financial Information, US Department of Commerce. Annual
Boundaries of the Latin American Republics: An Annotated List of Documents, 1493–1943. Department of State, Office of the Geographer. Washington, 1944
Burgin, M. (ed.) *Handbook of Latin American Studies.* Gainesville, Fla., 1935 ff.
Hirschman, A. O., *Latin American Issues:* [11] *Essays and Comments.* New York, 1961
Plaza, G., *The Organization of American States: Instrument for Hemispheric Development.*

Washington, 1969.—*Latin America Today and Tomorrow*. Washington, 1971
Steward, J. H. (ed.) *Handbook of the South American Indian*. 7 vols. Washington, 1946–59
Thomas, A. V. W. and A. J., *The Organization of American States*. Southern Methodist Univ. Press, 1963

LATIN AMERICAN ECONOMIC GROUPINGS

Latin American Integration Association (LAIA) /*Asociación Latinoamericano de Integración* (ALADI). The Association took over from the Latin American Free Trade Area (LAFTA) on 1 Jan. 1981 which was created in 1960 to further trade between the member states and promote regional integration. Members: Argentina, Bolivia, Brazil, Chile, Colombia, Ecuador, Mexico, Paraguay, Peru, Uruguay and Venezuela.

Headquarters: Cebollati 1461, Casilla 577, Montevideo, Uruguay.

Síntesis ALADI (monthly, Spanish)
Newsletter (six issues a year, Spanish)

Central American Common Market (CACM) /*Mercado Común Centroamericana*. In Dec. 1960 El Salvador, Guatemala, Honduras and Nicaragua concluded the General Treaty of Central American Economic Integration *(Tratado General de Integración Económica Centroamericana)* under the auspices of the Organization of Central American States (ODECA) in Managua. Costa Rica acceded in 1962. Members: Costa Rica, El Salvador, Guatemala, Honduras and Nicaragua.

Headquarters: 4a Avda 10–25, Zona 14, Apdo 1237, Guatemala City, Guatemala.

Carta Informativa (monthly)
Anuario Estadística Centroamericano de Comercio Exterior (annual)

The Andean Group (Grupo Andino). On 26 May 1969 an agreement was signed by Bolivia, Chile, Colombia, Ecuador and Peru creating the Andean Group. Venezuela was initially actively involved but did not sign the agreement until 1973. Chile withdrew from the Group in 1977. Members: Bolivia, Colombia, Ecuador, Peru and Venezuela.

Headquarters: Avda Paseo de la Republica 3895, Casilla 18–1177, Lima 27, Peru.

Latin American Economic System/Sistema Económico Latinoamericano (SELA). SELA was created by 25 Latin American and Caribbean countries (Suriname joined in 1979) meeting in Panama, 17 Oct. 1975. The System provides member countries with permanent institutional machinery for joint consultation, coordination, co-operation and promotion in economic and social matters at both intraregional and extraregional levels.

Headquarters: Apdo 17035, El Conde, Caracas 1010, Venezuela.

Latin American Association of Development Financing Institutions/Asociación Latinoamericana de Instituciones Financieros de Desarrollo (ALIDE). Founded in 1968 to promote co-operation among regional development financing organizations.

Headquarters: Paseo de la Republica 3211, POB 3988, Lima, Peru.

Latin American Banking Federation/Federación Latinoamericana de Bancos (FELABAN). Established to co-ordinate efforts towards a wider and accelerated economic development in Latin American countries.

Headquarters: Apdo Aereo 091959, Bogotá, DE8, Colombia.

Organization of the Cooperatives of America/Organización de las Cooperativas de América. Founded in 1963 to improve social, economic, cultural and moral conditions through the co-operative system.

Headquarters: POB 13568–24163, Calle 97A no. 11–31, Oficina 201, Bogotá, Colombia.

Cooperativa America (six times a year, Spanish)

Further Reading

British Bulletin of Publications on Latin America, the Caribbean, Portugal and Spain. London, from June 1949 (half-yearly)
South America, Central America and the Caribbean, 1988. London, 1987
The Latin America and Caribbean Review, 1989. Saffron Walden, 1988
Angarita, C. and Coffey, P., *Europe and the Andean Countries: A Comparison of Economic Policies and Institutions*. London, 1988
Box, B., (ed.) *1990 South American Handbook*. Bath (annual)
Bulmer-Thomas, V., *The Political Economy of Central America since 1920*. CUP, 1987.
—*Britain and Latin America: A Changing Relationship*, 1989
Duran, E., *European Interests in Latin America*. London, 1985
Ferguson, J. and Pearce, J., *The Thatcher Years: Britain and Latin America*. London, 1988
Inter-American Development Bank, *Economic and Social Progress in Latin America: Economic Integration*. Washington, 1984

CARIBBEAN COMMUNITY (CARICOM)

Establishment and Functions. The Treaty establishing the Caribbean Community, including the Caribbean Common Market, and the Agreement establishing the Common External Tariff for the Caribbean Common Market, was signed by the Prime Ministers of Barbados, Guyana, Jamaica and Trinidad and Tobago at Chaguaramas, Trinidad, on 4 July 1973, and entered into force on 1 Aug. 1973. Six less developed countries of CARIFTA signed the Treaty of Chaguaramas on 17 April 1974. They were Belize, Dominica, Grenada, Saint Lucia, St Vincent and Montserrat, and the Treaty came into effect for those countries on 1 May 1974. Antigua acceded to membership on 4 July 1974 and on 26 July the Associated State of St Kitts–Nevis–Anguilla signed the Treaty of Chaguaramas in Kingston, Jamaica, and became a member of the Caribbean Community, Bahamas became a member of the Community but not of the Common Market on 4 July 1983.

The Caribbean Community has 3 areas of activity: *(i)* economic co-operation through the Caribbean Common Market; *(ii)* co-ordination of foreign policy; *(iii)* functional co-operation in areas such as health, education and culture, youth and sports, science and technology, and tax administration.

The Caribbean Common Market provides for the establishment of a Common External Tariff, a common protective policy and the progressive co-ordination of external trade policies; the adoption of a scheme for the harmonization of fiscal incentives to industry; double taxation arrangements among member countries; the co-ordination of economic policies and development planning; and a special regime for the less developed countries of the community.

Membership: Antigua and Barbuda, Bahamas, Barbados, Belize, Dominica, Grenada, Guyana, Jamaica, Montserrat, St Kitts–Nevis, Saint Lucia, St Vincent and the Grenadines, and Trinidad and Tobago.

Structure: The *Conference of Heads of Government* is the principal organ of the Community, and its primary responsibility is to determine the policy of the Community. It is the final authority of the Community and the Common Market, and for the conclusion of treaties and relationships between the Community and international organizations and States. It is responsible for financial arrangements for meeting the expenses of the Community.

The *Common Market Council* is the principal organ of the Common Market and consists of a Minister of Government designated by each member state. Decisions in both the Conference and the Council are in the main taken on the basis of unanimity.

The *Secretariat*, successor to the Commonwealth Caribbean Regional Secretariat, is the principal administrative organ of the Community and of the Common Market. The Secretary-General is appointed by the Conference on the recommendation of the Council for a term not exceeding 5 years and may be reappointed. The Secretary-General shall act in that capacity in all meetings of the Conference, the Council, and of the institutions of the Community.

Institutions of the Community, established by the Heads of Government Conference, are: Conference of Ministers responsible for Health; Standing Committees of Ministers responsible for Education, Industry, Labour, Foreign Affairs, Finance, Agriculture, Energy, Mines and Natural Resources, Industry, Science and Technology, Transport and Legal Affairs, respectively.

Associate Institutions: Caribbean Development Bank; Caribbean Examinations Council; Council of Legal Education; University of the West Indies; University of Guyana; Caribbean Meteorological Organization.

Flag: Divided horizontally light blue over dark blue; in the centre a white disc bearing the linked letters CC in light blue and dark blue respectively.

Secretary-General: Roderick Rainford.

Deputy Secretary-General: Frank Abdulah.

Headquarters: Bank of Guyana Building, PO Box 10827, Georgetown, Guyana.

The language of the Community is English.

Further Reading

CARICOM Perspective. (3 times a year). *CARICOM Bibliography* (bi-annual)

The Caribbean Community in the 1980's. Caribbean Community Secretariat, 1982

Axline, A. W., *Caribbean Integration: The Politics of Regionalism.* London and New York, 1979

Cross, M. and Heuman, G., *Labour in the Caribbean.* London, 1988

Parry, J. H., *et. al. A Short History of the West Indies.* Rev. ed. London, 1987

Payne, A. J., *The Politics of the Caribbean Community 1961–79.* Manchester Univ. Press, 1980

SOUTH PACIFIC FORUM

The South Pacific Forum held its first meeting of Heads of Government in New Zealand in 1971. Membership: Australia, Cook Islands, Fiji, Kiribati, Nauru, New Zealand, Niue, Papua New Guinea, Solomon Islands, Tonga, Tuvalu, Vanuatu and Western Samoa. The Federated States of Micronesia have observer status.

In 1985 the Forum adopted a Treaty for a nuclear-free zone in the Pacific.

THE LEAGUE OF ARAB STATES

Origin. The formation of the League of Arab States in 1945 was largely inspired by the Arab awakening of the 19th century. This movement sought to re-create and reintegrate the Arab community which, though for 400 years a part of the Ottoman Empire, had preserved its identity as a separate national group held together by memories of a common past, a common religion and a common language, as well as by the consciousness of being part of a common cultural heritage. The leaders of the Arab movement in the 19th century and of the Arab revolt against Turkey in the First World War sought to achieve these aims through secession from the Ottoman Empire into a united and independent Arab state comprising all the Arab countries in Asia. However the 1919 peace settlement divided the Arab world in Asia (with the exception of Saudi Arabia and the Yemen) into British and French spheres of influence and established in them a number of separate states and administrations (Syria, Lebanon, Iraq, Jordan and Palestine) under temporary mandatory control.

By 1943, however, 7 of these countries had substantially achieved their independence. An Arab conference therefore met in Alexandria in the autumn of 1944; it formulated the 'Alexandria Protocol', which delineated the outlines of the Arab

League. It was found that neither a unitary state nor a federation could be achieved, but only a league of sovereign states. A covenant, establishing such a league, was signed in Cairo on 22 March 1945 by the representatives of Egypt, Iraq, Saudi Arabia, Syria, Lebanon, Jordan and Yemen. There were (1980) 21 members of the League: Algeria, Bahrain, Djibouti, Iraq, Jordan, Kuwait, Lebanon, Libya, Mauritania, Morocco, Oman, Palestine L.O., Qatar, Saudi Arabia, Somalia, Sudan, Syria, Tunisia, United Arab Emirates, P.D.R. of Yemen and Yemen Arab Republic.

In the Charter's Special Annex on Palestine, the signatories considered the special circumstances of Palestine and decided that until the country can effectively exercise its independence, the Council of the League should take charge in the selection of an Arab representative from Palestine to take part in its work.

Egypt's membership of the League was suspended, in accordance with a resolution passed at the Baghdad summit, in March 1979 and the secretariat moved from Cairo to Tunis. This action was taken in response to the signing of a bilateral peace treaty between Egypt and Israel. Egypt was readmitted in May 1989.

Organization. The machinery of the League consists of a Council, a number of Special Committees and a Permanent Secretariat. On the Council each state has one vote. The Council may meet in any of the Arab capitals. Its functions include mediation in any dispute between any of the League states or a League state and a country outside the League. The Council has a Political Committee consisting of the Foreign Ministers of the Arab states. There are also 22 specialized agencies.

The Permanent Secretariat of the League, under a Secretary-General (who enjoys, along with his senior colleagues, full diplomatic status), has its seat in Tunisia.

The League considers itself a regional organization within the framework of the United Nations at which its secretary-general is an observer.

Secretary-General: Chedli Klibi (Tunisia).

Flag: Dark green with the seal of the Arab League in white in the centre.

Arab Common Market. The Arab Common Market came into operation on 1 Jan. 1965. The agreement, reached on 13 Aug. 1964 and open to all the Arab League states, has been signed by Iraq, Jordan, Syria and Egypt. The agreement provides for the abolition of customs duties on agricultural products and natural resources within 5 years, by reducing tariffs at an annual rate of 20%. Customs duties on industrial products are to be reduced by 10% annually. The agreement also provides for the free movement of capital and labour between member countries, the establishment of common external tariffs, the co-ordination of economical development and the framing of a common foreign economic policy.

Further Reading

Arab Maritime Data, 1979–80. London, 1979
Gomaa, A. M., *The Foundation of the League of Arab States.* London, 1977

ORGANIZATION OF THE PETROLEUM EXPORTING COUNTRIES

Aims. The Organization was founded in Baghdad, Iraq, in 1960 with the following founder members, Iran, Iraq, Kuwait, Saudi Arabia and Venezuela. The principal aims are unifying the petroleum policies of member countries and determining the best means for safeguarding their interests, individually and collectively; to devise ways and means of ensuring the stabilization of prices in international oil markets with a view to eliminating harmful and unnecessary fluctuations; and to secure a steady income for the producing countries, an efficient, economic and regular supply of petroleum to consuming nations, and a fair return on their capital to those investing in the petroleum industry.

Membership (1989). Algeria, Ecuador, Gabon, Indonesia, Iran, Iraq, Kuwait, Libya, Nigeria, Qatar, Saudi Arabia, United Arab Emirates and Venezuela. Membership is open to any other country having substantial net exports of crude petroleum, which has fundamentally similar interests to those of member countries.

OPEC Fund for International Development: The Fund was established in 1976 to provide financial aid to developing countries, other than OPEC members, on advantageous terms.

Secretary-General: Dr Subroto.
Deputy Secretary-General: Vacant.

Headquarters: Obere Donaustrasse 93, A–1020 Vienna, Austria.

Flag: Light blue with the Opec logo in white in the centre.

Further Reading

OPEC publications include: *Annual Statistical Bulletin. Annual Report. OPEC Bulletin* (monthly). *OPEC Review* (quarterly).
Ahrari, M. E., *Opec: The Failing Giant.* Univ. Press of Kentucky, 1986
Al-Chalabi, F., *OPEC and the International Oil Industry: A Changing Structure.* OUP, 1980
El Mallakh, R., *OPEC: Twenty Years and Beyond.* London, 1982
Griffin, J. and Teece, D. J., *OPEC Behaviour and World Oil Prices.* London and Boston, 1982
Skeet, *OPEC: Twenty-five years of Prices and Policies.* CUP, 1988

ORGANIZATION OF AFRICAN UNITY

On 25 May 1963 the heads of state or government of 32 African countries, at a conference in Addis Ababa, signed a charter establishing an 'Organization of African Unity' *(Organisation de l'Unité Africaine).*

Its chief objects are the furtherance of African unity and solidarity; the co-ordination of the political, economic, cultural, health, scientific and defence policies and the elimination of colonialism in Africa.

The organs of the Organization are: (1) the assembly of the heads of state and government; (2) the council of ministers; (3) the general secretariat; (4) a commission of mediation, conciliation and arbitration. Arabic, French, Portuguese and English are recognized as working languages.

Chairman: Moussa Traore (Mali).
Secretary-General: Salim Ahmed Salim.
Headquarters: Addis Ababa.
Flag: Horizontally green, white, green, with the white fimbriated yellow, and the seal of the OAU in the centre.

DANUBE COMMISSION

The Danube Commission was constituted in 1949 based on the Convention regarding the regime of navigation on the Danube, which was signed in Belgrade on 18 Aug. 1948. The Belgrade Convention reaffirmed that navigation on the Danube from Ulm to the Black Sea, with access to the sea through the Sulina arm and the Sulina Canal, is equally free and open to the nationals, merchant shipping and merchandise of all states as to harbour and navigation fees as well as conditions of merchant navigation.

The Danube Commission is composed of representatives from the countries on the Danube (1 for each of these countries), namely, Austria, Bulgaria, Hungary, Romania, Czechoslovakia, USSR and Yugoslavia. Since 1957, representatives of the Ministry of Transport from the Federal Republic of Germany have attended the meetings of the Commission as guests of the Secretariat.

The functions of the Danube Commission are to check that the provisions of the Convention are carried out, to establish a uniform buoying system on all the Danube's navigable waterways and to establish the basic regulations for navigation on the river. The Commission co-ordinates the regulations for river, customs and sanitation control as well as the hydrometeorological service and collects statistical data concerning navigation on the Danube.

The Danube Commission enjoys legal status. It has its own seal and flag. The members of the Commission and elected officers enjoy diplomatic immunity. The Commission's official buildings, archives and documents are inviolable. French and Russian are the official languages of the Commission.

Since 1954 the headquarters of the Commission have been in Budapest.

Flag: Blue, with a red strip fimbriated white along the bottom edge, and the initials of the Commission within a wreath in the canton—Latin letters on obverse Cyrillic on reverse.

Further Reading

Danube Commission's publications include: Compilation of Agreements on Danube Navigation; Basic Regulations of Navigation; Recommendations relating to the establishment of the dimensions of the channel and hydrotechnical and other works (1969; 1975; 1979; 1988 Editions); Plan of basic works aiming at obtaining the dimensions of the channel and hydrotechnical and other works recommended on the Danube for the period 1980–1990 (1984 ed.); Danubian Bridges; Danubian Ships; Danube Maintenance; Danube Profile; Mileage Charts; Pilots' Charts; Sailing Direction; Hydrological Yearbooks; Hydrological Manuals; Statistical Yearbooks; Statistical Manuals; Recommendations on unified rules for sanitary, veterinary, plant protection and customs control; Rules of Procedure and other organization documents of the Danube Commission; Proceedings of Sessions; General Information on the Danube Commission and on its activity (with the text of the Convention regarding the regime of navigation on the Danube in annex).

PART II

COUNTRIES OF THE WORLD

A—Z

AFGHÁNISTÁN

Capital: Kábul
Population: 10–12m. (1988)
GNP per capita: US$250 (1985)

Jamhuria Afghanistan

HISTORY. A military *coup* on 17 July 1973 overthrew the monarchy of King Záhir Shàh. The *coup* was led by the King's cousin and brother-in-law Mohammad Daoud who declared a Republic. King Záhir abdicated on 24 Aug. 1973. President Daoud was killed in a military *coup* in April 1978 which led to the establishment of a pro-Soviet government of the People's Democratic Party of Afghánistán (PDPA).

AREA AND POPULATION. Afghánistán is bounded north by the USSR, east and south by Pakistan and west by Iran.

The area is 251,773 sq. miles (652,090 sq. km). Population, according to the (1979) census, is 15,551,358, of which some 2·5m. are nomadic tribes. Estimate (1988) 10–12m. Approximately 3m. Afghans have sought refuge in Pakistan, over 1m. in Iran and several hundred thousand have been killed since 1979. Infant mortality rates are as high as 200 per 1,000 live births in some areas. The population of Kábul is over 2m. There are no current reliable population figures for other cities and major towns.

Census (1979), Kábul 913,164; Kandahár, 178,409; Herát, 140,323; Mazár-i-Sharif, 103,372; Jalálábád, 53,915; Kunduz, 53,251; Baghlan, 39,228; Maimana, 38,251; Pul-i-Khumri, 31,101; Ghazni, 30,425; Charikar, 22,424; Shiberghan, 18,955; Gardez, 9,550; Faizabad, 9,098; Qala-i-nau, 5,340; Uiback, 4,938; Meterlam, 3,987; Cheghcherán, 2,974.

The main ethnic group are the Pathans. Other ethnic groups include the Tajiks, the Hazaras, the Turkomans and the Uzbeks.

CLIMATE. The climate is arid, with a big annual range of temperature and very little rain, apart from the period Jan. to April. Winters are very cold, with considerable snowfall, which may last the year round on mountain summits. Kábul. Jan. 27°F (–2·8°C), July 76°F (24·4°C). Annual rainfall 13" (338 mm).

CONSTITUTION AND GOVERNMENT. In Dec. 1979 Soviet troops invaded Afghánistán and Hafizullah Amin was deposed and replaced by Babrak Karmal. The pretext for the airlift of combat troops to Kábul was the Treaty of Friendship signed in Dec. 1978 between USSR and Afghánistán. In May 1986 Karmal was replaced as General Secretary of the PDPA by Dr Sayid Mohammed Najibullah who was elected President in Sept. 1987 at a special session of the Revolutionary Council. In early 1988 there were some 115,000 Soviet troops in Afghánistán but under the Geneva accords signed in April 1988 all USSR troops were withdrawn by 15 Feb. 1989.

A new Constitution was approved in Nov. 1987. The PDPA remains the leading political force in the country. It is governed by a Central Committee (112 full members and 63 alternate members), which elects a Political Bureau, currently of 14 full, and 4 alternate, members to decide policy. At that time, the name of the country was changed from the Democratic Republic of Afghánistán to the Republic of Afghánistán.

A State of Emergency was declared on 19 Feb. 1989 and a Military Council headed by President Najibullah was announced. On 20 Feb. the Prime Minister Dr Mohammed Hasan Sharq resigned when the 20-man Supreme Military Council for the Defence of the Homeland took over full control of economic, political and military policy.

On 23 Feb. 1989 Afghán rebels, meeting in Islamabad, Pakistan, elected Sibghatullah Mojaddidi as President of an interim government in exile.

The *Loya Jirga* (Grand Assembly) was convened on 21 May 1989 following elections on 17 May. President Najibullah appealed for active political involvement by opposition leaders. There was an attempted *coup* in March 1990.

National flag: Three equal horizontal stripes of red, black and green, with the national arms in the canton.

The official languages are Pushtu and Dari (Persian).

Local Government: There are 31 provinces each administered by an appointed governor.

DEFENCE. Conscription is currently for a period of 2 years, followed soon after by another period of 2 years for non-graduates.

Army. The Army is organized in 3 armoured and 14 infantry divisions, 1 special guard division, 1 mountain division, 1 mechanized infantry brigade, 1 artillery brigade, 2 commando brigades and 1 air defence artillery brigade. Equipment includes 50 T-34, 400 T-54/-55 and 170 T-62 battle tanks. Strength was (1990) about 50,000, but most units of the Army, effectively under Soviet control, are well below strength, largely as a result of desertions.

Air Force. The Air Force, which is Russian-equipped, had (1989) about 180 combat aircraft and 5,000 officers and men. Nominal strength comprises 3 squadrons of Su-7 and Su-20 attack aircraft, 3 squadrons of MiG-21 interceptors (about 40 aircraft), 3 squadrons of MiG-17s and 3 squadrons of MiG-23s, a helicopter attack force of at least 50 Mi-24s, a transport wing with 6-8 An-12s, 12 twin-turboprop An-26s, about 10 piston-engined An-2s, 50 Mi-8 and 10 Mi-4 helicopters and 2 turboprop Il-18s, and Yak-18, Aero L-39 and MiG-15UTI trainers. The main fighter station is Bagram, with facilities for the largest jet transports and bombers. There is a fighter-bomber station at Shindand, a training station at Mazár-i-Sharif and an air academy at Sherpur. Large numbers of SA-2 and SA-3 surface-to-air missiles are operational in Afghánistán. The Soviet Union is withdrawing its aviation units operated in Afghánistán but is leaving aircraft behind for the national Air Force.

Police and Militia. In addition to the Army and Air Force there are a number of paramilitary units, including a 50,000-strong gendarmerie, secret police and 'Defence of the Revolution' forces.

INTERNATIONAL RELATIONS

Membership. Afghánistán is a member of UN and of the Colombo Plan.

ECONOMY

Planning. A 5-year plan was adopted in 1986 to cover period 1986–1991. Emphasis is on reconstruction of agriculture and irrigation systems as well as exploitation of natural gas resources.

Budget. In 1983–84 the budget envisaged expenditure of Afs. 49,941m. and revenue of Afs. 34,120m.

Currency. The monetary system is on the silver standard. The unit is the *afgháni*, weighing 10 grammes of silver 0·900 fine, which is subdivided into 100 *puls*. Rates of exchange are fixed (1990) Afs. 99·25 = £1; Afs. 60·55 = US$1; unofficial rates are: Afs. 345 = £1; Afs. 225 = US$1.

Banking. The Afghán State Bank *(Da Afghánistán Bank)* is the largest of the 3 main banks and also undertakes the functions of a central bank, holding the exclusive right of note issue. Total assets of the 3 main banks were: Da Afghánistán Bánk (1981), Afs. 22,839m.; Pashtany Tejaraty Bánk (1981), Afs. 6,997m.; Bánk-i-Milli (1981), Afs. 3,087m.

Weights and Measures. Weights and measures used in Kábul are: Weights: 1 *khurd* = 0·244 lb.; 1 *pao* = 0·974 lb.; 1 *charak* = 3·896 lb.; 1 *sere* = 16 lb.; 1 *kharwár* = 1,280 lb. or 16 maunds of 80 lb. each. Long measure: 1 yard or *gaz* = 40 in. The metric system is in increasingly common use. Square measures: 1 *jaríb* = 60 x 60 kábuli yd or $^1/_2$ acre; 1 *kulbá* = 40 jaríbs (area in which $2^1/_2$ kharwárs of seed can be sown); 1 jaríb yd = 29 in. Local weights and measures are in use in the provinces.

ENERGY AND NATURAL RESOURCES

Electricity. Hydro-electric plants have been constructed at Sarobi, Nangarhár, Naghlu, Mahipár, Pul-i-Khumri and Kandahár. Production (1986) 1,390m. kwh. Supply 220 volts; 50 Hz.

Natural gas. Production (1985) 2,400m. cu. metres. Natural gas is found in northern Afghánistán around Shiberghan and Sar-i-Pol; over 2,000m. cu. metres, about 95% of production, is piped to the USSR annually.

Minerals. Mineral resources are scattered and little developed. Coal is mined at Karkar in Pul-i-Khumri, Ishpushta near Doshi, north of Kábul and Dar-i-Suf south of Mazar (total production, 1983–84, 145,300 tonnes). Rich, but as yet unexploited, deposits of iron ore exist in the Hajigak hills about 100 miles west of Kábul; beryllium has been found in the Kunar valley and barite in Bamian province. Other deposits include gold; silver (now unexploited, in the Panjshir valley); lapis lazuli (in the Panjshir valley and Badakhshán); asbestos; mica; sulphur (near Maimana); chrome (in the Logar valley and near Herát); and copper (in the north).

Agriculture. Although the greater part of Afghánistán is more or less mountainous and a good deal of the country is too dry and rocky for successful cultivation, there are many fertile plains and valleys, which, with the assistance of irrigation from small rivers or wells, yield very satisfactory crops of fruit, vegetables and cereals. It is estimated that there are 14m. hectares of cultivable land in the country, of which only 6% of the total land was being cultivated in 1982–83 (5·34m. hectares of this being irrigated land). Before 1979 Afghánistán was virtually self-supporting in foodstuffs but in 1989 it was estimated that 33% of the land had been destroyed by war. The castor-oil plant, madder and the asafœtida plant abound.

Fruit forms a staple food (with bread) of many people throughout the year, both in the fresh and preserved state, and in the latter condition is exported in great quantities. The fat-tailed sheep furnish the principal meat diet, and the grease of the tail is a substitute for butter. Wool and skins provide material for warm apparel and one of the more important articles of export. Persian lambskins (Karakuls) are one of the chief exports.

Production, 1988, in 1,000 tonnes: Wheat, 2,035; barley, 274; maize, 587; rice, 343.

Livestock (1988): Cattle, 2·7m.; horses, donkeys and mules (1986), 1·69m.; sheep, 19m.; goats (1986), 3m.; chickens, 5·9m.

INDUSTRY AND TRADE

Industry. At Kábul there are factories for the manufacture of cotton and woollen textiles, leather, boots, marble-ware, furniture, glass, bicycles, prefabricated houses and plastics. A large machine shop has been constructed and equipped by the USSR, with a capability of manufacturing motor spares. There is a wool factory and there are several cotton-ginning plants; a small cotton factory at Jabal-us-Seráj and a larger one at Pul-i-Khumri; a cotton-seed oil extraction plant at Lashkargah; a cotton textile factory at Gulbahar, and a cotton plant at Balkh.

An ordnance factory manufactures arms and ammunition, boots and clothing, etc. for the Army. There is a beet sugar plant at Baghlan (equipped with Soviet machinery) and a fruit-canning factory in Kandahár.

Industries include cement, coalmining, cotton textiles, small vehicle assembly plants, fruit canning, carpet making, leather tanning, footwear manufacture, sugar manufacture, preparation of hides and skins, and building. Most of these are relatively small and, with the exception of hides and skins, carpets and fruits, do not meet domestic requirements.

Commerce. Trade is supervised by the Government through the Ministries of Commerce and Finance and the Da Afghánistán Bánk. The Association of Afghán Chambers of Commerce works in close liaison with the Ministry of Commerce. The Government monopoly controls the import of petrol and oil, sugar, cigarettes and tobacco, motor vehicles and consignment goods from bilateral trading countries. The principal surface routes for imports to Afghánistán are *via* the Soviet rail system and the border posts at Torghundi and Hairatan; and from Karachi *via* the border post at Torkham.

In the year ended March 1985 Afghán imports totalled US$964·7m. and exports US$670·5m. Main export commodities were karakul skins (US$13·5m.), raw cotton (US$12·5m.), dried fruit and nuts (US$141m.), fresh fruit (US$53·3m.) and natural gas (US$302·4m.). Main items imported were petroleum products (US$164m.), textiles (US$122·5m.). Over 50% of trade is with the USSR.

Total trade between Afghánistán and UK (in £1,000 sterling, British Department of Trade returns):

	1985	*1986*	*1987*	*1988*	*1989*
Imports to UK	52,061	11,913	11,289	11,501	4,813
Exports and re-exports from UK	13,882	11,444	10,735	12,109	5,376

Tourism. Owing to internal political instability there has been negligible tourism since 1979.

COMMUNICATIONS

Roads. There were in 1986 22,000 km of roads. The Americans asphalted the Kandahár–Chaman and Kábul–Torkham roads. The Russians constructed a road and tunnel through the Salang pass (over 11,000 ft) which was opened in Sept. 1964 and cut 120 miles off the old road from Kábul to the north; they continued this road to Kunduz and Sherkhan Bandar (Qizil Qala) on the Oxus. In addition, the Americans in 1966 completed the road between Kábul and Kandahár and the Russians constructed a concrete road between Kandahár and Herát. In 1968 the Americans completed an asphalt road from Herát to the Iranian frontier at Islam Qala. With Soviet assistance a metalled road from Pul-i-Khumri to Mazár-i-Sharif was completed in 1969 and Mazár-i-Sharif to Shiberghán in 1971. A Soviet-built road and rail bridge across the Oxus (Amu Darya) River was opened in May 1982. There are about 90,000 cars and commercial vehicles registered in Kábul. All roads, particularly outside the towns, are in a very poor state of repair as a result of the war.

Railways. There are no railways in the country, but the Oxus bridge opened in 1982, brought Soviet Railways' track into the country. A 200 km line of 1,520 mm gauge has been authorized from Termez to Pul-i-Khumri.

Aviation. On 29 June 1956 Afghánistán signed an agreement with the USA for the development of civil aviation, including the construction of the international airport at Kandahár, comprising a loan of $5m. and a grant of $9·56m. Kábul airport has been expanded with Russian assistance. New runways at Kábul and Kandahár airports have been completed. Provincial all-weather airports have been constructed at Herát, Qunduz, Jalálábád and Mazár-i-Sharif.

Bakhtar Afghan Airlines (the domestic national airline) began operations on 8 Feb. 1968 and regularly serves the main internal airfields, which, from 1985 was merged with Ariana Afghan Airlines (the national airline) operating regular services to New Delhi, Prague, Tashkent and Moscow.

Shipping. There are practically no navigable rivers in Afghánistán, and timber is the only article of commerce conveyed by water, floated down the Kunar and Kábul rivers from Chitral on rafts. A port has been built at Qizil Qala on the Oxus; barge traffic is increasing on the Oxus. Three river ports on the Amu Darya have been built at Sherkhan Bandar, Tashguzar and Hairatan, linked by road to Kábul.

Post and Broadcasting. Telephones, installed in most of the large towns, numbered 31,200 in 1978. There is telegraphic communication between all the larger towns and with other parts of the world. Kábul Radio broadcasts in Pushtu, Persian,

Urdu, English, French, Russian and German. In 1986 there were 823,000 radio receivers and 12,800 television receivers.

Newspapers. In 1983 there were 3 daily newspapers with a circulation of 67,000.

JUSTICE, RELIGION, EDUCATION AND WELFARE

Justice. A Supreme Court was established in June 1978. If no provision exists in the Constitution or in the general laws of the State, the courts follow the Hanafi jurisprudence of Islamic law.

Religion. The predominant religion is Islam, mostly of the Sunni sect, though there is a minority of Shiah Moslems.

Education. There are elementary schools throughout the country, but secondary schools exist only in Kábul and provincial capitals. Both elementary and secondary education are free. In 1985 there were 580,000 pupils (16,000 teachers) in primary education and 105,000 pupils (5,700 teachers) in secondary education. There are 3 teacher-training institutions in Kábul and 11 elsewhere; UNESCO is supporting an expansion programme. Technical, art, commercial and medical schools exist for higher education. Kábul University was founded in 1932 and has 9 faculties (medicine, science, agriculture, engineering, law and political science, letters, economics, theology, pharmacology). The University of Nangarhar in Jalálábád was founded in 1963. A Polytechnic in Kábul was completed in 1968. In 1982 there were 13,115 students in higher education, 4,427 in teacher-training schools and 1,230 in technical schools.

Health. In 1982 there were 1,215 doctors and 6,875 hospital beds. Two-thirds of the doctors and half the beds were in Kábul.

DIPLOMATIC REPRESENTATIVES

Of Afghánistán in Great Britain (31 Prince's Gate, London, SW7 1QQ)
Chargé d'Affaires: Ahmad Sarwar.

Of Great Britain in Afghánistán (Karte Parwan, Kábul)
Staff temporarily withdrawn.

Of Afghánistán in the USA (2341 Wyoming Ave., NW, Washington, D.C., 20008)
Chargé d'Affaires: Alishah Masood.

Of the USA in Afghánistán (Wazir Akbar Khan Mina, Kábul)
Chargé d'Affaires: J. D. Glassman.

Of Afghánistán to the United Nations
Ambassador: Noor Ahmad Noor.

Further Reading

Arnold, A., *Afghanistan: The Soviet Invasion in Perspective.* Oxford and Stanford, 1981.—*Afghanistan's Two-Party Communism.* Oxford and Santa Barbara, 1983
Bradsher, H. S., *Afghanistan and the Soviet Union.* Duke Univ. Press, 1983
Chaliand, G., *Rapport sur la résistance afghane.* Paris, 1981.—*Report from Afghanistan.* New York, 1982
Ghaus, A. S., *The Fall of Afghanistan: An Insider's Account.* Oxford, 1988
Gilbertson, G. W., *Pakkhto Idiom Dictionary.* 2 vols. London, 1932
Giradet, E. R., *Afghanistan: The Soviet War.* London, 1985
Hammond, T. T., *Red Star over Afghanistan.* Boulder and London, 1984
Hanifi, M. J., *Historical and Cultural Dictionary of Afghanistan.* Metuchen, 1976
Hyman, A., *Afghanistan under Soviet Domination 1964–83.* London, 1984
Male, B., *Revolutionary Afghanistan.* London, 1982
Misra, K. P., *Afghanistan in Crisis.* London, 1981
Newell, N. P. and Newell, R. S., *The Struggle for Afghanistan.* Cornell Univ. Press, 1981
Roy, O., *Islam and Resistance in Afghanistan.* CUP, 1986
Saikal, A. and Maley, W., *The Soviet withdrawal from Afghanistan.* CUP, 1989
Sykes, P. M., *A History of Afghanistan.* 2 vols. New York, 1975

ALBANIA

Capital: Tirana
Population: 3·2m. (1989)
GNP per capita: US$930 (1986)

Republika Popullore Socialiste e Shqipërisë

HISTORY. For the history of Albania before the Second World War *see* THE STATESMAN'S YEAR-BOOK 1985–86, p. 66. During the years 1939–44 the country was overrun by Italians and Germans. The official Albanian date of the liberation is 29 Nov. 1944.

On 10 Nov. 1945 the British, US and USSR Governments recognized a Provisional Government under Gen. Enver Hoxha, on the understanding that it would hold free elections. The elections of 2 Dec. 1945 resulted in a Communist-controlled assembly, which on 11 Jan. 1946 proclaimed Albania a republic.

In 1946 Great Britain and the USA broke off relations with Albania and vetoed its admission to the UN. Albania was finally admitted in 1955.

Because of Albania's Stalinist and pro-Chinese attitudes diplomatic relations with USSR were broken off in 1961. In 1977 Albania terminated its special relationship with China. Since the death of Enver Hoxha on 11 April 1985 Albania has been moving out of its diplomatic isolation.

AREA AND POPULATION. Albania is bounded north and east by Yugoslavia, south by Greece and west by the Adriatic. The area of the country is 28,748 sq. km (11,101 sq. miles). By the peace treaty Italy restored the island of Sazan (Saseno) to Albania. At the census of 1982 the population was, 2,786,100. Population in 1989, 3·2m. (34% urban in 1987; density 107 per sq. km). The capital is Tirana (1983 population (in 1,000), 206); other large towns are Durrës (Durazzo) (72), Shkodër (Scutari) (71), Elbasan (70), Vlorë (Vlonë, Valona) (61), Korçë (Koritza) (57), Fier (37), Berat (37), Lushnjë (24), Kavajë (23) and Gjirokastër (Argyrocastro) (21).

Ethnic minorities (mainly Greeks) numbered some 300,000 in 1990.

Vital statistics, 1986 (per 1,000): Births, 25·3; deaths, 5·7; marriages, 9; divorces (1982), 0·8; natural increase, 21 per thousand. Growth rate, 1980–85, 2·1%. Life expectancy in 1987 was 72 years.

The country is administratively divided into 26 districts (*rreth*) (*see* map in THE STATESMAN'S YEAR-BOOK, 1962. N.B. The district of Ersekë has been renamed Kolonjë). Districts are subdivided into 3,315 *lokaliteteve*.

Districts	*Area (sq. km)*	*Population (in 1,000) (1982)*	*Districts*	*Area (sq. km)*	*Population (in 1,000) (1982)*
Berat	1,026	154·0	Lushnjë	712	115·4
Dibrë	1,569	134·8	Mat	1,028	67·0
Durrës	859	217·0	Mirditë	698	45·0
Elbasan	1,466	208·0	Permet	930	36·4
Fier	1,191	212·0	Pogradec	725	62·0
Gjirokastër	1,137	60·3	Pukë	969	45·0
Gramsh	695	38·0	Sarandë	1,097	76·7
Kolonjë	805	22·3	Shkodër	2,528	206·2
Korçë	2,181	199·0	Skrapar	775	42·0
Krujë	607	93·0	Tepelenë	817	45·2
Kukës	1,564	86·0	Tirana	1,222	310·0
Lezhë	479	53·0	Tropojë	1,043	39·8
Librazhd	1,013	63·0	Vlorë	1,609	155·0

Districts are named after their capitals; exceptions: Tropojë, capital—Bajram Curri; Mat—Burrel; Mirditë—Rrëshen; Skrapar—Çorovodë; Dibrë—Peshkopi; Kolonjë—Ersekë.

The Albanian language is divided into two dialects—Gheg, north of the river Shkumbi, and Tosk in the south. Many places therefore have two forms of name: Vlonë (Gheg), Vlorë (Tosk), etc., and many are known also by an Italian name, *e.g.*, Valona. Since 1945 the official language has been based on Tosk.

CLIMATE. Mediterranean-type, with rainfall mainly in winter, but thunderstorms are frequent and severe in the great heat of the plains in summer. Winters in the highlands can be severe, with much snow. Tirana. Jan. 44°F (6·8°C), July 75°F (23·9°C). Annual rainfall 54" (1,353 mm). Shkodër. Jan. 39°F (3·9°C), July 77°F (25°C). Annual rainfall 57" (1,425 mm).

CONSTITUTION AND GOVERNMENT. The political structure derived from the Constitution of 14 March 1946 as amended in 1950, 1955, 1960 and 1963. In Dec. 1976 a new Constitution was adopted, by which Albania became a 'Socialist People's Republic'. The supreme legislative body is the single-chamber People's Assembly of 250 deputies, which meets twice a year, and delegates its day-to-day functions to a Presidium. Election to the People's Assembly is by universal suffrage (at 18) every 4 years.

In the elections of 1 Feb. 1987 a 100% turnout of the electorate of 1,830,653 was claimed to vote for the 250 candidates (66 women) on the single list of the Democratic Front. (There was 1 vote against).

The Government consists of a Council of Ministers, of 22 members, including the Chairman (Prime Minister) and 3 Deputies. Effective rule is exercised by the Albanian Labour (*i.e.*, Communist) Party, founded 8 Nov. 1941, whose governing body is the Politburo.

In 1981 the Party had 122,600 full members and candidates (in 1979 37·5% workers, 29% farmers, 27% women).

Titular Head of State: Chairman of the Presidium of the People's Assembly: Ramiz Alia, elected Nov. 1982. In March 1990 the chief Party and Government posts were filled as follows: Full members of the Politburo: *First Secretary of the Central Committee of the Party:* Ramiz Alia, Adil Çarçani *(Prime Minister)*, Foto Çami, Prokop Murra *(Minister of Defence)*, Hekuran Isai, Besnik Bekteshi *(Minister of Industry)*, Pali Miska[1] *(Minister of Agriculture)*, Manush Myftiu[1] *(Chairman, State Control Commission)*, Rita Marko, Muho Asllani, Hajredin Celiku *(Minister of Transport)*; Simon Stefani[1] *(Minister of the Interior)*, Lenka Çuko. Candidate members: Llambi Gegprifti, Qirjako Mihali, Pirro Kondi, Kico Mustaqi, Vangjel Cerava.

Ministers not in the Politburo include: *Chairman, Council of Ministers:* Enver Halile. *Foreign Affairs:* Reiz Malile. *Foreign Trade:* Shane Korbeci. *Chairman, State Planning Commission:* Niko Gjyzari. *Finance:* Andrea Nako. *Education:* Skender Gjinush. *Health:* Ahmet Kamberi.

[1] Deputy Prime Minister.

Local Government is carried out by People's Councils at village, *lokalitet*, town and district level. Councillors are elected for 3 years.

National flag: Red, with a black double-headed eagle and a red, gold-edged 5-pointed star above it. *Mercantile flag:* Red, black, red (horizontal) with a red yellow-edged star in the centre.

National anthem: Rreth Flamurit te per bashkuar (The flag that united us in the struggle).

DEFENCE. Albania withdrew from the Warsaw Pact in 1968 in protest against the invasion of Czechoslovakia. The Constitution precludes the stationing of foreign troops in Albania. Conscription is for 2 years.

Army. The Army consists of 1 tank brigade, 4 infantry brigades, 1 engineer, and 3 artillery regiments. Equipment includes 190 T-34 and T-54 main battle tanks. Strength (1989) 31,500 (including 20,000 conscripts) and reserves number 150,000.

There are also paramilitary internal security forces (5,000 men) and frontier guards (7,000).

Navy. The combatant navy includes 2 submarines, 2 offshore patrol craft, 32 hydrofoil torpedo boats, 6 inshore patrol craft and 1 fleet minesweeper. Auxiliaries include 1 tanker and about 10 service craft. Navy personnel in 1989 totalled 2,000 officers and ratings, including 400 coastal defence guards. Service for ratings is 3 years. There are naval bases at Durrës and Vlorë. Navy personnel in 1989 totalled 2,000 officers and ratings, including 400 coastal defence guards.

Air Force. The Air Force, controlled by the Army, had (1989) about 7,200 officers and men, and in 1987 operated 80 combat aircraft received before relations with China were broken. The force included 20 Chinese-built F-7s and 30 F-6s, and 3 ground attack squadrons of F-2s and F-4s. Transport and training types include 3 Il-14s, 10 An-2s, Mi-4 helicopters, Yak-18s and MiG-15UTIs.

INTERNATIONAL RELATIONS

Membership. Albania is a member of UN.

ECONOMY

Planning. For the first seven 5-year plans *see* THE STATESMAN'S YEAR-BOOK, 1989–90. Cautious moves towards 'economic logic', a recognition of market forces were made in 1989. Targets of the eighth 5-year plan (1986–90): Social production, 30–32%; national income, 34–36%; industry, 29–31%; agriculture, 34–36%.

Budget. Budget figures for 1989: Revenue, 9,550m. leks; expenditure, 9,500m. leks. Defence expenditure (1986) 998m. leks.

Currency. The monetary unit is the *lek* of 100 *qintars*. It replaced the gold franc *(franc ar)* in July 1947. In Aug. 1965 a new *lek* was introduced: 10 old *leks* = 1 new *lek*. There are 5, 10, 20 and 50 *qintar* coins and a 1 *lek* coin; notes are for 1, 3, 5, 10, 25, 50 and 100 *leks*. Exchange rates, March 1990: US$1 = 6·09 *leks*; £1 = 9·98.

Banking. The Albanian State Bank was founded in 1925 with Italian aid. In 1970 savings deposits amounted to 572m. leks. In 1970 the Agricultural Bank was set up as a credit institution for agricultural co-operatives.

Weights and Measures. The metric system is in force.

ENERGY AND NATURAL RESOURCES

Electricity. Albania is rich in hydro-electric potential. Electric power production in 1985 was 4,700m. kwh., of which 53m. was from thermal plants. 2,000m. kwh. were exported in 1984 to Yugoslavia, Bulgaria, Romania and Greece.

Oil. Oil reserves are some 20m. tonnes. Output in 1989: Crude, 3m. tonnes; refined (1973), 1,596,000 tonnes. Refining capacity in 1970 was over 1m. tonnes. Oil is produced chiefly at Qytet Stalin which a pipeline connects to the port of Vlorë. Natural gas is extracted. Reserves: 8,000m. cu. metres; 1985 production, 420m. cu. metres.

Minerals. The mineral wealth of Albania is considerable and includes coal (not bituminous), oil, chrome and ferro-nickel ores but it is only recently being developed. Chromium ore output was some 1·5m. tonnes in 1986. Reserves are about 20m. tonnes. Salt is extracted near Vlorë and bitumen mined at Selenicë. Production in tonnes (1984): Copper ore, 168,000; nickel ore, 6,000; brown coal, 1·78m.; phosphate, 18,000; nitrogenous fertilizer, 75,000; cement, 1·1m.

Agriculture. The country for the greater part is rugged, wild and mountainous, the exceptions being along the Adriatic littoral and the Korçë (Koritza) Basin, which are fertile. In 1983 arable land comprised 709,800 hectares, 55% of which was irrigated.

Land is held by the State (largely forests and non-agricultural), state farms (50 in 1982 averaging 3,000 hectares of arable land) and co-operatives (460 in 1989 covering 75% of farm land). In 1989 co-operatives were permitted to fix their own prices and keep any profits surplus to plan. There is a pension scheme for collective farmers. In 1982 there were 31 machine and tractor stations.

Production of the main crops in 1988 was (in 1,000 tonnes): Wheat, 589; sugar-beet, 360; maize, 306; potatoes, 137; fruit, 216; grapes, 88; oats, 30; sorghum, 38; seed cotton, 14; barley, 40; sunflower seeds, 27; wine, 25; rice, 11; tobacco, 29.

Livestock, 1988: Cattle, 672,000; sheep, 1,432,000; goats, 979,000; pigs, 214,000; horses and mules, 64,000; poultry, 6m.

Forestry. 35% of the territory of Albania is forest land, mainly oak, elm, pine and birch. Some 40,000 hectares per annum are afforested or improved.

Fisheries. The catch in 1984 was 4,000 tonnes.

INDUSTRY AND TRADE

Industry. All industry is nationalized down to the smallest workshop. Output is small, and the principal industries are agricultural product processing, textiles, oil products and cement. Chemical and engineering industries are being built up. The metallurgical combine at Elbasan is being extended.

Labour. In 1978, 583,600 persons worked in the socialist sector of the national economy. In 1988, 47% of wage-earners were women.

Minimum wages may not fall below one-third of maximum. Hours of labour: 8-hour day, 6-day week and 12 days yearly paid holiday. Retirement age is 60 for men and 55 for women. Average monthly wage, 1989: 650 leks.

Commerce. Yugoslavia is Albania's main trading partner: in Nov. 1985 a 5-year agreement provided for a 20% increase in trade. Trade links with China were re-established in 1983, and a 5-year agreement was signed in Dec. 1985. Trade is conducted with the Comecon countries Bulgaria, Czechoslovakia, North Korea, Poland, and Vietnam; and also with Italy, France and India. The establishment of joint companies with, and the acceptance of credits from, capitalist firms is forbidden.

Exports which in 1983 were (estimate) US$500m. included crude oil, bitumen, chrome, nickel, copper, tobacco, fruit and vegetables.

Total trade between Albania and UK (British Department of Trade returns, in £1,000 sterling):

	1985	*1986*	*1987*	*1988*	*1989*
Imports to UK	212	129	91	2,764	605
Exports and re-exports from UK	5,252	2,887	2,565	1,126	1,957

COMMUNICATIONS

Roads. There were, in 1981, 21,000 km of roads suitable for motor traffic. The mountain districts of the north are still mostly inaccessible for wheeled vehicles, and communications are still by means of pack ponies or donkeys. Motor vehicles in 1970: Cars, 3,500; lorries and buses, 11,000. Road traffic carried 8·6m. passengers in 1970; goods carried, 34m. tonnes. There are no private cars.

Railways. Total length, in 1988 was 417 km. They comprise the lines from Durrës to Tirana, Vlorë, Ballsh, Korcë, Shkodër and across the Yugoslav border to Titograd. In 1987 the Milot-Rrëshen section of the Milot-Klos line was completed.

Aviation. There are regular scheduled flights from Tirana (Rinas Airport) to Belgrade, Bucharest, Budapest, East Berlin and Zurich. Olympic Airways operate a weekly flight from Athens to Tirana.

Shipping. In 1986 there were 20 ships totalling 56,133 GRT. The main ports are the Enver Hoxha Port of Durrës, Vlorë and Sarandë. A ferry service from Trieste to Durrës opened in Nov. 1983.

Post and Broadcasting. Number of post and telegraph offices (1970), 292; telephones (1963), 10,150. There are 17 broadcasting stations, including Tirana and Korçë. Radio Tirana operates a foreign service in 18 languages. Radio receiving sets (1983), 210,000; television sets, 20,500. Regular television broadcasting began in 1971. There were 7 TV stations in 1984.

Cinemas and Theatres. In 1975 there were 410 cinemas (including mobile) and in 1973 27 theatres with an attendance of 1·6m. 14 full-length films were produced in 1980.

Newspapers and Books. In 1978 there were 30 newspapers with an annual circulation of 57m. The Party paper is *Zëri i Popullit* (Voice of the People) (daily circulation, 105,000). 1,043 book titles were published in 1981.

JUSTICE, RELIGION, EDUCATION AND WELFARE

Justice is administered by People's Courts. Minor crimes are tried by tribunals. Judges of the Supreme Court are elected by the People's Assembly for 4-year terms. The Office of the Procurator-General oversees the administration of justice. In 1983 an Investigator's Office was set up, separate from the Ministry of the Interior and answerable to the People's Assembly.

Religion. Albania is constitutionally an atheist state. In 1967 the Government closed all mosques and churches. For details of the situation before 1967 *see* THE STATESMAN'S YEAR-BOOK, 1969–70. The population had been 70% Moslem.

Education. Primary education is free and compulsory in 8-year schools from 7 to 15 years. Secondary education is available in 12-year (general), technical-professional or lower vocational schools. Periods of productive work and military service are intermingled with full-time education. There were, in 1979–80, 2,541 kindergartens with 83,697 pupils and 3,920 teachers and in 1984–85, 721,057 primary and secondary school children with 35,846 teachers. In 1979–80 there were 116 technical–professional schools with 69,700 pupils and (in 1969–70) 36 institutes of higher education with 36,525 students and 941 teachers, including the Enver Hoxha University of Tirana (founded 1957), a polytechnic, an agricultural college, a medical school, 5 teachers' training colleges and an institute of science. In 1985–86 there were 820 teachers and some 12,000 students at Tirana University. An Albanian Academy was founded in 1972.

Health. Medical services are free, though medicines are charged for. In 1986 there were 797 hospitals and 3,307 outpatient clinics. In 1983 there were 4,967 doctors and dentists, and 17,600 hospital beds. In 1986 there were 710 maternity hospitals or hospital sections and 256 dental clinics.

DIPLOMATIC REPRESENTATIVE

Of Albania to the United Nations
Ambassador: Bashkim Pitarka.

Further Reading

Vjetari Statistikor (Statistical Yearbook). Tirana, irregular, 1959–72
35 vjet Shqipëri socialiste (statistical handbook). Tirana, 1979
History of the Labour Party of Albania 1966–1980. Tirana, 1981
Portrait of Albania. Tirana, 1982
Bertolino, J., *Albanie: la Citadelle de Staline*. Paris, 1979
Bland, W. B., *Albania*. [Bibliography] Oxford and Santa Barbara, 1988
Duro, I. and Hysa, R., *Albanian-English Dictionary*. Tirana, 1981
Fischer, B. J., *King Zog and the Struggle for Stability in Albania*. Boulder, 1984
Halliday, J., (ed.) *The Artful Albanian: The Memoirs of Enver Hoxha*. London, 1986
Hetzer, A. and Roman, V. S. *Albania: A Bibliographic Research Survey*. Munich, 1983

Hoxha, E., *Speeches, Conversations and Articles, 1969–1970*. Tirana, 1980.—*The Khrushchevites: Memoirs*. Tirana, 1980.—*The Anglo-American Threat to Albania*. Tirana, 1982.—*Selected works*. Tirana, 1982.

Lendvai, P., *Das einsame Albanien*. Zurich, 1985

Logoreci, A., *The Albanians: Europe's Forgotten Survivors*. London, 1977

Marmullaku, R., *Albania and the Albanians*. London, 1975

Martin, N., *La Forteresse Albanaise: un Communisme National*. Paris, 1979

Pollo, S. and Arben, P., *The History of Albania*. London, 1981

Prifti, P. R., *Socialist Albania since 1944*. Cambridge, Mass., 1978

Russ, W., *Der Entwicklungsweg Albaniens*. Meisenheim-am-Glan, 1979

Schnytzer, A., *Stalinist Economic Strategy in Practice: The Case of Albania*. OUP, 1982

ALGERIA

Capital: Algiers
Population: 23·85m. (1988)
GNP per capita: US$2,450 (1988)

al-Jumhuriya al-Jazairiya ad-Dimuqratiya ash-Shabiya

HISTORY. On 1 Nov. 1954 the National Liberation Front (FLN) went over to open warfare against the French administration and armed forces. For details of history 1958–62 *see* p. 76 THE STATESMAN'S YEAR-BOOK, 1982–83. A cease-fire agreement was reached on 18 March 1962, and Gen. de Gaulle declared Algeria independent on 3 July 1962; the Republic was declared on 25 Sept. 1962.

The Government was overthrown by a junta of army officers which, on 19 June 1965, established a Revolutionary Council under Col. Houari Boumédienne.

AREA AND POPULATION. Algeria is bounded west by Morocco and Western Sahara, south-west by Mauritania and Mali, south-east by Niger, east by Libya and Tunisia, and north by the Mediterranean Sea. It has an area of 2,381,741 sq. km (919,595 sq. miles). Population (census 1987) 22,971,558; estimate (1988) 23·85m.

In 1987, 49% lived in urban areas and 46% were under 15 years of age. 83% speak Arabic, the official language, while 17% are Berber.

The populations (1987 Census) of the 48 *wilayat* were as follows:

Adrar	216,931	Mila	511,047
Ain Defla	536,205	Mostaganem	504,124
Ain Témouchent	271,454	M'Sila	605,578
Annaba (Bône)	453,951	Naâma	112,858
Batna	757,059	Ouahran (Oran)	916,578
al-Bayadh	155,494	Ouargla	286,696
Béchar	183,896	al-Oued	379,512
Béjaia (Bougie)	697,669	Oum al-Bouaghi	402,683
Biskra	429,217	Qacentina (Constantine)	662,330
Bordj Bou Arreridj	429,009	Relizane	545,061
Bouira	525,460	Saida	235,240
al-Boulaida (Blida)	704,462	Setif	997,482
Boumerdes	646,870	Sidi bel-Abbès	444,047
Cheliff (Orléansville)	679,717	Skikda	619,094
Djelfa	490,240	Souk Ahras	298,236
Guelma	353,329	Tamanrasset	94,219
Ghardaia	215,955	at-Tarf	276,836
Illizi	19,698	Tébessa	409,317
al-Jaza'ir (Algiers)	1,687,579	Tiaret	574,786
Jijel	471,319	Tindouf	16,339[1]
Khenchela	243,733	Tipaza	615,140
Laghouat	215,183	Tissemsilt	227,542
Mascara	562,806	Tizi-Ouzou	931,501
Médéa	650,623	Tlemcen	707,453

[1] Excluding Saharawi refugees (170,000 in 1988) in camps.

The chief towns (1983) are as follows: Algiers, 1,721,607; Oran, 663,504; Constantine, 448,578; Annaba, 348,322; Blida, 191,314; Sétif, 186,978; Sidi-Bel-Abbès, 186,978; Tlemcen, 146,089; Skikda, 141,159; Bejaia, 124,122; Batna, 122,788; al Asnam, 118,996; Tizi-Ouzou, 100,749; Médéa, 84,292.

CLIMATE. Coastal areas have a warm temperate climate, with most rain in winter, which is mild, while summers are hot and dry. Inland, conditions become more arid beyond the Atlas Mountains. Algiers. Jan. 54°F (12·2°C), July 76°F (24·4°C). Annual rainfall 30" (762 mm). Biskra. Jan. 52°F (11·1°C), July 93°F (33·9°C). Annual rainfall 6" (158 mm). Oran. Jan. 54°F (12·2°C), July 76°F (24·4°C). Annual rainfall 15" (376 mm).

CONSTITUTION AND GOVERNMENT. A Constitution was approved by referendum in Feb. 1989. There was a turnout of 83% and 92% of the voters approved of the constitutional reforms which included the beginning of the separation of the *Front de Libération Nationale* (FLN) from the State in that the Prime Minister is to be responsible to the National Assembly rather than the FLN. The ideals of socialism no longer exist in the new Constitution.

The President of the Republic is Head of State, Head of the Armed Forces, and Head of Government. He is elected by universal suffrage for 5-year terms (renewable).

President of the Republic, General Secretary of the FLN, Minister of Defence: Bendjedid Chadli (sworn in 9 Feb. 1979, re-elected in 1984 and 1989).

The President appoints a Prime Minister and other Ministers, and presides over meetings of the Council of Ministers.

The Council of Ministers, as in Sept. 1989, consisted of:

Prime Minister: Mouloud Hamrouche.

Foreign Affairs: Sid-Ahmed Ghozali. *Interior:* Mohammed Saleh Mohammedi. *Religious Affairs:* Said Chibane. *Economy:* Ghazi Hidouci. *Education:* Mohamed el-Mili Brahimi. *Youth:* Abdelkader Boudjemaa. *Justice:* Ali Benflis. *Social Affairs:* Mohamed Ghrib. *Industry:* Hassan Kahlouche. *Equipment:* Cherif Rahmani. *Mines:* Saddek Boussena. *Transport:* El-Hadi Khediri. *Agriculture:* Abdelkader Bendaoud. *Public Health:* Akli Kheddis. *Posts and Telecommunications:* Hamid Sidi Said. *Ministers Delegate:* Benali Henni (*Local Authorities*), Abdessalem Ali-Rachedi (*Universities*), Abdennour Keramane (*Professional Training*), Smail Goumeziane (*Organization of Commerce*), Amar Kara Mohamed (*Employment*). *Secretary of State for Maghreb Affairs:* Abdelaziz Khellef. *Secretary-General of the Government:* Ahmed Medjhouda.

Legislative power is held by the National People's Assembly, whose 295 members are elected for a 5-year term by universal suffrage from the single list of the FLN who nominate 3 candidates for each single-member seat. In 1989 the political system was being liberalized and there were then more than 30 political parties.

National flag: Vertically green and white, a red crescent and star over all in centre.

The official language is Arabic, French being the principal foreign language. Arabic is spoken by 83·5% of the population and Berber by 16·1%.

DEFENCE. Conscription is for a period of 6 months at the age of 19.

Army. The Army had a strength of 120,000 in 1990, organized in 3 armoured, 5 mechanized and 12 motorized brigades; 31 infantry, 4 paratroop, 5 artillery, 5 air defence and 4 engineer battalions; and 12 companies of desert troops. Equipment includes 113 T-34, 390 T-54/-55, 300 T-62 and 100 T-72 main battle tanks.

Navy. The Naval combatant force, largely supplied from the USSR, consists of 4 diesel powered patrol submarines, 3 frigates, 3 missile-armed corvettes, 11 fast missile craft, 6 fast patrol craft, 2 ocean minesweepers, 2 tank landing ships, and 1 tank landing craft. There are some 10 auxiliaries. An associated coastguard operates 16 fast cutters. Naval personnel in 1989 totalled 7,000. There are naval bases at Algiers, Annaba and Mers el Kebir.

Air Force. Five MiG-15 jet-fighters were delivered in 1962 as the nucleus of an Algerian Air Force. Since then many more aircraft of Soviet design have followed, and the Air Force had (1990) about 300 combat aircraft and 12,000 personnel. Training and technical assistance have been given by Egypt and the Soviet Union. There are 8 squadrons of MiG-21s, 3 squadrons of MiG-23 variable-geometry interceptors and fighter-bombers, 3 squadrons of Su-7 and Su-20 variable-geometry attack aircraft, 2 squadrons with MiG-25 fighter and reconnaissance aircraft, more than 40 Mi-24 assault helicopters and gunships, 17 C-130H Hercules, 3 F.27, 4 Il-76 and 6 An-12 transports, an Il-18 and a variety of smaller transports, a wing of 4 Mi-6, 30 Mi-8, about 30 Mi-4, 5 Puma, 6 Alouette III and 6 Hughes 269 helicopters, and training units equipped with CM.170 Magister armed jet counter-insurgency/trainers (20), 8 Beech Queen Air twin-engine/instrument trainers, MiG-15UTIs and MiG-17s, and two-seat versions of operational types. Surface-to-air missile units have Soviet-built 'Guidelines', 'Goas', 'Gainfuls' and 'Gaskins'.

INTERNATIONAL RELATIONS

Membership. Algeria is a member of UN, OAU, the Arab League and OPEC.

ECONOMY

Planning. The fourth development plan (1985–89) envisaged expenditure of DA 550,000m. primarily on housing, agriculture and water resources.

Budget. Administrative expenditure for 1988 was DA 63,000m.

Currency. The Algerian currency is the *dinar* (DA) divided into 100 *centimes*. There are in circulation banknotes of DA 5, 10, 50 and 100 and coins of 1, 2, 5, 20 and 50 centimes and DA 1, 5 and 10. In March 1990, £1 = 13·05 DA; US$1 = 7·96 DA.

Banking. The Banque Centrale d'Algérie is the government emission bank. Other banks operating in Algeria are Banque National d'Algérie, Crédit Populaire d'Algérie, Banque Extérieure d'Algérie, Caisse Algérienne de Développement, Banque Algérienne de Développement, Banque de l'Agriculture et du Développement.

Weights and Measures. The metric system is in use.

ENERGY AND NATURAL RESOURCES

Electricity. Production (1986) 12,410m. kwh. Supply 127 and 220 volts; 50 Hz.

Oil. Two large oilfields went into production in 1957 around Edjéle and Hassi Messaoud and in 1959 at El Gassi. In 1960 about 200 wells were productive. Natural gas was discovered at Djebel Berga in 1954 and at Hassi-R'Mel in 1956. Oil pipelines from Edjéle to Skirra (Tunisia) and from Hassi Messaoud to Béjaia, and a gas pipeline from Hassi Messaoud *via* Hassi-R'Mel to Mostaganem–Oran–Algiers, have been completed. Oil production in 1989, 52m. tonnes.

Gas. Production of natural gas in 1985 was 50,000m. cu. metres.

Minerals. Algeria possesses deposits of iron, zinc, lead, mercury, silver, copper and antimony. Kaolin, marble and onyx, salt and coal are also found. Mineral output in 1985 (1,000 tonnes): Iron ore, 3,370; zinc, 12; copper, 0·9; lead, 3·6; phosphates (1988), 1,207; barite, 100; clay, 58; sulphur, 10; coal, 8.

Agriculture. The greater part of Algeria is of limited value for agricultural purposes. In the northern portion the mountains are generally better adapted to grazing and forestry than agriculture, and a large portion of the native population is quite poor. In spite of the many excellent roads built by the Government, a considerable area of the mountainous region is without adequate means of communication and is accessible only with difficulty. There were an estimated 7·5m. hectares of agricultural land in 1978–79, of which 6·8m. hectares were arable; 200,000 hectares under vine and 31·7m. hectares pastures and brushlands.

The chief crops in 1988 were (in 1,000 tonnes): Wheat, 1,150; barley, 556; dates, 182; potatoes, 950; oranges, 190; mandarins and tangerines, 83; watermelons, 320; wine, 100; tomatoes, 490; olives, 170; onions, 175; oats, 58.

Livestock, 1988: 187,000 horses, 635,000 mules and asses, 361,000 cattle, 14,325,000 sheep, 3,570,000 goats and 130,000 camels.

Forestry. Forests cover 4·7m. hectares or 2% of the land area. The greater part of the state forests are mere brushwood, but there are very large areas covered with cork-oak trees, Aleppo pine, evergreen oak and cedar. The dwarf-palm is grown on the plains, alfa on the table-land. Timber is cut for firewood, also for industrial purposes, for railway sleepers, telegraph poles, etc., and for bark for tanning. Considerable portions of the forest area are also leased for tillage, or for pasturage for cattle and sheep.

Fisheries. There are extensive fisheries for sardines, anchovies, sprats, tunny fish, etc., and also shellfish. Fish taken in 1986 amounted to 70,000 tonnes.

INDUSTRY AND TRADE

Industry. In 1981, 10·5m. tonnes of petroleum products were refined. Production of cement (1981) 4·45m. tonnes, crude steel (1982) 842,000 tonnes.

Labour. In 1984 the economically active population was estimated at 3·7% of whom 40% were in the agricultural sector.

Trade Unions. The *Union Générale des Travailleurs Algériens* had in 1982 about 1m. members in 8 affiliated groups, while the *Union Nationale des Paysans Algériens* had 700,000.

Commerce. The foreign trade of Algeria was as follows (in DA 1m.):

	1984	*1985*	*1986*	*1987*
Imports	51,257	49,491	43,415	34,196
Exports	59,106	64,564	36,890	39,000

In 1986 imports came chiefly from France, Federal Republic of Germany and Italy. Exports went mainly to Federal Republic of Germany and France.

Total trade between Algeria and UK (British Department of Trade returns, in £1,000 sterling):

	1985	*1986*	*1987*	*1988*	*1989*
Imports to UK	251,462	140,860	172,927	159,748	177,546
Exports and re-exports from UK	176,596	129,624	73,115	86,615	74,368

Tourism. In 1986, there were 150,000 visitors.

COMMUNICATIONS

Roads. There were in 1986, 78,410 km of national highway including 45,070 km of concrete or bituminous roads. Motor vehicles in 1980 included 472,483 passenger cars and 283,966 commercial vehicles.

Railways. In 1988 there were 3,836 km of which 2,698 km is of 1,435mm gauge (299 km electrified) and 1,138 km of 1,055mm gauge railway open for traffic. In 1988 the railways carried 13·1m. tonnes of freight and 44·8m. passengers.

Aviation. There are 5 international airports as well as another 65 airfields controlled by government and 135 owned by petroleum companies. Air Algeria serves the main Algerian cities, and an international network. Algeria is also served by Swissair, Royal Air Maroc and United Arab Airline. In 1980 the airports handled 2·84m. passengers and 22,479 tonnes of freight.

Shipping. In 1982, 69·4m. tonnes of goods were handled at Algerian ports.

A state shipping line, Compagnie Nationale Algérienne de Navigation, was formed in Jan. 1964.

Post and Broadcasting. There were, in 1980, 1,534 post offices; number of telephones (1985), 769,000. In 1982 *Radiodiffusion Télévision Algérienne* broadcast in Arabic, French and Kabyle (Berber) from 16 radio stations to (1986) 3·3m. radio receivers and from 16 television stations to about (1986) 1·54m. receivers.

Newspapers (1989). There were 6 daily newspapers, with a combined circulation of 1m.

JUSTICE, RELIGION, EDUCATION AND WELFARE

Justice. There are appeal courts at Algiers, Constantine and Oran; and in the *arrondissements* are 17 courts of first instance. There are also commercial courts and justices of the peace with extensive powers. Criminal justice is organized as in France. The Supreme Court is at the same time Council of State and High Court of Appeal.

Religion. The overwhelming part of the population are Sunni Moslems. There are about 150,000 Christians, mainly Roman Catholic.

Education. In 1987 there were 11,692 state primary schools with 133,250 teachers and 3,625,000 pupils; 1,900 secondary schools with 95,000 teachers and 1,877,000 pupils; and 71 technical and teacher-training colleges with 2,528 teachers and (1982) 12,903 students in technical education and 1,124 teachers and 13,315 students in teacher-training.

In 1981 there were 72,200 students in higher education including universities at Algiers (with 17,086 students), Oran (9,000), Constantine (8,340), Annaba (6,126), Sétif (5,800) and Boumerdes. There are also Universities of Science and Technology at Algiers (11,500) and Oran (5,800) and university centres at Tlemcen, Tizi-Ouzou, Batna, Tiaret, Constantine, Mostaganem, Sidi-Bel-Abbés and Boulaida.

Health. There were in 1986, 49,280 hospital beds; there were 15,361 doctors. There were also 1,422 dispensaries and consulting rooms, 747 health centres and 175 specializing centres for tuberculosis, venereal disease and trachoma in 1980.

DIPLOMATIC REPRESENTATIVES

Of Algeria in Great Britain (54 Holland Park, London, W11 3RS)
Ambassador: Abdelkrim Gheraieb (accredited 12 Dec. 1989).

Of Great Britain in Algeria (Résidence Cassiopée, 7 Chemin des Glycines, Algiers)
Ambassador: C. C. R. Battiscombe.

Of Algeria in the USA (2118 Kalorama Rd., NW, Washington, D.C., 20008)
Ambassador: Abderrahmane Bensid.

Of the USA in Algeria (4 Chemin Cheich Bachir Ibrahimi, Algiers)
Ambassador: Christopher W. S. Ross.

Of Algeria to the United Nations
Ambassador: Hocine Djoudi.

Further Reading

Statistical Information: The Service de Statistique Générale publishes the annual *Statistique Générale de l'Algérie, Documents statistiques sur le commerce de l'Algérie* (from 1902).

Ageron, C.-R., *A History of Modern Algeria.* London, 1988
Bennoune, M., *The Making of Contempory Algeria, 1830–1987.* CUP, 1988
Horne, A., *A Savage War of Peace: Algeria 1954–1962.* London, 1977
Knapp, W., *North West Africa: A Political and Economic Survey.* OUP, 1977
Lawless, R. I., *Algeria.* [Bibliography] Oxford and Santa Barbara, 1981

ANDORRA

Capital: Andorre-la-Vieille
Population: 51,400 (1988)

Principat d'Andorra

HISTORY. The political status of Andorra was regulated by the *Paréage* of 1278 which placed Andorra under the joint suzerainty of the Comte de Foix and of the Bishop of Urgel. The rights vested in the house of Foix passed by marriage to that of Bearn and, on the accession of Henri IV, to the French crown.

AREA AND POPULATION. The co-principality of Andorra is situated in the eastern Pyrenees on the French–Spanish border. The country consists of gorges, narrow valleys and defiles, surrounded by high mountain peaks varying between 1,880 and 3,000 metres. Its maximum length is 30 km and its width 20 km; it has an area of 468 sq. km (181 sq. miles) and a population (census, 1986) of 46,976 (65% urban); estimate (1988) 51,400, scattered in 7 villages. The chief towns (1986) are Andorre-la-Vieille, the capital (15,639) and its suburb Les Escaldes (11,955).

Catalan is the official language and was spoken by 30% of the population in 1986 but 59% spoke Spanish and 6% French.

CLIMATE. Les Escaldes. Jan. 36°F (2·3°C), July 67°F (19·3°C). Annual rainfall 32" (808 mm).

CONSTITUTION AND GOVERNMENT. Sovereignty is exercised jointly by the President of the French Republic and the Bishop of Urgel. The co-princes are represented in Andorra by the *'Viguier français'* and the *'Viguier Episcopal'*. Each co-prince has set up a Permanent Delegation for Andorran affairs; the Prefect of the Eastern Pyrenees is the French Permanent Delegate.

The valleys pay every second year a due of 960 francs to France and 460 pesetas to the bishop.

A 'General Council of the Valleys' submits motions and proposals to the Permanent Delegations. Its 28 members are elected for 4 years; half of the council is renewed every 2 years. The council nominates a First Syndic *(Syndic Procureur Général)* and a Second Syndic from outside its members.

In Jan. 1982 an Executive Council was appointed, following elections held in Dec. 1981, and legislative and executive powers were separated.

First Syndic: Francesc Cerqueda-Pascuet.

Head of Government: Josef Pintat Solans (from 3 Jan. 1986).

Finance: Bonaventura Riberaygua Miquel. *Education and Culture:* Roc Rossell Dolcet. *Tourism and Sports:* Josep Miño Guitart. *Public Works:* Merce Sansa Reñe. *Agriculture, Commerce and Industry:* Luis Molne Armengol. *Labour and Social Welfare:* Maestre Campderros.

National flag: Three vertical strips of blue, yellow, red, with the arms of Andorra in the centre.

ECONOMY

Budget. In 1986 the budget balanced at 6,655m. pesetas.

Currency. French and Spanish currency are both in use.

ENERGY AND NATURAL RESOURCES

Electricity. Production (1986) 140m. kwh. Andorra imported another 200m. kwh from Spain.

Agriculture. In 1981, 472 tonnes of potatoes and 264 tonnes of tobacco were produced.

Livestock (1982): 9,000 sheep, 1,115 cattle, 217 horses.

TRADE. In 1986, imports amounted to 74,313m. pesetas (42% from Spain and 27% from France) and exports to 2,325m. pesetas (54% to France and 33% to Spain).

Total trade between Andorra and UK (British Department of Trade returns, in £1,000 sterling):

	1987	*1988*	*1989*
Imports to UK	200	46	236
Exports and re-exports from UK	10,976	10,780	10,493

Tourism. Tourism is the main industry, and over 6m. people visited Andorra in 1982.

COMMUNICATIONS

Roads. There are 220 km of roads (120 km paved). A good road connects the Spanish and French frontiers by way of Sant Julia, Andorre-la-Vieille, les Escaldes, Encamp, Canillo and Soldeu: it crosses the Col d'Envalira (2,400 metres). Another road connects Andorre-la-Vieille with La Massana and Ordino. Motor vehicles (1983) 24,789.

Aviation. The nearest airports are at Seo de Urgel, Barcelona and Perpignan.

Post and Broadcasting. Number of telephones (1982) 17,719. Number of receivers (1986), radio, 8,000; TV, 4,000.

JUSTICE, RELIGION, EDUCATION AND WELFARE

Justice. Judicial power is exercised in civil matters in the first instance, according to the plaintiff's choice, by either the *Bayle Français* or the *Bayle Episcopal*, who are nominated by the respective co-princes. The judge of appeal is nominated alternately for 5 years by each co-prince; the third instance *(Tercera Sala)* is either the supreme court of Andorra at Perpignan or the supreme court of the Bishop at Urgel.

Criminal justice is administered by the *Corts* consisting of the 2 Viguiers, the judge of appeal, 2 *rahonadors* elected by the general council of the valleys, a general attorney and an attorney nominated for 5 years alternatively by each of the co-princes. The accused may be assisted by a barrister.

Religion. The prevailing religious denomination is Roman Catholic.

Education. In 1986–87 there were 1,866 pupils at infant schools, 3,458 at primary schools, 3,271 at secondary schools, 230 at technical schools and 46 at special schools.

Health. In 1988 there were 112 doctors and 113 hospital beds.

Further Reading

Brutails, *La Coutume d'Andorre*. Paris, 1904
Corts Peyret, J., *Geografia e Historia de Andorra*. Barcelona, 1945
Llobet, S., *El medio y la vida en Andorra*. Barcelona, 1947
Riberaygua-Argelich, B., *Les Valls d'Andorra*. Barcelona, 1946

ANGOLA

Capital: Luanda
Population: 9·39m. (1988)
GNP per capita: US$500 (1985)

República Popular de Angola

HISTORY. The first Europeans to arrive in Angola were the Portuguese in 1482, and the first settlers arrived there in 1491. Luanda was founded in 1575. Apart from a brief period of Dutch occupation from 1641 to 1648, Angola remained a Portuguese colony until 11 June 1951, when it became an Overseas Province of Portugal. On 11 Nov. 1975 Angola became fully independent as the People's Republic of Angola.

AREA AND POPULATION. Angola is bounded by Congo on the north, Zaïre on the north and north-east, Zambia on the east, Namibia on the south and the Atlantic ocean on the west. The area is 1,246,700 sq. km (481,351 sq. miles) including the 7,107 sq. km province of Cabinda, an enclave of territory separated by 30 km of Zaïre. The population at census, 1970, was 5,646,166, of whom 14% urban. Estimate (1988) 9,387,000, including 114,000 in Cabinda. Urban population (1986) 30% of whom 38% speak Umbundu, 27% Kimbundu, 13% Lunda and 11% Kikongo. Portuguese remains the official language. There were (1986) about 27,000 Cubans and 30,000 Europeans (mostly Portuguese) in Angola. Refugees living in Angola totalled 90,458 (1988) of whom 69,000 were Namibians.

The most important towns (with 1970 populations) are Luanda, the capital (480,613; 1988, 1·2m.), Huambo (61,885), Lobito (59,258), Benguela (40,996), Lubango (31,674; 1984, 105,000), Malange (31,559) and Namibe (formerly Moçâmedes, 23,145; 1981, 100,000).

CLIMATE. The climate is tropical, with low rainfall in the west but increasing inland. Temperatures are constant over the year and most rain falls in March and April. Luanda. Jan. 78°F (25·6°C), July 69°F (20·6°C). Annual rainfall 13" (323 mm). Lobito. Jan. 77°F (25°C), July 68°F (20°C). Annual rainfall 14" (353 mm).

CONSTITUTION AND GOVERNMENT. Under the Constitution adopted at independence, the sole legal party is the *Movimento Popular de Libertação de Angola – Partido do Trabalho*. The supreme organ of state is the unicameral National People's Assembly, whose members were first elected in Aug. 1980 for a 3-year term. In 1987 the Assembly had 206 members. There is an executive President elected for renewable terms of 5 years, who appoints a Council of Ministers to assist him.

Substantial parts of the country are, however, under the control of the anti-government forces of the *União Nacional para a Independência Total de Angola* (UNITA).

The Council of Ministers in Nov. 1989 was as follows:

President: José Eduardo dos Santos (re-elected 9 Dec. 1985).

Ministers of State: Zeferino Kassa Yombo *(Petroleum and Energy)*, Kundi Paihama *(Inspection and Control, State Security)*.

Planning: António Henriques da Silva. *Defence:* Col.-Gen. Pedro Maria Tonha (Pedalé). *External Relations:* Lieut.-Col. Pedro de Castro Van-Dúnem. *Justice:* Fernando José França Van-Dúnem. *Education:* Augusto Lopes Teixeira (Tutu). *Health:* Flavio João Fernandes. *Finance:* Augusto Teixeira de Matos. *Foreign Trade:* Domingo das Chagas Simoes Rangel. *Internal Trade:* Joaquim Guerreiro

Dias. *Industry:* Henrique de Carvalho dos Santos (Onambwe). *Transport and Communications:* Carlos António Fernandes. *Labour and Social Security:* Diogo Jorge de Jesus. *Agriculture:* Fernando Faustino Muteka. *Interior:* Francisco Magalhaes Paiva. *Construction:* João Henriques Garcia. *Fisheries:* José Ramos da Cruz.

Flag: Horizontally red over black, with a star and an arc of cogwheel crossed by a machete, all yellow over all in the centre.

Local government: Angola is divided into 18 provinces divided into 139 districts – (Cabinda, Zaïre, Uíge, Luanda, Cuanza Norte, Cuanza Sul, Malange, Lunda Norte, Lunda Sul, Benguela, Huambo, Bié, Moxico, Cuando-Cubango, Namibe, Huíla, Cunene and Bengo) each under a Provincial Commissioner, appointed by the President and an elected legislative of from 55 to 85 members.

DEFENCE. Conscription is for a period of 2 years.

Army. The Army has 70 brigades, each with infantry, tank, armoured personnel carriers, artillery and anti-aircraft units; and 10 SAM batteries. Total strength (1990) 91,500. Equipment includes Soviet 100 T-34, 300 T-54/55 and more than 100 T-62 and PT-76 tanks.

Navy. Twenty Portuguese naval craft were transferred on independence in 1975 of which several have been discarded, and 9 vessels were acquired from the Soviet Navy in 1977-79. There are 6 fast missile boats, 5 fast torpedo boats, 4 patrol craft, 13 inshore patrol boats, 11 landing craft, and 11 auxiliary vessels. Naval personnel in 1989 totalled 1,500.

Air Force. The Angolan People's Air Force (FAPA) was formed in 1976. The combat force has been expanded since 1983 with Soviet assistance. It included (1989) 50 MiG-21, 30 MiG-23 and 40 Su-22 fighters, plus 25 Mi-24 and 6 Gazelle gunships. (The MiG-17 is being withdrawn from service.) There are 10 An-2, 20 An-26, 12 Islander, 4 Turbo-Porter, 8 Aviocar and 2 F.27 transports, 2 Embraer EMB-111 maritime surveillance aircraft, 4 PC-9,12 PC-7 and 3 MiG-15UTI trainers, and 40 Mi-8, 15 Mi-17, 6 Dauphin, 2 Lama and 40 Alouette III helicopters. Personnel (1990) 7,000.

INTERNATIONAL RELATIONS

Membership. Angola is a member of UN, OAU and is an ACP state of the EEC.

ECONOMY

Budget. The 1986 budget includes 90,400m. kwanza for capital and current expenditure and revenue at 78,500m. kwanza.

Currency. The currency is the *kwanza* divided into 100 *lwei*. Coins are of 50 *lwei*, 1, 2, 5, 10 and 20 *kwanza*; notes are of 20, 50, 100, 500 and 1,000 *kwanza*. In March 1990, £1 = 51·68 *kwanza*; US$1 = 30·41 *kwanza*.

Banking. All banking was nationalized in 1975. The *Banco Nacional de Angola* is the central bank and bank of issue, while the *Banco Popular de Angola* handles all commercial activities throughout the country.

Weights and Measures. The metric system is in force.

ENERGY AND NATURAL RESOURCES

Electricity. Production (1986) totalled 851m. kwh, mainly hydro-electricity. In Nov. 1984 an agreement was signed with Brazil and USSR to construct a hydroelectric plant at Kapanda on the river Kwanza, 250 miles south of Luanda.

Oil. Total production (1989) about 24m. tonnes.

Minerals. Production of diamonds during 1985 totalled 625,000 carats. Production (1985) of salt, 10,000 tonnes. There has been no production of iron ore since 1975, but the mines at Kassinga were restarted in 1985. Phosphate mining commenced in the north in 1981. Manganese and copper deposits exist.

Agriculture. The principal cash crops (with 1988 production, in 1,000 tonnes): Sugar-cane (330), coffee (15), bananas (280), palm oil (40), palm kernels (12), seed cotton (33); others include tobacco, citrus fruit and sisal. Food crops comprise cassava (1,980), maize (270), sweet potatoes (180) and dry beans (40).

Livestock (1988): 3·4m. cattle, 265,000 sheep, 975,000 goats, 480,000 pigs.

Forestry. In 1988 there were 53·1m. hectares of forests, representing 43% of the land area. Mahogany and other hardwoods are exported, chiefly from the tropical rain forests of the north, especially Cabinda. Production (1986) 10m. cu. metres.

Fisheries. Total catch (1984) 70,700 tonnes.

INDUSTRY AND TRADE

Industry. In 1985, 10,000 tonnes of steel were produced and 350,000 tonnes of cement.

Commerce. Imports and exports for 4 calendar years in 1m. Kwanza.

	1982	*1983*	*1984* [1]	*1985* [1]
Imports	25,946	20,197	19,448	41,240
Exports	48,736	54,508	60,112	59,280

[1] Provisional.

The chief imports are textiles, transport equipment, foodstuffs, pig-iron and steel; chief exports are crude oil, coffee, diamonds, sisal, fish, maize, palm-oil. In 1983, crude petroleum represented 85% of exports, petroleum products, 5·6%, coffee 3·9% and diamonds 5·6%. In 1985 Portugal provided 13% of imports, France 12%, the USA 11%, and Brazil 11%, while 45% of exports went to the USA, 14% to Spain and 11% (all diamonds) to the Bahamas.

Total trade between Angola and UK (British Department of Trade returns, in £1,000 sterling):

	1986	*1987*	*1988*	*1989*
Imports to UK	43,147	2,312	10,036	1,286
Exports and re-exports from UK	30,896	29,573	20,154	24,785

COMMUNICATIONS

Roads. There were, in 1986, 73,830 km of roads, and in 1984, 56,625 cars and 29,000 commercial vehicles.

Railways. The length of railways open for traffic in 1987 was 2,952 km comprising 2,798 km of 1,067 mm gauge and 154 km of 600 mm gauge. The Benguela Railway runs from Lobito to the Zaïre border at Dilolo where it connects with the National Railways of Zaïre. Other lines link Luanda with Malange; Gunza with Gabela; and Namibe with Menongue. In 1986 Angola's railways carried 4·1m. passengers and 2·5m. tonnes of freight.

Aviation. Luanda has international air links to Lisbon, Rome, Paris, Moscow, Budapest, Brazzaville, Saõ Tomé, Lusaka, Maputo, Sal (Cape Verde Islands), Havana, Kinshasa, Libreville, Berlin, Tripoli, Lagos, Algiers, Niamey, Sofia, Malta, Rio de Janeiro and São Paulo.

Shipping. In 1975, 2·85m. tonnes were discharged and 16m. tonnes loaded in Angolan ports. In 1986 there were 100 merchant vessels (over 100 GRT) totalling 127,000 GRT.

Post and Broadcasting. Angola is connected by cable with east, west and south African telegraph systems. There were, in 1973, 1,808 km of telegraph lines, 77 telephone stations (with 40,000 instruments in 1982), 162 telegraph stations and 31 wireless stations.

Rádio Nacional de Angola is the largest of the 18 stations operating on medium- and short-waves. *Rádio Nacional* transmits 3 programmes as well as operating 2 regional stations. Number of radio receivers (1988) 1·2m. and television receivers 200,000.

Cinemas. There were, in 1972, 47 cinemas with seating capacity of 35,142.

Newspaper. The national daily newspaper is *Jornal de Angola*, with a circulation of 41,000 in 1988.

JUSTICE, RELIGION, EDUCATION AND WELFARE

Justice. The Supreme Court and Court of Appeal are in Luanda.

Religion. Article 7 of the Constitution of the People's Republic of Angola states that: 'The People's Republic of Angola is a secular state, where there is a complete separation of religious institutions from the state'. All religions will be respected.

In 1980 55% of the population were Roman Catholic, 9% Protestant and 34% animist.

Education. In 1983 there were 2·4m. pupils in primary schools, 153,000 in secondary schools and 4,746 students in higher education. The *Universidade de Angola* (founded 1963) at Luanda with faculties at Huambo and Lubango, had 3,500 students in 1982.

Health. In 1980 there were 436 doctors and 20,700 hospital beds and in 1973, 87 pharmacists, 284 midwives and 3,115 nursing personnel.

DIPLOMATIC REPRESENTATIVES

Of Angola in Great Britain (87 Jermyn St., London, SW1Y 6JD)
Ambassador: Luis Neto-Kiambata.

Of Great Britain in Angola (Rua Diogo Cão, 4, Luanda)
Ambassador: (Vacant).

Of Angola to the United Nations
Ambassador: Manuel Pedro Pacavira.

Further Reading

Anuário Estatistico de Angola. Luanda, from 1897
Araújo, A. Correia de, *Aspectos do desenvolvimento económico e social de Angola*. Lisbon, 1964
Bender, G. J., *Angola under the Portuguese: Myth and Reality*. London, 1979
Bhagavan, M. R., *Angola's Political Economy 1975–1985*. Uppsala, 1986
Davidson, B., *In the Eye of the Storm*. London, 1972
Klinghoffer, A. J., *The Angolan War*. Boulder, 1980
Marcrum, J., *The Angolan Revolution*. (2 vols.) MIT Press, 1969 and 1978
Pélissier, R., *Les guerres grises*. Montamets, 1980.—*La Colonie du Minotaure*. Montamets, 1980.—*Le naufrage des coravelles*. Montamets, 1980
Somerville, K., *Angola: Politics, Economics and Society*. London and Boulder, 1986
Wheeler, D. L. and Pélissier, R., *Angola*. London, 1971
Zirka, A. K., *Angola Libre?* Paris, 1975

ANGUILLA

Capital: The Valley
Population: 7,019 (1989)

HISTORY. Anguilla was probably given its name by the Spaniards because of its eel-like shape. After British settlements in the 17th century, the territory was administered as part of the Leeward Islands. From 1825 it became more closely associated with St Kitts and ultimately incorporated in the colony of St Kitts-Nevis-Anguilla. Opposition to this association grew and finally in 1967 the island seceded unilaterally. Following direct intervention by the UK in 1969 Anguilla became *de facto* a separate dependency of Britain; and this was formalized on 19 Dec. 1980 under the Anguilla Act 1980. A new Constitution came into effect in April 1982.

AREA AND POPULATION. Anguilla is the most northerly of the Leeward Islands, some 70 miles (112 km) to the north-west of St Kitts and 5 miles (8 km) to the north of St Martin/St Maarten. The territory also comprises the island of Sombrero (on which there is an important lighthouse) and several other off-shore islets or cays. The total area of the territory is about 60 sq. miles (155 sq. km). Census population (1984) was 6,987. Estimate, 1989, 7,019. The capital is The Valley.

CONSTITUTION AND GOVERNMENT. The House of Assembly consists of a Speaker, 7 elected members, 2 nominated members and 2 official members.

Executive power is vested in the Governor who is appointed by HM The Queen. Apart from his special responsibilities (External Affairs, Defence, Internal Security, including the Police, and the Public Service) and his reserve powers in respect of legislation, the Governor discharges his executive powers on the advice of an Executive Council comprising a Chief Minister, 3 Ministers and 2 official members: Attorney-General and Permanent Secretary, Finance.

Governor: B. G. J. Canty.
Chief Minister: Emile Gumbs.

ECONOMY

Budget. In 1989, the budget was: Expenditure EC$26·76m.; revenue EC$28·2m. Anguilla finances its recurrent budget and a small part of its capital budget but for the most part aid for capital projects comes from UK and other donors.

Currency. The currency is the Eastern Caribbean *dollar*.

ENERGY AND NATURAL RESOURCES

Electricity. Production (1988) 4m. kwh.

Agriculture. Because of low rainfall agriculture potential is limited. Main crops are pigeon peas, corn and sweet potatoes. Livestock consists of sheep, goats, cattle and poultry.

Fisheries. Fishing is a thriving industry with exports to neighbouring islands.

INDUSTRY AND TRADE

Trade. Total trade between Anguilla and UK (British Department of Trade returns, in £1,000 sterling):

	1987	*1988*	*1989*
Imports to UK	188	68	1,402
Exports and re-exports from UK	1,328	1,372	1,952

Tourism. There are a few hotels of international standing and others are under construction. There are also several locally-owned hotels, guest houses and apartments. In 1988 there were 69,482 tourists, of which 41,275 were day visitors.

COMMUNICATIONS

Roads. There are about 43 miles of tarred roads and 25 miles of secondary roads. In 1985 there were 973 passenger cars and 239 commercial vehicles.

Aviation. There is a 3,600 ft surfaced runway at Wallblake Airport. Apart from regular air taxi and charter flights WINAIR (subsidiary of ALM) provides daily scheduled services between Juliana International Airport, St Martin and Anguilla. WINAIR, LIAT and American Eagle operate direct flights from San Juan, Puerto Rico. Air BVI flies from Tortola and St Thomas to Anguilla.

Shipping. The main seaports are Road Bay and Blowing Point, the latter serving passenger and cargo traffic to and from St Martin.

Post and Telecommunications. There is a modern internal telephone service with (1986–87) 1,825 exchange lines; and international telegraph, telex and telephone services, all operated by Cable & Wireless. In 1986 there were 2,200 radio receivers.

Newspapers. In 1988 there was 1 daily newspaper.

RELIGION, EDUCATION AND WELFARE

Religion. There were in 1988 Anglicans, Roman Catholics, Methodists, Seventh Day Adventists, Church of God and Baptists.

Education. There are 6 government primary schools with (1989) 1,290 pupils and 1 comprehensive school with (1989) 883 pupils. Tertiary education is provided at regional universities and similar institutions.

Health. There is a 24-bed cottage hospital, clinics and a modern dental clinic. There were (1987) 4 doctors and 1 dentist.

Further Reading

Petty, C. L., *Anguilla: Where there's a Will, there's a Way.* Anguilla, 1984

ANTIGUA AND BARBUDA

Capital: St John's
Population: 81,500 (1986)
GNP per capita: US$ 2,800 (1988)

HISTORY. Antigua was discovered by Colombus in 1493 and named by him after a church in Seville (Spain). It was first colonized by English settlers in 1632; nearby Barbuda was colonized in 1661 from Antigua. Formed part of the Leeward Islands Federation from 1871 until 30 June 1956, when Antigua became a separate Crown Colony, which was part of the West Indies Federation from 3 Jan. 1958 until 31 May 1962. It became an Associated State of the UK on 27 Feb. 1967 and obtained independence on 1 Nov. 1981.

AREA AND POPULATION. Antigua and Barbuda comprises 3 islands of the Lesser Antilles situated in the Eastern Caribbean with a total land area of 442 sq. km (171 sq. miles); it consists of Antigua (280 sq. km), Barbuda, 40 km to the north (161 sq. km) and uninhabited Redonda, 40 km to the southwest (1 sq. km).

The population at the Census of 7 April 1970 was 65,525. In 1986 the estimated population was 81,500 of whom 1,500 lived in Barbuda. The chief towns are St John's, the capital on Antigua (30,000 inhabitants in 1982) and Codrington, the only settlement on Barbuda.

CLIMATE. A tropical climate, but drier than most West Indies islands. The hot season is from May to Nov., when rainfall is greater. Mean annual rainfall is 40" (1,000 mm).

CONSTITUTION AND GOVERNMENT. H.M. Queen Elizabeth, as Head of State, is represented by a Governor-General appointed by her on the advice of the Prime Minister. There is a bicameral legislature, comprising a 17-member Senate appointed by the Governor-General and a 17-member House of Representatives elected by universal suffrage for a 5-year term. The Governor-General appoints a Prime Minister and, on the latter's advice, other members of the Cabinet.

Governor-General: Sir Wilfred Ebenezer Jacobs, GCMG, GCVO, OBE, QC.

Prime Minister and Finance: Right Hon. Vere C. Bird, Sen., PC.

Deputy Prime Minister, Foreign Affairs, Economic Development, Tourism and Energy: Lester Bryant Bird.

At the general elections held on 17 April 1984, the ruling Antigua Labour Party won all 16 seats on Antigua and there was one independent (representing Barbuda).

Flag: Red, with a triangle based on the top edge, divided horizontally black, blue, white, with a rising sun in gold on the black portion.

DEFENCE. The defence force has a strength of about 700. A coastguard service has been formed.

INTERNATIONAL RELATIONS

Membership. Antigua and Barbuda is a member of UN, the Commonwealth, CARICOM and is an ACP state of the EEC.

ECONOMY

Budget. The budget for 1988 envisaged revenue at EC$217m. and expenditure of EC$231·7m.

Currency. The Eastern Caribbean $. In March 1990, £1 = EC$4·44; US$1 = EC$2·71.

Banking. Barclays Bank International, Royal Bank of Canada, Canadian Imperial Bank of Commerce, the Virgin Islands National Bank, the Antilles International Trust Co. and the Bank of Nova Scotia have branches at St John's. There is also the Antigua Co-operative Bank and a government savings bank.

ENERGY AND NATURAL RESOURCES

Electricity. Production (1986) 63·8m. kwh.

Agriculture. Cotton and fruits are the main crops. Production (1988) of fruits, 10,000 tonnes. There were 70,000 tonnes of cotton produced in 1985.

Livestock (1988): Cattle, 18,000; pigs, 4,000; sheep, 13,000; goats, 13,000.

Fisheries. Catch (1983) 1,013 tonnes.

INDUSTRY AND TRADE

Industry. An oil refinery was opened in 1982. Manufactures include toilet tissue, stoves, refrigerators, blenders, fans, garments and rum (molasses imported from Guyana).

Labour. In 1985 the workforce numbered 32,254, and there was 21% unemployment.

Commerce. Imports in 1984 amounted to EC$356·1m. and exports to EC$47·5m. of which the major amount came from bunkering provided to ships. The main trading partners were the USA, the UK and Canada.

Total trade between Antigua and Barbuda and UK (British Department of Trade returns, in £1,000 sterling):

	1987	*1988*	*1989*
Imports to UK	4,271	10,845	3,447
Exports and re-exports from UK	19,334	20,755	23,954

Tourism. There were 149,000 tourists (excluding cruise passengers) in 1986.

COMMUNICATIONS

Roads. There are 600 miles of roads (150 miles main road). In 1985 there were 10,000 passenger cars and 15,000 commercial vehicles.

Aviation. There is an international airport (V. C. Bird) on Antigua, and a small airstrip at Codrington on Barbuda.

Shipping. The main harbour is the St John's deep water harbour. There are 2 tugs for the berthing of ships and all modern and efficient general cargo handling equipment. The harbour can also accommodate 3 large cruise ships simultaneously.

Post and Broadcasting. In 1983 there were 10,470 telephones. In 1983 there were 20,000 radios and 17,000 television sets.

RELIGION, EDUCATION AND WELFARE.

Religion. The vast majority of the population are Christian, preponderantly Anglican.

Education. In 1985 there were 10,551 pupils and 436 teachers in 48 primary schools, and 5,106 pupils and 304 teachers in (1983) 16 secondary schools.

Health. There is a general hospital (Holberton) with 215 beds, a mental hospital with 200 beds, a geriatric unit with 150 beds, 4 health centres and 16 dispensaries.

DIPLOMATIC REPRESENTATIVES

Of Antigua and Barbuda in Great Britain (15 Thayer St., London, W1M 5DL)
High Commissioner: James A. E. Thomas.

Of Great Britain in Antigua and Barbuda (38 St Mary's St., St John's)
High Commissioner: K. F. X. Burns, CMG (resides in Bridgetown).

Of Antigua and Barbuda in the USA (3400 International Dr., NW, Washington, D.C., 20008)
Ambassador: Edmund Hawkins Lake.

Of the USA in Antigua and Barbuda
Chargé d'Affaires: R. James McHugh.

Of Antigua and Barbuda to the United Nations
Ambassador: Lionel Alexander Hurst.

Further Reading

Dyde, B., *Antigua and Barbuda: The Heart of the Caribbean.* London, 1986

ARGENTINA

Capital: Buenos Aires
Population: 31·06m. (1986)
GNP per capita: US$2,640 (1988)

República Argentina

HISTORY. In 1515 Juan Díaz de Solis discovered the Río de La Plata. In 1534 Pedro de Mendoza was sent by the King of Spain to take charge of the 'Gobernación y Capitanía de las tierras del Rio de La Plata', and in Feb. 1536 he founded the city of the 'Puerto de Santa María del Buen Aire'. In 1810 the population rose against Spanish rule, and in 1816 Argentina proclaimed its independence. Civil wars and anarchy followed until, in 1853, stable government was established.

Military leaders supported by the Navy and Air Force staged a *coup d'état* on 24 March 1976, and The Junta of Commanders in Chief deposed Isobel Perón and her Government elected in 1972. The Commander in Chief of the Army, Lieut-Gen. Videla, was appointed President. The previous Constitution remained in force in so far as it was consistent with the statutes and objectives of the Junta. Return to civilian rule took place on 10 Dec. 1983. For details of earlier history and Constitutions *see* THE STATESMAN'S YEAR-BOOK, 1982–83 and 1985–86.

AREA AND POPULATION. The Argentine Republic is bounded in the north by Bolivia, in the north-east by Paraguay, in the east by Brazil, Uruguay and the Atlantic Ocean and the west by Chile. The republic consists of 22 provinces, 1 federal district and the National Territories of Tierra del Fuego, the Antarctic and the South Atlantic Islands (census of 1980) as follows:

Provinces	*Area: Sq. km. 1960*	*Population Estimate 1989*	*Capital*	*Population census, 1980 (1,000)*
Litoral				
Federal Capital	200	2,900,794	Buenos Aires	2,908
Buenos Aires	307,571	12,604,018	La Plata	455
Corrientes	88,199	748,834	Corrientes	180
Entre Ríos	78,781	1,005,885	Paraná	160
Chaco	99,633	824,447	Resistencia	218
Santa Fé	133,007	2,765,678	Santa Fé	287
Formosa	72,066	354,512	Formosa	95
Misiones	29,801	723,839	Posadas	140
Norte				
Jujuy	53,219	502,694	San Salvador de Jujuy	124
Salta	154,775	822,378	Salta	260
Santiago del Estero	135,254	641,273	Santiago del Estero	148
Tucumán	22,524	1,134,309	San Miguel de Tucumán	393
Centro				
Córdoba	168,766	2,748,006	Córdoba	969
La Pampa	143,440	237,386	Santa Rosa	52
San Luis	76,748	246,087	San Luis	71
Andina				
Catamarca	100,967	232,523	Catamarca	78
La Rioja	89,680	191,468	La Rioja	67
Mendoza	148,827	1,387,914	Mendoza	118
San Juan	89,651	528,838	San Juan	118
Neuquén	94,078	326,313	Neuquén	90

Provinces	Area: Sq. km. 1960	Population Estimate 1989	Capital	Population census, 1980 (1,000)
Patagonia				
Chubut	224,686	327,780	Rawson	13
Rio Negro	203,013	466,713	Viedma	24
Santa Cruz	243,943	147,928	Rio Gallegos	43
Tierra del Fuego [1]	21,263	27,358	Ushuaia	11

[1] The total area is 2,780,092 sq. km excluding the claimed 'Antarctic Sector' and the population at the 1980 Census was 27,947,446; estimate (1989) 31·93m. In 1980, 95% spoke the national language, Spanish, while 3% spoke Italian, 1% Guaraní and 1% other languages. In 1983, 83% lived in urban areas and 17% rural, while 98% were white and 2% mestizo (mixed).

The official census including the 'Antarctic Sector', and stated to comprise the 'Malvinas' (Falklands), South Orcadas (Orkneys), South Georgias, South Sandwich Islands and the 'sovereign territories of Argentina in the Antarctic': population 3,300.

The principal metropolitan areas (1980 Census) are Buenos Aires (9,927,404), Córdoba (982,018), Rosario (954,606), Mendoza (596,796), La Plata (560,341), San Miguel de Tucumán (496,914), Mar del Plata (407,024), and San Juan (290,479). The suburbs of Buenos Aires, outside the Federal District, include San Justo (946,715), Morón (596,769), Lomas de Zamora (508,620), General Sarmiento (499,648), Lanus (465,891), Quilmes (441,780), General San Martín (384,306), Caseros (340,343), Almirante Brown (332,548), Avellaneda (330,654), Vicente López (289,815), San Isidro (287,048), Merlo (282,828), Tigre (205,926), Berazategui (200,926), and Esteban Echeverría (187,969).

Other large cities (1980 Census) are Rosario (875,664), Mar del Plata (407,024), Bahía Blanca (220,765), Guaymallén (157,334), Godoy Cruz (141,553), Rio Cuarto (110,254), Comodoro Rivadavia (98,985), San Nicolás (96,313) and Concordia (93,618).

CLIMATE. The climate is warm temperate over the pampas, where rainfall occurs at all seasons, but diminishes towards the west. In the north and west, the climate is more arid, with high summer temperatures, while in the extreme south conditions are also dry, but much cooler. Buenos Aires. Jan. 74°F (23·3°C), July 50°F (10°C). Annual rainfall 37" (950 mm). Bahía Blanca. Jan. 74°F (23·3°C), July 48°F (8·9°C). Annual rainfall 21" (523 mm). Mendoza. Jan. 75°F (23·9°C), July 47°F (8·3°C). Annual rainfall 8" (190 mm). Rosario. Jan. 76°F (24·4°C), July 51°F (10·6°C). Annual rainfall 35" (869 mm). San Juan. Jan. 78°F (25·6°C), July 50°F (10°C). Annual rainfall 4" (89 mm). San Miguel de Tucumán. Jan. 79°F (26·1°C), July 56°F (13·3°C). Annual rainfall 38" (970 mm). Ushuaia. Jan. 50°F (10°C), July 34°F (1·1°C). Annual rainfall 19" (475 mm).

CONSTITUTION AND GOVERNMENT. Presidential, congressional and municipal elections took place on 30 Oct. 1983 and a return to civilian rule took place on 10 Dec. 1983. With the return to constitutional rule the Constitution of 1853 (as amended up to 1898) is again in effect. The President and Vice-President are elected by a 600-member electoral college (directly elected by popular vote) for 6-year terms; both must be Roman Catholics of Argentine birth. The President is Commander-in-Chief of the Armed Services, and appoints to all civil and judicial offices.

The following is a list of Presidents from 1973 onwards:

Gen. Juan Domingo Perón. 12 Oct. 1973–1 July 1974.
Maria Estela (Isabel) Martinez Perón. 1 July 1974 (*a.i.* from 29 June 1974)–23 March 1976. (Deposed.)
Gen. Jorge Rafael Videla. 29 March 1976–29 March 1981.
Gen. Roberto Viola, 29 March–22 Dec. 1981.
Gen. Leopoldo Fortunato Galtieri, 22 Dec. 1981–17 June 1982.
Gen. Reynaldo Benito Antonio Bignone, 1 July 1982–10 Dec. 1983.
Dr Raúl Alfonsín, 10 Dec. 1983–30 June 1989.

The National Congress consists of a Senate and a House of Deputies: The Senate comprises 46 members, 2 nominated by each provincial legislature and 2 from the Federal District for 9 years (one-third retiring every 3 years). The House of Deputies comprises 254 members directly elected by universal suffrage (at age 18).

In the presidential elections held on 14 May 1989 Carlos Saúl Menem of the Justicalist Party won the support of 310 electors in the 600-member electoral college.

President of the Republic: Carlos Saúl Menem (sworn in 8 July 1989).

Vice-President: Eduardo Duhalde.

The Cabinet in Jan. 1990 was composed as follows:

Defence: (Vacant). *Economy:* Antonio Erman Gonzalez. *Education:* Antonio Francisco Salonia. *Foreign Relations:* Domingo Cavello. *Interior:* Eduardo Bauãá. *Labour and Social Security:* Alberto Jorge Triaca. *Public Health and Social Action:* (Vacant). *Public Works and Services:* José Roberto Dromi. *Secretary-General of the Presidency:* Alberto Kohan. *Justice:* Julio Oyhanarte.

National flag: Three horizontal stripes of light blue, white and light blue, with the gold Sun of May in the centre.

National anthem: Oid, mortales, el grito sagrado Libertad (words by V. López y Planes, 1813; tune by J. Blas Parera).

Local Government. In Oct. 1983 the governors were elected by the people.

DEFENCE

Army. There are 5 military regions. The Army is organized in 4 army corps; it consists of 2 armoured, 2 mechanized, 2 mountain, 1 jungle and 1 mixed infantry brigades; 2 engineering, 1 aviation and 1 air defence battalions.

In 1989 the Army was 55,000 strong, of whom 31,300 were conscripts.

The trained reserve numbers about 250,000, of whom 200,000 belong to the National Guard and 50,000 to the Territorial Guard.

Navy. The flagship of the Armada Republica Argentina is the light aircraft carrier *Veinticinco de Mayo* displacing 20,200 tonnes full load, and embarking an air group of 4 Super-Etendard, 3 S-2 Tracker and 4 S-61D Sea King aircraft. Originally the British *Venerable* (completed in 1948) she served in the Royal Netherlands Navy as *Karel Doorman*, from 1956 to 1968. She is currently undergoing major refit including re-engining. Of the two cruisers, the *General Belgrano*, *ex-Phoenix*, purchased from the USA in 1951 was sunk by the British submarine *Conqueror* in May 1982, while her sister ship *Nueve de Julio* (*ex*-USS *Bloise*) was withdrawn from service in 1980.

Other combatant forces include 4 German-built diesel submarines, 4 modern German-built destroyers, 2 British-built guided missile destroyers (Type 42), 4 German-designed and 3 French-built frigates, 2 old training frigates, 2 fast torpedo craft, 11 patrol ships, 4 coastal minesweepers, 2 minehunters and 1 tank landing ship. Auxiliaries include 2 survey ships, 2 training ships, 3 transports, 1 icebreaker and numerous harbour and service craft.

The new construction programme includes 2 diesel submarines (both building – but slowly) and 2 small frigates.

The Naval Aviation Service has some 62 combat aircraft and helicopters with (1989) 2,000 personnel, in 6 wings. Aircraft include 14 Super-Etendard strike aircraft, 5 A-4Q Skyhawk attack bombers, 11 EMB-326 and 5 EMB-339A light jet armed trainers, 4 Lockheed Electra maritime surveillance aircraft and 6 S-2E carrier-based Tracker anti-submarine aircraft, plus varied training, transport and general purpose aircraft. There is a squadron of S-60 ASW helicopters plus some 8 Alouettes. A variable mix of Super Etendards, Skyhawks and Trackers plus Sea King and Alouette helicopters will operate from the aircraft carrier when her refit is completed.

Main bases are at Buenos Aires, Puerto Belgrano (HQ and Dockyard), Mar del Plata and Ushuaia.

The active personnel of the navy in 1989 comprised 25,000, 4,000 of whom were conscripts, and including 5,000 marines.

The Prefectura Naval Argentina (PNA) for Coast Guard and rescue duties operates 5 new 910-tonne corvettes with helicopter and hangar, an *ex*-whaler of 700 tonnes, and 23 patrol vessels.

Air Force. The Air Force is organized into Air Operations, Air Regions, Materiel and Personnel Commands. Air Operations Command, responsible for all operational flying, is made up of air brigades, each with 1 to 4 squadrons, usually operating from a single base. No. I Air Brigade is a military air transport service, with responsibility also for LADE (state airline) operations into areas of Argentina not served by civilian companies. Its equipment includes 6 C-130E/H Hercules and 10 F.27 Friendship/Troopship turboprop transports, 2 KC-130H Hercules tanker/transports, 4 twin-turbofan F.28 Fellowship freighters, 7 Twin Otters, 15 Guarani IIs, the Presidential Boeing 707-320B and 707-320C, 4 more 707s, 2 VIP Fellowships, and many older or smaller types. No. II Air Brigade has 4 Canberra twin-jet bombers and 2 Canberra trainers; a photographic squadron with Guarani IIs and Learjets. No. III Air Brigade has 2 squadrons of IA 58 Pucara twin-turboprop COIN aircraft. No. IV Air Brigade comprises 2 ground attack squadrons equipped with about 30 Paris light jet combat and liaison aircraft, now being replaced by IA 63 Pampas, and one squadron with Mirage IIIs. No. V Air Brigade comprises 2 squadrons with a total of about 30 A-4P Skyhawk strike aircraft. No. VI Air Brigade has 40 Dagger (Israeli-built Mirage III) fighters, equipping 2 squadrons, and 1 squadron with 15 Mirage IIIE fighter-bombers and 4 Mirage IIID trainers. No. VII Air Brigade has 2 helicopter squadrons with 12 armed Hughes 500M, 8 Bell 212, 6 Bell UH-1 and 2 Chinook helicopters. No. X Air Brigade has 1 squadron of Mirage IIIC/5 fighters. There is a flying school at Córdoba, equipped with turboprop-powered Embraer Tucanos and Paris jets. There were (1990) about 15,000 personnel and about 150 combat aircraft.

INTERNATIONAL RELATIONS

Membership. Argentina is a member of UN, OAS and LAIA (formerly LAFTA).

ECONOMY

Budget. The financial year commences on 1 Jan. Budget receipts in 1988 151,208m. australes and expenditure 156,029m. australes.

Currency. The monetary unit is the *austral* divided into 100 cents. Circulation consists chiefly of paper notes (issued since 1897) ranging from 50,000 *australes* down to 1 *austral*. The coins actually circulating, 1988, were steel-nickel, 1, 5, 10 and 50 centavos. In March 1990, US$1 = 5,443 *austral*; £1 = 8,921 *austral*.

Banking. In 1988 there were 36 government banks, 109 private banks and 33 foreign banks. Total foreign debt (31 Dec. 1987) US$58,324m.

Weights and Measures. Since 1 Jan. 1887 the use of the metric system has been compulsory.

ENERGY AND NATURAL RESOURCES

Electricity. Electric power production (1988) was 48,965m. kwh. Supply 220 volts; 50 Hz.

Oil. Crude oil production (1989) 23m. tonnes. The oil industry aims at achieving self-sufficiency.

Gas. Natural gas production (1983) 13,500,000m. cu. metres. New offshore fields were reported in 1988.

Minerals. Argentina produced 505,000 tonnes of washed coal in 1988. Gold, silver and copper are worked in Catamarca, where there are also 2 tin-mines, and gold and copper in San Juan, La Rioja and the south-western territories. Iron ore (654,800 tonnes in 1988), tungsten, beryllium, clay, marble, lead (39,400 tonnes in 1988), barites, zinc (73,300 tonnes in 1988), borate (245,000 tonnes in 1988), bentonite and granite are produced.

Agriculture. Argentina has an area of about 670,251,000 acres, of which about 41% is pasture land, 32% woodland and 11% (73·73m. acres) cultivated.

Livestock (1988): Cattle 50,782,000; sheep, 29,202,000; pigs, 4·1m.; horses, 3·1m. The Province of Buenos Aires has 37% of the cattle. Wool production, 1988, was 138,000 tonnes.

Wheat production (1988) 7,769,000 tonnes from 4,617,000 hectares.

Argentina's meat exports are calculated in terms of actual weight; not 'carcase weight', as is the international practice.

Cotton, potatoes, vine, tobacco, citrus fruit, olives, rice, soya, and yerba maté (Paraguayan tea) are also cultivated. There are 36 cane-sugar mills and 1 beet-sugar factory; cane-sugar production, 1988, 14,773,000 tonnes. Potato production, 1988, amounted to 2·19m. tonnes. The area under tobacco, 1988, was 55,000 hectares; output 74,000 tonnes.

Sunflower seed (production (1988) 2,915,000 tonnes), first grown by Russian immigrants in 1900, now furnishes the country's most popular edible oil. There are more than 10m. olive trees. 443,000 tonnes of groundnuts were produced in 1988 (mainly in Córdoba). Argentina is the world's largest source of tannin.

Forestry. In 1989 woodland covered 22% of the land area (59·5m. hectares).

Fisheries. Fish landings in 1986 amounted to 420,300 tonnes.

INDUSTRY AND TRADE

Industry. Production (1988 in tonnes) Paper, 761,393; steel (1986), 2·85m.; sulphuric acid, 258,024; cement (1987), 6,302,065. Motor vehicles produced totalled, 131,253; television receivers, 454,429.

Commerce. Import values include charges for carriage, insurance and freight; export values are on a f.o.b. basis. Real values of foreign trade (in US$1m.):

	1986	*1987*	*1988*
Imports	4,724	5,818	5,322
Exports	6,852	6,360	9,135

Total trade between Argentina and UK (British Department of Trade returns, in £1,000 sterling):

	1985	*1986*	*1987*	*1988*	*1989*
Imports to UK	2,032	28,635	64,595	66,281	98,490
Exports and re-exports from UK	3,815	10,115	10,267	12,991	13,585

Tourism. In 1988, 2,119,140 tourists visited Argentina.

COMMUNICATIONS

Roads. In 1983 there were 220,093 km of national and provincial highways. The 4 main roads constituting Argentina's portion of the Pan-American Highway were opened to traffic in 1942. In 1985 there were 5·08m. cars and commercial vehicles.

Railways. The system based on the 1949 amalgamation of 18 government, British and French-owned railways, comprises 7 railways with a total route-km in 1987 of 34,172 km (210 km electrified) on metre, 1,435 mm and 1,676 mm gauges. In 1987 railways carried 7,977m. tonne-km and 11,966m. passenger-km. In 1988 parts of the network were being prepared for privatization.

Aviation. There were (1986) 10 international airports and 54 other airports. Scheduled services between Argentina and UK resumed in 1990.

Shipping. The merchant fleet, 1988, consisted of 451 vessels of 2,834,000 DWT.

Post and Broadcasting. In 1949 the telephone service was nationalized; instruments numbered 3,250,000 in 1984. There were (1984) 122 radio stations and 4 television channels in Buenos Aires. In 1986 there were 6m. radio receivers and 5·9m. television receivers.

Newspapers (1985). Daily newspapers numbered 227 with a circulation of 2·7m.

JUSTICE, RELIGION, EDUCATION AND WELFARE

Justice. Justice is administered by federal and provincial courts. The former deal only with cases of a national character, or in which different provinces or inhabitants of different provinces are parties. The chief federal court is the Supreme Court, with 5 judges at Buenos Aires. Other federal courts are the appeal courts, at Buenos Aires, Bahía Blanca, La Plata, Córdoba, Mendoza, Tucumán and Resistencia. Each province has its own judicial system, with a Supreme Court (generally so designated) and several minor chambers. Trial by jury is established by the Constitution for criminal cases, but never practised, except occasionally in the provinces of Buenos Aires and Córdoba.

The death penalty was re-introduced in 1976 for the killing of government, military police and judicial officials, and for participation in terrorist activities.

The police force is centralized under the Federal Security Council.

Religion. The Roman Catholic religion is supported by the State and membership was 26m. in 1986. There are several Protestant denominations with a total congregation (1983) of 500,000. The Jewish congregation numbered 300,000 in 1983.

Education. In 1984 the primary schools had 218,520 teachers and 4,430,513 pupils; secondary schools had 86,874 teachers and 656,521 pupils, vocational schools had 119,309 teachers and 905,755 pupils.

There are National Universities at Buenos Aires (2), Córdoba (2), La Plata, Tucumán, Santa Fé (Litoral), Rosario, Corrientes (Nordeste), Mendoza (Cuyo), Bahía Blanca (Sur), Catamarca, Tandil, Neuquén (Comahue), San Salvador de Jujuy, Salta, Santa Rosa (La Pampa), Mar del Plata, Comodoro Rivadavia (Patagonia), Río Cuarto, Entre Ríos, Resistencia, San Juan and Santiago del Estero. There are also private universities in Buenos Aires (6), Mendoza (3), Córdoba, Comodoro Rivadavia, La Plata, Morón, Tucumán, Salta, Santa Fé and Santiago del Estero. In 1981 universities had 525,688 students and 54,039 lecturers.

Health. Free medical attention is obtainable from public hospitals. Many trade unions provide medical, dental and maternity services for their members and dependants. In 1980 there were 151,568 hospital beds and 72,762 doctors.

DIPLOMATIC REPRESENTATIVES

Diplomatic links with Argentina were broken by Great Britain in April 1982 following the invasion of the Falkland Islands but Consular activity was resumed in Dec. 1989 and full diplomatic activity resumed in Feb. 1990.

Of Argentina in Great Britian
Ambassador: Mario Campora.

Of Argentina in the USA (1600 New Hampshire Ave., NW, Washington, D.C., 20009)
Ambassador: Guido José Maria di Tella.

Of the USA in Argentina (4300 Colombia, 1425, Buenos Aires)
Ambassador: Terence A. Todman.

Of Argentina to the United Nations
Ambassador: Dr Jorge Vazquez.

Further Reading

Boletin del comercio exterio Argentino y estadisticas económicas retrospectivas. Annual
Anuario de comercio exterior de la República Argentina. Annual
Economic Review, Banco de la Nación. Buenos Aires
Sintesis Estadistica Mensual. Dirección General de Estadistica. Buenos Aires, 1947 ff.
Boletin Internacional de Bibliografia Argentina. Ministry of Foreign Relations. Buenos Aires. Monthly
Geografia de la República Argentino. Ed. by the Sociedad Argentina de Estudios Geográficos. 7 vols. Buenos Aires. 1945–53
Bridges, E. L., *Uttermost Part of the Earth* [*Tierra del Fuego*]. New York, 1949
Crawley, E., *A House Divided: Argentina 1880–1980.* London, 1984
Ferns, H. S., *Britain and Argentina in the 19th Century.* OUP, 1960.—*The Argentine Republic 1516–1971.* Newton Abbot, 1973
Graham-Yooll, A., *The Forgotten Colony: A History of the English-Speaking Communities in Argentina.* London, 1981
Rock, D., *Argentina 1516–1982.* London, 1986
Santillán, Diego A. de (ed.) *Gran Enciclopedia Argentina.* 9 vols. 1956–64
Simpson, J. and Bennett, J., *The Disappeared: Voices from a Secret War.* London, 1985
Wynia, G. W., *Argentina.* Hoddesdon, 1986

AUSTRALIA

Capital: Canberra
Population: 16·8m. (1989)
GNP per capita: US$12,390 (1988)

Commonwealth of Australia

HISTORY. On 1 Jan. 1901 the former British colonies of New South Wales, Victoria, Queensland, South Australia, Western Australia and Tasmania were federated under the name of the 'Commonwealth of Australia', the designation of 'colonies' being at the same time changed into that of 'states'—except in the case of Northern Territory, which was transferred from South Australia to the Commonwealth as a 'territory' on 1 Jan. 1911.

In 1911 the Commonwealth acquired from the State of New South Wales the Canberra site for the Australian capital.

Territories under the administration of Australia in Jan. 1987, but not included in it, comprise Norfolk Island, the territory of Ashmore and Cartier Islands, and the Australian Antarctic Territory (acquired 24 Aug. 1936), comprising all the islands and territory, other than Adélie Land, situated south of 60° S. lat. and between 160° and 45° E. long. The Coral Sea Islands became an External Territory in 1969.

The British Government transferred sovereignty in the Heard Island and McDonald Islands to the Australian Government on 26 Dec. 1947. Cocos (Keeling) Islands on 23 Nov. 1955 and Christmas Island on 1 Oct. 1958 were also transferred to Australian jurisdiction.

AREA AND POPULATION. Australia, including Tasmania but excluding external territories, covers a land area of 7,682,300 sq. km, extending from Cape York (10° 41' S) in the north some 3,680 km to Tasmania (43° 39' S), and from Cape Byron (153° 39' E) in the east some 4,000 km west to Western Australia (113° 9' E). Growth in Census population has been:

1901	3,774,310	1947	7,579,358	1971	12,755,638
1911	4,455,005	1954	8,986,530	1976	13,915,500
1921	5,435,734	1961	10,508,186	1981	15,053,600
1933	6,629,839	1966	11,599,498	1986	15,763,000

Area and resident population (estimate), 30 June 1989, 16,806,730 (8,415,711 females), divided as follows:

States and Territories	*Area (sq. km)*	*Total*	*Per sq. km*
New South Wales (NSW)	801,600	5,761,919	7·0
Victoria (Vic.)	227,600	4,315,170	18·5
Queensland (Qld.)	1,727,200	2,830,198	1·5
South Australia (SA)	984,000	1,423,337	1·4
Western Australia (WA)	2,525,500	1,591,077	0·6
Tasmania (Tas.)	67,800	450,956	6·6
Northern Territory (NT)	1,346,200	156,147	0·1
Australian Capital Territory (ACT)	2,400	277,926	110·9
Total	7,682,300	16,806,730	2·2

85·4% of the population was urban in 1986. Resident population (estimate) in State capitals and other major cities (statistical districts), 30 June 1987:

Capitals	*State*	*Population*	*Statistical district*	*State*	*Population*
Canberra [1]	ACT	288,900	Darwin	NT	75,300
Sydney	NSW	3,531,000	Newcastle	NSW	419,200
Melbourne	Vic.	2,964,800	Wollongong	NSW	233,800
Brisbane	Qld.	1,215,300	Gold Coast [2]	Qld.	219,700
Adelaide	SA	1,013,000	Geelong	Vic.	149,300
Perth	WA	1,083,400	Townsville	Qld.	108,300
Hobart	Tas.	180,000			

[1] Includes Queanbeyan (20,450). [2] Includes Tweed Heads.

At 30 June 1987 the age-group distribution was: Under 15, 3,682,864; 15-44, 7,747,667; 45-64, 3,090,963; 65 and over, 1,741,825. Life expectancy in 1986 was 72·9 (males), 79·2 (females).

Australians born overseas (30 June 1989), 3·73m., of whom 1·2m. came from the UK and Ireland; 1·18m. from continental Europe; 730,570 from Asia and 273,894 from New Zealand.

Aboriginals have been included in population statistics only since 1967. At the 1986 census they numbered 227,645.

Vital statistics for 1987:

States and Territories	*Marriages*	*Divorces*	*Births*	*Deaths*	*Infant deaths*
New South Wales	41,319	11,661	84,018	42,167	759
Victoria	29,390	9,670	60,416	30,175	517
Queensland	18,030	7,042	40,165	17,861	351
South Australia	9,878	3,776	19,742	10,328	146
Western Australia	10,379	4,001	24,187	9,307	214
Tasmania	3,302	1,245	6,913	3,454	79
Northern Territory	759	381	3,307	661	53
Aust. Cap. Terr.	1,856	1,641	4,526	1,028	35
Total	114,913	39,417	234,274	114,981	2,154
Rate [1]	7·2	2·5	14·7	7·2	9·2 [2]

[1] Resident (estimate). [2] Per 1,000 live births registered.

Overseas arrivals and departures:

	1984–85	1985–86	1986–87
Arrivals	2·68m.	2·94m.	3·32m.
Long term and permanent	163,260	186,400	205,750
of whom, settlers	77,510	77,510	113,540
Departures	2·63m.	2·81m.	3·19m.
Long term and permanent	95,250	92,460	102,100
of whom, Australian residents leaving for good	51,710	49,690	49,360

Australian Bureau of Statistics, *Australian Demographic Statistics*. Quarterly. Canberra, June 1979 to date

National Population Inquiry, Population and Australia: Recent Demographic Trends and their Implications. Canberra, 1978

CLIMATE. Over most of the continent, four seasons may be recognised. Spring is from Sept. to Nov., Summer from Dec. to Feb., Autumn from March to May and Winter from June to Aug., but because of its great size there are climates that range from tropical monsoon to cool temperate, with large areas of desert as well. In Northern Australia there are only two seasons, the wet one lasting from Nov. to March, but rainfall amounts diminish markedly from the coast to the interior. Central and southern Queensland are subtropical, north and central New South Wales are warm temperate, as are parts of Victoria, Western Australia and Tasmania, where most rain falls in winter. Canberra. Jan. 68°F (20°C), July 42°F (5·6°C). Annual rainfall 23" (629 mm). Adelaide. Jan. 73°F (22·8°C), July 52°F (11·1°C). Annual rainfall 21" (528 mm). Brisbane. Jan. 77°F (25°C), July 58°F (14·4°C). Annual rainfall 45" (1,153 mm). Darwin. Jan. 83°F (28·3°C), July 77°F (25°C). Annual rainfall 59" (1,536 mm). Hobart. Jan. 62°F (16·7°C), July 46°F (7·8°C). Annual rainfall 24" (629 mm). Melbourne. Jan. 67°F (19·4°C), July 49°F (9·4°C). Annual rainfall 26" (659 mm). Perth. Jan. 74°F (23·3°C), July 55°F (12·8°C). Annual rainfall 35" (873 mm). Sydney. Jan. 71°F (21·7°C), July 53°F (11·7°C). Annual rainfall 47" (1,215 mm).

CONSTITUTION AND GOVERNMENT. *Federal Government:* Under the Constitution legislative power is vested in a Federal Parliament, consisting of the Queen, represented by a Governor-General, a Senate and a House of Representatives. Under the terms of the constitution there must be a session of parliament at least once a year.

The Senate comprises 76 Senators (12 for each State voting as one electorate and as from Aug. 1974, 2 Senators respectively for the Australian Capital Territory and the Northern Territory). Senators representing the States are chosen for 6 years. The terms of Senators representing the Territories expire at the close of the day next preceding the polling day for the general elections of the House of Representatives. In general, the Senate is renewed to the extent of one-half every 3 years, but in case of disagreement with the House of Representatives, it, together with the House of Representatives, may be dissolved, and an entirely new Senate elected. The House of Representatives consists, as nearly as practicable, of twice as many Members as there are Senators, the numbers chosen in the several States being in proportion to population as shown by the latest statistics, but not less than 5 for any original State. The numerical size of the House after the election in 1987 was 148, including the Members for Northern Territory and the Australian Capital Territory. The Northern Territory has been represented by 1 Member in the House of Representatives since 1922, and the Australian Capital Territory by 1 Member since 1949 and 2 Members since May 1974. The Member for the Australian Capital Territory was given full voting rights as from the Parliament elected in Nov. 1966. The Member for the Northern Territory was given full voting rights in 1968. The House of Representatives continues for 3 years from the date of its first meeting, unless sooner dissolved.

Every Senator or Member of the House of Representatives must be a subject of the Queen, be of full age, possess electoral qualifications and have resided for 3 years within Australia. The franchise for both Houses is the same and is based on universal (males and females aged 18 years) suffrage. Compulsory voting was introduced in 1925. If a Member of a State Parliament wishes to be a candidate in a federal election, he must first resign his State seat.

Executive power is vested in the Governor-General advised by an Executive Council. The Governor-General presides over the Council, and its members hold office at his pleasure. All Ministers of State, who are members of the party or parties commanding a majority in the lower House, are members of the Executive Council under summons. A record of proceedings of meetings is kept by the Secretary to the Council. At Executive Council meetings the decisions of the Cabinet are (where necessary) given legal form, appointments made, resignations accepted, proclamations, regulations and the like made.

The policy of a ministry is, in practice, determined by the Ministers of State meeting without the Governor-General under the chairmanship of the Prime Minister. This group is known as the Cabinet. There are 11 Standing Committees of the Cabinet comprising varying numbers of Cabinet and non-Cabinet Ministers. In Labour Governments all Ministers have been members of Cabinet. In Liberal and National Country Party Governments, only the senior ministers. Cabinet meetings are private and deliberative and records of meetings are not made public. The Cabinet does not form part of the legal mechanisms of Government; the decisions it takes have, in themselves, no legal effect. The Cabinet substantially controls, in ordinary circumstances, not only the general legislative programme of Parliament but the whole course of Parliamentary proceedings. In effect, though not in form, the Cabinet, by reason of the fact that all Ministers are members of the Executive Council, is also the dominant element in the executive government of the country.

The legislative powers of the Federal Parliament embrace trade and commerce, shipping, etc.; taxation, finance, banking, currency, bills of exchange, bankruptcy, insurance; defence; external affairs, naturalization and aliens, quarantine, immigration and emigration; the people of any race for whom it is deemed necessary to make special laws; postal, telegraph and like services; census and statistics; weights and measures; astronomical and meteorological observations; copyrights; railways; conciliation and arbitration in disputes extending beyond the limits of any one State; social services; marriage, divorce etc.; service and execution of the civil and criminal process; recognition of the laws, Acts and records, and judicial proceedings of the States. The Senate may not originate or amend money bills; and disagreement with the House of Representatives may result in dissolution and, in the last resort, a joint sitting of the two Houses. No religion may be established by the Commonwealth. The Federal Parliament has limited and enumerated powers, the several State parliaments retaining the residuary power of government over their respective territories. If a State law is inconsistent with a Commonwealth law, the latter prevails.

The Constitution also provides for the admission or creation of new States. Proposed laws for the alteration of the Constitution must be submitted to the electors, and they can be enacted only if approved by a majority of the States and by a majority of all the electors voting.

The Australia Acts 1986 removed residual powers of the British government to intervene in the government of Australia or the individual states.

The 35th Parliament was elected in July 1987.

General Elections were called for 24 March 1990.

House of Representatives (1990): Australian Labor Party, 78 seats; Liberal Party, 55; National Party, 4; independent, 1.

Senate (1989): Australian Labor Party, 32; Liberal Party, 27; Australian Democratic Party, 7; National Party, 7; others, 3.

Governor-General: William George Hayden.

The following is a list of former Governors-General of the Commonwealth:

Earl of Hopetoun	1901–02	HRH the Duke of Gloucester	1945–47
Lord Tennyson	1902–04	Sir William McKell	1947–53
Lord Northcote	1904–08	Viscount Slim	1953–60
Earl of Dudley	1908–11	Viscount Dunrossil	1960–61
Lord Denman	1911–14	Viscount De L'Isle	1961–65
Viscount Novar	1914–20	Lord Casey	1965–69
Lord Forster	1920–25	Sir Paul Hasluck	1969–74
Lord Stonehaven	1925–31	Sir John Kerr	1974–77
Sir Isaac Isaacs	1931–36	Sir Zelman Cowen	1977–82
Earl Gowrie	1936–45	Sir Ninian Stephen	1982–89

National flag: The British Blue Ensign with a large star of 7 points beneath the Union Flag, and in the fly 5 stars of the Southern Cross, all in white.

National Anthem: 'Advance Australia Fair' (adopted 19 April 1984). The 'Royal Anthem' (i.e. 'God Save the Queen') is used in the presence of the British Royal Family.

The cabinet of the Labour administration in Feb. 1989 was composed as follows:

Prime Minister: Robert Hawke.
Deputy Prime Minister and Attorney-General: Lionel Bowen.
Industry, Technology and Commerce: John Button.
Community Services and Health: Neil Blewett.
Industrial Relations: Peter Morris.
Treasurer: Paul Keating.
Immigration, Local Government and Ethnic Affairs: Robert Ray.
Finance: Peter Walsh.
Foreign Affairs and Trade: Gareth Evans.
Special Minister of State: Susan Ryan.
Transport and Communications: Ralph Willis.
Employment, Education and Training: John Dawkins.
Primary Industry and Energy: John Kerin.
Administrative Services: Stewart West.
Defence: Kim Beazley.
Social Security and Social Justice: Brian Howe.
Arts, Sport, Environment, Tourism and Territories: Graham Richardson.
Science and Small Business: Barry Jones.
Aboriginal Affairs: Gerry Hand.
Veterans' Affairs: Ben Humphries.
Consumer Affairs: Peter Staples.

The Acts of the Parliament of the Commonwealth of Australia Passed from 1901 to 1973. 12 vols. Annual volumes, 1974 to date

The Australian Constitution Annotated. Attorney-General's Department, Canberra, 1980
Parliamentary Handbook of the Commonwealth of Australia. Canberra, 1915 to date
Commonwealth of Australia Directory [1921–1958 The Federal Guide; 1961–72 *Commonwealth Directory;* 1973–75 *Australian Government Directory*]. Prime Minister's Department. Canberra, 1924 to date
Crisp, L. F., *Australian National Government.* 3rd ed. Melbourne and London, 1975
Hughes, C. A. and Graham, B. D., *A Handbook of Australian Government and Politics.* Canberra, 1968
Odgers, J. R., *Australian Senate Practice.* 5th ed. Canberra, 1976
Paton, Sir George (ed.) *The Commonwealth of Australia: its Laws and Constitution.* London, 1952
Pettifer, J. A., *House of Representatives Practice.* Canberra, 1981
Sawer, G., *Australian Federal Politics and Law 1901–1929, 1929–1949.* 2 vols. Melbourne, 1974.—*Australian Government To-day.* 11th ed. Melbourne, 1973
Wynes, W. A., *Executive and Judicial Powers in Australia.* 5th ed. Sydney, 1976

State Government: In each of the 6 States (New South Wales, Victoria, Queensland, South Australia, Western Australia, Tasmania) there is a State government whose constitution, powers and laws continue, subject to changes embodied in the Australian Constitution and subsequent alterations and agreements, as they were before federation. The system of government is basically the same as that described above for the Commonwealth—*i.e.*, the Sovereign, her representative (in this case a Governor), an upper and lower house of Parliament (except in Queensland, where the upper house was abolished in 1922), a cabinet led by the Premier and an Executive Council. Among the more important functions of the State governments are those relating to education, health, hospitals and charities, law, order and public safety, business undertakings such as railways and tramways, and public utilities such as water supply and sewerage. In the domains of education, hospitals, justice, the police, penal establishments, and railway and tramway operation, State government activity predominates. Care of the public health and recreative activities are shared with local government authorities and the Federal Government, social services other than those referred to above are now primarily the concern of the Federal Government, and the operation of public utilities is shared with local and semi-government authorities.

Administration of Territories. Since 1911, responsibility for administration and development of the Australian Capital Territory (ACT) has been vested in Federal Ministers and Departments. The ACT became self-governing on 11 May 1989.

The ACT House of Assembly has been accorded the forms of a legislature, but continues to perform an advisory function for the Minister for the Capital Territory.

On 1 July 1978 the Northern Territory of Australia became a self-governing Territory with expenditure responsibilities and revenue-raising powers broadly approximating those of a State.

Local Government. The system of municipal government is broadly the same throughout Australia, although local government legislation is a State matter.

Each State is sub-divided into areas known variously as municipalities, cities, boroughs, towns, shires or district councils, totalling about 900. Within these areas the management of road, street and bridge construction, health, sanitary and garbage services, water supply and sewerage, and electric light and gas undertakings, hospitals, fire brigades, tramways and omnibus services and harbours is generally part of the functions of elected aldermen and councillors. The scope of their duties, however, differs considerably, for in all States the State Government, either directly or through semi-government authorities, also carries out some or all of these types of services.

In some instances, *e.g.*, in New South Wales, a number of local government authorities combine to conduct a public undertaking such as the supply of water or electricity.

DEFENCE. The Minister for Defence has responsibility under legislation for the control and administration of the Defence Force. The Chief of Defence Force Staff is vested with command of the Defence Force. He is the principal military adviser to the Minister. The Secretary, Department of Defence is the Permanent Head of the Department. He is the principal civilian adviser to the Minister and has statutory responsibility for financial administration of the Defence outlay. The Chief of Defence Force Staff and the Secretary are jointly responsible for the administration of the Defence Force except with respect to matters falling within the command of the Defence Force or any other matter specified by the Minister.

The Chief of Naval Staff, the Chief of the General Staff and the Chief of the Air Staff command the Navy, Army and Air Force respectively. They have delegated authority from the Chief of Defence Force Staff and the Secretary to administer matters relating to their particular Service.

The structure of Defence is characterized by 3 organizational types: *(i)* A Central Office comprising 5 groups of functional orientated Divisions: Strategic Policy and Force Development; Supply and Support; Manpower and Financial Services; Management and Infrastructure Services; and, Defence Science and Technology; *(ii)* the 3 Armed Services of the Defence Force, each having a Service Office element in addition to the command structure; and *(iii)* a small number of outrider organizations concerned with such specialist fields as intelligence and natural disasters.

Defence Support. The Department of Defence Support purchases goods and services for defence purposes; provides technical expertise and other assistance to the defence industry; involves Australian industry in defence equipment to the maximum practical extent; administers the Australian Offsets Program so as to stimulate technological advancement and broaden the capabilities of strategic industries; within overall defence policies helps the capacity, efficiency and capability of Australian industry to design and export defence materiel; manages the Government's munitions and aircraft factories, and dockyards; markets defence and allied products and services to help maintain strategic industries.

In 1988 the Department employed 14,189 civilians.

Army. Overall organization and financial control of the Australian Army is vested in the Chief of General Staff. Under the Defence Force Re-organisation Act, which received the Royal Assent on 9 Sept. 1975, the Military Board, which was previously the controlling body of the Army, was abolished. The Act became effective on 1 Feb. 1976. A functional command structure, Headquarters Field Force Command, Headquarters Logistic Command, and Headquarters Training Command, with Headquarters in military districts, was introduced in 1973.

The strength of the Army was 31,300 in 1990. The Command troops consist of 1 regiment each of Air Defence, engineering, aviation and Special Air Service; the 1 infantry division is composed of 1 mechanized and 2 infantry brigades, 4 artillery regiments, and 1 regiment each of reconnaissance, armoured personnel carriers, engineering and aviation. The Army Aviation Corps has 24 N22 Missionmaster and 14 Turbo-Porter transports, and 106 helicopters.

The effective strength of the Army Reserve in 1989 was 25,000.

Staff and command training is carried out at the Command and Staff College, Queenscliff, Victoria, and the Land Warfare Centre, Canungra, Queensland.

In Jan. 1986 the Australian Defence Force Academy, Canberra, accepted its first officer cadets for the 3 Services. Cadets will study at the academy for degrees in arts, science and engineering. During semester breaks they will carry out military training with their particular Services.

At the end of 3 years at the academy, army officer cadets will undertake a year of military training at the Royal Military College, Duntroon. This will culminate with commissioning as a lieutenant.

From 1986 the Royal Military College have taken officer cadets for commssioning who previously would have attended the Officer Cadet School, Portsea, and the Women's Officer Cadet School, Sydney.

Navy. The Chief of Naval Staff is assisted by the Deputy Chief of Naval Staff and Assistant Chiefs for Personnel, Operational Requirements and Plans, Material and Logistics. The command, operation and administration of the Fleet is now vested in the Maritime Commander, Australia (previously known as the Commander, Australian Fleet) headquartered at Sydney.

Combatants include 6 UK-built Oxley class diesel submarines, 3 US-built guided missile destroyers, 4 US-built guided missile frigates, commissioned 1980-84 and 5 older frigates, 3 minehunters, 1 tank landing ship, 3 tank landing craft and 22 in-shore patrol craft. Major auxiliaries include 1 destroyer depot ship, 2 fleet replenishment tankers, 1 training ship, 3 survey ships, and there are some 85 minor auxiliaries and service craft.

New procurement includes 6 replacement submarines of Swedish design, with construction of the first starting in 1990 and 8 German designed frigates construction of which will start about a year later.

The Fleet Air Arm operates a shore-based ASW helicopter squadron of 10 Sea King, and is acquiring S-70B Lamps-III helicopters for deployment to the Guided Missile frigates which are having their flight decks extended to operate them. There are additionally 2 transport aircraft and 16 transport and utility helicopters.

The fleet main base is at Sydney, with subsidiary bases at Garden Island, Cairns and Darwin.

The all-volunteer Navy was (1989) 15,700 strong including 1,200 Fleet Air Arm.

Air Force. Command of the Royal Australian Air Force is vested in the Chief of the Air Staff (CAS) assisted by the Deputy Chief of the Air Staff, Chief of Air Force Operations and Plans, Chief of Air Force Materiel, Chief of Air Force Personnel, Chief of Air Force Technical Services, Director-General Supply—Air Force and Assistant Secretary Resources Planning.

The CAS administers and controls RAAF units through two commands: Operational Command and Support Command. Operational Command is responsible to the CAS for the command of operational units and the conduct of their operations within Australia and overseas. Support Command is responsible to the CAS for training of personnel, and the supply and maintenance of service equipment.

Flying establishment comprises 16 squadrons, of which 2 are equipped with 24 F-111 strike/reconnaissance aircraft. Of the others, 3 are equipped with missile-armed F-18 Hornet interceptors and 2 with Orion maritime reconnaissance aircraft. There are eight transport squadrons, 2 with Hercules turboprop transports, 2 with Caribou STOL transports, 1 with a mix of Ecureuil and Iroquois helicopters, 1 with Boeing Vertol CH-47C medium lift helicopters, 1 with Black Hawk helicopters, and a special transport squadron equipped with BAC One-Eleven, Mystère 20 and HS 748 aircraft. There is also one squadron operating B707 aircraft. Training aircraft include piston-engined Airtrainers, built in New Zealand, Aermacchi MB 326H jets for pilot training, and HS 748 aircraft for navigator training. A training unit has F-18 Hornets for crew conversion.

Training for commissioned rank is carried out at the RAAF Academy and Officers' Training School, both located at Point Cook, Victoria. Other major training activities which lead to commissioned rank include basic aircrew training and technical and commercial cadet schemes. Basic ground training to tradesman level is conducted at RAAF technical training schools. Higher command and staff training is, in the main, carried out at the RAAF Staff College, Fairbairn, ACT.

Personnel (1990) 22,600. There is also an Australian Air Force Reserve.

Long, G. (ed.) *Australia in the War of 1939–45*. 22 vols. Canberra, 1952 ff.

O'Neil, R. and Horner, D. M., *Australian Defence Policy for the 1980s*. Univ. of Queensland Press, 1983

INTERNATIONAL RELATIONS

Membership. Australia is a member of the UN, the Commonwealth, GATT, OECD, Colombo Plan, the South Pacific Commission and the South Pacific Bureau for Economic Co-operation.

ECONOMY

Financial relations with the States. Since 1942 the Federal Government alone has levied taxes on incomes. In return for vacating this field of taxation, the State

Governments are reimbursed by grants from the Federal Government out of revenue received. Payments to the States represent about one-third of Federal Government outlays, and in turn the payments State Governments receive from the Federal Government account for nearly half of their revenues.

The Financial Agreement of 1927 established the Australian Loan Council which represents the Federal and six State Governments, and co-ordinates domestic and overseas borrowings by these governments, including annual borrowing programmes. The Federal Government acts as a central borrowing agency in raising loans to finance the major part of those programmes. The Loan Council in 1984 agreed upon arrangements for the co-ordination of borrowings by semi-government and local authorities and government-owned companies.

Budget. In 1929, under a financial agreement between the Federal Government and States, approved by a referendum, the Federal Government took over all State debts existing on 30 June 1927 and agreed to pay $A15·17m. a year for 58 years towards the interest charges thereon, and to make substantial contributions towards a sinking fund on State debt. The Sinking Fund arrangements were revised under an amendment to the agreement in 1976.

Outlays and revenues of the Commonwealth Government for years ending 30 June (in $A1m.):

	1987–88	*1988-89*	*1989–90* [1]
Total outlays	78,764	82,128	86,753
including			
Assistance to States and NT	14,248	12,543	12,825
Assistance to the aged	7,240	7,870	8,786
Interest	5,850	5,370	5,328
Assistance to the disabled	2,481	2,736	3,015
Medical services and benefits	3,455	3,723	4,181
Hospitals	1,695	3,740	4,026
Assistance to unemployed and sick	3,886	3,689	3,794
Assistance to veterans	3,128	3,187	3,404
Defence personnel	3,102	3,290	3,384
Tertiary education	2,841	2,913	3,369
Schools	1,950	2,120	2,190
Total revenue	80,829	88,030	95,875
including			
PAYE income tax	37,751	43,976	46,730
Company tax	8,801	10,265	11,360
Sales tax	7,547	9,402	10,500
Other individual tax	8,251	7,712	9,300
Excise duty	9,668	8,603	9,264
Customs duty	3,683	3,802	4,082

[1]Estimates.

Foreign currency reserves were $A20,410m. in 1989.
Gross foreign debt at 30 June 1989 was $A37,046m.
The Consumer Price Index rose by 8% over the year to Sept. 1989.

Australian National Accounts. Australian Bureau of Statistics. 1953–54 to date
Public Authority Finance: Commonwealth Government Finance, Australia. Australian Bureau of Statistics, 1962–63 to date
Public Authority Finance: State and Local Government Finance, Australia. Australian Bureau of Statistics, 1971–72 to date
National Income and Expenditure. Australian Bureau of Statistics. Canberra, 1946 to date

Treasury Information Bulletin (and Supplements). Canberra Treasury Dept., 1956 to date (quarterly)
Hagger, A. J., *A Guide to Australian Economic and Social Statistics*. Sydney, 1983

Currency. On 14 Feb. 1966 Australia adopted a system of decimal currency. The currency unit, the *dollar* ($) is divided into 100 *cents*. Decimal notes are issued in denominations of $1, 2, 5, 10, 20, 50 and 100. Coins are issued in denominations of 1, 2, 5, 10, 20 and 50 cents and $1.

Australian notes, issued by the note-issue department of the Reserve Bank, are legal tender throughout Australia. The total value of notes in circulation on 30 June 1987 was $A9,838m., of which $A8,900m. were held by the public. In March 1990, US$1 = 1·36 *dollars*; £1 = 2·12 *dollars*.

The underlying inflation rate for the year ending Sept. 1989 was 5·8%.

Banking. The banking system in Australia comprises:

(a) The Reserve Bank of Australia is the central bank and bank of issue. Its Rural Credits Department provides short-term credit for the marketing of primary produce. Its assets were $A26,073m. in June 1987 and its liabilities $A26,541m., of which notes on issue, $9,801m.; deposits by trading banks, $3,472m.; deposits by Commonwealth Government, $2,090m.; assets $26,541m. of which gold and foreign exchange (including IMF Special Drawing Rights), $17,120m., treasury notes $1,657m., other Commonwealth Government securities $6,638m. Its functions and responsibilities derive from the Reserve Bank Act 1959, the Banking Act 1959, and the Financial Corporations Act 1974. For the history of the Reserve Bank *see* THE STATESMAN'S YEAR-BOOK 1986–87, p. 104.

(b) Four major trading banks: (i) The Commonwealth Bank of Australia; (ii) 3 private trading banks: The Australia and New Zealand Banking Group Ltd, Westpac Banking Corporation and the National Commercial Banking Corporation of Australia Ltd.

(c) Other trading banks: (i) 3 State Government banks—The State Bank of New South Wales, The State Bank of South Australia, and the Rural and Industries Bank of Western Australia; (ii) one joint stock bank—The Bank of Queensland Ltd, formerly The Brisbane Permanent Building and Banking Co. Ltd, which has specialized business in one district only; (iii) The Australian Bank Ltd; (iv) branches of 17 overseas banks—the restrictions on foreign banks operating in Australia, and on foreign investment in the merchant banks, were lifted in 1984–85.

(d) The Commonwealth Development Bank of Australia commenced operations on 14 Jan. 1960. Its function is to provide finance for primary production and small business.

(e) The Australian Resources Development Bank Ltd opened on 29 March 1968, to assist Australian enterprises in developing Australia's natural resources, through direct loans and equity investment or by re-financing loans made by trading banks. The bank is jointly owned by the 4 major Australian trading banks.

(f) The Primary Industry Bank of Australia Ltd commenced operations on 22 Sept. 1978. The equity capital of the bank consists of eight shares. Seven shares are held by the Australian Government and the major trading banks while the eighth share is held equally by the 4 State banks. The main objective of the bank is to facilitate the provision of loans to primary producers on longer terms than are otherwise generally available. The role of the bank is restricted to re-financing loans made by banks and other financial institutions.

(g) Savings banks, with total deposits of $52,495m. at 30 June 1987 ($42,614m. in 1986). In 1989 16 savings banks were operating in Australia. These comprise subsidiaries of the four major trading banks; four State-owned banks, six private banks, one trustee bank and one overseas bank. At 30 June 1988 these savings banks had 6,005 branches and 8,028 agencies.

Treasury Information Bulletin. Department of the Treasury. Canberra, 1956 to date (quarterly)

At June 30 1987 there were 62 building societies with assets of $S20,083m.

Weights and Measures. Conversion to the metric system is in progress.

ENERGY AND NATURAL RESOURCES

Electricity. Electricity supply is the responsibility of the State governments. Production 1987–88, 136,840m. kwh (13,949m. hydro-electric). Supply 240 and 250 volts; 50 Hz.

Oil and gas. The main fields are Gippsland (Vic.) and Carnarvon (WA). Crude oil production was 31,264m. litres in 1987-88, natural gas, 15,249,000m. litres.

Minerals. Australia is the world's leading producer of bauxite (36·6% of world production in 1987) and diamonds (31·3%). Coal is Australia's major source of energy. Reserves are large (1987 estimate: 50,000m. tonnes) and easily worked. The main fields are in New South Wales and Queensland. Production in 1987-88 was 136m. tonnes. Brown coal (lignite) reserves are mainly in Victoria and were estimated 41,900m. tonnes in 1988. Production, 1987-88: 44·3m. tonnes.

Production of other major minerals in 1987-88 (1,000 tonnes): Bauxite, 35,142; copper ore, 23,748; iron ore, 102,202; lead-copper concentrate, 32,763; lead-zinc concentrate, 178,694; manganese ore, 1,060; tungsten, 2,001; nickel ore, 2,039; silver concentrate, 4,780; tin concentrate, 13,667; uranium concentrate, 4,193; 167,486 kg of gold bullion. Gross value of coal and lignite production, 1987-88, $A4,842m.; metallic minerals, $A7,834m.; oil and gas, $A4,139m.

Agriculture. In 1987 there were about 169,700 farms and ranches, covering 471m. hectares (61·3% of the land area). 424m. hectares were grazing or fallow, 20m. hectares sown to crops, of which the most important are wheat (10m. tonnes from 8·9m. hectares in 1987); sugar cane (25m. from 306,000); barley (3·29m.); oats (1·86m.) and rice (780,000). Vineyards (57,000 hectares) produced 372m. litres from 512,000 tonnes. The livestock farms produced beef and veal (1·5m. tonnes); mutton and lamb (583,000); pigmeats (282,000); poultry-meats (384m.); wool (887,000); whole milk (6,162m. litres).

Gross value of agricultural production in 1986-87, $A17,272m.; including (in $A1m.):

	NSW	*Vic.*	*Q'ld*	*SA*	*WA*	*Tas.*	*Aust.*[1]
Wheat	723·8	428·2	128·4	390	858·9	0·7	2,530
Sugar cane	27·4		558·9				586·4
Barley	73·5	63·8	36·9	183·8	71·3	3·3	432·6
Oats	58·1	43·8	2·5	15·6	43·5	1·3	164·8
Rice	80·5		4·6				85·1
Grapes	55·6	117·8	4·3	82	12	0·4	272·2
Cotton	308·1		64·4				372·5
Fruit	232·4	203·6	191·1	120·2	58·9	29·8	837·2
Vegetables	149·9	227·4	252·4	98·8	89·2	62·3	885·4
Livestock disposals	1,244·7	1,066·6	1,349·5	326·4	407·9	111·1	4,611·1
Wool	1,098·7	726·3	292·4	389·3	716·3	108·7	3,333·6
Whole milk	250·2	643·8	159·6	80·8	59	64	1,257·4

[1] Includes Northern Territory and Australian Capital Territory.

Livestock (in 1,000) at 31 March 1987:

	NSW	*Vic.*	*Q'ld*	*SA*	*WA*	*Tas.*	*N. Terr.*	*ACT*	*Australia*
Cattle	4,868	3,478	9,011	912	1,660	535	1,439	12	21,915
Sheep	52,192	26,586	14,627	17,234	33,463	4,954	1	100	149,157
Pigs	830	432	579	422	295	46	7	—	2,611

Forestry. The Department of Primary Industries and Energy is responsible for forestry at the national level. Each State is responsible for the management of publicly-owned forests. Total forest area was 41·3m. hectares at 30 June 1986, of which 30·2m. hectares were publicly-owned. The major part of wood supplies derives from coniferous plantations, of which there were 832,172 hectares at 31 March 1986. Timber production was 3·09m. cu. metres in 1986-87.

INDUSTRY AND TRADE

Industry. Statistics of the manufacturing industries in Australia in 1986–87: Number of establishments, 28,795; workers employed, 1,022,700; salaries and wages paid, $A21,415·7m.; value-added, $A45,420·7m. (excludes small single-establishment enterprises employing less than 4 persons).

Manufacturing by sector, 1986–87:

Sector	*Employment*	*Value Added ($A1m.)*
Food, beverages and tobacco	167,500	8,394·2
Meat products	45,100	1,663·7
Textiles	34,400	1,409·0
Clothing and footwear	74,200	1,982·0
Wood and products	45,700	1,617·3
Printing and allied	85,500	3,777·5
Chemical, petroleum and coal products	53,500	4,115·3
Basic metals and products	73,600	4,379·7
Fabricated metal	97,300	3,522·4
Transport equipment	112,300	4,188·4
Other machinery and equipment	127,500	5,134·1

Labour. In Aug. 1988 the civilian labour force (persons aged 15 and over) numbered (in 1,000s) 7,869, including women, 3,199 (of whom married, 1,909) and over 65, 89·5. In 1988 the labour force included 378,900 employers, 6,143,000 wage and salary earners and 741,700 self-employed. The majority of wage and salary earners have their minimum wages and conditions of work prescribed in awards of industrial arbitration authorities established under federal and State legislation. However, in some States, some conditions of work (*e.g.*, normal weekly hours of work, long-service leave, annual leave) are set down in State legislation. In Sept. 1987 it was estimated that the average weekly earnings of all employees were $A393.20. Average working week, 1988: 36 hours (males 40·6; females 29·3).

Employees in all States are covered by workers' compensation legislation and by certain industrial award provisions relating to work injuries.

During 1987 industrial disputes involving stoppages of work of 10 man-days or more accounted for 1,316,400 working days lost. In these disputes 605,300 workers were involved.

The following table shows the distribution of employed persons by industry in 1988, by sex and average weekly hours worked, and total persons in 1989:

	1988				*1989*
Industry	*Numbers (in 1,000)*		*Hours worked*		
	Persons	*(Females)*	*Persons*	*(Females)*	*Persons*
Agriculture, forestry, fishing and hunting	431·0	(123·8)	42·0	(27·3)	432·4
Mining	96·7	(8·0)	41·2	(37·2)	98·0
Manufacturing	1,199·4	(316·4)	38·5	(33·0)	185·2
Food, beverages and tobacco	163·3	(48·1)	37·5	(32·6)	203·7
Metal products	205·9	(23·1)	40·4	(31·9)	829·6
Other manufacturing	830·2	(245·2)	38·2	(33·1)	1,218·5
Electricity, gas and water	113·8	(11·4)	33·5	(30·0)	119·4
Construction	526·2	(66·9)	38·0	(21·1)	567·5
Wholesale and retail trade	1,496·1	(660·9)	35·1	(27·5)	1,552·7
Transport and storage	376·7	(73·1)	38·3	(30·2)	384·6
Communication	134·2	(35·4)	33·2	(29·8)	137·8
Finance, property and business services	801·1	(400·0)	36·7	(31·3)	830·0
Public administration and defence	321·6	(121·6)	34·4	(31·4)	324·9
Community services	1,304·9	(844·0)	32·9	(29·5)	1,330·4
Recreation, personal and other services	528·3	(304·4)	32·4	(27·6)	539·9
Totals	7,330·1	(2,965·8)	36·0	(29·3)	7,540·3

In June 1988 1,739,800 wage and salary earners worked in the public sector and 4,198,900 in the private sector.

The following table shows the distribution of employed persons in 1988 according to the *Australian Standard Classification of Occupations*:

Occupation	*Employed persons (in 1,000)* *Persons*	*(Females)*
Managers and administrators	820·5	(163·0)
Professionals	905·3	(361·2)
Para-professionals	444·9	(188·3)
Tradespersons	1,171·4	(105·9)
Clerks	1,255·1	(698·5)
Salespersons and personnel service	1,025·0	(660·5)
Plant and machine operators, and drivers	584·1	(102·0)
Labourers and related workers	1,123·7	(383·2)
	7,330·1	(2,965·8)

In Aug. 1988 445,900 persons (7·1% of the labour force) were unemployed, (including 166,000 females and 47,700 persons aged 15-19). A further 92,900 persons were seeking part-time work. Of all these, 153,400 had been unemployed for more than one year. In May 1988 there were 58,500 job vacancies. In the year ended June 1988 743,674 unemployment beneficiaries received a total of $A3,374·88m., 154,963 sickness beneficiaries received $A511·04m. and 127,433 special beneficiaries received $A150·8m.

Trade Unions. In June 1988 there were 308 trade unions with 3,213,000 members (1,122,300 females). About 53% of wage and salary earners (43% females) were estimated to be members of unions. In 1988 there were 37 unions with fewer than 100 members and 9 unions with 80,000 or more members. Many of the larger trade unions are affiliated with central labour organizations, the oldest and by far the largest being the Australian Council of Trade Unions formed in 1927.

Labour Statistics 1987. Australian Bureau of Statistics. Canberra, 1988
Portus, J. H., *The Development of Australian Trade Union Law*. Melbourne, 1958
Rawson, D. W., *A Handbook of Australian Trade Unions and Employees' Associations*. Canberra, 1977

Commerce. Throughout Australia there are uniform customs duties, and trade between the States and Territories is free.

Merchandise imports and exports for years ending 30 June, in $A1m.:

	Imports	*Exports*
1986–87	37,159	35,423
1987–88	40,386	40,541
1988–89	47,055	42,963

The Australian customs tariff provides for preferences to goods produced in and shipped from certain countries as a result of reciprocal trade agreements. These include UK, New Zealand, Canada and Ireland.

Exports and imports, 1987-88 (in $A1m.):

	Exports	*Imports*
Live animals	295·3	147·3
Meat and preparations	2,552·5	19·2
Dairy goods and eggs	503·2	87·4
Fish, shellfish and their preparations	729·9	409·3
Cereals and preparations	2,310·0	73·4
Vegetables and fruit	601·2	282·2
Sugar and honey	734·6	33·6
Coffee, tea, cocoa, spices and their manufacturers	63·8	378·2
Animal feed (excl. unmilled cereal)	247·1	50·6
Miscellaneous edible products	75·5	186·7
Beverages	225·3	234·0
Tobacco and manufactures	24·8	110·6
Raw hides and skins	685·0	9·9
Oil seeds and fruit	31·5	18·6

	Exports	*Imports*
Crude rubber (incl. synthetic and reclaimed)	7·2	99·5
Cork and wood	394·8	382·5
Pulp and waste paper	31·4	224·8
Textile fibres (not wool tops)	5,600·0	165·0
Crude fertilizers, minerals (not coal, petroleum, gems)	173·8	248·4
Metal ores and scrap	5,224·5	68·9
Crude animal and vegetable materials	117·3	104·3
Coal, coke and briquettes	4,833·6	5·1
Petroleum and products	1,943·4	2,036·4
Gas, natural and manufactured	245·2	4·8
Animal oils and fats	117·6	1·5
Fixed vegetable oils and fats	12·7	89·7
Processed oils and fats, waxes thereof	8·4	17·2
Organic chemicals	96·0	105·9
Inorganic chemicals	79·0	518·6
Dyeing, colouring and tanning materials	81·4	194·6
Medicinal and pharmaceutical products	204·2	647·3
Essential oils, perfume and cleansing preparations	76·0	269·2
Manufactured fertilizers	7·1	138·0
Explosives and pyrotechnic products	6·3	30·4
Artificial resins, plastic and cellulose materials	168·2	923·8
Other chemical materials and products	169·7	446·7
Leather and manufactures, dressed furskins	171·6	168·0
Rubber manufactures	68·4	571·0
Cork and wood manufactures (not furniture)	12·9	188·5
Paper, board and pulp	98·8	1,206·5
Textile yarn, fabrics and products	311·4	1,926·5
Non-metallic mineral goods	259·5	849·4
Iron and steel	504·1	836·1
Non-ferrous metals	3,223·2	249·7
Metal manufactures	276·0	130·6
Power generators	365·8	1,210·1
Special machinery, industrial	313·8	993·0
Metalworking machinery	38·0	385·7
General machinery and parts, industrial	285·4	2,284·2
Office machines and data-processing equipment	437·9	2,646·3
Telecommunications and sound equipment	116·2	1,503·1
Electrical machinery and parts	290·0	2,141·6
Road vehicles (inc. air-cushion vehicles)	524·4	3,139·5
Other transport equipment	374·4	1,060·4
Sanitary, plumbing, heating and lighting fittings	14·0	97·6
Furniture and parts	40·7	254·7
Travel goods, handbags etc.	4·3	186·6
Clothing and accessories	57·9	721·1
Footwear	10·1	269·8
Professional, scientific and controlling instruments	214·3	961·1
Photographic and optical goods, watches and clocks	278·0	716·5

	Exports	Imports
Miscellaneous manufactured articles	404·9	2,367·4
Commodities and transactions	3,452·3	1,759·0
Gold and other coin	118·1	1·9
Total trade	40,943·5	40,594·3

Trade in ($A1m.) with major partners:

	1986–87		1987–88	
From or to	Imports	Exports	Imports	Exports
Belgium–Luxembourg	311·9	297·6	319·9	367·2
Canada	750·5	637·1	863·4	701·6
China	588·8	1,590·5	850·5	1,281·0
Egypt	...	362·5	2·2	311·4
France	827·3	908·8	892·2	980·6
Germany, Federal Republic	2,782·1	1,101·1	2,918·1	1,074·7
Hong Kong	800·0	1,086·1	845·4	1,977·3
India	203·4	425·4	288·1	505·3
Indonesia	310·6	527·6	587·7	561·8
Iran	4·4	343·8	17·1	380·4
Italy	1,110·3	823·7	1,329·2	1,092·1
Japan	7,737·1	9,088·0	7,816·7	10,655·2
Korea, South	898·0	1,499·6	1,020·1	1,767·8
Malaysia	409·7	590·0	590·8	651·4
New Zealand	143·2	1,775·9	1,732·7	2,165·0
Pakistan	61·0	100·5	64·7	101·4
Papua New Guinea	189·7	651·1	109·1	744·6
Saudi Arabia	437·3	298·0	418·9	266·3
Singapore	755·9	779·8	898·3	1,172·6
Sweden	655·3	120·9	776·6	120·5
Taiwan	1,517·5	1,227·6	1,744·2	1,308·7
USSR	151·4	687·7	21·7	631·8
UK	2,705·5	1,374·9	3,012·3	1,775·0
USA	8,118·4	4,194·6	8,530·6	4,665·5
(European Economic Community	8,803·7	5,635·1	9,746·4	6,413·7)

Overseas Trade. Australian Bureau of Statistics. Canberra, 1906 to date

Total trade between UK and Australia (British Department of Trade returns, in £1,000 sterling):

	1985	1986	1987	1988	1989
Imports to UK	736,986	643,238	673,837	745,570	864,965
Exports and re-exports from UK	1,373,184	1,227,647	1,223,613	1,377,997	1,711,241

Tourism. During 1987, 1·7m. overseas visitors arrived in Australia intending to stay for less than 12 months; tourists spent $A3,700m.

Australian Bureau of Statistics, Canberra: *Rural Industries.* 1962–63 to date.—*Manufacturing Establishments: Details of Operations.* 1968–69 to date.—*Non-rural Primary Industries.* 1967–68 and 1968–69.—*Value of Production.* 1964–65 to 1968–69.—*Manufacturing Industry.* 1963–64 to 1967–68.—*Manufacturing Commodities.* 1963–64 and 1964–65.— *Building and Construction.* 1964–65 to date

Quarterly Review of Agricultural Economics. Bureau of Agricultural Economics. Canberra, 1948 to date

Developments in Australian Manufacturing Industry. Department of Trade. Melbourne, 1954–55 to date (annual)

The Australian Mineral Industry Review. Department of National Development—Bureau of Mineral Resources, Geology and Geophysics. Canberra, 1948 to date

Australian Economy. Department of the Treasury. Canberra, 1956 to date

Australasian Institute of Mining and Metallurgy. *Proceedings: New Series.* Melbourne, 1912 to date

COMMUNICATIONS

Roads. In 1987 there were 38,124 km of state highways and freeways, 38,090 km of trunk roads, 31,673 km of ordinary main roads and 36,338 km of other roads.

At 30 June 1988, 7,243,600 cars, 1,977,600 vans, trucks and buses and 323,300 motor cycles were registered. New registrations, 1987-88, include 384,283 cars, 86,617 vans, trucks and buses and 18,532 motor cycles.

463·67m. passenger journeys were made by bus in 1986-87.

In 1986 there were 25,260 road accidents in which 2,888 persons were killed.

Railways. There are six government-owned railway systems with a total route length in 1989 of 7,315 km, comprising 3,628 km at standard 1,435 mm. gauge, 1,947 km at 1,600 mm and 1,740 km at 1,067 mm. Statistics for the year ended 30 June 1987:

System	*Route-km open* [4]	*Revenue train-km run, 1,000*	*Passenger journeys, 1,000*	*Goods and livestock, carried, 1,000 tonnes*	*Gross earnings, $A1m.*	*Working expenses, $A1,000*
State:						
New South Wales	9,907	72,011[5]	224,300	54,600	1,121·2	0,000,000
Victoria	5,257	28,399	97,822	10,597	481·3	000,000
Queensland	10,210	35,051	44,334	75,169	1,028·9	000,000
South Australia [3]	149	...	11,798	...	14·4	000,000
Western Australia	5,553	9,436	10,051	21,264	258·2	000,000
Australian National [1,2]	7,315	10,581	329	12,900	283·3	000,000

[1] The Australian National Railways operates services of the former Commonwealth Railways, the non-metropolitan South Australian Railways and the Tasmanian Railways.

[2] Excludes Adelaide metropolitan rail passenger services and the Tasmanian Region.

[3] The South Australian State Transport Authority operates services in the Adelaide metropolitan area.

[4] Inter system traffic is included in the total for each system over which it passes.

[5] Figures for 1985-86.

The State railway gauges are: New South Wales, 1,435 mm; Victoria, 1,600 mm (325 km 1,435 mm); Queensland, 1,067 mm (111 km 1,435 mm); South Australia, 1,600 mm for 2,533 km, 1,824 km 1,435 mm and the rest 1,067 mm; West Australia, 137 km, 1,435 mm and the rest 1,067 mm, and Tasmania, 1,067 mm. Of the Australian National Railways, the gauge of the Trans-Australian and Australian Capital Territory is 1,435 mm, and for the Central Australia 1,067 mm for 869 km and 1,435 mm for 350 km. Under various Commonwealth–State standardization agreements, all the State capitals are now linked by 1,435 mm gauge track. The Central Australia railway extends as far north as Alice Springs (now standard gauge on new alignment from Tarcoola to Alice Springs).

There are also private industrial and tourist railways.

Aviation. With effect from 1 July 1988 the Civil Aviation Authority has been responsible for aviation safety under the Civil Aviation Act, 1988.

In 1988 Australia had air service agreements with 26 countries, and 32 international airlines were operating scheduled services. Qantas Airways, Australia's international airline, operated 25 Boeing 747s and 7 Boeing 767s. All shares in Qantas are owned by the Commonwealth Government. In 1986-87 6·14m. passengers and 263,989 tonnes of freight were flown on international flights. The major international airports are Adelaide, Brisbane, Darwin, Melbourne, Perth, Sydney and Townsville.

Internal airlines carried 13·7m. passengers and 147,939 tonnes of freight in 1987-88.

At 30 June 1988 there were 430 licensed aerodromes (67 owned by the Commonwealth Government) and 9 helicopter pads.

Shipping. The chief ports are Sydney, Newcastle, Port Kembla (NSW); Melbourne, Geelong, Westernport (Vic.); Hay Point, Gladstone, Brisbane (Qld.); Port Hedland, Dampier, Port Walcott, Fremantle (WA). As at 30 June 1988 the Australian merchant marine (vessels of 150 tonnes gross and over) consisted of 63 coastal vessels of 876,276 tonnes gross and 30 overseas vessels of 1,293,187 tonnes gross.

Entrances and clearances of vessels engaged in overseas trade:

	Entrances			Clearances		
	No.	DWT (1,000 tonnes)	Cargo discharged (1,000 tonnes gross)	No.	DWT (1,000 tonnes)	Cargo loaded (1,000 tonnes gross)
1985–86	6,824	307,406	22,055	6,622	304,839	234,688
1986-87	6,707	300,348	23,418	6,507	296,952	233,747

46·89m. tonnes of cargo were carried by coastal shipping in 1986-87.

Post and Broadcasting. Postal services are operated by Australia Post, established by the Postal Services Act, 1975. Revenue was $A1,656·4m. in 1987-88, expenditure $A1,601·4m. There were 4,489 post offices and other agencies in 1988. 3,662m. postal items were handled.

Telecommunications are operated by Telecom Australia under the Telecommunications Act, 1975. Revenue was $A7,199·5m. in 1987-88, expenditure $A6,423·3m. There were 7,091,549 telephones. Services to other countries are operated by the Overseas Telecommunications Commission Australia (OTC), established by the Overseas Telecommmunications Act, 1946.

Australia's National Satellite System is owned and operated by AUSSAT Pty Ltd under the Satellite Communications Act, 1984. 75% of its shares are owned by the Commonwealth Government and the rest by Telecom Australia; 3 satellites are in orbit covering the entire continent.

Broadcasting is regulated by the Broadcasting Act, 1942 and the Broadcasting Ownership and Control Acts, 1987. The National Broadcasting Service is provided by the Australian Broadcasting Corporation (ABC), which at 30 June 1988 operated 100 MW, 141 FM and 6 high-frequency radio stations. In addition, 133 MW and 9 FM, commercial stations and 9 MW and 66 public stations were operating. The short-wave international service Radio Australia broadcasts in English, Bahasa Malay, Cantonese, Chinese, French, Japanese, Thai, Tok Pisin and Vietnamese.

The National Television Service is provided by the ABC, which at 30 June 1988 operated 366 transmitter stations. In addition, 50 commercial companies operated 288 transmitters.

In 1989 there were estimated to be 7·17m. radios and 6m. TV sets in use.

Cinemas (1971). There were 976 cinemas including 241 drive-in cinemas, with a total seating capacity of about 478,000.

Newspapers (1981). There was 1 national newspaper (average daily circulation 126,000) and 14 metropolitan daily newspapers in Australia with a combined daily circulation of 3·6m. Of these, 3 papers published in Melbourne accounted for 1·3m. and 4 published in Sydney for 1·2m.

Australian Transport. Sydney, Institute of Transport, 1937 to date (quarterly)

JUSTICE, RELIGION, EDUCATION AND WELFARE

Justice. The judicial power of the Commonwealth of Australia is vested in the High Court of Australia (the Federal Supreme Court), in the Federal courts created by the Federal Parliament (the Federal Court of Australia and the Family Court of Australia) and in the State courts invested by Parliament with Federal jurisdiction.

High Court. The High Court consists of a Chief Justice and 6 other Justices, appointed by the Governor-General in Council. The Constitution confers on the High Court original jurisdiction, *inter alia*, in all matters arising under treaties or affecting consuls or other foreign representatives, matters between the States of the Commonwealth, matters to which the Commonwealth is a party and matters between residents of different States. Federal Parliament may make laws conferring original jurisdiction on the High Court, *inter alia*, in matters arising under the Constitution or under any laws made by the Parliament. It has in fact conferred jurisdiction on the High Court in matters arising under the Constitution and in matters arising under certain laws made by Parliament.

The High Court may hear and determine appeals from its own Justices exercising original jurisdiction, from any other Federal Court, from a Court exercising Federal jurisdiction and from the Supreme Courts of the States. It also has jurisdiction to hear and determine appeals from the Supreme Courts of the Territories. The right of appeal from the High Court to the Privy Council was abolished in 1986.

Other Federal Courts. Since 1924, 4 other Federal courts have been created to exercise special Federal jurisdiction, *i.e.* the Federal Court of Australia, the Family Court of Australia, the Australian Industrial Court and the Federal Court of Bankruptcy. The Federal Court of Australia was created by the Federal Court of Australia Act 1976 and began to exercise jurisdiction on 1 Feb. 1977. It exercises such original jurisdiction as is invested in it by laws made by the Federal Parliament including jurisdiction formerly exercised by the Australian Industrial Court and the Federal Court of Bankruptcy, and in some matters previously invested in either the High Court or State and Territory Supreme Courts. The Federal Court also acts as a court of appeal from State and Territory courts in relation to Federal matters. Appeal from the Federal Court to the High Court will be by way of special leave only. The State Supreme Courts have also been invested with Federal jurisdiction in bankruptcy.

State Courts. The general Federal jurisdiction of the State courts extends, subject to certain restrictions and exceptions, to all matters in which the High Court has jurisdiction or in which jurisdiction may be conferred upon it.

Industrial Tribunals. The major Federal industrial tribunal in Australia is the Australian Conciliation and Arbitration Commission, constituted by presidential members (with the status of judges) and commissioners. The Commission's functions include settling industrial disputes, making awards, determining the standard hours of work and wage fixation. Questions of law, the judicial interpretation of awards and imposition of penalties in relation to industrial matters, are now dealt with by the Federal Court.

Australian Digest of Reported Decisions of the Australian Courts and of Australian Appeals to the Privy Council. 2nd ed. Sydney, Law Book Co. 1963—Supplements 1964 ff.
Baalman, J., *Outline of Law in Australia.* 4th ed. Sydney, 1979
Bates, N., *Introduction to Legal Studies.* 3rd ed. Melbourne, 1980
Benjafield, D. G. and Whitmore, H., *Principles of Australian Administrative Law.* 3rd ed. Sydney, 1966
Cowen, Z., *Federal Jurisdiction in Australia.* 2nd ed. Melbourne, 1978
Fleming, J. G., *The Law of Torts.* 5th ed. Sydney, 1977
Gunn, J. A. L., *Australian Income Tax Law and Practice.* 9th ed. by F. C. Bock and E. F. Mannix, Sydney, 1969, and *Butterworth's Taxation Service* to date
Howard, C., *Criminal Law.* 3rd ed. Sydney, 1975
Mills, C. P. and Sorrell, G. H., *Federal Industrial Law. (Nolan and Cohen.)* 5th ed. Sydney, 1975
O'Connell, D. P. (ed.) *International Law in Australia.* Sydney, 1966
Paterson, W. E. and Ednie, H. H., *Australian Company Law.* 2nd ed. Sydney, 1976, and *Butterworth's Company Service* to date
Sawer, G., *The Australian and the Law.* Melbourne, 1976
Twyford, J., *The Layman and the Law in Australia.* 2nd ed. Sydney, 1980
Wynes, A., *Legislative, Executive and Judicial Powers in Australia.* 5th ed. Sydney, 1976
Yorston, R. K. and Fortescue, E. E., *Australian Mercantile Law.* 14th ed. Sydney, 1971

Religion. Under the Constitution the Commonwealth cannot make any law to establish any religion, to impose any religious observance or to prohibit the free exercise of any religion, nor can it require a religious test as qualification for office or public trust under the Commonwealth. The following percentages refer to those religions with the largest number of adherents at the census of 1986. The census question on religion was not obligatory, however.

Christian, 73% of population; Catholic, 26%; Anglican, 23·9%; Uniting, 7·6%; Presbyterian, 3·6%; Orthodox, 2·7%; Baptist, 1·3%; Lutheran, 1·3%; Church of Christ, 0·6%; Religion other than Christian 2·%, No religion 12·7%, No statement 12·3%.

Education. The Governments of the Australian States and the Northern Territory have the major responsibility for education, including the administration and substantial funding of primary, secondary, and technical and further education. In most States, a single Education Department is responsible for these three levels, but in New South Wales and South Australia there is a separate department responsible solely for technical and further education and in Victoria, a Technical and Further Education Board. Furthermore, in New South Wales an Education Commission advises the Minister on primary, secondary and post-secondary education.

The Australian Government is directly responsible for education services in the Australian Capital Territory, administered through an education authority, and for services to Norfolk Island, Christmas Island and the Cocos (Keeling) Islands. The Australian Government provides supplementary finance to the States and is responsible for the total funding of universities and colleges of advanced education. It also has special responsibilities for student assistance, education programmes for Aboriginal people and children from non-English-speaking backgrounds, and for international relations in education.

The Australian Constitution empowers the Federal Government to make grants to the States and to place conditions upon such grants. There are two national Education Commissions which advise the Federal Government on the financial needs of educational institutions. The Commonwealth Schools Commission, established in 1973, advises on financial assistance to the States for schools. The Commonwealth Tertiary Education Commission advises on providing the States with total funding for universities and colleges of advanced education, and supplementary assistance for their institutions of technical and further education.

In 1984 legislation was passed to reactivate the national Curriculum Development Centre (CDC) within the framework of the Commonwealth Schools Commission. The CDC's functions are to concentrate on co-ordination and dissemination and on sponsoring the development of materials through contract arrangements with other agencies.

School attendance is compulsory between the ages of 6 and 15 years (16 years in Tasmania), at either a government school or a recognized non-government educational institution. Many Australian children attend pre-schools for a year before entering school (usually in sessions of 2-3 hours, for 2-5 days per week). Government schools are usually co-educational and comprehensive. Non-government schools have been traditionally single-sex, particularly in secondary schools, but there is a trend towards co-education. Tuition is free at government schools, but fees are normally charged at non-government schools.

The following is a summary at July 1987 of primary and secondary school education:

	Schools		*Teachers* [1]		*Pupils* [2]	
States and Territories	*Government*	*Non-government*	*Government schools*	*Non-government schools*	*Government schools*	*Non-government schools*
New South Wales	2,210	852	47,323	16,580	755,084	275,903
Victoria	2,091	729	41,432	16,192	537,895	253,086
Queensland	1,322	386	23,996	6,889	375,810	119,249
South Australia	717	177	13,951	3,400	187,388	53,959
Western Australia	733	237	12,552	3,807	208,078	62,662
Tasmania	261	66	4,732	1,130	65,401	17,602
Northern Territory	143	22	2,158	346	26,707	5,176
Aust. Cap. Terr.	98	35	2,829	1,200	40,379	20,504
	7,575	2,504	148,972	49,543	2,196,742	808,141

[1] Full-time teachers plus the full-time equivalent of part-time teaching.
[2] Full-time pupils only.

In post-secondary education, tuition fees were abolished in 1974 and student allowances are provided for full-time students subject to a means test. Universities are autonomous institutions, as are the substantial majority of colleges of advanced education. While both offer degree courses, colleges also offer diploma and associate diploma courses; these tend to be vocational or of applied learning. The major part of technical and further education is provided in government-administered institutions known as TAFE.

Students enrolled at university (1985) 175,476 as follows:

Type of Course		*Type of Enrolment*	
Doctorate	7,805	Full-time internal	107,427
Master	16,749	Part-time internal	51,562
Bachelor	137,490	External	16,487
Non-degree	13,432		

University teaching staff, full-time and full-time equivalent in 1985, 10,539.

Other advanced education (1985) 195,231 students enrolled and 11,039 staff.

Type of institution and enrolment:

College of advanced education	184,335
Institute of advanced education within a university	2,960
Technical and further education institution	5,275
Other Commonwealth institution	312
Other institution	2,349
Full-time internal	97,360
Part-time internal	68,759
External	29,112

Teacher education usually takes place in colleges of advanced education, though a substantial number of secondary teachers and a few primary teachers receive their pre-service education in a university. Government school teachers are recruited by the State and Northern Territory departments of education, and in the Australian Capital Territory by the ACT Schools Authority and the Public Service Board. Non-government schools recruit their own teachers.

The Australian Government provides assistance for students. The Secondary Allowances Scheme aims to help parents with a limited income to keep their children at school for the final 2 years of secondary education. The Assistance for Isolated Children Scheme provides special support to families whose children are isolated from schooling or are handicapped. The Adult Secondary Education Assistance Scheme provides assistance for mature-age students undertaking a full-time one-year matriculation level programme or a two-year programme if studies beyond the tenth year in the Australian secondary school system have not previously been undertaken. The Tertiary Education Assistance Scheme is a means-tested scheme to assist students enrolled for full-time study in approved courses at post-secondary institutions. Allowances are also available for post-graduate study and overseas study. Aboriginal students are eligible for assistance under the Aboriginal Secondary Grants Scheme and the Aboriginal Study Grants Scheme. The States also offer various schemes of assistance, principally at the primary and secondary levels.

National bodies with a co-ordinating, planning or funding rôle include: the Australian Education Council, comprising the Federal and State Ministers of Education, the Conference of Directors-General of Education and an advisory body, the National Aboriginal Education Committee.

Total expenditure on education in Australia (public and private sectors) in 1983–84 was estimated at $A10,805m.

Australian Education Directory. Canberra, 1983
Directory of Higher Education Courses 1982. Canberra, 1982
Primary and Secondary Schooling in Australia. Canberra, 1977
Schools Commission, *Triennium 1982–84. Report for 1982*. Canberra, 1981
Tertiary Education Commission, *Report for 1982–84, Triennium Vol. 2: Recommendations for 1982*. Canberra, 1981

Health. In 1987 there were an average 5·4 hospital beds per 1,000 population. There were 1,053 hospitals (general). The Royal Flying Doctor Service serves remote areas.

Social Security and Welfare. All Commonwealth Government social security pensions, benefits and allowances are financed from the Commonwealth Government's general revenue. In addition, assistance is provided for welfare services.

Expenditure on main programmes, 1987–88, $A22,599m.

The following summarizes the conditions of the major benefits.

Age and invalid pensions—age pensions are payable to men 65 years of age or more and women 60 years of age or more who have lived in Australia for a specified period and, unless permanently blind, also satisfy an income test. Persons over 16 years of age who are permanently blind or permanently incapacitated for work to the extent of at least 85% may receive an invalid pension. There is no residence qualification for an invalid pension if the permanent incapacity or blindness occurred within Australia or during temporary absence from Australia. An income test must be satisfied for an invalid pension unless permanently blind. Additional amounts are paid to pensioners with dependent children. Supplementary assistance may be paid to a pensioner paying rent or private lodging subject to an income test. Remote area allowance is payable to pensioners living in income tax zone A, except for those aged 70 or more receiving the special rate of age pension. Supplementary assistance, additional pension for children, mother's/guardian's allowance and remote area allowance are not taxable.

In 1987-88 1,328,814 age pensioners received a total of $A6,972m., and 296,913 invalid pensioners received $A2,188m.

Wife's pension—payable to the wife of an age or invalid pensioner if she is not eligible for a pension in her own right. The maximum rate and the income test are identical to those for age and invalid pensioners.

Spouse carer's pension—payable to the husband of an age or invalid pensioner who is providing constant care and attention at home for his wife if he is not eligible for pension in his own right. The maximum rate and the income test are identical to those for age and invalid pensions.

Widow's pension—widows, divorcees, certain deserted wives, women who have been the dependant of a man for 3 years immediately prior to his death and women whose husbands have been convicted of an offence and have been imprisoned for not less than 6 months may, if they satisfy a residence requirement and an income test, receive a widow's pension. If they have any dependent children they also receive a mother's/ guardian's allowance plus an additional allowance for each child. Persons who pay private rent may also receive supplementary assistance subject to an income test. Pensions are subject to income tax, but not mother's allowances, additional pension for children, supplementary assistance, or remote area allowance.

In 1987-88 143,451 widow pensioners received a total of $A1,002m.

Supporting parents benefit—sole parents who have custody, care and control of any dependent children may, if they satisfy a residence requirement and an income test, receive supporting parents benefit. It is payable at the same rate as the widow's pension and is subject to the same income test. Mother's/guardian's allowance, additional pension for each dependent child, supplementary assistance and remote area allowance are also payable.

In 1987-88 182,007 beneficiaries received a total of $A1,525m.

Sheltered employment allowance—is payable to disabled persons under age—pension age engaged in approved sheltered employment who are qualified to receive invalid pension. The rates of payment and allowances and income test are the same as invalid pension.

Rehabilitation allowance—persons undertaking a rehabilitation programme with the Commonwealth Rehabilitation Service who are eligible for a social security pension or benefit are eligible to receive a non taxable rehabilitation allowance during treatment or training and for up to 6 months thereafter. The allowance is equivalent to the invalid pension and is subject to the same income test.

Family Allowance—is paid without income test to assist families with children under 16 years or dependent full-time students aged 16 years to under 25 years. It is not subject to income tax.

In 1987-88 1,948,234 families comprising 3,796,745 children received a total of $A1,356m.

Family income supplement—payable subject to an income test to families with one or more children eligible for family allowances so long as they are not in receipt of any Commonwealth pension, benefit or allowance which provides additional payment for dependent children; this is not taxable.

In 1987-88 141,336 families received a total $A214m.

Child disability allowance—payable to parents or guardians of severely physically or mentally handicapped children in the family home and needing constant care and attention. The allowance is free of an income test but is subject to a residence qualification similar to that for family allowance.

In 1987-88 32,071 allowances totalling $A33·8m. were paid.

Double orphan's pension—the guardian of a child under 16 years of age or of a full-time student under 25, both of whose parents are dead, or one of whose parents is dead and the whereabouts of the other parent unknown, and for refugee children where both parents are outside Australia, may receive double orphan's pension. The payment is not subject to an income test nor is it taxable.

Unemployment and sickness benefits—are paid, subject to an income test, to persons between the ages of 18 and 16 respectively and age pension age who are unemployed, able and willing to work and making efforts to obtain work, or temporarily unable to work because of sickness or injury. Job search allowance is payable to unemployed persons aged 16-17. To be granted benefit a person must have resided in Australia for at least 12 months preceding his claim or intend to remain in Australia permanently. For unemployment benefit purposes unemployment must not be due to industrial action by that person or by members of a union to which that person is a member. Special benefits may be granted to persons not qualified above. For numbers of beneficiaries and amounts paid *see* **Labour** p. 107.

Service Pensions are paid by the Department of Veterans' Affairs, similar to the age and invalid pensions provided by the Department of Social Security. Male Veterans who have reached the age of 60 years or are permanently unemployable, and who served in a theatre of war, are eligible subject to an income test. Female Veterans who served abroad and who have reached the age of 55 or are permanently unemployable, are also eligible. Wives of service pensioners are also eligible provided that they do not receive a pension from the Department of Social Security. *Disability pension* is a compensatory payment in respect of incapacity attributable to war service. It is paid at a rate commensurate with the degree of incapacity and is free of any income test. A separate allowance may be paid to dependents. In 1987-88 402,864 pensioners received a total of $A2,011m.

In addition to cash benefits, welfare services are provided either directly or through State and Local government authorities and voluntary agencies, for people with special needs.

Medicare. On 1 Feb. 1984 the Commonwealth Government introduced a universal health scheme known as Medicare. This covers: Automatic entitlement under a single public health fund to medical and optometrical benefits of 85% of the Medical Benefits Schedule fee, with a maximum patient payment for any service where the Schedule fee is charged; access without direct charge to public hospital accommodation and to inpatient and outpatient treatment by doctors appointed by the hospital; the restoration of funds for community health to approximately the same real level as 1975; a reduction in charges for private treatment in shared wards of public hospitals, and increases in the daily bed subsidy payable to private hospitals.

The Medicare programme is financed in part by a 1% levy on taxable incomes, with low income cut-off points, which were $A8,980 p.a. for a single person in 1989 and $A15,090 p.a. for a family with a $A2,100 reduction for each child. The

Commonwealth Government subsidises registered health insurance organizations by contributing to the Health Benefits, and makes an annual contribution to the Reinsurance Trust Fund of $A20m. for payments of benefits to patients with hospital treatment in excess of 35 days.

Medicare benefits are available to all persons ordinarily resident in Australia. Visitors from UK, New Zealand and Malta have immediate access to necessary medical treatment, as do all visitors staying more than 6 months.

Medical Benefits. The Health Insurance Act provides for a Medical Benefits Schedule which lists medical services and the Schedule (standard) fee applicable in each State in respect of each medical service. Schedule fees are set and updated by an independent fees tribunal appointed by the Government. The fees so determined are to apply for Medicare benefits purposes.

Home and Community Care Program was introduced in 1985 to provide support services to enable aged and disabled persons to live at home. It is jointly funded by the Commonwealth and State or Territory Governments. Commonwealth funding was $A168m. in 11987-88.

DIPLOMATIC REPRESENTATIVES

Of Australia in Great Britain (Australia House, Strand, London, WC2B 4LA)
High Commissioner: Douglas McClelland, AC.

Of Great Britain in Australia (Commonwealth Ave., Canberra)
High Commissioner: Sir John Coles, KCMG.

Of Australia in the USA (1601 Massachusetts Ave., NW, Washington, D.C., 20036)
Ambassador: Michael John Cork.

Of the USA in Australia (Moonah Pl., Canberra)
Ambassador: (Vacant).

Of Australia to the United Nations
Ambassador: Dr Peter Stephen Wilenski.

Further Reading

Statistical Information: The Australian Bureau of Statistics (Cameron Offices, Belconnen, A.C.T., 2616) was established in 1906. All the activities of the Bureau are covered by the Census and Statistics Act, which confers authority to collect information and contains secrecy provisions to ensure that individual particulars obtained are not divulged. Under the provisions of the Statistics (Arrangements with States) Act which became law on 12 May 1956, the statistical services of all the States have been integrated with the Australian Bureau. An outline of the development of statistics in Australia is published in the *Official Year Book*, No. 51, 1965. *Australian Statistician:* Dr Ian Castles.

The principal publications of the Bureau are:

Official Year Book of Australia. 1907 to date
Pocket Year Book Australia. 1913 to date
Monthly Summary of Statistics Australia. Oct. 1937 to date
Digest of Current Economic Statistics Australia. Aug. 1959 to date
Catalogue of Publications, 1976 to date

Other Official Publications

Atlas of Australian Resources. Dept. of Resources and Energy, Division of National Mapping
Climatological Atlas of Australia. Bureau of Meteorology. Melbourne, 1940
Norfolk Island—Annual Report. Dept. of Territories and Local Government
Cocos (Keeling) Islands—Annual Report. Dept. of Territories and Local Government
Christmas Island—Annual Report. Dept. of Territories and Local Government
Australian Books: Select List of Works About or Published in Australia. National Library of Australia, Canberra, 1934 to date
Australian National Bibliography. Canberra, 1936 to date
Historical Records of Australia. 34 vols. National Library, Canberra, 1914–25
Australia Handbook. Dept. of Administrative Services. Australian Information Services

Annual Report. Dept. of Foreign Affairs, Canberra, 1932 to date
Australian Foreign Affairs Record. Dept. of Foreign Affairs, Canberra, 1936 to date
Australian Treaty List. Dept. of Foreign Affairs, Canberra, consolidated volume from Federation to 1970 with supplements to date
Coxon, H., *Australian Official Publications*. Oxford, 1981
Documents on Australian Foreign Policy 1937–49. Vols. I–VI. Dept. of Foreign Affairs, Canberra, 1975–83
Diplomatic List. Dept. of Foreign Affairs, Canberra. 1949 to date
Consular and Trade Representatives. Dept. of Foreign Affairs, Canberra. 1936 to date

Non-Official Publications

Australian Encyclopædia. 12 vols. Sydney, 1983
Australian Quarterly: A Quarterly Review of Australian Affairs. Sydney, 1929 to date
Ball, D. and Langtry, J. O., *Civil Defence and Australia's Security in a Nuclear Age*. Sydney, 1984
Blainey, G., *The Tyranny of Distance: How Distance Shaped Australia's History*. Melbourne, 1982
Caves, P. E. and Krause, L. B., *The Australian Economy: A View from the North*. Sydney, 1984
Clark, M., *A Short History of Australia*. Melbourne, 1981
Deery, S. and Plowman, D., *Australian Industrial Relations*. Sydney, 1985
Dixson, M., *The Real Matilda: Women and Identity in Australia 1788 to the Present*. Melbourne, 1984
Gilbert, A. D. and Inglis, K. S. (eds.) *Australians: A Historical Library*. 5 vols. CUP, 1988
Howard, C., *Australia's Constitution*. Melbourne, 1985
Hurst, J., *Hawke P. M.* Sydney, 1983
Inglis, K., *This is the ABC: The Australian Broadcasting Commission*. Melbourne, 1983
Jupp, J., *Party Politics: Australia, 1966–1981*. Sydney, 1982
Kepars, I., *Australia*. [Bibliography] Oxford and Santa Barbara, 1984
Lucy, R., *The Australian Form of Government*. Melbourne, 1985
Moore, D. and Hall, R., *Australia: Image of a Nation*. London, 1983
Serle, P., *Dictionary of Australian Biography*. 2 vols. Sydney, 1949
Solomon, D., *Australia's Government and Parliament*. Melbourne, 1981
Spann, R. N., *Government Administration in Australia*. Sydney, 1979
Who's Who in Australia. Melbourne, 1906 to date
Wilson, R. K., *Australia's Resources and their Development*. Univ. of Sydney, 1980

National Library: The National Library, Canberra, A.C.T. *Director-General:* Harrison Bryan.

AUSTRALIAN TERRITORIES

AUSTRALIAN CAPITAL TERRITORY

HISTORY. The area, now the Australian Capital Territory (ACT), was first visited by Europeans in 1820 and settlement commenced in 1824. Until its selection as the seat of government it was a quiet pastoral and agricultural community.

AREA AND POPULATION. The area of the Australian Capital Territory is 2,432 sq. km (including Jervis Bay area). The population (estimate) at 31 March 1988 was 271,900. Previous census population:

	Males	*Females*	*Total*		*Males*	*Females*	*Total*
1911	992	722	1,714	1966	49,991	46,041	96,032
1921	1,567	1,005	2,572	1971	73,589	70,474	144,063
1933	4,805	4,142	8,947	1976	100,103	95,519	197,622
1947	9,092	7,813	16,905	1981	110,415	111,194	221,609
1954	16,229	14,086	30,315	1986	132,100	132,300	264,400
1961	30,858	27,970	58,828				

(Figures before 1961 exclude particulars of full-blood Aborigines.)

CONSTITUTION AND GOVERNMENT. The Constitution of Australia provided (Sec. 125) that the seat of government should be selected by parliament and that it should be within New South Wales, distance not less than 160 km from Sydney. The present area was surrendered by New South Wales and accepted by the Australian Government from 1 Jan. 1911. In 1915 an additional 73 sq. km at

Jervis Bay was transferred from New South Wales to serve as a port. In 1911 an international competition was held for the city plan. The plan chosen was that of W. Burley Griffin, of Chicago. Construction, delayed by the First World War, began in 1923 and on 9 May 1927 Parliament was opened and Canberra became the seat of government. Most Australian Government departments now have their headquarters in Canberra.

The general administration lies with the ACT Administration, responsible to the Federal Minister for the Arts, Sport, Environment, Tourism and Territories. The Administration provides all municipal and Territorial services except police and courts (responsibility of the Federal Attorney-General).

The Australian Capital Territory Representation (House of Representatives) Act, 1973, provided for the representation of residents of the Territory by 2 elected members in the House of Representatives. The Senate (Representation of Territories) Act 1973 provided for the election of 2 Senators from the Territory. Elections took place on 1 Dec. 1984. The ACT became self-governing on 11 May 1989.

FINANCE. In 1987–88 the ACT was given its own budget. It is treated equitably with the States regarding local revenue raising, expenditure and assistance by the Commonwealth government.

PRODUCTION. Outside Canberra the Territory is mainly reserved for forestry and nature conservation (Namadgi National Park is 94,000 hectares). A considerable amount of reafforestation (mostly pine) has been undertaken, the total area of coniferous plantations at 30 June 1988 being 16,194 hectares. Farming is mainly in grazing: Livestock (1988), 12,422 cattle, 116,851 sheep, and 1,948 horses.

EDUCATION. In July 1988 there were 98 government schools comprising 68 primary schools, 25 secondary schools and colleges, 1 combined primary/secondary school and 4 special schools. Non-government schools numbered 37 of which there were 22 primary schools, 5 secondary schools and 8 schools with both primary and secondary enrolments. Students enrolled full-time in government schools in 1987 numbered 22,200 and 18,206 in primary and secondary school levels respectively. Enrolments at non-government schools comprised 10,428 primary school students and 9,317 secondary school students. Pre-school education is provided at 73 centres with a total enrolment of 3,942 (1987). There is an Institute of Technical and Further Education and a Canberra Institute of the Arts.

The Canberra College of Advanced Education commenced operation in 1970. Enrolments (1988) 6,582. The Australian National University is situated in Canberra. Enrolments (1988) 6,645.

Further Reading

A.C.T. Statistical Summary. Australian Bureau of Statistics. From 1960

Wigmore, L., *Canberra: A History of Australia's National Capital*. 2nd ed. Canberra, 1971

NORTHERN TERRITORY

HISTORY. The Northern Territory, after forming part of New South Wales, was annexed on 6 July 1863 to South Australia and in 1901 entered the Commonwealth as a corporate part of South Australia. The Commonwealth Constitution Act of 1900 made provision for the surrender to the Commonwealth of any territory by any state, and under this provision an agreement was entered into on 7 Dec. 1907 for the transfer of the Northern Territory to the Commonwealth, and it formally passed under the control of the Commonwealth Government on 1 Jan. 1911. For details of Constitutional development until 1978 *see* THE STATESMAN'S YEAR-BOOK 1980–81 pp. 123–24. The Commonwealth Government retained responsibility until Self-Government was granted on 1 July 1978.

AREA AND POPULATION. The Northern Territory is bounded by the 26th parallel of S. lat. and 129° and 138° E. long. Its total area is 1,346, 200 sq. km. The coastline is about 6,200 km in length, and the Territory includes adjacent islands between 129° and 138° E. long. The greater part of the interior consists of a tableland rising gradually from the coast to a height of about 700 metres. On this tableland there are large areas of excellent pasturage. The southern part of the Territory is generally sandy and has a small rainfall, but water may be obtained by means of sub-artesian bores.

The population of the Territory in June 1987 was 156,700. The capital, seat of Government and principal port is Darwin, on the north coast; population 76,400 in June 1987. Other main centres include Katherine (6,100), 330 km south of Darwin; Alice Springs (22,900), in Central Australia; Tennant Creek (3,300), a rich mining centre 500 km north of Alice Springs; Nhulunbuy (3,800), a bauxite mining centre on the Gove Peninsula in eastern Arnhem Land; and Jabiru, a model town built to serve the rich Uranium Province in eastern Arnhem Land with a planned population of 6,000 (actual, 1986, 1,410). Palmerston is a Darwin satellite town (1986, 5,700); Yulara (estimate, 500) is a resort village serving Uluru National Park and Ayers Rock. There also are a number of large self-contained Aboriginal communities. Aboriginals were 29,087 at the 1981 Census. On 31 July 1984, 26,692,400 hectares were designated Aboriginal Land under the Aboriginal Land Rights (N.T.) Act 1976.

Vital statistics for 1983: Births, 3,127; deaths, 727; marriages, 776; divorces, 371.

CONSTITUTION AND GOVERNMENT. The Northern Territory (Self-Government) Act 1978 established the Northern Territory as a body politic as from 1 July 1978, with Ministers having control over and responsibility for Territory finances and the administration of the functions of government as specified by the Federal Government. Regulations have been made conferring executive authority for the bulk of administrative functions. At 31 Dec. 1979 the only important powers retained by the Commonwealth related to rights in respect of Aboriginal land, some significant National Parks and the mining of uranium and other substances prescribed in the Atomic Energy Act. Proposed laws passed by the Legislative Assembly require the assent of the Administrator, who may assent, withhold assent, return them with recommended amendments or reserve them for the Governor-General's pleasure. The Governor-General may disallow any law assented to by the Administrator within 6 months of the Administrator's assent.

The Northern Territory has federal representation, electing 1 member to the House of Representatives and 2 members to the Senate.

The Legislative Assembly has 25 members, directly elected for a period of 4 years. The Chief Minister, Deputy Chief Minister and Speaker are elected by, and from, the members. The Administrator appoints Ministers on the advice of the Leader of the majority party.

The Legislative Assembly, elected in 1987, is composed as follows: Country Liberal Party, 16; Australian Labor Party, 6; Northern Territory National Party, 1; Independents, 2.

The Country Liberal Party Cabinet was as follows in 1988:

Chief Minister and Treasurer: Marshall Perron.

Deputy Chief Minister, Mines and Energy and Industries and Development: Barry Coulter. *Attorney-General, Lands and Housing and Conservation:* Daryl Manzie. *Health and Community Services:* Don Dale. *Education and Minister Assisting the Chief Minister on Constitutional Development:* Tom Harris. *Transport and Works:* Fred Finch. *Labour, Administrative Services and Local Government:* Terry McCarthy. *Tourism and Minister Assisting the Chief Minister on Central Australian Affairs:* Eric Poole. *Primary Industry and Fisheries:* Mike Reed.

Local Government: Local government was established in Darwin in 1957 and later in 5 regional centres. These are each managed by a mayor and a municipal council elected at intervals of not more than 4 years by universal adult franchise. Provision has been made for a limited form of local government for smaller communities.

FINANCE. Budgets in $A1m.:

	1983–84	1984–85	1985–86	1986–86 [1]
Revenue	972·8	1,075·3	1,217·7	1,230·2
Expenditure	970·4	1,075·3	1,217·7	1,230·2

[1] Provisional.

The revenue in 1986–87 comprised $A977·1m. in grants and allowances to the Northern Territory from the Commonwealth, as established by agreement at the time of self-government, together with $A253m. raised by the Northern Territory which included $A113·1m. through state-like taxes.

Expenditure during 1986–87 included $A180·1m. for education; $A67·4m. for housing; $A123·3m. for health; $A86·3m. for law, order and public safety; $A136·8m. for energy and $A53·9m.on subsidies.

ENERGY AND NATURAL RESOURCES

Oil and Gas. Significant oil and gas reserves have been discovered offshore in the Joseph Bonaparte Gulf and Timor Sea areas and onshore in the Amadeus Basin. In Aug. 1988 4 wells in the offshore Jabiru field were producing 42,000 bbls a day. Crude oil production from the onshore Mereenie oil and gas field began in 1984. Natural gas is piped from the Amadeus Basin to Darwin.

Minerals. The most important natural resources are minerals, and mining is the largest industry. Gross value of output, $A1,086m. in 1987-88. Uranium oxide accounted for 45% of production in 1986.

At present there are five major mining organizations extracting bauxite, manganese, uranium, gold and copper; in addition, one firm is producing uranium oxide from stockpiled ore. Zinc, lead and silver are also mined, and rock, sand and gravel are produced as construction materials.

In 1988 Gove Peninsula bauxite reserves were estimated at 180m. tonnes with an average alumina content of 50%. Alumina is exported to Europe, the USA, Canada, USSR and to China.

In 1988 the manganese mine on Groote Eylandt had proved recoverable resources containing just over 40m. tonnes. Much of the ore was exported to Japan, western Europe, South Korea, the USSR and China.

Gold is mined in the Pine Creek and Tennant Creek areas and in the Tanami desert. In 1988 Cosmo Hawley Mine had *in situ* reserves of 4·2m. tonnes and Woolwonga 2·4m. tonnes. Nobles Nob produced gold from 1938 to 1985 and its treatment plant continues to operate. Copper is mined at the Gecko Mine in the Tennant Creek area.

Agriculture. Cattle and buffalo production constitutes the largest farming industry in the Northern Territory. Many buffalo are exported live to Indonesia. Value of live cattle exports, 1986-87, A$7·5m.; value of export beef, 1986-87, A$17·5m.

The USA is the largest importer of Territory beef, followed by Taiwan and Japan.

There are 243 pastoral stations in the Northern Territory which produce cattle for Australian and overseas markets. They vary from small stations of 270 sq. km. to huge properties like Wave Hill Station which runs cattle over 12,359 sq. km.

General agriculture is conducted on a small scale. Fruit, vegetables, eggs, dairy produce, poultry and cereals are produced. Properties in the Katherine, Douglas-Daly and Adelaide River districts produce the Territory's seven main crops – sorghum, maize, mung beans, soybeans, rice, sesame and peanuts. Area under crops, 1987–88, 8,800 hectares.

Forestry. A forest development programme which commenced in 1970 has continued the multiple use management of Northern Territory forested areas; this included a softwood programme of 400 hectares per year, the introduction of additional suitable tree species in both arid and higher rainfall areas, conservation and management of native forests for production and recreational purposes, survey and assessment of resources, fire control activities and the creation of training opportunities for Aboriginals in forestry and allied saw-milling activities.

Local production of sawn timber is mainly of Cypress pine.

Fisheries. The total value (*ex*-vessel) of commercial fish products landed in the Northern Territory in 1987 was $A40·33m. Of this, prawns contributed $A35·76m. and barramundi $A2m. Mud crabs, threadfin salmon, shark, mackerel, bay lobster and reef fish made up most of the remainder. A Pearl Industry Development Plan was implemented in 1988 to foster the culturing of pearls from shells harvested in waters adjacent to the Territory.

INDUSTRY AND TRADE. In 1984–85 value added in the manufacturing industry, from 137 factories (with 4 or more persons employed) was $A128·8m. 2,645 persons were employed in these factories. The labour force totalled 71,800 in June 1980. In 1984, 75 trade unions had 20,300 members.

Tourism. In 1987-88, 830,000 people travelled to the Territory and tourism generated approximately $A300m. to the economy.

National Parks and Reserves. There are 74 areas totalling more than 2,350,326 hectares set aside as National Parks or Conservation Reserves, and many other areas are managed by the Conservation Commission.

COMMUNICATIONS

Roads. There are now (1988) 5,528 km of sealed road and 5,450 km of gravel and crushed stone road within the Northern Territory. They include three major interstate links: The Stuart Highway from Darwin to Adelaide (1,486 km), the Barkly Highway, Tennant Creek to the Queensland border (636 km), and the Victoria Highway, Katherine to the Western Australian border (468 km). In addition to this there are 4,758 km of formed roads and 4,194 km of unformed roads or tracks, totalling approximately 19,931 km of roads. In 1984–85 registrations of new motor vehicles included 4,504 cars, 2,248 utilities etc., 294 trucks, 82 buses and 1,092 motor cycles.

Railways. In 1980 Alice Springs was linked to the Trans-continental network by a standard (1,435 mm) gauge railway to Tarcoola (831 km). Direct services from Sydney started in 1984. The standard gauge railway is to be extended to Darwin, providing Australia with its first north-south rail link.

Aviation. There are daily flights from Darwin to Alice Springs with connexions to all Australian capital cities by 2 major domestic carriers, Australian Airlines and Ansett Airlines. Darwin is a first port of call for international aircraft flying in from Asia and a departure point for flights to such places as Singapore, Bali, Brunei and Timor.

Shipping. Regular freight shipping services connect Darwin with Western Australia, the eastern States and overseas. Passenger vessels also call at Darwin at irregular intervals.

The Port of Darwin is 997 km in extent; it is equipped to handle bulk, container and roll-on-roll-off traffic. There is a cyclone shelter for fishing vessels.

The ports of Melville Bay (Gove) and Milner Bay (Groote Eylandt) are connected with Darwin, the eastern States and overseas by regular shipping freight services.

The inland and coastal communities around the coast are provided with regular freight barge services from Darwin. Some of these communities also receive a barge freight-transhipment service out of a Brisbane vessel which calls at Melville and Milner Bays.

Radio and Television. In 1984 there were 8,658 radio-communication stations, 8 radio broadcasting stations and 5 television stations.

EDUCATION AND WELFARE

Education. Education is compulsory from the age of 6-15 years. There were (1987) about 35,000 pre-school, primary and secondary students enrolled in about 165 Government and non-Government schools. The proportion of migrant and Aboriginal students in the Territory is high with the latter comprising about 30% of total school enrolments. Schools range from single classrooms and transportable units catering for the needs of small Aboriginal communities and pastoral properties to urban high schools for over 1,000 pupils. Bilingual programmes operate in Aboriginal communities where traditional Aboriginal culture prevails. Secondary education extends from school years 8 to 12. The Northern Territory University was founded in 1989 by amalgamating the existing University College of the Northern Territory and the Darwin Institute of Technology, with the technical and further education courses hitherto offered by the latter to be conducted by an Institute of Technical and Further Education within the new University. The Alice Springs College of TAFE, the Katherine Rural College, the Northern Territory Open College and the Batchelor College for Aboriginals offer a wide range of specialized courses.

Health. In 1984 there were 5 hospitals with 650 beds. Community health services are provided from urban and rural Health Centres including mobile units. Remote communities are served by the Aerial Medical Service and by resident Aboriginal health workers.

Further Reading

The Northern Territory: Annual Report. Dept. of Territories, Canberra, from 1911. Dept. of the Interior, Canberra, from 1966–67. Dept. of Northern Territory, from 1972
Australian Territories, Dept. of Territories, Canberra, 1960 to 1973. Dept. of Special Minister of State, Canberra, 1973–75. Department of Administrative Services, 1976
Northern Territory Statistical Summary. Australian Bureau of Statistics, Canberra, from 1960
Donovan, P. F., *A Land Full of Possibilities: A History of South Australia's Northern Territory 1863–1911.* 1981.—*At the Other End of Australia: The Commonwealth and the Northern Territory 1911–1978.* Univ. of Queensland Press, 1984
Heatley, A., *The Government of the Northern Territory.* Univ. of Queensland Press, 1979
Mills, C. M., *A Bibliography of the Northern Territory.* Canberra, 1977
Powell, A., *Far Country: A Short History of the Northern Territory.* Melbourne Univ. Press, 1982

AUSTRALIAN EXTERNAL TERRITORIES

AUSTRALIAN ANTARCTIC TERRITORY. An Imperial Order in Council of 7 Feb. 1933 placed under Australian authority all the islands and territories other than Adélie Land situated south of 60° S. lat. and lying between 160° E. long. and 45° E. long. The Order came into force with a Proclamation issued by the Governor-General on 24 Aug. 1936 after the passage of the Australian Antarctic Territory Acceptance Act 1933. The boundaries of Adélie Land were definitively fixed by a French Decree of 1 April 1938 as the islands and territories south of 60° S. lat. lying between 136° E. long. and 142° E. long. The Australian Antarctic Territory Act 1954 declared that the laws in force in the Australian Capital Territory are, so far as they are applicable and are not inconsistent with any ordinance made under the Act, in force in the Australian Antarctic Territory.

The area of the territory is estimated at 6,119,818 sq. km (2,362,875 sq. miles).

On 13 Feb. 1954 the Australian National Antarctic Research Expeditions (ANARE) established a station on MacRobertson Land at lat. 67° 37' S. and long. 62° 52' E. The station was named Mawson in honour of the late Sir Douglas Mawson. Meteorological and other scientific research is conducted at Mawson, which is the centre for coastal and inland survey expeditions.

A second Australian scientific research station was established on the coast of Princess Elizabeth Land on 13 Jan. 1957 at lat. 68° 34' S. and long. 77° 58' E. The station was named Davis in honour of Capt. John King Davis, Mawson's second-in-command on 2 expeditions. The station was temporarily closed down in Jan. 1965 and re-opened in Feb. 1969.

In Feb. 1959 the Australian Government accepted from the US Government custody of Wilkes Station, which was established by the US on 16 Jan. 1957 on the

Budd Coast of Wilkes Land, at lat. 66° 15' S. and long. 110° 32' E. The station was named in honour of Lieut. Charles Wilkes, who commanded the 1838–40 US expedition to the area, and was closed in Feb. 1969. Operations were then transferred to the new station, Casey. Construction commenced on Casey station in Jan. 1965 and was continued, mainly during summer visits, until Feb. 1969, when it was opened. The station, specially designed to withstand blizzard winds and prevent inundation by snow, is situated 2·4 km south of Wilkes at lat. 66° 17' S. and long. 110° 32' E. The Antarctic Division has also operated a station, since March 1948, at Macquarie Island, about 1,360 km south-east of Hobart. Macquarie Island is part of the State of Tasmania.

On 1 Dec. 1959 Australia signed the Antarctic Treaty with Argentina, Belgium, Chile, France, Japan, New Zealand, Norway, South Africa, the USSR, the UK and the USA. Poland, Czechoslovakia, German Democratic Republic, Netherlands, Romania, Brazil, Denmark, Bulgaria, Federal Republic of Germany, Italy, India, People's Republic of China, Spain, Papua New Guinea, Peru, Hungary and Uruguay have subsequently acceded to the Treaty. Poland became a full member of the Antarctic Treaty in 1977 and the Federal Republic of Germany in 1981 and India and Brazil in 1983. The Treaty reserves the Antarctic area south of 60° S. lat. for peaceful purposes, provides for international co-operation in scientific investigation and research, and preserves, for the duration of the Treaty, the *status quo* with regard to territorial sovereignty, rights and claims. The Treaty entered into force on 23 June 1961.

COCOS (KEELING) ISLANDS. The Cocos (Keeling) Islands are 2 separate atolls comprising some 27 small coral islands with a total area of about 14·2 sq. km, and are situated in the Indian Ocean at 12° 05' S. lat. and 96° 53' E. long. They lie 2,768 km north-west of Perth and 3,685 km west of Darwin, while Colombo is 2,255 km to the north-west of the group.

The main islands in this Australian Territory are West Island (the largest, about 10 km from north to south) on which is an airport and an animal quarantine station, and most of the European community; Home Island, occupied by the Cocos Malay community; Direction, South and Horsburgh Islands, and North Keeling Island, 24 km to the north of the group.

Although the islands were discovered in 1609 by Capt. William Keeling of the East India Company, they remained uninhabited until 1826, when the first settlement was established on the main atoll by an Englishman, Alexander Hare, with a group of followers, predominantly of Malay origin. Hare left the islands in 1831, by which time a second settlement had been formed on the main atoll by John Clunies-Ross, a Scottish seaman and adventurer, who began commercial development of the islands' coconut palms.

In 1857 the islands were annexed to the Crown; in 1878 responsibility was transferred from the Colonial Office to the Government of Ceylon, and in 1886 to the Government of the Straits Settlement. By indenture in 1886 Queen Victoria granted all land in the islands to George Clunies-Ross and his heirs in perpetuity (with certain rights reserved to the Crown). In 1903 the islands were incorporated in the Settlement of Singapore and in 1942–46 temporarily placed under the Governor of Ceylon. In 1946 a Resident Administrator, responsible to the Governor of Singapore, was appointed.

On 23 Nov. 1955 the Cocos Islands were placed under the authority of the Australian Government as the Territory of Cocos (Keeling) Islands. An Administrator, appointed by the Governor-General, is the Government's representative in the Territory and is responsible to the Minister for Territories and Local Government. The Cocos (Keeling) Islands Council, established as the elected body of the Cocos Malay community in July 1979, advises the Administrator on all issues affecting the Territory.

In 1978 the Australian Government purchased the Clunies-Ross family's entire interests in the islands, except for the family residence. A Cocos Malay co-operative has been established to take over the running of the Clunies-Ross copra plantation (118 tonnes of copra were exported in 1985–86) and to engage in other business with the Commonwealth in the Territory, including construction projects.

The population of the Territory at 30 June 1986 was 616, distributed between Home Island (414) and West Island (202).

The islands are low-lying, flat and thickly covered by coconut palms, and surround a lagoon in which ships drawing up to 7 metres may be anchored, but which is extremely difficult for navigation.

An equable and pleasant climate, affected for much of the year by the south-east trade winds. Temperatures range over the year from 68° F (20° C) to 88° F (31·1° C) and rainfall averages 80" (2,000 mm) a year.

The Cocos (Keeling) Islands Act 1955 is the basis of the Territory's administrative, legislative and judicial systems. Under section 8 of this Act, those laws which were in force in the Territory immediately before the transfer continued in force there.

Roads. There are 24 km of roads.

Post and Broadcasting. In 1986 there were 150 radio receivers and (1985) 180 telephones.

Religion. About 58% are Moslems and 22% Christians.

Education. In 1986 there were 2 primary schools (on Home Island and West Island) with 105 pupils and 8 teachers, a secondary school (on West Island) with 30 pupils and 5 staff, and a technical school with 9 pupils.

Health. In 1985 there was a doctor and 4 nursing personnel, with 5 beds in clinics.

Administrator: C. M. Stuart.

CHRISTMAS ISLAND is an isolated peak in the Indian Ocean, lat. 10° 25' 22" S., long. 105° 39' 59" E. It lies 360 km S., 8° E. of Java Head, and 417 km N. 79° E. from Cocos Islands, 1,310 km from Singapore and 2,623 km from Fremantle. Area about 135 sq. km. The climate is tropical with temperatures varying little over the year at 27° C. The wet season lasts from Nov. to April with an annual total of about 2,673 mm. The island was formally annexed by the UK on 6 June 1888, placed under the administration of the Governor of the Straits Settlements in 1889, and incorporated with the Settlement of Singapore in 1900. Sovereignty was transferred to the Australian Government on 1 Oct. 1958. The population (Census, 1981) was 2,871; estimate (1986) 2,000 of whom 1,300 were of Chinese, 600 of Malay and 100 of Australian/European origin.

The legislative, judicial and administrative systems are regulated by the Christmas Island Act, 1958–73. They are the responsibility of the Commonwealth Government and operated by an Administrator. The laws of Singapore which were in force before the transfer have been continued but can be amended, repealed or substituted by ordinances made by the Governor-General. The first Island Assembly was elected in Sept. 1985.

Extraction and export of rock phosphate dust was the island's only industry until 1987. In Dec. 1948 Australia and New Zealand bought the lease rights of the Christmas Island Phosphate Co. and set up the Christmas Island Phosphate Commission (CIPC), which conducted the mining operation until mid-1981. The Phosphate Mining Co. of Christmas Island Ltd (PMCI) acted as managing agents for the CIPC until the Commission was wound up and then mined in its own right. The Commonwealth Government appointed liquidators on 11 Nov. 1987, with a view to ending all mining.

Electricity. Production (1985) 33m. kwh.

Roads. There are 32 km of roads, 759 passenger cars and 383 commercial vehicles.

Railways. There is a 20 km railway to serve the phosphate mines.

Aviation. There are weekly flights to Perth (Western Australia) and to Singapore.

Shipping. In 1985, 1·2m. tonnes (mostly phosphates) were loaded and 46,000 tonnes discharged at the port.

Post and Broadcasting. There are 2 post offices and (1986) 2,500 radio receivers.

Religion. About 35% are Buddhists, 25% Muslims and 20% Christians.

Education. In 1985 there were 261 pupils in 2 primary schools, 114 pupils in a secondary school and 60 students in a technical school.

Health. In 1985 there were 2 doctors, a dentist, a pharmacist and a hospital with 35 beds.

Administrator: T. F. Paterson.

NORFOLK ISLAND. 29° 02' S. lat. 167° 57' E. long., area 3,455 hectares, population, (June 1986), 1,977. The island was formerly part of the colony of New South Wales and then of Van Diemen's Land. It was a penal colony 1788–1814 and 1825–55. In 1856 it received all 194 descendants of the *Bounty* mutineers from Pitcairn Island. It has been a distinct settlement since 1856, under the jurisdiction of the state of New South Wales; and finally by the passage of the Norfolk Island Act 1913, it was accepted as a Territory of the Australian Government. The Norfolk Island Act 1957 is the basis of the Territory's legislative, administrative and judicial systems. An Administrator, appointed by the Governor-General and responsible to the Minister for Territories and Local Government, is the senior government representative in the Territory.

The Norfolk Island Act 1979 gives Norfolk Island responsible legislative and executive government to enable it to run its own affairs to the greatest practicable extent. Wide powers are exercised by the Norfolk Island Legislative Assembly of 9 elected members, and by an Executive Council, comprising the executive members of the Legislative Assembly who have ministerial-type responsibilities. The seat of administration is Kingston, the only major settlement. The Act preserves the Commonwealth's responsibility for Norfolk Island as a Territory under its authority, indicating Parliament's intention that consideration would be given to an extension of the powers of the Legislative Assembly and the political and administrative institutions of Norfolk Island within 5 years. Some powers were transferred in 1985 and further transfers are being considered.

The Territory Administration is financed from local revenue which for 1987–88 totalled $A4,872,000; expenditure, $A4,840,128.

Public revenue is derived mainly from tourism, the sale of postage stamps, customs duties, liquor sales and company registration and licence fees. Residents are not liable for income tax on earnings within the Territory, nor are death and personal stamp duties levied.

In 1986, 29,428 visitors travelled to Norfolk. Descendants of the *Bounty* mutineer families constitute the 'original' settlers and are known locally as 'Islanders', while later settlers, mostly from Australia, New Zealand and UK, are identified as 'mainlanders'. Over the years the Islanders have preserved their own lifestyle and customs, and their language remains a mixture of West Country English, Gaelic and Tahitian.

Roads. There are 72 km of roads (53 km paved), 1,802 passenger cars and 90 commercial vehicles.

Post and Broadcasting. There is one post office and (1984) 1,090 telephones, 400 television and (1987) 1,500 radio receivers.

JUSTICE, RELIGION, EDUCATION AND WELFARE

Justice. The island's Supreme Court sits as required and a Court of Petty Sessions exercises both civil and criminal juristiction.

Religion. 40% of the population are Anglicans.

Education. In 1986 there were 2 primary schools with 120 pupils and a secondary school with 111 pupils.

Health. In 1985 there were 2 doctors, a pharmacist and a hospital with 20 beds.

Administrator: Commodore J. A. Matthew, CVO, MBE.
Chief Minister: David E. Buffett.

HEARD AND McDONALD ISLANDS. These islands, about 2,500 miles south-west of Fremantle, were transferred from UK to Australian control as from 26 Dec. 1947. Heard Island is about 43 km long and 21 km wide; Shag Island is about 8 km north of Heard. The total area is 412 sq. km (159 sq. miles). The McDonald Islands are 42 km to the west of Heard.

TERRITORY OF ASHMORE AND CARTIER ISLANDS. By Imperial Order in Council of 23 July 1931, Ashmore Islands (known as Middle, East and West Islands) and Cartier Island, situated in the Indian Ocean, some 320 km off the north-west coast of Australia (area, 5 sq. km), were placed under the authority of the Commonwealth.

Under the Ashmore and Cartier Islands Acceptance Act, 1933, the islands were accepted by the Commonwealth under the name of the Territory of Ashmore and Cartier Islands, and the effective date was proclaimed by the Governor-General to be 10 May 1934. It was the intention that the Territory should be administered by the State of Western Australia, but owing to administrative difficulties the Territory was annexed to and deemed to form part of the Northern Territory of Australia (by amendment to the Act in 1938) with relevant laws of the Northern Territory, applying to the Territory of Ashmore and Cartier Islands. Responsibility for the administration of Ashmore and Cartier Islands rests with the Minister for the Arts, Sport, the Environment, Tourism and Territories.

On 16 Aug. 1983 a national nature reserve was declared over Ashmore Reef and the area so declared is now known as Ashmore Reef National Nature Reserve.

The islands are uninhabited but Indonesian fishing boats, which have traditionally plied the area, fish within the Territory and land to collect water in accordance with an agreement between the governments of Australia and Indonesia.

Periodic visits are made to the islands by ships of the Royal Australian Navy, and aircraft of the Royal Australian Air Force make aerial surveys of the islands and neighbouring waters.

TERRITORY OF CORAL SEA ISLANDS. The Coral Sea Islands became a Territory of the Commonwealth of Australia under the Coral Sea Islands Act 1969. It comprises scattered reefs and islands over a sea area of about 1m. sq. km. The Territory is uninhabited apart from a manned meteorological station on Willis Island.

NEW SOUTH WALES

HISTORY. New South Wales became a British possession in 1770; the first settlement was established at Port Jackson in 1788; a partially elective Council was established in 1843, and responsible government in 1856. New South Wales federated with the other Australian states to form the Commonwealth of Australia in 1901.

AREA AND POPULATION. New South Wales is situated between the 28th and 38th parallels of S. lat. and 141st and 154th meridians of E. long., and comprises 309,433 sq. miles (801,428 sq. km), inclusive of Lord Howe Island, 6 sq. miles (17 sq. km), but exclusive of the Australian Capital Territory (911 sq. miles, 2,359 sq. km) and 28 sq. miles (73 sq. km) at Jervis Bay.

Lord Howe Island, 31° 33' 4" S., 159° 4' 26" E., which is part of New South Wales, is situated about 702 km north-east of Sydney; area, 1,654 hectares, of which only about 120 hectares are arable; resident population, estimate (30 June 1987), 290. The Island, which was discovered in 1788, is of volcanic origin. Mount Gower, the highest point, reaches a height of 866 metres.

The Lord Howe Island Board manages the affairs of the Island and supervises the Kentia palm-seed industry.

Census population of New South Wales (including full-blood Aboriginals from 1966):

	Males	*Females*	*Persons*	*Population per sq. km*	*Average annual increase % since previous census*
1901	710,264	645,091	1,355,355	2	1·86
1911	857,698	789,036	1,646,734	2	1·97
1921	1,071,501	1,028,870	2,100,371	3	2·46
1933	1,318,471	1,282,376	2,600,847	3	1·76
1947	1,492,211	1,492,627	2,984,838	4	0·99
1954	1,720,860	1,702,669	3,423,529	4	1·98
1961	1,972,909	1,944,104	3,917,013	5	1·94
1966	2,126,652	2,111,249	4,237,901	5	1·58
1971	2,307,210	2,293,970	4,601,180	6	1·66
1976	2,380,172	2,396,931	4,777,103	6	0·75
1981	2,548,984	2,577,233	5,126,217	6	1·42
1986	2,684,570	2,717,311	5,401,881	7	1·05

At 30 June 1988 the estimated resident population was 5,699,300 (2,860,000 female). 1987 (and 1985): Sydney Statistical Division, 3,525,850 (3,472,650); Newcastle Statistical Subdivision, 418,960 (416,120); Wollongong Statistical Subdivision, 233,650 (232,510). Population of principal municipalities outside Sydney: Albury, 39,610 (39,180); Armidale, 20,920 (20,680); Bathurst, 25,620 (25,300); Broken Hill, 24,170 (25,170); Casino, 10,820 (10,770); Cessnock, 43,170 (42,700); Dubbo, 31,290 (31,040); Goulburn, 21,700 (21,780); Grafton, 16,230 (16,380); Greater Lithgow, 20,070 (20,170); Greater Taree, 36,960 (36,310); Hastings, 42,220 (41,170); Kiama, 14,080 (13,740); Lake Macquarie, 159,300 (158,300); Lismore, 38,130 (37,480); Maitland, 46,130 (45,410); Newcastle, 132,240 (132,940); Orange, 32,520 (32,340); Queanbeyan, 23,880 (23,180); Shellharbour, 45,550 (45,250); Shoalhaven, 59,470 (57,670); Tamworth, 33,830 (33,710); Wagga Wagga, 50,930 (50,380); Wollongong, 174,020 (173,520).

Vital statistics for calendar years:

	Live births	*Marriages*	*Divorces*	*Deaths (excluding still-births)*	*Infantile mortality per 1,000 live births*
1985	87,786	41,183	11,871	44,264	9·8
1986	84,531	41,319	11,661	42,167	9·0
1987	86,093	40,650	12,044	42,192	8·5

The annual rates per 1,000 of mean estimated resident population in 1987 were: Births, 15·3; deaths, 7·5; marriages, 7·2.

CONSTITUTION AND GOVERNMENT. Within the State there are three levels of government: The Commonwealth Government, with authority derived from a written constitution; the State Government with residual powers; the local government authorities with powers based upon a State Act of Parliament, operating within incorporated areas extending over almost 90% of the State.

The Constitution of New South Wales is drawn from several diverse sources; certain Imperial statutes such as the Commonwealth of Australia Constitution Act (1900); the Australian States Constitution Act (1907); an element of inherited English law; amendments to the Commonwealth of Australia Constitution Act; the (State) Constitution Act; the Australia Acts of 1986; the Constitution (Amendment) Act 1987 and certain other State Statutes; numerous legal decisions; and a large amount of English and local convention.

The Parliament of New South Wales may legislate for the peace, welfare and good government of the State in all matters not specifically reserved to the Commonwealth Government.

The State Legislature consists of the Sovereign, represented by the Governor, and two Houses of Parliament, the Legislative Council (upper house) and the Legislative Assembly (lower house).

Australian citizens aged 18 and over, and other British subjects who were enrolled prior to 25 Jan. 1984, men and women aged 18 years and over, are entitled to the franchise. Voting is compulsory. The optional preferential method of voting is used for both houses.

The Legislative Council has 45 members elected for a term of office equivalent to three terms of the Legislative Assembly, with 15 members retiring at the same time as the Legislative Assembly elections. The whole State constitutes a single electoral district. In Oct. 1988, the Council consisted of the following parties: Australian Labor Party (ALP), 21; Liberal Party of Australia (Lib), 12; National Party of Australia (NP), 7; Call to Australia Group (CTA), 3; Australian Democrats (AD), 2.

The President of the Legislative Council has an annual salary (1988) of $A77,985; the Leader of the Opposition members, the Chairman of Committees and the Deputy Leader of the Government members (if not a Minister), $A58,771 each; the Deputy Leader of the Opposition members and Government and Opposition Whips, $A54,388 each. The President is paid an annual expense allowance of $A12,977; the Leader of the Opposition members, the Chairman of Committees, the Deputy Leader of the Government members (if not a Minister) and the Deputy Leader of the Opposition members (when a leader of a party), $A7,133 each; the Deputy Leader of the Opposition members (when not a leader of a party) and Government and Opposition Whips, $A2,861 each. Other members who are not Ministers receive an annual salary of $A48,750. All members receive an annual electoral allowance of $A16,180.

The Legislative Assembly has 109 members elected in single seat electoral districts for a maximum period of 4 years. The Legislative Assembly, elected on 19 March 1988, consisted in Oct. 1988 of the following parties: APL, 42; Lib, 39; NP, 20; Independent (Ind), 6; Vacant, 2.

The Speaker of the Legislative Assembly and the Leader of the Opposition members receive a salary of (1988) $A77,985 each; the Chairman of Committees and Deputy Leader of the Opposition members, $A58,771 each; Government and Opposition Whips, $A55,383 each. The Speaker and the Leader of the Opposition members also receive an expense allowance of $A12,977 each; the Chairman of Committees and Deputy Leader of the Opposition members, $A7,133 each; Government and Opposition Whips, and Deputy Leader of the National Party, $A3,367 each. Members who are not Ministers receive an annual salary of $A48,750. All members receive an annual electoral allowance ranging from $A16,180 to $A31,359 according to the location of their constituencies.

Executive power is vested in the Governor, who is appointed by the Crown, and an Executive Council consisting of members of the Cabinet. Ministers receive the following annual salaries (1988): Premier, $A96,946; Deputy Premier, $A87,585; the Leader of the Government members in the Legislative Council, $A88,537; Deputy Leader of Government members in the Legislative Council, $A84,477; other Ministers, $A82,869. Ministers also receive an expense allowance (Premier, $A27,777; Deputy Premier, $A13,888; other Ministers, $A12,977 each). Ministers also receive an electoral allowance ranging from $A16,180 to $A27,221 to members of the Legislative Assembly, according to the location of their electorate; and $A16,180 to each member of the Legislative Council.

Governor: Rear Admiral David James Martin, AO (sworn in 20 Jan. 1989).

The New South Wales Ministry, in Oct. 1988, was as follows:

Premier, Treasurer and Minister for Ethnic Affairs: The Hon. N. F. Greiner, MP.

Deputy Prime Minister, Minister for State Development and Minister for Public Works: The Hon. W. T. J. Murray, MP. *Minister for Health and Minister for the Arts:* The Hon. P. E. J. Collins, MP. *Minister for Agriculture and Rural Affairs:* The Hon. I. M. Armstrong, OBE, MP. *Attorney-General:* The Hon. J. R. A. Dowd, MP. *Minister for Housing:* The Hon. J. J. Schipp, MP. *Minister for the Environment and Assistant Minister for Transport:* The Hon. T. J. Moore, MP. *Chief Secretary and Minister for Tourism:* The Hon. G. B. West, MP. *Minister for Police and Emergency Services and Vice-President of the Executive Council:* The Hon. E. P. Pickering, MLC. *Minister for Sport, Recreation and Racing:* The Hon. R. B. R.

Smith, MLC. *Minister for Family and Community Services:* The Hon. Virginia Chadwick, MLC. *Minister for Education and Youth Affairs:* The Hon. T. A. Metherell, MP. *Minister for Transport:* The Hon. B. G. Baird, MP. *Minister for Administrative Services and Assistant Minister for Transport:* The Hon. Matthew Singleton, MP. *Minister for Business and Consumer Affairs:* The Hon. G. B. P. Peacocke, MP. *Minister for Mineral Resources and Minister for Energy:* The Hon. N. E. W. Pickard, MP. *Minister for Industrial Relations and Employment and Minister Assisting the Premier:* The Hon. J. J. Fahey, MP. *Minister for Natural Resources:* The Hon. I. R. Causley, MP. *Minister for Local Government and Minister for Planning:* The Hon. D. A. Hay, MP. *Minister for Corrective Services:* The Hon. M. R. Yabsley, MP.

Agent-General in London: Norman Brunsdon (66 Strand, WC2N 5LZ).

Local Government. A system of local government extends over most of the State, including the whole of the Eastern and Central land divisions and almost three-quarters of the sparsely populated Western division. At 26 Sept. 1988 there were 65 municipalities, and 110 corporate bodies called shires. A number of the municipalities and shires have combined to form 41 county councils, which administer electricity or water supply undertakings or render other services of common benefit.

ECONOMY

Budget. State Consolidated Fund: Statement of receipts and expenditure (in $A1m.) for financial years ending 30 June:

	1984–85	*1985–86*	*1986–87*	*1987–88*
Receipts: Recurrent	7,348	8,220	10,657	12,379
Capital	654	659	1,508	1,384
Total Receipts	8,002	8,879	12,165	13,763
Expenditure: Recurrent	7,511	8,305	10,634	11,871
Capital	491	573	1,531	1,592
Revenue Equalization	...	...	...	...
Total Expenditure	8,002	8,879	12,165	13,519
Surplus/deficit	—	—	—	245

State Government receipts (in $A1m.) for 1987–88 included receipts from loan raisings, 114; Commonwealth general revenue grant, 4,269; and state taxation, 5,423. Expenditure included capital works and services, 1,592; education, 2,646; health, 3,137; and public debt charges, 750.

Public Debt. The long term debt of the State has three components. Debt outstanding at 30 June 1988 (in $A1m.) for each of these components was:

Debt of statutory bodies under State Government guarantee	18,142·1
Loan liability to the Commonwealth under the 1927 Financial Agreement	5,962·7
Loan liability to the Commonwealth outside the Financial Agreement	3,178·0
Total debt	27,282·8

Since 1983, access to the capital markets for borrowings has been principally through the New South Wales Treasury Corporation which acts as the central borrowing authority of the State.

Banking. There were 27 trading banks operating in New South Wales at 30 June 1988, including the Commonwealth Bank of Australia and the State Bank of New South Wales (Government banks). The trading bank business is transacted chiefly by the Commonwealth Bank of Australia, the State Bank of New South Wales and 3 private banks. At 30 June 1988 the 27 banks operated 1,960 branches and 293 agencies in New South Wales.

The weekly average amount of deposits held in New South Wales by the 27 banks was $A25,778·7m. in June 1988, consisting of $A19,219·1m. bearing interest and $A6,559·6m. not bearing interest. Bank advances, overdrafts, bills discounted, etc., amounted to $A30,669·7m. A statement of other assets and liabilities of the banks in New South Wales is of little significance, as banking business is conducted on an Australia-wide basis.

Savings bank deposits at the end of June 1988 amounted to $A20,155·9m., representing $A3,548 per head of population.

ENERGY AND NATURAL RESOURCES

Minerals. New South Wales contains extensive mineral deposits. The most important minerals mined are: Coal (which accounts for 76% of the value of the State's mineral production); silver–lead–zinc (9%); construction materials (sand, gravel, stone, etc., 10%); and mineral sands (rutile, zircon, etc., 1%). At 30 June 1987, there were 449 mining establishments. The average employment on a whole year basis in the N.S.W. mining industry for 1986–87 was 26,005 persons. During 1986–87, wages and salaries paid were $A982m., and value added was $A2,315m. Mine production of coal and metallic minerals (gross content) is shown below:

	1984–85	*1985–86*	*1986–87*	*1987–88*
Antimony (tonnes)	1,409	1,264	1,202	1,203
Cadmium (tonnes)	1,735	1,216	1,113	...
Coal (1,000 tonnes)	70,034	77,186	88,507	63,945
Cobalt (tonnes)	66	55	55	...
Copper (tonnes)	23,038	26,733	32,400	32,287
Gold (kg)	1,464	1,015	2,227	5,421
Lead (tonnes)	251,595	233,270	206,139	223,435
Silver (kg)	355,827	367,751	408,829	424,362
Sulphur (tonnes)	248,681	253,800	264,631	289,043
Tin (tonnes)	1,306	1,280	249	8
Titanium dioxide (tonnes)	41,283	47,240	58,066	60,178
Zinc (tonnes)	385,075	355,443	362,180	115,175
Zircon (tonnes)	47,113	53,607	50,234	50,000

The value of output in mining and quarrying in 1987–88 was $A3,218m.

Agriculture. The area under cultivation in New South Wales during 3 years (ended 31 March) and the principal crops (in tonnes) produced were as follows (Data relates to farms whose estimated value of agricultural operations was $A20,000 or more at the census):

	1985	*1986*	*1987*
Area of crops (hectares)	5,712,279	5,925,308	5,325,305

		1985		*1986*		*1987*	
Principal crops		*Hectares*	*Production*	*Hectares*	*Production*	*Hectares*	*Production*
Wheat	Grain	3,549,945	5,589,059	3,647,637	5,898,015	3,098,826	4,855,244
	Hay	12,751	36,568	15,112	46,611	19,237	55,456
Barley	Grain	596,023	904,718	538,754	811,780	408,313	613,646
	Hay	1,403	2,435	1,393	3,277	1,801	4,574
Oats	Grain	304,278	393,580	422,249	530,726	482,257	635,185
	Hay	19,101	50,907	25,200	71,008	39,066	111,344
Grain Sorghum		204,031	316,511	159,407	298,380	188,062	391,582
Potatoes		6,415	107,962	5,840	108,085	6,225	121,573
Lucerne (hay)		58,718	279,667	63,731	309,325	71,710	341,859
Rice		117,676	844,515	102,805	701,472	92,281	589,074
Cotton		131,237	534,039	135,820	541,751	125,026	499,356
Oilseeds		200,351	183,851	205,589	206,711	149,760	156,452

In 1986–87, 13,701 hectares of sugar-cane were cut for crushing, the production being 1,276,084 tonnes. The total area under grapes was 11,969 (including 643 not bearing) hectares; the production of table grapes was 8,476 tonnes; of wine, 117,800 tonnes; of dried vine fruits, 9,115 tonnes.

In 1986–87, 4,376 hectares of banana plantations; production from 3,949 hectares, 79,478 tonnes; there were 30,278 hectares of orchard fruit.

At 31 March 1987 the State had 52m. sheep and lambs, 4,868,047 cattle and 829,833 pigs. The production of shorn and crutched wool in 1986–87 was 229·7m. kg (greasy). In the year ended 30 June 1988 production of butter was 1,057 tonnes; cheese, 13,145 tonnes, and bacon and ham, 32,343 tonnes.

Forestry. The estimated area of Crown and private lands is 15m. hectares. The total area of State forests amounts to 3·2m. hectares, and 223,000 hectares have been set apart as timber reserves.

In 1986–87, 3,466,000 cu. metres of timber (excluding firewood) were produced, including 1,214,000 cu. metres of forest hardwoood and 1,323,000 cu. metres of pulpwoods.

INDUSTRY AND TRADE

Industry. Approximately 17% of employed persons in New South Wales are employed in manufacturing industries.

A very wide range of manufacturing activities is undertaken in the Sydney area, and there are large iron and steel works and associated metal fabrication works in operation in proximity to the coalfields at Newcastle and Port Kembla.

The following table shows a summary of manufacturing industries' statistics for 1986–87:

Industry	*Establishments* [1] *No.*	*Employment* [2] *Males (1,000)*	*Females (1,000)*	*Wages and salaries* [3] *($A1m.)*	*Value added ($A1m.)*
Food, beverages and tobacco	959	34·5	16·1	1,111	2,699
Textiles	228	5·8	3·8	197	425
Clothing and footwear	745	5·0	16·1	306	571
Wood, wood products and furniture	1,310	18·7	3·7	404	773
Paper, paper products, printing and publishing	1,224	24·4	12·6	885	1,907
Chemical, petroleum and coal products	377	16·4	7·8	635	1,959
Non-metallic mineral products	599	11·5	1·6	316	741
Basic metal products	186	35·3	2·8	1,026	1,981
Fabricated metal products	1,632	27·7	6·5	715	1,291
Transport equipment	409	27·6	2·6	678	1,081
Other machinery and equipment	1,552	39·1	14·2	1,154	2,268
Miscellaneous manufacturing	835	14·2	7·0	442	875
Total manufacturing	10,026	260·0	94·8	7,869	16,570

[1] Operating at 30 June 1987. Excludes single-establishment manufacturing enterprises with less than 4 persons employed.
[2] Persons employed at 30 June 1987, including working proprietors.
[3] Excludes drawings of working proprietors.

Some of the principal articles manufactured in 1987–88 were:

Article	*Quantity*	*Article*	*Quantity*
Flour (1,000 tonnes)	561	Ready mixed concrete (1,000 cu. metres)	4,729
Footwear (1,000 pairs)	5,881	Clay bricks (1m.) [1]	713
Raw steel (1,000 tonnes)	4,728	Electricity (1m. kwh.) [1]	49,702

[1] Includes the Australian Capital Territory.

During 1986–87 the value of all building jobs commenced in New South Wales was $A5,528m. (of which jobs valued at $A1,359m. were being built for government ownership), jobs completed were valued at $A4,539m. ($A862m. for government ownership), and jobs under construction at the end of the period were valued at $A6,294m. ($A2,406m. for government ownership).

Labour. Two systems of industrial arbitration and conciliation for the adjustment of industrial relations between employers and employees are in operation—the State system which operates within the territorial limits of the State, and the Commonwealth system, which applies to industrial disputes extending beyond State borders.

The industrial tribunals are authorized to fix minimum rates of wages and other conditions of employment. Their awards may be enforced by law, as may be industrial agreements between employers and organizations of employees, when registered.

The principal State tribunal is the Industrial Commission of New South Wales. The Commission is empowered to exercise all the arbitration and conciliation powers conferred on subsidiary tribunals, and has in addition authority to determine any widely defined 'industrial matter', to adjudicate in case of illegal strikes and lockouts, etc., to investigate union ballots when irregularities are alleged and to hear appeals from subsidiary tribunals. Subsidiary tribunals are Conciliation Committees for various industries, each having an equal number representing employers and employees and a Conciliation Commissioner as chairman.

The chief industrial tribunals of the Commonwealth are the Industrial Division of the Federal Court of Australia, composed of judges, and the Australian Conciliation and Arbitration Commission, composed of presidential members, and commissioners.

Trade Unions. Registration of trade unions is effected under the New South Wales Trade Union Act 1881, which follows substantially the Trade Union Acts of 1871 and 1876 of England. Registration confers a quasi-corporate existence with power to hold property, to sue and be sued, etc., and the various classes of employees covered by the union are required to be prescribed by the constitution of the union. For the purpose of bringing an industry under the review of the State industrial tribunals, or participating in proceedings relating to disputes before Commonwealth tribunals, employees and employers must be registered as industrial unions, under State or Commonwealth industrial legislation respectively. At 30 June 1987, there were 186 trade unions with a total membership of 1,205,800. Approximately 59% (estimate) of wage and salary earners were members of trade unions.

Commerce. The external commerce of New South Wales, exclusive of interstate trade, is included in the statement of the commerce of Australia (*see* pp. 109–11). The overseas commerce of New South Wales is given in $A1,000 ending 30 June:

	Imports	*Exports*		*Imports*	*Exports*
1982–83	8,610,870	4,963,957	1985–86	15,130,137	7,329,298
1983–84	10,027,696	5,240,042	1986–87	16,195,265	8,355,713
1984–85	12,707,157	6,717,850	1987–88	18,103,870	10,609,887

The main exports from New South Wales of Australian produce in 1986–87 were coal (18·2%), textile fibres (17·3%), non-ferrous metals (8·2%), meat (5·5%), cereals (4·8%). Principal imports were office machines (12·4%), electrical machinery, apparatus and appliances (5·4%), road vehicles (5%), general industrial machinery (4·6%), telecommunications equipment (4·2%).

Principal destinations of all exports from New South Wales in 1986–87 were Japan (31·3%), EEC countries (12·1%), ASEAN countries (7·4%), USA (7·4%), Hong Kong (7·2%), Republic of Korea (6%), New Zealand (5·9%), Taiwan (4·4%). Major sources of supply were EEC countries (24·1%), USA (23·5%), Japan (18·6%), UK (8·2%), Federal Republic of Germany (6·5%), ASEAN countries (5·4%), New Zealand (4·6%).

COMMUNICATIONS

Roads. At 31 Dec. 1986 there were 195,005 km of roads and streets open for general traffic in New South Wales (excluding unincorporated and Lord Howe Island), comprising 76,355 km bitumen or concrete, 64,363 km gravel, crushed stone or other improved surface, 34,288 km earth formed and 19,999 km natural surface.

The principal bus services in Sydney and Newcastle are operated by the State Government.

The number of registered motor vehicles (excluding tractors and trailers) at 30 June 1988 was 3,064,145, including 1,931,925 cars, 374,710 station wagons, 181,976 utilities, 213,906 panel vans, 203,831 trucks, 54,166 buses and 103,631 motor cycles.

Railways. At 30 June 1987, 9,909 km of government railway were open (618 km electrified). The revenue (including supplements) in 1986–87 was $A1,446m.; the expenditure from revenue, $A1,446m.; the number of passengers carried, 224·2m. and 54·6m. tonnes of freight carried. Also open for traffic are 325 km of Victorian Government railways which extend over the border; 68 km of private railways (mainly in mining districts) and 53 km of Commonwealth Government-owned track.

Aviation. Sydney is the major airport in New South Wales and Australia's principal international air terminal. During the year ended 31 Dec. 1987 scheduled aircraft movements at Sydney totalled 114,632. Passengers totalled 7,006,689 on domestic services and 3,462,604 on international services. Freight handled on domestic and international services was 61,232 tonnes and 153,337 tonnes respectively.

Shipping. Arrivals of vessels engaged in overseas trade in the ports of New South Wales in 1986–87 numbered 2,805 and clearances numbered 2,756. The revenue tonnage of cargo discharged and loaded was 8·6m. and 49·8m. respectively. Sydney Harbour is the principal port of Australia. The number of overseas vessels which entered in 1986–87 was 1,185.

JUSTICE, RELIGION, EDUCATION AND WELFARE

Justice. Legal processes may be conducted in Local Courts presided over by magistrates or in higher courts (District Court or Supreme Court) presided over by judges. There is also an appellate jurisdiction. Persons charged with the more serious crimes must be tried before a higher court.

Children's Courts have been established with the object of removing children as far as possible from the atmosphere of a public court. There are also a number of tribunals exercising special jurisdiction, *e.g.*, the Industrial Commission and the Compensation Court.

At 30 June 1988 there were 4,190 persons (3,961 males; 229 females) in prison custody in New South Wales.

Religion. There is no established church in New South Wales, and freedom of worship is accorded to all.

The following table shows the statistics of the religious denominations in New South Wales at the census in 1986, and of ministers of religion registered for the celebration of marriages in 1987:

Denomination	*Ministers*	*Adherents*	*Denomination*	*Ministers*	*Adherents*
Catholic	1,701	1,529,176	Other Christian	1,496	288,865
Anglican	1,008	1,519,806	Muslim	11	57,551
Uniting Church	603	327,360	Jewish	29	28,236
Presbyterian	228	227,663	Other Non-Christian	38	57,079
Orthodox	66	165,659	Others	...	1,101,409 [1]
Baptist	443	67,187			
Lutheran	38	31,890	Total	5,661	5,401,881

[1] Comprises 539,467 'no religion' and 561,942 'religion not stated' or 'inadequately described' (this is not a compulsory question in the census schedule).

Education. The State Government maintains a system of primary and secondary education, and attendance at school is compulsory from 6 to 15 years of age. In all government schools education is free. Non-government schools are subject to government inspection.

In July 1987 there were 2,210 government schools, comprising 1,666 primary schools, 64 combined primary and secondary schools, 379 secondary schools and 101 special-purpose schools. Total enrolment was 755,084 students, including 433,201 receiving primary instruction and 320,297 receiving secondary instruction. There were 47,323 teachers (including the full-time equivalent of part-time teachers) in 1987.

In July 1987 there were 852 non-government schools with 16,580 teachers (including the full-time equivalent of part-time teachers) and 275,940 students. This included 608 Roman Catholic schools with 12,127 teachers and 213,899 students and 36 Anglican schools with 1,532 teachers and 20,887 students.

The University of Sydney, founded in 1850, had 17,961 students in 1987. There are 7 colleges providing residential facilities at the university. The University of New England at Armidale, previously affiliated with the University of Sydney, was incorporated in 1954, and in 1987 had 9,424 students.

The University of New South Wales was established in 1949. Enrolments in 1987 numbered 17,825. There are 7 colleges providing residential facilities at the university. The University of Newcastle, previously affiliated with the University of New South Wales, was granted autonomy from 1965, and in 1987 had 5,766 students. The University of Wollongong, also previously associated with the University of New South Wales, became autonomous in 1975, and in 1987 had 5,702 students. Macquarie University in Sydney, established in 1964, had 10,883 students in 1987.

Advanced education courses at colleges of advanced education and other institutions provide tertiary training with a vocational emphasis. In 1987 there were 59,643 students enrolled in these courses.

Post-school technical and further education is provided at State technical and further education colleges. Enrolments in 1986 totalled 402,572 (85% being part-time).

State Government expenditure (including capital expenditure and federal grants) on education in 1985–86 was $A3,787m.

Social Welfare. The Commonwealth Government makes provision for social benefits, such as age and invalid pensions, widows' pensions, supporting parents' benefits, family allowances, and unemployment, sickness and special benefits.

The number of age and invalid pensions (including wives' and carers' pensions) current in New South Wales on 30 June 1987 was: Age, 487,855; invalid, 127,552. Expenditure for the year ended 30 June 1987 was $A2,316m. for age pensions and $A651m. for invalid pensions.

In addition there were 53,726 widows' pensions current in New South Wales at 30 June 1987. Expenditure on widows' pensions totalled $A340m. in 1986–87. Supporting parents' benefits at 30 June 1987 numbered 66,379; expenditure in 1986–87 was $A525m.

Under the Family Allowance scheme, which commenced in 1976, payments to families and approved institutions for children under 16 years and full-time students under 18 years (under 25 in special circumstances) during 1986–87 amounted to $A497m. The scheme covered 1,402,413 children and students at 30 June 1987.

Unemployment, sickness and special benefits commenced in 1945. During the year 1986–87 claims totalling $A1,566m. were paid in New South Wales. At 30 June 1988 unemployment benefit was being paid to 181,445 persons, sickness benefits to 33,329 persons and special benefits to 9,379 persons.

Direct State Government social welfare services are limited, for the most part, to the assistance of persons not eligible for Commonwealth Government pensions or benefits and the provision of certain forms of assistance not available from the Commonwealth Government. The State also subsidizes many approved services for needy persons.

Further Reading

Statistical Information: The NSW Government Statistician's Office was established in 1886, and in 1957 was integrated with the Commonwealth Bureau of Census and Statistics (now called the Australian Bureau of Statistics). *Deputy Commonwealth Statistician:* John Wilson. Its principal publications are:

New South Wales Year Book (1886/87–1900/01 under the title *Wealth and Progress of New South Wales*): latest issue, 1988

Regional Statistics: latest issue, 1988

New South Wales Pocket Year Book. Published since 1913; latest issue, 1988

Monthly Summary of Statistics. Published since May 1931

New South Wales in Brief. 1988

New South Wales Dept. of Business and Consumer Affairs, *New South Wales Business Handbook.* Sydney, 1987

New South Wales Department of Environment and Planning, *Sydney Into Its Third Century: Metropolitan Strategy for the Sydney Region.* Sydney, 1988
New South Wales Government Information Service, *New South Wales Government Directory.* 5th ed. Sydney, 1987

State Library: The State Library of NSW, Macquarie St., Sydney. *State Librarian:* Alison Crook, BA (Hons), MBA, Dip Lib, Dip Ed, ALAA, AAIM.

QUEENSLAND

AREA AND POPULATION. Queensland comprises the whole northeastern portion of the Australian continent, including the adjacent islands in the Pacific Ocean and in the Gulf of Carpentaria. Estimated area 1,727,000 sq. km.

The increase in the population as shown by the censuses since 1901 has been as follows:

	Census counts			Intercensal increase	
Year	*Males*	*Females*	*Total*	*Numerical*	*Rate per annum %*
1901	277,003	221,126	498,129	—	—
1911	329,506	276,307	605,813	107,684	1·98
1921	398,969	357,003	755,972	150,159	2·24
1933	497,217	450,317	947,534	191,562	1·86
1947	567,471	538,944	1,106,415	158,881	1·11
1954	676,252	642,007	1,318,259	211,844	2·53
1961	774,579	744,249	1,518,828	200,569	2·04
1966	849,390 [1]	824,934 [1]	1,674,324 [1]	144,857	1·84
1971	921,665 [1]	905,400 [1]	1,827,065 [1]	152,741 [1]	1·76 [1]
1976	1,024,611 [1]	1,012,586 [1]	2,037,197 [1]	210,132 [1]	2·20 [1]
1981	1,153,404 [1]	1,141,719 [1]	2,295,123 [1]	257,926 [1]	2·41 [1]
1986	1,295,630 [1]	1,291,685 [1]	2,587,315 [1]	292,192 [1]	2·43 [1]

[1] Including Aboriginals.

Since the 1981 census, official population estimates are according to place of usual residence and are referred to as estimated resident population. Estimated resident population at 30 June 1989, 2,830,198.

Statistics on birthplaces from the 1986 census are as follows: Australia, 2,162,995 (83·6%); UK and Ireland, 158,949 (6·1%); other countries, 229,760 (8·9%); at sea and not stated, 35,611 (1·4%).

Vital statistics (including Aboriginals) for calendar years:

	Total births	*Marriages*	*Divorces*	*Deaths*
1986	40,371	18,030	7,042	17,861
1987	39,365	18,265	6,918	18,861
1988	40,561	18,850	7,690	18,803

The annual rates per 1,000 population in 1988 were: Marriages, 6·9; births, 14·8; deaths, 6·9. The infant death rate was 8·4 per 1,000 births.

Brisbane, the capital, had at 30 June 1988 (estimate) a resident population of 1,240,286 (Statistical Division). The resident populations of the other major centres (Statistical Districts) at the same date were: Gold Coast-Tweed, 207,966; Townsville, 109,699; Sunshine Coast, 95,683; Toowoomba, 79,934; Cairns, 76,475; Rockhampton, 61,124; Mackay, 50,301; Bundaberg, 43,837 and Gladstone, 30,623. Other cities included Mount Isa, 24,104; Maryborough, 22,986; Hervey Bay, 21,151.

CONSTITUTION AND GOVERNMENT. Queensland, formerly a portion of New South Wales, was formed into a separate colony in 1859, and responsible government was conferred. The power of making laws and imposing taxes is vested in a Parliament of one House—the Legislative Assembly, which comprises 89 members, returned from 4 electoral zones for 3 years, elected for single-member constituencies at compulsory ballot. Members are entitled to $A54,500 per annum, with individual electorate allowances for travelling, postage, etc., of from $A21,525 to $A43,884.

At the general election of 1 Nov. 1986 there were 1,563,294 persons registered as qualified to vote under the Elections Act 1983. This Act provides franchise for all males and females, 18 years of age and over, qualified by 6 months' residence in Australia and 3 months in the electoral district.

The Legislative Assembly, following the elections of 2 Dec. 1989 (according to preliminary figures), was composed of the following parties: Australian Labor Pary, 51; National Party, 29; Liberals, 3. Six seats were undecided.

State elections were held on 2 Dec. 1989 and the National Party failed to win a majority. The party had been in power since 1957. The election was won by the Australian Labor Party. The election was dominated by local issues in which the National Party were accused of widespread patronage and deliberate manipulation of electoral boundaries.

Governor of Queensland: Sir Walter Benjamin Campbell, QC (assumed office 22 July 1985).

Premier: Wayne Goss (sworn in on 7 Dec. 1989).

Ministers have a salary of $A88,229, the Premier receives $A111,524, the Deputy Premier, $A95,941, and the Leader of the Opposition, $A79,666.

Agent-General in London: Hon. D. T. McVeigh (392–3 Strand, WC2R 0LZ).

Local Government. Provision is made for local government by the subdivision of the State into cities, towns and shires. These are under the management of aldermen or councillors, who are elected by all persons 18 years and over. Local Authorities are charged with the control of all matters of a parochial nature, such as sewerage, cleansing and sanitary services, health services, domestic water supplies, and roads and bridges within their allotted areas. In addition to Government grants and subsidies, Local Authority revenue is derived from general rates, paid by landowners on the unimproved capital value of land, and by charging for some specific services.

For the year ended 30 June 1988, the receipts and expenditure (including loans) for the 134 Local Authorities were $A2,047·6m. and $A2,018·6m. respectively and their rateable values amounted to $A27,601·2m.

ECONOMY

Budget. Revenue and expenditure of the Consolidated Revenue Fund of Queensland during 5 years ending 30 June (in $A1,000):

	1983–84	*1984–85*	*1985–86*	*1986–87*	*1987–88*
Revenue	4,212,842	4,681,674	5,190,941	5,649,027	6,308,439
Expenditure	4,211,919	4,682,431	5,190,727	5,648,701	6,270,305

Total receipts of the Queensland Government Authorities in 1987–88 were $A8,116·2m., of which Taxation and Federal Government grants amounted to $A5,896·8m. Expenditure from these funds included: Education, $A1,959·9m.; fuel and energy, $A441m.; transport and communications, $A942·1m.; health, $A1,080m.

Revenue and expenditure of Commonwealth Government departments on account of Queensland are not included.

Debt. The public debt of the State at 30 June 1989 was $A2,420·3m.

Banking. The major national trading and savings banks dominate banking operations in Queensland. The Bank of Queensland, which is a privately owned bank with its head office in Queensland, and several licensed foreign banks also provide trading and savings bank facilities. In June 1989 the average of weekly deposits held in trading banks in Queensland amounted to $A10,197m. while the average of advances owing to the banks was $A9,321m. The total depositors' balances held in savings banks in Queensland at 30 June 1989 was $A9,687m.

ENERGY AND NATURAL RESOURCES

Electricity. During 1988–89, 96·7% of the State's generation of 23,774m. kwh was derived from coal-fuelled steam power stations. The hydro-electric stations located in north Queensland provided 3·2% of the State's electricity needs with the remainder being produced by gas turbine and internal combustion generation using light fuel oil and natural gas.

Minerals. Principal minerals produced during 1987–88 were: Copper, 158,000 tonnes; coal, 65,189,000 tonnes; lead, 202,000 tonnes; zinc, 242,000 tonnes; silver, 525,000 kg; tin, 386 tonnes; gold, 19,000 kg; bauxite, 8,449,000 tonnes; mineral sands concentrates, 464,000 tonnes; nickel, 29,000 tonnes; liquid petroleum, 1,685,000 kilolitres. Value of output, at the mine, was $A4,107m. The chief mines are at Mount Isa (copper, silver, lead, zinc), Weipa (bauxite), Kidston, Mount Leyshon, Mount Morgan, Red Dame, Pajingo and Cracow (gold), Moreton and Bowen Basin (coal), Greenvale (nickel), Cooper-Eromanga Basin (petroleum) and North Stradbroke Island (mineral sands).

Land Settlement. At 30 June 1989, of the 172·7m. hectares of the State, 121·5m. hectares was Crown leasehold, 20·5m. hectares was in process of freeholding and the remaining 30·7m. hectares was roads, reserves, freehold, mining tenures and vacant land.

In the western portion of the State water is comparatively easily found by sinking artesian bores. At 30 June 1988, 3,700 such bores had been drilled, of which 2,595 were flowing.

Agriculture. Livestock on farms and stations at 31 March 1988 numbered 8·83m. cattle, 14·37m. sheep and 617,000 pigs. The wool production (greasy) was, in 1987–88, 78m. kg, valued at $A477m. The total area under crops during 1987–88 was 2·9m. hectares.

	Area (hectares)		*Production (tonnes)*	
Crop	*1986–87*	*1987–88*	*1986–87*	*1987–88*
Sugar-cane, crushed	286,967	291,169	23,466,026	23,199,753
Wheat	794,582	646,140	833,138	718,395
Maize	38,348	36,930	118,017	124,209
Sorghum	624,902	565,174	1,018,807	1,213,117
Barley	167,917	169,427	275,855	244,173
Oats	20,315	19,486	18,793	13,566
Potatoes	6,335	6,617	132,729	120,048
Pumpkins	3,602	3,538	33,122	33,071
Tomatoes	3,570	3,424	78,778	81,411
Peanuts	32,843	31,137	44,470	35,651
Tobacco	2,942	2,816	7,572	7,105
Apples [1]	2,804	2,669	36,591	33,640
Grapes [2]	1,059	982	4,191	4,190
Citrus [1]	1,689	1,546	46,507	46,651
Bananas [2]	3,408	3,505	64,298	79,183
Pineapples [2]	3,758	3,764	142,288	146,463
Green fodder [3]	580,203	582,100	...	...
Hay (all kinds)	51,643	62,722	228,583	258,026
Cotton (raw)	30,996	80,918	40,248	72,099

[1] Area of trees 6 years and over. [2] Bearing area only.
[3] Excluding lucerne and other pastures.

Forestry. A considerable area consists of natural forest, eucalyptus, pine and cabinet woods being the timbers mostly in evidence; a large quantity of ornamental woods is utilized by cabinet makers. The amount of timber processed, including plantation and imported, in 1988–89 was (in cu. metres): Conifers, 947,768; hardwoods, structural timbers and cabinet woods, 620,760.

INDUSTRY AND TRADE

Industry. In 1987–88, there were 4,624 establishments, with four or more workers, employing 97,335 males and 30,209 females, and producing goods and services worth $A17,255m. The manufacturing establishments contributing most to the overall production during 1987–88 were those predominantly engaged in the processing of food, beverages and tobacco.

The gross value of Queensland agricultural commodity production (in $A1,000) during 1987–88, amounted to 3,935,009, which included crops, 1,824,024; livestock disposals, 1,405,716; livestock products, 705,270.

Labour. In 1989 the labour force comprised 1·4m. persons, 63% of the 2·2m. civilian population aged 15 years and older, and the unemployment rate was 6·6%. Major industries employing people were wholesale and retail trade (22%), community services (16%) and manufacturing (13%).

Trade Unions. Unions both of employees and employers must be registered with the State or Australian Commission. There were 130 trade unions operating at June 1988 with 435,400 members (about 50% of total employees).

Commerce. The overseas commerce of Queensland is included in the statement of the commerce of Australia (*see* pp. 108–10).

Total value of the direct overseas imports and exports of Queensland (in $A1,000) f.o.b. port of shipment for both imports and exports:

	1983–84	*1984–85*	*1985–86*	*1986–87*	*1987–88*	*1988–89*
Imports	2,114,900	2,315,492	2,649,953	2,503,854	2,844,208	3,788,296
Exports	5,559,161 [1]	6,602,936 [1]	7,737,046 [1]	7,928,406 [1]	8,289,659 [1]	9,083,994 [1]

[1] State of origin.

In 1988–89 interstate exports totalled $A3,532·7m. and imports $A8,317·8m. The chief exports overseas are minerals including alumina, coal, meat (preserved or frozen), sugar, wool, cereal grains, copper and lead, and manufactured goods. Principal overseas imports are machinery, motor vehicles, mineral fuels (including lubricants, etc.), chemicals and manufactured goods classified by material. Chief sources of imports in 1988–89 were Japan ($A961·1m.), USA ($A912·9m.), UK ($A157·9m.), EEC, excluding UK ($A362·4m.); exports went chiefly to Japan ($A3,371·6m.), USA ($A730·7m.), UK ($A556·8m.), EEC, excluding UK ($A875·1m.).

COMMUNICATIONS

Roads. At 30 June 1988 there were 169,589 km of roads; of these, 152,952 km were formed roads, of which 56,700 km were surfaced with sealed pavement.

At 30 June 1988 motor vehicles registered in Queensland totalled 1,616,201, comprising 1,159,196 cars and station wagons, 220,652 utilities, 86,918 panel vans, 9,998 buses, 71,756 trucks and 67,681 motor cycles.

Railways. Practically all the railways are owned by the State Government. Total length of line at 30 June 1989 was 10,089 km, of which 2,460 km electrified. In 1988–89, 49m. passengers and 81m. tonnes of goods and livestock were carried.

Aviation. Queensland is well served with a network of air services, with overseas and interstate connexions. Subsidiary companies provide planes for taxi and charter work, and the Flying Doctor Service operates throughout western Queensland.

Shipping. In 1987–88, cargo discharged was 2·6m. GWT and cargo loaded was 70·8m. GWT.

Broadcasting. At 30 June 1988, 113 broadcasting and 98 television and translator stations were in operation throughout Queensland.

JUSTICE, RELIGION, EDUCATION AND WELFARE

Justice. Justice is administered by Higher Courts (Supreme and District), Magistrates' Courts and Children's Courts. The Supreme Court comprises a Chief Justice, a senior puisne judge, 18 puisne judges and 2 masters; the District Courts, 24 district court judges of whom 1 is chairman. Stipendiary magistrates preside over the Magistrates' and Children's Courts, except in the smaller centres, where justices of the peace officiate. A parole board may recommend prisoners for release.

The total number of appearances resulting in conviction as the most serious outcome in the Higher Courts in 1987–88 was 2,817; summary convictions in Magistrates' Courts totalled 131,721 and proven offences in Children's Courts numbered 4,728. There were, at 30 June 1988, 5 prisons, 2 prison farms conducted on the honour system and 1 prison for criminally-insane patients, with 2,304 male and 114 female prisoners. The total police force was 5,322 at 30 June 1988.

Religion. There is no State Church. Membership, census 1986: Anglican, 640,867; Catholic, 628,906; Uniting Church, 255,287; Presbyterian, 120,239; Lutheran, 56,910; Baptist, 39,099; other Christian, 211,316; Buddhist, 5,769; Muslim, 3,731; Hebrew, 2,631; all others (including not stated and no religion), 622,560.

Education. Education in Queensland ranges from pre-school level through to tertiary level. In addition, child care, kindergarten and adult education facilities are available. Education is compulsory between the ages of 6 and 15 years and is provided free in government schools. Expenditure on education by State and local government authorities for 1986–87 was $A1,954·6m.

At July 1988, pre-school education and child care was provided at 1,397 centres with 4,803 staff and 80,381 children.

Primary and secondary education comprises 12 years of full-time formal schooling and is provided by both the government and non-government sectors. At July 1988, the State administered 1,002 primary, 69 primary/secondary, and 168 secondary schools with 233,312 primary students and 143,011 secondary students. In addition, 76 special schools provided educational programmes for 3,997 children. State education programmes were provided by 24,113 teachers. Non-government enrolments at July 1988 were 60,989 primary students and 61,702 secondary students at 239 primary, 64 primary/secondary and 87 secondary schools. Educational programmes were provided at 4 non-government special schools for 69 children. Educational programmes at non-government schools were provided by 7,921 teachers.

Post-secondary education in Queensland involves technical and further education, advanced education and university education. In 1987, enrolments in TAFE courses totalled 179,423. At 30 April 1988, 34,976 students were enrolled in advanced education courses and 27,816 students were enrolled in university courses.

Social Welfare. Public hospitals are maintained by State and Federal Government endowment, supplemented by fees from patients not in standard wards. Welfare institutions providing shelter and social care for the aged, the handicapped, and children, are maintained or assisted by the State. A child health service is provided throughout the State. Age, invalid, widows', disability and war service pensions, family allowances, and unemployment and sickness benefits are paid by the Federal Government. Age pensioners in the State at 30 June 1988 numbered 210,818; invalid pensioners, 44,313; disability and service pensioners, 144,784 (including dependants).

There were 22,744 widows' pensions current at 30 June 1988, and at the same date family allowances were being paid to 336,796 families in respect of 663,731 children under 16 years and eligible students aged 16 to 24 years. In addition, family allowances were paid to 2,907 children and students in institutions.

Further Reading

Statistical Information: The Statistical Office (313 Adelaide St., Brisbane) was set up in 1859. *Deputy Commonwealth Statistician:* J. K. Cornish. *A Queensland Official Year Book* was issued in 1901, the annual *ABC of Queensland Statistics* from 1905 to 1936 with exception of 1918 and 1922. Present publications include: *Queensland Year Book.* Annual, from 1937 (omitting 1942, 1943, 1944, 1987).—*Queensland Pocket Year Book.* Annual from 1950.—*Monthly Summary of Queensland Statistics.* From Jan. 1961

Australian Sugar Year Book. Brisbane, from 1941
Endean, R., *Australia's Great Barrier Reef.* Brisbane, 1982
Johnston, W. R., *A Bibliography of Queensland History.* Brisbane, 1981.—*The Call of the Land: A History of Queensland to the Present Day.* Brisbane, 1982
Johnston, W. R. and Zerner, M., *Guide to the History of Queensland.* Brisbane, 1985
Queensland State Public Relations Bureau, *Queensland Resources Atlas,* Brisbane, 1980
Queensland Department of Commercial and Industrial Development, *Resources and Industry of Far North Queensland,* Brisbane, 1980

State Library: The State Library of Queensland, Queensland Cultural Centre, South Bank, South Brisbane. *State Librarian:* D. H. Stephens.

SOUTH AUSTRALIA

AREA AND POPULATION. The total area of South Australia is 380,070 sq. miles (984,377 sq. km). The settled part is divided into counties and hundreds. There are 49 counties proclaimed, covering 23m. hectares, of which 19m. hectares are occupied. Outside this area there are extensive pastoral districts, covering 76m. hectares, 43m. of which are under pastoral leases.

Census population (exclusive of full-blood Aboriginals before 1966):

	Males	*Females*	*Total*		*Males*	*Females*	*Total*
1901	180,485	177,861	358,346	1966	550,196	544,788	1,094,984
1911	207,358	201,200	408,558	1971	586,051	587,656	1,173,707
1921	248,267	246,893	495,160	1976	620,162	624,594	1,244,756
1933	290,962	289,987	580,949	1981	635,696	649,337	1,285,033
1947	320,031	326,042	646,073	1986	665,960	679,985	1,345,945
1961	490,225	479,115	969,340				

The number of Aboriginals and Torres Strait Islanders (as reported on Census schedules) in the State at the Census of 30 June 1986 was 14,291.

Vital statistics for calendar years:

	Live Births	*Marriages*	*Divorces*	*Deaths*
1985	19,790	10,148	4,216	10,496
1986	19,741	9,878	3,776	10,328
1987	19,235	9,695	4,050	10,565
1988	19,155	10,128	4,031	10,690

The infant mortality rate in 1988 was 7·94 per 1,000 live births.

The Adelaide Statistical Division had 1,023,517 inhabitants at 30 June 1988 in 22 cities and 8 municipalities and other districts. Cities outside this area (with populations at 30 June 1988) are Whyalla (27,317), Mount Gambier (22,031), Port Augusta (16,006), Port Pirie (15,182) and Port Lincoln (12,909).

CONSTITUTION AND GOVERNMENT. South Australia was formed into a British province by letters patent of Feb. 1836, and a partially elective Legislative Council was established in 1851. The present Constitution bears date 24 Oct. 1856. It vests the legislative power in an elected Parliament, consisting of a Legislative Council and a House of Assembly. The former is composed of 22 members. Every 4 years half the members retire, and the resulting vacancies are filled at a general election on the basis of proportional representation with the State as one multi-member electorate. The qualifications of an elector are, to be an Australian citizen, or a British subject who on 25 Jan. 1984 was enrolled on a Commonwealth electoral roll and/or at some time between 26 Oct. 1983 and 25 Jan. 1984 inclusive was enrolled on an electoral roll for a South Australian Assembly district or a Commonwealth electoral roll in any State. The person must be of at least 18 years of age and have lived continuously in Australia for at least 6 months, in South Australia for at least 3 months and in the sub-division for which he is enrolled at least 1 month. War service may substitute for residential qualifications in some cases. By the Constitution Act Amendment Act, 1894, the franchise was extended to women, who voted for the first time at the general election of 25 April 1896. The qualifications for election as a member of both Houses are the same as for an elector. Certain persons are ineligible for election to either House.

The House of Assembly consists of 47 members elected for 4 years, representing single electorates. Election of members of both Houses takes place by preferential secret ballot. Voting is compulsory for those on the Electoral Roll.

The House of Assembly, elected on 25 Nov. 1989, consists (preliminary figures) of the following members: Liberal Party of Australia, 22; Australian Labor Party, 22;; Independent Labor, 2. The Legislative Council consists of 9 Liberal Party of Australia, 11 Labor and 2 Australian Democrat members.

Each member of Parliament receives $A48,803 per annum with allowances of $A12,335–39,095 according to location of electorate, a free pass over government railways and superannuation rights. Electors enrolled (May 1989) numbered 957,339.

The executive power is vested in a Governor appointed by the Crown and an Executive Council, consisting of the Governor and the Ministers of the Crown. The Governor has the power to dissolve the House of Assembly but not the Legislative Council unless that Chamber has twice consecutively with an election intervening defeated the same or substantially the same Bill passed in the House of Assembly by an absolute majority.

Governor: Lieut.-Gen. Sir Donald Dunstan, KBE, CB.

The South Australian Labor Ministry, in April 1989 was as follows:

Premier and Treasurer: John Charles Bannon, MP.

Deputy Premier, Minister of Health, Minister of Community Welfare and Minister for the Aged: Donald Jack Hopgood, MP. *Attorney-General, Minister of Consumer Affairs and Minister of Corporate Affairs:* Christopher John Sumner, MLC. *Minister of State Development and Technology, Minister of Agriculture, Minister of Fisheries and Minister of Ethnic Affairs:* Lynn Maurice Ferguson Arnold, MP. *Minister of Education and Minister of Children's Services:* Gregory John Crafter, MP. *Minister of Housing and Construction, Minister of Public Works and Minister of Aboriginal Affairs:* Terence Henry Hemmings, MP. *Minister of Transport, Minister of Correctional Services and Minister Assisting the Treasurer:* Frank Trevor Blevins, MP. *Minister of Tourism and Minister of State Services:* Barbara Jean Wiese, MLC. *Minister of Employment and Further Education, Minister of Youth Affairs and Minister of Recreation and Sport:* Milton Kym Mayes, MP. *Minister of Environment and Planning, Minister of Water Resources, Minister of Lands and Minister of Repatriation:* Susan Mary Lenehan, MP. *Minister of Emergency Services, Minister of Mines and Energy and Minister of Forests:* John Heinz Cornelis Klunder, MP. *Minister of Labour, Minister of Marine and Chief Secretary:* Robert John Gregory, MP. *Minister of Local Government and Minister for the Arts:* Judith Anne Winstanley Levy, MLC.

Ministers are jointly and individually responsible to the legislature for all their official acts, as in the UK.

Agent-General in London: G. Walls (50 Strand, WC2N 5LW).

Local Government. The closely settled part of the State (mainly near the sea-coast and the River Murray) is incorporated into local government areas, and sub-divided into district councils (rural areas only), municipal corporations (mainly metropolitan, but including larger country towns) and cities (more densely populated areas with a qualification of 15,000 residents in the Adelaide metropolitan area, and 10,000 in the country). The main functions of councils are the construction and maintenance of roads and bridges, sport and recreational facilities and garbage collection and disposal.

The number and area of the sub-divisions, together with expenditure (in $A1,000) for the year ended 30 June 1988, were:

	No.	*Area (1,000 hectares)*	*Roads and bridges*	*Recreation and culture*	*All other*	*Total expenditure*
Adelaide statistical division	30	189·3	60,904	65,953	225,551	352,408
Other municipal corporations and district councils	92	15,223·3	51,289	24,237	102,199	177,725
Total	122	15,412·6	112,193	90,190	327,750	530,133

ECONOMY

Budget. Recurrent revenue and expenditure (in $A1,000) for years ended 30 June:

	1984	*1985*	*1986*	*1987*	*1988*	*1989*
Revenue	2,160,679	2,639,937	2,966,345	3,217,176	4,225,669	4,123,056
Expenditure	2,190,399	2,626,240	2,955,350	3,214,926	4,215,265	4,206,418

Banking. In June 1989 the average weekly balance of deposits held by all trading banks was $A5,728m. The average weekly balance of loans, advances and bills discounted was $A6,536m.

The savings banks on 30 June 1989 had deposits amounting to $A3,594m.

NATURAL RESOURCES

Minerals. The value of minerals produced in 1987–88 was $A949·7m. The principal minerals produced are opals, natural gas, iron ore, copper, gypsum, salt, talc, clays, limestone, dolomite and sub-bituminous coal.

Agriculture. Of the total area of South Australia (984,377 sq. km), 259,649 sq. km were alienated, 490,668 sq. km were held under lease and 234,059 sq. km were unoccupied. Area used for agricultural purposes, at 31 March 1988, was 603,975 sq. km.

Soil Conservation. Under the direction of special officers in the Department of Agriculture, determined efforts are made to deal with the problems of erosion and soil conservation. Included in the programme are the planting of cereal rye, perennial rye and other grasses to check sand drifts; contour-furrowing and contour banking; contour planting with vines and fruit trees and several water-diversion schemes.

Irrigation. For the year ended 31 March 1987, 91,765 hectares were under irrigated culture, being used as follows: Vineyards, 16,418; orchards, 11,865; vegetables, 6,244, and other crops and pasture, 57,238. Most of these areas are along the river Murray.

Gross value of agricultural production (in $A1,000), 1987–88: Crops, 963,763; livestock slaughtering, 395,508; livestock products, 690,570. Total gross value, 2,049,841; local value (*i.e.* less marketing costs), 1,848,398.

	1986–87		*1987–88*	
Chief crops	*Hectares*	*Tonnes*	*Hectares*	*Tonnes*
Wheat	1,669,341	2,261,805	1,570,094	1,819,872
Barley	970,865	1,616,570	887,917	1,277,234
Oats	117,287	151,895	134,149	137,022
Hay	209,087	678,382	189,655	539,846
Vines	...	196,941,000 [1]	...	212,486,000 [1]

[1] Litres of wine.

Fruit culture is extensively carried on, and in 1987–88, 282,113 tonnes of fresh fruit were produced. Other products, in addition to all kinds of root crops and vegetables, are grass seeds and oil seeds. Livestock, March 1988: 997,737 cattle, 17,718,547 sheep and 445,432 pigs. In 1987–88, 122,420 tonnes of wool and 377m. litres of milk were produced.

INDUSTRY AND TRADE

Industry. The preliminary turnover for manufacturing industries for 1987–88 was $A11,085m.

Industry sub-division	*Establishments (No.)*	*Persons employed (No.)*	*Wages and salaries ($A1m.)*	*Turnover ($A1m.)*
Food, beverages and tobacco	387	15,816	312	2,157
Textiles	45	2,659	52	407
Clothing and footwear	95	4,118	66	241
Wood, wood products and furniture	377	7,147	129	599
Paper, paper products, printing and publishing	231	7,566	170	732
Chemical, petroleum and coal products	47	2,356	57	447
Non-metallic mineral products	150	3,542	87	476
Basic metal products	48	6,736	178	1,168
Fabricated metal products	404	8,268	156	709
Transport equipment	138	15,735	367	2,260
Other machinery and equipment	358	13,625	272	1,131
Miscellaneous manufacturing	225	7,600	158	757
Total	2,505	95,168	2,003	11,085

Practically all forms of secondary industry are to be found, the most important being, motor vehicle manufacture, saw-milling and the manufacture of household appliances, basic iron and steel, meat and meat products, and wine and brandy.

Labour. Two systems of industrial arbitration and conciliation for the adjustment of industrial relations between employers and employees are in operation—the State system, which operates when industrial disputes are confined to the territorial limits of the State, and the Federal system, which applies when disputes involve other parts of Australia as well as South Australia.

The industrial tribunals are authorized to fix minimum rates of wages and other conditions of employment, and their awards may be enforced by law. Industrial agreements between employers and organizations of employees, when registered, may be enforced in the same manner as awards. In March 1989 the minimum wage under State awards was $A204.10.

Commerce. The commerce of South Australia, exclusive of inter-state trade, is comprised in the statement of the commerce of Australia given under the heading of the Commonwealth, *see* pp. 108–10.

Overseas imports and exports in $A1m. (year ending 30 June):

	1984–85	*1985–86*	*1986–87*	*1987–88*	*1988–89*
Imports	1,603·2	1,737·5	1,503·4	1,804·6	1,861·4
Exports	1,921·4	1,987·3	2,044·2	2,263·3	2,441·3

Principal exports in 1988–89 were (in $A1m.): Wool, 394·8; wheat, 274·1; petroleum and petroleum products, 187·7; meat and meat preparations, 179·6; barley, 130·2; fish and crustaceans, 93·7.

Principal imports in 1988–89 were (in $A1m.): Transport equipment, 429·9; machinery, 404·6; petroleum and petroleum products, 169·3.

In 1988–89 the leading suppliers of imports were (in $A1m.): Japan (570), USA (320·9), Saudi Arabia (101·2), Federal Republic of Germany (92·5); main exports went to Japan (384·1), New Zealand (227·8), USA (171·5), USSR (136·9), Iran (110·5), Singapore (109·4).

Tourism. In June 1989 there were 350 hotels and motels with 9,396 rooms; 197 caravan parks had a total of 22,598 sites.

COMMUNICATIONS

Roads. At 30 June 1988, of the roads customarily used by the public, there were 2,462 km of national roads, 9,987 km of arterial roads and 83,530 km of local roads, totalling 95,979 km. Lengths of road classified by surface were as follows: Sealed,

23,474 km; unsealed, 72,505 km. Costs of construction and maintenance are shared by the State and Commonwealth governments and by the councils of the local areas. Motor vehicles registered at 30 June 1989 included 561,144 cars, 116,671 station wagons, 149,045 commercial vehicles and 29,599 cycles.

Railways. At 30 June 1988, Australian National Railways operated 6,345 km of railway in country areas. The State Transport Authority operated 127 km of railway in the metropolitan area of Adelaide, which carried 8·7m. passengers in 1987-88. All public freight and non-metropolitan passenger services are operated by Australian National.

Aviation. For the year ended 30 June 1988 there were 1,976,613 passengers and 22,715 tonnes of freight handled by 18,387 aircraft movements at Adelaide, South Australia's principal airport (excluding Adelaide International). On 30 June 1988 there were 7 government and 29 licensed aerodromes.

Shipping. There are several good harbours, of which Port Adelaide is the principal one. In 1986–87, 800 vessels conducting overseas trade entered South Australia with 1,839,000 import tonnes of cargo and left with 6,294,000 export tonnes.

Post and Broadcasting. At 30 June 1988, there were 533 post offices. Telephone services connected totalled 661,661 on 30 June 1988. There were 43 radio and 31 television stations at 30 June 1988.

JUSTICE, RELIGION, EDUCATION AND WELFARE

Justice. There is a Supreme Court, which incorporates admiralty, civil, criminal, land and valuation, and testamentary jurisdiction; district criminal courts, which have jurisdiction in many indictable offences; local courts and courts of summary jurisdiction. Circuit courts are held at several places. In the year ended 31 Dec. 1987, 3,096 criminal matters were proven in higher courts. During the year 1987 there were 1,353 sequestrations and schemes under the Bankruptcy Act. There were 3,039 prisoners received under sentence in 1987 with a daily average prison population of 632.

Religion. At the Census of 1986 the religious distribution of the population (as reported on Census schedules) was as follows: Catholic, 267,137; Anglican, 242,722; Uniting Church, 176,980; Lutheran, 64,851; Orthodox, 37,149; Baptist, 21,415; Presbyterian, 18,566; other Christians, 108,048; non-Christian, 13,843; indefinite, 5,458; no religion, 227,564; not stated, 162,212.

Education. Education is secular and is compulsory for children 6–15 years of age. Primary and secondary education at government schools is free. In 1988 there were 715 government schools, comprising 520 primary, 67 primary and secondary, 101 secondary schools and 26 special schools. There were 184,766 full-time students. The Department of Technical and Further Education is responsible for technical, adult and vocational education. In 1988 there were 21 colleges of technical and further education, among the facilities are an adult migrant education service, a further education, a centre for performing arts and schools of music, maritime and external studies. Tertiary education, including teacher education, is provided by the 2 universities and 3 colleges of advanced education. There were 178 non-government schools and colleges, most of which are associated with religious denominations (55,245 students). In 1988 there were 417 pre-school centres with an enrolment of 24,680 pre-school children.

Social Welfare. Age, invalidity, war, unemployment, etc., pensions are paid by the Commonwealth Government. The number of pensioners in South Australia at 30 June 1988 was: Disability and service, 74,184; age, 136,662; invalid, 31,183; unemployment, 50,619. There are schemes for family allowances, widows, supporting parents and sickness and hospital and pharmaceutical benefits.

Further Reading

Statistical Information: The State branch of the Australian Bureau of Statistics is at 41 Currie St., Adelaide (GPO Box 2272). *Deputy Commonwealth Statistician:* R. J. Rogers. Although the first printed statistical publication was the *Statistics of South Australia, 1854* with the title altered to *Statistical Register* in 1859, there is a written volume for each year back to 1838. These contain simple records of trade, demography, production, etc. and were prepared only for the use of the Colonial Office; one copy was retained in the State.

The publications of the State branch include the *South Australian Year Book*, the *Pocket Year Book of South Australia* and a *Monthly Summary of Statistics*, a quarterly bulletin of building activity, a quarterly bulletin of tourist accommodation and approximately 40 special bulletins issued each year as particulars of various sections of statistics become available.

South Australia: Premier's Department, Adelaide, 1980
Douglas, J., *South Australia from Space.* Adelaide, 1980
Finlayson, H. H., *The Red Centre: Man and Beast in the Heart of Australia.* 2nd ed. Sydney, 1952
Gibbs, R. M., *A History of South Australia: From Colonial Days to the Present.* Adelaide, 1984
Whitelock, D., *Adelaide, 1836–1976: A History of Difference.* Univ. of Queensland Press, 1977

State Library: The State Library of S.A., North Terrace, Adelaide. *State Librarian:* E. M. Miller, MA (Hons), Dip. NZLS, ANZLA, ALAA.

TASMANIA

HISTORY. Abel Janzoon Tasman discovered Van Diemen's Land (Tasmania) on 24 Nov. 1642. The island became a British settlement in 1803 as a dependency of New South Wales; in 1825 its connexion with New South Wales was terminated; in 1851 a partially elective Legislative Council was established, and in 1856 responsible government came into operation. On 1 Jan. 1901 Tasmania was federated with the other Australian states into the Commonwealth of Australia.

AREA AND POPULATION. Tasmania is an island separated from the mainland by the Bass Strait with an area (including islands) of 68,331 sq. km, or 6·83m. hectares, of which 6,441,000 hectares form the area of the main island. The population at 10 consecutive censuses was:

	Population	Increase % per annum		Population	Increase % per annum
1921	213,780	1·12	1966	371,436	1·18
1933	227,599	0·52	1971	398,100 [1]	0·99
1947	257,078	0·87	1976	412,300 [1]	0·70 [2]
1954	308,752	2·65	1981	427,200 [1]	0·72 [2]
1961	350,340	1·82	1986	436,353	...

[1] Resident population. [2] Not comparable with previous censuses.

At the census of 30 June 1986, 5·32% were born in the UK and Ireland, 2·68% in other European countries and 88·61% in Australia. The last full-blooded Tasmanian Aboriginal died in 1876.

Vital statistics for calendar years:

	Marriages	Divorces	Births	Deaths
1986	3,302	1,245	6,950	3,454
1987	3,141	1,115	6,753	3,596
1988	3,034	1,220	6,771	3,529

The largest cities and towns (with populations at the 1986 Census) are Hobart (175,082), Launceston (88,486), Devonport (1981, 21,424) and Burnie (20,585).

CONSTITUTION AND GOVERNMENT. Parliament consists of the Governor, the Legislative Council and the House of Assembly. The Council has 19 members, elected by adults with 6 months' residence. Members sit for 6 years, 3 retiring annually and 4 every sixth year. There is no power to dissolve the Council. Vacancies are filled by by-elections. The House of Assembly has 35 members; the maximum term for the House of Assembly is 4 years. Members of both Houses are paid a basic salary of $A43,064 (Oct. 1989), plus an electorate allowance, according to the division represented. The annual allowance payable is calculated as a percentage of basic salary. The amounts vary from $A4,737 (11%) to $A15,072 (35%). Women received the right to vote in 1903. Proportional representation was adopted in 1907, the method now being the single transferable vote in 7-member constituencies. Casual vacancies in the House of Assembly are determined by a transfer of the preference of the vacating member's ballot papers to consenting candidates who were unsuccessful at the last general election.

A Minister must have a seat in one of the two Houses; all present Ministers are members of the House of Assembly.

In addition to the salary paid to Ministers as members of either House, the following allowances are payable: Premier, in conjunction with a ministerial office, $A47,160; Deputy Premier, in conjunction with a ministerial office, $A32,069; other Ministers, $A26,410. The Leader of the Opposition in the House of Assembly receives an allowance of $A26,410. The holders of some other offices receive allowances ranging from $A2,264 to $A12,576.

An election in May 1989 resulted in a 'hung parliament' with 17 Liberals, 13 Labor and 5 Independents. The most likely result was predicted to be a minority Liberal government, however, the final outcome was a Labor Party Government in an alliance with the 5 Independents.

The Legislative Council is predominantly independent without formal party allegiance; 1 member is Labor-endorsed.

Governor: Gen. Sir Phillip Bennett, AC, KBE, DSO.

The Labor Party Cabinet was composed as follows in Aug. 1989:

Premier, Minister for Finance, Treasurer, Minister for State Development: M. W. Field.

Deputy Premier, Justice and Attorney-General, Education and the Arts: P. J. Patmore. *Environment and Planning, Employment, Industrial Relations and Training, Minister Assisting Premier on Youth Affairs:* M. A. Aird. *Administrative Services, Minister Assisting Premier on Status of Women:* F. M. Bladel. *Tourism, Sport and Recreation:* H. N. Holgate. *Community Services, Parks, Wildlife and Heritage:* J. L. Jackson. *Primary Industry, Forests:* D. E. Llewellyn. *Resources and Energy, Construction:* M. W. Weldon. *Health, Minister Assisting the Premier on Aboriginal Affairs and on Multicultural Affairs:* J. C. White. *Roads and Transport, Police and Emergency Services:* K. S. Wriedt.

Local Government. For the purposes of local government, the State is divided into 46 municipal areas comprising the cities of Hobart, Launceston, Glenorchy and Devonport and 42 municipalities. The number of municipalities was reduced from 45 in May 1985 because of the amalgamation of 2 municipalities with the City of Launceston. The cities and municipalities are managed by elected aldermen and councillors, respectively, with reference to local matters such as sanitation and health services, domestic water supplies and roads and bridges within each particular area. The chief source of revenue is rates (based on assessed annual value) levied on owners of property.

Tasmanian Islands. Three inhabited Tasmanian islands (Bruny, King and Flinders) are organized as municipalities. Nearly 1,360 km south-east lies Macquarie Island (230 sq. km), part of the State, and used only as an Australian research base and meteorological station.

ECONOMY

Budget. The revenue is derived chiefly from taxation (pay-roll, motor, lottery and land tax, business franchises and stamp duties), and from grants and reimbursements from the Commonwealth Government. Customs, excise, sales and income tax are levied by the Commonwealth Government, which makes grants to Tasmania for both revenue and capital purposes. Commonwealth payments to Tasmania in 1988–89 (estimate) totalled $A898·7m. These included General Revenue Funds, $A481·3m.; Specific Purpose Payments, $A362·1m. and Capital Funds, $A55·3m.

Specific Purpose Grants are mainly used to provide essential services such as hospitals, housing, roads and educational services, while General Purpose Revenue Funds have been paid since 1942 to compensate the State for the loss of income tax to the federal government.

Consolidated Revenue Fund receipts and expenditure, in $A1,000, for financial years ending 30 June:

	1983–84	*1984–85*	*1985–86*	*1986–87*	*1987–88*	*1988–89*
Revenue	853,107	953,209	1,024,697	1,107,870	1,201,397	1,259,754
Expenditure	855,006	952,922	1,036,954	1,106,608	1,201,175	1,258,945

The public debt at current exchange rates amounted to $A1,226m. at 30 June 1989.

In 1988–89 State taxation revenue amounted to $A360m., of which pay-roll tax provided $A105·7m.; motor tax, $A20m.; stamp duties, $A80·5m.; business franchises, $A65·3m., and lottery tax, $A17·1m.

Banking. Trading bank activity in Tasmania is divided between 3 private banks and the Commonwealth Trading Bank. For the month of Dec. 1988 liabilities represented by depositors' balances averaged $A749m. and assets represented by advances, $A929m. The 6 savings banks operating in Tasmania are the Commonwealth Savings Bank, 2 trustee savings banks and 3 private savings banks operated by trading banks. At 31 Dec. 1988 total savings bank deposits were $A1,761m.

ENERGY AND NATURAL RESOURCES

Electricity. Tasmania has good supplies of hydro-electric power because of assured rainfall and high level water storages (natural and artificial). The Hydro-Electric Commission, Tasmania's sole commercial supplier of electricity, has been surveying water power resources of the State for many years and it is estimated that about 3m. kw. can be economically developed. With the addition of the Reece Dam, 2,315,000 kw. of generating plant was in commission in 1988–89. In 1988–89 the peak loading was 1,450,500 kw. The Pieman River Power Development, comprising 3 stations, was completed in 1987. The Gordon River Power Development Stage 2 (the Gordon-below-Franklin scheme) was halted by a High Court decision.

Minerals. The assayed content of principal metallic minerals contained in locally produced concentrates for 1986–87 was (in tonnes): Zinc, 88,026; iron pellets, 1,218,000; copper, 27,313; lead, 35,226; tin, 6,864; gold, 2,399 kg; silver, 102,264 kg. Coal production, 374,600 tonnes.

Primary Industries. The estimated gross value of recorded production from agriculture in 1987–88 was (in $A1m.): Livestock products, 239·1; livestock slaughterings and other disposals, 120; crops, 188·2; total gross value, 547·2. Estimated gross value of fisheries was $A91m. in 1986-87.

Agriculture. From 1986–87 the scope of the Census includes only those establishments undertaking agricultural activity and having an EVAO (Estimated Value of Agricultural Operations) of $A20,000 or more. The scope of previous Censuses was establishments undertaking agricultural activity having an EVAO of $A2,500 or more.

The area occupied by the 3,504 holdings in 1987–88 totalled 1,870,500 hectares, of which 916,800 were devoted to crops and sown pasture. The following table shows the area and production, in tonnes, of the principal crops:

	1985–86		*1986–87*		*1987–88*	
	Hectares	*Production*	*Hectares*	*Production*	*Hectares*	*Production*
Wheat	1,837	4,014	1,729	4,739	1,179	3,815
Barley	12,209	27,722	8,487	20,681	8,024	21,549
Oats	10,264	16,530	7,765	11,215	9,560	15,552
Green peas	6,622	27,908	6,714	22,683	6,211	28,552
Potatoes	4,832	193,485	5,744	223,425	6,380	248,303
Hay	56,664	261,455	45,116	200,363	41,162	163,434
Hops (bearing) (dry)	835	1,178	854	1,165	821	1,563

Livestock at 31 March 1988: Sheep, 4·7m.; cattle, 541,700; pigs, 47,600.

Wool produced during 1987–88 was 23,519 tonnes, valued at $A162·4m. In 1987–88 butter production was 3,885 tonnes; cheese, 16,255 tonnes.

Forestry. Indigenous forests cover a considerable part of the State, and the sawmilling and woodchipping industries are very important. Production of sawn timber in 1987–88 was 327,700 cu. metres. 892,500 cu. metres of logs were used for milling in 1987–88 and a further 3,892,000 cu. metres were used for chipping, grinding or flaking. Newsprint and paper are produced from native hardwoods, principally eucalypts.

INDUSTRY AND TRADE

Industry. The most important manufactures for export are refined metals, newsprint and other paper manufactures, pigments, woollen goods, fruit pulp, confectionery, butter, cheese, preserved and dried vegetables, sawn timber, and processed fish products. The electrolytic-zinc works at Risdon near Hobart treat large quantities of local and imported ore, and produce zinc, sulphuric acid, superphosphate, sulphate of ammonia, cadmium and other by-products. At George Town, large-scale plants produce refined aluminium and manganese alloys. During 1987–88, 4,005,300 tonnes (green weight) of woodchips were produced. In 1986–87 the average employment in manufacturing establishments employing 4 or more persons was 24,327; wages and salaries (excluding proprietors' drawings), $A526m.; turnover, $A3,050m.; value added, $A1,236m.; and number operating at 30 June 1987, 633.

Labour. The Commonwealth Industrial Court (judicial powers) and Commonwealth Conciliation and Arbitration Commission (arbitral powers) have jurisdiction over federal unions, *i.e.*, with interstate membership. Most Tasmanian employees are covered by federal awards.

State Industrial Boards, established for the various trades by resolution of Parliament or proclamation of the Governor, cover most of the remaining employees. Each Board consists of a Chairman appointed by the Governor with equal representation of employers and employees. The Boards have authority over minimum rates for wages or piecework, number of working hours for which the wage is payable, conditions of apprenticeship, annual leave and adjustment of wage and piecework rates. Industrial Boards follow to a large extent the wage rates fixed by the Conciliation and Arbitration Commission.

Commerce. In 1987–88 exports totalled $A1,221,995,000 to overseas countries. The principal countries of destination (with values in $A1m.) for overseas exports were: Japan, 474; USA, 120·1; Malaysia, 73·1; Indonesia, 49·7; and Taiwan, 86·7. In 1987–88 imports totalled $A282,415,000 from overseas countries. The principal countries of origin (with values in $A1m.) for overseas imports were: Canada, 39·5; Japan, 33·6; USA, 35·4; New Zealand, 24; Taiwan 11·7; Federal Republic of Germany, 13·5; Singapore, 29·2; China, 3·5 and Malaysia, 0·66.

The main commodities by value (with values in $A1m.) exported to overseas countries during 1987–88 were: Non-ferrous metals (mainly copper, lead, tin and tungsten), 294; iron and steel, 40; metalliferous ores and metal scrap, 202; fish, crustaceans and molluscs, 72; and meat and meat preparations, 49. Other main exports, for which details are not available for separate publication were woodchips, newsprint, printing and writing papers, refined aluminium, ferro-alloys and chocolate confectionery. The main imports from overseas countries in 1987–88 (with values in $A1m.) were: Coffee, tea, cocoa and spices, 20; pulp and waste paper, 42; petroleum products, 14; road vehicles, 14; and chemicals and related products, 26.

Tourism. In 1988, 681,500 passengers arrived in Tasmania by sea and air from interstate and New Zealand of whom 406,000 or just over 59% were visitors.

COMMUNICATIONS

Roads. The total road length at 30 June 1987 was 22,715 km, consisting of a classified road system of 3,701 km maintained by the State Department of Main Roads, and the remainder maintained by local government authorities, the Forestry Commission and the Hydro-Electric Commission. Motor vehicles registered at 30 June 1988 comprised 209,400 cars and station wagons, 62,700 other vehicles and 6,000 motor cycles.

Railways. There is an 840-km network of 1,067-mm gauge lines linking Hobart and Launceston with coastal and country areas, formerly operated by Tasmanian Government Railways, but since 1 July 1975 worked by the Australian National Railways Commission. A private railway of 130 km, operated by the Emu Bay Railway Co. Ltd, connects Burnie with the mining settlements on the west coast.

Aviation. Regular daily passenger and freight air services connect the south, north and north-west of the State with the mainland of Australia. In 1988 there was a total of 31,809 scheduled aircraft movements at Tasmanian airports; a total of 1·13m. passengers and 39,153 tonnes of freight, including mail, was carried.

Shipping. In 1987–88 there were, 1,736 ship visits to Tasmania with 11,066,913 mass tonnes of cargo carried through Tasmanian ports.

For posts and telegraphs, *see* p. 113.

JUSTICE, RELIGION, EDUCATION AND WELFARE

Justice. The Supreme Court of Tasmania, with civil, criminal, ecclesiastical, admiralty and matrimonial jurisdiction, established by Royal Charter on 13 Oct. 1823, is a superior court of record, with both original and appellate jurisdiction, and consists of a Chief Justice and 6 puisne judges. There are also inferior civil courts with limited jurisdiction, licensing courts, mining courts, courts of petty sessions and coroners' courts.

During the year 1988, 25,145 offences were finalized in the lower courts, 828 in the higher courts and 3,797 in the children's courts. The total police force at Oct. 1989 was 1,073. There was 1 gaol, with 854 imprisonments in 1987-88.

Religion. There is no State Church. At the census of 1986 the following numbers of adherents of the principal religions were recorded:

Anglican Church	154,748	Other religions	33,625
Roman Catholic	80,479	No religion	47,852
Methodist Uniting Church	36,724	Not stated [1]	61,742
Presbyterian	12,084	Total	435,346
Baptist	8,092		

Education. Education is controlled by the State and is free, secular and compulsory between the ages of 6 and 16. At 1 July 1988 government schools had a total enrolment of 65,404 pupils, including 28,148 at secondary level; private schools had a total enrolment of 17,795 pupils, including 8,242 at secondary level.

Technical and further education is conducted at technical and community colleges in the major centres throughout the state. In 1987 there were 18,956 students enrolled in the Division of Technical and Further Education, 21,982 students in the Division of Adult Education.

Tertiary education is offered at the University of Tasmania in Hobart, the Tasmanian State Institute of Technology and the Australian Maritime College, in Launceston. The University (established 1890) had (1988) 3,712 full-time and 1,601 part-time students, and 375 full-time teachers. There were 2,015 full-time and 715 part-time students enrolled in advanced education courses in 1988.

Social Welfare. Old Age, Invalid, War Service and Widows' Pensions are paid by the Commonwealth Government. The number of pensioners in Tasmania on 30 June 1988 was: Age (including wife and carer pensioners), 38,434; invalid, 11,347; war (service), 15,960; widows, 4,556. Benefit payments totalled $A524m. (including payments to wives).

Further Reading

Statistical Information: The State Government Statistical Office (Commonwealth Government Centre, Hobart), established in 1877, became in 1924 the Tasmanian Office of the Australian Bureau of Statistics, but continues to serve State statistical needs as required.

Deputy Commonwealth Statistician and Government Statistician of Tasmania: Stuart Jackson.

Main publications: *Annual Statistical Bulletins (e.g., Demography, Courts, Agricultural Industry, Finance, Manufacturing Establishments* etc.).—*Pocket Year Book of Tasmania.* Annual (from 1913).—*Tasmanian Year Book.* Annual (from 1967).—*Monthly Summary of Statistics* (from July 1945).

Tasmanian Development Authority, *Tasmanian Manufacturers Directory.* Hobart, 1985
Angus, M., *The World of Olegas Truchanas.* Hobart, 1975
Green, F. C. (ed.) *A Century of Responsible Government.* Hobart, 1956
Phillips, D., *Making more Adequate Provisions: State Education in Tasmania 1839–1985.* Hobart, 1985
Robson, L., *A History of Tasmania. Volume 1: Van Diemen's Land from the Earliest Times to 1855.* Melbourne, 1983
Townsley, W. A., *The Government of Tasmania.* Brisbane, 1976

State Library: The State Library of Tasmania, Hobart. *State Librarian:* D. W. Dunstan.

VICTORIA

AREA AND POPULATION. The State has an area of 227,600 sq. km, and a resident population (estimate) of 4,183,500 at 31 Dec. 1986.

The resident population (estimate) of the Melbourne Statistical Division at 30 June 1986 was 2,942,600 or 71% of the population of the State. The resident population (estimate) of each statistical district in Victoria at 30 June 1986 was: Ballarat, 78,290; Bendigo, 64,790; Geelong, 148,270; Morwell, 18,090; Shepparton-Mooroopna, 39,540.

The census count (exclusive of full-blood aboriginals prior to 1971) was:

Date of census enumeration	*Males*	*Population Females*	*Total*	*On previous census Numerical increase*	*Increase %*
5 April 1891	598,222	541,866	1,140,088	278,522	32·33
31 March 1901	603,720	597,350	1,201,070	60,982	5·35
3 April 1911	655,591	659,960	1,315,551	114,481	9·53
4 April 1921	754,724	776,556	1,531,280	215,729	16·40
30 June 1933	903,244	917,017	1,820,261	288,981	18·87
30 June 1947	1,013,867	1,040,834	2,054,701	234,440	12·88
30 June 1954	1,231,099	1,221,242	2,452,341	397,640	19·35
30 June 1961	1,474,395	1,455,718	2,930,113	477,772	19·48
30 June 1966	1,614,240	1,605,977	3,220,217	290,104	9·90
30 June 1971	1,750,061	1,752,290	3,502,351	282,134	8·76
30 June 1976	1,814,783	1,832,192	3,646,975	144,624	4·13
30 June 1981	1,901,411	1,931,032	3,832,443	185,468	5·09
30 June 1986	1,991,469	2,028,009	4,019,478	187,035	4·88

The count for the Melbourne Statistical Division (S.D.) on 30 June 1986 was 2,942,600. The count for the Geelong S.D. was 139,792; Ballarat S.D., 75,210; Bendigo S.D., 62,380; Shepparton-Mooroopna S.D., 37,086; and the Victorian component of Albury-Wodonga S.D., 35,183. Other urban centres: Warrnambool, 22,706; Traralgon, 19,233; Morwell, 16,387; Wangaratta, 16,598; Mildura, 18,382; Sale, 13,559; Horsham, 12,174; Colac, 9,532; Hamilton, 9,969; Bairnsdale, 10,328; Portland, 10,934; Swan Hill, 8,831; Ararat, 8,015; Benalla, 8,490; Maryborough, 7,705; Castlemaine, 6,603.

Vital statistics for calendar years:

	Births	*Marriages*	*Divorces*	*Deaths*
1985	61,555	29,810	9,688	31,353
1986	60,152	29,390	9,670	30,175
1987	61,507	29,682	9,626	31,549

The annual rates per 1,000 of the mean resident population (estimate) in 1987 were: Marriages, 7·1; births, 14·6; deaths, 7·5; divorces, 2·3.

CONSTITUTION AND GOVERNMENT. Victoria, formerly a portion of New South Wales, was, in 1851, proclaimed a separate colony, with a partially elective Legislative Council. In 1856 responsible government was conferred, the legislative power being vested in a parliament of two Houses, the Legislative Council and the Legislative Assembly. At present the Council consists of 44 members who are elected for 2 terms of the Assembly, one-half retiring at each election. The Assembly consists of 88 members, elected for 4 years from the date of its first meeting unless sooner dissolved by the Governor. Members and electors of both Houses must be aged 18 years and Australian citizens or those British subjects previously enrolled as electors, according to the Constitution Act 1975. No property qualification is required, but judges, members of the Commonwealth Parliament, undischarged bankrupts and persons convicted of an offence which is punishable by life imprisonment, may not be members of either House. Single voting (one elector one vote) and compulsory preferential voting apply to Council and Assembly elections. Enrolment for Council and Assembly electors is compulsory. The Council may not initiate or amend money bills, but may suggest amendments in such bills other than amendments which would increase any charge. A bill shall not become law unless passed by both Houses.

Private members of both Houses receive salaries of $A54,500 per annum.

Members holding the following offices receive an additional salary and in some cases an expense allowance. The President of the Council, $A36,510 salary and $A5,355 expense allowance; the Speaker of the Assembly, $A36,510 salary and $A5,355 expense allowance; the Chairman of Committees of the Council, $A15,578 salary and $A1,947 expense allowance; the Chairman of Committees of the Assembly, $A15,578 salary and $A1,947 expense allowance; the Leader of the Opposition in the Assembly, $A36,510 salary and $A8,762 expense allowance; the Deputy Leader of the Opposition in the Assembly, $A15,578 salary and $A2,921 expense allowance; the Leader of the Third Party, $A15,578 salary and $A2,921 expense allowance; a member of either House who is the Parliamentary Secretary of the Cabinet, $A15,578 salary and $A2,921 expense allowance; the Government Whip in the Assembly, $A8,762 salary; the Whip of any recognized Party which consists of at least 12 members of Parliament, of which Party no member is a responsible Minister, $A8,762 salary. Members receive electorate allowances, residential allowances and allowances for attending Parliament and Parliamentary Standing Committees.

The Legislative Assembly, elected on 1 Oct. 1988, is composed as follows: Labor Party, 46; Liberal Party, 33; National Party, 9.

Governor: Dr J. Davis McCaughey, AC.

In the exercise of the executive power the Governor is advised by a Cabinet of responsible Ministers. Section 50 of the Constitution Act 1975 provides that the number of Ministers shall not at any one time exceed 18, of whom not more than 6 may sit in the Legislative Council and not more than 13 may sit in the Legislative

Assembly. No Minister may hold office for more than 3 months unless he or she is or becomes a member of the Council or the Assembly.

Responsible Ministers receive the following amounts: The Premier, $A48,680 salary and $A20,446 expense allowance; the Deputy Premier, $A41,378 salary and $A10,223 expense allowance; 16 other Ministers, $A36,510 salary and $A8,762 expense allowance. The President, Speaker, Chairman of Committees in the Assembly and in the Council, Parliamentary Secretary of the Cabinet, Leader and Deputy Leader of the Opposition in the Assembly, Leader of the Opposition in the Council and Leader in the Assembly of the Third Party, also receive a travelling allowance when travelling on official business. The Premier, Deputy Premier, a Minister or office holder or Member, also receive a travelling allowance when travelling on official business.

The Labor Party Government was as follows on 1 Nov. 1989:

Premier and Minister responsible for Women's Affairs: John Cain, MP.

Agriculture and Rural Affairs: B. J. Rowe, MLC. *Arts, Major Projects and Minister responsibile for Post-Secondary Education:* E. Walker, MLC. *Attorney-General and Ethnic Affairs:* A. McCutcheon, MP. *Community Services and Prices:* P. Spyker, MP. *Conservation, Forests and Lands:* K. Setches, MP. *Consumer Affairs, Planning and Environment and Minister responsible for Aboriginal Affairs:* T. W. Roper, MP. *Police and Emergency Services, Tourism and Minister responsible for Corrections:* S. M. Crabb, MP. *Education:* J. Kirner, MP. *Health:* C. Hogg, MLC. *Housing and Construction:* B. Pullen, MLC. *Industry, Technology and Resources and Minister assisting the Treasurer in Budget Expenditure:* D. R. White, MLC. *Labour and Minister responsible for Youth Affairs:* N. Pope, MP. *Treasurer:* R. A. Jolly, MP. *Property Services and Water Resources:* R. Walsh, MP. *Sport and Recreation and Minister responsible for the Olympic Games:* N. B. Trezise, MP. *Transport:* J. H. Kennan, MP. *Local Government and the Aged:* M. Lyster, MLC.

Agent-General in London: Ian Haig (Victoria House, Melbourne Place, Strand, London, WC28 4LG).

Local Government. With the exception of Yallourn Works area (26·9 sq. km) and the unincorporated areas—French Island (154 sq. km), Lady Julia Percy Island (1·3 sq. km), the Bass Strait Islands and part of Gippsland Lakes (312·8 sq. km) and Tower Hill Lake Reserve (5 sq. km), the State is divided (in Oct. 1988) into 210 municipal districts, namely 68 cities, 5 towns, 6 boroughs and 132 shires. The constitution of cities, towns, boroughs and shires is based on statutory requirements concerning population, rate revenue and net annual value of rateable property.

ECONOMY

Budget. The receipts and payments (in $A1m.) of the Consolidated Fund in the years shown (ended 30 June) were:

	1982–83	*1983–84*	*1984–85*	*1985–86*
Receipts	7,203	7,781	8,827	9,659
Payments	7,209	7,752	8,828	9,686

The Consolidated Fund is divided into two sectors: The Current Account and the Works and Services (capital account).

Total receipts for 1985–86 of the Current Account sector were 7,865. Principal receipt items were: State taxation, 3,095; Commonwealth tax sharing, 2,248; other Commonwealth payments, 821 and public authorities, 410.

The Works and Services sector contributed 1,793. Principal receipt items were: Commonwealth payments, 646; loan raisings, 360 and the State Development Account (an investment account receiving deposits from various State Authorities), 89.

Of total Consolidated Fund payments during 1985–86 7,894 was paid through the Current Account sector. Principal payment items were: Debt charges, 702; education, 2,503; health, 1,612 and transport, 1,633.

The remaining 1,763 paid through the Works and Services sector was appropriated into the Works and Services Account, from which the Victorian Government makes its capital expenditure. Principal payment items were: Education, 249; housing, 239; transport, 739 and water resources, 53.

The public debt of Victoria at 30 June 1985 was 4,385. Victoria had other liabilities due to the Commonwealth Government of 1,336 largely being advances for housing.

Banking. The State Bank of Victoria, the largest bank in the State, joined with the State Banks of New South Wales, South Australia and Western Australia to form the State Banks Association in Feb. 1984. The Bank provides a full range of domestic and international banking services for both business and personal customers and is the largest supplier of housing finance in Victoria, with approvals for owner-occupied dwellings totalling $A853m. in the year to June 1985.

There are 4 major trading banks in Victoria (Commonwealth Bank of Australia, Australia and New Zealand Banking Group Ltd, Westpac Banking Corporation and National Australia Bank) with a total of 1,218 branches and 168 agencies between them at 30 June 1987, and 4 other trading banks. Private savings banks had 1,102 branches and 246 agencies at 30 June 1987. On 30 June 1986 there were 8·8m. operative accounts (excluding school bank accounts) in savings banks in Victoria. The total credit due to depositors at 30 June 1987 amounted to $A19,670m., made up of State Savings Bank, $A9,197·4m.; Commonwealth Savings Bank, $A2,862·1m.; private savings banks, $A7,610·6m.

The weekly average of deposits and advances of trading banks operating in Victoria during June 1987 were as follows: Deposits, not bearing interest, $A3,874m.; deposits, bearing interest, $A9,791m.; total deposits, $A13,665m.; loans, advances, and bills discounted, $A15,427m. The weekly average of debits to customers' accounts (excluding debits to Federal and State Government accounts at City branches in State capitals) for the same period totalled $A26,514m.

ENERGY AND NATURAL RESOURCES

Electricity. All electricity in this State for public supply is generated by the largest electricity supply authority in Australia, the State Electricity Commission of Victoria. Through its network of 116,000 km of power lines the SEC supplies more than 1,424,000 customers. Another 277,800 customers take SEC power from 11 metropolitan councils which buy in bulk and distribute electricity through their own systems.

Electricity demand has almost doubled in 10 years and is now over 25,000 megawatt/hours a year. Generating capacity at 30 June 1985 was 6,603 megawatts compared with 3,863 in 1973. This includes capacity within Victoria and that available from New South Wales.

About 80% of the power generated for the state system is supplied by brown-coal fired generating stations, Yallourn, Morwell, Hazelwood and Loy Yang, located in the La Trobe Valley on one of the largest single brown coal deposits in the world 140 to 180 km east of Melbourne in Central Gippsland.

There are 2 other thermal stations and 3 hydro-electric stations in north east Victoria. Victoria is also entitled to approximately 30% of the output of the Snowy Mountains hydro-electric scheme and half the output of the Hume hydro-electric station, both of which are in New South Wales.

Oil and Natural Gas. Crude oil in commercially recoverable quantities was first discovered by the Esso/BHP partnership in 1967 in 2 large fields offshore in East Gippsland in Bass Strait between 65 and 80 km from land. These fields, Halibut and Kingfish, with 10 other fields since discovered—Marlin, Snapper, Barracouta, Mackerel, Tuna, Cobia, Flounder, Fortescue, Bream and Seahorse have been assessed as containing initial recoverable reserves of more than 2,930m. bbls of treated crude oil. Estimated reserves of crude oil (1986) 184m. cu. metres.

In 1987-88 Gippsland Basin produced 84% of Australia's crude oil and 39% of its natural gas. Depletion of production from the 2 major fields, Kingfish and

Halibut and the smaller Barracouta field, was expected to occur in the late-1980s. Production of crude oil (1987) 151,571,000m. bbls.

Natural gas was discovered offshore in East Gippsland in 1965. The initial recoverable reserves of treated gas are 220,400m. cu. metres. Reserves are sufficient for at least 30 years. Following an extensive development and distribution programme, natural gas was first connected to homes and industry in Victoria in April 1969. All gas consumers in Melbourne, Geelong, Ballarat, Bendigo, Shepparton, Euroa, Benalla, Wangaratta, Wodonga, Albury and a number of towns near Melbourne, in the La Trobe Valley and in East Gippsland, are now using natural gas. At 30 June 1985 a total of 1,013,455 consumers were being supplied with it.

Natural gas and crude oil are conveyed from the producing fields to a large treatment plant at Longford in East Gippsland from where both hydrocarbons are distributed by a network of transmission lines to tank farms and city gate distribution points.

The crude oil is then distributed to refineries in Victoria by pipeline and to other States by seagoing tankers. Natural gas is distributed to residential and industrial consumers through a network of approximately 20,289 km of mains.

Liquefied petroleum gas is now being produced after extraction of the propane and butane fractions from the untreated oil and gas.

Brown Coal. Major deposits of brown coal are located in the Central Gippsland region and comprise approximately 94% of the total resources in Victoria. The resource is estimated to be 202,000 megatonnes, of which about 31,000 megatonnes are regarded as readily accessible reserves. It is young and soft with a water content of 60% to 70%. In the La Trobe Valley section of the region, the thick brown coal seams underlie an area from 10 to 30 km wide extending over approximately 70 kilometres from Yallourn in the west to the south of Sale in the east. It can be won continuously in large quantities and at low cost by specialized mechanical plant.

The primary use of these reserves is to fuel the major base load electricity generating stations located at Morwell and Yallourn. Production of brown coal in 1986-87 was 39,124,000 tonnes, value $A268,303,000.

Minerals. Production of certain metals and minerals, 1986–87: Gold, 1,346 kg, value $A21,599,000; kaolin, 89,000 tonnes, value $A4,244,000; gypsum, 274,000 tonnes, value $A2,244,000; bauxite, 8,000 tonnes, value $A82,000.

Land Settlement. Of the total area of Victoria (22·76m. hectares), 13,973,915 hectares on 30 June 1984 were either alienated or in process of alienation. The remainder (8,786,085) constituted Crown land as follows: Perpetual leases, grazing and other leases and licences, 2,160,352; reservations including forest and timber reserves, water, catchment and drainage purposes, national parks, wildlife reserves, water frontages and other reserves, plus unoccupied and unreserved including areas set aside for roads, 6,625,733.

Agriculture. In 1986-87 the total area of land utilized for agricultural activity was 10,398,000 hectares, and the gross value of agricultural commodities produced was $A4,020,648. The following table shows the area under the principal crops and the produce of each for 3 seasons (in 1,000 units):

	Total crop area	*Wheat*		*Oats*		*Barley*		*Potatoes*		*Hay*	
Season	*Hectares*	*Hectares*	*Tonnes*	*Hectares*	*Tonnes*	*Hectares*	*Tonnes*	*Hectares*	*Tonnes*	*Hectares*	*Tonnes*
1984–85	2,569	1,523	2,666	228	343	486	638	15	379	387	1,516
1985–86	2,528	1,508	2,250	212	300	389	476	14	367	425	1,648
1986–87	2,340	1,364	2,795	215	356	265	444	13	364	483	1,932

In 1986–87 there were 18,954 hectares of vineyards with 17,827 hectares of bearing vines, yielding 67,133 tonnes of grapes for wine-making and 221,482 tonnes of grapes for drying or for table use. The area planted with fruit, nuts and berries was 19,752 hectares; production of nuts was 1,261 tonnes. Tobacco covered 1,819 hectares yielding 3,975 tonnes (dry) and hops, 336 hectares yield 579 tonnes (dried weight). Fruit production, 1987, included pears, 123,859 tonnes; apples, 99,801 tonnes; oranges, 68,028 tonnes, and strawberries, 1,619,267 kg.

At March 1987 there were in the State 3·5m. head of cattle, 26,586,000 sheep and 431,832 pigs. In 1986–87, mutton production was 75,000 tonnes; lamb, 130,000 tonnes. Wool produced in the season 1986–87 amounted to 157,919 tonnes. Milk production in 1987-88, 3,649m. litres; butter, 82,000 tonnes; cheese, 103,000 tonnes. Egg production, 1986-87, 46,369,871 dozen; honey, 1987, 3,107 tonnes.

INDUSTRY AND TRADE

Industry. At 30 June 1987 there were 9,107 manufacturing establishments employing 4 or more persons. Selected articles manufactured (1987–88, in tonnes): Beef and veal, 305,000; lamb, 125,000; butter, 82,128; cheese, 102,470; white flour, 249,095; cotton yarn, 9,934; wool yarn, 16,744; cotton cloth, 18,698,000 sq. metres; wool cloth, 3,419,000 sq. metres; 180,000 cars and station wagons; plastic and synthetic resins, 467,000; 427m. clay bricks; ready mixed concrete, 3,599,000 cu. metres.

Labour. In Aug. 1988 there were 1,935,500 employed persons (58% of the civilian population aged 15 years and over): Agriculture, forestry, fishing and hunting, 95,200; mining, 5,700; manufacturing, 408,700; electricity, gas and water, 33,900; construction, 132,500; wholesale and retail trade, 382,500; transport and storage, 90,100; communication, 35,000; finance, property and business services, 215,400; public administration and defence, 85,900; community services, 340,000; recreation, personal and other services, 111,000. There were 115,300 unemployed persons in Aug. 1988 (5·6% of the labour force).

Trade Unions. There were 159 trade unions with a total membership of 875,700 operating in Victoria in June 1987.

Commerce. The commerce of Victoria, exclusive of inter-state trade, is included in the statement of the commerce of Australia, *see* pp. 108–10.

The total value of the overseas imports and exports of Victoria, including bullion and specie but excluding inter-state trade, was as follows (in $A1,000):

	1981–82	*1982–83*	*1983–84*	*1984–85*	*1985–86* [1]	*1986–87*
Imports	7,175,776	6,989,815	8,185,717	10,084,483	12,409,575	13,751,000
Exports [2]	4,177,187	4,321,674	5,059,996	6,382,293	6,810,680	7,187,000

[1] Preliminary. [2] Includes re-exports.

The chief exports in 1986–87 (in $A1m.) were: Textile fibres and their wastes, 1,279; petroleum, petroleum products and related materials, 960; cereals and cereal preparations, 483; meat and meat preparations, 423; dairy products and birds' eggs, 397; vegetables and fruit, 304; road vehicles, 248; hides, skins, and fur skins (raw), 230; power generating machinery and equipment, 227. Exports in 1986–87 went mainly to Japan ($A2,104m.), USA ($A1,052m.) and New Zealand ($A586m.).

COMMUNICATIONS

Roads. In 1986–87 there were 159,376 km of roads open for general traffic, consisting of 7,584 km of state highways and freeways, 14,771 km of main roads, 1,848 km of tourist and forest roads and 135,173 km of other roads and streets. The number of registered motor vehicles (other than tractors) at 30 June 1987 was 2,529,400.

Railways. All the railways are the property of the State and are under the management of the State Transport Authority and the Metropolitan Transit Authority, responsible to the Victorian Government.

At 30 June 1988, 5,150 km of government railway were open. In 1987-88, 10·9m. tonnes of freight and 5·5m. passengers (non-urban) were carried. Melbourne's suburban railways carried 93·8m. passengers.

Aviation. There were (1987) 67,866 domestic and 13,630 international aircraft movements at Essendon and Melbourne airports. Passengers totalled (1987) 5,569,526 on domestic flights and 1,400,673 on international flights. Freight handled (1987) 88,977 tonnes on domestic flights and 80,102 tonnes on international flights.

Post and Broadcasting. In 1988 there were 2,772,000 telephones. In 1988 there were 52 broadcasting stations and 19 television stations.

JUSTICE, RELIGION, EDUCATION AND WELFARE

Justice. There is a Supreme Court with a Chief Justice and 21 puisne judges. There are a county court, magistrates' courts, a court of licensing, and a bankruptcy court, etc.

Major crime in Victoria during 1986-87: 283,666 offences were reported to the police; 67,479 offences were cleared and 36,082 people were proceeded against.

At 30 June 1988 there were 13 prisons and 2,064 prisoners in custody.

Religion. There is no State Church in Victoria, and no State assistance has been given to religion since 1875. At the date of the 1986 census the following were the enumerated numbers of each of the principal religions: Catholic,[1] 1,104,044; Church of England, 715,414; Uniting, 280,262 (including Methodist); Orthodox, 177,565; Presbyterian, 138,000; Protestant (undefined), 87,557; other Christian, 90,756; Moslem, 37,965; Hebrew, 32,387; no religion, 557,939; no reply, 574,712; other groups, 222,877.

[1] So described on individual census schedules.

Education. Education establishments in Victoria consist of 4 universities, established under special Acts and opened in 1855, 1961, 1967 and 1977; Colleges of Advanced Education; government schools (primary, primary-secondary, high and secondary technical, and further education colleges), and non-government schools.

Total full-time teaching and research staff at the 4 universities in 1987, 3,398. The University of Melbourne, founded in 1853, had, in 1987, 15,909 students: Monash University, founded in 1958 in an eastern suburb of Melbourne, had, in 1987, 14,003 students; La Trobe University, founded in 1964 in a northern suburb of Melbourne, had 9,997 students in 1987; Deakin University (1974) near Melbourne had 6,857 students in 1987.

On 1 July 1987 there were 2,091 government schools with 537,895 pupils and 41,432 full-time teaching staff plus full-time equivalents of part-time teaching staff: 293,948 pupils were in primary schools, 238,824 in secondary schools and 5,123 attended special schools. In 1987 there were 232,467 students (excluding adult education programmes) enrolled in technical and further education schools and colleges, and 66,548 students enrolled in advanced education courses.

Non-government Schools. There were at 1 July 1987, 729 non-government schools, excluding commercial colleges, with 16,192 teaching staff (FTE) and 253,086 pupils enrolled. Of these schools, more than 66% were Roman Catholic.

Health. At 30 June 1987 there were 285 approved hospitals with 20,978 beds, of which 119 with 6,132 beds were private.

Social Services. Victoria was the first State of Australia to make a statutory provision for the payment of Age Pensions. The Act providing for the payment of such pensions came into operation on 18 Jan. 1901, and continued until 1 July 1909, when the Australian Invalid and Old Age Pension Act came into force. The Social Services Consolidation Act, which came into operation on 1 July 1947, repealed the various legislative enactments relating to age (previously old-age) and invalid pensions, maternity allowances, child endowment, and unemployment, and sickness benefits and while following in general the Acts repealed, considerably liberalized many of their provisions: it has since been amended. On 30 June 1987 there were 347,606 aged and 79,230 invalid pensioners, and the amount paid in pensions, including payments to wives and spouse carers of invalid pensioners, during 1986–87 was $A2,103·1m.

The number of disability pensions (members of the forces and their dependants) payable in Victoria on 30 June 1986 was 100,245, and the number of service pensions was 97,517. The amount paid in war and service pensions by the Federal Government during 1985–86 was $A638m.

Under the Australian Unemployment and Sickness Benefit Act 1944, there were 197,959 unemployment, sickness, and special benefits granted during 1986-87 and the amount paid in benefits totalled $A723,910,000 during 1986-87. Unemployment benefits accounted for 81% of the benefits granted and 83% of the benefits paid.

The number of widows' pensions in force at 30 June 1987 was 40,410, and the total amount paid in allowances during 1986-87 was $A250m.

The number of family allowances in force in 1986-87 was 1,055,413. In addition, endowment was being paid in respect of 1,055,413 children who were being maintained in approved institutions. The total amount paid and family allowances in 1986-87 was $A355,773,000. In 1986-87, $A253,515,000 was paid in supporting parent's benefits to 34,081 beneficiaries, $A7,226,000 in handicapped child's allowances for 7,550 children in 7,215 families and $A13,612,000 in family income supplement to 6,872 families with 20,158 children.

Further Reading

Statistical Information: Australian Bureau of Statistics (The Rialto Building, 525 Collins Street, Melbourne, 3000). *Deputy Commonwealth Statistician:* Erle Bourke.

Victorian Year Book. (Annually since 1873)
Victorian Pocket Year Book. (Annually since 1956)
Victorian Statistical Register. (Annually from 1854 to 1916)
Monthly Summary of Statistics (from Jan. 1960)

Historical Records of Victoria. Victorian Government Printing Office, Melbourne (From 1981)
Victoria: The First Century. Official History of Victoria. Melbourne, 1934
Victorian Municipal Directory. Melbourne, (From 1866)
Broome, R., *The Victorians: Arriving.* New South Wales, 1984
Christie, M. F., *Aborigines in Colonial Victoria, 1835–86.* Sydney Univ. Press, 1979
Dingle, T., *The Victorians: Settling.* New South Wales, 1984
Dunstan, D., *Governing the Metropolis: Politics, Technology, and Social Change in a Victorian City: Melbourne 1850–1891.* Melbourne Univ. Press, 1984
Grant, J. and Serle, G., *The Melbourne Scene 1803–1956.* Melbourne Univ. Press, 1956
Pratt, A., *The Centenary History of Victoria.* Melbourne, 1934
Priestley, S., *The Victorians: Making Their Mark.* Melbourne, 1984

State Library: The State Library of Victoria, 328 Swanston St., Melbourne, 3000. *State Librarian:* W. Horton, BA, ALAA.

WESTERN AUSTRALIA

HISTORY. In 1791 Vancouver, in the *Discovery*, took formal possession of the country about King George Sound. In 1826 the Government of New South Wales sent 20 convicts and a detachment of soldiers to King George Sound and formed a settlement then called Frederickstown. In 1827 Captain (afterwards Sir) James Stirling surveyed the coast from King George Sound to the Swan River, and in May 1829 Captain (afterwards Sir) Charles Fremantle took possession of the territory. In June 1829 Captain Stirling, newly appointed Lieut.-Governor, founded the colony now known as the State of Western Australia. On 1 Jan. 1901 Western Australia became one of the 6 federated States within the Commonwealth of Australia.

AREA AND POPULATION. Western Australia lies between 113° 09' and 129° E. long. and 13° 44' and 35° 08' S. lat.; its area is 2,525,500 sq. km.

The population at each census from 1947 was as follows [1]:

	Males	Females	Total		Males	Females	Total
1947	258,076	244,404	502,480	1971	539,332	514,502	1,053,834
1954	330,358	309,413	639,771	1976	599,959	578,383	1,178,342
1961	375,452	361,177	736,629	1981	659,249	642,807	1,300,056
1966	432,569	415,531	848,100	1986	736,131	722,888	1,459,019

[1] 1961 and earlier exclude full-blood Aboriginals; from 1966 figures refer to total population (*i.e.*, including Aboriginals). Figures from 1971 are based on estimated resident population.

The population count at the 1986 census was 1,406,929 (707,569 males and 699,360 females). Of these 1,020,362 were born in Australia. Married persons numbered 617,382 (308,974 males and 308,408 females); widowers, 10,787; widows, 49,776; divorced, 23,505 males and 28,268 females; never married, 348,343 males and 294,771 females. The number of males under 21 was 247,826 and of females 235,620.

Perth, the capital, had an estimated resident population of 1,118,131 at June 1988. Of this, the area administered by the City of Perth had a population of 82,118 while the population in the area for which the City of Fremantle is responsible (which includes the chief port of the State) was 23,845.

Principal local government areas outside the metropolitan area, with population at 30 June 1988 (estimate): Bunbury, 25,823; Geraldton, 20,648; Mandurah, 21,717; Roebourne, 17,777; Port Hedland, 13,749; Albany, 14,783; Boulder, 14,431; Busselton, 12,955; Kalgoorlie, 11,657.

Vital statistics for calendar years [1]:

	Births	Ex-nuptial births	Marriages	Divorces	Deaths
1984	21,625	3,489	9,920	4,069	8,503
1985	23,109	3,886	10,398	4,039	8,836
1986	24,236	4,481	10,379	4,001	9,307
1987	23,332	4,623	10,150	4,044	8,880

[1] Figures are on State of usual residence basis.

CONSTITUTION AND GOVERNMENT. In 1870 partially representative government was instituted, and in 1890 the administration was vested in the Governor, a Legislative Council and a Legislative Assembly. The Legislative Council was, in the first instance, nominated by the Governor, but it was provided that in the event of the population of the colony reaching 60,000, it should be elective. In 1893 this limit of population being reached, the Colonial Parliament amended the Constitution accordingly.

The Legislative Council consists of 34 members, 2 members representing each of the 17 electoral regions. Each member is elected for a term of 4 years.

There are 57 members of the Legislative Assembly, each member representing one of the 57 electoral districts of the State. Members are elected for the duration of the Parliament, normally 4 years. The qualifications applying to candidates and electors are identical for the Legislative Council and the Legislative Assembly. A candidate must have resided in Western Australia for a minimum of 12 months, be at least 18 years of age and free from legal incapacity, be an Australian citizen, and be enrolled, or qualified for enrolment, as an elector. A judge of the Supreme Court, the Sheriff of Western Australia, an undischarged bankrupt or a debtor against whose estate there is a subsisting order in bankruptcy may not be elected to Parliament. No person may hold office as a member of the Legislative Assembly and the Legislative Council at the same time. An elector must be at least 18 years of age, be an Australian citizen free from legal incapacity, must have resided in the Commonwealth of Australia for 6 and in Western Australia for 3 months continuously and in the electoral district for which he claims enrolment for a continuous period of 1 month immediately preceding the date of his claim. Enrolment is compulsory for all qualified persons except Aboriginal natives of Australia, who are entitled but not required to enrol. Voting at elections is on the preferential system and is compulsory for all enrolled persons.

Ordinary members of the legislature are paid a salary of $A50,644 a year, with an additional electorate allowance, ranging from $A15,136 to $A28,248 according to location of the electorate. Members are entitled to free travel on Western Australian government railways, bus and ferry services, and, by arrangement, once every year on government railways in other States. All members of Parliament contribute to the parliamentary superannuation fund.

The Premier receives a salary, including electorate and expense allowances, of $A131,255, the Deputy Premier $A108,969, the Leader of the Government in the Legislative Council $A104,301, and other Ministers $A97,650—110,662 according to location of the electorate.

The Legislative Assembly, elected on 4 Feb. 1989, is composed as follows: Australian Labor Party, 31; Liberal Party, 20; National Party of Australia, 6. The Legislative Council is composed of 16 Australian Labor Party, 15 Liberal Party, 3 National Party of Australia.

Governor: Gordon Reid, AC.

Lieut-Governor and Administrator: Hon. Sir Francis Theodore Page Burt, AC, KCMG, QC.

The Australian Labor Party Cabinet was in 1990:

Premier, Public Sector Management, Women's Interests: Hon. Carmen Mary Lawrence, MLA.

Deputy Premier, Treasurer, Resources Development, The Arts: Hon. David Charles Parker, MLA. *Attorney General, Budget Management, Corrective Services, Leader of the Government in the Legislative Council:* Hon. Joseph Max Berinson, QC, MLC. *Local Government, Lands, The Family, The Aged, Minister assisting the Minister for Women's Interests, Deputy Leader of the Government in the Legislative Council:* Hon. Elsie Kay Hallahan, MLC. *Housing, Planning:* Hon. Pamela Anne Beggs, MLA. *Agriculture, Water Resources, North-West:* Hon. Ernest Francis Bridge, MLA. *Mines, Fuel and Energy, Mid-West:* Hon. Jeffrey Phillip Carr, MLA. *Racing and Gaming, Sport and Recreation, Youth:* Hon. Graham John Edwards, MLC. *Economic Development and Trade, Tourism:* Hon. Julian Fletcher Grill, MLA. *Consumer Affairs, Works and Services:* Hon. Yvonne Daphne Henderson, MLA. *Regional Development, Fisheries, Multicultural and Ethnic Affairs:* Hon. Gordon Leslie Hill, MLA. *Transport, Environment, Parliamentary and Electoral Reform, Leader of the House in the Legislative Assembly:* Hon. Robert John Pearce, MLA. *Community Services, Justice, South-West:* Hon. David Lawrence Smith, MLA. *Police and Emergency Services, Conservation and Land Management, Waterways:* Hon. Ian Frederick Taylor, MLA. *Labour, Employment and Training, Productivity, Minister assisting the Minister for Education with TAFE:* Hon. Gavan John Troy, MLA. *Health:* Hon. Keith James Wilson, MLA. *Parliamentary Secretary of the Cabinet:* William Ian Thomas, MLA.

Agent-General in London: D. Fischer (Western Australia House, 115 Strand, WC2R 0AJ).

Local Government. The only unincorporated area in mainland Western Australia is King's Park, a public reserve of about 403 hectares in Perth. Including the lord-mayoralty of Perth there were 15 cities, 11 towns and 113 shires at 30 June 1987. The executive body in each of these districts is normally an elective council, presided over by a mayor (city and town) or a president (shire), but in certain circumstances it may be a commissioner appointed by the Governor. Their functions include road construction and repair, the provision of parks and recreation grounds, the administration of building controls and local services such as health and library services. Finance is derived largely from rates levied on property owners as well as charges for services and government grants (mainly for road construction).

ECONOMY

Budget. The revenue and expenditure (in $A) of Western Australia, as reported in the Consolidated Revenue Fund, in years ended 30 June, are given as follows:

	1987	*1988*	*1989*	*1990* [1]
Revenue	3,284,233,136	3,810,401,671	4,270,268,532	4,824,300,000
Expenditure	3,277,526,154	3,807,340,069	4,269,990,881	4,824,300,000

[1] Estimates.

Main items of revenue in 1988–89: Railways ($A263,954,495), taxation ($A1,280,031,237), lands, timber and mining ($A299,800,144), public utilities other than railways ($A15,990,071), from Federal funds ($A1,607,719,729). Western Australia had a net public debt of $A1,554,144,943 on 30 June 1988, the charge for that year being $A202,807,982.

Banking. There are 20 trading banks in Western Australia including the Commonwealth Trading Bank and The Rural and Industries Bank of Western Australia. In Dec. 1988, the average of customers' balances was $A6,729m. and average advances $A6,798m.

At 31 Dec. 1988, the 8 savings banks held deposits of $A5,865m., in 2,666,229 accounts.

ENERGY AND NATURAL RESOURCES

Minerals. The mining industry has been for many years of considerable significance in the Western Australian economy. Until the mid-1960s the major mineral produced was gold. It was then replaced by iron ore in terms of value, and has at various times fallen behind nickel concentrates, bauxite, oil, mineral sands and salt. In the latter half of the 1980s it enjoyed a resurgence and was (1988) second only to iron ore.

The total ex-mine value of minerals from mining and quarrying in the State in 1986–87 was $A5,009·9m. Principal minerals produced in 1986–87 were: Iron ore, 92·5m. tonnes, value $A1,801·6m.; bauxite, 20·4m. tonnes; gold bullion, 75·4m. grammes, value $A1,295·9m.; mineral sands concentrates valued at $A196·9m.; nickel concentrates, 406,000 tonnes; tin concentrates, 731 tonnes; black coal, 3·8m. tonnes; crude oil, 2,174m.; natural gas, 3,377,000m. kilolitres; salt, 5·1m. tonnes, value $A107·4m.; diamonds, 32·2m. carats, value $A284·1m.

Agriculture.

	1986–87		*1987–88*	
Crop	*Area 1,000 hectares*	*Production 1,000 tonnes*	*Area 1,000 hectares*	*Production 1,000 tonnes*
Wheat	4,260	5,377	3,312	3,882
Oats	302	414	373	502
Barley	468	601	461	617
Hay	218	681	243	778
Potatoes	2	68	2	72
Cauliflower	1	16	1	14

	1986–87		*1987–87*	
Crop	*No. Trees (1,000)*	*Production Tonnes*	*No. Trees (1,000)*	*Production Tonnes*
Apples	699	34,470	702	40,196
Pears	128	7,107	132	6,604
Oranges	183	5,432	179	5,217

Irrigation has been established by the Government along the south-western coastal plain and in the north of the State. Reservoirs with an aggregate capacity of 6,207m. cu. metres provided irrigation water for 20,402 hectares in 6 districts during 1985–86.

Livestock at 31 March 1988 included 1,705,000 cattle, 33,951,000 sheep and 307,000 pigs.

The wool clip in 1987–88 was 188,500 tonnes.

Forestry. The area of State forests and timber reserves at 30 June 1988 was 1,965,220 hectares; 1987–88 production of sawn timber was 318,652 cu. metres, principally Jarrah and Karri hardwoods.

Fisheries. The catch of fish, crustaceans and molluscs in Western Australia in 1986–87 totalled 29,609 tonnes for a gross value of $A182·4m. Of this, rock lobsters, with a total catch of 7,718 tonnes accounted for $A119·5m.

Value of Agricultural Commodities Produced. The estimated gross values of Western Australian agricultural commodities during 1987–88 were: Crops and pastures, $A1,203·2m.; livestock slaughterings and other disposals, $A440·1m.; livestock products, $A1,348m.

INDUSTRY AND TRADE

Industry. Perhaps the most significant change in Western Australian manufacturing came when the basis for an integrated industrial complex was established with the opening of a large oil refinery at Kwinana in 1954. Two of the plants in the Kwinana complex are directly concerned with metals processing. An alumina refinery commenced operations in 1964 and a nickel refinery commenced operations in 1970. Major mineral processing plants outside Kwinana also contribute to Western Australia's manufacturing industry. A plant at Australind, near Bunbury, which extracts titanium dioxide from ilmenite has been in operation since 1963. A nickel smelter commenced operations at Kalgoorlie in 1973 and another alumina refinery, at Pinjarra, began operating in 1972. In addition, two new alumina refineries are now in operation, one at Wagerup and the other at Worsley.

Besides providing for heavy industry directly associated with minerals processing, the mining development of recent years, especially on the North West Shelf, has also given impetus to other manufacturing activity, particularly to industries associated with the provision of capital equipment and other manufactured goods for the major mining projects.

The following table shows preliminary manufacturing industry statistics for 1987–88 [1]:

Industry sub-division	*Number of establishments operating at 30 June*	*Persons employed [2] 1,000*	*Wages and salaries $Am.*	*Turnover $Am.*
Food, beverages and tobacco	376	12·7	293	2,112
Textiles	45	1·4	24	117
Clothing and footwear	74	1·8	25	72
Wood, wood products and furniture	451	9·0	161	787
Paper, paper products, printing and publishing	247	7·4	159	622
Chemical, petroleum and coal products	76	3·1	87	716
Non-metallic mineral products	199	4·8	116	668
Basic metal products	48	5·9	182	1,893
Fabricated metal products	430	9·4	200	945
Transport equipment	165	4·8	106	387
Other machinery and equipment	368	8·4	187	709
Miscellaneous manufacturing	196	3·4	64	389
Total	2,675	72·1	1,605	9,417

[1] Excludes single establishment enterprises with less than 4 persons employed.
[2] At 30 June. Includes working proprietors.

Labour. A Court of Arbitration was established in Western Australia in 1901 under the provisions of the 'Industrial Conciliation and Arbitration Act 1900'. The Court of Arbitration was replaced, with effect from 1 Feb. 1964, by the Western Australian Industrial Appeal Court and The Western Australian Industrial Commission, authorities constituted in terms of the *Industrial Arbitration Act 1912*. These authorities continue to operate under the provisions of the *Industrial Arbitration Act 1979* which was proclaimed on 1 March 1980.

The Western Australian Industrial Appeal Court consists of 3 Judges, one of whom is the Presiding Judge. The members are nominated by the Chief Justice of Western Australia. An appeal lies to the Court from decisions of the President of the Western Australian Industrial Commission, the Full Bench or the Commission in Court Session but only on the ground that the decision is erroneous in law or is in excess of jurisdiction.

The Western Australian Industrial Commission consists of a President, a Chief Industrial Commissioner, a Senior Commissioner, and 'such number of other Commissioners as may, from time to time, be necessary'. There were 9 'other Commissioners' at Nov. 1988. A person shall not be appointed as President unless he is qualified to be a Judge, and on appointment he is entitled to the status of a Puisne Judge. The President or a Commissioner sitting or acting alone constitutes the Commission and may exercise the appropriate powers of the Commission.

The Commission can inquire into any industrial matter and make an award, order or declaration relating to such matter. 'Industrial matter' means any matter affecting or relating to the work, privileges, rights, or duties of employers or employees in any industry and includes any matter relating to the wages, salaries, allowances, or other remuneration of employees or the prices to be paid in respect of their employment; the hours of employment, sex, age, qualification or status of employees and the mode, terms and conditions of employment including conditions which are to take effect after the termination of employment. The Commission may also make inquiries where industrial action has occurred or is likely to occur.

The Commission in Court Session is constituted by not less than 3 Commissioners sitting or acting together, and may make General Orders, hear matters referred by the Commission, and hear appeals from decisions of Boards of Reference.

The Full Bench is constituted by not less than 3 members of the Commission, 1 of whom is the President, and may hear matters referred by the Commission on questions of law, and appeals from decisions of the Commission and Industrial Magistrates.

The following table shows details of the number of industrial awards, unions and members registered with The Western Australian Industrial Commission.

At 30 June	*1985*	*1986*	*1987*	*1988*	*1989*
Awards in force	630	608	592	610	628
Employee organizations:					
Number	70	72	69	70	69
Membership	185,061	176,769	189,770	186,608	187,206
Employer organizations:					
Number	15	15	15	15	16
Membership	2,535	3,561	2,690	2,825	2,817

Commerce. The external commerce of Western Australia, exclusive of interstate trade, is comprised in the statement of the commerce of Australia, *see* pp. 108–10.

The total value of imports and exports, including interstate trade, but excluding interstate value of horses, in 5 years (30 June) is, in $A1m., as follows:

	1983–84	*1984–85*	*1986–87*	*1987–88*	*1988–89*
Imports	5,574·4	6,446·5	6,984·9	7,878·2	8,621·5
Exports [1]	6,466·3	7,535·8	8,149·6	8,721·4	9,300·3

[1] Including ships' stores.

Selected overseas exports (in $A) for 1988–89: Iron ore and concentrates, 1,718,621,000; wheat, 981,469,529; wool, 164,406,454; petroleum and petroleum products, 258,026,576; gold bullion, 414,024,621; live sheep and lambs, 62,256,210; beef and veal, 73,606,700; salt, 118,153,754; mutton and lamb, 38,009,713; barley, 60,780,944; prawns, 33,321,973; hides and skins (including fur skins), 32,054,789; whole rock lobsters, 112,334,629; fruit and nuts (fresh or dried), 8,157,541; oats, 29,151,850.

Selected overseas imports (in $A) for 1988–89: Petroleum and petroleum products, 490,658,974; machinery, 702,487,987; transport equipment, 650,498,077;

iron and steel, 81,587,370; chemicals, 312,551,783; food, 94,078,966; crude fertilizer, 33,948,056; rubber manufactures, 100,105,317.

The chief countries exporting to Western Australia in 1988–89 were (in $A): Japan, 753,739,437; USA, 510,431,400; UK, 339,285,957; United Arab Emirates, 259,131,776; Federal Republic of Germany, 171,378,240; Canada, 144,849,607; Singapore, 142,203,655. Western Australia's exports in 1988–89 (in $A) went chiefly to: Japan, 2,263,689,090; USA, 1,394,295,151; Singapore, 407,487,809; China, People's Republic of, 366,354,734; Republic of Korea, 362,477,407; USSR, 316,695,290; Indonesia, 272,711,750.

Tourism. In 1986–87, 216,000 international visitors contributed $A237m. to the economy; 444,200 interstate tourists contributed $274m.; 4,617,000 intrastate tourists contributed $A932m.

COMMUNICATIONS

Roads. At 30 June 1988 there were 122,380 km of prepared and formed roads in Western Australia, 41,585 km of bituminous surface, 40,635 km other constructed surfaces and 40,159 km formed but not metalled or otherwise prepared. In addition, there are 19,539 km of roads unprepared except for clearing which are used for general traffic.

New motor vehicles registered in Western Australia during the year ended 30 June 1989 were 60,771.

Railways. At 30 June 1988 the State had 5,553 km of State government railway and 731 km of Federal line, the latter being the western portion of the Trans-Australian line (Kalgoorlie–Port Pirie), which links the State railway system to those of the other States of the Commonwealth. At 30 June 1988, mining companies operated 1,193 km of private railways for the transport of ore to ports on the north-west coast. In 1987–88 state railways carried 22m. tonnes and 449,000 passengers. Perth suburban lines, controlled by a separate authority, carried 9·6m. passengers.

Aviation. An extensive system of regular air services operates in Western Australia for the transport of passengers, freight and mail. During the year ended 31 Dec. 1987, Perth Airport handled 21,309 aircraft movements and 2,075,562 passengers on domestic and international services.

Shipping. In 1987–88, the number of overseas direct vessels through the major ports was: Port of Fremantle, 1,025 entered, 1,004 cleared; Port Hedland, 405 entered, 395 cleared; other ports, 1,184 entered, 1,168 cleared. The gross weight (in tonnes) of overseas cargo through those ports was: Port of Fremantle, 25,854,495 discharged, 25,621,064 loaded; Port Hedland, 44,255,455 discharged, 42,839,438 loaded; other ports, 82,024 470 discharged, 82,233,328 loaded.

Post and Broadcasting. Postal, telephone and telegraph facilities are afforded at 400 offices. Telephone services connected totalled 635,786 at 30 June 1988.

There were 96 radio broadcasting and 96 television stations, including translator stations, in operation at 30 June 1988.

JUSTICE, RELIGION, EDUCATION AND WELFARE

Justice. In Western Australia justice is administered by a Supreme Court, consisting of a Chief Justice, 9 puisne judges and 2 masters at 30 June 1988; a District Court comprising a chief judge and 14 other judges and Magistrates' Courts exercising both civil and criminal jurisdiction. The lower courts are presided over by justices of the peace, except in the more important centres, where the court is constituted by a stipendiary magistrate. Juvenile offenders may be dealt with either by the Children's (Suspended Proceedings) Panel or by the Children's Court. The Panel is comprised of 1 representative from the Department for Community Services and 1 from the Police Department. It is empowered to deal with certain offences involving first offenders under the age of 16 years who have pleaded guilty. Other young offenders are dealt with by the Children's Court, which is presided over by a Magistrate.

Offences against law	*1984–85*	*1985–86*	*1986–87*	*1987–88*
Charges	115,739 [1]	...	211,966	...
Lower Court convictions [2]	105,025 [1]	...	190,372	...
Higher Court convictions	3,369	4,142	3,912	5,239

[1] Excludes Perth and East Perth Lower Courts.
[2] Includes convictions for traffic offences: 43,851 in 1984–85; 87,140 in 1986–87. In addition, small fines were imposed for minor traffic offences as follows: 1983, 348,009; 1984, 373,662; 1985, 416,774; 1986, 401,415; 1987, 533,012; 1988, 525,581

Persons in prison at 30 June 1989 numbered 1,494 males and 92 females.

Religion. There is no State Church, and freedom of worship is accorded to all. At the census, 30 June 1986, the principal denominations were: Anglican, 371,302; Catholic, 347,695; Uniting, 82,876; Presbyterian, 31,641; Baptist, 16,869; Orthodox, 16,722; other Christian, 110,922; Buddhist, 7,178; all other, including not stated and no religion, 421,724.

Education. School attendance is compulsory from the age of 6 until the end of the year in which the child attains 15 years. Pre-school education is provided by a kindergarten system partly financed from government subsidy. In 1988 there were 743 government primary and secondary schools providing free education to 210,083 students and 242 non-government primary and secondary schools providing education, for which fees are charged, to 65,330 students.

Technical education is available at a number of technical colleges, schools and centres, which are staffed and controlled by the Ministry of Education.

Tertiary Education at 30 April 1987:

	Teaching Staff [1]	*Students Enrolled*
University of Western Australia	600	9,625
Murdoch University	237	4,624
Curtin University of Technology	720	12,669
Western Australian College of Advanced Education	569	10,775

[1] Comprises full-time teaching staff and part-time staff on the basis of equivalent full-time staff.

State Government expenditure from consolidated revenue on education during the year ended 30 June 1988, amounted to $A851,930,578.

Social Welfare. At 30 June 1987 there were 44 general hospitals and 8 nursing homes maintained wholly by public funds and 43 general hospitals and 9 nursing homes partly assisted therefrom. In addition, there are numerous private hospitals.

The Health Department of Western Australia Psychiatric Services comprises 3 approved hospitals, 10 outpatient clinics for adults, 10 general rehabilitation units, 7 psychiatric extended care units and 1 rehabilitation hostel. Specifically for children are: 3 outpatient clinics and 3 residential units. The Authority for the Intellectually Handicapped comprises 24 hostels and 20 group homes.

The Department for Community Services is responsible for the provision of welfare and community services throughout the State. There were 10 directorates in the Department on 30 June 1986. Six were regionally based, 3 in the Perth metropolitan area and 3 were in the country. These are concerned with direct service delivery, which is provided through 20 divisional and 35 district offices.

Direct services provided to the community include emergency financial assistance, family and substitute care, and counselling and psychological services. The Department supervises children's Day Care Centres. There is a 24-hour emergency welfare service provided through the Crisis Care Unit. Specialist units work in the areas of child abuse, adoptions, youth activities and Family Court counselling.

The Department provides residential facilities for the temporary accommodation, care and training of children and is also responsible for young offenders recommended for detention or remand by a Court.

Age, invalid, widows', disability and service pensions, and unemployment benefits are paid by the Federal Government. The number of pensioners in Western Australia at 30 June 1986 was: Age, 103,085; invalid, 25,769; widows, 12,817; disability, 35,223 and service, 36,423. There were 55,089 recipients of unemployment benefits at 30 June 1986.

During 1985–86 the department provided emergency assistance in 102,734 cases. This assistance, valued at $A4,504,000, was in the form of cash, vouchers to purchase goods and services, and payment on behalf of individuals.

Further Reading

Statistical Information: The State Government Statistician's Office was established in 1897 and now functions as the Western Australian Office of the Australian Bureau of Statistics (Merlin Centre, 30 Terrace Road, Perth). *Deputy Commonwealth Statistician and Government Statistician:* B. N. Pink. Its principal publications are: *Western Australian Year Book* (new series, from 1957). *Western Australian Facts and Figures* (from 1989). *Monthly Summary of Statistics* (from 1958)

Battye, J. S., *Western Australia: A History from its Discovery to the Inauguration of the Commonwealth.* Oxford, 1924.—*The Cyclopedia of Western Australia.* Adelaide, Vol. 1 (1912), Vol. 2 (1913)
Crowley, F. K., *Australia's Western Third: A History of Western Australia from the First Settlements to Modern Times.* (Rev. ed.). Melbourne, 1970
Kimberly, W. B., *History of Western Australia: A Narrative of Her Past.* Melbourne, 1897
Stannage, C. T. (ed.) *A New History of Western Australia.* Perth, 1980
Stephenson, G. and Hepburn, J. A., *Plan for the Metropolitan Region: Perth and Fremantle.* Perth, 1955

State Library: Alexander Library Building, Perth. *State Librarian:* R. C. Sharman, BA, FLAA.

AUSTRIA

Capital: Vienna
Population: 7·6m. (1988)
GNP per capita: US$16,595 (1988)

Republik Österreich

HISTORY. Following the break-up of the Austro–Hungarian Empire, the Republic of Austria was proclaimed on 12 Nov. 1918. On 12 March 1938 Austria was forcibly absorbed in the German Reich as *Ostmark* until it was liberated by the Allied armies in 1945. On 27 April 1945 a provisional government was set up and was recognized by the Allies on 20 Oct. 1945. Austria recovered its full independence on 27 July 1955.

AREA AND POPULATION. Austria is a land-locked country bounded north by the Federal Republic of Germany and Czechoslovakia, east by Hungary, south by Yugoslavia and Italy, and west by Switzerland and Liechtenstein. It has an area of 83,857 sq. km (32,377 sq. miles) and its population at recent censuses has been as follows:

1923	6,534,481	1951	6,933,905	1971	7,456,403
1934	6,760,233	1961	7,073,807	1981	7,555,338

Estimate (1988) 7,596,100. In 1981, 55% were urban and 97% were German-speaking, with linguistic minorities of Turks (60,000), Slovenes and Croats (32,000), Slovaks (23,000), Hungarians (19,000) and Czechs (10,000). The areas, populations and capitals of the 9 federal states are as follows:

Federal States	*Area sq. km*	*Population (1988)*	*State capitals*
Vienna (Wien)	415	1,482,800	Vienna
Lower Austria (Niederösterreich)	19,174	1,428,700	St Pölten
Burgenland	3,965	266,800	Eisenstadt
Upper Austria (Oberösterreich)	11,980	1,300,300	Linz
Salzburg	7,154	464,600	Salzburg
Styria (Steiermark)	16,387	1,181,000	Graz
Carinthia (Kärnten)	9,533	541,800	Klagenfurt
Tirol	12,647	613,700	Innsbruck
Vorarlberg	2,601	316,300	Bregenz

Vital statistics for calendar years:

	Live births	*Still births*	*Deaths* [1]	*Marriages*	*Divorces*
1985	87,440	407	89,578	44,867	15,460
1986	86,964	385	87,071	45,821	14,679
1987	86,503	289	84,907	76,205	14,639
1988	88,052	325	83,263	35,361	14,924

[1] Excluding still births.

The populations of the principal towns (excluding Vienna), according to the census of 12 May 1981 (area, 1 Jan. 1988) were as follows:

Graz	243,166	Steyr	38,942	Feldkirch	23,745	Mödling	19,276
Linz	199,910	Dornbirn	38,641	Baden	23,140	Lustenau	17,401
Salzburg	139,426	Wiener Neustadt	35,006	Krems a.d.D.	23,056	Braunau am Inn	16,318
Innsbruck	117,287	Leoben	31,989	Klosterneuburg	22,975	Ternitz	16,104
Klagenfurt	87,321	Wolfsberg	28,097	Amstetten	21,989	Hallein	15,377
Villach	52,692	Kapfenberg	25,716	Traun	21,464	Bruck an der Mur	15,068
Wels	51,060	Bregenz	24,561	Leonding	19,389		
St Pölten	50,419						

CLIMATE. Climate ranges from cool temperate to mountain type according to situation. Winters are cold, with considerable snowfall, but summers are very warm. The wettest months are May to August.

Vienna, Jan. 28°F (–2°C), July 67°F (19·5°C). Annual rainfall 25·6" (640 mm). Graz, Jan. 28°F (–2°C), July 67°F (19·5°C). Annual rainfall 34" (849 mm). Innsbruck, Jan. 27°F (–2·7°C), July 66°F (18·8°C). Annual rainfall 34·7" (868 mm). Salzburg, Jan. 28°F (–2·0°C), July 65°F (18·3°C). Annual rainfall 50·6" (1,266 mm).

CONSTITUTION AND GOVERNMENT. Austria recovered its sovereignty and independence on 27 July 1955 by the coming into force of the Austrian State Treaty between the UK, the USA, the USSR and France on the one part and the Republic of Austria on the other part (signed on 15 May).

The Constitution of 1 Oct. 1920 was restored on 27 April 1945. Austria is a democratic federal republic comprising 9 states *(länder)*, with a federal President *(Bundespräsident)* directly elected for not more than 2 successive 6-year terms, and a bicameral National Assembly which comprises a National Council and a Federal Council.

The National Council *(Nationalrat)* comprises 183 members directly elected for a 4-year term by proportional representation on a national basis. At the General Elections held on 23 Nov. 1986 the *Sozialistische Partei Österreichs* (SPÖ) won 80 seats, the *Österreichische Volkspartei* (ÖVP) 77 seats, the *Freiheitliche Partei Österreichs* (FPÖ) 18 seats and the *Vereinigte Grüne Österreich* (VGÖ or ecologists) 8 seats. The Federal Council *(Bundesrat)* 63 members appointed by the 9 states for the duration of the individual State Assemblies' terms; in 1987 the ÖVP held 33 seats and the SPÖ 30 seats.

The head of government is a Federal Chancellor, who is appointed by the President from the party winning the most seats in National Council elections. The Chancellor nominates a Vice-Chancellor and other Ministers for the President to appoint to a Council of Ministers which the Chancellor leads.

Federal President: Dr Kurt Waldheim (elected 8 June 1986; took office 8 July).

The coalition government was formed on 25 Jan. 1987 by the SPÖ and ÖVP and in Oct. 1989 was composed as follows:

Chancellor: Dr Franz Vranitzky.

Vice Chancellor and Federalism and Administrative Reform: Dr Josef Riegler. *Foreign Affairs:* Dr Alois Mock. *Economic Affairs:* Dr Wolfgang Schüssel. *Employment and Social Affairs:* Dr Walter Geppert. *Finance:* Ferdinand Lacina. *Health and Public Service:* Harald Ettl. *Interior:* Dr Franz Löschnak. *Justice:* Dr Egmont Foregger. *National Defence:* Dr Robert Lichal. *Agriculture and Forestry:* Dr Franz Fischler. *Environment, Youth and Family:* Dr Marilies Flemming. *Education, The Arts and Sport:* Dr Hilde Hawlicek. *Public Economy and Transport:* Dr Rudolf Streicher. *Science and Research:* Dr Erhard Busek.

The Federal Council *(Bundesrat)* which represents the federal provinces has 63 members and (1987) the Socialist Party had 30 members and the People's Party 33. The *Nationalrat* and *Bundesrat* together form the National Assembly.

National flag: Three horizontal stripes of red, white, red.

National anthem: Land der Berge, Land am Strome (words by Paula Preradovic; tune by W. A. Mozart).

The official language is German.

Local Government. The Republic of Austria comprises 9 Federal States (Vienna, Lower Austria, Upper Austria, Salzburg, Styria, Carinthia, Tirol, Vorarlberg, Burgenland). There is in every province an elected Provincial Assembly.

Every community has a Council, which chooses one of its number to be head of the Community (burgomaster) and a committee for the administration and execution of its resolutions.

DEFENCE. Conscription is for a 6-month period, with liability for 60 days reservist refresher training spread over 15 years.

Army. The Army consists of an alert force *(Bereitschafts truppe)*, mainly the 1st Armoured Division organized in 3 armoured infantry brigades; 1 air-missile and mountain battalion; field units with 3 artillery, 2 anti-aircraft, 1 anti-tank and 2 engineering battalions; and territorial troops, comprising 26 regiments and security companies. Strength was (1990) 38,000 (25,000 conscripts).

Army Aviation. *(Heeresfliegerkräfte):* The Division comprises 10 squadrons with about 4,500 personnel and about 200 aircraft, organized in three Aviation Regiments each of which including air defence battalions. PC-7 Turbo-trainers are also in service. Some 24 Draken interceptors equip 2 squadrons of a surveillance wing responsible for defence of Austrian airspace and a fighter-bomber wing of two squadrons. Helicopters equip six squadrons for transport/support, communications, observation, search and rescue duties. Types in service include 24 Alouette III, 12 armed Kiowa, JetRanger, 36 Agusta-Bell AB.204, AB.206 and AB.212s. Fixed-wing transports comprise two Skyvans and 12 Turbo-Porters.

INTERNATIONAL RELATIONS

Membership. Austria is a member of UN, OECD and EFTA.

ECONOMY

Budget. The budget for calendar years provided revenue and expenditure (ordinary and extraordinary) as follows (in 1m. schilling):

	1984	*1985*	*1986*	*1987*	*1988*	*1989* [1]	*1990* [2]
Revenue	344,901	372,895	391,675	409,556	446,409	465,409	486,081
Expenditure	435,135	464,673	498,390	514,461	517,583	531,535	549,038

[1] Preliminary. [2] Estimates.

External debt. The budgetary external debt was (1989) 132,300m. schilling.

Currency. The Austrian unit of currency is the *schilling* of 100 *groschen.* The rate of exchange in March 1990, £1 = 19·65 *schilling*, US$1 = 11·99 *schilling*.

Banking. The National Bank of Austria, opened on 2 Jan. 1923, was taken over by the German Reichsbank on 17 March 1938. It was re-established on 3 July 1945. At 31 Dec. 1989 foreign exchange amounted to 94,296m. and note circulation to 112,761m. schilling.

Principal banks with total assets (in 1m. schilling 1988): Creditanstalt, 405,436; Girozentrale Und Bank der Österreichischen Sparkassen, 287,135; Österreichische National Bank, 223,194; Österreichische Länderbank, 213,869; Zentralsparkasse Und Kommerzialbank, 220,956; Österreichische Kontrollbank, 177,030; Bank für Arbeit und Wirtschaft, 185,656; Genossenschaftliche Zentralbank, 173,518; Österreichische Postsparkasse, 170,251; Die Erste Österreichische Spar-Casse-Bank, 143,687; Österreichische Volksbanken, 60,276; Österreichische Investitionskredit, 46,775; Bank Für Oberösterreich Und Salzburg, 43,501; Österreichisches Credit Institut, 38,551.

Weights and Measures. The metric system of weights and measures has been in force since 1872.

ENERGY AND NATURAL RESOURCES

Electricity. Electric energy produced (1m. kwh.): 1988, 49,013; 1987, 50,518; 1986, 44,653; 1985, 44,534; 1984, 42,382. Supply 220 volts; 50 Hz.

Oil. The commercial production of petroleum began in the early 1930s. Production of crude oil (in tonnes): 1960, 2,448,391; 1971, 2,798,237; 1985, 1,146,958; 1986, 1,115,924; 1987, 1,060,367; 1988, 1,175,186.

Gas. Production of natural gas (in 1,000 cu. metres): 1987, 1,167,340; 1988, 1,264,564.

Minerals. The mineral production (in tonnes) was as follows:

	1987	*1988*		*1987*	*1988*
Lignite	2,785,611	2,129,258	Pig-iron	3,450,714	3,664,805
Iron ore	3,050,000	2,300,000	Raw steel	4,301,165	4,560,072
Lead and zinc ore [1]	322,088	372,393	Rolled steel	3,432,451	3,751,956
Raw magnesite [1]	946,943	1,121,585	Gypsum	655,051	721,745

[1] Including recovery from slag.

Austria is one of the world's largest sources of high-grade graphite. Production, which averaged 20,000 tonnes yearly from 1929 to 1944, dropped to 246 in 1946, but rose to 102,237 in 1964, and fell again to 23,992 in 1970, 37,199 in 1980, 24,451 in 1982, 40,418 in 1983, 43,789 in 1984, 30,764 in 1985, 36,167 in 1986, 39,391 in 1987 and 7,577 in 1988.

Agriculture. In 1989 the total area cultivated amounted to 3,548,239 hectares.

The chief products (area in hectares, yield in tonnes) were as follows:

	1987		*1988*		*1989*	
	Area	*Yield*	*Area*	*Yield*	*Area*	*Yield*
Wheat	320,366	1,450,731	291,938	1,559,993	278,068	1,362,951
Rye	85,415	309,327	87,889	355,888	91,019	381,188
Barley	291,496	1,178,686	292,384	1,366,424	291,876	1,421,645
Oats	69,373	245,728	69,145	273,067	67,150	249,063
Potatoes	34,128	879,497	33,115	1,001,044	32,395	845,466

Production of raw sugar in 1949, 66,700; 1955, 219,300; 1960, 308,000; refined sugar: 1970, 298,000; 1980, 419,800; 1982, 563,472; 1983, 354,479; 1984, 426,544; 1985, 430,730; 1986, 282,576; 1987, 358,951; 1988, 327,270 tonnes.

Livestock (1988): Cattle, 2,541,405; pigs, 3,873,884; sheep, 255,623; goats, 44,350; horses, 45,179; poultry, 13,589,542.

Forestry. Forested area in 1988, 3·2m. hectares (39% of the land area) of which 75% coniferous. Felled timber, in cu. metres: 1960, 10,015,925; 1970, 11,122,896; 1980, 12,732,507; 1987, 11,759,643; 1988, 12,032,399.

INDUSTRY AND TRADE

Industry. On 26 July 1946 the Austrian parliament passed a government bill, nationalizing some 70 industrial concerns. As from 17 Sept. 1946 ownership of the 3 largest commercial banks, most oil-producing and refining companies and the principal firms in the following industries devolved upon the Austrian state: River navigation; coal extraction; non-ferrous mining and refining; iron-ore mining; pig-iron and steel production; manufacture of iron and steel products, including structural material, machinery, railroad equipment and repairs, and shipbuilding; electrical machinery and appliances. Six companies supplying electric power were nationalized in accordance with a law of 26 March 1947.

In 1988, 9,377 industrial establishments (including 2,056 sawmills) employed 541,985 persons, producing a value of 623,000m. schillings (excluding value added tax).

Commerce. Imports and exports are as follows (excluding coined gold):

	Imports			*Exports*		
	1986	*1987*	*1988*	*1986*	*1987*	*1988*
Quantity (1,000 tonnes)	38,910	39,680	40,974	18,050	18,718	20,038
Value (1m. sch.)	407,954	411,859	451,442	342,479	342,433	383,213

The total trade between Austria and UK (British Department of Trade returns, in £1,000 sterling):

	1985	*1986*	*1987*	*1988*	*1989*
Imports to UK	630,586	705,732	781,986	824,616	933,971
Exports and re-exports from UK	381,047	403,000	463,187	509,991	598,099

Tourism. Tourism is an important industry. In 1988, 20,260 hotels and boarding-houses had a total of 653,931 beds available; 16,571,289 foreigners visited Austria; of these 753,230 came from the UK and 620,078 from the USA.

COMMUNICATIONS

Roads. On 31 Dec. 1988 federal roads had a total length of 10,269 km, 1,405 km autobahn; provincial roads, 22,904 km. On 31 Dec. 1988 there were registered 4,059,084 motor vehicles, including 2,784,792 passenger cars, 234,611 lorries, 381,055 tractors and 310,512 trailers.

Railways. Austrian railways have been nationalized since before the First World War. Length of route (Dec. 1988), 5,772 km, of which 3,210 km were electrified. Nineteen private railways have a total length of 566 km. Passengers in 1988 numbered 175m., and 63m. tonnes of freight were carried.

Aviation. Austria has 6 airports in Vienna (Schwechat), Linz, Salzburg, Graz, Klagenfurt and Innsbruck. In 1988, 104,381 commercial aircraft and 5,828 459 passengers arrived and departed at Austrian airports; 52,686 tonnes of freight, 14,651 tonnes of transit freight and 7,476 tonnes of mail were handled.

Shipping. Austria has no sea frontiers, but the Danube is an important waterway. Goods traffic (in tonnes): 8,093,854 in 1984;.7,619,115 in 1985; 7,708,311 in 1986; 8,027,360 in 1987; 8,832,907 in 1988. Ore and metal, coal and coke and iron ore comprise in bulk more than two-thirds of these cargoes. The Danube Steamship Co. (DDSG) is the main Austrian shipping company.

Post and Broadcasting. All postal, telegraph and telephone services are run by the State. In 1988 there were 3,001,319 telephones.

The 'Österreichische Rundfunk' transmits 2 national and 9 regional programmes. In the local area of Vienna there is an additional special service in English and French; there is also a 24 hour foreign service (short wave). All broadcasting is financed by licence payments and advertisements. There were 2·7m. registered listeners in Dec. 1988. Television was inaugurated in summer 1955 and 2 programmes are transmitted, both in colour, with 2·5m. licences in Dec. 1988.

Cinemas (1988). There were 413 cinemas.

Newspapers (1988). There were 34 daily newspapers (7 of them in Vienna) and a circulation of 2·7m. of all Austrian newspapers.

JUSTICE, RELIGION, EDUCATION AND WELFARE

Justice. The Supreme Court of Justice *(Oberster Gerichtshof)* in Vienna is the highest court in the land. Besides there are 4 higher provincial courts *(Oberlandesgerichte)*, 21 provincial and district courts *(Landes- und Kreisgerichte)* and 205 local courts *(Bezirksgerichte)* (1988).

Religion. In 1981 there were 6,372,645 Roman Catholics (84·3%), 423,162 Protestants (5·6%), 118,866 others (1·6%), 452,039 without religious allegiance (6%) and 79,017 (1%) unknown. The Roman Catholic Church has 2 archbishoprics and 7 bishoprics. There were (1988) 60,000 Moslems in Austria.

Education (1988–89). There were in Austria 5,110 elementary and special schools with 68,384 teachers and 469,697 pupils. Of all kinds of secondary schools there were 1,512 with 492,383 pupils.

There were also 114 commercial academies with 37,608 students and 4,636 teachers. There were 275 schools of technical and industrial training (including schools of hotel management and catering) with 6,341 teachers and 65,200 pupils; 52 higher schools of women's professions (secondary level) with 14,154 pupils; 9 training colleges of social workers with 631 pupils. 123 trade schools had 13,749 pupils.

Austria has 12 universities and 6 colleges of arts maintained by the State: Universities at Vienna (2,951 teachers, 61,878 students), Graz (1,155 teachers, 22,521 students), Innsbruck (1,445 teachers, 19,341 students) and Salzburg (519 teachers, 9,977 students). There are also technical universities at Vienna (1,069 teachers, 17,394 students) and Graz (648 teachers, 9,282 students), a mining university at Leoben (175 teachers, 1,884 students), an agricultural university at Vienna (325 teachers, 5,471 students), a veterinary university at Vienna (175 teachers, 2,485 students), a commercial university at Vienna (289 teachers, 18,202 students), a university for social and economic sciences at Linz (405 teachers, 9,458 students) and a university for educational science at Klagenfurt (156 teachers, 2,998 students). There is an academy of fine arts at Vienna (170 teachers, 496 students), a college of applied arts at Vienna (252 teachers, 1,003 students), 3 colleges of music and dramatic art at Vienna (558 teachers, 2,129 students), 'Mozarteum' Salzburg (335 teachers, 1,307 students) and Graz (315 teachers, 1,193 students); the college for industrial design at Linz (118 teachers, 413 students).

Health. In 1988 there were 23,907 doctors, 333 hospitals and 81,582 hospital beds.

DIPLOMATIC REPRESENTATIVES

Of Austria in Great Britain (18 Belgrave Mews West, London, SW1X 8HU)
Ambassador: Dr Walter F. Magrutsch (accredited 11 Feb. 1988).

Of Great Britain in Austria (Jaurèsgasse 12, 1030 Vienna)
Ambassador: Brian Lee Crowe, CMG (accredited 2 June 1989).

Of Austria in the USA (2343 Massachusetts Ave., NW, Washington, D.C., 20008)
Ambassador: Dr Friedrich Hoess (accredited 21 Dec. 1988).

Of the USA in Austria (Boltzmanngasse, 16, A-1091 Vienna)
Chargé d'Affaires: Michael J. Habib.

Of Austria to the United Nations
Ambassador: Dr Peter Hohenfellner (accredited 24 Feb. 1988).

Further Reading

Statistical Information: The Austrian Central Statistical Office was founded in 1829. *Address:* Hintere Zollamtsstrasze 2b, 1033 Vienna. *President:* Mag. Erich Bader.

Main publications:
Statistisches Handbuch für die Republik Österreich. New Series from 1950. Annually
Statistische Nachrichten. Monthly
Beiträge zur österreichischen Statistik (850 vols.)
Ergebnisse der Volkszählung vom 12 Mai 1981 (26 vols.)
Ergebnisse der Häuser- und Wohnungszählung vom 12 Mai 1981 (14 vols.)
Statistik in Österreich 1918–1938. [Bibliography] Vienna, 1985
Veröffentlichungen des Österr. Statist. Zentralamtes 1945-1985. [Bibliography] Vienna, 1986

Bobek, H. (ed.) *Atlas de Republik Österreich.* 3 vols. Vienna, 1961 ff.
Salt, D., *Austria.* [Bibliography] Oxford and Santa Barbara, 1986
Sotriffer, K., *Greater Austria: 100 Years of Intellectual and Social Life from 1800 to the Present Time.* Vienna, 1982
Waldheim, K., *In the Eye of the Storm.* London, 1985

National Library: Österreichische Nationalbibliothek, Vienna. *Director General:* Dr Magda Strebl.

THE COMMONWEALTH OF THE BAHAMAS

Capital: Nassau
Population: 236,171 (1986)
GNP per capita: US$10,570 (1988)

HISTORY. The Bahamas were discovered by Columbus in 1492 but the Spanish did not make a permanent settlement. British settlers arrived in the 17th century and it was occupied by Britain, except for a short period in the 18th century, until it gained independence. Internal self-government with cabinet responsibility was introduced on 7 Jan. 1964 and full independence achieved on 10 July 1973.

AREA AND POPULATION. The Commonwealth of The Bahamas consists of 700 islands and more than 1,000 cays off the south-east coast of Florida. They are the surface protuberances of two oceanic banks, the Little Bahama Bank and the Great Bahama Bank. Land area, 5,353 sq. miles (13,864 sq. km).

The areas and populations of the major islands are as follows:

	Sq. km	*1980*		*Sq. km*	*1980*
Grand Bahama	1,373	33,102	San Salvador	163	825
Abaco	1,681	7,271	Rum Cay	78	
Bimini Islands	23	1,411	Long Island	448	3,404
Berry Islands	31	509	Ragged Island	23	164
New Providence	207	135,437	Crooked Island	238	518
Andros	5,957	8,307	Long Cay	23	33
Eleuthera	518	8,331	Acklins Island	389	618
Cat Island	388	2,215	Mayaguana	110	464
Exuma Islands	290	3,670	Inagua Islands	1,671	924

The capital is Nassau on New Providence Island (135,437 inhabitants in 1980) and the only other large town is Freeport (24,423) on Grand Bahama. About 13% of the population were (1980) of British extraction, the rest being of African and mixed descent.

Vital statistics, 1987: Births, 4,018; deaths, 1,212 (excluding still-births); marriages, 1,830.

CLIMATE. Winters are mild and summers pleasantly warm. Most rain falls in May, June, Sept. and Oct., and thunderstorms are frequent in summer. Rainfall amounts vary over the islands from 30" (750 mm) to 60" (1,500 mm). Nassau. Jan. 71°F (21·7°C), July 81°F (27·2°C). Annual rainfall 47" (1,179 mm).

CONSTITUTION AND GOVERNMENT. The Commonwealth of The Bahamas is a free and democratic sovereign state. Executive power rests with Her Majesty the Queen, who appoints a Governor-General to represent her, advised by a Cabinet whom he appoints. There is a bicameral legislature. The Senate comprises 16 members all appointed by the Governor-General, 9 on the advice of the Prime Minister, 4 on the advice of the Leader of the Opposition, and 3 after consultation with both of them. The House of Assembly consists of 49 members elected from single-member constituencies for a maximum term of 5 years. At the general election of 19 June 1987, the Progressive Liberal Party obtained 31 seats, the Free National Movement 16 seats and 2 independents.

Independence from Britain took place on 10 July 1973.

Governor-General: Sir Henry Taylor.

The Cabinet in Nov. 1989 was composed as follows:

Prime Minister, Finance: Rt. Hon. Sir Lynden O. Pindling, KCMG.

Deputy Prime Minister, Tourism and Public Personnel: Sir Clement T. Maynard. *National Security, Education:* Paul L. Adderley. *Works and Lands:* Darrell E. Rolle. *Housing and National Insurance:* George W. Mackey. *Employment and Immigra-*

tion: Alfred T. Maycock. *Transport and Local Government:* Philip M. Bethel. *Health:* Norman R. Gay. *Agriculture, Trade and Industry:* Ervin Knowles. *Foreign Affairs:* Edward C. Carter. *Attorney-General:* Sean McWeeny. *Consumer Affairs:* Dr Bernard J. Nottage. *Youth, Sports and Community Affairs:* Peter Bethel.

National flag: Three horizontal stripes of aquamarine, gold, aquamarine, with a black triangle on the hoist.

DEFENCE. The Royal Bahamian Defence Force is a maritime force tasked with naval patrols and protection duties in the extensive waters of the archipelago. Equipment comprises 3 33 metre fast inshore patrol craft, 8 smaller inshore patrol craft and 6 boats, together with 2 small support craft. There are 3 Jetstream Commander light reconnaissance aircraft. Personnel (1989) 750, and the base is at Coral Harbour on New Providence Island.

INTERNATIONAL RELATIONS

Membership. The Commonwealth of The Bahamas is a member of UN, OAS, the Commonwealth, CARICOM and an ACP state of the EEC.

ECONOMY

Budget (in B$):

	1985	*1986*	*1987*
Revenue	401,160,713	435,547,873	468,849,335
Expenditure	416,512,806	420,616,320	478,199,453

The main sources of revenue were customs duties and receipts from fees, post office and public utilities.

Currency. A decimal system of currency was introduced in 1966. Bahamian $1.64 = £1 sterling (March 1990). Notes: $0.50, 1, 3, 5, 10, 20, 50, 100; coins: 1, 5, 10, 15, 25, 50 cents, $1, 2, 5. Sterling currency has been withdrawn. American currency is generally accepted.

Bank of England and Canadian notes are not accepted, except at the banks from travellers from the UK.

Banking. The Central Bank of The Bahamas was established in June 1974. At June 1989, it had assets of B$244·36m. and capital and reserves of B$55·76m. On 30 June 1989 there were 382 institutions licensed to carry on banking and/or trust business under the Bank and Trust Companies Regulations Act. There were 19 designated institutions by the Exchange Control Department as authorized dealers and agents. Among these were the Royal Bank of Canada, the Bank of Nova Scotia, the Bank of Bahamas, Chase Manhattan Bank, Barclays Bank, the Canadian Imperial Bank of Commerce and Citibank. While the majority of banks are located in Nassau, there are branches on several of the other islands. The Bahamas Development Bank was established in 1974 and began operations in Jan. 1978. At June 1989 it had total assets of B$20·3m. and paid-up capital of B$7·25m.

The Post Office Savings Bank, 31 Dec. 1984, had deposits of B$2·7m.

Weights and Measures. The UK (Imperial) system is in force.

ENERGY AND NATURAL RESOURCES

Electricity. Electricity is provided primarily by The Bahamas Electricity Corporation in conjunction with a few private franchises in the Family Islands. As at 31 Dec. 1987, total generated capacity was 306·1 mw; total units generated, 8,570 mwh and total number of consumers, 67,525. Supply 115 volts; 60 Hz.

Agriculture. In 1988 agricultural production was B$28·83m. (1973, B$17·5m.). Chicken and poultry production was estimated at 15·2m. lb in 1988, (16·9m. lb in 1987). Egg production (1988) declined to 3·6m. dozen. Production of sheep, goats and pigs in 1988: 129 sheep, 165 goats and 2,236 pigs were slaughtered. Beef production increased, with 27 beef cattle slaughtered.

Total agricultural production including fisheries was valued at B$62·1m. in 1988, with fisheries accounting for B$33·3m. Production, 1988 (in 1,000 tonnes): Sugarcane, 240; vegetables, 27; fruit, 14.

The quantity of meat derived from livestock in 1988 was: Mutton, 4,441 lb; goat meat, 6,559 lb; beef, 13,000 lb; pork, 158,770 lb.

Livestock (1988): Cattle, 5,000; sheep, 40,000; goats, 19,000; pigs, 20,000; poultry, 1m.

Fisheries. Studies were undertaken in 1986 to assess the viability of a stone crab industry. Aquaculture of red fish and marine shrimp have proved to be important. Exports of spiny lobster and snappers in 1988 were B$26,954,490. (B$24·6m. in 1987). Imports of fish in 1987 were B$4,971,284. (B$4·5m. in 1986).

INDUSTRY AND TRADE

Industry. Tourism is the major industry. Several light industries have been established on Grand Bahama and New Providence in response to special encouragement legislation; these include garment manufacturing, ice, furniture, purified water, plastic containers, perfumes, industrial gases, jewellery and others. Larger industrial activities in The Bahamas include manufacture of alcoholic beverages, pharmaceuticals, aragonite mining and solar salt production. Two industrial sites, one in New Providence and the other in Grand Bahama, have been developed as part of the industrialization programme.

Trade Unions. In 1986 there were 36 unions, the largest is The Bahamas Hotel Catering and Allied Workers' Union (5,000 members) and The Bahamas Public Services Union (over 4,000 members).

Commerce. The principal exports in 1985 were hormones, rum, salt, crawfish, cement and aragonite.

The principal imports in 1985 were: Food, drink and tobacco, raw materials and articles mainly unmanufactured and articles wholly or mainly manufactured.

Imports and exports (excluding bullion and specie) for 7 calendar years in B$:

	Imports	*Exports*		*Imports*	*Exports*
1980	5,506,577	4,836,366	1984	4,224,175	3,539,428
1981	4,203,000	3,515,000	1985	3,081,116	3,033,142
1982	3,051,000	2,444,000	1986	3,323,437	2,702,162
1983	4,616,251	3,970,319			

Total trade in £1,000 sterling, between Bahamas and UK (British Department of Trade returns):

	1985	*1986*	*1987*	*1988*	*1989*
Imports to UK	70,763	10,266	15,943	24,781	17,681
Exports and re-exports from UK	94,059	95,816	27,063	20,708	22,543

Tourism. Tourism is the most important industry in The Bahamas. In 1988 there were just under 3m. foreign arrivals in The Bahamas.

COMMUNICATIONS

Roads. There are 245 miles of paved roads in New Providence, and approximately 885 miles in Grand Bahama and the Family Islands. In 1987, 74,062 motor vehicles were registered. There are no railroads.

Aviation. Nassau international airport is located on the island of New Providence, about 10 miles from the city of Nassau. The other international airport is at Freeport on Grand Bahama Island. Scheduled flights—Air Canada: Once weekly from Toronto and Montreal. Bahamasair: 5 times daily to Miami, once daily to Newark, 3 times a week to Orlando and Tampa. Delta Airlines: Once daily from Nassau to Fort Lauderdale and Dallas; once daily to Atlanta and Boston and once daily to New York. Eastern Airlines: 4 flights daily from Nassau to Miami, 5 daily from Freeport to Miami. British Airways: Once weekly to Kingston and once weekly to Bermuda and London. Braniff Express: 5 flights weekly to Orlando. Henson Airlines: Once daily from Nassau to Fort Lauderdale and Tampa and 4 times daily from Freeport to West Palm Beach. Midway Airlines: Once daily from Nassau to Fort Lauderdale and Chicago. Piedmont Airlines: Once daily to Charlotte and once daily to Baltimore and Hartford. Pan American: Once daily to New York from

Nassau and twice daily from Freeport to Miami. Trans World Airlines: 5 flights weekly to New York and Boston from Nassau, 3 flights weekly from Freeport to New York and once weekly to St Louis. TCNA: Twice weekly from Nassau to Grand Turk, Providenciales and Cape Haitien. Comair: 4 flights daily from Freeport to Fort Lauderdale. Aero Coach: 4 flights daily from Freeport to Fort Lauderdale and 2 daily to West Palm Beach. Canadian Airlines: Twice weekly from Toronto to Treasure Cay, Governor's Harbour and Nassau. There are 58 airstrips on the various Family Islands. During 1986, 1,343,324 passengers landed at Nassau from 61,431 aircraft arrivals. At Freeport in 1986, 618,555 passengers landed from 33,157 aircraft arrivals.

Shipping. In 1987, 2,279 cruise liners cleared Nassau carrying 1,540,000 passengers. In 1984, 542 cargo vessels discharged 757,737 tons of cargo at Nassau. There are indirect cargo services with UK and Canada *via* the USA and passenger services with the USA only.

Post and Telecommunications. In 1985 there were 127 post offices. New Providence and most of the other major islands have modern automatic telephone systems in operation, interconnected by an extensive multi-channel radio network, while local distribution within the islands is by overhead and underground cables. The total number of telephones in use at 31 Dec. 1987 was approximately 119,061. International telecommunications service is provided by a submarine cable system to Florida, USA, and an INTELSAT Standard 'A' Earth Station. International operator assisted and direct dialling telephone services are available to all major countries. There is an automatic Telex system and a packet switching system for data transmission, and land mobile and marine telephone services. The Bahamas Broadcasting Corporation operates radio broadcasting stations on AM and FM in New Providence and Grand Bahama and a TV station in New Providence. In 1986 there were 40,000 television and 120,000 radio receivers.

Cinemas (1988). There are 4 cinemas.

Newspapers (1988). There are 2 daily and 1 weekly newspapers in Nassau.

JUSTICE, RELIGION, EDUCATION AND WELFARE

Justice (1986). 32,878 cases (traffic, 11,334; criminal, 17,970; civil, 2,178; domestic, 1,396) were dealt with in the magistrates' court, and civil, 1,561; divorce, 516; criminal, 200 in the Supreme Court. The strength of the police force (1988) was 1,665 officers and other ranks.

Religion. Over 94% of the population is Christian, with 26% being Roman Catholic, 21% Anglican and 48% other Protestants.

Education. Education is under the jurisdiction of the Ministry of Education and Culture. In 1986–87 there were 230 schools, and of these, 190 are fully maintained by Government and 39 are independent schools. Total school enrolment, 60,189. There are 38 government-owned schools in New Providence and 151 on the Family Islands. 26 independent schools are located on New Providence and 14 on the Family Islands. 280 students attended 5 special schools, 3 on New Providence and 2 on Grand Bahama; total staff, 49. Free education is available in ministry schools in New Providence and the Family Islands. Courses lead to the Bahamas Junior Certificate and the General Certificate of Education (GCE). Independent schools provide education at primary, secondary and higher levels.

The College of The Bahamas, officially opened in 1975, is the only publicly-funded tertiary level institution. It offers a wide range of programmes leading to the associate degree, advanced level GCE (London), college diplomas and certificates. Degree programmes in education are offered in conjunction with the University of the West Indies and the University of Miami. Total enrolment (1987) 5,866 with a staff of 128.

The Hotel Training College offers a wide range of subjects up to middle management level in aspects of hotel work. Enrolment in this institution includes Bahamian as well as regional and international students. Several schools of continuing education offer secretarial and academic courses. The Government-operated Princess Margaret Hospital offers a nursing course at two levels.

Health. In 1988 there was a government general hospital (454 beds) and a psychiatric/geriatric care centre (457 beds) in Nassau, and a hospital in Freeport (74 beds). The Family Islands, comprising 20 health districts, had 13 health centres, 38 main clinics and 52 satellite clinics. There was 1 private hospital (24 beds) in Nassau.

DIPLOMATIC REPRESENTATIVES

Of The Bahamas in Great Britain (10 Chesterfield St., London, W1X 8AH)
High Commissioner: Dr Patricia Rodgers.

Of Great Britain in The Bahamas (Bitco Bldg., East St., Nassau)
High Commissioner: Colin Mays, CMG.

Of The Bahamas in the USA (600 New Hampshire Ave., NW, Washington, D.C., 20037)
Ambassador: Margaret MacDonald, CVO, CBE.

Of the USA in The Bahamas (Queen St., Nassau)
Ambassador: Chic Hecht.

Of The Bahamas to the United Nations
Ambassador: James Moultrie.

Further Reading

Bahamas Handbook and Businessman's Annual (Annual)
Albury, P., *The Story of the Bahamas.* London, 1975.—*Paradise Island Story.* London, 1984
Barrett, P. J. H., *Grand Bahama.* London, 1982
Boultbee, P. G., *Bahamas.* [Bibliography] Oxford and Santa Barbara, 1989
Craton, M. A., *A History of the Bahamas.* London, 1962
Hughes, C. A., *Race and Politics in the Bahamas.* Univ. of Queensland Press, 1981
Hunte, G., *The Bahamas.* London, 1975
Stevenson, C. St. J., *The Bahamas Reference Annual.* Annual

Library: Nassau Public Library.

BAHRAIN

Dawlat al Bahrayn

Capital: Manama
Population: 421,040 (1988)
GNP per capita: US$6,610 (1987)

HISTORY. Treaties with Britain of 1882 and 1892 were replaced by a treaty of friendship which was signed on 15 Aug. 1971. Under the earlier treaties Britain had been responsible for Bahrain's defence and foreign relations. On the same day the State of Bahrain declared its independence.

AREA AND POPULATION. The State of Bahrain forms an archipelago of about 33 small islands in the Arabian Gulf, between the Qatar peninsula and the mainland of Saudi Arabia. The total area is about 265·5 sq. miles (687·75 sq. km). Bahrain ('Two Seas'), is 30 miles long and 10 miles wide (578 sq. km). It is connected by a causeway nearly 1·5 miles long, carrying a motor road, with the second largest island, Muharraq, 4 miles long and 1 mile wide, to the north-east, and by a causeway with Sitra, an island 3 miles long and 1 mile wide, to the east. In Nov. 1986 a causeway linking Bahrain with Saudi Arabia was officially opened. Other islands are Umm Al-Nassan, 3 miles by 2 miles, and Jidda, 1 mile by 0·5 mile, both to the west; Nabih Saleh, to the east; the Hawar group of 16 small islands off Qatar, to the south-east, and several islets, some uninhabited. From Sitra oil pipelines and a causeway carrying a road extend out to sea for 3 miles to a deep-water anchorage. The islands are low-lying, the highest ground being a hill in the centre of Bahrain, 450 ft. (122·4 metres) high.

The population in 1981 (census) was 350,798. Estimate (1988) 421,040. The majority of the people are Moslem arabs.

Arabic is the official language. English is widely used in business.

Manama, the capital of the state and the commercial centre, is situated at the northern end of the largest island and extends for 1·5 miles along the shore. It has a population 1988, of 151,500 (1981 census, 108,684). Other towns are Muharraq, 1988, 78,000 (46,061); Jidhafs, 48,000 (7,232); Rifa'a, 28,150 (22,408); Isa Town (21,275) and Hidd (7,111).

CLIMATE. The climate is pleasantly warm between Dec. and March but from June to Sept. the conditions are very hot and humid. The period June to Nov. is virtually rainless. Bahrain. Jan. 66°F (19°C), July 97°F (36°C). Annual rainfall 5·2" (130 mm).

CONSTITUTION AND GOVERNMENT. A Constitution was ratified in June 1973 providing for a National Assembly of 30 members, popularly elected for a 4-year term, together with all members of the Cabinet (appointed by the Amir). Elections took place in Dec. 1973, but in Aug. 1975 the Amir dissolved the Assembly and has since ruled through the Cabinet alone.

Reigning Amir: The ruling family is the Al Khalifa, an Arab dynasty, who have been in power since 1782. The present Amir, HH Shaikh Isa bin Sulman Al-Khalifa (born 1933) succeeded on 2 Nov. 1961. *Crown Prince:* Shaikh Hamad bin Isa Al-Khalifa.

In Jan. 1989 the cabinet was composed as follows:

Prime Minister: Shaikh Khalifa bin Sulman Al-Khalifa.

Defence: Shaikh Khalifa bin Ahmed Al-Khalifa. *Transport:* Ibrahim Mohammed Hassan Homaidan. *Housing:* Shaikh Khalid bin Abdulla Al-Khalifa. *Information:* Tariq Abdulrahman Almoayed. *Education:* Dr Ali Fakhro. *Health:* Jawad Salim Al-Arrayed. *Justice and Islamic Affairs:* Shaikh Abdullah bin Khalid Al-Khalifa. *Labour and Social Affairs:* Shaikh Khalifa bin Sulman bin Mohammed Al-Khalifa.

Works, Power and Water: Majid Jawad Al Jishi. *Interior:* Shaikh Mohammed bin Khalifa Al-Khalifa. *Foreign Affairs:* Shaikh Mohammed bin Mubarak Al-Khalifa. *Finance and National Economy:* Ibrahim Abdul-Karim. *Development and Industry:* Yousuf Ahmed Al-Shirawi. *Commerce and Agriculture:* Habib Ahmed Kassim. *Acting Minister of State for Cabinet Affairs:* Yousuf Ahmed Al-Shirawi. *Minister of State for Legal Affairs:* Dr Hussain Al Baharna.

Flag: Red, with white serrated vertical strip on hoist.

DEFENCE

Army. The Army consists of 2 infantry and 1 tank battalion, 1 armoured car squadron, 2 artillery and 2 mortar batteries with a personnel strength of 2,300 (1990). Equipment included 54 M-60 A3 main battle tanks, 8 Saladin armoured cars, 22 AML-90 and 8 Ferret scout cars.

Navy. The Naval force consists of 2 West-German-built missile corvettes with helicopter facilities, 4 fast missile craft and 7 fast patrol craft. Personnel in 1990 numbered 600. There is also a Coast Guard of 250 with 6 coastal patrol craft and 4 other vessels.

Air Force. An independent Air Force was created in 1985 as the successor to the Air Wing of the Army (Bahrain Defence Force). A fighter squadron operates 12 F-5E/F Tiger IIs, while 16 F-16s are on order for delivery in 1990–91. Three MBB BO 105 helicopters are also in use. Police and security forces both also operate helicopters. Personnel (1989) 200.

INTERNATIONAL RELATIONS

Membership. Bahrain is a member of UN, the Arab League, the Gulf Co-operation Council and OAPEC.

ECONOMY

Budget. The revenue of the State is derived from oil royalties and from customs duties, which are 10% *ad valorem* for luxury goods and 5% for essential goods. The exceptions are motor vehicles (20%); tobacco (30%); alcoholic beverages (100%); fresh fruit and vegetables (7%). Total revenues in 1988, BD 490m. (of which oil BD 252m.) and expenditure BD 365m.

On 2 Jan. 1958 Manama was declared a free transit port and the former 2% transit duty was abolished, but storage charges are levied.

Currency. The Bahrain *dinar* is divided into 1,000 *fils*. The Bahrain currency board issues notes of 20, 10, 5 and 1 *dinars*, and 500 *fils*, and coins of 100, 50, 25, 10, 5 and 1 *fils*. £1 = BD 0·621 in March 1990; US$1 = BD 0·379.

Banking. The Bahrain Monetary Agency has central banking powers. Since Nov. 1984 it has been responsible for licensing and monitoring the activities of money changers. There were (1988) 20 full commercial banks (including Bahrain Islamic Bank), 6 of which are locally incorporated and the rest branches of foreign banks. Total assets at 31 Dec. 1988, BD 2,184·9m. Two types of offshore banking units were operating in 1988: 15 locally incorporated banks (including 4 Islamic) with headquarters in Bahrain, and 50 branches of foreign banks. Total assets at 31 Dec. 1988 US$68,100m. There are 15 investment banks (3 Islamic), with assets of US$1,750m. in Dec. 1985. The state-owned Housing Bank provides financing for construction, development of real estate and reclamation of land.

Weights and Measures. The metric system of weights and measures is officially in use.

ENERGY AND NATURAL RESOURCES

Electricity. Production (1988) 2,996·1m. kwh. Supply 230 volts; 50 Hz.

Oil. In 1931 oil was discovered. Operations were conducted by the Bahrain Petroleum Co., registered in Canada but owned by US interests, under a concession granted by the Shaikh. Production of crude oil in 1989 was 2·15m. tonnes. A large oil refinery on Bahrain Island, besides treating crude oil produced locally, also processes oil from Saudi Arabia transported by pipeline.

In 1975 the Bahrain Government assumed a direct 60% interest in the Bahrain oilfield and related crude oil facilities of BAPCO.

Bahrain's proven oil reserves in 1988 were 150m. bbls.

Gas. There is an abundant supply of natural gas with known reserves of 7·1m. cu. ft. in 1987. Production, 1987, 252,431m. cu. ft. Bahrain's gas reserves are 100% government-owned.

Water. Water is obtained from artesian wells and desalination plants and there is a piped supply to Manama, Muharraq, Isa Town, Rifa'a and most villages. In 1987 total water production was about 60m. gallons per day; daily consumption 59·7m. gallons by Aug. 1987. A further desalination plant with a capacity of 10m. gallons per day was due on stream in 1988.

Agriculture. The 6-year agricultural plan, commissioned in 1982, aimed to increase food production from 6–16% of total domestic requirements and to improve conservation of natural water and irrigation techniques.

There are about 900 farms and small holdings (average 2·5 hectares) operated by about 2,500 farmers who produce a wide variety of fruits (49,000 tonnes in 1988) and vegetables (12,000 tonnes in 1988). The major crop is alfalfa for animal fodder. Ninety tonnes of dates a year are processed and a new processing plant produced a further 300 tonnes in 1986.

Thirty-two poultry farms produced about 3,000 tonnes of domestic poultry in 1987. 95% of egg requirements are met by domestic production of 90m. eggs a year, and 30% of broiler needs.

Livestock (1988): Cattle, 6,000; camels, 1,000; sheep, 8,000; goats, 16,000; poultry 1m.

Fisheries. The government operates a fleet of 2 large and 5 smaller trawlers. In 1987 total landings weighed 7,841·5 tonnes.

INDUSTRY AND TRADE

Industry. Bahrain is being developed as a major manufacturing state, the first important enterprise being the Aluminium Bahrain (ALBA), a company whose original shareholders included the Bahrain Government and British, Swedish, Federal German and US interests. In 1975, the government acquired a majority shareholding in the enterprise. The aluminium smelter operation is the largest non-oil industry in the Gulf; output, 1987, 180,000 tonnes. Ancillary industries developed around aluminium smelting include the production of aluminium powder. A plant producing aluminium alloys went on stream in 1987. The Gulf Aluminium Rolling Mill Company (GARMCO), a joint venture between Bahrain, Saudi Arabia, Kuwait, Iraq, Oman and Qatar, was inaugurated in Feb. 1986. The Arab Shipbuilding and Repair Yard (ASRY), commissioned in 1977, is now in service. The dry dock can handle up to 50 tankers (500,000 DWT each) annually. A US$207m. iron ore pelletizing plant was inaugurated in Dec. 1984 (output, 1985, 680,000 tonnes) and a US$400m. petrochemical complex started operations in 1985.

In addition to the traditional minor industries such as boat-building, weaving, pottery, etc., other modern industries have developed, which include electronics assembly and the production of building materials, furniture, syringes and other medical items, matches, asbestos pipes and plastics, foodstuffs and textiles.

The pearling industry for which Bahrain used to be famous has considerably declined.

Labour. Total work force in the private sector (estimate 1987) 85,979, of which 25·2% Bahraini. The non-national workforce (1987) was 79,550.

Commerce. In 1988 total imports were BD974·6m. and total exports were BD874·5m. Refined petroleum accounted for almost 78% of exports; crude oil accounted for 41·9% of merchandise imports.

The major non-oil imports in 1988 were machinery and transport, BD198·1m.; classified manufactured goods, including Alumina, BD111·5m.; chemicals, BD64·5m.; food and live animals, BD81·2m., and miscellaneous manufactured articles, BD78·2m. The chief sources of supply (in BD1,000) were UK (116,115); USA (62,566); Japan (58,850); Federal Republic of Germany (35,573), and Australia (33,615).

The chief non-oil exports in 1988 were classified manufactured goods, including aluminium, BD135·5m., and machinery and transport, BD31m. The main markets (in BD1m.) were Saudi Arabia (42·9); Japan (27·7); United Arab Emirates (26·3); USA (14·4), and Kuwait (11·3).

Import of arms and ammunition and telecommunication equipment is subject to special permission; the sale of alcoholic liquor is restricted and the import of cultured pearls is forbidden.

Total trade between Bahrain and UK (British Department of Trade returns, in £1,000 sterling):

	1985	*1986*	*1987*	*1988*	*1989*
Imports to UK	45,219	19,732	60,687	75,786	61,018
Exports and re-exports from UK	161,560	130,991	125,189	138,150	138,529

Tourism. More than 165,000 tourists from the Gulf area arrived in 1985.

COMMUNICATIONS

Roads. The 25 km causeway links Bahrain with Saudi Arabia. In 1987 there were 112,520 registered vehicles.

Aviation. The airport, situated at Muharraq, can take the largest aircraft and is considered one of the most modern and efficient in the Middle East, used by 2,486,582 arriving and 2,512,882 departing passengers in 1987. British Airways, Gulf Air, Middle East Airlines, Pakistan International Airways, Qantas, Kuwait Airways, Air India International, Singapore Airlines, UTA, Saudi Arabian Airlines, KLM, Air Lanka, Cathay Pacific Airways, Iraqi Airways, Korean Airways, Philippine Airlines, Thai Airways International, Trans-Mediterranean Airways, Egyptair, Alia, Cyprus Airways, Ethiopia Airlines and Sudan Airways also operate to and from Bahrain. Bahrain International Airport is the Arabian Gulf's main air communication centre.

Shipping. Bahrain's traditional position as the entrepôt of the Southern Gulf has been supplemented by the development of Mina Sulman—the new modern harbour—as a free transit and industrial area. Local and international companies have developed industries in this area, which is also used as a storage centre for firms selling elsewhere in the Gulf. The facilities offered by Mina Sulman include engineering and ship repairing yards; the Basrec slipway is probably the largest between Rotterdam and Hong Kong.

Post and Broadcasting. There were, at Dec. 1987, 120,000 telephones. There is a state-operated radio and television station and in 1983 there were 150,500 radio and 120,000 television receivers. There were 3 public service satellite stations in 1988.

Cinemas. There were 6 cinemas in 1987.

Newspapers. In 1988 there were several Arabic newspapers, and 1 English language daily newspaper, published in Manama.

JUSTICE, RELIGION, EDUCATION AND WELFARE

Justice. Criminal law is codified, based on English jurisprudence.

Religion. Islam is the State religion. In 1981 85% of the population were Moslem and 7·3% Christian. There are also Jews, Bahai, Hindu and Parsee minorities.

Education. Government schools provide free education from primary to technical college level. There were, in 1987, 143 schools for boys and girls with 4,967 teachers and 88,132 pupils. In 1984, 5 boys' general and commercial schools had 2,177 pupils; 3 boys' industrial schools at secondary level, had 1,306 pupils. In addition there were 7 private schools. The Men's Teacher Training College (established 1966) and the Women's Teacher Training College (established 1967) give 2-year courses. In 1987, 1,665 Bahrainis were in higher education abroad. The Gulf Technical College opened in Bahrain in Sept. 1968 and Bahrain University in 1978. In 1987, 6,922 adult education centres were open throughout Bahrain.

Health. There is a free medical service for all residents of Bahrain. In 1987, there were 4 government hospitals and 19 health centres, an American mission hospital, an oil company hospital, a military hospital and an international hospital.

Social Security. In Oct. 1976, pensions, sickness and industrial injury benefits, unemployment, maternity and family allowances were established.

DIPLOMATIC REPRESENTATIVES

Of Bahrain in Great Britain (98 Gloucester Rd., London, SW7 4AU)
Ambassador: Sulman Abdul Wahab Al Sabbagh (accredited 19 Dec. 1984).

Of Great Britain in Bahrain (21 Government Ave., P.O. Box 114, Manama)
Ambassador: J. A. Shepherd, CMG.

Of Bahrain in the USA (3502 International Dr., NW, Washington D.C., 20008)
Ambassador: Ghazi Mohammed Al-Gosaibi.

Of the USA in Bahrain (Shaikh Isa Road, P.O. Box 26431, Manama)
Ambassador: Charles W. Hostler.

Of Bahrain to the United Nations
Ambassador: Karim Ebrahim Al-Shakar.

Further Reading

Bahrain Business Directory. Manama (annual)
Statistical and General Information: Ministry of Information, PO Box 253, Manama
Statistical Abstract. Central Statistics Organisation (annual)

Lawson, F. H., *Bahrain: The Modernization of Autocracy*. Boulder, 1989
Rumaihi, M. G., *Bahrain: Social and Political Change since the First World War*. New York and London, 1976
Unwin, P. T. H., *Bahrain*. [Bibliography]. London and Santa Barbara, 1984

BANGLADESH

Capital: Dhaka
Population: 106·6m. (1988)
GNP per capita: US$170 (1988)

Gana Prajatantri Bangladesh —People's Republic of Bangladesh

HISTORY. The state was formerly the Eastern Province of Pakistan. In Dec. 1970 Sheikh Mujibur Rahman's Awami League Party gained 167 seats out of 300 at the Pakistan general election and immediately made known their wish for greater independence for the then Eastern Province. Martial law was imposed following disturbances in Dhaka, and civil war developed in March 1971. The war ended in Dec. 1971 and Bangladesh was proclaimed an independent state.

For developments between Jan. 1975 and March 1982, *see* THE STATESMAN'S YEAR-BOOK, 1986–87, pp. 186–187.

On 23 March 1982 there was a bloodless military *coup*, by which Lieut.-Gen. Hossain Mohammad Ershad became chief martial law administrator. President Sattar was deposed. The Constitution was suspended and parliament ceased to function. Assanuddin Chowdhury was sworn in as civilian president on 27 March. Lieut-Gen. Ershad assumed the presidency on 11 Dec. 1983. He was re-elected on 15 Oct. 1986.

Martial law ended on 10 Nov. 1986. The Constitution (Seventh Amendment) Act restored the constitution but protected the legality of President Ershad's decrees under martial law.

EVENTS. Extensive flooding in 1988 disrupted national life.

AREA AND POPULATION. Bangladesh is bounded west and north by India, east by India and Burma and south by the Bay of Bengal. The area is 55,598 sq. miles (143,998 sq. km). At the 1981 census the population was enumerated as 87,120,000. An adjustment for under enumeration produced a revised figure of 89,912,000 (46·3m. male, 14·09m. urban). Population estimate, 1988, 106·6m. (51·7m. female); density, 740 per sq. km. In 1987 the birth-rate was 33·3 per 1,000 population; death-rate, 11·85; marriage rate, 11·6; infant mortality, 111 per 1,000 live births. Growth rate was 2·8% in 1986-87. Life expectancy, 1987: Males, 55·6; females, 54·9. The capital is Dhaka (population, 1987, 4·77m. The other major cities are Chittagong (1·84m.), Khulna (860,000) and Rajshahi (430,000). The country is administratively divided into 4 divisions, subdivided into 21 regions of 64 districts:

		Area (sq. km)	*Population 1981*			*Area (sq. km)*	*Population 1981*
Dinajpur	(3 districts)	6,566	3,198,000	Kushtia	(3)	3,440	2,292,000
Rangpur	(5)	9,593	6,510,000	Jessore	(4)	6,573	4,020,000
Bogra	(2)	3,888	2,728,000	Khulna	(3)	12,168	4,329,000
Rajshahi	(4)	9,456	5,270,000	Barisal	(4)	7,299	4,667,000
Pabna	(2)	4,732	3,424,000	Patuakhali	(2)	4,095	1,843,000
Rajshahi division		*34,238*	*21,132,000*	Khulna division		*33,575*	*17,151,000*
Tangail	(1)	3,403	2,444,000	Sylhet	(4)	12,718	5,656,000
Mymensingh	(3)	9,668	6,568,000	Comilla	(3)	6,599	6,881,000
Jamalpur	(2)	3,349	2,452,000	Noakhali	(3)	5,460	3,816,000
Dhaka	(6)	7,470	10,014,000	Chittagong	(2)	7,457	5,491,000
Faridpur	(5)	6,882	4,764,000	Chittagong Hill Tracts	(2)	8,679	580,000
Dhaka division		*30,772*	*26,242,000*	Bandarban	(1)	4,501	171,000
				Chittagong division		*45,414*	*22,595,000*

The official language is Bangla. (Bengali). English is also in use for official, legal and commercial purposes.

CLIMATE. A tropical monsoon climate with heat, extreme humidity and heavyrainfall in the monsoon season, from June to Oct. The short winter season (Nov.-Feb.) is mild and dry. Rainfall varies between 50" (1,250 mm) in the west to 100" (2,500 mm) in the south-east and up to 200" (5,000 mm) in the north-east. Dhaka. Jan. 66°F (19°C), July 84°F (28·9°C). Annual rainfall 81" (2,025 mm). Chittagong. Jan. 66°F (19°C), July 81°F (27·2°C). Annual rainfall 108" (2,831 mm).

CONSTITUTION AND GOVERNMENT. Bangladesh is a unitary republic. The Constitution came into force on 16 Dec. 1972 and provides for a parliamentary democracy.

The head of state is the *President*, directly elected every five years. He appoints a *Vice-President*.

There is a *Council of Ministers* to assist and advise the President. The President appoints the Prime Minister from among the members of Parliament who appears to him to command the support of a majority of members; he also appoints the other ministers.

Parliament has one chamber of 300 members directly elected every 5 years by citizens over 18. There are 30 seats reserved for women members elected by Parliament.

In Jan. 1986 a National Executive Committee was formed and the National Party launched, composed of government supporters. The Party won the election of 3 March 1988, but there was a low turn-out and the result was disputed.

President, Minister for Defence: Lieut.-Gen. Hossain Mohammad Ershad.
Vice-President: Moudud Ahmed.
The Council of Ministers was as follows in Feb. 1990:
Prime Minister: Kazi Zafar Ahmed.
Deputy Prime Ministers: M. Abdul Matin *(Home Affairs)*, Shah Moazzam Hossain (*Labour*). *Health and Family Planning:* Mohammad Abdul Munim. *Agriculture:* Maj.-Gen. Mahmudul Hasan. *Shipping:* Korban Ali. *Foreign Affairs:* Anisul Islam Mahmud. *Relief:* Sirajul Hossain Khan. *Communication:* Anwar Hossain. *Jute:* A. K. M. Mayeedul Islam. *Planning:* Air Vice Marshal A. K. Khandakar. *Water:* Mahbubur Rahman. *Land:* Sunil Gupta. *Textiles:* Jafar Imam. *Education:* Sheikh Shahidul. *Commerce:* A. Sattar. *Fisheries and Livestock:* Sarder Amjad Hossain. *Energy and Minerals:* A. B. M. Ghulam Mustafa. *Works:* Mustafa Jamal Haider. *Social Welfare and Women's Affairs:* M. R. Hoque Chowdhury. *Finance:* Wahidal Hoque. *Food:* Iqbal Hussain Chowdhury. *Adviser on Tribal Affairs:* Benoy Kumar Dewan.

National flag: Bottle green with a red disc in the centre.

National anthem: Amar Sonar Bangla, ami tomay bhalobashi (My golden Bengal, I love you). Words by Rabindranath Tagore.

DEFENCE. The supreme command of defence services is vested in the President.

Army. There are 6 infantry divisional headquarters, with 14 infantry brigades, and 2 armoured and 6 artillery regiments, and 6 engineer battalions. Strength (1990) 90,000, with an additional 55,000 paramilitary volunteers, including an armed police reserve and the Bangladesh Rifles. Equipment includes 30 Soviet T-54 and 20 Chinese Type-59 tanks.

Navy. Naval bases are at Chittagong, Kaptai, Khulna and Dhaka.

The fleet comprises 3 *ex*-British frigates (formerly HM Ships *Jaguar*, *Lynx* and *Llandaff*), 8 new Chinese-built 390 tonne fast attack craft, 4 Chinese-built fast missile craft, 4 Chinese-built fast torpedo boats, 2 *ex*-Yugoslav 200 tonne patrol craft, 8 *ex*-Chinese-built 155 tonne fast gunboats, 2 *ex*-Indian 150 tonne patrol craft, 1 British-built 140 tonne patrol craft, 5 indigenously built 70 tonne river gunboats, 1 oiler, 1 repair vessel, 12 auxiliaries and 1 training ship of 710 tons.

The manpower of the Navy in 1989 was 7,500.

Air Force. Deliveries, from the Soviet Union and China successively, comprise 6

MiG-21 interceptors and about 20 J-6 (MiG-19) fighter-bombers; 1 An-24 and 3 An-26 turboprop transports; over 30 Mi-8, Bell 212, Bell 206L and Alouette III helicopters; 10 Chinese CJ-6 piston-engined primary trainers, FT-2 (MiG-15UTI) jet advanced trainers, 6 Magister armed jet trainers and some light aircraft. Personnel strength, (1990) 6,000.

INTERNATIONAL RELATIONS

Membership. Bangladesh is a member of the Commonwealth, the Asian Development Bank, the Organisation for South Asian Regional Co-operation, the UN and all its related agencies, the Colombo Plan and the Islamic Conference.

External Debt. Estimated debt, June 1985, US$6,000m. Most of this was in loans from the Western aid group through the World Bank.

Treaties. Bangladesh signed an economic and technical co-operation agreement with China on 4 Jan. 1977. The amended constitution of 1977 states that Bangladesh seeks fraternal relations with Moslem countries based on Islamic solidarity.

ECONOMY

Planning. The third 5-year development plan, 1985–90, envisages an annual growth rate of 5·4%, and an industrial growth rate of 10·1% annually; of industrial development funds, 55% is for the private sector. Agriculture receives 30% of total plan expenditure, and the plan aims at self-sufficiency in food by 1990.

Budget. In 1986-87 total Government receipts were Tk.92,764m., of which Tk.45,594m. were revenue receipts, and total expenditure was Tk.82,301m., divided into Tk.40,218m. revenue expenditure and Tk.42,083m. development expenditure. In 1987-88 revenue receipts were Tk.49,150m., revenue expenditure Tk.45,693m. and development expenditure Tk.42,083m. Revenue receipts included (in Tk.1m.) 40,731 from taxation (33,310 indirect). Expenditures: Education, 9,254; administration, 9,107; defence, 7,695; debt servicing, 5,179; justice, 3,992.

Currency. A new currency, the *taka*, of 100 *paisas*, was floated in 1976. There are 1, 5, 10, 25, 50 and 100 paisa coins and 1, 2, 5, 10, 20, 50, 100 and 500 taka notes. Money supply, 1988: Tk.50,477m. (of which Tk.24,150m. were in circulation). Foreign exchange reserves: Tk.26,963m. (Tk.51·00 = £1 and Tk.31·12 = US$1 in March 1990).

Banking. Bangladesh Bank is the central bank. There are 4 nationalized commercial banks, 9 private commercial banks, 3 specialized banks and 7 foreign commercial banks. In May 1988 the Bangladesh Bank had Tk.19,971m. deposits; Tk.25,886m. foreign liabilities, Tk.52,709m. assets. The scheduled banks had Tk.131,764m. deposits, Tk.32,210m. assets and Tk.24,313m. borrowings from the Bangladesh Bank. Post office savings deposits were Tk.1,070m. in 1987.

Weights and Measures. The metric system was introduced from July 1982, but imperial measures are still in use. Weight is in the *seer* (1 *seer* = 2 lb.); the *maund* (1 *maund* = 40 *seers*) and the ton.

ENERGY AND NATURAL RESOURCES

Electricity. Electric power is generated and distributed by the Bangladesh Power Development Board and the Rural Electrification Board. Installed capacity, June 1987, 1,757 mw.; electricity generated, 1986–87, 5,288·01m. kwh.; consumption, 3,479·38m. kwh. Supply 220 volts; 50 Hz.

Oil. Supplies have been located in the Bay of Bengal. Drilling is in progress.

Gas. There are 14 natural gas fields with recoverable reserves of 12,610,000m. cu. ft. Production, 1987–88, 147,454m. cu. ft. Consumption, 140,600 cu. ft.

Water. India and Bangladesh are working towards agreement on sharing the water of the river Ganges. The flow will be monitored daily at the Farakka barrage and two other points.

Minerals. The principal minerals are lignite, limestone, china clay and glass sand. Production, 1986–87: Limestone, 44,660m. tons (value Tk.13·34m.); china clay, 12,272m. tons (Tk.17·2m.).

Agriculture. At the 1983-84 census of agriculture there were 10·05m. farm holdings (7·07m. under 2·5 acres; 2·48m. of 2·5 to 7·5 acres; 496,000 over 7·5 acres. 28·3% of households had no cultivable land. Agriculture contributed 41% of GDP in 1987–88. The cultivable area was 22·84m. acres in 1987, of which 21·88m. acres were cropped (26·2m. under rice, 1·4m. wheat and 1·9m. jute). About 5·43m. acres (1987) is irrigated; 2·4m. by tubewells and another 1·63m. by power pump.

Bangladesh produces about 70% of the world's jute which is the principal foreign exchange earner. Production, 1987-88, 839,000 tonnes.

Rice is the most important food crop; production in 1987–88, 15·74m. tonnes. Other crops (1,000 tonnes): Sugar-cane, 7,093; wheat, 1,031; tobacco, 117; pulses, 530; oilseeds, 442; spices, 343; tea, 89·54m. lbs.; potatoes, 1,255.

Fertilizers used (1986–87), 1·32m. tonnes, of which 915m. tonnes was urea.

Livestock in 1988 (1,000): Poultry, 113,000; cattle, 22,789; goats, 10,700; sheep, 1,140; buffalo, 1,950. Livestock products in 1988 (tonnes): Beef and veal, 137,000; cow and buffalo milk, 750,000; goats' milk, 224,000; eggs, 110,000.

Forestry. The area under forests in 1988 was 2·1m. hectares (16% of the land area). Output of timber, 1986-87, was 12·76m. cu. ft.

Fisheries. Being bounded on the south by the Bay of Bengal and having numerous inland waterways, Bangladesh is a major producer of fish and products. In 1987-88 there were 497,000 sea- and 752,000 inland-fishermen, with 1,249 mechanized boats, including 52 trawlers, and 3,317 motor boats. Inland catch was 610,000 tonnes, sea, 227,000 tonnes.

INDUSTRY AND TRADE

Industry. Industry contributed 8·9% of GDP in 1987-88. The principal industries are jute and cotton textiles, tea, paper, newsprint, cement, chemical fertilizers and light engineering. In 1986-87 there were 4,386 factories (including 881 textile, 801 food and 564 chemical). New government policy in 1982 aimed to restore public-sector jute and textile mills to private ownership and encourage the private sector. Arms and ammunition, atomic energy, forestry, air transport, communications and electrical industries would remain in the public sector.

Production, 1987–88: Jute goods, 529,000 tonnes; cotton yarn, 103m. lb.; cotton cloth, 68m. yards; cement, 310,000 tonnes; sugar, 175,000 tonnes; vegetable products, 6,337 tonnes; fertilizer, 729,000 tonnes, newsprint, 49,000 tonnes; bicycles 19,749; 8,039 motor cycles; 121,000 radios.

Labour. In 1985–86, the labour force was 27·7m. (3·2m. female), of whom 27·4m. (3·1m.) were employed (2·8m. children between 10 and 14 years were also employed). 57·6% worked in agriculture and fishery, 11·5% in trade and 7·1% in production and transport. Average daily industrial wage, 1987-88: Skilled, Tk.49; unskilled, Tk.31.

Commerce. The main exports are jute and jute goods, tea, hides and skins, newsprint, fish and garments, and the main imports are machinery, transport equipment, manufactured goods, minerals, fuels and lubricants. In 1987–88 exports were valued at Tk.41,161m., and imports at Tk.91,588m.

Main sources of imports in 1987-88: Japan (mainly machinery and vehicles), Tk.10,098m.; USA (foodstuffs), Tk.8,161m.; Singapore (petroleum), Tk.6,327m.; Hong Kong, Tk.4,271m.; UK, 4,197m. Main export markets: USA, Tk.12,045m.; Italy, Tk.3,677m.; UK, Tk.2,433m. Federal Germany, Tk.2,306m.

Total trade between Bangladesh and UK (British Department of Trade returns, in £1,000 sterling):

	1986	*1987*	*1988*	*1989*
Imports to UK	34,117	35,454	50,249	52,527
Exports and re-exports from UK	48,218	54,382	64,018	78,270

Foreign investment is encouraged and legally protected. The Board of Investment must approve joint ventures if the foreign participation exceeds 49%. There is a duty-free Export Processing Zone at Chittagong.

Tourism. In 1987 there were 106,765 visitors to Bangladesh of whom 47,390 were from India. Foreign exchange earnings, Tk.192·4m.

COMMUNICATIONS

Roads. In 1986 there were 4,039 miles of roads with cement, concrete or bitumen surfaces. In 1987 there were 8,827 buses, 16,375 lorries and 27,120 private cars.

Railways. In 1988 there were 2,745 km of railways, comprising 923 km of 1,676 mm gauge and 1,822 km of metre gauge. They carried 2·5m. tonnes of freight and 53m. passengers.

Aviation. There are international airports at Dhaka (Zia), Chittagong and Sylhet, and 7 domestic airports. Bangladesh Biman (Bangladesh Airways) had 11 aircraft in 1988 and has domestic flights from Zia International Airport and services to Calcutta, Kathmandu, Bombay, Dubai, Abu Dhabi, Jeddah, Bangkok, Singapore, London, Doha, Kuwait, Amsterdam, Rome, Karachi, Kuala Lumpur, Bahrain, Tripoli, Athens and Muscat. In 1987 Zia handled 1·18m. passengers out of a total of 1·6m. Freight and mail handled, Zia, 32,413 tons; total, 34,376: Aircraft movements, Zia, 29,393; total, 55,051.

Shipping. There are sea ports at Chittagong and Mongla, and inland ports at Dhaka, Chandpur, Barisal, Khulna and five other towns. There are 5,000 miles of navigable channels. The three principle navigable rivers, the Padma, Brahmaputra and Meghna serve areas where railways cannot be economically constructed. The Bangladesh Shipping Corporation owned 21 ships in 1987. There are also 881 private cargo and 1,506 passenger vessels. In 1986–87 the port of Chittagong handled 5·8m. tons of imports and 402,000 tons of exports; total, all ports 7·4m. tons of imports and 1·1m. tons of exports. Vessels entered (all ports) 1,792 and cleared, 1,770. The Bangladesh Inland Water Transport Corporation had 430 vessels in 1988.

Post and Broadcasting. There were 7,810 post offices and 187,650 telephones in 1988. International communications are by the Indian Ocean Intelsat IV satellite.

There are radio and TV stations at Dhaka, Chittagong, Khulna, Rangpur, Sylhet, and Rangamati; radio stations at Comilla and Thakurgaon; and TV stations at Natore, Mymensingh, Noakhali, Satkhira and Cox's Bazar. Radio broadcasting is in Bangla, English, Urdu, Hindi, Arabic and Nepali. In 1987 there were 435,000 radios and 426,000 TV sets.

Cinema. In 1987 there were 681 cinemas with 363,000 seats. 75 full-length films were made.

Newspapers and Books. In 1987 there were 49 daily newspapers in Bangla with a circulation of 736,000 and 10 in English with a circualtion of 112,000. There were 171 other periodicals (15 in English) with a circulation of 737,000. Most papers are published in Dhaka. The Government has set up a paper *(Dainik Barta-at Rajshahi)* to stimulate a regional press. There is a Press Institute. In 1987 1,022 book titles were published (90 in English).

JUSTICE, RELIGION, EDUCATION AND WELFARE

Justice. The Supreme Court comprises an Appellate and a High court Division, the latter having control over all subordinate courts. There are benches at Comilla, Rangpur, Jessore, Barisal, Chittagong and Sylhet, and courts at District level. The Chief Justice and other judges of the High Court are appointed by the President and must retire at 62 years.

Religion. Islam is the State Religion. Some 80% of the population are Moslem and the rest Hindus, Buddhists and Christians.

Education. About 29·2% of the population over 15 was literate in 1989 (male 39·7%, female 18%). The Government has taken over school administration. The compulsory primary education scheme has been replaced by model primary education.

In 1987–88 there were 44,502 primary schools (6,864 private), with 11·08m. pupils (4·83m. female) and 186,597 teachers (33,575 female); 10,157 secondary schools (9,895 private), with 2·81m. pupils (927,000 female) and 116,835 teachers (11,432 female); 812 colleges of further education (630 private), with 792,000 students (183,000 female) and 17,215 teachers (2,268 female); and 77 technical colleges with 17,360 students (996 female) and 1,307 teachers (46 female). There is an Islamic University (891 students and 19 teachers in 1987-88) and universities at Dhaka (16,622 and 973), Rajshahi (11,755 and 469), Chittagong (6,025 and 420) and Jahingirnagar (2,660 and 181). There are also universities of agriculture (4,573 and 379) and engineering (3,758 and 349). There were 10 teacher-training colleges in 1987-88, with 3,624 students (1,040 female) and 160 teachers (47 female), and 53 primary training institutes with 6,893 students (4,122 female) and 532 teachers (106 female).

Health. In 1987 there were 608 state and 267 private hospitals with a total of 33,038 beds. There were 16,929 doctors. State expenditure on health, Tk.3,540m. There are 10 medical schools.

DIPLOMATIC REPRESENTATIVES

Of Bangladesh in Great Britain (28 Queen's Gate, London, SW7)
High Commissioner: Maj.-Gen. K. M. Safiullah.
(There are also Assistant High Commissioners in Birmingham and Manchester)

Of Great Britain in Bangladesh (Abu Bakr Hse., Gulshan, Dhaka)
High Commissioner: C. H. Imrey, CMG.

Of Bangladesh in the USA (2201 Wisconsin Ave., NW, Washington, D.C., 20007)
Ambassador: A. H. S. Ataul Karim.

Of the USA in Bangladesh (Madani Ave., Baridhara Model Town, Dhaka)
Ambassador: Willard A. DePree.

Of Bangladesh to the United Nations
Ambassador: A. H. S. Ataul Karim.

Further Reading

Official statistics are issued by the Bangladesh Bureau of Statistics (Director-General A. M. A. Rahim). Publications include: *Statistical Yearbook of Bangladesh.* 1976; 1979 to date. *Statistical Pocket Book of Bangladesh.* 1980 to date.

Bangladesh Planning Commission, *The First Five Year Plan—The Second Five Year Plan.*
Abdullah, T. and Zeidenstein, S., *Village Women of Bangladesh: Prospects for Change.* Oxford, 1981
Baxter, C., *Bangladesh: A New Nation in an Old Setting.* Boulder, 1986
Chowdhury, R., *The Genesis of Bangladesh.* London, 1972
Dutt, K., *Bangladesh Economy: An Analytical Study.* New Delhi, 1973
Franda, M., *Bangladesh: The First Decade.* New Delhi, 1982
Hartmann, B. and Boyce, J., *A Quiet Violence: View from a Bangladesh Village.* London, 1983
Kamal, K. A., *Sheikh Mujibur Rahman.* 2nd ed. Dhaka, 1970
Khan, A. R., *The Economy of Bangladesh.* London, 1972
de Lucia, R. J. and Jacoby, H. D., *Energy Planning for Developing Countries: A Study of Bangladesh.* John Hopkins Univ. Press, 1982
de Vylder, S., *Agriculture in Chains. Bangladesh: A Case Study in Contradictions and Constraints.* London, 1982
O'Donnell, C. P., *Bangladesh: Biography of a Muslim Nation.* Boulder, 1986
Rahman, M., *Bangladesh Today: An Indictment and a Lament.* London, 1978

BARBADOS

Capital: Bridgetown
Population: 253,881 (1987)
GNP per capita: US$5,990 (1988)

HISTORY. Barbados was occupied by the British in 1627 and during its colonial history never changed hands. Full internal self-government was attained in 1961. Barbados became an independent sovereign state within the Commonwealth on 30 Nov. 1966.

AREA AND POPULATION. Barbados lies to the east of the Windward Islands. Area 166 sq. miles (430 sq. km). In 1980 the census population was 248,983. Estimate (1987) 253,881. Bridgetown is the principal city: Population, 7,466.

CLIMATE. An equable climate in winter, but the wet season, from June to Nov., is more humid. Rainfall varies from 50" (1,250 mm) on the coast to 75" (1,875 mm) in the higher interior. Bridgetown. Jan. 76°F (24·4°C), July 80°F (26·7°C). Annual rainfall 51" (1,275 mm).

CONSTITUTION AND GOVERNMENT. The Legislature consists of the Governor-General, a Senate and a House of Assembly. The Senate comprises 21 members appointed by the Governor-General, 12 being appointed on the advice of the Prime Minister, 2 on the advice of the leader of the opposition and 7 in the Governor-General's discretion. The House of Assembly comprises 27 members elected every 5 years. In 1963 the voting age was reduced to 18.

The Privy Council is appointed by the Governor-General after consultation with the Prime Minister. It consists of 12 members and the Governor-General as chairman. It advises the Governor-General in the exercise of the royal prerogative of mercy and in the exercise of his disciplinary powers over members of the public and police services.

In the general election of May 1986 the Democratic Labour Party gained 24 seats and the Barbados Labour Party 3 seats.

Governor-General: Sir Hugh Springer, GCMG, CBE.

The Cabinet, in Jan. 1989, was composed as follows:

Prime Minister, Minister of Finance and Economic Affairs: Erskine Sandiford.

Deputy Prime Minister, International Transport, Immigration and Telecommunications, Leader of Government Business in the House of Assembly: Philip Greaves. *Attorney-General, Legal Affairs:* Maurice A. King, QC. *Employment, Labour Relations and Community Development:* Keith Simmons. *Foreign Affairs, Leader of the Senate:* Sir James Tudor. *Health:* Branford Taitt. *Housing and Lands:* Harold A. Blackman. *Tourism and Sport:* Wesley Hall. *Trade and Industry:* E. Evelyn Greaves. *Transport and Works:* Dr Don Blackman. *Education and Culture:* Cyril Walker. There were two Ministers of State.

National flag: Three vertical strips of blue, gold, blue, with a black trident in the centre.

INTERNATIONAL RELATIONS

Membership. Barbados is a member of UN, OAS, CARICOM, the Commonwealth and an ACP state of the EEC.

ECONOMY

Budget. The budget for 1987–88 envisaged capital expenditure of BD$176·5 and current expenditure of BD$814·1.

Currency. The monetary unit is the *Barbados dollar* (BD$) divided into 100 *cents*. In March 1990, £1 = BD$3.31; US$1 = 2.02.

Banking. Eight main commercial banks operate in Barbados including Barclays Bank International, the Royal Bank of Canada, Canadian Imperial Bank of Commerce, the Bank of Nova Scotia, Chase Manhattan Bank, Caribbean Commercial Bank, The Barbados National Bank, Bank of Credit and Commerce International.

Barbados is headquarters for the Caribbean Development Bank. The Barbados Development Bank opened on 15 April 1969 and Barbados became a member of the Inter-American Development Bank on 19 March 1969.

NATURAL RESOURCES

Electricity. Production (1987) 425m. kwh. Supply 150 volts; 50 Hz.

Oil. Crude oil production (1989) 60,000 tonnes and reserves (1987), 3·24m. bbls.

Gas. Output of gas (1987) 936m. cu. ft and reserves 18,618m. cu. metres.

Agriculture. Of the total area of 106,240 acres, about 55,000 acres are arable land. The land is intensely cultivated. In 1988, 12,000 hectares of sugar-cane were harvested. Cotton was successfully replanted in 1983 and 91 bales were harvested from 300 acres in 1985. The agricultural sector accounted for 7·1% (provisional) of GDP in 1985 (1946, 45%; 1967, 24%). In 1985, 6·9% of the total labour force were employed in agriculture. In 1988, 83,000 tonnes of sugar were produced. There are 6 sugar factories and 2 rum refineries in production. In 1988, 2,000 tonnes of yams and 4,000 tonnes of sweet potatoes were produced. Hot peppers, eggplants, watermelons, breadfruit and red ginger lilies are also grown for export.

Livestock (1988): Cattle, 18,000; sheep, 56,000; goats, 33,000; pigs, 49,000; poultry, 1m.

Fisheries. There are about 745 (1987) powered boats and many men and women are employed during the flying-fish season. Large numbers of these boats are laid up from July to Oct. The fish catch in 1987 was 9,800 tonnes.

INDUSTRY AND TRADE

Industry. Industrial establishments operating in Barbados in 1987 numbered approximately 330 and ranged from the manufacture of processed food to small specialized products such as garment manufacturing, furniture and household appliances, electrical components, plastic products and electronic parts.

Commerce. Total trade for calendar years in BD$1,000:

	1984	*1985*	*1986*	*1987*	*1988*
Domestic Imports [1]	1,324,623	1,221,595	1,181,075	1,035,891	1,170,316
Domestic Exports [1]	583,667	496,471	420,614	214,511	242,738

[1] Exclusive of bullion and specie.

In 1988 the principal imports (BD$1m.) were: Machinery and transport equipment, 275·7; manufactured goods, 360·5; food and live animals, 181·9; lubricants, mineral fuels, etc., 110·5; chemicals, 125·9; crude minerals, 36·2; beverages and tobacco, 29; animal and vegetable oils and fats, 12·9. In 1988 the principal domestic exports (BD$1m.) were: Sugar, 57·7; electronic components, 42·8; clothing, 30·4.

Total trade between Barbados and UK (British Department of Trade returns, in £1,000 sterling):

	1985	*1986*	*1987*	*1988*	*1989*
Imports from UK	13,512	11,661	23,320	19,487	22,304
Exports and re-exports to UK	36,856	38,338	33,067	32,061	38,136

Tourism. In 1988, 449,761 tourists visited Barbados spending BD$914·7m. The industry employs over 10,000 people.

COMMUNICATIONS

Roads. There are 1,035 miles of road open to traffic, of which 855 miles are all-weather roads. In Dec. 1987 there were 34,740 private cars, 2,266 hired cars and taxis, 470 buses including minibuses and 7,855 other vehicles including motorcycles.

Aviation. There is an international airport at Seawell, Christ Church, Barbados, served by British Airways, BWIA, Leeward Islands Air Transport, PANAM, American Airlines, Wardair, Air Martinique Cruziero (SC), Air Canada, Caribbean Airways and Eastern Airlines, Cubana Airlines, Venezuelan Airlines.

Shipping. A deep-water harbour opened in 1961 at Bridgetown provides 8 berths for ships 500–600 ft in length, including one specially designed for bulk sugar loading. The number of merchant vessels entering in 1986 was 1,961 of 6,452,000 net tons.

Post and Broadcasting. There is a general post office in Bridgetown and 16 branches on the island. In 1987 there were 94,338 telephones in service. In 1986 there were 200,000 radios and 62,000 television sets.

Cinemas. There were (1985) 3 cinemas and 2 drive-in cinemas for 600 cars.

Newspapers. In 1987 there were 2 daily newspapers with a total circulation of 41,000.

JUSTICE, RELIGION, EDUCATION AND WELFARE

Justice. Justice is administered by the Supreme Court and by magistrates' courts. All have both civil and criminal jurisdiction. There is a Chief Justice and 3 puisne judges of the Supreme Court and 8 magistrates.

Religion. The majority (about 70%) of the population are Anglicans, the remainder mainly Methodists, Moravians and Roman Catholics.

Education. In 1984–85 children in 105 government primary schools numbered 29,392; in 21 secondary schools, 21,501; in 5 vocational centres, 967; in 15 assisted private approved secondary schools, 4,227. There are 23 independent primary schools with 3,547 pupils and a number of independent schools for which no accurate figures are available. Education is free in all government-owned and maintained institutions from primary to university level.

The University of the West Indies in Barbados was opened in Sept. 1963 and Cave Hill campus in 1967 and in 1985 had 1,932 students. In 1984–85, 186 students attended Erdiston College and 1,617 students attended the Cave Hill campus. The Barbados Community College for higher education had in 1984–85, 1,806 students (full and part-time).

Health. In 1986 there were 2,054 hospital beds and 243 doctors.

DIPLOMATIC REPRESENTATIVES

Of Barbados in Great Britain (1 Great Russell St., London, WC1B 3NH)
High Commissioner: Sir Roy Marshall, CBE.

Of Great Britain in Barbados (Lower Collymore Rock, Bridgetown)
High Commissioner: K. F. X. Burns, CMG.

Of Barbados in the USA (2144 Wyoming Ave., NW, Washington, D.C. 20008)
Ambassador: Sir William Douglas, KCMG.

Of the USA in Barbados (PO Box 302, Bridgetown)
Ambassador: (Vacant)

Of Barbados to the United Nations
Ambassador: Dame Nita Barrow.

Further Reading

Statistical Information: The Barbados Statistical Service (NIS Bldg, Fairchild St, St Michael) produces selected monthly statistics and annual abstracts. *Director:* Eric Straughn.

Dann, G., *The Quality of Life in Barbados*. London, 1984
Hoyos, F. A., *Barbados: A History from the Amerindians to Independence*. London, 1978.—*Barbados: A Visitor's Guide*. London, 1983.—*Tom Adams: A Biography*. London, 1988
Potter, R. B. and Dann, G. M. S., *Barbados* [Bibliography]. Oxford and Santa Barbara, 1987
Warren, A. and Frazer, H., *The Barbados Carollna Connection*. London, 1989
Worrell, D., *The Economy of Barbados 1946–1980*. Bridgetown, 1982

Library: The Barbados Public Library, Bridgetown. *Acting Chief Librarian:* Edwin Ifill.

BELGIUM

Capital: Brussels
Population: 9·88m. (1987)
GNP per capita: US$14,550 (1988)

Royaume de Belgique— Koninkrijk België

HISTORY. The kingdom of Belgium formed itself into an independent state in 1830, having from 1815 been part of the Netherlands. The secession was decreed on 4 Oct. 1830 by a provisional government, established in consequence of a revolution which broke out at Brussels, on 25 Aug. 1830. A National Congress elected Prince Leopold of Saxe-Coburg King of the Belgians on 4 June 1831; he ascended the throne 21 July 1831.

By the Treaty of London, 15 Nov. 1831, the neutrality of Belgium was guaranteed by Austria, Russia, Great Britain and Prussia. It was not until after the signing of the Treaty of London, 19 April 1839, which established peace between King Leopold I and the King of the Netherlands, that all the states of Europe recognized the kingdom of Belgium. In the Treaty of Versailles (28 June 1919) it is stated that as the treaties of 1839 'no longer conform to the requirements of the situation', these are abrogated and will be replaced by other treaties.

AREA AND POPULATION. Belgium is bounded north by the Netherlands, north-west by the North Sea, west and south by France, east by Federal Republic of Germany and Luxembourg. Belgium has an area of 30,518 sq. km (11,778 sq. miles). The Belgian exclave of Baarle-Hertog in the Netherlands has an area of 7 sq. km, and a population (1 Jan. 1988) of 1,098 males and 1,014 females.

By an agreement, 23 Sept. 1956, the frontier with Germany was slightly readjusted.

Census	*Population*	*Increase % per annum*	*Census*	*Population*	*Increase % per annum*
1900	6,693,548	1·03	1947	8,512,195	0·36
1910	7,423,784	1·09	1961	9,189,741	0·52
1920	7,405,569	0·06	1970	9,650,944	0·55
1930	8,092,004	0·84	1981	9,848,647	0·18

Provinces	*Provincial capitals*	*Area (hectares)*	*Estimated population (31 Dec.)* 1970[1]	1985	1986	1987
Antwerp (Anvers)	Antwerp	286,726	1,533,249	1,582,786	1,585,163	1,587,450
Brabant	Brussels	335,811	2,176,373	2,218,349	2,219,272	2,221,818
Flanders West	Bruges	313,439	1,054,429	1,090,387	1,092,696	1,035,193
Flanders East	Ghent	298,167	1,310,117	1,328,805	1,328,931	1,328,779
Hainaut	Mons	378,669	1,317,453	1,277,939	1,274,034	1,271,649
Liège	Liège	386,213	1,008,905	991,535	991,089	992,068
Limbourg	Hasselt	242,231	652,547	731,875	734,382	736,981
Luxembourg	Arlon	444,114	217,310	224,988	225,563	226,452
Namur	Namur	366,501	380,561	412,231	413,621	415,326
Total		3,051,871	9,650,944	9,858,895	9,864,751	9,875,716

[1] Census.

In 1987 there were 4,821,803 males and 5,053,913 females.

Foreigners numbered 858,650 on 1 Jan. 1988.

Vital statistics for calendar years:

	Births	*Deaths*	*Marriages*	*Divorces*	*Immigration*	*Emigration*
1984	115,790	110,577	58,989	18,768	47,002	56,447
1985	114,283	112,691	57,630	18,530	47,042	54,021
1986	117,271	111,671	56,657	18,434	48,959	53,793
1987	117,448	105,840	56,588	19,830	49,750	57,033

	1984	1985	1986	1987
Of the total births excluding still-born	*115,790*	*114,283*	*117,271*	*117,448*
Boys	59,353	58,695	60,569	60,386
Girls	56,437	55,588	56,702	57,062

The most important towns, with estimated population on 1 Jan. 1988:

Brussels and suburbs [1]	970,346	St Niklaas (St Nicolas)	68,059
Antwerp (Antwerpen) [2]	476,044	Tournai (Doornik)	66,749
Ghent (Gent)	232,620	Hasselt	65,798
Charleroi	208,938	Genk	61,499
Liège (Luik)	200,312	Seraing	61,427
Brugge (Bruges)	117,857	Mouscron (Moeskroen)	53,543
Namur (Namen)	103,104	Verviers	53,355
Mons (Bergen)	89,515	Roeselare (Roulers)	52,132
Leuven (Louvain)	84,180	Turnhout	37,567
Aalst (Alost)	76,714	Herstal	36,919
Kortrijk (Courtrai)	76,314	Lokeren	34,488
La Louvière	76,291	Vilvoorde (Vilvorde)	32,893
Mechelen (Malines)	75,718	Lier (Lierre)	30,938
Oostende (Ostende)	68,397		

[1] The suburbs comprise 18 distinct communes, viz., Anderlecht, Etterbeek, Forest, Ixelles, Jette, Koekelberg, Molenbeek St Jean, St Gilles, St Josse-ten-Noode, Schaerbeek, Uccle, Woluwe-St Lambert, Auderghem, Watermael-Boitsfort, Woluwe-St Pierre, Berchem Ste Agathe, Evere and Ganshoren.
[2] Including Berchem, Borgerhout, Deurne, Hoboken, Merksem and Wilrijk.

CLIMATE. Cool temperate climate, influenced by the sea, giving mild winters and cool summers. Brussels. Jan. 36°F (2·2°C), July 64°F (17·8°C). Annual rainfall 33" (825 mm). Ostend. Jan. 38°F (3·3°C), July 62°F (16·7°C). Annual rainfall 31" (775 mm).

KING. Baudouin, born 7 Sept. 1930, succeeded his father, Leopold III, on 17 July 1951, when he took the oath on the constitution before the two Chambers: Married on 15 Dec. 1960 to Fabiola de Mora y Aragón, daughter of the Conde de Mora and Marqués de Casa Riera.

Brother and Sister of the King. (1) Josephine Charlotte, Princess of Belgium, born 11 Oct. 1927; married to Prince Jean of Luxembourg, 9 April 1953; (2) Albert, Prince of Liège, born 6 June 1934; married to Paola Ruffo di Calabria, 2 July 1959; *offspring:* Prince Philippe, born 15 April 1960; Princess Astrid, born 5 June 1962; married to Archduke Lorenz of Austria, 22 Sept. 1984; Prince Laurent, born 19 Oct. 1963. *Half-brother and half-sisters of the King.* Prince Alexandre, born 18 July 1942; Princess Marie Christine, born 6 Feb. 1951; Princess Maria-Esmeralda, born 30 Sept. 1956.

Aunt of the King. Princess Marie-José, born 4 Aug. 1906, married to Prince Umberto (King Umberto II of Italy in 1946) on 8 Jan. 1930.

BELGIAN SOVEREIGNS

Leopold I	1831–65	Leopold III	1934–44, 1950–51
Leopold II	1865–1909	Regency	1944–50
Albert	1909–34	Baudouin	1951–

CONSTITUTION AND GOVERNMENT. According to the constitution of 1831, Belgium is a constitutional, representative and hereditary monarchy. The legislative power is vested in the King, the Senate and the Chamber of Representatives. The royal succession is in direct male line in the order of primogeniture. By marriage without the King's consent, however, the right of succession is forfeited, but may be restored by the King with the consent of the two Chambers. No act of the King can have effect unless countersigned by one of his Ministers, who thus becomes responsible for it. The King convokes, prorogues and dissolves the Chambers. In default of male heirs, the King may nominate his successor with the consent of the Chambers. If the successor be under 18 years of age the two Chambers meet together for the purpose of nominating a regent during the minority.

National flag: Three vertical strips of black, yellow, red.

National anthem: Après des siècles d'esclavage (La Brabançonne; words by Jenneval, 1830; tune by F. van Campenhout, 1930).

French, Dutch and German are official languages.

Those sections of the Belgian Constitution which regulate the organization of the legislative power were revised in Oct. 1921. For both Senate and Chamber all elections are held on the principle of universal suffrage.

The Senate consists of members elected for 4 years, partly directly and partly indirectly. The number elected directly is equal to half the number of members of the Chamber of Representatives. The constituent body is similar to that which elects deputies to the Chamber; the minimum age of electors is 18 years. Women were given the suffrage at parliamentary elections on 24 March 1948. In the direct elections of members of both the Senate and Chamber of Representatives the principle of proportional representation was introduced by law of 29 Dec. 1899.

Senators are elected indirectly by the provincial councils, on the basis of 1 for 200,000 inhabitants. Every addition of 125,000 inhabitants gives the right to 1 senator more. Each provincial council elects at least 3 senators. There are at present 51 provincial senators. No one, during 2 years preceding the election, must have been a member of the council appointing him. Senators are elected by the Senate itself in the proportion of half the preceding category. The senators belonging to these two latter categories are also elected by the method of proportional representation. All senators must be at least 40 years of age. They receive about 2m. francs per annum. Sons of the King, or failing these, Belgian princes of the reigning branch of the royal family, are by right senators at the age of 18, but have no voice in the deliberations till the age of 25 years; this prerogative is hardly ever used.

The members of the Chamber of Representatives are elected by the electoral body. Their number, at present 212 (law of 3 April 1965), is proportional to the population, and cannot exceed one for every 40,000 inhabitants. They sit for 4 years. Deputies must be not less than 25 years of age, and resident in Belgium.

Each deputy has an annual allowance of about 2m. francs. Senators and deputies have also free railway passes.

The Senate and Chamber meet annually in October and must sit for at least 40 days; but the King has the power of convoking extraordinary sessions and of dissolving them either simultaneously or separately. In the latter case a new election must take place within 40 days and a meeting of the chambers within 2 months.

An adjournment cannot be made for a period exceeding 1 month without the consent of the Chambers.

After the revision of the Constitution by the laws of 24 Dec. 1970 and 28 July 1971 establishing three regions and two cultural councils, legislation on 'preparatory regionalization' was enacted in July 1974. Further revisions of the functions of the Cultural Councils took place on 8 and 9 Aug. 1980. The Cultural Councils became Community Councils with greater authority and the Regional Councils became competent on economic matters.

Elections were held on 13 Dec. 1987, the Flemish Christian Social Party (CVP) won 43 seats, Francophone Socialist Party (FS) 40, Flemish Socialist Party (SP) 32, Liberal Flemish Freedom and Progress Party (PVV) 25, Francophone Liberal Reform Party (PRL) 23, Francophone Christian Social Party (PSC) 19, Flemish Peoples' Union (VU) 16, Others, 14.

A 5-party coalition government was as follows in Dec. 1989:

Prime Minister: Wilfried Martens (CVP).

Deputy Prime Ministers: Philippe Moureaux, PS (Brussels Region and Institutional Reform); Willy Claes, SP *(Economic Affairs and Planning, National Education (Flemish))*; Jean-Luc Dehaene, CVP *(Communications and Institutional Reform)*; Melchior Wathelet, PSC *(Justice and Middle Classes)*; Hugo Schlitz, VU *(Budget and Scientific Policy)*. *Foreign Affairs:* Mark Eyskens (CVP). *Finance:*

Philippe Maystadt (PSC). *Foreign Trade:* Robert Urbain (PS). *Public Affairs:* Raymond Langendries (PSC). *Post and Telecommunications:* Marcel Colla (SP). *Social Affairs:* Philippe Busquin (PS). *National Defence:* Guy Coëme (PS). *Public Works:* Paula D'Hondt Van Opdenbosch (CVP). *Interior, Modernization of Public Services, and National Scientific and Cultural Institutions:* Louis Tobback (SP). *National Education (French):* Yvan Ylieff (PS). *Co-operation and Development:* (Vacant). *Pensions:* Alain Van der Biest (PS). *Employment and Work:* Luc Van den Brande (CVP).

There are thirteen Secretaries of State.

Local Government. Belgium has 9 provinces and since the so-called 'Amalgamation Law' of 30 Dec. 1975, 589 communes (instead of 2,359). They have a large measure of autonomous government. According to the law of 9 June 1982, all Belgians over 18 years of age, who are recorded in the registers of population of the commune have the right to vote in the communal elections. Proportional representation is applied to the communal elections, and communal councils are to be renewed every 6 years. In each commune there is a college composed of the burgomaster as the president and a certain number of aldermen.

DEFENCE. According to the Law of 30 April 1962, the Belgian Armed Forces are recruited by annual calls to the colours and by voluntary enlistments.

Military service is 10 months for conscripts serving in the Federal Republic of Germany and 12 months for those serving in Belgium, 13 months for voluntary reserve officers and 15 for the paracommando regiment. Duration of military obligation varies between 8 and 15 years for soldiers called for compulsory service.

The Medical Service has a strength of 5,785 personnel. Beside the medical units and detachments in the Armed Forces, the medical service manages 6 military hospitals and a central pharmacy.

Army. The Army comprises as major units 1 armoured and 3 mechanized brigades (2 of which are deployed as the Belgian divisions in the Belgian corps area in the Federal Republic of Germany) and 1 paracommando regiment. There are also 2 reconnaissance, 4 air defence, 1 missile, 4 engineering, 2 artillery and 2 tank battalions. Total strength (1990) 62,300. *Gendarmerie,* 15,900.

Equipment includes nearly 334 LEOPARD Main Battle Tanks, 133 SCORPION Light Tanks, 153 SCIMITAR Armoured Fighting Vehicles, 1,267 Armoured Personnel Carriers and 80 JPK 90mm Self-Propelled Anti-Tank Guns; Artillery Battalions are equipped with 155mm and 203mm Self-Propelled Howitzers, LANCE Surface-to-Surface Missiles, HAWK Surface-to-Air Missiles and GEPARD Armoured Vehicles with 35mm Anti-Aircraft Guns.

Other equipment in use: MILAN Anti-Tank Guided Weapon, STRIKER Armoured Fighting Vehicle with SWINGFIRE Anti-Tank Guided Weapon, Islander aircraft, Alouette II helicopters, Epervier Remotely Piloted Vehicle.

Navy. The naval forces include 4 frigates (Navy designed and Belgian built) completed in 1978, 6 ocean minehunters, 2 command and logistic support ships, 8 ASTER class minehunters (2 additional under construction), 4 coastal minesweepers, 11 inshore minesweepers, 2 research ships, 1 ammunition transport, 6 tugs and 2 service craft. Naval personnel in 1989 totalled 4,490 officers and ratings.

The naval air arm comprises 4 Alouette III general utility helicopters.

Air Force. The Air Force has a strength of (1990) 19,900 personnel and more than 230 aircraft in 12 operational squadrons and support units. There are 5 flying wings. The all-weather fighter wing consists of 2 squadrons of F-16s. One fighter-bomber wing has 2 squadrons of F-16s. Another fighter-bomber wing operates 2 squadrons of F-16s. The fourth wing operates Mirage 5, 1 squadron fighter bomber attack and 1 squadron tactical reconnaissance fighter. The transport wing consists of 1 squadron equipped with 12 C-130H Hercules turboprop transports, and 1 squadron flying 2 Boeing 727s, 3 HS 748 twin-turboprop transports, 5 Swearingen Merlin III light turboprop transports and 2 light twin-jet Falcons. Other types in service include Sea King Mk 48 search and rescue helicopters, SIAI-Marchetti SF.260M and

Alpha Jet training aircraft. Two surface-to-air missile squadrons, stationed in Germany, are equipped with Nike Hercules missiles.

INTERNATIONAL RELATIONS

Membership. Belgium is a member of UN, European Communities, Benelux Economic Union, Council of Europe, NATO, OECD and WEU.

ECONOMY

Budget. Revenue and expenditure for calendar years (in 1m. francs):

	1983	*1984*	*1985*	*1986*	*1987*	*1988*
Receipts						
Current	1,210,518	1,310,921	1,382,786	1,408,727	1,455,500	1,501,700
Capital	338,596	373,447	391,763	204,415	344,900	458,200
Total	1,549,114	1,684,368	1,774,549	1,614,142	1,800,400	1,959,900
Expenditure						
Current	1,611,881	1,710,302	1,803,661	1,840,903	1,804,300	1,833,700
Capital	216,147	166,317	170,839	173,352	154,400	151,400
Total	1,828,028	1,876,619	1,974,500	2,014,255	1,958,700	1,985,100

On 31 Dec. 1988 the Belgian public debt consisted of (in 1m. francs): Internal debt consolidated, 3,563,600; short and middle terms, 1,622,300; at sight, 88,900. External debt, 1,087,400.

Currency. The *franc* is the unit of currency.

No gold has been minted since 1882 (save only 5m. francs struck in 1914 and a limited number of new gold (50 Ecu) and silver (5 Ecu) coins issued in 1987). Note circulation 31 Dec. 1988, 430,442m. francs.

The official rate of exchange in March 1990 was US$1 = 38·39 francs; £1 = 58·00 francs.

Banking. The bank of issue in Belgium is the National Bank, instituted in 1850. It is the cashier of the State, and is authorized to carry on the usual banking operations. The articles of association of the National Bank of Belgium were modified on 13 Sept. 1948 so as to strengthen public control.

The savings banks are mainly operated by the *Caisse Générale d'Epargne et de Retraite* and by the private savings banks. *The Caisse Générale d'Epargne et de Retraite* (CGER), a state institution, consists of 2 parts: *the Caisse d'Epargne* which performs the whole range of banking activities and a further unit which embodies the funds engaged in social security and insurance activities; the CGER operates under the authority of the Minister of Finance. The *Commission bancaire* (bank commission) supervises the financial situation and the activities of the Caisse d'Epargne. It co-operates with the Belgian postal service, thus obviating any need of a postal-savings system. The savings deposits and savings bonds of the Caisse d'Epargne amounted to 1,048,739m. francs on 31 Dec. 1988. The private savings banks, whose liabilities expressed in savings accounts and bonds amounted to 1,144,702m. francs on 31 Dec. 1988, are controlled by the 'Commission bancaire'.

Weights and Measures. The metric system is in force.

ENERGY AND NATURAL RESOURCES

Electricity. The production of electricity (1m. kwh.) amounted to 51,015 in 1980; 48,179 in 1981; 47,936 in 1982; 49,912 in 1983; 51,850 in 1984; 54,184 in 1985; 57,505 in 1986; 59,999 in 1987; 61,913 in 1988. Supply 127 and 220 volts; 50 Hz.

Gas. Production of gas (in 1m. cu. metres): 675 in 1980; 690 in 1981; 594 in 1982; 623 in 1983; 717 in 1984; 716 in 1985; 636 in 1986; 674 in 1987; 689 in 1988.

Minerals. Output (in tonnes) for 4 calendar years:

	1985	*1986*	*1987*	*1988*
Coal	6,211,471	5,589,208	4,356,455	2,487,217
Coke	5,963,729	5,130,229	5,226,272	5,548,724
Cast iron	8,719,040	8,047,635	8,242,366	9,146,905
Wrought steel	10,687,461	9,764,551	9,786,422	11,220,497
Finished steel	8,072,766	7,359,316	7,415,200	8,771,198

Agriculture. Of the total area of 3,051,871 hectares, there were, in 1988, 1,369,380 hectares under cultivation, of which 348,714 were under cereals, 31,149 vegetables, 125,354 industrial plants, 147,265 root crops, 646,565 pastures and meadows.

Chief crops	*Area in hectares*			*Produce in tonnes*		
	1986	*1987*	*1988*	*1986*	*1987*	*1988*
Wheat	181,412	185,349	186,258	1,256,924	1,046,523	1,251,782
Barley	127,893	122,878	120,292	793,069	678,104	737,760
Oats	13,543	14,667	15,728	59,317	60,430	54,892
Rye	4,476	4,145	3,365	19,337	16,663	14,299
Potatoes	39,990	44,574	41,104	1,400,721	1,620,310	1,613,659
Beet (sugar)	112,763	106,189	109,316	5,886,234	5,425,174	6,108,603
Beet (fodder)	13,898	13,614	12,332	1,315,591	1,145,379	1,163,938
Tobacco	548	398	415	1,957	1,097	1,461

In 1988 there were 21,881 horses, 3,070,620 cattle, 186,730 sheep, 8,717 goats and 6,277,739 pigs.

Forestry. In 1988 the forest area covered 700,000 hectares, 21% of the land surface.

Fisheries. The total quantity of fish landed amounted to 31,370 tonnes valued at 2,867m. francs in 1988. The fishing fleet had a total tonnage of 24,620 gross tons at 31 Dec. 1988.

INDUSTRY AND TRADE

Industry (1988). Sugar factories and refineries, output 910,141 tonnes; 8 distilleries, output 47,471 hectolitres of alcohol; 119 breweries, output 13,792 hectolitres of beer; margarine factories, output 184,027 tonnes.

Six trusts control the greater part of Belgian industry: The Société Générale (founded in 1822) owns about 40% of coal, 50% of steel, 65% of non-ferrous metals and 35% of electricity; Brufina-Confinindus operates in steel, coal, electricity and heavy engineering; the Groupe Solvay rules the chemical industry; the Groupe Copée has interests in steel and coal; Empain controls tramways and electrical equipment; the Banque Lambert owns petroleum firms and their accessories.

Commerce. By the convention concluded at Brussels on 25 July 1921 between Belgium and Luxembourg and ratified on 5 March 1922 an economic union was formed by the two countries, and the customs frontier between them was abolished on 1 May 1922. Dissolved in Aug. 1940, the union was re-established on 1 May 1945. On 14 March 1947, in execution of an agreement signed in London on 5 Sept. 1944, there was concluded a customs union between Belgium and Luxembourg, on the one hand, and the Netherlands, on the other. The union came into force on 1 Jan. 1948, and is now known as the Benelux Economic Union. A joint tariff has been adopted and import duties are no longer levied at the Netherlands frontier, but import licences may still be required. A full economic union of the three countries came into operation on 1 Nov. 1960.

Benelux information is supplied by the Secretariat General of the Benelux Economic Union, Rue de la Régence, 39, 1000 Brussels. It publishes *Benelux. Bulletin Trimestriel de Statistique; Statistisch Kwartaalbericht* (1955 ff.).

Trade by selected countries (in 1,000 Belgian francs):

	Imports from			Exports to		
	1986	*1987*	*1988* [1]	*1986*	*1987*	*1988* [1]
France	485,654,709	487,806,590	522,017,828	614,836,278	633,879,572	675,428,913
USA	154,715,670	147,642,847	144,308,070	162,607,549	161,264,087	168,334,379
UK	255,845,998	244,250,202	258,982,640	267,140,182	261,011,649	315,503,055
Netherlands	547,563,309	533,407,032	602,058,448	461,130,695	465,960,727	496,597,430
German Dem. Rep.	7,903,247	7,190,164	7,275,266	5,335,897	4,760,106	5,637,680
Germany, Fed. Rep.	709,251,792	755,713,195	829,074,083	605,793,518	614,626,364	657,665,780
Argentina	10,466,223	7,321,373	9,621,813	2,574,133	2,557,859	2,725,186
Italy	129,985,407	132,439,516	144,480,019	179,133,742	197,522,718	210,426,308
Switzerland	67,528,998	60,519,623	61,273,525	72,607,130	70,898,295	77,240,373
Zaïre	27,831,948	23,934,164	31,286,766	12,231,661	10,425,291	11,312,419
Denmark	16,909,130	18,613,319	20,849,828	37,042,773	32,846,697	32,096,727
USSR	46,777,802	48,008,183	45,927,319	22,164,309	18,351,712	19,324,636
India	11,799,729	12,474,942	19,415,820	36,184,941	38,463,192	50,780,290
Rep. of S. Africa	16,093,835	14,362,466	20,687,750	9,351,499	10,205,743	13,541,472
Canada	16,054,286	21,623,568	23,241,765	18,434,189	15,070,357	17,205,073
Brazil	15,836,369	17,524,444	19,045,975	4,115,124	5,259,733	4,148,598
Australia	8,489,467	9,697,209	14,487,917	8,494,508	8,400,324	9,610,003

Imports and exports for 6 calendar years (in 1,000 Belgian francs):

	Imports	*Exports*		*Imports*	*Exports*
1983	2,820,864,806	2,851,340,902	1986	3,065,238,630	3,070,326,871
1984	3,195,768,712	2,992,116,161	1987	3,110,090,284	3,100,148,807
1985	3,317,811,996	3,167,691,043	1988 [1]	3,386,496,188	3,381,088,190

The total trade between Belgium and Luxembourg and UK was as follows (British Department of Trade returns, in £1,000 sterling):

	1985	*1986*	*1987*	*1988*	*1989*
Imports to UK	4,016,889	4,083,883	4,362,463	4,956,037	5,700,534
Exports and re-exports from UK	3,347,596	3,832,605	3,857,717	4,251,961	4,872,641

Principal Belgian-Luxembourg exports to UK in 1988[1] (tonnes; francs): Textiles (178,770; 31,778m.); metals (808,004; 30,528m.); chemical and pharmaceutical products (563,710; 26,924m.); precious stones and manufactures thereof (364; 32,977m.).

Principal Belgian-Luxembourg imports from the UK in 1988[1] (tonnes; francs): Machinery and electrical apparatus (83,285; 45,147m.); vehicles, chiefly motor cars, and aircraft (114,753; 20,652m.); textiles (43,378; 11,505m.); precious stones (104; 76,143m.); base metals and manufactures thereof (277,016; 13,775m.).

[1] Provisional.

Tourism. In 1988 receipts totalled 126·4m. francs.

COMMUNICATIONS

Roads. The total length of the roads in Belgium on 31 Dec. 1988 was as follows: State roads (including 1,613 km of motorway), 14,449 km; provincial roads, 1,358 km. The majority of roads are metalled. Number of motor vehicles in Belgium, 1 Aug. 1989, 4,439,889, including 3,736,317 passenger cars, 15,831 buses, 326,681 lorries, 35,198 non-agricultural tractors, 150,776 agricultural tractors, 134,211 motor cycles and 40,875 special vehicles.

Railways. The main Belgian lines were a State enterprise from their inception in 1834. In 1926 the *Société Nationale des Chemins de Fer Belges (SNCB)* was formed to take over the railways. The State is sole holder of the ordinary shares of SNCB, which carry the majority vote at General Meetings. The length of railway operated on 31 Dec. 1988 was 3,554 km, (electrified, 2,207 km). Revenue (1988), 65,680m. francs; expenditure, 66,058m. francs. In 1988, 65·8m. tonnes of freight and 143·1m. passengers were carried.

The *Société Nationale des Chemins de Vicinaux (SNCV)* operates electrified light railways around Charleroi (97 km) and from De Panne to Knokke (68 km). There is also a metro and tramway in Brussels, and tramways in Antwerp and Ghent.

Aviation. The national Belgian airline SABENA (*Société anonyme belge d'exploitation de la navigation aérienne*) was set up in 1923. Its capital is 750m. francs. In addition to its European network, SABENA operates different routes to North and South America, to North, Central and South Africa and to the Near, the Middle and the Far East. In 1987 its airfleet comprised 28 aircraft. In 1988 SABENA flew 64m. km, carrying 2,604,578 revenue passengers, 655m. ton-km of freight and 25m. ton-km of mail.

Shipping.[1] On 1 Jan. 1989 the Belgian merchant fleet was composed of 75 vessels of 2,014,873 tons. There were 40 shipping companies, of which the most important were the Compagnie Maritime Belge, with 11 ships, and the Belcan, SA, with 4 ships.

[1] Belgian shipping returns are given in the official 'Moorsom tons', which may be converted into net tons by deducting 19·85% from the Moorsom total.

The navigation at the port of Antwerp in 1988 was as follows: Number of vessels entered, 15,605; tonnage, 129,169,514. Number of vessels cleared, 15,752; tonnage, 130,456,747.

The total length of navigable waterways (rivers and canals) was 1,569·3 km in 1988.

Post and Broadcasting. On 31 Dec. 1988 there were 1,838 post offices. The gross revenue of the post office in the year 1988 amounted to 34,224m. francs.

In 1988 there were 4,841,110 telephones, 3,525,140 telephone subscribers, 21,086 mobile telephone subscribers, 40,053 subscribers to the paging service and 25,100 telex subscribers. As to data transmission, there were (1986) 50,226 modems connected to subscriber lines, 29,849 data transmission lines and 972 telegraph type lines.

Radio-Television belge de la Communauté française (RTBF) and *Belgische Radio en Televisie* (BRT) are public institutions broadcasting in French and Dutch respectively.

BRT has 5 radio programmes: BRT 1 is for service and information, documentary programmes, radio drama and light music; BRT 2 is for regional entertainment from each of the Flemish provinces. Both stations broadcast on medium-wave and on FM (stereo). BRT 3, on FM (stereo) is the cultural station; Studio Brussels (medium-wave and FM) gives information and light music for young listeners; the International Service (short-and medium-wave) aims at reaching the Fleming dwelling abroad and at presenting a picture of Flemish cultural life.

RTBF has 5 radio programmes: Radio I (medium-wave) for information; Radio II (FM stereo) for entertainment and local information; Radio III (FM stereo) for classical music; Radio 21 (FM stereo) a young people's popular music and news programme; *Radio quatre internationale* (short-wave) which broadcasts to Africa.

Each body has 2 television channels, one general and one mainly for sport, special events, cultural events, feature films; broadcasting is by PAL standards. Commercial advertising is not allowed on BRT radio or television, which are financed by the Flemish Council. In 1988 the Flemish community had 3·2m. radio receivers and 1·9m. television sets of which 85·5% were colour sets; the French-speaking community had 1·7m. radio receivers and 1·2m. television sets of which 72% were colour sets; 83·2% of the Flemish and 89% of the French-speaking households were connected to a television cable-network. Number of receivers (1988), radio, 2,066,630; TV, 3,258,127 (including 2,804,813 colour).

Cinemas (1988). There were 407 cinemas, with a seating capacity of 102,760.

Newspapers (1988). There are 35 daily newspapers (some of them only regional or local editions of larger dailies), of which 19 are in French, 15 in Dutch and 1 in German.

JUSTICE, RELIGION, EDUCATION AND WELFARE

Justice. Judges are appointed for life. There is a court of cassation, 5 courts of appeal, and assize courts for political and criminal cases. There are 27 judicial districts, each with a court of first instance. In each of the 222 cantons is a justice and judge of the peace. There are, besides, various special tribunals. There is trial by jury in assize courts.

Religion. Of the inhabitants professing a religion the majority are Roman Catholic, but no inquiry as to the profession of faith is now made at the censuses. There are, however, statistics concerning the clergy, and according to these there were in 1988: Roman Catholic higher clergy, 139; inferior clergy, 6,945; Protestant pastors, 95; Anglican Church, 12 chaplains; Jews (rabbis and ministers), 30. The State does not interfere in any way with the internal affairs of any church. There is full religious liberty, and part of the income of the ministers of all denominations is paid by the State. There are 8 Roman Catholic dioceses subdivided into 260 deaneries.

Estimated number of Protestants, 24,000; of Jews, 35,000; of Moslems, 285,000.

The Protestant (Evangelical) Church is under a synod. There is also a Central Jewish Consistory, a Central Committee of the Anglican Church and a Free Protestant Church.

Education. On 8 Nov. 1962/2 Aug. 1963 a linguistic frontier was fixed between the Dutch-speaking, French-speaking and German-speaking parts of Belgium. In the north, Dutch is recognized as the official language, in the south, French, and along the eastern border, German. The city and *arrondissement* of Brussels are bilingual. The percentage of the population in the Flemish, French, German and bilingual regions was 57·7, 31·8, 0·7, 9·8 on 1 Jan. 1988. (*See* map in THE STATESMAN'S YEAR-BOOK, 1967–68.)

Higher Education (1987–88). Higher education is given in state universities: Ghent (13,148 students), Liège (10,111 students), Mons (2,087 students), the Polytechnic Faculty in Mons (880 students), the Antwerp State University Centre (2,011 students), the Gembloux Faculty of Agronomical Sciences (987 students), the Royal Military School in Brussels (849 students) and in the private universities: Catholic University of Louvain (46,188 students), the Free University of Brussels (22,172), University Institution Antwerp (1,937 students), St Ignatius Antwerp (4,003 students), Our Lady of Peace in Namur (4,027 students), Catholic University Faculty in Mons (1,174 students), St Louis in Brussels (1,126 students), St Aloysius in Brussels (735 students), the Limbourg University Centre (760 students) and the Protestant Faculty of Theology in Brussels (136 students). The total number of students in university colleges, faculties and institutes was 112,331.

There are 5 royal academies of fine arts and 5 royal conservatoires at Brussels, Liège, Ghent, Antwerp and Mons.

Secondary Education. 2,004 (1987–88) middle schools had a total of 92,004 pupils in the general classes and 135,956 in the technical classes in the traditional system and 607,679 pupils in the new system.

Elementary Education. There were 4,636 (1987–88) primary schools, with 756,617 pupils and 4,214 (1987–88) infant schools, with 373,433 pupils.

Normal Schools. Under the French and German linguistic systems there were 23 (1987–88) schools for training secondary teachers (2,084 students) in 1987–88; 26 (1987–88) for training elementary teachers (2,028 students) in 1987–88, 20 technical normal schools in 1987–88 with 749 students and 17 normal infant schools with 1,715 students in 1987–88.

Health. In 1988 there were 31,718 physicians (including 456 dentists), 6,052 other dentists and 11,338 pharmacists. Hospital beds numbered 55,337 on 1 Jan. 1987.

Social Security. Social security is based on the law of Dec. 1944. It applies to all workers subject to an employment contract, and is administered by the Central National Office of Social Security (ONSS), which collects from employers and employees all contributions referring to family allowances, health insurance, old age insurance, holidays and unemployment. These sums are distributed by the Central Office to the various institutions concerned with these benefits. Insurance against unemployment is organized through a common fund, which also undertakes to retrain the unemployed for another employment while providing for their families. Since 1944 further laws have increased allowances, made fresh provisions for housing (1945), injuries while working, professional illnesses, etc. (1948).

Apart from private charity, the poor are assisted by the communes through the agency of the *Centre Public d'Aide Sociale* in French-speaking parts of the country and *Openbaar Centrum voor Maatschappelijk Welzijn* in Dutch-speaking areas. Provisions of a national character have been made for looking after war orphans and men disabled in the war. Certain other establishments, either state or provincial, provide for the needs of the deaf-mutes and the blind, and of children who are placed under the control of the courts. Provision is also made for repressing begging and providing shelter for the homeless.

DIPLOMATIC REPRESENTATIVES

Of Belgium in Great Britain (103 Eaton Sq., London, SW1W 9AB)
Ambassador: Jean-Paul Van Bellinghen (accredited 24 Feb. 1984).

Of Great Britain in Belgium (Britannia Hse., rue Joseph II 28, 1040 Brussels)
Ambassador: Robert James O'Neill, CMG.

Of Belgium in the USA (3330 Garfield St., NW, Washington, D.C., 20008)
Ambassador: Herman Dehennin.

Of the USA in Belgium (Blvd. du Régent 27, 1000 Brussels)
Ambassador: Maynard Wayne Glitman.

Of Belgium to the United Nations
Ambassador: P. Noterdaeme.

Further Reading

Statistical Information: The Institut National de Statistique (44 rue de Louvain, Brussels) was established on 24 Jan. 1831, under the designation of Bureau de Statistique Générale; after several changes, it received its present name on 2 May 1946. *Director-General (in charge):* L. Diels. *Main publications:*

Statistiques du commerce extérieur (monthly)
Bulletin de Statistique. Bi-monthly
Annuaire Statistique de la Belgique (from 1870).—*Annuaire statistique de poche* (from 1965)
Statistiques Agricoles. Irregular

Annuaire administratif et judiciaire de Belgique. Annual. Brussels
L'économie belge. Ministère des Affaires Economiques. Annual (from 1947)
Guide des Ministères: Revue de l'Administration Belge. Brussels, Annual
Riley, R. C., *Belgium.* [Bibliography] Oxford and Santa Barbara, 1989

BELIZE

Capital: Belmopan
Population: 179,800 (1988)
GNP per capita: US$1,460 (1988)

HISTORY. The early settlement of the territory was probably effected by British woodcutters about 1638; from that date to 1798, in spite of armed opposition from the Spaniards, settlers held their own and prospered. In 1780 the Home Government appointed a superintendent, and in 1862 the settlement was declared a colony, subordinate to Jamaica. It became an independent colony in 1884. Self-government was attained in 1964. Independence was achieved on 21 Sept. 1981.

AREA AND POPULATION. Belize is bounded north by Mexico, west and south by Guatemala and east by the Caribbean. Area, 22,963 sq. km. There are 6 districts:

	Sq. km	*Population census, 1980*		*Sq. km*	*Population census, 1980*
Corozal	1,860	22,902	Cayo	5,338	22,337
Belize	4,204	50,801	Stann Creek	2,176	14,181
Orange Walk	4,737	22,870	Toledo	4,649	11,762

Total population (census, 1980) 145,353. Estimate (1988) 179,800. In 1988 the birth rate per 1,000 was 37·3 and the death rate 4·8; infantile mortality 20·4 per 1,000 births and there were 1,072 marriages.

English is the official language. Spanish is spoken by 31·6% of the population. The main ethnic groups are Creole (African descent), Mestizo (Spanish-Maya) and Garifuna (Caribs).

Main city, Belize City; population, census 1980, 39,771. Estimate (1988) 49,700. Following the severe hurricane which struck the territory on 31 Oct. 1961 the capital Belmopan (population, 1988, 3,700) was moved to a new site 50 miles inland; construction began in Jan. 1967 and it became the seat of government on 3 Aug. 1970. *See* map in the 1978–79 edition of THE STATESMAN'S YEAR-BOOK.

CLIMATE. A tropical climate with high rainfall and small annual range of temperature. The driest months are Feb. and March. Belize. Jan. 74°F (23·3°C), July 81°F (27·2°C). Annual rainfall 76" (1,890 mm).

CONSTITUTION AND GOVERNMENT. Having achieved self-government in Jan. 1964 delays occurred in achieving independence because of the outstanding territorial claim by Guatemala. Attempts to reach agreement on the claim finally failed prior to independence being granted, but guarantees were given by Britain that a military force would remain.

The Constitution, which came into force on 21 Sept. 1981, provided for a National Assembly, with a 5-year term, comprising a 28-member House of Representatives elected by universal adult suffrage, and a Senate consisting of 8 members appointed by the Governor-General on the advice of the Prime Minister, 2 on the advice of the Leader of the Opposition and 1 on the advice of the Belize Advisory Council.

At the general election in Sept. 1989 the People's United Party won 15 seats in the House of Representatives and the United Democratic Party 13.

Governor-General: Dame Elmira Minita Gordon, GCMG, GCVO.

The cabinet in Oct. 1989 was composed as follows:

Prime Minister and Minister of Finance, Trade, Home Affairs and Defence: The Rt Hon. George Cadle Price.

Deputy Prime Minister and Minister of Industry and Natural Resources: Florencio Marin. *Foreign Affairs, Economic Development and Education:* Said Musa. *Housing and Co-operatives:* Valdemar Castillo. *Works:* Leopoldo Briceno. *Health and Urban Development:* Dr Theodore Aranda. *Attorney-General and Minister of*

Tourism and the Environment: Glenn Godfrey. *Social Services and Community Development:* Remijio Montejo. *Agriculture and Fisheries:* Michael Espat. *Labour, Public Service and Local Government:* Samuel Waight. *Energy and Communications:* Carlos Diaz.

There are 5 Ministers of State.

Flag: Blue with red band along the top and bottom edges. In the centre a white disc containing the coat of arms surrounded by a green garland.

DEFENCE. The Defence Force consists of 1 infantry battalion, with 4 active and 3 reserve companies. The Air Wing operates two twin-engined BN-2B Defenders for maritime patrol and transport duties. There is also a Maritime wing of the Belize Defence Force. It operates 2 armed Wasp patrol vessels and a number of smaller vessels utilized for anti-smuggling and coast guard duties. Naval personnel (1990) 50. British Forces in Belize number about 1,500, including a detachment of the Royal Air Force which deploys Harrier V/STOL ground attack/reconnaissance aircraft. Personnel (1990) 700.

INTERNATIONAL RELATIONS

Membership. Belize is a member of UN, the Commonwealth, CARICOM and is an ACP state of EEC.

ECONOMY

Budget. In 1989–90 envisaged expenditure of $B244·6m.

Public external debt, 31 Dec. 1988, US$116·1m.

Currency. There are notes of $B100, 20, 10, 5 and 1, and a subsidiary mixed metal coinage of 1-, 5-, 10-, 25- and 50-cent pieces. In March 1990, £1 = $B3·29 and US$1 = $B2.

Banking. A Central Bank was established in 1981. There were (1987) 4 commercial banks with a total of 14 branches: Belize Bank, Barclays Bank PLC, Bank of Nova Scotia and the locally incorporated Atlantic Bank. The Development Finance Corporation provides long-term credit for development of agriculture and industry. There were (1985) 7 government savings banks and 17 insurance companies, and (1989) 40 registered credit unions. Amendments to the Banking Ordinance permit offshore banking.

ENERGY AND NATURAL RESOURCES

Electricity. Production (1988) 90·5m. kwh. Supply 110 and 220 volts; 60 Hz.

Oil. Several oil companies were (1990) exploring for oil both off-shore and on-shore. Oil was discovered in the north in 1981 but not in commercial quantities.

Agriculture. In 1986 agriculture provided 65% of total foreign exchange earnings and employed 30% of the total labour force. The main agricultural export is sugar, followed by citrus fruit, chiefly grapefruit and oranges processed into oil, squash and concentrates. Citrus production, 1988, 1,338,000 boxes of oranges, 841,000 boxes of grapefruit. Sugar-cane production in 1988 was 777,000 tonnes. Bananas are the third export crop; production, 1988, 1,394,000 boxes. [Ed. note: Box of grapefruit, 80 lb., oranges, 90 lb., bananas, 42 lb.]. Cacao is becoming increasingly important as an export crop. Mangoes are also grown commercially; production, 1988, 854 tonnes. Main cultivated food crops (with production, 1988) are maize (50,973,000 lb), rice (12,237,000 lb) and red kidney beans (4,927,000 lb). Belize is self-sufficient in fresh beef and pork, poultry and eggs. A dairy plant (daily milk processing capacity 400 gallons) began operations in 1986. Beekeeping co-operatives produced 484,000 lb of honey in 1988.

Livestock (1988): Cattle, 51,578; sheep, 1,949; pigs, 21,555; poultry, 2·8m.

Forestry. 1m. hectares, 44% of the total land area, were under forests in 1988, which include mahogany, cedar, Santa Maria, pine and rosewood, and many secondary hardwoods of known or probable market value, as well as woods suitable for pulp production. Exports of forest produce in 1988 amounted to $B5·4m.

Fisheries. There were (1988) 8 registered fishing co-operatives. Food and game fish are plentiful, and domestic consumption is heavy. Main export markets for scale fish are in the USA, Mexico and Jamaica. Fish products exported in 1988 to the USA were valued at $B10.8m. Turtles—Hawksbill, Loggerhead and Green—are plentiful but as yet are not exported. There were 747 fishing vessels in 1988.

INDUSTRY AND TRADE

Industry. In 1988 production of the major commodities was: Sugar, 81,748 tonnes; molasses, 23,138 tonnes; cigarettes, 94·4m.; beer, 640,000 gallons; batteries, 8,835; wheat flour, 19·8m. lb.; rum 15,000 proof gallons; fertilizer, 8,572 tonnes; garments, 3,696,000; citrus concentrates, 1,653,000 gallons; soft drinks, 734,000 cases. The labour market alternates between full employment, often accompanied by local shortages in the citrus and sugar-cane harvesting (Jan.–July), and under-employment during the wet season (Aug.–Dec.), aggravated by the seasonal nature of the major industries.

Trade Unions. There are 14 accredited unions with an estimated membership of 8,200.

Commerce. In 1988 total imports amounted to $B361·9m. Total exports, $B232·5m. The principal domestic exports were timber ($B5·4m.), sugar ($B70m.), fish products ($B16·1m.), garments ($B37·3m.), bananas ($B17·2m.), citrus products ($B34·6m.), molasses ($B1m.) and honey ($B400,000).

Total trade between Belize and UK (British Department of Trade returns, in £1,000 sterling):

	1985	*1986*	*1987*	*1988*	*1989*
Imports to UK	15,050	17,954	22,757	22,461	24,272
Exports and re-exports from UK	8,329	8,232	7,543	12,064	11,842

Tourism. Tourists totalled 144,210 in 1988 spending $B55·99m.

COMMUNICATIONS

Roads. There are four major highways and all principal towns and villages are linked by road to Belmopan and Belize City. In 1988, there were 14,014 licensed vehicles.

Aviation. The Philip Goldson International Airport is 14 km from Belize City. In 1989, 3 airlines maintained international services to and from the USA, Central America and Mexico. In 1988, 765,430 passengers arrived and departed on international flights. Domestic air services provide connections to all main towns and 3 of the main offshore islands.

Shipping. The main port is Belize City, with a modern deep water port able to handle containerized shipping. During 1987-88, 232 port calls were made by cargo vessels carrying 234,315 short tons of cargo. The second largest port, Commerce Bight just south of Dangriga, can accommodate vessels up to 23 ft draft.

Post and Broadcasting. Number of telephones (1989), 14,000. Belize Telecommunications Ltd has instituted a country-wide fully automatic telephone dialling facility. There are 7 main post offices and 61 sub-post offices.

The Belize Broadcasting Network broadcasts daily, with 80% of its programmes in English and the remainder in Spanish. In 1989 there were 12 television stations.

Cinemas (1988). There were 5 cinemas with seating capacity of 5,000.

Newspapers. There were 4 weekly newspapers and 2 monthly magazines in 1990.

JUSTICE, RELIGION, EDUCATION AND WELFARE

Justice. Each of the 6 judicial districts has summary jurisdiction courts (criminal) and district courts (civil), both of which are presided over by magistrates. There is a

Supreme Court, a Court of Appeal and a Family Court was established in May 1989. There is a Director of Public Prosecutions, a Chief Justice and 3 Puisne Judges.

Religion. In 1986 about 62% of the population was Roman Catholic and 28% Protestant, including Anglican, Methodist, Seventh Day Adventist, Mennonite, Nazarene, Jehovah's Witness, Pentecostal and Baptist. There was a small group of Bahai.

Education. Education is compulsory for children between 6-14 years and primary education is free. In 1988, 226 primary schools had a total enrolment of 40,287 pupils with 1,575 teachers; 30 secondary schools, 7,376 pupils with 576 teachers; (1987) 8 other technical schools, 932 students with 69 teachers. The Belize Teachers' College offers courses for primary and secondary school teachers. The 2-year course leads to a teachers' diploma. The University College of Belize opened in 1986. There is 1 government-maintained special school for mentally handicapped and physically handicapped children. The University of the West Indies maintains an extra-mural department in Belize City.

Health. In 1989 there were 7 government hospitals (1 in Belmopan, 1 in Belize City and 1 in each of the other 5 districts) and an infirmary for geriatric and chronically ill patients, with 88 doctors and 583 hospital beds. Medical services in rural areas are provided by health care centres and mobile clinics.

DIPLOMATIC REPRESENTATIVES

Of Belize in Great Britain (200 Sutherland Ave., London, W9 1RX)
High Commissioner: Sir Edney Cain, OBE.

Of Great Britain in Belize (P.O. Box 91, Belmopan)
High Commissioner: P. A. B. Thomson, CVO.

Of Belize in the USA (3400 International Dr., NW, Washington, D.C., 20008)
Ambassador: Edward A. Laing.

Of the USA in Belize (Gabourel Lane and Hutson St., Belize City)
Ambassador: Richard G. Rich, Jr.

Of Belize to the United Nations
Ambassador: Carl Lindberg Rogers.

Further Reading

Abstract of Statistics 1981. Government Printer, Belize City, 1982
Bianchi, W. J., *Belize: The Controversy Between Guatemala and Great Britain.* New York, 1959
Dobson, D., *A History of Belize.* Belize, 1973
Fernandez, J., *Belize: Case Study for Democracy in Central America.* Aldershot, 1989
Grant, C. H., *The Making of Modern Belize.* CUP, 1976
Setzekorn, W. D., *Formerly British Honduras: A Profile of the New Nation of Belize.* Ohio Univ. Press, 1981
Woodward, R. L., Jr, *Belize.* [Bibliography] Oxford and Santa Barbara, 1980

BENIN

Capital: Porto-Novo
Population: 4·44m. (1988)
GNP per capita: US$340 (1988)

République Populaire du Bénin

HISTORY. The territory of the present State was occupied by France in 1892 and was constituted a division of French West Africa in 1904 under the name of Dahomey. It became an independent republic within the French Community on 4 Dec. 1958, and acquired full independence on 1 Aug. 1960.

In the sixth *coup* since independence, Maj. Mathieu (now Ahmed) Kerekou came to power on 26 Oct. 1972 and proclaimed a Marxist–Leninist state, whose name was altered from Dahomey to Benin on 1 Dec. 1975.

AREA AND POPULATION. Benin is bounded east by Nigeria, north by Niger and Burkina Faso, west by Togo and south by the Gulf of Guinea. The area is 112,622 sq. km, and the population, census 1979, 3,338,240. Estimate (1988) 4,444,000. In 1979, 48% of the inhabitants were male, 14·2% urban and 49% were under 15 years of age. The seat of government is Porto-Novo (208,258 inhabitants in 1982); the chief port and business centre is Cotonou (487,020 in 1982); other important towns (1982) are Parakou (65,945), Natitingou (50,800, 1979), Abomey (54,418), Kandi (53,000) and Ouidah. On 1 Jan. 1988 there were 3,033 refugees in Benin, primarily from Chad.

The areas, populations and capitals of the 6 provinces are as follows:

Province	*Sq. km*	*Census 1979*	*Estimate 1987*	*Capital*
Atakora	31,200	479,604	622,000	Natitingou
Borgou	51,000	490,669	630,000	Parakou
Zou	18,700	570,433	731,000	Abomey
Mono	3,800	477,378	610,000	Lokossa
Atlantique	3,200	686,258	909,000	Cotonou
Ouéme	4,700	626,868	806,000	Porto-Novo

French is the official language, while 47% of the people speak Fon, 12% Adja, 10% Bariba, 9% Yoruba, 6% Fulani, 5% Somba and 5% Aizo.

CLIMATE. In coastal parts there is an equatorial climate, with a long rainy season from March to July and a short rainy season in Oct. and Nov. The dry season increases in length from the coast, with inland areas having rain only between May and Sept. Porto Novo. Jan. 82°F (27·8°C), July 78°F (25·6°C). Annual rainfall 52" (1,300 mm). Cotonou. Jan. 81°F (27·2°C), July 77°F (25°C). Annual rainfall 53" (1,325 mm).

CONSTITUTION AND GOVERNMENT. Under a *Loi fondamentale* adopted in Aug. 1977, the sole political party is the *Parti de la Révolution Populaire du Bénin;* its Congress held in Nov. 1985 elected a Central Committee of 45 members to direct Party policy and to appoint the 11-member Political Bureau.

There is a unicameral legislature, the National Revolutionary Assembly of 196 People's Commissioners elected on 10 June 1984 for 5 years from the sole list of the PRPB. The Assembly elects the President for a 5-year term, and he appoints and leads a National Executive Council composed in Feb. 1989 as follows:

President, Minister of National Defence: Brig.-Gen. Mathieu Kerekou (re-elected 31 July 1984).

Ministers-Delegate to the Presidency: Maj. Edouard Zodehougan *(Interior, Security and Territorial Administration)*, Simon Ogouma *(Planning and Statistics). Rural Development and Co-operative Action:* Maj. Adolphe Biaou. *Equipment and Transport:* Soule Dankora. *Finance and Economy:* Hospice Antonio. *Commerce, Crafts and Tourism:* Girigissou Gado. *Nursery and Primary Education:* Capt. Philippe Akpo. *Secondary and Higher Education:* Vincent Guezodje. *Culture, Youth and Sports:* Ali Houdou. *Labour and Social Affairs:* Ireré Zindou. *Public Health:* Soule Dankoro. *Information and Communications:* Ousmane Batoko. *Foreign Affairs and Co-operation:* Guy Laudry Hazoume. *Justice, Inspection and Parastatal Enterprises:* Saliou Abdoudou.

National flag: Green with a red star in the canton.

Local Government. The 6 provinces, each governed by an appointed Prefect and a Provincial Revolutionary Council, are divided into 84 districts.

DEFENCE. National service is for a period of 18 months.

Army. The Army consists of 3 infantry, 1 para-commando and 1 engineer battalions, 1 armoured reconnaissance squadron and 1 artillery battery. Strength (1990) 3,800, with an additional 2,000-strong paramilitary gendarmerie.

Navy. A naval force was formed in 1979 with 2 Soviet torpedo craft and 4 inshore patrol craft. These are now believed unservicable, but a new French inshore patrol craft was delivered in 1987. Personnel in 1989 numbered 200, and the force is based at Cotonou.

Air Force. The Air Force had a strength of (1990) about 350 officers and men, 2 twin-turboprop An-26 and 2 C-47 transports, 1 Cessna Skymaster, 1 Aero Commander 500, 2 Broussard communications aircraft and 2 Ecureuil helicopters.

INTERNATIONAL RELATIONS

Membership. Benin is a member of UN, OAU and is an ACP state of EEC.

ECONOMY

Planning. A 10-year development plan (1981–90) envisaged an expenditure of 958,800m. francs CFA.

Budget. In 1987 revenue, 51,929m. francs CFA and expenditure, 53,737m. francs CFA.

Currency. The monetary unit is the *franc CFA (Communauté financiérè africaine)*, with a parity value of 50 *francs CFA* to 1 French *franc*. There are coins of 1, 2, 5, 10, 25, 50 and 100 *francs CFA*, and banknotes of 50, 100, 500, 1,000, 5,000 and 10,000 *francs CFA*. In March 1990, £1 = 472 *francs CFA*; US$1 = 288 *francs CFA*.

Banking. The *Banque Centrale des Etats de l'Afrique de l'Ouest* is the bank of issue and the central bank. The *Banque Commerciale du Bénin*, in Cotonou, conducts all government business.

ENERGY AND NATURAL RESOURCES

Electricity. *Société Béninoise d'Electricité et d'Eau*, produced 172m. kwh in 1985 from generating plants at Cotonou, Porto-Novo and Parakou. Major development of hydro-electric resources along the Mono river are being conducted jointly with Togo. Supply 220 volts; 50 Hz.

Oil. The Semé oilfield, located 10 miles offshore, was discovered in 1968. Production commenced in 1982 and reached 200,000 tonnes in 1989.

Agriculture. 90% of the population subsist by agriculture. The chief products, 1988 (in 1,000 tonnes) were: Cassava, 725; yams, 850; maize, 432; sorghum, 105; groundnuts, 67; dry beans, 45; rice, 9; and sweet potatoes, 34, while cash crops were palm kernels, 20, and palm oil, 40. Cotton cultivation has been successfully introduced in the north; coffee cultivation has given good results in the south.

Livestock (1988 in 1,000): Cattle (914), sheep (860), goats (960), pigs (648), poultry (23,000), horses (6), asses (1).

Forestry. There were (1988) 3·6m hectares of forest (43% of the land area), mainly in the north. Roundwood production in 1986 was 4·5m. cu. metres.

Fisheries. Total catch in 1986 was 23,500 tonnes (68% from inland and lagoon waters).

INDUSTRY AND TRADE

Industry. Industrial plants are few, limited mainly to palm-oil processing and brewing. There is a sugar complex at Savé, a cement plant at Onigbolo and textile mills at Cotonou and Parakou. Production (1985) included 51,000 tonnes of sugar, 37,000 tonnes of palm oil and 318,000 tonnes of cement.

Labour. In 1973 the small trade unions were amalgamated to form a single body, now named the *Union Nationale des Syndicats des Travailleurs du Bénin.*

Commerce. Imports in 1983, US$113m.; exports, US$78m. The main exports are palm oil and kernels, cocoa, cotton and sugar. In 1984, 32% of exports were to Spain, 21% to Federal Republic of Germany and 16% to France, which provided the largest share (23%) of imports.

Total trade between Benin and UK (British Department of Trade returns, in £1,000 sterling):

	1985	*1986*	*1987*	*1988*	*1989*
Imports to UK	7,390	4,910	2,930	2,450	356
Exports and re-exports from UK	8,362	6,728	7,207	8,169	7,294

Tourism. There were 72,000 foreign tourists in 1985.

COMMUNICATIONS

Roads. There were 7,445 km of roads in 1985, 2,740 passenger cars and 567 goods vehicles.

Railways. There are 579 km of metre-gauge railway. One line connects Cotonou with Parakou (438 km) and is being extended to Dosso (in Niger); the second runs from Cotonou *via* Porto-Novo to Pobé (107 km); and the third from Cotonou *via* Ouidah to Segboroué on the Togo frontier (34 km), continuing to Lomé. In 1986 1·5m. passengers and 456,000 tonnes of freight were carried.

Aviation. In 1981, 80,400 passengers and 9,763 tonnes of freight passed through Cotonou airport.There are other airports at Abomey, Natitingou, Kandi and Parakou.

Shipping. In 1983, 736,000 tonnes were unloaded and 64,400 tonnes loaded at the port of Cotonou. There were (1986) 15 vessels of 4,887 GRT registered in Benin.

Post and Broadcasting. There were, in 1985, 8,650 telephones. Telegraph lines connect Cotonou with Togo, Niger and Senegal. In 1984 there were 68,000 radios and 17,250 television receivers.

Cinemas. In 1976 there were 4 cinemas with a seating capacity of 4,400.

Newspapers. In 1984 there was 1 daily newspaper with a circulation of 12,000.

JUSTICE, RELIGION, EDUCATION AND WELFARE

Justice. The Supreme Court is at Cotonou. There are Magistrates Courts in Cotonou, Porto-Novo, Natitingou, Abomey, Kandi, Ouidah and Parakou, and a *tribunal de conciliation* in each district.

Religion. 61% of the population follow animist beliefs, chiefly Voodoo, about 22% are Christian, mainly Roman Catholic, and 15% Moslem.

Education. There were, in 1988, 471,016 pupils in 2,850 primary schools and 97,000 in 184 secondary schools. The University of Benin (Cotonou) had 6,302 students in 1983. Adult literacy (1980) 28%.

Health. In 1982 there were 6 hospitals, 31 health centres, 186 dispensaries and 65 maternity clinics with (1978, combined) 4,968 beds, and in 1979 there were 204 doctors, 13 dentists, 55 pharmacists and 1,294 midwives.

DIPLOMATIC REPRESENTATIVES

Of Benin in Great Britain
Ambassador: Souler Issoufou Idrissou (resides in Paris).

Of Great Britain in Benin
Ambassador: B. L. Barder (resides in Lagos).

Of Benin in the USA (2737 Cathedral Ave., NW, Washington, D.C., 20008)
Ambassador: Theophile Nata.

Of the USA in Benin (Rue Caporal Anani Bernard, Cotonou)
Ambassador: Walter E. Stadtler.

Of Benin to the United Nations
Ambassador: Gratien Tonakpon Capo-Chichi.

BERMUDA

Capital: Hamilton
Population: 58,616 (1988)
GNP per capita: US$20,500 (1988)

HISTORY. The Spaniards visited the islands in 1515, but, according to a 17th-century French cartographer, they were discovered in 1503 by Juan Bermudez, after whom they were named. No settlement was made, and they were uninhabited until a party of colonists under Sir George Somers was wrecked there in 1609. A company was formed for the 'Plantation of the Somers' Islands', as they were called at first, and in 1684 the Crown took over the government.

AREA AND POPULATION. Bermuda consists of a group of some 150 small islands (about 20 inhabited), situated in the western Atlantic (32° 18' N. lat., 64° 46' W. long.); the nearest point of the mainland, about 570 miles distant, is Cape Hatteras, N.C., and 690 miles from New York.

The area is 20·59 sq. miles (53·3 sq. km), of which 2·3 sq. miles were leased in 1941 for 99 years to the US Government for naval and air bases. The civil population (*i.e.*, excluding British and American military, naval and air force personnel) in 1980 (Census) was 54,893. Estimate (1988) 58,616.

Chief town, Hamilton; population, about 3,000.

In 1988 there were 935 live births, 868 marriages and 399 deaths; infantile mortality rate (1988) was 3·2 per 1,000 live births.

CLIMATE. A pleasantly warm and humid climate, with up to 60" (1,500 mm) of rain, spread evenly throughout the year. Hamilton. Jan. 63°F (17·2°C), July 79°F (26·1°C). Annual rainfall 58" (1,463 mm).

CONSTITUTION AND GOVERNMENT. Bermuda is a colony with representative government. Under the constitution of 8 June 1968 the Governor, appointed by the Crown, is normally bound to accept the advice of the Cabinet in matters other than external affairs, defence, internal security and the police, for which he retains special responsibility. The Cabinet is appointed from among members of the bicameral legislature, on the recommendation of the Premier. The Senate, of whom one or two members may serve on Cabinet, consists of 11 members. As a result of a Constitutional Conference held in Feb. 1979, it was decided that 5 Senators would be appointed by the Governor on the recommendation of the Premier, 3 by the Governor on the recommendation of the Opposition Leader and 3 by the Governor in his own discretion. The 40 members of the House of Assembly are elected 2 from each of 20 constituencies under full universal, adult suffrage. A general election was held in Feb. 1989. The United Bermuda Party won 23 seats, the Progressive Labour Party 15, and others, 2.

Governor: Sir Desmond Langley, KCVO, MBE.
Premier: Sir John W. D. Swan, KBE.
Flag: The British Red Ensign with the badge of the Colony in the fly.

DEFENCE. The Bermuda Regiment had 734 men and women in 1989.

ECONOMY

Budget. Revenue and expenditure in $B for years ending 31 March:

	1985–86	*1986–87*	*1987–88*	*1988–89*	*1989–90*
Revenue	214,800,000	231,508,700	251,550,300	297,639,200	307,439,000
Expenditure	190,362,000	200,706,300	220,172,000	245,542,700	274,738,000

Expenditure in $B1,000 (excluding capital items) was earmarked as follows:

	1985–86	*1986–87*	*1987–88*	*1988–89*	*1989–90*
Education	25,585	27,853	30,063	32,775	35,409
Health and Social Services	434,100	491,600	565,783	801,500	854,000
Public Works	20,195	21,427	25,713	27,226	30,958
Police	15,970	17,204	18,589	20,572	22,715
Tourism	17,793	19,383	22,316	25,508	26,230
Marine and Ports Services	5,127	5,852	6,809	7,246	7,527
Public Transportation	93,200	77,800	3,932	5,318	4,887
Agriculture and Fisheries	5,719	6,126	6,747	7,647	8,292
Post Office	5,022	5,991	6,724	6,828	7,804

The estimated chief sources of revenue in 1988–89 were: Customs duties, $115m.; employment tax, $23·9m.; land tax, $12m.; hospital levy, $30m.; vehicle licenses, $9,513,000; stamp duties, $13m.; passenger taxes, $10·4m. Public debt, as at 31 March 1989, was nil.

Currency. Decimal currency based on a *Bermuda dollar* of 100 *cents* was introduced 6 Feb. 1970. In March 1990 £1 = 1.64 Bermuda dollars and US$1 = 1 Bermuda dollar. The Bermuda Monetary Authority issues notes in denominations of $100, $50, $20, $10, $5 and $1, and coins in values of $5, $1, 50c, 25c, 10c, 5c and 1c.

Banking. There are 3 banks, the Bank of Bermuda, Ltd, the Bank of N. T. Butterfield and Son, Ltd, and the Bermuda Commercial Bank, Ltd, with correspondent banks and representatives in either New York, London, Canada or Hong Kong.

Weights and Measures. Metric, except that US and Imperial measures are used in certain fields.

ENERGY AND NATURAL RESOURCES

Electricity. Production (1988) 410m. kwh. Supply 115 volts; 60 Hz.

Agriculture. The chief products are fresh vegetables, bananas and citrus fruit. In 1988, 534 acres were under cultivation. In 1987 6,859 persons were employed in agriculture, fishing and quarrying.

In 1988, total value of agricultural products was $B10,960,000.

Livestock (1988): Cattle, 1,000; pigs, 2,000; goats, 1,000; poultry (1982), 47,000.

INDUSTRY AND TRADE

Trade Unions. Legislation providing for trade unions was enacted in Oct. 1946, and there are 9 trade unions with a total membership (1989) of 8,278.

Commerce. Imports and exports in $B:

	1987	*1988*	*1989*
Imports	419,939,867	488,285,238	534,409,715
Exports	29,218,856	30,815,235	50,398,458

The visible adverse balance of trade is more than compensated for by invisible exports, including tourism and off-shore insurance business.

Imports in 1988 from USA, $303m.; UK, $48m.; Canada, $31m; Japan, $29m.

In 1988 the principal imports were food, drink and tobacco ($98m.); electric equipment ($50m.); clothing ($37m.), transport equipment ($37m.). The bulk of exports comprise sales of fuel to aircraft and ships, and re-exports of pharmaceuticals.

Total trade between Bermuda and UK, in £1,000 sterling (British Department of Trade returns):

	1985	*1986*	*1987*	*1988*	*1989*
Imports to UK	6,394	1,262	1,208	6,767	4,517
Exports and re-exports from UK	28,024	26,180	25,383	24,995	77,122

Tourism. In 1988, 585,218 tourists visited Bermuda including those arriving by air and cruise ship.

COMMUNICATIONS

Roads. In 1948 the railway service was discontinued and a government-operated bus service introduced.

Between 1908 and Aug. 1946 the use of motor vehicles, with the exception of ambulances, fire engines and other essential services, was prohibited. In 1988, out of 44,518 registered vehicles 18,339 were private cars.

Aviation. Bermuda is served on a regularly scheduled basis by Air Canada, British Airways, American Airlines, Delta Airlines, Eastern Airlines, Pan American World Airways, Continental and Piedmont. Bermuda is connected by direct flights to Toronto, Canada; New York, Newark, Baltimore, Boston, Raleigh Durham, Tampa, Philadelphia and Atlanta in the USA; and London. The Caribbean is reached through scheduled connexions in the USA and Europe is reached through Gatwick.

Shipping. In 1989, there were 172 visits by cruise ships, 239 visits by cargo ships and 24 visits by oil and gas tankers.

Post and Broadcasting (1988). There are 15 post offices. The Bermuda Telephone Company is privately owned. There is International Direct Dialling to over 140 countries. Cable and Wireless Ltd provide external communications including telephone, telex, packet-switching, facsimile and electronic mail in conjunction with the Bermuda Telephone Company, and an International Database Access Service. Radio and television broadcasting is commercial.

Newspapers (1989). There is 1 daily newspaper with a circulation of 17,961 and 3 weeklies with a total circulation of 27,500.

JUSTICE, EDUCATION AND WELFARE

Justice. There are 3 magistrates' courts, 3 Supreme Courts and a court of appeal. The police had a strength of 476 men and women in 1989.

Education. Education is compulsory between the ages of 5 and 16, and government assistance is given by the payment of grants, and, where necessary, of school fees. In 1988, there were 18 primary schools, 14 secondary schools (of which 5 are private, including 2 denominational schools and one run by the US Armed Forces in Bermuda), 4 special schools at the primary and secondary levels which cater to blind, deaf, speech impaired and multiple handicapped persons aged 14–21, and 11 pre–schools. There were 428 full-time students attending the Bermuda College in 1988. There is no university, but extra-mural courses are available from Queen's University in Canada and the University of Maryland in the USA.

Health. In 1988 there were 2 hospitals, 57 doctors, 23 dentists, 643 professional nurses and 35 pharmacists.

Further Reading

Report of the Manpower Survey 1989. Hamilton, 1989
Bermuda Report, Second Edition 1985–88. Hamilton, 1988
Bermuda Historical Quarterly. 1944 ff.
Hayward, S. J., Holt-Gomez, V. and Sterrer, W., *Bermuda's Delicate Balance: People and the Environment*. Hamilton, 1981
Warwick, J. B., (ed.) *Who's Who in Bermuda 1980–81*. Hamilton, 1982
Wilkinson, H. C., *Bermuda from Sail to Steam*. OUP, 1973
Zuill, W. S., *The Story of Bermuda and Her People*. London, 1973

National Library: The Bermuda Library, Hamilton. *Head Librarian:* Cyril O. Packwood.

BHUTÁN

Capital: Thimphu
Population: 1·4m. (1988)
GNP per capita: US$160 (1987)

Druk-yul

HISTORY. In 1774 the East India Company concluded a treaty with the ruler of Bhután. Under a treaty signed in Nov. 1865 the Bhután Government was granted an annual subsidy. By an amending treaty concluded in Jan. 1910 the British Government undertook to exercise no interference in the internal affairs of Bhután, and the Bhután Government agreed to be guided by the advice of the British Government in regard to its external relations.

The Government of India concluded a fresh treaty with Bhután on 8 Aug. 1949. Under this treaty the Government of Bhután continues to be guided by the Government of India in regard to its external relations, and the Government of India have undertaken not to interfere in the internal administration of Bhután. The subsidy paid to Bhután has been increased to Rs 500,000, and the Government of India agreed to retrocede to Bhután an area of about 32 sq. miles in the territory known as Dewangiri, which was annexed in 1865.

AREA AND POPULATION. Bhután is situated in the eastern Himalayas, bordered north by China and on all other sides by India. Extreme length from east to west 190 miles: extreme breadth 90 miles. Area about 18,000 sq. miles (46,500 sq. km); population estimated at approximately 1,400,000 (1988). Hindus, of Nepálese origin, form 25%-30% of the population. Life expectancy (1985) was 48 years. The capital is at Thimphu (1987, 15,000 population).

CLIMATE. The climate is largely controlled by altitude. The mountainous north is cold, with perpetual snow on the summits, but the centre has a more moderate climate, though winters are cold, with rainfall under 40" (1,000 mm). In the south, the climate is humid sub-tropical and rainfall approaches 200" (5,000 mm).

KING. Jigme Singye Wangchuck, succeeded his father Jigme Dorji Wangchuck who died 21 July 1972.

GOVERNMENT. In 1907 the Tongsa Penlop (the governor of the province of Tongsa in central Bhután), Sir Ugyen Wangchuk, GCIE, KCSI, was elected as the first hereditary Maharaja of Bhután. The Bhutánese title is Druk Gyalpo, and his successor is now addressed as King of Bhután. From Oct. 1969 the absolute monarchy was changed to a form of 'democratic monarchy'. The National Assembly (*Tshogdu*) was reinstituted in 1953. It has 151 members and meets twice a year. Two-thirds are representatives of the people and are elected for a 3-year term. All Bhutánese over 25 years may be candidates. Ten monastic representatives are elected by the central and regional ecclesiastical bodies, while the remaining members are nominated by the King, and include members of the Council of Ministers (the Cabinet) and the Royal Advisory Council.

The official languages are Dzongkha, Lhotsam (Nepáli) and English.

National flag: Diagonally yellow over orange, over all in the centre a white dragon.

Local government: There are 18 districts, each under a district officer *(Dzongda)*.

DEFENCE

Army. There was (1990) an Army of 5,000 men.

INTERNATIONAL RELATIONS

Membership. Bhután is a member of UN.

ECONOMY

Planning. The 6th 5-year plan (1987–92), allows for expenditure of N8,811m.

Budget. The budget for 1988–89 envisaged expenditure of N2,157m. and internal revenue of N660m.

Currency. Paper currency has been introduced, known as the *Ngultrum*. Cupro-nickel and bronze currency is known as *Chetrum* (100 *Chetrum* = 1 *Ngultrum*). Indian currency is also legal tender. In March 1990, £1 = N27·60; US$1 = N16·84.

Banking. The Bank of Bhután was established in 1968. The headquarters are at Phuntsholing with 22 branches throughout the country. The Royal Monetary Authority, Thimphu, was founded in 1982 to act as Bhután's central bank. Deposits (Dec. 1987) N828m.

ENERGY AND NATURAL RESOURCES

Electricity. Production (1986) 1,950m. kwh, and 23 towns and 93 villages had electricity.

Minerals. Large deposits of limestone, marble, dolomite, graphite, lead, copper, slate, coal, talc, gypsum, beryl, mica, pyrites and tufa have been found.

Agriculture. The area under cultivation in 1984 was some 126,000 hectares. The chief products (1988 production in 1,000 tonnes) are rice (80), millet (7), wheat (16), barley (4), maize (81), cardamom, potatoes (50), oranges (51), apples (4), handloom cloth, timber and yaks. Extensive and valuable forests abound.

Livestock (1988): Cattle, 409,000; yaks (1985), 31,271; pigs, 63,000; sheep and goats, 59,000; poultry (1985), 179,521.

Forestry. In 1988, 3·3m. hectares were forested (70% of the land area).

INDUSTRY AND TRADE

Industry. In 1987 there were about 400 small-scale cottage and industrial units and also a cement plant, a fruit processing factory, a tea-chest ply veneer factory, a resin and turpentine factory, a salt iodization plant and 3 distilleries.

Commerce. Trade with India dominates but timber, cardamom and liquor are also exported to the Middle East, Singapore and Western Europe.

Total trade between Bhután and UK (British Department of Trade returns, in £1,000 sterling):

	1986	*1987*	*1988*	*1989*
Imports to UK	...	14	175	328
Exports and re-exports from UK	76	411	12,464	363

Tourism. Tourism is the largest source of foreign exchange (1987, US$2·04m. net). In 1988, 2,197 tourists visited Bhután.

COMMUNICATIONS

Roads. In 1988 there were about 2,200 km of roads. In 1986, there were 3,660 vehicles, of which 716 were private cars and 1,697 buses, Jeeps and trucks.

Aviation. (1987) There are 3 to 6 flights weekly by Druk-Air between Paro and Calcutta and a weekly return service from Paro to Dhaka.

Post and Broadcasting. A modern postal system was introduced in 1962. There are 56 general post offices and 30 branch post offices. In 1986 there were 943 km of telephone lines, 13 automatic exchanges and 1,945 telephones.

An international microwave link connects Thimphu to the Calcutta and Delhi satellite connexions. Thimphu and Phuntsholing are connected by telex to Delhi.

In 1986 there were 36 wireless stations for internal administrative communications, and 13 hydro-met stations, with an estimated 15,000 radio receivers. Bhután Broadcasting Service, Thimphu, broadcasts a daily programme in English, Sharchopkha, Dzongkha and Nepáli.

Newspapers. The only weekly newspaper, *Kuensel*, began publication in Aug. 1986 to replace the government weekly bulletin. It is published in 3 languages (English, Dzongkha and Nepáli). Total circulation (1988) about 12,500.

JUSTICE, RELIGION, EDUCATION AND WELFARE

Justice. The High Court consists of 8 judges (2 elected by the National Assembly for 5-year terms) appointed by the King. There is a Magistrate's Court in each district, under a *Thrimpon*, from which appeal is to the High Court at Thimphu.

Religion. In 1988 there were 1,160 monks in the Central Monastic Body (Thimphu and Punakha) and 2,120 in the District Monk Bodies. The monks are headed by an elected Je Khempo (Head Abbot). The majority of the people are Mahayana Buddhists of the Drukpa subsect of the Kagyud School which was first introduced from Tibet during the 12th century. Hindus of Nepálese origin represent approximately 25% of population.

Education. In 1988 there were 42,446 pupils and 1,513 teachers in primary schools, 16,350 pupils and 695 teachers in junior high and high schools and 1,761 pupils and 150 teachers in technical, vocational and tertiary-level schools. Many students receive higher technical training in India, as well as under the UN Development Programme, the Colombo Plan, etc., in Australia, the Federal Republic of Germany, New Zealand, Japan, Singapore, the USA and UK.

Health. There were (1986) 28 hospitals, 46 dispensaries, 67 basic health units, 4 indigenous dispensaries, 5 leprosy hospitals, 1 mobile hospital, 1 health school and 15 malaria eradication centres. In 1988 beds totalled 915; there were 134 doctors and 541 paramedics.

DIPLOMATIC REPRESENTATIVE

Of Bhután to the United Nations
Ambassador: Ugyen Tshering.

The Government of Bhután is in diplomatic relations with Bangladesh and India at ambassadorial level with resident missions in Thimphu. Honorary Consuls have also been appointed in Singapore, South Korea and Hong Kong (the latter also responsible for Macao).

Further Reading

Bhutan, Himalayan Kingdom. Bhután Government, Thimphu, 1979
Aris, M., *Bhutan: The Early History of an Himalayan Kingdom.* Warminster, 1979
Chakravarti, B., *A Cultural History of Bhutan.* 2nd rev. ed., 2 vols. Chitteranjan, 1981
Collister, P., *Bhutan and the British.* London, 1987
Das, N., *The Dragon Country.* New Delhi, 1973
Edmunds, T. O., *Bhutan: Land of the Thunder Dragon.* London, 1988.
Mehra, G. N., *Bhutan: Land of the Peaceful Dragon.* Rev. ed. New Delhi, 1985
Misra, H. N., *Bhutan: Problems and Policies.* New Delhi, 1988
Rahul, R., *Royal Bhutan.* New Delhi, 1983
Ronaldshay, the Earl of, *Lands of the Thunderbolt.* 2nd ed. London, 1931
Rose, L. E., *The Politics of Bhutan.* Cornell Univ. Press, 1977
Rustomji, N., *Bhutan: The Dragon Kingdom in Crisis.* OUP, 1978
Verma, R., *India's Role in the Emergence of Contemporary Bhutan.* Delhi, 1988

BOLIVIA

República de Bolivia

Capital: Sucre
Seat of Government: La Paz
Population: 7m. (1988)
GNP per capita: US$570 (1988)

HISTORY. Until 1884, when Bolivia was defeated by Chile, she had a strip bordering on the Pacific which contains extensive nitrate beds and at that time the port of Cobija (which no longer exists). She lost this area to Chile; but in Sept. 1953 Chile declared Arica a free port and, although it is no longer a free port for Bolivian imports, Bolivia still has certain privileges.

AREA AND POPULATION. Bolivia is a landlocked state bounded north and east by Brazil, south by Paraguay and Argentina and west by Chile and Peru, with an area of some 424,165 sq. miles (1,098,581 sq. km).

The following table shows the area and population of the departments (the capitals of each are given in brackets):

Departments	*Area (sq. km)*	*Census 1976*	*Census 1982* [1]	*Per sq. km 1975*
La Paz (La Paz)	133,985	1,456,078	1,913,184	12·50
Cochabamba (Cochabamba)	55,631	720,952	908,674	15·57
Potosí (Potosí)	118,218	657,743	823,485	7·98
Santa Cruz (Santa Cruz)	370,621	710,724	942,986	1·36
Chuquisaca (Sucre)	51,524	358,516	435,406	9·69
Tarija (Tarija)	37,623	186,704	246,691	5·95
Oruro (Oruro)	53,588	310,409	385,121	6·93
Beni (Trinidad)	213,564	168,367	217,700	0·99
Pando (Cobija)	63,827	34,493	42,594	0·55
Total	1,098,581	4,687,718	5,915,841	4·85

[1] Preliminary.

Total population (estimate 1988) 7m. of whom 49% urban.

Population (estimate 1985) of the principal towns: La Paz, 992,592; Santa Cruz, 441,717; Cochabamba, 317,251; Oruro, 178,393; Potosí, 113,000; Sucre, 86,609; Tarija (1982), 54,001.

Spanish is the official and commercial language, but the majority of Indians speak Aymará (25·2%) or Quechua (34·4%).

CLIMATE. The very varied geography of Bolivia produces several different climates. The two most significant are the low-lying areas in the Amazon Basin, which are very warm and damp throughout the year, with heavy rainfall from Nov. to March, and the alti-plano, which is generally dry between May and Nov. with abundant sunshine, but the nights are cold in June and July, while the months from Dec. to March are the wettest. La Paz. Jan. 53°F (11·7°C), July 47°F (8·3°C). Annual rainfall 23" (574 mm). Sucre. Jan. 55°F (13°C), July 49°F (9·4°C). Annual rainfall 27" (675 mm).

CONSTITUTION AND GOVERNMENT. The Republic of Bolivia was proclaimed on 6 Aug. 1825; its first constitution was adopted on 19 Nov. 1826.

La Paz is the actual capital and seat of the Government, but Sucre is the legal capital and the seat of the judiciary.

The following is a list of presidents since 1966 and the date on which they took office:

Gen. René Barrientos Ortuño (Constitutional President killed in air accident), 6 Aug. 1966–27 April 1969.
Dr Luis Adolfo Siles Salinas (deposed), 27 April 1969–26 Sept. 1969.
Gen. Alfredo Ovando Candia, 26 Sept. 1969–6 Oct. 1970.
Gen. Juan José Torres, 7 Oct. 1970–21 Aug. 1971.
Gen. Hugo Banzer Suarez, 21 Aug. 1971–21 July 1978.
Gen. Juan Pereda Asbun, 21 July 1978–24 Nov. 1978.
Gen. David Padilla Arancibia, 24 Nov. 1978–8 Aug. 1979.
Dr Walter Guevara Arze (deposed), 8 Aug. 1979–1 Nov. 1979.
Dr Lydia Gueiler Tejada (deposed), 16 Nov. 1979–17 July 1980.
Maj.-Gen. Luis García Meza Tejada (resigned), 18 July 1980–4 Aug. 1981.
Military Junta, 4 Aug. 1981–4 Sept. 1981.
Gen. Celso Torrelio Villa, (resigned), 4 Sept. 1981–19 July 1982.
Brig.-Gen. Guido Vildoso Calderón, 21 July 1982–10 Oct. 1982.
Dr Hernan Siles Zuazo, 10 Oct. 1982–6 Aug. 1985.
Dr Victor Paz Esstensoro, 6 Aug. 1985–6 Aug. 1989

For details of political history 1970–78 *see* THE STATESMAN'S YEAR-BOOK, 1980–81 and for the period 1978–1980 *see* THE STATESMAN'S YEAR-BOOK, 1983–84.

The President and Vice-President are elected by universal suffrage for a four year term. The President appoints the members of his Cabinet from candidates nominated by the Senate. There is a bicameral legislature; the Senate comprises 27 members, 3 from each department, and the Chamber of Deputies 130 members, all elected for 4 years.

The Cabinet was composed as follows in Jan. 1989:

President: Jaime Paz Zamora (sworn in 6 Aug. 1989).

Foreign Affairs and Worship: Carlos Iturralde Ballivían. *Interior, Migration and Justice:* Guillermo Capobianco Ribera. *Defence:* Héctor Ormachea Peñaranda. *Finance:* David Blanco Zavalo. *Planning and Co-operation:* Enrique Garcia Rodriquez. *Industry, Commerce and Tourism:* Guido Céspedes Argandoña. *Mining and Metallurgy:* Walter Soriano Lea Plaza. *Energy and Hydrocarbons:* Angel Zaniel Claros. *Agriculture and Peasant Affairs:* Mauro Bertero Gutiérrez. *Labour:* Oscar Zamora Medinacelli. *Information:* Manfredo Kempff Suárez. *Aeronautics:* Luis González Quintanilla. *Education and Culture:* Mariano Bapista Gumucio. *Housing and Urban Affairs:* Enrique Prado Abasto. *Transport and Communications:* Willy Vargas Vacaflor. *Without Portfolio:* Guillermo Fortún Suárez.

National flag: Three horizontal stripes of red, yellow, green, with the arms of Bolivia in the centre.

National anthem: Bolivianos, el hado propicio (words by I. de Sanjinés; tune by B. Vincenti).

Local Government: The republic is divided into 9 departments, established in Jan. 1826, with 98 provinces administered by sub-prefects, and 1,272 cantons administered by corregidores. The supreme authority in each department is vested in a prefect appointed by the President.

DEFENCE. Bolivia is divided into 6 military regions; regional HQ are located at La Paz, Sucre, Tarija, Potosí, Trinidad and Cobija. There is selective conscription for 12 months at the age of 18 years.

Army. The Army consists of 8 cavalry groups, 1 motorized infantry regiment, 22 infantry, 1 artillery, 1 airborne and 6 engineer battalions. Equipment, 36 Steyr SK105 light tanks and 24 EE-9 Cascavel armoured cars. Strength (1990) 20,000.

Navy. A small Navy exists for river and lake patrol comprising 10 patrol craft operating in Lake Titicaca, in the 6,000-mile Beni and Bolivia-Paraguay river systems. 1 ocean-going transport (a gift from Venezuela for use to and from Bolivian free zones in Argentina and Uruguay) and 2 17-tonne hospital craft on Lake Titicaca complete the inventory. There are two armed T-6 patrol aircraft and 2 Cessna light transports.

Personnel in 1989 totalled 4,000, including 1,000 marines. Most training of officers and petty officers is carried out in Argentina while junior ratings are almost entirely re-trained soldiers.

Air Force. The Air Force, established in 1923, has 3 combat-capable Groups, 2 equipped with T-33 armed jet trainers, and one with armed T-6s, SF.260s and Hughes 500 helicopters, for counter-insurgency operations. A search and rescue helicopter Group has 15 Brazilian-assembled Lamas and 20 UH-1 Iroquois. Other types in service include Brazilian T-23 Uirapuru and American T-41 primary trainers and Swiss turboprop-powered Pilatus PC-7 basic trainers, 1 Electra four-turboprop transport, 6 Fokker F.27 and 2 Israeli-built Arava twin-turboprop light transports, 2 Convair transports, 8 C-130H/L-100 Hercules, 6 C-47s, 15 Turbo-Porters and about 35 Cessna single- and twin-engined light aircraft. Personnel strength (1990) about 4,000.

INTERNATIONAL RELATIONS

Membership. Bolivia is a member of UN, OAS, LAIA (formerly LAFTA), the Andean Group and the Amazon Pact.

ECONOMY

Budget. Expenditure in 1984 was envisaged at 6,891,200m. *peso bolivanos.*

Currency. On 1 Jan. 1987 the *boliviano* ($b. equal to 1m. *pesos*) was introduced. Exchange rates were $b.3·06 = US$1 and $b.5·02 = £1 in March 1990.

Banking. In 1986 the principal banks were Banco Central de Bolivia, Banco del Estado, Banco de Santa Cruz de la Sierra, Banco Agricola de Bolivia, Banco Boliviano Americano, Banco Hipotecario Nacional, Banco Mercantil, Banco Minero de Bolivia, Banco Nacional de Bolivia, Banco do Brasil, Banco de la Nacion Argentina, Banco Popular del Peru, Banco Industrial S.A., First National City Bank, Banco del Progress Nacional, Bank of America and Bank of Boston.

Weights and Measures. The metric system of weights and measures is used by the administration and prescribed by law, but the old Spanish system is also employed.

ENERGY AND NATURAL RESOURCES

Electricity. Electric power production is expanding. Installed capacity was estimated at 490,000 kw. in 1985. Estimated production from all sources (1986), 2,080m. kwh. Supply 110 volts in La Paz but 220 volts in most other cities; 60 Hz.

Oil and Gas. There are petroleum and natural gas deposits in the Santa Cruz-Camiri areas. A pipeline for crude oil connects Caranda (Santa Cruz) with the Pacific coast at Arica (Chile) and a natural gas pipeline to Argentina was inaugurated in May 1972. All production, refining and internal distribution is now in the hands of *Yacimientos Petroliferos Fiscales Bolivianos* (the State Petroleum Organization). Total production of crude oil in 1989 was estimated at 900,000 tonnes. Production of natural gas in 1981 was estimated at 175,478m. cu. ft.

Minerals. Mining is the most important industry, accounting for about 69% of the foreign-exchange earnings. About half the mineral mined is tin. Tin mines are at altitudes of from 12,000 to 18,000 ft, where few except native Indians can stand the conditions; transport is costly. Bolivian tin is extracted by shaft-mining, frequently very deep; the ore yields only 0·7% or less of tin and is very refractory; tin is exported in concentrates called *barrilla,* through Pacific ports for refining. Smelting capacity was increased in 1980 and it is planned to smelt all the ores from the State Mining Co. but complex ores still have to be exported for smelting. Tin production in 1984 was 17,875 tonnes.

Alluvial gold deposits in the Alto Beni region are being exploited. Production (1987) 2·7 tonne.

Agriculture. The extensive and still largely undeveloped region east of the Andes comprises about three-quarters of the entire area of the country, and since the agrarian reform of 1953 sugar-cane, rice and cotton have been grown in this *Oriente* in increasing abundance, reaching self-sufficiency in all these products. Output in 1,000 tonnes in 1988 was: Sugar-cane, 2,000; rice, 171; coffee, 26; maize, 446; potatoes, 700; wheat, 63; cotton (lint), 4; cocoa, 3. Cocaine is by far the largest crop grown.

Livestock: In 1988 there were 5·45m. head of cattle, mostly in the Santa Cruz and Beni departments; some are exported to Peru; horses, 315,000; asses, 620,000; pigs, 1·75m.; sheep, 9·6m.; goats, 2·35m.; poultry, 12m.

Forestry. Forests cover 55·8m. hectares (51% of the land area). Tropical forests with woods ranging from the 'iron tree' to the light *palo de balsa* are beginning to be exploited.

INDUSTRY AND TRADE

Industry. There are few industrial establishments and the country relies on imports for the supply of many consumer goods. However a new investment law passed in 1971 provides incentives and protection for new investment, both foreign and domestic, and for reinvestment in various fields including manufacturing industry, mining, agriculture, construction and tourism.

Commerce. The value of imports and exports in US$1,000 has been as follows:

	1982	*1983*	*1984*	*1985*	*1986*	*1987*
Imports	496,300	451,100	713,800	551,900	711,500	776,000
Exports	898,500	786,700	609,500	672,500	637,500	569,600

Chief exports in 1983 (in US$1m.): Natural gas, 378·2; tin, 207·9; silver, 58·3; zinc, 33·4; wolfram, 20; coffee, 12·9; sugar, 12·3.

Chief imports in 1983 (in US$1m.): Raw materials for industry, 211·3; capital goods for industry, 152·4; consumer goods, 52·3; transport equipment, 52·2; construction materials, 38·4.

Imports and exports (in US$1m.), by country, 1984:

Country	*Imports*	*Exports*	*Country*	*Imports*	*Exports*
Argentina	97·2	271·1	Japan	22·9	—
Brazil	154·6	14·7	Korea	125·5	—
Chile	16·2	—	Peru	—	14·8
Federal Republic of Germany	31·5	38·6	UK	24·9	24·6
France	—	23·9	USA	116·1	145·1

Total exports, 1984, of all minerals, in concentrates, ingots or solder, were valued at US$363·9m.

Bolivia having no seaport, imports and exports pass chiefly through the ports of Arica and Antofagasta in Chile, Mollendo-Matarani in Peru, through La Quiaca on the Bolivian-Argentine border and through river-ports on the rivers flowing into the Amazon.

Total trade between Bolivia and UK (British Department of Trade returns in £1,000 sterling):

	1985	*1986*	*1987*	*1988*	*1989*
Imports to UK	14,434	10,225	14,799	13,224	17,666
Exports and re-exports from UK	10,443	3,663	3,658	6,029	6,148

Tourism. There were 133,000 visitors in 1986.

COMMUNICATIONS

Roads. A highway, in poor condition, 497 km long, runs from Cochabamba to the lowland farming region of Santa Cruz. La Paz and Oruro are also connected by a metalled road. Of other main highways (unmetalled) there is one from La Paz through Guaqui into Peru, another from La Paz, *via* Oruro, Potosí, Tarija and Bermejo, into Argentina, with branches to Cochabamba, Sucre and Camiri, passable throughout the year except at the height of the rainy season, and others from

Villazón to Villa Montes *via* Tarija, passable during the dry season. The total length of the road system is 41,000 km (1984). Motor vehicles in use in 1984, 168,600, including 43,677 cars.

Railways. In 1964 Bolivian National Railways (ENFE) was formed by the amalgamation of the Bolivian Government Railways, Bolivian Railway Co. and the Bolivian section of the Antofagasta (Chili) & Bolivia Railway. The Guaqui-La Paz Railway, formerly operated by Peru, became part of ENFE in 1973 and the privately-owned Marchacamarca Uncia mineral line was taken over in 1987. Access to the Pacific is by 3 routes: To Antofagasta and Arica in Chile, and to Mollendo in Peru *via* Guaqui, the Lake Titicaca train ferry to Puno (Peru), then rail to the coast. Construction began in 1978 of a 150-km line linking Puno with Desaguadero on the Bolivian border which would by-pass the train ferry, though gauge difference would still prevent through running to Peru. Current network totals 3,642 km of metre gauge, comprising unconnected Eastern (1,386 km) and Western (2,257 km) systems. In 1988 the railways carried 1m. passengers and 900,000 tonnes of freight.

Aviation. The 2 international airports are El Alto ($8^1/_2$ miles from La Paz) and Viru Viru (10 miles from Santa Cruz). The national airline is Lloyd Aéreo Boliviano. The airline runs regular services between La Paz and Lima, São Paulo, Buenos Aires, Miami, Caracas, Salta and Arica as well as many internal services. Eastern Airways runs regular flights between La Paz, Buenos Aires, Santiago and Asunción linking Bolivia to the USA. Lufthansa links Bolivia with Europe. Other airlines serving Bolivia are Aerolineas Argentinas, Cruzeiro, Aero Peru and Lan Chile.

Shipping. Traffic on Lake Titicaca between Guaqui and Puno is carried on by the steamers of the Peruvian Corporation. About 12,000 miles of rivers, in 4 main systems (Beni, Pilcomayo, Titicaca-Desaguadero, Mamoré), are open to navigation by light-draught vessels.

Post and Broadcasting. In Bolivia there were, in 1978, 458 post offices, of these, 205 provided telegraph and telephone services together with a further 245 offices for telegraph and telephone service only. There is telephone service in the cities of La Paz, Cochabamba, Oruro, Sucre, Potosí, Santa Cruz, Tarija, Camiri, Tupiza, Villazon, Riberalta and Trinidad with (1983), 204,747 telephones. There were (1987) about 85 radio stations, the majority of which are local and commercial. There is a commercial government television service. There are 4 private television stations and 1 University station (educational channel) in La Paz.

Cinemas. In 1986 there were 29 cinemas in La Paz and some 15 in other cities.

Newspapers. There were (1984) 7 daily newspapers in La Paz, 2 in Oruro, and 1 in Cochabamba. Several other towns have regular newspapers devoted to local news, but most of them appear only a few times a week. An economic monthly journal *Revista Economica* and 4 daily newspapers are produced in Santa Cruz.

JUSTICE, RELIGION, EDUCATION AND WELFARE

Justice. Justice is administered by the Supreme Court, superior district courts (of 5 or 7 judges) and courts of local justice. The Supreme Court, with headquarters at Sucre, is divided into two sections, civil and criminal, of 5 justices each, with the Chief Justice presiding over both. Members of the Supreme Court are chosen on a two-thirds vote of Congress.

Religion. The Roman Catholic is the recognized religion of the state; the free exercise of other forms of worship is permitted. The Catholic Church is under a cardinal (in Sucre), an archbishop (in La Paz), 6 bishops (Cochabamba, Santa Cruz, Oruro, Potosí, Riberalta and Tarija) and vicars apostolic (titular bishops resident in Cueva, Trinidad, San Ignacio de Velasco, Riberalta and Rurrenabaque).

By a law of 11 Oct. 1911 all marriages must be celebrated by the civil authorities. Divorce is permitted by a law enacted on 15 April 1932.

Education. Primary instruction is free and obligatory between the ages of 6 and 14 years. In 1986 there were 1·4m. pupils and 51,000 teachers in 9,093 primary and elementary schools, and 225,000 pupils, 10,400 teachers in 2,300 secondary schools.

At Sucre, Oruro, Potosí, Cochabamba, Santa Cruz, Tarija, Trinidad and La Paz are universities; La Paz is the most important of them while the San Francisco Xavier University at Sucre is one of the oldest in America, founded in 1624.

Health. In 1972 there were 2,143 doctors.

DIPLOMATIC REPRESENTATIVES

Of Bolivia in Great Britain (106 Eaton Sq., London, SW1W 9AD)
Ambassador: (Vacant).

Of Great Britain in Bolivia (Avenida Arce 2732–2754, La Paz)
Ambassador: M. F. Daley, CMG.

Of Bolivia in the USA (3014 Massachusetts Ave, NW, Washington, D.C., 20008)
Chargé d'Affaires: Horacio Bazoberry.

Of the USA in Bolivia (Banco Popular Del Peru Bldg, La Paz)
Ambassador: Robert S. Gelbard.

Of Bolivia to the United Nations
Ambassador: Hugo Navajas-Mogro.

Further Reading

Anuario Geográfico y Estadístico de la República de Bolivia
Anuario del Comercia Exterior de Bolivia
Boletín Mensual de Información Estadistica
Dunkerley, J., *Rebellion in the Veins: Political Struggle in Bolivia 1952–1982*. London, 1984
Fifer, J. V., *Bolivia: Land, Location and Politics Since 1825*. CUP, 1972
Guillermo, L., *A History of the Bolivian Labour Movement 1848–1971*. CUP, 1977
Klein, H., *Bolivia: The Evolution of a Multi-Ethnic Society*. OUP, 1982
Yeager, G. M., *Bolivia*. [Bibliography] Oxford and Santa Barbara, 1988

BOTSWANA

Capital: Gaborone
Population: 1·26m. (1989)
GNP per capita: US$1,050 (1988)

HISTORY. In 1885 the territory was declared to be within the British sphere; in 1889 it was included in the sphere of the British South Africa Company, but was never administered by the company; in 1890 a Resident Commissioner was appointed, and in 1895, on the annexation of the Crown Colony of British Bechuanaland to the Cape of Good Hope, the British Government was in favour of transferring the Protectorate to the BSA Company, but the three major chiefs of the Bakwena, the Bangwaketse and the Bamangwato went to England to protest against this proposal, and agreement was reached that their country should remain a British Protectorate if they ceded a strip of land on the eastern side of the country for railway construction. This railway was built in 1896–97.

On 30 Sept. 1966 the Bechuanaland Protectorate became an independent and sovereign member of the Commonwealth under the name of the Republic of Botswana.

AREA AND POPULATION. Botswana is bounded west and north by Namibia, north-east by Zambia and Zimbabwe and east and south by the Republic of South Africa. Area about 222,000 sq. miles (582,000 sq. km); population, estimate 1989, was 1,255,749 (census, 1981, 941,027).

The main business centres (with estimated population, 1989) are Gaborone (120,239), Mahalapye (104,450), Serowe (95,041), Tutume (86,405), Bobonong (55,060), Francistown (52,725), Selebi-Phikwe (49,542), Boteti (32,711), Lobatse (26,841), Palapye (16,959), Jwaneng (13,895), Tlokweng (11,760), Orapa (8,894).

The seat of government is at Gaborone.

The official language is English; the national language is Setswana.

CLIMATE. Most of the country is sub-tropical, but there are arid areas in the south and west. In winter, days are warm and nights cold, with occasional frosts. Summer heat is tempered by prevailing north-east winds. Rainfall comes mainly in summer, from Oct. to April, while the rest of the year is almost completely dry with very high sunshine amounts. Gaborone. Jan. 79°F (26·1°C), July 55°F (12·8°C). Annual rainfall 21" (538 mm).

CONSTITUTION AND GOVERNMENT. The Constitution adopted on 30 Sept. 1966 provides for a republican form of government headed by the President with 3 main organs: The Legislature, the Executive and the Judiciary.

The executive rests with the President of the Republic who is responsible to the National Assembly.

The National Assembly consists of 38 members, 34 elected by universal suffrage. The general election, held in Oct. 1989, returned 31 members of the Botswana Democratic Party and 3 Botswana National Front.

The President is an *ex-officio* member of the Assembly. If the President is already a member of the National Assembly, a by-election will be held in that constituency.

There is also a House of Chiefs to advise the Government. It consists of the Chiefs of the 8 tribes who were autonomous during the days of the British protectorate, and 4 members elected by and from among the sub-chiefs in 4 districts.

The first President of Botswana, who was re-elected 3 times, was Sir Seretse Khama, KBE, who died 13 July 1980.

President of the Republic: Dr Quett Ketumile Joni Masire (re-elected 1989).

In Dec. 1989 the Cabinet was as follows:

Vice President and Minister of Local Government and Lands: P. S. Mmusi. *Presidential Affairs and Public Administration:* Lieut.-Gen. Mompati Merafhe. *External Affairs:* Dr G. K. T. Chiepe. *Health:* Kebatlamang, P. Morake. *Works, Transport and Communications:* C. J. Butale. *Commerce and Industry:* Ponatshego Kedikilwe. *Mineral Resources and Water Affairs:* A. M. Mogwe. *Education:* Ray Molombo. *Finance and Development Planning:* Festus Mogae. *Labour and Home Affairs:* Patrick Balopi.

National flag: Light blue with a horizontal black stripe, edged white, across the centre.

Local Government. Local government is carried out by 9 district councils and 4 town councils. Revenue is obtained mainly from sales taxes; from rates in the towns and from central government subventions in the districts.

DEFENCE

Army. A defence force has been created for border control and comprises 5 infantry, 1 armoured car, 1 reconnaissance and 1 engineer companies. Personnel (1990) 4,500.

Air Force. Equipment includes 8 BAC Strikemaster light strike aircraft, 5 Britten-Norman Defender armed light transports for border patrol, counter-insurgency and casualty evacuation duties, 5 Bulldog piston-engined basic trainers, 2 CN-235 turboprop-powered medium transports, 2 Skyvan turboprop passenger/cargo transports, 2 Trislander 3-engined transports, 2 Ecureuil and 3 Bell 412 helicopters and 2 Cessna 152 light aircraft. Personnel (1989) about 150.

INTERNATIONAL RELATIONS

Membership. Botswana is a member of UN, OAU, SADCC, the Non-Aligned Movement, the Commonwealth and is an ACP state of EEC.

ECONOMY

Planning. Development Plan 1985–91 envisages capital expenditure of P1,200m.

Budget. The 1989–90 budget envisaged expenditure of P2,164m., revenue was envisaged at P1,032m.

Currency. The currency was formerly the South African Rand but in Aug. 1976 a new currency, the *pula*, was introduced (P3·09 = £1 sterling and P1·88 = US$1 in March 1990).

Banking. There were (1986) 3 commercial banks (Barclays Bank of Botswana Ltd, Standard Chartered Bank Botswana Ltd and Bank of Credit and Commerce (Botswana) Ltd) with 34 branches and sub-branches, and 44 agencies. The Bank of Botswana, established in 1976, is the central bank. The National Development Bank, founded in 1964, has 6 regional offices and agricultural, industrial and commercial development divisions. The government-owned Botswana Savings Bank operates through 64 post offices.

Total assets and liabilities of the 3 commercial banks at 31 March 1989, P897m. and of the Bank of Botswana, P4,785·1m.

ENERGY AND NATURAL RESOURCES

Electricity. The coal-fired power station at Morupule supplies all major cities. Production (1986) 533m. kwh. Supply 220 volts; 50 Hz.

Water. Surface water resources are about 18,000m. cu. metres a year. Nearly all flows into northern districts from Angola through the Okavango and Kwando river systems. The Zambezi, also in the north, provides irrigation in Chobe District. In the south-east, there are dams to exploit the ephemeral flow of the tributaries of the Limpopo. 80% of the land has no surface water, and must be served by boreholes.

Minerals. An important part of government revenue comes from the diamond mines at Orapa and Jwaneng and the nickel–copper complex at Selebi-Phikwe. An open-pit coalmine has been developed at Morupule. Mineral production 1988:

Diamonds, 15,229,000 carats; copper–nickel, 43,238 tonnes (value P81,374,000); coal, 612,713 tonnes (P11,300,000).

Mineral resources in north-east Botswana are being investigated, including salt and soda ash on the Sua Pan of the Makgadikgadi Salt Pans, nickel–copper at Selkirk and Phoenix, copper south of Maun and close to Ghanzi, and coal at Mmamabula.

Agriculture. Cattle-rearing is the chief industry, and the country is more a pastoral than an agricultural one, crops depending entirely upon the rainfall. In 1987, 295,000 hectares were planted with crops. In 1988 the number of cattle was 2·35m.; goats, 1m.; sheep, 220,000; poultry, 1m. Meat and meat products (1986) exported P144,157,165, sold locally P7,469,859.

Production (1988, in 1,000 tonnes): Maize, 12; sorghum, 40; groundnuts, 1; millet, 3; wheat, 1; roots and tubers, 7; sunflower seeds, 1; pulses, 14; seed cotton, 3; vegetables, 16; fruit, 11.

Forestry. There are forest nurseries and plantations. Concessions have been granted to harvest 7,500 cu. metres in Kasane and Chobe Forest Reserves and up to 2,500 cu. metres in the Masame area.

WILDLIFE. About 17% of land is set aside for wildlife preservation. In 1986 there were 4 national parks, 6 game reserves, 3 game sanctuaries and 40 controlled hunting areas for photographic and game viewing safaris and recreational (safari) and subsistence hunting.

INDUSTRY AND TRADE.

Labour. In 1987 there were 80,449 Batswana employed in the mines of the Republic of South Africa. The estimated total number of paid employees in all sectors in Botswana in Sept. 1987 was 150,200.

Commerce. In 1987 imports totalled P1,572,456 and exports P2,663,802. Of imports, 79·6% came from the South African customs area, 7·7% from other African countries. Exports are mainly diamonds (to Switzerland), copper–nickel matte (to USA), beef and beef products (to EEC).

Imports (1987 in P1,000) included vehicles and transport equipment, 242,785; food, beverages and tobacco, 253,422; machinery and electrical equipment, 260,370: Exports were mainly diamonds, 2,252,453. Imports in 1987 were mainly from the South African customs area (P1,250,954,000) and exports mainly to Europe (P2,412,152,000).

Botswana is a member of the South African customs union with Lesotho, the Republic of South Africa and Swaziland.

Total trade between Botswana and UK (British Department of Trade returns, in £1,000 sterling):

	1985	*1986*	*1987*	*1988*	*1989*
Imports to UK	20,998	16,652	11,836	6,942	13,135
Exports and re-exports from UK	6,680	8,629	10,275	26,763	34,582

Tourism. There were 432,323 foreign visitors in 1987.

COMMUNICATIONS

Roads. On 31 Dec. 1985, 1,914 km of road were bitumen-surfaced, 1,255 km gravel and about 4,860 km earth. In 1988 there were 46,560 registered motor vehicles including 14,199 cars, 16,350 light delivery vans and 6,895 lorries.

Railways. The main line from Mafikeng in Bophuthatswana to Bulawayo in Zimbabwe traverses Botswana. With two short branches the total was (1989) 705 km. These lines, formerly operated by National Railways of Zimbabwe, were taken over by the new Botswana Railways organization in 1987. In 1986–87 railways carried 1,203m. tonne-km and 284m. passenger-km.

Aviation. The Seretse Khama International Airport at Gaborone opened in 1984. Regular international flights are flown by Air Botswana, Air Zimbabwe, Royal

Swazi Air, Air Zambia, Air Tanzania, Air Malawi, Kenya Airways, Lesotho Airways, South African Airways and British Airways into Gaborone. In 1988, 77,250 passengers arrived by air, 65,519 departed and 4,056 were in transit.

Post and Broadcasting. In 1986 there were 66 post offices and 72 agencies. There were 12,511 telephones installed in 1987. Radio Botswana broadcasts 119 hours a week in English and Setswana.

Newspapers. In 1987 there was 1 daily newspaper, the bilingual (Setswana-English) *Daily News*, which is published by the Department of Information and Broadcasting; circulation, 36,000. There are 3 other privately-owned newspapers.

JUSTICE, RELIGION, EDUCATION AND WELFARE

Justice. The Botswana Court of Appeal was established in 1954. It has jurisdiction in respect of criminal and civil appeals emanating from the High Court of Botswana and has jurisdiction in all criminal and civil causes and proceedings. Subordinate courts and traditional courts are in each of the 12 administrative districts. The police force was 2,359 in 1985.

Religion. Freedom of worship is guaranteed under the Constitution. Christian denominations include the United Congregational Church of Southern Africa, the Catholic Church, Anglican, Lutheran, Dutch Reformed, Seventh Day Adventist, Assemblies of God, Methodist and Quaker groups. Non-Christian religions include Bahais, Moslems and Hindus.

Education. Primary education has been free since 1980 and secondary education from 1988. In 1988 enrolment in primary schools was 259,152 with (1987) 7,704 teachers, and in secondary schools 40,000 with (1987) 1,682 teachers. In 1987 there were 1,316 students with 78 teachers in teacher training colleges and 2,261 students with 328 instructors in vocational and technical training. There is a Polytechnic and an Auto Trades Training School. Throughout the country, Brigades provide lower level vocational training. The Department of Non-Formal Education offers secondary level correspondence courses and is the executing agency for the National Literacy Programme. The University of Botswana had 1,884 full-time students and 250 academic staff in 1987.

In 1987, 63% of those over 15 years could read and write.

Health (1986). There were 13 general hospitals, a mental hospital, 7 health centres, 81 clinics and 246 health posts. There were also 438 stops for mobile health teams. In 1986 there were 156 registered medical practitioners, 14 dentists, and 1,530 nurses. The health facilities are the concern of central and local government, medical missions, mining companies and voluntary organizations.

DIPLOMATIC REPRESENTATIVES

Of Botswana in Great Britain (6 Stratford Pl., London, W1N 9AE)
High Commissioner: Margaret Nasha.

Of Great Britain in Botswana (Private Bag 0023, Gaborone)
High Commissioner: Brian Smith, OBE.

Of Botswana in the USA (4301 Connecticut Ave., NW, Washington, D.C., 20008)
Ambassador: K. Sebele.

Of the USA in Botswana (PO Box 90, Gaborone)
Ambassador: John F. Kordek.

Of Botswana to the United Nations
Ambassador: Legwaila Joseph Legwaila.

Further Reading

General Information: The Director of Information and Broadcasting, PO Box 0060, Gaborone, Botswana publishes *Botswana Handbook*, the monthly *Kutlwano, The Botswana Daily News, Botswana in Brief* and *Botswana Up To Date*.

Botswana '86: An Official Handbook. Department of Information and Broadcasting, Gaborone, 1986
Statistical Bulletins. Quarterly. Central Statistical Office, Gaborone
Report on the Population Census, 1981. Government Printer, Gaborone, 1982
Campbell, A. C., *The Guide to Botswana*. Gaborone, 1980
Colclough, C. and McCarthy, S., *The Political Economy of Botswana*. OUP, 1980
Harvey, C., (ed.) *Papers on the Economy of Botswana*. London and Nairobi, 1981
Parson, J., *Botswana: Liberal Democracy and Labour Reserve in Southern Africa*. Aldershot, 1984

BRAZIL

Capital: Brasília, DF
Population: 147·4m. (1989)
GNP per capita: US$2,280 (1988)

República Federativa do Brasil

HISTORY. Brazil was discovered on 22 April 1500 by the Portuguese Admiral Pedro Alvares Cabral, and thus became a Portuguese settlement; in 1815 the colony was declared 'a kingdom', and it was proclaimed an independent Empire in 1822. The monarchy was overthrown in 1889 and a republic declared. Following a *coup* in 1964 the armed forces retained overall control until civilian government was restored on 15 March 1985.

AREA AND POPULATION. Brazil is bounded east by the Atlantic and on its northern, western and southern borders by all the South American countries except Chile and Ecuador. The area is 8,511,996 sq. km (3,286,485 sq. miles) including 55,457 sq. km of inland water. Population as at 1 Sept. 1980 (census) and 1 July 1989 (estimate):

Federal Unit and Capital	*Area (sq. km)*	*Census 1980*	*Estimate 1989*
North	3,851,560	5,880,268	9,566,564
Rondônia (Pôrto Velho)	238,379	491,069	1,057,237
Acre (Rio Branco)	153,698	301,303	406,787
Amazonas (Manaus)	1,567,954	1,430,089	1,948,508
Roraima (Boa Vista)	225,017	79,159	116,765
Pará (Belém)	1,246,833	3,403,391	4,862,775
Amapá (Macapá)	142,359	175,257	248,122
Tocantins (Miracema do Tocantins)	277,322	–	926,370
North-east	1,556,001 [1]	34,812,356	42,062,136
Maranhão (São Luís)	329,556	3,996,404	5,076,341
Piaui (Teresina)	251,273	2,139,021	2,616,927
Ceará (Fortaleza)	145,694	5,288,253	6,356,068
Rio Grande do Norte (Natal)	53,167	1,898,172	2,277,672
Paraíba (João Pessoa)	53,958	2,770,176	3,200,430
Pernambuco (Recife) [2]	101,023	6,141,993	7,238,280
Alagoas (Maceió)	29,107	1,982,591	2,381,522
Sergipe (Aracajú)	21,863	1,140,121	1,392,934
Bahia (Salvador)	566,979	9,454,346	11,521,962
South-east:	924,266	51,734,125	64,274,047
Minas Gerais (Belo Horizonte)	586,624	13,378,553	15,590,292
Espírito Santo [3] (Vitória)	45,733	2,023,340	2,476,811
Rio de Janeiro (Rio de Janeiro) [4]	43,653	11,291,520	13,845,243
São Paulo (São Paulo)	248,256	25,040,712	32,361,701
South	575,316	19,031,162	22,348,564
Parana (Curitiba)	199,324	7,629,392	8,935,142
Santa Catarina (Florianópolis)	95,318	3,627,933	4,386,697
Rio Grande do Sul (Pôrto Alegre)	280,674	7,773,837	9,026,725
Central West	1,604,852	7,544,795	9,153,064
Mato Grosso (Cuiabá) [5]	901,421	1,138,691	1,678,074
Mato Grosso do Sul (Campo Grande) [5]	357,472	1,369,567	1,755,763
Goiás (Goiânia)	340,166	3,859,602	3,915,749
Distrito Federal (Brasília)	5,794	1,176,935	1,803,478
Total	8,511,996	119,002,706	147,404,375

For notes *see* p. 230.

Population (1989) 147,404,375; density, 17 per sq. km. The 1980 census showed 59,123,361 males and 59,879,345 females. The urban population comprised 74·4% in 1989.

The language is Portuguese.

Population of principal cities (1980 census):

São Paulo	7,032,547	Brasília	410,999	São José dos Campos	268,034
Rio de Janeiro	5,090,700	Santos	410,933	Olinda	266,751
Salvador	1,491,642	Guarulhos	426,693	Londrina	257,899
Belo Horizonte	1,441,567	Niterói	382,736	Sorocaba	254,672
Recife	1,183,391	São Bernardo do Campo	381,097	Uberlândia	230,185
Pôrto Alegre	1,114,867	Natal	376,446	Diadema	228,660
Curitiba	842,818	Maceió	375,771	Feira de Santana	227,004
Belém	755,984	Teresina	339,042	Campina Grande	222,102
Goiânia	702,858	Duque de Caxias	306,243	Jundiaí	221,888
Fortaleza	647,917	Ribeirao Prêto	300,828	São Gonçalo	221,591
Manaus	611,763	Juiz de Fora	299,432	Joinville	216,986
Campinas	566,627	João Pessoa	290,247	Canoas	213,999
Santo André	549,556	Aracajú	287,934	São João de Meriti	210,574
Nova Iguaçu	491,766	Campo Grande	282,857	Mauá	205,740
Osasco	474,543				

The principal metropolitan areas (estimate, 1989) were São Paulo (16,832,285), Rio de Janeiro (11,140,933), Belo Horizonte (3,446,155), Recife (2,945,233), Porto Alegre (2,924,306), Salvador (2,362,449), Fortaleza (2,168,605), Curitiba (1,926,287) and Belém (1,296,209).

CLIMATE. Because of its latitude, the climate is predominantly tropical, but factors such as altitude, prevailing winds and distance from the sea cause certain variations, though temperatures are not notably extreme. In tropical parts, winters are dry and summers wet, while in Amazonia conditions are constantly warm and humid. The N.E. sertao is hot and arid, with frequent droughts. In the south and east, spring and autumn are sunny and warm, summers are hot, but winters can be cold when polar air-masses impinge. Brasilia. Jan. 72°F (22·2°C), July 64°F (17·8°C). Annual rainfall 64" (1,600 mm). Bahia. Jan. 80°F (26·7°C), July 74°F (23·3°C). Annual rainfall 76" (1,900 mm). Belém. Jan. 79°F (26°C), July 79°F (26°C). Annual rainfall 97" (2,438 mm). Manaus. Jan. 81°F (27·2°C), July 82°F (27·8°C). Annual rainfall 72" (1,811 mm). Recife. Jan. 81°F (27·2°C), July 75°F (24°C). Annual rainfall 64" (1,610 mm). Rio de Janeiro. Jan. 78°F (25·6°C), July 69°F (20·6°C). Annual rainfall 43" (1,082 mm).

CONSTITUTION AND GOVERNMENT. The present Constitution came into force on 5 Oct. 1988, the eighth since independence from the Portuguese in 1822. President and Vice-President are elected for a 5-year term and are not immediately re-eligible. To be elected candidates must secure 51% of the votes, otherwise a second round of voting is held to elect the President between the two most voted candidates. Voting is compulsory for men and women between the ages of 18 and 70 and optional for: illiterates, persons from 16 to 18 years old and persons over 70.

Congress consists of a 69-member Senate (3 Senators per state) and a Chamber of Deputies. The Senate is two-thirds directly elected (50% of these elected for 8 years in rotation) and one-third indirectly elected. The Chamber of Deputies is elected by

---

[1] Including litigious area between states of Piauí and Ceará (3,382 sq. km).

[2] The State of Fernando de Noronha (census 1980 population 1,279) was integrated into the State of Pernambuco by the Constitution of 1988.

[3] Including the islands of Trindade and Martin Vaz.

[4] The former States of Rio de Janeiro and Guanabara were consolidated, from 15 March 1975, into a single State of Rio de Janeiro.

[5] The former state of Mato Grosso was divided into 2 new states from 1 Jan 1979.

universal franchise for 4 years. At the General Election held on 15 Nov. 1986, the PMDB won 259 seats in the Chamber, the PFL 115 seats, and others 113 seats.

Voting is voluntary from 16 and compulsory for men and women between the ages of 18 and 65 and optional for persons over 65. Enlisted men (who numbered 339,849 at the 1980 census) may not vote. The Constitutional Amendment number 25 of 15 May 1985 granted illiterate persons (until then disenfranchised) the right to vote and also provided for the direct election of the President.

Former Presidents since 1961 have been as follows:

João Belchior Marques Goulart, 7 Sept. 1961–31 March 1964 (deposed).
Marshal Humberto de Alencar Castelo Branco, 15 April 1964–15 March 1967.
Marshal Artur da Costa e Silva, 15 March 1967–31 Aug. 1969 (resigned).
Gen. Emilio Garrastazu Medici, 30 Oct. 1969–15 March 1974.
Gen. Ernesto Geisel, 15 March 1974–15 March 1979.
Gen. João Baptista de Oliveira Figueiredo, 15 March 1979–15 March 1985.
José Sarney, 15 March 1985–15 March 1990.

President of the Republic: Fernando Collor de Mellor, assumed office 15 March 1990.

Ministers named by Feb. 1990:
Justice: Bernardo Cabral
Economy: Zelia Cardosa de Mello

National flag: Green, with yellow lozenge on which is placed a blue sphere, containing 24 white stars and crossed with a band bearing the motto *Ordem e Progresso.*

National anthem: Ouviram do Ipiranga. . . (words by J. O. Duque Estrada; tune by F. M. da Silva).

Local Government. Brazil consists of 23 states, 3 federal territories (Roraima, Amapá, Fernando de Noronha) and 1 federal district. Each state has its distinct administrative, legislative and judicial authorities, its own constitution and laws, which must, however, agree with the constitutional principles of the Union. Taxes on interstate commerce, levied by individual states, are prohibited. The governors and members of the legislatures are elected for 4-year terms, but magistrates are appointed and are not removable from office save by judicial sentence. The states and territories are sub-divided into 4,180 *municí pos*, each under an elected mayor *(prefeito)* and municipal council, and then further sub-divided into *distritos*. The Federal District is the national capital, inaugurated in 1960; it is divided into 8 administrative Regions the first Region being Brasília.

DEFENCE.

Army. The Army is organized in 8 divisions, each with 4 armoured, 4 mechanized cavalry brigades and 12 motorized infantry brigades; in addition there are 7 light 'jungle' infantry battalions, 28 artillery groups and 2 engineer groups; total strength (1990) over 223,000. An Aviation Corps is being formed.

Navy. The principal ship of the Brazilian Navy is the 20,200 tonne Light Aircraft Carrier *Minas Gerais*, formerly the British *Vengeance*, completed in 1945, purchased from the UK in 1956, and operating an air group of 8 S-2E Tracker ASW aircraft, and 8 ASH-3H ASW Sea King helicopters plus a few light utility helicopters.

There are also 7 diesel submarines (1 built in FR Germany, 3 British Oberon-class and 3 old *ex*-US), 11 frigates including 4 *ex*-US Garcia class leased in 1989 for 5 years, 6 built to two variants of a British design in the 1970s, and the first of a class of 4 locally designed and built. The fleet still includes 9 old *ex*-US Gearing class of 4 locally designed and built. The fleet still includes 9 old *ex*-US Gearing class destroyers, but some of these may be decommissioned following acquisition of the Garcias. There are also 6 coastal minesweepers and a patrol force of 9 tug/trawler types, 6 *ex*-US inshore craft and a number for work on the rivers. Major auxiliaries include 1 oiler, 1 repair ship, 4 transports, 5 survey and rescue, 1 training frigate and 5 tugs. There are some 70 minor auxiliaries. Amphibious forces consist of 2 tank landing ships. A further two diesel submarines and 3 small frigates are being built, and there is a long term project to build a nuclear powered submarine.

Fleet Air Arm personnel only fly helicopters, the 12 S-2E Tracker anti-submarine aircraft held for carrier operations and the 24 shore-based maritime patrol EMB-110A and EMB-111 being operated by the Air Force. Naval aircraft include 10 ASH-3 Sea King for carrier service, 8 Lynx, 7 Wasp and 8 Esquilo for embarkation in the smaller ships. Utility and SAR duties are performed by 16 Bell 206B Sea Ranger, and 4 Super Puma helicopters. Naval bases are at Rio de Janeiro, Aratu (Bahia), Belém, Natal, Recife, and Salvador, with river bases at Ladario and Rio Negro.

Active personnel in 1989 totalled 50,500, including 15,000 Marines and 700 Naval Aviation.

Air Force. The Air Force is organized in 6 zones, centred on Belém, Recife, Rio de Janeiro, São Paulo, Porto Alegre and Brasília. The 1a ALADA (air defence wing) has 16 Mirage IIIE fighters and 5 Mirage IIID trainers, integrated with Roland mobile short-range surface-to-air missile systems deployed by the Army, and a radar/communications/computer network. Two fighter groups have 3 squadrons of F-5E Tiger II supersonic fighter-bombers and two-seat F-5Bs; 4 others operate AT-26 (Aermacchi MB 326G) Xavante light jet attack/trainers, licence-built by Embraer in Brazil. Counter-insurgency squadrons are also equipped with Neiva Regente lightplanes, Universal armed piston-engined trainers, Super Puma transports and UH-1D/H Iroquois and armed Ecureuil helicopters for liaison and observation. There is an ASW group of S-2A/E Trackers for shore-based and carrier-based operations; a maritime patrol group (2 squadrons) with 12 EMB-111 (P-95) twin-turboprop aircraft developed from the Embraer Bandeirante transport and 3 Lear jets; and 2 air-sea rescue units with Bandeirantes. Equipment of transport units includes 1 squadron of C-130E/H Hercules transports; 1 squadron of Boeing 707 and KC-130H Hercules tanker/transports; 1 group made up of a squadron of HS 748 and a second squadron of Bandeirante turboprop transports; 2 troop-carrier groups with DHC-5 Buffaloes; 1 group with Bandeirantes; and 7 independent squadrons with Bandeirantes and Buffaloes. Light aircraft for liaison duties include 30 Embraer U-7s (licence-built Piper Senecas) and 7 Cessna Caravans. The VIP transport group has 2 Boeing 737s, 11 HS 125 twin-jet light transports, several Embraer Brasilias, 6 Embraer Xingu (VU-9) twin-turboprop pressurized transports and Ecureuil and JetRanger helicopters. Training is performed primarily on locally-built T-25 Universal and turboprop T-27 Tucano (EMB-312) basic trainers, and AT-26 Xavante armed jet basic trainers. New equipment will include 79 AM-X jet attack aircraft, produced jointly by Embraer and Aeritalia/Aermacchi of Italy, of which deliveries began late in 1989.

Personnel strength (1990) about 50,700, with more than 600 aircraft of all types.

INTERNATIONAL RELATIONS

Membership. Brazil is a member of UN, OAS and LAIA (formerly LAFTA).

ECONOMY

Budget. In 1988 the budget balanced at 4,667,963,808,000m. cruzeiros.

The foreign debt (including states and municipalities) of Brazil on 30 Sept. 1988 amounted to US$99,558·4m. Internal federal debt, Dec. 1988 was NCz$56,295·5m. Internal states and municipalities (main securities outstanding), Dec. 1988, NCz$3,834·2m.

Currency. The *new cruzado* (NCz$) is the monetary unit which was introduced in

Jan. 1989. 1 *new cruzado* = 1,000 *old cruzados*. The exchange rate was in March 1990 US$1 = NCz$31·40; £1 = NCz$51·46.

Banking. The Bank of Brazil (founded in 1853 and reorganized in 1906) is not a central bank of issue but a state-owned commercial bank; it had 2,535 branches in 1988 throughout the republic. On 31 Dec. 1987 deposits were Cr$837,912,257,000.

On 31 Dec. 1964 the Banco Central do Brasil was founded as the national bank of issue; assets (1985) Cr$639,424m.

Weights and Measures. The metric system has been compulsory since 1872.

ENERGY AND NATURAL RESOURCES

Electricity. Brazil's hydro-electric potential capacity for electric power production was estimated at 106,500 mw per year in Dec. 1987, one of the largest in the world, of which 34% belongs to the Amazon hydro-electric basin. Installed capacity (1988) 53,166 mw of which 45,871 mw hydro-electric. Production (1988) 231,951m. kwh (217,162m. kwh hydro-electric). Supply 110, 127 and 220 volts; 60 Hz.

Oil. There are 13 oil refineries, of which 11 are state owned. Crude oil production (1989) 30m. tonnes; (1988) 28·92m. tonnes of which 68% was from the continental shelf. Promising results have been obtained with the exploration of that area.

The country imported substantial amounts of oil in 1988: 31,700,745 tonnes (value f.o.b. US$3,194m.). Imports come mainly from Saudi Arabia and Iraq.

In Dec. 1984 a major oil field was reported on the fringes of the existing Campos Basin oil field; reserves are estimated at 4,000m. bbls. Total proven reserves (1986) 2,194m. bbls.

Gas. Production (1986) 5,686m. cu. metres; proven reserves (1986) 93,000m. cu. metres.

Minerals. Brazil is the only source of high-grade quartz crystal in commercial quantities; output, 1987, 209,034 tonnes raw, 7,062 tonnes processed. It is the largest western producer of chrome ore (reserves of 9·6m. tonnes; output, 1987, 829,739 tonnes); other minerals are mica (15 tonnes in 1987); zirconium, 26,040; beryllium 10; graphite 525,164; titanium ore 3,344,318 tonnes, and magnesite 860,163 tonnes. Along the coasts of the states of Rio de Janeiro, Espírito Santo and Bahia are found monazite sands containing thorium; output, 1987, 4,956 tonnes; reserves are estimated at 37,000 tonnes. Manganese ores of high content are important (reserves in 1987 were estimated at 75·3m. tonnes); output, 1987, 3,045,564 tonnes. Output of bauxite, 1987, 10,318,682 tonnes; mineral salt (1987), 951,645; tungsten ore, 346,557, unrough, 1,364; lead, 180,269; asbestos, 3,176,231; coal (1983), 21,367,472. Deposits of coal exist in Rio Grande do Sul, Santa Catarina, Parana and Minas Gerais. Total reserves were estimated at 4,159·5m. tonnes in 1984.

Iron is found chiefly in Minas Gerais, notably the Cauê Peak at Itabira. The Government is now opening up what is believed to be one of the richest iron-ore deposits in the world, situated in Carajás, in the northern state of Para, with estimated reserves of 35,000m. tonnes, representing the largest concentration of high-grade (66%) iron ore in the world. Total output of iron ore, 1987, mainly from the Cia. Vale do Rio Doce mine at Itabira, was 182,744,974 tonnes.

Production of tin ore (cassiterite, processed) was 40,324 tonnes in 1987. Output of barytes, 99,424 tonnes. Output of phosphate rock, 28·1m. tonnes.

Gold is chiefly from Pará (12,705 kg in 1985), Mato Grosso (5,914 kg) and Minas Gerais (4,642 kg); total production (1987), 34,996 kg processed. Silver output (processed in 1987) 2,064 kg. Diamond output in 1987 was 522,437 carats (200,000 carats in 1985 from Minas Gerais, 130,000 carats from Mato Grosso).

Agriculture. In 1985, 23,273,517 people were employed in agriculture, and there were 5·83m. farms. Production (in tonnes):

	1987	1988[1]		1987	1988[1]
Bananas (1,000 bunches)	513,115	515,585	Grapes	566,030	764,524
Beans	2,007,230	2,900,754	Coconut	329,266	374,868
Cassava	23,464,484	21,611,540	Coffee	4,405,416	2,704,216
Castor beans	103,568	145,478	Cotton	1,673,392	2,535,127
Oranges (1,000 fruits)	73,568,815	75,549,274	Jute	19,487	16,054
Potatoes	2,330,817	2,299,499	Maize	26,802,769	24,749,550
Rice	10,419,029	11,806,451	Soya	16,968,827	18,020,677
Sisal	191,279	189,654	Sugar-cane	268,741,059	258,448,735
Tomatoes	1,934,610	1,838,334	Wheat	6,034,586	5,751,219
			Tobacco	397,453	...

[1] Preliminary.

Harvested coffee area, 1988, 2,930,008 hectares, principally in the 4 states of São Paulo, Paraná, Espírito Santo and Minas Gerais. Harvested cocoa area, 1988, 662,823 hectares. Bahia furnished 82% of the output in 1987. Two crops a year are grown. Harvested castor-bean area, 1988, 274,060 hectares. Tobacco output was 397,453 tonnes in 1987 grown chiefly in Rio Grande do Sul and Santa Catarina.

Rubber is produced chiefly in the states of Acre, Amazonas, Rondônia and Pará. Output, 1987, 26,555 tonnes (natural). Brazilian consumption of rubber in 1987, was 415,332 tonnes. Jute output, 1988 (preliminary), 16,054 tonnes. Plantations of tung trees established in 1930 are beginning to yield tung oils in commercial quantities; output, 1987, 4,450 tonnes.

Livestock (in 1,000): 1988, 135,726 cattle, 32,480 swine, 19,860 sheep, 10,792 goats, 5,855 horses, 1,295 asses and 1,952 mules. In 1988, 11,906,000 cattle, 10,421,000 swine, 703,000 sheep and lambs, 501,000 goats and 786,583,000 poultry were slaughtered for meat.

Forestry. Roundwood production (1986) 237m. cu. metres.

Fisheries. The fishing industry had a 1987 catch of 934,408 tonnes.

INDUSTRY AND TRADE

Industry. The total number of persons engaged in industry (1984) was 4,215,751 and the value of production Cr$290,944,989m.

The National Iron and Steel Co. at Volta Redonda, State of Rio de Janeiro, furnishes a substantial part of Brazil's steel. Brazil's total output, 1987: Pig-iron, 21,334,721 tonnes; crude steel, 22,227,856 tonnes.

Cement output, 1988, was 25,328,769 tonnes. Brazil's output of paper, 1988, was 4,683,952 tonnes. Production (1988) of rubber tyres for motor vehicles, 27m. units; rubber tubes for motor vehicles, 16m. units.

Labour. The work force in 1988 numbered 61,047,954, of whom 14,233,308 were in agriculture.

Commerce. Imports and exports for calendar years in Cr$1m.:

	1985	1986	1987	1988
Imports	84,815,017	207,785,180	597,938,989	4,019,592,744
Exports	148,571,718	319,271,108	947,658,530	7,357,336,278

Principal imports in 1986 were (in US$1m.): Mineral products, 3,874; chemical products, 2,127; machinery and mechanical appliances, electrical equipment, 2,714; vegetable products, 1,195.

Principal exports in 1985 were (in US$1m.): Coffee (green), 2,369; soybean bran, 1,175; iron ore, 1,101; soya, 763; orange juice, 749; footwear, 571; cocoa beans, 361; pig iron, 268.

Of exports (in US$1m.) in 1986, USA took 6,315; Japan, 1,515; Netherlands, 1,303; Germany (Fed. Rep.), 1,101; Italy, 911; France, 720; Argentina, 682; UK, 647; China, 518. Of 1986 imports, USA furnished 3,228; Germany (Fed. Rep.), 1,285; Iraq, 960; Japan, 882; Saudi Arabia, 880; Argentina, 737; France, 569.

Total trade between Brazil and UK (according to British Department of Trade returns, in £1,000 sterling):

	1986	*1987*	*1988*	*1989*
Imports to UK	552,259	636,675	742,145	817,545
Exports and re-exports from UK	295,152	347,916	304,735	338,634

Tourism. In 1987, 1,929,053 tourists visited Brazil. 499,011 were Argentinian, 251,958 US citizens, 221,265 Uruguayan, 113,643 Paraguayan, 92,410 German, 79,497 Italian, 63,230 French, 55,721 Bolivian, 55,589 Spanish, 47,282 Chilean, 40,796 UK citizens, 37,802 Swiss, 33,666 Portuguese, 30,543 Japanese.

COMMUNICATIONS

Roads. There were (1988) 1,675,735 km of highways. In 1985 Brazil had 13,184,450 motor vehicles, including 9,494,193 passenger cars, 1,864,368 commercial vehicles, 130,064 buses and minibuses.

Railways. Public railways are operated by two administrations, the Federal Railways (RFFSA) formed in 1957 and São Paulo Railways (FEPASA) formed in 1971, which is confined to the state of São Paulo. RFFSA had a route-length of 22,067 km (82 km electrified) in 1988 and FEPASA 5,072 km (1,527 km electrified). An RFFSA subsidiary CBTU (the Brazilian Urban Train Company) runs passenger services in the principal cities. Principal gauges are metre (24,373 km) and 1,600 mm (3,449 km). Traffic moved by RFFSA in 1988 amounted to 80·8m. tonnes of freight and 514m. passengers. FEPASA carried 23·8m. tonnes and 109m. passengers.

There are several important independent freight railways, including the Vitoria à Minas (729 km with (1985) 103·1m. tonnes of freight), the Carajas (890 km, opened in 1985) and the Amapa (194 km). There are rapid-transit railways (metros) operating in São Paulo (from 1975), Rio de Janeiro city (1979), Belo Horizonte, Pôrto Alegre (both in 1985), and small systems in Fortaleza and Salvador.

Aviation. There were 34 companies (30 foreign) operating in 1985. The 4 Brazilian companies cover the whole territory and in 1987 they carried 16,144,000 passengers (14,067,000 in domestic traffic). Their commercial fleet consisted of 248 aircraft on 31 Dec. 1984. There were 243 taxiplane companies on 31 Dec. 1985. The 4 airlines are Viação Aérea Rio Grande do Sul (VARIG), Cruzeiro do Sul, Trans Brasil and VASP. In 1986 there were 126 airports with scheduled flights.

Shipping. Inland waterways, mostly rivers, are open to navigation over some 43,000 km; number of vessels in 1984, 1,348. Rio de Janeiro and Santos are the 2 leading ports; there are 19 other large ports. During 1988, 41,112 vessels entered and cleared the Brazilian ports.

The Lloyd Brasileiro is owned and operated by the Government; its fleet comprised (1984), 39 vessels of 604,733 DWT. Brazilian shipping, 1984 (registered with Lloyds) amounted to 1,636 vessels of 10,001,356 DWT. Petrobrás, the government oil monopoly, took over the government tanker fleet of 26 vessels in 1958; total tanker fleet in 1984 was 70 vessels of 5,090,494 DWT (private and government-owned).

Post and Broadcasting. Of the telegraph system of the country, about half, including all interstate lines, is under control of the Government. There were 12,687 post and telegraph offices in 1988. There were 9,081,649 telephones in 1988 (São Paulo, 3,336,959; Rio de Janeiro, 1,330,649; Brasília, 243,062). In 1986 there were 2,073 radio and 177 television stations, with 75m. radio and 34m. television receivers.

Cinemas (1985). Cinemas numbered 1,623.

Newspapers (1985). There were 322 daily newspapers with a total yearly circulation of 1,699m. Foreigners and corporations (except political parties) are not allowed to own or control newspapers or wireless stations.

JUSTICE, RELIGION, EDUCATION AND WELFARE

Justice. There is a Supreme Federal Court of Justice at Brasília composed of 11 judges, and a Supreme Court of Justice; all judges are appointed by the President with the approval of the Senate. There are also Labour Courts, Electoral Courts and Military Courts. There are Federal Courts in each state. Each state organizes its own judicial system in accordance with state law and with Brazilian Constitution.

Religion. At the 1980 census Roman Catholics numbered 105,861,113 (89% of the total), Protestants, 7,885,846 (6·6%) and Spiritualists, 1,538,230.

Education. Elementary education is compulsory. In 1986 there were 69,132,375 persons aged 15 years or over who could read and write; this was 80% of that age group (81·2% among men; 78·8% among women).

In 1984 there were 37,348 pre-primary schools with 2,493,381 pupils and 107,338 teachers. In 1985 there were 187,274 primary schools, with 24,769,736 pupils and 1,040,566 teachers; 9,260 secondary schools, with 3,016,138 pupils and 206,111 teachers; and 859 higher education institutions, with 1,367,609 pupils and 113,459 teachers: This tertiary level comprises 68 universities (including 20 private) and 791 other institutions (606 private).

Of the 35 Federal universities, the principal are at Rio de Janeiro (30,000 students), Niterói (20,713), Belo Horizonte (20,044), João Pessoa (19,849), Salvador (18,431), Pôrto Alegre (17,626), Recife (18,500), Manaus (17,000), Curitiba (14,882), Fortaleza (14,700) and Natal (14,000). Largest of the 10 State universities is that of São Paulo (44,159 students, founded 1934), and there are 2 Municipal universities.

The 20 private universities include 11 Catholic universities in Rio de Janeiro, São Paulo, Pôrto Alegre, Campinas, Recife, Belo Horizonte, Goiânia, Curitiba, Pelotas, Salvador and Petrópolis.

Health. In 1987 there were 32,450 hospitals and clinics (12,276 private) of which 7,062 were for inpatients (5,359 private). In 1987 there were 206,382 doctors, 28,772 dentists, 6,094 pharmacists and 29,082 nurses.

DIPLOMATIC REPRESENTATIVES

Of Brazil in Great Britain (32 Green St., London, W1Y 4AT)
Ambassador: Paula Tarso Flecha de Lima.

Of Great Britain in Brazil (Setor de Embaixadas Sul, Avedas Nações, Quadra 801, Conjunto K-70 408, Brasília, D.F.)
Ambassador: M. J. Newington, CMG.

Of Brazil in the USA (3006 Massachusetts Ave., NW, Washington, D.C., 20008)
Ambassador: Marcílio Marques Moreira.

Of the USA in Brazil (Ave das Nações, Lote 03, Brasília, D.F.)
Ambassador: Richard Melton.

Of Brazil to the United Nations
Ambassador: Paulo Nogueira Batista.

Further Reading

Anuário do Transporte Aéreo. Ministério da Aeronáutica, DAC. Rio de Janeiro, 1986
Anuário Estatístico do Brasil. Vol. 49. Fundação Instituto Brasileiro de Geografia e Estatística, Rio de Janeiro, 1989
Anuário Mineral Brasileiro. Departamento Nacional da Produção Mineral. Brasília, 1988
Boletim do Banco Central do Brasil. Banco Central do Brasil. Brasília. Monthly
Anuário Estatístico do Transporte Aquaviário. 1987
Indicadores – IBGE. Monthly
Estatísticas da Saúde – 1987 IBGE
Bruneau, T. C., *The Church in Brazil: The Politics of Religion.* Univ. of Texas Press, 1982
Bryant, S. V., *Brazil* [Bibliography] Oxford and Santa Barbara, 1985
Burns, E. B., *A History of Brazil.* 2nd ed. Columbia Univ. Press, 1980
Falk, P. S. and Fleischer, D. V., *Brazil's Economic and Political Future.* Boulder, 1988
Hanbury-Tenison, R., *A Question of Survival for the Indians of Brazil.* London, 1973
McDonough, P., *Power and Ideology in Brazil.* Princeton Univ. Press, 1981

Mainwaring, S., *The Catholic Church and Politics in Brazil, 1916–86*. Stanford Univ. Press, 1986
Micallef, J., (ed.) *Brazil: Country with a Future*. London, 1982
Moraes, R. Borba de., *Bibliographia Brasiliana (1504–1900)*. 2 vols. 1958
Trebat, T. J., *Brazil's State-Owned Enterprises*. CUP, 1983
Tyler, W. G., *The Brazilian Industrial Economy*. Aldershot, 1981
Young, J. M., *Brazil: Emerging World Power*. Malabar, 1982

National Library: Biblioteca Nacional Avenida Rio Branco 219–39, Rio de Janeiro, RJ.

BRITISH ANTARCTIC TERRITORY

HISTORY. The British Antarctic Territory was established on 3 March 1962, as a consequence of the entry into force of the Antarctic Treaty, to separate those areas of the then Falkland Islands Dependencies which lay within the Treaty area from those which did not (i.e. South Georgia and the South Sandwich Islands see p. 1113).

AREA AND POPULATION. The territory encompasses the lands and islands within the area south of 60°S latitude lying between 20°W and 80°W longitude (approximately due south of the Falkland Islands and the Dependencies). It covers an area of some 660,000 sq. miles, and its principal components are the South Orkney and South Shetland Islands, the Antarctic Peninsula (Palmer Land and Graham Land) the Filchner and Ronne Ice Shelves and Coats Land.

The British Antarctic Territory has no indigenous or permanently resident population. There is however an itinerant population of scientists and logistics staff of about 300, manning a number of research stations.

The territory was administered by a High Commissioner resident in Port Stanley, Falkland Islands until 1989. Designated personnel of the scientific stations of the British Antarctic Survey are also appointed to exercise certain legal and administrative functions.

Commissioner: M. S. Baker-Bates.
Administrator: Dr. J. A. Heap.

Fox, R., *Antarctica and the South Atlantic*. London, 1985
Parsons, A., *Antarctica: The Next Decade*. CUP, 1987

BRITISH INDIAN OCEAN TERRITORY

HISTORY. This territory was established by an Order in Council on 8 Nov. 1965, consisting then of the Chagos Archipelago (formerly administered from Mauritius) and the islands of Aldabra, Desroches and Farquhar (all formerly administered from Seychelles). The latter islands became part of Seychelles when that country achieved independence on 29 June 1976.

AREA AND POPULATION. The group, with a total land area of 23 sq. miles (60 sq. km) comprises 5 coral atolls (Diego Garcia, Peros Banhos, Salomon, Eagle and Egmont) of which the largest and southern-most, Diego Garcia, covers 17 sq. miles (44 sq. km) and lies 450 miles (724 km) south of the Maldives. The British Indian Ocean Territory was established to meet UK and US defence requirements in the Indian Ocean. In accordance with the terms of Exchanges of Notes between the UK and US governments in 1966 and 1976, a US Navy support facility has been established on Diego Garcia. There is no permanent population in the British Indian Ocean Territory.

Commissioner: R. J. S. Edis (non-resident).
Administrative Secretary: S. E. Turner (non-resident).
Commissioner's Representative: Cdr A. J. Tremelling, RN.

BRUNEI

Capital: Bandar Seri Begawan
Population: 241,400 (1988)
GNP per capita: US$14,120 (1987)

Negara Brunei Darussalam

HISTORY. The Sultanate of Brunei was a powerful state in the early 16th century, with authority over the whole of the island of Borneo and some parts of the Sulu Islands and the Philippines. At the end of the 16th century its power had begun to decline and various cessions were made to Great Britain, the Rajah of Sarawak and the British North Borneo Company in the 19th century to combat piracy and anarchy. By the middle of the 19th century the State had been reduced to its present limits. In 1847 the Sultan of Brunei entered into a treaty with Great Britain for the furtherance of commercial relations and the suppression of piracy, and in 1888, by a further treaty, the State was placed under the protection of Great Britain. As a result of negotiations in June 1978, the Sultan and the British Government signed a new treaty on 7 Jan. 1979 under which Brunei became a fully sovereign and independent State on 31 Dec. 1983.

AREA AND POPULATION. Brunei, on the northwest coast of Borneo, is bounded on all sides by Sarawak territory, which splits the State into two separate parts, with the smaller portion forming Temburong district. Area, about 2,226 sq. miles (5,765 sq. km), with a coastline of about 100 miles. Population (1981 census) was 192,832; estimate (1988) 241,400 (124,600 males and 116,800 females). Malays (105,700), Chinese (43,400). The 4 districts are Brunei/Muara (147,300), Belait (56,000), Tutong (28,500), Temburong (about 9,000). The capital is Bandar Seri Begawan (census, 1981) 49,902, 9 miles from the mouth of Brunei River; other large towns are Seria (23,415) and Kuala Belait (19,335). 50% of the population speak Malay and 26% Chinese.

CLIMATE. The climate is tropical marine, hot and moist, but nights are cool. Humidity is high and rainfall heavy, varying from 100" (2,500 mm) on the coast to 200" (5,000 mm) inland. There is no dry season. Bandar Seri Begawan. Jan. 80°F (26·7°C), July 82°F (27·8°C). Annual rainfall 131" (3,275 mm).

RULER. The Sultan and Yang Di Pertuan of Brunei Darussalam is HM Paduka Seri Baginda Sultan Haji Hassanal Bolkiah Mu'izzadin Waddaulah. He succeeded on 5 Oct. 1967 at his father's abdication and was crowned on 1 Aug. 1968.

CONSTITUTION AND GOVERNMENT. On 29 Sept. 1959 the Sultan promulgated a Constitution, but parts of it have been in abeyance since Dec. 1962. At independence, the Privy Council, Council of Ministers, and the posts of Chief Minister and State Secretary were abolished. There is no legislature (the 33-member Legislative Council was dissolved in Feb. 1984) and supreme political powers are vested in the Sultan.

The Council of Ministers was composed as follows in Dec. 1989:

Prime Minister, Minister of Defence: HM The Sultan and Yang Di Pertuan of Brunei Darussalam.

Foreign Affairs: Prince Haji Mohammad Bolkiah. *Finance:* Prince Haji Jefri Bolkiah. *Special Adviser to HM The Sultan and Yang Di Pertuan of Brunei Darussalam in the Prime Minister's Department, Home Affairs:* Pehin Dato Haji Isa. *Education:* Pehin Dato Haji Abdul Aziz. *Law:* Pengiran Haji Bahrin. *Industry and Primary Resources:* Pehin Dato Haji Abdul Rahman. *Religious Affairs:* Pehin Dato Dr Haji Mohammad Zain. *Development:* Pengiran Dato Dr Haji Ismail. *Culture, Youth and Sports:* Pehin Dato Haji Hussain. *Health:* Dato Dr Haji Johar. *Communications:* Dato Haji Zakaria.

The official language is Malay, but English may be used for other purposes. The Chinese community mainly use the Hokkien dialect.

Flag: Yellow, with 2 diagonal strips of white over black with the national arms in red placed over all in the centre.

DEFENCE

Army. The armed forces are known as the Task Force and contain the naval and air elements. Strength (1990) 3,700. Military units include 2 infantry battalions, 1 armoured reconnaissance squadron, 1 engineer squadron and 1 surface-to-air missile battalion. Equipment includes 16 Scorpion light tanks, 24 Sankey AT-104 armoured personnel carriers and 12 Rapier missiles.

Navy. The Royal Brunei Armed Forces Flotilla comprises 3 fast missile-armed attack craft of 200 tons and 3 coastal patrol boats all built by Vosper-Thorneycroft (Singapore). There are also 2 landing craft, 2 utility craft and 3 small patrol boats. The River Division operates 24 fast assault boats. An order for 3 much larger offshore patrol craft was awarded to Vosper-Thorneycroft (UK) in Nov. 1989. Personnel in 1989 numbered 500.

Two coastal patrol craft supplied in 1979 for the Marine Police operate with 7 smaller patrol boats.

Air Wing. The Air Wing of the Royal Brunei Armed Forces was formed in 1965. Current equipment includes 6 MBB BO 105, 2 Bell 206B JetRanger, 1 Bell 214, 2 Sikorsky S-70 and 11 Bell 212 helicopters, and 2 SF.260M piston-engined trainers. Personnel (1989) 300.

Police. Establishment provides over 1,900 officers and men (1989). In addition, there are 500 additional police officers mostly employed on static guard duties. The Marine Police has a fleet of fast coastal patrol boats for coastal policing and smaller boats for riverine duties. It has a major role in internal security and protection of economic installations.

INTERNATIONAL RELATIONS

Membership. Brunei is a member of the UN, the Commonwealth and ASEAN.

ECONOMY

Planning. A fifth Five-Year National Development Plan (1986–90) aimed to further improve the economic, social and cultural life of the people.

Budget. The budget for 1988 envisaged expenditure of B$2,487m. and revenue of B$2,721m.

Currency. The currency is the *Brunei dollar* with a par value of 0·290 299 gramme of gold. In March 1990, £1 = B$3·08; US$1 = B$1·88.

Banking. In 1988 there were 7 banks (1 incorporated in Brunei) with a total of 28 branches.

ENERGY AND NATURAL RESOURCES

Electricity. Electric power production (1988) was 1,114m. kwh. installed capacity, 387,000 kw, consumption, 1,081m. kwh. Supply 240 volts; 50 Hz.

Oil. The Seria oilfield, discovered in 1929, has passed its peak production. The high level of crude oil production is maintained through the increase of offshore oilfields production, which exceeds onshore oilfields production. There were 564 producing wells at 31 Dec. 1988. Production was 7·5m. tonnes in 1989. The crude oil is exported directly, and only a small amount is refined at Seria for domestic uses.

Gas. Natural gas is produced (8,544m. cu. metres in 1988) at one of the largest liquefied natural gas plants in the world and is exported to Japan.

Agriculture. The main crops produced in 1988 were, rice (1,422 tonnes), vegetables (848 tonnes), arable crops (523 tonnes) and fruits (3,300 tonnes).

Production, 1988 (in tonnes): Buffalo meat, 212; beef, 57; goat meat, 4·8; pork, 3,193; broilers, 3,750; and 59m. eggs.

Livestock in 1988: Cattle, 3,000; buffaloes, 10,000; pigs, 14,000; goats, 1,000; chickens, 2m.

Forestry. Most of the interior is under forest, containing large potential supplies of serviceable timber. In 1988 production of round timber was 140,800 cu. metres; sawn timber, 72,500 cu. metres.

INDUSTRY AND TRADE

Industry. Brunei depends primarily on its oil industry, which employs more than 7% of the entire working population. Other minor products are rubber, pepper, sawn timber, gravel and animal hides. Local industries include boat-building, cloth weaving and the manufacture of brass-and silverware.

Commerce. Liquefied natural gas accounts for 50% of the total value of the exports. The second main export is crude oil, which contributes 42% and petroleum products 6%. In 1988 (estimate) imports totalled B$1,451m.; exports (including re-exports), B$3,460m. In 1986 Singapore supplied 24% of imports, the USA 15·2% and Japan 20%. Japan took 68% of all exports.

Total trade between Brunei and UK (British Department of Trade returns, in £1,000 sterling):

	1985	*1986*	*1987*	*1988*	*1989*
Imports to UK	23,346	71,624	34,144	142,461	186,110
Exports and re-exports from UK	71,496	154,146	204,129	171,556	264,371

Tourism. There were 85,358 visitors in 1987.

COMMUNICATIONS

Roads. There were (1988) 1,956 km of road, of which 1,015 miles are bituminous surfaced. The main road connects Bandar Seri Begawan with Kuala Belait and Seria. In 1989 there were 93,000 passenger cars and 17,512 commercial vehicles.

Aviation. Brunei International Airport serves 400,000 passengers annually. Royal Brunei Airlines (RBA) and Singapore Airlines provide daily services linking Brunei and Singapore. RBA also operates services to Bangkok, Manila, Kuala Lumpur, Kuching, Kota Kinabalu, Hong Kong, Darwin, Jakarta, Taipei and Dubai (*via* Singapore). Cathay Pacific Airways also operates to Brunei and on to Western Australia from Hong Kong. British Airways provides a weekly service between Brunei and UK. Malaysian Airlines System has air connections from neighbouring regions. In 1985 Brunei International Airport handled 380,000 passengers and 8,500 tons of freight.

Shipping. Regular shipping services operate from Singapore, Hong Kong, and from ports in Sarawak and Sabah to Bandar Seri Begawan. Private companies operate a passenger ferry service between Bandar Seri Begawan and Labuan daily.

Post and Broadcasting. There are 12 post offices (1988) and a telephone network (44,619 telephones in 1988) linking the main centres. Radio Brunei, operates on medium- and shortwaves in Malay, English, Chinese and Nepali. Number of receivers (1988): Radio 87,000 and television 58,500.

JUSTICE, RELIGION, EDUCATION AND WELFARE

Justice. The Supreme Court comprises a High Court and a Court of Appeal and the Magistrates' Courts. The High Court receives appeals from subordinate courts in the districts and is itself a court of first instance for criminal and civil cases. Appeal from the High Court is to a Court of Appeal. The Judicial Committee of the Privy Council in London is the final court of appeal. Syariah Courts deal with Islamic law.

Religion. The official religion is Islam. In 1986, 66% of the population were Moslem (mostly Malays), 12% Buddhists and 9% Christian.

Education (1989). The government provides free education to all Brunei citizens from pre-school up to the highest level at local and overseas universities and institutions. In 1989 there were about 144 government schools and educational institutions (including one university) with about 53,000 students, and 40 non-government schools with about 16,000 students.

The University of Brunei Darussalam opened in 1985 with an enrolment of 176 students, and enables locals to pursue degree courses in the state. For courses not available at the university, scholarships are awarded to qualify Brunei citizns to study in Britain, the USA, New Zealand, Australia, Canada, Malaysia, Singapore and Egypt.

Health. Medical and health services are free to Brunei citizens and those in government service and their dependants. Citizens are sent overseas at government expense for medical care not available in Brunei. Flying medical services are provided to remote areas. In 1989 there were 8 hospitals with 893 beds; there were also 171 doctors, 31 dentists, 8 pharmacists, 185 midwives and 779 nursing personnel.

DIPLOMATIC REPRESENTATIVES

Of Brunei in Great Britain (49 Cromwell Rd, London, SW7 2ED)
High Commissioner: Pengiran Setia Raja Pengiran Haji Jaya bin Pengiran Haji Rajid (accredited 14 March 1984).

Of Great Britain in Brunei (Hong Kong Bank Chambers, Bandar Seri Begawan 2085)
High Commissioner: Roger Westbrook, CMG.

Of Brunei in the USA (2600 Virginia Ave., NW, Washington, D.C., 20037)
Ambassador: Pengiran Haji Idriss.

Of the USA in Brunei (Teck Guan Plaza, Bandar Seri Begawan 2085)
Ambassador: Christopher Phillip.

Of Brunei to the United Nations
Ambassador: Dato Paduka Haji Jaya Bin Abdul Latif.

Further Reading

Krausse, S. C. E. and G. H., *Brunei.* [Bibliography] Oxford and Santa Barbara, 1988

BULGARIA

Capital: Sofia
Population: 8·97m. (1988)
GNP per capita: US$6,460 (1985)

Narodna Republika Bulgaria

HISTORY. The Bulgarian state was founded in 681, but fell under Turkish rule in 1396. By the Treaty of Berlin (1878), the Principality of Bulgaria and the Autonomous Province of Eastern Rumelia, both under Turkish suzerainty, were constituted. In 1885 Rumelia was reunited with Bulgaria. On 5 Oct. 1908 Bulgaria declared her independence of Turkey.

In 1941 Bulgaria signed the Three Power Pact and the Anti-Comintern Pact. After a referendum which abolished the monarchy (for details *see* THE STATESMAN'S YEAR-BOOK, 1986–87) the Fatherland Front government asked for an armistice, which was signed on 28 Oct. 1944 by the USSR, the UK and the USA. A People's Republic was proclaimed on 15 Sept. 1946. The peace treaty was signed in Paris on 10 Feb. 1947. It restored the frontiers as on 1 Jan. 1941.

Following demonstrations in Sofia in Nov. 1989 which were occasioned by the Helsinki Agreement ecological conference, but broadened into demands for political reform, Todor Zhivkov was replaced as Communist Party leader and head of state by the foreign minister Petŭr Mladenov. In Dec. the National Assembly approved 21 measures of constitutional reform, including the abolition of the Communist Party's sole right to govern. The government resigned in Feb. 1990 but was succeeded by another Communist government as opposition parties declined to join a coalition.

AREA AND POPULATION. The area of Bulgaria is 110,994 sq. km (42,855 sq. miles) and is bounded in the north by Romania, east by the Black Sea, south by Turkey and Greece and west by Yugoslavia.

The country is divided into 9 regions (*oblast*) formed from amalgamations of 28 former provinces in 1987 (for these *see* THE STATESMAN'S YEAR-BOOK 1989-90, p. 243). Area and population in 1987:

Region	*Area (sq. km)*	*Pop. 1,000*	*Region*	*Area (sq. km)*	*Pop. 1,000*
Burgas	14,657	872·7	Razgrad	10,842	850·0
Khaskovo	13,892	1,044·4	Sofia (city)	1,331	1,208·2
Lovech	15,150	1,072·1	Sofia (region)	18,979	1,017·0
Mikhailovgrad	10,607	668·2	Varna	11,929	980·1
Plovdiv	13,628	1,258·0			

The capital, Sofia, has regional status. The population at the census of Dec. 1985 was 8,942,976 (females, 4,515,936). Population on 1 Jan. 1988 was 8,973,600 (4·4m. males; 66% urban). Population density 80·9 per sq. km.

Ethnic minorities are not identified officially, but there are some 1·2m. Moslem Turks. Attempts forcibly to Bulgarianise these from the mid 1980s led to an exodus of some 300,000 of them into Turkey in 1989 until Turkey closed its borders in Aug. There are also some 300,000 Moslem 'Pomaks' of Bulgarian origin. Both groups were granted linguistic and religious freedom in Dec. 1989. There are also Gipsies, Jews, Romanians and Armenians.

Population of principal towns (1987): Sofia, 1,128,859; Plovdiv, 356,596; Varna, 305,891; Ruse, 190,450; Burgas, 197,555; Stara Zagora, 156,441; Pleven, 133,747; Shumen, 106,496; Tolbukhin, 111,037; Sliven, 106,610; Pernik, 97,225; Yambol, 94,951; Khaskovo, 91,409; Gabrovo, 81,554; Pazardzhik, 81,513.

Vital statistics, 1987: Live births, 116,672; deaths, 107,213; marriages, 64,429; divorces, 11,687; birth rate, 13 per 1,000 population; death rate, 12; infant mortality, 14·7 per 1,000; growth rate, 1. Abortions, 1987: 134,097.

Expectation of life in 1986 was 71·19 years.

CLIMATE. The southern parts have a Mediterranean climate, with winters mild and moist and summers hot and dry, but further north the conditions become more continental, with a larger range of temperature and greater amounts of rainfall in summer and early autumn. Sofia. Jan. 28°F (–2·2°C), July 69°F (20·6°C). Annual rainfall 25·4" (635 mm).

CONSTITUTION AND GOVERNMENT. The 'Tŭrnovo' Constitution of 1879 was replaced by the 'Dimitrov' Constitution in 1947. This was in turn replaced by a new constitution on 18 May 1971. This vests supreme state power in a single-chamber National Assembly *(Narodno Sŭbranie)* which meets at least three times a year. Between sessions it delegates its powers to a Council of State elected from its members. The Assembly consists of 400 deputies elected from areas of equal population by direct, secret and universal suffrage (at 18) for a term of 5 years.

At the election on 27 Oct. 1946 the Fatherland Front, composed of the Workers (Communist), Agrarian, Socialist and Zveno Parties, and independents, obtained 364 seats (277 to the Communists) and the opposition 101. In 1947–48 the oppositional Agrarian Union and the Zveno Party were dissolved, the Socialists merged with the Communists, and the Fatherland Front became a mass organization with individual memberships, inside which there remained two political parties, the Bulgarian Communist Party (BCP) and the puppet Bulgarian People's Agrarian Union. The protest group Eco-Glasnost won legal recognition in Dec. 1989. A reconstituted Agrarian Party (130,000 members; leader Angel Dimitrov), a breakaway Nikola Petkov Agrarian Union and several other opposition groups formed a coalition, the Union of Democratic Forces (Petŭr Beron, Chairman), in Dec. 1989.

Elections to the National Assembly were held on 8 June 1986. 6,639,562 votes were stated to have been cast (from an electorate of 6,650,739) for the 400 candidates of the Fatherland Front (84 women; 276 Communists; 99 Agrarian Union; 25 independents). The speaker is Stanko Todorov.

A new general election was scheduled for June 1990.

In early 1990 the functions of the Head of State were performed by Petŭr Mladenov.

In March 1990 the Government included Andrei Lukanov *(Prime Minister)*; Aleksandŭr Chudomir *(Deputy Prime Minister)*; Kiril Zarev *(Deputy Prime Minister, Minister of the Economy and Planning)*, Belcho Belchev *(Finance)*, Boiko Dimitrov *(Foreign Affairs)*, Khristo Khristov *(Foreign Economic Relations)*, Ivan Shpatov *(Home Trade)*, Svetla Daskalova *(Justice)*, Gen. Dobri Dzhurov *(Defence)*, Georgi Pankov *(Ambassador to the USSR)*.

At an emergency congress in Feb. 1990, Petŭr Mladenov relinquished the leadership of the BCP in favour of Aleksandŭr Lilov, who was unanimously elected to the new office of President of the Presidium of the 131-member Supreme Party Council.

National flag: Three horizontal stripes of white, green, red, with the national emblem in the canton.

National anthem: An arrangement of Mila Rodino (Dear Fatherland), a popular patriotic song, was declared the national anthem in 1964.

Local Government. People's Councils for the 9 regions, 29 urban areas and 299 other districts are elected for 30 months. In addition to their civic functions they supervise the management of publicly owned enterprises. The Councils' executive organs are Permanent Committees. Elections were held on 28 Feb. 1988, for the first time with multiple candidacies; 25·87% of the 65,455 councillors elected were non-party, 23·75% women.

DEFENCE. There is a compulsory service of 2 years in the Army and Air Force (3 years in the Navy). Defence spending was cut by 12% in 1989.

Army. In 1989 the Army had a strength of 81,900, including 70,000 conscripts, and is organized in 8 motor rifle divisions and 5 tank brigades. Bulgaria is divided into 3 Military Districts, based on Sofia, Plovdiv and Sliven. Equipment includes 675 T-34, 1,200 T-54/-55, 200 T-72 and 125 T-62 tanks (in store). Paramilitary forces, including border guards, security police and People's Territorial Militia, number some 172,500.

Navy. Navy combatants, all *ex*-Soviet, comprise 4 'Romeo' class diesel submarines, 3 'Riga' class small frigates, 6 'Poti' class corvettes, 7'Osa' class missile craft, 6 patrol vessels, 6 torpedo craft, 5 coastal minesweepers and 28 inshore minesweepers. There are two medium landing ships and 23 craft. Major auxiliaries include 2 oilers, 2 research ships, an electronic intelligence gatherer and a training ship. There are some 20 minor auxiliaries and service craft. There are 2 regiments of coastal artillery including some missile-armed, and some 9 shore-based helicopters. The naval headquarters is at Varna, and there are bases at Burgas and Sozopol. Personnel in 1990 totalled 8,800 officers and ratings of whom 3,000 were conscripts.

Air Force. The large tactical Air Force had (1987) about 250 Soviet-built combat aircraft and (1990) 26,800 personnel. There are 3 regiments of MiG-21 and MiG-23 interceptors; 2 regiments of fighter/ground attack MiG-23s and MiG-17s; 2 reconnaissance squadrons of MiG-17s and MiG-21s; some Mi-24 helicopter gunships; a total of about 35 Tu-134, Il-14, An-2 and An-24/26 transport aircraft; a total of about 60 Mi-4, Mi-2, Ka-26, and Mi-8 helicopters; and L-29 Delfin, L-39 Albatros, MiG-15UTI, Zlin 42 and MiG-21UTI trainers. Soviet-built 'Guideline', 'Goa' and 'Ganef' surface-to-air missiles have also been supplied to Bulgaria.

INTERNATIONAL RELATIONS

Membership. Bulgaria is a member of UN, Comecon and the Warsaw Pact.

ECONOMY

Planning. State economic planning started in 1947. There were planning reforms in 1964, 1969, 1982, 1986 and 1987. An economic code of 1 Jan. 1988 provides for the self-management and self-accounting of all economic enterprises.

For the first eight 5-year plans *see* THE STATESMAN'S YEAR-BOOK for 1987–88. The ninth 5-year plan is running from 1986 to 1990. The emphasis is on technological development.

Budget. The revenue and expenditure of Bulgaria for calendar years were as follows (in 1m. leva):

	1977	*1980*	*1981*	*1982*	*1983*	*1984*	*1985*	*1986*	*1987*
Revenue	9,498	13,187	15,385	15,824	16,812	17,754	18,097	19,506	20,672
Expenditure	9,477	13,167	15,370	15,809	16,663	17,392	18,087	19,491	20,662

Of the 1984 revenue 92% came from the national economy. 1983 expenditure was: National economy, 8,630m. leva; education, 2,945m.; social security, 2,846m.

Currency. The unit of currency is the *lev* (pl. *leva*) divided into 100 *stotinki* (sing. *stotinka*). It has been linked to the Soviet rouble since May 1952. A new *lev*, equalling 10 old leva, was introduced on 1 Jan. 1962. The parity (clearing value) is 1 rouble = 1·30 *leva*. Official rate of exchange (March 1990) was £1 = 1·36 *leva*; US$1 = 0·87 *leva*. Rate of exchange for non-commercial transactions (1987): £1 = 2·40 leva; US$1 = 1·65 *leva*. Notes are issued for 1, 2, 5, 10 and 20 *leva* and coins for 1, 2, 5, 10, 20, 50 *stotinki* and 1, 2 and 5 *leva*.

Banking. Under a banking reform of 1987 the National Bank remains the central bank and is responsible for issuing currency. The Foreign Trade Bank (founded 1964) and the State Savings Bank also remain, the latter now serving local enterprises as well as the public. In 1986, 10·48m. depositors had savings totalling 13,954m. leva. Five commercial banks serving various specific industrial sectors, and three more broadly-based (the Economic Bank, the Agricultural Bank and the

Bank for Economic Initiative) have been set up. A Bavarian-Bulgarian Bank began operating in May 1987.

Weights and Measures. The metric system is in general use. On 1 April 1916 the Gregorian calendar came into force.

ENERGY AND NATURAL RESOURCES

Energy. Bulgaria has little oil, gas or high-grade coal and energy policy is based on the exploitation of its low-grade coal and hydro-electric resources, which produce 20% of the electricity supply. Supply 220 volts; 50 Hz.

Electricity. In 1987 there were 135 power stations with a potential of 10·7m. kw. (thermal, (46) 6·5m. kw.; hydroelectric, (88) 2m. kw.; nuclear, (1) 2·26m. kw.). Output, 1987, 43,464m. kwh. Domestic consumption was rationed in 1987–88.

Oil. Oil is extracted in the Balchik district on the Black Sea, in an area 100 km north of Varna and at Dolni Dubnik near Pleven. There are refineries at Burgas (annual capacity 5m. tonnes) and Dolni Dubnik (7m. tonnes). Total crude oil production (1989) 280,000 tonnes.

Minerals. Ore production 1987: Manganese, 10,900 tonnes; iron, 559,000 tonnes. 38·5m. tonnes of coal including 372,000 tonnes of hard coal and 31·4m. tonnes of lignite were mined in 1987. 92 tonnes of salt were extracted in 1987.

Agriculture. In 1987 agricultural land covered 6,165,300 hectares, of which 4,650,300 hectares were arable.

Size of private plots (maximum, 1 hectare) is based on the number of members of a household. Total area of private plots in 1987 was 616,300 hectares. Collective and state farms have been incorporated into 'agricultural-industrial complexes'. There were 285 of these in 1987. 146,351 tractors (in 15-h.p. units) were in use and 14,125 combine harvesters.

In 1982, 26 irrigation systems and 161 dams irrigated 1,169,900 hectares.

Production in 1988 (in 1,000 tonnes): Wheat, 4,713; maize, 1,625; barley, 1,306; sugar beet, 677; sunflower seed, 367; seed cotton, 14; tobacco, 117; tomatoes, 809; potatoes, 359; grapes, 929. Bulgaria produces 80% of the world supply of attar of roses; annual production, 1,200 kg.

Other products (in 1,000 tonnes) in 1988: Meat, 788; wool, 30·3; honey, 10·2; eggs, 162·2; milk, 2,585.

Livestock (1988, in 1,000s): 123 horses, 1,649 cattle, including 646 milch cows, 8,886 sheep, 4,034 pigs, 41,424 poultry and 608 beehives.

Forestry. Forest area, 1987, was 3,868,000 hectares (34% coniferous, 25% oak). 46,041 hectares were afforested in 1987 and 6·7m. cu. metres of timber were cut.

Fisheries. Catch, 1982: 115,600 tonnes (15,600 tonnes freshwater).

INDUSTRY AND TRADE

Industry. All industry was nationalized in 1947 and is divided into 11 associations of up to 150 linked enterprises. A Labour Code of 1986 provides for the self-management of enterprises and the election of management by the workforce.

Industrial production	*1982*	*1983*	*1984*	*1985*	*1986*	*1987*
Crude steel (1,000 tonnes)	2,584	2,831	2,878	2,944	2,965	3,045
Pig-iron (1,000 tonnes)	1,558	1,623	1,578	1,702	1,615	1,652
Cement (1,000 tonnes)	5,614	5,644	5,717	5,296	5,700	5,494
Sulphuric acid (1,000 tonnes)	916	861	908	810	807	689

In 1987 there were also produced (in 1,000 tonnes): Coke, 1,314; rolled steel, 3,325; artificial fertilizers, 2,003; calcinated soda, 689; sugar, 416; cotton fabrics, 352m. metres; woollens, 43m. metres.

Labour. There is 42½-hour 5-day working week. The average wage (excluding peasantry) was 2,791 leva per annum in 1987. Population of working age (males 16–60; females 16–55), 1985, 5·02m. (2·7m. males). The labour force (excluding peasantry) in 1987 was 4,112,674 (49·8% female), of whom 2,811,334 (44·9%)

were manual labourers. 1,422,215 worked in industry, 350,711 in building and 875,202 in agriculture and forestry.

An independent trade union movement, Podkrepa, was formed in Nov. 1989.

Commerce. Foreign trade is controlled by the Ministry of Foreign Trade. Bulgarian trade has developed as follows (in 1m. foreign exchange leva):

	1983	*1984*	*1985*	*1986*	*1987*
Imports	11,966	12,842	14,067	14,353	14,067
Exports	11,818	12,987	13,739	13,351	13,802

Proportion of major exports in 1987: Production machinery, 59%; foods, 11%; industrial consumer goods, 10%. Imports: Production machinery, 44%; fuels, 32%; chemicals, 6%.

Main exports are food products, tobacco, non-ferrous metals, cast iron, leather articles, textiles and (to Communist countries) machinery; main imports are machinery, oil, natural gas, steel, cellulose and timber.

81% of Bulgaria's trade is with the Communist countries (59% with USSR). Agreements with USSR envisage the co-ordination of Soviet and Bulgarian 5-year plans. Indebtedness to the West was US$9,000m. in 1989. Libya is Bulgaria's biggest non-Communist export market, the Federal Republic of Germany her major non-Communist supplier.

Total trade between Bulgaria and UK (British Department of Trade returns, in £1,000 sterling):

	1985	*1986*	*1987*	*1988*	*1989*
Imports to UK	22,291	32,459	24,249	28,068	34,272
Exports and re-exports from UK	109,970	80,504	88,761	82,156	86,209

Joint Western-Bulgarian industrial ventures have been permitted since 1980. Western share participation may exceed 50%.There were 6 in operation in 1985. In Oct. 1987 the Bulgarian government offered to repurchase Bulgarian bonds.

Tourism. Since 1988 5-year passports have been issued instead of ad hoc exeats. Bulgaria received 7·59m. foreign visitors in 1987 and 540,000 Bulgarians made visits abroad.

COMMUNICATIONS

Roads. In 1987 there were 36,908 km of roads, including 242 km of motorways and 2,938 km of main roads. 940m. passengers and 917m. tonnes of freight were carried.

Railways. In 1987 there were 4,294 km of standard gauge railway, including 2,510 km electrified. 110m. passengers and 83m. tonnes of freight were carried.

Aviation. BALKAN (Bulgarian Airlines) operates internal flights from Sofia (airport: Vrazhdebna) and international flights to Algiers, Amsterdam, Athens, Baghdad, Bratislava, Belgrade, Benghazi, Berlin, Brussels, Bucharest, Budapest, Cairo, Casablanca, Copenhagen, Damascus, Dresden, Frankfurt, Istanbul, London, Madrid, Moscow, Nicosia, Paris, Prague, Rome, Stockholm, Syktyvkar, Tunis, Vienna, Warsaw and Zurich. There are also flights from Burgas to Leningrad and Kiev, and from Varna to Leningrad, Kuwait, Athens and Stockholm. In 1987 BALKAN carried 2·8m. passengers and 24,213 tonnes of freight.

Shipping. Ports, shipping and shipbuilding are controlled by the Bulgarian United Shipping and Shipbuilding Corporation. In 1982 it had 194 ocean-going vessels with a loading capacity of 1·6m. DWT. Burgas is a fishing and oil-port open to tankers of 20,000 tons. Varna is the other important port. There is a rail ferry between Varna and Ilitchovsk (USSR). In 1987 Bulgaria set up an exclusive economic zone extending 200 miles into the Black Sea. In 1987, 460,000 passengers and 26m. tonnes of cargo were carried by sea-borne shipping, and 299,000 passengers and 4·08m. tonnes of freight by inland waterways.

Pipeline. Conveyed 21m. tonnes in 1987.

Post and Broadcasting. In 1987 there were 4,053 post and telecommunications offices, 2,228,681 telephones, 80 radio transmitters and 43 television transmitters. Radio Sofia transmits 2 TV programmes and 2 radio programmes on medium- and short-waves. A service for tourists is broadcast *via* the Varna II transmitter on 1,124 kHz. Advertisements are broadcast for half an hour a day. Bulgaria participates in the East European TV link 'Intervision'. Colour programmes by SECAM system. Radio receiving sets licensed in 1987, 1,982,929; television, 1,692,711.

Cinemas and Theatres (1987). There were 37 theatres, 20 puppet theatres, 8 opera houses, 1 operetta house and 3,305 cinemas. 705 films were made (35 full-length).

Newspapers and Books. In 1987 there were 17 dailies with a circulation of 2·2m. and 377 other periodicals. 3,786 book titles were published in 1987.

JUSTICE, RELIGION, EDUCATION AND WELFARE

Justice. A law of Nov. 1982 provides for the election (and recall) of all judges by the National Assembly. There are a Supreme Court, 28 provincial courts (including Sofia), 105 regional courts and 'Comrades' Courts' for minor offences. Jurors are elected at the local government elections.

The maximum term of imprisonment is 20 years. 'Exceptionally dangerous crimes' carry the death penalty. In 1985 harsh penalties were imposed for terrorist acts and drug smuggling following incidences of both.

The Prosecutor General who is elected by the National Assembly for 5 years and subordinate to it alone, exercises supreme control over the observance of the law by all government bodies, officials and citizens. He appoints and discharges all Prosecutors of every grade. The powers of this office were extended and redefined by a law of 1980 to put a greater emphasis on crime prevention and the rights of citizens.

Religion. 'The traditional church of the Bulgarian people' (as it is officially described), is that of the Eastern Orthodox Church. It was disestablished under the 1947 Constitution. In 1953 the Bulgarian Patriarchate was revived. The present Patriarch is Metropolitan Maksim of Lovech (enthroned 1971). The seat of the Patriarch is at Sofia. There are 11 dioceses, each under a Metropolitan, 10 bishops, 2,600 parishes, 1,700 priests, 400 monks and nuns, 3,700 churches and chapels, one seminary and one theological college.

The Constitution provides for freedom of conscience and belief but forbids propaganda against the Government. The State provides 17% of Church funds.

Churches may not maintain schools or colleges, except theological seminaries, or organize youth movements.

In 1987 there were some 60,000 Roman Catholics (including 10,000 Uniates) in 2 bishoprics with (in 1983) 42 priests (20 Uniates) in 50 parishes. In 1984 there were 5 Protestant groups: Pentecostals (10,000 members, 120 churches, 30 pastors); Baptists (1,000 members, 20 churches); Methodists; Congregationalists; Adventists. There were estimated to be about 700,000 practising Moslems in 1984 under a Chief Mufti elected by 7 regional muftis. There were about 1,000 mosques in 1987.

Education. Education is free, and compulsory for children between the ages of 7 and 16. The gradual introduction of unified secondary polytechnical schools offering compulsory education for all children from the ages of 7 to 17 was begun in 1973–74. Complete literacy is claimed. Schools are classified according to which years of schooling they offer: Elementary (1–3), primary (1–8), preparatory (4–8), secondary (9–11), complete secondary (1–11).

Educational statistics for 1987–88: 4,840 kindergartens (344,396 children, 28,652 teachers); 732 elementary schools; 2,159 primary schools; 44 preparatory schools; 72 secondary schcols; 482 complete secondary schools. Numbers of teachers and pupils: School years 1 to 3, 24,442 and 412,520; 4 to 8, 37,612 and 679,677; 9 to 11, 9,837 and 167,845. There were also 4 vocational-technical schools (51 teachers, 1,343 students), 261 secondary vocational-technical schools (7,405 teachers, 106,564 students), 248 technical colleges (10,619 teachers, 115,036 students), 16 post-secondary institutions (780 teachers, 11,019 students) and 30 institutes of higher education (15,941 teachers, 116,407 students). University entrance is by competitive examination. Failure rate was 65% in 1985. There are 3 universities:

the Kliment Ohrid University in Sofia (founded 1888) had 1,502 teachers and 15,501 students (in 1987–88); the Kirill i Metodii University in Veliko Tŭrnovo (founded 1971) had 417 teachers and 5,042 students and the Paisi Hilendarski University in Plovdiv (founded 1961) had 487 teachers and 5,117 students.

The Academy of Sciences was founded in 1869.

Social Welfare. Retirement and disablement pensions and temporary sick pay are calculated as a percentage of previous wages (respectively 55–80%, 35–100%, 69–90%) and according to the nature of the employment.

Monthly family allowances for children under 16: 15 leva for 1 child, 60 leva for 2 children and 115 leva for 3 children.

In 1986, 2·25m. persons received pensions totalling 2,650m. leva.

All medical services are free. In 1987 there were 185 hospitals (including 15 mental hospitals and addiction treatment centres) and 85,804 beds. There were 27,107 doctors and 5,229 dentists.

DIPLOMATIC REPRESENTATIVES

Of Bulgaria in Great Britain (186 Queen's Gate, London, SW7 5HL)
Ambassador: Dimitar Aleksandrov Zhulev (accredited 25 Feb. 1987).

Of Great Britain in Bulgaria (Blvd. Marshal Tolbukhin 65–67, Sofia)
Ambassador: Richard Thomas.

Of Bulgaria in the USA (1621 22nd St., NW, Washington, D.C., 20008)
Ambassador: Velichko Velichkov.

Of the USA in Bulgaria (1 Stamboliski Blvd., Sofia)
Ambassador: Sol Polansky.

Of Bulgaria to the United Nations
Ambassador: Aleksandŭr Strezov.

Further Reading

Kratka Bŭlgarska Entsiklopediia (Short Bulgarian Encyclopaedia), 5 vols. Sofia, 1963–69
Statistical Reference Book: PR of Bulgaria. Sofia, annual from 1988
Statisticheski Godishnik (Statistical Yearbook). Sofia from 1956
Constitution of the People's Republic of Bulgaria. Sofia, 1971
Information Bulgaria. Oxford, 1985
Modern Bulgaria: History, Politics, Economy, Culture. Sofia, 1981
Normative Acts of the Foreign Economic Relations of the People's Republic of Bulgaria. Sofia, 1982
Atanasova, T., *et al., Bulgarian-English Dictionary.* Sofia, 1975
Bell, J. D., *The Bulgarian Communist Party from Blagoev to Zhivkov.* Stanford, 1985
Crampton, R. J., *A Short History of Modern Bulgaria.* CUP, 1987.—*Bulgaria.* [Bibliography] Oxford and Santa Barbara, 1989
Feiwel, G. R., *Growth and Reforms in Centrally Planned Economies: the Lessons of the Bulgarian Experience.* New York, 1977
Lampe, J. R., *The Bulgarian Economy in the Twentieth Century.* London, 1986
Pundeff, M. V., *Bulgaria: A Bibliographic Guide.* Library of Congress, 1965
Zhivkov, T., *Modern Bulgaria: Problems and Tasks in Building an Advanced Socialist Society.* New York, 1974.—*Marxist Concepts and Practices.* Oxford, 1984.—*Statesman and Builder of New Bulgaria.* 2nd ed. Oxford, 1985

BURKINA FASO

Capital: Ouagadougou
Population: 8·53m. (1988)
GNP per capita: US$230 (1988)

HISTORY. A separate colony of Upper Volta was in 1919 carved out of the colony of Upper Senegal and Niger, which had been established in 1904. In 1932 it was abolished and most of its territory transferred to Ivory Coast, with small parts added to French Sudan and Niger, but it was re-constituted with its former borders on 4 Sept. 1947. Upper Volta became an autonomous republic within the French Community on 11 Dec. 1958 and reached full independence on 5 Aug. 1960.

On 3 Jan. 1966 the government of Maurice Yameogo was overthrown by a military *coup* led by Lieut-Col. Sangoulé Lamizana, who assumed the Presidency. In a further *coup* on 25 Nov. 1980, President Lamizana was overthrown and a military regime assumed power. Further *coups* took place on 7 Nov. 1982, 4 Aug. 1983 and 15 Oct. 1987 and 18 Sept. 1989. The name of the country was changed to Burkina Faso in 1984.

AREA AND POPULATION. Burkina Faso is bounded north and west by Mali, east by Niger, south by Benin, Togo, Ghana and the Côte d'Ivoire. The republic covers an area of 274,122 sq. km; population (census, 1985) 7,967,019 (3,846,518 males). Estimate (1988) 8·53m. The largest cities (1985 census) are Ouagadougou, the capital (442,223), Bobo-Dioulasso (231,162), Koudougou (51,670), Ouahigouya (38,604), Banfora (35,204), Kaya (25,799), Fada N'Gourma and Tenkodogo.

The areas and populations of the 30 provinces were:

Province	*Sq. km*	*Census 1985*	*Province*	*Sq. km*	*Census 1985*
Bam	4,017	164,263	Nahouri	3,843	105,273
Bazéga	5,313	306,976	Namentenga	7,755	198,798
Bougouriba	7,087	221,522	Oubritenga	4,693	303,229
Boulgou	9,033	403,358	Oudalan	10,046	105,715
Boulkiemde	4,138	363,594	Passoré	4,078	225,115
Comoé	18,393	250,510	Poni	10,361	234,501
Ganzourgou	4,087	196,006	Sanguie	5,165	218,289
Gnagna	8,600	229,249	Sanmatenga	9,213	368,365
Gourma	26,613	294,123	Sèno	13,473	230,043
Houet	16,472	585,031	Sissili	13,736	246,844
Kadiogo	1,169	459,138	Soum	13,350	190,464
Kénédougou	8,307	139,722	Sourou	9,487	267,770
Kossi	13,177	330,413	Tapoa	14,780	159,121
Kouritenga	1,627	197,027	Yatenga	12,292	537,205
Mouhoun	10,442	289,213	Zoundwéogo	3,453	155,142

The principal ethnic groups are the Mossi (48%), Fulani (10%), Lobi-Dagari (7%), Mandé (7%), Bobo (7%), Sénoufo (6%), Gourounsi (5%), Bissa (5%), Gourmantché (5%). French is the official language.

CLIMATE. A tropical climate with a wet season from May to Nov. and a dry season from Dec. to April. Rainfall decreases from south to north. Ouagadougou. Jan. 76°F (24·4°C), July 83°F (28·3°C). Annual rainfall 36" (894 mm).

CONSTITUTION AND GOVERNMENT. Following the *coup* of 15 Oct. 1987, when President Sankara was killed, the ruling National Recovery Council was dissolved and the government re-shuffled. A new Military Council was formed on 31 Oct. 1987

President of CNR, Head of State and Government: Capt. Blaise Compaoré.

The ruling Popular Front appointed a Council of Ministers, composed in Sept. 1988 as follows:

Popular Defence and Security: Maj. Jean-Baptiste Boukary Lingani. *External Relations:* Jean Marc Palm. *Justice:* Salif Sampegbo. *Economic Development:* Capt. Henri Zongo. *Health and Social Welfare:* Alain Zougba. *Secondary and Higher Education and Scientific Research:* Clément Oumarou Ouedraogo. *Planning and Co-operation:* Youssouf Ouedraogo. *Territorial Administration:* Jean-Léonard Compaoré. *Information and Culture:* Serge Théophile Balima. *Environment and Tourism:* Beatrice Damiba. *Commerce and People's Supply:* Frederic Korsaga. *Transport and Communications:* Issa Konate. *Peasant Co-operatives:* Capt. Laurent Sedgho. *Equipment:* Capt. Kambou Daprou. *Sports:* Capt. Hein Théodore Kilimite. *Labour, Social Security and Civil Service:* Nabou Kanidoua. *Finance:* Bintou Sanogo. *Agriculture and Livestock:* Albert Guigma. *Water Resources:* Alfred Nombre. *Primary Education and Mass Literacy:* Alice Tiendrebeogo. *Secretary-Gen. of the Revolutionary Committees:* Capt. Arsène Ye Bognessan. *Secretary-Gen. of the Council of Ministers:* Prosper Vocouma.

There are also 7 Secretaries of State.

National flag: Horizontally red over green with a yellow star over all in the centre.

Local government: The country is divided into 30 provinces and 250 districts.

DEFENCE

Army. The Army consists of 5 infantry regiments, 1 airborne regiment and tank, artillery and engineer support units. Equipment includes about 83 armoured cars. Strength (1990), 7,000 with a further 1,750 men in paramilitary forces.

Air Force. Creation of a small air arm to support the land forces began, with French assistance, in 1964. Combat equipment includes 5 MiG-21 fighters and MiG-21U trainers and 10 SF.260W Warrior light strike aircraft. Other equipment comprises 2 HS.748 twin-turboprop freighters, 1 C-47, 2 twin-turboprop Nord 262s, an Aero Commander 500, 2 Broussard and 1 Reims/Cessna Super Skymaster for transport and liaison duties, 1 Cessna 172 trainer, and 2 Dauphin and 1 Alouette III helicopters. Personnel total (1990) 200.

INTERNATIONAL RELATIONS

Membership. Burkina Faso is a member of UN, OAU and is an ACP state of the EEC.

ECONOMY

Planning. A 5-year Development Plan (1986–90) aimed at economic sufficiency and envisaged expenditure of 630,000m. francs CFA.

Budget. Government revenue in 1988 was 90,295m. francs CFA and expenditure 96,285m. francs CFA.

Currency. The unit of currency is the *franc* CFA with a parity rate of 50 *francs* CFA to 1 French *franc*. In March 1990, £1 = 471·63 *francs*; US$1 = 287·75 *francs*.

Banking. The *Banque Centrale des Etats de l'Afrique de l'Ouest* is the bank of issue. The main commercial bank is the *Banque Internationale du Burkina*. In Dec. 1982 it had deposits of 32,046m. *francs* CFA.

ENERGY AND NATURAL RESOURCES

Electricity. Production of electricity (1986) was 159m. kwh.

Minerals. There are deposits of manganese near Tambao in the north, but exploitation is limited by existing transport facilities. Magnetite, bauxite, zinc, lead, nickel and phosphates have been found in the same area. Gold was discovered in 1987 at Assakan, near the Malian border.

Agriculture. Production (1988, in 1,000 tonnes): Sorghum, 1,009; millet, 817; sugar-cane, 340; maize, 227; groundnuts, 161; rice, 39; seed cotton, 179; sesame, 9. Rice and groundnuts are of increasing importance.

Livestock (1988): 2,809,000 cattle, 2,972,000 sheep, 5,198,000 goats, 70,000 horses, 200,000 donkeys.

Forestry. In 1988, 25% of the land was forested, chiefly in the deep river valleys of the Mouhoun (Black Volta), Nakambe, (White Volta) and Nazinon (Red Volta). Production (1986), 6·93m. cu. metres.

Fisheries. River fishing produced 7,000 tonnes in 1986.

INDUSTRY AND TRADE

Industry. In 1982 gross manufacturing (including energy) was 68,146,600 francs CFA, of which textiles (3,666,600 francs CFA) and metal products (2,795,100 francs CFA).

Labour. In 1985 the labour force was 3,421,000. The trade union federation is the *Confédération syndicale burkinabe*.

Commerce. In 1986 imports totalled 139,640m. francs CFA and exports 28,665m. francs CFA. The major exports were cotton (37%) and karite nuts (7%). In 1983 France provided 28%, the Côte d'Ivoire 24% and USA 9% of imports, while the Côte d'Ivoire took 9%, France 12%, Taiwan 27%, China 11% and UK 8% of exports.

Total trade between Burkina Faso and UK (British Department of Trade returns, in £1,000 sterling):

	1986	*1987*	*1988*	*1989*
Imports to UK	1,369	462	546	954
Exports and re-exports from UK	3,104	4,168	3,732	4,647

Tourism. There were 68,304 tourists in 1987 spending 2,300m. francs CFA.

COMMUNICATIONS

Roads. The road system comprises 13,134 km, of which 4,396 km are national, 1,744 km departmental, 2,364 km regional and 1,940 km unclassified roads. In 1982 there were 33,769 vehicles, comprising 16,463 private cars, 419 buses, 14,852 commercial vehicles, 411 special vehicles and 1,123 tractors.

Railway. An independent Burkina Faso railway organization was established in 1988 to run the portion in Burkina (495 km of metre-gauge) of the former Abidjan-Niger Railway. An extension was under construction (1990) from the terminus at Ouagadougou to Kaya (107 km).

Aviation. Ouagadougou and Bobo-Dioulasso are regularly served by UTA and Air Afrique and in 1982 dealt with 120,684 passengers and 6,778 tonnes of freight. Air Burkina operates all internal flights to 47 domestic airports.

Post and Broadcasting. There were, in 1982, some 42 post offices and (1984) 14,000 telephones. There are radio stations at Ouagadougou and Bobo-Dioulasso and (1984) 116,000 receivers. The state television service, Télévision Nationale du Burkina, broadcasts 6 days a week in Ouagadougou; there were (1984) 20,000 receivers.

Cinemas. In 1982 there were 12 cinemas with 14,000 seats.

Newspapers. Four daily newspapers were published in Ouagadougou in 1986.

JUSTICE, RELIGION, EDUCATION AND WELFARE

Justice. There is a Supreme Court in Ouagadougou and Courts of Appeal at Ouagadougou and Bobo-Dioulasso. Revolutionary People's Tribunals have replaced the former lower courts.

Religion. In 1980 45% of the population followed animist religions; 43% were Moslem and 12% Christian (mainly Roman Catholic).

Education. There were (in 1986) 351,807 pupils and 6,091 teachers in 1,758 primary schools, 48,875 pupils and 1,514 teachers in 107 secondary schools, 4,808 students with 421 teachers in 18 technical schools and 347 students in a teacher-training establishment. The Université d'Ouagadougou had 3,869 students and 325 teaching staff in 1986.

Health (1980). There were 5 hospitals, 254 dispensaries, 11 medical centres, 65 regional clinics and 167 mobile clinics with a total of 4,587 beds. There were 119 doctors, 14 surgeons, 52 pharmacists, 163 health assistants, 229 midwives and 1,345 nursing personnel.

A 10-year health programme started in 1979, providing for 7,000 village health centres, 515 district health centres, regional and sub-regional medical centres, 10 departmental hospitals, 2 national hospitals and a university centre of health sciences in Ouagadougou.

DIPLOMATIC REPRESENTATIVES

Of Burkina Faso in Great Britain
Ambassador: Amadé Ouedraogo, resides in Brussels (accredited 11 July 1984).

Of Great Britain in Burkina Faso
Ambassador: V. E. Sutherland, CMG (resides in Abidjan).

Of Burkina Faso in the USA (2340 Massachusetts Ave., NW, Washington, D.C., 20008)
Ambassador: Paul-Désiré Kabore.

Of the USA in Burkina Faso (PO Box 35, Ouagadougou)
Ambassador: David H. Shinn.

Of Burkina Faso to the United Nations
Ambassador: Gaëtan Rimwanguiya Ouedraogo.

Further Reading

MacFarlane, D. M., *Historical Dictionary of Upper Volta*. Metuchen, 1978

BURMA

Capital: Rangoon
Population: 39·84m. (1988)
GNP per capita: US$200 (1986)

Pyidaungsu Myanma Naingngandaw

HISTORY. The Union of Burma came formally into existence on 4 Jan. 1948 and became the Socialist Republic of the Union of Burma in 1974. In 1948 Sir Hubert Rance, the last British Governor, handed over authority to Sao Shwe Thaike, the first President of the Burmese Republic, and Parliament ratified the treaty with Great Britain providing for the independence of Burma as a country not within His Britannic Majesty's dominions and not entitled to His Britannic Majesty's protection. This treaty was signed in London on 17 Oct. 1947 and enacted by the British Parliament on 10 Dec. 1947. On 19 June 1989 the military government changed the official name of the country in English to the Union of Myanmar.

For the history of Burma's connexion with Great Britain *see* THE STATESMAN'S YEAR-BOOK, 1950, p. 836.

AREA AND POPULATION. Burma is bounded east by China, Laos and Thailand, west by the Indian ocean, Bangladesh and India. The total area of the Union is 261,228 sq. miles (676,577 sq. km). The population in 1983 (census) was 35,313,905. Estimate (1988) 39,840,000. Birth rate (1977 estimate), 29·1; death rate, 10·4 per 1,000 population; infant deaths, 56·3 per 1,000 live births. The leading towns are: Rangoon (Yangon), the capital (1983), 2,458,712; other towns, Mandalay, 532,985; Moulmein, 219,991; Pegu, 150,447; Bassein, 144,092; Sittwe (Akyab), 107,907; Taunggye, 107,607; Monywa, 106,873.

The population of the 7 States and 7 Divisions at the 1983 census (provisional): Kachin State, 903,982; Kayah State, 168,355; Karen State, 1,057,505; Chin State, 368,985; Sagaing Division, 3,855,991; Tenasserim Division, 917,628; Pegu Division, 3,800,240; Magwe Division, 3,241,103; Mandalay Division, 4,580,923; Mon State, 1,682,041; Rakhine State, 2,045,891; Rangoon Division, 3,973,782; Shan State, 3,718,706; Irrawaddy Division, 4,991,057.

The Burmese belong to the Tibeto-Chinese (or Tibeto-Burman) family.

CLIMATE. The climate is equatorial in coastal areas, changing to tropical monsoon over most of the interior, but humid temperate in the extreme north, where there is a more significant range of temperature and a dry season lasting from Nov. to April. In coastal parts, the dry season is shorter. Very heavy rains occur in the monsoon months May to Sept. Rangoon. Jan. 77°F (25°C), July 80°F (26·7°C). Annual rainfall 104" (2,616 mm). Akyab. Jan. 70°F (21·1°C), July 81°F (27·2°C). Annual rainfall 206" (5,154 mm). Mandalay. Jan. 68°F (20°C), July 85°F (29·4°C). Annual rainfall 33" (828 mm).

CONSTITUTION AND GOVERNMENT. On 18 Sept. 1988, the Armed Forces, under Chief of Defence Staff Gen. Saw Maung, seized power and set up a State Law and Order Restoration Council, with Gen. Saw Maung as Chairman. The first elections for 30 years will be held on 27 May 1990.

A government was formed on 20 Sept. 1988, consisting of:

Prime Minister, Defence, Foreign Affairs: Gen. Saw Maung.

Planning and Finance, Energy, Mines: Rear-Adm. Maung Maung Khin. *Transport and Communications, Construction:* Maj.-Gen. Tin Tun. *Home and Religious Affairs, Information and Culture:* Maj.-Gen. Phone Myint. *Education, Social Welfare and Labour:* Brig.-Gen. Aung Ye Kyaw. *Industry:* Maj.-Gen. Sein Aung. *Co-operatives, Livestock Breeding and Fisheries, Agriculture and Fisheries:* Maj.-Gen. Chit Swe. *Trade:* Col. Abel. *Health:* Dr Pe Thein.

National flag: Red with a blue canton bearing 2 ears of rice within a cog-wheel and a ring of 14 stars, all in white.

Language: The official language is Burmese; the use of English is permitted.

Local government: Burma is divided into 7 states and 7 administrative divisions; these are sub-divided into 314 townships and thence into villages and wards.

DEFENCE

Army. The strength of the Army (1990) was 192,000. The Army is organized into 9 regional commands comprising 9 light infantry divisions. Combat units comprise 2 armoured, 175 independent infantry and 4 artillery battalions, and 1 anti-aircraft battery. Equipment includes over 26 Comet tanks, 40 Humber armoured cars and 45 Ferret scout cars. In addition, there are 2 paramilitary units: People's Police Force (38,000) and People's Militia (35,000).

Navy. The fleet includes 2 old escort patrol vessels (*ex*-USA PCE and MSF types), 2 small indigenously built coastal patrol craft, 21 partol craft, and 5 river gunboats. Auxiliaries include 1 patrol craft support ship, 1 survey ship and 13 small landing craft. Personnel in 1989 totalled 9,000 including 800 marines.

The Fishery protection service (under the people's Pearl and Fishery Department) operates 3 coastal and 9 inshore patrol craft.

Air Force. The Air Force is intended primarily for internal security duties. Its combat force comprises about 5 T-33A jet fighter/trainers supplied under MAP, supplemented by 15 SIAI-Marchetti SF.260W light piston-engined attack/ trainers. Other training aircraft include 20 turboprop Pilatus PC-7s and PC-9s, and 10 jet-powered T-37Cs. Transport and second-line units are equipped with 4 FH-227, 7 Turbo-Porter, 1 Citation and 6 Cessna 180 aircraft, 10 Japanese-built Bell 47 (H-13), 12 Bell UH-1, and 10 Alouette III helicopters. Personnel (1990) 9,000.

INTERNATIONAL RELATIONS

Membership. Burma is a member of the UN and Colombo Plan.

ECONOMY

Planning. The Development Plan, 1986–90, envisaged a total investment of K.14,000m.

Budget. The budget estimates (in K.1m.) for fiscal year 1 April 1988–31 March 1989 was revenue K.31,083m. and expenditure K.30,042m.

The largest items, in 1986–87, of revenue were commodities and service tax (K.5,778m.) and customs (K.4,208m.); of expenditure, processing and manufacturing (K.2,490m.); trade (K.1,000m.); mining (2,841m.).

Currency. The currency unit is now the *kyat* divided into 100 *pyas*. There are notes of *kyat* 90, 45, 15, 10, 5 and 1, and coins of *kyat* 1; *pyas* 100, 50, 25, 10, 5 and 1.

In March 1990, £1 = K.10·78 and US$1 = K.6·58.

Banking. Banks include the Union of Burma Bank, the Myanma Economic Bank, the Myanma Foreign Trade Bank and the Myanma Agricultural Bank, and the State Insurance Company is the Myanma Insurance Corporation.

ENERGY AND NATURAL RESOURCES

Electricity. In 1987–88 the total installed capacity of the Electric Power Corporation was 746,000 kw., of which 258,000 was hydro-electricity, 92,000 steam-turbine, 302,000 natural gas and 94,000 diesel. Production (1987–88) 2,279m. kwh. Supply 220 volts; 50 Hz.

Oil. Production (1989) of crude oil was 700,000 tonnes; natural gas (1988) 32,596m. cu. feet, petroleum (1986–87) 38,290m. cu. ft.

Minerals. Production in 1987–88 (in tonnes): Copper concentrates, 50,800; refined tin metal, 500; refined lead, 6,000; refined copper metal, 234; tin concentrates, 868; tungsten concentrates, 496; steel billets, 16,000; steel grinding balls, 3,000. Refined silver, 450,000 fine oz.; refined gold, 100 fine oz.

Agriculture. Production (1987–88) in 1,000 tonnes: Paddy, 13,722; sugar-cane, 2,969; maize, 277; jute, 41; cotton, 82; wheat, 241; butter beans, 122; soya beans, 24; rubber, 15.

Livestock (1987–88): Cattle, 9·9m.; buffaloes, 2·2m.; pigs, 3·1m.; sheep and goats, 1·5m.; poultry, 39·5m.

In 1987–88 the area irrigated by government-controlled irrigation works was 2,598,000 acres.

Forestry. The area of reserved forests in 1988 was 32·4m. hectares (49% of the land area). Teak extracted in 1987–88, 360,000 cu. tons; hardwood, 1,156,000 cu. tons. All the teak and about 60% of the hardwood is from the state sector. Other forest produce included 18,400,000 cu. tons of firewood and 867,000 cu. tons of charcoal.

Fisheries. In 1987–88 sea fishing produced 12,519,000 *viss* and freshwater fisheries 3,020,000 *viss*. [Ed. note 1 *viss* = 3·6 lb.].

INDUSTRY AND TRADE

Industry. Production (1987–88) in 1,000 tonnes: Cement, 490; sheet glass, 6·5; fertilizers, 326·4; sugar, 59·4; paper, 16·3; cotton yarn, 10·5. 2,300 motor cars, 700 tractors and 11,330 bicycles were produced in 1987–88.

Labour. Economically active (1987–88) 15·81m.

Commerce. All imports and exports are controlled by the government trading organizations.

Imports and exports (K.1m.) for 1987–88: Imports 4,100 and exports 2,098·7.

Total trade between Burma and UK (British Department of Trade returns, in £1,000 sterling):

	1985	*1986*	*1987*	*1988*	*1989*
Imports to UK	9,944	5,092	3,826	4,427	3,484
Exports and re-exports from UK	20,221	10,835	24,715	11,685	12,217

Tourism. There were 42,175 tourists in 1987.

COMMUNICATIONS

Roads. There were 14,533 miles of road in 1987–88, of which 2,452 miles were union highway.

Railways. In 1985 there were 2,774 miles of route on metre gauge. In 1987–88 the railway carried 2·28m. tons of freight and 65·9m. passengers.

Aviation. Burma Airways Corporation, formerly Union of Burma Airways, started its internal service in Sept. 1948 and its external service in Nov. 1950. Regular international services were (Nov. 1988) maintained only to Bangkok. There were, in 1987, 37 civil airfields.

Shipping. Burma has 60 miles of navigable canals. The Irrawaddy is navigable up to Myitkyina, 900 miles from the sea, and its tributary, the Chindwin, is navigable for 390 miles. The Irrawaddy delta has nearly 2,000 miles of navigable water. The Salween, the Attaran and the G'yne provide about 250 miles of navigable waters around Moulmein.

Post and Broadcasting. There were 1,113 post offices in 1987–88. Number of telephones was 61,872 in 1987–88. There were (1985) 7 radio stations and one television broadcasting station. In 1985 there were 725,000 radio and 35,000 television receivers.

Newspapers. In 1988 there were 2 daily newspapers, 1 Burmese language and 1 English language.

JUSTICE, RELIGION, EDUCATION AND WELFARE

Justice. The highest judicial authority is the Chief Judge, appointed by the State Law and Order Restoration Council.

Religion. Religious freedom is allowed. At the 1983 census, 68% of the population was Buddhist.

Education. The medium of instruction in all schools is Burmese; English is taught as a compulsory second language from kindergarten level.

Education is free in the primary, junior secondary and vocational schools; fees are charged in senior secondary schools and universities.

In 1986–87 there were 750 state high schools with 238,498 pupils, 1,772 state middle schools with 1,125,632 pupils and 33,499 state primary schools with 5,056,961 pupils; the total teaching staff was 218,206, of which 158,934 were in primary schools.

Beside the Arts and Science University, there are independent degree-giving institutes of engineering, education, medicine, agriculture, economics and commerce, and veterinary sciences. A foreign-languages institute in Rangoon had (1987) 1,127 students learning English, French, German, Russian, Japanese, Chinese and Italian.

There are intermediate colleges at Taunggyi, Magwe, Akyab and Myitkyina, and degree colleges at Moulmein and Bassein, and several technical and agricultural institutes at higher and middle level. 7,040 school teachers were being trained in 16 training colleges in 1986–87. Technical high schools had 5,414 students; agricultural schools, 1,675; other vocational colleges, 4,639, and university colleges 91,748.

Health. In 1986–87 there were 10,579 doctors and 636 hospitals with 26,839 beds.

DIPLOMATIC REPRESENTATIVES

Of Burma in Great Britain (19A Charles St., London, W1X 8ER)
Ambassador: U Tin Hlaing (accredited 15 June 1989).

Of Great Britain in Burma (80 Strand Rd., Rangoon)
Ambassador: Martin R. Morland, CMG.

Of Burma in the USA (2300 S. St., NW, Washington, D.C., 20008)
Ambassador: U Myo Aung.

Of the USA in Burma (581 Merchant St., Rangoon)
Ambassador: Burton Levin.

Of Burma to the United Nations
Ambassador: Kyaw Min.

Further Reading

Burma: Treaty between the Government of the United Kingdom and the Provisional Government of Burma. (Treaty Series No. 16, 1948.) HMSO, 1948
Cornyn, W. S. and Musgrave, J. K., *Burmese Glossary.* New York, 1958
Lehman, F. K., *The Structure of Chin Society.* Univ. of Illinois Press, 1963
Silverstein, J., *Burma: Military Rule and the Politics of Stagnation.* Cornell Univ. Press, 1978.
—*Burmese Politics: The Dilemma of National Unity.* Rutgers Univ. Press, 1980
Steinberg, D. I., *Burma.* Boulder, 1982
Stewart, J. A. and Dunn, C. W., *Burmese–English Dictionary.* London, 1940 ff.
Taylor, R. H., *The State of Burma.* London, 1988

BURUNDI

Capital: Bujumbura
Population: 5·54m. (1989)
GNP per capita: US$230 (1988)

Republika y'Uburundi

HISTORY. Tradition recounts the establishment of a Tutsi kingdom under successive Mwamis as early as the 16th century. German military occupation in 1890 incorporated the territory into German East Africa. From 1919 Burundi formed part of Ruanda-Urundi administered by the Belgians, first as a League of Nations mandate and then as a UN trust territory. Internal self-government was granted on 1 Jan. 1962, followed by independence on 1 July 1962.

On 8 July 1966 Prince Charles Ndizeye deposed his father Mwami Mwambutsa IV, suspended the constitution and made Capt. Michel Micombero Prime Minister. On 1 Sept. Prince Charles was enthroned as Mwami Ntare V. On 28 Nov., while the Mwami was attending a Head of States Conference in Kinshasa (Congo), Micombero declared Burundi a republic with himself as president.

On 31 March 1972 Prince Charles returned to Burundi from Uganda and was placed under house arrest. On 29 April 1972 President Micombero dissolved the Council of Ministers and took full power; that night heavy fighting broke out between rebels from both Burundi and neighbouring countries, and the ruling Tutsi, apparently with the intention of destroying the Tutsi hegemony. Prince Charles was killed during the fighting and it was estimated that up to 120,000 were killed. On 14 July 1972 President Micombero reinstated a Government with a Prime Minister. On 1 Nov. 1976 President Micombero was deposed by the Army. as was President Bagaza on 3 Sept. 1987.

AREA AND POPULATION. Burundi is bounded north by Rwanda, east and south by Tanzania and west by Zaïre, and has an area of 27,834 sq. km (10,759 sq. miles).

The population at the census in 1986 was 4,782,406; estimate (1989) 5·54m. There are three ethnic groups—Hutu (Bantu, forming over 83% of the total): Tutsi (Nilotic, less than 15%); Twa (pygmoids, less than 1%). There are some 3,500 Europeans and 1,500 Asians. In 1988 some 270,000 Tutsi refugees were living in Burundi, the majority from Rwanda.

Bujumbura, the capital, had (1986 census) 272,600 inhabitants. Gitega (95,300) was formerly the royal residence.

The local language is Kirundi, a Bantu language. French is also an official language. Kiswahili is spoken in the commercial centres.

CLIMATE. An equatorial climate, modified by altitude. The eastern plateau is generally cool, the easternmost savanna several degrees hotter. The wet seasons are from March to May and Sept. to Dec. Bujumbura. Jan. 73°F (22·8°C), July 73°F (22·8°C). Annual rainfall 33" (825 mm).

CONSTITUTION AND GOVERNMENT. A new Constitution was promulgated on 21 Nov. 1981 and provides for a one-party state. The 65-member National Assembly elected in Oct. 1982 comprised 52 members elected by universal suffrage from a list of 104 candidates nominated by UPRONA *(Parti de l'Unité et du Progrès National du Burundi)*, together with 13 members appointed by the President. President Bagaza became Party Chairman and Head of the Central Committee for a 5-year term in Jan. 1980 and was re-elected for a second 5-year term in Sept. 1984 but was deposed in Sept. 1987.

President of the Republic, Minister of Defence: Major Pierre Buyoya (assumed office 1 Oct. 1987).

Foreign Affairs and Co-operation: Cyprien Mbonimpa.

Finance: Gerard Niyibigira.

Flag: White diagonal cross dividing triangles of red and green, in the centre a white disc bearing 3 red green-bordered 6-pointed stars.

Local Government: There are 15 provinces, each under a military governor, and sub-divided into 114 districts and then into communes.

DEFENCE. The national armed forces total (1990), 7,200 (there are also about 1,500 in paramilitary units) and include a small naval flotilla and air force flight of 3 SF 260, 3 Cessna 150 and 1 DO27 liaison aircraft, 4 Alouette III and 2 armed Gazelle helicopters. The Army comprises 2 infantry battalions, 1 parachute battalion, 1 commando battalion and 1 armoured-car company.

INTERNATIONAL RELATIONS

Membership. Burundi is a member of UN and OAU and is an ACP state of EEC.

ECONOMY

Planning. The 5th, 5-year economic and social development plan, 1988-92 envisages investment of 159,000 Burundi francs.

Budget. The 1989 budget envisaged receipts of 28,679m. Burundi francs and expenditure at 34,790m. Burundi francs.

Currency. The currency is the *Burundi franc*. There are coins of 1, 5 and 10 *francs* and bank notes of 10, 20, 50, 100, 500, 1,000 and 5,000 *francs*. The exchange rate was 295·50 *Burundi francs* = £1 and 180·29 *Burundi francs* = US$1 in March 1990.

Banking. The Bank of the Republic of Burundi is the central bank and 4 commercial banks have headquarters in Bujumbura.

Weights and Measures. The metric system operates.

ENERGY AND NATURAL RESOURCES

Electricity. Electricity production was (1986) 44m. kwh. The majority of the electricity is supplied by Zaïre. Supply 220 volts; 50 Hz.

Minerals. Mineral ores such as bastnasite and cassenite were formerly mined but output is now insignificant. Gold is mined on a small scale. Deposits of nickel (280m. tonnes) and vanadium remain to be exploited.

Agriculture. The main economic activity and 85% of employment is subsistence agriculture. Beans, cassava, maize, sweet potatoes, groundnuts, peas, sorghum and bananas are grown according to the climate and the region.

The main cash crop is coffee, of which about 95% is arabica. It accounts for 90% of exports and taxes and levies on coffee constitute a major source of revenue. A coffee board (OCIBU) manages the grading and export of the crop. Production (1988) 33,000 tonnes. The main food crops (production 1988, in 1,000 tonnes) are cassava (620), yams (10), bananas (1,480), dry beans (316), maize (170), sorghum (251), groundnuts (85) and peas (40). Other cash crops are cotton (8) and tea (5).

Cattle play an important traditional role, and there were about 340,000 head in 1988. There were (1988) some 750,000 goats, 350,000 sheep and 80,000 pigs.

Forestry. Production (1985) 3·6m. cu. metres. For most of the population wood is the main form of energy.

Fisheries. There is a small commercial fishing industry on Lake Tanganyika. The catch in 1985 totalled 14,900 tonnes.

INDUSTRY AND TRADE

Industry. Industrial development is rudimentary. In Bujumbura there are plants for the processing of coffee and by-products of cotton, a brewery, cement works, a textile factory, a soap factory, a shoe factory and small metal workshops.

Commerce. The total value of exports in 1986 was US$184·6m., and of imports, US$245·4m. Main exports in 1986 were coffee and tea. Main imports, petrol products, food, vehicles and textiles. In 1984, 34% of exports were to the Federal Republic of Germany, while Belgium supplied 15% and France 14% of imports.

Total trade between Burundi and the UK (British Department of Trade returns, in £1,000 sterling):

	1985	*1986*	*1987*	*1988*	*1989*
Imports to UK	3,367	3,074	1,330	1,807	1,974
Exports and re-exports from UK	1,592	2,324	2,867	2,922	2,738

Tourism. Tourism is developing and there were 66,000 visitors in 1986.

COMMUNICATIONS

Roads. There is a road network of 5,144 km connecting with Rwanda, Zaïre and Tanzania. In 1984 there were 7,533 cars and 4,364 commercial vehicles.

Aviation. In 1984, 38,141 passengers arrived or departed through Bujumbura International airport, and there are local airports at Gitega, Nyanza-Lac, Kiofi and Nyakagunda.

Shipping. There are lake services from Bujumbura to Kigoma (Tanzania) and Kalémie (Zaïre). The main route for exports and imports is *via* Kigoma, and thence by rail to Dar es Salaam.

Post and Broadcasting. In 1983 there were 38 post offices and 6,033 telephones. In 1986 there were 4,000 television and 230,000 radio sets.

Cinemas. In 1980 there were 7 cinemas with 2,000 seats.

Newspapers. There was (1984) one daily newspaper *(Le Renouveau)* with a circulation of 20,000.

JUSTICE, RELIGION, EDUCATION AND WELFARE

Justice. There is a Supreme Court, an appeal court and a *tribunal de première instance* at Bujumbura and provincial tribunals in each provincial capital.

Religion. About 60% of the population is Roman Catholic; there is a Roman Catholic archbishop and 3 bishops. About 3% are Pentecostal, 1% Anglican and 1% Moslem, while the balance follow traditional tribal beliefs.

Education. In 1984 there were 387,710 pupils in 1,023 primary schools, 13,037 in 62 secondary schools, 12,902 in 47 technical schools and 2,783 students in higher education.

Health. In 1983 there were 216 doctors, 6 dentists, 24 pharmacists, 1,126 nursing personnel and 33 hospitals with 5,709 beds.

DIPLOMATIC REPRESENTATIVES

Of Burundi in Great Britain
Ambassador: Julien Nahayo, resides in Brussels (accredited 26 July 1989).

Of Great Britain in Burundi
Ambassador: R. L. B. Cormack, CMG (resides in Kinshasa).

Of Burundi in the USA (2233 Wisconsin Ave., NW, Washington, D.C., 20007)
Ambassador: Julien Kavakure.

Of the USA in Burundi (PO Box 1720, Ave. du Zaïre, Bujumbura)
Ambassador: James Daniel Phillips.

Of Burundi to the United Nations
Ambassador: (Vacant).

Further Reading

Lemarchand, R., *Rwanda and Burundi*. London, 1970
Weinstein, W., *Historical Dictionary of Burundi*. Metuchen, 1976

CAMBODIA

Capital: Phnom Penh
Population: 6·23m. (1985)
GNP per capita: No accurate estimate available (1989)

People's Republic of Kampuchea

Since April 1975 the situation in Cambodia has been such that it has been impossible to obtain reliable statistical and other information.

HISTORY. The recorded history of Cambodia starts at the beginning of the Christian era with the Kingdom of Fou-Nan, whose territories at one time included parts of Thailand, Malaya, Cochin-China and Laos. The religious, cultural and administrative inspirations of this state came from India. The Kingdom was absorbed at the end of the 6th century by the Khmers, under whose monarchs was built, between the 9th and 13th centuries, the splendid complex of shrines and temples at Angkor. Attacked on either side by the Vietnamese and the Thai from the 15th century on, Cambodia was saved from annihilation by the establishment of a French protectorate in 1863. Thailand eventually recognized the protectorate and renounced all claims to suzerainty in exchange for Cambodia's north-western provinces of Battambang and Siem Reap, which were, however, returned under a Franco-Thai convention of 1907, confirmed in the Franco-Thai treaty of 1937. In 1904 the province of Stung Treng, formerly administered as part of Laos, was attached to Cambodia. For history to 1969 *see* THE STATESMAN'S YEAR-BOOK, 1973–74, p. 1112.

Prince Sihanouk was deposed in March 1970 and on 9 Oct. 1970 the Kingdom of Cambodia became the Khmer Republic. From 1970 hostilities extended throughout most of the country involving North and South Vietnamese and US forces as well as Republican and anti-Republican Khmer troops. During 1973 direct American and North Vietnamese participation in the fighting came to an end, leaving a civil war situation which continued during 1974 with large-scale fighting between forces of the Khmer Republic supported by American arms and economic aid and the forces of the United National Cambodian Front including 'Khmer Rouge' communists supported by North Vietnam and China. After unsuccessful attempts to capture Phnom Penh in 1973 and 1974, the Khmer Rouge ended the 5-year war in April 1975, when the remnants of the republican forces surrendered the city. From April 1975 the Khmer Rouge instituted a harsh and highly regimented régime. They cut the country off from normal contact with the world and expelled all foreigners. All cities and towns were forcibly evacuated and the population were set to work in the fields.

The régime had difficulties with the Vietnamese from 1975 and this escalated into full-scale fighting in 1977–78. On 7 Jan. 1979, Phnom Penh was captured by the Vietnamese, and the Prime Minister, Pol Pot, fled. In Dec. 1985 the Khmer Rouge still had 30,000 guerrillas fighting the Vietnamese in Cambodia.

In June 1982 the Khmer Rouge (who claim to have abandoned their Communist ideology and to have disbanded their Communist Party) entered into a coalition with Son Sann's Khmer People's National Liberation Front and Prince Sihanouk's group. This government in exile is recognized by the UN.

In 1988 there were unofficial talks in Jakarta between the 4 Cambodian factions with the aim of obtaining a settlement of the political situation. From 30 July-30 Aug. 1989 an international conference, held in Paris, aiming to solve the political problems of Cambodia, was unsuccessful. The last Vietnamese forces withdrew in Sept. 1989.

Throughout 1989 attempts were made to find a peace settlement and in Feb. 1990 a meeting in Indonesia was held which aimed at solving the problems with UN help.

AREA AND POPULATION. Cambodia is bounded north by Laos and Thailand, in the west by Thailand, east by Vietnam and south by the Gulf of Thailand. It has an area of about 181,035 sq. km (69,898 sq. miles).

The total population was 5,756,141 (census, 1981) of whom 93% were Khmer, 4% Vietnamese and 3% Chinese. Estimate (1985) 6,232,000.

The capital, Phnom Penh is located at the junction of the Mekong and Tonle Sap rivers. Populations of major towns have fluctuated greatly since 1970 by flows of refugees from rural areas and from one town to another. Phnom Penh formerly had a population of at least 2·5m. but a 1983 estimate puts it at 500,000. Other cities are Kompong Cham and Battambang. Khmer is the official language.

CLIMATE. A tropical climate, with high temperatures all the year. Phnom Penh. Jan. 78°F (25·6°C), July 84°F (28·9°C). Annual rainfall 52" (1,308 mm).

CONSTITUTION AND GOVERNMENT. Following the ousting of the Khmer Rouge régime, the Vietnamese-backed Kampuchean National United Front for National Salvation (KNUFNS) on 8 Jan. 1979 proclaimed a People's Republic and established a People's Revolutionary Council to administer the country. A 117-member National Assembly was elected on 1 May 1981 for a 5-year term, which was extended by its own decision in Feb. 1986; in June 1981 it ratified a new Constitution under which it appointed a 7-member Council of State and a 16-member Council of Ministers, replacing the Revolutionary Council.

President of the Council of State: Heng Samrin.
Prime Minister: Hun Sen.

National flag: Divided red over blue with a depiction of the temple of Angkor Vat in yellow over all in the centre.

DEFENCE. Since April 1975 there has been no accurate data on defence and the three sections below should be treated with great reserve. There is conscription into the armed forces.

Army. Strength (1989) 42,500 including 6 infantry divisions and some 50 supporting units. Equipment reported includes 80 T-54/-55 and 10 PT-76 tanks. There are also provincial (22,500) and district (32,000) forces, and paramilitary local forces of some 50,000.

Navy. Little information was available in early 1990 on the Cambodian Navy which is believed to include 2 *ex*-Soviet hydrofoil torpedo craft, 9 inshore patrol craft and a miscellany of riverine and support craft.

Naval personnel in 1989 did not exceed 1,000.

Air Force. Aviation operations were resumed in 1988 under the aegis of the Army, equipment includes a newly-formed fighter squadron with MiG-21s and a small number of Mil Mi-8 transport helicopters and Mi-24 gunships.

ECONOMY

Currency. Under the Khmer Rouge money was abolished, but in 1980 the use of money was restored by the People's Republic of Kampuchea. There are coins of 5 *sen* and banknotes of 10, 20 and 50 *sen* and of 1, 5, 10, 20 and 50 *riel*. In March 1990, £1 = 355·54 *riel*; US$1 = 218 *riel*.

Banking. In 1964 all bank functions were taken over by government banks. In 1972 legislation permitted the re-opening of foreign banks but by the end of Dec. 1973 only a few representational offices had opened.

ENERGY AND NATURAL RESOURCES

Electricity. Production (1986) 142m. kwh. Supply 120 and 220 volts; 50 Hz.

Minerals. A phosphate factory, jointly controlled by the State and private interests, was set up in 1966 near a deposit of an estimated 350,000 tons. Another deposit of about the same size is earmarked for exploitation. High-grade iron-ore deposits (possibly as much as 2·5m. tons) exist in Northern Cambodia, but are not exploited commercially because of transportation difficulties. Some small-scale gold panning (6,687 troy oz. in 1963) and gem (mainly zircon) mining is carried out at Pailin where there is potential for considerable expansion.

Agriculture. The overwhelming majority of the population is normally engaged in agriculture, fishing and forestry. Of the country's total area of 44m. acres, about 20m. are cultivable and over 20m. are forest land. In 1980, 1·5m. hectares were cultivated. Before the spread of war the high productivity provided for a low, but well-fed standard of living for the peasant farmers, the majority of whom owned the land they worked. A relatively small proportion of the food production entered the cash economy. The war and unwise pricing policies have led to a disastrous reduction in production to a stage in which the country had become a net importer of rice.

A crop of about 2m. tonnes of paddy was produced in 1988. Rubber production in 1988 amounted to 25,000 tonnes. Production of other crops (1988 in tonnes): Maize, 100,000; dry beans, 36,000; soybeans, 2,000.

Livestock (1988): Cattle, 1·95m.; buffaloes, 700,000; sheep, 1,000; pigs, 1·5m.; horses, 15,000; poultry, 10m.

Forestry. Much of Cambodia's surface is covered by potentially valuable forests, 3·8m. hectares of which are reserved by the Government to be awarded to concessionaires, and are not at present worked to an appreciable extent. The remainder is available for exploitation by the local residents, and as a result some areas are over-exploited and conservation is not practised. There are substantial reserves of pitch pine. Roundwood production (1982) 5·1m. cu. metres.

Fisheries. Cambodia has the greatest freshwater fish resources in South-East Asia. Production in 1982 84,700 tonnes.

INDUSTRY AND TRADE

Industry. Some development of industry had taken place before the spread of open warfare in 1970. Industry established and in operation in Jan. 1970 included a motor-vehicle assembly plant, 3 cigarette manufacturing concerns, a modern factory, several metal fabricating concerns, a distillery, a saw-mill, textile, fish canning, plywood, paper, cement, sugar sack, tyre, pottery and glassware factories and a cotton-ginnery. In the private sector there are about 3,200 manufacturing enterprises, producing a wide range of goods; most of them are small family concerns.

Commerce. Principal imports by order of value (1972) were petroleum products, metals and machinery (including vehicles), general foodstuffs and chemicals.

The only recorded export in 1972 was 7,328 tonnes of rubber. Much of the country's trade is with Hong Kong and Singapore.

Total trade between Cambodia and UK (British Department of Trade returns, in £1,000 sterling):

	1985	*1986*	*1987*	*1988*	*1989*
Imports to UK	77	58	268	55	219
Exports and re-exports from UK	467	217	435	322	530

COMMUNICATIONS

Roads. There were, in 1981, 2,670 km of asphalt roads (including the 'Khmer-American Friendship Highway' from outside Phnom Penh to close to Kompong Som, built under the US aid programme and opened in July 1959), and 10,680 km of unsurfaced roads.

Railways. A line of 385 km (metre gauge) links Phnom Penh to Poipet (Thai frontier). In 1969 traffic amounted to 170m. passenger-km and 76m. ton-km. Work was completed during 1969 on a line Phnom Penh-Kompong Som *via* Takeo and Kampot. Total length, 649 km but by 1973 only a short stretch between Battambang and the Thai border remained in operation, the remainder having been closed by military action. Irregular passenger and freight trains were running over all the network in 1988.

Aviation. The Pochentong airport is 10 km from Phnom Penh. Air Kampuchea has 2 small aircraft.

Shipping. The port of Phnom Penh can be reached by the Mekong (through Vietnam) by ships of between 3,000 and 4,000 tons. In 1970, 97 ocean-going vessels imported 51,300 tons of cargo at Phnom Penh and exported 86,400 tons.

A new ocean port has been built under the French aid programme at Kompong Som (formerly Sihanoukville) on the Gulf of Siam and is being increasingly used by long-distance shipping.

Post and Broadcasting. There were 58 post offices functioning in 1968. There are telephone exchanges in all the main towns; number of telephones in 1981, 7,315. There is an International Telex network in Phnom Penh and direct telephone and telegraphic links with Singapore. In 1986 there were 6 radio stations and 200,000 receivers, and 2 television stations with 52,000 receivers.

Newspapers. In 1984 there were 16 daily newspapers.

RELIGION, EDUCATION AND WELFARE

Religion. In 1980 the majority of the population practised Theravada Buddhism. The Constitution of 1976 ended Buddhism as the State religion. There are small Roman Catholic and Moslem minorities.

Education. In 1984 there were 1,504,840 pupils in primary schools, 147,730 in secondary schools and 7,334 in vocational establishments. Phnom Penh University reopened in 1988.

Health. In 1984 there were 200 doctors, 130 pharmacists and 146 hospitals and clinics with 16,200 beds.

DIPLOMATIC REPRESENTATIVES

UK and USA Embassies have been closed as have Cambodian Embassies in London and Washington.

Of Democratic Kampuchea to the United Nations
Ambassador: Thiounn Prasith.

Further Reading

Ablin, D. A. and Hood, M., (eds.) *The Cambodian Agony*. London and New York, 1987
Barron, J. and Paul, A., *Murder of a Gentle Land*. New York, 1977.—*Peace with Horror*. London, 1977
Debré, F., *La Révolution de la Forét*. Paris, 1976
Etcheson, C., *The Rise and Demise of Democratic Kampuchea*. London, 1984
Kiljunen, K., (ed.) *Kampuchea: Decade of the Genocide*. London, 1984
McDonald, M., *Angkor*. London, 1958
Ponchaud, F., *Cambodia, Year Zero*. London, 1978
Vickery, M., *Cambodia: 1975–1982*. London, 1984

CAMEROON

Capital: Yaoundé
Population: 11m. (1988)
GNP per capita: US$1,010 (1988)

République du Cameroun

HISTORY. The former German colony of Kamerun was occupied by French and British troops in 1916. The greater portion of the territory (422,673 sq. km) was in 1919 placed under French administration, excluding the territory ceded to Germany in 1911, which reverted to French Equatorial Africa. The portion under French trusteeship was granted full internal autonomy on 1 Jan. 1959 and complete independence was proclaimed on 1 Jan. 1960.

The portion assigned to British trusteeship consisted of 2 parts where separate plebiscites were held in Feb. 1961. The northern part decided in favour of joining Nigeria, while the southern part decided to join the Cameroon Republic. This was implemented on 1 Oct. 1961 with the formation of a Federal Republic of Cameroon. As a result of a national referendum, Cameroon became a unitary republic on 2 June 1972. In Jan. 1984 the country was renamed the Republic of Cameroon.

AREA AND POPULATION. Cameroon is bounded west by the Gulf of Guinea, north-west by Nigeria and east by Chad, with Lake Chad at its northern tip, and the Central African Republic, and south by Congo, Gabon and Equatorial Guinea. The total area is 465,054 sq. km (179,558 sq. miles). Population (1976 census) 7,663,246 (28·5% urban). Estimate (1988) 11,082,000.

The areas, populations and chief towns of the 10 provinces were:

Province	*Sq. km*	*Census 1976*	*Chief town*	*Estimate 1981*
Adamaoua	63,691	359,227	Ngaoundéré	47,508
Centre	68,926	1,176,206	Yaoundé	653,670 [1]
Est	109,011	366,235	Bertoua	18,254
Extrême-Nord	34,246	1,394,958	Maroua	81,861
Littoral	20,239	935,166	Douala	1,029,731 [1]
Nord (Bénoué)	65,576	479,072	Garoua	77,856
Nord-Ouest	17,810	980,531	Bamenda	58,697
Ouest	13,872	1,035,597	Bafoussam	75,832
Sud	47,110	315,739	Ebolowa	22,222
Sud-Ouest	24,471	620,515	Buéa	29,953

[1] 1986.

Other large towns (1981): Nkongsamba (86,870), Kumba (53,823), Foumban (41,358), Limbe (32,917), Edéa (31,016), Mbalmayo (26,934) and Dschang (21,705).

The population is composed of Sudanic-speaking people in the north (Fulani, Sao and others) and Bantu-speaking groups, mainly Bamileke, Beti, Bulu, Tikar, Bassa, Duala, in the rest of the country. In Dec. 1987 there were 8,547 Chadian refugees living in Cameroon. The official languages are French and English.

CLIMATE. An equatorial climate, with high temperatures and plentiful rain, especially from March to June and Sept. to Nov. Further inland, rain occurs at all seasons. Yaoundé. Jan. 76°F (24·4°C), July 73°F (22·8°C). Annual rainfall 62" (1,555 mm). Douala. Jan. 79°F (26·1°C), July 75°F (23·9°C). Annual rainfall 160" (4,026 mm).

CONSTITUTION AND GOVERNMENT. The 1972 Constitution, subsequently amended, provides for a President as head of state and government and commander of the armed forces. He is directly elected for a 5-year term, and there is a Council of Ministers whose members must not be members of parliament.

The National Assembly, elected by universal adult suffrage for 5 years, consists of 180 representatives. Elections took place in April 1988. Since 1966 the sole legal party has been the Cameroon National Union. In March 1985 the UNC was renamed the Cameroon People's Democratic Movement and is administered by a 65-member Central Committee and a 12-member Political Bureau.

The Council of Ministers in Oct. 1989 comprised:

President: Paul Biya (assumed office 6 Nov. 1982, re-elected April 1988).

Minister-Delegate at the Presidency, Defence: Michel Meva'a M'Eboutou. *Territorial Administration:* Ibrahim Mbomo Njoya. *Social and Women's Affairs:* Aissatou Yaou. *Agriculture:* John Niba Ngu. *Special Duties at the Presidency:* Ogork Ebot Ntui. *Industrial and Commercial Development:* Joseph Tsanga Abanda. *National Education:* Joseph Mbui. *Livestock, Fisheries and Animal Industries:* Dr Hamadjoda Adjoudji. *Higher Education, Computer Services and Scientific Research:* Abdoulaye Babale. *Finance:* Sadou Hayatou. *Public Service and State Control:* Joseph Owona. *Information and Culture:* Henri Bandolo. *Youth and Sports:* Dr Joseph Fofe. *Justice, Keeper of the Seals:* Adolphe Moudiki. *Water Resources and Energy:* Francis Nkwain. *Plan and Regional Development:* Elisabeth Tankeu. *Posts and Telecommunications:* Oumarou Sanda. *External Relations:* Jacques-Roger Booh Booh. *Public Health:* Joseph Mbede. *Public Works and Transport:* Claude Tchepanou. *Labour and Social Welfare:* Jean Baptiste Bokam. *Town Planning and Housing:* Ferdinand Leopold Oyono. *Tourism:* Benjamin Itoue.

There were 7 Secretaries of State.

National flag: Three vertical strips of green, red, yellow, with a gold star in the centre.

National anthem: O Cameroon, Thou Cradle of our Fathers.

Local Government: The 10 provinces are each administered by a governor appointed by the President. They are sub-divided into 49 *départements* (each under a *préfet*) and then into *arrondissements* (each under a *sous-préfet*).

DEFENCE

Army. The Army consists of 1 armoured car, 1 para-commando, 1 engineer and 5 infantry battalions and 5 artillery and 1 anti-aircraft batteries. Equipment includes Ferret scout cars. Total strength (1990) 6,600, there are an additional 4,000 paramilitary troops.

Navy. The Navy, all French-built, operates 1 missile craft and 3 inshore patrol vessels. There are some 7 landing craft and 32 auxiliaries and service craft. Personnel in 1989 numbered 700.

The marine wing of the Gendarmerie operates 1 coastal and 12 inshore patrol craft.

Air Force. The Air Force has 3 C-130H Hercules turboprop transports, 4 Buffalo and 1 Caribou STOL transports, 3 C-47s for transport and communications duties, 3 Broussard liaison aircraft, 10 Magister armed jet basic trainers, 5 Alpha Jet close support/trainers, and 5 Alouette helicopters. Some of 4 Gazelle light helicopters are armed with anti-tank missiles. A small VIP transport fleet, maintained in civil markings, comprises 1 Boeing 727 jet aircraft, 1 Gulfstream III and 3 Aerospatiale helicopters. Radar-equipped Dornier 128-6 twin-turboprop aircraft serve for off-shore patrol. Personnel total (1990) 300.

INTERNATIONAL RELATIONS

Membership. Cameroon is a member of UN, OAU, the Non-Aligned Movement and is an ACP state of EEC.

ECONOMY

Planning. The Sixth 5-year Development Plan (from 1 July 1986 to 30 June 1991) gives priority to rural development and food self-sufficiency.

Budget. The budget for 1987–88 balanced at 650,000m. francs CFA.

Currency. The unit of currency is the *franc CFA*, with a parity rate of 50 *francs CFA* to 1 French *franc*. In March 1990, £1 = 471·63 *francs CFA*; US$1 = 287·75 *francs CFA*.

Banking. The Banque des Etats de l'Afrique Centrale is the sole bank of issue. The commercial banks are Banque Internationale pour l'Afrique Occidentale, Société Camerounaise de Banque, Société Générale de Banque au Cameroun, Banque International pour le Commerce et l'Industrie du Cameroun, Cameroon Bank, Banque Camerounaise de Développement, Bank of Credit and Commerce Cameroon, Paribas Cameroun, Boston Bank Cameroon Ltd, Chase Bank Cameroon Ltd and Bank of America Cameroon. Most of the banks operate in all the large cities and towns throughout the Republic.

ENERGY AND NATURAL RESOURCES

Electricity. There are 3 hydro-electric power stations at Edéa on the Sanaga river with a capacity of 180,000 kw. Total production (1986) 4,200m. kwh. Supply 127 and 220 volts; 50 Hz.

Oil. Production (estimate, 1989) mainly from Kole oilfield was 9m. tonnes.

Minerals. There are considerable deposits of bauxite and kyanite around Ngaoundéré. Further deposits of bauxite and cassiterite remain to be exploited in the Adamaoua plateau.

Agriculture. The main food crops (with 1988 production in 1,000 tonnes): Cassava, 680; millet, 410; maize, 380; plantains, 1,100; yams, 420; groundnuts, 142; bananas, 68. Cash crops include palm oil, 110; palm kernels, 27; cocoa, 130; coffee, 138; rubber, 26; cotton lint, 47; raw sugar, 80.

Livestock (1988): 4·5m. cattle, 2·9m. sheep, 2·9m. goats, 1·2m. pigs.

Forestry. Forests cover 24·9m. hectares, 53% of the land area, ranging from tropical rain forests in the south (producing hardwoods such as mahogany, ebony and sapele) to semi-deciduous forests in the centre and wooded savannah in the north. Production in 1986 amounted to 12·2m. cu. metres.

Fisheries. In 1986 the total catch was 84,000 tonnes.

INDUSTRY AND TRADE

Industry. There is a major aluminium smelting complex at Edéa; aluminium production in 1983 amounted to 77,600 tonnes. Production of cement totalled 227,000 tonnes in 1980. There are also factories producing shoes, beer, soap, oil and food products, cigarettes. Agro-industrial production (1984–85, in tonnes): Rubber, 17,679; palm-oil, 76,954; sugar, 73,717; oil palm, 14,849; tea, 2,279.

Labour. In 1982 the work-force numbered 3,543,000 of whom 73% were occupied in agriculture. The principal trade union federation is the *Organisation des syndicats des travailleurs camerounais* (OSTC) established on 7 Dec. 1985 to replace the former body, the UNTC.

Commerce. Imports and exports in 1m. francs CFA were as follows:

	1984–85	*1985–86*	*1986–87*
Imports	482,297	513,898	558,265
Exports	822,041	816,912	508,200

In 1984–85, exports (in 1m. francs CFA) went mainly to the Netherlands (136,057), France (127,966), Italy (58,333), Federal Republic of Germany (35,089), USA (30,098) and Spain (25,517), while imports were mainly from France (193,176), USA (51,687), Japan (36,354), Federal Republic of Germany (31,220) and Italy (26,610); the main exports were crude oils (123,398), coffee and by-products (111,201) and cocoa and by-products (105,858).

Total trade between Cameroon and UK (British Department of Trade returns, in £1,000 sterling):

	1985	*1986*	*1987*	*1988*	*1989*
Imports to UK	73,746	7,634	14,201	16,180	11,362
Exports and re-exports from UK	44,806	34,368	28,057	20,472	24,838

Tourism. There were an estimated 115,203 foreign visitors in 1987.

COMMUNICATIONS

Roads. In 1986 there were 66,910 km of roads, of which 2,922 km were tarmac. In 1984–85 there were 73,963 passenger cars and 43,165 commercial vehicles.

Railways. Cameroon Railways, *Regifercam* (1,115 km in 1985) link Douala with Nkongsamba and Ngaoundéré, with branches M'Banga–Kumba and Makak–M'Balmayo. In 1986–87 railways carried 2·3m. passengers and 1·4m. tonnes of freight.

Aviation. Douala is the main international airport; other airports are at Yaoundé and Garoua. Camair, the national airline, serve 7 domestic airports. In 1981–82, 644,000 passengers and 14,600 tonnes of freight passed through the airports.

Shipping. The merchant-marine consisted (1986) of 48 vessels (over 100 GRT) of 76,433 GRT. The major port of Douala handled (1984) 3m. tonnes of imports and 1m. tonnes of exports and in 1984–85, 671 cargo ships and 2,582 other ships entered the port. Timber is exported mainly through the south-west ports of Kribi and Campo. Other ports are Bota, Tiko, Limbe and Garoua.

Post and Broadcasting. There were (1975) 150 post offices supplemented by a mobile postal service; telephones (1984), 47,200; radio stations, 10 with 785,000 receivers. Television was introduced in 1985.

Cinemas. There were (1979) 52 cinemas with a capacity of 29,000 seats.

Newspapers. There was (1984) 1 daily newspaper with a circulation of 20,000.

JUSTICE, RELIGION, EDUCATION AND WELFARE

Justice. The Supreme Court sits at Yaoundé, as does the High Court of Justice (consisting of 9 titular judges and 6 surrogates all appointed by the National Assembly). There are magistrates' courts situated in the provinces.

Religion. In 1980, 21% of the population was Roman Catholic, 22% Moslem, 18% Protestant, while 39% followed traditional (animist) religions.

Education (1986–87). There were 1,795,254 pupils and 35,728 teachers in primary schools, 291,842 pupils and 9,017 teachers in general secondary schools and 90,666 pupils and 3,714 teachers in technical secondary schools. In 1984–85 there were 13,753 students and 572 teaching staff at higher education institutions of the University of Yaoundé.

Health. In 1981 there were 1,003 hospitals and health centres with 24,541 beds; there were also (1982) 604 doctors and 17 dentists, 96 pharmacists, 399 midwives and 1,086 nursing personnel.

DIPLOMATIC REPRESENTATIVES

Of Cameroon in Great Britain (84 Holland Pk., London, W11 3SB)
Ambassador: Dr Gibering Bol-Alima (accredited 12 May 1987).

Of Great Britain in Cameroon (Ave. Winston Churchill, BP 547, Yaoundé)
Ambassador: Martin Reith.

Of Cameroon in the USA (2349 Massachusetts Ave., NW, Washington, D.C., 20008)
Ambassador: Vincent Paul-Thomas Pondi.

Of the USA in Cameroon (Rue Nachtigal, BP 817, Yaoundé)
Ambassador: Mark L. Edelman.

Of Cameroon to the United Nations
Ambassador: Paul Bamela Engo.

Further Reading

Statistical Information: The Service de la Statistique Générale, at Douala, set up in 1945, publishes a monthly bulletin (from Nov. 1950)

DeLancey, M. W., *Cameroon: Dependence and Independence*. London, 1989
DeLancey, M. W. and Schraeder, P. J., *Cameroon*. [Bibliography] Oxford and Santa Barbara, 1986
Ndongko, W. A., *Planning for Economic Development in a Federal State: The Case of Cameroon, 1960–71*. New York, 1975
Rubin, N., *Cameroon*. New York, 1972

CANADA

Capital: Ottawa
Population: 26·2m. (1989)
GNP per capita: US$16,760 (1988)

HISTORY. The territories which now constitute Canada came under British power at various times by settlement, conquest or cession. Nova Scotia was occupied in 1628 by settlement at Port Royal, was ceded back to France in 1632 and was finally ceded by France in 1713 to England, by the Treaty of Utrecht; the Hudson's Bay Company's charter, conferring rights over all the territory draining into Hudson Bay, was granted in 1670; Canada, with all its dependencies, including New Brunswick and Prince Edward Island, was formally ceded to Great Britain by France in 1763; Vancouver Island was acknowledged to be British by the Oregon Boundary Treaty of 1846, and British Columbia was established as a separate colony in 1858. As originally constituted, Canada was composed of Upper and Lower Canada (now Ontario and Quebec), Nova Scotia and New Brunswick. They were united under an Act of the Imperial Parliament, 'The British North America Act, 1867', which came into operation on 1 July 1867 by royal proclamation. The Act provided that the constitution of Canada should be 'similar in principle to that of the United Kingdom'; that the executive authority shall be vested in the Sovereign, and carried on in his name by a Governor-General and Privy Council; and that the legislative power shall be exercised by a Parliament of two Houses, called the 'Senate' and the 'House of Commons'.

On 30 June 1931 the British House of Commons approved the enactment of the Statute of Westminster freeing the Provinces as well as the Dominion from the operation of the Colonial Laws Validity Act, and thus removing what legal limitations existed as regards Canada's legislative autonomy. A joint address of the Senate and the House of Commons was sent to the Governor-General for transmission to London on 10 July 1931. The statute received the royal assent on 12 Dec. 1931.

Provision was made in the British North America Act for the admission of British Columbia, Prince Edward Island, Newfoundland, Rupert's Land and Northwest Territory into the Union. In 1869 Rupert's Land, or the Northwest Territories, was purchased from the Hudson's Bay Company. On 15 July 1870, Rupert's Land and the Northwest Territory were annexed to Canada and named the Northwest Territories, Canada having agreed to pay the Hudson's Bay Company in cash and land for its relinquishing of claims to the territory. By the same action the Province of Manitoba was created from a small portion of this territory and they were admitted into the Confederation on 15 July 1870. On 20 July 1871 the province of British Columbia was admitted, and Prince Edward Island on 1 July 1873. The provinces of Alberta and Saskatchewan were formed from the provisional districts of Alberta, Athabaska, Assiniboia and Saskatchewan and originally parts of the Northwest Territories and admitted on 1 Sept. 1905. Newfoundland formally joined Canada as its tenth province on 31 March 1949.

In Feb. 1931 Norway formally recognized the Canadian title to the Sverdrup group of Arctic islands. Canada thus holds sovereignty in the whole Arctic sector north of the Canadian mainland.

In Nov. 1981 the Canadian government agreed on the provisions of an amended constitution, to the end that it should replace the British North America Act and that its future amendment should be the prerogative of Canada. These proposals were adopted by the Parliament of Canada and were enacted by the UK Parliament as the Canada Act of 1982.

The enactment of the Canada Act was the final act of the UK Parliament in Canadian constitutional development. The Act gave to Canada the power to amend the Constitution according to procedures determined by the Constitutional Act 1982, which was proclaimed in force by the Queen on 17 April 1982. The Constitution Act 1982 added to the Canadian Constitution a charter of Rights and Freedoms, and provisions which recognize the nation's multi-cultural heritage, affirm the existing rights of native peoples, confirm the principle of equalization of benefits among the provinces, and strengthen provincial ownership of natural resources.

AREA AND POPULATION. Canada is bounded north-west by the Beaufort Sea, north by the Arctic Ocean, north-east by Baffin Bay, east by the Davis Strait, Labrador Sea and Atlantic Ocean, south by the USA and west by the Pacific Ocean and USA (Alaska). Population of the area now included in Canada:

1851	2,436,297	1901	5,371,315	1951 [1]	4,009,429
1861	3,229,633	1911	7,206,643	1961	18,238,247
1871	3,689,257	1921	8,787,949	1971	21,568,311
1881	4,324,810	1931	10,376,786	1981	24,343,181
1891	4,833,239	1941	11,506,655		

[1] From 1951 figures include Newfoundland.

Population (census), 3 June 1986, was 25,354,064. Estimate (1989) 26·2m.

Areas of the provinces, etc. (in sq. km) and population at recent censuses:

Province	Land area	Fresh water area	Total land and fresh water area	Population, 1976	Population, 1981	Population, 1986 [1]
Newfoundland	371,690	34,030	405,720	557,725	567,681	568,349
Prince Edward Island	5,660	—	5,660	118,229	122,506	126,646
Nova Scotia	52,840	2,650	55,490	828,571	847,442	873,199
New Brunswick	72,090	1,350	73,440	677,250	696,403	710,442
Quebec	1,356,790	183,890	1,540,680	6,234,445	6,438,403	6,540,276
Ontario	891,190	177,390	1,068,580	8,264,465	8,625,107	9,113,515
Manitoba	548,360	101,590	649,950	1,021,506	1,026,241	1,071,232
Saskatchewan	570,700	81,630	652,330	921,323	968,313	1,010,198
Alberta	644,390	16,800	661,190	1,838,037	2,237,724	2,375,278
British Columbia	929,730	18,070	947,800	2,466,608	2,744,467	2,889,207
Yukon	478,970	4,480	483,450	21,836	23,153	23,504
Northwest Territories	3,293,020	133,300	3,426,320	42,609	45,471	52,238
Total	9,215,430	755,180	9,970,610	22,992,604	24,343,181	25,354,064

[1] Including estimates of incompletely enumerated Indian reserves and Indian settlements.

Of the total population in 1986, 21,113,855 were Canadian born, 3,908,150 foreign born, 282,025 of the latter being USA born and 2,435,100 European born.

The population (1986) born outside Canada in the provinces was in the following ratio (%): Newfoundland, 1·6; Prince Edward Island, 3·5; Nova Scotia, 4·7; New Brunswick, 3·8; Quebec, 8·3; Ontario, 23·1; Manitoba, 13·6; Saskatchewan, 7·2; Alberta, 15·6; British Columbia, 22·1; Yukon, 11·5; Northwest Territories, 5·4.

In 1986, figures for the population, according to origin, were [1]:

Single origins	18,035,665	Polish	222,260
Austrian	24,900	Portuguese	199,595
Belgian	28,395	Romanian	18,745
British [2]	6,332,725	Russian	32,080
Czech and Slovak [3]	55,535	Scandinavian [6]	171,715
Chinese	360,320	Spanish	57,125
Dutch (Netherlands)	351,765	Swiss	19,130
Finnish	40,565	Ukrainian	420,210
French [4]	6,093,160	Other single origins:	99,025
German	896,720		
Greek	143,780	*Multiple origins:* [7]	6,986,345
Magyar (Hungarian)	97,850	British and French	1,139,345
Italian	709,590	British and Other	2,262,525
Japanese	40,245	French and Other	325,655
Aboriginal Peoples [5]	373,265	Other multiple origins	616,000

[1] Data on ethnic origins for the 1986 Census excludes the population on incompletely enumerated Indian reserves and settlements. For Canada there were 136 such reserves and settlements and the total population was estimated to be about 45,000 in 1986.

[2] Includes the single origins of English, Irish, Scottish, Welsh, British, n.i.e. and other British.

[3] Includes the single origins of Czech, Czechoslovakian and Slovak.

[4] Includes the single origins of French, Acadian, French Canadian and Québécois.

[5] Includes the single origins of Inuit, Métis and North American Indian.

[6] Includes the single origins of Danish, Icelandic, Norwegian, Swedish and Scandinavian, n.i.e.

[7] Includes persons who report more than one origin.

The total aboriginal population single origins numbered 373,265 in 1986 and the Inuit population was 27,290 in 1986.

Populations of Census Metropolitan Areas (CMA) and Cities (proper), 1986 census:

	CMA	*City proper*
Toronto	3,427,168	612,289
Montreal	2,921,357	1,015,420
Vancouver	1,380,729	431,147
Ottawa-Hull	819,263	—
Ottawa	—	300,763
Hull	—	58,722
Edmonton	785,465	573,982
Calgary	671,326	636,104
Winnipeg	623,304	594,551
Quebec	603,267	164,580
Hamilton	557,029	306,728
St Catharines-Niagara	343,258	—
St Catharines	—	123,455
Niagara Falls	—	72,107
London	342,302	269,140
Kitchener	311,195	150,604

	CMA	*City proper*
Halifax	295,990	113,577
Victoria	255,547	66,303
Windsor	253,988	193,111
Oshawa	203,543	123,651
Saskatoon	200,665	177,641
Regina	186,521	175,064
St John's	161,901	96,216
Chicoutimi-Jonquière	158,468	—
Chicoutimi	—	61,083
Jonquière	—	58,467
Sudbury	148,877	88,717
Sherbrooke	129,960	74,438
Trois Rivières	128,888	50,122
Thunder Bay	122,217	112,272
Saint John	121,265	76,381

The total 'urban' population of Canada in 1986 was 19,352,085, against 18,435,927 in 1981.

While the registration of births, marriages and deaths is under provincial control, the statistics are compiled on a uniform system by Statistics Canada.

The following table gives the results for the year 1988:

Province	*Live births* *Number*	*Marriages* *Number*	*Deaths* *Number*
Newfoundland	7,941	3,380	3,578
Prince Edward Island	1,982	940	1,144
Nova Scotia	12,330	6,540	7,216
New Brunswick	9,884	4,910	5,568
Quebec	84,051	32,770	48,821
Ontario	135,568	73,900	69,382
Manitoba	17,065	7,740	8,866
Saskatchewan	16,946	6,620	7,746
Alberta	41,923	18,560	13,463
British Columbia	42,561	22,490	22,042
Yukon Territory	487	200	109
N.W. Territories	1,566	230	201
	372,304	178,280	188,136

Immigrant arrivals by country of last permanent residence:

Country	*1986*	*1987*	*1988*
UK	5,088	8,547	8,684
France	1,610	2,290	2,581
Germany	1,403	1,906	1,691
Netherlands	524	575	817
Greece	551	771	574
Italy	715	1,031	856
Portugal	1,970	5,977	4,148
Other Europe	10,848	16,466	20,704
Asia	41,600	67,337	80,215
Australia	338	530	517
USA	7,275	7,967	6,518
Caribbean	8,874	11,227	9,398
All other	18,423	27,474	23,440
Total	99,219	152,098	160,143

CLIMATE. The climate ranges from polar conditions in the north to cool temperate in the south, but with considerable differences between east coast, west coast and the interior, affecting temperatures, rainfall amounts and seasonal distribution.

Winters are very severe over much of the country, but summers can be very hot inland. *See* individual provinces for climatic details.

CONSTITUTION AND GOVERNMENT. The members of the Senate are appointed until age 75 by summons of the Governor-General under the Great Seal of Canada. Members appointed before 2 June 1965 may remain in office for life. The Senate consists of 104 senators, namely, 24 from Ontario, 24 from Quebec, 10 from Nova Scotia, 10 from New Brunswick, 4 from Prince Edward Island, 6 from Manitoba, 6 from British Columbia, 6 from Alberta, 6 from Saskatchewan, 6 from Newfoundland, 1 from the Yukon Territory and 1 from the Northwest Territories. Each senator must be at least 30 years of age, a born or naturalized subject of the Queen and must reside in the province for which he is appointed and his total net worth must be at least $4,000. The House of Commons is elected by the people, for 5 years, unless sooner dissolved. Women have the vote and are eligible. From 1867 to the election of 1945 representation was based on Quebec having 65 seats and the other provinces the same proportion of 65 which their population had to the population of Quebec. In the General Election of 1949 readjustments were based on the population of all the provinces taken as a whole. Generally speaking, this format for representation has prevailed in all subsequent elections with readjustments made after each decennial census. Under the Representation Act 1986, effective March 1986, the formula contained in section 51 of the Constitution Act, 1867[1] dealing with the number of seats in the House of Commons and their distribution throughout the country, was changed.

[1]The Constitution Act, 1986 (Representation). Redrawing of Electoral boundaries statutes of Canada 1984–86, Chap. 8.

The thirty-fourth Parliament, elected in Nov. 1988, comprises 295 members and the provincial and territorial representation are: Ontario, 99; Quebec, 75; Nova Scotia, 11; New Brunswick, 10; Manitoba, 14; British Columbia, 32; Prince Edward Island, 4; Saskatchewan 14; Alberta, 26; Newfoundland, 7; Yukon Territory, 1; Northwest Territories, 2.

State of parties in the Senate (Sept. 1989): Liberals, 56; Progressive Conservatives, 35; Independent, 5; Independent P.C., 1; Vacant, 7; total 104.

State of the parties in the House of Commons (Sept. 1989): Progressive Conservatives, 167; Liberals, 83; New Democratic Party, 43; Reform Party, 1; Vacant, 1; total, 295.

The following is a list of Governors-General of Canada:

Viscount Monck	1867–1868	Viscount Willington	1926–1931
Lord Lisgar	1868–1872	Earl of Bessborough	1931–1935
Earl of Dufferin	1872–1878	Lord Tweedsmuir	1935–1940
Marquess of Lorne	1878–1883	Earl of Athlone	1940–1946
Marquess of Lansdowne	1883–1888	Field-Marshal Viscount Alexander of Tunis	1946–1952
Lord Stanley of Preston	1888–1893	Vincent Massey	1952–1959
Earl of Aberdeen	1893–1898	Georges Philias Vanier	1959–1967
Earl of Minto	1898–1904	Roland Michener	1967–1974
Earl Grey	1904–1911	Jules Léger	1974–1979
HRH the Duke of Connaught	1911–1916	Edward Schreyer	1979–1984
Duke of Devonshire	1916–1921	Jeanne Sauvé	1984–1989
Viscount Byng of Vimy	1921–1926		

Governor-General: Hon. Ramon Hnatyshyn.

National flag: Vertically red, white, red with the white of double width and bearing a stylized red maple leaf.

The office and appointment of the Governor-General are regulated by letters patent, signed by the King on 8 Sept. 1947, which came into force on 1 Oct. 1947. In 1977 the Queen approved the transfer to the Governor-General of functions discharged by the Sovereign. He is assisted in his functions, under the provisions of the Act of 1867, by a Privy Council composed of Cabinet Ministers.

The following is the list of the Conservative Cabinet in July 1989, in order of precedence, which in Canada attaches generally rather to the person than to the office:

Prime Minister: The Rt. Hon. Martin Brian Mulroney.
Secretary of State for External Affairs: The Rt. Hon. Charles Joseph Clark.
Minister for International Trade: The Hon. John Carnell Crosbie.
Deputy Prime Minister, President of the Privy Council and Minister for Agriculture: The Hon. Donald Frank Mazankowski.
Minister of Public Works and Minister for the Atlantic Canada Opportunities Agency: The Hon. Elmer MacIntosh Mackay.
Minister of Energy, Mines and Resources: The Hon. Arthur Jacob Epp.
President of the Treasury Board: The Hon. Robert R. de Cotret.
Minister of Health and Welfare: The Hon. Henry Perrin Beatty.
Minister of Finance: The Hon. Michael Holcombe Wilson.
Minister of Regional Industrial Expansion, Minister of State for Science and Technology and Acting Minister of Consumer and Corporate Affairs: The Hon. Harvie Andre.
Minister of National Revenue: The Hon. Otto John Jelinek.
Minister of Fisheries and Oceans: The Hon. Thomas Edward Siddon.
Minister of Western Economic Diversification and Minister of State (Grains and Oilseeds): The Hon. Charles James Mayer.
Minister of National Defence: The Hon. William Hunter McKnight.
Minister of Transport: The Hon. Benoit Bouchard.
Minister of Communications: The Hon. Marcel Masse.
Minister of Employment and Immigration: The Hon. Barbara Jean McDougall.
Minister of Veterans Affairs: The Hon. Gerald S. Merrithew.
Minister of State (Employment and Immigration) and Minister of State (Seniors): The Hon. Monique Vezina.
Minister of State (Forestry): The Hon. Frank Oberle.
Leader of the Government in the Senate and Minister of State (Federal-Provincial Relations): The Hon. Lowell Murray.
Minister of Supply and Services: The Hon. Paul Wyatt Dick.
Minister of Indian Affairs and Northern Development: The Hon. Pierre H. Cadieux.
Minister of State (Youth), Minister of State (Fitness and Amateur Sport) and Deputy Leader of the Government in the House of Commons: The Hon. Jean J. Charest.
Minister of State (Small Businesses and Tourism): The Hon. Thomas Hockin.
Minister of External Relations: The Hon. Monique Landry.
Minister for Consumer and Corporate Affairs: The Hon. Bernard Valcourt.
Secretary of State of Canada and Minister of State (Multiculturalism and Citizenship): The Hon. Gerry Weiner.
Minister of Justice, Attorney-General of Canada and Leader of the Government in the House of Commons: The Hon. Douglas Grinsdale Lewis.
Solicitor-General of Canada and Minister of State (Agriculture): The Hon. Pierre Blais.
Minister of the Environment: The Hon. Lucien Bouchard.
Minister of State (Privatization and Regulatory Affairs): The Hon. John McDermid.
Minister of State (Transport): The Hon. Shirley Martin.
Associate Minister of National Defence: The Hon. Mary Collins.
Minister of State (Housing): The Hon. Alan Redway.
Minister of State (Science and Technology): The Hon. William Winegard.
Minister of State (Indian Affairs and Northern Development): The Hon. Kim Campbell.
Minister of Labour: The Hon. Jean Corbeil.
Minister of State (Finance): The Hon. Gilles Loiselle.

The salary of a member of the House of Commons (Jan. 1989) is $60,000 with a tax-free allowance ranging from $19,900 to $26,300. The salary of a senator is $60,000 with a tax-free allowance of $9,500. The salary and allowances of the Prime Minister total $150,500, that of the Speaker of the House of Commons is $129,700; of the Speaker of the Senate is $102,400; of the Opposition Leader is $127,700 and of the National Democratic Party Leader is $107,500.

An Act to provide retiring allowances, on a contributory basis, to members of the House of Commons was given the Royal Assent on 4 July 1952. Subsequent amendments provide allowances for surviving spouses and for former Prime Ministers or their surviving spouses.

Index to Federal Programs and Services 1988. Ninth edition. Supply and Services Canada. Annual, Ottawa

A consolidation of the *The Constitution Acts 1867 to 1982*. Department of Justice Canada. Ottawa, 1986

Bureaucracy in Canadian Government: selected readings. 2nd edition, edited by W. D. K. Kernashan, Toronto, 1973

Laskin's Canadian Constitutional Law. 5th ed., Vol. 2, Neil Finkelstein. Toronto: Carswell, 1986

Leading Constitutional decisions: Cases on the British North America Act. Edited and with an introduction by Peter H. Russell, 4th edition. Ottawa, 1987

The Canadian Parliamentary Guide. Annual. Ottawa

Report of the Royal Commission on Dominion–Provincial Relations, Canada 1867–1939. 3 vols. Ottawa, 1940

Bejermi, J., *Canadian Parliamentary Handbook*. Ottawa, 1986

Byers, R. B. (ed.) *Canada Challenged: The Viability of the Confederation*. Toronto, 1979

Cheffins, R. I. and Johnson, P. A., *The Revised Canadian Constitution, Politics as law*. Toronto, 1986

Fox, P. W., and White, G., *Politics Canada*. 6th ed. Toronto, 1987

Franks, C. E. S., *The Parliament of Canada*. Univ. of Toronto Press, 1987

Hogg, P. W., *Constitutional Law of Canada*. 2nd ed. Toronto, 1985

Kennedy, W. F. M., *Statutes, Treaties and Documents of the Canadian Constitutions, 1713–1929*. Toronto, 1939

Kernaghan, N. (ed.) *Bureaucracy in Canadian Government, Selected Readings*. Toronto, 1969

Morton, W. L., *The Kingdom of Canada; A General History From Earliest Times*. Toronto, 1969

Olmstead, R. A., *Decisions of the Judicial Committee of the Privy Council Relating to the British North America Act, 1867, and the Canadian Constitution, 1867–1954*. Ottawa, Queens' Printer, 1954

DEFENCE. The Department of National Defence was created by the National Defence Act, 1922, which established one civil Department of Government in place of the previous Departments of Militia and Defence, Naval Service and the Air Board. The Department now operates under authority of RSC 1970, c.N1-4. The Minister of National Defence has the control and management of the Canadian Forces and all matters relating to national defence establishments and works for the defence of Canada. He is the Minister responsible for presenting before the Cabinet, matters of major defence policy for which Cabinet direction is required. He is also responsible for the emergency measures organization known since 1 July 1986 as 'Emergency Preparedness Canada'.

In Dec. 1976, the Minister of National Defence was named as minister responsible for all aspects of air Search and Rescue (SAR) in the areas of Canadian SAR responsibility, and for the overall co-ordination of marine Search and Rescue including provision of air resources for marine SAR within Canadian territorial waters and in designated oceanic areas off the Pacific and Atlantic Coasts in accordance with agreements made with the United States Coast Guard. A group from Transport Canada, the Department of National Defence and the Department of Fisheries and Oceans was set up at the same time, as a co-ordinating body.

Since September 1985 the Minister has shared his responsibilities with an Associate Minister of National Defence.

The Canadian Forces (CF) are the military element of the Canadian government and are part of the Department of National Defence (DND). Government policy concerning the CF takes into account national and foreign policy. The roles of the CF are developed within this framework. They are:

- the protection of Canada and Canadian national interests at home and abroad; this includes the provision of aid of the civil power and national development;
- the defence of North America in co-operation with the United States' military forces;
- the fulfillment of such North Atlantic Treaty Organization (NATO) commitments to security as may be agreed upon; the performance of such international peacekeeping roles as Canada may from time to time assume.

Personnel and Budget

The 1988-89 Department of National Defence budget main estimate was $11,200m. or 9·4% of the government's budget. The estimate for 1989-90 was $11,300m. or 8·7% of the government's budget.

The strength of the Regular Force for 1989 was approximately 88,000.

Command Structure. The missions and roles of the CF are undertaken by functional and regional commands. Commands and major organizations report directly to National Defence Headquarters (NDHQ) in Ottawa, Ontario from headquarters situated as follows:

- Mobile Command, St Hubert, Quebec;
- Maritime Command, Halifax, Nova Scotia;
- Air Command, Winnipeg, Manitoba;
- Canadian Forces Training System, Trenton, Ontario;
- Canadian Forces Communication Command, Ottawa, Ontario;
- Canadian Forces Europe, Lahr, Federal Republic of Germany (FRG); and
- Northern Region, Yellowknife, NWT.

1. *Mobile Command*. Mobile Command (FMC) maintains combat ready land forces to meet Canada's defence commitments.

Defence of North America

Mobile Command is prepared to undertake defence of North America operations in conjunction with the forces of the United States. Under the Canada-United States Basic Defence Agreement, a number of mutual defence treaties exist. One that directly concerns Mobile Command is Canada-United States Land Operations (CANUS LANDOP). It is designed to provide the co-ordination of the land defence of Canada, Alaska, and the continental United States. Under this plan, Mobile Command is responsible for co-ordinating the land defence of Canada by both Canadian and US forces, if required, and must be prepared to assist US forces in the defence of Alaska and the United States. Both this and the National Security task force involves Mobile Command in maintaining a presence in the Canadian North through surveillance and patrols and numerous exercises.

NATO Commitment

Mobile Command (FMC) provides forces in support of several NATO commitments. FMC NATO commitments include:

(a) A division to Central Army Group (CENTAG) in Europe. In 1989 5e Groupe-brigade du Canada (5 GBC), located in Quebec, 4 Canadian Mechanized Brigade Group (4 CMBG) in Lahr, FRG, and various support groups were consolidated into 1 Canadian Division, committed to Central Europe. The commitment of the Canadian Air/Sea Transportable (CAST) Brigade to northern Norway ceased in 1989 with the operational tasking of 1 Canadian Division.

(b) An infantry battle group for operations with the Allied Command Europe Mobile Force (Land (AMF)L). The Canadian contingent is designated to deploy either to North Norway or to the Zeeland Group of Islands in Denmark. The contingent maintains a high degree of operational readiness for this purpose and exercises in its operational areas on a regular basis.

Although the land force units located in Europe are part of Canadian Forces Europe, FMC provides trained replacements through individual, sub-unit and unit rotations to sustain peacetime manning requirements.

International Peacekeeping or Stability Operations

Mobile Command is committed to providing forces for international peacekeeping or stability operations. In 1989, its UN involvement included commitments in Cyprus, on the Golan Heights and in Namibia, Iran-Iraq, and Afghánistán. Non-UN commitments included the Multi-National Peacekeeping Force (MFO) in the Sinai and a group of engineers in Pakistan teaching Afghan refugees mine recognition.

Budget and Personnel

In 1988–89, FMC budget was approximately $370m. for normal operations and maintenance costs. This excluded salaries. Expenditures in support of British, German and US Army units training on FMC bases were recovered from the nations concerned.

Personnel included approximately 21,100 Regular Force, 18,500 Militia and 5,500 civilians.

2. *Maritime Command.* The Maritime Command (MARCOM) role is to maintain combat-ready general purpose maritime forces to meet Canada's defence commitments. This role is fulfilled using MARCOM resources and designated Air Command aircraft under MARCOM control.

Maritime Command comprises operational maritime forces, headquarters and supporting units located primarily on the east and west coasts of Canada, but also extending as far north as Iqaluit, Northwest Territories and as far south as Bermuda.

Operational forces include 19 destroyers, 6 coastal patrol boats, 3 submarines, 2 mine counter-measures vessels, 3 operational support ships, 1 diving support ship, 3 research vessels and 12 tugboats. In addition there are more than 30 minor vessels located at Reserve Training Units on both coasts. The first of the new Canadian Patrol Frigates was scheduled for delivery in 1990.

Protection of Canada and National Interests

Maritime Command continues to conduct military surveillance of Canadian territorial waters on both coasts. Surveillance patrols in support of Canadian national interests are conducted in the 370 km economic zone by surface and air units. Fisheries patrols are conducted on both coasts.

Operations and Training

The air, surface and sub-surface resources of MARCOM maintain a high level of combat readiness through operations, tactical research, joint exercises and planned maintenance. Training was conducted on both coasts through exercises run by the destroyer squadrons. Advanced training, designed to maintain combat readiness and evaluate new tactics, was accomplished through Maritime co-ordinated exercises, one on each coast.

NATO Exercises

Canada is continuously represented in NATO's Standing Naval Force Atlantic (STANAVFORLANT) by a destroyer. This multi-national squadron provides a highly visible demonstration of NATO solidarity. The squadron visits ports throughout Europe, the Mediterranean and the east coast of North America, strengthening ties with NATO's member countries. East coast destroyers participate in the NATO Squadron and are involved in a number of exercises on both sides of the Atlantic. West coast ships conduct national exercises on a regular basis.

Personnel and Budget

MARCOM's budget for fiscal year 1988–89 was $237m. for operations and maintenance, naval reserve, cadets and miscellaneous. Personnel included approximately 10,000 Regular Force, 4,000 Naval Reserve and 7,000 civilians.

3. *Air Command.* Air Command's six functional groups provide combat-ready air forces to meet Canada's defence commitments.

Functional Organization

Air Command is divided into six functional air groups. The Commander, Air Command, delegates operational control to the commanders of the air groups over their assigned resources. The Commander retains responsibility for flight safety, as well as air doctrine and standards relating to flying operations throughout the Canadian Forces, including units located outside Canada. The air groups are:

(*a*) Fighter Group (North Bay, Ontario) maintains the sovereignty of Canada's airspace, supports Mobile and Maritime Command training and operations, and fulfills Canada's commitments to NATO and NORAD.

(*b*) Air Transport Group (Trenton, Ontario) provides airlift resources and Search and Rescue (SAR) forces for the CF.

(c) Maritime Air Group (MAG) (Halifax, Nova Scotia) provides operationally ready air forces to MARCOM in areas including anti-submarine warfare, surveillance, sovereignty, fisheries and pollution monitoring.

(d) 10 Tactical Air Group (St. Hubert, Quebec) provides combat-ready tactical aviation forces for operational employment in support of Mobile Command operations, training and other defence commitments.

(e) 14 Training Group (Winnipeg, Manitoba) trains aircrew and other air personnel to initial classification and trade specifications, and provides other training as directed.

(f) Air Reserve Group (Winnipeg, Manitoba) provides support to Air Command by provision of reserve operational units and individual augmentees.

Personnel and Budget

Air Command consists of 21,629 Regular Force members, 1,350 Air Reserves and 6,868 civilians for a total of 29,847 members. The operations and maintenance budget for 1988–89 was $510m. including aviation fuel and operations and maintenance costs.

4. *Canadian Forces Training System.* The Canadian Forces Training System headquarters is located at CFB Trenton, Ontario. Its functions include the planning and conduct of all recruit, trades, specialist and other officer classification training common to more than one command.

5. *Canadian Forces Communication Command (CFCC).* Canadian Forces Communication Command (CFCC) provides strategic communication services, including communications research message handling and data transfer, telephone systems and high frequency radio direction-finding services for the CF. To effect these services CFCC operates and maintains several data networks and voice communications systems.

It is implicit in the provision of strategic communications for the CF and emergency government that the organization be capable of extending services to the various military and civil headquarters during a national emergency. As well, it must supply reliable strategic communications from Canada to CF combat elements anywhere in the world. To these ends, Communication Command personnel exercise their equipment and procedures regularly.

Personnel and Budget

The Canadian Forces Communication Command's (CFCC) 5,700 personnel includes a regular force contingent of 3,300 members, a Communication Reserve of 1,800 and a civilian force of approximately 600.

The 1989 command budget was $117·4m. Of that budget, 77% was expended on strategic communications services with the remainder to operation of the Communication Reserve, command operations and maintenance and miscellaneous.

6. *Canadian Forces Europe (CFE).* Throughout 1989 Canadian Forces Europe (CFE) continued to provide, maintain and support European-based, combat-ready land and air forces to Supreme Allied Commander Europe in accordance with Canada's NATO commitment. The two formations stationed permanently in Central Europe, 4 Canadian Mechanized Brigade Group (4 CMBG) and 1 Canadian Air Group (1 CAG), completed challenging and realistic training programmes to maintain their operational readiness at the highest possible state. Support for the two formations was provided by Canadian Forces Bases Lahr and Baden-Soellingen, FRG.

Personnel and Budget

During 1989 service personnel at CFE numbered 8,000. There were approximately 4,400 civilian employees and a total of about 21,500 Canadian military and civilian personnel and their dependents.

During the fiscal year 1987–88, CFE was allocated an operations and maintenance budget of $190m, which includes civilian salaries but not military pay or new construction.

Regional organization. A regional structure is superimposed over the functional organization to most effectively respond to support requirements within Canada. This was accomplished by dividing Canada into six geographic regions and appointing the senior commander in each region as the region commander. Thus the following interrelationship of functional command/region/geographical area exists: *Maritime Command* – Atlantic Region (Newfoundland, New Brunswick, Nova Scotia and Prince Edward Island); *Mobile Command* – Eastern Region (Quebec); *Training System* – Central Region (Ontario); *Air Command* – Prairie Region (Manitoba, Saskatchewan, and Alberta); *Maritime Forces Pacific* – Pacific Region (British Columbia); and *Northern Region Headquarters* – Northern Region (Yukon and Northwest Territories). In 1989, a move was made to transfer the operational responsibilities from the regions to Mobile Command. Central Region operations was the first affected; others will be transferred in the future. Operational responsibilities include vital points defence, aid of the civil power, explosive ordinance disposal and many others. Responsibilities remaining with the regions include medical, dental, support to cadets, civilian personnel administration, etc.

7. *Northern Region Headquarters.* Situated in Yellowknife, NWT, the Northern Region Headquarters (NRHQ) was formed on 15 May 1970 to assist in maintaining Canadian sovereignty and support ongoing Canadian Forces activities in the North.

Training

During 1989, NRHQ continued to provide planning advice and liaison support to territorial governments and military units for exercises 'north of 60'. In all, 15 exercises were held in Northern Region in 1989, including *Amalgam Chief*, the largest-ever NORAD air exercise.

Personnel and Budget

NRHQ, including detachment personnel, is about 80 Regular Force, Reserve Force and civilian personnel located in Yellowknife and Whitehorse, NWT.

Seventy-two percent of the region's $2·6m. annual budget was used to support the ranger and cadet programme including National Cadet Camp Whitehorse. The remaining 28% was used for operations and maintenance.

The Reserve Force consists of officers and non-commissioned members who are enrolled for other than continuing full-time military service. The sub-components of the Reserve Force are the Primary Reserve, the Supplementary Ready Reserve, the Supplementary Holding Reserve, the Cadet Instructors List and the Canadian Rangers.

The elements of the Primary Reserve are the Naval Reserve, Militia, Air Reserve and Communication Reserve. Funded personnel levels for these four elements are 4,011, 18,768, 1,350 and 1,706, respectively. Officers and non-commissioned members of the Primary Reserve undergo part-time training at local armouries or collective training at central locations, often during the summer months.

The Supplementary Ready Reserve consists of former Regular and Reserve Force officers and non-commissioned members who are militarily fit and current, and prepared to report for duty when required in an emergency. The Supplementary Holding Reserve includes former members required to report for such duty only when the entire Supplementary Reserve was put on active service.

The Cadet Instructors List consists of commissioned officers whose primary duty is the supervision, administration and training of cadets.

The Canadian Rangers consists of officers and non-commissioned members who volunteer to hold themselves in readiness for service but are not required to undergo annual training. Their role is to provide a military force in sparsely settled, northern coastal and isolated areas of Canada.

Royal Canadian Mounted Police. The Royal Canadian Mounted Police is a civil force maintained by the federal government. It was established in 1873, as the North-West Mounted Police for service in what was then the North-West Territories and, in recognition of its services, was granted the use of the prefix 'Royal' by King Edward VII in 1904. Its sphere of operations was expanded in 1918 to include all of Canada west of Thunder Bay. In 1920 the force absorbed the Dominion Police, its headquarters was transferred from Regina to Ottawa, and its title was changed to Royal Canadian Mounted Police. The force is responsible to the Solicitor-General of Canada and is controlled and managed by a Commissioner who holds the rank and status of a Deputy Minister. The Commissioner is empowered under the Royal Canadian Mounted Police Act to appoint members to be peace officers in all provinces and territories of Canada.

The responsibilities of the Royal Canadian Mounted Police are national in scope. The administration of justice within the provinces, including the enforcement of the Criminal Code of Canada, is part of the power and duty delegated to the provincial governments.

All provinces except Ontario and Quebec have entered into contracts with the Royal Canadian Mounted Police to enforce criminal and provincial laws under the direction of the respective Attorneys-General. In addition, in these 8 provinces the Force is under agreement to provide police services to 191 municipalities, thereby assuming the enforcement responsibility of municipal as well as criminal and provincial laws within these communities. The Royal Canadian Mounted Police is also responsible for all police work in the Yukon and Northwest Territories enforcing federal law and territorial ordinances. The 15 Divisions, alphabetically designated, make up the strength of the Force across Canada; they comprise 52 sub-divisions which include 723 detachments. Headquarters Division, as well as the Office of the Commissioner, is located in Ottawa. The Force maintains liaison officers in 17 countries and represents Canada in the International Criminal Police Organization which has its headquarters in Paris.

Thorough training is emphasized for members of the Force. Recruits receive 6 months of basic training at the Royal Canadian Mounted Police Academy in Regina. This is followed by a further 6 months of supervised on-the-job training. The RCMP also operates the Canadian Police College at which its members and selected representatives of other Canadian and foreign police forces may study the latest advances in the fields of crime prevention and detection.

Many of these advances have been incorporated into the operation of the Force. A teletype system links the widespread divisional headquarters with the administrative centre at Ottawa and a network of fixed and mobile radio units operates within the provinces. The focal point of the criminal investigation work of the Force is the Directorate of Laboratories and Identification; its services, together with those of divisional and sub-divisional units, and of 8 Crime Detection Laboratories, are available to police forces throughout Canada. The Canadian Police Information Centre at RCMP Headquarters, a duplexed computer system, is staffed and operated by the Force. Law Enforcement agencies throughout Canada have access *via* a series of remote terminals of information on stolen vehicles, licences and wanted persons.

In Oct. 1989, the Force had a total strength of 20,398 including regular members, special constables, civilian members and public service employees. It maintained 6,984 motor vehicles, 87 police service dogs and 156 horses.

The Force has 13 divisions actively engaged in law enforcement, 1 Headquarters Division and 1 training division. Maritime services are divisional responsibilities and the Force currently has 394 boats at various points across Canada. The Air Directorate has stations throughout the country and maintains a fleet of 26 fixed-wing aircraft and 8 helicopters.

Eayrs, J., *In Defence of Canada: Growing up Allied.* Univ. of Toronto Press, 1980

INTERNATIONAL RELATIONS

Membership. Canada is a member of UN, the Commonwealth, OECD, NATO and Colombo Plan.

ECONOMY

Budget. Budgetary revenue and expenditure of the Government of Canada for years ended 31 March (in Canadian $1m.):

	1985–86	*1986–87*	*1987–88*	*1988–89*	*1989–90* [1]
Revenue	76,823	85,784	97,452	103,981	112,400
Expenditure	111,227	116,389	125,535	132,715	142,900

[1] Estimate.

Budgetary revenue, main items, 1988–89 (estimates in Canadian $1m.):

Unemployment contributions	11,268	Non-resident tax	1,578
Income tax, personal	46,026	Oil export charge	–
Income tax, corporation	11,730	Natural gas tax	1
Sales tax	15,645	Non-tax revenue Includes: on investment	7,343
Customs import duties	4,521		
Excise tax and gasoline and other non-tax revenue	2,174		

Details of budget estimates, 1988–89 (in Canadian $1m.):

Economic and regional development	13,341	External affairs and aid	3,557
Social development	59,091	Defence	11,025
Public debt charges	33,183	Services to government	4,149

On 31 March 1989 the net public debt was $320,918m.

Canadian Tax Foundation. *The National Finances: An Analysis of the Revenues and Expenditures of the Government of Canada.* Toronto. Annual

Currency. The denominations of money in the currency of Canada are dollars and cents. The cent is one-hundredth part of a dollar. Circulating coins are in denominations of 1, 5, 10, 25, 50 and 100 cents. The monetary standard is gold of 900 millesimal fineness (23·22 grains of pure gold equal to 1 gold dollar). The Currency Act provides for gold coins in the denominations of $5, $10 and $20, which are legal tender. The British and US gold coins are also legal tender, at the par rate of exchange. The legal equivalent of the British sovereign is $4.86⅔.

Since 1935 the Bank of Canada has the sole right to issue paper money for circulation in Canada. Restrictions introduced by the 1944 revisions of the Bank Act cancelled the right of chartered banks to issue or re-issue notes after 1 Jan. 1945; and in Jan. 1950 the chartered banks' liability for such of their notes as then remained outstanding was transferred to the Bank of Canada in return for payment of a like sum to the Bank of Canada. On 31 May 1970 the Canadian dollar which was stabilized at 92·50 US cents was allowed to fluctuate. The value of the US$ in Canadian funds was $1·19 and £1 sterling = Canadian $1·95 in March 1990.

The Bank of Canada bank notes in circulation are in denominations of $2, $5, $10, $20, $50, $100 and $1,000. On 25 March 1986, the Government of Canada announced the introduction of a circulating dollar coin with the eventual withdrawal of one dollar bank note in 1989.

The Ottawa Mint was established in 1908 as a branch of the Royal Mint, in pursuance of the Ottawa Mint Act, 1901. In Dec. 1931 control of the Mint was passed over to the Canadian Government, and since that time it has operated as the Royal Canadian Mint. The Mint issues nickel, bronze and cupronickel coins for circulation in Canada. In 1967, in celebration of Canada's Centennial of Confederation, a $20 gold piece was minted, the first gold coin struck since 1919. In 1935, on the occasion of His Majesty's Silver Jubilee, the Royal Canadian Mint issued the first Canadian silver dollar. Commemorative dollars were also issued in 1939 on the occasion of the visit of King George VI and Queen Elizabeth to Canada; in 1949, when Newfoundland became the tenth Province of Canada; in 1958, the one-hundredth anniversary of the establishment of the Colony of British Columbia; in 1964, the centennial of the Charlottetown and Quebec Conferences which paved the way to confederation. The silver dollar bearing the design of the canoe manned by an Indian and a Voyageur has been issued in the years 1935–38, 1945–48, 1950–57, 1959–63, 1965 and 1966. In 1968, the coin bore the same design but its composition changed from silver to nickel. This composition remained for all the following years. The design was used again in 1969, 1972, 1975–87. For centennial year the

Canada goose replaced the usual canoe design on the silver dollar. Because of a world-wide shortage of silver, the Government, in Aug. 1967, authorized the Mint to change the metal content of the 25-cent and 10-cent coins. Commencing in Sept. 1968, 10-cent, 25-cent, 50-cent and $1 coins were minted in pure nickel. Gold refining is one of the principal activities of the Mint. On average the Mint refines about 70% of Canada's total gold production. In 1987 the Mint processed over 3·8m. gross troy oz. of gold. Of this total, 2,862,489 troy oz. of rough bullion were received from Canadian gold mines for treatment, containing 2,282,724 troy oz. of fine gold and 400,260 troy oz. of fine silver. Coins issued (1987): Gold bullion 2,468,495 pieces.

Banking. Commercial banks in Canada are known as chartered banks and are incorporated under the terms of the Bank Act, which imposes strict conditions as to capital, returns to the Federal government, types of lending operations and other matters. In Aug. 1989 there were 66 chartered banks (8 domestic banks and 58 foreign bank subsidiaries) incorporated under the provisions of the Bank Act; the 8 had 6,829 branches serving 1,700 communities in all provinces in Canada and 233 branches in other countries. The foreign bank subsidiaries operate 295 offices in Canada including 57 head offices. The Bank Act is subject to revision by Parliament every 10 years. Bank charters expire every 10 years and are renewed at each decennial revision of the Bank Act. The chartered banks make detailed monthly and yearly returns to the Minister of Finance and are subject to periodic inspection by the Superintendent of Financial Institutions, an official appointed by the Government.

The Bank of Canada Act, effective from 3 July 1934, provided for the establishment of a central bank for the Dominion. This bank commenced operations on 11 March 1935 with a paid-up capital of $5m. By reason of certain changes introduced into the composition of stockholders of the bank (for which *see* THE STATESMAN'S YEAR-BOOK, 1944 pp. 322–23), the Minister of Finance on behalf of Canada is the sole registered owner of the capital stock of the bank. The revised Bank Act, which came into force on 1 Dec. 1980, requires chartered banks to maintain a statutory primary reserve of 10% on demand deposits, 3% on foreign-currency deposits and 2% on notice deposits, with an additional 1% on the portion of notice deposits exceeding $500m. This reserve is required to be maintained in the form of notes and deposits with the Bank of Canada. A secondary reserve of 4% in the form of treasury bills, government bonds, etc., is also required. All gold held in Canada by the chartered banks was transferred to the Bank of Canada along with the gold held by the Government as reserve against Dominion notes outstanding at the time of the commencement of operations of the Bank of Canada. The liability of the Dominion notes outstanding at the commencement of business of the Bank of Canada was assumed by the bank.

Weights and Measures. The legal weights and measures are in transition from the Imperial to the International system of units. The Metric Commission, established in June 1971, co-ordinates Canada's conversion to the metric system.

ENERGY AND NATURAL RESOURCES

Electricity. Electricity generation in 1988 was 490,672,000 mwh., of which 423,540,000 was used to meet domestic demand. Of the total, 62·1% was from hydro generation, 22% from thermal generation and 15·9% nuclear. Supply 115 volts; 60 Hz.

Oil and Natural Gas. Production of marketable crude oil, 1988, 92m. cu. metres; crude oil and equivalent exports, 41m. cu. metres; crude oil imports, 26m. cu. metres. Production of marketable natural gas, 1988, 88,000m. cu. metres, and natural gas by-products 22m. cu. metres; natural gas exports, 36,000m. cu. metres.

Minerals. Alberta and Ontario accounted for 59·5% of the value of all mineral products produced in 1988. Total value of minerals produced in 1988 (preliminary) was $37,081m. Principal minerals produced in 1988 (preliminary) were as follows:

	Quantity (1,000)	Value ($1,000)
Metallics		
Copper (kg)	721,588	2,317,018
Nickel (kg)	213,871	3,255,974
Zinc (kg)	1,253,580	2,064,647
Iron ore (tonnes)	38,742	1,388,129
Gold (grammes)	127,843	2,215,128
Lead (kg)	333,707	333,707
Silver (kg)	1,527	378,136
Molybdenum (kg)	12,388	107,737
Others	...	1,729,561
Total metallics	...	13,790,037
Non-metallics		
Asbestos (tonnes)	705	268,357
Potash (K_2O) (tonnes)	8,070	1,058,716
Salt (tonnes)	10,975	257,518
Sulphur, elemental (tonnes)	5,915	460,800
Gypsum (tonnes)	8,522	87,674
Others	...	545,015
Total non-metallics	...	2,678,080
Fuels		
Crude petroleum (cu. metres)	92,856	9,349,519
Natural gas (1,000 cu. metres)	87,893	4,973,307
Natural gas by-products (cu. metres)	22,332	1,609,518
Coal (tonnes)	69,500	1,907,800
Total fuels	...	17,840,144
Structural materials		
Cement (tonnes)	12,611	1,012,625
Sand and gravel (tonnes)	276,064	782,675
Stone (tonnes)	112,422	601,312
Clay products (bricks, tiles, etc.)	...	185,273
Lime (tonnes)	2,535	189,946
Total structural materials	...	2,771,831

Value (in Canadian $1,000) of mineral production by provinces:

Provinces	*1987*	*1988* [1]	*Provinces*	*1987*	*1988* [1]
Newfoundland	742,818	888,476	Saskatchewan	3,150,831	3,045,501
Pr. Ed. Island	2,541	2,625	Alberta	17,079,970	14,906,395
Nova Scotia	406,639	461,063	British Columbia	3,613,963	3,992,149
New Brunswick	622,231	831,055	Yukon Territory	437,199	465,530
Quebec	2,780,759	2,716,152	N.W. Territories	869,264	936,286
Ontario	5,636,085	7,154,383			
Manitoba	1,000,046	1,680,477	Total	36,342,345	37,080,092

[1] Preliminary.

Agriculture. According to the census of 1986 the total land area is 2,278·6m. acres of which 167·6m. acres are agricultural land.

Grain growing, dairy farming, fruit farming, ranching and fur farming are all carried on successfully. Total farm cash receipts (1988) $22,061·4m.

The following table shows the value of farm cash receipts for 1988, for selected agricultural commodities, in Canadian $1,000:

Wheat	2,566,156	Tobacco	212,933
Oats and barley	629,573	Cattle and calves	3,928,624
Canola	1,019,513	Hogs	1,778,378
Potatoes	340,452	Sheep and lambs	30,676
Vegetables	630,639	Dairy products	3,059,883
Fruit	346,154	Poultry and eggs	1,560,201

Number of occupied farms (census of 1986) was 293,089; average farm size, 571·8 acres.

Field Crops. The estimated acreage and yield of the principal field crops, by provinces, 1988 were:

	Wheat		*Tame hay*		*Oats*	
Provinces	*1,000 acres*	*1,000 bu.*	*1,000 acres*	*1,000 bu.*	*1,000 acres*	*1,000 bu.*
Newfoundland	—	—	11	24	—	—
Prince Edward Island	15	730	139	350	24	1,410
Nova Scotia	8	420	173	510	16	940
New Brunswick	10	510	174	420	30	1,700
Quebec	165	6,450	2,436	6,790	299	18,420
Ontario	770	40,900	2,560	7,300	300	14,000
Manitoba	4,820	88,200	1,600	1,900	400	14,500
Saskatchewan	19,200	252,000	2,050	1,900	800	31,000
Alberta	7,000	194,200	4,650	10,000	1,450	107,000
British Columbia	105	4,300	880	2,800	70	5,100
Total, Canada	32,093	587,710	14,673	31,994	3,389	194,070

	Barley		*Rye*		*Corn for Grain*	
Provinces	*1,000 acres*	*1,000 bu.*	*1,000 acres*	*1,000 bu.*	*1,000 acres*	*1,000 bu.*
Prince Edward Island	67	3,730	—	—	—	—
Nova Scotia	12	670	—	—	3	230
New Brunswick	29	1,630	—	—	—	—
Quebec	400	21,130	—	—	593	59,050
Ontario	490	23,000	55	1,600	1,740	147,000
Manitoba	1,400	50,000	120	2,300	80	4,100
Saskatchewan	3,050	96,000	290	3,500	—	—
Alberta	4,700	267,000	160	2,800	10	1,000
British Columbia	110	5,900	11	350	—	—
Total, Canada	10,258	469,060	636	10,550	2,426	211,380

	Canola		*Mixed grains*		*Soybeans*	
Provinces	*1,000 acres*	*1,000 bu.*	*1,000 acres*	*1,000 bu.*	*1,000 acres*	*1,000 bu.*
Prince Edward Island	—	—	57	3,380	—	—
Nova Scotia	—	—	—	—	—	—
New Brunswick	—	—	—	—	—	—
Quebec	—	—	69	3,674	37	1,051
Ontario	65	1,500	510	24,000	1,280	41,300
Manitoba	1,550	27,000	70	2,100	—	—
Saskatchewan	3,850	75,000	70	2,000	—	—
Alberta	3,500	84,000	175	10,000	—	—
British Columbia	110	2,600	4	220	—	—
Total, Canada	9,075	190,100	955	45,374	1,317	42,351

Livestock. In parts of Saskatchewan and Alberta stockraising is still carried on as a primary industry, but the livestock industry of the country at large is mainly a subsidiary of mixed farming. The following table shows the numbers of livestock (in 1,000) by provinces in July 1989:

Provinces	*Milch cows*	*Other cattle and calves*	*Sheep and lambs*	*Swine*
Newfoundland	4·2	3·9	7·4	16·5
Prince Edward Island	20·7	77·3	5·8	122·0
Nova Scotia	33·6	94·4	36·0	141·0
New Brunswick	26·5	76·5	9·0	103·0
Quebec	554·0	951·0	114·0	3,130·0
Ontario	465·0	1,795·0	212·0	3,115·0
Manitoba	66·0	999·0	23·0	1,230·0

Provinces	*Milch cows*	*Other cattle and calves*	*Sheep and lambs*	*Swine*
Saskatchewan	53·0	2,077·0	52·0	800·0
Alberta	123·0	4,067·0	212·0	1,750·0
British Columbia	75·0	633·0	57·0	227·0
Total	1,421·0	10,774·1	728·2	10,634·5

Net production of farm eggs in 1987, 475·5m. doz. ($492·6m.); 1988, 476·7m. doz. ($524·4m.).

Wool production (in tonnes), 1984, 1,306; 1985, 1,219; 1986, 1,143; 1987, 1,144; 1988, 1,094.

Dairying. In 1986 [1], the dairy products industry (which includes fluid milk industries and other dairy products industries) reported 393 for the number of establishments. The number of employees for the same period was 14,839. Production, 1988: Butter, 104,324 tonnes; cheddar cheese, 117,618 tonnes [2]; concentrated whole milk products, 68,920 tonnes; skim milk powder, 109,660 tonnes.

[1] The number of establishments/employees are based on the 1980 Standard Industrial Classification.

[2] Includes cheddar used to make processed cheese.

Fruit Farming. The value of fruit production (excluding apples) in 1988 was (in $1,000): Ontario, 79,124; British Columbia, 93,579; Quebec, 26,977; Nova Scotia, 19,594; New Brunswick, 7,407; Prince Edward Island, 1,999; Newfoundland, 1,906. Total apple production in Canada in 1988 was 486,229 tonnes, value $124,258,000.

Tobacco. Commercial production of tobacco is confined to Ontario, Quebec and the eastern provinces. Farm cash receipts for 1988 totalled $212·9m.

Forestry. As of 1986, the total area of land covered by forests is estimated at about 453·3m. hectares, of which 260·1m. hectares are classed as productive forest land.

Lumber production (in cu. metres) in 1986 was 53,059,380.

Lumber shipments from sawmills and planing mills in 1986 was valued at $6,019m. Pulp production was 20·3m. tonnes in 1986 and 20·2m. tonnes in 1985.

Fur Trade. In 1987–88, 4,640,276 pelts valued at $123,449,379, were taken. In wild-life pelt production marten led in total value. The most important animal raised on fur farms is mink. The value of mink pelts from fur farms in 1987-88 was $49,748,431. There were, in 1987–88, 1,040 fur farms reporting fox and 488 mink.

Fisheries. During 1987, landings in Canadian commercial fisheries reached 1,567,566 tonnes. The landed value was $1,647·7m. and the estimated market value was $3,351·1m. The landed value of principal fish in 1987 was (in $1,000): Salmon, 218,451; cod, 332,153; lobster, 283,045; herring, 141,433; scallops, 95,044; freshwater fish, 88,500; halibut, 39,584. Exports of fisheries' products, 1987, were valued at $2,772m.

Canadian Mines Handbook. Annual. Toronto, from 1931
Canadian Fisheries, Highlights 1987. Dept. of Fisheries and Oceans, 1988

INDUSTRY AND TRADE

Industry. Industry groups ranked by value of shipments, survey of 1986 (based on 1980 Standard Industrial Classification):

Industry	*Production workers*	*Wages ($1,000)*	*Cost of materials ($1,000)*	*Value of shipments ($1,000)*
Food industries	137,261	2,939,976	22,968,140	34,143,605
Beverage industries	17,200	516,127	2,144,602	5,045,073
Tobacco products	4,069	138,082	854,707	1,623,215
Rubber products	18,589	497,174	1,257,440	2,643,613
Plastic products	33,527	639,069	2,353,279	4,384,722
Leather and allied industries	20,192	302,557	660,889	1,324,840
Primary textile industries	20,011	421,166	1,514,506	2,957,500

Industry	Production workers	Wages ($1,000)	Cost of materials ($1,000)	Value of shipments ($1,000)
Textile products	27,011	459,052	1,616,227	2,892,955
Clothing industries	102,032	1,419,854	3,020,998	6,015,636
Wood industries	94,888	2,295,282	6,658,611	12,432,604
Furniture and fixtures	48,393	888,608	1,933,909	4,011,972
Paper and allied industries	88,880	2,892,539	9,357,461	20,066,737
Printing, publishing and allied industries	77,725	1,969,558	3,849,150	10,370,848
Primary metal industries	78,149	2,633,458	8,722,055	17,108,965
Metal fabricating industries	121,520	2,809,825	7,655,455	15,024,300
Machinery industries	57,510	1,399,526	4,080,054	8,098,978
Transport equipment industries	165,383	4,936,210	30,139,909	44,399,837
Electrical and electronic products	88,899	2,129,961	7,215,734	14,304,033
Non-metallic mineral products	42,011	1,121,461	2,630,675	6,632,011
Refined petroleum and coal prods.	6,359	265,156	12,798,291	15,756,364
Chemical and chemical prods.	47,288	1,356,794	9,109,639	18,639,240
Other manufacturing	54,666	1,050,258	2,794,417	5,533,506
All industries	1,351,563	33,081,693	143,336,148	253,410,556

Labour. In 1988 (annual average) the industrial distribution of the employed was estimated as follows (in 1,000): Community, business and personal services, 4,062; manufacturing, 2,104; trade, 2,168; transport, communication and other utilities, 904; construction, 726; public administration, 815; finance, insurance and real estate, 728; agriculture, 444; non-agriculture, 11,801; other primary industries, 294; total employed, 12,245; unemployed, 1,030. Union returns filed for 1987 in compliance with the Corporations and Returns Act (1962), show 459 labour organizations reporting on 15,173 local union branches in Canada. Union membership in 1987 was 3·67m. 51·8% of the membership in Canada belonged to national unions, with 58·6% of the Canadian membership affiliated with the Canadian Labour Congress. The membership share of international unions was 33·8%.

It is generally established by legislation, both federal and provincial, that a trade union to which the majority of employees in a unit suitable for collective bargaining belong, is given certain rights and duties. An employer is required to meet and negotiate with such a trade union to determine wage-rates and other working conditions of his employees. The employer, the trade union and the employees affected are bound by the resulting agreement. If an impasse is reached in negotiation conciliation services provided by the appropriate government board are available. Generally, work stoppages do not take place until an established conciliation or mediation procedure has been carried out and are prohibited while an agreement is in effect.

Freedom of association is a civil right in Canada, and under common law workers are at liberty to join unions and participate in their activities. This right has also been guaranteed by statutes which make it an offence to interfere with freedom of association.

Certain specific minimum standards in regard to working conditions are set by law, for the most part by provincial labour legislation. Minimum wages, maximum hours of work or an overtime rate of pay after a specified number of hours, minimum weekly rest periods, annual vacations with pay, statutory holidays, maternity protection and parental leave and notice of termination of employment are established for the majority of workers.

Dept. of Labour, *Working Conditions in Canadian Industry*. Annual, Ottawa

Commerce. Canada is one of the signatories of the General Agreement on Tariffs and Trade (GATT) and an active participant in the subsequent GATT negotiations. On 1 Jan. 1989, the Canada-US Free Trade Agreement came into effect. The Agreement, which provides for the phased removal of tariffs and other barriers, is consistent with Canada's obligation to its trading partners.

Imports and domestic exports (in Canadian $1,000) for calendar years:

	Imports	Exports
1960	5,842,695	5,255,575
1970	13,951,903	16,820,098
1980	69,273,844	74,445,976
1985	104,355,196	116,145,111
1986	112,511,445	116,733,385
1987	116,238,614	121,462,342
1988	131,554,000	137,695,000

Exports (domestic) by countries in 1988 (in Canadian $1m.):

Australia	893
Bahamas	39
Bahrain	4
Bangladesh	128
Barbados	43
Belize	7
Bermuda	41
Britain (UK)	3,545
Cyprus	5
Fiji	2
Ghana	40
Guyana	5
Hong Kong	1,003
India	396
Ireland	217
Jamaica	130
Kenya	7
Malaŵi	1
Malaysia	196
Malta	1
New Zealand	142
Nigeria	22
Pakistan	88
Qatar	5
Singapore	294
South Africa, Republic of [1]	135
Sri Lanka	26
Tanzania	25
Trinidad and Tobago	58
Uganda	1
Zambia	20
Albania	1
Algeria	287
Angola	3
Argentina	62
Austria	108
Belgium	1,162
Benin	1
Bolivia	5
Brazil	517
Cameroon Republic	17
Chile	141
China	2,599
Colombia	249
Costa Rica	29
Côte d'Ivoire	14
Cuba	226
Czechoslovakia	11
Denmark	136
Dominican Republic	60
Ecuador	44
Egypt (UAR)	73
El Salvador	23
Ethiopia	40
Finland	176
France	1,214
French Africa	10
French West Indies	7
Gabon	5
German Democratic Rep.	61
Germany, Fed. Rep. of	1,791
Greece	60
Greenland	9
Guatemala	18
Guinea	9
Haiti, Republic of	18
Honduras	19
Hungary	6
Iceland	12
Indonesia	299
Iran	142
Iraq	191
Israel	136
Italy	1,028
Japan	8,720
Jordan	13
Korea, North	5
Korea, South	1,216
Kuwait	32
Lebanon	14
Liberia	8
Libya	56
Luxembourg	7
Mauritania	2
Mexico	496
Morocco	278
Mozambique	20
Netherlands	1,433
Netherlands Antilles	17
Nicaragua	23
Norway	489
Panama	37
Paraguay	2
Peru	64
Philippines	133
Poland	22
Portugal	168
Puerto Rico	250
Romania	56
St Pierre and Miquelon	26
Saudi Arabia	207
Senegal	14
Spain	244
Sudan	15
Suriname	2
Sweden	325
Switzerland	707
Syria	4
Taiwan	995
Thailand	265
Togo	6
Tunisia	74
Turkey	181
USSR	1,152
United Arab Emirates	25

Exports *(continued)*

USA	100,614	Vietnam	4
US Oceania	8	Yemen (South)	5
US Virgin Islands	6	Yugoslavia	47
Uruguay	11	Zaïre	32
Venezuela	392	Zimbabwe	2

Imports by countries in 1988 (in Canadian $1m.):

Australia	662	France	2,857
Bahamas	20	French Africa	25
Bahrain	7	French Oceania	3
Bangladesh	30	Gabon	1
Barbados	6	German Democratic Rep.	54
Belize	13	Germany, Fed. Rep. of	3,836
Britain (UK)	4,631	Greece	68
Cyprus	1	Guatemala	38
Fiji	12	Guinea	15
Ghana	7	Haiti, Republic of	7
Guyana	15	Honduras	27
Hong Kong	1,154	Hungary	51
India	205	Iceland	13
Ireland	213	Indonesia	179
Jamaica	150	Iran	70
Kenya	16	Iraq	8
Leeward and Windward Islands	4	Israel	124
Malaŵi	2	Italy	1,948
Malaysia	323	Japan	9,253
Malta	66	Korea, South	2,271
Mauritius	23	Kuwait	2
New Zealand	224	Lebanon	6
Nigeria	310	Liberia	4
Pakistan	78	Libya	5
Sierra Leone	11	Luxembourg	21
Singapore	466	Madagascar	1
South Africa, Republic of [1]	156	Mexico	1,319
Sri Lanka	33	Morocco	46
Tanzania	2	Mozambique	2
Trinidad and Tobago	56	Netherlands	774
Uganda	6	Netherlands Antilles	20
		Nicaragua	64
Algeria	17	Norway	494
Angola	82	Panama	30
Argentina	123	Peru	85
Austria	282	Philippines	178
Belgium	588	Poland	83
Bolivia	22	Portugal	119
Brazil	1,180	Puerto Rico	246
Burma	2	Romania	70
Cameroon Republic	19	St Pierre and Miquelon	1
Chile	160	Saudi Arabia	95
China	955	Spain	708
Colombia	138	Sweden	932
Costa Rica	50	Switzerland	701
Côte d'Ivoire	31	Taiwan	2,258
Cuba	87	Thailand	343
Czechoslovakia	78	Togo	41
Denmark	259	Tunisia	3
Dominican Republic	36	Turkey	72
Ecuador	85	USSR	156
Egypt (UAR)	25	United Arab Emirates	46
El Salvador	41	USA	86,449
Ethiopia	6	US Virgin Islands	8
Finland	342	Uruguay	11

Imports *(continued)*

Venezuela	463	Zaïre	8
Vietnam	10	Zimbabwe	14
Yugoslavia	107		

[1] The Customs Union of Southern Africa for 1988 includes trade with Botswana, Lesotho, Swaziland, Namibia and the Republic of South Africa.

Categories of imports in 1988, estimate (in Canadian $1,000):

Live animals	118,201	Fabricated materials, inedible	24,687,152
Food, feed, beverages and tobacco	7,019,233	End products, inedible	89,114,083
Crude materials, inedible	7,425,729	Special transactions	2,717,415

Categories of exports (Canadian produce) in 1988, estimate (in Canadian $1,000):

Live animals	618,887	Fabricated materials, inedible	47,712,726
Food, feed, beverages and tobacco	11,110,421	End products, inedible	57,046,295
Crude materials, inedible	17,061,991	Special transactions	646,804

Total trade of Canada with UK (British Department of Trade returns, in £1,000 sterling):

	1985	*1986*	*1987*	*1988*	*1989*
Imports to UK	1,652,974	1,470,434	1,470,434	2,038,245	2,174,334
Exports and re-exports from UK	1,693,557	1,698,156	1,938,237	2,038,433	2,165,731

Tourism. The number of visitors to Canada in 1988 was 39,252,915 (1987, 39,595,250). In 1988, 36,147,055 came from USA (1987, 36,952,614).

COMMUNICATIONS

Roads. The total length of federal and provincial territorial roads and highways in Canada at the end of March 1986 was 280,251 km. Expenditures by these two levels of government on roads and highways during the fiscal year 1985–86 amounted to approximately $5,347·7m.

Federal expenditures were directed largely to the maintenance of national park highways, Indian Reserve roads and designated provincial/territorial highway construction in projects. In general highways are controlled and maintained by the provinces who also have the responsiblity of providing assistance to their municipalities and townships.

The Alaska Highway is part of the Canadian highway system. For the Trans-Canada Highway *see* map in THE STATESMAN'S YEAR-BOOK, 1962.

Registered motor vehicles totalled 15,794,050 in 1987; they included 11,686,439 passenger cars and taxis, 3,576,158 trucks and buses and 414,322 motor cycles.

Urban Transit. There are metros in Montreal, Toronto and Vancouver, and tram/light rail systems in Calgary, Edmonton and Toronto. In 1987 urban transit systems (urban and suburban passenger transport, electrical railway, trolley coach, bus or subway) carried 1,469,281,000 fare passengers 695,785,440 km for an operating revenue of $2,443,674,000. In 1987, intercity and rural bus operations carried 24,955,000 fare passengers 170,953,100 km, earning revenues of $346,873,000.

Railways. The total length of track operated during 1987 in Canada was 93,544 km. Mainline track, 38,589 km; branch line, 29,831 km; industrial and siding track, 25,124 km.

Canada has 2 great trans-continental systems: The Canadian National Railway system (CN), a government-owned body which operates 51,364 km (1987) of track, and the Canadian Pacific Railway, a joint-stock corporation operating 33,369 km (1987). From 1 April 1978, a government funded organization known as Via Rail took over passenger services formerly operated by CP and CN; 5·9m. passengers were carried in 1987.

Selected statistics of Canadian railways for 1987: Passenger revenue $245m.; freight revenue, $6,562m.; total railway operating revenues, $7,899·3m.; total operating expenses, $6,838·3m.

Aviation. Civil aviation in Canada is under the jurisdiction of the federal government. The technical and administrative aspects are supervised by Transport Canada, while the economic functions are assigned to the National Transportation agency.

In 1988 Canadian airports handled 48,258,628 revenue passengers on major scheduled services and 620,379 tonnes of cargo. Operating revenue for levels 1 through 4 Canadian commercial air carriers (1988) was $6,922·6m.; operating expenditure, $6,680·4m.

Shipping. Total vessel arrivals and departures at Canadian ports in domestic shipping was 60,474 in 1988, totalling a cumulative GRT of 282,335,037. A total of 60,902 vessel movements in international shipping at Canadian ports in 1988 loaded and unloaded 246m. tonnes of cargo.

The major canals in Canada are those of the St Lawrence–Great Lakes waterway with their 7 locks, providing navigation for vessels of 26-ft draught from Montreal to Lake Ontario; the Welland Canal by-passing the Niagara River between Lake Ontario and Lake Erie with its 8 locks; and the Sault Ste Marie Canal and lock between Lake Huron and Lake Superior. These 16 locks overcome a drop of 582 ft from the head of the lakes to Montreal. The St Lawrence Seaway was opened to navigation on 1 April 1959 (*see* map in THE STATESMAN'S YEAR-BOOK, 1957). In 1988, traffic on the Montreal–Lake Ontario Section of the Seaway numbered 3,142 transits carrying 40·5m. cargo tonnes; on the Welland Canal Section, 3,909 transits with 43·5m. cargo tonnes. Value of fixed assets was $544,711,000 and investments, $41,450,000 at 31 March 1989.

Coast Guard. The Canadian Coast Guard (formed in 1962) is responsible to the Minister of Transport. In 1988 it comprised 7 heavy icebreakers; 12 medium icebreakers; 1 light icebreaker/nav. aid tender; 7 ice strengthened/nav. aid tenders; 1 hydraulic survey and founding vessel; 76 search and rescue vessels (all types and sizes); 4 hovercraft; 35 helicopters and 1 fixed-wing aircraft (DC-3).

Post. In 1988–89 there were 14,972 retail postal outlets in operation and 8,268m. pieces of mail were processed. Total revenue (1988–89) was $3,508m.; total expenditure, $3,354m. (excluding amortization of extraordinary restructuring costs).

There were 13·9m. (estimate) telephone access lines reported by major telephone companies in 1988.

Broadcasting. There were 823 originating stations operating in Canada at 31 March 1989, of which 385 were AM radio stations, 303 FM radio stations and 135 television stations. Radio and television licence fees were abolished in 1953.

Cinemas (1986). There were 714 cinemas with a seating capacity of 501,422 and 183 drive-in theatres with a capacity of 101,268 cars.

Newspapers (1987). There were 119 daily newspapers, of which 102 were in English, 12 in French and 5 others.

JUSTICE, RELIGION, EDUCATION AND WELFARE

Justice. There is a Supreme Court in Ottawa, having general appellate jurisdiction in civil and criminal cases throughout Canada. There is an Exchequer Court, which is also a Court of Admiralty. There is a Superior Court in each province and county courts, with limited jurisdiction, in most of the provinces, all the judges in these courts being appointed by the Governor-General. Police, magistrates and justices of the peace are appointed by the provincial governments.

For the year ended 31 Dec. 1988, 2,392,419 Criminal Code Offences were reported and 419,258 adults were charged.

Canadian Legal and Directory. Toronto. Annual

Religion. Membership of the leading denominations in 1981:

Province	*Roman Catholic*	*United Church of Canada*	*Anglican Church of Canada*	*Presbyterian*	*Lutheran*
Newfoundland	204,430	104,835	153,530	2,700	460
Prince Edward Island	56,415	29,645	6,850	12,620	210
Nova Scotia	310,140	169,605	131,130	38,285	12,315
New Brunswick	371,100	87,460	66,260	12,070	1,810
Quebec	5,609,685	126,275	132,115	34,625	17,655
Ontario	2,986,175	1,655,550	1,164,315	517,020	254,175
Manitoba	269,070	240,395	108,220	23,910	58,830
Saskatchewan	279,840	263,375	77,725	16,065	88,785
Alberta	573,495	525,480	202,265	63,890	144,675
British Columbia	526,355	548,360	374,055	89,810	122,395
Yukon	5,470	3,310	4,665	615	915
Northwest Territories	18,215	3,725	15,295	505	665
Total, Canada	11,210,385	3,758,015	2,436,375	812,110	702,905

Other denominations: Baptist, 696,850; Greek Orthodox, 314,870; Jewish, 296,425; Ukrainian (Greek) Catholic, 190,585; Pentecostal, 338,790; Mennonite, 189,370; other, 3,136,815.

Education. Under the Constitution the various provincial legislatures have power over education. These powers are subject to certain qualifications respecting the rights of denominational and minority language schools. Newfoundland and Quebec legislations provide for Roman Catholic and Protestant school boards. School Acts in Ontario, Saskatchewan and Alberta provide tax support for both public and separate schools. School board revenues derive from local taxation on real property and government grants from general provincial revenue.

Enrolment for Indian and Inuit children, 1988-89: Federal schools, 13,783; band operated schools, 30,845; provincial schools, 40,954.

In 1988–89, 499,359 full-time regular students (graduates and undergraduates) were enrolled in universities. Approximately 103,775 received bachelor's or first professional degrees of which 16,196 were in education; 12,328 in humanities; 7,992 in engineering and applied sciences; 3,559 in fine and applied arts; 39,163 in social sciences; 7,210 in agriculture/biological sciences; 7,423 in health professions; 7,229 in mathematics/physical sciences; and 2,675 were unclassified.

The following statistics give information, for 1988–89 (estimates), about all elementary and secondary schools, public, federal and private:

Province	*Schools*	*Teachers*	*Pupils*
Newfoundland	567	7,780	132,910
Prince Edward Island	72	1,310	24,740
Nova Scotia	570	10,070	170,700
New Brunswick	478	7,565	138,400
Quebec	2,860	64,260	1,134,400
Ontario	5,560	103,180	1,917,800
Manitoba	838	12,570	219,400
Saskatchewan	1,022	11,480	216,100
Alberta	1,737	25,230	481,700
British Columbia	1,919	26,880	535,400
Yukon	25	300	5,000
Northwest Territories	73	710	13,400
National Defence (overseas)	9	255	3,650
Total	15,730	271,690	4,993,600

Health. Constitutional responsibility of health care services rests with the ten provinces and two territories of Canada. Accordingly, Canada's national health insurance system consists of an interlocking set of provincial and territorial hospital and medical insurance plans conforming to certain national standards rather than a single national programme. These national standards, which are set out in the

Canada Health Act, include: Provision of a comprehensive range of hospital and medical benefits; universal population coverage; access to necessary services on uniform terms and conditions; portability of benefits; and public administration of provincial and territorial insurance plans.

Provinces and territories satisfying these national standards are eligible for federal financial assistance according to the provisions of the Federal-Provincial Fiscal Arrangements and Federal Post-Secondary Education and Health Contributions Act. Under this Act, the provinces and territories are entitled to receive equal-per-capita federal health contributions escalated annually by the three year average increase in nominal Gross National Product. These federal contributions, estimated at $12,000m. in 1989, are paid in the form of a combination of tax point and cash transfers. Over and above these health transfers, the federal government also provides financial support for such provincial and territorial extended health care service programmes as nursing home care, certain home care services, ambulatory health care services and adult residential care services. These supplementary equal-per-capita cash payments, estimated at $1,300m. in 1989, are also escalated annually by increases to nominal GNP.

The national health insurance programmes were introduced in stages. The Hospital Insurance and Diagnostic Services Act was passed in 1958, providing prepaid coverage to all Canadians for in-patient and, at the option of each province and territory, out-patient hospital services. The Medical Care Act was introduced in 1968 to extend universal coverage to all medically equipped services provided by medical practitioners. The Canada Health Act, which took effect 1 April 1984, consolidated the original federal health insurance legislation and clarified the national standards provinces and territories are required to meet in order to qualify for full federal health contributions.

The approach taken by Canada is one of state-sponsored health insurance. Accordingly, the advent of insurance programmes produced little change in the ownership of hospitals, almost all of which are owned by non-government non-profit corporations, or in the rights and privileges of private medical practice. Patients are free to choose their own general practitioner. Except for 0·5% of the population whose care is provided for under other legislation (such as serving members of the Canadian Armed Forces and inmates of federal penitentiaries), all residents are eligible, regardless of whether they are in the work force. Benefits are available without upper limit so long as they are medically necessary, provided any registration obligations are met. Benefits are also portable during any temporary absence from Canada anywhere in the world—subject to any limitation a province or territory may impose upon treatment electively sought outside the particular province or territory without prior approval.

In addition to the benefits qualifying for federal contributions, provinces and territories provide additional benefits at their own discretion. All provinces and territories provide benefits covering a variety of services (*e.g.*, optometric care, children's dental care, drug benefits). Most fund their portion of health costs out of general provincial and territorial revenues. Two provinces levy health premiums which meet part of the provincial and territorial costs, 2 provinces impose a levy on employers, and 2 provinces utilize a tax or surcharge, based on personal income tax, for this purpose, and 1 province utilizes a payroll tax paid by employers. There are no co-charges for medically necessary short-term hospital care or medical care. Most provinces and territories have charges for long-term chronic hospital care geared, approximately, to the room and board portion of this OAS–GIS payment mentioned under Social Welfare. In 1988, total health expenditures were about $50·40m., representing 8·7% of GNP. Public sector spending accounts for about 75% of total national health expenditure.

Social Welfare. The social security system provides financial benefits and social services to individuals and their families through a variety of programmes administered by federal, provincial and municipal governments, and voluntary organizations. Federally, the Department of Health and Welfare Canada is responsible for research into the areas of health and social issues, provision of grants and contributions for various social services, improvement and construction of health facilities, the administration of several of Canada's income security programmes and the development and promotion of measures designed to improve the health and well-being of Canadians. These programmes are: The Family Allowances programme, introduced in 1945 and amended in 1973; the Old Age Security programme, introduced in 1952 and to which were added the Guaranteed Income Supplement in 1967 and the Spouse's Allowance in 1975; and the Canada Pension Plan and Canada Assistance Plan which came into being in 1966.

The 1973 Family Allowances Act provides for the payment of a monthly Family Allowance ($32.74 in 1989) in respect of a dependent child under the age of 18 who is a resident of Canada and is wholly or substantially maintained by a parent or guardian. At least one parent must be a Canadian citizen, or admitted to Canada as a permanent resident under the Immigration Act, or admitted to Canada for a period of not less than 1 year, if during that time his or her income is subject to Canadian income tax. Benefits are also paid under prescribed circumstances to Canadian citizens living abroad. Eligibility for Family Allowances (FA) is a precondition for receipt of the refundable Child Tax Credit discussed below. A Special Allowance ($48.84 monthly in 1989) is paid on behalf of a child under the age of 18 who is maintained by a welfare agency, a government department or an institution. In some cases, payment is made directly to a foster parent.

The Family Allowances Act specifies that a provincial government may request the federal government to vary the allowance rates payable within the province by age and/or family size subject to the fulfillment of stipulated conditions. Only the provinces of Alberta and Quebec have exercised this option. During the month of July 1989, close to 3·7m. Canadian families (including 6·6m. eligible children) received Family Allowances; the Special Allowance was paid on behalf of 31,000 of these children. The total bill for FA and Special Allowances for 1988–89 was $2,606m.

The Old Age Security (OAS) pension is payable to persons 65 years of age and over who satisfy the residence requirements stipulated in the Old Age Security Act. The amount payable, whether full or partial, is also governed by stipulated conditions, as is the payment of an OAS pension to a recipient who absents himself from Canada. OAS pensioners with little or no income apart from OAS may, upon application, receive a full or partial supplement known as the Guaranteed Income Supplement (GIS). Entitlement is normally based on the pensioner's income in the preceding year, calculated in accordance with the Income Tax Act. The spouse of an OAS pensioner, aged 60 to 64, meeting the same residence requirements as those stipulated for OAS, may be eligible for a full or partial Spouse's Allowance (SPA). SPA is payable, on application, depending on the annual combined income of the couple (not including the pensioner spouse's basic OAS pension or GIS). In 1979, the SPA programme was expanded to include a spouse, who is eligible for SPA in the month the pensioner spouse dies, until the age of 65 or until remarriage (Extended Spouse's Allowance). Since Sept. 1985, SPA has also been available to low income widow(er)s aged 60–64 regardless of the age of their spouse at death. For the fourth quarter of 1989, the basic OAS pension was $337·04 monthly; the maximum Guaranteed Income Supplement was $400·53 monthly for a single pensioner or a married pensioner whose spouse was not receiving a pension or a Spouse's Allowance, and $260·88 monthly for each spouse of a married couple where both were pensioners. The maximum Spouse's Allowance for the same quarter was $597·92 monthly (equal to the basic pension plus the maximum GIS married rate), and $660·11 for widow(er)s. Total OAS/GIS/SPA benefit expenditures for 1988–89 were $14,975m.; in July 1989, over 3m. Canadians received benefits through these programmes.

The Canada Pension Plan (CPP) is designed to provide workers with a basic level of income protection in the event of retirement, disability or death. Benefits may be payable to a contributor, a surviving spouse or an eligible child. As of 1 Jan. 1987, payment of actuarially adjusted retirement benefits may begin as early as age 60 or as late as age 70. Benefits are determined by the contributor's earnings and contributions made to the Plan. Contribution is compulsory for most employed and self-employed Canadians 18 to 65 years of age. The Canada Pension Plan does not operate in Quebec, which has exercised its constitutional prerogative to establish a similar plan, the Quebec Pension Plan (QPP), to operate in lieu of CPP; there is reciprocity between the two to ensure coverage for all adult Canadians in the labour force. In 1989, the maximum retirement pension payable under CPP and QPP was $556.25, the maximum disability pension was $681.23, and the maximum surviving spouse's pension was $333.75 (for survivors 65 years of age and over). For survivors under 65 years of age CPP pays a reduced flat rate while QPP pays varied rates depending on the age of the survivor. In 1989 both CPP and QPP were funded by equal contributions of 2·1% of pensionable earnings from the employer and 2·1% from the employee (self-employed persons contribute the full 4·2%), in addition to the interest on the investment of excess funds. In 1989, the range of yearly pensionable earnings was from $2,700 to $27,700; a person who earned and contributed at less than the maximum level receives monthly benefits at rates lower than the maximum allowable under CPP/QPP. In July 1989, over 3·2m. Canadians received Canada or Quebec Pension Plan benefits. Total expenditures in 1988–89 for both plans were about $11,109m.

Social security programme agreements co-ordinate the operation of the Old Age Security programme and the Canada Pension Plan with the comparable programmes of another country in order to accomplish four basic objectives: To remove restrictions, based on nationality, which may otherwise prevent Canadians from receiving benefits under the legislation of the other country; to ease or eliminate restrictions on the payment of social security benefits abroad; to eliminate situations in which a worker may have to contribute to the social security programmes of both countries for the same work; to assist migrants in qualifying for benefits based on the periods they have lived or worked in each country. Such agreements are in force with Italy, France, Portugal, the USA, Greece, Jamaica, Barbados, Belgium, Denmark, Norway, Sweden, Austria, St Lucia, Spain, Australia, Dominica, the Federal Republic of Germany, Finland and Iceland. In addition, agreements have been signed with Luxembourg and the Netherlands.

Ismael, J. S., (ed.) *Canadian Welfare State: Evolution and Transition*. Univ. of Alberta Press, 1987

DIPLOMATIC REPRESENTATIVES

Of Canada in Great Britain (Macdonald House., Grosvenor Sq., London, W1X 0AB)
High Commissioner: The Hon. Donald S. Macdonald, PC (accredited 11 Nov. 1988).

Of Great Britain in Canada (80 Elgin St., Ottawa, K1P 5K7)
High Commissioner: Brian J. P. Fall, CMG.

Of Canada in the USA (501 Pennsylvania Ave., NW, Washington, D.C., 20001)
Ambassador: Derek H. Burney.

Of the USA in Canada (100 Wellington St., Ottawa, K1P 5TI)
Ambassador: Edward M. Ney.

Of Canada to the United Nations
Ambassador: Yves Fortier, QC.

Further Reading

Statistical Information: Statistics Canada, Ottawa, has been the official central statistical organization for Canada since 1918. The Agency, which reports to Parliament through the Minister responsible for the Department of Regional Industrial Expansion, serves as the statistical agency for federal government departments; co-ordinates the statistics of the provincial governments along national lines; and channels all Canadian statistical data to internal organizations. *Chief Statistician of Canada:* Dr I. P. Felligi.

Publications of Statistics Canada are classified as periodical (issued more frequently than once a year), annual, biennial and occasional publications. The occasional publications frequently supplement the annual reports and usually contain historical information. A complete list is contained in the Statistics Canada catalogue 1988–89, available at a nominal cost. Reference publications include:

The Canada Year Book. Biennial, from 1905
Canada: A Portrait. Biennial, from 1980
Canadian Economic Observer. Monthly, with annual historical supplements, from 1988
Twelfth Decennial Census of Canada, 1981. Ottawa, 1982
Atlas and Gazetteer of Canada. Dept. of Energy, Mines and Resources. Ottawa, 1969
Cambridge History of the British Empire. Vol. VI. Canada and Newfoundland. Cambridge, 1930
Canadian Almanac and Directory. Toronto. Annual
Canadian Annual Review. Annual, from 1960
Canadian Dictionary: French–English. Toronto, 1970
Canadian Encyclopedia. 3 vols. Edmonton, 1985
Canadiana; A List of Publications of Canadian Interest. National Library, Ottawa. Monthly, with annual cumulation. 1951 ff.
Cook, R., *French-Canadian Nationalism; An Anthology*. Toronto, 1970.—*The Maple Leaf Forever; Essays on Nationalism and Politics in Canada*. Toronto, 1971
Creighton, D. G., *Canada's First Century*. Toronto, 1970.—*Towards the Discovery of Canada*. Toronto, 1974
Dewitt, D. B. and Kirton, J. J., *Canada as a Principal Power: A Study in Foreign Policy*. Toronto, 1983
Dictionnaire Bélisle de la langue française au Canada; dictionnaire Oxford. 1970
Dictionnaire canadien; français–anglais–français. Toronto, 1962
Encyclopedia Canadiana. 10 vols. Rev. ed. Ottawa, 1967
Granatstein, J. L., *Twentieth Century Canada*. Toronto, 1983
Hardy, W. G., *From Sea to Sea; Canada, 1850–1920: The Road to Nationhood*. Toronto, 1960
Harris, R. C., (ed.) *Historical Atlas of Canada*. Vol 1. Univ. of Toronto, 1987
Hockin, T. A., *Government in Canada*. London, 1976
Ingles, E., *Canada*. [Bibliography] Oxford and Santa Barbara, 1989
Kerr, D. G. G., *Historical Atlas of Canada*. Toronto, 1960
Leacy, F. H., (ed.) *Historical Statistics of Canada*. Government Printer, Ottawa, 1983
Lower, A. R. M., *Colony to Nation: A History of Canada*. 4th ed. Toronto, 1964
McCann, L. D., (ed.) *Heartland and Hinterland: A Geography of Canada*. Scarborough, Ontario, 1982
Mallory, J. R., *The Structure of Canadian Government*. Toronto, 1971
Moir, J. and Saunders, R., *Northern Destiny: A History of Canada*. Toronto, 1970
Newman, P. C., *Company of Adventurers: The Story of the Hudson's Bay Company*. Vol. 1, London, 1986
Nurgitz, N. and Segal, H., *No Small Measure: The Progressive Conservatives and the Constitution*. Ottawa, 1983
Smith, D. L., (ed.) *History of Canada: An Annotated Bibliography*. Oxford and Santa Barbara, 1983

National Library: The National Library of Canada, Ottawa, Ontario. *Librarian:* Marianne Scott.

CANADIAN PROVINCES

The 10 provinces have each a separate parliament and administration, with a Lieut.-Governor, appointed by the Governor-General in Council at the head of the executive. They have full powers to regulate their own local affairs and dispose of their revenues, provided only they do not interfere with the action and policy of the central administration. Among the subjects assigned exclusively to the provincial legislatures are: The amendment of the provincial constitution, except as regards the office of the Lieut.-Governor; property and civil rights; direct taxation for revenue purposes; borrowing; management and sale of Crown lands; provincial hospitals, reformatories, etc.; shop, saloon, tavern, auctioneer and other licences for local or provincial purposes; local works and undertakings, except lines of ships, railways, canals, telegraphs, etc., extending beyond the province or connecting with other provinces, and excepting also such works as the Dominion Parliament declares are for the general good; marriages, administration of justice within the province; education.

Local Government. Under the terms of the British North America Act the provinces are given full powers over local government. All local government institutions are, therefore, supervised by the provinces, and are incorporated and function under provincial acts.

The acts under which municipalities operate vary from province to province. A municipal corporation is usually administered by an elected council headed by a mayor or reeve, whose powers to administer affairs and to raise funds by taxation and other methods are set forth in provincial laws, as is the scope of its obligations to, and on behalf of, the citizens. Similarly, the types of municipal corporations, their official designations and the requirements for their incorporation vary between provinces. The following table sets out the classifications as at 1 Jan. 1988.

Type and size of group	*Nfld.*	*PEI*	*NS*	*NB*	*Que.*	*Ont.*	*Man.*
Type:							
Regional municipalities	—	—	—	—	98	39	—
Metropolitan and regional municipalities [1]	—	—	—	—	3	12	—
Counties and regional districts	—	—	—	—	95	27	—
Unitary municipalities	170	86	66	114	1,500	792	184
Cities [2]	3	1	3	6	65	50	5
Towns	167	8	39	25	193	145	35
Villages	—	—	—	83	233	119	39
Rural municipalities [3]	—	77	24	—	1,009	478	105
Quasi-municipalities [4]	143	—	—	—	—	8	17
Total	313	86	66	114	1,598	839	201
Population size group (1986 census):							
Unitary municipalities—							
Over 100,000	—	—	2	—	4	18	1
50,000 to 99,999	1	—	1	2	16	14	—
10,000 to 49,999	4	1	18	4	80	81	4
Under 10,000	165	85	45	108	1,400	679	179
Total	170	86	66	114	1,500	792	184

Type and size of group	*Sask.*	*Alta.*	*BC*	*YT*	*NWT*	*Canada*
Type:						
Regional municipalities	—	—	28	—	—	165
Metropolitan and regional municipalities [1]	—	—	—	—	—	15
Counties and regional districts	—	—	28	—	—	150
Unitary municipalities	821	345	144	8	8	4,238
Cities [2]	12	15	37	2	1	200
Towns	146	108	12	2	5	885
Villages	364	172	48	4	2	1,064
Rural municipalities [3]:	299	50	47	—	—	2,089
Quasi-municipalities [4]	14	19	—	—	30	231
Total	835	364	172	8	38	4,634
Population size group (1986 census):						
Unitary municipalities—						
Over 100,000	2	2	4	—	—	33
50,000 to 99,999	—	—	10	—	—	44
10,000 to 49,999	7	18	29	1	1	248
Under 10,000	812	325	101	7	7	3,913
Total	821	345	144	8	8	4,238

[1] Includes urban communities in Quebec; and Metropolitan Toronto, regional municipalities and the district municipality of Muskoka in Ontario. [2] Includes the borough of East York. [3] Includes municipalities in Nova Scotia; parishes, townships, united townships and municipalities without designation in Quebec; townships in Ontario; rural municipalities in Manitoba and Saskatchewan; municipal districts and counties in Alberta; and districts in British Columbia. [4] Includes local government communities and the metropolitan area in Newfoundland; improvement districts in Ontario and Alberta; local government districts in Manitoba; and hamlets in the Northwest Territories.

ALBERTA

HISTORY. The southern half of the province of Alberta was part of Rupert's land which was granted by royal charter in 1670 to the Hudson's Bay Company. The intervention by the North West Company in the fur trade after 1783 led to the establishment of trading posts. In 1869 Rupert's land was transferred from the Hudson's Bay Company (which had absorbed its rival in 1821) to the new Dominion, and in the following year this land was combined with the former Crown land of the North Western Territories to form the Northwest Territories.

In 1882 'Alberta' first appeared as a provisional 'district', consisting of the southern half of the present province. In 1905 the Athabasca district to the north was added when provincial status was granted to Alberta.

Four parties have held office: The Liberals 1905–21; the United Farmers 1921–35; Social Credit 1935–71, and Progressive Conservative since Sept. 1971.

AREA AND POPULATION. The area of the province is 661,185 sq. km; 644,389 sq. km being land area and 16,796 sq. km water area. The population (estimate 1 July 1989) was 2,432,400; the urban population (1986), centres of 1,000 or over, was 1,877,758 and the rural 488,067. Population of the cities (30 June 1989): Calgary, 671,138; Edmonton, 583,872; Lethbridge, 60,614; Red Deer, 55,947; Medicine Hat, 42,290; St Albert, 39,388; Fort McMurray, 33,698; Grande Prairie, 27,208; Leduc, 13,363; Camrose, 12,968; Spruce Grove, 12,332; Fort Saskatchewan, 11,983; Airdrie, 11,424; Lloydminster (Alberta portion), 10,201; Wetaskiwin, 10,103; Drumheller, 6,366.

Vital statistics, *see* p. 272.
Religion, *see* p. 291.

CLIMATE. A continental climate: Long, cold winters and mild summers. Rainfall amounts are greatest between May and Sept. Edmonton. Jan. 5°F (–15°C), July 63°F (17°C). Annual rainfall 13·6" (345·6 mm).

CONSTITUTION AND GOVERNMENT. The constitution of Alberta is contained in the British North America Act of 1867, and amending Acts; also in the Alberta Act of 1905, passed by the Parliament of the Dominion of Canada, which created the province out of the then Northwest Territories. All the provisions of the British North America Act, except those with respect to school lands and the public domain, were made to apply to Alberta as they apply to the older provinces of Canada. On 1 Oct. 1930 the natural resources were transferred from the Dominion to provincial government control. The province is represented by 6 members in the Senate and 26 in the House of Commons of Canada.

The executive is vested nominally in the Lieut.-Governor, who is appointed by the federal government, but actually in the Executive Council or the Cabinet of the legislature. Legislative power is vested in the Assembly in the name of the Queen.

Members of the Legislative Assembly are elected by the universal vote of adults over the age of 18 years.

There are 83 members in the legislature (elected 20 March 1989): 59 Progressive Conservative, 16 New Democratic Party, 8 Liberal.

Lieut.-Governor: Hon. Helen Hunley (sworn in 22 Jan. 1985).
Flag: Blue with the shield of the province in the centre.
The members of the Ministry were as follows in Oct. 1989:

Premier, President of Executive Council: Hon. D. R. Getty.
Deputy Premier and Minister of Federal and Intergovernmental Affairs: Hon. J. Horsman. *Transportation and Utilities:* Hon. J. A. Adair. *Consumer and Corporate Affairs:* Hon. D. Anderson. *Health:* Hon. N. Betkowski. *Education:* Hon. J. Dinning. *Economic Development and Trade:* Hon. J. Elzinga. *Forestry, Lands and Wildlife:* Hon. E. L. Fjordbotten. *Solicitor General:* Hon. D. Fowler. *Advanced Education:* Hon. J. Gogo. *Agriculture:* Hon. E. Isley. *Provincial Treasurer:* Hon. A. D.

Johnston. *Environment:* Hon. R. Klein. *Public Works, Supply and Services:* Hon. K. Kowalski. *Culture and Multiculturalism:* Hon. D. Main. *Labour:* Hon. E. McCoy. *Family and Social Services:* Hon. J. Oldring. *Energy:* Hon. R. Orman. *Attorney-General:* Hon. K. Rostad. *Tourism:* Hon. D. Sparrow. *Municipal Affairs:* Hon. R. Speaker. *Technology, Research and Telecommunications:* Hon. F. Stewart. *Occupational Health and Safety:* Hon. P. Trynchy. *Career Development and Employment:* Hon. N. Weiss. *Recreation and Parks:* Hon. S. West.

Local Government. The local government units are City, Town, New Town, Village, Summer Village, County, Municipal District and Improvement District.

There are 16 cities in Alberta, namely: Airdrie, Calgary, Camrose, Drumheller, Edmonton, Fort McMurray, Fort Saskatchewan, Grande Prairie, Leduc, Lethbridge, Lloydminster, Medicine Hat, Red Deer, St Albert, Spruce Grove and Wetaskiwin. These cities operate under the Municipal Government Act. The governing body consists of a mayor and a council of from 6 to 20 members. A city can be incorporated by order of the Lieut.-Governor-in-Council. A population of 10,000 is required.

There are no limits of area specified in the statutes for any of the different local government units. The population requirement for a Town as specified in the Municipal Government Act is 1,000 people, and the area at incorporation is that of the original village.

A Village must contain 75 separate and occupied dwellings. The Municipal Government Act requires each dwelling to have been occupied continuously for a period of at least 6 months. A Summer Village must contain 50 separate dwellings.

A rural county area is an area incorporated through an order of the Lieut.-Governor-in-Council under the provisions of the County Act. One board of councillors deal with both municipal and school affairs.

A rural Municipal District is an area which has been incorporated under the Municipal Government Act. In Municipal Districts separate boards control municipal and school affairs.

Areas not incorporated as counties or Municipal Districts are termed Improvement Districts or Special Areas. Sparsely populated, such districts are administered and taxed by the Department of Municipal Affairs of the provincial government. There are no requirements as to the minimum number of residents of a County or Municipal District.

FINANCE. The budgetary revenue and expenditure (in Canadian $) for years ending 31 March were as follows:

	1986–87	*1987–88*	*1988–89* [1]	*1989–90* [1]
Revenue [2]	7,168,269,000	9,466,000,000	9,819,000,000	10,181,000,000
Expenditure [2]	10,608,678,000	10,399,000,000	10,490,000,000	11,674,000,000

[1] Estimates.

[2] Excludes funds allocated to Alberta Heritage Savings Trust Fund for 1985–86 and 1986–87.

Personal income *per capita* (1988), $19,947.

ENERGY AND NATURAL RESOURCES

Oil. In 1988, 76,276,000 cu. metres of crude oil were produced with gross sales value of $7,724,165,000. Alberta produced 82% of Canada's crude petroleum output in 1988. Production of natural gas by-products was 21,489,000 cu. metres, valued at $1,559,096,000.

The 4 major deposits of oil sands are found in northern and eastern Alberta: The Athabasca, Cold Lake, Peace River and Buffalo Head Hills deposits; total area, 140,800 sq. km. A limited part of the deposits along the Athabasca River can be exploited through open-pit mining. The rest of the Athabasca, and all the deposits in the other areas, are deeper reserves which must be developed through in situ techniques. These reserves reach depths of 760 metres. By 31 Dec. 1986 there were 638 enhanced oil recovery projects operating. Production of bitumen was estimated at 12,000 cu. metres per day in Dec. 1985.

Two oil sands mining plants in the Fort McMurray area produced 10·5m. cu. metres of synthetic crude oil in 1987 and 6·1m. cu. metres of crude bitumen.

Gas. Natural gas is found in abundance in numerous localities. In 1988, 76,308m. cu. metres valued at $4,415,169,000 were produced.

Minerals. In 1987 the remaining in-place established resources of coal total about 75,000m. tonnes. Of this amount, about 31,000m. is considered to be recoverable by surface and underground methods. Production (1988) 29·27m. tonnes valued at $456m.

Value of total mineral production decreased from $17,079,970,000 in 1987 to $14,906,395,000 in 1988.

Agriculture. Total area of farms (1986) 51,040,463 acres; improved land, 31,891,516; (under crops, 22,641,092; improved pasture, 3,402,183; summer fallow, 5,255,965; other improved land, 592,276); unimproved land, 19,148,947; (unimproved pasture, 16,057,185; woodland, 713,699; other unimproved land, 2,378,063). Number of farms (1986) 57,777.

For particulars of agricultural production and livestock, *see under* CANADA, pp. 284–85. Farm cash receipts in 1988 totalled $4,440,807,000, of which crops contributed $1,634,191,000; livestock and products, $2,058,370,000, and direct payments, $748,246,000.

Forestry. Total forest lands, managed by the Crown, (1987–88) 331,000 sq. km, of which 182,000 sq. km were productive (supporting 2,300m. cu. metres of wood). In 1989 an additional 20,000 sq. km had the potential to produce forest products. In 1987–88, 8·3m. cu. metres of timber were harvested.

Fisheries. The largest catch in commercial fishing is whitefish. Perch, tullibee, walley, pike and lake trout are also caught in smaller quantities. In 1984 a provincial fish marketing policy was implemented and a new commercial fishery licensing system was implemented in 1987. Commercial fish production in 1987–88 was 2,841 tonnes, value $3·1m.

INDUSTRY. The leading manufacturing industries are food and beverages, petroleum refining, metal fabricating, wood industries, primary metal, chemical and chemical products and non-metallic mineral products industries. There were in 1986 approximately 2,747 manufacturing establishments, in which were employed 76,347 persons, who earned in salaries and wages $2,216,131,000.

Manufacturing shipments had a total value of $17·925m. in 1988. Chief among these shipments were: Food and beverages, $4·547m.; refined petroleum and coal products, $2·713m.; chemicals and chemical products, $3·258m.; fabricated metal products, $974m.; primary metals, $1·197m.; non-metallic mineral products, $571m.; printing, publishing and allied, $724m.; wood, $714m.; paper and allied products, $588m.; furniture and fixtures, $162m.; other, $228m.

Total retail sales (1988) $15,953,806,000.

Tourism is of increasing importance and in 1988 contributed $2,379m. to the economy.

COMMUNICATIONS

Roads. In 1989 there were 153,799 km of roads and highways, including 108,756 km gravelled and 20,155 km paved.

At 31 March 1989 there were 1,844,965 motor vehicles registered, including 1,385,371 passenger cars.

Railways. In 1989 the length of main railway lines was 9,459 km. In 1989 there was a modern rail rapid transit network in Edmonton (11·1 km) and Calgary (22·5 km).

Post and Telecommunications. Alberta's modern telephone system is owned and operated by the provincial government, except in the city of Edmonton (owned and operated by Edmonton) and some rural lines. There were 1,313,077 telephone subscriber lines in service in April 1989.

JUSTICE AND EDUCATION

Justice. The Supreme Judicial authority of the province is the Court of Appeal. Judges of the Court of Appeal and Court of Queen's Bench are appointed by the Federal Government and hold office until retirement at the age of 75. There are courts of lesser jurisdiction in both civil and criminal matters. The Court of Queen's Bench has full jurisdiction over civil proceedings. A Provincial Court which has jurisdiction in civil matters up to $2,000 is presided over by provincially appointed judges. Youth Courts have power to try boys and girls 12–17 years old inclusive for offences against the Young Offenders Act.

The jurisdiction of all criminal courts in Alberta is enacted in the provisions of the Criminal Code. The system of procedure in civil and criminal cases conforms as nearly as possible to the English system.

Education. Schools of all grades are included under the term of public school (including those in the separate school system which are publicly supported). The same board of trustees controls the schools from kindergarten to university entrance. In 1988–89 there were 446,235 pupils enrolled in grades 1-12, including private schools and special education programmes. The University of Alberta (in Edmonton), organized in 1907, had, in 1988–89, 24,603 full-time students. The University of Calgary, formerly part of the University of Alberta and autonomous from April 1966, had in 1988–89, 16,659 full-time students. The University of Lethbridge, organized in 1966, had in 1988–89, 2,935 full-time students. The Athabasca University had in 1988–89, 11,056 part-time students. Banff Centre for Continuing Education had in 1988–89, 1,340 part-time students. The full-time enrolment at Alberta's 11 public colleges totalled 19,708 students in 1988–89.

Further Reading

Statistical Information: The Alberta Bureau of Statistics (Dept. of Treasury, Edmonton), which was established in 1939, collects, compiles and distributes information relative to Alberta. Among its publications are: *Alberta Statistical Review* (Quarterly).—*Alberta Economic Accounts* (Annual).—*Alberta Facts* (Annual).—*Population Projections, Alberta* (Occasional).—*Alberta Population Growth* (Quarterly).

Dept. of Economic Development and Trade, *Alberta Industry and Resources Database.* Edmonton, (Biannual)

MacGregor, J. G., *A History of Alberta.* 2nd ed. Edmonton, 1981
Masson, J., *Alberta's Local Governments and their Politics.* Univ. of Alberta Press, 1985
Richards, J., *Prairie Capitalism: Power and Influence in the New West.* Toronto, 1979
Wiebe, Rudy., *Alberta, a Celebration.* Edmonton, 1979

BRITISH COLUMBIA

HISTORY. Vancouver Island was organized as a colony in 1849; the mainland as far as the watershed of the Rocky Mountains was organized as a colony following a gold rush on the Fraser River in 1859. The two were united as the colony of British Columbia in 1866; this became a Canadian Province in 1871.

AREA AND POPULATION. British Columbia has an area of 952,263 sq. km. The capital is Victoria. The province is bordered westerly by the Pacific ocean and Alaska Panhandle, northerly by the Yukon and Northwest Territories, easterly by the Province of Alberta and southerly by the USA along the 49th parallel. A chain of islands, the largest of which are Vancouver Island and the Queen Charlotte Islands, affords protection to the mainland coast.

The 1986 census population was 2,889,207; estimate (1989) 3,055,600.

The principal cities and their 1989 estimated populations are as follows: Metropolitan Vancouver, 1,498,980; Metropolitan Victoria, 273,242; Kelowna, 67,027; Prince George, 65,451; Kamloops, 62,261; Matsqui, 59,717; Nanaimo, 53,788; Chilliwack, 45,643; Penticton, 25,312; Vernon, 20,678; Campbell River, 19,501; Prince Rupert, 15,059; Cranbrook, 15,024; Fort St. John, 12,660.

Vital statistics, *see* p. 272.

Religion, *see* p. 291.

CLIMATE. The climate is cool temperate, but mountain influences affect temperatures and rainfall very considerably. Driest months occur in summer. Vancouver. Jan. 36°F (2·2°C), July 64°F (17·8°C). Annual rainfall 58" (1,458 mm).

CONSTITUTION AND GOVERNMENT. British Columbia (then known as New Caledonia) originally formed part of the Hudson's Bay Company's concession. In 1849 Vancouver Island and in 1858 British Columbia were constituted Crown Colonies; in 1866 the two colonies amalgamated. The British North America Act of 1867 provided for eventual admission into Canadian Confederation, and on 20 July 1871 British Columbia became the sixth province of the Dominion.

British Columbia has a unicameral legislature of 69 elected members. Government policy is determined by the Executive Council responsible to the Legislature. The Lieut.-Governor is appointed by the Governor-General of Canada, usually for a term of 5 years, and is the head of the executive government of the province.

Lieut.-Governor: The Hon. David See-Chai Lam.

Flag: A banner of the arms, *i.e.*, blue and white wavy stripes charged with a setting sun in gold, across the top of a Union Flag with a gold coronet in the centre.

The Legislative Assembly is elected for a maximum term of 5 years. Every male or female Canadian citizen 19 years and over, having resided a minimum of 6 months in the province, duly registered, is entitled to vote. Representation of the parties in Dec. 1989: Social Credit Party, 38; New Democratic Party, 26; Independent, 5.

The province is represented in the Federal Parliament by 28 members in the House of Commons, and 6 Senators.

The Executive Council was composed as follows, Jan. 1990:

Premier and President of the Executive Council: Hon. William N. Vander Zalm.

Advanced Education, Training and Technology: Hon. Bruce Strachan. *Agriculture and Fisheries:* Hon. John Savage. *Attorney-General:* Hon. Bud Smith, QC. *Crown Lands:* Hon. Dave Parker. *Education:* Hon. Tony Brummet. *Energy, Mines and Petroleum Resources:* Hon. Jack Davis. *Environment:* Hon. John Reynolds. *Finance and Corporate Relations:* Hon. Mel Couvelier. *Forests:* Hon. Claude Richmond. *Government Management Services and Minister responsible for Women's Programs:* Hon. Carol Gran. *Health:* Hon. John Jansen. *International Business and Immigration:* Hon. Elwood Veitch. *Labour and Consumer Services:* Hon. Norm Jacobsen. *Municipal Affairs, Recreation and Culture:* Hon. Lyall Hanson. *Native Affairs:* Hon. Jack Weisgerber. *Parks:* Hon. Ivan Messmer. *Provincial Secretary:* Hon. Howard Dirks. *Regional and Economic Development:* Hon. Stan Hagen. *Social Services and Housing:* Hon. Peter Dueck. *Solicitor General:* Hon. Russell Fraser. *Tourism:* Hon. Cliff Michael. *Transportation and Highways:* Hon. Rita Johnston.

Agent-General in London: Garde Gardom (British Columbia House, 1 Regent St., London, SW1Y 4NS).

Local Government. Vancouver City was incorporated by statute and operates under the provisions of the Vancouver Charter of 1953 and amendments. This is the only incorporated area in British Columbia not operating under the provisions of the Municipal Act. Under this Act municipalities are divided into the following classes:

(a) a village with a population between 500 and 2,500, governed by a council consisting of a mayor and 4 aldermen; *(b)* a town with a population between 2,500 and 5,000, governed by a council consisting of a mayor and 4 aldermen; *(c)* a city where the population exceeds 5,000 governed by a council consisting of a mayor and 6 or 8 aldermen depending on population; *(d)* a district where the area exceeds 810 hectares and the average density is less than 5 persons per hectare, governed by a council consisting of a mayor and 6 or 8 aldermen depending on population; *(e)* an Indian government district.

There are 3 other forms of local government: There are 8 Development Regions each represented in Cabinet by a Minister of State; the regional district covering a number of areas both incorporated and unincorporated, governed by a board of directors; and the improvement district governed by a board of 3 trustees.

Revenue for municipal services is derived mainly from real-property taxation, although additional revenue is derived from licence fees, business taxes, fines, public utility projects and grants-in-aid from the provincial government.

ECONOMY

Budget. Current provincial revenue and expenditure, including all capital expenditures, in Canadian $1m. for fiscal years ending 31 March:

	1986–87	*1987–88*	*1988–89*
Revenue	8,578·0	10,322·0	11,440·0
Expenditure	9,749·0	11,122·0	11,835·0

The main sources of current revenue are the income taxes, contributions from the federal government, and privileges, licences and natural resources taxes and royalties.

The main items of expenditure in 1989–90 (estimate) are as follows: Health, $4,309·1m.; education, $2,224·3m.; social services and housing, $1,609·7m.; transportation and highways, $1,016·2m.; advanced education and job training, $994·8m.; management of public funds and debt, $651·4m.; forests, $557·9m.; municipal affairs, recreation and culture, $535·6m.

Banking. On 31 Dec. 1988, Canadian chartered banks maintained 801 branches and had total assets of $38,497m. in British Columbia; credit unions at 280 locations had total assets of $7,995m. Several foreign banks have Canadian head offices in Vancouver and several others have branches.

ENERGY AND NATURAL RESOURCES

Electricity. Generation in 1988 totalled 60,943m. gwh. of which a net 9,215m. gwh. were exported. Consumption within the province was 54,078m. gwh.

Minerals. Copper, coal, natural gas, crude oil, gold and silver are the most important minerals produced. The 1988 total of mineral production was estimated at $3,838m. Total value of mineral fuels produced in 1988 was estimated at: Coal, $1,023·2m.; oil and gas, $672·3m.

Agriculture. Only 2·4m. hectares or 4% of the total land area is arable or potentially arable. Farm cash receipts, in 1988, were $1,118m. of which livestock and products $688m., crops, $383m.

Forestry. About 46% of British Columbia's land is productive forest land, with 43·3m. hectares bearing commercial forest. Over 94% of the forest area is owned or administered by the provincial government. The total cut from forests in 1988 was 86·8m. cu. metres. Output of forest-based products, 1988: Lumber, 36,737,000 cu. metres; plywood, 1,829,000 cu. metres; pulp, 6·97m. tonnes; paper and paperboard, 2,878,000 tonnes; newsprint, 1,648,000 tonnes.

Fisheries. In 1988, 200,000 tonnes of fish, value $447m., were landed.

INDUSTRY AND TRADE

Industry. The selling value of factory shipments from all manufacturing industries reached an estimated $25,173m. in 1988.

Labour. The labour force averaged 1,514,000 persons in 1988 with 1,358,000 employed, of which 484,000 were in service industries, 254,000 in trade, 166,000 in manufacturing, 107,000 in transportation, communication and other utilities, 91,000 in finance, insurance and real estate, 83,000 in public administration, 86,000 in construction, 33,000 in agriculture, 26,000 in forestry, 19,000 in mining and 8,000 in fishing and trapping.

Commerce. Exports of British Columbia origin during 1988 totalled $17,377·3m. in value, while imports amounted to $12,803·7m. USA is the largest market for products exported through British Columbia customs ports ($7,442·8m. in 1988) followed by Japan ($4,706·1m.).

The leading exports were: Lumber, $3,925·3m.; pulp, $3,348·9m.; coal, $1,457·1m.; paper and paperboard, $576·6m.

Tourism. In 1988, 18·7m. tourists spent $3,490m.

COMMUNICATIONS

Roads. At 31 March 1988 there were 47,024 km of provincial roads and rights of way in the province, of which 22,213 km were paved. In 1988, 1,341,000 passenger cars and 472,000 commercial vehicles were licensed.

Railways. The province is served by two transcontinental railways, the Canadian Pacific Railway and the Canadian National Railway. Passenger service is provided by VIA Rail, a Crown Corporation. British Columbia is also served by the publicly owned British Columbia Railway, the Railway Freight Service of the B.C. Hydro and Power Authority, the Northern Alberta Railways Company and the Burlington Northern Inc. The combined route-mileage of mainline track operated by the CPR, CNR and BCR totals 7,500 km. The system also includes CPR and CNR railcar barge connections to Vancouver Island, between Prince Rupert and Alaska, and interchanges with American railways at southern border points. A metro line was opened in Vancouver in 1986.

Aviation. International airports are located at Vancouver and Victoria. Daily interprovincial and intraprovincial flights serve all main population centres. Small public and private airstrips are located throughout the province. Total passenger arrivals and departures on scheduled services (1988) 9,233,000.

Shipping. The major ports are Vancouver, New Westminster, Victoria, Nanaimo and Prince Rupert. The volume of domestic cargo handled during 1987 was 46·4m. tonnes; international cargo, 86·5m. tonnes.

The British Columbia Ferries connect Vancouver Island with the mainland and also provide service to other coastal points; in 1988, 17·8m. passengers and 6·8m. vehicles were carried. Service by other ferry systems is also provided between Vancouver Island and the USA. The Alaska State Ferries connect Prince Rupert with centres in Alaska.

Post and Broadcasting. The British Columbia Telephone Company had (1988) approximately 1·7m. telephones in service. In March 1987 there were 79 radio and 11 television stations originating in British Columbia. In addition there were 575 rebroadcasting stations in the province.

JUSTICE, EDUCATION AND WELFARE

Justice. The judicial system is composed of the Court of Appeal, the Supreme Court, County Courts, and various Provincial Courts, including Magistrates' Courts and Small Claims Courts. The federal courts include the Supreme Court of Canada and the Federal Court of Canada.

Education. Education, free up to Grade XII levels, is financed jointly from municipal and provincial government revenues. Attendance is compulsory from the age of 7 to 15. There were 499,994 pupils enrolled in 1,563 public schools from kindergarten to Grade XII in Sept. 1988.

The universities had a full-time enrolment of approximately 37,392 for 1988–89. They include University of British Columbia, Vancouver; University of Victoria, Victoria and Simon Fraser University, Burnaby. The regional colleges are Camosun College, Victoria; Capilano College, North Vancouver; Cariboo College, Kamloops; College of New Caledonia, Prince George; Douglas College, New Westminister; East Kootenay Community College, Cranbrook; Fraser Valley College, Chilliwack/Abbotsford; Kwantlen College, Surrey; Malaspina College, Nanaimo; North Island College, Comox; Northern Lights College, Dawson Creek/Fort St John; Northwest Community College, Terrace/Prince Rupert; Okanagan College, Kelowna with branches at Salmon Arm and Vernon; Selkirk College, Castlegar; Vancouver Community College, Vancouver.

There are also the British Columbia Institute of Technology, Burnaby; Emily Carr College of Art and Design, Vancouver; Justice Institute of British Columbia, Vancouver; Open Learning Institute, Richmond; Pacific Marine Training Institute, North Vancouver; Pacific Vocational Institute, Burnaby/Maple Ridge/ Richmond. A televised distance education and special programmes through KNOW, the Knowledge Network of the West is provided.

Health. The Government operates a hospital insurance scheme giving universal coverage after a qualifying period of 3 months' residence in the province. The province has come under a national medicare scheme which is partially subsidized by the provincial government and partially by the federal government.

Further Reading

Statistical Information: Central Statistics Bureau (Ministry of Finance and Corporate Relations, Hon. Mel Couvelier—Minister, Parliament Buildings, Victoria, B.C., V8V 1X4), collects, compiles and distributes information relative to the Province.

Publications include *Manufacturers' Directory; External Trade Report* (annual); *British Columbia Facts and Statistics* (annual); *British Columbia Economic Accounts* (annual); *British Columbia Population Forecast* (annual).

Ministry of Finance, *British Columbia Economic and Statistical Review.* Victoria, B.C. (annual)

Morley, J. T., *The Reins of Power: Governing British Columbia.* Vancouver, 1983

Ormsby, M., *British Columbia: A History.* Vancouver, 1958

MANITOBA

HISTORY. The Hudson's Bay Company formed a colony on the Red River in 1812, which was part of territory annexed to Canada in 1870. The Metis colonists (part-Indian, mostly French-speaking, Catholic) objected to the arrangements for the purchase of the Company territory by Canada and the province of Manitoba was created to accommodate them. It was extended northwards and westwards in 1881 and to Hudson Bay in 1912.

AREA AND POPULATION. The area of the province is 250,946 sq. miles (649,046 sq. km), of which 211,721 sq. miles are land and 39,225 sq. miles water. From north to south it is 793 km and at the widest point it is 493 km.

The population (census, 1986) was 1,071,232. Estimate (1988), 1,084,800. Population of Winnipeg, the capital (June 1986), 625,304; other principal cities (census, 1986): Brandon, 38,708; Thompson, 14,701; Portage la Prairie, 13,198; Selkirk, 10,013; Flin Flon (Manitoba portion), 7,243.

Vital statistics, *see* p. 272.

Religion, *see* p. 291.

CLIMATE. The climate is cold continental, with very severe winters but pleasantly warm summers. Rainfall amounts are greatest in the months May to Sept. Winnipeg. Jan. –3°F (–19·3°C), July 67°F (19·6°C). Annual rainfall 21" (539 mm).

CONSTITUTION AND GOVERNMENT. Manitoba was known as the Red River Settlement before its entry into the Dominion in 1870. The provincial government is administered by a Lieut.-Governor assisted by an Executive Council (Cabinet) which is appointed from and responsible to a legislative assembly of 57 members elected for 5 years. Women were enfranchised in 1916. The Electoral Division Act, 1955, created 57 single-member constituencies and abolished the transferable vote. There are 28 rural electoral divisions, and 29 urban electoral divisions. The province is represented by 6 members in the Senate and 14 in the House of Commons of Canada.

Lieut.-Governor: Dr George Johnson (sworn in 12 Dec. 1986).
Flag: The British Red Ensign with the shield of the province in the fly.

State of parties in the Legislative Assembly in Nov. 1988: Progressive Conservative 24, Liberals 21, and New Democratic Party, 12.

The members of the Progressive Conservative Ministry (sworn in 9 May 1988) are as follows (Jan. 1990):

President of the Executive Council, Minister of Federal-Provincial Relations, Chairman of the Treasury Board: Gary Albert Filmon.

Northern Affairs, Minister responsible for Native Affairs, the Communities Economic Development Fund Act, Channel Area Loggers Ltd, Moose Lake Loggers Ltd, A. E. MacKenzie Company Ltd, Seniors: James Erwin Downey. *Health:* Donald Warder Orchard. *Highways and Transportation, Government Services:* Albert Driedger. *Finance, Minister responsible for the Crown Corporations Accountability Act, and the Manitoba Data Services Act:* Clayton Sidney Manness. *Family Services:* Charlotte Louise Oleson. *Deputy Premier, Minister responsible for the Manitoba Public Insurance Corporation Act, and Jobs Fund, Environment:* James Glen Cummings. *Justice and Attorney-General, Minister responsible for Corrections, Constitutional Affairs, Liquor Control Act, Keeper of the Great Seal:* James Collus McCrae. *Minister responsible for the Workers Compensation Act, Co-operative, Consumer and Corporate Affairs:* Edward James Connery. *Industry, Trade and Tourism, Minister responsible for the Development Corporation Act, Sport, Minister responsible for Fitness and Amateur Sport, Boxing and Wrestling Commission Act, Manitoba Forestry Resources Ltd:* James Arthur Ernst. *Agriculture, Minister responsible for the Manitoba Telephone Act:* Glen Marshall Findlay. *Education and Training:* Leonard Derkach. *Urban Affairs, Housing:* Gerald Ducharme. *Culture, Heritage and Recreation, Minister responsible for the Manitoba Lotteries Foundation Act:* Bonnie Elizabeth Mitchelson. *Rural Development:* John (Jack) Penner. *Energy and Mines, Minister responsible for the Manitoba Hydro Act:* Harold Johan Neufeld. *Labour, Minister responsible for the Status of Women, the Civil Service Superannuation Act, the Civil Service Special Supplementary Severance Benefit Act, the Public Servants Insurance Act:* Gerrie Hammond.

Local Government. Rural Manitoba is organized into rural municipalities which vary widely in size. Some have only 4 townships (a township is 36 sq. miles), while the largest has 22 townships. The province has 105 rural municipalities, as well as 35 incorporated towns, 39 incorporated villages and 5 incorporated cities.

On 1 Jan. 1972, the cities and towns comprising the metropolitan area of Winnipeg were amalgamated to form the City of Winnipeg. A mayor and council are elected to a central government, but councillors also sit on 'community committees' which represent the areas or wards they serve. These committees are advised by non-elected residents of the area on provision of municipal services within the community committee jurisdiction. Taxing powers and overall budgeting rest with the central council. The mayor is elected at the same time as the councillors in a city-wide vote. Revisions to the City of Winnipeg Act came into effect with the municipal elections held in Oct. 1977.

Since Jan. 1945, 17 Local Government Districts have been formed in the less densely populated areas of the province. They are administered by a provincially appointed person, who acts on the advice of locally elected councils.

In the extreme north, many communities have locally elected councils, while others are administered directly by the Department of Northern Affairs. This department provides most of the funding in all these northern settlements.

FINANCE. Provincial revenue and expenditure (current account) for fiscal years ending 31 March (in Canadian $):

	1984–85	*1985–86*	*1986–87* [1]	*1987–88* [2]	*1988–89*
Revenue	2,924,600,000	3,116,600,000	3,385,800,000	3,772,600,000	4,678,670,300
Expenditure	3,407,200,000	3,644,900,000	3,945,600,000	4,187,900,000	4,766,060,500

[1] Preliminary unaudited. [2] Budgeted.

ENERGY AND NATURAL RESOURCES

Electricity. The total generating capacity of Manitoba's power stations is 4·1m. kw. The Manitoba Hydro system, owned by the province, provides most of this power, while the city-owned Winnipeg Hydro provides about 190,000 kw. The systems have about 452,000 customers and consumption was 14·3m. kwh. in 1988.

Oil. Crude oil production in 1986 was valued at $195m. for the 825,000 cu. metres produced.

Minerals. Total value of minerals in 1988 was about $1,679m. Principal minerals mined are nickel, zinc, copper, and small quantities of gold and silver. Manitoba has the world's largest deposits of caesium ore.

Agriculture. Rich farmland is the main primary resource, although the area of Manitoba in farms is only about 14% of the total land area. In 1988 the total value of agricultural production in Manitoba was $1,800m., with $954m. from crops, $810m. from livestock and from the sale of other products including furs, hides and honey.

Forestry. About 51% of the land area is wooded, of which 334,440 sq. km is productive forest land. Total sales of wood-using industries (1988, estimate) $500m.

Fur Trade. Value of fur production to the trapper was $5m. in 1986.

Fisheries. From 57,000 sq. km of rivers and lakes fisheries production was about $28·3m. in 1987–88. Whitefish, sauger, pickerel and pike are the principal varieties of fish caught.

INDUSTRY AND TRADE

Industry. Manufacturing, the largest industry in the province, encompasses almost every major industrial activity in Canada. Estimated shipments in 1988 totalled $6,239m. Manufacturing employed about 63,000 persons. Due to the agricultural base of the province, the food and beverage group of industries is by far the largest, valued at $1,736m. in 1988. The next largest segments are transportation equipment, $608m., printing and publishing, $454m. and fabricated metals, $390m.

Trade. Products grown and manufactured in Manitoba find ready markets in other parts of Canada, in the USA, particularly the upper midwest region, and in other countries. Export shipments to foreign countries from Manitoba in 1988 were valued at $2,867m. Of total exports, $912·2m. were raw materials and $1,465·7m. processed and manufactured products.

Tourism. In 1986, non-Manitoban tourists numbered 2·4m. All tourists including Manitobans contributed $657m. to the economy.

COMMUNICATIONS

Roads. Highways and provincial roads totalled 19,721 km in 1989.

Railways. At 30 June 1988 the province had 6,600 km of track, not including industrial track, yards and sidings.

Aviation. A total of 108 licensed commercial air carriers operate from bases in Manitoba, as well as 5 regularly scheduled major national and international airlines.

Post. All of the Manitoba Telephone System's 535,000 (1988) telephones are dial-operated. There are some privately-owned fixtures and extension phones; all service is operated by MTS.

EDUCATION. Education is controlled through locally elected school divisions. There are about 199,000 children enrolled in the province's elementary and secondary schools. Manitoba has 3 universities with an enrolment of about 43,500 during the 1987–88 year; the University of Manitoba, founded in 1877, in Winnipeg, the University of Winnipeg, and Brandon University. Expenditure (estimate) on education in the 1987–88 fiscal year was $747m.

Three community colleges, in Brandon, The Pas and Winnipeg, offer 2-year diploma courses in a number of fields, as well as specialized training in many trades. They also give a large number and variety of shorter courses, both at their campuses and in many communities throughout the province.

Further Reading

General Information: Inquiries may be addressed to the Information Services Branch, Room 29, Legislative Building, Winnipeg, R3C OV8.

The Department of Agriculture publishes: *Year Book of Manitoba Agriculture*
Information Services Branch publishes: *Manitoba Facts*
Manitoba Statistical Review. Manitoba Bureau of Statistics, Quarterly
Twelfth Census of Canada: Manitoba. Statistics Canada, 1981
Jackson, J. A., *The Centennial History of Manitoba*. Toronto, 1970
Morton, W. L., *Manitoba: A History*. Univ. of Toronto Press, 1967

NEW BRUNSWICK

HISTORY. Touched by Jacques Cartier in 1534, New Brunswick was first explored by Samuel de Champlain in 1604. It was ceded by the French in the Treaty of Utrecht in 1713 and became a permanent British possession in 1763. It was separated from Nova Scotia and became a province in June 1784, as a result of the great influx of United Empire Loyalists. Responsible government came into being in 1848, and consisted of an executive council, a legislative council (later abolished) and a House of Assembly.

AREA AND POPULATION. The area of the province is 28,354 sq. miles (73,440 sq. km), of which 27,633 sq. miles (71,569 sq. km) are land area. The population (census 1986) was 710,422. Estimate (1989) 718,500. Of the individuals identifying a single ethnic origin (at the 1986 census), 46·9% were British and 33·3% French. Other significant ethnic groups were German, Dutch and Scandinavian. Among those who provided a multiple response 9·9% were of British and French descent and 4·3% British and other. In 1986 there were 9,375 Native People or Native People and other. Census 1986 population of urban centres: Saint John, 76,381; Moncton, 55,468; Fredericton (capital), 44,352; Bathurst, 14,683; Edmundston, 11,497; Campbellton, 9,073.

Vital statistics, *see* p. 272.
Religion, *see* p. 291.

CLIMATE. A cool temperate climate, with rain at all seasons but temperatures modified by the influence of the Gulf Stream. Saint John. Jan. 14°F (–10°C), July 63°F (17·2°C). Annual rainfall 51" (1,278 mm).

CONSTITUTION AND GOVERNMENT. The government is vested in a Lieut.-Governor and a Legislative Assembly of 58 members each of whom is individually elected to represent the voters in one constituency or riding. A simultaneous translation system is used in the Assembly. Any Canadian subject of full age and 6 months' residence is entitled to vote. As a result of the provincial election held on 13 Oct. 1987 and subsequent by-elections, the Assembly is composed of 58 Liberal Party members. The province has 10 members in the Canadian Senate and 10 members in the federal House of Commons.

Lieut.-Governor: Hon. Gilbert Finn (appointed Aug. 1987).

Flag: A banner of the Arms, *i.e.*, yellow charged with a black heraldic ship on wavy lines of blue and white; across the top a red band with a gold lion.

The members of the Liberal government are as follows (Sept. 1989):

Premier and Minister responsible for the Advisory Council on the Status of Women, and for Regional Development: Hon. Francis J. McKenna.

President of the Executive Council and Intergovernmental Affairs: Hon. Aldéa Landry.

Attorney General and Justice: Hon. James Lockyer. *Finance and responsibility for the New Brunswick Liquor Corporation:* Hon. Allan Maher. *Chairman of Board of Management:* Hon. Gérald Clavette. *Supply and Services:* Hon. Bruce Smith. *Transportation:* Hon. Sheldon Lee. *Natural Resources and Energy:* Hon. Morris Green. *Agriculture:* Hon. Alan Graham. *Health and Community Services:* Hon. Ray Frenette. *Income Assistance:* Hon. Laureen Jarrett. *Labour and responsibility for Multiculturalism:* Hon. Michael McKee. *Education:* Hon. Shirley Dysart. *Advanced Education and Training:* Hon. Russell King, MD. *Municipal Affairs:* Hon. Hubert Seamans. *Environment:* Hon. Vaughn Blaney. *Commerce and Technology:* Hon. A. W. Lacey. *Fisheries and Aquaculture:* Hon. Denis Losier. *Tourism, Recreation and Heritage:* Hon. Roland Beaulieu. *Housing:* Hon. Peter Trites. *Chairman of the New Brunswick Electric Power Commission:* Hon. Rayburn Doucett. *Solicitor General:* Hon. Conrad Landry. *Mines:* Hon. Edmond Blanchard. *Childhood Services:* Hon. Jane Barry.

Local Government. Under the reforms introduced in 1967 the province has assumed complete administrative and financial responsibility for education, health, welfare and administration of justice. Local government is now restricted to provision of services of a strictly local nature. Under the new municipal structure, units include existing and new cities, towns and villages. Counties have disappeared as municipal units. Areas with limited populations have become local service districts. The former local improvement districts have become towns, villages or local service districts depending on their size.

FINANCE. The ordinary budget (in Canadian $) is shown as follows (financial years ended 31 March):

	1986	*1987*	*1988*	*1989*
Gross revenue	2,662,864,912	2,770,035,356	3,024,858,732	3,322,730,180
Gross expenditure	2,714,257,315	2,890,963,016	3,131,700,768	3,253,858,361

Funded debt and capital loans outstanding (exclusive of Treasury Bills) as of 31 March 1989 was $4,330m. Sinking funds held by the province at 31 March 1988, $1,310m. The ordinary budget excludes capital spending.

ENERGY AND NATURAL RESOURCES

Electricity. Hydro-electric, thermal and nuclear generating stations of the New Brunswick Electric Power Commission had an installed capacity of 3,189,976 kw. at 31 March 1989, consisting of 14 generating stations. The Mactaquac hydro-electric development near Fredericton, has a name plate capacity of 653,400 kw. The largest thermal generating station, Coleson Cove, near Saint John, has over 1m. kw. of installed capacity. Atlantic Canada's first nuclear generating station, a 630,000 kw. CANDU plant built on a promontory jutting out in the Bay of Fundy, near Saint John, went into commercial operation in Jan. 1983. New Brunswick is electrically inter-connected with utilities in neighbouring provinces of Quebec, Nova Scotia and Prince Edward Island, as well as the New England States. Electricity export sales accounted for over 30% of revenue in 1988–89; energy purchases, mainly from the large Hydro Quebec system, supplied about 16% of in-province energy requirements.

Minerals. In 1988, a total of 22 different metals, minerals and commodities were produced. These included lead, zinc, copper, cadmium, bismuth, gold, silver, antimony, potash, salt, limestone, dolomite, gypsum, oil, gas, coal, oil shales, sand, gravel, clay, peat and marl. The total value of minerals produced in 1988 reached a record high of $831·1m., a 34% increase from $622·2m. in 1987. The largest contributors to mineral production are zinc, silver and lead accounting for over 60% of total value in 1988. These 3 minerals recorded significant increases in price in late 1986 which continued into 1988. In Canada in 1988, New Brunswick ranked first in the production of antimony and bismuth, second in lead, third in zinc, fourth in silver and fifth in the production of copper. Antimony is mined at Lake George and production resumed at the Durham Resources mine near Fredericton in 1985. Peat, rapidly becoming a major industry, is produced from 18 operations in the north. Two potash mines are in operation in the Sussex area, including the Denison-Potacan mine where production commenced in 1985. Oil and natural gas continue to be produced in the Stoney Creek and Hillsborough areas. Gordex Minerals produced its first gold in 1986 using the heap leach process. Coal is strip-mined at Grand Lake, producing some 530,000 tonnes annually. Not all of the province's minerals have been explored sufficiently and research continues. Provincial government programmes are being supplemented by a 5-year, $22m. Mineral Development Agreement between the Canada Department of Energy, Mines and Resources and the province. Federal and Provincial agencies are co-operating on field, laboratory and other projects.

Agriculture. The total area under crops is estimated at 129,475 hectares. Farms numbered 3,554 and averaged 115 hectares each (census 1986). Potatoes account for 22% of total farm cash income. Mixed farming is common throughout the province. Dairy farming is centred around the larger urban areas, and is located mainly along the Saint John River Valley and in the south-eastern sections of the province. Income from dairy operations provides about 23% of farm cash income. New Brunswick is self-sufficient in fluid milk and supplies a processing industry. For particulars of agricultural production and livestock, *see under* CANADA, pp. 284–85. Farm cash receipts in 1988 were $252m.

Forestry. New Brunswick contains some 62,000 sq. km of productive forest lands. The gross value of forest production was over $1,964·5m. in 1988, and it accounts for almost one-third of all goods produced in the province. The pulp and paper and allied industry group is the largest component of the industry contributing about 77% of the value of output. Timber-using plants employ about 16,000 people for all aspects of the forest industry, including harvesting, processing and transportation. Practically all forest products are exported from the province's numerous ports and harbours near which many of the mills are located or sent by road or rail to the USA.

Fisheries. Commercial fishing is one of the most important primary industries of the province, employing 7,903. Nearly 50 commercial species of fish and shellfish are landed, including scallop, shrimp, crab, herring and cod. Landings in 1988 (134,207 tonnes) amounted to $108·7m. In 1989 there were 157 fish processing plants employing nearly 14,000 people in peak periods. In 1988 molluscs and crustaceans ranked first with a value of $83·7m., 77% of the total landed value; pelagic fish second, 14·7%, and groundfish third, 8%. Exports (1988) $275m., mainly to the USA and Japan.

INDUSTRY. In 1989 there were 1,560 manufacturing and processing establishments, employing about 46,000 persons. New Brunswick's location, with deep-water harbours open throughout the year and container facilities at Saint John, makes it ideal for exporting. Industries include food and beverages, paper and allied industries, timber products. About 19% of the industrial labour force work in Saint John.

TOURISM. Tourism is one of the leading contributors to the economy. In 1988, 2·5m. non-resident and over 2m. resident travellers spent approximately $481m.

COMMUNICATIONS

Roads. There are about 1,541·9 km of arterial highways and 2,381·7 km of collector roads, all of which are hard-surfaced. 12,279·9 km of local roads provide access to most areas in the province. The main highway system, including 596·4 km of the Trans-Canada Highway, links the province with the principal roads in Quebec and Nova Scotia, and Prince Edward Island, as well as the Interstate Highway System in the eastern seaboard states of the USA. Passenger vehicles, 31 March 1989, numbered 300,836; commercial vehicles, 129,809; motor cycles, 11,290.

Railways. New Brunswick is served by main lines of both Canadian Pacific and Canadian National railways.

Post and Broadcasting. In 1988 the New Brunswick Telephone Co. Ltd had 502,987 telephones in service. The province is served by 21 radio stations. Sixteen are privately owned and 3 owned by the Canadian Broadcasting Corporation and 2 are university stations. Three stations broadcast in the French language, 3 are bilingual and the CBC International Service broadcasts in several languages from its station at Sackville. The province is served by 4 television stations, 1 of which broadcasts in French.

Newspapers. New Brunswick had (1988) 4 daily newspapers, 1 in French, and 24 weekly newspapers, 8 in French or bilingual.

EDUCATION. Public education is free and non-sectarian. There are 4 universities. The University of New Brunswick at Fredericton (founded 13 Dec. 1785 by the Loyalists, elevated to university status in 1823, reorganized as the University of New Brunswick in 1859) had 6,802 full-time students at the Fredericton campus and 1,232 full-time students at the Saint John campus (1988–89); Mount Allison University at Sackville had 1,846 full-time students; the Université de Moncton at Moncton, 3,536 full-time students, with 258 and 546 full-time students respectively at its satellite campuses at Shippegan and Edmundston; St Thomas University at Fredericton, 1,284 full-time students. During the period 1 July 1987 to 30 June 1988, there were 12,115 students enrolled full-time at 9 Community College campuses and at various campus training centres.

There were, in Sept. 1988, 136,287 students and 7,829 full-time (equivalent) teachers in the province's 428 schools. There are 42 school boards.

Further Reading

Industrial Information: Dept. of Commerce and Technology, Fredericton. *Economic Information:* Dept. of Finance, New Brunswick Statistics Agency, Fredericton. *General Information:* Communications New Brunswick, Fredericton.

Directory of Products and Manufacturers. Department of Commerce and Development; Annual

Thompson, C., *New Brunswick Inside Out*. Ottawa, 1977

Trueman, S., *The Fascinating World of New Brunswick*. Fredericton, 1973

NEWFOUNDLAND AND LABRADOR

HISTORY. Archaeological finds at L'Anse-au-Meadow in northern Newfoundland show that the Vikings had established a colony there at about A.D. 1000. This site is the only known Viking colony in North America. Newfoundland was discovered by John Cabot 24 June 1497, and was soon frequented in the summer months by the Portuguese, Spanish and French for its fisheries. It was formally occupied in Aug. 1583 by Sir Humphrey Gilbert on behalf of the English Crown, but various attempts to colonize the island remained unsuccessful. Although British sovereignty was recognized in 1713 by the Treaty of Utrecht, disputes over fishing rights with the French were not finally settled till 1904. By the Anglo-French Convention of 1904, France renounced her exclusive fishing rights along part of the coast, granted under the Treaty of Utrecht, but retained sovereignty of the offshore islands of St Pierre and Miquelon.

AREA AND POPULATION. Area, 143,501 sq. miles (371,690 sq. km) of which freshwater, 13,139 sq. miles (34,030 sq. km). In March 1927 the Privy Council decided the boundary between Canada and Newfoundland in Labrador. This area, now part of the Province of Newfoundland and Labrador, is 102,699 sq. miles. The coastline is extremely irregular. Bays, fiords and inlets are numerous and there are many good harbours with deep water close to shore. The coast is rugged with bold rocky cliffs from 200 to 400 ft high; in the Bay of Islands some of the islands rise 500 ft, with the adjacent shore 1,000 ft above tide level. The interior is a plateau of moderate elevation and the chief relief features trend north-east and south-west. Long Range, the most notable of these, begins at Cape Ray and extends north-east for 200 miles, the highest peak reaching 2,673 ft. Approximately one-third of the area is covered by water. Grand Lake, the largest body of water, has an area of about 200 sq. miles. The principal rivers flow towards the north-east. On the borders of the lakes and water-courses good land is generally found, particularly in the valleys of the Terra Nova River, the Gander River, the Exploits River and the Humber River, which are also heavily timbered.

Census population, 1986, was 568,349.

The capital of Newfoundland is the City of St John's (161,901, metropolitan area). The other cities are Corner Brook (22,719), Mt Pearl (20,293); important towns are Labrador City (8,664), Gander (10,207), Conception Bay South (15,531), Stephenville (7,994), Grand Falls (9,121), Happy Valley–Goose Bay (7,248), Marystown (6,660), Channel-Port aux Basques (5,901), Windsor (5,545), Carbonear (5,337), Bonavista (4,605), Wabana (4,057), Wabush (2,637).

Vital statistics, *see* p. 272.

Religion, *see* p. 291.

CLIMATE. The cool temperate climate is marked by heavy precipitation, distributed evenly over the year, a cool summer and frequent fogs in spring. St. John's. Jan. 23°F (–5°C), July 59°F (15°C). Annual rainfall 54" (1,367 mm).

CONSTITUTION AND GOVERNMENT. Until 1832 Newfoundland was ruled by the Governor under instructions of the Colonial Office. In that year a Legislature was brought into existence, but the Governor and his Executive Council were not responsible to it. Under the constitution of 1855, which lasted until its suspension in 1934, the government was administered by the Governor appointed by the Crown with an Executive Council responsible to the House of Assembly of 27 elected members and a Legislative Council of 24 members nominated for life by the Governor in Council. Women were enfranchised in 1925. At the Imperial Conference of 1917 Newfoundland was constituted as a Dominion.

In 1933 the financial situation had become so critical that the Government of Newfoundland asked the Government of the UK to appoint a Royal Commission to investigate conditions. On the strength of their recommendations, the parliamentary form of government was suspended and Government by Commission was inaugurated on 16 Feb. 1934.

A National Convention, elected in 1946, made, in 1948, recommendations to H.M. Government in Great Britain as to the possible forms of future government to be submitted to the people at a national referendum. Two referenda were held. In the first referendum (June 1948) the three forms of government submitted to the people were: Commission of government for 5 years, confederation with Canada and responsible government as it existed in 1933. No one form of government received a clear majority of the votes polled, and commission of government, receiving the fewest votes, was eliminated. In the second referendum (July 1948) confederation with Canada received 78,408 and responsible government 71,464 votes.

In the Canadian Senate on 18 Feb. 1949 Royal assent was given to the terms of union of Newfoundland and Labrador with Canada, and on 23 March 1949, in the House of Lords, London, Royal assent was given to an amendment to the British North America Act made necessary by the inclusion of Newfoundland and Labrador as the tenth Province of Canada.

Under the terms of union of Newfoundland and Labrador with Canada, which was signed at Ottawa on 11 Dec. 1948, the constitution of the Legislature of Newfoundland and Labrador as it existed immediately prior to 16 Feb. 1934 shall, subject to the terms of the British North America Acts, 1867 to 1946, continue as the constitution of the Legislature of the Province of Newfoundland and Labrador until altered under the authority of the said Acts.

The franchise was in 1965 extended to all male and female residents who have attained the age of 19 years and are otherwise qualified as electors.

The House of Assembly (Amendment) Act, 1979, established 52 electoral districts and 52 members of the Legislature.

In April 1989 there were 32 Liberals and 20 Progressive-Conservatives.

The province is represented by 6 members in the Senate and by 7 members in the House of Commons of Canada.

Lieut.-Governor: Hon. James W. McGrath (assumed office 5 Sept. 1986).

Flag: White, in the hoist 4 solid blue triangles; in the fly 2 red triangles voided white, and between them a yellow tongue bordered in red.

The Liberal Executive Council was, in May 1989, composed as follows:

Premier: Clyde Kirby Wells.

President of Executive Council and President of Treasury Board: Richard Winston Baker. *Fisheries:* Walter Carmichael Carter. *Employment and Labour Relations:* Patricia Anne Cowan. *Health:* Christopher Robert Decker. *Justice:* Paul David Dicks. *Social Services:* Reuben John Efford. *Forestry and Agriculture:* Graham Ralph Flight. *Development:* Charles Joseph Furey. *Mines and Energy:* Dr Rex Vincent Gibbons. *Works, Services and Transportation:* David Samuel Gilbert. *Municipal and Provincial Affairs:* Eric Augustus Gullage. *Environment and Lands:* Otto Paul James Kelland. *Finance:* Dr Hubert William Kitchen. *Education:* Dr Philip John Warren. *Speaker of the House of Assembly:* Thomas Lush.

Agent-General in London: H. Watson Jamer (60 Trafalgar Sq., WC2).

FINANCE. Budget[1] in Canadian $1,000 for fiscal years ended 31 March:

	1984–85	*1985–86*	*1986–87*	*1987–88*	*1988–89*[2]	*1989–90*[3]
Gross revenue	1,867,470	2,072,581	2,233,339	2,424,887	2,598,783	2,783,081
Gross expenditure	1,954,762	2,117,012	2,260,845	2,456,146	2,600,890	2,777,789

Capital account:

	1986–87	*1987–88*	*1988–89*	*1989–90*[3]
Gross revenue	49,888,000	120,670,000	65,495,000	111,500,000
Gross expenditure	252,932,000	287,235,000	291,107,000	370,231,000

[1] Current amount only. [2] Revised estimates. [3] Estimates.

Public debenture debt as at 31 March 1989 (preliminary) was $4,186·8m.; sinking fund, $1,409·8m.

ENERGY AND NATURAL RESOURCES

Electricity. The electrical energy requirements of the province are met mainly by hydro-electric power, with petroleum fuels being utilized to provide the balance. The total amount of energy generated in the province in 1987 was 40,089,415 mwh., of which 94% was derived from hydro-electric facilities. The greater part of the energy produced in 1987 (preliminary) came from Churchill Falls, of which 30,392,727 mwh. was sold to Hydro-Quebec under the terms of a long-term contract. Energy consumed in the province during 1987 (preliminary) totalled 9,696,688 mwh., with approximately 7,379,743 mwh., or 76%, coming from hydro-electric facilities.

At Dec. 1987 total electrical generating capacity in the province was 7,402 mw., with hydro-electric plants accounting for 6,644 mw., or 90%. It is estimated that potential additional hydro-electric generating capacity of up to 4·5m. kw. can be developed at various sites in Labrador.

Oil. In 1981 the province consumed refined petroleum at the rate of 39,000 bbls a day.

Since 1965, 137 wells have been drilled on the Continental Margin of the Province. In 1988 offshore exploration expenditures were $154m.

By 31 Dec. 1985 there had been 20 significant hydrocarbon discoveries off Newfoundland and delineation drilling had been initiated or was ongoing at 6: Terra Nova, Ben Nevis, Whiterose, North Ben Nevis and Mara. In 1986 only the Hibernia discovery had commercial capability and the Canada-Newfoundland Offshore Petroleum Board approved Mobil Oil Canada's development plan for the Hibernia Project, with production starting in the early 1990's.

In 1979, a discovery of oil was made on the Hibernia geological structure located 164 nautical miles east of Cape Spear. The discovery well, Hibernia P–15, tested medium gravity, sweet crude from several intervals with a reported total producing capability in excess of 20,000 bbls of oil per day.

By 31 Dec. 1985 there had been 20 significant hydrocarbon discoveries off Newfoundland but by Nov. 1986 only one (Hibernia) was considered commercially viable.

In June 1986, the Canada–Newfoundland Offshore Petroleum Board approved Mobil Oil Canada's development plan for the Hibernia Project. Production is currently expected to begin in the early 1990's.

Minerals. The mineral resources are vast but only partially documented. Large deposits of iron ore, with an ore reserve of over 5,000m. tons at Labrador City, Wabush City and in the Knob Lake area are supplying approximately half of Canada's production. Other large deposits of iron ore are known to exist in the Julienne Lake area.

There are a variety of other minerals being produced in the province in more limited amounts.

Uranium deposits in the Kaipokak Bay area near Makkovik in Labrador are presently being studied by Brinex. The Central Mineral Belt, which extends from the Smallwood Reservoir to the Atlantic coast near Makkovik, holds uranium, copper, beryllium and molybdenite potential.

In 1986 a gold mine was being developed at Hope Brook on the south coast east of Port aux Basques. Full production from an underground operation using conventional carbon-in-pulp gold processing is planned to start in late 1988.

Production in 1988 (preliminary): Iron ore, 20,044,000 tonnes ($726,574,000); zinc, 29,906,000 kg ($49,256,000); asbestos, 72,000 tonnes ($27,072,000); gypsum ($1,075,000); pyrophyllite and talc ($1·7m.); cement ($10,791,000); clay products ($1,225,000); sand and gravel, 3·44m. tonnes ($16,856,000); stone, 990,000 tonnes ($9,158,000); peat, 2,000 tonnes ($102,000).

Agriculture. The estimated value of agricultural products sold, including livestock, 1988, was $52·4m.

Forestry. The forestry economy in the province is mainly dependent on the operation of 3 newsprint mills. In 1988 the gross value of newsprint exported from these 3 mills totalled $505·7m. Lumber mills, saw-log operations produced 47m. f.b.m. in 1988–89.

Fisheries. The principal fish landings are cod, flounder, redfish, Queen crabs, lobster, salmon and herring. In 1988 (preliminary) a yearly average of some 10,400 persons were employed by the fish-processing industry and there were 29,023 licensed full-, part-time and casual fishermen engaged in harvesting operations. Approximately 224 processing operations were licensed in 1987. The production of fresh and frozen fish products was $760m. (estimate) in 1988.

The total catch in 1988 (preliminary) was 551,028 tonnes valued at $299,720,000, which comprised: Cod, 299,471 tonnes ($154,208,000); flounders and soles, 54,494 ($20,875,000); herring, 30,550 tonnes ($3,760,000); redfish, 17,342 ($6,158,000); lobster, 2,502 ($14,212,000); salmon, 947 ($3,939,000); capelin, 88,565 ($28,999,000); crab, 9,863 ($22,356,000); other, 47,294 ($45,213,000).

INDUSTRY. The total value of manufacturing shipments in 1988 was $1,511m. This consists largely of first-stage processing of primary resource products with two of the largest components being paper and fish products.

TRADE UNIONS. There were (1987) 487 unions representing 78,482 members of international and national unions and government employee associations.

COMMUNICATIONS

Roads. In 1987 there were 8,238 km, of which 5,671 were paved.

Railways. In 1981 there were 1,457·8 km of main track railway, of which the Canadian National Railways operated 1,130·6 (3 ft 6 in.), the Quebec North Shore and Labrador Railway 324·8 (4 ft 8½in.) and there were 2·4 km of private line. Car and passenger ferries operate from Port aux Basques and Argentia to North Sydney, Nova Scotia. On the island of Newfoundland, the Terra Transport operates a trans-island bus and rail freight service in addition to a coastal service for both passengers and freight. In 1988 CNR closed its Newfoundland operation. In the months that the Labrador coast is ice-free, usually from June to Nov., the CN Marine operates a scheduled coastal steamer service every week.

Aviation. The province is linked to the rest of Canada by regular air services provided by Air Canada, Canadian International Airways, Quebecair and a number of smaller air carriers.

Shipping. At 31 Dec. 1988 there were 1,564 ships registered in Newfoundland.

Post. There were 467 post offices open in 1988, and 2 telegraph offices in the Newfoundland and Labrador postal district. Telephone access lines in the province numbered 212,000 in 1987.

EDUCATION. The number of schools in 1988–89 was 555. The enrolment was 132,995; full-time teachers numbered 8,395. The Memorial University, offering courses in arts, science, engineering, education, nursing and medicine, had 16,064 full- and part-time students in 1987–88. Total expenditure for education by the Government in 1988–89 (estimate) was $615·5m.

Further Reading

Blackburn, R. H. (ed.) *Encyclopaedia of Canada: Newfoundland Supplement*. Toronto, 1949
Horwood, H., *Newfoundland*. Toronto, 1969
Loture, R. de, *Histoire de la grande pêche de Terre-Neuve*. Paris, 1949
Mercer, G. A., *The Province of Newfoundland and Labrador: Geographical Aspects*. Ottawa, 1970
Perlin, A. B., *The Story of Newfoundland, 1497–1959*. St John's, 1959

Tanner, V., *Outlines of Geography. Life and Customs of Newfoundland–Labrador.* 2 vols. Helsinki, 1944, and Toronto, 1947
Taylor, T. G., *Newfoundland: A Study of Settlement.* Toronto, 1946

NOVA SCOTIA

HISTORY. The first permanent settlement was made by the French early in the 17th century, and the province was called Acadia until finally ceded to the British by the Treaty of Utrecht in 1713.

AREA AND POPULATION. The area of the province is 21,425 sq. miles (55,000 sq. km), of which 20,401 sq. miles are land area, 1,024 sq. miles water area. The population (census 1986) was 873,199; (estimate 1989) 886,800.

Population of the principal cities and towns (census 1986): Halifax, 113,577; Dartmouth 65,243; Sydney, 27,754; Glace Bay, 20,467; Truro, 12,124; New Glasgow, 10,022; Amherst, 9,671; New Waterford, 8,326; Sydney Mines, 8,063; Bedford, 8,010; North Sydney, 7,472; Yarmouth, 7,617.

Vital statistics, *see* p. 272.

Religion, *see* p. 291.

CLIMATE. A cool temperate climate, with rainfall occurring evenly over the year. The Gulf Stream moderates the temperatures in winter so that ports remain ice-free. Halifax. Jan. 23°F (–5°C), July 64°F (17·8°C). Annual rainfall 56" (1,412 mm).

CONSTITUTION AND GOVERNMENT. Under the British North America Act of 1867 the legislature of Nova Scotia may exclusively make laws in relation to local matters, including direct taxation within the province, education and the administration of justice. The legislature of Nova Scotia consists of a Lieut.-Governor, appointed and paid by the federal government, and holding office for 5 years, and a House of Assembly of 52 members, chosen by popular vote at least every 5 years. The province is represented in the Canadian Senate by 10 members, and in the House of Commons by 11.

The franchise and eligibility to the legislature are granted to every person, male or female, if of age (19 years), a British subject or Canadian citizen, and a resident in the province for 1 year and 2 months before the date of the writ of election in the county or electoral district of which the polling district forms part, and if not by law otherwise disqualified. State of parties in Sept. 1989: 27 Progressive Conservatives, 22 Liberals, 2 New Democrats, 1 Independent.

Lieut.-Governor: Lloyd Crouse.

Flag: A banner of the Arms, *i.e.*, white with a blue diagonal cross, bearing in the centre the royal shield of Scotland.

The members of the Progressive Conservative Ministry were as follows in Nov. 1989:

Premier, President of the Executive Council, Minister Responsible for the Cabinet Secretariat, Chairman of the Policy Board: Hon. John M. Buchanan, QC.

Deputy Premier, Deputy President of the Executive Council, Minister of Housing, Minister responsible for the Emergency Measures Organization Act: Hon. Roger Bacon. *Mines and Energy, Chairman of the Senior Citizens Secretariat, Minister responsible for the Communications and Information Act:* Hon. Jack MacIsaac. *Tourism and Culture, Minister responsible for the Heritage Property Act:* Hon. Roland Thornhill. *Industry, Trade and Technology, Minister responsible for the Nova Scotia Research Foundation Corporation Act and the Advisory Council on Applied Science and Technology:* Hon. Donald Cameron. *Small Business Development, Minister Responsible for the Nova Scotia Business Capital Corporation Act:* Hon. Kenneth Streatch. *Education:* Hon. Ronald Giffin, QC. *Chairman of the Management Board, Government Services, Intergovernmental Affairs, Chairman of the Economic Development Committee of Cabinet, Minister responsible for the Civil*

Service Act: Hon. Terence Donohoe, QC. *Attorney-General, Minister responsible for the Administration of the Human Rights Act, Chairman of the Social Development Committee of Cabinet:* Hon. Thomas McInnis. *Advanced Education and Job Training:* Hon. Joel Matheson, QC. *Labour, Minister responsible for the Administration of the Liquor Control Act:* Hon. Ronald Russell. *Finance, Minister in charge of the Lottery Act:* Hon. Greg Kerr. *Environment:* Hon. John Leefe. *Transportation and Communications:* Hon. George Moody. *Health and Fitness, Registrar General, Minister in charge of the Administration of the Drug Dependency Act, Minister responsible for reporting on the Handicapped:* Hon. David Nantes. *Community Services, Minister responsible for Acadian Affairs:* Hon. Guy LeBlanc. *Municipal Affairs:* Hon. Brian Young. *Fisheries, Minister responsible for the Administration of the Advisory Council on the Status of Women Act:* Hon. Donald McInnes. *Consumer Affairs, Minister in charge of the Residential Tenancies Act:* Hon. Colin Stewart. *Agriculture and Marketing:* Hon. George Archibald. *Lands and Forests:* Hon. Charles MacNeil. *Solicitor General, Provincial Secretary, Minister in charge of the Regulations Act, Minister responsible for Youth:* Hon. Neil LeBlanc.

Agent-General in London: Donald M. Smith (14 Pall Mall, SW1Y 5LU).

Local Government. The main divisions of the province for governmental purposes are the 3 cities, the 39 towns and the 24 rural municipalities, each governed by a council and a mayor or warden. The cities have independent charters, and the various towns take their powers from and are limited by The Towns Act, and the various municipalities take their powers from and are limited by The Municipal Act as revised in 1967. The majority of municipalities comprise 1 county, but 6 counties are divided into 2 municipalities each. In no case do the boundaries of any municipality overlap county lines. The 18 counties as such have no administrative functions.

Any city (of which there are 3) or incorporated town (of which there are 39) that lies within the boundaries of a municipality is excluded from any jurisdiction by the municipal council and has its own government.

FINANCE. Revenue is derived from provincial sources, payments from the federal government under the Federal-Provincial Fiscal Arrangements and Established Programs Financing Act. Recoveries consist generally of amounts received under various federal cost-shared programmes. Main sources of provincial revenues include income and sales taxes.

Revenue, expenditure and debt (in Canadian $1m.) for fiscal years ending 31 March:

	1986	*1987*	*1988*	*1989*	*1990* [1]
Budgetary Transactions					
Current Expenditure	2,983·6	3,093·1	3,283·6	3,526·6	3,754·4
Current Revenues and Recoveries	2,714·6	2,903·9	3,164·5	3,465·5	3,706·0
Operating Deficit (Surplus)	269·0	189·2	119·1	61·1	48·4
Sinking Fund Instalments and Serial Retirements	77·2	87·3	86·5	90·9	98·5
Net Capital Expenditures	192·0	198·5	219·3	297·9	294·9
Net Budgetary Transactions	538·2	475·0	421·1	449·9	441·9
Non-Budgetary Transactions					
Capital Expenditures	2·7	0·9	2·5	2·7	2·6
Net Increase (Decrease) in Advances and Investments	(7·4)	28·1	(18·9)	7·8	42·5
Net Other Transactions	6·7	7·2	7·2	4·5	1·1
Non-Budgetary Transactions	2·0	36·2	(9·0)	15·0	46·2
	540·2	511·2	418·3	464·9	488·1

[1] Estimate.

Banking. All major Canadian banks are represented with numerous branch locations throughout the Province. In March 1989 total deposits with chartered banks in Nova Scotia totalled $4,024m.

NATURAL RESOURCES

Minerals. Principal minerals in 1988 were: Coal, 3·4m. tonnes, valued at $207·8m.; gypsum, 6·3m. tonnes, valued at $58·2m.; sand and gravel, 9·6m. tonnes, valued at $33·6m. Total value of mineral production in 1988 was about $461·1m.

Agriculture. Dairying, poultry and egg production, livestock and fruit growing are the most important branches. Farm cash receipts for 1988 were estimated at $307·3m., with an additional $4·6m. going to persons on farms as income in kind.

Cash receipts from sale of dairy products were $85m., with total milk production of 199,981,000 litres.

The production of poultry meat in 1988 was 25,589 tonnes, of which 20,502 tonnes were chickens and fowls and 3,087 tonnes were turkeys. Egg production was 19m. dozen.

The main 1988 fruit crops were apples, 80,014 tonnes; blueberries, 10,109 tonnes; and strawberries, 2,552 tonnes.

Forestry. The estimated forest area of Nova Scotia is 15,555 sq. miles (40,298 sq. km), of which about 25% is owned by the province. The principal trees are spruce, balsam fir, hemlock, pine, larch, birch, oak, maple, poplar and ash. 4,142,618 cu. metres of round forest products were produced in 1987.

Fisheries. The fisheries of the province in 1988 had a landed value of $413·8m. of sea fish including scallop fishery, $74·1m., and lobster fishery, $127·3m. In 1986 there were about 6,778 employees in the fish processing industry; the value of shipment of goods was $564·5m.

INDUSTRY. The number of manufacturing establishments was 820 in 1985; the number of employees was 35,149; wages and salaries, $774·6m.; value of shipments was $4,634·8m. The value of shipments in 1988, was $4,356m., and the leading industries were food, paper and allied industries and transportation equipment.

TRADE UNIONS. Total union membership during 1988 was 107,533 belonging to 94 unions comprised of 653 individual locals. The largest percentage of the total union membership was in the service sector followed by public administration and defence sector.

COMMUNICATIONS

Roads. In 1989 there were 26,053 km of highways; paved included 128 km freeway, 2,667 km arterial, 4,916 km collector and 5,454 km local. 12,888 km of highway are unpaved.

Railways. The province is covered with a network of 1,100 km of mainline track.

Aviation. There is direct air service to all major Canadian points and international scheduled service to Boston, New York, Bermuda, London, Glasgow, Amsterdam, Bombay and Singapore. In addition, there are winter charter services to Orlando, Tampa and other points.

Shipping. Ferry services connect Nova Scotia with Newfoundland, Prince Edward Island, New Brunswick and Maine. Direct service by container vessels is provided from the Port of Halifax to ports in the USA (east and west coast), Europe, Asia, Australia/New Zealand and the Caribbean.

JUSTICE AND EDUCATION

Justice. The Supreme Court (Trial Division and Appeal Division) is the superior court of Nova Scotia and has original and appellate jurisdiction in all civil and criminal matters unless they have been specifically assigned to another court by Statute. An appeal from the Supreme Court, Appeal Division, is to the Supreme Court of Canada. The other courts in the Province are the Provincial Court, which hears criminal matters only, the Small Claims Court, which has limited monetary jurisdiction, Probate Court, County Court, which has jurisdiction in criminal matters as well as original jurisdiction over actions not exceeding $50,000, and Family Court.

Young offenders are tried in Youth Court which in Nova Scotia is the Family Court or the Provincial Court.

For the year fiscal ending 31 March 1988 there were 4,301 admissions to provincial custody; of these, 2,912 were sentenced.

Education. Public education in Nova Scotia is free, compulsory and undenominational through elementary and high school. Attendance is compulsory to the age of 16. In addition to 534 public schools there are the Atlantic Provinces Resource Centres for the Hearing Handicapped and for the Visually Impaired; the Shelburne Youth Centre for young offenders and the Nova Scotia Residential Centre for delinquent children; and the Nova Scotia Youth Training Centre for mentally handicapped children. The province has 19 universities, colleges and technical institutions, of which the largest is Dalhousie University in Halifax. The Nova Scotia Agricultural College and the Nova Scotia Teachers' College are located at Truro. The Technical University of Nova Scotia at Halifax grants degrees in engineering and architecture.

The Department of Vocational and Technical Training administers 2 institutes of technology, a nautical institute and 14 other facilities under the system of Community colleges. It also provides in-school training for the Department of Labour Apprenticeship programme.

The Nova Scotia government offers financial support and organizational assistance to local school boards for provision of weekend and evening courses in academic and avocational subjects, and citizenship for new Canadians. It also provides local authorities with specialist support services to assist them in providing community workshops and it operates a correspondence study service for children and adults.

Total estimated expenditure on all levels of education for the year 1988-89 was $1,301·1m., of which 71% was borne by the provincial government. In 1988–89, classrooms operated in 530 elementary-secondary schools, with 10,000 teachers and 167,600 pupils.

Further Reading

Nova Scotia Fact Book. N.S. Department of Industry, Trade and Technology, Halifax, 1988
Nova Scotia Resource Atlas. N.S. Department of Industry, Trade and Technology, Halifax, 1986
Atlantic Provinces Economic Council. *The Atlantic Vision, 1990.* Halifax, 1979
Public Archives of Nova Scotia. *Place Names and Places of Nova Scotia.* Halifax, 1967
Beck, M., *The Evolution of Municipal Government in Nova Scotia, 1749–1973.* 1973
Fergusson, C. B., *Nova Scotia in Encyclopedia Canadiana,* Vol. VII. Toronto, 1968
Hamilton, W. B., *The Nova Scotia Traveller.* Toronto, 1981
McCormick, P., *A Guide to Halifax.* Tantallon, 1984
McCreath, P. and Leefe, J., *History of Early Nova Scotia.* Halifax, 1982
Vaison, R., *Nova Scotia Past and Present: A Bibliography and Guide.* Halifax, 1976

ONTARIO

HISTORY. The French explorer Samuel de Champlain explored the Ottawa River from 1613. The area was governed by the French, first under a joint stock company and then as a royal province, from 1627 and was ceded to Great Britain in 1763. A constitutional act of 1791 created there the province of Upper Canada, largely to accommodate loyalists of English descent who had immigrated after the United States war of independence. Upper Canada entered the Confederation as Ontario in 1867.

AREA AND POPULATION. The total area is about 412,582 sq. miles (1,068,630 sq. km), of which some 344,100 sq. miles (891,200 sq. km) are land area and some 64,490 sq. miles (189,196 sq. km) are lakes and fresh water rivers.

The province extends 1,050 miles (1,690 km) from east to west and 1,075 miles (1,730 km) from north to south.

Ontario is bounded on the north by the waters of Hudson and James Bay, on the east by Quebec, on the west by Manitoba, and on the south by the states of New York, Pennsylvania, Ohio, Michigan, Wisconsin and Minnesota.

The population of the province (census, 1 June 1981) was 8,625,107. Estimate (1988) 9·1m. Population of the principal cities (1985): Hamilton, 307,690 (city), 421,264 (metropolitan area); Kitchener, 147,439 (city), 287,801 (census metropolitan area); London, 276,000 (city); Ottawa (federal capital), 304,448 (city), 562,782 (census metropolitan area); Sudbury, 90,453 (city), 154,387 (regional municipality); Toronto (provincial capital), 606,247 (city), 2,998,947 (census metropolitan area); Windsor, 195,028 (city).

Vital statistics, *see* p. 272.

Religion, *see* p. 291.

CLIMATE. A temperate continental climate, but conditions are quite severe in winter, though proximity to the Great Lakes has a moderating influence on temperatures. Ottawa. Jan. 12°F (–11·1°C), July 69°F (20·6°C). Annual rainfall 35" (871 mm). Toronto. Jan. 23°F (–5°C), July 69°F (20·6°C). Annual rainfall 33" (815 mm).

CONSTITUTION AND GOVERNMENT. The provincial government is administered by a Lieut.-Governor, a cabinet and one chamber elected by a general franchise for a period of 5 years. Women were granted the right to vote and be elected to the chamber in 1917. The minimum voting age is 18 years.

In Aug. 1989 the provincial legislature was composed as follows: Liberals, 94; New Democrats, 19; Progressive Conservatives, 17; total 130.

Lieut.-Governor: Right Hon. Lincoln M. Alexander, PC, QC (appointed Sept. 1985).

Flag: The British Red Ensign with the shield of Ontario in the fly.

The members of the Executive Council in Oct. 1989 were as follows (all Liberals):

Premier and Minister of Intergovernmental Affairs: Hon. David R. Peterson.

Deputy Premier, Treasurer and Minister of Economics: Hon. Robert F. Nixon. *Agriculture and Food:* Hon. David Ramsay. *Attorney-General and Minister Responsible for Native Affairs:* Hon. Ian G. Scott, QC. *Citizenship, Minister Responsible for Race Relations and the Ontario Human Rights Commission:* Hon. Bob Wong. *Colleges and Universities, Education, and Skills Development:* Hon. Sean Conway. *Community and Social Services and Minister Responsible for Francophone Affairs:* Hon. Charles Beer. *Consumer and Commercial Relations:* Hon. Gregory Sorbara. *Correctional Services:* Hon. Richard Patten. *Culture and Communications:* Hon. Christine Hart. *Energy, and Natural Resources:* Hon. Lyn McLeod. *Environment:* Hon. James Bradley. *Financial Institutions, and Management Board of Cabinet:* Hon. Murray J. Elston. *Government Services:* Hon. Chris Ward. *Health:* Hon. Elinor Caplan. *Housing, and Municipal Affairs:* Hon. John Sweeney. *Industry, Trade and Technology:* Hon. Monte Kwinter. *Labour:* Hon. Gerry Phillips. *Mines:* Hon. Hugh O'Neil. *Northern Development:* Hon. René Fontaine. *Revenue:* Hon. Reno Mancini. *Solicitor General:* Hon. Steven Offer. *Tourism and Recreation:* Hon. Kenneth Black. *Transportation:* Hon. William Wrye. *Ministers Without Portfolio:* Hon. Shirley Collins (Responsible for Disabled Persons), Hon. Gilles E. Morin (Responsible for Senior Citizen's Affairs), Hon. Mavis Wilson (Responsible for Women's Issues).

Local Government. Local government in Ontario is divided into two branches, one covering municipal institutions and the other education.

The present municipal system dates from The Municipal Corporations Act enacted by The Province of Canada in 1849. It has been considerably modified in recent years with the creation of the Municipality of Metropolitan Toronto in 1954 and the launching of the Government of Ontario's local government restructuring programme in 1968. Generally, there are two levels of municipal government in Ontario. The upper level consists of 27 counties plus 12 restructured regional municipalities. The local level comprises more than 800 cities, towns and townships. Cities in the traditional county system function independently of the county in which they lie, as do 4 towns which have been separated for municipal purposes. There are no separated municipal units in regional governments.

Ontario's local municipalities are governed by councils elected by popular vote.

A city council usually consists of a mayor, aldermen and, sometimes, an executive committee known as a board of control.

Councils of towns, villages and townships usually consist of a mayor, reeve, deputy reeve, councillors and, in the case of the newer regional municipalities, one or more regional councillors who represent the area municipalities on the regional council.

County and regional government councils are federated assemblies.

A county council consists of the reeves and deputy reeves of the towns, villages and townships. The head of the county council is the warden, who is elected by the council from among its own members.

A regional council consists of the heads of council of the local municipalities, as well as a varying number of regional councillors, who are elected on the basis of representation, either directly or indirectly. The head of the regional council is the chairman who is elected by council but who, unlike a county warden, need not have been a council member.

No municipality in Ontario may incur long-term debts without the sanction of the tribunal created by the Provincial Legislature and known as the Ontario Municipal Board. Debenture obligations incurred by municipalities for utility undertakings (water-works and electric light and power systems) are discharged ordinarily out of revenues derived from the sale of utility services and do not fall upon the ratepayers.

Municipal councils have no jurisdiction for education beyond the collection of taxes for school purposes. Responsibility for providing, operating and maintaining school facilities, and for the supply of teachers, rests with local education authorities known as Boards of Education or School Boards. These Boards are now generally organized on a county or regional basis. Apart from some of the larger cities, local municipal school boards no longer exist.

Municipal institutions come under the jurisdiction of the Provincial Ministry of Intergovernmental Affairs. One of the principal functions of the Ministry is to advise and assist municipalities on such matters as accounting, reporting, auditing, budgeting and planning. Educational support and guidance at the provincial level is the responsibility of the Ministry of Education, which deals with the training of teachers and the formulation of curriculum. (At the university and community college level, education support services are provided by the Ministry of Colleges and Universities.)

There are considerable areas in the northernmost parts of Ontario where as yet there is little or no settlement of population. In such areas no municipal organization exists, and control for all purposes over such areas remains in the hands of the Provincial Government.

FINANCE. The gross revenue and expenditure and the net cash requirements (in Canadian $1,000) for years ending 31 March were as follows:

	1984–85	*1985–86*	*1986–87*	*1987–88*	*1989–90*
Gross revenue	23,765	26,228	28,454	33,866	40,713
Gross expenditure	26,430	32,562	31,031	34,846	41,290
Net cash requirement	1,701	2,134	1,544	980	577

Gross revenue and expenditure figures include all non-budgetary transactions, *i.e.*, the lending and investment activity of the Government to Crown corporations, agencies and municipalities as well as the repayment of these loans or recovery of investments. Transactions on behalf of Ontario Hydro are excluded.

ENERGY AND NATURAL RESOURCES

Electricity (1988). Ontario Hydro recorded for the calendar year an installed generating capacity of 30,385m. kw. and a net energy output generated and purchased of 139,413m. kwh.

Minerals (1988). The total value of shipments from mines was $7,200m. Important commodities (in $1m.) were: Nickel, 2,166; copper, 824; uranium, 523; gold, 1,003; zinc, 549. The mining industry employed about 25,000 people in 1988.

Agriculture. In 1988, 3·5m. hectares were under field crops with total farm receipts of $5,625m.

Forestry. According to the most recent inventory (1988) the total area of productive forest is 39·9m. hectares, comprising: Softwoods, 26·3m.; hardwoods, 13·6m. The growing stock equals 5,102m. cu. metres. The estimated value of shipments by the forest products industry (including logging) was (1988) $10,220m.

INDUSTRY AND TRADE

Industry (1988). Ontario is Canada's most highly industrialized province. About 73% of value added in commodity-producing industries is accounted for by manufacturing. Construction is next with 10%.

In 1988, the labour force was 5,118,000. Total labour income was $125,980m. The 1988 Gross Provincial Product (GPP) was $248,146m.

The leading manufacturing industries are motor vehicles and parts, iron and steel, meat and meat preparations, dairy products, paper and paperboard, chemical products, petroleum and coal products, machinery and equipment, metal stamping and pressing and communications equipment.

Trade. In 1988 Ontario exported 49% ($65,296m.) of Canada's total foreign trade.

COMMUNICATIONS

Roads. There were, in 1988, 155,075·3 km of roads. Motor licences (on the road) numbered (1988) 7,191,370, of which 4,577,803. were passenger cars, 1,059,092 commercial vehicles, 28,341 buses, 1,032,887 trailers, 138,869 motor cycles and 285,744 snow vehicles.

Railways. The provincially-owned Ontario Northland Railway has about 550 miles of track and the Algoma Central Railway 325 miles. The Canadian National and Canadian Pacific Railways operate a total of about 9,500 miles in Ontario. There is a metro and tramway network in Toronto.

Post (1987). Telephone service is provided by 30 independent systems (178,527 telephones) and Bell Canada (10m. telephones).

EDUCATION. There is a complete provincial system of elementary and secondary schools as well as private schools. In 1988 publicly financed elementary and secondary schools had a total enrolment of 1,857,921 pupils.

In 1965 Ontario established Colleges of Applied Arts and Technology (CAATS). There are now 22 of these publicly owned colleges with full-time enrolment (1987) of 95,043 in full-time academic courses.

The University of Toronto, founded in 1827 (full-time enrolment, 1988, 37,055), and 14 other major universities (total full-time enrolment, 1987, 200,914), all receive provincial grants. The general expenditure of the provincial ministries of education and colleges and universities for 1988-89 was $7,780m.

Further Reading

Statistical Information: Annual publications of the Ontario Ministry of Treasury and Economics include: *Ontario Statistics; Ontario Budget; Public Accounts; Financial Report.*
Guillet, E. C., *Pioneer Days in Upper Canada.* Toronto, 1933
McDonald, D. C. (ed.) *The Government and Politics of Ontario.* 2nd ed. Toronto, 1980
Middleton, J. E., *The Province of Ontario: A History 1615–1927.* Toronto, 1927, 4 vols.
Schull, J., *Ontario since 1867.* Toronto, 1978

PRINCE EDWARD ISLAND

HISTORY. The earliest discovery of the island is not satisfactorily known, but the first recorded visit was by Jacques Cartier in 1534, who named it Isle St-Jean; it was first settled by the French, but was taken from them in 1758. It was annexed to Nova Scotia in 1763, and constituted a separate colony in 1769. Prince Edward Island entered the Confederation on 1 July 1873.

AREA AND POPULATION. The province, which is the smallest in Canada, lies in the Gulf of St Lawrence, and is separated from the mainland of New Brunswick and Nova Scotia by Northumberland Strait. The area of the island is 2,185 sq. miles (5,660 sq. km). Total population (census, 1986), 126,646; (estimate, 1989), 130,200. Population of the principal cities: Charlottetown (capital), 15,776; Summerside, 8,020.

Vital statistics, *see* p. 272.
Religion, *see* p. 291.

CLIMATE. The cool temperate climate is affected in winter by the freezing of the St. Lawrence, which reduces winter temperatures. Charlottetown. Jan. 19°F (–7·2°C), July 67°F (19·4°C). Annual rainfall 43" (1,077 mm).

CONSTITUTION AND GOVERNMENT. The provincial government is administered by a Lieut.-Governor-in-Council (Cabinet) and a Legislative Assembly of 32 members who are elected for up to 5 years. In June 1989, parties in the Legislative Assembly were: Liberals, 30; Progressive Conservatives, 2.

Lieut.-Governor: Lloyd G. MacPhail (sworn in 1 Aug. 1985).
The Executive Council was composed as follows in Nov. 1989::

Premier, President of the Executive Council, Minister of Justice and Attorney-General: Hon. Joseph A. Ghiz, QC.

Finance and Environment: Hon. Gilbert R. Clements. *Community and Cultural Affairs and Fisheries and Aquaculture:* Hon. J. G. Leonce Bernard. *Industry:* Hon. Robert J. Morrissey. *Health and Social Services:* Hon. Wayne D. Cheverie, QC. *Transportation and Public Works:* Hon. Gordon MacInnis. *Agriculture:* Hon. Keith Milligan. *Education:* Hon. Paul Connolly. *Energy and Forestry:* Hon. Barry Hicken. *Tourism and Parks:* Hon. Nancy Guptill. *Labour:* Hon. Roberta Hubley.

Flag: A banner of the arms, *i.e.*, a white field bearing 3 small trees and a larger tree on a compartment, all green, and at the top a red band with a golden lion; on 3 sides a border of red and white rectangles.

Local Government. The Municipalities Act, 1983, provides for the incorporation of Towns and Communities. The City of Charlottetown and the town of Summerside are incorporated under private Acts of the Legislature.

FINANCE. Revenue and expenditure (in Canadian $) for 5 financial years ending 31 March:

	1985–86	*1986–87*	*1987–88*	*1988–89*	*1989–90*
Revenue	457,173,805	490,913,588	533,231,248	600,319,801	638,415,900
Expenditure	471,627,027	509,867,825	546,010,988	605,092,077	636,117,700

ENERGY AND NATURAL RESOURCES

Electricity. Electric power is supplied to 100% of the population. In 1988, total supply of electric energy was 703,964 mwh; net generation, 84,731 mwh. In 1977 the province completed the laying of an undersea power cable which links the island with New Brunswick and the Maritime Power Grid. In 1980, 30 miles of additional 138 kv transmission line was added to the PEI system; total received from other provinces, 619,511 mwh and delivered to other provinces, 278 mwh. In 1986, about 98% of power requirements were supplied through this system.

Agriculture. Total area of farms occupied approximately 673,196 acres in 1986 out of the total land area of 1,399,040 acres. Farm cash receipts in 1988 were $206·2m. with cash receipts from potatoes accounting for 30·5% of the total. Cash receipts from dairy products, cattle and hogs followed in importance. The land in forest covered 700,000 acres in 1986 and total value of forest products sold in 1986 was about $7m. For particulars of agricultural production and livestock, *see under* CANADA, pp. 284–85.

Fisheries. The fishery in 1988 had a landed value of $78·3m. Lobsters and shellfish accounted for 85·2% of the total. Value of groundfish landings accounted for 6%; pelagic and estuarial, 5·5%; Irish moss, 3·3%.

INDUSTRY AND TRADE

Industry. Value of manufacturing shipments for all industries in 1988 was $357·5m.

Labour. Per capita personal income rose from $12,031 in 1986 to $13,134 in 1987. The average weekly wage (industrial aggregate) rose from $362·39 in 1987 to $379·26 in 1988. The labour force averaged 62,000 in 1988, while employment averaged 54,000.

In 1988, provincial GDP for manufacturing was $77m.; construction, $109m. In 1988, total value of retail trade was $703·5m.

Tourism. The value of the tourist industry was estimated at $90m. in 1988 with 237,099 tourist parties.

COMMUNICATIONS

Roads. The province has a total of 5,292 km of road, including 3,766 km of paved highway.

Railways. Rail service was provided over 235 miles of track within the province and joined with the national railways system *via* the New Brunswick–Prince Edward Island ferry service but the rail service closed on 31 Dec. 1989.

Aviation. In 1987 air service for passengers, mail and cargo provided 15 flights daily in each direction between the province and various points in eastern Canada. A daily bus service operates between various centres in the province and 3 times daily to the mainland.

Shipping. A ferry service provides rail and highway communication with New Brunswick by means of 4 large ferries, 2 of which are powerful ice-breakers. Another ferry service employing 4 ferries operates between the province and Nova Scotia from April through Dec. A third ferry service employing 1 ferry operates between the province and Magdalen Islands, Quebec, during the open navigation season. The province has 4 ports accommodating marine shipping.

Telecommunications. In 1988 there were approximately 89,647 telephones.

EDUCATION (1988–89). Under the regional school boards there are 66 public schools, 1,395 teaching positions, 24,708 students. There is one undergraduate university (over 2,073 full-time students), and a veterinary college (143 students), both in Charlottetown. A college of applied arts and technology in centres across the province served 8,437 students (full-time and continuing education programmes), which equated to 2,971 full-time equivalent students. Total expenditure on education in the year ending 31 March 1989 was $134,195,600.

Further Reading

Baldwin, D. O., *Abegweit: Land of the Red Soil.* Charlottetown, 1985
Bolger, F. W. P., *Canada's Smallest Province.* Charlottetown, 1973
Clark, A. H., *Three Centuries and the Island.* Toronto, 1959
Hocking, A., *Prince Edward Island.* Toronto, 1978
MacKinnon, F., *The Government of Prince Edward Island.* Toronto, 1951

QUEBEC—QUÉBEC

HISTORY. Quebec was formerly known as New France or Canada from 1534 to 1763; as the province of Quebec from 1763 to 1790; as Lower Canada from 1791 to 1846; as Canada East from 1846 to 1867, and when, by the union of the four original provinces, the Confederation of the Dominion of Canada was formed, it again became known as the province of Quebec (Québec).

The Quebec Act, passed by the British Parliament in 1774, guaranteed to the people of the newly conquered French territory in North America security in their religion and language, their customs and tenures, under their own civil laws.

In the referendum held 20 May 1980, 59·5% voted against and 40·5% for 'separatism'.

AREA AND POPULATION. The area of Quebec (as amended by the Labrador Boundary Award) is 1,667,926 sq. km (594,860 sq. miles), of which 1,315,134 sq. km is land area and 352,792 sq. km water. Of this extent, 911,106 sq. km represent the Territory of Ungava, annexed in 1912 under the Quebec Boundaries Extension Act. The population (census 1986) was 6,532,461. Estimate (1988) 6,639,200.

Principal cities (1986): Quebec (capital), 164,580; Montreal, 1,015,420; Laval, 284,164; Sherbrooke, 74,438; Verdun, 60,246; Hull, 58,722; Trois-Rivières, 50,122.

Vital statistics, *see* p. 272.
Religion, *see* p. 291.

CLIMATE. Cool temperate in the south, but conditions are more extreme towards the north. Winters are severe and snowfall considerable, but summer temperatures are quite warm. Rain occurs at all seasons. Quebec. Jan. 10°F (–12·2°C), July 66°F (18·9°C). Annual rainfall 40" (1,008 mm). Montreal. Jan. 11°F (–11·7°C), July 67°F (19·4°C). Annual rainfall 30" (776 mm).

CONSTITUTION AND GOVERNMENT. There is a Legislative Assembly consisting of 122 members, elected in 122 electoral districts for 4 years. At the provincial general elections held 2 Dec. 1985, Liberals won 99 seats and *Parti Québecois*, 23. The Liberal Party was led by Robert Bourassa who failed to win a seat but did so at a subsequent by-election on 20 Jan. 1986.

Lieut.-Governor: The Hon. Gilles Lamontagne.

Flag: The Fleurdelysé flag, blue with a white cross, and in each quarter a white fleur-de-lis.

Senior members of the Executive Council as in Dec. 1988, were as follows:

Prime Minister: Robert Bourassa.

Deputy Prime Minister and Cultural Affairs: Lise Bacon. *Finance:* Gérard D. Lévesque. *Education:* Claude Ryan. *Justice:* Gil Rémillard.

General-delegate in London: Reed Scowen (59 Pall Mall, London SW1Y 5JH).
General-delegate in New York: Léo Paré (17 West 50th St., Rockefeller Center, New York 10020).
General-delegate in Paris: Jean-Louis Roy (66 Pergolèse, Paris 75116).

ECONOMY

Budget. Ordinary revenue and expenditure (in Canadian $1,000) for fiscal years ending 31 March:

	1983–84	*1984–85*	*1985–86*	*1986–87*	*1987–88*
Revenue	21,410,969	23,310,027	24,080,778	25,646,247	28,363,891
Expenditure	24,523,514	25,542,499	27,222,178	28,465,454	30,738,141

The total net debt at 31 March 1988 was $25,064,023,000.

ENERGY AND NATURAL RESOURCES

Electricity. Water power is one of the most important natural resources of the province of Quebec. Its turbine installation represents about 40% of the aggregate of Canada. At the end of 1987 the installed generating capacity was 32,661 mw. Production, 1988, was 149,005 gwh.

Minerals (1988). The estimated value of the mineral production (metal mines only) was $2,721,380,000. Chief minerals: Iron ore, (confidential); copper, $145,127,000; gold, $562,868,000; zinc, $120,956,000.

The second major iron-ore development in northern Quebec is, like the one at Knob Lake which gave birth to Schefferville, based on the Quebec–Labrador Trough which extends from Lac Jeannine to the northern tip of Ungava peninsula. The port of Sept-Iles and the railway connecting it with Schefferville allow easy shipment to the furnaces and steel mills of Canada, the USA and Europe.

Non-metallic minerals produced include: Asbestos ($190,285,000; about 75·6% of Canadian production), titane-dioxide (confidential), industrial lime, dolomite and brucite, quartz and pyrite. Among the building materials produced were: Stone, $219,762,000; cement, $194,850,000; sand and gravel, $74,404,000; lime, (confidential).

Agriculture. In 1988 the total area (estimate) of the principal field crops was 2,026,000 hectares. The yield of the principal crops was (1988 in 1,000 tonnes):

Crops	*Yield*	*Crops*	*Yield*
Tame hay	6,160	Fodder corn	1,940
Oats for grain	284	Maize for grain	1,500
Potatoes	385	Barley	460
Mixed grains	75	Buckwheat	12

The farm cash receipts from farming operations estimated in 1988 amounted to $3,385,869,000. The principal items being: Livestock and products, $2,385,978,000; crops, $535,408,000; dairy supplements payments, $135,656,000, forest and maple products, $121,543,000.

Forestry. Forests cover an area of 764,245 sq. km. About 545,703 sq. km are classified as productive forests, of which 649,468 sq. km are provincial crown land and 111,782 sq. km are privately owned. Quebec leads the Canadian provinces in pulpwood production, having nearly half of the Canadian estimated total.

In 1986 production of lumber was softwood and hardwood, 11,308,834 cu. metres; woodpulp, 6,119,546 tonnes.

Fisheries. The principal fish are cod, herring, red fish, lobster and salmon. Total catch of sea fish, 1988, 89,150 tonnes, valued at $97,610,000.

INDUSTRY AND TRADE

Industry. In 1986 there were 11,063 industrial establishments in the province; employees, 503,403; salaries and wages, $12,501,126,000; cost of materials,

$37,497,921,000; value of shipments, $66,711,585,000. Among the leading industries are petroleum refining, pulp and paper mills, smelting and refining, dairy products, slaughtering and meat processing, motor vehicle manufacturing, women's clothing, saw-mills and planing mills, iron and steel mills, commercial printing.

Commerce. In 1988 the value of Canadian exports through Quebec custom ports was $22,130,573,000; value of imports, $22,692,841,000.

COMMUNICATIONS

Roads. In 1988 there were 59,897 km of roads and 3,765,335 registered motor vehicles.

Railways. There were (1988) 8,660 km of railway. There is a metro system in Montreal.

Aviation. In 1988 Quebec had 2 international airports, Dorval (Montreal) with landing runway of 8·4 km and Mirabel (Montreal) with 7·3 km.

Post and Broadcasting. Telephones numbered 3,429,375 in 1987 and there were 32 television and 133 radio stations.

Newspapers (1989). There were 10 French- and 3 English-language daily newspapers.

EDUCATION. The province has 7 universities: 3 English-language universities, McGill (Montreal) founded in 1821, Bishop (Lennoxville) founded in 1845 and the Concordia University (Montreal) granted a charter in 1975; 4 French-language universities: Laval (Quebec) founded in 1852, Montreal University, opened in 1876 as a branch of Laval and became independent in 1920, Sherbrooke University founded in 1954 and University of Quebec founded in 1968.

In 1987–88 there were 116,501 full-time university students and 118,815 part-time students.

In 1987–88, in pre-kindergartens, there were 6,216 pupils; in kindergartens, 89,839; primary schools, 584,734; in secondary schools, 456,024; in colleges (post-secondary, non-university), 154,058; and in classes for children with special needs, 132,097. The school boards had a total of 59,966 teachers.

Expenditure of the Departments of Education for 1987–88, $7,569,267,000 net. This included $1,232,689,000 for universities, $4,704,461,000 for public primary and secondary schools, $242,099,000 for private primary and secondary schools and $1,069,013,000 for colleges.

Further Reading

Statistical Information: The Quebec Bureau of Statistics was established in 1912. The Bureau, which reports to the Finance Dept. since March 1983, collects, compiles and distributes statistical information relative to Quebec. *Director:* Luc Bessette.

A statistical information list is available on request. Among the most important publications are: *Le Québec Statistique, Statistiques* (quarterly), *Comptes économiques du Québec* (annual), *Situation démographique* (annual), *Commerce international du Québec* (annual), *Investissements privés et publics* (annual).

Baudoin, L., *Le Droit civil de la province de Québec*. Montreal, 1953
Blanchard, R., *Canada-français*. Paris, 1959
Hamelin, J., *Histoire du Québec*. St-Hyacinthe, 1978
Jacobs, J., *The Question of Separatism: Quebec and the Struggle for Sovereignty*. London, 1981
McWhinney, E., *Quebec and the Constitution*. Univ. of Toronto Press, 1979
Ouellet, F., *Histoire de la Chambre de Commerce de Québec, 1809–1959*. Québec, 1959
Raynauld, A., *Croissance et structure économiques de la province de Québec*. Québec, 1961
Trofimenkoff, S. M., *Action Française*. Univ. of Toronto Press, 1975
Wade, F. M., *The French Canadians, 1760–1967*. Toronto, 1968.—*Canadian Dualism: Studies of French–English Relations*. Quebec–Toronto, 1960

SASKATCHEWAN

HISTORY. Saskatchewan derives its name from its major river system, which the Cree Indians called 'Kis-is-ska-tche-wan', meaning 'swift flowing'. It officially became a province when it joined the Confederation on 1 Sept. 1905.

In 1670 King Charles II granted to Prince Rupert and his friends a charter covering exclusive trading rights in 'all the land drained by streams finding their outlet in the Hudson Bay'. This included what is now Saskatchewan. The trading company was first known as The Governor and Company of Adventurers of England; later as the Hudson's Bay Company. In 1869 the Northwest Territories was formed, and this included Saskatchewan. In 1882 the District of Saskatchewan was formed. By 1885 the North-West Mounted Police had been inaugurated, with headquarters in Regina (now the capital), and the Canadian Pacific Railway's transcontinental line had been completed, bringing a stream of immigrants to southern Saskatchewan. The Hudson's Bay Company surrendered its claim to territory in return for cash and land around the existing trading posts. Legislative government was introduced.

AREA AND POPULATION. Saskatchewan is bounded on the west by Alberta, on the east by Manitoba, to the north by the Northwest Territories; to the south it is bordered by the US states of Montana and North Dakota. The area of the province is 251,700 sq. miles (570,113 sq. km), of which 220,182 sq. miles is land area and 31,518 sq. miles is water. The population, 1986 census, was 1,010,198. Population of cities, 1986 census: Regina (capital), 175,064; Saskatoon, 177,641; Moose Jaw, 35,073; Prince Albert, 33,686; Yorkton, 15,574; Swift Current, 15,666; North Battleford, 14,876; Estevan, 10,161; Weyburn, 10,153; Lloydminster, 7,155; Melfort, 6,078; Melville, 5,123.

Vital statistics, *see* p. 272.

Religion, *see* p. 291.

CLIMATE. A cold continental climate, with severe winters and warm summers. Rainfall amounts are greatest from May to Aug. Regina. Jan. 0°F (–17·8°C), July 65°F (18·3°C). Annual rainfall 15" (373 mm).

CONSTITUTION AND GOVERNMENT. The provincial government is vested in a Lieut.-Governor, an Executive Council and a Legislative Assembly, elected for 5 years. Women were given the franchise in 1916 and are also eligible for election to the legislature. State of parties in Oct. 1989: Progressive Conservative, 38; New Democratic Party, 26.

Lieut.-Governor: Hon. Sylvia O. Fedoruk.

Flag: Green over gold, with the shield of the province in the canton, and a green and red prairie lily in the fly.

The Progressive Conservative Ministry in Nov. 1989 was composed as follows:

Premier, Agriculture and Food: Grant Divine.

Deputy Premier, Urban Affairs, Minister responsible for the Status of Women: Pat Smith. *Health:* George McLeod. *Finance, Public Participation:* Lorne Hepworth. *Provincial Secretary, Economic Development and Tourism:* Eric Berntson. *Justice and Attorney-General, Telephone:* Gary Lane. *Rural Development:* Neil Hardy. *Culture, Multiculturism and Recreation:* Colin Maxwell. *Environment and Public Safety, Indian and Native Affairs:* Grant Hodgins. *Human Resources, Labour and Employment, Consumer and Commercial Affairs:* Grant Schmidt. *Trade and Investment:* Jack Klein. *Education, Science and Technology:* Ray Meiklejohn. *Highways and Transportation:* Sherwin Peterson. *Energy and Mines:* Richard Swenson. *Parks and Renewable Resources, Northern Affairs:* Lorne Kopelchuk. *Family, Minister responsible for Seniors:* Beattie Martin. *Social Services:* William Neudorf.

Agent-General in London: Paul Rousseau, 21 Pall Mall, SW1Y 5LP.

Local Government. The organization of a city requires a minimum population of 5,000 persons; that of a town, 500; that of a village, 100 people. No requirements as to population exist for the rural municipality.

Cities, towns, villages and rural municipalities are governed by elected councils, which consist of a mayor and 6–20 aldermen in a city; a mayor and 6 councillors in a town; a mayor and 2 other members in a village; a reeve and a councillor for each division in a rural municipality (usually 6).

FINANCE. Budget and net assets (years ending 31 March) in Canadian $1,000:

	1986–87	*1987–88*	*1988–89*	*1989–90*
Budgetary revenue	3,358,742	3,202,508	3,607,683	4,083,400
Budgetary expenditure	3,747,892	3,779,743	3,935,896	4,309,460

ENERGY AND NATURAL RESOURCES. Agriculture used to dominate the history and economics of Saskatchewan, but the 'prairie province' is now a rapidly developing mining and manufacturing area. It is a major supplier of oil; has the world's largest deposits of potash; and net value of non-agricultural production accounts for (1987) 89·5% of the provincial economy.

Electricity. The Saskatchewan Power Corporation generated 12,617m. kwh. in 1988.

Minerals. The 1988 mineral sales were valued at $2,910,048,422, including (in $1m.): Petroleum, 1,044·2; natural gas, 206·1; coal and others, 110·3; gold, 20·9; copper, 6·1; zinc, 2·9; potash, 974·3; salt, 20·2; uranium, 463·3; sodium sulphate, 22·4.

Agriculture. Saskatchewan normally produces about two-thirds of Canada's wheat. Wheat production in 1988 (in 1,000 tonnes), was 6,858 from 19·2m. acres; oats, 478 from 800,000 acres; barley, 2,090 from 3·1m. acres; rye, 89 from 290,000 acres; rapeseed, 1,701 from 3·9m. acres; flax, 152 from 500,000 acres. Livestock (1 July 1988): Cattle and calves, 2·15m.; swine, 845,000; sheep and lambs, 51,000. Poultry in 1988: Chickens, 11,864,000; turkeys 708,000. Cash income from the sale of farm products in 1988 was $4,445m. At the June 1986 census there were 63,431 farms in the province, each being a holding of 1 acre or more with sales of agricultural products during the previous 12 months of $250 or more.

The South Saskatchewan River irrigation project, whose main feature is the Gardiner Dam, was completed in 1967. It will ultimately provide for an area of 200,000 to 500,000 acres of irrigated cultivation in Central Saskatchewan. As of 1988, 205,093 acres are irrigated. Total irrigated land in the province, 307,748 acres.

Forestry. Half of Saskatchewan's area is forested, but only 115,000 sq. km are of commercial value at present. Forest products valued at $259m. were produced in 1988. The province's first pulp-mill, at Prince Albert, went into production in 1968; its daily capacity is 1,000 tons of high-grade kraft pulp.

Fur Production. In 1987–88 wild fur production was estimated at $5,741,824. Ranch-raised fur production amounted to $155,800.

Fisheries. The lakeside value of the 1988–89 commercial fish catch of 3·3m. kg was $3·4m.

INDUSTRY. In 1986 Saskatchewan had 847 manufacturing establishments, employing 19,295 persons. Manufacturing contributed $1,135m., construction $796m. to the total gross domestic product at factor cost of $18,307m. in 1988.

TOURISM. An estimated 1·5m. out of province tourists spent $189m. in 1988.

COMMUNICATIONS

Roads. In 1988 there were 25,273 km of provincial highways, 157,896 km of municipal roads (including prairie trails). Motor vehicles registered totalled (1988) 728,698. Bus services are provided by 2 major lines.

Railways. There were (1988) approximately 11,746 km of main railway track.

Aviation. Saskatchewan had 2 major airports, 176 airports and landing strips in 1987.

Post and Broadcasting. There were (1988) 716 post offices (excluding sub-post offices), 82 TV and re-broadcasting stations and 50 AM and FM radio stations. 746,925 telephones were connected to the Saskatchewan Telecommunications system in 1988.

EDUCATION. The University of Saskatchewan was established at Saskatoon on 3 April 1907. In 1988–89 it had 13,978 full-time students, 3,513 part-time students and 995 full-time teaching staff. The University of Regina was established 1 July 1974; in 1988–89 it had 5,958 full-time and 4,072 part-time students and 386 full-time faculty members.

The Saskatchewan education system in 1988–89 consisted of 111 school divisions and 5 comprehensive school boards, of which 22 are Roman Catholic separate school divisions, serving 142,259 elementary pupils, 57,353 high-school students and 3,090 students enrolled in special classes. In addition, provincial technical and vocational schools had 27,876 students enrolled in 1988. In addition there are 10 community colleges with an enrolment of approximately 46,222 students in the 1988–89 school year.

Further Reading

Tourist and industrial publications, descriptive of the Government's programme, are obtainable from the Department of Industry and Commerce; other government publications from Government Information Services (Legislative Building, Regina).

Saskatchewan Economic Review. Executive Council, Regina. Annual

Archer, J. H., *Saskatchewan: A History*. Saskatoon, 1980

Arora, V., *The Saskatchewan Bibliography*. Regina, 1980

Richards, J. S. and Fung, K. I. (eds.) *Atlas of Saskatchewan*. Univ. of Saskatchewan, 1969

THE NORTHWEST TERRITORIES

HISTORY. The Territory was developed by the Hudson's Bay Company and the North West Company (of Montreal) from the 17th century. The Canadian Government bought out the Hudson's Bay Company in 1869 and the Territory was annexed to Canada in 1870. The Arctic Islands lying north of the Canadian mainland were annexed to Canada in 1880 by Queen Victoria.

AREA AND POPULATION. The total area of the Territories is 1,304,903 sq. miles (3,379,700 sq. km), divided into 5 administrative regions: Fort Smith, Inuvik, Kitikmeot, Keewatin and Baffin. The population in June 1986 was 51,384, 29,602 of whom were Inuit (Eskimo) or Dene (Indian) and Metis. When the transfer of governmental responsibility from Ottawa to the Territorial capital at Yellowknife took place in 1967, the population of Yellowknife increased by the influx of civil servants from 3,741 in 1966 to 11,077 in 1985. Main centres (June 1985): Inuvik (3,166), Fort Smith (2,468), Hay River (3,142), Iqaluit, formerly Frobisher Bay (2,954), Rankin Inlet (1,315), Cambridge Bay (902).

CLIMATE. Conditions range from cold continental to polar, with long hard winters and short cool summers. Precipitation is low. Yellowknife. Jan. –15°F (–26°C), July 61°F (16·1°C). Annual rainfall 10" (256 mm).

CONSTITUTION AND GOVERNMENT. The Northwest Territories comprises all that portion of Canada lying north of the 60th parallel of N. lat. except those portions within the Yukon Territory and the Provinces of Quebec and Newfoundland: It also includes the islands in Hudson Bay, James Bay and Ungava Bay except those within the Provinces of Manitoba, Ontario and Quebec.

The Northwest Territories is governed by a Government Leader, with a 7-member cabinet and a Legislative Assembly. The Assembly is composed of 24 members elected for a 4-year term of office. A Commissioner of the Northwest Territories acts as a lieutenant-governor and is the federal government's senior representative in the Territorial government. The seat of government was transferred from Ottawa to Yellowknife when it was named Territorial capital on 18 Jan. 1967.

Government Leader: Dennis Patterson.

Commissioner: J. H. Parker.

Flag: Vertically, blue, white, blue, with the white of double width and bearing the shield of the Territory.

Legislative powers are exercised by the Executive Council on such matters as taxation within the Territories in order to raise revenue, maintenance of justice, licences, solemnization of marriages, education, public health, property, civil rights and generally all matters of a local nature.

The Territorial Government has assumed most of the responsibility for the administration of the Northwest Territories but political control of Crown lands and non-renewable resources still rests with the Federal Government. On 6 Sept. 1988, the Federal and Territorial Governments signed an agreement for the transfer of management responsibilities for oil and gas resources, located on- and off-shore, in the Northwest Territories to the Territorial Government. In a Territory-wide plebiscite in April 1982, a majority of residents voted in favour of dividing the Northwest Territories into two jurisdictions, east and west. Two forums for each jurisdiction have been created to develop constitutions for the proposed new territories and to negotiate a dividing boundary.

ENERGY AND NATURAL RESOURCES

Oil and Gas. As of Dec. 1988, 27 licences for oil and gas exploration were held for 3·9m. hectares, 17 production licences were held for 62,245 hectares and 78 significant discovery licences were retained on 600,000 hectares.

Crude oil is produced at Norman Wells and piped to Alberta. In 1986, oil production was 117,520 cu. metres.

Minerals. Mineral production in 1987 was valued at $810,005,000, 7% of Canada's total. The Northwest Territories yielded 34% of lead, 25% of zinc, 10% of gold, 7% of cadmium and 8% of silver produced in Canada in 1987.

Trapping and Game. The 150,000 pelts, furs and hides sold by Northwest Territories hunters and trappers in the 1987–88 season were valued at $6·1m. The pelts of highest value are those of the marten, muskrat, polar bear and lynx. A herd of some 4,200 hybrid bison is protected in Wood Buffalo National Park. The only free-ranging herd of Wood Bison in the world is in the Mackenzie Bison Sanctuary. Barren ground caribou are abundant, totalling 1·5m.

Forestry. The principal trees are white and black spruce, jack-pine, tamarack, balsam poplar, aspen and birch. In 1987–88, 62,000 cu. metres of lumber, valued at $3·4m., was produced.

Fisheries. Commercial fishing, principally on Great Slave Lake, in 1987–88 produced 3·6m. lbs of fish valued at $2·7m., principally trout, arctic char and whitefish.

CO-OPERATIVES. There are 39 active co-operatives, including 2 housing co-operatives and one central organization to service local co-operatives, in the Northwest Territories. They are active in handicrafts, furs, fisheries, retail stores, hotels and print shops. Total revenue in 1988 was about $41m.

COMMUNICATIONS

Roads. The Mackenzie Route connects Grimshaw, Alberta, with Hay River, Pine Point, Fort Smith, Fort Providence, Rae-Edzo and Yellowknife. The Mackenzie Highway extension to Fort Simpson and a road between Pine Point and Fort Resolution have both been opened.

Highway service to Inuvik in the Mackenzie Delta was opened in spring 1980, extending north from Dawson, Yukon as the Dempster Highway. The Liard Highway connecting the communities of the Liard River valley to British Columbia opened in 1984.

Railways. There is one small railway system in the north which runs from the Pine Point site and Hay River, on the south shore of Great Slave Lake, 435 miles south to Grimshaw, Alberta, where it connects with the CN Rail's main system, but it was not in use in 1988.

Aviation (1988). Fourteen certified airports are operated by the federal Department of Transport and there are 25 certified and 13 uncertified airports operated by the Government of the Northwest Territories. Numerous certified and uncertified airports are operated privately in support of military operations, mining and resource exploration, and tourism. There are 20 privately-owned float plane bases. Major communities receive daily jet service to southern points. Most smaller communities are served by scheduled jet-prop air service several times weekly.

Shipping. A direct inland-water transportation route for about 1,700 miles is provided by the Mackenzie River and its tributaries, the Athabasca and Slave rivers. Subsidiary routes on Lake Athabasca, Great Slave Lake and Great Bear River and Lake total more than 800 miles.

Post and Broadcasting (1989). There were 60 post offices. The CBC northern service operated radio stations at Yellowknife, Inuvik, Frobisher Bay and Rankin Inlet. Virtually all communities of 150 or over were receiving television *via* satellite. Telephone service is provided by common carriers to nearly all communities in the Northwest Territories. Those few communities without service have high frequency or very high frequency radios for emergency use.

EDUCATION AND WELFARE

Education. In 1988-89 there were 3 divisional boards of education and several other regions were working towards divisional board status, which provides for more local and regional control of education. There were also 3 independent boards of education operating in Yellowknife: A separate school board, a public school board and a board of secondary education.

In 1988-89 there were 72 schools operating, with 762 teachers for 12,750 enrolled students. Residences in regional larger communities provide accommodation for students from smaller communities that cannot provide all education services up to grade 12. There is a full range of courses available in the school system: Academic, French immersion, native language and culture, commercial, technical and occupational training. Post secondary programmes include the 5-campus Arctic College, which offers a variety of certificate and diploma programmes, along with a first-year general arts university programme. Financial assistance (from the territorial government) is available to qualifying students for post-secondary studies.

Health. In April 1988 responsibility for health services was transferred to the territorial government by the Government of Canada. In 1989 the Department of Health, Government of the Northwest Territories, was responsible for 6 hospitals (Yellowknife, Hay River, Inuvik, Churchill, Winnepeg, Montreal), 6 public health centres (Yellowknife, Hay River, Inuvik, Rae, Fort Simpson, Fort Smith) and 6 satellite health centres.

Welfare. Welfare services are provided by professional social workers. Facilities included (1989) for children: 8 group homes, 1 receiving home, 3 residential treatment centres, 3 secure custody facilities for young offenders, 3 open custody young offender centres and 4 homes for the aged.

Further Reading

Annual Report of the Government of the Northwest Territories
Government Activities in the North, 1983–84. Indian and Northern Affairs, Canada
NWT Data Book 86/87. Yellowknife, 1986
Dawson, C. A., *The New North-West*. Toronto, 1947
MacKay, D., *The Honorable Company*. Toronto, 1949
Zaslow, M., *The Opening of the Canadian North 1870–1914*. Toronto, 1971

YUKON TERRITORY

HISTORY. Formerly part of the Northwest Territories, Yukon was joined to the Dominion as a separate territory on 13 June 1898.

AREA AND POPULATION. The Yukon Territory is situated in the extreme north-western section of Canada and comprises 482,515 sq. km. of which 4,481 fresh water. The census population in 1981 was 23,153; 1989 (estimate), 29,845. Principal centres are Whitehorse (capital), 20,706; Watson Lake, 1,744; Dawson City, 1,791; Faro, 1,606; Mayo-Elsa, 673.

Vital statistics, *see* p. 272.
Religion, *see* p. 291.

CLIMATE. A cold climate in winter with moderate temperatures in summer provide a considerable annual range of temperature and moderate rainfall. Whitehorse. Jan. 5°F (–15°C), July 56°F (13·3°C). Annual rainfall 10" (250 mm). Dawson City. Jan. –22°F (–30°C), July 57°F (13·9°C). Annual rainfall 13" (mm).

CONSTITUTION AND GOVERNMENT. The Yukon Territory was constituted a separate territory in June 1898. It is governed by a 5-member Executive Council (Cabinet) appointed from the majority party in the 16-member elected Legislative Assembly. The members are elected for a 4-year term. The seat of government is at Whitehorse. A federally appointed Commissioner has the final signing authority for all legislation passed by the Assembly.

Commissioner: Ken McKinnon (appointed 27 March 1986)

Flag: Vertically green, white, blue, in the proportions 2 : 3 : 2, charged in the centre with the arms of the Territory.

The legislative authority of the Assembly includes direct taxation, education, property and civil rights, territorial civil service, municipalities and generally all matters of local or private nature. All other major administration including federal Crown lands, income tax and natural resources is federally controlled. Discussions are continuing between the federal and territorial governments on the transfer of certain federal programmes to the Yukon government. A formula financing agreement allows the Yukon government to determine how it will spend funds transferred from the federal government.

ECONOMY

Planning. The three main sectors of the Yukon economy are government, mining and tourism. The economy has also seen significant growth in the renewable resource industries, with the annual value of raw and processed products of these industries estimated at $12m. to $15m. in 1988. There was also a large increase in activity in the manufacturing sector. Government expenditures were $472m. in 1987–88. The mining industry has made a strong recovery in all sectors. Curragh Resources reopened the large lead-zinc open-pit mine at Faro in 1986, employing 490 people in 1989. In 1988 gold production from Yukon's placer mines was $65m., setting a new 70 year record, and the Territory also had one hardrock gold mine, the Ketza River Mine, near the community of Ross River. The 1989 closing of the United Keno Hill Mine at Elsa was a significant loss to the economy and resulted in the shutdown of the community. Hardrock gold production in 1988 was $10m., silver $8m., lead $100m., zinc $195m., and exploration expenditures were $50m. The tourism industry remains strong with the development of new attractions and facilities, and expansion in the wilderness adventure sector.

Finance. The territorial revenue and expenditure (in Canadian $1,000) for fiscal years ended 31 March was:

	1986–87	*1987–88*	*1988–89*	*1989–90*
Revenue	262,279	276,000	305,000	334,699
Expenditure	266,513	278,800	322,800	334,004

ENERGY AND NATURAL RESOURCES

Electricity. Hydro generated power is supplied through plants at Whitehorse Rapids, Aishihik and Mayo. Thermal (diesel) generated power is supplied to several other communities (Dawson City, Watson Lake, Old Crow, Teslin). Current capacity is 78 mw hydro and 44 mw thermal generated power.

Oil. Dome Petroleum, Gulf, Esso Resources, Petro Canada and Shell had been exploring (1986) extensively for oil in the Beaufort Sea but falling world oil prices resulted in much of this exploration being curtailed after 1987.

Minerals. Mining remains the main industry. Lead, zinc, silver and gold are the chief minerals. Production figures for year ending 31 Dec. 1988 (provisional) in tonnes were: Lead, 100,000; zinc, 118,325; silver, 340; gold, 4. The value of mining production sales in 1988 was $455m. (provisional).

Agriculture. There are areas where the climate is suitable for the production of forage crops (occupying the largest acreage and used as feed for the estimated 2,500 horses), early maturing varieties of cereals and grains and vegetables. In 1984 cereal crop and forage fertility trials were initiated and the Yukon New Crop Development Project began in 1985. In 1987 there were 29 full time and 75 part-time farmers. The total improved acreage was 5,000 acres and the estimated value of agricultural products (farm gate not retail) $1·3m.

Forestry. The forests are part of the great Boreal forest region of Canada which stretches from the east coast of Canada into Alaska and north well above the Arctic Circle. Vast areas are covered by coniferous stands in the southern portion of Yukon with white spruce and lodgepole pine forming pure stands on wet sites and in northern aspects. Deciduous species form pure stands or occur mixed with conifers throughout forest areas.

The value of forest production in 1988 was approximately $3m.

Fisheries. Commercial fishing concentrates on chinook salmon, chum salmon, lake trout and whitefish. The value of fish processed in 1988 was between $3m. and $4m.

Game and Furs. The country abounds with big game, such as moose, goat, caribou, mountain sheep and bear (grizzly and black). The fur trapping industry is considered vital to rural and remote residents and especially native people wishing to maintain a traditional lifestyle. In 1988, 25,860 pelts were taken for a market value of $1,356,225. Marten was the most valuable fur and made up 69% of the total harvest bringing in $954,180 in revenues.

TOURISM. In 1988, 180,000 tourists visited Yukon and spent (estimate) $40m.

COMMUNICATIONS

Roads. The Alaska Highway and its side roads connect Yukon's main communities with Alaska and the provinces and with adjacent mining centres. Interior roads connect the mining communities of Elsa (silver–lead), Faro (lead–zinc–silver) and Dawson City (gold) and mineral exploration properties (lead–zinc and tungsten) north of Ross River. The 727 km Dempster Highway north of Dawson City connects with Inuvik, on the Arctic coast; this highway, the first public road to be built to the Arctic ocean, was opened in Aug. 1979. The Carcross–Skagway road was opened in May 1979, providing a new access to the Pacific Ocean. There are 4,688 km of roads in the Territory, of which about 250 km are paved. The other major roads, including the Alaska Highway, have received a new surface treatment which resembles pavement and the rest are all-weather gravel of which 1,364 km are accessible during the summer months only.

Railways. The 176-km White Pass and Yukon Railway connected Whitehorse with year-round ocean shipping at Skagway, Alaska, but was closed in 1982. A modified passenger service was restarted in 1988 to take cruise ship tourists from Skagway to the White Pass summit and back. There are no plans to run the service all the way to Whitehorse.

Aviation. In 1989 one commercial airline provided regular daily service between Whitehorse, Watson Lake, Edmonton and Vancouver. A second airline discontinued its winter service in 1989 and planned to resume a reduced summer service in 1990. Regularly scheduled air services extend from Whitehorse to interior communities of Faro, Mayo, Dawson City, Old Crow, Ross River, Watson Lake and Juneau, Alaska with connecting service to Anchorage, Seattle, Fairbanks and other points in Alaska. A Whitehorse charter company planned to start regularly scheduled service to Anchorage, Alaska and Edmonton, Alberta in 1990. There are several commercial bush plane operations for charter service.

Shipping. The majority of goods are shipped into the Territory by truck over the Alaska and Stewart–Cassiar Highways. Some goods are shipped by barge to Skagway and Haines, Alaska, and then trucked to Whitehorse, for distribution throughout the Territory. The majority of goods are transported by road within the Territory, while a modest amount is shipped by air. Although navigable, the rivers are no longer used for shipping.

Post and Broadcasting. There are 3 radio stations in Whitehorse and 13 low-power relay radio transmitters operated by CBC. CHON-FM, operated by Northern Native Broadcasting Society offers 12 hours of programming, 5 days a week, and is transmitted to virtually all Yukon communities by satellite. Dawson City has its own community run radio station, CFYT, which provides 15 hours of local programming 7 days a week. There are also 10 basic and 6 extended pay-cable TV channels in Whitehorse, and private cable operations in Faro and Watson Lake. Live CBC national television is provided by the Anik satellite to all communities in the Territory. All telephone and telecommunications in the Territory are provided by Northwestel, a subsidiary of Bell Canada Enterprizes. Microwave stations and satellite ground stations now provide most of the telephone transmissions services to the communities.

Newspapers. In 1989 there were 2 newspapers, 1 published 5 days a week and 1 twice a week, in Whitehorse. New monthly papers were established in Faro and Dawson City. *Dan Sha*, a publication for native people, is a monthly. Other publications include a monthly newspaper aimed at the Francophone population, a quarterly produced by a women's organization in Whitehorse, and a private monthly magazine which is distributed free.

EDUCATION AND WELFARE

Education. The Yukon Department of Education owns and operates all the schools. There are no private schools in the Territory. In Sept. 1989, the Territory had 25 schools with 339 teachers and 5,096 pupils attending classes from kindergarten to grade 12. In 1984 French schooling for francophone children was introduced, with a separate francophone school created in Sept. 1988. French immersion schooling is also offered at 2 schools. Virtually all post-secondary adult education, from trades and technical training to the first 2 years of university transfer programmes, is administered by Yukon College. A new college campus opened in Whitehorse in

Oct. 1988. In 1989 approximately 750 students were enrolled in full-time programmes and a further 2,600 were studying part-time at the main campus or at the College's 13 community campuses and 3 mobile classrooms. The Yukon government provides financial assistance to students whether they study at the College or outside the territory. Financial assistance is available to students of aboriginal descent from the federal Department of Indian Affairs and Northern Development.

Health. The health care system provides all residents with the care demanded by illness or accident. The federal government operates 1 general hospital at Whitehorse, 3 cottage hospitals, 2 nursing stations, with a total of 160 beds, 11 health centres and 4 health stations. The territorial government also operates a medical evacuation programme to send patients to Edmonton or Vancouver for specialized treatment not available in the Territory.

Further Reading

Annual Report of the Government of the Yukon.
Yukon Executive Council, *Statistical Review.*
Berton, P., *Klondike.* (Rev. ed.) Toronto, 1987
Coates, K. and Morrison, W., *Land of the Midnight Sun: A History of the Yukon.* Edmonton, 1988
Coults, R., *Yukon Places and Names.* Sidney, 1980
McClelland, C., *Part of the Land, Part of the Water.* Vancouver, 1987
Minter, R., *White Pass: Gateway to the Klondike.* Toronto, 1987

CAPE VERDE

Capital: Praia
Population: 359,000 (1988)
GNP per capita: US$460 (1986)

República de Cabo Verde

HISTORY. The Cape Verde Islands were discovered in 1460 by Diogo Gomes, the first settlers arriving in 1462. In 1587 its administration was unified under a Portuguese governor. The colony became an Overseas Province on 11 June 1951.

On 30 Dec. 1974 Portugal transferred power to a transitional government headed by the Portuguese High Commissioner. Full independence was granted on 5 July 1975.

AREA AND POPULATION. Cape Verde is situated in the Atlantic Ocean 620 km WNW of Senegal and consists of 10 islands and 5 islets. Praia is the capital. The islands are divided into 2 groups, named Barlavento (windward) and Sotavento (leeward). The total area is 4,033 sq. km (1,557 sq. miles). The population (census, 1980) was 295,703. Estimate (1988) 359,000. About 600,000 Cape Verdeans live abroad.

The areas and populations (1980, census) of the islands are:

	Sq. km	*Population*		*Sq. km*	*Population*
Santo Antão	779	43,321	Maio	269	4,098
São Vicente [1]	227	41,594	São Tiago	991	145,957
São Nicolau	388	13,572	Fogo	476	30,978
Sal	216	5,826	Brava	67	6,985
Boa Vista	620	3,372			
			Sotavento	1,803	188,018
Barlovento	2,230	107,685			
			Total	4,033	295,703

[1] Includes Santa Luzia which is uninhabited.

The main towns (1980 census) are Praia, the capital (37,676) on São Tiago; and Mindelo (36,746) on São Vicente. 70% of the inhabitants are of mixed origins, and another 28% are black. Crioulo serves as the common language of the islands, although the official language is Portuguese.

Vital statistics (1985): Births, 10,949; deaths, 2,804.

CLIMATE. The climate is arid, with a cool dry season from Dec. to June and warm dry conditions for the rest of the year. Rainfall is sparse, rarely exceeding 5" (127 mm) in the northern islands or 12" (304 mm) in the southern ones. There are periodic severe droughts. Praia. Jan. 72°F (22·2°C), July 77°F (25°C). Annual rainfall 10" (250 mm).

CONSTITUTION AND GOVERNMENT. The Constitution adopted on 12 Feb. 1981 removed all reference to possible future union with Guinea-Bissau, and the *Partido Africano da Independencia de Cabo Verde*, founded 20 Jan. 1981, became the sole legal party. The legislature consists of a unicameral People's National Assembly of 83 members elected for 5 years by universal suffrage; it elects the President, who appoints and leads a Council of Ministers. Elections were held on 7 Dec. 1985.

President: Arístides Maria Pereira (assumed office 5 July 1975; re-elected 1981 and 1986).

In Jan. 1990 the Council of Ministers comprised:

Prime Minister, Co-operation and Planning, Finance: Gen. Pedro Verona Rodrigues Pires.

Foreign Affairs: Col. Silvino Manuel da Luz. *Armed Forces and Security:* Col. Júlio de Carvalho. *Transport, Trade and Tourism:* Maj. Osvaldo Lopez da Silva. *Education:* André Corsino Tolentino. *Health, Labour and Social Welfare:* Dr Ireneu

Gomes. *Justice:* Dr José Eduardo Araújo. *Information, Culture and Sport:* Dr David Hopffer Cordeiro Almada. *Agriculture and Fisheries:* Commandant João Pereira Silva. *Local Government and Town Planning:* Tito Livio Santos de Oliveira Ramos. *Industry and Energy:* Adão Silva Rocha. *Public Works:* Adriano de Oliveira Lima. *Deputy Ministers:* Herculano Vieira *(to Prime Minister)*, Dr Arnaldo Vasconcellos Franca *(Finance)*. *Secretaries of State:* Virgilio Burgo Fernandes *(Trade and Tourism)*, Miguel Lima *(Fisheries)*, Aguinaldo Lisboa Ramos *(Foreign Affairs)*, Renato Cardoso *(Public Administration)*, João de Deus Maximiano *(Assistant to Prime Minister)*.

National flag: Horizontally yellow over green, with a vertical red strip in the hoist charged slightly above the centre with a black star surrounded by a wreath of maize, and beneath this a yellow clam shell.

Local government: The 2 *distritos* (Barlovento and Sotavento) are sub-divided into 14 *conçelhos* – Ribeira Grande, Paúl, Porto Novo (these 3 covering Santo Antão island), São Vicente (including Santa Luzia), São Nicolau, Sal, Boa Vista, Maio, Praia, Santa Catarina, Tarrafal, Santa Cruz (these 4 covering São Tiago island), Fogo and Brava.

DEFENCE

Army. The Popular Revolutionary Armed Forces had a strength of 1,000 in 1990.

Navy. There were (1989) 6 fast *ex*-Soviet patrol craft and 3 attack boats, all 6 *ex*-Soviet, and 1 small hydrographic survey vessel. Personnel (1989) 200.

Air Force. An embryo air force operates two survivors of three An-26 twin-turboprop transports and has (1990) under 100 personnel.

INTERNATIONAL RELATIONS

Membership. Cape Verde is a member of UN, OAU and an ACP state of EEC.

ECONOMY

Budget. In 1984, the budget included revenue of 1,630m. escudos Caboverdianos and expenditure, 2,134·5m.

Currency. *Escudo Caboverdiano* of 100 *centavos*. There are coins of 20 and 50 *centavos* and of 1, 2½, 10, 20 and 50 *escudos*, and banknotes of 100, 500 and 1,000 *escudos*. In March 1990, 118·86 *Escudo* = £1 and 72·52 *Escudo* = US$1.

Banking. The Banco de Cabo Verde is the bank of issue and commercial bank, with branches at Praia, Mindelo and Espargos airport (Sal).

ENERGY AND NATURAL RESOURCES

Electricity. Production in 1986 amounted to 18m. kwh; capacity (1986), 14,000 kw.

Minerals. Salt is obtained on the islands of Sal, Boa Vista and Maio. Volcanic rock (pozzolana) is mined for export.

Agriculture. Mostly confined to irrigated inland valleys, the chief crops (production, 1988, in 1,000 tonnes) are: Coconuts, 10; sugar-cane, 16; bananas, 5; potatoes, 3; cassava, 4; sweet potatoes, 6; maize, 8; beans, groundnuts and coffee. Bananas and coffee are mainly for export.

Livestock (1988): 80,000 goats, 13,000 cattle, 70,000 pigs and 6,000 asses.

Fisheries. The catch in 1985 was 10,200 tonnes, of which tuna comprised 46%. About 200 tonnes of lobsters are caught annually.

COMMERCE. Imports in 1985 totalled 7,445m. escudos Caboverdianos, of which 27% came from Portugal, 22% from the Netherlands; exports in 1985 totalled 462m. escudos Caboverdianos, of which 31% went to Algeria, 30% to

Portugal, 14% to Italy. In 1983, expatriated earnings from Cape Verdeans abroad totalled 2,800m. escudos Caboverdianos. Exports: Fish, salt and bananas.

Total trade of Cape Verde with UK (British Department of Trade returns, in £1,000 sterling):

	1985	*1986*	*1987*	*1988*	*1989*
Imports to UK	370	426	301	132	178
Exports and re-exports from UK	2,282	1,618	1,208	1,812	2,301

COMMUNICATIONS

Roads. There were 2,250 km of roads (660 km paved) in 1984 and there were 3,000 private cars and 750 commercial vehicles.

Aviation. Amilcar Cabral International Airport, at Espargos on Sal, is a major refuelling point on flights to Africa and South America. Transportes Aéros de Cabo Verde provides regular services to smaller airports on most of the other islands.

Shipping. The main ports are Mindelo and Praia. In 1982 the ports handled 371,812 tonnes of imports and 146,822 tonnes of exports. In 1986, the merchant marine comprised 25 vessels of 14,095 GRT.

Broadcasting. There are 2 radio stations, at Praia and Mindelo; both are government-owned. There were (1985) 50,000 radio and 500 television receivers and (1984) 2,384 telephones.

JUSTICE, RELIGION, EDUCATION AND WELFARE

Justice. There is a network of People's Tribunals, with a Supreme Court in Praia.

Religion. In 1982, over 98% of the population were Roman Catholic.

Education. In 1987 there were 49,703 pupils and 1,464 teachers at 347 primary schools, 10,304 pupils and 321 teachers at 16 preparatory schools, 5,026 pupils and 170 teachers at 4 secondary schools, and 531 students and 52 teachers at a technical school. There were 211 students and 53 teachers in 3 teacher-training colleges and about 500 students were at foreign universities.

In 1981, 49% of the adult population were literate.

Health. In 1980 there were 21 hospitals and dispensaries with 632 beds; there were also 51 doctors, 3 dentists, 7 pharmacists, 9 midwives and 184 nursing personnel.

DIPLOMATIC REPRESENTATIVES

Of Cape Verde in Great Britain
Ambassador: Luis Fonseca (resides in The Hague).

Of Great Britain in Cape Verde
Ambassador: J. E. C. Macrae, CMG (resides in Dakar).

Of Cape Verde in the USA (3415 Massachusetts Ave., NW, Washington, D.C., 20007)
Ambassador: José Luis Fernandes Lopes.

Of the USA in Cape Verde (Rua Hojl Ya Yenna 81, Praia)
Ambassador: Vernon D. Penner, Jr.

Of Cape Verde to the United Nations
Ambassador: Humberto Bettencourt Santos.

Further Reading

Annuario Estatistico de Cabo Verde. Praia. Annual
Carreira, A., *The People of the Cape Verde Islands*. London, 1982
Foy, C., *Cape Verde: Politics, Economics and Society*. London, 1988

CAYMAN ISLANDS

Capital: George Town
Population: 25,435 (1989)
GNP per capita: US$18,750 (1989)

HISTORY. The islands were discovered by Columbus on 10 May 1503 and (with Jamaica) were recognized as British possessions by the Treaty of Madrid in 1670. Grand Cayman was settled in 1734 and the other islands in 1833. They became a separate Crown Colony on 4 July 1959, administered by the same governor as Jamaica until the latter's independence on 6 Aug. 1962 when they received their own Administrator (From 1972 a governor).

AREA AND POPULATION. Cayman Islands consist of Grand Cayman, Little Cayman and Cayman Brac. Situated in the Caribbean Sea, about 200 miles NW of Jamaica. Area, 100 sq. miles (260 sq. km). Census population of 1979, 16,677 (11,282 Caymanians by birth); census (1989) 25,435. The spoken language is English. The chief town is George Town, estimate (1989) 13,700. Vital statistics (1988): Births, 380; marriages, 254; deaths, 110.

The areas and populations of the islands are:

	Sq. km	*Census 1979*	*Census 1989*
Grand Cayman	197	15,000	23,951
Cayman Brac	36	1,607	1,445
Little Cayman	26	70	33

CLIMATE. The climate is tropical maritime, with a cool season from Nov. to March and temperatures some 10°F warmer for the remaining months. Rainfall averages 56" (1,400 mm) a year at George Town. Hurricanes may be experienced between July and Nov.

CONSTITUTION AND GOVERNMENT. A new Constitution came into force in Aug. 1972. The Legislative Assembly consists of the Governor (as President), 3 official members, and 12 elected members.

The Executive Council consists of the Governor (as Chairman), the 3 official members and 4 elected members elected by the elected members of the Legislative Assembly.

Governor: A. J. Scott, CVO, CBE.

Flag: British Blue Ensign with the arms of the Colony on a white disc in the fly.

ECONOMY

Budget. Revenue 1990, CI$112m.; expenditure, CI$110·6m. Public debt (31 Dec. 1988), CI$19·4m.; total reserves, CI$11·2m.

Currency. The Cayman Island dollar (CI$) is divided into 100 cents. In March 1990, £1 = 1·36 CI$; US$1 = 0·83.

Banking. 534 commercial banks and trust companies held licences in Sept. 1989, which permit the holders to offer services to the public, over 30 domestically. Barclays Bank PLC has offices at George Town and Cayman Brac.

INDUSTRY AND TRADE

Electricity. Production (1988) 178·4m. kwh.

Industry. Finance and tourism are the main industries. In 1989 18,263 companies were registered in the islands.

Commerce. Exports, 1988 (f.o.b.), totalled CI$2m. Imports, (c.i.f.), CI$188m.; principally foodstuffs, manufactured items, textiles, building materials, automobiles and petroleum products.

Total trade between Cayman Islands and UK (British Department of Trade returns, in £1,000 sterling):

	1986	*1987*	*1988*	*1989*
Imports to UK	2,422	1,318	9,858	8,693
Exports and re-exports from UK	11,403	6,442	5,051	5,174

Tourism. Tourism is the chief industry of the islands, after financial services, and there were (1988) over 2,606 beds in hotels and over 2,552 in apartments, guest-houses and cottages. There were 534,294 visitors in 1988, including 218,709 by air, an increase of 5% over 1987.

COMMUNICATIONS

Roads. There were (1988) about 140 miles of road and 11,995 motor vehicles.

Aviation. Cayman Airways provides regular services between Grand Cayman and Miami, Houston, Tampa, Atlanta, New York and Jamaica. Pan American, American and Northwest Airlines provide a daily service between Miami and Grand Cayman. CAL provides a regular inter-island service. Air Jamaica also provides services between Grand Cayman and Jamaica.

Shipping. Motor vessels ply regularly between the Cayman Islands, Jamaica, Costa Rica and Florida. Shipping registered at George Town, 599 vessels (Dec. 1988).

Post and Broadcasting. There were 16,947 telephones in 1988 and there are 2 radio broadcasting stations in the islands, with (1988) 20,000 receivers.

Newspapers. The *Caymanian Compass* is published 5 days a week.

JUSTICE, RELIGION, EDUCATION AND WELFARE

Justice. There is a Grand Court, sitting 6 times a year at George Town under a Chief Justice and 2 puisne judges. 2 Summary Courts sit at other times.

Religion. There are Anglican, Roman Catholic, Presbyterian and other Christian communities represented in the islands.

Education. In 1988 there were 10 government primary schools with 1,340 pupils, 6 private elementary schools with 1,213 pupils and 3 private secondary schools with 109 pupils. Post-primary education at the government high schools and the government middle school was attended by 2,463 pupils. There was also a private institution for tertiary education and a government school for special educational needs.

Health. In 1989 there was a fully-equipped general hospital in George Town with 17 doctors, a dental clinic, 4 district clinics and a hospital in Cayman Brac.

Further Reading

Annual Report, 1988. Cayman Islands Government, 1989

Statistical Abstract of the Cayman Islands, 1988. Cayman Islands Government Statistics Unit, 1989

CENTRAL AFRICAN REPUBLIC

Capital: Bangui
Population: 2·9m. (1988)
GNP per capita: US$390 (1988)

République centrafricaine

HISTORY. Central African Republic became independent on 13 Aug. 1960, after having been one of the 4 territories of French Equatorial Africa (under the name of Ubangi Shari) and from 1 Dec. 1958 a member state of the French Community. A new Constitution was adopted in 1976 and it provided for the country to be a parliamentary democracy and to be known as the Central African Empire. President Bokassa became Emperor Bokassa I. The Emperor was overthrown in a *coup* on 20–21 Sept. 1979 and the empire was abolished. On 15 March 1981 David Dacko was re-elected President but Army Chief General André Kolingba took power in a bloodless *coup* on 1 Sept. 1981 at the head of a Military Committee for National Recovery (CMRN), which held supreme power until 21 Sept. 1985 when President Kolingba dissolved it and initiated a return towards constitutional rule.

AREA AND POPULATION. The Central African Republic is bounded north by Chad, east by Sudan, south by Zaïre and Congo, and west by Cameroon. The area covers 622,436 sq. km (240,324 sq. miles); its population in 1975 (census), 2,054,610 and estimate in 1988 was 2,899,376 of which 37% urban. The capital is Bangui (596,776 inhabitants in 1988).

The areas, populations and capitals of the prefectures are as follows:

Prefecture	*Sq. km*	*Estimate 1988*	*Capital*	*Estimate 1988*
Bangui [1]	67	596,776	Bangui	596,776
Ombella-M'poko	31,835	137,469	Boali	...
Lobaye	19,235	174,134	M'baiki	29,495
Sangha [2]	19,412	62,977	Nola	...
Haute-Sangha	30,203	253,717	Berbérati	45,432
Nana-Mambere	26,600	213,630	Bouar	49,166
Ouham-Pende	32,100	258,166	Bozoum	22,600
Ouham	50,250	292,132	Bossangoa	41,877
Gribingui [2]	19,996	92,558	Kaga-Bandoro	19,774
Bamingui-Bangoran	58,200	31,082	Ndele	...
Vakaga	46,500	25,629	Birao	...
Kemo-Gribingui	17,204	84,884	Sibut	22,214
Ouaka	49,900	235,277	Bambari	52,092
Basse-Kotto	17,604	199,830	Mobaye	...
Haute-Kotto	86,650	57,583	Bria	24,620
M'bomou	61,150	143,971	Bangassou	36,254
Haut-M'bomou	55,530	39,560	Obo	...

[1] Autonomous commune. [2] Economic prefecture.

French is the official language.

CLIMATE. A tropical climate with little variation in temperature. The wet months are May, June, Oct. and Nov. Bangui. Jan. 80°F (26·5°C), July 77°F (25°C). Annual rainfall 61" (1,525 mm). Ndele. Jan. 83°F (28·3°C), July 77°F (25°C). Annual rainfall 57" (1,417 mm).

CONSTITUTION AND GOVERNMENT. Under the Constitution adopted by a national referendum on 21 Nov. 1986, the sole legal political party is the *Rassemblement Démocratique Centrafricaine (RDC)*. Legislative elections for the 52-member National Assembly were held on 31 July 1987. The President is elected by popular vote for a term of 6 years, and appoints and leads a Council of Ministers.

The Council of Ministers in Jan. 1989 was composed as follows:

President of the Republic and of the RDC, Minister of Defence. Gen. André Kolingba (assumed office 1 Sept. 1981, re-elected 21 Nov. 1986).

Foreign Affairs: Michel Gbezera-Bria. *Interior, Territorial Administration:* Christophe Grelombe. *Economy, Finance, Planning and International Co-operation:* Dieudonné Wazoua. *National and Higher Education:* Jean Louis Psimhis. *Transport and Civil Aviation:* Pierre Gonifei-Ngaibounanou. *Civil Service, Labour, Social Security and Professional Training:* Daniel Sehoulia. *Justice, Keeper of the Seals:* Thomas Mapouka. *Public Health and Social Affairs:* Jean Willybiro-Sako. *Rural Development:* Théodore Bagayambo. *Energy and Mines, Geology and Hydrology:* Michel Salle. *Tourism, Water Resources, Forestry, Hunting and Fishing:* Raymond Mbitikon. *Trade and Industry, Small and Medium-sized Enterprises:* Thimothée Marboua. *Posts and Telecommunications:* Hugues Dobozendji. *Public Works and Territorial Planning:* Jacques Kithe. *Information, Arts and Culture:* Jean Bengue. *Parliamentary Relations, Secretary to Council of Ministers:* Edouard Franck.

There are also 5 Secretaries of State.

National flag: Four horizontal stripes of blue, white, green, yellow; over all in the centre a vertical red strip, and in the canton a yellow star.

Local Government: Central African Republic is divided into 14 prefectures (subdivided into 50 sub-prefectures); 2 'economic prefectures' and the autonomous commune of Bangui (the capital).

DEFENCE. Selective national service for a 2-year period is in force. There are some 6,500 personnel in the armed forces and the para-military Gendarmerie.

Army. The Army consisted (1989) of about 3,500 men, comprising a Republican Guard, a territorial defence and combined arms regiments. Equipment includes 4 T-55 tanks, 39 armoured personnel carriers and 10 Ferret scout cars.

Navy. The naval wing of the army has 9 river patrol craft and (1989) 85 personnel.

Air Force. The Air Force has 2 Rallye Guerrier armed light aircraft, 1 twin-jet Caravelle, 1 DC-4 and 2 C-47 transports, 2 Reims-Cessna 337, 6 Aermacchi AL.60 and 5 Broussard liaison aircraft, 1 Alouette and 1 Ecureuil helicopters. It also maintains and operates the government's Caravelle and Falcon 20 twin-jet VIP aircraft. Personnel strength (1989) about 300.

INTERNATIONAL RELATIONS

Membership. Central African Republic is a member of UN, OAU and an ACP state of EEC.

ECONOMY

Planning. The new recovery plan (1983–86) provided for expenditure of 31,300m. francs CFA for development of agriculture, transport and infrastructure.

Budget. The budget for 1987 provided for expenditure of 56,610m. francs CFA, and for revenue of 46,230m. francs CFA.

Currency. The unit of currency is the *franc CFA* with a parity of 50 *francs CFA* to 1 French *franc*. There are coins of 1, 2, 5, 10, 25, 50, 100 and 500 *francs CFA*, and banknotes of 100, 500, 1,000, 5,000 and 10,000 *francs CFA*. In March 1990, £1 = 471·63 *francs CFA*; US$1 = 287·75 *francs CFA*.

Banking. The *Banque des Etats de l'Afrique Centrale* is the bank of issue.

ENERGY AND NATURAL RESOURCES

Electricity. Production in 1987 totalled 92m. kwh. Supply 220 volts; 50 Hz.

Minerals. In 1986 258,701 carats of gem diamonds, 98,678 carats of industrial diamonds and (1987) 224 kg of gold were mined. There are significant regions of uranium in the Bakouma area.

Agriculture. Over 86% of the working population is occupied in subsistence agriculture. The main crops (production 1988, in 1,000 tonnes) are cassava, 400; groundnuts, 85; bananas, 86; plantains, 66; millet, 50; maize, 64; seed cotton, 43; coffee, 22; rice, 12.

Livestock (1988): Cattle, 2,313,000; goats, 1,159,000; sheep, 120,000; pigs, 382,000.

Forestry. There are 35·8m. hectares of forest, representing 58% of the land area. The extensive hardwood forests, particularly in the south-west, provide mahogany, obeche and limba for export. Production (1985) 3·42m. cu. metres.

Fisheries. Catch (1983) 13,000 tonnes.

INDUSTRY AND TRADE

Industry. The small industrial sector includes factories producing cotton fabrics, footwear, beer and radios.

Commerce. Imports and exports in 1m. francs CFA:

	1984	*1985*	*1986*	*1987*
Imports	77,700	90,370	96,677	...
Exports	50,057	58,720	44,960	39,180

In 1983, France took 30% of exports and provided 46% of imports. Of all exports, coffee comprised 29% (by value), diamonds 24%, timber 19% and cotton 13%.

Total trade of Central African Republic with UK (British Department of Trade returns, in £1,000 sterling):

	1986	*1987*	*1988*	*1989*
Imports to UK	1,452	233	195	418
Exports and re-exports from UK	787	1,127	733	1,630

Tourism. There were about 4,000 visitors in 1986.

COMMUNICATIONS

Roads. In 1986 there were 20,286 km of roads, of which 442 km bitumenized and (1984) 46,982 vehicles in use.

Railways. There are no railways, but a proposal existed (1985) for an 800 km line (1,435 mm gauge) from Bangui through Cameroon and Congo to connect with the Trans-Gabon railway at Belinga.

Aviation. There are international airports at Mpoko, near Bangui, and Berbérati. Air Centrafrique operates extensive internal services to several airstrips.

Shipping. Timber and barges are taken to Brazzaville (Congo).

Post and Broadcasting. There were (1982) 1,200 television and (1986) 125,000 radio receivers and 3,323 telephones.

Cinemas. In 1987 there were 5 cinemas.

Newspapers. In 1984 there was one daily newspaper.

JUSTICE, RELIGION, EDUCATION AND WELFARE

Justice. The Criminal Court and Supreme Court are situated in Bangui. There are 16 high courts throughout the country.

Religion. About 57% of the population follow animist beliefs, 20% are Roman Catholic, 15% Protestant and 8% Moslem.

Education. The University of Bangui was founded in 1970 and had 1,489 students in 1980. In 1986-87 there were 274,179 pupils at primary schools and 44,804 at secondary schools; technical schools (1984-85) had 2,514 students, while (1982) 327 were at the 2 teacher-training establishments.

Health. In 1984 there were 104 hospitals and health centres with 3,774 beds; there were also 112 doctors, 6 dentists, 16 pharmacists, 168 midwives and 710 nursing personnel.

DIPLOMATIC REPRESENTATIVES

Of Central African Republic in Great Britain
Ambassador: (Vacant).

Of Great Britain in Central African Republic
Ambassador: M. Reith (resides in Yaoundé).

Of Central African Republic in the USA (1618 22nd St., NW, Washington, D.C. 20008)
Ambassador: Jean-Pierre Sohahong-Kombet.

Of the USA in Central African Republic (Ave. President Dacko, Bangui)
Ambassador: David C. Fields.

Of Central African Republic to the United Nations
Ambassador: Christian Lingama-Toleque.

Further Reading

Kalck, H. P., *Historical Dictionary of the Central African Republic*. Metuchen, 1980

CHAD

République du Tchad

Capital: N'djaména
Population: 5·4m. (1988)
GNP per capita: US$160 (1988)

HISTORY. France proclaimed a protectorate over Chad on 5 Sept. 1900, and in July 1908 the territory was incorporated into French Equatorial Africa. It became a separate colony March 1920, and in 1946 one of the four constituent territories of French Equatorial Africa. On 28 Nov. 1958 Chad became an autonomous republic within the French Community and achieved full independence on 11 Aug. 1960, although the northern prefecture of Borkou-Ennedi-Tibesti remained under French military administration until 1965.

Conflicts between the central government and secessionist groups, particularly in the Moslem north and centre of Chad, began in 1965 and flared into a prolonged and confused civil war that continued under different protagonists, with occasional pauses during attempts at reconciliation. On 7 June 1982 the *Forces Armées du Nord* (FAN) led by Hissène Habré gained control of the country. In June 1983 the Libyan-backed forces of former President Goukouni Oueddei re-occupied Bourkou-Ennedi-Tibesti, but by April 1987 most of the rebels rallied to the government side, which then forced the Libyans back into the Aozou Strip, a 114,000 sq. km region in the extreme north of Chad occupied by Libyan forces since 1973. A ceasefire took effect on 11 Sept. 1987. There was an attempted coup on 1 April 1989.

AREA AND POPULATION. Chad is bounded west by Cameroon, Nigeria and Niger, north by Libya, east by Sudan and south by the Central African Republic. Area, 1,284,000 sq. km; its population in 1988 was estimated at 5,396,000 (census 1975, 4,029,917). The capital is N'djaména, formerly Fort Lamy with 511,700 inhabitants in 1986, other large towns (1985) being Sarh (124,000), Moundou (87,000), Abéché (71,000), Bongor (69,000) and Doba (64,000).

The areas, populations and chief towns of the 14 prefectures were:

Préfecture	*sq. km*	*Population Estimate 1984*	*Capital*
Borkou-Ennedi-Tibesti	600,350	103,000	Faya (Largeau)
Biltine	46,850	200,000	Biltine
Ouaddaï	76,240	411,000	Abéché
Batha	88,800	410,000	Ati
Kanem	114,520	234,000	Mao
Lac	22,320	158,000	Bol
Chari-Baguirmi	82,910	719,000	N'djaména
Guéra	58,950	234,000	Mongo
Salamat	63,000	121,000	Am Timan
Moyen-Chari	45,180	582,000	Sarh
Logone Oriental	28,035	350,000	Doba
Logone Occidental	8,695	324,000	Moundou
Tandjilé	18,045	341,000	Laï
Mayo-Kabbi	30,105	757,000	Bongor

The official language is French but more than 100 different languages and dialects are spoken. The largest ethnic group is the Sara of southern Chad. Arabic serves as a common language throughout the semi-tropical (Sahelian) centre and the Saharan north.

CLIMATE. A tropical climate, with adequate rainfall in the south, though Nov. to April are virtually rainless months. Further north, desert conditions prevail. N'djaména. Jan. 75°F (23·9°C), July 82°F (27·8°C). Annual rainfall 30" (744 mm).

CONSTITUTION AND GOVERNMENT. From June 1982 a State Council administered the country until 21 Oct. 1982, when Hissène Habré was sworn in as President and appointed a Council of Ministers to administer the country. A provisional constitution had been promulgated on 29 Sept. 1982, under which a new official political party was established on 22 June 1984, the *Union nationale pour l'independence et la révolution* (UNIR), administered by a 15-member Executive Bureau. A National Consultative Assembly was also formed on 21 Oct. 1982, comprising 2 representatives from each of the 14 prefectures and 2 from the capital, N'djaména. On 10 Dec. 1989, in a referendum, the electorate adopted a new Constitution and for the President to continue in office for a further 7 years.

President, Minister of Defence, Veterans and War Victims: Hissène Habré.
Foreign Affairs and Co-operation: Acheikh Ibn Oumar.
National flag: Three vertical strips of blue, yellow, red.
Local Government: The 14 *préfectures* are divided into 53 *sous-préfectures*.

DEFENCE

Army. The Army consists of 3 infantry and 1 armoured battalions with artillery support batteries. Equipment includes some 65 armoured fighting vehicles. In 1990 the strength was over 17,000 and there was a paramilitary force of 5,700.

Air Force. The Air Force has 3 C-130 Hercules, 1 VIP Caravelle, 1 C-54, 2 Aviocar and 6 C-47 transports, 4 Reims-Cessna F337 light aircraft, 2 Turbo-Porters, 2 Broussard communications aircraft, 2 Gazelle helicopters, 2 armed PC-7 aircraft and 2 SF.260W Warrior trainers. Personnel (1990) about 200.

INTERNATIONAL RELATIONS

Membership. Chad is a member of UN, OAU and is an ACP state of EEC.

ECONOMY

Budget. The budget for 1988 envisaged expenditure of 25,600m. francs CFA and revenue, 17,900m. francs CFA.

Currency. The unit of currency is the *franc CFA* with a parity value of 50 *francs CFA* to 1 French *franc*. In March 1990, £1 = 471·63 *francs*; US$1 = 287·75 *francs*.

Banking. The *Banque des Etats de l'Afrique Centrale* is the bank of issue, and the principal commercial banks are the *Banque de Développement du Tchad* and the *Banque Tchadienne de Crédit et de Dépôts*.

ENERGY AND NATURAL RESOURCES

Electricity. Production (1986) amounted to 66m. kwh. Supply 220 volts; 50 Hz.

Oil. The oilfield in Kanem préfecture has been linked by pipeline to a new refinery at Laï (in Tandjilé) but production has remained minimal due to war disruption.

Minerals. Salt (about 4,000 tonnes per annum) is mined around Lake Chad, and deposits of uranium, gold and bauxite are to be exploited.

Agriculture. Cotton growing (in the south) and animal husbandry (in the central zone) are the most important industries. Production (1988, in 1,000 tonnes) was: Millet, 690; sugar-cane, 290; yams, 240; seed cotton, 112; groundnuts, 78; cassava, 330; rice, 52; dry beans, 42; sweet potatoes, 46; mangoes, 32; dates, 32; maize, 47; cotton lint, 37; cotton seed, 68.

Livestock (1988): Cattle, 4,060,000; sheep, 2·25m.; goats, 2·25m.; chickens, 4m.

Fisheries. Fish production from Lake Chad and the Chari and Logone rivers, was estimated at 110,000 tonnes in 1986.

INDUSTRY AND TRADE

Industry. Cotton ginning is the principal activity, undertaken in some 22 mills. Sugar refineries produced 23,000 tonnes in 1984. A textile factory produced 13·1m. metres of woven fabric in 1980, a brewery 130,000 hectolitres of beer and a cigarette factory 259m. cigarettes. There are also rice and flour mills and other factories involved in food processing or light industry.

Commerce. Trade (in 1m. francs CFA):

	1981	*1982*	*1983*
Imports	29,349	35,701	74,802
Exports	22,665	18,968	48,563

The main trading partners are France and Nigeria. Cotton formed 91% of exports in 1983 as civil war has decimated other exporting industries.

Total trade with UK (British Department of Trade returns, in £1,000 sterling):

	1985	*1986*	*1987*	*1988*	*1989*
Imports to UK	1,099	2,806	1,101	1,764	822
Exports and re-exports from UK	1,847	1,250	1,006	639	3,462

COMMUNICATIONS

Roads. In 1983 there were 40,000 km of roads, of which only 400 km are surfaced. In 1985 there were 3,000 private cars and 4,000 lorries and buses.

Aviation. There is an international airport at N'djaména, from which UTA and Air Afrique run 4 flights per week to Paris; there are also flights to Douala, Bangui and Kinshasa. Air Tchad operates internal services to 12 secondary airports.

Post and Broadcasting. In 1978 there were 3,850 telephones and (1985), 1·1m. radios in use.

JUSTICE, RELIGION, EDUCATION AND WELFARE

Justice. There are criminal courts and magistrates courts in N'djaména, Moundou, Sarh and Abéché, with a Court of Appeal situated in N'djaména.

Religion. The northern and central parts of the country are predominantly Moslem (44% of the total population) and the southern part is mainly animist (38%) or Christian (17%).

Education. In 1987 there were 300,000 pupils in primary schools, 42,000 in secondary schools, and 4,000 in technical schools and teacher-training establishments. The University of Chad (founded 1971) at N'djaména had (1984) 1,643 students and 141 teaching staff.

Health. There were 33 hospitals with 3,353 beds in 1977 and in 1978 90 doctors, 4 dentists, 9 pharmacists, 98 midwives and 993 nursing personnel.

DIPLOMATIC REPRESENTATIVES

Of Chad in Great Britain
Ambassador: Abdoulaye Lamana (resides in Brussels).

Of Great Britain in Chad
Ambassador: C. S. Rycroft (resides in London).

Of Chad in the USA (2002 R. St., NW, Washington, D.C., 20009)
Ambassador: Mahamat Ali Adoum.

Of the USA in Chad (Ave., Felix Eboue, N'djaména)
Ambassador: Robert L. Pugh.

Of Chad to the United Nations
Ambassador: Mahamat Ali Adoum.

Further Reading

Kelley, M. P., *Conditions of the State's Survival.* Oxford, 1986
Thompson, V. and Adloff, R., *Conflict in Chad.* London and Berkeley, 1981
Westebbe, R., *Chad: Development Potential and Constraints.* Washington, D.C., 1974

CHILE

Capital: Santiago
Population: 12·68m. (1988)
GNP per capita: US$1,510 (1988)

República de Chile

HISTORY. The Republic of Chile threw off allegiance to the crown of Spain, constituting a national government on 18 Sept. 1810, finally freeing itself from Spanish rule in 1818.

AREA AND POPULATION. Chile is bounded north by Peru, east by Bolivia and Argentina, and south and west by the Pacific ocean.

Chile has an area of 736,905 sq. km (284,520 sq. miles) excluding the claimed Antarctic territory. Many islands to the west and south belong to Chile: The Islas Juan Fernández (179 sq. km with 516 inhabitants in 1982) lie about 600 km west of Valparaíso, and the volcanic Isla de Pascua (Easter Island or Rapa Nui, 118 sq. km with 1,867 inhabitants in 1982), discovered in 1722, lies about 3,000 km WNW of Valparaíso. Small uninhabited dependencies include Sala y Goméz (400 km east of Easter Is.), San Ambrosio and San Félix (1,000 km northwest of Valparaíso, and 20 km apart) and Islas Diego Ramírez (100 km SW of Cape Horn).

In 1940 Chile declared, and in each subsequent year has reaffirmed, its ownership of the sector of the Antarctic lying between 53° and 90° W. long.; and asserted that the British claim to the sector between the meridians 20° and 80° W. long. overlapped the Chilean by 27°. Seven Chilean bases exist in Antarctica. A law promulgated 21 July 1955 put the Intendente (*now* Gobernador) of the Province (*now* Region) of Magallanes in charge of the 'Chilean Antarctic Territory' which has an area of 1,269,723 sq. km. and a population (1982) 1,368.

The total population at the census in 1982 was 11,275,440. Estimate (31 March 1988) 12,683,000.

The areas of the 13 regions and their populations (census, 1982) were as follows:

Region	*Sq. km*	*Census 1982*	*Capital*	*Estimate 1987*
Tarapacá	58,786	273,427	Iquique	132,948
Antofagasta	125,253	341,203	Antofagasta	204,577
Atacama	74,705	183,071	Copiapó	70,241 [1]
Coquimbo	40,656	419,178	La Serena	106,617
Aconcagua	16,396	1,204,693	Valparaíso	278,762
Metropolitan	15,549	4,294,938	Santiago	4,858,342
Liberador	16,456	584,989	Rancagua	172,489
Maule	30,518	723,224	Talca	164,482
Bíobío	36,939	1,516,552	Concepción	294,375
Araucanía	31,946	692,924	Temuco	217,789
Los Lagos	67,247	843,430	Puerto Montt	113,488
Aisén	108,997	65,478	Coihaique	31,167 [1]
Magallanes	132,034	132,333	Punta Arenas	111,724

[1] Census, 1982

Vital statistics (1984): Birth rate 21·2 per 1,000 population; death rate, 6·3; marriage rate, 7 (1982); infantile mortality rate, 20·1 per 1,000 live births. Life expectancy (1981): Men, 65·4 years, women, 70·1.

Over 92% of the population is mixed or *mestizo*; only about 2% are European immigrants and their descendants, while the remainder are indigenous amerindians of the Araucanian, Fuegian and Chango groups. Language and culture remain of European origin, with the 675,000 Araucanian-speaking (mainly Mapuche) Indians the only sizeable minority.

Other large towns (estimate, 1987) are: Viña del Mar (297,294), Talcahuano (231,356), Arica (169,774), San Bernardo (168,534), Puente Alto (165,534),

Chillán (148,805), Los Angeles (126,122), Osorno (122,462), Valdívia (117,205), Calama (109,645), Coquimbo (105,252) and Quilpué (103,004).

CLIMATE. With its enormous range of latitude and the influence of the Andean Cordillera, the climate of Chile is very complex, ranging from extreme aridity in the north, through a Mediterranean climate in Central Chile, where winters are wet and summers dry, to a cool temperate zone in the south, with rain at all seasons. In the extreme south, conditions are very wet and stormy. Santiago. Jan. 67°F (19·5°C), July 46°F (8°C). Annual rainfall 15" (375 mm). Antofagasta. Jan. 69°F (20·6°C), July 57°F (14°C). Annual rainfall 0·5" (12·7 mm). Valparaíso. Jan. 64°F (17·8°C), July 53°F (11·7°C). Annual rainfall 20" (505 mm).

CONSTITUTION AND GOVERNMENT. The Marxist coalition government of President Salvador Allende Gossens was ousted on 11 Sept. 1973 by the 3 Armed Services and the *Carabineros* (para-military police). These forces formed a government headed by a Junta of the 4 Commanders-in-Chief. Gen. Augusto Pinochet Ugarte, Commander-in-Chief of the Army, took over the presidency. President Allende died on the day of the *coup*.

Marxist parties were outlawed and all political activities banned. The new Government assumed wide-ranging powers but the 'state of siege' ended in March 1978. A new Constitution was approved by 67·5% of the voters on 11 Sept. 1980 and came into force on 11 March 1981. It provided for a return to democracy after a minimum period of 8 years. Gen. Pinochet would remain in office during this period after which the Junta would nominate a single candidate for President.

A plebiscite was held on 5 Oct. 1988 with President Pinochet as the candidate to be approved or rejected by the people, to continue for 8 more years. Votes against 54·6%, votes in favour 43·31%.

National flag: Two horizontal bands, white, red, with a white star on blue square in top sixth next to staff.

National anthem: Dulce patria, recibe los votos (words by E. Lillo, 1847; tune by Ramón Carnicer, 1828).

The following is a list of the presidents since 1946:

Gabriel González Videla, 3 Nov. 1946–3 Nov. 1952.
Carlos Ibáñez del Campo, 3 Nov. 1952–3 Nov. 1958.
Jorge Alessandri Rodriguez, 3 Nov. 1958–3 Nov. 1964.
Eduardo Frei Montalva, 3 Nov. 1964–3 Nov. 1970.
Salvador Allende Gossens, 3 Nov. 1970–11 Sept. 1973 (deposed).
Gen. Augusto Pinochet, 17 Dec. 1974-11 March 1990.

President of the Republic: Patricio Aylwyn Azócar (assumed office 11 March 1990).

On 14 Dec. 1989 Patricio Aylwin Azócar obtained 55·2% of the popular votes in the presidential elections; Hernán Buchi, 29·4% and Francisco Javier Erraruriz, 15·3%.

Members of Cabinet announced in Jan. 1990

Finance: Alejandro Foxley.
Economics: Carlos Ominami.
Interior: Enrique Krauss.
Defence: Patricio Rojas.
Justice: Francisco Cumplido.

Local Government. For the purposes of local government the Military Junta in pursuance of its policy of administrative decentralization, has divided the republic into 13 regions (12 and Greater Santiago). Each Region is presided over by an *Intendente,* while the provinces (40) included in it are in charge of a *Gobernador* who represents the central government. The provinces are divided into municipalities under an *alcalde* (mayor). All these officials are appointed by the President.

DEFENCE. Military service is for a period of 2 years at the age of 19.

Army. The Army is organized in 6 divisions, each with infantry, armoured cavalry, artillery, mountain and engineer regiments; and 1 helicopter-borne ranger unit. Equipment includes 157 M-4A3 and 21 AMX-30 tanks, 110 light tanks and 330 armoured cars. The service operates over 50 aircraft including 6 Aviocar transports, 10 Puma, 2 Super Puma, 2 Iroquois, 2 Jet Ranger and 11 Lama helicopters, and communications aircraft and 16 Cessna Hawk XP trainers. Strength (1990) 57,000 (30,000 conscripts) and 100,000 reserves.

Navy. The principal ships of the Chilean Navy are the 1937-vintage *ex*-US cruiser *O'Higgins*, of 13,700 tonnes, armed with 9 152mm guns and 8 127mm. She carries one light helicopter. There are also the 4 *ex*-British 'County'-class guided missile armed destroyers *Norfolk, Antrim, Glamorgan* and *Fife* renamed *Capitan Prat, Almirante Cochrane, Almirante Latorre,* and *Blanco Encalada* respectively, purchased on their disposal from the Royal Navy between 1982 and 1987. The last named has had the Sea Slug launcher removed and replaced with an extended helicopter hangar and flight deck.

There are also 2 small modern West German-built diesel submarines, 2 British Oberon class submarines, 4 other destroyers (2 British-built in 1960, and 2 *ex*-US dating from 1944), 2 British Leander class frigates, 2 fast missile craft, 4 torpedo boats, 5 offshore patrol vessels and 26 coastal craft. There are 3 French-built medium landing ships. Major auxiliaries include 2 tankers, 1 submarine support vessel and 2 landing craft.

The Naval Air Service has 5 squadrons: 1 with Bandeirante and Aviocar transports; 1 with Alouette and JetRanger ASW helicopters; 1 with EMB-111 and Falcon maritime patrol aircraft; and 2 with Pilatus PC-7 trainers.

Naval personnel in 1988 totalled 29,000 all ranks including 5,200 marines and 500 in the maritime air service.

Air Force. Approximate strength (1990) is 15,000 personnel, with (1987) 105 first-line and 150 second-line aircraft, divided among 12 groups, each comprising 1 squadron, within 4 combat and support wings. Groups 1 and 12 have twin-jet A-37Bs, from a total of 34 acquired for light strike/reconnaissance duties. Group 2 is equipped for photo-reconnaissance with 2 Canberras. Group 4 has 13 Mirage 50 fighters. Group 5 has 14 Twin Otters for light transport and survey duties. Group 7 has 12 F-5E Tiger II fighter-bombers and 2 F-5F trainers. Groups 8 and 9 are also fighter-bomber units, with a total of 30 Hunter F.71s, *ex*-RAF FGA.9s, and T.72s. Group 10 is a transport wing, with 2 C-130H Hercules, 2 Boeing 707s, 3 Douglas piston-engined transports and various helicopters. An aerial survey unit has 2 Learjets and 3 Beech twin-engined aircraft. Training aircraft include piston-engined Piper Dakota and T-35 Pillan basic trainers and licence-built CASA C-101BB Aviojets. CASA C-101CC Aviojet light strike aircraft were being delivered in 1989.

INTERNATIONAL RELATIONS

Membership. Chile is a member of the UN, OAS and LAIA (formerly LAFTA).

ECONOMY

Budget. In 1987 revenue was US$8,469·8m. and expenditure, US$8,421·6m.

Currency. On 29 Sept. 1975 the currency became the *pesos* with a value of 1,000 escudos to the new peso.

In March 1990 there were 480·50 *pesos* = £1 and 293·17 *pesos* = US$1.

Banking. There is a Central Bank and State Bank and in 1988 18 domestic and 24 foreign banks were operating.

On 31 Dec. 1987 notes and coins in circulation were 161,337m. pesos; deposits in foreign currency totalled US$866·9m. and deposits in local currency 1,745,545m. pesos.

Weights and Measures. The metric system has been legally established in Chile since 1865, but the old Spanish weights and measures are still in use to some extent.

ENERGY AND NATURAL RESOURCES

Electricity. In 1987 production of electricity was 14,821m. kwh, of which 80% hydro-electric. Supply 220 volts; 50 Hz.

Oil. Petroleum was discovered in 1945 in the southern area of Magallanes. Production (1989) 1·25m. tonnes.

Gas. Production (1987) 4,352·6m. cu. metres.

Minerals. The wealth of the country consists chiefly in its minerals, especially in the northern provinces of Atacama and Tarapacá.

Copper is the most important source of foreign exchange (about 41% of exports in 1987) and government revenues (almost 40%). The copper industry's output in 1987 was 1,417,780 tonnes. Exports during 1987 were valued at US$2,100·5m. Copper production will increase by up to 30% in 1991 when the Escondida mine begins production.

Nitrate of soda is found in the Atacama deserts. Exports were US$98·8m. in 1987. Production was 870,000 tonnes in 1985. Iodine is a by-product: 1985 production totalled 2,760 tonnes. The use of solar evaporation as a means of reducing costs has developed the production of potassium salts as an additional by-product.

Iron ore, of which high-grade deposits estimated at over 1,000m. tonnes exist in the provinces of Atacama and Coquimbo, has overtaken nitrate as Chile's second mineral. Production in 1987 was 6,690,168 tonnes, plus 3,684,590 tonnes processed into pellet form.

Coal reserves exceed 2,000m. tons, partially low in thermal unit. Net 1987 production was 1,736,152 tonnes.

In 1987 other minerals included molybdenum (16,941 tonnes, pure), zinc (19,618 tonnes), manganese (31,803 tonnes), lead (829 tonnes).

Agriculture. Total area of land available for agricultural use in 1986 was 29m. hectares, of which 12% was sown crops, 38% grassland and 15% forested.

Some principal crops were as follows:

Crop	*Area harvested, 1,000 hectares 1988*	*Production, 1,000 tonnes 1988*	*Crop*	*Area harvested, 1,000 hectares 1988*	*Production, 1,000 tonnes 1988*
Wheat	577	1,874	Potatoes	62	727
Oats	61	127	Dry beans	77	81
Barley	24	48	Lentils	39	25
Maize	90	617	Green peas	7	24
Rice	39	147	Sugar-beet	47	2,650

In 1987 fruit plantations had expanded to 119,600 hectares with 9 types of fruit, mainly apples and table grapes. Production, 1988 (in 1,000 tonnes): Apples, 592; grapes, 440; pears, 80; peaches and nectarines, 78; plums, 72; oranges, 70; lemons and limes, 50. Exports in the season ended May 1988 totalled 90m. cases valued at US$527m.

Production of animal products in 1987 was (in 1,000 tonnes): Cattle, 174·6; sheep, 14·5; pork, 88·3; poultry, 89·5. Eggs, 1,790m.; milk, 1,100m. litres.

Livestock (1988): Cattle, 3,371,000; horses, 490,000; asses, 28,000; sheep, 6·54m.; goats, 600,000; pigs, 1·36m.; poultry, 21m.

Forestry. In 1987, there were 1,150,000 hectares of artificial forests from Maule to Magallanes, the most important species being the pine (*pinus radiata*) which covers almost 930,000 hectares. Eucalyptus and poplar cover some 92,000 hectares. Native species of importance amounted to 9·4m. hectares in 1983.

Production during 1988 amounted to about 2·7m. cu. metres of sawn timber. Exports of forestry products in 1987 were valued at US$587m.

Fisheries. Chile has 4,200 km of coastline and exclusive fishing rights to 1·6 m. sq.

km. There are 220 species of edible fish. Catch of fish and shellfish in 1987 was 4·9m. tonnes; shellfish, 167,000 tonnes. Exports of seafood in 1987 were US$654·3m., of which fishmeal accounted for US$375m. The industry employs 70,000 (1·5% of the working population).

INDUSTRY AND TRADE

Industry. A nationally-owned steel plant operates from Huachipato, near Concepción. Output, 1987, 689,800 tonnes of steel ingots. Cellulose and wood-pulp are two industries which are rapidly developing; in 1987, 673,100 tonnes of cellulose were produced. Cement (1·5m. tonnes) and fishmeal (469,400 tonnes) are also important.

Labour. In Dec. 1987 the total workforce numbered 4·01m., of which 837,000 were employed in agriculture, 208,000 in construction, 607,000 in manufacturing industries, 690,000 in trade, 81,000 in mining and 253,000 in transport and communications. A methanol plant with production capacity of 750,000 tonnes a year began operations in 1988 in Punta Arenas.

Trade unions began in the middle 1880s.

Commerce. Imports and exports in US$1m.:

	1982	*1983*	*1984*	*1985*	*1986*	*1987*
Imports	3,580	2,969	3,357	2,955	3,099	3,967
Exports	3,798	3,835	3,650	3,743	4,199	5,046

In 1987 imports (in US$1m.) from USA, were valued at 773; Venezuela, 144; Brazil, 380; Japan, 387; Federal Republic of Germany, 335; Argentina, 159; Spain, 117; France, 129; UK, 128; Italy, 96.

In 1987 the principal imports were (in US$1m.): Fuels, 460; chemicals, 740; industrial equipment, 718; transport equipment, 260; tools, 38, live animals, 4; foodstuffs, 40. The principal exports in 1987 were (in US$1m.): Copper, 2,100; paper and pulp, 365; gold, 165; fresh fruit, 527; fish meal, 375; nitrate, 99.

Total trade between Chile and UK (British Department of Trade returns, in £1,000 sterling):

	1985	*1986*	*1987*	*1988*	*1989*
Imports to UK	134,750	128,007	112,843	179,628	193,280
Exports and re-exports from UK	73,914	67,459	105,838	80,901	96,003

Tourism. Some 560,000 tourists visited Chile in 1987.

COMMUNICATIONS

Roads. In 1986 there were in Chile 78,025 km of highways. There were in 1986 (estimate), 850,000 automobiles, 185,000 goods vehicles and 22,500 buses.

Railways. The total length of state railway lines was (1988) 6,892 km, including 1,945 km electrified, of broad- and metre-gauge. In 1988 the State Railways carried 6·3m. tonnes and 6·8m. passengers. Further electrification is in progress between Concepción and Puerto Montt (600 km). An underground railway in Santiago was opened in Sept. 1975. The Antofagasta (Chili) and Bolivia Railway (702 km, metre-gauge) links the port of Antofagasta with Bolivia and Argentina and carried 1·4m. tonnes in 1987.

Aviation. There are 7 international airports, 16 domestic airports and about 300 landing grounds. Chile is served by 19 commercial air companies (2 Chilean). In 1986, 999,000 passengers were carried.

Shipping. The mercantile marine has consisted since 1982 of 60 ships of over 100 tons (825,076 DWT) but most of the fleet operates under flags of convenience. Valparaíso is the chief port. The free ports of Magallanes, Chiloé and Aysén serve the southern provinces.

Post and Broadcasting. There are 1,486 post offices and agencies. In 1983 there were 608,200 (Santiago, 360,053) telephones in use.

In 1988 there were 30m. radio receivers and 3·5m. television receivers.

Cinemas (1986). Cinemas numbered 170; 60 of them are in Santiago.

Newspapers (1986). There were 65 daily newspapers and 100 magazines.

JUSTICE, RELIGION, EDUCATION AND WELFARE

Justice. There are a High Court of Justice in the capital, 12 courts of appeal distributed over the republic, tribunals of first instance in the departmental capitals and second-class judges in the sub-delegations.

Religion. 89·5% of the population are Catholics. There are 1 cardinal-archbishop, 5 archbishops, 22 bishops and 2 vicars apostolic. Latest estimates show 6·7m. Roman Catholics, 880,500 Protestants and 25,000 Jews.

Education. Education is in 3 stages: Basic (6–14 years), Middle (15–18) and University (19–23). Enrolment (1987): 2,065,400 pupils in the basic schools, 752,000 pupils in the middle schools and 224,000 students in higher education, including universities.

University education is provided in the state university, University of Chile (founded in 1842), the Catholic University at Santiago (1888), the University of Concepción (1919), the Catholic University at Valparaíso (1928), the Universidad Técnica Federico Santa María at Valparaíso (1930), the Universidad Técnica del Estado (1952), Universidad Austral, Valdivia (1954) and Universidad del Norte, Antofagasta (1957).

Health. In 1982 there were 5,416 doctors, 1,644 dentists, 201 pharmacists, 1,930 midwives and 25,889 nursing personnel. 205 hospitals, 296 health centres and 888 emergency posts.

DIPLOMATIC REPRESENTATIVES

Of Chile in Great Britain (12 Devonshire St., London, W1N 2FS)
Ambassador: Juan Carlos Délano (accredited 26 Nov. 1987).

Of Great Britain in Chile (La Concepción 177, Casilla 72-D, Santiago)
Ambassador: Alan White, CMG, OBE.

Of Chile in the USA (1732 Massachusetts Ave., NW, Washington, D.C., 20036)
Ambassador: Octavio Errázuriz.

Of the USA in Chile (Agustinas 1343, Santiago)
Ambassador: Charles A. Gillespie Jr.

Of Chile to the United Nations
Ambassador: Pedro Daza.

Further Reading

Statistical Information: The Instituto Nacional de Estadística (Santiago), was founded 17 Sept. 1847. *Director General:* Alvaro Vial Donoso. Principal publications: *Anuario Estadística* and the bi-monthly *Estadística Chilena.*

Other sources are: *Geografía Económica,* by the Corporación de Fomento de la Production, and *Boletín Mensual*, by the Banco Central de Chile.

Blakemore, H., *Chile.* [Bibliography] Oxford and Santa Barbara, 1988
Davis, N., *The Last Two Years of Salvador Allende.* London, 1985
Falcoff, M., *et al Chile: Prospects for Democracy.* New York, 1988
Garretón, M. A., *The Chilean Political Process.* London and Boston, 1989
Heyerdahl, T., *Easter Island: The Mystery Solved.* New York and London, 1989
Horne, A., *Small Earthquake in Chile. A Visit to Allende's South America.* London, 1972
Smith, B. H., *Church and Politics in Chile: Challenges to Modern Catholicism.* Princeton Univ. Press, 1983

PEOPLE'S REPUBLIC OF CHINA

Capital: Beijing (Peking)
Population: 1,110m. (1990)
GNP per capita: US$330 (1988)

Zhonghua Renmin Gonghe Guo

HISTORY. In the course of 1949 the Communists obtained full control of the mainland of China, and in 1950 also over most islands off the coast (but not Taiwan, *see* p. 366-67).

On 1 Oct. 1949 Mao Zedong (Tse-tung) proclaimed the establishment of the People's Republic of China. In mid-1966 Mao launched the 'Great Proletarian Cultural Revolution', which lasted until April 1969. For details of the factional disputes which followed *see* THE STATESMAN'S YEAR-BOOK for 1989-90, p. 358. In April 1976 Hua Guofeng became Prime Minister and also, on the death of Mao on 9 Sept., Party Chairman (later General Secretary). Hua was replaced as Prime Minister by Zhao Ziyang in Sept. 1980 and as Party General Secretary by Hu Yaobang in June 1981. Hu was himself forced to resign following student demonstrations in Jan. 1987. Most prominent leader during this period was sometime Party Leader Deng Xiaoping, who resigned from the Politburo in Nov. 1987 and from the chairmanship of the Military Commissions in Nov.1989.

The funeral of Hu Yaobang on 15 April 1989 sparked off mass student demonstrations which escalated into a popular 'pro-democracy' movement in Beijing, Shanghai and other provincial centres demanding reforms. Despite Government appeals to disperse the demonstrations gathered strength during the summit visit of the Soviet President Gorbachev (15-17 May) and culminated in a sit-in in Tiananmen Square, Beijing. This was confronted by army units, at first peacefully. However, on 4 June troops opened fire on the demonstrators and tanks were sent in to disperse them. The official casualty figures are: 'over 200' demonstrators and 'dozens' of soldiers killed, and some 9,000 injured.

A hard-line faction assumed control in the Party Politburo which replaced Zhao Ziyang by Jiang Zemin as General Secretary. Martial law was imposed from May 1989 to Jan. 1990, and several prominent demonstrators were executed.

The visit of President Gorbachev marked the culmination of a process of gradual normalization of Sino-Soviet relations. It was announced that 'both sides favoured a reasonable settlement of the boundary question'.

AREA AND POPULATION. China is bounded north by the USSR and Mongolia, east by Korea, the Yellow Sea and the East China Sea, with Hong Kong and Macao as enclaves on the south-east coast; south by Vietnam, Laos, Burma, India, Bhután and Nepál; west by India, Pakistan, Afghánistán and the USSR.

The capital is Beijing (Peking).

See map in THE STATESMAN'S YEAR-BOOK, 1968–69.

The total area (including Taiwan) is estimated at 9,572,900 sq. km (3,696,100 sq. miles).

At the 1982 census population was 1,008,175,288. Han Chinese numbered 936·7m. There are 55 ethnic minorities; those numbering more than 3m. were with percentage of total population: Zhuang (1·3%), Hui (0·7%), Uighur (0·6%), Yi (0·54%), Miao (0·5%), Manchu (0·43%), Tibetan (0·39%) and Mongolian (0·34%).

1979 regulations restricting married couples to a single child, a policy enforced by compulsory abortions and economic sanctions, have been widely ignored, and it was admitted in 1988 that the population target of 1,200m. by 2000 would have to be revised to 1,270m. Since 1988 peasant couples have been permitted a second child after 4 years if the first born is a girl, a measure to combat infanticide.

Population, 1990: 1,110m. (1986: males, 530·11m.; urban, 382·44m.). Vital statistics, 1988: Birth rate (per 1,000), 20·78; death rate, 6·58; growth rate, 14·2. Population density, 113 per sq. km. in 1987. There were 8,290,588 marriages and 457,938 divorces in 1985. Expectation of life was 67 in 1985.

Estimates of persons of Chinese race outside China, Taiwan and Hong Kong in 1980 varied from 15m. to 20m. Since 1982 China has permitted the emigration of a limited number of persons to Hong Kong.

A number of widely divergent varieties of Chinese are spoken. The official 'Modern Standard Chinese' is based on the dialect of North China. The ideographic writing system of 'characters' is uniform throughout the country, and has undergone systematic simplification. In 1958 a phonetic alphabet (*Pinyin*) was devised to transcribe the characters, and in 1979 this was officially adopted for use in all texts in the Roman alphabet. The previous transcription scheme (Wade) is still used in Taiwan.

China is administratively divided into 21 provinces, 5 autonomous regions (originally entirely or largely inhabited by ethnic minorities, though in some regions now outnumbered by Han immigrants) and 3 government-controlled municipalities. These are in turn divided into 165 prefectures, 321 cities, 2,046 counties and 620 urban districts. (For earlier administrative divisions *see* THE STATESMAN'S YEAR-BOOK 1986–87).

Government-controlled municipalities	*Area (in 1,000 sq. km)*	*Population in 1987 (in 1,000s)*	*Density per sq. km*	*Capital*
Beijing	17·8	9,750	580	—
Tianjin	4·0	8,190	725	—
Shanghai	5·8	12,320	1,987	—
Provinces				
Hebei	202·7	56,170	299	Shijiazhuang
Shanxi	157·1	26,550	170	Taiyuan
Liaoning	151·0	37,260	256	Shenyang
Jilin	187·0	23,150	124	Changchun
Heilongjiang	463·6	33,320	71	Harbin
Jiangsu	102·2	62,130	611	Nanjing
Zhejiang	101·8	40,700	400	Hangzhou
Anhui	139·9	52,170	374	Hefei
Fujian	123·1	27,490	227	Fuzhou
Jiangxi	164·8	35,090	211	Nanchang
Shandong	153·3	77,760	507	Jinan
Henan	167·0	78,080	468	Zhengzhou
Hubei	187·5	49,890	266	Wuhan
Hunan	210·5	56,960	271	Changsha
Guangdong	231·4	63,640	299	Guangzhou
Sichuan	569·0	103,200	182	Chengdu
Guizhou	174·0	30,080	171	Guiyang
Yunnan	436·2	34,560	88	Kunming
Shaanxi	195·8	30,430	148	Xian
Gansu	530·0	20,710	46	Lanzhou
Qinghai	721·0	4,120	6	Xining
Autonomous regions				
Inner Mongolia	450·0	20,290	17	Hohhot
Guangxi	220·4	39,460	167	Nanning
Tibet [1]	1,221·6	2,030	2	Lhasa
Ningxia	170.0	4,240	64	Yinchuan
Xinjiang	1,646·8	13,840	9	Urumqi

[1] See also paragraph on Tibet below.

Population of largest cities in 1987: Shanghai, 7·1m.; Beijing (Peking), 5·97m.; Tianjin, 5·46m.; Shenyang, 4·29m.; Wuhan, 3·49m.; Guangzhou (Canton), 3·36m.; Chongqing, 2·83m.; Harbin, 2·67m.; Chengdu, 2·64m.; Xian, 2·39m.; Zibo, 2·33m.; Nanjing, 2·29m.; Taiyuan, 1·93m.; Changchun, 1·91m.; Dalian, 1·68m.; Zhengzhou,

1·61m.; Kunming, 1·52m.; Jinan, 1·46m.; Tangshan, 1·41m.; Guiyang, 1·4m.; Lanzhou, 1·39m.; Fushun, 1·3m.; Qiqihar, 1·3m.; Anshan, 1·27m.; Hangzhou, 1·27m.; Qingdao, 1·27m.; Fuzhou, 1·21m.; Changsha, 1·19m.; Shijazhuang, 1·19m.; Nanchang, 1·19m.; Jilin, 1·17m.; Baotau, 1·12m.; Huainan, 1·09.; Luoyang, 1·06m.; Urumqi, 1·04m.; Ningbo, 1·03m.; Datong, 1·02m.; Handan, 1·01m.

Tibet. For events before and after the revolt of 1959 *see* THE STATESMAN'S YEAR-BOOK, 1964–65 (under TIBET), and 1988–89. On 9 Sept. 1965 Tibet became an Autonomous Region. 301 delegates were elected to the first People's Congress, of whom 226 were Tibetans. The senior spiritual leader, the Dalai Lama, is in exile. He was awarded the Nobel Peace Prize in 1989. The Banqen Lama died in Jan. 1989. In 1988 the Tibetan population of Tibet was 2m., Han 73,000. Population of the capital, Lhasa, in 1987 was 130,000. Expectation of life was 45 years in 1985. 2m. Tibetans live outside Tibet, in China, and in India and Nepál. Chinese efforts to modernize Tibet include irrigation, road-building and the establishment of light industry: in 1985 296 small and medium-sized factories and mines were producing electric power, coal, building materials, lumber, textiles, chemicals and animal products.

In 1979, 1·6m. were engaged in agriculture, including 0·5m. nomadic herdsmen. By 1984, a large measure of autonomy for the peasantry had been re-introduced: Compulsory deliveries and some taxes were abolished and private ownership of livestock and 30-year disposition of land were granted. There were 23m. cattle in 1984. In 1975 Tibet became self-sufficient in grain. There are now 21,600 km of highways, and air routes link Lhasa with Chengdu, Xian and Kathmandu. Six more were opened in 1987. 30,000 tourists visited Tibet in 1986.

The borders were opened for trade with neighbouring countries in 1980. In July 1988 Tibetan was reinstated as a 'major official language', competence in which is required of all administrative officials.

Since 1980 178 monasteries and 743 shrines have been renovated and reopened. There were some 15,000 monks and nuns in 1987. In 1984 a Buddhist seminary in Lhasa opened with 200 students. Circulation of the Tibetan-language *Xizang Daily* now totals 38,000. In 1988 there were 2,437 primary schools, 67 secondary schools, 14 technical schools and 3 higher education institutes. The total number of students was 166,000. A university was established in 1985. In 1987 there were 7,048 medical personnel (of whom 59% were Tibetan) and 957 medical institutions, with a total of 4,738 beds.

Since 1987 there have been several anti-Chinese demonstrations in which a number of people have been killed. Martial law was declared on 8 March 1989.

Batchelor, S., *The Tibet Guide*. London, 1987
The Dalai Lama, *My Land and My People* (ed. D. Howarth). London, 1962
Grunfeld, A. T., *The Making of Modern Tibet*. London, 1987
Jäschke, H. A., *A Tibetan–English Dictionary*. London, 1934
Levenson, C. B., *The Dalai Lama: A Biography*. London, 1988
Shakabpa, T. W. D., *Tibet: A Political History*. New York, 1984
Sharabati, D., *Tibet and its History*. London, 1986

CLIMATE. Most of China has a temperate climate but, with such a large country, extending far inland and embracing a wide range of latitude as well as containing large areas at high altitude, many parts experience extremes of climate, especially in winter. Most rain falls during the summer, from May to Sept., though amounts decrease inland. Peking (Beijing). Jan. 24°F (–4·4°C), July 79°F (26°C). Annual rainfall 24·9" (623 mm). Chongqing. Jan. 45°F (7·2°C), July 84°F (28·9°C). Annual rainfall 43·7" (1,092 mm). Shanghai. Jan. 39°F (3·9°C), July 82°F (27·8°C). Annual rainfall 45·4" (1,135 mm). Tianjin. Jan. 24°F (–4·4°C), July 81°F (27·2°C). Annual rainfall 21·5" (533·4 mm).

CONSTITUTION AND GOVERNMENT. On 21 Sept. 1949 the 'Chinese People's Political Consultative Conference' met in Peking, convened by the Chinese Communist Party. The Conference adopted a 'Common Programme' of 60 articles and the 'Organic Law of the Central People's Government' (31 articles).

Both became the basis of the Constitution adopted on 20 Sept. 1954 by the 1st National People's Congress, the supreme legislative body. The Consultative Conference continued to exist after 1954 as an advisory body. In 1986 it had 2,021 members.

New Constitutions were adopted in 1975 and 1978 (for details *see* THE STATESMAN'S YEAR-BOOK 1986-87).

A further Constitution was adopted in 1982. It defines 'socialist modernisation' as China's basic task and restores the post of State President (*i.e.* Head of State). Constitutional amendments of 1988 legalized private companies and sanction the renting out of 'land-use' rights.

The National People's Congress can amend the Constitution, elects and has power to remove from office the highest State dignitaries, decides on the national economic plan, etc. The Congress elects a *Standing Committee* (which supervises the State Council) and the *State President* for a 5-year term: Yang Shangkun was elected in April 1988. *Vice-President:* Wang Zhen.

Congress is elected for a 5-year term and meets once a year for 2 or 3 weeks. When not in session, its business is carried on by its Standing Committee. It is composed of deputies elected on a constituency basis by direct secret ballot. Any voter, and certain organizations, may nominate candidates. Nominations may exceed seats by 50-100%. 2,839 deputies were elected to the 7th Congress in March-April 1988.

In 1989 there were 33 Ministries and 8 Commissions under the State Council. *Prime Minister, Chairman of the Commission for Economic Restructure:* Li Peng. *Deputy Prime Ministers:* Tian Jiyun, Yao Yilin, Wu Xueqian. Other ministers include: Qian Qichen *(Foreign Affairs)*, Zheng Tuobin *(Foreign Trade)*, Qin Jiwei *(Defence)*, Wang Bingqian *(Finance)*, Zou Jiahua *(Chairman, State Planning Commission)* and Wang Fang *(Public Security)*.

State emblem: 5 stars above Peking's Gate of Heavenly Peace, surrounded by a border of ears of grain entwined with drapings, which form a knot in the centre of a cogwheel at the base; the colours are red and gold.

National flag: Red with a large star and 4 smaller stars all in yellow in the canton.

National anthem: 'March of the Volunteers' composed 1935 by Tien Han. (Replacing the 1978 version).

De facto power is in the hands of the Communist Party of China, which had 48m. members in 1989. A purge of members was instituted following the events of June 1989 (*see* p. 354). There are 8 other parties, all members of the Chinese People's Political Consultative Conference. The members of the Politburo in March 1990 (the first 6 constituting its Standing Committee) were Jiang Zemin *(General Secretary)*, Li Peng, Qiao Shi, Song Ping, Li Ruihuan, Yao Yilin, Wan Li, Tian Jiyun, Li Tieying, Li Ximing, Yang Rudai, Yang Shangkun, Wu Xueqian, Qin Jiwei, Hu Qili; candidate member, Ding Guangen.

Local Government. There are 4 administrative levels: (1) Provinces, Autonomous Regions and the municipalities directly administered by the Government; (2) prefectures and autonomous prefectures (*zhou*); (3) counties, autonomous counties and municipalities; (4) towns. Local government organs ('congresses') exist at provincial, county and township levels and in national minority autonomous prefectures, but not in ordinary prefectures which are just agencies of the provincial government. Up to county level congresses are elected directly. Multiple candidacies are permitted at local elections.

DEFENCE. In Nov. 1989 Jiang Zemin took over from Deng Xiaoping as chairman of the State and Party's Military Commissions. China is divided into 7 military regions. The military commander also commands the air, naval and civilian militia forces assigned to each region.

Conscription is compulsory but for organizational reasons selective: Only some 10% of potential recruits are called up. Service is 3 years with the Army and 4 years with the Air Force and 5 years with the Navy.

A Defence University to train senior officers in modern warfare was established in 1985.

Army. The Army (PLA: 'People's Liberation Army') is divided into main and local forces. Main forces, administered by the 7 military regions in which they are stationed but commanded by the Ministry of Defence, are available for operation anywhere and are better equipped. Local forces concentrate on the defence of their own regions. There are 24 Integrated Group Armies comprising 80 infantry, 10 armoured and 6 artillery divisions; and 50 engineer regiments. Land-based missile forces consisted of (1989 estimate): 8 intercontinental and 60 intermediate range. Total strength in 1989 was 2·3m. including 1m. conscripts.

There is a para-military force of 12m., including 1,830,000 People's armed police.

Navy. The warship construction programme has slowed substantially as a result of financial pressure and technical difficulties, but the naval arm of the People's Liberation Army remains an important factor in the balance of power in the eastern hemisphere.

Strength comprises 1 nuclear powered ballistic missile armed submarine, 1 diesel trials submarine with ballistic missile tubes, 4 nuclear propelled fleet submarines, 1 diesel cruise missile submarine and some 85 old patrol submarines (of which probably no more than 40 are operational). Surface combatant forces include 19 destroyers, 37 frigates, some 215 missile craft and 160 torpedo craft. There is a mixed coastal and inshore patrol force of some 500 vessels and 50 riverine craft. The mine warfare force consists of 35 *ex*-Soviet offshore minesweepers, some 21 inshore, and about 60 unmanned drones. There are 58 landing ships of various types and some 400 craft. Major auxiliaries number over 100, including 3 oilers and 1 fleet stores ship, and there are several hundred minor auxiliaries, yard craft and service vessels.

The land-based naval air force of almost 900 combat aircraft, primarily for defensive and anti-submarine service is organized into 3 bomber and 6 fighter divisions. The force includes some 50 H-6 bombers and 130 H-5 torpedo bombers, about 100 Q-5 fighter/ground attack aircraft and 600 fighters including J-5 (MiG-17), J-6 (MiG-19), and J-7 (MiG-21) types. Maritime patrol tasks are performed by 10 Be-6 flying boats, and anti-submarine operations by 50 Z-5, and 12 Super Frelon helicopters from shore and about 6 Z-9 afloat. There are also about 60 communications, research, training and transport aircraft.

Main naval bases are at Qingdao (North Sea Fleet), Shanghai (East Sea Fleet), and Zhanjiang (South Sea Fleet).

Active personnel are reducing steadily as tasks are handed over to the militia; in 1989 there were some 260,000, including 30,000 in the naval air force and over 28,000 marines.

Air Force. In 1984 the Air Force was estimated at 4,500 front-line aircraft, organized in over 100 regiments of jet-fighters and about 12 regiments of tactical bombers, plus reconnaissance, transport and helicopter units. Each regiment is made up of 3 or 4 squadrons (each 12 aircraft), and 3 regiments form a division.

Equipment includes about 500 J-7 (MiG-21), 2,000 J-6 (MiG-19) and 750 J-4 and J-5 (MiG-17) interceptors and fighter-bombers, with about 500 H-5 (Il-28) jet-bombers, about 120 H-6 Chinese-built copies of the Soviet Tu-16 twin-jet strategic bomber, plus 500 Q-5 twin-jet fighter-bombers, evolved from the MiG-19. In service in small numbers is a locally-developed fighter designated J-8 (known in the west as 'Finback'). Transport aircraft include about 500 Y-5 (An-2), Y-8 (An-12), Y-12, An-24/26, Li-2, Il-14 and three-turbofan Trident fixed-wing types, plus 300 Z-5 (Mi-4) and Z-6 (Mi-8) helicopters. The MiG fighters and Antonov transports have been manufactured in China, initially under licence, and other types have been assembled there, including several hundred JJ-5 (2-seat MiG-17) trainers. Small quantities of Western aircraft have been procured in the past few years, including 24 Black Hawk and 6 Super Puma transport helicopters, 8 Gazelle armed helicopters and 5 Challenger VIP transports. The US Government is providing technical assistance in developing the J-8 fighter. Total strength (1989) 470,000, including 220,000 in air defence organization.

At least 27 nuclear tests have been made since 1964 and a nuclear force capable of reaching large parts of the USSR and Asia is operational. It was announced in

1986 that atmospheric nuclear testing had been abandoned. Land-based missile forces thought to be deployed consist of 4 intercontinental, 60 intermediate-range (approximately 3–5,000 km) and 50 medium-range (1,100 km) ballistic missiles. Missile forces are controlled by the Second Artillery, the missile arm of the PLA.

Joffe, E., *The Chinese Army after Mao*. London, 1987

INTERNATIONAL RELATIONS

Membership. The People's Republic of China is a member of UN (and its Security Council), the IMF, the Asian Development Bank, and is an observer at GATT.

ECONOMY

Planning. For planning history 1953–73 *see* THE STATESMAN'S YEAR-BOOK, 1973–74, p. 817.

A programme for fundamental reform of the urban economy was introduced in 1985. State planning was reduced in scope and enterprises gained a degree of freedom in deciding their production and marketing a portion of it. Wages were varied according to work performed, and prices adjusted to reflect market conditions. However, the end of 1988 saw a return to more central economic planning as a response to declining production, inflation, a foreign trade imbalance and unequal regional development. Further measures of state control were introduced in Dec. 1989. 'Key enterprises' (metals, coal, timber) are to be completely Government managed, and other firms not meeting production quotas will have their supplies reduced. A national economic plan published in Jan. 1990 aims to reduce inflation, balance state revenue and expenditure and reduce internal debt. Public sector industry receives preferential treatment in terms of subsidies and credit terms. The eighth 5-year plan is running from 1990 to 1994.

Budget. 1988 revenue was 258,780m. yuan; expenditure, 266,831m. yuan. Estimates for 1989: Revenue, 285,680m. yuan; expenditure, 293,080m. yuan.

Sources of revenue, 1989 (in million yuan): Tax receipts, 255,710; subsidies for enterprise losses, 52,140; construction funds, 20,500; foreign loans, 16,500. Expenditure: Capital construction, 62,790; education, science and health, 51,380; subsidies, 40,960; defence, 24,550; administration, 22,660; agriculture, 17,390; technical renovation of enterprises, 15,580; urban maintenance, 10,300; debt service, 9,560.

China's foreign exchange reserves in March 1988 were US$17,100m. Gold reserves in 1988 were 12·67m. troy oz. of gold. Inflation was 18·8% in 1989 (27·9% in 1988).

Currency. The currency is called Renminbi (RMB, *i.e.*, People's Currency). The unit of currency is the *yuan* which is divided into 10 *jiao*, the *jiao*, into 10 *fen*. In July 1986 the *yuan* was devalued by 15·8%. The official rate of exchange in March 1990 was £1 = 7·78 *yuan*; US$1 = 4·75 *yuan*.

Notes are issued for 1, 2 and 5 *jiao* and 1, 2, 5 and 10 *yuan* and coins for 1, 2 and 5 *fen*.

Banking. A re-organization of the banking system in 1983 resulted in the People's Bank of China assuming the role of a Central Bank (*Director:* Li Guixian). Its former commercial role has been taken over by the Industrial and Commercial Bank. Other specialized banks include the Agricultural Bank of China, the China Investment Bank and the Chinese People's Construction Bank. The Bank of China will continue to be responsible for foreign banking operations. It has branches in London, New York, Singapore, Luxembourg, Macao and Hong Kong, and agencies in Tokyo and Paris.

Savings bank deposits were 3,807,000m. yuan in 1988.

Weights and Measures. The metric system is in general use alongside traditional units of measurement, for which *see* THE STATESMAN'S YEAR-BOOK, 1975–76, p. 826 and 1954, pp. 877–88.

ENERGY AND NATURAL RESOURCES

Electricity. Sources of energy in 1987: Coal 72·6%; oil, 21%; hydroelectric power, 4·4%; gas, 2%. Hydroelectric potential is 676m. kw. Generating is not centralized; local units range between 30 and 60 mw of output. Output in 1987: 496,000m. kwh. Supply 220 volts; 50 Hz. There is a nuclear energy plant at Shanghai. Construction of a second plant at Daya Bay was abandoned in 1989. Plans to build further nuclear power plants were postponed in 1986 on economy grounds.

Oil. Exploration in the South China and Yellow Seas had not produced any commercially viable discoveries by 1986. There are on-shore fields at Daqing, Shengli, Dagang and Karamai, and 10 provinces south of the Yangtze River have been opened for exploration in co-operation with foreign companies. Crude oil production was 138m. tonnes in 1989.

Gas. Natural gas is available from fields near Canton and Shanghai and in Sichuan province. Production was 13,890m. cu. metres in 1987, but is only used locally.

Minerals. *Coal.* Most provinces contain coal, and there are 70 major production centres, of which the largest are in Hebei, Shanxi, Shandong, Jilin and Anhui. Coal reserves are estimated at 769,180m. tonnes. Coal production was 928m. tonnes in 1987.

Iron. Iron ore deposits are estimated at 496,410m. tonnes and are abundant in the anthracite field of Shanxi, in Hebei and in Shandong and are found in conjunction with coal and worked in the north-east. Estimated output of iron ore in 1984, 122m. tonnes. The biggest steel bases are at Anshan with a capacity of 6m. tons, Wuhan (capacity 3·5m. tonnes), Baotou and Maanshan (both 2·5m. tonnes) and Baoshan near Shanghai.

Tin. Tin ore is plentiful in Yunnan, where the tin-mining industry has long existed. Tin production was 15,000 tonnes in 1981.

Tungsten. China is the world's principal producer of wolfram (tungsten ore), producing 14,000 tonnes in 1981. Mining of wolfram is carried on in Hunan, Guangdong and Yunnan.

Production of other minerals in 1978 (in tonnes): Phosphate rock, 4·5m.; aluminium, 225,000; copper, 200,000; lead, 120,000; zinc, 125,000; antimony, 9,000; manganese, 2m.; (1973) sulphur, 130,000; (1967) bauxite, 350,000; (1973) salt, 18,000; (1969) asbestos, 160,000. Other minerals produced: Barite, bismuth, gold, graphite, gypsum, mercury, molybdenum, silver.

Agriculture. China remains essentially an agricultural country. 144m. hectares are sown to crops. Intensive agriculture and horticulture have been practised for millennia. Present-day policy aims to avert the traditional threats from floods and droughts by soil conservancy, afforestation, irrigation and drainage projects, and to increase the 'high stable yields' areas by introducing fertilizers, pesticides and improved crops. 44·4m. hectares were irrigated in 1987, and 21·42m. tonnes of chemical fertilizer were applied in 1988.

Agricultural communes have shed the administrative functions which they had in the Maoist period to become purely economic units. There were 2,124 state farms in 1987 with 5·13m. workers, and 180m. peasant households in 1989.

Since 1978 more flexible methods of management have been adopted comprising 'responsibility systems', whereby individual households or other small units are contracted to supply to the commune or government purchasing agency a quantity of crops to be produced from an allotted area of commune land. Any surplus is at the disposal of the household, to be consumed or marketed. In 1984 peasants were granted contracts to commune land with inheritance rights, and were permitted to hire up to 7 labourers. Initially production improved, but a fall in the 1985 total grain harvest to 380m. tonnes from the 1984 record of 407m. tonnes led to a policy of encouraging grain production in 1986. The 1988 harvest also fell short of targets. Reasons for the shortfall included the greater profitability in devoting land to cash crops and stock-breeding and the migration of 60m. peasants to industry. Net *per capita* annual peasant income, 1987: 460 yuan.

In 1988 there were 860,000 large and medium-sized tractors and in 1986 34,573 combine harvesters.

Agricultural production (in 1m. tonnes), 1988: Rice, 172·37; wheat, 87·5; maize, 73·82; soybeans, 10·92; roots and tubers, 144·93; tea, 0·57; cotton, 4·2; oilseed crops, 13·2; sugar-cane, 49·08; fruit, 16·62. The gross value of agricultural output in 1988 was 5,618,000m. yuan.

Livestock, 1988: Horses, 10,691,000; cattle, 73,963,000; goats, 77,894,000; pigs, 334,862,000; sheep, 102,655,000. Meat production in 1987 was 19·21m. tonnes.

Forestry. Forest area in 1988 was 116·6. hectares, including 2·6m. hectares of timber forest. Timber reserves were 102,600m. cu. metres in 1985. The chief forested areas are in Heilongjiang, Sichuan and Yunnan. Timber output in 1988 was 63m. cu. metres.

Fisheries. Total catch, 1988: 10·46m. tonnes. There were 172,582 motor fishing vessels in 1985.

INDUSTRY AND TRADE

Industry. 'Cottage' industries persist into the late 20th century. Modern industrial development began with the manufacture of cotton textiles, and the establishment of silk filatures, steel plants, flour-mills and match factories. In 1987 there were 494,000 industrial enterprises, of which 392,000 were collectives and 98,000 state-owned. 9,865 were classified as 'large and medium-sized'. A law of Aug. 1988 ends direct state control of factories and provides for the possibility of bankruptcy. In 1985 rural industries expanded by 53% and accounted for 20% of total industrial production. In 1988 there were 13·7m. 'small' and 115,000 'large' (more than 8 employees) private businesses accounting for 13% of retail sales. Labour is drawn from the rural surplus. Expanding sectors of manufacture are: Steel, chemicals, cement, agricultural implements, plastics and lorries.

Output of major products, 1988 (in tonnes): Cotton yarn, 4·54m.; paper, 12·1m.; sugar, 4·55m.; salt, 22m.; synthetic detergents, 1·29m.; aluminium ware, 87,500; steel, 59·18m.; rolled steel, 46·98m.; cement, 203m.; sulphuric acid, 10·98m.; chemical fertilizers, 17·67m.; civil shipping, 1·4m.; cotton cloth, 17,600m. metres; woollen fabrics, 265m. metres; bicycles, 41·22m.; TV sets, 24·85m.; tape recorders, 23·44m.; cameras, 2·92m.; washing machines, 10·46m.; refrigerators, 7·4m.; motor vehicles, 646,700; tractors, 52,100; locomotives, 843.

The gross value of industrial output in 1988 was 1,810,000m. yuan.

Labour. Workforce (excluding peasantry), 1987: 528m. (36·9% female), including 390m. rural workers, 93m. industrial workers, 27m. workers in service trades and commerce, 24·2m. in building and 13·7m. in transport and telecommunications. 19m. worked in private businesses in 1989. There were 2·8m. unemployed in 1987. Average annual non-agricultural wage in 1987: 1,459 yuan. There is a 6-day 48-hour working week. The All-China Federation of Trade Unions is headed by Zhu Houze.

Commerce. Foreign trade is being decentralized and has expanded rapidly since 1978. In 1980 4 Special Economic Zones were set up in the provinces of Guangdong and Fujian, in which concessions are made to foreign businessmen to encourage their investment. In 1984 14 coastal cities and Hainan Island were opened for technological imports, and in 1988 Hainan was also designated a Special Economic Zone. Since 1979 joint ventures with foreign firms have been permitted. By 1987 4,040 equity joint ventures, 4,864 contractual joint ventures and 176 wholly-owned foreign subsidiaries had been launched. About 80% of the investment was from Hong Kong. There is no maximum limit on the foreign share of the holdings; the minimum limit is 25%. Contracts between Chinese and foreign firms are only legally valid if in writing and approved by the appropriate higher authority. A Stock

Exchange was opened in Shanghai in 1986. Foreign indebtedness was US$2,500m. in 1987. In 1985 the IMF lent China US$3,000m. repayable over 5 years, but further loans of US$780m. were suspended after the events of June 1989.

Trade in 1988: Imports, US$5,525m.; exports, US$4,754m.

Major exports are textiles, oil and oil products, chemicals, light industrial goods and arms. Major imports are machinery and transport equipment, iron and steel, and chemicals.

Major exports in 1987 (in 1,000 tonnes): Crude oil, 32,170; grain, 7,080; tea, 174; raw silk, 9·2; tungsten ore, 23·1; cotton cloth, 2,342m. metres; imports: Wheat, 13,200; rolled steel, 12,400; motor vehicles, 90,239 units; chemical fertilizers, 10,900.

In 1984 only 7·2% of China's trade was with Communist countries (2·5% with the USSR), but trade with the USSR reached some US$2,800m. in 1988. A trade agreement covering 1986–90 was signed in 1985. Japan is China's biggest trading partner. Other major partners are Hong Kong, USA, Federal Republic of Germany and Canada. Customs duties with Taiwan were abolished in 1980.

Total trade between China and UK (British Department of Trade returns, in £1,000 sterling):

	1985	*1986*	*1987*	*1988*	*1989*
Imports to UK	307,963	327,032	391,766	443,698	530,720
Exports and re-exports from UK	396,156	535,943	416,012	411,563	417,911

China has agreed to settle by 1990 British claims for assets totalling £23·4m. confiscated by the present Chinese Government when it took power in 1949.

In April 1978 a most-favoured-nation agreement was signed with EEC, and in 1980 the EEC extended preferential tariffs to China.

China has most-favoured-nation status with the USA. In 1985 the UK and the USA signed nuclear power agreements with China. In May 1989 the UK and China signed a 6-year trade agreement worth US$3,000m.

In 1988 Japan and China signed an investment protection treaty, putting Japanese firms in China on the same footing as local firms.

Tourism. 31·69m. foreigners visited China in 1988. Tourist numbers dropped by 50% after the events of June 1989. Restrictions on Chinese wishing to travel abroad were eased in Feb. 1986.

COMMUNICATIONS

Roads. The total road length was 982,200 km in 1987. Highways are well graded but mostly unmetalled. In 1987 there were 2·7m. lorries and 1·11m. passenger vehicles. The use of bicycles is very widespread.

In 1988, 287·1 tonne/km of freight and 238·2 person/km were transported by road.

Railways. In 1987 there were 52,487 km of railway including 4,429 km electrified. Gauge is standard except for some 600 mm track in Yunnan.

The principal railways are:

(1) The great north–south trunk lines: (*a*) Beijing–Canton Railway (over 2,300 km), *via* Zhengzhou–Wuhan–Zhuzhou–Hengyang. (*b*) Tianjin–Shanghai Railway (1,500 km), *via* Pukow and Nanjing. (*c*) Baoji–Chongqing Railway, *via* Chengdu (1,174 km). Chongqing with the east–west route from Hengyang to the Vietnam border, and to Kunming, connecting there with the Yunnan Railway to the Vietnam border. Two further lines connect Baoji.

(2) Great east–west trunk lines: (*a*) Longhai Railway; Lianyungkang–Xuzhou–Zhengzhou (on the Beijing–Canton line) –Xian–Baoji–Tianshui–Lanzhou (1,500 km). (*b*) Lanzhou–Xinjiang Railway: Lanzhou–Yumen–Hami–Turfan–Urumqi (1,800 km); (c) Shanghai–Youyiguan (Vietnam border) *via* Hangzhou, Nanchang, Hengyang (on the Beijing–Canton line), Guilin, Liuzhou and Nanning. (*d*) Beijing–Lanzhou *via* Xining (from which a branch connects with the lines through Mongolia to the Trans–Siberian Railway), Dadong (from which a branch serves the province of Shanxi), Baotou and Yinchuan (Ningxia). (*e*) Zhuzhou–Guiyang (632 km). (*f*) Xiangfan–Chongqing.

Branches link coastal areas (*e.g.*, Fujian province) and the smaller inland centres with the main parts of the system. Surveys have been made for a new 500-km railway, linking the trunk line with the oilfield of Karamai in Xinjiang.

(3) The Manchurian system: (*a*) Chinese Eastern (Changchun) Railway (2,370 km), from Manzhouli on the Soviet border through northern Inner Mongolia and Manchuria *via* Qiqihar, Harbin and Mudanjiang to the Soviet border near Vladivostok. (*b*) South Manchuria Railway (705 km, 1,120 km with branches), Changchun–Shenyang–Luda. (*c*) Beijing–Shenyang Railway, with branches in Manchuria (854 km, 1,350 km with branches).

The Beijing–Lanzhou line connects through a branch with the Trans–Siberian Railway in the USSR. A line from Xinjiang across the border to Soviet Kazakhstan is due for completion in 1991.

In 1988, 820 km of double track railways were added and 419 km of single line, and 1,487 km were electrified.

In 1988 the railways carried 9,867 tonne/km of freight and 326 person/km.

Aviation. Since 1985 the Civil Aviation Administration of China has become the administrative body for 5 new airlines: Air China (based on Beijing); Eastern Airways (Shanghai); Southern Airways (Canton); South-Western Airways (Chengdu) and the Capital Helicopter Company. There are services to Pyongyang, Hanoi, Rangoon, Singapore, Bangkok, Karachi, Tokyo, Moscow, Ulan Bator, Teheran, Addis Ababa, Bucharest, Belgrade, Zürich, Paris, Frankfurt, Manila, New York, San Francisco, London, Sydney and Hong Kong. Route lengths in 1987, 389,100 km, of which 148,900 km were international. British Airways have a direct flight London-Beijing. Japan Airlines have a route from Tokyo to Beijing (*via* Osaka and Shanghai), Air France Paris to Beijing (*via* Athens and Karachi), Pakistan Airlines Karachi to Beijing, Aeroflot Moscow to Beijing, Ethiopian Airlines Addis Ababa to Shanghai, Tarom Bucharest to Beijing, Swissair Geneva to Beijing and Shanghai, Iran Air Paris to Beijing and PANAM Beijing *via* Tokyo. Singapore Airlines Singapore to Beijing and Thai Airways Bangkok to Beijing.

In 1988 CAAC carried 21·4 person/km and 0·74 tonne/km of freight.

Shipping. In 1980 the ocean-going merchant fleet consisted of 431 vessels with a total DWT of 7·92m.

Cargo handled by the major ports in 1985 (in tonnes): Shanghai, 113m.; Dalian, 44m.; Qinhuangdao, 44m.; Qingdao, 26m.; Huangpu, 18m.; Tianjin, 18m.; Zhanjiang, 12m. In 1987 79·8m. tonnes of freight were carried.

Inland waterways totalled 109,800 km in 1987. 858m. tonnes of freight and 458m. passengers were carried.

Pipeline. A pipeline links the Daqing oilfield to the port of Luda and to refineries in Peking. There is a pipeline from Lanzhou to Lhasa. There were 13,800 km of pipeline in 1987 which carried a load of 151·4m. tonnes.

Post and Broadcasting. There were 52,900 post offices in 1987. There were 8m. telephones and some 10,000 fax machines in 1989. The use of *Pinyin* transcription of place names has been requested for mail to addresses in China (*e.g.*, 'Beijing' *not* 'Peking').

In 1988 there were 461 radio and 422 television stations. In 1981 there were 9·02m. TV receivers.

Cinemas and Theatres. There were 8,331 cinemas, 135,719 film projection units and 2,094 theatres in 1987. 158 feature films were made in 1988.

Newspapers and books. In 1987 there were 850 newspapers with a circulation of 20,490m. and 5,687 periodicals. The Party newspaper is *Renmin Ribao* (People's Daily). In 1979 it had a daily circulation of 7m. 60,193 book titles were produced in 62,500m. copies in 1987. There were 2,479 public libraries in 1988.

JUSTICE, RELIGION, EDUCATION AND WELFARE

Justice. Six new codes of law (including criminal and electoral) came into force in 1980, to regularize the legal unorthodoxy of previous years. There is no provision for *habeas corpus*. An anti-crime campaign was launched in Aug. 1983 which, it was claimed in 1985, had cut the crime rate sharply; by 1986 624,000 sentences of death or long-term imprisonment had been imposed. The death penalty has been extended from treason and murder to include rape, embezzlement, smuggling, drug-dealing, bribery and robbery with violence. Courts will no longer be subject to the intervention of other state bodies, and their decisions will be reversible only by higher courts. 'People's courts' are divided into some 30 higher, 200 intermediate and 2,000 basic-level courts, and headed by the Supreme People's Court. The latter tries cases, hears appeals and supervises the people's courts.

People's courts are composed of a president, vice-presidents, judges and 'people's assessors' who are the equivalent of jurors. 'People's conciliation committees' are charged with settling minor disputes.

There are also special military courts.

Procuratorial powers and functions are exercised by the Supreme People's Procuracy and local procuracies.

Religion. Confucianism, Buddhism and Taoism have long been practised. Confucianism has no ecclesiastical organization and appears rather as a philosophy of ethics and government. Taoism—of Chinese origin—copied Buddhist ceremonial soon after the arrival of Buddhism two millennia ago. Buddhism in return adopted many Taoist beliefs and practices. It is no longer possible to estimate the number of adherents to these faiths. A more tolerant attitude towards religion had emerged by 1979, and the Government's Bureau of Religious Affairs was reactivated.

Ceremonies of reverence to ancestors have been observed by the whole population regardless of philosophical or religious beliefs.

Moslems are found in every province of China, being most numerous in the Ningxia–Hui Autonomous Region, Yunnan, Shaanxi, Gansu, Hebei, Honan, Shandong, Sichuan, Xinjiang and Shanxi. They totalled 14m. in 1986.

Roman Catholicism has had a footing in China for more than 3 centuries. In 1985 there were about 3m. Catholics who are members of the Patriotic Catholic Association, which declared its independence of Rome in 1958. In 1979 there were about 1,000 priests. In 1977 there were 78 bishops and 4 apostolic administrators, not all of whom were permitted to undertake religious activity. This figure included 46 'democratically elected' bishops not recognized by the Vatican. A bishop of Beijing was consecrated in 1979 without the consent of the Vatican and 2 auxiliary bishops of Shanghai in 1984. Archbishop Gong Pinmei, arrested in 1955, was freed in 1988. Protestants are members of the All-China Conference of Protestant Churches. 2 Protestant bishops were installed in 1988, the first for 30 years.

Education. In 1988 220m. people (70% women) were illiterate. In 1986 90% of school-age children attended school. In 1987 there were 176,775 kindergartens with 18·1m. children and 941,000 teachers. An educational reform of 1985 is phasing in compulsory 9-year education consisting of six years of primary schooling and three years of secondary schooling, to replace a previous 5-year system. In 1987 there were 807,406 primary schools with 6·09m. teachers and 128·4m. pupils, and 105,151 secondary schools, with 4·55m. teachers and 54·03m. pupils. There were 1,063 institutes of higher education, with 969,000 teachers and 1·95m. students.

University entry is dependent upon entrance examinations and students are funded by competitive scholarships. Following student demonstrations in Jan. 1987 political education courses and periods of labour service were restored to university curricula, and political criteria of selection re-applied. In 1989 the number of university places was cut by 30,000 to 610,000, and a compulsory year of military service inserted before student enrolment. First degree courses usually last 4 years. A further year of labour is obligatory before proceeding to postgraduate studies. In 1988 there were 149,000 full-time postgraduate and 670,000 undergraduate students.

There is an Academy of Sciences with provincial branches. An Academy of Social Sciences was established in 1977.

Among the universities are the following: People's University of China, Peking (founded 1912 by Dr Sun Yat-sen; reorganized 1950; about 3,000 students); Peking

University, Peking (1898, enlarged 1945; about 10,000 students); Xiamen University, Fujian (1921 and 1937); Fudan University, Shanghai (1905); Inner Mongolia University, Hohhot; Lanzhou University, Lanzhou (Gansu Prov.); Nankai University, Tianjin (1919); Nanjing University, Nanjing (1888 and 1928); Jilin University, Changchun (Jilin Prov.); North-West University, Xian (Shanxi Prov.); Shandong University, Qingdao (1926); Sun Yat-sen University, Canton (founded 1924 by Dr Sun Yat-sen); Sichuan University, Chengdu (1931); Qinghua University, Peking, Wuhan University, Wuhan (Hubei Prov.; 1905 and 1928); Yunnan University, Kunming. In 1987 some 36,000 students were studying abroad, but in 1988 the number has reduced to 3,000 a year (600 only to USA).

Chen, T. H., *Chinese Education since 1949*. Oxford, 1981
Heyhoe, R., (ed.) *Contemporary Chinese Education*. London, 1984

Health. Medical treatment is free only for certain groups of employees, but where costs are incurred they are partly borne by the patient's employing organization. In 1988 there were 1,618,000 doctors, of whom 1,096,000 practised Chinese medicine. About 10% of doctors are in private practice.

In 1987 there were 60,429 hospitals (including 348 mental hospitals) and in 1988 2·5m. hospital beds.

DIPLOMATIC REPRESENTATIVES

Of China in Great Britain (49 Portland Pl., London, W1N 3AH)
Ambassador: Ji Chaozhu (accredited Sept. 1987).

Of Great Britain in China (Guang Hua Lu 11, Jian Guo Men Wai, Beijing)
Ambassador: Sir Alan Donald, KCMG.

Of China in the USA (2300 Connecticut Ave., NW, Washington, D.C., 20008)
Ambassador: Zhu Qizhen (accredited July 1989).

Of the USA in China (Xiu Shui Bei Jie 3, Beijing)
Ambassador: James Lilley.

Of China to the United Nations
Ambassador: Li Luye.

Further Reading

Beijing Review. Beijing, weekly
China Daily [European ed.]. London, from 1986
China Directory [in Pinyin and Chinese]. Tokyo, annual
The China Quarterly. London, from 1960
China Reconstructs. Beijing, monthly
China's Foreign Trade. Bimonthly. Beijing, from 1966
People's Republic of China Yearbook. Beijing, from 1983
Statistical Yearbook of China. Beijing and Oxford, from 1981
The Population Atlas of China. OUP, 1988
Barnett, A. D., *The Making of Foreign Policy in China*. London, 1985
Barnett, A. D. and Clough, R., (eds.) *Modernizing China: Post-Mao Reform and Development*. Boulder, 1986
Bartke, W. (ed.) *Who's Who in the People's Republic of China*. 2nd ed. New York, 1986
Bartke, W. and Schier, P., *China's New Party Leadership: Biographies and Analysis*. London, 1985
Blecher, M., *China: Politics, Economics and Sociology*. London, 1986
Bonavia, D., *The Chinese*. New York, 1980.—*The Chinese: A Portrait*. London, 1981
Boorman, H. L. and Howard, R. C., (eds.) *Biographical Dictionary of Republican China*. 5 vols. Columbia Univ. Press, 1967–79
Brady, J. P., *Justice and Politics in People's China: Legal Order or Continuing Revolution?* London, 1982
Brown, D. G., *Partnership with China: Sino-foreign Joint Ventures in Historical Perspective*. Boulder, 1985
Bullard, M., *China's Political-Military Evolution*. Boulder, 1985
The Cambridge History of China. 14 vols. CUP, 1978 ff.
Chang, D. W., *China under Deng Xiao-ping: Political and Economic Reforms*. London, 1989

Cheng, P., *China.* [Bibliography] Oxford and Santa Barbara, 1983
Chow, G. C., *The Chinese Economy.* New York, 1985
Chu, G. C. and Hsu, F. L., (eds.) *China's New Social Fabric.* London, 1983
Cotterell, A., *China: A Concise Cultural History.* London, 1989
Deng Xiaoping, *Speeches and Writings.* 2nd ed. Oxford, 1987
Dietrich, C., *People's China: A Brief History.* OUP, 1986
Domes, J., *The Government and Politics of the PRC.* Boulder, 1985
Fairbank, J. K., *The Great Chinese Revolution 1800–1985.* London, 1987
Fathers, M. and Higgins, A., *Tiananmen: The Rape of Peking.* London and New York, 1989
Grummit, K., *China Economic Handbook.* London, 1986
Guide to China's Foreign Economic Relations and Trade. Hong Kong, 1984
Harding, H. (ed.) *China's Foreign Relations in the 1980's.* Yale UP, 1984.—*China's Second Revolution.* Washington, 1987
Hinton, H. C. (ed.) *The People's Republic of China 1949–1979.* 5 vols. Wilmington, 1980
Hook, B. (ed.) *The Cambridge Encyclopaedia of China.* CUP, 1982
Hsieh, C. M., *Atlas of China.* New York, 1973
Jingrong, W. (ed.) *The Pinyin-Chinese Dictionary.* Beijing and San Francisco, 1979
Kaplan, F. M. (ed.) *Encyclopedia of China Today.* 3rd ed. London, 1982
Kapur, H., *China and the European Economic Community.* Dordrecht, 1986
Kim, S. S. (ed.) *China and the World: Chinese Foreign Policy in the Post-Mao Era.* Boulder, 1984
Klein, D. W. and Clark, A. B., *Biographic Dictionary of Chinese Communism, 1921–1965.* Harvard U.P., 1971
Lamb, M., *Directory of Officials and Organizations in China, 1968–1983.* Armonk, 1984
Lardy, N. R., *Agriculture in China's Modern Economic Development.* CUP, 1983
Leeming, F., *Rural China Today.* London, 1985
Lippit, V. D., *The Economic Development of China.* Armonk, 1987
Mabbett, I., *Modern China: The Mirage of Modernity.* New York, 1985
Mancall, M., *China at the Center: 300 Years of Foreign Policy.* New York, 1984
Marshall, M., *Organizations and Growth in Rural China.* London, 1985
Mathews, R. H., *Chinese-English Dictionary.* Cambridge, Mass., 1943–47
Maxwell, N. and McFarlane, B. (eds.) *China's Changed Road to Development.* Oxford, 1984
Moise, E. E., *Modern China: A History.* London, 1986
Moser, L. J., *The Chinese Mosaic: the Peoples and Provinces of China.* Boulder, 1985
Nathan, A. J., *Chinese Democracy.* London, 1986
Pan, L., *The New Chinese Revolution.* London, 1987
Pannell, C. W. and Laurence, J. C., *China: the Geography of Development and Modernization.* London, 1983
Riskin, C., *China's Political Economy: The Quest for Development since 1949.* OUP, 1987
Rodzinski, W., *A History of China.* Oxford, 1981–84
Schram, S. R. (ed.) *The Scope of State Power in China.* London, 1985
Segal, G., *Defending China.* OUP, 1985
Segal, G. and Tow, W. T. (eds.) *Chinese Defence Policy.* London, 1984
Song, J., *et al, Population Control in China.* New York, 1985
Thornton, R. C., *China: A Political History, 1917–1980.* Boulder, 1982
The Times Atlas of China. London, 1974
Wong, K. and Chu, D. (eds.) *Modernization in China: The Case of the Shenzhen Special Economic Zone.* OUP, 1986
Yahuda, M. B., *Towards the End of Isolationism: China's Foreign Policy after Mao.* London, 1983
Yin, J., *Government of Socialist China.* Lanham, 1984
Young, G. (ed.) *China: Dilemmas of Modernisation.* London, 1985

TAIWAN[1]

'Republic of China'

Capital: Taipei
Population: 19·9m. (1988)
GNP per capita: US$6,053 (1988)

HISTORY. The island of Taiwan (Formosa) was ceded to Japan by China by the Treaty of Shimonoseki on 8 May 1895. After the Second World War the island was

[1] See note on transcription of names p. 355.

surrendered to Gen. Chiang Kai-shek in Sept. 1945 and was placed under Chinese administration on 25 Oct. 1945. USA broke off diplomatic relations with Taiwan on 1 Jan. 1979 on establishing diplomatic relations with the Peking Government. Relations between the USA and Taiwan are maintained through the American Institute on Taiwan and the Co-ordination Council for North American Affairs in the USA, set up in 1979 and accorded diplomatic status in Oct. 1980.

AREA AND POPULATION. Taiwan lies between the East and South China Seas about 100 miles from the coast of Fujian. The total area of Taiwan Island, the Penghu Archipelago and the Kinma area is 13,969 sq. miles (36,179 sq. km). Population (1988), 19·9m., of whom some 2m. are mainland Chinese who came with the Nationalist Government. There are also 335,287 aboriginals. Population density: 553 per sq. km.

In 1988, birth rate was 1·72%; death rate, 0·51%; rate of growth, 1·2% per annum (2000 target: 0·72% per annum). Life expectancy, 1988: Males, 71·3 years; females, 76·6 years.

Taiwan is divided into two special municipalities (Taipei, the capital, population 2·68m. in 1988 and Kaohsiung, population 1·3m. in 1988), 5 municipalities (Taichung, Keelung, Tainan, Chiayi and Hsinchu) and 16 counties (*hsien*): Changhwa, Chiayi, Hsinchu, Hualien, Ilan, Kaohsiung, Miaoli, Nantou, Penghu, Pingtung, Taichung, Tainan, Taipei, Taitung, Taoyuan, Yunlin. The seat of the provincial government is at Chunghsing New Village.

CLIMATE. A tropical climate with hot, humid conditions and heavy rainfall in the summer months but cooler from Nov. to March when rainfall amounts are not so great. Typhoons may be experienced. Taipei. Jan. 59°F (15·3°C), July 83°F (29·2°C). Annual rainfall 100" (2,500 mm).

CONSTITUTION AND GOVERNMENT. Taiwan is controlled by the remnants of the Nationalist Government. On 1 March 1950, Chiang Kai-shek resumed the presidency of the 'Republic of China'. He died 5 April 1975. His son Chiang Ching-kuo was president from March 1978 to his death in Jan. 1988. He was succeeded by Lee Teng-hui. Until 1986 there were 3 political parties: The ruling Kuomintang (KMT) (2·44m. members in 1987), which has a youth movement (China Youth Corps) of over 1m. members; the Young China Party, and the China Democratic Socialist Party. Opposition parties were banned.

The National Assembly was elected in 1947. In 1989 it had 940 delegates. Government is conducted through 5 councils (Executive, Legislative, Judicial, Examination, and Control *Yuan*). The highest administrative organ is the Executive Yuan, headed by the Prime Minister, which includes a number of ministers. The highest legislative body is the Legislative Yuan, elected in 1948, which in 1989 numbered 312 members. The National Assembly, Legislative Yuan and Control Yuan are elected bodies. Their terms of office have been extended indefinitely. As the number of original delegates dwindled, regulations introduced in 1966 and 1972 provided for the election of additional members to the National Assembly and Legislative Yuan, and elections were held in 1969, 1972, 1975, 1980, 1983 and 1986. Martial law, in force since 1949, was lifted in July 1987, and the ban on opposition parties was dropped in Jan. 1989. A new Democratic Progress Party (DPP)was formed in Oct. 1986 and a Democratic Liberal Party in Sept. 1987. In Dec. 1989 elections were held for 101 of the 261 seats in the Legislative Yuan. The KMT won 60% of the vote, the DPP 30%, the latter winning 21 seats. In simultaneous local elections for 21 county executives and city mayors, the DPP won 6 posts with 40% of the vote. At the local authority elections of 1986 the KMT won 1,002 out of 1,146 seats.

State emblem: A 12-pointed white sun in a blue sky.

National flag: Red with a blue first quarter bearing the state emblem in white.

National anthem: 'San Min Chu I', words by Dr Sun Yat-sen; tune by Cheng Mao-yun.

The cabinet included the following in March 1990:

Prime Minister: Lee Huan.

Vice-Premier: Shih Chi-yang. *Foreign Minister:* Lien Chan. *Minister of National Defence:* Cheng Wei-yuan. *Minister of the Interior:* Hsu Shui-teh. *Minister of Finance:* Shirley W. Y. Kuo. *Minister of Education:* Mao Kao-wen. *Minister of Economic Affairs:* Chen Li-an. *Minister of Communications:* Clement C. P. Chang. *Chairman, Mongolian and Tibetan Affairs Commission:* Wu Hua-peng. *Chairman, Overseas Chinese Affairs Commission:* Tseng Kwang-shun. The Governor of Taiwan Province was Chiu Chuang-huan.

DEFENCE

Army. The Army, which was formed on the forces which escaped to Taiwan under Chiang Kai-shek at the end of the civil war in 1949, numbered about 270,000 in 1989. It was reorganized, re-equipped and trained by the USA and in 1989 consisted of 12 heavy and 6 light infantry divisions, 2 armoured infantry and 1 airborne brigades, 4 tank groups, 20 field artillery and 5 SAM battalions. The aviation element has about 118 helicopters. There is a conscription system for 2 years and reserve liability. US supplies of military equipment were resumed in 1980 after a moratorium in 1979. US forces were withdrawn by 1 May 1979.

Navy. The Taiwan navy consists principally of former US Navy ships over 40 years old and well overdue for replacement. A major programme of replacement frigates in two classes has recently been initiated. Current fleet strength is 2 new Netherlands-built diesel submarines, 26 *ex*-US 1940s destroyers, 10 frigates, 3 corvettes (*ex*-fleet minesweepers), 52 fast missile craft and 8 coastal minesweepers. The amphibious force includes 1 amphibious flagship, 1 dock landing ship, 25 landing ships and over 250 amphibious craft. Auxiliary craft include 4 support tankers, 2 repair and 1 survey ship, 4 transport, 2 training ships and 1 Antarctic patrol ship. There are some 11 service craft and numerous boats.

The Naval Air Service has 4 squadrons: 1 with 6 EMB-111N and 3 Falcon maritime patrol aircraft, 1 with 3 Bandeirante, 2 Westwind and 3 Aviocar transports, 1 with 8 Alouette and 3 Jetranger anti-submarine helicopters, and 1 with 10 Pilatus PC-7 trainers.

Naval personnel in 1988 totalled 29,000 all ranks, of whom 3,000 were conscripts, including 5,200 marines and 500 in the naval air service.

A separate Coast Guard numbering 1,600 operates 13 patrol craft and a helicopter.

Air Force. The Nationalist Air Force is equipped mainly with aircraft of US design, including F-5E fighters built in Taiwan. It has 11 front-line squadrons of F-5E/F Tiger IIs, 3 of F-104G Starfighters and 1 tactical reconnaissance squadron of RF-104G Starfighters. The 6 transport squadrons are equipped with a VIP Boeing 720, 4 Boeing 727s, 12 Beech 1900s, 20 C-47s, about 40 C-119Gs, 12 C-130H Hercules and 10 C-123 Providers. There is a naval co-operation squadron with S-2A/E Trackers. Search and rescue units operate S-70 and Iroquois helicopters, and there are other helicopter and large training elements, some equipped with AT-3 twin-jet trainers designed and built in Taiwan and others with US-supplied T-34Cs. Total strength in 1989: 70,000 personnel and (1988) 400 combat aircraft.

INTERNATIONAL RELATIONS. By a treaty of 1 Dec. 1954 the USA was pledged to protect Taiwan, but this treaty lapsed 1 year after the USA established diplomatic relations with the People's Republic of China on 1 Jan. 1979. In April 1979 the Taiwan Relations Act was passed by the US Congress to maintain commercial, cultural and other relations between USA and Taiwan.

The People's Republic took over the China seat in the UN from the Nationalists on 25 Oct. 1971.

ECONOMY

Planning. There have been a series of development plans. The ninth (1986–89), aimed at an annual growth rate of 6·5% (industry 6·1%, agriculture 1·3%).

Budget. There are 2 budgets, the national together with a special defence budget (partly secret) and the provincial (*i.e.,* for Taiwan proper). For the fiscal year July 1989–June 1990 the national budget is scheduled for NT$680,444m. Expenditure planned: 31·2% on defence; 16% on economic development; 18·5% on welfare; 15·2% on education, science and culture. Foreign exchange reserves were US$70,326m. in June 1989.

Currency. The unit of currency is the New Taiwan dollar, divided into 100 cents. There are coins of NT$ 0·5, 1, 5 and 10 and notes of NT$ 10, 50, 100, 500 and 1,000. There are no cent coins or notes. Exchange rates (March 1990): £1 = NT$43·10; US$1 = NT$26·30.

Banking. The Central Bank of China (reactivated in 1961) regulates the money supply, manages foreign exchange and issues currency. *Governor:* Samuel Shieh.

The Bank of Taiwan is the largest commercial bank and the fiscal agent of the Government. In addition, there are 15 domestic commercial banks and 38 local branches of foreign banks.

ENERGY AND NATURAL RESOURCES

Electricity. Output of electricity in 1988 was 71,643m. kwh.; total generating capacity was 16·6m. kw. There are 3 nuclear power-stations (capacities 1m., 1m. and 0·6m. kw.) and a fourth is envisaged. Supply 110 volts; 60 Hz.

Minerals. There are reserves of coal (172m. tonnes), gold (5·5m. tonnes), copper (10m. tonnes), sulphur (2·2m. tonnes), oil (1·2m. kl.) and natural gas (20,028 cu. metres). In 1988, coal production was 1·2m. tonnes; refined oil, 2·1m. kl.; natural gas, 1,157m. cu. metres. Crude oil production (1989) 140,000 tonnes.

Agriculture. The cultivated area was 894,974 hectares in 1988, of which 483,514 hectares were paddy fields. Production in 1,000 tonnes, in 1988: Rice, 1,845; tea, 24; bananas, 229; pineapples, 228; sugar-cane, 6,767; sweet potatoes, 255; wheat, 3; soybeans, 14·6; peanuts, 83.

Livestock (1988): Cattle, 176,275; pigs, 6,954,322; goats, 195,869.

Forestry. Forest area, 1988: 1,865,141 hectares; forest reserves, 326,421,397 cu. metres; timber production, 310,370 cu. metres.

Fisheries. The fleet comprised 5,689 vessels over 20 GRT in 1988; the catch was 1,360,868 tonnes in 1988.

INDUSTRY AND TRADE

Industry. Output (in tonnes) in 1988 (and 1987): Steel bars, 3·6m. (3·1m.); pig-iron, 25,092 (87,180); shipbuilding, 662,508 (564,268); sugar, 575,403 (544,217); cement, 17·3m. (15·7m.); fertilizers, 1·24m. (1·8m.); paper, 787,617 (716,812); cotton fabrics, 745m. metres (729m.).

Labour. In 1988 the labour force was 8·11m., of whom 1·11m. worked in agriculture, forestry and fisheries, 3·45m. in industry (including 2·8m. in manufacturing and 590,000 in building), 1·54m. in commerce, 431,000 in transport and communications, and 1·57m. in other services. 139,000 were registered unemployed.

Commerce. Foreign trade affairs are handled by the China External Trade Development Council (founded 1970), which operates branches in 20 countries mostly under the name of Far East Trade Service. Principal exports: Textiles, electronic products, agricultural products, metal goods, plastic products. Principal imports: Oil, chemicals, machinery, electronic products. Total trade, in US$1m.:

	1983	*1984*	*1985*	*1986*	*1987*	*1988*
Imports	20,287	21,959	20,102	24,165	34,957	49,656
Exports	25,123	30,456	30,723	39,789	53,538	60,585

The USA, Japan and Hong Kong are Taiwan's major trade partners followed by the Federal Republic of Germany, UK and Canada. A mounting trade surplus has caused friction with the USA and a sharp appreciation of the Taiwan dollar. Economic liberalisation measures are being undertaken to improve the position.

Total trade between Taiwan and UK (British Department of Trade returns, in £1,000 sterling):

	1985	*1986*	*1987*	*1988*	*1989*
Imports to UK	582,904	705,775	1,006,880	1,150,392	1,351,695
Exports and re-exports from UK	164,776	192,492	292,275	355,786	407,432

Tourism. In 1988 1,935,134 tourists visited Taiwan, and 1,601,992 Taiwanese made visits abroad. The ban on Taiwanese travel to Communist China was lifted in 1987.

COMMUNICATIONS

Roads. In 1988 there were 19,981 km of roads (16,984 km surfaced). 8,930,878 motor vehicles were registered including 1,579,121 passenger cars, 21,955 buses, 520,189 trucks and 6,810,548 motor cycles. 2,008m. passengers and 240m. tonnes of freight were transported (excluding urban buses).

Railways. Total route length in 1988 was 2,526 km (1,067 mm to 762 mm gauge), of which a large proportion is owned by the Taiwan Sugar Corporation and other concerns. The state network consisted of 1,072 km. Freight traffic amounted to 18·2m. tonnes and passenger traffic to 132·2m.

Aviation. There are 2 international airports: Chiang Kai-shek at Taoyuan near Taipei, and Kaohsiung which operates daily flights to Hong Kong. There are 8 domestic airlines, including China Airlines (CAL), which also operates international services to Bangkok, Hong Kong, Jakarta, Kuala Lumpur, Manila, Seoul, Singapore, Amsterdam, Saudi Arabia, Japan and USA. In 1988 14·74m. passengers and 542,793 tonnes of freight were flown.

Shipping. The merchant marine in 1988 comprised 2 passenger ships, 78 container ships, 57 bulk carriers, 15 tankers and 102 mixed service ships, with a total DWT of 7·74m.

The 4 international ports, Kaohsiung, Keelung, Hwalien and Taichung, are being extensively redeveloped. The first two are container centres. Suao port is an auxiliary port to Keelung.

Post and Broadcasting. In 1988 there were 12,498 post offices. Number of telephones, 7,159,213. In 1986 there were more than 5m. TV receivers. There are 3 TV networks.

Cinemas (1988). Cinemas numbered 521.

Newspapers and Books. There were 124 daily papers and 3,748 periodicals in 1988. 8,980 book titles were published in 1987. A 36-year ban on the publication of new dailies was lifted on 1 Jan. 1988.

RELIGION, EDUCATION AND WELFARE

Religion. There were 2·35m. Taoists in 1988 with 7,461 temples and 24,832 priests, 4·1m. Buddhists with 3,345 temples and 6,360 priests, 421,605 Protestants and 289,231 Catholics.

Education. Since 1968 there has been free compulsory education for 9 years (6–15). In that year the curriculum was modernized to give more emphasis to science while retaining the traditional basis of Confucian ethics. Since 1983 school-leavers aged 15-18 receive part-time vocational education. There were, in 1988–89, 2,478 primary schools with 77,892 teachers and 2,407,166 pupils; 1,063 secondary schools with 80,062 teachers and 1,742,116 students; 109 schools of higher education, including 39 universities and colleges, with 23,809 full-time teachers and 496,530 students.

Health. In 1988 there were 84,271 medical personnel, including 18,193 doctors,

4,511 dentists and 2,397 doctors of Chinese medicine. There were 92 public hospitals with 32,641 beds and 821 private hospitals with 47,761 beds.

Further Reading

Statistical Yearbook of the Republic of China. Taipei, annual
Republic of China: A Reference Book. Taipei, annual
Taiwan Statistical Data Book. Taipei, annual
Annual Review of Government Administration, Republic of China. Taipei, annual
Gälli, A., *Taiwan ROC: A Chinese Challenge to the World*. London, 1987
Gold, T. B., *State and Society in the Taiwan Miracle*. Armonk, 1986
Hsieh, C. C., *Strategy for Survival: The Foreign Policy and External Relations of the Republic of China on Taiwan 1949–1979*. London, 1985
Kuo, S. W., *The Taiwan Economy in Transition*. Boulder, 1983
Liu, A. P. L., *Phoenix and the Lame Lion: Modernization in Taiwan and Mainland China, 1950–1980*. Stanford, 1987
Simon, D. F. S., *Taiwan, Technology Transfer, and Transnationalism*. Boulder, 1983

National Library: National Central Library, Taipei (established 1986). *Director:* Wang Chen-ku.

COLOMBIA

Capital: Bogotá
Population: 29·5m. (1985)
GNP per capita: US$1,240 (1988)

República de Colombia

HISTORY. The Vice-royalty of New Granada gained its independence of Spain in 1819, and was officially constituted 17 Dec. 1819, together with the present territories of Panama, Venezuela and Ecuador, as the state of 'Greater Colombia', which continued for about 12 years. It then split up into Venezuela, Ecuador and the republic of New Granada in 1830. The constitution of 22 May 1858 changed New Granada into a confederation of 8 states, under the name of Confederación Granadina. Under the constitution of 8 May 1863 the country was renamed 'Estados Unidos de Colombia', which were 9 in number. The revolution of 1885 led the National Council of Bogotá, composed of 2 delegates from each state, to promulgate the constitution of 5 Aug. 1886, forming the Republic of Colombia, which abolished the sovereignty of the states, converting them into departments, with governors appointed by the President of the Republic, though they retained some of their old rights, such as the management of their own finances.

AREA AND POPULATION. Colombia is bounded north by the Caribbean sea, north-west by Panama, west by the Pacific ocean, south-west by Ecuador and Peru, north-east by Venezuela and south-east by Brazil. The estimated area is 1,141,748 sq. km (440,829 sq. miles). It has a coastline of about 2,900 km, of which 1,600 km are on the Caribbean sea and 1,300 km on the Pacific ocean. Population census, (1985) 29,481,852. Bogotá, the capital, (census, 1985) 4,185,174.

Départmentos	*Area (sq. km)*	*Population census 1985*	*Capital*	*Population census 1985*
Antioquia	63,612	4,055,064	Medellín	1,506,050
Atlántico	3,388	1,461,925	Barranquilla	920,695
Bolívar	25,978	1,289,891	Cartagena	559,581
Boyacá	23,189	1,149,350	Tunja (M.E.)	95,503
Caldas	7,888	882,193	Manizales	309,821
Caquetá	88,965	254,777	Florencia	87,794
Cauca	29,308	848,603	Popayán	166,178
César (El)	22,905	646,088	Valledupar	208,741
Chocó	46,530	296,914	Quibdó	85,085
Córdoba	25,020	997,597	Montería	238,081
Cundinamarca [1]	22,478	1,481,573	Bogotá	4,185,174
Guajira (La)	20,848	303,110	Riohacha	83,956
Huila	19,890	671,112	Neiva	197,445
Magdalena	23,188	860,841	Santa Marta	225,936
Meta	85,635	443,755	Villavicencio	182,298
Nariño	33,268	1,048,480	Pasto	252,115
Norte de Santander	21,658	943,225	Cúcuta	407,236
Quindío	1,845	400,117	Armenia	199,459
Risaralda	4,140	659,292	Pereira	301,715
Santander	30,537	1,535,021	Bucaramanga	363,909
Sucre	10,917	560,886	Sincelejo	139,519
Tolima	23,562	1,114,990	Ibagué	306,078
Valle del Cauca	22,140	2,955,483	Cali	1,397,433

[1] Excluding Bogotá.

Intendencias	*Area (sq. km)*	*Population census 1985*	*Capital*	*Population census 1985*
Arauca	23,818	70,085	Arauca	21,279
Casanare	44,640	110,253	El Yopal	23,169
Putumayo	24,885	119,815	Mocoa	20,325
San Andrés y Providencia	44	35,936	San Andrés	32,282

Comisarías	*Area (sq. km)*	*Population census 1985*	*Capital*	*Population census 1985*
Amazonas	109,665	30,327	Leticia	19,245
Guainía	72,238	9,214	Obando (Puerto Inírida)	9,214
Guaviare	53,460	35,305	San José del Guaviare	31,082
Vaupés	54,135	18,935	Mitú	13,192
Vichada	100,242	13,770	Puerto Carreño	8,081

The bulk of the population lives at altitudes of from 4,000 to 9,000 ft above sea-level. It is divided broadly into: 68% mestizo, 20% white, 7% Indio and 5% Negro.

The official language is Spanish.

CLIMATE. The climate includes equatorial and tropical conditions, according to situation and altitude. In tropical areas, the wettest months are March to May and Oct. to Nov. Bogotá. Jan. 58°F (14·4°C), July 57°F (13·9°C). Annual rainfall 42" (1,052 mm). Baranquilla. Jan. 80°F (26·7°C), July 82°F (27·8°C). Annual rainfall 32" (799 mm). Cali. Jan. 75°F (23·9°C), July 75°F (23·9°C). Annual rainfall 37" (915 mm). Medellin. Jan. 71°F (21·7°C), July 72°F (22·2°C). Annual rainfall 64" (1,606 mm).

CONSTITUTION AND GOVERNMENT. The legislative power rests with a Congress of 2 houses, the Senate, of 112 members, and the House of Representatives, of 199 members, both elected for 4 years. Congress meets annually at Bogotá on 20 July. Women were given the vote, which is now open to citizens of either sex, over 18 years of age, on 25 Aug. 1954.

The President is elected by direct vote of the people for a term of 4 years, and is not eligible for re-election until 4 years afterwards. Congress elects, for a term of 2 years, one substitute to occupy the presidency in the event of a vacancy during a presidential term. There are 13 Ministries. The Governors of Departments and the Mayor of Bogotá are nominated by the national government.

A National Economic Council, functioning since May 1935, went through several transformations, becoming in 1954 a Directorate of Planning.

National Flag: Three horizontal stripes of yellow, blue, red with the yellow of double width.

National anthem: Oh! Gloria inmarcesible (words by R. Núñez; tune by O. Síndici).

The following is a list of presidents since 1953:

Gen. Gustavo Rojas Pinilla, 13 June 1953–10 May 1957.
Military Junta, Maj.-Gen. Gabriel París and 4 others, 10 May 1957–7 Aug. 1958.
Dr Alberto Lleras Camargo (Lib.), 7 Aug. 1958–7 Aug. 1962.
Dr Guillermo León Valencia (Cons.), 7 Aug. 1962–7 Aug. 1966.
Dr Carlos Lleras Restrepo (Lib.), 7 Aug. 1966–7 Aug. 1970.
Dr Misael Pastrana Borrero (Cons.), 7 Aug 1970–7 Aug. 1974.
Dr Alfonso López Michelsen (Cons./Lib.), 7 Aug. 1974–7 Aug. 1978.
Dr Julio Cesar Turbay Ayala (Lib.), 7 Aug. 1978–7 Aug. 1982.
Dr Belisario Betancur Cuartas (Cons.), 7 Aug. 1982–7 Aug. 1986.

President: Dr Virgilio Barco Vargas (Lib.). He was elected on 25 May 1986 and took office on 7 Aug. 1986.

The Cabinet was composed as follows in Sept. 1989:

Defence: Gen. Oscar Botero. *Interior:* Orlando Vásquez Velásquez. *Finance and Public Credit:* Luis Fernando Alarcón Mantilla. *Agriculture:* Gabriel Rosas Vega. *Economic Development:* Carlos Arturo Marulanda. *Labour and Social Security:* Maria Teresa Forero de Saade. *Health:* Eduardo Diaz Uribe. *Mines and Energy:* Margarita Mena de Quevado. *Education:* Manuel F. Becera. *Communications:* (Vacant). *Public Works and Transport:* Priscila Ceballos Ordoñez. *Government:* Raul Orujuela Bueno. *Justice:* Carlos Lemos Simmonds. *Foreign Affairs:* Julio Londoño Paredes.

Local government: The country is divided into 23 *départmentos*, 4 *intendencias*, 5 *comisarías* and a Special District. The governor of each is appointed by the President, but each has also a directly-elected legislature. The *départmentos* are subdivided into municipalities, each with a mayor appointed by the departmental governor.

DEFENCE. Men become liable for 1 year's military service at age 18, although the system is applied selectively. *Ex*-conscripts remain in the reserve, divided into 3 classes, until age 45.

Army. The Army consists of 14 infantry brigades, artillery, cavalry, engineer and motorized troops and the usual services. Personnel (1990) 111,400 men (conscripts, 38,000); reserves 100,000. Number of national police (1990) 80,000.

Navy. Colombia has 2 Federal German-built 1,200-ton diesel-electric powered patrol submarines completed in 1975, 2 Italian-built midget submarines; 4 small German-built missile-armed frigates with helicopter decks and 2 fast patrol craft. There are 3 river gunboats and 10 riverine patrol craft. Auxiliaries include 2 surveying vessels, 2 small transports, 1 training ship, 5 service craft and 10 tugs. Personnel in 1989 totalled 6,000, plus a brigade of marines numbering 6,000. An air arm was formed in 1984 and operates 4 BO-105 helicopters for ship-based ASW and SAR duties.

Air Force. Formed in 1922, the Air Force has been independent of the Army and Navy since 1943, when its reorganization began with US assistance. In 1986 it had about 300 aircraft, including a squadron of Mirage 5-COA fighter-bombers, 5-COR reconnaissance aircraft and 5-COD two-seat operational trainers; 2 squadrons of A-37B jets for counter-insurgency duties, a transport group equipped with 3 C-130, 12 C-47s, 3 C-54s, 4 DC-6s and a small number of Arava, Beaver and Turbo-Porter light transports; a presidential F-28 Fellowship jet transport; 1 Boeing 707, UH-1B/H utility helicopters; and a reconnaissance unit with Iroquois, Lama, Hughes OH-6A, 300C and TH-55 helicopters. Eight more C-47s, 2 C-54s, 1 F-28 and 4 HS.748 transports are flown by the Air Force operated airline SATENA. Thirty Cessna T-41D primary trainer/light transports were delivered in 1968 and were followed by 10 T-37C jet advanced trainers to supplement piston-engined T-34s and T-33A armed jet trainers. Total strength (1990) 7,000 personnel.

INTERNATIONAL RELATIONS

Membership. Colombia is a member of the UN, OAS, the Andean Group and LAIA (formerly LAFTA).

ECONOMY

Planning. The 1982–86 Development Plan gave priority to agriculture.

Budget. Revenue and expenditure of central government in 1986: Revenue, 945,419,000 pesos; expenditure, 901m. pesos. External public debt, 30 June 1988, US$12,926,000.

Currency. Coins include 1, 2, 5, 10, 20 and 50 *pesos*. There are also notes representing 100, 200, 500, 1,000, 2,000 and 5,000 *gold pesos*. Exchange rate March 1990, 746·90 *pesos* = £1 sterling; 455·70 *pesos* = US$1.

Banking. On 23 July 1923 the Banco República was inaugurated as a semi-official central bank, with the exclusive privilege of issuing bank-notes in Colombia; its charter, in 1951, was extended to 1973. Its note issues must be covered by a reserve in gold of foreign exchange of 25% of their value. Total assets (June 1988) 2,566,088m.

There are 25 commercial banks, of which 12 are privately owned, 8 jointly owned by Colombian and foreign interest and 5 official in nature, with total assets of 3,483,559 pesos as of June 1988.

Weights and Measures. The metric system was introduced in 1857, but in ordinary commerce Spanish weights and measures are generally used; according to new definitions by the Ministry of Development, *e.g.*, *botella* (750 grammes), *galón* (5 *botellas*), *vara* (70 cm), *arroba* (25 lb., of 500 grammes; 4 *arrobas* = 1 quintal).

ENERGY AND NATURAL RESOURCES

Electricity. Capacity of electric power (1986) was 7·19m. kw. Electric power produced in 1986, 29,580m. kwh. Supply 110, 120 and 150 volts; 60 Hz.

Oil. Production in 1989 was 20·3m. tonnes.

Minerals. Colombia is rich in minerals; gold is found chiefly in Antioquia and moderately in Cauca, Caldas, Tolima, Nariño and Chocó; output in 1987, 853,468 troy oz.

Other minerals are silver (167,277 troy oz. in 1987), copper, lead, mercury, manganese, emeralds and platinum; production of platinum, 1987, 22,530 troy oz. The chief emerald mines are those of Muzo and Chivor.

The Government holds the monopoly, which is leased to the Banco de la República, for extracting salts from the outstanding Zipaquirá mines (several hundred feet in depth and several hundred square miles in area) and for evaporating many sea salt pans; salt production in 1987 was 204,045 tonnes of land salt from the Zipaquirá mines and 616,971 tonnes of sea salt from Manaure and Galerazamba on the Caribe coast. Coal reserves were estimated at 16,500m. tonnes in 1983; production (1988, provisional) 19,595,000 tonnes.

Agriculture. Very little of the country is under cultivation, but much of the soil is fertile and is coming into use as roads improve. The range of climate and crops is extraordinary; the agricultural colleges have different courses for 'cold-climate farming' and 'warm-climate farming'. In 1988 there were 2,090,830 hectares under temporary cultivation and 1,208,020 under permanent.

Coffee area harvested (1988) 1m. hectares; production (1988) 6,565,000 60 kg. sacks. Crops are grown by smallholders, and are picked all the year round. Production (1988, in 1,000 tonnes): Potatoes, 2,491·9; rice, 1,784·9; maize, 880·5; sorghum, 681·1.

The rubber tree grows wild. Fibres are being exploited, notably the 'fique' fibre, which furnishes all the country's requirements for sacks and cordage; output (1988) 23,900 tonnes. Tolú balsam is cultivated, and copaiba trees are tapped but are not cultivated. Tanning is an important industry.

Livestock (1988): 24,307,000 cattle, 2,586,000 pigs, 2,652,000 sheep, 152·4m. poultry.

Fisheries. Total catch (1987) 83,569 tonnes.

INDUSTRY AND TRADE

Industry. Production (1988): Iron, 411,588 tons; cement, 4,219,611 tons; motor cars, 33,593; industrial vehicles, 8,609.

Commerce. Imports (c.i.f. values) and exports (f.o.b. values) (excluding export tax) for calendar years (in US$1m.):

	1984	*1985*	*1986*	*1987*
Imports	4,492	4,131	3,852	4,228
Exports	3,483	3,552	5,108	5,024

Important articles of export in 1987 (in US$1m.) were coffee (1,651), bananas (210), flowers (145), sugar (16), clothing and textiles (84). The chief imports are machinery, vehicles, tractors, metals and manufactures, rubber, chemical products, wheat, fertilizers and wool. It was reported (1987) that cocaine exports earn Colombia more than its main export, coffee.

Imports in 1987 (in US$1,000) from USA were valued at 1,494,100; Venezuela, 120,516; Japan, 386,165; Federal Republic of Germany, 334,524; Brazil, 150,496. Exports (in US$1,000) went to USA, 1,877,801; Federal Republic of Germany, 592,316; Netherlands, 212,107; Venezuela, 220,164; Italy, 68,298.

Total trade between Colombia and UK (British Department of Trade returns, in £1,000 sterling).

	1985	*1986*	*1987*	*1988*	*1989*
Imports to UK	112,486	94,112	65,331	61,835	70,715
Exports and re-exports from UK	82,639	58,084	61,385	53,132	61,733

Tourism. Foreign visitors totalled 732,000 in 1986.

COMMUNICATIONS

Roads. Owing to the mountainous character of the country, the construction of arterial roads and railways is costly and difficult. Total length of highways, about 75,000 km in 1983. Of the 2,300-mile Simón Bolívar highway, which runs from Caracas in Venezuela to Guayaquil in Ecuador, the Colombian portion is complete. Buenaventura and Cali are linked by a highway (Carreterra al Mar). Motor vehicles in 1986 numbered 1,242,650, of which 611,978 were passenger cars and 108,826 lorries.

Railways. There are 5 divisions of the State Railway with a total length of 2,622 km in 1985 and a gauge of 914 mm. The Pacific Railway connects Bogotá with the port of Buenaventura. The Atlantic line from Bogotá to Sta. Marta was opened in July 1961. Three connecting links are planned to improve the operating efficiency of the network. Total railway traffic, 1987, was 1,429,000 passengers and 1,055,000 tonnes of freight. A metro opened in Medellía in 1990.

Aviation. In civil aviation Colombia ranks perhaps second, after Brazil, among South American countries. There are 670 landing grounds of all kinds. In 1987 the national airports moved 5,524,000 passengers and 95,000 tonnes of cargo.

Shipping. Vessels entering Colombian ports in 1987 unloaded 6,101,000 tonnes of imports and loaded 17,543,000 tonnes of exports.

The Magdelena River is subject to drought, and navigation is always impeded during the dry season, but it is an important artery of passenger and goods traffic. The river is navigable for 900 miles; steamers ascend to La Dorada, 592 miles from Barranquilla.

Post and Broadcasting. The length of telephone lines in service is 705,852 km (Bogotá only); instruments in use, 1 Jan. 1984, 2,547,222. The cable company is government owned. Television was established in 1954 and in 1978 there were 1·75m. sets in use. In 1983 there were 485 radio stations, of which 50 were in Bogotá.

Cinemas (1987). There were 657 cinemas, of which 64 were in Bogotá.

Newspapers (1984). There were 31 daily newspapers, with daily circulation totalling 1·5m.

JUSTICE, RELIGION, EDUCATION AND WELFARE

Justice. The Supreme Court, at Bogotá, of 20 members, is divided into 3 chambers—civil cassation (6), criminal cassation (8), labour cassation (6). Each of the 61 judicial districts has a superior court with various sub-dependent tribunals of lower juridical grade. Communism was outlawed by government decree on 5 March 1956.

Religion. The religion is Roman Catholic, with the Cardinal Archbishop of Bogotá as Primate of Colombia and 7 other archbishops in Cartagena, Manizales, Medellín, Pamplona, Popayán, Cali and Tunja, 26 bishops, 1,546 parishes and 4,020 priests. Other forms of religion are permitted so long as their exercise is 'not contrary to Christian morals or to the law.

Education. Primaıy education is free but not compulsory, and facilities are limited. Schools are both state and privately controlled. In 1986 there were 6,640 pre-primary schools with 292,741 pupils, 34,520 primary schools with 3,740,379 pupils. In 5,181 secondary schools there were 1,684,731 pupils and (1987) in 232 higher education establishments there were 417,786 students.

In 1987 there were 61 institutes of higher education with 78,412 students, 37 technological institutes with 21,733 students and 62 institutes for professional training with 31,384 students.

There are 72 universities including the National University in Bogotá (founded 1886). In (1987) there were 303,094 students.

Health. In 1984 there were 753 hospitals and clinics. There were also 861 health centres.

DIPLOMATIC REPRESENTATIVES

Of Colombia in Great Britain (3 Hans Cres., London, SW1X 0LR)
Ambassador: Dr Fernando Cepeda (accredited 28 July 1988).

Of Great Britain in Colombia (Calle 98, No. 9–03 Piso 4, Bogotá)
Ambassador: Richard Neilson, CMG, LVO.

Of Colombia in the USA (2118 Leroy Pl., NW, Washington, D.C., 20008)
Ambassador: Victor Mosquera Chaux.

Of the USA in Colombia (Calle 38, 8-61, Bogotá)
Ambassador: Thomas E. McNamara.

Of Colombia to the United Nations
Ambassador: Dr Enrique Peñalosa.

Further Reading

Anuario General de Estadística de Colombia. Bogotá. Annual
Anuario de Comercio Exterior de Colombia. Annual
Anuario Estadístico Bogotá D. E. Annual
Boletín Mensual de Estadística. Monthly
Economía y Estadística. Occasional
Informe Financiero del Contralor General. Annual
Informe del Gerente de la Caja de Crédito Agrario, Industrial y Minero. Annual
Memorias (13) de los Ministros al Congreso Nacional. Annual
Braun, H., *The Assassination of Gaitán: Public Life and Urban Violence in Colombia.* Univ. of Wisconsin Press, 1985
Hartlyn, J., *The Politics of Coalition Rule in Colombia.* CUP, 1988
Morairetz, D., *Why the Emperor's New Clothes are not made in Colombia.* OUP, 1982

COMOROS

Capital: Moroni
Population: 422,500 (1987)
GNP per capita: US$440 (1988)

République fédérale islamique des Comores

HISTORY. The 3 islands forming the present state became French protectorates at the end of the 19th century, and were proclaimed colonies on 25 July 1912. With neighbouring Mayotte they were administratively attached to Madagascar from 1914 until 1947, when the 4 islands became a French Overseas Territory, achieving internal self-government in Dec. 1961.

In referenda held on each island on 22 Dec. 1974, the 3 western islands voted overwhelmingly for independence, while Mayotte voted to remain French. The Comoran Chamber of Deputies unilaterally declared the islands' independence on 6 July 1975, but Mayotte remained a French dependency.

The first government of Ahmed Abdallah was overthrown on 3 Aug. 1975 by a *coup* led by Ali Soilih (who assumed the Presidency on 2 Jan. 1976), but Ahmed Abdallah regained the Presidency after a second *coup* ousted Ali Soilih in May 1978. In Nov. 1989 President Abdallah was assassinated. The revolt was helped by mercenaries led by Bob Dinard who finally left the Comoros on 15 Dec. 1989.

AREA AND POPULATION. The Comoros consists of 3 islands in the Indian ocean between the African mainland and Madagascar with a total area of 1,862 sq. km (719 sq. miles). Population (estimate, 1988) 434,166.

	Area sq. km	*Population census 1980*	*Chief town*	*Population census 1980*
Njazídja (Grande Comore)	1,148	192,177	Moroni	20,112
Mwali (Mohéli)	290	17,194	Fomboni	5,663
Nzwani (Anjouan)	424	137,621	Mutsamudu	12,518
	1,862	346,992		

The indigenous population are a mixture of Malagasy, African, Malay and Arab peoples; the vast majority speak Comoran, an Arabised dialect of Swahili, but a small proportion speak Makua (a bantu language), French or Arabic. In 1985, 27% of the population were urban and 48% were under 15 years.

CLIMATE. There is a tropical climate, affected by Indian monsoon winds from the north, which gives a wet season from Nov. to April. Moroni. Jan. 81°F (27·2°C), July 75°F (23·9°C). Annual rainfall, 113" (2,825 mm).

CONSTITUTION AND GOVERNMENT. Under the new Constitution approved by referendum on 1 Oct. 1978 (amended 1983), the Comoros are a Federal Islamic Republic. Mayotte has the right to join when it so chooses.

The President is Head of State, directly elected for a 6-year term (renewable once). He appoints up to 9 other Ministers to form the Council of Government, on which each island's Governor has a non-voting seat. There is a 42-member unicameral Federal Assembly, directly elected for 5 years. Each of the 3 islands is administered by a Governor (nominated by the President), up to 4 Commissioners whom he appoints to assist him, and a Legislative Council directly elected for 5 years.

President: Said Mohamed Djohar, assumed office in March 1990.

National flag: Green with a crescent and 4 stars all in white in the centre, tilted towards the lower fly.

DEFENCE

Army. The army had a strength of about 700 in 1988.

Navy. An *ex*-British landing craft built in 1945 was transferred from France in 1976 and another vessel, with ramps, was purchased in 1981. Two small patrol boats were supplied by Japan in 1982.

Air Arm. In 1988 only 1 Cessna 402B communications aircraft and an Ecureuil helicopter were in operation.

INTERNATIONAL RELATIONS

Membership. Comoros is a member of UN and an ACP state of EEC.

ECONOMY

Budget. In 1986, current revenue amounted to 5,816m. Comorian francs and current expenditure to 10,380m. Comorian francs; the separate capital budget totalled 17,400m. Comorian francs revenue against 17,400m. Comorian francs expenditure.

Currency. The unit of currency is the *Comorian franc*. There are banknotes of 500, 1,000, and 5,000 *Comorian francs*. In March 1990, £1 = CF541·63; US$1 = CF314·72.

Banking. The Institut d'émission des Comores was established as the new bank of issue in 1975. The chief commercial banks are the Banque des Comores, established in 1974 by the separation of the former Comoran section of the Banque de Madagascar et des Comores and the Banque de Développement des Comores.

Weights and Measures. The metric system is in force.

ENERGY AND NATURAL RESOURCES

Electricity. Production (1986) 5m. kwh.

Agriculture. The chief product was formerly sugar-cane, but now vanilla, copra, maize and other food crops, cloves and essential oils (citronella, ylang, lemongrass) are the most important products. Production (1988 in tonnes): Cassava, 95,000; coconuts, 53,000; bananas, 39,000; sweet potatoes, 19,000; rice, 18,000; maize, 6,000 and copra, 3,000.

Livestock (1988): Cattle, 85,000; sheep, 10,000; goats, 96,000; asses, 4,000.

Forestry. Njazídja has a fine forest and produces timber for building.

Fisheries. In 1983 the catch was (estimate) 4,000 tonnes.

COMMERCE. Imports in 1985 amounted to 16,481m. Comorian francs, exports to 7,048m. Comorian francs. France provided 41% of imports and took 66% of exports. The main exports (1985) were vanilla (67% of value), cloves (20%), ylang-ylang (9%), essences, copra and coffee.

Trade between Comoros and UK (British Department of Trade returns, in £1,000 sterling):

	1985	*1986*	*1987*	*1988*	*1989*
Imports to UK	234	...	91	33	60
Exports and re-exports from UK	603	307	527	333	419

Tourism. In 1986 there were about 5,000 visitors.

COMMUNICATIONS

Roads. In 1983 there were 750 km of classified roads, of which 262 km were tarmac. There were 3,600 passenger cars and about 2,000 commercial vehicles.

Aviation. There is an international airport at Hahaya (on Njazídja). Air Comores have twice-weekly flights to Antananarivo, Dar es Salaam and Mombasa. Air

France and Air Madagascar also have twice-weekly flights to Antananarivo. Air Comores has daily internal flights between Moroni and Nzwani, and 5 per week between Moroni and Mwali.

Shipping. In 1982, vessels entering Comoran ports (excluding internal traffic) discharged 39,000 tonnes and loaded 15,000 tonnes.

Post and Broadcasting. There were 496 telephones in 1983. *Comores-Inter* broadcasts in French and Comorian on short-wave and FM for approximately 8 hours a day. Number of radios (1988) 40,000.

JUSTICE, RELIGION, EDUCATION AND WELFARE

Justice. French and Moslem law is in a new consolidated code.The Supreme Court comprises 7 members, 2 each appointed by the President and the Federal Assembly, and 1 by each island's Legislative Council.

Religion. Islam is the official religion, and over 99% of the population are Sunni Moslems; there are about 1,300 Christians.

Education. In 1981 there were 59,709 pupils and 1,292 teachers in 236 primary schools; 32 secondary schools had 13,528 pupils and 432 teachers, 2 technical schools held 151 students with 9 teachers, and a teacher-training college had 119 students and 8 teachers.

Health. In 1978 there were 20 doctors, 1 dentist, 2 pharmacists, 35 midwives and 124 nursing personnel. In 1980 there were 17 hospitals and clinics with 763 beds.

DIPLOMATIC REPRESENTATIVES

Of Great Britain in Comoros
Ambassador: M. E. Howell, CMG, OBE (resides in Port Louis).

Of the Comoros in the USA
Ambassador: Amini Al Moumin.

Of the USA in the Comoros
Ambassador: Harry K. Walker. (resides in Antananarivo).

Of the Comoros to the United Nations
Ambassador: Amini Al Moumin.

Further Reading

Newitt, N., *The Comoro Islands.* London, 1985

CONGO

Capital: Brazzaville
Population: 2·27m. (1988)
GNP per capita: US$930 (1988)

République Populaire du Congo

HISTORY. First occupied by France in 1882, the Congo became (as 'Middle Congo') a territory of French Equatorial Africa from 1910–58, when it became a member state of the French Community. It became an independent Republic on 15 Aug. 1960.

The first President, Fulbert Youlou, was deposed on 15 Aug. 1963 by a *coup* led by Alphonse Massemba-Débat, who became President on 19 Dec. Following a second *coup* in Aug. 1968, the Army took power under the leadership of Major Marien Ngouabi, whose colleague, Major Alfred Raoul, was appointed President from 3 Sept. until 1 Jan. 1969, when Ngouabi himself became President.

The country's present name was established on 3 Jan. 1970, when a Marxist-Leninist state was introduced. Ngouabi was assassinated on 18 March 1977, and succeeded by Col. Joachim Yhombi-Opango, who in turn was replaced on 5 Feb. 1979 by Col. Denis Sassou-Nguesso.

AREA AND POPULATION. The Congo is bounded by Cameroon and the Central African Republic in the north, Zaïre to the east and south, the Cabinda province of Angola and the Atlantic to the south-west and Gabon to the west, and covers 342,000 sq. km; census population (1984), 1,909,248. Estimate (1988) 2,266,000. The main towns (census, 1984) are Brazzaville, the capital (585,812), Pointe-Noire, the main port and oil centre (294,203), N'kayi (formerly Jacob) (35,540) and Loubomo (formerly Dolisie) (49,134). Over 51% were urban.

The areas, populations and capitals of the Regions in 1984 were:

Region	*Sq. km*	*1984*	*Capital*	*Region*	*Sq. km*	*1984*	*Capital*
Kouilou	13,694	369,073	Pointe-Noire	Fed. District	65	585,812	Brazzaville
Niari	25,942	173,606	Loubomo	Plateaux	38,400	109,663	Djambala
Lékoumou	20,950	68,287	Sibiti	Cuvette	74,850	135,744	Owando
Bouenza	12,265	187,143	N'kayi	Sangha	55,800	46,152	Ouesso
Pool	33,990	184,263	Kinkala	Likouala	66,044	49,505	Impfondo

In 1984, 45% spoke Kongo dialects, chiefly in the south and south-west; 20% were Teke (in the south-east); 15% Sanka and 16% Ubangi chiefly inhabit the north. There are also about 12,000 pygmies and 12,000 Europeans (mainly French). French is the official language, but 2 local *patois*, Monokutuba (west of Brazzaville) and Lingala (north of Brazzaville), serve as lingua francas.

CLIMATE. An equatorial climate, with moderate rainfall and a small range of temperature. There is a long dry season from May to Oct. in the S.W. plateaux, but the Congo Basin in the N.E. is more humid, with rainfall approaching 100" (2,500 mm). Brazzaville. Jan. 78°F (25·6°C), July 73°F (22·8°C). Annual rainfall 59" (1,473 mm).

CONSTITUTION AND GOVERNMENT. In July 1979 a new Constitution was approved by referendum. Executive power was vested in the President, elected for a 5-year term by the National Congress of the *Parti congolais du travail* (the sole legal party since 1969). The President is assisted by a Council of Ministers, appointed and led by him. The PCT Congress elects a Central Committee of 75 members and a Political Bureau of 10 to administer it; it nominates all candidates for the 153-member People's National Assembly and for the regional, district and local councils, all of which were last elected on 11 Aug. 1984. In 1984 a constitutional amendment made the President Head of Government and reduced the role of the Prime Minister to that of a co-ordinator.

The Council of Ministers in Aug. 1989 was composed as follows:

President, Head of Government, Minister of Defence and Security: Col. Denis Sassou-Nguesso.

Prime Minister: Alphonse Poaty-Souchalaty.

Planning and Economy: Pierre Moussa. *Youth and Rural Development:* Gabriel Oba-Apounou. *Ngollo Forestry:* Col. Raymond Damas. *Foreign Affairs and Co-operation:* Antoine Ndinga Oba. *Information:* Paul Ngatse. *Territorial Adminstration and People's Power:* Celestin Ngoma-Foutou. *Equipment, with responsibility for the Environment:* Florent Tsiba. *Health and Social Affairs:* Ossebi Douniam. *Mines and Energy, Posts and Telecommunications:* Aimé Emmanuel Yoka. *Secondary and Higher Education, with responsibility for Scientific Research:* Rodolphe Adada. *Basic Education and Literacy:* Pierre-Damien Bassoukou-Boumba. *Physical Education and Sport:* Jean-Claude Ganga. *Culture and Arts:* Jean-Baptiste Tati-Loutard. *Trade and Small and Medium-Sized Enterprises:* Alphonse Boudenesa. *Fishing, Industry and Handicrafts, with responsibility for Tourism:* Hilaire Babassana. *Labour and Social Security:* Jeanne Dambenzet. *Minister in the Presidency, with responbsibility for State Control:* Auxence Ickonga. *Finance and Budget:* Edouard Ngakosso. *Justice, Keeper of the Seals, with responsibility for Administrative Reforms:* Alphonse Nzoungou. *Transport and Civil Aviation:* François Bita.

National flag: Red, in the canton the national emblem of a crossed hoe and mattock, a green wreath and a gold star.

Local Government: The republic is divided into the capital district of Brazzaville and 9 regions (each under an appointed Commissioner and an elected Council), which are sub-divided into 46 districts.

DEFENCE

Army. The Army consists of 8 battalions, 2 armoured, 1 artillery and 3 infantry, 1 engineering, and 1 paracommando. Equipment includes 35 T-54/-55 and 15 T-59 tanks. Total personnel (1990) 8,000.

Navy. The combatant flotilla includes 3 modern Spanish-built, 7 *ex*-Soviet and 3 *ex*-Chinese inshore patrol craft. There are also 2 French-built tugs and numerous boats. Personnel in 1989 totalled 300.

Air Force. The Air Force had (1990) about 500 personnel, 15 MiG-17 jet fighters, 6 Antonov An-24/26 turboprop transports, 2 C-47, 2 Nord 262, and 2 Noratlas piston-engined transports, 3 Broussard communications aircraft, 4 L-39 jet trainers and 2 Alouette II and 2 Alouette III light helicopters.

INTERNATIONAL RELATIONS

Membership. Congo is a member of UN, OAU and is an ACP state of EEC.

ECONOMY

Budget. The 1988 Budget provided for revenue of 251,800m. francs CFA (over 50% from overseas funding) and expenditure of 283,976m. francs CFA, of which 252,800m. were for administration and 31,976m. for investment.

Currency. The unit of currency is the *franc CFA* with a parity value of 50 *francs CFA* to 1 French franc. There are coins of 1, 2, 5, 10, 25, 50, 100 and 500 *francs* CFA, and banknotes of 100, 500, 1,000, 5,000 and 10,000 *francs* CFA. In March 1990, £1 = 471·63 *francs*; US$1 = 287·75 *francs*.

Banking. The *Banque des États de l'Afrique Centrale* is the bank of issue. There are 4 commercial banks situated in Brazzaville, including the *Banque Commerciale Congolaise* and the *Union Congolaise de Banques*.

ENERGY AND NATURAL RESOURCES

Electricity. Production in 1985 was 306m. kwh from a hydro-electric plant at Djoué near Brazzaville and from about 6 thermal plants. Supply 220 volts; 50 Hz.

Oil. Oil reserves are estimated at 500–1,000m. tonnes. Output in 1989 was 6·75m. tonnes from the 26 offshore oil platforms operated by Elf Congo and Agip Congo. A refinery at Pointe-Noire came on stream in Dec. 1982.

Minerals. Lead, copper, zinc and gold (5 kg in 1985) are the main minerals. There are reserves of phosphates, bauxite and iron.

Agriculture. Production (1988, in 1,000 tonnes): Cassava, 700; sugar-cane, 400; pineapples, 114; bananas, 32; plantains, 65; yams, 15; maize, 9; groundnuts, 17; palm-oil, 16; coffee, 2; cocoa, 2; rice, 2; sweet potatoes, 14.

Livestock (1988): Cattle, 70,000; pigs, 48,000; sheep, 64,000; goats, 186,000; poultry, 1m.

Forestry. In 1988 equatorial forests cover 21m. hectares (62% of the total land area) from which (in 1983) 2,238,000 cu. metres of timber were produced, mainly okoumé from the south and sapele from the north. Hardwoods (mainly mahogany) are also exported.

Fisheries. In 1986 the catch amounted to 30,000 tonnes.

INDUSTRY AND TRADE

Industry. There is a growing manufacturing sector, located mainly in the 4 major towns, producing processed foods, textiles, cement (62,000 tonnes in 1985), metal industries and chemicals; in 1981 it employed 26% of the labour force.

Trade Unions. In 1964 the existing unions merged into one national body, the *Confédération Syndicale Congolaise*.

Commerce. Imports in 1985 totalled 306,198m. francs CFA (mainly machinery) and exports 488,366m. (of which petroleum 93%). In 1985 39% of imports were from France; 60% of exports were to USA, 14% to Spain and 11% to France.

Total trade between the Congo and UK (British Department of Trade returns, in £1,000 sterling):

	1985	*1986*	*1987*	*1988*	*1989*
Imports to UK	2,819	2,444	1,930	2,016	3,442
Exports and re-exports from UK	12,112	9,165	19,219	8,521	5,258

Tourism. There were 39,000 tourists in 1986.

COMMUNICATIONS

Roads. There were (1982) 8,246 km of all-weather roads, of which 849 km were paved. In 1982 there were 30,500 cars and 18,600 commercial vehicles.

Railways. A railway (517 km, 1,067 mm gauge) and a telegraph line connect Brazzaville with Pointe-Noire and a 200 km branch railway links Mont-Belo with Mbinda on the Gabon border. In 1986 railways carried 2·5m. passengers and 1·3m. tonnes of freight.

Aviation. The principal airports are at Maya Maya (near Brazzaville) and Pointe-Noire. In addition there are 22 airfields served by the local airline, Lina-Congo.

Shipping. Pointe-Noire handled (1979) 2·4m. tonnes of goods including manganese from Gabon. There were (1985) 21 vessels of 8,458 GWT registered. There are hydrofoil connexions from Brazzaville to Kinshasa (30 km across the river).

Post and Broadcasting. Telephones (1983) numbered 18,093. In 1985 there were 99,000 radios and 5,000 TV sets in use.

Newspapers. In 1986 there were 3 daily newspapers with a combined circulation of 24,000.

JUSTICE, RELIGION, EDUCATION AND WELFARE

Justice. The Supreme Court, Court of Appeal and a criminal court are situated in Brazzaville, with a network of *tribunaux de grande instance* and *tribunaux d'instance* in the regions.

Religion. In 1980, 54% of the population were Roman Catholic, 24% Protestant, 19% followed animist beliefs and 3% were Moslem.

Education. In 1985 there were 475,805 pupils and 7,745 teachers in 1,558 primary schools, 197,491 pupils and 4,773 teachers in secondary schools, 25,142 students with 1,549 teachers in technical schools and teacher-training establishments. The Université Marien-Ngouabi (founded 1972) in Brazzaville had 9,385 students and 565 teaching staff in 1985. Adult literacy (1980) 56%.

Health. There were (1978) 274 doctors, 2 dentists, 28 pharmacists, 413 midwives, 1,915 nursing personnel and 473 hospitals and dispensaries with 6,876 beds.

DIPLOMATIC REPRESENTATIVES

Of the Congo in Great Britain
Ambassador: Jean-Marie Ewengue (accredited 12 June 1986, resides in Paris).

Of Great Britain in the Congo (Ave. du General de Gaulle, Plateau, Brazzaville)
Ambassador: A. I. Glasby.

Of the Congo in the USA (4891 Colorado Ave., NW, Washington D.C., 20011)
Ambassador: Benjamin Bounkoulou.

Of the USA in the Congo (PO Box 1015, Brazzaville)
Ambassador: Leonard G. Shurtleff.

Of the Congo to the United Nations
Ambassador: Dr Martin Adouki.

Further Reading

Thompson, V. and Adloff, R., *Historical Dictionary of the People's Republic of the Congo*. 2nd ed. Metuchen, 1984

COSTA RICA

Capital: San José
Population: 2·89m. (1989)
GNP per capita: US$1,760 (1988)

República de Costa Rica

HISTORY. Part of the Spanish Viceroyalty of New Spain from 1540, Costa Rica (the 'Rich Coast') formed part of Central America when the latter acquired independence on 15 Sept. 1821. Central America seceded to Mexico on 5 Jan. 1822 until 1 July 1823, when it became an independent confederation as the United Provinces of Central America. The province of Guanacaste was acquired from Nicaragua in 1825. Costa Rica left the confederation and achieved full independence in 1838. The first Constitution was promulgated on 7 Dec. 1871.

AREA AND POPULATION. Costa Rica is bounded north by Nicaragua, east by the Caribbean, southeast by Panama, and south and west by the Pacific. The area is estimated at 51,100 sq. km (19,730 sq. miles). The population at the census of 1 June 1984 was 2,416,809. Estimate (1989) 2,886,990.

The area and census of population for 1 June 1984 was as follows:

Province	*Area (sq. km)*	*Population*	*Capital*	*Population*
San José	4,959·63	1,055,611	San José	284,550
Alajuela	9,753·23	512,886	Alajuela	42,047
Cartago	3,124·67	324,299	Cartago	28,588
Heredia	2,656·27	233,185	Heredia	25,812
Guanacaste	10,140·71	232.414	Liberia	27,637[1]
Puntarenas	11,276·97	321,920	Puntarenas	35,603[1]
Limón	9,188·52	206,675	Limón	64,406[1]

[1] District

In 1988, 44% lived in urban areas, and 36% were aged under 15; population density 56·5 per sq. km.

Vital statistics for calendar years:

	Marriages	*Births*	*Deaths*
1987	21,743	80,326	10,687
1988	22,918	81,376	10,944

The population of European descent, many of them of pure Spanish blood, dwell mostly around the capital of the republic, San José, and in the principal towns of the provinces. Limón, on the Caribbean coast, and Puntarenas, on the Pacific coast, are the chief commercial ports. The United Fruit Co., who in 1941 abandoned their banana plantations on the Atlantic coast in favour of large new plantations on the Pacific coast, have constructed ports at Quepos and Golfito. The Standard Fruit Co. and others have cleared land since 1958 in the Atlantic coast area. There are some 15,000 West Indians, mostly in Limón province. The indigenous Indian population is dwindling and is now estimated at 1,200. There were (1988) some 23,100 refugees (19,000 from Nicaragua).

Spanish is the language of the country.

CLIMATE. The climate is tropical, with a small range of temperature and abundant rains. The dry season is from Dec. to April. San José. Jan. 66°F (18·9°C), July 69°F (20·6°C). Annual rainfall 72" (1,793 mm).

CONSTITUTION AND GOVERNMENT. The Constitution was promulgated in Nov. 1949. It forbids the establishment or maintenance of an army. The legislative power is normally vested in a single chamber called the Legislative Assembly, which since 1962 consists of 57 deputies, 1 for every 49,000 inhabitants, elected for 4 years. The President and 2 Vice-Presidents are elected for 4 years; the candidate receiving the largest vote, provided it is over 40% of the total, is declared elected, but a second ballot is required if no candidate gets 40% of the total. Suffrage is universal, there being no exemption for reasons of economic status, race or sex. The vote is direct by secret ballot for all nationals of 18 years or over. Elections are normally held on the first Sunday in February. Voting for President, Deputies and Municipal Councillors is secret and compulsory for all men under 70 years of age. Independent non-party candidates are barred from the ballot.

Presidential elections took place on 4 Feb. 1990 and Rafael Angel Calderón of the Social Christian Unity Party defeated Dr Carlos Manuel Castillo of the ruling National Liberation Party by a 3% margin. President-elect Calderón had fought two previous presidential elections. He is the son of a former President and served as Foreign Minister in the 1970s.

President: Rafael Angel Calderón (assumed office 8 May 1990).

The powers of the President are limited by the constitution, which leaves him the power to appoint and remove at will members of his cabinet. All other public appointments are made jointly in the names of the President and of the minister in charge of the department concerned.

National flag: Five unequal stripes of blue, white, red, white, blue, with the national arms on a white disc near the hoist.

National anthem: Noble patria, tu hermosa bandera (words by J. M. Zeledón, 1903; tune by M. M. Gutiérrez, 1851).

DEFENCE

Army. The Army was abolished in 1948, and replaced by a Civil Guard reputed to be 4,500 strong. There has never been compulsory military service or training.

Navy. The para-military Civil Guard flotilla includes 1 fast patrol craft and 1 armed tug on the Atlantic coast and 5 small coastguard cutters on the Pacific coast. Personnel (1989) 100 officers and men.

Air Wing. The Civil Guard operates a small air wing equipped with about 15 lightplanes and helicopters.

INTERNATIONAL RELATIONS

Membership. Costa Rica is a member of UN, CACM and OAS.

ECONOMY

Budget. The 1985 Budget provided for revenue of 41,101·6m. colones and expenditure of 43,135·5m. colones.

External government debt on 31 Dec. 1985 was US$3,665m.

Currency. The unit of currency is the *colone* (₡). The official rate in March 1990 was ₡85·39 = US$1; 139·35 = £1. The official rate is used for all imports on an essential list and by the Government and autonomous institutions and a free rate is used for all other transactions.

The currency is chiefly notes. The Banco Central issue notes for 5, 10, 20, 50, 100, 500 and 1,000 colones. Silver coins of 1 colone, 50 centimos and 25 centimos were in 1935 replaced by coins (2 and 1 colones and 50 and 25 centimos) made up of 3 parts copper and 1 part nickel, and given the same value as the subsidiary silver currency. There are copper coins (and chromium stainless steel coins) of 10 and 5 centimos.

Banking. By a law passed on 28 Jan. 1950 a Central Bank was established for the organization and direction of the national monetary system and of dealings in foreign exchange, the promotion of facilities for credit and the supervision of all banking operations in the country. The bank has a board of 7 directors appointed by the Government, including *ex officio* the Minister of Finance and the Planning Office Director.

The National Insurance Institute *(Instituto Nacional de Seguros)* is a Government organization, created in 1924, which has a monopoly of new insurance business.

Weights and Measures. The metric system is legally established; but in the country districts the following old Spanish weights and measures are found: *libra* = 1·014 lb. avoirdupois; *arroba* = 25·35 lb. avoirdupois; *quintal* = 101·40 lb. avoirdupois, and *fanega* = 11 Imperial bushels.

ENERGY AND NATURAL RESOURCES

Electricity. Electricity, derived from water power in the highlands, is increasingly used as motive power. Output, 1986, was 2,770m. kwh. Supply 120 volts; 60 Hz.

Minerals. Gold output is about 3,000 troy oz. per year. Salt production from sea water is about 10,000 tonnes annually. Haematite ore was discovered on the Nicoya Peninsula late in 1960 and sulphur near San Carlos in 1966.

Agriculture. Agriculture is the principal industry. The cultivated area is about 1m. acres; grass lands cover 1·8m. acres. The principal agricultural products are coffee, bananas, sugar and cattle. Coffee normally accounts for about half the country's foreign-exchange earnings.

Coffee production in 1988 was 145,000 tonnes; sugar-cane, 2·73m.; bananas, 1·05m.; cocoa, 4,000; maize, 105,000; tobacco, 2,000; rice, 194,000; potatoes, 40,000.

In 1988 cattle numbered 2·19m. and pigs 223,000.

Forestry. In 1988 there were 1·6m. hectares of woodlands, representing 32% of the land surface. There are thousands of square miles of public lands that have never been cleared on which can be found quantities of rosewood, cedar, mahogany and other cabinet woods.

Fisheries. Total catch (1986) 21,000 tonnes.

INDUSTRY AND TRADE

Industry. The main manufactured goods are foodstuffs, textiles, fertilizers, pharmaceuticals, furniture, cement, tyres, canning, clothing, plastic goods, plywood and electrical equipment.

Labour. As Costa Rica is still essentially an agricultural country, the organization of labour has made progress only in the larger centres of population, and even there it is not a strong movement. There are two main trade unions, *Rerum Novarum* (anti-Communist) and *Confederación General de Trabajadores Costarricenses* (Communist).

Commerce. The value of imports into and exports from Costa Rica in 5 years was as follows in US$:

	1982	*1983*	*1984*	*1985*	*1986*
Imports	867,000,000	987,826,445	1,093,739,311	1,098,178,489	1,147,500,000
Exports	870,800,000	559,951,375	1,006,389,617	1,084,100,000	1,106,000,000

The values (in US$1m.) of the principal imports in 1984 were: Machinery, including transport equipment, 219·6; manufactures, 317·5; chemicals, 250·1; fuel and mineral oils, 166·7; foodstuffs, 9.

Chief exports (in US$1m.) in 1984 were: Manufactured goods and other products, 450·6; coffee, 267·8 (mostly to Federal Republic of Germany, USA, UK and Italy); bananas, 251 (to USA); sugar, 35·5; cocoa, 1·5.

Total trade between Costa Rica and UK (British Department of Trade returns in £1,000 sterling):

	1985	*1986*	*1987*	*1988*	*1989*
Imports to UK	22,646	30,318	16,752	16,902	24,113
Exports and re-exports from UK	14,413	12,007	14,407	11,390	12,780

Tourism. There was a total of 261,000 tourists in 1986.

COMMUNICATIONS

Roads. In 1987 there were about 35,000 km of all-weather motor roads open. On the Costa Rica section of the Inter-American Highway it is possible to motor to Panama during the dry season. The Pan-American Highway into Nicaragua is metalled for most of the way and there is now a good highway open almost to Puntarenas. Motor vehicles, 1985, numbered 186,046.

Railways. The nationalized railway system *(Incofer)*, totalling 828·5 km (128 km electrified) of 1,067 mm gauge, connects San José with Limón, the Atlantic port, and San José with Puntarenas, the Pacific port. Total railway traffic in 1988 was 1m. tonnes of freight and 1·3m. passengers.

Aviation. There were 92 airports (59 private) in service in 1984. Passenger movement in and out of Costa Rica is almost entirely by air *via* the local company, LACSA, PANAM and TACA. Passengers carried, 1984, 1,014,559. LACSA links San José by daily services with all the more important towns.

Shipping. In 1981, 1,221 ships entered and cleared the ports of the republic (Puerto Limón, Puntarenas and Golfito).

Post and Broadcasting. There were 281,042 telephones in 1983.

The commercial wireless telegraph stations are operated by *Cia Radiográfica Internacional de Costa Rica.* The stations are located at Cartago, Limón, Puntarenas, Quepos and Golfito. The Government has 19 wireless telegraph stations in its local network. The principal or central station at San José also maintains international radio-telegraph circuits to Nicaragua, Honduras, San Salvador and Mexico. The Government has 202 telegraph offices and 88 official telephone stations. In 1986 there were 200,000 radio and 470,000 television receivers.

Cinemas (1979). Cinemas numbered 106, with seating capacity of 105,000.

Newspapers (1984). There were 4 daily newspapers all published in San José.

JUSTICE, RELIGION, EDUCATION AND WELFARE

Justice. Justice is administered by the Supreme Court, 5 appeal courts divided into 5 chambers; the Court of Cassation, the Higher and Lower Criminal Courts, and the Higher and Lower Civil Courts. There are also subordinate courts in the separate provinces and local justices throughout the republic. Capital punishment may not be inflicted.

Religion. Roman Catholicism is the religion of the State, which contributes to its maintenance but controls the Church Patronage and insists on lay instruction in history, economics and similar subjects; there is entire religious liberty under the constitution, but religious appeals are forbidden in current political discussions. The Archbishop of Costa Rica has 4 bishops at Alajuela, Limón, San Isidro el General and Tilarán.

Protestants number about 40,000.

Education. Costa Rica has a very low illiteracy rate. Elementary instruction is compulsory and free; secondary education (since 1949) is also free. Elementary schools are provided and maintained by local school councils, while the national government pays the teachers, besides making subventions in aid of local funds. In 1986 there were 3,107 public primary schools with 13,500 teachers and administrative staff and 380,000 enrolled pupils; there were 241 public and private secondary schools with 8,926 teachers and 141,691 pupils. The University of Costa Rica, founded in San José in 1843, had (1980) 2,337 professors in 13 faculties and 38,629 students.

Health. In 1982 there were 1,929 doctors and 39 hospitals with 7,706 beds. In 1979 there were 239 dentists.

DIPLOMATIC REPRESENTATIVES

Of Costa Rica in Great Britain (14 Lancaster Gate, London, W2 3LW)
Ambassador: Miguel T. Yamuni.

Of Great Britain in Costa Rica (Edificio Centro Colon, Apartado 815, San José)
Ambassador and Consul-General: William Marsden.

Of Costa Rica in the USA (1825 Connecticut Ave., NW Washington D.C., 20009)
Ambassador: Danilo Jimenez.

Of the USA in Costa Rica (Pavas, San José)
Ambassador: Deane R. Hinton.

Of Costa Rica to the United Nations
Ambassador: Dr Carlos José Gutierrez.

Further Reading

Statistical Information: Official statistics are issued by the Director General de Estadística (Ministerio de Industria y Comercio, San José) as they become available. The compilation of statistics was started in 1861.

Ameringer, C. D., *Democracy in Costa Rica.* New York, 1982
Biesanz, R., *(et al), The Costa Ricans.* Hemel Hempstead, 1982
Bird, L., *Costa Rica: Unarmed Democracy.* London, 1984
Fernandez Guardia, L., *Historia de Costa Rica.* 2nd ed., 2 vols. San José, 1941
Seligson, M. A., *Peasants of Costa Rica and the Development of Agrarian Capitalism.* Univ. of Wisconsin Press, 1980
Stansifer, C., *Costa Rica.* [Bibliography] Oxford and Santa Barbara, 1988

CÔTE D'IVOIRE

Capital: Abidjan
Population: 11·63m. (1988)
GNP per capita: US$740 (1988)

République de la Côte d'Ivoire

HISTORY. France obtained rights on the coast in 1842, but did not actively and continuously occupy the territory till 1882. On 10 Jan. 1889 Ivory Coast was declared a French protectorate, and it became a colony on 10 March 1893; in 1904 it became a territory of French West Africa. On 1 Jan. 1933 most of the territory of Upper Volta was added to the Ivory Coast, but on 1 Jan. 1948 this area was returned to the re-constituted Upper Volta, now Burkina Faso. The Ivory Coast became an autonomous republic within the French Community on 4 Dec. 1958 and achieved full independence on 7 Aug. 1960. From 1 Jan. 1986 the French version of the name of the country became the only correct title.

AREA AND POPULATION. Côte d'Ivoire is bounded west by Liberia and Guinea, north by Mali and Burkina Faso, east by Ghana, and south by the Gulf of Guinea. It has an area of 322,463 sq. km and a population at the 1975 census of 6,702,866 (of whom 31·8% were urban). Estimate (1988) 11,634,000 (50% urban).

The areas and populations of the 34 departments were:

Department	*Sq. km*	*Census 1975*	*Department*	*Sq. km*	*Census 1975*
Abengourou	6,900	177,692	Ferkéssédougou	17,728	90,423
Abidjan	14,200	1,389,141	Gagnoa	4,500	174,018
Aboisso	6,250	148,823	Guiglo	14,150	137,672
Adzopé	5,230	162,837	Issia	3,590	104,081
Agboville	3,850	141,970	Katiola	9,420	77,875
Biankouma	4,950	75,711	Korhogo	12,500	276,816
Bondoukou	16,530	296,551	Lakota	2,730	76,105
Bongouanou	5,570	216,907	Man	7,050	278,659
Bouaflé	5,670	164,817	Mankono	10,660	82,358
Bouaké	23,800	808,048	Odienné	20,600	124,010
Bouna	21,470	84,290	Oumé	2,400	85,486
Boundiali	7,895	96,449	Sassandra	17,530	116,644
Dabakala	9,670	56,230	Séguéla	11,240	75,181
Daloa	11,610	265,529	Soubré	8,270	75,350
Danané	4,600	170,249	Tingréla	2,200	35,829
Dimbokro	8,530	258,116	Touba	8,720	77,786
Divo	7,920	202,511	Zuénoula	2,830	98,792

The principal cities (populations, census 1975) are the capital, Abidjan (951,216; estimate 1982, 1·85m.), Bouaké (175,264), Daloa (60,837), Man (50,288), Korhogo (45,250) and Gagnoa (42,362). The new capital will be at Yamoussoukro (120,000 in 1984).

The principal ethnic groups are the Akan-speaking peoples of the south-east (Baule, 12% and Anyi, 11%) and the Bete (20%) and Kru of the south-west; in the north-east are Voltaic groups including Senufo (14%), while Malinké (7%) and other Mandé peoples inhabit the north-west.

French is the official language and there were (1985) about 50,000 French residents.

CLIMATE. A tropical climate, affected by distance from the sea. In coastal areas, there are wet seasons from May to July and in Oct. and Nov., but in central areas the periods are March to May and July to Nov. In the north, there is one wet season from June to Oct. Abidjan. Jan. 81°F (27·2°C), July 75°F (23·9°C). Annual rainfall 84" (2,100 mm). Bouaké. Jan. 81°F (27·2°C), July 77°F (25°C). Annual rainfall 48" (1,200 mm).

CONSTITUTION AND GOVERNMENT. The 1960 Constitution was amended in 1971, 1975, 1980, 1985 and 1986. The sole legal Party is the *Parti Démocratique de la Côte d'Ivoire*. There is a 175-member National Assembly elected by universal suffrage (Elections were held in Nov. 1985) for a 5-year term. The President is also directly elected for a 5-year term (renewable). He appoints and leads a Council of Ministers who assist him.

The Government was in Sept. 1988 composed as follows:

President: Félix Houphouët-Boigny. (Re-elected for a sixth 5-year term in 1985).

Ministers of State: Auguste Denise, Mathieu Ekra, Camille Alliali, Maurice Seri Gnoleba, Emile Kéi Boguinard, Lamine Diabate, Lanzeni N. P. Coulibaly, Paul Gui Dibo, Amadou Thiam. *Public Health and Population:* Alphonse Djedje Mady. *Information and Culture:* Laurent Dona Fologo. *Commerce:* Nicolas Kouandi Angba. *Labour and 'Ivorization' of Personnel:* Albert Vanié Bi Tra. *Civil Service:* Jean-Jacques Bechio. *Tourism:* Jean-Claude Delafosse. *Social Affairs:* Yaya Ouattara. *Mining:* Yed Esai Angoran. *Internal Security:* Gen. Issouf Kone. *Justice, Keeper of the Seals:* Noël Neme. *Defence:* Jean Konan Banny. *Interior:* León Konan Koffi. *Foreign Affairs:* Siméon Ake. *Economy and Finance:* Abdoulaye Koné. *National Education, responsible for Secondary and Higher Education:* Dr Bala Keita *Drug Control:* Gen. Oumar N'Daw and 13 other ministers.

National flag: Three vertical strips of orange, white, green.

Local government: There are 34 departments, each under an appointed Prefect and an elected Conseil-Général, sub-divided into 163 sub-prefectures.

DEFENCE

Army. The Army consisted in 1989 of 1 armoured battalion, 3 infantry battalions and support units. Equipment includes 5 AMX-13 light tanks and 7 ERC-90 armoured cars. Total strength (1990), 5,500. Paramilitary forces, 7,800.

Navy. Offshore, riverine and coastal patrol squadrons include 2 fast missile craft, 2 patrol vessels, 1 riverine defence craft, 1 light transport, 4 fast assault boats and 2 minor landing craft. Personnel in 1989 totalled 700 and the force is based at Abidjan.

Air Force. The Air Force, formed in 1962, has 6 Alpha Jet advanced trainers, with combat potential, 1 turbofan Fokker 100, 1 Super-King Air, 1 Cessna 421, 1 Gulfstream transport, 2 Reims-Cessna 150s, 6 Beech F-33Cs and 4 SA330 Puma, 4 Dauphin 2, 1 Alouette III and 3 Gazelle helicopters. Personnel (1990) 900.

INTERNATIONAL RELATIONS

Membership. Côte d'Ivoire is a member of UN, OAU and is an ACP state of EEC.

ECONOMY

Budget. The budget for 1988 totalled 493,500m. francs CFA and for recurrent expenditure and 143,600m. francs CFA for investment. Capital expenditure 145,879 francs CFA.

Currency. The currency is the *franc CFA* with a parity rate of 50 *francs CFA* to 1 French *franc*. In March 1990, £1 sterling = 471·63 francs CFA; US$1 = 287·75 francs CFA.

Banking. The *Banque Centrale des Etats de l'Afrique de l'Ouest* is the bank of issue. Numerous foreign and domestic banks have offices in Abidjan, and *Société Générale de Banque, Société Ivoirienne de Banque, Banque Internationale pour le Commerce et l'Industrie de la Côte d'Ivoire* and *Banque Internationale pour l'Afrique Occidentale* maintain wide branch networks throughout the country.

ENERGY AND NATURAL RESOURCES

Electricity. Production in 1985 amounted to 2,162m. kwh mostly from new hydro-electric projects at Kassou and Taabo on the Bandama river, Buyo on the Sassandra river, and from 2 older dams on the Bia river. Supply 220 volts; 50 Hz.

Oil. Petroleum has been produced (offshore) since Oct. 1977. Production (1989) 350,000 tonnes.

Minerals. Diamond extraction was 700,000 carats in 1985. There are iron ore deposits at Bangolo and gold-mining began in Jan. 1990, reserves are estimated at 4,500 kg.

Agriculture. The main export crops (production 1988 in 1,000 tonnes) are coffee (187), cocoa (680), bananas (130), pineapples (265), palm oil (235), palm kernels (42), seed cotton (256) and rubber (54); food crops include yams (2,452), cassava (1,333), plantains (1,076), rice (597), maize (448), millet (42) and groundnuts (119). Sugar-cane (1·5m. tonnes in 1988) is grown on new plantations in the north at Ferkéssédougou and elsewhere.

Livestock, 1988: 960,000 cattle, 1·5m. sheep, 1·5m. goats, 450,000 pigs, 1,000 horses and 1,000 donkeys.

Forestry. Equatorial rain forests, especially in the south, cover 3m. hectares and produce over 30 commercially valuable species including teak, mahogany and ebony. Production in 1986 was 11·9m. cu. metres.

Fisheries. The catch in 1986 amounted to 97,200.

INDUSTRY AND TRADE

Industry. Industrialization has developed rapidly since independence, particularly food processing, textiles and sawmills. Several factories produce palm-oil, fruit preserves and fruit juice.

Labour. The main trade union is the *Union Générale des Travailleurs de Côte d'Ivoire*, with over 100,000 members.

Commerce. Trade for calendar years in 1m. francs CFA:

	1981	*1982*	*1983*	*1984*	*1985*
Imports	681,464	718,593	714,828	658,569	772,987
Exports	689,298	747,452	796,774	1,184,347	1,318,059

In 1985 exports of coffee furnished 21% of exports, cocoa 30%, timber 7% and petroleum products, 9%. Of the total 17% went to France, 17% to the Netherlands, 12% to the USA and 9% to Italy. Of the imports, France supplied 32% and Nigeria, 11%.

Total trade between the Côte d'Ivoire and UK (British Department of Trade returns, in £1,000 sterling):

	1985	*1986*	*1987*	*1988*	*1989*
Imports to UK	116,699	117,058	90,246	64,041	65,943
Exports and re-exports from UK	29,514	34,266	26,834	31,172	29,434

Tourism. In 1986 there were 187,000 foreign tourists.

COMMUNICATIONS

Roads. In 1984 roads totalled 53,736 km (including 128 km of motorway) and there were 182,956 private cars and 43,001 commercial vehicles.

Railways. From Abidjan a metre-gauge railway runs to Léraba on the border with Burkina Faso (655 km), and thence through Burkina Faso to Ouagadougou. Operation of the railway as a single entity ended in 1986, and in 1988 separate organizations were established in each country. In 1986–87 the railways carried 1·6m. passengers and 684,000 tonnes of freight.

Aviation. The international airport is at Abidjan-Port-Buet. In 1981 it handled 870,000 passengers and 33,000 tonnes of freight and mail. Air Ivoire provides regular domestic services to 10 regional airports and 15 landing strips.

Shipping. The main ports are Abidjan and San Pedro. In 1981 Abidjan port handled 5·8m. tonnes and San Pedro 1·5m. tonnes. In 1986 the merchant marine comprised 61 vessels of 141,674 tons gross.

Post and Broadcasting. There were 87,700 telephones in 1984 and 1,800 telex machines. In 1986 there were 550,000 television and 1·2m. radio receivers.

Newspapers. In 1984 there was 1 daily newspaper, *Fraternité-Matin.*

JUSTICE, RELIGION, EDUCATION AND WELFARE

Justice. There are 28 courts of first instance and 3 assize courts in Abidjan, Bouaké and Daloa, 2 courts of appeal in Abidjan and Bouaké, and a supreme court in Abidjan.

Religion. In 1980, 24% were Moslems (mainly in the north), 32% Christians (chiefly Roman Catholics in the south), and 44% animists.

Education. There were, in 1984, 1,179,456 pupils in primary schools, 245,342 pupils in secondary schools and (1979) 22,437 in technical schools. The *Université Nationale de Côte d'Ivoire,* at Abidjan (founded 1964), had 12,755 students in 1984.

Health. In 1978 there were 9,962 hospital beds, 429 doctors, 36 dentists, 615 midwives, 3,052 nurses and 76 pharmacists.

DIPLOMATIC REPRESENTATIVES

Of the Côte d'Ivoire in Great Britain (2 Upper Belgrave St., London, SW1X 8BJ)
Ambassador: Gervais Attoungbré (accredited 14 Dec. 1989).

Of Great Britain in the Côte d'Ivoire (Immeuble 'Les Harmonies', Blvd. Carde, Abidjan)
Ambassador: V. E. Sutherland, CMG.

Of the Côte d'Ivoire in the USA (2424 Massachusetts Ave., NW, Washington, D.C., 20008)
Ambassador: Charles Gomis.

Of the USA in the Côte d'Ivoire (5 Rue Jesse Owens, Abidjan)
Ambassador: Kenneth L. Brown.

Of the Côte d'Ivoire to the United Nations
Ambassador: Amara Essy.

Further Reading

Statistical Information: Service de la Statistique, Abidjan. It publishes *Bulletin Statistique Mensuel and Inventoire Économique de la Côte d'Ivoire.*

Zartman, I. W. and Delgado, C., *The Political Economy of Ivory Coast.* New York, 1984
Zolberg, A. R., *One-Party Government in the Ivory Coast.* Rev. ed. Princeton Univ. Press, 1974

CUBA

Capital: Havana
Population: 10·24m. (1986)
GNP per capita: US$2,696 (1981)

República de Cuba

HISTORY. Cuba, except for the brief British occupancy in 1762–63, remained a Spanish possession from its discovery by Columbus in 1492 until 10 Dec. 1898, when the sovereignty was relinquished under the terms of the Treaty of Paris, which ended the struggle of the Cubans against Spanish rule. Cuba thus became an independent republic, but the United States stipulated under the 'Platt Amendment' (abrogated by Roosevelt in 1934) that Cuba must enter into no treaty relations with a foreign power, which might endanger its independence.

The revolutionary movement against the Batista dictatorship, led by Dr Fidel Castro, started on 26 July 1953 (now a national holiday). It achieved power on 1 Jan. 1959 when Batista fled the country.

An invasion force of émigrés and adventurers landed in Cuba on 17 April 1961; the main body was defeated at the Bay of Pigs (Mantanzas province) and mopped up by 20 April.

The US Navy blockaded Cuba from 22 Oct. to 22 Nov. 1962.

AREA AND POPULATION. The island of Cuba forms the largest and most westerly of the Greater Antilles group and lies 135 miles south of the tip of Florida, USA. It has an area of 44,206 sq. miles (114,524 sq. km); the Isle of Youth (formerly Isle of Pines) has 1,180 sq. miles, and other islands about 1,350 sq. miles. Census (1981) 9,723,605; estimate in 1986 was 10·24m.

The area, population and density of population of the 14 provinces and the special Municipality of the Isle of Youth were as follows (1987 estimate):

	Area sq. km	*Population*		*Area sq. km.*	*Population*
Pinar del Río	10,860	669,500	Camagüey	14,134	711,200
La Habana	5,671	618,100	Las Tunas	6,373	467,600
Ciudad de La Habana	727	2,025,700	Holguín	9,105	957,800
Matanzas	11,669	586,600	Granma	8,452	765,700
Cienfuegos	4,149	346,600	Santiago de Cuba	6,343	954,000
Villa Clara	8,069	789,200	Guantánamo	6,366	478,000
Sancti Spíritus	6,737	415,600			
Ciego de Avila	6,485	345,200	Isla de la Juventud	2,199	68,700

The chief cities (1986, estimate) were Havana, the capital (2,014,800), Santiago de Cuba (358,800), Camagüey (260,800), Holguín (194,700), Santa Clara (178,300), Guantánamo (174,400), Cienfuegos (109,300), Matanzas (105,400), Bayamo (105,300), Pinar del Río (100,900), Las Tunas (91,400), Ciego de Avila (80,500) and Sancti Spíritus (75,600).

Infant mortality (1986) 13·6 per 1,000 live births.

CLIMATE. Situated in the sub-tropical zone, Cuba has a generally rainy climate, affected by the Gulf Stream and the N.E. Trades, though winters are comparatively dry after the heaviest rains in Sept. and Oct. Hurricanes are liable to occur between June and Nov. Havana. Jan. 72°F (22·2°C), July 82°F (27·8°C). Annual rainfall 48" (1,224 mm).

CONSTITUTION AND GOVERNMENT. The previous Constitution was suspended in Jan. 1959. The first socialist Constitution came into force on 24 Feb. 1976.

Since 1940 the following have been Presidents of the Republic:

	Took office		*Took office*
Gen. Fulgencio Batista y Zaldívar	10 Oct. 1940	Gen. Fulgencio Batista y Zaldívar	10 March 1952
Dr Ramón Grau San Martín	10 Oct. 1944	Dr Manuel Urratia Lleo	2 Jan. 1959
Dr Carlos Prío Socarrás	10 Oct. 1948	Osvaldo Dórticos Torrado	17 July 1959

Legislative power is vested in the National Assembly of People's Power, consisting of 499 deputies elected for a 5-year term by the Municipal Assemblies; elections were held in 1976, 1981 and 1986. The National Assembly elects a 31-member Council of State as its permanent organ. The Council of State's President, who is head of state and of government, nominates and leads a Council of Ministers approved by the National Assembly.

President: Dr Fidel Castro Ruz became President of the Council of State on 3 Dec. 1976. He is also President of the Council of Ministers, First Secretary of the Cuban Communist Party and C.-in-C. of the Revolutionary Armed Forces.

First Vice-President of the Council of State and of the Council of Ministers, Minister of the Revolutionary Armed Forces: Raúl Castro Ruz. *Foreign Affairs:* Isidoro Octavio Malmierca Peoli. *Interior:* Gen. Abelardo Colome. *Justice:* Juan Escalona Reguera. *Foreign Trade:* Ricardo Cabrisas Ruiz.

The Council of Ministers also includes 10 other Vice-Presidents, the Presidents of 10 State Planning Committees and 17 other Ministers.

Dr Castro on 2 Dec. 1961 proclaimed 'a Marxist–Leninist programme adapted to the precise objective conditions existing in our country'. The provisional *Organizaciones Revolucionarias Integradas* (ORI) were established as an intermediate stage towards a single (communist) party, and gave way to the *Partido Unido de la Revolución Socialista* (PURS). This brought together the *Partido Socialista Popular, Movimiento de 26 Julio* and (Students') *Directorio Revolucionario*. The PURS in turn became (3 Oct. 1965) the *Partido Comunista de Cuba*.

The Congress of the PCC elects a Central Committee of 146 full and 79 alternate (non-voting) members, which in turn appoints a Political Bureau comprising 14 full and 10 alternate members.

National flag: 3 blue, 2 white stripes (horizontal); a white 5-pointed star in a red triangle at the hoist.

National anthem: Al combate corred bayameses (words and tune by P. Figueredo, 1868).

Local Government. The country is divided into 14 provinces, the special Municipality (the Isle of Youth) and 169 municipalities. Local Government is the responsibility of the organizations of Peoples' Power. Elections were held in 1976, 1979, 1981, 1984 and 1987 for delegates to the Municipal Assemblies by universal suffrage for 2½ year terms; the Municipal Assemblies then elected the Provincial Assemblies for similar terms.

DEFENCE. On 13 Nov. 1963 conscription was introduced for all men between the ages of 16 and 45, later raised to 50 (3 years); women of the 17–35 age groups may volunteer (for 2 years).

Army. The strength was 145,000 officers and men (60,000 conscripts) in 1989. Reserves are estimated at 130,000.

The Army is organized in 4 corps, 3 armoured divisions, 9 mechanical divisions, 13 infantry divisions and air defence regiments. Equipment includes 800 T-54/-55, 300 T-62 tanks and 60 PT-76 light-tanks. Para-military forces total 69,000 and the new Territorial Militia, 1·3m. including reservists, all armed.

Navy. Naval combatants, all *ex*-Soviet, include 3 'Foxtrot' class diesel submarines, 3 'Koni' class frigates, 18 fast missile craft, 9 patrol hydrofoils, 31 inshore patrol craft, 4 coastal minehunters and 10 inshore minesweepers. There are 2 medium landing ships and 6 craft. The major auxiliaries include 1 tanker, 1 electronic intelligence gatherer, 1 survey ship, 1 tug and 1 training ship. Some 20 minor auxiliaries and service craft complete the total.

Personnel in 1989 totalled 13,500 including marines and coastguard. Main bases at Cienfuegos, Havana and Mariel. The USA is still in possession of the Guantánamo naval base, but the Cuban Government refuses to accept the nominal rent of US$5,000 per annum.

A separate coast guard division of the Frontier Guards operate 4 inshore patrol craft.

Air Force. The Air Force has been extensively re-equipped with aircraft supplied by USSR and in 1989 had a strength of some 22,000 officers and men and 300 combat aircraft. About 12 interceptor and 4 ground-attack squadrons fly MiG-23, MiG-21 and MiG-17 jet fighters. There is a squadron of An-26 twin-turboprop transports, some An-24 twin-turboprop transports, piston-engined Il-14s, and about 100 Mi-24 gunship, Mi-8 (some armed), Mi-17 and Mi-4 helicopters, Zlin 326 piston-engined trainers and L-39, MiG-15UTI, MiG-21U and MiG-23U jet trainers. An-2M biplanes are operated by the Air Force, mainly on agricultural and liaison duties. Soviet-built surface-to-air ('Guideline', 'Goa' and 'Gainful') and coastal defence ('Samlet') missiles are in service.

INTERNATIONAL RELATIONS

Membership. Cuba is a member of the UN, SELA, the Non-Aligned Movement and COMECON.

ECONOMY

Planning. The Cuban economy is now centrally planned. Since July 1972 Cuba has been a member of the Council for Mutual Economic Assistance (COMECON) and, since Jan. 1974, of the two COMECON international banks.

Budget. Revenue in 1989 11,900m. pesos and expenditure, 13,500m. pesos.

Currency. The *peso* is not a freely exchangeable currency but an official exchange rate is announced daily reflecting any changes in the strength of the US$. In March 1990, the sterling-peso rate was £1 = 1·31 *pesos*. US currency is accepted in tourist/hotel shops, but is not legal tender.

Copper-nickel coins of 1 *peso* and 20, 5, 2 and 1 *cent* are issued. Notes are for 100, 50, 20, 10, 5, 3 and 1 *peso*.

Banking. On 23 Dec. 1948 the president signed the law creating a central bank (with capital of US$10m.) and which began operating 27 April 1950.

On 14 Oct. 1960 all banks were nationalized, except the Royal Bank of Canada and the Bank of Nova Scotia, which were bought out later. All banking is now carried out by the National Bank of Cuba through its 250 agencies, or via the Banco Financiero.

All insurance business was nationalized in Jan. 1964. A National Savings Bank was established in 1983.

Weights and Measures. The metric system of weights and measures is legally compulsory, but the American and old Spanish systems are much used. The sugar industry uses the Spanish long ton (1·03 tonnes) and short ton (0·92 tonne). Cuba sugar sack = 329·59 lb. or 149·49 kg. Land is measured in *caballerías* (of 13·4 hectares or 33 acres).

ENERGY AND NATURAL RESOURCES

Electricity. Production in 1987 was 13,583m. kwh. Supply 115 and 120 volts; 60 Hz.

Oil. Crude oil production (1989) 800,000 tonnes.

Minerals. Iron ore abounds, with deposits estimated at 3,500m. tons, of which 90% were held as reserves by American steel interests but are now controlled by the Cuban Ministry of Basic Industry; output (tonnes), wrought iron (1980), 1,180; steel (1988), 320,500. Output of copper concentrate (1988) was 2,951·4 tonnes; refractory chrome (1987), 52,400 tonnes. Other minerals are nickel and cobalt (1988, 43,800 tonnes), silica and barytes. Gold and silver are also worked. Salt output from the solar evaporation of sea water was 122,300 tonnes in 1986.

Agriculture. In May 1959 all land over 30 *caballerías* was nationalized and has since been turned into state farms. In Oct. 1963 private holdings were reduced to a maximum of 5 *caballerías* (approximately 67 hectares).

In Sept. 1984 there were 1,472 co-operatives comprising 70,000 *caballerías* of land. The total cultivated land (1982) included state-owned, 3,398,200 hectares, and in the private sector, 475,400 hectares.

The most important product is sugar, of which Cuba is the world's second largest producer; with its by-products it furnishes nearly 50% by value of the national exports. The 1988-89 crop was estimated at 8·1m. tonnes. There are 164 mills, including 40 of the largest, which were taken over from US interests, and which represent 39% of total capacity. Tobacco, coffee, cotton, maize, rice, potatoes and citrus fruit are grown.

Production of other important crops in 1988 was (in tonnes): Tobacco, 38,400; rice, 488,000; maize, 95,000; coffee, 29,000.

Tobacco is grown mainly in the Vuelta–Abajo district, near Pinar del Río. Coffee is grown chiefly in the province of Oriente.

A fast-growing fibre, *kenaf*, originally from India, soft in texture, is replacing jute for sacking (production, 1986, 13,468 tonnes); the tobacco industry uses *majagua*, another local fibre, while a third fibre, *yarey*, from palms is also used. 277,000 tonnes of potatoes were produced in 1988. A nitrate plant has been built at Nuevitas and a large British-built urea plant at Cienfuegos. The principal fruits exported are pineapples, citrus fruit, tomatoes and pimentos. A rice cultivation plan began in 1967 in the south of Havana province. Cultivation is highly mechanized and the area so far sown produces two crops a year.

In 1987 citrus fruit production was 885,510 tonnes. In 1988 production of pineapples was 22,000 tonnes and tomatoes 331,000 tonnes.

In 1988 the livestock included 2·5m. pigs; 702,800 horses; 382,000 sheep; 110,000 goats; 4,984,000 head of cattle.

Forestry. Cuba has 2·7m hectares of forests representing 25% of the land area. These forests contain valuable cabinet woods, such as mahogany and cedar, besides dye-woods, fibres, gums, resins and oils. Cedar is used locally for cigar-boxes, and mahogany is exported. Cedars, mahogany, *majagua*, teca, etc., are also raised. In 1987 saplings planted included: Eucalyptus, 13m.; pine, 31·9m.; majagua, 4·6m.; mahogany, 3·3m.; cedar, 1·5m.; casuarina, 14·7m.

Fisheries. Fishing is the third most important export industry, after sugar and nickel. Catch (1987) 214,407·1 tonnes.

INDUSTRY AND TRADE

Industry. Production in 1988 was: Textiles, 260·1m. sq. metres; cement (1987), 3·5m. tonnes; wheat flour, 441,900 tonnes; fuel oil (1986), 3,314,000 tonnes; diesel oil (1986), 991,000 tonnes; 428,100 tyres; 350,100 inner tubes; leather shoes, 13·4m. pairs; paint (1986), 84,800 hectolitres; soft drinks (1985), 2,106,500 hectolitres; 269·7m. cigars; 16,885,200m. cigarettes; fertilizers, 840,400 tonnes; 2,537 buses; 153,000 radios; 65,100 TVs.

Trade Unions. All workers have a right to join a trade union. The Workers' Central Union of Cuba, to which 23 unions are affiliated, had 2m. members in 1978.

Commerce. Imports and exports (including bullion and specie) for calendar years (in 1m. pesos):

	1985	*1986*	*1987*	*1988*
Imports	7,983	7,569	7,612	4,549
Exports	7,209	6,702	5,401	5,518

Cuba's principal exports are sugar, minerals, tobacco and fish. The main imports from non-Communist countries are chemicals and engineering and electrical machinery and transport equipment.

In 1985 the USSR provided 67% of imports (by value) and took 75% of exports; in 1984 sugar formed 75% of all exports.

Total trade between Cuba and UK (British Department of Trade returns, in £1,000 sterling):

	1985	*1986*	*1987*	*1988*	*1989*
Imports to UK	7,273	8,555	12,776	28,489	34,388
Exports and re-exports from UK	59,332	58,760	41,510	31,162	53,255

Tourism. In 1988 there were 309,200 visitors (62,300 from socialist countries).

COMMUNICATIONS

Roads. In 1986 there were 16,740 km of paved highways open to traffic, traversing the island for 760 miles from Pinar del Río to Santiago. In 1983 there were 49,841 hire cars (including coaches and buses).

Railways. There were (1986) 4,881 km of public railway (mainly 1,435 mm gauge) of which 152 km is electrified. In 1987 it carried 2,189m. passenger-km and 13·2m. tonnes of freight. In addition, the large sugar estates have 7,773 km of lines on 1,435, 914 and 760 mm gauges.

Aviation. The state airline CUBANA operates all internal services, and from Havana to Mexico City, Madrid, Moscow and East Berlin, Montreal, Prague, Paris and Brussels, and also to Lima, Panama, Kingston, Bridgetown, Port of Spain, Georgetown and Managua. The other regular foreign services are Mexican, Spanish, Soviet, Czech, East German and Canadian.

Shipping. The coastline is over 3,500 miles long and has many fine harbours. The merchant marine, in 1987, consisted of 118 sea-going vessels of 1,427,916 DWT.

Post and Broadcasting. There are 3,545 miles of public and 8,902 miles of private telegraph wires. Cuba has 103 radio broadcasting stations and 2 television stations. Radio receiving sets, 1985, numbered 2·14m.; television sets, 1·53m. The national telephone system (1985) had 493,000 instruments.

Cinemas. In 1987 there were 535 (35mm) and 905 (16mm) cinemas.

Newspapers. In 1987 there were 29 newspapers of which 17 were daily newspapers.

JUSTICE, RELIGION, EDUCATION AND WELFARE

Justice. There is a Supreme Court in Havana and 7 regional courts of appeal. The provinces are divided into judicial districts, with courts for civil and criminal actions, with municipal courts for minor offences. The civil code guarantees aliens the same property and personal rights as are enjoyed by nationals.

The 1959 Agrarian Reform Law and the Urban Reform Law passed on 14 Oct. 1960 have placed certain restrictions on both. Revolutionary Summary Tribunals have wide powers.

Religion. There is no state Church, though Roman Catholics predominate. There is a bishop of the American Episcopal Church in Havana; there are congregations of Methodists in Havana and in the provinces as well as Baptists and other denominations.

Education. Education is compulsory (between the ages of 6 and 14) and free, and now available everywhere. In 1964 illiteracy was officially declared to have been completely eliminated.

In 1987–88 the universities had 262,225 students and 22,492 teaching staff. In 1987–88 there were 936,914 pupils and 73,874 teachers at primary schools, 1,143,137 pupils and 104,741 teachers at intermediate schools and 164,891 students at adult primary schools.

In 1989 there were 18,000 foreign pupils from over 30 developing countries attending international secondary/pre-university schools free of charge, including 7 Angolan schools (3,581 pupils) and 4 Mozambiquan schools (2,231 pupils), and about 30,000 foreign students attending polytechnics, teacher training colleges and universities at an annual cost of US$40m. Cuba sends teachers abroad to more than 40 countries.

Health. There were (1987) 28,060 doctors, 5,923 dentists and 264 hospitals with 71,106 beds. The 1989 health and education budget was 2,906·2m. pesos.

Free medical services are provided by the state polyclinics, though a few doctors still have private practices. All serious tropical diseases are effectively kept under control, and virtually all children under the age of 15 have been vaccinated against poliomyelitis.

DIPLOMATIC REPRESENTATIVES

Of Cuba in Great Britain (167 High Holborn, London, WC1)
Ambassador: (Vacant).

Of Great Britain in Cuba (Edificio Bolivar, Carcel 101–103, Havana)
Ambassador: A. D. Brighty, CMG, CVO.

Of Cuba to the United Nations
Ambassador: Dr Oscar Oramas Oliva.

The USA broke off diplomatic relations with Cuba on 3 Jan. 1961 but in 1977 Interest Sections were opened, officially attached to the Swiss Embassy in Havana and to the Czech Embassy in Washington respectively.

Further Reading

Anuario Estadístico de a República de Cuba. Havana
Boletín Oficial, Ministerio de Comercio. Monthly
Estadística General: Commercio Exterior. Quarterly and Annual.—*Movimiento de Población.* Monthly and Annual. Havana
Anuario azucarero de Cuba. Havana, from 1937
Brundenius, C., *Revolutionary Cuba: The Challenge of Economic Growth with Equity.* Oxford, 1984
Domínguez, J. I., *Cuba: Order and Revolution.* Harvard Univ. Press, 1978
Gravette, A. G., *Cuba: Official Guide.* London, 1988
Guerra y Sánchez, R. and others, *Historia de la Nación Cubana.* 10 vols. Havana, 1952
MacEwan, A., *Revolution and Economic Development in Cuba.* London, 1981
Mesa-Lago, C., *The Economy of Socialist Cuba: A Two-Decade Appraisal.* Univ. of New Mexico Press, 1981
O'Connor, J., *The Origins of Socialism in Cuba.* London, Cornell Univ. Press, 1970
Ritter, A. R. M., *The Economic Development of Revolutionary Cuba: Strategy and Performance.* New York, 1974
Thomas, H., *The Cuban Revolution: 25 Years Later.* Epping, 1984

CYPRUS

Kypriaki Dimokratia—Kibris Cumhuriyeti

Capital: Nicosia
Population: 687,500 (1988)
GNP per capita government controlled area: US$6,260 (1988)

HISTORY. About the middle of the 2nd millennium B.C. Greek colonies were established in Cyprus and later it formed part of the Persian, Roman and Byzantine empires. In 1193 it became a Frankish kingdom, in 1489 a Venetian dependency and in 1571 was conquered by the Turks. They retained possession of it until its cession to England for administrative purposes under a convention concluded with the Sultan at Constantinople, 4 June 1878. On 5 Nov. 1914 the island was annexed by Great Britain and on 1 May 1925 given the status of a Crown Colony.

For the history of Cyprus from 1931 to 1974 *see* THE STATESMAN'S YEAR-BOOK, 1958, pp. 237–38, 1959, p. 236, and 1983–84, p. 385.

On 15 July 1974 a *coup* was staged in Cyprus by the men of the Greek ruling junta, for the overthrow of President Makarios. The President left the island and the *coup* was short-lived. On 23 July power was handed over to the President of the House of Representatives, Glafcos Clerides, in accordance with the Constitution. He acted as President until the return of President Makarios on Dec. 7.

Turkey invaded the island on 20 July, eventually landing 40,000 troops supported with heavy armament and tanks. In two military operations 20–30 July and 14–16 Aug. the Turkish troops managed to occupy 40% of the northern part of Cyprus. As a result 200,000 Greek Cypriots fled to live as refugees in the south. The Cyprus crisis was raised in the UN and the General Assembly unanimously adopted resolutions calling for the withdrawal of all foreign troops from Cyprus and the return of refugees to their homes, but without result.

On 13 Feb. 1975 at a special meeting of the executive council and legislative assembly of the Autonomous Turkish Cypriot Administration a Turkish Cypriot Federated State was proclaimed. Rauf Denktash was appointed President and he declared that the state would not seek international recognition. The proclamation was denounced by President Makarios and the Greek Prime Minister but welcomed by the Turkish Prime Minister. In 1984 the UN Secretary-General initiated talks on a possible federal state but these failed in Jan. 1985. On 15 Sept. 1988 the first meeting between President Vassiliou and Rauf Denktash took place following a UN initiative in Aug. to restart substantive talks. A further initiative by the UN Secretary-General was made in July 1989, without success.

AREA AND POPULATION. The island lies in the eastern Mediterranean, about 50 miles off the south coast of Turkey and (at the nearest points) 65 miles off the coast of Syria. Area 3,572 sq. miles (9,251 sq. km); greatest length from east to west about 150 miles, and greatest breadth from north to south about 60 miles. The Turkish occupied area is 3,400 sq. km (about 37% of the total area). Population by ethnic group:

Ethnic group	*1946*	*1960*	*1973*	*1987*	*1988*
Greek Orthodox	361,199	441,656	498,511	544,700	550,400
Turkish Moslem	80,548	104,942	116,000	126,900	128,200
Others	8,367	26,968	17,267	8,800	8,900
Total	450,114	573,566	631,778	680,400	687,500

Population estimate (June 1988) 687,500, of which 80% are Greek Cypriot (Armenian, Maronite and Latin minorities included), 19% Turkish Cypriot and 1% other, mainly British. Principal towns with populations (Dec. 1988 estimate): Nicosia (the capital), 166,900 (Government controlled area); Limassol, 120,000; Larnaca, 53,600; Paphos, 22,900.

As a result of the Turkish invasion and the occupation of part of Cyprus, 200,000

Greek Cypriots were displaced and forced to find refuge in the south of the island. The urban centres of Famagusta, Kyrenia and Morphou were completely evacuated. See p. 406 for details of the 'Turkish Republic of Northern Cyprus'.

Vital statistics. The birth rate per 1,000 population in 1988 was 19·2; death rate, 8·8; infantile mortality per 1,000 live births, 11.

CLIMATE. The climate is Mediterranean, with very hot, dry summers and variable winters. Maximum temperatures may reach 112°F (44·5°C) in July and Aug., but minimum figures may fall to 22°F (–5·5°C) in the mountains in winter when snow is experienced. Rainfall is generally between 10" and 27" (250 and 675 mm) and occurs mainly in the winter months, but it may reach 48" (1,200 mm) in the Troodos mountains. Nicosia. Jan. 50°F (10·0°C), July 83°F (28·3°C). Annual rainfall 15" (371 mm).

CONSTITUTION AND GOVERNMENT. The legislative power is exercised by the House of Representatives of 80 members, of whom 56 were elected by the Greek community and 24 by the Turkish community. As from Dec. 1963 the Turkish members have ceased to attend.

On 13 Dec. 1959 Archbishop Makarios was elected President of the Republic. Dr Fazil Kuchuk was elected Vice-President unopposed; he resigned on 4 Jan. 1964. On 13 Feb. 1975, Rauf Denktash the Turkish-Cypriot leader announced the formation of a Turkish-Cypriot state within a federal republic and on 15 Nov. 1983 a unilateral declaration of independence, as the Turkish Republic of Northern Cyprus, was announced.

When President Makarios died in Aug. 1977 Spyros Kyprianou became acting President and was proclaimed President on 31 Aug. 1977 and was elected for a 5-year term in 1978 and re-elected in 1983. In 1988 George Vassiliou was installed as President following elections held on 14 Feb.

Flag: White with a copper-coloured outline of the island with 2 green olive-branches beneath.

The elections held on 8 Dec. 1985 returned 16 Democratic Party, 15 Akel Party (Communists), 6 EDEK (Socialist Party), 19 Democratic Rally. The Turks have not participated in the proceedings of the House since Dec. 1963.

The Council of Ministers in Jan. 1990 was as follows:

Foreign Affairs: George Iacovou. *Interior:* Christodoulos Veniamin. *Defence:* Andreas Aloneftis. *Agriculture and Natural Resources:* Andreas Gavrielides. *Commerce and Industry:* Takis Nemitsas. *Health:* Panikos Papageorgiou. *Communications and Works:* Nakos Protopapas. *Finance:* George Syrimis. *Education:* Andreas Philippou. *Labour and Social Insurance:* Takis Christofides. *Justice:* Christodoulos Chrysanthou.

DEFENCE

Army. Total strength (1989) 13,000 organized in 2 mechanized, 1 armoured, 1 artillery and 1 commando battalions. The National Guard has a twin-engined Maritime Islander light transport, 4 PC-9 trainers and 6 armed Gazelle helicopters. There is also a para-military force of 3,700 armed police.

The Turkish-Cypriot Security Force: 35,000 Turkish mainland troops, 5,000 Turkish Cypriots, and some T-34 tanks are stationed in occupied Cyprus (see p. 406).

INTERNATIONAL RELATIONS

Membership. Cyprus is a member of UN, the Commonwealth, the Council of Europe and the Non-Aligned Movement.

ECONOMY

Planning. A fourth emergency economic action plan (1982–86) envisaged expenditure of £C398m. for development projects.

Budget. Revenue and expenditure for calendar years (in £C1m.):

	1983	*1984*	*1985*	*1986*	*1987*	*1988*
Expenditure	368	418	448	491	535	600
Revenue	289	344	390	427	462	536

Main sources of ordinary revenue in 1988 (in £C1m.) were: Import duties, 103 (including 22 temporary refugee levy on imports); excise duties, 65; income tax, 101; rents, royalties and interest, 21; sales of goods and services, 26; other duties and taxes, 51; social security contributions, 88.

Main divisions of ordinary expenditure in 1988 (in £C1m.): Wages and salaries, 189; pensions and gratuities, 17; commodity subsidies, 32; expenditures on goods and services, 41; public debt charges, 199; social insurance benefits, 89.

Development expenditure for 1988 (in £C1m.) included 16 for water development, 5 for agriculture, forests and fisheries, 5 for rural development, 16 for roads and 1 for airports. (An independent Ports Authority with its own funds was set up in 1977.)

The outstanding long-term public debt as at 31 Dec. 1988 was £C616m. Outstanding loans as at 31 Dec. 1987 totalled £C60m. Foreign debt (1988) public and private, £C642m.

Currency. From Oct. 1983 the *Cyprus £* has been divided into 100 *cents*. Notes of the following denominations are in circulation: £10, £5, 50 *cents*. Coins in circulation: Cupro-zinc-nickel: 20, 5, 2, 1 *cent* and ½ cent in aluminium. Rate of exchange, March 1990: £1 = £C0·7825; US$1 = £C0·4774.

Banking. There is a Central and Issuing Bank exercising monetary functions, and the Cyprus Development Bank Ltd established by the Government as a major source of loan funds for industrial development. Commercial banks operating in Cyprus are: Bank of Cyprus Ltd, Turkish Bank Ltd, Cyprus Popular Bank Ltd, Barclays Bank International, National Bank of Greece, Hellenic Bank Ltd, Arab Bank Ltd and Turkiye Is Bankasi. There are 2 central co-operative banks (Co-operative Central Bank Ltd and the Cyprus Turkish Co-operative Central Bank) and 3 specialized financial institutions (Mortgage Bank of Cyprus Ltd, Lombard Natwest Banking Ltd and Housing Finance Corporation). Seventeen offshore banking units were in operation in 1989.

The Central Bank of Cyprus, established in 1963, is responsible for the issue of currency, the regulation of money supply and credit, administration of the exchange control law and the foreign-exchange reserves of the republic. The Bank also acts as a banker of the banks operating in Cyprus and of the Government and acts as supervisor of the banking system.

At the end of Dec. 1988 total deposits in banks were £C1,679m. The country's foreign exchange reserves at the end of Dec. 1988 were £C572m.

Weights and Measures. The metric (SI) system was introduced in 1986 and is now widely applied.

ENERGY AND NATURAL RESOURCES

Electricity. Production (1988) 1,667m. kwh. Supply 240 volts; 50 Hz.

Water Resources. In 1988 £C20·9m. was spent on water dams, water supplies, hydrological research and geophysical surveys. Existing dams had (1989) a capacity of 297m. cu. metres as against 6m. cu. metres before independence.

Minerals. The principal minerals exported during 1988 were (in tonnes): Asbestos, 15,776; flotation pyrites, 6,610; copper precipitates, 360. Mining products provided about 1% of domestic exports in 1988. Total value of minerals exported in 1988 was £C2·1m.

Agriculture. Chief agricultural products in 1988 (1,000 tonnes): Grapes, 198; potatoes, 164; milk, 122; cereals (wheat and barley), 158; citrus fruit, 132; meat, 57; carobs, 15; fresh fruit, 27; olives, 18; other vegetables, 114; eggs, 10m. dozen.

Of the island's 2·3m. acres, approximately 1m. are cultivated. About 13·8% (1988) of the economically active population are engaged in agriculture.

Livestock in 1988 (in 1,000): Cattle, 46; sheep, 300; goats, 205; pigs, 284; poultry, 2,500.

Forestry. By Dec. 1982, the reforesting of burnt areas in the Paphos Forest was completed and an area of 7,492 hectares (56,000 donums) was reforested. Reforestation work in other bare areas of state forests was carried out in an area of 6,464 hectares (42,318 donums). Total forest area, 1,340 sq. km.

In 1988 the chief forest products were timber, 45,943 cu. metres valued at £C697,000; firewood, £C170,000; figures relate to the area of Cyprus not occupied by Turkey.

Fisheries. Catch (1988) 2,575 tonnes.

INDUSTRY AND TRADE

Industry. The most important industries (in £C1m.) in 1988 were: Food, beverages and tobacco, 222·2; textiles, wearing apparel and leather, 203·5; chemicals and chemical petroleum, rubber and plastic products, 114·3; metal products, machinery and equipment, 100·9; wood and wood products including furniture, 68·9. Manufacturing industry in 1988 contributed about £C306·6m. to the GDP and gave employment to 47,000 of the economically active population.

The highest increases in output in 1987 were production of wearing apparel, metal products and machinery and equipment. Industrial exports rose to £C187·2m. in 1988 and accounted for 79% of total domestic exports.

Trade Unions and Associations. About 80% of the workforce is organized and the majority of workers belong either to the Pancyprian Federation of Labour or the Cyprus Workers Confederation.

Commerce. The commerce and the shipping, exclusive of coasting trade, for calendar years were (in £C1,000):

	1984	*1985*	*1986*	*1987*	*1988*
Imports	796,520	762,311	659,073	711,419	866,765
Exports [1]	336,826	290,611	260,158	297,992	330,861

[1] Including re-exports and ships' stores.

Chief civil imports, 1988 (in £C1m.):

Live animals and animal products	20·6
Vegetable products	33·7
Prepared foodstuffs, beverages and tobacco	56·2
Mineral products	81·5
Products of chemical or allied industries	62·4
Plastics and rubber and articles thereof	39·2
Pulp, waste paper and paperboard and articles thereof	35·2
Textiles and textile articles	93·6
Footwear, headgear, umbrellas, prepared feathers, etc.	5·5
Articles of stone, plaster, cement, etc., ceramic and glass products	20·8
Machinery, electrical equipment, sound and television recorders	167·3
Vehicles, aircraft, vessels and equipment	93·5
Optical, photographic, medical, musical and other instruments, clocks and watches	20·6
Raw hides and skins, leather and articles, travel goods	10·6
Wood and articles, charcoal, cork and articles, basketware, etc.	15·2
Pearls, precious stones and metals, semi-precious stones and articles	14·4

Chief domestic exports, 1988 (in £C1,000):

Grapes	3,819
Citrus fruit	13,782
Potatoes	16,178
Wine	4,548
Fruit, preserved and juices	8,148
Cigarettes	7,683
Paper products	3,398
Cement	5,896
Clothing	74,573
Footwear	16,480
Medicinal and pharmaceutical products	5,895

In 1988 the EEC countries supplied 54·5% of the imports; Arab countries, 4·8%; others, 40·7%. Of the exports (1988), 33·4% went to Arab countries; 42·8% to EEC countries; 4·1% to Eastern Europe and 19·7% to other countries.

Total trade between Cyprus and UK (British Department of Trade returns, in £1,000 sterling):

	1985	*1986*	*1987*	*1988*	*1989*
Imports to UK	93,689	124,198	118,250	121,828	145,047
Exports and re-exports from UK	150,921	140,387	141,129	159,788	173,092

Tourism. Foreign visitors (1988), 1,311,591 (1,111,818 tourists and 199,773 excursionists).

COMMUNICATIONS

Roads. In 1988 the total length of roads in the Government controlled area was 9,186 km, of which 4,838 km were bituminous and 4,348 km were earth or gravel roads. The asphalted roads maintained by the Ministry of Communications and Works (Public Works Department) by the end of 1988 totalled 2,860 km, of which 214 km were within the municipal areas. Roads improved or constructed and asphalted in 1988 totalled 138·4 km. On 31 Dec. 1988, there were 300,022 motor vehicles including 2,523 buses and 64,589 goods vehicles.

The area controlled by the Government of the Republic and that occupied by Turkey are now served by separate transport systems, and there are no services linking the two areas.

Aviation. Nicosia airport has been closed since Aug. 1974. In 1988, 31 international airlines operated scheduled services between Cyprus and Europe, Africa and the Middle East, and another 22 airlines operated non-scheduled services. A new airport opened in the 'Turkish Republic of Northern Cyprus' in 1986. During 1988, 2,580,000 persons travelled and 24,566 tonnes of commercial air-freight was handled through Larnaca and Paphos international airports.

Shipping. The 3 main ports are Limassol, Larnaca and Paphos. In 1988, 4,370 ships of 13,231,435 net tons entered Cyprus ports. Ships under Cyprus registry numbered 1,974 of 18,431 GRT. Famagusta has been closed to international traffic since Aug. 1974.

Post and Broadcasting. In 1988 there were 56 post offices and 705 postal agencies. Telephones (1988) 323,000. Wireless licences issued (1981) were 247,000, including television licences.

Cyprus Broadcasting Corporation broadcasts mainly in Greek, but also in Turkish, English, and Armenian on medium-waves. The corporation also broadcasts on one TV channel. There are also 2 foreign broadcasting stations.

Cinemas (1985). In the government-controlled area there were 59 cinemas.

Newspapers (1989). There were 10 Greek, 6 Turkish and 1 English daily newspapers and 6 Greek, 3 Turkish and 2 English weeklies.

JUSTICE, RELIGION, EDUCATION AND WELFARE

Justice. The administration of justice is exercised by separate and independent judiciary. Under the 1960 Constitution and other legislation in force there are the Supreme Court of the Republic, Assize Courts, District Courts, Ecclesiastical Courts and Turkish Family Courts.

The Supreme Court is composed of 13 judges one of whom is the President of the Court. There is an Assize Court and a District Court for each district. The Assize Courts have unlimited criminal jurisdiction and may order the payment of compensation up to £C3,000. The District Courts exercise original civil and criminal jurisdiction, the extent of which varies with the composition of the Bench.

There is a Supreme Council of Judicature, consisting of the President and Judges of the Supreme Court, entrusted with the appointment, promotion, transfers, termination of appointment and disciplinary control over all judicial officers, other than the Judges of the Supreme Court.

Religion. *See* Area and Population, p. 400.

Education. Until 31 March 1965 each community managed its own schooling through its respective Communal Chamber. Intercommunal education had been placed under the Minister of the Interior, assisted by a Board of Education for Intercommunal Schools, of which the Minister was the Chairman. In 1965 the Greek Communal Chamber was dissolved and a Ministry of Education was established to take its place. Intercommunal education has been placed under this Ministry.

Greek-Cypriot Education. Elementary education is compulsory and is provided free in 6 grades to children between $5\frac{1}{2}$ and $11\frac{1}{2}$ years of age. In some towns and large villages there are separate junior schools consisting of the first three grades. Apart from schools for the deaf and blind, there are also 9 schools for handicapped children. In 1988–89 the Ministry ran 201 kindergartens for children in the age group $2\frac{1}{2}$-3; there were 296 privately run pre-primary schools. There were 381 primary schools with 58,720 pupils and 2,689 teachers in 1988–89.

Secondary education is also free and attendance for the first cycle is compulsory. The secondary school is 6 years, 3 years at the gymnasium followed by 3 years at the lykeion. In 1978–79 the lyceums of optional subjects were introduced, in which students can choose one of the 5 main fields of specialization: Classical, science, economics, commercial/secretarial and foreign languages. There are 3-year technical schools. In 1988–89 there were 105 secondary schools with 3,405 teachers and 42,613 pupils.

Post-secondary education is provided at the Pedagogical Academy, which organizes 3-year courses for the training of pre-primary and primary school teachers, and at the Higher Technical Institute, which provides 3–4-year courses for technicians in civil, electrical, mechanical and marine engineering. There is also a 2-year Forestry College (administered by the Ministry of Agriculture), a Hotel and Catering Institute, the Mediterranean Institute of Management (Ministry of Labour and Social Insurance) and a 1–3-year Nurses' School (Ministry of Health). Adult education is conducted through youth centres in rural areas, foreign language institutes in the towns and private institutions offering courses in business administration and secretarial work.

In 1988–89, 9,410 students were studying in universities abroad, mainly in Greece, the USA, UK, Federal Republic of Germany and Italy.

Greek is the language of 82% of the population and Turkish of 18%. English is widely spoken. English and French are compulsory subjects in secondary schools. Illiteracy is largely confined to older people.

Social Security. The administration of the social-security services in Cyprus is in the hands of the Ministry of Labour and Social Insurance, with the Ministry of Health providing medical services through public clinics and hospitals on a means test, except medical treatment for employment accidents, which is given free to all insured employees and financed by the Social Insurance Scheme.

DIPLOMATIC REPRESENTATIVES

Of Cyprus in Great Britain (93 Park St., London, W1Y 4ET)
High Commissioner: Tasos Panayides, GCVO.

Of Great Britain in Cyprus (Alexander Pallis St., Nicosia)
High Commissioner: The Hon. H. J. H. Maud, CMG.

Of Cyprus in the USA (2211 R. St., NW, Washington, D.C., 20008)
Ambassador: Michael Sherifis.

Of the USA in Cyprus (Therissos St., Nicosia)
Ambassador: Bill K. Perrin.

Of Cyprus to the United Nations
Ambassador: Andreas Mavrommatis.

'TURKISH REPUBLIC OF NORTHERN CYPRUS'

HISTORY. *See* p. 400.

AREA AND POPULATION. The Turkish Republic of Northern Cyprus occupies 3,355 sq. km (about 37% of the island of Cyprus) and its population was estimated in 1986 to be 162,676. Population of principal towns (1985): Nicosia, 37,400; Famagusta, 19,428; Kyrenia, 6,902; Morphou, 10,179; Lefka, 3,785. Ethnic groups: Turks, 158,225; Greeks, 733; Maronites, 368; Others, 961.

CONSTITUTION AND GOVERNMENT. The Turkish Republic of Northern Cyprus was proclaimed on 15 Nov. 1983. The President is Rauf R. Denktash, and there is a Council of Ministers comprised in June 1988 of:

Prime Minister: Derviş Eroğlu.

Foreign Affairs and Defence: Kenan Atakol. *Economy and Finance:* Mehmet Bayram. *Interior, Village Affairs and Environment:* Olgun Paşalar. *Education and Culture:* Salih Djoşar. *Agriculture and Forests:* Aytaç Beşesler. *Communications, Works and Tourism:* Nazif Borman. *Trade and Industry:* Taşkent Atasayan. *Health and Social Welfare:* Dr Mustafa Erbilen. *Labour, Youth and Sports:* Günay Djaymaz. *Housing:* Mustafa Adaoghlu.

A 50-seat Legislative Assembly was elected in June 1985. In June 1988 the Ulusal Birlik Partisi (National Unity Party) had 25 seats, the Cumhuriyetçi Türk Partisi (Turkish Republican Party) 12 seats, the Toplumcu Kurtuluş Partisi (Communal Liberation Party) 9 seats and others 4 seats.

Flag: White with horizontal bars of red set near the top and bottom; between these a crescent and star in red.

Budget. The 1988 Budget balanced at 170,121m. Turkish lire.

Currency. The Turkish *lire* is used throughout Northern Cyprus.

Banking Turkish Bank Ltd, Turkiye Is Bankasi and the Cyprus Turkish Co-operative Central Bank Ltd are operating in the Turkish occupied area of the republic and consequently no control or supervision is exercised by the Central Bank of Cyprus.

Trade. Imports in 1986 amounted to 102,461m. and exports to 35,018m. Turkish lire.

Tourism. There were 150,000 tourists in 1987.

Education. In 1987 there were 20,781 pupils and 751 teachers in primary schools, 11,103 pupils and 706 teachers in secondary schools, 1,748 students and 192 teachers in technical schools, and 1,649 students with 84 teaching staff in higher education.

Health. In 1986 there were 118 doctors.

Further Reading

Statistical Information: Statistics and Research Department, Nicosia.
North Cyprus Almanack, London, 1987
Denktash, R., *The Cyprus Triangle.* London, 1982
Ertekün, N. M., *The Cyprus Dispute.* Nicosia North, 1984
Georghallides, G. S., *A Political and Administrative History of Cyprus 1918–1926.* Nicosia, 1979
Halil, K., *The Rape of Cyprus.* London, 1982
Hill, Sir George F., *A History of Cyprus.* 4 vols. Cambridge, 1940–52
Hitchins, C., *Cyprus.* London, 1984
Hunt, D., *Footprints in Cyprus.* London, 1982
Kitromilides, P. M. and Evriviades, M. L., *Cyprus,* [Bibliography]. Oxford and Santa Barbara, 1982
Kyle, K., *Cyprus.* London, 1984
Loizos, P., *The Heart Grows Bitter: A Chronicle of Cypriot War Refugees.* CUP, 1982
Mayes, S., *Makarios.* London, 1981
Necatigil, Z. M., *Our Republic in Perspective.* Nicosia, 1985
Reddaway, J., *Burdened With Cyprus.* London, 1986
St John-Jones, L. W., *The Population of Cyprus.* London, 1983

CZECHOSLOVAKIA

Česká a Slovenská Federátivní Republika

Capital: Prague
Population: 15·62m. (1989)
GNP per capita: US$8,700 (1985)

HISTORY. The Czechoslovak State came into existence on 28 Oct. 1918, when the Czech *Národni Výbor* (National Committee) took over the government of the Czech lands upon the dissolution of Austria–Hungary. Two days later the Slovak National Council manifested its desire to unite politically with the Czechs. On 14 Nov. 1918 the first Czechoslovak National Assembly declared the Czechoslovak State to be a republic with T. G. Masaryk as President (1918–35).

The Treaty of St Germain-en-Laye (1919) recognized the Czechoslovak Republic, consisting of the Czech lands (Bohemia, Moravia, part of Silesia) and Slovakia. To these lands were added as a trust the autonomous province of Subcarpathian Ruthenia.

This territory was broken up for the benefit of Germany, Poland and Hungary by the Munich agreement (29 Sept. 1938) between UK, France, Germany and Italy.

In March 1939 the German-sponsored Slovak government proclaimed Slovakia independent, and Germany incorporated the Czech lands into the Reich as the 'Protectorate of Bohemia and Moravia'. A government-in-exile, headed by Dr Beneš, was set up in London in July 1940.

Liberation by the Soviet Army and US Forces was completed by May 1945.

Territories taken by Germans, Poles and Hungarians were restored to Czechoslovak sovereignty. Subcarpathian Ruthenia was transferred to the USSR.

Elections were held in May 1946, at which the Communist Party obtained about 38% of the votes.

A coalition government under a Communist Prime Minister, Klement Gottwald, remained in power until 20 Feb. 1948, when 12 of the non-Communist ministers resigned in protest against infiltration of Communists into the police.

In Feb. a predominantly Communist government was formed by Gottwald. In May elections resulted in an 89% majority for the government and President Beneš resigned.

In 1968 pressure for liberalization culminated in the overthrow of the Stalinist leader, Antonín Novotný, and his associates. The Communist Party introduced an 'Action Programme' of far-reaching reforms.

Soviet pressure to abandon this programme was exerted between May and Aug. 1968, and finally, Warsaw Pact forces occupied Czechoslovakia on 21 Aug. The Czechoslovak government was compelled to accept a policy of 'normalization' (*i.e.*, abandonment of most reforms) and the stationing of Soviet forces.

A Czechoslovak–Soviet 20-year Treaty of Friendship was signed in 1970.

In 1974 the German Federal Republic and Czechoslovakia annulled the Munich agreement of 1938.

Mass demonstrations demanding political reform began in Nov. 1989. After the authorities' use of violence to break up a demonstration on 17 Nov., the Communist Party leader, Miloš Jakeš, and the entire Politburo resigned, and a new Government was formed on 3 Dec. The protest movement, focussed on the recently-established Civic Forum, in which prominent Charter 77 dissidents were active, continued to grow, however, and on 10 Dec. another Government was formed. Gustáv Husák resigned as President of the Republic, and was replaced by Václav Havel on the unanimous vote of 323 members of the Federal Assembly on 29 Dec.

In Dec. 1989 the Communist Party denounced the Warsaw Pact invasion of 1968 as 'unjustified and incorrect'.

AREA AND POPULATION. Czechoslovakia is bounded north-west by the German Democratic Republic, north by Poland, east by the USSR, south by Hungary and Austria and south-west by the Federal Republic of Germany. At the census of 11 Nov. 1980 the population was 15,283,095 (4,991,168 in Slovakia; 7·9m. females). Population in 1989, 15,624,021 (Slovakia, 5,263,541; females 8m. in 1987). There are 12 administrative regions *(Kraj)*, one of which is the capital, Prague (Praha) and one the capital of Slovakia, Bratislava.

Region	*Chief city*	*Area in sq. km*	*Population 1989*
Czech			
Prague	—	496	1,211,106
Středočeský	Prague (Praha)	10,994	1,122,023
Jihočeský	České Budějovice	11,345	697,785
Západočeský	Plzeň (Pilsen)	10,875	869,592
Severočeský	Ustí nad Labem	7,819	1,190,606
Východočeský	Hradec Králove	11,240	1,240,847
Jihomoravský	Brno	15,028	2,058,530
Severomoravský	Ostrava	11,067	1,969,991
Slovak			
Bratislava	—	368	435,499
Západoslovenský	Bratislava	14,492	1,725,766
Středoslovenský	Banská Bystrica	17,982	1,608,192
Východoslovenský	Košice	16,193	1,494,084

The area of Czechoslovakia is 127,899 sq. km (Slovakia, 49,035 sq. km). Population density in 1989: 122 per sq. km. Growth rate in 1988, 2·4 per 1,000. Expectation of life in 1985 was 67 (males); 74 (females).

Ethnic minorities have equal political and cultural rights. In 1987 there were (in 1,000): Czechs, 9,804; Slovaks, 4,953; Hungarians, 597; Poles, 73; Germans, 54; Ukrainians, 48; Russians, 7. There were 303,000 gipsies in 1983.

Official languages are Czech and Slovak.

The population of the principal towns in 1989 was as follows (in 1,000):

Prague (Praha)	1,211	Liberec	104	Gottwaldov	87
Bratislava	435	Hradec Králové	100	Banská Bystrica	87
Brno	390	České Budějovice	97	Kladno	73
Ostrava	331	Žilina	96	Trnava	72
Košice	232	Pardubice	96	Karviná	72
Plzeň	175	Havírov	92	Most	70
Olomouc	107	Nitra	89	Frýdek-Místek	65
Ustí nad Labem	106	Prešov	87	Martin	65

Vital statistics for calendar years:

	Live births	*Marriages*	*Divorces*	*Deaths*
1986	220,494	119,979	37,885	185,718
1987	214,927	122,168	39,522	179,224
1988 [1]	216,158	118,956	38,922	178,229

[1] Provisional

Infant mortality in 1988 (per 1,000 live births), 4·6. Abortion rate per 1,000 live births, in 1985: Czech Lands, 728; Slovakia, 504. Abortion law was liberalized in 1986.

CLIMATE. A humid continental climate, with warm summers and cold winters. Precipitation is generally greater in summer, with thunderstorms. Autumn, with dry, clear weather and spring, which is damp, are each of short duration. Prague. Jan. 29·5°F (–1·5°C), July 67°F (19·4°C). Annual rainfall 19·3" (483mm). Brno. Jan. 31°F (–0·6°C), July 67°F (19·4°C). Annual rainfall 21" (525mm).

CONSTITUTION AND GOVERNMENT. The 1960 constitution was amended in 1968. For details of previous constitutions, *see* THE STATESMAN'S YEAR-BOOK, 1968–69, pp. 927–28.

Since 1 Jan. 1969 Czechoslovakia has been a federal socialist republic consisting of two nations of equal rights: The Czech Socialist Republic (the Czech lands, previously Bohemia, Moravia and part of Silesia), and the Slovak Socialist Republic (Slovakia). Each Republic is governed by a National Council (the Czech with 200 deputies, the Slovak with 150), which delegates to an overall Federal

Assembly responsibility for constitutional and foreign affairs, defence and important economic decisions. The Federal Assembly consists of the Chamber of Nations, which has 75 Czech and 75 Slovak delegates, and the Chamber of the People, which has 200 deputies. Both Chambers are elected by direct universal suffrage for 5-year terms. Minimum age of voters is 18; of deputies, 21 years. At the elections of May 1986 a single list of National Front candidates was presented. Turnout was 99·39%. New elections were brought forward to 8 June 1990.

President of the Republic: Václav Havel, *Speaker of the Federal Assembly:* Alexander Dubček.

With the abolition by the Federal Assembly on 30 Nov. 1989 of the Communist Party's constitutional right to govern, two of the parties previously incorporated in the National Front resumed independent activity: the Socialist Party (SP), leader Bohuslav Kučera, and the People's Party (PP), leader Josef Bartončik, 44,000 members in Dec. 1989. Civic Forum was formed in Nov. 1989 as a focus for other opposition groups. The Communist Party (CP) in Dec. 1989 replaced its General-Secretary and Politburo with a Chairman (Ladislav Adamec), a First Secretary (Vasil Mohorita) and an Executive Committee. The CP had 1·69m. members in early 1989.

In March 1990 the Government consisted of: *Prime Minister:* Marian Čalfa (b.1946) (Ind.); *First Deputy Prime Ministers:* Valtr Komárek (Civic Forum), Ján Čarnogurský (Civic Forum); *Deputy Prime Ministers:* František Pitra (CP), Milán Čič (CP), Josef Hromadka (Ind.), Vladimír Dlouhý (Ind.) (also *Chairman, State Planning Committee*), František Reichel (PP) (also *Chairman, State Commission for Scientific, Technical and Investment Development*), Oldřich Burský (SP) (also *Minister of Agriculture*); *Foreign Minister,* Jiří Dienstbier (Civic Forum); *Defence,* Gen. Miroslav Vaček (CP); *Finance,* Václav Klaus (Civic Forum); *Foreign Trade,* Andřej Barčák (CP); *Labour and Social Affairs,* Petr Miller (Civic Forum); *Fuel and Power,* František Pinc (CP); *Transport and Telecommunications,* František Podlena (CP); *Metallurgy and Engineering,* Ladislav Vodrázka (CP); *Price Bureau,* Ladislav Dvořák (SP); *People's Control Committee,* Květoslava Korinková (Ind.); *Without portfolio,* Robert Martinko (Ind.), Richard Sacher (PP). The *Ministry of the Interior* was the joint responsibility of Marian Čalfa, Valtr Komárek and Ján Čarnogurský.

The Czech Prime Minister is Peter Pitárt; the Slovak, Iván Knotek.

Local government is carried on by National Committees consisting of deputies elected for 5-year terms. There are 10 regional Committees, 2 City Committees with the same status for Prague and Bratislava, 108 district Committees and 7,979 town and community Committees. Elections were held in 1986. 197,404 candidates were elected.

National flag: White and red (horizontal), with a blue triangle of full depth at the hoist, point to the fly.

National anthem: Kde domov můj (words by J. K. Tyl; tune by F. J. Škroup, 1834); combined with, Nad Tatru sa blyska (words by J. Matuška, 1844).

DEFENCE. Defence is the responsibility of the President of the Republic. Defence expenditure cuts of 15% were announced in 1989.

Soviet troops in the country, legalized by an agreement which followed the Warsaw Pact invasion of Aug. 1968, began to withdraw in 1990.

Military conscription is for one year.

Army. The Army had a strength (1990) of 148,600 (100,000 conscripts). It consists of 3 tank, 5 motor rifle and 1 artillery divisions; 2 anti-tank regiments, 3 *Scud*, 6 engineer and 1 airborne brigades and 5 regiments of Civil Defence troops. Equipment includes 4,585 T-54/-55/-72 tanks. There are also 2 paramilitary forces: Border Troops (11,000) and People's Militia (120,000).

Air Force. The Air Force is organized as a tactical force, under overall army command, and had a strength of some 51,100 personnel and 450 combat aircraft in 1990. Three interceptor regiments (each 3 squadrons of 14 aircraft) are equipped with MiG-29, MiG-23 and MiG-21 jets, and MiG-29 are coming into service. There are 4 regiments of Su-22, Su-25, MiG-23 and MiG-21 ground attack aircraft, as well as Mi-24 gunship helicopters. MiG-21s and modified L-39 Albatros jet trainers are used for tactical reconnaissance. Transport units have a total of 60 Let L-410, An-24/26, Il-14 and Tu-134 aircraft and about 100 Mil Mi-2 (some armed), Mi-4, Mi-8 and Mi-17 helicopters. Training units are equipped with 2-seat MiG-23s and MiG-21s and Czech-built aircraft, including L-29 and L-39 Albatros jet advanced trainers and Zlin primary trainers. Surface-to-air ('Guideline', 'Goa', 'Ganef', 'Gainful' and 'Gaskin') missile units are operational.

INTERNATIONAL RELATIONS

Membership. Czechoslovakia is a member of UN, COMECON and the Warsaw Pact.

ECONOMY

Planning. For the first six 5-year plans *see* THE STATESMAN'S YEAR-BOOK, 1985–86. In 1980 some rationalizations in the planning system, which have become known as the 'Set of measures', were applied. The 7th 5-year plan ran from 1981 to 1985. National income rose by 11%, industrial production by 13%, agricultural by 9% (Targets were 14%, 18% and 10%). The eighth 5-year plan covered 1986–90. Targets included a growth in national income of 18% and in agricultural production of 6%. Emphasis was laid on intensive rather than extensive development and a more efficient use of resources.

Budget. Budgets for calendar years (in Kčs. 1m.):

	1982	*1983*	*1984*	*1985*	*1986*	*1987*	*1988*
Revenue	314,203	324,127	343,805	359,692	368,696	383,732	404,045
Expenditure	314,046	323,890	342,192	358,028	365,949	382,151	401,199

Main items of the 1988 budget were (in Kčs. 1,000m.): Revenue: From the economy, 258; direct taxes, 47. Expenditure: National economy, 90; health and social services, 96; defence, 27; administration, 4.

Currency. The monetary unit in the Czechoslovak Republic is the *koruna* (Kčs.) or crown of 100 *haler*. Notes in circulation: Kčs. 10, 20, 50, 100, 500, 1,000. Coin: 5, 10, 20, 50 *halers*, and Kčs. 1, 2, 5. The *crown* is based on a gold content of 0·123426 gramme of pure gold and pegged on the rouble at Kčs. 1·80 = R.1. The IMF did not approve this change of the par value, and Czechoslovak membership was terminated in 1954. Foreign currency reserves were US$4,832m. in 1987; gold reserves were US$1,832m. The crown was devalued by 75% in Dec. 1989. Official rates of exchange (March 1990): £1 = Kčs. 28·30; US$1 = Kčs. 17·27. Tourist: £1 = Kčs. 60·60; US$1 = Kčs. 40·63.

The return of 18·4 tonnes of gold seized by Nazi Germany and held in London and New York since the nationalization of Western assets in 1948 was agreed in Jan. 1982 by the Czech, British and US governments.

Banking. For previous banking history *see* THE STATESMAN'S YEAR-BOOK, 1971–72, pp. 858–59. The central bank and bank of issue is the State Bank (Statni Banka), which controls foreign exchange reserves, and is a savings bank and a commercial credit bank to enterprises, except foreign trade enterprises. These are financed by the Commercial Bank (Obchodní Banka) which carries out all foreign trade transactions. The Trade Bank (Živnostenská Banka) provides banking services for private foreign clients, and maintains branches abroad. There is also an Investment Bank (Investiční Banka), one of whose functions is to manage foreign securities. 'Foreign exchange points' (*e.g.*, hotels) have partial foreign exchange authorization. There were 20·2m. savings accounts totalling 265,569m. Kčs in 1988.

Weights and Measures. The metric system is in force.

ENERGY AND NATURAL RESOURCES

Electricity. Production of electricity in 1988: 87,374m. kwh. In 1990 there were two nuclear power stations, producing 28% of all electricity. Two more were under construction. Supply 120 and 220 volts; 50 Hz.

Oil. Production (1989 estimate) 130,000 tonnes. There is an oil pipeline from the USSR with branches to Bratislava and Zaluzi.

Gas. A natural gas pipeline from the USSR supplies the German Federal and Democratic Republics, Austria and Italy as well as Czechoslovakia. A second is under construction.

Minerals. Czechoslovakia is not rich in minerals. There are hard and soft coal reserves (chief coalfields: Most, Chomutov, Kladno, Ostrava and Sokolov). There is also uranium, glass sand and salt, and small quantities of iron ore, graphite, copper and lead. Gold deposits were found near Prague in 1985. Production in 1988 (in 1,000 tonnes): Coal, 25,504; lignite and brown coal, 96,361.

Agriculture. In 1988 there were 6·8m. hectares of agricultural land (4·8m. hectares arable, 0·8m. meadow, 0·8m. pasture), of which 4·3m. were held by collective farms, 2·1m. by state farms and 67,000 as private plots (maximum size 1 hectare).

In 1988 there were 1,657 collective farms with 1,004,517 members and 238 state farms with 173,725 employees. Crop production in 1988 (in 1,000 tonnes): Sugar-beet, 5,418; wheat, 6,547; potatoes, 3,659; barley, 3,411; maize, 996; rye, 534.

Livestock. In 1988: Cattle, 5,075,000 (including 1,815,000 milch cows); horses, 44,000; pigs, 7,384,000; sheep, 1,047,000; poultry, 49m. In 1988 production of meat was 1,846,980 tonnes (live weight); milk, 6,754m. litres; 5,596m. eggs. In 1988 there were 141,191 tractors. 36,470 hectares were irrigated in 1988.

Forestry. Forest area in 1989 was 4,606,673 hectares (50% spruce, 16% beech and pine, 7% oak) representing 37% of the land area. The area reafforested in 1988 was 17,630 hectares. The timber yield was 18·1m. cu. metres in 1988.

Fisheries. Total catch was 21·25m. tonnes in 1988.

INDUSTRY AND TRADE

Industry. Industrialization is well developed and antedated the Communist régime. All industry was nationalized.

Output in 1988 (in 1,000 tonnes): Pig-iron, 9,706; crude steel, 15,319; coke, 10,586; rolled-steel products, 11,420; cement, 10,974; paper, 974; sulphuric acid, 1,249; nitrogenous fertilizers, 594; phosphate fertilizers, 313; plastics, 1,192; synthetic fibres, 204; sugar, 707; beer, 22·7m. hectolitres; cars, 163,834 (no.).

Textile production (in 1m. metres) in 1988: Cotton, 591; linen, 105; woollen, 59; shoes, 119·1m. pairs (55·3m. leather).

Labour. There were 8,882,691 persons of employable age in 1988 (*i.e.*, males, 15–59; females 15–54), of whom 7·5m. (46% women) were employed: 5·8m. in production (industry, 2·9m.; agriculture, 838,902; building, 694,425); and 2m. in services.

A 5-day 42-hour week with 4 weeks annual holiday is standard. A new wage system of norms and differentials linked to productivity was introduced in 1985. Average monthly wage in 1989: Kčs. 3,300. In 1988 the trade union movement had 7·7m. members; chairman, Miroslav Závadil.

Commerce. Total trade (in Kčs. 1m.) for calendar years:

	1983	*1984*	*1985*	*1986*	*1987*	*1988*
Imports	103,012	113,737	120,323	125,449	127,259	129,134
Exports	103,838	114,230	119,818	121,777	125,875	132,781

In 1988, trade with Communist countries amounted to 205,560m. Kčs. (109,200m. Kčs. with the USSR, 25,354m. Kčs. with the German Democratic Republic, 27,486m. Kčs. with Poland). The UK is Czechoslovakia's third biggest non-Communist trade partner after the Federal German Republic and Austria.

Major exports in 1986 (percentage of total): Machinery, 54; industrial consumer goods, 17·1; other finished products, 11·7. Imports: Machinery, 40; fuel, 38.

There are 11 foreign trade agencies (independent legal entities with their own capital run by state-appointed managers). Joint economic ventures with Western firms have been permitted since 1985. Foreign hard-currency indebtedness was US$4,000m. in 1989.

In 1972 an Anglo-Czech Agreement on Co-operation was signed. Under this an Anglo-Czech Joint Commission was established to further the development of trade and industrial and scientific co-operation.

UK-Czechoslovak trade has been conducted since 1 Jan. 1975 on the basis of autonomous EEC measures.

Total trade between Czechoslovakia and UK for calendar years (British Department of Trade returns, in £1,000 sterling):

	1985	*1986*	*1987*	*1988*	*1989*
Imports to UK	120,017	125,399	141,472	148,248	156,649
Exports and re-exports from UK	100,452	108,841	114,101	130,420	131,418

Tourism. In 1988, 14·03m. tourists visited Czechoslovakia (1·1m. from the West) and 6·3m. Czechoslovak tourists made visits abroad (346,000 to the West). Visa-free travel to the West has been permited since Dec. 1989.

COMMUNICATIONS

Roads. In 1988 there were 73,540 km of motorways and first-class roads (660 km of motorways in 1988). In 1984 there were 2,639,564 private cars (figures have not been given since). In 1988 state road transport carried 2,343m. passengers and 339m. tonnes of freight. In 1988 there were 109,521 accidents with 1,246 fatalities.

Railways. In 1988 the length of railway routes was 13,103 km. Of this, 3,798 km were electrified. In 1988, 415·4m. passengers and 294·8m. tonnes of freight were carried.

Aviation. Air transport is run by ČSA (Czechoslovak Airlines). The main airports are: Prague (Ruzyně), Brno (Cernovice), Bratislava (Vajnory), Olomouc (Holice), Košice (Barca). In 1988, 1·5m. passengers and 28,066 tonnes of freight were flown. There are 6 internal and 53 international flights from Prague. British Airways operates air traffic London–Prague, Air France Paris–Prague–Bucharest.

Shipping. In 1988 Czechoslovak Maritime Shipping had 14 freighters totalling 227,638 DWT, based on Szczecin. In 1988, 1·63m. tonnes of cargo were carried.

There are 475 km of inland waterways. Freight transport totalled 15·21m. tonnes in 1988. 537,000 passengers were carried in 1988.

Czechoslovak Danube Shipping operate 5 ships totalling 244,000 DWT in the Mediterranean from Bratislava, and Czechoslovak Elbe-Oder Shipping had a fleet of 284,500 DWT in 1985.

Post and Broadcasting. There were 5,137 post offices in 1988. Number of telephones in service in 1988 was 3,979,819. *Československy Rozhlas*, the governmental broadcasting station, broadcasts on 2 networks; 1 from Prague with 3 programmes in Czech and Slovak and 1 from Bratislava with 2 programmes in Slovak and additional broadcasts in Hungarian and Ukrainian. *Československa Televise* broadcast 2 television programmes nation-wide, including colour broadcasts. In 1988, 4·23m. people held radio and 4·66m. TV licences.

Cinemas and Theatres (1988). There were 2,778 cinemas and 86 theatres. 42 full-length films were made.

Newspapers and Books (1988). There were 30 daily newspapers, including 12 in Slovak, and 1,057 other periodicals. 6,977 book titles were published in 102·7m. copies. There were 9,014 public libraries.

JUSTICE, RELIGION, EDUCATION AND WELFARE

Justice. The criminal and criminal procedure codes date from 1 Jan. 1962, as amended in April 1973.

There is a Federal Supreme Court and federal military courts, with judges elected by the Federal Assembly. Both republics have Supreme Courts and a network of regional and district courts whose professional judges are elected by the republican National Councils. Lay judges are elected by regional or district local authorities. Local authorities and social organizations may participate in the decision-making of the courts. An amnesty for some 30,000 of the 40,000 persons in prison was announced in Jan. 1990.

Religion. Official surveys suggest that 20% of the population are religious believers. In 1987 there were 18 different faiths with 5,500 clergy and 7,500 churches. The largest single church is the Roman Catholic (3·7m. members, 4,336 parishes 5,085 churches and 3,175 priests, 1985): Its main support is in Slovakia. Cardinal František Tomašek was installed as archbishop of Prague in 1978. The archbishopric of Trnava is held by a bishop and that of Olomouc by an administrator. Most of the remaining 10 dioceses are directed by Government-appointed capitulary vicars but 3 bishops were consecrated in 1988, the first since 1973. There were 2 seminaries and 6 theological faculties in 1989.

In 1986 there were 1·3m. non-Catholic church members, including 475,000 Hussites, 81,000 Czech Brethren with 670 congregations, 370,000 Slovak Lutherans in 2 districts with 15 associations of parishes, 36,000 Silesian Lutherans and 120,000 Reformed Christians with 7 associations of parishes. In 1981 there were 15,000 Jews (mainly in Prague, where there is a synagogue and, since 1984, a rabbi). In 1986 there were 150,000 Orthodox with 100 congregations in 4 dioceses. The Uniate Church was suppressed in 1950 but maintained a clandestine existence.

Education. In 1988–89 there were 11,393 kindergartens for children from 3 to 6 years, with 50,483 teachers and 651,365 pupils. Education is free and compulsory for 10 years. Children of 6 to 14 years attend primary school (grades 1 to 9). Selection then takes place for secondary schools (4 years), vocational secondary schools (4 years) or apprentice centres (2-4 years). University entrance is mainly from secondary schools. In 1988–89 there were 6,216 primary schools with 2,013,910 pupils and 97,853 teachers, 349 secondary schools with 145,532 pupils and 10,378 teachers and 561 secondary vocational schools with 271,014 students and 16,857 teachers. In higher education in 1988–89, there were 136,656 (60,606 women) full-time students, and 20,434 teachers. There are 36 institutions of higher education, with 112 faculties. These include 5 universities—the Charles University in Prague (founded 1348); the Masaryk (formerly Purkyně) University in Brno (1919); the Comenius University in Bratislava (1919); the Palacký University in Olomouc (1573); the Šafárik University in Košice (1959); and 12 technical universities or institutes.

Welfare. Medical care is free. In 1988 Kčs. 32,190m. were spent on health insurance benefits. There were, in 1988, 231 hospitals with a total of 123,844 beds, and 57,112 doctors and dentists. Family allowances (Kčs. per month): 1 child, 200; 2 children, 650; 3, 1,210. Old age pensions averaging 67% of salary are paid at the age of 60 (men), 53–57 (women).

DIPLOMATIC REPRESENTATIVES

Of Czechoslovakia in Great Britain (25 Kensington Palace Gdns., London, W8 4QY)
Ambassador: Karel Duda.

Of Great Britain in Czechoslovakia (Thunovská 14, 11800 Prague 1)
Ambassador: P. L. O'Keeffe, CMG, CVO.

Of Czechoslovakia in the USA (3900 Linnean Ave., NW, Washington, D.C., 20008)
Ambassador: Rita Klimová.

Of the USA in Czechoslovakia (Tržiste 15–12548 Praha, Prague)
Ambassador: Shirley Temple Black.

Of Czechoslovakia to the United Nations
Ambassador: Evžen Zápotocký.

Further Reading

The Constitution of the Czechoslovak Socialist Republic. Prague, 1960
Statistická ročenka CSSR [Statistical Yearbook]. Prague, annual since 1958

Historická statistická ročenka ČSSR. Prague, 1985
Czechoslovak Foreign Trade. Prague, monthly
Batt, J., *Economic Reform and Political Change in Eastern Europe: A Comparison of the Czechoslovak and Hungarian Experiences*. Basingstoke, 1988
Bradley, J. F. N. *Politics in Czechoslovakia, 1945–1971*. Lanham, 1981
Czechoslovak Chamber of Commerce and Industry. *Facts on Czechoslovak Foreign Trade*. Prague, annual since 1965.—*Your Trade Partners in Czechoslovakia*. Prague, 1986
Demek, J. and others, *Geography of Czechoslovakia*. Prague, 1971
Hermann, A. H., *A History of the Czechs*. London, 1975
Hejzlar, Z. and Kusin, V. V., *Czechoslovakia, 1968–1969*. New York, 1975
Kalvoda, J., *The Genesis of Czechoslovakia*. New York, 1986
Kaplan, K., *The Communist Party in Power: A Profile of Party Politics in Czechoslovakia*. Boulder, 1987
Kolafova, V. and Slaba, D. *Czech-English and English-Czech dictionary*. Prague, 1979
Korbel, J., *Twentieth-Century Czechoslovakia: The Meanings of its History*. Columbia Univ. Press, 1977
Krystufek, Z., *The Soviet Régime in Czechoslovakia*. Columbia Univ. Press, 1981
Kusin, V. V., *From Dubček to Charter 77*. Edinburgh, 1978
Leff, C. S., *National Conflict in Czechoslovakia: The Making and Remaking of a State, 1918–1987*. Princeton, 1988
Mamatey, V. S. and Luža, R. (eds.) *A History of the Czechoslovak Republic 1918–1948*. Princeton Univ. Press, 1973
Mlynař, Z., *Night Frost in Prague: the End of Humane Socialism*. New York, 1980
Procházka, J., *English–Czech and Czech–English Dictionary*. 16th ed. London, 1959
Sejna, J. *We Will Bury You*. London, 1982
Short, D., *Czechoslovakia*. [Bibliography] Oxford and Santa Barbara, 1986
Sperling. W., *Tschechoslowakei: Beiträge zur Landeskunde Ostmitteleurapas*. Stuttgart, 1981
Stevens, J. N., *Czechoslovakia at the Crossroads: The Economic Dilemmas of Communism in Postwar Czechoslovakia*. Boulder, 1985
Stone, N. and Strouhal, E., (eds.) *Czechoslovakia: Crossroads and Crizes, 1918-88*. London, 1989
Suda, Z. L., *Zealots and Rebels: A History of the Communist Party in Czechoslovakia*. Stanford, 1980
Teichova, A., *The Czechoslovak Economy, 1918–1980*. London, 1988
Wallace, W. V., *Czechoslovakia*. London, 1977

DENMARK

Capital: Copenhagen
Population: 5·13m. (1989)
GNP per capita: US$18,470 (1988)

Kongeriget Danmark

HISTORY. First organized as a unified state in the 10th century, Denmark acquired approximately its present boundaries in 1815, having ceded Norway to Sweden and its north German territory to Prussia. Denmark became a constitutional monarchy in 1849.

AREA AND POPULATION. According to the census held on 9 Nov. 1970 the area of Denmark proper was 43,075 sq. km (16,631 sq. miles) and the population 4,937,579. Population, Jan. 1989: 5,129,778.

Administrative divisions		*Area (sq. km) 1989*	*Population 1970*	*Population 1989*	*Population 1989 per sq. km.*
København (Copenhagen)	(city)	88	622,773	467,850	5,301·4
Frederiksberg	(borough)	9	101,874	85,327	9,729·4
Københavns	(county)	526	615,343	602,046	1,144·7
Frederiksborg	,,	1,347	259,442	340,513	252·7
Roskilde	,,	891	153,199	215,993	242·3
Vestsjælland	,,	2,984	259,057	283,271	94·9
Storstrøm	,,	3,398	252,363	257,007	75·6
Bornholm	,,	588	47,239	46,105	78·4
Fyn	,,	3,486	432,699	458,111	131·4
Sønderjylland	,,	3,938	238,062	250,158	63·5
Ribe	,,	3,131	197,843	218,460	69·8
Vejle	,,	2,997	306,263	329,847	110·1
Ringkøbing	,,	4,853	241,327	266,834	55·0
Aarhus	,,	4,561	533,190	594,184	130·3
Viborg	,,	4,123	220,734	230,318	55·9
Nordjylland	,,	6,173	456,171	483,754	78·4
Total		43,093	4,937,579	5,129,778	119·0

The population is almost entirely Scandinavian; in Jan. 1989, of the inhabitants of Denmark proper, 95·9% were born in Denmark, including Faroe Islands and Greenland.

On 1 Jan. 1989 the population of the capital, Copenhagen (comprising Copenhagen, Frederiksberg and Gentofte municipalities), was 618,209 (including suburbs, 1,339,406); Aarhus, 259,493; Odense, 174,943; Aalborg, 154,547; Esbjerg, 81,480; Randers, 61,137; Kolding, 57,128; Helsingør, 56,754; Herning, 56,376; Horsens, 54,940.

Vital statistics for calendar years:

	Living births	*Still births*	*Marriages*	*Divorces*	*Deaths*	*Emigration*	*Immigration*
1984	51,800	230	28,624	14,490	57,109	25,053	29,035
1985	53,749	240	29,322	14,385	58,378	26,715	36,214
1986	55,312	242	30,773	14,490	58,100	27,928	38,932
1987	56,221	288	31,132	14,381	58,136	30,123	36,296
1988	58,904	292	32,080	14,717	59,034	34,544	35,051

Illegitimate births: 1983, 40·6%; 1984, 41·9%; 1985, 43%; 1986, 43·9%; 1987, 44·7%.

CLIMATE. The climate is much modified by marine influences, and the effect of the Gulf Stream, to give winters that are cold and cloudy but warm and sunny summers. In general, the east is drier than the west, though few places have more than 27" (675 mm) of rain a year. Long periods of calm weather are exceptional and windy conditions are common. Copenhagen. Jan. 33°F (0·5°C), July 63°F (17°C).

Annual rainfall 22·8" (571 mm). Esbjerg. Jan. 33°F (0·5°C), July 59°F (15°C). Annual rainfall 32" (800 mm).

REIGNING QUEEN. Margrethe II, born 16 April 1940; married 10 June 1967 to Prince Henrik, born Count de Monpezat; *offspring:* Crown Prince Frederik, born 26 May 1968; Prince Joachim, born 7 June 1969. She succeeded to the throne on the death of her father, King Frederik IX, on 14 Jan. 1972.

Mother of the Queen: Queen Ingrid, born Princess of Sweden, 28 March 1910. *Sisters of the Queen:* Princess Benedikte, born 29 April 1944 (married 3 Feb. 1968 to Prince Richard of Sayn-Wittgenstein-Berleburg); Princess Anne-Marie, born 30 Aug. 1946 (married 18 Sept. 1964 to King Constantine of Greece).

The crown of Denmark was elective from the earliest times. In 1448 after the death of the last male descendant of Swein Estridsen the Danish Diet elected to the throne Christian I, Count of Oldenburg, in whose family the royal dignity remained for more than 4 centuries, although the crown was not rendered hereditary by right till 1660. The direct male line of the house of Oldenburg became extinct with King Frederik VII on 15 Nov. 1863. In view of the death of the king, without direct heirs, the Great Powers signed a treaty at London on 8 May 1852, by the terms of which the succession to the crown of Denmark was made over to Prince Christian of Schleswig-Holstein-Sonderburg-Glücksburg, and to the direct male descendants of his union with the Princess Louise of Hesse-Cassel, niece of King Christian VIII of Denmark. In accordance with this treaty, a law concerning the succession to the Danish crown was adopted by the Diet, and obtained the royal sanction 31 July 1853. Linked to the constitution of 5 June 1953, a new law of succession, dated 27 March 1953, has come into force, which restricts the right of succession to the descendants of King Christian X and Queen Alexandrine, and admits the sovereign's daughters to the line of succession, ranking after the sovereign's sons.

Subjoined is a list of the kings of Denmark, with the dates of their accession, from the time of election of Christian I of Oldenburg:

House of Oldenburg

Christian I	1448	Christian IV	1588	Frederik V	1746
Hans	1481	Frederik III	1648	Christian VII	1766
Christian II	1513	Christian V	1670	Frederik VI	1808
Frederik I	1523	Frederik IV	1699	Christian VIII	1839
Christian III	1534	Christian VI	1730	Frederik VII	1848
Frederik II	1559				

House of Schleswig-Holstein-Sonderburg-Glücksburg

Christian IX	1863	Christian X	1912	Margrethe II	1972
Frederik VIII	1906	Frederik IX	1947		

CONSTITUTION AND GOVERNMENT. The present constitution of Denmark is founded upon the 'Grundlov' (charter) of 5 June 1953.

The legislative power lies with the Queen and the *Folketing* (Diet) jointly. The executive power is vested in the Queen, who exercises her authority through the ministers. The judicial power is with the courts. The Queen must be a member of the Evangelical-Lutheran Church, the official Church of the State. The Queen cannot assume major international obligations without the consent of the *Folketing*. The *Folketing* consists of one chamber. All men and women of Danish nationality of more than 18 years of age and permanently resident in Denmark possess the franchise and are eligible for election to the *Folketing*, which is at present composed of 179 members; 135 members are elected by the method of proportional representation in 17 constituencies. In order to attain an equal representation of the different parties, 40 *tillægsmandater* (additional seats) are divided among such parties which have not obtained sufficient returns at the constituency elections. Two members are elected for the Faroe Islands and 2 for Greenland. The term of the legislature is 4 years, but a general election may be called at any time.

The *Folketing* must meet every year on the first Tuesday in October. Besides its legislative functions, it appoints every 6 years judges who, together with the ordinary members of the Supreme Court *(Højesteret)*, form the *Rigsret*, a tribunal which can alone try parliamentary impeachments. The ministers have free access to the House, but can vote only if they are members.

Folketing, elected 10 May 1988: 55 Social Democrats, 10 Radical Liberals, 35 Conservatives, 24 Socialist People's Party, 9 Centre Democrats, 4 Christian People's Party, 22 Liberals, 16 Progress Party, 2 Faroe Islands and 2 Greenland representatives.

The executive (called the State Council *(Statsraadet)* when acting with the Queen presiding) is a minority non-Socialist coalition government, consisting of the Conservatives, the Liberals, the Centre Democrats and the Christian People's Party; it was in Jan. 1990 as follows:

Prime Minister: Poul Schlüter.

Foreign Affairs: Uffe Ellemann-Jensen. *Finance:* Henning Dyremose. *Economy:* Niels Helveg Petersen. *Justice:* Hans Engell. *Environment:* Lone Dybkjaer. *Education and Research:* Bertel Haarder. *Social Affairs:* Aase Olesen. *Ecclesiastical Affairs and Communications:* Torben Rechendorff. *Energy:* Jens Bilgrav Nielsen. *Labour:* Knud Erik Kirkegaard. *Fisheries:* Kent Kirk. *Industry:* Nils Wilhjelm. *Culture:* Ole Vig Jensen. *Taxation:* Anders Fogh Rasmussen. *Health:* Elsebeth Koch-Petersen. *Agriculture:* Laurits Toernaes. *Defence:* Knud Enggaard. *Housing:* Agnete Lausten. *Interior and Nordic Co-operation:* Thor Pedersen. *Public Works:* Knud Oestergaard.

The ministers are individually and collectively responsible for their acts, and if impeached and found guilty, cannot be pardoned without the consent of the *Folketing*.

In 1948 a separate legislature *(Lagting)* and executive *(Landsstyre)* were established for the Faroe Islands, to deal with specified local matters and in 1979 a separate legislature *(Landsting)* and executive *(Landsstyre)* were established for Greenland, also to deal with specified local matters.

National flag: Red with white Scandinavian cross (Dannebrog).

National anthems: Kong Kristian stod ved højen Mast (words by J. Ewald, 1778; tune by J. E. Hartmann, 1780) and Der er et yndigt land.

Local Government. For administrative purposes Denmark is divided into 275 municipalities *(kommuner)*; each of them has a district council of between 5 and 25 members, headed by an elected mayor. The city of Copenhagen forms a district by itself and is governed by a city council of 55 members, elected every 4 years, and an executive *(magistraten)*, consisting of the chief burgomaster *(overborgmesteren)* and 6 burgomasters, appointed by the city council for 4 years. There are 14 counties *(amtskommuner)*, each of which is administered by a county council *(amstråd)* of between 13 and 31 members, headed by an elected mayor. All councils are elected directly by universal suffrage and proportional representation for 4-year terms.

The counties and Copenhagen are superintended by the Ministry of Interior Affairs. The municipalities are superintended by 14 local supervision committees, headed by a state county prefect *(statsamtmand)* who is a civil servant appointed by the Queen.

DEFENCE. The Danish military defence is organized in accordance with the Defence Act of May 1982 and the overall organization of the Danish Armed Forces comprises the Defence Command, the Army, the Navy, the Air Force and inter-service authorities and institutions. To this should be added the Home Guard, which is an indispensable part of Danish military defence. The Home Guard is based on the Home Guard Act of May 1982.

In accordance with the Defence Act the Chief of Defence has full command of the three services: The Army, the Navy and the Air Force. The Chief of Defence, and the Defence Staff constitute the Defence Command. The Inspector Generals of the Army, the Navy and the Air Force are members of the Defence Staff.

The Minister of Defence is assisted by a Defence Council consisting of the Chief of Defence, the Chief of Defence Staff, the Chief of Danish Operational Forces, the Inspector Generals of the Army, the Navy and the Air Force and the Chief of the Home Guard.

The Constitution of 1849 declared it the duty of every fit man to contribute to the national defence, and this provision is still in force. According to the Personnel Act of May 1982, the military personnel comprises officers, n.c.o.s and privates. Private personnel are provided by enlistment and by recruiting of volunteers. Selection of conscripts takes place at the age of 18–19 years, and the conscripts are normally called up for service ½–1½ years later. Afterwards conscripts may be recalled for refresher training or musters. The initial training period for conscripts is between 4 and 12 months.

Army. The Army comprises field army formations and the local defence forces. The field army formations are organized in a covering force and in reserve units. The covering force numbers about 17,000 men and comprises a standing force (regulars and conscripts with more than six months' service), and a supplementary force consisting of men newly released from service. The standing force are organized in standing brigade units, headquarters units and support units. The brigade units are organized in 5 mechanized infantry brigades. The field army is equipped with 210 medium battle tanks, 52 light tanks and about 530 armoured personnel carriers as well as artillery including 76 self-propelled howitzers. The Army has 14 Hughes 500 helicopters and 8 Supporter aircraft for observation and liaison. The local defence units consist of about 18,000 men organized in 9 infantry battalions and some artillery battalions. The men of the latest annual service groups form the troops of the line, while those of the previous years form the local defence, the reserve and the reserve for the Home Guard. There are 55,000 Army reservists.

Navy. The Navy, in 1989, 7,700 strong (900 conscripts) is supported by 7,600 reservists and 4,900 Naval Home Guard. The fleet includes 3 small submarines, 3 frigates, 5 offshore patrol vessels, 4 coastal patrol craft, 10 fast missile craft, 6 torpedo craft, 4 ocean minelayers, 2 coastal minelayers and 3 coastal minesweepers. Two frigates are maintained in reserve. Major auxiliaries include 2 tankers, and the Royal Yacht; and there are some 12 minor auxiliaries. The Naval Air Arm comprises 8 Lynx helicopters (one is carried in each of the offshore patrol craft), and the Home Guard operates 37 inshore patrol craft.

Coastal Defence forces man 2 permanent fortresses armed with 150mm guns.

Additional forces of a para-military nature include 4 icebreakers maintained by the navy at the main base at Frederikshavn, and one coastal fishery protection vessel.

Air Force. The operational units of the Air Force comprise 8 surface-to-air missile squadrons and 6 flying squadrons.

The air defence force consists of the 8 Hawk surface-to-air missile squadrons and 4 all-weather air-defence squadrons with a total of 57 F-16s. All squadrons have an air-defence and a fighter-bomber rôle.

The fighter bomber force comprises 2 squadrons with a total of 32 F 35 Drakens, one unit having a secondary reconnaissance role.

In addition the Air Force has a number of supplementary units, including 1 transport squadron (C-130 Hercules and Gulfstream III), 1 helicopter rescue squadron (S-61As), and a control and warning system.

Total strength of the Air Force is about 9,400, and the mobilization force about 10,000 men.

Home Guard. The overall Home Guard organization comprises the Home Guard Command, the Army Home Guard, the Naval Home Guard and the Air Force Home Guard.

The personnel of the Home Guard is recruited on a voluntary basis. The personnel establishment of the Home Guard is at present about 71,400 persons (56,000 in the Army Home Guard, 4,700 in the Navy Home Guard and 10,700 in the Air Force Home Guard).

INTERNATIONAL RELATIONS

Membership. Denmark is a member of UN, NATO, OECD and the European Communities.

ECONOMY

Budget. The budget *(Finanslovforslag)* must be laid before the Parliament *(Folketing)* not later than 4 months before the beginning of a new fiscal year.

The following shows the actual revenue and expenditure as shown in central government accounts for the calendar years 1986, 1987 and 1988, the approved budget figures for 1989 and the budget for 1990 (in 1,000 kroner):

	1987	*1988*	*1989*	*1990*
Revenue	202,050,261	199,637,449	221,518,663	225,879,194
Expenditure	198,496,721	213,128,706	222,742,098	228,663,541

Receipts and expenditures of special government funds and expenditures on public works are included.

The 1990 budget envisages revenue of 123,465m. kroner from income and property taxes and 116,523m. from consumer taxes.

The central government debt on 31 Dec. 1988 amounted to 435,786m. kroner.

Currency. The monetary unit is the *krone* of 100 *øre*. In 1931 Denmark went off the gold standard, as established in 1873.

Small change: 10-kroner and 5-kroner pieces of copper-nickel, 1-krone pieces of copper-nickel; 25-øre pieces of copper–steel–copper clad. In March 1990, £1 = 10·71 *kroner*; US$1 = 6·54 *kroner*.

Banking. On 31 Dec. 1988 the accounts of the National Bank balanced at 148,871m. kroner. The assets included official net foreign reserves of 76,239m. kroner. The liabilities included notes and coin of 23,870m. kroner. On 31 Dec. 1988 there were 74 commercial banks, with deposits of 335,785m. kroner, and 140 savings banks, with deposits of 137,894m. kroner. Their advances amounted to 291,252m. kroner and 125,901m. kroner respectively. On 31 Dec. 1988 the money supply was 376,158m. kroner.

Weights and Measures. The use of the metric system of weights and measures has been obligatory in Denmark since 1 April 1912.

ENERGY AND NATURAL RESOURCES

Electricity. Production (1988) 25,789m. kwh. Supply 220 volts; Hz 50.

Oil. Production (1989) 5·4m. tonnes.

Agriculture. Land ownership is widely distributed. In June 1988 (census) there were 84,093 holdings with at least 5 hectares of agricultural area (or at least a production equivalent to that from 5 hectares of barley). About 8,000 holdings were below the sample threshold. There were 15,621 small holdings (with less than 10 hectares), 53,303 medium sized holdings (10–50 hectares) and 15,168 holdings with more than 50 hectares.

The number of agricultural workers declined from 120,442 in July 1961 to 23,691 in June 1988.

In June 1988 the cultivated area was utilized as follows (in 1,000 hectares): Grain, 1,587; peas and beans, 147; root crops, 211; other crops, 292; green fodder and grass, 550; fallow, 4; total cultivated area, 2,787.

	Area (1,000 hectares)			*Production (in 1,000 tonnes)*		
Chief crops	*1986*	*1987*	*1988*	*1986*	*1987*	*1988*
Wheat	353	399	308	2,177	2,285	2,080
Rye	120	137	80	546	512	366
Barley	1,078	954	1,154	5,134	4,292	5,419
Oats [1]	27	21	44	111	94	202
Potatoes	31	30	33	1,129	957	1,246
Other root crops	190	180	178	10,563	8,314	10,391

[1] Including mixed grain.

Livestock, 1988: Horses, 34,000; cattle, 2,262,000; pigs, 9,217,000; poultry, 14,768,000.

Production (in 1,000 tonnes) in 1988: Milk, 4,739; butter, 94; cheese, 260; beef, 236; pork and bacon, 1,218; eggs, 79.

In May 1987 farm tractors numbered 167,773 and harvester-threshers, 34,896.

Fisheries. The total value of the fish caught was (in 1m. kroner): 1950, 156; 1955, 252; 1960, 376; 1965, 650; 1970, 854; 1975, 1,442; 1980, 2,888; 1984, 3,645; 1985, 3,542; 1986, 3,576; 1987, 3,510; 1988, 3,407.

INDUSTRY AND TRADE

Industry. The following table sets forth the gross factor income (in 1m. kroner) by industrial origin in 3 calendar years:

	1986		*1987*		*1988*	
	Current Prices	*1980 Prices*	*Current Prices*	*1980 Prices*	*Current Prices*	*1980 Prices*
Agriculture, fur-farming, forestry, etc.	27,933	20,918	25,686	20,469	24,906	20,536
Fishing	2,430	1,596	2,561	1,568	2,569	1,738
Total	30,363	22,514	28,248	22,037	27,474	22,274
Mining and quarrying	3,972	6,819	3,447	8,439	2,768	8,671
Manufacturing	114,190	73,494	117,844	70,721	123,703	68,757
Electricity, gas and water	7,304	6,800	8,710	6,741	10,006	7,113
Construction	36,194	24,164	38,000	23,599	37,751	22,475
Total	161,660	111,277	168,001	109,500	174,228	107,016
Wholesale and retail trade	77,184	50,475	75,404	48,267	75,264	47,421
Restaurants and hotels	8,135	4,577	8,721	4,734	8,792	4,582
Transport and storage	34,317	20,776	36,975	22,823	41,410	25,205
Communication	10,124	6,281	9,502	5,669	9,782	5,442
Financing and insurance	22,203	14,020	21,221	12,781	21,831	12,645
Dwellings	49,557	29,942	53,664	30,363	59,499	31,225
Business services	31,063	20,066	32,309	20,236	34,685	20,551
Market services of education, health	6,689	4,440	6,962	4,258	7,337	4,291
Recreational and cultural services	5,300	3,650	5,473	3,582	5,964	3,646
Household services, incl. auto repair	15,557	9,637	18,466	9,943	20,007	10,064
Total	260,128	163,863	268,695	162,656	284,571	165,072
Other producers, excl. government	3,753	2,447	4,167	2,493	4,622	2,562
Producers of government services	119,810	83,090	131,477	83,260	141,623	83,896
Total	123,563	85,537	135,644	85,753	146,246	86,458
Imputed bank service charges	–22,850	–14,865	–22,047	–13,592	–23,093	–13,337
Gross domestic product at factor cost	552,864	368,327	578,542	366,354	609,425	367,485
Plus indirect taxes	130,839	70,666	135,935	69,515	139,379	66,623
Less subsidies	20,060		22,152		25,236	
Gross domestic product at market prices	663,643	438,993	692,325	435,869	723,568	434,108

According to the registration of business units for VAT settlement there were in 1985 a total of 37,000 manufacturing enterprises. In the following table 'number of wage-earners' refers to 7,200 establishments with 6 employees or more (1988), while 'gross-output' and 'value-added' cover 3,298 kind-of-activity units of enterprises with 20 employees or more (1987).

Branch of industry	*Number of wage-earners (1,000)*	*Gross output in factor values (1m. kroner)*	*Value added in factor values (1m. kroner)*
Mining and quarrying	0·9	810	613
Food products	50·5	84,852	22,242
Beverages	5·4	7,181	4,277
Tobacco	1·4	2,367	1,228
Textiles	10·5	8,440	3,870
Wearing apparel	7·2	3,660	1,797
Leather and products	0·5	403	173
Footwear	0·9	1,016	391
Wood products	8·0	5,735	2,644
Furniture and fixtures	11·3	6,556	3,428
Paper and products	7·0	7,002	3,351
Printing, publishing	15·3	13,722	8,853
Industrial chemicals	12·3	24,281	12,849
Other chemical products, petroleum refineries, petroleum coal products and rubber	2·9	8,242	2,247
Plastic products	7·5	5,688	3,114
Pottery, china, glass and products	3·2	1,669	1,018
Non-metal products	9·6	9,760	5,894
Iron, steel and non-ferrous metals	4·3	3,824	1,850
Metal products	27·5	18,712	9,693
Machinery	39·7	28,099	15,452
Electrical machinery	15·2	14,383	7,702
Transport equipment	16·5	12,620	5,567
Controlling equipment	6·5	5,290	3,347
Other industries	4·4	3,980	2,271
Total manufacturing	268·6	278,288	123,873

Labour. In 1989, 6% of the working population lived on agriculture, forestry and fishery, 20% on industries and handicrafts, 7% on construction, 14% on commerce, etc., 7% on transport and communication, and 46% on administration, professional services, etc.

Commerce. The following table shows the value, in 1,000 kroner, of special trade imports and exports (including trade with the Faroe Islands and Greenland) for calendar years:

	1984	*1985*	*1986*	*1987*	*1988* [1]
Imports	171,825,816	191,562,564	184,732,811	174,066,090	178,268,724
Exports	165,346,387	179,577,142	171,790,740	175,302,411	187,380,954

[1] Preliminary.

Imports and exports (in 1m. kroner) for calendar years:

	1987		*1988* [1]	
Leading commodities	*Imports*	*Exports*	*Imports*	*Exports*
Live animals, meat, etc.	920	18,513	1,149	18,880
Dairy products, eggs	652	6,568	890	6,464
Fish and fish preparations	5,684	11,260	5,634	11,333
Cereals and cereal preparations	1,430	4,148	1,212	4,522
Sugar and sugar preparations	655	1,173	743	1,341
Coffee, tea, cocoa, etc.	1,812	573	1,762	409
Feeding stuff for animals	3,634	1,188	4,006	1,694
Wood, lumber and cork	2,474	477	2,673	598
Textiles, fibres, yarns, fabrics, etc.	6,524	4,371	6,152	4,499
Fuels, lubricants, etc.	13,336	4,279	10,814	3,886

Leading commodities	1987 Imports	1987 Exports	1988[1] Imports	1988[1] Exports
Pharmaceutical products	2,617	5,745	2,883	6,231
Fertilizers, etc.	1,810	1,073	1,904	1,150
Metals, manufactures of metals	15,201	8,389	16,875	9,174
Machinery, electrical, equipment, etc.	37,471	35,710	37,745	38,149
Transport equipment	14,481	6,853	13,448	9,219

[1] Provisional.

Distribution of Danish foreign trade (in 1,000 kroner) according to countries of origin and destination, for calendar years:

Countries	Imports 1986	Imports 1987	Imports 1988[1]	Exports 1986	Exports 1987	Exports 1988[1]
Belgium	6,748,061	5,996,888	5,961,293	3,306,555	3,573,618	3,814,501
Finland	5,635,681	5,433,310	5,507,092	3,837,577	4,006,170	4,661,424
France	9,322,415	9,273,109	8,814,529	8,913,639	9,713,865	10,585,340
Germany (Fed. Rep.)	43,624,759	41,006,430	41,325,966	28,925,446	29,718,704	33,054,326
Norway	6,746,534	7,377,149	7,892,720	13,075,133	12,971,518	13,105,943
Sweden	22,784,336	21,267,090	21,840,830	19,480,514	20,114,801	21,544,852
Switzerland	3,956,279	3,730,737	3,888,221	3,559,544	4,094,550	4,303,161
UK	14,025,640	13,272,660	12,610,509	20,096,111	20,194,965	21,915,807
USA	9,700,211	9,305,670	9,297,642	14,558,022	12,385,059	10,842,544
Allied forces in Fed. Rep. Germany	—	—	365	193,114	187,811	180,515

[1] Provisional.

Total trade between Denmark (without the Faroe Islands) and UK (British Department of Trade returns, in £1,000 sterling):

	1985	1986	1987	1988	1989
Imports to UK	1,715,233	1,752,174	1,873,495	2,028,089	2,229,340
Exports and re-exports from UK	1,371,556	1,211,637	1,231,097	1,170,853	1,209,220

Tourism. In 1988, foreigners visiting Denmark spent some 14,232m. kroner. In 1988 foreigners spent 4·38m. nights in hotels and 3·21m. nights at camping sites.

Industrial Statistics. Danmarks Statistik. Copenhagen (annually)
Quarterly Statistics for the Industry: Commodity Statistics. Danmarks Statistik, Copenhagen
Statistics on Agriculture, Horticulture and Forestry. Danmarks Statistik. Copenhagen (annually)
Agricultural Statistics 1900–1965. Vol. I: *Agricultural Area and Harvest and Utilization of Fertilizers*.—Vol. II: *Livestock and Livestock Products, and Consumption of Feeding Stuffs*. Danmarks Statistik. Copenhagen, 1968–69
External Trade of Denmark. Danmarks Statistik, Copenhagen
Danish Industry in Facts and Figures. Federation of Danish Industries. Copenhagen (annually)
Energy Supply of Denmark, 1900–58 and *1948–65*. Danmarks Statistik. Copenhagen, 1959, 1967. Annual Supplements 1966–75 have been published in Statistical News
Report on Fisheries. Ministry of Fisheries, Copenhagen (annually)

COMMUNICATIONS

Roads. Denmark proper had (1 Jan. 1988), 599 km of motorways, 3,984 km of other state roads, 7,089 km of provincial roads and 58,816 km of commercial roads. Motor vehicles registered at 31 Dec. 1988 comprised 1,581,344 passenger cars, 293,543 lorries, 11,784 taxicabs (including 5,256 for private hire), 8,093 buses and 42,450 cycles.

Railways. In 1988 there were 2,344 km of State railways (199 km electrified), which carried 4,797m. passenger-km and 1,657m. tonne-km. There were also 494 km of private railways.

Aviation. On 1 Oct. 1950 the 3 Scandinavian airlines, Det Danske Luftfartsselskab, ABA and DNL, combined in Scandinavian Airlines System. In 1988 SAS flew 153m. km and carried 13,341,000 passengers.

SAS inaugurated its transpolar routes Copenhagen–Los Angeles on 15 Nov. 1954 and Copenhagen–Tokyo on 25 Feb. 1957, and its trans-Asian express route Copenhagen–Bangkok–Singapore *via* Tashkent on 4 Nov. 1967.

Shipping. On 31 Dec. 1987 the Danish merchant fleet consisted of 2,755 vessels (above 20 GRT) of 4,809,945 GRT.

In 1988, 35,479 vessels of 59m. GRT entered the Danish ports, unloading 41m. tonnes and loading 22m. tonnes of cargo; traffic by passenger ships and ferries is not included.

Post and Broadcasting. There were, in 1987, 1,292 post offices. On 31 Dec. 1987 the length of telephone circuits of private companies was 15,290,082 km. On 31 Dec. 1987 there were 4,248,862 telephone instruments. Postal revenues, 1987, 11,529m. kroner; expenditure, 9,538m. kroner.

Danmarks Radio is the government broadcasting station and is financed by licence fees. Television is broadcast by *Danmarks Radio* with colour programmes by PAL system. Number of receivers (1987): Combined radio and television, 1·94m., including 1·7m. colour sets; radio only, 0·09m.

Cinemas. In 1988 there were 381 cinema rooms with a seating capacity of 62,730.

Newspapers. In 1988 there were 46 daily newspapers with a combined circulation of 1·84m. on weekdays.

JUSTICE, RELIGION, EDUCATION AND WELFARE

Justice. The lowest courts of justice are organized in 82 tribunals *(byretter)*, where cases are dealt with by a single judge. The tribunals at Copenhagen have 34 judges, Aarhus 13, Odense 10, Aalborg 9, and the other tribunals have 1 to 6. Cases of greater consequence are dealt with by the superior courts *(Landsretterne)*; these courts are also courts of appeal for the above-named cases. Of superior courts there are two: *Østre Landsret* in Copenhagen with 46 judges, *Vestre Landret* in Viborg with 23 judges. From these an appeal lies to the Supreme Court *(Højesteret)* in Copenhagen, composed of 15 judges. Judges under 65 years of age can be removed only by judicial sentence.

In 1988, 14,853 men and 1,697 women were convicted of violations of the criminal code, fines not included. In 1988, the daily average population in penal institutions, local prisons, etc., was 3,283 men and 152 women, of whom 792 men and 52 women were on remand.

Religion. At the Reformation in 1536 the Danish Church ceased to exist as a legally independent unit, a part of the Roman Catholic Church, and became instead a Lutheran Church under the direction of the State. Since that time the State has, in one form or another, continued to exercise supreme authority in the affairs of the Church, and has regulated these by the passing of laws, by royal decree, or other appropriate means. The great majority of Danish citizens (about 90%) belongs to the National Church. Administratively, Denmark is divided into 10 dioceses each with a Bishop who, within the framework of the law, is the supreme diocesan authority in ecclesiastical affairs. The Bishop together with the Chief Administrative Officer of the county make up the diocesan governing body, responsible for all matters of ecclesiastical local finance and general administration. Bishops are appointed by the Crown after an election at which the clergy and parish council members of the diocese have had the opportunity of voting for the candidates nominated. Each diocese is divided into a number of deaneries (107 in the whole country) each with its Dean and Deanery Committee, who have certain financial powers. Local government at parish level (there are about 2,100 parishes in all) is in the hands of Parish Councils, who are elected for a 4-year period of office.

Since the Constitution of 1849 complete religious toleration is extended to every sect, and no civil disabilities attach to Dissenters.

Education. Education has been compulsory since 1814. The *folkeskole* (public primary and lower secondary school) comprises a pre-school class *(børnehaveklasse)*, a 9-year basic school corresponding to the period of compulsory education and a

1-year voluntary tenth form. Compulsory education may be fulfilled either through attending the *folkeskole* or private schools or through home-instruction, on the condition that the instruction given is comparable to that given in the *folkeskole*. The *folkeskole* is mainly a municipal school and no fees are paid. In the year 1987–88, 2,523 primary and lower secondary schools had 672,294 pupils and employed 63,400 teachers. 16% of the total number of schools were private schools and they were attended by 10% of the total number of pupils. The 9-year basic school is in practice not streamed. However, a certain differentiation may take place in the eighth and ninth forms.

On completion of the eighth and ninth forms the pupils may sit for the leaving examination of the *folkeskole (folkeskolens afgangsprøve)*. On completion of the tenth form the pupils may sit for either the leaving examination of the *folkeskole (folkeskolens afgangsprøve)* or the advanced leaving examination of the *folkeskole (folkeskolens udvidede afgangsprøve)*.

For 14–18 year olds there is an alternative of completing compulsory education at continuation schools, with the same leaving examinations as in the *folkeskole*. In the year 1987–88 there were 195 continuation schools with 15,019 pupils.

Under certain conditions the pupils may continue school either in the 3-year gymnasium (upper secondary school) or 2-year *studenterkursus* (adult upper secondary school) ending with *studentereksamen* (upper secondary school leaving examination) or in the 2-year higher preparatory examination course ending with the *højere forberedelseseksamen*. There were (1987–88) 161 of these upper secondary schools with 69,604 pupils.

Vocational education and training consists of apprenticeship training, *lærlingeuddannelse*; vocational education, *EFG-uddannelse*, consisting of a 1-year basic course, *EFG-basisår*, followed by a second part, *EFG-2.del*, and courses preparing for a vocation, leading to a diploma.

Vocational education and training cover courses in commerce and trade, iron and metal industry, chemical industry, construction industry, graphic industry, service trades, food industry, agriculture, horticulture, forestry and fishery, transport and communication, and health related auxiliary programmes.

In 1987–88 70,773 students were enrolled within trade and commerce, of whom 7,653 were in apprenticeship training and 45,755 in vocational education. 86,033 students were enrolled within technical education, of whom 36,311 were in apprenticeship training and 37,170 in vocational education. 17,365 students were admitted to the diploma courses within the field of trade and commerce, and 12,552 students were admitted to the technical diploma courses.

Tertiary education comprises all education after the 12th year of education, no matter whether the 3 years after the 9th form of the *folkeskole* have been spent on a course preparing for continued studies *(studentereksamen* or *højere forberedelseseksamen)*, or a course preparing for a vocation (*lærlingeuddannelse, EFG-uddannelse*, etc.). Tertiary education can be divided into 2 main groups, short courses of further education and long courses of higher education. There was a total of 27,180 students at short courses of further education.

There were 27 teacher-training colleges with 5,709 students and 26 colleges for training of teachers for kindergartens and leisure-time activities with 4,740 students.

Degree-courses in engineering: The Technical University of Denmark had 5,276 students. The Engineering Academy had 2,194 students and 8 engineering colleges had 6,261 students.

Universities: The University of Copenhagen (founded 1479) 23,918 students. The University of Aarhus (founded in 1928) 12,263 students. The University of Odense (founded in 1964) 5,634 students. Roskilde University Centre (founded in 1972) 2,647 students. Aalborg University Centre (founded in 1974) 5,328 students.

Other types of post-secondary education: The Royal Veterinary and Agricultural University had 2,509 students. The two dental colleges had 696 students. The Danish School of Pharmacy had 861 students. The 11 colleges of economics, business administration and modern languages had 23,067 students. The 2 schools of architecture had 1,677 students. Five academies of music had 827 students. Two schools of librarianship had 592 students. The Royal Danish School of Educational

Studies had 2,378 students. The 5 schools of social work had 741 students. The Danish School of Journalism had 766 students. Ten colleges of physical therapy had 1,374 students. Two schools of Midwifery Education had 117 students. Two colleges of home economics had 380 students. The School of Visual Arts had 147 students. Two schools of nursing had 397 students. Three military academies had 300 students.

Among adult education the most well-known are *Folkeskolehøjskoler*, folk high schools. Adult education in general programmes, single subjects (since 1978) and courses for semi-skilled workers and for skilled workers is organized by counties.

Andreseén, A., *The Danish Folk High School To-day*. Copenhagen, 1981
Struve, K., *Schools and Education in Denmark*. Copenhagen, 1981
Thorsen, L., *Public Libraries in Denmark*. English and French eds., Copenhagen, 1972

Social Security. The main body of Danish social welfare legislation is consolidated in 7 acts concerning (1) public health security, (2) sick-day benefits, (3) social pensions (for early retirement and old age), (4) employment injuries insurance, (5) employment services and unemployment insurance, (6) social assistance including assistance to handicapped, rehabilitation, child and juvenile guidance, day-care institutions, care of the aged and sick, and (7) family allowances.

Public health security, covering the entire population, provides free medical care, substantial subsidies for certain essential medicines together with some dental care and a funeral allowance. Hospitals are primarily municipal and the hospital treatment is normally free. All employed workers are granted daily sickness allowances, others can have limited daily sickness allowances. Daily cash benefits are granted in the case of temporary incapacity for work because of illness, injury or child-birth to all persons who earn an income derived from personal work. The benefit is paid at the rate of 90% of the average weekly earnings. There was a maximum rate of 2,397 kroner a week (July 1989).

Social pensions cover the entire population. Entitlement to old-age pensions at the full rates is subject to the condition that the beneficiary has been ordinarily resident in Denmark for a number of years (40). For a shorter period of residence, the benefits are reduced proportionally. The basic amount of the old-age pension in July 1989 was 82,488 kroner a year to married couples and 43,284 to single persons. Various supplementary allowances, depending on age and income, may be payable with the basic amount. Persons aged 55–66 may, depending on health and income, apply for an early-retirement pension. Persons over 67 years of age are entitled to the basic amount. The pensions to a married couple are calculated and paid to the husband and the wife separately. Early retirement pension to a disabled person is payable, having regard to the degree of disability, at a rate of up to 101,664 kroner to a single person. Early-retirement pensions may be subject to income regulation. The same applies to the basic amount of the old age pension to persons aged 67–69.

Employment injuries insurance provides for disablement or survivors' pensions and compensations. The scheme covers practically all employees.

Employment services are provided by regional public employment agencies. The insurance against unemployment provides daily allowances. The unemployment insurance funds had in Dec. 1989 a membership of 2,018,846.

The *Social Assistance Act* applies to the field of social legislation which rules the individually granted benefits in contrast to the other fields of social legislation which apply to fixed benefits.

Total social expenditure, including hospital and health services, statutory pensions, etc, amounted in the financial year 1986 to 185,440m. kroner.

Bibliography of Foreign Language Literature on Industrial Relations and Social Services in Denmark. Ministries of Labour and Social Affairs, Copenhagen, 1975
Social Conditions in Denmark. Vols. 1–8. Ministries of Labour and Social Affairs, Copenhagen
Marcussen, E., *Social Welfare in Denmark*. 4th ed. Copenhagen, 1980

THE FAROE ISLANDS
Føroyar/Færøerne

HISTORY. A Norwegian province to the peace treaty of 14 January 1814, the islands have been represented by 2 members in the Danish parliament since 1851, and in 1852 they obtained an elected assembly of their own, called *løgting*, which in 1948 secured a certain degree of home-rule within the Danish realm. The islands are not included in the EEC, but left EFTA together with Denmark on 31 Dec. 1972.

AREA AND POPULATION. The archipelago is situated due north of Scotland, 300 km from the Shetland Islands, 675 km from Norway and 450 km from Iceland, with a total land area of 1,399 sq. km (540 sq. miles). There are 17 inhabited islands (the main ones being Stremoy, Eysturoy, Vágoy, Suðuroy, Sandoy and Borðoy) and numerous islets, all mountainous and of volcanic origin. The census population in 1977 was 41,969; estimate (31 Dec. 1988) 47,663. The capital is Tórshavn (14,547 inhabitants on 31 Dec. 1988) on Stremoy. The inhabitants speak Faroese (føroyskt), a Scandinavian language which since 1948 has been the official language of the islands along with Danish.

CONSTITUTION AND GOVERNMENT. The parliament *(løgting)*, comprises 32 members elected by proportional representation by universal suffrage at age 18. The *løgting* elected on 8 Nov. 1988 consists of 8 People's Party, 7 Unionist Party, 7 Social-Democratic Party, 2 Autonomist Party, 6 Independence Party and 2 Christian People's Party. Parliament elects a government *(Landsstýri)* of at least 3 members which administers the home rule. Denmark is represented in the *løgting* by the chief administrator (*ríkisumboðsmaður*).

Chief Minister (Lømaður): Jøgvan Sundstein.

Local government is vested in the 50 *kommunur*, which have 29 or more inhabitants and income taxes of their own.

Flag: White with a red blue-edged Scandinavian cross.

ECONOMY

Budget. The 1988 Budget balanced at 3,151m. kr.

Currency. Since 1940 the currency has been the Faroese *krøna* (kr.) which remains freely interchangeable with the Danish krone.

ENERGY AND NATURAL RESOURCES

Electricity. There are 5 hydro-electric stations at Vestmanna on Stremoy and one at Eiði on Eysturoy. Total production (1988) 215·6m. kwh, of which hydro-electric 60·2m. kwh.

Agriculture. Only 2% of the surface is cultivated. The chief use is for grazing, the traditional mainstay of the economy. A small amount of potatoes is grown for home consumption. Livestock (1988): Sheep, 55,503; cattle, 2,176.

Fisheries. Deep sea fishing now forms the most important sector of the economy, primarily in the 200-mile exclusive zone but also off Greenland, Iceland, Svalbard and Newfoundland and in the Barents Sea. Total catch (1988) 357,000 tonnes, primarily cod, blue whiting, coalfish, prawns, mackerel and herring.

COMMERCE. The main industry is fishery. Exports, mainly fresh, frozen, filleted and salted fish, amounted to 2,345m. kr. in 1988; imports to 3,221m. kr. In 1988 Denmark supplied 39·6% of imports, Norway 21·1%, UK 8·2%, Sweden 6·3% and Federal Republic of Germany 5·8%; exports were mainly to Denmark (18·6%), UK (11·5%), Federal Republic of Germany (5·7%), USA (9·1%) and Norway (8%).

Total trade with UK (British Department of Trade returns, in £1,000 sterling):

	1985	*1986*	*1987*	*1988*	*1989*
Imports to UK	21,383	21,380	19,239	23,141	31,042
Exports and re-exports from UK	5,605	5,709	7,165	4,445	6,353

COMMUNICATIONS

Roads. In 1988 there were 433 km of roads, 14,232 passenger cars and 3,445 commercial vehicles.

Aviation. The airport is on Vágoy, from which there are regular services to Copenhagen and Reykjavík.

Shipping. The chief port is Tórshavn, with smaller ports at Klaksvik, Vestmanna, Skálafjørður, Tvøroyri, Vágur and Fuglafjørður.

Post and Broadcasting. In 1988 there were 20,816 telephones. *Utvarp Føroya* broadcasts from Tórshavn about 40 hours a week on 4 transmitters. In 1988 there were 17,000 radio and 11,000 television receivers.

RELIGION, EDUCATION AND WELFARE

Religion. About 80% are Evangelical Lutherans and 20% are Plymouth Brethren or belong to small communities of Roman Catholics, Pentecostal, Adventists, Jehovah Witnesses and Bahai.

Education. In 1988–89 there were 5,440 primary and 2,979 secondary school pupils with 601 teachers.

Health. In 1988 there were 87 doctors, 39 dentists, 10 pharmacists, 17 midwives and 344 nursing personnel. In 1989 there were 3 hospitals with 369 beds.

Further Reading

Årbog for Færøerne. 1986
Føroya landsstýri: Arsfrágreiðing 1988. Tórshavn 1989
Faroes in Figures. Thorshavn, annual, from 1956
Rutherford, G. K., (ed.) *The Physical Environment of the Færoe Islands.* The Hague, 1982
Wang, Z., *Stjórnmálafrøði.* Tórshavn, 1989
West, J. F., *Faroe.* London, 1973
Wylie, J., *The Faroe Islands: Interpretations of History.* Lexington, 1987
Young, G. V. C. and Clewer, C. R., *Faroese-English Dictionary.* Peel, 1985

GREENLAND
Grønland/Kalaallit Nunaat

HISTORY. A Danish possession since 1380, Greenland became on 5 June 1953 an integral part of the Danish kingdom. Following a referendum in Jan. 1979, home rule was introduced from 1 May 1979, and full internal self-government was attained in Jan. 1981 after a transitional period.

AREA AND POPULATION. Area 2,175,600 sq. km (840,000 sq. miles), made up of 1,833,900 sq. km of ice cap and 341,700 sq. km of ice-free land. The population, 1 Jan. 1989, numbered 55,171; West Greenland, 49,976; East Greenland, 3,425; North Greenland (Thule), 849, and 921 not belonging to any specific municipality. Of the total, 9,542 were born outside Greenland. Capital, Godthaab (Nuuk), 12,426.

CONSTITUTION. At the introduction of home rule, the council *(landsråd)* was replaced by a parliament *(landstinget)*. At the elections held on 26 May 1987 for the Parliament, the *Siumut* gained 11 seats, the *Atassut*, 11 seats, the *Inuit Ataqatigiit*, 4 seats and the *Isittup Partii-a* the remaining 1 seat. The Premier, Jonathan Motzfeldt, formed a 6-member administration, *Landsstyre*. Denmark is represented by an appointed commissioner.

ECONOMY

Budget. The Budget for 1987 balanced at 2,861m. kroner.

Currency. The Danish kroner remains the legal currency.

ENERGY AND NATURAL RESOURCES

Electricity. Production (1984) 181·7m. kwh.

Fisheries. In 1988 the catch totalled 133,500 tonnes.

INDUSTRY. Until the beginning of this century, the hunting of land and sea mammals, especially seals, was the main occupation of the population; now fishing is most important. Fish-processing industries, construction and trade are also important occupations.

Coal production ceased in 1972. A deposit of the valuable mineral cryolite has been mined at Ivigtut. The mine is now worked out. In 1973 the Danish company Greenex A/S began producing lead and zinc concentrate near Umanak. Annual production of lead and zinc concentrates was in 1988 about 34,000 tonnes and 136,000 tonnes respectively.

Public authorities are investigating possibilities of hydro-electric power and there are other private prospectors for various minerals.

COMMERCE. Imports (c.i.f. Greenland) (in 1m. kroner): 1979, 1,448; 1980, 1,848; 1981, 2,096; 1982, 2,319; 1983, 2,421; 1984, 2,836; 1985, 3,140; 1986, 2,951; 1987, 3,471; 1988 (provisional), 3,420. Exports (f.o.b. Greenland) (in 1m. kroner): 1979, 867; 1980, 1,199; 1981, 1,325; 1982, 1,432; 1983, 1,653; 1984, 1,751; 1985, 1,842; 1986, 2,101; 1987, 2,370; 1988 (provisional), 2,630. Trade is mainly with Denmark.

Total trade with UK (British Department of Trade returns, in £1,000 sterling):

	1985	*1986*	*1987*	*1988*	*1989*
Imports to UK	3,168	4,789	838	1,430	3,793
Exports and re-exports from UK	348	452	735	1,151	1,487

COMMUNICATIONS

Roads. There were (1970) 150 km of roads, of which 60 km were paved.

Aviation. There is an international airport at Søndre Srømfjord, and about 12 local airports with scheduled services.

Broadcasting. *Grønlands Radio* broadcasts in Greenlandic and Danish. The short wave transmitters are located at Godthaab. Several towns have local television stations. In 1988 there were 15,757 telephones, (1984) 10,000 television sets and (1984) 13,500 radio sets.

JUSTICE, RELIGION, EDUCATION AND WELFARE

Justice. The High Court *(Landsret)* in Godthaab comprises one professional judge and 2 lay magistrates, while there are 18 district courts under lay assessors.

Religion. About 98% of the population are Evangelical Lutherans.

Education. There were (1988–89) 8,967 pupils in primary comprehensive schools, of whom 7,459 were in the course of compulsory education (9 years). On 1 Sept. 1988, 2,297 students were enrolled in vocational training.

Health. The medical service is free to all inhabitants. There is a central hospital in Godthaab and 15 smaller district hospitals. In 1987 there were 65 doctors and 556 hospital beds.

Further Reading

Greenland. R. Danish Ministry of Greenland. Copenhagen. Annual from 1968

Indkomst-og erhvervsforholdene i Grønland ved Hjemmestyrets indførelse (Income and Business Conditions in Greenland at the Introduction of Home Rule), Statistiske Undersøgelser nr. 40, Danmarks Statistik 1984

Meddelelser om Grønland. Ed. Kommissionen for videnskabelige undersøgelser i Grønland. Copenhagen, 1899 ff. Since 1979 issued in 3 separate series: 'Bioscience', 'Geoscience' and 'Man and Society'

Statistiske Efterretninger (Statistical News), from 1983 special series: *Færøerne og Grønland* (Faroe Islands and Greenland)

Gad, F., *A History of Greenland.* Vol. 1. London, 1970.—Vol. 2. London, 1973

Hertling, K. (ed.) *Greenland Past and Present.* Copenhagen, 1970

DIPLOMATIC REPRESENTATIVES

Of Denmark in Great Britain (55 Sloane St., London, SW1X 9SR)
Ambassador: Rudolph Thorning-Petersen (accredited 1 Nov. 1989).

Of Great Britain in Denmark (36–40 Kastelsvej, DK-2100, Copenhagen)
Ambassador: N. C. R. Williams, CMG.

Of Denmark in the USA (3200 Whitehaven St., NW, Washington, D.C., 20008)
Ambassador: Peter Pedersen Dyvig.

Of the USA in Denmark (Dag Hammarskjolds Alle 24, Copenhagen)
Ambassador: Keith L. Brown.

Of Denmark to the United Nations
Ambassador: Kjeld Vilhelm Mortensen.

Further Reading

Statistical Information: Danmarks Statistik (Sejrøgade 11, 2100 Copenhagen Ø.) was founded in 1849 and reorganized in 1966 as an independent institution; it is administratively placed under the Minister of Economic Affairs. *Chief:* N. V. Skak-Nielsen. Its main publications are: *Statistisk Årbog* (Statistical Yearbook). From 1896; *Statistiske Efterretninger* (Statistical News). *Statistiske Månedsoversigt* Monthly Review of Statistics), *Statistisk hårsoversigt* (Statistical Ten-Year Review).

Ministry of Foreign Affairs, *Danish Foreign Office Journal. Commercial and General Review.—Denmark.* 1961.—*Economic Survey of Denmark* (annual).—*Facts About Denmark.* 1959.—Hæstrup, J., *From Occupied to Ally: the Danish Resistance Movement.* 1963

Bibliografi over Danmarks Offentlige Publikationer. Institut for International Udveksling, Copenhagen. Annual

Dania polyglotta. Annual Bibliography of Books ... in Foreign Languages Printed in Denmark. State Library, Copenhagen. Annual

Kongelig Dansk Hof og Statskalender. Copenhagen. Annual

Brynildsen, F., *A Dictionary of the English and Dano-Norwegian Languages.* 2 vols. Copenhagen, 1902–07

Danstrup, J., *History of Denmark.* 2nd ed. Copenhagen, 1949

Johansen, H. C., *The Danish Economy in the Twentieth Century.* London, 1987

Krabbe, L., *Histoire de Danemark.* Copenhagen and Paris, 1950

Miller, K. E., *Denmark.* [Bibliography] Oxford and Santa Barbara, 1987

Nielsen, B. K., *Engelsk–Dansk Ordbog.* Copenhagen, 1964

Trap, J. P., *Kongeriget Danmark.* 5th ed. 11 vols. Copenhagen, 1953 ff.

Vinterberg, H. and Bodelsen, C. A., *Dansk-Engelsk Ordbog.* Copenhagen, 1966

National Library: Det Kongelige Bibliotek, Copenhagen. *Librarian:* P. Birkelund.

DJIBOUTI

Capital: Djibouti
Population: 484,000 (1988)
GNP per capita: US$760 (1984)

Jumhouriyya Djibouti

HISTORY. At a referendum held on 19 March 1967, 60% of the electorate voted for continued association with France rather than independence and the new statute for the territory came into being on 5 July 1967. In Jan. 1976, following discussions between Ali Aref and President Giscard d'Estaing, it was announced that the French Government affirmed that the Territory of the Afars and the Issas was destined for independence but no date was fixed. Legislative elections were held on 8 May and independence as the Republic of Djibouti was achieved on 27 June 1977.

AREA AND POPULATION. Djibouti is bounded north-east by the Gulf of Aden, south-east by Somalia and all other sides by Ethiopia.

Djibouti has an area of 23,200 sq. km (8,958 sq. miles). The population was estimated in 1988 at 484,000, of whom 47% were Somali (Issa), 37% Afar, 8% European (mainly French) and 6% Arab. There were (1987) about 13,000 refugees from Ethiopia. Djibouti, the seat of government, had (1988) 290,000 inhabitants; other towns are Tadjoura, Obock, Dikhil and Ali-Sabieh. There are 5 administrative districts.

CLIMATE. Conditions are hot throughout the year, with very little rain. Djibouti. Jan. 78°F (25·6°C), July 96°F (35·6°C). Annual rainfall 5" (130 mm).

CONSTITUTION AND GOVERNMENT. Under an organic law approved by the Constituent Assembly on 10 Feb. 1981, the President is directly elected for a 6-year term (renewable once) and the Constituent Assembly became a 65-member Chamber of Deputies, with a 5-year term. In Oct. 1981, the Assembly declared Djibouti a one-Party state, the ruling Party being the *Rassemblement Populaire pour le Progrès*. Elections for the Chamber of Deputies were held 21 May 1982, when 26 Somali, 23 Afar and 16 Arab members were elected.

President: Hassan Gouled Aptidon (elected 1977 and re-elected 1981 and 1987).

The Council of Ministers in Oct. 1989 was composed as follows:

Prime Minister, Planning and Land Development: Barkat Gourad Hamadou.

Interior, Posts and Telecommunications: Khaireh Alleleh Hared. *Justice and Islamic Affairs:* Elaf Orbiss Ali. *Foreign Affairs and Co-operation:* Moumin Bahdon Farah. *Defence:* Hussein Barkad Siraj. *Commerce:* Moussa Bourale Roble. *Finance:* Muhammad Djama Elabe. *Civil Service:* Ismail Ali Youssouf. *Industry:* Salem Abdou. *Labour:* Ahmed Ibrahim Ardi. *Education:* Suleiman Farah Lodon. *Agriculture:* Muhammad Moussa Chehem. *Public Works:* Ahmed Aden Youssouf. *Health:* Ougoure Hassan Ibrahim. *Ports:* Bourhan Ali Warki. *Youth:* Omar Chirdon Abass.

National flag: Horisontally blue over green, with a white triangle based on the hoist charged with a red star.

DEFENCE

Army. The Army comprises 1 infantry battalion, 1 armoured squadron, 1 support battalion, 1 border commando battalion and 1 parachute company. Equipment includes 45 armoured cars. The strength of the Army (of which the Navy and Air Force form part) was (1990) 2,970 men. There is also a paramilitary gendarmerie of some 1,200 men.

Navy. A coastal patrol is maintained consisting of 3 minor landing craft and 5 inshore patrol craft. Personnel (1989) 60.

Air Force. There is a small air force, all equipment *via* French aid. There are 2 CASA Aviocar and 2 Noratlas transports, 1 Falcon 20 VIP aircraft, 1 Cessna 206 for liaison, 1 Rallye trainer, and 5 helicopters (Alouette II and Ecureuil). Personnel (1990) 100.

INTERNATIONAL RELATIONS

Membership. Djibouti is a member of UN, OAU, the Arab League and an ACP State of the EEC.

ECONOMY

Budget. Revenue for 1986 was 24,494m. Djibouti francs and expenditure 23,133m.

Currency. The currency is the *Djibouti franc*. In March 1990, £1 = 291 *Djibouti francs*; US$1 = 178 *Djibouti francs*.

Banking. The Banque Nationale de Djibouti is the bank of issue. There are 6 commercial banks.

ENERGY AND NATURAL RESOURCES

Electricity. Production (1986) 140m. kwh. Installed capacity 80,100 kw.

Minerals. Minerals supposed to exist are gypsum, mica, amethyst and sulphur.

Agriculture. Mainly market gardening at the oasis of Ambouli and near urban areas. Tomato production (1988) 1,000 tonnes. Livestock (1988): 70,000 cattle, 414,000 sheep, 500,000 goats, 8,000 donkeys, 58,000 camels.

Fisheries. The catch in 1984 was 426 tonnes.

INDUSTRY AND TRADE

Industry. In 1986 there were 2,134 persons employed in construction and 1,235 in manufacturing.

Commerce. The main economic activity is the operation of the port. The chief imports are cotton goods, sugar, cement, flour, fuel oil and vehicles; the chief exports are hides, cattle and coffee (transit from Ethiopia). Trade in 1m. Djibouti francs:

	1983	*1984*	*1985*	*1986*
Imports	39,307	39,425	35,670	33,106
Exports	1,919	2,362	2,488	3,628

Total trade between Djibouti and UK (British Department of Trade returns, in £1,000 sterling):

	1985	*1986*	*1987*	*1988*	*1989*
Imports to UK	293	53	175	169	489
Exports and re-exports from UK	21,546	12,537	12,501	8,479	10,555

Tourism. There were 21,790 visitors in 1987.

COMMUNICATIONS

Roads. There were (1987) 3,037 km of roads, of which 412 km were hard-surfaced. In 1987 there were 11,799 passenger cars and 1,501 commercial vehicles.

Railway. For the line Djibouti–Addis Ababa, of which 106 km lies within Djibouti *see* p. 464. In 1987 the railway carried 291,700 tonnes of freight and 1,295,000 passengers.

Aviation. Air Djibouti provides services to Addis Ababa, Nairobi, Jidda and the Gulf. Other airlines serving Djibouti international airport (Ambouli) are Ethiopian Airlines, Air France, Air Tanzania and Yemen Airways Corporation. In 1987,

67,856 passengers and 6,036 tonnes of freight arrived at Ambouli, and 61,518 passengers and 1,612 tonnes of freight departed.

Shipping. In 1986 there entered at Djibouti 1,723 vessels, unloading 466,000 tonnes and loading 155,000 tonnes of merchandise. In 1981 the merchant marine comprised 8 vessels of 3,185 GRT. Djibouti became a free port in 1981.

Post and Broadcasting. Number of telephones (1987), 4,452. *Radiodiffusion-Télévision de Djibouti* broadcasts on medium- and short-waves in French, Somali, Afar and Arabic. There is a television transmitter in Djibouti, broadcasting for 36 hours a week. Number of receivers (1985): Radio, 30,000; TV, 10,000.

JUSTICE, RELIGION, EDUCATION AND WELFARE

Justice. There is a Court of First Instance and a Court of Appeal in the capital. The judicial system is based on Islamic law.

Religion. The vast majority of the population is Moslem, with about 24,000 Roman Catholics.

Education. In 1987–88 there were 26,173 pupils and 592 teachers at primary schools, 6,327 pupils and 307 teachers at secondary and technical schools. There were 117 students in teacher training with 13 lecturers.

Health. In 1987 there were 29 hospitals and dispensaries with 1,285 beds, 89 physicians, 10 dentists and 15 pharmacists.

DIPLOMATIC REPRESENTATIVES

Of Djibouti in Great Britain
Chargé d'Affaires: Foudha Abdoulatif (resides in Paris).

Of Great Britain in Djibouti
Ambassador: M. A. Marshall (resides in San'a).

Of the USA in Djibouti (Plateau du Serpent Blvd., Djibouti)
Ambassador: Robert S. Barrett IV.

Of Djibouti to the United Nations and in the USA
Ambassador: Roble Olhaye.

Further Reading

Poinsot, J.-P., *Djibouti et la Côte française des Somalis.* Paris, 1965
Schraeder, P. J., *Djibouti.* [Bibliography] Oxford and Santa Barbara, 1989
Thompson, V. and Adloff, R., *Djibouti and the Horn of Africa.* Stanford Univ. Press, 1967

COMMONWEALTH OF DOMINICA

Capital: Roseau
Population: 81,200 (1988)
GNP per capita: US$1,650 (1988)

HISTORY. Dominica was discovered by Columbus. It was a British possession from 1805, a member of the Federation of the West Indies 1958–62, an Associated State of the UK, 1967–78 and became an independent republic as the Commonwealth of Dominica on 3 Nov. 1978.

AREA AND POPULATION. Dominica is an island in the Windward group of the West Indies situated between Martinique and Guadeloupe. It has an area of 751 sq. km (290 sq. miles) and a population at the 1981 Census of 74,851; estimate (1988) 81,200. The chief town, Roseau, had 8,279 inhabitants in 1981.

The population is mainly of Negro and mixed origins, with small white and Asian minorities. There is a Carib settlement of about 500, almost entirely of mixed blood.

CLIMATE. A tropical climate, with pleasant conditions between Dec. and March, but there is a rainy season from June to Oct., when hurricanes may occur. Rainfall is heavy, with coastal areas having 70" (1,750 mm) but the mountains may have up to 250" (6,250 mm). Roseau. Jan. 76°F (24·2°C), July 81°F (27·2°C). Annual rainfall 78" (1,956 mm).

CONSTITUTION AND GOVERNMENT. The House of Assembly has 21 elected and 9 nominated members. The Speaker is elected from among the members of the House or from outside. The Cabinet is presided over by the Prime Minister and consists of 6 other Ministers including the Attorney-General (official member). Elections were held in July 1985. The Dominica Freedom Party won 15 seats, the Dominica Labour Party 5 seats and the United Dominica Labour Party 1 seat.

President: Sir Clarence Seignoret.

The Cabinet in Nov. 1989 was composed as follows:

Prime Minister and Minister for Finance, Economic Development and External Affairs: Mary Eugenia Charles.

Attorney-General and Minister for Legal Affairs and Labour: Brian G. K. Alleyne. *Agriculture, Trade, Industry and Tourism:* Charles A. Maynard. *Health, Water, Sewerage and Fire:* Ronan David. *Community Development and Social Affairs:* Heskeith Alexander. *Education and Sports:* Henry George. *Housing, Communications and Works, Electricity, Telecommunications and Feeder Roads:* Alleyne Carbon.

National flag: Green with a cross over all of yellow, black, and white pieces, and in the centre a red disc charged with a Sisserou parrot in natural colours within a ring of 10 green yellow-bordered stars.

INTERNATIONAL RELATIONS

Membership. The Commonwealth of Dominica is a member of UN, OAS, CARICOM, the Commonwealth and is an ACP state of EEC.

ECONOMY

Budget. In 1988-89 revenue, EC$105·9m. and expenditure, EC$101·4m.

Currency. The French *franc,* the £ sterling and the East Caribbean *dollar* are legal tender. In March 1990, EC$2·71 = US$1 and EC$4·40 = £1.

Banking. Savings bank (Dec. 1982), 2,862 depositors, with $593,659 deposits. There are branches of Barclays Bank International and Royal Bank of Canada in

Roseau, and branches of Barclays and National Commercial and Development Bank at Portsmouth. The National Commercial and Development Bank was opened in 1977 and Banque Française Commerciale opened in 1979.

ENERGY AND NATURAL RESOURCES

Electricity. Production (1987) 16m. kwh.

Agriculture. Hurricanes in 1979 and 1980 devastated large agricultural areas and damaged infrastructure. Production (1988): Bananas, 66,000 tonnes; coconuts, 14,000; beef (1987) 439; pork (1987) 420. Livestock (1988): Cattle, 9,000; pigs, 5,000; sheep, 9,000; goats, 10,000; poultry (1986), 115,000.

INDUSTRY AND TRADE

Industry. The main industries are agriculture and tourism.

Commerce (1987). Imports, EC$179,215,824; exports and re-exports, EC$129,590,586. Chief products: Bananas, soap, fruit juices, essential oils, coconuts, vegetables, fruit and fruit preparations, and alcoholic drinks.

Total trade between Dominica and UK (British Department of Trade returns, in £1,000 sterling):

	1986	*1987*	*1988*	*1989*
Imports to UK	26,612	37,083	32,423	23,709
Exports and re-exports from UK	8,780	10,431	8,416	8,727

Tourism. Tourists (1987) totalled 41,200.

COMMUNICATIONS

Roads. In 1988 there were 470 miles of road and 280 miles of track. Vehicles totalled (Oct. 1988) 6,933.

Post and Broadcasting. Telephone lines, 210 route miles; number of telephones, 7,700 (Oct. 1988). Radio receivers (1982) 13,405.

Cinemas. In 1987 there was 1 cinema with a seating capacity of 1,000.

JUSTICE, RELIGION, EDUCATION AND WELFARE

Justice. There are 12 magistrates' courts. There is also a supreme court which dealt with 60 criminal and 307 civil cases in 1987–88. The police force consists of 10 officers and 431 other ranks.

Religion. 80% of the population is Roman Catholic.

Education. In 1987–88 there were 65 primary schools with 15,262 pupils and 10 secondary schools with 3,251 pupils, and 2 colleges of higher education.

Health. In Sept. 1988 there were 3 hospitals with 245 beds, 31 doctors, 4 dentists, 10 pharmacists, 273 nursing personnel, 7 health centres and 44 health clinics.

DIPLOMATIC REPRESENTATIVES

Of Great Britain in Dominica
High Commissioner: K. F. X. Burns, CMG (resides in Bridgetown).

Of Dominica in the USA
Ambassador: McDonald P. Benjamin.

Of Dominica in Great Britain and to the United Nations
High Comm. Ambassador: Franklin Andrew Baron (resides in Roseau).

Further Reading

Myres, R. A., *Dominica.* [Bibliography] Oxford and Santa Barbara, 1987

Library: Public Library, Roseau. *Librarian:* Mrs. C. Williams.

DOMINICAN REPUBLIC

Capital: Santo Domingo
Population: 6·7m. (1987)
GNP per capita: US$680 (1988)

República Dominicana

HISTORY. On 5 Dec. 1492 Columbus discovered the island of Santo Domingo, which he called La Española; for a time it was called Hispaniola. The city of Santo Domingo, founded by his brother, Bartholomew, in 1496, is the oldest city in the Americas. The western third of the island—now the Republic of Haiti—was later occupied and colonized by the French, to whom the Spanish colony of Santo Domingo was also ceded in 1795. In 1808 the Dominican population, under the command of Gen. Juan Sánchez Ramirez, routed an important French military force commanded by Gen. Ferrand, at the famous battle of Palo Hincado. This battle was the beginning of the end for French rule in Santo Domingo and culminated in the successful siege of the capital. Eventually, with the aid of a British naval squadron, the French were forced to capitulate and the colony returned again to Spanish rule, from which it declared its independence in 1821. It was invaded and held by the Haitians from 1822 to 1844, when they were expelled, and the Dominican Republic was founded and a constitution adopted. Independence day 27 Feb. 1844. Great Britain, in 1850, was the first country to recognize the Dominican Republic. The country was occupied by American Marines from 1916 until 1924. In 1936 the name of the capital city was changed from Santo Domingo to Ciudad Trujillo; and back again in 1961.

AREA AND POPULATION. The Dominican Republic occupies the eastern portion (about two-thirds) of the island of Hispaniola, Quisqueya or Santo Domingo, the western division forming the Republic of Haiti.

Area is 48,442 sq. km (18,700 sq. miles) with 870 miles of coastline, 193 miles of frontier line with Haiti (marked out in 1936).

The populations of the 26 provinces and National District at the 1981 census, and the 3 new provinces with estimates for 1987, were:

La Altagracia	100,112	Pedernales	17,006
Azua	142,770	Peravia	168,123
Bahoruco	78,636	Puerto Plata	206,757
Barahona	137,160	La Romana	109,769
Dajabón	57,709	Salcedo	99,191
Districto Nacional	1,550,739	Samaná	65,699
Duarte	235,544	Sánchez Ramírez	126,567
Espaillat	164,017	San Cristóbal	446,132
La Estrelleta	65,384	San Juan	239,957
Hato Mayor	76,023 [1]	San Pedro de Macorís	152,890
Independencia	38,768	Santiago	550,372
María Trinidad Sánchez	112,629	Santiago Rodríguez	55,411
Monseñor Nouel	121,906 [1]	El Seibo	157,866
Monte Cristi	83,407	Valverde	100,319
Monte Plata	170,758 [1]	La Vega	385,043

[1] Estimate, 1987.

Census (1981) 5,647,977. Estimate (1987) 6,708,000.

Population of the principal municipalities (Census 1981): Santo Domingo, the capital, 1,313,172; Santiago de los Caballeros, 278,638; La Romana, 91,571; San Pedro de Macoris, 78,562; San Francisco de Macoris, 64,906; La Vega, 52,432; San Juan de la Managuana, 49,764; Barahona, 49,334; Puerto Plata, 45,348.

The population is partly of Spanish descent, but is mainly composed of a mixed race of European and African blood.

CLIMATE. A tropical maritime climate with most rain falling in the summer months. The rainy season extends from May to Nov. and amounts are greatest in the north and east. Hurricanes may occur from June to Nov. Santo Domingo. Jan. 75°F (23·9°C), July 81°F (27·2°C). Annual rainfall 56" (1,400 mm).

CONSTITUTION AND GOVERNMENT. A new Constitution was promulgated on 28 Nov. 1966.

The President is elected for 4 years, by direct vote. In case of death, resignation or disability, he is succeeded by the Vice-president. There are 12 secretaries of state, a judicial adviser with secretary-of-state rank and 2 ministers without portfolio in charge of departments. Citizens are entitled to vote at the age of 18, or less when married.

At the general elections held in May 1986, 56 seats were won by the *Partido Reformista Social Cristiano*, 48 by the *Partido Revolucionario Dominicano*, and 16 seats by the *Partido de la Liberación Dominicana*.

There is a bicameral legislature, comprising a 27-member Senate and a 120-member Chamber of Deputies, both elected for 4-year terms at the same date as the President.

President: Dr Joaquín Balaguer (elected 16 May 1986; took office 16 Aug.).
Foreign Affairs: Joaquín Ricardo García.

National flag: Blue, red; quartered by a white cross.

National anthem: Quisqueyanos valientes, alzemos (words by E. Prud'homme; tune by J. Reyes, 1883).

Local Government: The republic consists of a National District (containing the capital, Santo Domingo, and surrounding areas) and 29 provinces, divided into 97 municipalities.

DEFENCE

Army. The Army has a strength (1989) of about 13,000. It is organized in 4 infantry brigades and 1 artillery, 1 engineer and 1 armoured battalions. There were (1989) some light tanks and armoured cars.

Navy. The Navy largely comprises former US vessels. The combatant force consists of 1 very old frigate (built 1944) acting as the staff flagship, 3 armed *ex*-US netlayers converted to offshore patrol, and 11 inshore patrol craft. There is 1 utility landing craft and support is provided by 2 oilers, 1 ocean tug, and some 12 harbour and service craft. Personnel in 1989 totalled 4,000 officers and men.

Air Force. The Air Force, with HQ at San Isidoro, has 1 combat squadron with 8 Cessna A-37s; 1 squadron with a total of about 12 Bell 205A-1, OH-6A and Alouette II/III helicopters; 1 transport squadron with 3 C-47s and some smaller communications aircraft; a Presidential Dauphin 2 helicopter; and an assortment of trainers, including 10 T-34B Mentors, 5 Cessna T-41s and 2 T-6 Texans. Personnel strength was (1990) 3,800.

INTERNATIONAL RELATIONS

Membership. The Dominican Republic is a member of UN and OAS.

ECONOMY

Budget. Expenditure (1986) RD$2,251m. and revenue RD$2,113m. In 1985 external debt was RD$3,551m.

Currency. In Oct. 1947 the *peso oro*, then equal to the US$, was formally made the unit of currency. In March 1990, £1 = RD$13·86; US$1 = RD$8·46.

There are silver coins for 50, 25 and 10 centavos, a copper-nickel 5-centavo piece and a copper 1-centavo piece.

Banking. There are 4 foreign banks—the Royal Bank of Canada with 12 branches, the Bank of Nova Scotia with 11 branches, the Citibank with 6 branches, the Chase Manhattan Bank with 7 branches and the Bank of America with 4 branches. An agricultural and mortgage bank, with paid-up capital of RD$500,000, was established in 1945; in 1950 its capital was increased to RD$5m. In 1947 the Central Bank of the Dominican Republic was established. A Banco Popular Dominicano, with an authorized capital of RD$5m., opened in Jan. 1964.

Weights and Measures. The metric system was nominally adopted on 1 Aug. 1913, but English and Spanish units have remained in common use in ordinary commercial transactions; on 17 Sept. 1954 a more drastic law requiring the decimal metric system was passed.

ENERGY AND NATURAL RESOURCES

Electricity. In 1986, 3,800m. kwh. of electricity was generated. Supply 110 and 220 volts; 60 Hz.

Minerals. Bauxite output in 1982 was 152,250 tonnes. Silver and platinum have been found, and near Neiba there are several hills of rock salt. Ferronickel production (1986) 58,000 tonnes. Production of gold (1986) 285,458 troy oz.; silver, 1,356,000.

Agriculture. Agriculture and its processing industries are the chief source of wealth, sugar cultivation being the principal industry. Of the total area (1984) meadows and pastures, 43%; permanant cultivation, 30%; forestry 13%.

Livestock in 1988: 2,129,000 cattle, 409,000 pigs, 100,000 sheep.

Sugar-cane production, 1988, was 8·3m. tonnes. Coffee is exported mainly to USA. Output, 1988, 54,000 tonnes. Production of rice for home consumption and export is fostered; output, 1988, 463,000 tonnes. Cocoa is the second principal crop and covers 2m. *tareas* (340,000 acres); output in 1988, 39,000 tonnes. There are useful crops of yucca and beans for local consumption. Scientific growing of bananas (1988: 391,000 tonnes) and of leaf tobacco (1988: 30,000 tonnes) is progressing.

Fisheries. The total catch (1986) was 17,200 tonnes.

INDUSTRY AND TRADE

Industry. Important products are sugar (89,100 of refined sugar in 1985), cement (960,000 tonnes in 1981). Value of textile manufactures (1983), RD$30·4m.; tobacco products, RD$63·5m.

Commerce. Total imports and exports in RD$1m. (equal to US$1m.):

	1981	*1982*	*1983*	*1984*	*1985*
Imports	1,450·2	1,255·8	1,297·0	1,257·1	1,285·9
Exports	1,188·0	767·7	785·9	868·1	739·3

The principal exports in 1983 were (in RD$1m.): Sugar, 263·5; coffee, 76·3; ferronickel, 83·5; Doré, 164·5.

Total trade between the Dominican Republic and UK (British Department of Trade returns, in £1,000 sterling):

	1985	*1986*	*1987*	*1988*	*1989*
Imports to UK	7,900	7,599	8,637	8,523	11,223
Exports and re-exports from UK	14,595	15,178	23,887	17,235	25,519

Tourism. About 1m. tourists visited the Dominican Republic in 1987.

COMMUNICATIONS

Roads. Total length of roads (1985) 17,120 km. There were 102,000 cars and 61,000 commercial vehicles in 1984.

Railways. Some 142 km of the Dominican Government Railway remains in use between La Vega and the port of Sánchez. Twelve lines, including the Central Romana Railway, exist to serve the sugar industry, totalling 1,600 km.

Aviation. The country is reached from the American continent and the Caribbean islands by 8 international airlines and in 1987 there were 4 airports. Two local aviation companies provide interior services and connect Santo Domingo with San Juan in Puerto Rico, Curaçao, Aruba and Miami.

Shipping. Santo Domingo is the leading port; Puerto Plata ranks next. In 1971, vessels of 9,833,000 tons entered the ports to discharge 3,009,000 tonnes of cargo, and vessels of 5,276,000 tons cleared the ports having loaded 1,986,000 tonnes.

Post and Broadcasting. Number of telephone instruments (1983), 175,054, of which 138,169 in Santo Domingo. The telegraph has a total length of about 500 km, privately owned; they have been leased to All-America Cables, Inc., which also controls submarine cables connecting, in the north, Puerto Plata with Puerto Rico and New York, and in the south, Santo Domingo with Puerto Rico, Cuba and Curaçao.

There were (1989) more than 90 broadcasting stations in Santo Domingo and other towns; this includes the 2 government stations. There are 4 television stations. In 1986 there were 800,000 radio and 500,000 television receivers.

Newspapers (1985). There were 9 daily newspapers with a circulation of 208,000.

JUSTICE, RELIGION, EDUCATION AND WELFARE

Justice. The judicial power resides in the Supreme Court of Justice, the courts of appeal, the courts of first instance, the communal courts and other tribunals created by special laws, such as the land courts. The Supreme Court consists of a president and 8 judges chosen by the Senate, and the procurator-general, appointed by the executive; it supervises the lower courts. Each province forms a judicial district, as does the *Distrito Nacional*, and each has its own procurator fiscal and court of first instance; these districts are subdivided, in all, into 72 municipalities and 18 municipal districts, each with one or more local justices. The death penalty was abolished in 1924.

Religion. The religion of the state is Roman Catholic; other forms of religion are permitted.

Education. Primary instruction (5,956 schools) is free and obligatory for children between 7 and 14 years of age; there are also secondary, normal, vocational and special schools, all of which are either wholly maintained by the State or state-aided; in 1985, primary schools had 28,000 teachers and 1,220,000 pupils and there were 11,754 teachers and 438,922 pupils in secondary schools.

The University of Santo Domingo (founded 1538) and 5 other universities had 88,000 students in 1985–86.

Health. There were, in 1980, 2,142 doctors and 8,953 hospital beds.

DIPLOMATIC REPRESENTATIVES

Of Dominican Republic in Great Britain
Ambassador: (Vacant).

Of Great Britain in the Dominican Republic
Ambassador: Giles Fitzherbert, CMG (resides in Caracas).

Of the Dominican Republic in the USA (1715 22nd St., NW, Washington, D.C., 20008)
Chargé d'Affaires: Dr Dario Suro.

Of the USA in the Dominican Republic (Calle Cesar Nicolas Penson, Santo Domingo)
Ambassador: Paul D. Taylor.

Of the Dominican Republic to the United Nations
Ambassador: Dr Rafael Pedro Gonzalez Pantaleon.

Further Reading

Anuario estadístico de la República Dominicana, 1944–45. Ciudad Trujillo. 1949. This has been succeeded by separate annual reports covering foreign trade, vital statistics, banking, insurance, housing and communications.

Official Guide to the Dominican Republic, 79–80. Tourist Information Center, Santo Domingo, 1980

Atkins, G. P., *Arms and Politics in the Dominican Republic.* London, 1981

Bell, I., *The Dominican Republic.* London, 1980

Black, J. K., *The Dominican Republic: Politics and Development in an Unsovereign State.* London, 1986

Diederich, B., *Trujillo: The Death of the Goat.* London, 1978

Wiarda, H. J. and Kryzanek, M. J., *The Dominican Republic: A Caribbean Crucible.* Boulder, 1982

ECUADOR

Capital: Quito
Population: 9·64m. (1986)
GNP per capita: US$681 (1988)

República del Ecuador

HISTORY. The Spaniards under Francisco Pizarro founded a colony after their victory at Cajamarca (16 Nov. 1532). Their rule was first challenged by the rising of 10 Aug. 1809. Marshal Sucre defeated the Spaniards at Pichincha in 1822, and in 1822 Bolívar persuaded the new republic to join the federation of Gran Colombia. The Presidency of Quito became the Republic of Ecuador by amicable secession 13 May 1830.

AREA AND POPULATION. Ecuador is bounded on the north by Colombia, on the east and south by Peru, on the west by the Pacific ocean. The frontier with Peru has long been a source of dispute between the two countries. The latest delimitation of it was in the treaty of Rio, 29 Jan. 1942, when, after being invaded by Peru, Ecuador lost over half her Amazonian territories. Ecuador unilaterally denounced this treaty in Sept. 1961. *See* map in THE STATESMAN'S YEAR-BOOK, 1942. Fighting between Peru and Ecuador began again in Jan. 1981 over this border issue but a ceasefire was agreed in early Feb.

No definite figure of the area of the country can yet be given, as a portion of the frontier has not been delimited. One estimate of the area of Ecuador is 270,670 sq. km, excluding the litigation zone between Peru and Ecuador, which is 190,807 sq. km, but including the Galápagos Islands (7,844 sq. km).

Mainland Ecuador has 3 distinct zones: the *Sierra* or uplands of the Andes, consisting of high mountain ridges with valleys, with 3·76m. of the population and high-priced farming land; the *Costa*, the coastal plain between the Andes and the Pacific, with 4·03m., whose permanent plantations furnish bananas, cacao, coffee, sugar-cane and many other crops; the *Oriente*, the upper Amazon basin on the east and the site of the main oilfields, consisting of tropical jungles threaded by large rivers (0·26m.).

The population is predominantly of Mestizos and Amerindians, with some proportion of people of European or African descent.

The official language is Spanish. The Amerindians of the highlands also speak the Quechua language; in the Oriental Region various tribes have languages of their own.

Census population in 1982, 8,072,702. Estimate (1986) 9·64m.

The population 28 Nov. 1982 was distributed by provinces as follows:

Province	*Sq. km*	*Census 1982*	*Capital*	*Census 1982*
Azuay	8,092	443,044	Cuenca	272,397
Bolívar	4,142	141,566	Guaranda	14,155 [1]
Cañar	3,481	174,674	Azogues	13,840 [1]
Carchi	3,744	125,452	Tulcán	33,635 [1]
Chimborazo	6,056	320,268	Riobamba	149,757
Cotopaxi	5,198	279,765	Latacunga	55,979
El Oro	5,908	337,818	Machala	117,243
Esmeraldas	15,162	247,311	Esmeraldas	141,030
Guayas	21,382	2,047,001	Guayaquil	1,300,868
Imbabura	4,976	245,745	Ibarra	60,719 [1]
Loja	11,472 [2]	358,952	Loja	86,196
Los Ríos	6,370	457,065	Babahoyo	42,583 [1]
Manabi	18,105	858,780	Portoviejo	167,070
Pichincha	16,587	1,376,831	Quito	1,110,248
Tungurahua	3,110	324,286	Ambato	221,392
Napo [3]	52,318 [2]	115,110	Tena	4,735 [1]
Pastaza [3]	30,269 [2]	31,779	Puyo	...
Morona-Santiago [3]	26,418 [2]	70,217	Macas	...
Zamora-Chinchipa [3]	18,394 [2]	46,691	Zamora	6,365
Colon (Galápagos)	7,994	6,119	Baquerizo Moreno	...

[1] 1983 estimate. [2] Excluding Peru-Ecuador litigation zone.
[3] Comprising 'Región Oriental'.

Vital statistics for calendar years: Births, (1985) 209,974; deaths, (1985) 51,134.

CLIMATE. The climate varies from equatorial, through warm temperate to mountain conditions, according to altitude which affects temperatures and rainfall. In coastal areas, the dry season is from May to Dec., but only from June to Sept. in mountainous parts, where temperatures may be 20°F colder than on the coast. Quito Jan. 59°F (15°C), July 58°F (14·4°C). Annual rainfall 44" (1,115 mm). Guayaquil. Jan. 79°F (26·1°C), July 75°F (23·9°C). Annual rainfall 39" (986 mm).

CONSTITUTION AND GOVERNMENT. A new Constitution came into force on 10 Aug. 1979. It provides for an executive President and a Vice-President to be directly elected for a non-renewable 4-year term by universal suffrage, with a further 'run-off' ballot being held between the two leading candidates where no-one has secured an absolute majority of the votes cast. The President appoints and leads a Council of Ministers.

Legislative power is vested in a unicameral 71-member National Congress, also directly elected for a 4-year term, 12 members on a national basis and 59 on a provincial basis. Voting is obligatory for all literate citizens of 18 years and over. At the most recent congressional elections in June 1986, 43 seats were won by the *Frente Progresista Democrática* and 27 by the *Frente de Reconstrucción Nacional*, with 1 independent.

The following is a list of the presidents and provisional executives since 1948:

Galo Plaza Lasso, 1 Sept. 1948–31 Aug. 1952.
Dr José María Velasco Ibarra, 1 Sept. 1952–31 Aug. 1956.
Dr Camilo Ponce Enríquez, 1 Sept. 1956–31 Aug. 1960.
Dr José María Velasco Ibarra, 1 Sept. 1960–8 Nov. 1961 (withdrew).
Dr Carlos Julio Arosemena Monroy, 8 Nov. 1961–11 July 1963 (deposed).
Military Junta, 11 July 1963–31 March 1966.
Clemente Yerovi Indaburu, 31 March–16 Nov. 1966 (interim).
Dr Otto Arosemena Gómez, 17 Nov. 1966–1 Sept. 1968.
Dr José María Velasco Ibarra, 1 Sept. 1968–15 Feb. 1972 (deposed).
Gen. Guillermo Rodriguez Lara, 16 Feb. 1972–11 Jan. 1976 (resigned).
Adm. Alfredo Poveda Burbano, 11 Jan. 1976–10 Aug. 1979.
Jaime Roldós Aguilera, 10 Aug. 1979–24 May 1981.
Osvaldo Hurtado Larrea, 24 May 1981–10 Aug. 1984.
León Febres Codero Rivadeneira, 10 Aug. 1984–10 Aug. 1988.

President: Rodrigo Borja Cevallos (elected 9 May 1988; installed 10 Aug. 1988).

The Cabinet in Oct. 1989 was composed as follows:

Government and Justice: Andrés Vallejo Arco. *Defence:* Gen. Jorge Félix Mena. *Education and Culture:* Alfredo Vera Arrata. *Agriculture and Livestock:* Mario Jalil. *Public Works and Communications:* Juan Neira. *Finance and Public Credit:* Jorge Gallardo. *Foreign Affairs:* Diego Cordóvez. *Industry, Commerce Integration and Fishing:* Jacinto Jouvin. *Public Health:* Plutarco Naranjo. *Social Welfare and Public Promotion:* Raúl Baco Carba. *Secretary General for Public Administration:* Washington Herrera. *Energy and Mines:* Diego Tamariz. *Labour and Human Resources:* César Verduga. *Secretary General for Public Information:* Gonzalo Ortiz.

National flag: Three horizontal stripes of yellow, blue, red, with the yellow of double width, and in the centre over all the national arms.

National anthem: Indignados tus hijos del yugo (words by J. L. Mera; music by A. Neumann, 1866).

Local Government. The country is divided politically into 21 provinces; 5 of them comprise the 'Región Oriental' and one the Archipelago of Galápagos, situated in the Pacific ocean about 600 miles to the west of Ecuador and comprising 15 islands. The provinces are administered by governors, appointed by the Government; their sub-divisions, or cantons, by political chiefs and elected cantonal councillors; and the parishes by political lieutenants. The Galápagos Archipelago is administered by the Ministry of National Defence. The 21 provinces are made up of 115 cantons, 212 urban parishes and 715 rural parishes.

DEFENCE. Military service is selective, with a 1-year period of conscription. The country is divided into 4 military zones, with headquarters at Quito, Guayaquil, Cuenca and Pastaza.

Army. The Army consists of 5 infantry, 1 armoured and 2 'jungle' brigades. Strength (1990) 35,000, with about 80,000 reservists. Equipment includes 45 American M-3 and 104 French AMX-13 light tanks. The aviation element has 4 survey aircraft, 3 Cessna light aircraft and 36 helicopters including 10 Super Pumas and 5 Pumas.

Navy. Navy combatant forces include 2 West German-built diesel submarines; 1 *ex*-US Gearing class destroyer, 1 old *ex*-US frigate, 6 Italian-built missile corvettes (with helicopter deck), 6 fast missile craft and 6 inshore patrol craft. Amphibious capability is 1 landing ship and 6 small craft. Auxiliaries consist of 1 small tanker, 1 survey ship, 2 tugs and a training ship plus some 8 harbour and service vessels. The Maritime Air Force has 10 aircraft, including 4 Cessna light aircraft, 3 T-34C trainers and 1 Alouette III helicopter. Naval personnel in 1989 totalled 4,000 officers and men including some 1,000 marines.

There are 6 inshore Coast Guard cutters and some 12 boats.

Air Force. The Air Force, formed with Italian assistance in 1920, was reorganized and re-equipped with US aircraft after Ecuador signed the Rio Pact of Mutual Defence in 1947 but latest equipment acquired from Europe and Brazil. 1990 strength of about 3,000 personnel and 70 combat aircraft includes a strike squadron equipped with 9 single-seat and 2 two-seat Jaguars; an interceptor squadron of 14 single-seat and 1 two-seat Mirage F.1; an interceptor squadron with 11 Kfirs; 3 counter-insurgency units equipped with 11 Cessna A-37B, 25T-33 and 12 Strikemaster light jet attack and training aircraft, 1 squadron with 2 C-130, 2 Buffalo and 4 HS 748 turboprop transports; Alouette III, AS 332 Super Puma, SA 330 Puma, Bell 47, Bell 212, UH-1 Iroquois and SA 315B Lama helicopters; and Cessna 150, T-34C-1 and T-41A/D trainers. Other transports are operated by the military airline TAME.

INTERNATIONAL RELATIONS

Membership. Ecuador is a member of UN, OAS, the Andean Group and LAIA (formerly LAFTA).

ECONOMY

Budget. Estimated revenue in 1988 was 812,000m. sucres and expenditure, 804,000m. sucres.

Net international reserves, 31 Dec. 1988, were US$176m.

Currency. The monetary unit is the *sucre,* divided into 100 *centavos*. In circulation are coins of 1, 5, 10, 20 and 50 *sucres*. The currency consists mainly of the notes of the Central Bank in denominations of 100, 500, 1,000 and 5,000 sucres. In March 1990, US$1 = 675; £1 = 1,106.

Banking. The Central Bank of Ecuador, at Quito, with a capital and reserves of 2,815m. sucres at 31 Aug. 1989, is modelled after the Federal Reserve Banks of US: through branches opened in 16 towns it now deals in mortgage bonds. All commercial banks must be affiliated to the Central Bank. American and European banks include the Bank of London and Canada with branches in Quito and Guayaquil.

Weights and Measures. By a law of 6 Dec. 1856 the metric system was made the legal standard but the Spanish measures are in general use. The quintal is equivalent to 101·4 lb.

The meridian of Quito has been adopted as the official time.

ENERGY AND NATURAL RESOURCES

Electricity. In 1988, total capacity of hydraulic and thermal plants was 1,805,400 kw. Estimated output was 5,352m. kwh. Supply 110,120 and 220 volts; 60 Hz.

Oil. Production of crude oil in 1989 was 14·7m. tonnes. In 1988 management of oil companies was taken over by the government.

Gas. In 1987, natural gas production was 460,778·9m. cu. metres.

Minerals. Production (1983): Silver, 3,137·6 troy oz; gold, 607·6 troy oz; copper, 7,900 kg; zinc, 14,820 kg. The country also has some iron, uranium, lead and coal.

Agriculture. Ecuador is divided into two agricultural zones: The coast and lower river valleys, where tropical farming is carried on in an average temperature of from 18° to 25°C.; and the Andean highlands with a temperate climate, adapted to grazing, dairying and the production of cereals, potatoes, pyrethrum and other flowers, and vegetables suitable to temperate climes. Some wheat has to be imported.

124,000 acres of rich virgin land in the Santo Domingo de los Colorados area has been set aside for settlement of smallholders.

Excepting the two agricultural zones and a few arid spots on the Pacific coast, Ecuador is a vast forest. Roughly estimated, 10,000 sq. miles on the Pacific slope extending from the sea to an altitude of 5,000 ft on the Andes, and the Amazon Basin below the same level containing 80,000 sq. miles, nearly all virgin forest, are rich in valuable timber, but much of it is still not commercially accessible.

The staple export products are bananas, cacao and coffee. Main crops, in 1,000 tonnes, in 1988: Rice, 420; potatoes, 301; maize, 387; coffee, 136; barley, 41; cocoa, 77; bananas, 2,238.

Livestock (1988): Cattle, 4,007,000; sheep, 1,707,000; pigs, 4·16m.; horses, 438,000; poultry, 48m.

Forestry. In 1988, 11·8m. hectares, 43% of the land area was forested. In 1981, 4·5m. cu. metres of timber were cut. Exports approximately US$10m. per annum.

Fisheries. Fisheries and fish product exports were valued at US$387·6m. in 1986 (268,000 tonnes).

INDUSTRY AND TRADE

Industry. Production in 1987: Sugar, 3,000 tonnes; cement 2·87m. tonnes.

Commerce. Imports and exports for calendar years, in US$1m.:

	1984	*1985*	*1986*	*1987*	*1988*
Imports (f.o.b.)	1,567	1,611	1,631	1,888	1,517
Exports (f.o.b.)	2,622	2,905	2,186	1,928	2,193

Of the total exports (1988); petroleum, US$875m.; bananas, US$298m.; cocoa, US$298m.; coffee, US$152m.

Total trade between Ecuador and UK (British Department of Trade returns, in £1,000 sterling):

	1985	*1986*	*1987*	*1988*	*1989*
Imports to UK	19,015	11,339	14,002	13,120	19,319
Exports and re-exports from UK	58,628	46,673	37,934	50,417	29,410

Tourism. There were 252,443 visitors in 1986, spending US$170m.

COMMUNICATIONS

Roads. In 1985, there were 36,187 km of roads of all types in this mountainous country. A trunk highway through the coastal plain is under construction which will link Machala in the extreme south-west with Esmeraldas in the north-west and with Quito and the northern section of the Pan-American Highway. In 1984, there were 314,360 cars and 32,379 commercial vehicles.

Railways. A 1,067 mm gauge line runs from San Lorenzo through Quito to Guayaquil and Cuenca, total 971 km.

Aviation. There are 2 international airports. The following international lines operate: Air France, Avianca, Eastern, Ecuatoriana de Aviación, KLM, Lufthansa, Pan-Am, Iberia, LAN Chile, Aerovías Peruanas, Aereolinas Argentinas, Air Panama and Varig. They connect Quito with North and Central America, other countries in South America and Europe. All the leading towns are connected by an almost daily service.

Shipping. Ecuador has 3 major seaports, of which Guayaquil is the chief and 6 minor ones. The merchant navy comprises 39,964 tons of seagoing and 21,232 tons of river craft. In 1980 ships totalling 26·58m. GRT entered Ecuadorean ports, unloading 2·28m. tons, and loading 8·59m. tons.

There is river communication, improved by dredging, throughout the principal agricultural districts on the low ground to the west of the Cordillera by the rivers Guayas, Daule and Vinces (navigable for 200 miles by river steamers in the rainy season).

Post and Broadcasting. In 1985 there were 339,040 telephones in use, 104,000 in Quito and 104,000 in Guayaquil; most were operated by the Government; 99% were automatic. Television was inaugurated in 1960 in Guayaquil, in 1961 in Quito and in 1967 in Cuenca. In 1985 there were 1·9m. radio receivers and 600,000 television receivers.

Newspapers (1984). There were 22 daily newspapers with an aggregate daily circulation of 526,000; 7 papers in Quito and Guayaquil have the bulk of the circulation.

JUSTICE, RELIGION, EDUCATION AND WELFARE

Justice. The Supreme Court in Quito, consisting of a President and 15 Justices, comprises 5 chambers each of 3 Justices. There is a Superior Court in each province, comprising chambers (as appointed by the Supreme Court) of 3 magistrates each. There are numerous lower and special courts. Capital punishment and all forms of torture are prohibited by the constitution, as are imprisonment for debt and contracts involving personal servitude or slavery.

Religion. The state recognizes no religion and grants freedom of worship to all. In 1984, 92% of the population were Roman Catholics. Divorce is permitted. Illegitimate children have the same rights as legitimate ones with respect to education and inheritance.

Education. Primary education is free and obligatory. Private schools, both primary and secondary, are under some state supervision. In 1986, 14,190 primary schools had 1·8m. pupils; 2,207 secondary schools with 744,000 pupils. There were (1989) 21 universities and polytechnics.

Health. In 1984 there were 11,000 doctors and 337 hospitals with 15,455 beds. In 1979 there were 795 dentists and 505 pharmacists.

DIPLOMATIC REPRESENTATIVES

Of Ecuador in Great Britain (3 Hans Cres., London, SW1X 0LS)
Ambassador: Dr José Antonio Correa (accredited 7 Feb. 1989).

Of Great Britain in Ecuador (Calle Gonzalez Suarez 111, Quito)
Ambassador: F. B. Wheeler.

Of Ecuador in the USA (2535 15th St., NW, Washington, D.C., 20009)
Ambassador: Jaime Moncayo García.

Of the USA in Ecuador (Avenida 12 de Octubre y Avenida Patria, Quito)
Ambassador: Richard N. Holwill.

Of Ecuador to the United Nations
Ambassador: Dr José Ayala Lasso.

Further Reading

Anuario de Legislación Ecuatoriana. Quito. Annual
Boletín del Banco Central. Quito
Boletín General de Estadistica. Tri-monthly
Boletín Mensual del Ministerio de Obras Públicas. Monthly
Informes Ministeriales. Quito. Annual
Bibliografia Nacional, 1756–1941. Quito, 1942
Invest in Ecuador. Banco Central del Ecuador, Quito, 1980
Buitrón, A. and Collier, Jr, J., *The Awakening Valley: Study of the Otavalo Indians*. New York, 1950
Corkhill, D., *Ecuador*. [Bibliography] Oxford and Santa Barbara, 1989
Cueva, A., *The Process of Political Domination in Ecuador*. London, 1982
Hickman, J., *The Enchanted Islands: The Galapagos Discovered*. Oswestry, 1985
Martz, J. D., *Ecuador: Conflicting Political Culture and the Quest for Progress*. Boston, 1972.—*Politics and Petroleum in Ecuador*. New Brunswick, 1987
Middleton, A., *Class, Power and the Distribution of Credit in Ecuador*. Glasgow, 1981

EGYPT

Capital: Cairo
Population: 50·74m. (1989)
GNP per capita: US$650 (1988)

Jumhuriyat Misr al-Arabiya

HISTORY. Part of the Ottoman Empire from 1517 until Dec. 1914 when it became a British protectorate, Egypt became an independent monarchy on 28 Feb. 1922. Following a revolution on 23 July 1952, a Republic was proclaimed on 18 June 1953. Egypt merged with Syria on 22 Feb. 1958 to form the United Arab Republic, retaining that name when Syria broke away from the union on 28 Sept. 1961, finally re-adopting the name of Egypt on 2 Sept. 1971.

AREA AND POPULATION. Egypt is bounded east by Israel, the Gulf of Aqaba and the Red Sea, south by Sudan, west by Libya and north by the Mediterranean. The total area is 1,002,000 sq. km (386,900 sq. miles), but the cultivated and settled area, that is, the Nile valley, delta and oases, covers only about 35,580 sq. km.

The area, population (1976 Census and 1985 estimate) and capitals of the governorates are:

Governorate	*Sq. km*	*1976 census*	*1985 estimate*	*Capital*
Sinai al-Janûbîya	33,140	10,104	24,000	At-Tur
Sinai ash-Shamâlîya	25,574		152,000	Al-Arish
Suez	17,840	194,001	254,000	Suez
Ismailia	1,442	351,889	465,000	Ismâilya
Port Said	72	262,620	374,000	Port Said
Sharqîya	4,180	2,621,208	3,318,000	Zaqâziq
Daqahlîya	3,471	2,732,756	3,469,000	Mansûra
Damietta	589	557,115	728,000	Damietta
Kafr el Sheikh	3,437	1,403,468	1,795,000	Kafr el-Sheikh
Alexandria	2,679	2,318,655	2,821,000	Alexandria
Behera	10,130	2,517,292	3,199,000	Damanhur
Gharbîya	1,942	2,294,303	2,847,000	Tanta
Menûfîya	1,532	1,710,982	2,157,000	Shibin el-Kom
Qalyûbîya	1,001	1,674,006	2,186,000	Benha
Cairo	214	5,084,463	6,205,000	Cairo
Gîza	85,105	2,419,247	3,159,000	Gîza
Faiyûm	1,827	1,140,245	1,495,000	Faiyûm
Beni Suef	1,322	1,108,615	1,424,000	Beni-Suef
Minya	2,262	2,055,739	2,692,000	Minyâ
Asyût	1,530	1,695,378	2,179,000	Asyût
Sohag	1,547	1,924,960	2,455,000	Sohag
Qena	1,851	1,705,594	2,159,000	Qinâ
Aswân	679	619,932	781,000	Aswân
al-Bahr al-Ahmar	203,685	56,191	70,000	Al-Ghurdaqah
al-Wadi al-Jadid	376,505	84,645	113,000	Al-Kharijah
Mersa Matruh	212,112	112,772	173,000	Matruh
Total		36,656,180	46,694,000	

The principal towns, with their (estimate) 1986 populations, were:

Cairo	6,325,000	Asyût	291,300	Sani Suwayf	162,500
Alexandria	2,893,000	Zagâziq	274,400	Uqsur (Luxor)	147,900
Gaza	1,670,800	Suez	265,000	Qinâ	141,700
Shubrâ al-Khayma	533,300	Kafr ad-Dawwar	240,000	Sawhâj	141,500
Mahalla al-Kubrâ	385,300	Ismâiliya	236,300	Shibin al-Kawm	135,900
Port Said	382,000	Fayyûm	227,300	Dumyât	121,200
Tantâ	373,500	Damanhûr	225,900	Banhâ	120,200
Mansûra	357,800	Minyâ	203,300	Kafr ash-Shaykh	104,200
Hulwan	352,300	Aswân	195,700		

Population (1989) 50·74m. and of Greater Cairo 13·3m.

The official language is Arabic, although French and English are widely spoken.

CLIMATE. The climate is mainly dry, but there are winter rains along the Mediterranean coast. Elsewhere, rainfall is very low and erratic in its distribution. Winter temperatures are everywhere comfortable, but summer temperatures are very high, especially in the south. Cairo. Jan. 56°F (13·3°C), July 83°F (28·3°C). Annual rainfall 1·2" (28 mm). Alexandria. Jan. 58°F (14·4°C), July 79°F (26·1°C). Annual rainfall 7" (178 mm). Aswân. Jan. 62°F (16·7°C), July 92°F (33·3°C). Annual rainfall trace. Giza. Jan. 55°F (12·8°C), July 78°F (25·6°C). Annual rainfall 16" (389 mm). Ismailia. Jan. 56°F (13·3°C), July 84°F (28·9°C). Annual rainfall 1·5" (37 mm). Luxor. Jan. 59°F (15°C), July 86°F (30°C). Annual rainfall trace. Port Said. Jan. 58°F (14·4°C), July 78°F (27·2°C). Annual rainfall 3" (76 mm).

CONSTITUTION AND GOVERNMENT. The Constitution was approved by referendum on 11 Sept. 1971. It defines Egypt as 'an Arab Republic with a democratic, socialist system' and the Egyptian people as 'part of the Arab nation' with Islam as the state religion and Arabic as the official language.

The President of the Republic is nominated by the People's Assembly and confirmed by plebiscite for a 6-year term. He is the supreme commander of the armed forces and presides over the defence council.

Presidents since the establishment of the Republic have been:

Gen. Mohamed Neguib, 18 June 1953–14 Nov. 1954 (deposed).

Col. Gamal Abdel Nasser, 14 Nov. 1954–28 Sept. 1970 (died).

Col. Muhammad Anwar Sadat, 28 Sept. 1970–6 Oct. 1981 (assassinated).

Lieut.-Gen. Muhammad Hosni Mubarak, 7 Oct. 1981–.

The People's Assembly is a unicameral legislature consisting of 448 members directly elected for a 5-year term; the President of the Republic may appoint up to 10 additional members. At the general elections held in April 1987, the National Democratic Party gained 346 seats, the New *Wafd* Party 35, SLP-led alliance 60, Independent 7.

The President may appoint one or more Vice-Presidents, and appoints a Prime Minister and a Council of Ministers, whom he may remove as he wishes.

A 210-member consultative body, the Shura Council, was established in 1980. Two-thirds of its members are elected and one-third appointed by the President.

President of the Republic: Hosni Mubarak, sworn in for second 6-year term Oct. 1987.

The Council of Ministers in Jan. 1990 was composed as follows:

Prime Minister: Dr Atef Mohamed Naguib Sidki.

Defence and Military Production: Gen. Youssef Sabri Abu Taleb. *Economy and Foreign Trade:* Youssri Mustafa. *Finance:* Mohammed Ahmed al Razaz. *Foreign Affairs and Deputy Prime Minister:* Ahmed Esmat Abdel Meguid. *Interior:* Mohammed Abdul-Halim Moussa.

National flag: Three horizontal stripes of red, white, black, with the national emblem in the centre in gold.

Local Government. There are 26 governorates: 16 provinces, 5 cities and 5 frontier districts.

DEFENCE. Conscription is for 3 years, between the ages of 20 and 35. Graduates serve for 1 year.

Army. The Army comprises 4 armoured, 6 mechanized infantry, and 2 infantry divisions; 1 Republican Guard, 2 independent armoured, 4 independent infantry, 2 airmobile, 1 parachute, 8 artillery and 2 heavy mortar brigades; 7 commando groups; and 2 surface-to-surface missile regiments. Strength (1990) 320,000 (180,000 conscripts) and about 500,000 reservists. Equipment includes 1,040 T-54/-55, 600 T-62 and 785 M-60A3 tanks.

Navy. About 6 of the current submarine force of 10 old *ex*-Soviet and *ex*-Chinese 'Romeo' class submarines are to be modernised under a US contract and 2 larger modernised *ex*-British Oberon class are to be added. Major surface combatants include 1 old destroyer, 2 Spanish-built and 2 Chinese-built missile armed frigates and one old training frigate. There are also 23 missile craft of mixed British, Soviet and Chinese origin and 18 coastal and inshore patrol craft. A small shore-based naval aviation branch operates 5 Sea King and 12 Gazelle helicopters. Mine warfare forces include 4 coastal and 2 inshore minesweepers. 3 *ex*-Soviet medium landing ships, provide amphibious lift supported by 11 minor landing craft. There are 7 major auxiliaries and some 14 minor service vessels.

There are Naval bases at Alexandria, Port Said, Mersa Matruh, Port Tewfik, Hurghada and Safaqa.

Naval personnel in 1989 totalled 18,000 plus reserves of 14,000. An associated para-military coastguard about 2,000 strong operates 32 inshore cutters and numerous boats.

Air Force. Until 1979, the Air Force was equipped largely with aircraft of USSR design, but subsequent re-equipment involves aircraft bought in the West, as well as some supplied by China. Strength (1990) is about 30,000 personnel and 500 combat aircraft, of which the interceptors are operated by an independent Air Defence Command, in conjunction with many 'Guideline', 'Goa', 'Gainful', Hawk and Crotale missile batteries. There are about 12 Tu-16 twin-jet strategic bombers, some equipped to carry 'Kelt' air-to-surface missiles. Other interceptor/ground attack fighter divisions are equipped with 75 F-16 Fighting Falcons, 50 Mirage 5s, 33 F-4E Phantoms, 20 Mirage 2000s, 80 F-6s (Chinese-built MiG-19s), 15 Alpha Jets, 50 Su-7s, more than 120 MiG-21s, and 60 F-7s (Chinese-built MiG-21s). Airborne early warning capability is provided by 5 E-2C Hawkeyes. Transport units have 19 C-130H Hercules turboprop heavy freighters, 12 An-12s, 9 twin-turboprop Buffaloes, 6 Beech 1900s, and up to 175 Gazelle, Mi-4, Mi-6, Mi-8, Sea King/Commando and Agusta-built CH-47C helicopters; some Commando helicopters and 2 EC-130H Hercules are equipped for electronic warfare duties. Training units are equipped with Gomhouria piston-engined trainers, Embraer Tucanos, Czech-built L-29 Delfin and French-designed Alpha Jet jet trainers, two-seat versions of the MiG-15, MiG-17s, two-seat FT-6s, Mirage 5s, MiG-21Us and Su-7Us, and UH-12E helicopters. Main aircrew training centre is the EAF Academy at Bilbeis.

INTERNATIONAL RELATIONS

Membership. Egypt is a member of UN, OAU, the Arab League and OAPEC.

ECONOMY

Planning. A 5-year development plan runs 1987/88–1991–92 and envisages investments totalling £E46,500m.

Budget. Ordinary revenue and expenditure for fiscal years ending 30 June, in £E1m.:

	1985–86	*1986–87*	*1987–88*
Revenue	15,010	14,451	17,910
Expenditure	19,910	20,246	23,060

Currency. By decree of 18 Oct. 1916 (20 Zi-El-Higga 1934), the monetary unit of Egypt is the gold Egyptian pound of 100 *piastres* of 1,000 *millièmes.* Coins in circulation are 20, 10, 5, 2 piastres (silver); 2, 1 piastre, 5 millièmes, 1 millième (bronze). Gold coins are no longer in circulation. Silver coin is legal tender only up to £E1, and bronze coins up to 10 piastres. The Treasury issues 5- and 10-piastre currency notes. Bank-notes are issued by the National Bank in denominations of 5, 10, 25 and 50 piastres, £E1, 5, 10, 20, and 100.

In March 1990, £1 sterling = £E4·32; US$1 = £E2·64.

Banking. On 18 Aug. 1960 a Central Bank of Egypt was established by decree. It manages the note issue, the Government's banking operations and the control of commercial banks. At the same date the National Bank founded in 1898 ceased to be the central bank and became a purely commercial bank. In 1986 there were 27 commercial banks, 33 business and investment banks (joint ventures and 22 foreign currency branches) and 4 specialized banks. There were also 29 representative offices of foreign banks.

Weights and Measures. In 1951 the metric system was made official with the exception of the feddân and its subdivisions.

Capacity. Kadah = 1/96th ardeb = 3·36 pints. *Rob* = 4 kadahs = 1·815 gallons. *Keila* = 8 kadahs = 3·63 gallons. *Ardeb* = 96 kadahs = 43·555 gallons, or 5·44439 bu., or 198 cu. decimetres.

Weights. Rotl = 144 dirhems = 0·9905 lb. *Oke* = 400 dirhems = 2·75137 lb. *Qantâr* or 100 rotls or 36 okes = 99·0493 lb. 1 *Qantâr* of unginned cotton = 315 lb. 1 *Qantâr* of ginned cotton = 99·05 lb. The approximate weight of the ardeb is as follows: Wheat, 150 kg; beans, 155 kg; barley, 120 kg; maize, 140 kg; cotton seed, 121 kg.

Surface. Feddân, the unit of measure for land = 4,200·8 sq. metres = 7,468·148 sq. pics = 1·03805 acres. 1 sq. pic = 6·0547 sq. ft = 0·5625 sq. metre.

ENERGY AND NATURAL RESOURCES

Electricity. Electricity generated in 1986 was 40,600m. kwh. Supply 110 and 220 volts; 50 Hz.

Oil. The first commercial discovery of oil in the Middle East outside Iran was made in Egypt in 1909, but production long remained low and often insufficient to meet Egypt's domestic requirements. Policy is controlled by the Egyptian General Petroleum Corporation (EGPC) a wholly state-owned corporation answerable to the Minister of Petroleum. EGPC is whole or part-owner of the various production and refining companies and controls supplies to the domestic marketing companies. With the agreement of EGPC several foreign oil companies were exploring for oil in 1986.

Production 1989, was 45m. tonnes of crude oil. Net oil earnings (1983–84) US$2,340m.

Gas. The first gas field, at Abu Madi in the Nile delta, became operational in 1974 and produced 4,306,000 tonnes in 1986. The 2 other fields are at Abu Gharadeq in the Western Desert and Abu Qir near Alexandria.

Water. The Aswân High Dam, completed in 1970, allows for a perennial irrigation system.

Minerals. Production (1986 in tonnes): Phosphate rock, 1·2m.; iron ore, 2,135,000; marine salt, 1,040,000. Other minerals discovered include manganese, chrome, tantalum, molybdenum and uranium.

Agriculture. The cultivated area of Egypt proper was estimated in 1982 at 11·17m. feddâns (1 feddân = 1·038 acres) and of this, 4,945,000 feddâns were under winter crops, 5,017,000 under summer crops, 818,000 under Nile crops and 390,000 under orchards.

Irrigation occupies a predominant place in the economic development of the country. An intricate irrigation system now reaches most cultivated areas but only about 6·5% of the total land area is arable. The 'vertical' development policy calls for improved methods, better drainage and the introduction of stiff penalties for encroachment of farmland. Under the first phase of the 'horizontal' expansion programme, which aims to add 2·8m. feddâns to the arable area over 20 years, 24,000 feddâns are being added near Alexandria. Export earnings from agriculture have fallen and Egypt is no longer self sufficient in food production partly due to the increase in population. No priority has been given in government planning and because of inadequate investment earnings have fallen for its three most important export crops, cotton, oranges and rice.

In 1985–86 the area sown with cotton rose 7% to 440,705 hectares; output increased 8% to 1,985,000 bales.

The major summer crops are cotton, rice, maize and sorghum. Berseem (Egyptian clover), wheat and beans are the main winter crops.

Production (1988, in 1,000 tonnes): Sugar cane, 9,750; maize, 4,088; tomatoes, 5,000; rice, 1,900; wheat, 2,839; potatoes, 1,700; oranges, 1,400; lint cotton, 348.

Livestock (1988): 1·92m. cattle, 2·6m. buffaloes, 1,165,000 sheep, 1·62m. goats, 70,000 camels and 15,000 pigs.

Forestry. In 1986 total removal of roundwood was 2·06m. cu. metres of which 2m. was fuel wood.

Fisheries. The catch of the Egyptian sea, Nile and lake fisheries in 1986 amounted to 138,800 tonnes.

INDUSTRY AND TRADE

Industry. (1987) Almost all large-scale enterprises are in the public sector and these account for about two-thirds of total output. The private sector, dominated by food processing and textiles, consists of about 150,000 small and medium businesses, most employing less than 50 workers. A car industry is being established.

Production in 1985–86 (in 1,000 tonnes) included: Phosphates, 766; fertilizer phosphates, 100·1; fertilizer nitrates, 4,482; cement, 7,735; cotton yarn, 225; cotton fabrics, 608,000 metres.

Trade Unions. Trade unions were first recognized in 1942.

Commerce. Imports and exports for 5 years (in £E1,000):

	1982	*1983*	*1984*	*1985*	*1986*
Imports	6,354,517	7,192,657	7,536,100	6,276,300	8,051,400
Exports	2,184,122	2,250,295	2,197,900	2,600,000	1,243,700

In 1985 major exports (in £E1m.) included: Crude petroleum, 1,402·1; refined petroleum, 362·5; cotton, 299. Major imports (1984–85) included: Machinery and transport equipment, 1,915·2; foodstuffs, 1,848·5.

Exports, 1985 (in US$1m.), were mainly to Italy (656·6), Israel (462), Romania (434·2), France (430), USSR (177·8), Netherlands (152·1), Greece (119·2), Japan (113·8), Spain (100·2) and Republic of Korea (99·7); imports were mainly from USA (1,295·7), Federal Republic of Germany (953·8), Italy (757·3), France (700·9), Japan (514·7), UK (425·3), Spain (390·1), Romania (369·7), Netherlands (356·5) and Australia (335·7).

Total trade between Egypt and UK (British Department of Trade returns, in £1,000 sterling):

	1985	*1986*	*1987*	*1988*	*1989*
Imports to UK	162,162	328,053	127,261	163,038	212,727
Exports and re-exports from UK	471,091	371,007	342,195	289,309	296,272

Tourism. In 1986 there were 1·36m. tourists (43% from Arab countries) spending £E251·3m.

COMMUNICATIONS

Roads. In 1980, the total length of roads was 21,637 km, of which 16,182 km were paved. Motor vehicles, in 1981, 580,000 private cars, 165,000 commercial vehicles (including buses).

Railways. In 1986 there were 4,321 km of state railways (1,435 mm gauge) which carried 28,340m. passenger-km and 8·6m. tonnes of freight. An underground rail system was opened in Cairo in 1987.

Aviation. There is an international airport at Cairo. There are 95 airfields (77 unusable). The national airline Egyptair operates scheduled flights connecting Cairo with Athens, Rome, Frankfurt, Zürich, London, Khartoum, Tokyo, Bombay, Aden, Jeddah, Doha, Dharan, Kuwait, Beirut, Baghdad, Tripoli, Benghazi, Algiers, Entebbe, Nairobi, Dar-es-Salaam, Kano, Lagos, Accra, Abidjan, Damascus,

Amman, Manilla, Paris, Munich, Copenhagen, Nicosia, Karachi, Aleppo, Bahrain, Abu Dhabi, Dubai, Sharjah, Sanaa and Vienna. In addition, Egyptair operates scheduled flights on a widespread domestic network connecting Cairo with Port Said, Mersa Matruh, Asyût, Luxor, Aswân. In 1982, 62,000 tonnes of cargo were carried.

Shipping. The Egyptian merchant navy in 1980 consisted of 75 steamers of 387,460 tons.

In 1977, 3,050 ships of 11,432,000 tons entered the port of Alexandria and 876 ships of 4,583,000 tons entered Port Said.

Suez Canal. The Suez Canal was opened for navigation on 17 Nov. 1869. By the convention of Constantinople of 29 Oct. 1888 the canal is open to vessels of all nations and is free from blockade, except in time of war, but the UAR Government did not allow Israeli ships to use the canal until May 1979, when the embargo was lifted. It is 173 km long (excluding 11 km of approach channels to the harbours), connecting the Mediterranean with the Red Sea. Its minimum width is 197 ft at a depth of 33 ft, and its depth permits the passage of vessels up to 38 ft draught.

In 1976 a 2-stage development project was started. The first stage which was completed in 1980 allowing vessels, of up to 150,000 tons, fully loaded, and up to 370,000 tons in ballast to pass through the canal and give a draught of 53 ft.

During the war with Israel in June 1967 the Canal was blocked. The canal was cleared and re-opened to shipping on 5 June 1975. This is part of a programme to develop and rebuild the whole area of Suez to make it one of the largest tax-free industrial zones. In 1987 17,541 vessels (347m. tons) went through the canal. The first tunnel below the canal, located 10 miles north of Suez City, was completed on 30 April 1980 and the first phase of a £E4,000m. development plan, to widen and deepen the canal, was completed in 1980.

Post and Broadcasting. There were, in 1980–81, 1,821 postal agencies, 1,812 mobile offices (1978), 1,747 government and 2,956 private post offices. Number of telephones in 1984, 600,000. Number of wireless licences in 1984, 12m. and 4m. TV licences.

The internal telecommunications system is owned and operated by the Telecommunications Organization. Government landlines connect with those of the Gaza sector and the Sudan.

Newspapers. In 1984 there were 11 dailies published in Cairo and 6 in Alexandria.

JUSTICE, RELIGION, EDUCATION AND WELFARE

Justice. The National Courts in 1981 were as follows: Court of Cassation with a bench of 5 judges which constitutes the highest court of appeal in both criminal and civil cases; Courts of Appeal with 3 judges situated in Cairo and 4 other cities; Assize Courts with 3 judges which deal with all cases of serious crime; Central Tribunals with 3 judges which deal with ordinary civil and commercial cases; Summary Tribunals presided over by a single judge which hear civil disputes in matters up to the value of £E3,250, and criminal offences punishable by a fine or imprisonment of up to 3 years.

Religion. In 1986 about 90% of the population were Moslems, mostly of the Sunni sect, and about 7% Coptic Christians, the remainder being Roman Catholics, Protestants or Greek Orthodox, with a small number of Jews.

There are in Egypt large numbers of native Christians connected with the various Oriental Churches; of these, the largest and most influential are the Copts, who adopted Christianity in the 1st century. Their head is the Coptic Patriarch. There are 25 metropolitans and bishops in Egypt; 4 metropolitans for Ethiopia, Jerusalem, Khartoum and Omdurman, and 12 bishops in Ethiopia. Priests must be married before ordination, but celibacy is imposed on monks and high dignitaries. The Copts use the Diocletian (or Martyrs') calendar, which begins in A.D. 284.

Education. Primary education (6 years) was made free in 1944, secondary and technical education in 1950. Compulsory education is provided in primary schools (6 years).

In 1982–83 there were 503 nurseries and kindergartens with 84,539 pupils. In 1982–83 there were in basic education (6–15 years) 5,036,608 primary stage pupils in 12,013 schools and 1,769,768 preparatory stage pupils in 3,151 schools. In secondary education there were 517,998 general secondary pupils in 823 schools; 441,636 commercial secondary pupils in 639 schools; 208,468 industrial secondary pupils in 170 schools and 84,527 agricultural secondary pupils in 65 schools. Ninety-two teacher training schools had 63,429 pupils and 144 rehabilitation schools had 8,215 pupils.

El Azhar institutes educate students who join the faculties of El Azhar University after graduation. In 1982–83, 1,287 institutes had 308,370 students.

Government experimental language schools, which teach in foreign languages, had 5,000 nursery and kindergarten pupils in 1982–83, and 2,700 primary stage pupils in 1983–84.

Higher education: In 1982, there were 64,870 students in 17 higher commercial institutes and 22,341 students in 16 industrial institutions.

There were 11 universities in Egypt (apart from El Azhar University), with 558,527 students and 74,945 graduates in 1980–81. El Azhar University had 65,451 students and 5,346 graduates in 1980–81.

Health. In 1983–84 there were about 73,300 doctors and 85,350 hospital beds.

DIPLOMATIC REPRESENTATIVES

Of Egypt in Great Britain (26 South St., London, W1Y 8EL)
Ambassador: Mohamed I. Shaker (accredited 27 Oct. 1988).

Of Great Britain in Egypt (Ahmed Ragheb St., Garden City, Cairo)
Ambassador: W. J. Adams, CMG.

Of Egypt in the USA (2310 Decatur Pl., NW, Washington, D.C., 20008)
Ambassador: Abdel Raouf El-Ridy.

Of the USA in Egypt (Lazougi St., Garden City, Cairo)
Ambassador: Frank G. Wisner.

Of Egypt to the United Nations
Ambassador: Abdel Halim Badawi.

Further Reading

The Egyptian Almanac. Annual
Le Mondain Egyptien (Who's Who). Cairo. Annual
Aliboni, R., *(et al) Egypt's Economic Potential.* London, 1984
Ansari, H., *Egypt: The Stalled Society.* New York, 1986
Hart, V., *Modern Egypt.* Cairo, 1984
Heikal, M., *Autumn of Fury: Assassination of Sadat.* London, 1983
Hopwood, D., *Egypt: Politics and Society 1945–1981.* London, 1982
Kepel, G., *Muslim Extremism in Egypt.* Univ. of California Press, 1986
McDermott, A., *Egypt: From Nasser to Mubarak.* London, 1988
Makar, R. N., *Egypt.* [Bibliography] Oxford and Santa Barbara, 1988
Waterbury, J., *The Egypt of Nasser and Sadat.* Princeton Univ. Press, 1983

EL SALVADOR

Capital: San Salvador
Population: 5m. (1987)
GNP per capita: US$950 (1988)

República de El Salvador

HISTORY. In 1839 the Central American Federation, which had comprised the states of Guatemala, El Salvador, Honduras, Nicaragua and Costa Rica, was dissolved, and El Salvador declared itself formally an independent republic in 1841.

AREA AND POPULATION. El Salvador is the smallest and most densely populated (256 inhabitants per sq. km) of the Central American states. Its area (including 247 sq. km of inland lakes) is estimated at 21,393 sq. km (8,236 sq. miles) with population estimate (1987) 5,009,000.

The republic is divided into 14 departments, each under an appointed governor. Their areas and populations in 1981 were:

Department	*Sq. km*	*1981*	*Chief town*	*1985*
Ahuachapán	1,281	241,323	Ahuachapán	71,846
Sonsonate	1,133	321,989	Sonsonate	47,489 [1]
Santa Ana	1,829	445,462	Santa Ana	208,322
La Libertad	1,650	388,538	Nueva San Salvador	52,226 [1]
San Salvador	892	979,683	San Salvador	972,810
Chalatenango	2,507	235,757	Chalatenango	28,675 [2]
Cuscatlán	766	203,978	Cojutepeque	31,108 [1]
La Paz	1,155	249,635	Zacatecoluca	81,035
San Vicente	1,175	206,959 [2]	San Vicente	65,462
Cabañas	1,075	179,909	Sensuntepeque	50,448 [2]
Usulután	1,780	399,912	Usulután	69,355
San Miguel	2,532	434,047	San Miguel	161,156
Morazàn	1,364	215,163	San Francisco	13,015 [2]
La Unión	1,738	309,879	La Unión	27,186 [1]

[1] 1984. [2] 1980.

CLIMATE. Despite its proximity to the equator, the climate is warm rather than hot and nights are cool inland. Light rains occur in the dry season from Nov. to April while the rest of the year has heavy rains, especially on the coastal plain. San Salvador. Jan. 71°F (21·7°C), July 75°F (23·9°C). Annual rainfall 71" (1,775 mm). San Miguel. Jan. 77°F (25°C), July 83°F (28·3°C). Annual rainfall 68" (1,700 mm).

CONSTITUTION AND GOVERNMENT. A new Constitution was enacted in Dec. 1983. The Executive Power is vested in a President elected for a non-renewable term of 5 years, with Ministers and Under-Secretaries appointed by him. The Legislative power is an Assembly of 60 members elected by universal suffrage and proportional representation for a term of 3 years. The judicial power is vested in a Supreme Court, of a President and 9 magistrates elected by the Legislative Assembly for renewable terms of 3 years; and subordinate courts. For governments, 1961–79 *see* THE STATESMAN'S YEAR-BOOK 1982–83, p. 436.

General elections were held on 20 March 1989. Of the 60 seats in the Legislative Assembly 31 were won by the Alianza Republicana Nacionalista, 23 by Partido Demócrata Cristiano, 6 by Partido de Conciliacíon Nacional.

President: Alfredo Felix Cristiani Burkard (sworn in 1 June 1989).

In Jan. 1990 the Cabinet was composed as follows:

Foreign Affairs: José Manuel Pacas Castro. *Planning and Co-ordination of Economic and Social Development:* Mirna Liévano de Márquez. *Interior:* Francisco Merino. *Justice:* Dr Oscar Santamaría. *Finance:* Rafael Alvarado Cano. *Economics:* Arturo Zablah. *Education:* Dr Réné Hernández Valiente. *Defence and Public Safety:* Humberto Larios. *Labour and Social Security:* Mauricio González Dubón.

Public Health and Social Welfare: Dr Lisandro Vásquez Sosa. *Agriculture and Livestock:* Antonio Cabrales. *Works:* Mauricio Stubig.

National flag: Blue, white, blue (horizontal): the white stripe charged with the arms of the republic.

National anthem: Saludemos la patria orgullosos (words by J. J. Cañas; tune by J. Aberle).

DEFENCE. There is selective national service for 2 years.

Army. The Army comprises 5 infantry brigades, 1 mechanized cavalry regiment, 1 artillery brigade, 1 engineer, 1 anti-aircraft, 1 parachute and 6 counter-insurgency battalions. Equipment includes 5 M-3A1 light tanks and 12 AML-90 armoured cars. Strength was (1990) 40,000. There are also National Guard, National Police and Treasury Police, paramilitary units, numbering (1990) about 12,000 and a territorial civil defence force of up to 12,500.

Navy. A small coastguard force based at Acajutla, with 700 (1990) personnel, operates 6 inshore patrol craft, 3 landing craft and numerous boats. There were also (1990) 1,300 marines, and 200 Commandos.

Air Force. The Air Force underwent a major re-equipment programme in 1974–75, with most aircraft coming from Israel and US aid for transport units, but lost 18 aircraft in a guerrilla attack in Jan. 1982. Counter-insurgency equipment includes 8 A-37B and 6 Magister attack aircraft, 6 armed C-47 transports and 4 Hughes 500MD helicopters. Other aircraft are 6 C-47, 3 Arava, 1 DC-6 and 2 C-123 transports, 6 Cessna O-2 patrol aircraft, plus 3 Lamas, 3 Alouette III and 50 UH-1H helicopters. Training types include about 15 piston-engined T-41Cs, T-6s and T-34s. Strength totalled about 2,200 personnel in 1990.

INTERNATIONAL RELATIONS

Membership. El Salvador is a member of UN, CACM and OAS.

ECONOMY

Planning. The development plan 1985–89 envisages investment of ₡6,294m.

Budget. Revenue and expenditure for fiscal years ending 31 Dec., in 1,000 cólones:

	1984	*1985*	*1986*	*1987*	*1988*
Revenue	2,817,730	2,391,010	3,508,159	3,232,628	3,175,573
Expenditure	2,685,009	2,276,052	3,481,152	3,397,276	3,428,129

External debt amounted to US$1,856m. in 1987.

Currency. The monetary unit is the *colón* (₡) of 100 *centavos*. The *colón* (₡) is issued in denominations of 1, 2, 5, 10, 25 and 100 *colónes*; 25 and 50 *centavos* and 1 *colón* (silver); 1, 2, 5 and 10 *centavos* (copper–nickel and copper–zinc); 1 centavo (nickel). In March 1990, £1 = ₡10·87; US$1 = ₡6·63.

Banking. There are 10 native commercial banks, including the Banco Salvadoreño (paid-up capital, 6m. colónes). The Citibank Bank of America and the Bank of Santander and Panama S. A. are the only foreign institutions. The Central Reserve Bank of El Salvador, constructed in 1934 out of the Banco Agricola Comercial, was nationalized on 20 April 1961.

Weights and Measures. On 1 Jan. 1886 the metric system was made obligatory. But other units are still commonly in use, of which the principal are as follows: *Libra* = 1·014 lb. av.; *quintal* = 101·4 lb. av.; *arroba* = 25·35 lb. av.; *fanega* = 1·5745 bushels.

ENERGY AND NATURAL RESOURCES

Electricity. A 200 ft high dam completed in 1954 was constructed across the (unnavigable) Lempa River, 35 miles north-east of San Salvador, with an annual capacity of 344m. kwh. The San Lorenzo dam, completed in 1983, has an annual capacity of 722m. kwh. Production in 1987, 1,971m. kwh.; consumption (1987), 1,672m. kwh. Supply 120 and 240 volts; 60 Hz.

Oil. Production of petroleum derivatives during 1988 totalled ₡1,076,639,000.

Minerals. The mineral output of the republic is now negligible, but the Ministry of Public Works has recently started to investigate 2 new silver mines in the department of Morazán.

Agriculture. El Salvador is predominantly agricultural; 32·5% of its total area is used for crops and 30·2% for pasture. Area devoted to coffee (1982–83) was about 516,615 acres, entirely owned by nationals. In 1981, 35·5% of the working population was engaged in farming.

Production (1988, in 1,000 tonnes): Coffee, 152; seed cotton, 27; maize, 589; dry beans, 56; rice, 57; sorghum, 152; sugar-cane, 3,407. A little rubber is exported.

Livestock (1988): 1,144,000 cattle, 442,000 pigs, 5,000 sheep, 15,000 goats.

Forestry. In the national forests are found dye woods and such woods as mahogany, cedar and walnut. Balsam trees also abound: El Salvador is the world's principal source of this medicinal gum. Sawn wood production, 1986, 38,000 cu. metres.

Fisheries. Total catch 1986, 12,500 tonnes.

INDUSTRY AND TRADE

Industry. Total production was valued at ₡4,579,322m. in 1984, which included (in 1,000 colones): Food, ₡1,827,983; textiles, ₡273,573; chemicals, ₡310,922; footwear and clothing, ₡218,287; beverages, ₡352,224.

Commerce. The imports (including parcels post) and exports have been as follows in calendar years in 1,000 colónes:

	1984	*1985*	*1986*	*1987*	*1988*
Imports	2,443,575	2,403,444	4,284,000	4,970,335	5,034,860
Exports	1,793,432	1,697,420	2,524,700	2,954,705	2,982,095

Of total exports (1988), coffee furnished about 34·9% by weight and 58·4% by value. The coffee is of the 'mild' variety; it is sold in bags of 60 kg, but trade statistics use a bag of 69 kg.

In 1988 US took 904,433,000 colónes of exports and furnished 1,417,720,000 colónes of the imports. The chief imports in 1988 were manufactured goods (28%), chemical and pharmaceutical products (18·1%), non-edible crude materials, mainly crude oil (8%), electric machinery, tools and appliances and transport equipment (25·6%). The other Central American Republics, the Federal Republic of Germany, Japan, Canada, Mexico, Spain, France and the Netherlands are also important trading partners.

Total trade between El Salvador and UK (British Department of Trade returns, in £1,000 sterling):

	1985	*1986*	*1987*	*1988*	*1989*
Imports to UK	1,662	1,323	1,890	2,961	2,133
Exports and re-exports from UK	8,507	6,917	9,595	8,186	9,594

Tourism. There were 125,000 visitors in 1987.

COMMUNICATIONS

Roads. In 1985 there were 12,164 km of national roads in the republic, including 1,706 km of main paved roads; 3,421 km main asphalted roads; other roads, 7,038 km. Vehicles registered, 1987: Cars, 138,000; buses, 7,000 and goods vehicles, 17,000.

Railways. All railways (602 km) came under the control of National Railways of El Salvador *(Fenadesal)* in 1975. Lines run from Acajutla to San Salvador; Cutuco to San Salvador; between San Salvador and Santa Ana, San Miguel and Sonsonate;

there is also a link to the Guatemalan system. Total railway traffic in 1986 was 51,000 tonnes of freight and 524,000 passengers.

Aviation. The airport at Ilopango, 8 km from San Salvador, now a military airport, and the new international airport at Cuscatlán, 40 km from San Salvador, opened in 1979. In 1985, 170,510 passengers arrived and 179,827 departed.

Shipping. The principal ports are La Unión, La Libertad and Acajutla, all on the Pacific. Passengers (and some freight) use the Guatemalan port of Puerto Barrios on the Atlantic, reaching El Salvador by rail or road.

Post and Broadcasting. The telephone and telegraph systems are government-owned; the radio-telephone systems are partly private, partly government-owned. Telephone instruments, 1985, 94,000. There were (1986) over 50 radio stations. Radio El Salvador is state-owned. There were (1988) 4 commercial television channels and 2 educational channels sponsored by the Ministry of Education. In 1985 there were 1·9m. radio receivers and (1986) 242,000 television sets.

Cinemas (1976). Cinemas numbered 65.

Newspapers (1990). There are 5 daily newspapers in San Salvador and 1 in Santa Ana.

JUSTICE, RELIGION, EDUCATION AND WELFARE

Justice. Justice is administered by the Supreme Court of Justice, courts of first and second instance, besides minor tribunals. Magistrates of the Supreme Court and courts of second instance are elected by the Legislative Assembly for a renewable 3-year term.

An anti-Communist law, effective 29 Sept. 1962, has made the propagation of totalitarian or Communist doctrines an offence punishable by imprisonment; supplementary offences, contrary to democratic principles, are punished by prison terms of from 3 to 7 years.

Religion. About 90% of the population is Roman Catholic. Under the 1962 Constitution churches are exempted from the property tax; the Catholic Church is recognized as a legal person, and other churches are entitled to secure similar recognition. There is an archbishop in San Salvador and bishops at Santa Ana, San Miguel, San Vicente, Santiago de María, Usulután, Sonsonate and Zacatecoluca. There are about 200,000 Protestants.

Education. Education is free and obligatory. In 1929 the State took over control of all schools, public and private, but the provision that the teaching in government schools must be wholly secular was removed in 1945.

In 1985 there were 62,500 pupils in nursery schools, 1,075,600 in primary and secondary schools, 60,994 students receiving higher education.

Social Welfare. The Social Security Institute now administers the sickness, old age and death insurance, covering industrial workers and employees earning up to ₡700 a month. Employees in other private institutions with salaries over this amount are included but are excluded from the medical and hospital benefits.

DIPLOMATIC REPRESENTATIVES

Of El Salvador in Great Britain (62 Welbeck St., London, W1)
Ambassador: Dr Mauricio Rosales-Rivera (accredited 26 Feb. 1986).

Of Great Britain in El Salvador
Ambassador and Consul General: P. J. Streams, CMG. (resides in Tegucigalpa).

Of El Salvador in the USA (2308 California St., NW, Washington, DC., 20008)
Ambassador: Dr Miguel Angel Salaverria.

Of the USA in El Salvador (25 Ave. Norte, Colonia Dueñas, San Salvador)
Ambassador: William G. Walker.

Of El Salvador to the United Nations
Ambassador: Dr Ricardo G. Castaneda-Cornejo.

Further Reading

Statistical Information: The Dirección General de Estadistica y Censos (Villa Fermina, Calle Arce, San Salvador) dates from 1937. *Director General:* Lieut.-Col. José Castro Meléndez. Its publications include *Anuario Estadistico.* Annual from 1911.—*Boletin Estadístico.* Quarterly.—*El Salvador en Gráficas.* Annual.—*Atlas Censal de El Salvador.* 1955 only.—Revista Mensual, Banco Central de Reserva de El Salvador.

Angel Gallardo, M., *Cuatro Constituciones Federales de Centro América y Las Constituciones Politicas de El Salvador.* San Salvador, 1945
Armstrong, R. and Shenk, J., *El Salvador: The Face of Revolution.* London, 1982
Baloyra, E. A., *El Salvador in Transition.* Univ. of North Carolina Press, 1982
Bevan, J., *El Salvador. Education and Repression.* London, 1981
Browning, D., *El Salvador: Landscape and Society.* OUP, 1971
Devire, F. J., *El Salvador: Embassy under Attack.* New York, 1981
Didion, J., *Salvador.* London, 1983
Erdozain, P., *Archbishop Romero: Martyr of El Salvador.* Guildford, 1981
Montgomery, T.S., *Revolution in El Salvador: Origins and Evolution.* Boulder, 1982
North, L., *Bitter Grounds: Roots of Revolt in El Salvador.* London, 1981
Schmidt, S. W., *El Salvador: America's Next Vietnam.* Salisbury (N.C.), 1983
Woodward, R. L., *El Salvador.* [Bibliography] Oxford and Santa Barbara, 1989

EQUATORIAL GUINEA

Capital: Malabo
Population: 336,000 (1988)
GNP per capita: US$350 (1988)

República de Guinea Ecuatorial

HISTORY. Equatorial Guinea was a Spanish colony (Territorios Españoles del Golfo de Guinea) until 1 April 1960, the territory was then divided into two Spanish provinces with a status comparable to the metropolitan provinces until 20 Dec. 1963, when they were re-joined as an autonomous Equatorial Region. It became an independent Republic on 12 Oct. 1968 as a federation of the two provinces, and a unitary state was established on 4 Aug. 1973. The first President, Francisco Macías Nguema, was declared President-for-Life on 14 July 1972, but was overthrown by a military *coup* on 3 Aug. 1979. A Supreme Military Council then created was the sole political body until constitutional rule was resumed on 12 Oct. 1982.

AREA AND POPULATION. The mainland part of Equatorial Guinea is bounded north by Cameroon, east and south by Gabon, and west by the Gulf of Guinea in which lie the islands of Bioko (formerly Macías Nguema, formerly Fernando Póo) and Annobón (called Pagalu from 1973 to 1979). The total area is 28,051 sq. km (10,831 sq. miles) and the population at the 1983 census was 300,000. Estimate (1988) 336,000. Another 110,000 are estimated to remain in exile abroad.

The 7 provinces are grouped into 3 regions with areas and populations as follows:

	Sq. km	*Census 1983*	*Chief town*
Annobón	17	2,006	Palé
Bioko Norte	776	46,221	Malabo
Bioko Sur	1,241	10,969	Luba
Centro Sur	9,931	52,393	Kogo
Kié-Ntem	3,943	70,202	Mikomeseng
Litoral	6,665 [1]	66,370	Bata
Wele-Nzas	5,478	51,839	Mongomo

[1] Including the adjacent islets of Corisco, Elobey Grande and Elobey Chico (17 sq. km).

In 1986 the largest towns were Bata (17,000) and the capital Malabo (10,000).

The main ethnic group on the mainland (Río Muni) is the Fang; there are several minority groups along the coast and adjacent islets. On Bioko the indigenous inhabitants (Bubis) constitute 60% of the population there, the balance being mainly Fang and coast people from Río Muni; the formerly numerous immigrant workers from Nigeria and Cameroon have mostly been repatriated. On Annobón the indigenous inhabitants are the descendents of Portuguese slaves and still speak a Portuguese patois. The official language is Spanish.

CLIMATE. The climate is equatorial, with alternate wet and dry seasons. In Río Muni, the wet season lasts from Dec. to Feb.

CONSTITUTION AND GOVERNMENT. A new Constitution was approved in Aug. 1982 by 95% of the votes cast in a plebiscite, which also confirmed the President in office for a further 7-year term. It provides for an 11-member Council of State, and for a 41-member House of Representatives of the People, the latter being directly elected on 28 Aug. 1983 for a 5-year term and re-elected on 10 July 1988. The President appoints and leads a Council of Ministers.

On 12 Oct. 1987 a single new political party was formed as the *Partido Democrático de Guinea Ecuatorial.*

President of the Supreme Military Council, Defence: Brig.-Gen. Teodoro Obiang Nguema Mbasogo.

Prime Minister: Cristino Seriche Bioko.

Foreign Affairs: Marcelino Nguema Ongueme. *Economy and Finance:* Antonio Fernando Nve. *Justice and Religion:* Angel Ndong Micha.

National flag: Three horizontal stripes of green, white, red; a blue triangle based on the hoist; in the centre the national arms.

DEFENCE. The Army consists of 3 infantry battalions with (1990) 1,100 personnel. There is also a paramilitary force of some 2,000.

INTERNATIONAL RELATIONS

Membership. Equatorial Guinea is a member of UN, OAU and is an ACP state of EEC.

ECONOMY

Budget. The 1988 budget envisaged income at 7,147m. francs CFA and expenditure at 7,894m. francs CFA.

Currency. On 2 Jan. 1985 the country joined the franc zone and the *Ekuele* was replaced by the *franc CFA* with a parity value of 50 *francs* CFA to 1 French franc. There are coins of 1, 2, 5, 10, 25, 50, 100 and 500 *francs* CFA, and banknotes of 100, 500, 1,000, 5,000 and 10,000 *francs* CFA. In March 1990, £1 = 472 *francs* CFA; US$1 = 288 *francs* CFA.

Banking. The *Banque des Etats de l'Afrique Centrale* became the bank of issue in Jan. 1985. There are 2 commercial banks.

ENERGY AND NATURAL RESOURCES

Electricity. Production (1986) 17m. kwh.

Agriculture. The chief products are cocoa (74,000 hectares in 1988), coffee (19,000 hectares) and wood; in 1988 production was about 17,000 tonnes of cocoa, most of it high-grade exported to Spain and the US. Coffee, of mediocre quality, is chiefly a Fang product. Production (1988) of coffee 7,000 tonnes; palm oil, 5,000; palm kernels, 3,000; bananas, 20,000. Food crops include cassava, 56,000; sweet potatoes, 37,000. Plantations in the hinterland have been abandoned by their Spanish owners and except for cocoa, commercial agriculture is under serious difficulties.

Livestock (1988): Cattle, 5,000; sheep, 35,000; goats, 8,000; pigs, 5,000.

Forestry. In 1988, 1·3m. hectares, 46% of the land area was forested. Wood was almost entirely exported from Río Muni to Spain and the Federal Republic of Germany. Production: 1981, 465,000 cu. metres.

Fisheries. Catch (1986) 4,400 tonnes.

INDUSTRY AND TRADE

Industry. Bioko has very few industries. Río Muni has no industry except lumbering. Post-independence political conditions have not been conducive to private investment.

Commerce. In 1981 imports amounted to 7,982m. Bikuele (of which 80% came from Spain) and exports to 2,502m. Bikuele (of which Spain took 87%). Cocoa amounted to 71% of all exports and timber to 24%.

Total trade between Equatorial Guinea and UK (British Department of Trade returns, in £1,000 sterling):

	1985	*1986*	*1987*	*1988*	*1989*
Imports to UK	...	1	...	...	2
Exports and re-exports from UK	191	633	1,572	1,029	640

COMMUNICATIONS

Roads. Length (1982) 2,760 km of which 330 km surfaced.

Aviation. There are international airports at Malabo and Bata. The line Madrid–Malabo–Bata is subsidized by Spain. Links with Douala (from Malabo) and Libreville (Gabon) exist.

Shipping. Malabo is the main port. The other ports are Luba, formerly San Carlos (bananas, cocoa) in Bioko and Bata, Kogo and Mbini (wood) in Río Muni. A new harbour in Bata has been completed. In 1981 47,731 tonnes were unloaded and 50,843 loaded.

Post and Broadcasting. In Feb. 1989 the radio stations began broadcasting in French in addition to Spanish. Estimated number of telephones (1969), 1,451. In 1985 there were 100,000 radio and 2,200 TV receivers.

JUSTICE, RELIGION, EDUCATION AND WELFARE

Justice. The Constitution guarantees an independent judiciary. The Supreme Tribunal is the highest court of appeal and is located at Malabo. There are Courts of First Instance and Courts of Appeal at Malabo and Bata.

Religion. The population of Equatorial Guinea is nominally Roman Catholic with influential Protestant groups in Malabo and Río Muni.

Education. There were in 1981 about 40,110 pupils and 647 teachers in 511 primary schools and 3,013 pupils and 288 teachers in 14 secondary schools.

DIPLOMATIC REPRESENTATIVES

Of Equatorial Guinea in Great Britain
Ambassador: (Vacant).

Of Great Britain in Equatorial Guinea
Ambassador and Consul-General: M. Reith (resides in Yaoundé).

Of the USA in Equatorial Guinea (Calle de Los Ministros, Malabo)
Ambassador: Chester E. Norris Jr.

Of Equatorial Guinea to the USA and the United Nations
Ambassador: Dámaso-Obiang Ndong.

Further Reading

Atlas Historico y Geográfico de Africa Española. Madrid, 1955

Plan de Desarrollo Económico de la Guinea Ecuatorial. Presidencia del Gobierno. Madrid, 1963

Berman, S., *Spanish Guinea: An Annotated Bibliography.* Microfilm Service, Catholic University. Washington, D.C. 1961

Liniger-Goumaz, M., *La Guinée équatoriale un pays méconnu.* Paris, 1980.—*Connaître la Guinée Equatoriale.* Paris, 1986

Pélissier, R., *Les Territoires espagnols d'Afrique.* Paris, 1963.—*Los territorios españoles de Africa.* Madrid, 1964.—*Etudes Hispano-Guinéennes.* Orgeval, 1969

ETHIOPIA

Capital: Addis Ababa
Population: 46m. (1987)
GNP per capita: US$120 (1988)

Hebretesebawit Ityopia

HISTORY. The ancient empire of Ethiopia has its legendary origin in the meeting of King Solomon and the Queen of Sheba. Historically, the empire developed in the centuries before and after the birth of Christ, at Aksum in the north, as a result of Semitic immigration from South Arabia. The immigrants imposed their language and culture on a basic Hamitic stock. Ethiopia's subsequent history is one of sporadic expansion southwards and eastwards, checked from the 16th to early 19th centuries by devastating wars with Moslems and Gallas. Modern Ethiopia dates from the reign of the Emperor Theodore (1855–68).

Menelik II (1889–1913) defeated the Italians in 1896 and thereby safeguarded the empire's independence in the scramble for Africa. By successful campaigns in neighbouring kingdoms within Ethiopia (Jimma, Kaffa, Harar, etc.) he united the country under his rule and created the empire as it is today.

In 1936 Ethiopia was conquered by the Italians, who were in turn defeated by the Allied forces in 1941 when the Emperor returned.

The former Italian colony of Eritrea, from 1941 under British military administration, was in accordance with a resolution of the General Assembly of the UN, dated 2 Dec. 1950, handed over to Ethiopia on 15 Sept. 1952. Eritrea thereby became an autonomous unit within the federation of Ethiopia and Eritrea.

This federation became a unitary state on 14 Nov. 1962 when Eritrea was fully integrated with Ethiopia. The Federation gave rise to an Eritrean secessionist movement which has since pursued a campaign of military resistance. It is the longest war in Africa. The government engaged in preliminary peace talks with the rebels in Sept. 1989 and former president Carter of the USA also acted as mediator. Fierce fighting took place in Tigre in late 1989 and many small towns in Wollo province fell to the rebels.

A provisional military government assumed power on 12 Sept. 1974 and deposed the Emperor. On 24 Nov. 1974 the Provisional Military Government announced that on 23 Nov. it had executed 60 former military and civilian leaders including Gen. Aman Andom who was Chairman of the Provisional Military Administrative Council.

On 3 Feb. 1977, Brig.-Gen. Teferi Bante, the Chairman of PMAC and 6 other members of the ruling military council were killed and Lieut.-Col. Mengistu Haile Mariam became Chairman.

For war with Somalia *see* THE STATESMAN'S YEAR-BOOK, 1989-90, p.462.

The poor harvest of 1989 threatened famine for Ethiopia in 1990.

AREA AND POPULATION. Ethiopia is bounded north-east by the Red Sea, east by Djibouti and Somalia, south by Kenya and west by Sudan. It has a total area of 1,221,900 sq. km (471,800 sq. miles). The first census was carried out in 1984: Population (preliminary) 42,019,418. Estimate (1987) 46m. There were 265,000 refugees in Ethiopia in Jan. 1988.

The dominant race of Ethiopia, the Amhara, inhabit the central Ethiopian highlands. To the north of them are the Tigréans, akin to the Amhara and belonging to the same Christian church, but speaking a different, though related, language. Both these races are of mixed Hamitic and Semitic origin, and further mixed by intermarriage with Oromo (Galla) and other races. The Oromos, some of whom are Christian, some Moslem and some pagan, comprise about 40% of the entire population, and are a pastoral and agricultural people of Hamitic origin. Somalis, another Hamitic race, inhabit the south-east of Ethiopia, in particular the Ogaden desert region. These like the closely related Afar people, are Moslem. The Afar stretch northwards from Wollo region into Eritrea.

Region	Area (sq. km)	Population May 1984	Chief town	Population May 1984
Addis Ababa	218	1,412,575	—	—
Arussi	23,500	1,662,233	Assela	36,720
Bale	124,600	1,006,491	Goba	22,963
Eritrea	117,600	2,614,700	Asmara	275,385
Gemu Gofa	39,500	1,248,034	Arba Minch	23,030
Gojjam	61,600	3,244,882	Debre Markos	39,808
Gondar (Begemdir)	74,200	2,905,362	Gondar	68,958
Hararge	259,700	4,151,706	Harar	62,160
Illubabor	47,400	963,327	Mattu	12,491
Kefa	54,600	2,450,369	Jimma	60,992
Shoa	85,200	8,090,565	—	—
Sidamo	117,300	3,790,579	Awassa	36,169
Tigre	65,900	2,409,700	Mekele	61,583
Wollega	71,200	2,369,677	Lekemti	28,824
Wollo	79,400	3,609,918	Dessie	68,848

Other large towns (population, May 1984): Dire Dawa, in Hararge, 98,104; Nazret, in Shoa, 76,284; Bahr Dar, 54,800; Debre Zeit, 51,143.

Local Government. From Sept. 1987 the country was divided into 24 administrative and 5 autonomous regions. Each region governed by a regional *shengo.*

CLIMATE. The wide range of latitude produces many climatic variations between the high, temperate plateaus and the hot, humid lowlands. The main rainy season lasts from June to Aug., with light rains from Feb. to April, but the country is very vulnerable to drought. Addis Ababa. Jan. 59°F (15°C), July 59°F (15°C). Annual rainfall 50" (1,237 mm). Harar. Jan. 65°F (18·3°C), July 64°F (17·8°C). Annual rainfall 35" (897 mm). Massawa. Jan. 78°F (25·6°C), July 94°F (34·4°C). Annual rainfall 8" (193 mm).

CONSTITUTION AND GOVERNMENT. The People's Democratic Republic of Ethiopia was inaugurated on 10 Sept. 1987 at the first meeting of the newly elected *Shengo* (National Assembly). A new Constitution, on a Marxist model, was approved on 1 Feb. 1987 in a referendum. On 14 June 1987 Ethiopia held its first parliamentary election when 813 members belonging to the single political party the Workers' Party of Ethiopia were elected to the new civilian legislature.

President: Mengistu Haile Mariam (elected Sept. 1987).
Vice President: Lieut.-Col. Fisseha Desta.
Prime Minister: Fikre Selassie Wogderess.

National flag: Three horizontal stripes of green, yellow and red.
National anthem: Ityopya, Ityopia Kidemi (tune by Daniel Yohannes, 1975).

DEFENCE. Ethiopia's revolutionary rulers have moved away from US military assistance since they came to power and from 1977 have relied on USSR for most of their military aid.

Army. The Army, comprises 26 infantry divisions, 4 mechanized divisions and 1 airborne division. Equipment includes 100 T-62, 600 T-54/-55, 20 T-34 and 30 M-47 tanks. Strength (1990) 313,000 including a People's Militia.

Navy. The Navy, almost all of Soviet origin, consists of 2 small frigates, 8 fast missile craft, 6 fast torpedo craft and 7 patrol craft. There are also 2 medium landing ships, and 6 craft. The major auxiliaries comprise 1 transport and a training ship (an *ex*-US Seaplane tender built in 1942).

The main base and training establishments are at Massawa, and there are other bases at Assab, and in the Dahlak Islands where the Soviet Navy maintains a forward support facility.

Personnel in 1989 totalled 1,800.

Air Force. The Air Force, trained originally by Swedish and American personnel, but now operating aircraft of Soviet origin, has its headquarters at Debre Zeit, near Addis Ababa. It includes a training school and a central workshop. Fighter equipment is understood to comprise 140 MiG-17s, MiG-21s and MiG-23s. There is a squadron of Mi-24 helicopter gunships, and a transport squadron equipped with An-12s, and An-26s. Training aircraft include two-seat MiG-21s and L-39 jet basic trainers. More than 30 Mi-8 helicopters are in service. Most equipment surviving from the 1960s and '70s (such as F-5 fighters, Canberra bombers and US-built transports) is in storage. However since 1984 India has delivered 10 Chetak (Alouette III) helicopters and Italy 21 SF-260TP turboprop trainers. Personnel, (1990) 4,000 officers and men.

INTERNATIONAL RELATIONS

Membership. Ethiopia is a member of UN, OAU and is an ACP state of EEC.

ECONOMY

Planning. The economy is centrally planned and organized. GDP growth 1974–85 averaged 1·2%.

Budget. Revenue for 1985–86 was EB4,356m. and expenditure EB4,392m.

Of the estimated revenue in 1985–86, EB1,620m. came from taxes.

Currency. The Ethiopian *birr*, divided into 100 cents, is the unit of currency; it is based on 5·52 grains of fine gold. It consists of notes of EB1, 2, 10, 50 and 100 denominations, and bronze 1-, 5-, 10-, 25- and 50-cent coins. In March 1990 *Birr* 3·37 = £1 sterling; *Birr* 2·06 = US$1.

Banking. The State Bank is the National Bank of Ethiopia. The Investment Bank of Ethiopia, was established in 1963 with a capital of EB10m., of which the Government held the majority of shares. In Sept. 1965 it became the Ethiopian Investment Corporation, which is a substantial shareholder in a number of industrial and other ventures. There is also the Agricultural and Industrial Development Bank, SC.

On 1 Jan. 1975 the Government nationalized all banks, mortgage and insurance companies.

Weights and Measures. The metric system of weights and measures is officially in use. Traditional weights and measures vary considerably in the various provinces: the principal ones are: *Frasilla* = approximately $37^1/_2$ lb.; *gasha*, the principal unit of land measure, which is normally about 100 acres but can vary between 80 and 300 acres, depending on the quality of the land.

ENERGY AND NATURAL RESOURCES

Electricity. Production in 1986 totalled 722m. kwh. Supply 220 volts; 50 Hz. Over 92% of energy supply is from firewood, charcoal, dung and crop residues. The main power source is hydro-electricity although imported fuel supplies 22% of public power systems.

Oil. A Russian built state-owned oil refinery at Assab came on stream in 1967 with a capacity of 750,000 tonnes of crude per annum.

Minerals. Ethiopia has little proved mineral wealth. Salt is produced mainly in Eritrea, while a placer goldmine is worked by the Government of Adola in the south. Gold production, in 1985–86, was 923 kg. A new mine was under development at Lega Dembi in 1989. Small quantities of other minerals are produced including platinum.

Agriculture. Coffee is by far the most important source of rural income accounting for 70% of foreign earnings in 1982. Harari coffee (long berry Mocha) is cultivated in the east.

Teff (*Eragrastis abyssinica*) is the principal food grain, followed by barley, wheat, maize and durra. Pulses and oilseeds are imported for local consumption and export. Cane sugar is an important crop.

Production (1988 in 1,000 tonnes): Maize, 1,650; sorghum, 1,100; barley, 1,050; pulses, 987.

Livestock (1988): 31m. cattle, 23·4m. sheep, 17·5m. goats; smaller numbers of donkeys, horses, mules and camels. Hides and skins and butter (ghee) are important for home consumption and export. Sheep, cattle and chickens are the main providers of meat. In 1986 79·3% of the population were engaged in agriculture, producing 44·7% of GDP. The continuing drought has had a devastating effect on production.

Forestry. In 1988 forests covered 27·4m. hectares, representing 25% of the land area. Sawnwood production (1983) 45,000 cu. metres.

Fisheries. Catch (1986) 4,100 tonnes.

INDUSTRY AND TRADE

Industry. Industrial output is controlled by the State and most public industrial enterprizes are controlled by the Ministry of Industry. Most individual activity is centred around Addis Ababa and Asmara, although Asmara has been severely hit by the civil war in Eritrea.

Commerce. Imports and exports (in EB1m.) for 4 years.

	1982	*1983*	*1984*	*1985*
Imports	1,529	1,810	1,601	1,734
Exports	835	863	866	689

Total trade between Ethiopia and UK (British Department of Trade returns, in £1,000 sterling):

	1985	*1986*	*1987*	*1988*	*1989*
Imports to UK	13,805	22,343	12,875	8,451	12,772
Exports and re-exports from UK	66,089	50,049	46,146	47,661	44,148

Tourism. There were 59,000 tourists in 1986.

COMMUNICATIONS

Roads. There were (1989) 3,508 km of ashphalt roads and 9,687 km of rural and gravel roads.

Motor vehicles (1984): Cars, 41,300; lorries and trucks, 8,800; buses, 3,041.

Railways. The former Franco-Ethiopian Railway Co. (782 km, metre-gauge) became the Ethiopian-Djibouti Railway Corp. in 1981, when the remaining France-owned shares were bought out. In 1986 the railway carried 370,000 tonnes of freight and 1m. passengers.

Aviation. Ethiopian Air Lines, formed in 1946, carried 375,000 passengers in 1984.

Shipping. A state shipping line was established in 1964. The ports unloaded 1·75m. tonnes in 1982 and loaded 547,000.

Post and Broadcasting. The postal system serves 301 offices, mainly by air-mail. All the main centres are connected with Addis Ababa by telephone or radio telegraph. International telephone services are available at certain hours to most countries in Europe, North America and India. Number of telephones (1986), 162,000.

The Ethiopian Broadcasting Service makes sound broadcasts on the medium and short waves in English, Amharic and in the vernacular languages spoken within the country. There were about 45,000 television sets and 2m. radio receivers in 1986.

Cinemas (1974). There were 31 cinemas, with seating capacity of about 25,600.

Newspapers. There were (1984) 3 government-controlled daily newspapers with a combined circulation of about 47,000.

JUSTICE, RELIGION, EDUCATION AND WELFARE

Justice. The legal system is said to be based on the Justinian Code. A new penal code came into force in 1958 and Special Penal Law in 1974. Codes of criminal procedure, civil, commercial and maritime codes have since been promulgated.

The extra-territorial rights formerly enjoyed by foreigners have been abolished, but any person accused in an Ethiopian court has the right to have his case transferred to the High Court, provided he asks for this before any evidence has been taken in the court of first instance.

Provincial and district courts have been established, and High Court judges visit the provincial courts on circuit. The Supreme Court at Addis Ababa is presided over by the Chief Justice.

Religion. About 45% of the population are Moslem and 40% Christian, mainly belonging to the Ethiopian Orthodox Church.

Education. Primary education commences at 7 years and continues with optional secondary education at 13 years. In the academic year 1988–89 there were more than 2·5m. pupils in primary schools and in secondary schools there were 500,000 students. Higher education is co-ordinated under the National University, chartered in 1961; in 1979–80, there were 14,562 students. The University College, the Engineering, Building and Theological Colleges are in Addis Ababa, the Agricultural College in Harar and the Public Health College in Gondar.

Health. In 1987 there were about 90 hospitals with 11,000 beds.

DIPLOMATIC REPRESENTATIVES

Of Ethiopia in Great Britain (17 Prince's Gate, London, SW7 1PZ)
Ambassador: Ato Teferra Haile-Selassie (accredited 24 June 1985).

Of Great Britain in Ethiopia (Fikre Mariam Abatechan St., Addis Ababa)
Ambassador: M. J. C. Glaze, CMG.

Of Ethiopia in the USA (2134 Kalorama Rd., NW, Washington D.C., 20008)
Chargé d'Affaires: Girma Amare.

Of the USA in Ethiopia (Entoto St., Addis Ababa)
Chargé d'Affaires: Robert G. Houdek.

Of Ethiopia to the United Nations
Ambassador: Tesfaye Tadesse.

Further Reading

Clapham, C., *Transformation and Continuity in Revolutionary Ethiopia.* CUP, 1988
Halliday, F. and Molyneaux, M., *The Ethiopian Revolution.* London, 1981
Hancock, G., *Ethiopia: The Challenge of Hunger.* London, 1985
Keller, E. J. *Revolutionary Ethiopia: From Empire to People's Republic.* Indiana Univ. Press, 1989
Pool, D., *Eritrea: Africa's Longest War.* London, 1982
Schwab, P., *Ethiopia: Politics, Economics and Society.* Boulder, 1985.

FALKLAND ISLANDS

Capital: Stanley
Population: 1,916 (1986)

HISTORY. France established a settlement in 1764 and Britain a second settlement in 1765. In 1770 Spain bought out the French and drove off the British. This action on the part of Spain brought that country and Britain to the verge of war. The Spanish restored the settlement to the British in 1771, but the settlement was withdrawn on economic grounds in 1774. In 1806 Spanish rule was overthrown in Argentina, and the Argentine claimed to succeed Spain in the French and British settlements in 1820. The British objected and reclaimed their settlement in 1832 as a Crown Colony.

On 2 April 1982 Argentine forces invaded the Falkland Islands and the Governor was expelled. At a meeting of the UN Security Council, held on 3 April, the voting was 10 to 1 in favour of the resolution calling for Argentina to withdraw. Britain regained possession on 14–15 June after the Argentine surrendered.

AREA AND POPULATION. The Crown Colony is situated in the South Atlantic Ocean about 480 miles north-east of Cape Horn. The numerous islands cover 4,700 sq. miles. The main East Falkland Island, 2,610 sq. miles; the West Falkland, 2,090 sq. miles, including the adjacent small islands.

The population of the Falkland Islands at census 1986 was 1,916. The only town is Stanley, in East Falkland, with a population of just over 1,200. The population of the Falkland Islands is nearly all of British descent, with about 67% born in the islands. A large garrison of British servicemen was stationed near Stanley in 1987.

CLIMATE. A cool temperate climate, much affected by strong winds, particularly in spring. Stanley. Jan. 49°F (9·4°C), July 35°F (1·7°C). Annual rainfall 27" (681 mm).

CONSTITUTION AND GOVERNMENT. A new Constitution came into force on 3 Oct. 1985. This incorporated a chapter protecting fundamental human rights and in the preamble recalled the provisions on the right of self-determination contained in international covenants.

Executive power is vested in the Governor who must consult the Executive Council except on urgent or trivial matters. He must consult the Commander British Forces on matters relating to defence and internal security (except police).

There is a Legislative Council consisting of 8 elected members and 2 *ex officio* members, the Chief Executive and Financial Secretary. Only elected members have a vote. The Commander British Forces has a right to attend and take part in its proceedings but has no vote. The Attorney General also has a similar right to take part in proceedings with the consent of the person presiding. The Governor presides over sittings. He also presides over sittings of the Executive Council which consists of 3 elected members (elected by and from the elected members of Legislative Council) and the Chief Executive and Financial Secretary (*ex officio*). The Commander British Forces and Attorney General have a right to attend but may not vote.

Offices in the Public Service are constituted by the Governor and he makes appointments and is responsible for discipline. The Constitution allows for the establishment of a public service commission.

Governor: W. H. Fullerton, CMG.
Chief Executive: R. Sampson.
Financial Secretary: J. H. Buckland-James.
Attorney General: D. G. Lang.
Government Secretary: C. F. Redston.

Flag: British Blue Ensign with arms of Colony on a white disc in the fly.

DEFENCE. Since 1982 the Islands have been defended by a large garrison of British servicemen. The Commander British Forces is responsible for all military matters in the Islands. He liaises with the Governor on civilian and political matters, and advises him on matters of defence and internal security, except police. In addition there is a local volunteer defence force.

ECONOMY

Budget. Revenue and expenditure (in £ sterling) for fiscal years ending 30 June:

	1983–84	*1984–85*	*1985–86*	*1986–87*	*1987–88* [1]	*1988–89* [1]
Revenue	5,314,000	5,163,000	6,003,315	19,646,310	22,774,680	35,761,900
Expenditure	3,867,000	4,358,000	5,344,048	12,212,805	21,968,150	28,646,190

[1] Estimate

Currency. The Falkland £ is at parity with the £ sterling.

Banking. On 1 Dec. 1983 the government savings bank was dissolved, and all savings bank deposits were transferred to the Standard Chartered Bank, which has a branch in Stanley, and provides a full range of banking facilities.

SHEEP FARMING. Much of the Colony is divided into large sheep runs. Subdivision into smaller family units is actively being pursued. Wool is the principal product, but hides are exported. In 1988 there were 704,602 sheep, 5,969 cattle and 1,837 horses in the islands.

DEVELOPMENT. The economy was formerly based solely on agriculture, principally sheep farming with a little dairy farming for domestic requirements and crops for winter fodder. Since the establishment of a 150-mile interim conservation and management zone around the Islands and the consequent introduction, on 1 Feb. 1987, of a licensing regime for vessels fishing within the zone the economy has diversified and income from the associated fishing activities is now the largest source of revenue. The Falkland Islands Development Corporation was established by statute in June 1984 with the aim of encouraging economic development. The first projects assisted by the Corporation include inshore and offshore fisheries surveys to establish potential catch size and value, agricultural improvement schemes to encourage investment in the land, a wool spinning and knitting factory to process a portion of the islands' main product, a new dairy and a hydroponic market garden.

TRADE. Total trade between the Falkland Islands and UK (British Department of Trade returns, in £1,000 sterling):

	1986	*1987*	*1988*	*1989*
Imports to UK	14,286	8,148	4,209	5,375
Exports and re-exports from UK	11,135	7,353	9,037	10,200

COMMUNICATIONS

Roads. There are 27 km of made-up roads in and around Stanley and another 54 km of all-weather road between Stanley and Mount Pleasant Airport. Other settlements outside Stanley are linked by tracks, which are passable, with high axle clearing four-wheel drive vehicles in all but the worst weather. Work has recently recommenced on the construction of an all-weather track linking the Estancia Farm with the Stanley to Mount Pleasant Road which help towards opening up the north of East Falkland. The Government is also providing assistance to farms which wish to improve tracks and bridges to their immediate area.

Aviation. Air communication is currently *via* Ascension Island. A new airport, completed in 1986, is sited at Mount Pleasant on East Falkland. RAF Tristar aircraft operate a twice-weekly service between the Falklands and the UK. Internal air links are provided by the government operated air service, which carries passengers, mail, freight and medical patients between the settlements and Stanley on non-scheduled flights in Islander aircraft.

Shipping. A charter vessel calls 4 or 5 times a year to/from the UK. There is occasional direct communication with South Georgia, the South Sandwich Islands and the British Antarctic Territory by the Royal research ships *John Biscoe* and *Bransfield* and by the ice-patrol vessel HMS *Endurance*. Vessels of the Royal Fleet Auxiliary run regularly to South Georgia. Sea links with Chile and Uruguay began in 1989.

Post and Broadcasting. Number of telephones (1987) 560. International direct dialling is available, as are international telex and facsimile links. Cable and Wireless plc signed a contract with the Falkland Islands Government in Sept. 1988 for the complete replacement of the telecommunications network with a modern system, which will allow confidential communications between the Camp (and Stanley) and the outside world for the first time. There is a government-operated broadcasting station at Stanley and television broadcasts began in 1988.

JUSTICE, EDUCATION AND WELFARE

Justice. There is a Supreme Court, and a Court of Appeal sits in the United Kingdom; appeals may go from that court to the judicial committee of the Privy Council. Judges have security of tenure and may only be removed for inability or misbehaviour on the advice of the judicial committee of the Privy Council. The senior resident judicial officer is the Senior Magistrate. There is an Attorney General and a Crown Counsel and a firm of solicitors established an office in Stanley in 1988.

Education. Education is compulsory between the ages of 5 and 15 years. In Sept. 1989 there were 375 children receiving education in the Colony. Almost 75% attended schools in Stanley, the others were taught in settlement schools or by itinerant teachers. 5 children were being educated abroad. Expenditure on education and training from own funds 1988-89 was £1,031,050.

Health. The Government Medical Department is responsible for all medical services to civilians. Expenditure (1988-89) £1,224,440. The Chief Medical Officer advises the Government on policy, and is chairman of the Board of Health responsible for public health. Medical services for the Islands are run from a temporary hospital; a new hospital and some sheltered accommodation was completed in March 1987. Services include all primary care for Stanley and the flying doctor service for outlying farm settlements.

WILD LIFE. The Falkland Islands are noted for their outstanding wild life, including penguin and seal. Four Nature Reserves have been declared and 18 Wild Animal and Bird Sanctuaries gazetted. The brown trout introduced between 1947 and 1952 can now be found in nearly all the rivers and there are good runs of sea-trout during spring and autumn.

Further Reading

Falkland Islands: The Facts. HMSO, London, 1982
Falkland Islands Journal. Stanley, from 1967
Falkland Islands Review [Franks Report] Cmnd. 8787. HMSO, London, 1983
Falklands/Malvinas, Whose Crisis? Latin American Bureau, London, 1982
Calvert, P., *The Falklands Crisis: The Rights and the Wrongs.* London, 1982
Hanrahan, B. and Fox, R., *'I counted them all out and I counted them all back'*. London, 1982
Hastings, M. and Jenkins, S., *The Battle for the Falklands.* London, 1983
Hoffmann, F. L. and Hoffmann, O. M., *Sovereignty in Dispute.* London, 1984
Phipps, C., *What Future for the Falklands?* London, 1977
Shackleton, E., *Falkland Islands Economic Study 1982.* HMSO, London, 1982
Strange, I. J., *The Falkland Islands.* 3rd ed. Newton Abbot, 1983.—*The Falkland Islands and their Natural History.* Newton Abbot, 1987

FIJI

Capital: Suva
Population: 727,104 (1989)
GNP per capita: US$1,540 (1988)

HISTORY. The Fiji Islands were discovered by Tasman in 1643 and visited by Capt. Cook in 1774, but first recorded in detail by Capt. Bligh after the mutiny of the *Bounty* (1789). In the 19th century the search for sandalwood, in which enormous profits were made, brought many ships. Deserters and shipwrecked men stayed on; firearms salvaged from wrecks were used in native wars, new diseases swept the islands, and rum and muskets became regular articles of trade. Tribal wars became bloody and general until Fiji was ceded to Britain on 10 Oct. 1874, after a previous offer of cession had been refused. British administrators produced order out of chaos, and since then there has been steady political, social and economic progress. Fiji gained independent status on 10 Oct. 1970.

AREA AND POPULATION. Fiji comprises about 332 islands and islets (about 110 inhabited) lying between 15° and 22° S. lat. and 174° E. and 177° W. long. The largest is Viti Levu, area 10,429 sq. km (4,027 sq. miles), next is Vanua Levu, area 5,556 sq. km (2,145 sq. miles). The island of Rotuma (47 sq. km, 18 sq. miles), about 12° 30' S. lat., 178° E. long., was added to the colony in 1881. Total area, 7,078 sq. miles (18,333 sq. km).

A population census is taken every 10 years. Total population (census, Aug. 1986), 715,375; average annual increase about 2%. The 1989 estimated total population of 727,104 consisted of the following: 351,966 (48·4%) Fijians; 337,557 (46·4%) Indians; 37,581 (5·2%) were of other races.

Suva, the capital, is on the south coast of Viti Levu; population (census, 1986), 71,608. Suva was proclaimed a city on 2 Oct. 1953. Lautoka had 28,728 in 1986.

Vital statistics, 1987: Crude birth rate per 1,000 population, Fijian, 30·7, Indian, 25·6; crude death rate per 1,000 population, Fijian, 5·4, Indian, 5·2. Average life expectancy (1989) 68 years.

CLIMATE. A tropical climate, but oceanic influences prevent undue extremes of heat or humidity. The S.E. Trades blow from May to Nov., during which time nights are cool and rainfall amounts least. Suva. Jan. 80°F (26·7°C), July 73°F (22·8°C). Annual rainfall 117" (2,974 mm).

CONSTITUTION AND GOVERNMENT. Following a military *coup* in May 1987 the government was removed from office by the Governor-General who took temporary control of the administration. A second *coup* led by Col. Rabuka took place in Sept. and Fiji was declared a Republic and membership of the Commonwealth lapsed.

President: Ratu Sir Penaia Ganilau, GCMG, KCVO, KBE, DSO.

Prime Minister and Minister for Home and Foreign Affairs: Ratu Sir Kamisese Mara, GCMG, KBE.

Attorney-General and Justice: Sailosi Kepa. *Finance and Economic Planning:* Josevata Kamikamica. *Education, Youth and Sport:* Filipe Bole. *Primary Industries and Co-operatives:* Viliame Gonelevu. *Health:* Dr Apenisa Kurisaqila. *Indian Affairs:* Irene Jai Narayan. *Fijian Affairs and Rural Development:* Col. Vatiliai Navunisaravi. *Tourism, Civil Aviation and Energy:* David Pickering. *Women and Social Welfare:* Adi Finau Tabakaucoro. *Forests:* Ratu Sir Josaia Tavaiqia. *Lands and Mineral Resources:* Ratu William Toganivalu. *Infrastructure and Public Utilities:* Apisai Tora. *Housing and Urban Development:* Tomasi Vakatora. *Employment and Industrial Relations:* Taniela Veitata. *Trade and Commerce:* Berenado Vunibobo. *Information, Broadcasting, Television and Telecommunications:* Ratu Inoke Kubuabola.

Flag: Light blue with the Union Flag in the canton and the shield of Fiji in the fly.

Local Government. Fiji is divided into 14 provinces, each with its own council under which 188 Tikina Councils have been established. The number of Tikina Councils within a province varies from 4 to 22. Tikina Councils have wide powers to make by-laws and levy rates to raise revenue. 50% of the rates collected is credited to the Provincial Council treasury for the running of the Council and 50% is used for the financing of the Tikina and village projects.

DEFENCE. The Fiji Military Forces are for the defence of Fiji, maintenance of law and order and provision of forces to international peace-keeping agencies overseas. The forces have two overseas battalions (in Egypt and Lebanon) and regular and territorial units at home. Total active strength (1989) 3,200 (reserves, 5,000).

Navy. A naval division of the armed forces formed in 1974 to perform miscellaneous offshore duties. Present strength is 3 *ex*-US coastal patrol craft (1 with a helicopter deck) and 2 inshore craft. There are also 2 small survey craft. Naval personnel in 1989 numbered 300 officers and ratings. The naval base is in Suva.

INTERNATIONAL RELATIONS

Membership. Fiji is a member of the UN, the Colombo Plan, the South Pacific Forum and is an ACP state of the EEC.

ECONOMY

Budget. The financial year corresponds with the calendar year. All figures are in $1m. Fijian.

	1985	*1986*	*1987*	*1988*	*1989*
Revenue	349·9	348·1	341·2	389·7	390·0
Expenditure	349·3	370·9	393·9	434·6	539·0

Currency. Fiji changed to decimal currency on 13 Jan. 1969, with the major unit being $F1. In March 1990, £1 = $F2·50; US$ = $F1·53.

Banking. The National Bank of Fiji had, in 1985, deposits amounting to $F62·3m. due to 241,375 accounts. The headquarters are at Suva, and there are 11 branches, 35 postal agencies and 9 private agencies throughout Fiji. The Westpac Banking Corporation has 9 branches, 2 sub-branches and 18 agencies; the Bank of New Zealand has 8 branches, and 18 agencies; the Australia and New Zealand Bank has 9 branches and 7 agencies and the Bank of Baroda has 8 branches and 3 agencies in Fiji.

ENERGY AND NATURAL RESOURCES

Electricity. Production (1986) 220m. kwh. Supply 240 volts; 50 Hz.

Agriculture. Some 600,000 acres of land are in agricultural use. Sugar-cane is the principal cash crop (production, 1988, 3·1m. tonnes), accounting for more than two-thirds of Fiji's export earnings; one quarter of the population depend on it directly for their livelihood. Copra, Fiji's second major cash crop (output, 1988, 13,000 tonnes), provides coconut oil and other products for export. Ginger is the third major export crop replacing bananas which has declined through disease and hurricane. Production, 1988 (in 1,000 tonnes): Rice, 31; maize, 2; fruit, 23; vegetables, 10. Tobacco and cocoa are also cultivated. There is a small, but fast developing, livestock industry.

Livestock (1988): Cattle, 159,000; horses, 42,000; goats, 60,000; pigs, 29,000; poultry, 2m.

Forestry. In 1987 there were 1·2m. hectares of forests and woodland; 65% of the land area. Fiji supplies the bulk of its own timber requirements. A comprehensive pine scheme has been implemented.

Fisheries. Catch (1985) 15,900 tonnes. Exports (1986) F$20m.

INDUSTRY AND TRADE

Industry. Major industries include 4 large sugar-mills, the goldmines (2,647 kg in 1987) and 2 mills which process copra into coconut oil and coconut meal. There is a great variety of light industries.

Trade Unions. In 1987 there were 46 trade unions operating with about 45,000 members.

Commerce. Exports in 1987, $F408,815,000 (including re-exports). Imports, $F465,583,000. Chief exports: Sugar, gold, molasses and canned fish.

Total trade between Fiji and UK (British Department of Trade returns, in £1,000 sterling):

	1985	*1986*	*1987*	*1988*	*1989*
Imports to UK	36,328	66,500	53,062	65,273	69,558
Exports and re-exports from UK	9,843	8,775	7,381	6,358	10,221

Tourism. In 1988, there were 208,155 visitors. Earnings (1988) $F180·6m.

COMMUNICATIONS

Roads. Total road mileage is 2,996, of which 376 are sealed (paved), 2,534 are gravelled and 86 are unimproved. In 1987, there were 70,206 vehicles including 29,262 private cars, 23,029 goods vehicles, 1,289 buses, 4,499 tractors, 2,236 taxis and 2,882 rental and hire cars and others.

Railway. Fiji Sugar Cane Corporation runs 600 mm gauge railways at four of its mills on Viti Levu and Vanua Levu, totalling 595 km.

Aviation. Fiji provides an essential staging point for long-haul trunk-route aircraft operating between North America, Australia and New Zealand. Under the South Pacific Air Transport Council, which comprises the UK, Australia, New Zealand and Fiji, the international airport at Nadi has been developed and administered. Eighteen other airports are in use for domestic services. In 1985, 257,646 passengers arrived at airports.

Shipping. The 3 ports of entry are Suva, Lautoka and Leuuka. In 1985, 1,313 vessels called at Suva, 780 at Lautoka and 1,004 at Leuuka. Local shipping provides services to scattered outer islands of the group.

Post and Broadcasting. There were (1988) 50 post offices and 185 postal agencies. Overseas telephone and telegram services are available through the Commonwealth cable to most countries except those in the South Pacific, which are served by direct radio circuits. The automatic telex network operates through New Zealand into the international telex system. There are ship-to-shore radio facilities. There were 60,017 telephones in 1987. In 1983 there were 400,000 radio receivers.

Newspapers. In 1988 there were 2 daily newspapers (circulation 40,000).

JUSTICE, RELIGION, EDUCATION AND WELFARE

Justice. An independent Judiciary is guaranteed under the Constitution of Fiji. The Constitution allows for a High Court of Fiji which has unlimited original jurisdiction to hear and determine any civil or criminal proceedings under any law.

The High Court also has jurisdiction to hear and determine constitutional and electoral questions including the membership of members of the House of Representatives.

The Chief Justice of Fiji is appointed by the President acting after consultation with the Prime Minister.

The Fiji Court of Appeal of which the Chief Justice is *ex officio* President is formed by three specially appointed Justices of Appeal. The Justices of Appeal are appointed by the President acting after consultation with the Judicial and Legal Services Commission. Generally any person convicted of any offence has a right of appeal from the High Court to the Fiji Court of Appeal. The final appellant court is the Supreme Court. Most matters coming before the Superior Courts originate in Magistrates' Courts.

Police. The Royal Fiji Police Force had (1987) a total strength of 1,561.

Religion. The 1986 census showed: Christians, 378,452; Hindus, 273,088; Sikhs, 4,674; Moslems, 56,001; Confucians, 82.

Education (1987). School attendance is not compulsory in Fiji. There were 815 schools scattered over 56 islands, staffed by 7,082 teachers, of whom about 99·3% were trained. There were also 236 pre-schools. The 674 primary and 141 secondary schools had 180,514 pupils. The technical and vocational schools had 4,039 students and the teachers' college 205. There were 3 teacher-training colleges, 1 medical and 2 agricultural schools.

The University of the South Pacific (USP) opened in Feb. 1968 at Laucala Bay in Suva. In 1987 there were about 2,344 students enrolled in courses on campus and about 4,085 enrolments in extension services. The University has an operating budget of $F12·13m. a year provided by the 11 countries it serves.

Total government expenditure on education in 1987 (including USP) was $F76,184,852.

Health. In 1987 there were 25 hospitals with 1,721 beds, 271 doctors, 48 dentists and 1,543 nurses.

DIPLOMATIC REPRESENTATIVES

Of Fiji in Great Britain (34 Hyde Park Gate, London, SW7 5DN)
Ambassador: Brig.-Gen. Ratu Epeli Nailatikau, LVO, OBE (accredited 8 June 1988).

Of Great Britain in Fiji (47 Gladstone Rd., Suva)
Ambassador: A. B. Peter Smart, CMG.

Of Fiji in the USA (2233 Wisconsin Ave., NW, Washington, D.C., 20007)
Chargé d'Affaires: Abdul Yusuf.

Of the USA in Fiji (31 Loftus St., Suva)
Ambassador: Evelyn I. H. Teegen.

Of Fiji to the United Nations
Ambassador: Winston Thompson.

Further Reading

Statistical Information: A Bureau of Statistics was set up in 1950 (Government Buildings, Suva).
Trade Report. Annual (from 1887 [covering 1883–86]). Bureau of Statistics, Suva.
Journal of the Fiji Legislative Council. Annual (from 1914 [under different title from 1885]). Suva
Fiji Today. Suva, Annual
Fiji Facts and Figures. Suva, 1986
Report of Commission of Inquiry Into Natural Resources and Population Trends in Fiji. Suva, Government Press, 1960
Ali, A., *Plantations to Politics, studies on Fiji Indians.* Suva, 1980
Bain, K., *Fiji at the Crossroads.* London, 1989
Capell, A., *New Fijian Dictionary.* 2nd ed. Glasgow, 1957
Ravuvu, A., *Vaka i Taukei: The Fijian Way of Life.* Suva, 1983
Scarr, D., *Fiji, A Short History.* Sydney, 1984
Wright, R., *On Fiji Islands.* London, 1987

FINLAND

Suomen Tasavalta—Republiken Finland

Capital: Helsinki
Population: 4·95m. (1988)
GNP per capita: US$21,143 (1988)

HISTORY. Since the Middle Ages Finland was a part of the realm of Sweden. In the 18th century parts of south-eastern Finland were conquered by Russia, and the rest of the country was ceded to Russia by the peace treaty of Hamina in 1809. Finland became an autonomous grand-duchy which retained its previous laws and institutions under its Grand Duke, the Emperor of Russia. After the Russian revolution Finland declared itself independent on 6 Dec. 1917. The Civil War began in Jan. 1918 between the 'whites' and 'reds', the latter being supported by Russian bolshevik troops. The defeat of the red guards in May 1918 consequently meant freeing the country from Russian troops. A peace treaty with Soviet Russia was signed in 1920.

On 30 Nov. 1939 Soviet troops invaded Finland, after Finland had rejected territorial concessions demanded by the USSR. These, however, had to be made in the peace treaty of 12 March 1940, amounting to 32,806 sq. km and including the Carelian Isthmus, Viipuri and the shores of Lake Ladoga.

When the German attack on the USSR was launched in June 1941 Finland again became involved in the war against the USSR. On 19 Sept. 1944 an armistice was signed in Moscow. Finland agreed to cede to Russia the Petsamo area in addition to cessions made in 1940 (total 42,934 sq. km) and to lease to Russia for 50 years the Porkkala headland to be used as a military base. Further, Finland undertook to pay 300m. gold dollars in reparations within 6 years (later extended to 8 years). The peace treaty was signed in Paris on 10 Feb. 1947. The payment of reparations was completed on 19 Sept. 1952. The military base of Porkkala was returned to Finland on 26 Jan. 1956.

AREA AND POPULATION. Finland is bounded north-west and north by Norway, east by the USSR, south by the Baltic Sea and west by the Gulf of Bothnia and Sweden. The area and the population of Finland on 31 Dec. 1988 (Swedish names in brackets):

Province	*Area (sq. km)* [1]	*Population* [2]	*Population per sq. km* [2]
Uusimaa (Nyland)	9,898	1,226,344	123·9
Turku-Pori (Åbo-Björneborg)	22,170	715,608	32·3
Ahvenanmaa (Åland)	1,527	24,045	15·7
Häme (Tavastehus)	17,010	684,431	40·2
Kymi (Kymmene)	10,783	335,922	31·2
Mikkeli (St Michel)	16,342	207,675	12·7
Pohjois-Karjala (Norra Karelen)	17,782	176,189	9·9
Kuopio	16,511	255,893	15·5
Keski-Suomi (Mellersta Finland)	16,230	249,504	15·4
Vaasa (Vasa)	26,447	444,060	6·8
Oulu (Uleåborg)	56,866	434,847	7·6
Lappi (Lappland)	93,057	199,841	2·1
Total	304,623	4,954,359	16·3

[1] Excluding inland water area which totals 33,522 sq. km. [2] Resident population.

The growth of the population, which was 421,500 in 1750, has been:

End of year	*Urban*	*Rural*	*Total*	*Percentage urban*
1800	46,600	786,100	832,700	5·6
1900	333,300	2,322,600	2,655,900	12·5
1950	1,302,400	2,727,400	4,029,800	32·3
1960	1,707,000	2,739,200	4,446,200	38·4
1970	2,340,300	2,258,000	4,598,300	50·9
1980	2,865,100	1,922,700	4,787,800	59·8
1988	3,060,700	1,893,700	4,954,400	61·8

The population on 31 Dec. 1988 by language primarily spoken: Finnish, 4,638,941; Swedish, 297,155; other languages, 16,535; Lappish, 1,728.

The principal towns with resident census population, 31 Dec. 1988, are (Swedish names in brackets):

Helsinki (Helsingfors)—capital	489,965	Kajaani	35,940
(metropolitan area)	987,009	Kokkola (Gamlakarleby)	34,409
Tampere (Tammerfors)	171,068	Imatra	34,143
(metropolitan area)	259,901	Rovaniemi	32,942
Turku (Åbo)	159,917	Kouvola	31,890
(metropolitan area)	263,308	Mikkeli (St Michel)	31,795
Espoo (Esbo)	167,734	Rauma (Raumo)	30,460
Vantaa (Vanda)	151,157	Savonlinna (Nyslott)	28,469
Oulu (Uleåborg)	98,933	Järvenpää	30,094
Lahti	93,251	Seinäjoki	27,233
Kuopio	79,495	Kerava	27,052
Pori (Björneborg)	76,789	Kemi	25,730
Jyväskylä	66,197	Nokia	25,344
Kotka	57,181	Varkaus	24,657
Vaasa (Vasa)	53,440	Riihimäki	24,862
Lappeenranta (Villmanstrand)	54,920	Iisalmi	23,724
Joensuu	47,089	Tornio	22,616
Hämeenlinna (Tavastehus)	42,760	Valkeakoski	22,242
Hyvinkää (Hyvinge)	39,808	Kuusankoski	21,746

Vital statistics in calendar years:

	Living births	*Of which illegitimate*	*Still-born*	*Marriages*	*Deaths (exclusive of still-born)*	*Emigration*
1981	63,469	8,431	260	30,100	44,404	10,042
1982	66,106	9,007	263	30,459	43,408	7,403
1983	66,076	9,386	268	29,474	45,388	6,822
1984	65,076	9,825	260	28,550	45,098	7,467
1985	62,796	10,931	241	25,751	48,198	7,739
1986	60,632	10,292	193	25,820	47,135	8,269
1987	59,827	11,467	314	26,267	47,949	8,475
1988	63,313	...	...	26,453	49,026	8,559

In 1987 the rate per 1,000 was: Births, 12·1; marriages, 5·3; deaths, 9·6, and infantile deaths (1985, per 1,000 live births), 6·2.

Population Census 1985. 5 vols. Helsinki, 1988
Population. Annual. Helsinki

CLIMATE. The climate is severe in winter, which lasts about 6 months, but mean temperatures in south and south-west are less harsh, 21°F (–6°C). In the north, mean temperatures may fall to 8·5°F (–13°C). Snow covers the ground for three months in the south and for over six months in the far north. Summers are short but quite warm, with occasional very hot days. Precipitation is light throughout the country, with one third falling as snow, the remainder mainly as convectional rain in summer and autumn. Helsinki (Helsingfors). Jan. 21°F (–6°C), July 62°F (16·5°C). Annual rainfall 24·7" (618 mm).

CONSTITUTION AND GOVERNMENT. Finland is a republic according to the Constitution of 17 July 1919.

Parliament consists of one chamber of 200 members chosen by direct and proportional election in which all Finnish citizens (men or women) who are 18 years have the vote (since 1972). The country is divided into 15 electoral districts with a representation proportional to their population. Every citizen over the age of 18 is eligible for Parliament, which is elected for 4 years, but can be dissolved sooner by the President.

The President is elected for 6 years by direct popular vote or, if no presidential candidate wins an absolute majority, by a college of 301 electors, elected by the votes of the citizens in the same way as the members of Parliament.

President of Finland: Dr Mauno Koivisto (elected 1982, re-elected 1988).

State of Parties for Parliament elected on 15–16 March 1987: Conservative 53; Swedish Party, 13 (including 1 for Coalition of Åland); Centre, 40; Rural, 9; Social Democratic Party, 56; People's Democratic League, 16; Christian League, 5; the Greens, 4; Democratic Alternative, 4.

The Council of State (Cabinet), composed as follows in March 1990:

Prime Minister: Harri Holkeri.

Foreign Affairs: Pertti Paasio. *Minister of State, Prime Minister's Office:* Ilkka Kanerva. *Finance:* Matti Louekoski. *Finance (Deputy):* Ulla Puolanne. *Education:* Christoffer Taxell. *Education (Deputy):* Anna-Liisa Kasurinen. *Social Affairs and Health:* Mauri Miettinen. *Social Affairs and Health (Deputy):* Tuulikki Hämäläinen. *Justice:* Tarja Halonen. *Agriculture and Forestry:* Toivo T. Pohjala. *Transport and Communication:* Raimo Vistbacka. *Labour:* Matti Puhakka. *Trade and Industry:* Ilkka Suominen. *Defence:* Ole Norrback. *Environment:* Kaj Bärlund. *Interior:* Jarmo Rantanen. *Foreign Trade:* Pertti Salolainen.

National flag: White with a blue Scandinavian cross.

National anthem: Maamme; Swedish: Vårt land (words by J. L. Runeberg, 1843; tune by F. Pacius, 1848).

Finnish and Swedish are the official languages of Finland.

Local Government. For administrative purposes Finland is divided into 12 provinces (*lääni*, Sw.: *län*). The administration of each province is entrusted to a governor (*maaherra*, Sw.: *landshövding*) appointed by the President. He directs the activities of the provincial office (*lääninhallitus*, Sw.: *länsstyrelse*) and of local sheriffs (*nimismies*, Sw.: *länsman*). In 1989 the number of sheriff districts was 224.

The unit of local government is the commune. Main fields of communal activities are local planning, roads and harbours, sanitary services, education, health services and social aid. The communes raise taxes independent from state taxation. Two different kinds of communes are distinguished: Urban communes (*kaupunki*, Sw.: *stad*) and rural communes. In 1990 there were altogether 460 communes of which 94 were urban and 366 rural. In all communes communal councils are elected for terms of 4 years; all inhabitants (men and women) of the commune who have reached their 18th year are entitled to vote and eligible. The executive power is in each commune vested in a board which consists of members elected by the council and one or a few chief officials of the commune. Several communes often form an association for the administration of some common institution, *e.g.*, a hospital or a vocational school.

The autonomous county *(landskap)* of Åland has a county council *(landsting)* of one chamber, elected according to rule corresponding to those for parliamentary elections. In addition to its provincial governor it has a county board with executive power in matters within the field of the autonomy of the county.

Constitution Act and Parliament Act of Finland. Helsinki, 1978

DEFENCE. The period of military training is 240, 285 or 330 days and refresher training obligation 40 to 100 days between conscript service and age 50 (officers and NCOs age 60). Total strength of trained and equipped reserves is about 700,000.

Army. The country is divided into 7 military areas. The Army consisted in 1990 of 1 armoured brigade, 5 infantry brigades, 7 independent infantry battalions, 3 independent field-artillery regiments, 1 independent field-artillery battalion, 1 coastal artillery regiment, 3 independent coastal artillery battalions, 3 anti-aircraft regiments, 1 independent anti-aircraft battalion, 2 engineering battalions, making a total strength in 1990, of about 30,000.

Navy. The Navy, which operates a mixture of indigenous and Soviet ships and weapons, is divided into 4 functional squadrons. About 50% of the combatant units are kept manned, with the others in short-notice reserve and re-activated on a regular basis. The inventory comprises 2 ASW corvettes, 8 missile craft (of which 4 are indigenous Helsinki class), 11 inshore patrol craft, 2 minelayers, and 6 inshore minesweepers. There are 14 landing craft of various types, and some 30 minor auxiliaries and tenders. There are also 9 civil-manned icebreakers.

Naval bases exist at Upinniemi (near Helsinki) and Turku. Total personnel strength is 1,400 of whom 600 are conscripts, and there are about 12,000 reserves.

Air Force. The Air Force has 3 fighter squadrons, 1 transport squadron, an air academy, a technical school, a signal school and a depot. The fighter squadrons have 60 MiG-21bis and Saab J35 Draken S and F aircraft. Other equipment includes 28 Valmet Vinka piston-engined primary trainers of Finnish design, 63 Hawk MK.51, MiG-21U and Saab J35B and C advanced jet trainers, 3 Fokker F.27 Friendship transport aircraft, 3 Gates Learjet 35A/S aircraft, Piper Arrow liaison aircraft, Piper Chieftain utility transports, and 7 Mi-8 and 2 Hughes 500 Ds helicopters. Personnel (1990) 3,000 officers and men.

Frontier Guard. Comprises 5 large patrol craft, 9 coastal craft and 34 coastal patrol boats. Personnel (1990) 4,200.

INTERNATIONAL RELATIONS

Membership. Finland is a member of UN, the Nordic Council, OECD, EFTA and the Council of Europe.

Treaties. A Treaty of friendship, co-operation and mutual assistance between Finland and the USSR was concluded in Moscow on 6 April 1948 for 10 years, extended on 19 Sept. 1955 to cover a period of 20 years, extended on 19 July 1970 for a further period of 20 years and extended again on 6 June 1983 for a further period of 20 years.

Treaty of Peace with Finland (10 Feb. 1947). Cmd. 7484

ECONOMY

Budget. Actual revenue and expenditure for the calendar years 1981–87, the ordinary budget for 1988 and the proposed budget for 1989 in 1m. marks:

	1983	*1984*	*1985*	*1986*	*1987*	*1988*	*1989*	*1990*
Revenue	76,354	86,611	96,408	96,769	108,650	119,551	124,174	139,676
Expenditure	77,190	85,748	95,803	95,172	106,988	117,275	124,171	136,675

Of the total revenue, 1988, 31% derived from sales tax, 29% from income and property tax, 12% from excise duties, 13% from other taxes and similar revenue, 1% from loans (net) and 14% from miscellaneous sources. Of the total expenditure, 1988, 17% went to education and culture, 19% to social security, 9% to transport, 9% to agriculture and forestry, 10% to general administration, public order and safety, 9% to health, 5% to communities and housing policy, 5% to defence, 5% to promotion of industry and 12% to other expenditures.

At the end of Dec. 1988 the foreign loans totalled 26,279m. marks. The internal loans amounted to 31,805m. marks, of which, 20,872m. were long-term loans. The cash surplus was 145m. marks. The total public debt was 58,084m. marks.

Currency. The unit of currency, starting 1 Jan. 1963, is the new *mark* of 100 *pennis*, equalling 100 old *marks*. The gold standard was suspended on 12 Oct. 1931. Aluminium bronze coins are 5 *marks* 50, 20 and 10 *pennis*; copper coins, 5 *pennis*; aluminium coins, 10 and 5 *pennis*; silver, 1 *mark* pieces. Exchange rate in March 1990: 6·58 marks = £1; 4·01 marks = US$1.

Banking. The Bank of Finland (founded in 1811) is owned by the State and under the guarantee and supervision of Parliament. It is the only bank of issue, and the limit of its right to issue notes is fixed equal to the value of its assets of gold and foreign holdings plus 500m. marks. Notes of 1,000, 500, 100, 50 and 10 marks are in circulation, and their total value at the end of 1987 was 9,117m. marks.

At the end of 1988 the deposits in banking institutions totalled 227,480m. marks and the loans granted by them 281,736m. marks. The most important groups of banking institutions in 1989 were:

	Number of institutions	*Number of offices*	*Deposits (1m. marks)*	*Loans (1m. marks)*
Commercial banks	7	1,011	105,243	125,724
Savings banks	211	1,313	65,716	68,680
Co-operative banks	367	1,217	55,269	62,401

Bank of Finland Monthly Bulletin. Helsinki, from 1926
Unitas. Quarterly Review, issued by Union Bank of Finland. Helsinki, from 1929
Economic Review (issued quarterly by Kansallis–Osake–Pankki). Helsinki, from 1948

Weights and Measures. The metric system of weights and measures was introduced in 1887 and is officially and universally employed.
Economic Survey of Finland. Annual

ENERGY AND NATURAL RESOURCES

Electricity. Electricity production was (in 1m. kwh.) 8,605 in 1960; 22,562 in 1970; 38,655 in 1980; 38,660 in 1982; 41,415 in 1983; 44,330 in 1984; 48,629 in 1985; 48,309 in 1986; 52,564 in 1987, of which 27% was hydro-electric; 51,156 in 1988 (preliminary). Supply 220 volts; 50 Hz.

Minerals. The most important mines are Outokumpu (copper, discovered in 1910) and Otanmäki (iron, discovered in 1953). In 1988 (preliminary) the metal content (in tonnes) of the output of copper concentrates was 18,420, of zinc concentrates 63,879, of nickel concentrates 10,434, of iron concentrates 374,000 and of lead concentrates 1,924.

Agriculture. The cultivated area covers only 9% of the land and of the economically active population 10% were employed in agriculture and forestry in 1988. The arable area was divided in 1987 into 192,244 farms, and the distribution of this area by the size of the farms was: Less than 5 hectares cultivated, 55,020 farms; 5–20 hectares, 102,404 farms; 20–50 hectares, 31,084 farms; 50–100 hectares, 3,338 farms; over 100 hectares, 398 farms.

The principal crops (area in 1,000 hectares, yield in tonnes) were in 1989:

Crop	*Area*	*Yield*	*Crop*	*Area*	*Yield*
Rye	69	195,900	Oats	440	1,443,800
Barley	517	1,629,900	Potatoes	45	981,300
Wheat	51	507,200	Hay	294	1,238,100

The total area under cultivation in 1989 was 2,051,500 hectares. Production of dairy butter in 1988 was 60,900 tonnes, and of cheese, 86,600 tonnes.

Livestock (1989): Horses, 14,900; cattle, 1,346,600; pigs, 1,290,700; poultry, 6,337,800; reindeer, 407,000.

Forestry. The total forest land amounts to 30–31m. hectares. The productive forest land covers 19·73m. hectares. The growing stock was valued at 1,660m. cu. metres in 1977–84 and the annual growth at 68·4m. cu. metres.

In 1987 there were exported: Round timber, 1,316m. cu. metres; sawn wood, 4,893m. cu. metres; plywood and veneers, 516m. cu. metres.

Monthly Review of Agriculture. Board of Agriculture
Agriculture 1982: Annual Statistics of Agriculture. Helsinki
Yearbook of Forest Statistics.

INDUSTRY AND TRADE

Industry. The following data cover establishments with a total personnel of 5 or more in 1988 [1]:

Industry	*Establishments* [2]	*Personnel* [3]	*Value of production: Gross (1m. marks)*	*Value of production: Value added (1m. marks)*
Mining and quarrying	145	4,707	2,632	1,432
Metal ore mining	8	1,627	979	557
Other mining	137	3,096	1,652	874
Manufacturing	6,574	455,936	256,167	94,313

[1] Preliminary. [2] 1987. [3] Working proprietors, salaried employees and wage earners.

Industry	Establishments [2]	Personnel [3]	Value of production Gross (1m. marks)	Value added (1m. marks)
Manufacture of food, beverages and tobacco	958	56,176	46,964	12,106
Textile, wearing apparel and leather industries	781	41,616	9,979	4,321
Manufacture of textiles	258	13,608	4,039	1,780
Manufacture of wearing apparel, except footwear	368	20,896	4,145	1,890
Manufacture of wood and wood products, incl. furniture	933	43,959	18,299	6,690
Manufacture of paper and paper prod., printing, publishing	870	83,044	60,205	22,964
Manufacture of paper and paper products	160	44,826	44,546	15,639
Printing, publishing, etc.	710	38,222	15,659	7,326
Manufacture of chemicals and chemical, petroleum, coal, rubber and plastic products	458	37,945	28,010	9,721
Manufacture of industrial chemicals	156	14,449	11,977	4,670
Manufacture of other chemical products	95	9,978	5,223	2,314
Petroleum refineries	2	2,824	6,807	746
Manufacture of non-metallic mineral products	407	19,708	8,605	4,199
Basic metal industries	82	17,703	19,650	5,006
Iron and steel basic industries	53	12,975	12,445	3,798
Non-ferrous metal basic industries	29	4,724	7,207	1,208
Manufacture of fabricated metal products, machinery, etc.	1,980	150,770	62,895	28,528
Manufacture of fabricated metal products, excl. machinery	739	31,774	12,162	5,769
Manufacture of machinery, except electrical	654	50,315	22,870	11,263
Manufacture of electrical machinery, apparatus, etc.	224	29,257	11,842	5,936
Manufacture of transport equipment	272	33,835	14,048	4,551
Other manufacturing industries	105	4,438	1,279	724
Electricity, gas and water	532	27,840	29,346	11,344
All industry	7,251	488,417	288,069	107,083

[2] 1987. [3] Working proprietors, salaried employees and wage earners.

GDP (at market prices) *per capita* (1988) 88,935 marks.

Industrial Statistics of Finland. Annual

Commerce. Imports and exports for calendar years, in 1m. marks:

	1984	*1985*	*1986*	*1987*	*1988*
Imports	74,682	81,520	77,602	86,696	88,229
Exports	80,904	84,028	82,579	87,564	90,854

The trade with some principal import and export countries was (in 1,000 marks):

Country	*Imports* 1987	1988	*Exports* 1987	1988
Australia	193,012	364,801	855,462	1,020,388
Austria	1,116,462	1,089,422	976,030	914,700
Belgium–Luxembourg	2,234,537	2,231,679	1,566,432	1,789,335
Brazil	498,217	566,311	236,654	220,441
Canada	448,754	637,535	996,499	1,099,169
China	449,628	567,532	688,804	463,440
Colombia	357,060	336,178	90,184	65,601
Czechoslovakia	448,417	449,647	334,278	278,851
Denmark	2,453,531	2,588,561	3,407,716	3,204,122
France	3,719,549	3,589,745	4,615,266	4,835,190
German Dem. Rep.	432,260	484,562	370,089	385,205
Germany (Fed. Rep.)	15,130,348	14,859,667	9,580,921	9,842,401
Greece	234,581	246,740	465,333	511,883
Hungary	325,970	370,389	264,024	276,384
Iran	17,513	8,808	190,430	169,065
Iraq	779	365	30,410	42,184
Ireland	322,321	381,773	495,158	536,005

Country	Imports 1987	Imports 1988	Exports 1987	Exports 1988
Israel	169,714	157,760	322,777	321,732
Italy	3,789,514	3,924,293	2,239,715	2,462,806
Japan	6,136,845	6,522,497	1,237,712	1,649,197
Netherlands	2,675,770	2,867,562	3,141,046	3,312,774
Norway	1,904,761	2,096,425	4,132,019	3,137,309
Poland	847,495	852,327	313,459	290,235
Portugal	804,374	759,403	294,035	392,304
Saudi Arabia	703,740	394,715	426,352	423,404
Spain	963,449	979,573	1,118,784	1,418,562
Sweden	11,205,449	11,765,250	13,090,417	12,835,219
Switzerland	1,743,071	1,639,199	1,564,687	1,553,718
USSR	12,461,880	10,592,193	13,522,520	11,863,809
UK	6,192,359	5,941,908	9,990,071	13,562,872
USA	4,539,359	5,615,962	4,523,448	5,245,131

Principal imports 1988 (in 1m. marks): Machinery, apparatus and appliances, 34,627; mineral fuels, lubricants, etc., 8,447; chemicals, 9,530; food and live animals, 4,362; road vehicles, 9,033; crude materials, inedible, except fuels, 5,549; textile yarn, fabrics, etc., 2,915; iron and steel, 2,958.

Principal exports in 1988 (in 1m. marks): Paper and paper-board, 25,131; machinery and transport equipment, 24,931; wood shaped or simply worked, 4,761; wood pulp, 4,697; ships, 4,427; clothing, 2,526; veneers, plywood, etc., and other wood manufactures, 2,264; food and live animals, 1,503; road vehicles, 3,267.

Total trade between Finland and UK (British Department of Trade returns, in £1,000 sterling):

	1985	1986	1987	1988	1989
Imports to UK	1,324,792	1,346,058	1,539,011	1,813,549	1,893,163
Exports and re-exports from UK	705,365	664,451	797,236	824,951	925,784

Foreign Trade. Annual

Tourism. In 1988 the total revenue from tourism was 4,257m. marks and the total expenditure 7,913m. marks.

COMMUNICATIONS

Roads. In Jan. 1989 there were 77,395 km of public roads, of which 44,965 km were paved. At the end of 1988 there were 1,795,908 registered cars, 52,736 lorries, 160,301 vans and pick-ups, 9,229 buses and coaches and 15,392 special automobiles.

Railways. On 31 Dec. 1988 the total length of the line operated was 5,863 km (1,636 km electrified), of which all was owned by the State. The gauge was 1,524 mm. In 1988 the number of passengers carried was 44m. and the amount of goods carried was 33m. tonnes. The total revenue in 1987 was 3,141m. marks and the total expenditure 4,149m. marks.

Aviation. The scheduled traffic of Finnish airlines covered 49m. km in 1988. The number of passengers was 4,009,000 and the number of passenger-km 4,034,000. The air transport of freight and mail amounted to 108m. tonne-km.

Shipping. The total registered mercantile marine on 31 Dec. 1988 was 415 vessels of 885,000 gross tons. In 1988 the total number of vessels arriving in Finland from abroad was 15,549 and the goods discharged amounted to 31·9m. tonnes. The goods loaded for export from Finland ports amounted to 23·4m. tonnes.

The lakes, rivers and canals are navigable for about 6,160 km. Timber floating is important, and there are about 9,400 km of floatable inland waterways. In 1988 bundle floating was about 4·3m. tonnes and free floating 1m. tonnes.

On 27 Aug. 1963 the USSR leased to Finland the Russian part of the canal connecting Lake Saimaa with the Gulf of Finland. After extensive rebuilding the canal was opened for traffic in 1968. The Saimaa Canal and deepwater channels on Lake Saimaa (770 km) can be used by vessels with dimensions not larger than as follows: Length 82 metres, width 11·8 metres, draught 4·2 metres and height of mast 24·5 metres.

Post and Broadcasting. In 1988 there were 3,382 post offices and 255 telecommunications offices. The total length of telegraph wires was 582,000 km and that of domestic trunk and net group telephone wires 9·6m. km. The number of telephone subscriber lines (1988), 2·47m. All post and telegraph systems are administered by the State jointly with a large part of the telephone services. The total revenues from postal services were 3,938m. marks and from (wire and radio) telegraph services 3,966m. marks.

On 31 Dec. 1988 the number of television licences was 1,862,479, of which licences for colour television, 1,677,207. *Oy Yleisradio AB* broadcasts 4 programmes (1 in Swedish), covering the whole country on long-, medium- and short-waves, and on FM. Four TV programmes (1 commercial) are broadcast.

Cinemas. In Dec. 1988 there were 344 cinema halls with a seating capacity of 70,000.

Newspapers. In 1988 the number of newspapers published more often than 3 times a week was 67, of which 9 were in Swedish.

JUSTICE, RELIGION, EDUCATION AND WELFARE

Justice. The lowest courts of justice are the municipal courts in towns and district courts in the country. Municipal courts are held by the burgomaster and at least 2 members of court, district court by judge and 5 jurors, the judge alone deciding, unless the jurors unanimously differ from him, when their decision prevails. From these courts an appeal lies to the courts of appeal *(Hovioikeus)* in Turku, Vaasa, Kuopio, Helsinki, Kouvola and Rovaniemi. The Supreme Court *(Korkein oikeus)* sits in Helsinki. Appeals from the decisions of administrative authorities are in the final instance decided by the Supreme Administrative Court *(Korkein hallintooikeus)*, also in Helsinki. Judges can be removed only by judicial sentence.

Two functionaries, the *Oikeuskansleri* or Chancellor of Justice, and the *Oikeusasiamies* (ombudsman), or Solicitor-General, exercise control over the administration of justice. The former acts also as counsel and public prosecutor for the Government; while the latter, who is appointed by the Parliament, exerts a general control over all courts of law and public administration.

At the end of 1988 the prison population numbered 3,599 men and 122 women; the preliminary number of convictions in 1987 was 365,312, of which 340,962 were for minor offences with maximum penalty of fines and 24,220 with penalty of imprisonment. 10,255 of the prison sentences were unconditional.

Religion. Liberty of conscience is guaranteed to members of all religions. National churches are the Lutheran National Church and the Greek Orthodox Church of Finland. The Lutheran Church is divided into 8 bishoprics (Turku being the archiepiscopal see), 79 provostships and 598 parishes. The Greek Orthodox Church is divided into 3 bishoprics (Kuopio being the archiepiscopal see) and 27 parishes, in addition to which there are a monastery and a convent.

Percentage of the total population at the end of 1988: Lutherans, 88·4; Greek Orthodox, 1·1; others, 0·6; not members of any religion, 9·9.

Education (1987–88). *Primary and Secondary Education:*

	Number of institutions	*Teachers*	*Students*
First-level Education (Lower sections of the comprehensive schools, grades I–VI)			390,469
Second-level Education General education (Upper sections of the comprehensive schools, grades VII–IX, and senior secondary schools)	5,340	47,045	287,490
Vocational education	536	16,846	111,577

Higher Education. Education at the third level (including universities and third level education at vocational colleges) was provided for 139,375 students. Education at universities was provided at 20 institutions with 7,538 teachers and 99,246 students.

University Education. Universities and similar types of institutions and the number of teachers and students are:

	Founded	*Teachers*	*Students Total*	*Students Women*
Universities				
Helsinki	1640	1,793	26,730	15,383
Turku (Swedish)	1919	308	4,515	2,577
Turku (Finnish)	1922	780	9,638	5,772
Jyväskylä	1958	536	6,856	4,362
Oulu	1958	827	8,238	3,939
Tampere	1966	585	9,979	6,094
Joensuu	1969	336	4,230	2,661
Kuopio	1972	285	2,410	1,509
Lapland	1979	114	1,259	651
Vaasa	1968	112	1,889	977
Universities of Technology				
Lappeenranta	1969	151	1,762	273
Helsinki	1849	586	9,207	1,590
Tampere	1972	263	3,644	500
College of Veterinary Medicine, Helsinki	1946	50	293	230
Schools of Economics and Business Administration				
Helsinki (Finnish)	1911	155	3,300	1,493
Helsinki (Swedish)	1927	96	1,763	760
Turku (Finnish)	1950	73	1,559	746
Universities of Art				
Sibelius Academy	1939	290	1,163	633
University of Industrial Arts	1949	137	960	617
Theatre Academy	1979	61	211	103

General adult education (at civic institutes, folk high schools and study centres) had 844,000 students.

General Education. Central Statistical Office, Helsinki (annual), *Higher Education.* Central Statistical Office, Helsinki (annual), *Vocational Education.* Helsinki (annual)

Health. In 1988 there were 9,614 physicians, 3,746 dentists and (1987) 67,246 hospital beds.

Social Security. The Social Insurance Institution administers general systems of old age pensions (to all persons over 65 years of age and disabled younger persons) and of health insurance. An additional system of compulsory old age pensions paid for by the employers is in force and works through the Central Pension Security Institute. Systems for child welfare, care of vagrants, alcoholics and drug addicts and other public aid are administered by the communes and supervised by the National Social Board and the Ministry of Social Affairs and Health.

The total cost of social security amounted to 105,718m. marks in 1987. Out of this 30,433m. (28·8%) was spent for health, 1,766m. (1·7%) for industrial accidents, 6,585m. (6·2%) for unemployment, 40,755m. (38·5%) old age and disability, 17,295m. (16·4%) for family allowances and child welfare, 1,221m. (1·4%) for general welfare purposes, 2,716m. (2·6%) for war-disabled, etc., 1,502m. (1·4%) as tax reductions for children. Out of the total expenditure 29% was financed by the State, 17% by local authorities, 42% by employers, 8% by the beneficiaries and 4% by users.

Labour Protection in Finland. Helsinki, 1980
Social Welfare in Finland. Helsinki, 1980
Social Security in the Nordic Countries 1981. Statistical Reports of the Nordic Countries, vol. 44. Helsinki, 1984

DIPLOMATIC REPRESENTATIVES

Of Finland in Great Britain (38 Chesham Pl., London, SW1X 8HW)
Ambassador: Ilkka Olavi Pastinen, KCMG (accredited 24 Feb. 1983).

Of Great Britain in Finland (16–20 Uudenmaankatu, Helsinki 00120)
Ambassador: G. Neil Smith.

Of Finland in the USA (3216 New Mexico Ave., NW, Washington, D.C., 20016)
Ambassador: Jukka Valtasaari.

Of the USA in Finland (Itäinen Puistotie 14A, Helsinki 00140)
Ambassador: John Giffen Weinmann.

Of Finland to the United Nations
Ambassador: Dr Klaus Törnudd.

Further Reading

Statistical Information: The Central Statistical Office (Tilastokeskus, Swedish: Statistikcentralen; address: PO Box 504, SF-00101 Helsinki 10) was founded in 1865 to replace earlier official statistical services dating from 1749 (in united Sweden–Finland). Statistics on foreign trade, agriculture, forestry, navigation, health and social welfare are produced by other state authorities. Its publications include: *Statistical Yearbook of Finland* (from 1879) and *Bulletin of Statistics* (monthly, from 1924). A bibliography of all official statistics of Finland was published in Finnish, Swedish and English in *Statistical publications 1856–1979*. Helsinki, 1980.

Constitution Act and Parliament Act of Finland. Helsinki, 1984
Suomen valtiokalenteri–Finlands statskalender (State Calendar of Finland). Helsinki. Annual
Facts About Finland. Helsinki. Annual (Union Bank of Finland)
Facts about Finland. Helsinki, 1988
Finland in Figures. Helsinki, Annual
Finland in Maps. Helsinki, 1979
Finnish Press Laws. Helsinki, 1984
Making and Applying Law in Finland. Ministry of Justice, 1983
Statistical Yearbook of Finland. Helsinki, Annual
Yearbook of Finnish Foreign Policy. Helsinki, Annual
The Finnish Banking System. Helsinki, 1987
Finnish Industry. Helsinki, 1988
Finnish Local Government. Helsinki, 1983
Health Care in Finland. Helsinki, 1987
Arter, D., *Politics and Policy-Making in Finland.* Brighton, 1987
Hurme-Malin-Syväoja, *Finnish-English General Dictionary.* Helsinki, 1984
Hurme-Pesonen, *English–Finnish General Dictionary.* Helsinki, 1982
Jakobson, M. *Myth and Reality.* Helsinki, 1987
Jutikkala, E. and Pirinen, K., *A History of Finland.* 3rd ed. New York, 1979
Kekkonen, U., *President's View.* London, 1982
Kirby, D. G., *Finland in the Twentieth Century.* 2nd ed. London, 1984
Klinge, M., *A Brief History of Finland.* Helsinki, 1987
Paasivirta, J., *Finland and Europe. The Period of Autonomy and the International Crises 1808–1914.* London, 1981
Polvinen, T., *Between East and West – Finland in International Politics 1944–1947.* Minnesota Univ. Press, 1986
Puntila, L. A., *The Political History of Finland, 1809–1966.* Helsinki, 1974
Screen, J. E. O., *Finland.* [Bibliography] Oxford and Santa Barbara, 1981
Singleton, F., *The Economy of Finland in the Twentieth Century.* Univ. of Bradford Press, 1987
University of Turku, *Political Parties in Finland.* Turku, 1987

FRANCE

Capital: Paris
Population: 56·18m. (1989)
GNP per capita: US$16,080 (1988)

République Française

HISTORY. The republic proclaimed on the fall of the Bourbon monarchy in 1792 lasted until the First Empire, under Napoleon I, was established in 1804. The Bourbon monarchy was restored in 1814 and (with an interval during 1815) lasted until the abdication of Louis Philippe in 1848. The Second Republic was established on 12 March 1848, the Second Empire (under Louis Napoleon) on 2 Dec. 1852. The Third Republic was established on 4 Sept. 1870 following the capture and imprisonment of Louis Napoleon in the Franco-Prussian war, and lasted until the German occupation of 1940. The Fourth Republic was established on 24 Dec. 1946 and lasted until 4 Oct. 1958.

AREA AND POPULATION. France is bounded north by the English Channel *(La Manche)*, north-east by Belgium and Luxembourg, east by Federal Republic of Germany, Switzerland and Italy, south by the Mediterranean (with Monaco as a coastal enclave), south-west by Spain and Andorra, and west by the Atlantic Ocean The total area is 543,965 sq. km (210,033 sq. miles).

The population (present in actual boundaries) at successive censuses has been:

1801	27,349,003	1881	37,672,048	Mar. 1946	40,506,639
1821	30,461,875	1891	38,342,948	May 1954	42,777,174
1841	34,230,178	1901	38,961,945	Mar. 1962	46,519,997
1861	37,386,313	1911	39,604,992	Mar. 1968	49,778,540
1866	38,067,064	1921	39,209,518	Feb. 1975	52,655,802
1872	36,102,921	1931	41,834,923	Mar. 1982	54,334,871

The 1982 total included 3,680,100 foreigners, of whom 795,920 were Algerian, 764,860 Portuguese, 431,120 Moroccan, 333,740 Italian and 321,440 Spanish.

Population estimate (Oct. 1989) is 56,184,000.

Vital statistics for calendar years:

	Marriages	*Live births*	*Deaths*
1985	269,300	768,431	552,500
1986	265,340	778,940	546,880
1987	265,177	767,828	527,466
1988	271,124	770,690	524,600

Live birth rate in 1988 was 13·8 per 1,000 inhabitants; death rate, 9·4; marriage rate, 4·9; divorce rate (1986), 2; infant mortality (1987), 7·6 per 1,000 live births. Life expectation at birth (1987); men, 72; women, 80·3. Population growth rate (1986), 4·2 per 1,000. Average density (1988) 102·7 persons per sq. km.

The areas, populations and chief towns of the 22 Metropolitan regions were as follows:

Regions	*Area (sq. km)*	*Census March 1982*	*Estimate Jan. 1987*	*Chief town*
Alsace	8,280	1,566,048	1,605,300	Strasbourg
Aquitaine	41,308	2,656,544	2,723,600	Bordeaux
Auvergne	26,013	1,332,678	1,329,200	Clermont-Ferrand
Basse-Normandie	17,589	1,350,979	1,379,400	Caen
Bourgogne (Burgundy)	31,582	1,596,054	1,610,600	Dijon
Bretagne (Brittany)	27,208	2,707,886	2,763,100	Rennes
Centre	39,151	2,264,164	2,333,800	Orléans
Champagne-Ardenne	25,606	1,345,935	1,357,900	Reims
Corse (Corsica)	8,680	240,178	246,000	Ajaccio
Franche-Comté	16,202	1,084,049	1,088,000	Besançon
Haute-Normandie	12,317	1,655,362	1,699,600	Rouen

Regions	Area (sq. km)	Census March 1982	Estimate Jan. 1987	Chief town
Ile-de-France	12,012	10,073,059	10,259,400	Paris
Languedoc-Roussillon	27,376	1,926,514	2,053,600	Montpellier
Limousin	16,942	737,153	734,700	Limoges
Lorraine	23,547	2,319,905	2,326,900	Nancy
Midi-Pyrénées	45,348	2,325,319	2,369,500	Toulouse
Nord-Pas-de-Calais	12,414	3,932,939	3,931,500	Lille
Pays de la Loire	32,082	2,930,398	3,042,500	Nantes
Picardie	19,399	1,740,321	1,776,400	Amiens
Poitou-Charentes	25,810	1,568,230	1,591,500	Poitiers
Provence-Alpes-Côte d'Azur	31,400	3,965,209	4,112,500	Marseille
Rhône-Alpes	43,698	5,015,947	5,174,800	Lyon

Populations of the principal conurbations and towns at Census 1982:

	Conurbation	Town		Conurbation	Town
Paris	8,706,963 [1]	2,188,918	Limoges	171,689	144,082
Lyon	1,220,844 [2]	418,476	Mantes-la-Jolie	170,265	43,585
Marseille	1,110,511	878,689	Amiens	154,498	136,358
Lille	936,295 [3]	174,039	Thionville	138,034	41,448
Bordeaux	640,012	211,197	Perpignan	137,915	113,646
Toulouse	541,271	354,289	Nîmes	132,343	129,924
Nantes	464,857	247,227	Pau	131,265	85,766
Nice	449,496	338,486	Saint-Nazaire	130,271	68,947
Toulon	410,393	181,985	Montbéliard	128,194	33,362
Grenoble	392,021	159,503	Bayonne	127,477	42,970
Rouen	379,879	105,083	Aix-en-Provence	126,552	124,550
Strasbourg	373,470	252,264	Troyes	125,240	64,769
Valenciennes	349,505	40,881	Besançon	120,772	119,687
Lens	327,383	38,307	Hagondange-Briey	119,669	9,091
Saint-Étienne	317,228	206,688	Annecy	112,632	51,593
Nancy	306,982	99,307	Valence	106,041	68,157
Cannes	295,525	72,787	Maubeuge	105,714	36,156
Tours	262,786	136,483	Lorient	104,025	64,675
Béthune	258,383	26,105	Angoulême	103,552	50,151
Clermont-Ferrand	256,189	151,092	Poitiers	103,204	82,884
Le Havre	254,595	200,411	La Rochelle	102,143	78,231
Rennes	234,418	200,390	Calais	100,823	76,935
Montpellier	221,307	201,067	Forbach	99,606	27,321
Mulhouse	220,613	113,794	Boulogne-sur-Mer	98,566	48,349
Orléans	220,478	105,589	Chambéry	96,163	54,896
Dijon	215,865	145,569	Bourges	92,202	79,408
Douai	202,366	44,515	Cherbourg	85,485	30,112
Brest	201,145	160,355	Saint-Brieuc	83,900	51,399
Reims	199,388	181,985	Creil	82,505	36,128
Angers	195,859	141,143	Melun	82,479	36,218
Dunkerque	195,705	73,618	Colmar	82,468	63,764
Le Mans	191,080	150,331	Saint-Chamond	82,059	40,571
Metz	186,437	118,502	Roanne	81,786	49,638
Caen	183,526	117,119	Béziers	81,347	78,477
Avignon	174,264	91,474	Arras	80,477	45,364

[1] Including towns of Boulogne-Billancourt (102,595), Argenteuil (96,045), Versailles (95,240), Montreuil (93,394), Saint-Denis (91,275), Nanterre (90,371) and Vitry-sur-Seine (85,820).
[2] Including towns of Villeurbanne (118,330) and Vénissieux (64,982).
[3] Including towns of Roubaix (101,836) and Tourcoing (97,121).

Recensement de la population de 1982. Paris, Institut National de la Statistique et des Etudes Economiques, 1983
Scargill, I., *Urban France*. London, 1983

CLIMATE. The north-west has a moderate maritime climate, with small temperature range and abundant rainfall, but inland, rainfall becomes more seasonal, with a summer maximum, and the annual range of temperature increases. Southern France has a Mediterranean climate, with mild moist winters and hot dry summers. Eastern France has a continental climate and a rainfall maximum in summer, with thunderstorms prevalent.

Paris. Jan. 37°F (3°C), July 64°F (18°C). Annual rainfall 22·9" (573 mm). Bordeaux. Jan. 41°F (5°C), July 68°F (20°C). Annual rainfall 31·4" (786 mm). Lyon. Jan. 37°F (3°C), July 68°F (20°C). Annual rainfall 31·8" (794 mm).

CONSTITUTION AND GOVERNMENT. The Constitution of the Fifth Republic, superseding that of 1946, came into force on 4 Oct. 1958. It consists of a preamble, dealing with the Rights of Man, and 92 articles.

France is a Republic, indivisible, secular, democratic and social; all citizens are equal before the law (Art. 2). National sovereignty resides with the people, who exercise it through their representatives and by referenda (Art. 3). Political parties carry out their activities freely, but must respect the principles of national sovereignty and democracy (Art. 4).

The President of the Republic sees that the Constitution is respected; he ensures the regular functioning of the public authorities, as well as the continuity of the state. He is the protector of national independence and territorial integrity (Art. 5). He is elected for 7 years by direct universal suffrage (Art. 6). He appoints a Prime Minister and, on the latter's advice, appoints and dismisses the other members of the Government (Art. 8). He presides over the Council of Ministers (Art. 9). He can dissolve the National Assembly, after consultation with the Prime Minister and the Presidents of the two Houses (Art. 12). He appoints to the civil and military offices of the state (Art. 13). In times of crisis, he may take such emergency powers as the circumstances demand; the National Assembly cannot be dissolved during such a period (Art. 16).

Previous Presidents of the Fifth Republic:

General Charles André Joseph de Gaulle, 8 Jan. 1959–28 April 1969 (resigned); Alain Poher (interim), 28 April 1969–20 June 1969; Georges Jean Raymond Pompidou, 20 June 1969–2 April 1974 (died); Alain Poher (interim), 2 April 1974–27 May 1974; Valéry Giscard d'Estaing, 27 May 1974–21 May 1981.

President of the Republic: François Mitterrand (elected 10 May 1981; took office 21 May 1981; re-elected 8 May 1988).

The government determines and conducts the policy of the nation (Art. 20). The Prime Minister directs the operation of the Government, is responsible for national defence and ensures the execution of laws (Art. 21). Members of the Government must not be members of Parliament (Art. 23).

The Council of Ministers was composed as follows in March 1990:

Prime Minister: Michel Rocard (PS).
National Education, Youth and Sport: Lionel Jospin (PS).
Economy, Finance and Budget: Pierre Bérégovoy (PS).
Equipment and Housing: Maurice Faure (MRG).
Foreign Affairs: Roland Dumas (PS).
Ministers:
Justice, Keeper of the Seals: Pierre Arpaillange (non-party).
Defence: Jean-Pierre Chevènement (PS).
Interior: Pierre Joxe (PS).
Industry and Regional Planning: Roger Fauroux (non-party).
European Affairs: Edith Cresson (PS).
Transport and Sea: Michel Delebarre (PS).
Civil Service and Administrative Reform: Michel Durafour (UDF-Rad.).
Labour, Employment and Vocational Training: Jean-Pierre Soisson (UDF-PR).
Co-operation and Overseas Development: Jacques Pelletier (UDF-Rad.).
Culture, Communication, Major Works and the Bicentenary: Jack Lang (PS).
Overseas Departments and Territories and Government Spokesman: Louis Le Pensec (PS).
Agriculture and Forestry: Henri Nallet (PS).
Postal Services, Telecommunications and Space: Paul Quilès (PS).
Relations with Parliament: Jean Poperen (PS).
Solidarity, Health and Social Protection: Claude Evin (PS).
Research and Technology: Hubert Curien (PS).

Foreign Trade: Jean-Marie Rausch (UDF-CDS).

Ministers-Delegate: Michel Charasse (PS) *(Budget)*, Olivier Stirn (PS) *(Tourism)*, Alain Decaux (non-party) *(Relations with Francophone countries)*, Jacques Mellick (PS) *(Sea)*, Jacques Chérèque (PS) *(Regional Planning and Redeployment)*, Théo Braun (PS) *(Elderly)*, Edwige Avice (PS) *(Foreign Affairs)*, François Doubin (MRG) *(Trade and Artisan Industries)*, Catherine Tasca (non-party) *(Communication)*.

There were also 17 Secretaries of State.

Parliament consists of the National Assembly and the Senate; the National Assembly is elected by direct suffrage and the Senate by indirect suffrage (Art. 24). It convenes as of right in two ordinary sessions per year, the first on 2 Oct. for 80 days and the second on 2 April for not more than 90 days (Art. 28).

The National Assembly comprises 577 Deputies, elected for a 5-year term from single-member constituencies – 555 in Metropolitan France and 22 in the various overseas departments and dependencies. The General Election, held in June 1988, resulted in a composition (by group, including 'affiliates') of 275 *Parti Socialiste* (including 9 *Mouvement des Radicaux de Gauche* and 6 other 'affiliates'), 40 *Union Du Centre (Centre des Démocrates Sociaux)*, 132 *Rassemblement Pour la République* (Gaullists), 90 *Union de la Démocracie Française* (of which 58 *Parti Republicaine)*, 25 *Parti Communiste Francaise* and 15 others.

The Senate comprises 319 Senators elected for 9-year terms (one-third every 3 years) by an electoral college in each Department or overseas dependency, made up of all members of the Departmental Council or its equivalent in overseas dependencies, together with all members of Municipal Councils within that area; there are 296 Senators for Metropolitan France, 13 for the Overseas Departments and dependencies, and 10 for French citizens residing outside France and its dependencies. Following the partial elections held in Sept. 1986, the Senate was composed of (by group, including 'affiliates') 154 UDF, 77 RPR, 73 *Groupe Socialiste* (including 9 MRG) and 15 *Groupe Communiste*.

The Constitutional Council is composed of 9 members whose term of office is 9 years (non-renewable), one-third every 3 years; 3 are appointed by the President of the Republic, 3 by the President of the National Assembly, and 3 by the President of the Senate; in addition, former Presidents of the Republic are, by right, life members of the Constitutional Council (Art. 56). It oversees the fairness of the elections of the President (Art. 58) and Parliament (Art. 59) and of referenda (Art. 60), and acts as a guardian of the Constitution (Art. 61).

The Economic and Social Council advises on Government and Private Members' Bills (Art. 69). It comprises representatives of employers', workers' and farmers' organizations in each Department and Overseas Territory.

National flag: The Tricolour of three vertical stripes of blue, white, red.

National anthem: La Marseillaise (words and music by C. Rouget de Lisle, 1792).

Local Government: France is divided into 22 regions for national development work, for planning and for budgetary policy. Under far-reaching legislation on decentralisation promulgated in March 1982, state-appointed Regional Prefects were abolished and their executive powers transferred to the Presidents of the Regional Councils, which are to be directly elected.

There are 96 *départements* within the 22 regions each governed by a directly-elected *Conseil Général*. From 1982 their Presidents' powers are greatly extended to take over local administration and expenditure from the former Departmental prefects, now called 'Commissioners of the Republic' with responsibility for public order. The *arrondissement* (325 in 1982) and the *canton* (3,714 in 1982), have little administrative significance.

The unit of local government is the *commune*, the size and population of which vary very much. There were, in 1982, in the 96 metropolitan departments, 36,433 communes. Most of them (31,122) had less than 1,500 inhabitants, and 16,144 had less than 300, while 227 communes had more than 30,000 inhabitants. The local affairs of the commune are under a Municipal Council, composed of from 9 to 36 members, elected by universal suffrage for 6 years by French citizens of 21 years or over after 6 months' residence. Each Municipal Council elects a mayor, who is both the representative of the commune and the agent of the central government.

In Paris the *Conseil de Paris* is composed of 109 members elected from the 20 *arrondissements*. It combines the functions of departmental *Conseil Général* and Municipal Council.

DEFENCE. The President of the Republic exercises command over the Armed Forces. He is assisted by the High Council of Defence *(Conseil Supérieur de Défense)*, which studies defence problems, and by two Committees *(Comité de Défense* and *Comité de Défense restreint)* which formulate directives. The Prime Minister is responsible for national defence; he exercises his military responsibilities and co-ordinates inter-ministry defence activities through the General Secretariat of National Defence (SGDN). Under the Prime Minister's authority, the Minister of Defence is responsible for the execution of military policy, in particular the organization and administration of the Armed Forces.

On 5 July 1969 the Ministry of Defence assumed responsibility from the former individual service Ministries for the Army, Air Force and Navy. The Ministry prepares general directives for negotiations relating to defence. The preparation and control of the Armed Forces is exercised by the Chief of Staff of the Armed Forces, the Chiefs of Staff of the 3 services—Army, Navy and Air—and the head of the *Gendarmerie*.

French forces are not formally under the NATO command structure. About 48,000 French service personnel are stationed in the Federal Republic of Germany, with a further 15,000 stationed in other overseas locations.

The General Directorate for Armament (DGA) is responsible for all aspects of the procurement of defence equipment. It employs about 73,000 personnel, and co-ordinates another 217,000 others employed in the defence industry.

Army. The Army consisted in 1990 of 292,500 personnel, of whom 6,000 were women and 183,000 are conscripts.

The Territorial Defence Forces consist of 7 zone brigades, 23 joint-services divisional regiments (RIAD), an infantry division and a Rhine division. They provide the main operational defence of French territory.

The peace-time tactical units comprise the Mechanized Armoured Corps (CBM) and the Rapid Intervention Force (FAR). The CBM forms the 1st Army of 170,000 men, with headquarters in Strasbourg, and is organized, equipped and trained for action in the Central Europe theatre; it consists of 6 armoured divisions, 2 light armoured divisions and 2 motorized rifle divisions, plus artillery, engineering, signals, parachute, transport, supply and naval infantry and artillery units. It also includes 5 nuclear artillery regiments equipped with 30 launchers for 'Pluton' missiles.

The headquarters of the FAR are at Maisons-Laffite. It comprises 47,000 men organized, equipped and trained for rapid engagement either in Europe or over large distances elsewhere; it includes a parachute division, an air-portable marine division, a light armoured division, an alpine division and an air-mobile division, together with various specialized units.

Equipment includes 1,400 AMX-30 and 230 AMX-13 main battle tanks, 284 AMX-10 armoured vehicles, 823 other armoured vehicles, 556 155-mm guns, 183 *Roland* anti-aircraft missile systems and 1,440 *Milan* anti-tank weapons.

The *Aviation Légère de l'Armée de Terre* (ALAT) with about 7,000 personnel is an integral part of the Army, equipped with 700 helicopters of various types for observation, reconnaissance, combat area transport, liaison and supply duties.

Gendarmerie. The para-military police force exists to ensure public security and maintain law and order, as well as participate in the operational defence of French territory as part of the armed forces. It consists of (1988) 87,497 personnel including 9,582 conscripts and 948 civilians. It comprises a mobile force of over 18,000 personnel and 120 departmental forces with over 51,000 personnel, together with specialised units. It is equipped with 28 VBC-90 armoured gun-carriers, 121 light armoured cars, 155 armoured vehicles and 33 troop transport vehicles, as well as 42 helicopters and 6 light aircraft.

Navy. The missions of the French Navy are to provide the prime element of the French independent nuclear deterrent through its force of strategic submarines, to assure the security of the French offshore zones so as to contribute to NATO's logistic transatlantic re-supply, and to provide on-station and deployment forces overseas in support of French interests.

French territorial seas and economic zones are organized into 3 maritime regions, each under the authority of a Maritime Prefect (with headquarters in Cherbourg, Brest and Toulon). Offshore, the seas and oceans are divided into 5 zones; Atlantic, Mediterranean, Indian Ocean, Pacific and Antilles-Guyana. Home based forces are commanded by Commanders-in-Chief based in Brest and Toulon, those in the Indian Ocean and Pacific by Flag Officers based afloat in the Indian Ocean, and at Nouméa. Naval forces in the Caribbean come under a joint force commander based at Cayenne.

The following is a summary of the strength of the fleet at the end of the years shown:

	1983	*1984*	*1985*	*1986*	*1987*	*1988*	*1989*
Aircraft carriers	2	2	2	2	2	2	2
Strat. submarines	5	6	6	6	6	6	6
Other submarines	18	20	16	17	18	16	14
Cruisers	2	2	2	2	2	2	2
Destroyers	5	4	4	4	4	4	4
Frigates	39	40	37	38	38	36	36

The Navy operates 6 nuclear-powered strategic missile submarines. The first 5 were of the Le Redoutable class, (*Redoutable, Terrible, Foudroyant, Indomptable* and *Tonnant*), 9,100 tonnes, completed between 1971 and 1980, and deploying 16 M-20 ballistic missiles. 2 have been, and a further 2 will be, converted to carry 16 M-4 missiles, which are also fitted in an intermediate ship, *L'Inflexible*, 9,100 tonnes, completed in 1985. A new, much larger class, (14,200 tonnes) is being built, of which the first, *Le Triomphant*, was laid down in 1988 for completion in 1995, and will deploy 16 M-4/5 missiles.

There are also 4 small (2,700 tonne) nuclear-powered submarines of the Rubis class commissioned 1983-87, and 14 diesel submarines.

The principal surface ships of the French Navy are the aircraft carriers *Clemenceau* and *Foch* of 33,300 tonnes each, completed in 1961 and 1963, and 2 cruisers. The 2 carriers embark an air group typically comprising 16 Super-Etendard strike aricraft, 2 Entandard recce, 7 F-8E Crusader, 6 Alize ASW and warning, plus a flight of 4 utility helicopters. They are due to be withdrawn from service in 1998 and 2002, when nuclear-powered replacements are planned. The first of these, *Charles de Gaulle*, was laid down at Brest in 1988. The guided missile cruiser *Colbert*, of 11,500 tonnes, completed in 1959, is armed with a twin Masurca surface to air missile launcher, 4 Exocet anti-ship missiles, and 4 100mm guns. The helicopter cruiser *Jeanne d'Arc*, of 12,600 tonnes completed in 1963 is used in peacetime as a training vessel, but could perform amphibious or ASW tasks in war. In these roles she could accommodate up to 8 Lynx helicopters, and 700 men. Her armament comprises 6 Exocet and 4 100mm guns.

Other surface combatants include 4 destroyers and 36 frigates. A modern mine countermeasure force consists of 10 tripartite coastal minehunters and 5 others, 5 old *ex*-US mine countermeasure vessels and 4 diver support vessels. The amphibious force includes 3 dock landing ships of which one is assigned to the Pacific nuclear test centre, 5 medium landing ships, and some 28 craft. Patrol forces include 1 ship (usually deployed in the South Indian Ocean), 21 coastal and 2 inshore patrol vessels. The Navy deploys a substantial support force includes 8 large and 2 small tankers, 16 other maintenance and logistic ships, 5 weapon system trials ships and 7 survey and research ships. There are several hundred minor auxiliaries.

All warships, and a proportion of naval weapons, are produced by the government armaments service, of which the naval element, *Direction des Constructions Navales*, operates the shipbuilding yards as well as dockyards. Building takes place at Cherbourg, Brest and Lorient. In addition to units already mentioned, 2 more nuclear-powered fleet submarines, 1 further guided missile destroyer, 1 frigate and 1 landing ship are being built. Fiscal restraints have caused many of these programmes to be slowed down.

The naval air arm, known as *Aeronavale*, numbers some 11,000. Operational aircraft include 40 Super-Etendard nuclear-capable strike aircraft, 20 Etendard reconnaissance aircraft, 8 US-built Crusader F-8E all-weather fighters, 28 Alize turboprop anti-submarine aircraft, 28 Atlantic and 5 Gardian maritime reconnaissance aircraft. The *Aeronavale* faces a problem with its fighter aircraft as the Crusaders' fatigue safe life expires in mid-1993, while the replacement, the maritime version of the Rafale, is unlikely to enter service before 1998. An interim solution is thus required to provide fleet air defence in the five-year gap. Rotary wing strength includes 16 commando Super Frelon, and 38 ASW and SAR Lynx helicopters. Numerous training, utility and transport aircraft bring the total strength to about 375 comprising 275 fixed-wing aircraft and 100 helicopters.

A small Marine force of 2,600 'Fusiliers Marins' provides 4 assault groups, plus numerous naval base protection units.

Personnel in 1989 numbered 65,500 including 19,200 conscripts (term of service 12 months) and a growing number of women, currently 1,700.

Air Force. Formed as the *Service Aéronautique* in April 1910, the *Armeé de l'Air* is organized in 7 major commands. The *Commandement des Forces Aériennes Stratégiques* (CFAS) commands the airborne nuclear deterrent force. The *Commandement de la Force Aérienne Tactique* (FATAC) directs the tactical air forces and is responsible for support of the ground forces. Under FATAC the 1st *Commandement Aérien Tactique* (1° CATAC) controls tactical air units based in eastern France; the 2nd *Commandement Aérien Tactique* (2° CATAC) controls the reserve forces and the air component of the *Force d'Intervention.* The *Commandement du Transport Aérien Militaire* (COTAM) is responsible for air transport operations and participates also in the training and transport of airborne forces. The *Commandement de la Défense Aérienne* (DA) controls French airspace. The *Commandement des Écoles de l'Armée de l'Air* (CEAA) is responsible for training the personnel for all branches of the Air Force. The *Commandement des Transmissions* has responsibility for communications and electronic warfare. Finally, the *Commandement du Génie de l'Air,* made up mainly of Army personnel, undertakes airbase construction and maintenance under Air Force control.

The home-based French Air Force is divided territorially among 4 metropolitan air regions (Metz, Villacoublay, Bordeaux, Aix-en-Provence); overseas, small air units are integrated into the local joint-service commands. There are about 40 combat squadrons plus about 30 transport, helicopter and support squadrons, and the Air Force uses a total of 60 bases.

The strategic, tactical and air defence forces are equipped entirely with jet aircraft. The CFAS has 20 Mirage IV supersonic nuclear bombers, deployed in 2 squadrons supported by 11 C-135F in-flight refuelling tanker transports. The FATAC deploys 6 wings (18 squadrons), with about 105 Mirage III-E and 5F ground-attack fighters, 30 Mirage 2000N, and 120 Jaguar strike aircraft, 3 reconnaissance squadrons with Mirage F1-CRs, and operational conversion units equipped with Mirage III-Bs and Jaguars. The air defence forces have 4 wings, comprising 8 squadrons with 120 Mirage F1-C and 4 squadrons with 60 Mirage 2000C interceptors. The COTAM is organized into 3 wings, equipped with 74 Transall C.160 turboprop transports, 5 DC-8s, 10 C-130s and 105 helicopters. Training aircraft include CAP-10/20/230 piston-engined primary trainers, Epsilon piston-engined and Fouga-Magister jet basic trainers, Mirage F1Bs, Mirage III-Bs, Mirage 2000Bs and two-seat Jaguars in wings for operational transformation; 25 Embraer 121-Xingus bought from Brazil are dual-purpose training/liaison aircraft. Total officers and other ranks (1990) 94,100; 450 combat aircraft.

INTERNATIONAL RELATIONS

Membership. France is a member of UN, the Council of Europe, NATO and the European Communities.

ECONOMY

Planning. For the history of planning in France from 1947 to 1980, *see* THE STATESMAN'S YEAR-BOOK, 1982–83, p. 474. The Eighth Plan, covering the 1981–85 period, was set aside after the change of government in May 1981 and replaced by an interim plan for 1982–83, followed by a new Ninth Plan for 1984–88.

Budget.

Receipts	*1987–88*
Taxation	1,179,633
Income tax	220,335
Corporation tax	121,240
Payroll tax	28,540
Taxes on consumption	
V.A.T.	522,887
Non fiscal receipts	74,430
Receipts from special allocations account	61,457
Internal taxes on petroleum products	106,041
Total gross budget receipts	1,134,930

Expenditure	*1987*	*%*	*1988*	*%*
Public authorities and general administration	133,888	12·2	142,038	12·3
Education and culture	250,377	22·7	260,820	22·6
Social affairs, health, employment	202,672	18·4	205,383	17·8
Agriculture and countryside	24,466	2·2	24,291	2·1
Housing and town planning	47,954	4·4	52,387	4·6
Transport and communications	47,568	4·3	47,142	4·1
Industry and services	49,939	4·5	51,049	4·4
External affairs	42,954	3·9	44,117	3·8
Defence	177,856	16·1	182,877	15·9
Miscellaneous expenditure	124,770	11·3	142,897	12·4
Total expenditure	1,102,444		1,153,001	

The accounts of revenue and expenditure are examined by a special administrative tribunal (*Cour des Comptes*), instituted in 1807.

Currency. The unit of currency is the *franc*. Coins are issued for 5, 10, 20 and 50 centimes, 1, 2, 5 and 10 francs; and bank-notes for 10, 20, 50, 100, 200 and 500 francs. In March 1990, £1 sterling = 9·43 *francs*; US$1 = 5·76 *francs*.

Banking. The *Banque de France*, founded in 1800, and nationalized on 2 Dec. 1945, has the monopoly (since 1848) of issuing bank-notes throughout France. Note circulation at 31 Dec. 1981 was 151,900m. francs. As a Central Bank, it puts monetary policy into effect and supervises its application.

The National Credit Council, formed in 1945 to regulate banking activity and consulted in all political decisions on monetary policy, comprises 45 members nominated by the Government; its president is the Minister for the Economy, its vice-president is the Governor of the *Banque de France*. Four principal deposit banks were nationalized in 1945 and the remainder in 1982 but the latter were privatized in 1987. The chief banks (1989) were the Crédit Lyonnais (founded 1863), Banque Nationale de Paris (founded by amalgamation 1966), Société Générale (founded 1864), Crédit Industriel et Commercial, Crédit Commercial de France, the Banque de Paris et des Pays-Bas (Paribas) and the Crédit du Nord. Total deposits and short- and medium-term held bills by the banks at 31 Dec. 1981 was 1,302,800m. francs. The rest of the banking system comprises the popular banks, the Crédit agricole, the Crédit mutuel, the Banque française du commerce exterieur and the various financial establishments.

The state savings organization (*Caisse nationale d'epargne*) is administered by the post office on a giro system. On 31 Dec. 1981 the private savings banks

(*Caisses d'epargne et de prévoyance*), numbering about 500 had 434,000m. francs in deposits; the state savings banks had 206,300m. francs in deposits. Deposited funds are centralized by a non-banking body, the *Caisse de Dépôts et Consignations*, which finances a large number of local authorities and state aided housing projects, and carries an important portfolio of transferable securities.

Weights and Measures. The metric system is in general use.

ENERGY AND NATURAL RESOURCES

Electricity. Production (in 1m. kwh.): 1986, 346,298, of which 64,444 was hydro-electric and 281,855 nuclear. Supply 127 and 220 volts; 50 Hz.

Oil. In 1989 3·2m. tonnes of crude oil were produced. The greater part came from the Parentis oilfield in the Landes. Reserves (1985) total 221m. bbls. France has an important oil-refining industry, chiefly utilizing imported crude oil. The principal plants are situated in Seine-Maritime and in Bouches-du-Rhône. In 1985, 72·49m. tonnes of petroleum products were refined. There are 7,802 km of pipelines.

There has been considerable development of the production of natural gas and sulphur in the region of Lacq in the foothills of the Pyrenees. Production of natural gas was 10,574m. cu. metres in 1984; reserves (1985) 41,000m. cu. metres.

Minerals. Principal minerals and metals produced in 1983, in 1,000 tonnes: Coal, 33,396; crude steel, 17,616; iron ore, 15,972; pig iron, 13,752; bauxite, 1,660; potash salts, 1,651.

Agriculture. Of the total area of France (54·9m. hectares) 18·2m. were under cultivation, 11·9m. were pasture, 1m. were under vines, 14·3m. were forests and 8·9m. were uncultivated land in 1986. In 1986 there were 1,484,900 tractors in use. In 1987 there were 981,722 holdings and 1,505,000 people (7% of the total working population) were employed in agriculture.

The following table shows the area under the leading crops and the production for 3 years:

	Area (1,000 hectares)			*Produce (1,000 tonnes)*		
	1986	*1987*	*1988*	*1986*	*1987*	*1988*
Wheat	4,859	4,932	4,825	26,475	27,415	29,677
Rye	81	82	79	229	299	276
Barley	2,090	1,992	1,916	10,063	10,489	10,086
Oats	312	281	273	1,066	1,122	1,074
Potatoes	201	197	183	6,267	6,720	6,344
Sugar-beet	448	446	432	25,830	26,471	28,606
Maize	1,884	1,743	1,936	11,641	12,470	13,996

Production (1988, in 1,000 tonnes): Centrifugal raw sugar, 4,424; wine, 6,379; beef and veal, 1,832; pork, 1,740; lamb and mutton, 152; poultry, 1,429; milk, 29,012.

The production of fruits (other than for cider making) for 3 years was (in 1,000 tonnes) as follows:

	1986	*1987*	*1988*		*1986*	*1987*	*1988*
Apples	2,739	2,424	2,357	Melons	274	286	275
Pears	370	439	355	Nuts	50	50	51
Plums	209	203	222	Grapes	9,340	9,164	7,419
Peaches	473	488	472	Strawberries	92	99	95
Apricots	121	98	97	Oranges	3	3	3

In 1988 the numbers of farm animals (in 1,000) were (figures for 1987 in brackets): Horses, 292 (300); cattle, 21,100 (22,803); sheep, 10,360 (10,580); goats, 1,150 (1,090); pigs, 12,577 (12,419); poultry, 220,000 (218,000).

Forestry. The total area of forested land (1988) was 139,000 sq. km, about 27% of the land area. Timber sold (1982), 28,342m. cu. metres valued at 7,581m. francs.

Fisheries. (1987). There were 23,426 fishermen, and 9,620 sailing-boats, steamers and motor-boats. Catch (in tonnes): Fish, total, 513,367; crustaceans, 24,111; shell fish, 226,890.

INDUSTRY AND TRADE

Industry. Industrial production (in 1,000 tonnes) for 3 years was as follows:

	1986	*1987*	*1988*
Sulphuric acid	3,956	3,960	4,081
Caustic acid	1,517	1,430	1,494
Sulphur	1,170	1,092	1,022
Polystyrene	501	527	536
Polyvinyl	880	933	1,017
Polyethylene	1,133	1,156	1,135
Wool	48	43	43
Cotton	139	136	136
Linen	1.2	1·2	1·0
Silk	66	67	73
Jute	4.8	4·9	4·6
Cheese	1,289	1,321	...
Chocolate	325	373	...
Biscuits	404	416	...
Sugar	3,410	3,655	...
Fish preparations	107	104	...
Jams and jellies	144	151	...
Cement and lime	22,596	23,557	30,863

Engineering production (in 1,000 units) for 3 years:

	1986	*1987*	*1988*
Motor vehicles	3,195	3,493	3,699
Television sets	1,869	2,015	2,081
Radio sets	...	2,132	1,983
Tyres	51,138	56,450	60,366

Labour (1987). Out of an economically active population of 24,084,300 persons, 1,465,300 were engaged in agriculture, forestry and fishing, 1,521,900 in building, 1,183,100 in manufacturing industries, 897,900 in transport, 602,300 in banking and insurance, 4,228,700 in services, 2,592,500 in commerce. At 31 Dec. 1987, there were 21,230,200 employed.

Trade Unions. The main confederations recognized as nationally representative are: the CGT (Confédération Générale du Travail), founded in 1895; the CGT-FO (Confédération Générale du Travail–Force Ouvrière) which broke away from the CGT in 1948 as a protest against Communist influence therein; the CFTC (Confédération Française des Travailleurs Chrétiens), which was founded in 1919 and divided in 1964, with a breakaway group retaining the old name and the main body continuing under the new name of CFDT (Confédération Française Démocratique du Travail); and the CGC (Confédération Générale des Cadres) formed in 1944 which only represents managerial and supervisory staff.

Membership is estimated because unions are not required to publish figures; but at elections held on 8 Dec. 1982 for labour tribunals, the CGT was supported by 2·8m. members, the CGT–FO by 1·4m., the CFDT by 1·8m., the CFTC by 650,000 and the CGC by 740,000. Except for the CGC unions operate within the framework of industries and not of trades.

Commerce. Imports (c.i.f.) and exports (f.o.b.) in 1m. francs for 5 calendar years were (including gold):

	1983	*1984*	*1985*	*1986*	*1987*
Imports	799,754	903,664	962,747	887,502	944,999
Exports	694,659	813,031	870,811	825,417	857,936

The chief imports for home use and exports of home goods are to and from the following countries, in 1m. francs (including gold):

Countries	Imports (c.i.f) 1986	Imports (c.i.f) 1987	Exports (f.o.b.) 1986	Exports (f.o.b.) 1987
Belgium-Luxembourg	83,917	88,681	74,895	79,873
Germany, Fed. Rep. of	172,324	186,666	133,107	142,713
Italy	103,289	110,811	97,059	103,637
Netherlands	32,204	36,063	11,157	13,225
Japan	50,997	53,270	40,665	43,602
Spain	36,941	41,241	33,781	45,500
Switzerland	22,167	23,624	37,727	36,787
UK	57,684	67,178	72,622	75,524
USA	66,995	67,592	61,091	62,527

Foreign trade by sector, 1987, in 1m. francs:

	Imports (c.i.f)	Exports (f.o.b.)
Agriculture and agri-food industry	119,036	148,570
Energy	100,274	18,540
Raw materials and semi-products	246,431	230,023
Capital goods	229,838	212,039
Surface transport equipment	92,852	115,769
Consumer goods	153,325	127,306

Total trade between France and UK (British Department of Trade returns, in £1,000 sterling):

	1985	1986	1987	1988	1989
Imports to UK	6,632,410	7,348,574	8,381,984	9,390,207	10,785,429
Exports and re-exports from UK	7,751,751	6,210,216	7,781,546	8,270,408	9,461,648

Tourism. In 1987 there were 31·9m. tourists.

COMMUNICATIONS

Roads. In 1986 there were 345,000 km of departmental road network and, in 1988, 36,800 km of national road network of which 8,590 km were motorway. In 1987 there were 5,364,251 registered vehicles, including 4,373,675 private and commercial vehicles, 6,988 coaches and buses, 600,000 lorries and vans and 231,035 motorcycles.

Railways. As from 1 Jan. 1938 all the independent railway companies were merged with the existing state railway system in a Société Nationale des Chemins de Fer Français, which became a public industrial and commercial establishment in 1983.

In 1988, the State railway totalled 34,570 km (12,433 km electrified) and carried 145m. tonnes of freight and 818m. passengers. A new railway for high-speed trains was completed in 1983 between Paris and Lyon and another opened in 1989 to serve Western France.

The Paris transport network consisted in 1988 of 548 km of underground railway (métro) and regional express railways and 2,212 km of bus routes. In 1988 it carried 1,483m. passengers on the métro and 793m. by bus.

Boring of the Channel tunnel began in March 1988. A network (TGV Nord) will be constructed linking Paris to the tunnel as well as to Lille, and this network will also connect Paris and the tunnel to Brussels and be extended to the Netherlands and the Federal Republic of Germany.

Aviation. Air France, UTA and Air Inter, the national airlines, had (31 Dec. 1987) a fleet of 318 aircraft, servicing Europe, North America, Central and South America, West and East Africa, Madagascar, the Near, Middle and Far East. There are local networks in the West Indies and Central America. In 1987 Air France, UTA and Air Inter flew 3,415m. tonne-km (excluding mail) and 44,343·9m. passenger-km. There were (1984) 60 airports with scheduled services.

Shipping. Merchant ships, in 1988, numbered 261 vessels of 4,389,000 GRT. During 1987, 186·87m. tonnes of cargo were unloaded, of which 92·2m. tonnes were crude and refined petroleum products, and 61·93m. tonnes were loaded; total passenger traffic, 21·5m.

In 1988 there were 8,500 km of navigable rivers, waterways and canals (of which 1,647 km accessible to vessels over 3,000 tons), with a total traffic in 1987 of 60·72m. tonnes.

Post and Broadcasting. On 31 Dec. 1987 the telephone system (government-owned) had 23,667,200 subscribers. In 1987 there were 17,187 post offices.

Radio and television broadcasting was reorganized under the Act of 7 Aug. 1974 which replaced the Office de Radiodiffusion Télévision Française with 4 broadcasting companies, a production company and an audio-visual institute. Organization, development, operation and the maintenance of networks and installations became the responsibility of the Public Broadcasting Establishment. In 1988 radio programmes are broadcast from 874 VHF transmitters of which 418 belong to 4 stations: *France Info, France Inter, France Musique* and *France Culture*. Television programmes are broadcast from 541 transmitters and 9,378 relay stations. There were about 20m. radio and 17·95m. TV sets in use in 1986.

Cinemas (1987). There were 5,063 cinemas; attendances totalled 132·5m.

Newspapers (1987). There were 72 daily papers published in the provinces with a circulation of 6·7m. copies, and 14 published in Paris with a national circulation of 2·5m. Among Paris dailies *France-Soir* sells 539,000; *Le Monde* 445,000; *Le Parisien Libéré* 421,000 and *Le Figaro* 465,000. Among provincial dailies *Ouest-France* (Rennes) sells 783,000; *Le Progrés* (Lyon) 447,000; *La Voix du Nord* (Lille) 372,000; *Sud-Ouest* (Bordeaux) 430,000; *La Dauphine Libérée* (Grenoble) 401,000 and *Le Provençal* (Marseilles) 345,000.

JUSTICE, RELIGION, EDUCATION AND WELFARE

Justice. Since 1958, 473 *tribunaux d'instance* (11 in overseas departments), under a single judge each and with increased material and territorial jurisdiction, have replaced the former *juges de paix* (1 in each canton); and 181 *tribunaux de grande instance* (6 in overseas departments) have taken the place of the former *tribunaux de première instance* (1 in each *arrondissement*).

The *tribunaux de grande instance* usually have a collegiate composition, however a law dated 10 July 1970 has allowed them to administer justice under a single judge in some civil cases.

All petty offences (*contraventions*) are disposed of in the Police Courts (*Tribunaux de Police*) presided over by a Judge on duty in the *tribunal d'instance*. The Correctional Tribunals pronounce upon all graver offences (*délits*), including cases involving imprisonment up to 5 years. They have no jury, and consist of 3 judges of the *tribunal de grande instance*, although in some cases, the correctional tribunal may consist of a single judge. In all cases of a *crime* and sometimes in cases of *délit* the preliminary inquiry is made in secrecy by an examining magistrate (*juge d'instruction*), who either dismisses the case or sends it for trial before a court where a public prosecutor (*Procureur*) endeavours to prove the charge.

The 282 Conciliation Boards (*Conseils de Prud'hommes*) each composed of an equal number of employers and employees, elected for 5 years deal with labour disputes. Commercial litigation goes to one of the 230 Commercial Courts (*Tribunaux de Commerce*) composed of tradesmen and manufacturers elected for 2 years initially and then for 4 years. Other local tribunals exist to deal with social security or rural holdings disputes.

When the decisions of any of these Tribunals are susceptible of appeal, the case goes to one of the 35 Courts of Appeal (*Cours d'Appel*), (including 3 in overseas departments and 2 in overseas territories), composed each of a president and a variable number of members.

The 103 Courts of Assizes are each composed of a President who is a member of the Court of Appeal, and 2 other magistrates, and assisted by a jury of 9 lay people, to try severe criminal offences (*crimes*) involving imprisonment of over 5 years. The decisions of the Courts of Appeal and the Courts of Assizes are final; however, the Court of Cassation (*Cour de Cassation*) has discretion to verify if the law has been correctly interpreted and if the rules of procedure have been followed exactly.

The Court of Cassation may annul any judgment, and the cases have to be tried again by a Court of Appeal or a Court of Assizes.

Capital punishment was abolished in Aug. 1981.

On 24 Jan. 1973 the first Ombudsman (*médiateur*) was appointed for a 6-year period.

The French penal institutions consist of: (1) *maisons d'arrêt* and *de correction*, where persons awaiting trial as well as those condemned to short periods of imprisonment are kept; (2) central prisons (*maisons centrales*) for those sentenced to long imprisonment; (3) special establishments, namely (*a*) schools for young adults, (*b*) hostels for old and disabled offenders, (*c*) hospitals for the sick and psychopaths. Special attention is being paid to classified treatment and the rehabilitation and vocational re-education of prisoners including work in open-air and semi-free establishments. There is 1 penal institution for women.

Juvenile delinquents go before special judges and courts; they are sent to public or private institutions of supervision and re-education.

The population at 31 Dec. 1989 of all penal establishments was 44,477 men and 2,038 women.

Religion. No religion is officially recognized by the State. Under the law promulgated on 9 Dec. 1905, which separated Church and State, the adherents of all creeds are authorized to form associations for public worship (*associations culturelles*). The law of 2 Jan. 1907 provided that, failing *associations culturelles*, the buildings for public worship, together with their furniture, would continue at the disposition of the ministers of religion and the worshippers for the exercise of their religion; but in each case there was required an administrative act drawn up by the *préfet* as regards buildings belonging to the State or the departments and by the *maire* as regards buildings belonging to the communes.

There were (1985) 125 archbishops and bishops of the Roman Catholic Church, with (1974) 43,557 clergy of various grades and (1986) 42·35m. members. The Protestants of the Augsburg confession are, in their religious affairs, governed by a General Consistory, while the Reformed Church is under a Council of Administration, the seat of which is in Paris. In 1988 there were about 800,000 Protestants and 1·9m. Moslems.

Education. The primary, secondary and higher state schools constitute the 'Université de France'. The Supreme Council of 84 members has deliberative, administrative and judiciary functions, and as a consultative committee advises respecting the working of the school system, the inspectors-general are in direct communication with the Minister. For local education administration France is divided into 25 academic areas, each of which has an Academic Council whose members include a certain number elected by the professors or teachers. The Academic Council deals with all grades of education. Each is under a Rector, and each is provided with academy inspectors, 1 for each department.

Compulsory education is now provided for children of 6–16. The educational stages are as follows:

1. Non-compulsory pre-school instruction for children aged 2–5, to be given in infant schools or infant classes attached to primary schools.

2. Compulsory elementary instruction for children aged 6–11, to be given in primary schools and certain classes of the *lycées*. It consists of 3 courses: Preparatory (1 year), elementary (2 years), intermediary (2 years). Physically or mentally handicapped children are cared for in special institutions or special classes of primary schools.

3. Lower secondary education (*Enseignement du premier cycle du Second Degré*) for pupils aged 11–15, consists of 4 years of study in the *lycées* (grammar schools), *Collèges d'Enseignement Secondaire* or *Collèges d'Enseignement Général*.

4. Upper secondary education (*Enseignement du second cycle du Second Degré*) for pupils aged 15–18:

Long, *général* or *professionel* provided by the *lycées* and leading to the *baccalauréat* or to the *baccalauréat de technicien* after 3 years.

Court, professional courses of 3, 2 and 1 year are taught in the *lycées d'enseignement professionel*, or the specialized sections of the *lycées*, CES or CEG.

The following table shows the number of schools in 1987–88 and the numbers of pupils in full-time education:

	State		Private	
	Schools	*Pupils*	*Schools*	*Pupils*
Nursery	17,900	5,732,931	385	930,853
Primary	40,235		6,038	
Secondary	7,342	4,481,797	3,905	1,192,813

Higher Instruction is supplied by the State in the universities and in special schools, and by private individuals in the free faculties and schools. The law of 12 July 1875 provided for higher education free of charge. This law was modified by that of 18 March 1880, which granted the state faculties the exclusive right to confer degrees. A decree of 28 Dec. 1885 created a general council of the faculties, and the creation of universities, each consisting of several faculties, was accomplished in 1897, in virtue of the law of 10 July 1896.

The law of 12 Nov. 1968 laying down future guidelines for higher education redefined the activities and working of universities. Bringing several disciplines together, 780 units for teaching and research (UER–Unités d'Enseignement et de Récherche) were formed which decided their own teaching activities, research programmes and procedures for checking the level of knowledge gained. They and the other parts of each university must respect the rules designed to maintain the national standard of qualifications.

The UERs form the basic units of 69 Universities and 3 National Polytechnic Institutes (with university status), grouped into 25 *académies* with 980,404 students in 1987.

There are also Catholic university facilities in Paris, Angers, Lille, Lyon and Toulouse with (1981–82) 34,118 students and private universities with (1984–85) 17,646 students.

Outside the university system, higher education (academic, professional and technical) is provided by over 400 schools and institutes, including the various Grand Écoles. In 1984–85 there were 139,827 students in state establishments and 61,996 in private establishments. In 1986–87 there were also 48,811 students in preparatory classes leading to the Grandes Écoles, 129,942 in the Sections de Techniciens Supérieurs and 47,300 in the Écoles d'ingénieurs; there were also (1984-85) 18,951 students in Écoles normales d'instituteurs (teacher-training).

Health. On 1 Jan. 1988 there were 138,825 doctors, (1987) 49,610 chemists, (1986) 34,946 dentists, (1986) 294,260 nurses and (1986) 9,725 midwives. On 1 Jan. 1987 there were 3,730 hospitals with 574,000 beds.

Social Welfare. An order of 4 Oct. 1945 laid down the framework of a comprehensive plan of Social Security and created a single organization which superseded the various laws relating to social insurance, workmen's compensation, health insurance, family allowances, etc. All previous matters relating to Social Security are dealt with in the Social Security Code, 1956; this has been revised several times.

Contributions. All wage-earning workers or those of equivalent status are insured regardless of the amount or the nature of the salary or earnings. The funds for the general scheme are raised mainly from professional contributions, these being fixed within the limits of a ceiling and calculated as a percentage of the salaries. The calculation of contributions payable for family allowances, old age and industrial injuries relates only to this amount; on the other hand, the amount payable for sickness, maternity expenses, disability and death is calculated partly within the limit of the 'ceiling' and partly on the whole salary. These contributions are the responsibility of both employer and employee, except in the case of family allowances or industrial injuries, where they are the sole responsibility of the employer.

Self-employed Workers. From 17 Jan. 1948 allowances and old-age pensions were paid to self-employed workers by independent insurance funds set up within their own profession, trade or business. Schemes of compulsory insurance for sickness were instituted in 1961 for farmers and in 1966, with modifications in 1970, for other non-wage-earning workers.

Social Insurance. The orders laid down in Aug. 1967 ensure that the whole population can benefit from the Social Security Scheme; at present all elderly persons who have been engaged in the professions, as well as the surviving spouse, are entitled to claim an old-age benefit.

Sickness Insurance refunds the costs of treatment required by the insured and the needs of dependants.

Maternity Insurance covers the costs of medical treatment relating to the pregnancy, confinement and lying-in period; the beneficiaries being the insured person or the spouse.

Insurance for Invalids is divided into 3 categories: (1) those who are capable of working; (2) those who cannot work; (3) those who, in addition, are in need of the help of another person. According to the category, the pension rate varies from 30 to 50% of the average salary for the last 10 years, with additional allowance for home help for the third category.

Old-age Pensions for workers were introduced in 1910 and are now fixed by the Social Security Code of 28 Jan. 1972. Since 1983 people who have paid insurance for at least $37^1/_2$ years (150 quarters) receive at 60 a pension equal to 60% of basic salary. People who have paid insurance for less than $37^1/_2$ years but no less than 15 years can expect a pension equal to as many 1/150ths of the full pension as their quarterly payments justify. In the event of death of the insured person, the husband or wife of the deceased person receives half the pension received by the latter. Compulsory supplementary schemes ensure benefits equal to 70% of previous earnings.

Family Allowances. The system comprises: (*a*) Family allowances proper, equivalent to 25·5% of the basic monthly salary (1,246 francs) for 2 dependent children, 46% for the third child, 41% for the fourth child, and 39% for the fifth and each subsequent child; a supplement equivalent to 9% of the basic monthly salary for the second and each subsequent dependent child more than 10 years old and 16% for each dependent child over 15 years. (*b*) Family supplement (519 francs) for persons with at least 3 children or one child aged less than 3 years. (*c*) Antenatal grants. (*d*) Maternity grant equal to 260% of basic salary; increase for multiple births or adoptions, 198%; increase for birth or adoption of third or subsequent child, 457%. (*e*) Allowance for specialized education of handicapped children. (*f*) Allowance for orphans. (*g*) Single parent allowance. (*h*) Allowance for opening of school term. (*i*) Allowance for accommodation, under certain circumstances. (*j*) Minimum family income for those with at least 3 children. Allowances (*b*), (*g*), (*h*) and (*j*) only apply to those whose annual income falls below a specified level.

Workmen's Compensation. The law passed by the National Assembly on 30 Oct. 1946 forms part of the Social Security Code and is administered by the Social Security Organization. Employers are invited to take preventive measures. The application of these measures is supervised by consulting engineers (assessors) of the local funds dealing with sickness insurance, who may compel employers who do not respect these measures to make additional contributions; they may, in like manner, grant rebates to employers who have in operation suitable preventive measures. The injured person receives free treatment, the insurance fund reimburses the practitioners, hospitals and suppliers chosen freely by the injured. In cases of temporary disablement the daily payments are equal to half the total daily wage received by the injured. In case of permanent disablement the injured person receives a pension, the amount of which varies according to the degree of disablement and the salary received during the past 12 months.

Unemployment Benefits vary according to circumstances (full or partial unemployment) which are means-tested. Since 1926 unemployment benefits have been paid from public funds.

DIPLOMATIC REPRESENTATIVES

Of France in Great Britain (58 Knightsbridge, London, SW1X 7JT)
Ambassador: Vicomte Luc de la Barre de Nanteuil (accredited 28 Feb. 1986).

Of Great Britain in France (35 rue du Faubourg St Honoré, 75383 Paris)
Ambassador: Sir Ewen Fergusson, KCMG.

Of France in the USA (4101 Reservoir Rd., NW, Washington, D.C., 20007)
Ambassador: Emmanuel de Margerie.

Of the USA in France (2 Ave. Gabriel, Paris)
Ambassador: Walter Curley.

Of France to the United Nations
Ambassador: Pierre-Louis Blanc.

Further Reading

Statistical Information: The Institut national de la Statistique et des Études économiques (18, Boulevard Adolphe Pinard, 75014 Paris) is the central office of statistics. It was established by a law of 27 April 1946, which amalgamated the Service National des Statistiques (created in 1941 by merging the Direction de la Statistique générale de la France and the Service de la Démographie) with the Institut de Conjoncture (set up in 1938) and some statistical services of the Ministry of National Economy. The Institut comprises the following departments: Metropolitan statistics, Overseas statistics, Market research and economic studies, Documentation, Research statistics and economics, Informatics, Foreign Economic Studies.

The main publications of the Institut include:

Annuaire statistique de la France (from 1878)
Annuaire statistique des Territoires d'Outre-Mer (from 1959)
Bulletin mensuel de statistique (monthly)
Documentation économique (bi-monthly)
Données statistiques africaines et Malgaches (quarterly)
Economie et Statistique (monthly)
Tableaux de l'Economie Française (biennially, from 1956)
Tendances de la Conjoncture (monthly)

Braudel, F., *The Identity of France: Vol 1, History and Environment*. London, 1988
Caron, F., *An Economic History of Modern France*. London, 1979
Chambers, F. J., *France*. [Bibliography] Oxford and Santa Barbara, (rev. ed.) 1990
Crozier, M., *A Strategy for Change: The Future of French Society*. MIT Press, 1982
Peyrefitte, A., *The Trouble with France*. New York, 1981
Pinchemel, P., *France: A Geographical, Social and Economic Survey*. CUP, 1987
Tuppen, J. N., *France*. Folkestone, 1981

OVERSEAS DEPARTMENTS

On 19 March 1946 the French colonies of Guadeloupe, French Guiana, Martinique and Réunion each became an Overseas Department of France, with the same status as the departments comprising Metropolitan France. The former territory of Saint Pierre and Miquelon held a similar status from July 1976 until June 1985, when it became a *collectivité territorial*.

GUADELOUPE

HISTORY. Discovered by Columbus in Nov. 1493, the two main islands were then known as *Karukera* (Isle of Beautiful Waters) to the Carib inhabitants, who resisted Spanish attempts to colonize. A French colony was established on 28 June

1635, and apart from short periods of occupancy by British forces, Guadeloupe has since remained a French possession. On 19 March 1946 Guadeloupe became an Overseas Department; in 1974 it additionally became an administrative region.

AREA AND POPULATION. Guadeloupe consists of a group of islands in the Lesser Antilles. The two main islands, Basse-Terre to the west and Grande-Terre to the east, are separated by a narrow channel, called Rivière Salée. Adjacent to these are the islands of Marie Galante *(Ceyre* to the Caribs) to the south-east, La Désirade to the east, and the Îles des Saintes to the south. The islands of St Martin and St Barthélemy lie 250 km to the north-west.

	Area in sq. km	*Census 1974*	*Census 1982*	*Chief town*
St Martin [1]	54 [2]	6,191	8,072	Marigot
St Barthélemy	21	2,491	3,059	Gustavia
Basse-Terre	848	135,746	135,341	Basse-Terre
Grande-Terre	590	159,424	163,668	Pointe-à-Pitre
Îles des Saintes	13	3,084	2,901	Terre-de-Bas
La Désirade	20	1,682	1,602	Grande Anse
Marie-Galante	158	15,912	13,757	Grand-Bourg
	1,705	324,530	328,400	

[1]Northern part only; the southern third is Dutch. [2]Includes uninhabited Tintamarre.

Population (estimate, 1988) 336,300. 77% are mulatto, 10% black and 10% mestizo, but the populations of St Barthélemy and Les Saintes are still mainly descended from 17th-century Breton and Norman settlers. French is the official language, but a Creole dialect is spoken by the vast majority except on St Martin.

The seat of government is Basse-Terre (13,656 inhabitants in 1982) at the south-west end of that island but the largest towns are Pointe-à-Pitre (25,310 inhabitants), the economic centre and main port, and its suburb, Les Abymes (51,837 inhabitants).

Vital statistics (1987): Live births, 6,855; deaths, 2,244; marriages, 1,880.

CLIMATE. Warm and humid. Pointe-à-Pitre. Jan. 74°F (23·4°C), July 80°F (26·7°C). Annual rainfall 71" (1,814 mm).

CONSTITUTION AND GOVERNMENT. Guadeloupe is administered by a *Conseil Général* of 42 members (assisted by an Economic and Social Committee of 40 members) and a Regional Council of 39 members, both directly elected for terms of 6 years. It is represented in the National Assembly by 4 deputies, in the Senate by 2 senators and on the Economic and Social Council by 2 councillors. There are 3 *arrondissements,* sub-divided into 34 communes, each administered by an elected municipal council. The French government is represented by an appointed Commissioner.

Commissioner: Yves Bonnet.

President of the Conseil Général: Dominique Larifla.

President of the Regional Council: Félix Proto.

ECONOMY

Budget. The budget for 1983 balanced at 1,633m. francs.

Banking. The main commercial banks are the Banque des Antilles Françaises (with 6 branches), the Banque Populaire de la Guadeloupe (with 6 branches), the Banque Nationale de Paris (14 branches), the Crédit Agricole (26), the Banque Française Commerciale (8), the Société Generale de Banque aux Antilles (5) and the Chase Manhattan Bank (1). The Caisse Centrale de Coopération économique is the official bank of the department and issues its bank-notes.

ENERGY AND NATURAL RESOURCES

Electricity. Production in 1986 totalled 315m. kwh.

Agriculture. Chief products (1988) are bananas (120,000 tonnes), sugar-cane (891,000 tonnes), rum (64,883 hectolitres of pure alcohol in 1984). Other fruits and vegetables are grown for domestic consumption. 11·8m. flowers were grown in 1984.

Livestock (1988): Cattle, 74,000; goats, 33,000; sheep, 4,000; pigs, 43,000.

Forestry. In 1985, there were 395 sq. km of forests. In 1984, 51,848 cu. metres of wood were produced.

Fisheries. The catch in 1984 was 8,500 tonnes; crustacea (120 tonnes), shell fish (300 tonnes).

COMMERCE. Trade for 1985 (in 1m. francs) was imports 5,745 and exports 669, 60% of imports were from France, while 63% of exports went to France and 18% to Martinique. In 1985 bananas formed 43% of the exports, sugar 10% and rum 7%. St Martin and St Barthélemy are free ports.

Toal trade between Guadeloupe and UK (British Department of Trade returns, £1,000 sterling):

	1989
Imports to UK	119
Exports and re-exports from UK	4,381

Tourism. In 1986 there were 212,000 tourists.

COMMUNICATIONS

Roads. In 1984 there were 3,500 km of roads. There were 87,785 passenger cars and 33,350 commercial vehicles in 1981.

Aviation. Air France and 7 other airlines call at Guadeloupe. In 1984 there were 31,451 arrivals and departures of aircraft and 1,325,500 passengers at Raizet (Pointe-à-Pitre) airport and, 6,682 aircraft movements and 116,000 passengers at Marie-Galante airport.

Shipping. Guadeloupe is in direct communication with France by means of 12 steam navigation companies. In 1983, 1,239 vessels arrived to disembark 74,921 passengers and 1,035,800 tonnes of freight and to embark 74,999 passengers and 470,600 tonnes of freight.

Post and Broadcasting. In 1984 there were 47 post offices and 64,916 telephones. RFO broadcasts for 17 hours a day in French and television broadcasts for 6 hours a day. There were (1983) 25,000 radio and (1981) 32,886 TV receivers.

Newspapers. There was (1984) 1 daily newspaper *(France-Antilles)* with a circulation of 25,000.

JUSTICE, RELIGION, EDUCATION AND WELFARE

Justice. There are 4 *tribunaux d'instance* and 2 *tribunaux de grande instance* at Basse-Terre and Pointe-à-Pitre; there is also a court of appeal and a court of assizes at Basse-Terre.

Religion. The majority of the population are Roman Catholic.

Education. In 1984 there were 62,303 pupils at 284 primary schools and 45,843 at secondary schools. The University Antilles-Guyane had 4,809 students in 1984–85, of which Guadeloupe itself had 1,870.

Health. The medical services in 1985 included 11 public hospitals (2,891 beds) and 18 private clinics (1,256 beds). There were 416 physicians, 127 dentists, 127 pharmacists, 70 midwives and 1,131 nursing personnel.

Further Reading

Information: Office du Tourisme du départemente, Point-à-Pitre. *Director:* Eric W. Rotin.

Lasserre, G., *La Guadeloupe, étude géographique*. 2 vols. Bordeaux, 1961

GUIANA
Guyane Française

HISTORY. A French settlement on the island of Cayenne was established in 1604 and the territory between the Maroni and Oyapock rivers finally became a French possession in 1817. Convicts settlements were established from 1852, that on off-shore Devil's Island being most notorious; all were closed by 1945. On 19 March 1946 the status of Guiana was changed to that of an Overseas Department and in 1974 also became an administrative region.

AREA AND POPULATION. French Guiana is situated on the north-east coast of South America, and has an area of about 83,533 sq. km (32,252 sq. miles) and a population at the 1982 Census of 73,800, of whom 3,000 were tribal Indians; estimate (1989) 93,540. The chief towns (1982 populations) are Cayenne, the capital (38,093), Kourou (7,061) and Saint-Laurent-du-Maroni (6,971). These figures exclude the floating population of miners, officials and troops and about 7,000 Surinamese refugees since 1986.

In 1982, 43% of the inhabitants were of Creole origin, 14% Chinese, 11% from Metropolitan France and 8% Haitian. 90% of the population speak Creole.

Vital statistics (1988): Live births, 2,700; deaths, 562; marriages (1987), 365.

CONSTITUTION AND GOVERNMENT. French Guiana is administered by a General Council of 19 members and a Regional Council of 31 members, both directly elected for terms of 6 years. It is represented in the National Assembly by 2 deputies and in the Senate by 1 senator. The French government is represented by a Prefect. There are 2 *arrondissements* (Cayenne and SaintLaurent-du-Maroni) subdivided into 21 communes.

Prefect: Jean-Pierre Lacroix.
President of the General Council: Elie Castor.
President of the Regional Council: Georges Othily.

ECONOMY

Budget. The budget for 1987 balanced at 847m. francs, excluding duplicated items and national expenditure.

Banking. The Banque de la Guyane has a capital of 10m. francs and reserve fund of 2·39m. francs. Loans totalled 2,762m. francs in 1987. Other banks include Banque National de Paris-Guyane, Crédit Populaire Guyanais and Banque Française Commerciale.

ENERGY AND NATURAL RESOURCES

Electricity. Production in 1988 totalled 243m. kwh. Supply 220 volts; 50 Hz.

Agriculture. Only 12,581 hectares are under cultivation. The crops (1988, in tonnes) consist of rice (14,000), manioc (6,263) and sugar-cane (1,740).

Livestock (1988): 15,000 cattle, 9,000 swine and (1987) 117,000 poultry.

Forestry. The country has immense forests (about 66,700 sq. km in 1988) rich in many kinds of timber. Roundwood production (1988) 101,273 cu. metres.

Fisheries. The fishing fleet for shrimps comprises 31 US and 41 French boats. The catch in 1988 totalled 4,256 tonnes of shrimps and 1,024 tonnes of fish. Production of *Macrobrachium Rosenbergii* (an edible river shrimp) totalled 62·8 tonnes.

COMMERCE. Trade in 1m. francs:

	1985	*1986*	*1987*	*1988*
Imports	2,287	2,065	2,371	2,742
Exports	300	255	323	325

In 1986, 8% of imports came from Trinidad and Tobago, 65% from France and 11% from the EEC, while 36% of exports went to the USA, 16% to Japan, 22% to the French West Indies and 23% to France. In 1985, shrimps formed 53% of exports and timber, 9%.

Total trade between Guiana and UK (British Department of Trade returns, in £1,000 sterling):

	1985	*1986*	*1987*	*1988*	*1989*
Imports to UK	124	55	380	1,148	9,009
Exports and re-exports from UK	1,146	1,052	1,134	4,232	4,559

TOURISM. There were 14,500 tourists in 1987.

COMMUNICATIONS

Roads. Three chief and some secondary roads connect the capital with most of the coastal area by motor-car services. There are (1986) 372 km of national and 341 km of departmental roads. In 1989 there were 23,520 passenger cars, 1,568 trucks and 121 buses. Connexions with the interior are made by waterways which, despite rapids, are navigable by local craft.

Aviation. In 1988, 123,792 passengers and 3,632 tonnes of freight arrived and 121,575 passengers and 1,572 tonnes of freight departed by air at Rochambeau International Airport (Cayenne). There are regular internal flights to 7 other airports.

The base of the European Space Agency (ESA) is located near Kourou and has been operational since 1979.

Shipping. The chief ports are: Cayenne, St-Laurent-du-Maroni and Kourou. Dégrad des Cannes (the port of Cayenne) is visited regularly by ships of the Compagnie Général Maritime, the Compagnie Maritime des Chargeurs Réunis and Marseille Fret. In 1988, 706 vessels arrived and departed. 189,000 tonnes of petroleum products arrived and 333,000 tonnes of other freight arrived and departed.

Post and Broadcasting. Number of telephones (1989), 26,146. There are wireless stations at Cayenne, Oyapoc, Régina, St-Laurent-du-Maroni and numerous other locations.

RFO-Guyane (Guiana Radio) broadcasts for 133 hours each week on medium- and short-waves and FM in French. Television is broadcast for 135 hours each week on 2 channels. In 1986 there were 44,000 radio and 6,500 TV receivers.

Newspapers. There was (1988) 1 daily newspaper *(Presse de la Guyane)* with a circulation of 1,000 and a paper published 4 times a week *(France-Guyane)* with a circulation of 5,500.

JUSTICE, RELIGION, EDUCATION AND WELFARE

Justice. At Cayenne there is a *tribunal d'instance* and a *tribunal de grande instance*, from which appeal is to the regional *cour d'appel* in Martinique.

Religion. In 1984, 77·6% of the population was Roman Catholic and 4% Protestant.

Education. Primary education has been free since 1889 in lay schools for the two sexes in the communes and many villages. In 1988 public primary schools had 18,024 pupils and (1986) 890 teachers, 10,897 pupils and (1986) 793, the *lycées* and *collèges d'enseignement secondaire*, 793 teachers and 9,085 pupils. Private schools had 152 teachers and 2,224 pupils. The *Institut Henri Visioz* forms part of the *Université des Antilles-Guyane,* with 253 students.

Health. There were (1986) 160 physicians, 44 dentists, 33 pharmacists, 29 midwives and 496 nursing personnel. In 1987 there were 3 hospitals with 748 beds and 3 private clinics with 162 beds.

MARTINIQUE

HISTORY. Discovered by Columbus in 1493, the island was known to its inhabitants as *Madinina*, from which its present name was corrupted. A French colony was established in 1635 and, apart from brief periods of British occupation the island has since remained under French control. On 19 March 1946 its status was altered to that of an Overseas Department, and in 1974 it also became an administrative region.

AREA AND POPULATION. The island, situated in the Lesser Antilles between Dominica and St Lucia, occupies an area of 1,079 sq. km (417 sq. miles). The population, 1982 Census, was 328,566 (estimate, 1988, 336,000), of whom 99,844 lived in Fort-de-France, the capital and chief commercial town, which has a land-locked harbour nearly 40 sq. km in extent. Other towns (1982) are Lamentin (26,367), Schoelcher (19,375) and La Trinité (10,076).

French is the official language, but the majority of the population use a Creole dialect.

Vital statistics (1988): Live births 6,397; deaths 2,099; marriages 1,537.

CLIMATE. Fort-de-France. Jan. 74°F (23·5°C), July 78°F (25·6°C). Annual rainfall 72" (1,840 mm).

CONSTITUTION AND GOVERNMENT. The island is administered by a General Council of 45 members and a Regional Council of 41 members, both directly elected for terms of 6 years. The French government is represented by an appointed Commissioner. There are 3 *arrondissements*, sub-divided into 34 communes, each administered by an elected municipal council. Martinique is represented in the National Assembly by 4 deputies, in the Senate by 2 senators and on the Economic and Social Council by 2 councillors.

Commissioner: Jean-Claude Roure.
President of the General Council: Émile Maurice.
President of the Regional Council: Camille Darsieres.

ECONOMY

Budget. The budget, 1988, balanced at 2,451m. francs.

Banking. The Institut d'Émission des Départements d'Outre-Mer is the official bank of the department. The Caisse Centrale de Coopération Économique is used by the Government in assisting the economic development of the department.

The Banque des Antilles Françaises (with a capital of 32·5m. francs), the Crédit Martiniquais (30·4m. francs), the Société Générale de Banque aux Antilles (15m. francs), the Banque Française Commerciale (49m. francs), the Banque Nationale de Paris and the Crédit Agricole are operating at Fort-de-France.

ENERGY AND NATURAL RESOURCES

Electricity. Production in 1987 totalled 513m. kwh.

Agriculture. Bananas, sugar and rum are the chief products, followed by pineapples, food and vegetables. In 1988 there were 3,458 hectares under sugar-cane, 8,290 hectares under bananas and 400 hectares under pineapples. Production (1988): Sugar, 7,500 tonnes; rum, 85,987 hectolitres; cane for sugar, 93,535 tonnes; cane for rum, 121,835 tonnes; bananas 200,000 tonnes; pineapples, 24,000 tonnes.

Livestock (1988): 43,000 cattle, 90,000 sheep, 48,000 pigs, 46,000 goats and 2,000 horses.

Forestry. Production (1985) 11,000 cu. metres. Forests comprise 26% of the land area.

Fisheries. The catch in 1988 was 3,000 tonnes.

COMMERCE. Trade in 1m. francs:

	1985	*1986*	*1987*	*1988*
Imports	6,050	6,065	6,708	7,722
Exports	1,300	1,496	1,163	1,172

In 1987 the main items of import were crude petroleum and foodstuffs; main items of export were petroleum products (14%), bananas (46%) and rum (13%); 65% of imports came from France and 64% of exports went to France and 24% to Guadeloupe.

Total trade between Martinique and UK (British Department of Trade returns, in £1,000 sterling):

	1985	*1986*	*1987*	*1988*	*1989*
Imports to UK	126	14	712	83	158
Exports and re-exports from UK	2,776	21,230	10,705	3,886	8,815

Tourism. In 1987 there were 261,139 tourists (67% from France).

COMMUNICATIONS

Roads. In 1987 there were 7 km of motorway, 274 km of national roads, 620 km of district roads and 1,013 km of local roads. In 1987 there were 10,065 passenger cars and 2,361 commercial vehicles registered.

Aviation. In 1988, 1,273,376 passengers arrived and departed by air at Fort-de-France–Lamentin airport.

Shipping. The island is visited regularly by French, American and other lines. In 1987, 1,330 commercial vessels called at Martinique and discharged 8,970 passengers and (1988) 1,573,400 tonnes of freight and embarked 7,744 passengers and (1988) 711,000 tonnes of freight, excluding about 150,000 passengers calling in transit.

Post and Broadcasting. There were, in 1985, 46 post offices and, 81,985 telephones. Radio-telephone service to Europe is available. In 1984 there were 46,000 radio and 42,500 TV receivers.

Newspapers. In 1989 there was 1 daily newspaper with a circulation of 19,000.

JUSTICE, RELIGION, EDUCATION AND WELFARE

Justice. Justice is administered by 2 *tribunaux d'instance*, a *tribunal de grande instance*, a regional court of appeal, a commercial court, a court of assizes and an administrative court.

Religion. In 1982, 94% of the population was Roman Catholic.

Education. Education is compulsory between the ages of 6 and 16 years. In 1988, there were 18,923 pupils in nursery schools, 32,986 pupils in primary schools, 31,234 pupils in comprehensive schools, 8,035 students at technical college and 7,000 pupils in sixth-form colleges. The *Institut Henri Visioz* forms part of the *Université des Antilles-Guyane*, which had (1986-87) 5,551 students.

Health. There were (1986) 18 hospitals with 3,427 beds, 519 doctors, 160 pharmacists, 110 dentists and 134 midwives.

Further Reading

Annuaire statistique I.N.S.E.E. 1977–80. Martinique, 1982
La Martinique en quelques chiffres. Martinique, 1982
Guide Economique des D.O.M.-T.O.M., Paris, 1982

RÉUNION

HISTORY. Réunion (formerly Île Bourbon) became a French possession in 1638 and remained so until 19 March 1946, when its status was altered to that of an Overseas Department; in 1974 it also became an administrative region.

AREA AND POPULATION. The island of Réunion lies in the Indian Ocean, about 640 km east of Madagascar and 180 km south west of Mauritius. It has an area of 2,512 sq. km (968·5 sq. miles) and population of 515,798 (March 1982 census); estimate (1988) 574,800. The capital is Saint-Denis (1982 census) 109,072; Saint-Pierre, 58,412. Most inhabitants speak a creole language, but French is official and Gujurati is also spoken.

Vital statistics (1987): Live births, 12,599; deaths, 3,090; marriages, 3,001.

The small islands of Juan de Nova, Europa, Bassas da India, Îles Glorieuses and Tromelin, with a combined area of 32 sq. km, are all uninhabited and lie at various points in the Indian Ocean adjacent to Madagascar. They remained French after Madagascar's independence in 1960, and are now administered by Réunion. Both Mauritius and the Seychelles claim Tromelin (transferred by the UK from the Seychelles to France in 1954), and Madagascar claims all 5 islands.

CLIMATE. A sub-tropical maritime climate, free from extremes of weather, though the island lies in the cyclone belt of the Indian Ocean. Conditions are generally humid and there is no well-defined dry season. Saint-Denis. Jan. 80°F (26·7°C), July 70°F (21·1°C). Annual rainfall 56" (1,400 mm).

CONSTITUTION AND GOVERNMENT. The island is administered by a *Conseil Général* of 36 members and a Regional Council of 45 members, both directly elected for terms of 6 years. Réunion is represented in the National Assembly by 5 deputies, in the Senate by 2 senators, and in the Economic and Social Council by 1 councillor. There are 4 *arrondissements*, sub-divided into 24 communes each administered by an elected municipal council. The French government is represented by an appointed Commissioner.

Commissioner: Jean Anciaux.
President of the Conseil Général: Eric Boyer.
President of the Conseil Régional: Pierre Lagourgue.

ECONOMY

Budget. The budget for 1987 balanced at 2,938m. French francs.

Banking. The Institut d'émission des Départements d'Outre-mer has the right to issue bank-notes. Banks operating in Réunion are the Banque de la Réunion (Crédit Lyonnais), the Banque Nationale de Paris Internationale, the Caisse Régionale de Crédit Agricole Mutuel de la Réunion, the Banque Française Commerciale (BFC) CCP, Trésorerie Générale, and the Banque de la Réunion pour l'Economie et la Développement.

ENERGY AND NATURAL RESOURCES

Electricity. Production (1986) 394m. kwh.

Agriculture (1988). The chief produce is sugar (250,000 tonnes), molasses (1984, 69,353 tonnes), bananas (5,000 tonnes), rum (1984, 98,037 hectolitres), maize (15,000 tonnes), potatoes (4,000 tonnes), onions (1984, 1,831 tonnes), cassava

(5,000 tonnes), pineapples (4,000 tonnes), tomatoes (4,000 tonnes), vanilla (1984, 168 tonnes), essences and tobacco.

Livestock (1988): 20,000 cattle, 75,000 pigs, 3,000 sheep, 44,000 goats and 4m. poultry.

Forestry. There were (1985) 103,330 hectares of forest. Roundwood production (1983) 33,000 cu. metres.

Fisheries. In 1985 the catch was 2,180 tonnes.

INDUSTRY AND TRADE

Industry (1985). Total number of workers (in 418 firms employing 10 or more) 16,000. The sugar industry employed 2,900.

Commerce. Trade in 1m. French francs:

	1980	*1981*	*1982*	*1983*	*1984*	*1985*
Imports	3,749	4,311	5,304	6,410	6,895	7,457
Exports	554	571	688	662	695	802

The chief export is sugar, forming (1985) 72% by value. In 1985 (by value) 65% of imports were from, and 53% of exports to, France.

Total trade between Réunion and UK (British Department of Trade returns, in £1,000 sterling):

	1986	*1987*	*1988*	*1989*
Imports to UK	12,259	1,056	1,372	4,389
Exports and re-exports from UK	4,225	8,624	8,536	7,529

Tourism. There were 93,476 tourists in 1986.

COMMUNICATIONS

Roads. There were, in 1984, 1,711 km of roads. There were 92,900 registered vehicles in 1984.

Railways. In 1984 there were 614 km of railways serving only the sugar plantations.

Aviation. Air France maintains an air service 6 times a week. In 1985, 210,121 passengers and 6,625 tonnes of freight arrived and 210,764 passengers and 3,666 tonnes of freight departed at Saint-Denis-Gillot airport.

Shipping. Four shipping lines serve the island. In 1985, 362 vessels visited the island to discharge 1,122,800 tonnes of freight and 1,900 passengers, and load 340,000 tonnes of freight and 1,900 passengers at Pointe-des-Galets.

Post and Broadcasting. There are telephone and telegraph connexions with Mauritius, Madagascar and metropolitan France. There are 38 post offices and a central telephone office; number of telephones (1984), 85,861.

France Régions 3 broadcast in French on medium- and short-waves for more than 18 hours a day. There are 2 television channels broadcasting for 70 hours a week. In 1984 there were 114,500 radio and 107,500 TV receivers.

Cinemas. In 1986 there were 25 cinemas with a seating capacity of 10,200.

Newspapers. There were (1985) 3 daily newspapers with a combined circulation of 70,000.

JUSTICE, RELIGION, EDUCATION AND WELFARE

Justice. There are 3 *tribunaux d'instance*, 2 *tribunaux de grande instance*, 1 *Cour d'Appel*, 1 *tribunal administratif* and 2 *conseils de prud'homme*.

Religion. In 1980, 96% of the population was Roman Catholic and 2% Moslem.

Education. Secondary education is provided in (1983–84) 6 *lycées*, 50 *collèges*, and 9 *lycées d'enseignement technique* with 66,653 pupils altogether and in 13 private secondary schools with 3,407 pupils. Primary education is given in 336 public schools with 4,018 teachers and 106,437 pupils; and in 28 private schools, with 306 teachers, and 8,827 pupils. The *Université Française de l'Océan Indien* (founded 1971) had 2,674 students and 82 teaching staff in 1984.

Health. In 1984 there were 21 hospitals with 3,879 beds; in 1984 there were 762 physicians, 183 dentists, 180 pharmacists, 102 midwives and 1,791 nursing personnel.

Further Reading

Bulletin de l'Académie de la Réunion. Biennial
Bulletin de la Chambre d'Agriculture de la Réunion
Panorama de l'Economie de la Reunion. 1983
Statistiques et Indicateurs Economiques. 1983

TERRITORIAL COLLECTIVITIES

MAYOTTE

HISTORY. Mayotte was a French colony from 1843 until 1914, when it was attached, with the other Comoro islands, to the government-general of Madagascar. The Comoro group was granted administrative autonomy within the French Republic and became an Overseas Territory.

When the other 3 islands voted to become independent (as the Comoro state) in 1974, Mayotte voted against this and remained a French dependency. In Dec. 1976, it became (following a further referendum) a Territorial Collectivity.

AREA AND POPULATION. Mayotte, east of the Comoro Islands, consists of a main island (362 sq. km) with 57,363 inhabitants at the 1985 Census, containing the chief town, Mamoundzou (12,119); and the smaller island of Pamanzi (11 sq. km) lying 2 km to the east, with 9,775 inhabitants in 1985, containing the old capital of Dzaoudzi (5,675). The whole territory covers 373 sq. km (144 sq. miles) and had a 1985 Census population of 67,138; estimate (1988) 77,300. The spoken language is Mahorian (akin to Comoran, an Arabized dialect of Swahili), but French remains the official and commercial language.

CONSTITUTION AND GOVERNMENT. The island is administered by a *Conseil Général* of 17 members, directly elected for a 6-year term. The French government is represented by an appointed Commissioner. Mayotte is represented by 1 deputy in the National Assembly and by 1 member in the Senate. There are 17 communes, including 2 on Pamanzi.

Commissioner: Akli Khider.
President of the Conseil Général: Younoussa Bamana.

ECONOMY

Budget. In 1984, revenue was 137·1m. francs (44% being subsidies from France) and expenditure 148·4m. francs. The 1985 Budget balanced at 313m. francs.

Currency. Since Feb. 1976 the currency has been the (metropolitan) *French franc.*

Banking. The *Institut d'Emission d'Outre-mer* and the *Banque Française Commerciale* both have branches in Dzaoudzi.

ENERGY AND NATURAL RESOURCES

Electricity. Production (1982) 5m. kwh.

Agriculture. The main food crops (1983 production in tonnes) are mangoes (1,500), bananas (1,300), breadfruit (700), cassava (500) and pineapples (200). The

chief cash crops are ylang-ylang, vanilla, coffee, copra, cinnamon and cloves.
Livestock (1982): Cattle, 3,000; goats, 10,000; pigs, 2,000.

Fisheries. A lobster and shrimp industry has recently been created. Annual catch is about 2,000 tonnes.

COMMERCE. In 1984, exports totalled 34m. francs (57% to France in 1983) and imports 182·8m. francs (53% from France). Ylang-ylang formed 48% of exports, vanilla 33% and coffee 12%. Total trade between Mayotte and UK (1984): Imports to UK, £67,000 and exports and re-exports from UK, £343,000.

Total trade between Mayotte and UK (British Department of Trade returns, in £1,000 sterling):

	1986	*1987*	*1988*	*1989*
Imports to UK	9	185	654	117
Exports and re-exports from UK	506	2,352	3,123	5,059

COMMUNICATIONS

Roads. In 1984 there were 93 km of main roads and 137 km of local roads, with 1,528 motor vehicles.

Aviation. In 1985, 17,426 passengers and 172 tonnes of freight arrived and departed by air.

Post and Broadcasting. In 1984 there were 6,000 radio receivers. Telephones (1981) 400.

Newspapers. There is 1 daily newspaper, *le Journal de Mayotte*.

JUSTICE, RELIGION, EDUCATION AND WELFARE

Justice. There is a *tribunal de première instance* and a *tribunal supérieur d'appel*.

Religion. The population is 97% Sunni Moslem, with a small Christian (mainly Roman Catholic) minority.

Education. In 1984 there were 14,992 pupils and 407 teachers in 72 primary schools; 1,374 pupils in 1 secondary school; and 475 students in 2 technical and teacher-training establishments.

Health. In 1980 there were 9 doctors, 1 dentist, 1 pharmacist, 2 midwives and 51 nursing personnel. In 1981 there were 2 hospitals with 86 beds.

ST PIERRE AND MIQUELON

Îles Saint-Pierre et Miquelon

HISTORY. The tiny remaining fragment of the once extensive French possessions in North America, the archipelago was settled from France in the 17th century and finally became a French territory from 1816 until July 1976, when its status was altered to that of an Overseas Department. In June 1985 it became a Territorial Collectivity.

AREA AND POPULATION. The archipelago consists of 8 small islands off the south coast of Newfoundland, with a total area of 242 sq. km, comprising the Saint-Pierre group (26 sq. km) and the Miquelon-Langlade group (216 sq. km). The population (census, 1982) was 6,041 of whom 5,415 were on Saint-Pierre and 626 on Miquelon; estimate (1988) 6,400. The chief town is St Pierre.

Vital statistics (1988): Births, 80; marriages, 27; deaths, 40.

CONSTITUTION AND GOVERNMENT. The dependency is administered by a *Conseil Général* of 19 members, directly elected for a 6-year term. It is represented in the National Assembly by 1 deputy, in the Senate by 1 senator and in the Economic and Social Council by 1 councillor. The French government is represented by an appointed Commissioner.

Commissioner: Jean-Pierre Marquie.
President of the Conseil Général: Marc Plantegenest.

ECONOMY

Budget. The ordinary budget for 1989 balanced at 82m. francs.

Banking. Banks include the Banque des Îles Saint-Pierre et Miquelon and the Crédit Saint-Pierrais.

ENERGY AND NATURAL RESOURCES

Electricity. Production (1988) 51m. kwh.

Agriculture. The islands, being mostly barren rock, are unsuited for agriculture, but some vegetables are grown and livestock kept for local consumption.

Fisheries. The catch (the islands' main industry) amounted in 1988 to 8,630 tonnes, chiefly cod.

COMMERCE. Trade in 1m. francs:

	1985	*1986*	*1987*	*1988*
Imports	358·4	348·3	343·5	366·7
Exports	106·7	163·1	186·7	143·5

In 1987, 85% of imports came from Canada, while 36% of exports were to USA, 27% to France and 11% to UK.

The main exports are fish (78%), shellfish (20%) and fishmeal (5%).

Total trade between St Pierre and Miquelon and UK (British Department of Trade returns in £1,000 sterling):

	1985	*1986*	*1987*	*1988*	*1989*
Imports to UK	497	474	77	159	164
Exports and re-exports from UK	370	367	604	470	533

Tourism. There were (1987) 16,193 visitors.

COMMUNICATIONS

Roads. In 1988 there were 120 km of roads, of which 50 km were paved. In 1988 there were 1,920 passenger cars and 774 commercial vehicles.

Aviation. Air Saint-Pierre connects St Pierre with Montreal, with Halifax and Sydney (Nova Scotia), and there are occasional flights to and from St John's (Newfoundland).

Shipping. St Pierre has regular services to Fortune (Newfoundland) and Halifax. In 1988, 97,459 tonnes of freight were unloaded and 62,640 tonnes loaded, while 1,085 ships (of 912,000 gross tonnage) entered the harbour.

Post and Broadcasting. There were 2,997 telephones in 1989. RFO broadcasts in French on medium-waves. St Pierre is connected by radio-telecommunication with most countries of the world.

Cinemas. There were (1988) 2 cinemas with a seating capacity of 760.

JUSTICE, RELIGION, EDUCATION AND WELFARE

Justice. There is a *tribunal de première instance* and a *tribunal supérieur d'appel* at St Pierre.

Religion. The population is chiefly Roman Catholic.

Education. Primary instruction is free. There were, in 1989, 8 nursery and 4 primary schools with 556 pupils and 4 secondary schools (including 2 technical schools) with 759 pupils.

Health. There was (1988) 1 hospital on St Pierre with 100 beds; 12 doctors and 4 dentists.

Further Reading

De Curton, E., *Saint-Pierre et Miquelon.* Paris, 1944
De La Rüe, E. A., *Saint-Pierre et Miquelon.* Paris, 1963
Ribault, J. Y., *Histoire de Saint-Pierre et Miquelon: Des Origines à 1814.* St Pierre, 1962

OVERSEAS TERRITORIES

Among the 7 French Overseas Territories remaining since Algerian independence in 1962, the Comoro Islands declared their independence on 6 July 1975 (recognized by France on 31 Dec.), but the island of Mayotte remained French and in Dec. 1976 was classed as a 'territorial collectivity'. The territory of Saint Pierre and Miquelon became a fifth Overseas Department in July 1976, but in June 1985 it acquired the same status as Mayotte. The former French Somaliland (subsequently Territory of the Afars and Issas) became independent on 27 June 1977 as the Republic of Djibouti. The remaining French Overseas Territories are New Caledonia (with its dependancies), French Polynesia, Wallis and Futuna, and the French Southern and Antarctic Territories.

SOUTHERN AND ANTARCTIC TERRITORIES

Terres Australes et Antarctiques Françaises

The Territory of the TAAF was created on 6 Aug. 1955. It comprises the Kerguelen and Crozet archipelagoes, the islands of Saint Paul and Amsterdam (formerly Nouvelle Amsterdam), all in the southern Indian ocean, and Terre Adélie.

The Administrator is assisted by a 7-member consultative council which meets twice yearly in Paris; its members are nominated by the Government for 5 years. The 12 members of the Scientific Council are appointed by the Senior Administrator after approval by the Minister in charge of scientific research. A 15-member Consultative Committee on the Environment, created in Nov. 1982, meets at least once a year to discuss all problems relating to the preservation of the environment. The administration has its seat in Paris.

Administrateur supérieur: Claude Corbier.

The staff of the permanent scientific stations of the TAAF (180 in 1989) is renewed annually and forms the only population.

Kerguelen islands, situated 48–50° S. lat., 68–70° E. long., consists of 1 large and 85 smaller islands and over 200 islets and rocks with a total area of 7,215 sq. km (2,786 sq. miles), of which Grande Terre occupies 6,675 sq. km (2,577 sq. miles). It was discovered in 1772 by Yves de Kerguelen, but was effectively occupied by France only in 1949. Port-aux-Français has several scientific research stations (75 members). Reindeer, trout and sheep have been acclimatized.

Crozet islands, situated 46° S. lat., 50–52° E. long., consists of 5 larger and 15 tiny islands, with a total area of 505 sq. km (195 sq. miles); the western group includes Apostles, Pigs and Penguins islands; the eastern group, Possession and Eastern islands. The archipelago was discovered in 1772 by Marion Dufresne, whose mate, Crozet, annexed it for Louis XV. A meteorological and scientific station (35 members) at Base Alfred-Faure on Possession Island was built in 1964.

Amsterdam Island and **Saint-Paul Island,** situated 38–39° S. lat., 77° E. long. Amsterdam, with an area of 54 sq. km (21 sq. miles) was discovered in 1522 by Magellan's companions; Saint-Paul, lying about 100 km to the south, with an area of 7 sq. km (2·7 sq. miles), was probably discovered in 1559 by Portuguese sailors. Both were first visited in 1633 by the Dutch explorer, Van Diemen, and were annexed by France in 1843. They are both extinct volcanoes. The only inhabitants are at Base Martin de Vivies, established in 1949 on Amsterdam Island, with several scientific research stations, hospital, communication and other facilities (35 members). Crayfish are caught commercially on Amsterdam.

Terre Adélie comprises that section of the Antarctic continent between 136° and 142° E. long., south of 60° S. lat. The ice-covered plateau has an area of about 432,000 sq. km (166,800 sq. miles), and was discovered in 1840 by Dumont d'Urville. A research station (30 members) is situated at Base Dumont d'Urville, which is maintained by the French Polar Expeditions.

NEW CALEDONIA

Nouvelle Calédonie et Dépendances

HISTORY. New Caledonia was annexed by France in 1853 and, together with most of its former dependencies, became an Overseas Territory in 1958.

AREA AND POPULATION. The territory comprises the island of New Caledonia and various outlying islands, all situated in the south-west Pacific with a total land area of 18,576 sq. km (7,172 sq. miles). In 1989 the population (census) was 164,173, including 55,085 Europeans (majority French), 73,598 Melanesians (Kanaks), 8,652 Vietnamese and Indonesians, 4,750 Polynesians, 14,186 Wallisians, 8,902 others. The capital, Nouméa had (1989) 65,110 inhabitants. Vital statistics (1987): Live births, 4,062; deaths, 904.

The main islands are:

1. The island of New Caledonia with an area of 16,372 sq. km, has a total length of about 400 km, and an average breadth of 50 km, and a population (census, 1983) of 127,885. The east coast is predominantly Melanesian, the Nouméa region predominantly European, and the rest of the west coast of mixed population.
2. The Loyalty Islands, 100 km (60 miles) east of New Caledonia, consisting of 3 large islands, Maré, Lifou and Uvéa, and many small islands with a total area of 1,981 sq. km and a population (census, 1989) of 17,912, nearly all Melanesians except on Uvéa, which is partly Polynesian. The chief culture in the islands is that of coconuts and the chief export, copra.
3. The Isle of Pines, 50 km (30 miles) to the south-east of Nouméa, with an area of 152 sq. km and a population of 1,465 (census 1989), is a tourist and fishing centre.
4. The Bélep Archipelago, about 50 km north-west of New Caledonia, with an area of 70 sq. km and a population of 745 (census 1989).

The remaining islands are all very small and none have permanent inhabitants. The largest are the Chesterfield Islands, a group of 11 well-wooded coral islets with a combined area of 10 sq. km, about 550 km west of the Bélep Archipelago. The Huon Islands, a group of 4 barren coral islets with a combined area of just 65 hectares, are 225 km north of the Bélep Archipelago. Walpole, a limestone coral island of 1 sq. km, lies 150 km east of the Isle of Pines; Matthew Island (20 hectares) and Hunter Island (2 sq. km), respectively 250 km and 330 km east of Walpole, are spasmodically active volcanic islands also claimed by Vanuatu.

CLIMATE. Nouméa. Jan. 78°F (25·6°C), July 67°F (19·4°C). Annual rainfall 43" (1,083 mm).

CONSTITUTION AND GOVERNMENT. Following constitutional changes introduced by the French government in 1985 and 1988, the Territory is administered by a High Commissioner assisted by a 4-member Consultative Committee, consisting of the President of the Territorial Congress (as President) and the Presidents of the 3 Provincial Assemblies. The French government is represented by the appointed High Commissioner. In Sept. 1987 the electorate voted in favour of remaining a French possession.

There is a 54-member Territorial Congress consisting of the complete membership of the 3 Provincial Assemblies.

New Caledonia is represented in the National Assembly by 2 deputies, in the Senate by 1 senator and in the Economic and Social Council by 1 councillor.

The Territory is divided into 3 provinces, Nord, Sud and Îles Loyauté, each under a directly-elected Regional Council. They are sub-divided into 32 communes administered by locally-elected councils and mayors.

Agreement was reached in June 1988 between the French government and representatives of both the European and Melanesian communities on New Caledonia, and confirmed in Nov. 1988 by plebiscites in both France and New Caledonia, under which the territory has been divided into 3 autonomous provinces, and a further referendum on full independence will be held in 1998.

High Commissioner: Bernard Grasset.

ECONOMY

Budget. The budget for 1989 balanced at 51,786m. francs CFP.

Currency. The unit of currency is the *franc* CFP, with a parity of CFP *francs* 18·18 to the French *franc*.

Banking. There are branches of the Banque de Indosuez, the Banque Nationale de Paris, the Banque de Paris et des Pays-Bas, and the Société Générale, and the Banque de la Nouvelle-Calédonie (Crédit Lyonnais).

ENERGY AND NATURAL RESOURCES

Electricity. In 1988, production totalled 1,662m. kwh.

Minerals. The mineral resources are very great; nickel, chrome and iron abound; silver, gold, cobalt, lead, manganese, iron and copper have been mined at different times. The nickel deposits are of special value, being without arsenic. Production of nickel ore in 1988, 3·39m. tonnes and chrome ore 112,236 tonnes. In 1988 the furnaces produced 10,470 tonnes of matte nickel and 37,352 tonnes of ferro-nickel.

Agriculture. 271,864 hectares are pasture land; about 10,035 hectares are commercially cultivated. The chief agricultural products are beef, pork, poultry, coffee, copra, maize, fruit and vegetables.

Livestock (1988): Cattle, 124,000; pigs, 47,000; goats, 21,000.

Forestry. There are about 250,000 hectares of forest. Roundwood production (1988) 5,118 cu. metres.

Fisheries. The catch in 1987 totalled 5,775 tonnes.

INDUSTRY AND TRADE

Industry. Local industries include chlorine and oxygen plants, cement, soft drinks, barbed wire, nails, pleasure and fishing boats, clothing, pasta, household cleaners and confectionery.

Labour. The working population (1983 census) was 58,000 of whom 19,700 worked in agriculture.

Commerce. Imports and exports in 1m. francs CFP for 5 years:

	1984	*1985*	*1986*	*1987*	*1988*
Imports	49,605	55,931	62,939	63,349	65,386
Exports	33,452	43,938	26,249	20,653	50,805

In 1988, 47·9% of the imports came from France and 10·3% from Australia, while 38·4% of the exports went to France. Refined minerals (mainly ferro-nickel and nickel) formed 81·2% of exports by value, nickel ore 10·2% and chrome ore 1·7%.

Tourism. In 1988 there were 63,715 tourists of which 27·9% French and 25·4% Japanese.

COMMUNICATIONS

Roads. There were, in 1987, 6,340 km of roads, of which 1,823·5 km were paved. There were (1987) 55,000 vehicles.

Aviation. New Caledonia is connected by air routes with France and Tahiti (by UTA and Minerve), Australia (UTA and Qantas), New Zealand (UTA and Air New Zealand), Fiji and Wallis and Futuna (by Air Cal International), Vanuatu (by UTA), and Nauru (by Air Nauru). In 1988, 103,719 passengers arrived and 104,993 departed *via* La Tontouta airport, near Nouméa. Internal services connect Nouméa with 21 domestic air fields.

Shipping. In 1988, 811 vessels entered Nouméa unloading 7,841,000 tonnes of goods and loading 1,547,900 tonnes of which 1m. tonnes comprised mineral exports.

Post and Broadcasting. There were (1988) 47 post offices and telex, telephone, radio and television services. There were (1988) 24,000 telephones. RFO broadcasts in French on medium- and short-wave radio (there are also 9 private stations) and on 2 television channels for 95 hours a week. Number of receivers (1986): Radio, 85,000; TV, 35,000.

Cinemas. In 1989 there were 11 cinemas.

Newspapers. In 1989 there was 1 daily newspaper with a circulation of 16,000.

JUSTICE, RELIGION, EDUCATION AND WELFARE

Justice. There is a *Tribunal de Première Instance* and a *Cour d'Appel* in Nouméa.

Religion. In 1980 over 72% of the population was Roman Catholic, 16% Protestant and 4% Moslem.

Education. In 1988, there were 33,108 pupils and 1,580 teachers in 282 primary schools, 13,655 pupils in 46 secondary schools, 6,008 students in 28 technical and vocational schools, and 701 students and 70 teaching staff in 4 higher education establishments.

Health. In 1988 there were 173 physicians, 37 dentists, 29 pharmacists, 20 midwives and 761 paramedical personnel; 6 hospitals and 24 dispensaries had a total of 1,081 beds.

Further Reading

Journal Officiel de la Nouvelle Calédonie
Tableaux de l'Economie Caledonienne, 1988
Information statistiques rapides. (monthly)

FRENCH POLYNESIA

Territoire de la Polynésie Française

HISTORY. French protectorates since 1843, these islands were annexed to France 1880–82 to form 'French Settlements in Oceania', which opted in Nov. 1958 for the status of an Overseas Territory within the French Community.

AREA AND POPULATION. The total land area of these 5 archipelagoes, scattered over a wide area in the Eastern Pacific is 3,265 sq. km (1,260 sq. miles). The population, Census, 1983, was 166,753; census (1988) 188,814.

The official languages are French and Tahitian.

Vital statistics (1987): Births, 5,384; marriages, 1,251; deaths, 980.

The islands are administratively divided into 5 *circonscriptions:*

1. The **Windward Islands** (Îles du Vent) (140,341 inhabitants in 1988) comprise Tahiti with an area of 1,042 sq. km and 115,820 inhabitants; Moorea with an area of 132 sq. km and 7,059 inhabitants; Maio (Tubuai Manu) with an area of 9 sq. km and 190 inhabitants, and the smaller Mehetia and Tetiaroa. The capital is Papeete (78,814 inhabitants including suburbs).

2. The **Leeward Islands** (Îles sous le Vent), comprise the volcanic islands of Raiatéa, Tahaa, Huahine, Bora-Bora and Maupiti, together with 4 small atolls, the group having a total land area of 404 sq. km and 22,232 inhabitants in 1988. The chief town is Uturoa on Raiatéa.

The Windward and Leeward Islands together are called the Society Archipelago (Archipel de la Société). Tahitian, a Polynesian language, is spoken throughout the archipelago and used as a *lingua franca* in the rest of the territory.

3. The **Tuamotu Archipelago**, consisting of two parallel ranges of 78 atolls lying north and east of the Society Archipelago, have a total area of 690 sq. km; the most populous atolls are Rangiroa, Hao and Turéia. Mururoa and Fangataufa atolls in the south-east of the group have been used by France for nuclear tests since 1966, having been ceded to France in 1964 by the Territorial Assembly.

The *circonscription* (12,374 inhabitants in 1988) also includes the **Gambier Islands** further east (of which Mangareva is the principal), with an area of 36 sq. km and a population of 582; the chief centre is Rikitea on Mangareva.

4. The **Austral or Tubuai Islands**, lying south of the Society Archipelago, comprise a 1,300 km chain of volcanic islands and reefs. They include Rimatara, Rurutu, Tubuai, Raivaevae and, 500 km to the south, Rapa-Iti, with a combined area of 148 sq. km and 6,509 (1988) inhabitants; the chief centre is Mataura on Tubuai.

5. The **Marquesas Islands**, lying north of the Tuamotu Archipelago, with a total area of 1,049 sq. km and 7,538 (1988) inhabitants, comprise Nukuhiva, Uapu, Uahuka, Hivaoa, Tahuata, Fatuhiva and 4 smaller (uninhabited) islands; the chief centre is Taiohae on Nukuhiva.

CLIMATE. Papeete. Jan. 81°F (27·1°C), July 75°F (24°C). Annual rainfall 83" (2,106 mm).

CONSTITUTION AND GOVERNMENT. Under the 1984 Constitution, the Territory is administered by a Council of Ministers, whose President is elected by the Territorial Assembly from among its own members; he appoints a Vice-President and 9 other ministers. There is an advisory Economic and Social Committee. French Polynesia is represented in the French Assembly by 2 deputies, in the Senate by 1 senator, and in the Economic and Social Council by 1 councillor. The French government is represented by a High Commissioner. The Territorial Assembly comprises 41 members elected every 5 years by universal suffrage.

At the elections held in March 1986, the *Tahoeraa Huiraatiraa* (Gaullists) won 22 seats, the *Amuitahiraa No Porinesia* 5 seats, Nationalists 5 seats and others 9 seats.

High Commissioner: Jean Montpezat.
President of the Council of Ministers: Alexandre Leontieff.

Flag: Three horizontal stripes of red, white, red, with the white of double width containing the emblem of French Polynesia in yellow.

ECONOMY

Budget. The ordinary budget for 1987 balanced at 52,135m. francs CFP.

Currency. The unit of currency is the *franc* CFP, with a parity of CFP *francs* 18·18 to the French *franc*.

Banking. There are 5 commercial banks, the Bank Indosuez, the Bank of Tahiti, the Banque de Polynésie, Paribas Pacifique and Société de Crédit et de Développement de l'Océanie.

ENERGY AND NATURAL RESOURCES

Electricity. Production in 1987 amounted to 265m. kwh (18% hydro-electric).

Agriculture. An important product is copra (coconut trees covering the coastal plains of the mountainous islands and the greater part of the low-lying islands), production (1988) 15,000 tonnes. Tropical fruits, such as bananas, pineapples, oranges, etc., are grown only for local consumption.

Livestock (1988): Cattle, 10,000; horses, 2,000; pigs, 54,000; sheep, 2,000; goats, 3,000; poultry, 1m.

Fisheries. The catch in 1986 amounted to 1,703 tonnes of fish.

COMMERCE. Trade in 1m. francs CFP:

	1983	*1984*	*1985*	*1986*	*1987*
Imports	74,241	85,622	88,864	92,666	90,544
Exports	4,823	5,084	6,564	5,106	8,986

Total trade between French Polynesia and UK (British Department of Trade returns, in £1,000 sterling):

	1985	*1986*	*1987*	*1988*	*1989*
Imports to UK	23	95	18	56	416
Exports and re-exports from UK	3,961	4,890	5,275	3,421	3,996

Chief exports are coconut oil and cultured pearls. In 1987, France provided 52% of imports and USA 13%, while (1985) 44% of exports went to France and 21% to USA.

Tourism. Tourism is very important, earning almost half as much as the visible exports. There were 143,000 tourists in 1987.

COMMUNICATIONS

Roads. In 1985 there were 797 km of roads and 44,000 vehicles.

Aviation. Seven international airlines connect Tahiti with Paris, Los Angeles and many Pacific locations. There is also a regular air service between Faaa airport (on Tahiti), Moorea and the Leeward Isles with occasional connexions to the other groups. In 1987, 194,218 international passengers arrived and 197,301 departed *via* the airports at Faaa and on Mooréa and Bora-Bora. Thirty other airfields have regular domestic services.

Shipping. Several shipping companies connect France, San Francisco, New Zealand, Japan, Australia, South East Asia and most Pacific locations with Papeete.

Post and Broadcasting. Number of telephones (1985), 28,192. *Radio Tele Tahiti* belongs to *Société de Radiodiffusion et de Télévision pour l'Outre-mer* (RFO) and broadcasts in French, Tahitian and English on medium- and short-waves and also broadcasts 1 television programme *via* 5 transmitters. There are also 9 private radio stations. Number of receivers (1986): Radio, 84,000; TV, 26,400.

Cinemas. In 1986 there were 8 cinemas in Papeete.

Newspapers. In 1988 there were 2 daily newspapers.

JUSTICE, RELIGION, EDUCATION AND WELFARE

Justice. There is a *tribunal de première instance* and a *cour d'appel* at Papeete.

Religion. In 1980 it was estimated that 46·5% of the inhabitants were Protestants, 39·4% Roman Catholic and 5·1% Mormon.

Education. There were, in 1987-88, 42,735 pupils in 264 primary schools, 15,002 pupils in 41 secondary schools, and 4,156 pupils in technical schools and teacher-training colleges.

Health. There were (1987) 273 physicians, 88 dentists, 35 pharmacists, 24 midwives and 464 nursing personnel. There was (1987) a main hospital at Mamao (on Tahiti), 7 secondary hospitals, 2 private clinics, 9 medical centres and 18 infirmaries, with together 1,048 beds.

DEPENDENCY. The uninhabited Clipperton Island, 1,000 km off the west coast of Mexico, is administered by the High Commissioner for French Polynesia but does not form part of the Territory; it is an atoll with an area of 5 sq. km.

Further Reading

Journal Officiel des Etablissements Françaises de l'Océanie, and *Supplement Containing Statistics of Commerce and Navigation*. Papeete
Andrews, E., *Comparative Dictionary of the Tahitian Language*. Chicago, 1944
Bounds, J. H., *Tahiti*. Bend, Oregon, 1978
Luke, Sir Harry, *The Islands of the South Pacific*. London, 1961
O'Reilly, P. and Reitman, E., *Bibliographie de Tahiti et de la Polynésie française*. Paris, 1967
O'Reilly, P. and Teissier, R., *Tahitiens. Répertoire bio-bibliographique de la Polynésie française*. Paris, 1963

WALLIS AND FUTUNA

HISTORY. French dependencies since 1842, the inhabitants of these islands voted on 22 Dec. 1959 by an overwhelming majority in favour of exchanging their status to that of an Overseas Territory, which took effect from 29 July 1961.

AREA AND POPULATION. The Territory comprises two groups of islands (total area 274 sq. km) in the central Pacific, The Iles de Hoorn lie 240 km north-east of Fiji and consist of 2 main islands–Futuna (64 sq. km) and uninhabited Alofi (51 sq. km). The Wallis Archipelago lies another 160 km further north-east, and comprises one main island – Uvea (159 sq. km), with a surrounding coral reef. The capital is Mata-Utu (815 inhabitants, 1983) on Uvea.

The resident population, census March 1982, was 11,943 (estimate, 1988, 15,400), comprising 7,843 on Uvea and 4,100 on Futuna. About 12,000 Wallisians and Futunians live abroad, mainly in New Caledonia. Wallisian and Futunian are distinct Polynesian languages.

CONSTITUTION AND GOVERNMENT. The Senior Administrator carries out the duties of Head of the Territory, assisted by a 20-member Territorial Assembly directly elected for a 5-year term. The territory is represented by 1 deputy in the National Assembly, by 1 senator in the Senate, and by 1 member on the Economic and Social Council. There are 3 districts: Singave and Alo (both on Futuna) and Wallis.

Administrateur supérieur: Jacques Le Ilénaff.
President of the Territorial Assembly: Falakiko Gata.

ECONOMY

Budget. The 1982 budget provided for expenditure of 303·8m. francs CFP.

Currency. The unit of currency is the *franc* CFP, with a parity of CFP *francs* 18·18 to the French *franc*.

AGRICULTURE. The chief products are copra, cassava, yams, taro roots and bananas.

Livestock: Pigs, 30,000 (1988); goats, 8,000 (1988).

COMMERCE. Imports (1981) amounted to 667m. francs CFP. There are few exports.

COMMUNICATIONS

Roads. In 1977 there were 100 km of roads on Uvea.

Aviation. In 1980 there were 581 aircraft arrivals and departures at Hihifo airport, on Uvea. There is a weekly flight *via* Vila (Vanuatu) to Nouméa (New Caledonia) and three flights each week to Futuna (Point Vele air strip).

Shipping. A regular service links wharves at Mata-Utu and at Singave (Futuna) with Nouméa (New Caledonia), Suva (Fiji) and Vila and Santo (Vanuatu).

Post and Broadcasting. In 1986 there were 2 radio stations and 6 post offices. In 1985 there were 340 telephones.

JUSTICE, RELIGION, EDUCATION AND WELFARE

Justice. There is a *tribunal de première instance*, from which appeals can be made to the *cours d'appel* in New Caledonia.

Religion. The majority of the population is Roman Catholic.

Education. In 1983, there were 3,962 pupils in 13 primary and lower secondary schools.

Health. In 1981 there were 4 physicians, 1 pharmacist, 1 dentist, 5 midwives and 27 nursing personnel. There were (1982) 3 hospitals with 92 beds.

GABON

Capital: Libreville
Population: 1·22m. (1988)
GNP per capita: US$2,970 (1988)

République Gabonaise

HISTORY. First colonized by France in the mid-19th century, Gabon was annexed to French Congo in 1888 and became a separate colony in 1910 as one of the 4 territories of French Equatorial Africa. It became an autonomous republic within the French Community on 28 Nov. 1958 and achieved independence on 17 Aug. 1960. The first President, Leon M'ba, died on 30 Nov. 1967 and was succeeded on 2 Dec. by his Vice-President, Albert-Bernard (now Omar) Bongo.

AREA AND POPULATION. Gabon is bounded west by the Atlantic ocean, north by Equatorial Guinea and Cameroon and east and south by Congo. The area covers 267,667 sq. km; its population at the 1970 census was 950,007; estimate (1988) is 1,226,000. The capital is Libreville (350,000 inhabitants, 1983), other large towns being Port-Gentil (123,300), Masuku (formerly Franceville, 38,030), Lambaréné (26,257 in 1978) and Mouanda (22,909 in 1978).

Vital statistics (1975): Birth rate, 3·22%; death rate, 2·22%.

Provincial areas, populations (estimate 1978, in 1,000) and capitals are as follows:

Province	*Sq. km*	*1978*	*Capital*	*Province*	*Sq. km*	*1978*	*Capital*
Estuaire	20,740	359	Libreville	Nyanga	21,285	98	Tchibanga
Woleu-Ntem	38,465	166	Oyem	Ngounié	37,750	118	Mouila
Ogooué-Ivindo	46,075	53	Makokou	Ogooué-Lolo	25,380	49	Koulamoutou
Moyen-Ogooué	18,535	49	Lambaréné	Haut-Ogooué	36,547	213	Masuku
Ogooué-Maritime	22,890	194	Port-Gentil				

The largest ethnic groups are the Fang (30%) in the north, Eshira (25%) in the south-west, and the Adouma (17%) in the south-east. French is the official language.

CLIMATE. The climate is equatorial, with high temperatures and considerable rainfall. Mid-May to mid-Sept. is the long dry season, followed by a short rainy season, then a dry season again from mid-Dec. to mid-Feb., and finally a long rainy season once more. Libreville. Jan. 80°F (26·7°C), July 75°F (23·9°C). Annual rainfall 99" (2,510 mm).

CONSTITUTION AND GOVERNMENT. The 1967 Constitution (as subsequently revised) provides for an Executive President directly elected for a 7-year term, who appoints a Council of Ministers to assist him. The unicameral National Assembly consists of 111 members, directly elected for a 5-year term (latest elections, Feb. 1985) and a further 9 members nominated by the President.

The sole legal political party is the *Parti democratique gabonais* founded in 1968. It is governed by a Central Committee of 297 members and a 44-member Political Bureau, both elected by the third party congress in Sept. 1986.

President: Omar Bongo (re-elected in 1973, 1979 and 1986).

The Council of Ministers was composed as follows in Oct. 1989:
Prime Minister: Léon Mébiame.

Deputy Prime Ministers: Georges Rawiri *(Fisheries, Water and Forestry)*, Guy-Etienne Mouvagha Tchioba *(Mining)*, Emile Kassa Mapsi *(Tourism, Social Communications and Leisure)*, Simon Essimengane *(Housing and Town Planning)*.

Ministers of State: Ali Bongo *(Foreign Affairs and Co-operation)*, Henri Minko *(Public Lands, Land Registration and Law of the Sea)*, René Radembino Coniquet *(Secretary-General to the Presidency)*, Jules Bourdes Ogouliguende *(Higher Education and Scientific Research)*, Etienne Moussirou *(Industry and Consumer Affairs, Aviation)*, Richard Nguema Bekale *(Civil Service and Administrative Reform, Mixed Economy Enterprises)*, Paul Biyoghe Mba *(Commerce, Technology Transfer and*

Rationalization), François Owono Nguema *(Culture, Arts and Popular Education)*, Zacharie Myboto *(Information, Posts and Telecommunications)*, Hervé Moutsinga *(Trans-Gabon Railway Office)*.

There are also 17 Ministers, Ministers-Delegate and 10 Secretaries of State.

Flag: Three horizontal stripes of green, yellow, blue.

Local government: The 9 provinces, each administered by a governor appointed by the President, are divided into 37 *départements*, each under a prefect.

DEFENCE

Army. The Army consists of 1 all-arms Presidential Guard battalion group with support units, totalling (1990), 3,200 men. There is also a paramilitary force of about 5,000 personnel, of whom 2,800 are coast guards with boats. France maintains a 550-strong marine infantry battalion.

Navy. The small naval flotilla in 1989 consisted of 1 French-built fast missile craft, 1 coastal and 4 inshore patrol craft. The flagship is a French-built medium landing ship, and there are about 3 minor service tenders. A separate Coast Guard operates some 10 small launches. Personnel in 1989 totalled 350 officers and men.

Air Force. The Air Force has 6 single-seat, 3 two-seat Mirage 5 and 3 Magister ground-attack aircraft, and 1 EMB-111 maritime patrol aircraft. Transport duties are performed primarily by 3 Hercules and 1 EMB-110 Bandeirante turboprop aircraft, 3 Nord 262s. Single Falcon 900, Gulfstream III DC-8 aircraft are used for VIP duties. Three T-34C-1 armed turboprop aircraft and an EMB-110 Bandeirante are operated for *La Garde Présidentiale*. Also in service are 2 Puma, 1 Bell 212, 1 Bel 412 and 2 Alouette III helicopters. Personnel (1990) 1,000.

INTERNATIONAL RELATIONS

Membership. Gabon is a member of UN, OAU and OPEC; it is an ACP state of the EEC.

ECONOMY.

Planning. The Fifth 5-year Plan (1984–88, later extended to 1990) envisaged public expenditure of 1,228,478m. francs CFA, of which 595,662m. were to develop the infrastructure.

Budget. The 1989 budget provided for expenditure of 358,000m. francs CFA and revenue of 260,000m.

Currency. The unit of currency is the franc CFA, with a parity value of 50 francs CFA to 1 French franc. There are coins of 1, 2, 5, 10, 25, 50, 100 and 500 *francs* CFA, and banknotes of 100, 500, 1,000, 5,000 and 10,000 *francs* CFA. In March 1990 £1 = 471·62 *francs* CFA; US$1 = 287·75 *francs* CFA.

Banking. The *Banque des États de l'Afrique Centrale* is the bank of issue. There are 9 commercial banks situated in Gabon. The *Banque Gabonaise de Développement* and the *Union Gabonaise de Banque* are Gabonese controlled.

ENERGY AND NATURAL RESOURCES

Electricity. The semi-public *Société d'energie et d'eau du Gabon* produced 886m. kwh. in 1986, mainly from thermal plants but increasingly from hydro-electric schemes at Kinguélé (near Libreville), Tchimbélé and Poubara (near Masuku). Supply 220 volts; 50 Hz.

Oil. Extraction from offshore fields totalled 11m. tonnes in 1989. Gabon operates 2 refineries, at Port-Gentil and at nearby Pointe Clairette. Proven reserves (1984) 490m. bbls.

Gas. Natural gas production (1985) was 201m. cu. metres.

Minerals. Production (1986) of manganese ore (from deposits around Moanda in the south-east) amounted to 3m. tonnes. Uranium is mined nearby at Mounana (850 tonnes in 1986). An estimated 850m. tonnes of iron ore deposits, discovered 1971 at Mékambo (near Bélinga in the north-east) await completion of the branch railway line to be exploited. Gold (18 kg in 1982), zinc and phosphates also occur.

Agriculture. The major crops (production, 1988, in 1,000 tonnes) are: Sugar-cane, 155; cassava, 265; plantains, 180; maize, 10; groundnuts, 9; bananas, 8; palm oil, 3·8; cocoa, 2; coffee, 2 and rice, 1.

Livestock (1988): 9,000 cattle, 84,000 sheep, 63,000 goats, 154,000 pigs.

Forestry. Gabon's equatorial forests covering 78% of the land area produced 1·38m. cu. metres of *okoumé* and other softwoods in 1985. Hardwoods (mahogany, ebony and walnut) are also exported.

Fisheries. The total catch (1986) amounted to 20,400 tonnes.

INDUSTRY AND TRADE

Industry. A sugar refinery at Masuku produced (1984) 15,000 tonnes raw sugar. Most manufacturing is based on the processing of food, timber and mineral resources.

Labour. The workforce in 1986 numbered 522,000 of whom 71% were agricultural.

Commerce. In 1985 imports totalled 384,000m. francs CFA and exports 876,000m. francs CFA. France and USA are Gabon's principal trading partners. In 1983 petroleum made up 83·5% of exports; metals, 7·5% and timber, 7%.

Total trade between Gabon and the UK (British Department of Trade returns, in £1,000 sterling):

	1985	*1986*	*1987*	*1988*	*1989*
Imports to UK	48,292	36,642	5,357	5,091	2,389
Exports and re-exports from UK	30,588	16,627	11,962	18,808	14,945

COMMUNICATIONS

Roads. There were (1987) 6,898 km of roads and in 1985 there were 16,093 passenger cars and 10,506 commercial vehicles.

Railways. A 1,435-mm gauge (Transgabonais) railway runs from Owendo *via* N'Djole to Booué and Lastourville, Mouanda and Masuku, opened throughout in 1986. Total 649 km of 1,437 mm gauge. In 1986, 134,000 passengers and 662,000 tonnes of freight were transported.

Aviation. There are 3 international airports at Port-Gentil, Masuku, and Libreville; internal services link these to 65 domestic airfields.

Shipping. Owendo (near Libreville), Mayumba and Port-Gentil are the main ports. In 1987 there were 23 merchant vessels of 97,967 GNT. In 1986, 5·9m. tonnes were loaded and 968,000 tonnes unloaded at the ports.

Post and Broadcasting. In 1985 there were 11,700 telephones, and (1986) 23,000 television and 117,000 radio licences.

Newspapers. There were (1984) 2 newspapers published in Libreville; *Gabon-Matin* (daily) has a circulation of 18,000 and *L'Union* (weekly) 15,000.

JUSTICE, RELIGION, EDUCATION AND WELFARE

Justice. There are *tribunaux de grande instance* at Libreville, Port-Gentil, Lambaréné, Mouila, Oyem, Masuku and Koulamoutou, from which cases move progressively to a central Criminal Court, Court of Appeal and Supreme Court, all 3 located in Libreville. Civil police number about 900.

Religion. 84% of the population is Christian (65% Roman Catholic), the majority of the balance following animist beliefs. There are about 10,000 Moslems.

Education. Education is compulsory between 6–16 years. In 1984–85 there were 178,111 pupils with 3,837 teachers in 940 primary schools; 25,815 pupils with

1,894 teachers in 51 secondary schools; 13,529 students with 720 teachers in 29 technical and teacher-training establishments.

The Université Omar Bongo, founded in 1970 in Libreville, had (1983–84) 3,228 students and 616 teaching staff.

Health. In 1985 there were 565 doctors, and in 1977, 20 dentists, 28 pharmacists, 99 midwives and 823 nursing personnel. In 1981 there were 16 hospitals and 87 medical centres, with a total of 4,815 beds, as well as 258 local dispensaries.

DIPLOMATIC REPRESENTATIVES

Of Gabon in Great Britain (48 Kensington Ct., London, W8 5DB)
Ambassador: Charles Mamadou Diop (accredited 20 Nov. 1986).

Of Great Britain in Gabon (Immeuble CK2, Blvd de l'Indépendence, Libreville)
Ambassador: M. A. Goodfellow.

Of Gabon in the USA (2034 20th St., NW, Washington, D.C., 20009)
Ambassador: Jean Robert Odzaga.

Of the USA in Gabon (Blvd de la Mer, Libreville)
Ambassador: Keith L. Wauchope.

Of Gabon to the United Nations
Ambassador: Denis Dangue Rewaka.

Further Reading

Bory, P., *The New Gabon*. Monaco, 1978
Remy, M., *Gabon Today*. Paris, 1977
Saint Paul, M. A., *Gabon: The Development of a Nation*. London, 1989

THE GAMBIA

Capital: Banjul
Population: 788,163 (1988)
GNP per capita: US$220 (1988)

HISTORY. The Gambia was discovered by the early Portuguese navigators, but they made no settlement. During the 17th century various companies of merchants obtained trading charters and established a settlement on the river, which, from 1807, was controlled from Sierra Leone; in 1843 it was made an independent Crown Colony; in 1866 it formed part of the West African Settlements, but in Dec. 1888 it again became a separate Crown Colony. The boundaries were delimited only after 1890. The Gambia achieved full internal self-government on 4 Oct. 1963 and became an independent member of the Commonwealth on 18 Feb. 1965. The Gambia became a republic within the Commonwealth on 24 April 1970. The Gambia, with Senegal formed the Confederation of Senegambia on 1 Feb. 1982.

AREA AND POPULATION. The Gambia is bounded west by the Atlantic ocean and on all other sides by Senegal. Area of Banjul (formerly Bathurst) and environs, 87·8 sq. km. In the provinces (area, 10,601·5 sq. km) the settled population (1971) was 275,469, not including temporary immigrants. Total population (census, April 1983), 687,817; (estimate, 1988) 788,163. The largest tribe is the Mandingo (251,997), followed by the Fulas (117,092), Woloffs (91,004), Jolas (64,494) and Sarahulis (51,137). The capital is Banjul, 1983 census (44,188), and the surrounding urban area, Kombo St Mary (101,504). Other principal towns are Serekunda (68,433), Bakau (19,309), Brikama (19,584), Sukuta (7,227), Gunjur (7,115) and Farafenni (10,168).

Birth rate (1983) 49 per 1,000; death rate, 21.

CLIMATE. The climate is characterized by two very different seasons. The dry season lasts from Nov. to May, when precipitation is very light and humidity moderate. Days are warm but nights quite cool. The SW monsoon is likely to set in with spectacular storms and produces considerable rainfall from July to Oct., with increased humidity. Banjul. Jan. 73°F (22·8°C), July 80°F (26·7°C). Annual rainfall 52" (1,295 mm).

CONSTITUTION AND GOVERNMENT. Parliament consists of the House of Representatives which consists of a Speaker, Deputy Speaker and 36 elected members; in addition, 5 Chiefs are elected by the Chiefs in Assembly; 5 nominated members are without votes and the Attorney-General is appointed and has no vote. *See* Senegal for details about Senegambia.

A general election was held March 1987. State of parties (Jan. 1988): The People's Progressive Party 31 and the National Convention Party 5.

The Government was in Oct. 1989 composed as follows:

President: Sir Dawda Kairaba Jawara.

Vice-President, Education, Youth, Sports and Culture: Bakary B. Darbo. *External Affairs:* Alhaji Omar Sey. *Finance and Trade:* Saikou Sabally. *Agriculture:* Omar A. Jallow. *Health, Labour, Social Welfare and Environment:* Louise Njie. *Works and Communications:* Alhaji Momodou Cadi Cham. *Economic Planning and Industrial Development:* Mbemba Jatta. *Justice and Attorney-General:* Hassan Jallow. *Water Resources:* Sarjo Touray. *Information and Tourism:* Dr Lamin Saho. *Interior:* Alhaji Lamin kiti Jabang. *Local Government and Lands:* Landing Jallow Sonko.

National flag: Three wide horizontal stripes of red, blue, green, with narrower stripes of white between them.

Local Administration. The Gambia is divided into 35 districts, each traditionally under a Chief, assisted by Village Heads and advisers. These districts are grouped into 6 Area Councils containing a majority of elected members, with the Chiefs of the district as *ex-officio* members. The city of Banjul is administered by a City Council.

DEFENCE. The Gambia National Army, 900 strong, has four infantry companies and an engineer squadron.

The marine branch of the Gambia Army at no stage integrated fully into the Senegambian forces. Some 100 personnel operate 2 *ex*-Chinese and 4 British built inshore patrol craft.

INTERNATIONAL RELATIONS

Membership. The Gambia is a member of UN, OAU, the Commonwealth, ECOWAS, the Non-Aligned Conference and is an ACP state of EEC.

ECONOMY

Budget. Revenue and expenditure for years ending 30 June are (in dalasi):

	1983–84	*1984–85*	*1985–86*	*1986–87*
Revenue	150,500,000	172,300,050	218,080,000	266,730,000
Expenditure	164,908,621	189,279,550	207,524,639	262,531,520

Currency. The currency is the *dalasi* and is divided into 100 *butut*. 13·69 *dalasi* = £1 sterling; 8·35 *dalasi* = US$1 (March 1990).

Banking. There are 4 banks in the Gambia, the Standard Bank of Gambia Ltd, Central Bank of the Gambia, Commercial and Development Bank and la Banque Internationale pour le Commerce et l'Industrie (BICI). On 30 Nov. 1978 the government savings bank had about 36,000 depositors holding approximately 992,496 dalasi.

ENERGY AND NATURAL RESOURCES

Electricity. Production (1986) 63m. kwh. Supply 230 volts; 50 Hz.

Minerals. Heavy minerals, including ilmenite, zircon and rutile, have been discovered (1m. tons up to 31 Dec. 1980) in Sanyang, Batokunku and Kartong areas.

Agriculture. Almost all commercial activity centres upon the marketing of groundnuts, which is the only export crop of financial significance; in 1988, 110,000 tonnes were produced. Cotton is also exported on a limited scale. Rice is of increasing importance for local consumption; production (1988) 30,000 tonnes.

Livestock (1988): 300,000 cattle, 200,000 goats, 200,000 sheep, 13,000 pigs and (1982) 300,000 poultry.

Forestry. Forests cover 200,000 hectares, 17% of the land area.

Fisheries. Total catch (1986) 10,700 tonnes, of which 2,700 tonnes were from inland waters.

TRADE. Chief items of imports are textiles and clothing, vehicles and machinery, metal goods and petroleum products.

Imports and exports, in 1,000 dalasi:

	1984–85	*1985–86*	*1986–87*	*1987–88* [1]
Imports	358,569	567,631	797,568	844,973
Exports	163,890	204,195	221,319	245,621

[1] Provisional.

Chief items of export (1985–86, in 1,000 dalasi): Groundnuts shelled, 33,570; groundnut oil, 15,132; groundnut cake, 4,142; cotton lint, 3,862; fish and fish preparations, 2,507; hides and skins, 1,652. Main imports: Food and live animals, 175,280; basic manufactured goods, 113,916; machinery and transport equipment, 97,850; mineral fuels and lubricants, 56,630.

Total trade between the Gambia and UK (British Department of Trade returns, in £1,000 sterling):

	1985	*1986*	*1987*	*1988*	*1989*
Imports to UK	2,823	2,273	3,038	2,927	2,340
Exports and re-exports from UK	11,918	16,707	19,765	19,236	16,583

TOURISM. In 1987–88, 80,469 tourists visited the Gambia.

COMMUNICATIONS

Roads. There are 2,990 km of motorable roads, of which 1,718 km rank as all-weather roads including 306 km of bituminous surface and 531 km of laterite gravel. Number of licensed motor vehicles (1985): 5,200 private cars, 700 buses, lorries and coaches, 2,000 motorcycles, scooters and mopeds.

Aviation. The Gambia is served by Gambia Air Shuttle, Minerve, British Airways, Ghana Airways and Nigeria Airways. The number of aircraft landing at Yundum Airport in 1984–85 was 1,576.

Shipping. The chief port is Banjul. In 1985–86, 125,959 tonnes of goods were loaded and 300,212 tonnes unloaded. Internal communication is maintained by steamers and launches. The Gambia River Development Organization was founded in 1978 as a joint project with Senegal to develop the river and its basin. Guinea and Guinea-Bissau were also members in 1984.

Post and Broadcasting. There are several post offices and agencies; postal facilities are also afforded to all river towns. Telephones numbered 3,476 in Jan. 1980.

Radio Gambia, a government station, broadcasts for about 15 hours a day; Radio Syd, a commercial station, broadcasts for 20 hours. Number of radio receivers (1986, estimate), 110,000.

Cinemas. In 1984 there were 14 cinemas.

Newspapers. There is an official newspaper and several news-sheets.

JUSTICE, RELIGION, EDUCATION AND WELFARE

Justice. Justice is administered by a Supreme Court consisting of a chief justice and puisne judges. It has unlimited jurisdiction but there is a Court of Appeal. Two magistrates' courts and divisional courts are supplemented by a system of resident divisional magistrates. There are also Moslem courts, group tribunals dealing with cases concerned with customs and traditions, and one juvenile court.

Religion. About 90% of the population is Moslem. Banjul is the seat of an Anglican and a Roman Catholic bishop. There are some Methodist missions. Some sections of the population retain their original animist beliefs.

Education (1984–85). There were 189 primary schools (2,640 teachers, 66,257 pupils), 16 secondary technical schools (502 teachers, 10,102 pupils), 8 secondary high schools (235 teachers, 4,348 pupils). In 1982–83 there were 8 post-secondary schools (179 teachers, 1,489 pupils). Gambia College, which replaced Yundum College as a teacher-training and vocational centre, opened for agricultural and health students in 1979.

Health. In 1980 there were 43 government doctors, 23 private doctors and about 635 hospital beds.

DIPLOMATIC REPRESENTATIVES

Of the Gambia in Great Britain (57 Kensington Ct., London, W8 5DG)
High Commissioner: Horace R. Monday, Jr.

Of Great Britain in the Gambia (48 Atlantic Rd., Fajara, Banjul)
High Commissioner: Alec Ibbott, CBE.

Of the USA in the Gambia (Fajara (East), Kairaba Ave., Banjul)
Ambassador: (Vacant).

Further Reading

The Gambia since Independence 1965–1980. Banjul, 1980
Gamble, D. P., *The Gambia.* [Bibliography] Oxford and Santa Barbara, 1988
Tomkinson, M., *The Gambia: A Holiday Guide.* London, 1983

GERMANY

POST-WAR HISTORY. Since the unconditional surrender of the German armed forces on 8 May 1945 there has been no central authority whose writ runs in the whole of Germany. Consequently no peace treaty has been signed with a government representing the whole of Germany, and the country is virtually partitioned between the Federal Republic of Germany (FRG) and the German Democratic Republic (GDR).

A Treaty was signed in East Berlin between the GDR and the FRG on 21 Dec. 1972 agreeing the basis of relations between the two countries.

By the Berlin Declaration of 5 June 1945 the governments of the USA, the UK, the USSR and France assumed supreme authority over Germany. Each of the 4 signatories was given a zone of occupation, in which the supreme power was to be exercised by the C.-in-C. in that zone (*see* map in THE STATESMAN'S YEAR-BOOK, 1947). Jointly these 4 Cs.-in-C. constituted the Allied Control Council in Berlin, which was to be competent in all 'matters affecting Germany as a whole'. The territory of Greater Berlin, divided into 4 sectors, was to be governed as an entity by the 4 occupying powers. The British Military Government in Berlin changed its name to British Mission Berlin in March 1990.

The agreements between the war-time allies concerning the occupation zones (12 Sept. 1944) and control of Germany (1 May 1945) were repudiated by the USSR on 27 Nov. 1958.

At the Potsdam Conference (17 July–2 Aug. 1945) the northern part of the Province of East Prussia, including its capital Königsberg (renamed Kaliningrad), was transferred to the Soviet Union, pending final ratification by a peace treaty; and it was agreed that, pending the final peace settlement, Poland should administer those parts of Germany lying east of a line running from the Baltic Sea immediately west of Swinemünde along the river Oder to its confluence with the Western Neisse and thence along the Western Neisse to the Czechoslovak frontier. This frontier was guaranteed by Federal Germany 'in the name of the West German people' by the Moscow Treaty of 1970. Federal German statements of 8 Nov. 1989 and 6 March 1990 have repeated this guarantee.

Following the reforms in the GDR in Nov. 1989 the Federal Chancellor Helmut Kohl issued a 10-point plan for German confederation.

The ambassadors of the war-time allies met in Berlin in Dec. 1989, the first such meeting since 1971. After talks with Chancellor Kohl on 11 Feb. 1990, President Gorbachev said the USSR had no objections to German re-unification in principle. On 13 Feb. the FRG, the GDR and the four war-time allies agreed a formula ('two plus four') for re-unification talks to begin after the GDR elections on 18 Mar.

GERMAN DEMOCRATIC REPUBLIC

Capital: Berlin (East)
Population: 16·68m. (1988)
GNP per capita: US$10,400 (1985)

Deutsche Demokratische Republik

HISTORY. For the immediate post-war history *see* p. 525. An agreement proclaiming the Oder–Neisse line the permanent frontier between Germany and Poland was concluded between the German Democratic Republic (GDR) and Poland on 6 July 1950. A protocol on the delimitation of the frontier was signed on 27 Jan. 1951.

Following public demonstrations in favour of the democratization of political life in the autumn of 1989, and a mounting exodus of refugees to Federal Germany, Erich Honecker was replaced as Communist Party leader on 18 Oct. by Egon Krenz.

Exit restrictions were progressively eased until the border with Federal Germany, including the Berlin Wall, was opened on 9 Nov. On 13 Nov. the People's Chamber elected Hans Modrow as Prime Minister in place of Willi Stoph, and other Communist leaders were replaced. On 30 Nov. Egon Krenz and the entire Communist Party leadership resigned, amidst revelations of corruption under the former régime. Gregor Gysi was elected Party leader on 11 Dec.

On 1 Feb. 1990 Hans Modrow said 'Germany should again become the unified fatherland of all citizens of the German nation'.

AREA AND POPULATION. The GDR is bounded north by the Baltic Sea, east by Poland, south-east by Czechoslovakia and west by Federal Germany. Its area is 108,333 sq. km. Population at the census of 31 Dec. 1981 was 16,705,635. Population in 1988, 16,674,632 (7·97m. male; 12·8m. urban). Population density: 154 per sq. km. There were some 110,000 Sorbs, a Slav minority, in 1985. Administratively, the country has been divided into 15 counties (*Bezirk*), subdivided into 38 urban districts, 189 rural districts and 7,563 communities. Berlin (East), the capital, has county status. Area and population, 1988:

Counties	*Area in sq. km*	*Population (1,000) Total*	*Female*	*Per sq. km*
Berlin (East)	403	1,284·5	674·4	3,187
Cottbus	8,262	884·7	455·2	107
Dresden	6,738	1,757·4	925·4	261
Erfurt	7,349	1,240·3	646·3	169
Frankfurt	7,186	713·8	366·0	99
Gera	4,004	742·0	388·0	185
Halle	8,771	1,776·5	927·9	203
Karl-Marx-Stadt	6,009	1,859·5	987·5	309
Leipzig	4,966	1,360·9	719·0	274
Magdeburg	11,526	1,249·5	651·8	108
Neubrandenburg	10,948	620·5	317·1	57
Potsdam	12,568	1,123·8	581·7	89
Rostock	7,075	916·5	468·8	130
Schwerin	8,672	595·2	307·1	69
Suhl	3,856	549·4	285·8	142

Resident population of the principal towns in 1988:

Berlin (East)	1,284,536	Rostock	253,990	Schwerin	130,685
Leipzig	545,307	Halle	236,044	Cottbus	128,639
Dresden	518,057	Erfurt	220,016	Zwickau	121,749
Karl-Marx-Stadt	311,765	Potsdam	142,862	Jena	108,010
Magdeburg	290,579	Gera	134,834	Dessau	103,867

Vital statistics:

	Live births	*Marriages*	*Divorces*	*Deaths*
1985	227,648	131,514	51,240	225,353
1986	222,269	137,208	52,439	223,536
1987	225,959	141,283	50,640	213,872
1988	215,734	137,165	49,380	213,111

Rates per 1,000, 1988: Birth, 12·9; marriage, 8·2; divorce, 3; death, 12·8; infant mortality: 5 stillborn, 8·1 under 1 year. Expectation of life, 1987: Men, 69·8; women, 75·9. 74,515 births were to unmarried mothers in 1987.

CLIMATE. The continental-type climate makes winters crisp and clear, but with cold easterly winds bringing very low temperatures and appreciable snowfall. Summers are hot, but with much convectional rainfall. Berlin. Jan. 31°F (–0·5°C), July 66°F (19°C). Annual rainfall 22·5" (563 mm). Dresden. Jan. 30°F (–1°C), July 65°F (18·5°C). Annual rainfall 27·2" (680 mm). Leipzig. Jan. 31°F (–0·6°C), July 65°F (18·5°C). Annual rainfall 24" (605 mm).

CONSTITUTION AND GOVERNMENT. Upon the establishment of the Federal Republic of Germany, the People's Council of the Soviet-occupied zone, appointed in 1948, was converted into a provisional People's Chamber, which on 7 Oct. 1949 enacted a constitution of the 'German Democratic Republic' (GDR).

A new 'socialist constitution' was approved by 94·5% of the electorate at a referendum on 6 April 1968. It was revised in 1974. Under it the People's Chamber (Volkskammer) is 'the supreme organ of state power'; it elects the Council of State, the Council of Ministers, the National Defence Council and the judges of the Supreme Court. At elections in June 1986 it was announced that 99·7% of the 12·43m. electorate had voted, and 99·94% of votes were for candidates of a National Front of Communists and allied parties and organizations. New elections were brought forward to 18 March 1990 for a People's Chamber of 400 members elected by proportional representation from 15 constituencies.

Council of State. The Council is authorized to issue decisions and to interpret existing laws. Its Chairman represents the GDR in international law. In March 1990 the Chairman was Manfred Gerlach (Liberal Democrat) *ad interim.*

In March 1990 the *Council of Ministers (Cabinet)* consisted of a Presidium, composed as follows:

Chairman (i.e. Premier): Hans Modrow (b.1928).

First Deputy Chairmen: Alfred Neumann, Werner Krolikowski.

Deputy Chairmen: Günther Kleiber, Wolfgang Rauchfuss *(Minister of Materials)*, Gerhard Schürer *(Chairman, State Planning Commission)*, Dr Herbert Weiz *(Minister of Science)*, Manfred Flegel, Kurt Wünsche *(Minister of Justice)*, Rudolph Schulze *(Minister for Posts and Telecommunications)*, Horst Sölle. *Members:* Walter Halbritter *(Director, Office of Prices)*, Ernst Höfner *(Minister of Finance)*; and 32 other ministers, including: Gen. Heinz Kessler *(Defence)*, Oskar Fischer *(Foreign Affairs)*, Gerhard Beil *(Foreign Trade)*, and Friedrich Dickel *(Interior)*.

In Dec. 1989 the Socialist Unity (*i.e.* Communist) Party renounced its constitutional monopoly of power and adopted the name Socialist Unity Party of Germany-Party of Democratic Socialism (SED-PDS). The Executive of the SED-PDS in March 1990 consisted of: Gregor Gysi (b.1948) *(Chairman)*; Wolfgang Berghofer, Hans Modrow, Wolfgang Pohl. Parties with which it was united in the National Front (1989 membership in brackets): the Christian Democratic Union (CDU) (137,000), Democratic Farmers Party (DB) (115,000), Liberal Democratic Party (LDP) (114,000) and the National Democratic Party (NDP) (110,000) began independent activity, and the umbrella organization New Forum emerged as a focus for opposition groups.

Some 40 parties prepared to contest the March 1990 elections, prominent amongst them (with sister parties in Federal Germany): The Social Democratic Party (SPD), leader Ibrahim Böhme (Social Democratic Party), and the German Social Union (DSU) (Christian Democratic Union).

National flag: Black, red, golden (horizontal); in the centre, on both sides, the coat of arms showing a hammer and compass with a wreath of grain entwined with a black, red and golden ribbon.

National hymn: Auferstanden aus Ruinen ('Risen from the Ruins') (tune by Hanns Eisler).

Local government is conducted by assemblies at county, district, town, borough and village level, elected every 5 years. It was announced in Feb. 1990 that the 1989 elections were fraudulent, and that fresh elections would be held on 6 May on the basis of the former *Länder*: Brandenburg, Mecklenburg, Saxony, Saxony-Anhalt and Thuringia.

DEFENCE. Conscription for men between 18 and 25 was introduced in 1962 (18 months in the army, reduced to 12 months in 1990, 2 years in the navy and air force). Conscientious objectors may be assigned to alternative duties.

In 1989 some 380,000 Soviet troops with about 3,000 tanks were stationed in the GDR in 6 tank divisions, 9 motorized rifle divisions and an artillery division, following reductions made in 1989–90. Defence budget cuts of 10% were made in 1989, chiefly along the Polish border.

Army. The Army, set up on 1 March 1956, is organized in 2 army corps, including 2 armoured divisions and 4 motorized infantry divisions. Operationally these divisions are subordinate to the Soviet formations of the Warsaw Pact forces. They are armed with about 3,000 tanks (mostly Soviet T-54, T-55, T-34 and T-72), 390 self-propelled guns and ground-to-air 'Guideline' missiles. The Border Police was taken out of the Army in 1974. Total army strength was (1990) 120,000 (71,500 conscripts) with a reserve of 250,000 men.

Police. The 'People's Police' *(Volkspolizei)* numbers 25,000 security and 46,500 border troops. There are also 400,000 militiamen organized in combat groups, who receive training from the People's Police.

Navy. The People's Navy (*Volksmarine*) operates a substantial surface combatant force including 19 small frigates, 5 missile corvettes, 13 fast missile craft, 20 torpedo craft, and 42 coastal minesweepers. Amphibious capability is provided by 12 medium landing ships, and support is provided by 3 intelligence collectors, 3 small tankers, 2 combat support ships, 6 logistic transports and one training ship, plus some 40 other auxiliaries. The Navy operates 25 Su-22 'Fitter' fighters and 12 Mi-12 'Haze' anti-submarine helicopters. Personnel in 1989 totalled 15,000 officers and men, including the Coastal Frontier Guards with 15 inshore patrol cutters. Bases exist at Peenemünde, Warnemünde, Dranske-Bug and Sassnitz.

Air Force. The *ex*-'air-police', set up in Nov. 1950, had in 1989 a strength of about 37,000 officers and men and 375 combat aircraft. Two air defence divisions consist respectively of 3 and 2 regiments (each with 3 squadrons of 12 aircraft), plus a fighter training division, equipped with MiG-21, MiG-23, and MiG-29 supersonic fighters. Tactical aircraft comprise a Regiment of MiG-23s and one equipped with Su-22s, backed up by 1 squadron of MiG-21 reconnaissance fighters. Mi-24 gunship helicopters have been delivered to the German Democratic Republic. Other units include a regiment of Mi-2, Mi-4 and Mi-8 helicopters, a regiment of An-2, Let L-410, Il-14, An-26 and Tu-134 transports and a Flight Training Division with Yak-18, Trener, L-29 Delfin, L-39 Albatross, MiG-15UTI and MiG-21U training aircraft. 'Guideline' and 'Goa' surface-to-air missile units are operational.

INTERNATIONAL RELATIONS

Membership. The GDR is a member of UN and Comecon.

ECONOMY

Policy. The economy, favoured by a special relationship with Federal Germany, had been one of the more successful of the centrally-planned type, but, acknowledging declining economic performance, the Government in 1990 began taking measures to establish a free-market economy.

Budget. The budget of the GDR was as follows (in M 1m.) for calendar years:

	1983	*1984*	*1985*	*1986*	*1987*	*1988*
Revenue	192,410	213,535	235,535	247,013	260,449	269,699
Expenditure	191,689	211,778	234,392	246,368	260,167	269,466

Of 1988 expenditure, M 49,811m. went on price subsidies, M 36,275m. on social benefits and pensions, M 19,376m. on education and culture, M 17,801m. on health and social services, M 15,654m. on defence. Revenue included M 20,816m. from taxes and M 18,822m. from social insurance.

Currency. The circulating Reichsmark notes were in June 1948 exchanged for 'Deutsche Mark' (East), renamed 'Mark of the German Bank of Issue' (MDN) from 1 Aug. 1964 and further renamed 'the Mark of the GDR' (M) from 1967. Money in circulation, 1988: M 15,623m. In March 1990, £1 = 2·79 M; US$1 = 1·70 M.

Banking. The most important banking institutions are the State Bank (*President*, Horst Kaminski), which is the bank of issue, the Foreign Trade Bank and the Industrial and Trade Bank. Savings in 1988 totalled M 151,590m.

Weights and Measures. The metric system is in force.

ENERGY AND NATURAL RESOURCES

Electricity. Sources of energy in 1988 included lignite, 85% (73% in 1989, with further reductions planned), nuclear power, 9·9% and hydroelectric power, 1·5%. Electricity generation (1988): 118,328 kwh. 5,759m. kwh. were imported. Domestic consumption, 14%. Supply 220 volts; 50 Hz.

Minerals. The GDR is the world's largest producer of lignite. (Production in 1989, 311m. tonnes) and there are extensive potash deposits. Otherwise mineral resources are few. There is some uranium, cobalt, bismuth, arsenic and antimony.

Water. 93·1% of households were connected to the mains supply in 1988. Average *per capita* consumption, 138 litres a day.

Agriculture. In 1989 the agricultural area was 6·2m. hectares including 4·7m. hectares arable and 1·26m. hectares grassland. There were 3,855 collective farms with 5·3m. hectares of arable land, and 465 state farms with 448,895 hectares of land in 1988. In 1987 private plots accounted for 9% of production. In 1988 there were 167,529 tractors and 18,404 combine harvesters.

The yield of the main crops in 1988 was as follows (in 1,000 tonnes): Potatoes, 11,546; sugar-beet, 4,625; barley, 3,798; wheat, 3,699; rye, 1,785; oats, 507.

Livestock (in 1,000) in 1988: Cattle, 5,710 (including 2,009 milch cows); pigs, 12,464; sheep, 2,634; poultry, 49,430. 2·8m. tonnes of meat, 8m. tonnes of milk and 5,720m. eggs were produced.

Forestry. In 1988 there were 2,981,303 hectares of forest. Timber production was 10·9m. cu. metres in 1988.

Fisheries. Total catch (1988) 244,900 tonnes. Inland catch was 26,524 tonnes.

INDUSTRY AND TRADE

Industry. Industry produced about 70% of the national income in 1989. The major industries are energy, chemicals, metallurgy, mechanical and electrical engineering, electronics and instruments. In 1990 trustees were appointed to supervise the eventual conversion of enterprises to joint-stock companies.

1988 production (in 1,000 tonnes): Rolled steel, 9,472; sulphuric acid, 799; chemical fertilizers, 5,192; petrol, 4,765; diesel fuel, 6,301; caustic soda, 627; plastics and synthetic resins, 1,149; cement, 12,510; antibiotics, 84·9 tonnes; passenger cars (no.), 218,045; television receivers (no.), 774,100; shoes, 91m. pairs.

Labour. In 1988 the workforce was 8·59m. (4·2m. females), of whom 7·59m. were employees, 629,100 worked on collective farms, 164,000 in co-operative workshops and 181,700 were self-employed. Workforce distribution by activity, 1988: Industry, 37·4%; services, 21·4%; agriculture, 10·8%; commerce, 10·3%; building, 6·6%; transport, 5·9%; handicrafts, 3·1%; posts and telecommunications, 1·5%; other products, 3%. There is a 5-day working week of 43¾ hours. Annual leave is 3 weeks and 3 days. Average monthly wage, 1988: M1,280. Unemployment benefit of 70% of previous year's wage was introduced in Feb. 1990.

Commerce. Trade in 1988 (and 1987) (in 1m. Valuta-Mark): Imports, 87,161 (86,646); exports, 90,176 (89,910).

In 1988 66% of trade was with Comecon countries. Largest trading partners: USSR (37%), Czechoslovakia, Poland, Federal Republic of Germany. Import categories included: Machinery, 37%; fuel and raw materials, 33·5%; semi-finished,14·1%; exports: Machinery, 47·6%; consumer durables, 16·4%; fuel and raw materials, 15·1%. Foreign debt was US$20,600m. in 1989.

The international Leipzig Trade Fair is held in March and Sept. Under new laws of 1990 foreign firms are permitted to set up branches, and foreign partners of joint ventures are guaranteed the transfer of earnings abroad.

Total trade between the German Democratic Republic and UK (British Department of Trade returns, in £1,000 sterling):

	1985	*1986*	*1987*	*1988*	*1989*
Imports to UK	204,293	195,513	180,299	152,977	168,742
Exports and re-exports from UK	63,797	81,276	81,489	113,239	106,445

COMMUNICATIONS

Roads. There were, in 1988, 47,203 km of classified roads including 1,855 km of motorways. 3,531m. passengers and 143m. tonnes of goods were carried by public road transport. There were 3,743,554 cars, 228,872 lorries, 1,318,571 motorcycles and 60,744 buses. There were 46,804 road accidents in 1988, with 1,441 fatalities.

Railways. There were, in 1988, 13,750 km of standard gauge line, of which 3,475 km were electrified. 600m. passengers and 349·4m. tonnes of freight were carried.

Aviation. Interflug operates services between Berlin and Prague, Warsaw, Budapest, Bucharest, Moscow, Sofia, Belgrade, Tirana, Cairo, Baghdad, Beirut and other capitals. Passengers carried (1988), 1,582,000; freight, 31,300 tonnes.

Shipping. In 1988 the merchant fleet had 164 vessels of 1,313,556 GRT. 13·7m. tonnes of freight were carried in 1988. Navigable inland waterways had a total length of 2,319 km. 8m. passengers and 20·3m. tonnes of freight were carried. There is a rail ferry from the Rügen Island to the ice-free Lithuanian port Klaipeda.

Pipeline. 1,323 km in 1988. Materials transported in 1988: 37m. tonnes.

Post and Broadcasting. In 1988 there were 11,971 post offices There were 3,976,844 telephone and 17,363 telex subscribers. The State Broadcasting Committee broadcasts 4 radio programmes on long-, medium-and short-waves, and on FM. The foreign service is broadcast in 11 languages on medium- and short-waves, using the name Radio Berlin International. GDR Television broadcasts 2 TV programmes in colour, using the SECAM-system. Number of wireless licences (1988), 6·78m.; TV licences, 6·2m. Hours broadcast in 1988: Radio, 94,145; TV, 9,194.

Cinemas and Theatres (1988). There were 808 cinemas with a seating capacity of 234,723, and 213 theatres with a capacity of 55,568.

Newspapers and Books. There were 542 newspapers and periodicals in 1988. 6,590 book titles were published in 149·6m. copies.

JUSTICE, RELIGION, EDUCATION AND WELFARE

Justice. There is a Supreme Court, responsible to the People's Chamber, and county, district and lay courts. Judges are elected by the people's representative organs. The administration of justice is overseen by the Prosecutor General who heads a hierarchy of public prosecutors' offices. The death penalty was abolished in July 1987. A general amnesty for all but the most serious crimes was announced in Dec. 1989.

Religion. According to the census of 1950, 80·5% of the population were Protestants and 11% were Roman Catholics. The Synod of Lutheran Churches was founded in 1969 and embraces 8 regional churches. There were some 1·5m. Lutherans in 1989 in 7,200 parishes with 4,300 priests. The Catholic Church is organized in 2 dioceses, 3 episcopal districts and one apostolic administration. In 1989 there were 1·05m. Catholics in 916 parishes with 1,155 priests. There were 300 monasteries. There were also 40 Free and other churches, including Methodists, Quakers and Seventh-Day Adventists. In 1989 there were 8 synagogues.

Education. 10-year comprehensive schooling is compulsory and free. 2-year apprenticeship or secondary schooling may follow: The pupil receives a grant. In 1988 764,423 children were in 13,402 pre-school educational institutions. General education schools numbered 5,907 with 167,207 teachers and 2,054,817 pupils. Of these schools 5,207 with 1,953,012 pupils offered 10 years schooling and the remainder 12.

In addition there were 955 vocational schools *(Berufsschulen)* with 16,256 teachers and 359,308 trainees, and 237 technical schools with 157,513 students. There were also 9 universities and 44 other higher education institutes with 132,423 full-time students, including 65,152 women. University entrance is 75% from secondary school and 25% from apprenticeships.

The Academy of Sciences comprises 72 institutes and has a staff of some 24,000.

Health and Welfare. Social insurance is funded by compulsory contributions from employees (10% of income) and firms and state subventions. Voluntary supplementary insurance is available. Disbursements of M31·11m. were made in 1988. Sick pay is 90% of wages for 6 weeks, reducing to 50%. Monthly child allowances in 1986 were M50 for a first child, M100 for a second, M150 for a third. Retirement pensions graduated according to years worked are paid at 60 (women) and 65 (men). Monthly average, 1989: M480. In 1988 there were 543 hospitals with 165,950 beds and 623 health centres. There were 41,639 doctors and 12,932 dentists. Medical care is free.

DIPLOMATIC REPRESENTATIVES

Of the German Democratic Republic in Great Britain (34 Belgrave Sq., London, SW1X 8QB)
Ambassador: Dr Joachhim Mitdank. (accredited 5 May 1989).

Of Great Britain in the German Democratic Republic (108 Berlin, Unter den Linden 32/34)
Ambassador: P. H. C. Eyers, CMG, LVO.

Of the German Democratic Republic in the USA (1717 Massachusetts Ave., NW, Washington, D.C., 20036)
Ambassador: Dr Gerhard Herder.

Of the USA in the German Democratic Republic (1080 Berlin, Neustädtische Kirchstrasse 4-5)
Ambassador: Richard C. Barclay.

Of the German Democratic Republic to the United Nations
Ambassador: Dr Siegfried Zachmann.

Further Reading

Statistical Information: The central statistical agency is the Staatliche Zentralverwaltung für Statistik (Hans-Beimler-Str. 70–72, 102, Berlin).

Statistisches Jahrbuch der Deutschen Demokratischen Republik, annual (from 1956).—*Statistical Pocket Book of the German Democratic Republic* (annual, from 1959).—*Statistische Praxis* (from 1946).

The Constitution of the German Democratic Republic. 3rd ed. Berlin, 1974
The German Democratic Republic, 1949-1989. East Berlin, 1989

Åslund, A., *Private Enterprise in Eastern Europe: The Non-Agricultural Private Sector in Poland and the GDR*. London, 1985
Beyme, K. von, and Zimmerman, H., (eds.) *Policy-making in the German Democratic Republic*. Aldershot, 1984
Buch, G., *Namen und Daten der wichtiger Personen der DDR*. 4th ed. West Berlin, 1987
Childs, D., *The GDR: Moscow's German Ally*. London, 1983.— (ed.), *Honecker's Germany*. London, 1985.—*East Germany to the 1990s: Can it resist Glasnost?* London, 1987
Dennis, M., *German Democratic Republic*. London, 1987
Edwards, G. E., *GDR Society and Social Institutions*. London, 1985
Honecker, E., *Reden und Aufsätze*. Berlin, 1975.—*The German Democratic Republic, Pillar of Peace and Socialism*. New York, 1979.—*Aus meinem Leben*. Berlin, 1980
Krisch, H., *The German Democratic Republic*. Boulder, 1985
McCauley, M., *The German Democratic Republic since 1945*. London, 1983
Simmons, M., *The Unloved Country: A Portrait of East Germany Today*. London, 1989
Staritz, D., *Geschichte der DDR, 1949–1985*. Frankfurt-am-Main, 1985
Thomaneck, J. and Mellis, J., (eds.) *Politics, Society and Government in the German Democratic Republic: Basic Documents*. Oxford, 1989
Wallace, I., *East Germany: The German Democratic Republic*. [Bibliography] Oxford and Santa Barbara, 1987
Weber, H., *Geschichte der DDR*. Munich, 1985

National Library: Deutsche Bücherei, Leipzig C.1. *Director:* Helmut Rötzsch.—Deutsche Staatsbibliothek, Berlin. *Director:* Dr Dieter Schmidmaier.

FEDERAL REPUBLIC OF GERMANY

Capital: Bonn
Population: 61·24m. (1988)
GNP per capita: US$20,311 (1988)

Bundesrepublik Deutschland

HISTORY. In June 1948 USA, UK and France agreed on a central government for the 3 western zones. An Occupation Statute, which came into force on 30 Sept. 1949, reduced the responsibilities of the occupation authorities. Formally, the Federal Republic of Germany came into existence on 21 Sept. 1949. The Petersberg Agreement of 22 Nov. 1949 freed the Federal Republic of numerous restrictions of the Occupation Statute. In 1951 USA, UK and France as well as other states terminated the state of war with Germany; the Soviet Union followed on 25 Jan. 1955. On 5 May 1955 the High Commissioners of USA, UK and France signed a proclamation revoking the Occupation Statute. On the same day, the Paris and London treaties, signed in Oct. 1954, came into force and the Federal Republic of Germany became a sovereign independent country.

AREA AND POPULATION. Federal Germany is bounded north by Denmark and the North and Baltic Seas, east by the German Democratic Republic (GDR), and Czechoslovakia, south-east and south by Austria, south by Switzerland and west by France, Luxembourg, Belgium and the Netherlands. Area: 248,706 sq. km. West Berlin is an enclave within the GDR. Population, 1988, 61,241,700 (31,820,800 females). There were 26·22m. households in 1987; 8·77m. were single-person, and 8·28m. had a female principal breadwinner. There were 778,000 unmarried couple households. 9·34m. persons were over 65 in 1987. Density 246 per sq. km.

The capital is Bonn.

The Federation comprises 11 Länder (states).

Area and population of the Länder at the 1987 census:

Länder	*Area in sq. km*	*Population (in 1,000's) (Females in brackets)*		*Per sq. km*
Schleswig-Holstein	15,727	2,554	(1,326)	162
Hamburg	755	1,593	(848)	2,110
Lower Saxony	47,438	7,162	(3,707)	151
Bremen	404	660	(348)	1,618
North Rhine-Westphalia	34,068	16,712	(8,701)	491
Hessen	21,115	5,508	(2,851)	261
Rhineland-Palatinate	19,848	3,631	(1,884)	183
Baden-Württemberg	35,751	9,286	(4,800)	260
Bavaria	70,553	10,903	(5,668)	155
Saarland	2,569	1,056	(550)	411
Berlin (West)	480	2,013	(1,078)	4,192

Vital statistics for calendar years:

	Marriages	*Live births*	*Of these to single parents*	*Deaths*	*Divorces*
1986	372,008	625,963	59,808	701,890	122,581
1987	382,564	642,010	62,358	687,419	129,850
1988	397,595	677,259	67,957	687,516	...

Crude birth rate in 1988 was 11 per 1,000 population; marriage rate, 6·5; death rate, 11·2; infantile mortality 7·6; growth rate, –0·2.

In 1988 there were 4,489,100 resident foreigners (1,956,200 female). 37,810 persons were naturalized in 1987.

In 1987 there were 400,932 emigrants and 614,603 immigrants. 842,227 refugees entered in 1989 (345,581 in 1988). These comprised 720,909 ethnic Germans (including 343,854 from GDR, 250,340 from Poland, 98,134 from USSR and 23,387 from Romania) and 121,318 non-Germans (mainly from Poland, Turkey, Yugoslavia, Sri Lanka, Lebanon and Iran).

Populations of towns of over 100,000 inhabitants in 1987 (in '000):

Town	*Land*	*Population*	*Town*	*Land*	*Population*
Berlin (West)	Berlin (West)	2,016·1	Mülheim a.d. Ruhr	N. Rhine-Westph.	176·1
Hamburg	Hamburg	1,593·6	Herne	N. Rhine-Westph.	174·2
Munich	Bavaria	1,188·8	Mainz	Rhinel.-Pal.	172·4
Cologne	N. Rhine-Westph.	927·5	Hamm	N. Rhine-Westph.	171·1
Essen	N. Rhine-Westph.	623·0	Solingen	N. Rhine-Westph.	159·1
Frankfurt am Main	Hessen	618·5	Ludwigshafen am Rhein	Rhinel.-Pal.	156·7
Dortmund	N. Rhine-Westph.	583·6	Leverkusen	N. Rhine-Westph.	154·7
Düsseldorf	N. Rhine-Westph.	563·4	Osnabrück	Lower Saxony	150·9
Stuttgart	Baden-Württ.	552·3	Neuss	N. Rhine-Westph.	142·2
Bremen	Bremen	533·4	Oldenburg	Lower Saxony	140·2
Duisburg	N. Rhine-Westph.	525·2	Darmstadt	Hessen.	134·2
Hanover	Lower Saxony	495·3	Heidelberg	Baden-Württ.	127·5
Nuremberg	Bavaria	471·8	Bremerhaven	Bremen	126·8
Bochum	N. Rhine-Westph.	386·2	Wolfsburg	Lower Saxony	124·9
Wuppertal	N. Rhine-Westph.	365·5	Würzburg	Bavaria	123·5
Bielefeld	N. Rhine-Westph.	305·6	Remscheid	N. Rhine-Westph.	120·1
Mannheim	Baden-Württ.	295·2	Recklinghausen	N. Rhine-Westph.	119·9
Gelsenkirchen	N. Rhine-Westph.	287·6	Regensburg	Bavaria	118·6
Bonn	N. Rhine-Westph.	276·5	Göttingen	Lower Saxony	114·9
Karlsruhe	Baden-Württ.	260·5	Bottrop	N. Rhine-Westph.	114·6
Braunschweig	Lower Saxony	252·2	Offenbach am Main	Hessen	111·3
Wiesbaden	Hessen	251·8	Salzgitter	Lower Saxony	111·1
Mönchengladbach	N. Rhine-Westph.	249·6	Heilbronn	Baden-Württ	110·9
Münster	N. Rhine-Westph.	246·3	Paderborn	N. Rhine-Westph.	110·8
Augsburg	Bavaria	243·0	Koblenz	Rhine-Pal.	108·2
Kiel	Schleswig-Holstein	237·8	Pforzheim	Baden-Württ.	106·6
Krefeld	N. Rhine-Westph.	232·3	Siegen	N. Rhine-Westph.	106·4
Aachen	N. Rhine-Westph.	229·8	Ulm	Baden-Württ.	103·6
Oberhausen	N. Rhine-Westph.	220·4	Hildesheim	Lower Saxony	103·4
Lübeck	Schleswig-Holstein	210·5	Witten	N. Rhine-Westph.	102·9
Hagen	N. Rhine-Westph.	209·2	Moers	N. Rhine-Westph.	100·9
Kassel	Hessen	188·5	Bergisch Gladbach	N. Rhine-Westph.	100·7
Saarbrücken	Saarland.	187·4			
Freiburg im Breisgau	Baden-Württ.	178·7			

CLIMATE. Oceanic influences are only found in the north-west where winters are quite mild but stormy. Elsewhere a continental climate is general. To the east and south, winter temperatures are lower, with bright frosty weather and considerable snowfall. Summer temperatures are fairly uniform throughout. Frankfurt. Jan. 33°F (0·6°C), July 66°F (18·9°C). Annual rainfall 24" (601 mm). Hamburg. Jan. 31°F (–0·6°C), July 63°F (17·2°C). Annual rainfall 29" (726 mm). Hanover. Jan. 33°F (0·6°C), July 64°F (17·8°C). Annual rainfall 24" (604 mm). Köln. Jan. 36°F (2·2°C), July 66°F (18·9°C). Annual rainfall 27" (676 mm). Munich. Jan. 28°F (–2·2°C), July 63°F (17·2°C). Annual rainfall 34" (855 mm). Stuttgart. Jan. 33°F (0·6°C), July 66°F (18·9°C). Annual rainfall 27" (677 mm).

CONSTITUTION. The Constituent Assembly (known as the 'Parliamentary Council') met in Bonn on 1 Sept. 1948, and worked out a Basic Law (*Grundgesetz*) which was approved by a two-thirds majority of the parliaments of the participating Länder and came into force on 23 May 1949. It is to remain in force until 'a constitution adopted by a free decision of the German people comes into being'.

The Basic Law consists of a preamble and 146 articles. There have been 35 amendments. The first section deals with the basic rights which are legally binding for legislation, administration and jurisdiction.

The Federal Republic is a democratic and social constitutional state on a parliamentary basis. The federation is constituted by the 11 Länder (states) (*see* p 533). In Berlin (West) the Basic Law applies with certain restrictions. The Basic Law decrees that the general rules of international law form part of the federal law. The constitutions of the Länder must conform to the principles of a republican, democratic and social state based on the rule of law. Executive power is vested in the Länder, unless the Basic Law prescribes or permits otherwise. Federal law takes precedence over state law.

Legislative power is vested in the Federal Assembly *(Bundestag)* and the Federal Council *(Bundesrat)*.

The Federal Assembly is composed of 520 members (including 22 for West Berlin with limited voting rights, and is elected in universal, direct, free, equal and secret elections for a term of 4 years.

The Federal Council consists of 45 members appointed by the governments of the Länder in proportions determined by the number of inhabitants. Each Land has at least 3 votes.

The Head of State is the Federal President *(Bundespräsident)* who is elected for a 5-year term by a Federal Convention specially convened for this purpose. This Convention consists of all the members of the Federal Assembly and an equal number of members elected by the Länder parliaments in accordance with party strengths, but who need not themselves be members of the parliaments. No president may serve more than two terms. Presidents since 1949: Theodor Heuss (1949-59); Heinrich Lübke (1959-69); Gustav Heinemann (1969-74); Walter Scheel (1974-1979).

Executive power is vested in the Federal Government, which consists of the Federal Chancellor, elected by the Federal Assembly on the proposal of the Federal President, and the Federal Ministers, who are appointed and dismissed by the Federal President upon the proposal of the Federal Chancellor.

The Federal Republic has exclusive legislation on: (1) foreign affairs (2) federal citizenship; (3) freedom of movement, passports, immigration and emigration, and extradition; (4) currency, money and coinage, weights and measures, and regulation of time and calendar; (5) customs, commercial and navigation agreements, traffic in goods and payments with foreign countries, including customs and frontier protection; (6) federal railways and air traffic; (7) post and telecommunications; (8) the legal status of persons in the employment of the Federation and of public law corporations under direct supervision of the Federal Government; (9) trade marks, copyright and publishing rights; (10) co-operation of the Federal Republic and the Länder in the criminal police and in matters concerning the protection of the constitution, the establishment of a Federal Office of Criminal Police, as well as the combating of international crime; (11) federal statistics.

For concurrent legislation in which the Länder have legislative rights if and as far as the Federal Republic does not exercise its legislative powers, *see* THE STATESMAN'S YEAR-BOOK, 1956, p. 1038.

Federal laws are passed by the Federal Assembly and after their adoption submitted to the Federal Council, which has a limited veto. The Basic Law may be amended only upon the approval of two-thirds of the members of the Federal Assembly and two-thirds of the votes of the Federal Council.

The foreign service, federal finance, railways, postal services, waterways and shipping are under direct federal administration.

In the field of finance the Federal Republic has exclusive legislation on customs and financial monopolies and concurrent legislation on: (1) excise taxes and taxes on transactions, in particular, taxes on real-estate acquisition, incremented value and on fire protection; (2) taxes on income, property, inheritance and donations; (3) real estate, industrial and trade taxes, with the exception of the determining of the tax rates.

The Federal Republic can, by federal law, claim part of the income and corporation taxes to cover its expenditures not covered by other revenues. Financial jurisdiction is uniformly regulated by federal legislation.

National flag: Three horizontal stripes of black, red, gold.

National anthem: Einigkeit und Recht und Freiheit (words by H. Hoffmann, 1841; tune by J. Haydn, 1797).

Local Government. Below *Land* level local government is carried on by elected councils to counties *(Landkreise)* and county boroughs *(Kreisfreie Städte)*, which form the electoral districts for the *Land* governments, and are subdivided into communities *(Gemeinden)*.

GOVERNMENT. The 11th Federal Assembly was elected 25 Jan. 1987. Electoral turnout was 84·4%. The government is formed by a coalition of the Christian Democrat/Christian Socialist (CDU/CSU) alliance with the Free Democrats (FDP). (The CSU is a Bavarian party where the CDU does not stand). Percentage votes, and seats gained (1983 electoral results in brackets): CDU/CSU 44·3%, 223 (48·8%, 244); Social Democratic Party (SPD), 37%, 186 (38·2%, 193); FDP, 9·1%, 46 (7%, 34); Greens, 8·3%, 42 (5·6%, 27). Date of next general election: 9 Dec. 1990.

Federal President: Dr Richard von Weizsäcker (sworn in 1 July 1984); elected for a second term 23 May 1989).
Speaker of the Federal Assembly: Rita Süssmuth (elected Nov. 1988).

The Cabinet, in March 1990, was as follows:

Chancellor: Dr Helmut Kohl (CDU).
Deputy Chancellor, Minister of Foreign Affairs: Hans-Dietrich Genscher (FDP).
Interior: Wolfgang Schäuble (CDU).
Justice: Hans A. Engelhard (FDP).
Finance: Theo Waigel (CSU).
Economy: Helmut Haussman (FDP).
Defence: Dr Gerhard Stoltenberg (CDU).
Transport: Dr Friedrich Zimmerman (CSU).
Government Spokesman: Hans Klein (CSU).
Minister at the Chancellery: Rudolf Seiters (CDU).
Intra-German Relations: Dorothée Wilms (CDU).
Food, Agriculture and Forestry: Ignaz Kiechle (CSU).
Labour and Social Affairs: Dr Norbert Blüm (CDU).
Youth, Family Affairs and Health: Ursula-Maria Lehr (CDU).
Environment, Nature Conservation and Reactor Safety: Klaus Töpfer (CDU).
Posts and Telecommunications: Dr Christian Schwarz-Schilling (CDU).
City Planning and Housing: Gerda Hasselfeldt (CSU).
Research and Technology: Dr Heinz Riesenhuber (CDU).
Education and Science: Jürgen Möllemann (FDP).
Economic Co-operation: Jürgen Warnke (CSU).

DEFENCE. The Paris Treaties, which entered into force in May 1955, stipulated a contribution of the Federal Republic to western defence within the framework of NATO and the Western European Union. The Federal Armed Forces *(Bundeswehr)* had a total strength (1988) of 488,400 all ranks (223,450 conscripts) and a further 750,000 reserves. Conscription is 15 months.

Army. The Army is divided into the Field Army, containing the units assigned to NATO in event of war, and the Territorial Army. The Field Army is organized in 3 corps, comprising 6 armoured, 4 armoured infantry, 1 mountain and 1 airborne divisions. Equipment includes 650 M-48, 2,130 Leopard I and 2,000 Leopard II tanks. An air component operates 210 BO 105P anti-armour helicopters, 108 CH-53G and 87 UH-1D Iroquois transport helicopters, plus 138 Alouette II and 97 BO 105M liaison/observation helicopters. The Territorial Army is organized into 5 Military Districts, under 3 Territorial Commands. Its main task is to defend rear areas and remains under national control even in wartime. Total strength was (1990) 340,700 (conscripts 175,900); Territorial Army 41,700.

Navy. The Federal Navy is tasked to maritime operations in support of the central European theatre in the Baltic and North Sea environments. The emphasis is thus on coastal and shallow-seas warfare. The Fleet Commander operates from a modern Maritime Headquarters at Glücksburg, close to the Danish border.

The fleet includes 24 diesel coastal submarines, 3 US-built guided-missile and 4 other destroyers, 7 frigates, 5 anti-submarine corvettes and 40 fast missile craft. There is a large mine-warfare force of 54 vessels, comprising 2 minelayer/transports, 34 coastal minesweepers and hunters of which 2 are new combined minelayer/hunters and 6 control ships for TROIKA minesweeping drones, and 18 inshore minesweepers. Major auxiliaries include 4 tankers, 2 repair ships, 9 oilers, 9 minesweeper/patrol craft support and HQ ships, 10 logistic transports, 8 large tugs, 3 intelligence collectors, 2 trial ships and a sail training vessel. There are several dozen minor auxiliaries and service craft.

The main naval bases are at Wilhemshaven, Bremerhaven, Kiel and Olpenitz, and there are several other lesser bases.

The Naval Air Arm, 6,700 strong, is unique among NATO navies in operating shore-based anti-ship strike squadrons comprising 95 missile-armed Tornado strike aircraft. 19 Atlantic long range, plus 19 Dornier-28 coastal patrol aircraft, 22 shore-based Sea King helicopters and 19 Lynx (12 frigate-based) complete the inventory.

Procurement of 5 new frigates and 18 further replacement mine warfare craft is in hand. The new submarine project has been deferred; the first is now due to commission in 1995. Modernization of the existing force proceeds.

Personnel numbered (1990) 39,000 including the Naval Air Arm (of whom 3,000 are assigned to central staffs).

Air Force. Since Oct. 1970, the *Luftwaffe* has comprised the following commands: German Air Force Tactical Command, German Air Force Support Command (including two German Air Force Regional Support Commands—North and South) and General Air Force Office. Its strength in 1989 was approximately 108,700 officers and other ranks and over 550 first-line combat aircraft. Combat units, including 12 heavy fighter-bomber squadrons, 7 light ground attack/reconnaissance squadrons, 4 reconnaissance squadrons, 8 surface-to-surface missile squadrons, and an air defence force of 4 interceptor squadrons, 24 batteries of *Nike-Hercules* and 36 batteries of *Improved Hawk* surface-to-air missiles, are assigned to NATO. There are 4 F-4F Phantom interceptor squadrons, 8 Tornado attack squadrons, 4 attack squadrons of F-4Fs, 4 RF-4E Phantom reconnaissance squadrons, and 7 light attack/reconnaissance squadrons of Alpha Jets. Four transport squadrons (each 15 aircraft) with turboprop Transall C-160 aircraft and 1 wing of 5 helicopter squadrons with UH-1D Iroquois add to the air mobility of the *Bundeswehr*. There are also VIP, support and light transport aircraft. Guided weapons in service include 8 squadrons of *Pershing* surface-to-surface missiles and 6 battalions of *Nike-Hercules* and 9 battalions of *Improved Hawk* surface-to-air missiles.

Pilots undergo basic and advanced training in USA.

INTERNATIONAL RELATIONS

Membership. The Federal Republic of Germany is a member of UN, OECD, European Communities, WEU, NATO and the Council of Europe.

ECONOMY

Budget. Since 1 Jan. 1979 tax revenues have been distributed as follows: Federal Government. Income tax, 42·5%; capital yield and corporation tax, 50%; turnover tax, 67·5%; trade tax, 15%; capital gains, insurance and accounts taxes, 100%; excise duties (other than on beer), 100%. Länder. Income tax, 42·5%; capital yield and corporation tax, 50%; turnover tax, 32·5%; trade tax, 15%; other taxes, 100%. Local authorities. Income tax, 15%; trade tax, 70%; local taxes, 100%. Income tax was reduced in 1990.

Budgets for 1988 and 1989 (in DM1m.):

Revenue	All public authorities 1988	1989	Federal portion 1988	1989
		Current		
Taxes	456,967	491,855	222,748	242,873
Economic activities	28,235	33,808	6,161	11,212
Interest	1,892	1,890	1,101	1,148
Current allocations and subsidies	110,338	110,209	1,516	1,226
Other receipts	32,297	33,301	4,591	4,495
minus equalising payments	99,346	103,069	...	...
	539,383	567,994	236,116	260,994
		Capital		
Sale of assets	9,083	5,102	2,698	444
Allocations for investment	23,068	25,570	13	27
Repayment of loans	5,585	5,033	2,965	2,690
Public sector borrowing	2,859	2,288	...	...
minus equalising payments	22,190	23,913	...	...
	18,405	14,080	5,676	3,161
Totals	557,788	582,286	241,792	264,155
Expenditure		*Current*		
Staff	190,807	196,561	40,116	41,519
Materials	92,880	96,714	39,694	41,279
Interest	60,034	62,419	32,284	32,356
Allocations and subsidies	270,863	286,585	131,287	141,035
minus equalising payments	99,346	103,069	...	...
	515,238	539,210	243,380	256,189
		Capital		
Construction	39,708	41,461	5,931	6,312
Acquisition of property	12,197	11,125	1,753	1,874
Allocations and subsidies	44,122	50,894	16,817	19,686
Loans	16,095	14,904	8,666	9,106
Acquisition of shares	3,331	2,894	2,564	2,346
Repayments in the public sector	1,437	1,554	...	...
minus equalising payments	22,190	23,913	...	...
	94,700	98,655	34,402	38,316
Totals	609,938	635,165	277,782	292,855

Major areas of expenditure in 1987 (and 1988) in DM1,000m.: Social, 87·2 (89·2); defence, 53·6 (53·9); transport and communications, 13·1 (12·9); economy, 10·2 (11·6).

Currency. 100 *pfennig* (pf.)=1 *deutsche Mark* (DM). There are 1, 2, 5, 10, 50 pf., 1, 2, 5 and 10 DM coins and 5, 10, 20, 50, 100, 500 and 1,000 DM notes. Money in circulation in 1988, DM 140,975m. In March 1990, £1 = 2·79 DM; US$1 = 1·70.

Banking. In 1948 the Bank deutscher Länder was established in Frankfurt as the central bank. The Länder and Berlin central banks were merged from 1 Aug. 1957 to form the Deutsche Bundesbank. Its assets were DM 268,925m. in 1988. The largest private banks are the Deutsche Bank, Dresdner Bank and Commerzbank. The public sector banks consist of 584 retail savings banks and 11 Landesbanken which represent them in the wholesale markets.

Savings deposits were DM 737,474m. in 1988.

Weights and Measures. The metric system is in force.

ENERGY AND NATURAL RESOURCES

Electricity. In 1989 some 50% of electricity was produced from coal, and 40% from nuclear power. In 1988, 431,200m. kwh. were produced. Supply 220 volts; 50 Hz.

Oil and Gas. The chief oilfields are in Emsland (Lower Saxony). In 1988, 13·94m. tonnes of crude, 9·72m. tonnes of petroleum, and 11·71m. tonnes of diesel oil were produced. Gas production was 14,783m. cu metres.

Minerals. The main production areas are: North Rhine-Westphalia (for coal, iron and metal smelting-works), Central Germany (for brown coal), and Lower Saxony (Salzgitter for iron ore; the Harz for metal ore).

Production (in 1,000 tonnes):

Minerals	*1983*	*1984*	*1985*	*1986*	*1987*	*1988*
Coal	82,202	79,426	82,398	80,801	76,300	73,304
Lignite	124,281	126,739	120,667	114,310	108,799	108,563
Potash	27,200	29,543	29,248	24,775	25,795	27,030

Production of iron and steel (in 1,000 tonnes):

	1983	*1984*	*1985*	*1986*	*1987*	*1988*
Pig-iron	26,598	30,203	31,919	29,443	28,918	33,016
Steel	35,729	39,389	40,497	37,134	36,248	41,023
Rolled products finished	26,063	27,962	28,919	27,409	27,437	30,385

Agriculture. Area cultivated, 1988: 11·81m. hectares (arable, 7·26m. in 1987; pasture, 4·42m.).

In 1987 the number of agricultural holdings classified by area farmed was:

	Total	*1–5 hectares*	*5–20 hectares*	*20–100 hectares*	*Over 100 hectares*
Schleswig-Holstein	29,036	6,206	5,327	16,089	1,414
Hamburg	1,202	717	272	199	14
Lower Saxony	102,602	26,372	27,708	46,286	2,236
Bremen	404	133	89	178	4
North Rhine-Westphalia	85,357	25,929	29,106	29,679	643
Hessen	50,361	17,880	19,261	12,914	306
Rhineland-Palatinate	50,193	20,401	17,871	11,678	243
Baden-Württemberg	112,769	44,147	44,263	15,946	413
Bavaria	229,848	58,430	112,912	57,832	674
Saarland	3,625	1,519	838	711	62
Berlin (West)	120	70	25	25	...
Federal Republic	*665,517*	*201,804*	*257,867*	*199,837*	*6,009*

Area (in 1,000 hectares) and yield (in 1,000 tonnes) of the main crops:

	Area				*Yield*			
	1985	*1986*	*1987*	*1988*	*1985*	*1986*	*1987*	*1988*
Wheat	1,618	1,648	1,671	1,743	9,866	10,406	9,932	11,922
Rye	424	414	412	378	1,821	1,768	1,599	1,579
Barley	1,944	1,947	1,849	1,836	9,690	9,377	8,571	9,588
Oats	582	506	459	474	2,807	2,276	2,008	2,039
Potatoes	218	210	206	199	7,905	7,390	6,836	7,433
Sugar-beet	403	391	376	379	20,813	20,260	19,049	18,590

4·52m. tonnes of fertilizers were used in Oct. 1987-Sept. 1988.

Wine production (in 1,000 hectolitres): 15,481 in 1987; 15,352 in 1988.

Livestock (in 1,000s), 1988: Cattle, 15,023 (including 4,986 milch cows); sheep, 1,895; pigs, 23,755; horses, 375; poultry, 72,035. Milk production was 3·65m. tonnes in 1988.

In 1987 there were 1·73m. tractors.

Forestry. Forestry is of great importance, conducted under the guidance of the State on scientific lines. In recent years enormous depredation has occurred through pollution with acid rain. Forest area in 1988 was 5·3m. hectares, of which 2·25m. were owned by the State. In 1987 28·69m. cu. metres of timber were cut.

Fisheries. In 1988 the yield of sea fishing was 142,207 tonnes live weight.

In 1988 the fishing fleet consisted of 17 trawlers (24,963 GRT) and 628 cutters.

INDUSTRY AND TRADE

Industry. Public limited companies are managed on the 'co-determination' principle, and have 3 statutory bodies: a board of directors, a works council elected by employees, and a supervisory council which includes employee representatives but has an in-built management majority.

In 1987 there were 50,981 manufacturing firms (with 20 and more employees) employing 8·26m. persons, made up of 282,000 in energy and water services, 206,000 in mining, 1·38m. in raw materials processing, 3·76m. in the manufacture of producers' goods, 1·26m. in the manufacture of consumer goods, 463,000 in food and tobacco and 909,000 in building.

Production of major industrial products:

Products (1,000 tonnes)	*1984*	*1985*	*1986*	*1987*	*1988*
Aluminium	777	745	765	793	753
Artificial fertilizers	1,691	1,651	1,425	1,449	1,274
Sulphuric acid, SO_3	3,518	3,428	3,351	3,323	3,308
Soda, Na_2CO_3	1,364	1,412	1,442	1,448	1,404
Cement	28,909	25,758	26,580	25,268	26,215
Plastics	7,505	7,666	7,941	8,546	9,277
Cotton yarn	194	131	128	142	126
Woollen yarn	49	42	41	40	38
Passenger cars (1,000)	3,505	3,867	3,952	4,008	3,980
TV sets (1,000)	...	3,738	3,895	3,537	3,737

Labour. 27·37m. persons were employed in 1988, including 10·61m. women and 1·96m. foreign workers. Major categories: Manufacturing industries, 11·24m.; services, 10·08m.; commerce and transport, 4·89m.; self-employed, 2·42m.; agriculture, forestry and fishing, 1·16m. Unemployed 2·24m.; unfilled vacancies, 188,621; part-time workers, 207,768.

Trade Unions. The majority of trade unions belong to the *Deutscher Gewerkschaftsbund* (DGB, German Trade Union Federation), which had (women in brackets) 7·8m. (1·83m.) members in 1989, including 5·19m. (878,844) manual workers, 1·8m. (785,064) white-collar workers and 805,755 (162,741) civil servants. DGB unions are organized in industrial branches such that only one union operates within each enterprise. Outside the DGB lie several smaller unions: The *Deutscher Beamtenbund* (DBB) or civil servants union with 786,948 (206,753) members, the *Deutsche Angestellten-Gewerkschaft* (DAG) or union of salaried staff with 496,832 (219,038) members and the *Christlicher Gewerkschaftsbund Deutschlands* (CGD, Christian Trade Union Federation of Germany) with 306,847 (76,216) members.

Strikes are not legal unless called by a union with the backing of 75% of members. Certain public service employees are contractually not permitted to strike. 41,880 working days were lost through strikes in 1988.

Commerce. Imports and exports in DM 1m.:

Imports				*Exports*			
1985	*1986*	*1987*	*1988*	*1985*	*1986*	*1987*	*1988*
463,811	413,744	409,641	439,768	537,164	526,363	527,377	567,750

Distribution of imports and exports by categories of countries in 1988 (in DM 1m.): EEC, 227,449, 308,232; developing countries, 54,760, 53,987; Communist countries, 20,465, 24,724 (USSR, 6,878, 9,424; China, 4,344, 4,919). Most important trading partners in 1988 (trade figures in DM 1m.) Imports: France, 53,045; Netherlands, 45,487; Italy, 40,221; Belgium with Luxembourg, 31,162; UK, 30,461; USA, 29,119; Japan, 28,388; Switzerland, 19,653; Austria, 18,917. Exports: France, 71,272; UK, 52,873; Italy, 51,653; Netherlands, 49,193; USA, 45,679; Belgium with Luxembourg, 42,071; Switzerland, 34,443; Austria, 31,871.

Distribution by commodities in 1988 (in DM 1m.) Imports and exports: Live animals, 714,736; foodstuffs, 44,735, 13,017; luxury foods and tobacco, 7,808, 4,552; raw materials, 27,820, 6,734; semi-finished products, 52,912, 32,226; manufactures, 298,146, 497,887.

Trade with the German Democratic Republic is not categorized as 'foreign'. In 1988 goods supplied were worth DM 7·23m. and goods received DM 6·79m.

Total trade between the Federal Republic of Germany and UK (British Department of Trade returns, in £1,000 sterling):

	1985	*1986*	*1987*	*1988*	*1989*
Imports to UK	12,601,387	14,139,097	15,783,904	17,667,097	20,005,276
Exports and re-exports from UK	8,947,055	8,542,196	9,404,257	9,521,851	11,110,623

Tourism. In 1988 there were 47,846 places of accommodation with 1·8m. beds (including 10,082 hotels with 559,786 beds). In the summer of 1988 151·28m. overnight stays (19·33 by foreigners) were registered.

COMMUNICATIONS

Roads. In 1988 the total length of classified roads was 173,590 km, including 8,618 km of motorway *(Autobahn)*, 35,279 km of federal highways, 63,393 km first-class and 70,383 km second-class country roads. Motor vehicles licensed on 1 July 1988: 33,764,200 (including 28,878,200 passenger cars, 1,372,100 trucks and 70,200 buses. In 1988 365m. tonnes of freight (106·23m. tonne-kilometres) and 5,442m. passengers were transported by long-distance road traffic.

Road casualties in 1988 totalled 448,223 injured and 8,213 killed.

Railways. Length of Federal Railway in 1988 was 27,278 km (1,435 mm gauge) of which 11,669 km was electrified. In 1988 it carried 1,009m. passengers and 271m. tonnes of freight. There were also 2,904 km of privately-owned and other minor railways.

Aviation. Deutsche Lufthansa was set up in 1953 with a capital of DM 900m. The Federal Republic owns 74·3%, Land North Rhine-Westphalia 2·2%, the Federal Railways, 0·9%, Federal Post 1·8%, Kreditanstalt für Wiederaufbau 3% and private industry 17·8%.

Lufthansa operate internal, European, African, North and South Atlantic, Near and Far East routes. British Airways and PanAm operate flights to West Berlin. Lufthansa opened a service to Leipzig (GDR) in 1989.

In 1988 civil aviation had 214 aircraft over 20 tonnes. There were 33·3m. passenger arrivals and 33·49m. departures. 53m. passengers were carried (15,701 person-kilometres), including 20·34m. to destinations abroad. Frankfurt am Main is the busiest airport, followed by Düsseldorf, Munich, Hamburg and West Berlin.

Shipping. On 31 Dec. 1987 the mercantile marine comprised 1,548 ocean-going vessels of 4,072,000 GRT.

The inland-waterways fleet on 31 Dec. 1987 included 2,101 motor freight vessels totalling 1·98m. tonnes and 441 tankers of 576,286 tonnes. The length of the navigable rivers and canals in use was 4,452 km.

Sea-going ships in 1988 carried 134·3m. tonnes of cargo. Inland waterways carried 220m. tonnes in 1987.

Pipeline. In 1988 there were 1,715 km of pipeline. 60·3m. tonnes of oil were transported.

Post and Broadcasting. Telecommunications were deregulated in 1989. In 1988 there were 17,533 post offices, 40·29m. telephones and 84,125 fax transmitters.

The post office savings banks had, in 1988, 22,001,000 depositors with DM 40,556m. to their credit.

In 1988 postal revenues amounted to DM 55,692m. and expenditure to DM 53,485m.

There are 9 regional broadcasting stations. The *Arbeitsgemeinschaft der öffentlich-rechtlichen Rundfunkanstalten der Bundesrepublik Deutschland* (ARD) organizes co-operation between them and also broadcasts a federal-wide TV programme of its own. Number of wireless licences, (1988) 26·89m.; of television licences, 23·74m.

Cinemas and Theatres. In 1987 there were 3,252 cinemas and 280 theatres with seating capacities of 631,588 and (in 1986) 148,049 respectively. 65 feature films were made in 1987.

Newspapers and Books. In 1987, 356 newspapers and 6,908 periodicals were published with respective circulations of 25·26m. and 275·49m. 65,680 book titles were published in 1987. In 1987 there were 1,029 learned libraries, and 11,386 public libraries, the latter with 6·72m. users.

JUSTICE, RELIGION, EDUCATION AND WELFARE

Justice. Justice is administered by the federal courts and by the courts of the Länder. In criminal procedures, civil cases and procedures of non-contentious jurisdiction the courts on the Land level are the local courts *(Amtsgerichte)*, the regional courts *(Landgerichte)* and the courts of appeal *(Oberlandesgerichte)*. Constitutional federal disputes are dealt with by the Federal Constitutional Court *(Bundesverfassungsgericht)* elected by the Federal Assembly and Federal Council. The Länder also have constitutional courts. In labour law disputes the courts of the first and second instance are the labour courts and the Land labour courts and in the third instance, the Federal Labour Court *(Bundesarbeitsgericht)*. Disputes about public law in matters of social security, unemployment insurance, maintenance of war victims and similar cases are dealt with in the first and second instances by the social courts and the Land social courts and in the third instance by the Federal Social Court *(Bundessozialgericht)*. In most tax matters the finance courts of the Länder are competent and in the second instance, the Federal Finance Court *(Bundesfinanzhof)*. Other controversies of public law in non-constitutional matters are decided in the first and second instance by the administrative and the higher administrative courts *(Observerwaltungsgerichte)* of the Länder, and in the third instance by the Federal Administrative Court *(Bundesverwaltungsgericht)*.

For the inquiry into maritime accidents the admiralty courts *(Seeämter)* are competent on the Land level and in the second instance the Federal Admiralty Court *(Bundesoberseeamt)* in Hamburg.

The death sentence has been abolished.

Religion. At the 1987 census there were 26,232,000 (13,822,000 female) Roman Catholics, 25,412,600 Protestants (13,784,000 female) and 1,651,000 Moslems (722,700 females).

The Evangelical (Protestant) Church consists of 18 member-churches in the Federal Republic and West Berlin (7 Lutheran Churches, 8 United-Lutheran-Reformed, 2 Reformed Churches and 1 Confederation of United member Churches: 'Church of the Union'). Its organs are the Synod, the Church Conference and the Council under the chairmanship of Bishop Dr Eduard Lohse (Hanover). There are also some 12 Evangelical Free Churches. In 1987 there were 10,714 parishes, 18,040 priests and 25·4m. members.

In 1987 there were 26·31m. Catholics. There are 5 Catholic archbishoprics (Bamberg, Cologne, Freiburg, Munich and Freising, Paderborn) and 17 bishoprics. Chairman of the German Bishops' Conference is Cardinal Joseph Höffner, Archbishop of Cologne. A concordat between Germany and the Holy See dates from 10 Sept. 1933.

There were 27,552 Jews in 1988 with 53 synagogues and 14 rabbis.

Taschenbuch der evangelischen Kirche in Deutschland. Frankfurt, 1980
Kirchliches Handbuch. Amtliches statistisches Jahrbuch der Katholischen Kirche Deutschlands
Alt-Katholisches Jahrbuch. Bonn, 1978

Education. Education is compulsory for children aged 6 to 15. After the first 4 (or 6) years at primary school *(Grundschulen)* children attend post-primary *(Hauptschulen)*, secondary modern *(Realschulen)*, grammar *(Gymnasien)*, or comprehensive schools *(Integrierte Gesamtschulen)*. Secondary modern school comprises 6, grammar school 9, years. Entry to higher education is by the final Grammar School Certificate (Abitur-Higher School Certificate). There are special schools *(Sonderschulen)* for handicapped or maladjusted children.

In 1987–88 there were 3,176 kindergartens with 65,921 pupils and 4,539 teachers, 13,665 primary schools with 2,304,017 pupils and 7,407 post-primary schools with 1,356,724 pupils. There were 230,470 teachers at primary and post-primary schools. There were also 2,816 special schools with 254,163 pupils and 41,986 teachers, 2,593 secondary modern schools with 915,253 pupils and 60,024 teachers; 2,455 grammar schools with 1,596,120 pupils and 123,488 teachers; 365 comprehensive schools with 244,222 pupils and 29,188 teachers.

Vocational education is provided in part-time, full-time and advanced vocational schools (*Berufs-*, *Berufsaufbau-*, *Berufsfach-* and *Fachschulen*, including *Fachschulen für Technik* and *Schulen des Gesundheitswesens*). Occupation-related, part-time vocational training of 6 to 12 hours per week is compulsory for all (including unemployed) up to the age of 18 years or until the completion of the practical vocational training. Full-time vocational schools comprise courses of at least one year. They prepare for commercial and domestic occupations as well as specialized occupations in the field of handicrafts. Advanced full-time vocational schools are attended by pupils over 18. Courses vary from 6 months to 3 or more years.

In 1987–88 there were 7,546 full- and part-time vocational schools with 2,508,515 pupils (1,132,127 female) and 90,343 teachers.

Higher Education. In 1988–89 there were 61 institutes of university status: Universities proper at Augsburg, Bamberg, Bayreuth, Berlin (West), Bielefeld, Bochum, Bonn, Bremen, Cologne, Dortmund, Düsseldorf, Erlangen-Nuremberg, Frankfurt am Main, Freiburg im Breisgau, Giessen, Göttingen, Hamburg, Hanover, Heidelberg, Hohenheim, Kaiserslautern, Karlsruhe, Kiel, Konstanz, Mainz, Mannheim, Marburg, Munich, Münster, Oldenburg, Osnabrück, Passau, Regensburg, Saarbrücken, Stuttgart, Trier, Tübingen, Ulm and Würzburg; technical universities at Berlin (West), Braunschweig, Clausthal, Hamburg-Harburg and Munich; military universities at Hamburg and Munich; a medical university at Lübeck; a Catholic university at Eichstatt; a private Nordic university at Flensburg; and advanced schools *(Hochschulen)* at Aachen, Cologne (sport), Darmstadt (technical), Hamburg (economics and politics), Hanover (medical, veterinary), Hildesheim, Koblenz (private business), Lüneberg, Rhineland-Palatinate (education), Speyer (administration) and Witten-Herdecke (private). There were 182 other institutes of higher education.

Academic staff in 1987/88: Universities including teacher training and theological colleges, 109,093; other institutes, 36,472.

Students in 1988–89: Universities, 989,805 (409,304 women); other institutes, 480,933.

Health. In 1988 there were 171,487 doctors (including 82,580 in hospitals) and 38,826 dentists. There were 3,071 hospitals (including 954 private) with 673,687 beds.

Social Welfare. *Social Health Insurance* (introduced in 1883). Wage-earners and apprentices, salaried employees with an income below a certain limit and social-insurance pensioners are compulsorily insured. Voluntary insurance is also possible.

Benefits: Medical treatment, medicines, hospital and nursing care, maternity benefits, death benefits for the insured and their families, sickness payments and out-patients' allowances.

36·72m. persons were insured in 1987 (21·56m. compulsorily) and 10·7m. persons (including 6·7m. women) were drawing pensions. Number of cases of incapacity for work totalled 25·84m., and 404·89m. working days were lost. Total disbursements DM 124,997m.

Accident Insurance (introduced in 1884). Those insured are all persons in employment or service, apprentices and the majority of the self-employed and the unpaid family workers.

Benefits in the case of industrial injuries and occupational diseases: Medical treatment and nursing care, sickness payments, pensions and other payments in cash and in kind, surviving dependants' pensions.

Number of insured in 1987, 38·85m.; number of current pensions, 946,698; total disbursements, DM 13,761m.

Workers' and Employees' Old-Age Insurance Scheme (introduced in 1889). All wage-earners and salaried employees, the members of certain liberal professions and—subject to certain conditions—self-employed craftsmen are compulsorily insured. The insured may voluntarily continue to insure when no longer liable to do so or increase the insurance.

Benefits: Measures designed to maintain, improve and restore the earning capacity; pensions paid to persons incapable of work, old age and surviving dependants' pensions.

Number of insured in 1988, 32·58m. (15·68m. women); number of current pensions, 1988: 13·88m.; pensions to widows and widowers, 3·95m. Total disbursements in 1987, DM 196,307m.

There are also special retirement and unemployment pension schemes for miners and farmers, assistance for war victims and compensation payments to members of German minorities in East European countries expelled after the Second World War and persons who suffered damage because of the war or in connexion with the currency reform.

Family Allowances. The monthly allowance for the first child is DM 50, for the second, DM 70-100 (varying according to income), for the third DM 140-220 and the fourth DM 140-240. DM 10,072m. were dispersed to 6·16m. recipients in 1988.

Unemployment Allowances. In 1988 947,000 persons (443,000 women) were receiving unemployment benefit and 528,000 (152,000 women) earnings-related benefit. Total expenditure on these and similar benefits (e.g. short-working supplement, job creation schemes) was DM 40,844m. in 1988.

Accommodation Allowances averaging DM 145 a month were paid in 1987 to 1·9m. persons.

Public Welfare (introduced in 1962). In 1987 DM 25·2m. were distributed to 3·14m. recipients (1·76m. women).

Public Youth Welfare. For supervision of foster children, official guardianship, assistance with adoptions and affiliations, social assistance in juvenile courts, educational assistance and correctional education under a court order. Total expenditure in 1987, DM 8,760m.

Arbeits- und Sozialstatistik. Bundesminister für Arbeit und Sozialordnung, Bonn (from 1950)
Fachserie 13 Sozialleistungen. Statistisches Bundesamt (from 1951)
Fachserie 12 Gesundheitswesen. Statistisches Bundesamt (from 1946)

DIPLOMATIC REPRESENTATIVES

Of the Federal Republic of Germany in Great Britain (23 Belgrave Sq., London, SW1X 8PZ)
Ambassador: Baron Hermann von Richthofen (accredited 16 Dec. 1988).

Of Great Britain in the Federal Republic of Germany (Friedrich-Ebert-Allee 77, 5300 Bonn 1)
Ambassador: Sir Christopher Mallaby, KCMG.

Of the Federal Republic of Germany in the USA (4645 Reservoir Rd, NW, Washington, D.C., 20007)
Ambassador: Juergen Ruhfus.

Of the USA in the Federal Republic of Germany (Deichmanns Ave., 5300, Bonn)
Ambassador: Gen. Vernon A. Walters.

Of the Federal Republic of Germany to the United Nations
Ambassador: Dr Otto Bräutigam.

Further Reading

Statistical Information: The central statistical agency is the Statistisches Bundesamt, 62 Wiesbaden 1, Gustav Stresemann Ring 11. *President:* Egon Hölder. Its publications include:

Statistisches Jahrbuch für die Bundesrepublik Deutschland; Wirtschaft und Statistik (monthly, from 1949); *Das Arbeitsgebiet der Bundesstatistik* (latest issue 1988; Abridged English version: *Survey of German Federal Statistics*).

Ardagh, J., *Germany and the Germans.* London, 1987
Bark, D. L. and Gress, D. R., *A History of West Germany, 1945-1988.* 2 vols. Oxford, 1989
Berghahn, V. R., *Modern Germany: Society, Economy and Politics in the Twentieth Century.* CUP, 1982

Beyme, K. von, *The Political System of the Federal Republic of Germany*. New York, 1983
Die Bundesrepublik Deutschland: Staatshandbuch. Cologne, annual
Burdick, C., *et al.* (eds.) *Contemporary Germany: Politics and Culture*, Boulder, 1984
Carr, J., *Helmut Schmidt, Helmsman of Germany*. London, 1985
Childs, D., *Germany since 1918*. 2nd ed. New York, 1980
Conradt, D. P., *The German Polity*. 2nd ed. New York, 1982
Craig, G. A., *Germany, 1866–1945*. OUP, 1981—*The Germans*. Harmondsworth, 1984
Detwiler, D. S. and Detwiler, I. E., *West Germany*. [Bibliography] Oxford and Santa Barbara, 1988
Dittmers, M., *The Green Party in West Germany*. 2nd ed. Buckingham, 1988
Edinger, L. J., *West German Politics*. New York, 1986
Eley, G., *From Unification to Nazism: Reinterpreting the German Past*. London, 1986
Friese, F-J., *Investment and Business Establishments in the Federal Republic of Germany: A Guide for the Foreign Investor*. Frankfurt-am-Main, 1988
Hardach, K., *The Political Economy of Germany in the Twentieth Century*. California Univ. Press, 1980
Hubatsch, W., *Studies in Medieval and Modern German History*. Basingstoke, 1985
Hucko, E. M. (ed.) *The Democratic Tradition* [Texts of German Constitutions]. Leamington Spa, 1987
Johnson, N., *State and Government in the Federal Republic of Germany: the Executive at Work*. 2nd ed. Oxford, 1983
Jonas, M., *The United States and Germany: A Diplomatic History*. Cornell Univ. Press, 1984
Koch, H. W., *A Constitutional History of Germany in the Nineteenth and Twentieth Centuries*. London, 1984
Kohl, W. L. and Basevi, G., *West Germany: A European and Global Power*. London, 1982
Kolinsky, E., *Parties, Opposition and Society in West Germany*. London, 1984
König, K., *et al.* (eds.) *Public Administration in the Federal Republic of Germany*. Boston, 1983
Laqueur, W., *Germany Today: a Personal Report*. London, 1985
Leaman, J., *The Political Economy of West Germany, 1945–1985*. Basingstoke, 1987
Markovits, A. S. (ed.) *The Political Economy of West Germany: Modell Deutschland*. New York, 1982
Marsh, D., *The Germans: Rich, Bothered and Divided*. London, 1989
Marshall, B., *The Origins of Post-War German Politics*. London, 1988
Moreton, E. (ed.) *Germany between East and West*. Cambridge Univ. Press, 1987
Pasley, M. (ed.) *Germany: a Companion to German Studies*. 2nd ed. London, 1982
Schweitzer, D.-C., (ed.) *Politics and Government in the Federal Republic of Germany: Basic Documents*. Leamington Spa, 1984
Smith, E. O., *The West German Economy*. London, 1983
Smith, G., *Democracy in Western Germany*. 3rd ed. Aldershot, 1986
Wallach, P. and Romoser, G. K. (eds.) *West German Politics in the Mid-Eighties: Crisis and Continuity*. New York, 1985
Weizsäcker, R. von, *A Voice from Germany: Speeches*. London, 1986
Who's Who in Germany, 1982–1983. Munich, 1983
Wild, T. (ed) *Urban and Rural Change in West Germany*. London, 1983

National Libraries: Deutsche Bibliothek, Zeppelinallee 4–8; Frankfurt-am-Main. *Director:* K.-D. Lehmann; (Berliner) Staatsbibliothek Preussischer Kulturbesitz, Potsdamer Str., Postfach 1407 D-1000 Berlin 30. *Director:* Dr. Richard Landwehrmeyer.

THE LÄNDER

BADEN–WÜRTTEMBERG

AREA AND POPULATION. Baden-Württemberg comprises 35,751 sq. km, with a population (at 1 Jan. 1989) of 9,432,709 (4,568,150 males, 4,864,559 females).

The Land is administratively divided into 4 areas, 9 urban and 35 rural districts, and numbers 1,111 communes. The capital is Stuttgart.

Vital statistics for calendar years:

	Live births	*Marriages*	*Divorces*	*Deaths*
1986	101,616	55,705	15,294	93,003
1987	103,590	56,780	16,781	91,587
1988	110,627	58,939	17,204	92,418

CONSTITUTION. The Land Baden-Württemberg is a merger of the 3 Länder, Baden, Württemberg-Baden and Württemberg-Hohenzollern, which were formed in 1945. The merger was approved by a plebiscite held on 9 Dec. 1951, when 70% of the population voted in its favour.

The Diet, elected on 20 March 1988, consists of 66 Christian Democrats, 42 Social Democrats, 7 Free Democrats, 10 Ecologists.

The Government is formed by Christian Democrats, with Lothar Späth (CDU) as Prime Minister.

AGRICULTURE. Area and yield of the most important crops:

	Area (in 1,000 hectares)			*Yield (in 1,000 tonnes)*		
	1986	*1987*	*1988*	*1986*	*1987*	*1988*
Rye	17·0	16·2	16·3	75·6	64·0	73·9
Wheat	216·3	220·1	214·0	1,166·0	1,071·0	1,326·8
Barley	197·4	190·2	202·7	810·7	809·8	1,025·4
Oats	77·7	74·2	77·6	329·4	332·9	406·5
Potatoes	14·9	14·0	12·4	807·1	304·6	399·6
Sugar-beet	23·3	22·4	22·6	1,293·5	1,219·7	1,215·1

Livestock (3 Dec. 1988): Cattle, 1,656,606 (including 612,129 milch cows); horses, 52,904; pigs, 2,251,479; sheep, 239,892; poultry, 5,925,231.

INDUSTRY. In 1988 9,255 establishments (with 20 and more employees) employed 1,433,567 persons; of these, 260,484 were employed in machine construction (excluding office machines, data processing equipment and facilities); 68,876 in textile industry; 251,174 in electrical engineering; 227,989 in car building.

LABOUR. The economically active persons totalled 4,414,900 at the 1%-EC-sample survey of April 1988. Of the total 516,200 were self-employed (including family workers), 3,898,700 employees; 184,600 were engaged in agriculture and forestry; 2,112,900 in power supply, mining, manufacturing and building, 655,200 in commerce and transport, 1,462,200 in other industries and services.

ROADS. On 1 Jan. 1989 there were 27,960 km of 'classified' roads, including 978 km of autobahn, 4,986 km of federal roads, 10,136 km of first-class and 11,860 km of second-class highways. Motor vehicles, at 1 Jan. 1989, numbered 5,462,694, including, 4,669,543 passenger cars, 8,813 buses, 202,239 lorries, 314,411 tractors and 204,660 motor cycles.

JUSTICE. There are a constitutional court *(Staatsgerichtshof)*, 2 courts of appeal, 17 regional courts, 108 local courts, a Land labour court, 9 labour courts, a Land social court, 8 social courts, a finance court, a higher administrative court *(Verwaltungsgerichtshof)*, 4 administrative courts.

RELIGION. On 25 May 1987, 40·7% of the population were Protestants and 45·3% Roman Catholics.

EDUCATION. In 1988–89 there were 3,644 primary schools *(Grund* and *Hauptschule)* with 31,729 teachers and 548,449 pupils; 574 special schools with 8,174 teachers and 42,483 pupils; 443 intermediate schools with 11,365 teachers and 173,291 pupils; 420 high schools with 18,787 teachers and 233,802 pupils; 28 *Freie Waldorf* schools with 1,183 teachers and 15,532 pupils. Other schools together had 776 teachers and 10,552 pupils; there were also 40 *Fachhochschulen* (colleges of engineering and others) with 47,414 students.

In the winter term 1988–89 there were 9 universities (Freiburg, 22,965 students; Heidelberg, 26,916; Konstanz, 7,732; Tübingen, 23,682; Karlsruhe, 19,619; Stuttgart, 19,892; Hohenheim, 5,569; Mannheim, 12,361; Ulm, 5,088); 6 teacher-training colleges with 7,893 students; 5 colleges of music with 2,872 students and 2 colleges of fine arts with 1,021 students.

Statistical Information: Statistisches Landesamt Baden-Württemberg (P.O.B. 10 60 33, D7000 Stuttgart 10) (*President:* Prof. Dr. Max Wingen), publishes: *'Baden-Württemberg in Wort und Zahl'* (monthly); *Jahrbücher für Statistik und Landeskunde von Baden-Württemberg; Statistik von Baden-Württemberg* (series); *Statistisch-prognostischer Bericht* (latest issue 1988–89); *Statistisches Taschenbuch* (latest issue 1988–89).

State Library: Württembergische Landesbibliothek, Konrad-Adenauer-Str. 8, 7000 Stuttgart 1. *Director:* Dr Hans-Peter Geh. Badische Landesbibliothek Karlsruhe, Lamm-Str. 16, 7500 Karlsruhe 1. *Director:* Dr Römer.

BAVARIA

Bayern

AREA AND POPULATION. Bavaria has an area of 70,553 sq. km. The capital is Munich. There are 7 areas, 96 urban and rural districts and 2,051 communes. The population (31 Dec. 1988) numbered 11,049,263 (5,322,555 males, 5,726,708 females).

Vital statistics for calendar years:

	Live births	*Marriages*	*Divorces*	*Deaths*
1986	118,439	67,061	18,352	120,489
1987	119,623	70,035	19,846	119,662
1988	126,409	71,742	19,496	118,450

CONSTITUTION. The Constituent Assembly, elected on 30 June 1946, passed a constitution on the lines of the democratic constitution of 1919, but with greater emphasis on state rights; this was agreed upon by the Christian Social Union and the Social Democrats.

The elections for the Diet, held on 12 Oct. 1986, had the following results: 128 Christian Social Union, 61 Social Democrats, 15 Green Party. The cabinet of the Christian Social Union is headed by Minister President Max Streibl (CSU).

AGRICULTURE. Area and yield of the most important products:

	Area (in 1,000 hectares)			*Yield (in 1,000 tonnes)*		
	1987	*1988*	*1989* [1]	*1987*	*1988*	*1989* [1]
Wheat	501·0	511·6	501·3	2,686·1	3,865·0	3,298·6
Rye	53·5	51·5	57·7	189·1	225·4	267·0
Barley	500·3	516·9	510·6	2,028·2	2,707·9	2,901·3
Oats	114·0	114·0	105·6	468·4	505·4	440·4
Potatoes	68·1	65·2	62·1	1,849·1	2,587·3	2,228·1
Sugar-beet	77·0	77·6	79·4	4,216·2	4,256·6	...

[1] Preliminary figures.

Livestock (2 Dec. 1988): 4,939,800 cattle (including 1,890,200 milch cows); 64,900 horses; 340,800 sheep; 3,781,900 pigs; 12,089,600 poultry.

INDUSTRY. In 1988, 9,290 establishments (with 20 or more employees) employed 1,355,802 persons; of these, 254,386 were employed in electrical engineering; 184,495 in mechanical engineering; 113,473 in clothing and textile industries.

LABOUR. The economically active persons totalled 5,344,800 at the 1% sample survey of the microcensus of April 1988. Of the total, 528,600 were self-employed, 255,500 unpaid family workers, 4,560,700 employees; 2,239,400 in power supply, mining, manufacturing and building; 880,900 in commerce and transport; 1,831,100 in other industries and services.

ROADS. There were, on 1 Jan. 1989, 41,154 km of 'classified' roads, including 2,015 km of autobahn, 7,126 km of federal roads, 13,800 km of first-class and 18,213 km of second-class highways. Number of motor vehicles, at 1 July 1989, was 6,725,647, including 5,489,445 passenger cars, 246,188 lorries, 13,441 buses, 586,006 tractors, 312,826 motor cycles.

JUSTICE. There are a constitutional court *(Verfassungsgerichtshof)*, a supreme Land court *(Oberstes Landesgericht)*, 3 courts of appeal, 22 regional courts, 72 local courts, 2 Land labour courts, 11 labour courts, a Land social court, 7 social courts, 2 finance courts, a higher administrative court *(Verwaltungsgerichtshof)*, 6 administrative courts.

RELIGION. At the census of 25 May 1987 there were 67·2% Roman Catholics and 23·9% Protestants.

EDUCATION. In 1988–89 there were 2,806 primary schools with 44,015 teachers and 716,178 pupils; 382 special schools with 6,294 teachers and 39,800 pupils; 336 intermediate schools with 8,787 teachers and 121,720 pupils; 395 high schools with 20,227 teachers and 269,102 pupils; 259 part-time vocational schools with 8,042 teachers and 327,852 pupils, including 51 special part-time vocational schools with 573 teachers and 8,162 pupils; 557 full-time vocational schools with 3,851 teachers and 49,874 pupils including 228 schools for public health occupations with 1,052 teachers and 15,498 pupils; 300 advanced full-time vocational schools with 2,294 teachers and 26,768 pupils; 84 vocational high schools *(Berufsoberschulen, Fachoberschulen)* with 1,913 teachers and 29,647 pupils.

In the winter term 1988–89 there were 11 universities with 175,971 students (Augsburg, 10,012; Bamberg, 6,036; Bayreuth, 6,437; Eichstätt, 2,113; Erlangen–Nürnberg, 27,066; München, 63,471; Passau, 6,160; Regensburg, 12,879; Würzburg, 17,803; the Technical University of München, 22,787; München University of the Federal Armed Forces (Universität der Bundeswehr), 2,162); the college of philosophy, München, 347 and 2 philosophical-theological colleges with together 442 students (Benediktbeuern, 132; Neuendettelsau, 310). There were also 2 colleges of music, 2 colleges of fine arts and 1 college of television and film, with together 2,408 students; 13 vocational colleges *(Fachhochschulen)* with 56,032 students including one for the civil service *(Bayerische Beamtenfachhochschule)* with 4,970 students.

Statistical Information: Bayerisches Landesamt für Statistik und Datenverarbeitung, 51 Neuhauser Str. 8000 Munich, was founded in 1833. *President:* Dr Hans Helmut Schiedermaier. It publishes: *Statistisches Jahrbuch für Bayern.* 1894 ff.—*Bayern in Zahlen.* Monthly (from Jan. 1947).—*Zeitschrift des Bayerischen Statistischen Landesamts.* July 1869–1943; 1948 ff.—*Beiträge zur Statistik Bayerns.* 1850 ff.—*Statistische Berichte.* 1951 ff.—*Schaubilderhefte.* 1951 ff.—*Kreisdaten.* 1972 ff.—*Gemeindedaten.* 1973 ff.

Nawiasky, H. and Luesser, C., *Die Verfassung des Freistaates Bayern vom 2. Dez. 1946.* Munich, 1948; supplement, by H. Nawiasky and H. Lechner, Munich, 1953

State Library: Bayerische Staatsbibliothek, Munich 22. *Director:* Dr Franz G. Kaltwasser.

BERLIN

GOVERNMENT. Greater Berlin was under quadripartite Allied government (Kommandatura) until 1 July 1948, when the Soviet element withdrew. On 30 Nov. 1948, a separate Municipal Government was set up in the Soviet Sector (*see* p. 525).

AREA. The total area of Berlin is 883 sq. km, of which Western Berlin covers 480 sq. km and the Soviet Sector 403 sq. km. The *British Sector* includes the administrative districts of Tiergarten, Charlottenburg, Wilmersdorf and Spandau; the *American Sector* those of Kreuzberg, Neukölln, Tempelhof, Schöneberg, Zehlendorf and Steglitz; the *French Sector* covers the administrative districts of Wedding and Reinickendorf, and the *Soviet Sector*, those of Mitte, Friedrichshain, Prenzlauer Berg, Pankow, Weissensee, Lichtenberg, Treptow and Köpenick. The British, American and French sectors form an administrative unit, called Berlin (West).

In 1961 the East German Government tried to stop the outflow of migrants, by erecting a heavily fortified barrier, the 'Berlin Wall', along the border. A minefield which accompanied it was removed in 1985.

BERLIN (WEST)

POPULATION. Population, 31 Dec. 1988, 2,068,313 (969,599 males, 1,098,714 females). In 1987, 1,079,000 were Protestants; 285,000 Roman Catholics; 50,000 Moslems and 6,000 Jews.

Vital statistics for calendar years:

	Live births	*Marriages*	*Divorces*	*Deaths*
1986	18,688	11,941	6,060	31,727
1987	19,554	11,961	6,230	30,719
1988	20,980	12,385	5,995	30,021

CONSTITUTION AND GOVERNMENT. According to the constitution of 1 Sept. 1950, Berlin is simultaneously a Land of the Federal Republic (though not yet formally incorporated) and a city. It is governed by a House of Representatives (at least 200 members); the executive power is vested in a Senate, consisting of the Governing Mayor, the Mayor and not more than 16 senators.

In the municipal elections, held on 29 Jan. 1989, the Christian Democrats obtained 48 seats; the Social Democrats, 47; the Alternative List, 15; the Republicans, 9.

Governing Mayor: Walter Homper (Social Democrat).

ECONOMY

Currency. The legal tender of Berlin (West) is the German Mark (DM).

Banking. On 20 March 1949 when the DM (West) became the only legal tender of the Western Sectors, the Zentralbank of Berlin was established. Its functions were similar to those of the Zentralbanks of the Länder of the Federal Republic. The Berlin Central Bank was merged with the Bank deutscher Länder as from 1 Aug. 1957, when the latter became the Deutsche Bundesbank. The legal tender for the Western Sectors of Berlin is being issued by the Deutsche Bundesbank (formerly Bank deutscher Länder).

AGRICULTURE. Agricultural area (April 1988), 1,318 hectares, including 948 hectares arable land and 93 hectares gardens, orchards, nurseries.

Livestock (Dec. 1988): Cattle, 657; pigs, 3,027; horses, 3,461; sheep, 1,241.

INDUSTRY. In 1988 (monthly averages), 1,045 establishments (with 20 or more employees) employed 161,977 persons; of these, 55,767 were employed in electrical engineering, 15,362 in machine construction, 12,849 in the manufacture of chemicals, 3,905 in steel construction and 3,632 in textiles.

LABOUR. The economically active persons totalled 969,900 at the 1%-sample survey of the microcensus of April 1988. Of the total, 83,700 were self-employed including unpaid family workers, 886,200 employees; 9,600 were engaged in agriculture and forestry; 287,400 in power supply, manufacturing and building; 156,400 in commerce and transport; 432,800 in other industries and services.

ROADS. There were, on 1 Jan. 1988, 145·6 km of 'classified' roads, including 44·3 km of autobahn and 101·3 km of federal roads. On 1 July 1988, 798,966 motor vehicles were registered, including 631,358 passenger cars, 44,306 lorries, 37,563 motor cycles, and 2,138 buses.

JUSTICE. There are a court of appeal *(Kammergericht)*, a regional court, 7 local courts, a Land Labour court, a labour court, a Land social court, a social court, a higher administrative court, an administrative court and a finance court.

EDUCATION. In 1988–89 (preliminary figures) there were 449 schools providing general education (excluding special schools) with 181,294 pupils; 56 special schools with 6,435 pupils. There were a further 175 vocational schools with 57,400 pupils.

In the winter term 1988–89 there was 1 university (58,463 students); 1 technical university (30,612); 1 theological (evangelical) college (537); 1 college of fine arts with 4,515 students; 1 vocational college (for economics) (1,628); 2 colleges for social work (1,288); 1 technical college (5,966), 1 college of the Federal postal administration (571) and 2 colleges for public administration (2,629).

Statistical Information: The Statistisches Landesamt Berlin was founded in 1862 (Fehrbelliner Platz 1, 1000 Berlin 31). *Director:* Prof. Günther Appel. It publishes: *Statistisches Jahrbuch* (from 1867): *Berliner Statistik* (monthly, from 1947).—*100 Jahre Berliner Statistik* (1962).

Childs, D. and Johnson, J., *West Berlin: Politics and Society.* London, 1981
Hillenbrand, M. J., *The Future of Berlin.* Monclair, 1981

State Library: Amerika-Gedenkbibliothek-Berliner Zentralbibliothek-, Blücherplatz 1, D1000 Berlin 61. *Director:* Dr Klaus Bock.

BREMEN

Freie Hansestadt Bremen

AREA AND POPULATION. The area of the Land, consisting of the towns and ports of Bremen and Bremerhaven, is 404 sq. km. Population, 31 Dec. 1988, 661,845 (313,750 males, 348,095 females).

Vital statistics for calendar years:

	Live births	*Marriages*	*Divorces*	*Deaths*
1986	5,745	3,904	1,680	8,707
1987	5,773	3,951	2,210	8,489
1988	6,420	4,230	2,037	8,712

CONSTITUTION. Political power is vested in the House of Burgesses *(Bürgerschaft)* which appoints the executive, called the Senate.

The elections of 13 Sept. 1987 had the following result: 54 Social Democratic Party, 25 Christian Democrats, 10 Free Democratic Party, 10 Die Grünen, 1 Deutsche Volksunion. The Senate is only formed by Social Democrats; its president is Klaus Wedemeier (Social Democrat).

AGRICULTURE. Agricultural area comprised (1987), 10,048 hectares: yield of grain crops (1987), 6,059 tonnes; potatoes, 155 tonnes.

Livestock (2 Dec. 1988): 15,588 cattle (including 4,464 milch cows); 3,859 pigs; 540 sheep; 1,045 horses; 22,970 poultry.

INDUSTRY. In 1988, 339 establishments (20 and more employees) employed 76,246 persons; of these, 7,896 were employed in shipbuilding (except naval engineering); 7,204 in machine construction; 9,236 in electrical engineering; 1,985 in coffee and tea processing.

LABOUR. The economically active persons totalled 271,000 at the census of May 1987. Of the total, 18,000 were self-employed, 253,000 employees; 89,000 in power supply, mining, manufacturing and building, 67,000 in commerce and transport, 113,000 in other industries and services, 2,000 in agriculture and fishing.

ROADS. On 1 Jan. 1988 there were 108 km of 'classified' roads, including 46 km of autobahn, 62 km of federal roads. Registered motor vehicles on 1 July 1988 numbered 296,676, including 267,243 passenger cars, 13,338 trucks, 2,487 tractors, 596 buses and 9,224 motor cycles.

SHIPPING. Vessels entered in 1988, 9,817 of 42,559,000 net tons; cleared, 9,685 of 42,591,000 net tons. Sea traffic, 1988, incoming 18,796,000 tonnes; outgoing, 12,314,000 tonnes.

JUSTICE. There are a constitutional court *(Staatsgerichtshof)*, a court of appeal, a regional court, 3 local courts, a Land labour court, 2 labour courts, a Land social court, a social court, a finance court, a higher administrative court, an administrative court.

RELIGION. On 25 May 1987 (census) there were 61% Protestants and 10% Roman Catholics.

EDUCATION. In 1988 there were 311 new system schools with 5,235 teachers and 63,910 pupils; 26 special schools with 557 teachers and 2,734 pupils; 24 part-time vocational schools with 28,384 pupils; 33 full-time vocational schools with 6,202 pupils; 7 advanced vocational schools (including institutions for the training of technicians) with 737 pupils; 14 schools for public health occupations with 964 pupils.

In the winter term 1988–89 about 11,160 students were enrolled at the university. In addition to the university there were 4 other colleges in 1988–89 with about 6,660 students.

Statistical Information: Statistisches Landesamt Bremen (An der Weide 14–16 (P.B. 101309), D2800 Bremen 1), founded in 1850. *Director:* Ltd Reg. Dir. Volker Hannemann. Its current publications include: *Statistische Mitteilungen Freie Hansestadt Bremen* (from 1948).—*Monatliche Zwischenberichte* (1949–53); *Statistische Monatsberichte* (from 1954).—*Statistische Berichte* (from 1956).—*Statistisches Handbuch für das Land Freie Hansestadt Bremen (1950–60*, 1961; *1960–64*, 1967; *1965–69*, 1971; *1970–74*, 1975; *1975–80*, 1982; *1981–85*, 1987).—*Bremen im statistischen Zeitvergleich 1950–1976*. 1977.—*Bremen in Zahlen*. 1989.

State and University Library: Bibliotheks Str., D2800 Bremen 33. *Director:* Prof. Dr Hans-Albrecht Koch.

HAMBURG

Freie und Hansestadt Hamburg

AREA AND POPULATION. In 1938 the territory of the town was re-organized by the amalgamation of the city and its 18 rural districts with 3 urban and 27 rural districts ceded by Prussia. Total area, 755·3 sq. km (1988), including the islands Neuwerk and Scharhörn (7·6 sq. km). Population (31 Dec. 1988), 1,603,070 (752,905 males, 850,165 females).

Vital statistics for calendar years:

	Live births	*Marriages*	*Divorces*	*Deaths*
1986	13,404	9,180	4,556	21,973
1987	14,259	9,565	4,825	21,516
1988	15,359	9,787	4,549	21,186

CONSTITUTION. The constitution of 6 June 1952 vests the supreme power in the House of Burgesses *(Bürgerschaft)* of 120 members. The executive is in the hands of the Senate, whose members are elected by the Bürgerschaft.

The elections of 17 May. 1987 had the following results: Social Democrats, 55; Christian Democrats, 49; Green Alternatives, 8; Free Democrats, 8. The First Burgomaster is Dr Henning Voscherau (Social Democrat).

The territory has been divided into 7 administrative districts.

AGRICULTURE. The agricultural area comprised 14,800 hectares in 1988. Yield, in tonnes, of cereals, 21,951; potatoes, 862.

Livestock (3 Dec. 1988): Cattle, 10,912 (including 2,500 milch cows); pigs, 5,101; horses, 2,748; sheep, 2,624; poultry, 57,497.

FISHERIES. In 1988 the yield of sea and coastal fishing was 457 tonnes valued at DM 1·1m.

INDUSTRY. In June 1988, 761 establishments (with 20 and more employees) employed 133,495 persons; of these, 20,732 were employed in electrical engineering; 16,517 in machine construction; 7,242 in shipbuilding (except naval engineering); 13,418 in chemical industry.

LABOUR. The economically active persons totalled 726,600 at the 0·1%-sample survey of the microcensus of April 1988. Of the total, 63,300 were self-employed, 5,600 unpaid family workers, 657,700 employees; 6,900 were engaged in agriculture and forestry, 183,600 in power supply, mining, manufacturing and building, 198,800 in commerce and transport, 337,300 in other industries and services.

ROADS. On 31 Dec. 1988 there were 3,889 km of roads, including 79 km of autobahn, 153 km of federal roads. Number of motor vehicles (1 July 1989), 733,614, including 660,754 passenger cars, 35,406 lorries, 1,535 buses, 5,168 tractors, 20,571 motor cycles and 10,360 other motor vehicles.

SHIPPING. Hamburg is the largest port in the Federal Republic.

Vessels		*1938*	*1958*	*1978*	*1987*
Entered:	Number	18,149	19,033	16,636	14,154
	Tonnage	20,567,311	27,454,640	61,785,643	55,192,622
Cleared:	Number	19,316	20,363	17,414	14,099
	Tonnage	20,547,148	27,579,914	62,028,141	54,975,740

JUSTICE. There is a constitutional court *(Verfassungsgericht)*, a court of appeal *(Oberlandesgericht)*, a regional court *(Landgericht)*, 6 local courts *(Amtsgerichte)*, a Land labour court, a labour court, a Land social court, a social court, a finance court, a higher administrative court, an administrative court.

RELIGION. On 25 May 1987 (census) Evangelical Church and Free Churches 50·2%, Roman Catholic Church 8·6%.

EDUCATION. In 1987 there were 369 schools of general education (not including *Internationale Schule*) with 8,264 teachers and 261,271 pupils; 61 special schools with 772 teachers and 6,658 pupils; 46 part-time vocational schools with 48,366 pupils; 22 schools with 1,609 pupils in their vocational preparatory year; 23 schools with 1,952 pupils in manual instruction classes; 59 full-time vocational schools with 11,068 pupils; 10 economic secondary schools with 2,433 pupils; 2 technical *Gymnasien* with 309 pupils; 24 advanced vocational schools with 4,045 pupils; 38 schools for public health occupations with 2,766 pupils; 6 vocational introducing schools with 255 pupils and 21 technical superior schools with 2,523 pupils; all these vocational and technical schools have a total number of 2,803 teachers.

In the summer term 1988 there was 1 university with 41,260 students; 1 technical university with 650 students; 1 college of music and 1 college of fine arts with together 1,575 students; 1 university of the *Bundeswehr* with 1,300 students; 1 professional high school *(Fachhochschule)* with 13,200 students; 1 high school for economics and politics with 1,970 students; 1 high school of public administration with 820 students, as well as 1 private professional high school with 150 students.

Statistical Information: The Statistisches Landesamt der Freien und Hansestadt Hamburg (Steckelhörn 12, D2000 Hamburg 11) publishes: *Hamburg in Zahlen, Statistische Berichte, Statistisches Taschenbuch, Statistik des Hamburgischen Staates.*

Klessmann, E., *Geschichte der Stadt Hamburg*. Hamburg, 1981
Meyer-Marwitz, B., *Das Hamburg Buch*. Hamburg, 1981
Möller, J., *Hamburg-Länderprofile*. Hamburg, 1985
Plagemann, V., *Industriekultur in Hamburg*. Hamburg, 1984
Studt, B. and Olsen, H., *Hamburg—eine kurzgefaßte Geschichte der Stadt*. Hamburg, 1964

State Library: Staats- und Universitätsbibliothek, Carl von Ossietzky, Von-Melle-Park 3, D2000 Hamburg 13. *Director:* Prof. Dr Horst Gronemeyer.

HESSEN

AREA AND POPULATION. The state of Hessen comprehends the areas of the former Prussian provinces Kurhessen and Nassau (excluding the exclaves belonging to Hessen and the rural counties of Westerwaldkreis and Rhine-Lahn) and of the former Volksstaat Hessen, the provinces Starkenburg (including the parts of Rheinhessen east of the river Rhine) and Oberhessen. Hessen has an area of 21,114 sq. km. Its capital is Wiesbaden. Since 1 Jan. 1981 there have been 3 areas with 5 urban and 21 rural districts and 421 communes. Population, 31 Dec 1988, was 5,568,892 (2,689,836 males, 2,879,056 females).

Vital statistics for calendar years:

	Live births	*Marriages*	*Divorces*	*Deaths*
1986	52,587	32,520	11,380	63,385
1987	54,814	33,705	12,448	61,698
1988	57,643	35,280	12,035	62,128

CONSTITUTION. The constitution was put into force by popular referendum on 1 Dec. 1946. The Diet, elected on 5 April 1987, consists of 44 Social Democrats, 47 Christian Democrats, 9 Free Democrats, 10 *Die Grünen*.

The Christian Democrat cabinet is headed by Minister President Walter Wallmann (CDU).

AGRICULTURE. Area and yield of the most important crops:

	Area (in 1,000 hectares)			*Yield (in 1,000 tonnes)*		
	1986	*1987*	*1988*	*1986*	*1987*	*1988*
Wheat	144·1	143·1	148·0	913·5	825·5	932·7
Rye	29·5	29·5	26·2	132·9	125·2	118·8
Barley	146·6	138·2	139·6	727·9	648·4	748·5
Oats	55·9	49·5	46·4	243·0	212·1	178·7
Potatoes	8·7	8·3	7·3	303·7	227·5	245·6
Sugar-beet	21·8	21·5	20·9	1,061·0	1,063·6	1,023·3

Livestock, Dec. 1988: Cattle, 752,189 (including 249,791 milch cows); pigs 1·08m.; sheep, 145,667; horses, 32,108; poultry, 3·24m.

INDUSTRY. In June 1989, 3,594 establishments (with 20 and more employees) employed 630,414 persons; of these, 99,622 were employed in chemical industry; 94,379 in electrical engineering; 91,325 in car building; 76,014 in machine construction; 30,597 in food industry.

LABOUR. The economically active persons totalled 2·54m. at the 1% sample survey of the microcensus of April 1988. Of the total, 203,300 were self-employed, 44,400 unpaid family workers, 2,296,700 employees; 63,500 were engaged in agriculture and forestry, 961,100 in power supply, mining, manufacturing and building, 523,600 in commerce and transport, 996,200 in other services.

ROADS. On 1 Jan. 1989 there were 16,626 km of 'classified' roads, including 929 km of autobahn, 3,497 km of federal highways, 7,149 km of first-class highways and 5,051 km of second-class highways. Motor vehicles licensed on 1 July 1989 totalled 3,264,778, including 2,850,993 passenger cars, 6,065 buses, 120,918 trucks, 141,440 tractors and 110,334 motor cycles.

JUSTICE. There are a constitutional court *(Staatsgerichtshof)*, a court of appeal, 9 regional courts, 58 local courts, a Land labour court, 12 labour courts, a Land social court, 7 social courts, a finance court, a higher administrative court *(Verwaltungsgerichtshof)*, 5 administrative courts.

RELIGION. In 1987 (census) there were 52·7% Protestants and 30·4% Roman Catholics.

EDUCATION. In 1988 there were 1,251 primary schools with 14,793 teachers and 258,133 pupils (including *Förderstufen*); 234 special schools with 2,675 teachers and 17,474 pupils; 161 intermediate schools with 2,422 teachers and 42,348 pupils; 156 high schools with 8,865 teachers and 119,041 pupils; 193 *Gesamtschulen* (comprehensive schools) with 10,613 teachers and 144,164 pupils; 120 part-time vocational schools with 4,626 teachers and 158,668 pupils; 255 full-time vocational schools with 2,416 teachers and 34,215 pupils; 102 advanced vocational schools with 627 teachers and 9,830 pupils; 168 schools for public health occupations with 9,295 pupils.

In the winter term 1988–89 there were 3 universities (Frankfurt/Main, 31,254 students; Giessen, 17,720; Marburg–Lahn, 14,533); 1 technical university in Darmstadt (14,996); 1 *Gesamthochschule* (11,535); 15 *Fachhochschulen* (40,117); 2 Roman Catholic theological colleges and 1 Protestant theological college with together 468 students; 1 college of music and 2 colleges of fine arts with together 1,336 students.

Statistical Information: The Hessisches Statistisches Landesamt (Rheinstr. 35–37, D6200 Wiesbaden). *President:* Götz Steppuhn. Main publications: *Statistisches Taschenbuch für das Land Hessen* (zweijährlich; 1980–81 ff.).—*Staat und Wirtschaft in Hessen* (monthly).—*Beiträge zur Statistik Hessens.—Statistische Berichte. —Hessische Gemeindestatistik 1960–61* (5 vols., 1963 ff.).—*Hessische Gemeindestatistik 1970* (5 vols., 1972 ff.).—*Hessische Gemeindestatistik* (annual, 1980 ff.).

State Library: Hessische Landesbibliothek, Rheinstr. 55–57, D6200 Wiesbaden.

LOWER SAXONY

Niedersachsen

AREA AND POPULATION. Lower Saxony (excluding the town of Bremerhaven, and the districts on the right bank of the Elbe in the Soviet Zone) comprises 47,439 sq. km, and is divided into 4 administrative districts, 38 rural districts, 9 towns and 1,019 communes; capital, Hanover.

Estimated population, on 31 Dec. 1988, was 7,184,943 (3,471,946 males, 3,712,997 females).

Vital statistics for calendar years:

	Live births	*Marriages*	*Divorces*	*Deaths*
1986	71,226	42,740	13,198	84,071
1987	73,037	43,730	13,780	82,964
1988	76,036	46,500	13,500	82,920

GOVERNMENT. The Land Niedersachsen was formed on 1 Nov. 1946 by merging the former Prussian province of Hanover and the *Länder* Brunswick, Oldenburg and Schaumburg-Lippe. The Diet, elected on 15 June 1986, consists of 69 Christian Democrats, 66 Social Democrats; Free Democrats, 9 and *Die Grünen*, 11.

The cabinet of the Christian Democratic Union is headed by Minister President Dr Ernst Albrecht (CDU).

AGRICULTURE. Area and yield of the most important crops:

	Area (in 1,000 hectares)			*Yield (in 1,000 tonnes)*		
	1986	*1987*	*1988*	*1986*	*1987*	*1988*
Wheat	280	301	347	2,119	2,066	2,293
Rye	176	178	155	747	690	587
Barley	454	425	411	2,290	2,071	1,983
Oats	110	95	99	519	448	379
Potatoes	79	82	83	3,011	3,282	3,019
Sugar-beet	146	139	140	6,850	6,264	5,929

Livestock, 3 Dec. 1988: Cattle, 3,203,979 (including 1,000,863 milch cows); horses, 77,073; pigs, 7,254,947; sheep, 207,099; poultry, 36,059,020.

FISHERIES. In 1986 the yield of sea and coastal fishing was 83,314 tonnes valued at DM 61m.

INDUSTRY. In Sept. 1988, 4,130 establishments (with 20 and more employees) employed 647,118 persons; of these 59,322 were employed in machine construction; 145,979 in car building; 65,865 in electrical engineering.

LABOUR. The economically active persons totalled 3,042,300 in 1988. Of the total 260,200 were self-employed, 90,300 unpaid family workers, 2,691,800 employees; 208,400 were engaged in agriculture and forestry, 1,149,200 in power supply, mining, manufacturing and building, 555,200 in commerce and transport, 1,129,500 in other industries and services.

ROADS. At 1 Jan. 1988 there were 27,957 km of 'classified' roads, including 1,139 km of autobahn, 4,912 km of federal roads, 8,736 km of first-class and 13,170 km of second-class highways.

Number of motor vehicles, 1 Jan. 1989, was 3,955,379 including 3,370,953 passenger cars, 149,526 lorries, 8,541 buses, 247,068 tractors, 135,693 motor cycles.

JUSTICE. There are a constitutional court *(Staatsgerichtshof)*, 3 courts of appeal, 11 regional courts, 79 local courts, a Land labour court, 15 labour courts, a Land social court, 8 social courts, a finance court, a higher administrative court (together with Schleswig-Holstein), 4 administrative courts.

RELIGION. On 25 May 1987 (census) there were 66·12% Protestants and 19·6% Roman Catholics.

EDUCATION. In 1987 there were 2,241 primary schools with 23,560 teachers and 363,145 pupils; 295 special schools with 4,540 teachers and 27,161 pupils; 325 stages of orientation with 7,403 teachers and 123,405 pupils; 269 intermediate schools with 7,756 teachers and 108,687 pupils; 242 grammar schools with 13,083 teachers and 156,633 pupils; 9 evening high schools with 197 teachers and 1,676 pupils; 24 integrated comprehensive schools with 2,013 teachers and 20,423 pupils; 17 co-operative comprehensive schools with 1,600 teachers and 18,651 pupils. In 1986 there were 139 part-time vocational schools with 225,189 pupils; 118 year of basic vocational training with 23,973 pupils; 538 full-time vocational schools with 38,008 pupils; 92 *Fachgymnasien* with 11,403 pupils; 142 *Fachoberschulen* with 8,151 pupils (full-time vocational schools leading up to vocational colleges); 36 vocational extension schools with 509 pupils; 196 advanced full-time vocational schools (including schools for technicians) with 9,439 pupils; 241 public health schools with 14,290 pupils.

In the winter term 1988–89 there were 4 universities (Göttingen, 29,740 students; Hanover, 26,891; Oldenburg, 8,854; Osnabrück, 9,421); 2 technical universities (Braunschweig, 15,641; Clausthal, 3,779); the medical college of Hanover (3,655), the veterinary college in Hanover (1,943) and the colleges of Hildesheim (2,366) and Lüneburg (2,663).

Statistical Information: The Niedersächsisches Landesverwaltungsamt—Statistik' (Geibelstr. 65, D3000 Hanover 1) fulfils the function of the 'Statistisches Landesamt für Niedersachsen'. *Head of Division:* Abteilungsdirektor Dr Günter Koop. Main publications are: *Statistisches Jahrbuch Niedersachsen* (from 1950).—*Statistische Monatshefte Niedersachsen* (from 1947).—*Statistik Niedersachsen.*

State Library: Niedersächsische Staats- und Universitätsbibliothek, Prinzenstr. 1, 3400, Göttingen. *Director:* Helmut Vogt; Niedersächsische Landesbibliothek, Waterloostr. 8, D3000 Hannover 1. *Director:* Dr W. Dittrich.

NORTH RHINE-WESTPHALIA

Nordrhein-Westfalen

AREA AND POPULATION. The Land comprises 34,070 sq. km. It is divided into 5 areas, 23 urban and 31 rural districts. Capital Düsseldorf. Population, 31 Dec. 1988, 16,874,059 (8,100,426 males, 8,773,633 females).

Vital statistics for calendar years:

	Live births	*Marriages*	*Divorces*	*Deaths*
1986	171,891	103,402	36,933	191,430
1987	177,109	105,446	37,810	185,565
1988	185,877	109,236	37,919	186,987

GOVERNMENT. The Land Nordrhein-Westfalen is governed by Social Democrats; Minister President, Johannes Rau (SPD). The Diet, elected on 12 May 1985, consists of 125 Social Democrats, 88 Christian Democrats and 14 Free Democrats.

AGRICULTURE. Area and yield of the most important crops:

	Area (in 1,000 hectares)			*Yield (in 1,000 tonnes)*		
	1986	*1987*	*1988*	*1986*	*1987*	*1988*
Wheat	236·6	240·9	257·8	1,636·3	1,551·3	1,772·7
Rye	50·9	52·9	53·0	235·1	228·5	224·6
Barley	338·7	328·3	305·1	1,871·0	1,677·1	1,694·9
Oats	71·1	66·1	66·0	333·2	296·8	263·5
Potatoes	17·6	17·4	16·5	643·3	702·0	720·7
Sugar-beet	80·5	78·1	78·7	4,019·4	3,997·6	4,195·8

Livestock, 2 Dec. 1988: Cattle, 1,954,598 (including 558,773 milch cows); pigs, 6,093,284; sheep, 180,280; horses, 82,301; poultry, 11,844,939.

INDUSTRY. In Sept. 1988, 10,835 establishments (with 20 and more employees) employed 1,958,507 persons; of these, 147,817 were employed in mining; 274,500 in machine construction; 132,895 in iron and steel production; 199,003 in chemical industry; 189,434 in electrical engineering; 57,828 in textile industry.

Output and/or production in 1,000 tonnes, 1988: Hard coal, 62,955; lignite, 103,509; pig-iron, 20,463; raw steel ingots, 23,730; rolled steel, 16,421; castings (iron and steel castings), 1,233; cement, 9,261; fireproof products, 1,141; sulphuric acid (including production of cokeries), 1,772; staple fibres and rayon, 303; metal-working machines, 94; equipment for smelting works and rolling mills, 87; machines for mining industry, 161; cranes and hoisting machinery, 60; installation implements, 1,525,954,391 (pieces); cables and electric lines, 260; springs of all kinds, 215; chains of all kinds, 85; locks and fittings, 400; spun yarns, 195; electric power, 165,049m. kwh. Of the total population, 11·7% were engaged in industry.

LABOUR. The economically active persons totalled 6,892,100 at the 1%-sample survey of the microcensus of April 1988. Of the total, 559,900 were self-employed, 80,100 unpaid family workers, 6,252,100 employees; 147,100 were engaged in agriculture and forestry, 3,027,500 in power supply, mining, manufacturing and building, 1,241,700 in commerce and transport, 2,475,800 in other industries and services.

ROADS. There were (1 Jan. 1989) 29,842 km of 'classified' roads, including 2,045 km of autobahn, 5,477 km of federal roads, 12,372 km of first-class and 9,938 km of second-class highways. Number of motor vehicles, 1 July 1989, 8,877,846, including 7,105,131 passenger cars, 809,362 lorries, 338,932 motor lorries/trucks, 16,930 buses, 212,464 tractors and 307,213 motor cycles.

JUSTICE. There are a constitutional court *(Verfassungsgerichtshof)*, 3 courts of appeal, 19 regional courts, 130 local courts, 3 Land labour courts, 30 labour courts, a Land social court, 8 social courts, 3 finance courts, a higher administrative court, 8 administrative courts.

RELIGION. On 25 May 1987 (census) there were 35·2% Protestants and 49·4% Roman Catholics.

EDUCATION. In 1988 there were 4,524 primary schools with 62,036 teachers and 995,344 pupils; 722 special schools with 12,216 teachers and 77,816 pupils;

536 intermediate schools with 15,281 teachers and 241,238 pupils; 149 *Gesamtschulen* (comprehensive schools) with 8,955 teachers and 97,386 pupils; 630 high schools with 36,902 teachers and 481,152 pupils; in 1988 there were 289 part-time vocational schools with 449,177 pupils; vocational preparatory year 204 schools with 12,244 pupils; 313 full-time vocational schools with 86,583 pupils; 7 schools offering upgrading courses to raise the general level of education and quality for vocational colleges with 162 pupils; 217 full-time vocational schools leading up to vocational colleges with 23,341 pupils; 165 advanced full-time vocational schools with 24,057 pupils; 578 schools for public health occupations with 11,192 teachers and 31,934 pupils; 24 schools within the scope of a pilot system of courses with 55,167 pupils and 2,193 teachers.

In the winter term 1988–89 there were 8 universities (Bielefeld, 13,582 students; Bochum, 32,933; Bonn, 38,302; Dortmund, 18,913; Düsseldorf, 15,664; Cologne, 49,226; Münster, 44,325; Witten, 366); the Technical University of Aachen (35,838); 4 Roman Catholic and 2 Protestant theological colleges with together 1,219 students. There were also 4 colleges of music, 2 colleges of fine arts and the college for physical education in Cologne with together 10,845 students; 20 *Fachhochschulen* (vocational colleges) with 101,993 students, and 6 *Universitäten-Gesamthochschulen* with together 89,811 students.

Statistical Information: The Landesamt für Datenverarbeitung und Statistik Nordrhein-Westfalen (Mauerstr. 51, D4000 Düsseldorf 30) was founded in 1946, by amalgamating the provincial statistical offices of Rhineland and Westphalia. *President:* A. Benker. The Landesamt publishes: *Statistisches Jahrbuch Nordrhein-Westfalen.* From 1946. More than 550 other publications yearly.

Först, Walter, *Kleine Geschichte Nordrhein-Westfalens.* Münster, 1986.

Land Library: Universitätsbibliothek, Universitätsstr. 1, D4000 Düsseldorf.

RHINELAND-PALATINATE

Rheinland-Pfalz

AREA AND POPULATION. Rhineland-Pfalz comprises 19,848 sq. km. Capital Mainz. Population (at 31 Dec. 1988), 3,653,155 (1,761,059 males, 1,892,096 females).

Vital statistics for calendar years:

	Live births	*Marriages*	*Divorces*	*Deaths*
1986	37,181	22,814	7,354	43,214
1987	37,778	23,905	7,516	42,016
1988	39,850	24,899	7,463	47,822

CONSTITUTION. The constitution of the Land Rheinland-Pfalz was approved by the Consultative Assembly on 25 April 1947 and by referendum on 18 May 1947, when 579,002 voted for and 514,338 against its acceptance.

The elections of 17 May 1987 returned 48 Christian Democrats, 40 Social Democrats, 7 Free Democrats and 5 Green Party.

The cabinet is headed by Carl Ludwig Wagner (Christian Democrat).

AGRICULTURE. Area and yield of the most important products:

	Area (1,000 hectares)			*Yield (1,000 tonnes)*		
	1986	*1987*	*1988*	*1986*	*1987*	*1988*
Wheat	105·7	103·8	100·3	557·8	552·5	601·8
Rye	28·1	27·7	25·0	115·3	108·5	109·7
Barley	137·3	128·4	141·0	617·8	541·0	657·1
Oats	38·4	35·7	36·1	151·2	140·4	142·6
Potatoes	12·4	11·4	10·9	381·5	336·8	334·2
Sugar-beet	22·7	21·8	22·0	1,213·0	1,234·6	1,177·2
Wine (1,000 hectolitres)	61·0	61·2	61·0	6,729·1	6,323·0	6,090·9

Livestock (3 Dec. 1988): Cattle, 564,300 (including 198,900 milch cows); horses, 20,900; sheep, 125,300; pigs, 544,700; poultry, 3,142,700.

INDUSTRY. In Sept. 1988, 2,614 establishments (with 20 and more employees) employed 372,576 persons; of these 76,957 were employed in chemical industry; electrical equipment, 18,562; 14,807 in production of leather goods and footwear; 49,473 in machine construction; 14,536 in processing stones and earthenware.

LABOUR. The economically active persons totalled 1,571,363 at the census of May 1987. Of the total, 140,854 were self-employed, 38,551 unpaid family workers, 1,391,958 employees; 71,949 were engaged in agriculture and forestry, 649,894 in power supply, mining, manufacturing and building, 264,485 in commerce and transport, 585,035 in other industries and services.

ROADS. There were (1 Jan. 1989) 18,374 km of 'classified' roads, including 779 km of autobahn, 3,214 km of federal roads, 6,978 km of first-class and 7,404 km of second-class highways. Number of motor vehicles, 1 July 1989, was 2,191,527, including 1,848,333 passenger cars, 81,071 lorries, 5,050 buses, 141,858 tractors and 89,415 motor cycles.

JUSTICE. There are a constitutional court *(Verfassungsgerichtshof)*, 2 courts of appeal, 8 regional courts, 47 local courts, a Land labour court, 5 labour courts, a Land social court, 4 social courts, a finance court, a higher administrative court, 4 administrative courts.

RELIGION. On 25 May 1987 (census) there were 87·7% Protestants and 54·7% Roman Catholics.

EDUCATION. In 1988 there were 1,186 primary schools with 14,077 teachers and 223,106 pupils; 154 special schools with 1,742 teachers and 11,840 pupils; 108 intermediate schools with 3,122 teachers and 47,047 pupils; 136 high schools with 6,936 teachers and 94,020 pupils; 91 vocational schools with 102,981 pupils; 150 advanced vocational schools and institutions for the training of technicians (full- and part-time) with 7,458 pupils; 109 schools for public health occupations with 347 teachers and 6,492 pupils.

In the winter term 1988–89 there were the University of Mainz (25,176 students), the University of Kaiserslautern (8,089 students), the University of Trier (7,874 students), the *Hochschule für Verwaltungswissenschaften* in Speyer (467 students), the Koblenz School of Corporate Management *(Wissenschaftliche Hochschule für Unternahmensführung Koblenz in Vallendar)* with 178 students, the Roman Catholic Theological College in Trier (217 students) and the Roman Catholic College in Vallendar (62 students). There were also the Teacher-Training College of the Land Rheinland-Pfalz *(Erziehungswissenschaftliche Hochschule)* with 3,197 students, the *Fachhochschule des Landes Rheinland-Pfalz* (college of engineering) with 16,893 students and 4 *Verwaltungsfachhochschulen* with 2,390 students; also 2 private colleges for social-pedagogy (878 students).

Statistical Information: The Statistisches Landesamt Rheinland-Pfalz (Mainzer Str., 14–16, D5427 Bad Ems) was established in 1948. *President:* Dr Weis. Its publications include: *Statistisches Jahrbuch für Rheinland-Pfalz* (from 1948); *Statistische Monatshefte Rheinland-Pfalz* (from 1958); *Statistik von Rheinland-Pfalz* (from 1949) 325 vols. to date; *Rheinland-Pfalz im Spiegel der Statistik* (from 1968); *Die kreisfreien Städte und Landkreise in Rheinland-Pfalz* (from 1977); *Rheinland-Pfalz heute* (from 1973); *Benutzerhandbuch des Landesinformationssystems* (1981); *Rheinland-Pfalz heute und morgen* (Mainz, 1985); *Raumordnungsbericht 1985 der Landesregierung Rheinland-Pfalz* (Mainz, 1985). *Landesentwicklungsprogramm 1980* (Mainz, 1980).

Klöpper, R. and Korber, J., *Rheinland-Pfalz in seiner Gliederung nach zentralörtlichen Bereichen.* Remagen, 1957

SAARLAND

HISTORY. In 1919 the Saar territory was placed under the control of the League of Nations. Following a plebiscite, the territory reverted to Germany in 1935. In 1945 the territory became part of the French Zone of occupation, and was in 1947 accorded an international status inside an economic union with France. In pursuance of the German–French agreement signed in Luxembourg on 27 Oct. 1956 the territory returned to Germany on 1 Jan. 1957. Its re-integration with Germany was completed by 5 July 1959.

AREA AND POPULATION. Saarland has an area of 2,570 sq. km. Population, 31 Dec. 1988, 1,054,142 (506,179 males, 547,963 females). The capital is Saarbrücken.

Vital statistics for calendar years:

	Live births	*Marriages*	*Divorces*	*Deaths*
1986	10,493	7,214	2,370	12,912
1987	10,517	7,021	2,481	12,318
1988	10,748	7,446	2,781	12,388

CONSTITUTION. Saarland now ranks as a *Land* of the Federal German Republic and is represented in the Federal Diet by 8 members. The constitution passed on 15 Dec. 1947 is being revised.

The Saar Diet, elected on 10 March 1985, is composed as follows: 26 Social Democrats, 20 Christian Democrats, 5 Free Democrats.

Saarland is governed by Social Democrats in Parliament. Minister President: Oskar Lafontaine (Social Democrat).

AGRICULTURE AND FORESTRY. The cultivated area (1989) occupied 119,658 hectares or 46·6% of the total area; the forest area comprises nearly 33% of the total (256,804 hectares).

Area and yield of the most important crops:

	Area (in 1,000 hectares)			*Yield (in 1,000 tonnes)*		
	1986	*1987*	*1988*	*1986*	*1987*	*1988*
Wheat	6·6	7·0	7·1	30·5	31·1	36·0
Rye	6·1	6·1	5·7	23·5	24·0	23·4
Barley	10·5	10·0	9·9	42·7	42·2	44·2
Oats	5·6	5·4	5·6	20·2	22·4	22·7
Potatoes	0·4	0·4	0·4	13·3	11·4	13·0

Livestock, Dec. 1988: Cattle, 68,188 (including 22,548 milch cows); pigs, 38,228; sheep, 13,789; horses, 3,958; poultry, 263,420.

INDUSTRY. In June 1989, 606 establishments (with 20 and more employees) employed 135,367 persons; of these 21,280 were engaged in coalmining, 20,939 in manufacturing motor vehicles, parts, accessories, 16,978 in iron and steel production, 13,042 in machine construction, 8,857 in electrical engineering, 7,385 in steel construction. In 1988 the coalmines produced 9·9m. tonnes of coal. Six blast furnaces and 7 steel furnaces produced 4·2m. tonnes of pig-iron and 4·9m. tonnes of crude steel.

LABOUR. The economically active persons totalled 419,900 at the 1%-sample survey of the microcensus of April 1988. Of the total, 30,800 were self-employed, 384,700 employees; 6,200 were engaged in agriculture and forestry, 177,100 in power supply, mining, manufacturing and building, 77,200 in commerce and transport, 157,100 in other industries and services.

ROADS. At 1 Jan. 1988 there were 2,192 km of 'classified' roads, including 221 km of autobahn, 388 km of federal roads, 792 km of first-class and 791 km of second-class highways. Number of motor vehicles, 31 Dec. 1988, 584,112, including 519,049 passenger cars, 22,257 lorries, 1,458 buses, 13,341 tractors and 22,830 motor cycles.

JUSTICE. There are a constitutional court *(Verfassungsgerichtshof)*, a court of appeal, a regional court, 11 local courts, a Land labour court, 3 labour courts, a Land social court, a social court, a finance court, a higher administrative court, an administrative court.

RELIGION. On 25 May 1987 (census) 72·7% of the population were Roman Catholics and 21·9% were Protestants.

EDUCATION. In 1988–89 there were 324 primary schools with 3,645 teachers and 57,350 pupils; 47 special schools with 430 teachers and 2,797 pupils; 35 intermediate schools with 1,026 teachers and 12,765 pupils; 36 high schools with 1,950 teachers and 23,615 pupils; 10 comprehensive high schools with 390 teachers and 4,183 pupils; 2 *Freie Waldorfschulen* with 64 teachers and 740 pupils; 4 Evening intermediate schools with 276 pupils; 2 Evening high schools and 1 *Saarland-Kolleg* with 20 teachers and 425 pupils; 43 part-time vocational schools with 27,803 pupils; year of commercial basic training: 81 institutions with 2,479 pupils; 21 advanced full-time vocational schools and schools for technicians with 3,243 pupils; 54 full-time vocational schools with 5,355 pupils; 11 *Berufsaufbauschulen* (vocational extension schools) with 591 pupils; 28 *Fachoberschulen* (full-time vocational schools leading up to vocational colleges) with 2,844 pupils; 44 schools for public health occupations with 2,148 pupils. The number of pupils visiting the vocational schools amounts to 44,463. They are instructed by 1,682 teachers.

In the winter term 1988–89 there was the University of the Saarland with 18,876 students; 1 music-conservatory with 297 students; 1 vocational college (economics, engineering and design) with 3,163 students; 1 vocational college for social affairs with 208 students; 1 vocational college for public administration with 148 students.

Statistical Information: The Statistisches Amt des Saarlandes (Hardenbergstrasse 3, D6600 Saarbrücken 1) was established on 1 April 1938. As from 1 June 1935, it was an independent agency; its predecessor, 1920–35, was the Statistical Office of the Government Commission of the Saar. *Chief:* Direktor Josef Mailänder. The most important publications are: *Statistisches Handbuch für das Saarland,* from 1950.—*Statistisches Taschenbuch für das Saarland,* from 1959.—*Saarländische Bevölkerungs-und Wirtschaftszahlen.* Quarterly, from 1949. —*Saarland in Zahlen* (special issues).—*Einzelschriften zur Statistik des Saarlandes,* from 1950—*Statistische Nachrichten,* from 1981.

Fischer, P., *Die Saar zwischen Deutschland und Frankreich.* Frankfurt, 1959
Osang, R.M., *Saarland ABC.* Saarbrücken, 1975
Schmidt, R. H., *Saarpolitik 1945–57.* 3 vols. Berlin, 1959–62

SCHLESWIG-HOLSTEIN

AREA AND POPULATION. The area of Schleswig-Holstein is 15,728 sq. km; it is divided into 4 urban and 11 rural districts and 1,131 communes. The capital is Kiel. The population (estimate, 31 Dec. 1988) numbered 2,564,565 (1,236,551 males, 1,328,014 females).

Vital statistics for calendar years:

	Live births	*Marriages*	*Divorces*	*Deaths*
1986	24,693	15,631	5,290	30,979
1987	25,956	16,464	5,937	30,885
1988	27,310	17,273	5,495	30,424

GOVERNMENT. The elections of 8 May 1988 gave the Christian Democrats 27, the Social Democratic Party 46 and the South Schleswig Association 1 seat.

Prime Minister: Björn Engholm.

AGRICULTURE. Area and yield of the most important crops:

	Area (in 1,000 hectares)			Yield (in 1,000 tonnes)		
	1986	1987	1988	1986	1987	1988
Wheat	154·6	152·8	176·6	1,230·0	1,135·4	1,394·6
Rye	48·0	47·3	44·5	221·8	164·6	210·7
Barley	139·6	127·6	113·0	849·3	743·7	740·5
Oats	24·4	18·2	29·3	132·6	85·1	137·8
Potatoes	4·1	3·9	3·6	151·8	120·9	113·3
Sugar-beet	17·2	15·9	16·7	768·9	493·6	756·5

Livestock, 2 Dec. 1988: 33,392 horses, 1,482,376 cattle (including 481,775 milch cows), 1,541,722 pigs, 199,207 sheep, 3,293,080 poultry.

FISHERIES. In 1988 the yield of small-scale deep-sea and inshore fisheries was 47,807 tonnes valued at DM76·3m.

INDUSTRY. In 1988 (average), 1,542 establishments (with 20 and more employees) employed 165,361 persons; of these, 8,588 were employed in shipbuilding (except naval engineering); 32,119 in machine construction; 22,551 in food and kindred industry; 17,372 in electrical engineering.

LABOUR. The economically active persons totalled 1,135,300 in 1988. Of the total, 107,300 were self-employed, 20,300 unpaid family workers, 1,007,700 employees; 56,700 were engaged in agriculture and forestry, 338,700 in power supply, mining, manufacturing and building, 235,200 in commerce and transport, 504,700 in other industries and services.

ROADS. There were (1 Jan. 1989) 9,845·5 km of 'classified' roads, including 393·2 km of autobahn, 1,958·3 km of federal roads, 3,521·5 km of first-class and 3,972·5 km of second-class highways. Number of motor vehicles, 1 Jan. 1989, was 1,393,208, including 1,195,903 passenger cars, 54,527 lorries, 2,840 buses, 73,794 tractors, 48,482 motor cycles.

SHIPPING. The Kiel Canal, 98·7 km (51 miles) long, is on Schleswig-Holstein territory. In 1938, 53,530 vessels of 22·6m. net tons passed through it; in 1981, 52,641 vessels of 53·3m. net tons; in 1982, 49,100 vessels of 52·7m. net tons; in 1983, 49,320 vessels of 50·9m. net tons; in 1984, 50,920 vessels of 53m. net tons; in 1985, 48,387 vessels of 53·5m. net tons; in 1986, 46,543 vessels of 47·5m. net tons; in 1987, 45,324 vessels of 45m. net tons; in 1988, 46,825 vessels of 43·8m. net tons.

JUSTICE. There are a court of appeal, 4 regional courts, 30 local courts, a Land labour court, 6 labour courts, a Land social court, 4 social courts, a finance court, an administrative court.

RELIGION. On 25 May 1987 (census) there were 73·3% Protestants and 6·2% Roman Catholics.

EDUCATION. In 1988–89 there were 687 primary schools with 4,898 teachers and 135,149 pupils; 164 special schools with 1,325 teachers and 12,756 pupils; 173 intermediate schools with 2,561 teachers and 51,370 pupils; 99 high schools with 3,764 teachers and 65,127 pupils; 7 *Integrierte Gesamtschulen* (comprehensive schools) with 289 teachers and 5,006 pupils; 42 part-time vocational schools with 1,562 teachers and 81,735 pupils; 139 full-time vocational schools with 454 teachers and 10,745 pupils; 56 advanced vocational schools for foreigners with 277 teachers and 5,606 pupils; 63 schools for public health occupations with 4,131 pupils; 58 vocational grammar schools with 384 teachers and 6,778 pupils; 6 *Fachhochschulen* (vocational colleges) with 13,534 pupils in the summer term 1989.

In the summer term 1989 the University of Kiel had 17,012 students, 2 teacher-training colleges had 1,953 students, 1 music college had 329 students, 1 *Medizin-*

ische University in Lübeck had 1,173 students and 1 *Nordische* University in Flensburg had 81 students.

Statistical Information: Statistisches Landesamt Schleswig-Holstein (Fröbel Str. 15–17, D2300 Kiel 1). *Director:* Dr Mohr. Publications: *Statistisches Taschenbuch Schleswig-Holstein,* since 1954.—*Statistisches Jahrbuch Schleswig-Holstein,* since 1951.—*Statistische Monatshefte Schleswig-Holstein,* since 1949.—*Statistische Berichte,* since 1947.—*Beitrage zur historischen Statistik Schleswig-Holstein,* from 1967.—*Lange Reihen,* from 1977.

Baxter, R. R., *The Law of International Waterways.* Harvard Univ. Press, 1964
Brandt, O., *Grundriss der Geschichte Schleswig-Holsteins.* 5th ed. Kiel, 1957
Handbuch für Schleswig-Holstein. 24th ed. Kiel, 1988

State Library: Schleswig-Holsteinische Landesbibliothek, Kiel, Schloss. *Director:* Prof. Dr Dieter Lohmeier.

GHANA

Capital: Accra
Population: 13·8m. (1988)
GNP per capita: US$400 (1988)

HISTORY. The State of Ghana came into existence on 6 March 1957 when the former Colony of the Gold Coast and the Trusteeship Territory of Togoland attained Dominion status. The name of the country recalls a powerful monarchy which from the 4th to the 13th century A.D. ruled the region of the middle Niger.

The Ghana Independence Act received the royal assent on 7 Feb. 1957. The General Assembly of the United Nations in Dec. 1956 approved the termination of British administration in Togoland and the union of Togoland with the Gold Coast on the latter's attainment of independence.

The country was declared a Republic within the Commonwealth on 1 July 1960 with Dr Kwame Nkrumah as the first President. On 24 Feb. 1966 the Nkrumah regime was overthrown in a military *coup* and ruled by the National Liberation Council until 1 Oct. 1969 when the military regime handed over power to a civilian regime under a new constitution. Dr K. A. Busia was the Prime Minister of the Second Republic. On 13 Jan. 1972 the armed forces and police took over power again from the civilian regime in a *coup*.

In Oct. 1975 the National Redemption Council was subordinated to a Supreme Military Council (SMC). In 1979 the SMC was toppled in a *coup* led by Flight-Lieut. J. J. Rawlings. The new government permitted elections already scheduled and these resulted in a victory for Dr Hilla Limann and his People's National Party. However on 31 Dec. 1981 another *coup* led by Flight-Lieut. Rawlings dismissed the government and Parliament, suspended the Constitution and established a Provisional National Defence Council to exercise all government powers.

AREA AND POPULATION. Ghana is bounded west by the Côte d'Ivoire, north by Burkina Faso, east by Togo and south by the Gulf of Guinea. The area of Ghana is 92,456 sq. miles (239,460 sq. km); census population 1984, 12,296,081. Estimate (1988) 13,812,000.

Ghana is divided into 10 regions:

Regions	*Area (sq. km)*	*Population census 1984*	*Capital*	*Population census 1984*
Eastern	19,977	1,680,890	Koforidua	58,731
Western	23,921	1,157,807	Sekondi-Takoradi	93,400
Central	9,826	1,142,335	Cape Coast	57,224
Ashanti	24,390	2,090,100	Kumasi	376,246
Brong-Ahafo	39,557	1,206,608	Sunyani	38,834
Northern	70,383	1,164,583	Tamale	135,952
Volta	20,572	1,211,907	Ho	37,777
Upper East	8,842	772,744	Bolgatanga	32,495
Upper West	18,477	438,008	Wa	...
Greater Accra	2,593	1,431,099	Accra	867,459

The capital is Accra, other chief towns (population, census, 1970); Asamankese, 101,144; Tema, 99,608 (1984); Nsawam, 57,350; Tarkwa, 50,570; Oda, 40,740; Obuasi, 40,001; Winneba, 36,104; Keta, 27,461; Agona Swedru, 23,843.

Vital statistics (1985): Birth rate, 47 per 1,000; death rate 15 per 1,000.

In the south and centre of Ghana, the people are of the Kwa ethno-linguistic group, mainly Akan (Ashanti, Fante, etc.), Ewe (in the Volta region) and Ga, while the 20% living in the north belong to Gur peoples (Dagbane, Gurma and Grusi).

CLIMATE. The climate ranges from the equatorial type on the coast to savannah in the north and is typified by the existence of well-marked dry and wet seasons. Temperatures are relatively high throughout the year. The amount, duration and seasonal distribution of rain is very marked, from the south, with over 80" (2,000 mm) to the north, with under 50" (1,250 mm). In the extreme north, the wet season is from March to Aug., but further south it lasts until Oct. Near Kumasi, two wet seasons occur, in May and June and again in Oct. and this is repeated, with greater amounts, along the coast of Ghana. Accra. Jan. 80°F (26·7°C), July 77°F (25°C). Annual rainfall 29" (724 mm). Kumasi. Jan. 77°F (25°C), July 76°F (24·4°C). Annual rainfall 58" (1,402 mm). Sekondi-Takoradi. Jan. 79°F (25°C), July 76°F (24·4°C). Annual rainfall 47" (1,181 mm). Tamale. Jan. 82°F (27·8°C), July 78°F (25·6°C). Annual rainfall 41" (1,026 mm).

CONSTITUTION AND GOVERNMENT. Since the *coup* of 31 Dec. 1981, supreme power is vested in the Provisional National Defence Council, which in Sept. 1989 consisted of: Chairman: Flight-Lieut. Jerry John Rawlings. *Vice Chairman:* Justice Daniel Annan. Aanaa Enin. Ebo Tawiah. Mahama Iddrisu. P. V. Obeng. Capt. Kojo Tsikata. Lieut.-Gen. Arnold Quainoo. Maj.-Gen. W. M. Mensa-Wood.

Committee of Secretaries: Foreign Affairs: Obed Y. Asamoah. *Internal Affairs:* Nii Okaija Adamafio. *Finance:* Dr Kwesi Botchwey. *Attorney-General:* E. G. Tanoh.

National flag: Red, gold, green (horizontal); a black star in the centre.
National anthem: Hail the name of Ghana.

Local government: The 10 Regions, each under a Regional Secretary appointed by the PNDC, are divided into 110 districts.

DEFENCE.

Army. The Ghana Army consists of 7 infantry battalions, 1 reconnaissance battalion, 1 field engineer battalion, 1 parachute battalion, 1 mortar battalion, with armoured cars and ancillary units. Total strength, (1990) 10,000.

Navy. The Ghana Navy, based at Sekondi and Tema comprises 2 small British-built corvettes, 2 German-built coastal patrol, 4 inshore patrol craft and 2 small service craft. Naval personnel in 1989 numbered 800.

Air Force. The Ghana Air Force was formed in 1959, when an Air Force Training School was established at Accra. Its first combat unit has 4 Italian-built Aermacchi M.B.326K light ground attack jets ordered in 1976. It has, for training, transport, search and rescue, and air survey operations, 4 Fokker Friendship twin-turboprop transports, a C-212 Aviocar and a twin-turbofan Fokker Fellowship for Presidential use, all built in the Netherlands, 8 Islander piston-engined light transports, 6 Shorts Skyvan twinturboprop STOL transports, and 10 Bulldog primary trainers, all built in the UK; 2 Bell 212 helicopters built in the US; 4 French-built Alouette III helicopters, and 5 Aermacchi M.B.326F and 2 M.B.339 jet trainers. There are air bases at Takoradi and Tamale. Personnel strength (1990) about 800.

INTERNATIONAL RELATIONS

Membership. Ghana is a member of UN, the Commonwealth, OAU, ECOWAS and is an ACP state of EEC.

ECONOMY

Budget. In 1989 budget provided for revenue estimated at ₵ 204,617m. and expenditure estimated at ₵ 196,191m.

Currency. The monetary unit is the *cedi* (₵), divided into 100 *pesewas* (P). Notes are issued of 1, 2, 5, 10, 50, 200 and 500 ₵; cupro-nickel coins of $2^1/_2$, 5, 10 and 20 P and 1₵. In March 1990, £1 = ₵ 515·35; US$1 = ₵ 314·43.

Banking. The Bank of Ghana was established in Feb. 1957 as the central bank of the country. The Ghana Commercial Bank, also established in Feb. 1957, is a purely commercial institution with agricultural financing as one of its priorities. It had 150 full branches in Sept. 1987, 1 in London and 1 subsidiary in Lomé (Togo). Barclays Bank of Ghana Ltd has 39 branches and agencies and the Standard Bank (Ghana) Ltd has 38 branches.

The National Investment Bank, established in 1963, is an autonomous joint state-private development finance institution. The former post office savings bank has been transformed into the National Savings and Credit Bank. The Bank for Housing and Construction opened in 1973; The Merchant Bank (Ghana) Ltd in 1972; The Ghana Co-operative Bank was established and re-organized in 1974; The Agricultural Development Bank in 1967; The Consolidated Discount House Ltd in Nov. 1987.

ENERGY AND NATURAL RESOURCES

Electricity. Production (1986) 4,372m. kwh, mainly from 2 hydro-electric stations operated by the Volta River Authority, Akosombo (6 units) and Kpong (4 units), with a total capacity of 1,072 mw. Supply 240 volts; 50 Hz.

Oil. The Government announced in Jan. 1978 that oil had been found in commercial quantities with known reserves (1980) 7m. bbls and in Oct. 1983 formed the Ghanaian National Petroleum Corporation with exploration rights in all areas not covered by existing agreements.

Minerals. In 1987 gold production was 323,496 fine oz.; diamonds, 396,720 carats; manganese, 235,123 tonnes; bauxite, 226,415 tonnes.

Agriculture. In southern and central Ghana main food crops are maize, rice, cassava, plantain, groundnuts, yam and cocoyam, and in northern Ghana groundnuts, rice, maize, sorghum, millet and yams.

Production of main food crops (1988 in 1,000 tonnes) was: Maize, 630; rice, 116; millet, 140; sorghum, 175; cassava, 3,300; cocoyam, 650; yam, 1,000; plantain, 700.

Cocoa is by far Ghana's main cash crop. Production (1988) 290,000 tonnes. Output has fallen considerably since the 1970s, and Ghana has lost its long-held position as the world's leading producer to the Côte d'Ivoire. While there is smuggling to that country, Ghana's low cocoa production was due to ageing trees and declining interest in cocoa growing because of poor prices. Since 1982 the PNDC has carried out a rehabilitation programme for cocoa as well as increased producer prices for farmers, which has halted the decline and raised production considerably.

Among other cash crops, tobacco and coffee are important, and improved types of palm oil and coconuts are being planted on an increased scale; progress has been made with clonal rubber in the south-west; pepper, ginger, pineapple, avocado, citrus and other crops are being grown for export, and efforts are being made to increase local supplies of cotton, kenaf, tobacco, palm oil, mango, pineapple and sugar-cane for local industries.

Livestock, 1988: Cattle, 1·3m.; sheep, 2·5m.; goats, 3m.; horses, 4,000; pigs, 750,000; poultry, 12m.

Forestry. In 1988 the closed forest zone covered 8,225,900 hectares (36% of the land area), of which 2,559,400 hectares were reserves and 46,600 hectares unreserved forest lands. In 1986, 221,000 cu. metres of logs and 104,000 cu. metres of sawn timber were exported. Production (1987) 493,543 cu. metres.

Fisheries. Catch (1987) 324,630 tonnes (54,630 from inland waters).

INDUSTRY AND TRADE

Industry. The aluminium smelter at Tema is the centre of industrial development, mainly concentrated on Accra/Tema, Kumasi and Takoradi/Sekondi. In 1984 the Volta Aluminium Company (VALCO), which operates the smelter, reached an agreement with the government on the use of Volta dam electricity. Production (1986) 120,000 tonnes.

Commerce. In 1989 exports were US$880m.; imports, US$1,200m. Exports went mainly to USA, UK, Japan and Federal Republic of Germany. Imports came from Nigeria, UK, USA and Federal Republic of Germany. Principal exports: Cocoa, timber and gold; imports were raw materials, capital equipment, petroleum and food.

Total trade between Ghana and UK (British Department of Trade returns, in £1,000 sterling):

	1985	*1986*	*1987*	*1988*	*1989*
Imports to UK	99,410	103,480	113,859	106,314	92,208
Exports and re-exports from UK	116,883	113,218	138,081	126,148	121,076

Tourism. In 1987 there were 103,440 tourists.

COMMUNICATIONS

Roads. In 1988 agencies of the Ministry of Roads and Highways maintained about 14,514 km of trunk roads, 14,000 km of feeder and 10,000 km of other rural roads, and 1,700 km of city and municipal roads. The number of vehicles in use (1986) was 54,196, of which private cars, 26,590.

Railways. Total length of railways open in 1985 was 953 km of 1,067 mm gauge. In 1987 railways carried 593,000 tonnes and 3·5m. passengers.

Aviation. There is an international airport at Accra, domestic airports at Takoradi, Kumasi, Tamale and Sunyani and airstrips at Wa, Navrongo and Ho. Services are operated by Ghana Airways, Nigeria Airways, Swissair, KLM, British Airways, Egypt Air, Air India, Aeroflot, Air Afrique and Bulgarian Airlines. Total aircraft freight in 1986 was 8,661,971 tonnes.

Shipping. The chief ports are Takoradi and Tema. In 1983, 1,299,146 tonnes of cargo were imported and 1,682,519 tonnes were exported by 663 ships.

Post and Broadcasting. There were 444 telephone exchanges and 666 call offices with (1987) 74,935 telephones in use. There are internal wireless stations at Accra, Kumasi, Bawku, Lawra, Kete-Krachi, Tamale, Yendi, Kpandu, Tumu and Sekondi-Takoradi. In 1988 there were over 2·9m. radio and 175,000 television receivers.

Cinemas. In 1987 there were 83 cinemas with an average seating capacity of 1,200.

Newspapers. There were (1989) 3 daily newspapers (circulation 180,000).

JUSTICE, RELIGION, EDUCATION AND WELFARE

Justice. The Courts were constituted as follows:

Supreme Court. The Supreme Court consists of the Chief Justice who is also the President and not less than 4 other Justices of the Supreme Court. The Supreme Court is the final court of appeal in Ghana. The final interpretation of the provisions of the constitution has been entrusted to the Supreme Court.

Court of Appeal. The Court of Appeal consists of the Chief Justice together with not less than 5 other Justices of the Appeal court and such other Justices of Superior Courts as the Chief Justice may nominate. The Court of Appeal is duly constituted by 3 Justices. The Court of Appeal is bound by its own previous decisions and all courts inferior to the Court of Appeal are bound to follow the decisions of the Court of Appeal on questions of law. Divisions of the Appeal Court may be created, subject to the discretion of the Chief Justice.

High Court of Justice. The Court has jurisdiction in civil and criminal matters as well as those relating to industrial and labour disputes including administrative complaints. The High Court of Justice has supervisory jurisdiction over all inferior Courts and any adjudicating authority and in exercise of its supervisory jurisdiction has power to issue such directions, orders or writs including writs or orders in the nature of habeas corpus, certiorari, mandamus, prohibition and quo qarrantto. The High Court of Justice has no jurisdiction in cases of treason. The High Court consists of the Chief Justice and not less than 12 other judges and such other Justices of the Superior Court as the Chief Justice may appoint.

The PNDC has established Public Tribunals in addition to the traditional courts of justice.

There is a Public Tribunal Board consisting of not less than 5 members and not more than 15 members of the public appointed by the PNDC, at least one of whom shall be a lawyer of not less than 5 years' standing as a lawyer. The Board is responsible for the administration of all tribunals.

A tribunal consists of at least three persons and not more than five persons, selected by the Board from among persons appointed by the Council as members of public tribunals.

Religion. In 1988 Christians represented 52% of the population (Protestant, 37%; Roman Catholic, 15%), Moslem, 13%, others, 30%.

Education. In 1985–86 there were 2,399 kindergartens for the age-groups 4–6 years with 171,182 pupils. Primary schools are free and attendance is compulsory. In 1985–86 there were 9,004 primary schools with 1,491,162 pupils. In 1986 there were 5,310 middle schools with 617,613 pupils; 110 junior secondary schools with 18,372 pupils and 233 secondary schools with 133,435 students. In 1986 there were 45 training colleges with 15,210 students and 26 vocational-technical schools with 19,547 students at the beginning of the academic year. In 1987–88 there were 8,847 students at the 3 universities (University of Ghana, the University of Science and Technology at Kumasi, and the University of Cape Coast). University education is free.

Health. In 1988 medical facilities included 46 government hospitals, 252 health centres and posts, 3 university hospitals, 3 mental hospitals, 35 mission hospitals, 34 mission clinics and 40 private hospitals. In addition, there are 26 nurses and midwives training schools. There were 600 doctors, 5,190 nurses and 2,830 midwives in 1986.

DIPLOMATIC REPRESENTATIVES

Of Ghana in Great Britain (13 Belgrave Sq., London, SW1X 8PR)
High Commissioner: Dr J. L. S. Abbey (accredited 15 Oct. 1986).

Of Great Britain in Ghana (Osu Link, off Gamel Abdul Nasser Ave., Accra)
High Commissioner: A. M. Goodenough.

Of Ghana in the USA (3512 International Dr., NW, Washington, D.C., 20008)
Ambassador: Eric K. Otoo.

Of the USA in Ghana (Ring Rd. East, Accra)
Ambassador: Raymond C. Ewing.

Of Ghana to the United Nations
Ambassador: James Victor Gbeho.

Further Reading

Digest of Statistics. Accra. Quarterly (from May 1953)
Ghana. Official Handbook. Annual
Davidson, B., *Black Star.* London, 1973
Jones, T., *Ghana's First Republic 1960–1966.* London, 1975
Killick, T., *Development Economics in Action: A Study of Economic Policies in Ghana.* London, 1978
Ray, D. I., *Ghana: Politics, Economics and Society.* London, 1986

GIBRALTAR

Population: 30,077 (1988)
GNP per capita: US$4,370 (1985)

HISTORY. The Rock of Gibraltar was settled by Moors in 711; they named it after their chief Jebel Tariq, 'the Mountain of Tarik'. In 1462 it was taken by the Spaniards, from Granada. It was captured by Admiral Sir George Rooke on 24 July 1704, and ceded to Great Britain by the Treaty of Utrecht, 1713. The cession was confirmed by the treaties of Paris (1763) and Versailles (1783).

On 10 Sept. 1967, in pursuance of a United Nations resolution on the decolonization of Gibraltar, a referendum was held in Gibraltar in order to ascertain whether the people of Gibraltar believed that their interests lay in retaining their link with Britain or in passing under Spanish sovereignty. Out of a total electorate of 12,762, 12,138 voted to retain the British connexion, while 44 voted for Spain.

On 15 Dec. 1982 the border between Gibraltar and Spain was re-opened for Spaniards and Gibraltarian pedestrians who are residents of Gibraltar. The border had been closed by Spain in June 1969. Following an agreement signed in Brussels in Nov. 1984 the border was fully opened on 5 Feb. 1985.

AREA AND POPULATION. Area, 2½ sq. miles (6·5 sq. km). Total population, including port and harbour (census, 1981), 28,719. Estimate (31 Dec. 1988) 30,077 (of which 20,236 were British Gibraltarian, 5,683 Other British and 4,158 Non-British). The population is mostly of Genoese, Portuguese and Maltese as well as Spanish descent.

Vital statistics (1988): Births, 523; marriages, 739; deaths, 293.

CLIMATE. The climate is warm temperate, with westerly winds in winter bringing rain. Summers are pleasantly warm and rainfall is low. Frost or snow is very rare. Jan. 57°F (13·9°C), July 75°F (23·9°C). Annual rainfall 23" (594 mm).

CONSTITUTION AND GOVERNMENT. Following a Constitutional Conference held in July 1968, a new Constitution was introduced in 1969. The Legislative and City Councils were merged to produce an enlarged legislature known as the Gibraltar House of Assembly. Executive authority is exercised by the Governor, who is also Commander-in-Chief. The Governor, while retaining certain reserved powers, is normally required to act in accordance with the advice of the Gibraltar Council, which consists of 4 *ex-officio* members (the Deputy Governor, the Deputy Fortress Commander, the Attorney-General and the Financial and Development Secretary) together with 5 elected members of the House of Assembly appointed by the Governor after consultation with the Chief Minister. Matters of primarily domestic concern are devolved to elected Ministers, with Britain responsible for other matters, including external affairs, defence and internal security. There is a Council of Ministers presided over by the Chief Minister.

The House of Assembly consists of a Speaker appointed by the Governor, 15 elected and 2 *ex-officio* members (the Attorney-General and the Financial and Development Secretary).

A Mayor of Gibraltar is elected by the elected members of the Assembly.

Governor and C.-in-C.: Adm. Sir Derek Reffell, KCB.

Chief Minister: Joseph John Bossano.

Flag: White with a red strip along the bottom, a red triple-towered castle with a gold key depending from the gateway.

DEFENCE. The Gibraltar Regiment is a part-time unit consisting of 1 infantry company, 1 battery of 105 mm light guns and an air defence troop equipped with blowpipe missiles with a small regular cadre. There is also a resident battalion from the British Army, an RAF Base and a Naval Base.

ECONOMY

Budget. Revenue and expenditure (in £ sterling):

	1986–87	*1987–88*	*1988–89*	*1989–90*
Revenue	75,387,665	78,343,477	81,730,000	81,552,000
Expenditure	72,868,043	82,063,600	86,103,000	86,439,000

Currency. The legal currency consists of Gibraltar government notes in denominations of £50, £20, £10, £5 and £1 and Gibraltar Government coinage. The amount of local currency notes in circulation at 31 March 1989 was £10·59m.

Banking. Domestic and offshore banking services are provided by 14 banks: Barclays Bank PLC (with 3 branches), Lloyds Bank PLC, Hambros Bank (Gibraltar) Ltd, Bank of Credit and Commerce Gibraltar Ltd, United Bank of Gibraltar Ltd, Algemene Bank Gibraltar Ltd, Banque Indosuez, Banco Espanol de Credito SA, Jyske Bank (Gibraltar) Ltd, Banco de Bilbao (Gibraltar) Ltd, Banco Central SA, National Westminster Bank PLC, National Westminster Bank Finance (Gibraltar) Ltd and Royal Bank of Scotland (Gibraltar) Ltd. In addition there are 8 offshore banks: Gibraltar and Iberian Bank Ltd, Hong Kong Bank and Trust Co. Ltd, Hambros Bank (Gibraltar) Ltd, Gibraltar Private Bank Ltd, Republic National Bank of New York (Gibraltar) Ltd, Gibraltar Trust Bank Ltd, Banco Hispano Americano SA and Abbey National (Gibraltar) Ltd. Total assets of commercial banks were £1,210·6m. in Dec. 1988.

INDUSTRY AND TRADE

Industry. There are a number of relatively small industrial concerns engaged in the bottling of beer and mineral waters, etc., mainly for local consumption. There is a small but important commercial ship-repair yard with 3 dry docks for vessels of up to 75,000 DWT, and a yacht repair yard.

Employment. The total insured labour force at 31 Dec. 1988, was 14,387. There were (1988) 9 registered trade unions and 9 employers associations. Approximately 50% of the local labour force is employed by the UK departments of the Gibraltar Government. In the private sector the main sources of employment are the construction industry, ship repairing, hotel and catering services, shipping services, trading agencies and retail distribution.

Commerce. Imports and exports (in £ sterling):

	1985	*1986*	*1987*	*1988*
Imports	113,200,000	111,700,000	140,962,000	144,787,000
Exports	48,300,000	44,300,000	51,731,000	46,093,000

Britain and the Commonwealth provide the bulk of imports, but fresh vegetables and fruit come mainly from Morocco and Spain. Foodstuffs accounted for 14% of total imports (about £20m.) in 1988. About 44% of non-fuel imports originate from the UK. Other sources include Japan, Spain and USA. Value of non-fuel imports, 1988, £116m. Exports are mainly re-exports of petroleum and petroleum products supplied to shipping. Gibraltar depends largely on tourism, offshore banking and other financial sector activity, the entrepôt trade and the provision of supplies to visiting ships. Exports of local produce are negligible.

Total trade between Gibraltar and UK (British Department of Trade returns, in £1,000 sterling):

	1986	*1987*	*1988*	*1989*
Imports to UK	6,021	3,367	4,537	4,560
Exports and re-exports from UK	46,200	49,986	67,944	69,350

Tourism. The number of tourists in 1988 was 3,770,619 of which 156,075 arrived by air, 85,539 by sea and 3,529,005 by land.

COMMUNICATIONS

Roads. There are 31 miles of roads including 4·25 miles of pedestrian way.

Aviation. There are regular flights between London and Gibraltar operated by GB Airways and British Airways. GB Airways operate daily flights between Gibraltar and Tangier. Air Europe operate regular flights between London and Gibraltar and Manchester and Gibraltar.

Shipping. Gibraltar has a government-owned ship repair yard of strategic importance. There is a deep Admiralty harbour of 440 acres. A total of 2,762 merchant ships, 44,112,541 GRT, entered the port during 1988, including 2,068 deep-sea ships of 43,922,783 GRT. In 1988, 5,014 calls were made by yachts, 152,678 GRT and 93 cruise liners called during 1988.

Post and Broadcasting. An automatic telephone system exists in the town; number of telephones (1987), 14,000. International direct dialling facilities are available to over 100 countries *via* the Gibraltar Telecommunications Ltd (Gibtel) Earth Station and other international circuits. Air-mail arrives daily. A direct air-mail service between Gibraltar and Tangier is run by GB Airways Ltd. Surface mails arrive direct and through France, Spain and Tangier. Radio Gibraltar broadcasts for 24 hours daily, in English and Spanish, and GBC Television operates for 5 hours daily in English. Number of receivers (31 Dec. 1988), TV, 7,280.

Newspapers. There were (1989) 2 dailies and 4 weeklies.

JUSTICE, RELIGION, EDUCATION AND WELFARE

Justice. The judicial system is based on the English system. There is a Court of Appeal, a Supreme Court, presided over by the Chief Justice, a court of first instance and a magistrates' court.

Religion. Religion of civil population mostly Roman Catholic; 1 Anglican and 1 Roman Catholic cathedral and 2 Anglican and 6 Roman Catholic churches; 1 Presbyterian and 1 Methodist church and 4 synagogues; annual subsidy to each communion, £500.

Education. Free compulsory education is provided for children between ages 4 and 15 years. Scholarships are made available for universities, teacher-training and other higher education in Britain. The comprehensive system was introduced in Sept. 1972. There were (1988) 12 primary and 2 comprehensive schools. Primary schools are mixed and divided into first schools for children aged 4-8 years and middle schools for children aged 8-12 years. The comprehensives are single-sex. In addition, there are 2 Services primary schools and 1 private primary school. A new purpose-built Special School for severely handicapped children aged 2-16 years was opened in 1977, and there are 3 Special Units for children with special educational needs (1 attached to a first school, 1 to a middle school and 1 at secondary level), 2 nurseries for children aged 3-4 years and an occupational therapy centre for handicapped adults. Technical education is available at the Gibraltar College of Further Education managed by the Gibraltar Government. In Sept. 1988, there were 1,353 pupils at government first schools, 1,412 at government middle schools, 172 at private and 648 at services schools; 19 at the special school; 837 at the boy's comprehensive school and 857 at the girls' comprehensive. In addition there were 114 full-time and 228 part-time students in the Gibraltar College of Further Education. Total full-time pupils in all educational institutions, 5,640. In 1987–88, government expenditure on education was £5,750,200.

Health. In 1988 there were 2 hospitals with 252 beds and 29 doctors. Total expenditure on medical and health services during year ended 31 March 1988 was £8,679,577.

Further Reading

Gibraltar Year Book. Gibraltar, (Annual)
Ellicott, D., *Our Gibraltar*. Gibraltar, 1975
Green, M. M., *A Gibraltar Bibliography*. London, 1980.—*Supplement*. London, 1982
Hills, G., *Rock of Contention: A History of Gibraltar*. London, 1974
Jackson, W. G. F., *The Rock of the Gibraltarians*. Farleigh Dickinson Univ. Press, 1987
Magauran, H. C., *Rock Siege: The Difficulties with Spain 1964–85*. Gibraltar, 1986
Shields, G. J., *Gibraltar*. [Bibliography] Oxford and Santa Barbara, 1988

GREECE

Capital: Athens
Population: 9·99m. (1987)
GNP per capita: US$5,213 (1988)

Elliniki Dimokratia

HISTORY. Greece gained her independence from Turkey in 1821–29, and by the Protocol of London, of 3 Feb. 1830, was declared a kingdom, under the guarantee of Great Britain, France and Russia. For details of the subsequent history to 1947 *see* THE STATESMAN'S YEAR-BOOK, 1957, pp. 1069–70 and for details of the monarchy *see* THE STATESMAN'S YEAR-BOOK, 1973–74, p. 1000.

AREA AND POPULATION. Greece is bounded north by Albania, Yugoslavia and Bulgaria, east by Turkey and the Aegean Sea, south by the Mediterranean and west by the Ionian Sea. The total area is 131,957 sq. km (50,949 sq. miles), of which the inhabited islands account for 25,042 sq. km (9,669 sq. miles).

The population was 9,740,417 according to the census of 5 April 1981. Estimate (1987) 9·99m.

Athens is the capital; population of Greater Athens, in 1981, 3,027,331.

The following table shows the prefectures *(Nomoi)* and their population:

Nomoi	*Area in sq. km*	*Population 1981*	*Capital*	*Population 1981*
Greater Athens [1]	*427*	*3,027,331*	Athens	885,737
			(Piraeus)	196,389
Central Greece and Euboea [2]	*24,391*	*1,099,841*		
Aetolia and Acarnania	5,461	219,764	Missolonghi	10,164
Attica [2]	3,381	342,093	Athens	885,737
Boeotia	2,952	117,175	Levadeia	16,864
Euboea	4,167	188,410	Chalcis	44,867
Evrytania	1,869	26,182	Karpenissi	5,100
Phthiotis	4,441	161,995	Lamia	41,667
Phokis	2,120	44,222	Amphissa	7,156
Peloponnesos	*21,379*	*1,012,528*		
Argolis	2,154	93,020	Nauplion	10,609
Arcadia	4,419	107,932	Tripolis	21,311
Akhaïa	3,271	275,193	Patras	141,529
Elia	2,618	160,305	Pyrgos	21,958
Korinthia	2,290	123,042	Korinthos	22,658
Lakonia	3,636	93,218	Sparte	11,911
Messenia	2,991	159,818	Calamata	41,911
Ionian Islands	*2,307*	*182,651*		
Zakynthos	406	30,014	Zante	9,764
Kerkyra	641	99,477	Kerkyra	33,561
Kefallenia	904	31,297	Argostolion	6,788
Levkas	356	21,863	Levkas	6,415
Epirus	*9,203*	*324,541*		
Arta	1,662	80,044	Arta	18,283
Thesprotia	1,515	41,278	Hegoumenitsa	5,879
Yannina	4,990	147,304	Yannina	44,829
Preveza	1,036	55,915	Preveza	12,662
Thessaly	*14,037*	*695,654*		
Karditsa	2,636	124,930	Karditsa	27,291
Larissa	5,381	254,295	Larissa	102,048
Magnessia	2,636	182,222	Volos	71,378
Trikkala	3,384	134,207	Trikkala	40,857

[1] Comprising parts of Attica (2,551,027) and Piraeus (476,304) prefectures.
[2] Excluding figures for the parts of Attica and Piraeus prefectures within Greater Athens.

Nomoi	Area in sq. km	Population 1981	Capital	Population 1981
Macedonia	*34,177*	*2,121,953*		
Grevena	2,291	36,421	Grevena	7,433
Drama	3,468	94,772	Drama	36,109
Imathia	1,701	133,750	Verria	37,087
Thessaloniki	3,683	871,580	Thessaloniki	406,413
Kavalla	2,111	135,218	Kavalla	56,375
Kastoria	1,720	53,169	Kastoria	17,133
Kilkis	2,519	81,562	Kilkis	11,148
Kozani	3,516	147,051	Kozani	30,994
Pella	2,506	132,386	Edessa	16,054
Pieria	1,516	106,859	Katerini	38,016
Serres	3,968	196,247	Serres	45,213
Florina	1,924	52,430	Florina	12,562
Khalkidiki	2,918	79,036	Polyghyros	4,075
Aghion Oros (Mount Athos)	336	1,472	Karyai (locality)	235
Thrace	*8,578*	*345,220*		
Evros	4,242	148,486	Alexandroupolis	34,535
Xanthi	1,793	88,777	Xanthi	31,541
Rodopi	2,543	107,957	Komotini	34,051
Aegean Islands	*9,122*	*428,533*		
Cyclades	2,572	88,458	Hermoupolis	13,876
Lesvos	2,154	104,620	Mitylini	24,115
Samos	778	40,519	Samos	5,575
Khios	904	49,865	Khios	24,070
Dodecanese	2,714	145,071	Rhodes	40,392
Crete	*8,336*	*502,165*		
Heraklion	2,641	243,622	Heraklion	101,634
Lassithi	1,823	70,053	Aghios Nikolaos	8,130
Rethymnon	1,496	62,634	Rethymnon	17,736
Canea	2,376	125,856	Canea	47,338

In 1981 cities (*i.e.*, communes of more than 10,000 inhabitants, including Greater Athens) had 5,475,997 inhabitants (56·2%), towns (*i.e.*, communes with between 2,000 and 9,999 inhabitants), 1,154,567 (11·9%), villages and rural communities (under 2,000 inhabitants), 3,109,853 (31·9%).

Mount Athos, the easternmost of the three prongs of the peninsula of Chalcidice, is a self-governing community composed of 20 monasteries. (*See* THE STATESMAN'S YEAR-BOOK, 1945, p. 983.) For centuries the peninsula has been administered by a Council of 4 members and an Assembly of 20 members, 1 deputy from each monastery. The Greek Government on 10 Sept. 1926 recognized this autonomous form of government; Articles 109–112 of the Constitution of 1927 gave legal sanction to the Charter of Mount Athos, drawn up by representatives of the 20 monasteries on 20 May 1924. Article 103 of the 1952 Constitution and Article 105 of the 1975 Constitution confirmed the special status of Mount Athos.

Vital statistics (1988): 107,505 live births; 736 still births; 2,219 illegitimate live births; 47,873 marriages; 92,407 deaths.

The Greek language consists of 2 branches, *katharevousa*, a conscious revival of classical Greek and *demotiki*. Demotiki is the official language both spoken and written.

CLIMATE. Coastal regions and the islands have typical Mediterranean conditions, with mild, rainy winters and hot, dry, sunny summers. Rainfall comes almost entirely in the winter months, though amounts vary widely according to position and relief. Continental conditions affect the northern mountainous areas, with severe winters, deep snow cover and heavy precipitation, but summers are hot. Athens. Jan. 48°F (8·6°C), July 82·5°F (28·2°C). Annual rainfall 16·6" (414·3 mm).

CONSTITUTION AND GOVERNMENT. A *coup d'état* took place on 21 April 1967, 'to avert the danger of a communist threat against the nation'. A Military Government was formed, which suspended the 1952 Constitution. Following the unsuccessful counter-*coup* in 1967, King Constantine went abroad.

Voting took place on 29 July 1973 in the referendum to change Greece from a Monarchy to a Republic and to elect a President. 77·2% of the valid votes were cast for a republican régime.

On 25 Nov. 1973, in a bloodless *coup*, President Papadopoulos was overthrown and Lieut.-Gen. Phaedon Ghizikis was sworn in. The military dictatorship collapsed on 23 July 1974 and the 1952 Constitution was reintroduced in a modified form. A new Constitution was introduced in June 1975. Parliamentary elections took place on 12 Nov. 1974. A further referendum on the Monarchy took place on 8 Dec. 1974 and 69·2% of the valid votes were cast for an 'uncrowned democracy'.

Elections were held on 5 Nov. 1989. The results were New Democracy, 148; Pasok, 128; Left Coalition, 21; Ecology, 1; Others, 2. Elections will take place in April 1990.

President: Christos Sartzetakis (elected President in March 1985).

The Cabinet in Nov. 1989:

Prime Minister: Xenophon Zolotas.

Minister to the Prime Minister: Niko Themelis. *National Defence and Tourism:* Tzannis Tzannetakis. *Foreign Affairs:* Antonis Samaras. *Interior:* Theodore Katrivanos. *National Economy:* George Yennimatas. *Finance:* George Souflias. *Agriculture:* Stavros Dimas. *Labour:* Apostolos Kaklamanis. *Health, Welfare and Social Security:* George Merikas. *Justice:* Constantine Stamatis. *Education and Religion:* Kostas Simitis. *Culture:* Sotiris Kouvelas. *Public Order:* Dimitris Manikas. *Macedonia-Thrace:* Yannis Deliyannis. *The Aegean:* Antonis Foussas. *Environment, Town Planning and Public Works:* Konstantino Liaskas. *Industry, Energy and Technology:* Anastasios Peponis. *Commerce:* Ioannis Varvitsiotis. *Transport and Communications:* Akis Tsochatzopoulos. *Merchant Marine:* Nikolaos Pappas.

National flag: Nine horizontal stripes of blue and white, with a canton of blue with a white cross.

National anthem: Hymn to Freedom, Imnos eis tin Eleftherian (words by Dionysios Solomos, 1824; tune by N. Mantzaros, 1828).

DEFENCE. In Aug. 1950 the Ministries of War, Marine and Military Aviation were fused into a single Ministry of National Defence. The General Staff of National Defence is directly responsible to the Minister on general defence questions, besides the special staffs for Army, Navy and Air Force. Military service in the Armed Forces is compulsory and universal. Liability begins in the 21st year and lasts up to the 50th. The normal terms of service are Army 21 months, Navy 25 months, Air Force 23 months, followed by 19 years in the First Reserve and 10 years in the Second Reserve.

Army. The Army is organized into 3 Military Regions, comprising 1 armoured, 1 mechanized, 1 para-commando, 6 parachute and 10 infantry divisions; 4 armoured brigades; 15 field artillery, 8 anti-aircraft, 2 surface-to-air missile, and 3 army aviation battalions; and 1 independent aviation company. Equipment includes 108 M-26, 359 M-47, 1,175 M-48, 190 AMX-30 and 109 Leopard I main battle tanks. Hellenic Army Aviation has over 150 helicopters, including 43 AB-205 and 64 UH-1H Iroquois, 8 Chinooks, 20 Nardi-Hughes 300s, and 15 Cessna U-17A observation aircraft, 2 Aero Commander and 2 Super King Air transports. Strength (1990) 160,000 (115,000 conscripts), with a further 350,000 reserves. There is also a paramiltary gendarmerie of 26,500 men.

Navy. The Hellenic Navy consists mostly of *ex*-US ships dating from the 1940s, includes 10 diesel submarines (8 German-built completed 1971-80), 14 destroyers, 7 frigates (2 built in the Netherlands, and commissioned 1981 and 1982) and 16 missile craft dating from the 1970s. Smaller units include 9 fast torpedo craft, 10 inshore patrol craft and 14 ex-US mine countermeasure vessels. Substantial amphibious lift is provided by 1 dock landing ship, 7 tank landing ships and 5 medium landing ships plus about 70 landing craft. Major auxiliaries include 2 small replenishment tankers, 1 ammunition transport, 1 water tanker and a purpose-built training ship. There are about 40 minor auxiliaries and service craft. Main bases are at Salamis, Patras, and Soudha Bay (Crete).

The Air Force operates 12 HU-16 Albatross maritime patrol amphibians on naval tasks; and the Navy 14 AB-212 anti-submarine helicopters and 4 Alouettes for SAR and liaison.

Future procurement plans include new frigates to the West German 'MEKO' design, new amphibious ships, and a modernization programme for the submarines.

Personnel in 1989 totalled 20,500 of whom 12,000 were conscripts, on 2 years compulsory service.

The Coastguard and Customs service, 4,000 strong, operate about 100 small patrol craft.

Air Force. The Hellenic Air Force had a strength (1989) of about 24,000 officers and men and 300 combat aircraft, consisting of 3 squadrons of F-4E Phantom air-superiority fighters, 2 squadrons of F-104G Starfighters, 2 squadrons of Mirage F.1 fighters, 3 squadrons of A-7H Corsair II attack aircraft, 3 squadrons of F-5 fighters, 1 squadron of RF-4E reconnaissance fighters and 1 squadron of HU-16B Albatross ASW amphibians (under Navy control). There are also transport squadrons equipped with C-130H Hercules (12), Noratlas, NAMC YS-11, DO28 and C-47 aircraft, 12 Canadair CL-215 twin-engined amphibians, 36 T-2E Buckeye training/attack aircraft, other training and helicopter equipment, and anti-aircraft units equipped with Nike-Hercules and Hawk surface-to-air missiles. Forty F-16 Fighting Falcon and 40 Mirage 2000 fighters are being delivered (1989-90).

The HAF is organized into Tactical, Training and Air Materiel Commands.

INTERNATIONAL RELATIONS

Membership. Greece is a member of UN, EEC, the Council of Europe and the military and political wings of NATO.

ECONOMY

Budget. The estimated revenue and expenditure for calendar years were as follows (in 1m. drachmai):

	1984	*1985*	*1986*	*1987*
Revenue	933,500	1,114,412	1,464,867	1,727,994
Expenditure	1,470,058	1,776,937	2,166,461	2,748,331

Currency. On 11 Nov. 1944 the Greek currency was stabilized at 1 new *drachma* equalling 50,000m. old *drachmai*. Further readjustments took place in 1946, 1949 and 1953. A 'new issue' of notes and coins was put into circulation on 1 May 1954, 1 new drachma equalling 1,000 old drachmai (72 drachmai = £1; 30 drachmai = US$1). The 'new issue' comprises notes of 50, 100, 500 and 1,000 drachmai and metal coins of 1, 2, 5, 10 and 20 drachmai and 10, 20 and 50 *lepta*. Rate of exchange, March 1990, £1 = 265·00 drachmai; US$1 = 161·68.

Banking. The Bank of Greece *(Trapeza Tis Ellados)* is the bank of issue.

The National Investment Bank for industrial development was set up in Dec. 1963; of its capital of 180m. drachmai, the National Bank provided 60%.

Other important banks are the Ionian and Popular Bank of Greece, the Commercial Bank of Greece, the National Mortgage Bank, the Hellenic Industrial Development Bank, the Investment Bank, the Commercial Credit Bank, the Agricultural Bank, the Bank of Central Greece and the General Bank of Greece.

Weights and Measures. The metric system was made obligatory in 1959; the use of other systems is prohibited. The Gregorian calendar was adopted in Feb. 1923.

ENERGY AND NATURAL RESOURCES

Electricity. Total installed capacity of the Public Power Corporation was 7,759,121 kw as at 31 Dec. 1986. Total net production in 1988 was 29,967m. kwh. Supply 220 volts; 50 Hz.

Minerals. Greece produces a variety of ores and minerals, including (with production, 1986, in tonnes) iron-pyrites (150,340), bauxite (2,231,360), nickel (2,196,843), magnesite (943,759), asbestos (3,928,030), chromite (217,979), barytes, marble (white and coloured) and various other earths, chiefly from the Laurium district, Thessaly, Euboea and the Aegean islands. There is little coal, and lignite of indifferent quality (38·41m. tonnes, 1986). Salt production (1986) 160,917 tonnes.

Agriculture. Of the total area (131,957 sq. km) 39,452 sq. km is arable and fallow. Another 52,550 sq. km is grazing land, 29,511 sq. km is forest.
Production (1988, in 1,000 tonnes):

Wheat	2,550	Grapes	1,565
Tobacco	142	Wine	450
Seed cotton	700	Citrus fruit	1,012
Sugar-beet	1,900	Other fruit	2,947
Raisins	160	Milk	1,704
Olive oil	290	Meat	524

Olive production (1988) about 1·5m. tonnes.

Rice is cultivated in Macedonia, the Peloponnese, Epirus and Central Greece. Successful experiments have been made in growing rice on alkaline land previously regarded as unfit for cultivation. The main kinds of cheese produced are white cheese in brine (commercially known as Fetta) and hard cheese, such as Kefalotyri.

Livestock (1988): 800,000 cattle, 1,000 buffaloes, 1,190,000 pigs, 10,816,000 sheep, 3,488,000 goats, 60,000 horses, 83,000 mules, 175,000 asses, 31m. poultry.

Fisheries. In 1987, 15,299 fishermen were active and landed 121,751 tonnes of fish. 10,000 kg of sponges were produced in 1987.

INDUSTRY AND TRADE

Industry. Manufacturing contributed 1,145,527m. drachmai to GDP in 1988. The main products are canned vegetables and fruit, fruit juice, beer, wine, alcoholic beverages, cigarettes, textiles, yarn, leather, shoes, synthetic timber, paper, plastics, rubber products, chemical acids, pigments, pharmaceutical products, cosmetics, soap, disinfectants, fertilizers, glassware, porcelain sanitary items, wire and power coils and household instruments.

Production, 1986 (1,000 tonnes): Textile yarns, 230; cement, 12,494; fertilizers, 1,448; ammonia, 294; iron (concrete-reinforcing bars), 857; alumina, 470; aluminium, 176; beer, 310; bottled wine, 112; chemical acids, 1,789; iron wire, 106; glass products, 141; packing materials, 200; cigarettes (1,000 pieces) 27,118; petroleum, 12,369; detergents, 127.

Labour. Of the economically active population in 1987, 970,700 were engaged in agriculture. 715,600 in manufacturing and 1,911,200 in other employment.

Trade Unions. The status of trade unions in Greece is regulated by the Associations Act 1914. Trade-union liberties are guaranteed under the Constitution, and a law of June 1982 altered the unions' right to strike.

The national body of trade unions in Greece is the Greek General Confederation of Labour.

Commerce. In 1987 exports totalled (in 1m. drachmai) 880,985·2 including: Clothing, 194,981·1; textile yarn, 51,067·3; petroleum products, 48,096·7; tobacco, 37,251·5; prepared fruits, 28,466·8; olive oil, 26,120·3; cements, 21,148·5. Imports totalling 1,758,951·4 including: Petroleum oils, crude, 203,311·6; meat, 101,001·9; iron and steel, 59,417·1; plastic materials, 48,366·6.

Exports in 1987 (in 1m. drachmai) were mainly to the Federal Republic of Germany (214,452·6), Italy (142,298·9), France (75,909·4), UK (72,521·7) and USA (59,861·9). Imports were mainly from the Federal Republic of Germany (389,888·6), Italy (215,568·8), France (137,573·7) and the Netherlands (123,752·3).

Total trade between Greece and UK (British Department of Trade returns, in £1,000 sterling):

	1985	*1986*	*1987*	*1988*	*1989*
Imports to UK	320,131	308,644	355,320	356,974	395,086
Exports and re-exports from UK	335,352	356,020	444,500	468,032	571,409

Tourism. Tourists visiting Greece in 1986 numbered 7,025,000. In 1988 they spent the equivalent of US$2,396m.

COMMUNICATIONS

Roads. There were, in 1987, 38,106 km of roads, of which 8,945 were national and 29,161 provincial roads.

Number of motor vehicles in Dec. 1988: 2,215,923, of which 1,507,952 were passenger cars, 688,894 goods vehicles, 19,077 buses.

Railways. In 1987 the State network, Hellenic Railways (OSE), totalled 2,479 km comprising 1,565 km of 1,435 mm gauge, 892 km of 1,000 mm gauge, and 22 km of 750 mm gauge, and carried 3·8m. tonnes of freight and 11·8m. passengers.

Aviation. Olympic Airways connects Athens with all important cities of the country, Europe, the Middle East and USA. Thirty-four foreign companies connect Athens with the principal cities of the world.

The principal airport is at Athens. In 1987, 239,508 aircraft departed and arrived; 11,059,000 passengers embarked and 10,999,000 disembarked.

Shipping. In Dec. 1988 the merchant navy comprised 2,015 vessels of 21,368,976 GRT. Greek-owned ships under foreign flags totalled 4,164,000 GRT in July 1988.

There is a canal (opened 9 Nov. 1893) across the Isthmus of Corinth (about 4 miles).

Post and Broadcasting. In 1988 there were 3,779 telephone exchanges and 4,300,634 telephones.

Elliniki Radiophonia Tileorasis (ERT), the Hellenic National Radio and Television Institute, is the government broadcasting station. ERT broadcasts 2 TV programmes. Number of receivers: Radio, 5m.; television, 1·4m.

Cinemas (1981). There were 1,150 cinemas.

Newspapers (1987). There were 33 daily newspapers published in Athens, 6 in Piraeus and 100 elsewhere.

JUSTICE, RELIGION, EDUCATION AND WELFARE

Justice. Under the 1975 Constitution judges are appointed for life by the President of the Republic, after consultation with the judicial council. Judges enjoy personal and functional independence. There are three divisions of the courts: Administrative, civil and criminal and they must not give decisions which are contrary to the Constitution. Final jurisdiction lies with a Special Supreme Tribunal.

Some laws, passed before the 1975 Constitution came into force, and which are not contrary to it, remain in force.

Religion. The Christian Eastern Orthodox faith is the established religion to which 98% of the population belong.

The Greek Orthodox Church is under an archbishop and 67 metropolitans, 1 archbishop and 7 metropolitans in Crete, and 4 metropolitans in the Dodecanese. The Roman Catholics have 3 archbishops (in Naxos and Corfu and, not recognized by the State, in Athens) and 1 bishop (for Syra and Santorin). The Exarchs of the Greek Catholics and the Armenians are not recognized by the State.

Complete religious freedom is recognized by the Constitution of 1968, but proselytizing from, and interference with, the Greek Orthodox Church is forbidden.

Education. Public education is provided in nursery, primary and secondary schools, starting at 6 years of age and since 1963 free at all levels.

In 1986–87 there were 5,281 nursery schools with 7,774 teachers and 155,527 pupils; 8,361 primary schools with 37,947 teachers and 865,660 pupils; 1,708 high schools with 25,821 teachers and 450,270 pupils; 1,057 lycea with 17,976 teachers and 267,138 pupils and 506 technical and vocational schools with 7,909 teachers and 118,437 pupils. There were also 7 teacher training schools with 60 teachers and 4,929 students; 12 technical education schools with 4,474 teachers and 73,150 students; 47 vocational and ecclesiastical schools with 675 teachers and 3,760 students and 16 higher education schools with 7,141 teachers and 115,969 students.

In 1982–83 there were 13 universities with 94,574 students and 7,638 lecturers.

Health (1987). There were 454 hospitals and sanatoria with a total of 51,745 beds. There were 33,290 doctors and 9,104 dentists.

DIPLOMATIC REPRESENTATIVES

Of Greece in Great Britain (1A Holland Park, London, W11 3TP)
Ambassador: (Vacant).

Of Great Britain in Greece (1 Ploutarchou St., 106 75 Athens)
Ambassador: Sir David Miers, KBE, CMG.

Of Greece in the USA (2221 Massachusetts Ave., NW, Washington, D.C., 20008)
Ambassador: Christos Zacharakis.

Of the USA in Greece (91 Vasilissis Sophias Blvd., 10160 Athens)
Ambassador: Michael G. Sotirhos.

Of Greece to the United Nations
Ambassador: Constantine Zepos.

Further Reading

Clogg, R., *Greece in the 1980s*. London, 1983

Clogg, M. J. and R., *Greece*. [Bibliography] Oxford and Santa Barbara, 1980

Freris, A. F., *The Greek Economy in the Twentieth Century*. London, 1986

Holden, D., *Greece Without Columns: The Making of the Modern Greeks*. London, 1972

Kousoulas, D. G., *Revolution and Defeat: The Story of the Greek Communist Party*. OUP, 1965

Kykkotis, I., *English–Modern Greek and Modern Greek–English Dictionary*. 3rd ed. London, 1957

Mouzelis, N. P., *Modern Greece*. London, 1978

Pring, J. T., *The Oxford Dictionary of Modern Greek, Greek-English, English-Greek*. OUP, 1965–82

Tsoukalis, L., *Greece and the European Community*. Farnborough, 1979

Woodhouse, C. M., *The Struggle for Greece, 1941–1949*. London, 1976.—*Karamanlis: The Restorer of Greek Democracy*. OUP, 1982

Xydis, S. G., *Greece and the Great Powers, 1944–47*. Thessaloniki, 1963

GRENADA

Capital: St George's
Population: 99,205 (1988)
GNP per capita: US$1,265 (1988)

HISTORY. Grenada became an independent nation within the Commonwealth on 7 Feb. 1974. Grenada was formerly an Associated State under the West Indies Act, 1967. The 1973 Constitution was suspended in 1979 following a revolution.

On 19 Oct. 1983 the army took control after a power struggle led to the killing of Maurice Bishop the Prime Minister. At the request of a group of Caribbean countries, Grenada was invaded by US-led forces on 24–28 Oct. On 1 Nov. a State of Emergency was imposed which ended on 15 Nov. when an interim government was installed.

AREA AND POPULATION. Grenada is the most southerly island of the Windward Islands with an area of 120 sq. miles (311 sq. km); the state also includes the Southern Grenadine Islands to the north, chiefly Carriacou and Petite Martinique, with an area of 13 sq. miles (34 sq. km). The total population (Census, 1988) was 99,205. The Borough of St. George's, the capital, had 29,369 inhabitants in 1981, but its urban area had a population of only 4,788. In 1983, 84% of the people were black and a further 12% of mixed origins.

Vital statistics (1987): Births, 3,102; deaths, 781.

CLIMATE. The tropical climate is very agreeable in the dry season, from Jan. to May, when days are warm and nights quite cool, but in the wet season there is very little difference between day and night temperatures. On the coast, annual rainfall is about 60" (1,500 mm) but it is as high as 150–200" (3,750–5,000 mm) in the mountains.

CONSTITUTION AND GOVERNMENT. The British sovereign is represented by an appointed Governor-General. There is a bicameral legislature, consisting of a 13-member Senate, appointed by the Governor-General, and a 15-member House of Representatives, elected by universal suffrage. Elections were held for the 15-seat House of Representatives on 3 Dec. 1984. The New National Party won 14 seats and the Grenada United Labour Party, 1.

Governor-General: Sir Paul Scoon, GCMG, GCVO, OBE.

Prime Minister: Hon. Ben Joseph Jones.

National flag: Divided into 4 triangles of yellow, top and bottom, and green, hoist and fly; in the centre a red disc bearing a gold star; along the top and bottom edged red stripes each bearing 3 gold stars; on the green triangle near the hoist a pod of nutmeg.

Local government: There are 7 district councils (including 1 for Carriacou/Petite Martinique) and the Borough Council of St. George's. Local Government Bills had their first reading in Parliament on 24 Oct. 1986. The second reading and final stages of the Bills were postponed. The Department of Local Government has subsequently submitted new proposals for the re-establishment of elected local councils in Grenada, Carriacou and Petite Martinique.

DEFENCE

Army. A People's Revolutionary Army was created in 1979. Personnel about 6,500 organized into 3 infantry battalions and an artillery battery.

INTERNATIONAL RELATIONS

Membership. Grenada is a member of the UN, OAS, Caricom, the Commonwealth and is an ACP state of EEC.

ECONOMY

Budget. The 1987 estimates balanced at EC$226·3m. Value added tax has replaced income tax.

Currency. The currency is the *Eastern Caribbean dollar*. In March 1990, £1 = EC$4·40; US$ = EC$2·71.

Banking. In 1987 there were 5 commercial banks in Grenada: The National Commercial Bank, Barclays Bank International, Grenada Bank of Commerce, Bank of Nova Scotia and the Grenada Co-operative Bank. The Grenada Agricultural Bank was established in 1965 to encourage agricultural development; in 1975 it became the Grenada Agricultural and Industrial Development Corporation. In 1987, bank deposits were EC$269·2m.

ENERGY AND NATURAL RESOURCES

Electricity. Production (1984) 40·5m. kwh.

Agriculture. The principal crops (1988 production in 1,000 lb.) are: Cocoa (3,665), nutmegs (5,510), bananas (21,116), mace (567) and coconuts (540); corn and pigeon peas, citrus, sugar-cane, root-crops and vegetables are also grown, in addition to small scattered cultivations of cotton, cloves, cinnamon, pimento, coffee and fruit trees.

Livestock (1988): Cattle, 5,000; sheep, 17,000; goats, 11,000; pigs, 11,000; poultry (1982), 260,000.

Fisheries. The catch (1988) was 2,204 tonnes.

COMMERCE (1987). Total value of imports, EC$239·4m. The exports are cocoa (EC$10·8m.), nutmegs (EC$39·4m.), bananas (EC$11·1m.), mace (EC$7·2m.) and fruit (EC$7m.).

Of exports in 1987, UK took 22·8%; Netherlands, 24·8%; Trinidad, 9·3%; Federal Republic of Germany, 17·9%, Canada, 3·5%; USA, 5%. Of 1987 imports, Trinidad furnished 11·9%; USA, 26·2%; UK, 16·9%; Canada, 6·5%; Netherlands, 2·5%; Federal Republic of Germany, 1·7%.

Total trade between Grenada and UK (British Department of Trade returns, in £1,000 sterling):

	1985	*1986*	*1987*	*1988*	*1989*
Imports to UK	6,735	7,011	6,302	6,115	5,924
Exports and re-exports to UK	8,820	8,628	8,772	7,162	9,058

TOURISM. In 1988, there were 200,632 visitors; including 135,980 cruise ship passengers.

COMMUNICATIONS

Roads. The scheduled road mileage is 577, of which 377 have an oiled surface and 210 are graded as third- and fourth-class roads. Vehicles registered (1988) 12,198.

Aviation. A new international airport was inaugurated in Oct. 1984 at Point Salines and has daily connexions to London, New York, Miami and South America *via* nearby islands. Pearls Airport is closed to international air traffic and is only occasionally used for crop spraying purposes. There is a small airstrip on Carriacou.

Shipping. Total shipping for 1987 was 1,004 motor and steamships and 140 sailing and auxiliary vessels, with a total net tonnage of 869,235 and 7,253 respectively.

Post and Broadcasting. A joint company was being formed in 1988 between the Government of Grenada and Cable and Wireless (W.I.) Ltd to replace both the Grenada Telephone Co. Ltd and the Cable and Wireless branch in Grenada. The system is fully digitalized. At 31 Oct. 1988 there were 6,199 lines and 9,340 stations connected. There were (1978) 63,500 radios.

JUSTICE, RELIGION, EDUCATION AND WELFARE

Justice. The Grenada Supreme Court, situated in St George's, comprises a High Court of Justice, a Court of Magisterial Appeal (which hears appeals from the lower Magistrates' Courts exercising summary jurisdiction) and an Itinerant Court of Appeal (to hear appeals from the High Court).

Religion. The majority of the population are Roman Catholic; the Anglican and Methodist churches are also well represented.

Education. In 1989 there were 71 pre-primary schools with 3,660 pupils, 58 primary schools with 19,963 pupils, 18 secondary schools with 6,437 pupils, 2 schools for special education and 5 day care centres. The Grenada National College, established in July 1988, incorporates the Institute for Further Education, the Grenada Teachers' College, the Grenada Technical and Vocational Institute, the School of Nursing, the Mirabeau Farm Institute, the Science and Technological Council, the Continuing Education Programme, the Public Service Training Division and the School of Pharmacy. There is also a branch of the University of the West Indies.

Health. In 1988 there were 5 hospitals and 29 clinics with 500 beds. In 1988 there were 37 doctors, 7 dentists, 24 pharmacists, 35 midwives and 296 nursing personnel.

DIPLOMATIC REPRESENTATIVES

Of Grenada in Great Britain (1 Collingham Gdns., London, SW5)
High Commissioner: O. M. Gibbs, CMG (accredited 15 March 1984).

Of Great Britain in Grenada
High Commissioner: K. F. X. Burns, CMG (resides in Bridgetown).

Of Grenada in the USA (1701 New Hampshire Ave., NW, Washington, D.C., 20009)
Ambassador: Albert O. Xavier.

Of the USA in Grenada (P.O. Box 54, St George's)
Chargé d'Affaires: James Ford Cooper.

Of Grenada to the United Nations
Ambassador: Dr Lamuel A. Stanislaus.

Further Reading

Davidson, J. S., *Grenada: A Study in Politics and the Limits of International Law*. London, 1987
Gilmore, W. G., *The Grenada Intervention: Analysis and Documentation*. London, 1984
Hodge, M. and Searle, C. (eds) *Is Freedom We Making*. Govt. Information Service, 1981
O'Shaughnessy, H., *Grenada: Revolution, Invasion and Aftermath*. London, 1984
Page, A., Sutton, P. and Thorndike, T., *Grenada and Invasion*. London, 1984
Sandford, G. and Vigilante, R., *Grenada: The Untold Story*. London, 1988
Searle, C., *Grenada: The Struggle against Destabilization*. London, 1983
Searle, C. and Rojas, D. (eds) *To Construct from Morning*. Grenada, 1982
Sinclair, N., *Grenada: Isle of Spice*. London, 1987
Thorndike, T., *Grenada: Politics, Economics and Society*. London, 1985
Wheaton, P. and Sunshine, C. (eds) *Grenada: The Peaceful Revolution*. Washington, 1982

GUATEMALA

Capital: Guatemala City
Population: 9m. (1989)
GNP per capita: US$880 (1988)

República de Guatemala

HISTORY. From 1524 to 1821 Guatemala was a Spanish captaincy-general, comprising the whole of Central America. It became independent from Spain in 1821 and formed part of the Confederation of Central America from 1823 to 1839, when Rafael Carrera dissolved the Confederation and Guatemala became independent.

AREA AND POPULATION. Guatemala is bounded on the north and west by Mexico, south by the Pacific ocean and east by El Salvador, Honduras and Belize, and the area is 108,889 sq. km (42,042 sq. miles). In March 1936 Guatemala, El Salvador and Honduras agreed to accept the peak of Mount Montecristo as the common boundary point.

The census population was 6,054,227 in 1981. Estimate (1989) 9m. In 1983, 53% were pure Indians, of 21 different groups descended from the Maya; most of the remainder are mixed Indian and Spanish. Density of population, 1985, 77 per sq. km.

Vital statistics, 1984: Births, 302,921; deaths, 75,462; marriages, 31,351.

Guatemala is administratively divided into 22 departments, each with a governor appointed by the President. Population, 1985:

Departments	*Area (sq. km)*	*Population*	*Departments*	*Area (sq. km)*	*Population*
Alta Verapaz	8,686	393,446	Petén	35,854	118,116
Baja Verapaz	3,124	160,567	Quezaltenango	1,951	478,030
Chimaltenango	1,979	283,887	Quiché	8,378	460,956
Chiquimula	2,376	220,067	Retalhuleu	1,858	228,563
El Progreso	1,922	106,115	Sacatepéquez	465	148,574
Escuintla	4,384	565,215	San Marcos	3,791	590,152
Guatemala	2,126	2,050,673	Santa Rosa	2,955	263,060
Huehuetenango	7,403	571,292	Sololá	1,061	181,816
Izabal	9,038	330,546	Suchitepéquez	2,510	327,763
Jalapa	2,063	171,542	Totonicapán	1,061	249,067
Jutiapa	3,219	348,032	Zacapa	2,690	155,496

The capital is Guatemala City with about 2m. inhabitants (1989). Other towns are Quezaltenango (246,000), Puerto Barrios (338,000), Mazatenango (38,319), Antigua (26,631), Zacapa (35,769) and Cobán (120,000).

CLIMATE. A tropical climate, with little variation in temperature and a well marked wet season from May to Oct. Guatemala City. Jan. 63°F (17·2°C), July 69°F (20·6°C). Annual rainfall 53" (1,316 mm).

CONSTITUTION AND GOVERNMENT. A new Constitution, drawn up by the Constituent Assembly elected on 1 July 1984, was promulgated in June 1985 and came into force on 14 Jan. 1986. The President and Vice-President are elected for a term of 5 years by direct election (with a second round of voting if no candidate secures 50% of the first-round votes). The unicameral Legislative Assembly comprises 100 members. Presidential, congressional and municipal elections were held on 3 Nov. 1985, with a second round of voting on 8 Dec. 1985.

President: Marco Vinicio Cerezo Arévalo (assumed office 14 Jan. 1986).

Vice-President: Roberto Carpio Nicolle.

Foreign Relations: Ariel Rivera Irias. *Finance:* Francisco Pinto Cassasola. *Defence:* Gen. Héctor Gramajo Morales.

National flag: Three vertical strips of blue, white, blue, with the national arms in the centre.

National anthem: ¡Guatemala! Feliz (words by J. J. Palma; tune by R. Alvarez).

DEFENCE. There is selective conscription into the armed forces for 30 months.

Army. The Army numbered (1990) 40,000, organized in 39 infantry, 2 airbourne, 2 air defence, 2 strategic reserve and 1 engineer battalions. Equipment includes light tanks and armoured cars. Reserves, 1990, 35,000. Territorial militia, 600,000.

Navy. A Naval element of the combined armed forces operates 9 inshore patrol craft, plus 30 river patrol boats. The force was (1989) 1,200 strong of whom 700 are marines for maintenance of riverine security. Main bases are Santo Tomás (on the Atlantic Coast), Puerto Quetzal and Puerto San José (Pacific).

Air Force. There is a small Air Force with 10 A-37B and 2 T-33 light attack aircraft, 1DC-6, 10 C-47, 3 F.27 and 7 Israeli-built Arava transports, 10 Pilatus PC-7 turboprop trainers, and a number of Cessna light aircraft and Bell helicopters, including a few armed UH-1 Iroquois. Strength was (1990) about 1,000 personnel and 80 aircraft.

INTERNATIONAL RELATIONS

Membership. Guatemala is a member of UN, OAS and CACM.

External Debt. On 31 Dec. 1988 the external debt was US$2,500m.

ECONOMY

Planning. The 1988 National Economic Development Plan, called 'Guatemala 2000', calls for sustained GDP growth of at least 6% per annum until 2000.

Budget. In 1989 expenditure was 3,500m. quetzales; revenue, 2,900m. quetzales

Currency. The *quetzal* was established 7 May 1925. There are coins of 25, 10, 5 and 1 *centavos* and there are also paper notes of 100, 50, 20, 10, 5, 1 and $^1/_2$ *quetzales* (50 *centavos*). In March 1990, £1 = Q.6·40; US$1 = Q.3·90.

Banking. On 4 Feb. 1946 the Central Bank of Guatemala (founded in 1926 as a mixed central and commercial bank) was superseded by a new institution, the Banco de Guatemala, to operate solely as a central bank. Savings and term deposits at commercial banks were Q.3,885·2m. at 31 July 1988. Total currency in circulation on 31 July 1989 was Q.1,785m.; total net international reserves amounted to Q.50m. on 31 July 1989.

There are 24 banks, including the Banco de Guatemala, Banco Nacional de Desarollo, set up in 1971 to promote agricultural development, its counterpart for small industries (Banco de los Trabajadores) set up in Jan. 1966 with initial capital of US$1·3m. and a subsidiary of Lloyds Bank plc.

Weights and Measures. The metric system has been officially adopted, but is little used in local commerce.

Libra of 16 oz.	=1·014 lb.	*League*	=3 miles
Arroba of 25 libras	=25·35 lb.	*Vara*	=32 in.
Quintal of 4 arrobas	=101·40 lb.	*Manzana*	=100 varas sq.
Tonelada of 20 quintals	=20·28 cwt	*Caballeria* of 64 manzanas	=110 acres
Fanega	=1$^1/_2$ Imp. bushels		

ENERGY AND NATURAL RESOURCES

Electricity. 2,800m. kwh. of electricity were generated in 1989. A large hydroelectric plant was inaugurated in Dec. 1985. Supply 110 and 220 volts; 60 Hz.

Oil. Guatemala began exporting crude oil in 1980; exports, 1984, were valued at US$34m. Production is from wells in Alta Verapaz department from where the oil is piped to Santo Tomas de Castilla. Further exploration is proceeding in the Petén.

Minerals. Mineral production includes zinc and lead concentrates, some antimony and tungsten, a small amount of cadmium and silver; some copper is also being mined. Exports (1988) Q.2m.

Agriculture. The Cordilleras divide Guatemala into two unequal drainage areas, of which the Atlantic is much the greater. The Pacific slope, though comparatively narrow, is exceptionally well watered and fertile between the altitudes of 1,000 and 5,000 ft, and is the most densely settled part of the republic. The Atlantic slope is sparsely populated, and has little of commercial importance beyond the chicle and timber-cutting of the Petén, coffee cultivation of Cobán region and banana-raising of the Motagua Valley and Lake Izabal district. Soil erosion is serious and a single week of heavy rains suffices to cause flooding of fields and much crop destruction.

The principal crop is coffee; there are about 12,000 coffee plantations with 138m. coffee trees on about 338,000 acres, but 80% of the crop comes from 1,500 large coffee farms employing 426,000 workers. Production (1988) 156,000 tonnes. Coffee exports in 1987 were valued at US$400m. mainly to USA and Federal Republic of Germany.

Bananas are still an important export crop, but exports have at times been seriously reduced, partly by labour troubles and by hurricanes. Production (1989) 780,000 tonnes. Exports 1987 were worth US$67m.

Cotton exports in 1984 were valued at US$70·4m. Cotton lint production (1988) 44,000 tonnes. Other important exports (1984) were sugar, US$74·5m.; beef, US$11·6m. Guatemala is, after Mexico, the largest producer of chicle gum (used for chewing-gum manufacture in USA). Rubber development schemes are under way, assisted by US funds. Guatemala is one of the largest sources of essential oils (citronella and lemon grass); exports in 1984 were valued at US$1·7m. Cardamom, exported mainly to the Arab countries, was valued at US$40m. in 1987.

Livestock (1988): Cattle, 2·14m.; pigs, 615,000; sheep, 660,000; horses, 112,000; poultry, 15m.

Forestry. The forest area had (1989) an extent of 4m. hectare, 37% of the land area. The department of Petén is rich in mahogany and other woods. Production (1980) 11·23m. cu. metres.

Fisheries. Exports were about Q.11·8m. in 1984.

INDUSTRY AND TRADE

Industry. The principal industries are food and beverages, tobacco, chemicals, hides and skins, textiles, garments and non-metallic minerals. New industries include electrical goods, plastic sheet and metal furniture.

Trade Unions. There are 3 federations for private sector workers.

Commerce. Values in Q.1,000 (1 quetzal =US$1) were:

	1985	*1986*	*1987*	*1988*
Imports (c.i.f.)	1,020,572	804,000	1,230,000	1,250,000
Exports (f.o.b.)	1,174,800	825,000	824,000	875,000

Total trade between Guatemala and UK (British Department of Trade returns, in £1,000 sterling):

	1985	*1986*	*1987*	*1988*	*1989*
Imports to UK	5,176	8,098	7,536	10,678	6,950
Exports and re-exports from UK	13,397	9,288	13,926	15,387	52,324

Tourism. There were 287,000 foreign visitors in 1986.

COMMUNICATIONS

Roads. In 1989 there were 18,000 km of roads, of which 2,850 are paved. There is a highway from coast to coast *via* Guatemala City. There are 2 highways from the Mexican to the Salvadorean frontier: the Pacific Highway serving the fertile coastal plain and the Pan-American Highway running through the highlands and Guatemala City. Motor vehicles numbered about 300,000 in 1989.

Railways. The principal railway system is the government-owned (since 1968) *Ferrocarriles de Guatemala*. All railways are of 914 mm gauge. Total length of all lines was (1989) 953 km. Passengers carried, 1986, numbered 379,789, and freight carried 650,000 tonnes.

Aviation. The government-owned airline, Aviateca, and 2 private airlines furnish both domestic and international services; 6 other airlines handle international traffic from La Aurora airport in Guatemala City.

Shipping. The chief ports on the Atlantic coast are Puerto Barrios and Santo Tomás de Castilla: on the Pacific coast, Puerto Quetzal and Champerico. Total tonnage handled was, 1987, 7m. tons.

Post and Broadcasting. The Government own and operate the telegraph and telephone services; there were 180,000 telephones in Sept. 1988. There are some 70 broadcasting stations. Radio receiving sets in use, 1988, numbered about 1m. There are 4 commercial TV stations, 1 government station and about 250,000 TV receivers. There is also reception by US television satellite.

Cinemas (1984). Cinemas numbered approximately 100.

Newspapers (1984). There are 4 daily newspapers.

JUSTICE, RELIGION, EDUCATION AND WELFARE

Justice. Justice is administered in a Constitution Court, a Supreme Court, 6 appeal courts and 28 courts of first instance. Supreme Court and appeal court judges are elected by Congress. Judges of first instance are appointed by the Supreme Court.

All holders of public office have to show on entering office, and again on leaving, a full account of their private property and income.

Religion. Roman Catholicism is the prevailing faith; but all other creeds have complete liberty of worship. Guatemala has a Roman Catholic archbishopric.

Education. In 1988 there were 11,587 schools with 45,611 teachers and an attendance of 1,331,294 pupils; these figures include private schools. There are 1,237 secondary and other schools having 13,891 teachers and an attendance of 194,484 pupils; the state-supported but autonomous University of San Carlos de Borromeo, founded in 1678, was reopened in 1910 with 7 faculties and schools and there are 4 private universities. Students at state university (1984) approximately 45,552. All education is in theory free, but owing to a grave shortage of state schools private schools flourish. The 1988 census estimates that 63% of those 10 years of age and older were illiterate.

Social Welfare. A comprehensive system of social security was outlined in a law of 30 Oct. 1946. Medical personnel include about 1,250 doctors and 275 dentists for the whole republic. There are about 60 public hospitals and about 100 dispensaries.

DIPLOMATIC REPRESENTATIVES

Of Guatemala in Great Britain (13 Fawcett St., London, SW10 9HN)
Ambassador: Dr Erwin Blandon.

Of Great Britain in Guatemala (7a Avenida 5-10, Zona 4, Guatemala City)
Ambassador: Bernard Everett.

Of Guatemala in the USA (2220 R. St., NW, Washington, D.C., 20008)
Ambassador: Rodolfo Rohrmoser Valdeavellano.

Of the USA in Guatemala (7–01 Avenida de la Reforma, Zone 10, Guatemala City)
Ambassador: Thomas Frank Stroock.

Of Guatemala to the United Nations
Ambassador: Francisco Villagrán DeLeon.

Further Reading

The official gazette is called *Diario de Centro America.*

Banco de Guatemala, *Memoria annual, Estudio económico* and *Boletín Estadístico*
Bloomfield, L. M., *The British Honduras–Guatemala Dispute*. Toronto, 1953
Franklin, W. B., *Guatemala*. [Bibliography] Oxford and Santa Barbara, 1981
Glassman, P., *Guatemala Guide*. Dallas, 1977
Immerman, R. H., *The CIA in Guatemala: The Foreign Policy of Intervention*. Univ. of Texas Press, 1982
Mendoza, J. L., *Britain and Her Treaties on Belize*. Guatemala, 1946
Morton, F., *Xeláhuh*. London, 1959
Plant, R., *Guatemala: Unnatural Disaster*. London, 1978
Schlesinger, S. and Kinzer, S., *Bitter Front: The Untold Story of the American Coup in Guatemala*. London and New York, 1982

National Library: Biblioteca Nacional, 5a Avenida y 8a Calle, Zona 1, Guatemala City.

GUINEA

Capital: Conakry
Population: 6·53m. (1988)
GNP per capita: US$350 (1988)

République de Guinée

HISTORY. Guinea was proclaimed a French protectorate in 1888 and a colony in 1893. It became a constituent territory of French West Africa in 1904. The independent republic of Guinea was proclaimed on 2 Oct. 1958, after the territory of French Guinea had decided at the referendum of 28 Sept. to leave the French Community. Following the death of the first President, Ahmed Sekou Touré on 27 March 1984, the armed forces staged a *coup* and dissolved the National Assembly.

AREA AND POPULATION. Guinea, a coastal state of West Africa, is bounded north-west by Guinea-Bissau and Senegal, north-east by Mali, south-east by the Côte d'Ivoire, south by Liberia and Sierra Leone, and west by the Atlantic Ocean.

The area is 245,857 sq. km (94,926 sq. miles), and the population, census, 1983, was 5,781,014; estimate, 1988, 6,533,000. The capital is Conakry. In 1985, 25% were urban.

The areas, populations and chief towns of the major divisions are:

	Sq. km	*Census 1983*	*Chief town*	*Census 1983*
Conakry (city)	308	705,280	Conakry	705,280
Guinée-Maritime	43,980	1,147,301	Kindia	55,904
Moyenne-Guinée	51,710	1,595,007	Labé	65,439
Haute-Guinée	92,535	1,086,679	Kankan	88,760
Guinée-Forestière	57,324	1,246,747	Nzérékoré	23,000 [1]

[1] 1972.

The ethnic composition is Fulani (40·3%, predominant in Moyenne-Guinée), Malinké (or Mandingo, 25·8%, prominent in Haute-Guinée), Susu (11%, prominent in Guinée-Maritime), Kissi (6·5%) and Kpelle (4·8%) in Guinée-Forestière, and Dialonka, Loma and others (11·6%).

CLIMATE. A tropical climate, with high rainfall near the coast and constant heat, but conditions are a little cooler on the plateau. The wet season on the coast lasts from May to Nov., but only to Oct. inland. Conakry. Jan. 80°F (26·7°C), July 77°F (25°C). Annual rainfall 172" (4,293 mm).

CONSTITUTION AND GOVERNMENT. Following the *coup* of 3 April 1984, supreme power rests with a *Comité Militaire de Redressement National*, ruling through a Council of Ministers appointed by the President composed as follows in 1989:

President and Head of CMRN: Brig-Gen. Lansana Conté.

Ministers-Delegate to Presidency: Major Henri Tofani *(National Defence)*, Hervé Vincent Bangoura *(Information, Culture and Tourism)*, Major Henri Foula *(Economy and Finance)*.

Resident (Regional) Ministers: Major Abou Camara *(Guinée-Maritime)*, Lieut.-Col. Sory Doumbouya *(Moyenne-Guinée)*, Major Alpha Oumar Barou Diallo *(Haute-Guinée)*, Major Alhousseini Fofana *(Guinée-Forestière)*.

Local Government: The administrative division comprises the capital Conakry and 29 provinces divided into 175 districts, grouped into 4 'supra-regions' which correspond to the 4 major geographical and ethnic areas: Guinée-Maritime; Moyenne-Guinée; Haute-Guinée and Guinée-Forestière.

National flag: Three vertical strips of red, gold, green.

Besides French, there are 8 official languages taught in schools: Fulani, Malinké, Susu, Kissi, Kpelle, Loma, Basari and Koniagi.

DEFENCE

Army. The Army of 8,500 men (1990), comprises 1 armoured, 5 infantry, 1 commando and 1 engineer, 1 artillery, 1 air defence and 1 special force battalions. Equipment includes 30 T-34 and 20 PT-76 tanks. There are also 3 paramilitary forces: People's Militia (7,000), Gendarmerie (1,000) and Republican Guard (1,600).

Navy. A small force of 600 men operate 2 French-built, 1 US-built and 6 Soviet-built inshore patrol craft, plus a number of riverine boats and 2 small landing craft; bases are at Conakry and Kakanda.

Air Force. The Air Force, formed with Soviet assistance, is reported to be equipped with 6 MiG-17 jet-fighters and 2 MiG-15UTI trainers, 4 An-14 and 4 Il-14 piston-engined transports and a Yak-40 jet aircraft for VIP duties, all Russian built, plus a few French-supplied helicopters, piston-engined Yak-18 and L-29 jet trainers. Personnel (1990) 800.

INTERNATIONAL RELATIONS

Membership. Guinea is a member of UN, OAU and is an ACP state of EEC.

ECONOMY

Budget. The budget for 1987: balanced at 377,000m. *Guinea francs*.

Currency. The monetary unit is the *Guinea franc*. There are banknotes of 25, 50, 100, 500, 1,000 and 5,000 *Guinea francs*. In March 1990, £1 = 493·35 *francs*; US$1 = 301·01 *francs*.

Banking. In 1986 the Central Bank was restructured and commercial banking returned to the private sector.

ENERGY AND NATURAL RESOURCES

Electricity. Production of electrical energy was 236m. kwh. in 1986.

Minerals. Bauxite is mined at Fria, Boké and Kindia; output (1986) 14·7m. tonnes, alumina 580,000 tonnes. Production of iron ore from the Nimba and Simandou mountains commenced in 1981, following exhaustion of the Kaloum peninsula deposits. Diamond mining output (1985) 105,000 carats of gem diamonds and 7,000 carats of industrial diamonds.

Agriculture. The chief crops (production, 1988, in 1,000 tonnes) are: Cassava, 530; rice, 486; plantains, 350; sugar-cane, 175; bananas, 110; groundnuts, 75; sweet potatoes, 75; yams, 62; maize, 45; palm-oil, 45; palm kernels, 40; pineapples, 20; pulses, 50; coffee, 15; coconuts, 15.

Livestock (1988): Cattle, 1·8m.; sheep, 460,000; goats, 460,000; pigs, 50,000.

Forestry: In 1988, 41% of the country was forested (10m. hectares). Round-wood production (1986) 4·4m. cu. metres.

Fisheries: Catch (1986) 30,000 tonnes.

COMMERCE. In 1984 imports totalled 7,542m. *Guinea francs* (32% from France) and exports 11,009m. *Guinea francs* (28% to the USA). Alumina forms about 30% and bauxite 58% of the exports.

Total trade between Guinea and the UK (British Department of Trade returns, in £1,000 sterling):

	1985	*1986*	*1987*	*1988*	*1989*
Imports to UK	9,064	23,892	19,538	7,582	10,657
Exports and re-exports from UK	10,301	10,679	10,675	10,106	13,937

COMMUNICATIONS

Roads. There are 29,000 km of roads and tracks, of which 520 km are bitumenized. In 1985 there were 106,000 cars and 113,000 commercial vehicles.

Railways. A railway connects Conakry with Kankan (662 km) and is to be extended to Bougouni in Mali. A line 134 km long linking bauxite deposits at Sangaredi with Port Kamsar was opened in 1973 and a third line links Conakry and Fria (144 km).

Aviation. There are airports at Conakry and Kankan; in 1982, 131,000 passengers disembarked and embarked.

Shipping. There are ports at Conakry and for bauxite exports at Kamsar (opened 1973). There were (1983) 18 vessels of 6,944 GRT registered in Guinea.

Post and Broadcasting. Telephones, 1981, numbered about 10,000. There were 200,000 radio receivers and 10,000 television receivers in 1986.

Newspapers. In 1979 there was 1 daily newspaper (circulation 20,000).

JUSTICE, RELIGION, EDUCATION AND WELFARE

Justice. There are *tribunaux du premier degré* at Conakry and Kankan, and a *juge de paix* at Nzérékoré. The High Court, Court of Appeal and Superior Tribunal of Cassation are at Conakry.

Religion. In 1980, about 69% of the population was Moslem, 1% Christian (mainly Roman Catholic) and 30% followed tribal religions.

Education. In 1987–88, 290,000 pupils and 7,239 teachers in primary schools, 76,000 pupils and 3,600 teachers in secondary schools, 4,700 students in technical schools and 1,200 in teacher-training colleges and 5,915 in higher education.

Health. In 1976 there were 314 hospitals and dispensaries with 7,650 beds; there were also 277 doctors, 21 dentists, 159 pharmacists, 394 midwives and 1,533 nursing personnel.

DIPLOMATIC REPRESENTATIVES

Of Guinea in Great Britain (resides in Paris)
Ambassador: Sekou Decazi Camara (accredited on 13 June 1985).

Of Great Britain in Guinea
Ambassador: J. E. C. Macrae, CMG (resides in Dakar).

Of Guinea in the USA (2112 Leroy Pl., NW, Washington, D.C., 20008)
Ambassador: Dr Kekoura Camara.

Of the USA in Guinea (2nd Blvd. and 9th Ave., Conakry)
Ambassador: Samuel E. Lupo.

Of Guinea to the United Nations
Ambassador: Zainoul Abidine Sanoussi.

Further Reading

Bulletin Statistique et Economique de la Guinée. Monthly. Conakry
Adamolekun, L., *Sékou Touré's Guinea.* London, 1976
Camara, S. S., *La Guinée sans la France.* Paris, 1976
Taylor, F. W., *A Fulani-English Dictionary.* Oxford, 1932

GUINEA-BISSAU

Capital: Bissau
Population: 932,000 (1988)
GNP per capita: US$160 (1987)

Republica da Guiné-Bissau

HISTORY. Guinea-Bissau, formerly Portuguese Guinea, on the coast of Guinea, was discovered in 1446 by Nuno Tristão. It became a separate colony in 1879. It is bounded by the limits fixed by the convention of 12 May 1886 with France. In 1951 Guinea-Bissau became an overseas province of Portugal. The struggle against colonial rule began in 1963. Independence was declared on 24 Sept. 1973. In 1974 Portugal formally recognized the independence of Guinea-Bissau.

AREA AND POPULATION. Guinea-Bissau is bounded by Senegal in the north, the Atlantic ocean in the west and by Guinea in the east and south. It includes the adjacent archipelago of Bijagós. Area, 36,125 sq. km (13,948 sq. miles); population (census, 1979), 767,739, of whom 125,000 (estimate, 1988) resided in the capital, Bissau; (estimate, 1988) 932,000.

The areas and populations (census 1979) of the regions were as follows:

Region	*Sq. km*	*Census 1979*	*Region*	*Sq. km*	*Census 1979*
Bissau City	78	109,214	Gabú	9,150	104,315
Bafatá	5,981	116,032	Oio	5,403	135,114
Biombo	838	56,463	Quinara	3,138	35,532
Bolama-Bijagós	2,624	25,473	Tombali	3,736	55,099
Cacheu	5,175	130,227			

In 1979, 14% of the population were urban, 48·2% were male and 44·3% were under the age of 15.

The main ethnic groups were (1979) the Balante (27%), Fulani (23%), Malinké 12%), Mandjako (11%) and Pepel (10%). Portuguese remains the official language, but Crioulo is spoken throughout the country.

CLIMATE. The tropical climate has a wet season from June to Nov., when rains are abundant, but the hot, dry Harmattan wind blows from Dec. to May. Bissau. Jan. 76°F (24·4°C), July 80°F (26·7°C). Annual rainfall 78" (1,950 mm).

CONSTITUTION AND GOVERNMENT. A new Constitution was promulgated on 16 May 1984. The Revolutionary Council, established following the 1980 *coup,* was replaced by a 15-member Council of State, while in April 1984 a new National People's Assembly was elected comprising 150 Representatives elected by and from the directly-elected regional councils. The sole political movement is the *Partido Africano da Independencia da Guiné e Cabo Verde* (PAIGC). The President is Head of State and Government, leading a Council of Ministers which in Oct. 1989 was composed as follows:

President: Brig-Gen. João Bernardo Vieira.

Ministers of State: Col. Iafai Camara *(Armed Forces)*, Dr Vasco Cabral *(Justice)*, Carlos Correia *(Rural Development and Fisheries)*, Tiago Alelua Lopes *(Presidency)*.

Foreign Affairs: Júlio Semedo. *Education, Culture and Sports:* Dr Fidelis Cabral d'Almada. *Commerce and Tourism:* Maj. Manuel dos Santos. *Public Works:* Avito da Silva. *National Security and Public Order:* Maj. José Pereira. *Natural Resources and Industry:* Filinto de Barros. *Finance:* Dr Vítor Freire Monteiro. *Public Health:* Adelino Nunes Correia. *Planning:* (Vacant). *Civil Service and Labour:* Henriqueta Godinho Gomes. *Information and Telecommunications:* Mussa Djassi. *Minister-Governor of Central Bank:* Dr Pedro A. Godinho Gomes.

There are 11 Secretaries of State.

National flag: Horizontally yellow over green with red vertical strip in the hoist bearing a black star.

Local government: The administrative division is divided into 3 provinces, 8 regions (each under an elected regional council), in turn subdivided into 37 sectors; and the city of Bissau, treated as a separate region.

DEFENCE

Army. The Army consisted in 1990 of 1 artillery and 5 infantry battalions, 1 engineer unit and 1 tank squadron. Equipment includes 10 T-34 tanks. Personnel, 6,800 men.

Navy. The naval flotilla, based at Bissau, is equipped with 12 inshore patrol craft of diverse origins; Soviet, Chinese and European. Personnel in 1989 totalled 300 officers and men.

Air Force. Formation of a small Air Force began in 1978 with the delivery of a French-built Cessna FTB-337 twin-engined counter-insurgency and general-purpose light transport. It has been followed by 2 Alouette III helicopters and 2 Dornier Do 27 utility aircraft. Personnel (1990) 100.

INTERNATIONAL RELATIONS

Membership. Guinea-Bissau is a member of UN, OAU and is an ACP state of EEC.

ECONOMY

Planning. The Development Plan ending 1990 aims at self-sufficiency in food.

Budget. The budget for 1985 balanced at 1,000m. pesos.

Currency. The monetary unit is the *peso* of 100 *centavos*. There are coins of 50 *centavos* and 1, 2, 5 and 20 *pesos*, and banknotes of 50, 100, 500 and 1,000 *pesos*. In March 1990, £1 = 1,068·92 *pesos*; US$1 = 648·85 *pesos*.

Banking. The Banco Nacional da Guiné-Bissau, founded 1976, is the bank of issue and also the commercial bank. There are also state-owned savings institutions. A private bank was planned to open in 1989.

ENERGY AND NATURAL RESOURCES

Electricity. Production (1986) 28m. kwh.

Minerals. Mining is very little developed although bauxite (200m. tonnes) has been located in the Boé area. Exploration for oil is taking place but no finds have been reported.

Agriculture. Chief crops (production, 1988, in 1,000 tonnes) are: Groundnuts, 30; sugar-cane, 6; plantains, 25; coconuts, 25; rice, 145; rubber, 23 (1981); palm kernels, 14; millet, 25; palm-oil, 3; sorghum, 35; maize, 15; cashew nuts, 10; timber, hides, seeds and wax.

Livestock (1988): Cattle, 340,000; sheep, 205,000; goats, 210,000; pigs, 290,000; poultry, 1m.

Forestry. Production (1985) 559,000 cu. metres. 33% of the country is forested.

Fisheries. Total catch (1986) 3,620 tonnes. Fishing is an important export industry.

COMMERCE. Imports in 1983, 1,586m. pesos of which 33% from Portugal; exports, 358m. of which 66% went to Portugal, 11% to Senegal and 10% to Guinea. In 1980, fish formed 33% of exports, groundnuts, 24% and coconuts, 17%.

Total trade between Guinea-Bissau and UK (British Department of Trade returns, in £1,000 sterling):

	1985	*1986*	*1987*	*1988*	*1989*
Imports to UK	2	214	17	22	29
Exports and re-exports from UK	1,209	1,319	1,152	925	1,185

COMMUNICATIONS

Roads. There were (1982) 5,058 km of roads and 4,100 vehicles.

Aviation. There is an international airport serving Bissau at Bissalanca.

Shipping. The main port is Bissau; minor ports are Boloma, Cacheu and Catió. In 1985 vessels entering the ports unloaded 129,000 tonnes.

Post. In 1986 there were 3,000 telephones and 26,000 radio receivers.

Cinemas. There were 4 cinemas (1988) with a seating capacity of 950.

Newspapers (1984). There was one weekly newspaper, with a circulation of 3,000.

RELIGION, EDUCATION AND WELFARE

Religion. In 1985 about 30% of the population were Moslem and about 5% Christian (mainly Roman Catholic).

Education. There were, in 1984, 81,444 pupils in 658 primary schools with 3,153 teachers; 11,710 pupils in 12 secondary schools with 718 teachers and 1,027 students in 4 technical schools and teacher-training establishments with 107 teachers.

Health. In 1981 there were 17 hospitals and clinics with 1,570 beds and in 1980 there were 108 doctors, 2 dentists, 3 pharmacists, 2 midwives and 56 nursing personnel.

DIPLOMATIC REPRESENTATIVES

Of Guinea-Bissau in Great Britain (resides in Brussels)
Ambassador: Bubacar Turé (accredited 26 Nov. 1986).

Of Great Britain in Guinea-Bissau
Ambassador: J. E. C. Macrae, CMG (resides in Dakar).

Of Guinea-Bissau in the USA
Ambassador: Alfredo Lopes Cabral.

Of the USA in Guinea-Bissau (Ave. Domingos Ramos, Bissau)
Ambassador: William L. Jacobsen, Jr.

Of Guinea-Bissau to the United Nations
Ambassador: Alfredo Lopes Cabral.

Further Reading

Relatório e Mapas do Movimento Comercial e Maritimo da Guiné. Bolama, Annual
Cabral, A., *Revolution in Guinea.* London, 1969.—*Return to the Source.* New York, 1973
Davidson, B., *Growing from the Grass Roots.* London, 1974
Gjerstad, O. and Sarrazin, C., *Sowing the First Harvest: National Reconstruction in Guinea-Bissau.* Oakland, 1978
Rudebeck, L., *Guinea-Bissau: A Study of Political Mobilization.* Uppsala, 1974

GUYANA

Capital: Georgetown
Population: 990,000 (1989)
GNP per capita: US$410 (1988)

HISTORY. The territory, including the counties of Demerara, Essequibo and Berbice, named from the 3 rivers, was first partially settled by the Dutch West Indian Company about 1620. The Dutch retained their hold until 1796, when it was captured by the English. It was finally ceded to Great Britain in 1814 and named British Guiana. On 26 May 1966 British Guiana became an independent member of the Commonwealth under the name of Guyana and the world's first Co-operative Republic on 23 Feb. 1970.

AREA AND POPULATION. Guyana is situated on the north-east coast of South America on the Atlantic ocean, with Suriname on the east, Venezuela on the west and Brazil on the south and west. Area, 83,000 sq. miles (214,969 sq. km). Estimated population (1989), 990,000. The official language is English, and in 1980 the population comprised 51% (East) Indians, 30% Africans, 10% mixed race, 5% Amerindian and 4% others. The capital is Georgetown, whose metropolitan area had 188,000 inhabitants in 1983; other towns are New Amsterdam, Linden, Rose Hall and Corriverton.

Vital statistics (1988): Birth rate 26·1%; death rate 8%.

Venezuela demanded the return of the Essequibo region in 1963. It was finally agreed in March 1983 that the UN Secretary-General should mediate. There was also an unresolved claim (1984) by Suriname for the return of an area between the New river and the Corentyne river.

CLIMATE. A tropical climate, with rainy seasons from April to July and Nov. to Jan. Humidity is high all the year but temperatures are moderated by sea-breezes. Rainfall increases from 90" (2,280 mm) on the coast to 140" (3,560 mm) in the forest zone. Georgetown. Jan. 79°F (26·1°C), July 81°F (27·2°C). Annual rainfall 87" (2,175 mm).

CONSTITUTION AND GOVERNMENT. A new Constitution was promulgated in Oct. 1980. The National Assembly consists of 65 elected members. Elections are held under the single-list system of proportional representation, with the whole of the country forming one electoral area and each voter casting his vote for a party list of candidates. The legislature is elected for 5 years unless earlier dissolved.

The elections held on 9 Dec. 1985 gave the People's National Congress 42 seats, the People's Progressive Party 8 seats, the United Force 2 seats and the Working People's Alliance 1 seat.

The Cabinet was in Jan. 1990 composed as follows:

President: H. Desmond Hoyte.

First Vice-President and Prime Minister: Hamilton Green.

Vice-President, Deputy Prime Minister, Culture and Social Affairs: Viola Burnham. *Attorney-General:* Keith Massiah. *Deputy Prime Ministers:* Robert H. O. Corbin (*Public Utilities*); William H. Parris (*Planning and Development*). *Foreign Affairs:* Rashleigh Jackson. *Finance:* Carl Greenidge. *Travel and Tourism:* Winston Murray.

National flag: Green with a yellow triangle based on the hoist, edged in white, charged with a red triangle edged in black.

Local government: There are 10 administrative regions: Barima/Waini, Pomeroon/Supernaam, Essequibo Islands/West Demerara, Demerara/Mahaica, Mahaica/Berbice, East Berbice/Corentyne, Cuyuni/Mazaruni, Potaro/Siparuni, Upper Takutu/Upper Essequibo, Upper Demerara/Berbice.

DEFENCE

Army. The Guyana Army had (1989) a strength of 5,300 (which includes airforce). It comprises 2 infantry, 1 guards, 1 special forces, 1 support weapons and 1 engineer battalions.

Navy. The Maritime Corps is an integral part of the Guyana Defence Force. In 1989 it had 150 personnel and comprised 3 fast inshore patrol craft and a utility landing craft.

Air Force. The Air Command is equipped with light aircraft and helicopters, including 1 Super King Air 200 twin-turboprop transport, 6 Islander twin-engined STOL transports, a Cessna U206F utility lightplane, and 4 Bell 206/212/412 and 2 Mi-8 helicopters. Personnel (1990) 300.

INTERNATIONAL RELATIONS

Membership. Guyana is a member of UN, the Commonwealth, Caricom, the Non-Aligned Movement and is an ACP state of the EEC.

ECONOMY

Budget. Revenue and expenditure for calendar years (in G$1,000):

	1984	*1985*	*1986*	*1987*	*1988*	*1989*
Revenue	1,537,928	1,200,208	1,667,708	2,004,391	2,296,587	7,012,345
Expenditure	1,585,840	1,562,858	2,551,380	2,976,517	3,528,120	8,796,129

Currency. The Bank of Guyana, established in 1965, issued Guyana dollar notes of $1, 5, 10, 20 and 100 and coins of 1-, 5-, 10-, 25- and 50-cent pieces. In March 1990: £1 = 49·15 G$; US$1 = 29·96 G$.

Banking. Of the 5 commercial banks operating in Guyana 2 are foreign-owned (Bank of Baroda and Bank of Nova Scotia) and 3 locally controlled (Guyana National Co-operative Bank, the National Bank of Industry and Commerce and the Republic Bank). The Guyana Agricultural and Industrial Development Bank (Gaibank) for farmers and agri-based industries and the Guyana Co-operative Mortgage Finance Bank for housing. Barclays Bank plc became Guyana Bank of Trade and Commerce in 1988.

ENERGY AND NATURAL RESOURCES

Electricity. Production (1986) 500m. kwh. Supply 110 volts; 60 Hz and 240 volts; 50 Hz.

Minerals. Placer gold mining commenced in 1884, and was followed by diamond mining in 1887. Output of gold was 18,803 oz. in 1988. Production of diamonds was 36,717 stones in 1988. Total production of the 4 grades of bauxite (calcined, chemical, metallurgical and abrasive) was 1·39m. tonnes in 1988. Full-scale production of manganese began in 1960 and other minerals include uranium, oil, copper and molybdenum.

Agriculture. Production, 1989: Sugar-cane, 2·3m. tonnes; rice, 133,900 tonnes. Important products are coconuts, 30,800 tonnes, 1989 and citrus, 7·4m. tonnes. Other tropical fruits and vegetables are grown mostly in scattered plantings; they include mangoes, papaws, avocado pears, melons, bananas and gooseberries. Other important crops are tomatoes, cabbages, black-eye peas, peanuts, carrots, onions, turmeric, ginger, pineapples, red kidney beans, soybeans, eschallot and tobacco. Large areas of unimproved land in the coastal region, which vary in width up to about 30 miles from the sea, are still available for agricultural and cattle-grazing projects.

Livestock estimate (1988): Cattle, 210,000; pigs, 185,000; sheep, 120,000; goats, 77,000; poultry, 15m.

Forestry. In 1988, 16·4m. hectares of the land area (83%) was forested. Production (1986) 4·7m. cu. ft.

Fisheries. Production (1989) of fish, 40,300 tons and shrimp, 1,872 tons.

COMMERCE. Imports and exports (in G$) for calendar years:

	1982	*1983*	*1984*	*1985*	*1986*
Imports	840,442,362	745,000,000	821,300,000	959,500,000	1,618,000,000
Exports	775,544,161	580,000,000	831,300,000	914,400,000	1,092,000,000

Chief imports (1983): Fuel and lubricants, 19,367,367 kg, $272,513,835; milk, 1,386,887 kg, $8,674,714.

Chief domestic exports (1983): Sugar, 210,734 tonnes, $195,814,993; rice, 41,721 tonnes, $64,939,971; bauxite, dried, 779,768 tonnes, $66,629,072; bauxite, calcined, 340,709 tonnes, $136,201,592; alumina, 29,301 tonnes, $7,019,133; rum, 20,442,180 litres, $6,987,107; timber, 49,720 cu. metres, $10,837,689; molasses, 53,938,864 litres, $2,019,371; shrimps, 7,318,145 kg, $14,067,860.

Imports (exclusive of transhipments), 1981, from CARICOM Territories, 35%; from USA, 25%; from UK, 16%; from Canada, 4%; exports (exclusive of transhipments) to UK, 26%; to CARICOM Territories, 17%; to Canada, 5%.

Total trade between Guyana and UK (British Department of Trade returns, in £1,000 sterling):

	1985	*1986*	*1987*	*1988*	*1989*
Imports to UK	52,377	55,535	58,502	43,518	54,523
Exports and re-exports from UK	18,406	13,737	15,371	10,590	13,216

COMMUNICATIONS

Roads. Roads and vehicular trails in the national, provincial and urban systems amount to 8,870 km. Motor vehicles, as of 31 Dec. 1987, totalled 53,446, including 8,401 passenger cars, 3,682 lorries and vans, 8,958 tractors and trailers, and 15,893 motor cycles. The main road on the Atlantic Coast, some 290 km (180 miles) long extends from Charity on the Pomeroon River to Crabwood Creek on the Corentyne, there are two unbridged gaps made by the Berbice and Essequibo Rivers, and the banks of the Demerara River are linked by a 1,853 metre (6,074 ft) floating bridge.

Railways. There is a government-owned railway in the North West District, while the Guyana Mining Enterprise operates a standard gauge railway of 133 km from Linden on the Demerara River to Ituni and Coomacka.

Aviation. Guyana Airways Corporation operates 11 flights weekly on its international service and 21 flights locally. In 1985 Guyana Airways Corporation carried 108,936 passengers on its international service and 59,113 passengers locally. Other services in operation: British Airways 4 times weekly to the Caribbean, Europe and North America: PANAM 3 times weekly to North, Central and South America: Air France, to and from Guadeloupe, Paramaribo and Cayenne 4 times a week; British West Indian Airways, Ltd, to and from Trinidad twice a week, providing direct connexion with New York and London; Cubana Airlines once a fortnight; Suriname Airways and Tropical Airways once weekly. The International Airport at Timehri serves Arrow Air Airlines, BWIA, Cubana Airways, and Suriname Airways.

Shipping. There are 217 nautical miles of river navigation. There are ferry services across the mouths of the Demerara, Berbice and Essequibo rivers, the last providing a link between the islands of Leguan and Wakenaam and the mainland at Adventure, and a number of coastal and river-boat services carrying both passengers and cargo. A number of launch services are operated in the more remote areas by private concerns.

Georgetown harbour, about ½ mile wide and 2½ miles long, has a minimum depth of 24 ft. New Amsterdam harbour is situated at the mouth of the Berbice River; there are wharves for coastal vessels only. Bauxite is loaded on ocean-going freighters at Mackenzie, 67 miles up the Demerara River, and at Everton on the Berbice River, about 10 miles from the mouth of the waterway. The Essequibo River has several timber-loading berths ranging from 20 to 40 ft. Springlands on the Corentyne River is the point of entry and departure of passengers travelling by launch services to and from Suriname. In 1984 the merchant marine comprised 84 vessels of 20,248 GRT.

Post and Broadcasting. The inland public telegraph and radio communication services are operated and maintained by the Telecommunication Corporation. On 31 Aug. 1988 there were 57 post offices and 28 agencies.

The telephone exchanges had at 31 Aug. 1988 a total of 28,450 direct exchange lines with (1988), 20,000 telephone instruments. The number of route miles in the coastal and inland areas was 2,982 km. 39 land-line stations were maintained at post offices in the coastal area, and 8 telegraph stations in the interior provide communication with the coastal area through a central telegraph office in Georgetown.

The Guyana Broadcasting Corporation, which came into operation on 1 July 1980, has 2 channels. In 1985 there were 350,000 radio receivers.

Cinemas (1989). There are 51 cinemas.

Newspapers (1989). There is 1 daily newspaper with a circulation of 60,000, 1 twice-weekly paper with an estimated circulation of 40,000 and 4 weekly papers with a combined circulation of 40,000.

JUSTICE, RELIGION, EDUCATION AND WELFARE

Justice. The law, both civil and criminal, is based on the common and statute law of England, save that the principles of the Roman–Dutch law have been retained in respect of the registration, conveyance and mortgaging of land.

The Supreme Court of Judicature consists of a Court of Appeal and a High Court.

Religion. In 1980, 34% of the population were Hindu, 34% Protestant, 18% Roman Catholic and 9% Moslem.

Education. In Sept. 1976 the Government assumed total responsibility for education from nursery school to university. Private education was abolished. In Sept. 1988, the total number of schools was 866: Nursery, 351; primary, 432; community high, 37; general secondary, 55.

There are now 3 technical and vocational schools and 2 schools for the teaching of home economics and domestic crafts. Training in co-operatives is provided by the Kuru-Kuru Co-operative College and agriculture by the Guyana School of Agriculture and there is one teacher training complex, the Cyril Potter College of Education. In 1986-87 there were 6,440 students at these post-secondary institutions. Higher education is also provided by the University of Guyana which was established in 1963 with faculties of medicine, natural science, social science, art, technology and education as well as first year students in law. There were 2,250 students in 1987–88. The total number of pupils in all schools was 211,315 in 1986-87.

Health. In 1989 there were 213 health facilities including hospitals. There were (1989) 111 doctors, 15 dentists, 29 pharmacists, 172 midwives and 854 nursing personnel.

DIPLOMATIC REPRESENTATIVES

Of Guyana in Great Britain (3 Palace Ct., London, W2 4LP)
High Commissioner: Cecil S. Pilgrim (accredited 5 Dec. 1986).

Of Great Britain in Guyana (44 Main St., Georgetown)
High Commissioner: D. P. Small, CMG, MBE.

Of Guyana in the USA (2490 Tracy Pl., NW, Washington, D.C., 20008)
Ambassador: Dr Cedric Hilburn Grant.

Of the USA in Guyana (31 Main St., Georgetown)
Ambassador: Theresa A. Tull.

Of Guyana to the United Nations
Ambassador: Samuel R. Insanally.

Further Reading

Baber, C. and Jeffrey, H. B., *Guyana: Politics, Economics and Society*. London, 1986
Braveboy-Wagner, J. A., *The Venezuela-Guyana Border Dispute: Britain's Colonial Legacy in Latin America*. London, 1984
Chambers, F., *Guyana*. [Bibliography] Oxford and Santa Barbara, 1989
Daly, P. H., *From Revolution to Republic*. Georgetown, 1970
Daly, V. T., *A Short History of the Guyanese People*. Rev. ed. London, 1975
Hope, K. R., *Development Policy in Guyana: Planning, Finance and Administration*. London, 1979
Latin American Bureau, *Guyana: Fraudulent Revolution*. London, 1984
Sanders, A., *The Powerless People*. London, 1987
Spinner, T. J., *A Political and Social History of Guyana, 1945–83*. Epping, 1985

HAITI

Capital: Port-au-Prince
Population: 5·7m. (1988)
GNP per capita: US$352 (1988)

République d'Haiti

HISTORY. Haiti occupies the western third of the large island of Hispaniola which was discovered by Christopher Columbus in 1492. The Spanish colony was ceded to France in 1697 and became her most prosperous colony. After the extirpation of the Indians by the Spaniards (by 1533) large numbers of African slaves were imported whose descendants now populate the country. The slaves obtained their liberation following the French Revolution, but subsequently Napoleon sent his brother-in-law, Gen. Leclerc, to restore French authority and re-impose slavery. Toussaint Louverture, the leader of the slaves who had been appointed a French general and governor, was kidnapped and sent to France, where he died in gaol. However, the reckless courage of the Negro troops and the ravages of yellow fever forced the French to evacuate the island and surrender to the blockading British squadron.

The country declared its independence on 1 Jan. 1804, and its successful leader, Gen. Jean-Jacques Dessalines, proclaimed himself Emperor of the newly-named Haiti. After the assassination of Dessalines (1806) a separate régime was set up in the north under Henri Christophe, a Negro general who in 1811 had himself proclaimed King Henry. In the south and west a republic was constituted, with the mulatto Alexander Pétion as its first President. Pétion died in 1818 and was succeeded by Jean-Pierre Boyer, under whom the country became re-united after Henry had committed suicide in 1820. From 1822 to 1844 Haiti and the eastern part of the island (later the Dominican Republic) were united. After one more monarchical interlude, under the Emperor Faustin (1847–59), Haiti has been a republic. From 1915 to 1934 Haiti was under United States occupation.

Following a military *coup* in 1950, and subsequent uprisings, Dr François Duvalier was elected President on 22 Oct. 1957 and subsequently became President for Life in 1964. He died on 21 April 1971 and was succeeded as president for life by his son, Jean-Claude Duvalier who fled the country on 7 Feb. 1986.

AREA AND POPULATION. The area is 27,750 sq. km (10,700 sq. miles), of which about three-quarters is mountainous. The population at the census in 1982 was 5,053,792 of which 21% urban and 48·5% male. Estimate (1988) 5,658,124, of which 28% urban.

The areas and populations of the 9 *départements* are as follows:

Département	*Sq. km*	*1988*	*Chief town*	*1988*
Nord-Ouest	2,094	326,361	Port-de-Paix	135,374
Nord	2,175	610,282	Cap Haïtien	133,233
Nord-Est	1,698	199,336	Fort-Liberté	34,043
L'Artibonite	4,895	801,115	Gonaïves	144,081
Centre	3,597	406,608	Hinche	122,003
Ouest	4,595	1,869,805	Port-au-Prince	1,143,626
Sud-Est	2,077	393,554	Jacmel	216,600
Sud	2,602	531,255	Les Cayes	214,606
Grande Anse	3,100	519,808	Jérémie	152,081

The Île de la Gonave, some 40 miles long, lies in the gulf of the same name. Among other islands is La Tortue, off the north peninsula. 95% of the population is black, with an important minority of mulattoes and only about 5,000 white residents, almost all foreign.

Haiti is the only French-speaking republic in the Americas. The standard French of government, parliament and the press is spoken by the small literate minority (about 10%), but the great majority of the people habitually speak the dialect known as Créole.

CLIMATE. A tropical climate, but the central mountains can cause semi-arid conditions in their lee. There are rainy seasons from April to June and Aug. to Nov. Hurricanes and severe thunderstorms can occur. The annual temperature range is small. Port-au-Prince. Jan. 77°F (25°C), July 84°F (28·9°C). Annual rainfall 53" (1,321 mm).

CONSTITUTION AND GOVERNMENT. Following the departure of President Jean-Claude Duvalier the 5-man Council of Government formed in Feb. 1986 was composed of Gen. Henry Namphy; Col. Max Valles, Commander of the Presidential Guard; Col. William Regala, Inspector-General; Alix Cinéas and Gérard Gourgue. Presidential elections were planned for 29 Nov. 1987 but were postponed because of violence. They took place on 17 Jan. 1988 and on 24 Jan. Leslie Manigat was declared elected President with 534,080 votes, 50·29% of the total cast. President Manigat was sworn in on 5 Feb. On 17 July 1988.

The 1987 Constitution, ratified by a referendum on 29 March 1987, provides for a bicameral legislature (Chambre des Députés, Sénat), and an executive President and Prime Minister. The Constitution was suspended in July 1987 by the military government under Gen. Henri Namphy, who seized power from elected President Leslie Manigat on 19 June 1988. A further *coup d'état* on 17 Sept. 1988 deposed Gen. Namphy, and a new military government under the presidency of Lieut.-Gen. Prosper Avril was formed. President Avril re-introduced the 1987 Constitution on 13 March 1989, with the exception of certain articles (relating to the legislative and executive powers) held in abeyance.

Gen. Avril resigned on 10 March 1990 and the new chief of the army, Gen. Herard Abraham took control of the country until on 13 March Ertha Pascal-Trouillot became head of the interim government. A Supreme Court judge she heads a 19-member advisory Council of State. Although an advisory body it possesses certain powers of veto. Her mandate is to organize elections and hand over to a new government by Feb. 1991.

National flag: Horizontally blue over red with the national arms on a white panel in the centre.

National anthem: 'La Dessalinienne': Pour le pays, pour les ancètres (words by J. Lhérisson; tune by N. Geffrard, 1903).

DEFENCE. The Haitian Defence Force (*Forces Armées d'Haiti*) totalling about 7,600 men, was divided into Army, Navy, and Air Force. The President is Commander-in-Chief and appoints the officers.

Army. Total strength, about 7,000 (1989), organized into 9 military departments. Three of the Departments are in Port-au-Prince and consist of the Presidential Guard, 1 infantry battalion, 1 airport security company, 2 artillery battalions and 6 artillery elements.

Navy. The Coast Guard of (1989) 150 personnel operates 3 coastal patrol craft and some boats; all are based at Port-au-Prince.

Air Force. Personnel strength was (1990) about 150, with (1987) about 30 aircraft of some 12 varieties. They include 7 Summit/Cessna O2-337 Sentry twin piston-engined counter-insurgency aircraft, 1 DC-3, 6 light transports, 14 training and liaison aircraft, including 4 S.211 jet trainers and 4 turboprop-powered SF.260 TPs.

INTERNATIONAL RELATIONS

Membership. Haiti is a member of UN and OAS and is an ACP state of the EEC.

ECONOMY

Budget. Revenue (fiscal year ending 30 Sept.) in US$1m. (5 gourdes = US$1), 1986–87, 305m.; expenditure, 350m.

Currency. The unit of currency is the *gourde* and its value fixed at 5 *gourdes* = US$1. In March 1990, £1 = 8·22 *gourdes*. There are copper–nickel coins for 50, 20, 10 and 5 *centimes* and copper–zinc–nickel coins of 10 and 5 centimes.

Banking. Banque Nationale de Credit, owned by the State, was established in 1982. US dollars may be included in the minimum required reserves. The Citibank, the Bank of Nova Scotia, the Bank of Boston, the Banque de l'Union Haitienne (mainly local capital with participation from American, Canadian and Dominican Republic Banks), Banque Nationale de Paris and Banque Nationale de la République d'Haiti (the central bank and has a monopoly of the note issue) all have branches in Port-au-Prince.

Weights and Measures. The metric system is officially accepted.

ENERGY AND NATURAL RESOURCES

Electricity. Production (1988) 337m. kwh. Supply 110 and 220 volts; 60 Hz.

Minerals. Copper exists but is at present uneconomic to exploit. Haiti may possess undeveloped mineral resources of oil, gold, silver, antimony, sulphur, coal and lignite, nickel, gypsum and porphyry.

Agriculture. Only one-third of the country is arable and most people own the tiny plots they farm; the resulting pressure of population is the main cause of rural poverty.

The occupations of Haiti are 90% agricultural, carried on in 7 large plains, from 200,000 to 25,000 acres, and in 15 smaller plains down to 2,000 acres. Irrigation is used in some areas. Haiti's most important product is coffee of good quality, classified as 'mild', and grown by peasants. Production in 1988 totalled about 31,000 tonnes. Second most important crop is sugar. Sisal is grown extensively. Much of the fibre is exported as or for cordage. New types of cotton are being tried with success. New varieties of rice should significantly boost future production, especially in the Artibonite Valley. Output of main crops in 1988 (in 1,000 tonnes) was: Sugar-cane, 3,000; mangoes, 355; plantains; 275; sweet potatoes, 300; cassava, 217; bananas, 230; maize, 145; sorghum, 90; rice, 103; sisal, 5; cotton, 6; cocoa, 5.

Rum and other spirits are distilled. Essential oils from vetiver, neroli and amyris are important. Cattle and horse breeding are encouraged.

Livestock (1988); Cattle, 1,545,000; sheep, 94,000; goats, 1·2m.; horses, 430,000; poultry, 12m.

Fisheries. Production (1986) 8,000 tonnes.

INDUSTRY AND TRADE

Industry. Light manufacturing industries assembling or finishing goods (mainly clothing, leather goods and electrical/electronic components) for re-export constitute the fastest growing sector. Soap factories produce laundry soap, toilet soap and detergent. A cement factory located near the capital produced 265,000 tonnes in 1987. A steel plant making rods, beams and angles was opened in 1974. There are also a pharmaceutical plant, a tannery, a plastics plant, 2 paint works, 5 shoe factories, a large factory producing enamel cookingware, 2 pastamaking factories, a tomato cannery and a flour-mill, all located in or near Port-au-Prince.

Commerce. In 1987 exports were US$160m. and imports, US$280m. The leading imports are petroleum products, foodstuffs, textiles, machinery, animal and vegetable oils, chemicals, pharmaceuticals, raw materials for transformation industries and vehicles.

Total trade between Haiti and UK (British Department of Trade returns, in £1,000 sterling):

	1985	*1986*	*1987*	*1988*	*1989*
Imports to UK	1,512	899	621	844	803
Exports and re-exports from UK	5,048	5,147	5,327	6,760	6,566

Tourism. In 1988, 85,000 tourists visited Haiti.

COMMUNICATIONS

Roads. Total length of roads is some 4,000 km, little of which is practicable in ordinary motors in the rainy season. There were (1984) about 50,000 vehicles in Haiti.

Railways. The only railway is owned by the Haitian American Sugar Company.

Aviation. An airport capable of handling jets was opened at Port-au-Prince in 1965. US and French carriers provide daily direct services to New York, Miami, Jamaica, Puerto Rico and the French Antilles. There are also services to the Dominican Republic and the Netherlands Antilles. A Haitian company provides a cargo service to the US and Puerto Rico. Air services connecting Port-au-Prince with other Haitian towns are operated by Haiti Air Inter.

Shipping. US, French, Federal Republic of Germany, Dutch, British, Canadian and Japanese lines connect Haiti with the US, Latin America (except Cuba), Canada, Jamaica, Europe and the Far East.

Post and Broadcasting. Most principal towns are connected by the government telegraph system, telephones and wireless.

The telephone company, of which the Haitian Government is now the majority stockholder, is in process of being modernized. Telephone subscribers totalled 34,000 in 1984.

In 1982 there were 105,000 radio and 65,000 television receivers.

Cinemas (1984). There were 10 cinemas in Port-au-Prince.

Newspapers (1989). There were 6 daily newspapers in Port-au-Prince, also a monthly in English and 1 weekly newspaper in Cap Haïtien.

JUSTICE, RELIGION, EDUCATION AND WELFARE

Justice. Judges, both of the lower courts and the court of appeal, are appointed by the President. The legal system is basically French. The divorce law has recently been amended to permit parties to obtain 'quick and painless' divorces at a moderate cost, in the hope of attracting the US trade, now that the Mexican 'divorce mills' have closed down. This has developed a useful flow of dollar revenue.

Police. The Police number about 1,200 in Port-au-Prince and are part of the armed forces.

Religion. Since the Concordat of 1860, the official religion is Roman Catholicism, under an archbishop with 5 suffragan bishops. There are still quite a number of foreigners, French and French Canadians mainly, among the clergy but the first Haitian archbishop took office in 1966. The Episcopal Church now has its first Haitian bishop who was consecrated in 1971. Other Christian churches number perhaps 10% of the population. The folk religion is Voodoo.

Education. Education is divided into primary (6 years, compulsory), secondary (7 years) and university/higher education. The school system is based on the French system and instruction is in French. In 1990 Educational Reform calling for basic schooling (9 years, compulsory) using Creole and French, with a 3-year secondary cycle, was being implemented.

In 1988 primary schools had 24,800 teachers and 983,000 pupils and 455 secondary schools had 8,400 teachers and 177,000 pupils.

Higher education is offered at the University of Haiti with 5,000 students in 1988.

Health. There were, in 1989, 944 doctors and 98 dentists in practice, and 87 hospitals and health centres with 4,566 beds.

DIPLOMATIC REPRESENTATIVES

Of Haiti in Great Britain. The Embassy closed on 30 March 1987.

Of Great Britain in Haiti
Ambassador: D. F. Milton (resides in Kingston).

Of Haiti in the USA (2311 Massachusetts Ave., NW, Washington, D.C., 20008)
Ambassador: Pierre François Benoit.

Of the USA in Haiti (Harry Truman Blvd., Port-au-Prince)
Ambassador: Alvin P. Adams, Jr.

Of Haiti to the United Nations
Ambassador: Glodys St.-Phard.

Further Reading

The official gazette is *Le Moniteur.*

Revue Agricole d'Haïti. From 1946. Quarterly
Bellegarde, D., *Histoire du Peuple Haïtien.* Port-au-Prince, 1953
Chambers, F. J., *Haiti.* [Bibliography] Oxford and Santa Barbara, 1983
Ferguson, J., *Papa Doc, Baby Doc: Haiti and the Duvaliers.* Oxford, 1987
Laguerre, M. S., *The Complete Haitiana.* [Bibliography] London and New York, 1982. — *Voodoo and Politics in Haiti*. London, 1989
Lundahl, M., *The Haitian Economy: Man, Land and Markets.* London, 1983
Nicholls, D., *From Dessalines to Duvalier: Race, Colour and National Independence in Haiti.* CUP, rev., 1988.—*Haiti in Caribbean Context: Ethnicity, Economy and Revolt.* London, 1985
Wilentz, A., *The Rainy Season: Haiti since Duvalier.* New York, 1989

National Library: Bibliothèque Nationale, Rue du Centre, Port-au-Prince.

HONDURAS

Capital: Tegucigalpa
Population: 4·3m. (1986)
GNP per capita: US$850 (1988)

República de Honduras

HISTORY. Honduras celebrates 15 Sept. 1821 as the anniversary of its national independence from Spain. On 5 Nov. 1838 Honduras declared itself an independent sovereign state, free from the Federation of Central America, of which it had formed a part.

AREA AND POPULATION. Honduras is bounded north by the Caribbean, east and south-east by Nicaragua, west by Guatemala, south-west by El Salvador and south by the Pacific ocean. Area is 112,088 sq. km (43,277 sq. miles), with a population, census (1974) of 2,656,948. Estimate (1986) 4·3m.

The chief cities (populations, 1986) were Tegucigalpa, the capital (604,600), San Pedro Sula (399,700), El Progreso (58,300), Choluteca (60,700), Danli (18,800) and the Atlantic coast ports of La Ceiba (63,800), Puerto Cortés (40,000) and Tela (30,100); other towns include Olanchito (13,000), Juticalpa (13,900), Comayagua (28,800), Signatepeque (30,100) and Santa Rosa de Copan (20,000).

The areas and populations of the 18 departments and federal district were as follows:

Department	*Sq. km*	*1983*	*Department*	*Sq. km*	*1983*
Atlántida	4,251	242,235	Intibucá	3,072	111,412
Choluteca	4,211	289,637	Islas de la Bahía	261	18,744
Colón	8,875	128,370	La Paz	2,331	86,627
Comayagua	5,196	211,465	Lempira	4,290	174,916
Copán	3,203	217,258	Ocotepeque	1,680	64,151
Cortés	3,954	624,090	Olancho	24,350	228,122
El Paraíso	7,218	206,601	Santa Bárbara	5,115	286,854
Federal District	1,648	604,600 [1]	Valle	1,565	125,640
Francisco Morazán	6,298	203,753	Yoro	7,939	304,310
Gracias a Dios	16,630	35,471			

[1] 1986.

Aboriginal tribes number over 35,000, principally Miskito, Payas and Xicaques Indians and Sambos (the latter a mixture of Miskito and Negro), each speaking a different dialect. The Spanish-speaking inhabitants are chiefly *mestizos*, Indians with an admixture of Spanish blood. Gracias a Dios is still largely unexplored and is inhabited by pure native races who speak little or no Spanish.

In 1985 the population growth rate was 3·1%; infant mortality rate 70 per 1,000 live births; life expectancy 62.

CLIMATE. The climate is tropical, with a small annual range of temperature but with high rainfall. Upland areas have two wet seasons, from May to July and in Sept. and Oct. The Caribbean Coast has most rain in Dec. and Jan. and temperatures are generally higher than inland. Tegucigalpa. Jan. 66°F (19°C), July 74°F (23·3°C). Annual rainfall 64" (1,621 mm).

CONSTITUTION AND GOVERNMENT. Presidential and Congressional elections were held on 24 Nov. 1985. A new Constitution was promulgated on 20 Jan. 1982. The President is directly elected for a 4-year term.

At the 1989 Presidential elections the National party's candidate obtained 50·2% of the vote.

President: Rafael Leonardo Callejas (sworn in 17 Jan. 1990).

The legislature is a 134-member Congress of Deputies, composed following the elections of 24 Nov. 1985 of 46 deputies of the official *Partido Liberal,* 63 of the

Partido Nacional and the remaining 25 seats were won by a rival Liberal Party faction and 2 smaller political parties.

National flag: Three horizontal stripes of blue, white, blue, with 5 blue stars in the centre.

National anthem: Tu bandera (words by A. C. Coello; tune by C. Hartling).

Local government: Honduras comprises a Federal District (containing the cities of Tegucigalpa and Comayaguela) and 18 departments (each administered by an appointed Governor), sub-divided into 282 municipalities.

DEFENCE. Conscription is for approximately 24 months.

Army. The Army consists of 4 infantry and 1 armed cavalry regiment, 1 artillery brigade and 1 engineer, 2 independent infantry, 1 special forces and 1 air defence battalions. Equipment includes 12 Scorpion light tanks. Strength (1990) 15,400 (11,000 conscripts). There is also a paramilitary Public Security Force of 4,500 men.

Navy. A small flotilla operates 5 US-built fast inshore patrol craft, some 6 other inshore craft, a tank landing craft and a number of boats. Personnel (1989) 1,200, of whom 900 are conscript, and the total includes 600 marines. Bases are at Puerto Cortés and Amapala.

Air Force. Equipment includes 12 F-5E/F Tiger IIs and a few F-86 fighters, 12 A-37B jet light attack aircraft, 4 Spanish-built CASA C-101BB armed jet trainers, 3 four-engined Douglas and Lockheed transports, 6 C-47, 4 Israeli-built Arava and 2 Westwind transports, about 30 helicopters and Tucano and T-41A trainers. Total strength was (1990) about 2,100 personnel, of whom many are civilian maintenance staff.

INTERNATIONAL RELATIONS

Membership. Honduras is a member of UN and OAS.

ECONOMY

Budget. In 1988 revenue (in 1m. lempiras) was 2,165 (1987, 1,932); expenditure, (1987) 2,059.

Total external debt (1986) was (in 1m. lempiras), 4,882 and net reserves of foreign currency, 280.

Currency. The unit of the monetary system is the *lempira* also known as a *peso*, comprising 100 *centavos*. Notes are issued by the Banco Central de Honduras which has the sole right to issue, in denominations of 100, 50, 20, 10, 5, 2 and 1 *lempiras*. Coins in circulation are 50 and 20 *centavos* in silver, 10 and 5 *centavos* in cupro-nickel and 2 and 1 *centavos* in copper.

Rate of exchange, March 1990: £1 = 3·39 *lempiras;* US$1 = 2·13 *lempiras*.

Banking. The central bank of issue is the Banco Central de Honduras. The Banco Atlántida has branches in Tegucigalpa, San Pedro Sula, Comayaguela, Puerto Cortés, La Ceiba, Tela, El Progreso, Choluteca and other towns. The Banco de Honduras which operates in many parts of the country is controlled by the Citibank. The Bank of London and Montreal has branches in Tegucigalpa, San Pedro Sula, Comayaguela and La Ceiba. The Central American Bank for Economic Integration has its head office in Tegucigalpa.

Weights and Measures. The metric system has been legal since 1 April 1897, but English pounds and yards and the old Spanish system are still in use: 1 *vara* = 32 in.; 1 *manzana* (10,000 sq. *varas*) = 700 sq. metres; 1 *arroba* = 25 lb.; 1 *quintal* = 100 lb.; 1 *tonelada* = 2,000 lb.

ENERGY AND NATURAL RESOURCES

Electricity. Production (1986) 1,400m. kwh. Supply 110 and 220 volts; 60 Hz.

Minerals. Mineral resources include gold, silver, lead, copper, zinc and iron ore, which are exported. There are probably reserves of other minerals which have not yet been exploited.

Agriculture. Although Honduras is essentially an agricultural country, less than a quarter of the total land area is cultivated and by far the larger portion of this is on the Caribbean and Pacific coastal plains. Agriculture employs 58·9% of the working population and provides 80% of the exports. The main agricultural crops are: Bananas, coffee, sugar and tobacco. Meat and lobster were important exports in 1987.

Livestock (1988): Cattle, 2,824,000; sheep, 7,000; pigs, 600,000; goats, 25,000; horses, 170,000; poultry, 8m.

Forestry. Forests in 1988 covered 31% of the total land area. Honduras has an abundance of hard- and soft-woods. Large stands of mahogany and other hardwoods — granadino, guayacán, walnut and rosewood—grow in the north-eastern part of the country, in the interior valleys, and near the southern coast. Stands of pine occur almost everywhere in the interior, but are severely damaged by bark beetle and fires. In 1985, total wood exports amounted to 200,000 cu. metres valued at 65·1m. lempiras.

Fisheries. Commercial fishing in territorial waters is restricted to Honduran nationals and Honduran companies in which the controlling share of the capital is owned by a Honduran national. Shrimps and lobsters are important catches; exports (1985) 102·4m. lempiras.

INDUSTRY AND TRADE

Industry. Small-scale local industries include beer and mineral waters, cement, flour, vegetable lard, coconut oil, sweets, cigarettes, cigars, textiles and clothing, panama hats, plastics, nails, matches, plywood, furniture, paper bags, soap, candles, fruit juices and household chemicals. Electricity from an important hydro-electric scheme, EL CAJON, built at Rio Lindo to serve the Central and North Coast regions, came on stream in 1985 (290 mw). The manufacturing industry employed 12% of the working population in 1985.

Labour. The organization of trade unions was begun in 1954 with the assistance of ORIT (Inter-American Regional Organization) sponsored by the USA trade unions. In 1988 there were 236 active trade unions with about 160,000 members. A 'Charter of Labour' was granted in Feb. 1955 and an advanced Labour Code and Social Security Bill passed into law in May 1959. A Ministry of 'Labour, Social Assistance and the Middle Class' was created in 1955; the last four words of its title were expunged in 1957.

Commerce. Imports in 1986 were valued at 1,940m. lempiras and exports at 1,800m. lempiras.

Imports (1985) in 1m. lempiras: Fuel and lubricants, (1986) 565; consumer goods, 426; raw materials, 576; capital goods, 432.

Exports (1986) in 1m. lempiras: Bananas, 530; coffee, 612; timber, 74; refrigerated meats, 40; shrimp and lobster, 88.

Trade with main countries in 1m. lempiras (1986) was: USA, 1,518·8; Japan, 302·2; Federal Republic of Germany, 297·2; Italy, 157·1; Netherlands, 89; Belgium, 85·6; Spain, 55·2; UK, 49.

Total trade between Honduras and UK (British Department of Trade returns, in £1,000 sterling):

	1985	*1986*	*1987*	*1988*	*1989*
Imports to UK	11,139	5,280	4,703	8,295	12,121
Exports and re-exports from UK	9,026	9,213	10,449	7,891	5,518

Tourism. There were 204,000 visitors in 1986.

COMMUNICATIONS

Roads. Honduras is connected with Guatemala, El Salvador and Nicaragua by the Pan-American Highway. Out of a total of 17,022 km of road (1985), 2,102 were asphalted and 8,366 were unpaved but of all-weather construction. There are good asphalted highways between Puerto Cortés in the north and Choluteca in the south passing through San Pedro Sula and Tegucigalpa with branches to Guatemala and El Salvador. In 1986 there were 114,675 motor vehicles.

Railways. Only 4 railways exist; they are confined to the north coastal region and are used mainly for transportation of bananas. Tegucigalpa, the capital, is not served by any railway, and there are no international railway connexions. The total railways operating in 1986 were 955 km of 1,067 mm and 914 mm gauge, which carried 1m. passengers and 1·2m. tonnes of freight.

Aviation. Over a large part of the country the aeroplane is the normal means of transport for both passengers and freight. There are international airports at Tegucigalpa, San Pedro Sula, La Ceiba and over 30 smaller airstrips in various parts of the country.

Shipping. Sailings to the Atlantic coast port of Puerto Cortés from Europe are frequent, mainly operated by the Harrison Line, Cia Generale Transatlantique, the Royal Netherlands Steamships Co., Hapag Lloyd and vessels owned or chartered by the Tela Railroad Co., a subsidiary of United Brands, and the Standard Fruit Co.

Post and Broadcasting. The Government in April 1972 operated 18,845 km of telephone lines and 12,526 km of telegraph lines. Number of telephones in use, 1986, 66,892; telephone exchanges, 56; number of telegraph offices, 364; combined telephone and telegraph offices, 119; radio stations, 259; commercial television channels, 6. There were (1979) about 27,000 receivers in use. Transmission in colour commenced mid-1973.

Cinemas (1982). Cinemas numbered about 60 with seating capacity of some 60,000.

Newspapers (1984). The 4 most important daily papers are *El Heraldo* and *La Tribuna* in Tegucigalpa, *La Prensa* and *El Tiempo* in San Pedro Sula. Several others exist but their circulation is low and their influence is very limited.

JUSTICE, RELIGION, EDUCATION AND WELFARE

Justice. Judicial power is vested in the Supreme Court, with 7 judges elected by the National Congress for 6 years; it appoints the judges of the courts of appeal, labour tribunals and the district attorneys who, in turn, name the justices of the peace.

Religion. Roman Catholicism is the prevailing religion, but the constitution guarantees freedom to all creeds, and the State does not contribute to the support of any. Evangelical movements from North America are fast spreading their influence.

Education. Instruction is free, compulsory (from 7 to 15 years of age) and secular. In 1986 the 6,710 primary schools had 805,504 children (20,732 teachers); the 354 secondary, normal and technical schools had 130,247 pupils (6,945 teachers); the teachers' training college had 3,389 students in 1986. In 1986, the three universities had a total of 31,455 students.

The illiteracy rate was 40% of those 10 years of age and older in 1983.

Health. In 1981 there were about 1,370 doctors. In 1987 there were 46 public hospitals and 25 private, with 5,601 beds, and 617 health centres.

DIPLOMATIC REPRESENTATIVES

Of Honduras in Great Britain (115 Gloucester Pl., London, W1H 3PJ)
Ambassador: Max Velásquez-Diaz (accredited 7 June 1984).

Of Great Britain in Honduras (Edificio Palmira, 3er Piso, Colonia Palmira, Tegucigalpa)
Ambassador: Peter John Streams, CMG (accredited 22 Aug. 1989).

Of Honduras in the USA (3007 Tilden St., NW, Washington, D.C., 20008)
Ambassador: Dr Jorge Ramón Hernandez Alcerro.

Of the USA in Honduras (Ave. La Paz, Tegucigalpa)
Ambassador: Cresencio S. Arcos.

Of Honduras to the United Nations
Ambassador: Roberto Martinez Ordoñez.

Further Reading

The *Anuario Estadístico* (latest issue, *Comercio Exterior de Honduras*, 1983) is published by the Dirección de Estadísticas y Censos, Tegucigalpa. *Director:* Elizabeth Zavala de Turcios.

Monthly Bulletin.—Honduras en Cifras. Banco Central de Honduras, 1980
Checchi, V. (and others), *Honduras, a Problem in Economic Development*. New York, 1959
Morris, J. A., *Honduras: Caudillo Politics and Military Rulers*. Boulder, 1984
Rubio Melhado, A., *Geografia General de la Republica de Honduras*. Tegucigalpa, 1953

HONG KONG

Population: 5·76m. (1989)
GDP per capita: US$9,642 (1988)

HISTORY. Hong Kong Island and the southern tip of the Kowloon peninsula were ceded by China to Britain after the first and second Anglo-Chinese Wars by the Treaty of Nanking 1842 and the Convention of Peking 1860. Northern Kowloon was leased to Britain for 99 years by China in 1898. Since then, Hong Kong has been under British administration, except from Dec. 1941 to Aug. 1945 during the Japanese occupation. Talks began in Sept. 1982 between Britain and China over the future of Hong Kong after the lease expiry in 1997. On 19 Dec. 1984, the two countries signed a joint declaration whereby China would recover sovereignty over Hong Kong (comprising Hong Kong Island, Kowloon and the New Territories) from 1 July 1997 and establish it as a Special Administrative Region where the existing social and economic systems, and the present life-style, would remain unchanged for another 50 years.

AREA AND POPULATION. Hong Kong island is 32 km east of the mouth of the Pearl River and 130 km south-east of Guangzhou. The area of the island is 79·45 sq. km. It is separated from the mainland by a fine natural harbour. On the opposite side is the peninsula of Kowloon (11·44 sq. km), which was added to the Territory by the Convention of Peking, 1860. By a further convention, signed at Peking on 9 June 1898, about 979·23 sq. km, consisting of all the immediately adjacent mainland and numerous islands in the vicinity, were leased to Great Britain by China for 99 years. This area is known as the New Territories. Total area of the Territory is 1,071 sq. km (including recent reclamations), a large part of it being steep and unproductive hillside. Some 40% of the Territory is conserved as country parks. Shortage of land suitable for development for housing and industry is a serious problem. Since 1945, the Government has reclaimed about 2,396·8 hectares from the sea, principally from the seafronts of Hong Kong and Kowloon, facing the harbour. In the New Territories, the new town of Tsuen Wan, incorporating Tsuen Wan, Kwai Chung and Tsing Yi, already houses 690,000 of its planned ultimate population of 860,000. The construction of 7 further new towns at Sha Tin, Tuen Mun, Tai Po, Fanling, Yuen Long, Tseung Kwan O and Tin Shui Wai is now well underway, with planned ultimate population of about 750,000, 562,000, 306,000, 280,000, 190,000, 440,000 and 140,000 respectively.

The population was 5,613,000 at 1987 census. Estimate (30 June 1989) 5,761,400. During the war years the population of Hong Kong fluctuated sharply. In Sept. 1945, at the end of the Japanese occupation, it was about 600,000. In mid-1950 it was estimated at 2·24m. From mid-1976 to mid-1989 the average annual growth rate has been 1·9%. Of the present population about 21·8% are under 15 years of age. About 59% of the population was born in Hong Kong. There were 56,810 Vietnamese refugees/boat people on 26 Oct. 1989.

CLIMATE. The climate is warm sub-tropical being much affected by monsoons, the winter being cool and dry and the summer hot and humid, May to Sept. being the wettest months. Jan. 60°F (15·6°C), July 83°F (28·6°C). Annual rainfall 85" (2,224·7 mm).

CONSTITUTION AND GOVERNMENT. The administration is in the hands of a Governor, aided by an Executive Council, composed of the Chief Secretary, the Commander British Forces, the Financial Secretary, the Attorney General (who are members *ex officio*) and such other members as may be appointed by the Queen upon the Governor's nomination. In Nov. 1989 there were, in addition to the 4 *ex-officio* members, 1 nominated official and 9 appointed members. There is also a Legislative Council, presided over by the Governor. In 1989 it consisted of 3 *ex-officio* members, namely the Chief Secretary, the Financial Secretary, the Attorney-General, 7 official members, 20 appointed members and 26 elected members. Chinese and English are the official languages. Two municipal councils with elected members are responsible on a regional basis for environmental hygiene, public health, recreational and cultural matters. District boards with elected members were set up in 1982 in the 19 administrative districts of Hong Kong. They have mainly an advisory role to perform and have a substantial influence over district affairs.

Governor and C.-in-C.: Sir David Wilson, KCMG.

Commander British Forces: Maj.-Gen. Peter Royson Duffell, CBE, MC.

Chief Secretary: Sir David Ford, KBE, LVO, JP.

Flag: British Blue Ensign with the arms of the Territory on a white disc in the fly.

DEFENCE. The Hong Kong garrison, under the Commander British Forces, comprises units of all three services. Its principal rôle is to assist the Hong Kong Government in maintaining security and stability.

Army. The Army constitutes the bulk of the garrison. It comprises a UK battalion, based at Stanley Fort, and 3 Gurkha infantry battalions, all based in the New Territories; supporting units include the Queen's Gurkha Engineers, the Queen's Gurkha Signals, the Gurkha Transport Regiment, and 660 Squadron Army Air Corps.

Navy. The Naval Base is at HMS *Tamar*. The Hong Kong Squadron comprises 3 Peacock class patrol craft which are specially designed for patrol duties during typhoons and perform Search and Rescue operation in both Hong Kong waters and international waters in the South China Sea. The vessels, HMS *Peacock*, HMS *Plover*, HMS *Starling*, were built by Hall Russell, Aberdeen, Scotland in 1984–85.

Air Force. The Royal Air Force is based at Shek Kong. No. 28 (Army Co-operation) Squadron operates Wessex helicopters. In addition to its operational rôle in support of the army and navy, the RAF carries out search and rescue and medical evacuation tasks. It is also responsible for air traffic control services at Shek Kong, and provides a territory-wide air traffic advisory service.

Auxiliary Forces. The local auxiliary defence units, consisting of the Royal Hong Kong Regiment and the Royal Hong Kong Auxiliary Air Force, are administered by the Hong Kong Government, but, if called out, would come under the command of the Commander British Forces. The Royal Hong Kong Regiment (The Volunteers) has a strength of about 950. It is fully mobile and its rôle is to operate in support of regular army battalions stationed in Hong Kong. The Royal Hong Kong Auxiliary Air Force is intended mainly for internal security and air-sea rescue duties. It has a strength of about 171, operating a fleet of 9 aircraft – 2 twin-engined Beech King Air 200s, 4 Slingsby T-67 trainers, and 3 Aérospatiale Dauphin 365C1 helicopters.

ECONOMY

Budget. The public revenue and expenditure for financial years ending 31 March were as follows (in HK$):

	1986–87	*1987–88*	*1988–89*	*1989–90* [1]
Revenue	43,870,000,000	55,641,000,000	72,658,000,000	80,539,000,000
Expenditure	39,928,000,000	44,022,000,000	56,591,000,000	69,065,000,000

[1] Estimate.

The revenue is derived chiefly from rates, licences, tax on earnings and profits, land sales, duties on tobacco, hydrocarbon oils, methyl alcohol, intoxicating liquor, non-intoxicating liquor, non-alcoholic beverages and cosmetics and various duties.

Currency. The unit of currency is the Hong Kong *dollar*. Banknotes (of denominations of $10 upwards) are issued by the Hongkong and Shanghai Banking Corporation, and the Standard Chartered Bank. Their combined note issue was, at 31 Dec. 1988, HK$31,826m. Subsidiary currency consisting of HK$5, HK$2, HK$1,

50-cent, 20-cent, 10-cent, 5-cent alloy coins and 1-cent notes is issued by the Hong Kong Government and at 31 Dec. 1988 totalled HK$1,889m.

Since Oct. 1983 the HK$ has been linked to the US$1 at a fixed exchange rate of US$1 = HK$7·84. In March 1990, £1 = HK$12·86.

The Hong Kong Government has issued a set of 14 Hong Kong commemorative HK$1,000 gold coins over the years. The set comprises 2 coins commemorating the Queen's visit to Hong Kong in 1975 and in 1986 and 12 coins depicting the animals of the Chinese lunar calendar. The last coin in the lunar series was issued in 1987 to commemorate the Year of the Rabbit.

Banking. At 31 Dec. 1988: There were 160 banks licensed under the Banking Ordinance with a total of 1,397 banking offices, and 152 representative offices of foreign banks; bank deposits were HK$778,989m. and loans and advances HK$866,486m.; there were 216 deposit taking companies registered, and 35 licensed, under the Banking Ordinance with total deposits of HK$66,531.

Weights and Measures. Metric, British Imperial, Chinese and US units are all in current use in Hong Kong. However Government departments have now effectively adopted metric units; all new legislation uses metric terminology and existing legislation is being progressively metricated. Metrication is also proceeding in the private sector.

The statutory equivalent for the *chek* is 14 5/8 inches. The variation of the size of the *chek* with usage still persists in Hong Kong but the *chek* and derived units are now used much less than in the past.

ENERGY AND NATURAL RESOURCES

Electricity. Production (1988) 23,956m. kwh. Supply 220 volts; 50 Hz.

Water. The provision of sufficient reservoir capacity to store the summer rainfall in order to meet supply requirements has always been a serious problem. Over the years no less than 17 impounding reservoirs have been constructed with a total capacity of 586m. cu. metres. The major among these are the Plover Cove Reservoir (230m. cu. metres) finally completed in 1973 and the High Island Reservoir (281m. cu. metres) completed in 1978, both involving the conversion of sea water inlets into fresh water lakes.

There are no sites remaining in Hong Kong suitable for development as storage reservoirs. Consequently the purchase of water from China has been of increasing importance and the future needs of Hong Kong will be met to a large extent from this source. In 1988-89 water purchased from China was in the order of 644m. cu. metres. The agreement with China allows for annual increases up to a total figure of 660m. cu. metres per annum by 1994–95 which will represent 60% of Hong Kong's demand.

These resources can be further supplemented when necessary by up to 181,000 cu. metres of fresh water a day from a desalting plant completed in 1976 and now considered as a reserve resource.

Agriculture. Only 9% of the total land area is suitable for crop farming and most vegetables are produced through intensive market gardening cultivation, with 34% self-sufficiency. In 1988, 132,000 tonnes of vegetables and 2,020 tonnes of fruit were produced. Poultry production was 42,890 tonnes, with 37% self-sufficiency. Livestock (1988): Cattle, 750; pigs, 629,110.

Fisheries. The fishing fleet of 4,900 vessels supplies 74% of fresh marine fish consumed locally. In 1988 the total catch was 228,100 tonnes, valued at HK$2,039m. Inland freshwater farming and coastal marine farming provided 6,640 tonnes of freshwater fish valued at HK$85m. and 3,280 tonnes of marine products valued at HK$222m.

INDUSTRY AND TRADE

Industry. An economic policy based on free enterprise and free trade; an industrious work force; an efficient and aggressive commercial infrastructure;

modern and efficient sea-port (including container shipping terminals) and airport facilities; its geographical position relative to markets in North America and its traditional trading links with Britain have all contributed to Hong Kong's success as a modern industrial territory.

In Dec. 1988, there were 49,843 factories employing 837,072 people out of a total population of over 5·7m. The type of factory involved ranges from the small sub-contractor type to large highly complex modern establishments. Given the scarcity of land it is most common for light industry to operate in multi-storey buildings specially designed for this purpose. The main industry is textiles and clothing, which employed 43% of the total industrial workforce and accounted for 38% of total domestic exports in 1988. Other major light manufacturing industries include electronic products, clocks and watches, toys, plastic products, electrical products, metalware, footwear, cameras and travel goods. Heavy industry includes ship-building, ship-repairing, aircraft engineering and the manufacture of machinery.

Labour. In 1988 the labour force totalled 2·78m., including 837,000 in manufacturing, 521,000 in wholesale, retail and export/import trade, 236,000 in finance, real estate and business services, and 191,000 in hotels and restaurants.

Commerce. Hong Kong's industries are mainly export oriented. The total value of domestic exports in 1988 was HK$217,664m. The major markets were USA (33·5%), China (17·5%), Federal Republic of Germany (7·4%), UK (7·1%), Japan (5·3%), Canada (2·7%), Netherlands (2·4%) and Singapore (2·3%). There is also a sizeable and flourishing entrepôt trade which accounted for another HK$275,405m. in 1988.

The total value of imports in 1988 was HK$498,798m., mainly from China (31·2%), Japan (18·6%), Taiwan (8·9%), USA (8·3%), Republic of Korea (5·3%) and Singapore (3·7%).

The chief import items were machinery and transport equipment (28·8%), manufactured goods (26·4%), chemicals (9%), foodstuffs (6·3%), mineral fuel, lubricants and related materials (1·9%).

Duties are levied only on tobacco, hydrocarbon oils, methyl alcohol, alcoholic liquors, non-alcoholic beverages and cosmetics, whether imported into or manufactured in Hong Kong for local consumption.

All imports (apart from foodstuffs, which are subject to a flat declaration charge irrespective of the value of the consignment) and exports are subject to an *ad valorem* declaration charge at the rate of HK50 cents for every $1,000 value (or part thereof) of the goods shipped.

Visible trade normally carries an adverse balance which is offset by a favourable balance of invisible trade, in particular transactions in connexion with air transportation, shipping, tourism and banking services.

Hong Kong has a free exchange market. Foreign merchants may remit profits or repatriate capital. Import and export controls are kept to the minimum, consistent with strategic requirements.

Total trade between Hong Kong and UK (British Department of Trade returns, in £1,000 sterling) is given as follows:

	1985	*1986*	*1987*	*1988*	*1989*
Imports to UK	1,175,984	1,530,786	1,531,681	1,788,631	2,036,976
Exports and re-exports from UK	949,180	960,956	1,013,038	1,030,725	1,111,517

Tourism. 5·6m. tourists spent HK$33,328·3m. in Hong Kong during 1988.

COMMUNICATIONS

Roads. In March 1989 there were 1,446 km of roads, distributed as follows: Hong Kong Island, 397; Kowloon, 372, and New Territories, 677. A cross-harbour tunnel, 1·8 km in length, opened to traffic in Aug. 1972, now links Hong Kong Island with the Kowloon peninsula. In Sept. 1989, another cross-harbour tunnel, the Eastern Harbour Tunnel, was opened, linking the eastern part of both Hong Kong Island and the Kowloon peninsula. The 1·4 km twin-tube Lion Rock Tunnel, which links Kowloon with Sha Tin New Town and other areas of the north-eastern New Territories, became fully operational in Oct. 1978. The 1·8 km twin-tube Aberdeen Tunnel, which connects Aberdeen and Wan Chai, became operational in March 1983.

Railways. There is an electric tramway with a total track length of 30·4 km, and a cable tramway connecting the Peak district with the lower levels in Victoria. The electrified Kowloon-Guangzhou Railway runs for 34 km from the terminus at Hung Hom in Kowloon to the border point at Lo Wu. It carried 153m. passengers and 4·5m. tonnes of freight in 1988. A light rail system operated by KCR opened in the Tuen Mun area in Sept. 1988.

An underground Mass Transit Railway system, comprising 43·2 km with 38 stations, is now in operation. The system consists of 4 lines, one linking the Central District of Hong Kong Island with Tsuen Wan in the west of Kowloon, the second linking Quarry Bay on Hong Kong Island with Kwun Tong in East Kowloon with Yau Ma Tei in Nathan Road, the third linking Sheung Wan and Chai Wan on Hong Kong Island. It carried 630m. passengers in 1988.

Aviation. Hong Kong International Airport is situated on the north shore of Kowloon Bay. It is regularly used by some 40 airlines and many charter airlines which provide frequent services throughout the Far East to Europe, North America, Africa, the Middle East, Australia and New Zealand. British Airways operates 17 flights per week via India or the Gulf to the UK. Cathay Pacific Airways, one of the two Hong Kong-based airlines, operates more than 400 passenger and cargo services weekly to Europe (including 14 passenger and 5 cargo services per week to the UK), the Far and Middle East, Australia and North America. Hong Kong Dragon Airlines Ltd, which was set up in July 1985, operates B-737 scheduled and non-scheduled services between Hong Kong and a number of cities in Asia, the People's Republic of China and Micronesia. Air Hong Kong, an all-cargo operator, provides a scheduled twice-weekly service to Manchester, UK, and operates non-scheduled services around the region. About 1,000 scheduled flights are operated weekly to and from Hong Kong by various airlines. In 1988, 8,700 aircraft arrived and departed on international flights, carrying 15·3m. passengers and 700,000 tonnes of freight.

Shipping. The port of Hong Kong, which ranks among the top three container ports in the world, handled 4·03m. 20-ft equivalent units in 1988. The Kwai Chung Container Port has 8 berths with more than 3,000 metres of quay backed by about 120 hectares of cargo handling area. In 1988, some 17,089 ocean-going vessels called at Hong Kong and loaded and discharged some 81m. tonnes of cargo.

Telecommunications, Post and Broadcasting. There were 106 post offices in 1988; postal revenue totalled HK$1,450·9m.; expenditure, HK$940·7m in the 1988–89 financial year; 747·9m. letters and parcels were handled. Telephone service is provided by the Hong Kong Telephone Co. Ltd. It provides local, and in association with Cable and Wireless (HK) Ltd., international voice, data and facsimile transmission services for Hong Kong. At 31 Dec. 1988 there were over 2·9m. telephones served by 2·2m. lines. Cable and Wireless (HK) Ltd. provides the international telecommunication services as well as local telegram and telex services. These include public telegram, telex, telephone, television programmes transmission and reception, leased circuits, facsimile, switched data, ship-shore and air-ground communications. International facilities are provided through submarine cables, microwave and satellite radio systems. Hong Kong Telephone Co. Ltd. and Cable and Wireless (HK) Ltd. are wholly-owned subsidiaries of Hong Kong Telecommunications Ltd. which is jointly owned by the Cable and Wireless World Wide Communications Group, Hong Kong Government and public shareholders.

There is a government broadcasting station, Radio Television Hong Kong, which broadcasts through 3 FM and 4 AM channels (3 Chinese, 1 English and 2 bi-lingual services and 1 dedicated to BBC world service), 4 of which provide 24-hour service. A commercial station, the Commercial Broadcasting Co. Ltd, transmits daily in English and Cantonese. It operates 3 channels which provide 24-hour service.

Television Broadcasts Ltd and Asia Television Ltd transmit commercial television in English and Chinese on 4 channels, in colour.

Cinemas. In Oct. 1989 there were 148 cinemas with a seating capacity in excess of 125,000.

Newspapers. In June 1989 there were 63 daily or weekly newspapers, registered and in circulation, including 15 English-language papers, one bilingual paper, 46 Chinese-language dailies, one Japanese-language paper and a number of news agency bulletins.

JUSTICE, EDUCATION AND WELFARE

Justice. There is a Supreme Court which comprises the Court of Appeal and the High Court. While the Court of Appeal hears appeals on all matters, civil and criminal from the lower courts, the High Court has unlimited jurisdiction in both civil and criminal matters including bankruptcy, company winding-up, adoptions, probate and lunacy matters. The District Court has civil jurisdiction to hear monetary claims up to HK$120,000 or, where the claims are for recovery of land, the annual rent or rateable value does not exceed HK$100,000. In its criminal jurisdiction, it may try more serious offences except murder, manslaughter and rape; the maximum term of imprisonment it can impose is seven years. The Magistrates' Court exercises criminal jurisdiction over a wide range of indictable and summary offences. Its powers of punishment are generally restricted to a maximum of two years' imprisonment, or a fine of HK$10,000, though cumulative sentences of imprisonment up to three years may be imposed. The Coroner's Court inquires into the identity of a deceased person and the cause of death. The Juvenile Court has jurisdiction to hear charges against young people aged under 16 for any offence other than homicide. Children under the age of seven are not deemed to have reached the age of criminal responsibility. The Lands Tribunal determines on statutory claims for compensation over land and certain landlord and tenant matters. The Labour Tribunal provides inexpensive and speedy settlements to individual monetary claims arising from disputes between employers and employees. The Small Claims Tribunal deals with monetary claims involving amounts not exceeding HK$15,000. The Obscene Articles Tribunal, established in 1987, has two judicial functions. It has exclusive jurisdiction to determine whether an article referred to it by a court or a magistrate is an obscene or indecent article and where the matter publicly displayed is indecent and it also has power to classify an article as Class I (neither obscene nor indecent), Class II (an indecent article) or Class III (an obscene article).

Police. At the end of 1989, the establishment of the Royal Hong Kong Police Force was 28,000. In addition, there were over 5,800 auxiliary officers. Overall crime has averaged about 80,000 reported for the past 10 years and the detection rate stands at 46·5%

The Marine Police Region is responsible for patrolling some 1,850 sq. km of territorial waters and involved in the control of some 33,000 local craft with a maritime population of about 100,000. At the end of 1989, it consisted of a disciplined staff of more than 3,200 and a fleet of over 150 vessels.

Education. The majority of schools have to be registered with the Education Department under the Education Ordinance. They are required to comply with regulations as to staff, building, fire and health requirements. From Sept. 1971, free and compulsory primary education was introduced in government and the majority of government-aided schools. Free junior secondary education of 3 years' duration was introduced in 1978 and it was made compulsory in Sept. 1979.

In Sept. 1988 there were 214,703 pupils in kindergartens (all private), another 535,037 in primary schools and 443,901 in secondary schools.

There are 8 technical institutes and 16 training centres with a total enrolment of 80,000, 1 technical teachers' college and 3 colleges of education with a total enrolment of 4,839.

The University of Hong Kong had a total enrolment of 8,654 students in academic year 1988-89 and the Chinese University of Hong Kong, inaugurated in Oct. 1963, had a total of 7,900 students. The Hong Kong University of Science and Technology, established in 1989, will admit its first intakes in 1991-92 with 700 students. The Hong Kong Polytechnic, 1988-89, had about 26,000 students. In Oct. 1984, the City Polytechnic of Hong Kong was opened and had a total of 6,900 students in 1988-89. The Hong Kong Baptist College had 2,700 full-time students in 1988-89.

Health. In March 1989 there were 5,636 doctors and about 25,057 hospital beds.

Social Security. The Government co-ordinates and implements expanding programmes in social welfare, which include social security, family services, child care, services for the elderly, youth and community work, probation and corrections and rehabilitation. 159 voluntary welfare agencies are subsidized by public funds.

The Government gives non-contributory cash assistance to needy families, unemployed able-bodied adults, the severely disabled and the elderly. Caseload in Sept. 1989 totalled 394,360. Victims of natural disasters, crimes of violence and traffic accidents are financially assisted.

Further Reading

Statistical Information: The Census and Statistics Department is responsible for the preparation and collation of Government statistics. These statistics are published mainly in the *Hong Kong Monthly Digest of Statistics* which is also available in a collected annual edition. The Department also publishes monthly trade statistics, economic indicators, annual review of overseas trade, etc. Statistical information is also published in the annual reports of Government departments. *Hong Kong 1989*, and other government publications, are available from the Hong Kong Government Publications Centre, GPO Building, Connaught Place, Hong Kong, and the Hong Kong Government Office in London, 6 Grafton Street, London, W1X 3LB.

The Hong Kong Trade Development Council, Convention Plaza, Tower Rd, Wan Chai, Hong Kong, issues a monthly *Hong Kong Enterprise* and other publications.

Hong Kong 1989. Hong Kong Government Press, 1989
Beazer, W. F., *The Commercial Future of Hong Kong*. New York, 1978
Benton, G., *The Hong Kong Crisis*. London, 1983
Bonavia, D., *Hong Kong 1997*. London, 1984
Cheng, J. Y. S. (ed.) *Hong Kong: In Search of a Future*. OUP, 1984
Chill, H., *et al* (eds.) *The Future of Hong Kong: Toward 1997 and Beyond*. Westport, 1987
Endacott, G. B., *A History of Hong Kong*. 2nd ed. OUP, 1973.–*Government and People in Hong Kong, 1841–1962. A Constitutional History*. OUP, 1965
Hopkins, K., *Hong Kong: The Industrial Colony*. OUP, 1971
Morris, J., *Hong Kong: Xianggang*. London, 1988
Patrikeeff, F., *Mouldering Pearl: Hong Kong at the Crossroads*. London, 1989
Tregear, E. R., *Land Use in Hong Kong*. Hong Kong Univ. Press, 1958.—*Hong Kong Gazetteer*. Hong Kong Univ. Press, 1958.—*The Development of Hong Kong as Told in Maps*. Hong Kong Univ. Press, 1959
Wacks, R., *Civil Liberties in Hong Kong*. OUP, 1988
Youngson, A. J., *Hong Kong: Economic Growth and Policy*. OUP, 1982

HUNGARY

Capital: Budapest
Population: 10·59m. (1989)
GNP per capita: US$2,460 (1988)

Magyar Köztársaság (Hungarian Republic)

HISTORY. Hungary first became an independent kingdom in 1001. For events to 1956 *see* THE STATESMAN'S YEAR-BOOK, 1957.

On 23 Oct. 1956 an anti-Stalinist revolution broke out, and the newly-formed coalition government of Imre Nagy on 1 Nov. withdrew from the Warsaw Pact and asked the UN for protection. János Kádár, formed a counter-government on 3 Nov. and asked the USSR for support. Soviet troops suppressed the revolution and abducted Nagy and his ministers; Nagy was secretly executed in 1958.

On 7 Sept. 1967 a second Soviet-Hungarian treaty of friendship was concluded for 20 years with subsequent automatic 5-year renewals.

A gathering reformist tendency within the Hungarian Socialist Workers' (i.e. Communist) Party led by Imre Pozsgay culminated in its self-dissolution in Oct. 1989 and reconstitution as the Hungarian Socialist Party.

Hungary was proclaimed the 'Hungarian Republic' on 23 Oct. 1989.

Nagy was reburied with state honours on 16 Aug. 1989.

AREA AND POPULATION. Hungary is bounded north by Czechoslovakia, north-east by the USSR, east by Romania, south by Yugoslavia and west by Austria. The peace treaty of 10 Feb. 1947 restored the frontiers as of 1 Jan. 1938. The area of Hungary is 93,032 sq. km (35,911 sq. miles).

The official language is Hungarian (Magyar).

At the census of 1 Jan. 1980 the population was 10,709,550 (5,195,300 males). Population in 1989: 10,590,000 (males, 5,107,000). Ethnic miorities, 1984: Germans, 1·6%; Slovaks, 1·1%; Romanians, 0·2%; others, 0·5%. There were 320,000 Gypsies in 1985 with a Gypsy Council.

60% of the population is urban (20% in Budapest). Population density, 114 per sq. km. Birth rate, 1988, 11·7 per 1,000; death rate, 13·1 per 1,000. Since 1981 the population has been decreasing, by 1·4 per 1,000 in 1988; expectation of life (1987): males, 66; females, 74. There is a world-wide Hungarian diaspora, of 1·5m. in 1988 (730,000 in US; 220,000 in Israel; 140,000 in Canada), and Hungarian minorities (3·5m. in 1988) in Romania, Yugoslavia and Czechoslovakia.

Vital statistics, 1988: Births, 124,348; marriages, 65,932 (of which 19,277 remarriages); divorces, 25,000 (estimate); deaths, 139,142; abortions, 87,000 (approx.); infant mortality, 15·8 per 1,000 live births. There were 4,494 suicides in 1988.

Hungary is divided into 19 counties (*megyék*) and the capital, Budapest, which has county status.

Area (in sq. km) and population (in 1,000) of counties and county towns:

Counties (1989)	*Area*	*Population*	*Chief town (1989)*	*Population*
Baranya	4,487	434	Pécs	183
Bács-Kiskun	8,362	552	Kecskemét	106
Békés	5,632	413	Békéscsaba	71
Borsod-Abaúj-Zemplén	7,247	772	Miskolc	208
Csongrád	4,263	456	Szeged	189
Fejér	4,373	426	Székesfehérvár	114
Győr-Sopron	4,012	426	Győr	132
Hajdú-Bihar	6,211	550	Debrecen	220
Heves	3,637	336	Eger	67
Komárom	2,251	320	Tatabánya	77
Nógrád	2,544	227	Salgótarján	49
Pest	6,394	989	Budapest	2,115
Somogy	6,036	348	Kaposvár	74
Szabolcs-Szatmár	5,938	564	Nyíregyháza	119
Szolnok	5,607	427	Szolnok	82
Tolna	3,704	262	Szekszárd	39

Counties (1989)	*Area*	*Population*	*Chief town (1989)*	*Population*
Vas	3,337	276	Szombathely	88
Veszprém	4,689	387	Veszprém	66
Zala	3,784	310	Zalaegerszeg	64
Budapest	525	2,115	(has county status)	

CLIMATE. A humid continental climate, with warm summers and cold winters. Precipitation is generally greater in summer, with thunderstorms. Dry, clear weather is likely in autumn, but spring is damp and both seasons are of short duration. Budapest. Jan. 32°F (0°C), July 71°F (21·5°C). Annual rainfall 25" (625 mm). Pécs. Jan. 30°F (–0·7°C), July 71°F (21·5°C). Annual rainfall 26·4" (661 mm).

CONSTITUTION AND GOVERNMENT. On 1 Feb. 1946 the National Assembly proclaimed a republic.

The People's Republic was established by the constitution of 18 Aug. 1949 (for details see THE STATESMAN'S YEAR-BOOK, 1989-90, p.615). In Jan. 1989 a reform programme involving electoral law, civil liberties and the enactment of a new constitution was approved by Parliament.

After a cabinet reshuffle in May 1989, the Prime Minister, Miklós Németh, announced that henceforth the Government would work independently and not just as the executive branch of the Communist Party.

On 18 Oct. 1989 Parliament approved by an 88% majority a new constitution which abolished the People's Republic. The preamble states 'The Hungarian Republic is an independent, democratic, law-based state in which the values of bourgeois democracy and democratic socialism hold good in equal measure. All power belongs to the people, which they exercise directly and through the elected representatives of popular sovereignty…No party may direct any organs of state'.

Ethnic minorities have equal rights and education in their own tongue.

National flag: Three horizontal stripes of red, white, green.

National anthem: God bless the Hungarians–Isten áldd meg a magyart (words by Ferenc Kölcsey, tune by Ferenc Erkel).

Chairman of the Presidential Council (Head of State): Imre Pozsgay, appointed June 1989. *Deputy Chairmen:* István Sárlos, Rezső Trautmann.

In 1949 the Hungarian Working People's Party (Communists), the Smallholders' Party, the National Peasant Party, the Trade Union Federation, and similar sectional federations were merged in the People's Independence (afterwards Patriotic) Front.

The Communist Party was reorganized after the 1956 revolution and changed its name to 'Hungarian Socialist Workers' Party' (HSWP). It had 888,000 members in 1988. János Kádár and other leaders associated with him were replaced in 1988.

Pressure for reform within the HSWP led by Imre Pozsgay's faction 'Movement for a Democratic Hungary' led the party to dissolve itself by 1,202 votes to 159 at its 14th Congress in Oct. 1989 and to reconstitute itself as the 'Hungarian Socialist Party' (HSP). The HSP declares itself the legal heir of the HSWP, but dissociates itself from the latter's 'crimes and mistakes'. Its founding document commits it to 'contributing to building a social market economy based on mixed ownership'.

Former HSWP members have to join the HSP anew; 20,000 had done so by the end of Oct. 1989.

The HSP has a presidium of 25 headed by Rezső Nyers, elected by an 80% majority. Other members include Imre Pozsgay, Míklós Németh and Gyula Horn.

Prominent members of the Government in March 1990 were:

Prime Minister: Miklós Németh.

Deputy Prime Ministers: Imre Pozsgay, Péter Medgyessy. *Finance:* László Békési. *Foreign Affairs:* Gyula Horn. *Defence:* Col.-Gen. Ferenc Kárpáti. *Justice:* Kálmán Kulcsár.

Parliament consists of 152 deputies elected by proportional representation from 20 regional lists, 176 deputies directly elected from constituencies, and 58 from a national list by transferable vote.

At a referendum on 26 Nov. 1989 it was decided, by a majority of some 6,000 votes, that the next President should be elected by Parliament after a general election, and not by direct ballot in Jan. 1990. 4·1m. votes were cast, a turn-out of 55%. Parliamentary elections were held on 25 Mar. 1990. 53 parties registered for the electoral campaign, including the Socialist Party (formerly Communist, with 50,000 members in Jan. 1990), Social Democratic Party, Democratic Forum, the Smallholders and the Alliance of Free Democrats.

Local Government. Counties are sub-divided into towns and boroughs. These are administered by a hierarchy of local councils which in turn elect Executive Committees to carry on day-to-day administration. There are 1,507 local council constituencies. Elections are held at the same time as general elections. Members of county councils are elected by the lower councils. At the June 1985 elections 42,731 councillors and 30,885 alternate councillors were elected.

DEFENCE. The President of the Republic is Commander-in-Chief of the armed forces.

Men between the ages of 18 and 23 are liable for 18 months' conscription in the Army, 24 months in the Air Force. Compulsory military service age-limits are 18 to 55 (18 to 45 women).

The Workers' Militia was disbanded in 1989.

The USSR has agreed to withdraw its forces by 1991.

Army. Hungary is divided into 4 army districts: Budapest, Debrecen, Kiskunfélegyháza, Pécs. The strength of the Army was (1990) 68,000 (including 40,000 conscripts). It is organized in 4 tank brigades, 12 motor rifle brigades, 1 artillery and 1 surface-to-surface missile brigade, 1 anti-aircraft regiment, 3 surface-to-air missile regiments and 1 airborne battalion. Equipment includes 1,300 T-54/-55 and 135 T-72 tanks.

Navy. The Danube Flotilla, the maritime wing of the Army, in 1989 consisted of some 500 personnel operating 10 river minesweepers and numerous boats and special-purpose vessels.

Air Force. The Air Force is an integral part of the Army, with a strength (1990) of about 23,000 officers and men and 200 combat aircraft. The combat aircraft strength comprises 1 regiment of MiG-23 fighters, 1 of MiG-21 interceptors, 1 of Su-22 fighter-bombers, 1 of Su-25 ground attack aircraft, and a regiment of Mi-8 and Mi-24 armed helicopters. Transport units are equipped with An-2, An-24 and An-26 aircraft. Other types in service include Ka-26, Mi-2 and Mi-8 helicopters and L-29 Delfin trainers. 'Guideline' and 'Goa' surface-to-air missiles are also operational.

INTERNATIONAL RELATIONS

Membership. Hungary is a member of UN, the Warsaw Pact and Comecon and, since 1982, IMF and IBRD.

External Debt. Hungary settled its debt to the UK in 1967. By an agreement of 6 March 1973 Hungary is to meet US claims of US$189m. arising from war damage and nationalization in 20 yearly instalments. Hungarian foreign indebtedness was some US$20,000m. in 1989.

ECONOMY

Policy. For planning under the Communist government *see* THE STATESMAN'S YEAR-BOOK, 1989-90, p. 616-17. An emergency budget in Dec. 1989 opened the economy to market mechanisms, and called for drastic cuts in Government spending, the abolition of price subsidies and the closure of loss-making state industries. It is envisaged that one-third of industry will be privatized by 1992. Enterprise councils, which were established in 1984, are being transformed into limited companies; the State retains 20% of shares while the rest are for sale. Income tax and VAT were introduced in Jan. 1988. Inflation was 18% in 1988. A State Property

Agency is overseeing privatization. Retail price index, 1989 (1987=100): House purchase, 123·4; rent, 114; clothing, 119·8; household energy, 112·4; food, 110·4; transport, 100.

Budget. The budget for calendar years was as follows (in 1,000 forints):

	1981	*1982*	*1983*	*1984*	*1985*	*1986*	*1987*
Revenue	472,600	485,792	543,735	572,920	632,800	682,000	760,600
Expenditure	482,400	498,007	549,822	576,580	646,600	727,300	795,000

1987 revenue included (1,000m. forints): Payments by enterprises, 469·4; consumer taxes, 122·3; payments by the population, 79·3. Expenditure included: Support of enterprises, 150·7; social security, 154·7; consumer price supports, 66·7; capital expenditure, 99·9; education and culture, 65·0; defence, 45·4. The defence budget was cut by 17% in 1989.

Currency. A decree of 26 July 1946 instituted a new monetary unit, the *forint* subdivided into 100 *fillér*. There are coins of 10, 20 and 50 fillér and 1, 2, 5, 10, 20 forints, and notes of 10, 20, 50, 100, 500, 1,000 and 5,000 forints. The forint was made partially convertible in 1989. It was devalued by 10% in Dec. 1989. The rate of exchange (March 1990) 109·54 forints to the £1 sterling, 66·83 forints = US$1.

Banking. In 1987 a two-tier system was established. The National Bank (*Director,* Ferenc Bartha) remained the central state financial institution, responsible for the circulation of money and foreign currency exchange, but also became a central clearing bank, with general (but not operational) control over 5 new second-tier commercial banks and 10 specialized development banks. 9 other commercial banks were set up in 1985 to finance development. In 1987 the State Development Institute was established to issue Government bonds to cover the budgetary deficit. A stock exchange was opened in Jan. 1989.

The Hungarian International Trade Bank opened in London in 1973. In 1980 the Central European International Bank was set up in Budapest with 7 Western banks holding 66% of the shares. The National Savings Bank handles local government as well as personal accounts. Deposits in 1988: 296,827m. forints.

Weights and Measures. The metric system is in use.

ENERGY AND NATURAL RESOURCES

Electricity. Supply 220 volts; 50 Hz. Sources of energy in 1988: Oil, 31·6%, gas, 26·8%; coal and lignite, 23·2%; others, 18·4%. Imported, 50·8%. Capacity of power stations was 7,092 mw. There is an 880-mw nuclear power station at Paks. A 750-kv power line links up with the Soviet grid. 29,217m. kwh were produced in 1988 (13,445 kwh by nuclear power), and 13,615m. kwh imported. In May 1989 Hungary withdrew from the Czech-Austrian-Hungarian hydroelectric project on the Danube at Nagymáros.

Oil. Oil and natural gas are found in the Szeged basin and Zala county. Production in 1989: Oil, 1·9m. tonnes; gas (1988), 6,327m. cu. m.

Minerals. Production in 1988 (in 1,000 tonnes): Coal, 2,255; lignite, 5,634; brown coal, 12,986; bauxite, 2,906.

Agriculture. Agricultural land was collectivised in 1950. A law of 1968 permits collectives to own land, and guarantees individuals' rights to private plots. Collectives meet in a National Council of Agricultural Co-operatives.

In 1988 the agricultural area was (in 1,000 hectares) 6,497, of which 4,712 were arable, 1,210 meadows and pastures, 338 market gardens, and 237 orchards and vineyards.

In 1988 there were 133 state farms (self-governing under the Ministry of Agriculture) with 905,200 hectares of land, 1,253 collective farms with 5m. hectares of land (including 281,500 hectares of household plots) and 1,375 private farms with 529,300 hectares. Structure of production, 1987: Co-operative, 48·4%; private,

36·4%; state, 15·2%. The irrigated area was 177,000 hectares; 53,000 tractors were in use.

Sown area, 1988: 4·64m. hectares (cereals, 2·8m.; industrial crops, 643,000; pulses, 165,000; potatoes, 48,000)

Crop production (in 1,000 tonnes) in 1988 (and 1987): Wheat, 6,962 (5,685); rye, 245 (182); barley, 1,168 (783); oats, 134 (95); maize, 6,027 (7,007); sugar-beet, 4,504 (4,255); sunflower seed, 705, (790); potatoes, 887 (694).

Livestock in 1988 was (in 1,000 head) as follows: Cattle, 1,690; pigs, 8,327; poultry, 35,607; sheep, 2,216; horses, 76,000.

Livestock products (1988): Eggs, 4,695m.; milk, 2,788m. litres; wool, 9,600 tonnes; animals for slaughter, 2,312,000 tonnes.

The north shore of Lake Balaton and the Tokaj area are important wine-producing districts. Wine production in 1988 (and 1987) was 430m. (320m.) litres.

Forestry. 18% of Hungary is under forest: 1·68m. hectares in 1988. 35,000 hectares were afforested and 7·96m. cu. metres of timber were cut.

Fisheries. There are fisheries in the rivers Danube and Tisza and Lake Balaton. In 1988 there were 26,500 hectares of commercial fishponds. Fish production was 25,000 tonnes.

INDUSTRY AND TRADE

Industry. In 1988 there were 1,156 state industrial enterprises (employing an average of 1,206 persons), 1,662 industrial co-operatives (195) and 46,995 private business (70). Creditors may proceed against insolvent companies which may be liquidated.

Production (in 1,000 tonnes) in 1988 (and 1987): Pig iron, 2,093 (2,107); steel, 6,373 (6,452); alumina, 873 (858); aluminium, 75 (74); aluminium semi-finished products, 192 (184); cement, 3,873 (4,153); sulphuric acid, 512 (573); petrol, 2,864 (2,977); plastics, 581 (545); chemical fertilizers, 922 (1,067); synthetic fibres, 38 (34); buses (units), 12,340 (12,956); lorries, 703 (577); TV receivers, 393,000 (446,000); refrigerators, 398,000 (399,000).

Labour. In 1988 there were 4,844,800 wage-earners (2,220,800 female) in the following categories: Working-class, 60·8%; white-collar, 26·3%; co-operative peasantry, 7·7%; self-employed tradesmen, 5·2%. 4,550,400 worked in the socialist sector. Percentage distributions of the workforce: Industry, 30·9; agriculture, 18·8; social and cultural services, 12·6; trade, 10·7; transport and communications, 8·3; building, 7·1. A 40-hour 5-day week was introduced in 1984. Average monthly wages in 1988: 7,015 forints. Minimum subsistence level, 1988, was 3,470 forints per month. There were some 30,000 unemployed in 1988. Unemployment benefit for one year became payable from Jan. 1989. Wilful unemployment is a criminal offence. Retirement age: Men, 60; women, 55. Leave entitlement, 15-24 days in 1985.

Trade Unions. Membership of the official National Council of Trade Unions (*Chairman:* Sándor Nagy) was 4·9m. in 1984, 3·9m. in 1988. Several independent trade unions have been founded since May 1988.

Commerce. The economy is heavily dependent on foreign trade. Trade for calendar years (in 1m. forints):

	1982	*1983*	*1984*	*1985*	*1986*	*1987*	*1988*
Imports	324,800	365,000	390,500	410,100	439,700	463,100	472,500
Exports	324,500	374,100	414,000	424,600	420,300	450,100	504,100

In 1988 Hungary's trade with communist countries (in 1,000m. forints): Imports, 231·6; exports, 254·9. In 1988 USSR was Hungary's major trading partner (25·0% of imports, 27·6% of exports), ahead of the Federal Republic of Germany (13·9%, 11·0%) and Austria (7·2%, 5·7%).

Commodity structure of foreign trade (%), 1988:

	Imports		*Exports*	
	Communist countries	*Other countries*	*Communist countries*	*Other countries*
Fuels and electricity	27·4	2·3	0·4	3·9
Raw materials	12·9	13·8	2·3	12·0
Semi-finished products	14·3	33·9	9·5	26·4
Spare parts	8·3	14·8	10·3	3·9
Machinery and capital goods	20·9	13·7	47·5	12·5
Industrial consumer goods	13·6	10·2	16·6	15·5
Agricultural produce	0·5	3·7	3·9	10·0
Food industry products	2·1	7·6	9·6	15·8

Enterprises may handle their own foreign trade relations, set up companies abroad and participate in foreign companies. The Marketexpo branch of the Hungarian National Market Research Institute will conduct research for foreign firms.

Joint ventures with Western firms holding up to 72% of the capital are encouraged, and may be declared duty-free zones. Foreign companies may set up offices in Hungary. In 1989 the US granted Hungary most-favoured-nation status. In 1988 a trade agreement was signed with the EEC which will lower quotas by 1995. An EEC loan of £700m. was granted in Oct. 1989.

Total trade between Hungary and UK (British Department of Trade returns, in £1,000 sterling):

	1985	*1986*	*1987*	*1988*	*1989*
Imports to UK	84,114	77,229	83,267	96,288	105,221
Exports and re-exports from UK	107,226	101,557	101,300	131,212	117,947

Tourism. In 1988, 17·97m. foreigners visited Hungary (6·38m. from the West), of whom 10·56m. were tourists (3·09m. from the West); and 10·78m. Hungarians travelled abroad (3·33m. to the West) of whom 6·75m. (1·27m.) were tourists. Restrictions on travel to the West were eased in Jan. 1988.

COMMUNICATIONS

Roads. In 1988 there were 29,701 km of roads, including motorways, 218 km; highways, 93 km and other first class main roads, 1,886 km. Passenger cars numbered 1,789,600 (1,747,300 private), lorries 179,203 and buses 26,569. 211m. tonnes of freight and 629m. passengers were transported by road (excluding intra-urban passengers). In 1988 there were 21,315 road accidents with 1,706 fatalities.

Railways. Route length of public lines in 1988, 7,770 km, of which 2.088 km were electrified. 112m. tonnes of freight and 226m. passengers were carried.

Aviation. Budapest airport (Ferihegy) handled 2·48m. passengers in 1988. In 1989 Hungarian Air Lines (Malév) had 22 aircraft and flew 40 routes to Europe, the Middle East and North America. 1·3m. passengers were carried. British Airways, PANAM, Air France, SABENA, Swissair, OS, Lufthansa and KLM as well as Aeroflot and East European lines have services to Budapest. TNT operates an express freight service.

Shipping. Navigable waterways have a length of 1,688 km. In 1988 5·34m. tonnes of cargo and 4·22m. passengers were carried. The Hungarian Shipping Company (MAHART) has agencies at Amsterdam, Alexandria, Algiers, Beirut, Rijeka and Trieste. It has 17 sea-going ships.

Pipeline. Length of network, 1988: Oil, 1,204 km; gas, 4,317. Quantity transported, 21·59m. tonnes (5,334m. tonne-kilometres).

Post and Broadcasting. In 1988 there were 3,196 post offices, 858,200 telephones, (593,100 private), and 12,614 telex subscribers. TV licences, (1987) 2,958,000. *Magyar Rádio és Televízió* broadcasts 3 programmes on medium-waves and FM and also regional programmes, including transmissions in German, Romanian and Serbo-Croat. Two TV programmes are broadcast, averaging 121 hours a week in 1988. Colour broadcasts are only transmitted in Budapest, using the SECAM system. Foreign commercials are accepted.

Cinemas and Theatres (1988). There were 2,943 cinemas; attendance 51m. 40 full-length feature films were made. There were 41 theatres; attendance 5·55m.

Newspapers and Publishing. In 1988 there were 29 dailies, circulating in 952m. copies and 1,692 other periodicals. 7,562 book titles were published in 1988 in 99·3m. copies.

JUSTICE, RELIGION, EDUCATION AND WELFARE

Justice. The administration of justice is the responsibility of the Procurator-General, elected by Parliament for 6 years. There are 108 regional courts and courts of labour, 20 county courts, 5 district courts and a Supreme Court. Criminal proceedings are dealt with by the regional courts through 3-member councils and by the county courts and the Supreme Court in 5-member councils. A new Civil Code was adopted in 1978 and a new Criminal Code in 1979.

Regional courts act as courts of first instance; county courts as either courts of first instance or of appeal. The Supreme Court acts normally as an appeal court, but may act as a court of first instance in cases submitted to it by the Public Prosecutor. All courts, when acting as courts of first instance, consist of 1 professional judge and 2 lay assessors, and, as courts of appeal, of 3 professional judges. Local government Executive Committees may try petty offences.

Regional and county judges and assessors are elected by the appropriate local councils; members of the Supreme Court by Parliament.

There are also military courts of the first instance. Military cases of the second instance go before the Supreme Court.

61,977 sentences were imposed on adults in 1988, including 22,820 of imprisonment. Juvenile convictions: 6,220.

Religion. There are 20 authorized religious denominations which share proportionally an annual state subsidy of 70m. forints. 8·5m. of the population professed a religious faith in 1976; the number of active church members was put between 1m. and 1·5m.

Senior church appointments require the consent of the Presidential Council. Lower ones are ratified by the State Office for Church Affairs. Certain appointments become valid if the Office makes no comment within 15 days, and for the most minor church appointments neither state consent nor prior notification is required. Ecclesiastics are required to take an oath of allegiance to the state.

In 1976 there were 5·25m. Roman Catholics with 4,400 churches, and 500,000 Uniates. In 1979 there were 3 seminaries and 1 Uniate seminary, a theological academy, and 8 secondary schools. There were 2,400 Roman Catholic priests in 1986. There are also lay co-operators of both sexes who perform some priestly duties. The Primate of Hungary is Archbishop László Pacskai, appointed Aug. 1986. There are 11 dioceses, all with bishops or archbishops. There is one Uniate bishopric.

In 1976 there were 2m. Calvinists with 4 dioceses, 1,300 ministers and 1,567 churches. There were 2 theological colleges (20% of students female) with 16 teachers, and 1 secondary school. There were 500,000 Lutherans with 16 dioceses, 374 ministers and 673 churches. There is a theological college with 6 teachers. The 10 denominations in the Association of Free Churches had 37,000 members, 230 ministers and 675 churches. There are 4 Orthodox denominations with 40,000 members in 1979. The Unitarian Church has 10,000 members, 11 ministers and 6 churches. In 1988 there were 80,000 Jews (825,000 in 1939) with 136 synagogues, 26 rabbis and a rabbinical college which enrols 10 students a year.

Education. Education is free and compulsory from 6 to 14. Primary schooling ends at 14; thereafter education may be continued at secondary, secondary technical or secondary vocational schools, which offer diplomas entitling students to apply for higher education, or at vocational training schools which offer tradesmen's diplomas. Students at the latter may also take the secondary school diploma examinations after 2 years of evening or correspondence study.

In 1988–89 there were 4,772 kindergartens with 33,876 teachers and 393,735 pupils; 3,526 primary schools with 90,620 teachers and 1,242,700 pupils; 645 secondary schools with 20,084 teachers and 248,300 pupils; and 294 vocational training schools with 11,745 teachers and 186,700 trainees. There are 4 universities proper (Budapest, Pécs, Szeged, Debrecen), and 14 specialized universities (6 technical, 4 medical, 3 arts, 1 economics). At these and at 40 other institutions of higher education there were 16,242 teachers and 71,700 full-time students (10% of the 18-22 year-old population).

Libraries and Museums. In 1988 there were 4,503 public and 4,456 trade union libraries. The Széchenyi Library is the national library. In 1988 there were 734 museums with 18·34m. visitors.

Health. In 1988 there were 36,059 doctors and dentists and 104,832 hospital beds. Main causes of death, 1988: Heart disease, 37,457; neoplasms, 28,997; cerebrovascular diseases, 21,219. 8 cases of AIDS were reported.

Average daily consumption per head of population, 1988: 13,750 kilojoules.

Social Security. Medical treatment is free. Patients bear 15% of the cost of medicines. Sickness benefit is 75% of wages, old age pensions (at 60 for men, 55 for women) 60–70%. In 1987, 162,000m. forints were paid out in social insurance benefits including 23,182m. in family allowances, 13,400m. in sick pay and 129,966m. in pensions. Benefits were raised in Dec. 1989. There were 2·42m. pensioners in 1988. In 1988 family allowances were paid to 1,327,000 families. Monthly allowances (in forints) are: One child, 1,620; two, 3,240; three, 5,250; four, 7,000 (more for single parents).

DIPLOMATIC REPRESENTATIVES

Of Hungary in Great Britain (35 Eaton Pl., London, SW1X 8BY)
Ambassador: Dr József Györke (accredited 2 Nov. 1989).

Of Great Britain in Hungary (Harmincad Utca 6, Budapest V)
Ambassador: J. A. Birch, CMG.

Of Hungary in the USA (3910 Shoemaker St., NW, Washington, D.C., 20008)
Ambassador: Dr Peter Varkonyi.

Of the USA in Hungary (Szabadság Tér 12, Budapest V)
Ambassador: (Vacant).

Of Hungary to the United Nations
Ambassador: Ferenc Esztergalyos.

Further Reading

Statisztikai Évkönyv. Budapest, annual; since 1871, abridged English version, *Statistical Year-Book*
Statistical Pocket Book of Hungary (in English). Budapest, annual from 1959
State Budget. Budapest, annual from 1983
Hungarian Digest. Budapest, 6 a year from 1980
The Hungarian Economy: a Quarterly Economic and Business Review. Budapest, since 1972
Hungary 66 (67 etc.). Budapest, annual from 1966
Managers in Hungary: A Biographical Directory. Budapest, 1986
Marketing in Hungary. Budapest, quarterly
Quarterly Review of the National Bank of Hungary. From 1983
Information Hungary. Budapest, 1980
The Constitution of the Hungarian People's Republic. Budapest, 1972
The 13th Congress of the Hungarian Workers' Party, March 25–28, 1985. Budapest, 1986

Andorka, R. and Bertalan, L. (eds.) *Economy and Society in Hungary*. Budapest, 1986
Bako, E., *Guide to Hungarian Studies*. 2 vols. Stanford Univ. Press, 1973
Batt, J., *Economic Reform and Political Change in Eastern Europe: A Comparison of the Czechoslovak and Hungarian Experiences*. Basingstoke, 1988
Berend, I. T. and Ranki, G., *Hungary: A Century of Economic Development*. New York and Newton Abbot, 1974.—*Underdevelopment and Economic Growth: Studies in Hungarian Social and Economic History*. Budapest, 1979.—*The Hungarian Economy in the Twentieth Century*. London, 1985

Bernat, T., (ed.) *An Economic Geography of Hungary*. Budapest, 1985
Bölöny, J., *Magyarország Kormányai, 1848–1975*. Budapest, 1978. [Lists governments and politicians]
Brown, D. M., *Towards a Radical Democracy: The Political Economy of the Budapest School*. Cambridge, 1988
Cave, M., *Alternative Approaches to Economic Planning*. London, 1981
Fekete, J., *Back to the Realities: Reflections of a Hungarian Banker*. Budapest, 1982
Gati, C., *Hungary and the Soviet Bloc*. Duke Univ. Press, 1986
Hare, P. G., and others (eds.) *Hungary: a Decade of Economic Reform*. London, 1981
Hegedüs, A., *The Structure of Socialist Society*. London, 1977
Heinrich, H.-G., *Hungary: Politics, Economics and Society*. London, 1986
Kabdebó, T., *Hungary*. [Bibliography] Oxford and Santa Barbara, 1980
Kádár, J., *For a Socialist Hungary*. Budapest, 1974.—*Socialism and Democracy in Hungary*. Budapest, 1984.—*János Kádár*. Oxford, 1985
Kovrig, B., *Communism in Hungary*. Stanford, 1979
Kozma, F., *Economic Integration and Economic Strategy*. The Hague, 1982
Kulcsár K., *Contemporary Hungarian Society*. Budapest, 1984
Lendvai, P., *Hungary: The Art of Survival*. London, 1989
Macartney, C. A., *Hungary: A Short History*. London, 1962
Németh, G. (ed.) *Hungary: A Comprehensive Guide*. Budapest, 1980
Országh, L., *Hungarian-English Dictionary*. Budapest, 1977.—*English-Hungarian Dictionary*. Budapest, 1970
Pamlényi, E. (ed.) *A History of Hungary*. Budapest, 1975
Pécsi, M. and Sárfalvi, B , *Physical and Economic Geography of Hungary*. 2nd ed. Budapest, 1979
Rába, A. and Schenk, K.-E., (eds.) *Investment System and Foreign Trade Implications in Hungary*. New York, 1987
Szoboszlai, G. (ed.) *Politics and Public Administration in Hungary*. Budapest, 1985
Vardy, S. B. and Vardy, A. H., (eds.) *Society in Change*. Boulder, 1983
Vasary, I., *Beyond the Plan: Social Change in a Hungarian Village*. Boulder, 1987

ICELAND

Lyðveldið Ísland

Capital: Reykjavík
Population: 253,482 (1989)
GNP per capita: US$20,160 (1988)

HISTORY. The first settlers came to Iceland in 874. Between 930 and 1264 Iceland was an independent republic, but by the 'Old Treaty' of 1263 the country recognized the rule of the King of Norway. In 1381 Iceland, together with Norway, came under the rule of the Danish kings, but when Norway was separated from Denmark in 1814, Iceland remained under the rule of Denmark. Since 1 Dec. 1918 it has been acknowledged as a sovereign state. It was united with Denmark only through the common sovereign until it was proclaimed an independent republic on 17 June 1944.

AREA AND POPULATION. Iceland is a large island in the North Atlantic, close to the Arctic Circle, and comprises an area of about 103,000 sq. km (39,758 sq. miles), with its extreme northern point (the Rifstangi) lying in 66° 32' N. lat., and its most southerly point (Kötlutangi) in 63° 23' N. lat., not including the islands north and south of the land; if these are included, the country extends from 67° 10' N. (the Kolbeinsey) to 63° 17' N. (Surtsey, one of the Westman Islands). It stretches from 13° 30' (the Gerpir) to 24° 32' W. long. (Látrabjarg). The skerry *Hvalbakur* (The Whaleback) lies 13° 16' W. long.

There are 8 regions:

Region	*Inhabited land (sq. km)*	*Mountain pasture (sq. km)*	*Waste-land (sq. km)*	*Total area (sq. km)*	*Population (1 Dec. 1988)*
Capital area Southwest Peninsula	1,266	716	—	1,982	141,938 14,949
West	5,011	3,415	275	8,711	14,817
Western Peninsula	4,130	3,698	1,652	9,470	10,097
Northland West	4,867	5,278	2,948	13,093	10,551
Northland East	9,890	6,727	5,751	22,368	26,075
East South	16,921	17,929	12,555	21,991 25,214	13,167 20,096
Iceland	42,085	37,553	23,181	102,819	251,690

The census population (1980) was 229,187. In 1988, 24,443 were domiciled in rural districts and 227,247 in towns and villages (of over 200 inhabitants). The population is almost entirely Icelandic.

In 1988 foreigners numbered 4,829; of these 1,154 were Danish, 816 US, 527 British, 337 Norwegian and 318 German nationals.

The capital, Reykjavík, had on 1 Dec. 1988, a population of 95,811; other towns were Akranes, 5,404; Akureyri, 13,972; Bolungarvík, 1,217; Dalvík, 1,430; Eskifjörður, 1,092; Garðabær, 6,843; Grindavík, 2,132; Hafnarfjörður, 14,199; Húsavík, 2,499; Ísafjörður, 3,458; Keflavík, 7,305; Kópavogur, 15,551; Neskaupstaður, 1,714; Njarðvík, 2,443; Ólafsfjörður, 1,179; Sauðárkrókur, 2,478; Selfoss, 3,774; Seltjarnarnes, 4,027; Seyðisfjörður, 996; Siglufjörður, 1,858; Vestmannaeyjar, 4,743.

Vital statistics for calendar years:

	Living births	*Still-born*	*Marriages*	*Divorces*	*Deaths*	*Infant deaths*
1986	3,881	18	1,229	498	1,598	21
1987	4,193	15	1,160	477	1,725	30
1988	4,673	18	1,294	459	1,818	29

The official language is Icelandic *(íslenska)*.

CLIMATE. The climate is cool temperate oceanic and rather changeable, but mild for its latitude because of the Gulf Stream and prevailing S.W. winds. Precipitation is high in upland areas, mainly in the form of snow. Reykjavik. Jan. 34°F (1°C), July 52°F (11°C). Annual rainfall 34" (860 mm).

CONSTITUTION AND GOVERNMENT. On 24 May 1944 the people of Iceland decided in a referendum to sever all ties with the Danish Crown. The voters were asked whether they were in favour of the abrogation of the Union Act, and whether they approved of the bill for a republican constitution: 70,725 voters were for severance of all political ties with Denmark and only 370 against it; 69,048 were in favour of the republican constitution, 1,042 against it and 2,505 votes were invalid. On 17 June 1944 the republic was formally proclaimed, and as the republic's first president the Alþingi elected Sveinn Björnsson for a 1-year term (re-elected 1945 and 1949; died 25 Jan. 1952). The President is now elected by direct, popular vote for a period of 4 years.

President of the Republic of Iceland: Vigdís Finnbogadóttir (elected 29 June 1980, with 43,611 out of 129,049 valid votes, inaugurated 1 Aug. 1980); re-elected unopposed in 1984; re-elected in 1988 with 94% of the valid votes.

National flag: Blue with a red white-bordered Scandinavian cross.

National anthem: Ó Guð vors lands (words by M. Jochumsson, 1874; tune by S. Sveinbjörnsson).

The *Alþingi* (Parliament) is divided into two Houses, the Upper House and the Lower House. The former is composed of one-third of the members elected by the whole Alþingi in common sitting. The remaining two-thirds of the members form the Lower House. The members of the Alþingi receive payment for their services.

The budget bills must be laid before the two Houses in joint session, but all other bills can be introduced in either of the Houses. If the Houses do not agree, they assemble in a common sitting and the final decision is given by a majority of two-thirds of the voters, with the exception of budget bills, where a simple majority is sufficient. The ministers have free access to both Houses, but can vote only in the House of which they are members.

The electoral law enacted in 1984 provides for an Alþingi of 63 members. Of these, 54 seats are distributed among the 8 constituencies as follows: 14 seats are allotted to Reykjavík, 8 to Reykjanes (i.e. the South-west excluding Reykjavík) and 5 or 6 to each of the remaining 6. From the 9 seats then left, 8 are divided beforehand among the constituencies according to the number of registered voters in the preceding elections. Finally, one seat is given to a constituency after the elections, to compensate the party with the fewest seats as compared to its number of votes.

At the elections held on 25 April 1987 the following parties were returned: Independence Party, 18; Progressives, 13; Social Democrats, 10; People's Alliance, 8; Citizen's Party, 7; Women's Alliance, 6; Association for Equality and Social Justice, 1.

The executive power is exercised under the President by the Cabinet. The coalition Cabinet, as constituted in Sept. 1989, was as follows:

Prime Minister: Steingrímur Hermannsson (Progress).

Foreign Affairs: Jón Baldvin Hannibalsson (Soc. Dem.). *Finance:* Ólafur Ragnar Grímsson (People's Alliance). *Social Affairs:* Jóhanna Sigurðardóttir (Soc. Dem.). *Fisheries:* Halldór Ásgrímsson (Progress). *Justice and Church:* Óli P. Guðbjartsson (Citizens' Party). *Agriculture and Communications:* Steingrímur J. Sigfússon (People's Alliance). *Health and Social Security:* Guðmundur Bjarnason (Progress). *Commerce, Energy and Industry:* Jón Sigurðsson (Soc. Dem.). *Education:* Svavar Gestsson (People's Alliance). *Statistical Bureau:* Júlíus Sólnes.

Local Administration. Iceland was on 1 Dec. 1988 divided into 217 communes, of which 29 had the status of a town. The commune councils are elected by universal suffrage (men and women 18 years of age and over), in towns and other urban communes by proportional representation, in rural communes by simple majority. For general co-operation the communes are free to form district councils. All the communes except 10 towns are members in 20 district councils. The communes appoint one or more representatives to the district councils according to their population size. The commune councils are supervised by the Ministry of Social Affairs. For national government there are 27 divisions (*lögsagnarumdæmi*), consisting of towns and counties, single or combined, with the exception of Keflavík Airport (also a

NATO base), which is a separate national government division consisting of parts of 5 communes. In the capital the different branches of national government are independent (jurisdictional power and executive power, i.e. courts, police, customs etc.), while in other national government divisions they are the charge of the sheriffs, also residing as the local magistrates.

DEFENCE. Iceland possesses neither an army nor a navy. Under the North Atlantic Treaty, US forces are stationed in Iceland as the Iceland Defence Force. Three armed fishery protection vessels are maintained by the Icelandic National Coastguard, with 1 patrol aircraft and 2 helicopters. Coastguard Service personnel in 1990 totalled about 150 officers and men.

INTERNATIONAL RELATIONS

Membership. Iceland is a member of UN, EFTA, OECD, the Council of Europe, NATO and the Nordic Council.

ECONOMY

Budget. Total revenue and expenditure for calendar years (in 1m. kr.):

	1983	*1984*	*1985*	*1986*	*1987*	*1988*
Revenue	16,282	22,088	28,746	40,176	52,324	71,287
Expenditure	17,717	20,474	30,617	46,374	53,582	73,415

Main items of the Treasury accounts for 1988 (in 1m. kr.):

Revenue		*Expenditure*	
Direct taxes	13,342	Administration, justice and police	6,606
Indirect taxes	53,272	Foreign service	573
Other	4,673	Education, culture and State Church	12,047
		Health and social security	30,791
		Subsidies	3,924
		Agriculture	2,990
		Fisheries	1,650
		Manufacturing and energy	1,338
		Communications	4,727
		Other	8,769

Central government debt was on 31 Dec. 1988, 68,273m. kr, of which the foreign debt amounted to 40,205m. kr.

Currency. The Icelandic monetary units are the *króna*, pl. *krónur* and the *eyrir*, pl. *aurar*. There are 100 *aurar* to the *króna*. In March 1990, US$1 = kr. 61·29; £1 = kr. 100·45. Note and coin circulation, 31 Dec. 1988, was 2,557m. kr.

Banking. The *Seðlabanki Íslands* (The Central Bank of Iceland), established in 1961, is responsible for note issue and carries out the central banking functions which before 1961 were carried out by the *Landsbanki Íslands* (The National Bank of Iceland, owned entirely by the State), currently (1990) the largest commercial bank. Between 1971 and 1989, 7 commercial banks (3 state-owned) operated in Iceland. In June 1989 the State agreed to sell its majority share in the *Útvegsbanki Íslands* (the Fisheries Bank of Iceland Ltd) to 3 private banks: *Iðnaðarbanki* (Industrial Bank of Iceland Ltd), *Verslunarbanki Íslands* (Iceland Bank of Commerce Ltd) and *Alþýðubanki* (The Union Bank Ltd). According to the argeement the 4 banks are to merge in 1990 to constitute the second largest commercial bank, *Íslandsbanki* (The Iceland Bank Ltd). Other banks operating are *Búnaðarbanki Íslands* (The Agricultural Bank of Iceland), a state bank founded in 1930, and *Samvinnubanki Íslands* (The Icelandic Co-operative Bank), established in 1963.

On 31 Dec. 1988 the accounts of the Central Bank balanced at 34,484m. kr.

At the end of 1988 there were 34 savings banks with deposits amounting to 13,261m. kr. and total deposits of the commercial banks amounted to 71,513m. kr.

Weights and Measures. The metric system of weights and measures is obligatory.

ENERGY AND NATURAL RESOURCES

Electricity. The installed capacity of public electrical power plants at the end of 1988 totalled 922,985 kw., of which 752,000 kw. comprised hydro-electric plants. Total electricity production in public-owned plants in 1988 amounted to 4,416m. kwh.; in privately-owned plants, 5m. kwh. Supply 220 volts; 50 Hz.

Agriculture. Of the total area of Iceland, about six-sevenths is unproductive, but only about 1·3% is under cultivation, which is largely confined to hay, potatoes and turnips. In 1988 the total hay crop was 3,279,531 cu. metres; the crop of potatoes, 10,288 tonnes, and of turnips (1987) 1,100 tonnes. At the end of 1988 the livestock was as follows: Horses, 63,531; cattle, 70,824 (including 32,005 milch cows); sheep, 586,887; pigs, 3,351; poultry, 229,733.

Fisheries. Fishing vessels at the end of 1988 numbered 956 with a gross tonnage of 119,690. Total catch in 1987, 1,632,000 tonnes; 1988, 1,758,000 tonnes.

The Icelandic Government announced that the fishery limits off Iceland were extended from 12 to 50 nautical miles from Sept. 1972. An interim agreement for 2 years signed by the UK and Iceland in Nov. 1973 expired in Nov. 1975.

On 15 July 1975 the Icelandic Government issued a decree that from 15 Oct. 1975 the fishery limits of Iceland were extended from 50 to 200 nautical miles. The Icelandic Government maintain that this extension is necessary to protect the fish stocks in Icelandic waters because the fishing industry is of vital importance to the national economy.

INDUSTRY AND TRADE

Industry. Production, 1988, in 1,000 tonnes: Aluminium, 82; diatomite, 25·1; fertilizer, 52·7; ferro-silcon, 65·4. Sales of cement, 1988, 100,200 tonnes.

Labour. In Aug. 1989, 1·3% of the total labour force was registered as unemployed.

Commerce. Total value of imports (c.i.f.) and exports (f.o.b.) in 1,000 kr.:

	1984	*1985*	*1986*	*1987*	*1988*
Imports	26,780,309	37,600,289	45,905,230	61,231,629	68,723,300
Exports	23,556,960	33,749,626	44,967,770	53,053,078	61,666,700

Leading exports (in 1,000 kg and 1,000 kr.):

	1987		*1988*	
	Quantity	*Value*	*Quantity*	*Value*
Marine products	638,277	40,322,027	689,735	43,826,200
Aluminium	89,081	5,080,422	81,071	6,626,400
Ferro-silicon	71,656	1,472,594	73,236	2,418,100

Leading imports (in 1,000 tonnes and 1,000 kr.):

	1987		*1988*	
	Quantity	*Value*	*Quantity*	*Value*
Ships (number)	20	3,279,600	34	5,427,600
Fuel oil	79,326	367,600	90,221	351,900
Gas oils	285,975	1,812,900	270,739	1,741,500
Jet fuel	98,228	703,500	69,085	469,100
Cereals	15,602	239,500	13,120	223,300
Animal feed	53,178	475,000	51,443	523,900
Gasoline	118,511	828,800	122,850	909,200
Motor vehicles (number)	24,681	6,385,200	14,702	5,115,700
Fishing nets and other gear	1,032	410,100	828	379,700

Value of trade with principal countries for 3 years (in 1,000 kr.):

	1986		*1987*		*1988*	
	Imports (c.i.f.)	*Exports (f.o.b.)*	*Imports (c.i.f.)*	*Exports (f.o.b.)*	*Imports (c.i.f.)*	*Exports (f.o.b.)*
Austria	322,485	38,691	460,175	43,839	474,100	63,500
Belgium	1,058,839	430,997	1,600,741	632,743	1,326,900	480,100
Brazil	296,787	43,897	303,435	57,002	250,500	70,900
Canada	183,245	135,477	253,273	155,191	290,900	174,000
Czechoslovakia	153,404	57,619	222,441	52,707	268,300	85,700

	1986 Imports (c.i.f.)	1986 Exports (f.o.b.)	1987 Imports (c.i.f.)	1987 Exports (f.o.b.)	1988 Imports (c.i.f.)	1988 Exports (f.o.b.)
Denmark	4,745,348	1,713,553	5,623,103	2,049,506	6,357,700	2,032,600
Faroe Islands	34,673	248,476	51,019	332,770	9,500	544,500
Finland	1,212,184	834,180	1,437,854	901,293	1,693,300	763,700
France	1,374,778	2,152,271	2,067,547	2,853,565	2,150,100	2,978,700
German Dem. Rep.	114,871	37,354	180,419	29,249	117,500	81,200
Germany, Fed. Rep. of	6,964,772	4,079,811	9,309,949	5,301,154	9,783,700	6,367,000
Greece	25,188	391,881	47,455	544,769	58,500	483,800
Hungary	15,007	9,008	17,822	13,875	23,100	118,100
India	30,845	—	33,958	—	56,900	—
Ireland	124,155	55,962	182,098	96,422	233,300	29,100
Israel	23,963	15,206	29,488	4,277	31,900	1,200
Italy	1,334,697	1,329,494	1,922,360	1,612,898	3,010,200	1,560,300
Japan	2,993,567	2,147,361	5,012,566	4,139,386	4,756,500	4,706,500
Netherlands	3,923,719	508,010	4,956,247	493,084	5,607,300	704,300
Nigeria	269	774,918	416	796,702	400	241,800
Norway	3,322,749	1,153,656	5,052,542	957,056	6,166,200	1,489,400
Poland	82,972	446,297	532,591	483,555	979,900	851,700
Portugal	439,552	2,915,100	485,120	4,967,089	611,200	5,240,100
Spain	532,291	1,592,764	643,754	1,575,506	651,100	2,113,000
Sweden	4,099,720	1,097,525	5,032,051	1,014,228	6,025,000	1,094,200
Switzerland	503,762	1,425,111	659,240	1,429,739	785,900	2,783,600
USSR	2,607,005	1,924,609	2,573,564	1,932,899	2,396,400	2,194,100
UK	3,754,209	9,177,626	5,032,757	10,321,470	5,608,000	14,340,900
USA	3,208,469	9,770,811	4,367,065	9,677,945	5,185,800	8,372,600

Total trade between Iceland and UK (British Department of Trade returns, in £1,000 sterling):

	1985	1986	1987	1988	1989
Imports to UK	128,281	173,140	178,314	198,365	196,678
Exports and re-exports from UK	76,194	73,640	84,866	87,100	69,497

TOURISM. There were 128,883 visitors to Iceland in 1988.

COMMUNICATIONS

Roads. On 31 Dec. 1988 the length of the public roads (including roads in towns) was 12,484 km. Of these 8,272 km were national main roads and 3,122 km were provincial roads. Total length of surfaced roads was 2,900 km. Motor vehicles registered at the end of 1988 numbered 139,395, of which 126,524 were passenger cars and 11,898 trucks; there were also 973 motor cycles.

Aviation. One large and some small companies maintain regular services between Reykjavík and various places in Iceland (the large one 1988: 257,939 passengers). The large company maintains regular services between Iceland and the UK, the Scandinavian countries, some other European countries and USA. In 1988 the company carried in scheduled foreign flights 534,887 passengers.

Shipping. Total registered vessels, 1,103 (205,000 GRT) on 31 Dec. 1988, of these 956 were sea-going fishing vessels.

Post and Broadcasting. At the end of 1988 the number of post offices was 129 and telephone and telegraph offices 83; number of telephone subscribers, 122,000. The State Broadcasting Service, *Rikisútvarpid*, broadcasts 2 radio channels and 1 TV channel. On 1 Jan. 1986 the state monopoly on broadcasting was abolished by law and the field opened to others, if they fulfilled certain conditions. Besides *Rikisútvarpid* 3 privately owned radio stations and 1 TV station were in operation in 1989. Number of licensed receivers (1989): Radio, about 85,000; television, about 78,000.

Cinemas (1988). In the capital area there were 6 cinemas (19 cinema halls) with a seating capacity of about 5,000.

Newspapers (1988). There are 6 daily newspapers, 5 in Reykjavík and one in Akureyri, with a combined circulation of about 100,000.

JUSTICE, RELIGION, EDUCATION AND WELFARE

Justice. The lower courts of justice are those of the provincial magistrates (*sýslumenn*) and town judges (*bæjarfógetar*). From these there is an appeal to the Supreme Court (*hæstiréttur*) in Reykjavík, which has 8 judges.

Religion. The national church, and the only one endowed by the State, is Evangelical Lutheran. But there is complete religious liberty, and no civil disabilities are attached to those not of the national religion. The affairs of the national church are under the superintendence of a bishop. In 1988, 5,832 persons (2·3%) were Dissenters and 3,335 persons (1·3%) did not belong to any religious community.

Education. Compulsory education for children began in 1907, and a university was founded in Reykjavík in 1911. There is in Reykjavík a teachers' training college and a technical high school; various specialized institutions of learning and a number of second-level schools are scattered throughout the country. There are many part-time schools of cultural activities, including music.

Compulsory education comprises 9 classes, 7-15 years of age. After completion of a facultative 9th class, attended by 93%-95% of the relevant age group, there is access to further schooling free of charge. Some 53%-74% of the age groups 16-19 years old attend schools. Around 15%-20% of each age group go into handicraft apprenticeship. About 30% pass matriculation examination, generally at the age of 20. Approximately one third-level student out of every four goes abroad for studies, two-thirds of them to Scandinavia, the rest mainly to English- and German-speaking countries.

Immatriculation in Iceland in autumn 1988: Preceding the first level, 4,500. First-level (1st-6th class) 25,400. Second-level first stage (7th-9th class) 12,700. Second-level second stage (4-year courses) 15,900. Third-level studies, 5,000.

Social Welfare. The main body of the Icelandic social welfare legislation is consolidated in six main acts:

(i) The social security legislation (a) health insurance, including sickness benefits; *(b)* social security pensions, mainly consisting of old age pension, disablement pension and widows' pension, and also children's pension; *(c)* employment injuries insurance.

(ii) The unemployment insurance legislation, where daily allowances are paid to those who have met certain conditions.

(iii) The subsistence legislation. This is controlled by municipal government, and social assistance is granted under special circumstances, when payments from other sources are not sufficient.

(iv) The tax legislation. Prior to 1988 children's support was included in the tax legislation, according to which a certain amount for each child in a family was subtracted from income taxes or paid out to the family. Since 1988 family allowances are paid directly to all children age 0-15 years. The amount is increased with the second child in the family, and children under the age of 7 get additional benefits. Single parents receive additional allowances.

(v) The rehabilitation legislation.

(vi) Child and juvenile guidance.

Health insurance covers the entire population. Citizenship is not demanded and there is no waiting period. Most hospitals are both municipally and state run, a few solely state run and all offer free medical help. Medical treatment out of hospitals is partly paid by the patient, the same applies to medicines, except medicines of life-long necessary use, which are paid in full by the health insurance. Dental care is free for the age groups 6-15, but is paid 75% for those five years or younger and the age group 16 but 50% for old age and disabled pensioners. Sickness benefits are paid to those who lose income because of periodical illness. The daily amount is fixed and paid from the 11th day of illness.

The pension system is composed of the public social security system and some 90 private pension funds. The social security system pays basic old age and disablement pensions of a fixed amount regardless of past or present income, as well as supplementary pensions to individuals with low present income. The pensions are index-linked, i.e. are changed in line with changes in wage and salary rates in the labour market. The private pension funds pay pensions that depend on past payments of premiums that are a fixed proportion of earnings. The payment of pension fund premiums is compulsory for all wage and salary earners. The pensions paid by the funds differ considerably between the individual funds, but are generally index-linked. In the public social security system, entitlement to old age and disablement pensions at the full rates is subject to the condition that the beneficiary has been resident in Iceland for 40 years at the age period of 16–67. For shorter period of residence, the benefits are reduced proportionally. Entitled to old age pension are all those who are 67 years old, and have been residents in Iceland for 3 years of the age period of 16–67. Entitled to disablement pension are those who have lost 75% of their working capacity and have been residents in Iceland for 3 years before application or have had full working capacity at the time when they became residents. Old age and disablement pension are of equally high amount, in the year 1986 the total sum was 74,028 kr. for an individual. Married pensioners are paid 90% of two individuals' pensions. In addition to the basic amount, supplementary allowances are paid according to social circumstances and income possibilities. Widows' pensions are the same amount as old age and disablement pension, provided the applicant is over 60 when she becomes widowed. Women at the age 50–60 get reduced pension. Women under 50 are not entitled to widows' pensions.

The employment injuries insurance covers medical care, daily allowances, disablement pension and survivors' pension and is applicable to practically all employees.

Social assistance is primarily municipal and granted in cases outside the social security legislation. Domestic assistance to old people and disabled is granted within this legislation, besides other services.

Child and juvenile guidance is performed by chosen committees according to special laws, such as home guidance and family assistance. In cases of parents' disablement the committees take over the guidance of the children involved.

DIPLOMATIC REPRESENTATIVES

Of Iceland in Great Britain (1 Eaton Terrace, London, SW1W 8EY)
Ambassador: Helgi Ágústsson (accredited 13 Dec. 1989).

Of Great Britain in Iceland (Laufásvegur 49, 101 Reykjavík)
Ambassador and Consul-General: Richard Best, CBE.

Of Iceland in the USA (2022 Connecticut Ave., NW, Washington, D.C., 20008)
Ambassador: Ingvi S. Ingvarsson.

Of the USA in Iceland (Laufásvegur 21, 101 Reykjavík)
Ambassador: Charles E. Cobb Jr.

Of Iceland to the United Nations
Ambassador: Hans G. Andersen.

Further Reading

Statistical Information: The Statistical Bureau of Iceland, Hagstofa Íslands (Reykjavík) was founded in 1914. *Director:* Hallgrímur Snorrason. Its main publications are:

Tölfræðihandbók. Statistical Abstract of Iceland (latest issue 1984)
Hagskýrslur Íslands. Statistics of Iceland (from 1912)
Hagtíðindi (Statistical Bulletin) (from 1916)
Hagtólur mánaðarins. Monthly Bulletin (from 1973). Central Bank of Iceland
Economic Statistics Quarterly. Central Bank of Iceland (quarterly from 1980)
Heilbrigðisskýrslur. Public Health in Iceland (latest issue for 1984-85; published 1989)
Yearbook of Nordic Statistics. Nordic Council of Ministers and the Nordic Statistical Secretariat, Copenhagen.
Cleasby, R., *An Icelandic-English Dictionary.* 2nd ed. Oxford, 1957
Einarsson, P. and Lacy, T. G., *Ensk-íslensk viðskiptaorðabók.* English-Icelandic Dictionary of Business Terms. Reykjavík, 1989
Foss, H. (ed.) *Directory of Iceland.* Annual. Reykjavík, 1907–40, 1948 ff.

Hermannsson, Halldór, *Islandica.* An annual relating to Iceland and the Fiske Icelandic Collection in Cornell University Library. Ithaca (from 1908)

Horton, J. J., *Iceland.* [Bibliography] Oxford and Santa Barbara, 1983

Magnússon, S. A., *Northern Sphinx: Iceland and the Icelanders from the Settlement to the Present.* London, 1977

Nordal, J. and Kristinsson, V. (eds) *Iceland 1986.* Central Bank of Iceland, Reykjavík, 1987

Þórðarson, Matthias, *The Althing, Iceland's Thousand-Year-Old Parliament, 930–1930.* Reykjavík, 1930

Zoëga, G. T., *Íslensk-ensk (and Ensk-íslensk) orðabók.* 3rd ed. 2 vols. Reykjavík, 1932–51

National Library: Landsbókasafnið, Reykjavík, *Librarian:* Dr Finnbogi Guðmundsson.

INDIA

Bharat

Capital: New Delhi
Population: 748m. (1984)
GDP per capita: US$330 (1988)

HISTORY. The Indus civilization was fully developed by *c.* 2500 B.C., and collapsed *c.* 1750 B.C. An Aryan civilization spread from the west as far as the Ganges valley by 500 B.C.; separate kingdoms were established and many of these were united under the Mauryan dynasty established by Chandragupta in *c.* 320 B.C. The Mauryan Empire was succeeded by numerous small kingdoms. The Gupta dynasty (A.D. 320–600) was followed by the first Arabic invasions of the north-west. Moslem, Hindu and Buddhist states developed together with frequent conflict until the establishment of the Mogul dynasty in 1526. The first settlements by the East India Company were made after 1600 and the company established a formal system of government for Bengal in 1700. During the decline of the Moguls frequent wars between the Company, the French and the native princes led to the Company's being brought under British Government control in 1784; the first Governor-General of India was appointed in 1786. The powers of the Company were abolished by the India Act, 1858, and its functions and forces transferred to the British Crown. Representative government was introduced in 1909, and the first parliament in 1919. The separate dominions of India and Pakistan became independent within the Commonwealth in 1947 and India became a republic in 1950.

AREA AND POPULATION. India is bounded north-west by Pakistan, north by China, Tibet, Nepál and Bhután, east by Burma, south-east, south and south west by the Indian ocean. The far eastern states and territories are almost separated from the rest by Bangladesh as it extends northwards from the Bay of Bengal. The area of the Indian Union (excluding the Pakistan and China-occupied parts of Jammu and Kashmir) is 3,166,829 sq. km. Its population according to the 1981 census was 685,184,692 (excluding the occupied area of Jammu and Kashmir); this represents an increase of 25% since 1971. Sex ratio was 933 females per 1,000 males (929 in 1971); density of population, 216 per sq. km. About 23·3% of the population was urban in 1981 (in Maharashtra, 35%; in Himachal Pradesh, 7·6%).

Many births and deaths go unregistered. Data from certain areas of better registration and field studies suggest that the birth rate for 1987 was about 32 per 1,000 population, the death rate 10.8 per 1,000. In 1981 (census) the age-group 0–14 years represented 39·5% of the population and only 6·5% were over 60. In 1981 expectation of life 54·4 years.

Marriages and divorces are not registered. The minimum age for a civil marriage is 18 for women and 21 for men; for a sacramental marriage, 14 for girls and 18 for youths.

The main details of the census of 1 March 1971 and of 1 March 1981 are:

Name of State	*Land area in sq. km (1981)*	*Population 1971*	*Population 1981*
States			
Andhra Pradesh	275,608	43,502,708	53,549,673
Assam	78,438	14,625,152	19,896,843
Bihar	173,877	56,353,369	69,914,734
Gujarat	195,024	26,697,475	34,085,799
Haryana	44,212	10,036,808	12,922,618
Himachal Pradesh	55,673	3,460,434	4,280,818
Jammu and Kashmir[1]	101,387	4,616,632	5,987,389
Karnataka	191,791	29,299,014	37,135,714
Kerala	38,863	21,347,375	25,453,680
Madhya Pradesh	443,446	41,654,119	52,178,844
Maharashtra	307,690	50,412,235	62,684,171
Manipur	22,429	1,072,753	1,420,953

[1] Excludes the Pakistan-occupied area.

Name of State	Land area in sq. km (1981)	Population 1971	Population 1981
Meghalaya	22,429	1,011,699	1,325,819
Nagaland	16,579	516,449	774,930
Orissa	155,707	21,944,615	26,370,271
Punjab	50,362	13,551,060	16,788,915
Rajasthan	342,239	25,765,806	34,261,862
Sikkim	7,096	209.845	316,385
Tamil Nadu	130,058	41,199,168	48,408,077
Tripura	10,486	1,556,342	2,053,058
Uttar Pradesh	294,411	88,341,144	110,862,013
West Bengal	87,852	44,312,011	54,580,647
Union Territories			
Andaman and Nicobar Islands	8,249	115,133	188,741
Arunachal Pradesh [1]	83,743	467,511	631,839
Chandigarh	114	257,251	450,610
Dadra and Nagar Haveli	491	74,170	103,676
Daman and Diu	112	62,648	78,981
Delhi	1,483	4,065,698	6,220,406
Goa [2]	3,702	795,123	1,007,749
Lakshadweep	32	31,810	40,249
Mizoram [1]	21,081	332,390	493,797
Pondicherry	492	471,707	604,471
Grand total	3,166,829	548,159,052	685,184,692

[1] Achieved statehood 1986. [2] Achieved statehood 1987.

Greatest density occurs in Delhi (4,194 per sq. km), Chandigarh (3,961), Lakshadweep (1,258) and Pondicherry (1,229). The lowest occurs in Arunachal Pradesh (8).

There were (1981) 343,930,423 males and 321,357,426 females.

In 1981, 525m. were rural (76·7%) and 160m. were urban.

Cities and Urban Agglomerations (with states in brackets) having more than 250,000 population at the 1981 census were (1,000):

City	Pop.	City	Pop.	City	Pop.
Agra (U.P.)	690	Erode (T.N.)	275	Nagpur (Mah.)	1,219
Ahmedabad (Guj.)	2,159	Faridabad agglomeration	331	Nasik (Mah.)	252
Ajmer (Raj.)	376	Ghaziabad (U.P)	276	New Delhi	273
Aligarh (U.P.)	321	Gorakhpur (U.P.)	308	Patna (Bih.)	814
Allahabad (U.P.)	620	Guntur (A.P.)	368	Pune (Mah.)	1,203
Amravati (Mah.)	261	Gwalior (M.P.)	539	Raipur (M.P.)	338
Amritsar (Pun.)	595	Hadra (W.B)	744	Rajahmundry (A.P.)	268
Aurangabad (Mah.)	299	Hubli-Dharwar (Kar.)	527	Rajkot (Guj.)	445
Bangalore (Kar.)	2,629	Hyderabad (A.P.)	2,157	Ranchi (Bih.)	490
Bareilly (U.P.)	395	Indore (M.P.)	829	Saharanpur (U.P.)	295
Bhatpara (W.B.)	265	Jabalpur (M.P.)	649	Salem (T.N.)	361
Belgaum (Kar.)	274	Jadavpur (W.B)	252	Sholapur (Mah.)	515
Bhavnagar (Guj.)	309	Jaipur (Raj.)	977	South Suburban (W.B)	395
Bhilainagar (M.P)	319	Jalandhar (Pun.)	408	Srinagar (J. & K.)	595[1]
Bhopal (M.P.)	671	Jamnagar (Guj.)	294	Surat (Guj.)	777
Bikaner (Raj.)	256	Jamshedpur (Bih.)	457	Thana (Mah.)	310
Bombay (Mah.)[2]	8,243	Jodhpur (Raj.)	506	Tiruchirapalli (T.N.)	362
Calcutta (W.B.)[3]	9,166	Kanpur (U.P.)	1,486	Tirunelveli (T.N.)	324
Calicut (Ker.)	394	Kolhapur (Mah.)	341	Trivandrum (Ker.)	500
Chandigarh (Ch.)	421	Kotah (Raj.)	358	Ujjain (M.P.)	282
Cochin (Ker.)	556	Lucknow (U.P.)	917	Ulhasnagar (Mah.)	274
Coimbatore (T.N.)	705	Ludhiana (Pun.)	607	Vadodara (Guj.)	734
Cuttack (Ori.)	295	Madras (T.N.)	3,277	Varanasi (U.P.)	721
Dehra Dun (U.P.)	221	Madurai (T.N.)	821	Vijayawada (A.P.)	462
Delhi	4,884	Meerut (U.P.)	417	Visakhapatnam (A.P.)	584
Dhanbad (Bih.)	677	Moradabad (U.P.)	330	Warangal (A.P.)	335
Durgapur (W.B.)	312	Mysore (Kar.)	479		
Durg-Bhilainagar (M.P.)	490				

[1] Estimate. [2] Greater Bombay. [3] Urban agglomeration.

Report of the Officials of the Government of India and the People's Republic of China on the Boundary Question. New Delhi, Ministry of External Affairs, 1961
Census of India: Reports and Papers, Decennial Series. (Government of India.)
Annual Report on the Working of Indian Migration. Government of India, from 1956
Report of the Commissioner for Scheduled Castes and Scheduled Tribes. Government of India. Annual
Public Health. Report of the Public Health Commission with the Government of India. Annual
Agarwala, S. N., *India's Population Problems.* New York, 1973

CLIMATE. India has a variety of climatic sub-divisions. In general, there are four seasons. The cool one lasts from Dec. to March, the hot season is in April and May, the rainy season is June to Sept., followed by a further dry season till Nov. Rainfall, however, varies considerably, from 4" (100 mm) in the N.W. desert to over 400" (10,000 mm) in parts of Assam.

Range of temperature and rainfall: New Delhi. Jan. 57°F (13·9°C), July 88°F (31·1°C). Annual rainfall 26" (640 mm). Bombay. Jan. 75°F (23·9°C), July 81°F (27·2°C). Annual rainfall 72" (1,809 mm). Calcutta. Jan. 67°F (19·4°C), July 84°F (28·9°C). Annual rainfall 64" (1,600 mm). Cherrapunji. Jan. 53°F (11·7°C), July 68°F (20°C). Annual rainfall 432" (10,798 mm). Cochin. Jan. 80°F (26·7°C), July 79°F (26·1°C). Annual rainfall 117" (2,929 mm). Darjeeling. Jan. 41°F (5°C), July 62°F (16·7°C). Annual rainfall 121" (3,035 mm). Hyderabad. Jan. 72°F (22·2°C), July 80°F (26·7°C). Annual rainfall 30" (752 mm). Madras. Jan. 76°F (24·4°C), July 87°F (30·6°C). Annual rainfall 51" (1,270 mm). Patna. Jan. 63°F (17·2°C), July 90°F (32·2°C). Annual rainfall 46" (1,150 mm).

CONSTITUTION AND GOVERNMENT. On 26 Jan. 1950 India became a sovereign democratic republic. India's relations with the British Commonwealth of Nations were defined at the London conference of Prime Ministers on 27 April 1949.

Unanimous agreement was reached to the effect that the Republic of India remains a full member of the Commonwealth and accepts the Queen as 'the symbol of the free association of its independent member nations and, as such, the head of the Commonwealth'. This agreement was ratified by the Constituent Assembly of India on 17 May 1949.

The constitution was passed by the Constituent Assembly on 26 Nov. 1949 and came into force on 26 Jan. 1950. It has since been amended 62 times.

India is a Union of States and comprises 25 States and 7 Union territories. Each State is administered by a Governor appointed by the President for a term of 5 years while each Union territory is administered by the President through an administrator appointed by him.

The capital is New Delhi.

Presidency. The head of the Union is the President in whom all executive power is vested, to be exercised on the advice of ministers responsible to Parliament. He is elected by an electoral college consisting of all the elected members of Parliament and of the various state legislative assemblies. He holds office for 5 years and is eligible for re-election. He must be an Indian citizen at least 35 years old and eligible for election to the Lower House. He can be removed from office by impeachment for violation of the constitution.

There is also a Vice-President who is *ex-officio* chairman of the Upper House of Parliament.

Central Legislature. The Parliament for the Union consists of the President, the Council of States *(Rajya Sabha)* and the House of the People *(Lok Sabha).* The Council of States, or the Upper House, consists of not more than 250 members; in Oct. 1989 there were 230 elected members and 12 members nominated by the President. The election to this house is indirect; the representatives of each State are elected by the elected members of the Legislative Assembly of that State. The Council of States is a permanent body not liable to dissolution, but one-third of the members retire every second year. The House of the People, or the Lower House, consists of 545 members, 530 directly elected on the basis of adult suffrage from territorial constituencies in the States, and 13 members to represent the Union territories, chosen in such manner as the Parliament may by law provide; in Dec. 1989 there were 525 elected members, 2 members nominated by the President and 2 vacancies. The House of the People unless sooner dissolved continues for a period of 5 years from the date appointed for its first meeting; in emergency, Parliament can extend the term by 1 year.

State Legislatures. For every State there is a legislature which consists of the Governor, and *(a)* 2 Houses, a Legislative Assembly and a Legislative Council, in the States of Bihar, Jammu and Kashmir, Karnataka, Madhya Pradesh (where it is provided for but not in operation), Maharashtra and Uttar Pradesh, and *(b)* 1 House, a Legislative Assembly, in the other States. Every Legislative Assembly, unless sooner dissolved, continues for 5 years from the date appointed for its first meeting. In emergency the term can be extended by 1 year. Every State Legislative Council is a permanent body and is not subject to dissolution, but one-third of the members retire every year. Parliament can, however, abolish an existing Legislative Council or create a new one, if the proposal is supported by a resolution of the Legislative Assembly concerned.

Legislation. The various subjects of legislation are enumerated in three lists in the seventh schedule to the constitution. List I, the Union List, consists of 97 subjects (including defence, foreign affairs, communications, currency and coinage, banking and customs) with respect to which the Union Parliament has exclusive power to make laws. The State legislature has exclusive power to make laws with respect to the 66 subjects in list II, the State List; these include police and public order, agriculture and irrigation, education, public health and local government. The powers to make laws with respect to the 47 subjects (including economic and social planning, legal questions and labour and price control) in list III, the Concurrent List, are held by both Union and State governments, though the former prevails. But Parliament may legislate with respect to any subject in the State List in circumstances when the subject assumes national importance or during emergencies.

Other provisions deal with the administrative relations between the Union and the States, interstate trade and commerce, distribution of revenues between the States and the Union, official language, etc.

Fundamental Rights. Two chapters of the constitution deal with fundamental rights and 'Directive Principles of State Policy'. 'Untouchability' is abolished, and its practice in any form is punishable. The fundamental rights can be enforced through the ordinary courts of law and through the Supreme Court of the Union. The directive principles cannot be enforced through the courts of law; they are nevertheless fundamental in the governance of the country.

Citizenship. Under the Constitution, every person who was on the 26 Jan. 1950, domiciled in India and *(a)* was born in India or *(b)* either of whose parents was born in India or *(c)* who has been ordinarily resident in the territory of India for not less than 5 years immediately preceding that date became a citizen of India. Special provision is made for migrants from Pakistan and for Indians resident abroad. Under the Citizenship Act, 1955, which supplemented the provisions of the Constitution, Indian citizenship is acquired by birth, by descent, by registration and by naturalization. The Act also provides for loss of citizenship by renunciation, termination and deprivation. The right to vote is granted to every person who is a citizen of India and who is not less than 21 years of age on a fixed date and is not otherwise disqualified.

Parliament. Parliament and the state legislatures are organized according to the following schedule (figures show distribution of seats in Dec. 1988):

	Parliament		State Legislatures	
	House of the People (Lok Sabha)	*Council of States (Rajya Sabha)*	*Legislative Assemblies (Vidhan Sabhas)*	*Legislative Councils (Vidhan Parishads)*
States:				
Andhra Pradesh	42	18	294	–
Arunachal Pradesh	2	1	30	–
Assam	14	7	126	–
Bihar	54	22	324	96
Goa	2	–	40	–
Gujarat	26	11	182	–
Haryana	10	5	90	–
Himachal Pradesh	4	3	68	–
Karnataka	28	12	224	75
Kerala	20	9	140	–
Madhya Pradesh	40	16	320	–
Maharashtra	48	19	288	63
Manipur	2	1	60	–
Meghalaya	2	1	60	–
Mizoram	1	1	30	–
Nagaland	1	1	60	–
Orissa	21	10	147	–
Punjab	13	7	117	–
Rajasthan	25	10	200	–
Sikkim	1	1	32	–
Tamil Nadu	39	18	234	–
Tripura	2	1	60	–
Uttar Pradesh	85	34	425	108
West Bengal	42	16	294	–
Jammu and Kashmir	6	4	76[2]	36[4]
Union Territories:				
Andaman and Nicobar Islands	1	–	–	–
Chandigarh	1	–	–	–
Dadra and Nagar Haveli	1	–	–	–
Delhi	7	3	56	–
Daman and Diu	1	–	–	–
Lakshadweep	1	–	–	–
Pondicherry	1	1	30	–
Nominated by the President under Article 80 (1) (a) of the Constitution	–	12	–	–
Total	545[1]	244	4,006	378

[1] Includes 2 nominated members to represent Anglo-Indians.
[2] Excludes 24 seats for Pakistan-occupied areas of the State which are in abeyance.
[3] Nominated by the President.
[4] Excludes seats for the Pakistan-occupied areas.

The number of seats allotted to scheduled castes and scheduled tribes in the House of the People is 79 and 40 respectively. Out of the 3,997 seats allotted to the Legislative Assemblies, 557 are reserved for scheduled castes and 315 for scheduled tribes.

Composition of the House of the People after the election held in Nov. 1989: Congress (I) 193; Janata Dal, 141; Bharatiya Janata Party, 88; CPI (Marxist, 32; CPI, 12; AIADMK (All India Anna DMK), 11; Akali Dal (Mann), 6; Revolutionary Socialist Party, 4; Bahujan Samaj Party, 3; Forward Bloc, 3; Jharkhand Murti Morcha, 3; J. & K. National Conference, 3; Muslim League, 2; Telegu Desam, 2; Independent and others, 22; nominated, 2; vacant, 18.

Composition of the Council of States in Jan. 1990: Congress (I) 136; CPI (Marxist), 17; All-India Anna DMK, 6; Janata Dal, 19; Bharatiya Janta, 4; Janata, 2; Telugu Desam, 14; Asom Gana Parishad, 3; Revolutionary Socialist Party, 2; J. & K. National Conference, 2; Communist Party, 3; Independent and others, 8; nominated, 5; vacant, 17.

National flag: Three horizontal stripes of saffron (orange), white and green, with the wheel of Asoka in the centre in blue.

National anthem: Jana-gana-mana (words by Rabindranath Tagore).

Indian Independence Act, 1947. (Ch. 30.) London, 1947
The Constitution of India (Modified up to 15 April 1967). Delhi, 1967
Appadorai, A., *Indian Political Thinking in the Twentieth Century: From Naoroji to Nehru.* OUP, 1971.—*Documents on Political Thought in Modern India.* OUP, 1974
Austin, G., *The Indian Constitution.* OUP, 1972
Mansergh, N., (ed.) *The Transfer of Power 1942–47.* 5 vols. HMSO, 1970–75
Pylee, M. V., *Constitutional Government in India.* 2nd ed. Bombay, 1965
Rao, K. V., *Parliamentary Democracy of India.* 2nd ed. Calcutta, 1965
Seervali, H. M., *Constitutional Law of India.* Bombay, 1967

Language. The Constitution provides that the official language of the Union shall be Hindi in the Devanagari script. It was originally provided that English should continue to be used for all official purposes until 1965. But the Official Languages Act 1963 provides that, after the expiry of this period of 15 years from the coming into force of the Constitution, English might continue to be used, in addition to Hindi, for all official purposes of the Union for which it was being used immediately before that day, and for the transaction of business in Parliament. According to the Official Languages (Use for official purposes of the Union) Rules 1976, an employee may record in Hindi or in English without being required to furnish a translation thereof in the other language and no employee possessing a working knowledge of Hindi may ask for an English translation of any document in Hindi except in the case of legal or technical documents.

The 56th amendment to the Constitution (26 Nov. 1987) authorised the preparation of a Constitution text in Hindi.

The following 15 languages are included in the Eighth Schedule to the Constitution: Assamese, Bengali, Gujarati, Hindi, Kannada, Kashmiri, Malayalam, Marathi, Oriya, Punjabi, Sanskrit, Sindhi, Tamil, Telugu, Urdu.

There are numerous mother tongues grouped under each language. Hindi, Bengali, Telugu, Tamil and Marathi languages (including mother tongues grouped under each) are spoken by 264·2m., 51·5m., 54·2m., 44·7m. and 49·6m. of the population respectively.

Ferozsons English–Urdu, Urdu–English Dictionary. 2 vols. 4th ed. Lahore, 1961
Fallon, S. W., *A New English–Hindustani Dictionary.* Lahore, 1941
Grierson, Sir G. A., *Linguistic Survey of India.* 11 vols. (in 19 parts). Delhi, 1903-28
Mitra, S. C., *Student's Bengali–English Dictionary.* 2nd ed. Calcutta, 1923
Scholberg, H. C., *Concise Grammar of the Hindi Language.* 3rd ed. London, 1955
University of Madras, *Tamil Lexicon.* 7 vols. Madras, 1924-39
Vyas, V. G. and Patel, S. G., *Standard English–Gujarati Dictionary.* 2 vols. Bombay, 1923

Government. *President of the Republic:* R. Venkataraman (sworn in 25 July 1987). Vice-President: Shankar Dayal Sharma (elected 4 Sept. 1987).

There is a Council of Ministers to aid and advise the President of the Republic in the exercise of his functions; this comprises Ministers who are members of the Cabinet and Ministers of State who are not. A Minister who for any period of 6 consecutive months is not a member of either House of Parliament ceases to be a Minister at the expiration of that period. The Prime Minister is appointed by the President; other Ministers are appointed by the President on the Prime Minister's advice.

The salary of each Minister is Rs 27,000 per annum, and that of each Deputy Minister is Rs 21,000 per annum. Each Minister is entitled to the free use of a furnished residence and a chauffeur-driven car throughout his term of office. A Cabinet Minister has a sumptuary allowance of Rs 1,000 per month, Ministers of State, Rs 500 and Deputy Ministers, Rs 300. At the administrative head of each Ministry is a Secretary of the Government.

The Cabinet was composed as follows in Jan. 1990:

Prime Minister: Vishwanath Pratap Singh.

Portfolios held by the Prime Minister assisted by Ministers of State:

Defence, Science and Technology, Atomic Energy, Personnel, Space, Environment and Forests.

Deputy Prime Minister and Agriculture: Devi Lal.
Industry: Ajit Singh.
Finance: Madhu Dandavate.
External Affairs: I. K. Gujral.
Commerce and Tourism: Arun Nehru.
Urban Development: Murasoli Maran.
Parliamentary Affairs, Information and Broadcasting: P. Upendra.
Steel and Mines, Law and Justice: Dinesh Goswami.
Home: Mufti Mohammad Sayeed.
Energy, Civil Aviation: Arif Mohammad Khan.
Surface Transport, Communications: K. P. Unnikrishnan.
Health, Family Welfare: Nilmani Routray.
Labour and Welfare: Ram Vilas Paswan.
Petroleum and Chemicals: M. S. Gurupadaswamy.
Food and Civil Supplies: Nathu Ram Mirdha.
Railways: George Fernandes.
Textiles, Food Processing Industries: Sharad Yadav.

There were also 3 Ministers of State.

Local Government. There were in 1981, 42 municipal corporations, 2,165 municipalities, 420 notified area committees and 59 cantonment boards (all figures exclude Assam). The municipal bodies have the care of the roads, water supply, drainage, sanitation, medical relief, vaccination and education. Their main sources of revenue are taxes on the annual rental value of land and buildings, octroi and terminal, vehicle and other taxes. The municipal councils enact their own bye-laws and frame their budgets, which in the case of municipal bodies other than corporations generally require the sanction of the State government. All municipal councils are elected on the principle of adult franchise.

For rural areas there is a 3-tier system of *panchayati raj* at village, block and district level, although the 3-tier structure may undergo some changes in State legislation to suit local conditions. All *panchayati raj* bodies are organically linked, and representation is given to special interests. Elected directly by and from among villagers, the *panchayats* are responsible for agricultural production, rural industries, medical relief, maternity and child welfare, common grazing grounds, village roads, tanks and wells, and maintenance of sanitation. In some places they also look after primary education, maintenance of village records and collection of land revenue. They have their own powers of taxation. There are some judicial *panchayats* or village courts.

Panchayati raj now cover all the States with the exception of Mizoram, Nagaland and Meghalaya, although Nagaland has area, range and tribal councils. They exist in all the Union Territories except Lakshadweep.

The powers and responsibilities of *panchayati raj* institutions are derived from State Legislatures, and from the executive orders of State governments.

NAGARLOK (Municipal Affairs Quarterly). Quarterly. Institute of Public Administration. Delhi
Proceedings of the 13th Meeting of the Central Council of Local Self Government. Delhi, 1970
Report of the Committee on Budgetary Reforms in Municipal Administration. Delhi, 1974
State Machinery for Municipal Supervision. Institute of Public Administration. Delhi, 1970
Statistical Abstract of India. Annual. Delhi.

DEFENCE. The Supreme Command of the Armed Forces vests in the President of the Indian Republic. Policy is decided at different levels by a number of committees, including the Political Affairs Committee presided over by the Prime Minister and the Defence Minister's Committee. Administrative and operational control rests in the respective Service Headquarters, under the control of the Ministry of Defence.

The Ministry of Defence is the central agency for formulating defence policy and for co-ordinating the work of the three services. Among the organizations directly administered by the Ministry are the Research and Development Organization, the Production Organization, the National Defence College, the National Cadet Corps and the Directorate-General of Armed Forces Medical Services.

The Research and Development Organization (headed by the Scientific Adviser to the Minister) has under it about 30 research establishments. The Production Organization controls 8 public-sector undertakings and 28 ordnance and 2 departmental factories.

The National Defence College, New Delhi, was established in 1960 on the pattern of the Imperial Defence College (UK): the 1-year course is for officers of the rank of brigadier or equivalent and for senior civil servants. The Defence Services Staff College, Wellington, trains officers of the three Services for higher command for staff appointments. There is an Armed Forces Medical College at Pune.

The National Defence Academy, Khadakvasla, gives a 3-year basic training course to officer cadets of the three Services prior to advanced training at the respective Service establishments.

Army. The Army Headquarters functioning directly under the Chief of the Army Staff is divided into the following main branches: General Staff Branch; Adjutant General's Branch; Quartermaster-General's Branch; Master-General of Ordnance Branch; Engineer-in-Chief's Branch; Military Secretary's Branch.

The Army is organized into 5 commands each divided into areas, which in turn are subdivided into sub-areas. Recruitment of permanent commissioned officers is through the Indian Military Academy, Dehra Dun. It conducts courses for ex-National Defence Academy, National Cadet Corps and direct-entry cadets, and for serving personnel and technical graduates.

The Territorial Army came into being in Sept. 1949, its role being to: (1) relieve the regular Army of static duties and, if required, support civil power; (2) provide anti-aircraft units, and (3) if and when called upon, provide units for the regular Army. The Territorial Army is composed of practically all arms of the Services.

The authorized strength of the Army was (1990) 1·1m., that of the Territorial Army, 160,000. There are 2 armoured, 1 mechanized, 19 infantry and 11 mountain divisions, 5 independent armoured brigades, 7 independent infantry, 3 independent artillery brigades, 1 parachute brigade, 1 mountain brigade, 6 air defence brigades and 4 independent engineer brigades. An Aviation Corps was formed in 1986 and operates locally-built Alouette and Lama helicopters.

Navy. The Indian Navy has 3 commands; Eastern, Western and Southern, the latter a training and support command. The fleet is divided into two elements, Eastern and Western; and well-trained, all volunteer personnel operate a unique mix of Soviet and Western vessels.

The principal ships of the Indian Navy are the two light aircraft carriers, *Viraat* and *Vikrant*. The *Viraat*, formerly HMS *Hermes*, is of 29,000 tonnes and was completed in 1959. Having earlier been converted to VSTOL aircraft operations, she was transferred to the Indian Navy in 1987. Her normal air group is 8 to 10 Sea Harrier fighters, and 8 Sea King ASW helicopters. *Vikrant*, substantially smaller at 19,800 tonnes, is the former British *Hercules*, transferred to India before her delayed completion as a conventional carrier in 1961. She is currently undergoing refit to the VSTOL role, and is expected to recommission, with an air group similar to Viraat, in late 1990. The two cruisers, *Delhi* and *Mysore*, were disposed of in 1979 and 1986 respectively.

In addition to the two carriers, there is a leased Soviet nuclear powered missile submarine, *Chakra*, of the Soviet 'Charlie-1' class; more are expected. The fleet also includes 6 'Kilo' and 8 'Foxtrot' Soviet-built diesel submarines and 2 smaller German-built. 5 new Soviet-built missile armed destroyers, 3 heavily modified and 6 rather less modified 'Leander' class frigates, all built in India, and 13 other frigates form the main suface force. Coastal forces include 8 Soviet-built missile corvettes, 13 fast missile craft and 11 inshore patrol craft. There are 12 Soviet-built offshore minesweepers, and 8 much smaller inshore vessels. Amphibious lift for the 1,000 strong marine force is provided by 1 landing ship tank and 9 medium landing ships, plus about 10 craft. Support forces include 3 tankers, 1 submarine depot ship, 1 transport, 10 survey and research, 2 tugs and one training ship.

The Naval Air force, 5,000 strong, operates 8 Sea Harriers, with further deliveries imminent, 3 Il-38 'May', 5 Tu-142M 'Bear' and 15 Britten-Norman Islander maritime patrol aircraft. The small squadron of 4 Alize ASW aircraft is now based ashore. Armed Helicopters include 10 Chetak, 5 Ka-25, 18 Ka-27 and 20 Sea King, and the inventory is completed with some 22 training and communications aircraft.

Main bases are at Bombay (HQ Western Fleet, and main dockyard), Goa, Vishakhapatnam (HQ Eastern Fleet) and Calcutta on the sub-continent, and Port Blair in the Andaman Islands.

Naval personnel in 1989 numbered 47,000 including 5,000 Naval Air Arm and 1,000 marines.

The Coast Guard is an independent para-military service currently 2,500 strong, which functions under Defence Ministry control, but is funded by the Revenue Department. All former frigates transferred from the Navy have now been disposed of, and the force comprises 6 offshore patrol vessels and 25 inshore patrol craft. Its 19 aircraft are of Dornier-228, Fokker F-27 and Britten-Norman Islander types.

Air Force. The Indian Air Force Act was passed in 1932, and the first flight was formed in 1933.

The Air Headquarters, under the Chief of Air Staff, consists of 4 main branches, viz., Air Staff, Administration, Policy and Plans, and Maintenance. Units of the IAF are organized into 5 operational commands–Western at Delhi, Central at Allahabad, Eastern at Shillong, Southern at Trivandrum and South-Western at Jodhpur. Training Command HQ is at Bangalore, Maintenance Command at Nagpur. Nominal strength in 1990 was 110,000 personnel and 735 aircraft of all types, in over 50 squadrons of aircraft and helicopters and about 30 squadrons of 'Guideline' and 'Goa' surface-to-air missiles, and close-range missiles such as 'Gainful' and Tigercat.

Air defence units include 2 squadrons of MiG-23 variable-geometry interceptors, 2 squadrons of MiG-29s, 18 squadrons of MiG-21s and 3 of Mirage 2000s. Initial delivery of MiG-21s from the Soviet Union was followed by large-scale licence production in India. Other combat units include 8 squadrons of MiG-27s, 2 of Canberras, 4 of Jaguars, 4 of MiG-23 supersonic fighter-bombers and one of MiG-25 reconnaissance aircraft plus a MiG-25U two seat trainer. Currently the main re-equipment programmes involve the licence-production of MiG-27 and Jaguar strike aircraft.

The large transport force includes An-12s, An-32s, Il-76s, Do 228s, HS 748s, 2 Boeing 737s, and smaller aircraft and helicopters for VIP and other duties. Helicopter units have Mi-8s and Mi-17s (10 squadrons), Mi-26s, and Mi-25 gunships, but the bulk of the Air Force's Chetaks (Alouette IIIs) and Cheetahs (Lamas) have been transferred to Army control, main training types are the Hindustan HPT-32 and Kiran, Polish-built TS-11 Iskra, Hunter T.66, MiG-21UT1 and MiG-23U.

Primary flying training is provided at the Elementary Flying School, Bidar, and advanced flying training at the Air Force Academy, Dundigal, Hyderabad. There is a Navigation and Signals School at Begumpet. The IAF Technical College, Jalahalli, imparts technical training, while the IAF Administrative College, Coimbatore, trains officers of the ground duty branch. There are also land-air warfare, flying instructors' and medical schools.

INTERNATIONAL RELATIONS

Membership. India is a member of the UN, the Commonwealth and the Colombo Plan.

External Debt. At the end of March 1989 India's external public debt was estimated at Rs 688,310m.

Treaties. India pursues a general policy of non-alignment; the exception is a Treaty of Peace, Friendship and Cooperation with the USSR, 1971; the parties agreed to mutual support short of force in the event of either being attacked by a third party.

ECONOMY

Planning. The sixth plan (1980–85) envisaged total investment of Rs 1,587,100m., of which Rs 975,000m. was for the public sector. The seventh plan (1985–89) aims at an annual 5·2% growth. The priority sections are power generation, irrigation and hydro carbons. Total planned outlay, Rs 3,200,000m., 56% from the public sector. Annual plan outlay (1987–88) Rs 446,980m.

Ministry of Agriculture. *Serving the Small Farmer: Policy Choices in Indian Agricultural Development.* 1975
Dutt, A. K. (ed.) *India: Resources, Potentialities and Planning.* Rev. ed. Dubuque, India, 1973
Singh, T., *India's Development Experience.* London, 1975

Budget. Revenue and expenditure (on revenue account) of the central government[1] for years ending 31 March, in crores of rupees:

	1988–89	*1989–90* [1]	*1990–91* [2]
Revenue	43,135	52,630	45,294
Expenditure	42,883	47,875	56,671

[1] Revised. [2] Budget estimates.

Important items of revenue and expenditure on the revenue account of the central government for 1990–91 (estimates), in Rs 1m.:

Revenue		*Expenditure*	
Net tax revenue	377,980	General Services	398,400
Non-tax revenue	118,370	Defence	109,480
		Major subsidies	85,160

Total capital account receipts (1990–91 budget), Rs 253,650m.; capital account disbursements, Rs 235,650m. Total (revenue and capital) receipts, Rs 873,290m.; disbursements, Rs 945,350m.

Under the Constitution (Part XII and 7th Schedule), the power to raise funds has been divided between the central government and the states. Generally, the sources of revenue are mutually exclusive. Certain taxes are levied by the Union for the sake of uniformity and distributed to the states. The Finance Commission (Art. 280 of the Constitution) advises the President on the distribution of the taxes which are distributable between the centre and the states, and on the principles on which grants should be made out of Union revenues to the states. The main sources of central revenue are: customs duties; those excise duties levied by the central government; corporation, income and wealth taxes; estate and succession duties on non-agricultural assets and property, and revenues from the railways and posts and telegraphs. The main heads of revenue in the states are: taxes and duties levied by the state governments (including land revenues and agricultural income tax); civil administration and civil works; state undertakings; taxes shared with the centre; and grants received from the centre.

Currency. A decimal system of coinage was introduced in 1957. The Indian *rupee* is divided into 100 *paise* (until 1964 officially described as *naye paise*), the decimal coins being 1, 2, 3, 5, 10, 20, 25 and 50 *paise*.

The rupee is valued in relation to a package of main currencies. The £ is the currency of intervention. In March 1990 Rs 27.60 = £1; Rs 16.84 = US$1.

The paper currency consists of: (1) Reserve Bank notes in denominations of Rs 2, 5, 10, 20, 50 and 100; and (2) Government of India currency notes of denominations of Re 1 deemed to be included in the expression 'rupee coin' for the purposes of the Reserve Bank of India Act, 1934.

According to the Reserve Bank of India, the total money supply with the public on the last Friday of Dec. 1988 was Rs 35,607 crores. Foreign exchange reserves, Dec. 1988, Rs 62,181m.

100,000 rupees are called 1 lakh; 100 lakhs are called 1 crore.

Banking. The Reserve Bank, the central bank for India, was established in 1934 and started functioning on 1 April 1935 as a shareholder's bank; it became a nationalized institution on 1 Jan. 1949. It has the sole right of issuing currency notes. The Bank acts as adviser to the Government on financial problems and is the banker for central and state governments, commercial banks and some other financial institutions. The Bank manages the rupee public debt of central and state governments. It is the custodian of the country's exchange reserve and supervises repatriation of export proceeds and payments for imports. The Bank gives short-term loans to state governments and scheduled banks and short and medium-term loans to state co-operative banks and industrial finance institutions. The Bank has extensive powers of regulation of the banking system, directly under the Banking Regulation Act, 1949, and indirectly by the use of variations in Bank rate, variation in reserve ratios, selective credit controls and open market operations. Bank rate was raised to 10% in July 1981.

Except refinance for food credit and export credit, the Reserve Bank's refinance facility to commercial banks has been placed on a discretionary basis. The net profit of the Reserve Bank of India for the year ended June 1986, after making the usual or necessary provisions, amounted to Rs 210 crores.

The commercial banking system consisted of 275 scheduled banks (*i.e.*, banks which are included in the 2nd schedule to the Reserve Bank Act) and 4 non-scheduled banks on 30 June 1986; scheduled banks included 194 Regional Rural Banks. Total deposits in commercial banks, Dec. 1990, stood at Rs 160,526 crores. The business of non-scheduled banks forms less than 0·1% of commercial bank business. Of the 275 scheduled banks, 21 are foreign banks which specialize in financing foreign trade but also compete for domestic business. The largest scheduled bank is the State Bank of India, constituted by nationalizing the Imperial Bank of India in 1955. The State Bank acts as the agent of the Reserve Bank and the subsidiaries of the State Bank act as the agents of the State Bank for transacting government business as well as undertaking commercial functions. Fourteen banks with aggregate deposits of not less than Rs 50 crores were nationalized on 19 July 1969. Six banks were nationalized in April 1980. The 28 public sector banks (which comprise the State Bank of India and its seven associate banks and 20 nationalised banks) account for over 90% of deposits and bank credit of all scheduled commercial banks.

Reserve Bank of India: Report on Currency and Finance.—Report on the Trend and Progress of Banking in India.—Report of the Central Board of Directors. Annual. Bombay

Weights and Measures. Uniform standards of weights and measures, based on the metric system, were established for the first time by the Standards of Weights and Measures Act, 1956, which provided for a transition period of 10 years. So far the system has been fully adopted in trade transactions but there are a few fields such as engineering, survey and land records and the building and construction industry where it has not; efforts are being made to complete the change as early as possible.

In order to align this legislation with the latest international trends an expert committee (Weights and Measures (Law Revision) Committee) was set up by the central government to suggest a revised Bill which was passed by Parliament in April 1976. The new Standards of Weights and Measures Act, 1976, has recognized the International System of Units and other units recommended by the General Conference on Weights and Measures and is in line with the recommendations of the International Organisation of Legal Metrology (OIML). The new Act also covers the system of numeration, the approval of models of weights and measures, regulation and control of inter-state trade in relation to weights and measures. The Act also protects consumers through proper indication of weight, quantity, identity, source, date and price on packaged goods. A draft Standards of Weights and Measures (Enforcement) Bill has also been prepared by the committee for adoption either by Parliament or State legislatures, as enforcement is now in the 'concurrent' list of legislation.

The provisions of the 1976 Act came into force in Sept. 1977, as did the accompanying Standards of Weights and Measures (Packaged Commodities) Rules, 1977.

While the Standards of Weights and Measures are laid down in the Central Act, enforcement of weights and measures laws is entrusted to the state governments; the central Directorate of Weights and Measures is responsible for co-ordinating activities so as to ensure national uniformity.

An Indian Institute of Legal Metrology trains officials of the Weights and

Measures departments of India and different developing countries. The Institute is being modernized with technical assistance from the Federal Republic of Germany.

There are 2 Regional Reference Standards laboratories at Ahmedabad and Bhubaneswar which (besides calibrating secondary standards of physical measurements) also provide testing facilities in metrological and industrial measurements. These laboratories are equipped with Standards next in line to the National Standards of physical measurements which are maintained at the National Physical Laboratory in New Delhi.

For weights previously in legal use under the Standards of Weight Act, 1956, *see* THE STATESMAN'S YEAR-BOOK, 1961, p. 171.

Calendar. The dates of the Saka era (named after the north Indian dynasty of the first century A.D.) are being used alongside Gregorian dates in issues of the *Gazette of India*, news broadcasts by All-India Radio and government-issued calendars, from 22 March 1957, a date which corresponds with the first day of the year 1879 in the Saka era.

ENERGY AND NATURAL RESOURCES

Electricity. In March 1986 about 68% of all villages had electricity. Production of electricity in 1987–88 was 201,890m. kwh., of which 154,490m. kwh. came from thermal and nuclear stations and 47,400m. kwh from hydro-electric stations. Supply 230 and 250 volts; 50 Hz.

Oil and Gas. The Oil and Natural Gas Commission, Oil India Ltd and the Assam Oil Co. are the only producers of crude oil. Production 1987-88, 30·36m. tonnes, about 60% of consumption. The main fields are in Assam and offshore in the Gulf of Cambay (the Bombay High field). Natural gas production, 1987–88, 11,467m. cu. metres.

Water. The net area of 63·3m. hectares (1987-88) under irrigation exceeds that of any other country except China, and equals about 38% of the total area under cultivation. Irrigation projects have formed an important part of all three Five-Year Plans. The possibilities of diverting rivers into canals being nearly exhausted, the emphasis is now on damming the monsoon surplus flow and diverting that. Ultimate potential of irrigation is assessed at 107m. hectares, total cultivated land being 142m. hectares. In 1985 India and Bangladesh reached an agreement to monitor the water of the Ganges at the Farakka barrage.

1987 was a year of severe drought, affecting both agriculture and water-supplies to cities.

Minerals. Bihar, West Bengal and Madhya Pradesh produce 42%, 25% and 19% of all coal, respectively. The coal industry was nationalized in 1973. Production, 1987–88, 180m. tonnes; reserves (including lignite) are estimated at 155,902m. tonnes. Production of other minerals, 1987-88 estimates (in 1,000 tonnes): Iron ore, 48,972; bauxite, 2,496; chromite 660; copper ore, 5,064; manganese ore, 1,284; gold, 1,872 kg. Other important minerals are lead, zinc, limestone, apatite and phosphorite, dolomite, magnesite and silver. Value of mineral production, 1986, Rs 96,410m. of which mineral fuels produced Rs 82,260m., metallic minerals Rs 6,440m. and non-metallic Rs 7,700m.

Agriculture. The chief industry of India has always been agriculture. About 70% of the people are dependent on the land for their living. In 1987-88 it provided 29·3% of NDP.

In 1984–85 agricultural commodities accounted for about 20% by value of Indian exports, while agricultural commodities, machinery and fertilizers accounted for about 20% of imports. Tea accounted for about 30% of agricultural exports.

An increase in food production of at least 2% per annum is necessary to keep pace with the rising population. Foodgrain production, 1988-89 (estimate) 172m. tonnes.

The Indian Council of Agricultural Research works through 41 institutes, 7 national research centres, 4 project directorates, and 68 national research projects. There are 4 national research bureaux and 23 agricultural universities.

The farming year runs from July to June through three crop seasons: Kharif (monsoon); rabi (winter) and summer.

Agricultural production, 1988-89 (in 1,000 tonnes): Rice, 70,667; wheat, 53,995; total foodgrains, 170,253; sugar-cane 204,626; oilseeds, 21,640; cotton, 8·7m. bales (of 180 kg); jute is grown in West Bengal (half total yield), Bihar and Assam, total yield, 6·6m. bales (of 180 kg); maize (1988), 7,500; pulses, 13,700. The coffee industry is growing: The main cash varieties are Arabica and Robusta (main growing areas Karnataka, Kerala and Tamil Nadu).

The tea industry is important, with production concentrated in Assam, West Bengal, Tamil Nadu and Kerala. Total crop in 1988–89, 703,200 tonnes from (1988) 403,000 hectares.

Livestock (1988): Cattle, 193m.; sheep, 51,684,000; pigs, 10·3m.; horses, 953,000; asses, 1,328,000m.; goats, 105m.; buffaloes, 72m.

Fertilizer consumption in 1987–88 was 9·01m. tonnes.

Land Tenure. There are three main traditional systems of land tenure: *Ryotwari* tenure, where the individual holders, usually peasant proprietors, are responsible for the payment of land revenues; *zamindari* tenure, where one or more persons own large estates and are responsible for payment (in this system there may be a number of intermediary holders); and *mahalwari* tenure, where village communities jointly hold an estate and are jointly and severally responsible for payment.

Agrarian reform, initiated in the first Five-Year Plan, being undertaken by the state governments includes: (1) The abolition of intermediaries under *zamindari* tenure. (2) Tenancy legislation designed to scale down rents to 1/4-1/5 of the value of the produce, to give permanent rights to tenants (subject to the landlord's right to resume a minimum holding for his personal cultivation), and to enable tenants to acquire ownership of their holdings (subject to the landlord's right of resumption for personal cultivation) on payment of compensation over a number of years. (3) Fixing of ceilings on existing holdings and on future acquisition; the holding of a family is between 4·05 and 7·28 hectares if it has assured irrigation to produce two crops a year; 10·93 hectares for land with irrigation facilities for only one crop a year; and 21·85 hectares for all other categories of land. Tea, coffee, cocoa and cardamom plantations have been exempted. (4) The consolidation of holdings in community project areas and the prevention of fragmentation of holdings by reform of inheritance laws. (5) Promotion of farming by co-operative village management (*see* p. 644).

The average size of holding for the whole of India is 2·63 hectares. Andhra Pradesh, 2·87; Assam, 1·46; Bihar, 1·53; Gujarat, 4·49; Jammu and Kashmir, 1·43; Karnataka, 4·11; Kerala, 0·75; Madhya Pradesh, 3·99; Maharashtra, 4·65; Orissa, 1·98; Punjab, 3·85; Rajasthan, 5·5; Tamil Nadu, 1·49; Uttar Pradesh, 1·78; West Bengal, 1·56.

Of the total 71m. rural households possessing operational holdings, 34% hold on the average less than 0·20 hectare of land each.

Opium. By international agreement the poppy is cultivated under licence, and all raw opium is sold to the central government. Opium, other than for wholly medical use, is available only to registered addicts.

Fisheries. Total catch (1987–88) was 2·96m. tons, of which Kerala, Tamil Nadu, and Maharashtra produced about half. Of the total catch, 1·66m. tonnes were marine fish. There were 160 deep-sea (20 metres and above) fishing boats in 1987-88. There were 23,500 mechanised boats (1987–88). There were 7,452 fishermen's co-operatives with 783,000 members in 1984–85; total sales, Rs 205·4m.

Forestry. The lands under the control of the state forest departments are classified as 'reserved forests' (forests intended to be permanently maintained for the supply of timber, etc., or for the protection of water supply, etc.), 'protected forests' and 'unclassed' forest land.

In 1988 the total forest area was 67·1m. hectares. Main types are teak and sal. About 16% of the area is inaccessible, of which about 45% is potentially productive. In 1985–86 3m. saplings were planted. Some states have encouraged planting small areas around villages.

INDUSTRY AND TRADE

Industries. Railways, air transport, armaments and atomic energy are government monopolies. In a number of industries (including the manufacture of iron and steel and mineral oils, shipbuilding and the mining of coal, iron and manganese ores, gypsum, gold and diamonds) new units are set up only by the state. In a further group of industries (road transport, manufacture of chemicals such as drugs, dyestuffs, plastics and fertilizers) the state established new undertakings, but private enterprise may develop either on its own or with state backing, which may take the form of loans or purchase of equity capital. Nationalized industries employed 4m. in 1981. Under the Industries (Development and Regulation) Act, 1951, as amended, industrial undertakings are required to be licensed; 162 industries are within the scope of the Act. The Government are authorized to examine the working of any undertaking, to issue directions to it and to take over its control if this be deemed necessary. A Central Advisory Council has been set up consisting of representatives of industry, labour, consumers and primary producers. There are Development Councils for individual industries and (1981) 4 national development banks.

Foreign investment is encouraged by a tax holiday on income up to 6% of capital employed for 5 years. There are special depreciation allowances, and customs and excise concessions for export industries.

Oil refinery installed capacity, April 1989, was 49·85m. tonnes; production of petroleum industry products (1987–88), 44·72m. tonnes. The Indian Oil Corporation was established in 1964 and had (1990) most of the market.

Industry, particularly steel, has suffered from a shortage of power and coal. There is expansion in petrochemicals, based on the oil and associated gas of the Bombay High field, and gas from Bassein field. Small industries (initial outlay on capital equipment of less than Rs 3·5m.) are important; they employ about 10·7m. and produced (1987–88) goods worth Rs 728,800m.

Industrial production, 1988-89 (in 1,000 tonnes): Pig-iron and ferro-alloys, 12,185; steel ingots, 13,580; finished steel, 10,384; aluminium, 332; 1,674,444 motor cycles, mopeds and scooters; 118,704 commercial vehicles; petroleum products, 45,660; cement, 41,760; board and paper, 2,072; nitrogen fertilizer, 6,600; phosphate fertilizer, 2,316; jute goods, 1,388; man-made fibre and yarn, 261; diesel engines, 1,707,600 engines; electric motors, 4·9m. h.p.

Lal, V. B., (et al) *The Aluminium Industry in India: Promise, Prospects, Constraints and Impact.* New Delhi, 1985

Labour. At the 1981 census there were 222·5m. workers, of whom 92·5m. were cultivators, 55·5m. agricultural labourers; in 1984 there were 7·4m. in manufacturing, 11·3m. in social, community and personal services, 1·5m. in construction and 3·53m. in transport, communications and storage. There were 36,606 registered trade unions. The bond labour system was abolished in 1975. Man-days lost by industrial disputes, 1986, 22·12m., of which 2·05m. were in the public sector. An ordnance of July 1981 gave the government power to ban strikes in essential services; the ordnance was to remain in force for six months and would then be renewable.

Companies. The total number of companies limited by shares at work in India, 31 March 1988, was 154,445; aggregate paid-up capital was Rs 46,447 crores. There were 18,459 public limited companies with an aggregate paid-up capital of Rs 17,947 crores, and 137,090 private limited companies (Rs 28,500 crores). There were also 309 companies with unlimited liability.

During 1987–88, 17,578 new limited companies were registered in the Indian Union under the Companies Act 1956 with a total authorized capital of Rs 6,396 crores; 953 were public limited companies (Rs 4,905 crores) and 16,625 were private limited companies (Rs 1,491 crores). There were 10 private companies with unlimited liability also registered in 1987–88. Of the new non-government limited companies, 283 had an authorized capital of Rs 1 crore and above, and 393 of between Rs 50 lakhs and Rs 1 crore. During 1987–88, 159 companies with an aggregate paid-up capital of Rs 18·10 crores went into liquidation and 49 companies (Rs 0·81 crores) were struck off the register.

On 31 March 1988 there were 1,104 government companies at work with a total paid-up capital of Rs 36,031 crores; 474 were public limited companies and 630 were private limited companies.

On 31 March 1988, 401 companies incorporated elsewhere were reported to have a place of business in India; 126 were of UK and 83 of USA origin.

Department of Company Affairs, Govt. of India. *Annual Report on the Working and Administration of the Companies Act, 1956*. New Delhi, 1988

Co-operative Movement. On 30 June 1988 there were about 350,000 co-operative societies with a total membership of about 145m. These included Primary Co-operative Marketing Societies, State Co-operative Marketing Federations and the National Agricultural Co-operative Marketing Federation of India. There were also State Co-operative Commodity Marketing Federations, and 29 general purpose and 16 Special Commodites Marketing Federations.

There were, on 30 June 1985, 28 State Co-operative Banks, 350 Central Co-operative Banks, 92,408 Primary Agricultural Societies, 19 State Land Development Banks, and 881 primary or district Land Development Banks/branches which provide long-term investment credit.

Total agricultural credit disbursed by Co-operatives in 1987–88 was Rs 4,280 crores including Rs 3,188 crores in short-term credit, Rs 380 crores in medium-term credit and Rs 712 crores in long-term credit.

Value of agricultural produce marketed by Co-operatives in 1987–88 was about Rs 4,000 crores.

In June 1987–88 there were 2,402 processing units; 211 sugar factories produced 5·26m. tons; 101 spinning mills (capacity 2·68m. spindles) produced 179m. kg. of yarn; there were 300 oil mills and similar units; total storage capacity was 8·49m. tons.

In 1987–88 there were 67,000 retail depots distributing 3m. tons of fertilizers.

Indian Labour Guide. Monthly. Delhi
Co-operative Movement in India, Statistical Statements Relating to. Annual. Reserve Bank of India, Bombay

Commerce. The external trade of India (excluding land-borne trade with Tibet and Bhután) was as follows (in 100,000 rupees):

	Imports	*Exports and Re-exports*
1985–86	1,965,769	1,089,459
1986–87	2,009,576	1,245,194
1987–88	2,239,897	1,574,123
1988-89[1]	2,769,287	2,028,092

[1]Provisional.

The distribution of commerce by countries and areas was as follows in the year ended 31 March 1988 (in 100,000 rupees):

Countries	*Exports to*	*Imports from*
Afghánistán	3,444	2,105
Argentina	230	3,640
Australia	18,110	49,683
Austria	3,805	9,650
Bahrain	3,366	4,989
Bangladesh	18,681	1,479
Belgium	48,442	140,359
Brazil	269	34,952
Bulgaria	4,682	1,777
Burma	99	5,663
Canada	14,948	30,559
Czechoslovakia	10,254	6,879
Denmark	5,797	6,198
Egypt	7,826	9,428
Finland	1,789	9,680
France	37,524	80,872
German Dem. Republic	10,633	9,459
Federal Rep. of Germany	106,119	217,844
Ghana	715	2,056
Hong Kong	45,315	12,434
Hungary	4,079	5,570
Indonesia	2,656	8,239
Iran	13,863	11,951
Iraq	1,734	37,332
Italy	50,238	50,452
Japan	161,492	211,962
Jordan	1,401	11,827
Kenya	3,569	689

Countries	Exports to	Imports from
Korea	14,082	32,940
Kuwait	10,565	48,328
Malaysia	8,917	81,993
Morocco	1,516	16,667
Nepál	9,368	4,466
Netherlands	28,245	44,541
New Zealand	2,705	5,175
Nigeria	5,101	967
Norway	2,250	8,877
Pakistan	2,012	3,059
Poland	20,120	5,636
Qatar	1,706	3,802
Romania	6,898	5,737
Saudi Arabia	29,591	138,696
Singapore	27,535	41,881
Spain	8,175	17,587
Sri Lanka	10,163	1,171
Sudan	2,125	212
Sweden	8,122	30,398
Switzerland	20,491	24,114
Tanzania	2,175	9,415
Thailand	8,161	6,389
Turkey	3,342	11,999
United Arab Emirates	31,414	78,334
USSR	197,149	127,890
UK	103,338	181,122
USA	290,765	202,497
Yugoslavia	5,553	16,636
Zaïre	227	4,092
Zambia	500	13,355

The value (in 100,000 rupees) of the leading articles of merchandise was as follows in the year ended 31 March 1988 (provisional):

Exports	*Value*
Meat and meat preparations	8,554
Fish, crustaceans, molluscs and preparations thereof	52,511
Rice	32,457
Vegetables and fruits	45,749
Coffee and coffee substitutes	26,322
Tea and mate	59,237
Spices	30,929
Oilcake	17,328
Tobacco unmanufactured and tobacco refuse	10,932
Raw cotton	9,549
Iron ore	54,276
Ores and minerals (excluding iron, mica and coal)	13,732
Cotton yarn, fabrics and madeup articles	106,378
Readymade garments	179,206
Jute manufactures including twist and yarn	24,282
Leather and leather manufactures	114,852
Gems and jewellery	261,360
Works of art	24,338
Handmade carpets	39,143
Engineering goods	143,304
Mineral fuel, lubricants and related products	64,869
Chemicals and allied products	77,429

Imports	*Value*
Wheat	350
Sugar	17,411
Pulp and waste paper	22,802
Crude rubber including synthetic and reclaimed	10,782
Synthetic and regenerated fibre	2,840
Fertilizers, crude	13,841
Sulphur and unroasted iron pyrites	17,624
Metalliferous ores and metal scrap	42,206
Petroleum, Petroleum products and related materials	408,275
Edible oil	92,004
Organic chemicals	65,245
Inorganic chemicals	39,807
Medical and pharmaceutical products	13,710
Fertilizers, manufactured	17,153
Artificial resins, plastic materials etc	54,844
Chemical materials and products	17,357
Paper, paper board and manufactures thereof	25,809
Textile yarn, fabrics and madeup articles	18,778
Pearls, precious and semi-precious stones	199,417

Imports	*Value*
Non-metallic mineral manufactures exclg. pearls	8,623
Iron and steel	127,319
Non-ferrous metal	57,611
Manufactures of metal	14,930
Machinery other than electric	428,011
Electrical machinery	111,516
Transport equipment	74,035
Professional, scientific, controlling instruments, photographic, optical goods, watches and clocks	49,059

Total trade between India and UK (British Department of Trade returns, in £1,000 sterling):

	1985	*1986*	*1987*	*1988*	*1989*
Imports to UK	431,785	440,681	536,704	559,684	701,985
Exports and re-exports from UK	894,708	941,169	1,090,146	1,111,740	1,382,436

Annual Statement of the Foreign Trade of India. 2 vols. Calcutta
Monthly Statistics of the Foreign Trade of India. Calcutta
Review of the Trade of India. Annual. Delhi
India–Handbook of Commercial Information. 3 vols. Calcutta
Guide to Official Statistics of Trade, Shipping, Customs and Excise Revenue of India. Rev. ed. Calcutta

Tourism. There were 1·24m. visitors (excluding nationals of Pakistan and Bangladesh) in 1988 bringing about Rs 21,000m. in foreign exchange; 200,509 from UK, 122,888 from USA, 70,640 from Sri Lanka.

COMMUNICATIONS

Roads. In 1988–89 there were about 2m. km of roads, of which about 840,000 km were surfaced. Roads are divided into 5 main administrative classes, namely, national highways, state highways, major district roads, other district roads and village roads. The national highways (33,612 km in 1989) connect capitals of states, major ports and foreign highways. The national highway system is linked with the ESCAP (Economic and Social Commission for Asia and the Pacific) international highway system. The state highways are the main trunk roads of the states, while the major district roads connect subsidiary areas of production and markets with distribution centres, and form the main link between headquarters and neighbouring districts.

There were (31 March 1989) 16,488,000 motor vehicles in India, comprising 2,284,000 private cars, taxis and jeeps, 10·7m. motor cycles and scooters, 293,000 buses and 1,140,000 goods vehicles.

Railways. The Indian railway system is government-owned and (under the control of the Railway Board) is divided into 9 zones; route-km at 31 March 1988:

Zone	*Headquarters*	*Route-km*
Central	Bombay	6,815 km (1,202 km elec.)
Eastern	Calcutta	4,291 km (1,246 km)
Northern	Delhi	10,980 km (884 km)
North Eastern	Gorakhpur	5,163 km
North East Frontier	Maligaon (Guwahati)	3,763 km
Southern	Madras	6,756 km (598 km)
South Central	Secunderabad	7,204 km (733 km)
South Eastern	Calcutta	7,113 km (2,065 km)
Western	Bombay	9,889 km (1,427 km)

Principal gauges are 1,676 mm. and metre, with networks also of 762 and 610 mm. gauge.

Passengers carried in 1987–88 were approximately 3,792m.; freight, 318·5m. tonnes. Revenue (1987–88) from passengers, Rs 2,058 crores; from goods, Rs 5,839 crores.

Indian Railways pay to the central government a fixed dividend of 4·5% on capital-at-charge. Railway finance in Rs 1m.:

Financial years	Gross traffic receipts	Working expenses	Net revenues (traffic and miscellaneous)	Net surplus or deficit (after dividend)
1986–87	75,057	69,006	6,051	+102
1987–88	84,353	78,030	6,323	+843

Aviation. The air transport industry in India was nationalized in 1953 with the formation of two Air Corporations: Air India for operating long-distance international air services, and Indian Airlines for operating air services within India and to adjacent countries. A third airline, Vayudoot, was formed in 1981 as an internal feeder airline. There are 93 airports.

Air India runs Boeing 747s and 707s, Airbus A-300 and A-310s; it operates from Bombay, Delhi, Madras, Trivandrum, Hyderabad, Bangalore, Goa and Calcutta to Africa (Nairobi, Lagos, Seychelles, Mauritius, Dar es Salaam, Lusaka and Harare); to Europe (London, Paris, Amsterdam, Frankfurt, Geneva, Zurich, Brussels, Moscow and Rome); to western Asia (Doha, Abu Dhabi, Dharan, Dubai, Bahrain, Kuwait, Muscat, Jeddah, Ras al Khaymah, Sharjah and Baghdad); to east Asia (Bangkok, Hong Kong, Tokyo, Osaka, Kuala Lumpur, Singapore and Sydney); to North America (New York). It carried 2·13m. passengers in 1987-88 and made a loss of Rs 273·4m.

Indian Airlines had a fleet of 53 aircraft consisting of Airbus A-300BS, Boeing 737, F-27 and HS-748 aircraft. During 1987–88 they carried 10·44m. passengers; net profit Rs 30·10 crores. Flights cover over 83,000 unduplicated route km. Vayudoot serves remote areas of India; it has a network of 94 stations.

The National Airports Authority maintains and operates 87 civil aerodromes and 28 civil enclaves. The management of the 4 international airports at Bombay, Calcutta, Delhi and Madras is vested in the International Airports Authority of India.

Shipping. In Sept. 1989, 394 ships totalling 5,751,998 GRT were on the Indian Register; of these, 149 ships of 469,049 GRT were engaged in coastal trade, and 245 ships of 5,282,949 GRT in overseas trade. Traffic of major ports, 1988–89, was as follows:

Port	Ships cleared	Imports (1m. tonnes)	Exports (1m. tonnes)
Kandla	911	16·4	1·4
Bombay	2,122	13·5	15·1
Mormugao	477	1·8	13·6
New Mangalore	426	1·6	5·5
Cochin	646	6·4	1·4
Tuticorin	461	4·9	0·3
Madras	1,371	14·8	9·1
Vizag	699	10·3	10·0
Paradip	270	2·8	3·2
Haldia	588	6·3	3·6
Calcutta	807	3·4	0·9

The Hindustan shipyard at Vishakhapatnam is capable of building vessels of a maximum of 42,750 DWT. Present capacity is about 118,250 DWT per year. The Mazagon dock in Bombay and Goa shipyard build vessels primarily for defence purposes. The Cochin Shipyard can build ships of 85,000 DWT each and repair ships up to 100,000 DWT. The installed capacity of the shipyard is 150,000 DWT new construction and 1m. GRT ship repair, per annum. Garden Reach Shipbuilders and Engineers are building bulk carriers of 26,000 DWT, ferry ships (6,000 DWT), hydrographic research ships, tugs and fast patrol craft.

There are about 5,200 km of major rivers navigable by motorized craft, of which 1,700 km are used. Canals, 4,300 km, of which 485 km are navigable by motorized craft (331 km are used).

Post and Broadcasting. On 1 April 1989 there were 147,377 post offices and 37,892 telegraph offices.

The telephone system is in the hands of the Telecommunications Department, except in Delhi, served by public corporation. In April 1989 the Department had 4·17m. telephones, 285 telex exchanges and 42,464 subscribers.

There were 96 radio stations on 31 Dec. 1988, and programmes were sent out from 167 transmitters. In 1990 television covered 83% of the population, through a network of 423 transmitters. Entertainment films occupy 27% of broadcasting time, news and current affairs, 45%. A communications satellite ('APPLE') went into operation in July 1981.

Cinemas. In 1987-88 there were 13,183 cinemas and about 750 feature films were produced.

Newspapers. In 1982 the total number of newspapers and periodicals was 19,937; about 30% were published in Delhi, Bombay, Calcutta and Madras. There were 1,334 daily and 5,898 weekly papers. Circulation of newspapers and periodicals (1984), 61·15m. Hindi papers have the highest number and circulation, followed by English, then Bengali, Urdu and Marathi.

Annual Report of the Register of Newspapers for India. New Delhi

JUSTICE, RELIGION, EDUCATION AND WELFARE

Justice. All courts form a single hierarchy, with the Supreme Court at the head, which constitutes the highest court of appeal. Immediately below it are the high courts and subordinate courts in each state. Every court in this chain, subject to the usual pecuniary and local limits, administers the whole law of the country, whether made by Parliament or by the state legislatures.

The states of Andhra Pradesh, Assam (in common with Nagaland, Meghalaya, Manipur, Mizoram, Tripura and Arunachal Pradesh), Bihar, Gujarat, Himachal Pradesh, Jammu and Kashmir, Karnataka, Kerala, Madhya Pradesh, Maharashtra, Orissa, Punjab (in common with the state of Haryana and the Union Territory of Chandigarh), Rajasthan, Tamil Nadu, Uttar Pradesh, West Bengal and Sikkim have each a High Court. The jurisdiction of Bombay High Court extends to the Territory of Goa. There is a separate High Court for Delhi. For the Andaman and Nicobar Islands the Calcutta High Court, for Pondicherry the High Court of Madras and for Lakshadweep the High Court of Kerala are the highest judicial authorities; in Dadra and Nagar Haveli and in Daman and Diu the High Court of Bombay is the relevant high court. The Allahabad High Court has a Bench at Lucknow, the Bombay High Court has Benches at Nagpur and Aurangabad, the Madhya Pradesh High Court has Benches at Gwalior and Indore, the Patna High Court has a Bench at Ranchi and the Rajasthan High Court has a Bench at Jaipur. Judges and Division Courts of the Gauhati High Court also sit in Meghalaya, Manipur, Nagaland and Tripura. Below the High Court each state is divided into a number of districts under the jurisdiction of district judges who preside over civil courts and courts of sessions. There are a number of judicial authorities subordinate to the district civil courts. On the criminal side magistrates of various classes act under the overall supervision of the High Court.

The Code of Criminal Procedure, 1898, has been replaced by the Code of Criminal Procedure, 1973 (2 of 1974), which came into force with effect from 1 April 1974. The new Code provides for complete separation of the Judiciary from the Executive throughout India.

Police. The states control their own police force through the state Home Ministers. The Home Minister of the central government co-ordinates the work of the states and controls the Central Detective Training School, the Central Forensic Laboratory, the Central Fingerprint Laboratory as well as the National Police Academy at Mount Abu (Rajasthan) where the Indian Police Service is trained. This service is recruited by competitive examination of university graduates and provides all senior officers for the state police forces. The Central Bureau of Investigation functions under the control of the Cabinet Secretariat.

The cities of Pune, Ahmedabad, Nagpur, Bangalore, Calcutta, Madras, Bombay and Hyderabad have separate police commissionerates.

Sarkar, P. C., *Civil Laws of India and Pakistan*. 2 vols. Calcutta, 1953.—*Criminal Laws of India and Pakistan*. 2nd ed. 2 vols. Calcutta, 1956
Setalvad, M. C., *The Common Law of India*. London, 1960
Sharma, S. R., *Supreme Court in the Indian Constitution*. Delhi, 1959

Religion. The principal religions in 1981 (census) were: Hindus, 549·7m. (82·63%); Moslems, 75·6m. (11·36%); Christians, 16·2m. (2·43%); Sikhs, 13·1m. (1·96%); Buddhists, 4·7m. (0·7%); Jains, 3·2m. (0·48%).

Education. Literacy. According to the 1981 census the literacy percentage in the country (excluding age-group, 0-4) was 36·23 (34·45 in 1971): 46·74% among males, 24·88% among females. Of the states and territories, Chandigarh and Kerala have the highest rates.

Educational Organization. Education is the concurrent responsibility of state and Union governments. In the union territories it is the responsibility of the central government. The Union Government is also directly responsible for the central universities and all institutions declared by parliament to be of national importance; the promotion of Hindi as the federal language; coordinating and maintaining standards in higher education, research, science and technology. Professional education rests with the Ministry or Department concerned, e.g., medical education, the Ministry or Department of Health. The Department of Education is a part of the Union Ministry of Human Resource Development, headed by a cabinet minister. There are several autonomous organizations attached to the Department of Education. These include the University Grants Commission, the National Institute of Educational Planning and Administration and the National Council of Educational Research and Training. There is a Central Advisory Board of Education to advise the Union and the State Governments on any educational question which may be referred to it.

School Education. The school system in India can be divided into four stages: Primary, middle, secondary and senior secondary.

Primary education is imparted either at independent primary (or junior basic) schools or primary classes attached to middle or secondary schools. The period of instruction in this stage varies from 4 to 5 years and the medium of instruction is in most cases the mother tongue of the child or the regional language. Free primary education is available for all children. Legislation for compulsory education has been passed by some state governments and Union Territories but it is not practicable to enforce compulsion when the reasons for non-attendance are socio-economic. Residential schools are planned for country children.

The period for the middle stage varies from 2 to 3 years.

Higher Education. Higher education is given in arts, science or professional colleges, universities and all-India educational or research institutions. In 1987–88 there were 142 universities, 10 institutions of national importance and 24 institutions deemed as universities. Of the universities, 9 are central: Aligarh Muslim University; Banaras Hindu University; University of Delhi; University of Hyderabad; Jawaharlal Nehru University; North Eastern Hill University; Visva Bharati; Pondicherry; Indira Gandhi National Open. The rest are state universities. Total enrolment at universities, 1985–86, 3·57m., of which 3·14m. were undergraduates. Women students, 1·05m.

Grants are paid through the University Grants Commission to the central universities and institutions deemed to be universities for their maintenance and development and to state universities for their development projects only; their maintenance is the concern of state governments. During 1985–86 the University Grants Commission sanctioned grants of Rs 192·37 crores.

Technical Education. The number of institutions awarding degrees in engineering and technology in 1987-88 was 262 (in 1947: 38), and those awarding diplomas in engineering and technology numbered 782 (in 1947: 53); the former admitted 190,779, the latter 243,389 students. Girls' Polytechnics had 36,173 students. For training high-level engineers and technologists 5 Institutes of Technology and the

Indian Institute of Science, Bangalore. There are (1986) 4 national Management Institutions and 42 other management units, admitting about 3,000 annually.

Adult Education. In spite of the improvement in the literacy rate, the number of adult illiterates over 14 was over 424·26m. in 1981. Adult education is, therefore, being accorded a high priority; it formed part of the Minimum Needs Programme under the seventh Five-Year Plan (1985–90). The National Literacy Mission aims to cover all illiterate persons in the age-group 15–35 by 1990. The Directorate of Adult Education, established in 1971, is the national resource centre; with state resource centres it is responsible for producing teaching/learning materials, training and orientation, monitoring and evaluating the programme.

Educational statistics for the year 1987–88:

Type of recognized institution	*No. of institutions*	*No. of students on rolls*	*No. of teachers*
Primary/junior basic schools	543,677	92,943,556	1,616,685
Middle/senior basic schools	141,014	29,914,499	1,014,162
High/higher secondary schools[1]	66,857	15,497,878	1,242,823
Training schools and colleges	1,475	184,925[2]	–
Arts, Science and Commerce colleges	4,329	3,433,012[3]	–

[1] Including Junior Colleges.
[2] Enrolment by stages of teachers' training courses at school and college level.
[3] Enrolment by stages of all post-graduate and graduate courses.

Expenditure. Total public expenditure on education 1988–89 is estimated at Rs 9,889 crores. Total public expenditure on education, sport, arts and youth welfare during the Seventh Plan, Rs 6,382·65 crores; Seventh Plan spending on adult education, Rs 130 crores in the central and Rs 230 crores in the state sectors.

Health. Health programmes are primarily the responsibility of the state governments. The Union Government has sponsored and supported major schemes for disease prevention and control which are implemented nationally. These include the prevention and control of malaria, filaria, tuberculosis, leprosy, venereal diseases, smallpox, trachoma and cancer. There are also Union Government schemes in connexion with water supply and sanitation, and with nutrition. The Nutrition Advisory Committee of the Indian Council of Medical Research sponsors schemes for research and advises the Government. The National Nutrition Advisory Committee is to formulate a national nutrition policy and recommend measures for improving national standards.

Medical relief and service is primarily the responsibility of the states. Medical education is also a state responsibility, but there is a co-ordinating Central Health Educational Bureau. Family planning is centrally sponsored and locally implemented. The goal is to reduce the birth-rate by means of education in family planning methods.

Total expenditure on health and family welfare in 1988-89 was Rs 5,048 crores.

DIPLOMATIC REPRESENTATIVES

Of India in Great Britain (India House, Aldwych, London, WC2B 4NA)
High Commissioner: Kuldip Nayar.

Of Great Britain in India (Chanakyapuri, New Delhi 1100-21)
High Commissioner: Sir David Goodall, KCMG.

Of India in the USA (2107 Massachusetts Ave., NW, Washington, D.C., 20008)
Ambassador: Dr Karan Singh.

Of the USA in India (Shanti Path, Chanakyapuri, New Delhi 21)
Ambassador: William Clark, Jr.

Of India to the United Nations
Ambassador: Chinmaya Rajaninath Gharekhan.

Further Reading

Special works relating to States are shown under their separate headings.

India: A Reference Annual. Delhi Govt. Printer. Annual
New Cambridge History of India. 3 vols. CUP, 1988
The Times of India Directory and Yearbook. Bombay and London. Annual
Akbar, M. J., *India: The Siege Within*. Harmondsworth, 1985
Balasubramanyam, V. N., *The Economy of India*. London, 1985
Bardham, P., *The Political Economy of Development in India*. Oxford, 1984
Brown, J., *Modern India: The Origins of an Asian Democracy*. OUP, 1985
Fishlock, T., *India File: Inside the Subcontinent*. London, 1983
von Fürer-Haimendorf, C., *Tribes of India: the Struggle for Survival*. Univ. of California Press, 1983
Kesavan, B. S. and Kulkarni, V. Y. (eds) *The National Bibliography of Indian Literature, 1901–53*, New Delhi, 1963 ff.
Gupta, B. K. and Kharbas, D. S., *India*. [Bibliography] Oxford and Santa Barbara, 1984
Hall, A., *The Emergence of Modern India*. Columbia Univ. Press, 1981
Hart, D., *Nuclear Power in India: a Comparative Analysis*. London, 1983
Majumdar, R. C., Raychandhuri, H. C. and Datta, K., *An Advanced History of India*. 2nd ed. London, 1950
Mehra, P., *A Dictionary of Modern Indian History, 1707–1947*. Delhi, 1987
Mitra, H. N., *The Indian Annual Register*. Calcutta, from 1953
Moon, P., *The British Conquest and Dominion of India*. London and Indiana Univ. Press, 1989
Moore, R. J., *Making the New Commonwealth*. Oxford, 1987
Nanda, B. R. (ed.) *Socialism in India*. Delhi, Bombay, Bangalore, Kanpur, London, 1972
Pachauri, R. K., *Energy and Economic Development in India*. New York, 1977
Philips, C. H. (ed.) *The Evolution of India and Pakistan: Select Documents*. OUP, 1962 ff.—*Politics and Society in India*. London, 1963
Poplai, S. L. (ed.) *India, 1947–50* (select documents). 2 vols. Bombay and London, 1959
Ray, R. K., *Industrialisation of India*. OUP, 1983
Roach, J. R., (ed.) *India 2000: The Next Fifteen Years*. Riverdale, My, 1986
Smith, V. E., *Oxford History of India*. 3rd ed. OUP, 1958
Spear, P., *India: A Modern History*. 2nd ed. Univ. of Michigan Press, 1972
Sutton, S. C., *Guide to the India Office Library (founded in 1801)*. HMSO, 1952
Thomas, R., *India's Emergence as an Industrial Power*. Royal Institute of International Affairs, London, 1982
Yasdani, C. (ed.) *Early History of the Deccan*. 2 vols. London, 1960

STATES AND TERRITORIES

The Republic of India is composed of the following 25 States and 7 centrally administered Union Territories:

States	*Capital*	*States*	*Capital*
Andhra Pradesh	Hyderabad	Manipur	Imphal
Arunachal Pradesh	Itanagar	Meghalaya	Shillong
Assam	Dispur	Mizoram	Aizawl
Bihar	Patna	Nagaland	Kohima
Goa	Panaji	Orissa	Bhubaneswar
Gujarat	Ahmedabad	Punjab	Chandigarh
Haryana	Chandigarh	Rajasthan	Jaipur
Himachal Pradesh	Shimla	Sikkim	Gangtok
Jammu and Kashmir	Srinagar	Tamil Nadu	Madras
Karnataka	Bangalore	Tripura	Agartala
Kerala	Trivandrum	Uttar Pradesh	Lucknow
Madhya Pradesh	Bhopal	West Bengal	Calcutta
Maharashtra	Bombay		

Union Territories

Andaman and Nicobar Islands; Chandigarh; Dadra and Nagar Haveli; Delhi; Daman and Diu; Lakshadweep; Pondicherry.

States Reorganization. The Constitution, which came into force on 26 Jan. 1950, provided for 9 Part A States (Assam, Bihar, Bombay, Madhya Pradesh, Madras, Orissa, Punjab, Uttar Pradesh and West Bengal) which corresponded to the previous governors' provinces; 8 Part B States (Hyderabad, Jammu and Kashmir,

Madhya Bharat, Mysore, Patalia-East Punjab (PEPSU), Rajasthan, Saurashtra and Travancore-Cochin) which corresponded to Indian states or unions of states; 10 Part C States (Ajmer, Bhopal, Bilaspur, Coorg, Delhi, Himachal Pradesh, Kutch, Manipur, Tripura and Vindhya Pradesh) which corresponded to the chief commissioners' provinces; and Part D Territories and other areas (*e.g.*, Andaman and Nicobar Island). Part A States (under governors) and Part B States (under rajpramukhs) had provincial autonomy with a ministry and elected assembly. Part C States (under chief commissioners) were the direct responsibility of the Union Government, although Kutch, Manipur and Tripura had legislatures with limited powers. Andhra was formed as a Part A State on its separation from Madras in 1953. Bilaspur was merged with Himachal Pradesh in 1954.

The States Reorganization Act, 1956, abolished the distinction between Parts A, B and C States and established two categories for the units of the Indian Union to be called States and Territories. The following were the main territorial changes: the Telugu districts of Hyderabad were merged with Andhra; Mysore absorbed the whole Kannada-speaking area (including Coorg, the greater part of 4 districts of Bombay, 3 districts of Hyderabad and 1 district of Madras); Bhopal, Vindhya Pradesh and Madhya Bharat were merged with Madhya Pradesh, which ceded 8 Marathi-speaking districts to Bombay; the new state of Kerala, comprising the majority of Malayalam-speaking peoples, was formed from Travancore-Cochin with a small area from Madras; Patalia-East Punjab was included in Punjab; Kutch and Saurashtra in Bombay; and Ajmer in Rajasthan; Hyderabad ceased to exist.

On 1 May 1960 Bombay State was divided into two parts: 17 districts (including Saurashtra and Kutch) in the north and west became the new state of Gujarat; the remainder was renamed the state of Maharashtra.

In Aug. 1961 the former Portuguese territories of Dadra and Nagar Haveli became a Union territory. The Portuguese territory of Goa and the smaller territories of Daman and Diu, occupied by India in Dec. 1961, were constituted a Union territory in March 1962. In Aug. 1962 the former French territories of Pondicherry, Karikal, Mahé and Yanaon were formally transferred to India and became a Union territory. In Sept. 1962 the Naga Hills Tuensang Area was constituted a separate state under the name of Nagaland. On 1 Nov. 1966, under the Punjab Reorganization Act 1966, a new state of Haryana and a new Union Territory of Chandigarh were created from parts of Punjab (India); for details, *see* pp. 662 and 695. On 26 Jan. 1971 Himachal Pradesh became a state. In 1972 the North East Frontier Agency and Mizo hill district were made Union territories (as Arunachal Pradesh and Mizoram) and Manipur, Meghalaya and Tripura full states. Sikkim became a state in 1975. Statehood for Mizoram was passed by parliament in July 1986; for Arunachal Pradesh in Dec. 1986; for Goa in May 1987.

Report of the States Reorganization Commission. Government of India. Delhi, 1956

ANDHRA PRADESH

HISTORY. Andhra was constituted a separate state on 1 Oct. 1953, on its partition from Madras, and consisted of the undisputed Telugu-speaking area of that state. To this region was added, on 1 Nov. 1956, the Telangana area of the former Hyderabad State, comprising the districts of Hyderabad, Medak, Nizamabad, Karimnaga, Warangal, Khammam, Nalgonda and Mahbubnaga, parts of the Adilabad district and some taluks of the Raichur, Gulbarga and Bidar districts, and some revenue circles of the Nanded district. On 1 April 1960, 221·4 sq. miles in the Chingleput and Salem districts of Madras were transferred to Andhra Pradesh in exchange for 410 sq. miles from Chittoor district. The district of Prakasam was formed on 2 Feb. 1970. Hyderabad was split into 2 districts on 15 Aug. 1978. A new district, Vizianagaram, was formed in 1979.

AREA AND POPULATION. Andhra Pradesh is in south India and is bounded south by Tamil Nadu, west by Karnataka, north and northwest by Maharashtra, northeast by Madhya Pradesh and Orissa, east by the Bay of Bengal.

The state has an area of 275,100 sq. km and a population (1981 census) of 53·5m. Density, 195 per sq. km. Growth rate 1971–81, 23·19%. The principal language is Telugu. Cities with over 250,000 population (1981 census), see p. 632. Other large cities (1981): Nellore (237,065); Kakinada (226,409); Kurnool (206,362); Nizamabad (183,061); Eluru (168,154); Machilipatnam (138,503); Anantapur (119,531); Tenali (119,257); Tirupati (115,292); Vizianagaram (114,806); Adoni (108,939); Proddatur (107,070); Cuddapah (103,125); Bheemavaram (101,894).

CONSTITUTION AND GOVERNMENT. Andhra Pradesh has a unicameral legislature; the Legislative Council was abolished in June 1985. There are 295 seats in the Legislative Assembly. At the election of Nov. 1989, the Congress I party took office.

For administrative purposes there are 23 districts in the state. The capital is Hyderabad.

Governor: Krishna Kant.
Chief Minister: Dr Marri Chenna Reddy.

BUDGET. The budget (estimate) for 1989–90 showed total receipts on revenue account of Rs 5,198·29 crores, and expenditure of Rs 5,382·71 crores.

ENERGY AND NATURAL RESOURCES

Electricity. There are 6 hydro-electric plants including Machkund, Upper Sileru and Nizam Sagar and 5 thermal stations including Nellore and Kothagudam. Installed capacity, 1988–89, 3,615 mw., power generated 13,850m. kwh. In 1988–89 there were 26,881 electrified villages and (1987-88) 828,000 electric pump sets.

Gas. Natural gas has been found in the Krishna–Godavari basin, where 3 gas-powered generating stations are proposed.

Water. In 1988–89, 15 large and 36 medium irrigation projects were in hand. The Telugu Ganga joint project with Tamil Nadu, now in execution, will irrigate about 233,000 hectares, besides supplying drinking water to Madras city (Tamil Nadu).

Minerals The state is an important producer of asbestos and barytes. Other important minerals are copper ore, coal, iron and limestone, steatite, mica and manganese.

Agriculture. There were (1987–88) about 12·1m. hectares of cropped land, of which 3·87m. hectares were under food-grains. Production (1987-88): Foodgrains, 9·7m. tonnes; rice, 7·7m.; wheat, 4,200; pulses, 644,000.

Livestock (1983 provisional): Cattle, 13·12m.; buffaloes, 8·7m.; goats, 5·5m.; sheep, 7·5m.

Forests. In 1989 it was estimated that forests occupy 23·2% of the total area of the state or 63,771 sq. km; main forest products are teak, eucalyuptus, cashew, casuarina, softwoods and bamboo.

Fisheries. Production 1986–87, 140,841 tonnes of marine fish and 107,950 tonnes of inland water fish. The state has a coastline of 974 km.

INDUSTRY. The main industries are textile manufacture, sugar-milling machine tools, pharmaceuticals, cement, chemicals, glass, fertilizers, electronic equipment, heavy electrical machinery, aircraft parts and paper-making. There is an oil refinery at Vishakhapatnam, where India's major shipbuilding yards are situated. In 1989 a steel plant was under construction at Vishakhapatnam and a railway repair shop at Tirupathi is functioning.

Cottage industry includes the manufacture of carpets, wooden and lacquer toys, brocades, bidriware, filigree and lace-work. The wooden toys of Nirmal and Kondapalli are particularly well known. Sericulture is developing rapidly. District Industries Centres have been set up to promote small-scale industry.

Tourism is growing; the main centres are Hyderabad, Nagarjunasagar, Warangal, Araku Valley, Horsley Hills and Tirupathi.

COMMUNICATIONS

Roads. On 31 March 1988 there were 2,352 km of national highways, 8,387 km of state highways, 25,487 km of major district roads, 85,156 km of other roads. Number of vehicles: 732,000 motor cycles and scooters, 71,190 cars and jeeps, 63,760 goods vehicles and 12,000 buses.

Railways. In 1988–89 there were 5,021 route-km of railway, of which 3,032 km were broad gauge.

Aviation. There are airports at Hyderabad, Tirupathi, Vijayawada and Vishakapatnam, with regular scheduled services to Bombay, Delhi, Calcutta, Bangalore and Madras. A feeder airline serves Rajahmundry and Cuddapah.

Shipping. The chief port is Vishakhapatnam. There are minor ports at Kakinada, Machilipatnam, Bheemunipatnam, Narsapur, Krishnapatnam, Vadarevu and Kalingapatnam.

JUSTICE, RELIGION, EDUCATION AND WELFARE

Justice. The high court of Judicature at Hyderabad has a Chief Justice and 25 puisne judges.

Religion. At the 1981 census Hindus numbered 47,525,681; Moslems, 4,533,700; Christians, 1,433,327; Jains 18,642; Sikhs, 16,222; Buddhists, 12,930.

Education. In 1981, 29·94% of the population were literate (39·13% of men and 20·52% of women). There were, in 1987–88 46,086 primary schools (7,095,199 students); 5,724 middle/senior basic (1,964,653); 5,186 high schools (836,258). Education is free for children up to 14.

There were in 1988–89, 365 degree colleges, 660 junior colleges and 13 universities: Osmania University, Hyderabad; Andhra University, Waltair; Sri Venkateswara University, Tirupathi; Kakatiya University, Warangal; Nagarjuna University, Guntur; Sri Jawaharlal Nehru Technological University, Hyderabad; Central Institute of English and Foreign Languages, Hyderabad; A.P. Agricultural University, Hyderabad; Sri Krishnadevaraya University, Anantapur; Smt. Padmarathi Mahila Vishwaridyalayam (University for Women), Tirupathi; A. P. Open University, Hyderabad; Telugu University, Hyderabad and A. P. Medical University, Vijayawada.

Health. There were (1987-88) 1,486 allopathic hospitals and dispensaries, 394 Ayurvedic dispensaries, 197 Unani and 280 homeopathy dispensaries. There were also 181 nature cure hospitals and 1,241 primary health centres. Number of beds in hospitals was 29,263.

ARUNACHAL PRADESH

HISTORY. In Jan. 1972 the former North East Frontier Agency of Assam was created a Union Territory. In Dec. 1986, by the Constitution (55th Amendment) and State of Arunachal Pradesh Acts, the Territory became the 24th state of India.

AREA AND POPULATION. The state is in north-east India and is bounded by Assam, Bhután, China and Burma; it comprises the former frontier divisions of Kameng, Tirap, Subansiri, Siang and Lohit; it has an area of 83,743 sq. km and a population (1981 census) of 631,839; growth, 1971–81, 34·34%; density, 7 per sq. km.

The state is mainly tribal; there are over 80 tribes using about 50 tribal dialects.

CONSTITUTION AND GOVERNMENT. There is a Legislative Assembly of 30 members. Elections were to be held during 1987. The capital is Itanagar.

Lieut.-Governor: R. D. Pradhan.
Chief Minister: Gegong Apang.

ENERGY AND NATURAL RESOURCES

Electricity. Power generated (1988): 42·01m. units. 1,042 out of 3,257 villages have electricity.

Oil and Coal. Crude oil reserves are estimated at 1·5m. tonnes and coal 850,000 tonnes.

Forestry. Area under forest, 51,540 sq. km; revenue from forestry (1988) Rs 141m.

Industries. The state has a light roofing-sheet factory, a fruit processing plant and a cement plant. There are 15 medium and 1,887 small industries. Most of the medium industries are forest-based.

Roads. Total length of roads maintained by the Public Works Department 7,923 km.

EDUCATION AND WELFARE

Education. There were (1988) 1,027 primary schools, 220 middle schools, 84 high and higher secondary schools and 4 colleges. Arunachal University was established in 1985.

Health. There are (1990) 13 hospials, 5 community health centres, 20 primary health centres and 125 sub-centres. There are also 2 TB hospitals and 4 leprosy hospitals. Total number of beds, 2,158.

ASSAM

HISTORY. Assam first became a British Protectorate at the close of the first Burmese War in 1826. In 1832 Cachar was annexed; in 1835 the Jaintia Hills were included in the East India Company's dominions, and in 1839 Assam was annexed to Bengal. In 1874 Assam was detached from Bengal and made a separate chief commissionership. On the partition of Bengal in 1905, it was united to the Eastern Districts of Bengal under a Lieut.-Governor. From 1912 the chief commissionership of Assam was revived, and in 1921 a governorship was created. On the partition of India almost the whole of the predominantly Moslem district of Sylhet was merged with East Bengal (Pakistan). Dewangiri in North Kamrup was ceded to Bhután in 1951. The Naga Hill district, administered by the Union Government since 1957, became part of Nagaland in 1962. The autonomous state of Meghalaya within Assam, comprising the districts of Garo Hills and Khasi and Jaintia Hills, came into existence on 2 April 1970, and achieved full independent statehood in Jan. 1972, when it was also decided to form a Union Territory, Mizoram (now a state), from the Mizo Hills district.

AREA AND POPULATION. Assam is in eastern India, almost separated from central India by Bangladesh. It is bounded west by West Bengal, north by Bhután and Arunachal Pradesh, east by Nagaland, Manipur and Burma, south by Meghalaya, Bangladesh, Mizoram and Tripura. The area of the state is now approximately 78,438 sq. km. Its population (1981 census) 19·9m. Density, 254 per sq. km. Growth rate since 1971, 36·09%. Principal towns with population (1971) are; Guwahati, 122,981; Dibrugarh, 80,344; Tinsukia, 55,392; Nowgong, 52,892; Silchar, 52,612. The principal language is Assamese.

The central government is surveying the line of a proposed boundary fence to prevent illegal entry from Bangladesh.

CONSTITUTION AND GOVERNMENT. Assam has a unicameral legislature of 126 members. In Dec. 1985 elections were held and an Asom Gana Parishad government was returned. The temporary capital is Dispur.

Governor: Shri H. Joshi.
Chief Minister: Prafulla Kumar Mahanta.

BUDGET. The budget estimates for 1988–89 showed receipts of Rs 1,968 crores and expenditure of Rs 2,025 crores. Plan allocation for 1990-91 is Rs 675 crores.

ENERGY AND NATURAL RESOURCES

Electricity. In 1987–88 there was an installed capacity of 503 mw and 17,897 villages (out of 21,995) with electricity. New power stations are under construction at Lakwa, and Karbi-Langpi hydro-electricity project.

Oil and Gas. Assam contains important oilfields and produces about 50% of India's crude oil. Production (1986-87): Crude oil, 4·97m. tonnes; gas, 1,003m. cu. metres.

Water. In 1987–88, 222,451 hectares were irrigated; 2 major and 11 medium projects were in hand.

Minerals. Coal production (1988), 1,017,103 tonnes. The state also has limestone, refractory clay, dolomite, and corundum.

Agriculture. There are 844 tea plantations, and growing tea is the principal industry. Production in 1985, 352m. kg, over 50% of Indian tea. Over 72% of the cultivated area is under food crops, of which the most important is rice. Total foodgrains, 1987–88, 2·9m. tonnes. Main cash crops: Jute, tea, cotton, oilseeds, sugarcane, fruit and potatoes. Wheat has been introduced recently and yielded 105,800 tonnes in 1987–88. Cattle are important.

Forestry. There are 17,423 sq. km of reserved forests under the administration of the Forest Department and 10,063·81 sq. km of unclassed forests, altogether about 30% of the total area of the state. Revenue from forests, 1987–88, Rs 1,721·66 lakhs.

INDUSTRY. Sericulture and hand-loom weaving, both silk and cotton, are important home industries together with the manufacture of brass, cane and bamboo articles. Hand-loom weaving of silk is stimulated by state and central development schemes. There are two silk-spinning mills and 26 cotton-mills. The main heavy industry is petro-chemicals; there are 3 oil refineries with 1 under construction in 1990. Other industries include manufacturing paper, nylon, fertilizers, sugar, jute and plywood products, rice and oil milling.

COMMUNICATIONS

Roads. In 1984–85 there were 26,352 km of road maintained by the Public Works Department in Assam, including national highway. There were 216,475 motor vehicles in the state in 1988.

Railways. The route km of railways in 1988 was 2,338 km, of which 262·09 km are broad gauge.

Aviation. Daily scheduled flights connect the principal towns with the rest of India. There are airports at Guwahati, Tezpur, Jorhat, North Lakhimpur, Silchar and Dibrugarh.

Shipping. Water transport is important in Lower Assam; the main waterway is the Brahmaputra River. Cargo carried in 1986 was 65,000 tonnes.

JUSTICE, RELIGION, EDUCATION AND WELFARE

Justice. The seat of the High Court is Guwahati. It has a Chief Justice and 6 puisne judges.

Religion. At the 1971 census Hindus numbered 10,604,618; Moslems, 3,592,124; Christians, 381,010; Buddhists, 22,565; Jains, 12,914; Sikhs, 11,920.

Education. In 1987–88 there were 26,670 primary/junior basic schools; 5,181 middle/senior basic; 2,745 high/higher secondary. There were 160 colleges for general education, 3 medical colleges, 3 engineering and 1 agricultural, 9 teacher-training colleges and 3 universities. There is a fisheries college at Raha.

Health. In 1988 there were 100 hospitals (9,520 beds) and 835 primary health centres.

BIHAR

The state contains the ethnic areas of North Bihar, Santhalpargana and Chota Nagpur. In 1956 certain areas of Purnea and Manbhum districts were transferred to West Bengal.

AREA AND POPULATION. Bihar is in north India and is bounded north by Nepál, east by West Bengal, south by Orissa, south-west by Madhya Pradesh and west by Uttar Pradesh. The area of Bihar is 173,877 sq. km and its population (1981 census), 69,914,734, a density of 402 per sq. km. Growth rate since 1971, 24·06%. Population of principal towns, *see* p. 632. Other large towns (1981): Muzaffarpur, 190,416; Darbhanga, 176,301; Biharsharif, 151,343; Munger, 129,260; Arrah, 125,111; Katihar, 122,005; Dhanbad, 120,221; Chapra, 111,564; Purnea, 109,649; Bermo, 101,502.

The official language is Hindi (55·8m. speakers at the 1981 census), the second, Urdu (6·9m.), the third, Bengali (2m.).

CONSTITUTION AND GOVERNMENT. Bihar has a bicameral legislature. The Legislative Assembly consists of 324 elected members and the Council, 96. After the elections in March 1985 a Congress government was returned. For the purposes of administration the state is divided into 10 divisions covering 39 districts. The capital is Patna.

Governor: Yunus Saleem.
Chief Minister: Dr Jagannath Mishra.

BUDGET. The budget estimates for 1989–90 show total receipts of Rs 37,346·7m and expenditure of Rs 37,574·7m. Plan allocation, 1989–90, Rs 18,000m.

ENERGY AND NATURAL RESOURCES

Electricity. Installed capacity (1985–86) 1,379·68 mw. Power generated (1987–88), 4,085m. kw.; there were 39,466 villages with electricity. Hydro-electric projects in hand will add about 149·2mw. capacity.

Minerals. Bihar is very rich in minerals, with about 40% of national production. There are huge deposits of copper, capatite and kyanite and sizeable deposits of coal, mica and china clay. Bihar is a principal producer of iron ore. Other important minerals: Manganese, limestone, graphite, chromite, asbestos, barytes, dolomite, feldspar, columbite, pyrites, saltpetre, glass sands, slate, lead, silver, building stones and radio-active minerals. Value of production (1987) Rs 16,280m.

Agriculture. About 26% of the cultivable area is irrigated. Cultivable land, 11·6m. hectares, of a total area of 17·4m. hectares. Total cropped area, 1987–88, 8·5m. hectares. Production (1987–88): Rice, 4·6m. tonnes; wheat, 2·8m.; total foodgrains, 9·1m. Other food crops are maize, rabi and pulses. Main cash crops are jute, sugarcane, oilseeds, tobacco and potato.

Forests in 1984 covered 30,896 hectares. There are 12 protected forests.

INDUSTRY. Main plants are the Tata Iron and Steel Co., the Tata Engineering and Locomotive Co., the steel plant at Bokaro, oil refinery at Barauni, Heavy Engineering Corporation and Foundry Forge project at Ranchi, and aluminium plant at Muri. Other important industries are machine tools, fertilizers, electrical engineering, sugar-milling, paper-milling, silk-spinning, manufacturing explosives and cement. There is a copper smelter at Ghatsila and a zinc plant at Tundo. There were 54,396 small industries in 1985.

TOURISM. The main tourist centres are Bodh Gaya, Patna, Nalanda, Jamshedpur, Sasaram, Betla, Hazaribagh and Vaishali.

COMMUNICATIONS

Roads. In 1983–84 the state had 84,185 km of highway. Passenger transport has been nationalized in 7 districts. There were 289,717 motor vehicles in March 1988.

Railways. The North Eastern, South Eastern and Eastern railways traverse the state; route-km, 1987–88, 5,305.

Aviation. There are airports at Patna and Ranchi with regular scheduled services to Calcutta and Delhi.

Shipping. The length of waterways open for navigation is 900 miles.

JUSTICE, RELIGION, EDUCATION AND WELFARE

Justice. There is a High Court (constituted in 1916) at Patna, and a bench at Ranchi, with a Chief Justice, 32 puisne judges and 4 additional judges.

Police. The police force is under a Director General of Police; in 1986 there were 1,036 police stations.

Religion. At the 1981 census Hindus numbered 58,011,070; Moslems, 9,874,993; Christians, 740,186; Sikhs, 77,704; Jains, 27,613; Buddhists, 3,003.

Education. At the census of 1981 the number of literates was 18·32m. (26·2%: males 38·11%; females, 13·62%). There were, 1987–88, 3,740 high and higher secondary schools with 779,580m. pupils, 12,164 middle schools with 1·97m. pupils, 51,391 primary schools with 8,145,536 pupils. Primary and middle schools had 103,130 teachers, higher secondary, high schools and junior colleges, 45,314. Education is free for children aged 6-11.

There were 9 universities in academic year 1987–88; Patna University (founded 1917) with 18,895 students (1984–85); Bihar University, Muzaffarpur (1952) with 60 constituent colleges, 7 affiliated colleges and 75,370 students (1984–85); Bhagalpur University (1960) with 50,473 students (1985–86); Ranchi University (1960) with 88,771 students (1985–86); Kameswar Singh Darbhanga Sanskrit University (1961); Magadha University, Gaya (1962) and Lalit Narayan Mithila University (1972), Darbhanga, Bisra Agricultural University, Ranchi (1980), Rajendra Agricultural University, Samastipur (1970).

Health. In 1985 there were 1,289 hospitals and dispensaries.

Das, A. N., *Agrarian Movements in India: Studies in 20th Century Bihar*. London, 1982

GOA

HISTORY. The coastal area was captured by the Portuguese in 1510 and the inland area was added in the 18th century. In Dec. 1961 Portuguese rule was ended and Goa incorporated into the Indian Union as a Territory together with Daman and Diu. Goa was granted statehood as a seperate unit on 30 May 1987. Daman and Diu remained Union Territories (see p. 696).

AREA AND POPULATION. Goa, bounded on the north by Maharashtra and on the east and south by Karnataka, has a coastline of 105 km. The area is 3,702 sq. km. (Population, 1981 census, 1,007,749). Density, 272 per sq. km. Panaji is the largest town; population (urban agglomeration, 1981) 76,839. The languages spoken are Konkani (official language), Marathi, Hindi, English.

GOVERNMENT. The Indian Parliament passed legislation in March 1962 by which Goa became a Union Territory with retrospective effect from 20 Dec. 1961.

On 30 May 1987 Goa attained statehood. It is represented by 2 elected and 2 nominated representatives in Parliament. There is a Legislative Assembly of 40 members. The Capital is Panaji. There are 183 village Panchayats.

Governor: Kurshid Alam Khan.
Chief Minister: Pratapsing Rane.

BUDGET. The total budget for 1988–89 was Rs 154·91 crores. Annual plan 1989–90, Rs 110 crores.

ENERGY AND NATURAL RESOURCES

Electricity. Eight towns and 397 villages were supplied with electric power by March 1989. Goa receives its power supply from the states of Maharashtra, Karnataka and Madhya Pradesh.

Minerals. Resources include manganese ore and iron ore, both of which are exported. Iron ore production (1977-78) 13·6m. tonnes. There are also reserves of bauxite, lime stone and clay.

Agriculture. Agriculture is the main occupation, important crops are rice, pulses, ragi, mango, cashew and coconuts. Area under paddy (1988–89) 43,274 hectares of high yielding grains (production 193,779 tonnes). Area under pulses 8,475, sugarcane 1,706, groundnut 570.

Government poultry and dairy farming schemes produced 30m. eggs and 35,000m. litres of milk in 1988–89.

Fisheries. Fish is the state's staple food. In 1988–89 the catch of seafish was 41,408·3 tonnes (value Rs 1144·53 lakhs). There is a coastline of about 104 km and about 3,453 active fishing vessels.

INDUSTRY. In 1988–89 there were 41 large and medium industrial projects and 4,231 small units registered. Production included: Nylon fishing nets, ready made clothing, pesticides, pharmaceuticals and footwear.

In 1989 46 small-scale industry units employed 25,124 persons.

ROADS. In 1988 there were 4,514·15 km of motorable roads (National Highway, 224 km).

JUSTICE, EDUCATION AND WELFARE

Justice. There is a bench of the Bombay High Court at Panaji.

Education. In 1987-88 there were 994 primary, 119 middle, 332 high and higher secondary schools. There were also 2 engineering colleges, 1 medical college, 1 teacher-training college and 11 other colleges. Goa University, Bambolin (1985) has 18 colleges affiliated to it.

Health. There were (1987-88) 115 hospitals (3,713 beds), 239 rural medical dispensaries, health and sub-health centres and 256 family planning units.

Hutt, A., *Goa: A Traveller's Historical and Architectural Guide*. Buckhurst Hill, 1988

GUJARAT

HISTORY. On 1 May 1960, as a result of the Bombay Reorganization Act, 1960, the state of Gujarat was formed from the north and west (predominantly Gujarati-speaking) portion of Bombay State, the remainder being renamed the state of Maharashtra. Gujarat consists of the following districts of the former state of Bombay: Banas Kantha, Mehsana, Sabar Kantha, Ahmedabad, Kaira, Panch Mahals, Vadodara, Bharuch, Surat, Dangs, Amreli, Surendranagar, Rajkot, Jamnagar, Junagadh, Bhavnagar, Kutch, Gandhinagar and Bulsar.

AREA AND POPULATION. Gujarat is in western India and is bounded north by Pakistan and Rajasthan, east by Madhya Pradesh, south-east by Maharashtra, south and west by the Indian ocean and Arabian sea. The area of the state is 196,024 sq. km and the population at the 1981 census (revised) was 34,086,000; a density of 174 per sq. km. Growth rate 1971–81, 27·2%. The chief cities, *see* p. 632. Gujarati and Hindi in the Devanagari script are the official languages.

CONSTITUTION AND GOVERNMENT. Gujarat has a unicameral legislature, the Legislative Assembly, which has 182 elected members. After the elections in March 1985 a Congress government was returned.

The capital is Gandhinagar. There are 19 districts.

Governor: Ram Krishna Trivedi.
Chief Minister: Madhavinh Solanki.

BUDGET. The budget estimates for 1989–90 showed receipts of Rs 3,219 crores and expenditure of Rs 3,500 crores.

ENERGY AND NATURAL RESOURCES

Electricity. In 1988 the total generating capacity was 3,526 mw of electricity, serving 338,046 towns and villages.

Water. The Karjan Dam, under construction, will provide a reservoir of 630m. cu. metres capacity; it is designed to irrigate 56,000 hectares through 2 main canals.

Oil and Gas. There were crude oil and gas reserves in 23 fields in 1982–83. Production: Crude oil, 4·53m. tonnes; gas, 685m. cu. metres in 1986.

Minerals. Chief minerals produced in 1986 (in tonnes) included lime stone (5·2m.), agate stone (849), calcite (1,089), quartz and silica (212,316), bauxite (467,447), crude china clay (15,427), refined china clays (7,233), dolomite (249,893), crude fluorite (121,262), calcareous and sea sand (537,000) and lignite (1·07m.). Value of production (1987) Rs 9,150m. Enormous reserves of coal were found under the Kalol and Mehsana oil and gas fields in May 1980. The deposit, mixed with crude petroleum, is estimated at 100,000m. tonnes, extending over 500 km.

Agriculture. In 1985–86 drought was exceptionally severe. Cropped area, 1983–84, was 11·9m. hectares. Area and production of principal crops, 1986–87 (in 1,000 hectares and 1,000 tonnes): Rice, 511 and 446; groundnuts, 1,825 and 1,292; cotton, 1,366 and 1,093,000 bales of 170 kg. Total cropped area 4·14m. hectares producing 3·1m. tonnes.

Livestock (1982): Buffaloes, 4·43m.; other cattle, 6·93m.; sheep, 2·33m.; goats, 3·26m.; horses and ponies, 24,000.

Fisheries. There were (1987) 80,204 people engaged in fisheries. There were 13,811 fishing vessels (5,313 motor vessels). The catch for 1986–87 (estimate) was 340,000 tonnes.

INDUSTRY. Gujarat is one of the 4 most industrialized states. In 1985 there were more than 70,000 small-scale units and 13,000 factories including 1,328 textile factories. There were 167 industrial estates. Principal industries are textiles, general and electrical engineering, petrochemicals, machine tools, heavy chemicals, pharmaceuticals, dyes, sugar, soda ash and cement. Large fertilizer plants have been set up and there is an oil refinery at Koyali near Vadodara, with a developing petrochemical complex.

State production of soda-ash is 90·4% of national output, and of salt, about 60%. Salt production (1986) 6·6m. tonnes; cement production, 2·4m. tonnes.

COMMUNICATIONS

Roads. In 1987 there were 61,560 km of roads. Gujarat State Transport Corporation operated 14,609 routes. Number of vehicles, 1,239,141.

Railways. In 1988 the state had 5,553 route km of railway line.

Aviation. Ahmedabad is the main airport. There are 5 services daily between

Ahmedabad and Bombay, Jaipur and Delhi. There are 8 other airports: Baroda, Bhavnagar, Bhuj, Jamnagar, Kandla, Keshod, Porbandar and Rajkot.

Shipping. The largest port is Kandla. There are 39 other ports, 11 intermediate, 28 minor.

Post. There were (March 1984–85) 9,000 post offices, 2,000 telegraph offices. Ahmedabad has direct dialling telephone connexion (or night S.T.D.) with 273 cities and 16 foreign countries. There were 227,000 telephone connexions in the state.

JUSTICE, RELIGION, EDUCATION AND WELFARE

Justice. The High Court of Judicature at Ahmedabad has a Chief Justice and 18 puisne judges.

Religion. At the 1971 census Hindus numbered 23,835,471; Moslems, 2,249,055; Jains, 451,578; Christians, 109,341; Sikhs, 18,233; Buddhists, 5,469.

Education. In 1981 the number of literates was 14·85m. (43·7%). Primary and secondary education up to Standard XI are free. Education above Standard XII is free for girls. In 1987–88 there were 12,950 primary schools and 16,000 middle/senior basic schools. There were 4,746 secondary schools including 1,298 higher secondary schools.

There are 9 universities in the state. Gujarat University, Ahmedabad, founded in 1949, is teaching and affiliating; it has 147 affiliated colleges. The Maharaja Sayajirao University of Vadodara (1949) is residential and teaching. The Sardar Patel University, Vallabh-Vidyanagar, (1955) has 16 constituent and affiliated colleges, Saurashtra University at Rajkot with 64 affiliated colleges, and South Gujarat at Surat with 39. Bhavnagar University (1978) is residential and teaching with 8 affiliated colleges. North Gujarat University was established at Patan in 1986. Gujarat Vidyapith at Ahmedabad is deemed a university under the University Grants Commission Act. There were also 1 agricultural and 1 Ayurvedic university.

There are 10 engineering colleges, 26 polytechnics, 6 medical colleges, 6 agricultural, 3 pharmaceutical and 2 veterinary. There are also 218 arts, science and commerce colleges and 39 teacher-training colleges.

Health. In 1987 there were 1,854 hospitals (22,595 beds), 457 primary health centres and 5,551 sub-centres.

Rushbrook Williams, L. F., *The Black Hills: Kutch in History and Legend*. London, 1958
Desai, I. F., *Untouchability in Rural Gujarat*. Bombay, 1977

HARYANA

HISTORY. The state of Haryana, created on 1 Nov. 1966 under the Punjab Reorganization Act, 1966, was formed from the Hindi-speaking parts of the state of Punjab (India). It comprises the districts of Hissar, Mohindergarh, Gurgaon, Rohtak and Karnal; Bhiwani, Faridabad, Jind, Kurukshetra, Sirsa, Sonipat, Ambala.

AREA AND POPULATION. Haryana is in north India and is bounded north by Himachal Pradesh, east by Uttar Pradesh, south and west by Rajasthan and north-west by Punjab. Delhi forms an enclave on its eastern boundary. The state has an area of 44,212 sq. km and a population (1981) of 12,922,618; density, 291 per sq. km. Growth rate, 1971–81, 28·75%. The principal language is Hindi.

CONSTITUTION AND GOVERNMENT. The state has a unicameral legislature with 90 members. In Dec. 1988 Lok Dal held 66 seats; Bharatiya Janata, 17; Congress (I), 4; others, 2; vacant, 1. The state shares with Punjab (India) a High Court, a university and certain public services. The capital (shared with Punjab) is Chandigarh (*see* p. 695). Its transfer to Punjab, intended for 1986, has been postponed. There are 12 districts.

Governor: Danik Lal Mandal.
Chief Minister: O. Prakash Chautala.

BUDGET. Budget estimates for 1989–90 show income of Rs 1,666 crores and expenditure of Rs 1,623 crores. Annual plan 1990–91, Rs 700 crores.

ENERGY AND NATURAL RESOURCES

Electricity. Approximately 1,000 mw are supplied to Haryana, mainly from the Bhakra Nangar system. In 1988–89 installed capacity was 2,177 mw and all the villages had electric power.

Minerals. Minerals include placer gold, barytes and rare earths. Value of production, 1987–88, Rs 40m.

Agriculture. Haryana has sandy soil and erratic rainfall, but the state shares the benefit of the Sutlej-Beas scheme. Agriculture employs over 82% of the working population; in 1981 there were about 900,000 holdings (average 3·7 hectares), and the gross irrigated area was 2·04m. hectares. Area under high-yielding varieties of foodgrains, 1988–89, 2·76m. hectares; foodgrain production was 9·46m. tonnes; sugar (gur), oilseeds, and wheat, are important.

Forests cover 3·3% of the state.

INDUSTRY. Haryana has a large market for consumer goods in neighbouring Delhi. In 1988–89 there were 394 large and medium scale industries employing 120,000 and producing goods worth over Rs 10,000m. There were 86,200 small units. The main industries are cotton textiles, agricultural machinery, woollen textiles, scientific instruments, glass, cement, paper and sugar milling, cars, tyres and tubes, motor cycles, bicycles, steel tubes, engineering goods, electrical and electronic goods. An oil refinery is being set up at Karnal, capital outlay, Rs 1,300 crores.

COMMUNICATIONS

Roads. There were (1988–89) 21,250 km of metalled roads, linking all villages. Road transport is nationalized. There were 139,890 motor vehicles in 1982–83.

Railways. The state is crossed by lines from Delhi to Agra, Ajmer, Ferozepur and Chandigarh. Route km, 1987–88, 1,500. The main stations are at Ambala and Kurukshetra.

Aviation. There is no airport within the state but Delhi is on its eastern boundary.

JUSTICE, EDUCATION AND WELFARE

Justice. Haryana shares the High Court of Punjab and Haryana at Chandigarh.

Education. In 1981 the number of literates was 4·67m. In 1987-88 there were 8,496 schools and colleges with 3,021,333 attending. This includes 5,048 primary schools, 2,094 high and higher secondary schools, 1,222 middle schools and 132 colleges of arts, science and commerce, 2 engineering colleges and 1 medical college. There are 3 universities.

Health. There were (1988-89) 77 hospitals (10,621 beds), 33 health centres, 124 dispensaries and 333 primary health centres.

HIMACHAL PRADESH

HISTORY. The territory came into being on 15 April 1948 and comprised 30 former Hill States. The state of Bilaspur was merged with Himachal Pradesh in 1954. The 6 districts were: Mahasu, Sirmur, Mandi, Chamba, Bilaspur and Kinnuar. On 1 Nov. 1966, under the Punjab Reorganization Act, 1966, certain parts of the State of Punjab (India) were transferred to Himachal Pradesh. These comprise the districts of Shimla, Kullu, Kangra, and Lahaul and Spiti; and parts of Hoshiarpur, Ambala and Gurdaspur districts.

AREA AND POPULATION. Himachal Pradesh is in north India and is bounded north by Kashmir, east by Tibet, south-east by Uttar Pradesh, south by Haryana, south-west and west by Punjab. The area of the state is 55,673 sq. km and it had a population at the 1981 census of 4,280,818. Density, 77 per sq. km. Growth rate, 1971–81, 23·71%. Principal languages are Hindi and Pahari.

CONSTITUTION AND GOVERNMENT. Full statehood was attained, as the 18th state of the Union, on 25 Jan. 1971.

On 1 Sept. 1972 districts were reorganized and 2 new districts created, Hamirpur and Una, making a total of 12. The capital is Shimla.

There is a unicameral legislature. After the elections in March 1985 a Congress government was returned.

Governor: B. Rachaiah.

Chief Minister: Virbhadra Singh.

BUDGET. Budget estimates for 1989–90 showed revenue receipts of Rs 817·82 (1988–89, Rs 790·43 crores) crores (including central assistance and centrally-sponsored schemes) and expenditure on revenue account of Rs 757·16 crores (Rs 494·79 crores). The capital account showed expenditure of Rs 264·14 crores (Rs 226·19 crores). Annual plan, 1989–90, Rs 300 crores.

ENERGY AND NATURAL RESOURCES

Electricity. In 1989, all the 16,916 villages had electricity. Power generation is the first priority of the 7th five-year plan.

Water. An artificial confluence of the Sutlej and Beas rivers has been made, directing their united flow into Govind Sagar Lake. Other major rivers are Ravi, Chenab and Yamuna.

Minerals. The state has rock salt, slate, gypsum, limestone, barytes, dolomite and pyrites.

Agriculture. Farming employs 71% of the people. Irrigated area is 17% of the area sown. Main crops are seed potatoes, wheat, maize, rice and fruits such as apples, peaches, apricots, nuts, pomegranates.

Production of foodgrains (1988-89) 1·34m. tonnes.

Livestock (1982 census): Buffaloes, 617,000; other cattle, 2,174,000; goats and sheep, 2·15m.

Forestry. (1989) Himachal Pradesh forests cover 38·3% of the state and supply the largest quantities of coniferous timber in northern India. The forests also ensure the safety of the catchment areas of the Yamuna, Sutlej, Beas, Ravi and Chenab rivers. Commercial felling of green trees has been totally halted and forest working nationalized. Efforts are being made to bring 50% of the area of the state under forests by the turn of the century.

INDUSTRY. The main sources of employment are the forests and their related industries; there are factories making turpentine and rosin. The state also makes fertilizers, cement and TV sets. There is a foundry and a brewery. Other industries include salt production and handicrafts, including weaving.

COMMUNICATIONS

Roads. The national highway from Chandigarh runs through Shimla; other main highways from Shimla serve Kullu, Manali, Kangra, Chemba and Pathankot. The rest are minor roads. Pathankot is also on national highways from Punjab to Kashmir. Length of roads (1987) 20,279 km, number of vehicles 5,194.

Railways. There is a line from Chandigarh to Shimla, and the Jammu-Delhi line runs through Pathankot. A Nangal-Talwara rail link has been approved by the central government and was in an advanced stage of completion in 1989.

Aviation. The state has airports at Bhuntar near Kullu and at Jubbarharthi near Shimla. Another airport, at Gaggal in Kangra district, was nearing completion in 1989.

JUSTICE, EDUCATION AND WELFARE

Justice. The state has its own High Court at Shimla.

Education. There were (1987-88) 7,009 primary schools, 1,075 middle schools, 930 high and higher secondary schools, 37 arts, science and commerce colleges, and 3 universities. The universities are Himachal Pradesh University, Shimla (1970) with 27 affiliated colleges, Himachal Pradesh Agricultural University, Palanpur (1978) and Dr Y. S. Parmar University of Horticulture and Forestry, Solan (1985). In 1981, 42·48% of the population was literate.

Health. There were (1987) 68 hospitals (7,036 beds), 180 primary health centres and 646 allopathic and Ayurvedic dispensaries.

JAMMU AND KASHMIR

HISTORY. The state of Jammu and Kashmir, which had earlier been under Hindu rulers and Moslem sultans, became part of the Mogul Empire under Akbar from 1586. After a period of Afghan rule from 1756, it was annexed to the Sikh kingdom of the Punjab in 1819. In 1820 Ranjit Singh made over the territory of Jammu to Gulab Singh. After the decisive battle of Sobraon in 1846 Kashmir also was made over to Gulab Singh under the Treaty of Amritsar. British supremacy was recognized until the Indian Independence Act, 1947, when all states decided on accession to India or Pakistan. Kashmir asked for standstill agreements with both. Pakistan agreed, but India desired further discussion with the Government of Jammu and Kashmir State. In the meantime the state became subject to armed attack from the territory of Pakistan and the Maharajah acceded to India on 26 Oct. 1947, by signing the Instrument of Accession. India approached the UN in Jan. 1948; India-Pakistan conflict ended by ceasefire in Jan. 1949. Further conflict in 1965 was followed by the Tashkent Declaration of Jan. 1966. Following further hostilities between India and Pakistan a ceasefire came into effect on 17 Dec. 1971, followed by the Simla Agreement in July 1972, whereby a new line of control was delineated bilaterally through negotiations between India and Pakistan and came into force on 17 Dec. 1972.

AREA AND POPULATION. The state is in the extreme north and is bounded north by China, east by Tibet, south by Himachal Pradesh and Punjab and west by Pakistan. The area is 222,236 sq. km, of which about 78,932 sq. km is occupied by Pakistan and 42,735 sq. km by China; the population of the territory on the Indian side of the line, 1981 census, was 5,987,389. Growth rate, 1971–81, 29·57%. The official language is Urdu; other commonly spoken languages are Kashmiri (3·1m. speakers at 1981 census), Hindi (1m.), Dogri, Balti, Ladakhi and Punjabi.

CONSTITUTION AND GOVERNMENT. The Maharajah's son, Yuvraj Karan Singh, took over as Regent in 1950 and, on the ending of hereditary rule (17 Oct. 1952), was sworn in as Sadar-i-Riyasat. On his father's death (26 April 1961) Yuvraj Karan Singh was recognized as Maharajah by the Indian Government; he decided not to use the title while he was elected head of state.

The permanent Constitution of the state came into force in part on 17 Nov. 1956 and fully on 26 Jan. 1957. There is a bicameral legislature; the Legislative Council has 36 members and the Legislative Assembly has 76. Since the 1967 elections the 6 representatives of Jammu and Kashmir in the central House of the People are directly elected; there are 4 representatives in the Council of States. After a period of President's rule, a National Conference–Indira Congress coalition government was formed in March 1987.

Kashmir Province has 8 districts and Jammu Province has 6 districts. Srinagar (population, 1981, 586,038) is the summer and Jammu (206,135) the winter capital.

Governor: (Vacant).
Chief Minister: (Vacant).

BUDGET. Expenditure (1989-90) Rs 806·60 crores; revenue, Rs 981·71 crores.

ENERGY AND NATURAL RESOURCES

Electricity. Installed capacity (1987–88) 212 mw.; 5,976 villages had electricity.

Minerals. Minerals include coal, bauxite and gypsum.

Agriculture. About 80% of the population are supported by agriculture. Rice, wheat and maize are the major cereals. The total area under food crops (1984-85) was estimated at 872,000 hectares. Total foodgrains produced, 1987–88, 966,400 tonnes. Fruit is important; production, 1985–86, 800,000 tonnes; exports, Rs 2,000m.

The Agrarian Reforms Act came into force in July 1978; the Debtors Relief Act and the Restriction of Mortgage Properties Act also alleviate rural distress. The redistribution of land to cultivators is continuing.

Livestock (1982): Cattle, 2,325,200; buffaloes, 5,631,000; goats, 1,003,900; sheep, 1,908,700; horses, 973,000, and poultry, 2,406,760.

Forestry. Forests cover about 20,891·89 sq. km., forming an important source of revenue, besides providing employment to a large section of the population. About 20,174 sq. km of forests yield valuable timber; state income in 1985–86 was Rs 477m.

INDUSTRY. There are 2 central public sector industries and 30 medium-scale (latter employing 6,468 in 1984). The largest industrial complex is the Bari Brahmara estate in Jammu which covers 320 acres and accommodates diverse manufacturing, as does the Khanmuh estate. The Sopore industrial area in Kashmir Division is intended for industries based on horticulture. There are 19,000 small units (1985–86) employing 86,713. The main traditional handicraft industries are silk spinning, wood-carving, papier-maché and carpet-weaving. Value of total industrial production, 1983–84, Rs 1,573m.

COMMUNICATIONS

Roads. Kashmir is linked with the rest of India by the motorable Jammu-Pathankot road. The Jawahar Tunnel, through the Banihal mountain, connects Srinagar and Jammu, and maintains road communication with the Kashmir Valley during the winter months. In 1985 there were 9,965 km of roads.

There were 58,000 motor vehicles in 1984–85.

Railways. Kashmir is linked with the Indian railway system by the line between Jammu and Pathankot; route km of railways in the state, 1987–88, 77 km.

Aviation. Major airports, with daily service from Delhi, are at Srinagar and Jammu. There is a third airport at Leh. Srinagar airport is being developed as an international airport.

Post. There were 1,457 post offices in 1985, 82 telephone exchanges and approximately 18,000 private telephones.

JUSTICE, RELIGION, EDUCATION AND WELFARE

Justice. The High Court, at Srinagar and Jammu, has a Chief Justice and 4 puisne judges.

Religion. The majority of the population, except in Jammu, are Moslems. At the 1981 census Moslems numbered 3,843,451; Hindus, 1,930,448; Sikhs, 133,675; Buddhists, 69,706; Christians, 8,481; Jains, 1,576.

Education. The proportion of literates was 27% in 1981. Education is free. There were (1987–88) 1,078 secondary schools, 2,282 middle and 8,610 primary schools. Jammu University (1969) has 3 constituent and 11 affiliated colleges, with 8,903 students (1985–86); Kashmir University (1948) has 6 constituent, 15 affiliated and 6 oriental institutions (11,900 students); the third university is Sher-E-Kashmir University of Agricultural Sciences and Technology. There are 2 medical colleges, 1 engineering and technology college, 2 polytechnics, 8 oriental colleges and an Ayurvedic college.

Health. In 1984–85 there were 50 hospitals, 93 primary health centres and 425 units, 679 clinics and dispensaries, and 483 other units. There were (1986) 3,442 doctors. There is a National Institute of Medical Sciences.

Bamzai, P. N. K., *A History of Kashmir.* Delhi, 1962
Gupta, S., *Kashmir: A Study in IndiaPakistan Relations.* London, 1967

KARNATAKA

HISTORY. The state of Karnataka, constituted as Mysore under the States Reorganization Act, 1956, brought together the Kannada-speaking people distributed in 5 states, and consisted of the territories of the old states of Mysore and Coorg, the Bijapur, Kanara and Dharwar districts and the Belgaum district (except one taluk) in former Bombay, the major portions of the Gulbarga, Raichur and Bidar districts in former Hyderabad, and South Kanara district (apart from the Kasaragod taluk) and the Kollegal taluk of the Coimbatore district in Madras. The state was renamed Karnataka in 1973.

AREA AND POPULATION. The state is in south India and is bounded north by Maharashtra, east by Andhra Pradesh, south by Tamil Nadu and Kerala, west by the Indian ocean and north-east by Goa. The area of the state is 191,791 sq. km, and its population (1981 census), 37,135,714, an increase of 26·43% since 1971. Density, 194 per sq. km. Kannada is the language of administration and is spoken by about 66% of the people. Other languages include Telugu (8·17%), Urdu (9%), Marathi (4·5%), Tamil (3·6%), Tulu and Konkani. Principal cities, *see* p. 632.

CONSTITUTION AND GOVERNMENT. Karnataka has a bicameral legislature. The Legislative Council has 75 members. The Legislative Assembly consists of 224 elected members. After elections in Nov. 1989 the Congress-I party formed a government.

The state has 20 districts (of which Bangalore Rural is one) in 4 divisions: Bangalore, Mysore, Belgaum and Gulbarga. The capital is Bangalore.

Governor: P. Venkatasubiah.
Chief Minister: Veerendra Patil.

BUDGET. Budget estimates for 1989–90 showed receipts, Rs 3,429·24 crores; expenditure, Rs, 3,551·41 crores. Plan allocation 1990-91, Rs 1,120 crores.

ENERGY AND NATURAL RESOURCES

Electricity. In 1987 the state's installed capacity was 2,530 mw. Electricity generated, 1987–88, 7,570m. kwh.

Water. About 2·25m. hectares were irrigated in 1986-87.

Minerals. Karnataka is an important source of gold and silver. The estimated reserves of high grade iron ore are 5,000m. tonnes. These reserves are found mainly in the Chitradurga belt. The National Mineral Development Corporation of India has indicated total reserves of nearly 1,000m. tonnes of magnesite and iron ore (with an iron content ranging from 25 to 40) which have been found in Kudremukh Ganga-Mula region in Chickmagalur District. Value of production (1987-88) Rs 138 crores. The estimated reserves of manganese are over 275m. tonnes.

Limestone is found in many regions; deposits (1986) are about 4,248m. tonnes.

Karnataka is the largest producer of chromite. It is one of the only two states of India producing magnesite. The other minerals of industrial importance are corundum and garnet.

Agriculture. Agriculture forms the main occupation of more than three-quarters of the population. Physically, Karnataka divides itself into four regions–the coastal region, the southern and northern 'maidan' or plain country, comprising roughly the districts of Bangalore, Tumkur, Chitaldrug, Kolar, Bellary, Mandya and Mysore, and the 'malnad' or hill country, comprising the districts of Chickmagalur, Hassan and Shimoga. Rainfall is heavy in the 'malnad' tracts, and in this area there is dense forest. The greater part of the 'maidan' country is cultivated. Coorg district is essentially agricultural.

The main food crops are rice and jowar, and ragi which is also about 30% of the national crop. Total foodgrains production (1987–88), 6·35m. tonnes of which rice, 1·90m. tonnes. Sugar, groundnut, castor-seed, safflower, mulberry silk and cotton are important cash crops. The state grows about 70% of the national coffee crop.

Production, 1987–88 (1,000 tonnes): Sugar-cane, 14,464; cotton, 576 bales (170 kg).

Livestock (1986): Buffaloes, 3,647,967; other cattle, 11,300,223; sheep, 4,791,650; goats, 4,546,928.

Forestry. Total forest in the state (1986–87) is 3,060,840 acres, producing sandal wood, bamboo and other timbers, and ivory.

INDUSTRY. There were 12,436 factories employing 803,285 in March 1988. The Vishweswaraya Iron and Steel Works is situated at Bhadravati, while at Bangalore are national undertakings for the manufacture of aircraft, machine tools, light engineering and electronics goods. Other industries include textiles, vehicle manufacture, cement, chemicals, sugar, paper, porcelain and soap. In addition, much of the world's sandalwood is processed, the oil being one of the most valuable productions of the state. Sericulture is a more important cottage industry giving employment, directly or indirectly, to about 2·7m. persons; production of raw silk, 1986–87, 4,671 tonnes, over two-thirds of national production.

COMMUNICATIONS

Roads. In 1987–88 the state had 113,094 km of roads. There were (31 March 1988) 1,031,131 motor vehicles.

Railways. In 1987 there were 3,029 km of railway (including 154 km of narrow gauge) in the state.

Aviation. There are airports at Bangalore, Mangalore, Bellary and Belgaum, with regular scheduled services to Bombay, Calcutta, Delhi and Madras.

Shipping. Mangalore is a deep-water port for the export of mineral ores. Karwar is being developed as an intermediate port.

JUSTICE, RELIGION, EDUCATION AND WELFARE

Justice. The seat of the High Court is at Bangalore. It has a Chief Justice and 24 puisne judges.

Religion. At the 1981 census there were 31,906,793 Hindus; 4,104,616 Moslems; 764,449 Christians; 297,974 Jains; 42,147 Buddhists; 6,401 Sikhs.

Education. The number of literates, according to the 1981 census, was 38·5m. In 1986–87 the state had 24,143 primary schools, 4,864 high schools, 173 polytechnic and 18 medical colleges, 50 engineering and technology colleges, 372 arts, science and commerce colleges and 8 universities. Education is free up to pre-university level.

Universities: Mysore (1916); Karnatak (1950) at Dharwar; University of Agricultural Sciences (1964) at Hebbal, Bangalore; Gulbarga, and Mangalore. Mysore has 6 university and 117 affiliated colleges (1983–84); Karnatak, 5 and 115; Bangalore, 126 affiliated; Hebbal, 8 constituent colleges.

The Indian Institute of Science, Bangalore, has the status of a university.

Health. There were in 1987, 2,872 hospitals, dispensaries and family welfare centres.

KERALA

HISTORY. The state of Kerala, created under the States Reorganization Act, 1956, consists of the previous state of Travancore-Cochin, except for 4 taluks of the Trivandrum district and a part of the Shencottah taluk of Quilon district. It took over the Malabar district (apart from the Laccadive and Minicoy Islands) and the Kasaragod taluk of South Kanara (apart from the Amindivi Islands) from Madras State.

AREA AND POPULATION. Kerala is in south India and is bounded north by Karnataka, east and south-east by Tamil Nadu, south-west and west by the Indian ocean. The state has an area of 38,863 sq. km. The 1981 census showed a population of 25,453,680; density of population was 655 per sq. km (highest of any state). Growth rate, 1971–81, 19%. Population of principal cities, *see* p. 632.

Languages spoken in the state are Malayalam, Tamil and Kannada.

The physical features of the land fall into three well-marked divisions: (1) the hilly tracts undulating from the Western Ghats in the east and marked by long spurs, extensive ravines and dense forests; (2) the cultivated plains intersected by numerous rivers and streams; and (3) the coastal belt with dense coconut plantations and rice fields.

CONSTITUTION AND GOVERNMENT. The state has a unicameral legislature of 140 elected (and one nominated) members including the Speaker. After the elections of March 1987 the Indian National (I) Congress Party and allies held 60 seats, the Left Front (CPI, CPI (M) and allies), 78.

The state has 14 districts. The capital is Trivandrum.

Governor: Dr Sarup Singh.
Chief Minister: E. K. Nayanar.

BUDGET. Budget estimates for 1989–90 showed total receipts of Rs 2,093·78 crores, expenditure Rs 2,265·53 crores. Annual Plan expenditure, 1989–90 Rs 526 crores.

ENERGY AND NATURAL RESOURCES

Electricity. Installed capacity (March 1988), 1,476·5 mw.; energy generated in 1987–88 was 4,094m. kw. The Idukki hydro-electric plant produced 2,314·4m. kwh, the Sabarigiri scheme 962·99m.

Minerals. The beach sands of Kerala contain monazite, ilmenite, rutile, zircon, sillimanite, etc. There are extensive whiteclay deposits; other minerals of commercial importance include mica, graphite, limestone, quartz sand and lignite. Iron ore has been found at Kozhikode (Calicut).

Agriculture. Area under irrigation in 1986-87 was 299,264 hectares, 19 irrigation projects were under execution in 1987-88. The chief agricultural products are rice, tapioca, coconut, arecanut, cashewnut, oilseeds, pepper, sugar-cane, rubber, tea, coffee and cardamom. About 98% of Indian black pepper and about 95% of Indian rubber is produced in Kerala. Area and production of principal crops, 1986–87 (in 1,000 hectares and 1,000 tonnes): Rice, 664, 1,134; black pepper, 129, 30·4; arecanut, 58, 10,563 (million nuts); coconuts, 706, 3,173 (million nuts); tea, 34·6, 50·33; coffee, 65·6, 23·5; rubber, 348, 202; tapioca, 194, 3,292.

Livestock (1982, provisional); Buffaloes, 408,584; other cattle, 3·1m.; goats, 2m. In 1985–86 milk production was 1·34m. tonnes. Egg production, 1,397m.

Forestry. Forest occupied 1,081,509 hectares in 1987. About 24% of the area is comprised of forests, including teak, sandal wood, ebony and blackwood and varieties of softwood. Net forest revenue, 1986–87, Rs 48·18 crores, from timber, bamboos, reeds and ivory.

Fisheries. Fishing is a flourishing industry; the catch in 1986-87 was about 334,400 tonnes. Fish exports, Rs 183·94 crores in 1987-88.

INDUSTRIES. Most of the major industrial concerns are either owned or sponsored by the Government. Among the privately owned factories are the numerous cashew and coir factories. Other important factory industries are rubber, tea, tiles, oil, textiles, ceramics, fertilizers and chemicals, zinc-smelting, sugar, cement, rayon, glass, matches, pencils, monazite, ilmenite, titanium oxide, rare earths, aluminium, electrical goods, paper, shark-liver oil, etc.

The number of factories registered under the Factories Act 1948 on 31 Dec. 1984 was 11,489, with daily average employment of 292,000.

Among the cottage industries, coir-spinning and handloom-weaving are the most important, forming the means of livelihood of a large section of the people. Other industries are the village oil industry, ivory carving, furniture-making, bell metal, brass and copper ware, leather goods, screw-pines, mat-making, rattan work, bee-keeping, pottery, etc. These have been organized on a co-operative basis.

COMMUNICATIONS

Roads. In 1986–87 there were 110,649 km of roads in the state; national highways, 839 km. There were 414,000 motor vehicles in 1986–87.

Railways. There is a coastal line from Mangalore (Karnataka) which serves Cannanore, Mahé, Kozhikode (Calicut), Ernakulam (for Cochin), Quilon and Trivandrum, and connects them with main towns in Tamil Nadu. In 1987–88 there were 927 route-km of track.

Aviation. There are airports at Calicut, Cochin and Trivandrum with regular scheduled services to Delhi, Bombay and Madras; international flights leave from Trivandrum.

Shipping. Port Cochin, administered by the central government, is one of India's major ports; in 1983 it became the out-port for the Inland Container Depot at Coimbatore (Tamil Nadu). There are 13 other ports and harbours.

JUSTICE, RELIGION, EDUCATION AND WELFARE

Justice. The High Court at Ernakulam has a Chief Justice and 14 puisne judges and 3 additional judges.

Religion. The majority are Hindus; other important faiths are Christianity and Islam. There are also some Jains.

Education. Kerala is the most literate Indian State with 17m. literates at the 1981 census (70·7%). Education is free up to the age of 14.

In 1987–88 there was a total school enrolment of 5·81m. students. There were 6,817 lower primary schools 2,885 middle schools and 2,542 high schools.

Kerala University (established 1937) at Trivandrum, is affiliating and teaching; in 1986–87 it had 43 affiliated arts and science colleges. The University of Cochin is federal, and for post-graduate studies only. The University of Calicut (established 1968) is teaching and affiliating and has 92 affiliated colleges. Kerala Agricultural University (established 1971) has 8 constituent colleges. Gandhiji University at Kottayam was established in 1983 and has 56 affiliated colleges.

Health. There were 141 allopathic, 97 Ayurvedic and 715 homeo hospitals, and 577 health centres in 1988.

MADHYA PRADESH

HISTORY. Under the provisions of the States Reorganization Act, 1956, the State of Madhya Pradesh was formed on 1 Nov. 1956. It consists of the 17 Hindi districts of the previous state of that name, the former state of Madhya Bharat (except the Sunel enclave of Mandsaur district), the former state of Bhopal and Vindhya Pradesh and the Sironj subdivision of Kotah district, which was an enclave of Rajasthan in Madhya Pradesh.

For information on the former states, *see* THE STATESMAN'S YEAR-BOOK , 1958, pp. 180–84.

AREA AND POPULATION. The state is in central India and is bounded north by Rajasthan and Uttar Pradesh, east by Bihar and Orissa, south by Andhra Pradesh and Maharashtra, west by Gujarat. Madhya Pradesh is the largest Indian state in size, with an area of 443,446 sq. km. In respect of population it ranks sixth. Population (1981 census), 52,178,844, an increase of 25·15% since 1971. Density, 118 per sq. km.

Cities with over 250,000 population, *see* p. 632. Other large cities (1981): Sagar, 174,770; Ratlam, 155,578; Burhanpur, 140,886; Durg, 118,507; Khandwa, 114,725; Rewa, 100,641.

The number of persons speaking each of the more prevalent languages (1981 census) were: Hindi, 43,870,242; Urdu, 1,131,288; Marathi, 1,184,128; Gujarati, 581,084.

CONSTITUTION AND GOVERNMENT. Madhya Pradesh is one of the 9 states for which the Constitution provides a bicameral legislature, but the Vidhan Parishad or Upper House (to consist of 90 members) has yet to be formed. The Vidhan Sabha or Lower House has 320 elected members. Following the election of March 1985, a Congress government was returned, with 250 out of 350 seats.

For administrative purposes the state has been split into 11 divisions with a Commissioner at the head of each; the headquarters of these are located at Bhopal, Bilaspur, Gwalior (2), Hoshangabad, Indore, Jabalpur, Raipur, Rewa, Sagar and Ujjain. There are 45 districts.

The seat of government is at Bhopal.

Governor: Mahmood Ali.

Chief Minister: Shyama Charan Shukla.

BUDGET. Budget estimates for 1989–90 showed total revenue of Rs 10,872·60 crores and expenditure of Rs 10,902·67 crores.

ENERGY AND NATURAL RESOURCES

Electricity. Madhya Pradesh is rich in low-grade coal suitable for power generation, and also has immense potential hydro-electric energy. Power generated, 12,460m. kwh. in 1986–87. The thermal power stations are at Korba in Bilaspur district, Amarkantak in Shahdol district and Satpura in Betul district; new stations are being built. The only hydro-electric power station is at Gandhi Sagar lake in Mandsaur district; this, with a maximum water surface of 165 sq. miles, is the biggest man-made lake in Asia.

Water. Major irrigation projects include the Chambal Valley scheme (started in 1952 with Rajasthan), the Tawa project in Hoshangabad district, the Barna and Hasdeo schemes, the Mahanadi canal system and schemes in the Narmada valley at Bargi and Narmadasagar.

Minerals. The state has extensive mineral deposits including coal (35% of national deposits), iron ore (30%) and manganese (50%), bauxite (44%), ochre, sillimanite, limestone, dolomite, rock phosphate, copper, lead, tin, fluorite, barytes, china clay and fireclay, corundum, gold, diamonds, pyrophyllite and diaspore, lepidolite, asbestos, vermiculite, mica, glass sand, quartz, felspars, bentonite and building stone. New and very large reserves of copper were found in the Malanjkhand area in 1986.

In 1987 the output of major minerals was (in tonnes): Coal, 34·2m.; limestone, 11·2m.; diamonds, 15,000 carats; iron ore, 7·7m.; manganese ore, 200,000. Value of production, 1987, Rs 11,120m.

Agriculture. Agriculture is the mainstay of the state's economy and 80% of the people are rural. Over 42% of the land area is cultivable, of which 14% is irrigated. The Malwa region abounds in rich black cotton soil, the low-lying areas of Gwalior, Bundelkhand and Baghelkhand and the Chhatisgarh plains have a lighter sandy soil, while the Narmada valley is formed of deep rich alluvial deposits. Production of principal crops, 1986–87 (in tonnes): Foodgrains, 13·52m. of which rice, 4·15m.; sugar, 70,000; oilseeds, 1·25m., and cotton, 240,000 bales of 170 kg each.

Livestock (1985–86): Buffaloes, 6,861,000; other cattle, 26,503,000; sheep, 1,120,000; goats, 7,636,000; horses and ponies, 112,000.

Forestry. In 1982 155,411 sq. km, or about 35% of the state's area was covered by forests. The forests are chiefly of sal, saja, bija, bamboo and teak. They are the chief source in India of best-quality teak; they also provide firewood for about 60% of domestic fuel needs, and form valuable watershed protection. Forest revenue, 1986–87, Rs 3,070m.

INDUSTRY. The major industries are the steel plant at Bhilai, Bharat Heavy Electricals at Bhopal, the aluminium plant at Korba, the security paper mills at Hoshangabad, the Bank Note Press at Dewas, the newsprint mill at Nepanagar and alkaloid factory at Neemuch, cement factories, vehicle factory, ordnance factory, and gun carriage factory. There are also 23 textile mills, 7 of them nationalized.

The Bhilai steel plant near Durg is one of the 6 major steel mills. A power station at Korba (Bilaspur) with a capacity of 420 mw serves Bhilai, the aluminium plant and the Korba coalfield.

The heavy electricals factory was set up by the Government of India at Bhopal during the second-plan period. This is India's first heavy electrical equipment factory and also one of the largest of its type in Asia. It makes a variety of highly complicated equipment required for generation, transmission, distribution and utilization of electric power.

Other industries include cement, sugar, straw board, paper, vegetable oil, refractories, potteries, textile machinery, steel casting and rerolling, industrial gases, synthetic fibres, drugs, biscuit manufacturing, engineering, tools, rayon and art silk. The number of heavy and medium industries in the state is 193, with 181 ancillary industries; the number of small-scale industries in production is 77,360. Thirty-nine out of 45 districts in the state are categorized as industrially backward districts.

The main industrial development agencies are Madhya Pradesh Financial Corporation, Madhya Pradesh Audyogik Vikas Nigam Ltd, Madhya Pradesh State Industries Corporation, Madhya Pradesh Laghu Udyog Nigam, Madhya Pradesh State Textile Corporation, Madhya Pradesh Handicrafts Board, Khadi and Village Industries Board and Madhya Pradesh State Mining Corporation.

The state is known for its traditional village and home crafts such as handloom weaving, best developed at Chanderi and Maheshwar, toys, pottery, lacework, woodwork, zari work, leather work and metal utensils. The ancillary industries of dyeing, calico printing and bleaching are centred in areas of textile production.

COMMUNICATIONS

Roads. Total length of roads in 1985–86 was 154,000 km, of which 58,230 km were surfaced. In 1985–86 there were 643,000 motor vehicles.

Railways. Bhopal, Bilaspur, Katni, Khandwar and Ratlam are important junctions for the central and northern networks. Route km of railways (1987–88), 5,764 km.

Aviation. There are airports at Bhopal, Indore, Jabalpur, Khajuraho and Raipur with regular scheduled services to Bombay, Calcutta and Delhi.

JUSTICE, RELIGION AND EDUCATION

Justice. The High Court of Judicature at Jabalpur has a Chief Justice and 21 puisne judges.

Religion. At the 1981 census Hindus numbered 48,504,575; Moslems, 2,501,919; Christians, 351,972; Buddhists, 75,312; Sikhs, 143,020, Jains, 444,960.

Education. The 1981 census showed 14·5m. people to be literate. Education is free for children aged up to 14.

In 1984–85 there were 377 higher educational institutions. Primary schools had 6·1m. pupils and higher secondary schools, 1,035,005 pupils.

There are 12 universities in Madhya Pradesh: Dr. Hari Singh Gour University (established 1946), at Sagar, had 73 affiliated colleges and 40,000 students in 1984–85; Rani Durgavati University (1957) had 28 affiliated colleges and 9,954 students; Vikram University (1957), at Ujjain, had 63 affiliated colleges and 34,425 students; Indira Kala Sangeet Vishwavidyalaya (1956), at Khairagarh, had 33 affiliated colleges and 6,720 students on roll (this university teaches music and fine arts); Devi Ahilya University (1964) had 26 affiliated colleges and 25,881 students; Jiwagi University (1963), at Gwalior, had 54 affiliated colleges and 46,696 students; Jawaharlal Nehru Krishi University (1964), at Jabalpur, had 11 constituent colleges and 2,994 students in 1985–86; Ravishankar University (1964), at Raipur, had 61 affiliated colleges. In 1987–88 there were 375 colleges of arts, science and commerce, 19 teacher-training colleges, and 11 engineering and technology colleges, 6 medical colleges, 14 polytechnics and 63 technical-industrial arts and craft schools.

MAHARASHTRA

HISTORY. Under the States Reorganization Act, 1956, Bombay State was formed by merging the states of Kutch and Saurashtra and the Marathi-speaking areas of Hyderabad (commonly known as Marathwada) and Madhya Pradesh (also called Vidarbha) in the old state of Bombay, after the transfer from that state of the Kannada-speaking areas of the Belgaum, Bijapur, Kanara and Dharwar districts which were added to the state of Mysore, and the Abu Road taluka of Banaskantha district, which went to the state of Rajasthan.

By the Bombay Reorganization Act, 1960, which came into force 1 May 1960, 17 districts (predominantly Gujarati-speaking) in the north and west of Bombay State became the new state of Gujarat, and the remainder was renamed Maharashtra.

The state of Maharashtra consists of the following districts of the former Bombay State: Ahmednagar, Akola, Amravati, Aurangabad, Bhandara, Bhir, Buldana, Chanda, Dhulia (West Khandesh), Greater Bombay, Jalgaon (East Khandesh), Kolaba, Kolhapur, Nagpur, Nanded, Nasik, Osmanabad, Parbhani, Pune, Ratnagiri, Sangli, Satara, Sholapur, Thana, Wardha, Yeotmal; certain portions of Thana and Dhulia districts have become part of Gujarat.

AREA AND POPULATION. Maharashtra is in central India and is bounded north and east by Madhya Pradesh, south by Andhra Pradesh, Karnataka and Goa, west by the Indian ocean and north-west by Daman and Gujarat. The state has an area of 307,690 sq. km. The population at the 1981 census (revised) was 62,784,171 (an increase of 24·36% since 1971), of whom about 30m. were Marathi-speaking. Density, 204 per sq. km. The area of Greater Bombay was 603 sq. km. and its population 8,227,000. For other principal cities, *see* p. 632.

CONSTITUTION AND GOVERNMENT. Maharashtra has a bicameral legislature. The Legislative Council has 78 members. The Legislative Assembly has 288 elected members and 1 member nominated by the Governor to represent the Anglo-Indian community. Following the election of March 1985 Congress (I) held 211 seats; Janata, 21; BJP, 16; Shetkari Karnagar Paksha, 13; Congress (S), 2; BCP, 2; MCP, 2; Independent, 20; other 1.

The Council of Ministers consists of the Chief Minister, 16 other Ministers, and 19 Ministers of State.

The capital is Bombay.

Governor: C. Subramaniam
Chief Minister: Sarad Pawar.

BUDGET. Budget estimates, 1989–90, show a deficit of Rs 212·55 crores.

ENERGY AND NATURAL RESOURCES

Electricity. Installed capacity, 31 March 1989, 7,658 mw. (5,634 mw. thermal, 1,436 mw. hydro-electricity and 160 mw. nuclear).

Minerals. Value of main mineral production, 1987, Rs 313 crores. The state has coal, silica, sand, dolomite, kyanite, sillimanite, limestone, iron ore, manganese, bauxite.

Agriculture. About 23·43% of the cropped area is irrigated. In 1988–89 there was heavy rain in 16 of the state's 30 districts. The monsoon-season harvest was feeble, and the winter-season harvest was good.

In normal seasons the main food crops are rice, wheat, jowar, bajri and pulses. Main cash crops: Cotton, sugar-cane, groundnuts.

Livestock (1982 census): Buffaloes, 3,972,000; other cattle, 16,162,000; sheep, 2,671,000; goats, 7,705,000; horses and ponies, 49,000; poultry, 19,844,000.

Forestry. Forests occupy 20·8% of the state.

INDUSTRY. Industry is concentrated mainly in Bombay, Pune and Thana. The main groups are chemicals and products, textiles, electrical and non-electrical machinery, petroleum and products, and food products. The state industrial development corporation had invested Rs 5,600 crores in 8,800 industrial units by 1989.

COMMUNICATIONS

Roads. On 31 March 1989 there were 169,921 km of roads, of which 121,207 km were surfaced. There were 2,056,357 motor vehicles on 31 March 1989, of which 557,142 were in Greater Bombay. Passenger and freight transport has been nationalized.

Railways. The total length of railway on 31 March 1988 was 5,440 km; 61% was broad gauge, 18% metre gauge and 20% narrow gauge. The main junctions and termini are Bombay, Manmad, Akola, Nagpur, Pune and Sholapur.

Aviation. The main airport is Bombay, which has national and international flights. Nagpur airport is on the route from Bombay to Calcutta and there are also airports at Pune and Aurangabad.

Shipping. Maharashtra has a coastline of 720 km. Bombay is the major port, and there are 48 minor ports.

JUSTICE, RELIGION, EDUCATION AND WELFARE

Justice. The High Court has a Chief Justice and 45 judges. The seat of the High Court is Bombay, but it has benches at Nagpur, Aurangabad and Panaji (Goa).

Religion. At the 1981 census Hindus numbered 51,109,457; Moslems, 5,805,785; Buddhists, 3,946,149; Christians, 795,464; Jains, 939,392; Sikhs, 107,255. Other religions, 155,692; religion not stated, 1,394.

Education. The number of literates, according to the 1981 census, was 29·6m.

The total number of recognized institutions in 1988–89 was 67,148, with 16,314,000 students. Higher and secondary schools numbered 10,274 with 6,287,000 pupils; primary schools, 56,173, with 9,948,000 pupils; pre-primary schools, 701 with 78,000.

Bombay University, founded in 1857, is mainly an affiliating university. It has 159 colleges with a total (1988–89) of 162,000 students. Colleges in Goa can affiliate to Bombay University. Nagpur University (1923) is both teaching and affiliating. It has 117 colleges with 55,000 students. Pune University, founded in 1948, is teaching and affiliating; it has 191 colleges and 97,000 students. The SNDT Women's University had 25 colleges with a total of 26,000 students. Marathwada University, Aurangabad, was founded in 1958 as a teaching and affiliating body to control colleges in the Marathwada or Marathi-speaking area, previously under Osmania University; it has 133 colleges and 55,000 students. Shiwaji University, Kolhapur, was established in 1963 to control affiliated colleges previously under Pune University. It has 138 colleges and 56,000 students. Amravarti University has 88 colleges and 35,000 students.

Health. In 1987 there were 768 hospitals (100,363 beds), 1,799 dispensaries and 1,539 primary health centres.

Statistical Information: The Director of Publicity, Sachivalaya, Bombay.
Tindall, G., *City of Gold*, London, 1982

MANIPUR

HISTORY. Formerly a state under the political control of the Government of India, Manipur, on 15 Aug. 1947, entered into interim arrangements with the Indian Union and the political agency was abolished. The administration was taken over by the Government of India on 15 Oct. 1949 under a merger agreement, and it is centrally administered by the Government of India through a Chief Commissioner. In 1950–51 an Advisory form of Government was introduced. In 1957 this was replaced by a Territorial Council of 30 elected and 2 nominated members. Later in 1963 a Legislative Assembly of 30 elected and 3 nominated members was established under the Government of Union Territories Act 1963. Because of the unstable party position in the Assembly, it had to be dissolved on 16 Oct. 1969 and President's Rule introduced. The status of the administrator was raised from Chief Commissioner to Lieut.-Governor with effect from 19 Dec. 1969. On the 21 Jan. 1972 Manipur became a state and the status of the administrator was changed from Lieut.-Governor to Governor.

AREA AND POPULATION. The state is in north-east India and is bounded north by Nagaland, east by Burma, south by Burma and Mizoram, and west by Assam. Manipur has an area of 22,327 sq. km and a population (1981) of 1,420,953. Density, 64 per sq. km. Growth rate, 1971–81, 32·46%. The valley, which is about 1,813 sq. km, is 2,600 ft above sea-level. The hills rise in places to nearly 10,000 ft, but are mostly about 5,000–6,000 ft. The average annual rainfall is 65 in. The hill areas are inhabited by various hill tribes who constitute about one-third of the total population of the state. There are about 40 tribes and sub-tribes falling into two main groups of Nagas and Kukis. Manipuri and English are the official languages. A large number of dialects are spoken, while Hindi is gradually becoming prevalent.

CONSTITUTION AND GOVERNMENT. With the attainment of statehood, Manipur has a Legislative Assembly of 60 members, of which 19 are from reserved tribal constituencies. There are 8 districts. Capital, Imphal (population, 1981, 155,639). Presidential rule was imposed in Feb. 1981.

Governor: Chintamani Panigrahi.
Chief Minister: R. K. Jaichandra Singh.

BUDGET. Budget estimates for 1988–89 show revenue of Rs 3,540m. and expenditure of Rs 3,460m. Plan allocation 1989–90, Rs 1,420m.

ENERGY AND NATURAL RESOURCES

Electricity. Installed capacity (1987) is 24·67 mw. from diesel and hydro-electric generators. This has been augmented since 1981 by the North Eastern Regional Grid. In May 1988 there were 887 villages with electricity.

Water. The main power, irrigation and flood-control schemes are the Loktak Lift Irrigation scheme (irrigation potential, 40,000 hectares; the Singda scheme (potential 4,000 hectares, and improved water supply for Imphal); the Thoubal scheme (potential 34,000 hectares, 7·5 mw. of electricity and 10 MGD of water supply), and four other large projects. By 1986–87 more than 43,500 hectares had been irrigated.

Agriculture. Rice is the principal crop; with wheat, maize and pulses. Total foodgrains, 1987–88, 323,100 tonnes.

Agricultural work force, about 348,000. Only 210,000 hectares are cultivable, of which 186,000 are under paddy. Fruit and vegetables are important in the valley, including pineapple, oranges, bananas, mangoes, pears, peaches and plums. Soil erosion, produced by shifting cultivation, is being halted by terracing.

Forests. Forests occupy about 15,154 sq km. The main products are teak, jurjan, pine; there are also large areas of bamboo and cane, especially in the Jiri and Barak river drainage areas, yielding about 300,000 tonnes annually. Total revenue from forests, 1987–88, Rs 17·1m.

Fisheries. Landings in 1981–82, 3,450 tonnes.

INDUSTRY. Handloom weaving is a popular industry. Larger-scale industries include sugar, cement, starch and glucose. Sericulture produces about 45 tonnes of raw silk annually. Estimated non-agricultural work force, 240,000.

COMMUNICATIONS. A national highway from Kazirangar (Assam) runs through Imphal to the Burmese frontier. There are no railways, but the highway runs through Dimapur which has a rail-head, 215 km from Imphal. There is an airport at Imphal with regular scheduled services to Delhi and Calcutta. Length of road (1987) 3,971 km; number of vehicles (1988) 29,760.

EDUCATION AND HEALTH

Education. The 1981 census gave the number of literates as 587,618. In 1987–88 there were 2,777 primary schools, 436 middle schools, 379 high and higher schools and 32 colleges, as well as Manipur University.

Health. In 1987–88 there were 11 hospitals, 52 dispensaries, 8 community health centres, 49 primary health centres and 389 sub-centres.

MEGHALAYA

HISTORY. The state was created under the Assam Reorganization (Meghalaya) Act 1969 and inaugurated on 2 April 1970. Its status was that of a state within the State of Assam until 21 Jan. 1972 when it became a fully independent state of the Union. It consists of the former Garo Hills district and United Khasi and Jaintia Hills district of Assam.

AREA AND POPULATION. Meghalaya is bounded north and east by Assam, south and west by Bangladesh. In 1981 (census figure) the area was 22,429 sq. km and the population 1,335,819. Density 60 per sq. km. Growth rate, 1971–81, 31·04%. The people are mainly of the Khasi, Jaintia and Garo tribes.

CONSTITUTION AND GOVERNMENT. Meghalaya has a unicameral legislature. The Legislative Assembly has 60 seats. Party position in summer 1984: Meghalaya Democratic Front, 37 (including 31 Congress I); opposition, 13.

There are 5 districts. The capital is Shillong (population, 1981, 109,244).

Governor: A. A. Rahim.
Chief Minister: Purno A. Sangma.

BUDGET. Budget estimates for 1986–87 showed revenue receipts of Rs 2,177m. and expenditure of Rs 1,639m. Annual Plan expenditure, 1990–91, Rs 175 crores.

ENERGY AND NATURAL RESOURCES

Electricity. Total installed capacity (1986–87) was 133·76 mw. 1,397 villages had electricity.

Minerals. The East and West Khasi and Jaintia Hills districts produce coal, sillimanite (95% of India's total output), limestone, fire clay, dolomite, felspar, quartz and glass sand. The state also has deposits of coal (estimated reserves 500m. tonnes), limestone (4,000m.), fire clay (100,000) and sandstone which are virtually untapped because of transport difficulties.

Agriculture. About 80% of the people depend on agriculture. Principal crops are rice, maize, potatoes, cotton, oranges, ginger, tezpata, areca nuts, jute, mesta, bananas and pineapples. Production 1986–87 (in tonnes): Foodgrains, 131,190; potatoes, 154,626; tapioca, 23,304; jute, 20,895 bales (of 180 kg); mesta, 16,885 bales (of 180 kg); pineapples, 60,580; citrus fruits, 36,297.

Forest products are the state's chief resources.

INDUSTRY. Apart from agriculture the main source of employment is the extraction and processing of minerals; there are also important timber processing mills. The state has a plywood factory, a cement factory (production capacity, 930 tonnes per day), a beverage plant and watch and match factories. Meghalaya Industrial Development Corporation has set up industrial units. There is a new industrial area in Byrnihat, and two industrial estates in Shillong and Mendipathar. Tantalum capacitors are manufactured in the Parapani Industrial Area near Shillong. In 1985–86 there were 58 registered factories and 671 small-scale industries.

COMMUNICATIONS. Three national highways run through the state. The state has no railways. Umroi airport (20 km from Shillong) connects the state with main air services. In March 1988 a helicopter passenger service was introduced between Shillong, Guwahti and Tura. In 1989 there were 461 km of national highway and (1986-87) 5,218 km of surfaced and unsurfaced roads.

JUSTICE, EDUCATION AND WELFARE

Justice. The Guwahti High Court is common to Assam, Meghalaya, Nagaland, Manipur, Mizoram, Tripura and Arunachal Pradesh. There is a branch of the Guwahti High Court at Shillong.

Education. In 1985–86 the state had 4,129 primary schools, 622 middle schools, 268 high and higher-secondary schools and 14 colleges. The North-eastern Hill University started functioning at Shillong in 1973.

Health. In 1986 there were 7 government hospitals, 39 primary health centres, 36 government dispensaries and 189 sub-centres. Total beds (hospitals and health centres), 1,422.

MIZORAM

HISTORY. On 21 Jan. 1972 the former Mizo Hills District of Assam was created a Union Territory. A long dispute between the Mizo National Front (originally Seperatist) and the central government was resolved in 1985. Mizoram became a state by the Constitution (53rd Amendment) and the State of Mizoram Acts, July 1986.

AREA AND POPULATION. Mizoram is one of the eastern-most Indian states, lying between Bangladesh and Burma, and having on its northern boundaries Tripura, Assam and Manipur. The area is 21,081 sq. km and the population (1981 census) 493,757. Density, 23 per sq. km; growth rate 1971–81, 48·55%.

CONSTITUTION AND GOVERNMENT. Mizoram has a unicameral Legislative Assembly with 40 seats: Congress I, 22; Mizo National Front, 14; others, 4. The capital is Aizawl.

Governor: Swaraj Kaushal.
Chief Minister: Lalthnahawla.

BUDGET. Annual plan outlay (1989-90) Rs 102 crores.

ELECTRICITY. Installed capacity (1986–87), 16,109 kw. Work was in progress (1988) on one diesel and two hydro-electric generators.

AGRICULTURE. About 90% of the people are engaged in agriculture, either on terraced holdings or in shifting cultivation. Area under rice paddy, 1986–87, 48,344 hectares; production, 68,746 tonnes.

Total forest area, 15,935 sq. km.

INDUSTRY. Hand loom weaving and other cottage industries are important.

COMMUNICATIONS. Aizawl is connected by road and air with Silchar in Assam.

RELIGION. The mainly tribal population is 83·81% Christian.

EDUCATION. In 1987–88 there were 1,003 primary, 477 middle and 162 high schools; there were 13 colleges and one university.

HEALTH. In 1986–87 there were 9 hospitals, 22 primary and 25 subsidiary health centres. Total beds, 893.

NAGALAND

HISTORY. The territory was constituted by the Union Government in Sept. 1962. It comprises the former Naga Hills district of Assam and the former Tuensang Frontier division of the North-East Frontier Agency; these had been made a Centrally Administered Area in 1957, administered by the President through the Governor of Assam. In Jan. 1961 the area was renamed and given the status of a state of the Indian Union, which was officially inaugurated on 1 Dec. 1963.

For some years a section of the Naga leaders sought independence. Military operations from 1960 and the prospect of self-government within the Indian Union led to a general reconciliation, but rebel activity continued. A 2-month amnesty in mid 1963 had little effect. A 'ceasefire' in Sept. 1964 was followed by talks between a Government of India delegation and rebel leaders. The peace period was extended and the 'Revolutionary Government of Nagaland' (a breakaway group from the Naga Federal Government) was dissolved in 1973. Further talks with the Naga underground movement resulted in the Shillong Peace Agreement of Nov. 1975.

AREA AND POPULATION. The state is in the extreme north-east and is bounded west and north by Assam, east by Burma and south by Manipur. Nagaland has an area of 16,579 sq. km and a population (1981) census of 774,930. Density 47 per sq. km. Growth rate, 1971–81, 50·05%. Towns include Kohima, Mokokchung, Tuensang and Dimapur. The chief tribes in numerical order are: Angami, Ao, Sema, Konyak, Chakhesang, Lotha, Phom, Khiamngan, Chang, Yimchunger, Zeliang-Kuki, Rengma and Sangtam.

CONSTITUTION AND GOVERNMENT. An Interim Body (Legislative Assembly) of 42 members elected by the Naga people and an Executive Council (Council of Ministers) of 5 members were formed in 1961, and continued until the State Assembly was elected in Jan. 1964. The Assembly has 60 members: Congress I, 36; Nagaland People's Council, 24. The Governor has extraordinary powers, which include special responsibility for law and order.

There are 17 cabinet ministers and 4 ministers of state.

The state has 7 districts (Kohima, Mon, Zunheboto, Wokha, Phek, Mokokchung and Tuensang). The capital is Kohima.

Governor: Dr Gopal Singh.
Chief Minister: S. C. Jamir.

BUDGET. Budget estimates 1988–89, revenue receipts, Rs 4,090m., expenditure, Rs 4,100m. Annual Plan, 1990–91, Rs 145 crores.

ENERGY AND NATURAL RESOURCES

Electricity. Installed capacity (1984) 5·12 mw; 80% of all towns and villages are electrified.

Agriculture. 90% of the people derive their livelihood from agriculture. The Angamis, in Kohima district, practise a fixed agriculture in the shape of terraced slopes, and wet paddy cultivation in the lowlands. In the other two districts a traditional form of shifting cultivation (*jhumming*) still predominates, but some farmers have begun tea and coffee plantations and horticulture. About 51,250 hectares were under terrace cultivation and 86,000 under *jhumming* in 1987–88. Production of rice (1985–86) was 83,200 tonnes.

Forests covered 2,875 sq. km in 1988.

INDUSTRY. There is a forest products factory at Tijit; a paper-mill (100 tonnes daily capacity) at Tuli, a distillery unit and a sugar-mill (1,000 tonnes daily capacity) at Dimapur. Bricks and TV sets are also made, and there are over 1,000 small units. Oil has been located in 3 districts. Other minerals include: Coal, limestone, clay, glass sand and slate.

COMMUNICATIONS. There is a national highway from Kaziranga (Assam) to Kohima and on to Manipur. There are state highways connecting Kohima with the district headquarters. Total surfaced roads, 1,538 km; unsurfaced, 5,287 km. (1987–88). Dimapur has a rail-head and a daily air service to Calcutta.

RELIGION, EDUCATION AND WELFARE

Religion. Christianity is the main religion; there are also Hindus, Moslems, and followers of indigenous faiths.

Education. The 1981 census records 329,000 literates, or 42·57%: 50·06% of men and 33·89% of women. In 1987 there were 3 government and 10 private colleges, 70 government and 50 private high schools, 226 government and 147 private middle schools and 1,150 government primary schools, 1 polytechnic, 1 agricultural college, 2 law colleges. The North Eastern Hill University opened at Kohima in 1978. Total enrollment in schools and colleges, 1987, 219,300.

Health. In 1988 there were 33 hospitals (1,409 beds), 23 primary and 3 community health centres, 73 dispensaries, 218 sub-centres.

Aram, M., *Peace in Nagaland,* New Delhi, 1974

ORISSA

HISTORY. Orissa, ceded to the Mahrattas by Alivardi Khan in 1751, was conquered by the British in 1803. In 1803 a board of 2 commissioners was appointed to administer the province, but in 1805 it was designated the district of Cuttack and was placed in charge of a collector, judge and magistrate. In 1829 it was split up into 3 regulation districts of Cuttack, Balasore and Puri, and the non-regulation tributary states which were administered by their own chiefs under the aegis of the British Government. Angul, one of these tributary states, was annexed in 1847, and with the Khondmals, ceded in 1835 by the tributary chief of the Boudh state, constituted a separate non-regulation district. Sambalpur was transferred from the Central Provinces to Orissa in 1905. These districts formed an outlying tract of the Bengal Presidency till 1912, when they were transferred to Bihar, constituting one of its divisions under a commissioner. Orissa was constituted a separate province on 1 April 1936, some portions of the Central Provinces and Madras being transferred to the old Orissa division.

The rulers of 25 Orissa states surrendered all jurisdiction and authority to the Government of India on 1 Jan. 1948, on which date the Provincial Government took over the administration. The administration of 2 states, viz., Saraikella and Kharswan, was transferred to the Government of Bihar in May 1948. By an agreement with the Dominion Government, Mayurbhanj State was finally merged with the province on 1 Jan. 1949. By the States Merger (Governors' Provinces) Order, 1949, the states were completely merged with the state of Orissa on 19 Aug. 1949.

AREA AND POPULATION. Orissa is in eastern India and is bounded north by Bihar, north-east by West Bengal, east by the Bay of Bengal, south by Andhra

Pradesh and west by Madhya Pradesh. The area of the state is 155,707 sq. km, and its population (1981 census), 26,370,271, density 169 per sq. km. Growth rate, 1971–81, 20·17%. The largest cities are Cuttack (295,268 in 1988), Rourkela (214,521) and Berhampur (162,550). The principal and official language is Oriya.

CONSTITUTION AND GOVERNMENT. The Legislative Assembly has 147 members. After the election in March 1985 a Congress government was returned.

The state consists of 13 districts.

The capital is Bhubaneswar (18 miles south of Cuttack).

Governor: Yagya Dutt Sharma.

Chief Minister: Hemananda Biswal.

BUDGET. Budget estimates, 1988–89 showed total revenue of Rs 2,288 crores and expenditure of Rs 2,291 crores. Annual plan outlay is Rs 925 crores.

ENERGY AND NATURAL RESOURCES

Electricity. The Hirakud Dam Project on the river Mahanadi irrigates 628,000 acres and has an installed capacity of 1,394 mw. There are other projects under construction: The upper Kolab; Indrabati; Rengali Dam; hydro-electric power is now serving a large part of the state. There were 29,186 electrified villages in 1988-89.

Minerals. Orissa is India's leading producer of chromite (95% of national output), dolomite (50%), manganese ore (25%), graphite (80%), iron ore (16%), fire-clay (34%), limestone (20%), and quartz-quartzite (18%). Production in 1986 (1,000 tonnes): Iron ore, 8,030; manganese ore, 464; chromite, 561; coal, 6,844; limestone, 2,954; dolomite, 980; bauxite, 239. Value of production in 1987 was Rs 329 crores.

Agriculture. The cultivation of rice is the principal occupation of nearly 75% of the population, and only a very small amount of other cereals is grown. Production of foodgrains (1988–89) totalled 7·4m. tonnes from 7m. hectares; oilseeds (906,000 tonnes) and sugar-cane (3·93m. tonnes) are also grown. Turmeric is cultivated in the uplands of the districts of Ganjam, Phulbani and Koraput, and is exported.

Livestock (1988): Buffaloes, 1·33m.; other cattle, 12·92m.; sheep, 1·98m.; goats, 4·93m.; 10·55m. poultry including ducks.

Forests. Forests occupy about 35·8% of the area of the state, the most important species being sal, teak, kendu, sandal, sisu, bija, kusum, kongada and bamboo.

Fisheries. There were, in 1985, 574 fishery co-operative societies. Fish production in 1988-89 was 129,865 tonnes. A fishing harbour has been developed at Dhamara.

INDUSTRY. 184 large and medium industries have been established (1988-89), mostly based on minerals, including the steel plant of Steel Authority of India Ltd at Rourkela, a pig-iron plant near Barbil, 3 ferrochrome plants, 2 ferromanganese plants at Joda and Rayagada, 1 ferrosilicon plant at Theruvelli and an aluminium smelter plant at Hirakud, 4 refractory plants and 2 cement plants. There are 3 large paper mills at Rayagada, Chowdwar and Brajrajnagar, three fertilizer plants, a caustic soda plant, a salt manufacturing unit and an industrial explosives plant. There are aluminium-alumina plants at Damanjodi and Angul.

Other industries of importance are sugar, glass, aluminium, heavy machine tools, a coach-repair factory, a re-rolling mill, textile mills and electronics. Also, there were 31,922 small-scale industries employing 245,000 persons. There were 771,686 cottage industries providing employment to 1·26m. persons; handloom weaving and the manufacture of baskets, wooden articles, hats and nets; silver filigree work and hand-woven fabrics are specially well known.

TOURISM. Tourist traffic is concentrated mainly on the 'Golden Triangle', Konark, Puri and Bhubaneswar, and its temples. Tourists also visit Gopalpur, the Similipal National Park, Nandankanan and Chilka Lake.

COMMUNICATIONS

Roads. On 31 March 1984–85 length of roads was: State highway, 2,846 km; national highway, 1,625 km; other Public Works Department roads, 61,330 km; council roads, 5,048 km. There were 183,888 motor vehicles in 1985. A 144-km expressway, part national highway, connects the Daitari mining area with Paradip Port.

Railways. The route-km of railway in 1987–88 was 1,982 km, of which 1,310 km was single line.

Aviation. There is an airport at Bhubaneswar with regular scheduled services to New Delhi, Calcutta, Visakhapatnam and Hyderabad.

Shipping. Paradip was declared a 'major' port in 1966 and has been developed to handle 4m. tons of traffic. Other minor ports at Chandbali and Gopalpur.

JUSTICE, RELIGION, EDUCATION AND WELFARE

Justice. The High Court of Judicature at Cuttack has a Chief Justice and 10 puisne judges.

Religion. There were in 1981: Hindus (including scheduled castes and scheduled tribes), 25,161,725; Christians, 480,426; Moslems, 422,266; Sikhs, 14,270; Buddhists, 8,028; Jains, 6,642.

Education. The percentage of literates in the population is 34·12% (males, 46·9%, females, 21·11%).

In 1987–88 there were 39,640 primary, 9,269 middle English and 4,036 high and higher secondary schools. There are 404 colleges.

Utkal University was established in 1943 at Cuttack and moved to Bhubaneswar in 1962; it is both teaching and affiliating. It has 2 university colleges (law) and 150 affiliated colleges. Berhampur University has 31 affiliated colleges and Orissa University of Agriculture and Technology 8 constituent colleges. Sambalpur University has 84 affiliated colleges. Sri Jagannath Sanskrit Viswavidyalaya University at Puri was established in 1981 for oriental studies.

Health. There were (1988) 13 district hospitals and 7,479 institutions for health care.

PUNJAB (INDIA)

HISTORY. The Punjab was constituted an autonomous province of India in 1937. In 1947, the province was partitioned between India and Pakistan into East and West Punjab respectively, under the Indian Independence Act, 1947, the boundaries being determined under the Radcliffe Award. The name of East Punjab was changed to Punjab (India) under the Constitution of India. On 1 Nov. 1956 the erstwhile states of Punjab and Patiala and East Punjab States Union (PEPSU) were integrated to form the state of Punjab. On 1 Nov. 1966, under the Punjab Reorganization Act, 1966, the state was reconstituted as a Punjabi-speaking state comprising the districts of Gurdaspur (excluding Dalhousie), Amritsar, Kapurthala, Jullundur, Ferozepore, Bhatinda, Patiala and Ludhiana; parts of Sangrur, Hoshiarpur and Ambala districts; and part of Kharar tehsil. The remaining area comprising an area of 18,000 sq. miles and an estimated (1967) population of 8·5m. was shared between the new state of Haryana and the Union Territory of Himachal Pradesh. The existing capital of Chandigarh was made joint capital of Punjab and Haryana; its transfer to Punjab alone (due in 1986) has been delayed while the two states seek agreement as to which Hindi-speaking districts shall be transfered to Haryana in exchange.

AREA AND POPULATION. The Punjab is in north India and is bounded at its northernmost point by Kashmir, north-east by Himachal Pradesh, south-east by Haryana, south by Rajasthan, west and north-west by Pakistan. The area of the state is 50,362 sq. km, with census (1981) population of 16,788,915. Density 333 per sq. km. Growth rate, 1971–81, 23·01%. The largest cities, *see* p. 632. The official language is Punjabi.

CONSTITUTION AND GOVERNMENT. Punjab (India) has a unicameral legislature, the Legislative Assembly, of 117 members. Presidential rule was imposed in May 1987 after outbreaks of communal violence. In March 1988 the Assembly was officially dissolved. By the 59th constitutional amendment the Union government was enabled to impose a state of emergency on the Punjab for a period of up to 3 years.

There are 12 districts. The capital is Chandigarh (*see* p. 695). There are 106 municipalities, 118 community development blocks and 9,331 elected village *panchayats.*

Governor: Nirmal Kumar Mukharji.

BUDGET. Budget estimates, 1989–90, showed receipts of Rs 1,980·86 crores and expenditure of Rs 2,041·57 crores. Plan outlay for 1989-90 was Rs 789 crores.

ENERGY AND NATURAL RESOURCES

Electricity. Installed capacity, 1987–88, was 2,661 mw; all villages had electricity.

Agriculture. About 75% of the population depends on agriculture which is technically advanced. The irrigated area rose from 2·21m. hectares in 1950–51 to 6·7m. hectares in 1986–87. In 1987–88,wheat production was 11m. tonnes, rice, 5·4m.; oilseeds, 178,000; maize, 366,000; cotton, 1·86m. bales.

Livestock (1977 census): Buffaloes, 4,110,000; other cattle, 3·31m.; sheep and goats, 1,219,600; horses and ponies, 75,900; poultry, 5·5m.

Forestry. In 1987–88 there were 267,644 hectares of forest land, of which 134,776 hectares belonged to the Forest Department.

INDUSTRY. In March 1987 the number of registered industrial units in the Punjab (India) was 122,766, employing about 800,000 people. On 31 March 1988 there were (provisional) 135,305 small industrial units, investment Rs 937 crores. The chief manufactures are textiles (especially hosiery), sewing machines, sports goods, sugar, bicycles, electronic goods, machine tools, hand tools, vehicle parts, surgical goods and vegetable oils. Recent (1989) large projects include food processing, electronics, diesel locomotives, paper and newsprint.

COMMUNICATIONS

Roads. The total length of metalled roads on 31 March 1987 was 35,501 km. State transport services cover 815,380 route km daily with a fleet of 3,422 buses carrying a daily average of over 1m. passengers. Coverage by private operators is estimated as 40%.

Railways. The Punjab possesses an extensive system of railway communications, served by the Northern Railway. Route-km (1988) 2,145 km.

Aviation. There is an airport at Amritsar, and Chandigarh airport is on the north-eastern boundary; both have regular scheduled services to Delhi, Jammu, Srinagar and Leh. There are also Vayudoot services to Ludhiana and Kulu.

JUSTICE, RELIGION, EDUCATION AND WELFARE

Justice. The Punjab and Haryana High Court exercises jurisdiction over the states of Punjab and Haryana and the territory of Chandigarh. It is located in Chandigarh. It consists (1988) of a Chief Justice and 21 puisne judges.

Religion. At the 1971 census Hindus numbered 5,037,235; Sikhs, 8,159,172; Moslems, 114,447; Christians, 162,202; Jains, 21,383; Buddhists, 1,374.

Education. Compulsory education was introduced in April 1961; at the same time free education was introduced up to 8th class for boys and 9th class for girls as well as fee concessions. The aim is education for all children of 6-11.

In 1988 there were 12,322 primary schools, 1,395 middle schools, 2,405 high schools and 324 senior secondary schools.

Punjab University was established in 1947 at Chandigarh as an examining, teaching and affiliating body. In 1962 Punjabi University was established at Patiala and an agricultural university at Ludhiana. Guru Nanak University has been established at Amritsar to mark the 500th anniversary celebrations for Guru Nanak Dev, first Guru of the Sikhs. Altogether there are 196 affiliated colleges, 170 for arts and science, 18 for teacher training, 5 medical, 3 engineering and 11 for other studies.

Health. Punjab claims the longest life expectancy (60·6 years for women, 60·7 for men) and lowest death rate (9 per 1,000). There were (1988) 268 hospitals, 528 Ayurvedic and Unani hospitals and dispensaries, 170 primary health centres, 2,702 sub-centres and 1,839 dispensaries.

Singh, Khushwant, *A History of the Sikhs*. 2 vols. Princeton and OUP, 1964–67

RAJASTHAN

HISTORY. As a result of the implementation of the States Reorganization Act, 1956, the erstwhile state of Ajmer, Abu Taluka of Bombay State and the Sunel Tappa enclave of the former state of Madhya Bharat were transferred to the state of Rajasthan on 1 Nov. 1956, whereas the Sironj subdivision of Rajasthan was transferred to the state of Madhya Pradesh.

EVENTS. An instance of *suttee* on 4 Sept. 1987 brought about state legislation (Rajasthan Sati (Prevention) Ordinance) promulgated on 1 Oct., and the central government's Sati Prevention Act (strengthening existing penalties) in Dec. 1987.

AREA AND POPULATION. Rajasthan is in north-west India and is bounded north by Punjab, north-east by Haryana and Uttar Pradesh, east by Madhya Pradesh, south by Gujarat and west by Pakistan. The area of the state is 342,239 sq. km and its population (census 1981, revised), 34,261,862, density 100 per sq. km. Growth rate, 1971–81, 32·36%. The chief cities, *see* p. 632.

CONSTITUTION AND GOVERNMENT. There is a unicameral legislature, the Legislative Assembly, having 200 members. After the election in March 1985 a Congress government was returned.

The capital is Jaipur. There are 27 districts.

Governor: Dr Debi Prasad Chattopadhyay.

Chief Minister: Harideo Joshi.

BUDGET. Estimates for 1989–90 show total revenue receipts of Rs 2,524 crores, and expenditure of Rs 2,524 crores. Annual plan 1989–90, Rs 795 crores.

ENERGY AND NATURAL RESOURCES

Electricity. Installed capacity in Feb. 1988, 1,978 mw.; 22,595 villages and 294,000 wells had electric power.

Water. In 1984 the Bhakra Canal irrigated 300,000 hectares, the Chambal Canal, 200,000 and the Rajasthan Canal, 450,000. The Rajasthan (now the Indira Gandhi canal) is the main canal system, of which (1984) 189 km. of main canal and 2,950 km of distributors had been built. Cost, at 1 March 1984, Rs 419 crores. There were 28,739 villages with drinking water in March 1987, out of 34,968.

Minerals. The state is rich in minerals. In 1987, 1·7m. tonnes of gypsum and 300,000 tonnes of rock phosphate were produced. Other minerals include silver (21,550 kg., 1987 estimate), asbestos, felspar, copper, limestone and salt. Total sale value of mineral production in 1987 (estimate) was about Rs 350 crores. Lead-zinc reserves have been found near Rampura-Agucha, estimated at 61m. tonnes.

Agriculture. The state has suffered drought and encroaching desert for several years. The cultivable area is (1985–86) about 26·6m. hectares, of which 4m. is irrigated. Production of principal crops (in 1,000 tonnes), 1986–87: Pulses, 879; sugarcane (gur), 1,291; total oilseeds, 882; cotton, 699,000 bales (of 180 kg). Total foodgrains (1986–87) 6,723.

Livestock (1983): Buffaloes, 6,034,743; other cattle, 13,466,474; sheep, 15,389,100; goats, 15,397,993; horses and ponies, 45,381; camels, 7,528,287.

INDUSTRY. In Dec. 1987 there were 9,665 registered factories and 122,304 small industrial units. There were 171 industrial estates. Total capital investment Rs 4,750·7m. Chief manufactures are textiles, cement, glass, sugar, sodium, oxygen and acetylene units, pesticides, insecticides, dyes, caustic soda, calcium, carbide, nylon tyre cords and refined copper.

COMMUNICATIONS

Roads. In 1988 there were 53,040 km of roads including 42,478 km of good and surfaced roads in Rajasthan; there were 12,521 km of national highway. Motor vehicles numbered 719,364 in Dec. 1987.

Railways. Jodhpur, Marwar, Udaipur, Ajmer, Jaipur, Kota, Bikaner and Sawai Madhopur are important junctions of the north-western network. Route km (1989) 5,611.

Aviation. There are airports at Jaipur, Jodhpur, Kota and Udaipur with regular scheduled services by Indian Airlines.

JUSTICE, RELIGION, EDUCATION AND WELFARE

Justice. The seat of the High Court is at Jodhpur. There is a Chief Justice and 11 puisne judges. There is also a bench of High Court judges at Jaipur.

Religion. At the 1971 census Hindus numbered 23,093,895; Moslems, 1,778,275; Jains, 513,548; Sikhs, 341,182; Christians, 30,202.

Education. The proportion of literates to the total population was 24·39% at the 1981 census.

In 1987–88 there were 36,862 primary and middle schools, 2,171 secondary and 897 higher secondary schools. Elementary education is free but not compulsory.

In 1987–88 there were 179 colleges. Rajasthan University, established at Jaipur in 1947, is teaching and affiliating (6 affiliated colleges); Jodhpur University and Udaipur University were founded in 1962. There are 8 other universities. There are also 5 medical and nursing colleges, 3 engineering colleges, 21,436 adult and other education centres, 32 sanskrit institutions, 33 teacher-training colleges and 14 polytechnics.

Health. In 1987 there were 899 hospitals and dispensaries, 498 primary health centres. In addition there were 3,228 Ayurvedic, Unani, homoepathic and naturopathy hospitals. There were 116 maternity centres.

SIKKIM

HISTORY. Sikkim became the twenty-second state of the Indian Union in May 1975. It is inhabited chiefly by the Lepchas, who are a tribe indigenous to Sikkim with their own dress and language, the Bhutias, who originally came from Tibet, and the Nepális, who entered from Nepál in large numbers in the late 19th and early 20th century. The main languages spoken are Bhutia, Lepcha and Nepáli. Being a small country Sikkim had frequently been involved in struggles over her territory, and as a result her boundaries have been very much reduced over the centuries. In particular the Darjeeling district was acquired from Sikkim by the British East India Company in 1839. The Namgyal dynasty had been ruling Sikkim since the 14th century; the first consecrated ruler was Phuntsog Namgya I who was consecrated in 1642 and given the title of 'Chogyal', meaning 'King ruling in accordance with religious laws', derived from Cho–religion and Gyalpo–king. The last Chogyal was deposed in 1975 and died in America in 1982.

Sikkim is a land of wide variation in altitude, climate and vegetation, and is known for the great number and variety of birds, butterflies, wild flowers and orchids to be found in the different regions. It is a fertile land and to the Sikkimese is known as Denjong, The Valley of Rice.

AREA AND POPULATION. Sikkim is in the Eastern Himalayas and is bounded north by Tibet, east by Tibet and Bhután, south by West Bengal and west Nepál. Area, 7,096 sq. km. Census population (1981), 316,385, of whom 36,768 lived in the capital, Gangtok. Density 43 per sq km. Growth rate, 1971–81, 50·01%.

CONSTITUTION AND GOVERNMENT. Sikkim was joined to the British Empire by a treaty in 1886 until 1947, but that relationship ceased when Britain withdrew from India in 1947. Thereafter there was a standstill agreement between India and Sikkim until a treaty was signed on 5 Dec. 1950 between India and Sikkim by which Sikkim became a protectorate of India and India undertook to be responsible for Sikkim's defence, external relations and strategic communications. The Chogyal had governed Sikkim with the help of the Sikkim Council, consisting of 18 elected members and 6 members nominated by the Chogyal. Sikkim parties represented were: National Party, Sikkim National Congress and, later, Sikkim Janta Congress.

Political reforms were demanded by the National Congress and the Janta Congress in March-April 1973 and Indian police took over control of law and order at the request of the Chogyal. On 13 April it was announced that the Chogyal had agreed to meet most of the political demands. Elections were held in April 1974 to a popularly-elected assembly. By the Government of Sikkim Act, June 1974, the Chogyal became a constitutional monarch with power of assent to the Assembly's legislation. By the Constitution (Thirty-Sixth Amendment) Act 1974 Sikkim became a state associated with the Indian Union. The office of Chogyal was abolished in April 1975. By the Constitution (Thirty-Eighth Amendment) Act 1975 Sikkim became the twenty-second state of the Indian Union. The Assembly has 32 members. After the election of Nov. 1989 the Sangram Parishad government continued in power.

Governor: Adm. R. H. Tahiliani.
Chief Minister: N. Bahadur Bhandari.

The official language of the Government is English. Lepcha, Bhutia, Nepáli and Limboo have also been declared official languages.

Sikkim is divided into 4 districts for administration purposes, Gangtok, Mangan, Namchi and Gyalshing being the headquarters for the Eastern, Northern, Southern and Western districts respectively. Each district is administered by a District Collector. Within this framework are the Panchayats or Village Councils.

ECONOMY

Budget. Budget estimates for 1989-90 show revenue receipt of Rs 157·40 crores and revenue expenditure of Rs 171·60 crores. Annual plan outlay for 1989-90 is Rs 710m.

ENERGY AND NATURAL RESOURCES

Electricity. There are 4 operational hydro-electric power stations; the Lagyap project is also being implemented by the Government of India as aid to meet the growing demand for electrical power for new industries. The first of its two 6 mv generators was commissioned 1 Sept. 1979.

Agriculture. The economy is mainly agricultural; main food crops are rice, maize, millet, wheat and barley; cash crops are cardamom (a spice), mandarin oranges, apples, potatoes, and buckwheat. Foodgrain production, 1988-89, 125,000 tonnes. A tea plantation has recently been started. Forests occupy about 1,000 sq. km. of the land area (excluding hill pastures) and the potential for a timber and wood-pulp industry is being explored. Some medicinal herbs are exported.

INDUSTRY AND TRADE

Industry. There is a state Industrial Development Investment Corporation and an Industrial Training Institute offering 7 trades. There are two cigarette factories (at Gangtok and Rangpo), two distilleries and a tannery at Rangpo and a fruit preserving factory at Singtam. Copper, zinc and lead are mined by the Sikkim Mining Corporation. A recent survey by the Geological Survey of India and the Indian Bureau of Mines has confirmed further deposits of copper, zinc, silver and gold in Dikchu, North Sikkim. There is a jewel-bearing factory for the production of industrial jewels. A watch factory has been set up in collaboration with Hindustan Machine Tools (India). A number of small manufacturing units for leather, wire nails, storage cells batteries, candles, safety matches and carpets, are already producing in the private sector. Local crafts include carpet weaving, making handmade paper, wood carving and silverwork. To encourage trading in indigenous products, particularly agricultural produce, the State Trading Corporation of Sikkim has been established.

Tourism. There is great potential for the tourist industry; a 78-bed lodge at Gangtok and a 50-bed tourist lodge in West Sikkim have been opened. Tourism has been stimulated by the opening of new roads from Pemayangtse to Yuksam in West Sikkim and from Yuksam to the Dzongri Glacier.

COMMUNICATIONS

Roads. There are 1,442 km. of roads, all on mountainous terrain, and 18 major bridges under the Public Works Department. Public transport and road haulage is nationalized.

Railways. The nearest railhead is at Siliguri (115 km from Gangtok).

Aviation. The nearest airport is at Bagdogra (128 km from Gangtok), linked to Gangtok by helicopter service.

Post and Broadcasting. There are 1,445 telephones (1987) and 37 wireless stations. A radio broadcasting station, Akashvani Gangtok, was built in 1982, and a permanent station in 1983. Gangtok also has a low-power TV transmitter.

RELIGION, EDUCATION AND WELFARE

Religion. The state religion is Mahayana Buddhism, but a large proportion of the population is Hindu. There are some Christians, Moslems and members of other religions.

Education. At the 1981 census there were 100,000 literates. Sikkim had (1987-88) 528 pre-primary schools, 489 primary schools, 123 junior high schools, 54 secondary and 14 higher secondary schools. Education is free up to class XII; text books are free up to class V. There are 500 adult education centres. There is also a training institute for primary teachers and a degree college.

Health. There are (1983) 4 district hospitals at Singtam, Gyalshing, Namchi and Mangan, and one central referral hospital at Gangtok, besides 20 primary health centres, 109 sub-centres and 8 dispensaries, a maternity ward, chest clinic and 2 blocks for tuberculosis patients. There is a blood bank at Gangtok. There are 110 doctors. Medical and hospital treatment is free; there is a health centre for every 20,000 of the population. Small-pox and Kala-azar have been completely eliminated and many schemes for the provision of safe drinking water to villages and bazaars have been implemented. A leprosy hospital (20 beds) was being built near Gangtok in 1987.

TAMIL NADU

HISTORY. The first trading establishment made by the British in the Madras State was at Peddapali (now Nizampatnam) in 1611 and then at Masulipatnam. In

1639 the English were permitted to make a settlement at the place which is now Madras, and Fort St George was founded. By 1801 the whole of the country from the Northern Circars to Cape Comorin (with the exception of certain French and Danish settlements) had been brought under British rule.

Under the provisions of the States Reorganization Act, 1956, the Malabar district (excluding the islands of Laccadive and Minicoy) and the Kasaragod district taluk of South Kanara were transferred to the new state of Kerala; the South Kanara district (excluding Kasaragod taluk and the Amindivi Islands) and the Kollegal taluk of the Coimbatore district were transferred to the new state of Mysore; and the Laccadive, Amindivi and Minicoy Islands were constituted a separate Territory. Four taluks of the Trivandrum district and the Shencottah taluk of Quilon district were transferred from Travancore-Cochin to the new Madras State. On 1 April 1960, 405 sq. miles from the Chittoor district of Andhra Pradesh were transferred to Madras in exchange for 326 sq. miles from the Chingleput and Salem districts. In Aug. 1968 the state was renamed Tamil Nadu.

AREA AND POPULATION. Tamil Nadu is in south India and is bounded north by Karnataka and Andhra Pradesh, east and south by the Indian ocean and west by Kerala. Area, 130,058 sq. km. Population (1981 census), 48,408,077, density of 372 per sq. km. Growth rate, 1971–81, 17·5%. Tamil is the principal language and has been adopted as the state language with effect from 14 Jan. 1958. The principal towns, *see* p. 632.

CONSTITUTION AND GOVERNMENT. The Governor is aided by a Council of 16 ministers. There is a unicameral legislature; the Legislative Assembly has 234 members: DMK, 148; AIADMK, 27; Congress I, 26; others, 33.

There are 20 districts. The capital is Madras.

Governor: P. C. Alexander.
Chief Minister: M. Karunanidhi.

BUDGET. Budget estimates for 1988-89, total receipts, Rs 4,041 crores, total expenditure, Rs 4,163 crores. Annual plan 1989–90, Rs 1,367 crores.

ENERGY AND NATURAL RESOURCES

Electricity. Installed capacity 1987–88 amounted to 4,558 mw of which 1,799 mw was hydro-electricity and 2,408 mw thermal. 99·9% of villages were supplied with electricity. The Kalpakkam nuclear power plant became operational in 1983; capacity, 350 mw.

Water. A joint project with Andhra Pradesh was agreed in 1983, to supply Madras with water from the Krishna river, also providing irrigation, *en route,* for Andhra Pradesh. In 1986–87 2·84m. hectares were irrigated.

Minerals. Value of mineral production, 1987, Rs 176 crores. The state has magnesite, salt, coal, chromite, bauxite, limestone, manganese, mica, quartz, gypsum and feldspar.

Agriculture. In 1981 there were 5·5m. cultivators and 5·9m. agricultural labourers. The land is a fertile plain watered by rivers flowing east from the Western Ghats, particularly the Cauvery and the Tambaraparani. Temperature ranges between 6°C. and 39°C., rainfall between 442 mm. and 1,307 mm. Of the total land area (13m. hectares), 6,508,349 hectares were cropped and 298,659 hectares of waste were cultivable. The staple food crops grown are paddy, maize, jawar, bajra, pulses and millets. Important commercial crops are sugar-cane, oilseeds, cashew-nuts, cotton, tobacco, coffee, tea, rubber and pepper. Production 1985–86, in 1,000 tons, (and area, 1,000 hectares): Rice 5,372 (2,264); small millet 148 (261); sugar-cane 2,000 (191); pulses 275 (582); cotton 3m. bales (169); oilseeds 1,130 (1,197).

Livestock (1982 census): Buffaloes, 3,212,242; other cattle, 10,365,500; sheep, 5,536,514; goats, 5,246,192; swine, 693,735; horses, ponies, mules, camels and donkeys, 90,632; poultry, 18,283,720.

Forestry. Forest area, 1985–86, 2,245,159 hectares, of which 1,844,779 were reserved forest. Forests cover about 27% of land area. Main products are teak, soft wood, wattle, sandalwood, pulp wood, cashew and cinchona bark.

Fisheries. There were 101,869 active marine fishermen working the 1,000 km coastline in 1986–87.

INDUSTRY AND TRADE

Industry. The number of working factories was 12,286 in 1986, employing 811,936 workers. The consumption of power in the industrial sector was 43% of total state consumption in 1982–83. The biggest central sector project is Salem steel plant.

Cotton textiles is one of the major industries. There are nearly 180 cotton textile mills and many spinning mills supplying yarn to the decentralized handloom industry. Other important industries are cement, sugar, manufacture of textile machinery, power-driven pumps, bicycles, electrical machinery, tractors, rubber tyres and tubes, bricks and tiles and silk.

Public sector undertakings include the Neyveli lignite complex, petrochemicals, integral coach factory, high-pressure boiler plant, photographic film factory, surgical instruments factory, teleprinter factory, oil refinery, continuous casting plant and defence vehicles manufacture. Main exports: Cotton goods, tea, coffee, spices, engineering goods, motor-car ancillaries.

In 1986 there were 4,386 registered trade unions. Man-days lost by strikes, 2,372,440; by lockouts, 1,080,684.

Tourism. In 1982, 229,000 foreign tourists visited the state.

COMMUNICATIONS

Roads. On 31 March 1986 the state had approximately 160,942 km of national and state highways, major and other district roads. In 1986–87 there were 958,269 registered motor vehicles.

Railways. On 31 March 1988 there were 6,451 km of railway track (3,937 route km). Madras and Madurai are the main centres.

Aviation. There are airports at Madras, Tiruchirapalli and Madurai, with regular scheduled services to Bombay, Calcutta and Delhi. Madras is the main centre of airline routes in South India.

Shipping. Madras and Tuticorin are the chief ports. Important minor ports are Cuddalore and Nagapattinam. Madras handled 23·9m. tonnes of cargo in 1988-89, Tuticorin, 5·2m. The Inland Container Depot at Coimbatore has a capacity of 50,000 tonnes of export traffic; it is linked to Cochin (Kerala).

JUSTICE, RELIGION, EDUCATION AND WELFARE

Justice. There is a High Court at Madras with a Chief Justice and 16 judges. *Police.* Strength of armed police, 1986, 12,723; there were 6,033 specials and 33,115 local police.

Religion. At the 1981 census Hindus numbered 43,016,546 (88·86%), Christians, 2,798,048 (5·78%); Moslems, 2,519,947 (5·21%).

Education. At the 1981 census 22·6m. people were literate (14·3m. males).

Education is free up to pre-university level. In 1986-87 there were 39,325 schools for general education, 10·2m. students and 290,000 teachers. There were 199 general colleges (200,000 students and 15,155 teachers); 80 professional colleges (38,313 and 5,519); 19 special education colleges (2,366 and 316).

There are 13 universities. Madras University (founded in 1857) is affiliating and teaching. Annamalai University, Annamalainagar (founded 1928) is residential; Madurai University (founded 1966) is an affiliating and teaching university; ten others include one agricultural and one rural university, and Mother Theresa Women's University.

Health. There were (1987) 410 hospitals, 728 dispensaries, 466 primary health centres and 7,390 health sub-centres.

Statistical Information: The Department of Statistics (Fort St George, Madras) was established in 1948 and reorganized in 1953. *Director:* D. S. Rajabushanam, MA. Main publications: *Annual Statistical Abstract; Decennial Statistical Atlas; Season and Crop Report; Quinquennial Wages Census; Quarterly Abstract of Statistics.*

TRIPURA

HISTORY. A Hindu state of great antiquity having been ruled by the Maharajahs for 1,300 years before its accession to the Indian Union on 15 Oct. 1949. With the reorganization of states on 1 Sept. 1956 Tripura became a Union Territory, and was so declared on 1 Nov. 1957. The Territory was made a State on 21 Jan. 1972.

EVENTS. Tripura National Volunteers (tribal guerillas) signed an agreement with Union and State governments in Aug. 1988, to end an 8-month campaign of insurgency.

AREA AND POPULATION. Tripura is bounded by Bangladesh, except in the north-east where it joins Assam and Mizoram. The major portion of the state is hilly and mainly jungle. It has an area of 10,486 sq. km and a population of 2,053,058 (1981 census); Density, 196 per sq. km. Growth rate, 1971-81, 32·37%.

The official languages are Bengali and Kokbarak. Manipuri is also spoken.

CONSTITUTION AND GOVERNMENT. There is a Legislative Assembly of 60 members. The election of Jan. 1983 was won by the Communist Party of India (Marxist). The territory has 3 districts, divided into 10 administrative subdivisions, namely, Sadar, Khowai, Kailasahar, Dharmanagar, Sonamura, Udaipur, Belonia, Kamalpur, Sabroom and Amarpur.

The capital is Agartala (population, 1981, 132,186).

Governor: Raghunath Reddy.
Chief Minister: Sudhir Ranjan Majumdar.

BUDGET. Budget estimates 1988-89, receipts Rs 428 crores and expenditure Rs 452 crores. Annual outlay for 1990-91 was Rs 200 crores.

ENERGY AND NATURAL RESOURCES

Electricity. Installed capacity (1988), 25 mw; there were (1988) 2,292 electrified villages.

Agriculture. About 24% of the land area is cultivable. The tribes practise shifting cultivation, but this is being replaced by modern methods. The main crops are rice, wheat, jute, mesta, potatoes, oilseeds and sugar-cane. Foodgrain production (1987-88), about 442,100 tonnes. There are 54 registered tea gardens producing 3,339,000 kg. per year, and employing 8,945.

Forestry. Forests cover about 55% of the land area. They have been much depleted by clearance for shifting cultivation and, recently, for refugee settlements of Bangladeshis. About 8% of the forest area still consists of dense natural forest; losses elsewhere are being replaced by plantation. Commercial rubber plantation has also been encouraged. In 1988, 7,597 hectares were under new rubber plantations.

INDUSTRY. Tea is the main industry. There is also a jute mill producing about 15 tonnes per day and employing about 2,000. The main small industries: Aluminium utensils, petrochemicals, rubber, saw-milling, soap, piping, fruit canning, handloom weaving and sericulture. Handloom weaving products (1983–84) were valued at Rs 9·75 crores.

COMMUNICATIONS

Roads. Total length of motorable roads (1988) 5,441 km, of which 3,320 km were surfaced. Vehicles registered, 31 March 1988, 13,963, of which 3,542 were lorries.

Railways. There is a railway between Dharmanagar and Kalkalighat (Assam).

Aviation. There is 1 airport and 2 airstrips. The airport (Agartala) has regular scheduled services to Calcutta.

EDUCATION AND WELFARE

Education. In 1987-88 there were 1,927 primary schools (362,462 pupils); 418 middle schools (108,651); 381 high and higher secondary schools (61,730). There were 11 colleges of general education, 9 institutions of professional and technical education and 1,203 social education centres.

Health. There were (1988) 21 hospitals, with 1,810 beds, 317 dispensaries, 539 doctors and 618 nurses. There were 47 primary health centres and 66 family planning centres.

UTTAR PRADESH

HISTORY. In 1833 the then Bengal Presidency was divided into two parts, one of which became the Presidency of Agra. In 1836 the Agra area was styled the North-West Province and placed under a Lieut.-Governor. The two provinces of Agra and Oudh were placed, in 1877, under one administrator, styled Lieut.-Governor of the North-West Province and Chief Commissioner of Oudh. In 1902 the name was changed to 'United Provinces of Agra and Oudh', under a Lieut.-Governor, and the Lieut.-Governorship was altered to a Governorship in 1921. In 1935 the name was shortened to 'United Provinces'. On Independence, the states of Rampur, Banaras and Tehri-Garwhal were merged with United Provinces. In 1950 the name of the United Provinces was changed to Uttar Pradesh.

AREA AND POPULATION. Uttar Pradesh is in north India and is bounded north by Himachal Pradesh, Tibet and Nepál, east by Bihar, south by Madhya Pradesh and west by Rajasthan, Haryana and Delhi. The area of the state is 294,411 sq. km. Population (1981 census), 110,862,013, a density of 377 per sq. km. Growth rate, 1971–81, 25·52%. Cities with more than 250,000 population, *see* p. 632. The official language is Hindi.

CONSTITUTION AND GOVERNMENT. Uttar Pradesh has had an autonomous system of government since 1937. There is a bicameral legislature. The Legislative Council has 108 members; the Legislative Assembly has 426, of which 425 are elected. After the elections in Nov. 1989 a Janata Dal government was returned.

There are 13 administrative divisions, each under a Commissioner, and 62 districts.

The capital is Lucknow.

Governor: B. Satya Narain Reddy.
Chief Minister: Mulayan Singh Yadav.

BUDGET. Budget estimates 1989–90 show revenue and capital receipts of Rs 9,635·03 crores; revenue and capital account expenditure, Rs 11,505·34 crores. Annual plan outlay (1989-90) Rs 2,800 crores.

ENERGY AND NATURAL RESOURCES

Electricity. The State Electricity Board had, 1987–88, an installed capacity of 4,566 mw. There were 75,749 villages with electricity in March 1988, out of a total 112,566.

Minerals. The state has magnesite, fire-clay, coal, copper, dolomite, limestone, soapstone, gypsum, bauxite, diaspore, ochre, phosphorite, pyrophyllite, silica sand and steatite among others.

Agriculture. Agriculture occupies 78% of the work force. 10·13m. hectares are irrigated. The state is India's largest producer of foodgrains; production (1987–88), 28·12m. tonnes; sugar-cane 8·82m.; oilseeds, 1·22m. The state is one of India's main producers of sugar. There were (1987-88) 1,605 veterinary centres for cattle.

Forests cover (1987) about 5·13m. sq. km.

The state government in 1985 began a management programme for the ravines of the Chambal river catchment area. The programme includes stabilizing ravines, soil conservation, afforestation, pasture development and ravine reclamation. Estimated cost of a six-year programme, Rs 453·96m.

INDUSTRY. Sugar production is important; other industries include edible oils, textiles, distilleries, brewing, leather working, agricultural engineering, paper and chemicals. There is an aluminium smelter at Renukoot. An oil refinery at Mathura has capacity of 6m. tonnes per annum. Large public-sector enterprises have been set up in electrical engineering, pharmaceuticals, locomotive building, general engineering, electronics and aeronautics. Village and small-scale industries are important; there were 130,061 small units in 1987-88. A petrochemical complex and a fertilizer complex are being implemented at Auriya and Shahjahanpur respectively. About one-third of cloth output is from hand-looms. Total working population (1981) 30·8m., of whom 6·8m. were non-agricultural.

COMMUNICATIONS

Roads. There were, 31 March 1987, 60,306 km of motorable roads. In 1987-88 there were 1,240,939 motor vehicles of which 829,230 were motorcycles.

Railways. Lucknow is the main junction of the northern network; other important junctions are Agra, Kanpur, Allahabad, Pant Nagar, Dehra Dun and Varanasi.

Aviation. There are airports at Lucknow, Kanpur, Varanasi, Allahabad, Agra and Gorakhpur.

JUSTICE, RELIGION, EDUCATION AND WELFARE

Justice. The High Court of Judicature at Allahabad (with a bench at Lucknow) has a Chief Justice and 49 puisne judges including additional judges. There are 56 sessions divisions in the state.

Religion. At the 1981 census Hindus numbered 92,365,968; Moslems, 17,657,735; Sikhs, 458,647; Christians, 162,199; Jains, 141,549; Buddhists, 54,542.

Education. At the 1981 census 30·1m. people were literate. In 1987–88 there were 74,480 junior basic schools, 16,582 senior basic schools and 2,364 high schools and 3,373 intermediate/junior colleges.

Uttar Pradesh has 20 universities: Allahabad University (founded 1887); Agra University (1927); the Banaras Hindu University, Varanasi (1916); Lucknow University (1921); Aligarh Muslim University (1920); Roorkee University (1948), formerly Thomason College of Civil Engineering (established in 1847); Gorakhpur University (1957); Sampurnanand Sanskrit Vishwavidyalaya, Varanasi (1958). Kanpur University and Meerut University were founded in 1966. Govind Ballabh Pant University of Agriculture and Technology, Pantnagar (1960); Garhwal University, Srinagar, (1973). Two universities of agriculture were founded in 1974–75 and Avadh, Kumaon, Rohilkhand and Bundelkhand Universities in 1975. Jaunpur University (Purvanchal Vishwavidyalaya) was founded in 1987.

There are also four institutions with university status: Gurukul Kangri and Dayal Bagh Educational Institute. There are 8 medical colleges, 3 engineering colleges, 13 teacher-training colleges and 403 arts, science and commerce colleges.

Health. In 1987–88 there were 4,034 allopathic, 2,448 ayurvedic and unani and 980 homoepathic hospitals. There were also TB hospitals and clinics.

WEST BENGAL

HISTORY. For the history of Bengal under British rule, from 1633 to 1947, *see* THE STATESMAN'S YEAR-BOOK , 1952, p. 183.

Under the terms of the Indian Independence Act, 1947, the Province of Bengal ceased to exist. The Moslem majority districts of East Bengal, consisting of the Chittagong and Dacca Divisions and portions of the Presidency and Rajshahi Divisions, became what was then East Pakistan (now Bangladesh).

EVENTS. Gorkha seperatists have campaigned for a Gorkha state in the hill areas; there has been strike and terrorist action. In Aug. 1988 an agreement was signed establishing a Darjeeling Gorka Hill Council with limited autonomy.

AREA AND POPULATION. West Bengal is in north-east India and is bounded north by Sikkim and Bhután, east by Assam and Bangladesh, south by the Bay of Bengal and Orissa, west by Bihar and north-west by Nepál. The total area of West Bengal is 88,752 sq. km. At the 1981 census its population was 54,580,647, an increase of 23·17% since 1971, the density of population 621 per sq. km. Population of chief cities, *see* p. 632. The principal language is Bengali.

CONSTITUTION AND GOVERNMENT. The state of West Bengal came into existence as a result of the Indian Independence Act, 1947. The territory of Cooch-Behar State was merged with West Bengal on 1 Jan. 1950, and the former French possession of Chandernagore became part of the state on 2 Oct. 1954. Under the States Reorganization Act, 1956, certain portions of Bihar State (an area of 3,157 sq. miles with a population of 1,446,385) were transferred to West Bengal.

The Legislative Assembly has 295 seats. Distribution March 1987: Communist Party of India (Marxist), 187; Forward Bloc, 26; Revolutionary Socialist Party, 18; Communist Party of India, 11; Revolutionary Communist Party of India, 1; Forward Bloc (Marxist), 2; Democratic Socialist Party, 2; Socialist Party, 4. Total 'Left Front', 251. Opposition: Indian National Congress, 40; others, 3; nominated, 1.

The capital is Calcutta.

For administrative purposes there are 3 divisions (Jalpaiguri, Burdwan and Presidency), under which there are 17 districts, including Calcutta. The Calcutta Metropolitan Development Authority has been set up to co-ordinate development in the metropolitan area (1,350 sq. km). For the purposes of local self-government there are 15 *zila parishads* (district boards) excluding Darjeeling, 339 *panchayat samities* (regional boards), and 3,320 *gram* (village) *panchayats*. There are 111 municipalities, 3 Corporations and 9 Notified Areas. The Calcutta Corporation has a mayor and deputy mayor, a commissioner, aldermen and standing committees.

Governor: Nurul Hasan.
Chief Minister: J. Basu.

BUDGET. Budget estimates for 1989–90, receipts Rs 3,734·04 crores and expenditure Rs 3,932·42 crores. Plan outlay for 1990-91 was Rs 1,328 crores.

ENERGY AND NATURAL RESOURCES

Electricity. Installed capacity, 1988–89, 3,616 mw; 23,485 villages had electricity at 31 March 1988.

Water. The major irrigation and power scheme at present under construction is (1987) the Teesta barrage. Major irrigation schemes are the Mayurakshi Reservoir, Kansabati Reservoir, Mahananda Barrage and Aqueduct and Damodar Valley. At March 1988 there were 10,896 tubewells and 3,198 riverlift irrigation schemes.

Minerals. Value of production, 1986, Rs 5,120m. The state has coal (the Raniganj field is one of the 3 biggest in India) including coking coal. Coal production (1987) 21·06m. tonnes.

Agriculture. About 5·5m. hectares were under rice-paddy in 1987-88. Total foodgrain production, 1987–88, 10·3m. tonnes; oilseeds, 505,800 tonnes; jute, 3·6m.

bales (180 kg); wheat, 673,900 tonnes; tea, 152·22m. kg. The state produces 54·3% of the national output of jute and *mesta*.

Livestock (1976 census): 11,968,000 cattle, 758,000 buffaloes; 1981 census, 758,000 sheep and goats, and 15,052,000 poultry.

Forests cover 13·4% of the state.

Fisheries. Landings, 1987–88, about 505,000 tonnes. During 1986–87 Rs 78m. was invested in fishery schemes.

INDUSTRY. The total number of registered factories, 1986, was 8,064; average daily employment in public sector industries, 1987, 1·7m. The coalmining industry, 1986, had 112 units with average daily employment of 121,000.

There is a large automobile factory at Uttarpara, and there are aluminium rolling-mills at Belur and Asansol. Durgapur has a large steel plant and other industries under the state sector—a thermal power plant, coke oven plant, fertilizer factory, alloy steel plant and ophthalmic glass plant. There are a locomotive factory and cable factory at Chittaranjan and Rupnarayanpur. A refinery and fertilizer factory are operating at Haldia.

Small industries are important; 301,214 units were registered at 31 Dec. 1988, (estimated employment, 1·6m.).

COMMUNICATIONS

Roads. In 1987–88 the length of national highway was 1,631 km, of state highway. On 31 March 1989 the state had 776,301 motor vehicles.

Railways. The route-km of railways within the state (1987–88) is 3,847 km. The main centres are Howrah, Sealdah, Kharagpur, Asansol and New Jalpaiguri. The Calcutta Metro was 75% complete by July 1987.

Aviation. The main airport is Calcutta which has national and international flights. The second airport is at Bagdogra in the extreme north, which has regular scheduled services to Calcutta. Vayudoot domestic airline flies between Calcutta and district headquarters.

Shipping. Calcutta is the chief port: A barrage has been built at Farakka to control the flow of the Ganges and to provide a rail and road link between North and South Bengal. A second port is being developed at Haldia, halfway between the present port and the sea, which is intended mainly for bulk cargoes. West Bengal possesses 779 km of navigable canals.

JUSTICE, RELIGION, EDUCATION AND WELFARE

Justice. The High Court of Judicature at Calcutta has a Chief Justice and 41 puisne judges. The Andaman and Nicobar Islands *(see below)* come under its jurisdiction.

Police. In 1989 the police force numbered 57,599, under a director-general and an inspector-general. Calcutta has a separate force under a commissioner directly responsible to the Government; its strength was 21,535 at 1 Oct. 1989.

Religion. At the 1981 census Hindus numbered 42,007,159; Moslems, 11,743,259; Christians, 319,670; Buddhists, 156,296; Sikhs, 49,054; Jains, 38,663.

Education. At the 1981 census 22·2m. people were literate. In 1987–88 there were 50,287 primary schools, 4,147 junior high and 6,801 high and higher secondary schools. Education is free up to higher secondary stage. There are 8 universities.

The University of Calcutta (founded 1857) is affiliating and teaching; in 1983–84 it had 150,000 students. Visva Bharati, Santiniketan, was established in 1951 and is residential and teaching; it had 3,943 students in 1985–86. The University of Jadavpur, Calcutta (1955), had 6,000 students in 1989–90. Burdwan University was established in 1960; in 1985–86 there were 84,095 students. Kalyani University was established in 1960 (2,306 students in 1985–86). The University of North Bengal (1962) had 22,504 students in 1984–85. Rabindra Bharati University had 4,273 students in 1985–86. Bidhan Chandra Krishi Viswavidyalaya (1974) had 540 students in 1985–86.

Health. There were (1987) 412 hospitals, 337 primary health centres, 837 subsidiary health centres, 7,665 sub-centres and 5 poly-clinics.

UNION TERRITORIES

ANDAMAN AND NICOBAR ISLANDS. The Andaman and Nicobar Islands are administered by the President of the Republic of India acting through a Lieut.-Governor. There is a 30-member Pradesh Council, 5 members of which are selected by the Administrator as advisory counsellors. The seat of administration is at Port Blair, which is connected with Calcutta (1,255 km away) and Madras (1,190 km) by steamer service which calls about every 10 days; there are air services from Calcutta and Madras. Roads in the islands, 733 km black-topped and 48 km others. There are 2 districts.

The population (1981 census) was 188,741; Area, 8,249 sq. km; density 23 per sq. km. Port Blair (1981), 49,634.

The climate is tropical, with little variation in temperature. Heavy rain (125" annually) is mainly brought by the south-west monsoon. Humidity is high.

Budget figures for 1988–89 show total revenue receipts of Rs 23·15 lakhs, and total expenditure on revenue account of Rs 17,979 lakhs.

On 31 March 1988 there were 314 educational institutions, including a B. Ed. college, another teachers' training college, and a polytechnic. Literacy (1981 census), 51·56%.

Lieut.-Governor: Lieut.-Gen. R. S. Dayal.

The **Andaman Islands** lie in the Bay of Bengal, 193 km from Cape Negrais in Burma, 1,255 from Calcutta and 1,190 from Madras. Five large islands grouped together are called the Great Andamans, and to the south is the island of Little Andaman. There are some 204 islets, the two principal groups being the Ritchie Archipelago and the Labyrinth Islands. The Great Andaman group is about 467 km long and, at the widest, 51 km broad.

The original inhabitants live in the forests by hunting and fishing; they are of a small Negrito type and their civilization is about that of the Stone Age. Their exact numbers are not known, as they avoid all contact with civilization. The total population of the Andaman Islands (including about 430 aboriginals) was 158,287 in 1981. Main aboriginal tribes, Andamanese, Onges, Jarawas and Sentinelese. Under a central government scheme started in 1953, some 4,000 displaced families, mostly from East Pakistan, had been settled in the islands by May 1967.

Japanese forces occupied the Andaman Islands on 23 March 1942. Civil administration of the islands was resumed on 8 Oct. 1945.

From 1857 to March 1942 the islands were used by the Government of India as a penal settlement for life and long-term convicts, but the penal settlement was abolished on re-occupation in Oct. 1945.

The Great Andaman group, densely wooded, contains many valuable trees, both hardwood and softwood. The best known of the hardwoods is the *padauk* or Andaman redwood; *gurjan* is in great demand for the manufacture of plywood. Large quantities of softwood are supplied to match factories. Annually the Forest Department export about 25,000 tons of timber to the mainland. Coconut, coffee and rubber are cultivated. The islands are slowly being made self-sufficient in paddy and rice, and now grow approximately half their annual requirements. Livestock (1982): 27,400 cattle, 9,720 buffaloes, 17,600 goats and 21,220 pigs. Fishing is important. There is a sawmill at Port Blair and a coconut-oil mill. Little Andaman has a palm-oil mill.

The islands possess a number of harbours and safe anchorages, notably Port Blair in the south, Port Cornwallis in the north and Elphinstone and Mayabandar in the middle.

The **Nicobar Islands** are situated to the south of the Andamans, 121 km from Little Andaman. The British were in possession 1869–1947. There are 19 islands, 7 uninhabited; total area, 1,953 sq. km. The islands are usually divided into 3 sub-groups (southern, central and northern), the chief islands in each being respectively, Great Nicobar, Camotra with Nancowrie and Car Nicobar. There is a fine land-locked harbour between the islands of Camotra and Nancowrie, known as Nancowrie Harbour.

The population numbered, in 1981, 30,454, including about 22,200 of Nicobarese and Shompen tribes. The coconut and arecanut are the main items of trade, and coconuts are a major item in the people's diet.

The Nicobar Islands were occupied by the Japanese in July 1942; and Car Nicobar was developed as a big supply base. The Allies reoccupied the islands on 8 Oct. 1945.

CHANDIGARH. On 1 Nov. 1966 the city of Chandigarh and the area surrounding it was constituted a Union Territory. Population (1981), 451,610; density, 3,948 per sq. km.; growth rate, 1971–81, 74·9%. Area, 114 sq. km. It serves as the joint capital of both Punjab (India) and the state of Haryana, and is the seat of a High Court and of a university serving both states. The city will ultimately be the capital of just the Punjab; joint status is to last while a new capital is built for Haryana.

There is some cultivated land and some forest (27·5% of the territory).

Administrator: Nirmal Kumar Mukharji.

DADRA AND NAGAR HAVELI. Formerly Portuguese, the territories of Dadra and Nagar Haveli were occupied in July 1954 by nationalists, and a pro-India administration was formed; this body made a request for incorporation into the Union, 1 June 1961. By the 10th amendment to the constitution the territories became a centrally administered Union Territory with effect from 11 Aug. 1961, forming an enclave at the southernmost point of the border between Gujarat and Maharashtra. Area 491 sq. km.; population (1981), 103,676 (males 52,515, females 51,161); density 211 per sq. km; growth rate, 1971–81, 39·78%. There is an Administrator appointed by the Government of India. The day-to-day business is done by various departments, co-ordinated by the Administrator's secretary and headed by a Collector. Headquarters are at Silvassa. The territory and 78·82% of the population is tribal and organized in 72 villages. Languages used are Bhilli, Gujarat, Bhilodi (91·1%), Marathi and Hindi.

Administrator: Khurshid Alam Khan.
Chief Secretary: R. P. Rai.

Electricity. Electricity is supplied by Gujarat, and all villages have been electrified.

Water. As the result of a joint project with the governments of Gujarat, Goa, Daman and Diu there is a reservoir at Damanganga with irrigation potential of 8,280 hectares.

Agriculture. Farming is the chief occupation, and about 25,000 hectares were under crops in 1988–89. Much of the land is terraced and there is a 100% subsidy for soil conservation. The major food crops are rice and ragi; wheat, small millets and pulses are also grown. There is little irrigation (1,280 hectares). There are 9 veterinary centres, a veterinary hospital, an agricultural research centre and breeding centres to improve strains of cattle and poultry. During 1988–89 the Administration distributed 250 tonnes of high yielding paddy seed, and high yielding wheat seed, and 611 tonnes of fertilizer.

Forests. About 20,311 hectares or 41·2% of the total area is forest, mainly of teak, sadad and khair. Timber production provides the largest simple contribution to the territory's revenue. There was (1985) a moratorium on commercial felling, to preserve the environmental function of the forests and ensure local supplies of firewood, timber and fodder.

Industry. There is no heavy industry, and the Territory is a ''No Industry District''. Industrial estates for small and medium units have been set up at Piparia, Masat and Khadoli. There were (1989) 322 small units, and 89 medium scale, employing about 7,000. Concessions (25% subsidy, 15 years' sales tax holiday) are available for small industries.

Communications. There are (1989) 326 km of motorable road. The railway line from Bombay to Ahmedabad runs through Vapi near Silvassa. The nearest airport is Bombay.

Tourism. The territory is a rural area between the industrial centres of Bombay and Surat-.Vapi. The Tourism Department is developing areas of natural beauty to promote acceptable tourism.

Justice. The territory is under the jurisdiction of the Bombay (Maharashtra) High Court. There is a District and Sessions Court and one Junior Division Civil Court at Silvassa.

Education. Literacy was 26·67% of the population at the 1981 census. In 1988–89 there were 150 adult education centres (4,500 students); there were 122 primary schools, 39 middle schools; 3 higher secondary schools and 5 high schools. Total primary enrolment was 18,331; high-school and higher secondary, 3,491.

Health. The territory had (1989) 1 cottage hospital, 5 primary health centres and 4 dispensaries; there is also a mobile dispensary.

DAMAN AND DIU. Daman (Damão) on the Gujarat coast, 100 miles (160 km) north of Bombay, was seized by the Portuguese in 1531 and ceded to them (1539) by the Shar of Gujarat. The island of Diu, captured in 1534, lies off the south-east coast of Kathiawar (Gujarat); there is a small coastal area. Former Portuguese forts on either side of the entrance to the Gulf of Cambay, in Dec. 1961 the territories were occupied by India and incorporated into the Indian Union; they were administered as one unit together with Goa, to which they were attached until 30 May 1987, when Goa was seperated from them and became a state.

Area and Population. Daman, 72 sq. km, population (1981) 48,560; Diu, 40 sq. km, population 30,421. The main language spoken is Gujarati.

The chief towns are Daman (population, 1981, 21,003) and Diu (8,020).

Daman and Diu have been governed as parts of a Union Territory since Dec. 1961, becoming the whole of that Territory on 30 May 1987.

The main activities are tourism, fishing and tapping the toddy palm. In Daman there is rice-growing, some wheat and dairying. Diu has fine tourist beaches, grows coconuts and pearl millet, and processes salt.

Administrator: Khurshid Alam Khan.

DELHI. Delhi became a Union Territory on 1 Nov. 1956.

Area and Population. The territory forms an enclave inside the eastern frontier of Haryana in north India. Delhi has an area of 1,483 sq. km. At the 1981 census its population was 6,220,406 (density per sq. km, 4,194). Estimate, 1 July 1987, 8·04m. Growth rate, 1971–81, 53%. In the rural area of Delhi there are 214 inhabited and 17 deserted villages and 27 census towns. They are distributed in 5 community development blocks.

Government. The Lieut-Governor is the Administrator, assisted by 4 Executive Councillors (1 Chief Executive Councillor and 3 Executive Councillors) appointed by the President of India on the recommendation of the Union Home Ministry. There is a Metropolitan Council of 61 members including 5 nominated by the President of India. The Territory is covered by 3 local bodies: Delhi Municipal Corporation, New Delhi Municipal Committee and Delhi Cantonment Board.

Lieut.-Governor: Air Chief Marshal Arjan Singh.
Chief Executive Councillor: J. Pravesh Chandra.

Budget. Revised estimates 1988–89 show total revenue of Rs 9,527m. and expenditure including plan expenditure: Rs 12,341m. of which plan, Rs 5,577m.; power, Rs 1,733m.; transport, Rs 789m.; water and sewerage, Rs 713m.; urban development, Rs 662m.; medical services and public health, Rs 434m. Plan outlay (1989-90) Rs 620 crores.

Agriculture. The contribution to the economy is not significant. In 1987-88 about 69,411 hectares are cropped (of which 60,090 are irrigated). Animal husbandry is increasing and mixed farms are common. Chief crops are wheat, jowar, bajra, grain, sugar-cane and vegetables.

Industry. The modern city is the largest commercial centre in northern India and an important industrial centre. Since 1947 a large number of industrial concerns have been established; these include factories for the manufacture of razor blades, sports goods, radios and television and parts, bicycles and parts, plastic and PVC goods including footwear, textiles, chemicals, fertilizers, medicines, hosiery, leather goods, soft drinks, hand tools. There is also metal forging, casting, galvanising and electroplating, and printing. The number of industrial units functioning was about 73,000 in 1987–88; average number of workers employed was 657,000. Production was worth Rs 38,500m. and investment was about Rs 14,200m.

Some traditional handicrafts, for which Delhi was formerly famous, still flourish; among them are ivory carving, miniature painting, gold and silver jewellery and papier mâché work. The handwoven textiles of Delhi are particularly fine; this craft is being successfully revived.

Delhi publishes major daily newspapers, including the *Times of India, Hindustan Times, The Hindu, Indian Express, National Herald, Patriot, Economic Times, Financial Express* and *Statesman* (all in English); *Nav Bharat Times, Jansatta* and *Hindustan* (in Hindi), and 3 Urdu dailies

Roads. Five national highways pass through the city. There were (1988) 1,415,931 registered motor vehicles in Delhi. The Transport Corporation had 4,248 buses in daily service in 1988-89.

Railways. Delhi is an important rail junction with three main stations: Delhi, New Delhi, Hazart Nizamuddin. There is an electric ring railway for commuters.

Aviation. Indira Gandhi International Airport operates international flights; Palam airport operates internal flights.

Religion. At the 1981 census Hindus numbered 5,200,432; Sikhs, 393,921; Moslems, 481,802; Jains, 73,917; Christians, 61,609; Buddhists, 7,117; others, 1,608.

Education. The proportion of literates to the total population was 61·54% at the 1981 census (68·4% of males and 53·07% of females).

The University of Delhi was founded in 1922; it had 66 constituent colleges and institutions in 1987–88, with a total of 121,445 students.There are also Jawaharlal Nehru university, Indira Gandhi National Open University and the Jamia Millia Islamia; the Indian Institute of Technology at Haus Khaz; the Indian Agricultural Research Institute at Pusa; the All India Institute of Medical Science at Ansari Nagar and the Indian Institute of Public Administration are deemed universities.

Health. In 1988 there were 79 hospitals including 43 general, 27 special, 5 Ayurvedic, 2 Unani, 2 Homeopathic. There were 609 dispensaries.

LAKSHADWEEP. The territory consists of an archipelago of 36 islands (10 inhabited), about 300 km off the west coat of Kerala. It was constituted a Union Territory in 1956 as the Laccadive, Minicoy and Amindivi Islands, and renamed in Nov. 1973. The total area of the islands is 32 sq. km. The northern portion is called the Amindivis. The remaining islands are called the Laccadives (except Minicoy Island). The inhabited islands are: Androth (the largest), Amini, Agatti, Bitra, Chetlat, Kadmat, Kalpeni, Kavaratti, Kiltan and Minicoy. Androth is 4·8 sq. km, and is nearest to Kerala. An Advisory Committee associated with the Union Home Minister and an Advisory Council to the Administrator assist in the administration of the islands; these are constituted annually. Population (1981 census), 40,249, nearly all Moslems. Density, 1,258 per sq. km.; growth rate, 1971–81, 26·53%. The language is Malayalam, but the language in Minicoy is Mahl. There were, in autumn 1988, 9 high schools and 9 nursery schools, 19 junior basic schools, 4 senior basic schools and 2 junior colleges. There are 2 hospitals and 7 primary health centres. The staple products are copra and fish. There is a tourist resort at Bangarem, an uninhabited island with an extensive lagoon. Headquarters of administration, Kavaratti Island. An airport, with Vayadoot services, opened on Agatti island in April 1988. The islands are also served by ship from the mainland and have helicopter inter-island services.

Administrator: Wajahat Habibullah.

PONDICHERRY. Formerly the chief French settlement in India, Pondicherry was founded by the French in 1674, taken by the Dutch in 1693 and restored to the French in 1699. The English took it in 1761, restored it in 1765, re-took it in 1778, restored it a second time in 1785, retook it a third time in 1793 and finally restored it to the French in 1814. Administration was transferred to India on 1 Nov. 1954. A Treaty of Cession (together with Karikal, Mahé and Yanam) was signed on 28 May 1956; instruments of ratification were signed on 16 Aug. 1962 from which date (by the 14th amendment to the Indian Constitution) Pondicherry, comprising the 4 territories, became a Union Territory.

Area and Population. The territory is composed of enclaves on the Coromandel Coast of Tamil Nadu and Andhra Pradesh, with Mahé forming an enclave on the coast of Kerala. The total area of Pondicherry is 492 sq. km, divided into 4 Districts. On Tamil Nadu coast: Pondicherry (293 sq. km; population, 1981 census, 444,417), Karikal (160; 120,010). On Kerala coast: Mahé (9; 28,413). On Andhra Pradesh coast: Yanam (30; 11,631). Total population (1981 census), 604,471; density, 1,228 per sq. km.; growth rate, 1971–81, 28·14%. Pondicherry Municipality had (1981) 162,639 inhabitants. The principal languages spoken are Tamil, Telegu, Malayalam, French and English.

Government. By the Government of Union Territories Act 1963 Pondicherry is governed by a Lieut.-Governor, appointed by the President, and a Council of Ministers responsible to a Legislative Assembly. The election in March 1985 returned a Congress (I) government.

Lieut.-Governor: Mrs Chandrawati.

Planning. Approved outlay for 1989–90 was Rs 630m. Of this, Rs 24m. was for agriculture, Rs 16m. for rural development, Rs 10m. for co-operatives, Rs 128m. for education, Rs 12m. for public works, Rs 85m. for electricity, Rs 12m. for fisheries.

Budget. Budget estimates for 1988–89 show revenue receipts of Rs 77·82 crores.

Electricity. Power is bought from neighbouring states. All 292 villages have electricity. Consumption, 1988–89, 361 units per head. Peak demand, 88 mw.; total consumption, 360·74m. units.

Agriculture. Nearly 45% of the population is engaged in agriculture and allied pursuits; 90% of the cultivated area is irrigated. The main food crop is rice. Foodgrain production, 62,663 tonnes from 31,315 hectares in 1986–87, of which 57,784 tonnes was paddy; cash crops include oilseeds, cotton (7,700 bales of 180 kg) and sugar-cane (325,325 tonnes).

Industry. There are (1989) 13 large and 42 medium-scale industries manufacturing consumer goods such as textiles, sugar, cotton yarn, paper, spirits and beer, potassium chlorate, rice bran oil, vehicle parts and soap. There were also 3,322 small industrial units engaged in varied manufacturing.

Roads. There were (1987) 402 km of roads of which 399 km were surfaced. Motor vehicles (1986) 47,817.

Railways. Pondicherry is connected to Villupuram Junction.

Aviation. The nearest airport is Madras.

Education. There were, in Sept. 1988, 110 pre-primary schools (7,289 pupils and

206 teachers), 351 primary schools (49,481 and 1,787), 101 middle schools (46,851 and 1,673), 72 high schools (46,201 and 1,664) and 24 higher secondary schools (26,886 and 980). There were 9 general education colleges (6,021 and 639); a medical college, a law college, a technical higher secondary school and a polytechnic had a total of 2,377 students.

Health. On 31 March 1988 there were 8 hospitals, 59 health centres and dispensaries and 70 sub-centres. In 1987 family schemes had reduced the birth rate to 22·4, the infant mortality rate to 35·5 per 1,000 live births.

INDONESIA

Republik Indonesia

Capital: Jakarta
Population: 175·6m. (1988)
GNP per capita: US$430 (1988)

HISTORY. In the 16th century Portuguese traders in quest of spices settled in some of the islands, but were ejected by the British, who in turn were ousted by the Dutch (1595). From 1602 the Netherlands East India Company conquered the Netherlands East Indies, and ruled them until the dissolution of the company in 1798. Thereafter the Netherlands Government ruled the colony from 1816 to 1941, when it was occupied by the Japanese until 1945. An independent republic was proclaimed by Dr Sukarno and Dr Hatta on 17 Aug. 1945.

Complete and unconditional sovereignty was transferred to the Republic of the United States of Indonesia on 27 Dec. 1949, except for the western part of New Guinea, the status of which was to be determined through negotiations between Indonesia and the Netherlands within one year after the transfer of sovereignty. A union was created to regulate the relationship between the two countries. A settlement of the New Guinea (Irian Jaya) question was, however, delayed until 15 Aug. 1962, when, through the good offices of the United Nations, an agreement was concluded for the transfer of the territory to Indonesia on 1 May 1963. In Feb. 1956 Indonesia abrogated the union and in Aug. 1956 repudiated Indonesia's debt to the Netherlands.

During 1950 the federal system which had sprung up in 1946–48 (*see* THE STATESMAN'S YEAR-BOOK, 1950, p. 1233) was abolished, and Indonesia was again made a unitary state. The provisional constitution was passed by the Provisional House of Representatives on 14 and came into force on 17 Aug. 1950. On 5 July 1959 by Presidential decree, the Constitution of 1945 was reinstated and the Constituent Assembly dissolved. For history 1960–66 *see* THE STATESMAN'S YEAR-BOOK, 1982–83, p. 678.

On 11–12 March 1966 the military commanders under the leadership of Lieut.-Gen. Suharto took over the executive power while leaving President Sukarno as the head of State. The Communist Party was at once outlawed and the National Front was dissolved in Oct. 1966. On 22 Feb. 1967 Sukarno handed over all his powers to Gen. Suharto.

AREA AND POPULATION. Indonesia, covering a total land area of 741,098 sq. miles (1,919,443 sq. km), consists of 13,677 islands (6,000 of which are inhabited) extending about 3,200 miles east to west through three time-zones (East, Central and West Indonesian Standard time) and 1,250 miles north to south. The largest islands are Sumatra, Java, Kalimantan (Indonesian Borneo), Sulawesi (Celebes) and Irian Jaya (the western part of New Guinea). Most of the smaller islands except Madura and Bali are grouped together. The two largest groups of islands are Maluku (the Moluccas) and Nusa Tenggara (the Lesser Sundas).

The total population in 1980 (census) was 147,490,298, distributed as follows:

Province	*Sq. km*	*Census 1980*	*Chief town*	*Census 1980*
Aceh (D.I.)	55,392	2,611,271	Banda Aceh	72,090
Sumatera Utara	70,787	8,360,894	Medan	1,378,955
Sumatera Barat	49,778	3,406,816	Padang	480,922
Riau	94,562	2,168,535	Pakanbaru	186,262
Jambi	44,924	1,445,994	Telanaipura	230,373
Sumatera Selatan	103,688	4,629,801	Palembang	787,187
Bengkulu	21,168	768,064	Bengkulu	64,783
Lampung	33,307	4,624,785	Tanjungkarang	284,275
Sumatera	473,606	28,016,160		

Province	*Sq. km*	*Census 1980*	*Chief town*	*Census 1980*
Jakarta Raya (D.C.I.)	590	6,503,449	Jakarta	6,503,449
Jawa Barat	46,300	27,453,525	Bandung	1,462,637
Jawa Tengah	34,206	25,372,889	Semarang	1,026,671
Yogyakarta (D.I.)	3,169	2,750,813	Yogyakarta	398,727
Jawa Timur	47,922	29,188,852	Surabaya	2,027,913
Jawa and Madura	132,187	91,269,528		
Kalimantan Barat	146,760	2,486,068	Pontianak	304,778
Kalimantan Tengah	152,600	954,353	Palangkaraya	60,447
Kalimantan Selatan	37,660	2,064,649	Banjarmasin	381,286
Kalimantan Timur	202,440	1,218,016	Samarinda	264,718
Kalimantan	539,460	6,723,086		
Sulawesi Utara	19,023	2,115,384	Menado	217,159
Sulawesi Tengah	69,726	1,289,635	Palu	298,584
Sulawesi Selatan	72,781	6,062,212	Ujung Padang	709,038
Sulawesi Tenggara	27,686	942,302	Kendari	41,021
Sulawesi	189,216	10,409,533		
Bali	5,561	2,469,930	Denpasar	261,263
Nusa Tenggara Barat	20,177	2,724,664	Mataram	68,964
Nusa Tenggara Timur	47,876	2,737,166	Kupang	403,110
Timor Timur [1]	14,874	555,350	Dili	60,150
Maluku	74,505	1,411,006	Amboina	208,898
Irian Jaya	421,981	1,173,875	Jayapura	149,618
Pulau–Pulau Lain	584,974	11,071,991		

[1] Formerly Portuguese East Timor.

Other major cities (census 1980): Malang, 511,780; Surakarta, 469,888; Bogor, 247,409; Cirebon, 223,776; Kediri, 221,830; Madiun, 150,562; Pematangsiantar, 150,376; Pekalongan, 132,558; Tegal, 131,728; Magelang, 123,484; Jember, 122,712; Sukabumi, 109,994 and Probolinggo, 100,296 (all on Java); Balikpapan (on Kalimantan), 280,875. Estimate (1988) 175·6m.

The principal ethnic groups are the Acehnese, Bataks and Minangkabaus in Sumatra, the Javanese and Sundanese in Java, the Madurese in Madura, the Balinese in Bali, the Sasaks in Lombok, the Menadonese, Minahasans, Torajas and Buginese in Sulawesi, the Dayaks in Kalimantan, Irianese in Irian Jaya, the Ambonese in the Moluccas and Timorese in Timor Timur.

Bahasa Indonesia, a Malay dialect, is the official language of the Republic although Dutch is spoken as an unofficial language.

CLIMATE. Conditions vary greatly over this spread of islands, but generally the climate is tropical monsoon, with a dry season from June to Sept. and a wet one from Oct. to April. Temperatures are high all the year and rainfall varies according to situation on lee or windward shores. Jakarta. Jan. 78°F (25·6°C), July 78°F (25·6°C). Annual rainfall 71" (1,775 mm). Padang. Jan. 79°F (26·7°C), July 79°F (26·7°C). Annual rainfall 177" (4,427 mm). Surabaya. Jan. 79°F (27·2°C), July 78°F (25·6°C). Annual rainfall 51" (1,285 mm).

CONSTITUTION AND GOVERNMENT. Indonesia is a sovereign, independent republic.

The People's Consultative Assembly is the supreme power. It has 1,000 members and it sits at least once every 5 years. The House of People's Representatives has 500 members, 400 of them elected, 100 as representatives from various groupings, and sits for a 5-year term.

General elections to the 400 elected seats in the House of Representatives were held on 23 April 1987 and 299 seats were won by the Golkar Party.

The Cabinet was as follows in Nov. 1989:

President, Prime Minister and Minister of Defence: Gen. Suharto, elected by the People's Consultative Assembly in 1968 and re-elected in 1973, 1978, 1983 and 1988.

Vice-President: Sudharmono. *Internal Affairs:* Rudini. *Foreign Affairs:* Ali Alatas. *Defence and Security:* L. B. Murdani. *Justice:* Ismail Saleh. *Information:* Harmoko. *Finance:* Dr J. B. Sumarlin. *Trade:* Dr Arifin Siregar. *Industry:* Hartarto. *Agriculture:* Wardoyo. *Mines and Energy:* Dr Ginandjar Kartasasmita. *Public Works:* Radinal Mochtar. *Communications:* Azwar Anas. *Co-operatives:* Bustanil Arifin. *Manpower:* Cosmas Batubara. *Transmigration:* Sugiarto. *Tourism, Post and Telecommunications:* Susilo Sudarman. *Education and Culture:* Dr Fuad Hassan. *Health:* Dr Adhyatma. *Religious Affairs:* H. Munawir Sjadzali. *Social Affairs:* Dr Haryati Soebadio. *Forestry:* Hasrul Harahap. *Co-ordinator Minister of Political and Security Affairs:* Sudomo. *Co-ordinator Minister of Economic, Financial and Industrial Affairs and Development Supervision:* Radius Prawiro. *Co-ordinator Minister of People's Welfare:* Supardjo Rustam. *State Minister and Secretary of State:* Moerdiono. *State Minister of National Development Planning and Chairman of the National Development Planning Board:* Dr Saleh Afiff. *State Minister of Population and Environment:* Dr Emil Salim. *State Minister of Housing Affairs:* Siswono Yudohusodo. *State Minister of Youth Affairs and Sports:* Akbar Tandjung. *State Minister for the Assessment and Application of Technology:* Dr B. J. Habibe. *State Minister of Utilization of the State Apparatus:* Sarwono Kusumaatmadja. *State Minister of Women's Affairs:* Sulasikin Murpratomo. *Commander-in-Chief of the Armed Forces:* Gen. Try Sutrisno. *Attorney-General:* Sukarton Marmosudjono. *Governor of Central Bank:* Dr Adrianus Moy.

There are 6 junior ministers.

National flag: Horizontally red over white.

National anthem: Indonesia Raya (tune by Wage Rudolf Supratman, 1928).

Local government: There are 27 provinces, 3 of which are special territories (the capital city of Jakarta, Yogyakarta and Aceh), each administered by a Governor appointed by the President; they are divided into 246 districts (*kabupatens*), each under a district head (*bupati*), and 55 municipalities (*kotamadya*), each under a mayor (*wali kota*). The districts are divided into 3,539 sub-districts (*kecamtans*), each headed by a *camat*. There are 66,437 villages.

DEFENCE. The Indonesian Armed Forces were formally set up on 5 Oct. 1945. On 11 Oct. 1967 the Army, Navy, Air Force and Police were integrated under the Department of Defence and Security. Their commanders no longer hold cabinet rank. There is selective military service.

Army. There are 2 infantry divisions and another forming: 1 armoured cavalry brigade, 3 infantry brigades, 3 airborne infantry brigades, 3 artillery regiments, 2 engineer battalions and 4 special warfare groups. There are 63 independent infantry battalions, 17 independent artillery battalions and 8 independent cavalry battalions. Equipment includes 100 AMX-13 and 41 PT-76 light tanks. The Army has over 80 aircraft, including 1 Islander, 2 C-47s and 25 other fixed-wing types, 16 Bell 205, 13 BO 105, 20 Hughes 300, 28 helicopters and locally-built Bell 412 helicopters. Total strength in 1990 was 215,000.

Navy. The Indonesian navy in 1989 numbered 43,000, including 12,000 in the Commando Corps, and 1,000 in the Naval Air Arm. Combatant strength includes 2 German-built diesel submarines and 15 frigates of which 5 are former Dutch Van Speijk class (the sixth expected in 1990), and 3 former British Ashanti class. There are also 4 fast missile craft, 1 torpedo-armed craft and 30 miscellaneous patrol craft including 5 hydrofoils as well as 2 Dutch-built tripartite coastal minehunters. Amphibious lift is provided by 15 tank landing ships (4 with helicopter facilities) and 64 craft. The auxiliary force includes 1 tanker, 8 surveying vessels, 2 command and submarine support ships, 1 repair ship, 3 training ships and some dozens of minor auxiliaries and service craft.

The Naval Air Arm operates 60 aircraft, including 18 Searchmaster maritime reconnaissance, and 12 ASW helicopters plus miscellaneous communications and utility aircraft.

A separate Military Sealift Command operates about 15 inter-island transport ships (which number includes 3 of the Tank Landing ships in the navy listing) totalling approximately 30,000 tonnes. The Maritime Security Agency operates 10 cutters, the Customs about 70 and the armed Marine Police 60 craft.

Air Force. Operational combat units comprise two squadrons of A-4E Skyhawk attack aircraft, and single squadrons of F-5E Tiger II and of F-16 fighters and OV-10F Bronco twin-turboprop counter-insurgency aircraft. There are 3 transport squadrons, equipped with turboprop C-130 Hercules, Nurtanio/CASA NC-212 Aviocar and F27 Friendship aircraft, and piston-engined C-47s, plus 3 specially-equipped Boeing 737 dual-purpose maritime surveillance/transports; and an assortment of other aircraft in transport, helicopter and training units including 16 Hawk attack/trainers, 25 T-34C-1 armed turboprop trainers, and 40 Swiss-built AS 202 Bravo piston-engined primary trainers. On order are 32 CN-235 twin-turboprop transports and Bell 412 helicopters, from IPTN of Indonesia. Personnel (1990) approximately 24,000.

INTERNATIONAL RELATIONS

Membership. Indonesia is a member of UN, OPEC and ASEAN.

ECONOMY

Planning. The fifth Five-Year Development Plan (1990-94) constitutes the final 5 years of the Government's first 25-Year Long Term Development Plan. It places emphasis on the structural diversification of the economy to reduce dependence on crude oil and, in particular, it places importance on the development of export-oriented and labour-intensive industries in the agricultural and manufacturing sectors.

Budget. The budget (in Rp.) in 1989–90, envisaged expenditure of 36,574,900m. (development 11,325,100m.) and expenditure revenue of 25,249,800m.

Currency. The monetary unit is the *rupiah* (abbreviated Rp.), divided into 100 *sen*. There are banknotes of 1, 2·5, 5, 10, 25, 50, 100, 500, 1,000, 5,000 and 10,000 rupiahs and aluminium coins of 1, 5, 10, 25 and cupro-nickel coins of 50 sen.

In March 1990 there were 2,997 rupiahs = £1 sterling; 1,828 rupiahs = US$1.

Banking. The Bank Indonesia, successor to De Javasche Bank established by the Dutch in 1828, was made the central bank of Indonesia on 1 July 1953. It had an original capital of Rp. 25m.; a reserve fund of Rp. 18m. and a special reserve of Rp. 84m. Total assets and liabilities at 31 March 1988, Rp. 36,252,000m.

There are 117 commercial banks, 28 development banks and other financial institutions, 8 development finance companies and 9 joint venture merchant banks. Commercial banking is dominated by 5 state-owned banks: Bank Rakyat Indonesia provides services to smallholder agriculture and rural development; Bank Bumi Daya, estate agriculture and forestry; Bank Negara Indonesia 1946, industry; Bank Dagang Negara, mining; and Bank Expor-Impor Indonesia, export commodity sector. All state banks are authorized to deal in foreign exchange.

There are 70 private commercial banks owned and operated by Indonesians. The 11 foreign banks, which specialize in foreign exchange transactions and direct lending operations to foreign joint ventures, include the Chartered Bank, the Hongkong and Shanghai Banking Corporation, the Bank of America, the City Bank, the Bank of Tokyo, Chase Manhattan and the American Express International Banking Corporation. The government owns one Savings Bank, Bank Tabungan Negara, and 1,000 Post Office Savings Banks. There are also over 3,500 rural and village savings bank and credit co-operatives.

Weights and Measures. The metric system of weights and measures was officially introduced in Feb. 1923, and came into full operation on 1 Jan. 1938.

The following are the old weights and measures: *Pikol* = 136·16 lb. avoirdupois; *Katti* = 1·36 lb. avoirdupois; *Bau* = 1·7536 acres; *Square Pal* = 227 hectares = 561·16 acres; *Jengkal* = 4 yd; *Pal* (Java) = 1,506 metres; *Pal* (Sumatra) = 1,852 metres.

ENERGY AND NATURAL RESOURCES

Electricity. Three large-scale hydro-electric plants are operating on the Jatiluhur and Brantas rivers in Java and on the Asahan River in Sumatra. Electricity produced (1986) 30,000m. kwh. Supply 127 and 220 volts; 50 Hz.

Oil. Indonesia is the principal producer of petroleum in the Far East, production coming from Sumatra, Kalimantan (Indonesian Borneo) and Java. Proven reserves (1986) 8,500m. bbls. The 1989 output of crude oil was 66m. tonnes.

Gas. Pertamina, the state oil company, started to pump natural gas to Jakarta in 1979. Production (1987–88) 1,771,300m. cu. ft.

Water. In 1987–88, 59,930 hectares of new irrigation networks had been constructed and 153,290 hectares rehabilitated and maintained.

Minerals. The high cost of extraction means that little of the large mineral resources outside Java is exploited; however, there is copper mining in Irian Jaya, nickel mining and processing on Sulawesi, aluminium smelting in northern Sumatra. Coal production (1987–88) 1,987,600 tonnes; bauxite (1987–88), 654,200 tonnes. Output (in 1,000 tonnes, 1987–88) of iron ore was 139·6; copper concentrate, 254·4; silver, 5,178·6 kg; gold, 710·6 kg; nickel ore, 1,860·4. In 1987–88 tin production was 25,700 tonnes.

Agriculture. Production (1988, in 1,000 tonnes): Rice, 41,769; cassava, 15,166; maize, 6,229; sweet potatoes, 2,166; sugar-cane, 20,800; coconuts and copra, 12,750; palm oil, 1,370; soybeans, 1,260; rubber, 1,094; coffee, 358; groundnuts, 585; vegetables, 3,180; fruits, 5,598; tea, 144; tobacco, 147.

Livestock (1988): Cattle, 6·5m.; buffaloes, 3m.; horses, 722,000; sheep, 5·4m.; goats, 12·7m.; pigs, 6·5m.; poultry, 439m.

Forestry. The forest area was (1988) 122m. hectares, 67% of the land area. Production (1987–88), provisional: Sawn timber, 7,566,000 cu. metres; plywood, 6,670,000 cu. metres. Exports (1987–88, provisional) of processed timber, 8,079,000 cu. metres.

Fisheries. In 1987 the catch of sea fish was 2,029,000 tonnes; inland fish was 638,000 tonnes. In 1987 there were 101,730 motorized and 218,190 other fishing vessels. Exports (1987, provisional) included 44·27m. tonnes of shrimps, 52·7m. tonnes of fresh fish and 530,000 tonnes of ornamental fish.

INDUSTRY AND TRADE

Industry. There are shipyards at Jakarta Raya, Surabaya, Semarang and Amboina. There were (1985) more than 2,000 textile factories (total production in 1987–88, 2,925·6m. metres), large paper factories (817,200 tonnes, 1986–87), match factories, automobile and bicycle assembly works, large construction works, tyre factories, glass factories, a caustic soda and other chemical factories. Production (1987–88): Cement, 22,419,000 tonnes; fertilizers, 5,811,000 tonnes; 160,372 motor vehicles and 249,573 motorcycles; 2·36m. boxes of matches; glasses and bottles, 126,060 tonnes; steel ingots, 1,337,000 tonnes; 640 TV sets and 159,020 refrigerators.

Labour. In 1985 there were 62,457,138 people employed: 34,141,809 in agriculture; 9,345,210 in commerce; 8,317,285 in public services; 5,795,919 in industry; 2,095,577 in construction; 1,958,333 in transport and communications; 415,512 in mining and quarrying; 250,481 in finance and insurance; 69,715 in electricity, gas and water.

Trade Unions. All unions must be affiliated to the All Indonesia Labour Federation

(FBSI). About 40% of the labour force belong to unions. Strikes are forbidden by law.

Commerce. Imports and exports (including oil) in US$1m. for year April–March:

	1984	*1985*	*1986*	*1987*
Imports	13,882	10,262	10,718	12,512
Exports	21,888	18,587	14,805	17,136

The main export items (in US$1m.) in 1987 were: Gas and oil, 8,556; forestry products, 2,504; manufactured goods, 1,262; rubber, 961; coffee, 535; fishery products, 430; copper, 159; tin, 155; pepper, 148; palm products, 144; tea, 119. Exports went mainly to Japan (43·1%), USA (19·5%), Singapore (8·4%), Netherlands (2·9%), Federal Republic of Germany (2·1%) and Australia (2·1%).

The main import items are non-crude oil, rice, consumer goods, fertilizer, chemicals, weaving yarn, iron and steel, industrial and business machinery. In 1987 imports came mainly from Japan (28·7%), USA (11·3%), Singapore (8·7%), Federal Republic of Germany (6·7%), Australia (4·4%), Taiwan (3·7%), China (3·3%) and France (3·1%).

Total trade between Indonesia and UK (British Department of Trade returns, in £1,000 sterling):

	1985	*1986*	*1987*	*1988*	*1989*
Imports to UK	155,934	141,242	144,819	233,807	273,102
Exports and re-exports from UK	172,818	196,629	236,027	203,275	184,032

Tourism. In 1987 1,060,800 tourists visited Indonesia.

COMMUNICATIONS

Roads. The total length of the artery and connecting road network in 1987-88 was 42,982 km, of which 26,086 km were in good condition. Motor vehicles, at 31 Dec. 1988, totalled 8,715,538.

Railways. In 1987 the State Railways totalled 6,458 km of 1,067 mm gauge, comprising 4,967 km on Java (of which 125 km electrified) and 1,491 km on Sumatra. They carried 48·3m. passengers and 7·9m. tonnes of freight. In addition some narrow gauge lines are still operated.

Aviation. In 1987-88 there were 788 aircraft in operation with 177 scheduled and 611 non-scheduled flights. The total number of passengers carried was 6,160,205, total freight 71,052 tonnes. Domestic airlines are operated by Garuda Indonesia, Merpati Nusantara, Mandala and Bouraq Indonesia Airlines.

Shipping. There are 16 ports for oceangoing ships, the largest of which is Tanjung Priok, which serves the Jakarta area and has a container terminal. The national shipping company Pelajaran Nasional Indonesia (PELNI) maintains interinsular communications. The Jakarta Lloyd maintains regular services between Jakarta, Amsterdam, Hamburg and London. In 1987–88, 35 ocean-going ships with a capacity of 446,980 DWT carried 16,470,859 tonnes of freight.

Post and Broadcasting. In 1979 the postal and telegraph services of Indonesia included 2,796 post offices. There were 660 telegraph offices which handled 3·9m. domestic and 488,000 international cables. Post offices handled 396·63m. letters, Rp. 388,700m. in money orders and 4,550,000m. in postal cheques in 1987–88. Deposits with post office savings accounts, Rp. 31,210m. Number of telephones (1988), 999,321.

Radio Republik Indonesia, under the Department of Information, operates 49 stations. In 1987–88 there were 8,948,195 TV receivers. In 1987, 54,318 public TV sets were placed in villages within reach of the state-owned Televisi Republik Indonesia telecast.

Newspapers (1986–87). There were about 252 newspaper publishers with estimated circulation (1987-88) of 9,765,817, of which 3,337,301 daily newspapers. There were 270 publishers of weekly papers and magazines with a circulation of 3·5m.

JUSTICE, RELIGION, EDUCATION AND WELFARE

Justice. There are courts of first instance, high courts of appeal in every provincial capital and a Supreme Court of Justice for the whole of Indonesia in Jakarta. Administrative matters on judicial organization are under the direction of the Department of Justice.

In civil law the population is divided into three main groups: Indonesians, Europeans and foreign Orientals, to whom different law systems are applicable. When, however, people from different groups are involved, a system of so-called 'intergentile' law is applied.

The present criminal law, which has been in force since 1918, is codified and is based on European penal law. This law is equally applicable to all groups of the population. For private and commercial law, however, there are various systems applicable for the various groups of the population. For the Indonesians, a system of private and agrarian law is applicable; this is called Adat Law, and is mainly uncodified. For the other groups the prevailing private and commercial law system is codified in the Private Law Act (1847) and the Commercial Law Act (1847). These Acts have their origins in the French *Code Civile* and *Code du Commerce* through the similar Dutch codifications. These Acts are entirely applicable to Indonesian citizens and to Europeans, whereas to foreign Orientals they are applicable with some exceptions, mainly in the fields of family law and inheritance. Penal law was in the process of being codified in 1981.

Religion. Religious liberty is granted to all denominations. About 87% of the Indonesians were Moslems in 1988 and 9% Christians. There are also about 1·6m. Buddhists, probably for the greater part Chinese. Hinduism has 3·5m. members, of whom 2·5m. are on Bali.

Education. In 1987–88 there were 30,960,000 pupils in primary schools, 6,687,000 students in junior high schools and 3,655,000 students in senior high schools, vocational schools, higher training and sports teachers' training colleges.

English is the first foreign language taught in schools. Literacy rate was 72% in 1984.

Total number of students in higher education (1987–88) 1,446,600 attending the 49 state, or 637 private universities and technical institutes.

Health. In 1988 there were 23,084 doctors, 64,087 nurses, 5,472 public health centres, 12,562 sub-public health centres and 3,521 mobile units.

DIPLOMATIC REPRESENTATIVES

Of Indonesia in Great Britain (38 Grosvenor Sq., London W1X 9AD)
Ambassador: T.M Hadi Thayeb.

Of Great Britain in Indonesia (Jalan M.H. Thamrin 75, Jakarta 10310)
Ambassador: W. K. K. White, CMG.

Of Indonesia in the USA (2020 Massachusetts Ave., NW, Washington, D.C., 20036)
Ambassador: A. R. Ramly.

Of the USA in Indonesia (Medan Merdeka Selatan 5, Jakarta)
Ambassador: John C. Monjo.

Of Indonesia to the United Nations
Ambassador: Nana Sutresna.

Further Reading

Indonesia 1989. Department of Information, Jakarta, 1989
Bee, O. J., *The Petroleum Resources of Indonesia.* OUP, 1982
Bemmelen, R. W. van, *Geology of Indonesia.* 2 vols. The Hague, 1949

Echols, J. M. and Shadily, H., *An Indonesian–English Dictionary*. 3rd ed. Cornell Univ. Press, 1989
International Commission of Jurists, *Indonesia and the Rule of Law*. London, 1987
Leifer, M., *Indonesia's Foreign Policy*. London, 1983
McDonald, H., *Suharto's Indonesia*. Univ. Press of Hawaii, 1981
Palmier, L., *Understanding Indonesia*. London, 1986
Papenek, G., *The Indonesian Economy*. Eastbourne, 1980
Polomka, P., *Indonesia Since Sukarno*. London, 1971
Robison, R., *Indonesia: The Rise of Capital*. Sydney, 1986
Thoolen, H., *Indonesia and the Rule of Law*. London, 1987

IRAN

Capital: Tehrán
Population: 53·92m. (1988)
GNP per capita: US$1,690 (1986)

Jomhori-e-Islami-e-Irân

HISTORY. Persia was ruled by the Shahs as an absolute monarchy until 30 Dec. 1906 when the first Constitution was granted. Reza Khan took control after a *coup d'état* on 31 Oct. 1925 deposed the last Shah of the Qajar Dynasty, and became Reza Shah Pahlavi on 12 Dec. 1925. The country's name was changed to Iran on 21 March 1935. Reza Shah abdicated on 16 Sept. 1941 in favour of his son, Mohammad Reza Pahlavi.

Following widespread civil unrest, the Shah left Iran on 17 Jan. 1979. The Ayatollah Ruhollah Khomeini, spiritual leader of the Shi'a Moslem community, returned from 15 years' exile on 1 Feb. 1979 and appointed a provisional government on 5 Feb. An Islamic Republic was proclaimed on 1 Apr. 1979.

In Sept. 1980 war began with Iraq with destruction of some Iranian towns and damage to the oil installations at Abadán. A UN-arranged ceasefire took place on 20 Aug. 1988 and UN-sponsored peace talks continued in 1989.

AREA AND POPULATION. Iran is bounded north by the USSR and the Caspian Sea, east by Afghánistán and Pakistan, south by the Gulf of Oman and the Persian Gulf, and west by Iraq and Turkey. It has an area of 1,648,000 sq. km (634,724 sq. miles), but a vast portion is desert, and the average density is only (1987) 31 inhabitants to the sq. km. Refugees in Iran (Jan. 1988) 2·6m. (of which 2·2m. Afgháns).

The population at recent censuses was as follows: (1956) 18,944,821; (1966) 25,781,090; (1976) 33,708,744; (1986) 49,445,010. Estimate (1988) 53·92m.

The areas, populations and capitals of the 24 provinces *(ostán)* were:

Province	*Area (sq. km)*	*Census 1976*	*Census 1986*	*Capital*
Azárbáiján, East	67,102	3,197,685	4,114,084	Tabriz
Azárbáiján, West	38,850	1,407,604	1,971,677	Orúmiyeh [2]
Bakhtárán [1]	23,667	1,030,714	1,462,965	Bakhtarán [3]
Boyer ahmadi and Kohkiluyeh	14,261	244,370	411,828	Yásúj
Búshehr	27,653	347,863	612,183	Búshehr
Chahár Mahál and Bakhtiári	14,870	394,357	631,179	Shahr-e-Kord
Esfáhán	104,650	2,176,694	3,294,916	Esfáhán
Fárs	133,298	2,035,582	3,193,769	Shiráz
Gilán	14,709	1,581,872	2,081,037	Rasht
Hamadán	19,784	1,088,024	1,505,826	Hamadan
Hormozgán	66,870	462,440	762,206	Bandár-e-Abbas
Ilám	19,044	246,024	382,091	Ilám
Kermán	179,916	1,091,148	1,622,958	Kermán
Khorásán	313,337	3,264,398	5,280,605	Mashhad
Khuzestán	67,282	2,187,118	2,681,978	Ahváz
Kordestán	24,998	782,440	1,078,415	Sánándáj
Lorestán	28,803	933,939	1,367,029	Khorramabád
Markazi	29,080	796,754	1,082,109	Arák
Mázándárán	46,456	2,387,171	3,419,346	Sári
Semnán	90,905	289,463	417,035	Semnán
Sistán and Balúchestan	181,578	664,292	1,197,059	Záhedán
Tehrán (formed from Markazi)	29,993	5,624,784	8,712,087	Tehrán
Yazd	70,011	356,849	574,028	Yazd
Zanján	36,398	1,117,157	1,588,600	Zanján

[1] Formerly Kermánsháhán. [2] Formerly Rezáyeh. [2] Formerly Kermánsháh.

The principal cities were:

	Census 1976	Census 1986		Census 1976	Census 1986
Tehrán	4,530,223	6,042,584	Ardabil	147,865	281,973
Esfáhán	661,510	986,753	Khorramshahr	140,490	...
Mashhad	667,770	1,463,508	Kermán	140,761	257,284
Tabriz	597,976	971,482	Karaj	137,926	275,100
Shiráz	425,813	848,289	Qazvin	139,258	248,591
Ahváz	334,399	579,826	Yazd	135,925	230,483
Abadán	294,068	...	Arák	116,832	265,349
Bakhtárán	290,600	560,514	Desful	121,251	151,420
Qom	247,219	543,139	Khorramábád	104,912	208,592
Rasht	188,957	290,897	Borujerd	101,345	183,879
Orúmiyeh	164,419	300,746	Zanján	100,351	215,261
Hamadán	165,785	272,499			

The national language is Farsi or Persian, spoken by 45% of the population. 23% spoke related languages, including Kurdish and Luri in the west and Baluchi in the south-east, while 26% spoke Turkic languages, primarily the Azerbáijáni-speaking peoples of the north-west and the Turkomen of Khorásan in the north-east.

CLIMATE. Mainly a desert climate, but with more temperate conditions on the shores of the Caspian Sea. Seasonal range of temperature is considerable. Abadán. Jan. 54°F (12·2°C), July 97°F (36·1°C). Annual rainfall 8" (204 mm). Tehrán. Jan. 36°F (2·2°C), July 85°F (29·4°C). Annual rainfall 10" (246 mm).

CONSTITUTION AND GOVERNMENT. The Constitution of the Islamic Republic was approved by a national referendum in Dec. 1979. It gives supreme authority to a religious leader (*wali faqih*), which position was held by Ayatollah Khomeini until his death on 3 June 1989. The Moslem clergy elected Seyed Ali Khamenei on 4 June 1989.

The President of the Republic is popularly-elected for a 4-year term and is head of the executive; he appoints a Prime Minister and other Ministers, subject to approval by the *Majlis*.

Presidents since the establishment of the Islamic Republic:

Abolhassan Bani-Sadr. 4 Feb. 1980–22 June 1981 (deposed).

Mohammad Ali Raja'i, 24 July 1981–30 Aug. 1981 (assassinated).

Sayed Ali Khamenei, 12 Oct. 1981-4 June 1989.

The Cabinet was composed as follows in 1988.

President: Hojatolislam Ali Akbar Hashemi Rafsanjani (sworn in on 3 Aug. 1989).

Vice President: Hassan Habibi.

Foreign Affairs: Ali Akbar Vellayati. *Oil:* Gholamreza Aghazadeh. *Interior:* Abdollah Nouri. *Economic Affairs and Finance:* Mohsen Nourbakhsh. *Agriculture and Rural Affairs:* Isa Kalantari. *Commerce:* Abdol-Hossein Vahaji. *Energy:* Namdar Zanganeh. *Roads and Transport:* Mohammed Saeedi Kya. *Construction Jihad:* Gholamreza Foruzesh. *Heavy Industries:* Mohammad Hadi Nezhad-Hosseinian. *Industry:* Mohammad Reza Nematzadeh. *Housing and Urban Development:* Sarajuddin Kazeruni. *Labour and Social Affairs:* Hossein Kamali. *Posts, Telephones and Telegraphs:* Mohammed Gharazi. *Health, Treatment and Medical Education:* Iraj Fazel. *Education and Training:* Mohammad Ali Najafi. *Higher Education and Culture:* Mostafa Moin. *Justice:* Hojatolislam Ismail Shostari. *Defence and Armed Forces Logistics:* Akbar Torkan. *Intelligence and Security:* Hojatolislam Ali Fallahiyan. *Culture and Islamic Guidance:* Seyyed Mohammad Khatami. *Mines and Metals:* Mohammad Hossein Mahloji.

Legislative power is held by a 270-member Islamic Consultative Assembly *(Majlis)*, directly elected for a 4-year term on 17 May 1984; but all legislation is subject to approval by a 12-member Council of Guardians who ensure it is in accordance with the Islamic code and with the Constitution. Six members of this constitutional Council are appointed by the *wali faqih* and six by the judiciary.

National flag: Three horizontal stripes of green, white and red; on the borders of the green and red stripes the legend *Allah Akbar* in white Kufi script repeated 22 times in all; in the centre of the white stripe the national emblem in red.

Local Government. The country is divided into 24 provinces *(ostán)*, these are sub-divided into 195 *shahrestán* (counties), each under a *farmándár* (governor) and thence into 500 *bakhsh* (districts), each under a *bakhshdár*. The districts are sub-divided into *dehistán* (groups of villages) each under a *dehdár*, each village having its elected *kadkhoda* (headman).

DEFENCE. Two years' military service is compulsory.

Army. The Army consisted (1990) of 305,000 men (about 250,000 conscripts), with some 350,000 reservists. It is organized in 4 mechanized, 1 special force, 6 infantry and 1 airborne divisions, and auxiliary units. Equipment includes T-54/-55/-62, T-72, Chieftain, M-47/-48 and M-60A1 main battle tanks. There is also a 300,000-strong Revolutionary Guard Corps. The Army operates 40 Cessna and some 500 helicopters but the full strength is not known.

Navy. Losses caused in the war with Iraq and clashes with the USN have left the navy in a weakened state, exacerbated by shortages of spares for its western-supplied fleet. Whilst precise figures of losses and serviceability are not known the combatant fleet is currently believed to comprise 1 *ex*-British 'Battle' class and 2 *ex*-US Sumner class destroyers, 3 UK-built frigates, 2 old *ex*-US patrol frigates and about 10 missile craft (for which there may be no missiles). Other units include 24 inshore patrol craft (some of them hovercraft), 3 small minesweepers and a substantial amphibious force of 7 tank landing ships and 4 tank landing craft. Auxiliaries include 3 tankers, 1 repair ship, 2 water tankers and 2 accommodation ships.

Naval Aviation comprises 1 ASW helicopter squadron with Sea King and AB-212 helicopters, an MCM squadron with RH-53D helicopters and a transport squadron with about a dozen various aircraft. Main naval bases are at Bandár-e-Abbas, Búshehr and Chah Bahar.

The naval forces of the Pasdaran are organizationally separate, but some integration may follow the appointment in Nov. 1989 of a former IRGC leader as Commander of the Navy, and integrated operations are now exercised. They operate some 40-60 fast boats armed with portable weapons, exercise control of the offshore oil rigs used as bases, and control coastal artillery and missile batteries.

Air Force. In Aug. 1955 the Air Force became a separate and independent arm, and had a strength of about 23 first-line squadrons (each 15 aircraft, plus reserves), with 100,000 personnel before the 1979 revolution. Strength (1990) was estimated at 35,000 personnel and 100 serviceable combat aircraft. The latter include some MiG-19/Chinese-built F-6 fighter-bombers, supplied via North Korea, and surviving US fighters that include F-14 Tomcat, F-5E Tiger II and F-4D/E Phantom II fighter-bombers, plus a few RF-4E reconnaissance-fighters. Transport aircraft include F27s, C-130 Hercules, PC-6 Turbo-Porters, Boeing 707s and 747s, some equipped as flight refuelling tankers. The status of the large fleet of CH-47C Chinook, Bell Model 214 and other helicopters is not known; but two P-3F Orion maritime patrol aircraft remain operational. Training aircraft include Bonanza basic trainers and 35 turboprop PC-7 Turbo-Trainers.

INTERNATIONAL RELATIONS

Membership. Iran is a member of UN, OPEC and the Colombo Plan.

ECONOMY

Budget. The budget for 1988–89 balanced at 9·8m. *rials*.

Currency. The Iranian unit of currency is the *rial* sub-divided into 100 *dinars*.

Notes in circulation are of denominations of 100, 200, 500, 1,000, 2,000, 5,000 and 10,000 *rials*. Coins in circulation are bronze–aluminium and copper, 50 *dinar*;

silver alloy, 1, 2, 5, 10, 20 and 50 *rials*. In March 1990, US$1 = 71·84 *rials*; £1 = 117·75 *rials*.

Banking. The *Bank Markazi Iran* was established in 1960 as the note-issuing authority and government bank of Iran. All other banks and insurance companies were nationalized in June 1979, and re-organized into 8 new state banking corporations. The 'Law for Usury-Free Banking' was given final approval in Aug.-Sept. 1983. From 21 March 1985 interest on accounts was abolished.

Weights and Measures. By a law passed on 8 Jan. 1933, the official weights and measures are those of the metric system.

The Iranian year is a solar year running from 21 March to 20 March; the Hejira year 1362 corresponds to the Christian year 21 March 1984–20 March 1985.

ENERGY AND NATURAL RESOURCES

Electricity. Capacity of generators installed at institutions affiliated to Ministry of Energy, 1985, was 12,369,000 kw., and 36,720m. kwh. was generated. Supply 220 volts; 50 Hz.

Oil. For a history of Iran's oil industry 1951–79, *see* THE STATESMAN'S YEAR-BOOK, 1982–83.

The petroleum industry was seriously disrupted by the 1979 revolution, and many facilities, including the vast refinery at Abadán, the new refinery at Bandár Khomeini and the tanker terminal at Kharg Island, have been destroyed or put out of action during the Gulf war with Iraq. All operating companies were nationalized in 1979 and operations are now run by the National Petrochemical Company.

Crude oil production, 145m. tonnes, 1989.

Gas. Natural gas production (1985) was 30,900m. cu. metres.

Minerals. Iran has substantial mineral deposits relatively underdeveloped. Production figures for 1985 (in 1,000 tonnes): Iron ore, 2,099; coal, 674; zinc and lead, 56; manganese, 46; chromite, 56; salt, 618.

Agriculture. In 1982, cultivatable land totalled 14,867,000 hectares, of which 5,664,000 were irrigated and 4,929,000 hectares fallow land. Forests totalled 12·7m. hectares and pastures 90m.

Crop production for 1988 (in 1,000 tonnes): Wheat, 8,200; barley, 2,500; rice, 1,757; sugar-beet, 3,500; sugar-cane, 2,035; tobacco, 22.

Wool comes principally from Khorásán, Bakhtarán, Mázandarán and Azárbáiján. Production, 1988, 16,000 tonnes greasy, 8,800 tonnes scoured.

Rice is grown largely on the Caspian shores.

Cigarette tobacco is grown mainly in Hormozgán, Bushehr and West Azárbáiján *ostáns*. It is purchased by the Tobacco Monopoly and manufactured in the government factory at Tehrán.

Opium, until 1955, was an important export commodity in Iran. On 7 Oct. 1955 an Act was approved by Parliament to prohibit the cultivation and usage of opium.

Livestock (1988): 34·5m. sheep, 13·62m. goats, 8·35m. cattle, 316,000 horses, 27,000 camels, (1984) 20,000 pigs, 230,000 buffaloes, and 1·8m. donkeys.

Fisheries. The Caspian Fisheries Co. (Shilát) is a government monopoly. Total catch (1986) 152,000 tonnes.

INDUSTRY AND TRADE

Industry. Production of industrial goods, 1984: Vegetable oil, 444,192 tonnes; sugar, 639,514 tonnes; finished cloth, 661,961,229 metres; footwear, 66,290,969 pairs; bricks, 10,824,612; cement, 12,064,027 tonnes; tractors, 14,513; combines, 612; tillers and threshers, 18,637; agricultural discs, 25,136; small vans, 68,644; trucks and small trucks, 14,932; private cars, 57,790; buses, 2,532; mini-buses, 8,170; ambulances, 559; motor cycles, 199,782. In 1984 there were 7,513 large-scale manufacturing establishments and the labour force was 619,332.

Commerce. Imports totalled 1,332,673m. rials in 1984–85. Exports totalled 33,041m. rials in 1984–85, excluding oil and hydrocarbon solvents obtained from oil.

Total trade between Iran and UK (British Department of Trade returns, in £1,000 sterling):

	1985	*1986*	*1987*	*1988*	*1989*
Imports to UK	63,317	100,303	187,572	140,207	250,548
Exports and re-exports from UK	525,589	399,373	307,853	247,768	257,149

Tourism. Total number of visitors (1987) 171,837.

COMMUNICATIONS

Roads. In 1985 the total length of roads was 139,368 km, of which 504 km were freeways, 16,346 km main roads, 35,930 km by-roads, 33,618 km rural roads and 52,366 km other roads.

In 1984 private motor vehicles numbered 2,246,143; rented vehicles, 377,745; government vehicles, 144,248.

Railways. The State Railways totalled 4,567 km of main lines in 1985, of which 146 km electrified. In 1986 the railways carried 4,638m. passenger-km and 7,316 tonne-km. Construction began in 1983 of a link from Kermán to Zahedán to connect the network to Pakistan.

Aviation. In 1985, 1,470,000 passengers arrived at Mehrabad Airport (1,157,000 on domestic flights and 313,000 on international flights) and 1,516,000 passengers departed (1,155,000 domestic and 361,000 international). The state airline carried 3,166,000 passengers and 52,303 tons of cargo and mail in 1983.

Shipping. In 1985, 1,345 ships, capacity 11,998,000 tonnes, entered commercial ports, unloading 12,660,000 tonnes and loading 447,000 tonnes of goods (excluding oil products).

Post and Broadcasting. Postal, telegraph and telephone services are administered by the Iranian Ministry of Posts, Telegraphs and Telephones.

In 1985 the number of telephones was 1,305,122, of which some 488,516 were in Tehrán province. Radio sets numbered 10m. in 1986, and television sets 2·1m.

Cinemas (1983). There were 277 cinemas with 174,366 seats.

Newspapers. There were in 1982, 17 daily papers in Tehrán and other cities. Their circulation is relatively small, *Ettela'át* and *Kayhán* leading with about 220,000 and 350,000 respectively. Two English-language and a French-language daily ceased publication in March 1979.

JUSTICE, RELIGION, EDUCATION AND WELFARE

Justice. A new legal system based on Islamic law was introduced by the new constitution in 1979. The President of the Supreme Court and the public Prosecutor-General are appointed by the *wali faqih* (Ayatollah Khomeini). The Supreme Court has 16 branches and 109 offences carry the death penalty.

Religion. The official religion is the Shi'a branch of Islam, known as the *Ithna-Ashariyya,* which recognizes 12 Imáms or spiritual successors of the Prophet Mohammad. Of the total population, 96% are Shi'a, 3% are Sunni and 1% non-Moslem.

Education. The great majority of primary and secondary schools are state schools. Elementary education in state schools and university education are free; small fees are charged for state-run secondary schools. Text-books are issued free of charge to pupils in the first 4 grades of elementary schools.

In 1984 there were 634,200 pupils in elementary schools, 2,021,520 in orientation schools and 901,056 in general secondary schools; there were 184,520 students in technical and vocational schools, 37,247 in teacher-training schools, 18,590 gifted children, and 182,239 in adult education courses. Universities and other institutes of higher education had 145,809 students in 1984. The Free Islamic University was established after the revolution and in 1983 the International University of Islamic Studies was being organized.

A literacy movement was established in 1981 and by 1985, 3m. citizens had participated.

Health. In 1984 70,152 hospital beds were available in 589 hospitals. Medical personnel included 15,945 physicians and 2,340 dentists in 1982.

DIPLOMATIC REPRESENTATIVES

Diplomatic links between Great Britain and Iran were broken in March 1989.

Of Iran in the USA (3005 Massachusetts Ave., NW, Washington, D.C., 20008)
Ambassador: (Vacant).

Of the USA in Iran (260 Takhte Jamshid Ave., Tehrán)
Ambassador: (Vacant).

Of Iran to the United Nations
Ambassador: Mahmoud Sadat Madarshahi.

Further Reading

Statistical Information. Statistical Centre of Iran, Dr Fakemi Avenue, Tehrán, Iran, 14144.

Afshar, H., *Iran: A Revolution in Turmoil.* London, 1985
Arberry, A. J. (ed.) *The Cambridge History of Iran.* 8 vols. CUP, 1968ff.
Bakhash, S., *The Reign of the Ayatollahs.* London, 1984
Benard, C. and Zalmay, K., *'The Government of God' Iran's Islamic Republic.* Columbia Univ. Press, 1984
Haim, S., *Shorter Persian–English Dictionary.* Tehrán, 1958
Heikal, M., *Iran: The Untold Story.* New York, 1982
Hiro, D., *Iran under the Ayatollahs.* London, 1985
Hussain, A., *Islamic Iran: Revolution and Counter-Revolution.* London, 1985
Katouzian, H., *The Political Economy of Iran.* London, 1981
Keddie, N., *Roots of Revolution.* Yale Univ. Press, 1981
Lambton, A. K. S., *Landlord and Peasant in Persia.* OUP, 1953.—*Persian Vocabulary.* CUP, 1954
Looney, R. E., *The Economic Development of Iran: A Recent Survey with Projections to 1981.* New York, 1973
Nashat, G., *Women and Revolution in Iran.* Boulder, 1983
Navabpour, A. R., *Iran.* [Bibliography] Oxford and Santa Barbara, 1988
Sick, G., *All Fall Down.* London, 1985
Steinglass, F. J., *A Comprehensive Persian–English Dictionary.* 2nd ed. London, 1930
Stempel, J. D., *Inside the Iranian Revolution.* Indiana Univ. Press, 1981
Sullivan, W. H., *Mission to Iran.* New York, 1981
Zabih, S., *Iran's Revolutionary Upheaval: An Interpretive Essay.* San Francisco, 1979.—*The Mosadegh Era: Roots of the Iranian Revolution.* Chicago, 1982.—*Iran since the Revolution.* London, 1982.—*The Left in Contemporary Iran.* London and Stamford, 1986

IRAQ

Capital: Baghdad
Population: 17·06m. (1988)
GNP per capita: US$2,140 (1986)

al Jumhouriya al 'Iraqia

HISTORY. Part of the Ottoman Empire from the 16th century, Iraq was captured by British forces in 1916 and became in 1921 a Kingdom under a League of Nations mandate, administered by Britain. It became independent on 3 Oct. 1932 under the Hashemite Dynasty, which was overthrown on 14 July 1958 by a military *coup* which established a Republic, controlled by a military-led Council of Sovereignty under Gen. Qassim. The republican régime terminated the adherence of Iraq to the Arab Federation (*see* THE STATESMAN'S YEAR-BOOK, 1958, p. 806). In 1963 Qassim was overthrown and Gen. Abdul Salam Aref became President, to be succeeded in 1966 by his brother Abdul Rahman Aref. In 1968 a successful *coup* was mounted by the Ba'th Party, which brought Gen. Ahmed Al Bakr to the Presidency. His Vice-President, from 1969, Saddam Hussein, became President in a peaceful transfer of power in 1979.

An attempt at succession by the Kurdish minority in the north-east of Iraq flared up in 1962, and fighting continued until the acceptance of a peace plan in June 1966. The Revolutionary Command Council formed after the 17 July 1968 *coup* announced in March 1970 a complete and constitutional settlement of the Kurdish issue. This was not, however, fully accepted by the Kurdish opposition leader.

In Sept. 1980 Iraq invaded Iran in a dispute over territorial rights in the Shatt-al-Arab waterway which developed into a full-scale war. A UN-arranged ceasefire took place on 20 Aug. 1988 and UN sponsored peace talks continued in 1989.

AREA AND POPULATION. Iraq is bounded north by Turkey, east by Iran, south-east by the Gulf, south by Kuwait and Saudi Arabia, and west by Jordan and Syria. The country has an area of 434,924 sq. km (167,925 sq. miles) and its population census (1977) was 12,000,497 and (estimate) 1988, 17,064,000.

The areas, populations (1977) and capitals of the governorates were:

Governorate	*sq. km*	*Estimate 1985*	*Capital*	*Estimate 1985*
Al-Anbar	137,723	582,058	Ar-Ramadi	137,388
Babil (Babylon)	5,258	739,031	Al-Hillah	215,249
Baghdad	5,159	4,648,609	Baghdad	4,648,609
al-Basrah	19,070	1,304,153	Al-Basrah	616,700
Dahuk [1]	6,120	330,356	Dahuk	19,736 [3]
Dhi Qar	13,626	725,913	an-Nasiriyah	138,842
Diyala	19,292	691,350	Ba'qubah	114,516
Irbil [1]	14,471	742,682	Irbil	333,903
Karbala	5,034	329,234	Karbala	184,574
Maysan	14,103	411,843	Al-Amarah	131,758
Al-Muthanna	51,029	253,816	As-Samawah	33,473 [2]
an-Najaf	27,844	472,103	An-Najaf	242,603
Ninawa (Nineveh)	37,698	1,358,082	Mosul	570,926
al-Qadisiyah	8,507	511,799	Ad-Diwaniyah	60,553 [2]
Salah ad-Din	29,004	442,782	Samarra	62,008 [3]
As-Sulaymaniyah [1]	15,756	906,495	As-Sulaymaniyah	279,424
Ta'mim	10,391	650,965	Kirkuk	207,852 [3]
Wasit	17,308	483,716	Al-Kut	58,647 [3]

[1] Forming Kurdish Autonomous Region. [2] Census 1965. [3] Estimate 1970.

The national language is Arabic, spoken by 81% of the population. There is a major minority group of Kurdish-speakers in the north-east (15·5%) and smaller groups speaking Turkic, Aramaic and Iranian languages.

CLIMATE. The climate is mainly arid, with small and unreliable rainfall and a large annual range of temperature. Summers are very hot and winters cold.

al-Basrah. Jan. 55°F (12·8°C), July 92°F (33·3°C). Annual rainfall 7" (175 mm). Baghdad. Jan. 50°F (10°C), July 95°F (35°C). Annual rainfall 6" (140 mm). Mosul. Jan. 44°F (6·7°C), July 90°F (32·2°C). Annual rainfall 15" (384 mm).

CONSTITUTION AND GOVERNMENT. The Provisional Constitution was published on 22 Sept. 1968 and promulgated on 16 July 1970. The highest state authority remains the 9-member Revolutionary Command Council (RCC) but some legislative power has now been given to the 250-member National Assembly, elected 20 June 1980 for a 4-year term.

The only legal political grouping is the National Progressive Front (founded July 1973) comprising the Arab Socialist Renaissance (Ba'th) Party and various Kurdish parties; the Iraqi Communist Party left the Front in March 1979. Elections were held in April 1989 and the main task of the new Assembly is to draft a new Constitution.

The President and Vice-President are elected by the RCC; the President appoints and leads a Council of Ministers responsible for administration.

President: Saddam Hussein at-Takriti (assumed office 17 July 1979).

National flag: Three horizontal stripes of red, white, black, with 3 green stars on the white stripe.

Local Government. Iraq is divided into 18 governorates *(liwa),* each administered by an appointed Governor; three of the governorates form a (Kurdish) Autonomous Region, with an elected 57-member Kurdish Legislative Council. Each governorate is divided into *qadhas* (under Qaimaqams) and *nahiyahs* (under Mudirs).

DEFENCE. Military training is compulsory for all men when they reach the age of 18. This consists of 21-24 months' service (extended for war) with the colours.

Army. The Army is organized into 5 armoured, 2 mechanized and 42 infantry divisions including People's Army and Reserve brigades; 6 Presidential Guard divisions, 20 special forces and missile brigades. Equipment includes 4,000 Soviet T-54/-55/-62/-72 and 1,500 Chinese Type-69 main battle tanks. Strength (1990 estimate) 955,000, including 480,000 active reserves.

Navy. At the outbreak of the Iran-Iraq war, the Iraqi navy was an insignificant force, and it played little part in the Iraqi campaign against Iranian oil exports. A major order for new ships was placed in Italy in 1981, and have been largely completed but not delivered, due to difficulties over payment, and the continuing unstable situation between Iraq and Iran. Including these ships the Navy comprises 4 new Italian-built frigates, 1 modern frigate/training ship, 4 new Italian-built missile corvettes (2 with helicopter decks), 8 *ex*-Soviet missile craft, 6 *ex*-Soviet torpedo boats, and 20 inshore patrol craft. There are also 3 Danish-built Ro-Ro ships used as tank landing ships, 3 medium landing ships, 1 oiler and 2 presidential yachts.

In 1989 naval personnel totalled 5,000 officers and ratings. The base at Basra probably remains unusable, due to mines and obstructions in the Shatt al 'Arab, but that at Um Qasr can be used.

Air Force. Except for some 40 Bell 214ST helicopters from the USA and 100 Mirage F.1E/B fighters, about 40 Alouette III, 10 Super Frelon, 40 Puma and 59 Gazelle helicopters acquired from France, the combat and transport squadrons are equipped primarily with aircraft of Soviet design, including 6 Tu-22 supersonic medium bombers, 30 Su-7 and 70 Su-20 fighter-bombers, some MiG-29 and 90 MiG-23 interceptors and fighter-bombers, and 100 Chinese-built F-7 and MiG-21 interceptors, 60 Chinese-built F-6 (MiG-19) fighters, 40 Mi-24 gunship helicopters, 100 Mi-8 helicopters, and four-turbofan Il-76, turboprop An-12 and An-24/26 transports. USSR was also reported (1987) to have supplied Su-25 ground attack aircraft. A few Il-14s and smaller types are used in a transport/communications role. L-29 Delfin and L-39 Albatross aircraft are employed for training, with Swiss-built Bravo piston-engined primary trainers, and Tucano and Pilatus PC-7 turboprop basic trainers, Soviet MiG-15UTI trainers and other types in the Air Force College and operational conversion units. Total strength (1990) 40,000 personnel and 500 combat aircraft. Soviet 'Guideline', 'Goa', 'Gainful', 'Gaskin' and Roland surface-to-air missiles are operational.

INTERNATIONAL RELATIONS

Membership. Iraq is a member of UN, Arab League and the Non-Aligned Movement.

ECONOMY

Budget. Revenue and expenditure (in 1,000 Iraqi dinars) for 1981 balanced at I.D. 19,250m.

Oil revenues account for nearly 50%, customs and excise for about 26% of the total revenue.

Currency. The monetary unit is the *Iraqi dinar* (I.D.) = 1,000 *fils* = *10 riyals* = *20 dirhams*. Silver alloy coins for 100 and 50 fils (*dirham*) and 25 fils are in circulation, and other coins for 10, 5 and 1 fils. Notes are for ¼, ½ and 1 dinar, and for 5 and 10 dinars. In March 1990, £1 = 0·5126 *dinar*; US$1 = 0·3127 *dinar*.

Banking. All banks were nationalized on 14 July 1964. The Central Bank of Iraq is the sole bank of issue. In 1941 the Rafidain Bank, financed by the Iraqi Government, was instituted to carry out normal banking transactions with head office in Baghdad and branches in the chief towns and abroad, including London. In addition, there are 4 government banks which are authorized to issue loans to companies and individuals: the Industrial Bank, the Agricultural Bank, the Estate Bank, and the Mortgage Bank.

Weights and Measures. The metric system is in general use.

ENERGY AND NATURAL RESOURCES

Electricity. Production in 1986 amounted to 22,560m. kwh. Supply 220 volts; 50 Hz.

Oil. Following the nationalization of the Iraqi oil industry in June 1972, the Iraqi National Oil Company (INOC) is responsible for the exploration, production, transport and marketing of Iraqi crude oil and oil products.

The total crude petroleum production was (1989) 138m. tonnes and of natural gas (1980) 1,760m. cu. ft. Oil exports are essential for the economy but oil terminals in the Gulf were destroyed in 1980 and the trans-Syria pipeline closed in 1982. Iraq is now wholly reliant on the 625 mile pipeline from Kirkuk to the Mediterranean *via* Turkey.

Agriculture. The chief winter crops (1988) are wheat, 1·2m. tonnes and barley, 1·25m. tonnes. The chief summer crop is rice, 250,000 tonnes. The date crop is important (350,000 tonnes), the country furnishing about 80% of the world's trade in dates; the chief producing area is the totally irrigated riverain belt of the Shatt-el-Arab. Wool and cotton are also important exports.

Livestock (1988): Cattle, 1·6m.; buffaloes, 145,000; sheep, 9·2m.; goats, 1·55m.; horses, 55,000; camels, 55,000; chickens, 76m.

Fisheries. Catch (1986) 20,600 tonnes.

INDUSTRY AND TRADE

Industry. Iraq is still relatively under-developed industrially but work has begun on new industrial plants which are being established with Soviet equipment and technical assistance.

Commerce. Imports and exports for 4 calendar years were (in US$1m.):

	1981	*1982*	*1983*	*1984*
Imports	10,530	10,250	9,785	11,260
Exports	20,922	21,728	12,275	11,720

In 1983, crude oil formed 98·6% of all exports, of which 23% to Brazil and

12·5% to Italy. 13·8% of imports came from Federal Republic of Germany and 11% from Kuwait.

Total trade between Iraq and UK (British Department of Trade returns, in £1,000 sterling):

	1985	*1986*	*1987*	*1988*	*1989*
Imports to UK	44,125	66,129	33,871	43,406	55,175
Exports and re-exports from UK	444,749	443,890	271,655	412,091	450,495

Tourism. About 1,004,000 tourists visited Iraq in 1986.

COMMUNICATIONS

Roads. There were 25,500 km of main roads in 1985. Vehicles registered in 1986 totalled 492,000 passenger cars and 246,000 commercial vehicles.

Railways. Following closure of metre-gauge operations in 1988, Iraqi Republic Railways comprises 1,721 km of 1,435 mm gauge route. In 1988 it carried 1,570m. passenger-km and 2,079m. tonne-km.

Aviation. Baghdad airport is served by British Airways, Lufthansa, Alitalia, SAS, Swissair, KLM, Middle East Air Lines, PIA, Iraqi Airways, Air Liban, United Arab Airlines and Aeroflot. In 1982 passenger-km were 1,476m. and cargo, 37·5m. tonne-km.

Shipping. The merchant fleet in 1980 comprised 142 vessels (over 100 gross tons) with a total tonnage of 1,465,949. The ports of Basra and Um Qasr have been closed since Sept. 1980.

Post and Broadcasting. Wireless telegraph services exist with UK, USA, UAR, Lebanon and Saudi Arabia, and wireless telephone services with UK, USA, Italy, UAR and USSR. Telephones, 1983, 624,685 (Baghdad, 302,219). In 1986 there were 2·5m. radio and 750,000 television receivers.

Newspapers (1983). In Baghdad there are 4 main daily newspapers (one of which is in English with a circulation of 200,000).

JUSTICE, RELIGION, EDUCATION AND WELFARE

Justice. The courts are established throughout the country as follows: For civil matters: The court of cassation in Baghdad; 6 courts of appeal at Baghdad (2), Basra, Babylon, Mosul and Kirkuk; 18 courts of first instance with unlimited powers and 150 courts of first instance with limited powers, all being courts of single judges. In addition, 6 peace courts have peace court jurisdiction only. Tribal law was abolished in Aug. 1958.

For *Shara'* (religious) matters: The Shara' courts at all places where there are civil courts, constituted in some places of specially appointed Qadhis (religious judges) and in other places of the judges of the civil courts. For criminal matters: The court of cassation; 6 sessions courts (2 being presided over by the judge of the local court of first instance and 4 being identical with the courts of appeal). Magistrates' courts at all places where there are civil courts, constituted of civil judges exercising magisterial powers of the first and second class. There are also a number of third-class magistrates' courts, powers for this purpose being granted to municipal councils and a number of administrative officials. Some administrative officials are granted the powers of a peace judge to deal with cases of debts due from cultivators.

Religion. In 1965 there were 7,711,712 Moslems, 232,406 Christians (1979), 2,500 Jews, 69,653 Yazidis and 14,262 Sabians.

Education. Primary and secondary education is free and primary education became compulsory in Sept. 1976. Primary school age is 6–12. Secondary education is for 6 years, of which the first 3 are termed intermediate. The medium of instruction is Arabic; Kurdish is used in primary schools in northern districts.

There were, in 1987, 8,210 primary schools with 2,917,474 pupils, and 2,315 secondary schools with 1,012,426 pupils. 245 vocational schools had 133,568 students and 43 teacher-training colleges had 28,164 students.

There were (1987) 6 universities with 110,173 students and 19 other higher educational establishments with 32,322 students.

Health. In 1981 there were 7,634 doctors, and 25,443 hospital beds.

DIPLOMATIC REPRESENTATIVES

Of Iraq in Great Britain (21 Queen's Gate, London, SW7 5JG)
Ambassador: Dr Azmi M. Shafiq Al-Salihi (accredited 8 Nov. 1989).

Of Great Britain in Iraq (Zukaq 12, Mahala 218, Hai Al Khelood, Baghdad)
Ambassador: H. B. Walker, CMG.

Of Iraq in the USA (1801 P. St., NW, Washington, D.C., 20036)
Ambassador: Dr Mohamed Sadiq Al-Mashat.

Of the USA in Iraq (PO Box 2447, Alwiyah, Baghdad)
Ambassador: April C. Glaspie.

Of Iraq to the United Nations
Ambassador: Dr Abdul Amir A. Al-Anbari.

Further Reading

Statistical Information: The Central Statistical Organization, Ministry of Planning, Baghdad *(President:* Dr Salah Al-Shaikhly) publishes an annual *Statistical Abstract* (latest issue 1973). Foreign Trade statistics are published annually by the Ministry of Planning.

Abdulrahman, A. J., *Iraq* [Bibliography]. Oxford and Santa Barbara, 1984
Axelgrad, F. W., *Iraq in Transition: A Political, Economic and Strategic Perspective.* London, 1986
Chubin, S. and Tripp, C., *Iran and Iraq at War.* London, 1988
Ghareeb, E., *The Kurdish Question in Iraq.* Syracuse Univ. Press, 1981
Postgate, E., *Iraq: International Relations and National Development.* London, 1983

IRELAND

Capital: Dublin
Population: 3·54m. (1988)
GNP per capita: US$7,480 (1988)

Éire

HISTORY. In April 1916 an insurrection against British rule took place and a republic was proclaimed. The armed struggle was renewed in 1919 and continued until 1921. The independence of Ireland was reaffirmed in Jan. 1919 by the National Parliament (*Dáil Éireann*), elected in Dec. 1918.

In 1920 an Act was passed by the British Parliament, under which separate Parliaments were set up for 'Southern Ireland' (26 counties) and 'Northern Ireland' (6 counties). The Unionists of the 6 counties accepted this scheme, and a Northern Parliament was duly elected on 24 May 1921. The rest of Ireland, however, ignored the Act.

On 6 Dec. 1921 a treaty was signed between Great Britain and Ireland by which Ireland accepted dominion status subject to the right of Northern Ireland to opt out. This right was exercised, and the border between *Saorstát Éireann* (26 counties) and Northern Ireland (6 counties) was fixed in Dec. 1925 as the outcome of an agreement between Great Britain, the Irish Free State and Northern Ireland. The agreement was ratified by the three parliaments.

Subsequently the constitutional links between *Saorstát Éireann* and the UK were gradually removed by the *Dáil*. The remaining formal association with the British Commonwealth by virtue of the External Relations Act, 1936, was severed when the Republic of Ireland Act, 1948, came into operation on 18 April 1949.

AREA AND POPULATION. The Republic of Ireland lies in the Atlantic ocean, separated from Great Britain by the Irish Sea to the east, and bounded northeast by Northern Ireland.

Counties and county boroughs	*Area in hectares* [1]	*Population, 1988* Males	Females	Total
Province of Leinster				
Carlow	89,635	20,816	20,172	40,988
Dublin County Borough	11,499	237,988	264,761	502,749
Dublin-Belgard	80,657 (Dublin-Belgard, Dublin-Fingal, Dun Laoghaire-Rathdown)	99,163	100,383	199,546
Dublin-Fingal		68,661	69,818	138,479
Dun Laoghaire-Rathdown		86,467	94,208	180,675
Kildare	169,425	59,542	56,705	116,247
Kilkenny	206,167	37,325	35,861	73,186
Laoighis	171,954	27,531	25,753	53,284
Longford	104,387	16,153	15,343	31,496
Louth	82,334	45,530	46,280	91,810
Meath	233,587	52,931	50,950	103,881
Offaly	199,774	30,819	29,016	59,835
Westmeath	176,290	32,048	31,331	63,379
Wexford	235,143	51,782	50,770	102,552
Wicklow	202,483	46,980	47,562	94,542
Total of Leinster	1,963,335	913,736	938,913	1,852,649
Province of Munster				
Clare	318,784	46,913	44,431	91,344
Cork County Borough	3,731	64,493	68,778	133,271
Cork	742,257	141,977	137,487	279,464
Kerry	470,142	63,293	60,866	124,159
Limerick County Borough	1,904	27,537	28,742	56,279
Limerick	266,676	55,149	53,141	108,290
Tipperary, N. R.	199,622	30,347	29,175	59,522
Tipperary, S. R.	225,836	39,381	37,716	77,097

[1] Exclusive of certain rivers, lakes and tideways.

Counties and county boroughs	Area in hectares [1]	Population, 1988 Males	Females	Total
Province of Munster—contd.				
Waterford County Borough	3,809	19,336	20,193	39,529
Waterford	179,977	26,282	25,340	51,622
Total of Munster	2,412,738	514,708	505,869	1,020,577
Province of Connacht				
Galway County Borough	...	22,578	24,526	47,104
Galway	593,966	68,047	63,401	131,448
Leitrim	152,476	14,205	12,830	27,035
Mayo	539,846	58,729	56,455	115,184
Roscommon	246,276	28,351	26,241	54,592
Sligo	179,608	28,184	27,862	56,046
Total of Connacht	1,712,172	220,094	211,315	431,409
Province of Ulster (part of)				
Cavan	189,060	28,202	25,763	53,965
Donegal	483,058	65,906	63,758	129,664
Monaghan	129,093	27,044	25,335	52,379
Total of Ulster (part of)	801,211	121,152	114,856	236,008
Total	6,889,456	1,769,690	1,770,953	3,540,643

[1] Exclusive of certain rivers, lakes and tideways.

Principal towns including suburbs (1986): Greater Dublin including Dún Laoghaire, 920,956; Cork, 173,694; Limerick, 76,557; Galway, 47,104; Waterford, 41,054.

Vital statistics for 6 calendar years:

	Births	Marriages	Deaths		Births	Marriages	Deaths
1983	67,117	19,467	32,976	1986	61,620	18,573	33,630
1984	64,062	18,513	32,076	1987	58,864	18,149	31,219
1985	62,388	18,791	33,213	1988	54,300	17,936	31,575

In 1988-89, 46,000 people emigrated. Total 1982-89 (estimate) 180,000.

CLIMATE. Influenced by the Gulf Stream, there is an equable climate with mild south-west winds, making temperatures almost uniform over the whole country. The coldest months are Jan. and Feb. (39–45°F, 4–7°C) and the warmest July and Aug. (57–61°F, 14–16°C). May and June are the sunniest months, averaging 5·5 to 6·5 hours each day, but over 7 hours in the extreme S.E. Rainfall is lowest along the eastern coastal strip. The central parts vary between 30–44" (750–1,125 mm), and up to 60" (1,500 mm) may be experienced in low-lying areas in the west. Dublin. Jan. 40°F (4·7°C), July 59°F (15°C). Annual rainfall 30" (750 mm). Cork. Jan. 42°F (5·6°C), July 61°F (16°C). Annual rainfall 41" (1,025 mm).

CONSTITUTION AND GOVERNMENT. Ireland is a sovereign independent, democratic republic. Its parliament exercises jurisdiction in 26 of the 32 counties of Ireland.

The first Constitution of the Irish Free State came into operation on 6 Dec. 1922. Certain provisions which were regarded as contrary to the national sentiments were gradually removed by successive amendments, with the result that at the end of 1936 the text differed considerably from the original document. On 14 June 1937 a new Constitution was approved by Parliament (*Dáil Éireann*) and enacted by a plebiscite on 1 July 1937. This Constitution came into operation on 29 Dec. 1937. Under it the name Ireland (Éire) was restored.

The Constitution provides that, pending the reintegration of the national territory, the laws enacted by the Parliament established by the Constitution shall have the same area and extent of application as those of the Irish Free State.

The *Oireachtas* or National Parliament consists of the President and two Houses, viz., a House of Representatives, called *Dáil Éireann*, and a Senate, called *Seanad*

Éireann, consisting of 60 members. The *Dáil*, consisting of 166 members, is elected by adult suffrage. Of the 60 members of the Senate, 11 are nominated by the *Taoiseach* (Prime Minister), 6 are elected by the universities and the remaining 43 are elected from 5 panels of candidates established on a vocational basis, representing the following public services and interests: (1) national language and culture, literature, art, education and such professional interests as may be defined by law for the purpose of this panel; (2) agricultural and allied interests, and fisheries; (3) labour, whether organized or unorganized; (4) industry and commerce, including banking, finance, accountancy, engineering and architecture; (5) public administration and social services, including voluntary social activities. The electing body is a college of about 1,109 members, comprising members of the *Dáil*, Senate, county boroughs and county councils.

A maximum period of 90 days is afforded to the Senate for the consideration or amendment of Bills sent to that House by the *Dáil*, but the Senate has no power to veto legislative proposals.

No amendment of the Constitution can be effected except with the approval of the people given at a referendum.

Irish is the first official language; English is recognized as a second official language. For further details of the Constitution *see* THE STATESMAN'S YEAR-BOOK , 1952, pp. 1123–34.

President: Pádraig Óhlighile (Patrick Hillery), installed on 3 Dec. 1976 and re-elected for a second 7-year term in 1983.

Former Presidents: Dr Douglas Hyde (1938–45); Seán T. O. Ceallaigh (1945–59; 2 terms); Éamon de Valéra (1959–73; 2 terms); Erskine Childers (1973–74; died in office); Cearbhall Ó Dálaigh (1974–76; resigned).

A general election was held in June 1989: Fianna Fáil, 77 (Feb. 1987 election, 81); Fine Gael, 55 (51); Labour Party, 15 (12); Progressive Democrats, 6 (14); Workers' Party, 7 (4); Others 6 (4).

There are no formal party divisions in the Senate.

The Government consisted of the following members in Nov. 1989:

Taoiseach (Prime Minister) and Minister for the Gaeltacht: Charles J. Haughey.

Tanaiste (Deputy Prime Minister) and Minister for Defence: Brian Lenihan. *Foreign Affairs:* Gerard Collins. *Finance:* Albert Reynolds. *Marine:* John Wilson. *Agriculture and Food:* Michael O'Kennedy. *Industry and Commerce:* Desmond O'Malley. *Labour:* Bertie Ahern. *Energy:* Bobby Molloy. *Social Welfare:* Dr Michael Woods. *Justice and Communications:* Ray Burke. *Environment:* Padraig Flynn. *Health:* Dr Rory O'Hanlon. *Education:* Mary O'Rourke. *Tourism and Transport:* Seamus Brennan. *Attorney-General:* John L. Murray.

There were 15 Ministers of State.

National flag: Three vertical strips of green, white, orange.

National anthem: The Soldier's Song (words by P. Kearney; music by P. Heaney).

Local Government. The elected local authorities comprise 27 county councils, 5 county borough corporations, 6 borough corporations, 49 urban district councils and 26 Boards of Town Commissioners. All the members of these authorities are elected under a system of proportional representation, normally every 5 years. All residents of an area who have reached the age of 18 are entitled to vote in the local election for their area. Elected members are not paid, but provision is made for the payment of travelling expenses and subsistence allowances.

The range of services for which local authorities are responsible is broken down into 4 main programme groups as follows: Housing, Roads, Environment and General Local Services, and Sanitary Services. Because of the small size of their administrative areas the functions carried out by town commissioners and some of the smaller urban district councils have tended to become increasingly limited, and the more important tasks of local government have tended to become the responsibility of the county councils.

The local authorities have a system of government which combines an elected council and a whole-time manager. The elected members have specific functions reserved to them which include the striking of rates (local tax), the borrowing of money, the adoption of development plans, the making, amending or revoking of bye-laws and the nomination of persons to other bodies. The managers, who are paid officers of their authorities, are responsible for the performance of all functions which are not reserved to the elected members, including the employment of staff, making of contracts, management of local authority property, collection of rates and rents and the day-to-day administration of local authority affairs. The manager for a county council is manager also for every borough corporation, urban district council and board of town commissioners whose functional area is wholly within the county.

DEFENCE. Under the direction of the President, and subject to the provisions of the Defence Act, 1954, the military command of the Defence Forces is exercisable by the Government through the Minister for Defence. To aid and counsel the Minister for Defence on all matters in relation to the business of the Department of Defence on which he may consult it, there is a Council of Defence consisting of the Minister for State at the Department of Defence, the Secretary of the Department of Defence, the Chief of Staff, the Adjutant-General and the Quartermaster-General. At present the Permanent Defence Force strength is approximately 13,000 all ranks including the Air Corps and the Naval Service. The Reserve Defence Force strength is approximately 16,700 all ranks. Recruitment is on a voluntary basis. The minimum terms of enlistment are 3 years in the Permanent Defence Force and 6 years in the Reserve.

Since May 1978 an Irish contingent has formed part of the United Nations force in Lebanon. The contingent now comprises 710 all ranks. 26 Irish officers are at present serving with the UN Truce Supervision Organization in the Middle East. Of these, 5 are seconded to the UN Good Offices Mission in Afghánistán and Pakistan (UNGOMAP) which was established early in 1988. 18 Irish officers are serving with the UN Iran Iraq Military Observer Group (UNIIMOG) established in Aug. 1988. 15 of the officers act as observers and 3 serve with the Military Police Company, which also includes 34 other ranks. 20 Irish officers have been serving with the UN Transition Assistance Group in Namibia since March 1989. There is a small detachment with the UN force in Cyprus.

Army. The Army has 4 brigades and an infantry force. Three of the brigades have 2 infantry battalions and 1 brigade has 3 infantry battalions. Each brigade has a field artillery regiment and a squadron/company size unit for each of the support corps. The infantry force has 2 infantry battalions. The current (1989) strength of the Army is approximately 11,250 all ranks.

Navy. The Naval Service comprises 6 offshore patrol vessels and 1 helicopter offshore patrol vessel. 5 of these ships were built in Cork. Two of the 5 AC Dauphin helicopters are for use on board the helicopter patrol vessel. The Naval Base is at Haulbowline Island in Cork Harbour. The current (1990) strength of the Naval Service is about 940 all ranks.

Air Corps. The Air Corps has a current (1990) strength of about 800 all ranks. It has a total of 42 aircraft, comprised of 6 Fouga Magister armed jet trainers, 9 SF 260W armed piston-engined trainers, 8 Rheims-Cessna Rockets, 8 Alouette III, 5 Dauphin and 2 Gazelle helicopters, 2 twin-turbo prop Beech Super Kingair for coastal fishery patrol, and 1 Beech Super Kingair and 1 British Aerospace HS-125/700 twin turbofan transports.

INTERNATIONAL RELATIONS

Membership. Ireland is a member of UN, OECD, the Council of Europe and the European Communities.

ECONOMY

Budget. Current revenue and expenditure (in IR£1m.):

Current revenue	*1988* [1]	*1989*
Customs duties	108	121
Excise duties	1,481	1,535
Capital taxes	62	45
Stamp duties	198	212
Income tax	3,055	2,697
Income levy	–	–
Corporation tax	334	320
Value-added tax	1,805	1,815
Agricultural levies (EC)	13	13
Motor vehicle duties	140	146
Youth employment levy	126	105
Non-Tax Revenue	368	322
Total	7,690	7,331
Current expenditure		
Debt service	2,141	2,244
Industry and Labour	227	210
Agriculture	401	383
Fisheries, Forestry, Tourism	53	52
Health	1,172	1,182
Education	1,162	1,231
Social Welfare	2,640	2,692
Less: Receipts, e.g. social security	(–)1,633	(–)1,611
Total (including other items)	6,163	6,383

[1]Includes exceptional once-off receipts from tax amnesty.

Capital expenditure amounted to IR£1,689m. in 1985, and IR£1,647m. in 1986.

On 31 Dec. 1988 the National Debt amounted to IR£24,611·2m. of which IR£15,112·8m. was denominated in Irish pounds and IR£9,498·4m. in foreign currencies and the official external reserves of the Central Bank of Ireland amounted to IR£3,161m.

Currency. The unit of currency is the Irish *pound* or *an punt Éireannach*. From 10 Sept. 1928 when the first Irish legal-tender notes were issued, the Irish currency was linked to Sterling on a one-for-one basis. This relationship was discontinued on 30 March 1979 when, following Ireland's adherence to the European Monetary System, it became inconsistent with Ireland's obligations under that system.

The Central Bank has the sole right of issuing legal tender notes; token coinage is issued by the Minister for Finance through the Bank. In March 1990, £1 = IR£1·05; US$ = IR£0·64.

The volume of legal-tender notes outstanding in June 1989 was £1,189m. Total notes and coins outstanding amounted to £1,260·6m.

Banking. The Central Bank, which was established as from 1 Feb. 1943, in accordance with the Central Bank Act, 1942, replaced the Currency Commission, which was set up under the Currency Act, 1927, and had been responsible *inter alia* for the regulation of the note issue. In addition to the powers and functions of the Currency Commission the Central Bank has the power of receiving deposits from banks and public authorities, of rediscounting Exchequer bills and bills of exchange, of making advances to banks against such bills or against Government securities, of fixing and publishing rates of interest for rediscounting bills, or buying and selling certain Government securities and securities of any international bank or financial institution formed wholly or mainly by governments. The Bank also collects and publishes information relating to monetary and credit matters. The Central Bank Acts, 1971 and 1989, give further powers to the Central Bank in the regulation of banking including licensing of banks, the supervision of their operations and control of liquidity and reserve ratios. The capital of the Bank is IR£40,000, of which IR£24,000 has been paid up and is held by the Minister for Finance.

The Board of Directors of the Central Bank consists of a Governor, appointed by the President on the advice of the Government, and 9 directors, all appointed by the Minister for Finance.

The principal independent commercial banks are Allied Irish Banks PLC., Bank of Ireland and two smaller banks, Ulster Bank and National Irish Bank. They operate the branch banking system; on 31 Aug. 1989 their total deposit and current accounts within Ireland amounted to IR£7,642·3m. and their total gross assets in Ireland, IR£15,200·5m.

There are also 30 Non-Associated Banks of which 20 are merchant and commercial banks and 10 are industrial banks whose main activity is instalment credit. Four of the merchant or commercial banks are subsidiaries of the Associated Banks; 8 are from other EC countries and 4 from outside the EC (mainly US) and the remainder are Irish. On 20 July 1989 their current and deposit accounts and interbank borrowings amounted to IR£9,545·7m. (46% of total bank resources) and their lending to IR£5,272·4m. (37·7% of lending to residents); total gross assets in Ireland, IR£11,092·8m.

There are two state-owned credit corporations, one industrial and one agricultural, and several building societies. There are 4 Trustee Savings Banks and the Post Office Savings Bank which together had deposits of IR£1,065m. in March 1988.

Weights and Measures. Conversion to the metric system is in progress; with some exceptions which are confined to the domestic market, all imperial units of measurement will cease to be legal, for general use, after 31 Dec. 1994.

ENERGY AND NATURAL RESOURCES

Electricity. The total generating capacity was (1988) 3,937 mw. In 1988 the total sales of electricity amounted to 10,615m. units supplied to 1,234,957 customers. Electricity generated by fuel source 1988: Coal, 41%; oil, 8%; gas, 27%; peat, 17%; hydro, 7%. Supply 220 volts; 50 Hz.

Oil. About 618,000 sq. km of the Irish continental shelf has been designated an exploration area; at the furthest point the limit of jurisdiction is 520 nautical miles from the coast. Since 1970, 106 exploratory offshore oil wells have been drilled. A number of encouraging oil and gas flows have been recorded. In 1989, 63 blocks were held under exclusive offshore exploration licences and offshore petroleum leases.

Gas. (1989) All of Ireland's natural gas requirements are met by the Kinsale Head gas field 50 km off the south coast. In March 1989 additional natural gas was discovered close to this field but assessment of commercially recoverable reserves has not yet been completed. Existing gas reserves should be depleted in approximately 15 years. Gas Transmission is controlled by the Irish Gas Board (BGE), which sells the gas into electricity generation, fertilizer production, and distribution systems for domestic, commercial and industrial use.

Peat. The country has very little indigenous coal, but possesses large reserves of peat, the development of which is handled largely by Bord na Mona (Peat Board). To date, the Board has acquired over 200,000 acres of bog and has 15 locations around the country. In the year ending 31 March, 1989, the Board sold 157,123 tonnes of sod peat to the domestic market and 68,437 tonnes for use in 4 sod peat electricity generating stations. The Board also sold 3,265,605 tonnes of milled peat for use in 7 milled peat generating stations. A further 967,517 tonnes was used by the Board in its factories to produce 363,000 tonnes of briquettes for sale to the domestic heating market. The Board also sold 1,311,597 cu. metres of horticultural peat.

Minerals. Lead and zinc concentrates are important. Metal content of production, 1988: Zinc, 176,500 tonnes; lead, 32,500 tonnes. Barytes, gypsum, limestone and aggregates are also important, and there is some coal, silver, quartz, dolomite, silica sand and marble. Exploration activity is centred on base metals, precious metals, industrial minerals and coal and about 45 companies are prospecting.

Agriculture. General distribution of surface (in hectares) in 1988: Crops and pasture, 4,670,000; other land, including grazed mountain, 2,219,200; total, 6,889,200.

Estimated area (hectares) under certain crops calculated from sample returns:

Crops	*Area* 1984	1985	1986	1987	1988
Wheat	77,200	78,100	76,100	56,900	60,400
Oats	24,900	23,300	20,900	20,400	19,600
Barley	304,300	298,400	282,800	276,000	266,100
Potatoes	35,700	33,000	30,500	30,300	28,100
Sugar-beet	34,900	33,900	37,000	37,100	33,300

Gross agricultural output (including value of changes in stocks) for the year 1988 was valued at £3,159·7m.

Livestock (1988): Cattle, 6,604,100; sheep, 6,656,300; pigs, 979,000; horses and ponies, 53,100; poultry, 8,940,900.

Forestry. The total area of state forests at 31 Dec. 1988 was 418,866 hectares, of which 342,839 was planted; 75,996 were reserve land for planting, the rest roads, water etc.

Fisheries. In 1989 approximately 13,500 people were engaged full- or part-time in the sea fishing industry; 5,850 full-time and 6,250 part-time in the fish catching, farming and processing industries. The number of vessels engaged in fishing in 1985 was 3,096, of which 1,116 accounted for the greater part of the fishing effort; men 7,778. The quantities and values of fish landed during 1987 were: Demersal fish, 41,805·8 tonnes, value IR£32,283,757; pelagic fish, 149,689·1 tonnes, value IR£18,980,194; shellfish, 25,544·3 tonnes, value IR£18,936,229. Total quantity: 217,039·2 tonnes; total value, IR£70,200,180.

INDUSTRY AND TRADE

Industry. The census of industrial production for 1986 gives the following details of the values (in IR£1m.) of gross and net output for the principal manufacturing industries. The figures for net output are those of gross output minus cost of materials, including fuel, light and power, repairs to plant and machinery and amounts paid to others in connexion with products made.

	Gross output	*Net output*
Slaughtering, preparing and preserving meat	1,567·3	250·4
Manufacture of dairy products	1,587·6	231·1
Bread, biscuit and flour confectionery	235·5	105·4
Cocoa, chocolate and sugar confectionery	233·9	71·6
Animal and poultry foods	460·5	87·0
Brewing and malting	286·8	191·9
Spirit distilling and compounding	144·7	79·6
Paper and paper products	204·9	80·2
Printing and publishing	348·8	224·9
Manufacture of metal articles	452·1	200·4
Manufacture of non-metallic mineral products	505·4	212·4
Chemicals, including manmade fibres	1,610·1	891·8
Mechanical engineering	363·0	175·3
Office machinery and data-processing machinery	1,636·3	744·6
Electrical engineering	932·9	488·6
Manufacture and assembly of motor vehicles, parts and accessories	96·0	39·8
Manufacture of other means of transport	148·6	76·0
Instrument engineering	374·4	212·1
Textiles	425·7	154·3
Manufacture of footwear and clothing	306·9	139·4
Timber and wooden furniture	262·6	104·9
Processing rubber and plastics	388·0	180·6
Mineral oil refining	173·8	16·8
Gas, water and electricity	992·7	695·9
All other industries	1,852·2	1,029·6
Total (all industries)	15,590·7	6,684·6

Labour. The total labour force at mid-April 1988 was about 1,310,000, of which about 219,000 persons were out of work. Of the estimated 1,091,000 persons at work, 166,000 were in the agricultural sector, 300,000 in industry and 626,000 in services.

The number of trade unions in Dec. 1988 was 73; total membership, 484,000. About 224,000 were organized in 4 general unions catering both for white collar and manual workers. There were 16 employers' associations holding negotiation licences, with membership of 11,400.

Commerce. Value of imports and exports of merchandise for calendar years (in IR£):

	1985	*1986*	*1987*	*1988*
Imports	9,428,197,691	8,621,291,016	9,155,206,863	10,213,064,564
Exports	9,743,037,929	9,374,310,355	10,723,497,879	12,300,704,602

The values of the chief imports and total exports are shown in the following table (in IR£1,000):

	Imports		*Exports*	
	1987	*1988*	*1987*	*1988*
Live animals and food	985,469	1,066,227	2,676,203	2,899,284
Raw materials	294,957	338,219	449,909	563,431
Mineral fuels and lubricants	676,514	566,399	77,210	64,539
Chemicals	1,126,241	1,292,744	1,307,169	1,612,787
Manufactured goods	1,442,726	1,637,533	942,246	1,035,857
Machinery and transport equipment	3,065,335	3,515,936	3,364,528	3,837,825
Manufactured articles [1]	1,172,788	1,345,681	1,304,260	1,606,281

[1] Not elsewhere specified.

Exports, in IR£1m., for 1988 (and 1987): UK, 4,349·1 (3,662·6); Federal Republic of Germany, 1,368·8 (1,202·6); France, 1,120·3 (994·4); USA, 949·5 (833·8); Netherlands, 859·7 (778·3); Belgium and Luxembourg, 545 (512·8); Italy, 463·9 (392·5); Sweden, 231·1 (205·4); Japan, 238·7 (181·2); Switzerland, 160·3 (168·1); Spain, 209·3 (164·2); Norway, 148·3 (123·6); Canada, 121·3 (110). Imports: UK, 4,301·8 (3,816); USA, 1,623 (1,555·4); Federal Republic of Germany, 880·8 (764·6); France, 416·8 (401·2); Japan, 496·9 (397·6); Netherlands, 407·5 (338·8); Italy, 259·5 (225); Belgium and Luxembourg, 214 (197·5); Sweden, 160·1 (139·5); Spain, 118·4 (118).

Total trade between Ireland and UK (British Department of Trade returns, in £1,000 sterling):

	1985	*1986*	*1987*	*1988*	*1989*
Imports to UK	2,816,007	3,053,807	3,488,406	3,876,630	4,279,202
Exports and re-exports from UK	3,642,844	3,558,372	3,831,737	4,057,046	4,714,780

Tourism. Total number of overseas tourists in 1988 was 2,425,000. These, together with cross-border visitors, spent IR£842m.

COMMUNICATIONS

Roads. At 31 Dec. 1988 there were 92,303 km of public roads, consisting of 8 km of motorway, 2,630 km of national primary roads, 2,625 km of national secondary roads, 10,566 km of regional roads, 73,975 km of county roads and 2,499 km of urban roads.

Number of licensed motor vehicles at 30 Sept. 1988: Private cars, 749,459; public-service vehicles, 8,653; goods vehicles, 118,764 agricultural vehicles, 66,850; motor cycles, 24,877; other vehicles, 12,693.

The total number of km run by road motor passenger vehicles of the omnibus type during 1986 was 94,069,000. Passengers carried numbered 230,206,000 and the gross receipts from passengers were IR£125,010,000.

Railways. The total length of railway open for traffic at 31 Dec. 1988 was 1,944 km (38 km electrified), all 1,600 mm gauge.

Railway statistics for years ending 31 Dec.	*1987*	*1988*
Passengers (no.)	24,895,000	24,043,000
Km run by coaching trains	9,692,000	9,288,000
Merchandise and mineral traffic conveyed (tonnes)	563,095,000	544,591,000
Km run by freight trains	4,232,000	3,942,000
Receipts (IR£)	132,083,000	134,220,000
Expenditure (IR£)	124,737,000	129,091,000

Aviation. Aer Lingus PLC is a state owned company. Incorporated in 1936, it operates air services within Ireland and between Ireland and Britain and Europe. Air services between Ireland and the USA are operated by Aerlinte Eireann PLC, a sister state owned company incorporated in 1947. Each company has a separate legal identity and board of directors. The management is common to both companies and their services are integrated under the marketing name of Aer Lingus as the national airline. During the year ended 31 March 1989 Aer Lingus carried 3,118,164 passengers and 26,409 tonnes of cargo/mail on its European services and 404,741 passengers and 18,948 tonnes of cargo/mail on its trans-Atlantic services.

In addition to Aer Lingus, there were in 1989 10 independent air transport operators, the largest of which, Ryanair, operates air services within Ireland and on a number of international routes (Ireland/UK, Ireland/Federal Republic of Germany).

Shipping. The Irish merchant fleet, of vessels of 100 gross tonnes or over, consisted of 76 vessels totalling 134,533 GRT at 30 June 1989. Total cargo traffic passing through the country's ports amounted to 24m. tonnes in 1988.

Inland Waterways. The principal inland waterways open to navigation are the Shannon Navigation (130 miles) and the Grand Canal and Barrow Navigation (156 miles). The Office of Public Works is responsible for the waterways system as a public amenity. Merchandise traffic has now ceased and navigation is confined to pleasure craft operated either privately or commercially.

Telecommunications. Telecommunication services are provided by Telecom Eireann, a statutory body set up under the Postal and Telecommunications Services Act, 1983. Number of working lines (July 1989), 872,000; telex lines, 5,153; data lines, over 8,000; Eirpac (public-switched network), 2,003 customers and Eircell (mobile telephone network), 7,566 customers.

Postal services are provided by An Post, a statutory body set up under the Postal and Telecommunications Services Act, 1983. Number of Post Offices as of Dec. 1988, 2,107. Delivery points, 1,150,000. Number of items delivered during year ended 31 Dec. 1988, 464·7m. An Post also offers a range of services throughout its Post Office network including National Savings Services and payment of Social Welfare Benefits/Pensions on an agency basis for the State.

Public service broadcasting is provided by Radio Telefis Eireann, a statutory body established under the Broadcasting Authority Acts 1960–79 to provide the national TV and radio services. RTE is financed by advertising and by TV licences. On 31 Dec. 1987 there were 787,501 holders of current TV licences. During 1988 new legislation was enacted to provide for the establishment of an independent commercial national radio service, an independent TV service and local radio services. In 1989 many of the radio services were in place and it was expected that the TV service would begin broadcasting in autumn 1990.

Cinemas. There were (1986) 124 cinemas and 169 (estimate) screens.

Newspapers (1986). There are 7 daily newspapers (all in English) with a combined circulation of 647,912; 5 of them are published in Dublin (circulation, 555,282).

JUSTICE, RELIGION, EDUCATION AND WELFARE

Justice. The Constitution provides that justice shall be administered in public in Courts established by law by Judges appointed by the President on the advice of the Government. The jurisdiction and organization of the Courts are dealt with in the Courts (Establishment and Constitution) Act, 1961, the Courts (Supplemental Provisions) Acts, 1961–88. These Courts consist of Courts of First Instance and a Court of Final Appeal, called the Supreme Court. The Courts of First Instance are the High Court with full original jurisdiction and the Circuit and the District Courts with local and limited jurisdiction. A judge may not be removed from office except for stated misbehaviour or incapacity and then only on resolutions passed by both Houses of the *Oireachtas*. Judges of the Supreme, High and Circuit Courts are appointed from among practising barristers. Judges of the District Court (called District Justices) may be appointed from among practising barristers or practising solicitors.

The Supreme Court, which consists of the Chief Justice (who is *ex officio* an additional judge of the High Court) and 4 ordinary judges, has appellate jurisdiction from all decisions of the High Court. The President may, after consultation with the Council of State, refer a Bill, which has been passed by both Houses of the *Oireachtas* (other than a money bill and certain other bills), to the Supreme Court for a decision on the question as to whether such Bill or any provision thereof is repugnant to the Constitution.

The High Court, which consists of a President (who is *ex officio* an additional Judge of the Supreme Court) and 15 ordinary judges, has full original jurisdiction in and power to determine all matters and questions, whether of law or fact, civil or criminal. In all cases in which questions arise concerning the validity of any law having regard to the provisions of the Constitution, the High Court alone exercises original jurisdiction. The High Court on Circuit acts as an appeal court from the Circuit Court.

The Court of Criminal Appeal consists of the Chief Justice or an ordinary Judge of the Supreme Court, together with either 2 ordinary judges of the High Court or the President and one ordinary judge of the High Court. It deals with appeals by persons convicted on indictment where the appellant obtains a certificate from the trial judge that the case is a fit one for appeal, or, in case such certificate is refused, where the court itself, on appeal from such refusal, grants leave to appeal. The decision of the Court of Criminal Appeal is final, unless that court or the Director of Public Prosecutions certifies that the decision involves a point of law of exceptional public importance, in which case an appeal is taken to the Supreme Court.

The Offences against the State Act, 1939 provides in Part V for the establishment of Special Criminal Courts. A Special Criminal Court sits without a jury. The rules of evidence that apply in proceedings before a Special Criminal Court are the same as those applicable in trials in the Central Criminal Court. A Special Criminal Court is authorised by the 1939 Act to make rules governing its own practice and procedure. An appeal against conviction or sentence by a Special Criminal Court may be taken to the Court of Criminal Appeal. On 30 May 1972 Orders were made establishing a Special Criminal Court and declaring that offences of a particular class or kind (as set out) were to be scheduled offences for the purposes of Part V of the Act, the effect of which was to give the Special Criminal Court jurisdiction to try persons charged with those offences.

The High Court exercising criminal jurisdiction is known as the Central Criminal Court. It consists of a judge or judges of the High Court, nominated by the President of the High Court. The Court sits in Dublin and tries criminal cases which are outside the jurisdiction of the Circuit Court.

The country is divided into a number of circuits for the purposes of the Circuit Court. The President of the Circuit Court is *ex officio* an additional judge of the High Court. The jurisdiction of the court in civil proceedings is limited to IR£15,000 in contract and tort, IR£15,000 in actions founded on hire-purchase and credit-sale agreements, IR£5,000 in equity and IR£5,000 in probate and administration, save by consent of the parties, in which event the jurisdiction is unlimited. In criminal matters it has jurisdiction in all cases except murder, treason, piracy and allied offences. The Circuit Court acts as an appeal court from the District Court.

The District Court has summary jurisdiction in a large number of criminal cases where the offence is not of a serious nature. In civil matters the Court has jurisdiction in contract and tort (except slander, libel, seduction, slander of title and false imprisonment) where the claim does not exceed IR£2,500; in proceedings founded on hire-purchase and credit-sale agreements, the jurisdiction is IR£2,500.

All criminal cases, except those of a minor nature, and those tried in the Special Criminal Court, are tried by a judge and a jury of 12. A majority vote of the jury (10 must agree) is necessary to determine a verdict.

Religion. According to the census of population taken in 1981 the principal religious professions were as follows:

	Leinster	*Munster*	*Connacht*	*Ulster (part of)*	*Total*
Roman Catholics	1,645,489	949,938	406,811	202,238	3,204,476
Church of Ireland	58,356	18,076	5,973	12,961	95,366

	Leinster	*Munster*	*Connacht*	*Ulster (part of)*	*Total*
Presbyterians	4,337	542	345	9,031	14,255
Methodists	3,339	1,285	324	842	5,790
Other religious denominations	9,148	2,586	753	483	12,970
Not stated or no religion	69,852	25,888	10,204	4,604	110,548

Education. *Elementary.* Elementary education is free and was given in about 3,387 national schools (including 118 special schools) in 1987-88. The total number of pupils on rolls in 1987–88 was 565,488, including pupils in special schools and classes; the number of teachers of all classes was about 21,217, including remedial teachers and teachers of special classes. The estimated state expenditure on elementary education for 1989 was IR£449,353,000, excluding the cost of administration.

Special provision is made for handicapped and deprived children in special schools which are recognized on the same basis as primary schools, in special classes attached to ordinary schools and in certain voluntary centres where educational services appropriate to the needs of the children are provided. Categories of children include visually handicapped, hearing impaired, physically handicapped, mentally handicapped, emotionally disturbed, travelling children and other socially disadvantaged children. Provision is also made, on an increasing scale, for children with dual or multiple handicaps. Each class in such schools is very much smaller than ordinary classes in a primary school and, because of the size of the catchment areas involved, an extensive system of school transport has been developed. Many handicapped children who have spent some years in a special school or class are integrated into normal schools for part of their school career, if necessary with special additional facilities such as nursing services, special equipment, etc. For others who cannot progress within the ordinary school system the special schools or classes provide both the primary and post-primary level of education. There are also part-time teaching facilities in hospitals, child guidance clinics, rehabilitation workshops, special 'Saturday-morning' centres and home teaching schemes.

Special schools (1987–88) numbered 118 with 8,575 pupils. There were 2,904 pupils enrolled in special classes attached to ordinary schools. 797 remedial teachers were employed for backward pupils in ordinary primary schools. 30 peripatetic teachers were employed for children with hearing or visual impairments, and for travelling children.

There are different types of post primary schools, as follows, in all of which pupils are prepared for the State examinations and for entrance to universities and institutes of further education.

Secondary. Voluntary secondary schools are under private control and are conducted in most cases by religious orders; all schools receive grants from the State and are open to inspection by the Department of Education. The number of recognized secondary schools during the school year 1988–89 was 496, and the number of pupils in attendance was 213,640.

Vocational Education Committee schools provide courses of general and technical education. The number of vocational schools during the school year 1988–89 was 251, full-time students, 84,442. These schools are controlled by the local Vocational Education Committees; they are financed mainly by state grants and also by local rating authorities and VECs.

Comprehensive Schools which are financed by the State combine academic and technical subjects in one broad curriculum so that each pupil may be offered educational options suited to his needs, abilities and interests. The number of comprehensive schools during the school year 1988–89 was 16 with 8,837 students.

Community Schools continue to be established through the amalgamation of existing voluntary secondary and Vocational Education Committee schools where this is found feasible and desirable and in new areas where a single larger school is considered preferable to 2 smaller schools under separate managements. These schools provide second-level education and also provide adult education facilities for their own areas. They also make facilities available to voluntary organizations and to the adult community generally. The number of community schools during the school year 1988–89 was 47 with 31,651 students.

The estimated State expenditure for post-primary education for 1989 was IR£461,840,000.

Regional Technical Colleges and Colleges of Technology. Apprentice, technician and professional courses (and some degree courses) are provided in the Dublin Institute of Technology under the auspices of the City of Dublin Vocational Education Committee; the Limerick College of Art, Commerce and Technology; the Cork School of Art and School of Music and 9 regional technical colleges at Athlone, Carlow, Cork, Dundalk, Galway, Letterkenny, Sligo, Tralee and Waterford. Students (full-time) 1988–89 (estimate) 23,000.

University Education is provided by the National University of Ireland, founded in Dublin in 1908, and by the University of Dublin (Trinity College), founded in 1592. The National University comprises 3 constituent colleges–University College, Dublin, University College, Cork, and University College, Galway.

St Patrick's College, Maynooth, Co. Kildare, is a national seminary for Catholic priests and a pontifical university with the power to confer degrees up to doctoral level in philosophy, theology and canon law. It also admits lay students (men and women) to the courses in arts, Celtic studies, science and education which it provides as a recognized college of the National University.

Besides the University medical schools, the Royal College of Surgeons in Ireland provides medical qualifications which are internationally recognized. Courses to degree level are available at the National College of Art and Design, Dublin.

There are six Colleges of Education for training primary school teachers. For degree awarding purposes, three of these colleges are associated with Trinity College, two with University College, Dublin, and one with University College, Cork. The Thomond College of Education, Limerick, trains post-primary teachers in physical education, rural and general science, metalwork and engineering science, woodwork and building science and commercial and secretarial subjects.

Third-level courses with a technological bias, leading to degree, diploma and certificate qualifications are also provided by the National Institutes for Higher Education, Limerick and Dublin. There are also 2 Home Economics Colleges, one associated with Trinity College and the other with University College, Galway.

Agricultural. Teagasc – the Agriculture and Food Development Authority is the agency responsible for providing agricultural advisory, training, research and development services. Full-time instruction in agriculture is provided for all sections of the farming community. There are 4 agricultural colleges for young people, administered by Teagasc, and 7 private Teagasc-aided agricultural colleges, at each of which a 1-year course in agriculture is given. A second-year course in farm machinery is provided at one college. Scholarships tenable at these colleges, all of which are residential, are awarded by Teagasc which also provides a comprehensive agricultural advisory service and operates an intensive programme of short courses for adult farmers in agriculture and horticulture at local centres.

Horticultural. Two of the agricultural colleges mentioned above also provide a commercial horticultural course. A third college aided by Teagasc also provides this course. A 3-year course in amenity horticulture is provided at the National Botanic Gardens in Dublin.

A comprehensive 3-year training programme for young entrants to farming leading to a 'Certificate in Farming', the main training programme for young people entering farming, involving both formal instruction and a period of supervised on-farm work experience, was introduced by ACOT in 1982. Students taking the Certificate in Farming can follow a course in general agriculture, pigs, poultry or horticulture. In the case of horticulture, the major part of this course is taken at one of the three horticultural colleges.

Health Services. There are 3 categories of entitlement, based on a person's income: *(i)* Persons on a low income and their dependants, who qualify for the full range of health services, free of charge, i.e. family doctor, drugs and medicines, hospital and specialist services as well as dental, aural and optical services. Maternity care and infant welfare services are also provided. There is no fixed limit, but guidelines laid down by health boards, determine eligibility – each application is considered on its merit. There is provision for hardship cases.

(ii) Persons whose income for the year ended 5 April 1989 was under IR£16,000. They and their dependants are entitled to hospital services, subject to certain charges, both as an in-patient and an out-patient, a full maternity and infant welfare service and assistance towards the cost of prescriptions. The latter limits the nett outlay on medicines used in a calendar month to IR£28.

(iii) Persons whose income for the year ended 5 April 1989 was IR£16,000 or more. They are entitled to in-patient and out-patient hospital services, subject to certain charges, but they are liable for the fees of consultants. They are also entitled to assistance towards the cost of prescriptions. Drugs and medicines are made available free of charge to all persons suffering from specified long-term ailments such as diabetes, multiple sclerosis, epilepsy, etc. Hospital in-patient and out-patient services are free of charge to all children under 16 years of age, suffering from specified long-term conditions such as cystic fibrosis, spina bifida, cerebral palsy, etc. Immunization and diagnostic services as well as hospital services are free of charge to everyone suffering from an infectious disease. A maintenance allowance is also payable in necessitous cases.

From 18 May 1987 persons in categories *(ii)* and *(iii)* are liable for in-patient and out-patient charge. A charge of IR£10 is made for each day or part of a day during which in-patient services are availed of subject to a maximum payment of IR£100 in any period of 12 consecutive months. A charge of IR£10 for out-patient services is made for the first and subsequent instances relating to the same matter. Persons in category *(i)*, women receiving service in respect of motherhood, children suffering from certain diseases etc. are not liable for these charges.

Services for Children: Health Boards are involved, with the co-operation of a wide network of voluntary organizations, in the provision of a range of child care services including adoption, fostering, residential care, day care and social work services for families in need of support.

Welfare Services: There are various services provided for the elderly, the chronic sick, the disabled and families in stress, such as social support service, day care services for children, home helps, home nursing, meals-on-wheels, day centres, cheap fuel, etc. Health Boards also provide disabled persons, without charge, with training for employment and place them in jobs.

Grants and Allowances: Disabled Persons' Maintenance Allowance is payable to the chronically disabled over the age of 16 who are not in long term care. Recipients are entitled to free travel and subject to certain conditions to electricity allowance, free TV licence, telephone rental and fuel vouchers. Mobility allowance is payable to severely disabled persons between 16 and 66 years who are unable to walk. Allowance for the Domiciliary Care of Severely Handicapped Children is payable to the mother of a severely handicapped child, maintained at home, but needing constant care and supervision. Blind welfare allowance: This allowance is in addition to the benefits for the blind operated by the Department of Social Welfare. Grants up to IR£1,500 are paid, subject to a means test, to disabled persons towards the purchase of a car, in order that they might obtain or retain employment.

Health contributions: A health contribution of 1·25% of income up to a ceiling of IR£16,000 is payable by all.

Social Security. Social-welfare services concerned primarily with income maintenance are under the general control of the Minister for Social Welfare. The services administered by the Department of Social Welfare are divided into Insurance and Assistance schemes.

Insurance Services. All employees irrespective of their level of earnings are compulsorily insured from age 16 to 66 years and are liable for pay-related social insurance contributions. The majority of employees pay a contribution of 7·75% of their earnings prescribed up to a ceiling of £16,000 while a contribution of 6·5% of their earnings continues to be deducted up to a ceiling of £16,700. Their employers pay a further 12·2% up to a prescribed ceiling of IR£18,000. (The insured population is approximately 1·2m.) Subject to appropriate statutory conditions (but without regard to the recipients' means) the following flat-rate insurance benefits are available: Disability benefit, invalidity pension, unemployment benefit, maternity benefit, widow's pension, deserted wife's benefit, orphan's allowance, treatment benefit, retirement pension payable at 65, old-age pension payable at 66 and a death grant. Pay-related benefit is payable with disability benefit, unemployment benefit and injury benefit to persons whose employment is insurable at certain class rates of pay-related social insurance contribution. The cost of the flat-rate and pay-related benefits is met by pay-related social insurance contributions from employers and employees and by a state grant.

The insurance services also provide for payment of benefits in respect of injury, disablement or death, as well as medical care resulting from an occupational accident or disease. These benefits are available to employees, irrespective of age, and are paid from an Occupational Injuries Fund which is financed by employers' contributions and income from investments.

In April 1988 compulsory social insurance was extended to self-employed persons. From 6 April 1989 the majority of the self-employed pay a contribution of 4% of income up to a ceiling of IR£16,700, subject to a minimum contribution of IR£208 each year. Self-employed persons on low incomes who are exempted from having to make a return of income for tax purposes, pay a flat rate contribution of IR£104 per year. Subject to the same statutory conditions as in the case of employees (and without regard to the recipient's means), the following flat rate insurance benefits are available under the scheme: Widow's pension, orphan's allowance and old age pension payable at 66.

Assistance Services. Child Benefit is payable without a means test in respect of each child under 16 years of age and children between 16 and 18 who are at school or incapacitated for a prolonged period. The following Assistance services are subject to a means test: Non-contributory widows' and orphans' pensions to the survivors of persons whose lack of insurance (or inadequate insurance record) precludes payment of contributory pensions; deserted wife's allowance to women who have been deserted by their husbands and for whom the deserted wife's benefit is similarly precluded; allowances for unmarried mothers, prisoners' wives and single women between the ages of 58 and 66 years; old age pensions payable at age 66 to persons not entitled to insurance pensions; blind pensions (under the same general conditions as apply to old age pensions) payable at age 18; unemployment assistance payable during unemployment to persons not entitled to receive unemployment benefit; supplementary welfare allowance, payable when a person has no other resources or when such resources are insufficient to meet his needs; family income supplement, payable to low income families with children where one or more parents are in employment.

DIPLOMATIC REPRESENTATIVES

Of Ireland in Great Britain (17 Grosvenor Pl., London, SW1X 7HR)
Ambassador: Andrew O'Rourke.

Of Great Britain in Ireland (33 Merrion Rd., Dublin, 4)
Ambassador: Sir Nicholas Fenn, KCMG.

Of Ireland in the USA (2234 Massachusetts Ave., NW, Washington, D.C., 20008)
Ambassador: Padraic N. MacKernan.

Of the USA in Ireland (42 Elgin Rd., Ballsbridge, Dublin)
Ambassador: Richard A. Moore.

Of Ireland to the United Nations
Ambassador: Francis Mahon Hayes.

Further Reading

Statistical Information: The Central Statistics Office (Earlsfort Terrace, Dublin, 2) was established in June 1949, and is attached to the Department of the Taoiseach. *Director:* T. P. Linehan, B.E., B.Sc.

Principal publications of the Central Statistics Office are *National Income and Expenditure* (annually), *Statistical Abstract* (annually), *Census of Population Reports, Census of Industrial Production Reports, Trade and Shipping Statistics* (annually and monthly), *Trend of Employment and Unemployment* (annually), *Reports on Vital Statistics* (annually and quarterly), *Irish Statistical Bulletin* (quarterly), *Labour Force Surveys* (annually), *Trade Statistics* (monthly), *Economic Series* (monthly).

Aspects of Ireland. (Series). Dublin Department of Foreign Affairs.
Atlas of Ireland. Royal Irish Academy, Dublin, 1979
Facts About Ireland. Dublin Department of Foreign Affairs, 6th ed. 1985
The Gill History of Ireland. 11 vols. Dublin
Bartholomew, P. C., *The Irish Judiciary.* Dublin, Institute of Public Administration, 1974
Chubb, B., *The Constitution and Constitutional Change in Ireland.* Dublin, reprinted 1988
Coolahan, J., *Irish Education: Its History and Structure.* Dublin, 1981
Eager, A. R., *A Guide to Irish Bibliographical Material.* 2nd ed. London, 1980
Encyclopaedia of Ireland. Dublin, 1968
Foster, R. F., *Modern Ireland 1600–1972.* London, 1988
Hensey, B., *The Health Services of Ireland.* 4th ed. Dublin, 1988
Hickey, D. J. and Doherty, J. E., *A Dictionary of Irish History since 1800.* Dublin, 1980
Johnston, T. J. and others, *A History of the Church of Ireland.* Dublin, 1953
Lee, J. J., *Ireland 1912-1985: Politics and Society.* CUP, 1989
McDunphy, Michael, *The President of Ireland: His Powers, Functions and Duties.* Dublin, 1945
Maher, D., *The Tortuous Path: The Course of Ireland's Entry into the EEC 1948–73.* Dublin, 1986
Miller, K. A., *Emigrants and Exiles: Ireland and the Irish Exodus to North America.* OUP, 1988
Page, R., *Sources of Economic Information: Ireland.* Dublin, 1985
Shannon, M. O., *Irish Republic.* [Bibliography] Oxford and Santa Barbara, 1986
Thom's Directory of Ireland. 2 vols. (Dublin, Street Directory, Commercial). Dublin, 1979–80
Tobin, F., *Ireland in the 1960s.* Dublin, 1984

ISRAEL

Capital: Jerusalem
Population: 4·48m. (1988)
GNP per capita: US$8,650 (1988)

Medinat Israel—State of Israel

HISTORY. The State of Israel was established on 14 May 1948. In 1967, following some years of uneasy peace, local clashes on the Israeli-Syrian border were followed by Egyptian mass concentration of forces on the borders of Israel. The UN emergency force was expelled and a blockade of shipping to and from Israel was imposed by Egypt in the Red Sea. Israel struck out at Egypt on land, in the air and by sea on 5–9 June 1967. Jordan joined in the conflict which spread to the Syrian borders. By 11 June the Israelis had occupied the Gaza Strip and the Sinai peninsula as far as the Suez Canal in Egypt, West Jordan as far as the Jordan valley and the heights east of the Sea of Galilee, including Quneitra in Syria.

A further war broke out on 6 Oct. 1973 when an Egyptian offensive was launched across the Suez Canal and Syrian forces struck on the Golan Heights. Following UN Security Council resolutions a ceasefire finally came into being on 24 Oct. In Dec. agreement was reached by Egypt and Israel on disengagement and a disengagement agreement was signed with Syria on 31 May 1974. A further disengagement agreement was signed between Israel and Egypt in Sept. 1975.

Developments in 1977 included President Sadat of Egypt's visit to Israel and peace inititative and in March 1978 Israeli troops entered southern Lebanon but later withdrew after the arrival of a UN peace-keeping force.

In Sept. 1978 President Carter convened the Camp David conference at which Egypt and Israel agreed on frameworks for peace in the Middle East with treaties to be negotiated between Israel and her neighbours. Negotiations began in USA between Egypt and Israel in Oct. 1978 and a peace treaty was signed in Washington 26 March 1979.

Under the Israel-Egypt peace treaty, Israel withdrew from the Sinai Desert in two phases, part was achieved on 26 Jan. 1980 and the final withdrawal by 26 April 1982.

AREA AND POPULATION. The area of Israel, within the boundaries defined by the 1949 armistice agreements with Egypt, Jordan, the Lebanon and Syria, is 20,770 sq. km (8,017 sq. miles), with a population (June 1983 census) of 4,037,600 (estimated, 1988, 4,476,800). Population of areas under Israeli administration as a result of the 6-day war was, in 1988: Judaea and Samaria (West Bank), 895,000, Gaza Strip, 589,000.

Crude birth rate per 1,000 population of Jewish population (1988), 20·2; non-Jewish: Moslems, 35·5; Christians, 22·9; Druzes and others, 30·5. Crude death rate, Jewish, 7·3; non-Jewish: Moslems, 3·5; Christians, 5·4; Druzes and others, 3·1. Infant mortality rate per 1,000 live births, Jewish, 7·7; non-Jewish: Moslems, 17; Christians, 10·5; Druzes and others, 18·7. Life expectancy (1987): Males, 73·6 years; females, 77.

Israel is administratively divided into 6 districts:

District	*Area (sq. km)*	*Population* [1]	*Chief town*
Northern	4,501	739,500	Nazareth
Haifa	854	602,800	Haifa
Central	1,242	938,600	Ramla
Tel Aviv	170	1,029,700	Tel Aviv
Jerusalem [2]	627	538,300	Jerusalem
Southern	14,107	529,300	Beersheba

[1] 1988. [2] Includes East Jerusalem.

On 23 Jan. 1950 the Knesset proclaimed Jerusalem the capital of the State and on 14 Dec. 1981 extended Israeli law into the Golan Heights. Population of the main towns (1988): Tel-Aviv/Jaffa, 317,800; Jerusalem, 493,500; Haifa, 222,600; Ramat Gan, 115,700; Bat-Yam, 133,100; Holon, 146,100; Petach-Tikva, 133,600; Beersheba, 113,200.

The official languages are Hebrew and Arabic.

Areas under Israeli occupation as a result of the 6-day war:

The **West Bank** has an area of 5,879 sq. km (2,270 sq. miles) and a population (1988) of 895,000, of whom 97% were Palestinian Arabs. Nearly 85% are Muslims, 7·4% Jewish and 8% Christian. In 1984, the birth rate was 3·9% and the death rate 8%. In 1987, there were 39,091 private cars and 13,710 commercial vehicles registered. There were (1988) 183,041 pupils in primary schools and 105,007 in secondary schools, while (1983) there were 7,066 students in higher education. In 1988 there were 16 hospitals and clinics with 1,336 beds.

The **Gaza Strip** has an area of 363 sq. km (140 sq. miles) and a population (1988) of 589,000. The chief town is Gaza itself, with (1979) 120,000 inhabitants. In 1984, over 98% of the population were Arabic-speaking Muslims; the birth rate was 4·8% and the death rate 0·8%. Citrus fruits, wheat and olives are grown, with farm land covering 193 sq. km (1980) and occupying most of the active workforce. Some 1,600 tonnes of fish (1984) was also caught. In 1987 there were 18,761 private cars and 4,374 commercial vehicles registered. There were (1988) 112,959 pupils in primary schools and 64,699 in secondary schools, with (1983) 2,387 students in higher education. In 1988 there were 7 hospitals and clinics with 895 beds.

Immigration. The following table shows the numbers of Jewish immigrants entering Palestine (Israel), including persons entering as travellers who subsequently registered as immigrants. For a year-by-year breakdown, *see* THE STATESMAN'S YEAR-BOOK, 1951, p. 1167.

1919–48	482,857	1958–68	384,870	1980–88	129,789
1948–57	905,740	1969–79	384,066		

During the period 1948–68, 45·5% of the immigrants came from Europe and America and 54·5% from Asia and Africa; in 1988, 74% came from Europe and America and 25·7% from Asia and Africa.

The Jewish Agency, which, in accordance with Article IV of the Palestine Mandate, played a leading role in laying the political, economic and social foundations on which the State of Israel was established, continues to be instrumental in organizing immigration.

CLIMATE. From April to Oct., the summers are long and hot, and almost rainless. From Nov. to March, the weather is generally mild, though colder in hilly areas, and this is the wet season. Jerusalem. Jan. 48°F (9°C), July 73°F (23°C). Annual rainfall 21" (528 mm). Tel Aviv. Jan. 57°F (14°C), July 81°F (27°C). Annual rainfall 22" (550 mm).

CONSTITUTION AND GOVERNMENT. Israel is an independent sovereign republic, established by proclamation on 14 May 1948. For the history of the British Mandate, *see* THE STATESMAN'S YEAR-BOOK, 1920–49, under PALESTINE.

In 1950 the Knesset (*Parliament*), which in 1949 had passed the Transition Law dealing in general terms with the powers of the Knesset, President and Cabinet, resolved to enact from time to time fundamental laws, which eventually, taken together, would form the Constitution. Fundamental laws that have been passed are: The Knesset (1958), Israel Lands (1960), the President (1964), the Government (1968), the State Economy (1975), the Army (1976), Jerusalem, capital of Israel (1980), and the Judicature (1984).

National flag: White with 2 horizontal blue stripes, the blue Shield of David in the centre.

National anthem: Hatikvah (The Hope). Words by N. N. Imber (1878); adopted as the Jewish National Anthem by the first Zionist Congress (1897).

The Knesset, a one-chamber Parliament, consists of 120 members. It is elected for a 4-year term by secret ballot and universal direct suffrage. The system of election is by proportional representation. After the Nov. 1988 elections the Knesset was composed as follows: Likud, 40; Labour Alignment, 39; Shas (Oriental Jew Religions), 6; National Religious Party, 5; Agudat Yisrael, 5; Citizens Rights Movement, 5; Communists, 4; Mapam, 3; Tehiya, 3; Shinui, 2; Moledet, 2; Degel Hatora, 2; Tsomet, 2; Arab Democratic List, 1; Progressive List for Peace, 1. The President is elected by the Knesset by secret ballot by a simple majority; his term of office is 5 years. He may be re-elected once.

Former Presidents of the State: Chaim Weizmann (1949–52); Izhak Ben-Zvi (1952–63); Zalman Shazar (1963–68); Ephraim Katzir (1968–78); Yitzhak Navon (1978–83).

President: Chaim Herzog, elected 1983; re-elected 1988.

The Cabinet in March 1990 was composed as follows but on 15 March the coalition government collapsed:

Prime Minister and Labour Minister: Yitzhak Shamir (Lik).

Vice Prime Minister and Minister of Finance: Shimon Peres (Lab). *Foreign Minister:* Moshe Arens (Lik). *Defence:* Yitzhak Rabin (Lab). *Deputy Prime Minister and Minister of Housing:* David Levy (Lik). *Deputy Prime Minister and Minister of Education and Culture:* Yitzhak Navon (Lab). *Transport:* Moshe Katzav (Lik). *Police:* Haim Bar-Lev (Lab). *Industry and Commerce:* Ariel Sharon (Lik). *Energy:* Moshe Shahal (Lab). *Justice:* Dan Meridor (Lik). *Agriculture:* Avraham Katz-Oz (Lab). *Tourism:* Gideon Patt (Lik). *Health:* Ya'acov Tsur (Lab). *Economics Planning:* Yitzhak Moda'i (Lik). *Communications:* Gad Ya'acobi (Lab). *Interior:* Arie Der'i (Shas). *Immigration:* Yitzhak Peretz (Shas). *Religious Affairs:* Zevulum Hammer (NRP). *Science:* Ezer Weizman (Lab). *Environmental Quality:* Ronni Milo (Lik). *Ministers Without Portfolio:* Moshe Nissim (Lik), Ehud Olmert (Lik), Mordechai Gur (Lab), Rafi Edri (Lab).

Local Government. Local authorities are of three kinds, namely, municipal corporations, local councils and regional councils. Their status, powers and duties are prescribed by statute. Regional councils are local authorities set up in agricultural areas and include all the agricultural settlements in the area under their jurisdiction. All local authorities exercise their authority mainly by means of bye-laws approved by the Minister of the Interior. Their revenue is derived from rates and a surcharge on income tax. Local authorities are elected for a 4-year term of office concurrently with general elections.

There were (1989) 42 municipalities (3 Arab), 136 local councils (63 Arab and Druze) and 54 regional councils.

DEFENCE. The Defence Service Law, provides a compulsory 36-month conscription for men (Jews and Druze only). Unmarried women (Jews only) serve 24 months.

The Israel Defence Force is a unified force, in which army, navy and air force are subordinate to a single chief-of-staff. The Minister of Defence is *de facto* commander-in-chief but from Oct. 1973 the cabinet formed a defence committee with authority to make decisions on military operations.

Army. The Army is organized in 3 armoured divisions, 3 infantry divisions, 5 mechanized infantry brigades, 3 artillery battalions and 1 surface-to-surface missile and 2 artillery battalions. The Reserves are organized in 9 armoured divisions, 1 mechanical (air mobile) division, 10 infantry and 4 artillery brigades. Equipment includes 3,794 main battle tanks and 6,000 other armoured fighting vehicles. Strength (1990) 104,000 (conscripts 88,000), rising to 598,000 on mobilization.

Navy. The Navy, tasked primarily for coastal protection and based at Haifa, Ashdod and Eilat, includes 3 small diesel submarines, 26 missile craft; 22 of which are of the evolving SA'AR types, from 250 to 500 tonnes, and 3 missile-armed hydrofoils. There are an additional 35 fast inshore patrol craft, 9 amphibious craft and a few minor auxiliaries.

The planned new construction programme includes 2 corvettes and 2 new submarines, to be built through the US foreign military sales programme.

Naval personnel in 1989 totalled 9,000 officers and men, of whom 3,000 are conscripts, including a Naval Cammando of 300. There are also 1,000 naval reservists available on mobilization.

Air Force. The Air Force has a personnel strength (1990) of 28,000, with about 629 first-line aircraft, all jets, of Israeli and US manufacture. There are 3 squadrons with about 50 F-15s, and 6 squadrons with the first 140 of a planned 250 F-16s in an interceptor role; 4 squadrons with 110 F-4E Phantoms, 4 squadrons with about 160 Kfirs, and 3 squadrons with A-4E/H/N Skyhawks in the fighter-bomber/attack role; and 15 RF-4E reconnaissance fighters; supported by 4 E-2C Hawkeye airborne early warning and control aircraft, RC-12 and RU-21 Elint aircraft. There are transport squadrons of turboprop C-130/KC-130 Hercules, C-47, Arava, Islander, and Boeing 707 (some equipped for tanker or ECM duties) aircraft, helicopter squadrons of CH-53, Super Frelon, AH-1 Huey-Cobra, Hughes 500MD/TOW Defender, JetRanger, Dauphin, Agusta-Bell 205, 206 and 212 aircraft, and training units with locally-built Magister jet trainers, which can be used also in a light ground attack role. Missiles in service include surface-to-air Hawks and surface-to-surface Lances.

INTERNATIONAL RELATIONS

Membership. Israel is a member of UN.

ECONOMY

Budget. The budget year runs from 1 April to 31 March. Government revenue in 1987-88 amounted to 44,539m. new shekels; expenditure, 44,021m. new shekels.

Currency. The unit of currency is the *new shekel* introduced in Jan. 1986 its value is 1,000 old *shekels*. Currency in circulation on 31 Dec. 1984 was I£161,651m. (bank-notes and coins). In March 1990, £1 = 3·23 *shekel*; US$ = 1·97 *shekel*.

Banking. The Bank of Israel was established by law in 1954 as Israel's central bank. Its Governor is appointed by the President on the recommendation of the Cabinet for a 5-year term. He acts as economic adviser to the Government and has ministerial status. There are 26 commercial banks headed by Bank Leumi Le Israel, Bank Hapoalim and Israel Discount Bank, 2 merchant banks, 1 foreign bank, 15 mortgage banks and 9 lending institutions specifically set up to aid industry and agriculture.

Weights and Measures. The metric system is in general use. The (metrical) *dunam* = 1,000 sq. metres (about 0·25 acre).

Jewish Year. The Jewish year 5749 corresponds to 12 Sept. 1988–29 Sept. 1989; 5750 30 Sept. 1989–19 Sept. 1990; 5751 20 Sept. 1990–8 Sept. 1991.

ENERGY AND NATURAL RESOURCES

Electricity. Electric-power production amounted during 1988 to 18,761m. kwh. Supply 230 volts; 50 Hz.

Oil and Gas. The only significant indigenous hydrocarbon known to be found is oil shale. In 1988 recoverable potential was estimated to be 250m. tons of oil.

Minerals. The most valuable natural resources of the country are the potash, bromine and other salt deposits of the Dead Sea, which are exploited by the Dead Sea Works, Ltd. Geological research and exploration of the natural resources in the Negev are undertaken by the Israel Mining Corporation. Potash production in 1986 was 2,035,000 tons.

Agriculture. In the coastal plain (Sharon, Emek Hefer and the Shephelah) mixed farming, poultry raising, citriculture and vineyards are the main agricultural activities. The Emek (the Valley of Jezreel) is the main agricultural centre of Israel. Mixed farming is to be found throughout the valleys; the sub-tropical Beisan and

Jordan plainlands are also centres of banana plantations and fish breeding. In Galilee mixed farming, olive and tobacco plantations prevail. The Hills of Ephraim are a vineyard centre; many parts of the hill country are under afforestation. In the northern Negev farming has been aided by the Yarkon–Negev water pipeline. This has become part of the overall project of the 'National Water Carrier', which is to take water from the Sea of Galilee (Lake Kinnereth) to the south. The plan includes a number of regional projects such as the Lake Kinnereth–Negev pipeline which came into operation in 1964; it has an annual capacity of 320m. cu. metres.

The area under cultivation (in 1,000 dunams) in 1988 was 4,317, of which 2,156 were under irrigation. Of the total cultivated area 2,361 dunams were under field crops, 422 under vegetables, potatoes, pumpkins and melons, 359 under citrus and plantations, 26 under fish ponds and the rest under miscellaneous crops, including auxiliary farms, nurseries, flowers, etc.

Industrial crops, such as cotton, have successfully been introduced. In 1988 the area under cotton totalled 503,000 dunams.

Production, 1988 (in 1,000 tonnes): Wheat, 211; barley, 20; maize, 25; potatoes, 207; pumpkins, 25; melons, 142; tomatoes, 236; citrus fruit, 1,282; seed cotton, 196.

Livestock (1988) included 307,000 cattle, 394,000 sheep, 125,000 goats, 130,000 pigs, 4,000 horses, 25m. poultry.

Characteristic types of rural settlement are, among others, the following: (1) The *Kibbutz* and *Kvutza* (communal collective settlement), where all property and earnings are collectively owned and work is collectively organized. (126,100 people lived in 270 settlements in 1988). (2) The *Moshav* (workers' co-operative smallholders' settlement) which is founded on the principles of mutual aid and equality of opportunity between the members, all farms being equal in size. (146, 500 in 409). (3) The *Moshav Shitufi* (co-operative settlement), which is based on collective ownership and economy as in the *Kibbutz,* but with each family having its own house and being responsible for its own domestic services. (11,300 in 47). (4) Other rural settlements in which land and property are privately owned and every resident is responsible for his own well-being. In 1988 there were 226 villages with a population of 112,000.

INDUSTRY AND TRADE

Industry. A wide range of products is manufactured, processed or finished in the country, including chemicals, metal products, textiles, tyres, diamonds, paper, plastics, leather goods, glass and ceramics, building materials, precision instruments, tobacco, foodstuffs, electrical and electronic equipment.

Labour. The General Federation of Labour (Histadrut) founded in 1920, had, in 1987, 1·6m. members (including 170,000 Arab and Druze members); including workers' families, this membership represents 71·5% of the population covering 87% of all wage-earners. Several trades unions also exist representing other political and religious groups.

Commerce. External trade, in US$1m., for calendar years:

	1984	*1985*	*1986*	*1987*	*1988*
Imports	8,257	8,202	9,550	11,916	12,960
Exports	6,242	6,682	7,712	8,475	9,739

The main exportable commodities are citrus fruit and by-products, fruit-juices, flowers, wines and liquor, sweets, polished diamonds, chemicals, tyres, textiles, metal products, machinery, electronic and transportation equipment. The main exports were, in 1988 (US$1m.): Diamonds, 2,837; chemical and oil products, 1,122·6; agricultural products including citrus fruit, 573; manufactured goods, machinery and transport equipment, 4,328. In 1987 64·1% of imports came from Europe, 17·2% from Canada and USA, 8·3% from Africa and Asia. Of exports, 36·4% went to Europe, 33·5% to Canada and USA, 14·2% to Africa and Asia.

Total trade between Israel and UK (British Department of Trade returns, in £1,000 sterling):

	1985	*1986*	*1987*	*1988*	*1989*
Imports to UK	403,952	385,164	437,014	460,289	479,840
Exports and re-exports from UK	434,470	452,407	523,591	487,255	502,411

Tourism. In 1988 there were about 1,165,000 tourists.

COMMUNICATIONS

Roads. There were 12,980 km of paved roads in 1988. Registered motor vehicles in 1988 totalled 952,786, including 8,693 buses, 143,805 trucks and 753,450 private cars.

Railways. Internal communications (1988) are provided by 575 km of standard gauge line. Construction is in progress of 215 km of new line linking Eilat on the Gulf of Aqaba with Sedom and the existing rail network. In 1988, 2·5m. passengers and 6·6m. tonnes of freight were carried.

Aviation. Air communications are centred in the airport of Ben Gurion, near Tel-Aviv. In 1988, 10,757 planes landed at Israeli airports on international flights; 1,705,000 passengers arrived, 1,726,000 departed. In 1988, 91,271 tons of freight were loaded and 82,458 tons unloaded. The Israeli airline El Al maintains regular flights to London, Paris, Rome, Amsterdam, Brussels, Cairo, Madrid, Lisbon, Bucharest, Athens, Vienna, New York, Montreal, Zurich, Munich, Istanbul, Johannesburg, Nairobi, Frankfurt and Copenhagen. In 1986–87 El Al carried 1·5m. passengers.

Shipping. Israel has 3 commercial ports, Haifa, Ashdod and Eilat. In 1987, 3,243 ships departed from Israeli ports; 19m. tons. of freight were handled. The merchant fleet consisted in 1988 of 72 vessels, totalling 1,573,000 GRT.

Post and Broadcasting. The Ministry of Communications controls the postal service, and a public company responsible to the Ministry administers the telecommunications service. In 1986 there were 594 post offices and postal agencies, 50 mobile post offices and (1988) 1·94m. telephones.

Israeli television and the state radio station, *Kol Israel* are controlled by the Israel Broadcasting Authority, established in 1965. Radio licences in 1985 numbered approximately 1·12m. and television licences (1986) 936,000.

Cinemas. In 1987 there were 162 cinemas.

Newspapers (1987). There were 23 daily newspapers.

JUSTICE, RELIGION, EDUCATION AND WELFARE

Justice. *Law.* Under the Law and Administration Ordinance, 5708/1948, the first law passed by the Provisional Council of State, the law of Israel is the law which was obtaining in Palestine on 14 May 1948 in so far as it is not in conflict with that Ordinance or any other law passed by the Israel legislature and with such modifications as result from the establishment of the State and its authorities.

Capital punishment was abolished in 1954, except for support given to the Nazis and for high treason.

The law of Palestine was derived from three main sources, namely, Ottoman law, English law (Common Law and Equity) and the law enacted by the Palestine legislature, which to a great extent was modelled on English law. The Ottoman law in its turn was derived from three main sources, namely, Moslem law which had survived in the Ottoman Empire, French law adapted by the Ottomans and the personal law of the non-Moslem communities.

Civil Courts. Municipal courts, established in certain municipal areas, have criminal jurisdiction over offences against municipal regulations and bye-laws and certain specified offences committed within a municipal area.

Magistrates courts, established in each district and sub-district, have limited jurisdiction in both civil and criminal matters.

District courts, sitting at Jerusalem, Tel-Aviv and Haifa, have jurisdiction, as courts of first instance, in all civil matters not within the jurisdiction of magistrates courts, and in all criminal matters, and as appellate courts from magistrates courts and municipal courts.

The Supreme Court has jurisdiction as a court of first instance (sitting as a High Court of Justice dealing mainly with administrative matters) and as an appellate court from the district courts (sitting as a Court of Civil or of Criminal Appeal).

In addition, there are various tribunals for special classes of cases, such as the Rents Tribunals and the Tribunals for the Prevention of Profiteering and Speculation. Settlement Officers deal with disputes with regard to the ownership or possession of land in settlement areas constituted under the Land (Settlement of Title) Ordinance.

Religious Courts. The rabbinical courts of the Jewish community have exclusive jurisdiction in matters of marriage and divorce, alimony and confirmation of wills of members of their community other than foreigners, concurrent jurisdiction with the civil courts in such matters of members of their community who are foreigners if they consent to the jurisdiction, and concurrent jurisdiction with the civil courts in all other matters of personal status of all members of their community, whether foreigners or not, with the consent of all parties to the action, save that such courts may not grant a decree of dissolution of marriage to a foreign subject.

The courts of the several recognized Christian communities have a similar jurisdiction over members of their respective communities.

The Moslem religious courts have exclusive jurisdiction in all matters of personal status over Moslems who are not foreigners, and over Moslems who are foreigners, if under the law of their nationality they are subject in such matters to the jurisdiction of Moslem religious courts.

Where any action of personal status involves persons of different religious communities, the President of the Supreme Court will decide which court shall have jurisdiction, and whenever a question arises as to whether or not a case is one of personal status within the exclusive jurisdiction of a religious court, the matter must be referred to a special tribunal composed of 2 judges of the Supreme Court and the president of the highest court of the religious community concerned in Israel.

Religion. Religious affairs are under the supervision of a special Ministry, with departments for the Christian and Moslem communities. The religious affairs of each community remain under the full control of the ecclesiastical authorities concerned: in the case of the Jews, the Sephardi and Ashkenazi Chief Rabbis, in the case of the Christians, the heads of the various communities, and in the case of the Moslems, the Qadis. The Druze were officially recognized in 1957 as an autonomous religious community.

In 1988 there were: Jews, 3,659,000; Moslems, 634,600; Christians, 105,000; Druze and others, 78,100.

The Jewish Sabbath and Holy Days are observed as days of rest in the public services. Full provision is, however, made for the free exercise of other faiths, and for the observance by their adherents of their respective days of rest and Holy Days.

Education. Laws passed by the Knesset in 1949 and 1978 provide for free and compulsory education from 5 to 16 years of age. There is free education until 18 years of age.

The State Education Law of 12 Aug. 1953 established a unified state-controlled elementary school system with a provision for special religious schools. The standard curriculum for all elementary schools is issued by the Ministry with a possibility of adding supplementary subjects comprising not more than 25% of the total syllabus. Most schools in towns are maintained by municipalities, a number are private and some are administered by teachers' co-operatives or trustees.

Statistics relating to schools under government supervision, 1988–89:

Type of School [1]	*Schools*	*Teachers*	*Pupils*
Hebrew Education			
Primary schools	1,323	32,197	482,215
Schools for handicapped children	191	3,162	11,434
Schools of intermediate division	304	13,274	120,339

Type of School [1]	*Schools*	*Teachers*	*Pupils*
Hebrew Education (cont'd)			
Secondary schools	536		202,261
Vocational schools	315	24,649	94,454
Agricultural schools	25		5,022
Arab Education			
Primary schools	312	6,424	138,074
Schools for handicapped children	15	220	1,146
Schools of intermediate division	63	1,868	27,230
Secondary schools	84		38,237
Vocational schools	42	2,542	6,516
Agricultural schools	2		718

[1] Schools providing more than one type of education are included more than once.

There are also a number of private schools maintained by religious foundations—Jewish, Christian and Moslem—and also by private societies.

The Hebrew University of Jerusalem, founded in 1925, comprises faculties of the humanities, social sciences, law, science, medicine and agriculture. In 1988–89 it had 16,000 students. The Technion in Haifa had 8,730 students. The Weizmann Institute of Science in Rehovoth, founded in 1949, had 650 students.

Tel Aviv University had 18,730 students. The religious Bar-Ilan University at Ramat Gan, opened in 1965 had 8,830 students. The Haifa University had 6,540 students. The Ben Gurion University had 5,410 students.

Health. In 1988 Israel had 161 hospitals with 27,842 beds and 9,500 doctors.

The National Insurance Law, which took effect in April 1954, provides for old-age pensions, survivors' insurance, work-injury insurance, maternity insurance, family allowances and unemployment benefits.

DIPLOMATIC REPRESENTATIVES

Of Israel in Great Britain (2 Palace Green, London, W8 4QB)
Ambassador: Yoav Biran (accredited 24 Nov. 1988).

Of Great Britain in Israel (192 Hayarkon St., Tel Aviv 63405)
Ambassador: Mark Elliott, CMG.

Of Israel in the USA (3514 International Dr., NW, Washington, D.C., 20008)
Ambassador: Moshe Arad.

Of the USA in Israel (71 Hayarkon St., Tel Aviv)
Ambassador: William A. Brown.

Of Israel to the United Nations
Ambassador: Yohanan Bein.

Further Reading

Statistical Information: There is a Central Bureau of Statistics at the Prime Minister's Office, Jerusalem. It publishes monthly bulletins of statistics (economic and social), foreign trade statistics and price statistics.

Atlas of Israel. 3rd ed. 1985

Government Yearbook. Government Printer, Jerusalem. 1951 ff. (latest issue, 1971/72)

Facts about Israel. Ministry of Foreign Affairs, Jerusalem, 1985

Statistical Abstract of Israel. Government Printer, Jerusalem (from 1949/50)

Israel Yearbook. Tel-Aviv, 1948–49 ff.

Statistical Bulletin of Israel. 1949 ff.

Reshumoth (Official Gazette)

Middle East Record, ed. Y. Oron. London, 1960 ff.

Laws of the State of Israel. Authorized translation. Government Printer, Jerusalem, 1958 ff.

Alkalay, R., *The Complete English–Hebrew Dictionary.* 4 vols. Tel-Aviv, 1959–61

Ben-Gurion, D., *Ben-Gurion Looks Back.* London, 1965.—*The Jews in Their Land.* London, 1966.—*Israel: A Personal History.* New York, 1971

Gilbert, M., *The Arab-Israeli Conflict: Its History in Maps.* 3rd ed. London, 1981

Harkabi, Y., *Israel's Fateful Decisions.* London, 1989

Harris, W., *Taking Root: Israeli Settlement in the West Bank, The Golan and Gaza Sinai 1967–1980.* Chichester, 1981

Kieval, G. R., *Party Politics in Israel and the Occupied Territories.* Westport, 1983
Louis, W. R. and Stookey, R. W., *The End of the Palestine Mandate.* London, 1986
O'Brien, C. C., *The Siege.* London, 1986
Peri, Y., *Between Battles and Ballots: Israeli Military in Politics.* CUP, 1983
Reich, B., *Israel: Land of Tradition and Conflict.* London, 1986
Sachar, H. M., *A History of Israel.* 2 vols. OUP, 1976 and 1987
Sager, S., *The Parliamentary System of Israel.* Syracuse Univ. Press, 1986
Segev, T., *1949: The First Israelis.* New York, 1986
Sharkansky, I., *The Political Economy of Israel.* Oxford and Santa Barbara, 1986
Shimshoni, D., *Israeli Democracy: The Middle of the Journey.* New York, 1982
Snyder, E. M. and Kreiner, E., *Israel.* [Bibliography] Oxford and Santa Barbara, 1985
Wolffsohn, M., *Politik in Israel.* Opladen, 1983

National Library: The Jewish National and University Library, Jerusalem.

ITALY

Capital: Rome
Population: 57·5m. (1988)
GNP per capita: US$13,320 (1988)

Repubblica Italiana

HISTORY. On 10 June 1946 Italy became a republic on the announcement by the Court of Cassation that a majority of the voters at the referendum held on 2 June had voted for a republic. The final figures, announced on 18 June, showed: For a republic, 12,718,641 (54·3% of the valid votes cast, which numbered 23,437,143); for the retention of the monarchy, 10,718,502 (45·7%); invalid and contested, 1,509,735. Total 24,946,878, or 89·1% of the registered electors, who numbered 28,005,449. For the results of the polling in the 13 leading cities, *see* THE STATESMAN'S YEAR-BOOK , 1951, p. 1175. Voting was compulsory, open to both men and women 21 years of age or older, including members of the Civil Service and the Armed Forces; former active Fascists and a few other categories were excluded.

On 18 June the then Provisional Government without specifically proclaiming the republic, issued an 'Order of the Day' decreeing that all court verdicts should in future be handed down 'in the name of the Italian people', that the *Gazzetta Ufficiale del Regno d'Italia* should be re-named *Gazzetta Ufficiale della Repubblica Italiana,* that all references to the monarchy should be deleted from legal and government statements and that the shield of the House of Savoy should be removed from the Italian flag.

Thus ended the reign of the House of Savoy, whose kings had ruled over Piedmont for 9 centuries and as Kings of Italy since 18 Feb. 1861. (For fuller account of the House of Savoy, *see* THE STATESMAN'S YEAR-BOOK, 1946, p. 1021.) The Crown Prince Umberto, son of King Victor Emmanuel III, became Lieut.-Gen. (*i.e.*, Regent) of the kingdom on 5 June 1944. Following the abdication and retirement to Egypt of his father on 9 May 1946, Umberto was declared King Umberto II; his reign lasted to 13 June, when he left the country. King Victor Emmanuel III died in Alexandria on 28 Dec. 1947.

AREA AND POPULATION. Italy is bounded north by Switzerland and Austria, east by Yugoslavia and the Adriatic Sea, south-east by the Ionian Sea, south by the Mediterranean Sea, south-west by the Tyrrhenian Sea and Ligurian Sea and west by France. The population (present in actual boundaries) at successive censuses were as follows:

31 Dec. 1881	29,277,927	21 April 1936	42,302,680
10 Feb. 1901	33,370,138	4 Nov. 1951	47,158,738
10 June 1911	35,694,582	15 Oct. 1961	49,903,878
1 Dec. 1921	37,403,956	24 Oct. 1971	53,744,737
21 April 1931	40,582,043	25 Oct. 1981	56,243,935

The following table gives area and population of the Regions (census 1981 and estimate, 1988):

Regions	*Area in sq. km (1981)*	*Resident pop. census, 1981*	*Resident pop. estimate, 1988*	*Density per sq. km (1981)*
Piemonte	25,399	4,479,031	4,365,911	175
Valle d'Aosta	3,262	112,353	114,760	35
Lombardia	23,856	8,891,652	8,898,951	373
Trentino-Alto Adige	13,613	873,413	884,039	64
Bolzano-Bozen	*7,400*	*430,568*	*438,009*	*58*
Trento	*6,213*	*442,845*	*446,030*	*71*
Veneto	18,364	4,345,047	4,380,587	235
Friuli-Venezia Giulia	7,846	1,233,984	1,206,362	157
Liguria	5,416	1,807,893	1,738,263	332
Emilia Romagna	22,123	3,957,513	3,921,281	178
Toscana	22,992	3,581,051	3,565,280	155
Umbria	8,456	807,552	819,562	95
Marche	9,694	1,412,404	1,429,223	145
Lazio	17,203	5,001,684	5,156,053	289
Abruzzi	10,794	1,217,791	1,262,692	113

Regions	Area in sq. km (1981)	Resident pop. census, 1981	Resident pop. estimate, 1988	Density per sq. km (1981)
Molise	4,438	328,371	335,211	73
Campania	13,595	5,463,134	5,773,067	398
Puglia	19,347	3,871,617	4,059,309	199
Basilicata	9,992	610,186	622,658	60
Calabria	15,080	2,061,182	2,151,351	135
Sicilia	25,708	4,906,878	5,164,266	189
Sardegna	24,090	1,594,175	1,655,859	66
Total	301,268	56,556,911	57,504,691	187

Vital statistics for calendar years:

		Living births				Deaths
	Marriages	Legitimate	Illegitimate	Total	Still-born	excl. of still-born
1982	312,486	590,042	29,055	619,097	4,757	534,935
1983	303,663	572,641	29,287	601,928	4,396	564,330
1984	300,889	557,773	30,098	587,871	4,175	534,676
1985	298,523	546,224	31,121	577,345	3,871	547,436
1986	296,539 [1]	523,876	31,569	555,445	3,584	544,489
1987 [1]	305,328	520,465	31,864	552,329	3,486	531,739
1988 [1]	315,447	535,266	33,025	568,291	3,504	536,701

[1] Provisional.

Emigrants to non-European countries, by sea and air: 1978, 23,589; 1979, 21,302; 1980, 20,360; 1981, 20,628; 1982, 22,324; 1983, 20,443; 1984, 16,776; 1985, 16,151; 1986, 13,215; 1987, 12,796. Since 1960 nearly nine-tenths of these emigrants have gone to Canada, USA and Australia.

Communes of more than 100,000 inhabitants, with population resident at the census of 25 Oct. 1981 and on 31 Dec. 1988:

	1981	1988		1981	1988
Roma (Rome)	2,840,259	2,816,474	Perugia	142,348	148,422
Milano (Milan)	1,604,773	1,464,127	Ravenna	138,034	136,306
Napoli (Naples)	1,212,387	1,202,582	Pescara	131,330	129,199
Torino (Turin)	1,117,154	1,012,180	Reggio nell'E.	130,376	130,093
Genova (Genoa)	762,895	714,641	Rimini	127,813	130,644
Palermo	701,782	731,483	Monza	123,145	122,846
Bologna	459,080	422,204	Bergamo	122,142	118,078
Firenze (Florence)	448,331	417,487	Sassari	119,596	119,734
Catania	380,328	370,679	Siracusa (Syracuse)	117,615	124,400
Bari	371,022	356,847	La Spezia	115,392	105,668
Venezia (Venice)	346,146	324,294	Vicenza	114,598	109,537
Verona	265,932	258,724	Terni	111,564	110,484
Messina	260,233	272,119	Forli	110,806	110,260
Trieste	252,369	235,014	Piacenza	109,039	104,432
Taranto	244,101	244,694	Cosenza	106,801	105,813
Padova (Padua)	234,678	222,163	Ancona	106,498	103,877
Cagliari	233,848	220,192	Bolzano	105,180	100,944
Brescia	206,661	197,821	Pisa	104,509	102,908
Modena	180,312	176,807	Torre del Greco	103,605	104,258
Parma	179,019	174,827	Novara	102,086	103,096
Livorno (Leghorn)	175,741	172,133	Udine	102,021	–
Reggio di C.	173,486	178,666	Catanzaro	100,832	103,174
Prato	160,220	165,524	Alessandria	100,523	–
Salerno	157,385	153,091	Trento	99,179	101,112
Foggia	156,467	159,236	Lecce	91,289	101,968
Ferrara	149,453	142,070			

CLIMATE. The climate varies considerably with latitude. In the south, it is warm temperate, with little rain in the summer months, but the north is cool temperate with rainfall more evenly distributed over the year.

Florence, Jan. 42°F (5·6°C), July 76°F (25°C). Annual rainfall 36" (901 mm). Milan, Jan. 35°F (2°C), July 75°F (24°C). Annual rainfall 32" (802 mm). Naples, Jan. 48°F (8·9°C), July 77°F (25·6°C). Annual rainfall 34" (850 mm). Palermo, Jan. 52°F (11·1°C), July 79°F (26·1°C). Annual rainfall 28" (702 mm). Rome, Jan. 44·5°F (7°C), July 77°F (25°C). Annual rainfall 26" (657 mm). Venice, Jan. 38°F (3·3°C), July 75°F (23·9°C). Annual rainfall 29" (725 mm).

CONSTITUTION AND GOVERNMENT. The new Constitution was passed by the constituent assembly by 453 votes to 62 on 22 Dec. 1947; it came into force on 1 Jan. 1948. The Constitution consists of 139 articles and 18 transitional clauses. Its main dispositions are as follows:

Italy is described as 'a democratic republic founded on work'. Parliament consists of the Chamber of Deputies and the Senate. The Chamber is elected for 5 years by universal and direct suffrage and it consists of 630 deputies. The Senate is elected for 5 years on a regional basis; each Region having at least 7 senators, consisting of 315 elected senators; the Valle d'Aosta is represented by 1 senator only. The President of the Republic can nominate 5 senators for life from eminent men in the social, scientific, artistic and literary spheres. On the expiry of his term of office, the President of the Republic becomes a senator by right and for life, unless he declines. The President of the Republic is elected in a joint session of Chamber and Senate, to which are added 3 delegates from each Regional Council (1 from the Valle d'Aosta). A two-thirds majority is required for the election, but after a third indecisive scrutiny the absolute majority of votes is sufficient. The President must be 50 years or over; his term lasts for 7 years. The President of the Senate acts as his deputy. The President can dissolve the chambers of parliament, except during the last 6 months of his term of office.

The Cabinet can be forced to resign only on a motivated motion of censure; the defeat of a government bill does not involve the resignation of the Government.

A Constitutional Court, consisting of 15 judges who are appointed, 5 each, by the President of the Republic, Parliament (in joint session) and the highest law and administrative courts, has rights similar to those of the Supreme Court of the USA. It can decide on the constitutionality of laws and decrees, define the powers of the State and Regions, judge conflicts between the State and Regions and between the Regions, and try the President of the Republic and the Ministers. The court was set up in Dec. 1955.

The reorganization of the Fascist Party is forbidden. Direct male descendants of King Victor Emmanuel are excluded from all public offices, have no right to vote or to be elected, and are banned from Italian territory; their estates are forfeit to the State. Titles of nobility are no longer recognized, but those existing before 28 Oct. 1922 are retained as part of the name.

National flag: Three vertical strips of green, white, red.

National anthem: Fratelli d'Italia (words by G. Mameli; tune by M. Novaro, 1847).

Head of State: On 3 July 1985 Chamber and Senate in joint session elected by an absolute majority (752 votes out of 977 votes cast) Francesco Cossiga (Christian Democrat; born 1928), President of the Republic.

Former Presidents of the Republic: Luigi Einaudi (1948–55); Giovanni Gronchi (1955–62); Antonio Segni (1962–64); Giuseppe Saragat (1964–71); Giovanni Leone (1971–78); Alessandro Pertini (1978–85).

General elections for the Senate and Chamber of Deputies took place on 22 July 1989.

Senate. Christian Democrats, 125; Communists, 101; Socialists, 36; Italian Social Movement, 16; Social Democrats, 5; Republicans, 8; Liberals, 3; other groups, 21. Total: 315.

Chamber. Christian Democrats, 234; Communists, 177; Socialists, 94; Italian Social Movement, 35; Republicans, 21; Social Democrats, 17; Liberals, 11; Radical Party, 13; Green Party, 13; other groups, 15. Total: 630.

The coalition government was composed as follows in Nov. 1989.

Prime Minister: Giulio Andreotti (DC).

Vice Prime Minister: Claudio Martelli (PSI).

Foreign Affairs: Gianni De Michelis (PSI).

Interior: Antonio Gava (DC).

Justice: Giuliano Vassalli (PSI).

Southern Affairs: Riccardo Misasi (DC).

Treasury: Guido Carli (DC).

Budget: Paolo Cirino Pomicino (DC).
Finance: Rino Formica (PSI).
Defence: Mino Martinazzoli (DC).
Education: Sergio Mattarella (DC).
Public Works: Giovanni Prandini (DC).
Agriculture: Calogero Mannino (DC).
Transport: Carlo Bernini (DC).
Post: Oscar Mammi (PRI).
Industry: Adolfo Battaglia (PRI).
Labour: Carlo Donat Cattin (DC).
Foreign Trade: Renato Ruggiero (PSI).
Merchant Navy: Carlo Vizzini (PSDI).
State Industry: Carlo Fracanzani (DC).
Health: Francesco De Lorenzo (PLI).
Tourism: Franco Carraro (PSI).
Culture: Ferdinando Facchiano (PSDI)
EEC Affairs: Pierluigi Romita (PSI).
Public Administration: Remo Gaspari (DC).
Scientific Research and Universities: Antonio Ruberti (PSI).
Regional and Institutional Affairs: Antonio Maccanico (PRI).
Relations with Parliament: Egidio Sterpa (PLI).
Civil Protection: Vito Lattanzio (DC).
Ecology: Giorgio Ruffolo (PSI).
Urban Problems: Carmelo Conte (PSI).
Special Affairs: Rosa Russo Jervolino (DC).

Regional Administration. Italy is administratively divided into regions (*regioni*), provinces (*province*) and municipalities (*comuni*).

Art. 116 of the 1948 constitution provided for the establishment of 5 autonomous regions with special statute (*regioni autonome con statuto speciale*) and 15 autonomous regions with ordinary statute (*regioni autonome con statuto normale*). The regions have their own parliaments (*consiglio regionale*) and governments (*giunta regionale e presidente*) with certain legislative and administrative functions adapted to the circumstances of each region.

A government commissioner co-ordinates regional and national activities. The results of the last regional elections were as follows:

Regions	*Election date*	*Christ-ian Demo-crats*	*Com-mun-ists*	*Social-ists*	*Social Move-ment*	*Social Demo-crats*	*Repub-licans*	*Lib-erals*	*Others*	*Total*
Piemonte	12 May 1985	19	18	8	3	3	3	3	3	60
Valle d'Aosta [1]	26 June 1988	7	5	3	1	–	1	–	18	35
Lombardia	12 May 1985	31	22	12	4	2	4	1	4	80
Trentino-Alto Adige [1]	20 Nov. 1988	20	4	5	5	1	1	1	32	70
Veneto	12 May 1985	30	12	8	2	1	2	1	4	60
Friuli-Venezia Giulia [1]	26 June 1988	24	11	12	3	2	1	1	8	62
Liguria	12 May 1985	13	15	4	2	1	2	1	2	40
Emilia-Romagna	12 May 1985	13	26	4	2	1	2	1	1	50
Toscana	12 May 1985	14	25	5	2	1	1	–	2	50
Umbria	12 May 1985	9	14	4	2	–	1	–	–	30
Marche	12 May 1985	15	15	4	2	1	1	1	1	40
Lazio	12 May 1985	21	18	7	6	2	2	1	3	60
Abruzzi	12 May 1985	19	11	5	2	1	1	1	–	40
Molise	12 May 1985	18	5	3	1	1	1	1	–	30
Campania	12 May 1985	24	14	9	5	3	2	1	2	60
Puglia	12 May 1985	20	13	8	5	2	1	1	–	50
Basilicata	12 May 1985	14	7	5	1	2	1	–	–	30
Calabria	12 May 1985	16	10	8	2	2	1	–	1	40
Sicilia [1]	22 June 1986	36	19	13	8	4	5	3	2	90
Sardegna [1]	11 June 1989	29	19	12	3	4	3	–	10	80

[1] Autonomous regions with special statute.

DEFENCE. Most of the restrictions imposed upon Italy in Part IV of the peace treaty signed on 10 Feb. 1947 were repudiated by the signatories on 21 Dec. 1951, only the USSR objecting.

Head of the armed forces is the Defence Chief of Staff. In 1947 the ministries of war, navy and air were merged into the ministry of defence. The technical and scientific council for defence directs all research activities.

National service lasts 12 months in the Army and Air Force, and 18 months in the Navy.

Army. The Army consists of 3 corps, one of which is alpine and others include mechanized, armoured and support brigades. In peninsular defence there are 2 independent motorized and 2 independent mechanized brigades. In addition there is a rapid intervention force, 2 amphibious battalions and a support brigade with missiles. Equipment includes 500 M-47, 300 M-60A1 and 920 Leopard I main battle tanks. The Army air corps operates 91 light aircraft and 326 helicopters. Strength (1990) 265,000 (215,000 conscripts), with 520,000 reserves. There is also the paramilitary Carabinieri of 105,000 men.

Navy. The principal ships of the Italian Navy are the light aircraft carrier *Giuseppe Garibaldi*, the helicopter carrying cruiser *Vittorio Veneto*, and 2 guided missile cruisers *Andrea Doria* and *Caio Duilio*. The *Giuseppe Garibaldi*, 13,450 tonnes, was completed in 1985 and currently operates an air group of 16 SH-3D Sea King ASW helicopters, but has a ski-jump bow which facilitates the operation of Harrier-type aircraft. She is also armed with 4 Teseo anti-ship missiles. The *Vittorio Veneto*, completed in 1969, is of 9,650 tonnes, and operates a squadron of 6 AB-212 ASW helicopters as well as a twin launcher for ASROC and US Standard SM-1 surface-to-air missiles, and 4 Teseo. The *Andrea Doria* and *Caio Duilio* displace 7,400 tonnes, were completed in 1964, are armed with Standard SM-1 missiles, and operate 3 AB-212 ASW helicopters.

The combatant forces also include 10 diesel submarines, 4 guided-missile destroyers armed with Standard SMI, 22 frigates, of which 14 carry one or more AB-212 helicopters, 3 corvettes and 7 missile-armed patrol hydrofoils. Mine countermeasure forces comprise 4 ocean minesweepers, 6 coastal minehunters and 5 coastal sweepers. There are 3 new offshore patrol vessels for EEZ work. Amphibious lift for the San Marco commando group (800 men) is provided by 2 dock landing ships and 33 craft. Auxiliaries include 2 replenishment oilers, 5 water carriers, 3 survey ships, 3 trial vessels, 2 training ships and 9 large tugs.

The Naval Air Arm operates 96 anti-submarine and training helicopters and budgetary provision has been made for a number of V/STOL aircraft for the *Giuseppe Garibaldi*. There is a Special Forces commando of some 600 assault swimmers (Commando Subacquei Incursori).

Main naval bases are at Spezia, Naples, Taranto and Ancona, with minor bases at Brindisi and Venice. The personnel of the Navy in 1989 numbered 52,000, including the naval air arm (1,500) and the marine battalion.

Paramilitary maritime tasks are carried out by the Financial Guards fleet of some 70 patrol craft and a Harbour control force with 25 inshore patrol craft and numerous boats.

Air Force. Control is exercised through 2 regional HQ near Taranto and Milan. Units assigned to NATO comprise the 1st air brigade of Nike-Hercules surface-to-air missiles, 5 fighter-bomber, 2 light attack, 8 interceptor and 2 tactical reconnaissance squadrons, with supporting transport, search and rescue, and training units. Two of the fighter-bomber squadrons have Tornados, others have Aeritalia G91Ys. The light attack squadrons operate AM-X Centauros and MB.339s. F-104S Starfighters have been standardized throughout the interceptor squadrons. The reconnaissance force operates RF-104G Starfighters. A total of 187 AM-X jet aircraft, built jointly by Aeritalia, Aermacchi and Embraer of Brazil, are replacing G91R, G91Y and F-104G/S aircraft in eight squadrons from 1989.

One transport squadron has turboprop C-130H Hercules aircraft; 2 others have turboprop Aeritalia G222s. There is a VIP and personnel transport squadron, equipped with AS-61, DC-9, Gulfstream III and Falcon 50 aircraft. Electronic warfare duties are performed by specially equipped G222s, PD-808s and MB 339s.

Two land-based anti-submarine squadrons operate Breguet Atlantics. Search and rescue are performed by 30 Agusta-Sikorsky HH-3F helicopters, Canadair CL-215 amphibians and smaller types. There are also strong support and training elements; some MB 339 jet trainers have armament provisions for secondary close air support and anti-helicopter roles.

Air Force strength in 1990 was about 73,000 officers and men, about 400 combat aircraft, 200 fixed-wing second-line aircraft and over 100 helicopters.

INTERNATIONAL RELATIONS

Membership. Italy is a member of UN, NATO and the European Communities.

ECONOMY

Budget. Total revenue and expenditure for fiscal years, in 1m. lire:

	Revenue	*Expenditure*		*Revenue*	*Expenditure*
1982	150,842,000	206,444,000	1985	218,973,000	319,099,000
1983	177,142,000	250,203,000	1986	266,301,009	384,344,429
1984	199,986,000	292,348,000	1987	283,875,850	442,965,463

In the revenue for 1987 turnover and other business taxes accounted for 63,838,450m. lire, customs duties and indirect taxes for 24,379,299m. lire.

The public debt at 31 Dec. 1987 totalled 798,539,164m. lire, including consolidated debt of 40,452m. lire and the floating debt 323,189,746m. lire.

Currency. The standard coin is the *lira*. From 30 March 1960 the gold standard was formally established as equal to 0·00142187 gramme of gold per lira.

State metal coins are of 5, 10, 20, 50, 100, 200, and 500 lire. There are in circulation bank-notes of 1,000, 2,000, 5,000, 10,000, 20,000, 50,000 and 100,000 lire; they are neither convertible into gold as foreign moneys nor exportable abroad, nor importable from abroad into Italy (except for certain specified small amounts).

Circulation of money at 31 Dec. 1988: State coins and notes, 1,248,900m. lire; bank-notes, 58,935,100m. lire.

In March 1990 the rate of exchange was 1,256 lire = US$1 and 2,059 lire = £1 sterling.

Banking. According to the law of 6 May 1926 there is only one bank of issue, the Banca d'Italia. Its gold reserve amounted to 37,242,000m. lire in Dec. 1988; the foreign credit reserves of the Exchange Bureau (*Ufficio Italiano Cambi*) amounted to 37,821,000m. lire at the same date.

Since 1936, all credit institutions have been under the control of a State organ, named 'Inspectorate of Credit'; the Bank of Italy has been converted into a 'public institution', whose capital is held exclusively by corporate bodies of a public nature. Other credit institutions, totalling 1,100, are classified as: (1) 6 chartered banks (Banco di Napoli, Banco di Sicilia, Banca Nazionale del Lavoro, Monte dei Paschi di Siena, Istituto di S. Paolo di Torino, Banca di Sardegna); (2) 3 banks of national interest (Banca Commerciale Italiana in Milan, Credito Italiano in Genoa and Banco di Roma); (3) banks and credit concerns in general, including 148 joint-stock banks and 127 co-operative banks; (4) 83 savings banks and Monti di pegno (institutions granting loans against personal chattels as security); (5) 728 *Casse rurali e agrarie* (agricultural banks, established as co-operative institutions with unlimited liability of associates); (6) 5 Istituti di Categoria.

At 31 Dec. 1988 there were 271 credit institutes handling 95% of all deposits and current accounts, with capital and reserves of 67,166,000m. lire.

On 31 Dec. 1988 the post office savings banks had deposits and current accounts of 130,450,000m. lire; credit institutions, 573,530,000m. lire.

Insurance. By a decree of 29 April 1923 life-assurance business is carried on only by the National Insurance Institute and by other institutions, national and foreign, authorized by the Government. At 31 Dec. 1987 the insurances vested in the *Istituto Nazionale delle Assicurazioni* amounted to 22,500,917m. lire, including the decuple of life annuities.

Weights and Measures. The metric system is in general use.

ENERGY AND NATURAL RESOURCES

Electricity. Italy has greatly developed her water-power resources. In 1988 the total power generated was 203,561m. kwh., of which 43,547m. kwh. were generated by hydro-electric plants. Supply 220 volts; 50 Hz and 120, 125, 160 and 260 volts; 60 Hz.

Oil. Production in 1988 amounted to 4,839,213 tonnes, of which 977,987 came from Sicily. Natural gas production (1988) 584,422m. cu. ft.

Minerals. The Italian mining industry is most developed in Sicily (Caltanissetta), in Tuscany (Arezzo, Florence and Grosseto), in Sardinia (Cagliari, Sassari and Iglesias), in Lombardy (particularly near Bergamo and Brescia) and in Piedmont.

Italy's fuel and mineral resources are wholly inadequate. Only sulphur and mercury outputs yield a substantial surplus for exports. In 1988 outputs, in tonnes, of raw steel were 23,760,369; rolled iron, 22,275,637; cast-iron ingots, 11,348,608.

Production of metals and minerals (in tonnes) was as follows:

	1983	*1984*	*1985*	*1986*	*1987*	*1988*
Iron pyrites	646,209	442,674	690,395	760,860	784,924	774,148
Iron ore	67,700	273,700	–	–	–	–
Manganese	7,205	9,528	8,621	6,396	3,802	9,701
Zinc	83,462	81,291	87,380	50,515	67,798	71,979
Crude sulphur	40,858	20,639	4,911	–	–	–
Bauxite	3,118	–	–	2,250	15,057	17,864
Lead	37,429	37,558	37,051	27,219	58,515	68,946
Aluminium	195,694	230,207	226,300	262,562	258,051	257,995

Agriculture. The area of Italy in 1988 comprised 301,278 sq. km, of which 262,780 sq. km was agricultural and forest land and 38,498 sq. km was unproductive; the former was mainly distributed as follows (in 1,000 hectares): Forage and pasture, 7,881; woods, 6,652; cereals, 4,590; vines, 1,165; olive trees, 994; garden produce, 680; leguminous plants, 289.

At the third general census of agriculture (24 Oct. 1982) agricultural holdings numbered 3,270,560 and covered 23,559,924 hectares. 3,063,010 owners (93·6%) farmed directly 16,597,798 hectares (70·4%); 152,250 owners (4·7%) worked with hired labour on 6,209,702 hectares (26·4%); 130,648 share-croppers (3·6%) tilled 1,271,485 hectares (5·1%); the remaining 55,300 holdings (1·7%) of 752,424 hectares (3·2%) were operated in other ways.

According to the labour force survey in July 1978 persons engaged in agriculture numbered 3·17m. (2·02m. males and 1·15m. females).

In 1987, 1,315,427 farm tractors were being used.

The production of the principal crops (in 1,000 metric quintals) in 1988: Sugar beet, 136,276; wheat, 79,450; maize, 63,194; tomatoes, 41,889; potatoes, 23,409; oranges, 21,699; rice, 10,935; barley, 15,607; lemons, 7,084; oats, 3,827; olive oil, 4,093; tangerines, 3,102; other citrus fruit, 253; rye, 180.

Production of wine, 1988, 61,010,000 hectolitres; of tobacco, 138,900 tonnes.

In 1987 consumption of chemical fertilizers in Italy was as follows (in 1,000 tons): Perphosphate, 764·2; nitrate of ammonia, 787·8; sulphate of ammonium, 337·2; potash salts, 229·2; nitrate of calcium 15/16, 83·3; deposed slags, 29·5.

Livestock estimated in 1988: Cattle, 8,736,000; pigs, 9,359,500; sheep, 11,622,900; goats, 1,214,300; horses, 256,000; donkeys, 81,000; mules, 47,000.

Fisheries. The Italian fishing fleet comprised in 1982, 23,385 motor boats (323,512 gross tons) and 11,694 sailing vessels (14,612 gross tons). The catch in 1984 was 428,691 tonnes.

INDUSTRY AND TRADE

Industry. The main branches of industry are: (% of industrial value added at factor cost in 1982) Textiles, clothing, leather and footwear (17·7%), food, beverages and tobacco (10·4%), energy products (7·9%), agricultural and industrial machines (7·7%), metal products except machines and means of transport (7%), mineral and non-metallic mineral products (7%), timber and wooden furniture (6·6%), electric plants and equipment (6·3%), chemicals and pharmaceuticals (6·2%), means of transport (6·1%).

Production, 1988: Steel, 22,275,637 tonnes; motor vehicles, 2,114,108; cement, 37,632,298 tonnes; artificial and synthetic fibres (including staple fibre and waste), 710,196 tonnes; polyethylene resins, 827,994 tonnes.

Labour. In 1988, 20·8m. persons were employed, 2m. unemployed (figures from a new series of statistics on the labour force, 1977, which is not comparable with previous series).

Trade Unions. There are 4 main groups: Confederazione Generale Italiana del Lavoro (Communist-dominated); Confederazione Italiana Sindacati Lavoratori (Catholic); Unione Italiana del Lavoro and Confederazione Italiana Sindacati Nazionali Lavoratori.

Commerce. The territory covered by foreign trade statistics includes Italy, the Republic of San Marino, but excludes the municipalities of Livigno and Campione.

The following table shows the value of Italy's foreign trade (in 1m. lire):

	1983	*1984*	*1985*	*1986*	*1987*	*1988*
Imports	121,978,334	148,162,029	172,809,202	148,993,862	161,596,640	180,064,049
Exports	110,530,106	129,026,980	149,723,608	145,331,231	150,454,324	167,189,222

The following table shows trade by countries in 1m. lire:

	Imports into Italy from			*Exports from Italy to*		
Countries	*1986*	*1987*	*1988*	*1986*	*1987*	*1988*
Argentina	530,980	447,774	591,995	453,949	498,648	453,033
Australia	905,845	862,113	1,272,254	1,049,527	1,135,914	1,298,182
Austria	3,188,037	3,730,502	4,320,180	3,445,688	3,793,928	4,129,405
Belgium-Luxembourg	6,920,226	8,032,085	8,801,012	4,842,513	5,078,461	5,712,674
France	21,654,420	23,592,402	26,733,833	22,704,291	24,570,821	27,677,255
Germany, Fed. Rep. of	30,506,735	34,076,283	39,217,256	26,355,260	27,958,933	30,211,166
Japan	3,119,645	3,457,826	4,549,940	1,966,167	2,403,860	3,165,492
Netherlands	8,771,001	9,035,325	10,299,944	4,755,267	4,640,120	5,136,207
Switzerland	6,485,310	7,718,373	8,062,673	6,607,199	7,082,240	7,868,418
USSR	3,464,909	3,676,009	4,091,736	2,410,783	2,847,165	2,733,745
UK	7,596,570	8,513,763	9,168,468	10,298,981	11,192,851	13,416,658
USA	8,495,617	8,618,939	10,053,542	15,604,645	14,456,025	14,834,391
Yugoslavia	2,004,412	2,367,747	2,959,017	2,020,347	1,867,069	2,041,451

In 1988 the main imports were maize, wood, greasy wool, metal scrap, pit-coal, petroleum, raw oils, meat, paper, rolled iron and steel, copper and alloys, mechanical and electric equipment, motor vehicles. The main exports were fruit and vegetables, fabrics, footwear and other clothing articles, rolled iron and steel, machinery, motor vehicles, plastic materials and petroleum by-products.

Italy's balance of trade (in 1,000m. lire) has been estimated as follows:

	Goods and services			*Income from investments and*	*Net*
	Export	*Import*	*Balance*	*work, balance*	*balance*
1980	83,705	94,276	−10,571	790	−9,781
1987	189,766	183,771	+5,995	−6,417	−422
1988	209,204	206,326	+2,878	−6,938	−4,060

Remittances from Italians abroad (in US$1m. until 1969 and then 1,000m. lire): 1950, 72; 1960, 214; 1970, 289; 1980, 1,059; 1988, 1,587.

Total trade between Italy and UK (British Department of Trade returns, in £1,000 sterling):

	1985	*1986*	*1987*	*1988*	*1989*
Imports to UK	4,293,941	4,658,036	5,216,751	5,817,445	6,701,683
Exports and re-exports from UK	3,466,495	3,472,364	4,145,659	4,106,417	4,630,896

Tourism. In 1987, 52·7m. foreigners visited Italy; they included 9·6m. German, 9m. Swiss, 10·5m. French, 5·5m. Austrian, 4·8m. Yugoslav, 2m. British, 1·4m. Dutch and 1·5m. US citizens. They spent about 15,782,808m. lire.

COMMUNICATIONS

Roads. Italy's roads totalled (31 Dec. 1987) 302,563 km, of which 51,840 km were state roads and highways, 109,027 km provincial roads, 141,666 km communal roads. Motor vehicles, Dec. 1986: Cars, 23·5m.; buses, 77,891; lorries, 1,930,182; motor cycles, light vans, etc., 6,219,133.

Railways. Railway history in Italy begins in 1839, with a line between Naples and Portici (8 km). Length of railways (31 Dec. 1988), 19,538 km, including 15,973 km of state railways, of which 6,873 had not yet been electrified. The first section of a new high-speed direct railway linking Rome and Florence opened in Feb. 1977. In 1988 the state railways carried 410m. passengers and 58m. tonnes of goods. The Rome Underground opened in Feb. 1980.

Aviation. The Italian airline Alitalia (with a capital of 585,000m. lire, of which 99·1% is owned by the State) operates flights to every part of the world. Airports include 25 international, 36 national and 75 club airports. Domestic and international traffic in 1988 registered 19,030,960 passengers arrived and 19,075,682 departed, while freight and mail (excluding luggage) amounted to 183,396 tonnes unloaded and 202,099 tonnes loaded.

Shipping. The mercantile marine at 31 Dec. 1986 consisted of 2,031 vessels of 8,060,067 gross tons, not including pleasure boats (yachts, etc.), sailing and motor vessels. There were 1,371 motor vessels of 100 gross tons and over.

In 1987, 269,225,000 tonnes of cargo were unloaded, and 97,207,000 tonnes of cargo were loaded in Italian ports.

Post and Broadcasting. On 31 Dec. 1985 there were 14,276 post offices and 13,759 telegraph offices. The maritime radio-telegraph service had 20 coast stations. On 1 Jan. 1987 the telephone service had 26,873,730 apparatus. *Radiotelevisione Italiana* broadcasts 3 programmes and additional regional programmes, including transmissions in English, French, German and Slovenian on medium- and short-waves and on FM. It also broadcasts 2 TV programmes. Radio licences numbered 184,084; television and radio licences, 14,717,013 in 1988.

Cinemas. There were 3,846 cinemas in 1988.

Newspapers. There were (1987) 72 daily newspapers with a combined circulation of 1,817,311 copies; of the papers 14 are published in Rome and 7 in Milan. One daily each is published in German and Slovene.

JUSTICE, RELIGION, EDUCATION AND WELFARE

Justice. Italy has 1 court of cassation, in Rome, and is divided for the administration of justice into 23 appeal court districts (and 3 detached sections), subdivided into 159 tribunal *circondari* (districts), and these again into *mandamenti* each with its own magistracy (*Pretura*), 899 in all. There are also 90 first degree assize courts and 26 assize courts of appeal. For civil business, besides the magistracy above mentioned, *Conciliatori* have jurisdiction in petty plaints (those to a maximum amount of 1m. lire).

On 31 Dec. 1983 there were 25,016 male and 1,448 female prisoners in establishments for preventive custody, 10,819 males and 409 females in penal establishments and 1,255 males and 98 females in establishments for the execution of safety measures.

Religion. The treaty between the Holy See and Italy, of 11 Feb. 1929, confirmed by article 7 of the Constitution of the republic, lays down that the Catholic Apostolic Roman Religion is the only religion of the State. Other creeds are permitted, provided they do not profess principles, or follow rites, contrary to public order or moral behaviour.

The appointment of archbishops and of bishops is made by the Holy See; but the Holy See submits to the Italian Government the name of the person to be appointed in order to obtain an assurance that the latter will not raise objections of a political nature.

Catholic religious teaching is given in elementary and intermediate schools. Marriages celebrated before a Catholic priest are automatically transferred to the civil register. Marriages celebrated by clergy of other denominations must be made valid before a registrar. In 1972 there were 279 dioceses with 28,154 parishes and 43,714 priests. There were 187,153 members (154,796 women) of about 20,000 religious houses.

In 1962 there were about 100,000 Protestants and about 50,000 Jews.

Education. Education is compulsory from 6 to 14 years of age. An optional pre-school education is given to the children between 3 and 5 years in the preparatory schools (kindergarten schools). Illiteracy of males over 6 years was 2·2% in 1981, of females 3·9%.

Compulsory education can be classified as primary education (5-year course) and junior secondary education (3-year course).

Senior secondary education is subdivided in classical (*ginnasio* and classical *liceo*), scientific (scientific *liceo*), language lyceum, professional institutes and technical education: agricultural, industrial, commercial, technical, nautical institutes, institutes for surveyors, institutes for girls (5-year course) and teacher-training institutes (4-year course).

University education is given in Universities and in University Higher Institutes (4, 5, 6 years, according to degree course).

Statistics for the academic year 1988–89:

Elementary schools	*No.*	*Pupils*
Kindergarten	28,303	1,550,283
Public elementary schools	23,810	2,991,943
Private elementary schools		
Private elementary recognized schools (*parificate*)	2,367	255,651

Government secondary schools		*Total students*
Junior secondary schools	10,031	2,843,637
Classical lyceum	735	220,172
Lyceum for science	1,003	420,873
Language lyceum	382	49,148
Teachers' schools	191	24,770
Teachers' institutes	657	161,806
Professional institutes	1,708	527,340
Technical institutes, of which:		
Industrial institutes	606	333,456
Commercial institutes	1,257	657,644
Surveyors' institutes	521	153,576
Agricultural institutes		
Nautical institutes		
Technical institutes for tourism	418	139,083
Managerial institutes		
Girls technical schools		
Artistic studies	272	90,816

Universities and higher institutes	*Date of foundation*	*Students 1987–88*	*Teachers 1987–88*	*Universities and higher institutes*	*Date of foundation*	*Students 1987–88*	*Teachers 1987–88*
Ancona	1965	6,892	384	Napoli	1224	114,914	4,406
Arezzo	1971	1,040	84	Padova	1222	37,425	2,311
Bari	1924	59,039	1,930	Palermo	1805	40,363	2,243
Bergamo	1970	4,035	124	Parma	1502	14,685	985
Bologna	1200	64,435	2,735	Pavia	1390	19,506	1,272
Brescia	1970	6,804	317	Perugia	1276	18,558	1,183
Cagliari	1626	21,548	1,165	Pescara	1965	10,771	241
Camerino				Piacenza	1924	624	102
(Macerata)	1727	3,761	240	Pisa	1338	30,020	1,993
Cassino				Potenza	1983	1,887	227
(Frosinone)	1968	4,770	140	Reggio di C.	1968	4,607	190
Catania	1434	32,693	1,578	Roma	1303	170,153	6,904
Catanzaro	1983	3,268	108	Salerno	1944	21,495	572
Chieti	1965	4,423	237	Sassari	1677	8,751	522
Cosenza	1972	6,666	524	Siena	1300	10,692	887
Feltre (Belluno)	1969	569	36	Teramo	1965	5,558	147
Ferrara	1391	4,688	500	Torino	1404	62,736	2,771
Firenze	1924	42,205	2,280	Trento	1965	5,367	418
Genova	1243	41,905	1,948	Trieste	1924	14,796	1,011
L'Aquila	1956	6,182	667	Udine	1969	5,027	433
Lecce	1959	9,740	373	Urbino	1564	14,629	517

Universities and higher institutes	Date of foundation	Students 1987–88	Teachers 1987–88	Universities and higher institutes	Date of foundation	Students 1987–88	Teachers 1987–88
Macerata	1290	5,396	178	Venezia	1868	23,895	721
Messina	1549	28,382	1,540	Verona	1969	9,783	538
Milano	1924	137,030	3,516	Viterbo	1980	1,633	179
Modena	1678	7,648	665				

Health. In 1986 there were 245,116 doctors and (1987) 440,187 hospital beds.

Social Security. Social expenditure is made up of transfers which the central public departments, local departments and social security departments, make to families. Payment is principally for pensions, family allowances and health services. Expenditure on subsidies, public assistance to various classes of people and people injured by political events or national disasters are also included.

DIPLOMATIC REPRESENTATIVES

Of Italy in Great Britain (14 Three Kings Yard, London, W1Y 2EH)
Ambassador: Boris Biancheri (accredited 11 Nov. 1987).

Of Great Britain in Italy (Via XX Settembre 80A, 00187, Rome)
Ambassador: Sir Stephen Egerton, KCMG.

Of Italy in the USA (1601 Fuller St., NW, Washington, D.C., 20009)
Ambassador: Rinaldo Petrignani.

Of the USA in Italy (Via Veneto 119/A, Rome)
Ambassador: Peter Secchia.

Of Italy to the United Nations
Ambassador: Giovanni Migiuolo.

Further Reading

Statistical Information: The Istituto Centrale di Statistica (16 Via Cesare Balbo 00100 Rome) was set up by law of 9 July 1926 as the central institute in charge of census and all statistical information. *President:* Prof. Guido Mario Rey. *Director-General:* Vincenzo Siesto. Its publications include:

Annuario statistico italiano. 1987, *Compendio statistico italiano.* 1988, *Bollettino mensile di statistica.* Monthly, from 1950, *Statistiche industriali.* 1987, *Statistiche demografiche.* 1987, *Statistica agrarie.* 1984, *Statistico della navigazione marittima.* 1988, *Statistico del commercio interno.* 1988, *Statistica annuale del commercio con l'estero.* 1988, *Statistica del commercio con l'estero.* Quarterly, *Statistiche del lavoro.* 1986, *Censimento generale dell'agricoltura.* 1982, *Censimento generale della popolazione, 1981.* Vol. I, II and III, *Censimento generale dell'industria e del commercio.* 1981 *Sommario di statistiche storiche, 1926–1985.*

Italy. Documents and Notes. Servizi delle Informazioni, Rome. 1952 ff.
Italian Books and Periodicals. Bimonthly from 1958
Banco di Roma, *Review of the Economic Condition in Italy* (in English). Bimonthly, 1947 ff.
Credito Italiano, *The Italian Economic Situation.* Bimonthly. Milan, from June 1961 (in Italian), from June 1962 (in English)
Compendio Economico Italiano. Rome, Unione Italiana delle Camere di Commercio. Annually from 1954
Clark, M., *Modern Italy 1871–1982.* London, 1984
Finer, S. E. and Mastropaolo, A. (eds.), *The Italian Party System, 1945–80.* London, 1985
Grindrod, M., *The Rebuilding of Italy, 1945–55.* R. Inst. of Int. Affairs, 1955
Nichols, P., *Italia, Italia.* London, 1974
Smith, D. M., *The Making of Italy 1796–1866.* London, 1988
Spotts, F. and Wieser, T., *Italy: A Difficult Democracy.* CUP, 1986
Woolfe, S. J. (ed.) *The Rebirth of Italy, 1943–50.* New York, 1972

National Library: Biblioteca Nazionale Centrale Vittorio Emanuele II Viale Castro Pretorio, Rome. *Director:* Dr L. M. Crisari.

JAMAICA

Capital: Kingston
Population: 2·4m. (1988)
GNP per capita: US$1,348 (1988)

HISTORY. Jamaica was discovered by Columbus in 1494, and was occupied by the Spaniards between 1509 and 1655, when the island was captured by the English; their possession was confirmed by the Treaty of Madrid, 1670. Self-government was introduced in 1944 and gradually extended until Jamaica achieved complete independence within the Commonwealth on 6 Aug. 1962.

AREA AND POPULATION. The island of Jamaica lies in the Caribbean Sea about 150 km south of Cuba. The area is 4,411 sq. miles (11,425 sq. km). The population at the census of 8 June 1982 was 2,095,878, distributed on the basis of the 14 parishes of the island as follows: Kingston and St Andrew, 565,487; St Thomas, 76,347; Portland, 70,787; St Mary, 101,442; St Ann, 132,475; Trelawny, 65,038; St James, 127,994; Hanover, 60,420; Westmoreland, 116,163; St Elizabeth, 132,353; Manchester, 136,517; St Catherine, 315,970; Clarendon, 194,885.

Chief towns (census, 1982): Kingston and St Andrew, 524,638, metropolitan area; Spanish Town, 89,097; Montego Bay, 70,265; May Pen, 40,962; Mandeville, 34,502.

Estimated population, in 1988, was 2·4m. The population is 76% of African ethnic origin, 3% European and 21% mixed and other groups.

Vital statistics (1988): Births, 53,600 (22·7 per 1,000 population); deaths, 12,200 (5·2); migration loss, 38,900.

CLIMATE. A tropical climate but with considerable variation. High temperatures on the coast are usually mitigated by sea breezes, while upland areas enjoy cooler and less humid conditions. Rainfall is plentiful over most of Jamaica, being heaviest in May and from Aug. to Nov. The island lies in the hurricane zone. Kingston. Jan. 76°F (24·4°C), July 81°F (27·2°C). Annual rainfall 32" (800 mm).

CONSTITUTION AND GOVERNMENT. Under the Constitution of Aug. 1962 the Crown is represented by a Governor-General appointed by the Crown on the advice of the Prime Minister. The Governor-General is assisted by a Privy Council. The Legislature comprises two chambers, an elected House and a nominated Senate. The executive is chosen from both chambers.

The Executive comprises the Prime Minister, who is the leader of the majority party, and Ministers appointed by the Prime Minister. Together they form the Cabinet, which is the highest executive power. An Attorney-General is a member of the House and is legal adviser to the Cabinet.

The Senate consists of 21 senators appointed by the Governor-General, 13 on the advice of the Prime Minister, 8 on the advice of the Leader of the Opposition. The House of Representatives (60 members, Dec. 1976) is elected by universal adult suffrage for a period not exceeding 5 years. Electors and elected must be Jamaican or Commonwealth citizens resident in Jamaica for at least 12 months before registration. The powers and procedure of Parliament correspond to those of the British Parliament.

The Privy Council consists of 6 members appointed by the Governor-General in consultation with the Prime Minister.

Governor-General: Sir Florizel Glasspole, GCMG, GCVO.

National flag: A yellow diagonal cross dividing triangles of green, top and bottom, and black, hoist and fly.

The elections to the House of Representatives, held on 9 Feb. 1989, returned 45 members of the People's National Party and the Jamaica Labour Party, 15 seats.

The Cabinet in Nov. 1989 was comprised as follows:
Prime Minister: Rt. Hon. Michael Manley, P.C.

Deputy Prime Minister and Minister of Development, Planning, and Production: P. J. Patterson, QC. *Foreign Affairs and Foreign Trade:* David Coore, QC. *Finance and The Public Service:* Seymour Mullings. *National Security:* K. D. Knight. *Justice and Attorney-General:* Carl Rattray, QC. *Education:* Carlyle Dunkley. *Health:* Easton Douglas. *Labour, Welfare and Sports:* Portia Simpson. *Construction:* O. D. Ramtallie. *Public Utilities and Transport:* Robert Pickersgill. *Agriculture:* Horace Clarke. *Local Government:* Ralph Brown. *Tourism:* Frank Pringle. *Mining and Energy:* Hugh Small, QC. *Industry and Commerce:* Claude Clarke. *Youth, Culture and Community Development:* Dr Douglas Manley. *Without Portfolio and Leader of the House (with special responsibility for Parliamentary Affairs):* Dr Ken McNeil. *Information:* Dr Paul Robertson.

There are 10 Ministers of State.

DEFENCE

Army. The Jamaica Defence Force consists of a Regular and a Reserve Force. The Regular Force is comprised of the 1st battalion, Jamaica Regiment and Support Services which include the Air Wing and Coast Guard. The Reserve Force consists of the 3rd battalion, Jamaica Regiment. Total strength (all services, 1990), 2,800. Reserves, 870.

Air Force. The Air Wing of the Jamaica Defence Force was formed in July 1963 and has since been expanded and trained successively by the British Army Air Corps and Canadian air force personnel. Equipment for army liaison, search and rescue, police co-operation, survey and transport duties includes 2 Defender armed STOL transports; 1 Beech King Air and 1 Cessna 337 light transports; 4 JetRanger and 2 Bell 212 helicopters. Personnel (1990) 150.

INTERNATIONAL RELATIONS

Membership. Jamaica is a member of UN, the Commonwealth, OAS, CARICOM and is an ACP state of EEC.

ECONOMY

Budget. Revenue and expenditure for fiscal years ending 31 March (in J$1m.):

	1985–86	*1986–87*	*1987–88*	*1988–89*
Revenue	3,207	4,467	5,429	6,020
Expenditure	4,529	5,631	6,509	8,199

The chief heads of recurrent revenue are income tax; consumption, customs and stamp duties. The other major share of current resources is generated by the Bauxite levy.The chief items of recurrent expenditure are public debt, education and health. Total external debt at 31 Dec. 1988, US$3,994·8m.

Currency. The currency is the *dollar*, divided into 100 cents. Currency circulation at 30 June 1989 was J$1,129·8m. In March 1990, £1 = J$11·24; US$1 = J$6·86.

Banking. On 1 May 1961 the Bank of Jamaica opened as Jamaica's Central Bank. It has the sole right to issue notes and coins in Jamaica, acts as Banker to the Government and to the commercial banks, and administers the island's external reserves and exchange control.

There are 10 commercial banks with about 171 branches and agencies in operation, with main offices in Kingston. Six of these banks are subsidiaries of major British and North American banks, of which 4 are incorporated locally. The Workers' Savings and Loan Bank is owned by the Government, Trade Unions and the private sector. The National Commercial Bank (Jamaica) Ltd, formerly Barclays Bank Jamaica Ltd, is 49% government-owned. The other 8 banks which operate are: The Bank of Nova Scotia (Jamaica) Ltd, City Bank of North America, Mutual Security Bank (formerly Royal Bank Jamaica Ltd), Canadian Imperial Bank of Commerce (formerly Bank of Commerce), Jamaica Citizens Bank Ltd, Eagle Commercial Bank, Bank of Credit and Commerce International and Century National Bank.

Total deposits in commercial banks, 30 June 1989, J$9,565·3m., of which J$2,342·7m. were time deposits and J$5,226·4m. (55%) were savings.

ENERGY AND NATURAL RESOURCES

Electricity. The Jamaica Public Service Co. is the public supplier of electricity. The bauxite companies, sugar estates and the Caribbean Cement Co. and Goodyear generate their own electricity. Total installed capacity, 1988, 485·4 mw. Production (1988) 1,652m. kwh. Supply 110 and 220 volts; 50 Hz.

Minerals. Bauxite, ceramic clays, marble, silica sand and gypsum are commercially viable. Jamaica has become the world's third largest producer of bauxite and alumina. The bauxite deposits are worked by a Canadian, an American and a Jamaican company. In 1988, 7·26m. tonnes of bauxite ore was mined; gypsum, 145,500 tonnes; marble, 2·7m. tonnes; sand and gravel, 810,000 cu. metres; industrial lime, 2,200 cu. metres.

Agriculture (1988). Production: Sugar-cane, 2,524,000 tons; sugar, 212,000 tons; rum, 4,588,000 proof gallons; molasses, 105,000 tons; bananas, 28,000 tons; citrus fruit, 446,000 boxes; cocoa, 2,350 tons; spices, 2,355 tons; copra, 3,239 short tons; domestic food crops, 427,772 short tons.

Livestock (1988): Cattle, 290,000; goats, 440,000; pigs, 250,000; poultry, 6m.

INDUSTRY AND TRADE

Industry. Three bauxite-mining companies also process bauxite into alumina; production, 1988, 1·5m. tonnes. From processing only a few agricultural products—sugar, rum, condensed milk, oils and fats, cigars and cigarettes—the island is now producing clothing, footwear, textiles, paints, building materials (including cement), agricultural machinery and toilet articles. There is an oil refinery in Kingston. In 1988 manufacturing contributed J$3,997·7m. to the total GDP at current prices.

Labour. Average total labour force (1988), 1,078,400, of whom 871,800 were employed. Government and other services employed 241,900; agriculture, forestry and fishing, 261,000; manufacturing, 131,100; construction and installation, 48,900.

Commerce. Value of imports and domestic exports for calendar years (in US$1m.):

	1985	*1986*	*1987*	*1988*
Imports	1,144	969	1,234	1,435
Domestic exports	535	567	692	812

Principal imports in 1988 (in US$1m.): Manufactured goods classified by materials, 307·3 (21·4%), with 42·1% of imports from USA; machinery and transport equipment, 305 (21·3%), with 37·5% from USA and 12·2% from Japan; food, 224 (15·6%); minerals, fuels, lubricants and related materials, 195·1 (13·6%); chemicals, 163·4 (11·4%).

Principal domestic exports in 1988 (in US$1m.): Crude materials, inedible oils except fuels, 423·1 (52·1%), of which alumina, 312·3 (38·5%) and bauxite, 104·9 (12·9%), with crude materials exports of 135·5 to USA, 108·6 to Canada and 87·1 to the Netherlands; food, 169·2 (20·8%), of which sugar, 91·9 (11·3%), with food exports of 117·9 to UK and 23·4 to USA; miscellaneous materials, 125·9 (15·5%).

Total trade between Jamaica and UK (British Department of Trade returns, in £1,000 sterling):

	1985	*1986*	*1987*	*1988*	*1989*
Imports to UK	89,684	87,416	85,655	89,693	95,516
Exports and re-exports from UK	44,290	43,378	54,644	48,855	61,355

Tourism. In 1988, 1,020,293 tourists arrived in Jamaica, spending about US$525m.

COMMUNICATIONS

Roads (1988). The island has 3,000 miles of main roads, and over 7,000 miles of secondary and tertiary roads. Main roads are constructed and maintained by the Ministry of Construction (Works), while other roads are constructed and maintained by parish councils. In 1988 there were 74,946 licensed vehicles.

Railways. There are 294 km of railway open of 1,435 mm gauge, operated by the Jamaica Railway Corporation, which also operates 31 km (Alcoa Mineral Railway) on behalf of one of the bauxite companies. In 1988 the railway carried 38,540 tonnes and 1·12m. passengers.

Aviation. Scheduled commercial international airlines operate through the Norman Manley and Sangster international airports at Palisadoes and Montego Bay. In 1988 Norman Manley airport had 32,532 aircraft movements, handled 1·19m. passengers and 32,430 tonnes of freight. Sangster had 29,351 movements, with 1·6m. passengers and 4,994 tonnes of freight. Trans-Jamaica Airlines Ltd operates internal flights; in 1987 it carried 37,600 passengers. Air Jamaica, originally set up in conjunction with BOAC and BWIA in 1966, became a new company, Air Jamaica (1968) Ltd, and is affiliated to Air Canada. In 1969 it began operations as Jamaica's national airline. In 1988 Air Jamaica carried 1·12m. passengers.

Shipping. In 1988 there were 2,198 visits to all ports; 11·03m. tons of cargo were handled. Kingston had 1,327 visits and handled 3·47m. tons. The outports had 871 visits and handled 7·56m. tons, of which 5·9m. was loaded and 1·6m. landed.

Post and Broadcasting. In 1988 there were 824 postal points. In Dec. 1988 there were 170,410 telephones.

There was (1988) 1 commercial and 1 publicly owned broadcasting stations; the latter also operates a television service.

Cinemas. In 1988 there were 34 cinemas and 2 drive-in cinemas.

JUSTICE, RELIGION, EDUCATION AND WELFARE

Justice. The Judicature comprises a Supreme Court, a court of appeal, resident magistrates' courts, petty sessional courts, coroners' courts, a traffic court and a family court which was instituted in 1975. The Chief Justice is head of the judiciary. All prosecutions are initiated by the Director of Public Prosecutions.

Police. The Constabulary Force in 1988 stood at approximately 5,426 officers, sub-officers and constables (men and women).

Religion. Freedom of worship is guaranteed under the Constitution. The main Christian denominations are Anglican, Baptist, Roman Catholic, Methodist, Church of God, United Church of Jamaica, and Grand Cayman (Presbyterian–Congregational) Moravian, Seventh-Day Adventists, Pentecostal, Salvation Army, Quaker, and Disciples of Christ. Pocomania is a mixture of Christianity and African survivals. Non-Christians include Hindus, Jews, Moslems and Bahai followers. There is also a growing number of Rastafarians who believe in the deity of the late Emperor Hailé Selassié of Ethiopia.

Education. In Sept. 1973 education became free for all government grant-aided schools (the majority of all schools) and for all Jamaicans entering the University of the West Indies, the College of Arts, Science and Technology and the Jamaica School of Agriculture. In 1987–88 there were 1,224 pre-primary schools and departments (124,344 pupils); 293 primary schools (170,736 pupils); 493 all-age schools (159,826 pupils).

There were 141 secondary and vocational schools (150,529 students). Teacher-training colleges had 3,094 students; community colleges had 15,097; the College of Arts, Science and Technology had 4,126; the College of Agriculture, 211 and the University of the West Indies, 4,917.

Health. In 1988 the public health service had 3,607 staff in medicine, nursing and pharmacology; 315 in dentistry; 300 public health inspectors; 49 in nutrition. In 1988 there were 361 primary health centres, 5,416 public hospital beds and 282 private beds.

DIPLOMATIC REPRESENTATIVES

Of Jamaica in Great Britain (1-2 Prince Consort Rd., London, SW7 2BZ)
High Commissioner: Ellen Bogle (accredited 27 Oct. 1989).

Of Great Britain in Jamaica (Trafalgar Rd., Kingston 10)
High Commissioner: Derek Milton.

Of Jamaica in the USA (1850 K. St., NW, Washington, D.C., 20006)
Ambassador: Keith Johnson.

Of the USA in Jamaica (2 Oxford Rd., Kingston 5)
Ambassador: Glen Holden.

Of Jamaica to the United Nations
Ambassador: Herbert S. Walker.

Further Reading

Statistical Information: The Department of Statistics, now Statistical Institute of Jamaica (25 Dominica Dr., Kingston), was set up in 1945—the nucleus being the Census Office, which undertook the operations of the 1943 Census of Jamaica and its Dependencies. *Director:* Vernon James. Publications of the Institute include the *Bulletin of Statistics on External Trade* and the *Annual Abstract of Statistics.*

Economic and Social Survey, Jamaica. Planning Institute of Jamaica, Kingston (Annual)
Social and Economic Studies. Institute of Social and Economic Research, Univ. of the West Indies. Quarterly
A Review of the Performance of the Jamaican Economy 1981–1983. Jamaica Information Service, 1985
Quarterly Economic Report. Planning Institute of Jamaica, Kingston
Beckford, G. and Witter, M., *Small Garden… Bitter Weed. The Political Struggle and Change in Jamaica.* 2nd ed. London, 1982
Cassidy, F. G. and Le Page, R. B., *Dictionary of Jamaican English.* CUP, 1966
Floyd, B., *Jamaica: An Island Microcosm.* London, 1979
Goulbourne, H., *Teachers, Education and Politics in Jamaica, 1892–1972.* London, 1988
Ingram, K. E., *Jamaica.* [Bibliography] Oxford and Santa Barbara, 1984
Manley, M., *A Voice at the Work Place.* London, 1975.—*Jamaica: Struggle in the Periphery.* London, 1983
Payne, A. J., *Politics in Jamaica.* London and New York, 1988
Post, K., *Strike the Iron, A Colony at War: Jamaica 1939–1945.* 2 vols. Atlantic Highlands, N.J., 1981
Sherlock, P., *Keeping Company with Jamaica.* London, 1984
Stephens, E. H. and Stephens, J. D., *Democratic Socialism in Jamaica.* London, 1986
Stone, C., *Class, Race and Political Behaviour in Urban Jamaica.* Kingston, 1973—*Democracy and Clientelism in Jamaica.* London and New Brunswick, N.J., 1981
Bibliography of Jamaica, 1900–1963. Jamaica Library Service, 1963

Libraries: National Library of Jamaica, Kingston. Jamaica Library Service, Kingston.

JAPAN

Nippon (*or* Nihon)

Capital: Tokyo
Population: 122·78m. (1988)
GNP per capita: US$21,040 (1988)

HISTORY. The house of Yamato, from about 500 B.C. the rulers of one of several kingdoms, in about A.D. 200 united the nation; the present imperial family are their direct descendants. From 1186 until 1867 successive families of Shoguns exercised the temporal power. In 1867 the Emperor Meiji recovered the imperial power after the abdication on 14 Oct. 1867 of the fifteenth and last Tokugawa Shogun Keiki (in different pronunciation: Yoshinobu). In 1871 the feudal system (Hoken Seido) was abolished; this was the beginning of the rapid westernization.

At San Francisco on 8 Sept. 1951 a Treaty of Peace was signed by Japan and representatives of 48 countries. For details *see* THE STATESMAN'S YEAR-BOOK, 1953, p. 1169. On 26 Oct. 1951 the Japanese Diet ratified the Treaty by 307 votes to 47 votes with 112 abstentions. On the same day the Diet ratified a Security Treaty with the US by 289 votes to 71 votes with 106 abstentions. The treaty provided for the stationing of American troops in Japan until she was able to undertake her own defence. The peace treaty came into force on 28 April 1952, when Japan regained her sovereignty. In 1960 Japan signed the Japan–US Mutual Security Treaty, valid for 10 years, which was renewed in 1970. Of the islands under US administration since 1945, the Bonin (Ogasawara), Volcano, and Daito groups and Marcus Island were returned to Japan in 1968, and the southern Ryukyu Islands (Okinawa) in 1972.

AREA AND POPULATION. Japan consists of 4 major islands, Honshu, Hokkaido, Kyushu and Shikoku, and many small islands, with an area of 377,835 sq. km. Census population (1 Oct. 1985) 121,047,196 (males 59,495,663, females 61,551,553). Estimate (1988) 122,783,000 (males 60,352,000, females 62,431,000). Foreigners registered 31 Dec. 1988 were 941,005, of whom 677,140 were Koreans, 129,269 Chinese, 32,766 Americans, 32,185 Filipinos, 8,523 British, 5,277 Thais, 4,763 Vietnamese, 4,159 Brazilians, 3,542 Malaysians, 3,510 Canadians, 3,222 West Germans, 1,658 stateless persons.

Japanese overseas, Oct. 1987, 518,318; of these 174,130 lived in USA, 115,252 in Brazil, 18,544 in Canada, 18,326 in the Federal Republic of Germany, 15,681 in Argentina, 14,327 in France, 10,396 in Hong Kong, 9,048 in Thailand, 9,063 in Australia, 8,496 in Singapore.

The areas, populations and chief cities of the principal islands (and regions) are:

Island/Region	*Sq. km*	*Census 1987*	*Chief cities*
Hokkaido	83,520	5,671,000	Sapporo
Honshu/Tohoku	66,971	9,745,000	Sendai
/Kanto	32,383	37,521,000	Tokyo
/Chubu	66,776	20,787,000	Nagoya
/Kinki	33,074	22,028,000	Osaka
/Chugoku	31,885	7,773,000	Hiroshima
Shikoku	18,808	4,227,000	Matsuyama
Kyushu	42,163	13,311,000	Fukuoka
Okinawa	2,255	1,202,000	Naha

The leading cities, with population, 31 March 1988 (in 1,000), are:

Akashi	261	Fukuyama	363	Ibaraki	250
Akita	295	Funabashi	515	Ichinomiya	259
Amagasaki	497	Gifu	408	Ichikawa	412
Aomori	292	Hachioji	433	Iwaki	357
Asahikawa	363	Hakodate	312	Kagoshima	528
Chiba	801	Hamamatsu	522	Kanazawa	423
Fujisawa	337	Higashiosaka	503	Kashiwa	291
Fukui	249	Himeji	450	Kasugai	259
Fukuoka	1,157	Hirakata	386	Kawagoe	291
Fukushima	271	Hiroshima	1,043	Kawaguchi	419

Kawasaki	1,114	Naha	310	Suita	342
Kitakyushu	1,035	Nara	339	Takamatsu	328
Kobe	1,427	Neyagawa	256	Takatsuki	354
Kochi	312	Niigata	470	Tokorozawa	289
Koriyama	303	Nishinomiya	412	Tokushima	258
Koshigaya	271	Oita	393	Tokyo	8,156
Kumamoto	555	Okayama	576	Toyama	316
Kurashiki	416	Okazaki	292	Toyohashi	326
Kyoto	1,419	Omiya	384	Toyonaka	406
Machida	335	Osaka	2,544	Toyota	315
Maebashi	281	Sagamihara	499	Urawa	392
Matsudo	439	Sakai	808	Utsunomiya	417
Matsuyama	434	Sapporo	1,582	Wakayama	401
Miyazaki	282	Sasebo	249	Yao	269
Nagano	341	Sendai	866	Yokkaichi	268
Nagasaki	446	Shimonoseki	260	Yokohama	3,122
Nagoya	2,100	Shizuoka	470	Yokosuka	431

Vital statistics (in 1,000) for calendar years:

	1981	*1982*	*1983*	*1984*	*1985*	*1986*	*1987*
Births	1,529	1,515	1,509	1,490	1,432	1,383	1,347
Deaths	720	712	740	740	752	751	751

Crude birth rate of Japanese nationals in present area, 1987, was 11·1 per 1,000 population (1947: 34·3); crude death rate, 6·2; crude marriage rate, 5·7; infant mortality rate per 1,000 live births, 6·7.

CLIMATE. The islands of Japan lie in the temperate zone, north-east of the main monsoon region of S.E. Asia. The climate is temperate with warm, humid summers and relatively mild winters except in the island of Hokkaido and northern parts of Honshu facing the Japan Sea. There is a month's rainy season in June-July, but the best seasons are spring and autumn, though Sept. may bring typhoons. There is a summer rainfall maximum. Tokyo. Jan. 40·5°F (4·7°C), July 77·4°F (25·2°C). Annual rainfall 63" (1,460 mm). Hiroshima. Jan. 39·7°F (4·3°C), July 78°F (25·6°C). Annual rainfall 61" (1,603 mm). Nagasaki. Jan. 43·5°F (6·4°C), July 79·7°F (26·5°C). Annual rainfall 77" (2,002 mm). Osaka. Jan. 42·1°F (5·6°C), July 80·6°F (27°C). Annual rainfall 53" (1,400 mm). Sapporo. Jan. 23·2°F (–4·9°C), July 68·4°F (20·2°C). Annual rainfall 47" (1,158 mm).

EMPEROR. The Emperor bears the title of Nihon-koku Tenno ('Emperor of Japan'). **Akihito,** born in Tokyo, 23 Dec. 1933; succeeded his father, Hirohito, 7 Jan. 1989; married 10 April 1959, to Michiko Shoda, born 20 Oct. 1934. *Offspring:* Crown Prince Naruhito (Hironomiya), born 23 Feb. 1960; Prince Fumihito (Ayanomiya), born 30 Nov. 1965; Princess Sayako (Norinomiya), born 18 April 1969.

By the Imperial House Law of 11 Feb. 1889, revised on 16 Jan. 1947, the succession to the throne was fixed upon the male descendants.

CONSTITUTION AND GOVERNMENT. Japan's Government is based upon the Constitution of 1947 which superseded the Meiji Constitution of 1889. In it the Japanese people pledge themselves to uphold the ideas of democracy and peace. The Emperor is the symbol of the States and of the unity of the people. Sovereign power rests with the people. The Emperor has no powers related to government. Japan renounces war as a sovereign right and the threat or the use of force as a means of settling disputes with other nations. Fundamental human rights are guaranteed.

National flag: White, with a red disc.

National anthem: Kimi ga yo wa (words 9th century, tune by Hiromori Hayashi, 1881).

Legislative power rests with the Diet, which consists of the House of Representatives (of 512 members), elected by men and women over 20 years of age for a 4-

year term, and the House of Councillors of 252 members (100 elected by party list system with proportional representation according to the d'Hondt method and 152 from prefectural districts), one-half of its members being elected every 3 years. The Lower House controls the budget and approves treaties with foreign powers.

The former House of Peers is replaced by the House of Councillors, whose members, like those of the House of Representatives, are elected as representatives of all the people. The House of Representatives has pre-eminence over the House of Councillors.

On 18 Jan. 1990 the House of Representatives consisted of 240 Liberal-Democrats, 114 Socialists, 31 Komeito, 18 Independents, 28 others.

The Cabinet, as constituted in 1990, was as follows:

Prime Minister: Toshiki Kaifu.
Justice: Shin Hasegawa.
Foreign Affairs: Taro Nakayama.
Finance: Ryutaro Hashimoto.
Education: Kasuke Hori.
Health and Welfare: Yuji Tsushima.
Agriculture, Forestry and Fishery: Tomio Yamamoto.
Trade and Industry: Kabun Muto.
Transport: Akira Ono.
Postal Service: Takashi Fukaya.
Labour: Shuni Tsukahara.
Construction: Tamisuke Watanuki.
Home Affairs: Keiwa Okuda.

Local Government. The country is divided into 47 prefectures (*Todofuken*), including Tokyo-to (the capital), Osaka-fu and Kyoto-fu, Hokkai-do, and 43 *Ken*. Each *Todofuken* has its governor (*Chiji*) elected by the voters in the area. The prefectural government of Tokyo-to is also responsible for the urban part (formerly Tokyo-shi) of the prefecture. Each prefecture, city, town and village has a representative assembly elected by the same franchise as in parliamentary elections.

New legislation, which came into effect on 1 July 1954, has given the central government complete control of the police throughout the country.

DEFENCE

Army. The 'Ground Self-Defence Force' had in 1990 an authorized strength of 156,000 uniformed personnel, plus a reserve of 46,000 men. The Army is organized in 12 infantry divisions, 1 armoured division, 1 airborne brigade, 2 air defence brigades, 1 artillery, 2 combined and 1 helicopter brigades in addition to 4 anti-aircraft artillery groups. Equipment includes 1,180 tanks, approximately 450 anti-tank guided weapons, observation and training helicopters, plus about 22 fixed-wing aircraft.

The Northern Army, stationed in Hokkaido, consists of 4 divisions (1 of which is armoured), an artillery brigade, an anti-aircraft artillery brigade, a tank group and an engineering brigade. The Western Army, stationed in Kyushu, consists of 2 divisions and 1 combined brigade. The North-Eastern Army (2 divisions), the Eastern Army (2 divisions and 1 airborne brigade), the Middle Army (3 divisions and 1 combined brigade). The infantry division establishment is approximately 9,000 with 4 infantry regiments or 7,000 (lower establishment) with 3 infantry regiments. Each infantry division has an artillery regiment, an anti-tank unit, a tank battalion and an engineering battalion in addition to administrative units.

Navy. The 'Maritime Self-Defence Force' is tasked with coastal protection and defence of the sea lanes to 1,000 nautical miles range from Japan. The modern and well-equipped combatant forces are mainly equipped with American weapon systems, which in many cases have been re-engineered and improved in Japan.

The combatant fleet, all home-built comprises 14 diesel submarines and one trials boat, 6 guided-missile destroyers armed with US Standard SM1-MR surface to air missiles, 20 helicopter-carrying frigates, with one or more Sea King ASW helicopters, and 37 other frigates of which 8 are employed on non-military tasks. Light forces comprise 5 torpedo craft and 9 small inshore patrol craft. There are 46 mine warfare vessels, 1 minelayer, 1 layer/command ship, 32 coastal minesweepers and 12 smaller vessels. A substantial amphibious capability is provided by 6 tank landing ships supported by some 40 smaller craft, but there are no specialist marines. 12 major auxiliaries include 2 combined oiler/ammunition ships, 5 survey vessels and 3 training support vessels, and there are several hundred minor auxiliaries and service craft.

The MSDF Air Arm, numbering 7 Air Wings, includes 80 Orion and Neptune ASW patrol aircraft, 10 US-1 flying boats for SAR, 60 Sea King ASW helicopters, 7 MCM helicopters plus numerous transport, training and utility aircraft.

The main elements of the fleet are organized into four escort flotillas based at Yokosuka (2), Sasebo and Maizuru. The submarines are based at Sasebo and Kure.

Personnel in 1989 numbered 44,000 including 12,000 Naval Air Arm.

The Maritime Safety Agancy regulates and safeguards all coastal navigation, providing a comprehensive SAR and navigation service. It operates 83 offshore patrol vessels, 10 coastal patrol vessels, and some 240 inshore patrol craft, plus numerous boats and service vessels. There are numerous shore command and support facilities, and 24 fixed-wing aircraft and 38 helicopers complete the equipment inventory. Personnel in 1987 numbered 12,000.

Air Force. An 'Air Self-Defence Force' was inaugurated on 1 July 1954. In 1989 its equipment included 5 interceptor squadrons of F-15J/DJ Eagles (total of 168 aircraft to be acquired by 1992) and 5 of F-4EJ Phantoms; 3 squadrons of Mitsubishi F-1 close-support fighters; 1 squadron of RF-4E reconnaissance fighters; 8 E-2C Hawkeye AWACS aircraft; ECM flight with 2 YS-11Es; 3 squadrons of turbofan Kawasaki C-1 and turboprop C-130H Hercules and NAMC YS-11 transports. About 55 helicopters, mostly KV-107s (to be replaced with CH-47 Chinooks), and MU-2 twin-turboprop aircraft perform search, rescue and general duties. Training units use piston-engined Fuji T-3 basic trainers, Fuji T-1 jet intermediate trainers, T-33 jet trainers and supersonic Mitsubishi T-2 jet advanced trainers. The T-33s are being replaced with Kawasaki T-4s from 1989. Six surface-to-air missile groups (19 squadrons) are in service. Total strength (1990) about 309 combat aircraft and 46,000 officers and men.

INTERNATIONAL RELATIONS

Membership. Japan is a member of UN, the Colombo Plan and OECD.

ECONOMY

Planning. The 1988–92 Plan envisages an onward real growth rate of 3·75% and a nominal 4·75%. The real growth rate for 1990 was envisaged at 4% and the nominal 5·2%.

Budget. Ordinary revenue and expenditure for fiscal year ending 31 March 1990 balanced at 60,414,200m. yen.

Of the proposed revenue in 1989, 51,010,000m. was to come from taxes and stamps, 711,100m. from public bonds. Main items of expenditure: Social security, 10,894,700m.; public works, 6,197,400m.; local government, 13,368,800m.; education, 4,937,100m.; defence, 3,919,800m.

The outstanding national debt incurred by public bonds was estimated in March 1988 to be 154,113,500m. yen, including 500m. yen of Japan's foreign currency bonds.

The estimated 1989 budgets of the prefectures and other local authorities forecast a total revenue of 62,773,000m. yen, to be made up partly by local taxes and partly by government grants and local loans.

Currency. Coins of 1, 5, 10, 50, 100 and 500 *yen* are in circulation as well as notes of the Bank of Japan, of 1,000, 5,000 and 10,000 *yen*. Bank-notes for 500 *yen* are still in circulation but are gradually being replaced by coins. In March 1990, £1 = 245·50 *yen*; US$1 = 149·79 *yen*.

In Dec. 1988 the currency in circulation consisted of 32,318,300m. yen Bank of Japan notes and 2,861,400m. yen subsidiary coins.

Banking. The modern banking system dates from 1872. The Nippon Ginko (Bank of Japan) was founded in 1882. The Bank of Japan has undertaken to finance the Government and the banks; its function is similar to that of a Central Bank in other countries. The Bank undertakes the actual management of Treasury funds and foreign exchange control.

Gold bullion and cash holdings of the Bank of Japan at 31 Dec. 1988 stood at 427,000m. yen.

There were on 31 Dec. 1988, 13 city banks, 64 regional banks, 7 trust banks, 3 long-term credit banks, 68 Sogo banks (mutual savings and loan banks), 455 Shinkin banks (credit associations), 419 credit co-operatives, and 82 foreign banks. There are also various governmental financial institutions, including postal savings which amounted to 130,503,500m. yen in Sept. 1989. Total savings by individuals, including insurance and securities, stood at 674,346,000m. yen on 30 Sept. 1989, and about 61% of these savings were deposited in banks and the post-office.

Many foreign banks operate branches in Japan including: Bank of Indo-China, Hongkong & Shanghai Banking Corporation, Chartered Bank of India, Australia and China, Bank of India, Mercantile Bank of India, Bank of Korea, Bank of China, Algemene Bank Nederland NV, National Handelsbank NV, Bank of America, National City Bank of New York, Chase Manhattan Bank, Bangkok Bank and American Express Co.

Weights and Measures. The metric system was made obligatory by a law passed in March 1921, and the period of grace for its compulsory use ended on 1 April 1966.

ENERGY AND NATURAL RESOURCES

Electricity. In 1987 generating facilities were capable of an output of 179,107,000 kw.; electricity produced was 719,068m. kwh. Supply 100 and 200 volts; 50 or 60 Hz.

Oil and Gas. Output of crude petroleum, 1988, was 650,000 tonnes, almost entirely from oilfields on the island of Honshu, but 194,515,000 tonnes crude oil had to be imported. Output of natural gas, 1987, 2,168m. cu. metres.

Minerals. Ore production in tonnes, 1987, of chromite, 11,815; coal, 13,049,000; iron, 266,054; zinc, 165,675; manganese (1986), 5,905; copper, 23,817; lead, 27,870; tungsten, 420; silver, 281,020 kg.; gold, 8,590 kg.

Agriculture. Agricultural workers in 1988 were 6,086,000, including 581,000 subsidiary and seasonal workers; 8·4% (1985) of the labour force as opposed to 24·7% in 1962. The arable land area in 1988 was 5,317,000 hectares (5,796,000 in 1970). Division of ordinary fields to non-agricultural use accounted largely for this decrease. Rice cultivation accounted for 2,146,000 hectares in 1987. The area planted with industrial crops such as rapeseed, tobacco, tea, rush, etc., was 248,400 hectares in 1987.

In 1988 there were 4,659,000 power cultivators and tractors in use together with 1,408,000 power sprayers, 1,674,000 power dusters and 2,199,000 rice power planters.

Output of rice was 10,366,000 tonnes in 1983, 11,878,000 in 1984, 11,662,000 in 1985, 11,647,000 in 1986, 10,627,000 in 1987 and 9,935,000 in 1988.

Production in 1988 (in 1,000 tonnes) of barley was 399; wheat, 1,021; soybeans (1987), 287. Sweet potatoes, which in the past mitigated the effects of rice famines, have, in view of rice over-production, decreased from 4,955,000 tonnes in 1965 to 1,423,000 tons in 1987. Domestic sugar-beet and sugar-cane production accounted for only 33·6% of requirement in 1987. In 1987, 1,758,000 tonnes were imported, 36·5% of this being imported from Australia, 23·5% from South Africa, 21·7% from Thailand, 17·1% from Cuba.

Fruit production, 1987 (in 1,000 tonnes): Mandarins, 2,518; apples, 998; pears, 477; grapes, 308; peaches, 212; and persimmons, 290.

Livestock (1988): 4,667,000 cattle (including about 2m. milch cows), 22,000 horses, 11,725,000 pigs, 29,000 sheep, 41,000 goats, 345m. chickens. Milk (1987), 7·34m. tonnes.

Forestry. Forests and grasslands cover about 25m. hectares (nearly 70% of the whole land area), with an estimated timber stand of 2,862m. cu. metres in 1984. In 1986, 40,154,000 cu. metres were felled.

Fisheries. Before the War, Japanese catch represented one-half to two-thirds of the world's total fishing, in 1986 it was 13·1%. The catch in 1987 was 12·47m. tonnes, excluding whaling.

INDUSTRY AND TRADE

Industry. Japan's industrial equipment, 1986, numbered 746,734 plants of all sizes, employing 11,549,000 production workers.

Since 1920 there has been a shift from light to heavy industries. The production of electrical appliances and electronic machinery has made great strides: Television sets (1988: 13,388,000), radio sets (1987: 10,496,000), cameras (1988: 16,608,000), computing machines and automation equipment are produced in increasing quantities. The chemical industry ranks third in production value after machinery and metals (1986). Production, 1987, included (in tonnes): Sulphuric acid, 6,541,000; caustic soda, 3,131,000; ammonium sulphate, 1,784,000; calcium superphosphate, 499,000.

Output (1987), in 1,000 tonnes, of pig iron was 73,418; crude steel, 98,513; ordinary rolled steel, 78,825.

In 1987 paper production was 12,807,000 tonnes; paperboard, 9,730,000 tonnes.

Japan's textile industry before the War had 13m. cotton-yarn spindles. After the War she resumed with 2·78m. spindles; in 1964, 8·42m. spindles were operating. Output of cotton yarn, 1987, 464,000 tonnes, and of cotton cloth, 1,837m. sq. metres.

In wool, Japan aims at wool exports sufficient to pay for the imports of raw wool. Output, 1987, 123,000 tonnes of woollen yarns and 331m. sq. metres of woollen fabrics.

Output, 1987, of rayon woven fabrics, 573m. sq. metres; synthetic woven fabrics, 2,678m. sq. metres; silk fabrics, 100m. sq. metres.

Shipbuilding has been decreasing and in 1987, 5,639,000 gross tons were launched, of which 1,780,000 GRT were tankers.

Labour. Total labour force, 1988, was 60·11m., of which 4·3m. were in agriculture and forestry, 400,000 in fishing, 70,000 in mining, 5·6m. in construction, 14·54m. in manufacturing, 16m. in commerce and finance, 3·84m. in transport and other public utilities, 12·84m. in services (including the professions) and 1·94m. in government work.

In 1988 there were 12,227,000 workers organized in 72,792 unions. The largest federation is the 'Japanese Private Sector Trade Union Confederation' (Rengo) with 5,327,000 members. The 'General Council of Japanese Trade Unions' (Sohyo) had 3,977,000 members. Rengo was organized in Nov. 1987 by dissolving the 'Japanese Confederation of Labour' (Domei Kaigi) and the 'Federation of Independent Unions' (Churitsu Roren).

In 1988, 1·55m. (2·5%) were unemployed. In 1988, 174,000 working days were lost in industrial stoppages.

Commerce. Trade (in US$1m.)

	1982	*1983*	*1984*	*1985*	*1986*	*1987*	*1988*
Imports	138,831	126,393	136,503	129,539	126,408	149,515	187,354
Exports	131,931	146,927	170,114	175,638	209,151	229,221	264,917

Distribution of trade by countries (customs clearance basis) (US$1m.):

	Exports 1987	Exports 1988	Imports 1987	Imports 1988
Africa	4,757	4,806	3,694	3,944
Australia	5,146	6,680	7,869	10,285
Canada	5,611	6,424	6,073	8,308
China	8,256	9,476	7,401	9,859
Fed. Rep. of Germany	12,833	15,793	6,150	8,101
Hong Kong	8,872	11,706	1,561	2,109
Latin America	8,760	9,297	6,355	8,313
South-east Asia	52,982	67,109	38,627	47,802
Korea, Republic of	13,229	15,441	8,075	11,811
Taiwan	11,346	14,354	7,128	8,743
USSR	2,563	3,130	2,352	2,766
UK	8,400	10,632	3,057	4,193
USA	83,580	89,634	31,490	42,037

Principal items in 1988, with value in 1m. yen were:

Imports, c.i.f.		*Exports, f.o.b.*	
Mineral fuels	4,909,000	Machinery and transport equipment	25,235,000
Foodstuffs	3,735,000	Metals and metal products	2,786,000
Metal ores and scrap	1,087,000	Textile products	885,000
Machinery and transport equipment	3,414,000	Chemicals	1,788,000

Total trade between Japan and UK (British Department of Trade returns, in £1,000 sterling):

	1985	*1986*	*1987*	*1988*	*1989*
Imports to UK	4,117,024	4,932,497	5,463,116	6,509,137	7,108,441
Exports and re-exports from UK	1,012,436	1,193,933	1,495,111	1,742,747	2,259,823

Tourism. In 1988, 2,414,447 foreigners visited Japan, 457,620 of whom came from USA, 149,954 from UK. Japanese travelling abroad totalled 8,426,867 in 1988.

COMMUNICATIONS

Roads. The total length of roads (including urban and other local roads) was 1,098,931 km at 1 April 1987; the 'national' roads extended 46,523 km, of which 40,419 km were paved. Motor vehicles, at 31 Dec. 1988, numbered 51,364,000, including 30,776,000 passenger cars and 20,350,000 commercial vehicles.

Railways. The first railway was completed in 1872, between Tokyo and Yokohama (29 km). In April 1987 the Japanese National Railways was reorganized into 7 private companies, the Japanese Railways (JR) Group – 6 passenger companies and 1 freight company. Total length of railways, in March 1987, was 25,782 km, of which the national railways had 19,639 km (9,367 km electrified) and private railways, 6,143 km (5,006 km electrified). In 1987 the JR carried 7,356m. passengers (other private, 12,616m.) and 56m. tons of freight (other private, 27m.). An undersea tunnel linking Honshu with Hokkaido was opened to rail services in 1988.

Aviation. The principal airlines are Japan Airlines and All Nippon Airways. Japan Airlines, founded in 1953, operate international services from Tokyo to the USA, Europe, the Middle East and Southeast Asia, including flights to London over the North Pole and to Moscow by way of Siberia. In 1986 Japanese companies carried 46,365,000 passengers in domestic services and 7,200,000 passengers in international services.

Shipping. On 1 July 1988 the merchant fleet consisted of 7,939 vessels of 100 gross tons and over; total tonnage 29m. gross tons; there were 701 ships for passenger transport (1,236,000 gross tons), 2,612 cargo ships (1,405,000 gross tons) and 1,277 oil tankers (9,275,000 gross tons).

Coastguard. The 'Maritime Safety Agency' (Coastguard) consists of 11 regional MS headquarters, 65 MS offices, 52 MS stations, 14 air stations, 1 special rescue station, 9 district communications centres, 3 traffic advisory service centres, 4 hydrographic observatories and 122 navigation aids offices (with 5,136 navigation aids facilities) and controls 46 large patrol vessels, 47 medium patrol vessels, 19 small patrol vessels, 233 patrol craft, 21 hydrographic service vessels, 5 firefighting vessels, 10 firefighting boats, 66 guard and rescue boats and 79 navigation aids service supply vessels. Personnel in 1989 numbered 12,104 officers and men.

The Coastguard aviation service includes 26 fixed-wing aircraft and 41 helicopters.

Post and Broadcasting. The telephone services, operated by a private company (NTT) since April 1985. In 1987 there were 47,977,000 instruments.

On 31 March 1988, 99% of all households owned colour television sets.

Cinemas (1988). Cinemas numbered 2,005 with an annual attendance of 145m. (1960: 1,014m.).

Newspapers (1987). Daily newspapers numbered 124 with aggregate circulation of 70,194,000, including 4 major English-language newspapers.

JUSTICE, RELIGION, EDUCATION AND WELFARE

Justice. The Supreme Court is composed of the Chief Justice and 14 other judges. The Chief Justice is appointed by the Emperor, the other judges by the Cabinet. Every 10 years a justice must submit himself to the electorate. All justices and judges of the lower courts serve until they are 70 years of age.

Below the Supreme Court are 8 regional higher courts, district courts (*Chihosaibansho*) in each prefecture (4 in Hokkaido) and the local courts.

The Supreme Court is authorized to declare unconstitutional any act of the Legislature or the Executive which violates the Constitution.

Religion. There has normally been religious freedom, but Shinto (literally, The Way of the Gods) was given the status of *quasi*-state-religion in the 1930s; in 1945 the Allied Supreme Command ordered the Government to discontinue state support of Shinto. State subsidies have ceased for all religions, and all religious teachings are forbidden in public schools.

In Dec. 1987 Shintoism claimed 112,203,000 adherents, Buddhism 93,396,000; these figures obviously overlap. Christians numbered 1,422,000.

Education. Education is compulsory and free between the ages of 6 and 15. Almost all national and municipal institutions are co-educational. On 1 May 1988 there were 15,021 kindergartens with 99,331 teachers and 2,041,820 pupils; 24,030 elementary schools with 445,222 teachers and 9,872,520 pupils; 11,173 junior high schools with 288,641 teachers and 5,896,080 pupils; 5,336 senior high schools with 280,325 teachers and 5,533,393 pupils; 571 junior colleges with 19,264 teachers and 450,436 pupils.

There were also 839 special schools for handicapped children (42,161 teachers, 95,825 pupils).

Japan has 7 main state universities, formerly known as the Imperial Universities: Tokyo University (1877); Kyoto University (1897); Tohoku University, Sendai (1907); Kyushu University, Fukuoka (1910); Hokkaido University, Sapporo (1918); Osaka University (1931), and Nagoya University (1939). In addition, there are various other state and municipal as well as private universities of high standing, such as Keio (founded in 1859), Waseda, Rikkyo, Meiji universities, and several women's universities, among which Tokyo and Ochanomizu are most notable. There are 490 colleges and universities with (1 May 1988) 1,994,616 students and 118,513 teachers.

Social Welfare. Hospitals on 1 Oct. 1987 numbered 9,841 with 1,582,393 beds. Physicians at the end of 1986 numbered 191,346; dentists, 66,797.

There are in force various types of social security schemes, such as health insurance, unemployment insurance and old-age pensions. The total population come under one or more of these schemes.

In 1987 15,193,510 persons and 8,565,895 households received some form of regular public assistance, the total of which came to 1,493,120m. yen.

DIPLOMATIC REPRESENTATIVES

Of Japan in Great Britain (101 Piccadilly, London, W1V 9FN)
Ambassador: Kazuo Chiba.

Of Great Britain in Japan (1 Ichiban-cho, Chiyoda-ku, Tokyo 102)
Ambassador: Sir John Whitehead, KCMG, CVO.

Of Japan in the USA (2520 Massachusetts Ave., NW, Washington, D.C., 20008)
Ambassador: Ryohei Murata.

Of the USA in Japan (10–1, Akasaka 1-chome, Minato-Ku, Tokyo)
Ambassador: Michael Armacost.

Of Japan to the United Nations
Ambassadors: Hideo Kagami and Katsumi Sezaki.

Further Reading

Statistics Bureau of the Prime Minister's Office: *Statistical Year-Book* (from 1949).—*Statistical Abstract* (from 1950).—*Statistical Handbook of Japan 1977.—Monthly Bulletin* (from April 1950)

Economic Planning Agency: *Economic Survey* (annual), *Economic Statistics* (monthly), *Economic Indicators* (monthly)

Ministry of International Trade: *Foreign Trade of Japan* (annual)

Kodansha Encyclopedia of Japan. 9 vols. Tokyo, 1983

Japan Times Year Book. (I. Year Book of Japan. II. Who's Who in Japan. III. Business Directory of Japan.) Tokyo, first issue 1933

Labor in Tokyo. Tokyo Metropolitan Government, 1986

Treaty of Peace with Japan. (Cmd. 8392). HMSO, 1951; (Cmd. 8601). HMSO, 1952

Allen, G. C., *The Japanese Economy.* London, 1981

Baerwald, H. H., *Japan's Parliament.* CUP, 1974.—*Party Politics in Japan.* Boston, 1986

Burks, A. W., *Japan: Profile of an Industrial Power.* Boulder, 1981

Kenkyusha's *New Japanese–English [and English–Japanese] Dictionary.* 2 vols. New ed. Cambridge, Mass., and Berkeley, Cal., 1960

Miyazaki, S., *The Japanese Dictionary Explained in English.* Tokyo, 1950

Morishima, U. *Why has Japan 'Succeeded'?* CUP, 1984

Murata, K., *An Industrial Geography of Japan.* London, 1980

Nippon: A Chartered Survey of Japan. Tsuneta Yano Memorial Society. Tokyo, annual

Okita, S., *The Developing Economics of Japan: Lessons in Growth.* Univ. of Tokyo Press, 1983

Prindl, A., *Japanese Finance: Guide to Banking in Japan.* Chichester, 1981

Sansom, G. B., *A History of Japan.* 3 vols. London, 1958–64

Shulman, F. J., *Japan.* [Bibliography] Oxford and Santa Barbara, 1988

Tsoukalis, L., (ed.) *Japan and Western Europe.* London, 1982

Vogel, E. F., *Japan as Number One.* Harvard Univ. Press, 1979

Ward, P., *Japanese Capitals.* Cambridge, 1985

THE HASHEMITE KINGDOM OF JORDAN

Capital: Amman
Population: 2·97m. (1988)
GNP per capita: US$1,500 (1988)

Al Mamlaka al Urduniya al Hashemiyah

HISTORY. By a Treaty, signed in London on 22 March 1946, Britain recognized Transjordan as a sovereign independent state. On 25 May 1946 the Amir Abdullah assumed the title of King, and when the treaty was ratified on 17 June 1946 the name of the territory was changed to that of 'The Hashemite Kingdom of Jordan' in 1949. A new Anglo-Transjordan treaty was signed in Amman on 15 March 1948. The treaty was to remain in force for 20 years, but by mutual consent was terminated on 13 March 1957.

The Arab Federation between the Kingdoms of Iraq and Jordan, which was concluded on 14 Feb. 1958, lapsed after the revolution in Iraq of 14 July 1958, and was officially terminated by royal decree on 1 Aug. 1958.

Since the occupation of the West Bank in June 1967 by Israeli forces, that part of Palestine has not been administratively controlled by the Jordanian government.

On 31 July 1988, King Hussein announced that Jordan was to abandon its efforts to administer the Israeli-occupied West Bank and surrendered its claims to the territory to the Palestine Liberation Organization.

AREA AND POPULATION. The part of Palestine remaining to the Arabs under the armistice with Israel on 3 April 1949, with the exception of the Gaza strip, was in Dec. 1949 placed under Jordanian rule and formally incorporated in Jordan on 24 April 1950. For the frontier lines *see* map in THE STATESMAN'S YEAR-BOOK, 1951. In June 1967 this territory, known as the West Bank, was occupied by Israeli forces. For details *see* p. 734.

The area formerly administered by the Jordanian government, known as the East Bank, comprised 89,206 sq. km (34,443 sq. miles) following an exchange of territory with Saudi Arabia on 10 Aug. 1965. Its population at the 1979 Census was 2,132,997; latest estimate (1988) 2·97m. The area and population of the 8 governates were:

Muhafaza	*1986*	*Muhafaza*	*1986*
Asimah	1,160,000	Ma'an	97,500
Balqa	193,800	Mafraq	98,600
Irbid	680,200	Tafilah	41,400
Karak	120,100	Zarqa	404,500

The largest towns with suburbs, with estimated population, 1986: Amman, the capital, 1,160,000; Irbid, 680,200; Zarqa, 404,500;.

In 1986 registered births numbered 112,451; deaths, 8,853; marriages, 19,397; divorces (1984), 2,652.

CLIMATE. Predominantly a Mediterranean climate, with hot dry summers and cool wet winters, but in hilly parts summers are cooler and winters colder. Those areas below sea-level are very hot in summer and warm in winter. Eastern parts have a desert climate. Amman. Jan. 46°F (7·5°C), July 77°F (24·9°C). Annual rainfall 12" (290 mm). Aqaba. Jan. 61°F (16°C), July 89°F (31·5°C). Annual rainfall 1·5" (35 mm).

KING. The Kingdom is a constitutional monarchy headed by HM King **Hussein**, GCVO, eldest son of King Talal, who, being incapacitated by mental illness, was deposed by Parliament on 11 Aug. 1952 and died 8 July 1972. The King was born 14 Nov. 1935, and married Princess Dina Abdul Hamid on 19 April 1955 (divorced 1957), Toni Avril Gardiner (Muna al Hussein) on 25 May 1961 (divorced 1972), Alia Toukan on 26 Dec. 1972 (died in air crash 1977) and Elizabeth Halaby on 15 June 1978. *Offspring:* Princess Alia, born 13 Feb. 1956; Prince Abdulla, born 30 Jan. 1962; Prince Faisal, born 11 Oct. 1963; Princesses Zein and Aisha, born 23 April 1968; Princess Haya, born 3 May 1974; Prince Ali, born 23 Dec. 1975; Prince Hamzah, born 1 April 1980; Prince Hashem, born 10 June 1981; Princess Iman, born 4 April 1983; Princess Raya, born 9 Feb. 1986. *Crown Prince* (appointed 1 April 1965): Prince Hassan, younger brother of the King.

CONSTITUTION AND GOVERNMENT. The Constitution passed on 7 Nov. 1951 provides that the Cabinet is responsible to Parliament.

The legislature consists of a lower house of 80 members elected by universal suffrage and a senate of 30 members nominated by the King.

On 5 Feb. 1976 both Houses of Parliament approved amendments to the Constitution by which the King was empowered to postpone calling elections until further notice. The lower house was dissolved. This step was taken because no elections could be held in the West Bank which has been under Israeli occupation since June 1967.

Parliament was reconvened on 9 Jan. 1984. By-elections were held in March 1984 and 6 members were nominated for the West Bank bringing Parliament to 60 members. Women voted for the first time in 1984. Elections were held on 8 Nov. 1989; the Moslem Brotherhood won 20 of the 80 seats.

Prime Minister and Defence: Modar Badran.

National flag: Three horizontal stripes of black, white, green, with a red triangle based on the hoist, bearing a white 7-pointed star.

The official language of the country is Arabic.

DEFENCE

Army. The Army is organized in 2 armoured and 2 mechanical infantry divisions, 1 Royal Guard and 1 special forces brigade, and 16 artillery battalions. Equipment includes some 1,130 main battle tanks. Total strength (1990) 74,000 men.

Navy. The Jordan Coastal Guard numbered (1989) 250 and operates 6 small patrol boats, with 3 larger craft on order.

Air Force. The Air Force has 2 interceptor and 3 ground attack squadrons equipped respectively with Mirage F1 and F-5E Tiger II fighters, and 2-seat F-5Fs, plus an OCU equipped with F-5A fighters and 2-seat F-5Bs. Two anti-armour squadrons have Bell AH-1S Huey Cobra helicopters. There are 6 C-130B/H Hercules and 2 CASA Aviocar turboprop transports, S-70 Blackhawk, S-76, Gazelle, Alouette III and Hughes 500D helicopters, piston-engined Bulldog basic trainers and CASA Aviojet jet trainers. Hawk surface-to-air missiles equip 14 batteries. Strength (1990) about 11,000 officers and men.

INTERNATIONAL RELATIONS

Membership. Jordan is a member of the UN and the Arab League.

ECONOMY

Planning. A 5-year plan (1986–90) aimed at improving agriculture and the development of water resources.

Budget. The budget estimates for the year 1989 provide for revenue of JD.907m. and expenditure of JD.1,106m. which included 209m. for defence. External public debt JD.1,868m.

Currency. The Jordan *dinar*, divided into 1,000 *fils*. The following bank-notes and coins are in circulation: 10, 5 dinars, 1 dinar, 500 fils (notes), 250, 100, 50, 25, 20 fils (cupronickel), 10, 5, 1 fils (bronze). In March 1990, £1 = JD.1·09,170; US$ = JD.0·6,676.

Banking. The Central Bank of Jordan was established in 1964. In 1986 there were 9 local commercial banks including Arab Bank (the largest, with a capital of JD.22m.), 8 foreign commercial banks including Grindlays Bank and 6 foreign banks with representative offices. In 1985 there were 2 investment banks, 5 finance companies, 3 Islamic institutions and 3 real estated-linked savings and loan associations.

Assets and liabilities of the Jordanian banking system (including the Central Bank, commercial banks and the Housing Bank) totalled JD.2,404·34m. in 1984.

Weights and Measures. The metric system is in force.

ENERGY AND NATURAL RESOURCES

Electricity. Production (1986) 2,955m. kwh. Supply 220 volts; 50 Hz.

Oil. Oil was discovered in 1982 at Azraq, 70 km east of Amman and 7 new wells were under development in 1985. Deposits of oil shale, estimated at 10,000m. tonnes, have been discovered at Lajjun.

Minerals. Phosphates production in 1987 was 6·85m. tonnes. Potash is found in the Dead Sea. Reserves, over 800m. tonnes. A potash plant built on the southeast shore to extract compounds by solar evaporation produced 1·2m. tonnes in 1987. Cement production (1987), 2·3m. tonnes.

Agriculture. The country east of the Hejaz Railway line is largely desert; north-western Jordan is potentially of agricultural value and an integrated Jordan Valley project began in 1973. The agricultural cropping pattern for irrigated vegetable cultivation was introduced in 1984 to regulate production and diversify the crops being cultivated. In 1987 Jordan was self-sufficient in the production of potatoes and onions. In 1986 the government began to lease state-owned land in the semi-arid southern regions for agricultural development by private investors, mostly for wheat and barley. Jordan is self-sufficient in poultry meat. The main crops are tomatoes and other vegetables, citrus fruit, wheat and olives.

Production in 1988 included (in tonnes): Tomatoes, 200,000; olives, 30,000; citrus fruit, 113,000; wheat, 80,000.

Livestock (1988): 1·22m. sheep; 460,000 goats; 29,000 cattle; 14,000 camels.

INDUSTRY AND TRADE

Industry. Production (1987, in tonnes): Phosphates, 6,841,000; petroleum products, 2,229,000; cement, 2,472,000; iron, 219,000; fertilizer, 1,656,000.

Other industries include cigarettes, cosmetics, textiles, shoes, batteries, plastic products, leather tanning, pharmaceutical products, iron pipes, detergents, aluminium and ceramics. Some 50% of industry is based in Amman.

Commerce. Imports in 1987 were valued at JD.915·54m. and exports and re-exports at JD.315·7m. Total remittances from Jordanians working abroad reached US$1,187·5m. in 1984.

Major exports in 1987 (in JD.1m.) included phosphates, 61; chemicals, 69·93; food and live animals, 248·77; manufactured goods, 37·34. Major imports included machinery and transport equipment, 186·29; crude oil, 118·59.

Exports in 1987 (in JD.1m.) were mainly to Iraq, 59·87; Saudi Arabia, 26·2 and India, 22. Imports were mainly from Saudi Arabia, 76·76 and the USA, 93·39.

Total trade between Jordan and UK (British Department of Trade returns, in £1,000 sterling):

	1985	*1986*	*1987*	*1988*	*1989*
Imports to UK	86,077	49,766	29,285	21,310	16,462
Exports and re-exports from UK	154,270	130,385	188,998	183,555	110,684

Tourism. In 1987 there were 1·9m. foreign visitors spending US$600m.

COMMUNICATIONS

Roads. Total length of public highways, 4,095 km. Motor vehicles in 1980 included 73,078 private passenger cars, 11,207 taxis, 1,415 buses, 29,517 goods vehicles, 4,888 motor cycles.

Railways. The 1,050 mm gauge Hejaz Jordan and Aqaba Railway runs from the Syrian border at Nassib to Ma'an and Naqb Ishtar and Aqaba Port (total, 618 km). In 1986 the railways carried 31,304 passengers and 2,789,524 tons of freight.

Aviation. The Queen Alia International airport, at Zizya, 30 km south of Amman was inaugurated in 1983. There are other international airports at Amman and Aqaba. Jordan is served by over 20 international airlines.

Shipping (1980). The port of Aqaba handled 6,598,591 tons of cargo. JD.65m. was spent between 1980–85 on developing facilities and US$1,000m. is to be provided under the 1986–90 plan on further developments including a special oil terminal and 4 new wharves.

Post and Broadcasting. In 1982 there were 791 post offices and (1987) 189,502 telephones. There were 250,000 TV receivers and 1·1m. radios in 1988.

Newspapers (1988). There were 4 daily (including 1 in English) and 3 weekly papers, with a total circulation (1987) of 188,000.

RELIGION, EDUCATION AND WELFARE

Religion. About 80% of the population are Sunni Moslems.

Education (1987). There were 411 pre-primary schools with 1,461 teachers and 31,827 pupils; 1,294 elementary schools with 18,448 teachers and 542,519 pupils; 1,124 preparatory schools with 10,495 teachers and 214,743 pupils; 510 secondary schools with 7,023 teachers and 98,786 pupils and 27 vocational educational schools with 2,180 teachers and 31,770 pupils. The University of Jordan, inaugurated on 15 Dec. 1962 had in 1987, 12,672 students. The Yarmouk University (Irbid) was inaugurated in 1976 with (1987) 11,603 students. The Mu'tah University was inaugurated in 1981 with (1987) 1,349 students. The Jordan University of Science and Technology was inaugurated in 1987 with 2,815 students.

Health (1987). There were 4,500 physicians, 1,041 dentists and 56 hospitals with 5,672 beds.

DIPLOMATIC REPRESENTATIVES

Of Jordan in Great Britain (6 Upper Phillimore Gdns., London, W8 7HB)
Ambassador: Dr Albert Butros.

Of Great Britain in Jordan (Abdoun, Amman)
Ambassador: Anthony Reeve, CMG.

Of Jordan in the USA (3504 International Dr., NW, Washington, D.C., 20008)
Ambassador: Hussein Hamami.

Of the USA in Jordan (Jebel Amman, Amman)
Ambassador: Roscoe S. Suddarth.

Of Jordan to the United Nations
Ambassador: Abdullah Salah.

Further Reading

The Department of Statistics, Ministry of National Economy, publishes a *Statistical Yearbook* (in Arabic and English), latest issue 1968, and a *Statistical Guide,* latest issue

1965.—*External Trade Statistics*, 1968.—*National Accounts and Input-Output Analysis, 1959–65*, 1967
The Constitution of the Hashemite Kingdom of Jordan. Amman, 1952
Gubser, P., *Jordan*. Boulder, 1982
Seccombe, I., *Jordan*. [Bibliography] Oxford and Santa Barbara, 1984
Seton, C. R. W., *Legislation of Transjordan, 1918-30*. London, 1931. [Continued by the Government of Jordan as an annual publication: *Jordan Legislation*. Amman, 1932 ff.]
Toni, Y. T. and Mousa, S., *Jordan: Land and People*. Amman, 1973
Wilson, M. C., *King Abdullah, Britain and the making of Jordan*. CUP, 1987

KENYA

Capital: Nairobi
Population: 22·8m. (1988)
GNP per capita: US$360 (1988)

Jamhuri ya Kenya

HISTORY. Until Kenya became independent on 12 Dec. 1963, it consisted of the colony and the protectorate. The protectorate comprised the mainland dominions of the Sultan of Zanzibar, viz., a coastal strip of territory 10 miles wide, to the northern branch of the Tana River; also Mau, Kipini and the Island of Lamu, and all adjacent islands between the rivers Umba and Tana. The Sultan on 8 Oct. 1963 ceded the coastal strip to Kenya with effect from 12 Dec. 1963.

The colony and protectorate, formerly known as the East African Protectorate were, on 1 April 1905, transferred from the Foreign Office to the Colonial Office and in Nov. 1906 the protectorate was placed under the control of a governor and C.-in-C. and (except the Sultan of Zanzibar's dominions) was annexed to the Crown as from 23 July 1920 under the name of the Colony of Kenya, thus becoming a Crown Colony.

The territories on the coast became the Kenya Protectorate.

A Treaty was signed (15 July 1924) with Italy under which Great Britain ceded to Italy the Juba River and a strip from 50 to 100 miles wide on the British side of the river. Cession took place on 29 June 1925. The northern boundary is defined by an agreement with Ethiopia in 1947. A Constitution conferring internal self-government was brought into force on 1 June 1963, and full independence was achieved on 12 Dec. 1963. On 12 Dec. 1964 Kenya became a republic.

AREA AND POPULATION. Kenya is bounded by Sudan and Ethiopia in the north, Uganda in the west, Tanzania in the south and the Somali Republic and the Indian ocean in the east. The total area is 224,960 sq. miles (582,600 sq. km), of which 219,790 sq. miles is land area. In the 1979 census, the population was 15,327,061, of which 15,101,540 were Africans, 78,600 Asians, 39,900 Europeans, 39,140 Arabs. Estimate (1988) 22·8m.

The land areas, populations and capitals of the provinces are:

Province	*Sq. km*	*Census 1979*	*Estimate 1987*	*Capital*	*Census 1979*
Rift Valley	171,108	3,240,402	4,702,400	Nakuru	92,851
Eastern	155,760	2,719,851	3,864,700	Embu	15,986
Nyanza	12,526	2,643,956	3,892,600	Kisumu	152,643
Central	13,173	2,345,833	3,284,800	Nyeri	35,753
Coast	83,040	1,342,794	1,904,100	Mombasa	425,634 [1]
Western	8,223	1,832,663	2,535,900	Kakamega	32,025
Nairobi District	684	827,775	1,288,700	Nairobi	1,103,554 [1]
North-Eastern	126,902	373,787	554,000	Garissa	14,076

[1] Estimate, 1984.

Other towns (1979): Machakos (84,320), Meru (70,439), Eldoret (59,503), Thika (41,324).

Kiswahili is the official language, but 21% speak Kikuyu as their mother tongue, 14% Luhya, 13% Luo, 11% Kamba, 11% Kalenjin, 6% Gusii, 5% Meru and 5% Mijikenda. English is spoken in commercial centres.

CLIMATE. The climate is tropical, with wet and dry seasons, but considerable differences in altitude make for varied conditions between the hot, coastal lowlands and the plateau, where temperatures are very much cooler. Heaviest rains occur in April and May, but in some parts there is a second wet season in Nov. and Dec. Nairobi. Jan. 65°F (18·3°C), July 60°F (15·6°C). Annual rainfall 39" (958 mm). Mombasa. Jan. 81°F (27·2°C), July 76°F (24·4°C). Annual rainfall 47" (1,201 mm).

CONSTITUTION AND GOVERNMENT. There is a unicameral National

Assembly of 203 members, comprising 188 elected by universal suffrage for a 5-year term, 12 members appointed by the President, and the Speaker and Attorney-General ex-officio. The President is also directly elected for 5 years; he appoints a Vice-President and other Ministers to a Cabinet over which he presides. The sole legal political party is the Kenya African National Union (KANU).

Elections to the National Assembly took place by secret ballot on 21 March 1988. Only 123 seats were contested, the rest were unopposed.

President: Daniel T. arap Moi (elected 1978, re-elected 1983 and 1988).
Vice-President and Minister of Finance: George Saitoti.

National flag: Three horizontal stripes of black, red, green, with the red edged in white; bearing in the centre an African shield in black and white with 2 crossed spears behind.

Administration. The country is divided into the Nairobi Area and 7 provinces and there are 40 districts.

DEFENCE

Army. The Army consists of 1 armoured, 1 engineer and 2 infantry brigades; 2 engineer, 1 air cavalry, airborne, 1 anti-aircraft and 5 infantry batallions. There are 30 Hughes Defender helicopters, of which 15 are armed with TOW missiles and 8 Hughes 500 ME helicopters. Total strength (1989) 19,000.

Navy. The Navy, based in Mombasa, in 1989 consisted of 2, 56-metre fast missile craft, 4 smaller missile craft, and 2 inshore patrol craft, all built in Britain, and 1 tug. Personnel in 1989 totalled 1,000.

The Marine police and Customs operate an additional 15 patrol boats.

Air Force. An air force, formed 1 June 1964, was built up with RAF assistance and is under Army command. Equipment includes 11 F-5E/F-5F supersonic combat aircraft/trainers, 12 Hawk and 5 BAC 167 Strikemaster light jet attack/trainers, 8 twin-turboprop Buffaloes for transport, air ambulance, anti-locust spraying and security duties, 7 Skyservant light twins, 12 Bulldog piston-engined primary trainers and Puma and Gazelle helicopters. Personnel (1990) 3,000.

INTERNATIONAL RELATIONS

Membership. Kenya is a member of UN, the Commonwealth, OAU and is an ACP state of EEC.

ECONOMY

Planning. The sixth national development plan (1989-93) aims to expand the economy and create 2m. jobs.

Budget. Ordinary revenue and expenditure for 1988–89: Revenue, KSh.36,298m.; expenditure, KSh.55,504m.

Currency. The monetary unit is the Kenya *Shilling* divided into 100 *cents*; 20 shillings = K£1. Notes of the Central Bank of Kenya are circulated in denominations of KSh.5, 10, 20, 50, 100, 200 and 500 and coins in denominations of 5, 10 and 50 cents and KSh.1 and 5. Currency in circulation at Dec. 1987: Notes, K£425,080,000; coins, K£13·7m. In March 1990, £1 = 36·99 *Shilling*; US$1 = 22·57 *Shilling*.

Banking. Banks operating in Kenya: The National & Grindlays Bank International, Ltd; the Standard Bank, Ltd; Barclays Bank of Kenya Ltd; Algemene Bank Nederland NV; Bank of India, Ltd; Bank of Baroda, Ltd; Habib Bank (Overseas), Ltd; Commercial Bank of Africa, Ltd; Citibank; The Co-operative Bank of Kenya, Ltd; National Bank of Kenya, Ltd; Agricultural Finance Corporation; The Kenya Commercial Bank; The Central Bank of Kenya. In Jan. 1985 there were 43 non-bank finance institutions.

The Kenya Post Office Savings Bank, a state savings bank established in 1978, had 1,250,000 ordinary savings accounts with total deposits of KSh.750m. at 31 Dec. 1984.

ENERGY AND NATURAL RESOURCES

Electricity. Installed generating capacity was 575 mw in 1987; two-thirds was provided by hydropower from power stations on the Tana river, 30% by oil-fired power stations and the rest by geothermal power. Production (1987) 2,454m. kwh. Supply 220 volts; 50 Hz.

Minerals. Production, 1987 (in 1,000 tonnes): Soda ash, 228; fluorspar ore, 47; salt, 72. Other minerals included gold, raw soda, lime and limestone, diatomite, garnets and vermiculite.

Agriculture. As agriculture is possible from sea-level to altitudes of over 9,000 ft, tropical, sub-tropical and temperate crops can be grown and mixed farming can be advocated. Four-fifths of the country is range-land which produces mainly livestock products and wild game which constitutes the major attraction of the country's tourist industry.

The main areas of crop production are the Central, Rift Valley, Western and Nyanza Provinces and parts of Eastern and Coastal Provinces. Coffee, tea, sisal, pyrethrum, maize and wheat are crops of major importance in the Highlands, while coconuts, cashew nuts, cotton, sugar, sisal and maize are the principal crops grown at the lower altitudes. Production, 1988 (in 1,000 tonnes), of principal food crops: Maize, 2,685; wheat, 240; rice, 26; barley, 20; millet, 60; sorghum, 120; potatoes, 740; sweet potatoes, 380; cassava, 560; sugar-cane, 4,730. Main cash crops (1988): Tobacco, 8; coffee, 125; tea, 164; vegetables, 479; fruit, 730; flowers (1987), 37; seed cotton, 24; pyrethrums (1987), 93; sisal, 40.

Livestock (1988): Cattle, 9·8m.; sheep, 7·2m.; goats, 8·5m.; pigs, 102,000; poultry, 23m.

Forestry. The total area of gazetted forest reserves in Kenya amounts to 16,800 sq. km, of which the greater part is situated between 6,000 and 11,000 ft above sea-level, mostly on Mount Kenya, the Aberdares, Mount Elgon, Tinderet, Londiani, Mau watershed, Elgeyo and Charangani ranges. These forests may be divided into coniferous, broad-leaved or hardwood and bamboo forests. The upper parts of these forests are mainly bamboo, which occurs mostly between altitudes of 8,000 and 10,000 ft and occupies some 10% of the high-altitude forests.

Fisheries. Landings in 1987 were 118,216 tonnes of fresh water fish, 6,096 tonnes of marine fish, 299 tonnes of crustaceans and 39 tonnes of other marine products; total value K£18,849,000.

INDUSTRY AND TRADE

Industry. In 1986 industry accounted for some 13% of GDP and employed about one-fifth of the wage-earning labour force. The main activities were textiles, chemicals, vehicle assembly and transport equipment, leather and footwear, printing and publishing, food and tobacco processing. An important sub-sector was the refining of crude petroleum at Mombasa.

Commerce. Total domestic exports (1987, provisional) K£753m.; imports K£1,431m.

Chief imports in 1987 were petroleum and petroleum products (19·7% of total), industrial supplies (32·8%), machinery and other capital equipment (22·4%), food and drink (6·9%) and transport equipment (13·3%). Chief exports were coffee (26%), tea (22%) and petroleum products (12·6%). By 1986 fresh vegetables, fruits and flowers became the fourth largest foreign exchange earner.

Imports in 1987 were mainly from the UK (17%), Japan (10·9%), Federal Republic of Germany (8%) and USA (7·1%). Exports were mainly to the UK (16·8%), Federal Republic of Germany (9·6%), Uganda (8·9%), USA (5·4%) and Pakistan (15·7%).

Total trade between Kenya and UK (British Department of Trade returns, in £1,000 sterling):

	1985	*1986*	*1987*	*1988*	*1989*
Imports to UK	185,622	163,745	129,236	142,455	154,313
Exports and re-exports from UK	160,651	170,671	199,059	202,094	208,464

Tourism. In 1987, about 662,100 tourists visited Kenya and spent KSh.5,840m.

COMMUNICATIONS

Roads. In 1987 there were 6,600 km of bitumen surfaced roads and 45,000 km of gravel-surfaced roads.

Railways. On 11 Feb. 1977 the independent Kenya Railways Corporation was formed following break-up of the East African Railways administration. The network totals 2,654 km of metre-gauge. In 1987, the railways carried 3·8m. passengers and 3m. tonnes of freight.

Aviation. Total number of passengers handled at the 3 main airports (1984) was 2,058,000. Jomo Kenyatta Airport, Nairobi, handles nearly 30 international airlines as well as Kenya Airways.

Shipping. A national shipping service is planned (1984) to be based in Mombasa, the Kenyan main port at Kilindini on the Indian Ocean. The port handles cargo freight both for Kenya as well as for the neighbouring East African states.

Post and Broadcasting. The Voice of Kenya operates 2 national services (Swahili–English) from Nairobi and regional services in Kisumu, Nairobi and Mombasa. The television service provides programmes mainly in English and Swahili. Telephones (1983) 216,674; television sets (1985) 250,000; radios (1985) 3·4m.

JUSTICE, RELIGION, EDUCATION AND WELFARE

Justice. The courts of Justice comprises the court of Appeal, the High Court and a large number of subsidiary courts.

The court of Appeal is the final Apellant court in the country and is based in Nairobi. It comprises of 7 Judges of Appeal. In the course of its Appellate duties the court of Appeal visits Mombasa, Kisumu, Nakuru and Nyeri.

The High court with full jurisdiction in both civil and criminal matters comprises of a total of 28 puisne Judges. Puisne Judges sit in Nairobi (16), Mombasa (2), Nakuru, Kisumu, Nyeri, Eldoret Meru and Kisii (1 each).

The Magistracy consists of approximately 300 magistrates of various cadres based in all provincial, district and some divisional centres. In addition to the above there are the Kadhi courts established in areas of concentrated Muslim populations: Mombasa, Nairobi, Malindi, Lamu, Garissa, Kisumu and Marsabit. They exercise limited jurisdiction in matters governed by Islamic Law.

Religion. In 1987, the Roman Catholic Church had nearly 6m. adherents (27% of the population), Protestants 4m. (19%) and other Christian churches over 6m. (27%), while Islam had 1·3m. (6%), traditional tribal religions 4m. (19%) and others 400,000 (2%).

Education. *Primary* (1987). 13,849 primary schools with 5·03m. pupils and 149,151 teachers.

Secondary (1987). There were 2,592 secondary schools with a total enrolment of 522,261 and 24,251 teachers.

Technical (1987). There were 17 Institutes of Science and Technology with 4,200 students and 433 teachers. Kenya, Mombasa and Eldoret Polytechnics and Jomo Kenyatta College of Agriculture and Technology had 7,100 students in 1987.

Teacher training (1987). 17,733 students were training as teachers in 22 colleges with 1,348 lecturers.

Higher Education. In 1987–88 there were 4 public universities and enrolments were: University of Nairobi (inaugurated 1970), 10,841; Moi University (opened 1985), 970; Kenyatta University, 5,135; Egerton University, 1,935 (592 undergraduates and 1,343 diploma students).

Health. In 1987 beds and cots in hospitals (including mission hospitals) totalled 31,356. 2,071 hospitals and health centres, including sub-centres and dispensaries, were in operation. Free medical service for all children and adult out-patients was launched in 1965.

DIPLOMATIC REPRESENTATIVES

Of Kenya in Great Britain (45 Portland Pl., London, W1)
High Commissioner: Dr Sally J. Kosgei.

Of Great Britain in Kenya (Bruce Hse., Standard St., Nairobi)
High Commissioner: Sir John Johnson, KCMG.

Of Kenya in the USA (2249 R. St., NW, Washington, D.C., 20008)
Ambassador: Denis D. Afande.

Of the USA in Kenya (Moi/Haile Selassie Ave., Nairobi)
Ambassador: Smith Hempstone, Jr.

Of Kenya to the United Nations
Ambassador: M. Okeyo.

Further Reading

Kenya Development Plan, 1984–88. Nairobi, 1984
Kenya Economic Survey, 1988. Nairobi, 1988
Statistical Abstract. Government Printer, Nairobi, 1982
Standard English–Swahili Dictionary. Ed. Inter-territorial Language Committee of East Africa. 2 vols. London, 1939
Who's Who in Kenya 1982–1983. London, 1983
Arnold, G., *Kenyatta and the Politics of Kenya.* London, 1974.—*Modern Kenya.* London, 1982
Bigsten, A., *Education and Income Distribution in Kenya.* Brookfield, Vermont, 1984
Collison, R. L., *Kenya.* [Bibliography] London and Santa Barbara, 1982
Harbeson, J. W., *Nation-Building in Kenya: The Role of Land Reform.* Northwestern Univ. Press, 1973
Hazlewood, A., *The Economy of Kenya: The Kenyatta Era.* OUP, 1980
Langdon, S. W., *Multinational Corporations in the Political Economy of Kenya.* London, 1981
Miller, N. N., *Kenya, the Quest for Prosperity.* Boulder and London, 1984
Tomkinson, M., *Kenya: A Holiday Guide.* 5th ed. London and Hammamet, 1981

KIRIBATI

Capital: Tarawa
Population: 66,250 (1987)
GNP per capita: US$650 (1988)

HISTORY. The Gilbert and Ellice Islands were proclaimed a protectorate in 1892 and annexed (at the request of the native governments) as the Gilbert and Ellice Islands Colony on 10 Nov. 1915 (effective on 12 Jan. 1916). On 1 Oct. 1975 the former Ellice Islands severed its constitutional links with the Gilbert Islands and took a new name Tuvalu.

Internal self-government was obtained on 1 Nov. 1976 and independence achieved on 12 July 1979 as the Republic of Kiribati.

AREA AND POPULATION. Kiribati (pronounced Kiribass) consists of 3 groups of coral atolls and one isolated volcanic island, spread over a large expanse of the Central Pacific with a total land area of 717·1 sq. km (276·9 sq. miles). It comprises Banaba or Ocean Island (5 sq. km), the 16 Gilbert Islands (295 sq. km), the 8 Phœnix Islands (55 sq. km), and 8 of the 11 Line Islands (329 sq. km), the other 3 Line Islands (Jarvis, Palmyra and Kingman Reef) being uninhabited dependencies of the US. Population, 1985 census, 63,848; estimate (1987) 66,250. It was announced in 1988 that 4,700 people are to be resettled on Teraina and Tabuaeran atolls because the main island group is overcrowded. Banaba, all 16 Gilbert Islands, and 3 atolls in the Line Islands (Teraina, Tabuaeran and Kiritimati—formerly Washington, Fanning and Christmas Islands respectively) are inhabited; their populations in 1985 (census) were as follows:

Banaba (Ocean Is.)	189	Abemama	2,966	Onotoa	1,927
Makin	1,777	Kuria	1,052	Tamana	1,348
Butaritari	3,622	Aranuki	984	Arorae	1,470
Marakei	2,693	Nonouti	2,930	Phœnix Island	24
Abaiang	4,386	Tabiteuea	4,493	Teraina	416
Tarawa	24,598	Beru	2,702	Tabuaeran	445
Maiana	2,141	Nikunau	2,061	Kiritimati	1,737

The remaining 13 atolls have no permanent population; the 8 Phœnix Islands comprise Birnie, Rawaki (formerly Phœnix), Enderbury, Kanton (or Abariringa), Manra (formerly Sydney), Orona (formerly Hull), McKean and Nikumaroro (formerly Gardner), while the others are Malden and Starbuck in the Central Line Islands and Caroline, Flint and Vostok in the Southern Line Islands. The population is almost entirely Micronesian.

CLIMATE. The Line Islands, Phœnix Islands and Banaba have a maritime equatorial climate, but the islands further north and south are tropical. Annual and daily ranges of temperature are small and mean annual rainfall ranges from 50" (1,250 mm) near the equator to 120" (3,000 mm) in the north. Tarawa. Jan. 83°F (28·3°C), July 82°F (27·8°C). Annual rainfall 79" (1,977 mm).

CONSTITUTION AND GOVERNMENT. Under the independence Constitution the republic has a unicameral legislature, comprising 36 members elected from 20 constituencies for a 4-year term. The *Beretitenti* (President) is both Head of State and of Government.

In Feb. 1989 the government was composed as follows:

President and Foreign Affairs: Ieremia Tabai, GCMG.

Vice-President, Finance and Economic Planning: Teatao Teannaki. *Home Affairs and Decentralization:* Babera Kirata, OBE. *Trade, Industry and Labour:* Raion Bataroma. *Health and Family Planning:* Rotaria Ataia. *Natural Resource Development:* Taomati Iuta, OBE. *Education:* Ataraoti Bwebwenibure. *Communications:* Uera Rabaua. *Minister for the Line and Phœnix Group of Islands:* Tekinaiti Kaiteie. *Works and Energy:* Ieruru Karotu. *Attorney-General:* Michael Takabwebwe.

National flag: Red, with blue and white wavy lines in base, and in the centre a gold rising sun and a flying frigate bird.

National anthem: Teirake Kain Kiribati.

INTERNATIONAL RELATIONS

Membership. Kiribati is a member of the Commonwealth, South Pacific Forum and is an ACP state of the EEC.

ECONOMY

Budget. Budget estimates for 1989 show revenue, $A20,648,000; principal items: Fishing licences, $A3·87m.; customs duties, $A5m.; direct taxation, $A2·5m. Expenditure amounted to $A20,648,000.

Currency. The currency in use is the Australian *dollar*.

ENERGY AND NATURAL RESOURCES

Electricity. Electric power production (1986) was 8m. kwh.

Minerals. Phosphate production was discontinued in 1979.

Agriculture. Land under agriculture and permanant cultivation, 50·7%; forest, 2·8%; other, 46·5%. The land is basically coral reefs upon which coral sand has built up, and then been enriched by humus from rotting vegetation and flotsam which has drifted ashore. The principal tree is the coconut, which grows prolifically on all the islands except some of the Phœnix Islands. Other food-bearing trees are the pandanus palm and the breadfruit. As the amount of soil is negligible, the only vegetable which grows in any quantity is a coarse calladium (alocasia) with the local name 'babai', which is cultivated most laboriously in deep pits. Pigs and fowls are kept throughout Kiribati.

Copra production is mainly in the hands of the individual landowner, who collects the coconut products from the trees on his own land. Production (1988) 12,000 tonnes; coconuts, 90,000 tonnes.

Livestock (1988): Pigs, 10,000; poultry (1982), 163,000.

Fisheries. Tuna fishing is an important industry and licenses have been granted to USSR fleets.

INDUSTRY AND TRADE

Commerce. The principal imports (1988, in A$1m.) are: Machinery and transport equipment, 9·3; food, 2·5; manufactured goods, 3·4; fuels, 1·23. The value of exports for 1988 amounted to $A6·7m. Exports are almost exclusively copra.

Total trade between Kiribati and UK (British Department of Trade returns, in £1,000 sterling):

	1986	*1987*	*1988*	*1989*
Imports to UK	4	8	128	26
Exports and re-exports from UK	179	301	522	378

Tourism. Tourism is in the early stages of development and in 1984 total income from the industry was US$1·4m.

COMMUNICATIONS

Roads. There were (1988) 640 km of roads, of which 483 km suitable for vehicles.

Shipping. The main port is at Betio (Tarawa). Other ports of entry are Christmas Island and Banaba. In 1988, 60 vessels were handled at Betio.

Aviation. Air Tungaru is the national carrier. It operates services from Tarawa to the other 15 outer Islands in the Gilbertese Group, services varying between one and four flights each week. There is a charter service weekly to Christmas Island, in the Line Islands, which continues to Honolulu. A fortnightly service operates to Funafuti and weekly to Majuro and Nandi. Air Nauru has a weekly flight between Nauru and Tarawa.

Post and Broadcasting. There were 911 telephones in 1987. Radio Tarawa transmits daily in English and I-Kiribati. A telephone line to Australia was installed in 1981. There were (1989 estimate) 25,000 radio receivers.

Cinemas. In 1989 there were 4 cinemas.

Newspapers. There was (1989) 1 bi-lingual weekly newspaper.

JUSTICE, RELIGION, EDUCATION AND WELFARE

Justice. In 1989 Kiribati had a police force of 232 under the command of a Commissioner of Police. The Commissioner of Police is also responsible for prisons, immigration, fire service (both domestic and airport) and firearms licensing.

Religion. The majority of the population belong to the Roman Catholic or Protestant (Congregational) church; there are small numbers of Seventh-day Adventist, Mormons, Baha'i and Church of God.

Education. In 1987 the government maintained boarding school had an enrolment of 470 pupils and there were 112 primary schools, with a total of 13,192 pupils, 6 secondary schools with 1,649 pupils, and 1 community high school with 232 pupils. The Government also maintains a teachers' training college with 56 students in 1987 and a marine training school which offers training for about 70 merchant seamen each year. The Tarawa Technical Institute at Betio offers a variety of part-time and evening technical and commercial courses and had 389 students in 1986.

In 1986, 85 islanders were in overseas countries for secondary and further education or training.

Welfare. Government maintains free medical and other services. There are few towns, and the people are almost without exception landed proprietors, thus eliminating child vagrancy and housing problems to a large extent, except in the Tarawa urban area. Destitution is almost unknown. There were 16 doctors in 1986. There is a general hospital on Tarawa and dispensaries on other islands, with 283 beds.

DIPLOMATIC REPRESENTATIVES

Of Kiribati in Great Britain
Acting High Commissioner: Peter T. Timeon (resides in Tarawa).

Of Great Britain in Kiribati (Tarawa)
High Commissioner: D. L. White.

Of Kiribati in the USA
Ambassador: Atanraoi Baiteke, OBE (resides in Tarawa).

Further Reading

Kiribati, Aspects of History. Univ. of South Pacific, 1979
Bailey, E., *The Christmas Island Story.* London, 1977
Cowell, R., *Structure of Gilbertese.* Suva, 1950
Grimble, Sir Arthur, *A Pattern of Islands.* London, 1953.—*Return to the Islands.* London, 1957
Maude, H. E., *Of Islands and Men.* London, 1968.—*Evolution of the Gilbertese Boti.* Suva, 1977
Sabatier, E., *Astride the Equator.* Melbourne, 1978
Whincup, T., *Nareau's Nation.* London, 1979

KOREA

Capital: Seoul
Population: 42·5m. (1989)
GNP per capita: US$3,450 (1988)

Han Kook

HISTORY. Korea was united in a single kingdom under the Silla dynasty from 668. China, which claimed a vague suzerainty over Korea, recognized Korea's independence in 1895. Korea concluded trade agreements with the USA (1882), Great Britain, Germany (1883). After the Russo-Japanese war of 1904–5 Korea was virtually a Japanese protectorate until it was formally annexed by Japan on 29 Aug. 1910 thus ending the rule of the Choson kingdom, which had begun in 1392.

Following the collapse of Japan in 1945, American and Russian forces entered Korea to enforce the surrender of the Japanese troops there, dividing the country for mutual military convenience into two portions separated by the 38th parallel of latitude. Negotiations between the Americans and Russians regarding the future of Korea broke down in May 1946.

On 25 June 1950 the North Korean forces crossed the 38th parallel and invaded South Korea. The same day, the Security Council of the United Nations asked all member states to render assistance to the Republic of Korea. When the UN forces had reached the Manchurian border Chinese troops entered the war on the side of the North Koreans on 26 Nov. 1950 and penetrated deep into the south. By the beginning of April 1951, however, the UN forces had regained the 38th parallel. On 23 June 1951 Y. A. Malik, President of the Security Council, suggested a cease-fire, and on 10 July representatives of Gen. Ridgway met representatives of the North Koreans and of the Chinese Volunteer Army. A cease-fire agreement was signed on 27 July 1953.

For the contributions of member-nations of the United Nations to the war, *see* THE STATESMAN'S YEAR-BOOK, 1954, p. 1195, and 1956, p. 1180.

On 16 Aug. 1953 the USA and Korea signed a mutual defence pact and on 28 Nov. 1956 a treaty of friendship, commerce and navigation.

On 4 July 1972 it was announced in Seoul and Pyongyang (North Korea) that talks had taken place aimed at 'the peaceful unification of the fatherland as early as possible'. In Nov. 1984 agreement was reached to form a joint economic committee.

A North Korean–UN agreement of 6 Sept. 1976 established a joint security area 850 metres in diameter, divided into 2 equal parts to ensure the separation of the two sides.

Several rounds of talks with North Korea have taken place since 1985.

AREA AND POPULATION. South Korea is bounded north by the demilitarized zone (separating it from North Korea), east by the Sea of Japan (East Sea), south by the Korea Strait (separating it from Japan) and west by the Yellow Sea. The area was (1988) 99,237 sq. km (38,315 sq. miles). The population (census, 1 Nov. 1985) was 40,466,577 (male, 20,280,857). Estimate (1989) 42,519,000 (male, 21,158,000).

The areas (in sq. km) and 1985 census populations of the Regions were as follows:

Region	*sq. km*	*1985*	*Region*	*sq. km*	*1985*
Seoul (city)	627	9,645,824	South Chungchong	8,807	3,001,538
Pusan (city)	433	3,516,768	North Cholla	8,052	2,202,218
Taegu (city)	455	2,030,649	South Cholla	12,189	3,748,442
Inchon (city)	201	1,387,475	North Kyongsang	19,427	3,013,276
Kyonggi	10,875	4,794,240	South Kyongsang	11,850	3,519,121
Kangwon	16,894	1,726,029	Cheju	1,825	489,458
North Chungchong	7,430	1,391,084			

The chief cities (populations, census 1985) are:

Seoul	9,645,824	Kwangchu	905,896	Masan	449,236
Pusan	3,516,768	Taejon	866,303	Seongnam	447,832
Taegu	2,030,649	Ulsan	551,219	Suweon	430,827
Inchon	1,387,475	Puch'on	456,311	Chonchu	426,490

CLIMATE. The extreme south has a humid warm temperate climate while the rest of the country experiences continental temperate conditions. Rainfall is concentrated in the period April to Sept. and ranges from 40" (1,020 mm) to 60" (1,520 mm). Pusan. Jan. 36°F (2·2°C), July 76°F (24·4°C). Annual rainfall 56" (1,407 mm). Seoul. Jan. 23°F (–5°C), July 77°F (25°C). Annual rainfall 50" (1,250 mm).

CONSTITUTION AND GOVERNMENT. A new constitution was approved by national referendum in Oct. 1987 and came into force on 25 Feb. 1988. It provides for a President, to be directly elected for a single 5-year term, a State Council of ministers whom he appoints and leads, and a National Assembly (299 members) directly elected for 4 years (224 from local constituencies and 75 by proportional representation).

The National Assembly elected on 26 April 1988 as of Oct. 1989 comprised 129 members of the Democratic Justice Party, 71 Party for Peace and Democracy, 60 Reunification Democratic Party, 35 New Democratic Republican Party and 4 independents.

President of the Republic: Roh Tae-woo (took office 25 Feb. 1988).

The Cabinet at Oct. 1989 was composed as follows:

Prime Minister: Kang Young-Hoon.

Deputy Prime Minister and Economic Planning: Cho Soon. *Foreign Affairs:* Choi Ho-Joong. *Home Affairs:* Kim Tae-Ho. *Finance:* Lee Kyu-Sung. *Justice:* Huh Hyong-Koo. *National Defence:* Lee Sang-Hoon. *Education:* Chung Won-Sik. *Sports:* Kim Jip. *Agriculture, Forestry and Fisheries:* Kim Sik. *Commerce and Industry:* Han Seung-Soo. *Energy and Resources:* Lee Bong-Suh. *Construction:* Kwon Yong-Gack. *Health and Social Affairs:* Kim Chong-In. *Labour Affairs:* Choi Young-Choul. *Transportation:* Kim Chang-Keun. *Communications:* Lee Woo-Jae. *Culture and Information:* Choe Byung Yul. *Government Administration:* Kim Yong-Nae. *Science and Technology:* Rhee Sang-Hi. *National Unification:* Lee Hong-Koo. *First Minister for State Affairs:* Park Chul-Un. *Second Minister for State Affairs:* Kim Yung-Chung. *Office of Legislation:* Hyun Hong-Joo. *Patriots and Veterans Affairs Agency:* Lee Sahng-Yeon.

National flag: White charged in the centre with the *yang-um* in red and blue and with 4 black *p'algwae* trigrams.

Local government: South Korea is divided into 9 provinces *(Do)* and 6 cities with provincial status (Seoul, Pusan, Taegu, Inchon, Kwangju and Taegeon); the provinces are sub-divided into 137 districts *(Gun)* and 67 cities *(Shi)*.

DEFENCE. Military service is compulsory for 30-36 months in all services.

Army. The Army is organized in 19 infantry divisions, 2 mechanized infantry divisions, 7 independent special forces brigades, 2 anti-aircraft artillery brigades, 2 surface-to-air missile brigades, 1 army aviation brigade and 2 surface-to-surface missile battalions. Equipment includes 350 M-47 and 950 M-48A5 main battle tanks. Army aviation equipment includes over 200 Hughes 500 and 25 AH-1 Cobra helicopters for anti-armour operations, observation and liaison, plus 60 UH-1 Iroquois transport helicopters. Strength (1990) 550,000, with a Regular Army Reserve of 1·5m. and a Homeland Reserve Defence Force of 3·3m. Para-military Civilian Defence Corps, 3·5m.

Navy. A substantial force of 60,000 (1,900 conscripts) including 25,000 marines, which has hitherto operated very old *ex*-US ships but is now modernizing rapidly. Current strength includes 3 midget submarines (175 tonnes), 11 aged (1943–46) *ex*-US destroyers, and 17 locally-built frigates with new US and European weapons,

11 fast missile craft, together with a patrol force of 68 inshore craft. There are 9 coastal minesweepers and an amphibious force of 8 tank landing ships, 7 medium landing ships, together with 37 amphibious craft. Major auxiliaries include 3 tankers, 2 large tugs, 4 survey vessels and 35 service craft. The Navy has a small aviation element with 25 shore-based S-2A/F Tracker anti-submarine aircraft and 25 Hughes 500MD and 12 Alouette helicopters, some of which embark in frigates and destroyers.

Three German-designed diesel submarines are under construction; and the squadron may in due course reach a total of 6.

Main bases are at Chinhae, Inchon and Pusan.

The Coastguard numbering some 12,000 (mostly shore based) operates 14 off-shore and 32 inshore patrol craft plus 9 light helicopters.

Air Force. With a 1990 strength of about 40,000 men, the Air Force is undergoing rapid expansion with US assistance. Its combat aircraft include 36 F-16C/D Fighting Falcons, about 120 F-4D/E Phantoms, 60 F-5A/B tactical fighters, more than 200 F-5E/F tactical fighters, 6 RF-5A reconnaissance fighters, 10 O-2A forward air control aircraft and 10 Hughes 500-D Defender helicopters. There are also 10 C-54 and 10 C-123 piston-engined transports, 4 C-130 Hercules turboprop-engined transports, 2 HS.748s, 1 Boeing 737 and 1 DC-6 for VIP transport; UH-1, Bell 212 and Bell 412 transport helicopters, and T-41, T-28, T-33 and T-37C trainers.

ECONOMY

Planning. Under the sixth 5-year social and economic plan (1987–91) the 1988 growth rate was 12·2% and the forecasted annual rate for 1989–91 is 7·3%.

Budget. The 1988 budget balanced at 17,464,400m. won of which 30·6% defence and 16·4% education.

Currency. Notes are issued by the Bank of Korea in denominations of 10,000, 5,000, 1,000 and 500 *won* and coins in denominations of 500, 100, 50, 10, 5 and 1 *won*. The exchange rate is determined daily by the Bank of Korea. In March 1990, 1,139·98 *won* = US$1; 695·53 *won* = £1 sterling.

Banking. State-run banks include the Bank of Korea, the Korean Development Bank, the Medium & Small Industry Bank, the Citizen's National Bank, the Korea Exchange Bank, the National Livestock Co-operatives Federation and the Federation of Fisheries Co-operatives serving as banking and credit institutions for farmers and fishermen, the Korea Housing Bank, the Export and Import Bank of Korea.

There are 8 commercial banks: The Bank of Seoul & Trust Co. Ltd, the Cho Heung Bank Ltd, the Commercial Bank of Korea, the Korea First Bank, the Hanil Bank, the Shinhan Bank, the Koram Bank, the Donghwa Bank; and 10 local banks. The Bank of Korea is the central bank and the only note-issuing bank, the authorized purchaser of domestically produced gold.

In addition, there are non-bank financial institutions consisting of 20 insurance companies, the Land Bank of Korea, the Credit Guarantee Fund, 32 short-term financial companies, 237 mutual credit companies, and the Merchant Banking Corporation.

ENERGY AND NATURAL RESOURCES

Electricity. Electricity generated (1988) was 85,462m. kwh. Supply 100 and 220 volts; 60 Hz.

Oil. The KODECO Energy Co. and the Indonesian state-run oil company Pertamin are developing an oil field off the coast of Indonesia's Madura Island. KODECO began drilling operations in 1982 and began producing oil in Sept. 1985 from the Madura field, which contains 22·1m. bbls of proven oil deposits. The state-run Korean Petroleum Development Corp. (PEDCO) and the US company Hadson Petroleum International are exploring for oil in the southern part of the Fifth Continental Shelf oil mining block off the coast of the Korean Peninsula. Oil worth US$3,788m. was imported in 1988.

Minerals. In 1986, 1,948 mining companies employed 94,811 people. Mineral deposits are mostly small, with the exception of tungsten; the Sangdong mine is one of the world's largest deposits of tungsten. Output, 1988, included (in tonnes): Anthracite coal, 22·7m.; iron ore, 666,000; tungsten ore, 3,433; limestone, 48·5m.; graphite, 104,384; lead ore, 25,806; silver, 12,809; zinc ore, 45,554.

Agriculture. The arable land in South Korea comprised 2,143,430 hectares in 1987, of which 1,351,657 hectares were rice paddies and 791,773 hectares dry fields.

Production (1987, in tonnes) of rice polished was 5,493,343; barley, 263,960; radishes, 1,972,683; Chinese cabbages, 2,433,981; apples, 556,160; grapes, 158,158; tobacco (leaf), 78,039.

Output of tobacco manufactures, a government monopoly, was 82,982 tonnes in 1986. In 1987 draft cattle numbered 1,923,121; milk cows, 463,330; pigs, 4,281,315; chickens, 59,323,977; ducks, 585,912.

Fisheries. Fishery exports (1987) US$1,731m. In 1987, 710 Korean deep-sea fishing vessels were operating overseas. In 1987, there was a total of 94,155 boats (911,958 gross tons). The fish catch (inland and marine) was 3,331,825 tonnes in 1987.

INDUSTRY AND TRADE

Industry. Manufacturing industry, which (1988) employed 4,667,000 persons, was concentrated primarily in 1988 on oil, petrochemicals, chemical fibres, construction, iron and steel, cement, machinery, shipbuilding, automobiles and electronics.

Commerce. In 1988 the total exports were US$59,648m., while imports were US$48,203m. In 1988 USA provided 26·5% and Japan 33% of imports; USA received 35·9% of exports, Japan 20·1%.

Major exports, 1988, included (in US$1m.): Heavy and chemical products, 32,913; light industrial products, 24,408. Major imports included: Crude oil and raw materials, 27,875; capital goods, 19,033; grain and other goods, 4,900.

Total trade between Korea and UK (British Department of Trade returns, in £1,000 sterling):

	1985	*1986*	*1987*	*1988*	*1989*
Imports to UK	480,448	661,975	936,038	1,135,107	1,164,723
Exports and re-exports from UK	247,887	288,421	427,229	1,742,747	493,945

Tourism. In 1989 there were 2,728,100 foreign tourists.

COMMUNICATIONS

Roads. In 1987 there were 54,689 km of roads. In 1988 motor vehicles totalled 2,035,448 including 635,445 trucks, 259,600 buses, 1,117,999 passenger cars.

Railways. In 1988 the National Railroad totalled 3,102 km of 1,435 mm gauge (525 km electrified) and 46 km of 762 mm gauge. In 1988 railways carried 564m. passengers and 61m. tonnes of freight.

Aviation. In 1989, 40 countries maintained aviation agreement with Korea and had 47 air routes with 28 cities in 18 countries. The Ministry of Transportation opened the Seoul-Singapore-Jakarta passenger route in 1989.

In Sept. 1989 Korea had 159 commercial aircraft (62 Korean Air passenger-cargo planes, 9 Asiana Airlines passenger-cargo planes, 38 light planes and 43 helicopters). In 1987, 4·73m. passengers and 337,139 tons of cargo and mail were carried on domestic routes and 5·24m. passengers on international routes.

Shipping. In Dec. 1987, there were 25 first-grade ports and 22 second-grade ports, and 8,852,000 gross tons in various vessels. Of the total tonnage, registered vessels accounted for 7,239,000 tons, chartered vessels for 1,613,000 tons. Passenger ships accounted for 54,000 tons, cargo vessels 6,932,000 tons and oil tankers 1,729,000 tons and others 146,000 tons.

Post and Telecommunications. Post offices total 3,199 (1988); telephones were

10,306,000 in 1988. The fifth satellite earth station was opened in June 1988, bringing the number of communications circuits *via* satellite to 2,866. There were 6·1m. television receivers in 1989.

Cinemas. In 1988 there were 696 with a seating capacity of 240,000.

Newspapers (1989). There were 68 daily papers, including 2 in English appearing in Seoul and 2 news agencies.

RELIGION, EDUCATION AND WELFARE

Religion. Basically the religions of Korea have been Shamanism, Buddhism (introduced A.D. 372) and Confucianism, which was the official faith from 1392 to 1910. Catholic converts from China introduced Christianity in the 18th century, but the ban on Roman Catholicism was not lifted until 1882. Protestantism was introduced in the late 19th century. The Christian population in 1985 was 8,343,455.

Education. In 1988 Korea had 4,819,857 pupils enrolled in 6,463 elementary schools, 2,523,515 pupils in 2,371 middle schools and 2,300,582 pupils in 1,653 high schools.

For higher education, 1,312,053 students attended 260 universities, colleges and junior colleges in 1988. There are 251 graduate schools granting master's degrees in 2 years and doctor's degrees in 3 years, where 75,177 students attended in 1988. There are 6 Open Universities.

The Korean language belongs to the Ural–Altaic group, is polysyllabic, agglutinative and highly developed syntactically. The modern Korean alphabet of 10 vowels and 14 consonants forms a script known as Han-gul.

Health. In 1987 there were 38,611 physicians, 4,426 oriental medical doctors, 6,761 dentists, 6,849 midwives, 186,177 nurses, and 32,855 pharmacists. There were 20,899 hospitals, clinics and health care centres in 1987 with 114,511 beds.

DIPLOMATIC REPRESENTATIVES

Of Korea in Great Britain (4 Palace Gate, London, W8 5NF)
Ambassador: Jay Hee Oh (accredited 16 Dec. 1987).

Of Great Britain in Korea (4 Chung-Dong, Chung-Ku, Seoul)
Ambassador: David J. Wright, LVO.

Of Korea in the USA (2370 Massachusetts Ave., NW, Washington, D.C., 20008)
Ambassador: Park Tong-Jin.

Of the USA in Korea (Sejong-Ro, Seoul)
Ambassador: Donald Gregg.

Further Reading

A Handbook of Korea. 4th ed. Seoul, 1982
Guide to Investment in Korea. Economic Planning Board. Seoul, 1980
Korea Annual 1983. 20th ed. Seoul, 1983
Korea Statistical Year Book. Seoul, 1981
Major Economic Indicators, 1979–80. Seoul, 1980
Monthly Statistics of Korea. Seoul
Hastings, M., *The Korean War.* London, 1987
Lew, H. J., *New Life Korean–English, English–Korean Dictionary.* 2 vols. Seoul, 1947–50
Martin, S. F. (ed.) *A Korean–English Dictionary.* Yale Univ. Press, 1968
Srivastava, M.P., *The Korean Conflict: Search for Unification.* New Delhi, 1982

NORTH KOREA

Capital: Pyongyang
Population: 22·42m. (1989)
GNP per capita: US$1,180 (1985)

Chosun Minchu-chui Inmin Konghwa-guk

HISTORY. In northern Korea the Russians, arriving on 8 Aug. 1945, one month ahead of the Americans, established a Communist-led 'Provisional Government'. The newly created Korean Communist Party merged in 1946 with the New National Party into the Korean Workers' Party. In July 1946 the KWP, with the remaining pro-Communist groups and non-party people, formed the United Democratic Patriotic Front. On 25 Aug. 1948 the Communists organized elections for a Supreme People's Assembly, both in Soviet-occupied North Korea (212 deputies) and in US-occupied South Korea (360 deputies, of whom a certain number went to the North and took their seats). A People's Democratic Republic was proclaimed on 9 Sept. 1948. Several proposals for talks between North and South Korea on reunification have been made since 1980, but have repeatedly broken down. North-South economic talks were held in 1985, and there was an exchange of family visits in 1989. Relations with the USSR have intensified since 1985. It was announced in March 1990 that President Kim Il Sung would hand over office to his son, Kim Jong Il, on 15 April.

AREA AND POPULATION. North Korea is bounded north by China, east by the sea of Japan, west by the Yellow Sea and south by South Korea, from which it is separated by a demilitarized zone of 1,262 sq. km. Its area is 120,538 sq. km. Population estimate in 1989, 22·42m. (64% urban). Population density, 186 per sq. km. Rate of population increase, 2·4% per annum; birth rate, 1985, 3%; death rate, 0·6%. Marriage is discouraged before the age of 32 for men and 29 for women. Expectation of life in 1987 was: Males, 65; females, 71 years. Large towns (estimate, 1984): Pyongyang, the capital (2,639,448); Chongjin (754,128); Nampo (691,284); Sinuiju (500,000); Wonsan (350,000); Kaesong (345,642); Kimchaek (281,000); Haeju (131,000); Sariwon (130,000); Hamhung (775,000 in 1981).

CLIMATE. There is a warm temperate climate, though winters can be very cold in the north. Rainfall is concentrated in the summer months. Pyongyang. Jan. 18°F (–7·8°C), July 75°F (23·9°C). Annual rainfall 37" (916 mm).

CONSTITUTION AND GOVERNMENT. The political structure is based upon the Constitution of 27 Dec. 1972. The head of state is the *President*, elected for 4-year terms. The Constitution provides for a Supreme People's Assembly elected every 4 years by universal suffrage. Citizens of 17 years and over can vote and be elected. Elections were held in 1948, 1957, 1962, 1972, 1977, 1982 and 2 Nov. 1986. At the latter it was claimed that 100% of the electorate voted for the list of single candidates presented. There are 579 deputies. The government consists of the Administration Council directed by the Central People's Committee (*Secretary*, Chi Chang Ik) which had 13 members in 1988.

In practice the country is ruled by the Korean Workers' (*i.e.*, Communist) Party which elects a Central Committee which in turn appoints a Politburo. In March 1990 this was composed of: Marshal Kim Il Sung, *(General Secretary of the Party, President of the Republic since 1971, last re-elected 1986, Chairman of the Central People's Committee, Supreme Commander of the Armed Forces)*; Kim Jong Il (Kim Il Sung's son and designated successor) *(Vice-President of the Republic)*; O Jin U *(Armed Forces' Minister)* (The latter 3 constituting the Politburo's Presidium); Kang Song San; Li Jong Ok *(Vice-President of the Republic)*; Pak Sung Chul *(Vice-President of the Republic)*; So Chol; Kim Yong Nam *(Deputy Prime Minister)*; Yun Ki Chong *(Foreign Minister)*; Kim Hwan *(Deputy Prime Minister, Minister of the*

Chemical Industry); Yi Kun Mo *(Prime Minister)*; O Guk Ryol; So Yun Sok; Ho Dam *(Deputy Prime Minister)*; Hong Song Nam *(First Deputy Prime Minister, Chairman, State Planning Commission)*; Kye Ung Tae. There were also 9 candidate members.

Ministers not full members of the Politburo include Kim Yun Hyok *(Deputy Prime Minister)*; Cho Se Ung *(Deputy Prime Minister)*; Yun Gi Jong *(Finance)*; Chong Song Nam *(Foreign Economic Affairs)*; Kim Bok Sin; Chong Jun Gi, Kim Yun Hyok, Kim Chang Ju *(Deputy Prime Ministers)*; Choe Jong Gun *(Foreign Trade)*; Paek Hak Rim *(Public Security)*.

In 1981 the Party had some 2m. members.

There are also the puppet religious Chongu and Korean Social Democratic Parties and various organizations combined in a Fatherland Front.

National flag: Blue, red and blue horizontal stripes separated by narrow white bands. The red stripe bears a white circle within which is a red 5-pointed star.

National anthem: 'A chi mun bin na ra i gang san' ('Shine bright, o dawn, on this land so fair'). Words by Pak Se Yong; music by Kim Won Gyun.

The country is divided into 13 administrative units: 4 cities (Pyongyang, Chongjin, Hamhung and Kaesong) and 9 provinces (capitals in brackets): South Pyongan (Nampo), North Pyongan (Sinuiju), Jagang (Kanggye), South Hwanghai (Haeju), North Hwanghai (Sariwon), Kangwon (Wonsan), South Hamgyong (Hamheung), North Hamgyong (Chongjin), Yanggang (Hyesan). These are sub-divided into 152 counties.

Local government: There are 26,539 deputies in People's Assemblies at city/province, county and commune level. Elections were on 15 Nov. 1987.

DEFENCE. Chief of the General Staff is Choe Gwang (appointed 1988). Military service is compulsory at the age of 16 for periods of 5-8 years in the Army and Navy and 3–4 years in the Air Force. In 1987 defence spending was 22% of GNP. North Korea adhered to the 1968 Non-Proliferation Treaty on nuclear weapons in 1985.

Army. The Army is organized in 31 infantry divisions; 15 armoured, 20 motorized infantry and 4 independent infantry brigades; 1 special purposes corps of 80,000 men; and an artillery corps with multiple rocket launchers and 6 surface-to-surface missile battalions. Equipment includes 3,000 T-34/-55/-62 and 175 Type-59 main battle tanks. Strength (1990) 930,000, with 500,000 reserves. There is also a paramilitary militia of some 3m. men and a ranger commando force of 115,000. The militia (men of 18–40 not in the armed forces or reserves, single women of 18–30) is estimated at 5m.

Navy. The Navy, principally tasked to coastal patrol and defence, comprises 23 diesel submarines (19 of Chinese design and 4 *ex*-Soviet). Surface forces include 2 small frigates, 29 missile craft, 173 fast torpedo craft, 6 anti-submarine patrol craft and some 150 inshore patrol craft. Amphibious forces consist of some 130 small craft. Support is provided by 2 *ex*-Soviet ocean tugs and 100 service craft. There is a coastal anised landing craft, 100 small assault landing craft, 30 trawlers and auxiliaries, 2 *ex*-Soviet ocean tugs and 100 service craft. There is a coastal defence element equipped with some 6 missile batteries and old 122 mm, 130 mm and 152 mm guns. Personnel in 1989 totalled 40,000 officers and men with 40,000 reserves.

Air Force. The Air Force had a total of about 854 combat aircraft and 53,000 personnel in 1989. Since 1985 the USSR has supplied 50 MiG-23 supersonic and 30 MiG-29 interceptors, 40 Su-25 fighter-bombers and 30 SA3 surface-to-air missiles. Other equipment is believed to include about 160 supersonic MiG-21 interceptors, more than 100 F-6s (Chinese-built MiG-19s), 150 MiG-17s for ground attack and reconnaissance, 30 Su-7 fighter-bombers, 40 Chinese-built A5 fighter-bombers, 60 Il-28 twin-jet light bombers, 200 An-2 light transport aircraft, 40 Mi-4 and Mi-8 transport helicopters and 80 US Hughes 300 and 500 helicopters.

INTERNATIONAL RELATIONS

North Korea is a member of WHO and Comecon and an observer at UN.

ECONOMY

Planning. For previous plans *see* THE STATESMAN'S YEAR-BOOK, 1987–88. After a hiatus it was announced in Oct. 1986 that a third 7-year plan would run from 1987 to 1993. Steel production targets have been reduced (to 10m. tonnes) and more emphasis placed on export items, non-ferrous metals and fishery products.

Budget (in 1m. won) for calendar years:

	1984	*1985*	*1986*	*1987*	*1988*
Revenue	26,305	27,439	28,539	30,337	31,852
Expenditure	26,158	27,329	28,396	30,085	31,852

Defence spending was 13·8% of the budget in 1987 (14% in 1986). Local government revenue in 1987: 4,185m. *won*; expenditure, 3,427m. *won*.

Currency. The monetary unit is the *won*, divided into 100 *jun*. There are coins of 1, 5, 10 and 50 *jun* and 1, 5, 10, 50 and 100 *won*. In March 1990, US$1 = 0·97 *won*; £1 = 1·60 *won*.

Weights and Measures. While the metric system is in force traditional measures are in frequent use. The *jungbo* = 1 hectare; the *ri* = 3,927 metres.

ENERGY AND NATURAL RESOURCES

Electricity. There are 3 thermal power stations and 4 hydro-electric plants. A nuclear power plant is being built with Soviet help. Output in 1986, was 50,000m. kwh (29,000m. kwh. hydro-electric). Installed capacity was 6·11m. kw in 1987. Hydro-electric potential exceeds 8m. kw. A hydro-electric plant and dam under construction on the Pukhan near Mount Kumgang has been denounced as a flood threat by the South Koreans, who constructed a defensive 'Peace Dam' in retaliation.

Oil. Oilwells went into production in 1957. An oil pipeline from China came on stream in 1976. Crude oil refining capacity was 70,000 barrels a year in 1986.

Minerals. North Korea is rich in minerals. Estimated reserves in tonnes: Iron ore, 3,300m.; copper, 2·15m.; lead, 6m.; zinc, 12m.; coal, 11,990m.; uranium, 26m.; manganese, 6,500m. 37·5m. tonnes of coal were mined in 1986, 8m. tonnes of iron ore and 15,000 tonnes of copper ore. 1986 production of gold was 160,000 fine troy oz; silver, 1·6m. fine troy oz; salt, 570,000 tonnes.

Agriculture. In 1987 there were 2·36m. hectares of arable land, including 635,000 hectares of paddy fields. In 1982, 38% of the population made a living from agriculture.

Collectivization took place between 1954 and 1958. 90% of the cultivated land is farmed by co-operatives. Land belongs either to the State or to co-operatives, and it is intended gradually to transform the latter into the former, but small individually-tended plots producing for 'farmers' markets' are tolerated as a 'transition measure'. Livestock farming is mainly carried on by large state farms.

There is a large-scale tideland reclamation project. There were 37,600 km of irrigation canals in 1976, making possible 2 rice harvests a year. In 1982 there were 133,000 tractors (15 h.p. units). The technical revolution in agriculture (nearly 95% of ploughing, etc., is mechanized) has considerably increased the yield of grain (sown on 2·3m. *jungbo* of land); rice production, 1988, was 6·35m. tonnes, maize, 2·95m. tonnes; potatoes, 1,975,000m. tonnes; soya beans, 448,000 tonnes.

Livestock, 1988: 1·25m. cattle, 3·1m. pigs, 20m. poultry.

Forestry. Between 1961 and 1970, 800,000 hectares were afforested. 4·6m. cu metres of timber were cut in 1986.

Fisheries. Catch in 1986: 1·7m. tonnes. There is a fishing fleet of 28,000 vessels including 19,000 motor vessels.

INDUSTRY AND TRADE

Industry. Industries were intensively developed by the Japanese, notably cotton spinning, hydro-electric power, cotton, silk and rayon weaving, and chemical fertilizers. Production (in tonnes) in 1982: Pig-iron, 4m.; crude steel, 4m.; rolled steel, 3·2m.; lead, 30,000; zinc, 140,000; copper, 48,000; ship-building, 400,000; chemical fertilizers, 620,000; chemicals, 20,000; synthetic resins, 90,000; cement (1986), 9,040; textiles (1986), 600m. metres; woven goods, 600m. metres; shoes, 40m. pairs; motor-cars (1986), 20,000; TV sets (1986), 240,000; refrigerators, 10,000. Annual steel production capacity was 4·3m. tonnes in 1987.

Labour. The economically-active population was 9m. (4·18m. females) in 1985. Industrial workers make up some 60% of the work force. Average monthly wage, 1984: 90 *won*.

Commerce. North Korea's largest trade partners have been USSR, China and Japan. Estimated exports, 1985: US$1,234·6m. (US$785·3m. to Communist countries); imports US$1,991·5m. (US$1,198·6m. from Communist countries). In Aug. 1987 140 Western banks declared North Korea in default on US$770m. in outstanding loans. In 1986 foreign debt was estimated at US$4,156m. The USA imposed sanctions in Jan. 1988 for alleged terrorist activities. The chief exports are metal ores and products, the chief imports machinery and petroleum products.

Joint ventures with foreign firms have been permitted since 1984.

Trade with the USSR is based on 5-year agreements, the last of which was signed in 1986.

Exports to the USSR in 1986 (and 1985) were worth 450·7m. (404·4m.) roubles; imports from the USSR, 757·2m. (654·8m.) roubles.

Total trade between North Korea and UK (British Department of Trade returns, in £1,000 sterling):

	1985	*1986*	*1987*	*1988*	*1989*
Imports to UK	1,983	1,374	641	824	1,095
Exports and re-exports from UK	2,608	3,331	2,198	3,125	3,087

Tourism. A 40-year ban on non-Communist tourists was lifted in 1986.

COMMUNICATIONS

Roads. There were 22,000 km of road in 1985, including 240 km of motorways. There were 180,000 motor cars in 1982. A 200 km 4-lane highway began construction in 1988 from Pyongyang to Kaesong.

Railways. The two trunk-lines Pyongyang–Sinuiju and Pyongyang–Myongchon are both electrified, and the Pyongyang–Sariwon trunk is in course of electrification. The 'Wonra' line runs from Wonsan to Rajin and is electrified from Myongchon to Rajin and beyond to Tumangang. The Namdokchon–Toknam line was opened in 1983. Lines are under construction from Pukchong to Toksong, from Palwon to Kujang and Kanggye *via* Hyesan to Musan. In 1987 the Unbong–Cha Song and Huju–Hyesan sections of this latter were opened. In 1988 there were 4,549 km of track, (2,706 km were electrified in 1984). In 1986, 89% of trains were hauled by electricity. In 1987 86% of all freight was transported by rail. A weekly service from Pyongyang to Beijing opened in 1983, and a twice-weekly service to Moscow in 1987.

Aviation. There are services to Moscow, Khabarovsk, Beijing and Hong Kong. An agreement envisaging a service from Pyongyang to Tokyo was signed in 1986. There are domestic flights from Pyongyang to Hamhung and Chongjin.

Shipping. The leading ports are Chongjin, Wonsan and Hungnam. Nampo, the port of Pyongyang, has been dredged and expanded. Pyongyang is connected to Nampo by railway and river. In 1987 the ocean-going merchant fleet numbered 71 vessels totalling 407,253 GRT.

The biggest navigable river is the Yalu, 698 km up to the Hyesan district.

Post and Broadcasting. There is a central TV station at Pyongyang and stations at

Kaesong and Mansudae. In 1986 there were some 250,000 television receivers. The central broadcasting station is Radio Pyongyang. There are several local stations and a station for overseas broadcasts. There were some 30,000 telephones in 1985.

Newspapers. There were 11 newspapers in 1984. The party newspaper is *Nodong* (or *Rodong*) *Sinmun* (Workers' Daily News). Circulation about 600,000.

JUSTICE, RELIGION, EDUCATION AND WELFARE

Justice. The judiciary consists of the Supreme Court, whose judges are elected by the Assembly for 3 years; provincial courts; and city or county people's courts. The procurator-general, appointed by the Assembly, has supervisory powers over the judiciary and the administration; the Supreme Court controls the judicial administration.

Religion. The Constitution provides for 'freedom of religion as well as the freedom of anti-religious propaganda'. In 1986 there were 3m. Chondoists, 400,000 Buddhists and 200,000 Christians. Another 3m. followed traditional beliefs.

Education. Free compulsory universal technical education lasts 11 years: 1 pre-school year, 4 years primary education starting at the age of 6, followed by 6 years secondary.

In 1988 there were 47,600 kindergartens. In 1980 there were some 10,000 11-year schools. In 1982–83 there were 5·2m. pupils and 110,000 teachers, and nearly 1m. students in higher education. In 1985 there were 216 institutes of higher education, including 3 universities—Kim Il Sung University (founded 1946), Kim Chaek Technical University, Pyongyang Medical School—and an Academy of Sciences (founded 1952).

In 1977–78 Kim Il Sung University had some 17,000 students.

Health. Medical treatment is free. In 1982 there were 1,531 general hospitals, 979 specialized hospitals and 5,414 clinics. There were 24 doctors and 130 hospital beds per 10,000 population in 1983.

DIPLOMATIC REPRESENTATIVE

Of North Korea to the United Nations
Ambassador: Pak Gil Yon.

Further Reading

North Korea Directory 1989. Tokyo, 1989
An, T. S., *North Korea in Transition*. Westport, 1983;–*North Korea: a Political Handbook*. Washington, 1983
Baik Bong, *Kim Il Sung: Biography*. 3 vols. New York, 1969–70
Chung, C.-S., (ed.) *North Korean Communism: A Comparative Analysis*. Seoul, 1980
Kihl, Y. W., *Politics and Policies in Divided Korea*. Boulder, 1984
Kim Han Gil, *Modern History of Korea*. Pyongyang, 1979
Kim Il Sung, *Works*. Pyongyang, 1980–83
Kim, Y. S., (ed.) *The Economy of the Korean Democratic People's Republic, 1945–1977*. Kiel, 1979
Koh, B. C., *The Foreign Policy Systems of North and South Korea*. Berkeley, 1984
Park, J. K. and Kim, J.-G., *The Politics of North Korea*. Boulder, 1979
Scalapino, R. A. and Lee, C.-S., *Communism in Korea. Part I: The Movement. Part II: The Society*. Univ. of Calif. Press, 1972—and Kim, J-Y. (eds.), *North Korea Today: Strategic and Domestic Issues*. Univ. of California Press, 1983
Suh, D.-S., *Korean Communism, 1945–1980: A Reference Guide to the Political System*. Honolulu, 1981
Yang, S. C., *Korea and Two Regimes: Kim Il Sung and Park Chung Hee*. Cambridge, Mass., 1981

KUWAIT

Dowlat al Kuwait

Capital: Kuwait
Population: 1·96m. (1988)
GNP per capita: US$13,680 (1988)

HISTORY. The ruling dynasty was founded by Shaikh Sabah al-Owel, who ruled from 1756 to 1772. In 1899 the then ruler Shaikh Mubarak concluded a treaty with Great Britain wherein, in return for the assurance of British protection, he undertook not to alienate any of his territory without the agreement of Her Majesty's Government. In 1914 the British Government recognized Kuwait as an independent government under British protection. On 19 June 1961 an agreement reaffirmed the independence and sovereignty of Kuwait and recognized the Government of Kuwait's responsibility for the conduct of internal and external affairs; the agreement of 1899 was terminated and Her Majesty's Government expressed their readiness to assist the Government of Kuwait should they request such assistance.

AREA AND POPULATION. Kuwait is bounded east by the Gulf, north and west by Iraq and south and south-west by Saudi Arabia, with an area of about 6,880 sq. miles (17,819 sq. km); the total population at the census of 1985 was 1,697,301, of which about 60% were non-Kuwaitis. Estimate (1988) 1·96m. Over 78% speak Arabic, the official language, while 10% speak Kurdish and 4% Iranian (Farsi). English is also used as a second language.

The country is divided into 4 governorates: The capital (comprising Kuwait City, Kuwait's 9 islands and territorial and shared territorial waters), with an area of 983 sq. km (population 167,750 at 1985 census); Hawalli, 620 sq. km (943,250); Ahmadi, 4,665 sq. km (304,662) and Jahra, 11,550 sq. km (279,466).

The chief cities were (census, 1985) Kuwait, the capital (44,335), and its suburbs Hawalli (145,126), as-Salimiya (153,369) and Jahra (111,222).

The Neutral Zone (3,560 sq. miles, 5,700 sq. km), jointly owned and administered by Kuwait and Saudi Arabia from 1922 to 1966, was partitioned between the two countries in May 1966, but the exploitation of the oil and other natural resources will continue to be shared.

CLIMATE. Kuwait has a dry, desert climate which is cool in winter but very hot and humid in summer. Rainfall is extremely light. Kuwait. Jan. 56°F (13·5°C), July 99°F (36·6°C). Annual rainfall 5" (125 mm).

RULER. HH Shaikh Jabir al-Ahmad al-Jabir al-Sabah the 13th Amir of Kuwait, succeeded on 31 Dec. 1977.

CONSTITUTION AND GOVERNMENT. In 1976 the Amir dissolved the Assembly and at the same time parts of the Constitution were suspended. Elections were held in Feb. 1985 for the 50-member National Assembly. Executive authority is vested in the Council of Ministers.

The Cabinet in Oct. 1989 was composed as follows:

Prime Minister: HRH Crown Prince Shaikh Saad al-Abdullah as Salim as Sabah.

Deputy Prime Minister, Foreign Affairs: Shaikh Sabah al Ahmad al Jabir as Sabah. *Finance and Economy:* Jassim Mohammed al Kharafi. *Education:* Anwar Abdullah al Nuri. *Waqfs and Islamic Affairs:* Khaled Ahmed Saad al Jasir. *Defence:* Shaikh Nawaf al Ahmad al Jabir as Sabah. *Justice, Legal and Administrative Affairs:* Dari Abdullah al Uthman. *Public Works:* Abdel Rahman Ibrahim al Houti. *Public Health:* Dr Abdurrahman Abdullah al Awadi. *Planning:* Mohammed Soleiman Said Ali. *Oil:* Shaikh Ali al Khalifa al Adhibi as Sabah. *Communications:* Khalid Jumayan Salim al Jumayan. *Electricity and Water:* Mohammed as Saad Abdel Moshin al Rifai. *Information:* Shaikh Nasser Mohammed al Ahmad al Jabir as Sabah. *Social Affairs and Labour:* Jabir Mubarak al Hamad. *Interior:* Shaikh Salim as Sabah as Salim as Sabah. *Trade and Industry:* Faisal Abdel Razzaq al Khaled.

There are 5 Ministers of State.

Flag: Three horizontal stripes of green, white, red, with a black trapezium based on the hoist.

DEFENCE. Military service is compulsory for 24 months (university students, 12 months).

Army. Kuwait maintains a small, well-equipped and mobile army of 2 armoured, 1 artillery and 1 mechanized infantry brigades and 1 surface-to-surface missile battalion. Equipment includes 70 Vickers Mk I, 40 Centurion and 165 Chieftain main battle tanks. Strength (1990) about 16,000 men.

Navy. The combatant flotilla comprises 2 missile craft, 6 smaller missile craft (all German-built), 15 inshore patrol craft and some 25 boats. 4 UK and 3 Singapore-built landing craft are used on logistic support tasks. In 1989 personnel totalled 2,100 and the force is based at El Adami (HQ) and As Shuwaikh.

Air Force. From a small initial combat force the Air Force has grown rapidly. It has 2 squadrons with 25 Mirage F1-C fighters and 4 Mirage F1-B 2-seat trainers; and 2 squadrons with 30 A-4KU/TA-4KU Skyhawk attack aircraft. Other equipment includes 2 DC-9 jet transports, 4 L-100-30 Hercules turboprop transports and 12 Hawk jet trainers, 10 Puma, 6 Exocet missile-armed Super Puma and 25 missile-armed Gazelle helicopters. Hawk surface-to-air missiles are in service. Personnel strength (1990) about 2,200.

INTERNATIONAL RELATIONS

Membership. Kuwait is a member of UN, the Arab League, Gulf Co-operation Council, OPEC and OAPEC.

ECONOMY

Planning. The 5-year development plan ran from 1986–90.

Budget. In 1985–86 revenue, KD1,979m.; expenditure, KD3,158m.

Currency. The Kuwait *dinar* of 1,000 *fils* replaced the Indian external rupee on 1 April 1961. Coins in circulation are, 1, 5, 10, 20, 50 and 100 fils and notes of KD, 20, 10, 5, 1, $^1/_2$ and $^1/_4$. In March 1990, £1 sterling = KD 0·491; US$1 = KD 0·294.

Banking. In addition to the Central Bank, 7 commercial banks (Bank of Kuwait and the Middle East, National Bank of Kuwait, Commercial Bank of Kuwait, Gulf Bank, Al-Ahli Bank, Burgan Bank and Bank of Bahrain and Kuwait) and 3 specialized banks (Credit and Savings Bank, Kuwait Real Estate Bank and Industrial Bank of Kuwait) operate in Kuwait. There is also the Kuwait Finance House, which is not subject to the control of the Central Bank.

Weights and Measures. The metric system was adopted in 1962.

ENERGY AND NATURAL RESOURCES

Electricity. 16,360m. kwh. were produced in 1986. Supply 240 volts; 50 Hz.

Oil. The Kuwait Petroleum Corporation (KPC) was set up in 1980 to reorganize, integrate and develop the oil sector. The functions of the operating oil companies have been reallocated: Kuwait Oil Company (KOC) specializes in exploration, drilling and production in all areas; Kuwait National Petroleum Company (KNPC) is responsible for refining, local marketing and gas liquefaction operations; Kuwait Oil Tankers Company (KOTC) is in charge of transporting crude oil, liquefied gas and oil products to various world markets; Petrochemical Industries Company is in charge of use of hydrocarbon resources to set up diverse petrochemical industries, and the International Marketing Department of KPC markets and sells oil and gas worldwide.

Oil revenues in 1983–84 were KD2,787·6m. Crude oil production in 1989, 91m. tonnes. As well as selling crude oil, Kuwait is refining, marketing refined products, and prospecting and producing abroad. Production of petroleum products in 1984, 24,266,000 tonnes.

Gas. Production (1983) 170,200m. cu. ft.

Water. In 1986 there were 5 distillation plants with a daily total capacity of 215m. gallons. Fresh mineral water is pumped and bottled at Rawdhatain. Underground brackish water is used for irrigation, street cleaning and livestock; production, 1985, 18,000m. gallons.

Agriculture. In 1985 the area of cultivated land was 20m. sq. metres and there were 27 dairy farms with a total production capacity of about 30,000 tonnes of fresh milk. Major crops (production, 1988, in tonnes) were melons (6,000), tomatoes (39,000), onions (25,000), dates (1,000), radishes, clover.

Livestock (1988): Cattle, 26,000; sheep, 300,000; goats, 20,000; poultry, 28m.

Fisheries. Shrimp fishing is becoming one of the important non-oil industries.

INDUSTRY AND TRADE

Industry. In 1985 there were 600 industrial establishments and 50,000 workers in the industrial sector. Industries, apart from oil, include boat building, fishing, food production, petrochemicals, gases and construction. The manufacture or import of alcoholic drinks is prohibited.

Trade Unions. In 1986 there were 16 trade unions and 17 labour federations.

Labour. In 1985 the labour force totalled 670,385, with 530,996 employed.

Commerce. The port of Kuwait formerly served mainly as an entrepôt for goods for the interior, for the export of skins and wool, and for pearl fishing. Entrepôt trade continues but, with the development of the oil industry, is declining in importance. Pearl fishing is now on a small scale. Dhows and launches of traditional construction are still built.

In 1986 total imports were valued at KD1,661m.; exports, (1984) KD3,632m. and oil accounted for 83·5% of exports at KD2,938m.

Major domestic exports include chemical fertilizers and other chemicals, shrimps, metal pipes and building materials, which represent about 33% of total non-oil products. The other 66% come from re-exports, particularly of machinery, transport equipment, foodstuffs and some industrial goods, which go mainly to neighbouring Arab countries.

Main imports include machinery, electrical generators, appliances, cars and medicines.

Total trade between Kuwait and UK (British Department of Trade returns, in £1,000 sterling):

	1985	*1986*	*1987*	*1988*	*1989*
Imports to UK [1]	156,912	58,517	81,530	72,318	150,354
Exports and re-exports from UK	347,915	300,586	225,168	237,515	228,711

[1] Including oil.

Tourism. There were 116,000 visitors in 1985.

COMMUNICATIONS

Roads. In 1986 there were 3,800 km of roads. Number of vehicles (1987) was 555,503 (private cars 440,142).

Aviation. There were 29,000 scheduled and unscheduled flights to and from Kuwait International Airport in 1985, carrying 2,257,000 passengers and 74,000 tonnes of freight. Kuwait Airways flew 5,000 flights in 1984, carrying about 1·5m. passengers and 8m. tonnes of cargo. Forty airlines operate at the airport.

Shipping. The largest oil terminal is at Mina Ahmade, which received 348 oil tankers in 1984. Three small oil ports lie to the south of Mina Ahmade: Mina Shuaiba (250 oil tankers in 1984); Mina Abdullah (25) and Mina Al-Zor (40). The main ports for other traffic are at Shuwaikh, where 1,585 ships docked in 1985, discharging 5m. tonnes of goods; Shuiaba, about 3·75m. tonnes were handled in 1985 (3·1m. imported, 650,000 exported), and Doha.

Post and Broadcasting. There were (1984), 419,200 telephones and there is a broadcasting and a television station. In 1986 there were 580,000 TV receivers and 750,000 radios.

Cinemas. In 1984 there were 14 cinemas, including 2 drive-ins.

Newspapers. In 1987 there were 5 daily newspapers in Arabic and 2 in English, with a combined circulation of about 418,000.

JUSTICE, RELIGION, EDUCATION AND WELFARE

Justice. In 1960 Kuwait adopted a unified judicial system covering all levels of courts. These are: Courts of Summary Justice, Courts of the First Instance, Supreme Court of Appeal, Court of Cassation, Constitutional Court and State Security Court. Islamic Sharia is a major source of legislation.

Religion. In 1980 about 78% of the population were Sunni Moslems, 14% Shia Moslems, 6% Christians and 2% others.

Education. In 1987–88 there were 33,375 pupils in kindergartens, 119,932 in primary schools, 120,961 in intermediate schools and 93,317 in secondary schools. In 1988 there were 836 students in the Religious Institute and 1,898 in special training institutes. The University of Kuwait had 15,990 students and 877 teachers in 1985–86.

Health. Medical services are free to all residents. There were (1985) 25 hospitals and sanatoria with 5,886 beds, 64 clinics and 25 health centres. In 1985 there were 2,692 doctors, 291 dentists and 8,557 nursing staff.

DIPLOMATIC REPRESENTATIVES

Of Kuwait in Great Britain (45 Queen's Gate, London, SW7)
Ambassador: Ghazi Mohammed Amin Al-Rayes (accredited 12 Feb. 1981).

Of Great Britain in Kuwait (Arabian Gulf St., Kuwait)
Ambassador: Michael Weston.

Of Kuwait in the USA (2940 Tilden St., NW, Washington, D.C., 20008)
Ambassador: Shaikh Saud Nasir Al-Sabah.

Of the USA in Kuwait (PO Box 77, Safat, Kuwait)
Ambassador: W. Nathaniel Howell.

Of Kuwait to the United Nations
Ambassador: Mohammad A. Abulhasan.

Further Reading

Arabian Year Book. Kuwait, 1978
Annual Statistical Abstract of Kuwait. Kuwait
Kuwait Facts and Figures 1986. Ministry of Information, 1987
Clements, F. A., *Kuwait.* [Bibliography] Oxford and Santa Barbara, 1985
Girgis, M., (ed.) *Industrial Progress in Small Oil-Exporting Countries: The Prospect for Kuwait.* Harlow, 1984
Sabah, Y. S. F., *The Oil Economy of Kuwait.* London, 1980

LAOS

Capital: Vientiane
Population: 3·83m. (1987)
GNP per capita: US$180 (1988)

HISTORY. The Lao People's Democratic Republic was founded on 2 Dec. 1975. Until that date Laos was a Kingdom, once called Lanxang (the land of a million elephants).

In 1893 Laos became a French protectorate and in 1907 acquired its present frontiers. In 1941 French authority was suppressed by the Japanese. When the Japanese withdrew in 1945 an independence movement known as Lao Issara (Free Laos) set up a government under Prince Phetsarath, the Viceroy of Luang Prabang. This government collapsed with the return of the French in 1946 and the leaders of the movement fled to Thailand.

Under a new Constitution of 1947 Laos became a constitutional monarchy under the Luang Prabang dynasty, and in 1949 became an independent sovereign state within the French Union. Most of the Lao Issara leaders returned to Laos but a few remained in dissidence under Prince Souphanouvong, who allied himself with the Vietminh and subsequently formed the 'Pathet Lao' (Lao State) rebel movement.

The war in Laos from 1953 to 1973 between the Royal Lao Government (supported by American bombing and Thai mercenaries) and the Patriotic Front *Pathet Lao* (supported by large numbers of North Vietnamese troops) ended in 1973 when an agreement and a protocol were signed. A provisional coalition government was formed by the two sides in 1974. However, after the communist victories in neighbouring Vietnam and Cambodia in April 1975, the *Pathet Lao* took over the running of the whole country, although maintaining the façade of a coalition. On 29 Nov. 1975 HM King Savang Vatthana signed a letter of abdication and the People's Congress proclaimed a People's Democratic Republic of Laos on 2 Dec. For the history of *Pathet Lao* and the military intervention of the Vietminh, *see* THE STATESMAN'S YEAR-BOOK, 1971–72, pp. 1126–28 and 1975–76 ed., pp. 1115–16.

AREA AND POPULATION. Laos is a landlocked country of about 91,400 sq. miles (236,800 sq. km) bordered on the north by China, the east by Vietnam, the south by Cambodia and the west by Thailand and Burma. Apart from the Mekong River plains along the border of Thailand, the country is mountainous, particularly in the north, and in places densely forested.

The population (census, 1986) was 3,722,000 (1,824,000 male); estimate (1987) 3·83m. The most heavily populated areas are the Mekong River plains by the Thailand border. Otherwise, the population is sparse and scattered, particularly in the northern provinces, and the eastern part of the country has been depopulated by war. The majority of the population is officially divided into 4 groups: about 56% Lao-Lum (Valley-Lao), 34% Lao-Theung (Lao of the mountain sides); and 9% Lao-Soung (Lao of the mountain tops), who comprise the Meo and Yaoe. Other minorities include Vietnamese, Chinese, Europeans, Indians and Pakistanis.

The Lao-Lum and Lao-Tai belong to the Lao branch of the Tai peoples, who migrated into South-East Asia at the time of the Mongol invasion of South China. The valley Lao are Buddhists, following the Hinayana (Theravada) form. The majority of the Lao-Theungma diverse group consisting of many tribes but mostly belonging to the Mon-Khmer group—are animists.

The Meo and Yaoe live in northern Laos. Far greater numbers live in both North Vietnam and China, having migrated over the last century. Their religions have strong Confucian and animistic features but some are Christians.

There are 17 provinces. Compared with other parts of Asia, Laos has few towns. The administrative capital and largest town is Vientiane, with a population of census (1985) 377,409. Other important towns (1973) are Luang Prabang, 44,244; Pakse, 44,860, in the extreme south, and Savannakhet, 50,690.

Language: Lao is the official language of the country. The liturgical language of Theravada Buddhism is Pali.

CLIMATE. A tropical monsoon climate, with high temperatures throughout the year and very heavy rains from May to Oct. Vientiane. Jan. 70°F (21·1°C), July 81°F (27·2°C). Annual rainfall 69" (1,715 mm).

CONSTITUTION AND GOVERNMENT. On 2 Dec. 1975 a national congress of 264 people's representatives met and declared Laos a People's Democratic Republic. A People's Supreme Council was appointed to draw up a new Constitution.

Acting President: Phoumi Vongvichit.

Prime Minister, Secretary General of the Central Committee of the Lao People's Revolutionary Party: Kaysone Phomvihane.

First Deputy Prime Minister, Deputy Secretary General of the Central Committee of the Lao People's Revolutionary Party: Nouhak Phounsavanh.

The Politbureau of the LPRP comprises the above 3 plus: Phoumi Vongvichit [1], Gen. Phoune Sipraseuth [1] *(Minister of Foreign Affairs),* Gen. Khamtai Siphandon [1] *(Minister of National Defence, Supreme Commander of the Lao People's Army)* and Sisomphon Lovansay *(Vice-President of the Supreme People's Assembly).* Ministers not in the Politbureau include Saly Vongkhamsao [1] *(Chairman of State Planning Committee).*

[1] Vice-Chairman of the Council of Ministers.

There are 4 deputy prime ministers.

National flag: Three horizontal stripes of red, blue, red, with blue of double width with in the centre a large white disc.

National anthem: Peng Sat Lao (Hymn of the Lao People).

Provincial Administration: All provincial administration is in the hands of the Lao People's Revolutionary Party. Orders come from the Central Committee through a series of 'People's Revolutionary Committees' at the province, town and village level.

DEFENCE. Military service is compulsory for 18 months.

Army. The Army is organized in 5 infantry divisions; 1 engineering regiment, 7 independent infantry regiments and 65 independent infantry companies; and 5 artillery and 9 anti-aircraft battalions. Equipment includes 30 T-34, T-55 main battle tanks. Strength (1990) about 52,500.

Navy. Little or no current information was available (1989) on the riverine force of about 650 personnel believed to be organized into 4 squadrons running some 40 river patrol craft for operations on the Mekong.

Air Force. Since 1975, the Air Force has received aircraft from the USSR, including 40 MiG-21 fighters, 6 An-24 and 3 An-26 turboprop transports and 10 Mi-8 helicopters. They may be supplemented by a few of the C-47 and C-123 transports, and UH-1 Iroquois, supplied by the USA to the former régime. Personnel strength, about 2,000 in 1990.

INTERNATIONAL RELATIONS

Membership. Laos is a member of UN.

Aid. Foreign aid in 1986, was US$44m.

ECONOMY

Planning. The priorities of the second Five Year Plan, 1986–90 continued to be infrastructure projects (telecommunications and transport), agriculture (crop diversification and improving paddy production), and agro-industrial processing. In

1988, in an attempt to stimulate the economy, the Government introduced an investment code designed to permit foreign companies to participate in Lao business ventures, and directives on the decentralization of decision-making in state/public enterprises and on the limited increase of private sector activities.

Budget. Total revenue 1986, K.14,127m.; total expenditure, K.24,900m. including capital expenditure of K.12,800m.

Currency. The currency is the new *kip*. 1 *kip* = 100 *att*. Coinage, 1, 2 and 5 *att*; banknotes, 1, 5, 10, 20, 50, 100 and 500 *kip*. The official rate of exchange was (March 1990) K.715 = US$1; £1 = K1,173.

ENERGY AND NATURAL RESOURCES

Electricity. Only a few towns in Laos have an electricity service. The Nam Ngum Dam situated about 45 miles north of Vientiane was inaugurated in Dec. 1971 with an initial installed capacity of 30,000 kw. and a planned ultimate capacity of 150,000 kw by 1985. Total installed capacity (1985) was 168,000 kw. Transmission lines to Vientiane and to Thailand have been constructed. Production (1986) 900m. kwh. Supply 127 and 220 volts; 50 Hz.

Minerals. Various minerals are found, but only tin is mined to any significant extent at present, and only at 2 mines. Production of tin concentrates (1986) 559 tonnes. There are extremely rich deposits of high-quality iron in Xieng Khouang province and potash near Vientiane.

Agriculture. The chief products are rice (production in 1988, 1,003,000 tonnes), maize (production 40,000 tonnes), tobacco (4,000 tonnes), seed-cotton (21,000 tonnes), citrus fruits, sticklack, benjohn tea and in the Boloven plateau coffee (8,000 tonnes), potatoes, cardamom and cinchara. Opium is produced but its manufacture is controlled by the state.

Livestock (1988): Cattle, 590,000; buffaloes, 1m. horses, 42,000; pigs, 1·52m. goats, 76,000; poultry, 9m.

Forestry. The forests, which cover 13m. hectares, representing 56% of the land area, produce valuable woods such as teak.

INDUSTRY AND TRADE

Industry. Industry is limited to beer, cigarettes, matches, soft drinks, plastic bags, saw-mills, rice-mills, weaving, pottery, distilleries, ice, plywood, bricks, etc. but most factories have been working at limited capacity in recent years. Plans for increased production are limited by lack of funds and skilled machine operators.

Commerce. In 1986 imports (estimate) amounted to US$216m. and exports to US$69·2m. The main imports were food and beverages, petroleum products and agricultural and other machinery. The chief supplying countries were Thailand and Japan. The main exports were timber and electricity.

Total trade between Laos and UK (British Department of Trade returns, in £1,000 sterling):

	1985	*1986*	*1987*	*1988*	*1989*
Imports to UK	6	150	621	2	1,369
Exports and re-exports from UK	523	1,460	1,742	1,332	908

COMMUNICATIONS

Roads. In 1986 the national road network, consisted of 2,350 km paved, 3,250 km gravel and 6,780 km earth roads.

Railways. There is no railway in Laos, but the Thai railway system extends to Nongkhai, on the Thai bank of the Mekong, which is connected by ferry with Thadeua about 12 miles east of Vientiane.

Aviation. Lao Aviation provides scheduled domestic air services linking major towns in Laos and international services to Bangkok, Phnom Penh and Hanoi. Thai International, Aeroflot and Air Vietnam provide flights from Bangkok, Hanoi, Rangoon, Ho Chi Min City and Moscow.

Shipping. The river Mekong and its tributaries are an important means of transport, but rapids, waterfalls and narrow channels often impede navigation and make transshipments necessary.

Telecommunications. There is a radio network in Laos as well as a limited TV service with the main station at Vientiane. There were (1988) about 400,000 radio and 32,000 television receivers. A ground station constructed near Vientiane under the Soviet aid programme enables USSR television programmes to be received in the capital. It also provides a telephone service to Hanoi and Eastern Europe.

In 1985 there were 8,136 telephones in Laos.

RELIGION, EDUCATION AND WELFARE

Religion. The majority of the population is Buddhist (Hinayana) but 34% follow tribal religions.

Education. In 1985–86 school year there were 8,000 elementary schools (523,000 pupils); 420 secondary schools (97,000 pupils); 60 senior high schools (4,900 pupils); and 55 vocational schools (6,800 students). There is 1 teachers' training college, 1 college of education, 1 school of medicine, 1 agricultural college and an advanced school of Pali.

Sisavangvong University in Vientiane (founded 1958) had 1,600 students in 1984, and there are regional technical colleges in Luang Prabang, Savannakhét and Champasak.

Health. In 1985 there were 430 doctors and 11,650 hospital beds.

DIPLOMATIC REPRESENTATIVES

Of Laos in Great Britain (resides in Paris)
Ambassador: Thongsay Bodhisane (accredited 17 Nov. 1988).

Of Great Britain in Laos
Ambassador: Ramsay Melhuish, CMG (resides in Bangkok).

Of Laos in USA (2222 S. St., NW, Washington, D.C., 20008)
Chargé d'Affaires: Done Somvorachit.

Of USA in Laos (Rue Bartholonie, Vientiane)
Chargé d'Affaires: Charles B. Salmon, Jr.

Of Laos to the United Nations
Ambassador: Saly Khamsy.

Further Reading

Cordell, H., *Laos.* [Bibliography] Oxford and Santa Barbara, 1990
Deuve, J., *Le royaume du Laos 1949–1965.* Paris, 1984
Stuart-Cox, M., *Contemporary Laos.* Univ. of Queensland Press, 1983.—*Laos: Politics, Economics and Society.* London, 1986
Zasloff, J. J., *The Pathet Lao: Leadership and Organization.* Lexington, Toronto and London, 1973

LEBANON

al-Jumhouriya al-Lubnaniya

Capital: Beirut
Population: 3·5m. (1984)
GNP per capita: No reliable figures available.

HISTORY. After 20 years' French mandatory regime, Lebanon was proclaimed independent at Beirut on 26 Nov. 1941. On 27 Dec. 1943 an agreement was signed between representatives of the French National Committee of Liberation and of Lebanon, by which most of the powers and capacities exercised hitherto by France were transferred as from 1 Jan. 1944 to the Lebanese Government. The evacuation of foreign troops was completed in Dec. 1946.

In early May 1958 the opposition to President Chamoun, consisting principally (though not entirely) of Moslem pro-Nasserist elements, rose in insurrection; and for 5 months the Moslem quarters of Beirut, Tripoli, Sidon and the northern Bekaa were in insurgent hands. On 15 July the US Government acceded to President Chamoun's request and landed a considerable force of army and marines who re-established the authority of the Government.

Israeli attacks on Lebanon resulted from the presence and activities of armed Palestinian resistance units. Internal problems, which had long been latent in Lebanese society, were exacerbated by the politically active Palestinian population and by the deeply divisive question of the Palestine problem itself. An attempt to regulate the activities of Palestinian fighters through the secret Cairo agreement of 1969 was frustrated both by the inability of the Government to enforce its provisions and by an influx of battle-hardened fighters expelled from Jordan in Sept. 1970. A further attempt to control the guerrillas in 1973 also failed. From March 1975, Lebanon was beset by civil disorder causing considerable loss of life and economic life was brought to a virtual standstill.

By Nov. 1976 however, large scale fighting had been brought to an end by the intervention of the Syrian-dominated Arab Deterrent Force which ensured sufficient security to permit Lebanon to establish quasi-normal conditions under President Sarkis. Large areas of the country, however, remained outside Governmental control, including West Beirut which was the scene of frequent conflict between opposing militia groups. The South, where the Arab Deterrent Force could not deploy, remained unsettled and subject to frequent Israeli attacks. In March 1978 there was an Israeli invasion following a Palestinian attack inside Israel. Israeli troops eventually withdrew in June, but instead of handing over all their positions to UN Peacekeeping Forces they installed Israeli-controlled Lebanese militia forces in border areas. Severe disruption continued in the South. In June 1982, following on the attempted assassination of the Israeli ambassador in London, Israeli forces once again invaded, this time in massive strength, and swept through the country, eventually laying siege to and devastatingly bombing Beirut. In Sept. Palestinian forces, together with the PLO leadership, evacuated Beirut. On 23 Aug. 1982 Bachir Gemayel was elected President of Lebanon. On 14 Sept. he was assassinated. His brother, Amin Gemayel, was elected in his place on 21 Sept. Since then there has been a state of 'no peace, no war' with intermittent clashes between the various *de facto* forces on the ground. Israeli forces started a complete withdrawal on 16 Feb. 1985. A peace agreement was signed by the leaders of the Druse, Amal and (Christian) Lebanese Forces to end the civil war on 28 Dec. 1985 but its terms were not implemented. Syrian forces were still acting as a peace keeping force between rival militias in early 1990.

The term of office of Amin Gemayel, as President, expired in Sept. 1989 and René Muaward was elected President on 5 Nov. 1989, but was assassinated on 22 Nov.

AREA AND POPULATION. Lebanon is a mountainous country about 135 miles long and varying between 20 and 35 miles wide, bounded on the north and east by Syria, on the west by the Mediterranean and on the south by Israel. Between the two parallel mountain ranges of Lebanon and Anti-Lebanon lies the fertile Bekaa Valley. About one-half of the country lies at an altitude of over 3,000 ft.

The area of Lebanon is estimated at 10,452 sq. km (4,036 sq. miles) and the population at 3·5m. (1984, estimate) but there are no reliable estimates. The principal towns, with estimated population (1980), are: Beirut (the capital), 702,000; Tripoli 175,000; Zahlé, 46,800; Saida (Sidon), 24,740; Tyre, 14,000.

The official language is Arabic. French and, increasingly, English are widely spoken in official and commercial circles.

CLIMATE. A Mediterranean climate with short, warm winters and long, hot and rainless summers, with high humidity in coastal areas. Rainfall is largely confined to the winter months and can be torrential, with snow on high ground. Beirut. Jan. 55°F (13°C), July 81°F (27°C). Annual rainfall 35·7" (893 mm).

CONSTITUTION AND GOVERNMENT. Lebanon is an independent republic. The first Constitution was established under the French Mandate on 23 May 1926. It has since been amended in 1927, 1929, 1943 (twice) and 1947. It is a written constitution based on the classical separation of powers, with a President, a single chamber elected by universal adult suffrage, and an independent judiciary. The Executive consists of the President and a Prime Minister and Cabinet appointed by him. The system is, however, adapted to the peculiar communal balance on which Lebanese political life depends. This is done by the electoral law which allocates deputies according to the confessional distribution of the population, and by a series of constitutional conventions whereby, *e.g.*, the President is always a Maronite Christian, the Prime Minister a Sunni Moslem and the Speaker of the Assembly a Shia Moslem. There is no highly developed party system other than on religious confessional lines.

President of the Republic: Elias Hrawi (elected 24 Nov. 1989).

National flag: Three horizontal stripes of red, white, red, with the white of double width and bearing in the centre a green cedar of Lebanon.

National anthem: Kulluna lil watan lil 'ula lil' alam (words by Rashid Nachleh, tune by Flaïfel brothers).

Local government: The 6 governorates (including the city of Beirut) are subdivided into 26 districts.

Since Sept. 1988 there have been 2 rival cabinets. General Michel Aoun has been acting Prime Minister of the Christian government and Dr Selim Hoss acting Prime Minister of the Moslem government.

DEFENCE

Army. The strength of the Army was about 21,000 in 1990 but it is in a state of flux and most of its units are well below strength. Its equipment includes 105 M-48, 32 AMX-13 tanks and Saladin armoured cars. In addition, there are numerous private militias under arms in Lebanon, divided between the Maronite-Christian factions, notably the Phalange of some 10,000 men, and the Moslem-Leftist groups.

Navy. The small Christian-controlled flotilla consists of 4 inshore patrol craft and 2 new French-built tank landing craft, the force numbering (1989) 500 officers and men.

Air Force. The Air Force had (1990) about 800 men and 50 aircraft. In addition to 5 Hunter jet fighter-bombers, it has (in storage) 9 Mirage III supersonic fighters and 1 Mirage 2-seat trainer. Other aircraft include 12 Alouette II and III, 4 Gazelle, 9 Puma and 8 Agusta-Bell 212 helicopters, and 5 Fouga Magister jet and 5 piston-engined Bulldog trainers. Serviceability of most aircraft is low because of the troubled national political situation.

INTERNATIONAL RELATIONS

Membership. Lebanon is a member of UN and the Arab League.

ECONOMY

Budget. The budget for 1986 provides for a total expenditure of £Leb.17,937m.

Currency. The Lebanese *pound*, divided into 100 *piastres*, is issued by the Banque du Liban, which commenced operations on 1 April 1964. There is a fluctuating official rate of exchange, fixed monthly (March 1990: £Leb.910·05 = £1 sterling; £Leb.555·25 US$1), this in practice is used only for the calculation of *ad-valorem* customs duties on Lebanese imports and for import statistics. For other purposes the free market is used.

Banking. Beirut was an important international financial centre, and there were about 80 banks registered with the central bank in 1979. As a result of the civil war, Beirut has lost much of its status as an international and regional banking centre; in general only local offices for banks remain.

Weights and Measures. The use of the metric system is legal and obligatory throughout the whole of the country. In outlying districts the former weights and measures may still be in use. They are: 1 *okiya* = 0·47 lb.; 6 *okiyas* = 1 *oke* = 2·82 lb.; 2 *okes* = 1 *rottol* = 5·64 lb.; 200 *okes* = 1 *kantar*.

ENERGY AND NATURAL RESOURCES

Electricity. Electric power production (1986) was 2,270m. kwh. Supply 110 and 120 volts; 50 Hz.

Oil. There are 2 oil refineries in Lebanon, one at Tripoli, which refines oil brought by ship from Iraq, and the other at Sidon, which refines oil brought from Saudi Arabia by a pipeline owned by the Trans-Arabian Pipeline Co. These refineries were not fully active in 1987 and the country depends on imports.

Minerals. Iron ore exists but is difficult to work. Other minerals known to exist are iron pyrites, copper, bituminous shales, asphalt, phosphates, ceramic clays and glass sand; but the available information is of doubtful value.

Agriculture. Lebanon is essentially an agricultural country, although owing to its physical character only about 38% of the total area of the country is at present cultivated.

The estimated production (in 1,000 tonnes) of the main crops in 1988 was as follows: Citrus fruits, 354; apples, 80; grapes, 159; potatoes, 210; sugar-beet, 4; wheat, 19; bananas, 23; olives, 75.

Livestock (estimated, 1988): Goats, 470,000; sheep, 141,000; cattle, 52,000; pigs, 22,000; horses, 2,000; donkeys, 11,000; mules, 4,000.

Forestry. The forests of the past have been denuded by exploitation and in 1988 covered 100,000 hectares, about 8% of the land area.

Fisheries. Total catch (1986) 1,600 tonnes.

INDUSTRY AND TRADE

Industry. Industry suffered badly during the civil war. The manufacturing industry was small but had doubled in size in the 10 years before the war. As a result of the war some industrial concerns have closed but others are working at reduced capacity.

Commerce. Foreign as well as local wholesale and retail trade is the principal source of income in Lebanon. Because of the protectionist policies followed in some neighbouring countries, this sector has been declining, the sectors to gain being those of banking, real estate, government and services.

Reliable trade figures have not been published in recent years.

Total trade between Lebanon and UK (British Department of Trade returns, in £1,000 sterling):

	1985	*1986*	*1987*	*1988*	*1989*
Imports to UK	7,888	9,845	9,528	14,172	11,054
Exports and re-exports from UK	52,751	55,867	40,707	55,575	48,474

Tourism. Receipts from tourism were £Leb.573m. in 1973; since 1975 they have been negligible, this sector having suffered badly as a result of the war.

COMMUNICATIONS

Roads. There were (1987) 7,000 km of roads of which main roads (2,000 km) are not good by international standards. The surface is normally of asphalt and they are well maintained in normal times. Roads between Beirut and the provinces were (1984) controlled by various militia.

In 1985 there were about 300,000 cars and taxis.

Railways. There are 3 railway lines in Lebanon, all operated by the *Office des Chemins de Fer de l'Etat Libanais* (CFL): (1) Nakoura–Beirut–Tripoli (standard gauge); the Nakoura–Sidon section has been idle since the establishment of Israel: (2) a narrow-gauge line running from Beirut to Riyak in the Bekaa Valley (now closed) and thence to Damascus, Syria; (3) a standard-gauge line from Tripoli to Homs and Aleppo in Syria, providing access to Ankara and Istanbul. From Homs a branch of the CFL line extends south and re-enters Lebanon, terminating at Riyak. Total length 417 km. Apart from a short section near Beirut these lines were idle in 1984–85 because of insecurity and large sections needed repairs.

Aviation. Beirut International Airport is used by a few international airlines. There are 2 national airlines, Middle East Airlines/Air Liban and Trans-Mediterranean Airways. Over the past few years Beirut airport was closed several times.

Shipping. Beirut is the largest port, followed by Tripoli, Jounieh and Sidon. Illegal ports have mushroomed on the coast, very much reducing the legal ports' activity. No reliable figures about tonnage were available in 1987.

Post and Broadcasting. There is an automatic telephone system in Beirut which is being extended to other parts of the country. There are no telegraph, postal or telephone communications with Israel. Number of telephones (1986), 150,000.

The state radio transmits in Arabic, French, English and Armenian. Teté-Liban, which is 50% government-owned was the only television station in operation in 1984. There were 450,000 TV sets in 1986 and 1·5m. radios.

Newspapers (1985). There were about 30 daily newspapers in Arabic, 2 in French, 1 in English and 4 in Armenian.

RELIGION, EDUCATION AND WELFARE

Religion. Probably less than half the population are Christians. The Christian faith has been indigenous since the earliest times. The Christians include the Maronites, Greek Orthodox, Armenians, Greek and Roman Catholics, Armenian Catholics and the Protestants. Moslems include the Sunnis, the Shiites and the Druzes. No reliable figures on the numbers of these communities are available. Most Jews left the country after the 1975 disturbances.

Education. Government schools in 1984 comprise primary and secondary schools. There were also private primary and secondary schools. There are also 5 universities, namely the Lebanese (State) University, the American University of Beirut, the French University of St Joseph (founded in 1875), the Arab University, a branch of Alexandria University and Beirut University College. The French Government runs the École Supérieure de Lettres and the Centre d'Études Mathématiques. The Maronite monks run the University of the Holy Spirit at Kaslik.

The Lebanese Academy of Fine Arts includes schools of architecture, art, music, political and social science.

Health. There are several government-run hospitals, and many private ones.

DIPLOMATIC REPRESENTATIVES

Of Lebanon in Great Britain (21 Kensington Palace Gdns., London, W8 4QM)
Ambassador: Gen. Ahmad al-Hajj (accredited 25 May 1983).

Of Great Britain in Lebanon (Shamma Bldg., Raouché, Ras Beirut)
Ambassador: D. E. Tatham.

Of Lebanon in the USA (2560 28th St., NW, Washington, D.C., 20008)
Ambassador: Dr Abdallah Bouhabib.

Of the USA in Lebanon
Ambassador: John T. McCarthy.

Of Lebanon to the United Nations
Acting Ambassador: Chawki Chouéry.

Further Reading

Statistical Information: Import and export figures are produced by the Conseil Supérieur des Douanes. The Service de Statistique Générale (M. A. G. Ayad, *Chef du Service*) publishes a quarterly bulletin (in French and Arabic) covering a wide range of subjects, including foreign trade, production statistics and estimates of the national income.

Cobban, H., *The Making of Modern Lebanon.* London, 1985
Deeb, M., *The Lebanese Civil War.* New York, 1980
Fisk, R., *Pity the Nation: Lebanon at War.* London, 1990
Gilmour, D., *Lebanon: The Fractured Country.* Oxford and New York, 1983
Gordon, D. C., *The Republic of Lebanon: Nation in Jeopardy.* London, 1983
Khairallah, S., *Lebanon.* [Bibliography] Oxford and Santa Barbara, 1979
Laffin, J., *The War of Desperation: Lebanon 1982–85.* London, 1985
Norton, A. R., *Amal and the Shi'a: Struggle for the Soul of Lebanon.* Univ. of Texas Press, 1987
Rabanovich, I., *The War for Lebanon, 1970–1983.* Cornell Univ. Press, 1984
Randal, J., *The Tragedy of Lebanon.* London, 1982
Shehadi, N. and Mills, D.H., *Lebanon: A History of Conflict and Concensus.* London, 1988
Weinberger, N. J., *Syrian Intervention in Lebanon.* New York, 1986

National Library: Dar el Kutub, Parliament Sq., Beirut.

LESOTHO

Capital: Maseru
Population: 1·67m. (1988)
GNP per capita: US$410 (1988)

HISTORY. Basutoland first received the protection of Britain in 1868 at the request of Moshoeshoe I, the first paramount chief. In 1871 the territory was annexed to the Cape Colony, but in 1884 it was restored to the direct control of the British Government through the High Commissioner for South Africa.

On 4 Oct. 1966 Basutoland became an independent and sovereign member of the Commonwealth under the name of the Kingdom of Lesotho.

AREA AND POPULATION. Lesotho, an enclave within the Republic of South Africa is bounded on the west by the Orange Free State, on the north by the Orange Free State and Natal, on the east by Natal, and on the south by Transkei. The altitude varies from 1,500 to 3,482 metres. The area is 11,720 sq. miles (30,355 sq. km). Lesotho is a purely African territory, and the few European residents are government officials, traders, missionaries and artisans.

The census in 1986 showed a total population of 1,577,536 persons. Estimate (1988) 1·67m. The capital is Maseru (population, 1986, 109,382).

The official languages are Sesotho and English.

CLIMATE. A healthy and pleasant climate, with variable rainfall, but averaging 29" (725 mm) a year over most of the country. The rain falls mainly in the summer months of Oct. to April, while the winters are dry and may produce heavy frosts in lowland areas and frequent snow in the highlands. Temperatures in the lowlands range from a maximum of 90°F (32·2°C) in summer to a minimum of 20°F (–6·7°C) in winter.

CONSTITUTION AND GOVERNMENT. Lesotho is a constitutional monarchy with HM the King as Head of State, but the constitution adopted at independence was suspended and the elections of 27 Jan. 1970 were declared invalid on 31 Jan. 1970. Parliamentary rule, with a National Assembly of nominated members, was reintroduced in April 1973, but the National Assembly was dissolved on 1 Jan. 1985 by the first Prime Minister, Chief Joseph Leabua Jonathan.

Chief Jonathan was deposed in a bloodless military *coup* on 20 Jan. 1986. HM the King, acts through a Council of Ministers on the advice of a Military Council. In March 1990 it was reported that the King was in dispute with the military government.

Ruler: Constantine Bereng Seeiso Motlotlehi Moshoeshoe II, Paramount Chief of the Sotho people since 1940, became King at independence on 4 Oct. 1966.

Chairman of the Military Council: Maj.-Gen. Justin Lekhanya.

The College of Chiefs settles the recognition and succession of Chiefs and adjudicates cases of inefficiency, criminality and absenteeism among them.

National flag: Diagonally white over blue over green with the white of double width charged with a brown Basotho shield in the upper hoist.

Local Government. The country is divided into 10 districts, subdivided into 22 wards, as follows: Maseru, Qacha's Nek, Mokhotlong, Leribe, Butha–Buthe, Teyateyaneng, Mafeteng, Mohale's Hoek, Quthing, Thaba–Tseka. Most of the wards are presided over by hereditary chiefs allied to the Moshoeshoe family.

DEFENCE

The Royal Lesotho Defence Force has 2,000 personnel. Formed in 1978, to facilitate deployment of men and equipment to less accessible regions, the service has a total of 6 Bell 412 and BO 105 helicopters.

INTERNATIONAL RELATIONS

Membership. Lesotho is a member of UN, OAU, the Commonwealth and is an ACP state of the EEC.

ECONOMY

Budget. Expenditure (1986–87) M463m.; revenue, M385m.

Currency. The currency is the *Loti* (plural *Maloti*) divided into 100 *Lisente* which is at par with the South African *Rand*. In March 1990, £1 = 4·24 *Maloti*; US$1 = 2·59 *Maloti*.

Banking. The Standard Bank of South Africa and Barclays Bank International have branches at Maseru, Mohale's Hoek and Leribe. The Lesotho Bank has branches throughout the country.

ENERGY AND NATURAL RESOURCES

Electricity. Production (1985) 1m. kwh. Supply 230 volts; 50 Hz.

Agriculture. The chief crops were (1988 production in 1,000 tonnes): Wheat, 21; maize, 126; sorghum, 55; barley, oats, beans, peas and other vegetables are also grown. Soil conservation and the improvement of crops and pasture are matters of vital importance.

Livestock (1988): Cattle, 525,000; horses, 119,000; donkeys, 126,000; pigs, 72,000; sheep, 1·43m.; goats, 1·03m.; mules, 1,000; poultry, 1m.

INDUSTRY AND TRADE

Industry. Industrial development is progressing under the National Development Corporation. Diamond mining ceased in 1982.

Commerce. Lesotho, Botswana and Swaziland are members of the South African customs union, by agreement dated 29 June 1910.

Total values of imports and exports into and from Lesotho (in Mm.):

	1983	*1984*	*1985*	*1986*
Imports	627	725	797	893
Exports	35	42	50	58

In 1981, 97% of imports came from within the Southern African customs union, while 47% of exports went to the same countries and 42% to Switzerland.

Principal imports were food, livestock, drink and tobacco, machinery and transport equipment, mineral fuels and lubricants; principal exports were wool and mohair and diamonds.

The majority of international trade is with the Republic of South Africa.

Total trade between Lesotho and UK (British Department of Trade returns, in £1,000 sterling):

	1985	*1986*	*1987*	*1988*	*1989*
Imports to UK	290	277	486	977	734
Exports and re-exports from UK	3,023	2,128	1,112	1,260	795

Tourism. In 1986 there were 213,000 visitors.

COMMUNICATIONS

Roads. There were (1988) 572 km of tarred roads and 2,300 km of gravel-surfaced roads. In addition to the main roads there were (1983) 931 km of food aid tracks leading to trading stations and missions. Communications into the mountainous interior are by means of bridlepaths suitable only for riding and pack animals, but a mountain road of 80 miles has been constructed, and some parts are accessible by air transport, which is being used increasingly. In 1983 there were 10,200 commercial vehicles and 4,359 passenger cars.

Railways. A railway built by the South African Railways, 1 mile long, connects Maseru with the Bloemfontein–Natal line at Marseilles.

Aviation. There is a scheduled passenger service between Maseru and Jan Smuts Airport, Johannesburg, operated jointly by Lesotho National Airways and SAA. There are also 30 airstrips for light aircraft.

Post and Broadcasting. There were 5,409 telephones in 1983. Radio Lesotho transmits daily in English and Sesotho. Radio receivers (1987), 400,000.

Newspapers. In 1985, 3 daily newspapers had a combined circulation of 44,000.

JUSTICE, RELIGION, EDUCATION AND WELFARE

Justice. The Lesotho High Court and the Court of Appeal are situated in Maseru, and there are Magistrates' Courts in the districts.

Religion. About 93% of the population are Christians, 44% being Roman Catholics.

Education. Education is largely in the hands of the 3 main missions (Paris Evangelical, Roman Catholic and English Church), under the direction of the Ministry of Education. In 1984–85 the total enrolment in 1,141 primary schools was 314,003; in 143 secondary schools, 35,423; in the National Teacher-Training College and 8 technical schools enrolment 2,221. University education is provided at the National University of Lesotho established in 1975 at Roma; enrolment in 1985, 1,119 and 146 teaching staff.

Health. The government medical staff of the territory consists of 1 Permanent Secretary for Health, 1 Director of Health Services, 1 medical superintendent, 8 district medical officers and a total of 102 doctors including 20 specialists.

There are 11 government hospitals staffed by 308 matrons, sisters and nurses. There is accommodation for 2,175 patients in government hospitals.

DIPLOMATIC REPRESENTATIVES

Of Lesotho in Great Britain (10 Collingham Rd., London, SW5 0NR)
High Commissioner: M. K. Tsekoa (accredited 15 Nov. 1989).

Of Great Britain in Lesotho (PO Box Ms 521, Maseru 100)
High Commissioner: J. C. Edwards, CMG.

Of Lesotho in the USA (2511 Massachusetts Ave., NW, Washington, D.C., 20008)
Ambassador: W. T. Van Tonder.

Of the USA in Lesotho (PO Box 333, Maseru, 100)
Ambassador: (Vacant).

Of Lesotho to the United Nations
Ambassador: Monyane P. Phoofolo.

Further Reading

Statistical Information: Bureau of Statistics, PO Box 455, Maseru, Lesotho.
Ashton, H., *The Basuto*. 2nd ed. OUP, 1967
Bardill, J. E. and Cobbe, J. H., *Lesotho: Dilemmas of Dependence in South Africa*. London, 1986
Murray, C., *Families Divided: The Impact of Migrant Labour in Lesotho*. OUP, 1981
Willet, S. M. and Ambrose, D. P., *Lesotho*. [Bibliography] Oxford and Santa Barbara, 1981

LIBERIA

Capital: Monrovia
Population: 2·44m. (1988)
GNP per capita: US$440 (1987)

HISTORY. The Republic of Liberia had its origin in the efforts of several American philanthropic societies to establish freed American slaves in a colony on the West African coast. In 1822 a settlement was formed near the spot where Monrovia now stands. On 26 July 1847 the State was constituted as the Free and Independent Republic of Liberia.

On 12 April 1980, President Tolbert was assassinated; his government was overthrown and the Constitution suspended. President Tolbert's party, the True Whig Party, was formed in 1860 and had been in power since 1870. In March 1980, the newly formed People's Progressive Party was banned and its leaders arrested. The *coup* was led by Master-Sergeant Doe who was later installed as Head of State and Commander-in-Chief of the army.

AREA AND POPULATION. Liberia has about 350 miles of coastline, extending from Sierra Leone, on the west, to the Côte d'Ivoire, on the east. It stretches inland to a distance, in some places, of about 250 miles and is bounded in the north by Guinea.

The total area is about 42,989 sq. miles (111,370 sq. km). At the census (1984) population 2,101,628. Estimate (1988) 2,436,000. English is the official language spoken by 15% of the population. The rest belong in the main to 3 linguistic groups: Mande, West Atlantic, and the Kwa. These are in turn subdivided into 16 ethnic groups: Bassa, Bella, Gbandi, Mende, Gio, Dey, Mano, Gola, Kpelle, Kissi, Krahn, Kru, Lorma, Mandingo, Vai and Grebo.

Monrovia, the capital, had (1984) a population of 425,000; other towns include Buchanan (24,000).

There are 11 counties and 2 territories, whose areas, populations (1984 census) and capitals are as follows:

County	*Sq. km*	*1984*	*Chief town*
Bomi [1]	1,955	66,420	Tubmanburg
Bong	8,099	255,813	Gbarnga
Grand Bassa	8,759	159,648	Buchanan
Grand Cape Mount	5,827	79,322	Robertsport
Grand Gedeh	17,029	102,810	Zwedru
Lofa	19,360	247,641	Voinjama
Margibi	3,263	97,992	Kakata
Maryland	5,351 [2]	132,058 [2]	Harper
Montserrado	2,740	544,878	Bensonville
Nimba	12,043	313,050	Saniquillie
Rivercess [1]	4,385	37,849	Rivercess
Sinoe	10,254	64,147	Greenville

[1] Territory. [2] Includes new county of Grand Kru (chief town, Barclayville).

CLIMATE. An equatorial climate, with constant high temperatures and plentiful rainfall, though Jan. to May is drier than the rest of the year. Monrovia. Jan. 79°F (26·1°C), July 76°F (24·4°C). Annual rainfall 206" (5,138 mm).

CONSTITUTION AND GOVERNMENT. A new Constitution was approved by referendum in July 1984 and came into force on 6 Jan. 1986. The National Assembly consists of a 26-member Senate and a 64-member House of Representatives. General elections were held on 15 Oct. 1985. The National Democratic Party of Liberia gained 21 seats in the Senate; the Liberal Action Party, 3 seats and the Liberian Unification Party and the Unity Party one each. In the House of Representatives, the NDPL won 45 seats and others 19 seats.

President and Commander-in-Chief: Samuel Kanyon Doe.
Vice President: Harry F. Moniba.

National flag: Six red and 5 white horizontal stripes alternating. In the upper corner, nearest the staff, is a square of blue covering a depth of 5 stripes. In the centre of this blue field is a 5-pointed white star.

National anthem: All hail, Liberia, hail! (words by President Warner; tune by O. Lucas, 1860).

DEFENCE

Army. The establishment organized on a militia basis numbers 5,300 (1990), divided into 6 infantry battalions with support units.

Navy. A coast-guard force of (1989) about 500 operates 5 inshore patrol craft, none exceeding 50 tonnes.

Air Force. The Air Reconnaissance Unit, supports the Liberian Army. Equipment includes 2 C-47 transports, 4 Israeli-built Arava twin-turboprop light transports, 1 Cessna 208 Caravan transport and a small number of Cessna 172, 185 and 337G light aircraft. Personnel (1990) about 250.

INTERNATIONAL RELATIONS

Membership. Liberia is a member of UN, OAU, ECOWAS and is an ACP state of EEC.

ECONOMY

Budget. Revenue and expenditure was as follows (in US$1,000):

	1984–85	*1985–86*	*1986–87*
Revenue	315,000	237,600	366,400
Expenditure	371,000	366,700	366,400

Currency. The legal currency of Liberia is the *dollar* which is equivalent to US$1 which itself has been in circulation since 3 Nov. 1942, but there is a Liberian coinage in silver and copper. Official accounts are kept in dollars and cents. The Liberian coins are as follows: Silver,$5, $1, 50-, 25-, 10- and 5-cent pieces; alloy, 2-cent and copper 1-cent pieces. The Government has not yet issued paper money. In March 1990, £1 = 1·64 Liberian $; US$1 = 1 Liberian $.

Banking. The First National City Bank (Liberia) was founded in 1935. An Italian bank, Tradevco, started business in 1955. The International Trust Co. of Liberia opened a commercial banking department at the end of 1960. The Liberian Bank of Development and Investment (LBDI) was founded in 1964 and began operations in 1965. The National Bank of Liberia opened on 22 July 1974, to act as a central bank. The National Housing and Savings Bank opened on 20 Jan. 1972. The Liberian Finance & Trust Corporation was incorporated Oct. 1976 and began operations in May 1977. The Liberian Agricultural and Co-operative Development Bank started operations in 1978. The Bank of Credit & Commerce International opened in Sept. 1978 and Meridien Bank of Liberia in July 1985.

Weights and Measures. Weights and measures are the same as in UK and USA.

ENERGY AND NATURAL RESOURCES

Electricity. Production (1986) was 655m. kwh. Supply 120 volts; 60 Hz.

Minerals. Iron ore production was 8·9m. tonnes in 1985. Gold production (1986) 21,125 oz valued at US$7·3m. and diamond production (1985) 66,000 carats.

Agriculture. Over 65% of the labour force is engaged in agriculture. The soil is productive, but due to excessive rainfall (from 160 to 180 in. per year), there are large swamp areas. Rice, cassava, coffee, citrus and sugar-cane are cultivated. The Government is negotiating the financing of large-scale investment in rice production aimed at making the country self-sufficient in rice production. Coffee, cocoa and palm-kernels are produced mainly by the traditional agricultural sector.

The Liberia Produce Marketing Corporation (LPMC) operates an oil-mill in Monrovia, processing most of the palm-kernels. There were 2 large commercial oil-palm plantations in the country. The Liberia Industrial Co-operative (LBINC) has 6,000 acres of oil-palm (of which 5,000 acres are in production) in Grand Bassa County, and West Africa Agricultural Co. (WAAC) has 4,020 acres in production in Grand Cape Mount County.

Production (1988, in 1,000 tonnes): Rice, 279; cassava, 310; coffee, 5; oranges, 7; sugar-cane, 225; cocoa, 5; palm-kernels, 8.

Livestock (1988): Cattle, 42,000; pigs, 140,000; sheep, 240,000; poultry, 4m.

Forestry. The Firestone Plantation Co. have large rubber plantations, employing over 40,000 men. Their concession comprises about 1m. acres and expires in the year 2025. About 100,000 acres have been planted. Independent producers have a further 65,000 acres planted.

Production in 1986 was 4·75m. cu. metres.

Fisheries. Catch (1986) 16,100 tonnes.

INDUSTRY AND TRADE

Industry. There are a number of small factories (brick and tile, soap, nails, mattresses, shoes, plastics, paint, oxygen, acetylene, tyre retreading, a brewery, soft drinks, cement, matches, candy and biscuits).

Commerce. Imports in 1986 totalled US$259,037,900 (1985, US$284,377,000) and exports US$408,374,099 (1985, US$435,570,000). Liberia's main trading partners are the USA and the Federal Republic of Germany.

In 1987, iron ore accounted for about 70% of total export earnings, rubber 15% and sawn timber over 5%. Other exports were coffee, cocoa, palm-kernel oil, diamonds and gold.

Total trade between Liberia and UK (British Department of Trade returns, in £1,000 sterling):

	1985	*1986*	*1987*	*1988*	*1989*
Imports to UK	7,967	7,574	7,284	9,574	12,776
Exports and re-exports from UK	15,957	22,056	13,538	11,684	15,148

The figures for exports from the UK include the value of shipping transferred to the Liberian flag; the genuine exports are considerably lower.

COMMUNICATIONS

Roads. In 1981, there were 4,794 miles of public roads (1,165 primary, 366 paved, 799 all-weather, 3,629 secondary and feeder) and 1,474 miles of private roads (93 paved, 1,381 laterite and earth). The principal highway connects Monrovia with the road system of Guinea, with branches leading into the Eastern and Western areas of Liberia. The latter branch reaches the Sierra Leone border and joins the Sierra Leone road system. A bridge over the St Paul River carries road traffic to the iron-ore mines at Bomi Hills.

Railway. A railway (for freight only) was built in 1951, connecting Monrovia with the Bomi Hills iron-ore mines about 69 km distant; this has been extended to the National Iron Ore Co. area by 79 km. There is a line from Nimba to Lower Buchanan and another line from Bong to Monrovia (78 km).

Aviation. The airport for Liberia is Roberts International Airport (30 miles from Monrovia). The James Spriggs Payne Airfield, 5 miles from Monrovia, can be used by light aircraft and mini jumbo jets. Air services are maintained by Ghana Airways, Swissair, British Caledonian, Air Guinea, SABENA, Iberia Airlines, Romanian Airlines and Air Liberia.

Shipping. Over 2,000 vessels enter Monrovia each year. The Liberian Government requires only a modest registration fee and an almost nominal annual charge and maintains no control over the operation of ships flying the Liberian flag.

Post and Broadcasting. There is cable communication with Europe and America *via* Dakar, and a wireless station is maintained by the Government at Monrovia. There is a telephone service (8,510 telephones, 1983), in Monrovia, which is gradually being extended over the whole country. There were (1988) 570,000 radio and 43,000 television receivers.

JUSTICE, RELIGION, EDUCATION AND WELFARE

Justice. Justice is administered by a Supreme Court of 5 judges, 14 circuit courts and lower courts.

Religion. The main denominations represented in Liberia are Methodist, Baptist, Episcopalian, African Methodist, Pentecostal, Seventh-day Adventist, Lutheran and Roman Catholic, working through missionaries and mission schools. There were (1985) about 670,000 Moslems.

Education. Schools are classified as: (1) Public schools, maintained and run by the Government; (2) Mission schools, supported by foreign Missions and subsidized by the Government, and operated by qualified Missionaries and Liberian teachers; (3) Private schools, maintained by endowments and sometimes subsidized by the Government.

In 1986 there were estimated to be 1,830 schools with 8,744 teachers and 443,786 pupils.

Health. There were 236 doctors in 1981 and about 3,000 hospital beds.

DIPLOMATIC REPRESENTATIVES

Of Liberia in Great Britain (2 Pembridge Pl., London, W2)
Ambassador: W. A. Givens.

Of Great Britain in Liberia (PO Box 10-0120, 1000, Monrovia)
Ambassador and Consul-General: M. E. J. Gore.

Of Liberia in the USA (5201 16th St., NW, Washington, D.C., 20011)
Ambassador: Eugenia Wordsworth-Stevenson.

Of the USA in Liberia (United Nations Drive, Monrovia)
Ambassador: James K. Bishop.

Of Liberia to the United Nations
Ambassador: Sylvester O. Jarrett.

Further Reading

Economic Survey of Liberia, 1981. Ministry of Planning and Economic Affairs
Dunn, D. E., *The Foreign Policy of Liberia during the Tubman Era, 1944–71*. London, 1979
Fraenkel, M., *Tribe and Class in Monrovia*. OUP, 1964
Wilson, C. M., *Liberia: Black Africa in Microcosm*. New York, 1971

LIBYA

Capital: Tripoli
Population: 3·96m. (1986)
GNP per capita: US$5,410 (1988)

Al-Jamahiriya Al-Arabiya Al-Libiya Al-Shabiya Al-Ishtirakiya Al-Uzma

HISTORY. Tripoli fell under Turkish domination in the 16th century, and though in 1711 the Arab population secured some measure of independence, the country was in 1835 proclaimed a Turkish vilayet. In Sept. 1911 Italy occupied Tripoli and on 19 Oct. 1912, by the Treaty of Ouchy, Turkey recognized the sovereignty of Italy in Tripoli.

After the expulsion of the Germans and Italians in 1942 and 1943, Tripolitania and Cyrenaica were placed under British, and the Fezzan under French, military administration. Britain recognized the Amir Mohammed Idris Al-Senussi as Amir of Cyrenaica in June 1949.

Libya became an independent, sovereign, federal kingdom under the Amir of Cyrenaica, Mohammed Idris Al-Senussi, as King of the United Kingdom of Libya, on 24 Dec. 1951, when the British Residents in Tripolitania and Cyrenaica and the French Resident in the Fezzan transferred their remaining powers to the federal government of Libya, in pursuance of decisions passed by the United Nations in 1949 and 1950.

On 1 Sept. 1969 King Idris was deposed by a group of army officers. Twelve of the group of officers formed the Revolutionary Command Council chaired by Col. Muammar Qadhafi and proclaimed a republic.

AREA AND POPULATION. Libya is bounded north by the Mediterranean Sea, east by Egypt and Sudan, south by Chad and Niger and west by Algeria and Tunisia. The area is estimated at 1,759,540 sq. km (679,358 sq. miles). The population, at the census on 31 July 1984, was 3,637,488; estimate (1986) 3,955,000.

In 1985, 65% of the population was urban. The chief cities (1981) were: Tripoli, the capital (858,000), Benghazi (368,000) and Misurata (117,000).

The populations (1984) of the municipalities were as follows:

Ajdabiya	100,547	Jabal al-Akhdar	120,662	Shati	46,749
Awbari	48,701	Khums	149,642	Surt	110,996
Aziziyah	85,068	Kufrah	25,139	Tarhunah	84,640
Benghazi	485,386	Marzuq	42,294	Tobruk	94,006
Derna	105,031	Misurata	178,295	Tripoli	990,697
Fatah	102,763	Niqat al-Khums	181,584	Yafran	73,420
Ghadames	52,247	Sabha	76,171	Zawia	220,075
Gharyan	117,073	Sawfajjin	45,195	Zlitan	101,107

CLIMATE. The coastal region has a warm temperate climate, with mild wet winters and hot dry summers, though most of the country suffers from aridity. Tripoli. Jan. 52°F (11·1°C), July 81°F (27·2°C). Annual rainfall 16" (400 mm). Benghazi. Jan. 56°F (13·3°C), July 77°F (25°C). Annual rainfall 11" (267 mm).

CONSTITUTION AND GOVERNMENT. In March 1977 a new form of direct democracy, the 'Jamahiriya' (state of the masses) was promulgated and the official name of the country was changed to Socialist Peoples Libyan Arab Jamahiriya. Under this system, every adult is supposed to be able to share in policy making through the Basic People's Congresses of which there are some 2,000 throughout Libya. These Congresses appoint Popular Committees to execute policy. Provincial and urban affairs are handled by Popular Committees responsible to

Municipality People's Congresses, of which there are 13. Officials of these Congresses and Committees form at national level the General People's Congress which now normally meets for about a week early each year (usually in March). This is the highest policy-making body in the country. The General People's Congress appoints its own General Secretariat and the General People's Committee, whose members (the equivalents of ministers under other forms of government) head the 10 government departments which execute policy at national level.

Until 1977 Libya was ruled by a Revolutionary Command Council headed by Col. Muammar Qadhafi. Upon its abolition in that year the 5 surviving members of the RCC became the General Secretariat of the General People's Congress, still under Qadhafi's direction. In 1979 they stood down to be replaced by elected officials. Since then, Col. Qadhafi has retained his position as Leader of the Revolution. But neither he nor his former RCC colleagues have any formal posts in the present administration, although they continue to wield considerable authority.

Arabic is the official language.

Secretary of the General People's Congress: Omar Mustafa al-Muntasir.
Foreign Affairs: Jadallah Azzuz al-Talhi.
National flag: Plain green.

DEFENCE. There is selective conscription for a 2 year period. Enrolment in the reserves, numbering about 40,000, continues until age 49. On 31 Aug. 1989 it was announced that the traditional armed forces were abolished and in future will be known as the 'Armed People'.

Army. The Army is organized into 1 tank and 2 mechanized infantry divisions in addition to 38 tank battalions, 54 mechanized infantry, 1 National Guard, 41 artillery, 2 anti-aircraft and 12 parachute commando battalions, 7 surface-to-surface and 3 surface-to-air brigades. Equipment includes 1,800 T-54/-55/-62 and 180 T-72 main battle tanks. The Army has an aviation component; equipped with 29 helicopters and about 10 O-1 Bird Dog observation aircraft. Strength (1990) 55,000. The paramilitary Pan-African Legion numbers approximately 2,500.

Navy. The fleet, a general mixture of Soviet and West European built ships, comprises 6 Soviet-built diesel submarines, 3 missile-armed frigates, 7 missile-armed corvettes, 24 fast missile craft, 1 coastal and 23 inshore patrol craft. There are 2 tank landing ships and 3 medium landing ships, plus 16 landing craft. Auxiliaries include 1 logistic support ship, 1 salvage ship, 1 transport and a diving support ship.

One Soviet-built missile corvette was sunk and one severely damaged by the USN in March 1986.

There is a small Naval Aviation wing operating 25 Flaze and 12 super-Frelon helicopters from shore bases.

Personnel in 1989 totalled 8,000, including coastguard. The forces are based at Tarabulus, Benghazi, Darnah, Tobruk, Sidi Bilal and Al Khums.

Air Force. The creation of an Air Force began in 1959. In 1974, delivery was completed of a total of 110 Mirage 5 combat aircraft and trainers, of which about 50 remain. They have been followed by 10 Tu-22 supersonic reconnaissance bombers, 70 MiG-25 interceptors and reconnaissance aircraft, 100 Su-22 ground attack fighters, 94 MiG-21s, and about 140 MiG-23 variable-geometry fighters and fighter-bombers from the USSR. In 1989 the first of 15 Su-2YD supersonic bombers were delivered. Other equipment includes 40 Mirage F1 fighters from France, 6 Mirage F1-B two-seat trainers, 20 Mi-24 gunship helicopters, Mi-14 anti-submarine helicopters, 10 C-130/L-100 Hercules and 20 Aeritalia G222T transports, 8 Super Frelon and 6 Agusta-built CH-47C Chinook heavy-lift helicopters, and a total of 16 Bell 212, Bell 47, Alouette III and Mi-8 helicopters. Training is performed on piston-engined SF.260Ms (some of which are armed for light attack duties) from Italy; L-39 Albatros, Galeb and Magister jet aircraft; and twin-engined L-410s built in Czechoslovakia. Personnel total (1990) about 22,000, with many of the combat aircraft operated by foreign aircrew.

INTERNATIONAL RELATIONS

Membership. Libya is a member of UN, OAU, OIC, OPEC, Arab Maghreb Union and the Arab League.

ECONOMY

Planning. Declining oil revenues (60% down on 1980 levels) has meant postponing of most projects envisaged in the 5-year development plan (1981–85) though the Great-Man-Made River Project has not been affected.

Budget. A development budget of LD1,174m. was announced for 1989.

Currency. The currency is the Libyan *dinar* which is divided into 1,000 *millemes*. Rate of exchange, March 1990: LD 0·4833 = £1; LD 0·2948 = US$1.

Banking. A National Bank of Libya was established in 1955; it was renamed the Central Bank of Libya in 1972. All foreign banks were nationalized by Dec. 1970. In 1972 the government set up the Libyan Arab Foreign Bank whose function is overseas investment and to participate in multinational banking corporations. The National Agricultural Bank, which has been set up to give loans and subsidies to farmers to develop their land and to assist them in marketing their crops, has offices in Tripoli, Benghazi, Sebha and other agricultural centres.

Weights and Measures. Although the metric system has been officially adopted and is obligatory for all contracts, the following weights and measures are still used: *oke* = 1·282 kg; *kantar* = 51·28 kg; *draa* = 46 cm; *handaza* = 68 cm.

ENERGY AND NATURAL RESOURCES

Electricity. Electricity capacity (1985) 5,615 mw. Production (1986) 2,126m. kwh. Supply 110, 115 and 220 volts; 50 Hz.

Oil. Production (1989) 53m. tonnes. Reserves (1988) 23,000m. bbls. The Libyan National Oil Corporation (NOC) was established in March 1970 to be the state's organization for the exploitation of Libya's oil resources. NOC does not participate in the production of oil but has a majority share in all the operating companies with the exception of two small producers Aquitaine-Libya and Wintershall Libya.

The largest producers are Waha (formerly Oasis, until the withdrawal of US oil companies at the end of June 1986) and AGECO who together produce more than 50% of total production. The other significant producers are Zuweitina (formerly Occidental Libya), AGIP, Sirte Oil Company, and Veba (also known as Mobil Oil Libya, although Mobil Inc. withdrew in July 1982 after EXXON's withdrawal from the Sirte Oil Company in Oct. 1981).

Gas. Reserves (1988) 620,000m. cu. metres. Production (1982) 29,000m. cu. metres. In 1983 a gas pipeline was under construction which will take gas from Brega, along the coast to Misurata. In 1987 agreement was reached with Algeria and Tunisia to construct a gas pipeline to supply western Libya with Algerian gas.

Water. Since 1984 a major project has been under way to bring water from wells in southern Libya to the coast. This scheme, called the 'Great Man-made River', is planned, on completion, to irrigate some 185,000 acres of land with water brought along some 4,000 km of pipes. It is planned that Phase I project will be operational in 1990 at a cost of US$3,300m; Phase II of the project (covering the west of Libya) was announced in Sept. 1989. This contract is valued at US$5,300m. and is expected to last 74 months.

Minerals. Cement production (1987) 2·7m. tonnes. Gypsum output (1982) 172,400 tonnes. Iron ore deposits have been found in the south and uranium has reportedly been found in the region of Ghat in the south-west.

Agriculture. Tripolitania has 3 zones from the coast inland—the Mediterranean, the sub-desert and the desert. The first, which covers an area of about 17,231 sq. miles, is the only one properly suited for agriculture, and may be further subdivided into: (1) the oases along the coast, the richest in North Africa, in which thrive the date palm, the olive, the orange, the peanut and the potato; (2) the steppe district, suitable for cereals (barley and wheat) and pasture; it has olive, almond, vine, orange and mulberry trees and ricinus plants; (3) the dunes, which are being gradually afforested with acacia, robinia, poplar and pine; (4) the Jebel (the mountain district, Tarhuna, Garian, Nalut-Yefren), in which thrive the olive, the fig, the vine and other fruit trees, and which on the east slopes down to the sea with the fertile hills of Msellata. Of some 25m. acres of productive land in Tripolitania, nearly 20m. are used for grazing and about 1m. for static farming. The sub-desert zone produces the alfa plant. The desert zone and the Fezzan contain some fertile oases, such as those of Ghadames, Ghat, Socna, Sebha, Brak.

Cyrenaica has about 10m. acres of potentially productive land, most of which, however, is suitable only for grazing. Certain areas, chief of which is the plateau known as the Barce Plain (about 1,000 ft above sea-level), are suitable for dry farming; in addition, grapes, olives and dates are grown. With improved irrigation, production, particularly of vegetables, could be increased, but stock raising and dry farming will remain of primary importance. About 143,000 acres are used for settled farming; about 272,000 acres are covered by natural forests. The Agricultural Development Authority plans to reclaim 6,000 hectares each year for agriculture. In the Fezzan there are about 6,700 acres of irrigated gardens and about 297,000 acres are planted with date palms.

Production (1988, in tonnes): Wheat, 193,000; barley, 99,000; milk, 143,000; meat, 154,000. Olive trees number about 3·4m. and productive date-palm trees about 3m.

Livestock (1988): 5·7m. sheep, 965,000 goats, 215,000 cattle, 37m. poultry.

Fisheries. The catch in 1986 was 7,800 tonnes.

INDUSTRY AND TRADE

Industry. Since the revolution there has been an ambitious programme of industrial development aimed at the local manufacture of building materials (steel and aluminium pipes and fittings, electric cables, cement, bricks, glass, etc.), foodstuffs (dairy products, flour, tinned fruits and vegetables, dates, fish processing and canning, etc.), textiles and footwear (ready-made clothing, woollen and cotton cloth, blankets, leather footwear, etc.) and development of mineral deposits (iron ore, phosphates, mineral salts). Many projects have been delayed or reduced in recent years, owing to fall in oil revenues since 1980. Small scale private sector industrialization in the form of partnerships is permitted. From 21 Sept. 1969 all businesses, except oil and banks, were Libyan-owned; subsequently all banks and most oil companies were nationalized.

Commerce. Total imports in 1987 were valued at US$4,969 (f.o.b.) and exports at US$6,612 (f.o.b.), virtually all crude oil. In 1987, 25% of imports came from Italy, while 33% of exports were to Italy, 16% to the Federal Republic of Germany and 11% to Spain.

Total trade between Libya and UK (British Department of Trade returns, in £1,000 sterling):

	1985	*1986*	*1987*	*1988*	*1989*
Imports to UK	311,764	136,390	133,649	111,812	104,546
Exports and re-exports from UK	237,639	260,529	220,626	235,957	239,191

Tourism. There were 100,000 visitors in 1984.

COMMUNICATIONS

Roads. In 1986 there were 25,675 km of roads. In 1982 there were 415,509 passenger cars and 334,405 commercial vehicles.

Railways. In 1989 there were no operating railways.

Aviation. A national airline, the Libyan Arab Airlines (LAA), was inaugurated on 30 Sept. 1965. Benghazi and Tripoli are linked by LAA and other international airlines to Athens, Rome, Madrid, Moscow, Frankfurt, Paris, Amsterdam, Vienna and Zurich.

Post and Broadcasting. Tripoli is connected by telegraph cable with Malta and by microwave link with Bengardane (Tunis). There are overseas wireless-telegraph stations at Benghazi and Tripoli, and radio-telephone services connect Libya with most countries of western Europe. In 1982 some 102,000 telephones were in use and in 1983 there were 165,000 radio sets and 170,000 television receivers.

Newspapers. There was (1989) one daily in Tripoli with a circulation of about 40,000.

JUSTICE, RELIGION, EDUCATION AND WELFARE

Justice. The Civil, Commercial and Criminal codes are based mainly on the Egyptian model. Matters of personal status of family or succession matters affecting Moslems are dealt with in special courts according to the Moslem law. All other matters, civil, commercial and criminal, are tried in the ordinary courts, which have jurisdiction over everyone.

There are civil and penal courts in Tripoli and Benghazi, with subsidiary courts at Misurata and Derna; courts of assize in Tripoli and Benghazi, and courts of appeal in Tripoli and Benghazi.

Religion. Islam is declared the State religion, but the right of others to practise their religions is provided for. In 1982, 97% were Sunni Moslems.

Education. There were (1981–82) 718,124 pupils in primary schools, 286,414 in preparatory and secondary schools, 44,789 pupils in technical schools and 25,700 students in higher education. There are 3 universities of Al Fatah (in Tripoli), Garyounes (in Benghazi) and Sabha.

Health. In 1981 there were 74 hospitals with 15,375 beds, 4,690 physicians, 314 dentists, 420 pharmacists, 1,080 midwives and 5,346 nursing personnel.

DIPLOMATIC REPRESENTATIVES

UK broke off diplomatic relations with Libya on 22 April 1984. Saudi Arabia looks after Libyan interests in UK and Italy looks after UK's interests in Libya.

USA suspended all embassy activities in Tripoli on 2 May 1980.

Of Libya to the United Nations
Ambassador: Dr Ali Treiki.

Further Reading

Allen, J. A., *Libya: The Experience of Oil*. London and Boulder, 1981.—*Libya since Independence*. London, 1982
Bearman, J., *Qadhafi's Libya*. London, 1986
Blundy, D. and Lycett, A., *Qadhafi and the Libyan Revolution*. London, 1987
Cooley, J. K., *Libyan Sandstorm: The Complete Account of Qaddafi's Revolution*. London and New York, 1983
Fergiani, M. B., *The Libyan Jamahiriya*. London, 1984
Hahn, L., *Historical Dictionary of Libya*. London, 1961
Harris, L. C., *Libya: Qadhafi's Revolution and the Modern State*. Boulder and London, 1986
Lawless, R. I., *Libya*. [Bibliography] Oxford and Santa Barbara, 1987
St John, R. B., *Qaddafi's World Design: Libyan Foreign Policy, 1969-1987*. London, 1987
Waddhams, F. C., *The Libyan Oil Industry*. London, 1980
Wright, J., *Libya: A Modern History*. London, 1982.— *Libya, Chad and the Central Sahara*. London, 1969

LIECHTENSTEIN

Capital: Vaduz
Population: 28,181 (1988)

HISTORY. The Principality of Liechtenstein, situated between the Austrian province of Vorarlberg and the Swiss cantons of St Gallen and Graubünden, is a sovereign state whose history dates back to 3 May 1342, when Count Hartmann III became ruler of the county of Vaduz. Additions were later made to the count's domains, and by 1434 the territory reached its present boundaries. It consists of the two former counties of Schellenberg and Vaduz (until 1806 immediate fiefs of the Roman Empire). The former in 1699 and the latter in 1712 came into the possession of the house of Liechtenstein and, by diploma of 23 Jan. 1719, granted by the Emperor Charles VI, the two counties were constituted as the Principality of Liechtenstein.

AREA AND POPULATION. Liechtenstein is bounded on the east by Austria and the west by Switzerland. Area, 160 sq. km (61·8 sq. miles); population, of Alemannic race (census 1980), 25,215; estimate, 1988, 28,181. In 1988 there were 416 births and 195 deaths. Population of Vaduz (census 1980), 4,606; estimate, 1988, 4,919. The language is German.

REIGNING PRINCE. Hans-Adam II, born 14 Feb. 1945; succeeded his father Prince Francis-Joseph, 13 Nov. 1989 (he exercised the prerogatives to which the Sovereign is entitled from 26 Aug. 1984); married on 30 July 1967 to Countess Marie Kinsky; there are 3 sons, Hereditary Prince Alois (born 11 June 1968), Prince Maximilian (born 16 May 1969) and Prince Constantin (born 15 March 1972), and one daughter, Princess Tatjana (born 10 April 1973). The monarchy is hereditary in the male line.

CONSTITUTION AND GOVERNMENT. Liechtenstein is a constitutional monarchy ruled by the princes of the House of Liechtenstein. The present constitution of 5 Oct. 1921 provided for a unicameral parliament (Diet) of 15 members elected for 4 years, but this was amended to 25 members in 1988. Election is on the basis of proportional representation. The prince can call and dismiss the parliament. On parliamentary recommendation, he appoints the prime minister and the 4 councillors for a 4-year term. Any group of 1,000 persons or any 3 communes may propose legislation (initiative). Bills passed by the parliament may be submitted to popular referendum. A law is valid when it receives a majority approval by the parliament and the prince's signed concurrence. The capital and seat of government is Vaduz and there are 10 more communes all connected by modern roads. The 11 communes are fully independent administrative bodies within the laws of the principality. They levy additional taxes to the state taxes. Since Feb. 1921 Liechtenstein has had the Swiss currency, and since 29 March 1923 has been united with Switzerland in a customs union.

At the elections for the Diet, on 5 March 1989, the Fatherland Union obtained 13 seats, the opposition Progressive Citizens' Party, 12 seats.

Head of Government: Hans Brunhart.

National flag: Horizontally blue over red, with a gold coronet in the first quarter.
National anthem: Oben am jungen Rhein (words by H. H. Jauch, 1850; tune, 'God save the Queen').

INTERNATIONAL RELATIONS

Membership. Liechtenstein is a member of EFTA, the Council of Europe and the International Court of Justice.

ECONOMY

Budget. Budget estimates for 1989: Revenue, 377,530,000 Swiss francs; expenditure, 371,193,000 Swiss francs. There is no public debt.

Currency. The Swiss *franc*.

Banking. There were (1989) 3 banks: Liechtensteinische Landesbank, Bank in Liechtenstein Ltd, Verwaltungs-und Privatbank Ltd.

Weights and Measures. The metric system is in force.

ENERGY AND NATURAL RESOURCES

Electricity. Electricity produced in 1988 was 60,082,000 kwh.

Agriculture. The rearing of cattle, for which the fine alpine pastures are well suited, is highly developed. In March 1989 there were 6,175 cattle (including 2,847 milk cows), 211 horses, 2,470 sheep, 176 goats, 2,698 pigs. Total production of dairy produce, 1988, 12,968,400 kg.

INDUSTRY AND TRADE

Industry. The country has a great variety of light industries (textiles, ceramics, steel screws, precision instruments, canned food, pharmaceutical products, heating appliances, etc.).

Since 1945 Liechtenstein has changed from a predominantly agricultural country to a highly industrialized country. The farming population has gone down from 70% in 1930 to only 2% in 1988. The rapid change-over has led to the immigration of foreign workers (Austrians, Germans, Italians, Spaniards). Industrial undertakings affiliated to the Liechtenstein Chamber of Industry and Commerce in 1988 employed 6,929 workers earning 356m. Swiss francs.

Commerce. Exports of home produce, for firms in membership of the Chamber of Commerce, in 1988 amounted to 1,876m. Swiss francs. 22·3% went to EFTA countries, of which Switzerland took 304m. (16·2%) and 39·6% went to EEC countries.

Total trade with UK is included with Switzerland from 1968.

Tourism. In 1988, 71,633 overnight visitors arrived in Liechtenstein.

COMMUNICATIONS

Roads. There are 250 km of roads. Postal buses are the chief means of public transportation within the country and to Austria and Switzerland.

Railways. The 18·5 km of main railway passing through the country is operated by Austrian Federal Railways.

Post and Broadcasting. In 1988 there were 14,612 telephones, 424 telex, 9,780 wireless sets and 9,155 television sets. The post and telegraphs are administered by Switzerland.

Cinemas. There were 2 cinemas in 1988.

Newspapers. In 1989 there were 2 daily newspapers with a total circulation of 16,350.

JUSTICE, RELIGION, EDUCATION AND WELFARE

Justice. The principality has its own civil and penal codes. The lowest court is the county court, *Landgericht*, presided over by one judge, which decides minor civil cases and summary criminal offences. The criminal court, *Kriminalgericht*, with a bench of 5 judges is for major crimes. Another court of mixed jurisdiction is the court of assizes (with 3 judges) for misdemeanours. Juvenile cases are treated in the Juvenile Court (with a bench of 3 judges). The superior court, *Obergericht*, and Supreme Court, *Oberster Gerichtshof*, are courts of appeal for civil and criminal cases (both with benches of 5 judges). An administrative court of appeal from government actions and the State Court determines the constitutionality of laws.

The death penalty was abolished in 1989.

Police. The principality has no army. Police force, 45; auxiliary police, 23 (1989).

Religion. In 1988, 87·3% of the population was Roman Catholic and 8·2% was Protestant.

Education (1989–90). In 14 primary, 3 upper, 5 secondary, 1 grammar and 2 (for backward children) schools there were 3,587 pupils and 264 teachers. There is also an evening technical school, a music school and a children's pedagogic-welfare day school.

Health. In 1989 there was 1 hospital, but Liechtenstein has an agreement with the Swiss cantons of St Gallen and Graubünden and the Austrian Federal State of Vorarlberg that her citizens may use certain hospitals.

DIPLOMATIC REPRESENTATIVES

In 1919, Switzerland agreed to represent the interests of Liechtenstein in countries where she has diplomatic missions and where Liechtenstein is not represented in her own right. In so doing Switzerland always acts only on the basis of mandates of a general or specific nature, which she may either accept or refuse, while Liechtenstein is free to enter into direct relations with foreign states or to set up her own additional diplomatic missions.

British Consul-General: A. H. Morgan (resident in Zürich).
USA Consul-General: L. Segesvary (resident in Zürich).

Further Reading

Statistical Information: Amt für Volkswirtschaft, Vaduz.

Rechenschaftsbericht der Fürstlichen Regierung. Vaduz. Annual, from 1922
Jahrbuch des Historischen Vereins. Vaduz. Annual since 1901
Batliner, E. H., *Das Geld- und Kreditwesen des Fürstentums Liechtenstein in Vergangenheit und Gegenwart.* 1959
Green, B., *Valley of Peace.* Vaduz, 1967
Larke, T. A. T., *Index and Thesaurus of Liechtenstein.* 2nd ed. Berkeley, 1984
Malin, G., *Kunstführer Fürstentum Liechtenstein.* Berne, 1977
Raton, P., *Liechtenstein: History and Institutions of the Principality.* Vaduz, 1970
Seger, O., *A Survey of Liechtenstein History.* 4th English ed. Vaduz, 1984
Steger, G., *Fürst und Landtag nach Liechtensteinischem Recht.* Vaduz, 1950

LUXEMBOURG

Grand-Duché de Luxembourg

Capital: Luxembourg
Population: 377,100 (1989)
GNP per capita: US$22,600 (1988)

HISTORY. The country formed part of the Holy Roman Empire until it was conquered by the French in 1795. In 1815 the Grand Duchy of Luxembourg was formed under the house of Orange-Nassau, also sovereigns of the Netherlands. In 1839 the Walloon-speaking area was joined to Belgium. In 1890 the personal union with the Netherlands ended with the accession of a member of another branch of the house of Nassau, Grand Duke Adolphe of Nassau-Weilburg.

AREA AND POPULATION. Luxembourg has an area of 2,586 sq. km (999 sq. miles) and is bounded on the west by Belgium, south by France, east by the Federal Republic of Germany. The population (1989) was 377,100. The capital, Luxembourg, had (1987) 76,640 inhabitants; Esch-Alzette, the centre of the mining district, 23,720; Differdange, 16,000; Dudelange, 14,060, and Petange, 11,590. In 1988 the foreign population was about 99,400.

Vital statistics (1988): 4,603 births, 3,840 deaths, 2,079 marriages.

CLIMATE. Cold, raw winters with snow covering the ground for up to a month are features of the upland areas. The remainder resembles Belgium in its climate, with rain evenly distributed throughout the year. Jan. 33·3°F (0·7°C), July 63·5°F (17·5°C). Annual rainfall 30·1" (764 mm).

REIGNING GRAND DUKE. Jean, born 5 Jan. 1921, son of the late Grand Duchess Charlotte and the late Prince Felix of Bourbon-Parma; succeeded 12 Nov. 1964 on the abdication of his mother; married to Princess Joséphine-Charlotte of Belgium, 9 April 1953. *Offspring:* Princess Marie-Astrid, born 17 Feb. 1954, married Christian of Habsbourg-Lorraine 6 Feb. 1982 (*Offspring:* Marie Christine, born 31 July 1983; Imre, born 8 Dec. 1985); Prince Henri, *heir apparent*, born 16 April 1955, married Maria Teresa Mestre 14 Feb. 1981; (*Offspring:* Prince Guillaume, born 11 Nov. 1981, Prince Felix, born 3 June 1984, Prince Louis, born 3 Aug. 1986). Prince Jean, born 15 May 1957, married Hélène Vestur; Princess Margaretha, born 15 May 1957, married Prince Nikolaus of Liechtenstein 20 March 1982; Prince Guillaume, born 1 May 1963.

The civil list is fixed at 300,000 gold francs per annum, to be reconsidered at the beginning of each reign.

On 28 Sept. 1919 a referendum was taken in Luxembourg to decide on the political and economic future of the country. The voting resulted as follows: For the reigning Grand Duchess, 66,811; for the continuance of the Nassau-Braganza dynasty under another Grand Duchess, 1,286; for another dynasty, 889; for a republic, 16,885; for an economic union with France, 60,133; for an economic union with Belgium, 22,242. But France refused in favour of Belgium, and on 22 Dec. 1921 the Chamber of the Grand Duchy passed a Bill for the economic union between Belgium and Luxembourg. The agreement, which is for 60 years, provides for the disappearance of the customs barrier between the two countries and the use of Belgian, in addition to Luxembourg, currency as legal tender in the Grand Duchy. It came into force on 1 May 1922.

The Grand Duchy was under German occupation from 10 May 1940 to 10 Sept. 1944. The Grand Duchess Charlotte and the Government carried on an independent administration in London. Civil government was restored in Oct. 1944.

National flag: Three horizontal stripes of red, white and light blue.

National anthem: Ons Hemecht (words by M. Lentz, 1859; tune by J. A. Zinnen).

CONSTITUTION AND GOVERNMENT. The Grand Duchy of Luxembourg is a constitutional monarchy, the hereditary sovereignty being in the Nassau family. The constitution of 17 Oct. 1868 was revised in 1919, 1948, 1956, 1972, 1979, 1983, 1988 and 1989. The revision of 1948 has abolished the 'perpetually neutral' status of the country and introduced the concepts of right to work, social security, health services, freedom of trade and industry, and recognition of trade unions. The revision of 1956 provides for the devolution of executive, legislative and judicial powers to international institutions.

The national language is Luxemburgish; French, German and English are widely used.

The country forms 4 electoral districts. An elector must be a citizen (male or female) of Luxembourg and have completed 18 years of age; to be eligible for election the citizen must have completed 21 years of age.

The Chamber of Deputies consists of 22 Christian Social, 18 Socialists, 11 Democrats, 1 Communist, 2 Green Alternatives, 2 Green Ecologists and 4 5/6 Action Committee (elections of 18 June 1989). A maximum of 60 members are elected for 5 years; they receive a salary and a travelling allowance.

The head of the state takes part in the legislative power, exercises the executive power and has a certain part in the judicial power. The constitution leaves to the sovereign the right to organize the Government, which consists of a Minister of State, who is President of the Government, and of at least 3 Ministers.

The Cabinet was, in Dec. 1989, composed as follows:

Prime Minister, Minister of State, Minister for Exchequer, Cultural Affairs: Jacques Santer.

Vice-Prime Minister, Foreign Affairs, Foreign Trade and Cooperation, Armed Forces: Jacques F. Poos. *Family Affairs and Social Solidarity, Middle Classes and Tourism:* Fernand Boden. *Interior, Housing and Town Planning:* Jean Spautz. *Finance, Labour:* Jean-Claude Juncker. *National Education, Justice, Civil Service:* Marc Fischbach. *Health, Social Security, Physical Education and Sports, Youth:* Johny Lahure. *Agriculture, Viticulture and Country Planning:* René Steichen. *Economy, Public Works, Transport:* Robert Goebbels. *Land Planning and Environment, Energy, Communications:* Alex Bodry. *Secretary of State for Foreign Affairs, Foreign Trade and Co-operation, Armed Forces:* Georges Wohlfart. *Secretary of State for Health, Social Security, Physical Education and Sports, Youth:* Mady Delvaux-Stehres.

Besides the Cabinet there is a Council of State. It deliberates on proposed laws and Bills, and on amendments; it also gives administrative decisions and expresses its opinion regarding any other question referred to it by the Grand Duke or the Government. The Council of State is composed of 21 members chosen for life by the sovereign, who also chooses a president from among them each year.

DEFENCE. A law passed by Parliament on 29 June 1967 abolished compulsory service and instituted a battalion-size army of volunteers enlisted for 3 years. Strength (1989) 800. The defence estimates for 1989 amounted to 2,346m. francs. Luxembourg is an original member of NATO and the battalion is committed to NATO ACE mobile force.

INTERNATIONAL RELATIONS

Membership. Luxembourg is a member of the UN, Benelux, the European Communities, OECD, the Council of Europe, NATO and WEU.

ECONOMY

Budget. Revenue and expenditure (including extraordinary) for years ending 30 April (in 1m. francs):

	1985	*1986*	*1987*	*1988*	*1989*	*1990* [1]
Revenue	81,363·8	82,385·3	86,313·0	85,047·5	89,593·5	97,162·7
Expenditure	79,536·8	81,863·3	86,239·7	88,913·8	89,250·0	94,414·5

[1] Provisional.

Consolidated debt at 31 Dec. 1988 amounted to 12,233m. francs (long-term) and 3,254m. francs (short-term).

Currency. On 14 Oct. 1944 the Luxembourg *franc* was fixed at par value with the Belgian franc. Notes of the Belgian National Bank are legal tender in Luxembourg.

Banking. On 31 Dec. 1988 depositors in the State Savings Bank with a total of 54,426m. francs to their credit. There were (June 1989) 156 banks and 24 non-bank credit institutions established in Luxembourg which has become an international financial centre.

Weights and Measures. The metric system is in force.

ENERGY AND NATURAL RESOURCES

Electricity. Power production was 1,334m. kwh. in 1988.

Minerals. In 1988 production (in tonnes) of pig-iron, 2,519,200; of steel, 3,660,890.

Agriculture. Agriculture is carried on by about 6,200 of the population on (1988) 5,059 farms with an average area of 36·15 hectares; 126,134 hectares were under cultivation in 1988. Production, 1988 (in tonnes) of main crops: Maize, 3,506,000; roots and tubers, 355,600; bread crops, 326,400; other crops, 981,500; forage crops, 710,700; pulses, 7,900; grassland, 1,376,300. Production, 1988 (in 1,000 tonnes) of meat, 22; milk, 276·3; butter, 6·3; cheese, 3·4. In 1988, 142,800 hectolitres of wine were produced from 1,199 hectares. In 1988 there were 8,867 tractors, 1,476 harvester-threshers, 2,670 manure spreaders and 2,747 gatherer-presses.

Livestock (1988): 1,806 horses, 214,255 cattle, 77,114 pigs, 6,936 sheep.

Forestry. In 1986 there were 88,600 hectares of forests, which produced 175,850 cu. metres of broadleaved and 151,800 cu. metres of coniferous wood.

INDUSTRY AND TRADE

Industry. Production, 1988 (in 1,000 tonnes); Steel, 3,661; rolled steel products, 4,019. At 30 June 1988 there were 3,714 industrial enteprises.

Commerce. By treaty of 5 Sept. 1944, signed in London, and the treaty of 14 March 1947, signed in The Hague, the Grand Duchy, together with Belgium and the Netherlands, became a party to the Benelux Customs Union, which came into force on 1 Jan. 1948. For further particulars *see* p. 199.

Total trade between Luxembourg and UK included with Belgium from 1974.

Tourism. In 1988 there were 760,300 tourists.

COMMUNICATIONS

Roads. In 1989 the network had a total of 5,085 km of which 75 km motorways. Motor vehicles registered in Luxembourg on 1 Jan. 1989 included 177,011 passenger cars, 10,614 trucks, 705 buses, 3,025 motorcycles, 19,821 tractors and special vehicles.

Railways. In 1988 there were 272 km of railway (standard gauge) of which 162 km electrified. It carried 639m. tonne-km and 277m. passenger-km.

Aviation. Findel is the airport for Luxembourg and 1,001,751 passengers and 113,657 tonnes of freight were handled in 1988.

Post and Broadcasting. In 1988 the telephone system had 919,799 km of subterranean telegraph and telephone line, 167,200 telephones, 107 post telegraph offices. *Compagnie Luxembourgeoise de Télédiffusion* broadcasts 1 programme in Luxembourgian on FM. Powerful transmitters on long-, medium-and short-waves are used for commercial and religious programmes in French, Dutch, German, English and Italian. Ten TV programmes are broadcast. Colour transmission by SECAM system.

Cinemas (1989). There were 15 cinemas.

Newspapers (1988). There were 6 daily newspapers with a circulation of 130,000.

RELIGION, EDUCATION AND WELFARE

Religion. The population is 95% Roman Catholic. The remaining 5% is mainly Protestant or Jewish, or does not belong to any religion. The Protestant Church is organized on an interdenominational basis.

Education. Education is compulsory for all children between the ages of 6 and 15. In 1986-87 the nursery schools had 8,315 pupils; primary schools, 24,381 pupils. In 1987-88 technical secondary schools had 14,790 pupils; secondary schools, 7,706 pupils; the Superior Institute of Technology, 265 pupils; pedagogic education, 146 pupils; university studies (1986–87), 397 pupils.

Health. In 1987 there were 666 doctors and 4,661 hospital beds.

DIPLOMATIC REPRESENTATIVES

Of Luxembourg in Great Britain (27 Wilton Crescent, London, SWIX 8SD)
Ambassador: Edouard Molitor, KCMG (accredited 13 June 1989).

Of Great Britain in Luxembourg (14 Blvd Roosevelt, Luxembourg)
Ambassador and Consul-General: Juliet J. d'A. Campbell, CMG.

Of Luxembourg in the USA (2200 Massachusetts Ave., NW, Washington, D.C., 20008)
Ambassador: André Philippe.

Of the USA in Luxembourg (22 Blvd. Emmanuel Servais, Luxembourg)
Ambassador: J. B. S. Gerard.

Of Luxembourg to the United Nations
Ambassador: Jean Feyder.

Further Reading

Statistical Information: The Service Central de la Statistique et des Études Économiques was founded in 1900 and reorganized in 1962 (19–21 boulevard Royal, C.P. 304 Luxembourg-City). *Director:* Georges Als. Main publications: *Bulletin du Statec.—Annuaire statistique.—Cahiers économiques.*

Bulletin de Documentation. Government Information Service. From 1945 (monthly)
The Institutions of the Grand Duchy of Luxembourg. Press and Information Service, Luxembourg, 1982
Als, G., *Le Luxembourg, en chiffres 1839-1989.* Luxembourg, 1989
Calmes, C., *The Making of a Nation from 1815 up to our Days.* Luxembourg, 1989
Heiderscheid, A., *Aspects de Sociologie Religieuse du Diocèse de Luxembourg.* 2 vols. Luxembourg, 1961
Hury, C. and Christophory, J., *Luxembourg.* [Bibliography] Oxford and Santa Barbara, 1981
Majerus, P., *Le Luxembourg independant.* Luxembourg, 1948.—*L'État Luxembourgeois.* Luxembourg, 1983
Newcomer, J., *The Grand Duchy of Luxembourg: The Evolution of Nationhood, 963 A.D. to 1983.* Washington, 1983
Trausch, G., *The Significance of the Historical Date of 1839.* Luxembourg, 1989

Archives of the State: Luxembourg-City. *Director:* Cornel Meder.
National Library: Luxembourg-City, 37 Boulevard Roosevelt. *Director:* Jules Christophory.

MADAGASCAR

Capital: Antananarivo
Population: 10·92m. (1988)
GNP per capita: US$280 (1988)

Repoblika Demokratika n'i Madagaskar

HISTORY. Madagascar was discovered by the Portuguese, Diego Diaz, in 1500. The island was unified under the Imérina monarchy between 1797 and 1861, but French claims to a protectorate led to hostilities culminating in the establishment of a protectorate on 30 Sept. 1895. Madagascar became a French Colony on 6 Aug. 1896 and the monachy was abolished on 26 Feb. 1897.

Madagascar became an Overseas Territory in 1946, and on 14 Oct. 1958, following a referendum, was proclaimed the autonomous Malagasy Republic within the French Community, achieving full independence on 26 June 1960.

The government of Philibert Tsiranana, President from independence, resigned on 18 May 1972 and executive powers were given to Maj.-Gen. Gabriel Ramanantsoa, who replaced Tsiranana as President on 11 Oct. 1972. On 5 Feb. 1975, Col. Richard Ratsimandrava became Head of State, but was assassinated 6 days later. A National Military Directorate under Brig.-Gen. Gilles Andriamahazo was established on 12 Feb. On 15 June it handed over power to a Supreme Revolutionary Council (SRC) under Didier Ratsiraka.

AREA AND POPULATION. Madagascar is situated off the south-east coast of Africa, from which it is separated by the Mozambique channel, the least distance between island and continent being 250 miles (400 km); its length is 980 miles (1,600 km); greatest breadth, 360 miles (570 km).

The area is 587,041 sq. km (226,658 sq. miles). In 1975 (census) the population was 7,603,790. Estimate (1988) 10,919,000.

Province	*Area in Sq. km*	*Population 1985*	*Chief town*	*Population 1986*
Antseranana	43,046	689,800	Antseranana	53,000
Mahajanga	150,023	1,075,300	Mahajanga	111,000
Toamasina	71,911	1,444,700	Toamasina	139,000
Antananarivo	58,283	3,195,800	Antananarivo	703,000
Fianarantsoa	102,373	2,209,700	Fianarantsoa	111,000
Toliary	161,405	1,396,700	Toliary	59,000

Vital statistics, 1984: Births, 456,000; deaths, 146,000.

The indigenous population are of Malayo-Polynesian stock, divided into 18 ethnic groups of which the principal are Merina (26%) of the central plateau, the Betsimisaraka (15%) of the east coast, and the Betsileo (12%) of the southern plateau. Foreign communities include Europeans, mainly French (30,000), Indians (15,000), Chinese (9,000), Comorians and Arabs.

CLIMATE. A tropical climate, but the mountains cause big variations in rainfall, which is very heavy in the east and very light in the west. Antananarivo. Jan. 70°F (21·1°C), July 59°F (15°C). Annual rainfall 54" (1,350 mm). Toamasina. Jan. 80°F (26·7°C), July 70°F (21·1°C). Annual rainfall 128" (3,256 mm).

CONSTITUTION AND GOVERNMENT. The new Constitution of the Democratic Republic of Madagascar was approved by referendum on 21 Dec. 1975 and came into force on 30 Dec. It provides for a National People's Assembly of 137 members elected by universal suffrage for a 5-year term from the single list of the *Front National pour la Défense de la Révolution Socialiste Malgache;* following the general elections held on 28 Aug. 1983, this comprised 117 members of the *Avant-garde de la Révolution Malgache*, 9 of the *Parti du Congrès de l'Indépendence* and

11 others. Executive power is vested in the President, directly elected for 7 years, who appoints a Council of Ministers to assist him, with the guidance of the 27-member Supreme Revolutionary Council.

President: Adm. Didier Ratsiraka (re-elected 12 March 1989).
The Council of Ministers in Nov. 1989 was composed as follows:

Prime Minister, Head of Government: Col. Victor Ramahatra.
Revolutionary Art and Culture: Gisèle Rabesahala. *Defence:* Brig.-Gen. Mahasampo Christophère Bien-Aimé Raveloson. *Keeper of the Seals, Justice:* Joseph Bedo. *Civil Service and Labour:* Georges Ruphin. *Information, Ideological Guidance and Co-operatives:* Jean-Claude Rahaga. *Health:* Dr Jean-Jacques Séraphin. *Planning and Economy:* Jean Robiarivony. *Animal Production, Water Resources and Forestry:* Maxime Zafera. *Finance and Budget:* Léon Rajaobelina. *Posts and Telecommunications:* Simon Pierre. *Interior:* Augustin Ampy Portos. *Higher Education:* Ignace Rakoto. *Commerce:* Georges Solofoson. *Foreign Affairs:* Jean Bemananjara. *Transport, Meteorology and Tourism:* Lucien Zasy. *Secondary and Basic Education:* Aristide Velompanahy. *Industry, Energy and Mines:* Vincent Radanielson. *Public Works:* Jean-Emile Tsaranazy. *Population, Social Welfare, Youth and Sport:* Badhroudine. *Agricultural Production, Agrarian Reform and Land Inheritance:* José Andrianoelison. *Scientific Research and Development:* Zafera Antoine Rabesa.

National flag: Horizontally red over green, in the hoist a vertical white strip.
National anthem: Ry tanindrazanay malala ô!

Malagasy, which is a language of Malayo-Polynesian origin, is the official language. French and English are understood and taught in Malagasy schools.

Local Government: The six provinces are sub-divided into 110 *Fivondronana*, which in turn are divided into 1,252 *Firaisana* and finally into 11,410 *Fokontany* (the traditional communal divisions). Each level is governed by an elected council.

DEFENCE

Army. The Army is organized in 2 battalion groups, and 1 engineer, 1 signals, 1 service and 7 construction regiments. Equipment includes PT-76 light tanks and M-8 armoured cars. Strength (1990) 20,000 and gendarmerie 7,500.

Navy. In 1989 the small maritime force had a strength of 500 (including 100 marines), and was equipped with 1 250 tonne patrol craft, 1 medium landing ship, a few small landing craft, together with a 600 tonne former trawler used for transport and training.

Air Force. Created in 1961, the Malagasy Air Force received its first combat equipment in 1978, with the arrival of 8 MiG-21 and 4 MiG-17 fighters, plus flying and ground staff instructors, from North Korea. Other equipment includes 5 An-26 turboprop transports, 1 Britten-Norman Defender armed transport, 2 C-47s, 1 HS. 748 and 1 Yak-40 for VIP use, 1 Aztec, 2 Cessna Skymasters, 4 Cessna 172Ms and 6 Mi-8 helicopters. Personnel (1990) 500.

INTERNATIONAL RELATIONS

Membership. Madagascar is a member of UN, OAU and is an ACP state of EEC.

ECONOMY

Planning. The 1984–87 agricultural plan aimed at food self-sufficiency and envisaged investment of US$219m.

Budget. The budget 1989, envisaged expenditure of 998,400m. FMG of which 464,400m. FMG was the operating budget, the remainder capital budget.

Currency. The Malagasy *franc* is the unit of currency. There are coins of 1, 2, 5, 10, 50 and 100 francs and banknotes of 50, 100, 500, 1,000, 5,000 and 10,000 francs. In March 1990, £1 = 2,171 FMG; US$1 = 1,324 FMG.

Banking. A Central Bank was formed in July 1973, replacing the former *Institut d'Emission Malgache* as the central bank of issue. All commercial banking and insurance was nationalized in June 1975 and privatized in 1988. Industrial development is financed through the *Bankin'ny Indostria,* and other commercial banking undertaken by the *Bankin'ny Tantsaha Mpamokatra* and the *Banky Fampandrosoana ny Varotra* and the *Banque Malgache de l'Océan Indien.*

Weights and Measures. The metric system is in use.

ENERGY AND NATURAL RESOURCES

Electricity. Production (1986) 479m. kwh. Supply 127 and 220 volts; 50 Hz.

Oil. The oil refinery at Toamasina has a capacity of 12,000 bbls a day.

Minerals. Mining production in 1986 included: Graphite, 161,788 tonnes; chromite, 82,910 tonnes; zircon (1985), 650 kg; beryl (1985), (industrial), 129,507 kg; mica, 1,775 kg; gold (1985), 181·6 grammes; industrial garnet (1985), 52·2 kg.

Agriculture. The principal agricultural products in 1988 were (in 1,000 tonnes): Rice, 2,100; cassava, 2,200; mangoes, 193; bananas, 260; potatoes, 268; sugar-cane, 2,000; maize, 150; sweet potatoes, 472; coffee, 81; oranges, 83; pineapples, 52; seed cotton, 46; groundnuts, 32; sisal, 20; tobacco, 5.

Cattle breeding and agriculture are the chief occupations. There were, in 1988, 10,600,000 cattle, 1·4m. pigs, 611,000 sheep, 1·08m. goats and 30m. poultry.

Forestry. The forests covered (1989) 14·7m. hectares (about 25% of the land surface) and contain many valuable woods, while gum, resins and plants for tanning, dyeing and medicinal purposes abound. Production (1984) 6·26m. cu. metres.

Fisheries. The fish catch in 1984 was 56,000 tonnes.

INDUSTRY AND TRADE

Industry. Industry, hitherto confined mainly to the processing of agricultural products, is now extending to cover other fields.

Commerce. Trade in 1m. FMG:

	1984	*1985*	*1986*	*1987*
Imports (c.i.f)	213,531	265,916	238,458	376,792
Exports (f.o.b)	192,267	181,630	205,875	348,025

The chief exports in 1985 were coffee (35%), cloves (15%) and vanilla (16%). France took 37% of exports, the USA, 14% and Japan, 11%, while France supplied 33% of imports, the USSR, 9%, Federal Republic of Germany, 6%, Qatar, 6% and the USA, 6%.

Total trade between Madagascar and UK (British Department of Trade returns, in £1,000 sterling):

	1986	*1987*	*1988*	*1989*
Imports to UK	6,432	6,925	7,154	5,865
Exports and re-exports from UK	6,872	6,382	4,747	3,352

Tourism. There were 27,000 tourists in 1986.

COMMUNICATIONS

Roads. In 1982 there were 49,637 km of roads of which 4,774 km bitumenized. In 1983 there were 23,412 private cars and 14,159 commercial vehicles.

Railways. In 1987 there were 883 km of railways, all metre gauge. In 1987, 2·7m. passengers and 596,000m. tonnes of cargo were transported.

Aviation. Air France and Air Madagascar connect Antananarivo (International airport, Ivato) with Paris, Alitalia connects with Rome. Several weekly services operated by Air Madagascar connect the capital with the ports and the chief inland towns. In 1985, 138,362 passengers and 5,144 tonnes of cargo arrived and departed.

Shipping. In 1986, 705,824 tonnes were loaded and 1,153,133 tonnes unloaded at Toamasina, Mahajanga and other ports. In 1980, registered merchant marine was 56 vessels (of more than 100 GRT) with a total of 91,211 GRT.

Post and Broadcasting. There were in 1978, 547 post offices and agencies. There were (1983) 37,100 telephone subscribers, and (1986) 2m. radio receivers and 96,000 television receivers.

Newspapers. In 1985 there were 7 daily newspapers with a total circulation of 68,000.

Cinemas. There were, in 1974, 31 cinemas with a seating capacity of 12,500.

JUSTICE, RELIGION, EDUCATION AND WELFARE

Justice. The Supreme Court and the Court of Appeal are in Antananarivo. In most towns there are Courts of First Instance for civil and commercial cases. For criminal cases there are ordinary criminal courts in most towns.

Religion. 47% of the population follow animist religions; 28% are Roman Catholic, 22% Protestant (mainly belonging to the Fiangonan'i Jesosy Kristy eto Madagaskar) and 3% Moslem.

Education. Education is compulsory from 6 to 14 years of age in the primary schools. In 1984 there were 1,608,722 pupils and 35,372 teachers in 13,973 primary schools, 275,000 pupils and 10,383 teachers in secondary schools and 11,041 students and 1,302 teachers in technical schools. The University of Madagascar has a main campus at Antananarivo and 5 university centres in the other provincial capitals, with 37,475 students in 1986. There are also 4 agricultural schools at Nanisana, Ambatondrazaka, Marovoay and Ivoloina.

Health. In 1978 there were 749 hospitals and dispensaries with 20,625 beds; there were (1981) 901 doctors, 52 dentists, 87 pharmacists, 839 midwives and 770 nursing personnel.

DIPLOMATIC REPRESENTATIVES

Of Madagascar in Great Britain
Ambassador: François de Paul Rabotoson (resides in Paris)

Of Great Britain in Madagascar (Immeuble Ny Havana, Cite de 67 Ha, Antananarivo)
Ambassador: D. O. Amy.

Of Madagascar in the USA (2374 Massachusetts Ave., NW, Washington, D.C., 20008)
Chargé d'Affaires: Jean René Tsiangalara.

Of the USA in Madagascar (14 rue Rainitovo, Antsahavola, Antananarivo)
Ambassador: Howard K. Walker.

Of Madagascar to the United Nations
Ambassador: Blaise Rabetafika.

Further Reading

Statistical Information: The Banque des Donnés de l'Etat in Antananarivo published the *Bulletin mensuel de Madagascar* (from 1971); continuation of the trimestrial *Bulletin de statistique générale* (1949–71), the *Revue de Madagascar*, the *Madagascar à travers ses provinces* (latest issue, 1953) and the *Statistiques du Commerce Extérieur de Madagascar*.
Bulletin de l'Académie Malgache (from 1902)
Brandt, H., *Guide to Madagascar*. Chalfont St Peter, 1988
Brown, M., *Madagascar Rediscovered*. London, 1978
Deschamps, H., *Histoire de Madagascar*. Paris, 4th ed. 1972

MALAWÎ

Capital: Lilongwe
Population: 7·1m. (1985)
GNP per capita: US$160 (1988)

HISTORY. Malawi was formerly the Nyasaland (until 1907 British Central Africa) Protectorate, constituted on 15 May 1891.

Nyasaland became a self-governing country on 1 Feb. 1963, and on 6 July 1964 an independent member of the Commonwealth under the name of Malawi. It became a republic on 6 July 1966.

AREA AND POPULATION. Malawi lies along the southern and western shores of Lake Malawi (the third largest lake in Africa), and is otherwise bounded north by Tanzania, south by Mozambique and west by Zambia. Land area (excluding inland water of Lakes Palombe, Chilwa and Chiuta) 36,325 sq. miles, divided into 3 regions and 24 districts, each administered by a District Commissioner.

Lake Malawi waters belonging to Malawi are 9,250 sq. miles and the whole Lake Malawi (including the waters under Mozambique by an agreement made between the two countries in 1950) is 11,650 sq. miles.

Population at census 1977, 5,547,460 (males, 2,673,589). Estimate (1985), 7,058,800. Over 90% of the population live in rural areas.

Population of main towns (estimate 1985) was as follows: Blantyre, 355,200; Lilongwe, 186,800; Mzuzu, 82,700; Zomba, 53,000.

Population of the regions, 1986 (and census 1977): Northern, 815,000 (648,853); Central, 2,938,300 (2,143,716); Southern, 3,525,600 (2,754,891).

The official languages are Chichewa, spoken by over 50% of the population, and English.

CLIMATE. The tropical climate is marked by a dry season from May to Oct. and a wet season for the remaining months. Rainfall amounts are variable, within the range of 29–100" (725–2,500 mm), and maximum temperatures average 75–89°F (24–32°C), and minimum temperatures 58–67°F (14·4–19·4°C). Lilongwe. Jan. 73°F (22·8°C), July 60°F (15·6°C). Annual rainfall 36" (900 mm). Blantyre. Jan. 75°F (23·9°C), July 63°F (17·2°C). Annual rainfall 45" (1,125 mm). Zomba. Jan. 73°F (22·8°C), July 63°F (17·2°C). Annual rainfall 54" (1,344 mm).

CONSTITUTION AND GOVERNMENT. The President of the republic is also head of Government and of the Malawi Congress Party. Malawi is a one-party state. Parliament is composed of 120 members: 104 elected for up to 5 years, and 16 nominated by the President.

Life President, External Affairs, Agriculture, Justice, Works: Ngwazi Dr H. Kamuzu Banda. (Took office 6 July 1966 and became Life President on 6 July 1971).

The Cabinet in Jan. 1990 was composed as follows:

Without Portfolio, Administrative Secretary of Malawi Congress Party: Maxwell Pashane. *Labour:* Wadson B. Deleza. *Health:* Edward Chitsulo Isaac Bwanali. *Trade, Industry and Tourism:* Robson W. Chirwa. *Finance:* Louis J. Chimango. *Forestry and Natural Resources:* Stanford Demba. *Transport and Communications:* Dalton S. Katopola. *Education and Culture:* Michael Mlambala. *Local Government:* Mfunjo Mwanjasi Mwakikunga.

National flag: Three equal horizontal stripes of black, red, green, with a red rising sun on the centre of the black stripe.

DEFENCE. All services form part of the Army and have a strength (1990) 7,250.

Army. The army is organized into 3 infantry battalions and 1 support battalion. Equipment includes scout cars.

Navy. There are 2 patrol craft and some 3 boats operated by about (1989) 100 personnel based at Chilumba on Lake Nyasa.

Air Wing. To support the infantry battalion, the Air Wing has 1 Do 28D Skyservant and 3 Do 228 light transports, and 2 Puma, 1 Ecureuil, 1 Dauphin, and 1 Alouette III helicopters. An HS 125 jet is used for VIP transport. Personnel (1990) 150.

INTERNATIONAL RELATIONS

Membership. Malaŵi is a member of UN, the Commonwealth, the Non-Aligned States, OAU, SADCC and is an ACP state of EEC.

ECONOMY

Planning. The Government of Malaŵi operates a 3-year 'rolling' public-sector investment programme, revised annually to take into account changing needs and the expected level of resources available. The greatest part of the development programme is annually financed from external aid, and priority in the use of resources has always been given to providing the counterpart contributions to funds received from external sources. The balance of these local resources is used for financing projects commanding high national priority for which no external funds can be secured.

Budget. Revenue Account receipts and expenditure (in K.1,000) for years ending 31 March:

	1985–86	*1986–87*	*1987–88*	*1988–89*
Revenue	450,200	512,300	583,382	681,800
Expenditure	523,600	547,000	728,834	784,300

Currency. The currency is the *kwacha* (dawn), which is subdivided into 100 *tambala* (cockerels). From 9 June 1975 the kwacha has been pegged to Special Drawing Rights. In March 1990: £1 sterling = K.4·34, US$1 = K.2·65.

Banking. In July 1964 the Reserve Bank of Malaŵi was set up with a capital of K.1m. to be responsible for the issue of currency and the holding of external reserves and to issue treasury bills and local registered stock on behalf of the Government. Since then, the Reserve Bank has fully assumed the responsibilities of a Central Bank.

The National Bank of Malaŵi has a total of 14 branches in major urban areas and 25 static and 41 mobile agencies in rural areas. The Commercial Bank of Malaŵi Ltd opened in 1970 and has branches at Limbe, Lilongwe, Mzuzu and Zomba and an agency in Dedza and headquarters at Blantyre. It has 4 permanent and 65 mobile agencies.

In 1972 The Investment Development Bank of Malaŵi was established in Blantyre. Its resources are derived from domestic and foreign official sources and its objective is to provide medium and long-term credits to private entities considered of importance to the economy.

The Post Office Savings Bank had (1985) 257 offices conducting savings business throughout the country, and the New Building Society has agencies in Limbe, Mzuzu, Zomba, Muloza and Blantyre with its head office in Lilongwe.

Weights and Measures. The metric system became fully operational in 1982.

ENERGY AND NATURAL RESOURCES

Electricity. The Electricity Supply Commission of Malaŵi is the sole supplier of electrical power and energy and the demand and supply of electricity and power on the inter-connected system was met from the hydro-electric generator sets installed at Tedzani Falls and Nkula Falls stations which together have a total capacity of 124 mw as at 1984. The inter-connected system extends from the Shire River hydro stations and covers most areas of the Southern and Central Regions, and part of the Northern Region. Production (1986) 466m. kwh. Supply 230 volts; 50 Hz.

Thermal plant of 23·8 mw capacity is available on the inter-connected system and there are stations at Blantyre, Lilongwe, Mtunthama, Kasungu, and Mzuzu. The capacity of the isolated station at Karonga was increased to 480 kw with the installation of 120 kw diesel generator set.

Minerals. The main product in 1976 was marble (149,254 tonnes) for the manufacture of cement. Coal mining began in 1985.

Agriculture. Malaŵi is predominantly an agricultural country. In 1983 agriculture contributed about 43% to the GDP, and agricultural produce accounted for 90% of total exports. Maize is the main subsistence crop and is grown by over 95% of all smallholders; production (1988) 1,455,000 tonnes. Tea cultivation is of growing importance; in 1988, 35,000 tonnes were produced. Almost all the surplus crops produced by smallholders are sold to the Agricultural Development and Marketing Corporation. Production (1988): Tobacco, 56,000 tonnes; sugar-cane, 1·7m. tonnes.

Livestock in 1988: Cattle, 1m.; sheep, 210,000; goats, 950,000; pigs, 210,000.

Forestry. There were (1989) 4·3m. hectares of forests; 46% of the land area. In 1983–84, 11,108 cu. metres of sawn timber were removed.

Fisheries. Landings in 1984 were 65,073 tonnes.

INDUSTRY AND TRADE

Industry. Index of manufacturing output in 1985 (1970 = 100): manufacturing for domestic consumption 419·7 (229·5 in 1980); of this consumer goods were at 183·4 (252·5) and intermediate goods mainly for building and construction were at 111·1 (150·4). Manufacturing for export, 236·3 (201·6).

Commerce. Exports 1985 (in K.1m.): Tobacco, 229·9; tea, 113·3; sugar, 28·9; pulses, 6·4; groundnuts, 1·1; rice, 3; other crops including manufactures, 53·4.

Trade statistics for calendar years are (in K.1m.):

	1984	*1985*	*1986*
Imports	381·5	492·5	480·0
Exports	446·2	419·6	445·9

Total trade between Malaŵi and UK (British Department of Trade returns, in £1,000 sterling):

	1986	*1987*	*1988*	*1989*
Imports to UK	56,983	44,223	30,183	27,890
Exports and re-exports from UK	28,557	18,069	27,618	30,604

Tourism. There were 41,145 visitors to Malaŵi in 1985.

COMMUNICATIONS

Roads. In 1988 there were 2,701 km of main road, of which 1,857 km were bitumen surfaced and 410 km gravel; 2,782 km of secondary roads, of which 285 km were surfaced and 239 km gravel; 5,354 km of district roads, of which 24 km were surfaced and 16 km gravel, and 8,008 km of earth roads. In 1987 there were 14,911 cars and 15,643 commercial vehicles.

Railways. Malaŵi Railways (789 km–1,067 mm gauge) operates a main line from Salima to the Mozambique border near Nsanje, from which running powers over the Trans-Zambezia Railway allow access to the port of Beira; a branch opened in 1970 runs eastwards from a point 16 km south of Balaka to the Mozambique border to give a direct route to the deep-water port of Nacala. The 26-km section from Nsanje to the border is operated by the Central Africa Railway Co. Ltd. An extension of 111 km from Salima to the new state capital of Lilongwe was opened in Feb. 1979, and a further extension to Mchinji on the Zambian border (120 km) was completed in 1981. In 1987–88, 414,995 tonnes were hauled and 1,709,983 passengers carried.

Aviation. In 1983 the Kamuzu International Airport at Lilongwe was inaugurated. It handled (1987) 225,620 passengers and 4,785·6 tonnes. In 1987 Chileka Airport handled 95,879 passengers and 675·7 tonnes of freight.

Shipping. In 1987–88 lake ships carried 210,103 passengers and 28,983 tonnes of freight.

Post and Broadcasting. Number of telephones (1987) 25,000. The Malaŵi Broadcasting Corporation broadcasts in English and Chichewa. There were 1m. radio sets in 1983.

Newspapers (1988). *The Daily Times* (English, Monday to Friday); 16,000 copies daily. *Malaŵi News* (English and Chichewa, Saturdays); 33,000 copies weekly. *Odini* (English and Chichewa); 8,500 copies fortnightly. *Boma Lathu* (Chichewa); 80,000 copies monthly.

JUSTICE, RELIGION, EDUCATION AND WELFARE

Justice. Justice is administered in the High Court, the magistrates' courts and traditional courts. There are 23 magistrates' courts, 176 traditional courts and 23 local appeal courts.

Appeals from traditional courts are dealt with in the traditional appeal courts and in the national traditional appeal court. Appeals from magistrates' courts lie to the High Court, and appeals from the High Court to Malaŵi's Supreme Court of Appeal.

Religion. In 1988 the Roman Catholic Church claimed 1·5m. members; Church of Central Africa Presbyterian, 500,000; Diocese of Southern Malaŵi and Lake Malaŵi (part of the Province of Central Africa (the Anglican Communion) (1983), 70,606; Seventh Day Adventist Church (1984), 59,319. Zambezi Evangelical Church (formerly Zambezi Industrial Mission) (1987), 30,000; Assembly of God, 13,740; Seventh Day Baptist (Central Africa Conference) (1987), 4,861; Church of Christ, 60,000; African Evangelical Church (1983), 6,000. Moslems were estimated to number about 500,000 in 1983.

Education In 1986–87 the number of pupils in primary schools was 1,022,765; in secondary schools, 25,681. There were 25,013 teachers in primary schools and 1,229 in secondary schools. The primary school course is of 8 years' duration, followed by a 4-year secondary course. English is taught from the 1st year and becomes the general medium of instruction from the 4th year. There were 1,802 students in teacher training schools and 777 in government technical schools.

The University of Malaŵi was inaugurated in 1965. In 1988–89 there were 2,323 students taking degree and diploma courses.

Health. In 1986 there were two central hospitals, one general hospital, one mental hospital, two leprosaria and 45 hospitals of which 21 were government district hospitals. There were 7,081 hospital beds of which 1,612 were for maternity.

DIPLOMATIC REPRESENTATIVES

Of Malaŵi in Great Britain (33 Grosvenor St., London, W1X 0DE)
High Commissioner: (Vacant).

Of Great Britain in Malaŵi (Lingadzi Hse., Lilongwe, 3)
High Commissioner: Dr D. G. Osborne, CMG.

Of Malaŵi in the USA (2408 Massachusetts Ave., NW, Washington, D.C., 20008)
Ambassador: R. Mbaya.

Of the USA in Malaŵi (PO Box 30016, Lilongwe, 3)
Ambassador: George A. Trail III.

Of Malaŵi to the United Nations
Ambassador: R. Mbaya.

Further Reading

General Information: The Chief Information Officer, PO Box 494, Blantyre.
Boeder, R. B., *Malawi.* [Bibliography] Oxford and Santa Barbara, 1980

MALAYSIA

Capital: Kuala Lumpur
Population: 17·4m. (1989)
GNP per capita: US$1,870 (1988)

HISTORY. On 16 Sept. 1963 Malaysia came into being, consisting of the Federation of Malaya, the State of Singapore and the colonies of North Borneo (renamed Sabah) and Sarawak. The agreement between the UK and the 4 territories was signed on 9 July (Cmnd. 2094); by it, the UK relinquished sovereignty over Singapore, North Borneo and Sarawak from independence day and extended the 1957 defence agreement with Malaya to apply to Malaysia. Malaysia became automatically a member of the Commonwealth of Nations. *See* map in THE STATESMAN'S YEAR-BOOK, 1964–65.

On 9 Aug. 1965, by a mutual agreement dated 7 Aug. 1965 between Malaysia and Singapore, Singapore seceded from Malaysia to become an independent Sovereign nation.

AREA AND POPULATION. Malaysia comprises 11 states and a federal territory in the Malay Peninsula (bounded north by Thailand), together with a further 2 states and a second federal territory lying on the island of Borneo (bounded south by Indonesia). Singapore and Brunei form enclaves along the coasts of these two 2arts.

The area of Malaysia is 329,759 sq. km (127,317 sq. miles) and the population (1989 estimate) is 17,363,000. The growth of Census population has been:

Year	*Peninsular Malaysia*	*Sarawak*	*Sabah/Labuan*	*Total Malaysia*
1970	8,809,557	975,918	655,295	10,440,770
1980	11,426,613	1,307,582	1,011,046	13,745,241

The areas, populations and chief towns of the states and federal territories are:

State	*Sq. km*	*Census 1980* [1]	*Capital*	*Census 1980*
Johor	18,985	1,638,229	Johor Baharu	249,880
Kedah	9,425	1,116,140	Alor Setar	71,682
Kelantan	14,931	893,753	Kota Baharu	170,559
Kuala Lumpur [2]	243	977,102	Kuala Lumpur	937,875
Melaka	1,658	464,754	Melaka	88,073
Negeri Sembilan	6,646	573,578	Seremban	136,252
Pahang	35,960	798,782	Kuantan	136,625
Perak	21,005	1,805,198	Ipoh	300,727
Perlis	795	148,276	Kangar	12,956
Pinang	1,033	954,638	Pinang (Georgetown)	250,578
Selangor	7,956	1,515,536	Shah Alam	24,138
Terengganu	12,955	540,627	Kuala Terengganu	186,608
Peninsular Malaysia	131,592	11,426,613		
Labuan [2]	98	12,219	Victoria	...
Sabah	73,613	998,827	Kota Kinabalu	55,997
Sarawak	124,449	1,307,582	Kuching	74,229
East Malaysia	198,160	2,318,628		

[1] Revised figures [2] Federal Territories.

Other large cities (1980 Census): Petaling Jaya (207,805), Kelang (192,080), Taiping (146,002), Sibu (85,231), Sandakan (70,420) and Miri (52,125).

Vital statistics (1987): Crude birth rate 29·5 per 1,000 population; crude death rate 4·7; infant mortality rate 15·24 per 1,000 live births.

Of the total population in 1980, 47% were Malay, 32% Chinese, 8% Indian and 13% others.

Over 58% speak *Bahasa Malaysia*, the official language, 9% Chinese, 4% Tamil and 3% Iban.

CLIMATE. Malaysia is affected by the monsoon climate. The N.E. monsoon prevails from Oct. to Feb., bringing rain to the east coast of the peninsula. The S.W. monsoon lasts from mid-May to Sept. and affects the opposite coastline the most. Temperatures are uniform throughout the year. Kuala Lumpur. Jan. 81°F (27·2°C), July 81°F (27·2°C). Annual rainfall 97·6" (2,441 mm). Penang. Jan. 82°F (27·8°C), July 82°F (27·8°C). Annual rainfall 109·4" (2,736 mm).

CONSTITUTION AND GOVERNMENT. The Constitution of Malaysia is based on the Constitution of the former Federation of Malaya, but includes safeguards for the special interests of Sabah and Sarawak. It was amended in 1983.

The federal capital is Kuala Lumpur, established on 1 Feb. 1974 with an area of approximately 94 sq. miles. The official language is Bahasa Malaysia.

The Constitution provides for one of the 9 Rulers of the Malay States to be elected from among themselves to be the *Yang di-Pertuan Agong* (Supreme Head of the Federation). He holds office for a period of 5 years. The Rulers also elect from among themselves a Deputy Supreme Head of State, also for a period of 5 years.

Supreme Head of State (Yang di-Pertuan Agong): HM Sultan Azlan Shah Muhibbuddin Shah ibni Almarhum Sultan Yussuf Izzuddin Ghafarullahu-lahu Shah, DK, DMN, PMN, SPCM, SPMP, elected as 9th *Yang di-Pertuan Agong* from 2 March 1989, succeeded 26 April 1989 and installed 18 Sept. 1989.

Raja of Perlis: HRH Tuanku Syed Putra ibni Al-Marhum Syed Hassan Jamalullail, DK, DKM, DMN, SMN, SPMP, SPDK, acceded 12 March 1949.

Sultan of Kedah: HRH Tuanku Haji Abdul Halim Mu'adzam Shah ibni Al-Marhum Sultan Badlishah, DK, DKH, DKM, DMN, DUK, SPMK, SSDK, acceded 20 Feb. 1959.

Sultan of Johor: HRH Sultan Mahmood Iskandar ibni Al-Marhum Sultan Ismail, DK, SPMJ, SPDK, DK (Brunei), SSIJ, PIS, BSI, acceded 11 May 1981 (Supreme Head of State from 26 April 1984 to 25 April 1989), returned as Sultan of Johor 26 April 1989.

Sultan of Selangor: HRH Sultan Salahuddin Abdul Aziz Shah ibni Al-Marhum Sultan Hisamuddin 'Alam Shah Al-Haj, DK, DMN, SPMS, SPDK, acceded 3 Sept. 1960.

Regent of Perak: HRH Raja Nazrin, appointed April 1989.

Yang di-Pertuan Besar of Negeri Sembilan: HRH Tuanku Ja'afar ibni Al-Marhum Tuanku Abdul Rahman, DMN, DK, acceded 8 April 1968.

Sultan of Kelantan: HRH Sultan Ismail Petra ibni Al-Marhum Sultan Yahya Petra, DK, SPMK, SJMK, SPSM, appointed 29 March 1979.

Sultan of Trengganu: HRH Sultan Mahmud Al-Marhum ibni Al-Marhum Tuanku Al-Sultan Ismail Nasiruddin Shah, DK, SPMT, SPCM, appointed 2 Sept. 1979.

Sultan of Pahang: Sultan Haji Ahmad Shah Al-Musta'in Billah ibni Al-Marhum Sultan Abu Bakar Ri'Ayatuddin Al-Mu'Adzam Shah, DKM, DKP, DK, SSAP, SPCM, SPMJ.

Yang di-Pertua Negeri Paau Pinang: HE Tun Haji Hamdan Sheikh Tahir, appointed 2 May 1989.

Yang di Pertua Negeri Melaka: HE Tun Datuk Seri Utama Syed Ahmad Al-Haj bin Syed Mahmud Shahabudin, SSM, PSM, DUNM, SPMK, SSDK, PGDK, PNBS, JMN, JP, appointed 4 Dec. 1984.

Yang di-Pertua Negeri Sarawak: HE Datuk Patinggi Haji Ahmad Zaidi Adruce bin Muhammed Noor, SSM, DP, DUNM, PNBS, BM Adipradana (Indonesia) appointed 2 April 1985.

Yang di-Pertua Negeri Sabah: HE Tan Sri Datuk Haji Mohd Said bin Keruak, PMN, SPDK, appointed 31 Dec. 1986.

Parliament consists of the *Yang di-Pertuan Agong* and two *Majlis* (Houses of Parliament) known as the *Dewan Negara* (Senate) of 69 members and *Dewan*

Rakyat (House of Representatives) of 177 members. There are 169 members from the states in Malaysia and 8 from the Federal Territory. Appointment to the Senate is for 3 years. The maximum life of the House of Representatives is 5 years, subject to its dissolution at any time by the *Yang di-Pertuan Agong* on the advice of his Ministers.

National flag: Fourteen horizontal stripes of red and white, with a blue quarter bearing a crescent and a star of 14 points, all in gold.

National Anthem: Negara-Ku.

The elections to the House of Representatives held on 2–3 Aug. 1986, returned the following members: National Front, 148; Democratic Action Party, 24; PAS, 1; Independent, 4. The Cabinet was in Dec. 1989 composed as follows:

Prime Minister and Minister for Home Affairs: Datuk Seri Dr Mahathir Mohamad, SSDK, SSAP, SPMS, SPMJ, DP(Sk), DUPN, SPNS, SPDK, SPCM, SSMT, DUMN.

Deputy Prime Minister and Minister for National and Rural Development: Encik Abdul Ghafar bin Baba. *Transport:* Dato Dr Ling Liong Sik. *Energy, Telecommunications and Posts:* Dato Seri S. Samy Vellu. *Primary Industries:* Dato Dr Lim Keng Yaik. *Defence:* Tnegku Dato Ahmad Rithaudeen Al-Haj bin Tengku Ismail. *Works:* Dato Leo Moggie anak Irok. *Trade and Industry:* Dato Seri Paduka Rafidah Aziz. *Ministers in the Prime Minister's Department:* Dato Dr Haji Sulaiman bin Haji Daud (*Justice*), Dato Dr Mohamad Yusof bin Haji Mohamed Nor. *Agriculture:* Datuk Seri Sanusi bin Junid. *Science, Technology and Environment:* Datuk Amar Stephen Yong Kuet Tze. *Education:* Encik Anwar bin Ibrahim. *Foreign Affairs:* Dato Abu Hassan bin Haji Omar. *Finance:* Dato Paduka Daim Zainuddin. *Housing and Local Government:* Encik Lee Kim Sai. *Youth and Sports:* Dato Seri Haji Mohd, Najib bin Tun Haji Abdul Razak. *Land and Regional Development:* Encik Kasitah bin Gaddam. *Health:* Encik Ng Cheng Kiat. *Information:* Dato Mohamed bin Rahmat. *Culture and Tourism:* Dato Sabbaruddin Chik. *Public Enterprizes:* Dato Napsiah binti Omar. *Social Services:* Encik Mustaffa bin Mohammad. *Labour:* Datuk Lim Ah Lek.

DEFENCE. The Malaysian Constitution provides for the *Yang di-Pertuan Agong* (Supreme Head of State) to be the Supreme Commander of the Armed Forces who exercises his powers and authority in accordance with the advice of the Cabinet. Under the general authority of the Yang di-Pertuan Agong and the Cabinet, there is the Armed Forces Council which is responsible for the command, discipline and administration of all other matters relating to the Armed Forces, other than those relating to their operational use.

The Armed Forces Council is chaired by the Minister of Defence and its membership consists of the chief of the Defence Forces, the 3 Service Chiefs and 2 other senior military officers, the Secretary-General of the Ministry of Defence, a representative of State Rulers and an appointed member.

The chief of the Armed Forces Staff is the professional head of the Armed Forces and the senior military member in the Armed Forces Council. He is the principal adviser to the Minister of Defence on the military aspects of all defence matters. The chief of the Armed Forces Staff's committee, established under the authority of the Armed Forces Council, is the highest level at which joint planning and coordination with the Armed Forces are carried out. The Committee is chaired by the chief of the Armed Forces Staff and its membership consists of the chief of the Army, Navy and Air Force, the chief of Personnel Staff, the chief of logistic Staff and the chief of Staff of the Ministry of Defence.

Army. The Army is organized into 4 divisions, comprising 9 infantry brigades made up of 36 infantry battalions; 4 armoured, 5 field artillery, 5 engineer and 5 signals regiments and 2 anti-aircraft battalions. There is also a special service regiment. Equipment includes 26 Scorpion light tanks. Strength (1990) about 97,000, with as reserves the Malaysian Territorial Army and the regular reservists who have completed their full-time service (45,000).

Navy. The Royal Malaysian Navy is commanded by the Chief of the Navy from the integrated Ministry of Defence in Kuala Lumpur. Main bases are at Lumut, and on Labuan Island which are also the headquarters for the Malay Peninsula and Borneo operational areas respectively. The peace-time tasks include fishery protection and anti-piracy patrols.

The combatants include 2 German-built and 2 British-built frigates all with helicopter platforms, 8 fast missile craft, 4 offshore and 27 inshore patrol craft. There are also 4 Italian-type offshore mine countermeasure vessels and 2 tank landing ships normally employed in support of patrol and missile craft. Auxiliaries include 2 multi-purpose support ships, 1 survey ship, a diving support ship and 33 amphibious craft.

A Naval aviation squadron was formed in 1988 and operates 6 *ex*-British Wasp helicopters. Navy personnel in 1989 totalled 12,500.

Paramilitary maritime forces include 50 armed patrol launches, 48 operated by the Royal Malaysian Police and 2 by the Government of Sabah which also operates 4 other patrol boats, 1 landing craft and a yacht.

Air Force. Formed on 1 June 1958, the Royal Malaysian Air Force is equipped primarily to provide air defence and air support for the Army, Navy and Police. Its secondary rôle is to render assistance to Government departments and civilian organizations. There were in late 1989 11 squadrons, of which 9 operated transport aircraft and helicopters. Some 35 A-4 Skyhawks, which previously equipped 2 squadrons, have been withdrawn from use and placed in storage. Other equipment includes 14 F-5E Tiger II jet fighterbombers, 2 RF-5E reconnaissance-fighters, and 3 F-5F trainers, 1 F.28 Fellowship and 1 Falcon 900 VIP transports, 9 C-130 Hercules four-engined transport and patrol aircraft, 15 Caribou twin-engined STOL transports, 2 HU-16 amphibians, 33 Sikorsky S-61A-4 Nuri heavy troop and cargo transport helicopters, 20 Alouette III, and 9 Bell 47 helicopters, 10 Cessna 402Bs for twin-engine training and liaison, 44 PC-7 Turbo-Trainers, 11 MB.339 jet trainers, 2 H.S. 125 Merpati twin-jet executive transports and 1 Super Puma VIP transport helicopter. Personnel (1990) totalled about 12,000.

Volunteer Forces. The Army Volunteer Force (Territorial Army) consists of first-line infantry, signals, engineer and logistics units able to take the field with the active army, and a second-line organization to provide local defence. There is also a small Naval Volunteer Reserve with Headquarters in Penang and Kuala Lumpur. The Royal Malaysian Air Force Volunteer Reserve has both air and ground elements.

INTERNATIONAL RELATIONS

Membership. Malaysia is a member of UN, the Commonwealth, Non-Aligned countries, the Colombo Plan, Organization of Islamic Conference and ASEAN.

ECONOMY

Planning. The fifth 5-year plan, 1986–90 envisaged an expenditure of M$74,000m. and aimed at stimulating economic growth through development of manufacturing industries, revitalization of agriculture and improvement of productivity in all sectors.

Budget. Revenue and expenditure for calendar years, in M$1m.:

	1985	*1986*	*1987*	*1988*	*1989*
Revenue	21,114	19,518	18,143	21,448	22,742
Operating expenditure	20,066	20,075	20,185	21,340	22,286
Development expenditure (net)	6,756	6,949	4,111	5,521	6,979

Currency. Bank Negara Malaysia (Central Bank of Malaysia) assumed sole currency issuing authority in Malaysia on 12 June 1967. The unit of currency issued by Bank Negara Malaysia is the Malaysian *ringgit* ($) which is divided into 100 *sen*. Currency notes are of denominations of $1, 5, 10, 20, 50, 100, 500 and $1,000. Coins are of denominations of 1 *sen*, 5, 10, 20, 50 *sen* and $1, $5 and $100. Total amount of currency in circulation at 30 June 1988, M$7,497m.

Rate of exchange, March 1990: 2·72 *ringgit* = US$1; 4·45 *ringgit* = £1.

Banking. Thirty-eight commercial banks were operating at 31 Dec. 1988; of these 22 were incorporated locally, with 911 banking offices. Total deposits with commercial banks at 31 Dec. 1988 were M$61,139m. There were 12 merchant banks at 31 Dec. 1988. Their total income was M$157m. in 1988. There were 47 finance companies with 486 offices in 1988.

The Islamic Bank of Malaysia began operations in July 1983. The National Savings Bank (formerly known as the post office savings bank) held M$973·8m. due to 3,600,948 depositors at 31 Dec. 1978.

Weights and Measures. The standard measures are the imperial yard, pound and gallon. The Weights and Measures Act of 1972 provides for a 10-year transition to the metric system, and was completed by 31 Dec. 1981.

ENERGY AND NATURAL RESOURCES

Oil. Production (1989) 28m. tonnes.

Gas. Natural gas reserves, 1987, 1,400,000m. cu. metres. Production of LNG in 1988 was approximately 6·2m. tonnes, most of which was exported to Japan.

Minerals. Production (1986, in 1,000 tonnes): Bauxite, 566; iron ore, 208; copper, 115; tin, 29.

Agriculture. Production (1988): Pineapples, 199,000 tonnes; tobacco leaves, 9,000 tonnes from 10,000 hectares; cocoa, 220,000 tonnes from 233,000 hectares, rubber, 1,612,000 tonnes; sugar-cane, 1·2m. tonnes from 19,000 hectares; tea, 18,000 tonnes from 8,000 hectares; coconuts, 1,186,000 tonnes; vegetables, 479,000 tonnes.

Livestock (1988): Cattle, 625,000, buffaloes, 220,000; sheep, 99,000; pigs, 2,258,000; goats, 347,000.

Forestry. In 1988 there were 19·6m. hectares of forests, 60% of the land area; the total output of saw logs was 34·3m. cu. metres; sawn timber, 6·6m. cu. metres.

Fisheries. Total landings of marine fish, 1987, 515,000 tonnes.

INDUSTRY AND TRADE

Industry. 1989: 6,287,700 were employed: 1,934,600 in agriculture, forestry and fishing; 1,065,900 in manufacturing; 852,700 in government services; 1,548,300 in other services; 38,300 in mining and quarrying; 361,800 in construction; 216,100 in finance, insurance, business services and real estate; 270,000 in transport, storage and communication.

Production, 1988 (1,000 tonnes): Rubber, 1,612; tin, 32; crude palm oil, 5,000; sawlogs, 33,600,000 cu. metres.

Commerce. In 1988 exports totalled M$54,422m. and imports M$42,880m.

Chief imports (1988, provisional): Machinery and transport equipment, M$17,485m.; manufactured goods, M$6,686m.; food, beverages and tobacco M$3,857m.; crude petroleum and related products, M$1,981m.

Chief exports (1988): Manufactured goods (M$26,347m.); crude petroleum (M$6,339m.); rubber (M$5,095m.); palm oil (M$4,625m.); saw logs (M$3,990m.); tin, M$938.

In 1987 imports (in M$1m.) came chiefly from Japan (6,926); USA (5,983) and Singapore (4,718). Exports went chiefly to Japan (8,828), Singapore (8,219) and USA (7,485).

Total trade of Malaysia with UK (British Department of Trade returns, in £1,000 sterling):

	1986	*1987*	*1988*	*1989*
Imports to UK	350,058	397,122	525,017	676,258
Exports and re-exports from UK	226,912	257,970	310,462	441,762

COMMUNICATIONS

Aviation. In 1989 there were 4 international airports and 15 other aerodromes at which regular public air transport was operated. About 20 international airlines operate through Kuala Lumpur linking Malaysia with the rest of the world. Malaysia Airlines, the national airline, operates domestic flights within Peninsular Malaysia as well as between Kuala Lumpur and Sabah and Sarawak, and flies to international destinations in Asia, Australia, Europe and the USA. In 1987 there were 204,155 landings and take-offs, carrying 5,445,610 passengers.

Shipping. The major ports are Port Kelang, Labuan, Pulau Pinang, Pasir Gudang, Kuantan, Kota Kinabalu, Sandakan, Kuching, Sibu and Bintulu. The Malaysian International Shipping Corporation operates a fleet of vessels (1,211,954 DWT).

Post and Broadcasting. The Postal Services in Malaysia are under the Ministry of Energy, Telecommunications and Post and are headed by the Director-General of Post, Malaysia. There were 1·2m. telephone subscribers in 1988. As at 31 Dec. 1986, 525 post offices, 1,586 postal agencies, 236 mobile post offices and 1 riverine postal office were operating in Malaysia.

In 1987, 378,314 radio licences and 1,658,566 television licences were issued.

Newspapers. Papers are published in Malay (1,226,000 daily sales in 1984), English (830,000), Chinese (387,000) and Tamil (19,000).

JUSTICE, RELIGION, EDUCATION AND WELFARE

Justice. By virtue of Art. 121(1) of the Federal Constitution judicial power in the Federation is vested on 2 High Courts of co-ordinate jurisdiction and status namely the High Court of Malaya and the High Court of Borneo, and the inferior courts. The Federal Court with its principal registry in Kuala Lumpur is the Supreme Court in the country.

The Lord President as the supreme head of the Judiciary, the 2 Chief Justices of the High Courts and 6 other Judges form the constitution of the Federal Court. Apart from having exclusive jurisdiction to determine appeals from the High Court the Federal Court is also conferred with such original and consultative jurisdiction as is laid out in Articles 128 and 130 of the Constitution.

A panel of 3 Judges or such greater uneven number as may be determined by the Lord President preside in every proceeding in the Federal Court.

The right of appeal to the Yang di-Pertuan Agong (who in turn refers the appeal to the Judicial Committee of the British Privy Council) from a decision of the Federal Court in respect of criminal and constitutional matters was abolished on 1 July 1978.

Religion. Islam is the official religion but there is freedom of worship.

Education. In 1988 there were 2,269,940 pupils enrolled in primary schools, 940,883 in lower secondary and 373,974 in upper secondary schools, 47,543 at pre-university level, 66,837 college students and 47,702 at university.

Health. In 1987 there were 5,794 private and government doctors (1986) 1,130 dentists, 10,601 government nurses, 101 hospitals and 4,370 clinics.

Social Security. The Employment Injury Insurance Scheme provides medical and cash benefits and the Invalidity Pension Scheme provides protection to employees against invalidity due to disease or injury from any cause. Other supplementary measures are the Employees' Provident Fund, the pension scheme for government employees, free medical benefits for all who are unable to pay and the provision of medical benefits particularly for workers under the Labour Code.

DIPLOMATIC REPRESENTATIVES

Of Malaysia in Great Britain (45 Belgrave Sq., London, SW1X 8QT)
High Commissioner: (Vacant)

Of Great Britain in Malaysia (185, Jalan Semantan, Ampang, Kuala Lumpur)
High Commissioner: J. Nicholas T. Spreckley, CMG.

Of Malaysia in the USA (2401 Massachusetts Ave., NW, Washington, D.C., 20008)
Ambassador: Albert S. Talalla.

Of the USA in Malaysia (376 Jalan Tun Razak, Kuala Lumpur)
Ambassador: Paul M. Cleveland.

Of Malaysia to the United Nations
Ambassador: Razali Ismail.

Further Reading

Statistical Information: The Department of Statistics, Malaysia, Kuala Lumpur, was set up in 1963, taking over from the Department of Statistics, States of Malaya. *Chief Statistician:* Khoo Teik Huat. Main publications: *Peninsular Malaysia Monthly* and *Annual Statistics of External Trade; Malaysia External Trade* (quarterly); *Peninsular Malaysia Statistical Bulletin* (monthly); *Rubber Statistics* (monthly); *Rubber Statistics Handbook* (annual); *Oil Palm Statistics* (monthly); *Oil Palm, Coconut and Tea Statistics* (annual). *Malaysia 1985*. The Department of Information, Kuala Lumpur, 1986

Anand, S., *Inequality and Poverty in Malaysia*. OUP, 1983
Brown, I. and Ampalavanar, R., *Malaysia.* [Bibliography] Oxford and Santa Barbara, 1986
Gullick, J., *Malaysia: Economic Expansion and National Unity*. Boulder and London, 1982
Meerman, J., *Public Expenditure in Malaysia*. OUP, 1980
Snodgrass, D. R., *Inequality and Economic Development in Malaysia*. OUP, 1982
Zakaria, A., *Government and Politics in Malaysia*. OUP, 1987

PENINSULAR MALAYSIA

AREA AND POPULATION. The total area of Peninsular Malaysia is about 50,810 sq. miles (131,598 sq. km). Population (1989 estimate) 14,303,000. The federal capital is Kuala Lumpur (244 sq. km).

CONSTITUTION AND GOVERNMENT. The States of the Federation of Malaya, now known as Peninsular Malaysia, comprises the 11 States of Johor, Pahang, Negeri Sembilan, Selangor, Perak, Kedah, Perlis, Kelantan, Trengganu, Penang and Melaka.

For earlier history of the States and Settlements *see* THE STATESMAN'S YEAR-BOOK, 1957, p. 241.

The Constitution is based on the agreements reached at the London conference of Jan.-Feb. 1956, between HM Government in the UK, the Rulers of the Malay states and the Alliance Party (which at the first federal elections on 27 July 1955 obtained 51 of the 52 elected members), and subsequently worked out by the Constitutional Commission appointed after that conference.

ECONOMY

Budget. See p. 834.

ENERGY AND NATURAL RESOURCES

Electricity. In 1987, 16,287m. kwh. were generated. Supply 240 volts; 50 Hz.

Oil. Production (1987) 23·6m. tonnes of crude oil.

Minerals. Production (in tonnes): Tin-in-concentrates: 1986, 29,134; 1987, 30,388. Iron ore: 1986, 207,963; 1987, 161,287. Bauxite: 1986, 566,170; 1987, 482,125. Copper: 1986, 115,304; 1987, 122,206. Gold: 1986, 2,221 troy oz.; 1987, 2,716.

Agriculture. Production in 1986 (in tonnes): Rice (1985), 1,122,400 from (1986) 627,000 hectares; rubber, 1·54m.; palm oil, 4·54m.; palm kernels, 1·34m.; cocoa, 102,000; coconuts, 33,900; (the following all 1985) copra, 216,000; vegetables, 481,000; fruit, 898,000; sugar-cane, 1·2m.; tea, 4,000; cassava, 370,000; sweet potatoes, 50,000; roots and tubers, 505,000; maize, 24,000.

Forestry (1984). Reserved forests, 4·7m. hectares. Production of logs (1986), 30m. cu. metres; sawn timber, 5·15m. cu. metres; plywood (1984), 630,000 cu. metres.

Fisheries. Landings in 1983 493,117 tonnes. Fishermen (1985) 87,000; 70% offshore.

INDUSTRY AND TRADE

Trade Unions. There were, in 1987, 311 trade unions with 560,800 members in Peninsular Malaysia.

Tourism. In 1987 there were 3,285,166 tourists.

COMMUNICATIONS

Roads. In 1986 the Public Works Department maintained 39,915 km of roads. In 1985 the 8-mile road bridge between the mainland and Penang island opened.

In 1987, 4,591,472 motor vehicles were registered, including 1,475,760 private cars, 22,134 buses, 316,846 lorries and vans, 2,611,584 motor cycles.

Railways. The Malayan Railway main line runs from Singapore to Butterworth opposite Penang Island. From Bukit Mertajam 8 miles south of Butterworth a branch line connects Peninsular Malaysia with the State Railways of Thailand at the frontier station of Padang Besar. Other branch lines connect the main line with Port of Klang, Teluk Anson, Port Dickson and Ampang. The east-coast line, branching off the main line at Gemas, runs for over 300 miles to Tumpat, Kelantan's northern-most coastal town; a 13-mile branch line linking Pasir Mas with Sungei Golok makes a second connexion with Thailand.

In 1988 there were 1,672 km (metre gauge) which carried 7,300m. passenger-km and 4m. tonnes of freight.

Aviation (1985). International air services are operated into Kuala Lumpur, Johor and Penang airports. The national carrier, Malaysian Airlines System (MAS), began operation on 1 Oct. 1972 to provide both domestic and international services.

Civil aviation statistics for airports in Peninsular Malaysia (1984): Aircraft movements, 97,890; terminal passengers, 6,078,273; freight, 80,232 tonnes; mail, 7,163 tonnes.

Shipping. The major ports of Peninsular Malaysia are Port Kelang, Penang, Johor and Kuantan. In 1984 Port Kelang handled 12,357,262 tonnes of cargo valued at M$16,318·4m., of which imports totalled 7,744,789 tonnes (M$9,532·9m.) and exports 4,612,473 tonnes (M$6,785·5m.). A total of 4,630 ships, GRT 35m. tonnes, called in 1984. In 1984 the Port of Penang handled 7,960,506 tonnes of cargo, of which 5,220,550 tonnes were imports and 2,739,956 tonnes exports. The total cargo handled in all ports during 1984 was 31,986,000 tonnes.

JUSTICE, RELIGION, EDUCATION AND WELFARE

Justice. Unlike the Federal Court and the High Court which were established under the Constitution, the subordinate courts in Peninsular Malaysia comprising the sessions court, the Magistrates' court and the Penghulu's court were established under a Federal Law (the subordinate Courts Act, 1948 (Revised 1972)).

All offences other than those punishable with death are tried before a Sessions Court President who is empowered to pass any sentence allowed by law other than the sentence of death. In civil matters, the sessions court has jurisdiction to hear all actions and suits where the amount in dispute does not exceed M$25,000.

A First Class Magistrate's criminal jurisdiction is limited to offences for which the maximum term provided by law does not exceed 10 years' imprisonment and to certain specified offences where the term of imprisonment provided for may be extended to 14 years' imprisonment or which are punishable with fine only.

Juvenile courts established under the Juvenile Courts Act, 1947 for juvenile offenders below the age of 18 are presided over by a First Class Magistrate assisted by 2 advisers. There are 30 penal institutions, including Borstal establishments and an open prison camp.

Religion. More than half the population are Moslems, and Islam is the official religion. In 1970 there were 4,673,670 Moslems, 765,250 Hindus, 220,897 Christians and 2,495,739 Buddhists.

Education. In 1987 there were 6,703 state assisted primary schools with 2,325,462 pupils and 103,983 teachers and in 1980, 208 private primary schools with 5,130 pupils and 224 teachers.

In 1986 there were 1,226 secondary schools with 1,329,399 pupils and 60,863 teachers.

There were (1980): 10 special schools with 1,312 pupils and 104 teachers; 401 classes for further education with 10,281 students and 997 teachers; 25 teacher training colleges with over 12,000 students.

In the academic year 1981–82 there were 10 institutions of higher learning:

	1981–82	
	Staff	*Students*
Ungku Omar Polytechnic, Ipoh	112	2,449
Kuantan Polytechnic, Kuantan	49	575
MARA Institute of Technology, Shah Alam	665	11,108
Tunku Ab. Rahman College, Kuala Lumpur	156	6,285
University of Malaya, Kuala Lumpur	1,085	9,310
University of Kebangsaan, Bangi	864	7,514
University of Science, Penang	417	4,387
University of Agriculture, Serdang	502	4,136
University of Technology, Kuala Lumpur	431	4,862

The International Islamic University opened in 1983.

Health. In 1987 there were 68 hospitals and 1,252 clinics. In 1983 there were 4,082 doctors, 774 dentists, 13,874 midwives and 17,916 nurses.

Further Reading

Morris, M. W., *Local Government in Peninsular Malaysia.* London, 1980
Wilkinson, R. J., *Malay-English Dictionary.* 2 vols. New ed. London, 1956
Winstedt, Sir R., *Malaya and Its History.* 3rd ed. London, 1953.—*An English–Malay Dictionary.* 3rd ed. Singapore, 1949.—*The Malays: A Cultural History.* London, 1959

SABAH

HISTORY. The territory now named Sabah, but until Sept. 1963 known as North Borneo, was in 1877-78 ceded by the Sultans of Brunei and Sulu and various other rulers to a British syndicate, which in 1881 was chartered as the British North Borneo (Chartered) Company. The Company's sovereign rights and assets were transferred to the Crown with effect from 15 July 1946. On that date, the island of Labuan (ceded to Britain in 1846 by the Sultan of Brunei) became part of the new Colony of North Borneo. On 16 Sept. 1963 North Borneo joined the new Federation of Malaysia and became the State of Sabah.

AREA AND POPULATION. Area, about 28,460 sq. miles (73,710 sq. km), with a coastline of 973 miles (1,577 km). The interior is mountainous, Mount Kinabalu being 13,455 ft (4,175 metres) high. Population, 1980 census 1,011,046, (1988 estimate, 1,371,000), of whom, 838,141 were Pribumis, 163,996 Chinese, 5,613 Indians, 3,296 others. The native population comprises Kadazans (largest and mainly agricultural), Bajaus and Bruneis (agriculture and fishing), Muruts (hill tribes), Suluks (mainly seafaring) and several smaller tribes.

The island of Labuan became Federal territory on 16 April 1984, 35 sq. miles (75 sq. km) in area, lying 6 miles (9·66 km) off the north-west coast of Borneo is a free port.

The principal towns are situated on or near the coast. They include Kota Kinabalu, the capital (formerly Jesselton), 1980 census population, 108,725, Tawau (113,708), Sandakan (113,496), Keningau in the hinterland (41,204), and Kudat (38,397).

CLIMATE. The climate is tropical monsoon, but on the whole is equable, with temperatures around 80°F (26·5°C) throughout the year. Annual rainfall varies, according to locality, from 10" (250 mm) to 148" (3,700 mm). The north-east monsoon lasts from Dec. to April and chiefly affects the east coast, while the south-west monsoon from May to Aug. gives the west coast its wet season.

CONSTITUTION AND GOVERNMENT. The Constitution of the State of Sabah provides for a Head of State, called the *Yang Dipertua Negeri Sabah*. Executive authority is vested in the State Cabinet headed by the Chief Minister.

Head of State: Tan Seri Mohamad Said Keruak.
Chief Minister: Datuk Joseph Pairin Kitingan.

Flag: Three horizontal stripes of blue, white and red with a large light blue canton bearing an outline of Mount Kinabalu in dark blue.

The Legislative Assembly consists of the Speaker, 48 elected members and not more than 6 nominated members.

The official language was English for a period of 10 years from Sept. 1963 but in Aug. 1973 Bahasa Malaysia was introduced and in 1974 was declared the official language. English is widely used especially for business.

ECONOMY

Budget. Budgets for calendar years, in M$1,000:

Ordinary Budget	*1984*	*1985* [1]	*1986* [1]	*1987* [1]	*1988* [1]
Revenue	1,336,171	1,156,431	1,099,475	1,411,509	2,037,913
Expenditure	1,437,179	1,037,226	1,017,981	1,061,724	1,715,387
Development Budget					
Revenue	195,099	202,861	219,067	183,680	333,574
Expenditure	299,889	239,231	206,510	212,710	306,325

[1] Excludes Federal Territory of Labuan.

Banking. There are branches of The Chartered Bank at Kota Kinabalu, Sandakan, Tawau, Labuan, Kudat, Tenom and Lahad Datu. The Hongkong and Shanghai Bank has branches at Kota Kinabalu, Sandakan, Labuan, Beaufort, Papar and Tawau. The Hock Hua Bank (S) has branches at Kota Kinabalu, Sandakan and Tawau. The Chung Khiaw Bank has branches at Kota Kinabalu, Tuaran and Sandakan. Malayan Banking Ltd has branches at Kota Kinabalu, Tawau, Semporna and Sandakan. United Overseas Bank and the Overseas Chinese Banking Corporation have each a branch at Kota Kinabalu. Bank Bumiputra Malaysia has branches at Kota Kinabalu. Lahad Datu, Sandakan and Keningau. Overseas Union Bank and the Development and Commercial Bank have each a branch at Sandakan. The Sabah Bank Berhad and Sabah Development Bank were established in Kota Kinabalu in 1979.

The National Savings Bank has taken over the functions of the post office savings bank as from 1 Dec. 1974 and had (1988) M$40·7m. due to depositors. It also provides additional services to depositors including the granting of loans for housing.

COMMERCE. The main imports are machinery, tobacco, provisions, petroleum products, metals, rice, textiles and apparel, vehicles, sugar, building material. Statistics for calendar years, in M$1,000:

	1984	*1985*	*1986*	*1987*	*1988*
Imports	3,647,744	4,037,766	3,432,768	3,604,801	4,122,993
Exports	5,522,111	5,546,967	4,967,423	6,477,242	6,814,997

Tourism. In 1988 some 46,908 tourists visited Sabah, excluding foreign visitors arriving *via* Peninsular Malaysia, Sarawak and Labuan.

COMMUNICATIONS

Roads (1988). There were 8,706 km of roads, of which 2,551 km were bitumen surfaced, 5,395 km gravel surfaced and 760 km of earth road. Work is in progress on a network of roads, notably the Kota Kinabalu-Sandakan and Sandakan-Lahad Datu road links.

Railways. A metre-gauge railway, 134 km, runs from Kota Kinabalu to Tenom in the interior. It carried 453,400 passengers and 154,300 tonnes of freight in 1988.

Aviation. External communications are provided from the international airport at Kota Kinabalu by Cathay Pacific Airways Ltd to Hong Kong; Malaysian Airways to Hong Kong, Manila, Brunei, Kuching, Singapore, Tokyo, Seoul and Kuala Lumpur; Brunei Airways to Brunei and Kuching and Philippine Airlines to Manila.

The total air traffic handled at Sabah airports during 1988 was 2,461,286 passengers, 19,601,200 kg freight and 4,174,889 kg mail.

Shipping (1988). Merchant shipping totalling 18,620,398 NRT used the ports, handling 18,659,182 tonnes of cargo.

Post. As at 31 Dec. 1988 there were 41 post offices, handling 382,479 parcels. There were 106,268 telephones on 31 Dec. 1988. As at 31 Dec. 1988, there were 34,902 wireless and 97,939 television licences issued.

JUSTICE, EDUCATION AND WELFARE

Justice. Pursuant to the Subordinate Courts Ordinance (Cap. 20) (1951) Courts of a Magistrate of the First Class, Second Class and Third Class were established to adjudicate upon the administration of civil and criminal law. The civil jurisdiction of a First Class Magistrate is limited to cases where the amount in dispute does not exceed M$1,000. but provision is made for the Chief Justice to enlarge that jurisdiction to M$3,000. This has been established so as to confer this jurisdiction on all stipendiary magistrates. A Second Class Magistrate can only try suits where the amount involved does not exceed M$500 and a Third Class Magistrate where it does not exceed M$100.

The criminal jurisdiction of these Magistrates' Courts is limited to offences of a less serious nature although stipendiary magistrates have enhanced jurisdiction. There are no Juvenile Courts.

There are also Native Courts with jurisdiction to try cases arising from breach of native law and custom (including Moslem Law and custom) where all parties are natives or one of the party is a native (if the matter is a religious, matrimonial or sexual one). Appeals from Native Courts lie to a District Judge or a Native Court of Appeal presided over by a Judge.

In 1988, 4,611 convictions were obtained in 1,006 cases taken to court.

Education. In 1988, there were 214,968 primary and 104,633 secondary pupils. There are 944 primary schools (770 government, 163 grant-aided and 11 private), and 126 general secondary schools (76 government, 37 grant-aided and 13 private) throughout the State. There were 4 teacher-training colleges, with (1988) 2,305 students.

The Government also runs 6 vocational schools offering carpentry, motor mechanics, electrical installation, fitting/turning, radio and television and heavy plant fitting.

The Department of Education also runs further education classes in most towns and districts. The main medium of instruction in primary schools is Bahasa Malaysia although there are some Chinese medium primary schools. Secondary education is principally English but this is being replaced by Bahasa Malaysia.

Health. The principal diseases are malaria, pulmonary tuberculosis and intestinal infestations. Specific control programmes for malaria and tuberculosis have drastically reduced the incidence of these two diseases.

As at 31 Dec. 1988 there were 16 hospitals (2,799 beds) and 265 clinics. Sixty-five fixed dispensaries in outlying districts providing in-patient and out-patient care are staffed by hospital assistants under the supervision of district medical officers. There is one mental hospital at Kota Kinabalu. There are 18 maternity and child health centres throughout the State.

Further Reading

Statistical Information: Director, Federal Department of Information, Kota Kinabalu.

Tregonning, K. G., *North Borneo.* HMSO, 1960

SARAWAK

HISTORY. The Government of part of the present territory was obtained on 24 Sept. 1841 by Sir James Brooke from the Sultan of Brunei. Various accessions were made between 1861 and 1905. In 1888 Sarawak was placed under British protection. On 16 Dec. 1941 Sarawak was occupied by the Japanese. After the liberation the Rajah took over his administration from the British military authorities on 15 April 1946. The Council Negeri, on 17 May 1946, authorized the Act of Cession to the British Crown by 19 to 16 votes, and the Rajah ceded Sarawak to the British Crown on 1 July 1946.

On 16 Sept. 1963 Sarawak joined the Federation of Malaysia.

AREA AND POPULATION. The area is about 48,250 sq. miles (124,449 sq. km), with a coastline of 450 miles and many navigable rivers.

The population at 1980 census was 1,294,753 (1988 estimate, 1·59m., including 471,073 Ibans; 329,613 Malays; 463,170 Chinese; 133,253 Bidayuhs; 91,704 Melanaus; 85,822 other indigenous; 18,465 others).

The capital, Kuching City, is about 34 km inland, on the Sarawak River (1988 population: 152,000). The other major towns (with 1988 population) are Sibu, 128 km up the Rejang River, which is navigable by large steamers (111,000) and Miri, the headquarters of the Sarawak Shell Ltd (86,000).

CONSTITUTION AND GOVERNMENT. On 24 Sept. 1941 the Rajah began to rule through a constitution. Since 1855 two bodies, known as Majlis Mesyuarat Kerajaan Negeri (Supreme Council) and the Dewan Undangan Negeri (State Legislature), had been in existence. By the constitution of 1941 they were given, by the Rajah, powers roughly corresponding to those of a colonial executive council and legislative council respectively. Sarawak has retained a considerable measure of local autonomy in state affairs. The State or Legislature consists of 56 elected members and sits for 5 years unless sooner dissolved.

A ministerial system of government was introduced in 1963. The Chief Minister presides over the Supreme Council, which contains no more than 8 other Council Negeri members, all of whom are Ministers.

Elections to the State Legislature on 15 and 16 April 1987 returned 28 members of the Sarawak Barisan Nasional comprising the Party Pesaka Bumiputera Bersatu (PBB), the Sarawak United Peoples' Party and the Sarawak National Party.

Sarawak has 24 seats in the Malaysia House of Representatives (154 members) and 5 seats in the Senate (58 members).

Sarawak has 9 divisions each under a Resident.

Head of State: Tun Datuk Patinggi Haji Ahmad Zaidi Adruce bin Muhammed Noor, SMN, SSM, DP, PNBS, Bintang Mahaputera Adipradana (Indonesia), PSLJ (Brunei).

Chief Minister: Datuk Patinggi Tan Sri Haji Abdul Taib Mahmud, DP, PSM, SPMJ, DGSM, PGDK, Kt. WE (Thailand) KOU (Korea), KEPN (Indonesia).

Deputy Chief Ministers: Datuk Amar Tan Sri Sim Kheng Hong, DA, PSM, PGDK, JMN. Datuk Amar Alfred Jabu Anak Numpang, DA, PNBS, KMN. *Environment and Tourism:* Datuk Amar James Wong Kim Min, DA, PNBS. *Infrastructure Development:* Datuk Amar Dr Wong Soon Kai, DA, PNBS, PBS. *Housing:* Datuk Celestine Ujang Anak Jilan, PNBS. *Industrial Development:* Abang Abdul Rahman Zohari bin Tun Datuk Abang Haji Openg, JBS. *Land Development:* Encik Adenan bin Haji Satem, JBS. *Special Functions:* Dr George Chan Hong Nam, KMN, PBS.

State Secretary: Datuk Amar Haji Bujang Mohd. Nor, DA, PNBS, JSM, AMN. *State Attorney-General:* Datuk Haji Mohammad Jemuri bin Serjan, PNBS, JMN, PPC. *State Financial Secretary:* Datuk Liang Kim Bang, PNBS, JBS, PPC, KMN.

The official language is Bahasa Malaysia. The use of English as official language in Sarawak was abolished in 1985.

Flag: Yellow with a diagonal stripe divided black over red charged with a yellow star of nine points.

ECONOMY

Planning. The revised fifth Malaysia 5-year development plan (1986-90) provides for Sarawak an expenditure of M$5,458·03m.; of this amount, 25·6% is allocated to energy and public utilities, 20·74% to transport and communication, 18·59% to agriculture and rural development and 10·43% to commerce, industry and urban development.

Budget. In 1989 State revenue was M$993,119,000.; expenditure, M$1,102,172,000. The revenue is mainly derived from royalties on oil, timber and gas.

Currency. The monetary unit is the Malaysian *ringgit.*

Banking. The National savings bank had 166,714 depositors in July 1988; the amount to their credit was M$75m. There are branches of Bank Negara Malaysia in Kuching, and branches of the Chartered Bank, the Hongkong & Shanghai Bank, Bank Bumiputera Malaysia, the Overseas Chinese Banking Corporation, the Malayan Bank.

Nine local banks have branches in major towns. Sibu is the centre for local commercial banking with Hock Hua Bank (established in 1951, 13 branches and assets of M$872·4m. in 1983) and Kwong Ming Bank (established in 1964, 8 branches and assets of M$170m. in 1983). Both are locally owned and have branches in Kuala Lumpur and other towns.

INDUSTRY AND TRADE

Industry. Industry includes petroleum and petroleum products, natural gas, timber and timber products and rubber. Emphasis is being given to the development of petro-chemical, timber-based and agro-based industries.

Commerce. The main exports were: Liquified natural gas, which accounted for 25·9% of the total, with 6,266,000 tonnes, value M$1,885m., all of which was exported to Japan; crude petroleum, 22·1% of the total, exported to Korea (29%), Japan (24·6%), Philippines (14%), Peninsular Malaysia (8·3%), Thailand (5·3%), Taiwan (5%) and Sri Lanka (3·9%). The other main exports in 1988 were sawn logs (25·4% of the total; 12,293,000 cu. metres, value M$1,849,707,000) and petroleum products (5·6% of the total). The major agricultural exports, which together accounted for M$377,477,000 or 5·2% of the total in 1988, were pepper, cocoa beans, palm oil and rubber.

Total import value, 1988, M$3,827,759,000.

Sarawak's major trading partners in 1988 were Japan (export, 45·7%; import, 14·9%), Peninsular Malaysia (export, 7·1%, import, 40·1%); Singapore (export, 7%, import, 5·7%); Korea (export, 10·9%, import, 0·6%); USA (export, 1·4%, import, 14·1%); Sabah (export, 5·8%, import, 1·2%).

Tourism. In 1988 there were 203,513 visitors.

COMMUNICATIONS

Roads. In 1988 there were 6,902 km of roads, consisting of 2,878 km of bitumen surfaced, 3,062 km of gravel or stone surfaced and 962 km of earth roads. There are no railways.

Aviation. There are daily Malaysian Airline System (MAS) B737 and Airbus flights between Kuching and Kuala Lumpur *via* Singapore, and also scheduled flights between Kuching, Brunei and Hong Kong. Major towns in Sarawak are linked up by internal air routes.

Shipping. In 1988 Sarawak ports handled a total of 25m. tonnes of cargo. Kuching wharf, operational since 1974, can accommodate vessels up to 15,000 tonnes. The Bintulu Port, the largest in the State, handled more than 11m. tonnes in 1988.

Post and Broadcasting. There are 54 post offices, 18 mobile offices and 209 postal agencies. The Telecommunications department was privatized in 1986 and renamed

Syarikat Telekoms Malaysia (STM). A telephone system with 65 automatic exchanges (86,000 telephones) covers the country. There are International Subscribers Dialling (ISD) links with 75 countries and Atur system was introduced in 1985. The government radio and television service had, in 1986, 245 electric radio, 28,693 battery radio and 92,739 TV registered receivers.

Newspapers (1989). There are 2 Malay bi-weekly, 3 English and 8 Chinese dailies. One Malay and 1 Iban monthly newspapers are published by Government.

JUSTICE, RELIGION, EDUCATION AND WELFARE

Justice (1987). In Sarawak there are the High Court and the Subordinate Court. High Court cases go on appeal to the Supreme Court which sits in Sarawak and Sabah twice a year. The Subordinate Courts (Amendment) Act 1987 was extended to Sarawak on 2 Sept. 1987 in which the jurisdiction of the Sessions Court judges and magistrates of the First Class and Second Class was enhanced.

In 1986 a Syariah Court was established.

Police. There is a Royal Malaysia Police, Sarawak Component, with a total establishment of about 9,000 regular officers and men.

Religion. There is a large Moslem population and many Buddhists. Islam is the national religion. There are Church of England, Roman Catholic, American Methodist, Seventh-day Adventist and Borneo Evangelical missions.

Education (1988). There were 1,271 government and government-aided primary schools with 218,547 pupils and 11,195 teachers, and 122 secondary schools with 121,933 pupils and 5,250 teachers. There were 3 teacher-training centres and an agricultural university campus conducting pre-university courses. The MARA Institute of Technology campus, established in 1973, had 960 students in 1987 and offers 3-year courses leading to diploma in accountancy, stenography and business studies and a 6-month pre-commerce course.

The Kuching Polytechnic campus, established in 1987, has 211 students and offers 2 and 3-year courses leading to diploma in accountancy and certificates in book-keeping, general mechanical, civil works, electronic and computer engineering and power engineering.

Health. In 1988 there were 17 government hospitals, 156 static and 119 travelling health centres, clinics and dispensaries, 155 public dental and school dental clinics and 165 maternal and child health centres. There were 358 doctors and 51 registered dentists.

Further Reading

Population and Housing Census of Malaysia, 1980. Dept. of Statistics, Kuala Lumpur
Sarawak Annual of Statistics. Dept. of Statistics, Kuching, 1981
Sarawak Annual External Trade Statistics. Dept. of Statistics, Kuching, 1982
1983 Sarawak Budget. Information Dept., Sarawak
Milne, R. S. and Ratnam, K. J., *Malaysia, New States in a New Nation: Political Development of Sarawak and Sabah in Malaysia.* London, 1974
Runciman, S., *The White Rajahs.* CUP, 1960
Scott, N. C., *Sea Dyak Dictionary.* Govt. Printing Office, Kuching, 1956

National Library: The Sarawak Central Library, Kuching.

MALDIVES

Capital: Malé
Population: 200,000 (1988)
GNP per capita: US$410 (1988)

Divehi Jumhuriya

HISTORY. The islands were under British protection from 1887 until complete independence was achieved on 26 July 1965. Maldives became a republic on 11 Nov. 1968. An attempted *coup* took place in Nov. 1988.

AREA AND POPULATION. The Republic of Maldives, some 400 miles to the south-west of Sri Lanka, consists of 1,200 low-lying coral islands (only 202 inhabited), grouped into 12 clearly defined clusters of atolls. Area 115 sq. miles (298 sq. km). Population (census 1985), 181,453, of which 45% under 15 years. Estimate (1988) 200,000. Capital, Malé (46,334).

CLIMATE. The islands are hot and humid, and affected by monsoons. Malé. Average temperature 81°F (27°C). Annual rainfall 59" (1,500 mm).

CONSTITUTION AND GOVERNMENT. The President is elected every 5 years by universal adult suffrage. He is assisted by the Ministers' *Majlis*, a cabinet of ministers of his own choice whom he may dismiss at will. There is also a Citizens' *Majlis* (Parliament) which consists of 48 members, 8 of whom are nominated by the President and 40 directly elected (2 each from Malé and the 19 administrative districts) for a term of 5 years. There are no political parties.

President, Minister of Defence, National Security and Defence: Maumoon Abdul Gayoom (re-elected unopposed for a third term on 23 Sept. 1988).

Justice: Mohammed Rasheed Ibrahim. *Home Affairs and Sports:* Umar Zahir. *Education:* Mohammed Zahir Hossain. *Health and Welfare:* Abdul Sattar Moosa Didi. *Fisheries and Agriculture:* Abdulla Jameel. *Transport and Shipping:* Abbas Ibrahim. *Tourism:* Ahmed Mujuthaba. *Public Works and Labour:* Abdulla Kamaaluddeen. *Foreign Affairs:* Fathulla Jameel. *Atolls Administration and the Speaker:* Abdullah Hameed. *Trade and Industries:* Ilyas Ibrahim. *Attorney-General:* Ahmed Zaki. *Chief Justice:* Moosa Sathy. *Iman of the Islamic Centre:* Ahmed Shathir.

There are 2 Ministers of State.

The official and spoken language is Divehi, which is akin to Elu or old Sinhalese.

National flag: Red with a green panel bearing a white crescent.

Local government: Maldives is divided into the capital and 19 other administrative districts, each under an appointed governor *(verin)* assisted by local chiefs *(katheebun)*, who are also appointed.

INTERNATIONAL RELATIONS

Membership. The Maldives is a member of UN and the Commonwealth.

ECONOMY

Budget. In 1987 revenue totalled 258·7m. rufiyaa and expenditure 364·2m. rufiyaa.

Currency. The *rufiyaa* is divided into 100 *laari*; there are notes of 1, 2, 5, 10, 20, 50 and 100 *rufiyaa*. In March 1990, £1 = 15·46 *rufiyaa*; US$1 = 9·43 *rufiyaa*.

ENERGY AND NATURAL RESOURCES

Electricity. Production, 1987, 14·8m. kwh.

Agriculture. The islands are covered with coconut palms and yield millet, cassava, yams, melons and other tropical fruit as well as coconut produce.

Production in 1988 included (in 1,000 tonnes): Coconuts, 12; copra, 2.

Fisheries. Catch, mainly tuna (1987) 56,900 tonnes.

INDUSTRY AND TRADE

Industry. The main industries are fishing, tourism, shipping, reedware, lacquer-work, coconut processing and garment manufacturing.

Commerce. In 1985 imports amounted to US$47·9m. and exports to US$23m. of which 29% was to Thailand, 24% to the USA and 20% to Sri Lanka. Bonito ('Maldive fish') is the main export commodity.

Total trade between the Republic of Maldives and UK (British Department of Trade returns, in £1,000 sterling):

	1985	*1986*	*1987*	*1988*	*1989*
Imports to UK	73	276	440	1,859	5,224
Exports and re-exports from UK	1,243	1,321	2,772	1,689	3,412

Tourism. There were 131,399 visitors in 1987.

COMMUNICATIONS

Roads. In 1987 there were 401 cars, 1,241 motorbikes, 648 handcarts, 16,681 bicycles and 485 other vehicles.

Aviation. In 1987, 2,975 aircraft, 292,903 passengers and 3,067,206 kg of freight were handled at Malé International Airport. There are 2 domestic airports. Air Maldives operates domestic flights only.

Shipping. The Maldives Shipping Line operated (1984) 32 vessels.

Post and Broadcasting. There were (1987) 2,965 telephones. There is one AM and one FM radio station broadcasting. There were (1988) 22,000 radio receivers and 4,136 television sets.

Newspapers. There were (1985) 2 daily newspapers, 1 weekly and 1 monthly magazine.

JUSTICE, RELIGION, EDUCATION AND WELFARE

Justice. Justice is based on the Islamic Shari'ah.

Religion. The State religion is Islam.

Education. In 1987 there were 300 primary schools with 53,412 pupils and 1,134 teachers and 6 secondary schools with 1,313 students and 116 teachers. Education is not compulsory.

Health. There is an 84-bed hospital in Malé and 4 regional hospitals. In 1987 there were 7 doctors, 1 dentist and 19 nurses.

DIPLOMATIC REPRESENTATIVES

Of Great Britain in the Republic of Maldives
High Commissioner: D. A. S. Gladstone, CMG (resides in Colombo).

Of the Republic of Maldives to the United Nations
Ambassador: Hussain Manikufaan.

Further Reading

Bell, H. C. P., *History, Archaeology and Epigraphy of the Maldive Islands.* Ceylon Govt. Press, Colombo, 1940

Bernini, F. and Corbin, G., *Maldives.* Turin, 1973

Forbes, A. D. W., *The Maldives.* [Bibliography] Oxford and Santa Barbara, 1989

MALI

Capital: Bamako
Population: 7·78m. (1988)
GNP per capita: US$230 (1988)

République du Mali

HISTORY. Annexed by France between 1881 and 1895, the region became the territory of French Sudan as a part of French West Africa. It became an autonomous state within the French Community on 24 Nov. 1958, and on 4 April 1959 joined with Senegal to form the Federation of Mali. The Federation achieved independence on 20 June 1960, but Senegal seceded on 22 Aug. and Mali proclaimed itself an independent republic on 22 Sept. The National Assembly was dissolved on 17 Jan. 1968 by President Modibo Keita, whose government was then overthrown by an Army *coup* on 19 Nov. 1968; power was assumed by a Military Committee for National Liberation led by Lieut. (now General) Moussa Traoré, who became President on 19 Sept. 1969.

AREA AND POPULATION. Mali is a landlocked state, consisting of the Middle and Upper Niger basin in the south, the Upper Senegal basin in the south-west, and the Sahara in the north. It is bounded west by Senegal, north-west by Mauritania, north-east by Algeria, east by Niger and south by Burkina Faso, Côte d'Ivoire and Guinea. The republic covers an area of 1,240,192 sq. km (478,841 sq. miles) and had a population of 7,620,225 at the 1987 Census; estimate (1988) 7,784,000. In 1985, 21% lived in urban areas.

The areas, populations and chief towns of the regions are:

Region	*Sq. km*	*Census 1987*	*Chief town*	*Census 1976*
Kayes	197,760	1,058,575	Kayes	44,736
Koulikoro	89,833	1,180,260	Koulikoro	16,876
Capital District	267	646,153	Bamako	404,022
Sikasso	76,480	1,308,828	Sikasso	47,030
Ségou	56,127	1,328,250	Ségou	64,890
Mopti	88,752	1,261,383	Mopti	53,885
Tombouctou	408,977	453,032	Tombouctou	20,483
Gao	321,996	383,734	Gao	30,714

The various indigenous languages belong chiefly to the Mande group; of these the principal are Bambara (spoken by 60% of the population), Soninké, Malinké and Dogon; non-Mande languages include Fulani, Songhai, Senufo and Tuareg. The official language is French.

CLIMATE. A tropical climate, with adequate rain in the south and west, but conditions become increasingly arid towards the north and east. Bamako. Jan. 76°F (24·4°C), July 80°F (26·7°C). Annual rainfall 45" (1,120 mm). Kayes. Jan. 76°F (24·4°C), July 93°F (33·9°C). Annual rainfall 29" (725 mm). Tombouctou. Jan. 71°F (21·7°C), July 90°F (32·2°C). Annual rainfall 9" (231 mm).

CONSTITUTION AND GOVERNMENT. A new constitution was announced on 26 April 1974 and approved by a national referendum on 2 June; it was amended by the National Assembly on 2 Sept. 1981. The sole legal party is the *Union démocratique du peuple malien* (UDPM), formally constituted on 30 March 1979 and governed by a 17-member Central Executive Bureau responsible to a 137-member National Council who nominate all candidates for election.

The President is directly elected for a term of 6 years. The 82-member National Assembly is also directly elected, for a term of 3 years. Elections were held on 26 June 1988.

The Council of Ministers in Sept. 1989 comprised:

President, Head of Government, Minister of National Defence: Gen. Moussa Traoré (assumed office Sept. 1969, re-elected June 1985).

Secretary-General to the Presidency: Diango Cissoko. *Public Health and Social Affairs:* Abdoulaye Diallo. *Foreign Affairs and International Co-operation:* Ngolo Traoré. *National Education:* Gen. Sékou Ly. *Transport and Tourism:* Zeini Moulaye. *Planning:* Souleymane Dembele. *Agriculture:* Moulaye Mohammed Haidara. *Environment and Animal Husbandry:* Morifing Kone. *Industry, Water Affairs and Energy:* Amadou Deme. *Public Works, Housing and Construction:* Cheikh Oumar Doumbia. *Territorial Administration and Basic Development:* Col. Issa Ongoiba. *Employment and Civil Service:* Diallo Lalla Sy. *Justice:* Mamadou Sissoko. *Information and Telecommunications:* Niamanto Diarra. *Finance and Trade:* Tiena Coulibaly. *Sports, Art and Culture:* Bakary Traoré. *Minister-Delegate for National Defence:* Gen. Abdoulaye Ouologuem.

National flag: Three vertical stripes of green, yellow, red.

Local Government: Mali is divided into the Capital District of Bamako and 7 regions, sub-divided into 46 *cercles* and then into 279 *arrondissements.*

DEFENCE. There is a selective system of 2 years' military service.

Army. The Army consists of 4 infantry battalions, 2 tank, 1 engineer, 1 parachute, 1 special force, 2 artillery battalions and support units. Equipment includes 21 T-34 tanks. Strength (1990) 6,900. There is also a paramilitary force of 7,800 men.

Air Force. The Air Force has 3 MiG-17 jet fighters, 1 MiG-15UTI jet trainer, some Yak-18 piston-engined trainers, 2 An-24, 2 An-26 and 2 An-2 transports, and 3 Mi-8 and Mi-4 helicopters from USSR. A twin-turbofan Corvette is used for VIP transport. Personnel (1990) total about 400.

INTERNATIONAL RELATIONS

Membership. Mali is a member of UN, OAU and is an ACP state of EEC.

ECONOMY

Budget. The budget for 1988 provided for revenue of 112,100m. francs CFA and expenditure of 146,500m. francs CFA.

Currency. Mali introduced its own currency, the *Mali franc*, in July 1962 but reverted to the *franc CFA* on 1 June 1984 at a rate of 2 *Mali francs* to 1 *franc CFA*. There are coins of 1, 2, 5, 10, 25, 50 and 100 *francs CFA*, and notes of 50, 100, 500, 1,000, 5,000 and 10,000 *francs CFA*.

Banking. The *Banque Centrale du Mali* (founded in 1968) is the bank of issue. There are 4 domestic and 2 French-owned banks.

ENERGY AND NATURAL RESOURCES

Electricity. Production (1986) totalled 161m. kwh. Supply 220 volts; 50 Hz.

Minerals. Mineral resources are limited, but marble (at Bafoulabé) and limestone (at Diamou) are being extracted in the Upper Senegal valley; iron ore deposits in this area await development. Salt is mined at Taoudenni in the far north (4,500 tonnes in 1986) and phosphates at Bouren (10,000 tonnes).

Agriculture. Production in 1988 included (in 1,000 tonnes): Millet, 1,900; sugar-cane, 220; groundnuts, 60; rice, 289; maize, 211; seed cotton, 187; cotton lint, 71; cassava, 73; sweet potatoes, 57.

Livestock, 1988: Cattle, 4,738,000; horses, 62,000; asses, 550,000; sheep, 5·5m.; goats, 5·5m.; camels, 241,000; chickens, 19m.

Forestry. Production (1986) 5·05m. cu. metres. 7% of the land is forested.

Fisheries. In 1986 60,000 tonnes of fish were caught in the rivers.

TRADE. Exports in 1985 totalled 77,200m. francs CFA. Chief imports are foodstuffs, automobiles, petrol, building material, sugar, salt and beer. France and Côte d'Ivoire are the main sources of imports. Cotton formed 41% of exports and livestock in 1983; 25% went to Belgium and 16% to France.

Total trade between Mali and UK (British Department of Trade returns, in £1,000 sterling):

	1985	*1986*	*1987*	*1988*	*1989*
Imports to UK	4,804	8,282	6,937	2,240	2,305
Exports and re-exports from UK	7,294	4,121	5,573	12,732	7,102

Tourism. There were 54,000 foreign tourists in 1986.

COMMUNICATIONS

Roads. There were (1985) 15,700 km of roads, 23,209 passenger cars and 6,802 commercial vehicles.

Railways. Mali has a railway from Kayes to Koulikoro by way of Bamako, a continuation of the Dakar–Kayes line in Senegal. Total length 642 km (metre-gauge) and in 1986 carried 756,000 passengers and 503,000 tonnes of freight.

Aviation. Air services connect the republic with Paris, Dakar and Abidjan. There are international airports at Bamako and Mopti, and Air Mali operates domestic services to 10 other airports.

Shipping. For about 7 months in the year small steamboats perform the service from Koulikoro to Tombouctou and Gao, and from Bamako to Kouroussa.

Post and Broadcasting. There were, in 1984, 9,537 telephones and (1986) 300,000 radio and 1,000 television receivers.

JUSTICE, RELIGION, EDUCATION AND WELFARE

Justice. The Supreme Court was established at Bamako in 1969 with both judicial and administrative powers. The Court of Appeal is also at Bamako, at the apex of a system of regional tribunals and local *juges de paix*.

Religion. In 1983, 90% of the population were Sunni Moslems, 9% animists and 1% Christians.

Education. In 1982–83 there were 364,382 pupils and 10,912 teachers in 1,558 primary and intermediate schools, 13,227 pupils and 890 teachers in 20 senior schools, 12,612 students in 11 technical schools. There were 5,792 students and 491 teaching staff in 7 higher educational establishments in 1979.

Health. In 1980 there were 12 hospitals, 327 health centres and 445 dispensaries, with a total of 3,200 beds; there were 319 doctors, 18 surgeons, 14 dentists (1978), 24 pharmacists (1978), 250 midwives and 1,312 nursing personnel.

DIPLOMATIC REPRESENTATIVES

Of Mali in Great Britain (resides in Brussels)
Ambassador: Lamine Keita (accredited 18 Feb. 1988).

Of Great Britain in Mali
Ambassador: John Macrae, CMG (resides in Dakar).

Of Mali in the USA (2130 R. St., NW, Washington, D.C., 20008)
Ambassador: Nouhoum Samassekou.

Of the USA in Mali (Rue Testard and Rue Mohamed V, Bamako)
Ambassador: Robert M. Pringle.

Of Mali to the United Nations
Ambassador: Noumou Diakite.

MALTA

Capital: Valletta
Population: 349,014 (1988)
GNP per capita: US$4,948 (1988)

Repubblika Ta' Malta

HISTORY. Malta was held in turn by Phoenicians, Carthaginians and Romans, and was conquered by Arabs in 870. From 1090 it was subject to the same rulers as Sicily until 1530, when it was handed over to the Knights of St John, who ruled until dispersed by Napoleon in 1798. The Maltese rose in rebellion against the French and the island was subsequently blockaded by the British aided by the Maltese from 1798 to 1800. The Maltese people freely requested the protection of the British Crown in 1802 on condition that their rights and privileges be preserved. The islands were finally annexed to the British Crown by the Treaty of Paris in 1814.

On 15 April 1942, in recognition of the steadfastness and fortitude of the people of Malta during the Second World War, King George VI awarded the George Cross to the island.

Malta became independent on 21 Sept. 1964 and became a republic within the Commonwealth on 13 Dec. 1974. For earlier constitutional and government history *see* THE STATESMAN'S YEAR-BOOK, 1980–81, p. 837.

In 1971 Malta began to follow a policy of non-alignment and closed the NATO base. In March 1972 agreement was reached on the phasing out of the British Military base which was closed down completely on 31 March 1979.

AREA AND POPULATION. The area of Malta is 246 sq. km (94·9 sq. miles); Gozo, 67 sq. km (25·9 sq. miles); Comino, 3 sq. km (1·1 sq. miles); total area, 316 sq. km (121·9 sq. miles). Population, census 16 Nov. 1985, 345,418; estimate (1988) 349,014. Malta, 323,530; Gozo and Comino, 25,484. Chief town and port, Valletta, population 9,210 but the urban harbour area, 101,210.

Vital statistics, 1988, estimate: Births, 5,533; deaths, 2,708; marriages, 2,531; emigrants, 561; returned emigrants, 936.

CLIMATE. The climate is Mediterranean, with hot, dry and sunny conditions in summer and very little rain from May to Aug. Rainfall is not excessive and falls mainly between Oct. and March. Average daily sunshine in winter is 6 hours and in summer over 10 hours. Valletta. Jan. 55°F (12·8°C), July 78°F (25·6°C). Annual rainfall 23" (578 mm).

CONSTITUTION AND GOVERNMENT. Malta is a democracy and the Constitution, provides for a President of the Republic, a House of Representatives of elected members and a Cabinet consisting of the Prime Minister and such number of Ministers as may be appointed. The Constitution which is founded on work, makes provision for the protection of fundamental rights and freedom of the individual, and ensures that all persons in Malta shall have full freedom of conscience and religious worship. In Jan. 1987 the 2 Political Parties agreed to amend the Constitution to provide that any political party winning more than 50% of all valid votes (but less than 50% of elected members) shall have the number of its members increased in order to have a majority in the House of Representatives. Elections were held in May 1987 in which the Nationalist Party obtained 50·91% of the votes but less seats than the Malta Labour Party. As a result of the above Amendment the Nationalist Party now commands a majority with 35 seats to the MLP 34 seats.

Maltese and English are the official languages.

Elections were held on 9 May 1987. State of parties on 31 Dec. 1988: Nationalist Party, 35; Malta Labour Party, 34.

President: Dr Censu Tabone (sworn in April 1989).

The Cabinet (Nationalist Party) was as at Dec. 1989:

Prime Minister and Minister of Foreign Affairs: Dr Edward Fenech Adami.

Deputy Prime Minister and Minister of the Interior and Justice: Dr Guido De Marco. *Education:* Dr Ugo Mifsud Bonnici. *Social Policy:* Dr Louis Galea. *Finance:* Dr George Bonello Dupuis. *Development of Infrastructure:* Michael Falzon. *Productive Development:* Lawrence Gatt. *Development of Tertiary Sector:* Dr Emmanuel Bonnici. *Gozo:* Anton Tabone.

There are 8 Parliamentary Secretaries.

National flag: Vertically white and red, with a representation of the George Cross medal in the canton.

DEFENCE. The Armed Forces of Malta total 1,500 officers and soldiers and are organized into a headquarters and depot, 1 Infantry battalion, 1 Engineers battalion and an airport security company. There is also a paramilitary force of 270 men. There is a Helicopter Flight equipped with 4 Augusta Bell 47G light helicopters and 1 AB206A Jet Ranger. A coastal patrol force of small craft is manned by AFM personnel and primarily employed as a coastguard. In 1989 it comprised 11 patrol craft.

INTERNATIONAL RELATIONS

Membership. Malta is a member of UN, the Commonwealth and the Council of Europe.

ECONOMY

Planning. National economic strategy aims especially at the attraction of new investment and the creation of new employment in the directly productive and market services (tertiary) sectors as a means of stimulating export-oriented growth. The objective is to promote the location in Malta of new manufacturing industry with higher skill production, develop the island as an offshore financial centre, and enter the EEC as a full member under suitable conditions. With this in mind an industrial incentive package has been announced, and a scheme introduced for the retraining of workers for productive employment in the private sector. Imports are being gradually liberalized, and plans are under way to turn Marsaxlokk all weather port into a free port zone for transhipment activities. Besides manufacturing (food, clothing, chemicals and electrical machinery parts), ship repair and shipbuilding and tourism are the mainstays of the economy.

Budget. Revenue and expenditure (in Lm):

	1985	*1986*	*1987*	*1988*
Revenue	220,548,390	225,853,367	221,160,214	308,747,572
Expenditure	227,644,950	240,463,682	263,619,931	274,003,588

The most important sources of revenue are customs duties, income tax, National Insurance contributions and receipts from the Central Bank of Malta.

Currency. The Maltese currency is (Lm) *Lira Maltija* (Maltese Lira). Central Bank of Malta notes of Lm2, Lm5, Lm10 and Lm20 denominations are in circulation. Malta coins are issued in the following denominations: Lm1, 50, 25, 10, 5, 2 and 1 cents; 5, 3 and 2 *mils.* Total notes and coins in circulation on 31 Sept. 1989, Lm322·6m. In March 1990, £1 sterling = Lm 0·549; US$1 = Lm 0·335.

Banking. The Central Bank of Malta was founded in 1968. Commercial banking facilities are provided by Bank of Valletta Ltd, Lombard Bank (Malta) Ltd and MidMed Bank Ltd. The other domestic banking institutions are the Investment Finance Bank (long-term industrial loans), the Apostleship of Prayer Savings Bank Ltd, Lohombus Corporation Ltd (house mortgage) and Melita Bank International Ltd (offshore bank).

ENERGY AND NATURAL RESOURCES

Electricity. Electricity is generated at 2 interconnected power stations located at Marsa, having a total available generating capacity of 252 mw. The larger station with an installed capacity of 235 mw is also equipped to produce potable water as a co-generation process. Supply 240 volts; 50 Hz.

The gross electricity generated in 1988–89 was 1,095m. kwh.

Oil. The government announced a new offshore exploration campaign in March 1988 and a number of companies were (1989) negotiating with the government for the acquisition of certain offshore blocks.

Agriculture. In 1988 agriculture and fisheries contributed Lm21·1m. to the Gross Domestic Product as against Lm21·4m. in 1987. (The 1988 figure represents a share of 3·9% in the GDP.) In 1983 there was a slight decrease in the cultivable area, which totalled 11,491 hectares as against 11,639 hectares in 1982. In 1988 agriculture employed 2,883 full-timers, representing 2·31% of the gainfully occupied population, and over 12,000 part-time farmers.

In 1988 the value of Malta's main agricultural exports reached Lm1,091,584. The 1987 exports consisted mainly of: Potatoes, Lm589,589; seeds, cut-flowers and plants, Lm518,774; wine, Lm21,458; hides and skins, Lm23,281.

Livestock (1989): Cattle, 20,644; pigs, 65,721; sheep, 5,945; goats 5,402; poultry, 598,460.

Fisheries. In 1987 the fishing industry occupied 1,232 power propelled and 153 other fishing boats, engaging 302 full-time and 1,144 part-time fishermen. The catch in 1987 was 1,311 tonnes valued at Lm956,415.

INDUSTRY AND TRADE

Industry. Foreign investors in industry in Malta are offered the following advantages: Political stability, excellent industrial relations, tax holidays, a strategic geographic location, a special association agreement with the EEC, eligibility for the generalized system of preferences operated by many industrialized countries including the USA and Japan, a fully developed and highly functional infrastructure, free repatriation of profits and capital, easily trainable and highly adaptable labour force, financing facilities at favourable rates of interest, ready-built factories at subsidized rents, training grants, soft loans. Over 300 state-aided manufacturing enterprises are in operation in various industrial sectors, of which the majority are foreign-owned or have foreign interests. The Malta Development Corporation is the Government agency responsible for promoting and implementing new industrial projects.

Labour. The total labour force in Dec. 1987 was 128,005; males, 96,150; females, 31,855, distributed as follows: Agriculture and fisheries, 3,203; manufacturing, 31,508; building, construction and quarrying, 6,736; services, 40,091; electricity, gas and drydocks, 6,215; government, 29,183; armed forces, 1,241; Dejma and auxiliary workers, 3,744. The number of registered unemployed under Part I of the Employment Register was 5,630, and under Part II, 454.

There were 23 trade unions registered as at 30 June 1989, with a total membership of 66,868 and 21 employers' associations with a total membership of 5,614.

Commerce. Imports and exports including bullion and specie (in Lm1,000):

	1983	*1984*	*1985*	*1986*	*1987*	*1988*
Imports	316,633	330,489	354,139	347,909	392,874	447,431
Exports	156,748	181,364	187,099	194,668	208,590	235,920

In 1988 the principal items of imports were: Semi-manufactures, Lm104·8m.; machinery and transport, Lm106·2m.; food, Lm46·8m.; fuels, Lm20·3m.; manufactures, Lm45·4m.; chemicals, Lm34·7m.; others, Lm29·2m. Of domestic exports: Manufactures, Lm90·2m.; machinery and transport, Lm83·6m.; semi-manufactures, Lm25·4m.; beverages and tobacco, Lm2·7m.; food, Lm4·9m.; chemicals, Lm2·5m.

In 1988, Lm99·7m. of the imports came from Italy, Lm79·9m. from UK, Lm66·2m. from Federal Republic of Germany, Lm42·7m. from USA, Lm36·5m.

from Asia, Lm13·8m. from the EFTA, Lm14·6m. from Africa, Lm1·8m. from Australia/Oceania, Lm29·1m. from other European countries; of domestic exports, Lm61·2m. to Federal Republic of Germany, Lm61·2m. to UK, Lm40m. to Italy, Lm15m. to Africa, Lm12·2m. to Asia, Lm25·8m. to USA, Lm3·8m. to EFTA and Lm4·9m. to other European countries.

Total trade between Malta and UK (British Department of Trade returns, in £1,000 sterling):

	1985	*1986*	*1987*	*1988*	*1989*
Imports to UK	51,794	49,197	52,105	40,189	42,194
Exports and re-exports from UK	101,247	101,877	107,941	121,696	132,287

Tourism. In 1988, 783,846 tourists visited Malta, 476.578 from UK, 50,678 from Italy, 22,533 from Scandinavia, 77,644 from Federal Republic of Germany, 37,133 from Libya, 23,927 from France, 17,831 from the Netherlands and 8,734 from USA. In 1988, gross income from tourism was Lm126m.

COMMUNICATIONS

Roads. Every town and village is served by motor omnibuses. There are ferry services running between Malta and Gozo; cars can be transported on the ferries. In 1988 there were 1,405 km of roads. Motor vehicles registered at 31 Dec. 1988 totalled 126,828, of which 94,108 were private cars, 3,542 hire cars, 20,075 commercial vehicles, 697 buses and minibuses and 8,406 motor cycles.

Aviation. In 1988 the main scheduled airlines, Air Malta, Alitalia, British Airways, Corse Air, Interflug, JAT, KLM, Lufthansa, Libyan Arab Airlines, Balkan Bulgarian Airlines, Czechoslovakian Airlines, Austrian Airlines, Swissair, Aeroflot and Tunisavia, operated scheduled services between Malta and UK, German Democratic Republic, Federal Republic of Germany, France, Italy, Libya, Netherlands, Switzerland, Yugoslavia, Bulgaria, Czechoslovakia, Austria, USSR, Tunisia, Greece and Hungary. In 1988 there were 19,068 civil aircraft movements at Luqa Airport. 1,671,759 passengers, 7,026 tonnes of freight and 700 tonnes of mail were handled. A new terminal at Luqa was under construction in 1990.

Shipping. The number of yachts and ships registered in Malta on 31 Dec. 1988 was 939; 3,408,095 GRT. Ships entering harbour, excluding yachts and fishing vessels, during 1988, 2,442.

Post and Telecommunications. Telephone services are administered by Telemalta Corporation with exchanges at Malta and Gozo. On 30 June 1989 there were 168,865 telephones, 134,501 television sets and (31 Dec. 1988) 27,226 radio sets.

Cinemas (1988). There were 13 cinemas with a seating capacity of 9,000.

Newspapers. There were (1989) 1 English, 2 Maltese daily newspapers and 7 weekly papers.

JUSTICE, RELIGION, EDUCATION AND WELFARE

Justice. The number of persons convicted of crimes in 1988 was 1,297; those convicted for contraventions against various laws and regulations numbered 7,272. Seventy-two were committed to prison and 2,937 were awarded fines.

Police. On 31 Dec. 1988 police numbered 71 officers and 1,584 other ranks, including 118 women police.

Religion. The majority of the population (96%) belong to the Roman Catholic Church.

Education. Education in Malta is compulsory between the ages of 5 and 16 and free in government schools. Kindergarten education is provided for 3- and 4-year old children. The primary level enrols children between 5 and 11 years in a 6-year course. In 1989, there were 25,142 children (13,095 boys and 12,047 girls) in 80 primary schools. Another 1,306 pupils were enrolled in preparatory (secondary) classes and classes for weaker pupils. Eight Junior Lyceums (6 in Malta and 2 in

Gozo) had a total of 8,044 students (3,171 boys, 4,873 girls). There were 28 other secondary schools with a total of 12,427 (6,717 boys, 5,710 girls). Secondary schools run 5-year courses leading to GCE 'O' level. Two-year GCE 'A' level courses leading to university entrance, during which students are paid an allowance and expected to gain work experience, are offered by the New Lyceums, *i.e.* upper secondary schools (2 in Malta and 1 in Gozo, with a total of 1,831 students). A higher Secondary School catering for students at GCE 'O' and 'A' level enrolled 736 students. Enrolment in vocational and technician courses in 3 technical institutes and 5 specialized training centres was 900. Trade schools provide a technical and vocational education at craft level and are open to students who finish their second year of secondary education. Extended skills training schemes are also available for trade school graduates. The number of students of all ages in special education was 441.

There were 80 private schools with a population of 4,385 at the nursery level, 10,200 at the primary level and 6,500 at the secondary level.

About 5,000 students attended evening courses in academic, commercial, technical and practical subjects established in various centres. Other schools run on a mainly part-time basis by the Education Department for adult students are the School of Art, the School of Music and the School of Art and Design.

The University of Malta consists of 10 faculties: Law; Medicine and Surgery; Architecture and Civil Engineering; Dental Surgery; Education; Economics, Management and Accountancy; Mechanical and Electrical Engineering; Theology; Arts; Science. There were 2,209 full-time students in 1989–90.

Social Security. The Social Security Act, 1987, provides cash benefits for marriage, maternity, sickness, unemployment, widowhood, orphanhood, invalidity, old age, children's allowances and industrial injuries.

The total number of persons in receipt of benefits on 31 Dec. 1988 was 90,393, viz., 984 in receipt of sickness benefit, 397 unemployment benefit, 157 special unemployment benefit, 89 injury benefit, 305 disablement benefit, 90 death benefit, 23,260 retirement pensions, 9,698 widows' pensions, 8 widows' special allowance, 9 orphan's allowance, 5,027 invalidity pensions, 49,943 children's allowances and 428 maternity benefit.

The Act further provides for the payment of social assistance, medical assistance and non-contributory pensions to persons over 60 years of age, to blind persons over the age of 14 years and to handicapped persons over the age of 16 years.

The number of households in receipt of social assistance and of medical assistance on 31 Dec. 1987 was 6,919 and 7,603 respectively, and the number of pensioners in receipt of a non-contributory pension was 6,746.

Health. In 1989 there were 760 doctors, 93 dentists, 373 pharmacists, 257 midwives, 3,774 nursing personnel and 7 hospitals with 3,259 beds.

DIPLOMATIC REPRESENTATIVES

Of Malta in Great Britain (16 Kensington Sq., London, W8 5HH)
High Commissioner: John A. Manduca.

Of Great Britain in Malta (7 St Anne St., Floriana)
High Commissioner: Brian Hitch, CMG, CVO.

Of Malta in the USA (2017 Connecticut Ave., NW, Washington, D.C., 20008)
Ambassador: Salv J. Stellini.

Of the USA in Malta (Development Hse., St Anne St., Floriana)
Ambassador: Sally J. Novetzke.

Of Malta to the United Nations
Ambassador: Dr Alexander Borg Olivier.

Further Reading

Statistical Information: The Central Office of Statistics (Auberge d'Italie, Valletta) was set up in 1947. It publishes *Statistical Abstracts of the Maltese Islands*, a quarterly digest of statistics, quarterly and annual trade returns, annual vital statistics and annual publications on shipping and aviation, education, agriculture and industry and National Accounts and Balance of Payments.

Government publications: Department of Information (Auberge de Castille, Malta), set up in 1955, publishes *The Malta Government Gazette* (twice weekly), *Malta Information, Economic Survey 1989, Heritage of an Island, Reports on the Working of Government Departments for the year 1988, Malta: Weekly Review of the Press, Report on the Organisation of the Public Service, Subsidiary Legislation for the year 1988, Laws of Malta.*

Annual Reports. Central Bank of Malta
Trade Directory. Chamber of Commerce (annual)
The Year Book. Sliema (annual)
Malta Independence Constitution (Cmnd 2406). HMSO, 1964
Constitution of the Republic of Malta. Information Division, 1975
Malta Manufacturers and Exporters. Department of Industry
Bannerman, D. A. and Vella-Gaffiero, J. A., *Birds of the Maltese Archipelago.* Valletta, 1976
Blouet, B., *The Story of Malta.* London, Rev. ed. 1981
Cremona, J. J., *The Malta Constitution of 1835 and its Historical Background.* Malta, 1959.—*The Constitutional Developments of Malta under British Rule.* Malta Univ. Press, 1963.—*Human Rights Documentation in Malta.* Malta Univ. Press, 1966
Gerada, E. and Zuber, C., *Malta: An Island Republic.* Paris, 1979
Haslam, S. M., Sell, P. D. and Wolseley, P. A., *A Flora of the Maltese Islands.* Malta Univ. Press, 1977
Luke, Sir Harry, *Malta.* 2nd ed. London, 1962
Price, G. A., *Malta and the Maltese: A Study in 19th-century Migration.* Melbourne, 1954
Thackrah, J. R., *Malta.* [Bibliography] Oxford and Santa Barbara, 1985

MAURITANIA

Capital: Nouakchott
Population: 1·89m. (1988)
GNP per capita: US$480 (1988)

République Islamique de Mauritanie

HISTORY. Mauritania became a French protectorate in 1903 and a colony in 1920. It became an autonomous republic within the French Community on 28 Nov. 1958 and achieved full independence on 28 Nov. 1960. Under its first President, Moktar Ould Daddah, Mauritania became a one-party state in 1964, but following his deposition by a military *coup* on 10 July 1978, the ruling *Parti du peuple mauritanien* was dissolved.

Following the Spanish withdrawal from Western Sahara on 28 Feb. 1976, Mauritania occupied the southern part (88,667 sq. km) of this territory and incorporated it under the name of Tiris el Gharbia. In Aug. 1979 Mauritania renounced sovereignty and withdrew from Tiris el Gharbia.

Following the *coup* of 10 July 1978, power was placed in the hands of a Military Committee for National Recovery (CMRN); the constitution was suspended and the 70-member National Assembly dissolved. On 6 April 1979 the CMRN was renamed the Military Committee for National Salvation (CMSN).

AREA AND POPULATION. Mauritania is bounded west by the Atlantic ocean, north by Western Sahara, north-east by Algeria, east and south-east by Mali, and south by Senegal. The total area is 1,030,700 sq. km (398,000 sq. miles) of which 47% is desert, and the population at the Census of 1976 was 1,419,939 including 12,897 in Tiris el Gharbia; latest estimate (1988) 1,894,000. The capital Nouakchott had a population of over 500,000 in 1985; other towns (1976) were Nouâdhibou (21,961), Kaédi (20,848), Zouérate (17,474), Rosso (16,466) and Atâr (16,326).

The areas and populations of the Capital District and 12 Regions are:

Region	*Sq. km*	*Estimate 1982*	*Region*	*Sq. km*	*Estimate 1982*
Nouakchott District	120	150,000	Adrar	215,300	60,000
Hodh ech-Chargui	182,700	235,000	Dakhlet Nouâdhibou	22,300	30,000
Hodh el-Gharbi	53,400	154,000	Tagant	95,200	84,000
Açâba	36,600	152,000	Guidimaka	10,300	102,000
Gorgol	13,600	169,000	Tiris Zemmour	252,900	28,000
Brakna	33,000	171,000	Inchiri	46,800	23,000
Trarza	67,800	242,000			

In 1983, 34% of the population were urban and 25% were nomadic. In 1980 81% of the inhabitants were Moorish, speaking the Hassaniyah dialect of Arabic, while the other 19% consist of Negro peoples, mainly Fulfulde-speaking Tukulor (8%) and Fulani (5%) who together with the Soninike (Sarakole) and Wolof groups all inhabit the Senegal valley in the extreme south.

The official languages are Arabic and French.

CLIMATE. A tropical climate, but conditions are generally arid, even near the coast, where the only appreciable rains come in July to Sept. Nouakchott. Jan. 71°F (21·7°C), July 82°F (27·8°C). Annual rainfall 6" (158 mm).

CONSTITUTION AND GOVERNMENT. The 24-member CMSN wields all executive and legislative powers, working through an appointed Council of Ministers composed as follows in Aug. 1989:

President, Prime Minister, Minister of Defence and Chairman of CMSN: Col. Moaouia Ould Sidi Mohamed Taya (assumed office 12 Dec. 1984).

Foreign Affairs: Maj. Cheikh Ahmed Ould Baba. *Finance:* Mohamed Ould Nany.

National flag: Green, with a crescent beneath a star in yellow in the centre.

Local Government: Mauritania is divided into a capital district and 12 regions and sub-divided into 49 *départements.*

DEFENCE

Army. The Army consists of 2 infantry, 1 parachute and 1 artillery battalion, 1 Camel Corps, 3 armoured car squadrons and support units; total strength, 10,400 in 1990.

Navy. The Navy, some 350 strong in 1989, is based at Noudhibou and consists of 4 fast patrol craft, and 4 smaller patrol vessels.

Air Force. The Air Force has 6 Britten-Norman Defender armed light transports, 2 Maritime Surveillance Cheyennes for coastal patrol, 2 Buffalo and 2 Skyvan transports, 4 Reims-Cessna 337 Milirole twin-engined counter-insurgency, forward air control and training aircraft and 4 Hughes 500 helicopters for communications. Personnel (1990) 250.

INTERNATIONAL RELATIONS

Membership. Mauritania is a member of UN, OAU, the Arab League and is an ACP state of EEC.

ECONOMY

Budget. The ordinary budget for 1989 balanced at 22,000m. ouguiyas.

Currency. The monetary unit is the *ouguiya* which is divided into 5 *khoums.* Banknotes of 1,000, 500, 200 and 100 *ouguiya* and coins of 20, 10, 5 and 1 *ouguiya* and 1 *khoum* are in circulation. In March 1990, £1 = 137·40 *ouguiya*; US$1 = 83·83 *ouguiya.*

Banking. *The Banque Centrale de Mauritanie* (created 1973) is the bank of issue, and there are 5 commercial banks situated in Nouakchott.

ENERGY AND NATURAL RESOURCES

Electricity. Production (1986) 74m. kwh.

Minerals. Iron ore production (1984) 9·5m. tonnes. Copper mining at Akjoujt (by the state-owned SOMIMA), suspended in 1978, resumed in 1983.

Agriculture. Agriculture is mainly confined to the south, in the Senegal river valley. Production in tonnes (1988) of millet, 89,000; dates, 13,000; potatoes, 1,000; maize, 8,000; sweet potatoes, 3,000; rice, 15,000; groundnuts, 2,000.

In 1988 there were 810,000 camels, 1·25m. cattle, 149,000 asses, 17,000 horses, 4·1m. sheep, 3·2m. goats.

Forestry. There were 15m. hectares of forests, chiefly in the southern regions, where wild acacias yield the main product, gum arabic.

Fisheries. Total catch (1986) 104,100 tonnes.

TRADE. In 1986 imports totalled 17,392m. ouguiya, and exports, 25,950 ouguiya of which iron ore comprised 40% of exports and salted and dried fish 60%; 24% of all exports went to Italy, 22% to Japan, 18% to Belgium and 15% to France, while France provided 22% of imports and Spain 20%.

Total trade between Mauritania and UK (British Department of Trade returns, in £1,000 sterling):

	1985	*1986*	*1987*	*1988*	*1989*
Imports to UK	6,311	2,184	8,724	7,259	15,387
Exports and re-exports from UK	2,069	2,495	3,862	3,048	4,005

Tourism. In 1986 there were 13,000 tourists.

COMMUNICATIONS

Roads. There were 8,900 km of roads in 1983. In 1985 there were 15,017 passenger cars and 2,188 commercial vehicles.

Railways. A 652-km railway links Zoué rate with the port of Point-Central, 10 km south of Nouâdhibou, and is used primarily for iron ore exports. In 1986 it carried 9·4m. tonnes and 19,353 passengers.

Aviation. There are international airports at Nouakchott, Nouâdhibou and Néma.

Shipping. The major ports are at Point-Central (for mineral exports), Nouakchott and Nouâdhibou.

Post and Broadcasting. There were, in 1985, 3,161 telephones and 200,000 radio receivers and about 1,000 television receivers.

JUSTICE, RELIGION, EDUCATION AND WELFARE

Justice. There are *tribunaux de première instance* at Nouakchott, Atâr, Kaédi, Aïoun el Atrouss and Kiffa. The Appeal Court and Supreme Court are situated in Nouakchott. Islamic jurisprudence was adopted in Feb. 1980.

Religion. Over 99% of Mauritanians are Sunni Moslem, mainly of the Qadiriyah sect.

Education. In 1986 there were 150,605 pupils in primary schools, 35,129 in secondary schools, 2,808 in technical schools and teacher-training establishments and 4,830 students in higher education. The University of Nouakchott (founded 1983) had 974 students in 1984.

Health. In 1984 there were 13 hospitals and clinics with 1,325 beds. In 1984 there were 170 doctors, 8 dentists, 16 pharmacists, 129 midwives and 582 nursing personnel.

DIPLOMATIC REPRESENTATIVES

Of Mauritania in Great Britain
Ambassador: Mohamed El Hanchi Ould Mohamed Saleh (resides in Paris).

Of Great Britain in Mauritania
Ambassador: John Macrae, CMG (resides in Dakar).

Of Mauritania in the USA
Ambassador: (Vacant).

Of the USA in Mauritania (PO Box 222, Nouakchott)
Ambassador: William H. Twaddell.

Of Mauritania to the United Nations
Ambassador: Mohamedou Ould Mohamed Mahmoud.

Further Reading

Stewart, C. C. and Stewart, E. K., *Islam and Social Order in Mauritania.* New York, 1970
Westebbe, R. M., *The Economy of Mauritania.* New York, 1971

MAURITIUS

Capital: Port Louis
Population: 1,077,187 (1988)
GNP per capita: US$1,810 (1988)

HISTORY. Mauritius was known to Arab navigators probably not later than the 10th century. It was probably visited by Malays in the 15th century, and was discovered by the Portuguese between 1507 and 1512, but the Dutch were the first settlers (1598). In 1710 they abandoned the island, which was occupied by the French under the name of Ile de France (1715). The British occupied the island in 1810, and it was formally ceded to Great Britain by the Treaty of Paris, 1814. Mauritius attained independence on 12 March 1968. In 1965 the Chagos Archipelago was transferred to the British Indian Ocean Territory.

AREA AND POPULATION. Mauritius, the main island, lies 500 miles (800 km) east of Madagascar. Rodrigues (formerly a dependency and now a part of Mauritius) is about 350 miles (560 km) east of Mauritius. The outer islands consist of Agalega and the St Brandon Group. Population estimate (1988) 1,077,187.

Island	*Area in sq. km*	*Census 1983*	*Estimate 1988*
Mauritius	1,865	966,863	1,040,222
Rodrigues	104	33,082	36,465
Dependencies			
Agalega	70	487	500
St Brandon	1	–	–
Total	2,040	1,000,432	1,077,187

Port Louis is the capital (139,038, 1987). Other towns, Beau Bassin-Rose Hill, 93,016; Curepipe, 64,687; Quatre Bornes, 64,668; Vascoas-Phoenix, 55,464.

Vital statistics, 1988: Births, 20,001 (19·1 per 1,000); marriages, 11,283; deaths, 6,699 (6·6 per 1,000).

The official language is English.

CLIMATE. The sub-tropical climate produces quite a difference between summer and winter, though conditions are generally humid. Most rain falls in the summer so that the pleasantest months are Sept. to Nov. Rainfall amounts vary between 40" (1,000 mm) on the coast to 200" (5,000 mm) on the central plateau, though the west coast only has 35" (875 mm). Mauritius lies in the cyclone belt, whose season runs from Nov. to April, but is seldom affected by intense storms. Port Louis. Jan. 73°F (22·8°C), July 81°F (27·2°C). Annual rainfall 40" (1,000 mm).

CONSTITUTION AND GOVERNMENT. Mauritius became an independent state and a monarchial member of the British Commonwealth on 12 March 1968 after 7 months of internal self-government. The Governor-General is the local representative of HM the Queen, who remains the Head of the State.

The Cabinet is presided over by the Prime Minister. Each of the other 18 members of the Cabinet is responsible for the administration of specified departments or subjects and is bound by the rule of collective responsibility. 10 Parliamentary Secretaries may also be appointed by the Governor-General on the advice of the Prime Minister.

The Legislative Assembly consists of a Speaker, elected from its own members, and 62 elected members (3 each for the 20 constituencies of Mauritius and 2 for Rodrigues) and 8 additional seats in order to ensure a fair and adequate representation of each community within the Assembly. General Elections are held every 5 years on the basis of universal adult suffrage.

The Constitution also provides for the Public Service Commission and the

Judicial and Legal Service Commission which have both assumed executive powers for appointments to the Public Service. An Ombudsman assumed office on 2 March 1970.

At the General Election held on 30 Aug. 1987, 41 of the 62 seats were won by the ruling *Alliance* (Mouvement Socialiste Mauricien, 26; Mauritius Labour Party, 9; Parti Mauricien Social-Démocrate, 4; Organisation du Peuple Rodriguais, 2) and 21 by the opposition *Union for the Future* (the Mouvement Militant Mauricien and its allies); of the 8 additional seats awarded to the highest losers in each community, 5 went to the *Alliance* and 3 to the *Union*.

Governor-General: Sir Veerasamy Ringadoo, GCMG, QC.

The Cabinet was composed as follows in Jan. 1990:

Prime Minister, Defence and Internal Security, Information, External Communications and the Outer Islands: Sir Anerood Jugnauth, QC.

Deputy Prime Minister, Attorney-General, Justice, External Affairs and Emigration: Sir Satcam Boolell, QC. *Deputy Prime Minister and Finance:* Seetanah Lutchmeenaraidoo. *Deputy Prime Minister and Economic Planning and Development:* Dr Beergoonath Ghurburrun. *Education, Arts and Culture:* Armoogum Parsuraman. *Trade and Shipping:* Dwarkanath Gungah. *Energy, Water Resources and Postal Services:* Mahyendrah Utchanah. *Labour and Industrial Relations, Women's Rights and Family Welfare:* Sheilabai Bappoo. *Youth and Sports and Tourism:* Michael James Kevin Glover. *Health:* Jagdishwar Goburdhun. *Agriculture, Fisheries and Natural Resources:* Murlidas Dulloo. *Social Security and Reform Institutions:* Dineshwar Ramjuttun. *Works:* Ramduth Jaddoo. *Rodrigues:* Serge Clair. *Housing, Lands and the Environment:* Sir Ramesh Jeewoolall. *Industry:* Clarel Malherbes. *Co-operatives:* V. Sajadah. *Local Government:* Regis Finette. *Civil Service Affairs and Employment:* Marie France Roussety.

National flag: Horizontally 4 stripes of red, blue, yellow and green.

DEFENCE. The Mauritius Police, which is responsible for defence, is equipped 2with arms; its strength was (1990) 6,584 officers and men.

INTERNATIONAL RELATIONS

Membership. Mauritius is a member of UN, the Commonwealth, OAU, the Non-Aligned Movement and is an ACP state of EEC.

ECONOMY

Budget. Revenue and expenditure (in Rs1m.) for years ending 30 June:

	1985–86	*1986–87*	*1987–88*	*1988–89*
Revenue	4,131	5,009	6,215	8,065
Expenditure	4,488	4,635	5,813	7,700

Principal sources of revenue, 1988–89 (estimate): Direct taxes, Rs 1,358·4m.; indirect taxes, Rs 5,278·3m.; receipts from public utilities, Rs 131·1m.; receipts from public services Rs 141·3m.; interest and reimbursement, Rs 119m. Capital expenditure was Rs 2,300m. Capital revenue, Rs 2,568·6m. On 30 June 1988 the public debt of Mauritius was Rs 10,335·9m.

Currency. The unit of currency is the Mauritius *Rupee*, divided into 100 *cents*.

The currency consists of: (i) Bank of Mauritius notes of Rs 500, 200, 100, 50, 25, 10 and 5; (ii) Cupro-nickel coins of 5 rupees and 1 rupee; (iii) nickel-plated steel coins of 50 cents and 20 cents; (iv) copper-plated steel coins of 5 cents and 1 cent. In March 1990, £1 = 24·40 *rupees*; US$1 = 14·89.

Banking. The Bank of Mauritius was established in 1966, with an authorized capital of Rs 10m., to exercise the function of a central bank. There are 13 commercial banks, the Mauritius Commercial Bank Ltd (established 1838), Barclays Bank PLC, the Bank of Baroda Ltd, The HongKong and Shanghai Banking Corporation, the Mauritius Co-operative Central Bank Ltd, Banque Nationale de Paris (Intercontinentale), the Habib Bank Ltd, the State Commercial Bank Ltd, the Bank of

Credit and Commerce International SA, Indian Ocean International Bank Ltd, Mauritius Commercial Bank Finance Corporation Ltd, Union International Bank Ltd and Habib Bank (Zurich). Other financial institutions include the Mauritius Housing Corporation, the Development Bank of Mauritius and the Post Office Savings Bank.

On 31 Dec. 1988 the Post Office Savings Bank held deposits amounting to Rs 228·4m., belonging to 246,660 depositors.

ENERGY AND NATURAL RESOURCES

Electricity. Electric power production (1988) was 545m. kwh. Supply 230 volts; 50 Hz.

Agriculture. In 1988 83,100 hectares were planted with sugar-cane. There were 19 factories and sugar production (1988 in tonnes) was 634,224, molasses, 179,622.

The main secondary crops in 1988 were tea (3,385 hectares from which 6,854 tonnes were produced), tobacco (967 tonnes), potatoes (12,770 tonnes) and maize (3,790 tonnes).

In 1988 poultry production totalled 9,500 tonnes, beef 780 tonnes, pork 660 tonnes and goat meat 138 tonnes.

Livestock (1988): Cattle, 30,000; goats, 95,000; poultry, 2m.

Forestry. The total forest area was estimated (1988) at 21,161 hectares including some 11,730 hectares of plantations. In 1988 production totalled 27,954 cu. metres of timber, poles and fuel wood.

Fisheries. Production (1988) 15,872 tonnes.

INDUSTRY AND TRADE

Industry. Manufactures include: Knitwear, clothing, footwear, diamond cutting, jewellery, furniture, watchstraps, sunglasses, plastic ware and chemical products. Total employment in manufacturing (March 1989) 106,765.

Labour. In 1987 the labour force was 440,000.

Trade Unions. In 1986 there were 291 registered trade unions and 11 federations with a total membership of 101,179.

Commerce. Total trade (in Rs1m.) for calendar years:

	1985	*1986*	*1987*	*1988*
Imports c.i.f.	8,119	9,199	13,042	17,247
Exports f.o.b.	6,644	9,063	11,497	13,454

In 1988, Rs 2,133m. of the imports came from France, Rs 1,482m. from the Republic of South Africa, Rs 1,259m. from UK, Rs 445m. from Australia. Rs 4,799m. of the exports went to UK, Rs 3,025m. to France, Rs 1,793m. to USA and Rs 1,273m. to Federal Republic of Germany.

Sugar exports in 1988 were 652,000 tonnes, Rs 4,449m. Other major exports (1987) included clothing, Rs 6,582m.; tea, Rs 88m. and toys, Rs 86m. Major imports, 1987, included textiles and fabrics, Rs 3,972m.; petroleum products, Rs 1,009m. and machinery and transport equipment, Rs 5,129m.

Total trade between Mauritius and UK (British Department of Trade returns, in £1,000 sterling):

	1985	*1986*	*1987*	*1988*	*1989*
Imports to UK	122,829	153,271	163,271	186,240	216,190
Exports and re-exports from UK	28,512	32,087	44,395	38,553	43,528

Tourism. In 1988, 239,210 tourists visited Mauritius.

COMMUNICATIONS

Roads. In 1988 there were 29 km of motorway, 856 km of main roads, 816 km of secondary and other roads. At 31 Dec. 1988 there were 30,283 cars, 1,771 buses, 9,912 motor cycles, 29,181 auto cycles and 10,322 lorries and vans.

Aviation. Mauritius is linked by air with Europe, Africa, Asia and Australia by the following airlines: Air France, Air India, Air Mauritius, British Airways, Lufthansa, Singapore Airlines, South African Airways and Zambia Airways. In addition to passenger services two weekly cargo flights are operated by Air France and Air Mauritius on the Mauritius–Paris route and the Mauritius–Amsterdam route respectively. In 1988, 343,940 passengers arrived at Plaisance airport and 7,500 tonnes of freight were unloaded. Air Mauritius operates a joint regional service with Air Madagascar on the Mauritius–Tananarive–Moroni–Nairobi route, a joint weekly service with Air India to Bombay, and services to Hong Kong, Réunion and Rodrigues.

Shipping. In 1988 940 vessels entered Port Louis with an average gross tonnage of 15,000 tonnes.

Post and Broadcasting. In 1988 there were 33 telephone exchanges and 72,259 individual telephone installations in Mauritius and Rodrigues. Communication with other parts of the world is established *via* satellite.

At 31 Dec. 1988 there were 138,000 television sets and (1984) 129,414 radio sets.

Cinemas (1988). There were 36 cinemas, with a seating capacity of about 40,000.

Newspapers. There were (1988) 5 French daily papers (with occasional articles in English) and 2 Chinese daily papers with a combined circulation of about 80,000.

RELIGION, EDUCATION AND WELFARE

Religion. At the 1983 Census (excluding Rodrigues) there were 247,723 Roman Catholics, 6,049 Protestants (Church of England and Church of Scotland), 506,270 Hindus and 160,190 Moslems.

Education. Primary education is free and not usually compulsory. About 96% of children aged 5 to 11 years attend schools. In 1989 there were 134,136 pupils at 273 primary schools and 72,389 pupils at 125 secondary schools. There were 8 special schools and 870 students in 3 technical institutions and 5 handicraft training centres and 501 teachers in training in 1989.

In 1989, 1,241 students were enrolled at the University of Mauritius.

Health. In 1988 there were 847 doctors, including 151 specialists, and 2,857 hospital beds.

DIPLOMATIC REPRESENTATIVES

Of Mauritius in Great Britain (32–33 Elvaston Pl., London, SW7)
High Commissioner: Dr Boodhun Teelock (accredited 23 Feb. 1989).

Of Great Britain in Mauritius (King George V Ave., Floreal, Port Louis)
High Commissioner: M. E. Howell, CMG, OBE.

Of Mauritius in the USA (4301 Connecticut Ave., NW, Washington, D.C., 20008)
Ambassador: Chitmansing Jesseramsing.

Of the USA in Mauritius (Rogers Bldg., John Kennedy St., Port Louis)
Ambassador: Penne Percy Korth.

Of Mauritius to the United Nations
Ambassador: Dr S. Peerthum.

Further Reading

Statistical Information: The Central Statistical Information Office (Rose Hill, Mauritius) was founded in July 1945. Its main publication is the *Bi-annual Digest of Statistics*.

Ministry of Information, *Fruits of Political and Social Democracy.—Mauritius Facts and Figures 1980.—The Mauritius Handbook 1989*

Simmons, A. S., *Modern Mauritius: The Politics of Decolonization.* Indiana Univ. Press, 1982

Library: The Mauritius Institute Public Library, Port Louis.

MEXICO

Capital: Mexico City
Population: 84·3m. (1989)
GNP per capita: US$1,820 (1988)

Estados Unidos Mexicanos

HISTORY. Mexico's history falls into four epochs: the era of the Indian empires (before 1521), the Spanish colonial phase (1521–1810), the period of national formation (1810–1910), which includes the war of independence (1810–21) and the long presidency of Porfirio Díaz (1876–80, 1884–1911), and the present period which began with the social revolution of 1910–21 and is regarded by Mexicans as the period of social and national consolidation.

AREA AND POPULATION. Mexico is at the southern extremity of North America and is bounded in the north by USA, west and south by the Pacific, south-east by Guatemala, Belize and the Caribbean, and north-east by the Gulf of Mexico. It comprises 1,958,201 sq. km (756,198 sq. miles), including uninhabited islands (5,073 sq. km) offshore.

The population at recent censuses has been as follows:

1900	13,607,272	1950	25,791,017	1970	48,225,238
1930	16,552,722	1960	34,923,129	1980	66,846,833

The areas (in sq. km), populations and capitals of the states are:

States	*Sq. km*	*Census 1980*	*Estimate 1989*	*Capital*
Aguascalientes	5,471	519,439	702,615	Aguascalientes
Baja California	69,921	1,177,886	1,408,774	Mexicali
Baja California Sur	73,475	215,139	327,389	La Paz
Campeche	50,812	420,553	617,133	Campeche
Chiapas	74,211	2,084,717	2,559,461	Tuxtla Gutiérrez
Chihuahua	244,938	2,005,477	2,253,975	Chihuahua
Coahuila	149,982	1,557,265	1,937,209	Saltillo
Colima	5,191	346,293	426,225	Colima
Distrito Federal	1,479	8,831,079	10,355,347	México City
Durango	123,181	1,182,320	1,402,782	Victoria de Durango
Guanajuato	30,491	3,006,110	3,593,210	Guanajuato
Guerrero	64,281	2,109,513	2,604,947	Chilpancingo
Hidalgo	20,813	1,547,493	1,847,259	Pachuca de Soto
Jalisco	80,836	4,371,998	5,269,816	Guadalajara
México	21,355	7,564,335	12,013,056	Toluca de Lerdo
Michoacán de Ocampo	59,928	2,868,824	3,424,235	Morelia
Morelos	4,950	947,089	1,288,875	Cuernavaca
Nayarit	26,979	726,120	857,359	Tepic
Nuevo Léon	64,924	2,513,044	3,202,434	Monterrey
Oaxaca	93,952	2,369,076	2,669,120	Oaxaca de Juárez
Puebla	33,902	3,347,685	4,139,609	Puebla de Zaragoza
Querétaro	11,449	739,605	976,548	Querétaro
Quintana Roo	50,212	225,985	414,301	Chetumal
San Luis Potosí	63,068	1,673,893	2,055,364	San Luis Potosí
Sinaloa	58,328	1,849,879	2,425,006	Culiacán Rosales
Sonora	182,052	1,513,731	1,828,390	Hermosillo
Tabasco	25,267	1,062,961	1,322,613	Villahermosa
Tamaulipas	79,384	1,924,484	2,294,680	Ciudad Victoria
Tlaxcala	4,016	556,597	676,446	Tlaxcala
Veracruz	71,699	5,387,680	6,798,109	Jalapa Enríquez
Yucatán	38,402	1,063,733	1,327,298	Mérida
Zacatecas	73,252	1,136,830	1,259,407	Zacatecas

At the 1980 census 33,039,307 were males, 33,807,526 females. Estimate (1989) 84,278,992. Urban population was 66·3% in 1988 and rural population 33·7%. The official language is Spanish, the mother tongue of over 92% of the population, but there are 5 indigenous language groups (Náhuatl, Maya, Zapotec, Otomi and Mixtec) from which are derived a total of 59 dialects spoken by 5,181,038 inhabitants (1980 census). In 1980, about 16% of the population were of European ethnic origin, 55% mestizo and 29% Amerindian.

The populations (1980 Census) of the largest cities were:

México [1]	12,932,116	Saltillo	321,758	Ensenada	175,425
Guadalajara [2]	2,244,715	Victoria de Durango	321,148	Poza Rica de Hidalgo	166,799
Monterrey [3]	1,916,472	Veracruz Llave	305,456	Tuxtla Gutiérrez	166,476
Puebla de Zaragoza	835,759	Querétaro	293,586	Ciudad Obregón	165,572
Léon de los Aldamas	655,809	Tampico	267,957	Salamanca	160,040
Ciudad Juárez	567,365	Villa Hermosa	250,903	Oaxaca de Juárez	157,284
Culiacán Rosales	560,011	Mazatlán	249,988	Ciudad Victoria	153,206
Mexicali	510,554	Irapuato	246,308	Campeche	151,805
Tijuana	461,257	Matamoros	238,840	Uruapan	146,998
Mérida	424,529	Cuernavaca	232,355	Minatitlán	145,268
Acapulco de Juárez	409,335	Celaya	219,010	Pachuca de Soto	135,248
Chihuahua	406,830	Jalapa Enríquez	212,769	Ciudad Madero	132,444
San Luis Potosí	406,630	Reynosa	211,412	Cordoba	126,179
Torreón	363,886	Nuevo Laredo	203,286	Los Mochis	122,531
Aguascalientes	359,454	Atizapán de Zaragoza	188,497	Monclova	119,609
Toluca de Lerdo	357,071	Coatzacoalcos	186,129	Gómez Palacio	116,967
Morelia	353,055	Tepic	177,007	Orizaba	114,848
Hermosillo	340,779				

[1] Metropolitan Area, including Netzahualcóyotl (1,341,230).
[2] Metropolitan Area, including Zapopan (345,390) and Tlaquepaque (135,500).
[3] Metropolitan Area, including Guadalupe (370,524) and San Nicolás de los Garzas (280,696).

Largest metropolitan areas (1986, estimate): Mexico City, 18,748,000; Guadalajara, 2,587,000; Monterrey, 2,335,000; Puebla de Zaragoza, 1,217,600; Léon de los Aldamas, 946,800; Torreón, 729,800; San Luis Potosí, 601,900; Ciudad Juárez, 595,700; Mérida, 580,300.

Vital statistics for calendar years:

	Births	*Deaths*	*Marriages*	*Divorces*
1984	2,511,894	410,550	498,698	32,170
1985	2,655,571	414,003	569,146	34,114

Crude birth rate in 1984 was 33·2 per 1,000 population; crude death rate, 5·4; marriage rate (1983) 6·8. In 1980 there were 73,260 permanent immigrants.

CLIMATE. Latitude and relief produce a variety of climates. Arid and semi-arid conditions are found in the north, with extreme temperatures, whereas in the south there is a humid tropical climate, with temperatures varying with altitude. Conditions on the shores of the Gulf of Mexico are very warm and humid. In general, the rainy season lasts from May to Nov. Mexico City. Jan. 55°F (12·6°C), July 61°F (16·1°C). Annual rainfall 30" (747 mm). Guadalajara. Jan. 59°F (15·2°C), July 69°F (20·5°C). Annual rainfall 36" (902 mm). La Paz. Jan. 64°F (17·8°C), July 85°F (29·4°C). Annual rainfall 6" (145 mm). Mazatlan Jan. 66°F (18·9°C), July 82°F (27·8°C). Annual rainfall 33" (828 mm). Merida. Jan. 72°F (22·2°C), July 83°F (28·3°C). Annual rainfall 38" (957 mm). Monterrey. Jan. 58°F (14·4°C), July 81°F (27·2°C). Annual rainfall 23" (588 mm). Puebla de Zaragoza. Jan. 54°F (12·2°C), July 63°F (17·2°C). Annual rainfall 34" (850 mm).

CONSTITUTION AND GOVERNMENT. A new Constitution was promulgated on 5 Feb. 1917 and has been amended from time to time. Mexico is a representative, democratic and federal republic, comprising 31 states and a federal district, each state being free and sovereign in all internal affairs, but united in a federation established according to the principals of the Fundamental Law. Citizenship, including the right of suffrage, is vested in all nationals of 18 years of age and older who have 'an honourable means of livelihood'.

There is complete separation of legislative, executive and judicial powers (Art. 49). Legislative power is vested in a General Congress of 2 chambers, a Chamber of Deputies and a Senate (Art.50). The Chamber of Deputies consists of 500 members directly elected for 3 years, 300 of them from single-member constituencies and 200 chosen under a system of proportional representation (Arts.51–55). At the general elections held on 7 July 1988, 234 of the single-member seats were won by the *Partido Revolucionario Institucional* (PRI), 38 by the *Partido de Acción Nacional* (PAN).

The Senate comprises 64 members, 2 from each state and 2 from the federal district, directly elected for 6 years (Arts.56–58). At the elections of 7 July 1988, the PRI won 60 seats and the FDN 4 seats. Members of both chambers are not immediately re-eligible for election (Art.59). Congress sits from 1 Sept. to 31 Dec. each year; during the recess there is a permanent committee of 15 deputies and 14 senators appointed by the respective chambers.

The President is the supreme executive authority. He appoints the members of the Council of Ministers and the senior military and civilian officers of the state. He is directly elected for a single 6-year term.

The names of the presidents from 1958 are as follows:

Adolfo López Mateos, 1 Dec. 1958–30 Nov. 1964.
Gustavo Díaz Ordaz, 1 Dec. 1964–30 Nov. 1970.
Luis Echeverría Alvarez, 1 Dec. 1970–30 Nov. 1976.
José López Portillo y Pacheco, 1 Dec. 1976–30 Nov. 1982.
Miguel de la Madrid Hurtado, 1 Dec. 1982–30 Nov. 1988.

President: Carlos Salinas de Gortari (assumed office 1 Dec. 1988).

In Nov. 1989 the Council of Ministers was composed as follows:

Government: Fernando Gutiérrez Barrios. *Foreign Relations:* Fernando Solana Morales. *Defence:* Gen. Antonio Riviello Bazan. *Navy:* Adm. Mauricio Scheleske Sánchez. *Finance and Public Credit:* Dr Pedro Aspe Armella. *Planning and Federal Budget:* Dr Ernesto Cedillo Ponce de León. *Comptroller-General:* María Elena Vásquez Nava. *Energy, Mines and Public Industries:* Fernando Hiriart Balderrama. *Commerce and Industrial Development:* Dr Jaime Serra Puche. *Agriculture and Water Resources:* Jorge de la Vega Dominguez. *Communications and Transport:* Andres Caso Lombardo. *Urban Development and Ecology:* Patricio Chirinos Calero. *Education:* Manuel Bartlett Diaz. *Health:* Dr Jesús Cumate Rodriguez. *Labour and Social Welfare:* Arsenio Farell Cubillas. *Agrarian Reform:* Victor Cervera Pacheco. *Tourism:* Carlos Hank González. *Fisheries:* Maria de los Angeles Moreno Iruegas. *Governor of Federal District:* Manuel Camacho Solis. *Attorney-General:* Enrique Alvárez del Castillo. *Attorney-General of the Federal District:* Ignacio Morales Lechuga. *Chief of the Presidential Staff:* Brig.-Gen. Arturo Cardona Marino. *Director-General of the Technical Cabinet Secretariat:* Dr José Córdoba Montoya. *Presidential Secretary:* Andrés Massieu Berlanga. *Director-General of Legal Affairs of the Presidency:* Ruben Valdés Abascal.

National flag: Three vertical strips of green, white, red, with the national arms in the centre.

National anthem: Mexicanos, al grito de guerra (words by F. González Bocanegra; tune by Jaime Nunó, 1854).

Local Government. Mexico is divided into 31 states and a Federal District. The latter is co-extensive with Mexico City and is administered by a Governor appointed by the President. Each state has its own constitution, with the right to legislate and to levy taxes (but not inter-state customs duties); its Governor is directly elected for 6 years and its unicameral legislature for 3 years; judicial officers are appointed by the state governments. Mexico City is sub-divided into 16 municipalities and the 31 states into 2,378 municipalities.

DEFENCE

Army. Enlistment into the regular army is voluntary, but there is also one year of conscription by lottery. The army consists of 3 infantry brigades (one of which is mechanized), 3 armoured regiments, a garrison for each of the country's 36 military zones (with motorized cavalry, artillery and infantry), and support units. Equipment includes 45 M-3/-8 tanks and some 140 armoured cars. Strength of the regular army (1989) 105,500; conscripts, 60,000.

Navy. The Navy is primarily equipped and organized for offshore and coastal patrol duties. It comprises 3 *ex*-US destroyers of second world war vintage, 7 modern offshore patrol vessels with small helicopter decks and hangars, and 37 older offshore ships, mostly *ex*-US. There are also 30 inshore patrol vessels and 20 riverine patrol craft. Auxiliaries include 4 survey ships, 1 repair ship, 2 training ships, 6 tugs plus some 24 service craft.

The naval air force, 500 strong, operates 10 Aviocars and 11 HU-16 Albatross amphibians for maritime patrol and SAR, there are 12 Bo-105 helicopters for service afloat, and some 21 fixed wing and 7 helicopters for transport and liaison duties.

Naval personnel in 1989 totalled 28,000, including naval air force and 8,000 marines.

Air Force. The Air Force had (1990) a strength of about 8,000 officers and men, and has nine operational groups, each with one or two squadrons. No. 1 Group comprises No. 208 Squadron with 9 IAI Aravas for transport, search and rescue and counter-insurgency duties; and No. 209 Squadron with Bell 205A, 206B JetRanger, Alouette III and Puma helicopters. No. 2 Group has two Squadrons (Nos. 206 and 207) of Swiss-built Pilatus PC-7 Turbo-Trainers for light attack duty. No. 3 Group (203 and 204 Squadrons) also operates PC-7s; No. 4 Group (201 and 205 Squadrons) is equipped with PC-7s. No. 5 Group consists of No. 101 communications Squadron and a photo-reconnaissance unit, both equipped with Aero Commander 500S piston-engined light twins. Nos. 301 and 302 Squadrons, in No. 6 Group, operate a total of 8 turboprop-powered Lockheed C-130 Hercules and 5 C-54, 2 C-118A and 1 DC-7 piston-engined transports. The main combat Group, No. 7, comprises No. 401 Squadron with 11 F-5E Tiger II and F-5F 2-seat fighters; and No. 202 Squadron with AT-33A jet trainer/fighter-bombers. No. 8 Group has 7 C-47s in a VIP transport squadron. No. 9 Group operates the Air Force's remaining 12 or more C-47s in Nos. 311 and 312 transport Squadrons. There is a Presidential Squadron with 7 Boeing 727s, 1 757, 2 737s, 1 HS.125, 1 Electra, 1 JetStar, 1 Islander, 2 Super Pumas and 1 Bell 212. Other training aircraft include 20 Mudry CAP-10Bs, 20 Beech Musketeers, 40 Bonanzas, over 30 T-28 Trojans and PC-7 Turbo-Trainers.

INTERNATIONAL RELATIONS

Membership. Mexico is a member of UN, OAS, SELA and LAIA.

ECONOMY

Planning. An economic development plan (1989-94) was announced in June 1989 aimed at restoring growth and improving living standards.

Budget. The 1988 budget provided for expenditure of 103,348,500m. pesos and revenue of 65,505,900m. pesos.

Currency. The monetary unit is the *peso*. There are coins of 1, 5, 10, 20, 50, 100, 200, 500, 1,000 and 5,000 *pesos*; and banknotes of 1,000, 2,000, 5,000 10,000, 20,000, and 50,000 *pesos*. Total currency in circulation (1988) was 13,164,400m. *pesos*.

Rate of exchange, March 1990: 2,740 pesos = US$1; 4,491 pesos = £1.

Banking. The Bank of Mexico, established 1 Sept. 1925, is the central bank of issue; it is modelled on the Federal Reserve system, with large powers to 'manage' the currency. On 1 Sept. 1982 the private banking sector was nationalized. The total external debt (1988) was US$96,700m.

Weights and Measures. The metric system was introduced in 1896, and its sole use is enjoined by law of 14 Dec. 1928.

ENERGY AND NATURAL RESOURCES

Electricity. In 1987 (preliminary) the 3,998 plants in service generated 26,124 mw of electric energy, of which 7,195 mw was hydro-electric and 18,929 mw thermo-electric. Supply 120 volts; 50 Hz and some 120 volts; 60 Hz.

Oil. Mexico has the largest oil deposits in Latin America. Crude petroleum output was 144·5m. tonnes in 1989.

Gas. Natural gas production 3,478m. cu. feet in 1988.

Minerals. Uranium deposits were discovered in the states of Chihuahua, Durango, Sonora and Queretaro in 1959, rich deposits have been located in Nuevo León. Total reserves (proven 1982) 15,000 tonnes of uranium 308; potential reserves, 150,000 tonnes. Silver output (tonnes) was 2,359 in 1988; gold 9,098 kg.

Mexico has large coal resources, calculated at 5,448m. tonnes, including 1,675m. tonnes (65% cokeable) high-grade coking coal in Coahuila.

Output, 1988 (in 1,000 tonnes): Lead, 171; copper, 268; zinc, 262; fluorite, 756; pig iron, 5,564; sulphur, 2,138; manganese, 169; gypsum, 2,649; phosphorite, 667; barite, 535; coal, 4,211; coke, 2,332; dolomite, 341.

Agriculture. In 1981 Mexico had 21·9m. hectares of arable land, 74·4m. hectares of meadows and pastures, 48·1m. hectares of forests, 1·6m. hectares of permanent crops and 40·6m. hectares of other land. Grains occupy most of the cultivated land, with about 43% given to maize, 10% to sorghum and 5% to wheat. In 1982 there were 146,083 tractors.

Livestock (1988): Cattle, 31·2m.; sheep, 6m.; pigs, 16·5m.; horses, 6·16m.; goats, 10·5m.; mules, 3·13m.; donkeys, 3,183,000; poultry, 243m.

Production of crops for 1988 was as follows (in 1,000 tonnes):

Crop	*1988*	*Crop*	*1988*	*Crop*	*1988*
Maize	11,800	Sugar-cane	41,500	Oranges	1,942
Sorghum	5,500	Tomatoes	1,494	Bananas	1,080
Wheat	3,700	Potatoes	960	Lemons	681
Barley	465	Dry beans	1,075	Pineapples	293
Rice	420	Soybeans	400	Apples	535
Chickpeas	150	Coconuts	1,006	Grapes	560
Seed cotton	700	Coffee	283	Mangoes	780

Forestry. Forests extended over 44m. hectares in 1984, representing 23% of the land area, containing pine, spruce, cedar, mahogany, logwood and rosewood. There are 14 forest reserves (nearly 800,000 hectares) and 47 national park forests of 750,000 hectares. In 1986 total roundwood production amounted to 8,958,542m. cu. metres.

Fisheries. Catch (1987, in tonnes): Sardines, 477,971; anchoveta, 161,268; shrimp and prawns, 83,882; oysters, 50,715; tunny, 102,566; shark, 16,662; sea perch (*mojarras*), 86,731; sea bass, 9,380. Total catch in 1987 was 1,464,841 tonnes.

INDUSTRY AND TRADE

Industry. In 1987, the primary sector (agriculture etc.) provided 9·2% of GDP, the mining, oil and petrochemical industry 5·1%, manufacturing and construction 29·4% and the service sector (commerce, transport and communications, power supply and other services) 56·3%.

Labour. In 1987 unemployment was estimated to be over 50%. Approximately 5m. people belong to trade unions, of whom 85% are affiliated to the *Congreso del Trabajo*.

Commerce. Trade for calendar years in US$1m.:

	1985	*1986*	*1987*	*1988*
Imports	14,014	11,432	12,223	18,903
Exports	21,866	16,030	20,656	20,657

Of total imports in 1985, 63·7% came from USA, 3·8% from Federal Republic of Germany and 5·2% from Japan. Leading imports were mechanical and transport equipment, machine tools, parts and spares.

Of total exports in 1985, 61·1% went to USA, 7·8% to Spain, 7·8% to Japan,

3·7% to France and 3·1% to UK. The main exports (1984) were crude petroleum (62%) vehicles (6%) and petroleum products (5%).

The 1,200 in-bond assembly plants situated along the US-Mexican border generate the second largest flow of foreign exchange after oil, earning US$1,300m. in 1986 and employing 300,000 people.

Total trade between Mexico and UK (British Department of Trade returns, in £1,000 sterling):

	1985	*1986*	*1987*	*1988*	*1989*
Imports to UK	236,811	116,078	244,719	144,947	165,295
Exports and re-exports from UK	203,404	162,328	198,992	190,011	205,130

Tourism. In 1988, there were 5,694,000 tourists; gross revenue, including border visitors, amounted to US$2,544m.

COMMUNICATIONS

Roads. Total length, (1986) 228,686 km, of which 45,399 km were main roads. Motor vehicles registered in 1986 comprised 454,176 passenger cars, 2,296,655 commercial vehicles and 251,327 motorcycles.

Railways. Following mergers completed in 1987, *Ferrocarriles Nacionales de Mexico* (NdeM) is now the only common-carrier railway. It comprises 20,119 km of 1,435 mm gauge and 90 km of 914 mm gauge, and in 1988 carried 56m. tonnes of freight and 19·4m. passengers. In Mexico City an urban railway system opened in 1969 had 141 km of route and 8 lines in 1988 and carried 1,476m. passengers.

Aviation. There are 32 international and 41 national airports. Each of the larger states has a local airline which links them with main airports. Thirty-four companies maintained international services, of which *Aeromexíco* and *Mexicana de Aviacíon* are Mexican. In 1986 commercial aircraft carried 18m. national and international passengers and some 164,076 tonnes of mail and freight.

Shipping. Mexico has 49 ocean ports, of which, on the Gulf coast, the most important include Coatzacoalcos, Carmen (Campeche), Tampico, Veracruz and Tuxpan. On the Pacific are Salina Cruz, Isla de Cedros, Guaymas, Santa Rosalia, Manzanillo, Lázaro Cárdenas and Mazatlán.

Merchant shipping loaded 82·8m. tonnes and unloaded 9m. tonnes of international traffic in 1986. Passengers (1982), embarked and disembarked 2·8m. In 1982, the merchant marine comprised 545 vessels (of over 100 GRT) with a total tonnage of 1,251,630 GRT.

Post and Broadcasting. In 1980 the telegraph and telephone system had 7,140 offices. *Teléfonos de México*, a state-controlled company, controls about 98% of all the telephone service. Telephones in use, Jan. 1985, 7,329,416.

In 1984 there were 823 commercial radio stations and 45 cultural government radio stations while (1986) 21m. homes had receiving sets. In 1984 commercial television stations numbered 118 and cultural stations 8; there were 9·5m. homes with receiving sets in 1988.

Cinemas (1983). Cinemas numbered 1,751 with annual attendance of 271·8m.

Newspapers (1982). There were 362 dailies and 36 weeklies, with an aggregate circulation of 9·5m. In Mexico City the main dailies are, *Excelsior, El Sol de México, Uno más Uno, La Prensa, El Heraldo de México, Novedades, El Universal* and *Esto,* with a combined circulation (1984) 1·8m.

JUSTICE, RELIGION, EDUCATION AND WELFARE

Justice. Magistrates of the Supreme Court are appointed for 6 years by the President and confirmed by the Senate; they can be removed only on impeachment. The courts include the Supreme Court with 21 magistrates, 12 collegiate circuit courts with 3 judges each and 9 unitary circuit courts with 1 judge each, and 68 district courts with 1 judge each.

The penal code of 1 Jan. 1930 abolished the death penalty, except for the armed forces.

Religion. The prevailing religion is the Roman Catholic (92·6% of the population in 1980); with (1983) 3 cardinals, 12 archbishops and 87 bishops, but by the constitution of 1857, the Church was separated from the State, and the constitution of 1917 provided strict regulation of this and all other religions. At the 1980 census there were also 3·3% Protestants, and 4·1% members of other religions.

Education. Primary and secondary education is free and compulsory, and secular. In 1987–88 there were:

	Establishments	*Teachers*	*Students*
Nursery	41,438	93,414	2,625,678
Primary	79,677	463,115	14,768,008
Secondary	20,636	251,578	4,793,805
Preparatory/Vocational	5,586	136,567	2,012,268
Teacher-training	477	12,289	132,100
Higher education	1,453	107,492	1,112,788

The most important university is the Universidad Nacional Autónoma de México (UNAM) in México City which, with its associated institutions, had, in 1982, 136,534 students (excluding post-graduates). UNAM was founded in 1551, reorganized in 1910, and granted full autonomy in 1920. Other universities of particular importance in México City are the Instituto Politécnico Nacional, specializing in technology and applied science, with 52,694 students, and the Universidad Autónoma Metropolitana with 27,452 students, opened in 1973.

Outside México City the principal universities are the Universidad de Guadalajara (in Guadalajara) with 65,799 students; the Universidad Veracruzana (in Jalapa) with 57,755 students; the Universidad Autónoma de Nueva León (in Monterrey) with 48,124 students; the Universidad Autónoma de Puebla (in Puebla) with 39,505 students; the Universidad Auto noma de Sinaloa (in Culiacán) with 33,366 students; and the Universidad Michoacana (in Morelia) with 23,935 students.

Health. In 1986 Mexico had 71,058 physicians; there were 11,072 state and private hospitals and clinics with 57,391 beds.

DIPLOMATIC REPRESENTATIVES

Of Mexico in Great Britain (8 Halkin St., London, SW1X 7DW)
Ambassador: Bernardo Sépulveda, GCMG.

Of Great Britain in Mexico (Lerma 71, Col. Cuauhtémoc, México City 06500, D.F.)
Ambassador: M. K. O. Simpson-Orlebar, CMG (accredited 13 July 1989).

Of Mexico in the USA (2829 16th St., NW, Washington, D.C., 20009)
Ambassador: Gustavo Petricioli.

Of the USA in Mexico (Paseo de la Reforma 305, México City 5, D.F.)
Ambassador: John D. Negroponte.

Of Mexico to the United Nations
Ambassador: Dr Jorge Montaño

Further Reading

Anuario Estadístico de los Estados Unidos Mexicanos. Annual
Revista de Estadística (Monthly); *Revista de Economia* (Monthly)
Banco de México S.A., Annual report
Banco Nacional de Comercio Exterior. *Comercio Exterior,* monthly.—*Mexico.* Annual (in Spanish or English)
Bailey, J. J., *Governing Mexico: The Statecraft of Crisis Management.* London and New York, 1988
Bazant, J., *A Concise History of Mexico.* CUP, 1977
Grayson, G. W., *Oil and Mexican Foreign Policy.* Univ. of Pittsburgh Press, 1988
Hamilton, N. and Harding, T. F., (eds.) *Mexico: State, Economy and Social Conflict.* London, 1986
Philip, G., (ed.) *Politics in Mexico.* London, 1985
Riding, A., *Distant Neighbours.* London, 1985.—*Mexico: Inside the Volcano.* London, 1987
Robbins, N. C., *Mexico.* [Bibliography] Oxford and Santa Barbara, 1984
Wyman, D. L., (ed) *Mexico's Economic Crisis: Challenges and Opportunities.* San Diego, 1983

MONACO

Capital: Monaco
Population: 28,000 (1989)

HISTORY. Monaco is a small Principality on the Mediterranean, surrounded by the French Department of Alpes Maritimes except on the side towards the sea. From 1297 it belonged to the house of Grimaldi. In 1731 it passed into the female line, Louise Hippolyte, daughter of Antoine I, heiress of Monaco, marrying Jacques de Goyon Matignon, Count of Torigni, who took the name and arms of Grimaldi. The Principality was placed under the protection of the Kingdom of Sardinia by the Treaty of Vienna, 1815, and under that of France in 1861. Prince Albert I (reigned 1889–1922) acquired fame as an oceanographer; and his son Louis II (1922–49) was instrumental in establishing the International Hydrographic Bureau.

AREA AND POPULATION. The area is 195 hectares or 481 acres. The Principality is divided into 4 districts: Monaco-Ville, la Condamine, Monte-Carlo and Fontvieille. Population (1989), 28,000, of which 5,813 Monegasques. The official language is French.

CLIMATE. A Mediterranean climate, with mild moist winters and hot dry summers. Monaco. Jan. 50°F (10°C), July 74°F (23·3°C). Annual rainfall 30" (758 mm).

REIGNING PRINCE. Rainier III, born 31 May 1923, son of Princess Charlotte, Duchess of Valentinois, daughter of Prince Louis II, 1898–1977 (married 19 March 1920 to Prince Pierre, Comte de Polignac, who had taken the name Grimaldi, from whom she was divorced 18 Feb. 1933). Prince Rainier succeeded his grandfather Louis II, who died on 9 May 1949. He married on 19 April 1956 Miss Grace Kelly, a citizen of the USA (died 14 Sept. 1982). *Issue:* Princess Caroline Louise Marguerite, born 23 Jan. 1957; married Philippe Junot on 28 June 1978, divorced, 9 Oct. 1980, married Stefano Casiraghi on 29 Dec. 1983, offspring: Andrea, born 8 June 1984, Charlotte, born 3 Aug. 1986, Pierre, born 7 Sept. 1987. Prince Albert Alexandre Louis Pierre, born 14 March 1958 *(heir apparent).* Princess Stephanie Marie Elisabeth, born 1 Feb. 1965.

CONSTITUTION AND GOVERNMENT. Prince Rainier III on 28 Jan. 1959 suspended the Constitution of 5 Jan. 1911, thereby dissolving the National Council and the Communal Council. On 28 March 1962 the National Council (18 members elected every 5 years, last elections 1988) and the Communal Council (15 members elected every 4 years, last elections 1987) were re-established as elected bodies. On 17 Dec. 1962 a new constitution was promulgated. It maintains the hereditary monarchy, though Prince Rainier renounces the principle of divine right. The supreme tribunal becomes the custodian of fundamental liberties, and guarantees are given for the right of association, trade union freedom and the right to strike. It provides for votes for women and the abolition of the death penalty.

The constitution can be modified only with the approval of the elected National Council. Women were given the vote in 1945.

Monegasque relations with France were based on a convention of neighbourhood and administrative assistance of 1951. This was terminated by France on 11 Oct. 1962, but has been replaced by several new conventions signed on 18 May 1963.

National flag: Horizontally red over white.

ECONOMY

Planning. A 55-acre site has been reclaimed from the sea at Fontvieille. This land has been earmarked for office and residential development. The present industrial zone is to be reorganized and developed with a view to attracting new light industry to the Principality.

Budget. The budget (in 1,000 francs) was as follows:

	1984	*1985*	*1986*	*1987*	*1988*
Revenue	1,842,237	1,964,790	2,139,305	2,232,032	2,542,175
Expenditure	1,460,102	1,550,748	1,999,764	2,229,806	2,494,307

Currency. The monetary unit is the French *franc* divided into 100 *centimes.*

Weights and Measures. The metric system is in use.

INDUSTRY AND TRADE

Trade Unions. Membership of trade unions is estimated at 2,000 out of a work force of 25,600 (1989).

Commerce. International trade is included with France.

Tourism. There were 214,149 overnight tourists in 1987.

COMMUNICATIONS

Roads. There were 50 km of roads in 1989.

Railways. The 1·6 km of main line passing through the country is operated by the French National Railways (SNCF).

Aviation. The nearest airport is at Nice, France and a heliport at Fontvieille.

Shipping. The harbour has an area of 40 acres, depth at the entrance 98 ft, and alongside the quay 23 ft at least.

Post and Broadcasting. Telephone subscribers numbered about 25,232 in 1989 and telex subscribers (1989), 720. Monaco issues its own postage stamps.

Radio Monte Carlo broadcasts FM commercial programmes in French (long- and medium-waves). Radio Monte Carlo owns 55% of Radio Monte Carlo Relay Station on Cyprus. The foreign service is dedicated exclusively to religious broadcasts and is maintained by free-will contributions. It operates in 36 languages under the name 'Trans World Radio' and has relay facilities on Bonaire, West Indies, and is planning to build relay facilities in the southern parts of Africa. *Télé Monté-Carlo* broadcasts TV programmes in French, Italian and English.

Cinemas. In 1986 there were 4 cinemas (one open air) with seating capacity of 1,000.

JUSTICE, RELIGION, EDUCATION AND WELFARE

Justice. There are the following courts, *Juge de Paix*, Tribunal of the First Instance, a Court of Appeal, Criminal Tribunal, *Cour de Révision Judiciaire* and a Supreme Tribunal.

Police: There is an independent police force *(Sûreté Publique)* which comprised (1989) 236 policemen and inspectors.

Religion. There has been since 1887 a Roman Catholic bishop elevated since 1982 to an archbishop, directly dependent on the Holy See.

Education. In 1990 there were 5,523 pupils with over 735 teachers.

Health. In 1990 there were 537 hospital beds and 80 physicians.

DIPLOMATIC REPRESENTATIVES

British Consul-General (resident in Marseille): T. E. J. Mound, OBE.
British Honorary Consul (resident in Nice): Lieut.-Col. R. W. Challoner, OBE.
Consul-General for Monaco in London: I. S. Ivanovic.

Further Reading

Journal de Monaco. Bulletin Officiel. 1858 ff.
Handley-Taylor, G., *Bibliography of Monaco.* London, 1968

MONGOLIA

Capital: Ulan Bator
Population: 2m. (1989)
GNP per capita: US$940 (1978)

Bügd Nayramdakh Mongol Ard Uls – Mongolian People's Republic

HISTORY. Outer Mongolia was a Chinese province from 1691 to 1911, an autonomous state under Russian protection from 1912 to 1919 and again a Chinese province from 1919 to 1921. On 13 March 1921 a Provisional People's Government was established which declared the independence of Mongolia and on 5 Nov. 1921 signed a treaty with Soviet Russia annulling all previous unequal treaties and establishing friendly relations. On 26 Nov. 1924 the Government proclaimed the country the Mongolian People's Republic.

On 5 Jan. 1946 China recognized the independence of Outer Mongolia after a plebiscite in Mongolia (20 Oct. 1945) had resulted in an overwhelming vote for independence. A Sino-Soviet treaty of 14 Feb. 1950 guaranteed this independence. In Aug. 1986 a consular agreement, in June 1987 a boundary agreement, and in Nov. 1988 a border treaty, were signed with China.

AREA AND POPULATION. Mongolia is bounded north by the USSR, east and south and west by China. Area, 1,567,000 sq. km (605,022 sq. miles). Population (1989 census); 2,001,000 (52% urban; 50% male). Density (1987), 1·28 per sq. km. Birth rate (1983), 36·2 per 1,000; death rate, 9·8 per 1,000; marriage rate, 5·7 per 1,000; divorce rate, 0·3 per 1,000. Rate of increase (1987), 27·5 per 1,000. The population is predominantly made up of Mongolian peoples (77·5% Khalkha). There is a Turkic Kazakh minority (5·3% of the population) and 8 Mongol minorities. The official language is Khalkha Mongol. Expectation of life in 1987 was 65 years. 45% of the population is under 16.

The republic is administratively divided into 3 cities (Ulan Bator, the capital, population 500,000 (1988), Darkhan, 80,000 (1988) and Erdenet 42,900 (1985)), and 18 provinces *(aimag)*. The provinces are sub-divided into 258 districts *(somon)*.

CLIMATE. A very extreme climate, with six months of mean temperatures below freezing, but much higher temperatures occur for a month or two in summer. Rainfall is very low and limited to the months mid-May to mid-Sept. Ulan Bator. Jan. –14°F (–25·6°C), July 61°F (16·1°C). Annual rainfall 8" (208 mm).

CONSTITUTION AND GOVERNMENT. According to the fourth Constitution (1960) legislative power is vested in the *Great People's Khural* of deputies elected for 5 years by universal suffrage of voters over 18 years of age on a basis of 1 deputy per 2,500 inhabitants. It elects from its number 9 members of the Presidium, which carries on current state affairs.

At the election of 22 June 1986 it was stated that turn-out was 99·99%, and 99·99% of votes were cast for the 370 deputies (92 women).

Sole power was in the hands of the Mongolian People's Revolutionary (*i.e.*, Communist) Party (MPRP), which had 89,588 members in 1987, but an opposition Mongolian Democratic Party, founded in Dec. 1989, achieved tacit recognition and held its first congress in Feb. 1990. Following demonstrations and hunger-strikes, on 12 March the entire MPRP Politburo resigned and was replaced by a 5-member Politburo headed by Gombojavyn Ochirbat (b. 1929) as *General-Secretary*. Political opposition was legalized in March 1990 and multi-party elections brought forward to summer 1990. On 21 March 1990 Punsalmaagiyn Ochirbat (b. 1943) replaced Jambyn Batmunkh as *Chairman of the Presidium of the Great People's Khural* (head of state); Sharavyn Gungaadorj became *Prime Minister*.

National flag: Red–sky-blue–red (vertical), with a golden 5-pointed star and under it the golden *soyombo* emblem on the red stripe nearest to the flagpole.

Local government is administered by People's Deputies' *khurals*. Elections to the 380 *khurals* took place in June 1984. Turn-out was announced to be 99·99% of the electorate. There are some 15,000 councillors. White-collar, 50%; collective farmers, 30%; industrial workers, 20%; Communist Party members, 60%; women, 33%; under-30, 20%, first term of office, 50%.

DEFENCE. Military service is 3 years.

Army. The Army comprises 4 motorized infantry divisions. Equipment includes 650 T-54/-55/-62 main battle tanks. Strength (1990) 21,000, with reserves of 200,000. There is a paramilitary Ministry of Public Security force of about 10,000 men. A civil defence force was set up in 1970.

There were some 50,000 Soviet service personnel in Mongolia, but the USSR has announced it will reduce this number to 15,000 by 1991.

Air Force. The Air Force has about 100 pilots and more than 70 aircraft, including 12 MiG-21 and 10 MiG-17 fighters; a total of about 30 An-2, An-24 and An-26 transports used mainly on civil air services; 3 Wilga utility aircraft; 6 Mi-4 and 10 Mi-8 helicopters; and Yakovlev trainers. Personnel (1989) 3,500.

INTERNATIONAL RELATIONS

Membership. Mongolia is a member of UN and Comecon.

Aid. Mongolia receives economic aid from the USSR and other communist countries. There is also a UN development aid programme running at US$2m. per annum.

Treaties. Relations with the USSR are based on a 15-year treaty of economic and technical co-operation (1985).

Sino-Mongolian relations deteriorated after the estrangement between China and USSR, but have improved recently.

ECONOMY

Planning. Mongolia has had for centuries a traditional nomadic pastoral economy, which the Government aims to transform into an 'agricultural–industrial economy'. The eighth 5-year plan is running from 1986 to 1990. For earlier plans *see* THE STATESMAN'S YEAR-BOOK, 1987–88.

Budget (in 1m. tugriks):

	1978	*1980*	*1982*	*1983*	*1984*	*1985*
Revenue	3,660	4,070	4,830	5,255	...	5,743
Expenditure	3,650	4,058	3,131	3,356	...	5,693

Sources of revenue, 1983: Turnover tax, 64%; profits tax, 28%; social insurance, 3·5%. Expenditure: Economy, 40%; social and cultural, 40%.

Currency. 100 *möngö* = 1 *tugrik*. Notes are issued for 1, 3, 5, 10, 20, 50 and 100 *tugriks*; and coins for 1, 3, 5, 10, 15, 20, 50 *möngö* and 1 *tugrik*. In March 1990, £1 = 5·52 *tugriks*; US$1 = 3·35 *tugriks*.

Banking. The Mongolian State Bank (established 1924) is the sole bank, being at once a bank of issue and a commercial, savings and development bank. It has 21 main branches.

Weights and Measures. The metric system is in use.

ENERGY AND NATURAL RESOURCES

Electricity. There are 6 thermal electric power stations. Production of electricity, 1986, 2,800m. kwh.

Minerals. There are large deposits of copper, nickel, zinc, molybdenum, phosphorites, tin, wolfram and fluorspar; production of the latter in 1984, 747,000 tonnes, entirely exported to the USSR. The copper/molybdenum ore-dressing plant at Erdenet was completed in 1981. Coal reserves are 17,000m. tonnes. Coal accounted for 74·6% of energy production in 1980. There are major coalmines near Ulan Bator and Darkhan. Coal (mainly lignite) production in 1984 was 5·4m. tonnes.

Agriculture. 68% of agricultural production derives from cattle-raising. In 1988 there were 2,047,000 horses, 2,526,000 cattle, 13,234,000 sheep, 547,000 camels and 4,388,000 goats.

Ownership of livestock (in 1m.) in 1983:

	Collective farms	*State farms*	*Private*
Cattle	1·14	0·02	0·98
Camels	0·48	0·01	0·08
Horses	1·11	0·08	0·73
Sheep	10·92	1·04	1·93
Goats	3·55	0·07	0·91

In 1988 there were 120,000 pigs and (1983) 240,200 poultry. 230,300 tonnes of meat and 6·5m. litres of fermented mare's milk were produced in 1984. Milk production was 44·7m. litres in 1986. In 1983 there were 255 collective farms, 39 interfarm associations, 14 fodder supply farms and 51 state farms.

All cultivated land belongs to collective or state farms. The total agricultural area in 1983 was 124·98m. hectares, of which 1·3m. were arable (1·2m. sown) and 12·37m. meadows and pastures. 78·5% of the sown area belongs to state farms, 21·2% to collectives. In 1985 81% was sown to cereals, 17% to fodder and 2% to vegetables. The 1988 crop was 814,300 tonnes of wheat; 1,700 tonnes of rye (1980); 50,000 tonnes of oats; 146,000 tonnes of barley. In 1988, 103,000 tonnes of potatoes were harvested. In 1981 there were 7,500 tractors (15 h.p. units) and 2,000 combine harvesters.

Forestry. Forests, chiefly larch, cedar, fir and birch, occupy 15·2m. hectares, 10% of the land area. Production, 1983: 683,100 cu. metres of timber.

INDUSTRY AND TRADE

Industry. Industry though still small in scale and local in character, is being vigorously developed and now accounts for a greater share of GNP than agriculture. The food industry accounts for 20% of industrial production. The main industrial centre is Ulan Bator; others are at Erdenet and Baga-Nuur, and a northern territorial industrial complex is being developed based on Darkhan and Erdenet to produce copper and molybdenium concentrates, lime, cement, machinery and wood- and metal-worked products. Production figures (1983): Wool, 12,100 tonnes; cement, 165,300 tonnes; leather footwear, 2·2m. pairs; meat, 64,400 tonnes; soap, 10,800 tonnes.

Employment. The labour force was 365,000 in 1983, including 82,200 in industry, 41,200 in agriculture, 26,700 in building, 39,700 in transport and communications and 38,900 in trade. In 1988 48% of the labour force was female. Average wage was 450 tugriks per month in 1988. Trade union membership was 530,000 in 1988. There is a labour shortage necessitating the employment of military personnel, and workers from the USSR and Eastern Europe.

Commerce. Since 1989 some enterprizes have been able to trade directly abroad and joint ventures with foreign firms have been permitted. Trade figures for 1983 (in 1m. tugriks): Exports, 1,816; imports, 2,764. Exports in 1988 included 40% minerals and fuels, 28% food and consumer goods and 20% non-food raw materials. 97% of foreign trade is with communist countries. Main imports are machinery and fuel. Imports from the USSR totalled 1,014·6m. roubles in 1984, exports to the USSR, 387·4m. roubles. The main non-Communist trading partner is Japan.

Total trade between Mongolia and UK (British Department of Trade returns, in £1,000 sterling):

	1986	*1987*	*1988*	*1989*
Imports to UK	4,750	3,847	1,857	405
Exports and re-exports from UK	1,031	941	1,637	979

Tourism. 9,700 tourists visited Mongolia in 1988.

COMMUNICATIONS

Roads. There are fewer than 1,000 km of surfaced roads running around Ulan Bator, from Ulan Bator to Darkhan, at points on the frontier with USSR and towards the south. Truck services run where there are no surfaced roads. 30·8m. tonnes of freight were carried in 1983, and 144·9m. passengers.

Railways. The Trans-Mongolian Railway (1,423 km in 1983) connects Ulan Bator with the Soviet Union and China. The Moscow–Ulan Bator–Beijing express runs each way once a week, and there are services to Irkutsk, Moscow and Beijing. There are spur lines to Erdenet and to the coalmines at Nalaykh and Sharin Gol. A separate line connects Choybalsan in the east with Borzya on the Trans-Siberian railway. 1·9m. passengers and 12m. tonnes of freight were carried in 1983.

Aviation. Mongolian Airlines (MIAT) operates internal services, a flight to Irkutsk which links with the Soviet airlines (Aeroflot) stopping service to Moscow, and (with Aeroflot) a daily non-stop service to Moscow from Ulan Bator. A weekly flight to Beijing operates in summer. 10,000 tons of freight were carried in 1983 and 500,000 passengers. Ulan Bator airport (Buyant Uhaa) was modernized and expanded in 1985.

Shipping. There is a steamer service on the Selenge River and a tug and barge service on Hobsgol Lake. 3,000 tonnes of freight were carried in 1976.

Post and Broadcasting. There were, in 1983, 414 post offices and 264 telephone exchanges. Number of telephones (1983), 44,600.

There are wireless stations at Ulan Bator, Gobi Altai and Olgiy. In 1983 there were 186,600 radio and 70,700 television receivers. Television services began in 1967. A Mongolian television station opened in 1970. Mongolia is a member of the international TV organization Intervision.

Cinemas. In 1983 there were 26 cinemas, 493 mobile cinemas and 20 theatres.

Newspapers and books. In 1983, 37 newspapers and 39 journals were published. The Party daily paper *Ünen* ('Truth') had a circulation of 112,000 in 1978. 400 book titles were published in 1982 in 70m. copies

JUSTICE, RELIGION, EDUCATION AND WELFARE

Justice. The Procurator-General is appointed, and the Supreme Court elected, by the *Khural* for 5 years. There are also courts at province, town and district level. Lay assessors sit with professional judges.

Religion. Tibetan Buddhist Lamaism was the prevalent form of religion. It was suppressed in the 1930s, and only one functioning monastery exists today, at Ulan Bator, with about 100 lamas.

Education. In 1985 there were 680 nurseries with 62,500 children. Schooling begins at the age of 7. In 1984-85 there were 911 general education schools with 444,000 pupils and 15,900 teachers, 28 specialized secondary schools with 23,000 students and 1,200 teachers and 40 vocational technical schools with 25,000 pupils. There is a state university (founded 1942) at Ulan Bator (40 professors, 240 lecturers and 10,000 students in 1982), and 7 other institutes of higher learning (teacher training, medicine, agriculture, economics, etc.) with 26,000 students in

1983 and 1,400 teachers under the supervision of an Academy of Sciences (founded 1961) which has 15 institutes and 190 research workers. Some 6,000 students a year are sent to study abroad, principally in the USSR.

In 1946 the Mongolian alphabet was replaced by Cyrillic, but its teaching has now been resumed.

Health and Welfare. In 1983 68·3m. tugriks were spent on maternity benefits.

Annual average per capita consumption (in kilogrammes) of foodstuffs over 1981–83: Meat, 91·4; milk and products, 147·7; sugar, 21·3; flour, 97·7; potatoes, 17·9; fresh vegetables, 14·5. In 1987 there were 24 doctors and 111 hospital beds per 10,000 population.

DIPLOMATIC REPRESENTATIVES

Of Mongolia in Great Britain (7 Kensington Ct., London, W8 5DL)
Ambassador: Ishetsogyin Ochirbal.

Of Great Britain in Mongolia (30 Enkh Taivny Gudamzh, Ulan Bator)
Ambassador: D. K. Sprague, MVO.

Of Mongolia in the USA
Ambassador: Gendengiin Nyamdoo.

Of the USA in Mongolia
Ambassador: Richard Williams (accredited 18 Sept. 1988).

Of Mongolia to the United Nations
Ambassador: Mangalyn Dugersuren.

Further Reading

The Central Statistical Office: *National Economy of the MPR, 1924–1984: Anniversary Statistical Collection*. Ulan Bator, 1984

Bawden, C. R., *The Modern History of Mongolia*. London, 1968

Boberg, F., *Mongolian–English, English–Mongolian Dictionary*. 3 vols. Stockholm, 1954–55

Butler, W. E., (ed.) *The Mongolian Legal System: Contemporary Legislation and Documentation*. The Hague, 1982

Haltod, M. (ed.) *Mongolian–English Dictionary*. Berkeley, Cal., 1961

Jagchid, S. and Hyer, P., *Mongolia's Culture and Society*. Folkestone, 1979

Lattimore, O., *Nationalism and Revolution in Mongolia*. Leiden, 1955.—*Nomads and Commissars*. OUP, 1963

Lörinc, L., *Histoire de la Mongolie des Origines à nos Jours*. Budapest, 1984

Mongol'skaia Narodnaia Respublika: Spravochnik. Moscow, 1986

News from Mongolia. Ulan Bator, fortnightly, Jan. 1980

Rupen, R. A., *How Mongolia is Really Ruled: A Political History of the Mongolian People's Republic, 1900–1978*. Stanford, 1979

Sanders, A. J. K., *The People's Republic of Mongolia: A General Reference Guide*. OUP, 1968.—*Mongolia: Politics, Economics and Society*. London, 1987

Shirendev, B. and Sanjdorj, M. (eds.) *History of the Mongolian People's Republic*. Vol. 3 (vols. 1 and 2 not translated). Harvard Univ. Press, 1976

Socialist Mongolia. Ulan Bator, 1981

MONTSERRAT

Capital: Plymouth
Population: 11,852 (1985)
GNP per capita: US$3,127 (1985)

HISTORY. Montserrat was discovered by Columbus in 1493 and colonized by Britain in 1632 who brought Irish settlers to the island. Montserrat formed part of the federal colony of the Leeward Islands from 1871 until 1956, when it became a separate colony following the dissolution of the Federation. The island's Constitution came into force in 1960 and the title Administrator was changed to that of Governor in 1971.

EVENTS. On 17 Sept. 1989 hurricane 'Hugo' caused devastating damage to the island.

AREA AND POPULATION. Montserrat is situated in the Caribbean Sea 25 miles south-west of Antigua. The area is 39·5 sq. miles (106 sq. km). Population, 1985, 11,852. Chief town, Plymouth, 3,500 inhabitants.

CLIMATE. A tropical climate but with no well-defined rainy season, though July to Dec. shows slightly more rainfall, with the average for the year being about 60" (1,500 mm). Dec. to March is the cooler season while June to Nov. is the hotter season, when hurricanes may occur. Plymouth. Jan. 76°F (24·4°C), July 81°F (27·2°C). Annual rainfall 65" (1,628 mm).

CONSTITUTION AND GOVERNMENT. Montserrat is a crown colony. The Executive Council is composed of 4 elected Ministers (the Chief Minister and 3 other Ministers) and 2 civil service officials (Attorney-General and Financial Secretary). The Legislative Council consists of 7 elected and 2 civil service officials (the Attorney-General and Financial Secretary) and 2 nominated members. The Executive Council is presided over by the Governor and the Legislative Council by the Speaker.

In elections to the Legislative Council in 1987, 4 seats were won by the People's Liberation Movement, 2 by the National Development Party and 1 by the Progressive Democratic Party.

Governor: David Taylor.

Chief Minister: Hon. J. A. Osborne.

Flag: The British Blue Ensign with the shield of Montserrat in the fly.

ECONOMY

Budget. In 1988 the budget expenditure was at EC$31m. of which EC$8·64m. was capital expenditure. In 1981 the territorial budget ceased to be grant-aided by the British Government.

Currency. 100 cents = 1 Eastern Caribbean dollar (EC$). Coins: 1, 2, 5, 25, 50 cents. Notes: 1, 5, 10, 20 and 100 dollars.

Banking. There are 6 recognized banks on Montserrat. These are Barclays Bank, the Royal Bank of Canada, The First American Bank, the Government Savings Bank, the Bank of Montserrat and the Montserrat Building Society.

ENERGY AND NATURAL RESOURCES

Electricity. Production (1987) 16·3m. kwh.

Agriculture. Self-sufficiency in fruit, ground provisions and vegetables though canned and preserved foodstuffs were imported was achieved in 1988. The processing and packaging of tropical fruits and herbal teas for export are being encouraged together with the growing of ornamental plants for export.

Livestock (1988); Cattle, 3,000; pigs, 1,000; sheep and goats, 11,005; poultry, 50,500.

Fisheries. Catch (1988) 100 tonnes.

INDUSTRY AND TRADE

Industry. Manufacturing contributes about 6% to GDP and accounts for 10% of employment, but is responsible for up to 85% of exports. It is limited to small scale industries producing light consumer goods such as electronic components, plastic bags, leather goods and various items made from locally grown cotton.

Commerce. Imports in 1988 totalled EC$72m.; domestic exports, EC$6m. Chief imports were manufactured goods, food and beverages, machinery and transport equipment and fuel. Chief exports were cotton clothing, electronic parts and lighting fittings.

Total trade between Montserrat and UK (British Department of Trade returns, in £1,000 sterling):

	1985	*1986*	*1987*	*1988*	*1989*
Imports to UK	414	358	139	125	494
Exports and re-exports from UK	2,330	3,926	2,432	2,524	3,092

Tourism. In 1988, 29,736 tourists arrived in Montserrat.

COMMUNICATIONS

Roads. In 1987 there were 290 km of roads, 212 km paved, 1,368 passenger cars and 270 commercial vehicles.

Aviation. At Blackburne airport 4,447 aircraft landed in 1988, disembarking 30,272 passengers and 214 tonnes of cargo.

Shipping. In 1988, 270 cargo vessels arrived, landing 47,026 and loading (1987) 663 tonnes of cargo.

Post and Broadcasting. Number of telephones (1988), 3,938; telex, 46 and 44 facsimile subscribers. In 1984 there were 4,000 radio and 1,100 TV receivers.

JUSTICE, RELIGION, EDUCATION AND WELFARE

Justice. There are 2 magistrates' courts, at Plymouth and Cudjoe Head. Strength of the police force (1987), 2 gazetted officers, 3 inspectorate and 89 other ranks.

Religion. In 1980 (census) there were 1,368 Roman Catholics, 3,676 Anglicans, 2,742 Methodists, 1,041 Seventh Day Adventists, 1,503 Pentecostals and 285 members of the Church of God. There is also a Christian Council of Churches.

Education. There were (1989) 2 day-care centres, 12 nursery schools, 12 primary schools, a comprehensive secondary school with 3 campuses, and a technical training college. Schools are run by the Government, the churches and the private sector. In 1988 there were 460 pupils at nursery schools; 1,403 at primary school, 1,043 at secondary school and 72 at the technical training college. There is an Extra Mural Department of the University of the West Indies in Plymouth with about 200 students and 15 part-time and 1 full-time lecturers.

Health. In 1985 there were 8 doctors and 67 hospital beds.

Further Reading

Population Census 1980. Montserrat
Overseas Trade 1983. Montserrat Government
Vital Statistics Report. Montserrat Government, 1983
Statistical Digest 1984. Montserrat Government
Fergus, H.A., *Montserrat: Emerald Isle of the Caribbean*. London, 1983

Library: Public Library, Plymouth. *Librarian:* Miss Ruth Allen.

MOROCCO

Capital: Rabat
Population: 23m. (1987)
GNP per capita: US$750 (1988)

al-Mamlaka al-Maghrebia

HISTORY. From 1912 to 1956 Morocco was divided into a French protectorate (established by the treaty of Fez concluded between France and the Sultan on 30 March 1912), a Spanish protectorate (established by the Franco-Spanish convention of 27 Nov. 1912) and the international zone of Tangier (set up by France, Spain and Great Britain on 18 Dec. 1923).

On 2 March 1956 France and the Sultan terminated the treaty of Fez; on 7 April 1956 Spain relinquished her protectorate, and on 29 Oct. 1956 France, Spain, Great Britain, Italy, USA, Belgium, the Netherlands, Sweden and Portugal abolished the international status of the Tangier Zone. The northern strip of Spanish Sahara was ceded by Spain on 10 April 1958, and on 30 June 1969 the former Spanish province of Ifni was returned to Morocco.

A tripartite agreement was announced on 14 Nov. 1975 providing for the transfer of power from Spanish Sahara (Western Sahara) to the Moroccan and Mauritanean governments on 28 Feb. 1976. Spanish troops left El Aaiún on 20 Dec. 1975. On 14 April 1976 a Convention was signed by Mauritania and Morocco in which the 2 countries agreed to partition the former Spanish territory, but on 14 Aug. 1979 Mauritania renounced its claim to its share of the territory (Tiris El-Gharbiya) which was added by Morocco to its area.

AREA AND POPULATION. Morocco is bounded by Algeria to the east and south-east, Western Sahara to the south-west, the Atlantic ocean to the north-west and the Mediterranean to the north. Excluding the Western Saharan territory claimed and occupied since 1976 by Morocco, the total area is 458,730 sq. km and its total population at the Sept. 1982 census was 20,255,687; the latest estimate (1987) is 23,557,000.

The areas (in sq. km) and populations (census 1982) of the provinces are:

Province	*Sq. km*	*1982*
Agadir	5,910	579,741
Taroudant	16,460	558,501
Al-Hoceima	3,550	311,298
Azilal	10,050	387,115
Beni Mellal	7,075	668,703
Ben Slimane	2,760	174,464
Boulemane	14,395	131,470
Casablanca-Anfa [1]		923,630
Aïn Chok-Hay Hassani [1]		298,376
Ben Msik-Sidi Othmane [1]	1,615	639,558
Hay Mohamed-Aïn Sebâa [1]		421,272
Mohamedia-Znata [1]		153,828
Chechaouèn	4,350	309,024
El Jadida	6,000	763,351
El Kelâa-Srarhna	10,070	577,595
Er Rachidia	59,585	421,207
Es Saouira	6,335	393,683
Fez	5,400	805,464
Figuig	55,990	101,359
Guelmim	28,750	128,676
Kénitra	4,745	715,967
Sidi Kacem	4,060	514,127
Khémisset	8,305	405,836
Khénifra	12,320	363,716
Khouribga	4,250	437,002
Marrakesh	14,755	1,266,695
Meknès	3,995	626,868
Ifrane	3,310	100,255

Province	*Sq. km*	*1982*
Nador	6,130	593,255
Ouarzazate	41,550	533,892
Oujda	20,700	780,762
Rabat-Salé [1]	1,275	1,020,001
Safi	7,285	706,618
Settat	9,750	692,359
Tangier	1,195	436,227
Tan-Tan	17,295	47,040
Taounate	5,585	535,972
Tata	25,925	99,950
Taza	15,020	613,485
Tétouan	6,025	704,205
Tiznit	6,960	313,140
Morocco	458,730	20,255,687
Boujdour (Bojador)	100,120	8,481
Es Semara (Smara)	61,760	20,480
Laâyoune (Al Aaiún)	39,360	113,411
Oued Ed Dahab	50,880	21,496
Sahara	252,120	163,868

[1] Urban prefectures

The chief cities (with Census populations, 1982) are as follows:

Casablanca	2,139,204	Tangier	266,346	Agadir	110,479
Rabat	518,616	Oujda	260,082	Mohammedia	105,120
Fez	448,823	Tétouan	199,615	Beni Mellal	95,003
Marrakesh	439,728	Safi	197,616	Al Jadida	81,455
Meknès	319,783	Kénitra	188,194	Taza	77,216
Salé	289,391	Khouribga	127,181	Ksar al Kabir	73,541

The official language is Arabic, spoken by 75% of the population; the remainder speak Berber. French and Spanish are considered subsidiary languages.

CLIMATE. The climate ranges from semi-arid in the south to warm temperate Mediterranean conditions in the north, but cooler temperatures occur in the mountains. Rabat. Jan. 55°F (12·9°C), July 72°F (22·2°C). Annual rainfall 23" (564 mm). Agadir. Jan. 57°F (13·9°C), July 72°F (22·2°C). Annual rainfall 9" (224 mm). Casablanca. Jan. 54°F (12·2°C), July 72°F (22·2°C). Annual rainfall 16" (404 mm). Marrakesh. Jan. 52°F (11·1°C), July 84°F (28·9°C). Annual rainfall 10" (239 mm). Tangier. Jan. 53°F (11·7°C), July 72°F (22·2°C). Annual rainfall 36" (897 mm).

REIGNING KING. Hassan II, born on 9 July 1929, succeeded on 3 March 1961, on the death of his father Mohammed V, who reigned 1927–61. The royal style was changed from 'His Sherifian Majesty the Sultan' to 'His Majesty the King' on 18 Aug. 1957. *Heir apparent:* Crown Prince Sidi Mohammed, born 21 Aug. 1963.

The King holds supreme civil and religious authority; the latter in his capacity of Emir-el-Muminin or Commander of the Faithful. He resides usually at Rabat, but occasionally in one of the other traditional capitals, Fez (founded in 808), Marrakesh (founded in 1062), or at Skhirat.

CONSTITUTION AND GOVERNMENT. A new Constitution was approved by referendum in March 1972 and amendments were approved by referendum in May 1980. The Kingdom of Morocco is a constitutional monarchy with a legislature of a single chamber composed of 306 deputies. Deputies for 102 seats are elected by indirect vote through an electoral college representing the town councils, the regional assemblies, the chambers of commerce, industry and agriculture, and the trade unions. Deputies for the remaining 204 seats are by general election. The King, as sovereign head of State, appoints the Prime Minister and other Ministers, has the right to dissolve Parliament and approves legislation.

In the General Elections held on 14 Sept. 1984, the new *Union constitutionelle* (founded Jan. 1983) won 83 seats, the *Rassemblement nationale des indépendants* 61 seats, the *Union socialiste des forces populaires* 36 seats, the *Mouvement populaire* 47 seats, *Istiqlal* (Independence) 41 seats; others 38 seats.

National flag: Red, with a green pentacle star in the centre.

The cabinet in 1989 was composed as follows:

Prime Minister: N. Azzeddine Laraki.

Justice: Moulay Mustapha Belarbi Alaoui. *Interior:* Driss Basri. *Foreign Affairs, Co-operation and Information:* Abdellatif Filali. *Planning:* Rachid Ghazouani. *National Education:* Mohamed Hilali. *Economic Affairs:* Moulay Zine Zahidi. *Finance:* Abdellatif Jouahri. *Trade, Industry and Tourism:* Abdallah al-Azmani. *Handicrafts and Social Affairs:* Mohamed Labied. *Transport:* Mohamed Bouamoud. *Energy and Mining:* Mohamed Fettah. *Health:* Tayeb Bencheikh. *Maritime Fishing and Merchant Navy:* Bensalem Smili. *Secretary-General of the Government:* Abbas Kaissi. *Cultural Affairs:* Mohamed Benaissa. *Housing and Land Management:* Abderrahmane Boufettas. *Equipment, Executive and Professional Training:* Mohamed Kabbaj. *Posts and Telecommunications:* Mohand Laensar. *Agriculture and Land Reform:* Otman Demnati. *Relations with Parliament:* Tahar Afifi. *Youth and Sports:* Abdellatif Semlali. *Labour:* Hassan Abbadi. *Islamic Affairs:* Abdelkbar Alaoui Medaghri. *Administrative Affairs:* Abderrahim Ben

Abdeljalil. *Saharan Province:* Khali H. Ould Rachid. *Relations with the European Community:* Azzedine Guessous. There was 1 Minister of State.

Local Government: The country is administratively divided into 39 provinces and 8 urban prefectures.

DEFENCE. Military service is compulsory for 18 months.

Army. The Army comprises 1 mechanized infantry and 2 motorized infantry; 6 mechanized infantry regiments; 11 artillery groups; 7 armoured, 1 Royal Guard, 3 camel corps, 3 desert cavalry, 1 mountain, 4 commando and 17 engineer battalions. Equipment includes 224 M-48A5 main battle tanks, 50 light tanks and many armoured cars. Strength (1990) 170,000 men. There are also 40,000 paramilitary troops.

Navy. The Navy includes 1 missile-armed Spanish-built frigate, 4 fast missile craft, 9 coastal patrol craft and 10 inshore patrol craft. There are additionally 3 medium landing ships of French origin, 2 transports and 1 Ro-Ro ferry in naval use. Personnel in 1989 numbered 6,500, including a 1,500 strong brigade of Naval Infantry. Bases are located at Casablanca, Agadir, Al-Hoceima and Dakhla.

There were also 13 small customs cutters and 24 more building.

Air Force. The Air Force was formed in Nov. 1956. Equipment in current use is mainly of US and West European origin. It includes 40 Mirage F1s, a total of 30 F-5A/B/E/F fighter-bombers and RF-5A reconnaissance-fighters, 3 OV-10 Bronco counter-insurgency aircraft, 2 Falcon 20s for electronic warfare, and 24 Gazelle armed helicopters, 24 Alpha Jet advanced trainers, 22 Magister armed jet basic trainers, 12 T-34C-1 turboprop basic trainers, 10 Swiss-built Bravo primary trainers, 2 Mudry CAP 10B aerobatic trainers, 4 Broussard liaison aircraft, 90 Agusta-Bell 205 and 212, Puma and JetRanger helicopters, 2 Do 28D Skyservants for coastal patrol, 11 CH-47C heavy-lift helicopters, 18 C-130H turboprop transport aircraft, 2 KC-130H tanker/transports, a Falcon 50 and a Gulfstream II VIP transport, 2 Boeing 707s and 8 turboprop King Air light transports. Personnel strength (1990) about 16,000.

INTERNATIONAL RELATIONS

Membership. Morocco is a member of UN, the Non-Aligned Movement, the Islamic Conference and the Arab League.

ECONOMY

Budget. The budget for 1988 envisaged revenue of 50,547m. DH and expenditure of 59,736m. DH.

Debt. In April 1985 foreign debt was estimated at US$12,500m. (£9,800m.).

Currency. In Oct. 1959, a national currency was introduced. Its unit is the *dirham* (abbreviated DH), equalling 100 *centimes*. Notes: 10, 50, 100 DH; coins: 0·10, 0·20, 0·50, 1 DH. The exchange rate in March 1990 was £1 sterling = 13·21 DH; US$1 = 8·06 DH.

Banking. The central bank is the Banque al Maghrib. Authorized banks are: La Banque Marocaine du Commerce Extérieur, La Banque Marocaine pour le Commerce et l'Industrie, La Banque Commerciale du Maroc, Compagnie Marocaine du Crédit et de Banque, Société Générale Marocaine de Banque, Crédit du Maroc, Union Marocaine de Banque, Société de dépôt et de crédits, Arab Bank Ltd, Bank of America, Banco Espagnol en Maruecos, Banque de Paris et des Pays-Bas, First National City Bank, Société Hollandaise de Banque et de Gestion, The British Bank of the Middle East, Société de Dépôt et de Crédits, Wafabank, Citibank, Algemene Bank Nederland and Banque Américano-Suisse pour le Maroc. The Banque Centrale Populaire and regional Banques populaires also provide banking services for small and medium businesses. There are 3 development banks: Banque Nationale du Development Economique, whose major area of investment has been industry;

Credit Industrial et Hotelier, which finances housing on easy terms; Caisse Nationale du Credit Agricole, which specializes in agriculture. La Banque National pour le Développement économique grants loans to the industrial sector. Le Crédit Immobilier et Hôtelier grants loans for construction. La Caisse de Dépôt et de Gestion is responsible for the centralization of savings and their management.

Weights and Measures. The metric system of weights and measures is the sole legal system.

ENERGY AND NATURAL RESOURCES

Electricity. Electric power-plants produced 6,920m. kwh. in 1986. Supply 110, 127 and 220 volts; 50 Hz.

Oil. Crude oil production, 17,500 tonnes 1981. Refined oil production (including imported crude), 4·5m. tonnes in 1983.

Minerals. The principal mineral exploited is phosphate, the output of which was 21·4m. tonnes in 1986. Other important minerals (in tonnes, 1985) are: Anthracite (774,500), iron ore (190,258), lead (153,636), copper (59,245), zinc (27,153), manganese (43,690), baryt (463,380), fluorine (74,350), salt (118,173).

Agriculture. Land suitable for cultivation, 1984, 7·7m. hectares, of which (in 1,000 hectares): Cereals, 4,500; leguminous vegetables, 400; market gardening, 150; oil-producing and industrial cultivation, 130; fodder, 110; dense fruit plantations, 400; fallows, 2,000.

Production in 1988 (in 1,000 tonnes): Wheat, 4,035; barley, 3,501; maize, 355; fruit, 1,787 (of which citrus fruits, 1,275); pulses, 450; sunflower seeds, 88; groundnuts, 32; sugar beets, 2,770; sugar-cane, 800; olives, 360; potatoes, 550; tomatoes, 400; onions, 272.

Dairy production in 1988 included: Milk, 923,000 tonnes; butter, 13,629 tonnes; cheese, 7,221 tonnes. Meat production (1988) 369,000 tonnes.

Livestock (in 1,000 heads), 1988: Cattle, 3,300; sheep, 15,700; goats, 5,800.

Forestry. Forests covered (1988) 5m. hectares (12% of land area) and employed (1984) 50,000. They produce mainly firewood, building and industrial timber, some cork and charcoal.

Fisheries. The industry employed 83,000 workers in 1987. Total catch in 1986 was 591,000 tonnes, value 2,442,404,000 DH. The value of fish exports in 1986 was 2,860,552,000 DH.

INDUSTRY AND TRADE

Industry. In 1984 industry represented 14% of the GNP. Manufacturing industries are concentrated in Casablanca (metallurgy, car assembly, sugar-producing and pharmaceutical products), Fez, Rabat, Muhammadia (textile), Safi (chemicals, manure, fish treatment) and Agadir (fish treatment, canning factories). There are 8 cement factories, with an output of 3,848,200 tonnes in 1983, when self-sufficiency was achieved.

The agricultural and food industries produce 40% of the whole industrial output. The sugar industry meets 76% of the country's needs and produced 426,800 tonnes of crude sugar in 1983.

Trade Unions. In 1984 there were 8 trade unions.

Commerce. Imports and exports were (in DH1m.):

	1985	*1986*	*1987*
Imports	38,675	34,608	35,271
Exports	21,740	22,103	23,390

Exports (1986) of phosphates 13·7m. tonnes, value DH3,840m.

Exports in 1985 went mainly to France (24%), Spain (7%), Federal Republic of Germany (7%), Italy (6%) and UK (3%). Imports were mainly from France (25%), Spain (14%), Federal Republic of Germany (8%), Italy (6%) and UK (3%).

Total trade between Morocco and UK (British Department of Trade returns, in £1,000 sterling):

	1985	*1986*	*1987*	*1988*	*1989*
Imports to UK	74,820	65,419	61,108	78,896	96,138
Exports and re-exports from UK	92,658	84,510	94,487	79,017	84,475

Tourism. In 1986, 1·47m. visitors came to Morocco, spending (1985) DH6,200m.

COMMUNICATIONS

Roads. In 1983 there were 57,592 km of classified roads, of which 19,099 km were surfaced. A motorway links Rabat to Casablanca. In 1987 there were in use 207,000 commercial vehicles, 554,000 private cars and 19,000 motor cycles.

Railways. In 1987 there were 1,893 km of railways, of which 974 km were electrified. The principal standard-gauge lines are from Casablanca eastward to the Algerian border, forming part of the continuous rail line to Tunis; Casablanca to Marrakesh with 2 important branches, one eastward to Oued Zem tapping the Khouribga phosphate mines, the other westward to the port of Safi. Another branch serves the manganese mines at Bou Arfa. Two new double-track electrified lines are to serve a new deep-water port at Jorf Lasfar.

In 1988 the railways carried 2,092m. passenger-km and 5,706 tonne-km of freight.

Aviation. There are 15 international airports as well as national airports. The most important, Mohamed V airport in Casablanca, handled 18,154 flights with 1,367,548 passengers and 24,968·8 tonnes of freight including mail in 1983. Total flights, 1983, 44,606 with 3,176,648 passengers and 29,882·7 tonnes of freight including mail.

Shipping. In 1983, 17,555 vessels entered and cleared the ports of Morocco and 19,393,000 tonnes of merchandise, including 13,891,500 tonnes of phosphate, were loaded and 11,260,000 tonnes unloaded.

Post and Broadcasting. In 1983 there were 359 post offices. Telephone subscribers totalled 265,672 in 1983.

There are broadcasts in Arabic, Berber, French, Spanish and English from Rabat and Tangier; television in Arabic and French began in 1962. In 1988 there were 4·4m. radio receivers and 1·2m. television receivers.

Newspapers. In 1984 there were 12 daily newspapers (7 Arabic, 5 French) and 18 main weeklies and monthlies (10 Arabic, 8 French).

JUSTICE, RELIGION, EDUCATION AND WELFARE

Justice. A uniform legal system is being organized, based mainly on French and Islamic law codes and French legal procedure. The judiciary consists of a Supreme Court, courts of appeal, regional tribunals and magistrates' courts.

Religion. Islam is the established state religion. 98% are Sunni Moslems of the Malekite school and 2% are Christians, mainly Roman Catholic.

Education. In 1959 a standardization of the various school systems (French, Spanish, Israeli, Moslem, etc.) was begun. Education is compulsory from the age of 7 to 13.

In 1984 there were 2,550,000 pupils and 75,094 teachers in 3,144 state primary schools; 1,050,000 pupils and 51,711 teachers in secondary schools; 10,020 (1981) students in technical schools and 16,148 (1981) students in teacher-training establishments.

The language of instruction in primary and secondary schools is Arabic. Some scientific courses were (1985) still taught in French.

Professional and vocational colleges had 6,942 students in 1983. There were 30,000 students abroad.

There are six universities, Mohamed V at Rabat, Hassan II at Casablanca, Mohamed Ben Abdallah at Fez, Quaraouyine at Fez, Mohamed I at Oujda and Cadi

Ayyad at Marrakesh with a total enrolment of 99,637 students and 3,146 teaching staff in 1984.

Health. In the public sector, 1984, there were 1,048 medical centres and dispensaries, 5,258 doctors, 63 chemists and 4,424 (1983) registered nurses. In the private sector, 1984, there were 1,971 doctors, 6,713 (1983) chemists and 709 registered nurses. There were 14,847 qualified nurses in 1983.

DIPLOMATIC REPRESENTATIVES

Of Morocco in Great Britain (49 Queen's Gate Gdns., London, SW7 5NE)
Ambassador: Abdeslam Zenined, GCVO.

Of Great Britain in Morocco (17 Blvd de la Tour Hassan, Rabat)
Ambassador: J. W. R. Shakespeare, CMG, LVO.

Of Morocco in the USA (1601 21st St., NW, Washington, D.C., 20009)
Ambassador: Ali Bengelloun.

Of the USA in Morocco (2 Ave. de Marrakech, Rabat)
Ambassador: E. Michael Ussery.

Of Morocco to the United Nations
Ambassador: Driss Slaoui.

Further Reading

Statistical Information: The Service Central des Statistiques (BP 178, Rabat) was established in 1942. Its publications include: *Annuaire de Statistique Générale.—La Conjoncture Économique Marocaine* (monthly; with annual synthesis).—*Bulletin économique et social du Maroc* (trimestral)

Bulletin Official (in Arabic and French). Rabat. Weekly

Findlay, A. M. and A. M. and Lawless, R. I., *Morocco.* [Bibliography] Oxford and Santa Barbara, 1984

Kinross, Lord and Hales-Gary, D., *Morocco.* London, 1971

National Library: Bibliothèque Générale et Archives, Rabat.

MOZAMBIQUE

Capital: Maputo
Population: 14·9m. (1988)
GNP per capita: US$100 (1988)

República Popular de Moçambique

HISTORY. Trading settlements were established by Arab merchants at Sofala (Beira), Quelimane, Angoche and Mozambique Island in the fifteenth century. Mozambique Island was visited by Vasco da Gamba's fleet on 2 March 1498, and Sofala was occupied by Portuguese in 1506. At first ruled as part of Portuguese India, a separate administration was created in 1752, and on 11 June 1951 Mozambique became an Overseas Province of Portugal. Following a decade of guerrilla activity, Portugal and the nationalists jointly established a transitional government on 20 Sept. 1974. Independence was achieved on 25 June 1975. In March 1984 the Republic of South Africa and Mozambique signed a non-agression pact.

AREA AND POPULATION. Mozambique is bounded east by the Indian ocean, south by South Africa, south-west by Swaziland, west by South Africa and Zimbabwe and north by Zambia, Malaŵi and Tanzania. It has an area of 799,380 sq. km (308,642 sq. miles) and a population, according to the census of 1980, of 11,673,725. Estimate (1988) 14,907,000 of whom (1986) 882,814 lived in the capital, Maputo. Other chief cities are Beira (1986 population, 269,700) and Nampula (182,553). The areas, populations and capitals of the provinces are:

Province	*Sq. km*	*Census 1980*	*Estimate 1987*	*Capital*
Cabo Delgado	82,625	940,000	1,109,921	Pemba
Niassa	129,056	514,100	607,670	Lichinga
Nampula	81,606	2,402,700	2,837,856	Nampula
Zambézia	105,008	2,500,200	2,952,251	Quelimane
Tete	100,724	831,000	981,319	Tete
Manica	61,661	641,200	756,886	Chimoio
Sofala	68,018	1,065,200	1,257,710	Beira
Inhambane	68,615	997,600	1,167,022	Inhambane
Gaza	75,709	990,900	1,138,724	Xaixai
Province of Maputo	25,756	491,800	544,692	Maputo
City of Maputo	602	755,300	1,006,765	

The main ethnolinguistic groups are the Makua/Lomwe (52% of the population), mainly in the 4 provinces in the north, the Malaŵi (12%), Shona (6%) and Yao (3%) in Tete, Manica and Sofala, and the Thonga (24%) in the 3 provinces in the south. Portuguese remains the official language, but vernaculars are widely spoken throughout the country.

CLIMATE. A humid tropical climate, with a dry season from June to Sept. In general, temperatures and rainfall decrease from north to south. Maputo. Jan. 78°F (25·6°C), July 65°F (18·3°C). Annual rainfall 30" (760 mm). Beira. Jan. 82°F (27·8°C), July 69°F (20·6°C). Annual rainfall 60" (1,522 mm).

CONSTITUTION AND GOVERNMENT. Under the Constitution adopted at independence on 25 June 1975, the directing power of the state is vested in the *Frente de Libertação de Moçambique* (FRELIMO), the liberation movement, which in Feb. 1977 was reconstituted as sole political Party. A new Constitution was under discussion in 1987. The legislative organ is the People's Assembly of 250 members, elected in Dec. 1986.

The Council of Ministers in June 1989 consisted of:

President, and Commander-in-Chief of the Armed Forces: Joaquim Alberto Chissano.

Prime Minister: Mário da Graça Machungo.

Foreign Affairs: Pascoal Manuel Mocumbi. *Finance:* Abdul Magid Osman. *Defence:* Gen. Alberto Chipande.

National flag: Horizontally green, black, yellow with the black fimbriated in white; a red triangle based on the hoist, charged with a yellow star surmounted by an open white book and a crossed rifle and hoe in black.

Local Government. The capital of Maputo and 10 provinces, each under a Governor who is automatically a member of the Council of Ministers, are sub-divided into 112 districts.

DEFENCE. Selective conscription for 2 years is in force.

Army. The Army consists of 1 tank brigade and 7 infantry brigades, 7 anti-aircraft artillery battalions and many support units. Equipment includes T-34/-54/-55 main battle tanks. Strength (1990) 60,000. There are also 6,000 Border Guards and various militias.

Navy. The small flotilla based principally at Maputo, with subsidiary bases at Beira, Nacala, Pemba and Inhambane comprises 26 inshore patrol craft of mixed origins, 3 *ex*-Soviet inshore minesweepers and 2 landing craft. Four of the patrol craft are based at Metangula on Lake Nyasa. Naval personnel in 1989 totalled 750.

Air Force. The Air Force is reported to have about 20 MiG-17 and 30 MiG-21 fighters, probably flown by Cuban pilots, An-26 turboprop transports, and a few C-47 piston-engined transports. About 6 Mi-24 armed helicopters and 10 Mi-8 transport helicopters, a small number of L-39 jet trainers, Zlin 326 primary trainers and a few *ex*-Portuguese Air Force Alouette liaison helicopters. Personnel (1990) 4,250.

INTERNATIONAL RELATIONS

Membership. Mozambique is a member of UN, OAU, SADCC and is an ACP state of EEC.

ECONOMY

Planning. The Economic Recovery Programme (1987–90) aimed to stimulate production and to restore the real value of wages and earnings as an incentive to productivity in industry and agriculture.

Budget. In 1987 the revenue was US$277·87m.; expenditure, US$427·91m. Foreign debt (1986) US$3,200m.

Currency. In June 1980 the currency became the *metical* (pl. *meticais*) divided into 100 *centavos*. The *metical* was established at par with the former *escudo*. In March 1990, £1 = 1,458 *meticais*; US$1 = 889 *meticais*.

Banking. Most banks had been nationalized by 1979. The *Banco de Moçambique* (bank of issue) and the *Banco Popular de Desenvolvimento* (state investment bank) each have a capital of 1,000m. meticais.

Weights and Measures. The metric system is in force.

ENERGY AND NATURAL RESOURCES

Electricity. Production (1986) 1,640m. kwh. Capacity (1986) 2,225,000 kw. Supply 220 volts; 50 Hz. The hydro-electric dam at Cabora Bassa on the Zambezi is the largest producer in Africa.

Minerals. Coal is the main mineral being exploited. Output was 380,000 tonnes in 1983. Coal reserves (estimate) 400m. tonnes. Small quantities of bauxite, gold, titanium, fluorite and colombo-tantalite are produced. Iron ore deposits and natural gas are known to exist.

Agriculture. Production in tonnes (1988): Cereals, 530,000; tea, 5,000; maize,

334,000; bananas, 82,000; sisal, 3,000; rice, 55,000; groundnuts, 65,000; copra, 69,000; vegetables, 198,000; citrus, 42,000; potatoes, 65,000; cashews, 30,000; sunflower seed, 20,000; cotton (lint), 32,000; sugar, 50,000.

Livestock 1988: 1·36m. cattle, 375,000 goats, 119,000 sheep, 160,000 pigs, 20,000 asses.

Forestry. Forests covered (1988) 19% of land area. Production (1985) 35,000 cu. metres of cut timber.

Fisheries. In 1984 the prawn catch was 5,800 tonnes; other fish (1986) 31,900 tonnes.

INDUSTRY AND TRADE

Industry. Although the country is overwhelmingly rural, there is some substantial industry in and around Maputo (steel, engineering, textiles, processing, docks and railways).

Commerce. Imports in 1987 totalled US$645m. and exports US$96m. In 1986 12% of imports came from the USSR, 12% from the Republic of South Africa and 12% from the USA. 21% of exports were to Spain, 22% to the USA and 23% to Japan. Shrimps made up 48% of exports; cashews, 12%; sugar, 10%; copra, 3% and petroleum products, 5%.

Total trade between Mozambique and UK (British Department of Trade returns, in £1,000 sterling):

	1985	*1986*	*1987*	*1988*	*1989*
Imports to UK	6,908	1,335	6,580	5,574	14,582
Exports and re-exports from UK	11,343	13,175	21,168	24,218	20,268

COMMUNICATIONS

Roads. There were, in 1984, 20,000 km of roads, of which 5,000 km were tarred. Motor vehicles, in 1980, included 99,400 passenger cars and 24,700 lorries and buses. The Government is devoting effort to constructing a new North/South road link, and to improving provincial rural feeder road systems.

Railways. The Mozambique State Railways consist of 5 independent networks known as the Maputo, Mozambique, Sofala (Beira), Inhambane and Gaza, and Quelimane systems. The Maputo system has a link at Komatipoort with the Republic of South Africa, Swaziland and Zimbabwe railways; the Sofala system links with Zimbabwe at Machipanda (near Umtali); and the Mozambique system links with Malaŵi at Entre Lagos. Total route-km (1986), 2,988 km (1,067 mm gauge), and 143 km (762 mm gauge). In 1986, 6·8m. passengers and 301m. tonne-km of goods were carried.

Aviation. There are international airports at Maputo, Beira and Nampula with regular services to European and Southern African destination by several foreign airlines and by *Linhas Aéreas de Moçambique*, who also serve 13 domestic airports.

Shipping. The total tonnage handled by Mozambique ports (1987) was 2·7m. The principal ports are Maputo, Beira, Nacala and Quelimane.

Post and Broadcasting. Maputo is connected by telegraph with the Transvaal system. Quelimane has telegraphic communication with Chiromo. Number of telephones (1983), 59,000.

Radio Moçambique broadcasts 5 programmes in Portuguese, English and Tsonga as well as 4 regional programmes in 8 languages. Number of receivers (1986): Radio, 500,000; TV 02, 20,000.

Newspapers. There were (1984) 2 daily newspapers in Mozambique: *Noticias,* published in Maputo (circulation, 45,000), and *Diario de Mozambique* in Beira (15,000).

JUSTICE, RELIGION, EDUCATION AND WELFARE

Justice. A system of People's Courts exists at all levels.

Religion. About 60% of the population follow traditional animist religions, while some 18% are Christian (mainly Roman Catholic) and 16% Moslem.

Education. In 1987 there were 1,370,528 pupils in 4,105 primary schools and (1986) 144,015 in 171 secondary schools. The *Universidade Eduardo Mondlane* had 2,500 students in 1985. Literacy rate (1986) 30%.

Health. There were (1987) 1,156 hospitals and medical centres with 11,671 beds; there were 327 doctors, 1,112 midwives and 2,871 nursing personnel. In 1987 there were 138 dentists and 301 pharmacists.

DIPLOMATIC REPRESENTATIVES

Of Mozambique in Great Britain (21 Fitzroy Sq., London W1P 5HJ)
Ambassador: Armado Alexandre Panguene.

Of Great Britain in Mozambique (Ave. Vladimir 1 Lenine 310, Maputo)
Ambassador: Maeve G. Fort, CMG.

Of Mozambique in the USA (1990 M. St., NW, Washington, D.C., 20036)
Ambassador: Valeriano Ferrao.

Of the USA in Mozambique (Ave Kaunda 193, Maputo)
Ambassador: Melissa F. Wells.

Of Mozambique to the United Nations
Ambassador: Pedro Comissario Afonso.

Further Reading

Darch, C., *Mozambique.* [Bibliography] Oxford and Santa Barbara, 1987
Hanlon, J., *Mozambique: The Revolution under Fire.* London, 1984
Henriksen, T. H., *Mozambique: A History.* London and Cape Town, 1978
Houser, G. and Shore, H., *Mozambique: Dream the Size of Freedom.* New York, 1975
Isaacman, A., *A Luta Continua: Building a New Society in Mozambique.* New York, 1978.
—*Mozambique: From Colonization to Revolution, 1900–1982.* Aldershot and Boulder, 1984
Mondlane, E., *The Struggle for Mozambique.* London, 1983
Munslow, B., *Mozambique: The Revolution and its Origins.* London and New York, 1983

NAMIBIA

Capital: Windhoek
Population: 1·29m. (1988)
GNP per capita: US$1,020 (1986)

Suidwes-Afrika—South West Africa

HISTORY. Britain annexed Walvis Bay in 1878, and incorporated it in the Cape of Good Hope in 1884. In 1884 South West Africa was declared a German protectorate. In 1915 the Union of South Africa occupied German South West Africa at the request of the Allied powers. On 17 Dec. 1920 the League of Nations entrusted South West Africa as a Mandate to the Union of South Africa, to be administered under the laws of the mandatory power. After World War II South Africa refused to place the territory under the UN Trusteeship system, and formally applied for its annexation to the Union. On 18 July 1966 the International Court of Justice decided that Ethiopia and Liberia had no legal right in applying for a decision on the international status of South West Africa, but in Oct. 1966 the General Assembly of the UN terminated South Africa's mandate, and established a UN Council for South West Africa in May 1967. However, South Africa continued to administer the territory, in defiance of various UN resolutions. It speeded up the implementation of the Odendaal Plan (1964), which required massive development aid and the formation of enlarged homelands for the various ethnic groups. In June 1968 the UN changed the name of the territory to Namibia. In 1971 the International Court of Justice ruled in an advisory opinion that South Africa's presence in Namibia was illegal. In Dec. 1973 the UN appointed a UN Commissioner for Namibia.

After negotiations between South Africa and the UN, a multi-racial Advisory Council was appointed in 1973. Representatives of all the population groups assembled in the Turnhalle in Windhoek for the Constitutional Conference, which on 17 Aug. 1976 decided that a multi-racial interim government was to be formed by early 1977, and that the country should become independent by 31 Dec. 1978. This interim government was rejected by the Western Five, (USA, Britain, Federal Republic of Germany, France and Canada), after which South Africa agreed to universal suffrage elections. An Administrator-General was appointed in Sept. 1977 to govern the territory until independence, and he moved to abolish all laws based on racial discrimination – a precondition for elections. In April 1978 South Africa accepted a plan for UN-supervised elections leading to independence, which was endorsed in UN Security Council Resolution 435 of 27 July 1978. After the final plans for the UN-supervised elections were published, South Africa announced on 20 Sept. 1978 that it was going ahead with internally sponsored elections for a Constitutent Assembly. In the elections held on 4-8 Dec. 1978 the Democratic Turnhalle Alliance (DTA) gained 41 of the 50 seats in a percentage poll of 82%, in spite of the fact that the South West Africa People's Organisation (SWAPO) instructed its members not to take part in the elections.

A 12-member Ministers' Council was instituted, and in Sept. 1981 it was enlarged to 15 members and given executive authority on all matters except constitutional issues, security and foreign affairs. On 11-13 Nov. 1980 elections were held for the second-tier Representative Authorities, which each control certain administrative functions for a specific ethnic group, but no specific geographical area. In Jan. 1983 the Ministers' Council and the National Assembly were dissolved and executive and legislative powers reverted to the Administrator-General.

On 13 Sept. 1983 the Multi-Party Conference (MPC) was formed. In May 1984 talks were held in Lusaka between the MPC and SWAPO, which were followed in July 1984 by talks between the Administrator-General and SWAPO. SWAPO was again invited to take part in constitutional talks with the MPC, but again refused. The MPC then petitioned the Republic of South Africa for a form of self-government for Namibia, and on 17 June 1985 the Transitional Government of

National Unity was installed. Negotiations began again in May and July 1988 between Angola, Cuba and the Republic of South Africa. A peaceful settlement was agreed and the Geneva Protocol was signed on 5 Aug. 1988. In Dec. it was agreed that Cuban troops should withdraw from Angola and South African troops from Namibia by 1 April 1989. The Transitional Government of National Unity resigned on 28 Feb. 1988 to make provision for the implementation of UN Security Council Resolution 435. The UN Transition Group (UNTAG) was established in Namibia to supervise elections for the constituent assembly in Nov. 1989. Independence was achieved on 21 March 1990.

AREA AND POPULATION. The total area of the Territory, including the Caprivi-Zipfel, is 318,261 sq. miles (824,269 sq. km); this figure includes that of the enclave of Walvis Bay, administered by the Republic of South Africa, 434 sq. miles (1,124 sq. km).

The country is bounded on the north by Angola and Zambia, on the west by the Atlantic ocean, on the south and south-east by South Africa and on the east by Botswana. The Caprivi Strip, about 300 km long, extends eastwards up to the Zambezi river, projecting into Zambia and Botswana and touching Zimbabwe. The rainfall increases steadily from less than 50 mm. in the west and south-west up to 600 mm. in the Caprivi Strip.

The Kunene River and the Okavango, which form portions of the northern border of the country, the Zambesi, which forms the eastern boundary of the Caprivi-Zipfel, the Kwando or Mashi, which flows through the Caprivi-Zipfel from the north between the Okavango and the Zambesi, and the Orange River in the south, are the only permanently running streams. But there is a system of great, sandy, dry river-beds throughout the country, in which water can generally be obtained by sinking shallow wells. In the Grootfontein area there are large supplies of underground water, but except for a few springs, mostly hot, there is no surface water in the country.

The population at the censuses in 1970 and 1981 and estimates 1988, were:

	1970	*1981*	*1988*
Ovambos	342,455	506,114	641,000
Whites	90,658	76,430	82,000
Damaras	64,973	76,179	97,000
Hereros	55,670	76,296	97,000
Namas	32,853	48,541	62,000
Kavangos	49,577	95,055	120,000
Caprivians	25,009	38,594	48,000
Coloureds	28,275	42,254	52,000
Basters	16,474	25,181	32,000
Bushmen	21,909	29,443	37,000
Tswanas	4,407	6,706	8,000
Other	. . .	12,403	12,000
	732,260	1,033,196	1,288,000

The capital is Windhoek (population 114,500, estimate 1988). Other large towns: Swakopmund, 15,500; Rehoboth, 15,000; Rundu, 15,000; Keetmanshoop, 14,000; Tsumeb, 13,500; Otjiwarongo, 11,000; Grootfontein, 9,000; Okahandja, 8,000; Mariental, 6,500; Gobabis, 6,500; Khorixas, 6,500; Lüderitz, 6,000. (Others all have populations under 5,000).

English and Afrikaans are the official languages.

ADMINISTRATION AND GOVERNMENT. For history of the administration from 1949–1985 *see* THE STATESMAN'S YEAR-BOOK 1986–87 p. 1087. Legislative authority is the National Assembly in Windhoek consisting of 62 members nominated by the six political groups represented in the Transitional Government of National Unity; 22 members for the Democratic Turnhalle Alliance, which consists of 11 parties, and 8 members for each of the other parties. Certain administrative functions for nine of the ethnic groups are controlled by second-tier Representative Authorities first elected in 1980. These are the administrations for

Ovambos, Namas, Damaras, Kavangos, Hereros, Whites, Basters, Coloureds and Tswanas. In the case of the Bushmen and Caprivians, these functions are handled by a commissioner and advisory council.

At the elections 7–11 Nov. 1989 voting was for the 72 seats in the Constituent Assembly. South West Africa People's Organization (SWAPO) won 41 seats; Democratic Turnhalle Alliance (DTA) 21; United Democratic Front, 4; Action Christian Nation (ACN) 3; Namibia Patriotic Front (NPF) 1; Federal Convention of Namibia (FCN) 1; Namibia National Front (NNF) 1. Swapo-Democrats (SWAPO-D), Christian Democratic Action (CDA) and Namibia National Democratic Party (NNDP) won no seats.

On 9 Feb 1990 with a unanimous vote the Constituent Assembly approved the Constitution which stipulated a multi-party republic, an independent judiciary and an executive President who may serve a maximum of 2 5-year terms. On 21 March 1990 Namibia achieved independence and became a member of the Commonwealth.

President: Sam Nujoma.

Prime Minister: Hage Geingob. *Foreign Affairs:* Theo-Ben Gurirab. *Finance:* Otto Herrigel.

ECONOMY

Budget. In 1988-89 revenue and expenditure balanced at R1945·4m. Expenditure 1989-89, R2238·9m.

Currency. The monetary unit is the South African *Rand.* In March 1990, £1 = R4·24; US$1 = R2·59.

Banking. The South African Reserve Bank branch in Windhoek performs the functions of a central bank. Commercial banks represented in the Territory include First National Bank, Boland Bank, Nedbank, Standard Bank, Bank of South West Africa/Namibia and Bank of Windhoek Ltd (the only locally-owned bank). There is a Land and Agricultural Bank in Windhoek.

A Post Office Savings Bank was established in 1916. The number of accounts opened in 1985–86 was 3,398. The balance due to holders as at 31 March 1986 amounted to R2,983,790.

ENERGY AND NATURAL RESOURCES

Electricity. Production (1986) 692m. kwh.

Water. The 12 most important dams have a total capacity of 589·2m. cu. metres.

Minerals. Diamonds of 1,009,520 carats were recovered in 1986 from open cast mines north of the Orange river. A new open-cast diamond mining area will start production here in 1990, with another to be developed near Elizabeth Bay, south of Lüderitz. The largest open groove uranium mine in the world started operations near Swakopmund in 1976. The mine has a production capacity of 5,000 short tons of uranium oxide concentrate per year and an estimated average of 60m. tons of ore has been processed annually since 1979. Total value of mineral exports, 1988, R1,542·6m.; diamonds, R653·5m.

Agriculture. Namibia is essentially a stock-raising country, the scarcity of water and poor rainfall rendering crop-farming, except in the northern and north-eastern parts, almost impossible. Generally speaking, the southern half is suited for the raising of small stock, while the central and northern parts are more suited for cattle. In 1986 there were 314 registered hunting farms, 25 guest farms and 20 safari farms. Guano is harvested from the coast, converted into fertilizer in the Republic of South Africa and most of it exported to Europe. In 1986, 16% of the active labour force worked in the agricultural sector, while 70% of the population was directly or indirectly dependent on agriculture for their living.

Livestock (1988): 2·05m. cattle, 6·4m. sheep, 2·5m. goats. In 1987, 246,163 head of cattle, 102,037 beef carcasses and 786,611 head of small stock were exported, and 770,627 karakul pelts were produced.

In 1988, 70,000 tonnes of cows' milk and 70,000 tonnes of cheese were produced. Principal crops (1988 in tonnes): Wheat, 1,000; maize, 48,000; sunflower seed (1987), 525, sorghum; 7,000; vegetables, 28,000.

Forestry. Forests cover 18m. hectares (22% of the land area).

Fisheries. Value of catches, 1988-89: Pelagic fish, R182·7m.; crayfish, R53,298,968.

INDUSTRY AND TRADE

Industry. Of the estimated total of 350 undertakings (66% of which are in Windhoek), the most important are meat processing, the supply of specialized equipment to the mining industry, the assembly of goods from predominantly imported materials and the manufacture of metal products and construction material. Small industries, including home industries, textile mills, leather and steel goods, have expanded. Products manufactured locally include chocolates, beer, leather shoes and delicatessen meats and game meat products.

Labour. In 1988 there were 184,983 economically active persons, 67·2% male. The estimated unemployment rate was 20%. The main employers were government services, agriculture and mining.

Commerce. Total imports, R1,712,900 and exports R1,809,800 in 1987.

The bulk of the direct imports into the country is landed at Walvis Bay which handles 750,000 tons of cargo a year.

Total trade between Namibia and UK (British Department of Trade returns, in £1,000 sterling):

	1985	*1986*	*1987*	*1988*	*1989*
Imports to UK	21,920	6,826	7,681	10,729	4,568
Exports and re-exports from UK	4,084	2,915	3,909	3,259	4,264

COMMUNICATIONS

Roads. In 1988 the total national road network was 41,762 km, including 4,500 km of tarred roads. In 1986 there were 103,715 registered motor vehicles.

Railways. The Namibia system connects with the main system of the South African Railways at De Aar. The total length of the line inside Namibia is 2,383 km of 1,065 mm gauge in 1989. In 1988 railways carried 300,000 passengers and 2·4m. tonnes of freight.

Aviation. In 1987–88 the Territory's 2 major airports handled about 190,217 passengers and 2·2m. kg of freight on international flights and 10,000 passengers and 88,000 kg of freight on internal flights.

Shipping. In 1985 Walvis Bay harbour handled 764 vessels and Luderitz, 152 vessels.

Post and Broadcasting. In 1987 there were 71 post offices and 16 postal agencies, and 1,070 private bag services distributed by rail or road transport.

There were (1987) 69,273 telephones. There were 1,012 telex users.

In 1987, 57,683 radio licences and 28,500 television licences were issued.

Newspapers (1989). There are 5 daily and 6 weekly newspapers.

JUSTICE, RELIGION, EDUCATION AND WELFARE

Justice. Namibia is divided into 24 magisterial districts (with the exception of Rehoboth). There are magistrate's courts and offices in all the districts and resident magistrates in Windhoek and 10 other centres.

Religion. About 90% of the population is Christian.

Education (1988). In 1989–90, R143·6m. was spent on education. There were 1,153 schools for all races, 374,269 pupils and 12,525 teachers. This included 1,118 primary and senior secondary schools, 3 centres for the handicapped, 1 technical school and 2 agricultural schools, 3 technical institutes and 3 agricultural colleges. There were 4 teachers' training colleges and an academy.

Health (1988). There were 68 hospitals and 171 clinics. The ratio of beds per population was 5·5 per 1,000. There were 270 general practitioners, 30 specialists and 40 dentists. Nursing staff numbered 4,350.

Further Reading

Namibia Information Services, *Namibia: The Economy*. Windhoek, 1987
Human Rights and Namibia. London, 1986
Herbstein, D. and Evenston, J., *The Devils are Among Us: The War for Namibia*. London, 1989
Katjavivi, P.H., *A History of Resistance in Namibia*. London, 1988
Rotberg, R. I., *Namibia: Political and Economic Prospects*. Lexington, 1983
Schoeman, E. R. and H. S., *Namibia*. [Bibliography] Oxford and Santa Barbara, 1984
Soggot, D., *Namibia: The Violent Heritage*. New York, 1986
Thomas, W. H., *Economic Development in Namibia*. Munich, 1978
van der Merwe, J. H., *National Atlas of South West Africa*. Windhoek, 1983

NAURU

Population: 8,100 (1983)
GNP per capita: US$9,091 (1985)

HISTORY. The island was discovered by Capt. Fearn in 1798, annexed by Germany in Oct. 1888, and surrendered to the Australian forces in 1914. It was administered under a mandate, effective from 17 Dec. 1920, conferred on the British Empire and approved by the League of Nations until 1 Nov. 1947, when the United Nations General Assembly approved a trusteeship agreement with the governments of Australia, New Zealand and UK as joint administering authority. Independence was gained in 1968.

AREA AND POPULATION. The island is situated 0° 32' S. lat. and 166° 56' E. long. Area, 5,263 acres (2,130 hectares). It is an oval-shaped upheaval coral island of approximately 12 miles in circumference, surrounded by a reef which is exposed at low tide. There is no deep water harbour but offshore moorings, reputedly the deepest in the world, are capable of holding medium-sized vessels, including 30,000 tonne capacity bulk carriers. On the seaward side the reef dips abruptly into the deep waters of the Pacific at an angle of 45°. On the landward side of the reef there is a sandy beach interspersed with coral pinnacles. From the sandy beach the ground rises gradually, forming a fertile section ranging in width from 150 to 300 yd and completely encircling the island. There is an extensive plateau bearing phosphate of a high grade, the mining rights of which were vested in the British Phosphate Commissioners until 1 July 1970, subject to the rights of the Nauruan landowners. In July 1970 the Nauru Phosphate Corporation assumed control and management of the enterprise. It is chiefly on the fertile section of land between the sandy beach and the plateau that the Nauruans have established themselves. With the exception of a small fringe round a shallow lagoon, about 1 mile inland, the plateau, which contains the phosphate deposits, has few foodbearing trees and is not settled by the Nauruans.

At the census held on 13 May 1983 the population totalled 8,100, of whom 5,285 were Nauruans.

Vital statistics, 1982: Births, 286 (224 Nauruan); deaths, 77 (42 Nauruan).

CLIMATE. A tropical climate, tempered by sea breezes, but with a high and irregular rainfall, averaging 82" (2,060 mm). Jan. 81°F (27·2°C), July 82°F (27·8°C). Annual rainfall 75" (1,862 mm).

CONSTITUTION AND GOVERNMENT. A Legislative Council was established by the Nauru Act, passed by the Australian Parliament in Dec. 1965 and was inaugurated on 31 Jan. 1966. The trusteeship agreement terminated on 31 Jan. 1968, on which day Nauru became an independent republic but having special relationship with the Commonwealth. An 18-member Parliament is elected on a 3-yearly basis.

President and Minister for Foreign Affairs: Kenas Aroi.

National flag: Blue with a narrow horizontal gold stripe across the centre, beneath this near the hoist a white star of 12 points.

FINANCE. Revenue and expenditure (in $A) for financial year ending 30 June 1989 (estimate): revenue, 57,350,000; expenditure, 59,230,000 (health, 3,120,000; education, 3,500,000).

The interests in the phosphate deposits were purchased in 1919 from the Pacific Phosphate Company by the governments of the UK, the Commonwealth of Australia and New Zealand at a cost of £Stg3·5m., and a Board of Commissioners representing the 3 governments was appointed to manage and control the working of the deposits. In May 1967, in Canberra, the British Phosphate Corporation agreed to hand over the phosphate industry to Nauru and on 15 June 1967 agreement was reached that the Nauruans could buy the assets of the B.P.C. for approximately

$A20m. over 3 years. It is estimated that the deposits will be exhausted by 1993. Phosphate sales (1984–85) $A100m. In May 1989 Nauru filed a claim against Australia for environmental damage caused by the mining.

COMMERCE. The export trade consists almost entirely of phosphate shipped to Australia, New Zealand and Japan. The imports consist almost entirely of food supplies, building construction materials and machinery for the phosphate industry.

Total trade between Nauru and UK (British Department of Trade returns, in £1,000 sterling):

	1985	*1986*	*1987*	*1988*	*1989*
Imports to UK	479	148	674	642	662
Exports from UK	1,199	1,239	394	759	549

COMMUNICATIONS

Aviation. There is an airfield on the island capable of accepting medium size jet aircraft. Air Nauru, a wholly owned government subsidiary, operates services with Boeing 727 and 737 aircraft.

Shipping. The Nauru Local Government Council, through its agency the Nauru Pacific Shipping Line, owns 6 ships and 2 fishing boats. These ships ply between Australia, Pacific Islands, west coast of USA, New Zealand, Japan, Singapore etc. Other shipping coming to the island consists of those under charter to the phosphate industry.

Telecommunications. Number of telephones (1978) 1,500 and (1984) 5,500 radio receivers. Direct daily high frequency service is maintained with Tarawa and both long- and short-wave transmissions with merchant shipping. A separate tele-radio service exists between Nauru and Ocean Island.

Cinemas. In 1989 there were 3 cinemas with seating capacity of 500.

JUSTICE, RELIGION AND EDUCATION

Justice. The highest Court is the Supreme Court of Nauru. It is the Superior Court of record and has the jurisdiction to deal with constitutional matters in addition to its other jurisdiction. There is also a District Court which is presided over by the Resident Magistrate who is also the Chairman of the Family Court and the Registrar of Supreme Court. The laws applicable in Nauru are its own Acts of Parliament and a large number of British statutes and the common law have been adopted for Nauru.

Religion. The population is mainly Roman Catholic or Protestant.

Education. Attendance at school is compulsory for all children between the ages of 6 and 17. In June 1989 there were 10 infant and primary schools and 2 secondary schools. There were 165 teachers and 2,707 pupils in infant, primary and secondary schools. In addition, there is a trade school with 4 instructors and an enrolment of 88 trainees. Scholarships are available for Nauruan children to receive secondary and higher education and vocational training in Australia and New Zealand. In 1989, 99 Nauruans were receiving secondary and tertiary education abroad.

DIPLOMATIC REPRESENTATIVES

Of Great Britain in Nauru
High Commisioner: A. B. P. Smart (resides in Suva).

Of Nauru in the USA
Ambassador: T. W. Star (resides in Melbourne).

Further Reading

Packett, C. N., *Guide to the Republic of Nauru.* Bradford, 1970
Pittman, G. A., *Nauru, the Phosphate Island.* London, 1959
Viviani, N., *Phosphate and Political Progress.* Canberra, 1970

NEPÁL

Capital: Káthmándu
Population: 16·63m. (1985)
GNP per capita: US$170 (1988)

Nepal Adhirajya

HISTORY. From 1846 to 1951 Nepál was virtually ruled by theRáná family, a member of which always held the office of prime minister, the succession being determined by special rules. The last Ráná prime minister (and, until 18 Feb. 1951, Supreme C.-in-C.) was HH Máháràja Mohan Shumsher Jung Bahádur Ráná, who resigned in Nov. 1951.

AREA AND POPULATION. Nepál, is bounded on the north by Tibet, on the east by Sikkim and West Bengal, on the south and west by Bihar and Uttar Pradesh. There are 3 geographical regions: The fertile Tarai plain in the south; a central belt containing the Mahabharat Lekh and Churia Hills and the basins of the Inner Tarai; and the Himalayas in the north. Area 56,827 sq. miles (147,181 sq. km); population (estimate, 1985), 16,625,439; (census, 1981) 15,022,839 of whom 52·4% were Nepali-speaking and 18·5% Bihari-speaking.

Capital, Káthmándu, 75 miles from the Indian frontier; population (census 1981) 235,160. Other towns include Pátan (also called Lalitpur), 79,875; Moráng (Biratnagar), 93,544; Bhádgáon (Bhaktapur), 48,472.

The aboriginal stock is Mongolian with a considerable admixture of Hindu blood from India. They were originally divided into numerous hill clans and petty principalities, one of which, Gorkha or Gurkha, became predominant in 1559 and has since given its name to men from all parts of Nepál. The 15 feudal chieftainships were integrated into the kingdom on 10 April 1961.

CLIMATE. The rainfall is high, with maximum amounts from May to Sept., but conditions are very dry from Nov. to Jan. The range of temperature is moderate. Káthmándu. Jan. 50°F (10°C), July 76°F (24·4°C). Annual rainfall 57" (1,428 mm).

RULING KING. The sovereign is HM Mahárájádhirája **Birendra Bir Bikram Sháh Dev**, who succeeded his father Mahendra Bir Bikram Sháh Dev on 31 Jan. 1972.

CONSTITUTION AND GOVERNMENT. On 18 Feb. 1951 the King proclaimed a constitutional monarchy, and on 16 Dec. 1962 a new Constitution of the 'Constitutional Monarchical Hindu State'. The village and town *panchayat*, recognized as the basic units of democracy, elect the district *panchayat*, these elect the zonal *panchayat*, and these finally the 112 members of the national *panchayat*. The Constitution was amended in 1975 and 1980. In addition, 28 representatives of professional organizations and royal nominees not exceeding 15% of the elected members, will be included in the national *panchayat*. The executive power is vested in the King, who appoints a council of ministers from the national *panchayat*. A state council will advise the King and proclaim the successor or, if the heir is a minor, a regency council. Art. 81 empowers the King to declare a state of emergency and to suspend the Constitution. In April 1990 democratic rights were restored to the people following a long struggle which reached its climax in Feb. 1990 when 200 people died.

Prime Minister: Krishna Prasad Bhattarai.

National flag: Two triangular parts of red, with a blue border all round, bearing symbols of the moon and the sun in white.

National anthem: 'May glory crown our illustrious sovereign' (1952).

Local Government: The country is administratively divided into 14 zones (Bágmati, Bheri, Dhaulagiri, Gandaki, Janakpur, Karnali, Kosi, Lumbini,

Mahakali, Mechi, Nárâyani, Rápti, Sagarmatha and Seti) and thence into 75 districts and over 3,500 villages.

DEFENCE

Army. The Army consists of 1 Royal Guard, 7 infantry brigades, and single artillery, engineer, signals, parachute and transport battalions. Equipment includes 25 Ferrets. Strength of all services (1990) about 35,000, and there is also a 28,000-strong paramilitary police force.

Air Force. Independent of the army since 1979, the Air Force has 3 Skyvan transport aircraft, 1 Puma helicopter and 2 Chetak helicopters. An H.S. 748 turboprop transport and 1 Super Puma and 1 Puma helicopter are operated by the Royal Flight.

INTERNATIONAL RELATIONS

Membership. Nepál is a member of UN and the Colombo Plan.

ECONOMY

Budget. The general budget for the fiscal year 1987–88 envisaged current expenditure of NRs 4,307m. Domestic revenue were estimated at NRs 5,875m.

Currency. The Nepalese *rupee* is 171 grains in weight, as compared with the Indian rupee, which weighs 180 grains. The rate of exchange is 135 Nepalese rupees for 100 Indian rupees. 100 Nepalese *pice* = 1 Nepalese rupee. Coins of all denominations are minted. The Rástra Bank also issues notes of 1, 5, 10, 100 and 1,000 rupees. In March 1990, US$1 = 28·50 *rupees*; £1 = 46·70 *rupees*.

ENERGY AND NATURAL RESOURCES

Electricity. Production (1986) 395m. kwh. A hydro-electric power scheme on the Karnali river costing US$4,500m. was being planned in 1986.

Agriculture. Nepál has valuable forests in the southern part of the country. In the northern part, on the slopes of the Himálayas, there grow large quantities of medicinal herbs which find a world-wide market. Forests covered (1988) 2·3m. hectares, 17% of the land area; 5·4m. acres is covered by perpetual snow; 9·6m. acres is under paddy, 2·9m. maize and millet, 800,000 wheat. Production (1988 in 1,000 tonnes): Rice, 2,787; maize, 890; wheat, 745; sugar-cane, 816; potatoes, 566; millet, 160.

Livestock (1988); Cattle, 6,374,000, including about 675,000 cows; 2·9m. buffaloes; sheep, 833,000; goats, 5,125,000; pigs, 479,000; poultry, 10m.

Fisheries. Catch (1986) 9,400 tonnes.

INDUSTRY AND TRADE

Industry. Industries, such as jute- and sugar-mills, match, leather, cigarette, and shoe factories, and chemical works have been established, including two industrial estates at Pátan and Balaju. Production (1986 in 1,000 tonnes): Jute goods, 20·5; sugar, 18·5; cement, 10·4.

Commerce. The principal articles of export are food grains, jute, timber, oilseeds, ghee (clarified butter), potatoes, medicinal herbs, hides and skins, cattle. The chief imports are textiles, cigarettes, salt, petrol and kerosene, sugar, machinery, medicines, boots and shoes, paper, cement, iron and steel, tea.

Imports and exports in NRs 1,000:

	1985	*1986*	*1987*	*1988*
Imports	7,742,000	9,341,200	11,020,300	13,940,000
Exports	2,741,000	3,079,000	3,059,700	4,080,000

Total trade between Nepál and UK (British Department of Trade returns, in £1,000 sterling):

	1985	*1986*	*1987*	*1988*	*1989*
Imports to UK	9,347	5,966	8,331	9,384	8,306
Exports and re-exports from UK	7,835	4,672	8,707	4,968	7,802

Tourism. There were 248,000 tourists in 1987.

COMMUNICATIONS

Roads. With the co-operation of India and the USA 900 miles of motorable roads are being constructed, including the East-West Highway through southern Nepál. A road from the Tibetan border to Káthmándu was recently completed with Chinese aid. There are about 1,300 miles motorable roads. A ropeway for the carriage of goods covers the 14 miles from Dhursing above Bhimphedi into the Káthmándu valley. A road connects Káthmándu with Birgung.

Railways. Railways (762 mm gauge) connect Jayanagar on the North Eastern Indian Railway with Janakpur and thence with Bizalpura (54 km).

Aviation. The Royal Nepál Airline Corporation has linked Káthmándu, the capital, with 11 districts of Nepál; and in 1984, 30 airfields were in regular use. The airline carried 424,000 passengers and 2,900 tonnes of freight in 1983–84. The Royal Nepalese Airline Corporation has services between Káthmándu and Calcutta, Patna, New Delhi, Bangkok, Rangoon and Dacca, employing Boeing 727 jet aircraft.

Post and Broadcasting. Káthmándu is connected by telephone with Birganj and Raxaul (North Eastern Indian Railway) on the southern frontier with Bihar; and with the eastern part of the Terai foothills; an extension to the western districts is being completed. Number of telephones (1980) 11,800. Under an agreement with India and the USA, a network of 91 wireless stations exists in Nepál, with further stations in Calcutta and New Delhi. Radio Nepál at Káthmándu broadcasts in Nepáli and English. In 1986 there were 2m. radio receivers and 27,000 television receivers.

Newspapers. In 1987 there were 58 daily newspapers.

JUSTICE, RELIGION, EDUCATION AND WELFARE

Justice. The Supreme Court Act, established a uniform judicial system, culminating in a supreme court of a Chief Justice and no more than 6 judges. Special courts to deal with minor offences may be established at the discretion of the Government.

Religion. Hinduism is the religion of 90% of the people. Buddhists comprise 5% and Moslems 3%. Christian missions are permitted, but conversion is forbidden.

Education. In 1985 there were 1,818,668 primary school pupils, 501,063 secondary school pupils and in 1984, 55,555 students at the Tribhuvan University (founded 1960).

In 1981, 23% of the population were literate.

Health. There were about 420 doctors and 2,586 hospital beds in 1979.

DIPLOMATIC REPRESENTATIVES

Of Nepál in Great Britain (12a Kensington Palace Gdns., London, W8 4QU)
Ambassador: Maj.-Gen. Bharat Kesher Simha (accredited 14 July 1988).

Of Great Britain in Nepál (Láincháur, Káthmándu)
Ambassador: R. E. G. Burges Watson, CMG.

Of Nepál in the USA (2131 Leroy Pl., NW, Washington, D.C., 20008)
Ambassador: Mohan Man Sainju.

Of the USA in Nepál (Pani Pokhari, Káthmándu)
Ambassador: Julia Chang Bloch.

Of Nepál to the United Nations
Ambassador: Jai Pratap Rana.

Further Reading

Statistical Information: A Department of Statistics was set up in Káthmándu in 1950.

Baral, L. S., *Political Development in Nepal.* London, 1980
Bezruchka, S., *A Guide to Trekking in Nepal.* Leicester, 1981
Turner, R. L., *Nepali Dictionary.* 1980.
Wadhwa, D. N., *Nepal.* [Bibliography] Oxford and Santa Barbara, 1986

THE NETHERLANDS

Capital: Amsterdam
Seat of Government: The Hague
Population: 14·8m. (1989)
GNP per capita: US$14,530 (1988)

Koninkrijk der Nederlanden

HISTORY. William of Orange (1533–84), as the German count of Nassau, inherited vast possessions in the Netherlands and the Princedom of Orange in France. He was the initiator of the struggle for independence from Spain (1568–1648); in the Republic of the United Netherlands he and his successors became the 'first servants of the Republic' with the title of 'Stadhouder' (governor). In 1689 William III acceded to the throne of England, becoming joint sovereign with Mary II, his wife. William III died in 1702 without issue, and after a stadhouderless period a member of the Frisian branch of Orange–Nassau was nominated hereditary stadhouder in 1747; but his successor, Willem V, had to take refuge in England, in 1795, at the invasion of the French Army. In Nov. 1813 the United Provinces were freed from French domination.

The Congress of Vienna joined the Belgian provinces, the 'Austrian Netherlands' before the French Revolution, to the Northern Netherlands. The son of the former stadhouder Willem V was proclaimed King of the Netherlands at The Hague on 16 March 1815 as Willem I. The union was dissolved by the Belgian revolution of 1830, and the treaty of London, 19 April 1839, constituted Belgium an independent kingdom.

Netherlands Sovereigns

Willem I	1815–1840 (died 1843)	Wilhelmina	1890–1948 (died 1962)
Willem II	1840–1849	Juliana	1948–1980
Willem III	1849–1890	Beatrix	1980–

AREA AND POPULATION. The Netherlands is bounded north and west by the North Sea, south by Belgium and east by the Federal Republic of Germany.

The total area of the Netherlands is 41,863 sq. km (16,163 sq. miles), of which 33,934 sq. km (13,102 sq. miles) is land area.

On 14 June 1918 a law was passed concerning the reclamation of the Zuiderzee. The work was begun in 1920; the following sections have been completed: 1. The Noordholland–Wieringen Barrage (2·5 km), 1924; 2. The Wieringermeer Polder (210 sq. km), 1930 (inundated by the Germans in 1945, but drained again in the same year); 3. The Wieringen–Friesland Barrage (30 km), 1932; 4. The Noordoost Polder (501 sq. km), 1942; 5. Oost Flevoland (604 sq. km), 1957; 6. Zuidelijk Flevoland (499 sq. km), 1967.

The reclamation of the Markerwaard is still a subject of political discussion. A portion of what used to be the Zuiderzee behind the barrage will remain a freshwater lake: Ijsselmeer (1,400 sq. km). The 'Delta-project', completed in 1986, comprises (semi) enclosure dams in the estuaries between the islands in the southwestern part of the country, excluding the sea-entrances to the ports of Rotterdam and Antwerp. *See* map in THE STATESMAN'S YEAR-BOOK, 1959.

Growth of census population:

1829	2,613,298	1909	5,858,175	1960	11,461,964
1849	3,056,879	1920	6,865,314	1971	13,060,115
1869	3,579,529	1930	7,935,565		
1889	4,511,415	1947	9,625,499		

Area, density and estimated population on 1 Jan. 1977 and 1989:

Province	Land area (in sq. km) 1989	Population 1977	Population 1989	Density per sq. km 1989
Groningen	2,345·79	544,264	555,200	237
Friesland	3,359·00	566,042	599,190	178
Drenthe	2,655·46	409,874	439,066	165
Overijssel	3,339·65	948,009	1,014,949	304
Flevoland [1]	1,411·50	85,619	202,678	144
Gelderland	5,014·76	1,653,516	1,794,678	358
Utrecht	1,363·37	873,753	1,004,632	737
Noord-Holland	2,662·79	2,299,410	2,365,160	889
Zuid-Holland	2,876·62	3,049,570	3,200,408	1,113
Zeeland	1,792·57	335,624	355,585	198
Noord-Brabant	4,942·55	1,991,176	2,172,604	440
Limburg	2,169·16	1,055,619	1,099,622	507
Central Population Register [2]	—	1,468	1,468	—
Total	33,933·22	13,814,495	14,805,240	436

[1] The new province Flevoland, former Ijsselmeerpolders, established on 1 Jan. 1986. The Noordoostpolder (drained in 1942) and the Zuidelijke Ijsselmeerpolders (drained in 1957) are parts of the former Zuiderzee, now called Ijsselmeer.

[2] The Central Population Register includes persons who are residents of the Netherlands but who have no fixed residence in any particular municipality (living in caravans and houseboats, population on inland vessels, etc.).

Of the total population on 1 Jan. 1989, 7,316,590 were males, 7,488,650 females.

Vital statistics for calendar years:

	Live births Total	Live births Illegitimate	Still births	Marriages	Divorces	Deaths	Net migration
1984	174,436	13,445	1,036	81,655	34,068	119,812	+ 8,053
1985	178,136	14,766	1,054	82,747	34,044	122,704	+ 24,147
1986	184,513	16,220	1,060	87,337	29,836	125,307	+ 32,669
1987	186,667	17,385	1,036	87,400	27,788	122,199	+ 43,924
1988	186,647	18,951	1,038	87,843	27,870	124,163	+ 35,102

Population of principal municipalities on 31 Dec. 1988:

Aalsmeer	21,954
Achtkarspelen	27,479
Alkmaar	88,571
Almelo	62,008
Almere	63,785
Alphen a/d Rijn	59,586
Amersfoort	96,072
Amstelveen	69,505
Amsterdam	694,888
Apeldoorn	147,270
Arnhem	128,946
Assen	49,398
Baarn	24,897
Barneveld	41,649
Bergen op Zoom	46,842
Best	21,857
Beuningen	21,617
Beverwijk	35,126
De Bilt	31,729
Borne	21,261
Borsele	20,144
Boxtel	24,951
Breda	121,362
Brummen	20,802
Brunssum	29,799
Bussum	31,988
Capelle a/d Ijssel	57,423
Castricum	22,433
Culemborg	21,116
Delft	88,135
Delfzijl	23,472
Deurne	29,308
Deventer	66,398
Doetinchem	41,260
Dongen	21,124
Dongeradeel	24,572
Dordrecht	108,519
Dronten	24,281
Edam-Volendam	24,572
Ede	92,293
Eindhoven	190,736
Elburg	20,537
Emmen	92,422
Enschede	145,223
Epe	33,872
Ermelo	25,644
Etten-Leur	32,010
Franekeradeel	20,931
Geldermalsen	22,017
Geldrop	25,817
Geleen	33,756
Gendringen	20,186
Gilze en Rijen	22,577
Goes	31,815
Gorinchem	28,222
Gouda	63,232
's-Gravenhage	443,845
Groningen	167,779
Haaksbergen	22,690
Haarlem	149,198
Haarlemmermeer	93,427
Hardenberg	32,065
Harderwijk	34,600
Heemskerk	32,910
Heemstede	26,308
Heerenveen	37,700
Heerhugowaard	35,522
Heerlen	94,149
Heiloo	20,467
Den Helder	62,094
Hellendoorn	34,287
Hellevoetsluis	34,276
Helmond	66,791
Hengelo (O.)	76,175
's-Hertogenbosch	90,584
Hillegom	20,001
Hilversum	84,983
Hoogeveen	45,601
Hoogezand-Sappemeer	34,618
Hoorn	56,474
Houten	23,644
Huizen	41,823
Kampen	32,769
Katwijk	39,441
Kerkrade	52,994
Krimpen a/d Ijssel	27,638
Landgraaf	40,131
Leeuwarden	85,296
Leiden	109,254
Leiderdorp	22,303
Leidschendam	32,628

Lelystad	58,125	Rheden	46,088	Veendam	28,234
Leusden	27,302	Ridderkerk	46,163	Veenendaal	47,258
Lisse	20,826	Rijssen	23,927	Veghel	25,701
Loon op Zand	21,372	Rijswijk	48,189	Veldhoven	38,644
Losser	22,526	Roermond	38,486	Velsen	57,608
Maarssen	37,629	Roosendaal en Nispen	59,237	Venlo	63,607
Maassluis	33,155			Venray	34,172
Maastricht	116,380	Rosmalen	27,040	Vlaardingen	74,480
Meerssen	20,462	Rotterdam	576,232	Vlissingen	44,022
Meppel	23,452	Rucphen	21,085	Voorburg	40,455
Middelburg	39,462	Schiedam	69,438	Voorschoten	22,267
Naaldwijk	27,683	Schijndel	21,397	Voorst	23,678
Nieuwegein	58,330	Sittard	44,894	Vught	23,718
Nijkerk	25,613	Skarsterlân	23,809	Waalwijk	28,674
Nijmegen	145,405	Sliedrecht	22,833	Waddinxveen	24,652
Noordoostpolder	37,829	Smallingerland	50,434	Wageningen	32,370
Noordwijk	24,996	Sneek	29,408	Wassenaar	25,972
Nuenen c.a.	20,859	Soest	41,598	Weert	40,068
Nunspeet	24,573	Spijkenisse	65,208	Weststellingwerf	24,426
Oldebroek	21,353	Stadskanaal	33,047	Wierden	22,200
Oldenzaal	29,680	Steenwijk	20,907	Wijchen	33,606
Oosterhout	48,157	Stein	26,569	Winterswijk	28,024
Ooststellingwerf	24,837	Terneuzen	35,043	Woerden	28,139
Opsterland	26,433	Tiel	31,394	Zaanstad	129,653
Oss	50,987	Tilburg	155,110	Zeist	59,431
Oud-Bijerland	20,385	Tytsjerksteradiel	30,082	Zevenaar	26,848
Papendrecht	27,056	Uden	35,057	Zoetermeer	92,542
Purmerend	56,233	Uithoorn	22,205	Zutphen	31,144
Putten	20,898	Utrecht	230,634	Zwijndrecht	41,357
Raalte	26,883	Valkenswaard	29,811	Zwolle	92,517
Renkum	33,841				

Urban agglomerations as at 1 Jan. 1989: Rotterdam, 1,039,566; Amsterdam, 1,038,382; The Hague, 683,631; Utrecht, 525,989; Eindhoven, 381,788; Arnhem, 299,310; Heerlen-Kerkrade, 267,156; Enschede-Hengelo, 250,189; Nijmegen, 241,981; Tilburg, 227,050; Haarlem, 213,963; Groningen, 206,415; Dordrecht-Zwijndrecht, 204,429; 's-Hertogenbosch, 194,759; Leiden, 185,478; Geleen-Sittard, 178,842; Maastricht, 161,281; Breda, 157,331; Zaanstreek, 141,834; Velsen-Beverwijk, 125,644; Hilversum, 102,603.

CLIMATE. A cool temperate maritime climate, marked by mild winters and cool summers, but with occasional continental influences. Coastal temperatures vary from 37°F (3°C) in winter to 61°F (16°C) in summer, but inland the winters are slightly colder and the summers slightly warmer. Rainfall is least in the months Feb. to May, but inland there is a well-defined summer maximum in July and Aug.

The Hague. Jan. 37°F (2·7°C), July 61°F (16·3°C). Annual rainfall 32·8" (820 mm). Amsterdam. Jan. 36°F (2·3°C), July 62°F (16·5°C). Annual rainfall 34" (850 mm). Rotterdam. Jan. 36·5°F (2·6°C), July 62°F (16·6°C). Annual rainfall 32" (800 mm).

REIGNING QUEEN. Beatrix Wilhelmina Armgard, born 31 Jan. 1938 daughter of Queen Juliana and Prince Bernhard; married to Claus von Amsberg on 10 March 1966; succeeded to the crown on 1 May 1980, on the abdication of her mother. *Offspring:* Prince Willem-Alexander, born 27 April 1967; Prince Johan Friso, born 25 Sept. 1968; Prince Constantijn, born 11 Oct. 1969.

Mother of the Queen: Queen Juliana Louise Emma Marie Wilhelmina, born 30 April 1909, daughter of Queen Wilhelmina (born 31 Aug. 1880, died 28 Nov. 1962) and Prince Henry of Mecklenburg-Schwerin (born 19 April 1876, died 3 July 1934); married to Prince Bernhard Leopold Frederick Everhard Julius Coert Karel Godfried Pieter of Lippe-Biesterfeld (born 29 June 1911) on 7 Jan. 1937. Abdicated in favour of her daughter, the Reigning Queen, on 30 April 1980.

Sisters of the Queen: Princess Irene Emma Elisabeth, born 5 Aug. 1939, married to

Prince Charles Hugues de Bourbon-Parma on 29 April 1964, divorced 1981 (*sons:* Prince Carlos Javier Bernardo, born 27 Jan. 1970; Prince Jaime Bernardo, born 13 Oct. 1972; *daughters:* Princess Margarita Maria Beatriz, born 13 Oct. 1972; Princess Maria Carolina Christina, born 23 June 1974); Princess Margriet Francisca, born in Ottawa, 19 Jan. 1943, married to Pieter van Vollenhoven on 10 Jan. 1967 (*sons:* Prince Maurits, born 17 April 1968; Prince Bernhard, born 25 Dec. 1969; Prince Pieter-Christiaan, born 22 March 1972; Prince Floris, born 10 April 1975); Princess Maria Christina, born 18 Feb. 1947, married to Jorge Guillermo on 28 June 1975 (*sons:* Bernardo, born 17 June 1977; Nicolas Daniel Mauricio, born 6 July 1979; *daughter:* Juliana, born 8 Oct. 1981).

CONSTITUTION AND GOVERNMENT. According to the Constitution of the Kingdom of the Netherlands, the Kingdom consists of the Netherlands, Aruba and the Netherlands Antilles. Their relations are regulated by the 'Statute' for the Kingdom, which came into force on 29 Dec. 1954. Each part enjoys full autonomy; they are united, on a footing of equality, for mutual assistance and the protection of their common interests.

The first Constitution of the Netherlands after its restoration as a Sovereign State was promulgated in 1814. It was revised in 1815 (after the addition of the Belgian provinces, and the assumption by the Sovereign of the title of King), 1840 (after the secession of the Belgian provinces), 1848, 1884, 1887, 1917, 1922, 1938, 1946, 1948, 1953, 1956, 1963, 1972 and 1983.

The Netherlands is a constitutional and hereditary monarchy. The royal succession is in the direct male or female line in the order of primogeniture. The Sovereign comes of age on reaching his/her 18th year. During his/her minority the royal power is vested in a Regent—designated by law—and in some cases in the Council of State.

The central executive power of the State rests with the Crown, while the central legislative power is vested in the Crown and Parliament (the *Staten-Generaal*), consisting of 2 Chambers. After the 1956 revision of the Constitution the Upper or First Chamber is composed of 75 members, elected by the members of the Provincial States, and the Second Chamber consists of 150 deputies, who are elected directly from all Netherlands nationals who are aged 18 or over on polling day. Members of the States-General must be Netherlanders or recognized as Netherlands subjects and 21 years of age or over; they may be men or women. They receive an allowance.

First Chamber (as constituted in 1987): Labour Party, 26; Christian Democratic Appeal, 26; People's Party for Freedom and Democracy, 12; Democrats '66, 5; Party of Political Radicals, 1; Communist Party, 1; Pacifist Socialist Party, 1; Calvinist Party, 1; Reformed Political Federation, 1; Calvinist Political Union, 1.

Second Chamber (elected on 6 Sept. 1989): Christian Democratic Appeal, 54; Labour Party, 49; People's Party for Freedom and Democracy, 22; Democrats, 66, 12; Green Left, 6; Calvinist Party, 3; Reformed Political Federation, 1; Calvinist Political Union, 2; Centre Democrats, 1.

The revised Constitution of 1917 has introduced an electoral system based on universal suffrage and proportional representation. Under its provisions, members of the Second Chamber are directly elected by citizens of both sexes who are Netherlands subjects not under 18 years (since 1972).

The members of the First Chamber and of the Second Chamber are elected for 4 years, and retire in a body. The Sovereign has the power to dissolve both Chambers of Parliament, or one of them, subject to the condition that new elections take place within 40 days, and the new House or Houses be convoked within 3 months.

Both the Government and the Second Chamber may propose Bills; the First Chamber can only approve or reject them without inserting amendments. The meetings of both Chambers are public, though each of them may by a majority vote decide on a secret session. It is a fixed custom, that Ministers and Secretaries of State, on their own initiative or upon invitation of the Parliament, attend the sessions to defend their policy, their budget, their proposals of Bills, etc., when these are in discussion. A Minister or Secretary of State, however, cannot be a member of Parliament at the same time.

The Constitution can be revised only by a Bill declaring that there is reason for introducing such revision and containing the proposed alterations. The passing of this Bill is followed by a dissolution of both Chambers and a second confirmation by the new States-General by two-thirds of the votes. Unless it is expressly stated, all laws concern only the realm in Europe, and not the oversea part of the kingdom, the Netherlands Antilles.

Every act of the Sovereign has to be covered by a responsible Minister.

The Ministry, a coalition of Christian Democrats and Liberals, was composed as follows in Jan. 1990:

Prime Minister: Ruud Lubbers (CDA).

Deputy Prime Minister and Finance: Wim Kok (PVDA). *Foreign Affairs:* Hans van den Broek (CDA). *Economic Affairs:* J. Andriessen (CDA). *Defence:* Relus ter Beek (PVDA). *Development Aid Co-operation:* Jan Pronk (PVDA). *Home Affairs:* Ien Dales (PVDA). *Justice:* E. Hirsch-Ballin (CDA). *Agriculture and Fisheries:* Gerrit Braks (CDA). *Welfare, Public Health and Culture:* Hedy d'Ancona (PVDA). *Education and Science:* Jo Ritzen (PVDA). *Transport and Public Works:* Hanja Maij-Weggen (CDA). *Housing, Physical Planning and Environment:* Hans Alders (PVDA). *Social Affairs and Employment:* Bert de Vries (CDA).

There are also 11 state secretaries.

The Council of State *(Raad van State)*, appointed by the Crown, is composed of a vice-president and not more than 28 members. The Queen is president, but the day-to-day running of the council is in the hands of the vice-president. The Council can be consulted on all legislative matters. Decisions of the Crown in administrative disputes are prepared by a special section of the Council.

The Hague is the seat of the Court, Government and Parliament; Amsterdam is the capital.

National flag: Three horizontal stripes of red, white, blue.

National anthem: Wilhelmus van Nassoue (words by Philip Marnix van St Aldegonde, *c.* 1570).

Local Government. The kingdom is divided in 12 provinces and 714 municipalities. Each province has its own representative body, the Provincial States. The members must be 21 years of age or over; they are elected for 4 years, directly from the Netherlands inhabitants of the province who are 18 years of age or over. The electoral register is the same as for the Second Chamber. The members retire in a body and are subject to re-election. The number of members varies according to the population of the province, from 83 for Zuid-Holland to 39 for Flevoland (a new province in the Zuiderzee area). The Provincial States are entitled to issue ordinances concerning the welfare of the province, and to raise taxes pursuant to legal provisions. The provincial budgets and the provincial ordinances and resolutions relating to provincial property, loans, taxes, etc., must be approved by the Crown. The members of the Provincial States elect the First Chamber of the States-General. They meet twice a year, as a rule in public. A permanent commission composed of 6 of their members, called the 'Deputy States', is charged with the executive power and, if required, with the enforcement of the law in the province. Deputy as well as Provincial States are presided over by a Commissioner of the Queen, appointed by the Crown, who in the former assembly has a deciding vote, but attends the latter in only a deliberative capacity. He is the chief magistrate in the province. The Commissioner and the members of the Deputy States receive an allowance.

Each municipality forms a Corporation with its own interests and rights, subject to the general law, and is governed by a Municipal Council, directly elected from the Netherlands inhabitants, and, under certain circumstances, non-Netherlands inhabitants of the municipality who are 18 years of age or over, for 4 years. All Netherlands inhabitants and non-Netherlands inhabitants who meet certain requirements aged 21 or over are eligible, the number of members varying from 7 to 45, according to the population. The Municipal Council has the right to issue bye-laws concerning the communal welfare. The Council may levy taxes pursuant to legal provisions; these ordinances must be approved by the Crown. All bye-laws may be vetoed by the Crown. The Municipal Budget and resolutions to alienate municipal property require the approbation of the Deputy States of the province. The Council meets in public as often as may be necessary, and is presided over by a Burgomaster, appointed by the Crown. The day-to-day administration is carried out by the Burgomaster and 2–7 Aldermen *(wethouders)*, elected by and from the Council; this body is also charged with the enforcement of the law. The Burgomaster may suspend the execution of a resolution of the council for 30 days, but is bound to notify the Deputy States of the province. In maintaining public order, the Burgomaster acts as the chief of police. The Burgomaster and Aldermen receive allowances.

DEFENCE. The Netherlands are bordered on the south by Belgium, on the east by the Federal Republic of Germany. On both sides the country is quite level and has no natural defences, except the barriers of some large rivers, running east to west and south to north. The country has an excellent roadnet and a vast railway system, enabling rapid movement. The western part of the country is densely populated.

Army. Service is partly voluntary and partly compulsory; the voluntary enlistments are of small proportion to the compulsory. The total peacetime strength amounts to 69,900, including Military Police. The number of regulars is 25,000. The Army also employs 13,000 civilians. The legal period of active service for national servicemen is 22–24 months; the actual service period is 16 months for reserve-officers and n.c.o.s and 14 months for other ranks. The balance is spent as 'short leave'. After their period of actual service or short leave, conscript personnel are granted long leave. However, they will be liable to being called up for refresher training or in case of mobilization until they have reached the age of 35 (n.c.o.s 40, reserve officers 45).

The 1st Netherlands Army Corps is assigned to NATO. It consists of 10 brigades and Corps troops. The active part of the Corps comprises 2 armoured brigades and 4 armoured infantry brigades, grouped in two divisions and 40% of the Corps troops. Part of this force is stationed in the Federal Republic of Germany. The peacetime strength of the active brigades is 80% of the war-authorized strength.

The mobilizable part of the Corps comprises 1 armoured brigade, 2 armoured infantry brigades, 1 infantry brigade and the remaining Corps troops.

The mechanized brigades comprise tank battalions (Leopard I improved and Leopard 2), armoured infantry battalions (YP-408 and YPR-765), medium artillery battalions (155 mm self-propelled), armoured engineer units and armoured anti armour units. The Corps troops comprise headquarters units, combat-support units, including Engineer and Corps artillery (203 mm, 155 mm and Lance) and service-support units. Helicopter squadrons are also available.

The National Territorial Command forces consist of territorial brigades, security forces, some logistical units and staffs. The major part of these units is mobilizable. Some units in the Netherlands are earmarked for assignment to the United Nations as peace-keeping forces. The army is responsible for the training of these units. In time of war, the civil defence operations will be closely co-ordinated with the local civilian authorities.

Navy. The principal headquarters and main base of the Royal Netherlands Navy is at Den Helder, with minor bases at Flushing, Curaçao (Netherlands Antilles) and Oranjestad (Aruba).

The modern and combatant fleet, all built in home shipyards, and largey equipped with indigenous sensors and imported weapons, comprises 6 diesel submarines including the first of the new Zeeleeuw class, 4 guided missile destroyers armed with US Standard SM1-MR surface-to-air missiles, 10 frigates each with 1 or 2 Lynx ASW helicopters, 15 coastal minehunters and 11 coastal minesweepers. There are 2 multi-purpose support ships (each carrying up to 3 helicopters), 3 survey ships, 2 training ships and a torpedo tender, plus numerous service vessels.

The last of the 6 Van Speijk class frigates is also held pending her sale to Indonesia to join the other 5. Transfer was expected in late 1990. The first of a new class of frigate, *Karel Doorman*, is expected to commence sea trials in 1990.

The Marine corps has 12 small amphibious craft, but is integrated operationally with the UK Marines for its NATO tasks.

The Naval air service operates 13 Orion P-3C, 17 Westland Lynx SH-14B/C for embarked service and 5 Lynx UH-14A for SAR, utility and transport.

In 1989 personnel totalled 16,900 officers and other ranks, including 1,400 in the Naval Air Service, 560 women (who serve in all classes of ships except submarines) and 2,800 in the Royal Netherlands Marine Corps.

Air Force. The Royal Netherlands Air Force (RNLAF) was established 1 July 1913. Its strength (1990) was 18,200 personnel and it has a first-line combat force of 9 squadrons of aircraft and 3 groups of surface-to-air missiles in the Federal Republic of Germany. All squadrons are operated by Tactical Air Command. Aircraft operated are F-16A/B (6 squadrons for air defence and ground attack, 1 for tactical reconnaissance), and NF-5A/B fighter-bombers (2 squadrons, to be re-equipped with F-16s by 1993). Also under control of Tactical Air Command is 1 squadron of the USAF, flying F-15C/D Eagles in the air defence role. 3 squadrons of Alouette III and Bölkow Bö 105C helicopters are under control of the Royal Netherlands Army, but flown and maintained by the RNLAF for use in the communications and observation roles. Also operated is 1 squadron of F.27 Friendship/Troopship transport aircraft, and another (based in Curaçao) with F.27 maritime patrol aircraft.

Training of RNLAF pilots is undertaken in the USA, Belgium and the Netherlands. The surface-to-air missile force consists of 1 group of Nike Hercules (to be disbanded in 1988), 1 group of Hawk and Patriot missile systems and 1 group of Hawk (to be partly re-equipped with Patriot as of 1989). Hawk missiles are also used for air defence in the Netherlands.

INTERNATIONAL RELATIONS

Membership. The Netherlands is a member of UN, the European Communities, OECD, the Council of Europe and NATO.

ECONOMY

Budget. The revenue and expenditure of the central government (ordinary and extraordinary) were, in 1m. guilders, for calendar years:

	1982	*1983*	*1984*	*1985*	*1986*	*1987*	*1988*
Revenue [1]	113,967	115,002	127,918	138,605	159,689	156,111	150,724
Expenditure[2]	142,586	146,622	157,709	162,085	167,321	170,275	171,977

[1] Without the revenue of loans. [2] Without redemption of loans.

The revenue and expenditure of the Agriculture Equalization Fund, the Fund for Central Government roads, the Property Acquisition Fund and of the Investment Account Fund (established in 1978) have been incorporated in the general budget.

The national debt, in 1m. guilders, was on 31 Dec.:

	1984	*1985*	*1986*	*1987*	*1988*
Internal funded debt	183,312	208,484	219,466	234,474	263,949
„ floating „	19,806	19,799	19,969	16,683	10,524
Total	203,118	228,283	239,435	251,157	274,473

Currency. The monetary unit is the *gulden* (guilder, florin) of 100 *cents*. In March 1990 the rate of exchange was US$1 = 1·92 guilders; £1 = 3·14 guilders.

Legal tender are bank-notes, silver 10-guilder pieces, 5-guilder pieces, nickel 2½- and 1-guilder pieces, 25-cent, 10-cent pieces and bronze 5-cent pieces.

Banking. The Netherlands Bank, founded as a private institution, was nationalized on 1 Aug. 1948, the shareholders receiving, for a share of 1,000 guilders, a security of 2,000 guilders on the 2½% National Debt. Since 1863 the bank has the sole right of issuing bank-notes. The capital amounts to 75m. guilders.

Weights and Measures. The metric system of weights and measures was adopted in the Netherlands in 1820.

ENERGY AND NATURAL RESOURCES

Electricity. The total production of electrical energy (in 1m. kwh.) amounted in 1938 to 3,688; 1958, 13,854; 1970, 40,859; 1980, 64,806; 1985, 62,936; 1986, 67,148; 1987, 68,437; 1988, 69,016. Supply 220 volts; 50 Hz.

Gas. Production of manufactured gas (milliard k joule): 1978, 181,033; 1979, 233,553; 1980, 210,011; 1981, 197,586; 1982, 244,438; 1983, 258,515; 1984, 267,643. Production of natural gas in 1950, 8m. cu. metres; 1955, 139; 1960, 384; 1970, 31,688; 1980, 91,153; 1985, 80,721; 1986, 74,037; 1987, 74,247; 1988, 65,610.

Minerals. On 1 Jan. 1975 all coalmines were closed.

The production of crude petroleum (in 1,000 tonnes) amounted in 1943 (first year) to 0·2; 1953, 820; 1970, 1,919; 1978, 1,402; 1979, 1,316; 1980, 1,280; 1981, 1,348; 1982, 1,637; 1983, 2,589; 1984, 3,102; 1985, 3,729; 1986, 4,628; 1987, 4,291; 1988, 3,909.

There are saltmines at Hengelo and Delfzijl; production (in 1,000 tonnes), 1950, 412·6; 1960, 1,096; 1970, 2,871; 1978, 2,939; 1979, 3,951; 1980, 3,464; 1981, 3,578; 1982, 3,191; 1983, 3,124; 1984, 3,674; 1985, 4,154; 1986, 3,763; 1987, 3,979; 1988, 3,693.

Agriculture. The net area of all holdings was divided as follows (in hectares):

	1985	*1986*	*1987*	*1988*	*1989*
Field crops	749,722	763,068	787,078	789,798	795,822
Grass	1,164,290	1,141,978	1,124,472	1,114,009	1,098,823
Market gardening	72,288	72,352	66,971	70,415	71,281
Land for flower bulbs	15,055	15,564	16,432	16,420	16,698
Flower cultivation	5,965	6,216	6,377	6,623	7,054
Nurseries	6,738	7,037	7,523	7,911	8,478
Fallow land	4,965	6,367	5,410	6,493	5,722
Total	2,019,023	2,012,589	2,014,263	2,011,669	2,003,878

The net areas under special crops were as follows (in hectares):

Products	*1988*	*1989*	*Products*	*1988*	*1989*
Autumn wheat	104,182	130,738	Colza	7,272	6,275
Spring wheat	10,279	8,894	Flax	4,487	5,258
Rye	6,592	6,826	Agricultural seeds	24,631	25,696
Autumn barley	6,277	7,806	Potatoes, edible [1]	104,157	104,919
Spring barley	56,397	42,393	Potatoes, industrial [2]	56,673	60,204
Oats	13,167	7,787	Sugar-beet	123,374	123,757
Peas	28,210	15,913	Fodder-beet	2,078	2,532

[1] Including early and seed pototoes. [2] Including seed potatoes.

The yield of the more important products, in tonnes, was as follows:

Crop	*Average 1960–69*	*Average 1970–79*	*1987*	*1988*	*1989* [1]
Wheat	630,054	701,934	768,250	827,139	1,069,349
Rye	289,503	103,442	24,661	28,271	31,601
Barley	388,444	327,345	261,847	302,290	262,504
Oats	385,164	144,855	47,088	59,541	36,105
Field beans	1,847	...	48,091	56,791	...
Peas	61,808	19,972	121,552	107,518	70,286
Colza	11,763	32,797	30,963	24,153	24,984
Flax, unrippled	159,257	43,620	31,745	31,967	33,015
Potatoes, edible [2]	2,508,369	3,084,356	4,955,081	4,413,192	4,730,850
Potatoes, industrial	1,469,799	2,554,555	2,522,446	...	...
Sugar-beet	4,045,153	5,546,689	6,920,023	...	...
Fodder-beet	1,678,285	348,117	166,075	...	...

[1] 1989 figures provisional. [2] Including early potatoes.

Livestock, May 1989: 4,771,829 cattle, 13,729,209 pigs; 66,674 horses and ponies; 1,404,348 sheep, 91,822,620 poultry.

In 1988 the production of butter, under state control, declined to 169,877 tonnes; that of cheese, under state control, increased to 581,757 tonnes. Export value (processed and unprocessed) of arable crops amounted to 17,501m. guilders; animal produce, 19,100m. guilders and horticultural produce, 12,487m. guilders.

Fisheries. The total produce of fish landed from the sea and inshore fisheries in 1981 was valued at 595m. guilders; the total weight amounted to 399,438 tonnes. In 1981 the herring fishery had a value of 26m. guilders and a weight of 16,710 tonnes. The quantity of oysters produced in 1981 amounted to 573 tonnes (10m. guilders).

INDUSTRY AND TRADE

Industry. Numbers employed (in 1,000) and turnover (in 1m. guilders) in manufacturing enterprises with 10 employees and more, excluding building:

Class in industry	*Numbers employed* 1987	1988[1]	*Turnover* 1987	1988[1]
Mining and quarrying	17·8	14·7	9·3	9·5
Manufacturing industry	238·2	253·8	811·2	814·2
Foodstuffs and tobacco products	67·3	69·7	132·6	133·3
Textile industry	5·0	5·1	23·0	22·2
Clothing	1·4	1·4	9·7	9·9
Leather and footwear	0·9	0·9	5·8	5·4
Wood and furniture industry	4·5	4·9	25·3	26·7
Paper industry	7·1	7·7	24·7	24·9
Graphic industry, publishers	13·3	14·2	64·0	65·2
Petroleum industry	16·7	14·7	9·3	8·9
Chemical industry, artificial yarns and fibre industry	36·7	41·4	87·6	87·9
Rubber and synthetic materials processing industry	6·9	7·3	28·1	28·8
Building industry, earthenware and glass	6·4	7·4	29·2	29·9
Basic metal industry	7·8	9·8	30·0	29·7
Metal products (excl. machinery and means of transport)	12·6	14·2	72·4	75·9
Machinery	14·3	14·7	78·7	80·4
Electrical industry	23·5	24·4	121·5	117·2
Means of transport	12·2	14·1	57·8	55·9
Instrument making and optical industry	1.0	1·1	7·2	7·4
Other industries	0·7	0·8	4·4	4·9
Public utilities	18·5	16·3	...	...

[1] Provisional.

Commerce. On 5 Sept. 1944 and 14 March 1947 the Netherlands signed agreements with Belgium and Luxembourg for the establishment of a customs union. On 1 Jan. 1948 this union came into force and the existing customs tariffs of the Belgium–Luxembourg Economic Union and of the Netherlands were superseded by the joint Benelux Customs Union Tariff. It applies to imports into the 3 countries from outside sources, and exempts from customs duties all imports into each of the 3 countries from the other two. The Benelux tariff has 991 items and 2,400 separate specifications.

Returns of special imports and special exports for calendar years (in 1,000 guilders):

	Imports	*Exports*		*Imports*	*Exports*
1949	5,331,569	3,851,126	1985	216,008,008	226,017,400
1959	14,968,454	13,702,927	1986	185,052,790	197,286,108
1969	39,955,406	36,205,110	1987	184,477,026	187,574,394
1979	134,885,386	127,689,416	1988	196,348,717	203,728,967

Value of the trade with leading countries (in 1,000 guilders):

Country	*Imports* 1986	1987	1988	*Exports* 1986	1987	1988
Belgium–Luxembourg	26,286,181	26,684,158	28,806,310	28,057,567	27,252,200	29,953,362
France	13,319,119	13,452,421	14,949,836	21,253,869	20,430,214	21,925,480
Germany (Fed. Rep.)	48,888,290	49,086,298	51,650,397	55,687,427	51,425,867	53,402,641
Indonesia	630,571	632,363	813,967	664,440	513,545	827,272
Italy	7,034,169	6,933,599	7,395,160	12,474,524	12,098,113	13,038,894
Kuwait	1,517,250	1,789,889	1,943,455	298,297	214,530	202,754
Sweden	4,077,128	4,040,116	4,350,203	3,538,996	3,612,041	3,826,853
UK	15,213,018	14,150,914	15,106,871	20,093,817	19,365,426	21,939,246
USA	14,569,326	13,331,612	15,003,921	9,333,552	8,162,911	8,745,545
Venezuela	83,963	178,534	128,588	268,014	205,416	307,226

Total trade between the Netherlands and UK (British Department of Trade returns, in £1,000 sterling):

	1985	*1986*	*1987*	*1988*	*1989*
Imports to UK	6,550,735	6,615,851	7,148,036	8,279,747	9,585,699
Exports and re-exports from UK	7,344,681	5,442,503	5,856,164	5,583,280	6,515,325

Tourism. There were 3,114,000 foreign visitors in 1987 (hotels only). 604,000 came from the Federal Republic of Germany, 556,000 from UK and 396,000 from USA. Total income from tourism (1988) US$2,858m.

COMMUNICATIONS

Roads. In 1988 the length of the Netherlands network of surfaced inter-urban roads was 55,100 km, of which 2,060 km were motor highways. Number of private cars (1988), 5·3m.

Railways. All railways are run by the mixed company 'N.V. Nederlandse Spoorwegen'. Length of line in 1988 was 2,929 km, of which 1,957 km were electrified. Passengers carried (1988), 230m.; goods transported, 19·6m. tonnes.

Aviation. The Royal Dutch Airlines (KLM) was founded on 7 Oct. 1919. Revenue traffic, 1988–89: Passengers, 6·9m.; freight, 423m. kg; mail, 20m. kg.

Sea-going Shipping. Survey of the Netherlands mercantile marine as at 1 Jan. (capacity in 1,000 GRT):

	1988		*1989*	
Ships under Netherlands flag	*Number*	*Capacity*	*Number*	*Capacity*
Passenger ships [1]	4	77	4	77
Freighters (100 GRT and over)	410	2,138	367	2,060
Tankers	59	678	57	668
	473	2,892	428	2,804

[1] With accommodation for 13 or more cabin passengers.

In 1988, 44,588 sea-going ships of 380m. gross tons entered Netherlands ports.

Total goods traffic by sea-going ships in 1988 (with 1987 figures in brackets), in 1m. tonnes, amounted to 267 (250) unloaded, of which 121 (118) tankshipping, and 88 (83) loaded, of which 31 (30) tankshipping. The total seaborne freight traffic at Rotterdam was 274m. (254m.) and at Amsterdam 28m. (29m.) tonnes.

The number of containers (including flats) at Rotterdam in 1988 (with 1987 figures in brackets) was: Unloaded from ships, 1,062,661 (976,666), of which 252,955 (241,677) from North America, and 1,122,541 (1,010,178) loaded into ships, of which 215,760 (175,583) to North America.

Inland Shipping. The total length of navigable rivers and canals is 5,016 km, of which about 2,391 km is for ships with a capacity of 1,000 and more tonnes. On 1 Jan. 1988 the Netherlands inland fleet actually used for transport (with carrying capacity in 1,000 tonnes) was composed as follows:

	Number	*Capacity*
Self-propelled barges	5,244	3,979
Dumb barges	349	239
Pushed barges	620	1,330
	6,213	5,647

In 1988, 275m. (1987: 273m.) tonnes of goods were transported on rivers and canals, of which 184m. (183m.) was international traffic. Goods transport on the Rhine across the Dutch–German frontier near Lobith amounted to 125m. (119m.) tonnes.

Post and Broadcasting. On 1 Jan. 1989 there were 6·5m. telephone connexions (44 per 100 inhabitants). Number of telex lines, 33,000. *Nederlandse Omroep Stichting* (NOS) provides 5 programmes on medium-waves and FM in co-operation with broadcasting organizations. Regional programmes are also broadcast.

Advertisements are transmitted. NOS broadcasts 3 TV programmes. Advertisements, 1986–87 were restricted to 5·5% of the transmission time in the evening. Television sets (1 Jan. 1988) totalled 4·7m.; holders of television licences may, in addition, have wireless receiving sets.

Cinemas (end 1988). There were 443 cinemas with a seating capacity of 104,000.

Newspapers (Sept. 1986). There were 85 daily newspapers with a total circulation of nearly 4·6m.

JUSTICE, RELIGION, EDUCATION AND WELFARE

Justice. Justice is administered by the High Court of the Netherlands (Court of Cassation), by 5 courts of justice (Courts of Appeal), by 19 district courts and by 62 cantonal courts; trial by jury is unknown. The Cantonal Court, which deals with minor offences, is formed by a single judge; the more serious cases are tried by the district courts, formed as a rule by 3 judges (in some cases one judge is sufficient); the courts of appeal are constituted of 3 and the High Court of 5 judges. All judges are appointed for life by the Sovereign (the judges of the High Court from a list prepared by the Second Chamber of the States-General). They can be removed only by a decision of the High Court.

At the district court the juvenile judge is specially appointed to try children's civil cases and at the same time charged with administration of justice for criminal actions committed by young persons between 12 and 18 years old, unless imprisonment of more than 6 months ought to be inflicted; such cases are tried by 3 judges.

Number of sentences, and cases in which prosecution was evaded by paying a fine to the public prosecutor (excluding violation of economic and tax laws):

Major offences		*Minor offences*	
1986	93,148	1986	823,328
1987	97,361	1987	915,329
1988	102,348	1988[1]	819,837

In addition, prosecution was evaded by paying a fine to the police in about 1·95m. cases in 1988.

[1] Provisional.

Police. There are both State and Municipal Police. In 1988 the State Police, about 8,500 men strong, served 566, and the Municipal Police, about 20,300 men strong, served 148 municipalities. The State Police includes ordinary as well as water, mounted and motor police. The State Police Corps is under the jurisdiction of the Police Department of the Ministry of Justice, which also includes the Central Criminal Investigation Office, which deals with serious crimes throughout the country, and the International Criminal Investigation Office, which informs foreign countries of international crimes.

Religion. Entire liberty of conscience is granted to the members of all denominations. The royal family belong to the Dutch Reformed Church.

The number of adherents of the Churches according to survey estimates of 1988 was: Roman Catholics, 5,297,000; Dutch Reformed Church, 2,751,000; Reformed Churches, 1,177,000; other creeds, 824,000; no religion, 4,723,000.

The government of the Reformed Church is Presbyterian. On 1 July 1972 the Dutch Reformed Church had 1 synod, 11 provincial districts, 54 classes, 147 districts and 1,905 parishes.

Their clergy numbered 2,000. The Roman Catholic Church had, Jan. 1973, 1 archbishop (of Utrecht), 6 bishops and 1,815 parishes and rectorships. The Old Catholics had (1 July 1972) 1 archbishop (Utrecht), 2 bishops and 29 parishes. The Jews had, in 1970, 46 communities.

Education. Statistics for the scholastic year 1987–88:

	Full-time Pupils/Students			Part-time[1] Pupils/Students		
	Schools	Total	Female	Schools	Total	Female
Basic schools	8,499	1,431,428	707,155	—	—	—
Special schools	1,001	106,306	33,897	—	—	—
Secondary general schools	1,338	747,119	393,141	80	95,829	68,686
Secondary vocational schools:						
Junior—						
Technical, nautical	385	124,520	5,746	4	144	1
Agricultural	130	28,783	8,544	83	1,255	392
Domestic science	488	66,869	63,218	—	—	—
Other	248	79,351	40,968	—	—	—
Senior—						
Technical, nautical	131	82,897	8,500	45	7,842	342
Agricultural	66	19,381	3,753	42	7,521	1,244
Service trade and health care training	133	74,710	67,189	73	10,452	7,140
Other	215	118,613	56,308	—	177,353	67,195
Third level non-university training:						
Technical, nautical	68	40,358	4,731	17	4,329	462
Agricultural	13	7,864	1,739	1	282	35
Arts	50	16,700	9,393	31	4,890	2,573
Teachers' training	88	26,492	17,229	101	25,044	12,812
Other	138	68,930	40,205	65	23,244	11,777

[1] Including apprenticeship schemes, young workers' educational institutes.

Academic Year 1987–88

	Schools	Full-time Students		Part-time Students	
		Total	Female	Total	Female
University education:					
Humanities	21	28,280	17,207	1,207	656
Social sciences		71,770	29,391	10,540	4,229
Natural sciences		14,303	3,760	218	51
Technical sciences		24,904	2,536	...	...
Medical sciences		17,393	8,279	157	106
Agricultural sciences		6,473	2,431	88	43

Health. On 1 Jan. 1989 there were 35,853 doctors and about 66,647 licensed hospital beds.

DIPLOMATIC REPRESENTATIVES

Of the Netherlands in Great Britain (38 Hyde Park Gate, London, SW7 5DP)
Ambassador: Hans Jonkman, GCVO (accredited 20 Feb. 1987).

Of Great Britain in the Netherlands (Lange Voorhout, 10, The Hague)
Ambassador: Sir Michael Heald, KCMG.

Of the Netherlands in the USA (4200 Linnean Ave., NW, Washington, D.C., 20008)
Ambassador: Richard H. Fein.

Of the USA in the Netherlands (Lange Voorhout, 102, The Hague)
Ambassador: C. Howard Wilkins Jr.

Of the Netherlands to the United Nations
Ambassador: Robert J. Van Schaik.

Further Reading

Statistical Information: The 'Centraal Bureau voor de Statistiek' at Voorburg and Heerlen, is the official Netherlands statistical service. *Director-General of Statistics:* Prof. Dr W. Begeer.

The Bureau was founded in 1899. Prior to that year, statistical publications were compiled by the 'Centrale commissie voor de statistiek', the 'Vereniging voor staathuishoudkunde en statistiek' and various government departments. These activities have gradually been taken over and co-ordinated by the Central Bureau, which now compiles practically all government statistics.

Its current publications include:

Statistical Yearbook of the Netherlands. From 1923/24 (preceded by *Jaarcijfers voor het Koninkrijk der Nederlanden, 1898–1922);* latest issue, 1987 (in English)
Statistisch zakboek (Pocket Year Book). From 1899/1924 (1 vol.); latest issue, 1987
CBS Select (Statistical Essays). From 1980; latest issue, 1987
Statistisch Bulletin (From 1945; weekly statistical bulletin)
Maandschrift (From 1944; monthly bulletin)
85 Jaren Statistiek In Tijdreeksen (historical series of the Netherlands 1899–1984)
Nationale Rekeningen (National Accounts). From 1948–50; latest issue, 1987
Statistisch Magazine. From 1981
Statistische onderzoekingen. From 1977
Statistical Studies. From 1953
Regionaal Statistisch Zakboek (Regional Pocket Yearbook). From 1972, latest issue 1986
Environmental Statistics of the Netherlands, 1987 (in English)

Other Official Publications

Central Economic Plan. Centraal Plan bureau, The Hague (Dutch text), annually, from 1946
Netherlands. Organization for Economic Co-operation and Development. Paris, annual from 1964
Staatsalmanak voor het Koninkrijk der Nederlanden. Annual. The Hague, from 1814
Staatsblad van het Koninkrijk der Nederlanden. The Hague, from 1814
Staatscourant (State Gazette). The Hague, from 1813
Atlas van Nederland. Government Printing Office, The Hague, 1970 and supplements up to and including 1973
Basic Guide to the Establishing of Industrial Operations in the Netherlands 1976. Ministry of Economic Affairs, The Hague, 1976

Non-Official Publications

Jansonius, H., *Nieuw Groot Nederlands—Engels Woordenboek Voor Studie en Praktijk.* 3 vols. Leiden, 1973 (Vols. 1–3)
King, P. K. and Wintle, M., *The Netherlands.* [Bibliography] Oxford and Santa Barbara, 1988
Pyttersen's Nederlandse Almanak. Zaltbommel, annual, from 1899
A Compact Geography of the Netherlands. Utrecht, 1980
National Library: De Koninklijke Bibliotheek, Prinz Willem Alexanderhof 5, The Hague. *Director:* Dr C. Reedijk.

ARUBA

HISTORY. Discovered by Alonzo de Ojeda in 1499, the island of Aruba was claimed for Spain but not settled. It was acquired by the Dutch in 1634, but apart from garrisons was left to the indigenous Caiquetios (Arawak) Indians until the 19th century. From 1828 it formed part of the Dutch West Indies and, from 1845, part of the Netherlands Antilles, with which on 29 Dec. 1954 it achieved internal self-government.

Following a referendum in March 1977, the Dutch government announced on 28 Oct. 1981 that Aruba would proceed to independence separately from the other islands. Aruba was constitutionally separated from the Netherlands Antilles from 1 Jan. 1986, and full independence has been promised by the Netherlands after a 10-year period.

AREA AND POPULATION. The island, which lies in the southern Caribbean 24 km north of the Venezuelan coast and 68 km west of Curaçao, has an area of 193 sq. km (75 sq. miles) and a population at the 1981 census of 60,312; estimate (1988) 62,500. The chief towns are Oranjestad, the capital (20,000) and Sint Nicolaas, site of the former oil refinery (17,000). Dutch is the official language, but the language usually spoken is Papiamento, a creole language. Unlike other Caribbean islands, over half the population is of Indian stock, with the balance chiefly of Dutch, Spanish and mestizo origin.

CLIMATE. Aruba has a tropical marine climate, with a brief rainy season from Oct. to Dec. Oranjestad. Jan. 79°F (26·0°C), July 84°F (29·0°C). Annual rainfall 17" (432 mm).

CONSTITUTION AND GOVERNMENT. Under the separate constitution inaugurated on 1 Jan. 1986, Aruba is an autonomous part of the Kingdom of the Netherlands with its own legislature, government, judiciary, civil service and police force. The Netherlands is represented by a Governor appointed by the monarch. The unicameral legislature *(Staten)* consists of 21 members; at the general elections held on 6 Jan. 1989, 10 seats were won by the *(Movimento Electoral di Pueblo*, 8 by the *Arubaanse Volks Partij*, and 1 each by 3 smaller parties with whom the AVP formed a coalition government.

Governor: Felipe B. Tromp.
Prime Minister, Minister of General Affairs: Nelson O. Oduber.
Deputy Prime Minister, Public Works and Health: Pedro P. Kelly.
Economic Affairs and Tourism: Daniel I. Leo. *Justice:* Hendrik S. Croes. *Social Affairs and Education:* Fredis J. Refunjol. *Transport and Communications:* Euladio D. Nicolaas. *Finance:* Guillermo P. Trinidad.

Flag: Blue, with 2 narrow horizontal yellow stripes, and in the canton a red 4-pointed star fimbriated in white.

ECONOMY

Budget. The 1984 budget totalled 207m. guilders revenue and 278m. guilders expenditure.

Currency. From 1 Jan. 1986 the currency has been the Aruban florin, at par with the Netherlands Antilles guilder. In March 1990, £1 = 2·94 *Aruban florins*; US$1 = 1·80 *Aruban florins*.

Banking. As well as the Aruba Bank, there are local branches of the Algemene Bank Nederland, Barclays Bank International, Caribbean Mercantile Bank and Citibank.

ENERGY AND NATURAL RESOURCES

Electricity. Generating capacity totals 310,000 kw. Production (1986) 945m. kwh.

Oil. The Exxon refinery dominated the economy from 1929–85, when it was closed, resulting in unemployment reaching 40% by the end of 1985.

Minerals. Gold, first discovered in 1825, is still found but in uneconomic quantities.

INDUSTRY AND TRADE

Trade. Total trade between Aruba and UK (British Department of Trade returns, in £1,000 sterling):

	1987	*1988*	*1989*
Imports to UK	296	133	653
Exports and re-exports from UK	5,652	7,315	12,751

Tourism. Tourism is now the main economic sector. In 1986 there were 181,000 tourists.

COMMUNICATIONS

Roads. In 1984 there were 380 km of surfaced highways. In 1984 there were 23,409 passenger cars and 582 commercial vehicles.

Aviation. There is an international airport (Prinses Beatrix) served by numerous airlines.

Post and Broadcasting. In 1983 there were 5 radio stations and 1 television station. In 1983 there were 17,000 telephones.

JUSTICE RELIGION, EDUCATION AND WELFARE

Justice. The Aruban judiciary is now separated from that of the Netherlands Antilles. There is a Court of First Instance and a Court of Appeal situated in Oranjestad.

Religion. In 1981, 89% of the population were Roman Catholic and 7% Protestant.

Education. In 1983 there were 33 elementary schools with 6,763 pupils, 10 junior high schools with 3,082 pupils and 4 senior schools and colleges with 881 students.

Health. In 1985 there were 59 doctors, 16 dentists, 9 pharmacists, 189 nursing personnel and one hospital with 279 beds.

THE NETHERLANDS ANTILLES

De Nederlandse Antillen

HISTORY. Bonaire and Curaçao islands, originally populated by Caiquetios Indians, were discovered in 1499 by Amerigo Vespucci and Alonso de Ojeda respectively, and claimed for Spain. They were settled in 1527, and the indigenous population exterminated and replaced by a slave-worked plantation economy. The 3 Windward Islands, inhabited by Caribs, were discovered by Columbus in 1493. They were taken by the Dutch in 1632 (Saba and Sint Eustatius), 1634 (Curaçao and Bonaire) and 1648 (the southern part of Sint Maarten, with France acquiring the northern part). With Aruba, the islands formed part of the Dutch West Indies from 1828, and the Netherlands Antilles from 1845, with internal self-government being granted on 29 Dec. 1954. Aruba was separated from 1 Jan. 1986.

AREA AND POPULATION. The Netherlands Antilles comprise two groups of islands, the Leeward group (Curaçao and Bonaire) being situated 100 km north of the Venezuelan coast and the Windward Islands situated 800 km away to the north-east, at the northern end of the Lesser Antilles. The total area is 800 sq. km (308 sq. miles) and the Census population in 1981 was 235,707. Estimate (1988) 192,866 (excluding Aruba). Willemstad is the capital.

The areas, populations and chief towns of the islands are:

Island	*Sq. km*	*1988 Estimate*	*Chief town*	*1981 Census*
Bonaire	288	10,610	Kralendijk	1,200
Curaçao	444	152,240	Willemstad	50,000
Saba	13	1,133	The Bottom	–
Sint Eustatius	21	1,889	Oranjestad	–
Sint Maarten [1]	34	26,994	Philipsburg	6,000

[1] The southern part belongs to the Netherlands Antilles, the northern to France.

Dutch is the official language, but the languages usually spoken are Papiamento (a creole language) on Curaçao and Bonaire, and English in the Windward Islands.

Vital statistics (1988: Live births, 3,456; marriages, 1,275; deaths, 1,219.

CLIMATE. All the islands have a tropical marine climate, with very little difference in temperatures over the year. There is a short rainy season from Oct. to Jan. Willemstad. Jan. 79°F (26·1°C), July 82°F (27·8°C). Annual rainfall 23" (582 mm).

CONSTITUTION AND GOVERNMENT. On 29 Dec. 1954, the Netherlands Antilles became an integral part of the Kingdom of the Netherlands but are fully autonomous in internal affairs, and constitutionally equal with the Netherlands and Aruba. The Sovereign of the Kingdom of the Netherlands is Head of State and Government, and is represented by a Governor.

The executive power in internal affairs rests with the Governor and the Council of Ministers, who together form the Government. The Ministers are responsible to a unicameral legislature *(Staten)* consisting of 22 members (since 1985, 14 from Curaçao, 3 from Bonaire, 3 from Sint Maarten, and 1 each from Saba and Sint

Eustatius) elected by universal suffrage. In general elections held on 22 Nov. 1985, 9 seats were won by the *Democratische Partij*, 6 by the *Nationale Volks Partij*, 4 by the *Movimento Antijas Nobo*, and 1 each by three smaller parties.

The executive power in external affairs is vested in the Council of Ministers of the Kingdom, in which the Antilles is represented by a Minister Plenipotentiary with full voting powers. On each of the insular communities, local autonomous power is divided between an Island Council (elected by universal suffrage), the Executive Council and the Lieut.-Governor, responsible for law and order.

Governor: Dr Rene A. Römer.

The Cabinet in May 1989 was composed as follows:
Prime Minister: Maria Liberia Peters.

Deputy Prime Minister, Transport, Communications and Health: Louis Gumbs. *Justice:* Ivo Knoppel. *Finance:* Gilbert de Paula. *Economic Affairs:* Chuchu Smits. *Social and Labour Affairs:* Stanley Inderson. *Development:* Franklin Christian. *Education:* Ellis Woodley.

Flag: White, with a red vertical strip crossed by a blue horizontal strip bearing 5 white stars.

ECONOMY

Budget. The central budget for 1988 envisaged 342·8m. NA guilders revenue and 368·9m. guilders expenditure.

Currency. The currency is the *Netherlands Antilles guilder* of 100 cents. There are notes of 250, 100, 50, 25, 10, 5, 2½ and 1 *guilder*, and coins of 2½ and 1 *guilder* and 25, 10, 5, 2½ and 1 *cent*. The official rate of exchange was £1 = 2·94 *NA guilder*; US$1 = 1·79 *NA guilder* in March 1990.

Banking. At 31 Dec. 1988 the Bank of the Netherlands Antilles had total assets and liabilities of 679·4m. NA guilders; commercial banks, 2,573·7m. NA guilders.

Post office savings banks had deposits of 6,837m. NA guilders in 1987.

ENERGY AND NATURAL RESOURCES

Electricity. Production (1988) totalled 695m. kwh.

Oil. The economy was formerly based largely on oil refining at the Shell refinery on Curaçao, but following an announcement by Shell that closure was imminent, this was sold to the Netherlands Antilles government in Sept. 1985, and leased to Petróleos de Venezuela to operate on a reduced scale.

Minerals. About 100,000 tons of calcium phosphate are mined annually. Calcium carbonate (limestone) has been mined since 1980, when mining of calcium phosphate ceased. Production, 1988, 375,000 tons.

Agriculture. Livestock (1988): Cattle, 8,000; goats, 23,000. Figures include Aruba.

Fisheries. Catch (1982) 11,000 tonnes.

INDUSTRY AND TRADE

Industry. Curaçao has one of the largest ship-repair dry docks in the western hemisphere. Curaçao has a paint factory, 2 cigarette factories, a textile factory, a brewery and some smaller industries. Bonaire has a textile factory and a modern equipped salt plant. Sint Maarten has a rum factory and fishing is important. Sint Eustatius and Saba are of less economic importance.

Labour. In 1988 the economically active population numbered 74,467, the working population 59,625.

Commerce (1987). Total imports amounted to 2,703m. (crude and petroleum products, 1,889m.) NA guilders, total exports to 2,354m. (crude and petroleum products, 2,241m.) NA guilders.

Total trade between the Netherlands Antilles and UK (British Department of Trade returns, in £1,000 sterling):

	1985	*1986* [1]	*1987* [1]	*1988*	*1989*
Imports to UK	163,236	78,509	5,133	7,823 [1]	5,115
Exports and re-exports from UK	19,844	17,260	19,635	20,089	19,396

[1] Excluding Aruba.

Tourism. In 1988, 618,000 tourists visited the islands (Sint Maarten, 429,000; Curaçao, 155,000; Bonaire, 34,000) excluding 586,000 cruise passengers (Curaçao, 124,000; Sint Maarten, 451,000; Bonair, 11,000).

COMMUNICATIONS

Roads. In 1984, the Netherlands Antilles had 820 km of surfaced highway distributed as follows: Curaçao, 550; Bonaire, 210; Sint Maarten, 3. Number of motor vehicles (31 Dec. 1986): 51,462.

Aviation. There are international airports on Curaçao (Hato Airport), Bonaire (Flamingo Field) and Sint Maarten (Princess Juliana Airport). In 1988 Curaçao handled 769,000 passengers, Bonaire 200,000, Sint Maarten 951,000, Sint Eustatius 28,772 and Saba 15,392.

Shipping (1988). 4,756 ships (totalling 31,108,000 GRT) entered the port of Curaçao; 1,069 ships (9,507,000 GRT) entered the port of Bonaire. In 1986 Curaçao handled 172,904 passengers, Bonaire 3,898 and Sint Maarten 1,021,896.

Post and Broadcasting. Number of telephones, 1987, 43,754. At 31 Dec. 1986 there were 17 radio transmitters (6 on Bonaire, 8 on Curaçao and 1 each on Saba, Sint Eustatius and Sint Maarten) and 6 TV channels (5 on Curaçao, 1 on Sint Maarten). These stations broadcast in *Papiamento*, Dutch, English and Spanish and are mainly financed by income from advertisements. In addition, Radio Nederland and Trans World Radio have powerful relay stations operating on medium- and short-waves from Bonaire. There were (1984, including Aruba) 160,000 radio and 57,000 TV receivers.

Newspapers. In 1988 there were 7 daily newspapers with a total circulation of 94,000.

JUSTICE, RELIGION, EDUCATION AND WELFARE

Justice. There is a Court of First Instance, which sits in each island, and a Court of Appeal in Willemstad.

Religion. In 1981, 85% of the population were Roman Catholics, 9·7% were Protestants (Sint Maarten and Sint Eustatius being chiefly Protestant).

Education. In 1987 there were 22,073 pupils in primary schools, 9,396 pupils in general secondary schools, 4,962 pupils in junior and senior secondary vocational schools, and 803 students in vocational colleges and universities.

Health. In 1988 there were 227 doctors, 55 dentists and 1,596 hospital beds; (1987) 1,465 nursing personnel.

DIPLOMATIC REPRESENTATIVE

USA Consul-General: Sharon Wilkinson.

Further Reading

Statistical Information: Statistical publications (on population, trade, cost of living, etc., are obtainable on request from the Statistical Office, Willemstad, Curaçao. *Statistical Jaarboek 1970* (text in Dutch, English and Spanish).

De West Indische Gids. The Hague. Monthly from 1919

NEW ZEALAND

Capital: Wellington
Population: 3·4m. (1989)
GNP per capita: US$11,126 (1988)

HISTORY. The first European to discover New Zealand was Tasman in 1642. The coast was explored by Capt. Cook in 1769. From about 1800 onwards, New Zealand became a resort for whalers and traders, chiefly from Australia. By the Treaty of Waitangi, in 1840, between Governor William Hobson and the representatives of the Maori race, the Maori chiefs ceded the sovereignty to the British Crown and the islands became a British colony. Then followed a steady stream of British settlers.

The Maoris are a branch of the Polynesian race, having emigrated from the eastern Pacific before and during the 14th century. Between 1845 and 1848, and between 1860 and 1870, misunderstandings over land led to war, but peace was permanently established in 1871, and the development of New Zealand has been marked by racial harmony and integration.

EVENTS. The cyclone 'Bola' devastated a large area of North Island in March 1988 causing damage of more than NZ$1,000m.

AREA AND POPULATION. New Zealand lies south-east of Australia in the south Pacific, Wellington being 1,983 km from Sydney by sea. There are two principal islands, the North and South Islands, besides Stewart Island, Chatham Islands and small outlying islands, as well as the territories overseas (*see* pp. 930–32).

New Zealand (*i.e.*, North, South and Stewart Islands) extends over 1,750 km from north to south. Area, excluding territories overseas, 267,844 sq. km comprising North Island, 114,821 sq. km; South Island, 149,463 sq. km; Stewart Island, 1,746 sq. km; Chatham Islands, 963 sq. km; minor islands, 833 sq. km. Growth in census population, exclusive of territories overseas:

	Total population	*Average annual increase %*		*Total population*	*Average annual increase %*
1858	115,462	—	1926	1,408,139	2·06
1874	344,984	—	1936	1,573,810	1·13
1878	458,007	7·33	1945[1]	1,702,298	0·83
1881	534,030	5·10	1951[1]	1,939,472	2·37
1886	620,451	3·05	1956[1]	2,174,062	2·31
1891	668,632	1·50	1961[1]	2,414,984	2·12
1896	743,207	2·13	1966[1]	2,676,919	2·10
1901[1]	815,853	1·89	1971[1]	2,862,631	1·34
1906	936,304	2·75	1976[1]	3,129,383	1·71
1911	1,058,308	2·52	1981[1]	3,175,737	0·20
1916[1]	1,149,225	1·50	1986[1]	3,307,084	0·82
1921	1,271,644	2·27			

The census of New Zealand is quinquennial, but the census falling in 1931 was abandoned as an act of national economy, and owing to war conditions the census due in 1941 was not taken until 25 Sept. 1945. [1] Excluding members of the Armed Forces overseas.

The areas and populations of local government regions (with principal centres) at 4 March 1986 were as follows [1]:

Local Government Region (and principal centre)	*Area [2] (sq. km)*	*Total Population 1981 census*	*1986 census*	*Intercensal change (%)*
Northland (Whangarei)	12,604	113,994	126,999	11·4
Auckland (Auckland) [1]	5,201	827,408	887,448	7·3
Thames Valley (Thames–Coromandel)	4,666	54,343	58,665	8·0
Bay of Plenty (Tauranga)	9,126	172,480	187,462	8·7
Waikato (Hamilton)	13,241	221,850	228,303	2·9
Tongariro (Taupo)	12,085	40,089	40,793	1·8
East Cape (Gisborne)	11,461	53,295	53,968	1·3
Hawke's Bay (Napier, Hastings)	12,396	137,840	140,709	2·1
Taranaki (New Plymouth)	7,876	103,798	107,600	3·7
Wanganui (Wanganui)	9,171	68,702	69,439	1·1

Local Government Region (and principal centre)	*Area*[2] *(sq. km)*	*Total Population 1981 census*	*Total Population 1986 census*	*Intercensal change (%)*
Manawatu (Palmerston North)	6,669	113,238	115,500	2·0
Horowhenua (Levin)	1,614	49,296	53,592	8·7
Wellington (Wellington)	1,379	323,162	328,163	1·5
Wairarapa (Masterton)	6,894	39,689	39,608	−0·2
Total, North Island[2]	*114,383*	*2,319,184*	*2,438,249*	*5·1*
Nelson Bays (Nelson)	10,197	65,934	69,648	5·6
Marlborough (Blenheim)	12,882	37,557	38,225	1·8
West Coast (Greymouth)	22,893	34,178	34,942	2·2
Canterbury (Christchurch)	17,465	336,846	348,712	3·5
Aorangi (Timaru)	19,910	84,772	81,294	−4·1
Clutha–Central Otago	28,982	45,402	48,771	7·4
Coastal–North Otago (Dunedin)	10,590	138,164	137,393	−0·6
Southland (Invercargill)	27,716	107,905	104,618	−3·0
Total, South Island[2]	*150,635*	*850,758*	*863,603*	*1·3*
Total, New Zealand[2]	265,018	3,169,942	3,301,852	4·2

[1] Excludes Great Barrier Island and Chatham Island Counties.
[2] Excludes Extra County Islands.

New Zealand-born residents made up 84·5% of the population at the 1986 census. Foreign-born (provisional): UK, 196,872; Australia, 46,839; Netherlands, 24,159; Samoa, 33,864; Cook Islands, 15,540; others (including USA and Ireland), 187,644.

Maori population: 1896, 42,113; 1936, 82,326; 1945, 98,744; 1951, 115,676; 1961, 171,553; 1971, 227,414; 1976, 270,035; 1981, 279,255; 1986, 294,201.

Populations of main urban areas as at 31 March 1989 were as follows:

Auckland	850,900	Invercargill	51,800
Christchurch	301,500	Nelson	45,400
Dunedin	106,400	New Plymouth	47,900
Hamilton	104,100	Rotorua	53,600
Napier–Hastings	107,700	Tauranga	62,700
Palmerston North	67,400	Timaru	28,300
Wellington	324,600	Wanganui	41,000
Gisborne	31,800	Whangarei	43,800

Vital statistics for calendar years:

	Total live births	*Ex-nuptial births*	*Deaths*	*Marriages*	*Divorces (decrees absolute)*
1986	52,824	14,237	27,045	24,037	8,753
1987	55,254	15,798	27,419	24,443	8,709
1988	57,546	17,623	27,408	23,485	8,674

Birth rate, 1988, 17·3 per 1,000; death rate, 8·24 per 1,000; marriage rate, 7 per 1,000; infant mortality, 10·77 per 1,000 live births.

External migration (exclusive of crews and through passengers) for years ended 31 March:

	Arrivals	*Departures*		*Arrivals*	*Departures*
1982	946,287	951,030	1986	1,111,926	1,130,444
1983	915,463	900,021	1987	1,321,729	1,317,372
1984	922,868	912,311	1988	1,554,992	1,555,949
1985	1,017,212	1,016,995	1989	1,669,637	1,687,935

Population and Migration: Part B—External Migration. Dept. of Statistics, Wellington, Annually

CLIMATE. Lying in the cool temperate zone, New Zealand enjoys very mild winters for its latitude owing to its oceanic situation, and only the extreme south has cold winters. The situation of the mountain chain produces much sharper climatic contrasts between east and west than in a north-south direction. Observations for 1983: Auckland. Jan. 65·5°F (18·6°C), July 50°F (10·2°C). Annual rainfall 41·5" (1,053 mm). Christchurch. Jan. 61·3°F (16·3°C), July 42·4°F (5·8°C). Annual rainfall 29" (737 mm). Dunedin. Jan. 57·4°F (14·1°C), July 43·2°F (6·2°C). Annual rainfall 38·1" (968 mm). Hokitika. Jan. 56·1°F (13·4°C), July 43·5°F (6·4°C). Annual rainfall 132·2" (3,357 mm). Rotorua. Jan. 61·2°F (16·2°C), July 43·7°F (6·5°C). Annual rainfall 49·9" (1,268 mm). Wellington. Jan. 59·9°F (15·5°C), July 46·4°F (8·0°C). Annual rainfall 51·2" (1,300 mm).

CONSTITUTION AND GOVERNMENT. Definition was given to the status of New Zealand by the (Imperial) Statute of Westminster of Dec. 1931, which had received the antecedent approval of the New Zealand Parliament in July 1931. The Governor-General's assent was given to the Statute of Westminster Adoption Bill on 25 Nov. 1947.

The powers, duties and responsibilities of the Governor-General and the Executive Council under the present system of responsible government are set out in Royal Letters Patent and Instructions thereunder of 11 May 1917, published in the *New Zealand Gazette* of 24 April 1919. In the execution of the powers vested in him the Governor-General must be guided by the advice of the Executive Council.

The following is a list of Governors-General, the title prior to June 1917 being Governor:

Earl of Liverpool	1917–20	Viscount Cobham	1957–62
Viscount Jellicoe	1920–24	Sir Bernard Fergusson	1962–67
Sir Charles Fergusson, Bt	1924–30	Sir Arthur Porrit, Bt	1967–72
Lord Bledisloe	1930–35	Sir Denis Blundell	1972–77
Viscount Galway	1935–41	Sir Keith Holyoake	1977–80
Sir Cyril Newall	1941–46	Sir David Beattie	1980–85
Lord Freyberg, VC	1946–52	Sir Paul Reeves	1985–90
Lord Norrie	1952–57		

National flag: The British Blue Ensign with 4 stars of the Southern Cross in red, edged in white, in the fly.

National anthems: God Save the Queen; God Defend New Zealand (words by Thomas Bracken, music by John J. Woods).

Since Nov. 1977 both 'God Save the Queen' and 'God Defend New Zealand' have equal status as national anthems.

Parliament consists of the House of Representatives, the former Legislative Council having been abolished since 1 Jan. 1951.

The statute law on elections and the life of Parliament is contained in the Electoral Act, 1956. In 1974 the voting age was reduced from 20 to 18 years.

The House of Representatives from Aug. 1987 consists of 97 members, including 4 members representing Maori electorates, elected by the people for 3 years. The 4 Maori electoral districts cover the whole country and adult Maoris of half or more Maori descent are the electors. From 1976 a descendant of a Maori is entitled to register either for a general or a Maori electoral district. Women's suffrage was instituted in 1893: Women became eligible as members of the House of Representatives in 1919. The House in 1987 included 12 women members.

During Parliamentary sittings the proceedings of the House are broadcast regularly on sound radio.

House of Representatives as composed Dec. 1989: Labour, 57; National Party, 40.

The Executive Council was composed as follows in Aug. 1989:

Governor-General: Dame Catherine Tizard, DBE.

Prime Minister, Environment, Security Intelligence Service: Geoffrey Palmer.

Deputy Prime Minister, Health, Labour: Helen Clark.

External Relations and Trade, Overseas Trade and Marketing: M. K. Moore.

Finance: D. F. Caygill.

State Owned Enterprises, Police, Railways and Pacific Island Affairs: R. W. Prebble.

Maori Affairs: K. T. Wetere.

Social Welfare: Dr Michael Cullen.

Education: P. B. Goff.

Housing and Communications: Jonathan L. Hunt.

Justice, Transport, Civil Aviation and Meteorological Services: W. P. Jeffries.

Consumer Affairs, Statistics and Women's Affairs: Margaret Shields.

Defence, Lands, Recreation and Sport: P. Tapsell.
Commerce and Energy: D. Butcher.
Employment, Youth Affairs and Immigration: Annette King.
Disarmament and Arms Control, Tourism: Fran Wilde.
Conservation and Local Government: P. T. E. Woollaston.
Customs, Works and Development, Revenue: P. Neilson.
Agriculture and Forestry: J. R. Sutton.
Science and State Services: Clive Matthewson.
Internal Affairs, Arts and Culture, Civil Defence, Research, Science and Technology: Margaret Austin.
Attorney-General: David R. Lange.
Regional Development: P. F. Dunne.
Fisheries: Ken Shirley.
Without Portfolio: Noel Scott, F. Gerbic, Ralph Maxwell.

Ministers not in Cabinet but on Executive Council: D. R. Lange, Fran Wilde, Philip T. E. Woollaston, Peter Neilson, Noel Scott.

The Prime Minister (provided with residence) had in 1989 a salary of NZ$147,000 plus a tax-free expense allowance of $26,000 per annum; Ministers with portfolio, $103,000 plus a tax-free expense allowance of $10,750 per annum; Minister without portfolio, $83,000 plus a tax-free expense allowance of $8,500 per annum; Parliamentary Under-Secretaries, $80,000 plus an expense allowance of $8,500 per annum. In addition, Ministers and Parliamentary Under-Secretaries not provided with residence at the seat of Government receive $2,000 per annum house allowance. An allowance of up to $220 per day while travelling within New Zealand on public service is payable to Ministers.

The Speaker of the House of Representatives receives $97,000 plus an expense allowance of $14,250 per annum in addition to his electorate allowance, and residential quarters in Parliament House, and the Leader of the Opposition $103,000 plus expense allowance of $10,750 per annum, and allowances for travelling and housing.

Members were paid $57,000 per annum, plus an expense allowance of $5,500 plus an electoral allowance varying from $7,600 to $18,600 according to the area of electorate represented.

There is a compulsory contributory superannuation scheme for members; retiring allowances are payable to a member after 9 years' service and the attainment of 45 years of age.

Dollimore, H. N., *The Parliament of New Zealand and Parliament House*. 3rd ed. Wellington, 1973
Scott, K. J., *The New Zealand Constitution*. OUP, 1962

Local Government. New Zealand is divided into 14 regions, excluding the Chatham Islands and various uninhabited minor islands. New Zealand is also divided into 14 cities and 59 districts. A city must have a minimum of 50,000 persons, be predominantly urban in character, be a distinct entity and a major centre of activity within the region. A district, on the other hand, serves a combination of rural and urban communities. There is no distinction in structural status or responsibility between a city council and a district council. There are a few other local authorities created for specific functions.

DEFENCE. The control and co-ordination of defence activities is obtained through the Ministry of Defence. This is a unitary department combining not only all joint-Service functions but also the former Departments of Army, Navy and Air.

Army. The Chief of the General Staff commands the Army, assisted by the General Staff and the staffs of Defence Headquarters. A regular force battalion is stationed in Singapore.

There are 2 infantry battalions, 1 artillery battery, 1 light armoured squadron.

Regular personnel, in 1990, totalled 5,748, territorial personnel totalled 5,741.

Navy. The Royal New Zealand Navy is 2,500 strong (with 500 Reserves) and includes 4 frigates of British Leander type, 1 12,400 tonne fleet replenishment ship with helicopter facilities, 6 inshore patrol craft, 2 survey vessels, and 1 diver support ship. The 7 Wasp helicopters for embarked service are Air Force owned and operated. The main base and Fleet headquarters is at Auckland.

Personnel, in 1990, totalled 2,600 officers and ratings and 500 in the naval reserve.

Air Force. The Chief of Air Staff and Air Officer Commanding the RNZAF exercises command and administration of the RNZAF. Maritime (P-3B Orion), long and medium-range transport (Boeing 727, C-130H Hercules, Andover, F.27 Friendship) and helicopter (Iroquois, Wasp) squadrons are based at RNZAF Base Auckland, and Hobsonville; and offensive support (A-4 Skyhawk) at RNZAF Base Ohakea. Flying training units (Airtrainer, Strikemaster, TA-4 Skyhawks, Sioux) are located at RNZAF Bases Wigram and Ohakea; ground training is carried out at RNZAF Bases Auckland, Woodbourne and Wigram.

The strength in 1990 was 4,200 regular personnel, 1,034 reserves.

INTERNATIONAL RELATIONS

Membership. New Zealand is a member of UN, the Commonwealth, OECD, South Pacific Forum and the Colombo Plan.

ECONOMY

Budget. The following tables of revenue and expenditure relate to the Consolidated Account, which covers the ordinary revenue and expenditure of the government—*i.e.*, apart from capital items, commercial and special undertakings, advances, etc. Total revenue and expenditure of the Consolidated Account, which covers ordinary revenue and expenditure of the New Zealand government (*i.e.* apart from capital items, commercial and special undertakings, advances, etc.), in NZ$1m., year ended 31 March:

	1988	*1989*
Revenue	29,871·7	32,150·6
Expenditure	30,476·8	32,151·2

Taxation receipts in 1988–89 for all purposes amounted to $22,864m., giving an average of $6,807 per head of mean population. Included in the total taxation is $561m. National Roads Fund taxation.

The gross public debt at 31 March 1989 was $39,601m., of which $23,008m. was held in New Zealand, $3,569m. in Europe, $7,323m. in USA and $5,701m. in Canada, Australia and other sources. The gross annual interest charge on the public debt at 31 March 1989 was $4,487m.

New Zealand System of National Accounts. This replaces the National Income and Expenditure Accounts which have been produced since 1948.

National Accounts aggregates for 4 years are given in the following table (in NZ$1m.):

Year ended 31 March	*Gross domestic product*	*Gross national product*	*National income*
1985	38,838	36,934	33,800
1986	44,861	42,817	39,180
1987	53,079	50,865	46,768
1988	59,257	56,506	51,944

Currency. The monetary unit is the New Zealand *dollar*, divided into 100 *cents*. In March 1990, £1 = 2·08NZ$; US$1 = 1·71NZ$.

Banking. The Reserve Bank is the sole issuer of notes and coin, issuing notes in denominations of: NZ$1, 2, 5, 10, 20, 50, 100 and coin in denominations of 5c, 10c, 20c and 50c.

The New Zealand financial system comprises a central bank, the Reserve Bank of New Zealand, registered banks, and a range of other financial institutions. Registered banks include the former commercial or trading banks, and other institutions, including banks from abroad, which have satisfied certain capital adequacy and managerial quality requirements. The other financial institutions include the regional trustee banks, now grouped under Trust Bank, building societies, finance companies, merchant banks and stock and station agents. The number of registered banks (1990, 20) grows as other financial institutions apply for, and satisfy the requirements for registration as a bank.

The primary functions of the Reserve Bank are the formulation and implementation of monetary policy to achieve the economic objectives set by the Government, and the promotion of the efficiency and soundness of the financial system, through the registration of banks, and supervision of financial institutions.

On 31 March 1989 the funding (financial liabilities including deposits) and claims (financial assets including loans) for each institutional group were in NZ$ millions:

	Funding		*Claims*	
Institutional Group	*NZ$*	*Foreign Currency*	*NZ$*	*Foreign Currency*
Registered banks	30,808	5,374	29,249	3,740
Other financial institutions	*20,924*	*3,857*	*23,370*	*1,627*
Total (net of inter-institutional claims and funds)	*45,777*	*9,231*	*45,253*	*5,367*

Weights and Measures. The metric system of weights and measures operates.

ENERGY AND NATURAL RESOURCES

Electricity. On 1 April 1987 the former Electricity Division of the Ministry of Energy became a state-owned enterprise, the Electricity Corporation of N.Z. Ltd., which has 39 power stations (30 hydro-electric and 9 thermal, with a total nominal capacity of 7,247 mw) producing 96% of the country's electricity. The other 4% comes from supply authorities' own generation schemes. Supply 230 volts; 50 Hz.

Statistics for 4 years ended 31 March are:

	1986	*1987*	*1988*	*1989*
Total sales revenue ($1m.)	1,022	1,196	1,317	1,434
Total sales volume (gwh)	24,241	25,187	25,772	26,436
Generation (gwh) (nett)	25,957	26,948	27,498	28,189
Number of employees	5,107	5,079	4,403	4,106
Production/total staff employed (gwh/person)	5·15	5·30	5·80	6·63

Natural Gas. In 1989 there were 4 gasfields in production: Kapuni (on stream 1970), Maui (1979), McKee (mainly crude oil) (1984), Kaimiro (1984).

Minerals. New Zealand's production of minerals in 1988 included 2,404 kg of gold, 1,255 tonnes of bentonite, 87,892 tonnes of clay for bricks, tiles, etc., 29,649 tonnes of potters' clays, 2,351,000 tonnes of iron sand concentrate, 708,404 tonnes of limestone for agriculture and 310,577 tonnes of limestone for industry, 1,255,720 tonnes of limestone, marl, etc., for cement, 25,000 tonnes of pumice, 16,000 tonnes of serpentine, 55,000 tonnes of silica sand. Mineral fuel production amounted to 2,401,000 tonnes of coal.

Agriculture. Two-thirds of the surface of New Zealand is suitable for agriculture and grazing. The total area under cultivation at 30 June 1988 was 17,746,065 hectares (including residential area and domestic orchards). There were 13,770,601 hectares of grassland, lucerne and tussock, 88,961 hectares of land for horticulture, 330,676 hectares of grain or fodder crops and 1,265,104 hectares of plantations.

The largest freehold estates are held in the South Island. The extent of occupied holdings as at 30 June 1988 (exclusive of holdings within borough boundaries) was as follows:

Size of holdings (hectares)	*Number of farms*	*Area (hectares)*	*Size of holdings (hectares)*	*Number of farms*	*Aggregate area (hectares)*
Under 5	10,851	31,182	400–799	4,395	2,389,912
5–19	16,477	157,622	800–1,199	1,211	1,160,296
20–39	8,596	235,550	1,200–1,999	921	1,398,745
40–59	7,487	359,649	2,000–3,999	564	1,544,234
60–99	10,073	777,712	4,000 and over	484	5,415,761
100–199	11,447	1,639,339			
200–399	9,557	2,685,111	Total	82,063	17,795,113

The area and yield for each of the principal crops are given as follows (area and yield for threshing only, not including that grown for chaff, hay, silage, etc.):

	Wheat		*Maize*		*Barley*	
Crop years	*Area (1,000 hectares)*	*Yield (1,000 tonnes)*	*Area (1,000 hectares)*	*Yield (1,000 tonnes)*	*Area (1,000 hectares)*	*Yield (1,000 tonnes)*
1985	71·8	309·6	17·8	174·6	152·3	644·4
1986	91·4	379·7	19·5	187·7	138·6	556·2
1987 [1]	83·0	336·8	19·0	176·1	102·5	400·6
1988 [1]	50·6	206·0	16·0	136·9	83·0	356·1

[1] Area sown.

Private air companies are carrying out such aerial work as top-dressing, spraying and crop-dusting, seed-sowing, rabbit poisoning, aerial photography and surveying, and dropping supplies to deer cullers and dropping fencing materials in remote areas. In 1988, 1,723,485 tonnes of fertilizer was spread.

Livestock 1988: 8,058,000 cattle, 64·6m. sheep and 414,000 pigs, 606,000 deer and 1·3m. goats. Total meat produced in the year ended 30 Sept. 1988 was estimated at 1·21m. tonnes (including 554,000 tonnes of beef and 417,700 tonnes of lamb). Total liquid milk produced in the year ended 31 May 1988 was 6,921m. litres.

Production of wool for 1987–88, 346,400 tonnes.

Agricultural Statistics. Dept. of Statistics, Wellington. Annual.

Forestry. Of the 6·2m. hectares of indigenous forest, most is protected in National Parks or State Forests. Declining quantities of indigenous timber are being produced from restricted areas of State Forest and from privately owned forest. There are just over 1m. hectares of productive exotic forest, and this produces far more timber than the indigenous forests. Introduced pines form the bulk of the large exotic forest estate and among these radiata pine is the best multi-purpose tree, reaching log size in 25–30 years. Other species planted are Douglas fir and Eucalyptus species. The table below shows production of rough sawn timber in 1,000 cu. metres for years ending 31 March:

	Indigenous			*Exotic*			*All Species*
	Rimu and Miro	*Beech*	*Total*	*Exotic Pines*	*Douglas Fir*	*Total*	*Total*
1985–86	96	13	133	2,044	183	2,265	2,398
1986–87	85	8	112	1,764	174	1,966	2,079
1987–88	62	9	85	1,557	163	1,737	1,822

Forest industries consist of 300 saw-mills, 6 plywood and veneer plants, 3 particle board mills, 8 pulp and paper mills and 4 fibreboard mills.

The basic products of the pulp and paper mills are mechanical and chemical pulp which are converted into newsprint, kraft and other papers, paperboard and fibreboard. Production of woodpulp, 31 March 1988, amounted to 1·21m. tonnes and of paper (including newsprint paper and paperboard) to 699,000 tonnes.

Fisheries. The total value of New Zealand Fisheries exports during the year ended 30 June 1989 was $789·9m., an increase of $178·9m. over the previous year.

	Exports, 1988		*Exports, 1989*	
	Quantity tonnes	*Value $ (1m.)*	*Quantity tonnes*	*Value $ (1m.)*
Fish	109,054	406·2	150,025	537·1
Squid	32,038	54·2	79,083	124·2
Crayfish	2,424	88·5	2,446	73·3
Mussels	5,496	21·7	6,119	26·6
Other fish	...	40·4	...	28·7
Total	149,012	611·0	237,673	789·9

INDUSTRY AND TRADE

Industry. Major industrial developments in recent years have included the establishment of an oil refinery, an iron and steel industry using New Zealand iron sands, a petro-chemical industry and an aluminium smelter using hydro-electric power.

Statistics of manufacturing industries:

Production year	*Persons engaged*	*Salaries and wages paid (NZ$1,000)*	*Cost of materials (NZ$1,000)*	*Sales and other income (NZ$1,000)*	*Value added (NZ$1,000)*
1986–87	300,063	6,091,996	17,068,922	33,331,340	10,571,806

The following is a statement of the provisional value of the products (including repairs) of the principal industries for the year 1986–87 (in NZ$1,000):

Industry group	*Purchases & operating expenses*	*Sales and other income*	*Value added*	*Additions to fixed tangible assets*
		(NZ$1,000)		
Food, beverage and tobacco manufacturing	8,819,221	9,203,149	2,558,848	558,534
Textile, wearing apparel, leather industries	2,895,136	3,050,800	1,022,716	90,679
Wood and wood products (including furniture)	2,049,450	2,164,985	742,505	86,216
Paper and paper products, printing and publishing	3,373,133	3,632,622	1,305,913	286,007
Chemicals and chemical, petroleum, coal, rubber and plastic products	3,749,973	4,196,454	1,511,459	1,590,900
Non-metallic mineral products	1,137,708	1,260,637	429,018	63,904
Basic metal industries	1,321,356	1,305,817	338,752	343,073
Fabricated metal products, machinery and equipment	7,622,760	8,154,538	2,545,426	396,190
Other manufacturing industries	3,333,346	362,338	117,169	19,914
Total	31,302,084	33,331,340	10,571,806	3,435,417

Economy Wide Census. Dept. of Statistics, Wellington.

Labour. In March 1989 there were 168 industrial unions of workers with a total of 649,857 members.

By the Accident Compensation Act 1982 immediate compensation without proof of fault is provided for every injured person and wherever the accident occurred. Compensation is paid both for permanent physical disability and also—in the case of earners—for income losses on an income related basis. Regular adjustment in the level of payment is provided for in accordance with variations in the value of money. Non-earners such as tourists, housewives, children, students, retired people do not normally qualify for earnings related compensation but are eligible for all other benefits. These are not taxable. Housewives—including visiting women from overseas—who are non-earners are eligible for the benefits available to non-earners and home help can be paid for or the husband compensated for loss of earnings while he is looking after the home until the injured wife can resume her duties.

After the first week's incapacity and for the ensuing 4 weeks the earner can be paid 80% of his average earnings for the 28 days preceding the accident; after that the 80% is related to average earnings over the 12 preceding months. In addition—for earners—lump sums are payable for impairment, pain and disfigurement and for funeral expenses and weekly sums and lump payments to their widows and dependent children. All employees are covered by the Accident Compensation Act 1982.

Commerce. Trade (excluding specie and bullion) in NZ$1m. for 12 months ended 30 June:

	Total merchandise imported (v.f.d.) [1]	*Exports of domestic produce*	*Re-exports*	*Total merchandise exported (f.o.b.)*
1985–86	10,468·3	10,139·0	432·7	10,571·7
1986–87	10,803·4	11,723·9	383·3	12,107·2
1987–88	10,625·1	12,104·1	347·4	12,451·5
1988-89	11,402·4	14,484·7	422·5	14,907·2

[1] Value for duty.

The principal imports for the 12 months ended 30 June 1989:

Commodity	Value (NZ$1m. v.f.d.)
Fruit	92·4
Sugar and sugar confectionery	77·0
Beer, wine and spirits	83·9
Crude petroleum oil	432·8
Inorganic chemicals (excluding aluminium oxide)	122·4
Aluminium oxide	191·5
Knitted or crocheted fabrics and articles	94·8
Glass and glassware	91·5
Iron and steel	243·9
Articles of iron and steel	162·9
Copper and articles of copper	111·3
Aluminium and articles of aluminium	126·2
Tools, implements and articles of base metals	146·3
Machinery and mechanical appliances	1,769·2
Organic chemicals	195·4
Pharmaceutical products	286·3
Plastics and articles of plastic	547·9
Rubber and articles of rubber	149·6
Paper, paperboard and articles thereof	263·8
Printed books, newspapers etc.	215·1
Cotton yarn and fabrics	104·5
Man-made filaments and fibres	197·4
Electrical machinery and equipment	1,252·6
Motor cars, station wagons, utilities	844·5
Trucks, buses and vans	192·6
Aircraft	224·5
Ships and boats	77·3
Optical, photographic, technical and surgical equipment	420·9

The principal exports of New Zealand produce for the 12 months ended 30 June 1989 were:

Commodity	Value (NZ$1m.f.o.b.)	Commodity	Value (NZ$1m.f.o.b.)
Live animals	212·1	Fresh apples	154·9
Meat, fresh, chilled or frozen		Forest products	
Beef and veal	1,279·6	Sawn timber and logs	316·8
Lamb and mutton	1,007·9	Paper and paper products	265·9
Dairy products		Wood pulp	398·8
Milk, cream and yoghurt	934·3	Aluminium and articles thereof	339·2
Butter	609·2	Casein and caseinates	878·4
Cheese	319·8	Plastic materials and articles thereof	135·3
Raw hides, skins and leather	725·2	Iron and steel and articles thereof	316·9
Wool	1,795·3	Machinery and mechanical appliances	329·8
Sausage casings	122·5	Electrical machinery and equipment	183·3
Fish, fresh, chilled or frozen	537·2		
Vegetables	166·1		
Fresh kiwifruit	455·1		

The following table shows the trade with different countries for the year ended 30 June (in NZ$1m.):

Countries	Imports v.f.d. from 1988	Imports v.f.d. from 1989	Exports and re-exports f.o.b. to 1988	Exports and re-exports f.o.b. to 1989
Australia	2,266·6	2,459·9	2,073·8	2,609·6
Bahrain	9·2	3·3	8·4	–
Belgium	83·2	75·3	257·6	272·1
Canada	181·2	227·7	216·9	261·2
China	112·2	125·2	435·3	539·1
Fiji	16·1	–	88·5	141·6
France	177·6	165·8	188·7	204·8
Germany, Fed. Rep. of	597·9	497·0	294·3	307·6
Greece	6·8	–	60·7	–
Hong Kong	178·6	202·6	177·6	247·8
India	38·1	–	51·4	–
Iran	34·3	–	207·0	130·6

Countries	Imports v.f.d. from 1988	1989	Exports and re-exports f.o.b. to 1988	1989
Italy	209·4	196·0	250·7	316·8
Japan	1,864·9	2,109·6	2,078·2	2,661·2
Korea, Republic of	199·0	280·0	287·5	468·8
Kuwait	20·0	–	15·3	–
Malaysia	57·6	72·2	163·6	247·5
Netherlands	158·2	124·7	170·7	171·1
Peru	–	–	–	22·9
Philippines	19·4	–	90·8	159·7
Saudi Arabia	247·6	343·9	99·7	–
Singapore	128·4	138·2	160·8	174·9
Sweden	121·8	169·7	26·6	–
Switzerland	–	106·5	–	–
Taiwan	–	372·8	–	281·4
UK	1,014·6	882·6	1,062·2	1,036·4
USSR	11·0	–	146·6	351·4
USA	1,683·0	1,906·0	1,803·0	2,008·2
Venezuela	–	–	–	114·4

Total trade between New Zealand and UK was as follows (British Department of Trade returns, in £1,000 sterling):

	1985	1986	1987	1988	1989
Imports to UK	533,047	455,694	487,332	443,081	436,772
Exports and re-exports from UK	396,595	343,145	378,368	300,016	399,295

Tourism. The country has a growing tourist industry. In the year ended 31 March 1989, 901,078 travellers visited New Zealand, compared with 855,492 in 1988.

COMMUNICATIONS

Roads. Total length of formed roads and streets in New Zealand at 31 March 1989 was 92,974 km. There were 14,057 bridges of over 3 metres in length with a total length of 314,000 metres at 31 March 1989. The network of state highways comprised, at 31 March 1989, 11,523 km, including the principal arterial traffic routes.

Total expenditure on roads, streets and bridges by the central government and local authorities combined for the financial year 1988–89 amounted to $849m.

At 31 March 1989 motor vehicles licensed numbered 2,217,259, of which 1,438,704 were cars and 10,633 omnibuses, public taxis and service vehicles. Included in the remaining numbers were 89,459 motor cycles, 1,211 power cycles, 289,225 trucks, 341,280 trailers and caravans and 7,904 farm tractors and other farm equipment.

Railways. On 31 March 1988 there were 4,202 km of 1,067 mm gauge railway open for traffic (525 km electrified). In 1988–89, railways carried 8·8m. tonnes and 26·9m. passengers. Operating revenue during 1987–88, $646,821,000 and operating expenses $684,117,000. Three rail/road ferries maintain a regular service between the North and South Islands.

Aviation. International services are operated to and from New Zealand by a previously stateowned company, Air New Zealand Ltd, and by a number of overseas companies. Air New Zealand Ltd, Mt Cook Airlines and Ansett are the major domestic carriers.

Domestic scheduled services during the 12 months ended Dec. 1987: Passengers carried, 3,782,000. International services: Passengers carried, 3,001,000; mail, 4,385 tonnes; freight, 117,769 tonnes.

Shipping. Container ships operate from all major New Zealand ports, serving all the major trading areas.

Entrances and clearances of vessels from overseas:

	Entrances		Clearances	
	No.	Tons	No.	Tons
1985	2,932	14,607,000	2,935	14,613,000
1986	2,519	13,388,000	2,527	13,365,000
1987	3,060	14,113,000	3,050	14,107,000
1988	3,298	27,844,000	3,334	27,247,000

Post and Broadcasting. The provision of postal and telecommunication services is the responsibility of two state-owned enterprizes: New Zealand Post, which began operations on 1 April 1987, and the Telecom Corporation of New Zealand, formed in 1987. In 1989 there were 470 post offices, and 336 post shops with 8,700 staff.

There are 2 TV channels both operated by the New Zealand Broadcasting Corporation, which also operates most of the broadcasting stations. A third, privately-owned TV channel commenced in Nov. 1989. Over 85% of New Zealand households have TV sets. There are (1990) 59 medium-wave broadcasting stations, 28 FM broadcasting transmitters and 1 100 kw short-wave transmitter. Some commercial material is broadcast by both sound and TV services. Number of TV receiving licences at 31 March 1988 was 949,810.

Cinemas. There were in 1987, 121 cinemas.

Newspapers. There were (1987), 34 daily newspapers (10 morning and 24 evening) with a combined circulation of 1,134,835. Seven of these newspapers (2 each in Auckland, Wellington and Christchurch and 1 in Dunedin) had a circulation of 711,538.

JUSTICE, RELIGION, EDUCATION AND WELFARE

Justice. The judiciary consists of the Court of Appeal, the High Court and District Courts. All exercise both civil and criminal jurisdiction. Other special courts include the Maori Land Court, Family Courts and Children's and Young Persons' Courts. At the end of Dec. 1988 the prisons and corrective training institutions contained 3,318 prisoners, 3,173 males and 145 females. The death penalty for murder was replaced by life imprisonment in 1961.

The Criminal Injuries Compensation Act, 1963, which came into force on 1 Jan. 1964, provided for compensation of persons injured by certain criminal acts and the dependants of persons killed by such acts. However, this has now been phased out in favour of the Accident Compensation Act, 1972, except in the residual area of property damage caused by escapers. The Offenders Legal Aid Act 1954 provides that any person charged or convicted of any offence may apply for legal aid which may be granted depending on the person's means and the gravity of the offence etc. Since 1970 legal aid in civil proceedings (except divorce) has been available for persons of small or moderate means.

Police. The police in New Zealand are a national body maintained wholly by the central government. The total authorized establishment at 31 March 1989 was 5,328, the proportion of police to population being 1 to 625. The total cost of police services for the year 1988–89 was NZ$479m., equivalent to $144 per head of population. In New Zealand the police do not control traffic.

Ombudsmen. The office of Ombudsman was created in 1962. From 1975 additional Ombudsmen have been authorized. There are currently two. Ombudsmen's functions are to investigate complaints under the Ombudsman Act, the Official Information Act and the Local Government Official Information and Meetings Act from members of the public relating to administrative decisions of central, regional and local government.

During the year ended 31 March 1989, a total of 3,511 complaints were received, 593 of which were sustained.

Religion. No direct state aid is given to any form of religion. For the Church of England the country is divided into 7 dioceses, with a separate bishopric (Aotearoa) for the Maoris. The Presbyterian Church is divided into 23 presbyteries and the Maori Synod. The Moderator is elected annually. The Methodist Church is divided into 10 districts; the President is elected annually. The Roman Catholic Church is divided into 4 dioceses, with the Archbishop of Wellington as Metropolitan Archbishop.

Religious denomination	*Number of clergy (April 1977)*	*Number of adherents 1981 census*	*Number of adherents 1986 census* [1]
Church of England	780	814,740	784,059
Presbyterian	686	523,221	586,530
Roman Catholic (including 'Catholic' undefined)	931	456,858	495,300
Methodist	349	148,512	152,955
Baptist	254	50,043	67,716
Brethren	187	24,324	
Ratana	142	35,781	
Protestant (undefined)	—	16,986	
Salvation Army	241	20,490	
Latter-day Saints (Mormon)	162	37,686	
Congregationalist	10	3,825	
Seventh-day Adventist	55	11,523	871,689
Ringatu	88	6,114	
Christian (undefined)	—	101,901	
Jehovah's Witnesses	125	13,737	
Hebrew	7	3,360	
All other religious professions	—	279,768	
Agnostic	—	24,201	
Atheist	—	21,528	
Not specified	—	108,015	59,385
Object to state	—	473,115	244,152
Total	4,712	3,175,737	3,261,786

[1] Provisional.

Education. New Zealand has 7 universities, the University of Auckland, University of Waikato (at Hamilton), Victoria University of Wellington, Massey University (at Palmerston North), the University of Canterbury (at Christchurch), the University of Otago (at Dunedin) and Lincoln University (near Christchurch). The number of students in 1988 was 72,313. There were 6 teachers' training colleges with 4,502 students in 1988.

At 1 July 1988 there were 315 state secondary schools with 14,506 full-time teachers and 217,272 pupils. There were also 35 area high schools with 3,208 scholars in the secondary division. At 1 July 1988, 70,045 part-time pupils attended technical classes, and 33,601 received part-time instruction from the technical correspondence institute. At 1 July 1988, 1,171 pupils received tuition from the secondary department of the correspondence school. There were 18 registered private secondary schools with 451 teachers and 12,132 pupils.

At 1 July 1988, there were 2,316 state primary schools (including intermediate schools and departments), with 398,189 pupils; the number of teachers was 18,214. A correspondence school for children in remote areas and those otherwise unable to attend school had 1,683 primary pupils. There were 78 registered private primary schools with 356 teachers and 12,053 pupils.

Education is compulsory between the ages of 6 and 15. Children aged 3 and 4 years may enrol at the 568 free kindergartens maintained by Free Kindergarten Associations, which receive government assistance. There are also 644 play centres which also receive government subsidy. In July 1988 there were 42,537 and 14,628 children on the rolls respectively. There are also 618 childcare centres with 15,701 children, 534 *kohanga reo* (providing early childhood education in the Maori language) with 11,125 children, and a number of other smaller providers of early childhood care and education.

Total budgeted expenditure in 1988–89 on education was NZ$3,568m.

The universities are autonomous bodies. All state-funded primary and secondary schools are controlled by boards of trustees. Education in state schools is free for children under 19 years of age. All educational institutions are reviewed every 3 years by teams of educational reviewers.

Report of the Minister of Education ('E.1. Report'). Annually. Wellington, Government Printer

NZ Committee on Secondary Education. *Towards Partnership.* Dept. of Education, 1976

Health. At 30 June 1988 there were 8,980 doctors on the medical register. At 31 March 1988 there were 23,744 public hospital beds, of which 2,052 were for maternity cases.

Social Welfare. New Zealand's record for progressive legislation reaches back to 1898, when it was second only to Denmark in introducing non-contributory old-age pensions.

The present system came into operation from 1 April 1972. It provides for retirement, unemployment, widowhood, invalidity and sickness, as well as hospital and other medical care. Since 1 April 1969 the scheme has been financed from general taxation. Previously there was a special social security tax on virtually all income of individuals and companies in excess of $4 a week which met approximately three-quarters of the cost of the scheme, the balance being met from general taxation.

At 31 March 1988 the current weekly rates of widows', invalids', sickness, domestic purposes, unemployment and miners' benefits were $252·46 for a married couple, $151·48 for an unmarried person aged 18 years or over, and $122·57 for those under 18 years.

There are additional payments for dependent children.

All benefits except superannuation and family allowances are subject to an income test.

Family Benefit. A family benefit of $6 a week is payable for each dependent child.

Unemployment Benefit. The payment is subject to the condition that the applicant is capable and willing to undertake suitable employment.

Sickness Benefit. Payment is subject to medical evidence of incapacity of a person who has suffered a loss of weekly earnings as a result.

Other benefits include emergency benefits and additional benefits for those in need but who either do not qualify for one of the standard benefits or who have special needs or commitments for which a benefit at the standard rate is insufficient.

Medical, Hospital and Related Benefits. Medical, hospital and other related benefits are also provided under the Social Welfare scheme. These consist mainly of the payment of certain fees for medical attention by private practitioners, free treatment in public and mental hospitals, certain fees for treatment in private hospitals, maternity benefits (including ante-natal and post-natal treatment and services of doctors and nurses at confinements), pharmaceutical benefits (medicines, drugs, etc., prescribed by medical practitioners), etc. There are also benefits in connexion with dental services up to the age of 16, X-ray diagnosis, massage, home-nursing, artificial aids, etc.

Pensions. Provision is made for the payment of pensions and allowances to members or dependants of disabled, deceased or missing members, of the New Zealand Forces who served in the South African War, the two World Wars, the Korean War and the Vietnam War, to members of the New Zealand Mercantile Marine during the Second World War, or in connexion with any emergency whether arising out of the obligations undertaken by New Zealand in the Charter of the United Nations or otherwise. Principal rates are: War pensions are payable to widows at a rate of $151·48 a week, together with a mother's allowance of $93·46 a week, increased by $16 a week for each additional child, in addition to the normal child allowances of $6 per week for each child. These rates may be increased by an amount not exceeding $65·57 per week if the pensioner is suffering from total blindness, two or more serious disabilities or one extremely severe disability.

An 'economic pension' is defined as a supplementary pension granted on economic grounds and is additional to any pension payable as of right in respect of death or disablement. The maximum weekly rates are $252·46 to a married person (if unmarried, $151·48); to the widow or dependent widowed mother of a member, $149·23.

War veterans' allowances are $151·48 weekly for a single person and $126·23 for a married person, plus an equal amount to a wife, increased by $1.50 a week each at age 65, subject to income qualifications.

Domestic Purposes Benefit. A domestic purposes benefit is payable to unsupported male and female solo parents including divorced, separated and unmarried persons, prisoners' spouses and also to those who are required to give full-time care to a person (other than their spouse) who would otherwise have to be admitted to hospital.

Death Benefit. A death benefit of $1,260 is payable to a widow or widower if totally dependent on the deceased plus $630 for each dependent child.

Social Welfare Benefits and War Pensions:

Benefits	*Number in force at 31 March 1988*	*Total payments 1987–88 (NZ$1,000)*
SOCIAL WELFARE:		
Monetary—		
Retirement pension	479,985	3,986,544
Widows	12,862	104,170
Family	436,066	290,556
Invalids	24,379	196,051
Miners and orphans	1,546	6,243
Unemployment	86,782	672,694
Sickness	13,132	159,850
Domestic purposes	74,862	808,787
Total	1,129,614	6,224,895

Benefits	*Total payments 1987–88 (NZ$1,000)*
SOCIAL WELFARE (*contd.*):	
Health, etc.—	
Medical	92,178
Hospital	53,776
Maternity	30,543
Pharmaceutical	439,601
Supplementary	67,554
Total	683,652

WAR PENSIONS as at 31 March 1988:

Type of Pension	*Number in Force*	*Dependent Wives Included*	*Annual Value (NZ$ 1,000)*
War disablement	21,212	–	43,417
Dependants of disabled	40	–	263
Widows	4,225	–	18,551
Other dependants of deceased	26		
Economic	1,160	41	9,232
War service	1,648	959	18,196
War veteran's allowance	563	247	6,201
Police	32	–	73
Total	28,906	1,247	95,933

Reciprocity with Other Countries. There are reciprocal arrangements between New Zealand and Australia in respect of age, invalids', widows', family, unemployment and sickness benefits, and between New Zealand and the UK in respect of family, age, superannuation, widows', orphans', invalids', sickness and unemployment benefits.

Superannuation. Following the change of Government in Dec. 1975 the earnings-related superannuation scheme described in THE STATESMAN'S YEAR-BOOK, 1977–78, was abolished. Under the new system (operative from Feb. 1977) superannuation is payable to all New Zealanders on reaching the age of 60. It is taxable but not subject to an income test. The rates are based on the national average wage, of which married couples now receive 80% and single persons 60% of the married rate.

MINOR ISLANDS

The minor islands (total area, 320 sq. miles, 829 sq. km) included within the geographical boundaries of New Zealand (but not within any local government area) are the following: Kermadec Islands (34 sq. km), Three Kings Islands (8 sq. km), Auckland Islands (62 sq. km), Campbell Island (114 sq. km), Antipodes Islands (606 sq. km), Bounty Islands (1 sq. km), Snares Islands (3 sq. km), Solander Island (1 sq. km). With the exception of meteorological station staff on Raoul Island in the Kermadec Group (5 in 1986) and Campbell Island (10 in 1986) there are no inhabitants.

The **Kermadec Islands** were annexed to New Zealand in 1887, have no separate administration and all New Zealand laws apply to them. Situation, 29° 10' to 31° 30' S. lat., 177° 45' to 179° W. long., 1,000 miles NNE of New Zealand. The largest of the group is Raoul or Sunday Island, 29 sq. km, smaller islands being Macaulay and Curtis, while Macaulay Island is 3 miles in circuit.

TERRITORIES OVERSEAS

Territories Overseas coming within the jurisdiction of New Zealand consist of Tokelau and the Ross Dependency.

Tokelau. Situated some 480 km to the north of Western Samoa between 8° and 10° S. lat., and between 171° and 173° W. long., are the 3 atoll islands of Atafu, Nukunonu and Fakaofo of the Tokelau (Union) group. Formerly part of the Gilbert and Ellice Islands Colony, the group was transferred to the jurisdiction of New Zealand on 11 Feb. 1926. By legislation enacted in 1948, the Tokelau Islands were declared part of New Zealand as from 1 Jan. 1949. The area of the group is 1,011 hectares; the population at 10 Oct. 1986 was 1,690.

By the Tokelau Islands Act 1948 the Tokelau Group was included within the territorial boundaries of New Zealand; legislative powers are now invested in the Governor-General in Council. The inhabitants are British subjects and New Zealand citizens. In Dec. 1976 the territory was officially renamed 'Tokelau', the name by which it has customarily been known to its inhabitants.

From 8 Nov. 1974 the office of Administrator was invested in the Secretary of Foreign Affairs. Certain powers are delegated to the district officer in Apia, Western Samoa.

Because of the very restricted economic and social future in the atolls, the islanders agreed to a proposal put to them by the Minister of Island Territories in 1965 that over a period of years most of the population be resettled in New Zealand. Up to March 1975, 528 migrants entered New Zealand as permanent residents under Government sponsorship. At the request of the people the scheme has now been suspended.

New Zealand Government aid to Tokelau totalled $3·3m. for the year ended 31 March 1987.

Ross Dependency. By Imperial Order in Council, dated 30 July 1923, the territories between 160° E. long. and 150° W. long. and south of 60° S. lat. were brought within the jurisdiction of the New Zealand Government. The region was named the Ross Dependency. From time to time laws for the Dependency have been made by regulations promulgated by the Governor-General of New Zealand.

The mainland area is estimated at 400,000–450,000 sq. km and is mostly ice-covered. In Jan. 1957 a New Zealand expedition under Sir Edmund Hillary established a base in the Dependency. In Jan. 1958 Sir Edmund Hillary and 4 other New Zealanders reached the South Pole.

The main base—Scott Base—at Pram Point, Ross Island—is manned throughout the year, about 12 people being present during winter. Vanda Station in the dry ice-free Wright Valley is manned every summer.

Quartermain, L. B., *New Zealand and the Antarctic*. Wellington, 1971

SELF-GOVERNING TERRITORIES OVERSEAS

THE COOK ISLANDS

HISTORY. The Cook Islands, which lie between 8° and 23° S. lat., and 156° and 167° W. long., were proclaimed a British protectorate in 1888, and on 11 June 1901 were annexed and proclaimed part of New Zealand. In 1965 the Cook Islands became a self-governing territory in 'free association' with New Zealand.

AREA AND POPULATION. The islands within the territory fall roughly into two groups—the scattered islands towards the north (Northern group) and the islands towards the south known as the Lower group. The names of the islands with their populations as at the census of 1986 were as follows:

Lower Group—	*Area sq. km*	*Population*	*Northern Group—*	*Area sq. km*	*Population*
Rarotonga	67·2	9,281	Nassau	1·2	119
Mangaia	51·8	1,270	Palmerston (Avarau)	2·0	66
Atiu	26·9	1,040	Penrhyn (Tongareva)	9·8	496
Aitutaki	18·0	2,400	Manihiki (Humphrey)	5·4	505
Mauke (Parry Is.)	18·4	693	Rakahanga (Reirson)	4·1	276
Mitiaro	22·3	265	Pukapuka (Danger)	5·1	761
Manuae and Te au-o-tu	6·2	–	Suwarrow (Anchorage)	0·4	—
Takutea	1·3	–			
			Total	293	17,185

Vital statistics (1985): Births, 418; marriages, 105; deaths, 117.

CONSTITUTION AND GOVERNMENT. The Cook Islands Constitution Act 1964, which provides for the establishment of internal self-government in the Cook Islands, came into force on 4 Aug. 1965.

The Act establishes the Cook Islands as fully self-governing but linked to New Zealand by a common Head of State, the Queen, and a common citizenship, that of New Zealand. It provides for a ministerial system of government with a Cabinet consisting of a Premier and 6 other Ministers. The New Zealand Government is represented by a New Zealand Representative and the position of a Queen's Representative has recently been created by changes in the Constitution. New Zealand continues to be responsible for the external affairs and defence of the Cook Islands, subject to consultation between the New Zealand Prime Minister and the Prime Minister. The changed status of the Islands does not affect the consideration of subsidies or the right of free entry into New Zealand for exports from the group. The capital is Rarotonga, which was devastated by a hurricane in Jan. 1987.

The unicameral Parliament comprises 24 members elected for a term of 5 years; at general elections held in Nov. 1983, the Democratic Party won 13 seats and the Cook Islands Party 11 seats. There is also an advisory council composed of hereditary chiefs, the 15-member House of Ariki, without legislative powers.

Prime Minister: Dr Pupuke Robati.

ECONOMY AND TRADE

Budget. Budget 1987–88, NZ$40,104,700. Revenue is derived chiefly from customs duties which follow the New Zealand customs tariff, income tax and stamp sales.

Grants from New Zealand, mainly for medical, educational and general administrative purposes totalled NZ$7m. in 1982–83.

Currency. The Cook Island *dollar* is at par with the New Zealand *dollar*.

Agriculture. Livestock (1988): Pigs, 18,000; goats, 3,000.

Fisheries. Catch (1984) 800 tonnes.

Commerce. Exports, mainly to New Zealand, were valued at $6·5m. in 1984. Main items of export were fresh fruit and vegetables, fruit juice, copra and clothing. Imports totalled $30m. in 1984. The main items were foodstuffs, manufactured goods (including transport equipment), petrol and petroleum products.

COMMUNICATIONS

Roads. In 1984 there were 280 km of roads and 1,417 vehicles.

Aviation. New Zealand has financed the construction of an international airport at Rarotonga which became operational for jet services in Sept. 1973.

Shipping. A fortnightly cargo shipping service is provided between New Zealand, Niue and Rarotonga.

Telecommunications. Wireless stations are maintained at all the permanently inhabited islands. In 1983 there were 2,052 telephones. There are 2 radio stations on Rarotonga with (1983) 10,000 receivers.

Newspapers. The *Cook Islands News* (circulation 2,000) is the sole daily newspaper.

JUSTICE, RELIGION, EDUCATION AND HEALTH

Justice. There is a High Court and a Court of Appeal, from which further appeal is to the Privy Council in the UK.

Religion. Some 60% of the population belong to the Cook Islands Congregational Church, about 20% are Roman Catholics, and the rest chiefly Mormons and Seventh-Day Adventists.

Education. In 1986 there were 30 primary schools with 165 teachers and 3,183 pupils, and 8 secondary schools with 146 teachers and 2,156 pupils on Rarotonga, Aitutaki, Mangaia, Atiu, Mauke and Pukapuka.

Health. All Cook Islanders receive free medical and surgical treatment in their villages, the hospital and the tuberculosis sanatorium. Cook Islands Maori patients in the hospital and the sanatorium and all schoolchildren receive free dental treatment. In 1982 there were 18 doctors, 8 dentists and 65 nursing personnel. In 1981 there were 8 hospitals and clinics with 154 beds.

NIUE

History. Captain James Cook sighted Niue in 1774 but was repulsed by rock throwing warriors, their teeth painted red. Cook called the island Savage Island. Christian missionaries arrived in 1846. Niue became a British Protectorate in 1900 and was annexed to New Zealand in 1901. Internal self-government was achieved in free association with New Zealand on 19 Oct. 1974, New Zealand taking responsibility for external affairs and defence.

Area and Population.. Niue is the largest uplifted coral island in the world. Distance from Auckland, New Zealand, 1,343 miles; from Rarotonga, 580 miles. Area, 258 sq. km; height above sea-level, 220 ft. Population (census, 1986) 2,531; estimate 31 Dec. 1988 was 2,190. During 1988 births registered numbered 55, deaths 14. Migration to New Zealand is the main factor in population change. The capital is Alofi (811 inhabitants in census, 1986).

Constitution and Government. There is a Legislative Assembly of 20 members, 14 elected from 14 constituencies and 6 elected by all constituencies.

Premier: Sir Robert R. Rex, CMG, OBE.

Budget. Financial aid from New Zealand, 1987–88, totalled $8,500,000.

Agriculture. The most important products of the island are coconuts, honey, limes and root crops.

Trade. Exports, 1985, $175,924 (main export, coconut cream); imports, $3,753,384.

Communications. There is a wireless station at Alofi, the port of the island. A weekly commercial air service links Niue with New Zealand. Telephones (1986) 460.

Justice. There is a High Court under a Chief Justice, with a right of appeal to the New Zealand Supreme Court.

Religion. 75% of the population belong to the Congregational (Ekalesia Niue); 10% are Mormons and 5% Roman Catholics.

Education. There were 7 government schools with 702 pupils in 1987.

Health. In 1986 there were 3 doctors, 3 dentists, 7 midwives and 27 nursing personnel. There is a 25-bed hospital at Alofi.

DIPLOMATIC REPRESENTATIVES

Of New Zealand in Great Britain (New Zealand Hse, Haymarket, London, SW1Y 4TQ)
High Commissioner: Bryce Harland.

Of Great Britain in New Zealand (Reserve Bank of New Zealand Bldg., 2 The Terrace, Wellington, 1)
High Commissioner: R. A. C. Byatt, CMG.

Of New Zealand in the USA (37 Observatory Cir., NW, Washington, D.C., 20008)
Ambassador: H. H. (Tim) Francis.

Of the USA in New Zealand (29 Fitzherbert Terrace, Wellington)
Ambassador: Della M. Newman.

Of New Zealand to the United Nations
Ambassador: Terence O'Brien.

Further Reading

Statistical Information: The central statistical office for New Zealand is the Department of Statistics (Wellington, 1).

The beginning of a statistical service may be seen in the early 'Blue books' prepared annually from 1840 onwards under the direction of the Colonial Secretary, and designed primarily for the information of the Colonial Office in England. A permanent statistical authority was created in 1858. The Department of Statistics functions under the Statistics Act 1975 and reports to Parliament through the Minister of Statistics. A comprehensive statistical service has been developed to meet national requirements, and close contact is maintained with the United Nations Statistical Office and other international statistical organizations; through the Conference of Asian Statisticians assistance is being given with the development of statistics in the region. The oldest publications consist of *(a)* census results from 1858 onwards and *(b)* annual volumes of statistics (first published 1858 but covering years back to 1853). Main current publications:

New Zealand Official Yearbook. Annual, from 1893
Catalogue of New Zealand Statistics. 1972
Statistical Reports of New Zealand. Annual
Monthly Abstract of Statistics. From 1914
Pocket Digest of Statistics. Annual, 1927–31, 1938 ff.

Parliamentary Reports of Government Departments. Annual

Encyclopaedia of New Zealand. 3 vols. Wellington, 1966
National Bibliography. Wellington, 1968
Alley, R., *New Zealand and the Pacific*. Boulder, 1984
Bedggood, D., *Rich and Poor in New Zealand*. Sydney, 1980
Bush, G., *Local Government and Politics in New Zealand*. Sydney, 1980
Easton, B., *Social Policy and the Welfare State in New Zealand*. Auckland, 1980
Grover, R. R., *New Zealand*. [Bibliography] Oxford and Santa Barbara, 1981
Hawke, G. R., *The Making of New Zealand: An Economic History*. CUP, 1985
Morrell, W. P. and Hall, D. O. W., *A History of New Zealand Life*. Christchurch and London, 1957
Oliver, W. H. (ed.) *The Oxford History of New Zealand*. OUP, 1981
Robson, J. L. (ed.) *New Zealand: The Development of its Laws and Constitution*. 2nd ed. London, 1967
Sinclair, K., *A History of New Zealand*. Rev. ed. London, 1980
Thakur, R., *In Defence of New Zealand*. Wellington, 1984
Wards, I., *A Descriptive Atlas of New Zealand*. Wellington, Government Printer, 1976

NICARAGUA

Capital: Managua
Population: 3·5m. (1987)
GNP per capita: US$830 (1987)

República de Nicaragua

HISTORY. Active colonization of the Pacific coast was undertaken by Spaniards from Panama, beginning in 1523. After links with other Central American territories, and Mexico, Nicaragua became completely independent in 1838, but subject to a prolonged feud between the 'Liberals' of León and the 'Conservatives' of Granada. Mosquitia remained an autonomous kingdom on the Atlantic coast, under British protection until 1860.

On 5 Aug. 1914 the Bryan–Chamarro treaty between Nicaragua and the US was signed, under which the US in return for US$3m. acquired a permanent option for a canal route through Nicaragua and a 99-year option for a naval base in the Bay of Fonseca on the Pacific coast and Corn Islands on the Atlantic coast. It was ratified by Nicaragua on 7 April 1916 and by the US on 22 June 1916. US Marines finally left in 1933. The Bryan–Chamarro treaty was abrogated on 14 July 1970 and the Corn Islands handed back in 1971.

The 46-year political domination of Nicaragua by the Somoza family ended on 17 July 1979, after the 17 years long struggle by the Sandinista National Liberation Front flared into civil war. A Government Junta of National Reconstruction was established by the revolutionary government on 20 July 1979 and a 51-member Council of State later created; both were dissolved on 10 Jan. 1985 following new Presidential and legislative elections.

On 9 Jan. 1987 the President signed the new Constitution, but immediately reimposed a state of emergency, suspending many of the liberties granted under the Constitution.

In Nov. 1989, following infiltration into Nicaragua by some 2,000 contras, the ceasefire was ended. On 7 Nov. 1989 the Security Council of the UN voted to establish a UN Observer Group in Central America.

AREA AND POPULATION. Nicaragua is bounded north by Honduras, east by the Caribbean, south by Costa Rica and west by the Pacific. Area 127,849 sq. km (49,363 sq. miles) or 118,558 sq. km (45,775 sq. miles) if the lakes are excluded. The coastline runs 540 km on the Atlantic and 350 km on the Pacific. Population at the census of April 1971 was 1,877,972. Estimate (1987) 3·5m.

Nicaragua is the largest in area and most thinly populated of the Central American republics, 30 inhabitants per sq. km in 1987. In 1984, births, 139,800; marriages, 13,600; deaths, 30,700.

The people of the western half of the republic are principally of mixed Spanish and Indian extraction, some of pure Spanish descent and many Indians. The population of the eastern half is composed mainly of Mosquito and other Indians and Zambos, and Negroes from Jamaica and other islands of the Caribbean. The main ethnic groups in 1980 were: Mestizo, 69%; white, 14%; black, 8%; amerindian, 4%.

The areas, estimated populations (1985) and capitals of the 6 regions and 3 special zones are as follows:

Region	*Capital*	*Sq. km*	*1985*
1	Estelí	7,598	334,717
2	León	9,896	545,321
3	Managua	3,597	903,998
4	Jinotepe	4,726	514,113
5	Juigalpa	9,929	209,218
6	Matagalpa	16,370	406,913

Special Zone	*Capital*	*Sq. km*	*1985*
Zelaya Norte	Rosita	59,094	325,454
Zelaya Sur	Bluefields	[1]	[1]
Rio San Juan	San Carlos	7,448	34,330

[1] Included in Zelaya Norte.

The capital is Managua, situated on the lake of the same name, 180 ft above sea level, with (1985) 682,111 inhabitants. Other cities: León, 100,982; Granada,

88,636; Masaya, 74,946; Chinandega, 67,792; Matagalpa, 36,983; Esteli, 30,635; Tipitapa, 30,078; Chichigalpa, 28,889; Juigalpa, 25,625; Corinto, 24,250; Jinotepe, 23,538.

CLIMATE. The climate is tropical, with a wet season from May to Jan. Temperatures vary with altitude. Managua. Jan. 79°F (26°C), July 86°F (30°C). Annual rainfall 45" (1,140 mm).

CONSTITUTION AND GOVERNMENT. The National Assembly drafted and approved on 19 Nov. 1986 the new Constitution which was promulgated on 9 Jan. 1987. It provided for a unicameral National Assembly comprising 90 members directly elected by proportional representation, together with unsuccessful presidential election candidates obtaining a minimum level of votes.

The President and Vice-President are directly elected for a 6-year term commencing on the 10 Jan. following their date of election.

Under Article 185 of the Constitution, the President is empowered to declare a state of emergency and suspend certain of the civil rights provisions enshrined therein; this was done by the President immediately upon the promulgation of the Constitution.

Elections were held on 25 Feb 1990 and Violeta Barrios de Chamorro of the National Opposition Union (UNO) defeated Daniel Ortega Saavedra of the Sandinista National Liberation Front (FSLN). Provisional figures showed the UNO would have 52 seats in the National Assembly and FSLN 38 seats.

President: Violeta Barrios de Chamorro (elected 25 Feb. 1990, took office 25 April 1990).

National flag: Three horizontal stripes of blue, white, blue, with the national arms in the centre.

National anthem: Salve a ti Nicaragua (words by S. Ibarra Mayorga, 1937).

Local government. Since 26 July 1982 the country has been divided into 6 administrative regions and 3 special zones. Article 181 of the new Constitution provides for autonomous governments for Zelaya Norte and Zelaya Sur to offer self-government for the ethnic minorities who chiefly inhabit the Atlantic coast – Miskitos, Sumos, Ramos, creoles, garifunas (mixed black and amerindian) and mestizos.

DEFENCE. Conscription for 2 years was introduced in 1983 for men between 17 and 22 years.

Army. The Army is organized into 2 armoured, 2 motorized infantry, 2 frontier and 1 artillery brigades, 20 infantry and 4 engineer battalions. Equipment includes 130 T-54/-55 main battle tanks. Strength (1990) 73,500; 76,000 reservists and 58,000 Militia.

Navy. The Marina de Guerra Sandinista was (1989) some 600 strong and operates 18 inshore patrol craft of mixed Soviet and North Korean origins, 8 small inshore minesweepers and 3 minor landing craft.

Air Force. Formed in June 1938 as the Nicaraguan Army Air Force, the Air Force has been semi-independent since 1947. Its combat units are reported to have 4 L-39 Albatros light jet attack/trainers, 4 T-33 armed jet trainers, and 3 T-28 armed piston-engined trainers but confirmation is not available. Other equipment includes 2 C-47s, 2 Spanish-built Aviocar transports and smaller communications aircraft and helicopters, including 20 Mi-8/17s, 2 Mi-2s and 5 Mi-24 gunships and 6 SF.260s for counter-insurgency duties. Personnel (1990) 3,000.

INTERNATIONAL RELATIONS

Membership. Nicaragua is a member of the UN, OAS and the CACM.

ECONOMY

Budget. Revenue in 1986 was 147,000m. córdobas and expenditure 209.000m. córdobas.

Currency. The monetary unit is the new *córdoba* (C$), divided into 100 *centavos*. Bills form the greater part of the currency, in denominations from 1,000 córdobas to 1 córdoba. Coins are 5 and 1 *córdobas* and 50, 25, 10 and 5 *centavos*. March 1990, US$1 = 41,498 new *córdobas*; £1 = 68,015 new *córdobas*.

Banking. The Central Bank of Nicaragua came into operation on 1 Jan. 1961 as an autonomous bank of issue, absorbing the issue department of the National Bank. In July 1979 private financial banking was nationalized and branches of foreign banks were prohibited from receiving deposits.

Weights and Measures. Since 1893 the metric system of weights and measures has been recommended.

ENERGY AND NATURAL RESOURCES

Electricity. Installed capacity for electric energy was 398,000 kw. in 1986 and 1,200 kwh. was produced. Supply 120 volts; 60 Hz.

Minerals. Production of gold in 1980 was 67,000 troy oz.; of silver, 167,000 troy oz.; of copper, 3,000 tonnes. Large deposits of tungsten in Nueva Segovia were reported in 1961.

Agriculture. Agriculture is the principal source of national wealth, finding work for 65% of the labour force.

Of the total land area (about 36·5m. acres), about 17·5m. acres are under timber 900,000 acres are used for grazing and 2·1m. acres are arable. The unit of area used locally is the *manzana* (= 1·73 acres). Of the arable only 1·2m. acres are actively cultivated, 780,000 in annual crops such as cotton and rice and the remainder in perennial crops such as coffee and sugar-cane, or in two harvests a year in the cases of maize, sorghum and beans.

The products of the western half are varied, the most important being cotton, coffee, now under the aegis of the new *Instituto del Café*, sugar-cane, cocoa, maize, sesame and beans. Production (1988): Coffee, 43,000 tonnes; sugar-cane, 1,932,000 tonnes; seed cotton, 130,000 tonnes.

There were about 1·7m. head of cattle in 1988 and 745,000 pigs.

Forestry. Timber production has been declining, though the forests, which cover 10m. acres, contain mahogany and cedar, which were formerly largely exported, three varieties of rosewoods, guayacán (*lignum vitae*) and dye-woods. Production of sawn wood in 1983, 222,000 tonnes.

Fisheries. On the Atlantic coast fisheries are an important subsistence activity. Catch (1984) 4,300 tonnes.

INDUSTRY AND TRADE

Industry. Chief local industries are cane sugar, cooking oil, cigarettes, beer, leather products, plastics, textiles, chemical products, metal products, cement (100,000 tonnes in 1982), strong and soft drinks, soluble coffee, dairy products, meat, plywood. Production of oil products (1983) 489,000 tonnes.

Labour. In 1980 there were some 813,000 persons gainfully employed.

Commerce. The foreign trade of Nicaragua, in US$1m. (1984): Exports, 390m. consisting of cotton, coffee, chemical products, meat, sugar; imports, 750m.

Total trade between Nicaragua and UK (British Department of Trade returns, in £1,000 sterling):

	1985	*1986*	*1987*	*1988*	*1989*
Imports to UK	1,324	1,307	717	725	918
Exports and re-exports from UK	6,368	7,349	7,883	6,856	6,985

Tourism. In 1985 there were about 100,000 visitors, mainly from the USA.

COMMUNICATIONS

Roads. In 1984, 4,000 km were paved, out of a total of 25,000 km. The whole 368·5 km of the Nicaraguan section of the Pan-American Highway is now paved. The all-weather Roosevelt Highway linking Managua with the river port Rama was completed in 1968, to provide the first overland link with the Atlantic coast. There are paved roads to San Juan del Sur, Puerto Sandino and Corinto. In 1986 there were 78,000 vehicles in use including 46,000 cars.

Railways. The Pacific Railroad of Nicaragua, owned and operated by the Government, has a total length of 334 km, all single-track, and connects Corinto, Chinandega, León, Managua, Masaya and Granada. Passengers carried (1986) 3·5m. and 2·5m. tonnes of freight.

Aviation. LANICA, the Nicaraguan airline has daily flights to Miami and 6 flights a week to Guatemala and to the inner cities of Blue fields, Puerto Cabezas and the mining towns of Siuna and Bonanza. PANAM and TACA (Transportes Aéreos Centroamericanos), COPA (Compañía Panameña de Aviacíon), have daily services to Panama, Mexico, the other Central American countries and USA. SAM (Servicio Aéreo de Medellín) has 3 flights a week to Nicaragua and Colombia.

Shipping. The Pacific ports are Corinto (the largest), San Juan del Sur and Puerto Sandino through which pass most of the external trade. The chief eastern ports are El Bluff (for Bluefields) and Puerto Cabezas. The merchant marine consists solely of the Mamenic Line with 8 vessels. In 1980, 471,000 tonnes of goods were loaded and 1·14m. tonnes unloaded at Nicaraguan ports.

Post and Broadcasting. In 1984 there were 51,237 telephones.

The Tropical Radio Telegraph Company maintains a powerful station at Managua, and branch stations at Bluefields and Puerto Cabezas. The Government operates the National Radio with 47 broadcasting stations: There are 31 commercial stations and some 70 others. Number of radio sets in 1986 was 870,000 and television sets 200,000. There are 2 television stations at Managua.

Newspapers. In 1984 there were 3 daily newspapers (2 in Managua and 1 in León), with a total circulation of about 105,000.

JUSTICE, RELIGION, EDUCATION AND WELFARE

Justice. The judicial power is vested in a Supreme Court of Justice at Managua, 5 chambers of second instance (León, Masaya, Granada, Matagalpa and Bluefields) and 153 judges of inferior tribunals.

Religion. The prevailing form of religion is Roman Catholic, but religious liberty is guaranteed by the Constitution. The republic constitutes 1 archbishopric (seat at Managua) and 7 bishoprics (León, Granada, Estelí, Matagalpa, Juigalpa, Masaya and Puerto Cabezas). Protestants, established principally on the Atlantic coast, numbered 54,100 in 1966.

Education. There were, in 1986, 4,526 primary schools, with a total of 556,684 pupils and 17,199 teachers; and 119,000 pupils in secondary schools. The illiteracy rate was 12% in 1983. In 1987 there were 26,878 students in higher education.

Health. In 1984 there were 2,172 doctors, 222 dentists, 5,649 nursing personnel and 49 hospitals with 5,045 beds.

DIPLOMATIC REPRESENTATIVES

Of Nicaragua in Great Britain (8 Gloucester Rd., London, SW7 4PP)
Ambassador: Francisco d'Escoto.

Of Great Britain in Nicaragua
Ambassador and Consul-General: W. Marsden (resides in San José).

Of Nicaragua in the USA (1627 New Hampshire Ave., NW, Washington, D.C., 20009)
Chargé d'Affaires: Leonor de Huper.

Of the USA in Nicaragua (Km. 4½ Carretera Sur., Managua)
Ambassador: (Vacant).

Of Nicaragua to the United Nations
Ambassador: Dr Alejandro Serrana Caldera.

Further Reading

Dirección General Estadística y Censos, *Boletín de Estadística* (irregular intervals); and *Indicadores Economicos.*
Boletín de la Superintendencia de Bancos. Banco Central, Managua
Booth, J. A., *The End of the Beginning: The Nicaraguan Revolution.* Boulder, 1982
Christian, S., *Nicaragua: Revolution in the Family.* New York, 1985
Gilbert, D., *Sandinistas: The Party and the Revolution.* Oxford, 1988
McGinnis, J., *Solidarity with the People of Nicaragua.* New York, 1985
Rosset, P. and Vandermeer, J., (eds.) *The Nicaragua Reader: Documents of a Revolution under Fire.* New York, 1984
Spalding, R. J., *The Political Economics of Revolutionary Nicaragua.* London, 1987
Walker, T. W., *Nicaragua: The Land of Sandino.* Boulder, 1982.—*Nicaragua: The First Five Years.* New York, 1985
Woodward, R. L., *Nicaragua.* [Bibliography] Oxford and Santa Barbara, 1983

National Library: Biblioteca Nacional, Managua, D.N.

NIGER

Capital: Niamey
Population: 7·19m. (1988)
GNP per capita: US$310 (1988)

République du Niger

HISTORY. Niger was occupied by France between 1883 and 1899, and constituted a military territory in 1901, which became a part of French West Africa in 1904. It became an autonomous republic within the French Community on 18 Dec. 1958 and achieved full independence on 3 Aug. 1960.

On 15 April 1974 the first President, Hamani Diori, was overthrown in a military *coup* led by Lieut.-Col. Seyni Kountché, who suspended the constitution, dissolved the National Assembly and banned political groups.

AREA AND POPULATION. Niger is bounded north by Algeria and Libya, east by Chad, south by Nigeria, south-west by Benin and Burkina Faso, and west by Mali. Area, 1,186,408 sq. km (458,075 sq. miles), with a population at the 1977 census of 5,098,657. Estimate (1988) 7·19m. of which 20% live in urban areas. The major towns (populations 1983) are: Niamey, the capital (399,100 inhabitants), Zinder (82,800), Maradi (65,100), Tahoua (41,900), Agadez (27,000). Arlit (28,000), Akouta (26,000). In 1987, 20% of the population was urban. The population is composed chiefly of Hausa (54%), Songhai and Djerma (23%), Fulani (10%), Beriberi-Manga (9%) and Tuareg (3%).

The official language is French but Hausa is understood by 85% of the population.

Vital statistics (1985): Births, 330,000; deaths, 150,000.

CLIMATE. Precipitation determines the geographical division into a southern zone of agriculture, a central zone of pasturage and a desert-like northern zone. The country lacks water, with the exception of the south-western districts, which are watered by the Niger and its tributaries, and the southern zone, where there are a number of wells. Niamey, 95°F (35°C). Annual rainfall varies from 22" (560 mm) in the south to 7" (180 mm) in the Sahara zone.

CONSTITUTION AND GOVERNMENT. The country is administered by a Supreme Military Council of 12 officers led by the President, who appoints a Council of Ministers to assist him. A system of elected Development Councils at all levels has been created, culminating in a 150-member National Development Council with limited legislative powers charged with drafting a new constitution.

The Council of Ministers, in July 1989, comprised:

Head of State, President of SMC, Defence and Interior: Col. Ali Seybou (took office 14 Nov. 1987).
Prime Minister: Mamane Oumarou.
Foreign Affairs and Co-operation: Mahamat Sani Bako.

National flag: Three horizontal strips of orange, white and green, with an orange disc in the middle of the white strip.

Local government: Niger is divided into 7 *départements* (Agadez, Diffa, Dosso, Maradi, Niamey, Tahoua and Zinder), each under a prefect, sub-divided into 32 *arrondissements*, each under a sub-prefect, and some 150 communes.

DEFENCE. Selective military service for 2 years operates.

Army. The Army consists of 2 armoured reconnaissance squadrons, 6 infantry, 1 engineer, 1 parachute and 1 support company. Equipment includes 10 M-8, 18 AML-90 and 18 AML-60-7 armoured cars. Strength (1990) 3,200. There are additional paramilitary forces of some 4,500 men.

Air Force. The Air Force had (1990) over 100 officers and men, 2 C-130H and 3 Noratlas transports, 1 Boeing 737 VIP transport, 2 Cessna Skymasters and 3 Do 28D Skyservants and 1 Do 228 for communications duties.

INTERNATIONAL RELATIONS

Membership. Niger is a member of UN, OAU and is an ACP state of the EEC.

ECONOMY

Planning. The 10-year plan (1981–90) provided for an investment of 520,000m. francs CFA in the first phase (1981–85) with a prime aim of obtaining self-sufficiency in food and developing the mining sector.

Budget. The 1988 budget balanced at 114,310 francs CFA.

Currency. The unit of currency is the *franc CFA*, with a parity rate of 50 francs CFA to 1 French franc.

Banking. The *Banque Centrale des États de l'Afrique de l'Ouest* is the bank of issue, and there are 9 commercial banks in Niamey.

ENERGY AND NATURAL RESOURCES

Electricity. Production (1986) amounted to 265m. kwh. Supply 220 volts; 50 Hz.

Minerals. Large uranium deposits are mined at Arlit and Akouta. Concentrate production (1986) 3,108 tonnes. Phosphates are mined in the Niger valley, and coal reserves are being exploited by open-cast mining (production, 1985, 61,000 tonnes). Salt and natron are produced at Manga and Agadez, tin ore in Aïr, iron ore at Say.

Agriculture. The chief foodcrops in 1988 (in 1,000 tonnes) were: Millet, 1,783; rice, 50; sorghum, 603; cassava, 212; sugar-cane, 112; onions, 126. The main cash crops are ground-nuts (41), cotton and gum arabic.

Livestock (1988): Cattle, 3·5m.; horses, 296,000; asses, 512,000; sheep, 3·5m.; goats, 7·55m.; camels, 417,000; chickens, 17m.

Forestry. There were (1988) 2·5m. hectares of forest. Production (1986) 4·01m. cu. metres.

Fisheries. Catch (1986) 2,400 tonnes.

INDUSTRY AND TRADE

Industry. Some small manufacturing industries, mainly in Niamey, produce textiles, food products, furniture and chemicals.

Trade Unions. The sole national body is the *Union Nationale des Travailleurs du Niger*, which has 15,000 members in 31 unions.

Commerce. Imports in 1983 were valued at 123,288m. francs CFA and exports at 113,896m. francs CFA of which uranium formed 83%. France provided 33% of imports and Nigeria 32%, while 48% of exports went to France, 23% to Japan and 11% to Nigeria.

Total trade between Niger and UK (British Department of Trade returns, in £1,000 sterling):

	1985	*1986*	*1987*	*1988*	*1989*
Imports to UK	399	848	10,556	1,359	1,472
Exports and re-exports from UK	12,076	10,367	7,026	7,552	6,862

Tourism. There were 27,000 tourists in 1986.

COMMUNICATIONS

Roads. In 1987 there were 19,000 km of roads. Niamey and Zinder are the termini of two trans-Sahara motor routes; the Hoggar–Aïr–Zinder road extends to Kano and the Tanezrouft-Gao-Niamey road to Benin. A 648-km 'uranium road' runs from

Arlit to Tahoua. There were (1987), 9,000 private cars and 21,000 goods vehicles and vans.

Aviation. There are international airports at Niamey, Zinder and Maradi. Air Niger operates domestic services to over 20 other public airports.

Shipping. Sea-going vessels can reach Niamey (300 km. inside the country) between Sept. and March.

Post and Broadcasting. There were (1983) 159 post offices and (1985) 11,824 telephones. In 1986 there were 300,000 radio and 25,000 television receivers.

Newspapers. In 1986 there was 1 daily newspaper, *Le Sahel*, with a circulation of 3,000.

JUSTICE, RELIGION, EDUCATION AND WELFARE

Justice. There are Magistrates' and Assize Courts at Niamey, Zinder and Maradi, and justices of the peace in smaller centres. The Court of Appeal is at Niamey.

Religion. In 1983, 97% of the population was Sunni Moslem and the remainder mainly followed animist beliefs. There were about 30,000 Christians.

Education. There were, in 1986, 294,000 pupils and 7,600 teachers in 2,000 primary schools, 51,000 and 1,900 teachers in secondary schools, and 2,400 students and 120 teachers in the technical and teacher-training colleges. In 1984 there were 2,863 students and 314 teaching staff at the University of Niamey.

Health. In 1982 there were 2 hospitals, 36 medical centres and 116 dispensaries. In 1980 there were 136 doctors, and (in 1978) 10 dentists, 12 pharmacists, 88 midwives and 1,080 nursing personnel.

DIPLOMATIC REPRESENTATIVES

Of Niger in Great Britain
Ambassador: Ibrahim Bare Mainassara (resides in Paris).

Of Great Britain in Niger
Ambassador and Consul-General: V. E. Sutherland, CMG (resides in Abidjan).

Of Niger in the USA (2204 R. St., NW, Washington, D.C., 20008)
Ambassador: Col. Moumouni Adamou Djermakoye.

Of the USA in Niger (PO Box 11201, Niamey)
Ambassador: Carl C. Cundiff.

Of Niger to the United Nations
Ambassador: Col. Moumouni Adamo Djermakoye.

Further Reading

Bonardi, P., *La République du Niger*. Paris, 1960
Fugelstad, F., *A History of Niger, 1850–1960*. OUP, 1984
Séré de Rivières, E., *Histoire du Niger*. Paris, 1965

NIGERIA

Capital: Lagos
Population: 118·7m. (1988)
GNP per capita: US$290 (1988)

Federal Republic of Nigeria

HISTORY. The Federal Republic comprises a number of areas formerly under separate administrations. Lagos, ceded in Aug. 1861 by King Dosunmu, was placed under the Governor of Sierra Leone in 1866. In 1874 it was detached, together with Gold Coast Colony, and formed part of the latter until Jan. 1886, when a separate 'colony and protectorate of Lagos' was constituted. Meanwhile the United African Company had established British interests in the Niger valley, and in July 1886 the company obtained a charter under the name of the Royal Niger Company. This company surrendered its charter to the Crown on 31 Dec. 1899, and on 1 Jan. 1900 the greater part of its territories was formed into the protectorate of Northern Nigeria. Along the coast the Oil Rivers protectorate had been declared in June 1885. This was enlarged and renamed the Niger Coast protectorate in 1893; and on 1 Jan. 1900, on its absorbing the remainder of the territories of the Royal Niger Company, it became the protectorate of Southern Nigeria. In Feb. 1906 Lagos and Southern Nigeria were united into the 'colony and protectorate of Southern Nigeria', and on 1 Jan. 1914 the latter was amalgamated with the protectorate of Northern Nigeria to form the 'colony and protectorate of Nigeria', under a Governor. On 1 Oct. 1954 Nigeria became a federation under a Governor-General. In 1967, 12 states were created and in 1976 this was increased to 19 and to 21 in 1987. On 1 Oct. 1960 Nigeria became sovereign and independent and a member of the Commonwealth and on 1 Oct. 1963 Nigeria became a republic.

For the history of Nigeria from 1961 to 1978, see THE STATESMAN'S YEAR-BOOK, 1979–80, pp. 923-924.

AREA AND POPULATION. Nigeria is bounded north by Niger, east by Chad and Cameroon, south by the Gulf of Guinea and west by Benin. It has an area of 356,669 sq. miles (923,773 sq. km). Census population, Nov. 1963, 55,670,052. The results of the 1973 census have been officially repudiated. There is considerable uncertainty over the total population, but one estimate based on electoral registration in 1978 is 95m. Estimate (1988) 118·7m.

There were (1988) 21 states and a Federal Capital Territory (Abuja):

States	*Area (in sq. km)*	*Population 1988*	*States*	*Area (in sq. km)*	*Population 1988*
Akwa Ibom	7,081	5,077,540	Katsima	24,192	5,389,950
Anambra	17,675	7,879,900	Kwara	66,869	3,685,100
Bauchi	64,605	5,326,800	Lagos	3,345	4,569,400
Bendel	35,500	5,391,700	Niger	65,037	2,214,700
Benue	45,174	5,317,500	Ogun	16,762	3,397,900
Borno	116,400	6,567,200	Ondo	20,959	5,980,700
Cross River	20,156	2,505,766	Oyo	37,705	11,412,300
Gongola	91,390	5,708,200	Plateau	58,030	4,385,100
Imo	11,850	8,046,500	Rivers	21,850	3,768,100
Kaduna	46,053	3,689,850	Sokoto	102,535	9,944,100
Kano	43,285	12,351,100	Abuja (FCT)	7,315	523,900

The populations (1983) of the largest towns were as follows:

Lagos	1,097,000	Abeokuta	308,800	Kaduna	247,100
Ibadan	1,060,000	Port Harcourt	296,200	Mushin	240,700
Uyo	1,000,000 [1]	Zaria	274,000	Maiduguri	230,900
Ogbomosho	527,400	Ilesha	273,400	Enugu	228,400
Kano	487,100	Onitsha	268,700	Ede	221,900
Oshogbo	344,500	Ado-Ekiti	265,800	Aba	216,000
Ilorin	343,900	Iwo	261,600	Ife	214,500

[1] 1988.

Ila	189,700	Offa	142,300	Effon-Alaiye	110,600
Oyo	185,300	Owo	132,600	Kumo	107,000
Ikerre-Ekiti	176,800	Calabar	126,000	Shomolu	106,800
Benin City	165,900	Shaki	125,800	Oka-Akoko	103,500
Iseyin	157,000	Ondo	122,600	Ikare	101,700
Katsina	149,300	Akure	117,300	Sapele	100,600
Jos	149,000	Gusau	114,100	Minna	98,900
Sokoto	148,000	Ijebu-Ode	113,100	Warri	91,100
Ilobu	143,800				

It was announced in Feb. 1976 that the federal capital would be moved from Lagos to the Abuja area and, in Sept. 1982, Abuja was established as the future capital.

CLIMATE. Lying wholly within the tropics, temperatures everywhere are high. Rainfall varies very much, but decreases from the coast to the interior. The main rains occur from April to Oct. Lagos. Jan. 81°F (27·2°C), July 78°F (25·6°C). Annual rainfall 72" (1,836 mm). Ibadan. Jan. 80°F (26·7°C), July 76°F (24·4°C). Annual rainfall 45" (1,120 mm). Kano. Jan. 70°F (21·1°C), July 79°F (26·1°C). Annual rainfall 35" (869 mm). Port Harcourt. Jan. 79°F (26·1°C), July 77°F (25°C). Annual rainfall 100" (2,497 mm).

CONSTITUTION AND GOVERNMENT. Under the Constitution drafted and ratified in 1977–78, Nigeria is a sovereign, federal republic comprising 19 states and a federal capital district. Elections were held in Aug. 1983 and President Shagari was returned with 48% of the vote but in Dec. 1983 the military again took over control in a *coup* and in Jan. 1984 a Supreme Military Council under Maj.-Gen. Mohammed Buhari took office. In Aug. 1985 there was a *coup* following which a 29-member Armed Forces Ruling Council was sworn in on 30 Aug. 1985. Return to civilian rule is envisaged for 1992.

President, Defence, Chairman of AFRC and C.-in-C. of the Armed Forces: Gen. Ibrahim Badamisi Babangida.

On 12 Sept. 1985 the AFRC appointed a National Council of Ministers comprising the following in Jan. 1990:

Agriculture and Natural Resources: Ismaila Mamman. *Aviation:* T. O. Graham-Douglas. *Budget and Planning:* Abubakar Alhaji. *Culture and Social Welfare:* Mamman Ankah. *Education:* Babs Fafunwa. *External Affairs:* Rilwanu Lukman. *Finance and Economic Development:* Olu Falae. *Information:* Tony Momoh. *Internal Affairs:* Cmdre. Lamba Dung Gwom. *Petroleum Resources:* Jubril Aminu. *Science and Technology:* Gordian Ezekwe. *Youth and Sports:* Air-Cmdre. A. Ikazobor. *Water Resources:* Bunu Sheriff. *Communications:* Col. David Mark. *Employment, Labour and Productivity:* Abubakakar Umar. *Federal Capital Territory:* Maj.-Gen. Mohammed Nasko. *Health:* Olikoye Ransome-Kuti. *Industries:* Air Vice-Marshall Mohammed Yahaya. *Justice:* Bola Ajibola Mines. *Power and Steel:* Air Vice-Marshal Nura Imam. *Trade:* S. J. Ukpanah. *Transport:* Alani Akinrinade. *Works and Housing:* Brig. Mamman Kontagora. *Special Duties:* Hamza Abdullahi.

National flag: Three vertical strips of green, white, green.

Local Government: Each of the 21 states is administered by a military governor, who appoints and presides over a State Executive Council.

DEFENCE

Army. The Army consists of 1 armoured division, 2 mechanized divisions and 1 airborne and amphibious forces division, each with supporting artillery and engineer and reconnaissance units. Equipment includes 60 T-55 and 72 Vickers Mk 3 main battle tanks. Strength (1990) 80,000 men.

Navy. The Nigerian Navy comprises 1 German-built M-type frigate with a helicopter and one frigate-type training ship, 3 British-built corvettes, 6 fast missile craft, 2 minehunters, and some 4 inshore patrol craft. There are also 2 German-built tank landing ships, 1 survey ship and some 15 service craft. The Navy has a small aviation element equipped with 3 Lynx anti-submarine helicopters. Naval personnel in 1989 totalled 5,000.

An ambitious new construction programme of armed light forces to contain continuing maritime lawlessness off the Nigerian coast appears not to be proceeding. However the problem remains.

The Nigerian police also operate about 80 small patrol launches.

Air Force. The Nigerian Air Force was established in Jan. 1964. Pilots were trained initially in Canada, India and Ethiopia. The Air Force was built up subsequently with the aid of a Federal Republic of Germany mission; much first-line equipment has since been received from the Soviet Union.

It has 14 MiG-21 supersonic jetfighters, 15 Jaguar attack aircraft and MiG-21U fighter-trainers, and 22 Alpha Jet light attack/trainers. About 20 BO 105 twin-turbine helicopters have been acquired from the Federal Republic of Germany for search and rescue, while 2 F.27MPAs are used for maritime patrol. Transport units operate 9 C-130H-30 and C-130H Hercules 4-turboprop heavy transports, 5 twin-turboprop Aeritalia G222s, 2 Puma and 2 Super Puma helicopters, 3 DO 228s, a Boeing 727 and a Gulfstream II for VIP use, 18 Dornier 128-6 twin-turboprop and 18 DO 28D twin-piston utility aircraft, 2 Navajos and a Navajo Chieftain. Training types include 25 Bulldog primary trainers, 12 MB 339 jets for instrument training, and 22 L-39 Albatros advanced trainers. Personnel (1990) total about 9,500.

INTERNATIONAL RELATIONS

Membership. Nigeria is a member of UN, the Commonwealth, ECOWAS, OAU, OPEC and is an ACP state of EEC.

ECONOMY

Budget. The 1989 budget provided for expenditure (capital and recurrent) of ₦30,107m. and revenue of ₦17,707m.

Currency. Since 1 Jan. 1973 a decimal currency has been issued by the Central Bank of Nigeria, consisting of *Naira* (₦) and divided into 100 *kobo* (k). Notes in circulation ₦20, ₦10, ₦5, ₦1, 50k. Coins, 25k, 10k, 5k, 1k, ½k.

In March 1990, £1 = ₦12·94; US$1 = ₦7·90. The currency is unconvertible and subject to stringent exchange controls.

Banking. There were (1989) 28 commercial banks, 8 merchant banks, 3 development banks, 1 mortgage bank and 1 savings bank.

Weights and Measures. The metric system is in force.

ENERGY AND NATURAL RESOURCES

Electricity. The National Electric Power Authority generated 10,730m. kwh. in 1986. Supply 230 volts; 50 Hz.

Oil. There are refineries at Port Harcourt, Warri and at Kaduna. Oil represents 95% of exports. Production, 1989, 81m. tonnes.

Gas. Natural gas is being used at electric power stations at Afam, Ughelli and Utorogu. Reserves: 4,000,000m. cu. metres.

Water. Eleven River Basin Development Authorities have been established for water resources development.

Minerals. Production: Tin, 1980, 2,527 tonnes; columbite, 1977 (the world's largest producer), 800 tonnes; coal (1981) 114,875 tonnes. There are large deposits of iron ore, coal (reserves estimate 245m. tonnes), lead and zinc. There are small quantities of gold and uranium.

Agriculture. Of the total land mass, 75% is suitable for agriculture, including arable farming, forestry, livestock husbandry and fisheries. Main food crops are millet and sorghum in the north, plantains and oil palms in the south, and maize, yams, cassava and rice in much of the country, the north being, however, the main food producing area. Production, 1988 (in 1,000 tonnes) were: Millet, 4,000; sorghum, 4,940; plantains, 1,800; maize, 1,500; yams, 16,000; cassava, 14,000; rice, 1,400.

Groundnut production in 1988 was 720,000 tonnes. Cotton lint production (1988) 57,000 tonnes. Cocoa production has declined in recent years, to 140,000 tonnes in 1988; palm kernel was 370,000 tonnes and palm oil, 750,000 tonnes.

Livestock (1988). There were 12·2m. cattle, 13·2m. sheep, 26m. goats, 1·3m. pigs and 190m. poultry.

Forestry. In 1988 there were 14m. hectares of woodland 16% of the total land area. There are plywood factories at Epe, Sapele and Calabar, and numerous saw-mills. The most important timber species include mahogany, iroko, obeche, abwa, ebony and camwood.

Fisheries. The total catch (1984) was 373,800 tonnes.

INDUSTRY AND TRADE

Industry. Timber and hides and skins are major export commodities. Industrial products include soap, cigarettes, beer, margarine, groundnut oil, meat and cake, concentrated fruit juices, soft drinks, canned food, metal containers, ply-wood, textiles, ceramic products and cement (3m. tonnes, 1985). Of growing importance is the local assembly of motor vehicles, bicycles, radio equipment, electrical goods and sewing machines. In 1982, the Delta Steel Plant opened at Ovwian—Aladja.

Two petrochemical plants (one at Ekpan near Warri in Bendel State producing about 35,000 tonnes of polypropylene and 18,000 tonnes of carbon black annually, and one at Kaduna producing 30,000 tonnes of linear-alkyl benzene annually) were commissioned in 1988.

Trade Unions. There is a central labour Trade Union, the Nigerian Labour Congress.

Commerce. There is a great deal of internal commerce in local foodstuffs and imported goods moving by rail, lorry and pack animals overland, and by launches, rafts and canoes along an extensive and complex network of inland waterways.

Total trade in ₦m. for 4 years; oil 97% of exports in 1988.

	1984	*1985*	*1986*	*1987*
Imports (c.i.f.)	7,200	8,300	6,700	15,694
Exports and re-exports (f.o.b.)	8,700	12,600	6,800	29,578

Total trade between Nigeria and UK (according to British Department of Trade returns, in £1,000 sterling):

	1985	*1986*	*1987*	*1988*	*1989*
Imports to UK	660,410	329,036	159,386	128,123	129,406
Exports and re-exports from UK	960,703	566,176	481,568	330,476	388,777

Tourism. There were 340,000 foreign visitors in 1985.

COMMUNICATIONS

Roads (1980). There were 108,000 km of maintained roads and 633,268 vehicles were registered.

Railways. There are 3,505 route-km of line 1,067 mm gauge, which in 1984 ran 1,246m. tonne-km and carried 15·3m. passengers.

Aviation. There is an extensive system of internal and international air routes, serving Europe, USA, Middle East and South and West Africa. Regular services are operated by Nigerian Airways (WAAC), British Caledonian, UTA, KLM, SABENA, Swissair, PANAM and other lines. In 1981, 2·3m. passengers were carried on domestic and international routes.

Shipping. The principal ports are Lagos, Port Harcourt, Warri and Calabar.

Post and Broadcasting. Postal facilities are provided at 1,667 offices and agencies; telegraph, money order and savings bank services are provided at 280 of these. Most internal letter mail is carried by air at normal postage rates. External telegraph services are owned and operated by Nigerian External Telecommunications (NITEL), at Lagos, from which telegraphic communication is maintained with all parts of the world. There were 708,390 telephones in use in 1982, of which 249,150 were in Lagos and 33,138 in Ibadan. There is also a telex service.

Federal and some state governments have established commercial corporations for sound and television broadcasting, which are widely used in schools. In 1985 there were 15·7m. radio and 500,000 television receivers.

Cinemas (1974). There were 120 cinemas, with a seating capacity of 60,000. Mobile cinemas are used by the Federal and States Information Services.

Newspapers. In 1989 there were 18 daily and 30 weekly newspapers. The aggregate circulation is about 1m., of which the *Daily Times* (Lagos) has about 400,000. (Another 4 dailies were published in Lagos, 4 in Ikeja, 3 in Enugu, and 4 in Ibadan.)

JUSTICE, RELIGION, EDUCATION AND WELFARE

Justice. The highest court is the Federal Supreme Court, which consists of the Chief Justice of the Republic, and up to 15 Justices appointed by AFRC. It has original jurisdiction in any dispute between the Federal Republic and any State or between States; and to hear and determine appeals from the Federal Court of Appeal, which acts as an intermediate appellate Court to consider appeals from the High Court.

High Courts, presided over by a Chief Justice, are established in each state. All judges are appointed by the AFRC. Magistrates' courts are established throughout the Republic, and customary law courts in southern Nigeria. In each of the northern States of Nigeria there are the Sharia Court of Appeal and the Court of Resolution. Moslem Law has been codified in a Penal Code and is applied through Alkali courts.

Religion. Moslems, 48%; Christians, 34% (17% Protestants and 17% Roman Catholic); others, 18%. Northern Nigeria is mainly Moslem; Southern Nigeria is predominantly Christian and Western Nigeria is evenly divided between Christians, Moslems and animists.

Education. In 1982–83 there were 15,021,100 primary school pupils, and 2,421,625 secondary grammar/commercial school pupils.

In 1989 there were 9 teacher training colleges, 41 government 'Unity' colleges and 10 polytechnics.

In 1989 there were 16 federal and 8 state universities.

Health. Most tropical diseases are endemic to Nigeria. Blindness, yaws, leprosy, sleeping sickness, worm infections, malaria are major health problems which, however, are yielding to remedial and preventative measures. In co-operation with the World Health Organization river blindness and malaria are being tackled on a large scale, while annual campaigns are undertaken against the danger of smallpox epidemics. Dispensaries and travelling dispensaries are found in most parts of the country.

In 1980 there were 8,000 doctors and 75,000 hospital beds.

DIPLOMATIC REPRESENTATIVES

Of Nigeria in Great Britain (9 Northumberland Ave., London, WC2 5BX)
High Commissioner: George Dove-Edwin, GCVO (accredited 29 May 1986).

Of Great Britain in Nigeria (11 Eleke Cres., Victoria Island, Lagos)
High Commissioner: B. L. Barder.

Of Nigeria in the USA (2201 M. St., NW, Washington, D.C., 20037)
Ambassador: Hamzat Ahmadu.

Of the USA in Nigeria (2 Eleke Cres., Lagos)
Ambassador: Lannon Walker.

Of Nigeria to the United Nations
Ambassador: Maj.-Gen. Joseph N. Garba.

Further Reading

Nigeria Digest of Statistics. Lagos, 1951 ff. (quarterly)
Annual Abstract of Statistics. Federal Office of Statistics. Lagos, 1960 ff.
Nigeria Trade Journal. Federal Ministry of Commerce and Industries (quarterly)
Achebe, C., *The Trouble with Nigeria*. London, 1984
Adamolekun, L., *Politics and Administration in Nigeria*. Ibadan, 1986
Barbour, K. M. (ed.) *Nigeria in Maps*. London, 1982
Burns, A., *History of Nigeria*. 8th ed. London, 1978
Crowder, M. and Abdullahi, G., *Nigeria, an Introduction to its History*. London, 1979
Ikoku, S. G., *Nigeria's Fourth Coup: Options for Modern Statehood*. Enugu, 1984
Kirk-Greene, A. and Rimmer, D., *Nigeria since 1970*. London, 1981
Myers, R. A., *Nigeria*. [Bibliography] Oxford and Santa Barbara, 1989
Nwabueze, B. O., *The Presidential Constitution of Nigeria*. Lagos and London, 1982
Oyediran, O., *Nigerian Government and Politics under Military Rule, 1966–1979*. New York, 1980
Oyovbaine, S.E., *Federalism in Nigeria: A Study in the Development of the Nigerian State*. London, 1985
Shaw, T. M. and Aluko, O., *Nigerian Foreign Policy: Alternative Perceptions and Projections*. London, 1984
Simmons, M. and Obe, O. A., *Nigerian Handbook 1982–83*. London, 1982
Tijjani, A. and Williams, D. (eds.) *Shehu Shagari: My Vision of Nigeria*. London, 1981
Van Apeldoorn, G. J., *Perspectives on Drought and Famine in Nigeria*. London, 1981
Williams, D., *President and Power in Nigeria*. London, 1982
Zartman, I. W., *The Political Economy of Nigeria*. New York, 1983

NORWAY

Capital: Oslo
Population: 4·2m. (1989)
GNP per capita: US$20,020 (1988)

Kongeriket Norge

HISTORY. By the Treaty of 14 Jan. 1814 Norway was ceded to the King of Sweden by the King of Denmark, but the Norwegian people declared themselves independent and elected Prince Christian Frederik of Denmark as their king. The foreign Powers refused to recognize this election, and on 14 Aug. a convention proclaimed the independence of Norway in a personal union with Sweden. This was followed on 4 Nov. by the election of Karl XIII (II) as King of Norway. Norway declared this union dissolved, 7 June 1905, and Sweden agreed to the repeal of the union on 26 Oct. 1905. The throne was offered to a prince of the reigning house of Sweden, who declined. After a plebiscite, Prince Carl of Denmark was formally elected King on 18 Nov. 1905, and took the name of Haakon VII.

Norwegian Sovereigns

Inge Baardssøn	1204	Erik of Pomerania	1389
Haakon Haakonssøn	1217	Kristofer af Bavaria	1442
Magnus Lagabøter	1263	Karl Knutssøn	1449
Eirik Magnussøn	1280	Same Sovereigns as in Denmark	1450–1814
Haakon V Magnussøn	1299	Christian Frederik	1814
Magnus Erikssøn	1319	Same Sovereigns as in Sweden	1814–1905
Haakon VI Magnussøn	1343	Haakon VII	1905
Olav Haakonssøn	1381	Olav V	1957
Margrete	1388		

AREA AND POPULATION. Norway is bounded north by the Arctic ocean, east by the USSR, Finland and Sweden, south by the Skagerrak Straits and west by the North Sea.

Fylker (counties)	*Area (sq. km)*	*Census population 1 Nov. 1980*	*Population 1 Jan. 1989*	*Pop. per sq. km (total area) 1989*
Oslo (City)	454·0	452,023	456,124	1,004·7
Akershus	4,916·5	369,193	410,881	83·6
Østfold	4,183·4	233,301	237,997	56·9
Hedmark	27,388·4	187,223	186,806	6·8
Oppland	25,259·7	180,765	182,510	7·2
Buskerud	14,927·3	214,571	224,578	15·0
Vestfold	2,215·9	186,691	196,099	88·5
Telemark	15,315·1	162,050	163,205	10·7
Aust-Agder	9,211·7	90,629	96,567	10·5
Vest-Agder	7,280·3	136,718	143,350	19·7
Rogaland	9,140·7	305,490	333,351	36·5
Hordaland	15,633·8	391,463	407,926	26·1
Sogn og Fjordane	18,633·5	105,924	106,338	5·7
Møre og Romsdal	15,104·2	236,062	238,287	15·8
Sør-Trøndelag	18,831·4	244,760	249,624	13·3
Nord-Trøndelag	22,463·4	125,835	126,750	5·6
Nordland	38,327·1	244,493	239,611	6·3
Troms	25,953·8	146,818	146,648	5·7
Finnmark	48,637·3	78,331	74,034	1·5
Mainland total	323,877·5 [1]	4,092,340	4,220,686	13·0

Svalbard and Jan Mayen have an area of 63,080 sq. km. Persons staying on Svalbard and Jan Mayen are registered as residents of their home Norwegian municipality.

[1] 125,049 sq. miles.

On 1 Nov. 1980, 2,874,990 persons lived in densely populated areas and 1,197,939 in sparsely populated areas.

Population of the principal towns at 1 Jan. 1989:

Oslo	456,124	Sandnes	43,636	Gjøvik	26,136
Bergen	211,095	Sandefjord	35,853	Halden	25,841
Trondheim	136,601	Bodø	35,851	Moss	24,720
Stavanger	96,948	Ålesund	35,633	Lillehammer	22,564
Kristiansand	64,395	Porsgrunn	31,238	Harstad	22,340
Drammen	51,957	Haugesund	27,229	Molde	22,012
Tromsø	50,228	Ringerike	27,108	Kongsberg	21,217
Skien	47,553	Fredrikstad	26,525	Steinkjer	20,439

Vital statistics for calendar years:

	Marriages	*Divorces*	*Births*	*Still-born*	*Illegitimate* [1]	*Deaths*
1985	20,221	8,090	51,134	279	13,203	44,372
1986	20,513	7,891	52,514	268	14,673	43,560
1987	21,081	8,417	54,027	237	16,705	44,959
1988	21,744	8,772	57,526	270	19,407	45,354

[1] Excluding still-born.

CLIMATE. There is considerable variation in the climate because of the extent of latitude, the topography and the varying effectiveness of prevailing westerly winds and the Gulf Stream. Winters along the whole west coast are exceptionally mild but precipitation is considerable. Oslo. Jan. 24°F (–4·7°C), July 63°F (17·3°C). Annual rainfall 29·1" (740 mm). Bergen. Jan. 35°F (1·4°C), July 60°F (15·3°C). Annual rainfall 83" (2,108 mm). Trondheim. Jan. 26°F (–3·5°C), July 57°F (14°C). Annual rainfall 32·1" (870 mm).

REIGNING KING. Olav V, born 2 July 1903, married on 21 March 1929 to Princess Märtha of Sweden (born 28 March 1901, died 5 April 1954), daughter of the late Prince Carl (son of King Oscar II). He succeeded on the death of his father, King Haakon VII, on 21 Sept. 1957. *Offspring:* Princess Ragnhild Alexandra, born 9 June 1930 (married, 1953, Erling Lorentzen); Princess Astrid Maud Ingeborg, born 12 Feb. 1932 (married, 12 Jan. 1961, Hr. Johan Martin Ferner); Crown Prince Harald, born 21 Feb. 1937, married, 29 Aug. 1968, Sonja Haraldsen. *Offspring:* Princess Märtha Louise, born 22 Sept. 1971; Prince Haakon Magnus, born 20 July 1973.

CONSTITUTION AND GOVERNMENT. Norway is a constitutional and hereditary monarchy. The royal succession is in direct male line in the order of primogeniture. In default of male heirs the King may propose a successor to the Storting, but this assembly has the right to nominate another, if it does not agree with the proposal.

The Constitution, voted by the constituent assembly at Eidsvoll on 17 May 1814 and modified at various times, vests the legislative power of the realm in the Storting (Parliament). The royal veto may be exercised; but if the same Bill passes two Stortings formed by separate and subsequent elections it becomes the law of the land without the assent of the sovereign. The King has the command of the land, sea and air forces, and makes all appointments.

Since June 1938 all branches of the Government service, including the state church, are open to women.

National flag: Red with a blue white-bordered Scandinavian cross.

National anthem: Ja, vi elsker dette landet (words by B. Bjørnson, 1865; tune by R. Nordraak, 1865).

The Storting assembles every year. The meetings take place *suo jure*, and not by any writ from the King or the executive. They begin on the first weekday in Oct. each year, until June the following year. Every Norwegian subject of 18 years of age is entitled to vote, unless he is disqualified for a special cause. Women are, since 1913, entitled to vote under the same conditions as men. The mode of election is direct and the method of election is proportional. The country is divided into 19 districts, each electing from 4 to 15 representatives.

At the elections for the Storting held in 1989 the following parties were elected:

Labour, 63; Conservative, 37; Centre Party, 11; Christian Democratic Party, 14; Socialist Left Party, 17; Party of Progress, 22; Future for Finmark, 1

The Storting, when assembled, divides itself by election into the *Lagting* and the *Odelsting*. The former is composed of one-fourth of the members of the Storting, and the other of the remaining three-fourths. Each Ting (the Storting, the Odelsting and the Lagting) nominates its own president. Most questions are decided by the Storting, but questions relating to legislation must be considered and decided by the Odelsting and the Lagting separately. Only when the Odelsting and the Lagting disagree, the Bill has to be considered by the Storting in plenary sitting, and a new law can then only be decided by a majority of two-thirds of the voters. The same majority is required for alterations of the Constitution, which can only be decided by the Storting in plenary sitting. The Storting elects 5 delegates, whose duty it is to revise the public accounts. The Lagting and the ordinary members of the Supreme Court of Justice (the *Høyesterett*) form a High Court of the Realm (the *Riksrett*) for the trial of ministers, members of the *Høyesterett* and members of the Storting. The impeachment before the *Riksrett* can only be decided by the Odelsting.

The executive is represented by the King, who exercises his authority through the Cabinet or Council of State *(Statsråd)*, composed of a Prime Minister (*Statsminster*) and (at present) 17 ministers *(Statsråder)*. The ministers are entitled to be present in the Storting and to take part in the discussions, but without a vote.

A Coalition Government was formed and took office on 16 Oct. 1989. The members of the Government were in Oct. 1989:

Prime Minister: Jan P. Syse.

Foreign Affairs: Kjell Magne Bondevik. *Cultural Affairs and Church:* Eleonore Bjartveit. *Environment:* Kristin Hille Valla. *Industry:* Petter Thomassen. *Petroleum and Energy:* Eivind Reiten. *Local Government and Labour:* Johan J. Jakobsen. *Development Cooperation:* Tom Vraalsen. *Trade and Shipping:* Kaci Kullmann Five. *Fisheries:* Svein Munkejord. *Defence:* Per Ditlev-Simonsen. *Transport and Communications:* Lars Gunnar Lie. *Justice and the Police:* Else Bugge Fougner. *Finance:* Arne Skauge. *Family and Education:* Einar Steensnæs. *Health and Social Affairs:* Wenche Frogn Sellæg. *Agriculture:* Anne Vik. *Consumer Affairs:* Solveig Sollie. *Government Administration:* Kristin Clemet.

The official languages are Bokmål (or Riksmål) and Nynorsk (or Landsmål).

Local Government. For the purposes of administration the country is divided into 19 counties *(fylker)*, in each of which the central government is represented by a county governor *(fylkesmannen)*. The counties are divided into 448 municipalities, each of which usually corresponds in size to a parish *(prestegjeld)*. The municipalities are administered by municipal councils *(kommunestyrer)*, whose membership may vary between 13 and 85 councillors, and by a committee *(formannskap)* which is elected by and from the members of the council. The council is four times the size of the committee. The council elects a chairman and a vice-chairman from among the committee members.

Each of the 18 counties forms a county district *(fylkeskommune)*, while the remaining one, Oslo, comprises an urban district. The supreme authority in a county district is the county council *(fylkesting)*. The members of the county council are elected directly by the electors of the county and the number of representatives varies between 25 and 85. In a county district the county committee *(fylkesutvalg)* occupies a position corresponding to that of the committee *(formannskap)* in the primary districts. The county committee is elected by and from among the members of the county council. The number of county committee members is one-fourth of the membership of the county council, but must be not more than 15. The county council elects from among the members of the county committee a county sheriff *(fylkesordfører)* and a deputy sheriff.

DEFENCE. Service is universal and compulsory, liability in peace-time commencing at the age of 19 and continuing till the age of 44. The training period in the Army, Coastal Artillery and Anti-air Artillery is 12 months, and periodic refresher training, in the Navy and Air Force, 15 months and limited refresher training. The Norwegian Defence forces are organized into 2 integrated regional commands.

Army. In Northern Command the largest standing element is Brigade North. There are also 2 infantry battalions and 1 tank platoon, 1 SP field artillery battery and 1 AD battery in the North. Southern Command comprises 1 infantry battalion, 1 tank company and 1 self-propelled field artillery battery. Equipment includes 80 Leopard I and 37 M-48A5 main battle tanks. Strength (1990) 19,000 (including 13,000 conscripts). The fast mobilization force numbers about 146,000, organized in 12 brigades and a number of independent battalions and other units. There is also a Land Home Guard of 75,000.

Navy. The Royal Norwegian Navy has three components: The Navy, Coast Guard and Coastal Artillery. Main Naval combatants include 12 coastal submarines (including the first of a new German-built class, Ula, which entered service in 1989), 5 frigates, 2 corvettes, 36 missile craft, 7 coastal minesweepers, 1 minehunter and 2 minelayers. Auxiliaries comprise 1 submarine/missile craft support ship, 1 Royal Yacht and some 10 small general-purpose tenders. The Coastal Artillery man 32 coastal batteries and other static defence systems.

The personnel of the navy totals 5,300, of whom 3,500 are conscripts, and 2,000 serve in coast artillery. The main naval base is at Bergen (Håkonsvern), with subsidiary bases at Horten, Ramsund and Tromsø.

Finally, the naval elements of the Home Guard on mobilization can muster some 7,000 personnel, and man 2 tank landing craft and about 400 requisitioned fishing vessels.

The 13 Coast Guard offshore patrol vessels (of which 3 are armed, and of frigate capability) are Navy-subordinated, and assist other government agencies in rescue service, environmental patrols, surveillance and police duties. The coast guard numbers 700.

Air Force. The Royal Norwegian Air Force comprises the Air Force and the Anti-air Artillery. The Air Force consists of 4 squadrons of F-16 Fighting Falcons, 1 squadron of F-5 fighter-bombers, 1 maritime patrol squadron of P-3C Orions, 1 squadron of C-130H Hercules transports and Falcon 20s equipped for EW duties, 1 squadron with Twin Otter light transports and 2 squadrons of Bell 412SP helicopters. The Anti-air Artillery deploy 4 Nike surface-to-air missile batteries and several light anti-aircraft artillery units. Noah (Norwegian adapted Hawk missiles) batteries have been introduced to provide area and airfield defence. Nine Westland Sea King helicopters are used for search and rescue duties; 5 Lynx helicopters are operated for the Coast Guard; 18 O-1 Bird Dogs provide artillery spotting for the Army.

Total strength (1990) is about 9,100 personnel, including 5,300 conscripts.

Home Guard. The Home Guard is organized in small units equipped and trained for special tasks. Service after basic training is 1 week a year. The total strength is approximately 85,000.

INTERNATIONAL RELATIONS

Membership. Norway is a member of UN, NATO, EFTA, OECD, the Council of Europe and the Nordic Council.

ECONOMY

Budget. Current revenue and expenditure for years ending 31 Dec. (in 1,000 kroner):

	1984 [1]	*1985* [1]	*1986* [1]	*1987* [1]	*1988* [1]	*1989* [1 2]
Revenue	192,896,000	222,994,000	246,466,000	256,991,000	268,317,000	288,193,000
Expenditure	171,369,000	198,332,000	225,143,000	248,689,000	263,745,000	283,333,000

[1] Including National Insurance. [2] Voted budget.

National debt [1] for years ending 31 Dec. (in 1,000 kroner):

1980	106,908,000	1983	92,406,100	1986	194,287,500
1981	107,662,000	1984	115,805,000	1987	165,248,000
1982	103,799,400	1985	142,392,600	1988	166,471,000

[1] At the rate of par on foreign loans: including treasury bills (in 1m. kroner) which amounted to 14,600 in 1980, 35,111 in 1985, 48,975 in 1986, 24,644 in 1987, and 22,980 in 1988.

Currency. The Norwegian *krone*, of 100 øre, is of the value of about 11 *kroner* to £1 sterling. National bank-notes of 50, 100, 500 and 1,000 *kroner* are legal means of payment. March 1990, US$1 = 6·57 *kroner*; £1 = 10·77 *kroner*.

On 31 Aug. 1988 the nominal value of the coin in circulation was 1,199m. kroner; notes in circulation, 26,443m. kroner.

Banking. Norges Bank is the central bank. Supreme authority is vested in the Executive Board consisting of 7 members appointed by the King and the Supervisory Council consisting of 15 members elected by the Storting. It is the only bank of issue.

At the end of 1988 there were 29 private joint-stock banks. Their total amount of capital and funds was 13,318m. kroner (capital 8,121m., funds 5,197m.). Deposits amounted to 228,990m. kroner, of which 85,596m. kroner were at call and notice, and 143,394m. kroner on time.

The number of savings banks at the end of 1988 was 159. The total amount of funds of the savings banks amounted to 9,712m. kroner, and total deposits 178,119m. kroner, of which 74,797m. kroner were on ordinary terms and 103,322m. kroner on special terms.

Weights and Measures. The metric system of weights and measures has been obligatory since 1875.

ENERGY AND NATURAL RESOURCES

Electricity. Norway is a large producer of hydro-electric energy. The potential total hydro-electric power at regulated mean water flow is estimated at 170,000m. kwh. annually.

By the end of 1987 the capacity of the installations for production of thermo-electric energy was 252 mw. and the capacity for production of hydro-electric energy was 25,426 mw. In 1988 the total production of electricity amounted to 110,063m. kwh. of which 99·6% was produced by hydro-electric plants.

Most of the electricity is used for industrial purposes, especially by the chemical and basic metal industries for production of nitrate of calcium and other nitrogen products, carbide, ferrosilicon and other ferro-alloys, aluminium and zinc. The paper and pulp industries are also big consumers of electricity. Supply 130, 150, 220 and 230 volts; 50 Hz.

Oil. In 1963 sovereignty was proclaimed over the Norwegian continental shelf and in 1966 the first exploration well was drilled. By 1988 production was almost 7 times the domestic consumption of petroleum and is valued at about 10% of the GNP. Production (1989) 74m. tonnes.

Gas. Production (1988) 1,058,504m. cu. ft.

Minerals. Production and value of the chief concentrates, metals and alloys were:

	1986		*1987*	
Concentrates and minerals	*Tonnes*	*1,000 kroner*	*Tonnes*	*1,000 kroner*
Copper concentrates	116,943	225,018	102,471	303,282
Pyrites	379,934	80,062	355,686	77,819
Titanium ore	802,476	...	852,323	...
Zinc and lead concentrates	61,643	92,392	47,471	69,369
Metals and alloys				
Copper	35,202	...	30,101	...
Nickel	38,202	...	44,564	...
Aluminium	725,813	7,079,165	853,213	8,880,670
Ferro-alloys	195,257	546,659	193,748	564,045
Pig-iron	560,743	...	377,671	...
Zinc	90,475	...	116,593	...
Lead and tin	17	...	17	...

Agriculture. Norway, including Svalbard and Jan Mayen, is a barren and mountainous country. The arable soil is found in comparatively narrow strips, gathered in deep and narrow valleys and around fiords and lakes. Large, continuous tracts fit for cultivation do not exist. Of the total area, 79·3% is unproductive, 18% productive forest and 2·7% under cultivation.

Principal crops	Area [1] (hectares) 1986	1987	1988	Produce [1] (tonnes) 1986	1987	1988
Wheat	39,600	57,980	43,610	158,500	249,000	148,300
Rye	1,000	960	720	3,100	3,600	2,100
Barley	174,370	162,740	172,960	545,100	566,500	542,000
Oats	127,300	122,310	126,950	400,600	465,900	373,700
Potatoes	17,130	17,610	18,540	398,400	370,300	482,600
Hay	424,860	422,560	426,050	2,881,300	2,889,400	3,010,200

Livestock, 1988 [1]: 17,200 horses, 931,900 cattle (335,600 milch cows), 2,209,700 sheep, 91,500 goats, 745,300 pigs, 3,930,900 hens.

Fur production in 1987–88 was as follows (1986–87 in brackets): Silver fox, 223,300 (153,500); silver-blue fox, 170,300 (88,500); blue fox, 295,700 (376,000); mink, 509,000 (550,000).

[1] Holdings with at least 5 decares agricultural area in use.

Forestry. About 80% of the productive forest area consists of conifers and 20% of broadleaves. The annual increment (estimate, 1987) is about 19m. cu. metres with bark. The area of productive forests is 66,600 sq. km. Forests in public ownership cover 8,470 sq. km of this area. Between 1978–79 and 1987–88 an annual average of 8·9m. cu. metres was cut for sale: 8·6m. for industrial use, 300,000 for fuel. Of industrial use, 4·6m. cu. metres in the lumber industry, 3·4m. as pulp, 200,000 as particle board, about 400,000 in other industries or exported. About 700,000 cu. metres are consumed annually on farms.

Fisheries. The total number of registered fishermen in 1988 was 29,350, of whom 7,302 had another chief occupation. In 1988, the number of fishing vessels (all with motor) was 22,935, and of these, 12,039 were open boats.

The value of sea fisheries in 1m. kroner in 1988 was: Cod, 1,704; capelin, 57; mackerel, 306; coal-fish (saithe), 432; deep-water prawn, 702; haddock, 309; herring, 391; dogfish, 4. The catch totalled in 1988, 1·9m. tons, valued at 4,942m. kroner.

Fish farming is a growth industry, exports (1987) 2,309m. kroner.

INDUSTRY AND TRADE

Industry. Industry is chiefly based on raw materials produced within the country (wood, fish, etc.) and on water power, of which the country possesses a large amount. Crude petroleum and natural gas production, the manufacture of paper and paper products, industrial chemicals and basic metals are the most important export manufactures. In the following table are given figures for industrial establishments in 1987, excluding one-man units. Electrical plants, construction and building industry are not included. The values are given in 1m. kroner.

Industries	Establishments	Number of Employees	Gross value of production	Value added
Coalmining	1	676	197·7	40·0
Crude petroleum and natural gas	12	13,825	72,692·9	55,044·1
Metal-mining	12	2,666	1,388·9	453·7
Other-mining	429	3,282	2,440·2	1,113·1
Food manufacturing	2,221	50,049	56,828·0	7,166·9
Beverages	59	4,700	5,295·8	3,394·5
Tobacco	4	956	3,052·8	2,533·2
Textiles	427	8,343	3,535·1	1,297·4
Clothing, etc.	277	4,065	1,382·1	544·4
Footwear	31	612	207·0	94·1
Leather	51	699	322·0	101·0
Wood	1,448	20,262	14,161·8	4,295·5
Furniture and fixtures	512	8,977	4,887·3	1,667·0
Pulp and paper	132	13,100	15,201·7	3,834·9
Printing and publishing	1,922	36,919	19,620·9	8,569·1
Chemical, industrial	62	8,979	13,631·6	4,626·2
Chemical, other	161	6,171	5,888·9	2,181·3

Industries	*Establish-ments*	*Number of Employees*	*Gross value of produc-tion*	*Value added*
Petroleum, refined	3	1,034	9,506·7	439·7
Petroleum and coal	71	1,676	2,178·0	566·9
Rubber	72	1,599	925·4	382·1
Plastics	336	6,995	4,653·7	1,641·3
Ceramics	31	1,067	301·1	185·5
Glass	69	2,072	1,279·1	554·2
Other mineral products	522	8,339	7,429·9	2,672·4
Iron, steel and ferro-alloys	50	9,870	8,726·2	2,130·1
Non-ferrous metals	56	12,988	16,895·8	5,143·4
Metal products, except machinery	1,774	27,682	13,433·8	5,566·5
Machinery and equipment	1,354	42,747	39,611·2	10,637·6
Electrical apparatus and supplies	491	21,312	14,745·0	5,716·3
Transport equipment	914	25,655	17,115·8	5,310·9
Professional and scientific instruments, photographic and optical goods	76	1,656	1,007·1	424·9
Other manufacturing industries	297	3,075	1,309·8	555·5
Total (all included)	13,877	352,048	359,853·1	138,883·8

Income at factor cost (in 1m. kroner):

	1986	*1987*	*1988*
Net domestic product	441,157	480,497	501,942
Less Indirect taxes	99,922	107,059	107,042
Add Subsidies	29,569	31,515	33,638
	370,804	404,953	428,538
Industries			
Agriculture	10,198	11,684	11,175
Forestry	2,788	3,182	3,675
Fishing and fish breeding	3,519	3,187	3,707
Crude petroleum and natural gas production	27,066	24,755	15,529
Manufacturing, mining and quarrying	71,366	78,011	87,361
Electricity supply	11,429	12,385	14,659
Construction	25,374	32,534	33,593
Wholesale and retail trade	41,649	43,919	44,275
Hotels and restaurants	7,709	8,730	9,413
Financial services	24,287	29,691	29,875
Business services	22,292	25,008	27,450

Labour. Distribution of employed persons by occupation in 1988 showed 461,000 (22%) in technical, physical science, humanistic and artistic work; 135,000 (6%) administration; 239,000 (11%) clerical; 219,000 (10%) sales; 133,000 (6%) agriculture, forestry, fishing etc.; 8,000 (0·4%) mining and quarrying; 139,000 (7%) transport and communication; 463,000 (22%) manufacturing; 275,000 (13%) service, and 43,000 (2%) military and occupations not specified.

Source: Labour Force Sample Surveys.

Commerce. Total imports and exports in calendar years (in 1,000 kroner):

	1984	*1985*	*1986*	*1987*	*1988*
Imports	113,102,212	132,563,356	150,052,325	152,041,081	151,100,812
Exports	154,034,540	170,732,779	133,847,404	144,543,413	146,165,546

Trading according to countries was as follows (in 1,000 kroner):

	1987		*1988*	
Countries	*Imports*	*Exports*	*Imports*	*Exports*
Argentina	156,365	40,702	230,536	116,193
Australia and New Zealand	583,185	698,483	660,973	795,834
Belgium and Luxembourg	4,378,640	1,945,872	3,634,589	3,607,838
Brazil	773,523	376,506	877,436	421,891
Canada	1,877,465	1,166,056	2,546,566	2,114,310
China	1,157,868	559,516	712,908	438,419
Czechoslovakia	277,549	188,473	264,969	220,631

Countries	1987 Imports	1987 Exports	1988 Imports	1988 Exports
Denmark	11,734,081	7,394,155	11,430,379	7,777,145
Fed. Republic of Germany	23,555,899	21,448,057	20,517,675	18,105,178
Finland	6,603,609	2,842,569	5,259,429	3,321,102
France	5,618,155	7,338,247	5,012,644	10,525,918
Hong Kong	1,284,515	302,611	1,666,557	434,156
India	174,786	342,575	219,566	354,319
Italy	5,993,298	3,314,647	5,044,164	3,926,226
Japan	8,670,003	1,792,078	6,904,203	2,780,334
Korea	1,452,164	515,306	1,398,557	574,534
Netherlands	5,842,929	10,342,481	5,912,971	9,884,347
Panama	897,344	1,933,675	2,776,003	464,413
Poland	507,140	382,643	384,114	517,154
Portugal	1,474,040	798,568	1,454,868	949,742
Spain	1,736,538	874,777	1,829,012	1,265,969
Sweden	28,758,135	16,111,028	26,539,775	17,250,450
Switzerland	2,527,298	1,420,862	2,456,967	1,505,305
UK	13,617,861	38,638,438	11,721,879	38,130,979
USA	9,813,513	8,244,390	10,002,548	8,854,188
USSR	981,538	618,474	1,114,382	895,783

Principal items of import in 1988 (in 1,000 kroner): Machinery, transport equipment, etc., 59,892,269; fuel oil, etc., 5,540,479; base metals and manufactures thereof, 14,950,475; chemicals and related products, 12,385,267; textiles, 3,538,608.

Principal items of export in 1988 (in 1,000 kroner): Machinery and transport equipment, 21,923,731; base metals and manufactures thereof, 26,580,803; crude oil and natural gas, 48,513,043; edible animal products, 10,577,726; pulp and paper, 8,181,719.

Total trade between Norway and UK (British Department of Trade returns, in £1,000 sterling):

	1985	1986	1987	1988	1989
Imports to UK	4,367,154	3,265,157	3,290,339	3,074,000	3,637,119
Exports and re-exports from UK	1,140,376	1,147,790	1,220,844	1,053,613	1,056,506

COMMUNICATIONS

Roads. On 31 Dec. 1988 the length of the public roads (including roads in towns) was 87,578 km. Of these, 52,875 km were main roads; 59,928 km had some kind of paving, mostly bituminous and oil-gravel treatment, the rest being gravel-surfaced.

Number of registered motor vehicles (31 Dec. 1988) was 2,343,087, including 1,621,955 passenger cars (including taxis), 294,102 lorries and vans, 19,771 buses, 202,852 motor cycles and mopeds. The scheduled bus and lorry services in 1987 drove 4,199m. passenger-km.

Railways. The length of state railways on 31 Dec. 1988 was 4,168 km; of private companies, 16 km. On 2,422 km of state and 16 km of private railways electric traction is installed. Total receipts of the state railways and road traffic in 1988 were 3,099m. kroner; total expenses (excluding depreciation and interest on capital), 4,266m. kroner. The state railways carried 22·8m. tonnes of freight (of which 14m. was iron ore on the Ofoten railway) and 34·1m. passengers.

Aviation. Det Norske Luftfartselskap (DNL) started its post-war activities on 1 April 1946. On 1 Aug. 1946 DNL, together with DDL (Danish Airlines) and ABA/SILA (Swedish Airlines), formed the 'Scandinavian Airlines System'—SAS. The 3 companies remained independent units, but all services were co-ordinated. In 1951 a new agreement was signed (retroactive from 1 Oct. 1950) according to which the 3 national companies became holding partners in a new organization which took over the entire operational system. Denmark and Norway hold each two-sevenths and Sweden three-sevenths of the capital, but they have joint responsibility towards third parties.

On 31 Dec. 1988 there were 868 registered engine-driven aircraft. Scheduled air services are run by SAS, Braathens South-American and Far East Air transport service (SAFE) and Wideroes Flyveselskap service. The Norwegian share of the scheduled air service run by SAS is two-sevenths of the SAS service on international routes and the total SAS service in Norway.

Air transport on domestic routes only:

	1,000 km flown	*Passengers carried*	*1,000 passenger-km*	*Post, luggage, freight and passengers (1,000 ton-km) Total*	*Of which post*
1985	37,014	5,207,949	2,091	196,000	7,000
1986	44,171	5,764,926	2,271	210,000	8,000
1987	45,882	6,360,417	2,495	231,000	8,000
1988	47,436	6,421,708	2,553	239,000	8,000

Shipping. The total registered mercantile marine on 1 Jan. 1989 was 1,532 vessels, 13m. gross tons (steam and motor vessels above 100 gross tons). These figures do not include fishing and catching boats, tugs, salvage vessels, icebreakers and similar special types of vessels, totalling 787 vessels of 370,000 gross tons.

Vessels entering Norway from foreign countries 1985	*Total No.*	*Net tons*
Norwegian	6,970	17,470
Foreign	10,013	31,264
Total entered	16,983	48,734

Goods (in 1,000 tonnes) in 1988 discharged, 18,799; loaded, 63,707, of which 11,726 was Swedish iron ore shipped from Narvik.

Telecommunications and Broadcasting. Number of telephone connexions on 31 Dec. 1988 was 2,016,213 (47·8 per 100 of population). Receipts, 13,884·3m. kroner; expenses, 12,405·3m. kroner (interest on capital included) for State Telecommunications. *Norsk Rikskringkasting* is a non-commercial enterprise operated by an independent state organization and broadcasts 1 programme (P1) on long-, medium-, and short-waves and on FM and 1 programme (P2) on FM. Local programmes are also broadcast. It broadcasts 1 TV programme from 2,259 transmitters. Colour programmes are broadcast by PAL system. Number of television licences, 1,471,967.

Cinemas. There were 426 cinemas with a seating capacity of 110,913 in 1987.

Newspapers. There were 61 daily newspapers with a combined circulation of 2,087,737 in 1988.

JUSTICE, RELIGION, EDUCATION AND WELFARE

Justice. The judicature is common to civil and criminal cases. The same professional judges, who are legally educated, preside over both kinds of cases. These judges are as such state officials. The participation of lay judges and jurors, both summoned for the individual case, varies according to the kind of court and kind of case.

The ordinary Court of First Instance *(Herredsrett* and *Byrett)* is in criminal cases composed of one professional judge and 2 lay judges, chosen by ballot from a panel elected by the district council. In civil cases 2 lay judges may participate. The ordinary Court of First Instance is in general competent in all kinds of cases with the exception of criminal cases where the maximum penalty prescribed in the Criminal Code for the offence in question exceeds five years imprisonment. Altogether there are about 100 ordinary courts of first instance.

In every community there is a Conciliation Council *(Forliksråd)* composed of 3 lay persons elected by the district council. A civil lawsuit usually begins with mediation in the council which also has judicial authority in minor civil cases.

The ordinary Courts of Second Instance *(Lagmannsrett)*, of which there are 5, are composed of 3 professional judges. Additionally, in civil cases 2 or 4 lay judges may be summoned. In criminal cases a jury of 10 lay persons is summoned to determine whether the defendant is guilty according to the charge. Four lay persons take part in the assessment of the punishment. In civil cases, the Court of Second Instance is an ordinary court of appeal. In criminal cases in which the lower court does not have judicial authority, it is itself the court of first instance. In other criminal cases it is an appeal court as far as the appeal is based on an attack against the lower court's assessment of the facts when determining the guilt of the defendant. An appeal based on any other alleged mistakes is brought directly before the Supreme Court.

The Supreme Court *(Høyesterett)* is the court of last resort. There are 18 Supreme Court judges. Each individual case is heard by 5 judges. Some major cases are determined in plenary session. The Supreme Court may in general examine every aspect of the case and the handling of it by the lower courts. However, in criminal cases the Court may not overrule the lower court's assessment of the facts as far as the guilt of the defendant is concerned.

The Court of Impeachment *(Riksretten)* is composed of 5 judges of the Supreme Court and 10 members of Parliament.

All serious offences are prosecuted by the State. The Public Prosecution Authority *(Påtalemyndigheten)* consists of the Attorney General *(Riksadvokaten)*, the district attorneys *(statsadvokater)* and legally qualified officers of the ordinary police force. Counsel for the defence is in general provided for by the State.

Religion. There is complete freedom of religion, the Evangelical Lutheran Church, however, being the national church, endowed by the State. Its clergy are nominated by the King. Ecclesiastically Norway is divided into 11 *Bispedømmer* (bishoprics), 93 *Prostier* (provostships or archdeaconries) and 623 *Prestegjeld* (clerical districts). There were 190,322 members of registered and unregistered religious communities outside the Evangelical Lutheran Church, subsidized by central government and local authorities in 1989. The Roman Catholics are under a Bishop at Oslo, a Vicar Apostolic at Trondheim and a Vicar Apostolic at Tromsø.

Education. In Norway the children normally start their school attendance the year they are 7 years of age and finish compulsory school the year they complete 16 years of age.

On 1 Sept. 1988 the number of primary schools and pupils were as follows: 3,475 primary schools, 492,769 pupils; 85 special schools for the handicapped, 2,583 pupils.

On 1 Oct. 1987 the number of pupils in upper secondary schools, *i.e.*, folk high schools, secondary general schools and vocational schools, was 200,476.

There are in Norway 4 universities and 11 institutions equivalent to universities. In autumn 1988 the total number of students was 48,328. The University of Oslo, founded in 1811, had 20,886 students. The University of Bergen, founded in 1948, had 9,843 students. The University of Trondheim consists of the Norwegian Institute of Technology, founded in 1910, and the College of Arts and Science, founded in 1925. At each of them the number of students was in autumn 1987, 6,247 and 3,854 respectively. The University of Tromsø was established in 1968; 2,503 students were registered in autumn 1987. The other university institutions had 4,995 students.

On 1 Oct. 1987 there were at other schools of higher education, 61,044 students. These included 13,660 at colleges for teachers, 7,694 at colleges for engineers and 9,221 at district colleges.

In 1985–86 there were 6,673 Norwegian students and pupils attending foreign universities and schools.

Health. In 1986 there were 9,443 doctors and (1987) 66,373 hospital beds.

Social Security. In 1988, about 108,000m. kroner were paid under different social insurance schemes, amounting to approximately 21% of the net national income.

The National Insurance Act of 17 June 1966, which came into force on 1 Jan. 1967, replaced the schemes relating to old age pensions, disability benefits, widows' and mothers' pensions, benefits to unmarried women, 'survivors' benefit for children and rehabilitation aid. Schemes relating to health insurance, unemployment insurance and occupational injury insurance were revised and incorporated in National Insurance Scheme on 1 Jan. 1971. As from 1 Jan. 1981, benefits to divorced and separated supporters also are covered by the National Insurance Scheme.

The following conspectus gives a survey of schemes established by law. Many municipalities grant additional benefits to old-age, disablement and survivor's pensions.

Type of scheme	*Introduced*[1]	*Scope*	*Principal benefits as from 1 Oct. 1989*
National insurance	1967 (1989)		
Medical care and sickness cash benefits[2]	1911	All residents	Medical benefits: all hospital expenses; cost share of expense of medical consultation, important medicines, travel expenses, etc. (such costs exceeding 950kr. a calendar year are paid in full by the National Insurance).
		Nearly all wage-earners	Daily sickness allowances: kr. 63 to 755 per day cash (5 days a week). The present sickness allowance scheme (established 1978) entitles employees to a daily allowance equal to 100% of their gross earned income (within certain limits) from and including the first day of absence; self-employed persons, ordinarily 65% of gross earned income as from the 15th day. Supplementary insurance available
		All female residents giving birth	Maternity allowances: same as sickness allowances for 120 days (time sharing with the father is possible) or a lump sum of kr. 6,147 per child
Unemployment benefits[2]	1939	Nearly all wage-earners	Daily allowance during unemployment kr. 50 to 392 per day, excluding supplement for supported child(ren) (six days a week). Contributions to training and retraining, removal expenses, wage subsidies
Rehabilitation benefits[3]	1961	Persons unfit for work because of disablement and persons who have a substantially limited general functional capacity	Training; treatment; rehabilitation allowance grants and loans Full rehabilitation allowance equals old age pension (however, no special supplement is granted, see below.)
Disability benefits[3]	1961	All residents	*A basic grant* and *an assistance grant* to persons with special needs. Basic grant: kr. 4,584 to kr. 15,276 per annum. Assistance grant: kr. 7,632, may be increased for children below 18 years of age to a maximum of kr. 42,744 per annum
		All residents between 16 and 67 years of age	*Disability pension* to persons between 16 and 67 years of age, occupationally disabled by at least 50%, unfit for rehabilitation Full disability pension equals old age pension

For notes *see* p. 961.

Type of scheme	Intro-duced [1]	Scope	Principal benefits as from 1 Oct. 1989
Occupational injury benefits [2] (industrial workers 1895; fishermen 1909; seamen 1913; military personnel 1953, combined in the act of occupational injury insurance 1960)	1960	All employed persons, drafted military personnel, school children and students; self-employed on a voluntary basis	The ordinary benefits of the National Insurance, alternative calculation of pensions etc. which in many cases are more favourable for the insured person—or his survivors than the ordinary rules *An occupational injury compensation,* alone or in addition to a disability pension
Old age pensions [3]	1937	All persons above 67 years of age	Basic pensions: Single, kr. 32,700; couples, kr. 49,050 per annum; supplementary pensions based on previous pensionable income; supplement for supported spouse kr. 16,350 per annum; supplement for supported child(ren) kr. 8,175 to kr. 4,088 per child per annum; *see below* under 'Special supplement' and 'Compensation supplement'
Death grants	1967	All residents	A certain amount fixed by the Storting, for the time being kr. 4,000
Survivors' benefits [3]	1965	All residents	Full pension = kr. 32,700 per annum + 55% of the supplementary pension due to the deceased, *transitional benefits,* child care allowance and educational allowances (*see below* under 'Special supplement' and 'Compensation supplement')
Children's pension [3]	1958	Under 18 (20) years of age, after loss of one or both parents	40% of basic amount (kr. 13,080) for first child, 25% (kr. 8,175) for each additional child. If both parents are dead, full survivors' pension for first, 40% of basic amount for second, 25% third, etc., child
Benefits to unmarried supporters [3]	1965	Unmarried mothers or fathers	An additional maternity benefit of kr. 9,261, transitional benefit, full amount kr. 32,700 per annum, child care allowance and educational allowances (*see below* under 'Special supplement' and 'Family allowances')
Benefits to divorced and separated supporters [4]	1972	Divorced and separated supporters	Same kind of benefits as unmarried supporters above
Benefits to unmarried persons forced to live at home [3]	1965	Unmarried persons under 67 years of age having stayed at home for at least 5 years to give necessary care and attention to parents or other near relatives	Transitional benefit or a pension kr. 32,700 per annum, educational allowances (*see below* under 'Special supplement' and 'Compensation supplement')

For notes *see* p. 961.

Type of scheme	*Introduced* [1]	*Scope*	*Principal benefits as from 1 Oct. 1989*
Special supplement to National Insurance pensions or transitional benefits	1969 (1989)	Pensioners and persons with transitional allowance on basic rates	Full special supplement, 57% of basic amount, *i.e.* kr. 18,639. For a married pensioner the rate may be different. If the pensioner supports a spouse who is 60 years or older, the rate is 104·5%, *i.e.*kr. 34,172. If the spouse has a pension of his/her own, the rate is 52·25%, *i.e.*kr. 7,086
Compensation supplement to National Insurance pensions or transitional benefits	1970 (1989)	Pensioners, persons with transitional benefits (except unmarried, divorced and separated supporters) or rehabilitation allowances	Full compensation supplement kr. 500 for single persons and kr. 750 for married couples per annum
Family allowances	1946 (1989)	All families with children under 16 years of age	Kr. 7,836 per annum for the first child, kr. 8,328 for the second, kr. 9,744 for the third, kr. 10,368 for the fourth and kr. 10,752 for the fifth and each additional child. Single supporters receive benefits for one child more than the actual number. Families resident in certain districts north of the Arctic Circle receive an additional amount of kr. 2,400 per child
War pensions	1946 (1989)	War victims, 1939–45	Pensions up to kr. 144,960 per annum for single pensioners/couples (excluding supplement for supported child(ren); widows' and children's pensions)
Special pension schemes:		Persons with at least: [5]	Maximum old-age pension:
Forestry workers	1952 (1989)	750 premium weeks (1,500 „ „)	Kr. 32,700 per annum (for supported spouse an additional 33⅓%, 10% supplement per child, maximum 5 children)
Fishermen	1958 (1989)	750 premium weeks (1,500 „ „)	Kr. 32,700 per annum (for supported spouse an additional 50%, 30% supplement per child)
Seamen	1948 (1989)	150 months service (360 „ „)	Kr. 107,150 [6] per annum (officers) Kr. 76,536 [6] „ „ (others) (no spouse supplement, an additional 10% per child)

[1] Date of latest revision of law in brackets.
[2] Transferred to national insurance scheme and revised in 1971.
[3] Transferred to national insurance scheme and revised in 1967.
[4] Transferred to national insurance scheme and revised in 1981.
[5] Requirements for maximum pensions in brackets.
[6] Supplements for service during war not included.

Provisions have been laid down for the integration of more than one benefit, pension, etc., so as to limit the total amount.

As a main rule all running benefits are taxable, while lump sums are not taxed. Certain tax modifications apply to all pensioners and pensioners with no other income than minimum benefits are not charged for tax.

SVALBARD

An archipelago situated between 10° and 35° E. long. and between 74° and 81° N. lat. Total area, 62,000 sq. km (24,000 sq. miles).

The main islands of the archipelago are Spitsbergen (formerly called Vestspitsbergen), Nordaustlandet, Edgeøya, Barentsøya, Prins Karls Forland, Bjørnøya, Hopen, Kong Karls Land, Kvitøya, and many small islands. The arctic climate is tempered by mild winds from the Atlantic.

The archipelago was probably discovered by Norsemen in 1194 and rediscovered by the Dutch navigator Barents in 1596. In the 17th century the very lucrative whale-hunting caused rival Dutch, British and Danish–Norwegian claims to sovereignty and quarrels about the hunting-places. But when in the 18th century the whale-hunting ended, the question of the sovereignty of Svalbard lost its significance; it was again raised in the 20th century, owing to the discovery and exploitation of coalfields. By a treaty, signed on 9 Feb. 1920 in Paris, Norway's sovereignty over the archipelago was recognized. On 14 Aug. 1925 the archipelago was officially incorporated in Norway.

Coal is the principal product. Of the 3 Norwegian and 3 Soviet mining camps, 2 Norwegian and 2 Soviet camps are operating. Total population on 31 Dec. 1988 was 3,646, of which 1,055 were Norwegians, 2,579 Soviet citizens, and 12 Poles. In 1987, 473,279 tonnes of coal were exported from the Norwegian and 462,942 tonnes from the Soviet mines.

Norwegian and foreign companies have been prospecting for oil. So far 5 deep drillings have been made, but oil and gas finds have not been reported.

There are Norwegian meteorological and/or radio stations at the following places: Bjørnøya (since 1920), Hopen (1945), Isfjord Radio (1933), Longyearbyen (1930), Svalbard Lufthavn (1975) and Ny-Ålesund (1961). A research station, administered by Norsk Polarinstitutt, was erected at Ny-Ålesund in 1968 for various observations and investigations. An airport near Longyearbyen (Svalbard Lufthavn) opened in 1975.

Norsk Polarinstitutt, Skrifter, Oslo, from 1948 (under different titles from 1922)
Greve, T., *Svalbard: Norway in the Arctic.* Oslo, 1975
Hisdal, V., *Geography of Svalbard.* Norsk Polarinstitutt, Oslo, rev. ed., 1984
Orvin, A. K., 'Twenty-five Years of Norwegian Sovereignty in Svalbard 1925–1950' (in *The Polar Record,* 1951)

JAN MAYEN

This bleak, desolate and mountainous island of volcanic origin and partly covered by glaciers, is situated 71° N. lat. and 8° 30' W. long., 300 miles NNE of Iceland. The total area is 380 sq. km (147 sq. miles). Beerenberg, its highest peak, reaches a height of 2,277 metres. Volcanic activity, which had been dormant, was reactivated in Sept. 1970.

The island was possibly discovered by Henry Hudson in 1608, and it was first named Hudson's Tutches (Touches). It was again and again rediscovered and renamed. Its present name derives from the Dutch whaling captain Jan Jacobsz May, who indisputably discovered the island in 1614. It was uninhabited, but occasionally visited by seal hunters and trappers, until 1921 when Norway established a radio and meteorological station. On 8 May 1929 Jan Mayen was officially proclaimed as incorporated in the Kingdom of Norway. Its relation to Norway was finally settled by law of 27 Feb. 1930. A LORAN station (1959) and a CONSOL station (1968) have been established.

BOUVET ISLAND

Bouvetøya

This uninhabited volcanic island, mostly covered by glaciers and situated 54° 25' S. lat. and 3° 21' E. long., was discovered in 1739 by a French naval officer, Jean Baptiste Loziert Bouvet, but no flag was hoisted till, in 1825, Capt. Norris raised the Union Jack. In 1928 Great Britain waived its claim to the island in favour of Norway, which in Dec. 1927 had occupied it. A law of 27 Feb. 1930 declared Bouvetøya a Norwegian dependency. The area is 50 sq. km (19 sq. miles). From 1977 Norway has had an automatic meteorological station on the island, and 5 men operated a meteorological station there during the 1978–79 season.

PETER I ISLAND
Peter I Øy

This uninhabited island, situated 68° 48' S. lat. and 90° 35' W. long., was sighted in 1821 by the Russian explorer, Admiral von Bellingshausen. The first landing was made in 1929 by a Norwegian expedition which hoisted the Norwegian flag. On 1 May 1931 Peter I Island was placed under Norwegian sovereignty, and on 24 March 1933 it was incorporated in Norway as a dependency. The area is 180 sq. km (69 sq. miles).

QUEEN MAUD LAND
Dronning Maud Land

On 14 Jan. 1939 the Norwegian Cabinet placed that part of the Antarctic Continent from the border of Falkland Islands dependencies in the west to the border of the Australian Antarctic Dependency in the east (between 20° W. and 45° E.) under Norwegian sovereignty. The territory had been explored only by Norwegians and hitherto been ownerless. Since 1949 expeditions from various countries have explored the area. In 1957 Dronning Maud Land was given the status of a Norwegian dependency.

DIPLOMATIC REPRESENTATIVES

Of Norway in Great Britain (25 Belgrave Sq., London, SW1X 8QD)
Ambassador: Kjell Eliassen, GCMG (accredited 15 Feb. 1989).

Of Great Britain in Norway (Thomas Heftyesgate 8, 0244 Oslo, 2)
Ambassador: David Ratford.

Of Norway in the USA (2720 34th St., NW, Washington, D.C., 20008)
Ambassador: Kjeld Vibe.

Of the USA in Norway (Drammensveien 18, 0244 Oslo, 2)
Ambassador: Loret Miller Ruppe.

Of Norway to the United Nations
Ambassador: Tom Eric Vraalsen.

Further Reading

Statistical Information: The Central Bureau of Statistics, Statistisk Sentralbyrå (Skippergaten 15, P.B.8131 Dep.N-0033, Oslo 1), was founded in 1876 as an independent state institution. *Acting director general:* Arne Øien. The earliest census of population was taken in 1769. The Sentralbyrå publishes the series *Norges Offisielle Statistikk,* Norway's official statistics (from 1828), and *Social Economic Studies* (from 1954). The main publications are:

- *Statistisk Årbok for Norge* (annual, from 1880; from 1952 bilingual Norwegian–English)
- *Economic survey* annual, from 1935; with English summary from 1952, now published in *Økonomiske Analyser* (annual)
- *Historisk Statistikk 1978* (historical statistics; bilingual Norwegian–English)
- *Statistisk Månedshefte* (monthly, from 1880; with English index)
- *Sosialt Utsyn 1989* (social survey). Irregular
- *Miljöstatistikk 1988* (environmental statistics). Irregular

Norges Statskalender. From 1816; annual from 1877

Facts about Norway. Ed. by Aftenposten. 20th ed. Oslo, 1986–87
Arntzen, J. G. and Knudsen, B. B., *Political Life and Institutions in Norway*. Oslo, 1981
Derry, T. K., *A History of Modern Norway, 1814–1972*. OUP, 1973.—*A History of Scandinavia*. London, 1979
Glässer, E., *Norwegen* [Bibliography] Darmstadt, 1978
Gleditsch, Th., *Engelsk–norsk ordbok*, 2nd ed. Oslo, 1948
Greve, T., *Haakon VI of Norway, Founder of a New Monarchy*. London, 1983
Grønland, E., *Norway in English, Books on Norway . . . 1742–1959*. Oslo, 1961
Haugen, E., *Norwegian–English Dictionary*, Oslo, 1965
Helvig, M., *Norway: Land, People, Industries, a Brief Geography*. 3rd ed. Oslo, 1970
Holtedahl, O. (ed.) *Geology of Norway*. Oslo, 1960
Hornby, A. S. and Svenkerud, H., *Oxford engelsk-norsk ordbok*. Oslo, 1983
Hove, O., *The System of Education*. Oslo, 1968
Imber, W., *Norway*. Oslo, 1980
Knudsen, O., *Norway at Work*. Oslo, 1972
Larsen, K., *A History of Norway*. New York, 1948
Midgaard, J., *A Brief History of Norway*. Oslo, 1969
Nielsen, K. and Nesheim, A., *Lapp Dictionary: Lapp–English–Norwegian*. 5 vols., Oslo 1963
Orvik, N. (ed.) *Fears and Expectations: Norwegian Attitudes Toward European Integration*. Oslo, 1972
Paine, R., *Coast Lapp Society*. 2 vols. Tromsø, 1957–65
Popperwell, R. G., *Norway*. London, 1972
Sather, L. B., *Norway*. [Bibliography] Oxford and Santa Barbara, 1986
Selbyg, A., *Norway Today: An Introduction to Modern Norwegian Society*. Oslo, 1986

National Library: The University Library, Drammensvein 42b, 0255 Oslo. *Director:* Ben Rugaas.

OMAN

Capital: Muscat
Population: 1·3m. (1987)
GNP per capita: US$5,070 (1988)

Sultanate of Oman

HISTORY. Oman was dominated by Portugal from 1507–1649. The Al-Busaid family assumed power in 1744 and have ruled to the present day. The Sultanate of Oman, known as the Sultanate of Muscat and Oman until 1970, is an independent sovereign state, situated in south-east Arabia.

AREA AND POPULATION. Its coastline is over 1,000 miles long and extends from the Ras al Khaimah Emirate near Bukha on the west side of the Musandum Peninsula to Fujairah Emirate on the east side, then again from the southern boundary of Fujairah to Ras Dharbat Ali, which marks the boundary between Oman and the territory of the People's Democratic Republic of Yemen. The Sultanate extends inland to the borders of the Rub' al Khali ('Empty Quarter') across three geographical divisions—a coastal plain, a range of hills and a plateau. The coastal plain varies in width from 10 miles near Suwaiq to practically nothing in the vicinity of Mutrah and Muscat towns, where the hills descend abruptly into the sea. These hills are for the most part barren except at the highest part of the mountainous region of the Jebel Akhdar (summit 9,998 ft) where there is some cultivation. The plateau has an average height of 1,000 ft. With the exception of oases there is little or no cultivation. North-west of Muscat the coastal plain, known as the Batinah, is fertile and prosperous. The date gardens extend for over 150 miles. Whereas the coastline between the capital, Muscat, and the southern province of Dhofar is barren, Dhofar itself is highly fertile. Its principal town is Salalah on the coast which is served by the port of Raysut.

The area has been estimated at about 105,000 sq. miles (300,000 sq. km) and the population (1987) 1·3m., chiefly Arabs; of these, some 40,000 live in Dhofar. The town of Muscat is the capital which, while formerly of some commercial importance, has now lost most of its trade to the adjacent port of Mutrah, the starting point for the trade routes into the interior. The population of both towns consists of pure Arabs, Indians, Pakistanis and Negroes; numerous merchants are Khojas (from Sind and Kutch) and Hindus (mostly from Gujarat and Bombay). Estimated population of the Capital area (comprising Muscat, Mutrah, Ruwi and Seeb), 1987, 400,000. Other principal towns are Nizwa, 10,000 and Salalah, 10,000. Other ports are Sohar, Khaburah and Sur on the Gulf of Oman and Raysut in the south; only Raysut affords shelter from bad weather.

The port of Gwadur and a small tract of country on the Balúchistán coast of the Gulf of Oman were handed over to Pakistan on 8 Sept. 1958.

The **Kuria Muria** islands were ceded to the UK in 1854 by the Sultan of Muscat and Oman. On 30 Nov. 1967 the islands were retroceded to the Sultan of Muscat and Oman, in accordance with the wishes of the population.

CLIMATE. Oman has a desert climate, with exceptionally hot and humid months from April to Oct., when temperatures may reach 117°F (47°C). From Dec. to the end of March, the climate is more pleasant. Light monsoon rains fall in the south from June to Sept., with highest amounts in the western highland region. Muscat. Jan. 72°F (22·2°C), July 91°F (33·3°C). Annual rainfall 4·0" (99·1 mm). Salalah. Jan. 72°F (22·2°C), July 78°F (25·6°C). Annual rainfall 3·3" (81·3 mm).

RULER. The present Sultan is Qaboos bin Said (born Nov. 1940). He took over from his father Said bin Taimur, on 23 July 1970 in a Palace *coup*.

CONSTITUTION AND GOVERNMENT. Oman is an absolute monarchy and there is no formal constitution. The Sultan legislates by decree and appoints a

Cabinet to assist him; and he is nominally Prime Minister and Minister of Foreign Affairs, Defence and Finance. The other Ministers were in Oct. 1989:

Deputy Prime Ministers: Sayyid Fahr bin Taimur bin Faisal Al Said (*Security and Defence*), Sayyid Fahd bin Mahmud bin Muhammad Al Said (*Legal Affairs*), Qais bin Abdul Mun'im al Zawawi (*Financial and Economic Affairs*). *Agriculture and Fisheries:* Muhammed bin Abdullah bin Zaher al Hinai. *Civil Service:* Ahmad bin Abdul Nabi Macki. *Commerce and Industry:* Salim bin Abdullah al Ghazali. *Communications:* Hamud bin Abdullah al Harthy. *Education and Youth:* Yahya bin Mahfudh al Manthari. *Electricity and Water:* Khalfan bin Nasr al Wahaibi. *Environment:* Sayyid Shabib bin Taimur Al Said. *Health:* Ali bin Muhammed bin Musa al Raisi. *Housing:* Malik bin Sulaiman al Ma'mari. *Information:* Abdul Aziz bin Muhammed al Rowas. *Interior:* Sayyid Badr bin Saud bin Harib Al Bu Saidi. *Justice, Awqaf and Islamic Affairs:* Sayyid Hilal bin Saud bin Harib Al Bu Saidi. *National Heritage and Culture:* Sayyid Faisal bin Ali Al Said. *Petroleum and Minerals:* Said bin Ahmad al Shanfari. *Posts, Telegraphs and Telephones:* Ahmad bin Suweidan al Baluchi. *Regional Municipalities:* Muhammed bin Ali al Qatabi. *Social Affairs and Labour:* Shaikh Mustahail bin Ahmed al Ma'shani. *Minister of State for Foreign Affairs:* Yousuf bin Alawi bin Abdullah. *Minister of State and Wali of Dhofar:* Sayyid Musallim bin Ali Al Bu Saidi. *President, Diwan of the Royal Court:* Sayyid Saif bin Hamad bin Saud. *President of the Palace Office;* Maj.-Gen. Ali bin Majid al Mamari.

In Oct. 1981 the Sultan issued three decrees establishing a 45-member State Consultative Council. The number of Council members was increased to 55 in 1983.

National flag: Red, with a white panel in the upper fly and a green one in the lower fly, and in the canton the national emblem in white.

Local government: Oman is divided into 7 regions *(liwas)* and sub-divided into 51 governates *(wilayats)* each under a governor *(wali)*.

DEFENCE

Army. The Army consists of 2 headquarter brigades; 1 armoured, 1 reconnaissance and 3 artillery regiments; 8 infantry battalions; 1 special force, 1 engineer regiment and 1 parachute regiment. Equipment includes 6 M-60A1 and 33 Chieftain main battle tanks. Strength (1989) about 20,000.

Navy. The Navy, which is based principally at Seeb (HQ) and Wudam comprises 4 fast missile craft, 4 coastal and 4 inshore patrol craft. Auxiliaries include 1 training ship, 1 logistic support ship, 1 troop transport and 1 survey craft. There are also 2 specially adapted amphibious ships and 3 craft. Naval personnel in 1989 totalled 2,500.

The marine police operate 12 coastal patrol boats, 2 logistics support craft, 3 inshore patrol boats and 8 launches.

The wholly separate Royal Yacht Squadron consists of a 3,800 tonne yacht and an 11,000 tonne support ship.

Air Force. The Air Force, formed in 1959, had in 1987 two strike/interceptor squadrons of Jaguars, a ground attack/interceptor squadron of Hunters, a squadron of Strikemaster light jet training/attack aircraft, 1 DC-8, 3 BAC One-Eleven and 2 Gulfstream VIP transports, 3 C-130H Hercules, 6 Defender and 15 Skyvan light transports, 35 Agusta-Bell 205, 212, 214B and JetRanger, and Bell 214 ST helicopters for security duties, 2 Super Puma VIP helicopters and 2 Bravo piston-engined trainers. Air defence force has batteries of Rapier low-level surface-to-air missiles. Personnel (1990) about 3,000.

INTERNATIONAL RELATIONS

Membership. Oman is a member of UN, the Arab League, the Islamic Conference Organisation and the Gulf Co-operation Council.

Treaties. The Treaty of Friendship, Commerce and Navigation between Britain and the Sultan signed on 20 Dec. 1951, reaffirmed the close ties which have existed between the British Government and the Sultanate of Oman for over a century and a half. A Memorandum of Understanding signed in June 1982 provided for regular consultations on international and bilateral issues.

ECONOMY

Planning. The third 5-year plan (1986–90) envisages expenditure of R.O. 9,250m.

Budget. Revenue (1989) R.O. 1,209m. (75% from oil); expenditure, 1,617m.

Currency. The *Rial Omani* was introduced in Nov. 1972 replacing the *Rial Saidi*. It is divided into 1,000 *baiza*. There are notes of 100, 200 and 500 *baiza* and 1, 5, 10, 20 and 50 *Rial Omani* and coins of 2, 5, 10, 25, 50, 100, 250 and 500 *baiza*. The exchange rate in March 1990 was £1 = 634 *baiza*; US$1 = 387 *baiza*.

Banking. In Dec. 1986 there were 22 commercial banks operating in Oman, of which 13 were foreign institutions. There are 3 specialized banks: The Oman Development Bank, the Oman Housing Bank and the Oman Bank for Agriculture and Fisheries. The Central Bank of Oman commenced operations in 1975.

Weights and Measures. The metric system of measurement is in operation. Transactions in the former measurements are now illegal.

ENERGY AND NATURAL RESOURCES

Electricity. Production (1988) 3,541m. kwh. Supply 240 volts; 50 Hz.

Oil. The economy of Oman is dominated by the oil industry, which provides nearly all Government revenue. In 1937 Petroleum Concessions (Oman) Ltd, a subsidiary of the Iraq Petroleum Co., was granted a 75-year oil concession extending over the whole of Oman, although it relinquished Dhofar in 1950. In 1951 the company's name was changed to Petroleum Development (Oman) Ltd. The company (PDO) regained the Dhofar concession area in 1969. When some of the IPC partners withdrew from Oman in 1960, Shell took over the management of PDO with an 85% interest (minority interests were held by Compagnie Française des Pétroles, 10% and Gulbenkian, 5%). At the beginning of 1974 the Oman Government bought a 25% share in PDO, increasing this retroactively to 60% in July. A Joint Management Committee was established. Other companies active in exploration activities in Oman, with mixed success, include Amoco, Elf-Acquitaine and a consortium of Deminex, Agip and Hispanoil with BP as operator.

Oil in commercial quantities was discovered in 1964 and production began in 1967. Production in 1989 was 28·5m. tonnes. Total proven reserves were estimated in 1988 to be 4,071m. bbls, or sufficient for 19 years at the current rate of production. Since the first oil refinery became operational in 1982, Oman has been self-sufficient in most oil-derived products.

Oman is not a member of OPEC or OAPEC.

Gas. Production (1988) 7m. cu. metres per day. In 1989 reserves were estimated at 283,000m. cu. metres.

Water Resources. Oman relies on a combination of water and desalination plants for its water. Two desalination plants at Ghubriah, built in 1972 and 1982, provide most of the water needs of the capital area.

Minerals. Production of refined copper at the smelter at Sohar was about 15,500 tonnes in 1987.

Agriculture. About 41,000 hectares are under cultivation. In the valleys of the interior, as well as on the Batinah, date cultivation has reached a high level, and there are possibilities of agricultural development subject to present water resources and soil surveys. The crop of dates was 97,000 tonnes in 1988, most of which is exported to India. Other main crops are limes, bananas, coconuts, mangoes and alfalfa. Camels (82,000 in 1988) are bred in large numbers by the inland tribes.

Fisheries. Catch (1987) 115,000 tonnes.

INDUSTRY AND TRADE

Industry. Manufacturing accounts for 3% of GDP and apart from oil production, copper mining and smelting and cement production there are no industries of any importance. Fishing, water resources, soil and agricultural surveys are being undertaken. The government gives priority to import substitute industries.

Commerce. The total imports for 1987 were valued at R.O. 700·7m., including machinery and transport equipment (255m.), manufactured goods (120m.), food and live animals (130m.), petroleum products (21m.) and chemicals (48m.).

Total exports 1988, R.O. 1,256·7m. of which oil R.O. 1,101·7m.

Total trade between Oman and UK (British Department of Trade returns, in £1,000 sterling):

	1985	*1986*	*1987*	*1988*	*1989*
Imports to UK	69,015	87,235	49,487	146,751	84,009
Exports and re-exports from UK	489,926	399,647	249,916	344,875	298,974

COMMUNICATIONS

Roads. A network of adequate graded roads links all the main sectors of population, and only a few mountain villages are not accessible by Land-Rover. In Dec. 1989 there were 4,000 km of paved roads and over 19,000 km of graded roads. In 1988 there were 185,636 vehicles.

Aviation. Gulf Air run regional services in and out of Seeb international airport (20 miles from Muscat) to Bahrain, Doha, Abu Dhabi, Dubai, Karachi, Bombay and operate daily flights to and from London. Other airlines serving Muscat are British Airways, KLM, Thai International, British Caledonian, Air Tanzania, MEA, Kuwait Airlines, PIA, Air India, Iran Air, TMA (cargo) and Trade Winds (cargo). Domestic flights are provided by Oman Aviation Services.

Shipping. In Mutrah a deep-water port (named Mina Qaboos) was completed in 1974 at a cost of R.O. 18·2m. It provides 12 berths, 9 of which are deep-water berths, warehousing facilities and a harbour for dhows and coastal vessels. The annual handling capacity has been raised to 1·5m. tons. Mina Raysut, the port of Salalah, has a capacity of 1m. tons per year.

Post and Broadcasting. In 1988 there were 70 post offices and sub-post offices. Omantel maintain a telegraph office at Muscat and an automatic telephone exchange (23,000 lines, 1984) which includes Mutrah, Bait-al-Falaj and Mina al-Fahal, the oil company terminal. A high-frequency radio link with Bahrain was opened in Aug. 1972 providing communications with other parts of the world. Internally, there are radio telephone, telex and telegraph services direct between Salalah and Muscat, and a VHF radio link between Seeb international airport and Muscat. The airport is also served by a SITA telex system. Radio Oman broadcasts daily for 17 hours in Arabic and 2 hours in English.

A colour television service covering Muscat and the surrounding area started transmission in Nov. 1974. A television service for Dhofar opened in 1975. Total number of televisions, 23,500 and radios, 800,000 in 1985.

Newspapers. There were (1989) 2 Arabic and 1 English daily newspapers and 1 English weekly newspaper.

EDUCATION AND WELFARE

Education. In 1987, there were 649 schools with 247,546 pupils and 11,142 teachers. Plans have been implemented for the development of technical and agricultural training and craft training at intermediate and secondary level. Oman's first university, the Sultan Qaboos University, opened in Sept. 1986 and in 1989 there were 1,819 students and 262 teachers. There are also programmes to combat adult illiteracy.

Health. In 1988 there were 47 hospitals with 3,304 beds, 86 health centres, 1,371 doctors, 96 dentists, 235 pharmacists and 3,810 nursing staff.

DIPLOMATIC REPRESENTATIVES

Of Oman in Great Britain (44A Montpelier Sq., London, SW7 1JJ)
Ambassador: (Vacant).

Of Great Britain in Oman (PO Box 300, Muscat)
Ambassador: T. J. Clark.

Of Oman in the USA (2342 Massachusetts Ave., NW, Washington, D.C., 20008)
Ambassador: Awadh Bader Al-Shanfari.

Of the USA in Oman (PO Box 50202 Madinat Qabos, Muscat)
Ambassador: Richard Boehm.

Of Oman to the United Nations
Ambassador: Salim Bin Mohammed Al-Khussaiby.

Further Reading

Oman in 10 years. Ministry of Information. Oman, 1980
Oman: A MEED Practical Guide. London, 1984
Carter, J. R. L., *Tribes of Oman.* London, 1981
Clements, F. A., *Oman: The Reborn Land.* London and New York, 1980.—*Oman.* [Bibliography] Oxford and Santa Barbara, 1981
Graz, L., *The Omani's: Sentinels of the Gulf.* London, 1982
Hawley, D., *Oman and its Rennaissance.* London, 1977
Peterson, J. E., *Oman in the Twentieth Century.* London and New York, 1978
Peyton, W. D., *Oman before 1970: The End of an Era.* London, 1985
Pridham, B. R., (ed.) *Oman: Economic, Social and Strategic Developments.* London, 1987
Shannon, M. O., *Oman and South-eastern Arabia: A Bibliographic Survey.* Boston, 1978
Skeet, I., *Muscat and Oman: The End of an Era.* London, 1974
Thesiger, W., *Arabian Sands.* London, 1959
Townsend, J., *Oman.* London, 1977
Ward, P., *Travels in Oman.* Cambridge, 1987
Wikan, U., *Behind the Veil in Arabia: Women in Oman.* Johns Hopkins Univ. Press, 1982
Wilkinson, J. C., *The Imanate Tradition of Oman.* CUP, 1987

PAKISTAN

Capital: Islamabad
Population: 105·4m. (1989)
GNP per capita: US$350 (1988)

Islamic Republic of Pakistan

HISTORY. Pakistan was constituted as a Dominion on 14 Aug. 1947, under the provisions of the Indian Independence Act, 1947, which received the royal assent on 18 July 1947. The Dominion consisted of the following former territories of British India: Balúchistán, East Bengal (including almost the whole of Sylhet, a former district of Assam), North-West Frontier, West Punjab and Sind; and those States which had acceded to Pakistan.

On 23 March 1956 an Islamic republic was proclaimed after the Constituent Assembly had adopted the draft constitution on 29 Feb.

On 7 Oct. 1958 President Mirza declared martial law in Pakistan, dismissed the central and provincial Governments, abolished all political parties and abrogated the constitution of 23 March 1956. Field Marshal Mohammad Ayub Khan, the Army Commander-in-Chief, was appointed as chief martial law administrator and assumed office on 28 Oct. 1958, after Maj.-Gen. Iskander Mirza had handed all powers to him. His authority was confirmed by a ballot in Feb. 1960. He proclaimed a new constitution on 1 March 1962.

On 25 March 1969 President Ayub Khan resigned and handed over power to the army under the leadership of Maj.-Gen. Agha Muhammad Yahya Khan who immediately proclaimed martial law throughout the country, appointing himself chief martial law administrator on the same day. On 29 March 1970 the Legal Framework Order was published, defining a new constitution: Pakistan to be a federal republic with a Moslem Head of State; the National Assembly and Provincial Assemblies to be elected in free and periodical elections, the first of which was held on 7 Dec. 1970.

At the general election the Awami League based in East Pakistan and led by Sheikh Mujibur Rahman gained 167 seats and the Peoples' Party 90. Martial law continued pending the settlement of differences between East and West, which developed into civil war in March 1971. The war ended in Dec. 1971 and the Eastern province declared itself an independent state, Bangladesh. On 20 Dec. 1971 President Yahya Khan resigned and Mr Z. A. Bhutto became President and chief martial law administrator. On 30 Jan. 1972, Pakistan withdrew from the Commonwealth, rejoining on 1 Oct. 1989.

A new Constitution was adopted by the National Assembly on 10 April 1973 and enforced on 14 Aug. 1973. It provided for a federal parliamentary system with the President as constitutional head and the Prime Minister as chief executive. President Bhutto stepped down to become Prime Minister and Fazal Elahi Chaudhry was elected President.

The Chief of the Army Staff, Gen. M. Zia-ul-Haq, proclaimed martial law on 5 July 1977 and the armed forces took control of the administration; scheduled elections were postponed. Mr Bhutto was hanged (for conspiracy to murder) on 4 April 1979. Gen. M. Zia-ul-Haq succeeded Fazal Elahi Chaudhry as President in Sept. 1978.

With the proclamation of martial law the Constitution was kept in abeyance, but not abrogated.

National elections were held in Feb. 1985 on the basis of the 1973 Constitution, amended to provide wider presidential powers. On 19 Dec. 1984 a referendum had been held to determine whether the President should continue in office for a 5-year term, following the elections; results were announced as 98% in favour.

The Pakistan People's Party won 47 seats in the new Assembly, the Muslim League 17 and the Jamaat Islami Party, 9. In March 1985 the President set up a new

National Security Council, led by himself; he assumed power to appoint and dismiss ministers and retained the final decision on legislation.

In April 1985 the Council was replaced by a Federal Cabinet. On 30 Dec. 1985 martial law ended.

Governors-General of Pakistan: Quaid-I-Azam Mohammed Ali Jinnah (14 Aug. 1947–11 Sept. 1948); Khawaja Nazimuddin (14 Sept. 1948–18 Oct. 1951; took over the premiership after the assassination of Liaquat Ali Khan); Ghulam Mohammad (19 Oct. 1951–6 Aug. 1955); Maj.-Gen. Iskander Mirza (assumed office of President on 6 Oct. 1955, elected President on 5 March 1956).

Presidents of Pakistan: Maj.-Gen. Iskander Mirza (23 March 1956–28 Oct. 1958); Field Marshal Mohammad Ayub Khan (28 Oct. 1958–25 March 1969); Maj.-Gen. Agha Muhammad Yahya Khan (31 March 1969–20 Dec. 1971); Zulfiqar Ali Bhutto (20 Dec.1971–14 Aug. 1973); Fazal Elahi Chaudhry (14 Aug. 1973–16 Sept. 1978); Gen. Mohammad Zia ul-Haq (16 Sept. 1978–17 Aug. 1988); Ghulam Ishaq Khan (acting 17 Aug. 1988, confirmed 12 Dec. 1988).

AREA AND POPULATION. Pakistan is bounded north-west by Afghánistán, north by the USSR and China, east by India and south by the Arabian Sea. The total area of Pakistan is 307,293 sq. miles (796,095 sq. km); population (1981 census), 84·25m.; males, 44,232,000; females, 40,021,000. Density, 105·8 per sq. km. Estimate (1989) 105·4m. Urban population (1987), 28·3%.

The population of the principal cities is:

Census of 1981

Islamabad	201,000	Multan	730,000	Jhang	195,000
Karachi	5,103,000	Gujranwala	597,000	Sukkur	191,000
Lahore	2,922,000	Peshawar	555,000	Bahawalpur	178,000
Faisalabad	1,092,000	Sialkot	296,000	Kasur	155,000
Rawalpindi	928,000	Sargodha	294,000	Gujrat	154,000
Hyderabad	795,000	Quetta	285,000	Okara	154,000

Population of the provinces (census of 1981) was (1,000):

	Area (sq. km)	*1981 census population Total*	*Male*	*Female*	*Urban*	*1981 density per sq. km (number)*	*Estimated total 1985*
North-west Frontier Province	74,521	11,061	5,761	5,300	1,665	148	12,287
Federally admin. Tribal Areas	27,219	2,199	1,143	1,056	–	81	2,467
Fed. Cap. Territory Islamabad	907	340	185	155	204	376	379
Punjab	205,344	47,292	24,860	22,432	13,051	230	53,840
Sind	140,914	19,029	9,999	9,030	8,243	135	21,682
Balúchistán	347,190	4,332	2,284	2,048	677	12	4,908

By Jan. 1987 there were 3m. Afghan refugees in Pakistan, of whom most were in the North-west Frontier Province, and small numbers in Balúchistán and the Punjab.

Language. The commonest languages are Urdu and Punjabi. Urdu is the national language while English is used in business and in central government. Provincial languages are Punjabi, Sindhi, Pushtu (North-West Frontier Province), Baluchi and Brahvi.

CLIMATE. A weak form of tropical monsoon climate occurs over much of the country, with arid conditions in the north and west, where the wet season is only from Dec. to March. Elsewhere, rain comes mainly in the summer. Summer temperatures are high everywhere, but winters can be cold in the mountainous north. Islamabad. Jan. 50°F (10°C), July 90°F (32·2°C). Annual rainfall 36" (900 mm). Karachi. Jan. 61°F (16·1°C), July 86°F (30°C). Annual rainfall 8" (196 mm). Lahore. Jan. 53°F (11·7°C), July 89°F (31·7°C). Annual rainfall 18" (452 mm). Multan. Jan. 51°F (10·6°C), July 93°F (33·9°C). Annual rainfall 7" (170 mm). Quetta. Jan. 38°F (3·3°C), July 80°F (26·7°C). Annual rainfall 10" (239 mm).

CONSTITUTION AND GOVERNMENT. Under the Constitution of 1973 Parliament is bi-cameral, comprising a Senate of 63 members (14 from each province, 5 from Federally Administered Tribal Areas and 2 from the federal capital area, elected by the members of the Provincial Assemblies), and a National Assembly of 207 directly elected Moslem males, 20 women elected by the National Assembly and 10 religious minority representatives.

The Constitution obliges the Government to use such ways and means as may enable the people to order their lives collectively and individually in accordance with the principles of Islam. The Constitution (Ninth Amendment) Bill, 1986, consolidated Islam as the basis of law. An Ombudsman was appointed in Jan. 1983.

Elections to the National Assembly on 16 Nov. 1988 returned the Pakistan People's Party as the largest single group (92 seats) followed by the Islamic Democratic Alliance (55).

President, Head of State: Ghulam Ishaq Khan.

In Nov. 1989 the Government included the following ministers:

Prime Minister, Defence, Finance: Benazir Bhutto.

Senior Minister without Portfolio: Nusrat Bhutto. *Interior:* Aitzaz Ahsan. *Law and Justice:* S. I. H. Gilani. *Education:* S. G. I. Shar. *Foreign Affairs:* S. Yaqub Khan. *Railways:* Z. Leghari. *Industries:* A. Nawaz Shah. *States, Frontier Regions and Kashmiri Affairs, Housing and Construction:* M. Hanif Khan. *Labour, Overseas Pakistani Affairs:* M. Ahmad Awan. *Water:* S. F. Laghari. *Religious Affairs:* Khan Bahadur Khan. *Parlimentary Affairs:* K. A. T. Rahime. *Communications:* M. A. Faheem. *Culture:* A. Tariq Khan. *Youth Affairs:* P. Ali Shah. *Food, Agriculture and Co-operatives:* R. S. Iqbal. *Tourism:* Y. R. Gilani. *Commerce, Local Government and Rural Development:* S. F. Saleh Hayat. *Welfare:* S. A. H. Kazmi. *Science and Technology:* J. Badar.

National flag: Green, charged at the centre, with a white crescent and white 5-pointed star, a white vertical stripe at the mast to one-quarter of the flag.

Local Government. Pakistan comprises the Federal Capital Territory (Islamabad), the provinces of the Punjab, the North-West Frontier, Sind and Balúchistán, and the tribal areas of the north-west. The provincial capitals are Peshawar (NWFP), Lahore (Punjab), Karachi (Sind) and Quetta (Balúchistán). Provincial governors are appointed by the President and are assisted by elected provincial councils.

Within the provinces there are divisions administered by Commissioners appointed by the President; the divisions are divided into districts and agencies administered by Deputy Commissioners or Political Agents who are responsible to the Provincial Governments.

The tribal areas (Khyber, Kurram, Malakand, Mohmand, North Waziristan, South Waziristan) are administered by political agents responsible to the federal government.

Kashmir. Pakistan controls the northern and western portions of Kashmir, an area of about 84,160 sq. km with a population of about 2·8m. in 1985. Under a United Nations resolution of 1949 its future was to be decided by plebiscite; it is still a disputed territory.

The people of Azad Kashmir (the west) have their own Assembly (42 members including 2 women), their own Council (of 14 members), High Court and Supreme Court. There is a Parliamentary form of Government with a Prime Minister as the executive head and the President as the Constitutional head. Elections to the Legislative's 40 general seats are to be held within 10 days of the general elections in Pakistan, according to a presidential proclamation of 8 Oct. 1977. The seat of government is Muzaffarabad.

The Pakistan Government is directly responsible for Gilgit, Diamir and Baltistan (the north).

DEFENCE

Army. The Army consists of 2 armoured and 14 infantry divisions; 5 independent armoured, 4 independent infantry, 8 artillery and 3 anti-aircraft brigades; 6 armoured reconnaissance regiments and 1 Special Services Group. Equipment includes 500 M-47/-48, 51 T-54/-55 and 1,200 Chinese Type-59 main battle tanks. The Army has an air component with about 150 fixed-wing aircraft for transport, reconnaissance and observation duties and 120 helicopters for anti-armour operations, transport, liaison and training. Strength (1990) 480,000, with a further 500,000 reservists. There are also 164,000 men in paramilitary units: National Guard, Frontier Corps, Pakistan Rangers, Coast Guard and Frontier Constabulary.

Navy. The Pakistani Navy has been transformed in 1988-89 by the addition, through purchase or lease, of 10 frigates from the US and British navies. It is anticipated that more of the old *ex*-US destroyers will now be withdrawn from service. The smaller craft are mostly of Chinese origin.

The combatant fleet comprises 6 French-built diesel submarines, about 6 midget submarines for swimmer delivery, 1 UK-built 'County' class destroyer, *Babur*, converted to carry up to to 4 Sea King ASW helicopters, 4 *ex*-US World War 2 vintage destroyers, 4 *ex*-US Brooke class guided missile frigates armed with Standard SM-1 surface-to-air missiles, 6 other frigates, 8 fast missile craft, 4 hydrofoil torpedo craft, 4 coastal and 12 inshore patrol craft, and 3 coastal minesweepers. Auxiliaries include 2 fleet replenishment tankers, 1 survey ship and 1 salvage tug, plus a static *ex*-US repair ship. There are about a dozen minor auxiliaries.

The Air force operates 4 Atlantic and 1 Fokker F-27 Friendship for maritime patrol and transport duties, whilst the Navy operates 6 Sea King helicopters and 4 Alouette III ASW and liaison helicopters. All destroyers and frigates have helicopter decks capable of operating an Alouette.

The principal naval base and dockyard are at Karachi. Naval personnel in 1989 totalled 15,000.

A navy-subordinated Maritime Safety Agency operates 4 fast inshore patrol craft on EEZ protection duties.

Air Force. The Pakistan Air Force came into being on 14 Aug. 1947. It has its headquarters at Peshawar and is organized within 3 air defence sectors, in the northern, central and southern areas of the country. Air defence units include 2 squadrons of F-16 Fighting Falcons, 2 squadrons of F-7P Skybolts and at least 6 squadrons of Chinese-built F-6s (MiG-19). Tactical units include 5 squadrons of Mirage III-EP/5 supersonic fighters and 6 with A-5 fighter-bombers, 1 squadron equipped with Mirage III-RP reconnaissance aircraft, and 1 with C-130 Hercules turboprop transports. Flying training schools are equipped with Masshaq (Saab Supporter) armed piston-engined primary trainers, T-37B/C jet trainers supplied by the USA, Mirage III-DPs and Chinese-built FT-5s (two-seat MiG-17s) and FT-6s (two-seat MiG-19s). A VIP transport squadron operates the Presidential F27 turboprop aircraft, 3 four-jet Boing 707s, 3 twin-jet Falcon 20s and a Puma helicopter. There is a flying college at Risalpur and an aeronautical engineering college at Korangi Creek. Total strength in 1990 was about 400 combat aircraft and 25,000 all ranks.

INTERNATIONAL RELATIONS

Membership. Pakistan is a member of the UN, the Commonwealth, the Colombo Plan, and Regional Co-operation for Development.

External Debt (30 June 1989), US$19,983·17m.

ECONOMY

Planning. The sixth 5-year plan (1983–88) envisaged a total fixed investment of Rs 495,000m. including Rs 77,000m. for industry, of which Rs 62,000m. would be spent in the private sector. Real growth in GDP was planned at 6·5% annually (agriculture 5%; industry 9%). Expenditure was to be met mainly (75%) from internal resources. Allocations: For energy (Rs 116,000m.), agriculture and irrigation (Rs 88,000m.), special development programmes (Rs 22,000m.) and family planning (Rs 1,800m.).

Budget. The following table shows the budget for the years 1987–88 and 1988–89 in Rs 1m.:

	Revised	1988–89 Budget
Revenue receipts	121,239·8	134,993·9
of which taxes	89,018·6	98,611·9
Capital receipts	71,704·4	66,414·3
of which External	27,515·6	32,040·4
Revenue expenditure	146,233·4	158,606·9
Capital expenditure	39,068·7	43,884·3

Main items of expenditure on revenue account (Rs 1m.):

	Revised	1988–89 Budget
Defence	45,295·1	48,321·5
Debt servicing	29,343·5	34,201·2
Development	25,628·4	26,776·0
Administration	5,210·6	5,925·9
Social, including health and education	4,538·2	5,853·5

Currency. The monetary unit is the Pakistan *rupee*. In March 1990 Rs 34·60 = £1; Rs 21·11 = US$1. Decimal coinage was introduced on 1 Jan. 1961. The rupee, which previously consisted of 64 *pice*, now consists of 100 *paisas*. The notes are of Rs 100, 50, 10 and 5 denominations issued by the State Bank in the name of the Government, and Rs 1 issued by the State Bank incurring no liability; the coinage in the decimal series is 0·5, 0·25, 0·1, 0·05 and 0·01 rupee.

Total monetary assets on 30 June 1988 amounted to Rs 269,437m. Currency in circulation, Rs 87,782m.

Banking. As from 1 Jan. 1985, banks and other financial institutions will abandon the payment of interest on new transactions. This does not apply to international business, but does apply to the domestic business of foreign banks operating in Pakistan. Investment partnerships, between bank and customer, are to replace straight loans at interest. The aim is to bring all domestic financial transactions into conformity with Islamic teaching. The State Bank of Pakistan has prepared a schedule of acceptable practice.

The State Bank of Pakistan is the central bank; it came into operation as the Central Bank on 1 July 1948 with an authorized capital of Rs 30m. and was nationalized in Jan. 1974. At end June 1988 total assets or liabilities of the issue department amounted to Rs 91,206m. and those of the banking department Rs 82,253m.; total deposits, Rs 68,163m. It is the sole bank of issue for Pakistan, custodian of foreign exchange reserves and banker for the federal and provincial governments and for scheduled banks. It also manages the rupee public debt of federal and provincial governments. It provides short-term loans to the Government and commercial banks and shortand medium-term loans to specialized banks. The Bank's subsidiary Federal Bank for Co-operatives makes loans to provincial co-operative banks.

There were 37 scheduled banks in Pakistan on 30 June 1988. Of these 9 were Pakistani (nationalized since 1974). Total liabilities or assets of all scheduled banks stood at Rs 481,456·7m., of which time liabilities, Rs 115,184·8m., on the last working day of June, 1988. The National Bank of Pakistan acts as an agent of the State Bank for transacting Government business and managing currency chests at places where the State Bank has no offices of its own.

Weights and Measures. The metric system is in general use.

ENERGY AND NATURAL RESOURCES

Electricity. Installed capacity of the state power system (1986–87) by type of generation: Thermal 3,263 mw., hydro-electric, 2,898 mw.; the Karachi Electric Supply Corporation had 17·9%. Total generated electrical energy in 1986–87, 28,236m. kwh; 15,241m. kwh of this was hydro-electricity, the main source being the Tarbela Dam. By June 1986 21,846 villages (of a total 43,244) had access to electric power. Supply 230 volts; 50 Hz.

Oil. Oil comes mainly from the Potowar Plain, from fields at Meyal, Tut, Balkassar, Joya Mair and Dhullian. Production in 1989 was 2·6m. tonnes. Oil reserves were also found at Dhodak in Dec. 1976. Exploitation is mainly through government incentives and concessions to foreign private sector companies. The Pak-Arab refinery pipeline runs 865 km. from Karachi to Multan; capacity, 4·5m. tonnes of oil annually.

Gas. Gas pipelines from Sui to Karachi (345 miles) and Multan (200) supply natural gas to industry and domestic consumers. A pipeline between Quetta and Shikarpur was constructed in 1982. There are 4 other productive fields. Reserves (1983), 500,000m. cu. metres; production in 1987–88 was 12,383m. cu. metres.

Water. The Indus water treaty of 1960, concluded between India and Pakistan, has created the basis for a large-scale development programme. The Indus Basin Development Fund Agreement has been subscribed by Australia, Canada, Federal Republic of Germany, New Zealand, UK and USA and is administered by the International Bank; the works to be constructed call for expenditure of US$1,000m. The main purpose of the treaty is the division of the water power of the Indus and its 5 tributaries between India and Pakistan. After the construction of some 460 miles of canals, the Indus and the 2 western tributaries will serve Pakistan and the entire flow of the 3 eastern tributaries will be released for use in India.

The largest project is the construction of the Tarbela Dam, an earth-and-rock filled dam on the river Indus, 485 ft high, which has a gross storage capacity of 11·1m. acre feet of water for irrigation.

The Lloyd Barrage and Canal Construction Scheme, consists of a barrage across the river Indus at Sukkur and 7 canals—4 on the left and 3 on the right bank. Another barrage across the Indus, $4^1/_2$ miles north of Kotri, called the Ghulam Muhammad Barrage, was completed in 1955. The Taunsa barrage on the Indus, 80 miles downstream of Kalabagh, was completed in 1958. The Gudu barrage, 10 miles from Kashmore, was completed in 1962.

The province of the Punjab set up in 1949 the Thal Development Authority to colonize the Thal desert between the Indus and Jhelum rivers.

The Chashma canal will carry water 172 miles across Dera Ismail Khan from the Chashma barrage on the Indus. The Mangla Dam on the Jhelum was inaugurated in Nov. 1967.

Minerals. The main agencies are the Pakistan Mineral Development Corporation, the Resource Development Corporation and the Gemstone Corporation of Pakistan. Coal is mined at Sharigh and Harnai on the Sind–Pishin railway and in the Bolan pass, also in Sor Range and Degari in the Quetta–Pishin district and in the Punjab; total recoverable reserves, about 480m. tonnes, mainly low-grade. A further 55m. tonnes was found at Lakhra in 1980 and reserves of over 500m. tonnes were found in the 300 sq. mile Thatta Sadha field in 1981. Copper ore reserves at Saindak, in Balúchistán, 412m. tons, containing (1984 estimate) 1·69m. tons of copper; 2·24m. oz. of gold; 2·2m. oz. of silver. Chromite is extracted in and near Muslimbagh. Limestone is quarried generally. Gypsum is mined in the Sibi district and elsewhere; reserves (1983), about 370m. tonnes. Iron ore is being worked in Kalabagh and elsewhere; reserves, about 400m. tonnes, low-grade. A further 18m. tonnes, high-grade, has been found in Balúchistán. Uranium has been found in Dera Ghazi Khan.

Production (tonnes, 1987–88): Coal, 2·73m.; chromite, 8,628; limestone, 7·61m.; gypsum, 404,042; rock salt, 502,281; fire clay, 133,869. Other minerals of which useful deposits have been found are magnesite, sulphur, barites, marble, bauxite, antimony ore, bentonite, celestite, dolomite, fireclay, fluorite, fuller's earth, phosphate rock, silica sand and soapstone.

Agriculture. The entire area in the north and west is covered by great mountain ranges. The rest of the country consists of a fertile plain watered by 5 big rivers and their tributaries. Agriculture is dependent almost entirely on the irrigation system based on these rivers. Areas irrigated, 1987: Punjab, 11·8m. hectares; Sind, 3·3m.; NWFP, 840,000; Balúchistán, 520,000. It employs (1987) about 50% of labour and provides about 22% of GNP. The main crops are wheat, cotton, maize, sugar-cane and rice, while the Quetta and Kalat divisions (Balúchistán) are known for their fruits and dates.

Pakistan is self-sufficient in wheat, rice and sugar. Areas harvested, 1987–88: Wheat, 7·3m. hectares; rice, 1·96m.; sugar, 841,600.

Production, 1987–88, in 1,000 tonnes: Rice (cleaned), 3,240·9; wheat, 12,675·1; sugar-cane, 33,013·4; cotton, 1,468·5; cottonseed, 2,937; maize, 1,126·9; potatoes, 563·2.

An ordinance of Jan. 1977 reduced the upper limit of land holding to 100 irrigated or 200 non-irrigated acres; it also replaced the former land revenue system with a new agricultural income tax, from which holders of up to 25 irrigated or 50 unirrigated acres are exempt. Of about 4m. farms, 89% are of less than 25 acres. Of the surveyed area of 156m. acres, cultivated land accounts for 63m. acres, of which 11m. acres consist of fallow land, so that the net area sown is 52m. acres.

Livestock (estimate, 1988): Cattle, 17,156,000; buffaloes, 14·02m.; sheep, 27,479,000; goats, 33,018,000; poultry, 151m.

Forestry. In 1986–87 the forest area was 2·9m. hectares. 14·4m. cu. ft of timber and 19·2m. cu. ft of firewood were produced. Forest lands are also used as national parks, wildlife and game reserves.

Fisheries. In 1987 landings were 336,100 tonnes of marine and 96,100 of inland water fish.

INDUSTRY AND TRADE

Industry. Industry employs about 10% of the population. Manufacturing (1987–88) contributed about 17% to GNP. In 1972 public sector companies were re-organized under a Board of Industrial Management. Government policy since 1977 has been to encourage private industry, particularly small industry. The public sector, however, is still dominant in large industries. Steel, cement, fertilizer and vegetable ghee are the most valuable public sector industries.

A public sector steel-mill (Pakistan Steel) has been built at Port Qasim near Karachi, capacity 1·1m. tonnes; production of coke and pig-iron began in autumn 1981 and of steel in 1983.

Production 1987–88 (tonnes): Refined sugar, 1·77m.; vegetable products, 685,549; jute textiles, 113,602; soda ash, 134,106; sulphuric acid, 78,723; caustic soda, 61,344; chip board and paper board, 70,027; bicycles, 661,183 units; cotton cloth, 280·9m. sq. metres; cotton yarn, 685·5m. kg.; cement, 7·04m.; steel billets 271,367; hot-rolled steel sheets and coils, 475,621; cold-rolled, 154,550; mild steel products, 867,565.

Labour. The 1981 census gave the total work force as 22·62m. Estimates (1985–86) give 28·9m., employed workforce 27·86m. In 1988 51·15% were engaged in agriculture, forestry and fishing, 12·69% in manufacturing; the textile industry was the largest single manufacturing employer. Services employed 11·39%; commerce, 11·92%; construction, 6·38%; transport, storage and communication, 4·89%.

Commerce. Total value of exports during 1987–88 amounted to Rs 78,444·6m., and the total value of imports to Rs 111,381·9m. (In 1986–87, exports were Rs 63,267·9m., imports, Rs 92,430·8m.). The value of the chief articles imported into and exported from Pakistan (in Rs 1m.):

Imports	*1986–87*	*1987–88*
Minerals, fuels, lubricants	14,806·2	18,057·5
Machinery and transport equipment	27,543·5	32,869·0
Edible oils	5,003·4	8,977·0
Chemicals	15,773·1	17,612·5
Raw cotton	7,675·8	10,758·6

Exports	*1986–87*	*1987–88*
Cotton cloth	5,931·1	8,539·5
Cotton yarns	8,765·6	9,597·4
Rice	5,052·6	6,404·4
Leather	...	5,041·5
Carpets, tapestries	3,419·5	4,418·2

Of exports (1987–88), Rs 24,530·4m. went to the European Community; Rs 9,582·3m. to the middle east, of which Rs 3,892·1m. was to Saudi Arabia; Rs 8,603·4m. went to USA. Of imports, Rs 29,379·8m. came from the European Community; Rs 12,471·3m. from USA; Rs 20,898·5m. from the middle east, of which Rs 5,621·8m. was from Saudi Arabia.

Total trade between Pakistan and UK (British Department of Trade returns, in £1,000 sterling):

	1985	*1986*	*1987*	*1988*	*1989*
Imports to UK	119,006	131,296	167,315	175,337	216,110
Exports and re-exports from UK	255,419	227,064	252,978	263,300	233,532

Tourism. In 1987 there were 424,900 tourist arrivals spending US$172·8m.; 189,300 came from India; 110,200 from Europe, including 73,000 from UK.

COMMUNICATIONS

Roads. In 1987–88 Pakistan had 108,530 km of roads, of which 46,143 km were all-weather roads. The Karakoram highway to the Chinese border, through Kohistan and the Hunza valley, was opened in 1978. An all-weather road linking Skardu and the remote NE Indus valley to the highway was built in 1980.

In 1987 there were 2·22m. vehicles registered, including 1·06m. motor-cycles and 514,837 cars, jeeps and station wagons.

Railways. Pakistan Railways had (1988) a route length of 8,775 km (of which 290 km electrified) mainly on 1,676 mm. gauge, with some metre gauge and narrow gauge line. In 1987–88 there were 81·2m. passengers and 11·6m. tonnes of freight.

Aviation. Karachi is served by British Airways, KLM, PANAM, Lufthansa, Swissair, SAS, Iran National Airlines, Air France, Garuda, Gulf Air and by Philippine, Japanese, Chinese, East African, Syrian, Iraqi, Kuwait, Jordanian, Saudi Arabian, Romanian, Egyptian and Soviet airlines.

Pakistan International Airlines (founded 1955; 62% of shares are held by the Government) had 8 Boeing 747s, 8 Airbus A300-B4s, 6 Boeing 707s, 6 Boeing 737-300s, 9 Fokker F-27s, 2 Twin Otters and 5 Cessna Trainers in 1987. Services operate to 30 home and 38 international airports, including London, New York, Frankfurt, Paris, Amsterdam, Copenhagen, İstanbul, Athens, Rome, Cairo, Tripoli, Nairobi, Dhahran, Damascus, Amman, Baghdad, Riyadh, Tokyo, Peking (Beijing), Zahedan, Singapore, Manila, Kuala Lumpur, Bangkok, Colombo, Bombay, Delhi, Dacca, Tehrán, Káthmándu, the Maldive Islands and Jiddah.

At Pakistan airports, 1987–88, there were 10m. passengers (including 6·3m. on domestic flights) and 180,577 tonnes of cargo (61,294).

Shipping. There is a seaport at Karachi, dry-cargo-handling capacity 6m. tonnes a year, oil-handling, 10m. The second port, 26 miles east of Karachi, is Port Muhammad Bin Qasim; it has iron and coal berths for Pakistan Steel Mills, multi-purpose berths, bulk-cargo handling, oil and container-traffic terminals. International shipping entered and cleared (1987–88): Karachi 1,901 and 1,888 vessels; Port Qasim 152 and 154. Cargo handled: Karachi 17·7m. tonnes, Port Qasim 3·72m. Coastal shipping (Pakistani and Arabian craft), total 823 vessels entered (239·1m. NRT), 793 cleared (298·4m.). The Pakistan National Shipping Corporation had 26 vessels in 1988, of 410,234 DWT. National flag carriers now operate between Pakistan and UK; USA and Canada; the Far East; the (Persian) Gulf, Arabian Gulf, Red Sea, Black Sea and Mekran Coast; Continental Europe and the Middle East. The Karachi Shipyard and Engineering Works Ltd construct all types of vessels up to 27,000 DWT and repairs all types; dry-dock and under-water repairs can be done on vessels up to 29,000 DWT, above-water repairs on vessels and drilling rigs of all sizes.

Post and Broadcasting. The telegraph and telephone system is government-owned. Telephones, 1988, numbered 740,000; a nationwide dialling system is in operation between 46 cities. In 1988 there were 12,226 post offices. Pakistan has international telephone connections by 102 satellite, 7 HF, 4 microwave and 10 carrier circuits, and an international direct-dialling exchange. The Pakistan Broadcasting Corporation had 18 radio stations in 1988 and 5 TV stations (Lahore, Karachi, Peshawar, Quetta and Rawalpindi–Islamabad). In 1988 there were 1·51m. radio licences and 1·51m. TV sets, and 235,100 video recorders were in use..

Cinemas (1986). There were about 850 cinemas.

Newspapers. Newspapers and periodicals numbered 1,826 in 1988; 177 were dailies, 368 weeklies, 126 twice-weeklies, 776 monthlies and 374 quarterlies. Titles by language (and average circulation) in 1988: Urdu, 1,343 (263m.); English, 379 (387,741); Sindhi, 72 (64,823). Titles are also published in Pushtu, Punjabi, Baluchi and Brahvi.

JUSTICE, RELIGION, EDUCATION AND WELFARE

Justice. The Central Judiciary consists of the Supreme Court of Pakistan, which is a court of record and has three-fold jurisdiction, namely, original, appellate and advisory. There are 4 High Courts in Lahore, Peshawar, Quetta and Karachi. Under the Constitution, each has power to issue directions of writs of *Habeas Corpus, Mandamus, Certiorari* and others. Under them are district and sessions courts of first instance in each division; they have also some appellate jurisdiction. Criminal cases not being sessions cases are tried by district magistrates and subordinate magistrates. There are subordinate civil courts also.

The Constitution provides for an independent judiciary, as the greatest safeguard of citizens' rights. The Laws (Continuance in Force) (Eleventh Amendment) Order, 1980, prescribed the date of 14 Aug. 1981 by which the judiciary shall be separated from the executive. There is an Attorney-General, appointed by the President, who has right of audience in all courts.

A Federal Shariat Court at the Supreme Court level has been established to decide whether any law is wholly or partially un-Islamic. Islamic law is to be enforced as the law of the state; penalties for offences involving intoxicating liquor, offences against property and sexual offences have been specified. Imprisonment remains as a penalty in general use, but some offences in all the above categories are liable to whipping and some property offences, to amputation.

Religion. Religious groups (1981 census): Moslems, 96·68%; Christians, 1·55%; Hindus, 1·51%; Parsees, Buddhists, and others. There is a Minorities Wing at the Religious Affairs Ministry to safeguard the constitutional rights of religious minorities.

Education. At the census of 1981, 23·3% of the population were able to read and write. Estimate (1985), 26%. Adult literacy programmes have been established.

The principle of free and compulsory primary education has been accepted as the responsibility of the state; duration has been fixed provisionally at 5 years. About 49% of children aged 5-9 are enrolled at school. Present policy stresses vocational and technical education, disseminating a common culture based on Islamic ideology. Figures for 1987–88 in 1,000:

	Total pupils	*Female pupils*	*Total teachers*	*Women teachers*	*Institutions*
Primary	7,606	2,498	186·3	59·4	83,872
Middle	2,133	594	61·2	18·5	6,458
High	695	190	82·2	25·7	5,008
Colleges	502	153	35·2	14·4	680
Universities	65	10	4·0	0·6	22

Health. In 1988 there were 710 hospitals and 3,616 dispensaries (52,866 beds) and 55,346 doctors. There were 998 maternity and child welfare centres.

Distribution by province:

	Hospitals	*Dispensaries*	*Mother and child centres*
Punjab	258	1,154	448
Sind	251	1,557	154
NWFP	152	590	325
Balúchistán	45	267	68

DIPLOMATIC REPRESENTATIVES

Of Pakistan in Great Britain (35 Lowndes Sq., London, SW1X 9JN)
High Commissioner: Shaharyar M. Khan (accredited 26 Feb. 1987).

Of Great Britain in Pakistan (Diplomatic Enclave, Ramna 5, Islamabad)
High Commissioner: N. J. Barrington, CMG, CVO.

Of Pakistan in the USA (2315 Massachusetts Ave., NW, Washington, D.C., 20008)
Ambassador: Zulfiqar Ali Khan.

Of the USA in Pakistan (Diplomatic Enclave, Ramna, 5, Islamabad)
Ambassador: Robert B. Oakley.

Of Pakistan to the United Nations
Ambassador: Nasim Ahmed.

Further Reading

Pakistan Statistical Yearbook. Karachi
Pakistan Yearbook., Karachi
Ahmed, A. S., *Religion and Politics in Muslim Society: Order and Conflict in Pakistan*. CUP, 1973
Ali, T., *Can Pakistan Survive? The Death of the State*. Harmondsworth, 1983
Bhutto, B., *Daughter of the East*. London, 1988
Burki, S. J., *Pakistan Under Bhutto*. London, 1980
Choudbury, G. W., *Pakistan: Transition from Military to Civilian Rule*. London, 1988
Gilmartin, D., *Empire and Islam: Punjab and the making of Pakistan*. London, 1988
Hyman, A. *et al Pakistan: Zia and After*. London, 1989
Jennings, Sir Ivor, *Constitutional Problems in Pakistan*. CUP, 1957
Noman, O., *The Political Economy of Pakistan, 1947-85*. London and New York, 1988
Taylor, D., *Pakistan*. [Bibliography] Oxford and Santa Barbara, 1989
Waseem, N., *Pakistan under Martial Law, 1977-85*. Lahore, 1987

PANAMA

Capital: Panama City
Population: 2·42m. (1990)
GNP per capita: US$2,240 (1987)

República de Panamá

HISTORY. A revolution, supported by the USA, led to the separation of Panama from the United States of Colombia and the declaration of its independence on 3 Nov. 1903. The *de facto* Government was on 5 Nov. recognized by the USA, and soon afterwards by the other Powers. In 1924 Colombia agreed to recognize the independence of Panama. On 8 May 1924 diplomatic relations between Colombia and Panama were established. On 1 Oct. 1979 Panama assumed sovereignty over what was previously known as the Panama Canal Zone and now called the Canal Area. For the treaties regulating the relations between Panama and the USA *see* pp. 983–84.

Elections, the first to be held in Panama for 16 years, were held in May 1984. Nicholas Barletta was elected president and took office in Nov. 1984, but he resigned in Sept. 1985 and was succeeded by one of his vice-presidents.

AREA AND POPULATION. Panama is bounded north by the Caribbean, east by Colombia, south by the Pacific and west by Costa Rica. Extreme length is about 480 miles (772 km); breadth between 37 (60) and 110 miles (177 km); coastline, 726 miles (1,160 km) on the Atlantic and 1,060 (1,697 km) on the Pacific; total area is 29,761 sq. miles (77,082 sq. km); population according to the census of 11 May 1980 was 1,830,175. Estimate (1990) 2,417,955. Over 75% are of mixed blood and the remainder Indians, negroid, white and Asiatic. In 1986, 53% were urban. Over 93% speak Spanish, the official language, 3% speak Guaymí and 2% Cuna (both Amerindian languages).

The largest towns (census, 1980) are Panama City, the capital on the Pacific coast (386,393); its suburb San Miguelito (156,361); Colón, the port on the Atlantic coast (59,043); and David (50,621).

The areas and populations of the 9 provinces and the Special Territory were:

Province	*Sq. km*	*Census 1980*	*Estimate 1990*	*Capital*
Bocas del Toro	9,506	53,579	83,926	Bocas del Toro
Chiriquí	8,924	287,801	382,311	David
Veraguas	11,226	173,195	218,867	Santiago
Herrera	2,185	81,866	105,844	Chitré
Los Santos	4,587	70,200	82,311	Las Tablas
Coclé	4,981	140,320	172,475	Penonomé
Colón	7,205	166,439	214,922	Colón
Terr. de San Blas	3,206			El Porvenir
Panama	11,400	830,278	1,115,058	Panama City
Darién	15,458	26,497	42,241	La Palma

Vital statistics (1987): Births, 56,991; marriages, 10,091; deaths, 8,813.

CLIMATE. A tropical climate, unvaryingly with high temperatures and only a short dry season from Jan. to April. Rainfall amounts are much higher on the north side of the isthmus. Panama City. Jan. 79°F (26·1°C), July 81°F (27·2°C). Annual rainfall 70" (1,770 mm). Colón. Jan. 80°F (26·7°C), July 80°F (26·7°C). Annual rainfall 127" (3,175 mm). Balboa Heights. Jan. 80°F (26·7°C), July 81°F (27·2°C). Annual rainfall 70" (1,759 mm). Cristóbal. Jan. 80°F (26·7°C), July 81°F (27·2°C). Annual rainfall 130" (3,255 mm).

CONSTITUTION AND GOVERNMENT. The 1972 Constitution, as amended in 1978 and 1983, provides a president and two vice-presidents to be elected by direct popular vote and a 67 seat Legislative Assembly to be elected on a party basis; in 28 of the 40 constituencies the party winning the vote obtaining one seat; in the other 12, the 39 remaining seats being allocated on a system of proportional party representation. There are also 505 Representatives elected, one member for each electoral district.

On 26 Feb. 1988 the Legislative Assembly deposed Eric Arturo Delvalle and appointed Manuel Solis Palma as acting President in his place. Elections on 9 May 1989 were annulled by the Electoral Court. The Council of State elected Francisco Rodríguez and Dr Carlos Ozores as Provisional President and Vice-President. They were sworn in on 1 Sept. 1989 but Gen. Manuel Noriega remained *de facto* leader.

In May 1989 a further 2,000 US troops were sent to Panama and a US-backed *coup* attempt in Oct. failed. On 15 Dec. Gen. Noriega declared a 'state of war' with the US. On 20 Dec. the US invaded Panama to remove Gen. Noriega from power and he surrendered on 3 Jan. 1990. US troops started to withdraw on 2 Jan. A President was sworn in by an electoral tribunal on 27 Dec. 1989.

President: Guillermo Endara Gallimany.

Vice President: Arias Calderón.

National flag: Quarterly: first a white panel with a blue star, second red, third blue, fourth white with a red star.

National anthem: Alcanzamos por fin la victoria (words by J. de la Ossa; tune by Santos Jorge, 1903).

Local government: The 9 provinces and a Special Territory (another is envisaged) are sub-divided into 65 municipal districts and are further sub-divided into 505 *corregimientos* (electoral districts).

DEFENCE

Army. The Army (National Guard) numbered (1990) 3,500 men organized in 8 light infantry companies, equipped with 16 V-150 and 13 V-300 armoured cars. There is one air-borne group. There was (1990) a para-military force of 11,000.

Navy. Divided between both coasts, the flotilla comprises 2 patrol craft, 2 small craft, 1 medium landing ship, 3 utility landing craft and 1 logistic support vessel. In 1989 personnel totalled 400.

Air Force. The status of the Air Force since the US intervention in late 1989 is unclear, but immediately prior to this the service had 5 CASA 212, 2 Islander, 1 CN-235 and 2 Twin Otter transports, 4 Cessna and 2 DHC-3 Otter liaison aircraft, a Falcon 20 and 2 Boeing 727s for VIP transport, 25 UH-1B/H Iroquois and twin-engined UH-1N helicopters plus a Super Puma for official use. Four Chilean-built Pillan trainers were used for training. Personnel (1990) 500.

INTERNATIONAL RELATIONS

Membership. Panama is a member of UN, OAS and Non-aligned Countries.

ECONOMY

Budget. The 1987 budget provided for expenditure of 1,705m. balboas and revenue of 1,405m. balboas. Public sector debt was US$3,691m. in 1985.

Currency. The monetary unit is the *balboa*. Other coins are the half-balboa (equal to 50 cents US); the quarter and tenth of a balboa piece; a cupro-nickel coin of 5 cents, and a copper coin of 1 cent. US coinage is also legal tender. The only paper currency used is that of the USA. In March 1990, US$1 = 1 *balboa*; £1 = 1·64 *balboas*.

Banking. There is no statutory central bank. The Government accounts are handled through the *Banco Nacional de Panama*. The number of commercial banks was 132 in June 1986. Leading banks are the Citibank, Lloyds Bank International (Bahamas) Ltd., and the Chase Manhattan Bank of New York. Other foreign-owned banks include the Bank of America, as well as Canadian.

Weights and Measures. English weights and measures are in general use; the metric system is the official system.

ENERGY AND NATURAL RESOURCES

Electricity. Production (1986) 3,120m. kwh. Supply 110 and 120 volts; 60 Hz.

Minerals. There are known to be copper deposits in the provinces of Chiriquí, Colón and Darien. The most important, containing possibly the largest undeveloped reserves in the world, is Cerro Colorado (Chiriquí) on which a feasibility study was undertaken by the Rio Tinto Zinc Corporation Ltd. If it is eventually decided to develop the mine, it is expected that the annual production of copper will reach 260,000 to 280,000 tonnes within a few years. The deposit has estimated reserves of 1,300m. tonnes, with an average grade of 0·76% copper.

Agriculture. Of the whole area (1981) 15·6% is cultivated, 57·6% is natural or artificial pasture land and 8·6% is fallow. Of the remainder only a small part is cultivated, though the land is rich in resources. About 60% of the country's food requirements are imported. Production in 1988 totalled 900,000 tonnes of bananas and 107,000 tonnes of raw sugar. Oranges (36,000 tonnes) and mangoes (28,000 tonnes) are also produced. Most important food crop, for home consumption, is rice, grown on 80% of the farms; Panama's *per capita* consumption is very high. Production of rice was 166,000 tonnes in 1988. Other products are maize (97,000 tonnes in 1988), cocoa (1,000 tonnes), coffee (13,000 tonnes) and coconuts (22,000 tonnes). Beer, whisky, rum, 'seco', anise and gin are produced. Coffee is mainly grown in the province of Chiriquí, near the Costa Rican frontier. The country has great timber resources, notably mahogany. Livestock (1988): 1,502,000 cattle, 240,000 pigs and 7m. poultry.

Forestry. Production (1986) 2·05m. cu. metres.

Fisheries. The catch in 1988 was 92,951 tonnes.

INDUSTRY AND TRADE

Industry. Local industries include cigarettes, clothing, food processing, shoes, soap, cement factories; foreign firms are being encouraged to establish industries, and a petrol refinery is operating at Colón.

Commerce. The imports and exports (including re-exports) for the Republic of Panama, for 4 calendar years are as follows (in 1,000 balboas; 1 balboa = US$1):

	Imports	*Exports*		*Imports*	*Exports*
1984	1,423,000	251,500	1986	1,275,245	1,306,183
1985	1,391,218	301,076	1987	326,864	338,167

Total trade between Panama (including Colón Free Zone) and UK (British Department of Trade returns, in £1,000 sterling):

	1985	*1986*	*1987*	*1988*	*1989*
Imports to UK	14,612	4,950	4,919	12,230	6,818
Exports and re-exports from UK [1]	55,424	44,975	40,020	32,497	32,875

[1] Including new ships built for foreign owners and registered in Panama.

Tourism. In 1987, 283,000 people visited Panama.

COMMUNICATIONS

Roads. Panama had in 1985, 9,694 km of roads. The road from Panama City westward to the cities of David and Concepción and to the Costa Rican frontier, with several branches, is part of the Pan-American Highway. A concrete highway connects Panama City and Colón.

On 1 Jan. 1981 registered motor vehicles, private and commercial, numbered 166,498.

Railways. The *Ferrocarril de Panama* (Panama Railroad) (1,524 mm gauge) (through the Canal area), which connects Ancón on the Pacific with Cristóbal on the Atlantic, is the principal railway. It is 190 km long and runs along the banks of the Canal. As most vessels unload their cargo at Cristóbal (Colón), on the Atlantic side, the greater portion of the merchandise destined for Panama City is brought overland by the *Ferrocarril de Panama*. The United Brands Company runs 376 km of railway, and the Chiriquí National Railroad 171 km.

Aviation. Eastern Airlines, Swissair, Varig, JAL, Alitalia, KLM, Iberia Airlines, Aeromexico, VIASA, Air France and other international companies operate at Gen. Omar Torrijos Airport, 12 miles from Panama City. Air Panama provides services between Panama City and New York, Los Angeles, Miami, Central America and some countries in South America. The *Compañía Panameña de Aviación* (COPA) and *Aerolineas Las Perlas* provide a local service between Panama City and the provincial towns. COPA also provides an international service to Central America.

Shipping. Ships under Panamanian registry in 1988 numbered 12,094 of 67·2m. gross tons; most of these ships elect Panamanian registry because fees are low and labour laws lenient. All the international maritime traffic for Colón and Panama runs through the Canal ports of Cristóbal, Balboa and Bahia Las Minas (Colón); Almirante is used for both the provincial and international trade. There is an oil transfer terminal at Puerto Armuelles on the Pacific coast.

Panama Canal. On 18 Nov. 1903 a treaty between the USA and the Republic of Panama was signed making it possible for the US to build and operate a canal connecting the Atlantic and Pacific oceans through the Isthmus of Panama. The treaty granted the US in perpetuity the use, occupation and control of a Canal Zone, approximately 10 miles wide, in which the US would possess full sovereign rights 'to the entire exclusion of the exercise by the Republic of Panama of any such sovereign rights, power or authority'. In return the US guaranteed the independence of the republic and agreed to pay the republic $10m. and an annuity of $250,000. The US purchased the French rights and properties—the French had been labouring from 1879 to 1899 in an effort to build the Canal—for $40m. and in addition, paid private landholders within what would be the Canal Zone a mutually agreeable price for their properties.

Two new treaties between Panama and USA were agreed on 10 Aug. and signed on 7 Sept. 1977. One deals with the operation and defence of the canal until the end of 1999 and the other guarantees permanent neutrality.

The USA maintains operational control over all lands, waters and installations, including military bases, necessary to manage, operate and defend the canal until 31 Dec. 1999. A new agency of the US Government, the Panama Canal Commission, operates the canal, replacing the Panama Canal Co. A policy-making board of 5 US citizens and 4 Panamanians serves on the Commission's board of directors. Until 31 Dec. 1989 the canal administrator was a US citizen and the deputy was Panamanian. After that date the position was reversed.

Six months after the exchange of instruments of ratification Panama assumed general territorial jurisdiction over the former Canal Zone and became able to use portions of the area not needed for the operation and defence of the canal. Panamanian penal and civil codes became applicable. At the same time Panama assumed responsibility for commercial ship repairs and supplies, railway and pier operations, passengers, police and courts, all of which were among other areas formerly administered by the Panama Canal Company and the Canal Zone Government.

66% of the electorate of Panama agreed to the ratification of the treaties when a referendum was held on 23 Oct. 1977 and on 18 April 1978 the treaty was ratified by the US Congress. The treaty went into effect on 1 Oct. 1979.

At the end of 1962 the US completed the construction of a high-level bridge over the Pacific entrance to the Canal, and the flags of Panama and the US were flown jointly over areas of the Canal Zone under civilian authority. Following the devaluation of the dollar in 1972 and 1973, the annuity was adjusted proportionally to US$2·1m. and US$2·33m. respectively.

In 1986 a tripartite commission, formed by Japan, Panama and the USA, began studies on alternatives to the Panama Canal. Options are: To build a sea-level canal, to enlarge the existing canal with more locks, to improve the canal alongside upgraded rail and road facilities, to continue with the existing facilities.

The Panama Canal Commission, a US Government Agency, is concerned primarily with the actual operation of the Canal. On 8 July 1974, 18 Nov. 1976, 10 Oct. 1979 and 12 March 1983 tolls were increased. These were the first increases of toll rates in the history of the Canal. Tolls were raised again on 1 Oct. 1989. The new rates are US$2.01 a Panama Canal ton for vessels carrying passengers or cargo and US$1·60 per ton for vessels in transit in ballast. A Panama Canal ton is equivalent to 100 cu. ft of actual earning capacity. The new toll rate for warships, hospital ships and supply ships, which pay on a displacement basis, is US$1·12 a ton.

The changes were designed to continue the approximately break-even financial operating results after paying its own expenses and paying interest on the net direct investment of the US in the Canal.

Administrator of the Panama Canal Commission: Adolfo Altamirano Duque.

US military personnel assigned permanently in Panama in Sept. 1989 were approximately 10,000. The total permanent workforce employed by the Panama Canal Commission in Sept. 1989 was 7,602, comprising 993 US citizens, 6,513 Panamanians and 96 others.

The Canal was opened to commerce on 15 Aug. 1914. It is 85 ft above sea-level. It is 51·2 statute miles in length from deep water in the Caribbean Sea to deep water in the Pacific Ocean, and 36 statute miles from shore to shore. The channel ranges in bottom-width from 500 to 1,000 ft; the widening of Gaillard Cut to a minimum width of 500 ft was completed in 1969. Normally, the average time of a vessel in Canal waters is about 24 hours, 8–12 of which are in transit through the Canal proper. A map showing the Panama, Suez and Kiel canals on the same scale will be found in THE STATESMAN'S YEAR-BOOK, 1959 and a further map in the 1978–79 edition.

Particulars of the ocean-going commercial traffic through the canal are given as follows (vessels of 300 tons Panama Canal net and 500 displacement tons and over; cargo in long tons):

Fiscal year ending 30 Sept.	*North-bound (Pacific to Atlantic)*		*South-bound (Atlantic to Pacific)*		*Total*		*Tolls levied*[1] *(in US$)*
	Vessels	*Cargo*	*Vessels*	*Cargo*	*Vessels*	*Cargo*	
1986	5,712	67,229,841	6,214	72,580,652	11,926	139,810,493	322,734,202
1987	5,766	61,683,921	6,464	87,006,459	12,230	148,690,380	329,858,775
1988	5,807	65,504,306	6,427	90,978,335	12,234	156,482,641	339,319,326
1989	5,678	63,360,524	6,311	88,275,589	11,989	151,636,113	329,696,838

[1] All annual tolls figures have been revised to show total tolls collected instead of oceangoing commercial tolls.

In the fiscal year ending 30 Sept. 1989, 13,389 ships passed through the Canal. Transits by flag included 2,423 Panamanian; 1,090 Liberian; 640 Japanese; 636 US; 542 Greek; 597 Russian; 322 Ecuadorian; 435 British; 614 Cyprian; 374 Filippino; 377 Norwegian; 327 Bahamian.

Statistical Information: The Panama Canal Commission Office of Public Affairs.

Annual Reports on the Panama Canal, by the Administrator of the Panama Canal Commission.
Rules and Regulations Governing Navigation of the Panama Canal. The Panama Canal Commission, Miami, Florida *or* Washington, DC
Cameron, I., *The Impossible Dream.* London, 1972
Le Feber, W., *The Panama Canal: The Crisis in Historical Perspective.* OUP, 1978
McCullough, D., *The Path Between the Seas.* New York and London, 1978

Post and Broadcasting. There are telegraph cables from Panama to North America and Central and South American ports, and from Colón to the USA and Europe. There is also inter-continental communication by satellite. There were (1985) 97 licensed commercial broadcasting stations, nearly all operated by private companies, one of which functions in the canal. There are 6 television stations, one of them run by the US Army at Fort Clayton. In 1985 there were 295,000 radio and 400,000 television sets. On 1 Jan. 1983 there were 202,627 telephones.

Newspapers. There were (1989) 1 English language and 5 Spanish language daily morning newspapers and 1 English/Spanish evening newspaper.

JUSTICE, RELIGION, EDUCATION AND WELFARE

Justice. The Supreme Court consists of 9 justices appointed by the executive. There is no death penalty.

Religion. 85% of the population is Roman Catholic, 5% Protestant, 4·5% Moslem. There is freedom of religious worship and separation of Church and State. Clergymen may teach in the schools but may not hold public office.

Education. Elementary education is compulsory for all children from 7 to 15 years of age, with an estimated 552,172 students in schools in 1985. The University of Panama at Panama City, inaugurated on 7 Oct. 1935, had a total enrolment (1985) of 55,000 students. The Catholic university Sta. Maria La Antigua, inaugurated on 27 May 1965, had 1,916 students in Sept. 1978.

Health. In 1986 there were 2,596 doctors, 519 dentists, 2,923 nursing personnel and 50 hospitals with 7,799 beds.

DIPLOMATIC REPRESENTATIVES

Of Panama in Great Britain (119 Crawford St., London, W1H 1AF)
Ambassador: Guillermo Vega (accredited 29 May 1984).

Of Great Britain in Panama (Calle 53, Panama City 1)
Ambassador: John Grant MacDonald.

Of Panama in the USA (2862 McGill Terr., NW, Washington, D.C., 20008)
Ambassador: (Vacant).

Of the USA in Panama (Apartado 6959, Panama City 5)
Ambassador: Arthur Davis.

Of Panama to the United Nations
Ambassador: Leonardo Kam.

Further Reading

Statistical Information: The Comptroller-General of the Republic (Contraloria General de la República, Calle 35 y Avenida 6, Panama City) publishes an annual report and other statistical publications.

Jorden, W. J., *Panama Odyssey*. Univ. of Texas Press, 1984
Langstaff, E. DeS., *Panama*. [Bibliography] Oxford and Santa Barbara 1982
Ropp, S. C., *Panamanian Politics*. New York, 1982

National Library: Biblioteca Nacional, Departamento de Información. Calle 22, Panama.

PAPUA NEW GUINEA

Capital: Port Moresby
Population: 3·59m. (1989)
GNP per capita: US$770 (1988)

HISTORY. To prevent that portion of the island of New Guinea not claimed by the Netherlands or Germany from passing into the hands of a foreign power, the Government of Queensland annexed Papua in 1883. This step was not sanctioned by the Imperial Government, but on 6 Nov. 1884 a British Protectorate was proclaimed over the southern portion of the eastern half of New Guinea, and in 1887 Queensland, New South Wales and Victoria undertook to defray the cost of administration, and the territory was annexed to the Crown the following year. The federal government took over the control in 1901; the political transfer was completed by the Papua Act of the federal parliament in Nov. 1905, and on 1 Sept. 1906 a proclamation was issued by the Governor-General of Australia declaring that British New Guinea was to be known henceforth as the Territory of Papua. The northern portion of New Guinea was a German colony until the First World War. It became a League of Nations mandated territory in 1921, administered by Australia, and later a UN Trust Territory (of New Guinea).

The Papua New Guinea Act 1949–1972 provides for the administration of the UN Australian Trust Territory of New Guinea in an administrative union with the Territory of Papua, in accordance with Art. 5 of the New Guinea Trusteeship Agreement, under the title of Papua New Guinea.

Australia granted Papua New Guinea self-government on 1 Dec. 1973 and, on 16 Sept. 1975, Papua New Guinea became a fully independent state.

AREA AND POPULATION. Papua New Guinea extends from the equator to Cape Baganowa in the Louisiade Archipelago to 11° 40' S. lat. and from the border of West Irian to 160° E. long. with a total area of 462,840 sq. km. According to the census the 1980 population was 3,010,727. Estimate (1989) 3·59m. Port Moresby, 152,100; Lae, 79,600; Rabaul (1980), 14,954; Madang, 24,700; Wewak, 23,200; Goroka, 21,800; Mount Hagen (1980), 13,441. Area and population of the provinces:

Provinces	*Sq.km*	*Census 1980*	*Estimate 1987*	*Capital*
Milne Bay	14,000	127,975	153,800	Alotau
Northern	22,800	77,442	92,200	Popondetta
Central	29,500	116,964	135,000	Port Moresby
National Capital District	240	123,624	145,300	—
Gulf	34,500	64,120	72,600	Kerema
Western	99,300	78,575	93,600	Daru
Southern Highlands	23,800	236,052	262,400	Mendi
Enga	12,800	164,534	180,100	Wabag
Western Highlands	8,500	265,656	304,800	Mount Hagen
Chimbu	6,100	178,290	186,800	Kundiawa
Eastern Highlands	11,200	276,726	310,300	Goroka
Morobe	34,500	310,622	364,400	Lae
Madang	29,000	211,069	251,100	Madang
East Sepik	42,800	221,890	260,000	Wewak
West Sepik	36,300	114,192	130,100	Vanimo
Manus	2,100	26,036	30,500	Lorengau
West New Britain	21,000	88,941	110,600	Kimbe
East New Britain	15,500	133,197	157,800	Rabaul
New Ireland	9,600	66,028	78,900	Kavieng
North Solomons	9,300	128,794	159,100	Arawa

Vital statistics (1987, estimate): Crude birth rate, 35 per 1,000; crude death rate, 13.

CLIMATE. There is a monsoon climate, with high temperatures and humidity the year round. Port Moresby is in a rain shadow and is not typical of the rest of Papua New Guinea. Jan. 82°F (27·8°C), July 78°F (25·6°C). Annual rainfall 40" (1,011 mm).

CONSTITUTION AND GOVERNMENT. Papua New Guinea has a Westminster type of government. A single legislative house, known as the National Parliament, is made up of 109 members from all parts of the country. The members are elected under universal suffrage and general elections are held every 5 years. All persons over the age of 18 who are Papua New Guinea citizens are eligible to vote and stand for election. Voting is by secret ballot and follows the preferential system.

The first Legislative Council was established in 1951. It was abolished in 1964 and replaced with the House of Assembly. In 1950 the first village council was formed which established the basis of an extensive local government system. A system of provincial government was introduced in 1976 and, since then, the importance of lower-level local government has diminished.

In the general elections held in June-July 1987, 26 seats were won by the Pangu Party, 18 by the People's Democratic Movement, 12 by the National Party, 32 by other parties and 21 by independents. A PDM-led government held office until 4 July 1988, when it was defeated in Parliament and replaced by one led by the Pangu Party.

Governor-General: Sir Serei Eri.

The Cabinet in Sept. 1989 was as follows:

Prime Minister: Rt. Hon. Rabbie Namaliu.

Deputy Prime Minister, Public Service: Akoka Doi. *Agriculture and Livestock:* Galen Lang. *Finance and Planning:* Paul Pora. *Tourism and Culture:* Beona Motawiya. *Minerals and Energy:* Patterson Lowa. *Forests:* Karl Stack. *Provincial Affairs:* John Momis. *Transport:* Anthony Temo. *Justice:* Bernard Narakobi. *Education:* Jack Genia. *Defence:* Benias Sabumei. *Communications:* Brown Sinamoi. *Works and Supply:* Paul Wanjik. *Fisheries and Marine Resources:* Allan Ebu. *Environment and Conservation:* Jim Waim. *Foreign Affairs:* Michael Somare. *Lands and Physical Planning:* Karl Swokin. *Health:* Robert Suckling. *Labour and Employment:* Peter Garong. *Police:* Mathias Ijape. *Home Affairs and Youth:* Timothy Bonga. *Trade and Industry:* Galeva Kwarara. *Correctional Services:* Melchior Pep. *Housing:* Gerard Sigulogo. *Administrative Services:* Theodore Tuyo. *Minister for State, Assisting the Prime Minister:* Ted Diro. *Civil Aviation:* Bernard Vogae.

The seat of the Government is at Port Moresby.

National flag: Diagonally ochre-red over black, on the red a bird of paradise in gold, and on the black 5 stars of the Southern Cross in white.

DEFENCE. The Papua New Guinea Defence Force has a total strength of 3,200 (1989) consisting of land, maritime and air elements. The Army is organized in 2 infantry and 1 engineer battalions. The Navy, based at Port Moresby and Manus, is all of Australian build and comprises 5 inshore patrol craft and 2 tank landing craft. Personnel number 200. The Defence Force has an Air Transport Squadron with (1990) about 100 personnel. Current equipment comprises 5 C-47 transports, and 4 Australian-built N22B Nomads and 3 Israeli-built Aravas for both transport and border patrol duties. The Aravas were being offered for sale late in 1989.

INTERNATIONAL RELATIONS

Membership. Papua New Guinea is a member of UN, the Commonwealth, the Colombo Plan, the South Pacific Commission and is an ACP state of EEC.

ECONOMY

Budget. Revenue (in K1,000) for calendar years was:

Source	*1987*	*1988*	*1989*
Customs, excise and export tax	229,867	246,000	301,000
Other taxes	234,422	263,000	266,160
Foreign government grants [1]	184,250	192,000	201,100
Loans	89,493	167,563	176,770
Other revenue	178,295	107,341	122,000
Total	916,327	975,904	1,067,030

[1] Mainly from Australia.

Expenditure (in K1,000) for the same periods:

Source	*1986*	*1987*	*1988*
Consumption	513,350	538,250	530,590
Capital	138,830	71,438	81,042
Other expenditure [1]	178,930	254,317	298,501
Total	831,100	864,005	910,133

[1] Includes transfers to provincial governments.

Currency. The unit of currency is the *kina* divided into 100 *toea* and is the sole legal tender. In March 1990, £1 = K1·60; US$1 = K0·98.

Banking. The Bank of Papua New Guinea assumed the central banking functions formerly undertaken by the Reserve Bank of Australia on 1 Nov. 1973.

A national banking institution which has been named the Papua New Guinea Banking Corporation, has been established. This bank has assumed the Papua New Guinea business of the Commonwealth Trading Bank of Australia except where certain accounts give rise to special financial or contractual problems.

The subsidiaries of 3 Australian commercial banks also operate in Papua New Guinea. These are the Australia and New Zealand Banking Group (PNG) Ltd, the Bank of New South Wales (PNG) Ltd, and the Bank of South Pacific Ltd, all of which offer trading and savings facilities. As from 1 Nov. 1973 these banks operated under Papua New Guinea banking legislation.

In 1983, two additional commercial banks Indosuez Niugini Bank Ltd and Niugini Lloyds International Bank Ltd began operating, each with 51% national ownership, and the remaining 49% held by the affiliate of a major international bank.

In addition to these five commercial banks, the Agriculture Bank of Papua New Guinea (formerly the Development Bank) has provided long-term development finance with a particular attention to the needs of small-scale enterprises since 1967. The country's first merchant bank, Resources and Investment Finance Ltd (RIFL), specializing in large-scale financial services began business in late 1979. Its shares are owned by the Hong Kong and Shanghai Banking Corporation, the Commonwealth Trading Bank of Australia and the Papua New Guinea Banking Corporation.

On 30 June 1987 commercial banks deposits totalled K762·2m.

Weights and Measures. The metric system is in force.

ENERGY AND NATURAL RESOURCES

Electricity. In 1986 installed capacity was 494,300 mw, production 1,602·4m. kwh.

Oil. The Iagifu field in the Southern Highlands had (1988) potential recoverable reserves of 500m. bbls.

Minerals. Copper is the main mineral product. Gold, copper and silver are the only minerals produced in quantity. The Misima open-pit gold mine, first mined in 1888, was opened in 1989. Production is forecast at 210,000 oz a year with a life of 10 years. Major copper deposits in the Kieta district of Bougainville have proved reserves of about 800m. tonnes and have been worked by Bougainville Copper Ltd since 1972. Copper and gold deposits in the Star Mountains of the Western Province are being developed by Ok Tedi Mining Ltd at the Mt. Fubilan mine. Production of gold commenced in 1984 and of copper concentrates in 1987. In 1986, B.C.L. produced 586,552 tonnes of copper concentrate containing approximately 178,593 tonnes of copper, 16,367 kg of gold and 50,385 kg of silver; Ok Tedi Mining Ltd produced 18,277 kg of gold and 5,677 kg of silver.

Agriculture. At 31 Dec. 1983, the total area of larger holdings was 397,081 hectares, of which 180,000 hectares were for agricultural purposes, the principal crops being coffee, copra, cocoa and palm oil. Minor commercial crops include pyrethrum, tea, peanuts and spices. Locally consumed food crops include sweet potatoes, maize, taro, bananas, rice and sago. Tropical fruits grow abundantly. There is extensive grassland. A newly-established sugar industry has made the country self-sufficient in this commodity while a beef-cattle industry is being developed.

Production (1988, in 1,000 tonnes): Coffee, 72; copra, 155; cocoa beans, 36; palm oil, 156.

Livestock (1988): Cattle, 101,000; pigs, 1·7m.; goats, 12,000; poultry, 3m.

Forestry. Timber production is of growing importance for both local consumption and export. In 1986, 1·7m. cu. metres of logs were harvested; logs exported, 1·3m. cu. metres.

Production of sawn timber, 1986, 84,000 cu. metres, exports, 7,438 cu. metres; exports of woodchips, 81,037 tonnes.

Fisheries. Tuna, both skipjack and yellowfin species, is the major fisheries resource; in 1980 the catch was 33,000 tonnes but has diminished sharply since then due to oversupply conditions on world markets. Exports of various crustacea, 1986, 1,575 tonnes, value K10·47m.

INDUSTRY AND TRADE

Industry. Secondary and service industries are expanding for the local market. The main industries were (1988) food processing, beverages, tobacco, timber products, wood, and fabricated metal products. In 1985 there were 707 factories employing 27,195 persons. Value of output K695m.

Labour. In 1980 about 733,000 were gainfully employed.

Commerce. Imports (in K1,000) for calendar years:

	1985	*1986*	*1987*
Food and live animals	153,460	162,809	171,524
Beverages and tobacco	9,605	8,481	11,888
Crude materials, inedible, except fuels	6,206	6,945	7,824
Mineral fuels, lubricants and related materials	153,806	93,444	112,047
Oils and fats (animal and vegetable)	3,402	3,453	3,608
Chemicals	65,838	81,568	84,595
Manufactured goods, chiefly by material	132,432	149,046	181,570
Machinery and transport equipment	248,350	307,997	339,631
Miscellaneous manufactured articles	83,210	75,973	87,636
Commodities and transactions of merchandise trade, not elsewhere specified	10,590	12,353	12,550
Total imports	866,898	902,069	1,012,874

Exports (in K1,000) for calendar years:

	1986	*1987*	*1988*
Coconut and copra products—			
Copra	10,154	15,113	19,486
Copra (coconut) oil	10,887	14,486	17,456
Copra cake and pellets	888	1,034	1,262
Total	21,929	30,633	38,204
Coffee beans	203,505	134,643	116,355
Cocoa beans	56,183	56,359	46,023
Crude rubber	3,860	3,078	4,401
Tea	7,133	5,571	6,439
Pyrethrum extract	484	249	148
Forest and timber products			
Logs	62,303	103,645	90,421
Sawn timber	1,800	1,259	1,018
Plywood	–	–	–
Other	5,010	6,825	5,704
Total	69,113	111,729	97,143

	1986	1987	1988
Crocodile skins	2,475	1,879	877
Crayfish and prawns	10,472	10,509	7,321
Gold	220,542	140,573	112,096
Copper concentrate	357,559	538,315	702,756
Other domestic produce	45,972	35,726	37,640
Total domestic produce	999,227	1,069,262	1,169,253
Re-exports	17,885	17,665	34,484
Total exports	1,017,111	1,086,927	1,203,737

Of exports in 1988, Japan took 41%, Federal Republic of Germany, 22% and Australia, 6%; of imports (1987), Australia furnished about 43%, Singapore, 7% and Japan, 19%.

Total trade between Papua New Guinea and UK (British Department of Trade returns, in £1,000 sterling):

	1985	1986	1987	1988	1989
Imports to UK	59,642	38,474	46,045	44,291	47,839
Exports and re-exports from UK	12,592	12,084	16,693	20,521	15,822

Tourism. In 1988, there were 40,529 visitors of which 10,648 were tourists.

COMMUNICATIONS

Roads. In 1985 there were approximately 19,736 km of roads including approximately 1,200 km paved. Motor vehicles numbered (1986) 45,713 including 16,499 cars and station wagons.

Aviation. Frequent air services operate to and from Australia (Sydney, Brisbane and Cairns), and there are regular flights to Djayapura (Indonesia), Manila and Singapore. A service is also maintained to Honiara in the Solomon Islands. In addition to Air Niugini, the national flag carrier, Qantas operates in and out of Papua New Guinea. There are a total of 177 airports and airstrips with scheduled services.

Shipping. There are regular shipping services between Australia and Papua New Guinea ports, and also services to New Zealand, Japan, Hong Kong, US west coast, Singapore, Solomon Islands, Vanuatu, Taiwan, Philippines and Europe. Small coastal vessels run between the various ports. In 1985 cargo discharged from overseas was 1·5m. tonnes; cargo loaded for overseas was 2·1m. tonnes.

Post and Broadcasting. Telephones numbered 63,212 on 31 Dec. 1986. The National Broadcasting Commission operates three networks. A national service is relayed throughout the country by a series of transmitters on medium- and short-wave bands. Local services operate in each of the 19 provinces, mainly on short-wave, while the larger urban centres are also covered by a commercial FM network relayed from Port Moresby. Two commercial television stations broadcast to Port Moresby which had plans (1987) to extend their services to other areas. In 1985 there were 230,000 television and (1986) 225,000 radio receivers.

Newspapers. In 1986 there was one daily newspaper with a circulation of 28,000.

JUSTICE, RELIGION, EDUCATION AND WELFARE

Justice. In 1983, over 1,500 criminal and civil cases were heard in the National Court and an estimated 120,000 cases in district and local courts.

Police. Total uniformed strength at 31 Dec. 1986, 4,756.

Religion. At the 1980 Census, Protestants formed 64% of the population and Roman Catholics 33%.

Education. At 30 June 1986 about 374,950 children attended 2,461 primary schools and 60,052 enrolled in 234 secondary, technical and vocational schools. The University of Papua New Guinea and the Papua New Guinea University of Technology had 3,029 students enrolled in full-time courses in 1986.

Health. In 1986, there were 19 hospitals, 459 health centres, 2,231 aid posts and 283 doctors.

DIPLOMATIC REPRESENTATIVES

Of Papua New Guinea in Great Britain (14 Waterloo Pl., London, SW1R 4AR)
High Commissioner: Philip Bouraga, CBE.

Of Great Britain in Papua New Guinea (Kiroki St., Port Moresby)
High Commissioner: E. J. Sharland.

Of Papua New Guinea in the USA (1330 Connecticut Ave., NW, Washington D.C., 20036)
Ambassador: Margaret Taylor.

Of the USA in Papua New Guinea (Armit St., Port Moresby)
Ambassador: (Vacant).

Of Papua New Guinea to the United Nations
Ambassador: Renagi Lohia.

Further Reading

The Territory of Papua. Annual Report. Commonwealth of Australia. 1906–1940–41 and from 1945–46
The Territory of New Guinea. Annual Report. Commonwealth of Australia. 1914–1940–41 and from 1946–47
Papua New Guinea, Annual Report. From 1970–71
Hasluck, P., *A Time for Building.* Melbourne Univ. Press, 1976
McConnell, F., *Papua New Guinea.* [Bibliography] Oxford and Santa Barbara, 1988
Ross, A. C. and Langmore, J., *Alternative Strategies for Papua New Guinea.* OUP, 1974
Ryan, P. (ed.) *Encyclopaedia of Papua and New Guinea.* Melbourne Univ. Press, 1972
Skeldon, R. (ed.) *The Demography of Papua New Guinea.* Institute of Applied Social and Economic Research, 1979

PARAGUAY

Capital: Asunción
Population: 4·04m. (1988)
GNP per capita: US$1,180 (1988)

República del Paraguay

HISTORY. The Republic of Paraguay gained its independence from Spain on 14 May 1811. In 1814 Dr José Gaspar Rodríguez de Francia was elected dictator, and in 1816 perpetual dictator by the National Assembly. He died 20 Sept. 1840. In 1844 a new constitution was adopted, under which Carlos Antonio López (first elected in 1842, died 10 Sept. 1862) and his son, Francisco Solano López, ruled until 1870. During the devastating war against Brazil, Argentina and Uruguay (1865–70) Paraguay's population was reduced from about 600,000 to 232,000. Argentina, in Aug. 1942, and Brazil, in May 1943, voided the reparations which Paraguay had never paid. Further severe losses were incurred during the war with Bolivia (1932–35) over territorial claims in the Chaco. A peace treaty by which Paraguay obtained most of the area her troops had conquered was signed in July 1938.

AREA AND POPULATION. Paraguay is bounded north-west by Bolivia, north-east and east by Brazil, south-east, south and south-west by Argentina. The area of the Oriental province is officially estimated at 159,827 sq. km (61,705 sq. miles) and the Occidental province at 246,925 sq. km (95,337 sq. miles), making the total area of the republic 406,752 sq. km (157,042 sq. miles).

The population (Census 1982) was 3,035,360; estimate (1988) 4,039,161. In 1984 the capital, Asunción (and metropolitan area), had 729,307 inhabitants; other principal cities: Presidente Stroessner (110,000), Pedro Juan Caballero (80,000), Encarnación (31,445), Pilar (26,352), Concepción (25,607).

The capital district and 19 departments had the following populations in 1982:

Asunción (city) Central	729,307	Misiones	79,278
		Neembucu	70,689
Caaguazú	299,227	Amambay	68,422
Itapua	263,021	Canendiyú	65,807
Paraguari	202,152	*Oriente*	*2,959,568*
Cordillera	194,826	Presidente Hayes	43,787
San Pedro	189,751	Boquerón	14,685
Alto Paraná	188,351	Alto Paraguay	4,535
Guairá	143,374	Chaco	286
Concepción	135,068	Nueva Asunción	231
Caazapá	109,510	*Occidente*	*63,524*

Number of births, 1986, was 109,626; deaths, 11,519.

The population is overwhelmingly *mestizo* (mixed Spanish and Guaraní Indian) forming a homogeneous stock. There are some 46,700 unassimilated Indians of other tribal origin, in the Chaco and the forests of eastern Paraguay. There are some small traces of Negro descent. 40·1% of the population speak only Guaraní; 48·2% are bilingual (Spanish/Guaraní); and 6·4% speak only Spanish.

Mennonites who arrived in 3 groups (1927, 1930 and 1947) are settled in the Chaco and Oriental Paraguay and were estimated in 1969 to number 13,000, of whom 2,000 came from Canada and 11,000 from Germany. The Japanese colonists in the Oriental section, who first came in 1935, were reckoned to number 7,000 in 1983. An agreement with Korea was signed in 1966 and there were (1988) about 7,575 Korean families living in Paraguay.

CLIMATE. A tropical climate, with abundant rainfall and only a short dry season from July to Sept., when temperatures are lowest. Asunción. Jan. 81°F (30°C), July 64°F (17·8°C). Annual rainfall 53" (1,316 mm).

CONSTITUTION AND GOVERNMENT. A new constitution replacing that of 1940 was drawn up by a Constituent Convention in which all legally recognized political parties were represented and was signed into law on 25 Aug. 1967. It provides for a two-chamber parliament consisting of a 36-seat Senate and a 72-seat House of Deputies, each elected for a 5-year term. Two-thirds of the seats in each House are allocated to the majority party (since 1954 the *Partido Colorado)* and the remaining one-third shared among the minority parties in proportion to the votes cast. Voting is compulsory for all citizens over 18. The President is directly elected for a 5-year (renewable) term; he appoints the Cabinet and during parliamentary recess can govern by decree through the Council of State, the members of which are representatives of the Government, the armed forces and other bodies. Gen. Stroessner was deposed in a *coup* on 3 Feb. 1989. At the presidential elections held on 1 May 1989 Gen. Rodríguez received 74·18% of the vote.

President: Gen. Andrés Rodríguez, assumed office 3 Feb. 1989; inaugurated after election on 15 May 1989.

The following is a list of past presidents since 1948, with the date on which each took office:

Dr J. Natalicio González, 15 Aug. 1948 (deposed).
Gen. Raimundo Rolón, 30 Jan. 1949.
Dr Felipe Molas López, 26 Feb. 1949[1] (resigned).
Dr Federico Chávez, 16 July 1950 (resigned).
Tomás Romero Pereira, 4 May 1954.
Gen. Alfredo Stroessner, 11 July 1954 (deposed).

[1] Provisional, *i.e.*, following a *coup d'état.*

The Cabinet in Jan. 1990 was composed as follows:

Foreign Affairs: Dr Luis M. Argaña. *Interior:* Gen. Orlando Machuca Vargas. *Finance:* Enzo Debernardi. *Public Health and Social Welfare:* Cynthia Prieto. *Justice and Labour:* Dr Alexis Frutos Vaesken. *Public Works and Communications:* Gen. Porfirio Pereira Ruiz Díaz. *Industry and Commerce:* Antonio Zuccolillo. *Education and Worship:* Dr Dionisio González Torres. *Without Portfolio:* Dr Juan R. Chaves. *Defence:* Brig.-Gen. Angel Juan Souto Hernández. *Agriculture and Livestock:* Hernando Bertoni Argón. *Secretary-General of the Presidency:* Conrado Pappalardo.

National flag: Red, white, blue (horizontal); the white stripe charged with the arms of the republic on the obverse, and, on the reverse, with a lion and the inscription *Paz y Justicia*—the only flag in the world with different obverse and reverse.

National anthem: ¡Paraguayos, república o muerte! (words by F. Acuña de Figueroa; tune by F. Dupey).

The country is divided into 2 provinces: the 'Oriental', east of Paraguay River, and the 'Occidental', west of the same river. The Oriental section is divided into 14 departments and the capital. The more important departments are supervised by a *Delegado* appointed by and directly responsible to the central government. The Occidental province, or Chaco, is divided into 5 departments.

DEFENCE. The army, navy and air forces are separate services under a single command. The President of the Republic is the active Commander-in-Chief. The armed forces totalled (1989) about 16,000 officers and men.

Army. The Army consists of 1 cavalry division, 8 infantry divisions and supporting artillery, engineer and signals units. Equipment includes 3 M-4A3 main battle and 18 M-3A1 light tanks. Strength (1990) 12,500 (including 8,600 conscripts), and there are 30,500 reserves.

Navy. The flotilla comprises 6 armoured river defence gunboats (the average age of which exceeds 40 years), 1 converted landing ship with helicopter deck, 7 river patrol boats, 1 ocean-going transport and training ship, and about 12 service craft. There are 2 AT-6G naval counter-insurgency aircraft, 1 Dakota transport and 3 helicopters. Personnel in 1989 totalled 2,500 including 500 marines, of whom 1,000 were conscripts.

Air Force. The Air Force came into being in the early thirties. After operating only transport and training aircraft for a number of years, it received 9 Xavante light jet strike/training aircraft from Brazil in 1980. Other types in service include about 6 C-47 and 4 Aviocar twin-engined transports, 1 Convair C-131A, a Twin Otter, an Otter, 8 Brazilian-built Uirapuru primary trainers, 12 T-6 Texan, 5 Brazilian-supplied Universal armed basic trainers, 5 Tucano advanced trainers and a number of light aircraft and helicopters. HQ and flying school are at Campo Grande, Asunción. Personnel (1989) 1,000.

INTERNATIONAL RELATIONS

Membership. Paraguay is a member of UN, OAS and LAIA.

ECONOMY

Budget. In 1988 budget balanced at Gs. 859,410,496,826.

Currency. The *guaraní* was established on 5 Oct. 1943 equal to 100 old paper pesos. Total monetary circulation was Gs.81,531m. in Dec. 1983. There were (1988) two official rates of exchange; a rate Gs.400 for the import of oil and by-products and Gs.550 for other goods.

Rate of exchange, March 1990: 1,321 *guaraníes* = US$1; 2,165 *guaraníes* = £1.

Banking. The Banco Central del Paraguay opened 1 July 1952 to take over the central banking functions previously assigned to the National Bank of Paraguay, which had opened in March 1943 and been reorganized as the Banco del Paraguay in Sept. 1944 with a monetary, a banking and a mortgage department. The Banco del Paraguay closed in Nov. 1961 and has been replaced, with the aid of a US loan of US$3m., by the Banco Nacional de Fomento.

The Banco Nacional de Fomento, Lloyds Bank, Banco Exterior do Brasil, Citibank, Banco de Asunción, Banco Exterior SA, Banco Unión SA, Banco Paraguayo de Comercio, Banco Real del Paraguay SA, Banco Aleman Transatlantico, Banco Holandés Unido, Banco Nacional del Estado de São Paulo, Yegros y Azara, Interbanco, Banco Paraná and Banco de Inversiones all have agencies in Asunción and branches in some main towns.

Weights and Measures. The metric system was officially adopted on 1 Jan. 1901.

ENERGY AND NATURAL RESOURCES

Electricity. Electricity requirements are supplied by Acaray hydro-electric power plant. Production in 1988 was 13,535m. kwh. Supply 220 volts; 50 Hz.

Itaipú, the largest hydro-electric dam in the world, a joint effort of the governments of Brazil and Paraguay, was inaugurated in 1982 and it is estimated that the whole project will be completed in 1990. Eventually it will have 18 turbogenerators, each with a capacity of 700,000 kw. In 1984 the first turbine started generating power.

The Yacyretá project is being carried out by the Binational Commission Yacyretá which was created by a treaty between the governments of Argentina and Paraguay. Work is being carried out on this project and it is hoped that the plant will be in full operation by the end of this decade. Initially 20 turbines each of 135,000 kw generating capacity will be installed giving the plant an initial output of 2·7m. kw.

Oil. The oil refinery at Villa Elisa, which has been in operation since 1966, has a production of about 3,500 bbls a day. Exploration for petroleum in the Chaco yielded negative results but prospecting was continuing in 1988.

Minerals. Iron, manganese and other minerals have been reported but have not been shown to be commercially exploitable. There are large deposits of limestone, and also salt, kaolin and apatite. National and international firms have acquired licences to prospect for oil and natural gas in the Chaco.

Agriculture. In 1981 it was estimated that agriculture absorbs some 51·4m. hectares. In 1988, the main agricultural products (in 1,000 tonnes) were: Mandioca (cassava), 3,891; soybeans, 1,407; maize, 1,200; cotton, 537; wheat, 318; rice, 81; tobacco, 14; sugar-cane, 3,382; poroto (green beans), 49; tártago (spurge), 49.

Wheat, soybeans, cotton, sugar, tobacco, coffee are increasing in importance, as are also essential oils and oilseeds. *Yerba maté*, or strongly flavoured Paraguayan tea, continues to be produced but is declining in importance.

Livestock (1988). Paraguay had about 7,780,000 cattle, 328,000 horses, 2,108,000 pigs, 430,000 sheep.

Forestry. In 1988, 39% of the land area was forested (15·6m. hectares). In the Oriental section there are reserves of hardwoods and cedars that have scarcely been exploited. Palms, tung and other trees are exploited for their oils. The Japanese are experimenting with mulberries for silk growing. Pines and firs have been introduced under a UN project. In 1986, 181,355 tons of timber were exported.

INDUSTRY AND TRADE

Industry. Production, 1988 (1,000 tons): Frozen meat, 15·5; cotton fibre, 187·4; sugar, 98·1; rice, 34·8; wheat flour, 104·5; edible oil, 39·7; industrial oil, 12·9; tung oil, 6·9; sawn timber, 629·7; cement, 255·6; soybean, peanut and coconut flour, 405; cigarettes (1m. packets), 46,598; matches (1,000 boxes), 8,979. There are 3 meat-packing plants and other factories producing vegetable oils. A textile industry in Pilar and Asunción meets a large part of local needs.

Labour. Trade unionists number about 30,000 (*Confederación Paraguaya de Trabajadores* and *Confederación Cristiana de Trabajadores*).

Commerce. Imports and exports (in US$1m.):

	1984	*1985*	*1986*	*1987*	*1988*
Imports	513·0	442·3	509·3	592·3	573·9
Exports	334·5	303·9	232·5	353·4	511·9

Chief exports in 1988 included (in US$1,000): Cotton, 209,621; soybeans, 153,816; vegetable oil, 12,604; sawn wood, 16,056; expellers, 27,532; tobacco, 5,970; cattle hides, 16,807; tannin extract, 4,409; processed meat, 23,007; essential oils, 4,700.

Chief imports 1988 (in US$1,000): Fuels and lubricants, 92,225; machinery, 113,095; chemical and pharmaceutical products, 39,534; transport and accessories, 52,296; drinks and tobacco, 50,122; foodstuffs, 11,969; iron and manufactures, 19,845; agricultural implements and accessories, 9,416; textiles and clothing, 12,377; paper, cardboard and paper products, 13,065; metal and metal products, 6,624.

Imports and exports (in US$), by country, 1988:

Country	*Imports*	*Exports*
Algeria	37,074	...
Argentina	58,677	33,588
Belgium	3,462	24,410
Brazil	150,593	117,121
Federal Republic of Germany	30,820	19,417
France	10,276	6,782
Italy	8,636	12,686
Japan	36,859	...
Netherlands	2,906	67,972
Spain	8,056	15,132
Sweden	2,020	...
Switzerland	6,542	38,908
UK	34,837	2,635
Uruguay	5,691	4,430
USA	49,786	18,884

Total trade between Paraguay and UK (British Department of Trade returns, in £1,000 sterling):

	1985	*1986*	*1987*	*1988*	*1989*
Imports to UK	2,086	1,455	1,409	1,950	8,898
Exports and re-exports from UK	15,540	31,010	25,409	22,024	19,282

Tourism. Visitors numbered 200,000 in 1986.

COMMUNICATIONS

Roads. In 1986 there were 23,606 km of roads, of which 2,159 were paved. The principal paved roads are Route No. 2/7 running from Asunción to the bridge over the Paraná at Puerto Presidente Stroessner, and thence down to the ocean at Paranaguá; and Route No. 1 to Encarnación in the south. The other main arteries are Coronel Oviedo-Pedro Juan Caballero road (unpaved from Coronel Oviedo) in the north and the Trans-Chaco road which starts from the bridge across the river Paraguay north of Asunción and ends at Nueva Asunción on the Bolivian border. Unpaved roads are closed when it rains. In the Argentine, a paved road starts from Pilcomayo, opposite Asunción, and provides good communication with Buenos Aires. In 1987 there were 90,000 vehicles (36,900 cars, 24,300 lorries, 2,700 buses and 26,100 jeeps and taxis).

Railways. The President Carlos Antonio López (formerly Paraguay Central) Railway runs from Asunción to Encarnación, on the Río Alto Paraná, with a length of 441 km (1,435 mm gauge). In 1986, traffic amounted to 156,231 tonnes and 348,535 passengers.

Aviation. International services are operated by 8 airlines (1 domestic and 7 foreign) and internal routes by military airlines and some small private lines.

Shipping. In flood the Paraguay River, which divides the country into two distinct parts, is navigable for 12ft-draught vessels as far as Concepción, 180 miles north of Asunción, and for smaller vessels for a further distance of 600 miles northward. Drought conditions often restrict navigation to lighter traffic. The Paraná River is navigable by large boats from Corrientes up to Puerto Aguirre, at the mouth of the Yguazú River. Boats of a few hundred tons capacity navigate the tributary rivers.

Asunción, the chief port, is 950 miles from the sea. The cargo fleet includes 25 vessels of 300–1,000 tons, 3 tankers of 1,100–1,700 tons, 2 passenger river boats and 1 ocean-going freighter of 713 tons.

Post and Broadcasting. In 1985 there were 382 postal offices and 88,730 telephones. In Dec. 1984 there were 266,200 television and 624,000 radio receivers. There are 4 television stations.

Cinemas (1986). Cinemas numbered 6 in Asunción. The larger country towns usually have an outdoor cinema.

Newspapers (1988). There were 5 daily newspapers in Asunción.

JUSTICE, RELIGION, EDUCATION AND WELFARE

Justice. The highest court is the Supreme Court with 5 members. There are special Chambers of Appeal for civil and commercial cases, and criminal cases. Judges of first instance deal with civil, commercial and criminal cases in 6 departments. Minor cases are dealt with by Justices of the Peace.

The Attorney-General represents the State in all jurisdictions, with representatives in each judicial department and in every jurisdiction. In matters of revenue, taxes, etc., the State is represented by the *Abogado del Tesoro*.

Religion. Religious liberty is guaranteed by the 1967 constitution. Article 6 thereof recognizes Roman Catholicism as the official religion of the country. The same article states that relations between Paraguay and the Holy See shall be regulated by concordats or other bilateral agreements, but no such agreements have yet been negotiated.

The Roman Catholic Church is organized into the Archdiocese of Asunción, 3 other dioceses (San Juan Bautista de las Misiones, Concepción and Villarrica); 4 Prelatures (Coronel Oviedo, Encarnación, Alto Paraná and Caacupé); and 2 Vicariates Apostolic (Chaco and Pilcomayo). The bishops meet in a Conference of Paraguayan Bishops. Only civil marriages are legally valid. There are numerous non-catholic communities, the largest of whom are the Mennonites. There is a small Anglican church in Asunción, with missions in the Chaco, which comes under the jurisdiction of an Anglican Bishop resident in Asunción.

Education. Education is free and nominally compulsory. In 1987 there were 4,101 primary schools (public and private) with 579,687 pupils and 28,136 teachers. In 1985 there were 740 secondary schools with (1987) 148,516 students and (1982) 2,448 teachers. The National University in Asunción had, in 1987, 18,711 students and (1985) 2,694 professors; the Catholic University had 10,409 students and (1984) 900 professors.

Health. In 1982 there were 2,201 doctors. In 1979 there were 855 dentists, 860 pharmacists, 783 midwives and 2,636 nursing personnel. In 1985 there were 3,380 hospital beds.

DIPLOMATIC REPRESENTATIVES

Of Paraguay in Great Britain (51 Cornwall Gdns, London, SW7 4AQ)
Ambassador: (Vacant).

Of Great Britain in Paraguay (Calle Presidente Franco, 706, Asunción)
Ambassador and Consul-General: T. H. Steggle, CMG.

Of Paraguay in the USA (2400 Massachusetts Ave., NW, Washington, D.C., 20008)
Ambassador: Dr Marcos Martínez Mendieta.

Of the USA in Paraguay (1776 Mariscal López Ave., Asunción)
Ambassador: Timothy Towell.

Of Paraguay to the United Nations
Ambassador: Alfredo Cañete.

Further Reading

Gaceta Official, published by Imprenta Nacional, Estrella y Estero Bellaco, Asunción
Anuario Daumas. Asunción
Anuario Estadístico de la República del Paraguay. Asunción. Annual
Lewis, P. H., *Paraguay under Stroessner.* Univ. of North Carolina Press, 1980
Maybury-Lewis, D. and Howe, J., *The Indian Peoples of Paraguay: Their Plight and Their Prospects.* Cambridge, Mass., 1980
Nickson, R. A., *Paraguay.* [Bibliography] Oxford and Santa Barbara, 1987

National Library: Biblioteca Nacional, De la Rosidenta, Asunción.

PERU

República del Perú

Capital: Lima
Population: 21·3m. (1988)
GNP per capita: US$1,470 (1987)

HISTORY. The Republic of Peru, formerly the most important of the Spanish vice-royalties in South America, declared its independence on 28 July 1821; but it was not till after a war, protracted till 1824, that the country gained its actual freedom.

AREA AND POPULATION. Peru is bounded north by Ecuador and Colombia, east by Brazil and Bolivia, south by Chile and west by the Pacific Ocean. Area 1,285,216 sq. km (496,093 sq. miles).

The long-standing dispute with Chile over the provinces of Tacna and Arica (*see* THE STATESMAN'S YEAR-BOOK, 1928, p. 1198) reached an amicable settlement on 3 June 1929 at Lima, Tacna going to Peru and Arica to Chile. In response to demands by Bolivia for permanent access to the Pacific Coast, proposals for a Bolivian corridor to the sea and a new Bolivian port to be built in the disputed area have been put forward by Chile and Peru. To date, little progress has been made. One result has been increased tension along the Chilean–Peruvian border, there is no sign of a settlement of the border dispute, and the armed forces of both countries remain on the alert in the disputed border area. Fighting broke out between Peruvian and Ecuadorean Forces, in early 1981, along part of the disputed border (the Cordillera del Condor) which has to date not been adequately mapped. A number of proposals for settling the issue permanently have been put forward but a final settlement is unlikely to be reached in the near future. For an account of the settlement of other boundary disputes, *see* THE STATESMAN'S YEAR-BOOK, 1948, p. 1173.

The census taken in 1981 gave the population as 17,005,210. Estimate (1988) 21,255,900 (10,707,400 male). Lima, the capital, had (1983) 5,258,600 population. Birth rate per 1,000 population (1988), 34·2; death rate, 9; infant mortality rate per 1,000 live births, 85·8.

The area and population of the 24 departments and the constitutional province of Callao, together with their capitals, are shown below:

Department	*Sq. km*	*Estimate 1988*	*Capital*	*Estimate 1988*
Amazonas	41,297	319,500	Chachapoyas	12,800
Ancash	36,669	951,800	Huaraz	61,200
Apurimac	20,550	364,800	Abancay	27,000
Arequipa	63,528	910,500	Arequipa	591,700
Ayacucho	44,181	557,600	Ayacucho	94,200
Cajamarca	34,930	1,222,600	Cajamarca	85,600
Callao [1]	148	560,000	Callao	318,300
Cuzco	76,329	1,000,400	Cuzco	255,300
Huancavelica	21,079	372,900	Huancavelica	24,700
Huánuco	34,094	583,800	Huánuco	85,500
Ica	21,251	519,500	Ica	144,000
Junín	41,296	1,062,600	Huancayo	199,200
La Libertad	23,241	1,180,800	Trujillo	491,100
Lambayeque	13,737	881,000	Chiclayo	394,800
Lima	33,821	6,313,000	Lima	417,900 [3]
Loreto	379,025	621,800	Iquitos	247,900
Madre de Dios	78,403	46,000	Puerto Maldonado	19,500
Moquegua	15,709	126,900	Moquegua	29,400
Pasco	24,035	270,800	Cerro de Pasco	72,100
Piura	36,403	1,413,600	Piura	297,200
Puno	72,382 [2]	997,400	Puno	92,700
San Martín	52,309	429,500	Moyobamba	22,900
Tacna	15,232	195,500	Tacna	137,500
Tumbes	4,732	135,900	Tumbes	61,100
Ucayali	100,831	217,700	Pucallpa	140,700

[1] Constitutional province.
[2] Includes Peruvian zone of Lake Titicaca (4,996 sq. km).
[3] Municipality proper; Lima/Callao metropolitan area 4,605,043.

The official languages are Spanish (spoken by 68% of the population) and Quechua (spoken by 27%); 3% speak Aymara.

CLIMATE. There is a very wide variety of climate, ranging from equatorial to desert, (or perpetual snow on the high mountains). In coastal areas, temperatures vary very little, either daily or annually, though humidity and cloudiness show considerable variation, with highest humidity from May to Sept. Little rain is experienced in that period. In the Sierra, temperatures remain fairly constant over the year, but the daily range is considerable. There the dry season is from April to Nov. Desert conditions occur in the extreme south, where the climate is uniformly dry, with a few heavy showers falling between Jan. and March. Lima. Jan. 74°F (23·3°C), July 62°F (16·7°C). Annual rainfall 2" (48 mm). Cuzco. Jan. 56°F (13·3°C), July 50°F (10°C). Annual rainfall 32" (804 mm).

CONSTITUTION AND GOVERNMENT. On 3 Oct. 1968 a military junta overthrew the government of President Fernando Belaúnde Terry and installed Gen. Juan Velasco Alvarado as President of a 'Revolutionary Government' with a cabinet composed entirely of officers of the armed services. Gen. Velasco was ousted in bloodless *coup* in Aug. 1975 and was replaced by Gen. Francisco Morales Bermudez.

The new Constitution, which became effective when a civilian government was installed in July 1980, provides for a Legislature consisting of a Senate (60 members) and a Chamber of Deputies (180 members) and an Executive formed of the President of the Republic and a Council of Ministers appointed by him. Elections were held in April 1985. They are held every 5 years with the President and Congress elected, at the same time, by separate ballots.

All Peruvians over the age of 18 are eligible to vote; in May 1980 the number of registered voters was over 6m., including 1m. in Lima province. Voting is compulsory; women were fully enfranchised in 1955.

Presidential elections will take place on 8 April 1990. See Addenda.

Presidents since 1962 were:

Gen. Ricardo Pérez Godoy, 18 July 1962–3 March 1963.[1]
Gen. Nicolás Lindley López, 3 March–28 July 1963.
Fernando Belaúnde Terry, 28 July 1963–3 Oct. 1968.[1]
Gen. Juan Velasco Alvarado, 3 Oct. 1968–29 Aug. 1975.[1]
Gen. Francisco Morales Bermudez, 29 Aug. 1975–28 July 1980.
Fernando Belaúnde Terry, 28 July 1980–28 July 1985.

[1] Deposed.

President: Alan García Pérez (sworn in 28 July 1985).

The Cabinet was in Nov. 1988 composed as follows:

Prime Minister and Foreign Affars: Guillermo Larco Cox.

Defence: Gen. Julio Velasquez Giacarini. *Economy and Finance:* César Vasquez Bazán. *Education:* Efrain Obregoso Rodriguez. *Justice:* María Angelíca Bocko Heredia. *Labour:* Wifredo Echaque Villanueva.

There are 24 departments divided into 179 provinces (plus the constitutional province of Callao) and 1,764 districts; the province of Callao has some of the functions of a department.

National flag: Three vertical strips of red, white, red, with the national arms in the centre.

National anthem: Somos Libres, seámoslo siempre (words by J. de la Torre Ugarte; tune by J. B. Alcedo, 1821).

DEFENCE

Army. While military service is compulsory youths are only conscripted to fill the annual quota. The term of service is 2 years and all males of 20–25 years of age are liable. The country is divided into 5 military regions.

The Army comprises (1990) approximately 80,000 men (including 60,000 conscripts). There are 5 military regions with 2 armoured, 1 cavalry, 8 infantry, 1 airborne and 1 jungle divisions with supporting artillery, engineer and helicopter battalions. There is an air element of 35 Mil Mi-8 and Mi-17, 2 Mi-6 and 1 Alouette III helicopter, plus about a dozen fixed-wing transport and liaison aircraft. Equipment consists of approximately 450 tanks (T-54/-55 and AMX-13), over 300 light armoured fighting vehicles and 105-mm./130-mm./155-mm. field artillery.

There is a para-military national police force of 70,000 personnel.

Navy. The principal ships of the Peruvian Navy are the former Netherlands cruisers *Almirante Grau* (*ex-De Zeven Provincien*) and *Aguirre* (formerly *De Ruyter*) built in 1953. *Almirante Grau*'s main armament remains her 8 152 mm guns plus 8 Otomat surface-to-surface missiles. *Aguirre* has been converted to a helicopter cruiser and mounts only 4 152 mm guns, the after two turrets having been removed in favour of a hangar and flight deck capable of supporting 3 SH-3D Sea King helicopters. (Confusion sometimes exists over Peruvian ship names because of the tradition that the flagship always bears the name *Almirante Grau*. Thus when this ship is in refit the name is temporarily re-assigned to another). The two former British cruisers *ex-Newfoundland* and *ex-Ceylon* have both been retired.

There are 11 diesel submarines, 6 built in West Germany (1974-82), and 5 *ex*-US all over 30 years old (a sixth was sunk in collision in 1988). Other combatants include 2 much-modernized former British Daring class and 4 *ex*-Netherlands Friesland class destroyers of 1950s vintage, 4 Italian Lupo class frigates (2 built in Italy and 2 in Peru), 6 French-built fast missile craft and 4 tank landing ships. Major auxiliaries include 5 tankers, 2 transports, 1 survey ship and an ocean tug, and there are about 30 minor auxiliaries and service craft. A river flotilla of 10 patrol craft police the Upper Amazon, based at Madre de Dios and Iquitos.

The Naval Aviation branch comprises 8 S-2 Trackers and 3 Super-King Air ASW aircraft based ashore, 6 Sea King and 6 AB-212 ASW helicopters for service afloat plus 15 miscellaneous transport and utility aircraft.

Callao is the main base, where the dockyard is located and most training takes place. Smaller ocean bases exist at Paita and Talara.

Naval personnel in 1989 totalled 25,000 (12,000 conscripts) including the Naval Air Arm and 2,500 Marines.

The Coast Guard, 600 strong includes 6 coastal patrol craft, 5 inshore and 10 river patrol craft.

Air Force. The operational force consists of 5 combat groups. No. 6 Group has 2 squadrons of Mirage 5 jet fighters; No. 9 Group has 2 squadrons of Canberra light jet bombers; No. 7 Group has 2 squadrons of A-37B light attack aircraft; No. 12 Group has Soviet-built Su-22 variable-geometry fighter bombers in 2 operational squadrons; No. 11 Group has one squadron of Su-22s and one with Mirage 2000s. Other aircraft in service include medium transports (1 F.28 Fellowship, 15 An-32, 14 C-130/L-100 Hercules), light transports (16 Twin Otter, 1 twin-jet Falcon and 12 Turbo-Porter), helicopters (2 Mi-6 and 6 Mi-8, 24 Mi-24 gunships, Bell 47G, 206, 212, 214ST, 412 and UH-1, BO 105 and Alouette III), 70 training aircraft (including Aermacchi MB 339, T-37 and T-41D) and a small number of miscellaneous types for photographic and communications duties. There are military airfields at Talara, Chiclayo, Piura, Pisco, Lima (2), Iquitos and La Joya, and a seaplane base at Iquitos. All officers and pilots are trained at the Air Academy at Lima (Las Palmas). The approximate strength of the Peruvian Air Force (1990) 15,000 personnel and 120 combat aircraft.

INTERNATIONAL RELATIONS

Membership. Peru is a member of UN, OAS, Andean Group and LAIA (formerly LAFTA).

ECONOMY

Budget. The budget for 1987 envisaged expenditure of 92,539m. intis and revenue of 66,424m. intis.

Currency. The monetary unit is the *inti* introduced 1986. One *inti* = 1,000 *soles*. In March 1990, £1 = 21,754 *inti*; US$1 = 13,372 *inti*.

Banking. The government bank of issue is the Banco Central de la Reserva del Perú, which was established in 1922. The Government's fiscal agent is the Banco de la Nación.

There were in 1987, 12 commercial banks (of which 7 state-owned), 5 foreign commercial banks, 4 development banks, 6 regional commercial banks and a savings bank.

Weights and Measures. The metric system of weights and measures was established by law in 1869, and since 1916 has come into general use.

ENERGY AND NATURAL RESOURCES

Electricity. In 1987 the production of electric energy was 13,951m. kwh (10,809m. kwh hydro-electric). Supply 220 volts; 60 Hz.

Oil. Proven oil reserves in the jungle region amount to about 900m. bbls. The new 850 km pipeline, linking the new jungle oilfields to coastal terminals, was opened in 1977. Output amounted to 5·9m. tonnes in 1989 and Peru became an oil exporter in 1985.

Minerals. Peru's mining industry produces 13 metals and 25 non-metallic minerals. Lead, copper, iron, silver, zinc and petroleum are the chief minerals exploited. In 1984 prospecting for uranium was in progress. Mineral production (in 1,000 tonnes, 1987) of iron, 3,305; zinc, 612; copper, 406; lead, 204; silver, 2,054,000 kg; gold, 5·6m. kg.

Agriculture. There are 4 natural zones: The coast strip, with an average width of 80 km; the Sierra or Uplands, formed by the coast range of mountains and the Andes proper; the Montaña or high wooded region which lies on the eastern slopes of the Andes, and the jungle in the Amazon Basin, known as the Selva. In 1984 irrigation was increasing the amount of cultivable acreage in the arid coastal sections of the country, using the abundance of water flowing from the Andes mountains.

Production in 1988 (in 1,000 tonnes): Sugar-cane, 6,200; potatoes, 1,960; seed cotton, 280; coffee, 103; rice, 1,080; maize, 880.

Livestock (1988): 2·48m. (1987) alpacas, 25,000 (1987) vicuna, 3·9m. cattle, 13·32m. sheep, 2·4m. pigs, 52m. poultry.

Forestry. There are 209m. acres of forests containing valuable hardwoods; oak and cedar account for about 40%. In 1986, total roundwood removals totalled 7·7m. cu metres.

Fisheries. Production (1987 in tonnes) 4,274,000, including anchoveta, 1,640,700; sardine (1986), 1,721,000.

INDUSTRY AND TRADE

Industry. About 70% of Peru's manufacturing industries are located in or around the Lima/Callao metropolitan area. Products include pig-iron, blooms, billets, largets, round and round-deformed bars, wire rod, black and galvanized sheets and galvanized roofing sheets. Refractories are manufactured at Lima.

The Government has a monopoly of the import and/or local manufacture and sale of guano, salt, alcohol and explosives.

Labour. In 1988 the total labour force was considered to number 7,205,500 persons. The population was distributed as follows: Agriculture, forestry, hunting and fishing, 2,507,500; manufacturing industry, 742,200; commerce, 1,080,800; construction, 259,400; mining, 172,900; services, 1,923,900; others, 518,800.

Trade Unions. Trade unions have about 2m. members (approximately 1·5m. in peasant organizations and 500,000 in industrial). The major trade union organization is the *Confederación de Trabajadores del Perú*, which was reconstituted in

1959 after being in abeyance for some years. The other labour organizations recognized by the Government are the *Confederación General de Trabajadores del Perú*, the *Confederación Nacional de Trabajadores* and the *Central de Trabajadores de la Revolución Peruana.*

Commerce. The value of trade has been as follows (in US$1m.):

	1982	*1983*	*1984*	*1985*	*1986*	*1987*
Imports	3,722	2,722	2,140	1,806	2,596	3,068
Exports	3,293	3,015	3,147	2,978	2,531	2,605

In 1987, imports (in US$1,000) were mainly from the USA (563,264), Federal Republic of Germany (233,205) and Japan (209,926); exports were mainly to the USA (541,799) and Japan (162,447). In 1986 the chief export was minerals, US$1,023,000.

Total trade between Peru and UK (British Department of Trade returns, in £1,000 sterling):

	1986	*1987*	*1988*	*1989*
Imports to UK	82,141	91,689	90,844	125,538
Exports and re-exports from UK	48,275	49,324	31,384	29,707

Tourism. There were 320,000 visitors in 1988.

COMMUNICATIONS

Roads. In 1986 there were 69,942 km, of which 7,459 km were paved and 13,538 km gravel. In 1987 there were 610,813 registered motor vehicles.

Railways. Total length (1986), 1,672 km on 1,435- and 914-mm gauges. In 1986 railways carried 2·3m. tonnes of freight and 3·3m. passengers.

Aviation. In 1986 there were 30 airports.

Shipping. In 1983, 23·5m. tonnes of goods were loaded and unloaded, including 10·4m. coastal traffic.

Post and Broadcasting. An earth satellite ground communication station at Lurin connects Peru through Intelsat. III to the US and Europe. In 1986 there were 628,643 telephones, 419,164 in Lima. Radio-telephone circuits connect Lima with distant towns. There are 153 broadcasting stations, of which 29 are in Lima. Radio receivers (1987) 5·2m. and television receivers 1·6m.

Newspapers. The main Lima newspapers are *El Comercio, Expreso, República, Hoy, La Voz, Ojo, El Popular El Diario, La Tercera, Extra, El Nacional* and *La Crónica.*

JUSTICE, RELIGION, EDUCATION AND WELFARE

Justice. The Peruvian judicial system is a pyramid at the base of which are the justices of the peace who decide minor criminal cases and civil cases involving small sums of money. The apex is the Supreme Court with a President and 12 members; in between are the judges of first instance, who usually sit in the provincial capitals, and the superior courts.

Religion. Religious liberty exists, but the Roman Catholic religion is protected by the State, and since 1929 only Roman Catholic religious instruction is permitted in schools, state or private. In 1972 there were 1 Roman Catholic cardinal, 7 archbishops, 14 bishops, 3 vicars-general, 8 vicars apostolic, 2,672 priests, 506 cloistered monks and 4,558 members of religious orders.

Education. Elementary education is compulsory and free for both sexes between the ages of 7 and 16; secondary education is also free.

In 1987 there were 3,763,730 pupils in primary schools and 1,732,466 pupils in secondary schools.

In 1987 the total number of students at 35 universities was 409,654.

Health. There were in 1986, 353 hospitals and 920 health centres.

DIPLOMATIC REPRESENTATIVES

Of Peru in Great Britain (52 Sloane St., London, SW1X 9SP)
Ambassador: Felipe Valdivieso - Belaúnde (accredited 20 July 1989).

Of Great Britain in Peru (Edificio El Pacifico Washington, Ave. Arequipa, Lima)
Ambassador: D. Keith Haskell, CVO.

Of Peru in the USA (1700 Massachusetts Ave., NW, Washington, D.C., 20036)
Ambassador: Cesar G. Atala.

Of the USA in Peru (PO Box 1995, Lima)
Ambassador: Anthony C. E. Quainton.

Of Peru to the United Nations
Ambassador: Dr Ricardo V. Luna.

Further Reading

The official gazette is *El Peruano*, Lima.

Anario Estadistico del Perú. Annual.—*Perú: Compendio Estadístico.* Annual.—*Boletin de Estadistica Peruana.* Quarterly.—*Demarcación Política del Perú.* (Dirección Nacional de Estadística), Lima
Estadística del Comercio Exterior (*Superintendencia de Aduanas*). Lima
Banco Central de Reserva. Monthly Bulletin.—*Renta Nacional del Perú.* Annual, Lima

Figueroa, A., *Capitalist Development and the Peasant Economy of Peru.* CUP, 1984
Hemming, J., *The Conquest of the Incas.* London, 1970
McClintock, C. and Lowental, A. F., (eds.) *The Peruvian Experiment Reconsidered.* Princeton Univ. Press, 1983
Mejía Baca, J. and Tauro, A., *Diccionário Enciclopédico del Perú.* 3 vols. 1966
Thorpe, R. and Bertram, G., *Peru 1890–1977: Growth and Policy in an Open Economy.* London, 1978

National Library: Avenida Abancay, Lima.

PHILIPPINES

Capital: Manila
Population: 60m. (1989)
GNP per capita: US$630 (1988)

Republika ng Pilipinas

HISTORY. Before the Spanish discovery of the Philippines, the native Filipinos came in contact with India, China and Arabia. According to the early records of China, 'some Filipinos from the country of Ma-i arrived in Canton and sold their merchandise' as early as 982. The Philippine islands were discovered by Magellan in 1521 and conquered by Spain in 1565. Following the Spanish–American war, the islands were ceded to the USA on 10 Dec. 1898, after the Filipinos had tried in vain to establish an independent republic in 1896.

The Philippines acquired self-government as a Commonwealth of the USA by Act of Congress signed by President Roosevelt on 24 March 1934 and ratified by plebiscite on 14 May 1935. This provided for independence after a 10-year transitional period, at the end of which the Philippines became completely independent on 4 July 1946.

AREA AND POPULATION. The Philippines is situated between 21° 25' and 4° 23' N. lat. and between 116° and 127° E. long. It is composed of 7,100 islands and islets, 2,773 of which are named. Approximate land area, 115,830 sq. miles (300,000 sq. km). The largest islands (in sq. km) are Luzon (104,684), Mindanao (94,627), Samar (13,079), Negros (12,706), Palawan (11,784), Panay (11,515), Mindoro (9,735), Leyte (7,215), Cebu (4,421), Bohol (3,864), Masbate (3,268).

Census population 1980 was 48,098,460; 36% urban. Estimate (1989) 60,096,988. (41% urban in 1987).

The area and population of the 13 regions are as follows (from north to south):

Region	*Sq. km*	*Estimate 1988*	*Region*	*Sq. km*	*Estimate 1988*
Ilocos	21,568	4,133,684	Central Visayas	14,951	4,446,456
Cagayan Valley	36,403	2,712,698	Eastern Visayas	21,432	3,242,836
Central Luzon	18,231	5,862,990	Northern Mindanao	28,328	3,437,549
National Capital	636	7,561,413	Southern Mindanao	31,693	4,132,019
Southern Luzon	46,924	7,691,855	Central Mindanao	23,293	2,802,001
Bicol	17,633	4,197,973	Western Mindanao	18,685	3,060,825
Western Visayas	20,223	5,438,994			

The major cities (with 1980 census populations) are as follows; all on Luzon unless indicated in parenthesis.

Manila	1,630,485 [1]	Batangas	143,570
Quezon City	1,165,865 [1]	Cabanatuan	138,298
Davao (Mindanao)	610,375	San Pablo	131,655
Cebu (Cebu)	490,281	San Juan del Monte	130,088 [1]
Caloocan	467,816 [1]	Cadiz (Negros)	129,632
Makati	372,631 [1]	Navotas	126,146 [1]
Zamboanga (Mindanao)	343,722	Lipa	121,166
Pasay	287,770 [1]	Baguio	119,009
Pasig	268,570 [1]	Silay (Negros)	111,131
Bacolod (Negros)	262,415	Mandaue (Cebu)	110,590
Iloilo (Panay)	244,827	Lucena	107,880
Cagayan de Oro (Mindanao)	227,312	Calbayog (Samar)	106,719
Valenzuela	212,363 [1]	Ormoc (Leyte)	104,978
Marikina	211,613 [1]	Tacloban (Leyte)	102,523
Parañaque	208,552 [1]	San Carlos (Luzon)	101,243
Mandaluyong	205,366 [1]	Legaspi	99,766
Angeles	188,834	Dagupan	98,344
Butuan (Mindanao)	172,489	Malolos	95,699
Iligan (Mindanao)	167,358	San Carlos (Negros)	91,627
Olongapo	156,430	Naga	90,712
General Santos (Mindanao)	149,396		

[1] City within Metropolitan Manila (total population 5,925,884).

In 1980 the national language, Pilipino (based on Tagalog, a Malayan dialect) was spoken by 55% of the population, but as a mother tongue by only 23·8%; among the 76 other indigenous languages spoken, all of the Malayo-Polynesian family, Cebuano was spoken as a mother tongue by 24·4%, Ilocano by 11·1%, Hiligaynon by 8% and Bikol by 5%.

CLIMATE. Some areas have an equatorial climate while others experience tropical monsoon conditions, with a wet season extending from May to Nov. Mean temperatures are high all year, with very little variation. Manila. Jan. 77°F (25°C), July 82°F (27·8°C). Annual rainfall 82" (2,083 mm).

CONSTITUTION AND GOVERNMENT. Presidential elections were held on 7 Feb. 1986. Ferdinand E. Marcos was opposed by Corazón Aquino. The elections proved to be fraudulent and although Marcos was proclaimed President, by the National Assembly, on 15 Feb., on 25 Feb. he fled the country. President Corazón Aquino was sworn in on 25 Feb.

On 25 March 1986 the President abolished the Parliament and declared a provisional government. A new Constitution was ratified by referendum in 1987 with 78·5% of the voters endorsing it. It aims 'to secure to ourselves and our posterity the blessings of independence and democracy under the rule of law and a regime of truth, justice, freedom, love, equality and peace'.

At congressional elections held on 11 May 1987, 24 senators were elected in the Upper House and 200 congressmen in the House of Representatives.

President: Corazón Aquino.

Vice President: Salvador Laurel.

Executive Secretary, Presidential Co-ordinator for Political and Security Affairs: Catalino Macarait. *Defence:* Fidel Ramos. *Local Government:* Luis Santos. *Foreign Affairs:* Raul Manglapus. *Justice:* Franklin Drilon. *Finance:* Jesus Estanislao. *Trade:* José Concepcion. *Public Works and Highways:* Fiorello Estuar. *Agrarian Reform:* Florencio Abad. *Agriculture:* Senen Bacani. *Social Welfare:* Mita Pardo de Tavera. *Transport and Communications:* Oscar Orbos. *Education:* Isidro Carino. *Tourism:* Peter Garrucho. *Science:* Ceferino Follosco. *Budget:* Guillermo Carague. *Press:* Tomas Gomez. *Economic Planning (acting):* Cayetano Pedranga. *Labour (acting):* Dionisio de la Serna. *Presidential Spokesman:* Adolfo Azcuna. *Presidential Co-ordinator for Economic and Financial Affairs:* Vicente Jayme. *Presidential Co-ordinator for Resource and Welfare Affairs:* José de Jesus.

National flag: Horizontally blue over red, with a white triangle based on the hoist bearing a gold sun of 8 rays and 3 gold stars.

National hymn: 'Land of the Morning', lyric in English by M. A. Sane and C. Osias, tune by Julian Felipe (1898); 'Pambansang Awit ng Pilipinas', Tagalog lyric by the Institute of National Language, music by Julian Felipe.

Local Government. The country is administratively divided into 14 regions, 73 provinces, 60 cities, 1,532 municipalities, 21 municipal districts and 40,904 *barangays.* On 14 Nov. 1975 the name of provincial boards and city or municipal boards or councils was changed into *Sangguniang Bayan.*

DEFENCE. On 14 March 1947 the Philippine and US Governments signed a 99-year military-base arrangement since reduced to 25 years and will end in 1991. The USA was granted the use of a series of army, navy and air bases, with the right to use a number of others on mutual agreement. On 21 March a second agreement provided for a US Military Advisory Group as well as military assistance. A treaty of mutual assistance was signed in Washington on 30 Aug. 1951; the instruments of ratification were exchanged in Manila on 27 Aug. 1952. The Philippines is also a signatory of the S.E. Asia Collective Defence Treaty.

The Chief of Staff of the Armed Forces has overall command over the Army, Air Force, Navy and Constabulary.

Army. The Army comprises 6 infantry divisions, 1 ranger regiment, 3 engineer brigades, 1 light armoured regiment and 8 artillery battalions. Equipment includes 41 Scorpion light tanks. Strength (1990) 68,000, with reserves totalling 80,000. There are also paramilitary forces; the Philippine Constabulary (38,000) and the Civil Home Defence Force (45,000).

Navy. The Philippine navy consists principally of *ex*-US ships completed in 1944 and 1945, and serviceability and spares are a problem. A modernization programme, based on acquisition of a substantial number of much smaller patrol craft of US design is planned, but the first had not yet arrived in 1989.

The fleet in 1989, includes 2 *ex*-US frigates, 8 offshore patrol vesels (*ex*-US minesweepers and escorts), 4 *ex*-US coastal patrol craft, and about 40 inshore patrol craft. There are 24 tank landing ships and 4 medium landing ships, (of which only 10 are serviceable) and some 70 landing craft. Auxiliaries include 3 repair ships, 2 oilers, 2 yachts/SAR craft and 1 transport, plus some 20 minor auxiliaries. There are 65 patrol craft and SAR craft in the coastguard.

Navy personnel in 1989 totalled 28,000 including 10,000 marines and 2,000 in the coastguard.

Air Force. The Air Force had (1990) a strength of 16,000 officers and men, with 330 aircraft, and was built up with US assistance. Its fighter-bomber wing is equipped with 1 squadron of F-5As. A strike wing is equipped with armed trainers, 2 squadrons having T-28s and 1 squadron SF.260WPs. Other units include a maritime patrol squadron with F27 Maritimes and HU-16 Albatross amphibians and 7 transport squadrons (1 with C-130/L-100 Hercules, 1 with F27s, 1 with Nomads, 1 with C-47s, 2 with UH-1 Iroquois helicopters and 1 with S-76 helicopters). Training aircraft include T-41s, T-34s and T-33 jets, plus S. 211s from Italy being delivered 1989-90. Two S-70 helicopters are used as VIP transports.

Police. Public order is maintained partly through the Philippine constabulary and partly through the local police forces. The constabulary now forms part of the Armed Forces and has 27,000 personnel.

INTERNATIONAL RELATIONS

Membership. The Republic of the Philippines is a member of UN and the Colombo Plan.

External Debt. At July 1988 the external debt (monetary and non-monetary) amounted to US$28,039m.

ECONOMY

Planning. A development plan, 1987–92, aimed at an average growth rate of 6·8%.

Budget. The revenues and expenditures of the central government for calendar years were, in 1m. Philippine pesos, as follows:

	1985	*1986*	*1987*	*1988*	*1989*
Revenue	68,961	79,245	103,214	128,253	146,946
Expenditure	80,148	114,505	155,503	190,689	228,940

Expenditure (1989) included (in 1m. pesos): National defence, 20,770; education, health and social services, 43,988; economic development, 44,754; debt service, 97,712.

At Oct. 1988 the total internal public debt outstanding of the national and local governments and monetary institutions, including those of the government corporations, stood at P.204,225·2m.

Currency. Total money supply, July 1989, was P.59,500m., of which P.36,600m. was currency in circulation and P.22,900m. were demand deposits. The coins used are: 5 *peso*, 1 *peso*, one-half *peso*, quarter *peso*, media *peseta* (10 *centavos*), all contain 70 grammes copper, 18 grammes zinc and 12 grammes nickel; 5 *centavo* in copper and zinc, and 1 *centavo* in aluminium and magnesium zinc. Central Bank notes are issued in 2, 5, 10, 20, 50, 100, 500 *pesos* denominations.

In March 1990, £1 = 35·70 *pesos*; US$1 = 21·78 *pesos*.

Banking. In June 1988 there were 29 head offices and 1,714 branches of commercial banks, with 4 overseas, 1 each in New York, Hong Kong, Taipei and London. Agencies exist in Honolulu, San Francisco and Los Angeles. Total deposits of the commercial banks at 31 Dec. 1988 were P.197,611·9m. Total number of Philippine banking institutions, 31 Dec. 1988, 3,562 with total assets P.742,004·7m. at 31 Dec. 1988 and total deposits of P.225,662·4m. in 1988.

Under the law passed 15 June 1948 the Central Bank of the Philippines was created to have sole control of the credit and monetary supply, independent of the Treasury. It has a capital of P.10m. furnished solely by the Government. Its total assets, at 31 Dec. 1987 were P.325,185·1m. Central Bank's total assets at March 1988 were P.326,446·5m.

Weights and Measures. The metric system of weights and measures was established by law in 1869, and since 1916 has come into general use but there are local units including the picul (63·25 kg) for sugar and fibres, and the cavan (16·5 gallons) for cereals.

ENERGY AND NATURAL RESOURCES

Electricity. Government and private electric systems furnish the Philippines with electric power, with total installed capacity of 5,796m. mw (1988); production 20,865m. kwh. Supply 110 and 220 volts; 60 Hz.

Minerals. Mineral production in 1988 (in tonnes): Nickel metal (1987), 8,510; zinc metal (1987), 1,128; copper metal, 824,200; cobalt metal (1986), 90; coal, 1,336,000; salt, 466,427; gold, 30,500 kg; silver, 54,600 kg; silica sand, 213,407. Other minerals include chromite, cement, rock asphalt, sand and gravel.

Agriculture. Of the total area of 30m. hectares, 7·04m. hectares are commercial forests; 5·4m. hectares non-commercial forests; 794,000 hectares open grassland; 115,000 hectares mangrove and marshes; 14,794,000 hectares cultivated.

About 98·4% of the total cultivated area is owned by Filipinos; the average size of the farm was 2·63 hectares in 1980. The principal products are unhusked rice (palay), copra, sugar-cane, maize and root crops, bananas and pineapples. As of Oct. 1987 9,940,000 persons were employed in agriculture (47·8% of the working population).

The products (in 1,000 tonnes) are (1988, provisional): Rough rice, 8,971; coconuts, 10,800; sugar (centrifugal muscovado and molasses), 1,883; shelled corn, 4,428; bananas, 3,645; tobacco, 58; abaca fibre, 84.

Minor crops are fruits, nuts, vegetables, onions, beans, coffee, cacao, peanuts, ramie, rubber, maguey, kapok, abaca and tobacco.

Livestock, estimated in 1988: 2,890,030 carabaos (water buffaloes), 1,700,010 cattle, 7,580,410 pigs, 2,120,110 goats and 66,344,350 poultry.

Forestry. The forests covered 6·79m. hectares in 1987. Log production, 1988, 3,809,200 cu. metres.

Fisheries. Fish production from all sources was 2,269,700 tonnes in 1988.

INDUSTRY AND TRADE

Industry. Manufacturing is a major source of economic development contributing 25·18% to GNP in 1988. Leading growth sectors were food manufacturing, textile, footwear and wearing apparel, machinery except electrical, fabricated metal products, wood and cork products, industrial chemicals and other chemical products, furniture and fixtures and publishing and allied industries. In 1987 (annual survey), there were 5,000 large manufacturing establishments, of which 1,165 were engaged in food; 414 wearing apparel; 111 footwear; 297 textile; 366 publishing and allied industries; 300 machinery except electrical; 258 fabricated metal products; 295 industrial chemicals and other chemical products; 254 wood and cork products; 162 plastic products and 145 transport equipment. The non-agricultural labour force as of Oct. 1988 was 10,163,000 out of a total of 22,937,000 employed.

Commerce. The values of imports and exports (f.o.b.) for calendar years are stated as follows in US$1m.:

	1985	*1986*	*1987*	*1988*
Imports	5,111	5,044	6,737	8,159
Exports	4,629	4,842	5,720	7,074

The principal exports in 1988 were (in US$1m.): Garments, 1,317; electronics, 1,318; coconut oil (crude), 408; bars, rods and slabs of copper, 295; shrimps and prawns, 250; lumber, 157; bananas, 121; copper concentrates, 109.

Main imports in 1988 (in US$1m.): Petroleum products and related materials, 1,025; textile yarns, fabrics, made-up articles and related products, 324; electric machinery, apparatus and appliances, 472; cereals and cereal preparations, 228; iron and steel, 475; industrial machinery, equipment and machine parts, 211; organic chemicals, 255; artificial resins and plastic materials, 230; machinery specialized for particular industries, 316.

For over a half-century the foreign trade has been chiefly with the USA.

Total trade between the Philippines and UK (British Department of Trade returns, in £1,000 sterling):

	1985	*1986*	*1987*	*1988*	*1989*
Imports to UK	179,979	182,852	202,707	223,571	233,128
Exports and re-exports from UK	94,370	79,809	113,784	123,974	137,367

Tourism. In 1988, 1,043,114 tourists visited the Philippines spending US$1,400m.

COMMUNICATIONS

Roads. In 1988 highways totalled 157,448 km; of this, 9,804 km were concrete; 12,524, asphalt; 9,068, earth; 126,051, macadam. In 1988 there were registered 1,270,483 motor vehicles of all types.

Railways. The National Railways totals 1,027 km of 1,067 mm gauge on Luzon. In 1987, 1,177,763 passengers and 57,020 tonnes of freight were carried by PNR and 101,292,990 passengers by LRT.

Aviation. The Philippine Air Lines, Inc., in 1988-89 carried 1,794,124 international and 4,033,020 domestic passengers. In 1988 there were 75 national and 112 private airports.

Shipping. In 1988 there were 166 public and 286 private ports. In 1988, 80,512 vessels of 69,562,000 net tons entered and 80,610 vessels of 69,064,000 net tons cleared all ports.

Post and Broadcasting. In 1988 there were in operation 2,085 post offices. The Philippine Long Distance Telephone Co. had 926,006 telephones in service (company-owned and subscriber-owned) in 1988. Other major operators had 57,780 connexions in 1988.

Radio stations in 1987 numbered 28,020.

Newspapers (1986). There were 472 registered publications (288 published in Manila), 20 of which were dailies in 1986.

JUSTICE, RELIGION, EDUCATION AND WELFARE

Justice. There is a Supreme Court which is composed of a chief justice and 14 associate justices; it can declare a law or treaty unconstitutional by the concurrent votes of the majority sitting. There is an intermediate appellate court, which consists of a presiding appellate justice and 49 associate appellate justices. There are 13 regional trial courts, one for each judicial region, with a presiding regional trial judge in its 720 branches. There is a metropolitan trial court in each metropolitan area established by law, a municipal trial court in each of the other cities or municipalities and a municipal circuit trial court in each area defined as a municipal circuit comprising one or more cities and/or one or more municipalities.

The Supreme Court may designate certain branches of the regional trial courts to handle exclusively criminal cases, juvenile and domestic relations cases, agrarian cases, urban land reform cases which do not fall under the jurisdiction of quasijudicial bodies and agencies and/or such other special cases as the Supreme Court may determine.

Religion. In 1970 there were 31,169,488 Roman Catholics, 1,434,688 Aglipayans, 1,584,963 Moslems, 1,122,999 Protestants, 475,407 members of the Iglesia ni Kristo, 33,639 Buddhists and 863,302 others.

The Roman Catholics are organized in 12 archbishoprics, 30 bishoprics, 12 prelatures nullius, 4 apostolic vicariates, 4 apostolic prefectures and some 1,633 parishes. The Philippine Independent Church, founded in 1902, and comprising about 3·9% of the population, denies the spiritual authority of the Roman Pontiff. It is divided into two groups, one of which has accepted ordinations by the Episcopalian Church.

Education. Formal education consists of 3 levels: Elementary, secondary and further education. Public elementary education is free and public elementary schools are established in almost every *barangay* or *barrio*. The majority of the secondary and post-secondary schools are private, sectarian or non-sectarian. The number of years required to complete the elementary and secondary levels are 6 and 4 years respectively, while the tertiary level requires at least 4 years for an academic degree. Pre-school education is also offered mostly in private schools to children from ages 3–6.

Non-formal education consists of adult literacy classes, agricultural and farming training programmes, occupation skills training, youth clubs, and community programmes of instructions in health, nutrition, family planning and co-operatives.

Public and private schools in 1987–88 enrolled 9,601,322 pupils in primary schools, 3,494,460 in secondary schools and 1,460,545 students in further education. The University of the Philippines (founded in 1908) had 15,316 students in 1984.

Health. In 1985 there were 51,461 registered physicians and (1987) 87,697 hospital beds.

DIPLOMATIC REPRESENTATIVES

Of the Philippines in Great Britain (9A Palace Green, London, W8 4QE)
Ambassador: Tomas T. Syquia.

Of Great Britain in the Philippines (115 Esteban St., Manila)
Ambassador: Keith MacInnes, CMG.

Of the Philippines in the USA (1617 Massachusetts Ave., NW, Washington, D.C., 20036)
Ambassador: Emmanuel N. Pelaez.

Of the USA in the Philippines (1201 Roxas Blvd., Manila)
Ambassador: Nicholas Platt.

Of the Philippines to the United Nations
Ambassador: Claudio Teehankee.

Further Reading

Philippine Yearbook 1987. National Statistics Office, Manila, 1987
Bresnan, J. (ed.) *Crisis in the Philippines: The Marcos Era and Beyond.* Princeton Univ. Press, 1986
Karnow, S., *In Our Image: America's Empire in the Philippines.* New York, 1989
May, R. J. and Nemenzo, F. (eds.), *The Philippines after Marcos.* London and Sydney, 1985
Poole, F. and Vanzi, M., *Revolution in the Philippines.* New York, 1984
Richardson, J. A., *Philippines.* [Bibliography] Oxford and Santa Barbara, 1989
Seagrove, S., *The Marcos Dynasty:* London, 1989

PITCAIRN ISLAND

Only settlement: Adamstown
Population: 54 (1989)

HISTORY. It was discovered by Carteret in 1767, but remained uninhabited until 1790, when it was occupied by 9 mutineers of HMS *Bounty*, with 12 women and 6 men from Tahiti. Nothing was known of their existence until the island was visited in 1808. In 1856 the population having become too large for the island's resources, the inhabitants (194 in number) were, at their own request, removed to Norfolk Island; but 43 of them returned in 1859–64.

AREA AND POPULATION. Pitcairn Island (1·75 sq. miles; 4·6 sq. km) is situated in the Pacific Ocean, nearly equidistant from New Zealand and Panama (25° 04' S. lat., 130° 06' W. long.). Adamstown is the only settlement. The population on 31 Dec. 1989 was 54.

The uninhabited islands of Henderson (12 sq. miles), Ducie (1½ sq. miles) and Oeno (2 sq. miles) were annexed in 1902 and are included in the Pitcairn group.

CLIMATE. An equable climate, with average annual rainfall of 80" (2,000 mm), spread evenly throughout the year. Mean monthly temperatures range from 75°F (24°C) in Jan. to 66°F (19°C) in July.

CONSTITUTION. Pitcairn was brought within the jurisdiction of the High Commissioner for the Western Pacific in 1898 and transferred to the Governor of Fiji in 1952. When Fiji became independent in Oct. 1970, the British High Commissioner in New Zealand was appointed Governor.

The Local Government Ordinance of 1964 constitutes a Council of 10 members, of whom 4 are elected, 5 are nominated (3 by the 4 elected members and 2 by the Governor) and the Island Secretary is an *ex-officio* member. The Island Magistrate, who is elected triennially, presides over the Council; other members hold office for only 1 year. Liaison between Governor and Council is through a Commissioner in the Auckland, New Zealand, office of the British Consulate-General.

Governor: R. A. C. Byatt, CMG (resides in Wellington).
Island Magistrate: Brian Young (elected Dec. 1987).

Flag: British Blue Ensign with the whole arms of Pitcairn in the fly.

TRADE. Fruit, vegetables and curios are sold to passing ships; fuel oil, machinery, building materials, flour, sugar and other foodstuffs are imported.

ROADS. There were (1989) 6 km of roads. In Aug. 1989 motor cycles provided the sole means of personal automotive transport; there were 4 2-wheelers, 16 3-wheelers and four 4-wheeled motor cycles.

JUSTICE. The Island Court consists of the Island Magistrate and 2 assessors.

EDUCATION. In 1989 there was 1 teacher and 11 pupils.

Further Reading

A Guide to Pitcairn. Pitcairn Island Administration, Auckland, revised ed. 1982
Ball, I., *Pitcairn: Children of the Bounty.* London, 1973
Ross, A. S. C. and Moverly, A. W., *The Pitcairnese Language.* London, 1964

POLAND

Capital: Warsaw
Population: 37·78m. (1989)
GNP per capita: US$1,850 (1988)

Polska Rzeczpospolita—Polish Republic

HISTORY. In 1966 Poland celebrated its millennium, but modern Polish history begins with the partitions of the once-powerful kingdom between Russia, Austria and Prussia in 1772, 1793 and 1795. For 19th century events *see* THE STATESMAN'S YEAR-BOOK 1980–81.

On 10 Nov. 1918 independence was proclaimed by Józef Piłsudski, the founder of the Polish Legions during the war. On 28 June 1919 the Treaty of Versailles recognized the independence of Poland.

On 1 Sept. 1939 Germany invaded Poland, on 17 Sept. 1939 Soviet troops entered eastern Poland, and on 29 Sept. 1939 the fourth partition of Poland took place. After the German attack on the USSR, Germany occupied the whole of Poland. By March 1945 the country had been liberated by the USSR.

In 1970 the Federal Republic of Germany recognized Poland's western boundary as laid down by the Potsdam Conference of 1945 (the 'Oder–Neisse line'), and reaffirmed this recognition in Nov. 1989 and March 1990.

In July 1944 the USSR recognized the Polish Committee of National Liberation *(Polski Komitet Wyzwolenia Narodowego)* established in Lublin as an executive organ of the National Council of the Homeland *(Krajowa Rada Narodowa).* The Committee was transformed into the Provisional Government in Dec. 1944, and on 28 June 1945, supplemented by members of the Polish Government in London (which had been recognized by the UK and USA), it was re-established—in Moscow—as the Polish Provisional Government of National Unity and on 6 July recognized as such by the UK and USA.

Elections were held on 19 Jan. 1947. Of the 12·7m. votes cast, 11·24m. were recognized as valid and 9m. were given for the Communist-dominated 'Democratic Bloc'.

After riots in Poznań in June 1956 nationalist anti-Stalinist elements gained control of the Communist Party, under the leadership of Władysław Gomułka. In Dec. 1970 strikes and riots in Gdańsk, Szczecin and Gdynia led to the replacement of Gomułka by Edward Gierek. The raising of meat prices on 1 July 1980 resulted in a wave of strikes which broadened into generalized wage demands and eventually acquired a political character. Workers in Gdańsk, Gdynia and Sopot elected a joint strike committee, led by Lech Wałęsa. On 31 Aug. the Government and Wałęsa signed the 'Gdańsk Agreements' permitting the formation of independent trade unions.

On 5 Sept. Gierek was replaced by Stanisław Kania. On 17 Sept. various trade unions decided to form a national confederation ('Solidarity') and applied for legal status, which was granted on 24 Oct.

On 9 Feb. 1981 the Defence Minister, Gen. Wojciech Jaruzelski, became Prime Minister. At Solidarity's first national congress (4–10 Sept. and 2–8 Oct. 1981) Wałęsa was re-elected chairman and a radical programme of action was adopted. On 18 Oct. Kania was replaced as Party leader by Jaruzelski. On 13 Dec. 1981 the Government imposed martial law (*stan wojenny*) and set up a 20-member Military Council of National Salvation (WRON). Solidarity was proscribed and its leaders detained. Martial law was approved by the Sejm on 26 Jan. 1982. Wałęsa was released in Nov. 1982. On 8 Oct. the Sejm voted a law dissolving all registered trade unions including Solidarity. These were replaced by workplace unions.

Martial law was lifted in July 1983. An amnesty of 21 July 1984 freed 35,000 common and 652 political prisoners. In Nov. 1985 Jaruzelski resigned the Prime Ministership in favour of Zbigniew Messner, and was elected Chairman of the

Council of State. In 1986 the Government granted an amnesty to political prisoners. Following strikes and demands for the reinstatement of Solidarity, Messner and his government resigned in Sept. 1988. Mieczysław Rakowski was appointed Prime Minister on 27 Sept.

After the parliamentary elections of June 1989 Czesław Kiszczak was elected Prime Minister on 2 Aug. 1989, but was unable to form a government against the opposition of Solidarity, and resigned on 14 Aug. Tadeusz Mazowiecki, a Solidarity member, was elected Prime Minister by the Sejm on 24 Aug. by 378 votes to 4, with 41 abstentions.

AREA AND POPULATION. Poland is bounded north by the Baltic and the RSFSR, east by Lithuania, White Russia and the Ukraine, south by Czechoslovakia and west by the German Democratic Republic. Poland comprises an area of 312,683 sq. km (120,628 sq. miles). The country is divided into 49 voivodships (*wojewodztwo*) and these in turn are divided into 822 towns and 2,121 wards (*gmina*). The capital is Warsaw (Warszawa).

Area (in sq. km) and population (in 1,000) in 1989 (1984 % urban in brackets).

Voivodship	*Area*	*Population*		*Voivodship*	*Area*	*Population*	
Biała Podlaska	5,348	303	(32·5)	Opole	8,535	1,008	(50·9)
Białystok	10,055	685	(57·7)	Ostrołęka	6,498	391	(30·9)
Bielsko–Biała	3,704	890	(48·9)	Piła	8,205	473	(53·9)
Bydgoszcz	10,349	1,098	(62·8)	Piotrków	6,266	638	(45·3)
Chełm	3,866	244	(39·9)	Płock	5,117	512	(45·7)
Ciechanów	6,362	424	(33·0)	Poznan	8,151	1,317	(69·7)
Czestochowa	6,182	773	(51·2)	Przemyśl	4,437	402	(35·7)
Elblag	6,103	474	(58·6)	Radom	7,294	743	(44·5)
Gdańsk	7,394	1,411	(76·2)	Rzeszów	4,397	711	(37·7)
Gorzów	8,484	494	(60·4)	Siedlce	8,499	646	(28·7)
Jelenia Góra	4,378	515	(65·3)	Sieradz	4,869	407	(33·1)
Kalisz	6,512	704	(44·5)	Skierniewice	3,960	415	(42·2)
Katowice	6,650	3,932	(87·7)	Słupsk	7,453	407	(53·8)
Kielce	9,211	1,123	(44·4)	Suwałki	10,490	463	(49·9)
Konin	5,139	465	(38·6)	Szczecin	9,981	958	(73·9)
Koszalin	8,470	499	(61·0)	Tarnobrzeg	6,283	591	(34·6)
Kraków (Cracow)	3,254	1,220	(69·1)	Tarnów	4,151	661	(34·2)
Krosno	5,702	488	(32·8)	Torun	5,348	653	(60·8)
Legnica	4,037	505	(66·6)	Wałbrzych	4,168	738	(88·5)
Leszno	4,154	381	(46·1)	Warsaw	3,788	2,413	(73·0)
Łódź	1,523	1,141	(91·4)	Włocławek	4,402	427	(44·9)
Łomża	6,684	344	(35·7)	Wrocław	6,287	1,119	(72·4)
Lublin	6,792	1,006	(55·5)	Zamosc	6,980	489	(24·9)
Nowy Sącz	5,576	685	(35·5)	Zielona Góra	8,868	651	(59·0)
Olsztyn	12,327	741	(56·4)				

Population (in 1,000) of the largest towns (1985):

Warsaw	1,649	Bydgoszcz	361	Gliwice	213
Łódź	849	Lublin	324	Kielce	201
Kraków (Cracow)	716	Sosnowiec	255	Zabrze	198
Wrocław (Breslau)	636	Częstochowa	247	Toruń	186
Poznań	553	Białystok	245	Tychy	182
Gdańsk (Danzig)	467	Gdynia	243	Bielsko-Biala	174
Szczecin (Stettin)	391	Bytom	239	Ruda Słaska	165
Katowice	363	Radom	214	Olsztyn	147

At the census of 6 Dec. 1984 the population was 37,026,000 (18m. males; 60% urban). Population on 31 Dec. 1988, 37,775,000 (19·35m. females; 23·13m. urban), density, 121 per sq. km. Vital statistics, 1988 (per 1,000): Marriages, 6·5; divorces, 1·3; live births, 15·5; deaths, 9·8; infant mortality (per 1,000 live births), 16·1.

The rate of natural growth, 1988, 5·7 per 1,000. Expectation of life in 1984 was 66·8 years. In 1984, 55% of the population was under 30.

Ethnic minorities are not identified. There were estimated to be 1·2m. Germans in 1984. In 1982 there were 900 immigrants and 32,100 emigrants. In 1983 19,200 Germans emigrated. There is a large Polish diaspora, some 65% in USA. About 250,000 Poles settled abroad between 1981 and 1988, 153,000 illegally.

CLIMATE. Climate is continental, marked by long and severe winters. Rainfall amounts are moderate, with a marked summer maximum. Warsaw. Jan. 25°F (−3·9°C), July 66°F (18·9°C). Annual rainfall 22·1" (550 mm). Gdańsk. Jan. 29°F (−1·7°C), July 63°F (17·2°C). Annual rainfall 22" (559 mm). Kraków. Jan. 27°F (−2·8°C), July 67°F (19·4°C). Annual rainfall 29" (729 mm). Poznań. Jan. 30°F (−1·1°C), July 67°F (19·4°C). Annual rainfall 21" (523 mm). Szezecin. Jan. 30°F (−1·1°C), July 65°F (18·3°C). Annual rainfall 22" (550 mm). Wrocław. Jan. 30°F (−1·1°C), July 66°F (18·9°C). Annual rainfall 23" (574 mm).

CONSTITUTION AND GOVERNMENT. The present Constitution was adopted on 22 July 1952. Amendments were adopted in 1976 and 1983.

The authority of the republic is vested in the *Sejm* (Parliament of 460 members), elected for 4 years by all citizens over 18. The Sejm elects a *Council of State* and a *Council of Ministers.*

The titular head of state is the President, Wojciech Jaruzelski, elected for a 6-year term on 19 July 1989 by 270 votes in the Sejm (a majority of one vote).

Talks between the Communist Party (PUWP), Solidarity and others in Feb.–March 1989 resulted in proposals for reform which were approved by Parliament in April 1989. These included the establishment of a 100-member upper house (Senate), the legalization of Solidarity and Rural Solidarity, and the holding of parliamentary elections at which Solidarity and other opposition groups would be free to contest all the seats in the Senate and 35% of seats in the Sejm. The Senate has power of veto which only a two-thirds majority of the Sejm can overrule.

At the elections of 4 and 18 June 1989 Solidarity (S) won 99 seats in the Senate and 161 in the Sejm. Only 2 of a government-sponsored 'National List' of 35 candidates qualified for election by gaining more than 50% of votes. The PUWP were allotted 173 seats, and their coalition partners the United Peasant's Party (UPP) 76; the Democratic Party (DP), 27; the Christian Democrats, 23.

In March 1990 the Cabinet comprised the following Ministers:

Prime Minister: Tadeusz Mazowiecki (S); *Deputy Prime Ministers:* Leszek Balcerowicz (S) (*Finance*); Czesław Kiszczak (PUWP) Czesław Janicki (UPP) (*Agriculture*); Jan Janowski (DP) (*Scientific Development*); *Defence:* Gen. Florian Siwicki (PUWP); *Foreign:* Krzysztof Skubiszewski (S); *Justice:* Aleksander Bentkowski (UPP); *Industry:* Tadeusz Syryjczyk (S); *Council of Ministers:* Jacek Ambroziak (S); *Environment:* Bronisław Kamiński (UPP); *Housing:* Aleksander Paszyński (S); *Transport:* Adam Wieładek (PUWP); *Home Trade:* Aleksander Mackiewicz (DP); *Labour and Social Policy:* Jacek Kuroń (S); *Education:* Henryk Samsonowicz (S); *Health:* Andrzej Kosiniak-Kamysz (UPP); *Foreign Trade:* Marcin Święcicki (PUWP); *Culture:* Izabella Cywińska (S); *Communications:* Marek Kucharski (DP); *Central Planning:* Jerzy Osiatyński (S); *Chairman of Economic Council:* Witold Trzeciakowski (S); *Agricultural Development:* Artur Balazs (S); *Contact with Non-Parliamentary Opposition:* Aleksander Hall (S).

In Jan. 1990 the PUWP dissolved itself and formed a new party, the Social Democracy of the Polish Republic. *Chairman:* Aleksander Kwaśniewski (b. 1964); *Secretary:* Leszek Miller. A breakaway Social Democratic Union, led by Tadeusz Fiszbach, was also formed.

Local government is carried out by People's Councils elected every 4 years at voivodship and community level. 256,632 candidates stood at the elections of 19 June 1988; turn-out was claimed to be 56%. It was admitted in 1990 that these were undemocratic, and new elections were fixed for 27 May.

National flag: Horizontally white over red.

National anthem: Jeszcze Polska nie zginęła ('Poland has not yet perished'; words by J. Wybicki, 1797; tune by M. Ogiński, 1796).

DEFENCE. A National Defence Committee was set up in Nov. 1983 with Gen. Jaruzelski at its head. Poland is divided into 3 military districts: Warsaw (the eastern part of Poland); Pomerania (Baltic coast, part of central Poland; headquarters at Bydgoszcz); Silesia (Silesia and southern Poland; headquarters at Wrocław).

Armed forces are on Soviet lines and divided into army and air force (18 months conscription), navy (3 years), anti-aircraft, rocket and radio-technological units (3 years) and internal security forces (2 years). The military age extends from the 19th to the 50th year. The strength of the armed forces was (1988) 394,000, plus 87,000 security and frontier forces. Security forces include armoured brigades.

3-year civilian duty as a conscientious alternative to conscription was introduced in 1988. Reductions in defence spending and personnel were announced in 1989.

Army. The Army consists of 5 armoured, 8 mechanized divisions, 1 airborne and 1 amphibious assault, 5 artillery brigades; 3 anti-tank regiments; 4 surface-to-surface missile brigades; 1 air defence brigade. Equipment includes 2,700 T-54/-55 and 360 T-72 main battle tanks. Strength (1989) 217,000 (including 168,000 conscripts).

Navy. The fleet comprises 3 *ex*-Soviet diesel submarines, 1 *ex*-Soviet guided missile destroyer armed with SA-N-1 Goa surface-to-air and SS-N-2C Styx anti-ship missiles, 1 new frigate, 4 missile corvettes, 12 smaller fast missile craft, 9 inshore patrol craft, 21 coastal and 11 inshore minesweepers, 24 medium landing ships, plus 16 landing craft. Auxiliaries include 2 intelligence vessels, 3 survey vessels, and 2 training ships together with about 60 minor auxiliaries.

The Fleet Air Arm operates 11 shore-based Mi-14 Haze anti-submarine helicopters and a further 25 transport and utility helicopters. Naval-manned coast defences provide 6 artillery battalions and 3 missile batteries.

Personnel in 1989 totalled 25,000 including 6,000 conscripts. 2,300 of these serve in naval aviation and 4,000 in coast defence. Bases are at Gdynia, Gdańsk and Świnoujście.

A para-military border guard service operates 18 inshore patrol craft and some 30 boats.

Air Force. The Air Force had a strength (1990) of some 105,000 officers and men and 650 first-line jet aircraft of Soviet design, forming 4 air divisions. There are 11 air defence regiments (33 squadrons) with about 400 MiG-21, MiG-23 and MiG-29 supersonic interceptors, and 6 regiments (18 squadrons) operating variable-geometry MiG-23BM and Su-20 close-support fighters. There are also reconnaissance, ECM, transport, helicopter (including Mi-2s for observation and Mi-24 gunships) and training units. Soviet 'Guideline' 'Goa', 'Ganef', 'Gainful' and 'Gaskin' surface-to-air missiles are operational.

Two Soviet armoured divisions are stationed on Polish territory.

INTERNATIONAL RELATIONS

Membership. Poland is a member of UN, Comecon and the Warsaw Pact and was readmitted to IMF in May 1986.

ECONOMY

Policy. For planning history until 1989 *see* THE STATESMAN'S YEAR-BOOK 1989–90, p.1012-13. Wide-ranging measures to convert the economy into a market-oriented system were passed by Parliament in Dec. 1989, including the privatization of much of industry, the commercialization of interest and exchange rates, the abolition of price subsidies, the termination of wages indexation and the encouragement of foreign investment.

Budget. Budget in 1m. złotys, for calendar years:

	1983	*1984*	*1985*	*1986*	*1987*	*1988*
Revenue	2,629,100	3,299,700	3,854,200	4,902,700	5,850,400	10,080,800
Expenditure	2,654,400	3,367,800	3,979,200	4,193,200	5,029,800	8,423,000

Main items of 1988 revenue (in 1m. złotys): State enterprises, 8,661,100; finance and insurance, 349,600; non-socialized economy and taxes, 470,900. Expenditure: The economy, 4,187,300; welfare, 1,094,000; education, 804,700; defence, 742,200. 1990 budget estimates halve subsidies but increase allocations to health, education and the environment.

Currency. The currency unit is the *złoty*, divided into 100 *groszy*. The currency consists of notes of 10, 20, 50, 100, 500, 1,000, 2,000 and 5,000 złotys; and of coins of 10, 20 and 50 groszy and 1, 2, 5, 10, 20 and 50 złotys. The złoty was substantially devalued in 1989. Inflation was 900% in Jan. 1990. In March 1990, £1 sterling = 16,102 złotys, US$1 = 9,824 złotys. In Dec. 1989 a US$1,000m. Currency Stabilization Fund was established with the agreement of the IMF. The złoty became convertible on 1 Jan. 1990.

Banking. The National Bank of Poland (established 1945) is the central bank and bank of issue. The banking system is being commercialized with IMF advice. The General Savings Bank (Powszechna Kasa Oszczędności) exercises central control over savings activities.

In addition to the National Bank of Poland other authorized foreign-exchange banks are the Polish Welfare Bank (Bank Polska Kasa Opieki SA) and the Commercial Bank of Warsaw (Bank Handlowy w Warszawie SA). An Export Development Bank was established in 1986.

Deposits in savings institutions amounted to 3,691·8m. złotys in 1988.

Weights and Measures. The metric system is in general use.

ENERGY AND NATURAL RESOURCES

Electricity. Electricity production (1988) 144,000m. kwh. In 1989, 70% of electricity was produced by coal-powered thermal plants. Supply 127 and 220 volts; 50 Hz. A nuclear power station is being built at Zarnowiec.

Minerals. Poland is a major producer of coal (reserves of some 120,000m. tonnes), copper (56m. tonnes) and sulphur. Production in 1988 (in tonnes): Coal, 193m.; brown coal, 73·5m.; copper ore 401,000; silver, 1,063. Oil was discovered 80 km off the port of Leba in 1985. Total oil reserves amount to some 100m. tonnes. Crude oil production was 130,000 tonnes in 1989, natural gas 5,714m. cu. metres.

Agriculture. In 1988 there were 18·8m. hectares of agricultural land, of which 14·3m. hectares were in private hands, 3·5m. in state farms, 701,000 in co-operatives and 59,000 in agricultural associations. 14·5m. hectares were arable, 238,000 orchards, 2·5m. meadows, 1·6m. pasture lands.

Although collectivization had been largely abandoned by the Communist government, procurement remained a state monopoly, and prices were centrally-fixed. There were 2,207 co-operatives in 1988, 1,226 state farms and 396 agricultural associations. In Dec. 1987 a private, Catholic, Foundation for the Development of Polish Agriculture was set up to aid farmers with Western finance. Rural Solidarity (*Chairman:* Josef Slisz) was re-legalized in 1989). A compulsory contributory pension scheme was introduced in 1978 for farmers who turn over their farms to their successors or the State. Private holdings may not exceed 100 hectares. There were 2·73m. in 1988, of which 809,000 were less than 2 hectares.

Crops	*Area (1,000 hectares)* 1987	1988	*Total Yield (1,000 tonnes)* 1987	1988	*(from private plots)*
Wheat	2,132	2,179	7,942	7,528	(5,290)
Rye	2,647	2,325	6,816	5,501	(4,762)
Barley	1,286	1,250	4,335	3,804	(2,642)
Oats	856	850	2,428	2,222	(1,723)
Potatoes	1,934	1,866	36,252	34,707	(31,683)
Sugar-beet	422	412	13,987	14,069	(11,747)

Livestock (1988, in thousands): 10,322 cattle (4,806 cows), 19,605 pigs, 4,377 sheep, 1,051 horses, 00,000 poultry. Milk production was 15,029m. litres, meat, 3·18m. tonnes.

Tractors in use in 1988: 1,101,000 (in 15-h.p. units).

Forestry. In 1988, 8·7m. hectares were forests (predominantly coniferous). 70,000 hectares were afforested, and 24·26m. cu. metres of timber gained.

Fisheries. In 1985 the fishing fleet had 93 deep-sea vessels totalling 314,000 GRT. The catch was 650,600 tonnes.

INDUSTRY AND TRADE

Industry. Production in 1988 (in 1,000 tonnes): Coke, 17,100; rolled steel, 12,420; cement, 17,000; sulphuric acid (100%), 5,004; fertilizers, 2,718; electrolytic copper, 401; zinc, 177; salt, 4,865 in 1985; sugar, 1,684; plastics, 720. In 1988, 224 ships over 100 DWT were built (325 in 1987), 293,000 cars, 46,800 lorries and 10,300 buses.

Output of light industry in 1988: Cotton fabrics, 781m. metres; woollen fabrics, 101m. metres; synthetic fibres, 720,000 tonnes; shoes, 168m. pairs; household glass, 68,900 tonnes; paper, 1,448,000 tonnes; washing machines 761,000, refrigerators 486,000, and TV sets 756,000.

Labour. In 1988 the total number in employment was 17·12m., of whom 4·92m. worked in the private sector, and including in industry 4·9m. agriculture, 4·73m.; trade, 1·48m., building 1·35m. and transport and communications 1m. There were 5,000 'seeking jobs'. Founded in Aug. 1980 the 'independent self-governing union' organization Solidarity (Chairman Lech Wałęsa) was dissolved in Oct. 1982 along with all other trade unions. New official unions (OPZZ) established in 1983 took over Solidarity's funds in 1985. OPZZ (Chairman, Alfred Miodowicz) had 5m. members in 1988. There are also some 4,000 small unions not affiliated to OPZZ. Solidarity was re-legalized in May 1989 and successfully contested the parliamentary elections in June. It has 3m. members. Average wage in 1989, 208,200 złotys per month. Unemployment benefit of an initial 70% of previous wages was introduced in Dec. 1989. Workers made redundant are entitled to one month's wages. There is a statutory 42-hour working week which may be compulsorily extended in certain workplaces, with 38 free Saturdays a year.

Commerce. Trade statistics for calendar years (in 1m. złotys; trade with convertible currency areas in brackets):

	1984	*1985*	*1986*	*1987*	*1988*	
Imports	1,209,695	1,594,900	1,964,000	2,875,600	5,272,300	(3,145,700)
Exports	1,336,125	1,691,000	2,115,600	3,236,500	6,011,700	(3,611,800)

Main imports in 1988 (in tonnes): Petroleum, 15m.; iron ore, 16·64m.; fertilizers, 5·83m.; wheat, 2·3m.; passenger cars, 38,700 units; machinery and electronic equipment.

Main exports in 1988 (in tonnes): Coal, 32·2m.; coke, 2·84m.; copper, 167,000; sulphur, 3·88m.; ships, 45,000 DWT.

Foreign trade deals should be made directly with the appropriate foreign trade enterprise. Information may be obtained from the Polish Chamber of Foreign Trade, Trebacka 4, 00–950 Warsaw. Joint ventures with Western firms are encouraged both at home and abroad. Since Jan. 1989 Western investors may own 100% of companies on Polish soil.

41% of Poland's trade was with Comecon countries in 1988. A trade agreement with the USSR for 1986–90 gave the USSR a wide role in the Polish economy, particularly in the supply of oil, and rescheduled Poland's 5,000m. rouble debt beyond 1990. Soviet exports include plant and equipment and raw materials; Polish exports, machinery, ships, coal, chemicals and consumer goods. Federal Germany and UK are Poland's major non-communist trading partners.

In Feb. 1990 the IMF granted a loan of US$725m., and Western creditor nations agreed to a rescheduling of debts. Polish indebtedness to the West was US$39,200m. in 1989. Offers of aid to the Solidarity government in 1989 included DM3,000m. from Federal Germany, US$200m. from USA and US$150m. from UK. Poland does not accept liability for the £495,000 debts of pre-war Danzig (Gdańsk).

Total trade between Poland and UK (British Department of Trade returns £1,000 sterling):

	1985	*1986*	*1987*	*1988*	*1989*
Imports to UK	320,276	309,746	303,418	328,013	330,163
Exports and re-exports from UK	184,143	182,841	181,451	175,685	196,446

In Feb. 1987 the US restored Poland's most-favoured-nation status. A trade agreement was signed with the European Community in Sept. 1989.

Tourism. In 1988, 4,196,000 tourists visited Poland (1,104,000 from the West) and 6,924,000 Polish citizens made visits abroad (1,665,000 to the West). More liberal passport regulations were introduced for Polish citizens in 1987.

COMMUNICATIONS

Roads. In 1988 Poland had 156,500 km of hard-surfaced roads. There were 4·52m. passenger cars (4·45m. private), 922,000 lorries (395,000 private) 90,000 buses and 1·46m. motor cycles. Public road transport carried 2,504m. passengers and 105m. tonnes of freight. There were 36,433 road accidents in 1987 (4,625 fatal).

Railways. Length of standard gauge routes was 24,309 km (10,508 km electrified) in 1988 and 981m. passengers and 421m. tonnes of freight were carried.

Aviation. In 1985 the state airline 'Lot' had 39 aircraft including 5 Il-62s, operated 9 internal and 34 international routes. 2·02m. passengers were flown in 1988. There are British Airways, SABENA, KLM, PANAM, Alitalia, Swissair, Air France, Austrian Airlines and Lufthansa services to Okęcie (Warsaw) airport.

Shipping. The principal ports are Gdynia, Gdańsk (Danzig) and Szczecin (Stettin). Ocean-going services are grouped into Polish Ocean Lines based on Gdynia and operating regular liner services, and the Polish Shipping Company based on Szczecin and operating cargo services. Poland also has a share in the Gdynia America Line. 30·8m. tonnes of freight and 453,000 passengers were carried in 1988.

In 1988 the merchant marine had 256 vessels totalling 4·1m. GRT (including 46 container ships, 9 ferries and 8 tankers and 16 vessels over 30,000 tons). There are regular lines to London, Hull, China, Indonesia, Australia, Vietnam and some African and Latin-American countries.

There are 3,997 km of navigable inland waterways. 15·5m. tonnes of freight and 6·5m. passengers were carried in 1988.

Pipeline. In 1988 there were 2,021 km of oil pipeline; 43m. tonnes were transported.

Post and Broadcasting. In 1988 there were 8,405 post offices. There were 2·63m. telephones of which 1·98m. were private and 32,000 telex subscribers in 1987.

Polskie Radio i Telewizja broadcasts 3 radio programmes and 2 TV programmes. Colour programmes are transmitted by the SECAM system. Links with the West are provided through the Eutelstat satellite. There were 84 transmitting stations in 1988. Radio licences in 1988, 11·08m.; TV licences, 10·03m.

Cinemas and Theatres. In 1988 there were 1,877 cinemas, 101 theatres and 50 concert halls. Cinema attendance was 85·5m.; theatre, 7·8m. 32 full-length films were made.

Newspapers and Books. In 1988 there were 97 newspapers with an overall circulation of 10·05m. and 3,011 other periodicals. The Communist Party newspaper is *Trybuna*. Solidarity's newspaper, *Gazeta Wyborcza* (Election News), had the largest circulation in 1990. 10,728 book titles were published in 1988 in 245·3m copies.

JUSTICE, RELIGION, EDUCATION AND WELFARE

Justice. The penal code was adopted in 1969. Espionage and treason carry the severest penalties. For minor crimes there is provision for probation sentences and fines.

There exist the following courts: The Supreme Court; voivodship, district and special courts. Judges and lay assessors are elected. The State Council elects the judges of the Supreme Court for a term of 5 years, and appoints the Prosecutor-General. The office of the Prosecutor-General is separate from the judiciary. An ombudsman's office was established in 1987.

Family courts were established (1977) for cases involving divorce and domestic relations. Crimes reported in 1983 (and 1984) 466,205 (538,930) including 478 (593) homicides and 1,875 (2,184) rapes.

Religion. In 1978, 93% of the population was baptized into the Catholic Church, and 78% of the population attended church regularly. According to a survey published in the Communist Party journal *Nowe drogi* in 1985, 90% of the population held religious beliefs. Church–State relations are regulated by three laws of May 1989 which guarantee religious freedom, grant the Church radio and TV programmes and permit it to run schools, hospitals and old age homes. The Church has a university (Lublin), an Academy of Catholic Theology and in 1983 46 seminaries. Religious education of children is conducted in 'catechism centres' of which there were some 20,000 in 1985.

The archbishop of Warsaw and Gniezno is the primate of Poland (since 1981, Cardinal Józef Glemp). The Vatican considers the archbishoprics of Lwów and Vilnius (incorporated in the USSR in 1940) as still being under Polish jurisdiction. In 1983 there were 5 archbishoprics, 27 dioceses and 7,496 parishes, 84 bishops, 37,132 monks and nuns and 14,498 churches and 4,201 chapels. In 1986 there were 3 cardinals and 22,381 priests. In Oct. 1978 Cardinal Karol Wojtyla, archbishop of Cracow, was elected Pope as John Paul II.

On 28 June 1972 the Vatican adjusted the Church boundaries, to coincide with the State's western frontier ('Oder–Neisse line') and the 4 apostolic administrators in the former German territories became bishops.

Figures for other churches in 1983: Polish Autocephalous Orthodox, 5 dioceses, 218 parishes, 301 churches, 226 priests, 1 monastery, 1 nunnery, 600,000 adherents. Lutheran, 6 dioceses, 121 parishes, 173 churches, 153 chapels, 100 parsons (100,000 adherents in 1975). Uniate, 3 dioceses, 85 parishes, 98 churches, 90 priests (200,000 adherents in 1975). Old-Catholic Mariavite, 3 dioceses, 42 parishes, 55 churches, 29 priests (30,000 adherents in 1975). Methodist, 5 districts, 60 parishes, 57 chapels, 36 parsons (4,133 adherents in 1975). United Evangelical, 200 congregations, 56 chapels, 180 parsons. Seventh-day Adventist, 123 communities, 123 churches, 61 parsons. Baptist, 128 congregations, 58 chapels, 58 parsons (2,300 adherents in 1975). Jews, 16 congregations, 10 synagogues (12,000 adherents in 1978). Epiphany World Mission, 9 chapels and 426 priests. In 1985 there were 2,500 Moslems with 3 mosques and 5 priests.

Education. Basic education from 7 to 15 is free and compulsory. Free secondary education is then optional in general or vocational schools. Primary schools are organized in complexes based on wards under one director ('gmina collective schools'). In 1988–89 there were: Kindergartens, 26,343 with 1·39m. pupils and 90,000 teachers; primary schools, 18,241 with 5,185,000 pupils and 273,000 teachers; secondary schools, 1,146 with 444,000 pupils and 23,000 teachers; vocational schools, 9,382 with 1,714,000 pupils and 83,000 teachers, and 92 institutions of higher education (including 11 universities, 18 polytechnics, 9 agricultural schools, 6 schools of economics, 10 teachers' training colleges and 11 medical schools) with 352,800 students and 59,003 teaching staff.

In 1984 administration of schools was transferred from central to local government.

Health. In 1988 there were 716 hospitals (including 43 mental hospitals) with 250,000 beds, 6,649 dispensaries and 3,311 health centres. There were 78,800 doctors, 17,600 dentists, 16,300 pharmacists and 194,600 nurses.

Social Security. In 1984, 76,955m. złotys were paid in family allowances and 77,830m. złotys in sick pay. In 1987 2·21m. retirement pensions were paid (monthly average 18,808 złotys), 2·05m. disability pensions (14,236 złotys), 951,000 dependants' pensions (14,107 złotys) and 1·2m. farmers' retirement pensions (11,598 złotys).

DIPLOMATIC REPRESENTATIVES

Of Poland in Great Britain (47 Portland Pl., London, W1N 3AG)
Ambassador: Tadeusz de Virion

Of Great Britain in Poland (Aleje Roz No. 1, Warsaw)
Ambassador: S. J. Barrett, CMG.

Of Poland in the USA (2640 16th St., NW, Washington, D.C., 20009)
Ambassador: Jan Kinast.

Of the USA in Poland (Aleje Ujazdowskie 29/31, Warsaw)
Ambassador: John R. Davis, Jr.

Of Poland to the United Nations
Ambassador: Stanislaw Pawlak.

Further Reading

Statistical Information: The Central Statistical Office, Warsaw (Wawelska 1–3), publishes *Rocznik statystyczny* (annual, 1930–39; 1947–); *Concise Statistical Yearbook of Poland* (1959–); *Poland: Statistical Data.* (annual, 1977–); *Statystyka Polski* (irreg., 1947–); *Biuletyn statystyczny* (monthly, 1957–).

Constitution of the Polish People's Republic. Warsaw, 1964
Ascherson, N., *The Struggles for Poland.* London, 1987
Ash, T. G., *The Polish Revolution: Solidarity 1980–82.* London, 1983
Beneš, V. L. and Pounds, N. G. J., *Poland.* London, 1970
Bielasiak, J. and Simon, M. D. (eds.) *Polish Politics: Edge of the Abyss.* New York, 1984
Brandys, K., *Warsaw Diary 1978–1981.* New York, 1984
Bromke, A., *Poland: the Protracted Crisis.* Oakville (Ontario), 1983.—*The Meaning and Uses of Polish History.* New York, 1987
Brumberg, A., *Poland: Genesis of a Revolution.* New York, 1983
Bulas, K. and others, *English–Polish and Polish–English Dictionary.* 2 vols. The Hague, 1959
Burda, A., *Parliament of the Polish People's Republic.* Wrocław, 1978
Davies, N., *Poland, Past and Present: A Select Bibliography of Works in English.* Newtonville, 1977.—*God's Playground: A History of Poland.* 2 vols. OUP, 1981.—*Heart of Europe: a Short History of Poland.* OUP, 1984
De Weydenthal, J. B., et al. *The Polish Drama, 1980–1982.* Lexington, 1983
Dziewanowski, M. K., *Poland in the Twentieth Century.* Columbia Univ. Press, 1977
Eringer, R., *Strike for Freedom: The Story of Lech Wałęsa and Polish Solidarity.* New York, 1982
Gieysztor, A., and others, *History of Poland. 2nd ed. Warsaw, 1979*
Halecki, O., *A History of Poland.* 4th ed. London, 1983
Jaruzelski, W., *Jaruzelski, Prime Minister of Poland: Selected Speeches.* Oxford, 1985
Kanka, A. G., *Poland: An Annotated Bibliography of Books in English.* New York, 1988
Karpiński, J., *Countdown: the Polish Upheavals of 1956, 1968, 1970, 1976, 1980.* New York, 1982
Kieniewicz, S. (ed.) *History of Poland.* 2nd ed. Warsaw, 1979
Landau, Z., *The Polish Economy in the Twentieth Century.* London, 1985
Leslie, R. F., (ed.) *The History of Poland since 1863.* CUP, 1980
Lewanski, R. C., *Poland.* [Bibliography] Oxford and Santa Barbara, 1984
Lipski, J. J., *KOR: A History of the Workers' Defense Committee in Poland, 1976–1981.* Univ. of California Press, 1985
Michnik, A., *Letters from Prison and Other Essays.* London, 1985
Misztal, B., (ed.) *Poland after Solidarity.* New Brunswick, 1985
Potel, J.-I., *The Summer Before the Frost: Solidarity in Poland.* London, 1982
Preibisz, J. M., (ed.) *Polish Dissident Publications: An Annotated Bibliography.* New York, 1982
Raina P., *Independent Social Movements in Poland.* London, 1981.—*Poland 1981: Towards Social Renewal.* London, 1985
Ruane, K., *The Polish Challenge.* London, 1982
Singer, D., *The Road to Gdańsk: Poland and the USSR.* New York and London, 1981
Staniszkis, J., *Poland's Self-Limiting Revolution.* Princeton, 1984
Steven, S., *The Poles.* London, 1982
Szczypiorski, A., *The Polish Ordeal: The View from Within.* London, 1982
Taras, R., *Poland: Socialist State, Rebellious Nation.* Boulder, 1986
Wałęsa, L., *A Path of Hope.* London, 1989
Wedel, J., *The Private Poland.* New York, 1986
Weschler, L., *Solidarity: Poland in the Season of its Passion.* New York, 1982
Who's Who in Poland. New York, 1983
Wielka Encyklopedia Powszechna. 13 vols. Warsaw, 1962–70
Woodall, J., (ed.) *Policy and Politics in Contemporary Poland: Reform, Failure and Crisis.* London, 1982

National Library: Biblioteka Narodowa, Rakowiecka 6, Warsaw.

PORTUGAL

Capital: Lisbon
Population: 10·27m. (1987)
GNP per capita: US$3,670 (1988)

República Portuguesa

HISTORY. Portugal has been an independent state since the 12th century, apart from one period of Spanish rule (1580–1640). The monarchy was deposed on 5 Oct. 1910 and a republic established.

A *coup* on 28 May 1926 established a military provisional government from 1 June. A corporatist constitution was adopted on 19 March 1933 under which a civil dictatorship governed until a fresh *coup* on 25 April 1974 established a Junta of National Salvation.

Following an attempted revolt on 11 March 1975, the Junta was dissolved and a Supreme Revolutionary Council formed which ruled until 25 April 1976 when constitutional government was resumed; the SRC was renamed the Council of the Revolution, becoming a consultative body until its abolition in 1982.

AREA AND POPULATION. Mainland Portugal is bounded north and east by Spain and south and west by the Atlantic ocean. The Atlantic archipelagoes of the Azores and of Madeira form autonomous but integral parts of the republic, which has a total area of 91,985 sq. km (35,516 sq. miles) and census populations:

1940	7,755,423	1960	8,889,392	1981	9,833,014
1950	8,510,240	1970	8,648,369		

The areas and populations of the districts and Autonomous Regions are:

Districts:	*sq. km*	*Census 1981*	*Estimate 31 Dec. 1987*	*Districts:*	*sq. km*	*Census 1981*	*Estimate 31 Dec. 1987*
Aveiro	2,808	622,988	665,500	Porto	2,395	1,562,287	1,670,600
Beja	10,225	188,420	177,700	Santarém	6,747	454,123	460,600
Braga	2,673	708,924	771,400	Setúbal	5,064	658,326	779,600
Bragança	6,608	184,252	184,700	Viana de Castelo	2,225	256,814	266,400
Castelo Branco	6,675	234,230	223,700	Vila Real	4,328	264,381	262,900
Coimbra	3,947	436,324	446,500	Viseu	5,007	423,648	423,300
Evora	7,393	180,277	174,300	Total mainland	88,944	9,336,760	9,744,400
Faro	4,960	323,534	341,200	*Autonomous Regions:*			
Guarda	5,518	205,631	196,200				
Leiria	3,515	420,229	435,900				
Lisboa	2,761	2,069,467	2,126,400	Azores	2,247	243,410	254,200
Portalegre	6,065	142,905	137,500	Madeira	794	252,844	271,400

At the 1981 census, 29·7% of the population was urban (living in towns of 10,000 and more) and 48·2% were male. The chief cities at 31 Dec. 1987 (and census, 1981) are Lisbon, the capital 830,500 (817,627) and Porto 350,000 (330,199); other population aggregates are Amadora 95,518 (93,663), Setúbal 77,885 (76,812), Coimbra 74,616 (71,782), Braga 63,033 (63,771), Vila Nova de Gaia 62,469 (60,962), Barreiro 50,863 (50,745), Funchal 44,111 (48,638), Almada 42,607 (41,468), Queluz 42,241 (41,112), Odivelas 38,322 (38,546), Evora 34,851 (34,072), Agualva-Cacem 34,341 (34,041) and Oeiras 32,529 (32,046).

The Azores islands lie in the mid-Atlantic ocean, between 1,200 and 1,600 km west of Lisbon. They are divided into 3 widely separated groups with clear channels between, São Miguel (759 sq. km) together with Santa Maria (97 sq. km) being the most easterly; about 100 miles north-west of them lies the central cluster of Terceira (382 sq. km), Graciosa (62 sq. km), São Jorge (246 sq. km), Pico (446 sq. km) and Faial (173 sq. km); still another 150 miles to the north-west are Flores (143 sq. km) and Corvo (17 sq. km), the latter being the most isolated and primitive of the islands. São Miguel contains over half the total population of the archipelago.

Madeira comprises the island of Madeira (745 sq. km), containing the capital, Funchal; the smaller island of Porto Santo (40 sq. km), lying 46 km. to the northeast of Madeira; and two groups of uninhabited islets, Ilhas Desertas (15 sq. km), being 20 km. south-east of Funchal and Ilhas Selvagens (4 sq. m), near the Canaries.

Vital statistics for calendar years:

	Live-births	*Still-births*	*Marriages*	*Divorces*	*Deaths*	*Emigrants*
1983	144,327	1,791	74,417	7,837	96,150	7,096
1984	142,805	1,664	69,875	7,034	97,227	6,556
1985	130,492	1,510	68,461	8,988	97,339	7,149
1986	126,748	1,390	69,271	8,411	95,828	6,253
1987	123,218	1,230	71,656	8,948	95,423	8,108

In 1987 the births included 63,572 boys and 59,646 girls; deaths, 49,828 males and 45,595 females. In 1987, 167 emigrants went to France, 2,643 to USA and 1,346 to Oceania.

CLIMATE. Because of westerly winds and the effect of the Gulf Stream, the climate ranges from the cool, damp Atlantic type in the north to a warmer and drier Mediterranean type in the south. July and Aug. are virtually rainless everywhere. Inland areas in the north have greater temperature variation, with continental winds blowing from the interior. Lisbon. Jan. 52°F (11°C), July 72°F (22°C). Annual rainfall 27·4" (686 mm). Porto. Jan. 48°F (8·9°C), July 67°F (19·4°C). Annual rainfall 46" (1,151 mm).

CONSTITUTION AND GOVERNMENT. A new Constitution, replacing that of 1976, was approved by the Assembly of the Republic (by 197 votes to 40) on 12 Aug. 1982 and promulgated in Sept. It abolished the (military) Council of the Revolution and reduced the role of the President of the Republic.

Portugal is a sovereign, unitary republic with all citizens possessing fundamental rights and duties before the law. Executive power is vested in the President of the Republic, directly elected for a 5-year term (for a maximum of 2 consecutive terms). Presidents since 1926:

Marshal António Oscar de Fragoso Carmona, 29 Nov. 1926–18 April 1951 (died).
Dr Antonio de Oliveira Salazar (acting), 18 April 1951–22 July 1951.
Marshal Francisco Higino Craveiro Lopez, 22 July 1951–9 Aug. 1958.
Rear-Adm. Américo Deus Rodrigues Tomaz, 9 Aug. 1958–25 April 1974. (deposed).
Gen. Antonio Sebastião Ribeiro de Spinola, 25 April 1974–30 Sept. 1974 (resigned).
Gen. Francisco da Costa Gomes, 30 Sept. 1974–14 July 1976.
Gen. Antonio Ramalho Eanes, 14 July 1976–9 March 1986.

President of the Republic: Mario Soares, elected 16 Feb. 1986 (took office 9 March 1986).

The President appoints a Prime Minister and, upon the latter's nomination, other members of the Council of Ministers, as well as Secretaries and Under-Secretaries of State, who are outside the Council.

The Social Democrat government was composed in Jan. 1990:

Prime Minister: Anibal Cavaço Silva.

Deputy Prime Minister, Defence: Carlos Brito. *Minister of State and Justice:* Fernando Nogueira. *Parliamentary Affairs:* Antonio Capucho. *Finance:* Miguel Beleza. *Planning and Territorial Administration:* Luis Valente de Oliveira. *Interior:* Manuel Pereira Godinho. *Foreign Affairs:* João de Deus Pinheiro. *Agriculture, Fisheries and Alimentation:* Arlindo Cunha. *Industry and Energy:* Luis Mira Amaral. *Education:* Roberto Carneiro. *Public Works, Transport and Communication:* João Oliveira Martins. *Health:* Arlindo Carvalho. *Labour and Social Security:* José Silva Peneda. *Trade and Tourism:* Joaquim Ferreira do Amaral. *Youth:* Antonio Couto dos Santos. *Environment:* Ferrando Ferreira Real.

There is a unicameral legislature, the Assembly of the Republic, comprising 250 deputies elected for 4 years by universal adult suffrage under a system of proportional representation. At the General Election of 19 July 1987, there were 148 seats won by the *Partido Social Democrata* (PSD), 60 by the *Partido Socialista* (PS), 7 by the Democratic Renewal Party, 31 by the Communist Party and 4 by the Christian Democrats.

National flag: Vertical green and red, with the red of double width, and over all on the dividing line the national arms.

National anthem: A Portuguesa (words by Lopes de Mendonça, 1890; tune by Alfredo Keil).

Local government: Since 1976, the archipelagoes of the Azores and of Madeira are Autonomous Regions with their own legislatures and governments. Pending the formation of other regional governments, Continental Portugal is divided into 18 districts. Regions and districts are divided into 305 municipal authorities *(concelhos)* and sub-divided into 4,050 parishes. Each level is governed by an assembly elected by direct universal suffrage under a system of proportional representation, with an executive body responsible to the assembly.

DEFENCE. Military service is compulsory for 12–15 months in the Army and 18–20 months in the Navy and Air Force. Reserves for all services number about 190,000.

Army. The Army consists of 1 brigade, 2 cavalry regiments, 1 armoured regiment, 14 infantry regiments, 1 commando regiment and 3 independent battalions, 1 special forces brigade, 1 field, 1 air-defence and 1 coast artillery regiments, 2 engineer and 1 signals regiments and 1 regiment of military police. Equipment includes 60 M-48A5 main battle tanks and 105 M113 armed personnel carriers. Strength (1989) 44,000 (including 35,000 conscripts). Security forces are National Republic Guard (19,000), Public Security Police (17,000), and the Border Guard (8,500).

Navy. The Portuguese Navy is organized into 3 commands: Continental based at Lisbon and Portimão, Azores, and Madeira. The combatant fleet comprises 3 French-built Daphne class diesel submarines, 14 small frigates, 4 coastal patrol vessels and 7 inshore patrol craft. Auxiliaries include 1 tanker, 1 transport, 1 survey ship, a sail training ship and an ocean tug. There are 3 tank landing craft, 9 smaller amphibious craft and some 20 service vessels. The building programme includes 3 frigates to the ubiquitous West German MEKO design. Naval personnel in 1989 totalled 16,000 (5,900 conscripts) including 2,800 marines.

Air Force. Formed in 1912, the Air Force has been independent since 1952, when it was combined with the naval air service and given equal status with the Army and Navy. In 1990, it had a strength of about 15,200 officers and men.

Equipment comprises 2 strike squadrons with 40 A-7P Corsair IIs; 2 squadrons of G.91Rs for ground attack; 1 squadron of P-3P Orion maritime patrol aircraft now forming; 1 squadron of 5 C-130H Hercules and 4 squadrons of CASA 212 Aviocars for transport and search and rescue operations; 32 Cessna 337 Skymasters and a force of Puma and Alouette III helicopters. Other aircraft in service include Chipmunk piston-engined trainers, T-37C jet basic trainers, T-33, T-38A Talon and G.91T jet advanced trainers. Delivery of 18 Epsilon trainers (to replace the Chipmunks) began early in 1989.

INTERNATIONAL RELATIONS

Membership. Portugal is a member of UN, the European Communities, OECD, NATO and the Council of Europe.

ECONOMY

Planning. The main objective of the 1989-92 medium-term plan is the modernization of the economy and society.

Budget. Revenue in 1988, 1,694m.; expenditure, 2,170m. (in escudos).

Currency. The unit of currency is the *escudo* of 100 *centavos*, which contains 0·06651 gramme of fine gold. It was stabilized on 9 June 1931, and the paper currency re-linked to gold when the notes of the Bank of Portugal became payable in gold or its equivalent in foreign currency. 1,000 *escudos* is called a *conto*.

In 1987 there were bank notes of 5,000, 1,000, 500 and 100 *escudos*; cupronickel coins of 50, 25, 20, 5 and $2^1/_2$ *escudos*; nickel-brass coins of 1 *escudo*; bronze coins of $^1/_2$ *escudo*. In March 1990, £1 = 244·80 *escudos*; US$1 = 149·36 *escudos*.

Banking. Since 1931, the central bank for Portugal and the only bank of issue for the country (including the Azores and Madeira) has been the Banco de Portugal, founded 19 Nov. 1846 and nationalized on 13 Sept. 1974. Its capital is fixed at 200m. escudos. All other Portuguese banks and insurance companies were nationalized on 14 March 1975 but from Feb. 1984 new private banks were allowed to operate.

The National Development Bank began operations on 4 Jan. 1960. Its total capital (1985) is 10,500m. escudos.

In March 1988 there were 27 banks (9 foreign) operating in Portugal: 22 commercial banks, 2 investment banks and 3 savings banks. In March 1988 commercial banks' total credits were 1,777,184m. escudos and deposits 3,730,027m. escudos; investment banks' total credits 266,675m. escudos and deposits 163,822m. escudos; savings banks' total credits 1,335,841m. escudos and deposits 1,886,075m. escudos.

The 9 foreign banks were, the Bank of Brazil, Lloyds Bank International Ltd., Manufactures Hanover (Portugal), Chase Manhattan, Citibank-Portugal, Crédit Franco-Portugais, Barclays Bank International Ltd, Banque Nationale de Paris and General Bank.

Weights and Measures. The metric system is the legal standard. The arroba (of 14·69 kg) is sometimes used locally.

ENERGY AND NATURAL RESOURCES

Electricity. Total production of electrical power in 1986 was 20,355m. kwh.; the installed capacity totalled 7,730,645 kva. of which 3,350,106 was hydro-electric. Supply 110 and 220 volts; 50 Hz.

Minerals. Portugal possesses considerable mineral wealth. Production in tonnes:

	1985	*1986*	*1987*		*1985*	*1986*	*1987*
Coal	238,414	209,501	228,648	Gold (refined)	0·229	0·303	0·320
Cupriferous pyrites	355,519	321,514	279,061	Uranium	139	131	167
Tin ores	379	300	90	Wolframite	2,977	2,764	2,011
Kaolin	104,055	70,567	66,736				

Uranium mining commenced in Aug. 1979. Annual production, 115 tonnes; reserves, 7,000 tonnes.

Agriculture. About 30% of the workforce is engaged in agriculture. The following figures show the area (in 1,000 hectares) and production (in 1,000 tonnes) of the chief crops:

	1986		*1987*		*1988*	
Crop	*Area*	*Quantity*	*Area*	*Quantity*	*Area*	*Quantity*
Wheat	315·0	499·7	323·0	532·5	275	401
Maize	252·7	611·4	256·9	640·4	230	663
Oats	194·1	152·7	196·9	155·2	168	76
Barley	87·1	89·6	83·7	79·4	73	48
Rye	124·4	99·9	128·4	108·2	124	73
Rice	32·3	149·4	32·2	144·4	33	151
Dried beans	198·4	44·4	195·5	44·1	162	47
Potatoes	118·8	1,067·2	123·0	1,112·4	124	795

Wine production (in tonnes), 1988, 368,000; olive oil (tonnes), 22,000. In 1987, 76,839 tonnes of port wine were exported.

Livestock (1988). 29,000 horses, 90,000 mules, 175,000 asses, 1,387,000 cattle, 745,000 goats, 5·22m. sheep and 2·8m. pigs.

Forestry. Forest area covers 3m. hectares, of which 1·38m. are pine, 680,390 cork oak, 534,370 other oak, 243,180 eucalyptus, 30,230 chestnut and 160,890 other species.

Portugal surpasses the rest of the world in the production of cork; 79,357 tonnes in 1987. Most of it is exported crude. Production of resin was 108,439 tonnes in 1986; more than two-thirds are exported.

Fisheries. The fishing industry for the continent and adjacent isles is of importance. At 31 Dec. 1987 there were 41,844 men and boys employed, with 17,980 registered boats. The sardine catch, 1987, was 90,416 tonnes valued at 2,881,221 contos; The most important centres of the sardine industry are at Matosinhos, Figueira di Foz, Peniche, Setúbal, Portimão and Olhão.

INDUSTRY AND TRADE

Industry. The main groups are textiles, shoes, leather goods, wood and cork products and ceramics; these are produced mainly by small companies. Nationalized steel, oil and engineering industries employed about 5% of the industrial workforce in 1983.

Trade Unions. 331 unions had in 1976 a membership of 1,436,142.

Commerce. Imports for consumption and exports (exclusive of coin and bullion and re-exports) for calendar years, in 1m. escudos:

	1983	*1984*	*1985*	*1986*	*1987*
Imports	899,340	1,160,633	1,326,528	1,442,493	1,965,315
Exports	508,568	760,580	971,747	1,082,261	1,311,003

The principal exports in 1985 were clothing (18% by value), textile yarns and fabrics (12%), machinery and transport equipment (6%), petroleum products (4%), chemicals (7%), cork and cork products (4%), footwear (5%), pulp and waste paper (5%) and wine (3%).

The distribution of the imports and exports (in 1m. escudos):

	Imports (c.i.f.)			*Exports (f.o.b.)*		
From or to	*1985*	*1986*	*1987*	*1985*	*1986*	*1987*
Angola	14,000	11,196	5,614	26,720	13,785	14,612
Belgium-Lux.	28,431	41,682	63,628	34,740	37,037	39,106
France	106,751	145,157	220,721	123,743	164,235	207,268
Germany, Fed. Rep. of	152,421	205,420	294,270	133,339	158,627	200,948
Italy	68,628	114,487	171,591	38,318	42,915	51,727
Mozambique	1,029	389	1,361	3,743	3,073	4,486
Netherlands	42,051	57,053	79,636	67,086	72,232	84,983
Spain	97,971	157,060	230,601	40,250	71,681	118,438
UK	100,078	108,281	158,468	141,454	154,010	184,451
USA	128,961	100,592	94,777	89,635	75,557	84,325

Total trade between Portugal (excluding the Azores and Madeira) and UK (British Department of Trade returns, in £1,000 sterling):

	1985	*1986*	*1987*	*1988*	*1989*
Imports to UK	695,744	768,470	847,980	928,015	1,040,706
Exports and re-exports from UK	439,499	472,078	699,915	810,537	915,682

Tourism. Tourism is of increasing importance for the invisible balance of payments. In 1988 there were 16,076,681 visitors.

COMMUNICATIONS

Roads (1987). There were 22,375 km of road. There were registered in continental Portugal in 1987, 2,425,106 motor vehicles (excluding 113,254 motor cycles, 165,357 tractors and vehicles used by the armed forces).

Railways. In 1987 total railway length was 3,607 km (1,668 mm and metre gauges), of which 461 km of broad-gauge was electrified. In 1987, 5,907m. passenger-km were carried and 1,615m. tonne-km of merchandise transported.

Aviation. There are international airports at Portela (Lisbon), Pedras Rubras (Porto), Faro (Algarve), Santa Maria and Lages (Azores) and Funchal (Madeira). Services connect Lisbon with most major centres in North and South America, Western Europe and Africa. Airlines in 1987 carried 3m. passengers and 46,916 tonnes of freight. The national airline changed its name to Air Portugal in 1979.

Shipping. In 1987, 12,885 vessels of 71·5m. tons entered the ports (continental and islands), of which 4,637 (20·9m. tons) were Portuguese, 338 (3·1m. tons) British and 601 (2·8m. tons) Spanish. In 1986 the merchant marine consisted of 65 transport vessels of 1,469,051 gross tons.

Post and Broadcasting (1987). The number of post offices was 17,835. The State owned 7,693,529 km of telephone line through the *Telefones de Lisboa e Porto* (nationalized in 1977). Number of telephones was 2,071,544 (1987).

Radio Difusão Portuguesa broadcasts 3 programmes on medium-waves and on FM as well as 3 regional services. *Radiotelevisão Portuguesa* broadcasts 2 commercial TV programmes. *Radio Renancença* is a commercial, nationwide network. In addition there are 6 local, commercial stations, operating on medium-waves. Radio Trans Europe is a high-powered short-wave station, retransmitting programmes of different broadcasting organizations, *e.g.*, IBRA, Radio Canada and Deutsche Welle. Radio Free Europe also has relay facilities on short-waves in Portugal. Number of receivers: Radio (1984), 2,155,000; TV (1987), 1,618,313.

Cinemas (1987). There were 358 cinemas with a seating capacity of 163,112.

Newspapers (1987). There were 31 daily newspapers with a combined circulation of 162,649m.; 14 of these, with a combined circulation of 103,458m., appeared in Lisbon.

JUSTICE, RELIGION, EDUCATION AND WELFARE

Justice. Portuguese law distinguishes civil (including commercial) and penal, labour, military, administrative and fiscal branches, having low courts and high courts.

The republic is divided for civil and penal cases into 217 *comarcas*; in every comarca there is at least one court or tribunal. In the comarca of Lisbon there are 39 lower sub divisional courts *(juizos)* (22 for criminal procedure and 17 for civil or commercial cases); in the comarca of Porto there are 20 such courts (11 for criminal and 9 for civil or commercial cases); at Braga, Coimbra, Loures, Setúbal, Sintra and Vila Nova de Gaia there are 4 functioning courts; at Almada, Cascais, Funchal, Guimarães, Leiria, Matosinhos, Oeiras, Santarém, Torres Vedras, Viana do Castelo, Vila do Conde, Vila da Feira and Viseu there are 3 courts; 22 comarcas have 2 courts each. There are 4 courts of appeal *(Tribunal de Relação)* at Lisbon, Coimbra, Evora and Porto, and a Supreme Court in Lisbon *(Supremo Tribunal de Justiça).*

Capital punishment was abolished completely in the Constitution of 1976.

The prison population as at 31 Dec. 1986 was 8,353.

Religion. In 1981, 94·5% of the population were Roman Catholic, but there is freedom of worship, both in public and private, with the exception of creeds incompatible with morals and the life and physical integrity of the people.

Education. Compulsory education has been in force since 1911. In 1985–86 there were 10,188 public primary schools with 790,947 pupils and 39,881 teachers. In 1985–86 private elementary schools numbered 662 with 55,371 pupils and 2,851 teachers. Basic preparatory schools numbered 1,891 with 391,794 pupils and 30,611 teachers. In 1985–86 there were 499 secondary schools, with 647,391 pupils and 53,881 teachers. There were also 27 schools which taught art activities (cinema, music and theatre) with 15,165 students. There are 18 universities, of which 8 are in Lisbon: The University of Lisbon (1930), the private Portuguese Catholic University, also with faculties and sections at Braga, Porto and Viseu (1968), the New University of Lisbon (1973), the private International University (1984), the private Autonomous University of Lisbon 'Luis de Camoes' (1986), the private Lusiada University (1986) and the Open University (1988); the other 10 are Coimbra (founded 1290), Porto (1911), Aveiro (1973), Minho, at Braga and Guimaraes (1973), Evora (1979), Azores, at Agra do Heróismo, Horto and Ponta Delgado (1980) and Algarve, at Faro (1983) Beira Interior, at Covilha (1986), Tras-os-Montes e Alto Douro, at Vila Real (1986) and the private Portucaleuse University, at Porto (1986). Including other colleges, there were 107,485 students in higher education in 1985–86 with 12,749 teaching staff.

Health. In 1987 there were 229 hospitals, 366 health centres, 26,381 doctors, 392 dentists, 607 stomatologists, 4,728 pharmacists and 25,777 nursing personnel.

DIPLOMATIC REPRESENTATIVES

Of Portugal in Great Britain (11 Belgrave Sq., London, SW1X 8PP)
Ambassador: António Vaz-Pereira LVO (accredited 12 July 1989).

Of Great Britain in Portugal (35-37 Rua de S. Domingos à Lapa, Lisbon)
Ambassador: H. J. Arbuthnott, CMG.

Of Portugal in the USA (2125 Kalorama Rd., NW, Washington, D.C., 20008)
Ambassador: João Eduardo M. Pereira Bastos.

Of the USA in Portugal (Ave. das Forcas Armadas, 1600 Lisbon)
Ambassador: Edward Rowell.

Of Portugal to the United Nations
Ambassador: Fernando José Reino.

Further Reading

Statistical Information: The Instituto Nacional de Estatistica (Avenida António José de Almeida, Lisbon) was set up in 1935 in succession to the Direcção-Geral de Estatistica. The Centro de Estudos Económicos and the Centro de Estudos Demográficos were affiliated to the Instituto in 1944. The main publications are:

Anuário Estatistíco. Annuaire statistique. Annual, from 1875
Estatísticas do Comércio Externo. 2 vols. Annual from 1967 (replacing *Comércio Externo,* 1936–66, and *Estatística Comercial*, 1865–1935)
Censo da População de Portugal. 1864 ff. Decennial (latest ed. 1972)
Estatística da Organização Corporativa. 1938–49. Estatísticas da Organização Corporativa e Previdência Social. 1950 ff.
Estatísticas das Finanças, Publicas and *Estatísticas Nometárias.* 1969 ff. (replacing *Estatísticas Financeiras.* 1947–68 and *Situação Bancária*, 1919–46)
Estatísticas Agrícolas. Statistique Agricole. 1943–64; replaced by *Estatísticas Agri colas e Alimentares.* From 1965. Annual
Estatísticas Industrials. 1967 ff. (replacing *Estatística Industrial. Statistique Industrielle.* 1943–66)
Estatísticas Demográficas. From 1967 (replacing *Anuário Demográfico*, 1929–66)
Boletim Mensal do Instituto Nacional de Estatística. Monthly since 1929
Centro de Estudos Económicos. Revista. 1945 ff.
Centro de Estudos Demográficos. Revista. 1945 ff.
Estatísticas das Contribuições e Impostos. Annual from 1967 (replacing *Anuário Estatístico das Contribuições e Impostos*, 1936–66)
Estatisticas da Cultura, Reveio e Resporto, 1979 ff.
Estatísticas da Educação. 1940 ff.
Estatísticas da Justica. 1968 ff. (replacing *Estatísticas Judiciária.* 1936–66)
Estatísticas das Sociedades. 1939 ff.
Estatísticas da Saúde, 1969 ff.
Estatísticas do Turismo. 1969 ff.
Estatísticas do Energia. 1969 ff.

Azevedo, Gonzaga de, *Historia de Portugal.* 6 vols. Lisbon, 1935–44
Ferreira, H. G. and Marshall, M. W., *Portugal's Revolution: Ten Years On.* CUP, 1986
Ferreira, J. A., *Dictionario inglês-portugês.* 2 vols. Porto, 1948
Gallagher, T., *Portugal: A Twentieth Century Interpretation.* Manchester Univ. Press, 1983
Graham, L. S. and Wheeler, D. L., (eds.) *In Search of Modern Portugal: The Revolution and its Consequences.* Univ. of Wisconsin Press, 1983
Harvey R., *Portugal: Birth of a Democracy.* London, 1978
Robertson, I., *Blue Guide: Portugal.* London, 1982
Rogers, F. M., *Atlantic Islanders of the Azores and Madeiras.* North Quincy, 1979
Taylor, J. L., *Portuguese-English Dictionary.* London, 1959
Unwin, P. T. H., *Portugal.* [Bibliography] Oxford and Santa Barbara, 1987

National Library: Biblioteca Nacional de Lisboa, Campo Grande, Lisbon. *Director:* A. H. C. Marques.

MACAO

HISTORY. Macao was visited by Portuguese traders from 1513 and became a Portuguese colony in 1557; it remains a Portuguese-administered territory by virtue of a Sino-Portuguese treaty of 1 Dec. 1887. It was an Overseas Province of Portugal, 1961–74. Discussions on the future of Macao were taking place with the People's Republic of China in 1986–87 and in 1999 Macao will be handed to China.

AREA AND POPULATION. The territory, which lies at the mouth of the Canton (Pearl) River, comprises a peninsula (6·05 sq. km) connected by a narrow isthmus to the People's Republic of China, on which is built the city of Santa Nome de Deus de Macao, and the islands of Taipa (3·78 sq. km), linked to Macao by a 2-km bridge, and Colôane (7·09 sq. km) linked to Taipa by a 2-km causeway (total area, 16·92 sq. km (6 sq. miles). The population (Census, 1981) was 261,680, Estimate (1987) 434,300, of which 51·8% are males and (1984) 91·5% live in the city of Macao. The official language is Portuguese, but Cantonese is used by virtually the entire population.

Vital statistics (1987): Births, 7,565; marriages, 2,472; deaths, 1,321.

CONSTITUTION AND GOVERNMENT. By agreement with Beijing in 1974, Macao is a Chinese territory under Portuguese administration. An 'organic statute' was published on 17 Feb. 1976. It defined the territory as a collective entity, *pessoa colectiva,* with internal legislative authority which, while remaining subject to Portuguese constitutional laws, would otherwise enjoy administrative, economic and financial autonomy. The Governor is appointed by the Portuguese President, who also appoints up to 5 Secretaries-Adjunct on the Governor's nomination. The Legislative Assembly of 17 deputies, chosen for a 3-year term, comprises 6 members directly elected by universal suffrage, 6 indirectly elected by economic, cultural and social bodies and 5 appointed by the Governor.

Governor: Carlos Melancia.

ECONOMY

Budget. In 1987, revenue was 2,488,700,000 *patacas* and expenditure 2,390,800,000 *patacas.*

Currency. The unit of currency is the *pataca,* of 100 *avos* which is tied to the *HongKong dollar* at the rate of 103 *patacas* = HK$100. In March 1990, £1 = 13·27 *patacas*; US$1 = 8·09 *patacas.*

Banking. The bank of issue is the Instituto Emissor de Macau. Commercial business is handled (1987) by 22 banks with 94 branches in Macao, 8 of which are local (with 81·5% of total resident deposits and 67·4% of total domestic credit at 31 Dec. 1984) and 14 foreign (including 4 offshore banking units). Total banks' deposits, 1987, 14,111·5m. patacas.

INDUSTRY AND TRADE

Industry. In 1985 the number of establishments for food products was 74 and output in 1,000 patavos was 108,853; textiles (130) 1,330,626; clothing (444) 2,836,832; plastics (67) 523,128.

Labour. The estimated total labour force in 1984 was 178,000, 44% of whom were employed in manufacturing, 33% in commerce and services and 8% in construction.

Commerce. The trade, mostly transit, is handled by Chinese merchants. Imports, in 1987, were 9,107·1m. patacas and exports, 11,233·5m. patacas.

In 1987, 43% of imports came from Hong Kong and 21% from China. 33% of exports went to USA, 36% to EEC (mainly Federal Republic of Germany, France and UK); clothing and textiles accounted for 73·5% of exports, toys 9·9%.

Total trade between Macao and UK (British Department of Trade returns, in £1,000 sterling):

	1985	*1986*	*1987*	*1988*	*1989*
Imports to UK	36,509	45,286	45,896	41,116	45,299
Exports and re-exports from UK	1,595	6,522	5,617	4,348	7,498

Tourism. There were 5,100,500 visitors in 1987. 82·2% were from Hong Kong and 5·1% from Japan.

COMMUNICATIONS

Roads. In 1984 there were 90 km of roads. In 1987 there were 35,925 vehicles, of which 20,391 were passenger cars and 4,099 commercial vehicles.

Shipping. Macao is served by Portuguese, British and Dutch steamship lines. In 1987, 39,239 vessels of 11·5m. gross tons entered the port. In 1987, 4·84m passengers embarked and 4·7m disembarked. Regular services connect Macao with Hong Kong, 65 km to the north-east.

Post and Broadcasting. The territory has 1,577 km of telephone line (55,643 instruments in 1987). One government and 1 private commercial radio station are in operation on medium-waves broadcasting in Portuguese and Chinese. Number of receivers (1977), 70,000. Macao receives television broadcasts from Hong Kong and in 1984 a public bilingual TV station began operating. There were (1979) 50,000 receivers.

Newspapers. In 1987, there were 8 newspapers (2 in Portugese and 6 in Chinese).

JUSTICE, RELIGION, EDUCATION AND WELFARE

Justice. There is a court of First Instance, from which there is appeal to the Court of Appeal and then the Supreme Court, both in Lisbon.

In 1987 there were 4,717 cases of crimes known to the police, of which 3,454 were against property. There were 29,558 cases in courts pending on 1 Jan. and presented during 1987, of which 4,840 were in district court, 10,195 in criminal court and 3,467 in administrative court. At 31 Dec. 1987 there were 326 prisoners, and 37 addicts in the centre for rehabilitation of drugs-abusers.

Religion. The majority of the Chinese population are Buddhists. About 6% are Roman Catholic.

Education. In 1986–87 education was provided at 60 kindergartens (16,516 pupils; 458 teachers), 74 primary schools (31,914; 1,118), 30 secondary schools (14,913; 851), 5 special schools (88; 31), 5 teacher-training schools (61; 26), 5 higher schools (6,891; 70) and 88 adult schools (23,088; 629). The University of East Asia, established in 1981 on Taipa, had 1,165 students in 1983.

Health. In 1987 there were 2 hospitals with 1,242 beds; there were 179 doctors and (1982) 26 pharmacists, 10 midwives and 315 nursing personnel.

Further Reading

Anuário Estatístico de Macau. Macao, Annual
Macau in Figures. Macao, Annual.
Education Survey, 1984–85, Macao, 1986
Brazáo, E., *Macau.* Lisbon, 1957
Edmonds, R.L., *Macau.* [Bibliography] Oxford and Santa Barbara, 1989

QATAR

Capital: Doha
Population: 371,863 (1987)
GNP per capita: US$11,610 (1988)

Dawlat Qatar

HISTORY. The State of Qatar declared its independence from Britain on 3 Sept. 1971, ending the Treaty of 3 Nov. 1916 which was replaced by a Treaty of friendship between the 2 countries.

AREA AND POPULATION. The State of Qatar, which includes the whole of the Qatar peninsula, extends on the landward side from Khor al Odeid to the boundaries of the Saudi Arabian province of Hasa. The territory includes a number of islands in the coastal waters of the peninsula, the most important of which is Halul, the storage and export terminal for the offshore oilfields. Area, 11,437 sq. km; population census (1981) 244,534; estimate in 1987 371,863. In 1987 only 25% were Qatari, with a large majority coming from Pakistan and India.

The capital is Doha (population 1986, 217,294), which is the main port. Other towns are Dukhan, the centre of oil production, Umm Said, oil-terminal of Qatar, and Ruwais, Wakra, Al-Khour, Umm Salal Mohammad and Umm-Bab.

Vital statistics (1988): Live births, 10,842; deaths, 861; marriages, 1,333; divorces, 385.

The official language is Arabic.

CLIMATE. The climate is hot and humid. Doha. Jan. 62°F (16·7°C), July 98°F (36·7°C). Annual rainfall 2·5" (62 mm).

RULER. *The Amir:* HH Shaikh Khalifa bin Hamad Al-Thani, assumed power on 22 Feb. 1972. On 31 May 1977, HH Shaikh Hamad bin Khalifa Al-Thani was appointed Heir Apparent of the State of Qatar, and the portfolio of Minister of Defence was added to his existing responsibility of Commander-in-Chief of the Armed Forces.

Minister of Foreign Affairs: Abdullah bin Khalifa al-Attiyah.

There is no Parliament, but the Council of Ministers is assisted by a 30-member nominated Advisory Council.

Local government: Qatar is divided into 9 municipalities.

Flag: Maroon, with white serrated border on hoist.

DEFENCE

Army. The Army consists of 1 Royal Guard regiment, 1 tank and 3 mechanized infantry battalions, 1 artillery regiment and 1 surface-to-air missile battery. Equipment includes 24 AMX-30 tanks. Personnel (1990) 6,000.

Navy. The navy has 3 French-built fast missile craft and 6 British-built 33 metre inshore patrol craft, 1 tank landing craft and some 30 boats. There are also 3 quadruple shore-based Exocet missile batteries. Personnel in 1989 totalled 700.

Air Force. The Air Force has 1 squadron of Mirage F1 fighters and 12 Commando, 16 Gazelle and 6 Super Puma helicopters and 6 Alpha Jet armed trainers and Tigercat surface-to-air missile systems. Personnel (1990) 300.

INTERNATIONAL RELATIONS

Membership. Qatar is a member of UN and the Arab League.

ECONOMY

Budget. Revenue (1987–88) 6,745m. riyals; expenditure 12,217m. riyals.

Currency. On 13 May 1973 the Qatar *Riyal* (of 100 *dirhams*) was introduced. There are coins of 1, 5, 10, 25 and 50 *dirhams*, and banknotes of 1, 5, 10, 50, 100 and 500 *riyals*. In March 1990, £1 = 5·99 *riyals*, US$1 = 3·66 *riyals*.

Banking. The 13 banks operating in Qatar in 1989, included 5 national banks: Qatar National Bank, The Commercial Bank of Qatar, Doha Bank, the Islamic Bank of Qatar and Al Ahli Bank. There are 2 Arab banks: Arab Bank Limited and Bank of Oman. The other 6 foreign banks were: Banque Paribas, the British Bank of the Middle East, Chartered Bank, Bank Saderat Iran, Grindlays Bank and the United Bank. The Qatar National Bank was established in 1965 with capital of 56m. riyals, 50% of which was contributed by the Government and 50% by the private sector. Deposits in commercial banks were 1,241·8m. riyals by Dec. 1987. Government deposits 331m. riyals and private sector's savings deposits 1,240·1m. riyals in 1987.

Weights and Measures. The metric system is in general use.

ENERGY AND NATURAL RESOURCES

Electricity. Production (1988) 4,592·3m. kwh (generation of Abu Samra not included). Supply 240 volts; 50 Hz.

Oil. On 9 Feb. 1977 Qatar gained national control over its 2 natural resources, oil and gas, with the signing of an agreement with Shell Qatar over the procedure for the transfer to the State of the company's remaining 40% share. A similar agreement had been reached with the Qatar Petroleum Co. on 16 Sept. 1976.

The Qatar General Petroleum Corporation (QGPC) had been established by decree in July 1974 to assume overall responsibility for the State's domestic and foreign oil interests and operations. On 16 Oct. 1976 the Qatar Petroleum Producing Authority (QPPA) was established to serve as the executive arm of the QGPC—but in 1980 it was merged into the QGPC, which now directly oversees oil production through two operational divisions, Onshore and Offshore. The National Oil Distribution Company (NODCO) had a daily throughput capacity of 62,000 bbls a day in 1984 following the opening of a 50,000 bbls a day refinery at Umm Said to supplement the existing refinery.

Production, 1989, 20m. tonnes. Proven reserves (1986) 3,300m. bbls.

Gas. The North West Dome oilfield is being developed which contains 12% of the known world gas reserves. Production (1986) 229,100m. cu. ft.

Water Resources. Two main desalination stations, at Ras Abu Aboud and Ras Abu Fontas, together have a daily capacity of 167·6m. gallons of potable water. A third station is planned at Al Wasil, with a capacity of 40m. gallons a day. Total water production 1988 (well field and distillate) 17,542·5m. gallons.

Agriculture. 10% of the working population is engaged in agriculture. The Ministry of Agriculture is implementing a long-term policy aimed at ensuring self-sufficiency in agricultural products. The number of farms rose from 120 in 1960 to 841 in 1985. Production (1988) in tonnes: Cereals, 3,224; fruits and dates, 8,409; vegetables, 20,927; green fodder, 72,612; meat, 1,734 milk, 18,501; eggs, 1,522.

Livestock (1988): Cattle, 9,516; camels, 22,706; sheep, 122,259; goats, 87,396; chickens, 1,786,467; horses, 1,041; deer (1987), 3,463.

Fisheries. The produce of local fisheries in 1984 met 77·2% of Qatar's requirements. The state-owned Qatar National Fishing Company has 3 trawlers and its refrigeration unit processes 10 tonnes of shrimps a day. Catch (1988) 2,880 tonnes; value (1987) 19·55m riyals.

INDUSTRY AND TRADE

Industry. The Qatar Fertiliser Co. plant was opened in 1974 (production, 1988, 724,900 tonnes of ammonia and 779,600 tonnes of urea), the Qatar Steel Co. factory in 1978 (output, 1987, 483,833 tonnes of steel, 482,270 tonnes of sponge iron and (1988) 533,000 tonnes of reinforcing steel bars) and the Qatar Petrochemicals Co. plant in 1981 (production, 1988, 256,500 tonnes of ethylene, 171,400 tonnes of polyethylene and 37,000 tonnes of sulphur), all in the Umm Said industrial zone. Other production (1987, in tonnes): Cement, 791,200; unslaked lime, 13,500; flour, 26,200; bran, 6,600; organic fertilizer, 27,700. Two natural gas liquids plants produced 315,724 tonnes of propane, 223,384 tonnes of butane and 182,592 tonnes of gasoline in 1987.

Labour. The economically active population (15 years and above) in March 1986 totalled 200,238, of whom 6,283 were engaged in agriculture and fishing, 4,807 in mining and quarrying, 13,914 in manufacturing, 5,266 in electricity, gas and water, 40,523 in building and construction, 21,964 in trade, restaurants and hotels, 7,357 in transport and communications, 3,157 in finance, insurance and real estate and 96,466 in social and community services.

Commerce. In 1987 exports totalled 7,224m. riyals, and imports, 4,000m. riyals, (1988, 4,613m. riyals). Main imports in 1987 (in 1,000 riyals) were machinery and transport equipment (1,666,892), manufactured goods (1,218,517) and food and live animals (706,201). In 1987 Japan provided 16·3% of imports, the UK 16%, the USA 11·9% and the Federal Republic of Germany 7·2%.

Total trade between Qatar and UK (British Department of Trade returns, in £1,000 sterling):

	1985	*1986*	*1987*	*1988*	*1989*
Imports to UK	32,607	29,587	13,765	3,888	4,342
Exports and re-exports from UK	142,065	112,143	105,087	88,920	89,256

Tourism. In 1988 tourists stayed 226,134 nights in hotels.

COMMUNICATIONS

Roads. In 1981 there were about 800 miles of road. In 1988 there were 154,963 registered vehicles including 2,502 motorcycles.

Aviation. Gulf Air (owned equally by Qatar, Bahrain, Oman and the UAE), operates daily services from Bahrain; British Airways, Middle East and about 15 other airlines operate regular international flights from Doha airport. In 1988, 520,478 passengers arrived, 508,843 departed and 453,126 were in transit; 9,996 aircraft arrived and 9,996 departed.

Shipping. In 1987, 395 vessels, 1,101,925 tonnes of cargo and 1,854 containers were handled.

Post and Telecommunications. There were 26 post offices in Doha and other towns in 1988. Qatar Broadcasting Service, using 12 transmission stations, broadcasts for 41 hours a day in Arabic, English, French and Urdu. Telephone and radiotelephone services connect Qatar with Europe and America; there were 129,291 telephones in 1988. In 1987 there were 75,000 radios and 111,000 television receivers.

Cinemas. In 1987 there were 4 cinemas.

Newspapers. In 1987 there were 4 daily and 2 weekly newspapers and 6 magazines.

JUSTICE, RELIGION, EDUCATION AND WELFARE

Justice. The Judiciary System is administered by the Ministry of Justice which comprises three main departments: Legal affairs, courts of justice and land and real estate register. There are 5 Courts of Justice proclaiming sentences in the name of H. H. the Amir: The Court of Appeal, the Labour Court, the Higher Criminal Court, the Civil Court and the Lower Criminal Court.

All issues related to personal affairs of Moslems under Islamic Law embodied in the Holy Quran and Sunna are decided by Sharia Courts.

Religion. The population is almost entirely Moslem.

Education. There were, in 1988, 35,133 pupils at 97 primary schools, 12,817 pupils at 43 preparatory schools, 8,064 pupils at 29 secondary schools and 894 male students at 3 specialist schools. There were 48 Arab and foreign private schools with 18,346 pupils in 1987–88. The University of Qatar had 5,621 students in 1989.

Students abroad (1988) numbered 881. In 1986–87, 3,435 men and 2,507 women attended evening classes.

Health. There were 3 hospitals (including 1 for women and 1 for gynaecology and obstetrics) with a total of 937 beds in 1987. There were 21 health centres in 1988. In 1987 there were 560 doctors, 62 dentists, 140 pharmacists and 1,418 qualified nurses.

DIPLOMATIC REPRESENTATIVES

Of Qatar in Great Britain (27 Chesham Pl., London, SWIX 8HG)
Ambassador: Abdulrahman Abdulla Al-Whaibi (accredited 20 Dec. 1989).

Of Great Britain in Qatar (Doha, Qatar)
Ambassador and Consul-General: G. H. Boyce.

Of Qatar in the USA (600 New Hampshire Ave., NW, Washington, D.C., 20037)
Chargé d'Affaires: Saleh Mohammed Al-Khalifa.

Of the USA in Qatar (Fariq Bin Omran, Doha)
Ambassador: Marc Hambley.

Of Qatar to the United Nations
Ambassador: Dr Hassan Ali Hussain Alni'ma.

Further Reading

Annual Statistical Abstract. 8th ed. Doha, 1988
El Mallakh, R., *Qatar: The Development of an Oil Economy.* New York, 1979
Unwin, P. T. H., *Qatar.* [Bibliography] Oxford and Santa Barbara, 1982

ROMANIA

Capital: Bucharest
Population: 23m. (1990)
GNP per capita: US$2,540 (1981)

HISTORY. 1918 is celebrated as the year of foundation of the 'unitary national Romanian state'. For the history and constitution of Romania from 1859 to 1947, *see* THE STATESMAN'S YEAR-BOOK, 1947, pp. 1187–89. On 30 Dec. 1947 King Michael abdicated under Communist pressure and parliament proclaimed the 'People's Republic'. The former king now lives in exile.

Since the accession to power in 1965 of Nicolae Ceauşescu Romania had been taking a relatively independent stand in foreign affairs while becoming increasingly repressive and impoverished domestically.

An attempt by the authorities on 16 Dec. 1989 to evict a protestant pastor, László Tőkés, from his home in Timişoara provoked a popular protest which escalated into a mass demonstration against the government. Despite the use of armed force against the demonstrators, the uprising spread to other areas. On 21 Dec. the government called for an official rally in Bucharest, but this turned against the régime. A state of emergency was declared, but the Army went over to the uprising, and Nicolae and Elena Ceauşescu fled the capital. A dissident group which had been active before the uprising, the National Salvation Front (NSF), proclaimed itself the provisional government. Suggestions of Soviet involvement have been denied.

The Ceauşescus were captured, and after a secret two-hour trial by military tribunal, summarily executed on 25 Dec. on four charges of genocide, undermining the power of the state, undermining the economy and embezzlement. Fighting by pro-Ceauşescu 'Securitate' forces continued until 27 Dec. It is estimated that 7,689 people were killed in the uprising.

On 26 Dec. Ion Iliescu, leader of the NSF, and Petre Român, were sworn in as President and Prime Minister respectively. The Provisional Government was at once recognized by many countries throughout the world, including the UK, USA and USSR.

AREA AND POPULATION. Romania is bounded north and north-east by the USSR, east by the Black Sea, south by Bulgaria, south-west by Yugoslavia and north-west by Hungary. The area of Romania is 237,500 sq. km (91,699 sq. miles). Pre-war Romania had an area of 113,918 sq. miles. Population at censuses: 1930, 18,057,208 (14,280,729 within present-day Romania); 1948, 15,872,624 (48·3% male); 1966, 19,103,163 (49% male, 38·2% urban); 1977, 21,559,910 (49·3% male, 47·5% urban).

In 1987 the population was 22,940,430 (49·3% male; 51·3% urban), density per sq. km, 96. Vital statistics, 1985 (per 1,000 population): Live births, 15·8; deaths, 10·9; marriages, 7·1; divorces, 1·43; stillborn (per 1,000 live births), 7·8; infant mortality (per 1,000 live births), 25·6. Expectation of life in 1984, 66·9 years. Measures designed to raise the birthrate were immediately abolished by the post-Ceauşescu government, and abortion and contraception legalized. Population growth rate per 1,000 was 4·9 in 1985 and 5·2 in 1984.

Administratively, Romania is divided into 41 counties (*judeţ*), 237 towns (*oraş*) (of which 55 are municipalities) and 2,705 local authorities (*comune*). The capital is Bucharest (Bucureşti), a municipality with county status.

District	*Area in sq. km*	*Population 1987*	*Capital*	*Population 1985*
Alba	6,231	425,903	Alba Iulia	64,369
Arad	7,652	504,556	Arad	185,892
Argeş	6,801	671,954	Piteşti	154,112
Bacău	6,606	717,946	Bacău	175,299
Bihor	7,535	657,707	Oradea	208,507
Bistriţa-Năsăud	5,305	322,501	Bistriţa	73,429
Botoşani	4,965	460,211	Botoşani	104,836

District	Area in sq. km	Population 1987	Capital	Population 1985
Braşov	5,351	695,160	Braşov	346,640
Brăila	4,724	400,832	Brăila	234,600
Buzău	6,072	522,685	Buzău	132,311
Caraş-Severin	8,503	407,402	Reşiţa	104,362
Călăraşi	5,075	347,312	Călăraşi	68,226
Cluj	6,650	740,929	Cluj-Napoca	309,843
Constanţa	7,055	726,059	Constanţa	323,236
Covasna	3,705	233,049	Sf. Gheorghe	65,868
Dîmboviţa	4,035	563,621	Tîrgovişte	88,663
Dolj	7,413	771,971	Craiova	275,098
Galaţi	4,425	635,425	Galaţi	292,805
Giurgiu	3,810	325,150	Giurgiu	65,792
Gorj	5,641	380,582	Tîrgu Jiu	85,058
Harghita	6,610	359,205	Miercurea-Ciuc	45,651
Hunedoara	7,016	559,619	Deva	76,934
Ialomiţa	4,449	304,809	Slobozia	44,797
Iaşi	5,469	793,369	Iaşi	314,156
Maramureş	6,215	546,035	Baia Mare	135,536
Mehedinţi	4,900	327,309	Drobeta-Turnu Severin	97,862
Mureş	6,696	616,401	Tîrgu Mureş	157,411
Neamţ	5,890	570,204	Piatra-Neamţ	107,581
Olt	5,507	531,323	Slatina	73,982
Prahova	4,694	868,779	Ploieşti	234,021
Satu Mare	4,405	412,227	Satu Mare	128,115
Sălaj	3,850	267,517	Zalău	54,676
Sibiu	5,422	507,850	Sibiu	176,928
Suceava	8,555	685,661	Suceava	92,690
Teleorman	5,760	504,623	Alexandria	51,267
Timiş	8,692	731,667	Timişoara	318,955
Tulcea	8,430	269,808	Tulcea	84,353
Vaslui	5,297	457,699	Vaslui	62,372
Vîlcea	5,705	427,059	Rîmnicu Vîlcea	93,271
Vrancea	4,863	390,055	Focşani	83,562
Bucharest [1]	1,521	2,298,256	Bucharest [2]	1,975,808

[1] Total conurbation. [2] Central area.

The last official figures on the size of the ethnic minorities were published in 1977. Estimates for 1989: Hungarians, 2m. (mainly in Transylvania); Germans, 280,000; Gypsies, 2·3m.; Jews, 30,000. The agricultural 'systematisation' (*see* Agriculture, p. 1036) bore particularly hardly upon ethnic Hungarians, who had not been allowed to emigrate. Some 120,000 Germans had emigrated by 1988. The official language is Romanian.

CLIMATE. A continental climate with a large annual range of temperature and rainfall showing a slight summer maximum.

Bucharest. Jan. 27°F (–2·7°C), July 74°F (23·5°C). Annual rainfall 23·1" (579 mm). Constanţa. Jan. 31°F (–0·6°C), July 71°F (21·7°C). Annual rainfall 15" (371 mm).

CONSTITUTION AND GOVERNMENT. For the Communist Constitution and government *see* THE STATESMAN'S YEAR-BOOK, 1989-90, pp. 1033-34.

The head of state is the *President*, elected by direct vote. The supreme legislative body is the bi-cameral *Grand National Assembly*, for which elections were due on 20 May 1990. It was announced that a new draft constitution would be submitted for the Assembly's approval.

The Provisional Government constituted by the National Salvation Front (NSF) on 1 Feb. 1990 agreed to share power with opposition parties in a 180-member Provisional Council for National Unity which also included regional representatives and co-opted specialists. In March 1990 the Council's Executive Bureau included: Ion Iliescu (*President of the Republic*); Jelu Voicăn (*Vice-President*), Petre Român (*Prime Minister*), Gen. Anastase Stănculescu (*Minister of Defence*).

More than 30 parties compaigned for the May 1990 elections, including the NSF (reconstituted as a party), the National Peasant Party (*Chairman:* Corneliu Coposu) and the National Liberal Party (*Chairman:* Radu Campeanu).

Local government is carried out by People's Councils at the administrative levels mentioned on p. 1033. 57,584 councillors were elected from among 117,349 candidates on 15 Nov. 1987.

National flag: Three vertical strips of blue, yellow and red.

National anthem: Trei culori ('Three colours'). A new anthem is under consideration.

DEFENCE.

Military service is compulsory for 16 months in the Army and Air Force and 24 months in the Navy.

Army. The 4 Army Areas consist of 2 tank and 8 motor rifle divisions; 4 mountain, 2 artillery, 4 anti-aircraft and 2 surface-to-surface missile brigades; and 4 artillery, 5 anti-tank and 4 airborne regiments. Equipment includes 3,200 T-34, T-54/-55, T-72 and M-77 main battle tanks. Strength (1990) 128,000 (including 95,000 conscripts), and 178,000 reservists. There are a further 40,000 men in paramilitary border guard and internal security forces.

Navy. The fleet comprises 1 *ex*-Soviet diesel submarine, 1 Romanian-built missile-armed destroyer with hangar for 2 helicopters, 4 frigates, 3 corvettes, 6 fast missile craft, 42 fast torpedo craft, 4 offshore, 3 coastal and 4 inshore patrol vessels, 2 minelayer/mine countermeasure support ships and 40 small minesweepers. The Danube flotilla counts 3 river monitors (100 mm guns) and some 40 river patrol craft. Auxiliaries include 2 logistic ships, 1 oceanographic ship, 1 training ship and 2 tugs.

There is a substantial coastal defence force organized into 10 batteries of artillery with about 100 guns (130 mm, 150 mm and 152 mm).

Headquarters of the Navy is at Mangalia, and of the Danube flotilla at Brăila. Personnel in 1989 totalled 9,000 (2,500 conscripts) including 2,000 in Coastal Defence.

Air Force. The Air Force numbered some 34,000 men, with 295 combat aircraft in 3 air divisions (7 regiments) in 1990. These were organized into 12 interceptor squadrons with MiG-21 and MiG-23 fighters, 6 ground-attack and close-support squadrons with MiG-17 fighters, and 1 reconnaissance squadron of Il-28s. There were also more than 150 training aircraft, 20 An-24/26/30 transports and more than 150 helicopters (Mi-2, Mi-4, Mi-8, Mi-14, Alouette and Puma). Under delivery were 185 IAR-93 close-support/interceptors to replace the MiG-17s and Skyfox anti-armour helicopters. 'Guideline' and 'Gainful' surface-to-air missiles were operational, and short-range surface-to-surface missiles have been displayed.

INTERNATIONAL RELATIONS

Membership. Romania is a member of UN, IMF, Comecon and the Warsaw Pact.

ECONOMY

Planning. For planning under Ceauşescu *see* THE STATESMAN'S YEAR-BOOK, 1989–90, p. 1035). Romania was committed to intensive industrialization and agriculture had been neglected. Severe shortages have resulted from the diversion of resources to pay off foreign debt.

Budget. Revenue and expenditure (in 1m. lei) for calendar years:

	1982	*1983*	*1984*	*1985*	*1986* [1]	*1988* [1]
Revenue	288,511	301,908	308,917	363,180	340,914	433,094
Expenditure	288,511	301,908	308,917	342,545	340,914	433,094

[1] Estimates.

In 1985 sources of revenue (in 1m. lei) included: Profit payments of state enterprises 29,527; turnover tax, 93,666; personal taxes, 4,251; insurance contributions,

40,009; taxes on enterprise wage funds, 47,125. Expenditure: National economy, 172,559; social and cultural, 90,412; defence, 12,113.

Revenue and expenditure of local councils (included above) was 63,054m. lei and 60,560m. lei in 1985.

Romania has settled UK claims arising out of the peace treaty and on defaulted bonds.

Currency. The monetary unit is the *leu*, pl.*lei* (of 100 *bani*). On 1 Feb. 1954 the gold content of the leu was to 0·148112 gramme of fine gold. Exchange rates (March 1990): £1 = 35·30 lei; US$1 = 21·54 lei.

Bank-notes of 1, 5, 10, 25, 50 and 100 *lei* are issued by the National Bank, and there are coins of 5, 10, 15 and 25 *bani* and 1, 3 and 5 *lei*.

Banking. The National Bank of Romania (founded 1880, nationalized 1946) is the State Bank under the Minister of Finance. Half its profits are allotted to the State budget. There are also a Bank of Investments, a Foreign Trade Bank, an Agriculture and Food Industry Bank and a Savings Bank. The US Export-Import Bank withdrew Romania's borrowing rights as a sanction in 1988. In 1974 the American bank Manufactures Hanover Trust Co. opened a branch in Bucharest, the first Western bank to do so in a Communist country.

Weights and measures. The Gregorian calendar was adopted in 1919. The metric system is in use. Tubes and pipes are measured in *tol* (= 1 inch).

ENERGY AND NATURAL RESOURCES

Electricity. Installed electric power 1984: 18,829,000 kw.; output, 1987, 74,079m. kwh (11,209m. kwh hydroelectric). Supply 220 volts; 50 Hz. There are two joint Romanian–Yugoslav hydro-electric power plants on the Danube at the 'Iron Gates' with a combined yearly output of 22,250m. kwh. A nuclear power programme has been subject to cut-backs and delays. A nuclear powere plant is under construction at Cernăvoda. In Oct. 1985 a state of emergency was declared in the energy sector and its administration handed over to the military. This was still in force in 1989.

Oil. The oilfields are in the Prahova, Băcau, Gorj, Crişana and Argeş districts. Oil production in 1989 was 9m. tonnes. Oil reserves are expected to be exhausted by the mid-1990s. Refining capacity was enlarged from 16m. tonnes per annum in 1970 to 30m. tonnes in 1985. Crude oil has to be imported.

Minerals. The principal minerals are oil and natural gas, salt, brown coal, lignite, iron and copper ores, bauxite, chromium, manganese and uranium. Salt is mined in the lower Carpathians and in Transylvania; production in 1987 was 5·4m. tonnes.

Output, 1987 (and 1986) (in 1,000 tonnes): Iron ore, 2,281 (2,431); coal, 51,524 including lignite, 41,579 (47,518, including lignite 38,012); methane gas (cu. metres), 25,301m. (26,763m.).

Agriculture. There were 15·09m. hectares of agricultural land in 1987, including (in 1,000 hectares): Arable, 10,080; meadows and pasture, 4,407; vineyards and fruit trees, 606. In 1985 there were 2·7m. hectares of irrigated land.

Production in 1988 (in 1,000 tonnes): Wheat, 9,000; rye, 60; barley, 2,200; maize, 19,500; potatoes, 8,000; sunflower seeds, 1,190; sugar-beet, 6,500.

Livestock (1988, in 1,000's): 7,182 cattle, 15,224 pigs, 18,793 sheep, 135,956 poultry, 693 horses. The number of horses had fallen to some 200,000 by Feb. 1986, but it was then decided to increase the herd and allow the tractor park to reduce by 30%. Romania is the largest sheep-rearing country in Europe after the UK.

In 1985 there were 4,363 collective farms, with 9·1m. hectares of land (7·2m. arable; 1·4m. private plots). State farms numbered 419, with 2m. hectares of land, of which 1·65m. hectares were arable. A further 2·4m. hectares of land were in the hands of other state agricultural organizations. There were 573 agriculture mechanization stations. Total tractor force, 1987: 187,850. Since 1984 production quotas on private plots had to be met on pain of confiscation. Private leasing of land from collectives and private marketing of produce were permitted by the Provisional Government in Jan. 1990. The 1988 programme of 'systematisation' to replace more than 50% of traditional villages by apartment blocks was rescinded by the Provisional Government in Dec. 1989.

Forestry. Total forest area was 6·34m. hectares in 1988, representing 28% of the land area.

INDUSTRY AND TRADE

Industry. Output of main products in 1987 (and 1986) (in tonnes): Pig-iron, 8,673 (9,329); steel, 13,885 (14,276); steel tubes, 1,394 (1,565); coke, 5,826 (5,182); rolled steel, 9,675 (10,207); chemical fertilizers, 2,897 (3,278); washing soda, 894 (895); caustic soda, 817 (846); paper, 712 (768); cement, 13,583 (14,216); sugar, 646 (489); edible oils, 392 (339). Fabrics (in 1m. sq. metres): Cotton, 710 (731); woollens, 139 (140); man-made fibres, 286,818 (302,681). In 1,000 units: Radio sets, 618 (580); TV sets, 484 (530); washing machines, 242 (263); motor cars, 129,330 (124,372).

Labour. The employed population in 1986 was 10·7m., of whom 3m. worked in agriculture and 4·8m. industry and building. In 1985 39·4% of the total workforce, and 42·6% of the industrial workforce, were women. The average monthly wage was 2,827 lei in 1985. Wages were increased by 10% in 1988. A 5-day working week was introduced in Dec. 1989. Men retire at 62, women at 57.

Commerce. In 1985 exports totalled 192,295m. lei and imports 148,362m. lei.

Principal exports in 1985 were (in 1,000 tonnes): Petroleum products, 9,691; cement, 2,477; cereals, 842; oilfield equipment, 6,110m. lei; equipment for cement mills, 274m. lei; equipment for chemical factories, 904m. lei; shipbuilding, 966m. lei. Principal imports (in 1,000 tonnes): Iron ore, 15,207; industrial coke, 1,898; rolled ferrous metals, 696; electrical equipment, 4,809m. lei; motor cars, 1,303 units, and industrial and agricultural equipment.

In 1985 Romania's main trading partners (trade in 1m. lei) were: USSR, 74,333; Egypt, 22,304; Federal Republic of Germany, 19,486; Italy, 16,866; Iran, 16,758; German Democratic Republic, 16,737; USA, 15,645.

Total trade between Romania and UK (British Department of Trade returns, in £1,000 sterling):

	1985	*1986*	*1987*	*1988*	*1989*
Imports to UK	102,946	86,730	92,526	100,906	117,685
Exports and re-exports from UK	78,474	82,011	55,688	50,111	38,141

Both the UK and the USA have joint economic commissions with Romania. The US Congress abolished Romania's most-favoured nation status in 1988. In May 1986 Romania and the USSR signed a co-operation agreement for a 15-year programme of economic, scientific and technical development.

It was announced in April 1989 that all foreign debts had been paid off, and further foreign credit was prohibited.

Joint companies with Western firms are permitted; at least 51% of the capital must be in Romanian hands. The 'Romconsult' and 'Publicom' agencies will carry out respectively market research and publicity campaigns on behalf of foreign firms. Romania has a trade link with EEC under the generalized preference system. Agreements with the EEC on industrial products and establishing a joint economic commission were reached in March 1980.

On 1 Jan. 1975 a 2-tier tariff system was introduced, graded according to the grant of most-favoured nation status to Romania.

Tourism. In Jan. 1990 citizens were granted the right to travel freely.

COMMUNICATIONS

Roads. There were in 1985, 14,666 km of national roads of which 12,239 km were modernized. Freight carried, 362m. tonnes; passengers, 837m.

Railways. Length of standard-gauge route in 1987 was 11,275 km, of which 3,411 km were electrified. In 1985 there were 472 km of narrow-gauge lines. Freight carried in 1985, 283m. tonnes; passengers, 460m.

Aviation. TAROM (*Transporturi Aeriene Române*), the state airline, operates all internal services, and also services to Amsterdam, Athens, Beirut, Belgrade, Berlin, Brussels, Budapest, Cairo, Cologne, Copenhagen, Düsseldorf, Frankfurt, Istanbul, London, Moscow, Paris, Prague, Rome, Sofia, Tel-Aviv, Vienna, Warsaw and Zürich. Bucharest is also served by British Airways, PANAM, SABENA, Aeroflot, Air France, Interflug, CSA, MALEV, Austrian Air Lines, SAS, Lot, TABSO, El Al, Alitalia, Lufthansa and Swissair. An air agreement with China was signed in 1973.

Bucharest's airports are at Băneasa (internal flights) and Otopeni (international flights; 12 miles from Bucharest). Air transport in 1985 carried 2·5m. passengers and 29,000 tonnes of freight.

Shipping. The main ports are Constanța on the Black Sea and Galați and Brăila on the Danube. A new port has been constructed at Agigea on the Black Sea and the 64 km canal between the Danube and the Black Sea was opened in 1984. The largest shipyard is at Galați.

In 1985 the mercantile marine (NAVROM) owned some 200 sea-going ships. In 1985 sea-going transport carried 25·72m. tonnes of freight; river transport, 18·4m. tonnes and 1·84m. passengers.

Post and Broadcasting. There were 4,979 post offices in 1985. Number of telephone subscribers, 1·96m. *Radio-televiziunea Româna* broadcasts 3 programmes on medium-waves and FM. There are also 6 regional programmes, and radio and TV transmission in Hungarian and German (restored since Dec. 1989). As a result of the energy crisis in 1984 TV broadcasting was reduced to 22 hours a week, but had been increased to 80 hours a week by Feb. 1990. Links with the West are provided by Eutelsat satellite. Radio receiving sets in 1986 3·19m.; TV sets, 3·86m.

Cinemas and Theatres. There were, in 1987, 5,454 cinemas and 150 theatres and concert halls. 27 full-length feature films were made in 1985.

Newspapers and Books. There were, in 1987, 36 daily and 24 weekly newspapers and 435 periodicals, including 11 dailies and 3 weeklies in minority languages. There were 7,181 public libraries in 1987. 3,063 book titles were published in 1985 in 66·3m. copies. (376 titles in minority languages).

JUSTICE, RELIGION, EDUCATION AND WELFARE

Justice. Justice is administered by the Supreme Court, the 41 county courts, and lower courts. Lay assessors (elected for 4 years) participate in most court trials, collaborating with the judges. The Procurator-General exercises 'supreme supervisory power to ensure the observance of the law' by all authorities, central and local, and all citizens. The Procurator-General in 1990 was Gheorghe Robu. The Procurator's Office and its organs are independent of any organs of justice or administration, and only responsible to the Grand National Assembly (which appoints the Procurator-General for 4 years) and between its sessions, to the State Council. The Ministry of the Interior is responsible for ordinary police work. State security is the responsibility of the State Security Council. A new penal code came into force on 1 Jan. 1969. An amnesty of Jan. 1988 abolished or reduced the sentences of all convicts. All political prisoners were released on 23 Dec. 1989. The death penalty was abolished in Dec. 1989.

Religion. Churches are organized and function in accordance with art. 30 of the Constitution. Churches administer their own affairs and run seminaries for the training of priests. Expenses and salaries are paid by the State. There are 14 Churches, all under the control of the 'Department of Cults'. The largest is the Romanian Orthodox Church, which claimed some 16m. members in 1985. It is autocephalous, but retains dogmatic unity with the Eastern Orthodox Church. It is administered by the consultative Holy Synod and National Ecclesiastical Assembly and the executive National Ecclesiastical Council and Patriarchal Administration. It is organized into 12 dioceses grouped into 5 metropolitan bishoprics (Hungaro-Wallachia;

Moldavia-Suceava; Transylvania; Olt; Banat) and headed by Patriarch Teoctist Arapaşu. There are some 11,800 churches, 2 theological colleges and 6 'schools of cantors', as well as seminaries.

The Uniate (Greek Catholic) Church (which severed its connexion with the Vatican in 1698) was suppressed in 1948. It had 1·6m. adherents and 1,818 priests. Estimates for 1973: 700,000 adherents and 600 priests.

Other churches: Serbs have a Serbian Orthodox Vicariate at Timişoara. In 1986 there were 1·2m. Roman Catholics, mainly among the Hungarian and German minorities. There are 8 dioceses. In 1985 6 were vacant. There is a bishop of Alba Iulia and an Apostolic Administrator was appointed to Bucharest in Oct. 1984. There were 734 priests in 1982. The Church has not secured approval for a Statute and has no hierarchical ties with the Vatican.

Calvinists (600,000; mainly Hungarian) have bishoprics at Cluj and Oradea; Lutherans (150,000, mainly Germans) a bishopric at Sibiu and Unitarians (60,000, Hungarians) a bishopric at Cluj. These sects share a seminary at Cluj. In 1987 there were about 200,000 Baptists and 300,000 other neo-Protestants.

In 1989 there were 20,000 Jews under a Chief Rabbi. There were 120 synagogues in 1987.

There were 40,000 Moslems in 1983 and they have a Muftiate at Constanţa.

Education. Education is free and compulsory from 6 to 16, consisting of 8 years of primary school and 2 years of secondary (gymnasium). Further secondary education is available at *lycées*, professional schools or advanced technical schools.

In 1987–88 there were 12,291 kindergartens with 31,300 teachers and 828,079 children; 13,895 primary and secondary schools with 141,609 teachers and 3,027,196 pupils; 981 *lycées* with 43,805 teachers and 1,228,490 pupils; 764 professional schools with 2,419 teachers and 278,003 pupils; and 322 advanced technical schools with 1,146 teachers and 22,879 pupils. In 1983–84 there were 3,130 schools for 340,773 pupils of ethnic minorities with 15,922 teachers.

There are universities at Iaşi (founded 1860), Bucharest (1864), Cluj (1919), Timişoara (1962), Craiova (1965) and Braşov (1971). In 1987– 88 there were in all 44 institutes of higher education, with 157,041 (7,062 foreign) students and 12,036 teachers. In 1983–84 there were 11,568 students at institutes of higher education for ethnic minorities with some 1,000 teachers.

The Academy, with seat at Bucharest, has 2 branches at Iaşi and Cluj.

Health. In 1987 there were 214,253 hospital beds and 48,271 doctors (including 7,212 dentists). Under the Ceauşescu régime health standards severely declined and medical services were neglected.

Social Security. In 1987 3·26m. pensioners drew an average monthly pension of 2,106 lei.

DIPLOMATIC REPRESENTATIVES

Of Romania in Great Britain (4 Palace Green, London, W8 4QD)
Ambassador: (Vacant).

Of Great Britain in Romania (24 Strada Jules Michelet, Bucharest)
Ambassador: M. W. Atkinson, CMG, MBE.

Of Romania in the USA (1607 23rd St., NW, Washington, D.C., 20008)
Ambassador: Ion Stoichici.

Of the USA in Romania (7–9 Strada Tudor Arghezi, Bucharest)
Ambassador: Alan Green, Jr.

Of Romania to the United Nations
Ambassador: Petre Tanasie.

Further Reading

Anuarul Statistic al R.S.R. Bucharest, annual
Atlas Geografic Republica Socialistă Romania. Bucharest, 1965

Dicţionar Enciclopedic Român. Bucharest, 1962–66
Economic and Commercial Guide to Romania. Bucharest, annual since 1969
Mic Dicţionar Enciclopedic. Bucharest, 1973
Revista de Statistică. Bucharest, monthly
Romania: An Encyclopaedic Survey. Bucharest, 1980
Romania, the Industrialization of an Agrarian Economy under Socialist Planning: Report of a Mission sent to Romania by the World Bank. Washington, 1979
Academia Republicii Socialiste România. *Dicţionar Englez-Român.* Bucharest, 1974
Ceauçescu, N., *Romania on the Way of Completing Socialist Construction.* 3 vols. Bucharest, 1968–69.—*Romania on the Way of Completing the Many-sided Developed Socialist Society.* Bucharest, 1970 *ff.*
Deletant, A. and D., *Romania* [Bibliography]. Oxford and Santa Barbara, 1985
Fischer-Galati, S. A., *Rumania: A Bibliographical Guide.* Library of Congress, 1963.—*The New Rumania.* Mass. Inst. of Technology, 1968.—*The Socialist Republic of Rumania.* Baltimore, 1969.—*Twentieth Century Rumania.* New York, 1970
Giurescu, C. C. (ed.) *Chronological History of Romania.* 2nd ed. Bucharest, 1974
Ionescu, A. (ed.) *The Grand National Assembly of the Socialist Republic of Romania: A Brief Outline.* Bucharest, 1974
King, R. R., *History of the Romanian Communist Party.* Stanford, 1980
Leviţchi, L., *Dicţionar Român-Englez.* 2nd ed. Bucharest, 1965
Morariu, T., *et al, The Geography of Rumania.* 2nd ed. Bucharest, 1969
Pacepa, I., *Red Horizons.* London, 1988
Shafir, M., *Romania: Politics, Economics and Society.* London, 1985
Stanciu, I. G. and Cernovodeanu, P., *Distant Lands: The Genesis and Evolution of Romanian–American Relations.* Boulder, 1985
Turnock, D., *An Economic Geography of Romania.* London, 1974.—*The Romanian Economy in the Twentieth Century.* London 1986

RWANDA

Capital: Kigali
Population: 6·71m. (1988)
GNP per capita: US$310 (1988)

Republika y'u Rwanda

HISTORY. From the 16th century to 1959 the Tutsi kingdom of Rwanda shared the history of Burundi (*see* p. 258). In 1959 an uprising of the Hutu destroyed the Tutsi feudal hierarchy and led to the departure of the Mwami Kigeri V. Elections and a referendum under the auspices of the United Nations in Sept. 1961 resulted in an overwhelming majority for the republican party, the Parmehutu (*Parti du Mouvement de l'Emancipation du Bahutu*), and the rejection of the institution of the Mwami. The republic proclaimed by the Parmehutu on 28 Jan. 1961 was recognized by the Belgian administration (but not by the United Nations) in Oct. 1961. Internal self-government was granted on 1 Jan. 1962, and by decision of the General Assembly of the UN the Republic of Rwanda became independent on 1 July 1962. The first President, Gregoire Kayibanda, was deposed in a *coup* on 5 July 1973.

AREA AND POPULATION. Rwanda is bounded south by Burundi, west by Zaïre, north by Uganda and east by Tanzania. A mountainous state of 26,338 sq. km (10,169 sq. miles), its western third drains to Lake Kivu on the border with Zaïre and thence to the Congo river, while the rest is drained by the Kagera river into the Nile system.

The population was 4,819,317 at the 1978 Census, of whom over 90% were Hutu, 9% Tutsi and 1% Twa (pygmy); latest estimate (1988) 6,710,000. In 1988 there were about 20,000 refugees in Rwanda, all from Burundi.

The areas and populations (1978 Census) of the 10 prefectures are:

Prefecture	*Sq. km*	*Census 1978*	*Prefecture*	*Sq. km*	*Census 1978*
Cyangugu	2,226	331,380	Kigali	3,251	698,063
Kibuye	1,320	337,729	Kibungo	4,134	360,934
Gisenyi	2,395	468,786	Gitarama	2,241	602,752
Ruhengeri	1,762	528,649	Gikongoro	2,192	369,891
Byumba	4,987	519,968	Butare	1,830	601,165

Kigali, the capital, had 156,650 inhabitants in 1981; other towns (1978) being Butare (21,691), Ruhengeri (16,025) and Gisenyi (12,436). Kinyarwanda, the language of the entire population, and French are official languages, and Kiswahili is spoken in the commercial centres, where most of the 1,200 Europeans and 750 Asians reside.

Vital statistics (1975): Live births, 113,154; deaths, 41,385; marriages, 13,899.

CLIMATE. Despite the equatorial situation, there is a highland tropical climate. The wet seasons are from Oct. to Dec. and March to May. Highest rainfall occurs in the west, at around 70" (1,770 mm), decreasing to 40–55" (1,020–1,400 mm) in the central uplands and to 30" (760 mm) in the north and east. Kigali. Jan. 67°F (19·4°C), July 70°F (21·1°C). Annual rainfall 40" (1,000 mm).

CONSTITUTION AND GOVERNMENT. A new Constitution was approved by referendum on 17 Dec. 1978; under it, the *Mouvement revolutionnaire national pour le développement* (MRND) founded 5 July 1975 becomes the sole political organization. Executive power is vested in a President, elected by universal suffrage for a (renewable) 5-year term. He presides over a Council of Ministers, whom he appoints and dismisses.

Legislative power rests with a National Development Council of 70 deputies, elected for a 5-year term; elections were held on 26 Dec. 1983.

President: Maj.-Gen. Junéval Habyarimana (took office July 1975; elected Dec. 1978 and re-elected Dec. 1983).

Foreign Affairs and Co-operation: Casimir Bizimungu.

National flag: Three equal vertical panels of red, yellow and green (left to right), the letter 'R' in black superimposed on the centre panel.

Local government: The 10 prefectures, each under an appointed Prefect, are divided into 143 communes, each with an appointed Burgomaster and an elected Council.

DEFENCE

Army. The Army consists of 1 commando battalion, 1 reconnaissance, 8 infantry and 1 engineer companies. Equipment includes 12 AML-60/-90 armoured cars. Strength (1990) about 5,000.

Air Force. The Air Force currently operates 2 Guerrier armed light aircraft, 2 Noratlas, 2 Islander light transports, 6 Gazelle and 4 Alouette III helicopters. A Caravelle is operated on VIP duties. Personnel (1990) 200.

INTERNATIONAL RELATIONS

Membership. Rwanda is a member of UN, OAU and is an ACP state of EEC. With Burundi and Zaïre it forms part of the Economic Community of Countries of the Great Lakes.

ECONOMY

Budget. The budget for 1989 balanced at 27,500m. Rwanda francs.

Currency. The currency is the *Rwanda franc*. The official rate of Rwanda francs 131·11 = £1; 79·99 = US$1 (March 1990).

Banking. The Development Bank of Rwanda *(Banque Rwandaise de Développement—BRD)* had a capital (1983) of 1,000m. Rwanda francs. Other banks are the Central Bank *(Banque Nationale du Rwanda)*; 2 commercial banks which are majority foreign owned—the *Banque Commerciale du Rwanda* and the *Banque de Kigali*; the People's Bank, the Savings Association and the *Caisse Hypothécaire*.

ENERGY AND NATURAL RESOURCES

Electricity. 4 hydro-electric installations and 1 thermal plant produced 110m. kwh in 1986, but over half of the country's needs come from Zaïre. Supply 220 volts; 50 Hz.

Minerals. Cassiterite and wolframite are mined east of Lake Kivu. Production (1983): Cassiterite, 1,526 tonnes; wolfram, 429 tonnes. About 1m. cu. metres of natural gas are obtained from under the lake each year.

Agriculture. Subsistence agriculture accounts for most of the gross national product. Staple food crops (production 1988, in 1,000 tonnes) are sweet potatoes (800), cassava (390), dry beans (143), sorghum (177), potatoes (183), maize (88), peas and groundnuts. The main cash crops are *aravica* coffee (42), tea (8) and pyrethrum. There is a pilot rice-growing project.

Long-horned Ankole cattle, 639,000 head in 1980, play an important traditional role. Efforts are being made to improve their present negligible economic value. There were (1988) 660,000 cattle, 1·2m. goats, 360,000 sheep and 92,000 pigs.

INDUSTRY AND TRADE

Industry. There are about 100 small-sized modern manufacturing enterprises in the country. Food manufacturing is the dominant industrial activity (64%) followed by construction (15·3%) and mining (9%). There is a large modern brewery.

Commerce. In 1984 imports amounted to 27,122m. Rwanda francs and exports to 15,543m. of which coffee comprised 83%, tea 4% and tin 6%; Belgium provided 14% of imports, Kenya 13% and Japan 10%.

Total trade between Rwanda and UK (British Department of Trade returns, in £1,000 sterling):

	1985	*1986*	*1987*	*1988*	*1989*
Imports to UK	3,998	7,487	4,291	8,434	2,991
Exports and re-exports from UK	3,565	1,681	2,526	1,636	1,790

Tourism. In 1984 there were 20,000 visitors to national parks.

COMMUNICATIONS

Roads. There were (1982) 6,760 km of roads. There are road links with Burundi, Uganda, Tanzania and Zaïre. There were in 1982 6,188 cars and 7,168 commercial vehicles.

Aviation. There are international airports at Kanombe, for Kigali, and at Kamembe, with services to Bujumbura, Bukavu, Entebbe, Goma, Lubumbashi, Athens and Brussels.

Post and Broadcasting. Telephones (1983) 6,598. In 1983 there were 2 radio stations and 155,000 receivers.

JUSTICE, RELIGION, EDUCATION AND WELFARE

Justice. A system of Courts of First Instance and provincial courts refer appeals to Courts of Appeal and a Court of Cassation situated in Kigali.

Religion. The population was (1983) predominantly Roman Catholic (56%); there is an archbishop (Kigali) and 3 bishops. 23% of the population follow traditional religions, 12% are Protestants and 9% Moslems.

Education. In 1985 there were 790,198 pupils attending primary schools with 14,005 teachers. There were secondary, technical and teacher-training schools with 45,000 students and 1,082 teachers. The National University, opened at Butare, with sites at Butare and Ruhengeri, in 1963, had 1,577 students in 1984.

Health. In 1983 there were 170 hospitals and health centres with (1980) 9,015 beds; there were also 164 doctors, 1 dentist, 10 pharmacists, 464 midwives and 525 nursing personnel.

DIPLOMATIC REPRESENTATIVES

Of Rwanda in Great Britain
Ambassador: (Vacant).

Of Great Britain in Rwanda
Ambassador: R. L. B. Cormack, CMG (resides in Kinshasa).

Of Rwanda in the USA (1714 New Hampshire Ave, NW, Washington, D.C., 20009)
Ambassador: Aloys Uwimana.

Of the USA in Rwanda (Blvd. de la Revolution, Kigali)
Ambassador: Leonard H. O. Spearman, Sr.

Of Rwanda to the United Nations
Ambassador: Oswald Rukashaza.

ST CHRISTOPHER (ST KITTS)—NEVIS

Capital: Basseterre
Population: 43,410 (1987)
GNP capita: US$2,770 (1988)

HISTORY. St Christopher (known to its Carib inhabitants as *Liamuiga*) and Nevis were discovered and named by Columbus in 1493. They were settled by Britain in 1623 and 1628 respectively, but ownership was disputed with France until 1713. They formed part of the Leeward Islands Federation from 1871 to 1956, and part of the Federation of the West Indies from 1958 to 1962. In Feb. 1967 the colonial status was replaced by an 'association' with Britain, giving the islands full internal self-government, while Britain remained responsible for defence and foreign affairs. St Christopher–Nevis became fully independent on 19 Sept. 1983.

AREA AND POPULATION. The islands form part of the Lesser Antilles in Eastern Caribbean. Population, estimate (1986) 43,700.

	sq. km	*Census 1980*	*Chief town*	*Census 1980*
St Christopher	174	33,881	Basseterre	14,283
Nevis	93	9,428	Charlestown	1,243
	267	43,309		

In 1980, 94% of the population were black and 36% were urban. English is the official and spoken language.

CLIMATE. A pleasantly healthy climate, with a cool breeze throughout the year, low humidity and no recognized rainy season. Average annual rainfall is about 55" (1,375 mm).

CONSTITUTION AND GOVERNMENT. The 1983 Constitution described the country as 'a sovereign democratic federal state'. It allowed for a unicameral Parliament consisting of 11 elected Members (8 from St Kitts and 3 from Nevis) and 3 appointed Senators. Nevis was given its own Island Assembly and the right to secession from St Kitts. At the General Elections held on 21 March 1989, 6 seats in St Kitts were won by the People's Action Movement and 2 by the Labour Party, and in Nevis 2 seats were won by the Nevis Reformation Party and 1 by the Concerned Citizens Movement.

Governor-General: Sir Clement Athelston Arrindell, GCMG, GCVO.

Prime Minister: Rt. Hon. Dr Kennedy Alphonse Simmonds.

Flag: Diagonally green, black, red, with the black fimbriated in yellow and charged with two white stars.

INTERNATIONAL RELATIONS

Membership. St Christopher–Nevis is a member of the UN, the OAS, the Commonwealth and is an ACP state of EEC.

ECONOMY

Budget. The 1989 budget envisaged expenditure at EC$86,973,030 and revenue at EC$86,966,246

Currency. The East Caribbean *dollar* (of 100 *cents*) is in use. In March 1990, £1 = EC$4·40; US$1 = EC$2·71.

Banking. The National Bank operates 4 branches in St. Kitts and Nevis. The main office is located in Basseterre. Other banks include Barclay's Bank International, with a sub-branch in Nevis, Royal Bank of Canada, and the Nevis Co-operative Banking Co. Ltd and the Bank of Nevis in Charlestown. Branches of the Bank of Nova Scotia are located in Basseterre and Charlestown. Commercial banks' assets (1988) EC$418·6m.; deposits EC$289·8m.

ENERGY AND NATURAL RESOURCES

Electricity. Production (1984) 34m. kwh.

Agriculture. The main crops are sugar and cotton. There are 30 sugar estates and 124 acres of cotton. Most of the farms are small-holdings and there are a number of coconut estates amounting to some 1,000 acres under public and private ownership. Sugar production (1989) 24,777 long tonnes. 35,185 lbs of cotton and 287,020 lbs of copra were produced in 1987, and 6,587 lbs of cotton lint in 1988-89.

Livestock (1988): Cattle, 7,000; pigs, 10,000; sheep, 15,000; goats, 10,000; donkeys, (1987) 1,116; poultry, (1987) 50,116.

Fisheries. Catch (1988) 2·5m. lbs.

INDUSTRY AND TRADE

Industry. The main employer of labour is the sugar industry. In 1989 construction was a major industry. Other industries are clothing and assembly of electronic equipment.

Commerce. Imports, (1988) EC$255·7m. mainly from the USA and UK; exports, EC$76·6m. Chief export was sugar, with 14,873 long tons (EC$20,717,387) to the UK and 6,895 long tons (EC$9,005,747). to the USA

Total trade between St Christopher (St Kitts)–Nevis and UK (British Department of Trade returns, in £1,000 sterling):

	1986	*1987*	*1988*	*1989*
Imports to UK	4,429	4,677	4,271	4,866
Exports and re-exports from UK	6,008	7,041	8,025	5,887

Tourism. In 1988, there were 123,200 tourists, 53,600 arriving by sea. In 1989 there were 22 hotels with 1,353 beds.

COMMUNICATIONS

Roads. There were (1983) about 305 km of roads, and (1988) 4,903 licensed vehicles.

Railways. There are 36 km of railway operated by the sugar industry.

Aviation. There is an airport at Golden Rock (St Kitts). 98,263 passengers arrived by air in 1987. There is an airfield on Nevis (Newcastle).

Shipping. A deep water port was opened in 1981 at Bird Rock with accommodation for cargo, tourist, roll-on-roll-off ships and bulk sugar and molasses loading. 1,428 tourists arrived by sea in 1985.

Post and Telecommunications. There is a general post office in Basseterre. Five branches are on the island. Charlestown has a general post office, and there are two branches in Nevis. There were 7,000 telephones in 1988. In 1985 there were 5,000 television and 21,000 radio receivers.

JUSTICE, RELIGION, EDUCATION AND WELFARE

Justice. Justice is administered by the Supreme Court and by Magistrates' Courts.They have both civil and criminal jurisdiction.

Religion. In 1985, 36·2% were Anglican, 32·3% Methodist, 7·9% other Protestant, and 10·7% Roman Catholic.

Education. Primary education is compulsory for all children between the ages of 5 and 14, but no pupil is required to leave school before the age of 16 years. There is an Extra-Mural Department of the University of the West Indies, a Technical College and a Teachers' Training College.

In 1988 there were 1,357 pupils in nurseries and pre-schools, 7,473 pupils in primary schools, 4,273 in secondary schools, and (1989) 211 students in the Technical and Teacher's Training Colleges.

Health. In 1987 there were 22 doctors, 4 hospitals with 258 beds and 17 health clinics.

DIPLOMATIC REPRESENTATIVES

Of St Christopher and Nevis in Great Britain (10 Kensington Ct., London W8)
High Commissioner: Richard Gunn.

Of Great Britain in St Christopher and Nevis
High Commissioner: K. F. X. Burns, CMG (resides in Bridgetown).

Of St Christopher and Nevis in the USA (2501 M. St., NW, Washington, D.C., 20037)
Chargé d'Affaires: Erstein M. Edwards.

Of St Christopher and Nevis to the United Nations
Ambassador: Dr William Herbert.

Further Reading

National Accounts. Statistics Division, Ministry of Development (annual)
St Kitts and Nevis Quarterly. Statistics Division, Ministry of Development

Gordon, J., *Nevis: Queen of the Caribees*. London, 1985

Library: Public Library, Basseterre. *Librarian:* Miss V. Archibald.

ST HELENA

Capital: Jamestown
Population: 5,564 (1988)

HISTORY. The island was administered by the East India Company from 1659 and became a British colony in 1834.

AREA AND POPULATION. St Helena, of volcanic origin, is 1,200 miles from the west coast of Africa. Area, 47 sq. miles (121·7 sq. km), with a cultivable area of about 600 acres (243 hectares). Population (1988) 5,564. The port of the island is Jamestown, population (1976) 1,516.

In 1982 there were: Births, 123; deaths, 52; marriages, 26.

CLIMATE. A mild climate, with little variation. Temperatures range from 75–85°F (24–29°C) in summer to 65–75°F (18–24°C) in winter. Rainfall varies between 13" (325 mm) and 37" (925 mm) according to altitude and situation.

GOVERNMENT. The Government of St Helena is administered by a Governor, with the aid of a Legislative Council consisting of the Governor, 2 *ex-officio* members (the Government Secretary and the Treasurer) and 12 elected members. Committees of the Legislative Council are responsible for the general oversight of the activities of government departments and have, in addition, statutory and administrative functions.

The Governor is also assisted by an Executive Council consisting of the 2 *ex-officio* members and the chairmen of the 6 Council committees.

Governor and C.-in-C.: R. F. Stimson.
Government Secretary: E. C. Brooks, OBE.

Flag: The British Blue Ensign with the shield of the colony in the fly.

FINANCE AND TRADE

Budget. In 1984 revenue was £4·34m. and expediture £3·91m.

Commerce. Total trade between Ascension and St Helena and UK (British Department of Trade returns, in £1,000 sterling):

	1985	*1986*	*1987*	*1988*	*1989*
Imports to UK	4,515	380	189	205	504
Exports and re-exports from UK	7,914	8,196	8,065	6,103	7,208

Banking. Savings-bank deposits on 31 Dec. 1982, £1,467,079, belonging to 3,800 depositors.

COMMUNICATIONS

Roads. There were (1988) 94 km of all-weather motor roads. There were 1,301 vehicles in 1987.

Shipping. The number of merchant vessels that called in 1987 was 154.

Post and Broadcasting. The Cable & Wireless Ltd cable connects St Helena with Cape Town and Ascension Island. There is a telephone service with 85 miles of wire and (1982), 310 telephones.

St Helena Government Broadcasting Station broadcasts in English on medium-waves. Number of radio receivers (1988), 2,400.

JUSTICE, RELIGION, EDUCATION AND WELFARE

Justice. Police force, 32; cases dealt with by police magistrate, 205 in 1981.

Religion. There are 10 Anglican churches, 4 Baptist chapels, 3 Salvation Army halls, 1 Seventh Day Adventist church and 1 Roman Catholic church.

Education. Three pre-school playgroups, 7 primary, 3 senior and 1 secondary schools controlled by the Government had 1,188 pupils in 1987.

Health. There were 3 doctors, 1 dentist and 54 hospital beds in 1982.

Ascension is a small island of volcanic origin, of 34 sq. miles (88 sq. km), 700 miles north-west of St Helena. In Nov. 1922 the administration was transferred from the Admiralty to the Colonial Office and annexed to the colony of St Helena. There are 120 hectares providing fresh meat, vegetables and fruit. Population, 31 March 1988, was 1,007 (excluding military personnel).

The island is the resort of sea turtles, which come to lay their eggs in the sand annually between Jan. and May. Rabbits are more or less numerous on the island, which is, besides, the breeding ground of the sooty tern or 'wideawake', these birds coming in vast numbers to lay their eggs every eighth month. There is also a small herd of feral donkeys.

Cable & Wireless Ltd own and operate a cable station, connecting the island with St Helena, Sierra Leone, St Vincent, Rio de Janeiro and Buenos Aires. There is an airstrip (Miracle Mile) near the settlement of Georgetown which was being extended in 1985.

Administrator: M. T. S. Blick.

Tristan da Cunha, is the largest of a small group of islands in the South Atlantic lying 1,320 miles (2,124 sq. km) south-west of St Helena, of which they became dependencies on 12 Jan. 1938. Tristan da Cunha has an area of 98 sq. km and a population (1988) of 313, all living in the settlement of Edinburgh. Inaccessible Island (10 sq. km) lies 20 miles west and the 3 Nightingale Islands (2 sq. km) lie 20 miles south of Tristan da Cunha; they are uninhabited. Gough Island (90 sq. km) is 220 miles south of Tristan and has a meteorological station.

Tristan consists of a volcano rising to a height of 6,760 ft, with a circumference at its base of 21 miles. The volcano, believed to be extinct, erupted unexpectedly early in Oct. 1961. The whole population was evacuated without loss and settled temporarily in the UK. In 1963 they returned to Tristan where they all dwell in the settlement of Edinburgh. Before the disaster occurred the habitable area was a small plateau on the north west side of about 12 sq. miles, 100 ft above sea-level. Only about 30 acres was under cultivation, three-quarters of it for potatoes. There were apple and peach trees. Potatoes remain the chief crop, cattle, sheep and pigs are now reared, and fish are plentiful.

Population in 1880, 109; in 1988, 306. The original inhabitants were shipwrecked sailors and soldiers who remained behind when the garrison from St Helena was withdrawn in 1817.

At the end of April 1942 Tristan da Cunha was commissioned as HMS *Atlantic Isle*, and became an important meteorological and radio station. In Jan. 1949 a South African company commenced crawfishing operations. An Administrator was appointed at the end of 1948 and a body of basic law brought into operation. The Island Council, which was set up in 1932, in 1982 consisted of a Chief Islander, 3 nominated and 7 elected members under the chairmanship of the Administrator.

Administrator: R. Perry.

Further Reading

Crawford, A., *Tristan da Cunha and the Roaring Forties*. Edinburgh, 1982
Cross, A., *Saint Helena*. Newton Abbot, 1980
Munch, P. A., *Sociology of Tristan da Cunha*. Oslo, 1945.—*Crisis in Utopia*. New York, 1971

ST LUCIA

Capital: Castries
Population: 146,600 (1988)
GNP per capita: US$1,540 (1988)

HISTORY. St Lucia was discovered about 1500 A.D. Attempts to colonize the island by the English took place in 1605 and 1638. The French settled in 1650 and St Lucia was ceded to Britain in 1814. Self-government was achieved in 1967 and independence on 22 Feb. 1979.

AREA AND POPULATION. St Lucia is a small island of the Lesser Antilles situated in the Eastern Caribbean between Martinique and St Vincent, with an area of 238 sq. miles (617 sq. km); population (census, 1980) 120,300. Estimate (1988) 146,600. The capital is Castries (population, 1988, 52,868), and Vieux Fort, the second town and port 12,951 in 1984. Life expectancy (1985) was 68·6 (men) and 75·5 (women).

CLIMATE. The climate is tropical, with a dry season lasting from Jan. to April, a wet season from May to Aug., followed by an Indian summer for two months, but most rain falls in Nov. and Dec. Amounts vary over the year, according to altitude, from 60" (1,500 mm) to 138" (3,450 mm). Temperatures are uniform at about 80°F (26·7°C).

CONSTITUTION AND GOVERNMENT. There is a 17-seat House of Assembly elected for 5 years; an 11-seat Senate appointed by the Governor-General, 6 on the advice of the Prime Minister, 3 on the advice of the Leader of the Opposition, and 2 'after consultation with appropriate religious, economic or social bodies or associations'.

At the elections in April 1987, the United Workers' Party gained 9 seats, and the St Lucia Labour Party, 8.

Acting Governor-General: Stanislaus James.

Prime Minister: Rt Hon. John George Melvin Compton.

Flag: Blue with a design of a black triangle edged in white, bearing a smaller yellow triangle, in the centre.

Local government: In 1986 the 10 *quartiers* were replaced by 8 administrative regions.

INTERNATIONAL RELATIONS

Membership. St Lucia is a member of UN, OAS, Caricom, the Commonwealth and is an ACP state of the EEC.

ECONOMY

Planning. The aim of the Development Plan, 1977–90, was to develop agriculture to diversify production and to contain rural-urban drift.

Budget. The budget in 1989–90 amounted to EC$370·3m. expenditure; revenue, EC$358·7m.

Banking. There are Barclays Bank International with 4 branches and 2 agencies, the Royal Bank of Canada with 1 branch, the Bank of Nova Scotia with 3 branches, the Canadian Imperial Bank of Commerce and the St Lucia Co-operative bank with 2 branches each, the National Development Bank with 1 branch and the National Commercial Bank with 3 branches.

INDUSTRY AND TRADE

Industry. In 1990, laundry soap, coconut meal, rum, beverages, electronic assembly and clothing were the chief products.

Agriculture. Bananas, cocoa, coconuts, mace, nutmeg and citrus fruit are the chief products. Livestock (1988): Cattle, 13,000; pigs, 12,000; sheep, 15,000; goats, 12,000.

Commerce. Value of imports (1986), EC$419·3m.; of exports, EC$213·2m., including coconut oil, cocoa beans, copra and bananas. Main items of imports were artificial silk and cotton piece-goods, cement, plastic goods, iron and steel products, hardware, motor vehicles, agricultural machinery, fertilizers, wheat flour, codfish and rice, meat and meat preparations.

Total trade between St Lucia and UK (British Department of Trade returns, in £1,000 sterling):

	1986	*1987*	*1988*	*1989*
Imports to UK	59,855	40,908	58,385	48,746
Exports and re-exports from UK	12,441	13,196	19,750	19,601

Tourism. The total number of visitors during 1987 was 202,336.

COMMUNICATIONS

Roads. The island has 500 miles of main and secondary roads, and 2,084 commercial vehicles and 8,629 cars in 1986.

Aviation. The island is served on a scheduled basis by Leeward Islands Air Transport, British West Indian Airways, Eastern Airline, British Airways, Pan Am, Caribbean Airways and Air Canada. There are 2 airfields—Hewanorra International Airport, with 9,000 ft runway, and Vigie.

Shipping. There are 2 ports, Castries and Vieux Fort.

Post and Broadcasting. There were (1986) 13,654 telephone instruments coupled to 7,960 exchange lines; 157 telex machines, and telegram service. There were 5,000 TV and 99,000 radio receivers in 1988.

Cinemas. There were 8 cinemas in 1986.

JUSTICE, RELIGION, EDUCATION AND WELFARE

Justice. The island is divided into 2 judicial districts, and there are 9 magistrates' courts. Appeals lie with the Eastern Caribbean Supreme Court of Appeal.

Religion. In 1989 over 82% of the population was Roman Catholic.

Education (1985–86). 79 primary schools, with 32,273 pupils on roll. Primary education is free and compulsory by law, but the legislation is not enforced. There are 12 secondary schools with 5,665 pupils. There is 1 technical college with (1985–86) 223 students and 1 teachers' college with (1985–86) 123 students.

Health. Victoria Hospital (in Castries) has 213 beds; there is also a 162-bed mental hospital, 3 other hospitals (150 beds) and 29 health centres. In 1984 there were 58 doctors, 5 dentists and 236 nursing personnel.

DIPLOMATIC REPRESENTATIVES

Of St Lucia in Great Britain (10 Kensington Ct., London, W8)
High Commissioner: Richard Gunn.

Of Great Britain in St Lucia
High Commissioner: K. F. X. Burns, CMG (resides in Bridgetown).

Of St Lucia in the USA and to the United Nations
Ambassador: Dr Charles S. Flemming.

Further Reading

Ellis, G., *St Lucia: Helen of the West Indies.* London, 1985

Library: The Central Library, Castries. *Acting Librarian:* Frances Niles.

ST VINCENT AND THE GRENADINES

Capital: Kingstown
Population: 112,614 (1987)
GNP per capita: US$1,100 (1988)

HISTORY. The date of discovery of St Vincent was 22 Jan. 1498. In 1969 St Vincent became a self-governing Associated State of UK and acquired full independence on 27 Oct. 1979.

AREA AND POPULATION. St Vincent is an island of the Lesser Antilles, situated in the Eastern Caribbean between St Lucia and Grenada, from which latter it is separated by a chain of small islands known as the Grenadines. The total area of 388 sq. km (150 sq. miles) comprises the island of St Vincent itself (345 sq. km) and the Northern Grenadines (43 sq. km) of which the largest are Bequia, Mustique, Canouan, Mayreau and Union.

The population at the 1980 Census was 97,845; latest estimate (1987) was 112,614 of whom 5,451 lived on the Northern Grenadines. The capital, Kingstown, had 28,942 inhabitants in 1987 (including suburbs). The population is mainly of black (82%) and mixed (13·9%) origin, with small white, Asian and Amerindian minorities.

Vital statistics (1987): Live births, 2,639; deaths, 608; marriages, 416.

CLIMATE. The climate is tropical marine, with north-east Trades predominating and rainfall ranging from 150" (3,750 mm) a year in the mountains to 60" (1,500 mm) on the south-east coast. The rainy season is from June to Dec., and temperatures are equable throughout the year.

CONSTITUTION AND GOVERNMENT. The House of Assembly consists of 13 elected members, directly elected for a 5-year term from single-member constituencies, the Attorney-General (elected) and 6 Senators appointed by the Governor-General (4 on the advice of the Prime Minister and 2 on the advice of the Leader of the Opposition). At the General Elections held 16 May 1989, the New Democratic Party won all 21 seats in the House of Assembly.

Acting Governor-General: Henry Harvey Williams.
Prime Minister: Rt. Hon. James Fitz-Allen Mitchell.
Agriculture, Industry and Labour: Allan Cruickshank. *Education, Youth and Women's Affairs:* John Horne. *Housing, Community Development and Local Government:* Louis Jones. *Health and Environment:* Burton Williams. *Information, Legal Affairs, Attorney General:* Parnell Campbell. *Communications and Works:* Jeremiah Scott. *Trade and Tourism:* Herbert Young.

There are 2 Ministers of State.

National Flag: Three vertical stripes of blue, yellow, green, with the yellow of double width and charged with three green diamonds.

INTERNATIONAL RELATIONS

Membership. St Vincent and the Grenadines is a member of UN, OAS, Caricom, the Commonwealth and is an ACP state of the EEC.

ECONOMY

Budget. Revenue (estimate), 1988–89, $123,693,070; expenditure, $123,621,279. Public debt at the end of the financial year 1985–86 was $57,905,110.

Currency. The currency is the Eastern Caribbean *dollar*. In March 1990, £1 = EC$4·40; US$1 = EC$2·71.

Banking. There are branches of Barclays Bank PLC, the Caribbean Banking Corporation, the Canadian Imperial Bank of Commerce, the Bank of Nova Scotia. Locally-owned banks: the National Commercial Bank, St Vincent Co-operative Bank and the St Vincent Agricultural Credit and Loan Bank.

ENERGY AND NATURAL RESOURCES

Electricity. Production (1987) 35m. kwh. Supply 230 volts; 50 Hz.

Agriculture. Agriculture accounted for 20·8% of GDP in 1987. According to the 1985–86 census of agriculture, 29,649 acres of the total acreage of 85,120 were classified as agricultural lands; 5,500 acres were under forest and woodland and all other lands accounted for 1,030 acres. The total arable land was about 8,932 acres, of which 4,016 acres were under temporary crops, 2,256 acres under temporary pasture, 2,289 acres under temporary fallow and other arable land covering 371 acres. 16,062 acres were under permanent crops, of which approximately 5,500 acres were under coconuts and 7,224 acres under bananas; the remainder produce cocoa, citrus, mangoes, avocado pears, guavas and miscellaneous crops. The sugar industry was closed down in 1985 although some sugar-cane will be grown for rum production. Production (1988, in tonnes): Coconuts, 25,000; bananas, 40,000.

Livestock (1988): Cattle, 7,000; pigs, 9,000; sheep, 15,000; goats, 5,000.

INDUSTRY AND TRADE

Industry. Industries include assembly of electronic equipment, manufacture of garments, electrical products, animal feeds and flour, corrugated galvanized sheets, exhaust systems, industrial gases, concrete blocks, plastics, soft drinks, beer and rum, wood products and furniture, and processing of milk, fruit juices and food items.

Commerce (1987). Imports, EC$264,301,919; exports, EC$139,569,582.

Principal exports, 1987 in EC$: Arrowroot, 1,155,492; eddoes and dasheen, 11,288,471; sweet potatoes, 5,978,280; tannias, 4,434,584; bananas, 53,049,346; galvanized sheets, 4,850,654; yams, 848,965; plantain, 2,670,207; ginger, 740,884; flour, 16,722,941.

Total trade between St Vincent and the Grenadines and UK (British Department of Trade returns, in £1,000 sterling):

	1986	*1987*	*1988*	*1989*
Imports to UK	21,161	20,208	29,709	31,570
Exports and re-exports from UK	8,288	8,529	8,011	11,075

Labour (1987). The Department of Labour is charged with looking after the interest and welfare of all categories of workers, including providing advice and guidance to employers/employees and their organizations and enforcing the labour laws.

Tourism. There were 127,776 visitors in 1987.

COMMUNICATIONS

Roads. There were (1987) 620 km of all-weather roads, 453 km of rough motorable roads and 180 km of tracks. Vehicles registered (1987) 8,500.

Aviation. Scheduled services are operated daily by LIAT and Air Martinique. Non-scheduled services are operated by Mustique Airways, Tropical Air Services, Aero-Services and St Lucia Airways. Passengers are able to travel daily through the chain of islands stretching as far north as San Juan, Puerto Rico and south to Trinidad. Connexions to the USA, Canada, South America and Europe are possible *via* Barbados, Antigua, Trinidad and St Lucia.

Shipping (1987): 36 auxiliary sailing vessels of 1,510 NRT entered and cleared. 659 motor vessels of 805,261 NRT entered and cleared. 47 tankers of 41,798 NRT bringing 18,925·13 tons of fuel entered.

Post and Broadcasting. There is a General Post Office at Kingstown and 49 district post offices. There is an automatic telephone system with (1987), 6,145 subscribers; 7,950 stations and a digital radio link to Bequia, Mustique and Union

Island; VHF links Petit St Vincent and Palm Island. In 1987 there were 12,000 TV and 60,000 radio receivers.

Cinemas. There were 2 cinemas in 1987 with a seating capacity of 1,825.

JUSTICE, RELIGION, EDUCATION AND WELFARE

Justice (1986). There were 3,699 criminal matters disposed of in the 3 magisterial districts which comprise 11 courts. 192 cases were dealt with in the 1987 Criminal Assizes in the High Court. Strength of police force (1982), 525 (including 12 officers).

Religion. At the 1980 Census, 42% of the population was Anglican, 21% Methodist and 12% Roman Catholic.

Education (1987). Sixty-one primary schools; pupils on roll, 25,152. Expenditure on primary education, $13,937,403. There is also a secondary school for girls (703 pupils), a co-educational school (592 pupils), as well as 12 assisted secondary schools (3,667 pupils) and 7 rural secondary schools with 1,820 pupils. Expenditure on secondary education, $3,937,703. There is a private secondary school with 298 pupils.

Health. There were (1987) a General Hospital in Kingstown (204 beds), 5 rural hospitals at Chateaubelair, Georgetown, Mesopotamia, Bequia and Union Island; 1 psychiatric hospital (120 beds); 1 geriatric hospital (120 beds); 35 medical clinics and 1 private hospital (10 beds). In 1987 there were 39 doctors, 2 dentists, 80 technical staff, 236 trained nursing personnel and 85 community health aides.

Library: St Vincent Public Library, Kingstown. *Librarian:* Mrs Lorna Small.

DIPLOMATIC REPRESENTATIVES

Of St Vincent and the Grenadines in Great Britain (10 Kensington Ct, London, W8)
High Commissioner: Richard Gunn.

Of Great Britain in St Vincent and the Grenadines
High Commissioner: K. F. X. Burns, CMG (resides in Bridgetown).

Of St Vincent and the Grenadines to the UN
Ambassador: (Vacant).

Further Reading

Price, N., *Behind the Planter's Back.* London, 1988

SAN MARINO

Capital: San Marino
Population: 22,746 (1988)

Repubblica di San Marino

HISTORY. On 22 March 1862 San Marino concluded a treaty of friendship and co-operation, including a *de facto* customs union with the kingdom of Italy, preserving the independence of the ancient republic, although completely surrounded by Italian territory. The treaty was renewed on 27 March 1872, 28 June 1897 and 31 March 1939, with several amendments 1942–85.

The republic has extradition treaties with Belgium, France, the Netherlands, UK and USA.

AREA AND POPULATION. San Marino is a land-locked state in central Italy, 20 km from the Adriatic. The frontier line is 38·6 km in length, area is 61·19 sq. km (24·1 sq. miles) and the population (31 Dec. 1988), 22,746; some 11,000 citizens live abroad. The capital, San Marino, had 4,363 inhabitants (1986); the largest town is Serravalle (7,109), an industrial centre in the north.

CONSTITUTION AND GOVERNMENT. The legislative power is vested in the Great and General Council of 60 members elected every 5 years by popular vote, 2 of whom are appointed every 6 months to act as regents *(Capitani reggenti).*

The elections held on 29 May 1988 gave 27 seats to the Christian Democrats, 18 to the Communists, 15 to Socialist parties.

The regents (who are Heads of State) exercise executive power together with the Congress of State *(Congresso di Stato)*, which comprises the regents, 3 secretaries of state and 7 ministers, and through Commissions on social welfare, public works, etc.

National flag: Horizontally white over light blue, with the national arms over all in the centre.

DEFENCE. Military service is not obligatory, but all citizens between the ages of 16 and 55 can be called upon to defend the State. They may also serve as volunteers in the Military Corps.

ECONOMY. The budget (ordinary and extraordinary) for the financial year ending 31 Dec. 1989 balanced at 259,275,271,797 lire.

Wheat, barley, maize and vines are grown. The chief exports are wood machinery, chemicals, wine, textiles, tiles, varnishes and ceramics.

Italian currency is in general use, but the republic issues its own postage stamps and coins.

In 1987, 3m. tourists visited San Marino.

COMMUNICATIONS

Roads. A bus service connects San Marino with Rimini. There are 237 km of roads and (1987) 16,540 passenger cars and 3,225 commercial vehicles.

Post and Broadcasting. In 1986 there were 11,707 telephones. In 1983 there were 8 post offices. In 1987 there were 10,600 radio and 6,608 television receivers.

Cinemas. In 1987 there were 7 cinemas with a seating capacity of 1,000.

JUSTICE, RELIGION, EDUCATION AND WELFARE

Justice. Law is administered by a Commissioner for civil cases and a Commissioner for criminal cases (acting with a penal judge), from whom appeals can be made to a civil appeals judge and a criminal appeals judge respectively. The highest legal authority is, in certain cases, the *Consiglio dei XII*. Civil marriage was instituted in Sept. 1953 and divorce allowed in April 1986.

Religion. 95% of the population are Roman Catholic.

Education. In 1985 there were 13 elementary schools with 1,411 pupils and 158 teachers, 4 secondary schools with 1,248 pupils and 183 teachers. There is also a foreign languages school, a technical school and a trade and handicraft school.

Health. In 1987 there were 149 hospital beds and 60 doctors.

DIPLOMATIC REPRESENTATIVES

British Consul-General (resides at Florence): M. L. Croll.
Consul-General in London: Lord Forte.

Further Reading

Information: Office of Cultural Affairs and Information of the Department of Foreign Affairs.

Garbelotto, A., *Evoluzione storica della costituzione di S. Marino.* Milan, 1956
Matteini, N., *The Republic of San Marino.* San Marino, 1981
Packett, C. N., *Guide to the Republic of San Marino.* Bradford, 1970
Rossi, G., *San Marino.* San Marino, 1954

SÃO TOMÉ E PRÍNCIPE

Capital: São Tomé
Population: 115,600 (1988)
GNP per capita: US$280 (1987)

HISTORY. The islands of São Tomé and Príncipe, were discovered in 1471 by Pedro Escobar and João Gomes, and from 1522 constituted a Portugese colony. On 11 June 1951 it became an overseas province of Portugal.

On 26 Nov. 1974 the Government of Portugal and the liberation movement of São Tomé e Príncipe signed an agreement granting independence to the archipelago on 12 July 1975.

AREA AND POPULATION. The republic, which lies about 200 km off the west coast of Gabon, in the Gulf of Guinea, comprises the main islands of São Tomé (845 sq. km) and Príncipe and several smaller islets including Pedras Tinhosas and Rolas. It has a total area of 1,001 sq. km (387 sq. miles). Total population (census, 1981) 96,611. Estimate (1988) 115,600.

The areas and populations of the 2 provinces were as follows:

Province	*Sq. km*	*Census 1981*	*Estimate 1987*	*Chief town*	*Estimate 1984*
São Tomé	859	91,356	106,900	São Tomé	34,997
Príncipe	142	5,255	6,100	São António	1,000

The official language is Portuguese, but 90% speak Fang, a Bantu language.

Vital statistics (1985): Births, 3,700; deaths, 900.

CLIMATE. The tropical climate is modified by altitude and the effect of the cool Benguela current. The wet season is generally from Oct. to May, but rainfall varies very much, from 40" (1,000 mm) in the hot and humid north-east to 150–200" (3,800–5,000 mm) on the plateau. São Tomé Jan. 79°F (26·1°C), July 75°F (23·9°C). Annual rainfall 38" (951 mm).

CONSTITUTION AND GOVERNMENT. A new constitution was approved by the Constitutional Assembly (elected 6 July 1975) on 12 Dec. 1975. Under it, the sole legal party is the *Movimento de Libertação de São Tomé e Príncipe*, who nominate candidates for the Presidency and People's Assembly. The President is elected by the People's Assembly for a 4-year term; he is also head of government and appoints a Cabinet of Ministers to assist him. The 40-member People's Assembly is also elected for 4 years.

President, Commander-in-Chief: Dr Manuel Pinto da Costa (re-elected 30 Sept. 1985).

Prime Minister: Celestino Rochas da Costa.

Foreign Affairs: Carlos da Graça.

Flag: Three horizontal stripes of green, yellow, green, with the yellow of double width and bearing 2 black stars; in the hoist a red triangle over all.

Local government: São Tomé province comprises 6 districts, while Príncipe province forms a seventh district.

DEFENCE. About 700 Angolan and 200 Cuban military personnel are stationed on the islands.

INTERNATIONAL RELATIONS

Membership. São Tomé e Príncipe is a member of UN, OAU and is an ACP state of EEC.

ECONOMY

Budget. In 1986 the budget balanced at 1,092m. dobra.

Currency. The currency is the *dobra*, introduced in 1977, divided into 100 *centavos*. In March 1990, £1 = 173·66 *dobra*; US$1 = 105·95 *dobra*.

Banking. *Banco Nacional de São Tomé e Príncipe* (established, 1975) is the central bank.

ENERGY AND NATURAL RESOURCES

Electricity. Production (1986) 3m. kwh.

Agriculture. About 38% of the area is under cultivation. Production (1988 in tonnes): Coconuts, 37,000; copra, 4,000; bananas, 3,000; palm oil, 250. Food crops include cassava, sweet potatoes and yams. In 1988 there were 4,000 goats, 2,000 sheep, 3,000 pigs and 3,000 cattle.

Fisheries. The fishing industry is being developed, to exploit the rich tuna shoals. Catch (1986) 2,800 tonnes.

COMMERCE. Imports in 1984 amounted to 485·9m. dobras and exports to 539·6m. dobras the main exports being cocoa (80%), copra (15%), coffee, bananas and palm-oil. Portugal provided 30% of imports while the German Democratic Republic took 35% of exports, the Netherlands 18% and Portugal 15%.

Total trade between São Tomé e Príncipe and UK (British Department of Trade returns, in £1,000 sterling):

	1985	*1986*	*1987*	*1988*	*1989*
Imports to UK	197	327	205	20	4
Exports and re-exports from UK	824	455	329	416	819

COMMUNICATIONS

Roads. There were 288 km of roads (198 paved) in 1975.

Aviation. São Tomé airport is linked by regular services to Douala, Lisbon, Luanda, Cabinda, Libreville, Malabo and Brazil, as well as to Príncipe.

Post and Broadcasting. There were (1986) 28,000 radio receivers and 2,200 telephones.

Newspapers. In 1986 there were 2 weekly newspapers.

JUSTICE, RELIGION, EDUCATION AND WELFARE.

Justice. Members of the Supreme Court are appointed by the People's Assembly.

Religion. About 80% of the population are Roman Catholic.

Education. In 1984 there were 19,086 pupils and 517 teachers in 63 primary schools, 6,186 pupils and 300 teachers in 11 secondary schools, and 370 students and 35 teachers in 2 technical schools.

Health. In 1981 there were 38 doctors and 118 nursing personnel.

DIPLOMATIC REPRESENTATIVES

Of São Tomé and Príncipe to Great Britain
Ambassador: Maria Manuela Margarido (resides in Brussels).

Of Great Britain in São Tomé and Príncipe
Ambassador: (Vacant).

Of São Tomé and Príncipe in the USA and to the United Nations
Ambassador: Joaquim Rafael Branco.

SAUDI ARABIA

Capital: Riyadh
Population: 12m. (1988)
GNP per capita: US$6,170 (1988)

al-Mamlaka al-'Arabiya as-Sa'udiya

HISTORY. Saudi Arabia was founded by Abdul Aziz ibn Abdur-Rahman al-Faisal Al Sa'ud, GCB, GCIE (born about 1880; died 9 Nov. 1953), who had been proclaimed King of the Hejaz on 8 Jan. 1926 and had in 1927 changed his title of Sultan of Nejd and its Dependencies to that of king, thus becoming 'King of the Hejaz and of Nejd and its Dependencies'. On 20 May 1927 a treaty was signed at Jiddah between Great Britain and Ibn Sa'ud, by which the former recognized the complete independence of the dominions of the latter. The name of the State was changed to 'The Saudi Arabian Kingdom' by decree of 23 Sept. 1932.

AREA AND POPULATION. Saudi Arabia, which occupies over 70% of the Arabian peninsula, is bounded west by the Red Sea, east by the Gulf and the United Arab Emirates, north by Jordan, Iraq and Kuwait, south by the Yemen Arab Republic, the People's Democratic Republic of Yemen and Oman. The total area is estimated to be 849,400 sq. miles (2·2m. sq. km).

The principal cities of the Western Province (formerly *Hejaz*) are Jiddah (561,104 inhabitants at the 1974 Census; estimate (1986) 1·4m.), Mecca (618,006), Taif (204,857) and Medina (500,000); of the Central Province (formerly *Nejd*) are Riyadh, the national capital (666,840; estimate, 1988, 2m.), Buraidah (184,000), Ha'il (40,502), Uneiza and Al-Kharj; of the Northern Province are Tabouk (99,000), Al-Jawf and Sakaka; of the Eastern Province (formerly *Al-Hasa*) are Dammam (127,844), Hofuf (101,271), Haradh (100,000), Al-Mobarraz (54,325), Al-Khobar (48,817) and Qatif; and of the Southern Province (formerly *Asir*) are Khamis-Mushait (49,581), Najran (47,501), Jisan (32,814) and Abha (155,406). New industrial cities are being built at Jubail and Yanbu on the Gulf. Taif, about 3,800ft above sea-level and some 50 miles from Mecca, is a summer resort.

The total population was (1974 census) 7,012,642, of which 5,128,655 were categorized as settled and 1,883,987 as nomadic. Estimate (1988) 12m.

CLIMATE. A desert climate, with very little rain and none at all from June to Dec. The months May to Sept. are very hot and humid, but winter temperatures are quite pleasant. Riyadh. Jan. 58°F (14·4°C), July 108°F (42°C). Annual rainfall 4" (100 mm). Jiddah. Jan. 73°F (22·8°C), July 87°F (30·6°C). Annual rainfall 3" (81 mm).

KING. Fahd ibn Abdul Aziz, custodian of the two Holy Mosques, succeeded in May 1982, after King Khalid's death. *Crown Prince:* Prince Abdullah ibn Abdul Aziz, First Deputy Prime Minister, Head of the National Guard, brother of the King.

National flag: Green, with the text 'There is no God but Allah and Mohammed is his prophet' in white Arabic script, and beneath this a white sabre.

CONSTITUTION AND GOVERNMENT. The Kingdom has been welded together from Hejaz, Nejd, Asir and Al-Hasa. Riyadh is the political capital and Mecca the religious capital. There is no formal Constitution.

The King has the post of Prime Minister.

First Deputy Prime Minister and Head of the National Guard: Prince Abdullah ibn Abdul Aziz.
Second Deputy Prime Minister and Minister of Defence and Aviation, and Inspector General: Prince Sultan ibn Abdul Aziz.

Public Works and Housing: Prince Miteb ibn Abdul Aziz. *Interior:* Prince Naif ibn Abdul Aziz. *Foreign Affairs:* Prince Saud al Faisal. *Labour and Social Affairs:* Muhammad al-Ali al-Fayiz. *Communications:* Hussein Ibrahim al Mansouri. *Finance and National Economy:* Muhammad Ali Aba'l Khail. *Information:* Ali ibn Hasan al-Shaer. *Industry and Electricity:* Dr Abdul Aziz al Zamil. *Commerce:* Dr Sulaiman Abdul Aziz al Sulaim. *Justice:* Muhammad ibn Jubair. *Education and Acting Higher Education:* Dr Abdul Aziz al Abdullah al Khuwaiter. *Petroleum and Mineral Resources and Planning:* Hisham Nazer. *Haj Affairs, Waqfs:* Abdul Wahhab Ahmad Abdul Wasi. *Municipal and Rural Affairs:* Ibrahim ibn Abdullah al Angari. *Agriculture and Water:* Dr Abdul Rahman ibn Abdul Aziz ibn Hasan al Shaikh. *Health:* Faisal ibn Abdul Aziz al Hejailan. *Posts and Telecommunications:* Dr Alawi Darwish Kayyal. *Without Portfolio:* Fayez Badr. *Pilgrimage and Endowments:* Abdul Wahhab Ahmed Abdul Wasi. There are 6 Ministers of State.

There are provisions for the setting up of certain advisory councils, comprising a consultative Legislative Assembly in Mecca, municipal councils in each of the towns of Mecca, Medina and Jiddah, and village and tribal councils throughout the provinces. The country is divided for administrative purposes into 14 Regions (Emirates).

DEFENCE. The US maintains a Military Mission (with an Air Force element) as do France and Pakistan. Personnel are trained in Saudi Arabia, France, Pakistan, UK and the USA. The UK has training missions with the Army and the Navy.

Army. The Army comprises 2 armoured brigades, 4 mechanized brigades, 1 airborne brigade, 1 Royal Guard regiment, 23 artillery battalions and 1 infantry brigade. Equipment is mainly US or French (M101, M109 and M198 artillery, M113 APCs, M60 tanks, AMX30 tanks. There are surface-to-air batteries with Stinger and Redeye. Six Dauphin helicopters are in service. Total strength of Army (1989) approximately 38,000. There are para-military forces with the Ministry of Interior; Frontier Force (approximately 8,500).

Navy. The Royal Saudi Naval Forces, comprise 4 French-built 2,900 tons frigates armed with Otomat anti-ship missiles, 4 smaller US-built missile frigates, 9 fast missile craft, 3 German-built torpedo craft and 4 US-built coastal minesweepers. Auxiliaries include 2 French-built replenishment tankers each embarking 2 helicopters, 3 ocean tugs and a Royal Yacht. There are numerous minor auxiliaries and boats.

Naval Aviation forces operate 24 Dauphin helicopters, both ship and shore based, and there is a small newly-formed regiment of some 1,200 marines.

The main naval bases are at Jiddah (Red Sea) and Jubail (The Gulf). Naval personnel in 1989 totalled 7,200 including marines.

The Frontier Force operates some 40 inshore patrol craft, 24 hovercraft and over 300 boats of various types.

Air Force. Formed as a small army support unit in 1932, the Air Force has been built up considerably with British and US assistance since 1946. Complete re-equipment began in 1966 and delivery of 45 F-15 Eagles to equip 3 air superiority squadrons was made in 1982–84; they operate in conjunction with 5 E-3A Sentry AWACS aircraft and 8 KC-707 flight refuelling tankers. Current combat units include 3 squadrons of F-5E Tiger II supersonic fighter-bombers and RF-5E Tigereye reconnaissance aircraft, supported by a conversion unit with F-5B/F combat trainers. One squadron has formed with Tornado strike aircraft, of which 48 are on order, plus an air defence unit with the first of 24 Tornado interceptors. Two squadrons of Strikemaster light jet attack/trainers are based at the King Faisal Air Academy, Riyadh, together with 12 Reims/Cessna FR172 piston-engined primary trainers, PC-9 basic trainers, Hawk advanced trainers and Jetstream navigation trainers. Other types in current service include 50 C-130E/H and KC-130H Hercules transports and tankers, 1 Boeing 747 SP, 1 Boeing 747-200, 1 Boeing 737, 3 Boeing 707, 4 CN-235s and 2 JetStar VIP jet transports, more than 60 Agusta-Bell 205, 212 and JetRanger helicopters, 2 Agusta AS-61A-4 VIP transport helicopters and communications aircraft. Personnel (1989), about 16,500.

Air Defence Force. This separate Command was formerly part of the Army, which retains a point air defence capability. In 1989 there were French and Pakistani training missions. Equipment comprises approximately 18 Crotale missile systems, 15 batteries of Improved Hawk surface-to-air missiles, 30 mm Oerlikon and 20 mm Vulcan guns.

National Guard. The National Guard comprises 2 mechanized brigades (trained by the US), 1 ceremonial cavalry squadron. Additionally there are a number of regular and irregular units, the total strength of the National Guard amounting to approximately 56,000 (10,000 active). The National Guard's primary role is the protection of the Royal Family and vital points in the Kingdom. It does not come under command of the Ministry of Defence and Aviation. UK provides small advisory teams to the National Guard in the fields of general training and communications.

INTERNATIONAL RELATIONS

Membership. Saudi Arabia is a member of UN, the Arab League, the Gulf Co-operation Council and OPEC.

ECONOMY

Planning. The fourth 5-year development plan (1985–90) aims to increase manpower by an overall 3·8% and emphasizes industrial growth and economic development.

Budget. In 1986 the financial year became the calendar year. The 1988 budget provided for expenditure of 141,200m. rials and revenue of 105,300m. rials.

There is no public debt.

Currency. The paper *rial* is divided into 100 *halalas*. In March 1990, £1 = 6·17 *rials*; US$1 = 3·77 *rials*.

Banking. The Saudi Arabian Monetary Agency, established in 1953, is the central bank and the government's fiscal agent. There were 637 commercial banks in mid 1987. The Saudi Arabian Agricultural Bank with 70 branches and offices extended 1,019m. rials in credit services to farmers during 1987. In 1985 total deposits in commercial banks were US$111,000m. and total assets were 143,000m. rials.

ENERGY AND NATURAL RESOURCES

Electricity. 49,925m. kwh. was generated by the main electricity companies in 1985. A programme of research and development of solar energy has produced a photovoltaic power system with a capacity in 1988 of 50 kw to provide electricity for 2 villages. Supply 127 and 220 volts; 50 and 60 Hz.

Oil. The first general geologic–geographical survey of Saudi Arabia was completed in 1961 under the joint sponsorship of the Saudi Arabian and US governments but surveying continues. Proven reserves (1988) 169,000m. bbls.

Oil production began in 1938 by Aramco, which is now 100% state-owned and accounts for about 97% of total crude oil production, with Getty and the Arabian Oil Co. accounting for the remainder.

Crude oil production in 1989 was 255m. tonnes. Crude oil exports in 1985 were 1,216m. bbls, of which Aramco provided 97·4%, Arabian Oil 1·94% and Getty Oil 0·6%. 1985 oil exports earned US$30,000m. (95m. for crude) and Aramco earned 98% of this total.

Production comes from 14 major oilfields, mostly in the Eastern Region, the most important of which are Ghawar (believed to be the world's largest oilfield), Abqaiq, Safaniyah (the largest offshore field) and Berri.

New fields have been discovered onshore at Farhah and Assahba and deeper pools offshore at Marjan, Safaniya and Zuluf, and during 1984 117 new wells were drilled and 4 seismic explorations conducted.

In 1981 a pipeline from the eastern oilfields to the Red Sea oil terminal at Yanbu was completed and a link to the Iraqi oilfields was completed in 1985.

In early 1986 there were 5 domestic refineries: Ras Tanura, refining capacity 450,000 bbls per day (Aramco); Riyadh, 120,000 bbls per day, Jiddah, 96,000 bbls per day and Yanbu, 170,000 bbls per day (Petromin); Rasal-Khafji, 13,000 bbls per day (Arabian Oil Co.); as well as 3 joint venture export refineries: Yanbu, 250,000 bbls per day (Petromin/Mobil Oil); Jubail, 250,000 bbls per day (Petromin/Shell Saudi Arabia); Rabigh, 325,000 bbls per day (Petromin/Petrola International). Aramco has added a 300 tonne a day sulphur plant to Ras Tanura and operates a 400 tonnes a day desulphurization plant at Jubail.

Gas. In 1984 production of liquefied natural gas from oilfield associated and dissolved gas was 355,059 bbls per day.

Water Resources. Intensive efforts are under-way to provide adequate supplies of water for urban, industrial, rural and agricultural use. Most investment however has gone into seawater desalination. By early 1985 22 plants in 21 towns had the capacity to produce 509m. cu. metres a day.

Minerals. Commercial production was scheduled to begin in 1988 at Mahd Al-Dahab gold mine. Deposits of iron, phosphate, bauxite, uranium and copper have been found.

Agriculture. Since 1970 the Government has spent substantially on desert reclamation, irrigation schemes, drainage and control of surface water and control of moving sands. Undeveloped land has been distributed to farmers and there are research and extension programmes. Large scale private investment has concentrated on wheat, poultry and dairy production.

Production, 1988 (in 1,000 tonnes): Dates, 517; tomatoes, 465; water melons, 745; wheat, 3,000; barley, 186; grapes, 112; milk, 508; poultry meat, 248; eggs, 455.

Livestock estimates for 1988 include 630,000 cattle, 200,000 camels, 4m. sheep and 2·6m. goats.

Fisheries. Saudi Fisheries, established in 1981, has introduced a wide variety of fish to the domestic market and opened up a thriving export business in shrimps. Annual catch about 10,000 tonnes.

INDUSTRY AND TRADE

Industry. The Government actively encourages the establishment of manufacturing industries in the country. The policy includes the provision of industrial estates and loans covering 50% of capital investment. The Government has also established two industrial poles at Jubail and Yanbu, linked by gas and oil pipelines, to be the focus of heavy industrial development. Both have petrochemical complexes producing ethylene and methanol. In 1988 there were 12 major industries (petrochemical, urea and ammonia fertilizer, steel, gas and plastics) and over 65 support and light manufacturing businesses in operation in Jubail, and 8 heavy industries (natural gas liquids fractionation, refining, petrochemical, lube additives, crude oil and chemical terminals) and 21 light and support industries in operation in Yanbu.

Labour. The expatriate labour force grew by an average of 11·7% a year between 1980 and 1985. The proportion of non-Saudis in the total labour force rose from 28·2% in 1975 to 60% by 1985. In 1988, 95% of the total labour force was employed in the non-oil sector.

Commerce. Exports in 1988 (in 1m. rials) 88,896 of which crude oil, 62%; refined oil, 23%; petro-chemicals, 11%. Total imports (1988) 81,582m. rials. Major export destinations in 1988 included: Japan, USA, Singapore. Major import sources in 1984 included: USA, Japan, UK, Federal Republic of Germany, Italy and France.

Total trade between Saudi Arabia and UK (British Department of Trade returns, in £1,000 sterling):

	1985	*1986*	*1987*	*1988*	*1989*
Imports to UK	483,634	435,930	383,143	614,144	502,416
Exports and re-exports from UK	1,256,081	1,507,062	1,978,440	1,713,423	2,432,941

Tourism. In 1989 there were nearly 774,560 pilgrims to Mecca from abroad.

COMMUNICATIONS

Roads. All the main regions and population centres of the Kingdom are linked by asphalted roads, of which there were 33,576 km in 1987 and 59,226 km of graded, unpaved agricultural roads. An additional 2,021 km of roads were under construction including the Trans-Peninsula Expressway. There are road links with Yemen, Jordan, Kuwait and Qatar, and a causeway link to Bahrain. In 1986 there were 2·25m. passenger cars, 2·25m. commercial vehicles and about 41,000 buses.

Railways. A railway from Riyadh to Dammam on the Gulf (571 km, 1,435 mm gauge) *via* Dhahran and the oilfields Abqaiq, Ithmaniya (near Hofuf) and Haradh was completed in Oct. 1951. A 'dry port' at Riyadh station opened in 1981, and a new 465 km Dammam-Riyadh direct line was opened throughout in 1985. There are plans to extend the line *via* Medina to Jiddah. That section of the Hejaz Railway which is in Saudi Arabian territory is not now in working order, but studies have been initiated to restore the whole line from Damascus to Medina. In 1988 railways carried 121m. passenger-km and 801m. tonne-km.

Aviation. Saudi Arabian Air Lines, a government-owned company operates regular internal air services, and international routes to Africa, the Middle East, Europe and the Far East, as well as special flights for pilgrims. There are 3 major international airports at Jiddah, Dhahran and Riyadh and 20 domestic airports. King Fahd International Airport in Eastern Province is due to be completed in 1990. In 1987, 21m. passengers and 332,000 tonnes of cargo were carried.

Shipping. The ports of Dammam and Jubail on the Gulf and Jiddah, Yanbu and Jizan on the Red Sea had 143 deep-water piers by 1985 and discharged 35·9m. freight tonnes. Aramco operates a deepwater oil terminal at Ras Tanura.

Post and Broadcasting. Number of telephones (1988), 1,099,000. Number of post offices (1988) 603. In 1988 there were (estimate) 3·2m. radio receivers and 3·6m. television receivers.

Newspapers. In 1988 there were 8 daily newspapers in Arabic and 3 in English and 15 weekly or monthly magazines.

JUSTICE, RELIGION, EDUCATION AND WELFARE

Justice. The religious law of Islam is the common law of the land, and is administered by religious courts, at the head of which is a chief judge, who is responsible for the Department of Sharia (legal) Affairs. Sharia courts are concerned primarily with family inheritance and property matters. The Committee for the Settlement of Commercial Disputes is the commercial court. Other specialized courts or committees include one dealing exclusively with labour and employment matters; the Negotiable Instruments Committee, which deals with cases relating to cheques, bills of exchange and promissory notes, and the Board of Grievances, whose preserve is disputes with the government or its agencies and which also has jurisdiction in trademark-infringement cases and is the authority for enforcing foreign court judgements.

Religion. About 85% are Sunni Moslems and 15% Shiites.

Education. Schooling is in three stages, primary, intermediate and secondary which is to prepare older pupils for university; pre-primary schools are being introduced. Education is free in all these stages; monthly scholarships are paid to students in higher education and certain allowances are paid at general education level. Girls' education is administered separately. In 1987 there were 512 pre-primary schools with 60,590 pupils, 4,662 primary schools with 1,460,283 pupils and 90,535 teachers, and 3,526 intermediate/secondary schools with 635,606 students and 43,361 teachers. In 1988 there were 3,526 pupils in 30 special education institutes for mentally retarded and physically handicapped children. In 1986–87 there were 64,888 students in 1,305 schools in the programme to combat illiteracy.

In 1987 there were 27 vocational centres, where 2,820 primary school graduates were instructed in basic trades. There were also 8 technical and 22 commercial secondary schools, taking 11,310 intermediate school graduates, and 2 technical and 3 commercial higher institutes (649 students), 21 more advanced industrial, commercial and agricultural education institutes.

University courses concentrating on science, engineering, agriculture and medicine, but also covering education, commerce and arts, are available at the King Abdul Aziz University, Jiddah, King Saud University, Riyadh and King Faisal University, Dammam and Hofuf. There are two branches of King Saud University at Abha and Qaseem. King Abdul Aziz University had a branch campus at Taif. Specialized engineering studies are available at the King Faud University of Petroleum and Minerals, Dhahran, and Arabic and Sharia law studies at the Islamic University, Medina, Imam Mohammad bin Saud University, Riyadh and the Um-AlQura University, Makkah. There were 113,939 university students (46,355 women) and 5,500 post-graduate students in 1986–87.

Welfare. The Ministry of Health is responsible for medical services, serving both Saudi citizens, foreign residents and pilgrims. In 1988 there were 224 hospitals with 35,797 beds, 2,258 primary health care centres and in 1988, 18,048 doctors, 38,434 nurses and midwives, 8,858 technical assistants. There were also 73 private hospitals (10,244 beds) employing 6,096 doctors. The Jiddah Quarantine Centre, designed by WHO and primarily for pilgrims, can take 2,400 patients.

DIPLOMATIC REPRESENTATIVES

Of Saudi Arabia in Great Britain (30 Belgrave Sq., London, SW1X 8QB)
Ambassador; Sheikh Nasser H. Almanqour, GCVO.

Of Great Britain in Saudi Arabia (PO Box 94351, Riyadh)
Ambassador: Sir Alan Munro, KCMG.

Of Saudi Arabia in the USA (601 New Hampshire Ave., NW, Washington, D.C., 20037)
Ambassador: HRH Prince Bandar bin Sultan.

Of the USA in Saudi Arabia (PO Box 9041, Riyadh)
Ambassador: Charles W. Freeman, Jr.

Of Saudi Arabia to the United Nations
Ambassador: Samir Shihabi.

Further Reading

Anderson, N., *The Kingdom of Saudi Arabia*. (Rev. ed.). London, 1982
Clements, F. A., *Saudi Arabia*. [Bibliography] Oxford and Santa Barbara, 1988
Hajrah, H. H., *Land Distribution in Saudi Arabia*. London, 1982
Holden, D. and Johns, R., *The House of Saud*. London and New York, 1981
Looney, R. E., *Saudi Arabia's Development Potential*. Lexington, 1982
McMaster, B., *The Definitive Guide to Living in Saudi Arabia*. London, 1980
Niblock, T., *State, Society and Economy in Saudi Arabia*. New York, 1981
Presley, J. R., *A Guide to the Saudi Arabian Economy*. London, 1984
Quandt, W. B., *Saudi Arabia in the 1980's: Foreign Policy, Security and Oil*. Washington, 1981
Safran, N., *Saudi Arabia: The Ceaseless Quest for Security*. Harvard Univ. Press, 1985

SENEGAL

Capital: Dakar
Population: 6·98m. (1988)
GNP per capita: US$630 (1988)

République du Sénégal

HISTORY. France established a fort at Saint-Louis in 1659 and later acquired other coastal settlements from the Dutch; the interior was occupied in 1854–65. Senegal became a territory of French West Africa in 1902 and an autonomous state within the French Community on 25 Nov. 1958. On 4 April 1959 Senegal joined with French Sudan to form the Federation of Mali, which achieved independence on 20 June 1960, but on 22 Aug. Senegal withdrew from the Federation and became a separate independent republic. Senegal was a one-Party state from 1966 until 1974, when a pluralist system was re-established. Léopold Sédar Senghor, President since independence, resigned on 31 Dec. 1980 and was succeeded by his Prime Minister, Abdou Diouf. From 1 Feb. 1982 Senegal joined with Gambia to form a Confederation of Senegambia.

AREA AND POPULATION. Senegal is bounded by Mauritania to the north and north-east, Mali to the east, Guinea and Guinea-Bissau to the south and the Atlantic to the west with The Gambia forming an enclave along that shore. The republic has a total area of 196,192 sq. km; the population (census, 1976) 4,907,507 (estimate, 1988) 6,982,000. In 1988 there were 5,200 refugees in Senegal, of whom 5,000 from Guinea-Bissau.

The areas (in sq. km), Census populations and capitals of the 10 regions are:

Region	*sq. km*	*1984 Estimate*	*Capital*	*1985 Estimate*
Dakar	550	1,380,700	Dakar	1,382,000
Diourbel	4,359	501,000	Diourbel	55,307 [1]
Fatick	7,935	506,500	Fatick	...
Kaolack	16,010	741,600	Kaolack	132,400
Kolda	21,011	517,600	Kolda	...
Louga	29,188	493,900	Louga	37,665 [2]
Saint-Louis	44,127	612,100	Saint-Louis	91,500
Tambacounda	57,602	355,000	Tambacounda	29,054 [1]
Thiès	6,601	837,900	Thiès	156,200
Ziguinchor	7,339	361,000	Ziguinchor	79,464 [1]

[1] 1976 [2] 1979.

Ethnic groups are the Wolof (36% of the population), Serer (19%), Fulani (13%), Tukulor (9%), Diola (8%), Malinké (6%), Bambara (6%) and Sarakole (2%).

Vital statistics (1984): Births, 306,500 (birth rate 4·9%); deaths, 116,700 (death rate 1·9%).

CLIMATE. A tropical climate with wet and dry seasons. The rains fall almost exclusively in the hot season, from June to Oct., with high humidity. Dakar. Jan. 72°F (22·2°C), July 82°F (27·8°C). Annual rainfall 22" (541 mm).

CONSTITUTION AND GOVERNMENT. Under the Constitution promulgated on 7 Mar. 1963 (as subsequently amended) there are simultaneous elections by universal adult suffrage for 5-year terms for both the Presidency and for the unicameral 120-member National Assembly; for the latter 60 members are elected in single-member constituencies and 60 by a form of proportional representation.

In the general election of Feb. 1983 the *Parti socialiste* gained 111 seats, the *Parti démocratique sénégalais* 8 seats and the *Rassemblement national démocratique* 1.

On 14 Nov. 1981, President Diouf of Senegal and President Jawara of The Gambia issued a joint communiqué proposing the establishment of a confederation, to be known as Senegambia. Both parliaments ratified the agreement at the end of the year. The instruments of ratification were exchanged in Banjul on 11 Jan. 1982 and the Confederation formally came into existence on 1 Feb.

The agreement stated that each confederal state shall maintain its independence and sovereignty and calls for the integration of the armed security forces, economic and monetary union, co-operation in the fields of communications and external relations, and the establishment of joint institutions (*i.e.* President, Vice President, Council of Ministers, Confederal Parliament). The President of the Confederation would be President Diouf, and the Vice President President Jawara, The Confederal Parliament would have one third Gambian representation and two thirds Senegalese.

President Jawara said in Nov. 1981 that 'the Confederation would not compromise any of the agreements which link The Gambia direct to Britain and the rest of the Commonwealth'.

President of the Republic: Abdou Diouf (took office in Jan. 1981, re-elected 1983 and 1988).

The Council of Ministers was composed as follows in June 1989:

Foreign Affairs: Ibrahima Fall. *Defence:* Medoune Fall. *Interior:* André Sonko. *Economy and Finance:* Serigne Lamine Diop. *Culture:* Moustapha Kâ. *National Education:* Ibrahima Niang. *Higher Education:* Hakhir Thiam. *Rural Development:* Cheikh Abdoul Khadre Cissokho. *Industrial Development and Handicrafts:* Famara Ibrahima Sagna. *Housing and Urban Affairs:* Momodou Abbas Bâ. *Commerce:* Seydina Oumar Sy. *Planning and Co-operation:* Djibo Kâ. *Communications:* Robert Sagna. *Justice, Keeper of the Seals:* Seydou Madani Sy. *Civil Service and Labour:* Moussa N'Doye. *Public Health:* Mme. Therese King. *Social Development:* Ndioro Ndiaye. *Water Resources:* Samba Yella Diop. *Youth and Sports:* Abdoulaye Makhtar Diop. *Equipment:* Alassane Dialy Ndiaye. *Tourism:* Malik Sy.

Ministers-Delegate: Farba Lo *(Relations with National Assembly)*, Fatou Ndongo Dieng *(Emigration)*, Moussa Toure *(Finance and Economy)*, Mbaye Diouf *(Rural Development, Animal Resources)*, Moctar Kebe *(Rural Development, Protection of the Environment)*.

National flag: Three vertical strips of green, yellow, red, with a green star in the centre.

The official language is French.

Local Government. Senegal is divided into 10 *régions*, each with an appointed governor and an elected regional assembly. They are divided into 30 *départements*, each under an appointed *Préfet*, and thence into 99 *arrondissements*.

DEFENCE. There is selective conscription.

Army. The Army had a strength of 8,500 (1989), organized in 5 infantry battalions, 1 engineer, 1 armoured, 1 airborne, 1 commando and 1 artillery battalions, and minor units. Equipment includes about 70 armoured cars. There is also a paramilitary force of gendarmarie and customs.

Navy. The flotilla includes 2 coastal patrol craft, 6 inshore patrol craft, 2 tank landing craft, 2 smaller amphibious craft, and about 6 service craft. Personnel (1989) totalled 700, and bases are at Dakar and Casamance.

Air Force. The Senegal Air Force, formed with French assistance, has 4 Rallye Guerrier and 5 Magister armed trainers and 1 Twin Otter for maritime patrol, 1 Boeing 727 transport, 6 F.27 twin-turboprop transports, 2 Broussard and 1 Cessna 337 liaison aircraft, 2 Puma, 1 Gazelle and 2 Alouette II helicopters, plus 4 Rallye trainers. Personnel (1990) 500.

INTERNATIONAL RELATIONS

Membership. Senegal is a member of UN, OAU and is an ACP state of EEC.

ECONOMY

Planning. The Seventh 4-year Development Plan (1985–89) provided 645,000m. francs CFA for investment in the productive sector, improved infrastructure and for reducing foreign debt.

Budget. The budget for 1987–88 balanced at 337,660m. francs CFA.

Currency. The currency is the *franc* CFA, with a parity value of 50 *francs* CFA to 1 French *franc*.

Banking. The bank of issue is the *Banque Centrale des États de l'Afrique de l'Ouest*. The principal commercial bank is the *Union Sénégalaise de la Banque pour le Commerce et l'Industrie* (established 1961 with assistance from Crédit Lyonnais) in which the Senegalese government has the majority share-holding; also state controlled is the *Banque Nationale de Développement du Sénégal*. There are 3 private banks.

ENERGY AND NATURAL RESOURCES

Electricity. Production (1986) was 737m. kwh. Supply 110 volts; 50 Hz.

Minerals. Production of phosphates (1987) 2,022,300 tonnes. Titanium ores and zirconium are extracted from coastal (sand) deposits. Iron ore deposits amounting to an estimated 980m. tonnes have been located at La Faleme.

Agriculture. Of the total area (19·7m. hectares), 5·35m. were under cultivation, 5·84m. were pasture, 5·45m. were forested and 3·03m. were uncultivated land in 1981. Production, 1989 (in tonnes): Groundnuts for oil, 703,362; groundnuts for consumption, 19,536; cotton, 45,000; sorghum, 594,200; rice paddy, 146,405; maize, 123,327; manioc, 54,885.

Livestock (1988): 3,792,000 sheep, 1·15m. goats, 2,608,000 cattle, 470,000 pigs, 210,000 asses, 8,000 camels and 208,000 horses.

Forestry. There were (1988) 5·9m. hectares of forest representing 31% of the land area. Production (1986) amounted to 4·1m. cu. metres.

Fisheries. The 1986 catch totalled 255,400 tonnes.

INDUSTRY AND TRADE

Industry. Dakar has numerous industrial works. A major ship-repairing complex has been constructed there for vessels of up to 28,000 tonnes. Cement production (1983) 395,300 tonnes; petroleum products, 336,000; groundnut oil, 217,000.

Trade Unions. There are two major unions, the *Union Nationale des Travailleurs Sénégalais* (government-controlled) and the *Conféderation Nationale des Travailleurs Sénégalais* (independent) which broke away from the former in 1969.

Commerce. In 1986 imports totalled 332,929m. francs CFA and exports 214,793m. francs CFA; 30% of imports came from France and 30% of exports went to France. In 1985 petroleum products provided 22% of exports, fisheries 22%, phosphates 10% and cotton fabrics 4%.

Total trade between Senegal and UK (British Department of Trade returns, in £1,000 sterling):

	1985	*1986*	*1987*	*1988*	*1989*
Imports to UK	17,671	13,881	11,307	11,284	6,820
Exports and re-exports from UK	13,514	12,328	11,878	14,840	13,448

Tourism. In 1987, 235,466 tourists visited Senegal.

COMMUNICATIONS

Roads. The length of roads (1989) was 9,971 km of which 3,476 km was bitumenized. In 1984 there were 73,665 passenger cars and 36,144 commercial vehicles.

Railways. There are 4 railway lines: Dakar-Kidira (continuing in Mali), Thiès-Saint-Louis (193 km), Guinguinéo-Kaolack (22 km), and Diourbel-Touba (46 km). Total length (1986), 905 km (metre gauge). In 1986–87 railways carried 800,000 passengers and 1·4m. tonnes of freight.

Aviation. In 1984 230m. passenger-km and 17·4m. tonne-km of freight were flown. There are major airports at Yoff, Saint-Louis, Tambacounda and Ziguinchor.

Shipping. In 1986 the merchant marine numbered 148 vessels of 41,651 DWT. There is a river service on the Senegal from Saint-Louis to Podor (363 km) open throughout the year, and to Kayes (924 km) open from July to Oct. The Senegal River is closed to foreign flags. The Saloum River is navigable as far as Kaolack, the Casamance River as far as Ziguinchor.

Post and Broadcasting. There were, in 1983, 530 post offices. Telephones in 1986 numbered 54,000. In 1985 there were 11 radio stations with 450,000 radio receivers and 2 television stations with 55,000 receivers.

Newspapers. The main daily is *Le Soleil,* circulation (1989) 30,000.

JUSTICE, RELIGION, EDUCATION AND WELFARE

Justice. There are *juges de paix* in each *département* and a court of first instance in each region. Assize courts are situated in Dakar, Kaolack, Saint-Louis and Ziguinchor, while the Court of Appeal resides in Dakar.

Religion. The population (1980) was 91% Moslem, 6% Christian (mainly Roman Catholic) and 3% animist.

Education. In 1986-87 there were 610,946 pupils in elementary schools, 102,771 pupils in middle schools (general and technical) and 34,098 pupils in secondary schools (general, 30,005; technical, 4,093). In 1986-87 there were 12,028 teachers in private and public schools. The University in Dakar, established on 24 Feb. 1957, had 15,324 students in 1987. A second university was being built (1985) at St Louis.

Health. In 1978 there were 44 hospitals with 7,092 beds; and in 1981, 449 doctors, 70 dentists, 139 pharmacists, 326 midwives and 1,766 state nursing personnel.

DIPLOMATIC REPRESENTATIVES

Of Senegal in Great Britain (11 Phillimore Gdns., London, W8 7QG)
Ambassador: Gen. Idrissa Fall, GCVO, MBE (accredited 1 Nov. 1984)

Of Great Britain in Senegal (20 Rue du Docteur Guillet, Dakar)
Ambassador: John Macrae, CMG.

Of Senegal in the USA (2112 Wyoming Ave., NW, Washington, D.C., 20008)
Ambassador: Ibra Deguene Ka.

Of the USA in Senegal (Ave. Jean XXIII, Dakar)
Ambassador: George E. Moose.

Of Senegal to the United Nations
Ambassador: Absa Claude Diallo.

Further Reading

Crowder, M., *Senegal: A Study in French Assimilation.* OUP, 1962
Gellar, S., *Senegal.* Boulder, 1982.—*Senegal: An African Nation between Islam and the West.* Aldershot, 1983
Samb, M. (ed.) *Spotlight on Senegal.* Dakar, 1972

SEYCHELLES

Capital: Victoria
Population: 67,305 (1988)
GNP per capita: US$3,590 (1988)

HISTORY. The islands were first colonized by the French in 1756, in order to establish plantations of spices to compete with the Dutch monopoly. They were captured by the English in 1794 and incorporated as a dependency of Mauritius in 1814. In Nov. 1903 the Seychelles archipelago became a separate colony. Internal self-government was achieved on 1 Oct. 1975 and independence as a republic within the Commonwealth on 29 June 1976. The first President, James Mancham, was deposed in a *coup* on 5 June 1977 and replaced by his Prime Minister.

AREA AND POPULATION. The Seychelles consists of 115 islands and islets in the Indian ocean, north of Madagascar, with a combined area of 175 sq. miles (455 sq. km) within two distinct groups. The Mahé or Granitic group of 41 islands cover 92 sq. miles (239 sq. km); the principal island is Mahé, with 59 sq. miles (153 sq. km) and 59,500 inhabitants at the 1987 census, the other inhabited islands of the group being Praslin, La Digue, Silhouette, Fregate and North, which together have 7,100 inhabitants.

The Outer or Coralline group comprises 74 islands spread over a wide area of ocean between the Mahé group and Madagascar, with a total land area of 83 sq. miles (214 sq. km) and a population of about 400. The main islands are the Amirante Isles (including Desroches, Poivre, Daros and Alphonse), Coetivy Island and Platte Island, all lying south of the Mahé group; the Farquhar, St Pierre and Providence Islands, north of Madagascar; and Aldabra, Astove, Assumption and the Cosmoledo Islands, about 1,000 km south-west of the Mahé group. Aldabra (whose lagoon covers 55 sq. miles), Farquhar and Desroches were transferred to the new British Indian Ocean Territory in 1965, but were returned by Britain to the Seychelles on the latter's independence in 1976. Population (1988, estimate) 67,305. Vital statistics (1989): Births, 1,600; deaths, 563.

The official languages are Creole, English and French but 95% of the population speak Creole.

CLIMATE. Though close to the equator, the climate is tropical. The hot, wet season is from Dec. to May, when conditions are humid, but south-east trades bring cooler conditions from June to Nov. Temperatures are high throughout the year, but the islands lie outside the cyclone belt. Victoria. Jan. 80°F (26·7°C), July 78°F (25·6°C). Annual rainfall 95" (2,375 mm).

CONSTITUTION AND GOVERNMENT. A new Constitution came into force on 5 June 1979, under which the Seychelles People's Progressive Front is the sole legal Party and nominates all candidates for election. There is a unicameral People's Assembly comprising 23 members elected for 5 years with 2 further nominated members. There is an Executive President directly elected for a 5-year term, who nominates and leads a Council of Ministers.

President: France Albert René (re-elected for a 3rd, 5-year term June 1989).

Education: Simon Testa. *Information, Culture and Sport:* Sylvette Frichot. *Tourism and Transport:* Jacques Hodoul. *Finance:* James Michel. *Health:* Ralph Adam. *Social Services:* William Herminie. *Agriculture and Fisheries:* Jeremy Bonnelame. *Planning and External Relations:* Danielle De St Jorre. *Manpower:* Joseph Belmont. *Community Development:* Esme Jumeau.

National flag: Divided horizontally red over green by a wavy white stripe, with red of double width.

DEFENCE. The Defence Force comprises all services. Personnel (1989) 1,300 organized in 1 infantry battalion, 2 artillery troops and a marine group, 200 strong, based at Port Victoria, which operates 5 fast inshore patrol craft and a tank landing craft. The Air Wing with 2 Islanders, 1 Defender and 1 Merlin IIB for transport and 2 Chetak helicopters. There is also a People's Militia (5,000).

INTERNATIONAL RELATIONS

Membership. Seychelles is a member of UN, the Commonwealth, OAU, Non-Aligned Movement and is an ACP state of EEC.

ECONOMY

Budget, in 1m. rupees, for calendar years:

	1985	*1986*	*1987*	*1988*
Recurrent revenue	476·4	515·6	639·2	763·8
Recurrent expenditure	543·6	591·1	641·8	744·0

Currency. The currency is the Seychelles *rupee* divided into 100 cents. In March 1990, £1 = 8·95 *rupees;* US$1 = 5·46 *rupees.*

Banking. Central Bank of Seychelles, Development Bank of Seychelles and Seychelles Savings Bank have head offices and Barclays Bank, Standard Bank, Bank of Credit and Commerce International, Banque Francaise Commerçiale, Habib Bank and Bank of Baroda, have branches in Victoria and Mahé.

ENERGY AND NATURAL RESOURCES

Electricity. Production (1988) 83·4m. kwh.

Agriculture. Coconuts are the main cash crop (production, 1988, 19,000 tonnes). Other main crops produced for export are cinnamon bark (1988, 225 tonnes) and copra (1988, 1,138 tonnes). Tea production, 1988, 106 tonnes. Crops grown for local consumption include cassava, sweet potatoes, yams, sugar-cane, bananas and vegetables. The staple food crop, rice, is imported.

Livestock (1988): Cattle, 2,000; pigs, 15,000; goats, 4,000.

Fisheries. The fishing industry is being expanded for home consumption and export. Catch (1988) 4,344 tonnes.

INDUSTRY AND TRADE

Industry. Local industry is expanding, the largest development in recent years being the brewery (output, 1988, 5,007,000 litres). Other main activities include production of soft drinks (4,696,000 litres in 1988), cigarettes (61m. in 1988) and paints, dairy, processing of cinnamon and coconuts.

Commerce. Total trade, in rupees, for calendar years:

	1985	*1986*	*1987*	*1988*
Imports (less re-exports)	704,700,000	652,000,000	633,900,000	823,000,000
Domestic exports	21,900,000	13,900,000	35,800,000	73,900,000

Principal imports (1987): Manufactured goods, Rs 197·8m.; food, beverages and tobacco, Rs 134·6m.; petroleum products, Rs 94·9m., machinery and transport equipment, Rs 156·3m. mainly (1985) from UK (15%), Italy (10%), France (9%) and the Republic of South Africa (9%). Principal exports (1987): Copra, Rs 3·2m.; fresh and frozen fish, Rs 7·9m.; cinnamon bark, Rs 1·6m.; canned tuna, Rs 20·8m. mainly (1985) to Pakistan (35%), Japan (31%) and Réunion (12%).

Total trade between Seychelles and UK (British Department of Trade returns, in £1,000 sterling):

	1986	*1987*	*1988*	*1989*
Imports to UK	938	884	1,297	993
Exports and re-exports from UK	9,639	10,770	10,478	10,741

Tourism. Visitor numbers declined to 55,867 in 1983 but were 86,000 in 1989.

COMMUNICATIONS

Roads. There is a good system of tarmac (187 km) and earth roads (82 km) in Mahé; extensive roadmaking is being undertaken.

Aviation. Air Seychelles operates 4 services a week between Europe and Seychelles, regular services from Mahé to Praslin and Fregate Islands and a weekly service to Singapore. British Airways operates 2 services a week between London, Bahrain, Mauritius and Seychelles. Air France operates 3 services a week. Kenya Airways operates a service twice a week. Aeroflot has 2 flights a month. Lesotho and Adria Airways operate weekly flights. In 1988 aircraft movements were 1,937; passenger movements, 396,000 (including domestic flights); freight loaded, 356 tonnes, unloaded, 1,483 tonnes.

Shipping. The main port is Victoria. Shipping (1988), goods unloaded, 279,900 tonnes, goods loaded, 8,700 tonnes. There are regular cargo vessels from Australia and the Far East, South Africa and Europe. The vessel *Cinq Juin* travels to and from Mauritius and visits the outlying islands.

Post and Broadcasting. Services operated by Cable & Wireless Ltd provide telegraphic communications with all parts of the world by satellite. Telephones in Jan. 1983 numbered 4,512. There are 2 radio stations and (1983) 18,000 receivers. There were 3,500 television sets in 1987 and Radio Television Seychelles runs radio and television services in Creole, English and French.

Cinema. In 1989 there was 1 cinema with seating capacity of 200.

Newspaper. In 1990 there was 1 daily newspaper.

JUSTICE, RELIGION, EDUCATION AND WELFARE

Justice. The police force numbered 492 all ranks and 69 special constabulary.

Religion. 90% of the inhabitants are Roman Catholic and 8% Anglican.

Education. Equality of educational opportunity exists for all children for a minimum of 9 years. In 1989 there were 14,484 pupils and 766 teachers in primary schools, 2,576 pupils and 153 teachers in secondary schools and 1,476 students and 176 teachers in the Polytechnic. In 1983, a total of 239 students were undergoing training overseas, mainly in the UK; 153 were in university, 39 teacher-training and 6 nursing.

Health. In 1987 there were 57 doctors, 9 dentists, 275 nurses and 373 hospital beds.

DIPLOMATIC REPRESENTATIVES

Of Seychelles in Great Britain (111 Baker St., London, W1M 1FE)
Acting High Commissioner: Sylvestre Radegonde.

Of Great Britain in Seychelles (Victoria Hse., Victoria, Mahé)
High Commissioner: G. W. P. Hart, OBE.

Of Seychelles in the USA and to the United Nations
Ambassador: (Vacant).

Of the USA in Seychelles (Victoria Hse., Victoria, Mahé)
Ambassador: James B. Moran.

Further Reading

Statistical Information: Information Office, 52 Kingsgate House, Victoria, Mahé.
Agricultural Survey 1980. Government Printer
Seychelles in Figures. Statistics Division, Mahé, 1986
Benedict, M. and Benedict, B., *Men, Women and Money in Seychelles.* Univ. of California Press, 1983
Franda, M., *The Seychelles: Unquiet Islands*. Boulder, 1982
Lionnet, G., *The Seychelles*. Newton Abbot, 1972
Mancham, J. R., *Paradise Raped: Life, Love and Power in the Seychelles*. London, 1983

SIERRA LEONE

Capital: Freetown
Population: 3·88m. (1988)
GNP per capita: US$240 (1988)

HISTORY. The Colony of Sierra Leone originated in the sale and cession, in 1787, by native chiefs to English settlers, of a piece of land intended as a home for natives of Africa who were waifs in London, and later it was used as a settlement for Africans rescued from slave-ships. The hinterland was declared a British protectorate on 21 Aug. 1896. Sierra Leone became independent as a member state of the Commonwealth on 27 April 1961, and a republic on 19 April 1971.

AREA AND POPULATION. Sierra Leone is bounded on the north-west, north and north-east by the Republic of Guinea, on the south-east by Liberia and on the south-west by the Atlantic ocean. The coastline extends from the boundary of the Republic of Guinea to the north of the mouth of the Great Scarcies River to the boundary of Liberia at the mouth of the Mano River, a distance of about 212 miles (341 km). The area of Sierra Leone is 27,925 sq. miles (73,326 sq. km). Population (census 1985), 3,517,530, of whom about 2,000 are Europeans, 3,500 Asiatics and 30,000 non-native Africans. Estimate (1988) 3,875,000. The capital is Freetown, with 469,776 inhabitants.

Vital statistics (1986); Live births, 75,862; deaths, 6,272.

Sierra Leone is divided into 3 provinces and the Western Area:

	Sq. km	*Census 1985*	*Capital*	*Estimate 1988*
Western Area	557	554,243	Freetown	469,776
Southern province	19,694	740,510	Bo	26,000
Eastern province	15,553	960,551	Kenema	13,000
Northern province	35,936	1,262,226	Makeni	12,000

The principal peoples are the Mendes (34% of the total) in the south, the Temnes (31%) in the north and centre, the Konos, Fulanis, Bulloms, Korankos, Limbas and Kissis.

CLIMATE. A tropical climate, with marked wet and dry seasons and high temperatures throughout the year. The rainy season lasts from about April to Nov., when humidity can be very high. Thunderstorms are common from April to June and in Sept. and Oct. Rainfall is particularly heavy at Freetown because of the effect of neighbouring relief. Freetown. Jan. 80°F (26·7°C), July 78°F (25·6°C). Annual rainfall 135" (3,434 mm).

CONSTITUTION AND GOVERNMENT. For earlier Constitutional history *see* THE STATESMAN'S YEAR-BOOK 1978–79, p. 1046. Following a referendum in June 1978, a new Constitution was instituted under which the ruling All People's Congress (APC) became the sole legal Party. The 124-member Parliament comprises 105 members directly elected for a 5-year term (latest elections, 31 May 1986), together with 12 Paramount Chiefs representing the 12 districts and 7 members appointed by the President. The President is elected for a 7-year term by the National Delegates' Conference of the APC; he appoints and leads a Council of Ministers.

President: Maj.-Gen. Dr Joseph Saidu Momoh.
First Vice-President, Minister of Lands, Housing and Planning: Abu B. Kamara.
Finance: Hassan Ghassay Kanu. *Foreign Affairs:* Abdul Karim Koroma.

National flag: Three horizontal stripes of green, white, blue.

Local Government. The provinces are administered through the Ministry of Internal Affairs and divided into 148 Chiefdoms, each under the control of a Paramount

Chief and Council of Elders known as the Tribal Authorities, who are responsible for the maintenance of law and order and for the administration of justice (except for serious crimes). All of these Chiefdoms have been organized into local government units, empowered to raise and disburse funds for the development of the Chiefdom concerned.

DEFENCE

Army. The Army consists of 2 infantry battalions, 2 artillery batteries and 1 engineer squadron. Strength (1989), 3,000 officers and men.

Navy. The small flotilla comprises 2 *ex*-Chinese fast inshore patrol craft, 3 very small inshore craft and 3 landing craft. Personnel in 1989 totalled 150.

Air Force. The Air Wing of the Defence Force appears to be inactive, although the Defence Ministry operates 1 BO 105 and 2 AS.355 Ecureuil helicopters carrying civil registrations. Personnel, about 30.

INTERNATIONAL RELATIONS

Membership. Sierra Leone is a member of UN, OAU, ECOWAS, the Commonwealth, the Mano River Union and is an ACP state of EEC.

ECONOMY

Budget. Revenue and expenditure (in 1,000 leone) for years ending 30 June:

	1985–86	*1986–87*	*1987–88*	*1988–89*
Revenue	375,500	1,254,500	1,990,400	3,500,000
Expenditure	566,400	1,828,300	3,960,800	6,630,000

Currency. The Bank of Sierra Leone, which was established on 4 Aug. 1964, is responsible for providing the currency in the country. It introduced on 4 Aug. 1964 a decimal currency, the *leone* and the *cent*. The paper currency consists of 1, 2, 5, 10 and 20 *leone* and 50-*cent* notes; the coinage of 1, 5, 10, 20 and 50 *cents*.

At 30 June 1982 total Sierra Leone notes and coins in circulation was Le. 91·75m. In March 1990, £1 = 193·30 *leone*; US$1 = 117·94 *leone*.

Banking. The Standard Chartered Bank Sierra Leone, the National Commercial Bank, International Bank of Credit and Commerce, International Bank of Trade and Industry and Barclays Bank Sierra Leone have their headquarters at Freetown; the Standard Chartered Bank has 14, Barclays Bank 12 and the National Commercial Bank, 8 branches and agencies.

The Post Office Savings Bank had 94,910 depositors with total credit balance of nearly Le. 3,455,469 in 1983.

ENERGY AND NATURAL RESOURCES

Electricity. Production (1986) 85m. kwh. Supply 230 volts; 50 Hz.

Minerals. The chief minerals mined are diamonds (314,000 carats, 1987), bauxite (1·3m. tonnes), and rutile (113,900 tonnes). Molybdenite is being prospected.

Agriculture. In the western area farming is largely confined to the production of cassava and garden crops, such as maize, vegetables and mangoes, for local consumption. In the regions the principal products include rice, which is the staple food of the country, cassava, groundnuts and export crops such as palm-kernels, cocoa beans, coffee, ginger and piassava. Cattle production is important in the northern part of the country, and most of the poultry, eggs and pork are produced in the Western Area. Production (1988, in 1,000 tonnes): Rice, 430; cassava, 116; palm oil, 44; palm kernels, 30; coffee, 9; cocoa, 11.

Livestock (1988): Cattle, 330,000; goats, 180,000; sheep, 330,000; chickens, 6m.

Fisheries. The estimated tonnage of catch of all species of fish during 1986 was 53,000 tonnes.

INDUSTRY AND TRADE

Industry. Four pioneer oil-mills for the expressing of palm-oil are operated by the

Sierra Leone Produce Marketing Board. Government also operates 4 rice-mills, and there are a number of privately owned mills. At Kenema the Government Forest Industries Corporation produces sawn timber, joinery products (including prefabricated buildings) and high-class furniture. In addition, there is a smaller privately owned saw-mill at Panguma, Kenema and Hangha, and several small furniture workshops are used internally. Village industries include fishing, fish curing and smoking, weaving and hand methods of expressing palm-oil and cracking palm kernels.

Labour. A large proportion of the population is engaged in agriculture and about 125,000 workers are in wage-earning employment. The number of workers in establishments employing 6 or more persons was 64,092 in 1982, distributed as follows: Services, 24,142; mining and quarrying, 6,170; transport, storage and communications, 4,814; construction, 9,721; commerce, 6,870; manufacturing, 9,407; agriculture, forestry and fishing, 5,834; electricity and water services, 24,142.

Commerce. Total trade (in 1,000 leone) for 1988: Imports, 5,215; exports, 3,317.

Total trade between Sierra Leone and UK (British Department of Trade returns, in £1,000 sterling):

	1985	*1986*	*1987*	*1988*	*1989*
Imports to UK	17,435	11,599	12,679	14,462	15,899
Exports and re-exports from UK	23,620	17,403	16,221	14,256	20,402

Tourism. Tourism is being developed and is a major growth industry. In 1986 there were 194,000 tourists.

COMMUNICATIONS

Roads. There were (1978) about 7,500 miles of main roads, of which 1,000 miles are surfaced with bitumen. A programme to improve the road system was initiated in 1988.

Motor vehicles licensed in 1987, passenger cars, 25,000; commercial vehicles, 18,200.

Railways. The government railway closed in 1974, though in 1987 there were plans to resume operations, and an 84-km mineral line of 1,067-mm gauge connecting Marampa with the port of Pepel has been rehabilitated.

Aviation. Freetown Airport (Lungi), situated north of Freetown in the Port Loko District, is the only international airport in Sierra Leone.

The airport is served by Sierra Leone Airlines, Ghana/Nigeria Airways, Union de Transport Aériens, KLM, Air Afrique and Aeroflot.

Sierra Leone Airlines provide domestic flights daily (except Sundays) from Hastings (14 miles from Freetown) to Gbangbatoke, Bo, Kenema, Yengema; twice weekly to Bonthe, and occasional charter flights to Marampa and Port Loko. Domestic air taxi services also operate.

Shipping. During 1986 the total imports handled by the port of Freetown amounted to 1,990 tonnes and exports 990 tonnes.

Bonthe-Sherbro, 80 miles south of Freetown, is used for the shipment of rutile and bauxite. Pepel lies some 12 miles from Freetown and exports iron ore.

Post and Broadcasting. Number of telephones (1981) 220,000. Telegraphic facilities are provided at 58 offices.

There were (1983) 37 post offices and 76 postal agencies.

The number of private wireless-licence holders (1986, estimate) was 820,000 and 31,000 television sets.

Newspapers. In 1987 there was one daily newspaper with a circulation of 12,000.

JUSTICE, RELIGION, EDUCATION AND WELFARE

Justice. The High Court has jurisdiction in civil and criminal matters. Subordinate courts are held by magistrates in the various districts. Native Courts, headed by court Chairmen, apply native law and custom under a criminal and civil jurisdiction. Appeals from the decisions of magistrates' courts are heard by the High Court.

Appeals from the decisions of the High Court are heard by the Sierra Leone Court of Appeal. Appeal lies from the Sierra Leone Court of Appeal to the Supreme Court which is the highest court.

Religion. The Moslem community was estimated to comprise 39% of the population in 1980, while 52% followed traditional tribal religions; Protestants were 6% and Roman Catholics 2% of the total. The Temne people are mainly Moslem and the Mende chiefly animists. Spiritualist churches were growing in 1985.

Education (1984). There were over 1,267 registered primary schools; total enrolment (1982) 276,911. Primary education is partially free but not compulsory though parents and guardians are urged to send their children and wards to school. School attendance varies considerably in different parts of the country. There were (1984) 184 secondary schools with (1982) 66,464 pupils; 71 of these schools are fully assisted by the Government. Technical education was provided in 4 technical institutes, 2 trade centres and in the technical training establishments of the mining companies. There is also a rural institute.

Fourah Bay College (1,400 students) and Njala University College are the 2 constituent colleges of the University of Sierra Leone. The Institute of Education, which is part of the University, is now responsible for teacher education, educational research and curriculum development in the country.

There is a paramedical school at Bo in the Southern region.

Health (1984). In the Western Area there are 13 government hospitals (1,108 beds and 217 cots), including a maternity hospital, a children's hospital and an infectious diseases hospital near Freetown. There are 6 government health centres in the Western Area. Three private hospitals are located in Freetown with 108 beds. A mental hospital at Kissy has accommodation for 224 patients. In the provinces there are 14 government hospitals, 6 hospitals associated with mining companies and 7 mission hospitals. There is a school of nursing in Freetown. There are 156 government dispensaries and health treatment centres and two military hospitals with 124 beds.

DIPLOMATIC REPRESENTATIVES

Of Sierra Leone in Great Britain (33 Portland Pl., London, W1N 3AG)
High Commissioner: Caleb Aubee.

Of Great Britain in Sierra Leone (Standard Chartered Bank of Sierra Leone Ltd Bldg., Lightfoot Boston St., Freetown)
High Commissioner: D. W. Partridge, CMG.

Of Sierra Leone in the USA (1701 19th St., NW, Washington, D.C., 20009)
Ambassador: Dr George Carew.

Of the USA in Sierra Leone (Corner Walpole and Siaka Stevens St., Freetown)
Ambassador: Johnny Young.

Of Sierra Leone to the United Nations
Ambassador: Dr Thomas Kargbo.

Further Reading

Atlas of Sierra Leone. Ed. Survey and Lands Dept. Freetown, 1953
Background to Sierra Leone. Freetown, 1980
Cole, B. P., *Sierra Leone Directory of Commerce, Industry and Tourism.* 1985
Fyfe, C., *A History of Sierra Leone.* OUP, 1962.—Fyfe, C. and Jones, E. (ed.) *Freetown.* Sierra Leone Univ. Press and OUP, 1968
Fyfe, C. N. and Jones, E. D., *A Krio–English Dictionary.* OUP and Sierra Leone Univ. Press, 1980
Kup, A. P., *Sierra Leone.* Newton Abbot, 1975
Porter, A. T., *Creoledom: A Study in the Development of Freetown Society.* OUP, 1963
Riley, S. P., *Sierra Leone.* [Bibliography] Oxford and Santa Barbara, 1989

REPUBLIC OF SINGAPORE

Population: 2·65m. (1988)
GNP per capita: US$8,782 (1988)

HISTORY. For the early history of the settlement (1819) and colony (1867) *see* THE STATESMAN'S YEAR-BOOK, 1959, pp. 246 f.

By an agreement entered into between the Governments of Malaysia and of the State of Singapore on 7 Aug. 1965, effective on 9 Aug. 1965, Singapore ceased to be one of the 14 states of the Federation of Malaysia and became an independent sovereign state. On 22 Dec. 1965 it became a republic. The separation was ratified by the Constitution and Malaysia (Singapore Amendment) Act of the Malaysian Parliament on 9 Aug. The 2 governments agreed to enter into a treaty on external defence and mutual assistance. The Singapore Government retains its executive authority and legislative powers under its State Constitution and took over the powers of the Malaysian Government under the Malaysian Constitution in Singapore. The sovereignty and jurisdiction of the head of the Malaysian State was transferred to the Singapore Government. Civil servants working in Singapore for the Federal Departments became Singapore civil servants. Singapore citizens ceased to be Malaysian citizens.

Singapore accepted responsibility for international agreements entered into by the Malaysian Government on its behalf.

AREA AND POPULATION. The Republic of Singapore consists of Singapore Island itself, and some 58 islets.

Singapore Island is situated off the southern extremity of the Malay peninsula, to which it is joined by a 1,056-metre causeway carrying a road, railway and water pipeline. The Straits of Johore between the island and the mainland are about three-quarters of a mile wide. The island is some 26·1 miles (42 km) in length and 14·3 miles (23 km) in breadth, and about 240·4 sq. miles (625·6 sq. km) in area, including some 58 adjacent islets, 20 of which are inhabited.

Census of population (1980): 1,856,237 Chinese, 351,508 Malays, 154,632 Indians and 51,568 others; total 2,413,945. Estimate (June 1988), 2,011,300 Chinese, 401,200 Malays, 171,800 Indians and 62,800 others; total 2,647,100.

Report on the Census of Population 1980. Dept. of Statistics, Singapore, 1980

CLIMATE. The climate is equatorial, with uniformly high temperatures and no defined wet or dry season, rain being plentiful throughout the year, especially from Nov. to Jan., generally the cooler months. Jan. 78·1°F (25·6°C), July 80·8°F (27·1°C). Annual rainfall 102·3" (2,599 mm).

CONSTITUTION AND GOVERNMENT. By a constitutional amendment the name of the state was changed to 'Republic of Singapore', the head of state was named 'President of Singapore' and the legislative assembly was renamed 'Parliament'.

Parliament is unicameral consisting of 81 members, elected by secret ballot from single-member and group representation constituencies and 1 non-constituency member of Parliament, and is presided over by a Speaker, chosen by Parliament from its own members who are neither ministers nor parliamentary secretaries or from among persons who are not members of Parliament but who are qualified for election as members of Parliament. In the latter case, the Speaker has no vote. The present Speaker is an elected Member of Parliament. With the customary exception of those serving criminal sentences, all citizens over 21 are eligible to vote irrespective of sex, race, education or property qualification. Voting in an election is compulsory. For the general election held on 3 Sept. 1988, Singapore was divided into 55 electoral divisions, of which 42 were single-member constituencies and 13 were group representation constituencies (GRC). Each GRC returned 3 Members of Parliament, one of whom must be from the Malay community, the Indian and other minority communities. There is a common roll without communal electorates. Citizenship is acquired by birth and descent; it can also be acquired by registration or by naturalization.

A Presidential Council for minority rights was established under Part IVA of the Constitution enacted on 9 Jan. 1970. The general function of the Council is to consider and report on matters affecting persons of any racial or religious community in Singapore as referred to it by Parliament or the Government. The Council will draw attention to any bill or subsidiary legislation which in its opinion is a differentiating measure.

Parliament is composed of 80 People's Action Party members, 1 Singapore Social Democratic Party member and 1 non-constituency member of Parliament from the Workers' Party.

President of Singapore: Wee Kim Wee (re-elected for a second term, Sept. 1989).

The People's Action Party Cabinet at Nov. 1989 was composed as follows:
Prime Minister: Lee Kuan Yew.

First Deputy Prime Minister and Minister for Defence: Goh Chok Tong. *Second Deputy Prime Minister:* Ong Teng Cheong. *National Development:* S. Dhanabalan. *Education:* Dr Tony Tan Keng Yam. *Environment:* Dr Ahmad Mattar. *Communications and Information, Second Minister for Defence (Policy):* Dr Yeo Ning Hong. *Law and Home Affairs:* S. Jayakumar. *Finance:* Dr Richard Hu Tsu Tau. *Labour:* Lee Yock Suan. *Foreign Affairs and Community Development:* Wong Kan Seng. *Trade and Industry and Second Minister for Defence (Services):* Brig.-Gen. Lee Hsien Loong. *Acting Minister for Health:* Dr Yeo Cheow Tong.

There are 7 Ministers of State.

National flag: Horizontally red over white, charged in the upper left canton with a crescent and a circle of 5 stars, all in white.

Malay, Chinese (Mandarin), Tamil and English are the official languages; Malay is the national language and English is the language of administration.

DEFENCE. The Ministry of Defence is responsible for national defence and security through the promotion of defence consciousness among the population, the development of military and the command and control of the armed forces. It comprises 5 major divisions, *i.e.*, the general staff, manpower, logistic, security and intelligence and finance divisions. Compulsory military service in peace-time for all male citizens and permanent residents was introduced in 1967. Periods of service are officers/n.c.o.s. 30 months, other ranks 24 months. Reserve liability is to 40 for men, 50 for officers.

Singapore also concluded a Five-Power Defence Agreement with Malaysia, UK, Australia and New Zealand.

Army. The Army consists of the 1st and 2nd People's Defence Force (PDF) Commando and 3 divisions: The 3rd (Tiger) division, the 6th (Cobra) division and the 9th (Panther) division, the latter 2 being reservist formations. Standard infantry weapons are the SAR-80 assault rifle, AR-15 (M-16) rifle, Ultimax 100 light machine gun, 60 mm and 81 mm mortars, 84 mm Carl Gustav anti-tank guns and the Jeep-mounted 106 mm recoilless guns. Most of these weapons and the ammunition are manufactured locally. Strength (1989) 45,000 (including 30,000 conscripts) and 170,000 reserves. Paramilitary forces number 37,500.

Navy. The small, relatively modern Navy operates 2 fast missile corvettes, 6 German-designed fast missile craft, 20 inshore patrol craft, 2 old *ex*-US coastal minesweepers, 6 *ex*-US tank landing ships and 10 small landing craft. A further 4 missile corvettes are under construction in Singapore. Naval personnel number 4,500 of whom 1,800 are conscripts and the naval base is on Pulau Brani.

The Marine Police operates some 60 patrol boats, some armed.

Air Defence Command. The formation of an Air Defence Command began in 1968. The Republic of Singapore Air Force now has 2 squadrons of F-5E supersonic fighters supported by 2-seat F-5Fs; 4 fighter-bomber squadrons equipped with A-4S Skyhawks, supported by TA-4S two-seat trainers; 1 squadron of Hawker Hunter jet fighters and reconnaissance-fighters, supported by Hunter 2-seat trainers; a squadron of Strikemaster armed trainers; a radar unit, anti-aircraft guns and Bloodhound, Rapier and Hawk surface-to-air missile squadrons; a transport squadron of C-130 Hercules (including 4 equipped as flight refuelling tankers); a squadron of Skyvans equipped for search and rescue; a squadron of Bell UH-1s and AS 332M Super Pumas helicopters; and training units equipped with SF.260MS piston-engined basic trainers, a fleet of new-generation trainers, the SIAI-Marchetti S.211 jets, AS 350 Ecureuil helicopters, plus four E-2C Hawkeye AWACS aircraft. Eight F-16 Fighting Falcons will enter service in mid-1989. Personnel strength (1989) about 6,000.

INTERNATIONAL RELATIONS

Membership. Singapore is a member of UN, the Commonwealth, the Colombo Plan and ASEAN.

ECONOMY

Planning. The GNP in 1988, at current cost was S$49,864·5m., an increase of 3·9% over 1987.

Budget. Public revenue and expenditure for financial years (in S$1m.):

	1985	*1986*	*1987*	*1988*
Revenue	10,829·4	10,970·4	10,470·9	13,775·9
Expenditure [1]	6,678·3	6,281·9	8,465·9	7,202·3

[1] Payments from Consolidated Revenue Account.

Currency. The *Singapore dollar* (S$) is divided in 100 *cents*. Gross circulation in Dec. 1988 was S$6,720·17m. In March 1990, £1 = 3·08 *dollars*; US$1 = 1·88 dollars.

Banking. The functions of the Commissioner of Banking have been assumed from 1 Jan. 1971 by the Monetary Authority of Singapore, which performs all the functions normally associated with a central bank, except the issuing of currency which is the responsibility of the Board of Commissioner of Currency.

The Development Bank of Singapore was established as a fully licensed bank in 1968, and is the largest local bank in terms of assets. Primarily it provides long-term financing of manufacturing and other industries. At 31 Dec. 1988 it had a paid up capital of S$419·1m. and shareholders' funds amounting to S$2,495·3m.

There were 134 commercial banks with 408 banking offices operating in Singapore in 1988. The total assets/liabilities amounted to S$96,400m. as at Dec. 1988. Total deposits of non-bank customers amounted to S$42,500m. while loans and advances including bills financing, totalled S$41,800m.

There were 64 merchant banks operating in Singapore at 31 Dec. 1988. Of these, 63 had an Asian Currency Unit each and were engaged actively in Asian dollars transactions. Their main functions included underwriting, portfolio fund management, financial advisory services and loan syndication.

In Dec. 1988, the Singapore Post Office Savings Bank had 3,454,705 savings accounts and a total deposit balance of all accounts of S$12,140m.

Weights and Measures. The metric system or the International System of Units (SI) was introduced in 1971.

ENERGY AND NATURAL RESOURCES

Electricity. The Public Utilities Board is responsible for the provision of electricity, piped gas and water. Electrical power is generated by 4 oil-fired power stations, with a total generating capacity of 3,371 mw at the end of 1988. Production (1988) 13,017m. kwh. Supply 230 volts; 50 Hz.

Oil. Singapore is the largest oil refining centre in Asia.

Agriculture. Only 3% of Singapore's total area is used for farming. Agriculture contributed less than 0·5% of GDP and employed only 1% of the labour force in 1988. Most food is imported but Singapore is self-sufficient in eggs and pork, and 10,000 tonnes (5·6%) of vegetables were produced for domestic consumption in 1988. Orchids are a valuable export, amounting to S$15m. in 1988.

Fisheries. As the prospect of increasing fish production from inshore waters is poor, in 1967 various projects were introduced with the aim of making Singapore self-sufficient in fish as well as a major fishing base in the region.

The Jurong fishing port and fish market began operating 26 Feb. 1969. A Fishery Training Institute was established at Changi with the assistance of the United Nations Development Programme (Special Fund) to train youths and fishermen in modern fishing techniques. At Changi, too, a Marine Fisheries Research Department was set up under the sponsorship of the South-East Asian Fisheries Development Centre. Research on fish culture and ornamental fish was carried out at the Freshwater Fisheries Laboratory at Sembawang. The ornamental fish industry is a valuable foreign exchange earner. Export of aquarium fish in 1988, S$59·7m. The total local supply of fresh fish in 1988 was 13,152 tonnes.

INDUSTRY AND TRADE

Industry. The largest industrial area is the Jurong Industrial Estate with 1,877 factories employing 105,957 workers in March 1988.

Production, 1988 (in S$1m.), totalled 55,524·1, including machinery and appliances, 25,738·1; petroleum, 7,765·3; food and beverages, 2,500·2; chemical products, 4,629·9; transport equipment, 2,543·7; fabricated metal products, 2,425·8; paper products and printing, 1,966; wearing apparel, 1,729·3; rubber processing, 226·6.

Labour. In June 1988, 1,238,500 persons were employed, of whom 1,057,400 were employees, 61,000 were employers, 98,400 were self-employed and 21,700 were unpaid family workers. The majority were working in manufacturing, 352,600; trade, 283,600.

The Employment Act and the Industrial Relations Act provide principal terms and conditions of employment such as hours of work, sick leave and other fringe benefits. A new labour legislation was introduced allowing youths of 14-16 years to work in industrial establishments, and also children from 12-14 years to be employed in approved apprenticeship schemes. A trade dispute may be referred to the Industrial Arbitration Court which was established in 1960.

The Ministry of Labour operates an employment service to assist job seekers to obtain employment and employers to recruit workers. In addition it provides the handicapped with specialized on-the-job training. The Central Provident Fund was established in 1955 to make provision for employees in their old age. On 31 Dec. 1988 there were 2·1m. members with S$32,500m. standing to their credit in the fund. The total number of contributors to the fund in 1988 was 963,800.

Trade Unions. There were 89 registered trade unions comprising 83 employee unions, 5 employer unions and 1 federation of employee unions at 31 Dec. 1988. The total membership of employee unions numbered 210,918, of whom 208,625 belonged to 70 employee unions and 4 co-operatives affiliated to the National Trades Union Congress. Members of employer unions numbered 1,203.

Commerce.

Imports and exports (in S$1m.), by country, 1988:

	Imports (c.i.f.)	*Exports (f.o.b.)*
Australia	1,744·0	2,141·7
China	3,385·6	2,368·6
France	1,586·2	1,312·3
Germany, Federal Republic of	3,265·0	2,747·7
Hong Kong	2,431·5	4,943·7
Italy	1,317·2	1,142·6
Japan	19,364·5	6,827·8

	Imports (c.i.f.)	*Exports (f.o.b.)*
Malaysia	12,928·7	10,721·1
Saudi Arabia	3,873·2	555·6
Taiwan	3,996·7	2,234·9
Thailand	2,386·3	4,311·2
UK	2,561·8	2,301·7
USA	13,718·4	18,826·0

The major trading countries for 1988 were US (19·5%), Japan (15·7%), Malaysia (14·1%) and the EEC (12·5%). In 1988, imports (S$88,226·7m.) increased by 29%. Exports increased by 31·2% from S$60,265·7m. in 1987 to S$79,051·3m. in 1988.

Exports (1988, in S$1m.): Machinery and transport equipment, 37,938·7 (of which electrical machinery, 9,415·2; transport equipment, 2,168·3); mineral fuels, 10,147; crude materials, 4,046·7 (of which rubber, 2,290·5); chemicals, 5,198·9; food, beverages and tobacco, 3,837·9; clothing, 2,495·4; animal and vegetable oils, 885·5; textiles, 1,386·5; scientific and optical instruments, 1,558·3; metal goods, 857·3; iron and steel, 721.

Imports (1988, in S$1m.): Machinery and transport equipment, 38,298.8; mineral fuels, 12,422·2; food, beverages and tobacco, 5,397; chemicals, 5,808·5; crude materials, 2,999·1 (of which rubber, 1,698·7); textiles, 2,951·5; iron and steel, 2,665·5; animal and vegetable oils, 941; metal goods, 1,673·3; scientific and optical instruments, 2,359·1; non-metal mineral goods, 1,254·1; paper and paperboard and related articles, 1,134·4.

In the following table (British Department of Trade returns, in £1,000 sterling) the imports include produce from Sabah, Sarawak and other eastern places, transhipped at Singapore, which is thus entered as the place of export:

	1985	*1986*	*1987*	*1988*	*1989*
Imports to UK	441,345	462,878	473,814	579,368	903,248
Exports and re-exports from UK	612,920	547,419	602,627	632,452	773,866

Tourism. There were 4,186,091 visitors in 1988, spending S$4,828·3m. The average length of stay was 3·4 days. In 1988 there were 68 gazetted hotels with a total of 24,669 rooms.

COMMUNICATIONS

Roads. There were (1989) 2,810 km of public roads, of which 2,725 km are asphalt-paved. In Dec. 1988 motor vehicles numbered 491,808, of which 238,984 were private cars, 8,733 buses, 116,476 motor cycles and scooters, 13,633 public cars including taxis, school taxis and private hire cars.

Railways. A 16-mile (25·8-km) main line runs through Singapore, connecting with the States of Malaysia and as far as Bangkok. Branch lines serve the port of Singapore and the industrial estate at Jurong. A metro opened in 1987.

Aviation. The new international airport at Changi was completed and operational from 1 July 1981. Forty-nine international airlines operated 1,500 scheduled flights a week, totalling 79,037 commercial aircraft movements at Singapore International Airport in Changi in 1988. Freight handled (1988) 511,541 tonnes and there were 12,569,788 passengers.

Shipping. A total of 35,966 vessels of 236m. NRT entered Singapore during 1988.

Post and Telecommunications. In March 1988, 88 post offices and 44 postal agencies were in operation. Telephones numbered 1·3m. in 1988.

Cinemas (1988). There were 46 cinemas with a total seating capacity of 48,379.

Newspapers (1988). There were 7 daily newspapers, in 4 languages, with a total daily circulation of 743,334.

JUSTICE, RELIGION, EDUCATION AND WELFARE

Justice. There is a Supreme Court in Singapore which consists of the High Court, the Court of Appeal and the Court of Criminal Appeal. The Supreme Court is composed of a Chief Justice and 7 Judges. An appeal from the High Court lies to the Court of Appeal in civil matters and to the Court of Criminal Appeal in criminal matters. Further appeal can in certain cases be made to the Judicial Committee of the Privy Council which is the final appellate Court of Singapore although the proceedings are conducted in the UK. The High Court has original civil and criminal jurisdiction as well as appellate civil and criminal jurisdiction in respect of appeals from the Subordinate Courts. There are 12 district courts, 14 magistrates' courts, 1 juvenile and 1 coroner's court and a small claims tribunal.

Penalties for drug trafficking and abuse are severe. The death penalty is mandatory for possession of morphine in excess of 30 grammes or diamorphine in excess of 15 grammes.

Religion. In Aug. 1988, 41·7% of the population aged 15 years and above were Buddhists and Taoists, 18·7% Christians, 16% Moslems and 4·9% Hindus.

Education. Statistics of schools in 1988:

	Schools	Pupils	Teachers
Primary			
Government schools	166	198,429	7,958
Government-aided schools	54	60,688	2,234
Private schools	1	153	9
Secondary			
Government schools	113	147,596	6,806
Government-aided schools	44	52,589	2,161
Private schools	4	1,570	73

The National University of Singapore was established on 8 Aug. 1980 following the merger of the University of Singapore and the Nanyang University. The National University of Singapore has 8 faculties: Arts and social sciences, law, science, medicine, dentistry, engineering, architecture and building, and business administration. Post-graduate studies are offered in all the faculties and there are 3 post-graduate schools for medical, dental and management studies. Total enrolment for 1988–89 was 14,317 students.

The Nanyang Technological Institute, situated in the former Nanyang University, was established on 8 Aug. 1981. The institute had an enrolment of 4,440 students in 1988–89. It will be developed into the Nanyang Technological University by 1991. The Singapore Polytechnic had 9,824 students and the Ngee Ann Polytechnic 10,498 students in 1988–89. The Institute of Education, established on 1 April 1973, is now the only institution responsible for teacher education in Singapore and for promoting research in education. There were 3,389 students in 1988.

The Adult Education Board and the Industrial Training Board were merged to form the Vocational and Industrial Training Board, on 1 April 1979. The VITB has taken over all the functions and responsibilities in vocational training and continuing education. The VITB runs 15 training institutes and centres offering full-time and part-time courses. The total student enrolment for 1988 was 16,978.

Health. There were 10 government hospitals with a total of 7,971 beds in 1988. There were 3,162 doctors and 8,994 nurses registered. There are 11 private hospitals with 1,839 beds.

DIPLOMATIC REPRESENTATIVES

Of Singapore in Great Britain (2 Wilton Cres., London, SW1X 8RW)
High Commissioner: Abdul Aziz Mahmood.

Of Great Britain in Singapore (Tanglin Rd, Singapore, 1024)
High Commissioner: Michael E. Pike, CMG.

Of Singapore in the USA (1824 R. St., NW, Washington, D.C., 20009)
Ambassador: Tommy T. B. Koh.

Of the USA in Singapore (30 Hill St., Singapore, 0617)
Ambassador: Robert D. Orr.

Of Singapore to the United Nations
Ambassador: Dr Chan Heng Chee.

Further Reading

Statistical Information: The Department of Statistics (PO Box 3010, Maxwell Road, Singapore 9050) was established 1 Jan. 1922. Its publications include: *Singapore Trade Statistics: Imports and Exports* (monthly), *Monthly Digest of Statistics, Yearbook of Statistics, Singapore Demographic Bulletin* (monthly), *Census of Population 1980. Singapore Yearbook of Labour Statistics. Chief Statistician:* Khoo Chian Kim.

National Library. *Books About Singapore*. Singapore. Biennial
Singapore. Constitution. The Constitution of Singapore. Singapore, 1966
The Budget for the Financial Year 1988–89. Singapore, 1988
Singapore. Economic Committee, The Singapore Economy: new directions: report of the Economic Committee, Ministry of Trade and Industry, Singapore, 1986
Singapore Yearbook. Singapore, Information Division, Ministry of Communications and Information
Singapore. Government Gazette (published weekly with supplement)
Economic Survey of Singapore. Ministry of Trade and Industry, Singapore (Quarterly and Annual)
Singapore Facts and Pictures. Singapore, Information Division, Ministry of Communications and Information
Singapore Government Directory. Singapore, Information Division, Ministry of Communications and Information
Singapore: An Illustrated history, 1941–48. Ministry of Culture, Singapore, 1984
The Statutes of the Republic of Singapore. Rev. 12 vols., 1985 (with annual supplements). Singapore, Law Revision Commission, 1986—.
Clammer, J. R., *Singapore: Ideology, Society, Culture*. Singapore, 1985
Drysdale, J., *Singapore: Struggle for Success*. Singapore, 1984
Josey, A., *Lee Kuan Yew, The Struggle for Singapore*. London, 1980.—*Singapore: Its Past, Present and Future*. Singapore, 1979
Krause, L. B., *The Singapore Economy Reconsidered*. Singapore, 1988
Lim, L., *Trade, Employment and Industrialisation in Singapore*. Singapore, 1989
Myint, S., *The Principles of Singapore Law*. Singapore, 1987
Quah, J. S. T., *Government and Politics of Singapore*. OUP, 1985
Quah, S. T. and Quah, J. S. T., *Singapore* [Bibliography] Oxford and Santa Barbara, 1988
Saw, S. H., *New Population and Labour Force Projections and Policy Implications for Singapore*. Singapore, 1987
Soon, T. W., *Singapore's New Education System; Education Reform for National Development*. Singapore, 1988
Tan, C. H., *Financial Institutions in Singapore*. 4th ed. Singapore, 1985
Turnbull, C. M., *A History of Singapore, 1819–1975*. OUP, 1977
You, P. S. and Lim, C. Y. (eds.) *Singapore: Twenty-five years of Development*. Singapore, 1984

National Library: National Library, Stamford Rd, Singapore, 0617. *Director:* Mrs Yoke-Lan Wicks.

SOLOMON ISLANDS

Capital: Honiara
Population: 285,796 (1986)
GNP per capita: US$430 (1988)

HISTORY. The Solomon Islands were discovered in 1568 by Alvaro de Mendana, on a voyage of discovery from Peru; 200 years passed before European contact was again made with the Solomons. The southern Solomon Islands were placed under British protection in 1893; the eastern and southern outliers were added in 1898 and 1899. Santa Isabel and the other islands to the north were ceded by Germany in 1900. Full internal self-government was achieved on 2 Jan. 1976 and independence on 7 July 1978.

AREA AND POPULATION. The Solomon Islands lie within the area 5° to 12° 30' S. lat. and 155° 30' to 169° 45' E. long. The group includes the main islands of Guadalcanal, Malaita, New Georgia, San Cristobal (now Makira), Santa Isabel and Choiseul; the smaller Florida and Russell groups; the Shortland, Mono (or Treasury), Vella La Vella, Kolombangara, Ranongga, Gizo and Rendova Islands; to the east, Santa Cruz, Tikopia, the Reef and Duff groups; Rennell and Bellona in the south; Ontong Java or Lord Howe to the north; and innumerable smaller islands. The land area of the Solomons is estimated at 10,640 sq. miles (27,556 sq. km). The larger islands are mountainous and forest clad, with flood-prone rivers of considerable energy potential. Guadalcanal has the largest land area and the greatest amount of flat coastal plain.

Population of the Solomon Islands was (census, 1986) 285,796. Growth rate (1988) 3·4%.

The islands are administratively divided into 7 provinces. These provinces are (with 1987 estimated population): Western Province (62,300), Guadalcanal, including Honiara (71,300), Central (20,600), Malaita (80,700), Makira and Ulawa (20,800), Temotu (15,300), Isabel (15,500).

The capital, Honiara, on Guadalcanal, is the largest urban area, with estimated population in 1986 of 30,499.

English is the official language but there are at least 87 vernacular languages.

CLIMATE. An equatorial climate with only small seasonal variations. South-east winds cause cooler conditions from April to Nov., but north-west winds for the rest of the year bring higher temperatures and greater rainfall, with annual totals ranging between 80" (2,000 mm) and 120" (3,000 mm).

CONSTITUTION AND GOVERNMENT. The Solomon Islands is a constitutional monarchy with the British Sovereign (represented locally by a Governor-General, who must be a Solomon Island citizen) as Head of State, while legislative power is vested in the unicameral National Parliament composed of 38 members, elected by universal adult suffrage for four years (subject to dissolution), and executive authority is effectively held by the Cabinet, led by the Prime Minister.

The Governor-General is appointed for up to five years, on the advice of Parliament, and acts in almost all matters on the advice of the Cabinet. The Prime Minister is elected by and from members of Parliament. Other Ministers are appointed by the Governor-General on the Prime Minister's recommendation, from members of Parliament. The Cabinet is responsible to Parliament. Emphasis is laid on the devolution of power to provincial governments, and traditional chiefs and leaders have a special role within the arrangement.

Governor General: Sir George Lepping, GCMG, MBE.
Prime Minister: Solomon Mamaloni.
National flag: Divided blue over green by a diagonal yellow band, and in the canton 5 white stars.

INTERNATIONAL RELATIONS

Membership. The Solomon Islands is a member of UN, the Commonwealth and is an ACP state of EEC.

ECONOMY

Budget. The budget for 1989 envisaged expenditure of SI$115m. and revenue of SI$110·5m.

Currency. The *Solomon Island dollar* (SI$) was introduced in 1977. In March 1990, US$1 = 2·43 *dollars*; £1 = 4·05 *dollars*.

Banking. In 1988 there were 3 commercial banks: Australia and New Zealand Banking Group, National Bank of Solomon Islands and Westpac Banking Corporation.

Weights and Measures. The metric system is in force.

ENERGY AND NATURAL RESOURCES

Electricity. Production (1987) 24,205,117 kwh. Supply 240 volts; 50 Hz.

Minerals. There are reserves of bauxite and phosphate, and there is a small industry extracting gold (65,807 grams refined, in 1986) and silver (70,158) by panning.

Agriculture. Land is held either as customary land (88% of holdings) or registered land. Customary land rights depend on clan membership or kinship. Only Solomon Islanders own customary land; only Islanders or government members may hold perpetual estates of registered land. Coconuts, cocoa, rice and other minor crops are grown. Main food crops coconut, cassava, sweet potato, yam, taro and banana: Solomon Islands Plantations Ltd has a plantation of about 40,000 hectares of oil-palm, near Honiara. Production of copra (1988), 25,000 tonnes; palm oil, 15,000; cocoa, 3,000; palm kernels, 3,000.

Rice-cropping in 1983 yielded 4,608 tonnes of milled rice. Rice has been imported since the 1986 cyclone. Production, 1988, 6,000 tonnes.

Livestock (1988): Cattle, 13,000; pigs, 52,000.

Forestry. Forests cover about 2·4m. hectares, with (1987) an estimated 10·4m. cu. metres of commercial timber. Production (1987) of logs, 301,700 cu. metres and sawn timber, 17,600 cu. metres; total exports, 285,650 cu. metres.

Fisheries. Catch of tuna (1987) 32,210 tonnes.

INDUSTRY AND TRADE

Industry. Industries include palm oil milling, rice milling, fish canning, fish freezing, saw milling, food, tobacco and soft drinks. Other products include wood and rattan furniture, fibreglass articles, boats, clothing and spices.

Commerce. Total exports (1987) SI$128·3m. The main imports (1987, in SI$1m.) were machinery and transport equipment, 39·28; mineral fuels and lubricants, 19·88; manufactured goods, 27·7; food, 20·23. Total imports SI$134,944,000. Main exports included fish products, 52·58; wood products, 37·17; cocoa beans, 9·54; copra, 10·26; palm oil products, 7·63. In 1987 imports were mainly from Australia (41%), Japan (19%), Singapore (9%), New Zealand (8%) and the UK (4%); exports were mainly to Japan (36%), Thailand (32%), UK (14%) and USA (5%), on a regional basis South East Asia accounted for 57%, EEC, 22% and Oceania, 12%.

Total trade between Solomon Islands and UK (British Department of Trade returns, in £1,000 sterling):

	1986	*1987*	*1988*	*1989*
Imports to UK	4,074	4,461	5,153	6,404
Exports and re-exports from UK	1,618	1,566	2,576	1,088

Tourism. In 1987, there were 12,555 visitors of whom 60·1% were tourists.

COMMUNICATIONS

Roads. In 1987 there were 1,300 km of motorable roads of which 100 km of bitumen-topped roads; the rest were coral or gravel. In 1986 there were 3,629 vehicles, of which about 1,827 were commercial vehicles.

Aviation. (1988) An international airport 13 km from Honiara is served by Air Nauru, Air Niugini, Air Pacific and Solomon Islands Airline. There are 27 airfields. Solomon Islands Airline also provides inter-island transport and scheduled flights to Kieta in Papua New Guinea.

Shipping. International seaports are Honiara, and Yandina in the Russell group. Shipping services are maintained with Australia, New Zealand, UK and the Far East. Honiara port handles about 250 overseas vessels annually. In 1987 the merchant marine comprised 26 vessels of 5,811 GRT.

Post and Broadcasting. In addition to the general post office, there are 9 post offices, 4 sub post offices and 95 Postal Agencies. Number of telephones (1988), 2,500. Solomon Islands Broadcasting Corp. transmits 118 hours a week from Honiara, Gizo and Lata. In 1987 there were about 35,000 radio receivers.

Newspapers. In 1988 there were 3 weekly newspapers.

JUSTICE, RELIGION, EDUCATION AND WELFARE

Justice. Civil and criminal jurisdiction is exercised by the High Court of Solomon Islands, constituted 1975. A Solomon Islands Court of Appeal was established in 1982. Jurisdiction is based on the principles of English law (as applying on 1 Jan. 1981). Magistrates' courts can try civil cases on claims not exceeding $2,000, and criminal cases with penalties not exceeding 14 years' imprisonment. Certain crimes, such as burglary and arson, where the maximum sentence is for life, may also be tried by magistrates. There are also local courts, which decide matters concerning customary titles to land; decisions may be put to the Customary Land Appeal Court. There is no capital punishment.

Religion. At the 1986 census, 33·9% of the population were Anglican, 19·2% Roman Catholic, 17·6% South Sea Evangelical and 23·5% other Protestant.

Education. In 1987 there were 42,374 pupils and 2,124 teachers in 462 primary schools, and 5,604 pupils and 300 teachers in 12 provincial and 8 national secondary schools.

Training of teachers and trade and vocational training is carried out at the college of Higher Education. There were 413 students on overseas scholarships in 1987.

Health. In 1988 there were 8 hospitals, 31 doctors, 464 registered nurses and 283 nursing aides.

DIPLOMATIC REPRESENTATIVES

Of the Solomon Islands in Great Britain (resides in Honiara).
High Commissioner: Wilson Ifunaoa (accredited 12 Feb. 1987).

Of Great Britain in the Solomon Islands (Soltel House, Mendana Ave., Honiara)
High Commissioner: D. Junor Young.

Of the USA in the Solomon Islands
Ambassador: (Vacant).

Of the Solomon Islands in the USA and to the United Nations
Ambassador: (Vacant).

Further Reading

Solomon Islands Hand Book 1983. Government Information Service, Honiara, 1983
Bennett, J. A., *Wealth of the Solomons: A History of a Pacific Archipelago, 1800–1978*. Univ. of Hawaii Press, 1987
Kent, J., *The Solomon Islands*. Newton Abbot, 1972

SOMALIA

Capital: Mogadishu
Population: 6·26m. (1988)
GNP per capita: US$170 (1988)

Jamhuriyadda Dimugradiga Somaliya

HISTORY. The Somali Republic came into being on 1 July 1960 as a result of the merger of the British Somaliland Protectorate, which became independent on 26 June 1960, and the Italian Trusteeship Territory of Somalia.

On 21 Oct. 1969 Maj.-Gen. Mohammed Siyad Barre took power in a *coup,* suspended the Constitution and formed a Supreme Revolutionary Council to administer the country, which was renamed the Somali Democratic Republic. Constitutional government was re-established on 23 Sept. 1979.

AREA AND POPULATION. Somalia is bounded north by the Gulf of Aden, east and south by the Indian ocean, and west by Kenya, Ethiopia and Djibouti. Total area 637,657 sq. km (246,201 sq. miles). Census population (1975) 3,253,024 of whom 15% urban. Estimate (1988) 6·22m. In Aug. 1987 there were 700,000 refugees from Ethiopia.

The capital is Mogadishu (1m. including a floating population of about 250,000), other large towns being Hargeisa (400,000), Baidoa (300,000), Burao (300,000), Kismaayo (200,000), Merca (100,000), Kisimayu (70,000) and Berbera (65,000).

CLIMATE. Much of the country is arid, though rainfall is more adequate towards the south. Temperatures are very high on the northern coasts. Mogadishu. Jan. 79°F (26·1°C), July 78°F (25·6°C). Annual rainfall 17" (429 mm). Berbera. Jan. 76°F (24·4°C), July 97°F (36·1°C). Annual rainfall 2" (51 mm).

CONSTITUTION AND GOVERNMENT. The Constitution came into force on 23 Sept. and was amended in Dec. 1984. The sole legal Party (since 1 July 1976) is the Somali Revolutionary Socialist Party, administered by a 51-member Central Committee, but a move to a multi-party system is envisaged for 1990. There is an Executive President nominated by the Central Committee and elected for a 7-year term by direct popular vote; legislative power resides with a People's Assembly consisting of 171 members directly elected for a 5-year term from a single list of 171 SRSP candidates, together with a further 6 members appointed by the President. The President appoints and leads a Council of Ministers.

President: Maj.-Gen. Mohammed Siyad Barre (elected 1980, and re-elected in 1986).

National flag: Light blue with a white star in the centre.

The national language is Somali. Arabic is also an official language and English and Italian are extensively spoken.

Local Government. There are 18 regions, sub-divided into 84 districts.

DEFENCE

Army. The Army consists of 4 tank, 45 mechanized and infantry, 4 commando and 1 surface-to-air missile, 3 field artillery brigades. Equipment includes 140 T-34/-54/-55, 123 M-47 and 30 Centurion main battle tanks. Strength (1990) 61,300. There are additional paramilitary forces: Police (8,000), Border Guards (1,500) and People's Militia (20,000).

Navy. The flotilla includes 2 fast missile craft, 4 fast torpedo boats, 5 inshore patrol craft, 1 medium landing ship and 4 minor landing craft. All are former Soviet naval units, and serviceability is now poor. Personnel totalled 1,200 in 1989. Bases are at Mogadishu, Berbera and Kisimayu.

Air Force. Formed with a nucleus of aircraft taken over from the former Italian Air Corps of Somalia, in 1960, the Air Corps was built up with Soviet aid. Current equipment includes 6 MiG-21 and 20 F-6 (Chinese-built MiG-19) supersonic fighters, 8 Hunter fighter-bombers (including 1 trainer), about 8 MiG-17 jetfighters and 2 MiG-15UTI two-seat advanced trainers, and small transport, helicopter and training units. Support equipment includes 2 Aeritalia G222, 6 Aviocar and 2 An-26 twin-turboprop transports, 5 SIAI-Marchetti SF.260W armed trainers and 4 Agusta-Bell 212 helicopters from Italy, plus 3 Islander and 2 P-166 light transports. Serviceability of most aircraft is reported to be low. Personnel (1990) 2,500.

INTERNATIONAL RELATIONS

Membership. Somalia is a member of UN, OAU, the Arab League, the Islamic League and is an ACP state of EEC.

ECONOMY

Budget. The budget for 1989 balanced at Som.Sh.18,055m..

Currency. The currency is the *Somali shilling*, divided into 100 cents. The money is issued in notes of 5, 10, 20 and 100 shillings and coins of 1, 5, 10, 50 cents and 1 shilling. In March 1990 £1 = 674·25 Som.Sh.; US$1 = 411·38 Som.Sh.

Banking. The bank of issue is the Central Bank of Somalia (founded in 1960 as the Somali National Bank). All foreign banks were nationalized in May 1970, and the Commercial and Savings Bank of Somalia and the Somali Development Bank, both state-owned, are the only other banks.

Weights and Measures. The metric system is in use.

ENERGY AND NATURAL RESOURCES

Electricity. Electricity production (1986) was 137m. kwh. Supply 220 volts; 50 Hz.

Minerals. Deposits of iron ore in the south and gypsum in the north are known to exist. Beryl and columbite are also found in the north. None are commercially exploited. Several firms hold exploration and drilling licences for oil. Uranium is found in the Juba area.

Agriculture. Somalia is essentially a pastoral country, and about 80% of the inhabitants depend on livestock-rearing (cattle, sheep, goats and camels). In Southern Somalia, especially along the Shebeli and Juba rivers, there are banana and sugar-cane plantations with a cultivated area of some 90,000 hectares. Estimated production, 1988 (in 1,000 tonnes): Sugar-cane, 450; bananas, 120; maize, 260; sorghum, 220; grapefruit, 28; seed cotton, 6. Fresh fruit and oil seeds are grown in increasing quantities.

Livestock (1988): 20m. goats; 13·5m. sheep; 6·68m. camels; 5m. cattle; 1,000 horses, 25,000 asses and 23,000 mules.

Forestry. Production (1986) 4·5m. cu. metres.

Fisheries. 21 co-operatives, including 4,000 full-time and 10,000 part-time fishermen, caught some 16,500 tonnes in 1986.

INDUSTRY AND TRADE

Industry. A few small industries existed in 1986 including sugar refining, food processing, textile and petroleum refining. Production (1985): Textiles, 3·4m. yards; sugar, 39,400 tonnes; flour and pasta, 11,700 tonnes.

Commerce. In 1983 imports were Som.Sh.2,844m. and exports Som.Sh.1,423m. The chief exports are fresh fruit, livestock, hides and skins.

In 1984, 20% of imports came from Italy, 20% from USA and 13% from Saudi Arabia, while 59% of exports went to Saudi Arabia.

Total trade between the Somali Republic and UK (British Department of Trade returns, in £1,000 sterling):

	1985	*1986*	*1987*	*1988*	*1989*
Imports to UK	1,448	740	825	1,151	508
Exports and re-exports from UK	8,646	9,139	11,417	10,379	10,508

COMMUNICATIONS

Roads. Somalia has no developed transport system. Internal freight and passenger transport is almost entirely by means of road haulage. In 1985 there were 17,215 km of roads (2,500 km were paved), 17,754 passenger cars and 9,533 commercial vehicles.

Aviation. There is a commercial national airline, Somali Airlines. Mogadishu airport is used by Alitalia, Alyemda, Air Tanzania, PIA, Saudi Airways and Kenya Airways.

Shipping. There are 4 deep-water harbours at Kisimayu, Berbera, Marka and Mogadishu. The merchant fleet (1985) amounted to 26 vessels of 28,053 gross tons.

Post and Broadcasting. Number of telephones (1985), about 6,000. The state radio stations transmit in Somali, Arabic, English and Italian from Mogadishu, and Hargeisa. There were 250,000 radios in 1986.

JUSTICE, RELIGION, EDUCATION AND WELFARE

Justice. There are 84 district courts, each with a civil and a criminal section. There are 8 regional courts and 2 Courts of Appeal (at Mogadishu and Hargeisa), each with a general section and an assize section. The Supreme Court is in Mogadishu.

Religion. The population is almost entirely Sunni Moslems.

Education. The nomadic life of a large percentage of the population inhibits education progress. In 1985 there were 194,335 pupils and 9,676 teachers in primary schools, there were 37,181 pupils and 2,320 teachers in secondary schools, and in 1984 613 students with 30 teachers at teacher-training establishments. The National University of Somalia in Mogadishu (founded 1959) had 15,562 students in 1986.

Health. In 1986 there were 450 doctors, 180 pharmacists, 2 dentists, 556 midwives and 1,834 nursing personnel.

DIPLOMATIC REPRESENTATIVES

Of Somalia in Great Britain (60 Portland Pl., London, W1N 3DG)
Ambassador: (Vacant).

Of Great Britain in Somalia (Waddada Xasan Geedd Abtoow 7/8, Mogadishu)
Ambassador: Ian McCluney.

Of Somalia in the USA (600 New Hampshire Ave., NW, Washington, D.C., 20037)
Chargé d'Affaires: Abdi Awale Jama.

Of USA in Somalia (Corso Primo Luglio, Mogadishu)
Ambassador: T. Frank Crigler.

Of Somalia to the United Nations
Ambassador: Abdillahi Said Osman.

Further Reading

Background to the Liberation Struggle of the Western Somalis. Ministry of Foreign Affairs, Mogadishu, 1978

DeLancey, M. W., *et al. Somalia.* [Bibliography] Oxford and Santa Barbara, 1988

Legum, C. and Lee, B., *Conflict in the Horn of Africa.* London, 1977

REPUBLIC OF SOUTH AFRICA

Capital: Pretoria
Population: 30·19m. (1989)
GNP per capita: US$2,290 (1988)

Republiek van Suid-Afrika

HISTORY. The Union of South Africa was formed in 1910 and comprised the former self-governing British colonies of the Cape of Good Hope, Natal, the Transvaal and the Orange Free State.

The Union remained a member of the British Commonwealth until it became a republic on 31 May 1961.

A state of emergency has been reimposed annually since 12 June 1986.

Some of the restrictions of apartheid have been gradually removed, and the government has announced its willingness to consider the extension of Black South Africans' political rights. In Feb. 1990 a 30-year ban on the African National Congress was lifted and its leader, Nelson Mandela, released from prison.

In March 1990 there was violent unrest in some homelands associated with demands for re-integration into South Africa; in Ciskei President Sebe was deposed.

AREA AND POPULATION. South Africa is bounded north by Namibia, Botswana and Zimbabwe, north-east by Mozambique and Swaziland, east by the Indian ocean, south and west by the South Atlantic. Lesotho forms an enclave between the Orange Free State and Natal. Area without the 'independent' homelands (Transkei, Bophuthatswana, Venda and Ciskei) was (1989) 347,860 sq. miles (1,127,200 sq. km), divided between the provinces as follows: Cape Province, 198,760 (644,060); Natal, 28,310 (91,740); Transvaal, 81,930 (265,470); Orange Free State, 38,860 (125,930).

On 25 Dec. 1947 the Union formally took possession of Prince Edward Island and, on 30 Dec., of Marion Island, about 1,200 miles south-east of Cape Town.

The census taken in 1904 in each of the 4 colonies was the first simultaneous census taken in South Africa. In 1911 the first Union census was taken.

	All races			*Whites*		*Non-whites*	
	Total	*Whites*	*Non-Whites*	*Males*	*Females*	*Males*	*Females*
1904	5,174,827	1,117,234	4,057,593	635,317	481,917	2,046,370	2,011,223
1911	5,972,757	1,276,319	4,696,438	685,206	591,113	2,383,879	2,312,559
1921	6,927,403	1,521,343	5,406,060	783,006	738,337	2,753,188	2,652,872
1936	9,587,863	2,003,334	7,584,529	1,017,557	985,777	3,818,211	3,766,318
1946	11,415,925	2,372,044	9,043,881	1,194,201	1,177,843	4,610,862	4,433,019
1951	12,671,452	2,641,689	10,029,763	1,322,754	1,318,935	5,109,331	4,920,432
1960	15,994,181	3,080,159	12,914,022	1,534,923	1,545,236	6,504,317	6,409,705
1970	21,402,470	3,726,540	17,675,930	1,856,180	1,870,360	8,689,920	8,986,010
1980[1]	24,885,960	4,528,100	20,357,860	2,265,400	2,262,700	10,393,780	9,964,080
1985[2]	23,391,245	4,574,339	18,816,906	2,254,801	2,319,538	9,293,081	9,523,825
1986[2]	27,607,000	4,832,000	...	...	...	...	...

[1] Excludes the 'independent' homelands except Ciskei (677,820).
[2] Excludes the 'independent' homelands.

Official population estimates (without the 'independent' homelands), 30 June 1989, (in 1,000; females in brackets): Whites, 4,979 (2,508); Coloureds, 3,168 (1,610): Asians, 941 (474); Blacks; 21,105 (10,131). The numerically leading Black nations (1980) are the Zulu (5,682,520), Xhosa (2,987,340), Sepedi (North Sotho) (2,347,600), Seshoeshoe (South Sotho) (1,742,060), Tswana (1,357,360). Population, (1985) of the Black national areas: Kwa Zulu, 3,738,334; Gazankulu, 496,200; Lebowa, 1,833,144; Qwaqwa, 180,924; Ka Ngwane, 391,205; Kwa Ndebele, 235,511. These places are included in the land area figures for the provinces where they lie, but their inhabitants are not included in the provincial population figures. Annual growth rate 1980–89, 2·1% (Black, 2·39%; Coloured, 1·82%; Asian, 1·74%; White, 1·08%). Urban population was 56% in 1985.

Vital statistics for calendar years:

	Whites			Immi-		Asians and Coloureds		
	Births	*Deaths*	*Marriages*	*grants*	*Emigrants*	*Births*	*Deaths*	*Marriages*
1986	72,938	38,241	41,575	6,994	13,711	101,331	28,714	28,276
1987	70,431	40,194	41,033	...	...	103,642	33,867	24,433
1988	...	...	...	10,400	7,767	...	...	...

Marriages and divorces in 1988: Whites, 41,219 and 18,432; Coloureds, 16,088 and 4,907; Asians, 5,791 and 1,251; Mixed, 1,076 and 168.

Births in 1988: Whites, 69,184 (females, 33,734); Coloureds, 77,751 (38,544); Asians, 19,525 (9,597).

Deaths in 1988: Whites, 40,194 (females, 18,231); Coloureds, 27,059 (11,466); Asians, 5,476 (2,187). Infant deaths: Whites, 914; Coloureds, 4,467; Asians, 340.

Of the 6,994 immigrants in 1986, 3,818 were from Europe (of whom 2,012, UK); 2,433 from Africa (of whom 1,859, Zimbabwe); 359 from the Americas and 232 from Asia: Of the 13,711 emigrants 6,741 went to Europe (of whom 5,407 to UK); 3,978 to Australia; 747 to Africa.

The registration of Black essential data was introduced on a compulsory basis many years ago. However, despite serious efforts on the part of the registering authorities, the Blacks are still largely reluctant to have their essential data registered. Consequently no complete vital statistics are available for this population group.

Urban areas, according to the 1985 census:

Urban Area	*Total*	*White*	*Coloured*	*Asian*	*Black*
Johannesburg/Randburg	1,609,408	515,670	121,860	57,775	914,103
Cape Peninsula	1,911,521	542,705	1,068,921	18,389	281,506
Durban/Pinetown/Inanda	982,075	307,930	59,925	490,857	123,363
East Rand	1,038,108	399,445	33,390	17,472	587,801
Pretoria/Wonderboom/ Soshanguve	822,925	432,267	21,215	18,017	351,426
Port Elizabeth/Uitenhage	651,993	173,273	172,186	7,346	299,188
West Rand	647,334	233,460	19,206	7,631	387,037
Vanderbijlpark/Vereeniging/ Sasolburg	540,142	167,905	15,321	4,529	352,387
Bloemfontein	232,984	95,271	20,152	35	117,526
Pietermaritzburg	192,417	60,161	13,771	57,006	61,479
Free State Goldfields	320,319	69,387	6,246	2	244,184
Kimberley	149,667	33,782	50,214	1,202	64,469
East London/King William's Town	193,819	77,827	29,008	2,921	84,063

In 1986 (estimate), of the 4·8m. Whites Afrikaans was spoken by 2·7m., English by 1·75m. The remainder included Portuguese, 70,000; German, 43,000; Greek, 20,000; Italian, 15,000; Dutch, 14,000. Nguni languages (mainly Zulu, Xhosa, Swazi and South Ndebele) are spoken by about 13·6m.; Sotho languages (Southern, Northern or Sepedi and Western or Tswana) by about 8m.; Tsongo languages by about 1·2m. and Venda by 550,000. Fanakilo is a pidgin language developed mainly on the mines.

Afrikaans and English are the official languages.

CLIMATE. The climate is healthy and invigorating, with abundant sunshine and relatively low rainfall. The factors controlling this include the latitudinal position, the oceanic location of much of the country, and the existence of high plateaus. The south-west has a Mediterranean climate, with rain mainly in winter, but most of the country has a summer maximum, though quantities show a clear decrease from east to west. Temperatures are remarkably uniform over the whole country. Pretoria. Jan. 70°F (21·1°C), July 52°F (11·1°C). Annual rainfall 31" (785 mm). Bloemfontein. Jan. 73°F (22·8°C), July 47°F (8·3°C). Annual rainfall 23" (564 mm). Cape Town. Jan. 69°F (20·6°C), July 54°F (12·2°C). Annual rainfall 20" (508 mm). Durban. Jan. 75°F (23·9°C), July 62°F (16·7°C). Annual rainfall 40" (1,008 mm). Johannesburg. Jan. 68°F (20°C), July 51°F (10·6°C). Annual rainfall 28" (709 mm).

CONSTITUTION AND GOVERNMENT. On 2 Nov. 1983 a referendum among white voters approved the South Africa Constitution Bill which had previously been passed in the House of Assembly by 119 votes to 35. Turnout for the referendum was 2,062,469 (76·02%), of whom 1,360,223 voted in favour.

The new constitution became effective on 4 Sept. 1984. It provides for a tricameral parliament: The House of Assembly with 178 members of whom 166 are directly elected and 8 indirectly elected by White voters; the House of Representatives with 85 members of whom 80 are directly elected by Coloured voters; the House of Delegates with 45 members of whom 40 are directly elected by Indian voters. The term for all members is 5 years.

These houses choose (from their majority parties) respectively 50 White, 25 Coloured and 13 Indian members of an electoral college which elects an executive President. The President initiates legislation and resolves disputes between houses. He is helped by a 60-member President's Council: 20 members are elected by the House of Assembly, 10 by the House of Representatives and 5 by the House of Delegates; 15 are MPs nominated by himself and 10 are MPs nominated by Opposition parties.

The President appoints a Ministers' Council for each house, choosing 5 members from the majority party; a member chosen from outside the house must become a member of it within one year, and enjoy majority-party support. The Councils handle the affairs of their own population group and administer the departments established for that group. The President also appoints a Cabinet; any member appointed from outside Parliament must become a member of one of the three houses within one year. Any Ministers' Council member may be appointed a Cabinet member for a specific purpose or for an indefinite period. Any Ministers' Council may co-opt a Cabinet member in the same way, providing that member qualifies as a member of the Council in question.

Each house legislates on its own community affairs; the three houses have co-responsibility for national affairs. The State President, on the Cabinet's advice, decides whether a certain matter is a community or a national affair.

To hold an office of profit under the State (with certain exceptions) is a disqualification for membership of either House, as are also insolvency, crime and insanity. Pretoria is the seat of government, and Cape Town is the seat of legislature.

The state of the parties on 4 Sept. 1984: in the House of Assembly, National Party, 114; Progressive Federal Party, 26; Conservative Party, 17; New Republic Party, 8; South African Party, 3. In the House of Representatives, Labour Party, 76; others, 4. In the House of Delegates, National People's Party 18; Solidarity, 17; others, 5.

Indians voting in the elections to the new House of Delegates in Aug. 1984, 20·3% of registered voters; Coloured voters to the new House of Representatives, 30·9%.

At the House of Assembly elections of 6 Sept. 1989, the Nationalist Party won 93 seats; the Conservative Party, 39; and the Democratic Party (formed from a merger of the Progressive Federal Party, the New Republic Party and Independents), 33.

President: Frederik Willem de Klerk (sworn in, 20 Sept. 1989).

The Cabinet in March 1990 was in order of seniority as follows:

Foreign Affairs: R. F. 'Pik' Botha. *Constitutional Development and Planning and National Education:* Gerrit Viljoen. *Defence:* Gen. Magnus Malan. *Mineral and Energy Affairs and Public Enterpises:* Dawie de Villiers. *Justice:* Kobie Coetsee. *Finance:* Barend du Plessis. *Manpower:* Eli Louw. *Law and Order:* Adriaan Vlok. *Environment and Water:* Gert Kotze. *Education and Development Aid:* Stoffel van der Merwe. *Home Affairs:* Gene Louw. *Trade and Industry and Tourism:* Kent Durr. *Transport and Public Works and Land Affairs:* George Bartlett. *Planning and Provincial Affairs:* Hernus Kriel. *National Health and Population Development:* Rina Venter. *Agriculture:* Jacob de Villers. *Administration and Privatization:* W. J. 'Wim' de Villiers.

The Chairman of the President's Council is Willie van Niekerk.

The Prime Minister receives an annual salary of R43,000 and a reimbursive allowance of R20,000; a member of the Cabinet an annual salary of R23,500 and a reimbursive allowance of R6,500; and a Deputy Minister an annual salary of R19,000 and a reimbursive allowance of R6,500.

The English and Afrikaans languages are both official, subject to amendments carried by a two-thirds majority in joint session of both Houses of Parliament.

National flag: Three horizontal stripes of orange, white, blue, with the flags of the Orange Free State and the Transvaal, and the Union Jack side by side in the centre.

National anthem: The Call of South Africa/Die Stem van Suid-Afrika (words by C. J. Langenhoven, 1918; tune by M. L. de Villiers, 1921).

Provincial Administration. In each of the 4 provinces there is an Administrator appointed by the State President-in-Council for 5 years. Until 1986 there were provincial councils, each council electing an executive committee of 4 (either members or not of the council), the Administrator acting as chairman. Provincial councils were abolished in 1986; local governments remain, comprising municipal councils, management boards and other local committees, all of which have authority to deal with local matters, of which provincial finance, education (primary and secondary, other than higher education and technical education), hospitals, roads and bridges, townships, horse and other racing, and game and fish preservation are the most important. All ordinances passed by the local councils are subject to the veto of the State President-in-Council.

Black Administration. In 1959 the main ethnic groups received legislative recognition by the passing of the Promotion of Bantu Self-Government Act, which provided *inter alia* for the various ethnic groups to develop into self-governing national units.

As the Act envisaged eventual political autonomy for each of the various national units and representation in the highest White governing bodies was regarded as a retarding factor, the representation of Blacks by Whites in Parliament and the Cape Provincial Administration was abolished with effect from 30 June 1960.

Territorial Authorities were established between 1968 and 1970, and were converted to Legislative Assemblies in 1971.

Each national unit also has an Executive Council. These Councils, each headed by a Chief Councillor, consist of 6 members, except in the case of the South Sotho, where there are only 4. Each of these Councillors is responsible for the administration of a Department. A civil service has been established in each instance, staffed by citizens of the respective homelands. White officials will serve the homeland governments on secondment, until trained Black citizens are able to take over all duties.

There are (1989) 10 homelands of which 4 are recognised by the South African government as Independent:

The Transkei, territory of the Xhosa nation, became independent on 26 Oct. 1976 (*see* p. 1107), Bophuthatswana on 6 Dec. 1977 (*see* p. 1105), Venda on 13 Sept. 1979 (*see* p. 1108) and Ciskei on 4 Dec. 1981 (*see* p. 1111).

There are (1989) 6 territories with a degree of self-government but still forming part of the Republic: Kwa Zulu, Gazankulu (Machangana-Tsonga people), Lebowa (North Sotho), Qwaqwa (South Sotho), Ka Ngwane (Swazi) and Kwa Ndebele (Southern Ndebele).

DEFENCE. The South African Defence Force comprises a Permanent Force, a Citizen Force and a Commando organization. The Permanent Force consists of professional soldiers, airmen and seamen who are responsible for the administration and training of the whole Defence Force in peace-time, but who are gradually absorbed into the Citizen Force in time of war. The Permanent Force and the Citizen Force consist of Army, Air Force and Naval components; the Commando organization is an army and air organization.

Every white male citizen between 18 and 65 is liable to undergo training and to render personal service in time of war. Those between the ages of 16 and 25 are liable to undergo a compulsory course of peace training.

The S.A. Defence Force is administered by the Chief of the Defence Force, his advisers being the Chief of the Army, Chief of the Air Force and Chief of the Navy,

Chief of Staff Operations, Chief of Staff Personnel, the Chief of Staff Management Services and the Surgeon-General.

Army. South Africa is divided into 11 territorial Commands. Within the various Commands are training units, of which members of the Permanent Force form the permanent staff. Courses of various types are held also at the S.A. Military College. The Army includes 1 armoured, 1 mechanized, 4 motorized and 1 parachute brigade; 1 special reconnaissance regiment and supporting artillery, engineer and signals units. Equipment includes some 250 Centurion/Olifant main battle tanks. Strength (1989) 75,000 (including 55,000 conscripts) with an Active Reserve of 150,000. Paramilitary forces are Commandos (130,000) and in 1987 the total staff complement of the South African Police was 60,950 men and women, of whom 32,754 were Whites and 28,196 Blacks, Coloureds and Indians. In 1987 there were 28 police stations manned by Blacks only, 14 by Coloureds only and 6 by Asians.

Navy. The South African Navy has its headquarters at Pretoria, and is operationally divided into two commands: Eastern, based at Durban, and Western, based at Simonstown. The navy includes 3 French-built diesel submarines, 9 fast missile armed patrol craft, 9 coastal minesweepers, 1 British-built survey ship, 2 fleet replenishment ships and a naval-manned Antarctic supply ship, the latter three all with helicopter facilities. There are additionally some 6 service craft. The Marine force of 900 is principally employed on port security duties for which it is equipped with 24 fast armed launches, but has recently exercised amphibious raiding operations. The 2 British-built frigates are still held in reserve but are unlikely to be reactivated.

Navy personnel in 1989 totalled 6,500 (1,500 conscripts) including marines.

Air Force. There is 1 bomber squadron with 5 Canberra B.12 and 2 Canberra T.4; 1 bomber squadron with 6 Buccaneer Mk.50; 1 coastal patrol squadron with 18 Piaggio P.166S; 1 coastal patrol squadron with C-47s; 1 fighter-bomber squadron with 30 Mirage F1-AZ ground attack aircraft; 2 fighter-bomber squadrons with Atlas Cheetahs (locally modified Mirage IIIs) including some equipped for reconnaissance; and 1 squadron with Mirage F1-CZ interceptors. Transport squadrons have 9 Transall C-160s, 7 C-130B Hercules, more than 40 C-47s, 7 C-54s, 4 Boeing 707s, 1 Viscount, 4 twin-jet HS.125s and 4 twin-turboprop Merlin IVA light transports. Four helicopter squadrons and No. 22 Flight have more than 80 Alouette IIIs, 60 Pumas, 8 Wasps, and 14 Super Frelons. T-6Gs are used for primary training, followed by advanced training on Impalas, Atlas Cheetahs and Mirage IIIEZ/DZ, weapons training on Impalas, and multi-engine/crew training on C-47s. Built under licence in the Republic of South Africa, about 150 two-seat Impala Mk. 1s have been followed by 75 single-seat Impala Mk. 2s, based on the Aermacchi MB.326M and 326K respectively. Three squadrons operate C4M Kudu and AM.3C Bosbok liaison aircraft. South African industry is currently modernizing the Mirage combat aircraft (under the name 'Cheetah') and developing an armed helicopter derived from the Puma.

The Citizen Force has 3 squadrons of Impalas for counter-insurgency duties and C4M Kudu and AM.3C Bosbok liaison aircraft. CF personnel have additional functions in regular SAAF squadrons, notably those equipped with C-47 transports and P.166 light transport/coastal patrol aircraft. Total strength (1990) was about 11,000 regular officers and men.

INTERNATIONAL RELATIONS

Membership. The Republic of South Africa is a member of UN.

ECONOMY

Budget. Total revenue and expenditure of the central government's State Revenue Account in R1m.:

	1986–87	*1987–88*	*1988-89* [1]
Revenue	34,611	38,794	...
Expenditure	40,213	46,319	59,923

[1] Estimate.

The main sources of State Revenue 1987–88 were income tax, R21,887m.; general sales tax, R9,954m.; excise duties, R1,920m.; customs duties, R1,540m. Main expenditure: Education, R8,617m.; defence, R7,018m.; economic services, R6,248m.; interest on public debt, R6,098m.; health, R4,339m.; other social, R4,274m.

Public debt on 31 March 1987, R47,619m., of which R3,220m. was foreign debt; internal debt, R44,399m.

Currency. Decimal coinage was introduced in 1959, the units being the *rand* (abbreviated as R) and the *cent* (abbreviated as c). The rand/cent coinage system came into operation on 14 Feb. 1961. The decimal coins are: *Gold coins.* 2 rand; 1 rand. *Silver coins.* 50 cents; 20 cents; 10 cents; 5 cents. *Bronze coins.* 2 cents; 1 cent. In March 1990, £1 = R4·24; US$1 = R2·59.

Banking. In Dec. 1920 a Central Reserve Bank was established at Pretoria. It commenced operations in June 1921, and began to issue notes in April 1922. The bank has branches in Pretoria (Head Office), Johannesburg, Cape Town, Durban, Port Elizabeth, East London, Bloemfontein, Pietermaritzburg and Windhoek (Namibia). Total deposits, 31 March 1987, R3,957m.; assets, R12,158m.

At 31 Dec. 1987 there were 15 commercial banks with total liabilities, R51,764m.; 24 general banks (formerly hire-purchase and savings banks), R397m.; 8 merchant banks, R6,038m.; 4 discount houses, R862m. The Land and Agricultural Bank had (March 1987) R8,342m. total liabilities; Post Office Savings Bank deposits, R3,356m.

Weights and Measures. The Measuring Units and National Measuring Standards Act, 1973, confirmed the adoption of the international metric system.

ENERGY AND NATURAL RESOURCES

Electricity. The total capacity of the power plants controlled by the Electricity Supply Commission was 28,086,000 kw at the end of 1986. There were 21 coal-fired stations, 3 hydro-electric stations and 3 gas-turbine stations. Production (1986) 145,394m. kwh of which ESCOM generated 133,644m. kwh. Net production (sent out from plants for consumption), 133,293, of which ESCOM, 123,643. Supply 220 and 240 volts; 50 Hz.

Oil. In 1987 reserves were found to be sufficient to yield 25,000 bbls of diesel and petrol a day for 30 years from gas produced at sea and converted on land.

Water. Government activities are governed by the Water Act, 1956 (as amended), which is administered by the Directorate of Water Affairs. A Water Research Commission was established in 1971 to co-ordinate and promote research; it is responsible for hydrological research, major water resource development, water pollution control. The combined average flow of South Africa's rivers is about 53,500m. cu. metres annually, most of it lost by evaporation and spillage.

In 1989, 2 major storage dams controlled 7,300m. cu. metres of the annual flow of 7,500m. cu. metres. An 82·5 km long tunnel to transfer water from the Orange River to the Great Fish River valley had been completed.

In Oct. 1986 South Africa signed a treaty with Lesotho to allow damming the Orange River head waters within Lesotho and diverting the collected water through tunnels into the Vaal River system of the OFS. Lesotho is to receive royalties and hydro-electric power in exchange.

Minerals. Value of the main mineral production sales (in R1,000):

	1983	*1984*	*1985*	*1986*
Asbestos	113,279	101,207	102,453	99,064
Chrome ore	71,453	121,627	231,669	212,794
Coal	2,539,731	3,348,058	4,962,285	5,245,943
Copper	351,137	365,761	535,853	550,178
Diamonds	525,217	463,019	702,648	647,996
Fluorspar	30,744	49,209	56,510	62,104
Gold	10,180,209	11,556,315	15,296,931	17,287,356

	1983	*1984*	*1985*	*1986*
Iron ore	309,919	372,728	472,353	473,510
Lime and limestone	162,493	182,831	203,975	237,311
Manganese	110,219	202,566	298,761	271,024
Phosphate	74,271	97,962	118,855	150,287
Silver	79,342	64,332	78,248	72,087

Total value of all minerals sold (1986), R29,240·1m.

Mineral production (tonnes) 1986: Coal, 170m.; iron ore, 24·5m.; phosphates, 2·9m.; manganese ore, 3·7m.; chromite, 3m.; asbestos, 138,000; copper, 196,000; lime and limestone, 14·3m.; fluorspar, 334,000; gold, 635,233 kg; silver, 216,599 kg; diamonds, 10·1m. carats.

South Africa is the world's largest producer of gold. Reserves were estimated at US$1,275m. in 1989.

At 31 Dec. 1986 the number of persons engaged in mining was 752,264. Of these, 553,668 were engaged in goldmining.

Minerals. A Quarterly Report of Production and Sales. Department of Mineral and Energy Affairs. Pretoria, from 1936

Mining Statistics. Department of Mineral and Energy Affairs, Pretoria, from 1966

Agriculture. Much of the land suitable for mechanical farming has unreliable rainfall. Good rainfall in 1989 followed 7 years of drought and crop failure. Of the total area natural pasture occupies 58% (71·3m. hectares); about 14m. hectares are suitable for dry-land farming, of which 10·6m. are actually cultivated. There are some 65,000 farms.

In 1987, agriculture, forestry and fisheries contributed approximately 5·6% to GDP.

Production (1988, in 1,000 tonnes): Maize, 6,900; sorghum, 482; wheat, 3,400; groundnuts, 231; sunflower seed, 419; sugar-cane, 20,332; oranges, 520; potatoes, 956; vegetables, 1,886; grapes, 1,411; apples, 446.

Livestock, in 1,000 (1988): 11,820 cattle, 29,800 sheep, 5,840 goats, 1,460 pigs.

The 1988 production of red meat was 947,000 tonnes, poultry meat 364,000 tonnes, wool, 92,400 tonnes, eggs, 190,000 tonnes, milk, 2·6m. tonnes.

Cotton-growing is now undertaken by many farmers, the plant being found a better drought resistant than either tobacco or maize. Viticulture and fruit-growing are important. Gross value of production (1986–87), R127·7m.

In 1986–87 the gross value of agricultural production was R12,677m. (field crops, R4,787m.; livestock products, R5,825m.; horticultural products, R2,365m.).

Forestry. The commercial forests occupy about 1·62m. hectares, of which 148,000 hectares are indigenous trees and the rest exotic trees (pine, gum, wattle). On 31 March 1986 there were 613,747 hectares of pines and other softwoods, 387,236 hectares of eucalypts, 124,228 hectares of wattle and 8,013 hectares of other hardwoods.

Production, 1985-86, of sawn timber, 1·66m. cu. metres (value R313m.); pulp, paper and paperboard, 1·39m. tonnes (R1,227m.).

Local production meets South Africa's needs of mining timber, firewood, round poles, wooden boxes, crates, particle boards, fibre board and sawn softwood, 30% of its requirements for sawn hardwood and more than 80% of its paper requirements. Rayon pulp, newsprint, other pulp and paper products, pulpwood chips and wattle tanning extract are the main exports.

The Republic is self-sufficient in newsprint and exports pulp and paper.

Fisheries. In 1986 sea fisheries landed 573,000 tons, of which 390,000 tons were pelagic shoal fish, 78% anchovy; trawl fisheries caught 191,000 tons, 72% hake. Total output, wholesale value, R585m. The fishing fleet consists of about 4,420 vessels. About 22,000 people are employed in the fishing industry and its ancillary activities. 10,100 seal pups and 321 bulls were culled in 1986.

INDUSTRY AND TRADE

Industry. Net value of sales of the principal groups of industries (in R1m.) in 1986: Processed food, 13,667; beverages and tobacco, 3,426; vehicles, 5,318; basic metals, 9,463·3; chemicals and products, 17,756; non-electrical machinery, 4,331; electrical machinery, 3,876; fabricated metal products except machinery, 5,555; printing and publishing, 1,795; wood and cork products except furniture, 1,357; clothing, 1,947; paper and products, 3,785; textiles, 3,497; total net value including other groups, 86,055. Manufacturing industry contributed R28,321m. to gross domestic product of R128,524m. in 1986.

In 1989 the workforce (excluding the 'independent' homelands of Transkei, Bophuthatswana, Venda and Ciskei) numbered (in 1,000; females in brackets): Whites, 2,033 (654); Coloureds, 1,223 (509); Asians, 344 (97); Blacks, 7,256 (2,351).

Industrial employment (except mining) at 28 Feb. 1987: Manufacturing employed 1,322,100 workers; construction, 295,600; trade and accommodation services, 742,917 (31 Dec. 1986).

Average monthly earnings of white employee, 1984, R1,402; of black, R364.

Trade Unions. In 1988 there were 209 registered trade unions in 10 federations with an estimated total membership of 2,084,323. There were 40 White unions, 26 Coloured and Asian and 28 Black. Ninety-three unions were mixed and 22 did not specify their composition.

The Industrial Conciliation Amendment Act (1979) provides for freedom of association to all workers irrespective of race. Unions were barred from political activity in Feb. 1988. Secondary and repeat strikes are banned, and unions are financially liable for illegal strike action. Work-days lost through strikes: 1987, 5·82m.; 1988, 914,000.

Commerce. South Africa, Botswana, Lesotho, Swaziland and Transkei are members of a customs union and the foreign trade statistics shown below represent the combined imports and exports of these countries. The total value of the imports and exports was as follows (in R1m.):

	Imports		*Exports*
1985	22,989·1	1985	36,474·2
1986	26,893·7	1986	41,796·7
1987	28,735·7	1987	42,716·9

The principal commodity groups of imports and exports (in R1m.) in 1987 were:

Imports		*Exports*	
Machinery	7,839·9	Minerals and products	3,868·7
Vehicles and aircraft	3,821·2	Base metals	4,696·2
Chemical products	3,148·1	Precious stones, metals and coins	3,717·8
Base metals	1,407·0	Textiles	943·4
Scientific and special equipment	1,420·7	Chemical products	1,150·4
Resins and plastics	1,311·6	Food, beverages and tobacco	1,039·6
Textiles	1,198·4	Vegetable products	1,244·5

Gold exports totaled US$8,527·5m. in 1988, some 40% of all exports.

In 1987 Japan was South Africa's main export market, with 11·6% of all exports, and Federal Germany the major source of imports (18·3%). In 1986 the geographical origin of South Africa's imports and the Direction of its export trade were mainly as follows:

	Imports %	*Exports %*
Africa	2	4
Europe	42	23
USA	13	9
Japan	10	8

Total trade between South Africa and UK (British Department of Trade returns, in £1,000 sterling):

	1985	*1986*	*1987*	*1988*	*1989*
Imports to UK	989,757	829,305	658,162	807,669	884,607
Exports and re-exports from UK	1,009,629	849,557	948,584	1,074,826	1,038,342

Tourism. In 1988, 804,985 tourists visited the Republic of South Africa; in 1987, 703,351, of whom 368,555 were from African countries and 237,709 from Europe

(97,286 from the UK and 56,260 from the Federal Republic of Germany).

COMMUNICATIONS

Roads. The railway administration operates the long-distance road motor services, together with private operators.

There were at 31 March 1987, 228,268 km of roads, of which 182,968 km were national and provincial roads (52,504 km surfaced) and 45,300 km municipal roads and streets (36,200 surfaced).

South African Transport Services carried 11·7m. passengers and 4·12m. tonnes of goods by road in 1986-87.

Motor vehicles in operation on 30 June 1987 included 3,107,031 passenger cars, 1,189,641 commercial vehicles, 144,339 minibuses, 27,573 buses and 322,842 motorcycles.

Railways. Railway history in South Africa begins in 1860 with the line Durban–Point. With the formation of the Union in 1910, the state-owned lines in the 4 provinces (12,194 km) were amalgamated into one state undertaking, which also took over the control of the harbours–the South African Railways and Harbours Administration now known as South African Transport Services. In 1990, SATS became a public company with the government as the only shareholder, as a prelude to possible privatization.

In 1988-89 there were 23,259 km of 1,065 mm gauge (8,440 km electrified) and 360 km of 762 mm gauge. Railways caried 568m. passengers and 165m. tonnes of freight.

Aviation. Civil aviation in South Africa is controlled by the Department of Transport, which administers the following state-owned airports: Jan Smuts Airport, Johannesburg; D. F. Malan Airport, Cape Town; Louis Botha Airport, Durban; J. B. M. Hertzog Airport, Bloemfontein; Ben Schoeman Airport, East London; H. F. Verwoerd Airport, Port Elizabeth; B. J. Vorster Airport, Kimberley; P. W. Botha Airport, George; Pierre van Ryneveld Airport, Upington. At other airports the Department provides air navigation services.

South African Airways, as the national air carrier, operate scheduled international air services within Africa and to Europe, South America, Israel and the Far East. Twenty independent operators provide internal flights which link up with SAA's internal network.

During 1986-87 South African Airways carried 4,220,317 passengers (3,741,963 on internal flights) and 75,269 tonnes of freight and mail (25,596).

In Sept. 1987 there were 264 licensed aerodromes, of which 156 were public and 108 private, and 76 approved helistops.

Shipping. The main ports are Durban, Cape Town, Saldanha, Richards Bay, Port Elizabeth and East London. Smaller ports are Mossel Bay, Port Nolloth, Walvis Bay and Lüderitz. During 1987 main ports handled 93m. tons of cargo.

Post and Broadcasting. On 31 March 1986 there were in South Africa 2,183 money-order post offices and postal agencies.

In March 1988 the international telex switchboard served 31,604 telex subscribers in South Africa. Line capacity of automatic telephone exchanges, 2·1m.; there were (1986) 4m. telephones.

The South African Broadcasting Corporation broadcasts (1989) 23 radio services in 19 languages and 4 television services in 7 languages. There were (1988) about 2m. television viewers.

Cinemas (1989). There were 400 including 100 drive-ins.

Newspapers (1987). There are 39 main newspapers, of which 10 were Afrikaans, 27 English, 1 Zulu and English and 1 Xhosa and English. There were 6 Afrikaans and 14 English daily newspapers.

JUSTICE, RELIGION, EDUCATION AND WELFARE

Justice. The common law of the republic is the Roman–Dutch law—that is, the uncodified law of Holland as it was at the date of the cession of the Cape in 1806.

The law of England as such is not recognized as authoritative, though by statute the principles of English law relating to evidence and to mercantile matters, *e.g.*, companies, patents, trademarks, insolvency and the like, have been introduced. In shipping and insurance, English law is followed in the Cape Province, and it has also largely influenced civil and criminal procedure throughout the republic. In all other matters, family relations, property, succession, contract, etc., Roman–Dutch law rules, English decisions being valued only so far as they agree therewith.

The Supreme Court of South Africa is constituted as follows: (i) The Appellate Division, consisting of the Chief Justice and as many Judges of Appeal as the State President may stipulate, is the highest court and its decisions are binding on all courts. It has no original jurisdiction, but is purely a Court of Appeal. (ii) The Provincial Divisions: In each province there is a provincial division of the Supreme Court, while in the Cape there are three such divisions possessing both original and appellate jurisdiction. (iii) The Local Divisions: There is a local division each in the Transvaal and Natal exercising the same original jurisdiction within limited areas as the provincial divisions. The judges hold office till they attain the age of 70 years. No judge can be removed from office except by the State President upon an address from both Houses of Parliament on the ground of misbehaviour or incapacity. The circuit system is fully developed.

The Black appeal courts and 3 Black divorce courts have jurisdiction to some extent concurrent with and in certain respects exclusive of that of the Supreme Court in cases in which the parties are Black.

Each province is further divided into districts with a magistrate's court having a prescribed civil and criminal jurisdiction. From this court there is an appeal to the provincial divisions of the Supreme Court, and thence to the appellate division. Magistrates' convictions carrying sentences above a prescribed limit are subject to automatic review by a judge. In addition, several regional divisions consisting of a number of districts have been constituted. Convictions of such courts are not subject to automatic review by a judge.

Courts of Black affairs commissioners have been constituted in defined areas to hear all civil cases and matters between Black and Black only. An appeal lies to the Black appeal court, whose decision is final, unless the court consents to an appeal to the appellate division of the Supreme Court on a point stated by the court itself. Black affairs commissioners have concurrent criminal jurisdiction with magistrates' courts in respect of certain offences committed by Blacks, while a limited civil and criminal jurisdiction is conferred upon the Black chief or headman over his own tribe.

Religion. A sample tabulation of the 1980 census results as regards religious denominations shows the following: *Whites:* Nederduits Gereformeerde Kerk, 1,693,640; Anglicans, 456,020; Methodists, 414,080; Roman Catholics, 393,640; Nederduits Hervormde Kerk, 246,340; Presbyterians, 128,920; Gereformeerde Kerk, 128,360; Apostolics, 125,920; other Christians, 566,640; Jews, 119,220; others, 255,320. *Blacks:* Methodists, 11,554,280; Black independent churches, 4,954,000; Nederduits Gereformeerde Kerk, 1,103,560; Roman Catholics, 1,676,680; Anglican, 797,040; Lutheran, 698,400; other Christian churches, 1,760,860; non-Christian churches, 101,700; others, 4,277,240. *Coloureds and Asians:* Nederduits Gereformeerde Kerk, 678,380; Hindus, 512,360; Anglican, 360,380; Roman Catholic, 285,980; Islam 318,000; others, 1,279,020.

Membership of the white branch of the Nederduits Gereformeerde Kerk was opened to all races in 1986.

Education. Primary and secondary public education, other than that specifically provided elsewhere, falls under the Provincial Administration. In terms of the National Education Policy Act, 1967, the Minister of Education, Arts and Science may, after consultation with the Provincial Administrators and the National Advisory Education Council, determine general educational policy within the framework of the Act. Black education is the responsibility of the Department of Black Education and Training, while education for Coloureds and Indians is controlled by the Department of Internal Affairs.

Public primary and secondary schools in 1987: Schools for Whites had 951,594 pupils and 71,657 teachers. For Coloureds, 822,767 pupils and 43,689 teachers. For Indians, 235,424 pupils and 12,787 teachers. For Blacks, 4,674,565 pupils and 137,442 teachers. A non-racial school (100 pupils) opened near Durban in 1987. Special schools (1987) for 4,465 Black pupils had 3,073 teachers; for 13,832 White pupils, 4,336 teachers; for 5,641 Coloured pupils, 1,256 teachers; for 1,929 Indian pupils, 738 teachers.

Private Schools. To a certain extent the activities of private schools are controlled by government regulations. Their pupils generally sit for the state schools' examinations. These schools make provision for kindergarten, elementary and preparatory, general primary, secondary and commercial education.

Higher Education. In March 1987 tertiary-level students included 247,035 whites (5% of white population), 31,488 coloureds (1%), 25,183 Indians (2·7%) and 95,119 Blacks (0·45%).

Of these, 164,634 whites, 24,012 coloureds, 19,802 Indians and 82,675 Blacks were at university and Colleges of Education. There are 17 universities in the republic: (1) The University of Cape Town. (2) The University of Natal in Durban and Pietermaritzburg. (3) The University of the Orange Free State at Bloemfontein (teaching in Afrikaans). (4) Potchefstroom University for Christian Higher Education, Potchefstroom (Afrikaans). (5) The University of Pretoria (Afrikaans). (6) Rhodes University, Grahamstown, C.P. (7) The University of Stellenbosch (Afrikaans). (8) The University of the Witwatersrand, Johannesburg. (9) The University of South Africa, with its seat in Pretoria, which conducts a Division of External Studies by means of correspondence and vacation courses (English and Afrikaans); it is also an examining body. (10) The University of Port Elizabeth (English and Afrikaans). (11) Rand Afrikaans University, Johannesburg (All may enrol, white, black, coloured or Asian students).

The University of Fort Hare (12), the University of the North (13) near Pietersburg and the University of Zululand (14) near Empangeni, Natal, are operated by the Department of Education and Training and provide education at university level for Blacks, the University of the Western Cape (15), Bellville (Cape), offers university facilities to the Coloured population and is administered by the Department of Internal Affairs as is the University for Indians (16), the University of Durban-Westville, at Durban. The Medical University of South Africa (17) is for Black students.

Technical and Vocational Education. Technical, vocational and special education for persons other than those for whom specific provision is made: The Department of National Education is responsible for the maintenance, management and control of or the payment of subsidies to colleges for advanced technical education, technical colleges, technical institutes, special schools, schools of industries and reform schools. Colleges for advanced technical education provide education on an advanced level for a variety of technical, commercial and general courses of study as well as secondary education on a part-time basis. Technical colleges and technical institutes are mainly responsible for the training of apprentices and the education, on a part-time basis, of persons not subject to compulsory school attendance. Special schools for handicapped children cater for the educational needs of those who are blind, partially sighted, deaf, hard of hearing, epileptic, cerebral palsied and physically handicapped. Children found to be in need of care by a children's court, are admitted to schools of industries and reform schools.

The Department of Internal Affairs has taken over all schools of this nature for Coloureds.

In 1987, technical and training colleges (except Colleges of Education) had 82,401 white students; 7,476 coloured; 5,381 Indian; 12,444 black.

Health. In 1987 there were 20,174 medical practitioners of whom 5,532 were specialists, 3,892 dental specialists and dentists, 134,574 nurses. In 1984 there were 629 hospitals. In 1983 there were 14,333 beds in psychiatric hospitals; 652,054 mentally ill were treated as out-patients, and others treated in psychiatric wards in general hospitals.

All public health services rendered by government bodies are free, or charged according to the patient's means.

Social Welfare. Under the Social Pensions Act, 1973, pensions and allowances are made to aged, blind, disabled and war veterans, subject to a means test. Family allowances are paid to families with 3 or more children and inadequate income, and to mothers alone with one or more children and inadequate income.

Welfare Services. South Africa is not a welfare state, yet provides many services for the community. Welfare work on behalf of the Government is done by the Departments of Health and Welfare, Co-operation and Development, and Internal Affairs.

In 1989 there were over 1,600 voluntary organizations. The work of all these bodies is co-ordinated by the South African Welfare Council and regional welfare boards set up under the National Welfare Act, 1978.

The Child Care Act, 1983 which superseded the Children's Act, 1960 is designed to protect children against neglect, abuse, ill-treatment and exploitation. The Act provides for preventive child care services, foster care, adoption and residential care, and also for various children's alowances and financial assistance to children's homes and creches.

Welfare services for the aged are mainly provided by voluntary bodies with government subsidies; the same principle applies to the care of the handicapped, but there are State settlements for the permanently handicapped, and State sheltered-employment programmes for handicapped adults.

The National Advisory Board on Rehabilitation Matters advises and brings together the voluntary and government agencies working on drug abuse and alcoholism.

In all fields of welfare, State subsidies enable voluntary bodies to employ professional social workers.

DIPLOMATIC REPRESENTATIVES

Of South Africa in Great Britain (South Africa Hse., Trafalgar Sq., London, WC2N 5DP)
Ambassador: P. R. Killen.

Of Great Britain in South Africa (255 Hill St., Arcadia, Pretoria, 0002)
Ambassador: Sir Robin Renwick, KCMG.

Of South Africa in the USA (3051 Massachusetts Ave., NW, Washington, D.C., 20008)
Ambassador: Piet G. Koornhof.

Of the USA in South Africa (225 Pretorius St., Pretoria)
Ambassador: William L. Swing.

Of South Africa to the United Nations
Ambassador: Jeremy B. Shearar.

Further Reading

Statistical Information: The Bureau (formerly Office) of Census and Statistics (Schoeman St., Pretoria)

The Customs and Excise Office, Pretoria, publishes *Monthly Abstract of Trade Statistics* (from 1946) and *Trade and Shipping of the Union of South Africa* (annually, 1910–55); *Foreign Trade Statistics* (annually, from 1956)

Benson, M. *Nelson Mandela: The Man and the Movement.* New York, 1986
Bindman, G., (ed.) *South Africa: Human Rights and the Rule of Law.* London, 1988
Bissell, R. E. and Crocker, C. A., *South Africa in the 1980s.* Boulder, 1979
Böhning, W. R., *Black Migration to South Africa.* Geneva, 1981
Branford, J., *A Dictionary of South African English.* Rev. ed. OUP, 1980
Davenport, T. R. H., *South Africa: A Modern History.* 3rd ed. CUP, 1986
de Villiers, L., *South Africa: A Skunk Among Nations.* London, 1975
Gann, L. H. and Duignan, P., *Why South Africa will Survive.* London, 1981
Goldenhuys, D., *The Diplomacy of Isolation: South African Foreign Policy Making.* Johannesburg, 1984

Hill, C. R., *Change in South Africa: Blind Alleys and New Directions.* London, 1983
Lewis, S. R., *The Economics of Apartheid.* New York, 1989
Meli, F., *South Africa belongs to us.* Indiana Univ. Press, 1989
Musiker, R., *South Africa,* [Bibliography] Oxford and Santa Barbara, 1980
Oxford History of South Africa. OUP, Vol. 1, 1969; Vol. 2 1971
Thompson, L., *The Political Mythology of Apartheid.* Yale Univ. Press, 1985
Venter, D. J., *South Africa, Sanctions and Multinationals.* London, 1989

PROVINCE OF THE CAPE OF GOOD HOPE

Kaapprovinsie

HISTORY. The colony of the Cape of Good Hope was founded by the Dutch in the year 1652. Britain took possession of it from 1795 to 1803 and again in 1806, and it was formally ceded to Great Britain by the Convention of London, 13 Aug. 1814. Letters patent issued in 1850 declared that in the colony there should be a Parliament which should consist of the Governor, a Legislative Council and a House of Assembly. On 31 May 1910 the colony was merged in the Union of South Africa, thereafter forming an original province of the Union.

AREA AND POPULATION. The following table gives the population of the Cape of Good Hope [1] (area (1980) 646,332 sq. km) at the last census:

	All races			*Whites*		*Non-Whites*	
	Total	*Males*	*Females*	*Males*	*Females*	*Males*	*Females*
1936	3,527,865	1,663,169	1,864,796	396,058	394,993	1,267,011	1,469,803
1946	4,051,424	1,924,334	2,127,090	433,849	436,300	1,490,485	1,690,790
1951	4,426,726	2,110,674	2,316,052	463,917	471,168	1,646,757	1,844,884
1960	5,360,234	2,553,245	2,806,989	493,370	507,398	2,059,875	2,299,591
1970 [2]	4,293,726	2,151,629	2,142,097	546,761	567,448	1,604,868	1,579,649
1980 [3]	5,091,360	2,575,460	2,515,900	624,680	639,360	1,950,780	1,876,540
1986 [1]	4,901,261	2,371,906	2,529,355	...	...	...	...

[1] Including Walvis Bay (699 sq. km). [2] Excluding Transkei.
[3] Excluding Transkei, Ciskei and Bophuthatswana.

Present area, 641,379 sq. km (247,637 sq. miles), including the enclave of Walvis Bay 1,124 sq. km (434 sq. miles) on the coast of South West Africa (Namibia) which forms an administrative part of the Cape Province.

Of the non-White population in 1980, 32,120 were Asians, 1,569,040 were Blacks and 2,226,160 Coloureds.

Vital statistics for calendar years:

	Births	*Deaths*	*Marriages*
1979	80,900	32,185	34,243
1980	80,546	34,162	29,334
1983	73,654	39,164	39,162
1984	74,122	41,345	40,165

ADMINISTRATION. In June 1986 the provincial councils were abolished.

Cape Town is the seat of the provincial administration.

Administrator: Eugene Louw.

The province is divided into 111 magisterial districts and 35 divisions. Each division has a council of at least 6 members (15 in the Cape Division) elected quinquennially by the owners or occupiers of immovable property. The duties devolving upon divisional councils include the construction and maintenance of roads and bridges, local rating, vehicle taxation (except motor vehicle taxation) and preservation of public health. There are 216 municipalities, each governed by a mayor and councillors. Municipal elections are held biennially.

FINANCE. In 1984–85 revenue amounted to R1,996,920,000 and expenditure to R1,987,920,000.

MINING. For mineral production, *see* p. 1093-94.

AGRICULTURE. Viticulture in the republic is almost exclusively confined to the Cape Province, but practically all other forms of agricultural and pastoral activity are pursued.

INDUSTRY. The province has brick, tile and pottery works, saw-mills, engineering works, foundries, grain-mills, distilleries and wineries, clothing factories, furniture, boot and shoe factories, etc.

RELIGION. Sample tabulation, 1980 census. Nederduits Gereformeerde Kerk, 1,110,516; Gereformeerde Kerk, 12,714; Nederduits Hervormde Kerk, 115,012; Anglican, 430,102; Presbyterian, 35,126; Methodist, 112,961; Roman Catholic, 251,000; Apostolic, 73,140; Lutheran, 89,134; Islam, 183,000; Hindu, 7,000; Independent Churches, 94,103; other Christian Churches, 440,000; Jews, 31,621; Agnostics, 55,000.

EDUCATION. On 1 April 1986 the Education Department came within the jurisdiction of the Central Government. Education is compulsory for all White children. Primary and secondary education is free to the end of the calendar year in which the age of 19 years is attained.

Whites (1985). There were 828 government and aided schools with 14,205 teachers and 238,853 pupils; 8 teacher-training colleges with 291 lecturers and 1,841 students; 53 private schools with 13,859 pupils.

Coloureds (1985). There were 1,776 government and aided schools with 26,583 teachers and 657,391 pupils; 13 teacher-training colleges with 6,709 students; 18 private schools with 2,652 pupils.

Black (1985). There were 1,137 government schools with 7,105 teachers and 318,541 pupils and 17 private schools with 118 teachers and 6,120 pupils.

Asians (1985). There were 8 government schools with 201 teachers and 5,400 pupils.

PROVINCE OF NATAL

HISTORY. Natal was annexed to Cape Colony in 1844, placed under separate government in 1845, and on 15 July 1856 established as a separate colony. By this charter partially representative institutions were established, and in 1893 the colony attained responsible government. The province of Zululand was annexed to Natal on 30 Dec. 1897. The districts of Vryheid, Utrecht and part of Wakkerstroom, formerly belonging to the Transvaal, were annexed in Jan. 1903. On 31 May 1910 the colony was merged in the Union of South Africa as an original province of the Union.

AREA AND POPULATION. The province (including Kwa Zulu, 36,073 sq. km) has an area of 91,785 sq. km, with a seaboard of about 576 km. The climate is sub-tropical on the coast and somewhat colder inland. The province is divided into 45 magisterial districts.

The census returns of population (excluding Kwa Zulu) were:

	All races			*Whites*		*Non-Whites*	
	Total	*Males*	*Females*	*Males*	*Females*	*Males*	*Females*
1960	2,979,034	1,443,561	1,535,473	166,404	222,750	1,227,157	1,362,468
1970	4,236,770	2,009,410	2,227,360	171,005	214,960	1,794,430	2,004,610
1980	2,676,340	1,360,600	1,315,740	276,240	285,620	1,084,360	1,030,120
1985	2,145,018	1,072,426	1,072,592	274,987	285,234	797,629	787,358

Of the non-White population in 1980, 665,340 were Asians, 91,020 Coloureds and 1,358,120 Blacks. Population of Kwa Zulu, *see* p. 1088.

ADMINISTRATION. State of parties Oct. 1985: New Republic Party, 14; National Party, 5; Progressive Federal Party, 1.

The seat of provincial government in Natal is Pietermaritzburg. In April 1978 the area of East Griqualand was transferred to Natal from Cape Province.

Administrator: The Hon. Radclyffe Macbeth Cadman.

FINANCE. In 1988–89 revenue amounted to R1,478,605,796 and expenditure to R1,434,163,171.

MINING. The province is rich in mineral wealth, particularly coal. For figures of mineral production, *see* p. 1093-94.

AGRICULTURE. Sugar and citrus growing are of major importance. On the coast and in Zululand there are vast plantations of sugar-cane (about 375,000 hectares), producing, in 1985, 20,756,000 tons. Cereals of all kinds (especially maize), fruits, vegetables, the *Acacia molissima* (the bark of which is much used for tanning purposes) and other crops are produced. Large areas are devoted to timber plantations and forestry.

INDUSTRY. Natal is highly industrialized. There are metallurgical, chemical, paper, rayon and food-processing plants, iron and steel foundries, petrol refineries, pulp-mills, explosives and fertilizer plants, milk- and meat-canning factories.

EDUCATION. The Department of Education and Culture controls primary and secondary education for Whites. Control was transferred from the province to central government on 1 April 1986, and the classification of government-aided schools changed to private although they continue to receive a subsidy.

Whites (1989). There were 261 government schools with 98,966 pupils; 2 residential teacher-training colleges with 893 students; 1 correspondence teacher-training college with 458 pupils; 52 private schools with 11,290 pupils; 11 special schools and training centres with 1,426 pupils and 9 technical colleges with 3,668 pupils.

Coloureds (1989). There were 65 state and state-aided schools with 1,386 teachers and 30,565 pupils; 18 state subsidized pre-primary schools with 15 teachers and 1,000 pupils; 4 special schools with 155 pupils and 22 teachers; 1 teacher-training college with 301 students and 32 lecturers; 1 technical college with 42 full-time lecturers and 14 part-time lecturers.

Blacks (1989). There were 1,086 schools with 5,809 teachers and 214,364 pupils. These schools are situated in the white area of Natal and the south-eastern Transvaal.

Asians (1989). There were 439 state and state-aided schools with 11,458 teachers and 249,331 pupils; 35 pre-primary schools with 2,446 children; 2 schools of industries with 216 pupils; 16 special schools and training centres with 1,578 pupils; 3 technical colleges with 2,396 full-time students and 5,170 part-time students; 2 Colleges of Education with 682 students and 1 pre-vocational school with 240 pupils.

PROVINCE OF THE TRANSVAAL

HISTORY. The Transvaal was one of the territories colonized by the Boers who left the Cape Colony during the Great Trek in 1834 and following years. In 1852, by the Sand River Treaty, Great Britain recognized the independence of the Transvaal, which, in 1853, took the name of the South African Republic. In 1877 the republic was annexed by Great Britain, but the Boers took up arms towards the end of 1880. In 1881 peace was made and self-government, subject to British suzerainty and certain stipulated restrictions, was restored to the Boers. The London Convention of 1884 removed the suzerainty and a number of these restrictions but reserved to Great Britain the right of approval of the Transvaal's foreign relations, excepting with regard to the Orange Free State. In 1886 gold was discovered on the Witwatersrand, and this discovery, together with the great influx of foreigners which it occasioned, gave rise to many grave problems. Eventually, in 1899, war broke out between Great Britain and the Transvaal. Peace was concluded on 31 May 1902, the Transvaal and the Orange Free State both losing their independence. The Transvaal was governed as a crown colony until 12 Jan. 1907, when responsible government came into force. On 31 May 1910 the Transvaal became one of the four provinces of the Union.

AREA AND POPULATION. The area of the province is 262,499 sq. km or 101,351 sq. miles, including Gazankulu, Lebowa, Ka Ngwane and Kwa Ndebele. The province is divided into 53 districts. The following table shows the population, excluding Gazankulu, Lebowa, Ka Ngwane and Kwa Ndebele in 1985, at each of the last censuses:

		All races		*Whites*		*Non-Whites*	
	Total	*Males*	*Females*	*Males*	*Females*	*Males*	*Females*
1936	3,341,470	1,846,576	1,494,894	424,470	396,286	1,422,108	1,098,608
1946	4,283,038	2,374,323	1,908,715	541,053	522,068	1,833,270	1,386,647
1951	4,812,838	2,619,314	2,193,524	737,194	731,111	2,575,119	2,230,053
1960	6,270,711	3,310,948	2,959,763	735,845	729,730	2,575,103	2,230,034
1970	6,478,904	3,507,753	2,971,151	957,291	946,802	2,550,462	2,024,349
1980	8,376,042	4,581,054	3,794,988	1,192,484	1,176,055	3,388,570	2,618,933
1985	7,532,179	4,008,070	3,524,109	1,224,064	1,237,300	2,784,006	2,286,809

Of the non-White population in 1985, 4,674,290 were Black, 126,201 Asians and 270,324 Coloureds. Population of Gazankulu, Lebowa, Ka Ngwane and Kwa Ndebele, *see* p. 1088.

Important towns of the province are listed on p. 1089.

ADMINISTRATION. The seat of provincial government is at Pretoria, which is also the administrative capital of the Republic of South Africa.

Administrator: D. J. Hough.

FINANCE. In 1988–89 revenue amounted to R2,075,960,000 and expenditure to R2,116,552,000.

MINING. For mineral production, *see* p. 1093-94. Gold output in 1983 was 15,807,760 oz. worth R7,483,932,210.

AGRICULTURE. The province is in the main a stock-raising country, though there are considerable areas well adapted for agriculture, including the growing of tropical crops.

INDUSTRY. The province has iron and brass foundries and engineering works, grain-mills, breweries, brick, tile and pottery works, tobacco, soap, and candle factories, coach and wagon works, clothing factories, etc.

RELIGION. 1980 population census. *Whites:* Christians, 1,927,646; Jews, 76,913; other non-Christians, 4,265.

Non-Whites: Christians, 4,692,362; Moslems, 74,504; Hindus, 37,249; other non-Christians, 15,668.

EDUCATION. All education for Whites except that of universities is under the provincial authority. The province has been divided for the purposes of local control and management into 21 school districts. Instruction in government schools, both primary and secondary, is free. The medium of instruction is the home language of the pupil. The teaching of the other language begins at the earliest stage at which it is appropriate on educational grounds. Both languages are taught as examination subjects to every pupil.

Whites (1988). There were 984 public schools with 27,400 teachers and 504,032 pupils; 6 teacher-training colleges with 7,560 students; 115 private schools with 2,187 teachers and 33,831 pupils.

Coloureds (1988). There were 103 state and state-aided schools with 2,956 teachers and 74,607 pupils; 1 teacher-training college with 562 students.

Asians (1988). There were 81 public schools with 1,409 teachers and 32,412 pupils; 1 teacher-training college with 31 teachers and 126 students.

Blacks (1988). There were 4,295 public and private school sections with 25,779 teachers and 957,322 pupils (homelands excluded).

PROVINCE OF THE ORANGE FREE STATE

Oranje-Vrystaat

HISTORY. The Orange River was first crossed by Europeans in the middle of the 18th century. Between 1810 and 1820, settlements were made in the southern parts of the Orange Free State, and the Great Trek greatly increased the number of settlers during and after 1836. In 1848, Sir Harry Smith proclaimed the whole territory between the Orange and Vaal rivers as a British possession called the 'Orange River Sovereignty'. However, in 1854, by the Convention of Bloemfontein, British sovereignty was withdrawn and the independence of the country was recognized.

During the first 5 years of its existence the Orange Free State was much harassed by incessant raids by the Basutos. These were at length conquered, but, owing to the intervention of the British Government, the treaty of Aliwal North incorporated only part of the territory of the Basutos in the Orange Free State.

On account of the treaty with the South African Republic, the Orange Free State took a prominent part in the South African War (1899–1902) and was annexed on 28 May 1900 as the Orange River Colony. Crown colony government continued until 1907, when responsible government was introduced. On 31 May 1910 the Orange River Colony was merged in the Union of South Africa as the province of the Orange Free State, and on 31 May 1961 became a province of the Republic of South Africa.

AREA AND POPULATION. The area of the province is 127,993 sq. km or 49,418 sq. miles, including Qwaqwa. The province is divided into 43 administrative and 49 magisterial districts. The population has varied as follows:

	All races			*Whites*		*Non-Whites*	
	Total	*Males*	*Females*	*Males*	*Females*	*Males*	*Females*
1936	772,060	381,903	390,157	101,872	99,106	280,031	291,051
1946	879,071	432,896	446,175	101,874	100,203	331,022	345,972
1951	1,016,570	519,166	497,404	115,637	112,015	403,529	385,389
1960	1,386,202	731,486	654,716	139,304	137,103	601,182	553,613
1970	1,716,350	899,140	817,210	148,110	148,030	751,030	669,180
1980	1,931,860	1,039,220	892,640	166,380	159,840	872,840	732,800
1989	2,349,556	1,246,523	1,103,033	183,679	188,219	1,062,844	914,814

Of the non-White population in 1989, 1,908,414 were Black, 69,184 Coloureds and 60 Indians.

ADMINISTRATION. Provincial councils were abolished on 30 June 1986.

For the Whites there are 71 municipal councils and 6 village management boards. For the coloured 9 management committees and for the Blacks, 4 city councils, 8 town councils, 56 village committees and 2 local authority committees.

Administrator: L. J. Botha.

FINANCE. In 1988–89 revenue was R957m. and expenditure R871m.

MINING. For mineral statistics, *see* p. 0000. The output of gold in 1988 was 171,512 kg valued at R5,462·7m.

AGRICULTURE. The province consists of undulating plains, affording excellent grazing and wide tracts for agricultural purposes. The rainfall is moderate. The Orange Free State is the largest grain-producing province in the Republic and is also an important sheep- and cattle-farming region.

INDUSTRY. The more important manufacturing industries in the province are the oil-from-coal factory at Sasolburg (as well as industries based on its by-products); grain mills and brick, tile and pottery works. Fertilizers, agricultural implements, blankets, woollen products, clothing, hosiery, cement and pharmaceutical products are also manufactured.

EDUCATION. Primary, secondary and vocational education and the training of teachers are controlled and financed by the Department of Education and Culture Administration: House of Assembly for Whites and Administration; House of Representatives for Coloureds; Department of Education and Training for Blacks.

Education is free in all public schools up to the university matriculation standard. Attendance is compulsory for White and Coloured between the ages of 7 and 16, but exemption may be granted in special cases. Attendance is not compulsory for Black children, except in areas/communities/towns where a request for compulsory education had been made. In these cases education is compulsory up to Standard 5 or the age of 16. The home language of the pupil is the medium of instruction up to Standard 2; thereafter he has an option of Afrikaans, English or his home language in Black schools.

Further education and training are given at 2 universities (UOFS and Vista), 3 teachers' training colleges, 1 technikon, 1 agricultural college, 2 nursing colleges, 5 technical colleges and numerous training centres.

Whites (1989). There were 211 government and aided schools with 4,460 teachers and 75,711 pupils.

Coloureds (1989). There were 47 government and aided schools with 750 teachers and 17,381 pupils.

Blacks (1989). There were 2,687 government schools with 10,574 teachers and 414,329 pupils.

BOPHUTHATSWANA

HISTORY. Bophuthatswana was first to obtain self-government under the Bantu Homeland Constitution Act of 1971 and was the second black homeland to ask the Republic of South Africa for full independence, which was granted on 6 Dec. 1977.

AREA AND POPULATION. The total area is 44,000 sq. km.

In 1985 there was a *de jure* population of 3·2m., of which 47% lived in the White areas. The remaining 53% (1,740,600) lived in the homeland. Estimate (1989) 2·3m. The capital is Mmabatho.

CONSTITUTION AND GOVERNMENT. The Bophuthatswana Government is a compromise between the traditional chief-in-council system and a democratic electoral system. There are 72 elected and 24 nominated members in the Legislative Assembly. Self-government was granted in 1972. Each regional authority (coinciding with the 12 districts of the country) nominates 2 members, and each district elects 6 members to the National Assembly and 12 designated by the President on account of their special knowledge, qualifications or experience.

Executive power vests in the President, who is directly elected by general suffrage of persons who are registered as voters, and he elects his Cabinet.

The first general election was held in Oct. 1972, 2 political parties taking part. Kgosi Lucas Mangope's Bophuthatswana National Party (BNP) won 20 of the 24 contested seats, but in 1974 he formed the Bophuthatswana Democratic Party which in the 1987 elections won 66 seats; the People's Progressive Party, 6 seats.

Members of regional authorities are elected from among the tribal and community authorities in their areas.

The Cabinet in Nov. 1989 consisted of:

President, Minister of Law and Order, Audit and Public Service: Dr Kgosi Lucas Manyane Mangope (took office 6 Dec. 1977; re-elected for another 7 years as from 11 Nov. 1984).

Population Development: T. M. Molatlhwa. *Internal Affairs:* Kgosi V. S. Suping Motsatsi. *Finance:* L. G. Young. *Posts and Telecommunications and Broadcasting:* K. C. V. A. Sehume. *Manpower and Coordination:* S. M. Seodi. *State Affairs and Civil Aviation:* R. Cronje. *Foreign Affairs:* S. L. L. Rathebe. *Health and Social Welfare:* Dr N. C. O. B. Khaole. *Water Affairs:* T. M. Tlhabane. *Economic Planning, Energy Affairs and Mines:* E. B. Keikelame. *Agriculture and Natural Resources:* P. H. Moeketsi. *Parliamentary Affairs, Local Government and Housing:* H. F. Tlou. *Education:* G. S. Nkau. *Justice and Transport:* S. G. Mothibe. *Public Works:* S. C. Kgobokoe.

There were 8 Deputy Ministers.

Flag: Blue, crossed by a diagonal orange stripe, and in the canton a white disc charged with a leopard's face in black and white.

DEFENCE. The Air Wing of the Defence Force has 2 Partenavia P-68 patrol aircraft, 2 Aviocar transports, and 1 Alouette III, 2 BK-117 and 1 Ecureuil helicopters. There is an Army Force of 3,100 with 2 infantry battalions.

INTERNATIONAL RELATIONS

Aid. The Republic of South Africa granted aid of R530m. in 1989–90.

ECONOMY

Budget. The 1989–90 budget balanced at R2,300m.

Currency. South African Rand.

Banking. The financial system is controlled by legislation inherited from South Africa on independence, and commercial banks have strong direct links with South African banks which in certain instances are controlled by overseas banking companies.

In 1988 there were 3 commercial banks with branches in all major commercial and agricultural centres offering a full range of banking services. The Agricultural Bank of Bophuthatswana provides finance to farmers. The government-funded Agricultural Development Fund provides loan finance and subsidy support to agricultural co-operative societies. The Bophuthatswana Building Society grants loans for house building.

NATURAL RESOURCES

Water. The Department of Water Affairs controls and maintains 2,833 reservoirs, 6,845 boreholes and 648 earth dams.

Minerals. The territory is particularly rich in minerals. In 1988 there were 20 mines employing 56,000 people. Minerals include platinum, asbestos, gold, calcite, granite, chrome, vanadium, limestone and diamonds.

Exploration for more platinum, chrome and coal is currently being carried out both by the private sector and by the Mining and Geological Survey Division of the Department of Economic Planning. The platinum mines around Rustenburg produce about 66% of the free world's total production. The major chrome mines are near Rustenburg and Marico, while vanadium is mined in the Odi district near Brits. The Rustenburg, Western and Impala Platinum mines which are shared with the Republic of South Africa produce about 1·9m. oz. a year.

AGRICULTURE. Bophuthatswana is a semi-arid area of bushveld and grass veld suitable for stock farming. The annual rainfall is 300 mm in the west and 700 mm in the east and there are 4 river catchment areas—those of the Molopo, Ngotwane, Sehujwane (Limpopo) and Madikwe (Vaal) rivers.

Although the land tenure system militates against establishing large farms, some land which is suitable for farming is leased by the Government to successful farmers.

Livestock (1988): Cattle, 467,355; sheep, 268,351; goats, 530,430; pigs, 8,039; poultry, 196,396.

Only 6·6% of the territory is suited to dryland farming, but crop yields have shown a steady improvement in recent years. In Ditsobotla district, 36,926 hectares of fertile land has been developed by 3 primary co-operatives comprising 190 Batswana farmers. Silkworm farming was being tried in 1983. By 1981 the country was self sufficient in maize and exported the surplus. Three rice projects are successfully expanding and vegetable production was flourishing in 1987. The budget for 1989–90 is R145m.

INDUSTRY. The first industries were started on an agency basis at Babelegi; the fastest growing industrial area in the homeland, in 1977 it covered 183 hectares and by March 1985 more than R234m. had been invested in the project. Other industries are situated at Mmabatho, Garankuwa, Selosesha, Mafikeng and Mogwase. South African border industries are also promoted by the government, notably at Rosslyn where 128 industries had been established by Dec. 1975.

COMMUNICATIONS

Roads. Total length (1988) 6,300 km, of which 1,300 km are tarred.

Aviation. Mmabatho International Airport was opened in 1984.

Post and Broadcasting. There were 23,473 telephones at 30 April 1988, and 44 post offices.In 1989 there was 1 television station and 2 radio stations (Radio-Bop broadcasts in English and Radio Mmabatho in Setswana).

EDUCATION AND WELFARE

Education. Education is not compulsory but is free apart from nominal contributions to school funds and hostel fees at post-primary schools. Medium of instruction from Grade I to Standard 2 is in Setswana; from Standard 3 to senior standards is in English. Afrikaans is taught as a subject. The education is controlled by the Department of Education with a budget of R417m. in 1989-90.

In 1988 there were 28,439 children in kindergartens, 356,585 in primary schools, 125,372 in middle schools, 71,891 in high schools, 984 in schools for the mentally handicapped, 677 for the physically handicapped, 4,056 in colleges of education, 2,773 in technical schools and university. The number of teachers was 16,178 excluding lecturers.

Health. In 1987 there were 11 hospitals, 152 static clinics, 6,303 hospital and clinic beds, 106 doctors and 2,672 nurses. The health budget in 1987–88 was R103m.

Further Reading

Five Years of Independence: Republic of Bophuthatswana. Mafikeng, 1983
A Nation on the March
Bophuthatswana at a Glance

TRANSKEI

HISTORY. Transkei is the homeland of the Xhosa nation and was granted self-government by the Republic of South Africa in 1963. Over 1·5m. Transkeians live permanently in the Republic of South Africa but were deprived of their South African citizenship on independence.

AREA AND POPULATION. The total area is 16,910 sq. miles (43,798 sq. km). Population (1985 estimate) 2,876,122. The capital is Umtata (population (1976) 24,805; 20,196 Blacks, 1,067 Coloured and 3,542 Whites). Other towns include Gcuwa, Kwabhaca, Umzimvubu and Lusikisiki.

CONSTITUTION AND GOVERNMENT. The Status of Transkei Bill of 1976 gave Transkei a unicameral National Assembly instead of the then existing Legislative Assembly. Independence was achieved 26 Oct. 1976.

General elections were held on 29 Sept. 1976 and the Transkei National Independence Party gained 69 of the 75 elective seats in the National Assembly. Members were elected for a 5-year period. In addition there are 75 traditional (co-opted) members (70 chiefs and 5 paramount chiefs).

President: Paramount Chief T. N. Ndamase.

In Sept. 1987 Chief George Mantanzima the Prime Minister, resigned and was succeeded by Stella Sigcau who in turn was ousted in a bloodless military coup, led by Major-Gen. Bantu Holomisa in Jan. 1988.

Flag: Three horizontal stripes of ochre, white, green.

FINANCE. In 1985 government income was R872m. and expenditure R984m.

MINERALS. Coal, titanium and black granite are mined.

AGRICULTURE. Notable examples of successful commercial enterprises in agriculture are the Magwa and Majola tea estates, with approximately 1,700 hectares planted, and various fibre plantations. 70,000 hectares of land are under indigenous forests and 61,000 hectares have been put under exotic plantations. There are 28 sawmills in the country.

Livestock (1976): Cattle, 1·3m.; sheep, 2·5m.; goats, 1·25m.

COMMUNICATIONS

Roads. There are above 8,800 km of roads.

Railways. There is a 209 km railway line linking Umtata with the port of East London in the Republic of South Africa.

Aviation. An international airport exists at Umtata.

Shipping. A start was made in 1978 on a 'free port' at Mnganzana but has since been abandoned.

Post. There were 11,498 telephones in 1978.

EDUCATION AND WELFARE

Education. In 1985 there were 690,000 pupils in primary schools and 193,000 pupils in secondary schools. The national university was inaugurated in Umtata in 1977 and has a brance in Butterworth.

Health. There were (1987) 31 hospitals with a total of 7,561 beds.

DIPLOMATIC REPRESENTATIVES

No country, other than the Republic of South Africa, has recognized Transkei as an independent state.

VENDA

HISTORY. Traditionally the territory of the Vhavenda, the country was granted self-government in 1973, and became the third Black homeland to be granted independence by the Republic of South Africa on 13 Sept. 1979.

AREA AND POPULATION. The total area is 7,460 sq. km. In 1985, census, the *de jure* population of Venda was estimated at 651,393, the *de facto* population at 459,986. The capital is Thohoyandou. The other main towns are Sibasa, Makwarela, Makhado, Vuwani, Mutale and Masisi.

Vital statistics, 1987: Birth rate was 39·1 per 1,000 population; crude death rate, 10·3; infant mortality rate 56·9 per 1,000 live births.

CONSTITUTION AND GOVERNMENT. Executive power is vested in the President, who is elected for the duration of each Parliament, which consists of the President and the National Assembly; legislative power is vested in Parliament. In addition to the National Assembly there is an Executive Council, or Cabinet, and a judiciary independent of the Executive. The National Assembly consists of 45 members elected by popular vote, 15 members designated by 5 district councils, 6 members nominated by the President and 27 chiefs as *ex officio* members, and a representative of the Paramount Chief. A new Assembly must be elected after every 5 years, but it may be dissolved at any time by the President. All existing tribal, community and regional councils were retained with their status and powers unchanged, like those of the tribal leaders.

The first general election was held in Aug. 1973; the sole political party, the Venda Independence People's Party (VIPP) won 10 of the 18 contested seats. Shortly after, the Chief Minister, Chief Mphephu, formed the Venda National Party (VNP); in the second general election of July 1978 the VIPP won 31 of the 42 contested seats, VNP the remaining 11. Chief Mphephu was re-elected Chief Minister.

President: F. N. Ravele.

Internal Affairs and Manpower: Chief J. R. Rambuda. *Agriculture and Forestry, National Assembly and Local Government:* Chief A. M. Madzivhandila. *Water Affairs:* (Vacant). *Foreirn Affairs, Information and Broadcasting and Public Service Commission:* Chief C. A. Nelwamondo. *Finance, Commerce, Industry and Tourism:* Headman E. R. B. Nesengani. *Education and Culture:* Headman R. R. Sumbana. *Transport, Public Works and Posts and Telecommunications:* G. M. Ramabulana. *Urban Affairs and Land Tenure:* Chief M. M. Mphaphuli. *Justice and Prisons:* N. A. Mashila. *Health, Social Welfare and Pensions:* Chief T. A. Mulima.

Flag: Three horizontal stripes of green, yellow, and brown, with a brown V on the yellow stripe, and a blue vertical strip in the hoist.

DEFENCE. The Venda Defence Force was formed in 1983. It includes a small aviation component operating 1 Alouette III and 1 BK-117 helicopters.

INTERNATIONAL RELATIONS

Aid. The Republic of South Africa granted aid of R45m. in 1981–82.

ECONOMY

Budget. The 1989–90 budget envisaged expenditure of R776m.

Currency. South African Rand.

NATURAL RESOURCES

Water. In 1989 there were 4 major dams with a total capacity of 26·1m. cu. metres, and a purification plant.

Minerals. Venda is relatively poor in mineral resources, although there are large supplies of stone for construction. Coal is the most important mineral; there are large deposits in the west near Makhado. In 1988 further development was planned of the trial coal mine in the east at Tshikondeni to increase production from 208,000 to 750,000 tons a year.

Agriculture. About 85% of Venda is suitable only for the raising of livestock because of insufficient rainfall and poor soils, while some 10% is suited to dry-land crop production. Over 10,965 hectares have been given over to forest, mainly pine and eucalyptus. Eighteen irrigation schemes are being developed and there is extensive reclamation and conservation of eroded or overgrazed land. Only maize is grown on a comparatively large scale, but tea, sisal, groundnuts, coffee and sub-tropical fruits are increasing in importance. Over 80% of the working population are engaged in agriculture.

INDUSTRY AND TRADE

Industry. Industrial development is still in its early stages, and since Venda's location is unfavourable, the Government is concentrating on the promotion of agro-industries utilizing local produce, and small-scale industries. A chutney factory has recently been established, in addition to a tea processing plant, a furniture factory and several saw-mills. A copper-chrome arsenate preservation plant has been established at Phiphidi. At Shayandima a 20-hectare industrial area has been prepared. In 1989 the 460-hectare Shayandima industrial area at Thohoyandou had over 70 developed sites with 43 industries, and 21 new factories under construction. There was a second major industrial area at Muraleni, and commercial complexes at Makhado. In 1986 there were 159 manufacturing establishments, mainly small labour-intensive firms with a total employment of 3,016 and 906 commercial establishments with employment of 3,803.

Labour. In 1986, 45,000 migrant workers earned R180m. in the Republic of South Africa. In 1985 an estimated 6,500 border commuters worked in the Republic of South Africa, income R26m.

Commerce. Venda is a member of the South African Customs Union and trade is mainly with the Republic of South Africa. Exports include sub-tropical fruit, tea, coffee, timber, clothing, furniture and pottery. Petroleum products, machinery, motor vehicles, food, clothing and furniture are imported.

Tourism. In 1989 there were 3 National Parks, 2 caravan parks and 2 holiday resorts.

COMMUNICATIONS

Roads. There were (1989) 2,100 km of roads, of which 300 km had a permanent surface.

Aviation. An airline, inaugurated in 1981, operates between Nwangundu in Thohoyandu and Johannesburg *via* Pietersburg and Pretoria.

Post and Broadcasting. In 1989 there were 17 post offices, 21 postal agencies and 14 money order offices, and telex and fax facilities in all urban areas. There were 3 automatic and 13 manual telephone exchanges, and 15 telephone agencies. In 1989 the government-owned Radio Thohoyandou broadcast 24 hours daily in Venda and English on MW and FM, and South African television programmes were received through its transposers.

Newspapers. In 1989 there was 1 newspaper published weekly in Venda and English, with a circulation of 33,000.

JUSTICE, EDUCATION AND WELFARE

Justice. The Supreme Court acts as the Court of Appeal for the 5 magistrates' courts and 2 sub-offices, 2 periodical courts and the one Regional Court. Appeals from the Supreme Court are heard in the Republic of South Africa Appeal Court.

Education. The Department of Education assumed responsibility for education on independence. Education is free up to Standard 2, and pupils are taught in the native tongue, Luvenda, for the first 4 years (up to Standard 2), after which English is gradually introduced. Secondary education comprises Standards 6 to 10.

In 1989 there were 661 schools with 227,569 pupils and (1988) 7,200 teachers, 4 teacher training colleges, 3 trade schools, 1 technical high school and 1 special school. The University of Venda was established in 1981; 4,500 students (1988).

Health. In 1989 there were 3 general hospitals (1,433 beds), 2 maternity hospitals

(38 beds), 2 health centres (80 beds), 51 clinics, 1 chronic ill-health institution (412 beds) and 508 rural care groups. There were about 35 doctors in the general hospitals and 15 private doctors in different areas, and 1,411 nurses.

Welfare. In 1986-87 the Government spent R20·6m. on social pension payments to 34,388 pensioners; civil pensions' payments were R1,982,127 to 301 beneficiaries.

Further Reading

Venda 1983. Dept. of Information and Broadcasting. Sibasa, 1984

CISKEI

HISTORY. On 4 Dec. 1981 the Republic of South Africa gave independence to Ciskei, the fourth of the tribal homelands.

AREA AND POPULATION. Ciskei lies between latitudes 32° and 33°35' and longitudes 26°20' and 27°48', and has a coastal boundary between East London and Port Alfred. The total area is about 9,000 sq. km. The population was (1987) 2m. but only 1m. live in Ciskei. The remainder are resident and workers in the Republic of South Africa.

Populations of towns (1987): Mdantsane, 350,000; Zwelitsha, 55,000; Sada, 38,000; Dimbaza, 25,000 and Litha, 9,500. The capital, Bisho, houses 8,000 people, although the development is still going on.

CONSTITUTION AND GOVERNMENT. In 1981 Ciskei became an independent democratic republic. In 1988 the Government consisted of a President and an Executive Council consisting of 15 Ministers appointed by the President. The legislature is a National Assembly consisting of (1988) 45 Hereditary Chiefs, 16 elected and 5 nominated Members and the Paramount Chief's representatives of 37 are traditional leaders, the others being elected on the basis of adult suffrage every five years. On 4 March 1990, in a bloodless coup, the President-for-life, Dr Lennox Sebe was deposed. The Constitution was suspended. The coup was led by Brig. O. J. Gqozo.

Flag: Blue, a broad diagonal band from lower hoist to upper fly, charged with a black crane.

National Anthem: Nkosi Sikelel' i Afrika, composed by Enoch Sontonga.

DEFENCE. There is a Ciskei Defence Force. Its aviation element is equipped with 2 Skyvan and 3 Islander transports, and 3 BK-117 and 1 BO 105 helicopters, plus 2 Cessna 152 trainers.

ECONOMY

Budget. The 1987–88 budget balanced at R859m.

Currency. South African Rand.

ENERGY AND NATURAL RESOURCES

Electricity. Ciskei is totally dependent on power supply lines maintained by the Republic of South Africa.

Minerals. Mineral resources are mainly undeveloped and in 1988 only two mines existed in Ciskei, one producing dolorite, the other rutile ilmenite, leucoxene and zircon.

Agriculture. In 1977–78, total agricultural production was valued at R8·26m.

In 1986, the dryland products included (in tons): Maize, 3,125; wheat, 131; sorghum, 325; sunflower, 8·7. Horticultural crops included (1986, in tons): Potatoes, 979·9; cabbage, 5,135·8; carrots, 981·1; brussel sprouts, 356; onions, 4·8; pumpkins, 102·4; cauliflower, 11·6; peas, 28; dry beans, 83·3; spinach, 1·9; beetroot, 8·5.

Livestock (1986): 11,442 cattle, 76,294 sheep, 77,568 goats, 3,743 pigs, 14,742,814 poultry.

Forestry. In 1983–84, 5,500 hectares were planted mainly with conifers. The indigenous forest covered some 18,000 hectares. In 1984–85 (estimate), production of timber was valued at R600,000.

INDUSTRY AND TRADE

Industry. In 1988 total investment was R467m. The chief manufactures include textiles, timber products, electronic components, steel products, food and leather goods.

Commerce. International trade is mainly with the Republic of South Africa and no separate figures are available. The main exports are pineapples, timber and manufactured goods.

Tourism. Tourism is an important and developing industry.

COMMUNICATIONS

Roads. In 1988 there were 448 km of tarred roads and 2,556 km of gravel roads.

Railways. There are two main railway lines serving the southern part of Ciskei.

Aviation. Ciskei uses East London's airport and there is a new international airport at Bulembu, near Bisho.

Shipping. Ciskei has no harbour of its own but has full access to the facilities of East London in the Republic of South Africa.

Post and Broadcasting. All major centres have post offices and manual and automatic telephone exchanges; telex facilities are available. There were (1987–88) 21,095 telephones. Radio Ciskei broadcasts from Bisho daily.

Newspapers (1988). There were three Ciskeian newspapers: *Umthombo*; *Imvo*, first published in 1884; *Umtha*, an agricultural newspaper.

JUSTICE, RELIGION, EDUCATION AND WELFARE

Justice. The Supreme Court acts as Court of Appeal for the eight Magistrates' Courts, which in turn act as Courts of Appeal for the Chiefs' Courts. Appeals from the Supreme Court are heard by the Appellate Division of Ciskei in Bisho.

Religion. In 1988 (estimate) the population was 27% Methodists, 20% Independent, 16% Presbyterian, 12% Anglicans, 7% Roman Catholics and 5% Dutch Reformed Church.

Education. In 1986–87 there were 545 primary schools with 200,752 pupils and 4,369 teachers; 158 post primary schools with 59,414 students and 1,809 teachers; 3 training colleges with 1,677 students and 97 teachers and 1 vocational school with 174 students and 20 teachers. The University of Fort Hare had a total of 2,304 students in 1981.

Health. In 1987–88, there were 8 hospitals with 2,910 beds, and a total of 2,952 nursing staff.

Social Welfare. Pensions paid in 1984–85:

	Beneficiaries	*Amount (R1,000)*
Old age	42,573	20,435
Blind	564	270
Disability	5,421	2,602
War veterans	72	38
Leprosy	11	5

Further Reading

Charlton, N., *Ciskei: Economics and Politics of Dependence in a South African Homeland.* London, 1980
Pauw, B. A., *Christianity and the Xhosa Tradition.* OUP, 1975
Van der Kooy, R. (ed.) *The Republic of Ciskei: A Nation in Transition.* Pretoria, 1981

SOUTH GEORGIA AND SOUTH SANDWICH ISLANDS

HISTORY. South Georgia was probably first sighted by a London merchant, Antonio de la Roche, and then in 1756 by a Spanish Captain, Gregorie Jerez. The first landing and exploration was undertaken by Captain James Cook, who formally took possession in the name of George III on 17 Jan. 1775. British sealers arrived in 1788 and American sealers in 1791. Sealing reached its peak in 1800. A German team was the first to carry out scientific studies there in 1882–83. Whaling began in 1904 when the Compania Argentina de Pesca formed by C. A. Larsen, a Norwegian, established a station at Grytviken. Six other stations were established up to 1912. Whaling ceased in 1966 and the civil administration was withdrawn. Argentine forces invaded South Georgia on 3 April 1982. A British naval task force recovered the Island on 25 April 1982.

AREA AND POPULATION. South Georgia lies 800 miles south-east of the Falkland Islands and has an area of 1,450 sq. miles. The South Sandwich Islands are 470 miles south-east of South Georgia and have an area of 130 sq. miles. There has been no permanent population in South Georgia since the whaling station at Leith was abandoned in 1966. There is a small military garrison. The British Antarctic Survey have a biological station on Bird Island. The South Sandwich Islands are uninhabited.

CLIMATE. The climate is wet and cold with strong winds and little seasonal variation. 15°C is occasionally reached on a windless day. Temperatures below –15°C at sea level are unusual.

CONSTITUTION AND GOVERNMENT. Under the new Constitution which came into force on 3 Oct. 1985 the Territories ceased to be dependencies of the Falkland Islands. Executive power is vested in a Commissioner who is the officer for the time being administering the Government of the Falkland Islands. The Commissioner is obliged to consult the officer for the time being commanding Her Majesty's British Forces in the South Atlantic on matters relating to defence and internal security (except police). The Commissioner whenever practicable consults the Executive Council of the Falkland Islands on the exercise of functions that in his opinion might affect the Falkland Islands. There is no Legislative Council. Laws are made by the Commissioner.

Commissioner: W. H. Fullerton, CMG.

Economy. The total revenue of the Territories (estimate, 1988–89) £268,240, mainly from philatelic sales and investment income. Expenditure estimate £194,260.

Communications. There is occasional direct sea communication between the Falkland Islands and South Georgia and the South Sandwich Islands by means of the Royal Research Ships *John Biscoe* and *Bransfield* and the ice patrol vessel *HMS Endurance*. Royal Fleet Auxiliary ships, which serve the garrison, run regularly to South Georgia. Mail is dropped from military aircraft.

Justice. There is a Supreme Court for the Territories and a Court of Appeal in the United Kingdom. Appeals may go from that court to the Judicial Committee of the Privy Council. There is no magistrate permanently in residence. The Officer Commanding the garrison is usually appointed a magistrate.

Further Reading

Headland, R. K., *The Island of South Georgia.* CUP, 1985

SPAIN

Capital: Madrid
Population: 39·2m. (1988)
GNP per capita: US$7,740 (1988)

España

HISTORY. Although Spain has traditionally been a monarchy there have been two Republics, the first in 1873, which lasted for 11 months, and the second 1931–39; both were democratically and peacefully proclaimed. Part of the army rebelled against the republican government on 18 July 1936, thus beginning the Spanish Civil War, *see* THE STATESMAN'S YEAR-BOOK, 1939, pp. 1325–26. The new regime was led by Gen. Franco, who had been proclaimed Head of State and Government in 1936, and its institutions were based on single party rule, with the *Falange* as the only legal political organization.

In July 1969, Prince Don Juan Carlos de Borbón y Borbón, grandson of Alfonso XIII, was sworn in as successor to the Head of State and he had the title of HRH Prince of Spain until he became King.

Gen. Francisco Franco y Bahamonde died on 20 Nov. 1975 and on 22 Nov. Prince Juan Carlos de Borbón y Borbón took the oath as Juan Carlos I, King of Spain.

On 23 Feb. 1981 there was an attempted military *coup*. For 18 hours the deputies of the lower house of Parliament and the Cabinet were held hostage. The King, the only high authority who kept his liberty, obtained the surrender of the rebels without bloodshed.

AREA AND POPULATION. Spain is bounded north by the Bay of Biscay and the Pyrenees (which form the frontier with France and Andorra), east and south by the Mediterranean and the Straits of Gibraltar, south-west by the Atlantic and west by Portugal and the Atlantic. Continental Spain has an area of 492,592 sq. km, and including the Balearic and Canary Islands and the towns of Ceuta and Melilla 504,750 sq. km (194,884 sq. miles). Population (mid-decennial census, 1986), 38,891,313. Estimate (1988) 39,217,804.

The growth of the population has been as follows:

Census year	*Population*	*Rate of annual increase*	*Census year*	*Population*	*Rate of annual increase*
1860	15,655,467	0·34	1950	27,976,755	0·81
1910	19,927,150	0·72	1960	30,903,137	0·88
1920	21,303,162	0·69	1970	33,823,918	0·94
1930	23,563,867	1·06	1981	37,746,260	1·15
1940	25,877,971	0·98			

Area and population of the autonomous communities and provinces, mid-decennial census of 1 April 1986:

Autonomous community Province	*Area (sq. km)*	*Population*	*Per sq. km*	*Autonomous community Province*	*Area (sq. km)*	*Population*	*Per sq. km*
Andalusia	*87,268*	*6,875,628*	*78*	Zaragoza	17,194	845,832	49
Almería	8,774	448,592	51	*Asturias*	*10,565*	*1,114,115*	*106*
Cádiz	7,385	1,054,503	142	*Baleares*	*5,014*	*754,777*	*151*
Córdoba	13,718	745,175	54	*Basque*			
Granada	12,531	796,857	63	*Country, The*	*7,261*	*2,133,002*	*296*
Huelva	10,085	430,918	43	Álava	3,047	275,703	92
Jaén	13,498	633,612	47	Guipúzcoa	1,997	688,894	344
Málaga	7,276	1,215,479	168	Vizcaya	2,217	1,168,405	531
Sevilla	14,001	1,550,492	110	*Canary Islands*	*7,273*	*1,614,882*	*221*
Aragón	*47,669*	*1,214,729*	*25*	Palmas, Las	4,065	855,494	213
Huesca	15,671	220,824	14	Santa Cruz			
Teruel	14,804	148,073	10	de Tenerife	3,208	759,388	237

Autonomous community Province	*Area (sq. km)*	*Population*	*Per sq. km*	*Autonomous community Province*	*Area (sq. km)*	*Population*	*Per sq. km*
Cantabria	*5,289*	*524,670*	*99*	Tarragona	6,283	531,281	84
Castilla-La Mancha	*79,226*	*1,665,029*	*21*	*Extremadura*	*41,602*	*1,088,543*	*26*
Albacete	14,858	342,278	23	Badajoz	21,657	664,516	30
Ciudad Real	19,749	477,967	24	Cáceres	19,945	424,027	21
Cuenca	17,061	210,932	12	*Galicia*	*29,434*	*2,785,394*	*94*
Guadalajara	12,190	146,008	12	Coruña, La	7,876	1,102,376	141
Toledo	15,368	487,844	31	Lugo	9,803	399,232	40
Castilla-León	*94,147*	*2,600,330*	*27*	Orense	7,278	399,378	55
Ávila	8,048	179,207	22	Pontevedra	4,477	884,408	197
Burgos	14,269	363,530	25	*Madrid*	*7,995*	*4,854,616*	*607*
León	15,468	528,502	34	*Murcia*	*11,317*	*1,014,285*	*89*
Palencia	8,029	188,472	23	*Navarra*	*10,421*	*512,676*	*49*
Salamanca	12,336	366,668	29	*Rioja, La*	*5,034*	*262,611*	*52*
Segovia	6,949	151,520	21	*Valencian Community*	*23,305*	*3,772,002*	*161*
Soria	10,287	97,565	9	Alicante	5,863	1,254,920	216
Valladolid	8,202	503,306	61	Castellón	6,679	437,320	66
Zamora	10,559	221,560	21	Valencia	10,763	2,079,762	194
Catalonia	*31,930*	*5,977,008*	*187*	*Ceuta* [1]	*18*	*71,403*	*3,996*
Barcelona	7,773	4,598,249	591	*Melilla* [1]	*14*	*55,613*	*3,972*
Gerona	5,886	490,667	83				
Lérida	12,028	356,811	29	*Total*	*504,750*	*38,891,313*	*77*

[1] Ceuta and Melilla are municipalities located in the northern coast of Morocco.

The capitals of the autonomous communities are as follows: Andalusia, cap. Sevilla (Seville); Aragón, cap. Zaragoza (Saragossa); Asturias, cap. Oviedo; Baleares (Balearic Islands), cap. Palma de Mallorca; The Basque Country, cap. Vitoria; Canary Islands, dual and alternative capital, Las Palmas and Santa Cruz de Tenerife; Cantabria, cap. Santander; Castilla-León, cap. Valladolid; Catalonia, cap. Barcelona; Extremadura, cap. Mérida; Galicia, cap. Santiago de Compostela; Madrid, cap. Madrid; Murcia, cap. Murcia (but regional parliament in Cartagena); Navarra, cap. Pamplona; La Rioja, cap. Logroño; Valencian Community, cap. Valencia. Castilla-La Mancha had not chosen (1989) a capital town; the actual seat of its legislature and executive is at Toledo.

The capitals of the provinces are in the towns from which they take the name, except in Álava (capital Vitoria), Asturias (Oviedo), Baleares (Palma de Mallorca), Cantabria (Santander), Guipúzcoa (San Sebastián), La Rioja (Logroño), Navarra (Pamplona) and Vizcaya (Bilbao).

On 1 April 1986 there were 19,771,007 females and 19,120,306 males.

By decree of 21 Sept. 1927 the islands which form the Canary Archipelago were divided into 2 provinces, under the name of their respective capitals: Santa Cruz de Tenerife and Las Palmas de Gran Canaria. The province of Santa Cruz de Tenerife is constituted by the islands of Tenerife, La Palma, Gomera and Hierro, and that of Las Palmas by Gran Canaria, Lanzarote and Fuerteventura, with the small barren islands of Alegranza, Roque del Este, Roque del Oeste, Graciosa, Montaña Clara and Lobos. The area of the islands is 7,273 sq. km; population (mid-decennial census 1986), 1,614,882. Places under Spanish sovereignty in Morocco are: Alhucemas, Ceuta, Chafarinas, Melilla and Peñón de Vélez.

The following were the registered populations of principal towns at mid-decennial census 1986:

Town	*Population*	*Town*	*Population*	*Town*	*Population*
Albacete	127,169	Badalona	223,444	Castellón	129,813
Alcalá de Henares	150,221	Baracaldo	112,854	Córdoba	304,826
Alcorcón	137,225	Barcelona	1,694,064	Cornellá	86,467
Algeciras	97,213	Bilbao	378,221	Coruña, La	241,808
Alicante	265,543	Burgos	163,910	Elche	173,392
Almería	156,838	Cáceres	79,342	Ferrol, El	88,101
Avila	44,618	Cádiz	154,051	Fuenlabrada	119,463
Badajoz	126,340	Cartagena	168,809	Gerona	67,578

Town	Population	Town	Population	Town	Population
Getafe	130,971	Mataró	99,642	Santa Coloma de Gramanet	133,515
Gijón	259,226	Móstoles	175,802	Santa Cruz de Tenerife	211,389
Granada	280,592	Murcia	309,504	Santander	188,539
Hospitalet	276,865	Orense	102,455	Santiago de Compostela	104,045
Huelva	135,427	Oviedo	190,651	Sevilla	668,356
Jerez de la Frontera	180,444	Palencia	76,707	Tarragona	109,557
Jaén	102,826	Palma de Mallorca	321,112	Tarrasa	159,530
Laguna, La	114,223	Palmas, Las	372,270	Torrejón de Ardoz	79,877
Leganés	167,088	Pamplona	183,703	Valencia	738,575
León	137,414	Reus	83,251	Valladolid	341,194
Lérida	111,507	Sabadell	185,960	Vigo	263,998
Logroño	118,770	Salamanca	166,615	Vitoria	207,501
Lugo	77,728	San Baudilio del Llobregat	75,388	Zaragoza	596,080
Madrid	3,123,713	San Fernando	84,940		
Málaga	595,264	San Sebastián	180,043		

Vital statistics for calendar years:

	Marriages	*Births*	*Deaths*
1983	183,068	477,291	296,188
1984	192,406	465,709	295,425
1985	193,128	451,373	308,430
1986	203,394	434,490	306,613
1987	210,098	421,799	309,364

On 31 Dec. 1987 the number of foreigners legally registered was 334,935 (largest foreign community, British, 55,318).

Languages. The Constitution states that 'Castilian is the Spanish official language of the State', but also that 'All other Spanish languages will also be official in the corresponding Autonomous Communities'.

Catalan is spoken by a majority of people in Catalonia (64%, 1986) and Baleares (70·8%), and by one half in Valencian Community (49%, where it is frequently called Valencian); in Aragón, a narrow strip close to Catalonia and Valencian Community boundaries, speaks Catalan.

Galician, a language very close to Portuguese, is spoken by a majority of people in Galicia (90%, 1986); Basque, by a significant minority in the Basque Country (24·5%). Basque is also spoken by a small minority in north-west Navarra (12%).

In bilingual communities, both Spanish and the regional language are taught in the schools and universities.

CLIMATE. Most of Spain has a form of Mediterranean climate with mild, moist winters and hot, dry summers, but the northern coastal region has a moist, equable climate, with rainfall well-distributed throughout the year, mild winters and warm summers, though having less sunshine than the rest of Spain.

Madrid. Jan. 41°F (5°C), July 77°F (25°C). Annual rainfall 16·8" (419 mm). Barcelona. Jan. 46°F (8°C), July 74°F (23·5°C). Annual rainfall 21" (525 mm). Cartagena. Jan. 51°F (10·5°C), July 75°F (24°C). Annual rainfall 14·9" (373 mm). La Coruña. Jan. 51°F (10·5°C), July 66°F (19°C). Annual rainfall 32" (800 mm). Sevilla. Jan. 51°F (10·5°C), July 85°F (29·5°C). Annual rainfall 19·5" (486 mm). Palma de Mallorca (Balearic Islands). Jan. 51°F (11°C), July 77°F (25°C). Annual rainfall 13·6" (347 mm). Santa Cruz de Tenerife (Canary Islands). Jan. 64°F (17·9°C), July 76°F (24·4°C). Annual rainfall 7·72" (196 mm).

KING. Juan Carlos I, born 5 Jan. 1938. The eldest son of Don Juan, Conde de Barcelona. Juan Carlos was given precedence over his father as pretender to the Spanish throne in an agreement in 1954 between Don Juan and Gen. Franco. Don Juan resigned his claims to the throne in May 1977. King (then Prince) Juan Carlos married, in 1962, Princess Sophia of Greece, daughter of the late King Paul of the Hellenes and Queen Frederika. *Offspring:* Elena, born 20 Dec. 1963; Cristina, 13 June 1965; Felipe, Prince of Asturias, Heir to the throne, 30 Jan. 1968.

CONSTITUTION AND GOVERNMENT. The *Cortes* (Parliament) was freely elected on 15 June 1977. The text of the new Constitution was approved by referendum on 6 Dec. 1978, and came into force 29 Dec. 1978. It established a parliamentary monarchy, with King Juan Carlos I as head of state. Legislative power is vested in the *Cortes*, a bicameral parliament composed of the Congress of Deputies (lower house) and the Senate (upper house). The Congress of Deputies has not less than 300 nor more than 400 members (350 in the general elections of 1977, 1979, 1982, 1986 and 1989), all elected in a proportional system regarding the population of every province. The members of the Senate are elected in a majority system: The 47 peninsular provinces elect 4 senators each, regardless of population; the insular provinces electing 5 (Baleares, Las Palmas) or 6 (Santa Cruz de Tenerife); and Ceuta and Melilla, 2 senators each. There are 208 senators, to whom are added some other members of the upper house elected by the parliaments of the autonomous communities. Deputies and senators are elected in universal (but not compulsory), direct, free, equal and secret suffrage, for a term of 4 years, liable to dissolution. Executive power is vested in the President of the Government (prime minister), with his Cabinet; he is elected by the Congress of Deputies.

A general election took place on 29 Oct. 1989.

Congress of Deputies (350 members): Spanish Workers Socialist Party (PSOE), 175; Popular Party (PP, conservative), 106; United Left (IU, communist dominated coalition), 18; Convergence and Union (CiU, Catalan nationalists), 18; Social and Democratic Centre (CDS, centrist), 14; Basque Nationalist Party (PNV), 5; Herri Batasuna (HB, Basque independentists), 4; Andalusian Party (PA, Andalusian regionalists), 2; Eusko Alkartasuna (EA) and Euskadiko Eskerra (EE), both non-radical Basque independentists, 2 each; Valencian Union (UV, Valencian regionalists), 2; two conservative regional parties from Aragón and the Canaries, 1 each. *Presidente* (speaker) of the Congress of Deputies, Félix Pons Irazazábal (PSOE).

Senate: 208 members, excluding those elected by regional parliaments (250 including them): PSOE, 108; PP, 76; CiU, 10; PNV, 4; HB, 3; CDS, 2; IU, 1; four different insular groups from the Canaries, 4 in all. *Presidente* (speaker) of the Senate, Juan José Laborda (PSOE).

The Council of Ministers was composed as follows in March 1990:

President of the Government (Prime Minister): Felipe González Márquez (Secretary-General of PSOE).

Vice-President of the Government (Deputy Premier): Alfonso Guerra González. *Foreign Affairs:* Francisco Fernández Ordóñez. *Economy, Finance and Commerce:* Carlos Solchaga Catalán. *Industry and Energy:* Claudio Aranzadi Martínez. *Interior:* José Luis Corcuera. *Defence:* Narcís Serra i Serra. *Public Administration:* Joaquín Almunia Amann. *Education and Science:* Javier Solana Madariaga. *Public Works:* Javier Sáez de Cosculluela. *Justice:* Enrique Múgica Herzog. *Culture:* Jorge Semprún. *Agriculture, Fisheries and Food:* Carlos Romero Herrero. *Health and Consumers Affairs:* Julián García Vargas. *Labour and Social Security:* Manuel Chaves. *Transport, Tourism and Communications:* José Barrionuevo. *Social Affairs:* Matilde Fernández. *Minister, Government Spokeswoman:* Rosa Conde. *Relations with the Cortes and Secretary of the Cabinet:* Virgilio Zapatero.

All ministers are members of PSOE, except Aranzadi and Semprún, who are independents.

National flag: Three horizontal stripes of red, yellow, red, with the yellow of double width, and charged near the hoist with the national arms.

National anthem: Marcha real.

Regional and local government. The Constitution of 1978 establishes a semi-federal system of regional administration, with the autonomous community *(Comunidad Autónoma)* as its basic element. There are 17 autonomous communities, each of them having a Parliament, elected by universal vote, and a regional government; all possess exclusive legislative and executive power in many matters, as listed in the national Constitution and in their own fundamental law *(estatuto de autonomía)*. The Basque Country and Catalonia elected their first parliaments in

March 1980, Galicia in Oct. 1981 and Andalusia in May 1982. All others in May 1983. Further elections were held in the autonomous communities 1984–89.

There are 7 autonomous communities composed of one only province, i.e., Asturias (*ex*-Oviedo province), Cantabria (*ex*-Santander province), La Rioja (*ex*-Logroño province), Navarra, Baleares, Murcia and Madrid. The other 10 are formed by 2 or more provinces. In all, there are in Spain 50 provinces, since the administrative division established in 1833; Ceuta and Melilla, municipalities in the northern coast of Morocco, are not part of any province. The provincial council *(Diputación Provincial)* is the administrative organ of the province, except in the 7 autonomous communities composed of one only province, where there are only the regional legislative and executive powers. The provincial council is indirectly elected. Each of the 7 main islands of the Canaries (provinces of Las Palmas and Santa Cruz de Tenerife) has a directly elected corporation, the *Cabildo Insular*, to rule its special interests; in the main islands of the Balearics there is also an elected *Consell Insular*.

The provinces are constituted by the association of municipalities (8,063 on 10 June 1987). Municipalities are autonomous in their own sphere. At their head stands the municipal council *(Ayuntamiento)*, members of which are elected in a universal ballot every 4 years, and they, in turn, elect one of them as Mayor *(Alcalde)*.

DEFENCE. On 26 Sept. 1953 the US and Spain signed three agreements covering the construction and use of military facilities in Spain by the US, economic assistance, and military end-item assistance. These agreements were renewed several times, the last in July 1982. The American naval and air base at Rota (near Cádiz) is connected by pipelines with the American bomber bases at Morón de la Frontera (near Seville), Torrejón (near Madrid) and Zaragoza. The US will withdraw from Torrejón in 1991 (withdrawal began in Aug. 1988).

Length of service is 12 months and 16 months for volunteers. Since early 1989 women are accepted in all sections of the armed forces.

In March 1986 a referendum was conducted to establish whether Spain should remain in NATO. 52·5% of the voters were for the resolution.

Army. The Army is divided into 2 principal parts: 8 Regional Operation Commands and the General Reserve Force. The former consist of 1 armoured, 1 mechanized, 2 mountain and 1 motorized divisions; 2 armoured cavalry, 1 parachute and 1 air-portable brigades; 1 infantry regiment and supporting artillery, engineer and signals units. The General Reserve Force comprises an airborne brigade with air defence, artillery and engineer units. There are also the Royal Guard unit, and the Army Aviation forces. Equipment includes 299 AMX-30, 329 M-47E and 164 M-48 tanks. The aviation element of the Army consists of about 200 helicopters, including 70 BO 105s, 60 UH-1 Iroquois and 6 AB.212s. Strength (1990) 285,000 (including 210,000 conscripts). Of these 5,600 are stationed on the Balearic Islands, 10,000 on the Canary Islands and 15,800 in Ceuta/Melilla. The paramilitary Civil Guard number 64,000 men and the National Police, 47,000.

Navy. The accession of Spain to NATO, even though not fully integrated into the military structure, has provided the Navy with a key operational role in support of NATO sea lines of communication on the Canaries-Gibraltar-Balearics axis. The main task force, 'Grupo Alfa', is centred on the flagship, *Principe de Asturias*, escorted by new and modernized frigates. This group played a major part in the 1989 NATO major naval exercise, Sharp Spear, in autumn 1989, working around the north of Scotland and into the North Sea.

The new flagship, the 17,000 tonne *Principe de Asturias*, a light V/STOL aircraft carrier built to a US design, commissioned in May 1989. Her predecessor the *Dedalo* (*ex*-USS *Cabot*) has been returned to the USA where she is to become a maritime museum. The *Principe de Asturias*' air group comprises 8 AV-8B Matador (Harrier-II), 8 Sea King ASW helicopters, 2 Sea King early warning helicopters and about 4 AB-212 light helicopters.

There are also 8 French-designed submarines (4 Daphne class, 4 Agosta class), 4 old *ex*-US destroyers, 3 US-design Santa Maria guided missile frigates with Standard SM-1 surface-to-air missiles, 5 other guided missile frigates with Standard, and 6 smaller frigates, 4 offshore patrol vessels, 18 coastal and 37 inshore patrol craft, 4 ocean minesweepers, 8 coastal minesweepers, 2 amphibious troop transports, 3 tank landing ships and 11 landing craft. Major auxiliaries include 1 transport, 6 ocean tugs, 2 training ships, 1 royal yacht, 4 water carriers and 6 survey ships. There are about 80 minor auxiliaries and service craft.

The Spanish Navy is being renewed and modernized: One further new guided-missile frigate joins the fleet in 1990 and several more will be required to replace the last few old destroyers. A new fleet replenishment ship is being designed in co-operation with the Netherlands, and new mine countermeasures vessels will start building shortly to the British Sandown class design.

The Naval Air Service operates 23 EAV-8 and EAV-8B Harrier-type attack aircraft, 39 Sea King, AB-212 and Hughes 500 ASW helicopters, 3 radar early warning Sea Kings and a few additional training and utility aircraft. The Air force operates 6 Orion maritime patrol aircraft on ASW tasks.

There are 8,500 marines, who provide 1 amphibious regiment and garrison regiments at the main bases. Main naval bases are at Ferrol, Rota, Cádiz, Cartagena, Palma de Mallorca, Mahón and Las Palmas (Canary Islands).

In 1989 personnel totalled 39,000 (24,500 conscripts) including marines.

Air Force. The Air Force is organized as an independent service, dating from 1939. It is administered through 4 operational commands. These comprise Air Combat Command which controls interceptor squadrons (including USAF elements) and the control and warning radar network, Tactical and Transport Commands, and Air Command of the Canaries. Strength (1990) 40,000 and 215 combat aircraft.

The Tactical Air Command has 2 fighter-bomber squadrons of Spanish-built Northrop SF-5s, 1 aero-naval co-operation squadron with P-3 Orion anti-submarine aircraft, and a liaison flight at Tablada with CASA 127s. Air Combat Command has 2 squadrons of Mirage III-Es, 1 squadron of RF-4C Phantom IIs, 3 squadrons of F-18 Hornets and 2 squadrons of Mirage F1-Cs, plus a flight of CASA/Dornier Do27/127 liaison aircraft. Five KC-130H tankers support the fighter squadrons. Three wings of Air Transport Command operate C-130 Hercules, Caribou and Spanish-built CASA Aviocars. Air Command of the Canaries has 3 squadrons, equipped with Aviocar transports; Mirage F1 fighter-bombers; F27 Maritime aircraft and Super Puma helicopters for search and rescue. Other equipment includes 2 Boeing 707s, 2 CN-235s, 5 Falcons and helicopters for VIP transport; and aircraft for photographic, firefighting, target towing and research duties. Air-sea rescue units have Aviocars and Super Puma helicopters.

American-built F33 Bonanza and Chilean-built Pillan piston-engined aircraft are used for basic training, after which pupil pilots progress to CASA C-101 jet aircraft. Two-seat versions of operational types are used as advanced trainers. Other training types include Beechcraft Barons for instrument flying and liaison duties.

INTERNATIONAL RELATIONS

Membership. Spain is a member of UN, the Council of Europe, NATO, WEU, the European Communities and OECD.

ECONOMY

Budget. Revenue and expenditure in 1m. pesetas:

	1985	*1986*	*1987*	*1988*	*1989*
Revenue	6,113,086	7,164,232	8,113,442	8,939,237	10,644,507
Expenditure	6,113,086	7,164,232	8,113,442	8,939,237	10,644,507

The budget is made up as follows (in 1m. pesetas):

Revenue (1989)	
Direct taxes	4,002,900
Indirect taxes	3,751,161
Levies and various revenues	295,800
Current transactions	338,434

Revenue (1989) continued	
Real estate income	113,382
Miscellaneous income	235,003
Deficit (financed with public debt, treasury loans, etc)	1,907,827

Expenditure (1989)		*Expenditure (1989) continued*	
H.M. House	750	Ministry of Education and Science	858,738
Cortes (Parliament)	11,496	„ Labour and Social Security	900,950
Court of Accounts	2,594	„ Industry and Energy	216,428
Constitutional Court	1,042	„ Agriculture and Food	183,094
Council of State	518	„ Transport, Tourism and Communications	533,898
Public Debt	1,386,330	„ Culture	42,953
Civil Service Pensions	480,174	„ Public Administration	33,593
General Council of the Judicial Power	1,368	„ Health and Consumer Affairs	1,137,516
Relations with the Cortes and Secretariat of the Cabinet	22,165	„ Social Affairs	24,764
Ministry of Foreign Affairs	57,896	„ the Government Spokeswoman	1,574
„ Justice	158,270	Regional governments	1,600,334
„ Defence	817,913	Regional Compensation Fund	208,070
„ Finance	295,924	Expenses in several ministries	454,572
„ Interior	387,610	Financial relations with EEC	323,708
„ Public Works and Housing	500,255		

Currency. The *peseta* is divided into 100 *céntimos*; but *céntimos* are no longer in legal use since 1 July 1984.

Bank-notes of 10,000, 5,000, 2,000, 1,000, 500, 200 and 100 *pesetas* and coins of 1 *peseta* (copper and aluminium), 2, 5, 10, 25, 50, 100, 200 and 500 *pesetas* (nickel and copper) are in circulation. In Sept. 1987 the circulation of bank-notes was 2,699,700m. *pesetas* and of coins, 159,200m. *pesetas*.

In March 1990, £1 = 179·50 *pesetas*; US$1 = 109·52.

Inflation rate in Dec. 1987, 4·6%; 1988, 5·8%; 1989, 6·9%.

Banking. On 1 Jan. 1922 the Bank of Spain came under the Bank Ordinance Law, according to which the Government participate in its net profits.

The 9 largest banks are: Banco Bilbao Vizcaya; Banco Central; Banco Español de Crédito; Banco Hispano Americano; Banco de Santander; Banco Popular Español; Banco Exterior de España; Banco Pastor; Banco de Sabadell. All are privately owned except the Banco Exterior de España.

Spanish banks deposits, 30 June 1988, amounted to 19,053,135m pesetas; foreign banks, 402,405m.; savings banks, 14,152,285m.; rural (farmers) savings banks, 698,896m.

Weights and Measures. On 1 Jan. 1859 the metric system of weights and measures was introduced.

ENERGY AND NATURAL RESOURCES

Electricity. Electric power-stations in 1988 had a total installed capacity of 44·5m. kw. The total output 1988, amounted to 139,010m. kwh of which 36,080m. hydro-electric and 50,410m. nuclear. There were 10 nuclear power stations, with a net capacity of 7·5m. kw (Jan. 1989). Supply 110 and 220 volts; 50 Hz.

Oil. Crude oil production (1989) 1·1m. tonnes.

Gas. Production of natural gas in 1988 was 919m. cu. metres.

Minerals. Spain has a relatively wide range of minerals but most of them are found in small or moderate quantities. Production of the principal minerals (in 1,000 tonnes; net metal content):

	1987	*1988*		*1987*	*1988*
Anthracite	5,512	5,271	Lead	78	71
Coal	8,903	9,211	Zinc	225	247
Lignite	21,961	17,288	Tin [1]	71	59
Uranium [1]	380	306	Wolfram [1]	64	101
Iron	2,042	1,940	Fluorspar	196	151
Pyrites	992	1,060	Potassium salts	1,612	1,360
Copper	11	9			

[1] Tonnes.

Agriculture. In 1987 the total value of agricultural produce was 1,610·5m. pesetas; of livestock, 1,068m.; of forestry, 116·4m. Land under cultivation in 1988 (in 1,000 hectares) included: Cereals, 7,696; vegetables, 419; potatoes, 280. In 1988, 670,000 tractors and 53,500 harvesters were in use.

Principal crops	*Area (in 1,000 hectares)*				*Yield (in 1,000 tonnes)*			
	1985	*1986*	*1987*	*1988*	*1985*	*1986*	*1987*	*1988*
Wheat	2,025	2,096	2,174	2,332	5,326	4,292	5,774	6,514
Barley	4,155	4,334	4,377	4,175	10,680	7,331	9,533	12,070
Oats	465	384	378	335	719	422	502	537
Rye	222	223	222	222	295	220	321	357
Rice	74	79	78	80	459	494	482	499
Maize	516	525	526	535	3,331	3,405	3,338	3,577
Potatoes	327	289	303	280	5,770	4,857	5,550	4,578
Sugar-beet	178	195	184	194	7,349	7,629	7,638	9,056
Sunflower	1,125	936	978	894	915	844	926	1,123

In 1986, 1,574,000 hectares were under vines; production of wine was (1988) 22·6m. hectolitres. The area of onions was (1988) 32,000 hectares, yielding (1988) 1,146,000 tonnes. Production of oranges and mandarines was 3,345,000 tonnes, lemons, 679,000. Other products are esparto, flax, hemp and pulse. Spain has important industries connected with the preparation of wine and fruits.

Industrial crops (1988 in 1,000 tonnes): Cotton, 353; olive oil, 356; tobacco, 42 (1985).

Livestock products (1988 in 1,000 tonnes): Pork, 1,630; beef, 454; mutton, 219; poultry meat, 756; goat meat, 19; rabbit meat, 82; cows' milk, 5,700m. litres; sheep's milk, 287m. litres; goats' milk, 492m. litres; eggs, 904m. dozen.

Livestock (1988): Horses, 250,000; asses, 131,000; mules, 110,000; cattle, 4·98m.; sheep, 17,894,000; goats, 2·9m.; pigs, 16,941,000; poultry, 55m.

Forestry. Total forests (1989) 15·7m. hectares; production, 1986, 15,635,000 cu. metres of wood. Other forest products (1986 in tonnes): Resins, 23,955; cork, 73,541; esparto, 5,872.

Fisheries. The total catch amounted in 1988 to 1,047,620 tonnes, including 79,874 tonnes of molluscs, 30,622 of crustaceans and 111,987 from nurseries; total value, 231,582m. pesetas. The main fishing region is the North-West (Galicia), with 60·2% of the catch. The Spanish fishing fleet in 1986 consisted of 17,464 vessels of 649,457 tonnes, with a total crew of 94,246.

INDUSTRY AND TRADE

Industry. The industrial sector represented 72·3% of export value, 38·6% of GNP and 24·2% of employment in 1987. In 1983, the principal textile productions were (in 1,000 tonnes): Wool yarn, 33; cotton yarn, 106; fabrics yarn, 128; wool cloth, 9; cotton cloth, 88; fabrics cloth, 69. In 1983, 2·4m. tonnes of writing, printing, packing and other paper were produced. The production of cement reached 24,372,000 tonnes in 1988. Steel production (1988) 11,859,000 tonnes; the three great blast-furnaces concentrations are in Bilbao area, Avilés (Asturias) and Sagunto (Valencia). The chemical industry is located in the areas of Madrid, Barcelona and Bilbao; sulphuric acid production (1982), 2m. tonnes; nitrogenous fertilizers, 822,000 tonnes; plastics (1988), 1,878,000 tonnes. The 9 oil refineries refined (1988) 48·7m. tonnes of crude oil. In 1982 900,000 TV sets (550,000 colour sets) were manufactured. 953,067 refrigerators and 1,354,000 washing machines were manufactured in 1988. Spain has important toy and shoe industries, toys especially in Alicante and Barcelona provinces and shoes in Alicante province and the Balearic islands.

Spanish shipyards launched 140,160 BRT in 1988. In 1988, 1,498,000 cars and 368,000 industrial and commercial vehicles were built.

Labour. The monthly minimum wage for workers was 50,010 pesetas (Jan. 1990).

The economically active population numbered 14,632,800 in Dec. 1988. Of these, 11,780,600 were employed: 1,694,300 in agriculture and fishing, 2,804,500 in manufactures, 1,020,600 in construction industry and 6,261,600 in trade, transport and other public and personal services. 18·5% of the active population was unemployed at the end of 1988 (2,701,200 persons).

Trade Unions. The Constitution guarantees the establishment and activities of trade unions provided they have a democratic structure. The two most important trade unions are *Unión General de Trabajadores* (UGT), founded in 1888 by Pablo Iglesias (who had founded in 1879 the Spanish Workers Socialist Party, PSOE), and *Comisiones Obreras*, which was gradually established 1958–63, then as a clandestine labour organization.

Commerce. Foreign trade of Spain (Peninsula, Baleares, Canaries, Ceuta, Melilla) (in 1m. pesetas):

	1984	*1985*	*1986*	*1987*	*1988*
Imports	4,628,991	5,073,239	4,890,768	6,029,838	7,039,516
Exports	3,778,071	4,104,143	3,800,225	4,195,623	4,686,376

In 1988 the most important items of import were (in 1m. pesetas): Crude petroleum, 564,240 (8·01% of total); vehicle parts, 238,275 (3·38%); vehicles 384,995 (5·47%); computers, 193,172 (2·74%); petroleum products, 127,306 (1·81%); inner combustion motors, 161,841 (2·3%); aircraft, 109,620 (1·56%); telecommunications equipment, 108,173 (1·54%); electrical machinery and tools, 101,754 (1·45%); paper and paperboard, 104,866 (1·49%).

The most important exports in 1988 (in 1m. pesetas) were: Vehicles, 501,620 (10·7% of total); petroleum products, 187,205 (4%); fresh fruit and nuts, 220,657 (4·71%); vehicle parts, 190,191 (4·06%); footwear, 133,498 (2·85%); vegetables, 113,681 (2·42%); iron and steel bars, 96,188 (2·05%); tyres, 84,878 (1·81%); aircraft, 74,306 (1·59%); lorries and buses, 97,414 (2·08%).

Distribution of Spanish foreign trade (in 1m. pesetas) according to main origin and destination, for calendar years:

	Imports		*Exports*	
	1987	*1988*	*1987*	*1988*
EEC	3,292,037	3,998,825	2,676,714	3,074,843
Germany, Federal Republic	970,299	1,138,357	503,380	561,996
France	773,993	947,517	786,869	865,142
Italy	532,650	675,484	371,852	453,721
UK	421,774	499,423	398,029	458,931
Netherlands	195,090	243,869	225,738	229,762
Belgium–Luxembourg	193,790	230,178	126,476	158,899
Portugal	100,707	146,224	189,893	262,128
USA	499,075	626,439	341,672	368,871
Japan	270,245	361,057	46,319	55,565
Latin America	373,620	375,305	182,086	142,188
Mexico	176,973	128,642	21,630	27,429
EFTA	217,049	376,828	1,187,631	195,758
Sweden	105,922	131,912	46,628	45,645
Switzerland	101,613	105,876	75,145	30,775
COMECON	155,976	180,892	66,940	61,844
USSR	109,114	129,494	36,386	31,104
Nigeria	102,172	109,334	15,593	13,122
Libya	100,618	77,075	15,982	14,347
Saudi Arabia	85,091	53,060	43,952	51,869
Iraq	82,272	48,060	2,140	18,010
Iran	81,828	56,643	12,549	8,895

Total trade between Spain and UK (British Department of Trade returns, in £1,000 sterling):

	1986	*1987*	*1988*	*1989*
Imports to UK	1,777,341	2,099,139	2,482,360	2,772,011
Exports and re-exports from UK	1,905,479	2,164,221	2,691,662	3,137,941

Total trade of the Spanish territories and UK (British Department of Trade returns, in £1,000 sterling):

	Imports to UK			*Exports from UK*		
	1987	*1988*	*1989*	*1987*	*1988*	*1989*
Canary Islands	77,191	77,491	74,532	86,185	90,834	89,852
North Africa	...	34	57	3,831	3,599	4,640

Tourism. In 1988, 54,172,700 tourists visited Spain (from France, 22·3%; Portugal, 18·6%; Federal Republic of Germany, 12·7%; UK, 14·1%; Morocco, 5·1%). Receipts of foreign currency (1988) US$16·78m. Hotel and similar beds, 1,784,900 (1987).

COMMUNICATIONS

Roads. In 1986 the total length of highways and roads of all classes was 318,225 km. The main network comprised 2,155 km of motorways (1,798 km toll motorways), 619 km of other four-lane highways and 17,760 km of first class roads. Number of cars (1988) was 10,788,975, lorries and vans, 2,034,728, buses, 44,178 and motorcycles (1987), 845,612. There were in Dec. 1986 12,345,589 driving licences (3,370,450 drivers were women).

Railways. The total length of the state railways in 1987 was 12,721 km, mostly 1,676-mm gauge (6,226 km electrified). On 1 Feb. 1941 the Spanish railways, of broad gauge only, passed into state ownership; they are under a board known as the *Red Nacional de Ferrocarriles Españoles* (RENFE). The gauge of the principal Spanish railways has, for strategic reasons, been kept different from that of France; passengers therefore must change trains at the French frontier stations except by certain trains having variable gauge axles. In 1988 freight carried was 36·6m. tonnes and 194·5m. passengers. There are several regional railways including Basque, Catalan and FEVE (narrow gauge) railways.

Aviation. The most important Spanish airline is 'Iberia': it maintains a regular service with Europe, America, Africa and the Middle and Far East. Its fleet included 6 B-747s (for 430 passengers each), 8 DC-10s (for 266), 6 Airbus-300Bs (for 253), 35 B-727s (for 161) and 30 DC-9s (for 110) in 1985. 'Aviaco' operates mainly internal flights. There are 43 airports open to civil traffic; those of Madrid, Palma de Mallorca and Barcelona are the most active. A small airport in Seo de Urgel, in the Pyrenees, used especially for the air service of Andorra was opened in 1982.

Aircraft movements in 1987, 309,385 internal and 293,177 international, carrying 25·7m. passengers on internal and 37·2m. on international flights, and 348,056 tonnes of merchandise.

Shipping. The merchant navy in 1988 had 463 vessels of a gross tonnage of 3·5m.

In 1987, 82,174 ships entered Spanish ports, carrying 14·1m. passengers and discharging and loading 215·7m. tonnes of cargo.

Post and Broadcasting. The receipts of the post office in 1986 were 87,396m. pesetas; expenses, 99,892m. pesetas. There were in 1986, 13,292 post offices and (Nov. 1987) 15,350,464 telephones, these all privately operated.

Radio Nacional de España broadcasts 5 programmes on medium-waves and FM, as well as many regional programmes; it does not broadcast advertising. The greatest radio audience is that of a private network, *Sociedad Española de Radiodifusión* (SER); *Cadena de Ondas Populares Españolas* (COPE) belongs to the Roman Catholic church. Two private broadcasting networks were established in 1982 covering the whole of Spain, *Antena 3* and *Radio 80*. *Televisión Española* broadcasts 2 programmes. There were (1989) the following regional TV networks: *TV3* (1983) and *Canal 33* (1989), both broadcasting in Catalan; *ETB1* (1983) and *ETB2* (1987), both Basque, the first one broadcasting in Basque; *Televisión de Galicia* (1985), in Galician; *TM3* (1989), for the area of Madrid; *RTVV* (1989), mostly in Valencian (Catalan); and *Tele-Sur* (1989), for Andalusia. Colour transmissions are carried by PAL system. Number of receivers (1986): Radio, 11·5m.; television, 12·5m. (about 90% colour sets).

Cinemas (1986). There were 2,640 cinemas with an audience of 87·3m.

Newspapers (1986). There were about 75 daily newspapers with a total daily circulation of about 5m. copies. In 1987 the following dailies had a daily circulation of more than 100,000 copies: *El País* (Madrid, 372,141), *La Vanguardia* (Barcelona, 201,015), *ABC* (Madrid, 247,225), *As* (Madrid, [sports], 156,534), *El Periódico* (Barcelona, 153,735), *Diario 16* (Madrid, 136,099) and *El Correo Español-El Pueblo Vasco* (Bilbao, 123,123).

JUSTICE, RELIGION, EDUCATION AND WELFARE

Justice. Justice is administered by *Tribunales* and *Juzgados* (Tribunals and Courts), which conjointly form the *Poder Judicial* (Judicial Power). Judges and magistrates cannot be removed, suspended or transferred except as set forth by law. The Constitution of 1978 has established a new organ, the *Consejo General del Poder Judicial* (CGPJ, General Council of the Judicial Power), formed by 1 President and 20 magistrates, judges, attorneys and lawyers, governing the Judicial Power in full independence from the other two powers of the State, the Legislative (Cortes) and the Executive (President of the Government and his Cabinet); all members of the CGPJ, magistrates, etc., have been appointed by the Cortes since 1985. Its President is that of the *Tribunal Supremo*.

The Judicature is composed of the *Tribunal Supremo* (Supreme High Court); 17 *Tribunales Superiores de Justicia* (Upper Courts of Justice, 1 for each autonomous community); 52 *Audiencias Provinciales* (Provincial High Courts); *Juzgados de Primera Instancia* (Courts of First Instance), *Juzgados de Instrucción* (Courts of Judicial Proceedings, not passing sentences) and *Juzgados de lo Penal* (Penal Courts, passing sentences).

The *Tribunal Supremo* consists of a President (appointed by the King, on proposal from the *Consejo General del Poder Judicial*) and various judges distributed among 7 chambers: 1 for trying civil matters, 3 for administrative purposes, 1 for criminal trials, 1 for social matters and 1 for military cases. The *Tribunal Supremo* has disciplinary faculties; is court of cassation in all criminal trials; for administrative purposes decides in first and second instance disputes arising between private individuals and the State, and in social matters resolves in the last instance.

The jury system, re-established by the art. 125 of the Constitution, had not been applied by Jan. 1990, pending its parliamentary regulation.

The *Tribunal Constitucional* (Constitutional Court) has power to solve conflicts between the State and the Autonomous Communities, to determine if legislation passed by the Cortes is contrary to the Constitution and to protect constitutional rights of the individuals violated by any authority. Its 12 members are appointed by the King in the following way: 4, on proposal of the Congress of Deputies; 4, on proposal of the Senate; 2 on proposal of the *Consejo General del Poder Judicial;* and 2 on proposal of the Cabinet. It has a 9 year term, a third of the membership renewed every 3 years.

The death penalty was abolished in 1978 by the Constitution (art. 15). Divorce is again legal since July 1981 and abortion since Aug. 1985.

The prison population was, on 6 Nov. 1988, 30,250.

Religion. Roman Catholicism is the religion of the majority. There are 11 metropolitan sees and 52 suffragan sees, the chief being Toledo, where the Primate resides.

The archdioceses of Madrid-Alcalá and Barcelona depend directly from the Vatican.

The Constitution guarantees full religious freedom and states that no religion has an established legal condition (art. 16); so, since 29 Dec. 1978 there has been no official religion in Spain. A report issued in 1982 by the Episcopal Conference of the Roman Catholic Church claims that 82·76% of all children born in 1981 were baptized in that church.

There are about 250,000 other Christians, including several Protestant denominations, Jehovah Witnesses (about 60,000) and Mormons. The British and Foreign Bible Society was, on 10 March 1963, allowed to resume its activities.

The first synagogue since the expulsion of the Jews in 1492 was opened in Madrid on 2 Oct. 1959. The number of Jews is estimated at about 13,000.

There is a growing Moslem community, with about 450,000 members. Most of them are foreign citizens, but there are also Spanish Moslems, mainly in Ceuta and Melilla.

Education. Primary education is compulsory and free between 6 and 14 years of age.

In 1986–87 pre-primary education (under 6 years) was undertaken by 39,190 schools, with 39,105 teachers and 1,326,917 pupils. Primary or basic education (6 to 14 years): 185,658 schools, 192,217 teachers and 6,649,521 pupils. Secondary education (14-17 years) is conducted on two branches: Middle schools *(Institutos)*, and vocational and technical centres *(Formación Profesional)*, with 2,638 and 2,199 school units, 77,163 and 50,480 teachers and 1,263,841 and 727,212 pupils. For adult education there were (in 1986–87) 602 school units, with 543 teachers and (1985–86) 145,062 students. For the physically or mentally disabled there were (1986–87) 4,817 school units, with 5,146 teachers and 42,620 pupils.

In 1989 there were in all 35 universities: 24 State Universities, in Madrid, Barcelona, Valencia, Granada, Sevilla, Santiago de Compostela, Zaragoza, Bilbao (University of the Basque Country), Oviedo, Valladolid, Salamanca (founded in 1215), La Laguna (Canaries), Murcia, Málaga, Córdoba, Badajoz-Cáceres (University of Extremadura), Cádiz, León, Santander, Alicante, Palma de Mallorca, Albacete–Ciudad Real (University of Castilla–La Mancha), Alcalá de Henares and in the southern area of Madrid (Carlos III University, 1989); 4 Polytechnic Universities, in Madrid, Barcelona, Valencia and Las Palmas (Canaries); 2 Autonomous Universities, in Madrid and Barcelona; 4 private (catholic) universities, in Deusto (Bilbao), Pamplona, Salamanca and Madrid (University of Comillas); and the *Universidad Nacional de Educación a Distancia* (National University for Education at Home), which teaches by mail, radio and TV, with its central seat at Madrid (53,717 students, 1987–88). There were 966,007 university students (1987–88) including 31,156 students at private universities.

Health. In 1987 there were 131,080 doctors, 5,722 dentists, 31,118 pharmacists, 147,462 nurses, 6,103 midwives and 935 hospitals with 179,192 beds.

Social Security. The social services budget was 5,467,797m. pesetas in 1989, and covered retirement pensions (59·3% of that budget), health and hospital services (29·7%) and other allowances and aids. There is a minimum pension for every retired citizen with yearly earnings under 520,000 pesetas.

In 1989 the system of contributions to the social security and employment scheme was: For pensions, sickness, invalidity, maternity and children, a contribution of 28·8% of the basic wage (24% paid by the employer, 4·8% by the employee); for unemployment benefit, a contribution of 6·3% (5·2% paid by the employer, 1·1% by the employee). There are also minor contributions for a Fund of Guaranteed Salaries, working accidents and professional sicknesses, and vocational training.

DIPLOMATIC REPRESENTATIVES

Of Spain in Great Britain (24 Belgrave Sq., London SW1X 8QA)
Ambassador: Felipe de la Morena.

Of Great Britain in Spain (Calle de Fernando el Santo, 16, Madrid, 4)
Ambassador: Robin Fearn, CMG.

Of Spain in the USA (2700 15th St., NW, Washington, D.C., 20009)
Ambassador: Julián Santamaría.

Of the USA in Spain (Serrano 75, Madrid)
Ambassador: Joseph Zappala.

Of Spain to the United Nations
Ambassador: Francisco Villar Ortiz de Urbina.

Further Reading

Statistical Information: The Instituto Nacional de Estadistica (Paseo de la Castellana, 183, Madrid) combines the administrative work of a government department attached to the Presidency of the Government with a centre of statistical studies.

Bell, D. (ed.) *Democratic Politics in Spain: Spanish Politics after Franco*. London, 1983
Carr, R., *Modern Spain, 1875–1980*. OUP, 1980
Collins, R., *The Basques*. Oxford, 1986
Donaghy, P. J. and Newton, M. T., *Spain: A Guide to Political and Economic Institutions*. CUP, 1987

Enciclopedia Universal Ilustrada. 70 vols., 10 appendices, 10 supplements. Madrid
Gunther, R. (et al) *Spain after Franco: The Making of a Competitive Party System*. Univ. of California Press, 1986
Harrison, J., *The Spanish Economy in the Twentieth Century*. London, 1985
Hooper, J., *The Spaniards: A Portrait of The New Spain*. London, 1986
Maravall, J., *The Transition to Democracy in Spain*. London, 1982
Morris, J., *Spain*. London, 1979
Preston, P., *The Triumph of Democracy in Spain*. London and New York, 1986
Shields, G. J., *Spain*. [Bibliography] Oxford and Santa Barbara, 1985

National Library: Biblioteca Nacional, Madrid.

FORMER PROVINCE IN AFRICA (WESTERN SAHARA)

The colony of Spanish Sahara became a Spanish province in July 1958. On 14 Nov. 1975 Spain, Morocco and Mauritania had reached agreement on the transfer of power over Western Sahara to Morocco and Mauritania on 28 Feb. 1976. Morocco occupied al-Aaiún in late Nov. and on 12 Jan. 1976 the Spanish army withdrew from Western Sahara which had ceased to be a Spanish province on 31 Dec. 1975. The country was partitioned by Morocco and Mauritania on 28 Feb. 1976; Morocco reorganized its sector into 3 provinces. In Aug. 1979 Mauritania withdrew from the territory it took over in 1976. The area was taken over by Morocco and reorganized into a fourth province.

A liberation movement, *Frente Polisario*, launched an armed struggle against Spanish rule on 20 May 1973 and, in spite of occupation of all western centres by Moroccan troops, Saharawi guerrillas based in Algeria continue to attempt to liberate their country. They have renamed it the Saharawi Arab Democratic Republic and hold most of the desert beyond a defensive line built by Moroccan troops encompassing Smara, Bu Craa and Laâyoune. A ceasefire was agreed in Aug. 1988. In Sept. 1989 Polisario's guerrillas ended the lull in fighting with battles on 7 and 11 Oct. – Morocco and Polisario failed to agree on how the referendum (part of UN plan) should be held.

In 1982 the Saharawi Arab Democratic Republic became a member of the Organization of African Unity (OAU).

President: Mohammed Abdelaziz.

Area 266,769 sq. km (102,680 sq. miles). The population at the census held by Morocco in Sept. 1982 was 163,868; estimate (1986) 180,000. Another estimated 165,000 Saharawis live in refugee camps around Tindouf in south-west Algeria. The main towns (1982 census) are Laâyoune (al-Aaiún), the capital (96,784), Dakhla (17,822) and as-Smara (17,753). The population is Arabic-speaking, and virtually entirely Sunni Moslem.

Rich phosphate deposits were discovered in 1963 at Bu Craa. Morocco holds 65% of the shares of the former Spanish state-controlled company. While production reached 5·6m. tonnes in 1975, exploitation has been severely reduced by guerrilla activity but in 1984 produced 1m. tonnes. After a nearly complete collapse, production and transportation of phosphate resumed in 1978, ceased again, and then resumed in 1982. There are about 6,100 km of motorable tracks, but only about 500 km of paved roads. There are airports at Laâyoune and Dakhla. As most of the land is desert, less than 19% is in agricultural use, with about 2,000 tonnes of grain produced annually. There are (1983) about 22,000 sheep, as well as goats and camels raised. Electricity produced (1983) 78m. kwh.

Further Reading

Damis, J., *Conflict in Northwest Africa: The Western Sahara Dispute*. Stanford, 1983
Hodges, T., *Western Sahara: The Roots of a Desert War*. London and Westport, 1984
Sipe, L. F., *Western Sahara: A Comprehensive Bibliography*. New York, 1984
Thompson, V. and Adloff, R., *The Western Saharans: Background to Conflict*. London, 1980

SRI LANKA

Capital: Colombo
Population: 16·6m. (1988)
GNP per capita: US$420 (1988)

Ceylon

HISTORY. According to the Mahawansa chronicle, an Indian prince from the valley of the Ganges, named Vijaya, arrived in the 6th century B.C. and became the first king of the Sinhalese. The monarchical form of government continued until the beginning of the 19th century when the British subjugated the Kandyan Kingdom in the central highlands.

In 1505 the Portuguese formed settlements on the west and south, which were taken from them about the middle of the next century by the Dutch. In 1796 the British Government annexed the foreign settlements to the presidency of Madras. In 1802 Ceylon was constituted a separate colony.

Ceylon became an independent Commonwealth state when the Ceylon Independence Act, 1947, came into force on 4 Feb. 1948. Sri Lanka became a republic in 1972. War between northern Tamil separatists and government forces began in 1983; the state of emergency ended on 11 Jan. 1989, but violence continued.

AREA AND POPULATION. Sri Lanka is an island in the Indian Ocean, south of the Indian peninsula from which it is separated by the Palk Strait. On 28 June 1974 the frontier between India and Sri Lanka in the Palk Strait was redefined, giving to Sri Lanka the island of Kachchativu. Area (in sq. km.) and census population on 17 March 1981.

Provinces	*Area*	*Population*	*Provinces*	*Area*	*Population*
Western	3,708·61	3,919,807	North-Central	10,723·59	849,492
Central	5,583·50	2,009,248	Uva	8,487·91	914,522
Southern	5,559·15	1,882,661	Sabaragamuwa	4,901·55	1,482,031
Northern	8,882·11	1,109,404			
Eastern	9,951·26	975,251	Total	65,609·86	14,846,750
North-Western	7,812·18	1,704,334			

Population (1981 census), 14,846,750, an increase of 17% since 1971. Population (in 1,000) according to ethnic group and nationality at the 1981 census: 10,980 Sinhalese, 1,887 Sri Lanka Tamils, 1,047 Sri Lanka Moors, 39 Burghers, 47 Malays, 819 Indian Tamils, 28 others. Non-nationals of Sri Lanka totalled 635,150.

Vital statistics, 1988 (provisional): Birth-rate (per 1,000 population), 20·7; death-rate, 5·8; infant death-rate (per 1,000 live births) (1987, provisional), 24.

The urban population was 21·5% of the total in 1981. The principal towns and their population according to the census of 1981 are: Colombo (the capital), 587,647; Dehiwela-Mt. Lavinia, 173,529; Moratuwa, 134,826; Jaffna, 118,224; Kotte, 101,039; Kandy, 97,872; Galle, 76,863; Negombo, 60,762; Trincomalee, 44,313; Batticaloa, 42,963; Matara, 38,843; Ratnapura, 37,497; Anuradhapura, 35,981; Badulla, 33,068; Kalutara, 31,503. Population of the Greater Colombo area, 1980, about 1m.

The national languages are Sinhala, English and Tamil; Sinhala is the official language and Tamil is used in the northern and eastern provinces.

CLIMATE. Sri Lanka has an equatorial climate with low annual temperature variations, but it is affected by the north-east Monsoon (Dec. to Feb.) and the south-west Monsoon (May to Sept.). Rainfall is generally heavy but never lasts long; it is heaviest in the south-west and central highlands while the north and east are relatively dry. Thirty-year averages, 1951–80: Colombo. Jan. 79·7°F (26·5°C), July 81·1°F (27·3°C). Annual rainfall 99·5" (2,527 mm). Trincomalee. Jan. 78·6°F (25·9°C), July 86·2°F (30·1°C). Annual rainfall 63·60" (1,615 mm). Kandy. Jan. 73·9°F (23·3°C), July 75·9°F (24·4°C). Annual rainfall 76·6" (1,947 mm). Nuwara

Eliya. Jan. 58·5°F (14·7°C), July 60·3°F (15·7°C). Annual rainfall 80·04" (2,044 mm).

CONSTITUTION AND GOVERNMENT. A new constitution for the Democratic Socialist Republic of Sri Lanka was promulgated in Sept. 1978.

The Executive President is directly elected by the people and has to receive more than one-half of the valid votes cast. His term of office is six years and he shall not hold the office for more than two consecutive terms. He is the Head of the State, the Head of the Executive and of the Government and the Commander-in-chief of the Armed Forces. He does not have any veto power over legislation; even in a time of public emergency, he must act with Parliamentary control and approval.

Parliament consists of one chamber, composed of 225 members (196 elected and 29 from the National List). The Senate was abolished by constitutional amendment in Oct. 1971.

The term of Parliament is six years. In Nov. 1982 Parliament voted to extend its present term (expiring Aug. 1983) for a further six years. The vote was subject to national referendum on 20 Dec. 1982; 71% of the electorate voted and 55% approved the extension.

The Prime Minister and other Ministers, who must be members of Parliament, are appointed by the President. The President is head of the Cabinet.

The electorate consists of all who are 18 years of age and over.

National flag: A yellow field bearing 2 panels: In the hoist 2 vertical strips of green and orange; in the fly, dark red with a gold lion holding a sword and in each corner a gold 'bo' leaf.

The Cabinet was as follows in Dec. 1989:

President, Buddha Sasana, Defence, Policy Planning and Implementation: Ranasinghe Premadasa.

Prime Minister, Finance: D. B. Wijeratne.

Tourism: A. M. S. Adikari. *Post and Telecommunications:* Alick Aluvihare. *Labour and Social Welfare:* Dr Ranjith Atapattu. *Agriculture, Food and Co-operatives:* Lalith Athulath Mudali. *Housing and Construction:* B. Sirisena Cooray. *Lands, Irrigation and Majaweli Development:* P. Dayaratne. *Plantation Industries:* Gamini Dissanayake. *Higher Education, Science and Technology:* A. C. S. Hameed. *Health and Women's Affairs:* Renuka Herath. *Education, Cultural Affairs and Information:* W. J. M. Lokubandara. *Youth Affairs and Sports:* C. Nanda Mathew. *Transport and Highways:* Wijayapala Mendis. *Trade and Shipping:* A. R. Munsoor. *Power and Energy:* Festus Perera. *Fisheries and Aquatic Resources:* M. Joseph Michael Perera. *Justice and Parliamentary Affairs and Chief Govenment Whip:* M. Vincent Perera. *Textiles and Rural Industrial Development:* S. Thondaman. *Industries and Leader of the House:* Ranil Wickremasinghe. *Public Administration, Provincial Councils and Home Affairs:* U. B. Wijekoon. *Foreign Affairs:* Ranjan Wijeratne.

For purposes of general administration, the island is divided into 25 districts, administered by government agents. There are 12 Municipal Councils and 24 District Councils.

DEFENCE

Army. The Army was constituted on 16 Oct. 1949. It consists of 5 infantry brigades, 2 reconnaissance, 2 field artillery and 1 engineer regiment, and 1 signals battalion. Equipment includes 18 Saladin armoured cars and 15 Ferret scout cars. Strength (1990) 34,000 including active reservists. There are also paramilitary forces: Police Force (28,000), Volunteer Force (eventually 18,000, when fully mobilized).

Navy. The naval force comprises 3 Surveillance Command Ships (*ex*-mercantile), 2 locally-built coastal patrol craft, 34 inshore patrol craft of varying types plus about 30 small fast patrol boats and service craft. There are 2 mechanized landing craft of 270 tonnes full load. The main naval base is at Trincomalee. Personnel in 1989 numbered 5,500, with a reserve of about 1,000.

Air Force. The Air Force was formed on 10 Oct. 1950. Its flying bases are at Katunayake and China Bay, Trincomalee. Equipment of 4 squadrons comprises 9 SF.260 and 4 Cessna 150/152 trainers, 3 HS748, 6 Chinese-built Y-12s, 2 Chinese-built Y-8s (An-12s), 1 Super King Air, 3 Cessna Skymasters, 1 Cessna 421 and a Cessna Cardinal for general transport and utility purposes; and 2 Dauphin, 10 Bell 212, 4 Bell 412 and 8 JetRanger helicopters for internal security operations. Total strength (1990) about 3,700 officers and airmen. There is also an Air Force Reserve.

INTERNATIONAL RELATIONS

Membership. Sri Lanka is a member of UN, the Commonwealth, the Non-Aligned Movement, the South Asian Association for Regional Co-operation and the Colombo Plan.

External debt. External debt in Dec. 1986 was Rs 86,208·2m. (provisional).

ECONOMY

Planning. The 1988–92 plan aims at 5·3% annual growth rate. Investment allocated is mainly for education, agriculture, food and nutrition, the plantation sector, power, telecommunications and road repairs. Total public investment, about Rs164,300m.

Budget. Revenue and expenditure of central government in Rs 1m. for financial years ending 31 Dec.:

		Expenditure		
Year	*Revenue*	*Recurrent*	*Capital*	*Total*
1986	41,644	34,772	27,589	62,361
1987	44,900	38,816	29,013	67,829
1988 [1]	45,675	49,093	41,794	90,887

[1] Estimate.

The principal sources of revenue in 1988 were (in Rs 1m.): General sales and tax, 12,320; import levies, 11,599; export duties, 1,574; selective sales taxes, 4,685.

The principal items of recurrent expenditure in 1988 (in Rs 1m.): Finance and planning, 17,713; defence, 6,584; education, 4,823; administration, 4,083; social services, 3,769. Capital expenditure on finance and planning, 6,697; defence, 6,408; Mahaweli development, 550; power and energy, 4,620; rehabilitation, 2,555.

Currency. The Monetary Law Act provides that the standard monetary unit is the Sri Lankan *rupee*.

The Central Bank of Sri Lanka is the sole authority for the issue of currency and all currency notes and coins issued by the Central Bank are legal tender for the payment of any amount, except notes of Rs 50 and Rs 100 dated before 25 Oct. 1970. Currency notes are issued in the denominations of Rs 2, 5, 10, 20, 50, 100, 500 and 1,000. Coins are issued in the denominations of 1, 2, 5, 10, 25 and 50 cents; Rs 1, 2 and 5. The total circulation was Rs 29,371·3m. on 31 Dec. 1988. In March 1990, £1 = Rs 65·00; US$1 = Rs 39·66.

Banking. The narrow money supply (M1) at 31 Dec. 1988 stood at Rs 32,379·3m.

The main commercial banks in Sri Lanka are: The Bank of Ceylon and the People's Bank (state-managed), the State Bank of India, Grindlays Bank, the Hongkong and Shanghai Banking Corporation, the Standard Chartered Bank, the Commercial Bank of Ceylon Ltd., the Hatton National Bank Ltd., the Habib Bank (Overseas) Ltd., Indo-Suez Bank, Bank of Credit and Commerce International Ltd., American Express Bank Ltd., the Indian Overseas Bank Ltd., Citibank NA, Sampath Bank Ltd., Seylan Trust Bank Ltd., Algemene Bank Nederlands NV, Amsterdam-Rotterdam Bank NV, Bank of Oman Ltd., Deutsche Bank AG, Habib Bank AG, Zurich, Indian Bank, Middle East Bank Ltd., Overseas Trust Bank Ltd and Emirates Bank International Ltd. Total assets of 25 commercial banks at 31 Dec. 1988, Rs 95,814·5m.

The monopoly in all insurance business enjoyed by the state-owned Ceylon Insurance Corporation and the National Insurance Corporation is broad based with the participation of a large number of assurance companies in this business.

Sri Lanka National Savings Bank at 31 Dec. 1988 had a balance to depositors' credit of Rs 18,002·2m. Sri Lanka State Mortgage and Investment Bank, National Development Bank, Development Finance Corporation, the National Housing Authority and the Housing Development Finance Corporation of Sri Lanka Ltd. are the main long-term credit institutions.

Weights and Measures. The metric system has been established by the Weights and Measures (Amendment) Law No. 24 of 1974, and subsequent legislation.

ENERGY AND NATURAL RESOURCES

Electricity. Installed capacity of electric energy (1988), 1,208,450 kw. Energy produced, 2,799m. kwh; the main source was thermal power as the water levels of the reservoirs were not sufficient to operate the hydro power plants at full capacity. Supply 230 volts; 50 Hz.

Water. The Mahaweli Ganga irrigation scheme is (1987) irrigating 41,000 hectares of new land and 77,000 hectares of land already cultivated. There is a Water Resources Board (set up in 1966) and a National Water Supply and Drainage Board (1974). Water supply to the city and area of Colombo comes from the Labugama and Kalatuwawa reservoirs. Consumption within Colombo city limits is estimated at 10,000m. gallons a year.

Minerals. Gems are among the chief minerals mined and exported. Precious and semi-precious stones are found mainly in the Ratnapura district in the south-east. The most important are sapphire, ruby, crysoberyl, beryl, topaz, spinel, garnet, zircon and tourmaline. Value of gemstones exported in 1988, Rs 2,070m.

Graphite is also important. The State Graphite Corporation was set up in 1971. There were 3 large mines (Bogala, Kahatagaha and Kalangaha), and several smaller mines. Graphite produced (tonnes), 1985, 7,413; 1986, 7,708; 1987, 6,718.

The Ceylon Mineral Sands Corporation was established in 1957, mainly to extract ilmenite. Production of ilmenite, 1987, 132,427 tonnes. Some rutile is also produced (7,238 tonnes in 1987).

Salt extraction is the oldest industry in Sri Lanka and is now controlled by the National Salt Corporation. The method is solar evaporation of sea-water. Production, 1987, 115,274 tonnes.

Agriculture. The area of the island is 6,561,000 hectares, of which about 2m. hectares are under cultivation. Agriculture engages about 45% of the labour force. The main crops in 1988 were as follows: Paddy (2,477,000 tonnes from 815,561 hectares), rubber (122,000 tonnes), tea (226,000 tonnes) and coconuts (1,933m. nuts).

Livestock in 1988 (estimate): 1,788,000 cattle, 953,400 buffaloes, 94,900 swine, 538,200 goats and sheep, 8,645,000 poultry.

Fisheries. Production for 1988 was 197,536 tonnes including 155,099 tonnes of coastal water fish, 38,012 tonnes of fresh water fish and 4,425 tonnes from deep-sea fisheries. In 1988 there were 29,728 fishing craft, of which 14,877 were not motorized.

INDUSTRY AND TRADE

Industry. The main industries are food, beverages and tobacco; textiles, clothing and leather goods; chemicals, petroleum, rubber and plastics.

The Greater Colombo Economic Commission has two Investment Promotion Zones: Katunayake and Biyagama.

Trade Unions. The registration and control of trade unions are regulated by the Trade Unions Ordinance (Ch. 138 of the Legislative Enactments). In 1985 there were 957 registered trade unions with a membership of 1,565,394.

Commerce. The values of total imports and exports (imports excluding bullion, specie and postal articles; exports, including re-exports and ship's stores) for calendar years (in Rs 1,000):

	1984	*1985*	*1986*	*1987*	*1988*
Imports	46,913,266	49,068,542	51,281,508	59,749,717	70,320,427
Exports	36,540,767	35,034,947	34,092,261	39,860,638	47,092,044

Principal exports (domestic) in 1988 (in Rs 1m.): Tea, 12,299; rubber, 3,706; copra, coconut oil and desiccated coconut, 895; other crops, 1,561; textiles and garments, 14,260; precious and semi-precious stones, 2,614.

Principal imports (Rs 1m.) in 1988 were petroleum, 7,839m.; machinery and equipment, 7,047m.; vehicles and transport equipment, 1,409; food and beverages, 10,201.

In 1988 the principal sources of imports were (in Rs 1m.): Saudi Arabia, 445; Japan, 9,705; UK, 4,025; USA, 4,857; India, 2,894; Iran, 3,238; Singapore, 2,955; Federal Republic of Germany, 3,265; South Korea, 2,843.

Principal export destinations 1988 were (in Rs 1m.): UK, 2,535; USA, 11,664; Japan, 2,665; Pakistan, 1,667; Federal Republic of Germany, 3,302; Saudi Arabia, 1,156.

Total trade between Sri Lanka and UK (British Department of Trade returns, in £1,000 sterling):

	1985	*1986*	*1987*	*1988*	*1989*
Imports to UK	73,956	51,860	53,817	56,661	63,527
Exports and re-exports from UK	79,234	83,315	84,680	92,528	92,465

Tourism. 182,662 tourists visited the country in 1988.

COMMUNICATIONS

Roads. There are 25,680 km. of motorable roads, of which 82% are blacktopped. Number of motor vehicles, 31 Dec. 1985, 523,723, including 148,587 private cars and cabs, 98,859 lorries, 75,474 tractors, 161,373 motor cycles, 38,309 buses.

Railways. In 1988 there were about 1,453 km of railway open, of which 1,394 km were 1,676 mm gauge and 59 762 mm gauge. In 1988 railways ran 1,859·1m. passenger-km and 197·5m. tonne-km.

Aviation. Air Lanka operates international services. Foreign airlines which operate scheduled services to Sri Lanka are Indian Airlines, Aeroflot, KLM, Singapore Airlines, Thai Airways International, Pakistan International Airlines, Gulf Air, Kuwait Airways, Saudi Air, Emirates, UTA French Airlines, Royal Jordanian Airlines and Balkan Bulgarian Airlines; various others operate charter services.

Internal services are operated by Upali, Air Taxis and Consolidated Engineering.

Shipping. In 1988, merchant vessels totalling 24·5m. GRT entered the ports of Sri Lanka. The Sri Lanka Shipping Corporation began functioning as ship-owners, charterers, brokers and shipping agents in 1971. The Sri Lanka Port Authority was established in 1979.

Post and Broadcasting. In 1986 there were 487 post offices and 3,221 sub-post offices. In 1982 there were 1,900 telegraph offices and 109,900 telephones. Throughout the Greater Colombo Area inter-dialling facilities are now available between 52 stations.

The Overseas Telecommunication Service operates telegraph and telephone services to most parts of the world. Broadcasting is provided by the Sri Lanka Broadcasting Corporation, which assumed the functions of Radio Ceylon on 5 Jan. 1967.

Cinemas. In 1987 there were 274 cinemas. The National Film Corporation established in 1971 has exclusive rights to import films and arrange distribution of foreign and local films. Films released, 1987, 172.

Newspapers. There are 5 main newspaper groups: Associated Newspapers of Ceylon Ltd (5 daily and 3 weekly papers and other periodicals); Express Newspapers (Ceylon) Ltd (2 daily and 2 weekly papers); Independent Newspapers Ltd. (3 daily and 3 weekly papers and other periodicals); Upali Newspapers Ltd. (2 daily, 2 weekly papers and other periodicals); Wijeya Publications (2 weekly papers and other periodicals).

There are 6 daily and 5 weekly papers in Sinhala; 5 daily and 4 weekly in Tamil; 4 daily and 4 weekly in English.

JUSTICE, RELIGION, EDUCATION AND WELFARE

Justice. The systems of law which obtain in Sri Lanka are the Roman-Dutch law, the English law, the Tesawalamai, the Moslem law and the Kandyan law.

The Kandyan law applies to the Kandyan Sinhalese in respect of all matters relating to inheritance, matrimonial rights and donations. The law of Tesawalamai is applied to all inhabitants of Jaffna, in all matters relating to inheritance, marriages, gifts, donations, purchases and sales of land. The Moslem law is applied to all Moslems in respect of succession, donations, marriage, divorce and maintenance. These customary and religious laws have been modified in many respects by local enactments.

The courts of original jurisdiction are the High Court, District Courts, Magistrates' Courts and Primary Courts. The High Court tries major crimes and also exercises admiralty jurisdiction. The 13th Amendment to the Constitution established Provincial High Courts which exercise original criminal jurisdiction of the High Court in respect of offences committed within the province and appellate and revisionary jurisdiction in respect of appeals from the Magistrates' Courts and the Primary Courts within the province. The Provincial High Courts also have the power to issue orders in the nature of Habeas Corpus, in respect of persons illegally detained within the province and issue Writs of Certiorari, Prohibition, Procedendo, Mandamus and Quo Warranto pertaining to matters within the province. The District Court has unlimited civil jurisdiction in civil, revenue, trust, insolvency and testamentary matters, over persons and estates of persons of unsound mind, and wards. The Magistrates' Courts exercise criminal jurisdiction carrying the power to impose terms of imprisonment not exceeding 2 years and fines not exceeding Rs 1,500. The Primary Courts which were established in 1978 exercise civil jurisdiction where the value of the subject matter does not exceed Rs 1,500 and also have jurisdiction in respect of by-laws of local authorities and matters relating to the recovery of revenue of such local authorities. Primary Courts exercise exclusive criminal jurisdiction in respect of offences which may be prescribed by regulation by the Minister. The Primary Courts have the power to impose sentences of imprisonment not exceeding three months and fines not exceeding Rs 250.

The Constitution of 1978 provided for the establishment of two superior courts, the Supreme Court and the Court of Appeal.

The Supreme Court is the highest and final superior court of record and exercises jurisdiction in respect of constitutional matters, jurisdiction for the protection of fundamental rights, final appellate jurisdiction in election petitions and jurisdiction in respect of any breach of the privileges of Parliament. Parliament may provide by law that the Supreme Court exercises the power to grant and issue any of the orders in the nature of Writs of Certiorari, Prohibition, Procedendo, Mandamus or Quo Warranto. The Court of Appeal has appellate jurisdiction to correct all errors in fact or law committed by any court, tribunal or institution; it can grant and issue orders in the nature of the above Writs, and of Writs of Habeas Corpus and injunctions; it can also try election petitions in respect of election of members of Parliament.

Police. The strength of the police service in 1988 was 25,791.

Religion. Buddhism was introduced from India in the 3rd century B.C. and is the religion of 69·3% of the inhabitants. There were (1981) 10,288,325 Buddhists, 2,297,806 Hindus, 1,130,568 Christians, 1,121,717 Moslems and 8,334 others.

Education. Education is free from school year 1 to university and is imparted in the medium of the mother tongue. In 1981 about 87% of the population (10 years old and older) was literate.

In 1987 there were 10,207 schools including 9,709 government schools and 427 Pirivenas; the rest were private schools. The government schools had 140,385 teachers and 3·85m. students from year 1 to 12. Ministry of Education expenditure (1987), Rs 4,313·6m. Education is now administered by 8 provisional education directors.

The overall control of the education regions is vested in the Ministry of Education, Cultural Affairs and Information.

There are 9 Universities: Peradeniya, Colombo, Jaffna, Sri Jayawardenepura, Moratuwa, Kelaniya, Eastern, Ruhuna and an Open University. Dumbara Campus comes under Peradeniya University. There are 9 Institutes (5 for postgraduate and 4 for undergraduate studies).

In 1987 there were 24,668 students and 1,962 teachers in the 8 Universities excluding the Open University, which had 15,802 students. Postgraduate Institutes had 700 students, the others, 1,696. There were 28 institutions for technical education, 11 of which had grade I status; total enrolment (1987), 20,673.

Health. In 1988 there were 498 hospitals, including 85 maternity homes, and 350 central dispensaries. Hospitals had 45,406 beds and there were 2,316 Department of Health doctors. Total state budget expenditure on health, 1988, Rs 3,836m.

Social Security. The activities of the Department of Social Services include:

(1) Payment of Public Assistance, monthly allowance, tuberculosis assistance and leprosy allowance to all needy persons.

(2) Relief for those affected by widespread distress, such as floods, drought, cyclone.

(3) Custodial care and welfare services to the elderly and infirm.

(4) Vocational training, rehabilitation, aids and appliances for the physically handicapped.

(5) Custodial care, vocational training and rehabilitation for socially handicapped persons.

(6) Distribution of Food Stamps.

(7) Financial assistance to voluntary institutions that provide welfare services.

DIPLOMATIC REPRESENTATIVES

Of Sri Lanka in Great Britain (13 Hyde Park Gdns., London, W2 2LU)
High Commissioner: Chandra Monerawela (accredited 15 May 1984).

Of Great Britain in Sri Lanka (190 Galle Rd., Kollupitiya, Colombo 3)
High Commissioner: D. A. S. Gladstone, CMG.

Of Sri Lanka in the USA (2148 Wyoming Ave., NW, Washington, D.C., 20008)
Ambassador: W. S. L. De Alwis.

Of the USA in Sri Lanka (210 Galle Rd., Kollupitiya, Colombo 3)
Ambassador: Marion V. Creekmore, Jr.

Of Sri Lanka to the United Nations
Ambassador: Daya Perera.

Further Reading

The Sri Lanka Year Book. Department of Census and Statistics. Colombo, Annual
Census Publications from 1871
Economic Atlas. Department of Census and Statistics. Colombo, 1980
Performance 1985. Ministry of Plan Implementation, Colombo. 1985
Review of the Economy. Central Bank of Ceylon. Annual
Statistical Pocket-Book. Department of Census and Statistics. Colombo, 1984
Statistical Abstract. Department of Census and Statistics, Colombo, 1982

Coomaraswamy, R., *Sri Lanka: The Crisis of the Anglo-American Constitutional Traditions in a Developing Society.* Colombo, 1984
de Silva, K. M. (ed.) *Sri Lanka: A Survey.* London, 1977.—*A History of Sri Lanka.* London, repr. 1982.—*Managing Ethnic Tensions in Multi-Ethnic Societies: Sri Lanka 1880–1985.* New York, 1986
Ferguson's *Ceylon Directory.* Annual (from 1858)

International Commission of Jurists, ed., *Sri Lanka: A Mounting Tragedy of Errors.* London, 1984
Johnson, B. L. C. and Scrivenor, M. le M., *Sri Lanka: Land, People and Economy.* London, 1981
Manogaran, C., *Ethnic Conflict and Reconciliation in Sri Lanka.* Univ. Hawaii Press, 1987
Manor, J., *Sri Lanka: In Change and Crisis.* London, 1984
Moore, M., *The State and Peasant Politics in Sri Lanka.* CUP, 1985
Piyadasa, L., *Sri Lanka: The Holocaust and After.* London, 1984
Poonambalam, S., *Dependent Capitalism in Crisis: The Sri Lankan Economy 1948–80.* London, 1981
Ratnasuriya, M. D. and Wijeratne, P. B. F., *Shorter Sinhalese-English Dictionary.* Colombo, 1949
Richards, P. and Gooneratne, W., *Basic Needs, Poverty and Government Policies in Sri Lanka.* Geneva, 1981
Samaraweera, V., *Sri Lanka.* [Bibliography] Oxford and Santa Barbara, 1987
Schwarz, W., *The Tamils of Sri Lanka.* London, 1983
Tambiah, S. J., *Sri Lanka: Ethnic Fratricide and the Dismantling of Democracy.* London, 1986
Wilson, A. J., *Politics in Sri Lanka 1947-73.* London, 1974.—*The Gaullist System in Asia: the Constitution of Sri Lanka.* London, 1980.—*The Break-Up of Sri Lanka: The Sinhalese-Tamil Conflict.* London, 1988

SUDAN

Capital: Khartoum
Population: 25·56m. (1987)
GNP per capita: US$340 (1988)

Jamhuryat es-Sudan

HISTORY. Sudan was proclaimed a sovereign independent republic on 1 Jan. 1956. On 19 Dec. 1955 the Sudanese parliament passed unanimously a declaration that a fully independent state should be set up forthwith, and that a Council of State of 5 should temporarily assume the duties of Head of State. The Codomini, the UK and Egypt, gave their assent on 31 Dec. 1955.

For the history of the Condominium and the steps leading to independence, *see* THE STATESMAN'S YEAR-BOOK, 1955, pp. 340–341.

On 8 July 1965 the Constituent Assembly elected Ismail El-Azhari as President of the Supreme Council. Following a crisis in the coalition Cabinet the Prime Minister, Mohammed Ahmed Mahgoub resigned on 23 April 1969. For political history *see* THE STATESMAN'S YEAR-BOOK, 1973–74, p. 1333. The Government was taken over by a 10-man Revolutionary Council on 25 May 1969 under the Chairmanship of Col. Jaafar M. al Nemery. This Council was dissolved in 1972.

AREA AND POPULATION. Sudan is bounded north by Egypt, north-east by the Red Sea, east by Eritrea and Ethiopia, south by Kenya, Uganda and Zaïre, west by the Central African Republic and Chad, north-west by Libya. Sudan covers an area of 967,500 sq. miles (2,505,813 sq. km) and the population at the census of 14 Feb. 1983 was 20,564,364; latest estimate (1987) 25·56m. The chief cities (census, 1983) are the capital, Khartoum (476,218), its suburbs Omdurman (526,287) and Khartoum North (341,146), Port Sudan (206,727), Wadi Medani (141,065), al-Obeid (140,024), Kassala (98,751 in 1973), Atbara (73,009), al-Qadarif (66,465 in 1973), Kosti (65,257 in 1973) and Juba (56,737 in 1973).

The northern and central thirds of the country are populated by Arab and Nubian peoples, while the southern third is inhabited by Nilotic and Negro peoples; Arabic, the official language, is spoken by 51%, Darfurian by 6% and other northern languages by 12%, while Nilotic languages (chiefly Dinka and Nuer) are spoken by 18%, Nilo-Hamitic by 5%, Sudanic by 5% and others by 3%. In 1987 there were 975,000 refugees in Sudan (337,544 from Ethiopia).

The area and population (census, 1983) of the regions are as follows:

Region	*Sq. km*	*1983*	*Region*	*Sq. km*	*1983*
Northern	183,941	1,083,024	Dafur	196,555	3,093,699
Eastern	129,086	2,208,209	Equatoria [1]	76,495	1,406,181
Central	53,716	4,012,543	Bahr al-Ghazal [1]	77,625	2,265,510
Kurdufan	146,932	3,093,294	Upper Nile [1]	92,269	1,599,605
Khartoum (province)	10,883	1,802,299			

[1] Re-united in 1985 as Southern Region.

Local government: Sudan is divided into Khartoum Province (centrally administered) and 6 Regions, each with an elected Regional Assembly and government, and sub-divided into 18 more Provinces.

CLIMATE. Lying wholly within the tropics, the country has a continental climate and only the Red Sea coast experiences maritime influences. Temperatures are generally high throughout the year, with May and June the hottest months. Winters are virtually cloudless and night temperatures are consequently cool. Summer is the rainy season inland, with amounts increasing from north to south, but the northern areas are virtually a desert region. On the Red Sea coast, most rain falls in winter. Khartoum. Jan. 74°F (23·3°C), July 89°F (31·7°C). Annual rainfall 6" (157 mm). Juba. Jan. 83°F (28·3°C), July 78°F (25·6°C). Annual rainfall 39" (968 mm). Port

Sudan. Jan. 74°F (23·3°C), July 94°F (34·4°C). Annual rainfall 4" (94 mm). Wadi Halfa. Jan. 60°F (15·6°C), July 90°F (32·2°C). Annual rainfall 0·1" (2·5 mm).

CONSTITUTION AND GOVERNMENT. President Nemery was deposed in a military *coup* on 6 April 1985 and the Constitution of 1973 was suspended. A transitional Constitution was approved in Oct. 1985. A Military Council was established to which the Cabinet was responsible prior to elections held in April 1986 for the 301-seat National Assembly.

On 30 June 1989 Brig.-Gen. (later Lieut.-Gen.) Omar Hassan Ahmad al-Bashir led a military *coup* against the civilian government and suspended the Constitution. This was the third time since independence in 1956 that the armed forces have overthrown a military government. Gen. Bashir pledged himself to ending the 6-year civil war.

Prime Minister, Defence: Lieut.-Gen. Omar Hassan Ahmad al-Bashir.

Deputy Prime Minister: Brig.-Gen. Zubir Mohammed Saleh. *Foreign Affairs:* Ali Sahlul. *Finance:* Sayed Ali Zaki.

National flag: Three horizontal stripes of red, white, black, with a green triangle based on the hoist.

DEFENCE

Army. The Army is organized in 1 Republican Guard brigade, 2 armoured, 1 parachute, 1 airborne and 12 infantry brigades, with 3 artillery and 1 engineer regiments, and 3 Air Defence brigades (including 1 surface-to-air missile). Equipment includes 155 T-54 and T-55, 70 Chinese Type-62 and 20 M-60A3 main battle tanks. Strength (1990) 65,000. Paramilitary forces are National Guard (500) and Border Guard (2,500).

Navy. The Navy operates in the Red Sea and also on the River Nile. It comprises 6 inshore patrol craft transferred in the 1970s from the Iranian coastguard, and 2 *ex*-Yugoslav landing craft. The flotilla suffers from lack of maintenance and spares. Personnel in 1989 totalled 750.

Air Force. The Air Force was built up with Soviet and Chinese assistance, and is now receiving equipment from the USA. Two combat squadrons are equipped with about 10 MiG-21 fighters, 6 Northrop F-5E, 2 MiG-23, 10 F-6 (Chinese-built MiG-19) and 12 F-5 (Chinese-built MiG-17) fighter-bombers. There is 1 transport squadron, with 5 C-130H Hercules, 6 Aviocars and 3 DHC-5D Buffalo turboprop transports; 2 helicopter squadrons have 12 AB.212s, 12 Romanian-built Pumas, 6 Mi-8s; there are 3 Jet Provost, 3 Strikemaster and 1 F-5F jet armed trainers, and some Chinese-built FT-2 (MiG/ISUII) advanced trainers. Personnel totalled (1990) about 6,000.

INTERNATIONAL RELATIONS

Membership. Sudan is a member of UN, OAU, the Arab League and is an ACP state of EEC.

ECONOMY

Budget. The 1989–90 budget envisages revenue of £S8,600m. and expenditure of £S21,600m.

Currency. The monetary unit is the Sudanese *pound* (£S) divided into 100 *piastres* and 1,000 *milliemes*. Sudanese bank-notes of £S10, £S5, £S1, 50 and 25 *piastres* and Sudanese coins of P. 10, 5, 2; m/ms 10, 5, 2, 1 are in circulation. In March 1990, £1 = £S18·83; US$1 = £S11·49.

Banking. The Bank of Sudan opened in Feb. 1960 with an authorized capital of £S1·5m. as the central bank of the country; it has the sole right to issue currency. All foreign banks were nationalized in 1970.

Weights and Measures. The metric system is in use.

ENERGY AND NATURAL RESOURCES

Electricity. Production (1986) 1,210m. kwh. Supply 240 volts; 50 Hz.

Oil. Two oil wells in the south-west produce 15,000 bbls per day of high quality oil. Production of petrol products (1985) 1,019 tonnes.

Minerals. Minerals known to exist include: Gold, graphite, sulphur, chromium-ore (estimate, 9,900m. tonnes in 1982), iron-ore, manganese-ore, copper-ore, zinc-ore, fluorspar, natron, gypsum and anhydrite, magnesite, asbestos, talc, halite, kaolin, white mica, coal, diatomite (kieselguhr), limestone and dolomite, pumice, lead-ore, wollastonite, black sands, vermiculite pyrites.

Gold is being exploited on a small scale at Gabeit and at Abirkateib (in Kassala Province); alluvial gold is occasionally exploited in Southern Fung and Equatoria. Iron-ore was discovered in Red Sea area in 1976.

Manganese mining activities started in the 1950s but this industry did not develop well and in 1982 only 200 tonnes was produced. Processed and scrap white mica have been mined since the late fifties; it went out of production for almost a decade, but started again in 1970 when 170 tonnes were produced; 1982, 200 tonnes. A big deposit of vermiculite and a medium-sized deposit of pyrophyllite are known to occur in the Sinkat District. Reserves of metallurgical grade chromite occur in the Ingessana Hills, Blue Nile Province. Huge reserves of chrysotile asbestos are proved in this vicinity and also in Qala El Nahal area, Kassala Province. Deposits of magnesite, with or without talc, are known to occur in the Ingessana Hills and Qala El Nahal areas in addition to other occurrences in the Halaib area, Red Sea Province.

Agriculture. The Sudan is a predominantly agricultural country. Cotton is by far the most important cash crop on which the Sudan depends for earning foreign currency. The two types of cotton grown in the Sudan are: (*a*) long staple sakellaridis and sakel types (derivatives of sakellaridis), grown in Gezira, White Nile, Abdel Magid and private pump schemes; (*b*) short staple, mainly American types, in Equatoria and Nuba Mountains, generally by rain cultivation.

Production (1988) in 1,000 tonnes: Sorghum, 4,640; sugar-cane, 4,500; groundnuts, 527; seed cotton, 394; millet, 550; wheat, 181; sesame, 278; cotton seed, 290.

One of the largest sugar complexes in the world was opened at Kenana in March 1981. It is capable of processing 330,000 tonnes a year.

Livestock (1988): Cattle, 22·5m.; sheep, 18·5m.; goats, 13·5m.; poultry, 29m.

Forestry. Gum arabic, mainly hashab gum from *Acacia senegal*, is the sole forest produce exported on a major scale. Production (1983) 38·16m. cu. metres.

COMMERCE. Total trade for calendar years, in US$1,000:

	1984	*1985*	*1986*
Imports	556,000	1,237,000	1,055,000
Exports	519,000	544,000	497,000

In 1983, Saudi Arabia provided 14·3% of imports and the UK 10%, while 17·1% of exports went to Saudi Arabia and 10% to Italy; cotton formed 49% by value of exports and groundnuts 2%, sesame 9% and gum arabic 9%.

Total trade between Sudan and UK (British Department of Trade returns, in £1,000 sterling):

	1985	*1986*	*1987*	*1988*	*1989*
Imports to UK	21,323	12,826	18,850	9,910	9,532
Exports and re-exports from UK	103,635	83,335	75,322	86,480	60,602

Tourism. There were 42,000 visitors in 1986.

COMMUNICATIONS

Roads. In 1982 there were about 3,000 km of tarmac roads, including the new 1,190 km road from Khartoum to Port Sudan, and 45,000 km of tracks. There were 99,400 passenger cars and 17,500 commercial vehicles in 1985.

Railways. The main railway lines run from Khartoum to El Obeid *via* Wadi Medani, Sennar Junction, Kosti and El Rahad (701 km); El Rahad to Nyala *via* Abu Zabad, Babanousa and Ed-Daein (698 km); Sennar Junction to Kassala *via* Gedaref (455 km) and to Roseires *via* Singa (220 km); Kassala to Port Sudan *via* Haiya Junction and Sinkat (550 km); Khartoum to Wadi Halfa *via* Shendi, El Dammer, Atbara, Berber and Abu Hamad Junction (924 km); Abu Hamad to Karima (248 km); Atbara to Haiya Junction (271 km); Babanousa to Wau (444 km). The main flow of exports and imports is to and from Port Sudan *via* Atbara and Kassala. The total length of line open for traffic (1982) was 4,786 km. The gauge is 1,067 mm. In 1987, the railways carried 357m. passenger-km and 699m. tonne-km of freight.

Aviation. Sudan Airways is a government-owned airline, with its headquarters in Khartoum, operating domestic and international services. In 1980 Sudan Airways carried 519,000 passengers and 6·8m. ton-kg of mail and freight.

Shipping. Supplementing the railways are regular river steamer services of the Sudan Railways, between Karima and Dongola, 319 km; from Khartoum to Kosti, 319 km; from Kosti to Juba, 1,436 km, and from Kosti to Gambeila, 1,069 km. Port Sudan is the country's only seaport; it is equipped with 13 berths.

Post and Broadcasting Number of telephones in 1983 was 68,838 (44,756 in Greater Khartoum). Radio receivers (1982) 5m. The television service broadcasts for 35 hours per week. There were (1982) 1m. TV receivers.

Cinemas. In 1975 there were 58, seating capacity 112,000 and also 43 mobile units.

Newspapers. In 1985 there were 2 daily newspapers with a circulation of 120,000.

JUSTICE, RELIGION, EDUCATION AND WELFARE

Justice. The judiciary is a separate and independent department of state directly and solely responsible to the President of the Republic. The general administrative supervision and control of the judiciary is vested in the High Judicial Council.

Civil Justice is administered by the courts constituted under the Civil Justice Ordinance, namely the High Court of Justice—consisting of the Court of Appeal and Judges of the High Court, sitting as courts of original jurisdiction—and Province Courts—consisting of the Courts of Province and District Judges. The law administered is 'justice, equity and good conscience' in all cases where there is no special enactment. Procedure is governed by the Civil Justice Ordinance.

Justice in personal matters for the Moslem population is administered by the Mohammedan law courts, which form the Sharia Divisions of the Court of Appeal, High Courts and Kadis Courts; President of the Sharia Division is the Grand Kadi. The religious law of Islam is administered by these courts in the matters of inheritance, marriage, divorce, family relationship and charitable trusts.

Criminal Justice is administered by the courts constituted under the Code of Criminal Procedure, namely major courts, minor courts and magistrates' courts. Serious crimes are tried by major courts, which are composed of a President and 2 members and have the power to pass the death sentence. Major Courts are, as a rule, presided over by a Judge of the High Court appointed to a Provincial Circuit or a Province Judge. There is a right of appeal to the Chief Justice against any decision or order of a Major Court, and all its findings and sentences are subject to confirmation by him.

Lesser crimes are tried by Minor Courts consisting of 3 Magistrates and presided over by a Second Class Magistrate, and by Magistrates' Courts.

Religion. In 1980 about 73% of the population was Moslem. The population of the 12 northern provinces is almost entirely Moslem (Sunni), while the majority of the 6 southern provinces are animist (18%) or Christian (9%).

Education (1985). 6,707 primary schools had 1·7m. pupils; there were 490,583 pupils in 2,167 secondary schools and 28,985 in tertiary education. In 1979 Khartoum University with 10 faculties had 8,777 students. The Khartoum branch of Cairo University with 4 faculties had about 5,000 students and the Islamic University of Omdurman with 3 faculties had 1,472 students. Juba University, founded in 1975 with 5 faculties had 425 students.

Health. In 1981 the Ministry of Health maintained 158 hospitals (with 17,205 beds), 887 dispensaries, 1,619 dressing stations and 220 health centres. There were 2,122 doctors and 12,871 nurses.

DIPLOMATIC REPRESENTATIVES

Of Sudan in Great Britain (3 Cleveland Row, London, SW1A 1DD)
Ambassador: El Rashid Abushama (accredited 6 Dec. 1989).

Of Great Britain in Sudan (PO Box No. 801, Khartoum)
Ambassador: Allan Ramsay.

Of Sudan in the USA (2210 Massachusetts Ave., NW, Washington, D.C., 20008)
Ambassador: Hassan Elamin El-Bashir.

Of the USA in Sudan (Sharia Ali Abdul Latif, Khartoum)
Ambassador: James R. Cheek.

Of Sudan to the United Nations
Ambassador: Amin M. Abdoun.

Further Reading

Sudan Almanac. Khartoum (annual)
Daly, M. W., *Sudan.* [Bibliography] Oxford and Santa Barbara, 1983
Gurdon, C., *Sudan in Transition: A Political Risk Analysis.* London, 1986
Halasa, A. *et al The Return to Democracy in Sudan.* Geneva, 1986
Holt, P. M., *A Modern History of the Sudan.* New York, 3rd ed. 1979
Iten, O., *Le Soudan.* Zurich, 1983

SURINAME

Capital: Paramaribo
Population: 415,000 (1987)
GNP per capita: US$2,450 (1988)

HISTORY. At the peace of Breda (1667) between Great Britain and the United Netherlands, Suriname was assigned to the Netherlands in exchange for the colony of New Netherland in North America, and this was confirmed by the treaty of Westminster of Feb. 1674. Since then Suriname has been twice in British possession, 1799–1802 (when it was restored to the Batavian Republic at the peace of Amiens) and 1804–16, when it was returned to the Kingdom of the Netherlands according to the convention of London of 13 Aug. 1814, confirmed at the peace of Paris of 20 Nov. 1815. On 25 Nov. 1975, Suriname gained full independence and was admitted to the UN on 4 Dec. 1975. On 25 Feb. 1980 the Government was ousted in a *coup*, and a National Military Council (NMC) established. A further *coup* on 13 Aug. replaced several members of the NMC, and the State President. Other attempted coups took place in 1981 and 1982, with the NMC retaining control. Suriname returned to democracy in Jan. 1988 following elections held in Nov. 1987.

AREA AND POPULATION. Suriname is situated on the north coast of South America and bounded on the north by the Atlantic ocean, on the east by the Marowijne River, which separates it from French Guiana, on the west by the Corantijn River, which separates it from Guyana, and on the south by forests and savannas, which separate it from Brazil.

Area, 163,820 sq. km. Census population (1980), 354,860. Estimate (1987) 415,000. The capital, Paramaribo, had (1988 estimate) 192,109 inhabitants.

Suriname is divided into 9 districts (populations census 1980): Paramaribo (urban district), 67,905; Commewijne,14,351; Coronie, 2,777; Marowijne, 23,402; Nickerie, 34,480; Saramacca, 10,335; Suriname, 166,494; Brokopondo, 20,249 and Para, 14,867.

The official languages are Dutch and English. English is widely spoken next to Hindi, Javanese and Chinese as inter-group communication. A vernacular, called 'Sranan Tongo' or 'Surinamese', is used as a lingua franca. In 1976 it was announced that Spanish would become the nation's principal working language.

CLIMATE. The climate is equatorial, with uniformly high temperatures and rainfall. There is no recognized dry season. Paramaribo. Jan. 80°F (26·7°C), July 81°F (27·2°C). Annual rainfall 89" (2,225 mm).

CONSTITUTION AND GOVERNMENT. A new Constitution was approved by referendum in Sept. 1980. Elections took place 25 Nov. 1987. The Front for Democracy and Development won (provisional) 40 of the 51 seats in the National Assembly.

President: Ramsewak Shankar (elected for a 5-year term in Jan. 1988).

Flag: Horizontally green, red, green with the red of double width with yellow 5-pointed star in centre of red bar.

DEFENCE

Army. Armed forces of the Republic of Suriname consist of 1 infantry and 1 military police battalions with a strength of about 2,700 in 1990. Equipment includes 2 PC-7 armed trainers, 3 Defender twin-engined light transports operated alongside 1 Bell 205, 2 Alouette III and 1 Cessna 206 liaison aircraft. Officers' ranks were abolished in Feb. 1986.

Navy. The flotilla comprises 3 32m and 3 22m inshore patrol craft, plus 3 river patrol boats, all built in the Netherlands. In 1989 personnel totalled 200.

INTERNATIONAL RELATIONS

Membership. Suriname is a member of UN, OAS and is an ACP state of the EEC.

ECONOMY

Planning. For 15 years from independence approximately 3,500m. guilders is available from the Netherlands to carry out an extensive social and economic development programme.

Budget. The revenues and expenditures (derived from import, export and excise duties, taxes on houses and estates, personal imports and some indirect taxes) were as follows (in 1m. Suriname guilders) in 1989: Revenue, 856; expenditure, 705.

External public debt in 1985, US$24m.

Currency. Notes ranging from 5 to 1,000 *Suriname guilders* are legal tender. Currency notes of 1·00 and 2·50 guilders are issued by the Government. In March 1990, US$1 = 1·79 *Suriname guilders*; £1 sterling = 2·93 *Suriname guilders*.

Banking. The Central Bank of Suriname is a bankers' bank and also a bank of issue; the Surinaamsche Bank, the Algemene Bank Nederland and the Handels-, Kredieten Industriebank, are commercial banks; the Suriname People's Credit Bank operates under the auspices of the Government; Surinaamse Postspaarbank (postal savings bank); Surinaamse Hypotheekbank NV (mortgage bank); Surinaamse Investerings Mij. NV (investment bank); Agentschap van de Maatschappij tot financiering van het Nationaal Herstel NV (long-term investments); National Development Bank; The Agrarian Bank.

Weights and Measures. The metric system is in force.

ENERGY AND NATURAL RESOURCES

Electricity. Production (1986) 1,610m. kwh.

Minerals. Bauxite is the most important mineral; it is being mined in the Suriname and Marowijne districts but in 1987 several mines have been closed by attacks by anti-government rebels. Fresh deposits have been found in the western areas. The ore is exported mainly to USA and the Dominican Republic, but partly processed locally into alumina and aluminium. Production (1987 in 1,000 tonnes): Bauxite, 2,522.

Agriculture. Agriculture is restricted to the alluvial coastal zone; cultivated area in 1982, 87,442 hectares. The staple food crop is rice; 72,571 hectares of paddy were planted in 1982, chiefly in the Nickerie, Commewijne, Saramacca and Coronie districts.

Production (1988, in 1,000 tonnes): Sugar-cane, 45; rice, 300; oranges, 9; grapefruit, 2; coconuts, 11; palm oil, 6·8; cassava, 3.

Livestock (1988): 74,000 head of cattle, 4,000 sheep, 6,000 goats, 20,000 pigs, 6m. poultry.

Forestry. Forests cover 14·9 hectares, 42% of the land area. Production in 1986 196,000 cu. metres.

Fisheries. The fish catch in 1987 amounted to 2,321 tonnes.

INDUSTRY AND TRADE

Industry. In 1981, there were 3 large bauxite plants, 1 alumina and 1 aluminium smelting plants, sugar- and rice-mills, 3 paint factories, 2 fruit-juice plants, 3 shrimp freezing plants, a plywood factory, timber-mills, a milk pasteurization plant, a butter and margarine factory and a number of various medium and small industries. Shortage of skilled personnel inhibits expansion.

Commerce. In 1987 imports totalled 525·4m. Suriname guilders and exports, 542·7m.

Principal exports in 1982 (in 1,000 Suriname guilders): Alumina, 411,500; bauxite, 52,400; aluminium, 124,000; rice, 72,100; shrimp, 53,300; wood and wood products, 20,600; bananas, 13,200.

Principal imports in 1982 (in 1,000 Suriname guilders): Raw and auxiliary materials, 356,700; fuels and lubricants, 209,900; investment goods, 117,800; food-stuffs, cars and motorcycles, 73,100; textile yarn and fabrics, 9,600.

Total trade between Suriname and UK (British Department of Trade returns, in £1,000 sterling):

	1985	*1986*	*1987*	*1988*	*1989*
Imports to UK	15,405	15,554	12,488	11,256	16,366
Exports and re-exports from UK	9,398	9,743	7,974	6,107	6,777

Tourism. Visitors totalled 8,440 in 1987.

COMMUNICATIONS

Roads. There are 1,335 km of main roads. Two of them lead from Paramaribo to the bauxite centres of Smalkalden (29 km) and Paranam (30 km) and to the airport of Zanderij (49 km). Another main road runs across the districts of Saramacca (71 km) and Coronie (68 km), a fourth across the Commewijne district (41 km) and a fifth in the Marowijne district, from the bauxite centre Moengo to Albina (45 km). The 'East–West connexion' is almost completed, linking the Corantijn and the Marowijne rivers (375 km).

In 1987 there were 32,000 passenger cars, 11,000 trucks, 2,000 buses and 1,100 motor cycles.

Railways. There is a single-track railway, running from Onverwacht to Bronsweg (86 km); part of the track, from Paramaribo to Onverwacht (34 km) has been removed. Another single-track railway runs from Apoera to the Bakhuis Mountains.

Aviation. Regular air services are maintained by KLM, SLM, Aero Cubano and Cruzeiro do Sul. The international airfield at Zanderij is capable of handling all types of planes.

Suriname Airways Ltd provides daily services between all major districts and maintains also a charter service.

Shipping. The Royal Netherlands Steamship Co. plies between Amsterdam, Rotterdam, Antwerp, Hamburg and Paramaribo, and New York, Baltimore, New Orleans and Paramaribo. Regular sailings are made to Georgetown, Ciudad Bolivar and most Caribbean ports. The Suriname Navigation Co. maintains services from Paramaribo to Georgetown and Cayenne, and once a month to the Caribbean area. A French and an Italian company maintain passenger services to Europe. The Alcoa Steamship Co. has a fortnightly service to New York, Baltimore, Mobile and New Orleans; a Japanese line sails once a month from Hong Kong and Yokohama to Paramaribo; the Boomerang Line maintains a monthly freight and passenger service between Suriname and Australia.

Post and Broadcasting. In 1985 there were 36,000 telephones. Wireless telephone connects Suriname with the Netherlands, USA, Curaçao, Guyana, French Guiana and Trinidad. There are 6 broadcasting and 1 television stations. In 1986 there were 246,000 radios and 48,000 TV sets.

Cinemas. In 1981 there were 18 cinemas and 1 drive-in cinema.

Newspapers (1987). There are 2 daily newspapers.

JUSTICE, RELIGION, EDUCATION AND WELFARE

Justice. There is a court of justice, whose members are nominated by the President. There are 3 cantonal courts.

Religion. There is entire religious liberty. At the end of 1983 the main religious bodies were: Hindus, 97,170; Roman Catholics, 80,922; Moslems, 69,638;

Moravian Brethren, 55,625; Reformed, 6,265; Lutheran, 2,695; Jehovah's Witnesses, 1,626; Seventh Day Adventists, 1,061; others, 24,627.

Education. In 1986–87 there were 301 primary schools with 3,954 teachers and 59,633 pupils, and there were 1,588 teachers and 23,217 pupils at 89 secondary schools. There was also a University with (1986) 1,070 students and a teacher training college with 1,500 students.

Health. There were (1985) 1,964 hospital beds and 219 physicians.

DIPLOMATIC REPRESENTATIVES

Of Suriname in Great Britain
Ambassador: Cyrill Bisoendat Ramkisor.

Of Great Britain in Suriname
Ambassador: D. P. Small, CMG, MBE (resides in Georgetown).

Of Suriname in the USA (4301 Connecticut Ave., NW, Washington, D.C., 20008)
Ambassador: Willem A. Udenhout.

Of the USA in Suriname (Dr Sophie Redmondstraat 129, Paramaribo)
Ambassador: Richard C. Howland.

Of Suriname to the United Nations
Ambassador: Kriesnadath Nandoe.

Further Reading

Statistical Information: The General Bureau of Statistics in Paramaribo was established on 1 Jan. 1947. Its publications comprise trade statistics, *Suriname in Figures* (including, from 1953, the former *Handelsstatistiek*) and *Statistische Berichten.*

Economische Voorlichting Suriname. Ministry of Economic Affairs, Paramaribo
Annual Report of the Central Bank of Suriname

SWAZILAND

Capital: Mbabane
Population: 681,059 (1986)
GNP per capita: US$790 (1988)

HISTORY. The Swazi migrated into the country to which they have given their name, in the last half of the 18th century. They settled first in what is now southern Swaziland, but moved northwards under their chief, Sobhuza, known also to the Swazi as Somhlolo. Sobhuza died in 1838 and was succeeded by Mswati. The further order of succession has been Mbandzeni and Bhunu, whose son, Sobhuza II, was installed as King of the Swazi nation in 1921 after a long minority.

The independence of the Swazis was guaranteed in the conventions of 1881 and 1884 between the British Government and the Government of the South African Republic. In 1890, soon after the death of Mbandzeni, a provisional government was established representative of the Swazis, the British and the South African Republic Governments. In 1894 the South African Republic was given powers of protection and administration. In 1902, after the conclusion of the Boer War, a special commissioner took charge, and under an order-in-council in 1903 the Governor of the Transvaal administered the territory, through the Special Commissioner. Swaziland became independent on 6 Sept. 1968.

On 25 April 1967 the British Government gave the country internal self-government. It changed the country's status to that of a protected state with the Ngwenyama, Sobhuza II, recognized as King of Swaziland and head of state. King Sobhuza died on 21 Aug. 1982. On 25 April 1986, King Mswati III was installed as King of Swaziland.

AREA AND POPULATION. Swaziland is bounded on the north, west and south by the Transvaal Province, and on the east by Mozambique and Zululand. The area is 6,705 sq. miles (17,400 sq. km).

The country is divided geographically into 4 longitudinal regions running from north to south; 3 of roughly equal width—Highveld (westernmost), Middleveld, Lowveld—and the Lubombo plateau in the east. The mountainous region on the west rises to an altitude of over 6,000 ft (1,800 metres). The Middleveld is mostly between 1,700 and 3,000 ft, while the Lowveld has an average height of not more than 1,000 ft (300 metres).

Population (census 1986), 681,059. Mbabane, the administrative capital (1986, 38,290). The main urban areas with 1986 census populations are: Manzini (18,084); Big Bend (9,676); Mhlume (6,509); Havelock Mine (4,850); Nhlangano (4,107); Pigg's Peak (3,223) and Siteki (2,271). 31,072 citizens abroad. In early 1988 there were 14,550 refugees living in the country.

CLIMATE. A temperate climate with two seasons. Nov. to March is the wet season, when temperatures range from mild to hot, with frequent thunderstorms. The cool, dry season from May to Sept. is characterised by clear, bright sunny days. Mbabane. Jan. 68°F (20°C), July 54°F (12·2°C). Annual rainfall 56" (1,402 mm).

CONSTITUTION AND GOVERNMENT. Britain's protection ended at independence, when a Constitution similar to the 1967 Constitution was brought into force. The general elections (by universal adult franchise) in April 1967 gave the royalist and traditional Imbokodvo National Movement all 24 seats. The Parliament consists of a House of Assembly, with 24 elected and 6 nominated members and the Attorney-General, who has no vote, and a Senate comprising 12 members, 6 of whom are elected by the House of Assembly and 6 appointed by the King. The executive authority is vested in the King and exercised through a Cabinet presided over by the Prime Minister, and consisting of the Prime Minister, the Deputy Prime Minister and up to 8 other ministers. In April 1973 the King assumed supreme power and the Constitution was suspended and in 1976 it was abolished.

On 28 Oct. 1983 a general election took place to elect an electoral college of 80 members.

His Majesty the King: Mswati III (crowned 25 April 1986).

In Nov. 1989, the Cabinet was composed as follows:

Prime Minister: Obed M. Dlamini.

Foreign Affairs: G. M. Mamba. *Labour and Public Service:* B. M. Nsibandze. *Agriculture and Co-operatives:* H. S. Mamba. *Commerce, Industry and Tourism:* N. D. Ntiwane. *Works and Communications:* W. C. Mkhonta. *Education:* Chief Sipho Shongwe. *Finance:* B.S. Dlamini. *Health:* Dr F. Friedman. *Justice:* R. Dladla. *Interior and Immigration:* E. S. Shabalala. *Natural Resources, Land Utilization and Energy:* Prince Nqaba Dlamini.

National flag. Horizontally 5 unequal stripes of blue, yellow, crimson, yellow, blue; in the centre of the crimson strip an African shield of black and white, behind which are 2 assegais and a staff, all laid horizontally.

Local Government. The country is divided into the 4 regions of Shiselweni, Lubombo, Manzini and Hhohho. They are administered by Regional Administrators.

DEFENCE

Army Air Wing. First military aircraft acquired by Swaziland, in mid-1979, were 2 Israeli-built Arava light twin-turboprop transports with underwing weapon attachments for light attack duties.

INTERNATIONAL RELATIONS

Membership. Swaziland is a member of UN, OAU, the Commonwealth and is an ACP state of EEC.

ECONOMY

Budget. Revenue and expenditure (in 1,000 emalangeni) for financial years ending 31 March:

	1987–88	*1988–89* [1]	1989–90 [1]
Revenue	337,310	361,052	449,211
Expenditure	315,726	370,568	450,234

[1]Estimate.

Currency. The currency in circulation in Swaziland is the *emalangeni,* but remains in the rand monetary area. In March 1990, £1 = 4·24 *emalangeni;* US$1 = 2·59 *emalangeni.*

Banking. Barclays Bank International and the Standard Bank Ltd maintain branches at Mbabane and Manzini; sub-branches and agencies are operated in 17 other places. Bank rates are those in force throughout South Africa and are prescribed by the main South African offices of the 2 banks. The Swaziland Credit and Savings Bank, now known as The Swazi Bank, a statutory body, was opened in 1965. It specializes in credit for agriculture and low-cost housing. Its head office is in Mbabane and it has branches or agencies at 3 other places. A fourth bank, The Bank of Credit and Commerce International opened in Sept. 1978; its head office is in Manzini and it has a branch in Mbabane.

ENERGY AND NATURAL RESOURCES

Electricity. Production (1986) 120m. kwh. Supply 230 volts; 50 Hz.

Minerals. Swaziland produces asbestos from the Havelock Mine (22,804 tonnes in 1988). Coal is mined at Mpaka (164,845 tonnes in 1988). Quarry stone is also mined (107,205 cu. metres in 1988).

A railway has been built from the Ngwenya haematite deposits to Goba, in Mozambique, chiefly for the transportation of iron ore. The extensive deposits of low-volatile bituminous coal in the Lowveld are being worked to provide coal for the railway, sugar-mills and export.

Agriculture. In 1987–88 the cultivated area was 165,464 hectares, the grazing area 1,105,274 hectares and the commercial forest area 102,625 hectares. Production (1987–88, in 1,000 tonnes): Sugar-cane, 3,870; citrus, 68; rice, 4; seed cotton, 26; maize, 113; sorghum, 1; pineapples, 35; tomatoes, 4; potatoes, 6. Tobacco is also grown. It is usually necessary to import maize from South Africa. Sugar, first produced in 1958, and woodpulp and other forest products are the two main agricultural exports.

Livestock (1988): Cattle, 640,000; goats, 284,000; sheep, 26,000; poultry, 1m.

COMMERCE. By agreement with the Republic of South Africa, Swaziland is united in a customs union with the republic and receives a *pro rata* share of the customs dues collected.

Total exports (1987-88) amounted to E826,244,100. The chief items were (in E1,000): Sugar, 272,839; unbleached woodpulp, 129,852; canned fruit, 32,722; asbestos, 23,810.

Total imports (1987-88) amounted to E916,079,000. The chief items were (in E1,000): Machinery and transport equipment, 164,003; minerals, fuels and lubricants, 129,438; manufactured items, 127,005; food, 119,727.

Total trade between Swaziland and UK (British Department of Trade returns, in £1,000 sterling):

	1985	*1986*	*1987*	*1988*	*1989*
Imports to UK	41,281	48,194	36,901	27,973	31,368
Exports and re-exports from UK	3,122	3,922	2,257	1,564	1,358

Tourism. There were 256,000 visitors in 1986.

COMMUNICATIONS

Roads. There is daily communication by railway motor-buses and interstate transport between Swaziland and South Africa. There are also Swazi owned taxis and buses which operate between the two countries. Total length of roads (1987) 2,758 km of which 689 km were tarred.

Railways. In 1987 the system comprised 370 km of route, and carried 2,633,000 tonnes of freight.

Aviation. The country's chief airport is at Matsapa, near Manzini. It is served by Royal Swazi National Airways connecting with Johannesburg, Durban, Lusaka, Nairobi, Harare and Gaborone. Lesotho National Airways flies to Harare and Maputo through Matsapa. In 1986 Zambian Airways inaugurated their weekly flight to Matsapa *via* Gaborone.

Post and Broadcasting. There were (1987) 71 post offices, 2 telegraph stations and 29 postal agencies. There were, 31 Dec. 1987, 21,100 telephones, 9,820 exchange connexions and 297 telex exchange connexions. In 1986 there were over 96,000 radio sets and over 12,000 television receivers.

Cinemas. There were 5 cinemas in 1980 with a total seating capacity of 1,625.

Newspapers. There were in 1987 two daily newspapers.

JUSTICE, RELIGION, EDUCATION AND WELFARE

Justice. The judiciary is headed by the Chief Justice. A High Court having full jurisdiction and subordinate courts presided over by Magistrates and District Officers are in existence.

There is a Court of Appeal with a President and 3 Judges. It deals with appeals from the High Court. There are 16 Swazi courts of first instance, 2 Swazi courts of appeal and a Higher Swazi Court of Appeal. The channel of appeal lies from Swazi Court of first instance to Swazi Court of Appeal, to Higher Swazi Court of Appeal, to the Judicial Commissioner and thence to the High Court of Swaziland.

Religion. In 1984 there were about 120,000 Christians and about 30,000 adults holding traditional beliefs. A large number of churches and missionary societies are established throughout the country and, in addition to evangelism, are doing important work in the fields of education and medicine. In the larger centres there are churches of several denominations—Protestant, Roman Catholics and others.

Education. In 1988 there were 606 schools with 152,895 pupils in primary classes and 35,278 in secondary and high school classes. The then Swaziland Agricultural College and University Centre at Luyengo was opened in Oct. 1966. The College is now the Faculty of Agriculture at the University of Swaziland, which is situated in Matsapa. Technical and vocational training classes are run at the Government Swaziland College of Technology (SCOT), the Swaziland Institute of Management and Public Administration (SIMPA), the Gwamile Vocational Commercial Training Institute (VOCTIM), Mpaka Vocational Centre and the Manzini Industrial Training Centre. The Government also operates a Police College, Institute of Health Sciences, the Nazarene Prison College and the Nursing College which trains paramedical staff for the hospitals and clinics. There were 3 teacher training colleges with 501 students in 1987–88. There were 1,313 students enrolled in all the vocational centres except SIMPA, and 1,427 at the University of Swaziland, in 1987–88.

Health. In 1984 there were 80 doctors, 13 dentists and 1,608 hospital beds.

DIPLOMATIC REPRESENTATIVES

Of Swaziland in Great Britain (58 Pont St., London SW1X 0AE)
High Commissioner: M. N. Dlamini.

Of Great Britain in Swaziland (Allister Miller St., Mbabane)
High Commissioner: J. G. Flynn.

Of Swaziland in the USA (3400 International Dr., NW, Washington, D.C., 20008)
Ambassador: A. V. Mamba.

Of the USA in Swaziland (PO Box 199, Mbabane)
Ambassador: Mary Ryan.

Of Swaziland to the United Nations
Ambassador: Dr Timothy L. L. Dlamini.

Further Reading

Booth, A., *Swaziland: Tradition and Change in a Southern African Kingdom.* Aldershot and Boulder, 1984
Grotpeter, J. J., *Historical Dictionary of Swaziland.* Metuchen, 1975
Jones, D., *Aid and Development in Southern Africa.* London, 1977
Matsebula, J. S. M., *A History of Swaziland.* London, 1972
Nyeko, B., *Swaziland.* [Bibliography] Oxford and Santa Barbara, 1982

SWEDEN

Konungariket Sverige

Capital: Stockholm
Population: 8·5m. (1988)
GNP per capita: US$21,078 (1988)

HISTORY. Organized as an independent unified state in the 10th century, Sweden became a constitutional monarchy in 1809. In 1809 she also ceded Finland to Russia. In 1815 German possessions were ceded to Prussia and Sweden was united with Norway, which union lasted until 1905.

AREA AND POPULATION. Sweden is bounded west and north-west by Norway, east by Finland and the Gulf of Bothnia, south-east by the Baltic Sea and south-west by the Kattegat. The first census took place in 1749, and it was repeated at first every third year, and, after 1775, every fifth year. Since 1860 a general census has been taken every 10 years and, in addition, in 1935, 1945, 1965, 1975 and 1985.

Latest census figures: 1940, 6,371,432 (annual increase since 1935: 0·38%); 1950, 7,041,829 (1·1% since 1945); 1960, 7,495,316 (0·64% since 1950); 1965, 7,766,424 (1·04% since 1960); 1970, 8,076,903 (1·04% since 1965); 1975, 8,208,544 (1·02% since 1970); 1980, 8,320,438 (1·01% since 1975); 1985, 8,360,178.

Counties (Län)	*Land area: sq. km*	*Census population 1 Nov. 1985*	*Estimated population 31 Dec. 1988*	*Pop. per sq. km 31 Dec. 1988*
Stockholm	6,488	1,577,596	1,617,038	249
Uppsala	6,989	251,754	260,476	37
Södermanland	6,060	249,885	251,423	41
Östergötland	10,562	393,668	396,919	38
Jönköping	9,944	300,892	304,021	31
Kronoberg	8,458	174,025	175,427	21
Kalmar	11,170	238,406	237,781	21
Gotland	3,140	56,180	56,383	18
Blekinge	2,941	151,055	149,544	51
Kristianstad	6,089	280,516	283,818	47
Malmöhus	4,938	750,294	763,349	155
Halland	5,454	240,090	247,417	45
Göteborg and Bohus	5,141	715,831	729,629	142
Älvsborg	11,395	426,769	433,417	38
Skaraborg	7,938	270,530	272,126	34
Värmland	17,583	279,503	280,694	16
Örebro	8,519	270,384	270,031	32
Västmanland	6,302	254,858	254,847	40
Kopparberg	28,194	284,029	284,407	10
Gävleborg	18,191	289,452	287,004	16
Västernorrland	21,678	262,555	259,964	12
Jämtland	49,443	134,161	134,116	3
Västerbotten	55,401	245,302	247,521	4
Norrbotten	98,911	262,443	261,536	3
Total	410,928[1]	8,360,178	8,458,888	21

[1] Total area of Sweden, 449,964 sq. km.

On 31 Dec. 1988 there were 4,175,880 males and 4,283,008 females.

On 31 Dec. 1988 aliens in Sweden numbered 421,023. Of these, 127,939 were Finns, 38,930 Yugoslavs, 28,605 Norwegians, 28,420 Iranians; 25,664 Danes, 22,968 Turks, 14,333 Poles, 14,067 Chileans, 11,859 West Germans, 9,342 Britons, 7,128 Greeks, 7,079 Americans, 4,935 Iraqis, 4,375 Ethiopians and 3,912 Italians.

Vital statistics for calendar years:

	Total living births	To mothers single, divorced or widowed	Stillborn	Marriages	Divorces	Deaths exclusive of still-born
1985	98,463	45,640	388	38,297	19,763	94,032
1986	101,950	49,324	423	38,906	19,107	93,295
1987	104,699	52,218	412	41,223	18,426	93,307
1988	112,080	57,090	422	44,229	17,746	96,743

Immigration: 1983, 27,495; 1984, 31,486; 1985, 33,134; 1986, 39,487; 1987, 42,688; 1988, 51,092. Emigration: 1983, 25,269; 1984, 22,825; 1985, 22,041; 1986, 24,495; 1987, 20,679; 1988, 21,461.

In 1860 the urban population numbered 435,000 (11% of the total population) and on 31 Dec. 1965, 4,177,212 (54%); including other densely populated areas, the urbanized population in 1965 was 77·4%.

On 15 Sept. 1980, population in densely populated areas was 6,910,431 (83·1%).

Population of largest communities, 31 Dec. 1988:

Stockholm	669,485	Halmstad	78,607	Kalmar	55,129
Göteborg	430,763	Karlstad	75,412	Falun	52,448
Malmö	231,575	Skellefteå	74,127	Kungsbacka	52,027
Uppsala	161,828	Huddinge	71,921	Mölndal	51,106
Örebro	119,824	Kristianstad	70,491	Solna	50,964
Norrköping	119,370	Växjö	68,499	Trollhättan	50,296
Linköping	119,167	Botkyrka	68,167	Sollentuna	50,242
Västerås	117,717	Luleå	67,443	Hässleholm	48,658
Jönköping	109,890	Nyköping	64,739	Varberg	47,566
Helsingborg	107,443	Nacka	61,931	Skövde	46,712
Borås	100,795	Haninge	61,551	Uddevalla	46,489
Sundsvall	92,983	Örnsköldsvik	58,967	Borlänge	46,343
Eskilstuna	88,850	Karlskrona	58,634	Norrtälje	43,741
Umeå	88,726	Östersund	57,281	Motala	41,502
Gävle	87,747	Järfälla	56,402	Sandviken	39,740
Lund	85,150	Gotland	56,383	Västervik	39,522
Södertälje	80,660	Täby	56,339		

Befolkningsförändringar (Population Changes). Annual. 3 vols. Statistics Sweden, Stockholm
Folkmängd 31 Dec. (Population). Annual. 2 vols. Statistics Sweden, Stockholm

CLIMATE. North Sweden suffers from severe winters, with snow lying for 4–7 months. Summers are fine but cool, with long daylight hours. Further south, winters are less cold, summers are warm and rainfall generally well-distributed over the year, though with a slight summer maximum. Stockholm. Jan. 24·4°F (–4·1°C), July 59·9°F (17·3°C). Annual rainfall 25" (622 mm).

REIGNING KING. Carl XVI Gustaf, born 30 April 1946, succeeded on the death of his grandfather Gustaf VI Adolf, 15 Sept. 1973, married 19 June 1976 to *Silvia* Renate Sommerlath, born 23 Dec. 1943 (Queen of Sweden). *Daughter* and *Heir Apparent:* Crown Princess Victoria Ingrid Alice Désirée, Duchess of Västergötland, born 14 July 1977; *son:* Prince Carl Philip Edmund Bertil, Duke of Värmland, born 13 May 1979; *daughter:* Princess Madeleine Thérèse Amelie Josephine, Duchess of Hälsingland and Gästrikland, born 10 June 1982.

Sisters of the King. Princess Margaretha, born 31 Oct. 1934, married 30 June 1964 to Mr John Ambler; Princess Birgitta (Princess of Sweden), born 19 Jan. 1937, married 25 May 1961 (civil marriage) and 30 May 1961 (religious ceremony) to Johann Georg, Prince of Hohenzollern; Princess Désirée, born 2 June 1938, married 5 June 1964 to Baron Niclas Silfverschiöld; Princess Christina, born 3 Aug. 1943, married 15 June 1974 to Tord Magnuson.

Uncles of the King. Sigvard, Count of Wisborg, born on 7 June 1907; Prince Bertil, Duke of Halland, born on 28 Feb. 1912, married 7 Dec. 1976 to Lilian May Davies, born 30 Aug. 1915 (Princess of Sweden, Duchess of Halland); Carl Johan, Count of Wisborg, born on 31 Oct. 1916.

Aunt of the King. Princess Ingrid (Princess of Sweden), born 28 March 1910, married 24 May 1935 to Frederik, Crown Prince of Denmark (King Frederik IX), died 14 Jan. 1972.

The following is a list of the kings and queens of Sweden, with the dates of their accession from the accession of the House of Vasa:

House of Vasa	
Gustaf I	1521
Eric XIV	1560
Johan III	1568
Sigismund	1592
Carl IX	1599
Gustaf II Adolf	1611
Christina	1632
House of Pfalz-Zweibrücken	
Carl X Gustaf	1654
Carl XI	1660
House of Pfalz-Zweibrücken (contd.)	
Carl XII	1697
Ulrica Eleonora	1719
House of Hesse	
Fredrik I	1720
House of Holstein-Gottorp	
Adolf Fredrik	1751
Gustaf III	1771
Gustaf IV Adolf	1792
Carl XIII	1809
House of Bernadotte	
Carl XIV Johan	1818
Oscar I	1844
Carl XV	1859
Oscar II	1872
Gustaf V	1907
Gustaf VI Adolf	1950
Carl XVI Gustaf	1973

The royal family of Sweden have a civil list of 16·75m. kronor; this does not include the maintenance of the royal palaces.

CONSTITUTION AND GOVERNMENT. Sweden's present Constitution came into force in 1975 and replaced the 1809 Constitution. Under the present Constitution Sweden is a representative and parliamentary democracy. Parliament (*Riksdag*) is declared to be the central organ of government. The executive power of the country is vested in the Government, which is responsible to Parliament. The King is Head of State, but he does not participate in the government of the country. Since 1971 Parliament has consisted of one chamber. It has 349 members, who are elected for a period of 3 years in direct, general elections.

Every man and woman who has reached the age of 18 years on election-day itself, and who is not under wardship has the right to vote and to stand for election.

The manner of election to the *Riksdag* is proportional. The country is divided into 28 constituencies. In these constituencies 310 members are elected. The remaining 39 seats constitute a nation-wide pool intended to give absolute proportionality to parties that receive at least 4% of the votes. A party receiving less than 4% of the votes in the country is, however, entitled to participate in the distribution of seats in a constituency, if it has obtained at least 12% of the votes cast there.

The *Riksdag*, elected 1988, has 156 Social Democrats, 66 Conservatives, 42 Centre Party, 44 Liberals, 21 Communists and 20 Green Party.

The Social Democratic Cabinet was composed as follows in Jan. 1990:

Prime Minister: Ingvar Carlsson.

Finance: Kjell-Olof Feldt. *Health and Social Affairs:* Ingela Thalen. *Special responsibility for international development co-operation, Ministry of Foreign Affairs:* Lena Hjelm-Wallén. *Foreign Affairs:* Sten Andersson. *Higher Education, with special responsibility for cultural affairs and the mass media:* Bengt Göransson. *Foreign Trade:* Anita Gradin. *Environment:* Birgitta Dahl. *Defence:* Roine Carlsson. *Agriculture:* Mats Hellström. *Public Administration:* Bengt Johansson. *Transport and Communications:* Georg Andersson. *Special responsibility for family policy, the disabled and elderly, Ministry of Health and Social Affairs:* Bengt Lindqvist. *Labour, with special responsibility for immigrant affairs:* Maj-Lis Lööw. *Housing:* Ulf Lönnqvist. *Labour:* Mona Sahlin. *Industry and Energy:* Rune Molin. *Assistant Minister of Finance:* Odd Engström. *Justice:* Laila Freivalds. *Special responsibility for church, equality and consumer affairs, Ministry of Public Administration:* Margot Wallström. *Special responsibility for comprehensive schools, adult education, Ministry of Education:* Göran Persson.

Ministerial decisions are formally made by the Cabinet collectively and not (with some exceptions) by individual ministers.

Public administration in Sweden is characterized by a unique degree of functional decentralization. The Ministries are not really administrative agencies. Their main function is to prepare the decisions of the Cabinet; such decisions may concern bills for the *Riksdag*, general government directives and higher appointments. Only to a small extent does the Cabinet make individual administrative decisions. The routine administrative work is attended to by the central boards (*centrala ämbetsverk*). Each board is in principle subordinate to the government; its sphere of activity depends on the appropriations granted by the *Riksdag*. The Government often asks the boards' opinion on proposed measures.

National flag: Blue with a yellow Scandinavian cross.

National anthem: Du gamla, du fria, du fjällhöga nord (words by R. Dybeck, 1844; folk-tune).

The official language is Swedish. The capital is Stockholm.

Regional and Local Government. For national administrative purposes Sweden is divided into 24 counties (*län*), in each of which the central government is represented by a state county administrative board (*länsstyrelse*). The governor (*landshövding*), appointed by the government, is chairman of the board, which in addition to the governor has 14 members elected by the county council.

Local government and the levying of local taxes are based on the Instrument of Government (the Swedish Constitution) and are regulated by the local government act and special acts. According to the local government act Sweden is divided into municipalities in which all men and women who have reached the age of 18 on election-day itself, and not under wardship, are entitled to elect the municipal council. These councils are named *kommunfullmäktige*. The number of municipalities has, since 1951, been reduced from about 2,500 to 284. The municipalities deal with a great variety of different tasks such as social welfare, education and culture, public health, town planning, housing etc. Each county, except Gotland, which consists of only one municipality, has a county council (*landsting*) elected by men and women who enjoy local suffrage. The county councils chiefly administer the health services and medical care. The municipalities of Gothenburg and Malmö do not belong to county councils. The parishes, 2,600 in 1990, are the local units of the Church of Sweden and have the same status in public law as the municipalities. The parochial church council (*kyrkofullmäktige*) is the supreme decision-making body in most parishes, whose members are publicly elected. Small parishes have instead the parish meeting, a form of direct democracy.

Boalt, G., *The Political Process.* Stockholm, 1984
Gustafsson, A., *Local Government in Sweden.* Stockholm, 1988
Gustafsson, G., *Local Government Reform in Sweden.* Stockholm, 1980
Hadenius, S., *Swedish Politics During the 20th Century.* Stockholm, 1988
Lewin, L., Jansson, B. and Sörbom, D., *The Swedish Electorate 1887–1968.* Stockholm, 1972
Lindström, E., *The Swedish Parliamentary System.* Stockholm, 1983
Strömberg, L. and Westerstahl, J., *The New Swedish Communes.* Gothenburg, 1984
Vinde, P., *Swedish Government Administration.* 2nd rev. ed. Stockholm, 1978

DEFENCE. A Supreme Commander is, under the Government, in command of the three services. He is assisted by the Defence Staff under a chief of staff.

The military forces are recruited on the principle of national service, supplemented by voluntarily enlisted personnel who form the permanent cadres for training purposes, staff duties, etc.

Liability to service commences at the age of 18, and lasts till the end of the 47th year. The period of training for the Army and Navy is $7^1/_2$-12 months and for the Airforce 8-12 months.

The territorial organization consists of 6 military commands each one under a general officer commanding.

Army. The C.-in-C. of the Swedish Army has at his disposal the Army Staff under a chief of staff. The peace-time Army consists for training purposes of 16 infantry, 2 cavalry, 7 armour, 6 artillery, 5 AA, 3 engineer, 2 signal and 3 Army Service Corps units, most of which are called 'regiments' (*regementen*). The Army Aviation Corps comprises 2 Battalions operating 6 Bulldog aircraft and 18 JetRanger helicopters for observation, 20 armed BO 105 helicopters, 12 AB.204B transport helicopters, plus 26 Hughes 300C helicopters and 2 DO 27 aircraft for training and observation duties.

The Army is organized and equipped with regard to the varying geographical and climatic conditions of the country. The voluntary Home Guard (*Hemvärnet*) with a total strength of more than 100,000 men ready for action within 2 hours, raised during the War continues to be in force.

Sweden's ground forces, total 850,000 men (including the voluntary Home Guard), can be said to consist of an Army which for the most part is on indefinite leave, but which on short notice can be ready for action. One of the basic principles of the Swedish system of mobilization is the local recruitment of as many units as possible. The storage of equipment and supplies is decentralized on more than 3,000 places.

The active personnel of the Army comprises (1990) about 47,000, including 37,700 conscripts doing basic training.

Navy. The C.-in-C. of the Swedish Navy is assisted by the Chief of Naval Staff and the Chief of Naval Material. THe main operational commander is the Commander-in-Chief, Coastal Fleet. Naval forces are divided between two branches, the Navy and Coastal Defence Artillery. There are 4 Naval Command Areas, covering southern, eastern, western and northern coasts. The coastal defence areas are the Stockholm archipelago, Blekinge, Gothenburg, Gotland and Norrland, covered by a coastal artillery brigade each.

The Navy operates 11 small diesel submarines, 2 50m Stockholm class missile craft, (which act as leaders for smaller craft), 28 other missile craft, 11 inshore patrol craft, 3 minelayers, 6 minehunters, 4 coastal minesweepers and 18 inshore minesweepers. Auxiliaries include 1 MCM support ship, 1 electronic intelligence gatherer, 1 surveying vessel, 6 icebreakers, 2 tugs and 1 salvage vessel, plus numerous service craft and boats.

As well as an extensive inventory of artillery up to 120 mm calibre, and coast defence missiles, the coastal defence artillery also operate 9 coastal and 16 inshore minelayers, 18 small patrol craft and some 140 amphibious craft.

The Naval Air Arm comprises 14 Boeing Vertol 107 helicopters and 9 AB-206 Jet-Ranger helicopters, plus 1 Aviocar fixed-wing aircraft for anti-submarine warfare and electronic surveillance.

The personnel of the navy and coast artillery in 1989 totalled 12,000 (6,300 conscripts) of whom 2,700 serve in coastal artillery.

A separate civil Coast Guard, 550 strong, operate some 70 inshore cutters, patrol boats and service craft and lists 4 aircraft.

Air Force. The C-in-C. of the Swedish Air Force has at his disposal the Air Staff under a chief of staff.

The combat force consists of 3 fighter-interceptor, 3 ground-attack and 3 mixed interceptor/reconnaissance wings (*flottiljer*), each with 2-3 squadrons of 12-15 aircraft, including 6 reconnaissance squadrons (*divisioner*). Total peace-time strength of the combat units is 16 squadrons with nearly 400 first-line aircraft.

Night and all-weather fighters are the Swedish-built Saab J35 Draken, equipping 3 squadrons, and JA37 Viggen, equipping 8 squadrons. The ground-attack wings have 6 squadrons of Saab AJ37 Viggens, and there is provision for 4 light ground-attack squadrons of twin-jet Saab-105s (Sk60s), which could be drawn in wartime from training units. The 3 reconnaissance squadrons have SF37 (photo) and SH37 (maritime, radar) Viggen reconnaissance aircraft; and there are transport, helicopter and other support units. The Sk60 is the Air Force's standard advanced trainer, to which pupils progress after initial training on piston-engined Bulldogs. Other trainers in service include the Sk61 Bulldog, Sk35C Draken and Sk37 Viggen.

Active strength (1990) 8,000 personnel, including 5,000 conscripts.

INTERNATIONAL RELATIONS

Membership. Sweden is a member of UN and EFTA.

ECONOMY

Budget. Revenue and expenditure of the total budget (Current and Capital) for financial years ending 30 June (in 1m. kr.):

	Revenue	Expenditure		Revenue	Expenditure
1982–83	191,280	277,031	1985–86	275,099	322,241
1983–84	221,165	297,881	1986–87	320,105	334,996
1984–85	260,596	330,281	1987–88	332,552	336,669

The preliminary revenue and expenditure for the financial year 1 July 1988 to 30 June 1989 was as follows (in 1m. kr.):

Revenue		*Expenditure*	
Taxes:		Royal Household and residences	44
Taxes on income, capital gains and profits	103,487	Justice	12,544
		Foreign Affairs	12,236
		Defence	30,761
Statutory social security fees	52,349	Health and Social Affairs	98,491
		Transport and Communications	13,717
Taxes on property	19,383	Ministry of Finance	23,230
Value-added tax	86,637	Education and Cultural Affairs	46,115
Other taxes on goods and services	62,037	Agriculture	6,012
		Labour	23,999
Total revenue from taxes	323,893	Housing and Physical Planning	16,853
		Industry	5,640
Non-tax revenue	33,043	Civil Service Affairs	3,071
Capital revenue	209	Ministry of Environment and Energy	2,428
Loan repayment	6,759		
Computed revenue	2,865	Parliament and agencies	586
Total revenue	366,769	Interest on National Debt, etc.	53,179
		Unforeseen expenditure	20
		Total expenditure	348,926

On 31 Dec. 1988 the national debt amounted to 609,940m. kr.

Riksgäldskontoret (National Debt Office), *årsbok*. Annual. Stockholm, from 1920
Riksskatteverket (National Tax Board), *årsbok*. Annual. Stockholm, from 1971
The Swedish Budget. Ministry of Economic Affairs and Ministry of the Budget, from 1962/63

Currency. The monetary unit is the Swedish *krona*, of 100 *öre*. In March 1990, £1 = 10·07 *krona*; US$1 = 6·15 *krona*.

Gold coins do not exist as a currency. Central banknotes for 5, 10, 50, 100, 500, 1,000 and 10,000 kr. are legal means of payment.

Banking. The Riksbank, or Central Bank of Sweden, belongs entirely to the State and is managed by directors elected for 3 years by the Parliament, except the chairman, who is designated by the Government. The bank is under the guarantee of the Parliament, its capital and reserve capital are fixed by its constitution. Since 1904, only the Riksbank has the right to issue notes. On 31 Dec. 1987 its note circulation amounted to 56,303m. kr.; its gold and foreign-exchange reserves totalled 50,288m. kr. There are 25 commercial banks. On 31 Dec. 1987 their total deposits amounted to 290,276m. kr.; advances to the public amounted to 344,024m. kr.

On 31 Dec. 1987 there were 116 savings banks; their total deposits amounted to 135,351m. kr.; advances to the public were 109,416m. kr. Co-operative banks had total deposits of 36,479m. kr.; advances to the public were 26,481m. kr.

Sveriges Riksbank, årsbok. Annual. Stockholm, from 1908
Skandinaviska Enskilda Banken, Kvartalskrift. Quarterly Review (in English). Stockholm, from 1920
Bosworth, B. and Rivlin, A. M., (eds.) *The Swedish Economy*. Washington, D.C., 1987

Weights and Measures. The metric system is obligatory.

ENERGY AND NATURAL RESOURCES

Electricity. Sweden is rich in hydro-power resources. The total electric energy net production in 1987 was 141,521m. kwh. About 50% of this energy was produced in hydro-electric plants and 45% in nuclear power plants. The remaining 5% was produced in conventional thermal power plants. Supply 220 volts; 50 Hz.

Minerals. Sweden is one of the leading exporters of iron ore. The largest deposits are found north of the polar circle in the area of Kiruna and Gällivare-Malmberget.

The ore is exported *via* the Norwegian port of Narvik and the Swedish port of Luleå. There are also important resources of iron ore in southern Sweden (Bergslagen). The most important fields are Grängesberg and Stråssa and the ores are shipped *via* the port of Oxelösund. Some of the southern deposits have, in contrast to the fields in North Sweden, a low phosphorus content.

There are also some deposits of copper, lead and zinc ores especially in the Boliden area in the north of Sweden. These ores are often found together with pyrites. Non-ferrous ores, except zinc ores, are used in the Swedish metal industry and barely satisfy domestic needs.

The total production of iron ores amounted to 19·1m. tons in 1987 and exports to 17·2m. tons. The production of copper ore was 356,700 tons, of lead ore 133,074 tons, of zinc ore 392,494 tons.

There are also deposits of raw materials for aluminium not worked at present. In southern Sweden there are big resources of alum shale, containing oil and uranium.

Agriculture. According to the farm register which is revised annually the following data was provided for 1988. The number of farms in cultivation of more than 2 hectares of arable land, was 100,906; of these there were 57,987 of 2-20 hectares; 39,120 of 20-100 hectares; 3,799 of above 100 hectares. Of the total land area of Sweden (41,161,500 hectares), 2,872,319 [1] hectares were arable land, 332,363[1] hectares cultivated pastures and (1981) 22,742,235 hectares forests.

	Area (1,000 hectares) [1]			*Production (1,000 tonnes)*		
Chief crops	*1986*	*1987*	*1988*	*1986*	*1987*	*1988*
Wheat	321·4	335·6	258·9	1,731	1,558	1,296
Rye	40·4	42·2	35·3	154	137	128
Barley	680·9	580·5	566·7	2,327	1,907	1,879
Oats	486·8	424·6	446·6	1,486	1,440	1,330
Mixed grain	50·0	45·8	38·3	...	...	...
Peas and vetches	41·0	59·0	45·4	...	...	...
Potatoes	37·5	37·9	38·8	1,209	958	1,283
Sugarbeet	51·3	51·3	51·3	2,187	1,699	2,439
Tame hay	671·0	676·6	699·0	3,981	4,488	4,435
Oil seed	175·8	169·7	149·8	374	296	293

Area of rotation meadows for pasture was (in 1,000 hectares[1]): 1984, 182; 1985, 181; 1986, 180; 1987, 175; 1988, 182.

Total production of milk (in 1,000 tonnes): 1984, 3,821; 1985, 3,724; 1986, 3,566; 1987, 3,513; 1988, 3,498. Butter production in the same years was (in 1,000 tonnes): 78, 75, 68, 66, 62; and cheese 116, 115, 113, 114; 123.

Livestock (1988): Cattle, 1·7m.; sheep, 395,000; pigs, 2·3m.; poultry, 11m.

Number of farm tractors in 1986, 183,828; combines in 1986, 47,089.

The number of pelts produced in 1987–88 was as follows: Fox, 29,779; mink, 1·57m.; others, 9,576.

[1] Figures refer to holdings of more than 2 hectares of arable land.

Forestry. In 1983–87 the forests covered an area of 23·6m. hectares, *i.e.* roughly 58% of the country's land area. Municipal and State ownership accounts for one-fourth of the forests, companies own another fourth, and the remaining half is in private hands. In the felling seasons, 1985–86 and 1986–87 respectively, 52·1m. and 53m. cu. metres (solid volume excluding bark) of wood were removed from the forests in Sweden. The sawmill, wood pulp and paper industries are all of great importance. The number of sawmills in 1984 was about 2,500, producing 12·1m. cu. metres of sawn wood. In 1988 the production of sawn soft-wood was about 11·3m. cu. metres. The total production amounted to 10·3m. tons (including dissolving pulp) (dry weight).

Fisheries. In 1987 the total catch of the sea fisheries was 197,307 tons, landed weight, value 746m. kr.

INDUSTRY AND TRADE

Industry. The most important sector of Swedish manufacturing is the production of metals, metal products, machinery and transport equipment, covering almost half of the total value added by manufacturing. Production of high-quality steel is an old Swedish speciality. A large part of this production is exported. The production of ordinary steel is slightly decreasing and is still short of domestic demand. The total production of steel amounted to 4·1m. tons in 1983. There is also a large production of other metals (aluminium, lead, copper) and rolled semi-manufactured goods of these metals.

These basic metal industries are an important basis for the production of more developed metal products, machinery and equipment, which are to a large extent sold on the world market, *i.e.*, hand tools, mining drills, ball-bearings, turbines, pneumatic machinery, refrigerating equipment, machinery for pulp and paper industries, etc., sewing machines, machine tools, office machinery, high-voltage electric machinery, telephone equipment, cars and trucks, ships and aeroplanes.

Another important manufacturing sector is based on Sweden's forest resources. This sector includes saw-mills, plywood factories, joinery industries, pulp- and paper-mills, wallboard and particle board factories, accounting for about 20% of the total value of manufacturing. A fast increasing sector is the chemical industry, especially the petro-chemical branch. Minerals industries include production of building materials, decorative arts products of glass and china.

Industry groups	*No. of establishments* 1986	1987	*Average no. of wage-earners* 1986	1987	*Sales value of production (gross) in 1m. kr.* 1986	1987
Mining and quarrying	*107*	*100*	*8,075*	*7,249*	*5,820*	*5,601*
Metal-ore mining	35	34	6,997	6,198	5,068	4,867
Other mining	72	66	1,098	1,051	752	735
Manufacturing	*9,022*	*9,012*	*531,228*	*531,100*	*527,322*	*560,874*
Manufacture of food, beverages and tobacco	818	817	51,227	50,638	74,501	76,453
Textile, wearing apparel and leather industries	607	592	23,224	22,414	11,046	11,463
Manufacture of wood products including furniture	1,372	1,335	44,532	45,268	34,993	38,224
Manufacture of paper and paper products, printing and publishing	1,080	1,077	65,580	65,383	76,161	85,781
Manufacture of chemicals and chemical, petroleum, coal, rubber and plastic products	724	719	42,081	43,100	70,216	73,669
Manufacture of non-metallic mineral products, except products of petroleum and coal	378	368	15,829	15,898	11,309	12,752
Basic metal industries	160	161	35,436	34,267	38,961	40,040
Manufacture of fabricated metal products, machinery and equipment	3,788	3,847	250,698	251,495	208,657	220,953
Other manufacturing industries	95	96	2,621	2,637	1,479	1,538
Electricity, gas and water [1]	*702*	*691*	*10,292*	*10,165*	*76,888*	*79,442*
Electricity, gas and steam	702	691	10,292	10,165	76,888	79,442

[1] Excluding water, 1986.

Arbetsmarknadsstatistik (Labour Market Statistics). Monthly. National Labour Market Board, Stockholm, from 1963

Arbetsmarknadsstatistisk Årsbok (Year Book of Labour Statistics). Statistics Sweden, Stockholm, from 1973

Johansson, Ö., *The Gross Domestic Product of Sweden and its Composition 1861–1955.* Stockholm, 1967

Thalberg, B. and Marno, N., eds., *Economic Growth, Welfare and Industrial Relations: A Comparative Study of Japan and Sweden.* Tokyo, 1984

Jordbruksekonomiska meddelanden (Journal of Agricultural Economics, published monthly by the National Agricultural Market Board). Stockholm, from 1939

Jordbruksstatistisk årsbok (Yearbook of Agricultural Statistics). Statistics Sweden, Stockholm, from 1965

The Swedish Economy. Ministry of Economic Affairs and National Institute of Economic Research. Stockholm, from 1960

Trade Unions. The Swedish Federation of Trade Unions (LO) had 24 member unions with a total membership of 2,279,885 in 1987; the Swedish Central Organization of Salaried Employees (TCO) had 21, with 1,250,073; the Swedish Confederation of Professional Associations (SACO-SR) had 25, with 300,084.

Commerce. The imports and exports of Sweden, unwrought gold and coin not included, have been as follows (in 1m. kr.):

	1982	*1983*	*1984*	*1985*	*1986*	*1987*	*1988*
Imports	173,932	200,368	218,569	244,654	232,614	257,870	279,663
Exports	168,134	210,516	242,811	260,481	265,103	281,433	304,782

Imports and exports by products (in 1m. kr.):

	Imports		*Exports*	
	1987	*1988*	*1987*	*1988*
Food and live animals chiefly for food	14,556	15,518	4,694	4,816
Cereals and cereal preparations	829	931	1,209	1,160
Vegetables and fruit	5,183	5,369	395	467
Coffee, tea, cocoa, spices and manufactures thereof	2,707	2,737	632	686
Feeding stuff for animals (not including unmilled cereals)	971	1,190	155	128
Beverages and tobacco	1,952	2,139	338	371
Crude materials, inedible, except fuels	10,988	12,753	25,911	28,148
Hides, skins and furskins, raw	613	615	850	1,105
Crude rubber (including synthetic and reclaimed)	471	506	158	199
Cork and wood	3,293	3,450	9,970	9,934
Pulp and waste paper	582	669	10,449	12,119
Textile fibres (other than wool tops and other combed wool) and their wastes (not manufactured into yarn or fabric)	368	376	225	216
Crude fertilizers and crude minerals (excluding coal, petroleum and precious stones)	1,473	1,545	468	465
Metalliferous ores and metal scrap	2,466	3,725	3,535	3,757
Mineral fuels, lubricants and related materials	22,981	19,146	8,176	6,641
Coal, coke and briquettes	1,329	1,388	196	114
Petroleum, petroleum products and related materials	20,814	16,806	7,379	5,762
Chemicals and related products, n.e.s.	24,970	28,096	19,283	21,805
Artificial resins and plastic materials, and cellulose esters and ethers	7,364	8,847	5,491	6,456
Manufactured goods classified chiefly by material	41,425	47,062	73,639	81,240
Paper, paperboard, and articles of paper pulp, of paper or of paperboard	3,307	3,753	30,434	33,824
Textile yarn, fabrics, made-up articles, n.e.s., and related products	7,107	7,157	3,635	3,444
Non-metallic mineral manufactures, n.e.s.	4,170	4,466	3,149	3,099
Iron and steel	8,597	10,173	16,284	19,301
Non-ferrous metals	4,830	6,972	4,906	6,148
Machinery and transport equipment	99,208	110,709	121,832	130,591
Power generating machinery and equipment	6,079	6,370	7,795	9,164
Machinery specialized for particular industries	9,082	9,950	13,880	15,225
Metal working machinery	3,063	3,176	2,693	3,210
General industrial machinery and equipment, n.e.s. and machine parts, n.e.s.	14,523	15,430	19,695	21,123
Office machines and automatic data processing machines	11,556	13,988	7,982	8,382
Telecommunications and sound recording and reproducing apparatus and equipment	7,040	8,164	9,615	12,308

	Imports		*Exports*	
	1987	*1988*	*1987*	*1988*
Electrical machinery apparatus and appliances, n.e.s., and electrical parts thereof (including non-electrical counterparts, n.e.s., of electrical household type equipment)	15,896	17,882	11,858	12,927
Road vehicles (including air cushion vehicles)	27,632	30,835	43,322	43,706
Other transport equipment	4,337	4,914	4,993	4,546
Miscellaneous manufactured articles	40,396	42,360	26,187	28,762

Principal import and export countries (in 1m. kr.):

	Imports from		*Exports to*	
	1987	*1988*	*1987*	*1988*
Belgium-Luxembourg	7,667	9,061	11,653	12,662
Denmark	17,360	18,610	20,894	21,064
Federal Republic of Germany	56,260	59,439	33,351	36,986
Finland	17,840	19,512	17,533	20,026
France	13,259	14,033	15,061	16,088
Italy	10,751	11,279	10,593	12,107
Netherlands	10,588	11,359	13,801	14,612
Norway	15,175	16,949	30,270	28,512
Switzerland	5,410	5,528	6,321	7,197
USSR	4,882	4,512	1,826	1,756
UK	23,545	24,045	28,674	34,230
USA	17,793	20,968	30,067	30,064

Total trade between Sweden and UK (British Department of Trade returns, in £1,000 sterling):

	1985	*1986*	*1987*	*1988*	*1989*
Imports to UK	2,465,582	2,756,536	2,952,453	3,366,524	3,747,600
Exports and re-exports from UK	3,006,890	2,307,900	2,322,235	2,195,032	2,350,122

Historisk Statistik för Sverige, 3: Utrikeshandel [Foreign Trade], *1732–1970*. Statistics Sweden, Stockholm, 1972

Utrikeshandel, årsstatistik [Foreign Trade, Annual Bulletin]. Statistics Sweden, Stockholm. 5 vols. Statistical Reports, Series H

Utrikeshandel, månadsstatistik [Foreign Trade, Monthly Bulletin]. Statistics Sweden, Stockholm.

Utrikeshandel, kvartalsstatistik [Foreign Trade, Quarterly Bulletin]. Statistics Sweden, Stockholm. January – December. Exports respectively imports. Statistical Reports, Series H

Utrikeshandel, års statistik [Foreign Trade, Annual]. Official Statistics of Sweden, Statistics Sweden, Stockholm. Imports and exports. Distribution by country and commodity according to the SITC

Utrikeshandel, årsstatistik [Foreign Trade, Annual]. Official Statistics of Sweden, Statistics Sweden, Stockholm. Imports and exports. Commodities according to the CCCN.

Tourism. In 1987 foreign visitors spent 12,881m. kr., and stayed 3,243,324 nights in hotels, 909,706 in holiday villages and youth hostels and 2,936,216 camping. Earnings from tourism (1987) 12·88m. kr.

COMMUNICATIONS

Roads. On 1 Jan. 1988 there were 200,000 km of public roads comprising State-administered roads, 98,441 km, municipal, 32,000 km, private roads with subsidies, 77,031 km, of which 68,762 km were surfaced. Motor vehicles on 31 Dec. 1987 included 3,366,570 passenger cars, 259,576 buses and lorries and 31,016 motor cycles (all in use).

Railways. At the end of 1988 the total length of railways was 11,194 km; 6,995 km were electrified which carried 72m. passengers and 52·6m. tonnes of freight.

Aviation. Commercial air traffic is maintained in (1) Sweden and other parts of the world by Scandinavian Airlines System (SAS), of which AB Aerotransport (ABA = Swedish Air Lines) is the Swedish partner (DDL = Danish Air Lines and DNL = Norwegian Air Lines being the other two); (2) only within Sweden by Linjeflyg AB. Scandinavian Airlines System have a joint paid-up capital of about Sw. kronor 9,187m. Capitalization of ABA, Sw. kronor 2,212m., of which 50% is owned by the Government and 50% by private enterprises. Capitalization of Linjeflyg, Sw. kronor 758m., of which 50% is owned by SAS and 50% by ABA.

In scheduled air traffic during 1988 the total number of km flown was 102·8m.; passenger-km, 7,829·9m.; goods, 171·2m. ton-km; mail, 20·4m. ton-km. These figures represent the Swedish share of the SAS traffic (Swedish domestic and three-sevenths of international traffic) and the Linjeflyg traffic.

Shipping. The Swedish mercantile marine consisted on 30 June 1989 of 416 vessels of 2m. gross tons (only vessels of at least 100 gross tons, and excluding fishing vessels and tugs). Stockholm and Göteborg, with together 165 vessels of 1·4m. gross tons in Dec. 1988, are the two major home ports for the Swedish mercantile marine.

Vessels entered from and cleared for foreign countries, exclusive of passenger liners and ferries, with cargoes and in ballast, in 1988, are as follows (only vessels of at least a gross tonnage of 75): With cargoes, 28,101 with a gross tonnage of 118·8m.; in ballast, 14,482 with a gross tonnage of 54·6m.

Post and Broadcasting. On 1 Jan. 1988 there were 5,480,000 main telephone lines.

Number of combined radio and television reception fees paid at the end of 1987 was 3,293,000, of which 3m. included extra fees for colour television. As from 1 April 1978, special sound broadcasting licences were discontinued.

Sveriges Radio AB is a non-commercial semi-governmental corporation, transmitting 3 programmes on long-, medium-, and short-waves and on FM. There are also regional programmes. It also broadcasts 2 TV programmes. Colour programmes are broadcast by PAL system.

The overseas radio-telegraph and radio-telephone services are conducted by the Swedish Telecommunications Administration.

The number of post offices at the end of 1986 was 2,164. For receipts of the post and telecommunication services *see* the section on Economy.

Cinemas (1987). There were 1,112 cinemas.

Newspapers (1987). There were 178 daily newspapers with a total circulation of 4·9m.

JUSTICE, RELIGION, EDUCATION AND WELFARE

Justice. The administration of justice is entirely independent of the Government. The *Justitiekansler*, or Attorney General (a royal appointment) and the *Justitieombudsmän* (Parliamentary Commissioners appointed by the Diet), exercise a check on the administration. In 1968 a reform was carried through which meant that the offices of the former *Justitieombudsman* (Ombudsman for civil affairs) and the *Militieombudsman* (Ombudsman for military affairs) were turned into one sole institution with 3 Ombudsmen, each styled *Justitieombudsman*. They exert a general supervision over all courts of law, the civil service, military laws and the military services. In 1988–89 they received altogether 3,054 cases; of these, 163 were instituted on their own initiative and 2,855 on complaints.

The *Riksåklagaren* (a royal appointment) is the chief public prosecutor.

The kingdom has a Supreme Court of Judicature and is divided into 6 Courts of Appeal districts (*hovrätter*) and 97 district-court divisions (*tingsrätter*). There is also a Housing Appeal Court and 12 rent and tenancy tribunals.

Of the district courts 27 also serve as real estate courts and 6 as water rights courts.

These district courts (or courts of first instance) deal with both civil and criminal cases. Each member of the court has an individual vote and is legally responsible for the decision. In the voting, the majority rules. When the votes are evenly divided in a criminal case, the opinion implying the least severe sentence applies, and in cases where there is no opinion that could be considered the mildest, the Chair has the casting vote, as is also the case in family civil cases and matters; petty cases are tried by the judge alone. Civil cases are tried as a rule by 3 to 4 judges or in minor cases by 1 judge. Disputes of greater consequence relating to the Marriage Code or the Code relating to Parenthood and Guardianship are tried by a judge and a *nämnd* of 3-4 lay assessors. When cases concerning real estate are being tried the court consists of 2 qualified lawyers, 1 specialist on technical matters and 2 lay assessors.

Criminal cases are tried by a judge and a jury of 5 members (lay assessors) in felony cases, and of 3 members in misdemeanour cases. The cases in Courts of Appeal are generally tried by 4 or 5 judges, but the same cases, which are tried with a judge and a *nämnd* in the first instance, are tried by 3 or 4 judges and a *nämnd* of 2-3 members. In cases concerning real estate the court consists of a specialist on technical matters in place of one of the judges and in water-right cases of 3 or 4 judges and 1 or 2 specialists on technical water matters.

Those with low incomes can receive free legal aid out of public funds. In criminal cases a suspected person has the right to a defence counsel, paid out of public funds.

The Attorney-General (*Justitiekanslern*) and the Parliamentary Commissioner (*Justitieombudsmannen*) for the Judiciary and Civil Administration supervise the application in the public sector of acts of parliament and regulations. The Attorney-General is the Government's legal adviser and also the Public Prosecutor.

The holders of the office of Parliamentary Commissioner are 4 in number.

There were 77 penal and correctional institutions for offenders in 1988 with an average population of 4,473 male and 254 female inmates (including offenders in remand prison). Besides, there were 456 children or young people registered for care in treatment and/or residential homes on 31 Dec. 1988, admitted under the 'Care of Young Persons' Act.

Anderman, S., (ed.) *Law and the Weaker Party: An Anglo-Swedish Comparative Study*. Abingdon, 1981–83
Bruzelius, A. and Ginsburg, R. B., *The Swedish Code of Judicial Procedure*. South Hackensack, Rev. ed., 1979
Strömholm, S., *An Introduction to Swedish Law*. Stockholm, 1981
al-Wahab, I., *The Swedish Institution of Ombudsmen*. Stockholm, 1979
Justitieombudsmännens ämbetsberättelse avgiven till Riksdagen. Annual. Stockholm
The Penal Code of Sweden: As Amended 1 Jan. 1972. South Hackensack, 1972
Rättsstatistisk årsbok (Year Book of Legal Statistics). Statistics Sweden, Stockholm, from 1975

Religion. The overwhelming majority of the population belong to the Evangelical Lutheran Church, which is the established national church. In 1988 there were 13 bishoprics (Uppsala being the metropolitan see) and 2,565 parishes. The clergy are chiefly supported from the parishes and the proceeds of the church lands. The nonconformists mostly still adhere to the national church. The largest denominations, on 1 Jan. 1987, were: Pentecost Movement, 100,442; The Mission Covenant Church of Sweden, 78,325; Salvation Army, 28,691; Swedish Evangelical Mission, 23,169; Swedish Baptist Church, 20,741; Orebro Missionary Society, 22,328; Swedish Alliance Missionary Society, 13,503; Holiness Mission, 6,087.

There were also 129,403 Roman Catholics (under a Bishop resident at Stockholm).

Parliament and Convocation (*Kyrkomötet*) decided in 1958 to admit women to ordination as priests.

Education. By the Swedish Higher Educational Act of 1977 a unified educational system was created by integrating institutions which had previously been administered separately. This new *högskola* includes not only traditional university studies but also those of various former professional colleges as well as a number of study programmes earlier offered by the secondary school system. One of the goals of the 1977 university reform was to introduce an increased element of vocational training into part of Swedish higher education and to widen admission. A Certificate of Education (B.Sc., M.Sc., U.C. etc.) is awarded on completion of a general study programme. This certificate states the number of courses taken as well as the points and grades obtained on each course in the study programme.

In autumn 1988 there were, in these new integrated institutions for higher education, *högskola*, about 166,200 enrolled for undergraduate studies of whom 113,600 were distributed by sector as follows: Education for technical professions, 32,700; education for social work, economic and administrative professions, 34,900; education for medical and paramedical professions, 21,600; education for the teaching professions, 18,400; and education for information, communication and cultural professions, 6,000. The number of students enrolled for post-graduate studies was 12,900.

In autumn term in the school year 1988–89 there were 580,200 pupils in primary education (grades 1–6 in compulsory comprehensive schools). Secondary education at the lower stage (grades 7–9 in compulsory comprehensive schools) comprised 325,400 pupils. In secondary education at the higher stage (the integrated upper secondary school), there were 245,900 pupils (excluding about 8,700 pupils in the fourth year of the technical line regarded as third-level education). The folk high schools, 'people's colleges', had 14,000 pupils in courses of more than 15 weeks.

In municipal adult education there were 129,000 pupils (corresponding to a gross number of 273,000 participants). Basic education for adults had 22,100 pupils.

There are also special schools for pupils with visual and hearing handicaps (about 660 in 1988–89) and for those who are mentally retarded (about 10,300 pupils).

Education Policy for Planning: Goals for Educational Policy in Sweden. OECD, Paris, 1980
Science and Technology Policies in Sweden. Ministry of Education and Cultural Affairs, Stockholm, 1986
The Swedish Folk High School. Swedish National Board of Education, Stockholm, 1986
Yearbook of Educational Statistics 1986, Statistics Sweden, Stockholm, 1986
Boucher, L., *Tradition and Change in Swedish education.* OUP, 1982
Düring, A., *Swedish Research.* Stockholm, 1985
Götberg, B. and Svärd, S., *The Swedish 'Folk High School': Its Background and its Present Situation.*
Kim, L., *Widened Admission to Higher Education in Sweden.* Stockholm, 1982
Marklund, S., *Educational Administration and Educational Development.* Univ. of Stockholm, 1979.—*The Democratization of Education in Sweden.* Univ. of Stockholm, 1980
Paulston, C. B., *Swedish Research and Debate about Bilingualism.* Stockholm, 1983
Stenholm, B., *The Swedish School System.* Stockholm, 1984
Sundgvist, A., *New Rules for Swedish Study Circles.* Stockholm, 1983
Ueberschlag, G., *La Folkhögskola.* Paris, 1981

Social Welfare. The social security schemes are greatly expanding. Supported by a referendum, the Diet in 1958 and 1959 decided that the national pensions should be increased successively until 1968 and supplementary pensions paid from 1963. These pensions are of invariable value. In 1969 the Diet decided that as from 1 July 1969 an increment to the basic pension was to be paid to persons without supplementary pensions, and this amount is to be successively increased in a 10-year period. The basic and supplementary pensions consist of old-age and family pensions, as well as pensions paid to the disabled. The financing of the supplementary system is based on the current-cost method.

The most important social welfare schemes are described in the conspectus below.

Type of scheme	*Introduced*	*Scope*	*Principal benefits*
Sickness insurance (compulsory–current law, 1962)	1955	All residents	Hospital fees, most private doctors charge the insured person normally 60 kr., district physicians and doctors in hospitals charge the insured person only 50 kr. for full medical treatment, some reimbursement of cost of transportation as well as costs of physiotherapy, convalescent care, etc., medicines at reduced prices or free of charge. During sickness daily allowance 90% of the yearly income in between 6,000 and 193,500 kr. There is generally no maximum benefit period. Dental care is available to all residents from 20 years of age, the maximum payable by the patient being 60% up to 2,500 kr. and 25% thereafter. Before 20 years of age dental care is given free through the national dental service.

Type of scheme	*Introduced*	*Scope*	*Principal benefits*
Employment injury insurance (compulsory–current law, 1976)	*1901*	All employed persons	Medical treatment, medicine and medical appliances, hospital care, sickness benefit 100% of the yearly income in between 6,000 and 193,500 kr. (first 90 days covered by sickness insurance), disability annuities, funeral benefit and survivor's pensions.
Unemployment insurance (current law, 1973)	1935	Members of recognized unemployment insurance societies (about 70% of all employees)	149-425 kr. per day subject to tax.
Basic pensions (current law, 1962)			
Old-age	1914	All citizens	Payable from the age of 65 or, at a reduced rate, from the age of 60. 65,274 kr. per annum for married couples, 37,152 kr. for others (including the special increment of 24,768 kr. and 12,384 kr. respectively for those without supplementary pension); about half of them receive municipal housing supplement.
Disability	1914	All citizens	Payable before the age of 65. Full pension 49,536 kr. per annum (including the special increment of 24,768 kr.).
Survivors	1948	All citizens	Widow's pension is payable before the age of 65. The pension is 37,152 kr. (including the special increment of 12,384 kr.) but less for those who have become widows before the age of 50 and have no child below 16. Many of them receive municipal housing supplements. Child pension is payable before the age of 18. The pension amounts to 10,578 kr. (fatherless or motherless) and 15,996 kr. (orphans).
Supplementary pensions (current law, 1962)			
Old-age	1960	All gainfully occupied persons	Payable from the same age as the basic pension (*see above*). The pension is in principle 60% of the insured person's average annual earnings during the best 15 years except an amount corresponding to the basic pension and subject to a ceiling.
Disability	1960	All gainfully occupied persons	Payable before the age of 65. Full pension corresponds in principle to supplementary old-age pension.

Type of scheme	*Intro-duced*	*Scope*	*Principal benefits*
Survivors	1960	All gainfully occupied persons	Payable to widow and children, before the age of 19, of a deceased person as a certain percentage of the deceased's supplementary pension.
Partial pensions (current law, 1979)	1976	All employees between 60–65 years of age	The pension is payable between 60-65 years of age. The insured must have reduced his working time by 5 hours on an average a week and the part-time work must thereafter comprise at least 17 hours per week. Furthermore the insured must have worked during at least 5 of the last 12 months and achieved a right to supplementary pension for 10 years after the age of 45. The partial pension is paid out by 65% of the loss of income in connection with the change-over to part-time work.
Parents benefit	1974	All resident parents in connection with confinement	Parents cash benefit of 60 kr. a day during 360 days until the child reaches 4 years of age. Employed parents entitled to daily parents cash benefit of 90% of the daily income (in between 6,000–193,500 kr. yearly) for 270 days. Maximum daily parents cash benefit 477 kr. and for the last 90 days 60 kr. a day will be paid.
Temporary parents benefit	1974	All resident parents	Temporary parents cash benefit with the same amount as for parents cash benefit for care of each child which is ill during 60 days for the parents together until the child reaches 12 years of age.
Children's allowances	1948	All children below 16	From 1 Jan. 1987 5,820 kr. per annum. An additional allowance is paid out for the third child with one-half of an allowance and 160% of a full allowance for each additional child.
		Children at school 16–18	485 kr. per month during school-courses.

Total social expenditure, including also hygiene, care of the sick and social assistance, amounted to 295,888m. kr. in 1986, representing 32% of the GDP.

The Cost and Financing of the Social Services in Sweden, 1981. Stockholm, 1983

Ministry of Health and Social Affairs, *The Evolution of the Swedish Health Insurance*. Stockholm, 1978

Socialnytt (Official Journal of the National Board of Health and Welfare). Stockholm, from 1968

Social Insurance Statistics. Facts 1986. National Social Insurance Board, Stockholm, 1986

The Swedish Health Services in the 1990s. The National Board of Health and Welfare, Stockholm, 1985

Forsberg, M., *The Evolution of Social Welfare Policy in Sweden*. Stockholm, 1984

Heclo, H., *Modern Social Politics in Britain and Sweden: From Relief to Income Maintenance*. New Haven, 1974

Lagerström, L., *Pension Systems in Sweden*. Stockholm, 1976.—*Social Security in Sweden*. Stockholm, 1976

DIPLOMATIC REPRESENTATIVES

Of Sweden in Great Britain (11 Montagu Pl., London, W1H 2AL)
Ambassador: Leif Leifland, GCVO (accredited on 10 Nov. 1982).

Of Great Britain in Sweden (Skarpögatan 6-8, 115 27 Stockholm)
Ambassador: Sir John Ure, KCMG, LVO.

Of Sweden in the USA (600 New Hampshire Ave., NW, Washington, D.C., 20037)
Ambassador: Anders Thunborg.

Of the USA in Sweden (Strandvägen 101, 115 27 Stockholm)
Ambassador: Charles E. Redman.

Of Sweden to the United Nations
Ambassador: Jan Eliasson.

Further Reading

Statistical Information: Statistics Sweden, (Statistiska, Centralbyrån, S-11581 Stockholm) was founded in 1858, in succession to the Kungl. Tabellkommissionen, which had been set up in 1756. *Director-General:* Sten Johansson. Its Publications include:

Levnadsförhållanden, årsbok (Living Conditions). Annual. From 1975.—*Rapport*. From 1976
Statistisk årsbok för Sverige (Statistical Abstract of Sweden). From 1914
Siffror om Sverige (Sweden). From 1971. Also in English as *Sweden*
Historisk statistik för Sverige (Historical Statistics of Sweden). 1955 ff. (4 vols. to date)
Allmän månadsstatistik (Monthly Digest of Swedish Statistics). From 1963
Statistiska meddelanden (Statistical Reports). From 1963

Andersson, L., *A History of Sweden*. Stockholm, 1962
Atlas över Sverige. Stockholm, 1953–71. [Publ. in separate parts dealing with population, economics, etc.]
Publications on Sweden. Stockholm, 1988
Documents on Swedish Foreign Policy. Stockholm, Annual.
Grosskopf, G., *The Swedish Tax System*. Stockholm, 1986
Gullberg, I. E., *Swedish–English Dictionary of Technical Terms.—Svensk-Engelsk Fackordbok*. Stockholm, 2nd ed. 1977
Hadenius, S., *Swedish Politics during the Twentieth Century*. Stockholm, 1985
Hansson, I., Jonung, L., Myhrman, J. and Söderström, H. T., *Sweden – the Road to Stability*. Stockholm, 1985
Heelo, H. and Madsen, H., *Policy and Politics in Sweden: Principled Pragmatism*. Philadelphia, 1987
Hellberg, T. and Jansson, L. M., *Alfred Nobel*. Stockholm, 1984
Linton, M., *The Swedish Road to Socialism*. London, 1985
Meyerson, P-M., *Eurosclerosis, The Case of Sweden*. Stockholm, 1985
Nordic Council, *Yearbook of Nordic Statistics*. From 1962 (in English and one Nordic Language)
Olivecrona, G., (ed.) *Sweden In Fact*. Stockholm, 1986
Sather, L. B. and Swanson, A., *Sweden*. [Bibliography] Oxford and Santa Barbara, 1987
Scott, F. D., *Sweden: The Nation's History*. Univ. of Minnesota Press, 1983
Söderström, H. T., *Getting Sweden Back to Work*. Stockholm, 1986
Turner, B., *Sweden*. London, 1976
Sveriges statskalender. Published by Vetenskapsakademien. Annual, from 1813

National Library: Kungliga Biblioteket, Stockholm. *Director:* Lars Tynell.

SWITZERLAND

Capital: Bern
Population: 6·6m. (1988)
GNP per capita: US$27,260 (1988)

Schweiz—Suisse—Svizzera

HISTORY. On 1 Aug. 1291 the men of Uri, Schwyz and Unterwalden entered into a defensive league. In 1353 the league included 8 members and in 1513, 13. Various territories were acquired either by single cantons or by several in common, and in 1648 the league became formally independent of the Holy Roman Empire, but no addition was made to the number of cantons till 1798. In that year, under the influence of France, the unified Helvetic Republic was formed. This failed to satisfy the Swiss, and in 1803 Napoleon Bonaparte, in the Act of Mediation, gave a new Constitution, and out of the lands formerly allied or subject increased the number of cantons to 19. In 1815 the perpetual neutrality of Switzerland and the inviolability of her territory were guaranteed by Austria, France, Great Britain, Portugal, Prussia, Russia, Spain and Sweden, and the Federal Pact, which included 3 new cantons, was accepted by the Congress of Vienna. In 1848 a new Constitution was passed. The 22 cantons set up a Federal Government (consisting of a Federal Parliament and a Federal Council) and a Federal Tribunal. This Constitution, in turn, was on 29 May 1874 superseded by the present Constitution. In a national referendum held in Sept. 1978, 69·9% voted in favour of the establishment of a new canton, Jura, which was established on 1 Jan. 1979.

AREA AND POPULATION. Switzerland is bounded west and north-west by France, north by the Federal Republic of Germany, east by Austria and south by Italy. Area and population, according to the census held on 1 Dec. 1980 and estimate 31 Dec. 1988.

Canton	*Area (sq. km)*	*Census 1 Dec. 1980*	*Estimate 31 Dec. 1988*	*Pop. per sq. km 1980*
Zürich (Zurich) (1351)	1,729	1,122,839	1,141,494	650
Bern (Berne) (1553)	6,049	912,022	932,577	151
Luzern (Lucerne) (1332)	1,492	296,159	311,761	198
Uri (1291)	1,076	33,883	33,544	31
Schwyz (1291)	908	97,354	106,409	107
Obwalden (Obwald) (1291)	491	25,865	27,896	53
Nidwalden (Nidwald) (1291)	276	28,617	31,619	104
Glarus (Glaris) (1352)	685	36,718	36,953	54
Zug (Zoug) (1352)	239	75,930	83,419	318
Fribourg (Freiburg) (1481)	1,670	185,246	200,166	111
Solothurn (Soleure) (1481)	791	218,102	221,464	276
Basel-Stadt (Bâle-V.) (1501)	37	203,915	190,854	5,485
Basel-Landschaft (Bâle-C.) (1501)	428	219,822	228,151	513
Schaffhausen (Schaffhouse) (1501)	298	69,413	70,317	233
Appenzell A.-Rh. (Rh.-Ext.) (1513)	243	47,611	50,328	196
Appenzell I.-Rh. (Rh.-Int.) (1513)	172	12,844	13,333	75
St Gallen (St Gall) (1803)	2,014	391,995	410,773	195
Graubünden (Grisons) (1803)	7,106	164,641	167,904	23
Aargau (Argovie) (1803)	1,405	453,442	484,308	323
Thurgau (Thurgovie) (1803)	1,013	183,795	198,371	181
Ticino (Tessin) (1803)	2,811	265,899	280,630	95
Vaud (Waadt) (1803)	3,218	528,747	565,181	164
Valais (Wallis) (1815)	5,226	218,707	239,048	42
Neuchâtel (Neuenburg) (1815)	797	158,368	157,436	199
Genève (Genf) (1815)	282	349,040	371,356	1,237
Jura (1979)	837	64,986	64,681	78
Total	41,293[1]	6,365,960	6,619,973	154

[1] 15,943 sq. miles.

The German language is spoken by the majority of inhabitants in 19 of the 26 cantons above (French names given in brackets), the French in 6 (Fribourg, Vaud, Valais, Neuchâtel, Jura and Genève, for which the German names are given in brackets), the Italian in 1 (Ticino). In 1980, 65% spoke German, 18·4% French, 9·8% Italian, 0·8% Romansch and 6% other languages; counting only Swiss nationals, the percentages were 73·5, 20·1, 4·5, 0·9 and 1. On 8 July 1937 Romansch was made the fourth national language; it is spoken mostly in Graubünden.

At the end of 1988 the 5 largest cities were Zürich (346,800); Basel (171,600); Geneva (161,500); Berne (136,300); Lausanne (124,000). At the end of 1988 the population figures of the '*agglomérations*' or conurbations were as follows: Zürich, 838,700; Basel, 358,500; Geneva, 389,000; Bern, 298,700; Lausanne, 262,900; other towns 1985, (and their conurbations, 1986), were Winterthur, 84,400 (107,812); St Gallen, 73,200 (125,879); Luzern, 60,600 (160,594); Biel, 52,000 (82,544).

The number of foreigners resident in Switzerland in Dec. 1988 was 1,032,714. Of these, in 1985, 186,600 were in Zürich canton, 109,100 in Vaud and 122,900 in Geneva.

Vital statistics for calendar years:

	Live births					
	Total	*Illegitimate*	*Marriages*	*Divorces*	*Still births*	*Deaths*
1985	74,700	4,200	38,800	11,400	340	59,600
1986	76,300	4,300	40,200	11,400	330	60,100
1987	76,500	4,500	43,000	11,600	340	59,500
1988	80,300	...	45,700	12,700	...	60,600

In 1983 there were 91,300 emigrants and 88,000 immigrants; in 1984, 85,000 and 97,000; in 1985, 85,000 and 99,000; in 1986, 85,000 and 107,000; in 1987, 86,300 and 112,700; in 1988, 91,500 and 125,000.

CLIMATE. The climate is largely dictated by relief and altitude and includes continental and mountain types. Summers are generally warm, with quite considerable rainfall; winters are fine, with clear, cold air. Bern. Jan. 32°F (0°C), July, 65°F (18·5°C). Annual rainfall 39·4" (986 mm).

CONSTITUTION AND GOVERNMENT. Switzerland is a republic. The highest authority is vested in the electorate, *i.e.*, all Swiss citizens of over 20. This electorate—besides electing its representatives to the Parliament—has the voting power on amendments to, or on the revision of, the Constitution. It also takes decisions on laws and international treaties if requested by 50,000 voters or 8 cantons (facultative referendum), and it has the right of initiating constitutional amendments, the support required for such demands being 100,000 voters (popular initiative).

The Federal Government is supreme in matters of peace, war and treaties; it regulates the army, the railway, telecommunication systems, the coining of money, the issue and repayment of bank-notes and the weights and measures of the republic. It also legislates on matters of copyright, bankruptcy, patents, sanitary policy in dangerous epidemics, and it may create and subsidize, besides the Polytechnic School at Zürich and at Lausanne, 2 federal universities and other educational institutions. There has also been entrusted to it the authority to decide concerning public works for the whole or great part of Switzerland, such as those relating to rivers, forests and the construction of national highways and railways. By referendum of 13 Nov. 1898 it is also the authority in the entire spheres of common law. In 1957 the Federation was empowered to legislate on atomic energy matters and in 1961 on the construction of pipelines of petroleum and gas.

National flag: Red with a white couped cross.

National anthem: Trittst im Morgenrot daher (words by Leonard Widmer, 1808–68; tune by Alberik Zwyssig, 1808–54); adopted by the Federal Council in 1962.

The legislative authority is vested in a parliament of 2 chambers, a *Ständerat*, or Council of States, and a *Nationalrat*, or National Council.

The *Ständerat* is composed of 46 members, chosen and paid by the 23 cantons of the Confederation, 2 for each canton. The mode of their election and the term of membership depend entirely on the canton. Three of the cantons are politically divided—Basel into Stadt and Land, Appenzell into Ausser-Rhoden and Inner-Rhoden, and Unterwalden into Obwalden and Nidwalden. Each of these 'half-cantons' sends 1 member to the State Council.

The *Nationalrat*—after the referendum taken on 4 Nov. 1962—consists of 200 National Councillors, directly elected for 4 years, in proportion to the population of the cantons, with the proviso that each canton or half-canton is represented by at least 1 member. The members are paid from federal funds at the rate of 150 francs for each day during the session and a nominal sum of 10,000 francs per annum.

In 1987 the 200 members were distributed among the cantons [1] as follows:

Zürich (Zurich)	35	Appenzell—Outer- and Inner-Rhoden	3
Bern (Berne)	29	St Gallen (St Gall)	12
Luzern (Lucerne)	9	Graubünden (Grisons)	5
Uri	1	Aargau (Argovie)	14
Schwyz	3	Thurgau (Thurgovie)	6
Unterwalden–Upper and Lower	2	Ticino (Tessin)	8
Glarus (Glaris)	1	Vaud (Waadt)	17
Zug (Zoug)	2	Valais (Wallis)	7
Fribourg (Freiburg)	6	Neuchâtel (Neuenburg)	5
Solothurn (Soleure)	7	Genève (Genf)	11
Basel (Bâle)—town and country	13	Jura	2
Schaffhausen (Schaffhouse)	2		

[1] The name of the canton is given in German, French or Italian, according to the language most spoken in it, and alternative names are given in brackets.

Composition of the National Council in 1987: Social Democrats, 42; Radicals, 51; Christian-Democratic People's Party, 42; Swiss People's Party, 25; Liberals, 9; Independents, 8; National Campaign/Vigilance, 3; Evangelical Party, 3; Progressive Organizations, 4; Environmentalists, 9; Others, 4.

Council of States (1987): Christian Democrats, 19; Radicals, 14; Social Democrats, 5; Swiss People's Party, 4; Liberals, 3; Independents, 1.

A general election takes place by ballot every 4 years. Every citizen of the republic who has entered on his 20th year is entitled to a vote, and any voter, not a clergyman, may be elected a deputy. Laws passed by both chambers may be submitted to direct popular vote, when 50,000 citizens or 8 cantons demand it; the vote can be only 'Yes' or 'No'. This principle, called the *referendum*, is frequently acted on.

Women's suffrage, although advocated by the Federal Council and the Federal Assembly, was on 1 Feb. 1959 rejected, but in a subsequent referendum, held on 7 Feb. 1971, women's suffrage was carried.

The chief executive authority is deputed to the *Bundesrat*, or Federal Council, consisting of 7 members, elected from 7 different cantons for 4 years by the *Vereinigte Bundesversammlung*, *i.e.*, joint sessions of both chambers. The members of this council must not hold any other office in the Confederation or cantons, nor engage in any calling or business. In the Federal Parliament legislation may be introduced either by a member, or by either House, or by the Federal Council (but not by the people). Every citizen who has a vote for the National Council is eligible for becoming a member of the executive.

The President of the Federal Council (called President of the Confederation) and the Vice-President are the first magistrates of the Confederation. Both are elected by the Federal Assembly for 1 calendar year and are not immediately re-eligible to the same offices. The Vice-President, however, may be, and usually is, elected to succeed the outgoing President.

President of the Confederation. (1990): Arnold Koller.

The 7 members of the Federal Council—each of whom has a salary of 203,000 francs per annum, while the President has 215,000 francs—act as ministers, or chiefs of the 7 administrative departments of the republic. The city of Berne is the seat of the Federal Council and the central administrative authorities.

The Federal Council was composed as follows in 1990:

Foreign Affairs: René Felber.
Interior: Flavio Cotti.
Justice and Police: Arnold Koller.
Military: Kaspar Villiger.
Finance: Otto Stich.
Public Economy: Jean-Pascal Delamuraz.
Transport, Communications and Energy: Adolf Ogi.

Local Government. Each of the cantons and demi-cantons is sovereign, so far as its independence and legislative powers are not restricted by the federal constitution; all cantonal governments, though different in organization (membership varies from 5 to 11, and terms of office from 1 to 5 years), are based on the principle of sovereignty of the people.

In all cantons a body chosen by universal suffrage, usually called *der Grosse Rat*, or *Kantonsrat*, exercises the functions of a parliament. In all the cantonal constitutions, however, except those of the cantons which have a *Landsgemeinde*, the referendum has a place. By this principle, where it is most fully developed, as in Zürich, all laws and concordats, or agreements with other cantons, and the chief matters of finance, as well as all revisions of the Constitution, must be submitted to the popular vote. In Appenzell, Glarus and Unterwalden the people exercise their powers direct in the *Landsgemeinde*, *i.e.*, the assembly in the open air of all male citizens of full age. In all the cantons the *popular initiative* for constitutional affairs, as well as for legislation, has been introduced, except in Lucerne, where the *initiative* exists only for constitutional affairs. In most cantons there are districts (*Amtsbezirke*) consisting of a number of communes grouped together, each district having a Prefect (*Regierungsstatthalter*) representing the cantonal government. In the larger communes, for local affairs, there is an Assembly (legislative) and a Council (executive) with a president, maire or syndic, and not less than 4 other members. In the smaller communes there is a council only, with its proper officials.

DEFENCE. There are fortifications in all entrances to the Alps and on the important passes crossing the Alps and the Jura. Large-scale destructions of bridges, tunnels and defiles are prepared for an emergency.

Army. Switzerland depends for defence upon a *national militia.* Service in this force is compulsory and universal, with few exemptions except for physical disability. Those excused or rejected pay certain taxes in lieu. Liability extends from the 20th to the end of the 50th year for soldiers and of the 55th year for officers. The first 12 years are spent in the first line, called the *Auszug*, or *Élite*, the next 10 in the *Landwehr* and 8 in the *Landsturm*. The unarmed *Hilfsdienst* comprises all other males between 20 and 50 whose services can be made available for non-combatant duties of any description.

The initial training of the Swiss militia soldier is carried out in recruits' schools, and the periods are 118 days for infantry, engineers, artillery, etc. The subsequent trainings, called 'repetition courses', are 20 days annually; but after going through 8 courses further attendance is excused for all under the rank of sergeant. The *Landwehr* men are called up for training courses of 13 days every 2 years, and the *Landsturm* men have to undergo a refresher course of 13 days.

The Army is divided into 3 field corps each of 1 armoured and 2 infantry divisions and support groups, a corps with 3 mountain divisions, and independent redoubt-, fortress- and territorial-brigades. Strength on mobilization (1990): 565,000, and 400,000 reserves.

The administration of the Swiss Army is partly in the hands of the Cantonal authorities, who can promote officers up to the rank of captain. But the Federal Government is concerned with all general questions and makes all the higher appointments.

In peace-time the Swiss Army has no general; only in time of war the Federal Assembly in joint session of both Houses appoints a general.

The Swiss infantry are armed with the Swiss automatic rifle and with machine-guns, bazookas and mortars. The field artillery is armed with a Q.F. shielded 10·5 Bofors and field howitzers of 10·5 cm calibre. The heavy artillery is armed with guns of 10·5 cm and howitzers of 15 cm calibre. Equipment includes 130 Leopard, 150 Centurian and P3-61/-68 tanks and 1,350 M-63/-73/-64 armoured personnel carriers.

Air Force. The Air Force has 3 flying regiments, with about 270 combat aircraft. The fighter squadrons are equipped with Swiss-built F-5E Tiger IIs (7 squadrons), Mirage IIIS supersonic interceptor/ground-attack (2 squadrons), Mirage IIIRS fighter/reconnaissance (1 squadron), and Hunter interceptor/ground-attack (9 squadrons) aircraft. Bloodhound surface-to-air missile batteries are operational.

Training aircraft are Pilatus P-3 and PC-7 Turbo-Trainer and Vampire; there are also communications and transport aircraft and helicopters. The Vampires were being replaced, in 1989, by Hawk trainers. Personnel (1990), 60,000 on mobilization.

INTERNATIONAL RELATIONS

Membership. Switzerland is a member of OECD, EFTA and the Council of Europe. In a referendum in 1986 the electorate voted against joining the UN.

ECONOMY

Budget. Revenue and expenditure of the Confederation, in 1m. francs, for calendar years:

	1983	*1984*	*1985*	*1986*	*1987*	*1988*
Revenue	19,400	20,770	22,200	25,200	24,900	27,200
Expenditure	20,300	21,400	22,900	23,200	23,900	26,000

The public debt, including internal debt, of the Confederation in 1980 amounted to 24,409m. francs; 1981, 24,677m.; 1982, 24,968m.; 1983, 25,249m.; 1984, 27,700m.; 1985, 29,300m.; 1986, 28,200m.; 1987, 27,200m.

Schweizerisches Finanz-Jahrbuch. Bern. Annual. From 1899

Currency. The *franc* of 100 *Rappen* or *centimes* is the monetary unit. On 10 May 1971 there was a revaluation to 0·21759 gramme of fine gold.

The legal gold coins are 20- and 10-franc pieces; cupro-nickel coins are 5, 2, 1 and ½ franc, 20, 10 and 5 centimes; bronze, 2 and 1 centime. Notes are of 1,000, 500, 100, 50, 20, 10 and 5 francs.

On 10 July 1981 the notes in circulation (of francs of nominal value) was as follows: In 1,000 franc notes, 8,685·1m. francs; in 500, 4,201·9m. francs; in 100, 6,687·3m. francs; in 50, 1,058·3m. francs, and in lower denominations 1,195·8m.

In March 1990, £1 = 2·46 *francs*; US$1 = 1·50 *francs*.

Banking. The National Bank, with headquarters divided between Bern and Zürich, opened on 20 June 1907. It has the exclusive right to issue bank-notes. In 1984 the condition of the bank was as follows (in 1m. francs): Gold, 11,904, foreign exchange (currency), 38,800; currency in circulation, 26,500.

On 31 Dec. 1988 there were 1,675 banking institutions with total assets of 915,800m. Swiss francs. They included 29 cantonal banks (179,700m. francs), 5 big banks (483,500m.), 213 regional and saving banks (82,400m.), 1,243 loan and *Raiffeisen* banks (28,100m.), 205 other banks (142,100m.).

On 31 Dec. 1988 the total amount of savings deposits, deposit and investment accounts in Swiss banks was 197,600m. francs.

National Bank: Bulletin mensuel.—Das schweizerische Bankwesen. Yearly. From 1920

Weights and Measures. The metric system of weights and measures was made compulsory by the federal law on 3 July 1875 and since 1 Jan. 1887 only metric units have been legal. By the federal law of 24 June 1909 the international electric units were also adopted.

ENERGY AND NATURAL RESOURCES

Electricity. The total production of energy amounted to 57,519m kwh. in 1988 of which 36,439m. kwh. were generated by hydro-electric plants. Supply 220 volts; 50 Hz.

Gas. The production of gas in 1986 was 54·52m. cu. metres.

Minerals. There are 2 salt-mining districts; that in Bex (Vaud) belongs to the canton, but is worked by a private company, and those at Schweizerhalle, Rheinfelden and Ryburg are worked by a joint-stock company formed by the cantons interested. The output of salt of all kinds in 1982 was 361,964 tonnes.

Agriculture. Of the total area of the country of 4,129,315 hectares, about 1,057,794 hectares (25·6%) are unproductive. Of the productive area of 3,071,521 hectares, 1,051,991 hectares are wooded. The agricultural area, in 1985, totalled 1,076,339 hectares, of which 287,049 hectares arable land, 13,450 hectares vineyards, 7,229 hectares intensive fruit growing and 642,194 hectares permanent meadow and pasture land. In 1985 there were 119,731 farms. The gross value of agricultural products was estimated at 7,243·1m. francs in 1980 and 8,775m. francs in 1986.

Area harvested, 1988 (in 1,000 hectares): Cereals, 186; coarse grains, 92; potatoes, 19; sugar-beet, 15. Production, 1988 (in 1,000 tonnes): Potatoes, 748; sugar-beet, 923; wheat, 553; barley, 299; maize, 237; tobacco, 1.

The fruit production (in 1,000 tonnes) in 1988 was: Apples, 540; pears, 229; plums, 33; cherries, 35; nuts, 6.

Wine is produced in 18 of the cantons. In 1988 Swiss vineyards yielded 117 tonnes of wine.

Livestock (1988): 49,000 horses, 367,000 sheep, 1,837,000 cattle (including about 798,000 milch cows), 1,940,000 pigs, (1985) 6m. poultry.

Forestry. Of the forest area of 999,795 hectares, 56,876 were owned by the Federation or the cantons, 636,069 by communes and 306,850 by private persons or companies in 1982. Production (1987) 4,570 cu. metres of softwood and 1,158 cu. metres of hardwood.

INDUSTRY AND TRADE

Industry. The chief food producing industries, based on Swiss agriculture, are the manufacture of cheese, butter, sugar and meat. The production in 1986 was (in tonnes): Cheese, 130,900; butter, 37,300; sugar, 9,800; meat, 37,600. There are 46 breweries, producing in 1978, 4·05m. hectolitres of beer. Tobacco products in 1986: Cigars, 278m.; cigarettes (1982), 26,497m.

Among the other industries, the manufacture of textiles, wearing apparel and footwear, chemicals and pharmaceutical products, bricks, glass and cement, the manufacture of basic iron and steel and of other metal products, the production of machinery (including electrical machinery and scientific and optical instruments) and watch and clock making are the most important. In 1981 there were 8,738 factories with 693,243 workers. In 1982, 41,200 were working in textile industries, 45,000 in the manufacture of clothing and footwear, 70,200 in chemical works, 194,700 in the construction industry, 168,600 in manufacture of metal products, 252,000 in the manufacture of machinery and 55,300 in watch and clock making and in the manufacture of jewellery.

Production in 1982 was: Woollen and blended yarn, 15,467 tonnes; woollen and blended cloth, 7,534 metres; footwear (1981), 5·87m. pairs; cement, 4,099,874 tonnes; raw aluminium, 75,256 tonnes; chocolate, 76,605 tonnes, 25·38m. watches and clocks were exported (1981).

Labour. In 1988, the total working population was 3,572,300, of which 208,600 were active in agriculture and forestry, 1,230,200 in manufacture and construction and 2,133,600 in services.

The foreign labour force with permit of temporary residence was 788,000 in Aug. 1986. Of the number recorded 284,000 were Italians, 91,000 Spaniards, 83,000 Frenchmen, 71,000 Germans and 29,000 Austrians.

The Swiss Federal Union of Administrative and Public Service Workers had, in 1985, a membership of 123,300. The Federation of Trade Unions had about 443,000 members.

Commerce. The special commerce, excluding gold (bullion and coins) and silver (coins), was (in 1m. Swiss francs) as follows:

	1981	*1982*	*1983*	*1984*	*1985*	*1986*	*1987*	*1988*
Imports	60,094	58,060	61,064	69,024	74,750	73,513	75,171	82,399
Exports	52,822	52,659	53,724	60,654	66,624	67,004	67,477	74,064

The following table, in 1m. francs, shows the distribution of the special trade of Switzerland among the principal countries:

	Imports from				*Exports to*			
Countries	*1985*	*1986*	*1987*	*1988*	*1985*	*1986*	*1987*	*1988*
Federal Rep. of Germany	22,912·7	24,267·1	25,806·0	28,056·0	13,103·2	14,146·2	14,367·8	15,481·3
France	8,344·2	8,423·6	8,109·1	8,745·7	5,552·5	6,065·0	6,166·1	6,935·8
Italy	7,243·0	7,487·4	7,641·9	8,356·5	4,956·4	5,161·3	5,568·0	6,159·7
Netherlands	3,412·6	3,069·9	3,015·9	3,465·3	1,767·4	1,829·8	1,880·0	2,059·0
Belgium–Luxembourg	3,009·4	2,593·1	2,570·4	2,779·8	1,344·5	1,450·8	1,629·4	1,639·5
UK	5,425·2	5,375·0	4,577·8	4,691·4	5,298·9	5,182·1	5,038·5	5,820·0
Denmark	677·6	713·0	787·8	834·2	889·8	904·3	817·7	893·5
Portugal	244·1	271·6	276·0	298·1	377·8	413·2	462·6	535·4
Ireland	354·2	402·9	409·0	361·5	153·1	150·2	118·2	162·0
Spain	1,089·8	944·5	925·6	1,014·8	1,186·4	1,098·7	1,200·2	1,390·2
Greece	135·1	127·4	113·6	114·8	406·0	348·4	347·8	375·2
EEC Total	51,514·0	53,675·5	54,233·0	58,718·1	33,471·7	36,750·0	37,596·2	41,451·7
Austria	2,666·1	2,896·9	2,903·3	3,181·8	2,582·6	2,605·2	2,558·1	2,693·1
Norway	302·5	285·0	360·3	383·9	560·0	586·0	493·4	491·8
Sweden	1,377·2	1,330·6	1,483·4	1,699·0	1,317·3	1,300·2	1,327·8	1,363·4
Finland	418·5	454·0	484·9	536·4	530·0	562·9	573·9	607·9
Iceland	66·9	64·5	81·0	106·0	20·3	19·6	20·3	24·2
EFTA	5,075·4	5,031·0	5,312·7	5,907·2	5,388·0	5,073·8	4,973·5	5,180·4
Gibraltar, Malta	4·1	5·4	10·8	4·6	25·0	24·5	20·8	24·1
German Dem. Republic	133·3	129·4	115·1	131·8	189·8	243·0	352·4	492·0
Poland	134·2	101·3	104·9	104·3	300·2	264·3	261·1	291·5
Czechoslovakia	194·6	163·4	152·1	166·1	310·2	324·4	310·2	355·2
Hungary	351·2	271·1	237·8	234·2	335·1	321·7	318·3	325·2
Yugoslavia	197·7	167·9	163·1	157·3	462·3	512·4	424·2	456·2
Bulgaria	33·4	23·2	18·3	21·1	233·3	279·2	229·5	181·4
Romania	48·9	38·9	29·8	26·0	84·8	52·3	29·0	17·7
USSR	1,196·4	722·0	409·5	300·0	636·5	535·2	710·3	810·8
Turkey	200·1	228·6	201·7	198·3	590·1	667·9	677·6	666·0
Other European countries	23·2	14·4	12·4	11·0	45·1	38·6	44·2	49·7
Europe Total	60,196·3	60,572·1	61,001·3	65,980·2	43,258·5	45,087·3	45,947·4	50,301·9
Egypt	58·2	27·0	21·4	21·1	395·9	291·3	278·6	282·4
Sudan	2·9	1·7	...	6·4	44·9	36·5	...	51·9
Libya	949·1	410·7	409·0	292·5	170·4	117·4	113·8	87·5
Tunisia	21·6	33·5	...	43·9	52·0	50·2	...	38·8
Algeria	417·6	166·3	154·0	92·1	242·3	200·7	125·6	139·4
Morocco	23·6	25·2	...	30·8	90·2	81·1	...	118·7
Côte d'Ivoire	67·3	56·5	...	32·5	46·2	55·3	...	37·6
Guinea	1·8	0·2	...	1·1	11·4	8·2	...	4·6
Ghana	30·3	30·1	...	28·0	21·5	32·8	...	19·9
Nigeria	439·0	147·8	112·7	40·8	344·6	279·7	153·5	248·2
Zaïre	6·2	10·0	...	7·0	38·0	41·2	...	26·5
Angola	6·4	5·6	...	4·0	37·3	23·0	...	14·6
S Africa, Rep. of	171·4	154·3	395·4	800·3	482·9	430·9	404·7	470·6

Countries	Imports from 1985	1986	1987	1988	Exports to 1985	1986	1987	1988
Zambia	5·7	10·6	…	20·2	19·2	8·0	…	12·2
Zimbabwe	34·3	19·4	…	12·9	32·8	37·1	…	21·1
Tanzania	3·9	1·7	…	4·3	26·6	22·9	…	18·8
Kenya	35·0	40·7	…	23·2	35·6	43·7	…	45·9
Other African countries	117·5	101·2	…	97·3	216·4	223·4	…	199·1
Africa Total	2,391·8	1,242·5	1,393·2	1,558·5	2,308·2	1,983·4	1,679·5	1,837·7
Syria	3·1	6·5	…	1·9	95·3	59·1	…	40·5
Lebanon	55·4	93·2	…	105·3	81·4	75·5	…	135·1
Israel	260·3	233·6	235·7	262·7	843·0	749·3	797·7	1,028·0
Iraq	1·2	1·1	…	0·5	256·5	169·0	…	265·9
Kuwait	2·4	1·2	…	1·6	189·1	111·3	…	103·6
Iran	66·7	87·4	77·1	75·4	475·6	420·0	327·5	290·3
Saudi Arabia	307·7	188·7	192·1	288·2	1,410·7	981·6	1,073·5	919·9
UAE	96·3	7·1	40·6	14·0	342·0	224·3	205·2	243·0
Pakistan	46·9	54·0	…	60·1	197·8	259·2	…	234·1
India	173·8	173·3	185·4	197·8	381·4	549·9	354·5	355·2
Thailand	155·7	200·7	…	208·4	248·5	201·8	…	401·5
Malaysia	72·2	54·9	…	64·1	142·2	144·0	…	119·2
Singapore	93·8	87·1	116·0	137·4	457·7	415·6	482·6	582·7
China	218·0	185·3	238·7	297·6	589·1	738·3	613·6	596·7
Hong Kong	802·7	722·1	772·2	873·5	1,086·4	1,305·7	1,392·3	1,730·0
Taiwan	233·7	277·1	…	534·4	265·6	260·7	…	501·6
Korea, Rep. of	227·9	244·7	…	415·4	252·8	280·5	…	410·2
Korea, Dem. People's Rep.	…	…	…	2·1	…	…	…	7·2
Japan	2,960·2	3,418·6	3,448·4	4,117·0	1,122·2	2,171·5	2,573·8	3,184·3
Philippines	41·0	31·7	…	31·2	101·2	104·6	…	115·0
Indonesia	70·2	64·4	…	50·1	155·9	193·6	…	223·3
Other Asian countries	73·6	97·4	…	200·2	543·4	464·6	…	456·3
Asia Total	5,962·8	6,230·1	6,664·4	7,939·0	10,237·8	9,880·1	10,448·4	11,943·5
Canada	274·7	240·9	293·5	305·6	759·8	719·5	633·8	757·4
USA	4,390·9	3,970·1	3,993·6	4,560·7	6,870·8	6,343·0	5,917·5	6,294·4
Mexico	43·6	40·4	38·8	56·1	358·5	341·3	242·8	327·1
Guatemala	47·3	55·3	…	28·8	28·1	17·2	…	21·0
Honduras	50·5	43·6	…	32·1	20·2	15·5	…	25·1
Costa Rica	68·4	63·3	…	46·5	15·2	17·6	…	14·0
Panama	217·8	161·6	258·0	144·5	233·6	176·9	185·8	150·2
Cuba	14·5	14·4	…	13·6	65·8	40·7	…	44·0
Colombia	140·6	145·2	…	87·2	160·9	127·1	…	134·4
Venezuela	17·3	9·2	9·2	13·6	190·0	215·2	181·7	276·2
Brazil	421·9	304·6	291·4	363·5	473·5	557·1	489·3	544·8
Uruguay	24·0	29·3	…	25·9	29·3	27·3	…	24·9
Argentina	132·0	83·5	74·3	102·3	293·1	223·7	242·3	184·9
Chile	18·1	21·2	…	11·2	83·0	95·0	…	100·7
Bolivia	2·5	0·7	…	1·0	9·4	11·9	…	6·0
Peru	35·7	34·8	…	25·6	86·0	126·4	…	75·7
Ecuador	23·5	20·0	…	13·9	68·4	67·4	…	60·7
Other American countries	126·7	89·1	…	958·0	338·5	230·9	…	262·3
Australia and Oceania	149·5	140·6	133·6	130·9	735·1	699·5	689·3	676·9

Custom receipts (in 1,000 francs): 1980, 3,170,700; 1981, 3,243,631; 1982, 3,243,000; 1983, 3,382,000; 1984, 3,393,000; 1985, 3,449,000.

Total trade between Switzerland (including Liechtenstein) and UK for calendar years (British Department of Trade, in £1,000 sterling):

	1985	*1986*	*1987*	*1988*	*1989*
Imports to UK	2,371,090	2,989,112	3,298,009	3,840,643	4,125,731
Exports and re-exports from UK	1,306,757	1,575,247	1,835,851	1,854,918	2,245,354

Federal Customs Office, *Statistique mensuelle du commerce extérieur de la Suisse*. From 1925.—*Statistique annuelle du commerce extérieur de la Suisse*. 2 vols. From 1840. —*Rapport annuel de la statistique du commerce Suisse*. From 1889

Tourism. Tourism is an important industry. In 1988, overnight stays in hotels and sanatoria were 35,239,000 and in other accommodation 39,266,000 (34,496,000 by foreign visitors).

COMMUNICATIONS

Roads. There were (1983) 70,848 km of main roads, including 1,300 km of 'national roads' for motor cars only. Motor vehicles, as at 30 Sept. 1988, numbered 3,345,000, including 2,761,000 private cars, 228,000 trucks, 153,000 motor cycles, 11,000 buses and 192,000 commercial and agricultural vehicles.

Railways. Railway history in Switzerland begins in 1847. In 1986 the length of the general traffic railways was 5,034 km, and of special lines (funiculars etc.), 814 km. The operating receipts of general traffic lines amounted to (1986) 4,504,500,000 francs; operating expenses, 5,074,800,000 francs. Traffic (1987) was 12,494m. passenger-km and 7,184 tonnes-km of goods were carried.

There are many privately-owned lines, the most important of which are the Bern–Lotschberg–Simplon (115 km) and Rhaetian (363 km) networks.

Aviation. In 1985 Swiss aviation on domestic and international routes carried 7,498,000 passengers.

The air transport organization Swissair (founded in 1931) in 1982 carried 189,139 tonnes of freight and 7,168,567 passengers. Swissair had a capital of 422m. francs on 15 May 1977. Its fleet consisted of 53 aircraft in Jan. 1983.

Shipping. A merchant marine was created by a decree of the Swiss Government dated 9 April 1941, the place of registry of its vessels being Basel. In 1985 it consisted of 39 vessels with a total of 225,434 GRT. In 1981, 8,277,359 tonnes of goods were handled in the port of Basel.

Post and Broadcasting. In 1985 there were 3,880 post offices. On 1 Jan. 1988 there were 5,879,200 telephones, all integrated in one dial system.

Wireless communication is furnished by 3 main medium-wave stations and 1 short-wave station. There are 3 television studios and more than 100 transmitters. TV programmes are financed by licence fees and advertisements. Advertisements are limited to 15 minutes each day. All stations are operated by the Federal Post, Telephone and Telegraph (PTT) services. Radio-telegraph circuits are operated by Radio Suisse SA, radio-telephone circuits by the PTT. Radio licences, 1988, 2,590,200; television licences, 2,338,300.

The total expenditure of the PTT in 1985 was 7,812·4m. francs, the total gross receipts 8,098·3m. francs.

Cinemas (1986). There were 428 cinemas with a seating capacity of 122,000.

Newspapers (1988). There were 112 daily newspapers (85 German language, 19 French, 7 Italian and 1 multi-lingual).

JUSTICE, RELIGION, EDUCATION AND WELFARE

Justice. The Federal Tribunal (*Bundes-Gericht*), which sits at Lausanne, consists of 26-28 members, with 11-13 supplementary judges, appointed by the Federal Assembly for 6 years and eligible for re-election; the President and Vice-President serve for 2 years and cannot be re-elected. The President has a salary of 170,000 francs a year, and the other members 158,000 francs. The Tribunal has original and final jurisdiction in suits between the Confederation and cantons; between cantons and cantons; between the Confederation or cantons and corporations or individuals, the value in dispute being not less than 8,000 francs; between parties who refer their case to it, the value in dispute being at least 20,000 francs; in such suits as the constitution or legislation of cantons places within its authority; and in many classes of railway suits. It is a court of appeal against decisions of other federal authorities, and of cantonal authorities applying federal laws. The Tribunal also tries persons accused of treason or other offences against the Confederation. For this purpose it is divided into 4 chambers: Chamber of Accusation, Criminal Chamber (*Cour d'Assises*), Federal Penal Court and Court of Cassation. The jurors who serve in the Assize Courts are elected by the people, and are paid 100 francs a day when serving.

On 3 July 1938 the Swiss electorate accepted a new federal penal code, to take the place of the separate cantonal penal codes. The new code, which abolished capital punishment, came into force on 1 Jan. 1942.

Religion. There is complete and absolute liberty of conscience and of creed. No one is bound to pay taxes specially appropriated to defraying the expenses of a creed to which he does not belong. No bishoprics can be created on Swiss territory without the approbation of the Confederation.

According to the census of 1 Dec. 1980 Roman Catholics numbered 3,030,069 (47·6%) of the population; Protestants, 2,822,266 (44·3%) and others, 513,625 (8·1%). In 1960 Protestants were in a majority in 10 of the cantons and Catholics in 12. Of the more populous cantons, Zürich, Bern, Vaud, Neuchâtel and Basel (town and land) were mainly Protestant, while Luzern, Fribourg, Ticino, Valais and the Forest Cantons are mainly Catholic. The Roman Catholics are under 6 Bishops, viz., of Basel (resident at Solothurn), Chur, St Gallen, Lugano, Lausanne–Geneva–Fribourg (resident at Fribourg) and Sitten (Sion), all of them immediately subject to the Holy See. The Old Catholics have a theological faculty at the university of Bern.

Education. Education is administered by the cantons and is compulsory. Before the year 1848 most of the cantons had organized a system of primary schools, and since that year elementary education has steadily advanced. In 1874 it was made obligatory for the whole country (the school age varying in the different cantons) and placed under the civil authority. In some cantons the cost falls almost entirely on the communes, in others it is divided between the canton and communes. In all the cantons primary instruction is free. In 1988–89 there were 134,804 pupils in nursery schools and 696,516 in primary schools.

In most cantons there are also secondary schools for youths of from 12 to 15, gymnasia, higher schools for girls, teachers' seminaries, commercial and administrative schools, trade schools, art schools, technical schools, schools for the instruction of girls in domestic economy and other subjects, agricultural schools, schools for horticulture, for viticulture, for arboriculture and for dairy management. There are also institutions for the blind, the deaf and dumb and feeble-minded. In 1988–89 there were 308,189 pupils in secondary schools.

There are 7 universities in Switzerland. These universities are organized on the model of those of Germany, governed by a rector and a senate, and divided into faculties (theology, jurisprudence, philosophy, medicine, etc.). In 1988–89 the Federal Institute of Technology at Zürich (founded in 1855) had 11,004 matriculated students; the Federal Institute of Technology at Lausanne, independent of the university since 1946, had 3,431 students; the St Gall School of Economics and Social Sciences, founded in 1899, had 3,845 matriculated students.

University statistics in the winter of 1986–87:

	Theology	*Humanities etc*	*Law*	*Economics*	*Medicine*	*Science*	*Teaching staff (1985–86)*
Basel (1460)	223	1,687	881	848	1,761	1,275	625
Zürich (1523 & 1833)	358	7,463	3,138	2,239	3,354	2,101	1,661
Bern (1528 & 1834)	374	2,696	1,657	848	1,798	1,628	723
Genève (1559[1] & 1873[1])	130	4,578	995	2,411	1,506	1,645	913
Lausanne (1537[1] & 1890[2])	85	1,678	889	1,405	1,503	875	476
Fribourg (1889)	504	1,999	995	1,129	225	506	548
Neuchâtel (1866 & 1909)	52	870	310	444	57	524	240

[1] Founded as an academy. [2] Reorganized as a university.

These numbers are exclusive of 'visitors', but inclusive of women students. In 1988–89 there were 80,629 students attending universities.

Health. In 1988 there were 18,667 doctors, 37,360 (1980) nurses, 4,750 dentists and 12,300 physiotherapists. There were (1988) 435 hospitals and 1,417 pharmacies.

Social Security. The Federal Insurance Law against illness and accident, of 13 June 1911, entitles all Swiss citizens to insurance against illness; foreigners may be admitted to the benefits. Compulsory insurance against illness does not exist as yet, but cantons and communities are entitled to declare insurance obligatory for certain classes or to establish public benefit (sick fund) associations, and to make employers responsible for the payment of the premiums of their employees.

Unemployment insurance is based since 13 June 1976 upon a Constitution amendment which stipulates unemployment insurance as compulsory for all wage-earners.

Insurance against accident is compulsory for all officials, employees and workmen of all the factories, trades, etc., which are under the federal liability law.

On 6 July 1947 a federal law was accepted by a referendum, providing compulsory old age and widows and widowers insurance for the whole population, as from 1 Jan. 1948. In March 1985 the number of normal pensioners was 1,033,000.

DIPLOMATIC REPRESENTATIVES

Of Switzerland in Great Britain (16–18 Montagu Pl., London, W1H 2BQ)
Ambassador: Franz E. Muheim (accredited 14 June 1989).

Of Great Britain in Switzerland (Thunstrasse 50, 3005 Bern)
Ambassador: Christopher Long, CMG.

Of Switzerland in the USA (2900 Cathedral Ave., NW, Washington, D.C., 20008)
Ambassador: Edouard Brunner.

Of the USA in Switzerland (Jubilaeumstrasse 93, 3005, Bern)
Ambassador: Joseph Gildenhorn.

Further Reading

Statistical Information: Bureau fédéral de statistique (Hallwylstr. 15, 3003 Bern) was established in 1860. *Director:* Carlo Malaguerra. Its principal publications are:

Annuaire statistique de la Suisse. Bâle. From 1891
Bibliographie Suisse de statistique et d'économie politique. Annual, from 1937
Reflêts de l'économie (monthly)

Swiss Confederation
Annuaire; Budget; Message du Budget; Compte d'Etat (annual) *Feuille Fédérale; Recueil des Lois fédérales* (weekly)
Recueil systématique des lois et ordonnances, 1848–1947 (in German, French and Italian). Bern, 1951
Sammlung der Bundes- und Kantonsverfassungen (in German, French and Italian). Bern, 1937

Federal Department of Economics
La vie économique (and supplements). Monthly. From 1928
Legislation sociale de la Suisse. Annual, from 1928

Schwarz, U., *The Eye of the Hurricane: Switzerland in World War Two*. Boulder, 1980
Wildblood, R., *What makes Switzerland tick?* London, 1988

National Library: Bibliothèque Nationale Suisse, Hallwylstr.15, 3003, Bern. *Director:* Dr Jean Frédéric Janslin.

SYRIA

Capital: Damascus
Population: 11·3m. (1988)
GNP per capita: US$1,670 (1988)

al-Jumhuriya al-Arabya as-Suriya

HISTORY. For the history of Syria from 1920 to 1946 *see* THE STATESMAN'S YEAR-BOOK , 1957, pp. 1408 f. Complete independence was achieved on 12 Apr. 1946. Syria merged with Egypt to form the United Arab Republic from 2 Feb. 1958 until 29 Sept. 1961, when independence was resumed following a *coup* the previous day. Lieut.-Gen. Hafez al-Assad became Prime Minister following the fifth *coup* of that decade on 13 Nov. 1970, and assumed the Presidency on 22 Feb. 1971.

AREA AND POPULATION. Syria is bounded by the Mediterranean and Lebanon on the west, by Israel and Jordan on the south, by Iraq on the east and by Turkey on the north. The frontier between Syria and Turkey (Nisibim-Jeziret ibn Omar) was settled by the Franco-Turkish agreement of 22 June 1929.

The area of Syria is 185,180 sq. km (71,498 sq. miles), of which 35,000 sq. km have been surveyed. The census of 1981 gave a total population of 9,046,144 (47% urban). Estimate (1988) 11,338,000. of whom 50% were urban. There were 282,673 registered Palestinian refugees in 1987

The areas and populations (1981 Census) of the 14 *mohafaza* (districts) are:

	Sq. km	*1981 Census*		*Sq. km*	*1981 Census*
City of Damascus	105	1,112,214	Idlib	6,097	579,581
Dimashq (Damascus)	18,032	917,364	Hasakah	23,334	669,887
Aleppo	18,500	1,878,701	Raqqah	19,616	348,383
Homs	42,223	812,517	Suwaydá	5,550	199,114
Hama	8,883	736,412	Dará	3,730	362,969
Lattakia	2,297	554,384	Tartous	1,892	443,290
Dayr az-Zawr	33,060	409,130	Qunaytirah	1,861	26,258

Principal towns (census 1981), Damascus, 1,251,028; Aleppo, 976,727; Homs, 354,508; Lattakia, 196,791; Hama, 176,640.

Vital statistics, 1987: Births, 421,328; deaths, 43,571; marriages, 102,626; divorces, 7,249.

Arabic is the official language, spoken by 89% of the population, while 6% speak Kurdish (chiefly Hasakah governorate), 3% Armenian and 2% other languages.

CLIMATE. The climate is Mediterranean in type, with mild wet winters and dry, hot summers, though there are variations in temperatures and rainfall between the coastal regions and the interior, which even includes desert conditions. The more mountainous parts are subject to snowfall. Damascus. Jan. 45°F (7°C), July 81°F (27°C). Annual rainfall 9" (225 mm). Aleppo. Jan. 43°F (6·1°C), July 83°F (28·3°C). Annual rainfall 16" (401 mm). Homs. Jan. 45°F (7·2°C), July 83°F (28·3°C). Annual rainfall 12" (300 mm).

CONSTITUTION AND GOVERNMENT. A new Constitution was approved by plebiscite on 12 March 1973 and promulgated on 14 March. It confirmed the Arab Socialist Renaissance *(Ba'ath)* Party, in power since 1963, as the 'leading party in the State and society'. Legislative power is held by a 195-member People's Council, elected for a 4-year term. At the elections on 10 Nov. 1981, all seats were won by the National Progressive Front, a coalition of the Ba'ath Party and 4 smaller ones.

President: Lieut.-Gen. Hafez al-Assad (re-elected for further 7-year terms in 1978 and 1985).

First Vice-President: Abdul Halim Khaddam *(Political and Foreign Affairs). Second Vice-President:* Rifaat al-Assad *(Defence and Security). Third Vice-President:* Mohammed Zuhair Mashrqa *(Party Affairs).*

Prime Minister: Mahmoud Zubi.

Deputy Prime Ministers: Gen. Mustafa Tlass *(Defence)*; Salim Yassin *(Economic Affairs)*; Mahmud Qaddur *(Public Affairs). Education:* Ghassan Halabi. *Higher Education:* Kamal Sharaf. *Interior:* Mohammad Harbah. *Transport:* Yusuf al-Ahmed. *Information:* Mohammad Salman. *Local Administration:* Ahmed Diab. *Supply and Internal Trade:* Hassan Saqqa. *Economy and Foreign Trade:* Mohammad al-Imadi. *Culture:* Najah al-Attar. *Foreign Affairs:* Farooq ash-Shar'. *Tourism:* Adnan Quli. *Health:* Iyad al-Shatti. *Waqfs (Religious Endowments):* Abdel-Majid Tarabulsi. *Irrigation:* Abd ar-Rahman Madani. *Electricity:* Kamil al-Baba. *Oil and Mineral Resources:* Antonios Habib. *Construction:* Marwan Farra. *Housing and Utilities:* Mohammad Nur Antabi. *Agriculture and Agrarian Reform:* Mohammad Ghabbash. *Finance:* Khaled al-Mahayni. *Industry:* Antoine Jubran. *Communications:* Murad Quwatli. *Justice:* Khalid Ansari. *Presidential Affairs:* Wahib Fadil. *Labour and Social Affairs:* Haydar Buzu.

There are 7 Ministers of State.

National flag: Three horizontal stripes of red, white, black, with 2 green stars on the white stripe.

Local Government: Syria is administratively divided into 14 districts *(Mohafaza)*, including the Governorate of Damascus City: At 31 Dec. 1987 the other 13 were divided into 59 *Mantika*, which were further divided into 179 smaller administrative units *(Nahia)*, each covering a number of villages.

DEFENCE. Military service is compulsory for a period of 30 months.

Army. The Army is organized into 5 armoured and 3 mechanized divisions, 1 special forces division, 7 independent special forces regiments, 2 artillery, 3 surface-to-surface missile brigades and 3 coastal defence brigades. Strength (1989) about 300,000 (including 130,000 conscripts) and reserves 50,000. There are a further 25,000 men in paramilitary forces. Equipment includes 2,100 T-54/-55, 1,000 T-62 and 950 T-72/-72M main battle tanks.

Navy. The Navy includes 3 *ex*-Soviet 'Romeo'-class diesel submarines, 2 small frigates, 12 fast missile craft, 3 minesweepers, 6 inshore minesweepers, 6 inshore patrol craft and 3 medium landing ships (all *ex*-Soviet). A small naval aviation branch operates 17 Soviet type ASW helicopters. Personnel in 1989 totalled 4,000, and the main base is at Tartus, which also provides facilities for the Soviet Mediterranean Squadron.

Air Force. The Air Force, including Air Defence Command, was believed (1990) to have about 40,000 personnel and over 500 first-line jet combat aircraft, made up of about 200 MiG-21, 80 MiG-23 and 30 MiG-25 supersonic interceptors, 60 MiG-23, 40 Su-7, 60 Su-22 and 50 MiG-17 fighter-bombers, plus some MiG-25 reconnaissance aircraft. Sixty MiG-29 interceptors are being delivered by the USSR. Training units have Spanish-built Flamingo piston-engined primary trainers and Czechoslovakian L-29 Delfin and L-39 jet basic trainers. There are also transport units with Il-76, An-12, An-24/26, Il-14 and other types, and helicopter units with Soviet-built Mi-6s, Mi-8s, Mi-14s and Mi-24 gunships, and French-built Gazelles. 'Guideline', 'Goa', 'Gainful' and 'Gaskin' surface-to-air missiles are widely deployed in Syria by Air Defence Command, and 'Gammon' long-range surface-to-air missiles in Lebanon.

INTERNATIONAL RELATIONS

Membership. Syria is a member of UN and the Arab League.

ECONOMY

Budget. The ordinary budget for the calendar year 1988 balanced at £Syr.51,545m.

Currency. The monetary unit is the Syrian *pound*, divided into 100 *piastres*. In March 1990, £1 = £Syr.34·53; US$1 = £Syr.20·96.

Banking. The Central Bank has the sole right of issuing currency. Other banks were nationalized in March 1963. Number of branches, 1 Jan. 1987: Central Bank of Syria,10; Commercial Bank of Syria, 35; Industrial Bank, 11; Agricultural Co-operative Bank, 64; Real Estate Bank, 13; Popular Credit Bank, 44. Total deposits at specialized banks, 1987 (in £Syr.1m.): Commercial Bank of Syria, 23,403·3; Industrial Bank, 1,369; Agricultural Co-operative Bank, 1,882; Real Estate Bank, 5,810·1; Popular Credit Bank, 4,298·7.

Weights and Measures. A decree dated 22 Aug. 1935 makes the use of the metric system legal and obligatory throughout the whole of the country. In outlying districts the former weights and measures may still be in use. They are: 1 *okiya* = 0·47 lb.; 6 *okiyas* = 1 *oke* = 2·82 lb.; 2 *okes* = 1 *rottol* = 5·64 lb.; 200 *okes* = 1 *kantar*.

ENERGY AND NATURAL RESOURCES

Electricity. Production (1987) 7,161m. kwh.

Oil. A branch of the Iraq Petroleum Co.'s oil pipeline from Kirkuk crosses Syria between Makaleb in the east and Nahr el Kebir valley in the west. The Iraq Petroleum Co. has constructed a new pipeline from Kirkuk to the small fishing port of Banias (south of Lattakia), which came into use in April 1952; the Trans-Arabian Pipeline Co.'s line to Sidon crosses southern Syria. Crude oil production (1989) 16m. tonnes. Reserves (1983) 1,521m. bbls.

Gas. Gas reserves (1982) 700,000m. cubic ft. Production (1983) 75·86m. cu. metres.

Water. In 1987 there were 3 main dams, at Al-Rastan (storage capacity 250m. cu. metres), Mouhardeh (50m. cu. metres) and Taldo (15m. cu. metres), and 29 surface dams. Production of drinking water, 1987, 486,207,000 cu. metres.

Minerals. Phosphate deposits have been discovered at two places near al-Shargiya and at Khneifis. Production, 1987, 1,985,000 tonnes; other minerals were salt, 81,000 tonnes and gypsum 248,000 tonnes. There are indications of lead, copper, antimony, nickel, chrome and other minerals widely distributed. Sodium chloride and bitumen deposits are being worked.

Agriculture. In 1987, 129,000 hectares were under cotton, 1,183,000 hectares under wheat and 1,570,000 hectares under barley. The cultivable area in 1987 was 6,133,000 hectares, and there were 534,000 hectares of forest and 8,277,000 hectares of steppe and pasture. In 1987 there were 52,400 tractors.

Production of principal crops, 1988 (in 1,000 tonnes): Wheat, 2,067; barley, 2,836; maize, 105; seed cotton, 446; olives, 439; lentils, 171; millet, 6; sugar-beet, 368; potatoes, 353; tomatoes, 517; grapes, 515.

Production, of animal products 1987 (in tonnes): Milk, 1,108,000; butter, 2,924; cheese, 62,181; chicken meat, 64,250; wool, 13,284; hair, 688; honey, 590; silk cocoons, 84; 1,283m. eggs.

Livestock (1988): Cattle, 723,000; horses, 43,000; mules, 30,000; asses, 200,000; sheep, 13,304,000; goats, 1,078,000; poultry, 12m.

Forestry. In 1987 the artificial forestry area was 25,586 hectares, producing 30,406,000 woody plants, 1,509 tonnes of charcoal, 57,660 tonnes of firewood and 26,900 tonnes of industrial wood.

Fisheries. The total catch in 1986 was 4,800 tonnes.

INDUSTRY AND TRADE

Industry. Public sector industrial production in 1987 included (in tonnes): Cotton yarn, 39,340; cotton and mixed textiles, 21,441; mixed woollen yarn, 1,817; manufactured tobacco, 19,143; cement, 3,870; iron bars, 32,186; asbestos, 21,684;

vegetable oil, 22,801; 55,025 electrical engines; 20,889 refrigerators; 70,000 water meters; 1,198 tractors; wollen carpets, 595,000 sq. metres. In 1987, 137,941 people were employed in the industrial public sector..

Trade Unions. In 1987 there were 198 trade unions with 312,003 members.

Labour. In 1984 the labour force was 2,356,000 (out of a total population of 9,616,000), of whom 2,246,000 were employed (1,329,000 urban).

Commerce. Trade in calendar years in £Syr.1m. was as follows:

	1984	*1985*	*1986*	*1987*
Imports	16,154	15,570	10,709	27,915
Exports	7,275	6,427	5,199	15,192

Main imports, 1987 (in £Syr.1,000) included: Petroleum and products, 5,343,278; wheat, 730,764; iron tubes and pipes (not cast iron), 706,174; refined sugar, 637,898; yarn of continuous synthetic fibres, 549,272; direct current generators, 531,584; special purpose motor lorries, trucks and vans, 511,372. Main exports included: Petroleum and products, 7,871,220; raw cotton, 877,224; printed woven cotton fabrics, 577,433.

In 1987, imports (in £Syr.1,000) came mainly from France, 2,737,676; USSR, 2,317,606, Iran, 2,294,879; Federal Republic of Germany, 2,284,403; Italy, 1,883,869; Libya, 1,575,212; USA, 1,470,980. Exports went mainly to Italy, 4,718,628; USSR, 3,165,821; France, 1,507,082; Romania, 1,311,369.

Total trade between Syria and UK (British Department of Trade returns, in £1,000 sterling):

	1985	*1986*	*1987*	*1988*	*1989*
Imports to UK	78,575	31,298	24,937	36,100	55,258
Exports and re-exports from UK	80,901	55,511	34,053	24,647	38,537

Tourism. In 1987, there were 1,217,564 visitors.

COMMUNICATIONS

Roads. In 1987 there were 22,538 km of asphalted roads, 6,018 km of paved non-asphalted road and 1,652 km of earth roads. The first-class roads are capable of carrying all types of modern motor transport and are usable all the year round, while the second-class roads are usable during the dry season only, *i.e.*, for about 9 months. In 1987 there were 314,729 motor vehicles, including 112,595 cars and taxis, 4,646 buses, 8,010 micro buses, 41,758 goods vehicles and 67,139 motor-cycles.

Railways. Network totals 1,686 km of 1,435 mm gauge (Syrian Railways) and 246 km of 1,050 mm gauge (Hedjaz-Syrian Railway). In 1987 the Syrian Railways network carried 4,052,000 passengers and 5,639,000 tonnes of freight.

Aviation. In 1987, 10,079 aircraft arrived at Damascus, Aleppo, Al-Kamishli, Lattakia and Deir Ez-zor airports; 595,335 passengers arrived, 624,149 departed and 99,858 were in transit; 2,281,719 kg of freight was unloaded and 3,280,192 kg loaded.

Shipping. The amount of cargo discharged in 1980 was 2·6m. tons and the amount loaded 430,000 tons.

Post and Broadcasting. Number of telephones (1987), 495,629; of these, 179,808 were in Damascus and 79,903 in Aleppo. There were 2m. radio sets in 1985 and 400,000 television receivers.

Cinemas. In 1985 there were 85 cinemas with 47,840 seats.

Newspapers. There were (1984) 3 national daily newspapers in Damascus; other dailies and periodicals appear in Hama, Homs, Aleppo and Lattakia.

JUSTICE, RELIGION, EDUCATION AND WELFARE

Justice. Syrian law is based on both Islamic and French jurisprudence. There are 2 courts of first instance in each district, one for civil and 1 for criminal cases. There is also a Summary Court in each sub-district, under Justices of the Peace. There is a Court of Appeal in the capital of each governorate, with a Court of Cassation in Damascus.

Religion. The population is composed 90% of Sunni Moslems and there are also Shiites and Ismailis. There are also Druzes and Alawites. Christians include Greek Orthodox, Greek Catholics, Armenian Orthodox, Syrian Orthodox, Armenian Catholics, Protestants, Maronites, Syrian Catholics, Latins, Nestorians and Assyrians. There are also Jews and Yezides.

Education. The Syrian University was founded in 1924, although the faculties of law and of medicine had existed previously. In 1986-87 there were 4 universities with 138,743 students.

In 1986-87 there were 766 kindergartens with 70,859 children; 9,315 primary schools with 85,583 teachers and 2,158,594 pupils; 1,922 intermediate and secondary schools with 37,541 teachers and 855,453 pupils. In 1987, 21 teachers' colleges had 1,167 teachers and 10,076 students; 143 schools for professional education had 7,245 teachers and 56,664 students.

Health. In 1987 there were 12,606 hospital beds (1 per 870 persons) in 206 hospitals, and 566 health centres; there were also 8,146 doctors, 2,456 dentists, 2,960 pharmacists, 3,049 midwives and 9,786 nursing personnel.

DIPLOMATIC REPRESENTATIVES

Of Syria in the USA (2215 Wyoming Ave., NW, Washington, D.C., 20008)
Chargé d'Affaires: Bushra Kanafani.

Of the USA in Syria (Abu Rumaneh, Al Mansur St., Damascus)
Ambassador: Edward P. Djerejian.

Of Syria to the United Nations
Ambassador: Ahmad Fathi Al-Masri.

Diplomatic relations with Syria were broken off by the UK on 31 Oct. 1986.

Further Reading

Statistical Information: There is a Central Statistics Bureau affiliated to the Council of Ministers, Damascus. It publishes a monthly summary and an annual Statistical Abstract (in Arabic and English).

Abd-Allah, U. F., *The Islamic Struggle in Syria.* Berkeley, 1983
Barthélemy, A., *Dictionnaire arabe-français. Dialectes de Syrie.* 4 vols. Paris, 1935–50
Devlin, J. F., *Syria: Modern State in an Ancient Land.* Boulder, 1983
Maoz, M. and Yaniv, A., *Syria under Assad.* New York, 1986
Seale, P., *The Struggle for Syria.* London, 1986.—*Asad of Syria: The Struggle for the Middle East.* London, 1989
Seccombe, I. J., *Syria.* [Bibliography] Oxford and Santa Barbara, 1987

TANZANIA

Capital: Dodoma
Population: 23·2m. (1987)
GNP per capita: US$160 (1988)

Jamhuri ya Muungano wa Tanzania

HISTORY. German East Africa was occupied by German colonialists from 1884 and placed under the protection of the German Empire in 1891. It was conquered in the First World War and subsequently divided between the British and Belgians. The latter received the territories of Ruanda and Urundi and the British the remainder, except for the Kionga triangle, which went to Portugal. The country was administered as a League of Nations mandate until 1946 and then as a UN trusteeship territory until 9 Dec. 1961.

Tanganyika achieved responsible government in Sept. 1960 and full self-government on 1 May 1961. On 9 Dec. 1961 Tanganyika became a sovereign independent member state of the Commonwealth of Nations. It adopted a republican form of government on 9 Dec. 1962. For history from the end of the 17th century until 1884 *see* THE STATESMAN'S YEAR-BOOK 1982–83, p. 1170.

On 24 June 1963 Zanzibar became an internal self-governing state and on 9 Dec. 1963 she became independent. On 24 June 1963 the Legislative Council was replaced by a National Assembly.

On 12 Jan. 1964 the sultanate was overthrown and the sultan sent into exile by a revolt of the Afro-Shirazi Party leaders who established the People's Republic of Zanzibar.

On 26 April 1964 Tanganyika, Zanzibar and Pemba combined to form the United Republic of Tanganyika and Zanzibar (named Tanzania on 29 Oct.).

AREA AND POPULATION. Tanzania is bounded north-east by Kenya, north by Lake Victoria and Uganda, north-west by Rwanda and Burundi, west by Lake Tanganyika, south-west by Zambia and Malaŵi and south by Mozambique. Total area 945,037 sq. km (364,881 sq. miles including the offshore islands of Zanzibar (1,660 sq. km) and Pemba (984 sq. km) and inland water surfaces (59,050 sq. km)). The census of Aug. 1978 gave 17,551,925 for the United Republic, of which 17,076,270 were counted in mainland Tanzania and 475,655 in Zanzibar and Pemba. Estimate (1987) 23·2m.

The chief towns (1978 census populations) are Dar es Salaam, the chief port and former capital (757,346), Zanzibar Town (110,669), Mwanza (110,611), Dodoma, the capital (45,703), Tanga (103,409), Arusha (55,281), Mbeya (76,606), Morogoro (61,890), Mtwara (48,510), Tabora (67,392), Iringa (57,182), and Kigoma (50,044).

The United Republic is divided into 25 administrative regions of which 20 are in mainland Tanzania, 3 in Zanzibar and 2 in Pemba. The 1985 estimated population of the islands was 571,000, of which 45% (256,950) were in Pemba and 55% (314,050) in Zanzibar.

The estimated populations of the 20 mainland regions were as follows in 1985:

Region	Population	Region	Population	Region	Population
Arusha	1,183,000	Lindi	604,000	Rukwa	603,000
Dar es Salaam	1,394,000	Mara	862,000	Ruvuma	691,000
Dodoma	1,171,000	Mbeya	1,335,000	Shinyanga	1,662,000
Iringa	1,100,000	Morogoro	1,134,000	Singida	730,000
Kagera	1,298,000	Mtwara	878,000	Tabora	1,089,000
Kigoma	782,000	Mwanza	1,736,000	Tanga	1,236,000
Kilimanjaro	1,093,000	Pwani	578,000		

Kiswahili is the national language and English is the official language.

CLIMATE. The climate is very varied and is controlled very largely by altitude and distance from the sea. There are three climatic zones: the hot and humid coast, the drier central plateau with seasonal variations of temperature, and the semi-temperate mountains. Dodoma. Jan. 75°F (23·9°C), July 67°F (19·4°C). Annual rainfall 23" (572 mm). Dar es Salaam. Jan. 82°F (27·8°C), July 74°F (23·3°C). Annual rainfall 43" (1,064 mm).

CONSTITUTION AND GOVERNMENT. A permanent Constitution was approved in April 1977. The country is a one-party state. The Tanganyika African National Union and the Afro-Shirazi Party in Zanzibar merged into one revolutionary party, *Chama cha Mapinduzi,* in Feb. 1977.

The President of the United Republic is head of state, chairman of the party and commander-in-chief of the armed forces. The second vice-president is head of the executive in Zanzibar.The Prime Minister and first vice-president is also the leader of government business in the National Assembly.

According to the Constitution of 1977, as amended in Oct. 1984, the National Assembly is composed of a total of 244 members: 169 Members of Parliament elected from the Constituencies (119 from the mainland and 50 from Zanzibar); 15 National Members elected by the National Assembly; 15 women members elected by the National Assembly, 5 from Zanzibar; 5 members elected by the House of Representatives in Zanzibar; 25 ex-officio Members (20 Regional Commissioners from the mainland and 5 from Zanzibar) and 15 Nominated Members (by the President), 5 from Zanzibar.

In Dec. 1979 a separate Constitution for Zanzibar was approved. Although at present (1981) under the same Constitution as Tanzania, Zanzibar has, in fact, been ruled by decree since 1964.

The Government was in Nov. 1989 composed as follows:

President of the United Republic: Ndugu Ali Hassan Mwinyi (sworn in 5 Nov. 1985 for 5-year term).

Prime Minister and First Vice President: Joseph S. Warioba.

President of Zanzibar and Second Vice President: Idris A. Wakil. *Without Portfolio:* Rashidi Kawawa, Getrude Mongella. *Deputy Prime Minister, Defence and National Service:* Salim Ahmed Salim. *Finance, Economic Affairs and Planning:* Cleopa D. Msuya *Foreign Affairs:* Benjamin Mkapa. *Agriculture and Livestock Development:* Jackson Makwetta. *Local Government, Co-operatives and Marketing:* Paul Bomani. *Communications and Works:* Mustafa Nyang'anyi. *Labour and Manpower Development:* Christian Kisanji. *Home Affairs:* Muhiddin Kimario. *Education:* Kighoma Malima. *Mineral Resources and Energy:* Al Noor Kassum. *Lands, Natural Resources and Tourism:* Arcado Ntagazwa. *Industries and Trade:* Joseph Rwegasira. *Health and Social Welfare:* Dr Aaron Chiduo. *Attorney General and Justice:* Damian Lubuva. *Water:* Dr Pius Ng'wandu. *Community Development, Culture, Youth and Sports:* Fatma Saidi Ali. There are 7 Ministers of State and 10 Deputy Ministers.

National flag: Divided diagonally green, black, blue, with the black strip edged in yellow.

DEFENCE

Army. The Army consists of 8 infantry, 1 tank brigade; 2 artillery, 2 anti-aircraft, 2 mortar, 1 surface-to-air missile, 2 anti-tank and 2 signals battalions. Equipment includes 30 Chinese Type-59 main battle tanks. Strength (1990) 45,000. There is also a Citizen's Militia of 100,000 men.

Navy. There are 4 *ex*-Chinese torpedo-armed hydrofoils and 10 inshore patrol craft of mixed Chinese and North Korean origins. 4 further British-built inshore patrol craft are based permanently in Zanzibar and 4 armed patrol boats on Lake Victoria Nyanza. Personnel in 1989 totalled some 700.

Air Force. The Tanzanian People's Defence Force Air Wing was built up initially with the help of Canada, but combat equipment has been acquired from China. Personnel totalled about 1,000 in 1990, with about 10 F-7 (MiG-21), 10 F-6 (MiG-19) and 8 F-4 (MiG-17) jet fighters; 1 F28 Fellowship VIP transport; 5 Buffalo twin-engined STOL transports; 4 HS 748 turboprop transports; 2 Cessna 404 and 6 Cessna 310 liaison aircraft; 4 Agusta-Bell AB.205 transport helicopters, and 2 JetRanger and 2 Bell 47G light helicopters; and Piper Cherokee and FT-2 (Chinese-built MiG-15 UTI) trainers.

INTERNATIONAL RELATIONS

Membership. Tanzania is a member of UN, OAU, the Commonwealth, Non-Aligned Movement and is an ACP state of EEC.

ECONOMY

Budget. In 1988–89 revenue US$627m., capital expenditure US$284m. and recurrent expenditure US$903m.

Currency. The monetary unit is the *Tanzanian shilling* divided into 100 *cents*. The Tanzanian coinage has denominations of 5, 10, 20, 50 cents, 1 Sh., 5 Sh., 20 Sh. and 1,500 Sh.; notes, 10 Sh., 20 Sh., 50 Sh., 100 Sh. and 200 Sh. In March 1990, £1 = Sh. 317·60; US$ = Sh. 193·78.

Banking. On 14 June 1966 the central bank called the Bank of Tanzania, with a government-owned capital of Sh. 20m., began operations.

On 6 Feb. 1967 all commercial banks with the exception of National Co-operative Banks were nationalized and their interests vested in the National Bank of Commerce on the mainland and the Peoples' Bank in Zanzibar.

Weights. The metric system is in force.

ENERGY AND NATURAL RESOURCES

Electricity. Production (1986) 830m. kwh. Supply 230 volts; 50 Hz.

Minerals. Production (1986): Diamonds, 38,000 grammes; gold, 46,900 grammes; salt, 15,300 tonnes. Large deposits of coal and tin exist but mining is on a small scale. Exploration is going on to establish economic deposits of copper, cobalt and nickel, and feasibility studies to exploit iron ore deposits in south-western Tanzania.

Agriculture. Production of main agricultural crops in 1988 (in 1,000 tonnes) was: Sisal, 28; seed cotton, 245; sugar-cane, 1,190; coffee, 51; tobacco, 13; maize, 2,339; wheat, 79; cashew nuts, 25; citrus, 33. Production of sisal has been declining since 1967. The Tanganyika Sisal Corporation has embarked on a diversification programme by introducing various new crops. Crops already planned are cardamom, beans, cashew nuts, citrus, cocoa, coconuts, cotton, maize and timber. Cattle ranching, dairying and twine spinning have also been introduced.

Zanzibar used to provide the greater part of the world's supply of cloves, but in 1989 only contributed 10% of world production.

A 10-year programme to rehabilitate the coconut industry started in 1980. By 1985 over 23m. trees were under plantation on the mainland and Zanzibar. Chillies, cocoa, limes, other tropical fruits and coil tobacco are also cultivated. The chief food crops are rice, bananas, cassava, pulses, maize and sorghum.

Livestock (1988, including Zanzibar): 13·5m. cattle, 4·7m. sheep, 6·6m. goats, 30m. poultry.

Forestry. Total forested land 43m. hectares (48% of the land area). Total production (1983) 114,900 cu. metres.

Fisheries. A Fisheries Development Co. is catching sardines and tuna for export. Catch (1986) 309,900 tonnes of which, inland waters, 265,800 tonnes.

INDUSTRY AND TRADE

Industry. Industry is limited and is mainly textiles, petroleum and chemical products, food processing, tobacco, brewing and paper manufacturing.

Commerce. Total trade (in Sh. 1m.):

	1982	*1983*	*1984*	*1985*	*1986*	*1987*
Imports	7,781	8,877	11,953	17,962	30,270	57,971
Exports	4,117	4,138	5,661	5,937	10,963	18,512

Imports and exports (in Tanzanian Sh. 1m.), by country, 1987:

Country	*Imports*	*Exports*	*Country*	*Imports*	*Exports*
Bahrain	1,279·6	23·0	India	1,181·3	1,119·7
Belgium	1,056·0	359·6	Italy	5,195·9	609·8
China	557·4	18·8	Japan	6,533·9	726·1
Denmark	2,813·6	15·5	Netherlands	2,842·2	1,426·5
Federal Republic of Germany	7,217·9	2,267·1	Singapore	444·3	590·5
			Thailand	3·8	119·3

Major export items 1987 (in Sh. 1m.): Coffee, 5,792·6; cotton, 2,831·8; sisal, 321·7; cloves, 264·7; tea, 825·4; tobacco, 864·2; cashew nuts, 439; diamonds, 576·9.

Total trade between Tanzania and UK (British Department of Trade returns, in £1,000 sterling):

	1986	*1987*	*1988*	*1989*
Imports to UK	40,268	26,400	26,386	22,641
Exports and re-exports from UK	62,869	91,874	88,686	93,036

Tourism. In 1987 about 103,000 visitors.

COMMUNICATIONS

Roads. In 1988 there were 82,000 km of roads and (1983) 43,248 cars and 12,579 licensed commercial vehicles of which 11,290 were trucks and 1,289 buses.

Railways. On 23 Sept. 1977 the independent Tanzanian Railway Corporation was formed following the break-up of the East African Railways administration. The network totals 2,600 km (metre-gauge), excluding the Tan-Zam Railway 969 km in Tanzania (1,067 mm gauge) operated by a separate administration. In 1986, the state railway carried 3m. passengers and 989,000 tonnes of freight while the Tan-Zam Railway carried 1m. tonnes of freight and 1·2m. passengers.

Aviation. There are 53 aerodromes and landing strips maintained or licensed by Government; of these, 2 are of international standards category (Dar es Salaam and Kilimanjaro) and 18 are suitable for Dakotas. Air Tanzania Corporation provide regular and frequent services to all the more important towns within the territory and to Mozambique, Zambia, Seychelles, Comoro, Rwanda, Burundi and Madagascar.

There is an all-weather landing-ground in Zanzibar and a smaller all-weather landing-ground in Pemba.

Shipping. In 1985, 635,000 tonnes of freight were loaded and 2·6m. unloaded.

Post and Broadcasting. In 1988 there were 63,000 direct telephone lines and 1,400 telex lines. There are 2 broadcasting stations (1 for mainland Tanzania and 1 for Zanzibar) and colour television operates in Zanzibar. In 1986 there were 13,000 television receivers (on Zanzibar only) and 2m. radio receivers.

Newspapers (1985). There were 3 dailies, 2 weeklies and several monthly magazines.

JUSTICE, RELIGION, EDUCATION AND WELFARE

Justice. The Judiciary is independent in both judicial and administrative matters and is composed of a 4-tier system of Courts: Primary Courts; District and Resident Magistrates' Courts; the High Court and the Court of Appeal. The Chief Justice is head of the Court of Appeal and the Judiciary Department. The Court's main registry is at Dar es Salaam; its jurisdiction includes Zanzibar. The Principal Judge is head of the High Court, also headquartered at Dar es Salaam, which has resident judges at 7 regional centres.

Religion. In 1984 some 40% were Christian, including Roman Catholics under the Archbishops of Dar es Salaam and Tabora, Anglicans under the Archbishop of

Tanzania, and Lutherans. Moslems amount to 33%, but reach 66% in the coastal towns; Zanzibar is 96% Moslem and 4% Hindu. Some 23% follow traditional religions.

Education. In 1987 there were 10,302 primary schools with 3,169,202 pupils, and 288 (1988) secondary schools (175 private) with 127,703 students.

Technical and vocational education is provided at several secondary and technical schools and at the Dar es Salaam Technical College.

There were, in 1987, 63 teachers' colleges, including the college at Chang'ombe for secondary-school teachers, with 11,667 students.

The University of Dar es Salaam, independent since 1970, has faculties of law, arts, social sciences, medicine, engineering, commerce and management. Sokoine University of Agriculture, established in 1984, has faculties of agriculture, forestry and veterinary medicine. The total number of students in both universities was 3,395 in 1987.

Health. In 1984 there were 1,065 doctors and 152 hospitals with 22,800 beds.

DIPLOMATIC REPRESENTATIVES

Of Tanzania in Great Britain (43 Hertford St., London, W1)
High Commissioner: John S. Malecela (accredited 17 Oct. 1989).

Of Great Britain in Tanzania (Hifadhi Hse., Samora Ave., Dar es Salaam)
High Commissioner: J. T. Masefield, CMG.

Of Tanzania in the USA (2139 R. St., NW, Washington, D.C., 20008)
Ambassador: Asterius M. Hyera.

Of the USA in Tanzania (36 Laibon Rd., Dar es Salaam)
Ambassador: Edward DeJarnette, Jr.

Of Tanzania to the United Nations
Ambassador: Anthony B. Nyakyi.

Further Reading

Atlas of Tanganyika. 3rd ed. Dar es Salaam, 1956
Tanganyika Notes and Records. Tanganyika Society, Dar es Salaam. (Twice yearly, from 1936) *The Economic Development of Tanganyika. Report... by the International Bank.* Johns Hopkins Univ. Press and OUP, 1961
Ayany, S. G., *A History of Zanzibar.* Nairobi, 1970
Coulson, A., *Tanzania: A Political Economy.* OUP, 1982
Darch, C., *Tanzania.* [Bibliography] Oxford and Santa Barbara, 1985
Hood, M., (ed.) *Tanzania and Nyerere.* London, 1988
Nyerere, J., *Freedom and Development.* New York, 1976
Resnick, I. N., *The Long Transition: Building Socialism in Tanzania.* New York and London, 1981
Yeager, R., *Tanzania: An African Experiment.* Aldershot, 1982

THAILAND

Capital: Bangkok
Population: 54·5m. (1988)
GNP per capita: US$1,000 (1988)

Prathes Thai, or Muang-Thai

HISTORY. Until 24 June 1932 Siam was an absolute monarchy. On that date a *coup d' état* was effected and a Provisional Constitution Act was promulgated on 27 June. This was replaced by the constitution of 10 Dec. 1932, which in turn was superseded by new constitutions.

AREA AND POPULATION. Thailand is bounded west by Burma, north and east by Laos and south-east by Cambodia. In the south it becomes a peninsula bounded west by the Indian Ocean, south by Malaysia and east by the Gulf of Thailand. Area is 513,115 sq. km (198,456 sq. miles).

At the census taken in 1980 the registration gave a population of 46,961,338, of whom 30·4% lived in the Central region, 35·2% in the North-East region, 12·5% in the South region, 21·9% in the North region. Estimate (1988) 54,465,056 (27,112,981 females).

Vital statistics, 1984: Births, 956,680 (467,566 females); deaths, 225,282 (94,433 females).

Thailand is divided into 73 provinces. Provinces with over 1m. population 1987 were Nakhon Rajchasima (2,298,024), Ubon Rajchathani (1,810,846), Udorn Thani (1,740,650), Khon Kaen (1,638,260), Buriram (1,382,451), Nakhon Si Thammaraj (1,376,926), Chiangmai (1,313,859), Sri Saket (1,261,694), Surin (1,237,770), Roi Et (1,184,070), Nakhon Sawan (1,059,909) and Songkhla (1,044,244).

Bangkok Metropolis is the capital (population 1987, 5,609,352). Other towns (1980 census) are Changmai (101,595), Hat Yai (93,519), Khon Kaen, (85,863), Phitsanulok (79,942), Nakhon Rajchasima (78,246), Udorn Thani (71,142), Songkhla (67,945), Nakhon Sawan (63,935), Nakhon Si Thammaraj (63,162), Ubon Rajchathani (50,788), Ayutthaya (47,189), Nakhon Pathom (45,242), Lampang (42,301) and Ratchaburi (40,404).

Thai is the national language. Several Chinese dialects are also spoken in Bangkok and the north and some Malay in the south. English, French and German are increasingly used in tourist areas.

CLIMATE. The climate is tropical, with high temperatures and humidity. Over most of the country, 3 seasons may be recognized. The rainy season is June to Oct., the cool season from Nov. to Feb. and the hot season is March to May. Rainfall is generally heaviest in the south and lightest in the north east.

Bangkok. Jan. 78°F (25·6°C), July 83°F (28·3°C). Annual rainfall 56" (1,400 mm).

REIGNING KING. Bhumibol Adulyadej, born 5 Dec. 1927, younger brother of King Ananda Mahidol, who died on 9 June 1946. King Bhumibol married on 28 April 1950 Princess Sirikit, and was crowned 5 May 1950. Children: Princess Ubol Ratana (born 5 April 1951, married Aug. 1972 Peter Ladd Jensen), Crown-Prince Vajiralongkorn (born 28 July 1952, married 3 Jan. 1977 Soamsawali Kitiyakra), Princess Maha Chakri Sirindhorn (born 2 April 1955), Princess Chulabhorn (born 4 July 1957, married 7 Jan. 1982 Virayudth Didyasarin).

CONSTITUTION AND GOVERNMENT. The military government resigned on 14 Oct. 1973 and a new government was formed. A new Constitution was promulgated in Dec. 1978. A general election was held on 24 July 1988. Of the 357 seats in Parliament, the Chart Thai Party won 87, the Social Action Party 54, the Democrat Party 48, Ruam Thai Party 35.

The cabinet in Jan. 1990 was composed as follows:

Prime Minister and Minister of Defence: Gen. Chatichai Choonhavan.

Deputy Prime Ministers: Pong Sarasin, Bhichai Rattakul, Gen. Tienchai Sirisumpan. *Ministers to the Prime Minister's Office:* Meechai Ruchupan, Booneua Prasertsuwan, Korn Dabbaransi, Anuwat Wattanapongsiri, Chaisiri Ruangkanchanasetr, Supatra Masdit, Col. Phon Rerngprasertvit, Capt. Chalerm Yoobamrung. *Finance:* Pramual Sabhavasu. *Foreign Affairs:* Air Chief Marshal Siddhi Savetsila. *Agriculture and Cooperatives:* Lieut.-Col. Sanan Khajornprasat. *Communications:* Montree Pongpanit. *Commerce:* Dr Subin Pinkhayan. *Interior:* Banharn Silpa-Archa. *Justice:* Lieut.-Gen. Chamras Mangklarat. *Science, Technology and Energy:* Prachuab Chaiyasan. *Education:* Gen. Mana Ratanakoses. *Public Health:* Chuan Leekpai. *Industry:* Maj.-Gen. Pramarn Adireksarn. *University Affairs:* Tavich Klinpratoom.

National flag: Five horizontal stripes of red, white, blue, white, red, with the blue of double width.

Local Government. Thailand is divided into 73 provinces *(changwads)*, each under the control of a *changwad* governor. The *changwads* are subdivided into 655 districts *(amphurs)* and 83 sub-districts *(king amphurs)*, 6,633 communes *(tambons)* and 58,623 villages *(moobans)*.

DEFENCE. Under the Military Service Act of 1954 every able-bodied man between the ages of 21 and 30 is liable to serve 2 years with the colours; 7 years in the first reserve; 10 years in the second reserve; 6 years in the third reserve.

Army. The Army is organized in 4 Regions and consists of 2 cavalry, 1 armoured, 6 infantry, 2 special forces, 1 artillery and 1 anti-aircraft divisions; 19 engineer and 8 independent infantry battalions; and 4 reconnaissance companies. Equipment includes 64 M-48A5, 60 Chinese Type-69 and 200 M-41 main battle tanks. There is also an Army Aviation force including about 100 transport helicopters, and over 62 O-1 Bird Dog observation aircraft and 4 C-47 and 1 Short 330 twin-turboprop transport. Strength (1990) 190,000 (with 500,000 reserves for all armed forces).

Navy. The Royal Thai Navy is, next to the Chinese, the most significant naval force in the South China Sea. The combatant fleet includes 5 small frigates, 2 modern missile-armed 950t corvettes, 6 German and Italian-built fast missile craft, 14 coastal and 30 inshore patrol craft, and about 40 riverine patrol boats. There is 1 MCM support vessel, 2 coastal minehunters and 4 coastal minesweepers. Amphibious capability is provided by 7 tank landing ships and 3 medium landing ships plus 39 landing craft. Major auxiliaries are 1 small tanker, 2 surveying ships, and 2 training ships. Minor auxiliaries and service craft number about 12.

The Naval air element, all shore based includes 9 S-2F ASW Trackers, 3 F-27 Friendship, 5 N24A Nomad and 2 CL-215s for maritime patrol, 5 C-47s and 2 F-27s for transport duties, 9 Cessna T-337 armed light transports and 13 Bell utility and SAR helicopters.

Naval personnel in 1989 totalled 50,000 including 20,000 marines and 900 Naval Air Arm, and the main bases are at Bangkok, Sattahip, Songkla and Phan Nga, with the riverine forces based at Nakhon Pathom.

A separate coast guard force, the Royal Thai Marine Police, numbers 1,700 and operates 3 coastal patrol craft, 32 riverine and inshore craft and numerous boats.

Air Force. The Royal Thai Air Force was reorganized with the assistance of a US Military Air Advisory Group. It had a strength (1990) 43,000 personnel, and is made up of a headquarters and Combat, Logistics Support, Training and Special Services Groups. Combat units comprise 1 squadron of F-16 and 2 squadrons of F-5E/F interceptors, 1 squadron of F-5A/B fighter-bombers and RF-5A reconnaissance aircraft, 1 squadron with A-37B light jet attack aircraft, 2 with OV-10 Bronco light reconnaissance/ attack aircraft, and 1 with AU-23A Peacemakers and 1 squadron with C-47s for security duties. Three Aravas are used for electronic intelligence gathering and 3 Learjets for combat support. There are transport units equipped with a total of about 70 C-130H/H-30 Hercules, HS 748, C-123B Provider, C-47 and smaller aircraft, including 20 Australian-built Missionmasters; there are 25 UH-1H and 17 S-58T helicopters; 20 O-1 Bird Dog observation aircraft; training units with Airtrainer CT/4 primary trainers built in New Zealand, Italian-built SF.260MTs, T-37 and Fantrainer intermediate and T-33A advanced trainers.

INTERNATIONAL RELATIONS

Membership. Thailand is a member of UN, ASEAN and the Colombo Plan.

ECONOMY

Planning. The Sixth 5-year Development Plan (1987–91) envisages emphasis on development of the production system, with specific attention being paid to providing employment and expanding the industrial base.

Budget. Expenditure (1988, 1m. baht) 223,089: Economic services, 30,924; social services, 65,647; defence, 44,149; general administration and services, 28,059; unallocatable items, 54,310. Revenue, 258,231 (1m. baht).

Currency. The unit of currency is the *baht*, which is divided into 100 *satang*. Only nickel, copper, tin and bronze coins are now minted, in denominations of 1, 2, 5 *baht*, 25, 50 *satang*. Currency notes now comprise, 5, 10, 20, 50, 100, 500 *baht* notes.

On 31 March 1989 the total amount of notes in circulation was 113,949m. baht. In March 1990, £1 = 41·80 *baht*; US$1 = 25·50 *baht*.

Banking. In 1942 the Bank of Thailand was established under the Bank of Thailand Act, B.E. 2485 (1942) and began operations on 10 Dec. 1942, with the functions of a central bank; total assets and liabilities of the Bank of Thailand at 31 March 1989, 322,120·6m. baht. The Bank has its banking activities entirely separate from the management of the note issue.

The Bank also took over the note issue previously performed by the Treasury Department of the Ministry of Finance. Although the entire capital is owned by the Government, the Bank is an independent body.

Banks incorporated under Thai law include the Bangkok Bank Ltd, the Bangkok Bank of Commerce Ltd, the Bank of Asia for Industry & Commerce Ltd, the Bank of Ayudhya Ltd, Bangkok Metropolitan Bank Ltd, the Laem Thong Bank Ltd, the Siam City Bank Ltd, the Siam Commercial Bank Ltd, First Bangkok City Bank Ltd, Union Bank of Bangkok Ltd, the Bank of Agriculture and Agricultural Co-operatives, the Government Housing Bank, the Sayam Bank and the Wang Lee Chan Bank Ltd. Foreign banks include the Chartered Bank, the Hongkong and Shanghai Banking Corporation, the Citibank, Banque de l'Indochine, Bank of Canton Ltd, Bank of China Ltd, Bank of America, N.T. & S.A., the Mitsui Bank Ltd, The Asia Trust Bank Ltd, Bharat Overseas Bank Ltd, The Chase Manhattan Bank, United Malayan Banking Corporation and the Bank of Tokyo Ltd, Nakornthon Bank, Thai Farmers' Bank, Thai Military Bank, Thai Danu Bank.

Total assets and liabilities of commercial banks at 31 March 1989, 1,200,589·9m. baht.

Weights and Measures. The metric system was made compulsory by a law promulgated on 17 Dec. 1923. The actual weights and measures prescribed by law are: Units of weight: 1 *standard picul* = 60 kg; 1 *standard catty* (1/100 picul) = 600 grammes; 1 *standard carat* = 20 centigrammes. Units of length: 1 *sen* = 40 metres; 1 *wah* (1/20 sen) = 2 metres; 1 *sauk* (1/2 wah) = 0·50 metre; 1 *keup* (1/2 sauk) = 0·25 metre. Units of square measure: 1 *rai* (1 sq. sen) = 1,600 sq. metres: 1 *ngan* (1/4 rai) = 400 sq. metres; 1 *sq. wah* (1/100 ngan) = 4 sq. metres. Units of capacity: 1 *standard kwien* = 2,000 litres; 1 *standard ban* (1/2 kwien) = 1,000 litres; 1 *standard sat* (1/50 ban) = 20 litres; 1 *standard tannan* (1/20 sat) = 1 litre.

Legislation passed in 1940 provided that the calendar year shall coincide with the Christian Year, and that the year of the Buddhist era 2484 shall begin on 1 Jan. 1941. (The New Year's Day was previously 1 April.).

ENERGY AND NATURAL RESOURCES

Electricity. In 1987 the principal sources of energy generation were natural gas (50%), lignite (24%), hydro (17%) and heavy oil (7%). Installed capacity was 55% thermal, 30% hydro, 11% combined cycle and 4% gas turbine. Annual hydro capacity, 26,204 mw. Supply 220 volts; 50 Hz.

Oil. There is extensive oil and gas exploration in the Gulf of Thailand. In 1987 the Sirikit oil field, which came on stream in 1983, remained Thailand's only significant find. Proven oil reserves in 1987 were less than 160m. bbls. Production of crude oil (1989) 1·85m. tonnes providing 15% of needs.

Gas. Production of natural gas (1988) 212,641m. cu. ft. Estimated reserves, 1986, 12,922,000m. cu. ft.

Minerals. The mineral resources include cassiterite (tin ore), wolfram, scheelite, antimony, coal, copper, gold, iron, lead, manganese, molybdenum, rubies, sapphires, silver, zinc and zircons. Production, 1986 (in 1,000 tonnes): Iron ore, 14·5; manganese ore, 5; tin concentrates, 23·2; lead ore, 61·9; antimony ore, 1·7; zinc ore, 384·5; lignite, 4,542·2; gypsum, 1,665·6; wolfram ore (tungsten), 1; fluorite ore, 335·2; barite, 142·2; phosphate, 6·9.

Agriculture. The chief produce of the country is rice, which forms the national food and the staple article of export. The area under paddy is about 18m. acres. In 1987 40% of the total land area was cultivated.

Output of the major crops in 1988 was (in 1,000 tonnes): Paddy, 19,460; maize, 4,880; sugar-cane, 27,500; jute and kenaf, 204; tobacco, 27; tapioca-root, 22,180; soybeans, 380; coconut, 780; mung beans, 310; cotton, 92; groundnuts, 147; sesame, 35; castor seeds, 30; kapok and bambax fibre, 35.

Livestock, 1988 (in 1,000): Horses, 19; buffaloes, 6,000; cattle, 5,000; pigs, 4,260; sheep, 95; goats, 80; poultry, 101,000.

Forestry. About 28% of the land area (14·4m. hectares) of Thailand was under forest in 1988. In the north, mixed deciduous forests with teak *(Tectona grandis, Linn.)*, growing in mixture with several other species, predominate. In the north-eastern section hardwood of the *Dipterocarpus* species, especially *Shorea obtusa* and *Pentacme Siamensis, Kurz* exist in most parts. In all other regions of the country tropical evergreen forests are found, with the well-known timber of commerce, Yang (*Dipterocarpus alatus, Roxb* and *Dipterocarpus* spp.) as the outstanding crops. Most of the teak timber exploited in northern Thailand is floated down to Bangkok.

Output of main forestry products in 1987: Teak, 38,100 cu. metres; yang and other woods, 2,110,900 cu. metres. By-products in 1987: Firewood, 873,700 cu. metres; charcoal, 463,900 cu. metres; 16m. bamboo (1985) and 139,711 decalitres of yang oil (1984).

Rubber production (in 1,000 tonnes), 1980, 501; 1988, 970.

Fisheries. In 1986 the catch of sea fish was 2,348,600 tonnes including marine prawns and shrimps, 141,200 tonnes; of freshwater fish, 187,800 tonnes.

INDUSTRY AND TRADE

Industry. Production of manufactured goods in 1988 included 11,514,000 tonnes of cement, 130,261,000 litres of beer, 1,836m. bottles of soft drinks, 33,992 tonnes of cigarettes and tobacco, 387,571 iron rods, 189,996 galvanized iron sheets, 147,337 tin plates, 154,183 automobiles, 488,669 motorcycles and 50,787 tonnes of tyres.

Labour. In 1988, 28·2m. persons out of a labour force of 29·9m. were employed: 17·9m. in agriculture and 2·8m. in manufacturing.

Commerce. The foreign trade (in 1m. baht) was as follows:

	1984	*1985*	*1986*	*1987*	*1988*
Imports (c.i.f.)	245,155	251,169	245,900	341,900	500,000
Exports (f.o.b.)	175,237	193,366	231,000	298,100	400,000

In 1987 exports (in 1m. baht) included: Garments, 35,900; rice, 22,668; tapioca, 20,719; rubber, 20,392; jewellery, 19,722; integrated circuits, 15,173; canned sea-food, 13,220; fabrics, 8,683; sugar, 8,583; footwear, 5,918.

1987 imports (in 1m. baht) included: Chemicals, 36,045; iron and steel, 23,693; non-electrical machinery and parts, 49,485; electrical machinery and parts, 31,988; vehicles and parts, 15,240; fuel and lubricants, 44,457.

Total trade between Thailand and UK (British Department of Trade returns, in £1,000 sterling):

	1985	*1986*	*1987*	*1988*	*1989*
Imports to UK	131,806	182,756	239,430	321,241	443,144
Exports and re-exports from UK	157,723	158,195	206,571	279,717	427,484

Tourism. In 1988 4,231,000 foreigners visited Thailand. Earnings (1985) 31·768m. baht.

COMMUNICATIONS

Roads. In 1985 the total length of roads was 156,776 km, of which 44,534 km (29%) were national highways and 112,242 km (71%) provincial roads. Motor vehicles registered in 1982 included 492,742 passenger cars, 32,114 buses (1979), 419,143 lorries (1979) and 1,401,918 motor cycles.

Railways. In 1988 the State Railway totalled 3,924 km (metre gauge) and carried 82·7m. passengers and 6·2m. tonnes of freight.

Aviation. There are international airports at Bangkok, Changmai in the north and Phuket and Hat Yai in the south. Thai Airways Co. Ltd (TAC), is the sole Thai air transport enterprise. The Company operates 11 domestic routes and 3 international routes and carried more than 1m. passengers in 1984. In 1959 Thai Airways and the Scandinavian Airlines System set up a new company, Thai Airways International, to operate the international air services from Thailand. In 1984, more than 2·7m. passengers were carried.

Shipping. In 1983, 3,137 vessels of 14,174,828 NRT entered and 2,648 of 11,663,452 NRT cleared the port of Bangkok.

The port of Bangkok, about 30 km from the mouth of the Chao Phya River, is capable of berthing ocean-going vessels of 10,000 gross tons and 28 ft draught. Bangkok is now a port of entry for Laos, and goods arriving in transit are sent up by rail to Nong Khai and ferried across the river Mekhong to Vientiane.

Post and Broadcasting. In 1985 there were 576,082 telephones, of which 389,096 were in Bangkok.

In 1985, there were 275 radio stations and 11 television stations,7,629,998 radios and 4,122,000 televisions.

Cinemas (1983). There were 651 cinemas with a seating capacity of 438,787.

Newspapers (1989). There are 23 daily newspapers in Bangkok, including 2 in English and 7 in Chinese, with a combined circulation of about 2m.

JUSTICE, RELIGION, EDUCATION AND WELFARE

Justice. The judicial power is exercised in the name of the King, by *(a)* courts of first instance, *(b)* the court of appeal *(Uthorn)* and *(c)* the Supreme Court *(Dika)*. The King appoints, transfers and dismisses judges, who are independent in conducting trials and giving judgment in accordance with the law.

Courts of first instance are subdivided into 20 magistrates' courts *(Kwaeng)* with limited civil and minor criminal jurisdiction; 85 provincial courts *(Changwad)* with unlimited civil and criminal jurisdiction; the criminal and civil courts with exclusive jurisdiction in Bangkok; the central juvenile courts for persons under 18 years of age in Bangkok.

The court of appeal exercises appellate jurisdiction in civil and criminal cases from all courts of first instance. From it appeals lie to Dika Court on any point of law and, in certain cases, on questions of fact.

The Supreme Court is the supreme tribunal of the land. Besides its normal appellate jurisdiction in civil and criminal matters, it has semi-original jurisdiction over general election petitions. The decisions of Dika Court are final. Every person has the right to present a petition to the Government who will deal with all matters of grievance.

Religion. In 1983 there were 47,049,223 Buddhists, 1,869,427 Moslems, 267,381 Christians and 64,369 Hindus, Sikhs and others.

Education. Primary education is compulsory for children between the ages of 7–14 and free in local municipal schools. In 1984 there were 532,097 students enrolled at pre-primary level, 7,229,064 at primary level, 1,304,520 at lower secondary level, 945,260 at upper secondary level and 361,819 in higher education. In 1980 there were 36 teachers' training colleges with 5,317 teachers and 63,983 students and about 180 government vocational schools and colleges with 11,240 teachers and 208,088 students. There are 8 schools for deaf children, 2 for the blind, 1 for multiple-handicapped and 2 for the mentally retarded. In 1984 the 36 teacher training colleges were regionally consolidated into 8 United Colleges also offering 4-year programmes in science and technology, management, social development, agriculture, arts and journalism. In 1986 there were 14 universities 3 of which were private: Chulalongkorn University (1916), Thammasat University (1934), Universities of Medical Science, Agriculture and Fine Arts; Ramkamhaeng University (1971)—all in Bangkok; Chiengmai University (1964), the Khon Kaen University (1966) in the north-east and Prince of Songkhla University (1968) in the south.

Health. The Primary Health Care Programme had provided health services in 95% of villages in 1986. In 1982 there were 434 hospitals and 6,496 health centres. In 1982 there were 6,550 physicians, 1,122 dentists and (1981) 2,680 pharmacists.

DIPLOMATIC REPRESENTATIVES

Of Thailand in Great Britain (30 Queen's Gate, London, SW7 5JB)
Ambassador: Sudhee Prasasvinitchai (accredited 4 Nov. 1986).

Of Great Britain in Thailand (Wireless Rd., Bangkok)
Ambassador: M. R. Melhuish, CMG.

Of Thailand in the USA (2300 Kalorama Rd., NW, Washington, D.C., 20008)
Ambassador: Vitthya Vejjajiva.

Of the USA in Thailand (95 Wireless Rd., Bangkok)
Ambassador: Daniel A. O'Donohue.

Of Thailand to the United Nations
Ambassador: Nitya Pibulsonggram.

Further Reading

Thailand Statistical Yearbook. National Statistical Office, Bangkok
Thailand in Brief. 7th ed. Bangkok, 1985
Girling, J. I. S., *Thailand: Society and Politics.* Cornell Univ. Press, 1981
Morrell, D. and Samudavanija, C., *Political Conflict in Thailand.* Cambridge, Mass., 1981
Watts, M., *Thailand.* [Bibliography] Oxford and Santa Barbara, 1986

TOGO

République Togolaise

Capital: Lomé
Population: 3·25m. (1988)
GNP per capita: US$370 (1988)

HISTORY. A German protectorate from July 1884, Togo was occupied by British and French forces in Aug. 1914 and subsequently partitioned between the two countries on 20 July 1922 under a League of Nations mandate. British Togo subsequently joined Ghana. The French mandate was renewed by the UN as a trusteeship on 14 Dec. 1946. On 28 Oct. 1956 a plebiscite was held to determine the status of the territory. Out of 438,175 registered voters, 313,458 voted for an autonomous republic within the French Union and the end of the trusteeship system. The trusteeship was abolished on the achievement of independence on 27 April 1960.

On 13 Jan. 1963 the first President Sylvanus Olympio was murdered by n.c.o.s. of the army. Nicolas Grunitzky, a former prime minister and Olympio's brother-in-law, was appointed President. On 13 Jan. 1967 in a bloodless *coup* the army under Lieut.-Col. Etienne Eyadéma made President Grunitzky 'voluntarily withdraw'. On 14 April 1967 Col. Eyadéma assumed the Presidency. There was a return to constitutional government on 13 Jan. 1980.

AREA AND POPULATION. Togo is bounded west by Ghana, north by Burkina Faso, east by Benin and south by the Gulf of Guinea. The area is 56,785 sq. km. The population of Togo in 1981 (census) was 2,700,982; 1988 (estimate) 3,246,000. The capital is Lomé (population, 1983, 366,476), other towns (1981, population) being Sokodé (48,098), Kpalimé (31,800), Atakpamé (27,100), Bassar (21,800), Tsévié (17,000) and Aného (14,000).

The areas, populations and chief towns of the 5 regions are:

Region	*Sq. km*	*Census 1981*	*Chief town*
Des Savanes	8,602	326,826	Dapaong
De La Kara	11,630	432,626	Kara
Centrale	13,182	269,174	Sokodé
Des Plateaux	16,975	561,656	Atakpamé
Maritime	6,396	1,039,700	Lomé

The south is largely populated by Ewe-speaking peoples (forming 47% of the population) and related groups, while the north is mainly inhabited by Hamitic groups speaking Voltaic (Gur) languages such as Kabre (22%), Gurma (14%) and Tem (4%). The official language is French but Ewe and Kabre are also taught in schools. In 1984, 27% lived in urban areas and (1981) 48% were male.

Vital statistics, 1984: Live birth rate, 4·5%; death rate, 1·6%.

CLIMATE. The tropical climate produces wet seasons from March to July and from Oct. to Nov. in the south. The north has one wet season, from April to July. The heaviest rainfall occurs in the mountains of the west, south-west and centre. Lomé. Jan. 81°F (27·2°C), July 76°F (24·4°C). Annual rainfall 35" (875 mm).

CONSTITUTION AND GOVERNMENT. Following approval in a referendum on 30 Dec. 1979, a new Constitution came into force on 13 Jan. 1980, when the Third Togolese Republic was proclaimed. It provides for an Executive President, directly elected for a 7-year term, and for a National Assembly of 77 deputies, elected on a regional list system for a 5-year term. Elections to the Assembly were held on 24 March 1985.

All candidates are approved by the *Rassemblement du peuple togolais*, the sole legal Party since 1969; it is administered by a 46-member Central Committee and a 13-member Political Bureau elected at its fourth Party Congress in Dec. 1986.

The government in Nov. 1989 was composed as follows:

President, Minister of Defence: Gen. Gnassingbé Eyadéma (re-elected for a further 7-year term in Dec. 1986).

Foreign Affairs and Co-operation: Yaovi Adodo. *Rural Development:* Koffi Walla. *Economy and Finance:* Komlan Alipui. *Planning and Mines:* Barry Moussa Barque. *Posts and Telecommunications:* Ayeva Nassirou. *Public Works, Labour and Civil Service:* Bitokotipou Yagninim. *Minister-Delegate to Presidency in charge of Information:* Gbegnon Amegboh. *Youth, Sports and Culture:* Messan Agbeyome Kodjo. *National Education and Scientific Research:* Tchalim Tcha Koza. *Interior:* Yao Mawulikplimi Amegi. *Public Health, Social and Women's Affairs:* Dr Ayissah Agbetra. *Industry and State Enterprises:* Koffi Djondo. *Technical and Professional Training:* Koffi Edoh. *Environment and Tourism:* Yao Komlavi.

National flag: Five horizontal stripes of green and yellow, a red quarter with a white star.

Local Government: There are 5 regions, each under an inspector appointed by the President; they are divided into 21 *prefectures,* each administered by a district chief assisted by an elected district council.

DEFENCE. Armed forces numbered (1989) about 5,900, all forming part of the Army.

Army. The Army consists of 2 infantry, 1 Presidential Guard commando and 1 para-commando regiments, with artillery and logistic support units. Equipment includes 9 Scorpion and 2 T-54/-55 main battle tanks. Strength (1990) 4,000, with a further 1,550 men in a paramilitary force.

Navy. In 1989 the Naval wing of the Army operated 2 inshore patrol craft from the naval base at Lomé. Naval personnel number 100.

Air Force. An Air Force, established with French assistance, has 6 Brazilian-built EMB-326 Xavante (Aermacchi MB.326) armed jet trainers; 5 Alpha Jet advanced trainers, with strike capability, 1 Boeing 707, 1 DC-8 and 1 twin-turbofan F28 Fellowship for VIP use, 2 turboprop Buffalo transports; 2 Beech Barons and 2 Cessna 337s for liaison; 3 Epsilon basic trainers; 1 Puma and 2 Lama helicopters. Personnel (1990) 250.

INTERNATIONAL RELATIONS

Membership. Togo is a member of UN, OAU and ECOWAS, and is an ACP state of EEC.

ECONOMY

Budget. The ordinary budget for 1988 balanced at 89,692m. francs CFA.

Currency. The unit of currency is the *franc* CFA with a parity rate of 50 *francs* CFA to 1 French *franc*. The rate of exchange (March 1990) was 471·63 francs CFA to £1; US$1 = 287·75.

Banking. The bank of issue is the *Banque Centrale des Etats de l'Afrique de l'Ouest.* Seven commercial and 3 development banks are based in Lomé.

ENERGY AND NATURAL RESOURCES

Electricity. Production (1986) 203m. kwh. There is a hydro-electric plant at Kpalime. Supply 127 and 220 volts; 50 Hz.

Minerals. A Mines Department was set up in 1953 after the discovery of very rich deposits of phosphate and bauxite; mining began in 1961. Output of phosphate rock (1985) 2·5m. tonnes. Other mineral deposits are limestone, estimated at 200m. tons; iron ore, estimated at 550m. tons with iron content varying between 40% and 55%, and marble estimated at 20m. tonnes. Salt production (1982) 600,000 tonnes.

Agriculture. Inland the country is hilly, rising to 3,600 ft, with streams and waterfalls. There are long stretches of forest and brushwood, while dry plains alternate with arable land. Maize, yams, cassava, plantains, groundnuts, etc., are cultivated; oil palms and dye-woods grow in the forests; but the main commerce is based on coffee, cocoa, palm-oil, palm-kernels, copra, groundnuts, cotton, manioc. There are considerable plantations of oil and cocoa palms, coffee, cacao, kola, cassava and cotton. Production, 1988 (in 1,000 tonnes): Cassava, 410; tomatoes, 7; yams 378; maize, 296; sorghum, 120; millet, 50; seed cotton, 67; rice, 27; groundnuts, 17; coffee, 11.

Livestock (1988): Cattle, 290,000; sheep, 1m.; swine, 300,000; horses, 1,000; asses, 3,000; goats, 900,000.

Forestry. In 1988 forests covered 25% of the land surface (1·4m. hectares). Roundwood production (1987) 813,000 cu. metres.

Fisheries. Catch (1986) 14,800 tonnes.

INDUSTRY AND TRADE

Industry. There is a cement works (production, 1983; 232,000 tonnes); a second is being built in co-operation with Ghana and Côte d'Ivoire with a capacity of 1·2m. tonnes per annum. An oil refinery of 1m. tonne capacity opened in Lomé in 1978 and a steel mill (20,000 tonne capacity) in 1979. Industry, though small, is developing and there are about 40 medium sized enterprises in the public and private sectors, including textile and food processing plants.

Commerce (in 1m. francs CFA):

	1981	*1982*	*1983*	*1984*	*1985*
Imports	117,769	128,354	108,141	118,460	129,406
Exports	56,241	58,173	61,921	83,588	85,380

In 1985, of the exports, phosphates amounted to 38%, cotton 11%, coffee 11% and cocoa beans 6% by value; 22% of exports went to France and 18% to the Netherlands. Of the imports, France supplied 27%, the Netherlands, 11% and UK, 10%.

Total trade between Togo and UK (British Department of Trade returns, in £1,000 sterling):

	1985	*1986*	*1987*	*1988*	*1989*
Imports to UK	4,597	5,008	2,579	690	2,022
Exports and re-exports from UK	17,034	17,488	15,431	22,231	15,009

Tourism. There were about 121,000 tourists in 1988.

COMMUNICATIONS

Roads. There were, in 1986, 7,850 km of roads, of which 1,500 km were paved. In Dec. 1987 there were 44,120 passenger cars and 22,000 commercial vehicles.

Railways. There are 4 metre-gauge railways connecting Lomé, with Anécho (continuing to Cotonou in Benin), Kpalime, Tabligbo and (*via* Atakpamé) Blitta; total length 525 km. In 1986 the railways carried 6·3m. tonne-km and 60m. passenger-km.

Aviation: Air services connect Tokoin airport, near Lomé, with Paris, Dakar, Abidjan, Douala, Accra, Lagos, Cotonou and Niamey and by internal services with Sokodé, Mango, Dapaong, Atakpamé and Niamtougou.

Shipping. In 1983, vessels landed 654,000 tonnes and cleared 683,000 tonnes at Lomé; 31,058 containers passed through the port in 1981. The merchant marine comprised (1985) 11 vessels of 77,989 DWT. In 1981 some 2·2m. tonnes of phosphate were loaded at the port of Kpéme.

Post and Broadcasting. There were (1983) 388 post offices and 11,105 telephones. Togo is connected by telegraph and telephone with Ghana, Benin, Côte d'Ivoire and Senegal, and by wireless telegraphy with Europe and America. There were 16,000 television receivers and 680,000 radio receivers in 1986.

Newspapers. There was (1989) 1 daily newspaper (circulation 10,000).

JUSTICE, RELIGION, EDUCATION AND WELFARE

Justice. The Supreme Court and two Appeal Courts are in Lomé, one for criminal cases and one for civil and commercial cases. Each receives appeal from a series of local tribunals.

Religion. In 1980, 28% of the population were Catholics, 17% Moslem (chiefly in the north) and 9% Protestant; while 46% follow animist religions.

Education. In 1986 there were 474,998 pupils and 10,209 teachers in 2,345 primary schools, 86,327 pupils in secondary schools, and 5,050 students and 198 teachers in technical schools and 374 students and 22 teachers at the teacher-training college. The University of Benin at Lomé (founded in 1970) had 4,500 students and 308 teaching staff in 1986.

Health. In 1981 there were 61 hospitals with 4,500 beds; and in 1985, 168 doctors, 7 dentists, 51 pharmacists, 559 midwives (1980) and 1,116 nursing staff.

DIPLOMATIC REPRESENTATIVES

Of Togo in Great Britain (30 Sloane St., London, SW1)
Chargé d'Affaires: Djibril Akanga.

Of Great Britain in Togo
Ambassador and Consul-General: A. M. Goodenough (resides in Accra).

Of Togo in the USA (2208 Massachusetts Ave., NW, Washington, D.C., 20008)
Ambassador: Ellom-Kodjo Schuppius.

Of the USA in Togo (Rue Pelletier Caventou, Lomé)
Ambassador: Rush W. Taylor, Jr.

Of Togo to the United Nations
Ambassador: Adjuyi Koffi.

Further Reading

Cornevin, R., *Histoire du Togo.* 3rd ed., Paris, 1969
Feuillet, C., *Le Togo en general.* Paris, 1976
Piraux, M., *Le Togo aujourd'hui.* Paris, 1977

TONGA

Capital: Nuku'alofa
Population: 95,200 (1988)
GNP per capita: US$800 (1988)

Friendly Islands

HISTORY. The Kingdom of Tonga attained unity under Taufa'ahau Tupou (George I) who became ruler of his native Ha'apai in 1820, of Vava'u in 1833 and of Tongatapu in 1845. By 1860 the Kingdom had become converted to Christianity (George himself having been baptized in 1831). In 1862 the King granted freedom to the people from arbitrary rule of minor chiefs and gave them the right to the allocation of land for their own needs. These institutional changes, together with the establishment of a parliament of chiefs, paved the way towards the democratic constitution under which the Kingdom is now governed, and provided a background of stability against which Tonga was able to develop her agricultural economy.

The Kingdom continued up to 1899 to be a neutral region in accordance with the Declaration of Berlin, 6 April 1886. By the Anglo-German Agreement of 14 Nov. 1899 subsequently accepted by the USA, the Tonga Islands were left under the Protectorate of Great Britain. A protectorate was proclaimed on 18 May 1900, and a British Agent and Consul appointed. On 4 June 1970 the UK Government ceased to have any responsibility for the external relations of Tonga.

The Tongatapu group was discovered by Tasman in 1643.

AREA AND POPULATION. The Kingdom consists of some 169 islands and islets with a total area of 289 sq. miles (748 sq. km; including inland waters), and lies between 15° and 23° 30' S. lat and 173° and 177° W. long., its western boundary being the eastern boundary of Fiji. The islands are split up into the following groups reading from north to south: The Niuas, Vava'u, Ha'apai, Tongatapu and 'Eua. The 3 main groups, both from historical and administrative significance, are Tongatapu in the south, Ha'apai in the centre and Vava'u in the north.

The capital is Nuku'alofa on Tongatapu, population (1986) 29,018.

There are 5 divisions comprising 23 districts:

Division	*Sq. km*	*Census 1986*	*Capital*
Niuas	72	2,368	Hihifo
Vava'u	119	15,175	Neiafu
Ha'apai	110	8,919	Pangai
Tongatapu	261	63,794	Nuku'alofa
'Eua	87	4,393	Ohonua

Census population (1986) 94,649 (males, 47,611); estimate (1988) 95,200.

CLIMATE. Generally a healthy climate, though Jan. to March is hot and humid, with temperatures of 90°F (32·2°C). Rainfall amounts are comparatively high, being greatest from Dec. to March. Nuku'alofa. Jan. 78°F (25·6°C), July 70°F (21·1°C). Annual rainfall 63" (1,576 mm). Vava'u. Jan. 80°F (26·7°C), July 73°F (22·8°C). Annual rainfall 110" (2,750 mm).

CONSTITUTION AND GOVERNMENT. The present Constitution is almost identical with that granted in 1875 by King George Tupou I. There is a Privy Council, Cabinet, Legislative Assembly and Judiciary. The legislative assembly, which meets annually, is composed of 9 nobles elected by their peers, 9 elected representatives of the people and the Privy Councillors (numbering 11); the King appoints one of the 9 nobles to be the Speaker. The elections are held triennially. In 1960, women voted for the first time.

King: HM King Taufa'ahau Tupou IV, GCVO, GCMG, KBE, born 4 July 1918, succeeded on 16 Dec. 1965 on the death of his mother, Queen Salote Tupou III; his coronation took place on 4 July 1967.

Prime Minister: HRH Prince Fatafehi Tu'ipelehake, KCMG, KBE, younger brother of the King.
Acting Deputy Prime Minister: Hon. Baron Vaea.
Foreign Affairs and Defence: HRH Crown Prince Tupouto'a.

National flag: Red with a white quarter bearing a red couped cross.

INTERNATIONAL RELATIONS

Membership. Tonga is a member of the Commonwealth and is an ACP state of EEC.

ECONOMY

Budget. Recurrent revenue and expenditure in T$1,000:

	1987–88 [1]	*1988–89* [1]	*1989–90* [1]
Revenue	29,846	35,860	43,720
Expenditure	29,846	35,957	43,720

[1] Estimate.

The principal sources of revenue are import dues, income tax, sales tax, port and service tax, wharfage and philatelic revenue.
Public debt at 30 June 1987, T$44·5m. of which T$40·9m. was external debt.

Currency. There is a government note issue of *pa'anga* (T$) 50, 20, 10, 5, 2 and 1 and coin issue of T$2, T$1 and *seniti* 50, 20, 10, 5, 2 and 1. In March 1990, £1 = 2·17 *pa'anga*; US$1 = 1·33 *pa'anga*.

Banking. The Bank of Tonga and the Tonga Development Bank are both situated in Nuku'alofa (Tongatapu) with branches in the main islands 'Eua, Ha'apai, Vava'u and the Niuas.

ENERGY AND NATURAL RESOURCES

Electricity. Production (1986) 8m. kwh. Supply 230 volts; 50 Hz.

Agriculture. Production (1988, in 1,000 tonnes) consisted of coconuts (53), fruit and vegetables (21), copra (6) and cassava (17).
Livestock (1988): Cattle, 8,000; horses, 9,000; pigs, 65,000; goats, 11,000; poultry (1982), 175,000.

Fisheries. Catch (1982) 2,500 tonnes.

INDUSTRY AND TRADE

Commerce. In 1988, imports were valued at T$70,688,883 while exports and re-exports were T$9,502,664 and T$1,052,628.
Main imports (1988, in T$): Food 17,740,693, beverages and tobacco 3,302,660, crude materials 2,635,054, fuel and lubricants 6,853,259, oils and fats 178,927, chemicals 4,603,950, manufactured goods 13,453,825, machinery and transport equipment 15,472,034, miscellaneous manufactured articles 6,028,649.
Main exports (1988, in T$): Coconut oil 1,101,656, vanilla beans 1,384,837, bananas 658,362, dessicated coconut 403,250, water melons 19,169, knitted clothes 733,219, tarotaruas 99,286; fish 2,295,046, cassava 157,584, yams, 253,379, footwear 105,806, tapa cloth 102,345.
Principal destinations for Tongan exports/re-exports in 1988 were: New Zealand (T$3,313,202), Australia (T$1,738,191), USA (T$1,729,788), UK (T$28,170). Of 1988 imports (in T$), New Zealand furnished 21,313,446; Australia, 20,184,246; Japan, 5,401,330; Singapore, 3,451,779; USA, 5,338,115; Fiji, 7,190,968; China (Mainland), 2,068,269; UK, 766,370.
Total trade between Tonga and UK (British Department of Trade returns, in £1,000 sterling):

	1986	*1987*	*1988*	*1989*
Imports to UK	86	100	145	28
Exports and re-exports from UK	936	2,013	856	831

Tourism. There were 39,550 visitors in 1987.

COMMUNICATIONS

Roads. In 1987–88 there were over 5,000 registered motor vehicles and (1988) 1,242 km of roads (291 km paved).

Aviation. International air service connexions to Tongatapúare now provided by Air New Zealand, Polynesian Airlines, Air Pacific and Hawaiian Air with 4 flights per week to Auckland, 3 to Apia, 4 to Suva and 2 to Nadi. Hawaiian Air provides a twice weekly service to Hawaii via Pagopago. Internal air service flights are operated during the week to 'Eua, Ha'apai, Vava'u and Niuatoputapu by Friendly Island Airways.

Shipping. Pacific Forum Line maintains a four weekly service New Zealand–Fiji–Samoas–Tonga from Sydney, Australia–Noumea–Fiji–Samoas–Tonga. Warner Pacific Line maintains a monthly service New Zealand–Tonga–Samoas–Tonga–New Zealand and a monthly service Tonga–New Zealand–Australia–Funufuti–Tarawa–Samoas–Tonga.

Post and Telecommunications. The Kingdom has its own issue of postage stamps. Telephones numbered 3,500 in 1986 and there were 65,000 radio receivers. The operation of the International Telecommunication Services is undertaken by Cable and Wireless, under an agreement between the Company and the Government. The operation and development of the National Telecommunication Network and Services and the responsibilities of the Tonga Telecommunication Commission.

JUSTICE, RELIGION, EDUCATION AND WELFARE

Justice. Since the lapse of British extra-territorial jurisdiction British and foreign nationals charged with an offence against the laws of Tonga (the enforcement of which is a responsibility of the Minister of Police) are fully subject to the jurisdiction of the Tongan courts to which they are already subject in all civil matters.

Religion. The Tongans are Christian, 40,516 (1986) being adherents of the Free Wesleyan Church.

Education. In 1987 there were 102 government and 11 denominational primary schools, with a total of 16,715 pupils. There were 8 government and 48 mission schools and 1 private school offering secondary education, with a total roll of 14,137. There was one government teacher-training college; 5 government technical and vocational schools and 3 non-government technical and vocational schools. 201 students were undertaking tertiary training overseas under an official scholarship in 1985.

Health. In 1988–89 there were 45 doctors, 11 dentists, 2 pharmacists, 37 midwives, 266 nursing personnel and 4 hospitals with 307 beds.

DIPLOMATIC REPRESENTATIVES

Of Tonga in Great Britain (New Zealand Hse., Haymarket, London, SW1Y 4TE)
High Commissioner: S. M. Tuita (accredited 6 June 1989).

Of Great Britain in Tonga (Nuku'alofa)
High Commissioner: W. L. Cordiner.

Further Reading

Churchward, C. M., *Tongan Dictionary*. London, 1959
Luke, Sir Harry, *Queen Salote and Her Kingdom*. London, 1954
Packett, C. N., *Travel and Holiday Guide to Tongatapu Island*. Bradford, 1984

TRINIDAD AND TOBAGO

Capital: Port-of-Spain
Population: 1·24m. (1988)
GNP per capita: US$3,350 (1988)

HISTORY. Trinidad was discovered by Columbus in 1498 and colonized by the Spaniards in the 16th century. During the French Revolution a large number of French families settled in the island. In 1797, Great Britain being at war with Spain, Trinidad was occupied by the British and ceded to Great Britain by the Treaty of Amiens in 1802. Trinidad and Tobago were joined in 1889.

Under the Bases Agreement concluded between the governments of the UK and the USA on 27 March 1941, and the concomitant Trinidad–US Bases Lease of 22 April 1941, defence bases were leased to the US Government for 99 years. On 8 Dec. 1960 the US agreed to abandon 21,000 acres of leased land and the US has since given up the remaining territory, except for a small tracking station.

On 31 Aug. 1962 Trinidad and Tobago became an independent member state of the British Commonwealth. A Republican Constitution was adopted on 1 Aug. 1976.

AREA AND POPULATION. The island of Trinidad is situated in the Caribbean Sea, about 12 km off the north-east coast of Venezuela; several islets, the largest being Chacachacare, Huevos, Monos and Gaspar Grande, lie in the Gulf of Paria which separates Trinidad from Venezuela. The smaller island of Tobago lies about 31 km further to the north-east. Altogether, the islands cover 5,124 sq. km (1,978 sq. miles) of which Trinidad (including the islets) has 4,821 sq. km (1,861 sq. miles) and Tobago 303 sq. km (117 sq. miles). Population (census 1980): 1,079,800. (Trinidad, 1,039,100; Tobago, 40,700); estimate (1988) 1,243,000 (Trinidad, 1,198,000, Tobago, 45,000). Capital, Port-of-Spain, 58,400; other important towns, San Fernando (34,200) and Arima (24,600). Those of African descent are 40·8% of the population, Indians, 40·7%, mixed races, 16·3%, European, Chinese and others, 2·2%. English is spoken generally. Estimated population in 1987, 1·22m.

Vital statistics (rate per 1,000), 1983: Births, 29·2; deaths, 6·6; infant deaths, 12·6. Proportion of population under 15 years (1984) 39·2%.

Tobago is situated about 30·7 km north-east of Trinidad. Main town is Scarborough.

Principal goods shipped from Tobago to Trinidad are copra, cocoa, livestock and poultry, fresh vegetables, coconut oil and coconut fibre.

CLIMATE. A tropical climate whose dry season runs from Jan. to June, with a wet season for the rest of the year. Temperatures are uniformly high the year round. Port-of-Spain. Jan. 78°F (25·6°C), July 79°F (26·1°C). Annual rainfall 65" (1,631 mm).

CONSTITUTION AND GOVERNMENT. The 1976 Constitution provides for a bicameral legislature of a Senate and a House of Representatives. The Senate consists of 31 members, 16 being appointed by the President on the advice of the Prime Minister, 6 on the advice of the Leader of the Opposition and 9 at the discretion of the President.

Tobago has a 15-man House of Assembly (with limited powers).

The House of Representatives consists of 36 (34 for Trinidad and 2 for Tobago) elected members and a Speaker elected from within or outside the House.

The Cabinet consists of the Prime Minister, appointed by the President, and other Ministers, including the Attorney-General.

At the general elections in Dec. 1986 the National Alliance for Reconstruction won 33 seats; the People's National Movement won 3 seats.

President: Noor Mohammed Hassanali.
Prime Minister and Minister of Finance and Economy: A. N. R. Robinson.

Local Government: Trinidad is divided into a city (the capital), 3 boroughs and 6 counties; Tobago has since 1980 had a 15-member elected House of Assembly with limited powers of self-government.

National flag: Red with a diagonal black strip edged in white.

DEFENCE. The Defence Force has a regular and a reserve infantry battalion and a support battalion equipped with 81mm mortars, and there is also a small air element, equipped with 1 Cessna 402 light transport. Personnel in 1990 totalled 2,650.

In 1989 there were 2 Swedish (Karlskrona)-built patrol vessels, 2 British (Vosper, Portsmouth)-built patrol craft, 7 minor patrol boats, 1 survey vessel, 2 research craft and 1 sail training ship. A Commodore is Chief of Defence Staff while a Commander directs the Coast Guard. Of total defence personnel (1989) 600 were coastguard. The Police operate 2 coastal patrol cutters.

INTERNATIONAL RELATIONS

Membership. Trinidad and Tobago is a member of UN, the Commonwealth, OAS, Caricom and is an ACP state of EEC.

ECONOMY

Budget. The 1989 budget envisaged current expenditure (in TT$) as 4,627·9m. and capital expenditure at 1,324·6m.

Total external debt at 31 Dec. 1986, TT$5,600m.

Currency. The currency is the *Trinidad and Tobago dollar* of 100 *cents.* There are coins of 1, 5, 10, 25 and 50 cents and TT$1, and banknotes of TT$1, 5, 10, 20 and 100. £1 = TT$6·99; US$1 = TT$4·26 (March 1990).

Banking. Banks operating: Republic Bank of Trinidad and Tobago Ltd; Royal Bank of Trinidad and Tobago Ltd; Bank of Commerce, Trinidad and Tobago Ltd; Bank of Nova Scotia; United Bank of Trinidad and Tobago Ltd; National Commercial Bank of Trinidad and Tobago; Workers' Bank of Trinidad and Tobago; Trinidad Co-operative Bank Ltd. A Central Bank began operations in Dec. 1964.

Government savings banks are established in 69 offices, with a head office in Port-of-Spain.

ENERGY AND NATURAL RESOURCES

Electricity. In 1986, 3,182m. kwh was generated. Supply 115 and 230 volts; 60 Hz.

Oil. Oil production is one of Trinidad's leading industries and represented (1986) 71·6% of exports. Commercial production began in 1909; production of crude oil in 1989 was 7·8m. tonnes. Trinidad also possesses 2 refineries, with rated distillation capacity of 305,000 bbls annually; crude oil is imported from Venezuela, Indonesia, Ecuador, Nigeria, Brazil, and Saudi Arabia and refined in Trinidad. The 'Pitch Lake' is an important source of asphalt; production, 1986, 5,360,700 cu. metres.

Gas. In 1985 production was 7,413m. cu. ft., of which 1,601m. cu. ft. was flared and lost.

Agriculture. Hectares under cultivation and care include (1984): Cocoa, 21,000; sugar, 18,000. Sugar production in 1988 was 91,000 (1987: 85,000) tonnes. The territory is still largely dependent on imported food supplies, especially flour, dairy products, meat and rice. Areas have been irrigated for rice, and soil and forest conservation is practised.

Livestock (1988): Cattle, 78,000; sheep, 12,000; goats, 50,000; pigs, 84,000; poultry, 8m.

Fisheries. The catch in 1986, 14,800 tonnes.

INDUSTRY AND TRADE

Industry. In 1985, 474,300 tonnes of iron and steel were produced at the first integrated steelworks to be constructed in the Caribbean which was opened in 1981. Other manufacturing includes ammonia (production, 1985, 1,323,500 tonnes), fertilizers (1986 production, 1,888,000 tonnes), cement (338,000 tonnes, 1986), rum (2,307,000 proof gallons, 1986), beer (20,716 litres, 1986), cigarettes (920,000 kg, 1986).

Labour. The working population in 1986 was 471,300 and unemployment was about 17%; about 30% of the labour force belong to unions.

Commerce. Exports in 1986 were TT$4,962·2m. of which TT$3,504·4m. was mineral fuels and products and chemicals, TT$766·8m. USA took 61·5% of exports. Imports totalled TT$4,902·8m. of which TT$1,792·9m. was for machinery and transport of which the USA supplied 41·8%.

Total trade of Trinidad and Tobago with UK (British Department of Trade returns, in £1,000 sterling):

	1985	*1986*	*1987*	*1988*	*1989*
Imports to UK	81,719	41,662	38,600	35,728	37,426
Exports and re-exports from UK	93,897	79,029	57,016	39,868	45,881

Tourism. In 1986, 182,640 foreigners visited Trinidad and Tobago spending (estimate) TT$293·9m.

COMMUNICATIONS

Roads. There were (1985) about 6,435 km of main and local roads. Motor vehicles registered in 1985 totalled 336,769, including 127,716 private cars, 26,392 hired and rented cars, and 33,846 goods vehicles.

Aviation. The following airlines operate scheduled passenger, mail and freight services. British West Indian Airways, Ltd, Air Canada, PANAM, KLM, Linea Aeropostal Venezolana, Leeward Islands Air Transport, Caribair, British Airways, American Airlines, Guyana Airways, ALM Antillean Airline, Cruzeiro (Brazil), Eastern Airlines, Caribbean Airways and Viasa.

Shipping. In 1985 12·6m. tons of cargo were handled.

Post and Broadcasting. International communications to all parts of the world are provided by Trinidad and Tobago External Telecommunications Co. Ltd (TEXTEL) by means of a satellite earth station and various high quality radio circuits. The marine radio service is also maintained by TEXTEL. Number of post offices (1984), 69; postal agencies, 166; number of telephones (1986), 182,325. Four wireless stations are maintained by the Trinidad Government and 3 by airline companies. There were 500,000 radio and 300,000 television receivers in 1985. A meteorological station is maintained at Piarco airport.

Cinemas (1986). There are 57 cinemas and 3 drive-in cinemas.

Newspapers (1986). There are 4 daily newspapers with a total daily circulation (1984) of 166,380, 2 Sunday newspapers with a total circulation (1984) of 161,832, and 3 weekly newspapers.

JUSTICE, RELIGION, EDUCATION AND WELFARE

Justice. The High Court consists of the Chief Justice and 11 puisne judges. In criminal cases a judge of the High Court sits with a jury of 12 in cases of treason and murder, and with 9 jurors in other cases. The Court of Appeal consists of the Chief Justice and 3 Justices of Appeal; there is a limited right of appeal from it to the Privy Council. There are 3 High Courts and 12 magistrates' courts.

Religion. In 1980, 15% of the population were Anglicans (under the Bishop of Trinidad and Tobago), 33·6% Roman Catholics (under the Archbishop of Port-of-Spain), 25% Hindus and 5·9% Moslems.

Education. In 1985–86 there were 172,424 pupils enrolled in primary schools, 12,622 in government secondary schools, 17,576 in assisted secondary schools, 39,188 in junior secondary schools, 21,614 in senior comprehensive schools, 3,564 in composite schools and 4,419 in technical and vocational schools. The University of the West Indies campus in St Augustine had 2,684 full- and part-time students in 1984–85.

Health. In 1985 there were 1,103 physicians, 129 dentists, 496 pharmacists and 31 hospitals and nursing homes with 4,087 beds. There were 3,344 nurses and midwives and 980 nursing assistants in government institutions.

DIPLOMATIC REPRESENTATIVES

Of Trinidad and Tobago in Great Britain (42 Belgrave Sq., London, SW1X 8NT)
High Commissioner: Mervyn Assam.

Of Great Britain in Trinidad and Tobago (Furness Hse., 90 Independence Sq., Port-of-Spain)
High Commissioner: Sir Martin Berthoud, KCVO, CMG.

Of Trinidad and Tobago in the USA (1708 Massachusetts Ave., NW, Washington, D.C., 20036)
Ambassador: Angus Albert Khan.

Of the USA in Trinidad and Tobago (15 Queen's Park West, Port-of-Spain)
Ambassador: Charles A. Gargano.

Of Trinidad and Tobago to the United Nations
Ambassador: Dr Marjorie R. Thorpe.

Further Reading

Statistical Information: The Central Statistical Office, Government of Trinidad and Tobago, 2 Edward St., Port-of-Spain. *Director:* J. Harewood. Publications include *Annual Statistical Digest, Quarterly Economic Report, Annual Overseas Trade Report, Population and Vital Statistics Annual Report, Report on Education Statistics.*

Facts on Trinidad and Tobago. Ministry of Information, Port-of-Spain, 1983
Immigration Guidelines. Government Printer, Port-of-Spain, 1980
Oil and Energy, Trinidad and Tobago. Government Printer, Port-of-Spain, 1980
Trinidad and Tobago Year Book. Port-of-Spain. Annual (from 1865)
Chambers, F., *Trinidad and Tobago.* [Bibliography] Oxford and Santa Barbara, 1986
Cooper, St G. C. and Bacon, P. R. (eds.) *The Natural Resources of Trinidad and Tobago.* London, 1981

Central Library: The Central Library of Trinidad and Tobago, Queen's Park East, Port-of-Spain. *Acting Librarian:* Mrs L. Hutchinson.

TUNISIA

Capital: Tunis
Population: 7·75m. (1988)
GNP per capita: US$1,230 (1988)

al-Jumhuriya at-Tunisiya

HISTORY. Tunisia was a French protectorate from 1883 and achieved independence on 20 March 1956. The Constituent Assembly, elected on 25 March 1956, abolished the monarchy (of the Bey of Tunis) on 25 July 1957 and proclaimed a republic.

AREA AND POPULATION. The boundaries are on the north and east the Mediterranean Sea, on the west Algeria and on the south Libya. The area is about 164,150 sq. km (63,378 sq. miles), including that portion of the Sahara which is to the east of the Djerid (salt marsh), extending towards Ghadamès.

At the census of 30 March 1984 there were 6,966,173 inhabitants (3,547,487 males and 3,419,026 females) of whom 52·8% were urban. Estimate (1988) 7,745,500.

The census populations of the 23 *gouvernorats* were as follows as at 30 March 1984:

	Sq. km	*1984*		*Sq. km*	*1984*
Aryanah	1,558	374,192	Qasrayn (Kassérine)	8,066	297,959
Bajah (Béja)	3,558	274,706	Qayrawan (Kairouan)	6,712	421,607
Banzart (Bizerta)	3,685	394,670	Qibili (Kebili)	22,084	95,371
Bin Arus	761	246,193	Safaqis (Sfax)	7,545	577,992
Jundubah (Jendouba)	3,102	359,429	Sidi Bu Zayd		
Kaf (Le Kef)	4,965	247,672	(Sidi Bouzid)	6,994	288,528
Madaniyin (Médénine)	8,588	295,889	Silyanah (Siliana)	4,631	222,038
Mahdiyah (Mahdia)	2,966	270,435	Susah (Sousse)	2,621	322,491
Munastir (Monastir)	1,019	278,478	Tatawin (Tataouine)	38,889	100,329
Nabul (Nabeul)	2,788	461,405	Tawzar (Tozeur)	4,719	67,943
Qabis (Gabès)	7,175	240,016	Tunis	346	774,364
Qafsah (Gafsa)	8,990	235,723	Zaghwan (Zaghouan)	2,768	118,743

Tunis, the capital, had (census, 1984) 596,654 inhabitants: Sfax, 231,911; Aryanah, 98,655; Bizerta, 94,509; Djerba, 92,269; Gabès, 92,258; Sousse, 83,509; Kairouan, a holy city of the Moslems, 72,254; Bardo, 65,669; La Goulette, 61,609; Gafsa, 60,970; Béja, 46,708; Kasserine, 47,606; Nabeul, 39,531; Mahdia, 36,828; Monastir, 35,546; Le Kef, 34,509; Tataouine, 30,371; Medenine, 26,602; Jendouba, 23,249; Tozeur, 21,604; Sidi Bouzid, 19,218; Siliana, 12,433; Kébili, 11,780; Zaghouan, 10,149.

Vital statistics (1986). Birth rate, 31·7 per 1,000 population; death rate, 6·7 per 1,000.

The official language is Arabic but the use of French is widespread.

CLIMATE. The climate ranges from warm temperate in the north, where winters are mild and wet and the summers hot and dry, to desert in the south. Tunis. Jan. 48°F (8·9°C), July 78°F (25·6°C). Annual rainfall 16" (400 mm). Bizerta. Jan. 52°F (11·1°C), July 77°F (25°C). Annual rainfall 25" (622 mm). Sfax. Jan. 52°F (11·1°C), July 78°F (25·6°C). Annual rainfall 8" (196 mm).

CONSTITUTION AND GOVERNMENT. The Constitution of the republic was promulgated on 1 June 1959. The President and the National Assembly are elected simultaneously by direct universal suffrage for a period of 5 years. The President cannot be re-elected more than 3 times consecutively.

Elections were held on 2 Nov. 1986, when all 125 seats in the Chamber of Deputies were won by the *Front National*, an alliance of the ruling *Parti Socialiste Destourien*, renamed Rassemblement Constitutionnel Democratique, and the *Union générale des travailleurs tunisiens*. The elections were boycotted by opposition parties. General and presidential elections will be held on 9 Nov. 1989.

President of the Republic: Zine El Abidine Ben Ali (appointed 2 April 1989).

The Cabinet in 1989 was composed as follows:

Prime Minister: Hamed Karoui.

Justice: Mustapha Bouaziz. *Foreign Affairs:* Abdelhamid Escheikh. *Secretary General of the Presidency:* Mohamed El Jeri. *National Defence:* Abdallah Kallal. *Interior:* Chedly Neffati. *Planning and Finance:* Mohamed Ghannouchi. *National Economy:* Moncef Belaid. *Agriculture:* Nouri Zorgati. *Equipment and Housing:* Ahmed Friaa. *Transport:* Ahmed Smaoui. *Tourism and Handicrafts:* Mohamed Jegham. *Communications:* Sadok Rabah. *Education, Higher Education and Scientific Research:* Mohamed Charfi. *Culture and Information:* Habib Boulares. *Public Health:* Daly Jazi. *Social Affairs:* Moncer Rouissi. *Youth and Infancy:* Hamouda Ben Slama. *Secretary General of the Government:* Taoufik Cheikhrouhou.

There were 12 Secretaries of State.

Local Government. The country is divided into 23 *gouvernorats*, sub-divided into 199 districts and then into *communes and imadas*.

Flag: Red with a white circle in the middle, on which is a 5-pointed red star encircled by a red crescent.

DEFENCE. Selective military service is 1 year. Officer-cadets are being trained in France.

Army. The Army consists of 2 mechanized, 1 Sahara and 1 para-commando brigades; 1 armoured reconnaissance, 1 field, 2 anti-aircraft, 1 anti-tank and 1 engineer regiments. Equipment includes 14 M-48 and 54 M-60A3 main battle, and 40 AMX-13 and 10 M-41 light tanks. Strength (1990) 30,000. There are also the paramilitary gendarmerie (3,500 men) and National Guard (10,000 men).

Navy. The Navy consists of 1 frigate (*ex*-US, vintage 1943), 3 1985-built fast missile craft and 3 older craft with short range missiles, 2 *ex*-US-coastal minesweepers used as patrol ships, 14 inshore patrol craft and 1 large tug. In 1989 naval personnel totalled 4,500 (700 conscripts). Forces are based at Bizerta, Sfax and Kelibia.

Air Force. Equipment of the Air Force, acquired from various Western sources, includes 1 squadron of Aermacchi M.B.326K/L jet light attack aircraft; 1 squadron of F-5E/F Tiger II fighters; 12 SF.260W piston-engined light trainer/attack aircraft; 2 C-130H Hercules transports, 2 S.208 liaison aircraft, 6 SF.260M trainers, 7 M.B.326B jet trainers, 6 UH-1H, 18 AB.205, 6 Ecureuil and about 12 Alouette II and III helicopters. Personnel (1990) about 3,500.

INTERNATIONAL RELATIONS

Membership. Tunisia is a member of UN, OAU, the Islamic Conference and the Arab League.

ECONOMY

Planning. A seventh development plan (1987–91) envisaged investment of 8,000m. dinars.

Budget (in dinars). Budget estimates, 1988, revenue, 3,287m.; expenditure, 3,148m.

Currency. On 1 Nov. 1958 a new currency, the *dinar*, divided into 1,000 *millimes*, was established. Note circulation, Aug. 1980, was 910m. *dinars*.

Currency consists of coins of 1, 2, 5, 10, 20, 50, 100 and 500 *millimes*, and notes of 500 *millimes*, 1 *dinar*, 5 and 10 *dinars*. £1 = 1·50 *dinar*; US$1 = 0·92 *dinar* (March 1990).

Banking. The Central Bank of Tunisia is the bank of issue. In 1988 there were 9 development banks, 10 deposit banks and 9 off-shore banks.

Weights and Measures. The metric system of weights and measures has almost entirely taken the place of those of Tunisia, but corn is still sold in *kaffis* and *wibas*. The *kfiz* (of 16 *wiba*, each of 12 *sa'*) = 16 bushels. The *ounce* = 31·487 grammes.

The principal measure of length is the metre.

ENERGY AND NATURAL RESOURCES

Electricity. Electrical energy generated was 3,820m. kwh. in 1986. Supply 127 and 220 volts; 50 Hz.

Oil. Crude oil production (1989) 4·8m. tonnes.

Gas. Natural gas production (1984) 430m. cu. metres.

Water. In 1989 there were 15 dams (total capacity 945m. cu. metres) and 3 were being built (259m. cu. metres). In 1986, 257,000 hecatres were irrigated.

Minerals. Mineral production (in 1,000 tonnes) in 1987: Calcium phosphate, 6,200; iron ore, 291; lead ore (concentrated), 3·4; zinc ore (concentrated), 10·7; salt, 422; barytine, 18; spath fluor, 43.

Agriculture. Tunisia may be divided into 5 districts—the north, characterized by its mountainous formation, having large and fertile valleys (*e.g.*, the valley of the Medjerdah and the plains of Mornag, Mateur and Béja); the north-east, with the peninsula of Cap Bon, the soil being specially suited for the cultivation of oranges, lemons and tangerines; the Sahel, where olive trees abound; the centre, the region of high table lands and pastures, and the desert of the south, famous for its oases and gardens, where dates grow in profusion.

Agriculture is the chief industry, and large estates predominate. Of the total area of 15,583,000 hectares, about 9m. hectares are productive, including 2m. under cereals, 3·6m. used as pasturage, 900,000 forests and 1·3m. uncultivated. Production, 1988 (in 1,000 tonnes): Wheat, 225; barley, 63; olive oil, 71; olives, 320; citrus fruits, 214; dates, 40; almonds, 35; potatoes, 180; tomatoes, 370; pimentoes, 160; melons, 354; chickpeas, 21; sugar-beet, 267; tobacco, 5. Wine (1988) 49,000 tonnes.

Other products are apricots, pears, apples, peaches, plums, figs, pomegranates, almonds, shaddocks, pistachios, esparto grass, henna and cork.

Livestock (1988): Horses, 56,000; asses, 220,000; mules, 76,000; cattle, 612,000; sheep, 5·9m.; goats, 1,115,000; camels, 184,000; pigs, 4,000.

Fisheries. In 1980, 6,209 boats with 22,555 men were engaged in fishing. In 1987 the catch amounted to 99,180 tonnes.

INDUSTRY AND TRADE

Industry. Production, 1987 (in 1,000 tonnes): Superphosphate, 1,030; phosphoric acid, 593; cement, 3,215; lime, 527. 2,010 cars, 450 lorries, 1,240 vans, 220 buses and coaches, 330 tractors, 23,320 radio and 58,460 television sets were produced in 1987.

Trade Unions. The Union Générale des Travailleurs Tunisiens won 27 seats in the parliamentary elections (1 Nov. 1981). There are also the Union Tunisienne de l'Industrie, du Commerce et de l'Artisanat (UTICA, the employers' union) and the Union National des Agriculteurs (UNA, farmers' union).

Commerce. The imports and exports for calendar years (in 1,000 dinars) were as follows:

	1982	*1983*	*1984*	*1985*	*1986*	*1987*
Imports	2,008,000	2,116,100	2,472,500	2,287,000	2,308,300	2,509,000
Exports	1,188,000	1,263,900	1,396,800	1,443,000	1,387,600	1,770,600

Exports to France in 1987 totalled 384·1m. dinars, and imports from France, 687·2m. dinars and exports to USA were valued at 32·1m. dinars and imports from USA were valued at 149·1m. dinars.

In 1987 the main exports (in 1m. dinars) were: Clothing, 354·5; hosiery, 90·3; phosphoric acid, 69·8; electric machines, 66·8; fish and molluscs, 66·7; olive oil, 65·6.

Total trade between Tunisia and UK (British Department of Trade returns, in £1,000 sterling):

	1985	*1986*	*1987*	*1988*	*1989*
Imports to UK	39,826	17,292	14,714	36,062	43,266
Exports and re-exports from UK	43,209	39,824	24,943	30,780	31,148

Tourism. In 1986, there were 1,874,734. tourists.

COMMUNICATIONS

Roads. In 1987 there were 18,952 km of roads. Number of motor vehicles, 1987, 506,000.

Railways. In 1987 there were 2,167 km of railways (465 km of 1,435 mm gauge and 1,689 km of 1,000 mm gauge), of which 21 km electrified and carried 413m. passengers and 24m. tonnes of freight. A suburban railway links Tunis and La Marsa, and a light rail network opened in Tunis in 1985.

Aviation. The national airline is Tunis-Air. There are 5 international airports, the main one is at Tunis-Carthage. In 1987, 4,429,000 passengers and 21,688 tonnes of freight were carried.

Shipping. The main port is Tunis, and its outer port is Tunis-Goulette. These two ports and Sfax, Sousse and Bizerta are directly accessible to ocean going vessels. The ports of La Skhirra and Gabès are used for the shipping of Algerian and Tunisian oil.

In 1983, 5,370 ships of 19,224,000 tons entered Tunisian ports.

Post and Broadcasting. There were, in 1983, 218,808 telephones. There were, in 1978, 403 post offices, and 6 wireless transmitting stations. Wireless sets in use in 1985 were 1·15m. Television began in 1966 and in 1985 there were 400,000 sets.

Cinemas (1987). There were 80 cinemas.

Newspapers. There were (1987) 2 Arabic and 4 French daily newspapers.

JUSTICE, RELIGION, EDUCATION AND WELFARE

Justice. There are 51 magistrates' courts, 13 courts of first instance, 3 courts of appeal (in Tunis, Sfax and Sousse) and the High Court in Tunis.

A Personal Status Code was promulgated on 13 Aug. 1956 and applied to Tunisians from 1 Jan. 1957. This raised the status of women, made divorce subject to a court decision, abolished polygamy and decreed a minimum marriage age.

Religion. The constitution recognizes Islam as the state religion. There are about 20,000 Roman Catholics, under the Prelate of Tunis. The Greek Church, the French Protestants and the English Church are also represented.

Education. All education was in 1956 made dependent on the Ministry of National Education. The 208 independent koranic schools have been nationalized and the distinction between religious and public schools has been abolished. All education is free from primary schools to university. A teachers' training college (*école normale supérieure*) was established in 1955. There are also a high school of law, 2 centres of economic studies, 2 schools of engineering, 2 medical schools, a faculty of agriculture, 2 institutes of business administration and one school of dentistry.

In 1987–88 there were 3,605 primary schools with 43,189 teachers and 1,338,905 pupils; 436 secondary schools with 22,373 teachers and 437,604 pupils. In 1980–81 there were 60,137 students at technical and vocational schools and 4,101 students in teacher-training. In 1988 there were 3 universities: The University of Tunis (38,829 students and 5,019 teaching staff in 1984–85), the University of Sousse and the University of Sfax.

Health. In 1987 there were 36 general hospitals (22 university and 14 regional), 20 specialized institutions, centres and university hospitals, and (1988) 92 district hospitals. In 1986 there were 15,814 beds.

Social Security. A system of social security was set up in 1950 (amended 1963, 1964 and 1970).

DIPLOMATIC REPRESENTATIVES

Of Tunisia in Great Britain (29 Prince's Gate, London, SW7 1QG)
Ambassador: Abdelwahab Abdallah (accredited 18 Oct. 1988).

Of Great Britain in Tunisia (5 Place de la Victoire, Tunis)
Ambassador and Consul-General: S. P. Day, CMG.

Of Tunisia in the USA (1515 Massachusetts Ave., NW, Washington, D.C., 20005)
Ambassador: Dr Abdelaziz Hamzaoui.

Of the USA in Tunisia (144 Ave. de la Liberté, Tunis)
Ambassador: Robert H. Pelletreau, Jr.

Of Tunisia to the United Nations
Ambassador: Ahmed Ghezal.

Further Reading

Statistical Information: Institut National de la Statistique (27 Rue de Liban, Tunis) was set up in 1947. Its main publications are: *Annuaire statistique de la Tunisie* (latest issue, 1975).

Lawless R. I., Findlay, Allan M. and Findlay, A. M. *Tunisia.* [Bibliography] Oxford and Santa Barbara, 1982

Ling, D. L., *Tunisia: From Protectorate to Republic.* Indiana Univ. Press, 1967

Rudebeck, L., *The Tunisian Experience: Party and People.* London, 1970

Salem, N., *Habib Bourguiba, Islam and the Creation of Tunisia.* London, 1984

Tomkinson, M., *Tunisia: A Holiday Guide.* London and Hammamet, 1984

TURKEY

Capital: Ankara
Population: 50·67m. (1985)
GNP per capita: US$1,295 (1988)

Türkiye Cumhuriyeti

HISTORY. The Turkish War of Independence (1919–22), following the disintegration of the Ottoman Empire, was led and won by Mustafa Kemal (Atatürk) on behalf of the Grand National Assembly which first met in Ankara on 23 April 1920. On 20 Jan. 1921 the Grand National Assembly voted a constitution which declared that all sovereignty belonged to the people and vested all power, both executive and legislative, in the Grand National Assembly. The name 'Ottoman Empire' was later replaced by 'Turkey'. On 1 Nov. 1922 the Grand National Assembly abolished the office of Sultan and Turkey became a republic on 29 Oct. 1923.

Religious courts were abolished in 1924, Islam ceased to be the official state religion in 1928, women were given the franchise and western-style surnames were adopted in 1934.

On 27 May 1960 the Turkish Army, directed by a National Unity Committee under the leadership of Gen. Cemal Gürsel, overthrew the government of the Democratic Party. The Grand National Assembly was dissolved and party activities were suspended. Party activities were legally resumed on 12 Jan. 1961. A new constitution was approved in a referendum held on 9 July 1961 and general elections were held the same year.

On 12 Sept. 1980, the Turkish armed forces overthrew the Demirel Government (Justice Party). Parliament was dissolved and all activities of political parties were suspended. The Constituent Assembly was convened in Oct. 1981, and prepared a new Constitution which was enforced after a national referendum on 7 Nov. 1982.

AREA AND POPULATION. Turkey is bounded west by the Aegean Sea and by Greece, north by Bulgaria and the Black Sea, east by the USSR and Iran, and south by Iraq, Syria and the Mediterranean.

The area (including lakes) is 779,452 sq. km (300,947 sq. miles). Area in Europe (Trakya), 23,764 sq. km. Area in Asia (Anadolu), 755,688 sq. km; population (census 1985), 50,664,458.

The census population is given as follows:

	Total		*Total*		*Total*
1927	13,648,270	1950	20,947,188	1970	35,605,176
1935	16,158,018	1955	24,064,763	1975	40,347,719
1940	17,820,950	1960	27,754,820	1980	44,736,957
1945	18,790,174	1965	31,391,421	1985	50,664,458

The population of the provinces, at the census in 1985, was as follows:

Adana	1,725,940	Çankırı	263,964	İzmir	2,317,829
Adıyaman	430,728	Çorum	599,204	Kahramanmaraş	840,472
Afyonkarahisar	666,978	Denizli	667,478	Kars	722,431
Ağri	421,131	Diyarbakir	934,505	Kastamonu	450,353
Amasya	358,289	Edirne	389,638	Kayseri	864,060
Ankara	3,306,327	Elâziğ	483,715	Kırklareli	297,098
Antalya	891,149	Erzincan	299,985	Kirşehir	260,156
Artvin	226,338	Erzurum	856,175	Kocaeli	742,245
Aydin	743,419	Eskişehir	597,397	Konya	1,769,050
Balıkesir	910,282	Gaziantep	966,490	Kütahya	543,384
Bilecik	160,909	Gireşun	502,151	Malatya	665,809
Bingöl	241,548	Gümüşhane	283,753	Manisa	1,050,130
Bitlis	300,843	Hakkari	182,645	Mardin	652,069
Bolu	504,778	Hatay	1,002,252	Muğla	486,290
Burdur	248,002	Isparta	382,844	Muş	339,492
Bursa	1,324,015	İçel	1,034,085	Nevşehir	278,129
Çanakkale	417,121	İstanbul	5,842,985	Niğde	560,386

Ordu	763,857	Sinop	280,140	Tunceli	151,906
Rize	374,206	Sivas	772,209	Uşak	271,261
Sakarya	610,500	Tekirdağ	402,721	Van	547,216
Samsun	1,108,710	Tokat	679,071	Yozgat	545,301
Şanliurfa	795,034	Trabzon	786,194	Zonguldak	1,044,945
Siirt	524,741				

The population of towns of over 100,000 inhabitants, at the census of Oct. 1985, was as follows:

Istanbul	5,494,916	Diyarbakir	305,259	Denizli	171,360
Ankara	2,251,533	Samsun	280,068	Trabzon	155,960
Izmir	1,489,817	Antalya	258,139	Sakarya	155,041
Adana	776,000	Erzurum	252,648	Balikesir	152,402
Bursa	614,133	Malatya	251,257	Manisa	126,319
Gaziantep	466,302	Kocaeli	236,144	Van	121,306
Konya	438,859	K. Maraş	212,206	Kütahya	120,354
Kayseri	378,458	Şanliurfa	206,385	Zonguldak	119,125
Eskişehir	367,328	Sivas	197,266	Hatay	109,233
Içel	314,105	Elaziğ	181,253	Isparta	101,784

CLIMATE. Coastal regions have a Mediterranean climate, with mild, moist winters and hot, dry summers. The interior plateau has more extreme conditions, with low and irregular rainfall, cold and snowy winters and hot, almost rainless summers. Ankara. Jan. 32·5°F (0·3°C), July 73°F (23°C). Annual rainfall 14·7" (367 mm). Istanbul. Jan. 41°F (5°C), July 73°F (23°C). Annual rainfall 28·9" (723 mm). Izmir. Jan. 46°F (8°C), July 81°F (27°C). Annual rainfall 28" (700 mm).

CONSTITUTION AND GOVERNMENT. The Turkish Grand National Assembly was dissolved on 12 Sept. 1980. The National Security Council took over its functions and powers. On 23 Oct. 1981 a Consultative Assembly was inaugurated, to prepare a new Constitution to replace that of 1961. The Assembly began its work in Oct. 1981 under the presidency of Sadi Irmak and on 7 Nov. 1982 a national referendum established that 98% of the electorate were in favour of the new Constitution.

Turkish men and women are entitled to vote at the age of 21 to elect members of a single-chamber parliament.

Elections were held on 29 Nov. 1987. Of the 450 seats in the Grand National Assembly the Motherland Party won 292; The Social Democratic Populist Party, 99; The True Path Party, 59.

President: Turgut Özal.

The Cabinet in Nov. 1989 was composed as follows:

Prime Minister: Yildirim Akbulut.

Deputy Prime Minister and Minister of State: Ali Bozer. *Justice:* Oltan Sungurlu. *Defence:* Safa Giray. *Interior:* Abdulkadir Aksu. *Foreign Affairs:* Mesut Yilmaz. *Customs and Finance:* Ekrem Pakdemirli. *Education:* Avni Akyol. *Public Works and Housing:* Cengiz Altinkaya. *Health:* Halil Sivgin. *Labour:* Imren Aykut. *Transportation and Communications:* Cengiz Tuncer. *Agriculture, Forestry and Rural Affairs:* Lutfullah Kayalar. *Industry and Commerce:* Sükrü Yürür. *Energy and Natural Resources:* Fahrettin Kurt. *Tourism:* Ilhan Akuzum. *Culture:* Namik Kemal Zeybek.

There are 14 Ministers of State.

National flag: A white crescent and star on red.

National anthem: Korkma! Sönmez bu şafaklarda yüzen al sancak (words by Mehmed Akif Ersoy; tune by Zeki Güngör; adopted 12 March 1921).

Local Government. The Constitution of 1921 provided for the administrative division of the country into *I,* (province, now 67 in number), divided into *Ilçe* (district), subdivided in their turn into *Bucak* (township or commune). At the head of each Il is a Vali representing the Government. Each Il has its own elective council.

The Ilçe is regarded as a mere grouping of Bucaks for certain purposes of general administration. The Bucak or commune is an autonomous entity and possesses an elective council charged with the administration of such matters as are not reserved to the State.

According to the municipal law passed in 1930, Turkish women have the right to be electors and to be elected at local and national elections.

DEFENCE. Several bills for the reorganization of the armed forces were passed in June 1961 by the Grand National Assembly. One of these placed all organizations connected with national defence under the authority of the Minister of National Defence. Another created a Supreme Council of National Security, under the chairmanship of the Prime Minister, with the object of co-ordinating the resources of the country in case of war. Besides the Minister of National Defence and the Chief of the General Staff, the heads of economic Ministries are members of this council.

Military service in Army, Air Force and Navy is 18 months. Men are called up when they reach the age of 20.

Army. The Army consists of 12 infantry, 2 mechanized and 1 armoured divisions, 11 infantry, 1 parachute and 2 commando brigades; 5 coastal defence battalions. Equipment includes 1,615 M-48, 900 M-47 and 77 Leopard main battle tanks. Army Aviation has over 500 aircraft and helicopters, including about 100 Bell transport helicopters. Strength (1990) 650,900 (including 575,800 conscripts), and reserves number 808,000. There is also a paramilitary force of 125,000 men including an active gendarmerie, 75,000.

Navy. Current strength includes 15 diesel submarines (6 of German design built 1975-89 and 9 *ex*-US built 1944-45, 12*ex*-US destroyers (1943-46), 10 frigates of which 4 are modern German MEKO-type, 4 *ex*-German Type 120 Köln class, and 2 locally built in the 1970s. Light forces comprise 16 fast missile craft, 4 fast torpedo craft, 7 coastal and 21 inshore patrol craft. Mine warfare forces include 6 minelayers, 22 coastal and 11 inshore minesweepers. Amphibious lift is provided by 7 tank landing ships and over 70 smaller craft. Major auxiliaries in service are 1 replenishment and 6 support tankers, 5 depot ships, 3 salvage/rescue ships, 1 survey ship and 1 training ship. Minor auxiliaries, coastal freighters and service craft number about 120.

The main naval bases are at Gölcük in the Gulf of Izmit, at Iskenderun, at Taskizak (Istanbul) and at Izmir.

The naval air component operates 22 S-2A/E/TS-2A mixed Air Force and Naval-manned Tracker ASW aircraft and 9 helicopters for anti-submarine and patrol duties. There is a Marine Brigade some 4,000 strong.

Personnel in 1989 totalled 55,000, of whom 42,000 were conscripts, including marines.

The separate Coast Guard numbers about 1,000 and performs coastal police duties with a force of 28 inshore patrol vessels, 4 transports and numerous boats.

Air Force. The Air Force is under the control of the General Staff and, operationally, under 6 ATAF. It is organized as 2 tactical air forces, with headquarters at Eskisehir and Diyarbakir, each having a flight of C-47s, UH-1H helicopters, T-33s. Combat aircraft comprise F-104G and F-104S Starfighters in 7 squadrons; F-5As in 3 squadrons; F-16A/Bs in 2 squadrons; RF-5As in 1 squadron; F-4E and RF-4E Phantoms in 6 squadrons; plus Nike-Hercules surface-to-air missile batteries. The 4 transport squadrons are equipped with Transall C-160, C-130 Hercules, Citation, Viscount and C-47 aircraft, and UH-IH helicopters. Training types include T-33A, T-37 and T-38 advanced trainers, T-34 basic and T-41 primary trainers. Personnel strength (1990) 67,400, with over 320 combat aircraft. Delivery of 160 F-16 Fighting Falcons began late in 1987.

INTERNATIONAL RELATIONS

Membership. Turkey is a member of UN, OECD, NATO and Council of Europe and an Associate of EEC.

ECONOMY

Planning. The development plan 1985–90 envisaged an investment of TL14,412,900m.

Budget. The budget for 1988–89 envisaged expenditure of TL20,800,000m. and revenue of TL18,400,000m.

Currency. The Turkish *Lira* (TL) is divided into 100 *kuruş (piastres).* Coins in general circulation are of the following values: 5, 10, 25, 50, 100 and 500 *Lira.* Banknotes in circulation are as follows: 1,000, 5,000, 10,000, 20,000 and 50,000 *Lira*. In March 1990, US$1 = 2,470 *Lira*; £1 = 4,048.

Banking. The Turkish banking system is composed of the Central Bank of the Republic of Turkey (Merkez Bankası), 3 state banks and 58 private banks. The assets and liabilities of deposit money banks in 1987 were TL37,027,597m.

Weights and Measures. The metric system came into force on 1 Jan. 1934. On 24 May 1928 the Grand National Assembly made European numerals obligatory as from 1 June 1929.

On 1 March 1917 the Gregorian calendar was introduced into Turkey, to be used side by side with the Hegira calendar, while as from 26 Dec. 1925 it was decided finally to adopt the Gregorian calendar alone.

ENERGY AND NATURAL RESOURCES

Electricity. The potential hydro-electric power in Turkey is estimated at 56,000m. kwh. In 1986 the electrical power plants (hydro-electric or thermal) produced 38,490m. kwh. Supply 220 volts; 50 Hz.

Oil. Oil is being produced in Garzan and Raman by the Turkish Petroleum Co. Under the oil law of 14 Oct. 1954 private companies can explore and produce oil. Crude oil production (1989) was 2·6m. tonnes. The 3 refineries refined 12m. tons of crude oil in 1975. With a fourth refinery, introduced in 1973, total refining capacity now reaches 24m. tons a year. The oil pipeline Batman–Iskenderun (494 km) was opened on 4 Jan. 1967. Imports (refined locally) in 1983 were 14·3m. tonnes.

Minerals. The Turkish provinces, especially those in Asia, are reported rich in minerals. Turkey is one of the four principal producers of chrome in the world.

Production of principal minerals (in 1,000 tonnes) was:

	1985	*1986*	*1987*
Coal	7,260	7,015	7,084
Lignite	39,437	45,470	46,481
Chrome	877	1,040	1,049
Copper concentrate	136	...	...
Refined sulphur	43	40	...
Iron	3,995	5,249	5,366
Boron	1,543	1,636	1,629

Of the Government organizations producing these ores, Zonguldak coal mines operate under the Turkish State Coal Exploitation; while the copper mines at Murgul and Ergani, the Eastern chromite mines, Keçiborlu sulphur, Emet colemanite, Küre pyrite and cupriferous pyrite, Keban argentiferous lead mines operate under the Etibank.

Agriculture. The number of people aged 15 and over engaged in agriculture in 1980 was 10,482,856.

In 1987, 24,318,000 hectares were crop land, 18,744,000 hectares of it sown and 5,574,000 hectares fallow; vineyards, fruit orchards and olive groves occupied 2,963,000 hectares; forest occupied 20,199,000 hectares.

The soil for the most part is very fertile; the principal products are cotton, tobacco, cereals (especially wheat), figs, silk, dried fruits, liquorice root, nuts, almonds, mohair, skins and hides, furs, wool, gums, canary seed, linseed and sesame. The principal tobacco districts are Samsun, Bafra, Çarsamba, Izmit and Izmir. Two-thirds of the exports of leaf tobacco goes to the USA. The principal centre for silk production is Bursa. The production of olives for olive oil, mainly confined to the Ils of Aydın and Balıkesir, is very important (1·1m. tonnes in 1988). Sugar production (refined) in 1985 was 1,429,586 tonnes. Agricultural production (in tonnes) in 1988 included 3·35m. grapes, 754,000 oranges and 370,000 lemons, 362,000 hazelnuts, 1,954,000 apples, 1·1m. olives, 4·35m. potatoes. Tea production (fresh leaves, 1987) was 660,690 tonnes.

Turkey produced 1,000 tonnes of flax fibre and 5,000 tonnes of hemp fibre in 1988. Cotton lint production was 577,000 tonnes in 1988. Agricultural tractors numbered 637,449 in 1987.

Production (in 1,000 tonnes) of principal crops:

	1984	*1985*	*1986*	*1987*	*1988*
Wheat	17,200	17,000	19,000	18,900	20,500
Barley	6,500	6,500	7,000	6,900	7,500
Maize	1,500	1,900	2,300	2,400	2,100
Rye	360	360	350	380	293
Tobacco	178	170	158	182	212
Oats	316	314	300	325	276
Rice	168	162	165	165	263

Livestock (1988): 40m. sheep, 13·1m. goats, 12m. cattle, 1·2m. asses, 620,000 horses, 540,000 buffaloes.

In 1988 Turkey produced 62,000 tonnes of wool, 245,000 tonnes of cattle meat and 305,000 tonnes of sheep meat and 290,000 tonnes of poultry.

Forestry. The most wooded Ils are Kastamonu, Aydın, Bursa, Bolu, Trabzon, Konya and Balikesir. In 1987 total forest land was 20,199,000 hectares, 26% of the land area. Produce (1,000 cu. metres) in 1987: Logs, 3,950; pit props, 652; industrial wood, 500; poles, 186. Also 4,956,000 tonnes of firewood.

Fisheries. Catch (1987): Sea fish, 562,697 tonnes; crustaceans and molluscs, 20,156 tonnes; fresh water fish, 41,760 tonnes. Aquaculture production, 1987, 3,300 tonnes (mainly carp and trout). There were (1987) 8,594 fishing boats.

INDUSTRY AND TRADE

Industry. In 1987 Turkey produced (in tonnes) 8·15m. of fuel oil; 6,584,000 of motor oil; 4·1m. of crude iron; 338,000 of pig iron; 7m. of steel ingots; 3,649,000 of super phosphate; 3,017,000 of coke; 21·98m. of cement and 532,412 of paper. In 1987, 107,185 passenger cars were produced and 35,995 tractors. There are steel works at Karabük, Ereğli and Iskenderun.

Trade Unions. The trade-union movement began in 1947. There are 4 national confederations (including Türk-Iş and Disk) and 6 federations. There are 35 unions affiliated to Türk-Iş and 17 employers' federations affiliated to Disk, whose activities were banned on 12 Sept. 1980. In 1987, labour unions totalled 91 and employers' unions, 48.

Economically active population aged 12 and over, 1985, 20,556,786, of whom 12,118,533 were engaged in agriculture, forestry, hunting and fishing, 2,185,369 in manufacturing, 1,382,636 in trade, restaurants and hotels and 2,847,289 in services.

Commerce. Imports and exports (in US$1m.) for calendar years:

	1985	*1986*	*1987*
Imports	11,343	11,105	14,158
Exports	7,958	7,457	10,190

Exports (1988) in US$1m.: Textiles, 3,201; iron and steel products, 1,457; chemical products, 734; leather clothing, 514; plastic material and rubber, 351; hazelnuts, 351; machinery, 332; petroleum products, 331; electrical machinery, 294; tobacco, 266.

Imports (1988) in US$1m.: Crude oil, 2,434; machinery, 2,400; chemical products, 1,984; iron and steel products, 1,655; electrical equipment, 1,075; transport equipment, 690; plastic material and rubber, 525; other metallic assets, 411; petroleum products, 343; coal, 251.

In 1988 imports (in US$1m.) were: From Federal Republic of Germany, 2,054·4; USA, 1,519·7; Iraq, 1,440·8; Italy, 1,005·7; France, 828·8; UK, 739·1; Iran, 659·8; Japan, 554·8; Belgium, 477·8; USSR, 442·6. Exports: Federal Republic of Germany, 2,149; Iraq, 986·1; Italy, 954·7; USA, 760·6; UK, 576·1; Iran, 545·7; France, 498·5; Saudi Arabia, 355·2; Netherlands, 351·1; USSR, 291·4.

Total trade between Turkey and UK (British Department of Trade returns, in £1,000 sterling):

	1985	*1986*	*1987*	*1988*	*1989*
Imports to UK	538,462	406,605	579,366	509,636	533,769
Exports and re-exports from UK	460,220	433,753	513,479	477,539	434,562

Tourism. The number of foreign visitors was 4,249,641 in 1988; earnings from tourism in 1987, US$1,028m.

COMMUNICATIONS

Roads. In 1987 there were 31,062 km of state highways (including 125 km of motorway in 1989) and 27,853 km of provincial roads; 55,946 km were surfaced. In 1987 there were 1,193,021 cars, 459,352 trucks and pick-ups, 159,868 buses and minibuses and 369,894 motorcycles.

Railways. Total length of railway lines in 1987 was 8,439 km (1,435 mm gauge) of which 479 km electrified; 130m. passengers and 13·9m. tonnes of freight were carried.

Aviation. In 1986 Turkish Airlines fleet of 31 planes flew 2,746,000 passengers and carried 37,952 tons of freight.

Shipping. In 1985 the gross tonnage of cargo ships totalled 690,784; passenger ships 131,325 and tankers 186,267. The main ports are: Istanbul, Izmir, Samsun, Mersin, Iskenderun and Trabzon.

Coastal shipping, 1986: 25,543 vessels handled; 632,004 passengers entered, 626,602 cleared; 23·3m. tons of goods entered, 20·6m. cleared. International shipping: 12,383 vessels handled; 385,628 passengers entered, 380,440 cleared; 3,717m. tons of goods entered, 58·5m. cleared.

Post and Broadcasting. Number of telephones in 1986 was 2·28m.; İstanbul, 566,745; Ankara, 248,824.

In 1984 there were 6,023,000 licensed radio sets. There were 6,933,285 television receivers.

Newspapers. In 1988, 13 dailies were published in Ankara, 29 dailies in İstanbul, 5 dailies in Izmir, 4 dailies in Bursa and 3 dailies in Konya.

JUSTICE, RELIGION, EDUCATION AND WELFARE

Justice. The unified legal system consists of: (1) justices of the peace (single judges with limited but summary penal and civil jurisdiction); (2) courts of first instance (single judges, dealing with cases outside the jurisdiction of (3) and (4)); (3) central criminal courts (a president and 2 judges, dealing with cases where the crime is punishable by imprisonment over 5 years); (4) commercial courts (3 judges); (5) state security courts, to prosecute offences against the integrity of the state (a president and 4 judges, 2 of the latter being military).

The civil and military Courts of Cassation sit at Ankara.

The Council of State is the highest administration tribunal; it consists of 5 chambers. Its 31 judges are nominated from among high-ranking personalities in politics, economy, law, the army, etc.

The Military Court of Cassation in Ankara is the highest military tribunal. The Military Administrative Court deals with the judicial control of administrative acts and deeds concerning military personnel.

The Constitutional Court, set up under the Constitution, can review and annul legislation and try the President of the Republic, Ministers and senior judges. It consists of 15 regular and 5 alternate members.

The Civil Code and the Code of Obligations have been adapted from the corresponding Swiss codes. The Penal Code is largely based upon the Italian Penal Code, and the Code of Civil Procedure closely resembles that of the Canton of Neuchâtel. The Commercial Code is based on the German.

Religion. Freedom of religion is guaranteed by the Constitution. Although Islam is not the official state religion of Turkey, Moslems form 98·2% of the population. The administration of the Moslem religious organizations is in charge of the Presidency of Religious Affairs, attached to the Prime Minister's office. The Turkish Republic is a secular state.

Istanbul is the seat of the (Ecumenical Patriarch, who is the head of the Orthodox Church in Turkey. The Armenian Church (Gregorian) is ruled by a Patriarch in Istanbul who is subordinate to the Katholikos of Etchmiadzin, the spiritual head of all Armenians. The Armenian Apostolic Church is ruled by the Patriarch of Cilicia. The Chaldeans (Nestorian Uniats) have a Bishop at Mardin. The Syrian Uniats have a See of Mardin and Amida, but it is united with their Patriarchate of Antioch (residence, Damascus). Greek Uniats (Byzantine Rite) have as their Ordinary in Istanbul, the Titular Bishop of Gratianopolis. The Latins have an Apostolic Delegate in Istanbul and an Archbishop in Izmir, but their Patriarch of Istanbul is titular and non-resident. There is a Grand Rabbi (Hahambaşi) in Istanbul for the Jews, who are nearly all Sephardim.

A law passed in Dec. 1934 forbids the wearing of clerical garb for those other than religious leaders except in places of worship and during divine service. The constitution forbids the political exploitation of religion or any impairment of the secular character of the republic.

Education. Elementary education is compulsory and co-educational and, in state schools, free. All children from 7 to 12 are to receive primary instruction, which may be given in state schools, schools maintained by communities, or private schools, or, subject to certain tests, at home. The state schools are under the direct control of the Ministry of Education. They include primary schools, secondary or middle schools, and *lycées* or secondary schools of a superior kind. There are also training schools for male and female teachers, and technical schools. In 1986–87 there were 28 universities and over 100 other institutes of higher education. The important non-Moslem communities in Istanbul maintain their own schools, which, like all 'private' schools, are subject to the supervision of the Ministry of Education.

Literacy of the population of 6 years and over was 10·6% in 1927, 19·2% in 1935, 29% in 1945, 40·9% in 1955, 48·7% in 1965, 49% in 1970, 61·7% in 1975, 67·5% in 1980.

Religious instruction in schools, hitherto prohibited, was made optional in elementary and middle schools in May 1948. There are many training schools for Moslem clergy as well as a Faculty of Theology in Ankara.

Statistics for 1986–87	*Number*	*Teachers*	*Students*
Primary schools (state and private)	49,718	216,889	6,703,895
Secondary schools (state and private)	4,753	42,246	1,761,794
High schools (state and private)	1,344	55,065	672,574
Vocational and technical schools	2,131	45,219	666,319
Faculties (university and higher education)	322	24,382	481,600

In 1989 there were 29 universities with 5,600 teaching staff and 550,000 students.

Health. Public health is the responsibility of the Ministry of Health and Social Welfare, established in 1920; social insurance for workers comes under the Workers' Insurance Institution attached to the Ministry of Labour. A law promulgated in 1961 and implemented from 1963 provided for the nationalization of the health services within 15 years. In 1986, 2·8m. workers and employees were covered by social insurance, including free medical care.

In 1988 there were 38,829 doctors (1986), 8,410 dentists and 127,025 beds in 798 hospitals and 95 health centres.

DIPLOMATIC REPRESENTATIVES

Of Turkey in Great Britain (43 Belgrave Sq., London, SW1X 8PA)
Ambassador: Nurver Nureş (accredited 16 Feb. 1989).

Of Great Britain in Turkey (Sehit Ersan Caddesi 46/A, Cankaya, Ankara)
Ambassador: Sir Timothy Daunt, KCMG.

Of Turkey in the USA (1606 23rd St., NW, Washington, D.C., 20008)
Ambassador: Nüzhet Kandemir.

Of the USA in Turkey (110 Ataturk Blvd., Ankara)
Ambassador: Morton Abramowitz.

Of Turkey to the United Nations
Ambassador: Mustafa Akşin.

Further Reading

Statistical Information: The State Institute of Statistics in Ankara consists of a research bureau and 10 sections dealing with agriculture, education, foreign trade, etc. It published an *Annuaire Statistique/Istatistik Yiliği* (1928–53) and *Aylık Istatistik Bülteni*, Monthly Bulletin of Statistics.

The Turkish Constitution, 1971. Ankara, 1972
Resmî Gazete, Official Gazette. Ankara
Konjonktür. Ministry of Commerce (three times a year, from 1940)
Banque Centrale de la République de Turquie. *Bulletin Mensuel* (from Jan. 1953)
Barchard, D., *Turkey and the West*. London, 1985
Dodd, C. H., *The Crisis of Turkish Democracy*. Beverley, 1983
Goodwin, G., *A History of Ottoman Architecture*. London, 1971
Güclü, M., *Turkey*. [Bibliography] Oxford and Santa Barbara, 1981
Hale, W., *The Political and Economic Development of Modern Turkey*. London, 1981
Hesper, M., *The State Tradition in Turkey*. Beverley, 1985
Kazancigil, A. and Ozbudun, E., (eds.) *Atatürk: Founder of a Modern State*. London, 1981
Kinross, Lord, *Atatürk*. London, 1964
Lewis, B., *The Emergence of Modern Turkey*. OUP, 1968
Mackenzie, K., *Turkey in Transition: The West's Neglected Ally*. London, 1984
Rustow, D. A., *Turkey: America's Forgotten Ally*. New York, 1987
Sezer, D. B., *Turkey's Security Policies*. London, 1981
Tachau, F., *Turkey: The Politics of Authority, Democracy and Development*. New York, 1984
Weiker W., *The Modernization of Turkey*. New York, 1981

State Library: MilliKütüphane Müdürlügü, Ankara.

THE TURKS AND CAICOS ISLANDS

Capital: Grand Turk
Population: 13,000 (1989)

HISTORY. After a long period of rival French and Spanish claims the islands were eventually secured to the British Crown by the appointment in 1766 of a Resident British Agent, and became a separate colony in 1973 after association at various times with the colonies of the Bahamas and Jamaica.

AREA AND POPULATION. The Turks and Caicos Islands are geographically part of the Bahamas extremity, of which they form the south-eastern archipelago. There are upwards of 30 small cays; area 192 sq. miles (430 sq. km). Only 6 are inhabited; the largest, Grand Caicos, is 30 miles long by 2 to 3 miles broad. The seat of government is at Grand Turk, 7 miles long by 1·25 broad; 3,098 inhabitants. Population, 1980 census, 7,436; South Caicos, 1,380; Middle Caicos, 396; North Caicos, 1,278; Providenciales, 977; Salt Cay, 284. Estimate (1989) 13,000.

Vital statistics (1985): Births, 217; marriages, 49; deaths, 72.

CLIMATE. An equable and healthy climate as a result of regular trade winds, though hurricanes are sometimes experienced. Grand Turk. Jan. 76°F (24·4°C), July 83°F (28·3°C). Annual rainfall 29" (725 mm).

CONSTITUTION AND GOVERNMENT. A new Constitution was introduced in Aug. 1976, providing for an Executive Council and a Legislative Council. The Governor retains responsibility for external affairs, internal security, defence and certain other matters. The Executive Council comprises 3 official members: The Chief Secretary, the Financial Secretary and the Attorney-General; a Chief Minister and 3 other ministers from among the elected members of the Legislative Council; and is presided over by the Governor. The Legislative Council consists of a Speaker, the 3 official members of the Executive Council, 13 elected members and 2 appointed members. At general elections held on 3 March 1988 for the 13 elective seats on the Legislative Council, 11 seats were won by the People's Democratic Movement.

Governor: M. J. Bradley, QC.
Chief Minister: Oswald Skipping

Flag: British Blue Ensign with the shield of the Colony in the fly.

ECONOMY

Budget. 1989–90 total revenue US$44,360m. and expenditure, US$43,990m.

Currency. The currency in circulation is US$.

Banking. In 1988 there were 3 commercial banks. Barclays Bank, Bank of Nova Scotia and Turks and Caicos Banking Company have offices in Grand Turk.

COMMERCE (1985–86). Exports, US$3,509,224, and imports, US$29,106,090. Principal imports, food, drink, manufactured goods. Origin of imports (1985–86 in US$1): USA, 26,149,337; UK, 558,378. The main exports are crawfish (US$1·08m. in 1985–86), dried and fresh frozen conch (US$2·4m. in 1985–86). All crawfish, conch and other fish exports go to the USA after processing in plants in South Caicos and Providenciales.

Total trade between Turks and Caicos Islands and UK (British Department of Trade returns, in £1,000 sterling):

	1985	*1986*	*1987*	*1988*	*1989*
Imports to UK	6	86	31	66	74
Exports and re-exports from UK	1,063	1,025	496	710	731

Tourism. Number of hotels and guest houses, 34 (700 rooms/units) including the 346 room Club Mediterranée. Number of visitors, 1988, 47,000.

COMMUNICATIONS

Aviation. There is a 6,335 ft paved airfield on Grand Turk. On South Caicos there is a 6,000 ft paved airfield and on Providenciales a 7,000 ft paved airstrip. There are small paved and unpaved airstrips on the other 3 inhabited islands. Pan American World Airways operate passenger services to Miami. Turks and Caicos National Airlines operates daily service to the islands and a number of flights a week to Cap Haitien (Haiti), the Dominican Republic and the Bahamas. Turks Air Ltd and Caicos Caribbean operate regular weekly cargo services from Miami. There are 5 local charter operators, operating charters to the Bahamas and the Caribbean.

Shipping. Registered shipping (1985), 168 sailing vessels of 2,445 tons and 49 motor vessels of 5,517 tons.

Post and Broadcasting. Air-mail is received 4 times weekly from Miami and dispatched twice weekly to Miami. Surface mail from all parts of the world is routed *via* the US arriving weekly from Miami, Florida. There is no regular outgoing surface mail and this is sent as accumulated. Cable & Wireless (West Indies) provide internal and international cable, telephone, telex, telegraph and facsimile services. There were (1988) 1,359 telephones. North Caicos and Salt Cay are linked with the Providenciales and Grand Turk exchanges respectively. The Government operates a radio broadcasting service from Grand Turk to the Islands, call sign Radio Turks and Caicos (RTC), for a total of 98 hours a week on 1,460 KHZ medium wave. Number of receivers, approximately 12,000.

Newspapers. The *Turks and Caicos News* is published weekly.

JUSTICE, RELIGION, EDUCATION AND WELFARE

Justice. Laws are a mixture of Statute and Common Law. There is a Magistrates Court and a Supreme Court. Appeals lie from the Supreme Court to the Court of Appeal which sits in Nassau, Bahamas. There is a further appeal in certain cases to the Privy Council in London.

Religion. The Christian faith predominates with Anglican, Methodist, Baptist. Church of God of Prophecy and New Testament Church of God being the largest group.

Education. Education is free and compulsory up to 15 years of age in the 14 government primary and 3 government secondary schools. There are also 2 private primary schools. Pupils at Turks and Caicos High School, 371; South Caicos, 174; Providenciales, 103; North Caicos, 224. Expenditure on education 1988–89 was US$1,878,003.

Health. In 1987 there were 5 doctors and 30 hospital beds.

TUVALU

Capital: Fongafale
Population: 8,229 (1985)
GNP per capita: US$500 (1984)

HISTORY. Formerly the Ellice Islands, a British Protectorate since 1892. On the recommendation of a Commissioner, appointed by the British Government, to consider requests that the island group be separated from the Gilbert Islands, a referendum was held in 1974. There was a large majority in favour of separation and this took place in Oct. 1975. Independence was achieved on 1 Oct. 1978.

AREA AND POPULATION. Tuvalu (formerly the Ellice Islands) lies between 5° 30' and 11° S. lat. and 176° and 180° E. long. and comprise Nanumea, Nanumanga, Niutao, Nui, Vaitupu, Nukufetau, Funafuti (administrative centre), Nukulaelae and Niulakita. Population (census 1985) 8,229 and 1,500 work abroad, mainly in Nauru. Area approximately 9$^1/_2$ sq. miles (24 sq. km). The population is of a Polynesian race.

CLIMATE. A pleasant but monotonous climate with temperatures averaging 86°F (30°C), though trade winds from the east moderate conditions for much of the year. Rainfall ranges from 120" (3,000 mm) to over 160" (4,000 mm). Funafuti. Jan. 84°F (28·9°C), July 81°F (27·2°C). Annual rainfall 160" (4,003 mm).

CONSTITUTION AND GOVERNMENT. The Constitution provides for a Prime Minister and 4 other Ministers to be elected from among the 12 elected members of the House of Parliament, for which general elections took place in Sept. 1985. The Cabinet, chaired by the Prime Minister, consists of the 4 ministers and 2 *ex-officio* members, the Attorney-General and the Secretary to Government, who are also *ex-officio* members of the House of Assembly.

Governor-General: Sir Tupua Leupena,GCVO, MBE.
Prime Minister: Bikenibeu Paeniu.
Finance: Kitiseni Lopati. *Social Services:* Telava Tevasa. *Commerce and Natural Resources:* Lale Seluka. *Works and Communications:* Solomona M. Tealof.

National flag: Light blue with the Union Jack in the canton, and 9 gold stars in the fly arranged in the same pattern as the 9 islands.

Local Government. There is a town council on Funafuti and island councils on the 7 other atolls, each consisting of 6 elected members including a president. Since 1966 Members of Parliament have been *ex-officio* members of Island Councils. The island of Niulakita is administered as part of Niutao.

INTERNATIONAL RELATIONS

Membership. Tuvalu is a member of the Commonwealth and is an ACP state of EEC.

ECONOMY

Budget. In 1988 the budget envisaged revenue of $A4,701,594.

Currency. The unit of currency is the Australian *dollar* although Tuvaluan coins up to $A1 are in local circulation.

Banking. The Tuvalu National Bank was established at Funafuti in 1980 and is a joint venture between the Tuvalu Government and Wespac International.

ENERGY AND NATURAL RESOURCES

Electricity. Production (1986) 3m. kwh.

Agriculture. Coconut palms are the main crop. Production of coconuts (1988), 3,000 tonnes. Fruit and vegetables are grown for local consumption.

Fisheries. Sea fishing is excellent but is largely unexploited although (1988) Japanese, Taiwanese and South Korean vessels have been granted licences to fish. The USSR was refused a licence.

INDUSTRY AND TRADE

Industry. The main sources of income are from overseas remittances from Tuvaluans working abroad, philatelic and copra sales, and handicrafts.

Employment. A significant number of the population are employed in the phosphate industry on Nauru. The remainder are engaged in harvesting coconuts and fishing.

Commerce. Commerce is dominated by co-operative societies, the Tuvalu Co-operative Wholesale Society being the main importer. Imports (1984) $A3·96m.

Total trade between Tuvalu and UK (British Department of Trade returns, in £1,000 sterling):

	1985	*1986*	*1987*	*1988*	*1989*
Imports to UK	—	88	2	1	—
Exports and re-exports from UK	87	78	106	105	162

Tourism. In 1979 there were 474 visitors.

COMMUNICATIONS

Aviation. Tuvalu is linked to the outside world by Fiji Air which operates three times a week, on Monday, Wednesday and Friday, and Air Marshal once a week on Saturdays from Kiribati and Sundays from Fiji.

Shipping. Funafuti is the only port and a deep-water wharf was opened in 1980. Inter-island communication is by ship.

Post and Broadcasting. The Tuvalu Broadcasting Service transmits daily in Tuvaluan and English and all islands have daily radio communication with Funafuti. There were 120 telephones and 2,500 radio receivers in 1985.

JUSTICE, RELIGION, EDUCATION AND WELFARE

Justice. There is a High Court presided over by the Chief Justice of Fiji. Appeals lie to the Fiji Court of Appeal.

Religion. The majority of the population are Christians mainly Protestant but with small groups of Roman Catholics, Seventh Day Adventists, Jehovah's Witnesses, Mormons and Bahai's. There are some Moslems.

Education. In 1985 there was 1 secondary school jointly administered by the Government and the Church with 250 pupils. In addition there were 9 primary schools with (1985, inclusive of 326 pupils in community training centres) 924 pupils run by Island Councils and subsidized by the central government. In 1979, a maritime school was opened on Amatuku islet. Tuvaluans requiring further education must seek it abroad.

Health. In 1984 there was 1 central hospital with 36 beds situated at Funafuti. There were 4 doctors.

DIPLOMATIC REPRESENTATIVES

Of Great Britain in Tuvalu
High Commissioner: A. B. P. Smart (resides in Suva).

Of Tuvalu in the USA
Ambassador: Gregory Polson (resides in Tuvalu).

UGANDA

Capital: Kampala
Population: 17m. (1989)
GNP per capita: US$280 (1988)

HISTORY. Uganda became a British Protectorate in 1894, the province of Buganda being recognized as a native kingdom under its Kabaka. In 1961 Uganda was granted internal self-government with federal status for Buganda.

Uganda became a fully independent member of the Commonwealth on 9 Oct. 1962 after nearly 70 years of British rule. Full sovereign status was granted by the Uganda Independence Act, 1962, and the Constitution was embodied in the Uganda (Independence) Order in Council, 1962. The post of Governor-General was on 9 Oct. 1963 replaced by that of President as head of state, elected by the National Assembly for a 5-year term. Uganda became a republic on 8 Sept. 1967.

In 1971, Dr A. Milton Obote was overthrown by troops led by Gen. Idi Amin.

In April 1979 a force of the Tanzanian Army and Ugandan exiles advanced into Uganda taking Kampala on 11 April. On 14 April Dr Yusuf Lule was sworn in as President and the country was administered, initially, by the Uganda National Liberation Front.

The former Attorney-General, Godfrey Lukongwa Binaisa, QC, was appointed President by the National Consultative Council on 20 June 1979. Dr Lule subsequently left the country. G. L. Binaisa was subsequently overthrown in May 1980 by the Military Commission, the military arm of Uganda National Liberation Front.

At the elections held on 10–11 Dec. 1980, the Uganda People's Congress, led by Dr A. Milton Obote, was declared to have held 72 of the 124 elective seats in the new Parliament, the Democratic Party 51 seats, and the Uganda Patriotic Movement 1 seat. There were 17 specially elected members.

On 27 July 1985 President Obote was overthrown, the Constitution suspended and the borders closed. Lieut.-Gen. Tito Okello became head of State on 29 July but on the following day the National Resistance Army stated that it was not prepared to co-operate with the new regime. A ceasefire between the NRA and government forces was agreed on 17 Dec. 1985 and President Museveni was installed as President on 27 Jan. 1986.

AREA AND POPULATION. Uganda is bounded on the north by Sudan, on the east by Kenya, on the south by Tanzania and Rwanda, and the west by Zaïre. Total area 91,343 sq. miles (236,860 sq. km), including 15,217 sq. miles (39,459 sq. km) of swamp and water.

The population was (census 1980) 12,630,076; (estimate 1989) 17m. In 1980, 12% lived in urban areas, the largest towns (1980 Census) being Kampala, the capital (458,423), Jinja (45,060), Masaka (29,123), Mbale (28,039), Mbarara (23,155), Entebbe (20,472) and Gulu (14,958). The areas, populations and capitals of the 10 provinces are:

Province	*Sq. km*	*Census 1980*	*Capital*
Busoga	13,340	1,221,872	Jinja
Central	6,270	1,117,648	Kampala
Eastern	22,260	2,015,530	Mbale
Karamoja	26,960	350,908	Moroto
Nile	15,730	811,755	Arua
North Buganda	27,010	1,554,371	Bombo
Northern	41,520	1,261,364	Gulu
South Buganda	15,970	905,754	Masaka
Southern	21,280	1,963,428	Mbarara
Western	30,980	1,427,446	Fort Portal

About 70% of the population (10·7m. inhabitants in 1986) speak Bantu languages, the major groups being the Baganda (18%), Banyoro (14%), Banyankole (8%), Bagisu (10%), Basoga (8%) and Bachiga (7%). About 16% were Nilotic groups in the north, chiefly the Lango (6·5%) and Acholi (4%), and the rest mainly Nilo-Hamitic, predominantly Teso (8%) and Karamojong (3%) in the northeast. The official language is English, but Kiswahili is also widely used as a lingua franca.

CLIMATE. Although in equatorial latitudes, the climate is more tropical, because of its elevation, and is characterized the year round by hot sunshine, cool breezes and showers of rain. The wettest months are March to June and there is no dry season. Temperatures vary little over the year. Kampala. Jan. 74°F (23·3°C), July 70°F (21·1°C). Annual rainfall 46" (1,150 mm). Entebbe. Jan. 72°F (22·2°C), July 69°F (20·6°C). Annual rainfall 60" (1,506 mm).

CONSTITUTION AND GOVERNMENT. The National Resistance Council was enlarged to include representatives from every county. A new Constitution was being drafted in 1990. Elections were held in Feb.-March 1989 and there were 278 members in the National Resistance Council in Nov. 1989. In Nov. 1989 the government was composed as follows:

President, Minister of Defence: Yoweri Museveni (sworn in 27 Jan. 1986).
Prime Minister: Dr Samson Kisekka.
First Deputy Prime Minister: E. Kategaya. *Second Deputy Prime Minister, Minister of Foreign and Regional Affairs:* Dr P. K. Semwogerere. *Third Deputy Prime Minister:* Abu Mayanja. *Finance:* Dr C. Kiyonga. *Co-operatives and Marketing:* J. F. Wapakhabulo. *Animal Industry and Fisheries:* Dr M. Kagonyera. *Health:* Z. Kaheru. *Public Service and Cabinet Affairs:* Tom Rubale. *Industry and Technology:* Dr E. T. Adriko. *Works:* Dan Kigozi. *Internal Affairs:* Ibrahim Mukiibi. *Information and Broadcasting:* Kintu Musoke. *Planning and Economic Development:* Joshua Mayanja Nkangi. *Commerce:* Paul Etyang. *Rehabilitation:* Adoko Nekyon. *Lands and Surveys:* Ben Okello Luwum. *Water and Mineral Development:* Kajura Henry. *Justice and Attorney-General:* Dr G. Kanyeihamba. *Tourism and Wildlife:* Sebagereka Sam. *Education:* Amanya Mushega. *Agriculture:* J. Sekitoleko. *Transport and Communications:* Dr Ruhakana Rugunda. *Energy:* Richard Kaijuka. *Youth, Culture and Sports:* Brig. Moses Ali. *Labour:* Stanley Okurut. *Environment Protection:* Moses Kintu. *Constitutional Affairs:* S. K. Njuba. *Housing and Urban Development:* Sebana Kizito. *Local Government:* Jaberi Bidandi Ssali.

National flag: Six horizontal stripes of black, yellow, red, black, yellow, red, in the centre a small white disc bearing a representation of a Balearic Crested Crane.

Local government: There are 34 districts divided into 152 counties, which are in turn divided into sub-counties which form the basic administrative units.

DEFENCE

Army. The National Resistance Army had a strength of about 70,000 in 1990 and is loosely organized in 6 brigades and some battalions. Equipment includes some BTR-60 armoured personnel carriers and 7 helicopters.

Navy. A small lake patrol was initiated in 1977.

Air Force. Since 1979, the service has been in a period of decline. As far as is known in early 1989, the equipment received from the East Bloc (MiG-17 and MiG-21 combat aircraft and L-29 jet trainers) is in storage. It is understood that some aircraft of Western European origin are still serviceable, including a small number of AS.202 Bravo and SF.260 trainers and about 6 Agusta-Bell helicopters, plus 3 Mi-8 transport helicopters, donated by Libya. The Police Air Wing still operates 2 fixed-wing aircraft and 7 Bell helicopters.

INTERNATIONAL RELATIONS

Membership. Uganda is a member of UN, OAU, Islamic Conference Organization, the Non-Aligned Movement, the Commonwealth and is an ACP state of EEC.

ECONOMY

Budget. In 1988–89 revenue was 56,690m. Uganda Sh. and expenditure, 88,240m. Uganda Sh.

Currency. The monetary unit is the *Uganda shilling* divided into 100 *cents*. In May 1987 a new 'heavy' shilling was introduced worth 100 old shillings. In March 1990, £1 = 627·51 Uganda shillings; US$1 = 382·86 Uganda shillings.

Banking. The Bank of Uganda was established on 16 May 1966. The Uganda Credit and Savings Bank, established in 1950, was on 9 Oct. 1965 reconstituted as the Uganda Commercial Bank, with its capital fully owned by the Government.

Barclays Bank of Uganda Ltd. has 4 branches, Standard Bank Uganda Ltd. has 1 branch, Bank of Baroda Uganda Ltd. has 3 branches and the Libyan Arab Uganda Bank for Foreign Trade and Development has 3 branches, the Uganda Commercial Bank has 184 branches. The Co-operative Bank is owned by the Co-operative Movement. There are 2 Development Banks; the East African Development Bank and the Uganda Development Bank.

ENERGY AND NATURAL RESOURCES

Electricity. Industrial expansion is based on hydro-electric power provided by the Owen Falls scheme, which has a capacity of 150,000 kwh. Production (1986) 287m. kwh.

Minerals. Production, 1988: Gold, 26·3 grammes; tin, 63·8 tonnes.

Agriculture. In 1989, agriculture was one of the priority areas for increased production, with many projects funded both locally and externally. Coffee, cotton, tea and tobacco are the principal exports. Production (1988) in 1,000 tonnes: Tobacco, 4; coffee, 184; cotton seed, 18; tea, 2; sugar-cane, 900.

Livestock (1988): Cattle, 3·91m.; sheep, 1·74m.; goats, 2·8m.; pigs, 440,000; poultry, 15m.

Forestry. Woodland covers 29% of the land area (5·7m. hectares) and exploitable forests consist almost entirely of hardwoods. 40% of the hardwood timber is used locally and 30% is exported to Kenya, Rwanda and the UK. There is also a small percentage of mature softwood plantation out of which 10% of softwood timber is exported to Rwanda and 20% used locally.

Fisheries. With its 13,600 sq. miles of lakes and many rivers, Uganda possesses one of the largest fresh-water fisheries in the world. In 1988 fish production was 214,700 tonnes of which 50% came from Lake Victoria. Fish farming (especially carp and tilapia) is a growing industry.

COMMERCE. In 1987 imports were US$605·5m. and exports, US$319·4m.

Total trade between Uganda and UK (British Department of Trade returns, in £1,000 sterling):

	1985	*1986*	*1987*	*1988*	*1989*
Imports to UK	48,571	50,870	37,076	30,487	20,985
Exports and re-exports from UK	39,925	26,046	38,545	35,340	39,218

Tourism. There were 35,000 tourists in 1986.

COMMUNICATIONS

Roads. There were (1985) 7,582 km of all-weather roads maintained by the Ministry of Works, of which 1,934 km are two-lane bitumenized highways, and some 19,640 km of other roads, maintained by district governments.

Railways. On 26 Aug. 1977 Uganda Railways was formed following break-up of the East African Railways administration. The network totals 1,286 km (metre gauge). In 1986 railways carried 1·5m. passengers and 315,819 tonnes of freight.

Aviation. The International Airport, at Entebbe, has direct flights to Europe, Zimbabwe, Sudan, Kenya, Burundi, Ghana, Ethiopia, Zaïre, Nigeria, USSR, and Rwanda by Sudan Airways, Air Congo, SABENA, Air France, Ethiopian Airlines,

Air Zaïre and Aeroflot. Eleven other government airfields are used for internal communications.

Posts and Broadcasting. There were 54,400 telephones in use in 1983. There were 600,000 radio receivers and about 90,000 television sets in 1986.

Newspapers. There were 5 daily newspapers in 1989 with a circulation of 35,000.

JUSTICE, RELIGION, EDUCATION AND WELFARE

Justice. The High Court of Uganda, presided over by the Chief Justice and 15 puisne judges, exercises original and appellate jurisdiction throughout Uganda. Subordinate courts, presided over by Chief Magistrates and Magistrates of the first, second and third grade, are established in all areas: Jurisdiction varies with the grade of Magistrate. Chief and first-grade Magistrates are professionally qualified; second- and third-grade Magistrates are trained to diploma level at the Law School, Entebbe. Chief Magistrates exercise supervision over and hear appeals from second- and third-grade courts.

The Supreme Court of Uganda hears appeals from the High Court.

Religion. About 62% of the population are Christian and 6% Moslem.

Education. In 1989 there were 2,633,764 pupils in 7,905 primary schools (of which 7,420 were Government-aided schools and 485 private schools); 240,334 students in 774 secondary schools; 13,174 students in 94 primary teacher training colleges; 3,208 students in 24 technical institutes; 1,819 students in 10 national teachers colleges; 1,009 students in technical colleges; 1,628 students in 5 colleges of commerce; 1,037 students in the Institute of Teacher Education, Kyambogo; 504 students in the Uganda Polytechnic, Kyambogo; 800 students in the National College of Business Studies, Nakawa; 5,565 students in Makerere University, Kampala; 163 in the Islamic University, Mbale; 50 students in the University of Science and Technology, Mbarara. There are also 3 agricultural colleges, 1 forestry college, 1 fisheries institute, 1 land survey school and training institutes under different ministries which offer pre-service courses in different fields.

Health. In 1989 there were 81 hospitals and 20,136 hospital beds. The Ministry of Health has 16 schools for training nurses, midwives, medical assistants, environmental and laboratory personnel, and other health staff, 105 health centres, 89 dispensaries with maternity units, 87 dispensaries, 35 maternity units, 371 sub-dispensaries, 14 leprosy centres and 169 aid posts.

DIPLOMATIC REPRESENTATIVES

Of Uganda in Great Britain (Uganda Hse., Trafalgar Sq., London, WC2N 5DX)
High Commissioner: William S. K. Matovu (accredited 7 July 1988).

Of Great Britain in Uganda (10/12 Parliament Ave., Kampala)
High Commissioner: Charles A. K. Cullimore.

Of Uganda in the USA (5909 16th St., NW, Washington, D.C., 20011)
Ambassador: Stephen K. Katenta Apuuli.

Of the USA in Uganda (Parliament Ave., Kampala)
Ambassador: John A. Burroughs Jr.

Of Uganda to the United Nations
Ambassador: Perez Karukubiro Kamunanwire.

Further Reading

Collison, R. L., *Uganda.* [Bibliography] Oxford and Santa Barbara, 1981
Jørgensen, J. J., *Uganda: A Modern History.* London, 1981
Kitching, A. L. and Blackledge, G. R., *A Luganda–English and English–Luganda Dictionary.* Kampala, 1925

UNION OF SOVIET SOCIALIST REPUBLICS

Capital: Moscow
Population: 286·7m. (1989)

Soyuz Sovyetskikh Sotsialisticheskikh Respublik

POST-REVOLUTION HISTORY. Up to 12 March 1917 the territory now forming the USSR, together with that of Finland, Poland and certain tracts ceded in 1918 to Turkey, but less the territories then forming part of the German, Austro-Hungarian and Japanese empires–East Prussia, Eastern Galicia, Transcarpathia, Bukovina, South Sakhalin and Kurile Islands–which were acquired during and after the Second World War, was constituted as the Russian Empire. It was governed as an autocracy under the Tsar, with the aid of Ministers responsible to himself and a State Duma with limited legislative powers, elected by provincial assemblies chosen by indirect elections on a restricted franchise.

On 8 March 1917 a revolution broke out. The Duma parties, on 12 March, set up a Provisional Committee of the State Duma, while the factory workmen and the insurgent garrison of Petrograd elected a Council (Soviet) of Workers' and Soldiers' Deputies. Soviets were also elected by the workmen in other towns, in the Army and Navy and, as time went on, by the peasantry. On 15 March 1917 the Tsar abdicated, and the Provisional Committee, by agreement with the Petrograd Soviet, appointed a Provisional Government and, on 14 Sept., proclaimed a republic. However, a political struggle went on between the supporters of the Provisional Government–the Mensheviks and the Socialist Revolutionaries–and the Bolsheviks, who advocated the assumption of power by the Soviets. When they had won majorities in the Soviets of the principal cities and of the armed forces on several fronts, the Bolsheviks organized an insurrection through a Military-Revolutionary Committee of the Petrograd Soviet. On 7 Nov. 1917 the Committee arrested the Provisional Government and transferred power to the second All-Russian Congress of Soviets. This elected a new government, the Council of People's Commissars, headed by Lenin.

On 25 Jan. 1918 the third All-Russian Congress of Soviets issued a Declaration of Rights of the Toiling and Exploited People, which proclaimed Russia a Republic of Soviets of Workers', Soldiers' and Peasants' Deputies; and on 10 July 1918 the fifth Congress adopted a Constitution for the Russian Soviet Federal Socialist Republic. In the course of the civil war other Soviet Republics were set up in the Ukraine, Belorussia and Transcaucasia. These first entered into treaty relations with the RSFSR and then, in 1922, joined with it in a closely integrated Union.

AREA AND POPULATION. The total area of the Soviet Union in April 1989 was 22·4m. sq. km (8·65m. sq. miles). The census population on 15 Jan. 1970 was 241·7m. (111·4m. males, 130·3m. females; 136m. urban, 105·7m. rural). The census population on 12 Jan. 1989 was 286·7m. (135·5m. males, 151·2m. females, 188·8m. urban, 97·9m. rural). The increase of 25·2m. in urban population between 1979 and 1989 was due to natural increase (14·6m.) and migration from rural areas and the urbanization of large rural centres (10·6m.). Consequently, despite a natural increase in rural areas, there was a net decrease of 0·9m. over this period. Population at 1 Jan. 1989, 286·7m. (135·5m. males, 151·2m. females; 188·8m. urban; 97·9m. rural).

The Soviet social structure is officially described as consisting of two friendly social classes–workers and collective farm peasantry–and a social stratum, the intelligentsia, who are engaged in mental rather than manual labour. In 1987 workers (in industry and state-owned agriculture) accounted for 61·8% of total population, collective farmers for 12% and intelligentsia for 26·2%.

The areas (in 1,000 sq. km) and population (in 1m., in Jan. 1989) of the constituent republics are as follows (capitals in brackets):

Constituent Republics	*Area*	*Population*	*Constituent Republics*	*Area*	*Population*
RSFSR (Moscow)	17,075	147·4	Tadzhikistan (Dushanbe)	143	5·1
Ukraine (Kiev)	604	51·7	Kirgizia (Frunze)	199	4·3
Uzbekistan (Tashkent)	447	19·9	Lithuania (Vilnius)	65	3·7
Kazakhstan (Alma-Ata)	2,717	16·5	Armenia (Yerevan)	30	3·3
Belorussia (Minsk)	208	10·2	Turkmenistan (Ashkhabad)	488	3·5
Azerbaijan (Baku)	87	7·0	Latvia (Riga)	64	2·7
Georgia (Tbilisi)	70	5·5	Estonia (Tallinn)	45	1·6
Moldavia (Kishinev)	34	4·3			

Nationalities. The most numerous nationalities at the 1979 census were: 137·4m. Russians, 42·3m. Ukrainians, 12·5m. Uzbeks, 9·5m. Belorussians, 6·6m. Kazakhs, 6·3m. Tatars, 5·5m. Azerbaijanians, 4·1m. Armenians, 3·6m. Georgians, 3m. Moldavians, 2·9m. Tadzhiks, 2·9m. Lithuanians, 2m. Turkmenians, 1·9m. Germans, 1·9m. Kirgiz, 1·8m. Jews, 1·8m. Chuvashes, 1·4m. Latvians, 1·4m. Bashkirs, 1·2m. Mordovians, 1·2m. Poles, 1m. Estonians. The great majority (in each case 73-99%) indicated the language of their nationality as their native tongue; exceptions were the Bashkirs (67%), Germans (57%), Poles (29%) and Jews (14%).

Estimated losses of population in the Second World War, 20m., of which 7m. were military losses.

The following tables show the growth of the population in Russia:

1897 (Russian Empire)	126,900,000	1959 (census)	208,826,650
1913 (Russian Empire)	170,900,000	1970 (census)	241,720,134
1913 (present frontiers)	159,153,000	1979 (census)	262,436,227
1939 (census)	170,557,093	1989 (census)	286,717,000

The following was the population on 1 Jan. 1989 of the larger towns (in 1,000):

Astrakhan	509	Kishinev	565	Riga	915
Baku	1,757	Krasnodar	620	Rostov-on-Don	1,020
Barnaul	602	Krasnoyarsk	912	Ryazan	515
Chelyabinsk	1,143	Krivoi Rog	713	Saratov	905
Dnepropetrovsk	1,179	Kuibyshev	1,257	Sverdlovsk	1,367
Donetsk	1,110	Leningrad	5,020	Tashkent	2,073
Dushanbe	595	Lvov	790	Togliatti	630
Frunze	616	Minsk	1,589	Tomsk	502
Gomel	500	Moscow	8,967	Tula	540
Gorky	1,438	Naberezhnye Chelny	501	Ufa	1,083
Irkutsk	626	Nikolayev	503	Ulyanovsk	625
Izhevsk	635	Novokuznetsk	600	Vilnius	582
Karaganda	614	Novosibirsk	1,436	Vladivostok	648
Kazan	1,094	Odessa	1,115	Volgograd	999
Kemerovo	520	Omsk	1,148	Voronezh	887
Khabarovsk	601	Orenburg	547	Yaroslavl	633
Kharkov	1,611	Penza	543	Yerevan	1,199
Kiev	2,587	Perm	1,091	Zaporozhye	884

Narodnoe khozyaistvo SSSR. Moscow, annual
Ezhegodnik Bol' shoi Sovetskoi Entsiklopedii. Moscow, annual
Itogi Vsesoyuznoi perepisi naseleniya 1970 goda, 7 vols. Moscow, 1972–74
Chislennost' i sostav naseleniya SSSR po dannym Vsesoyuznoi perepisi 1979 goda. Moscow, 1984
Naselenie SSSR 1987. Moscow, 1988
Sovetskii Soyuz. Geograficheskoe opisanie, 22 vols. Moscow, 1966–72
Cole, J. P., *Geography of the Soviet Union*. London, 1984
Howe, G. Melvyn, *The Soviet Union: a Geographical Survey* (2nd ed.). London, 1983
Symons, L., (ed.) *The Soviet Union: a Systematic Geography*. London, 1983
Wixman, R., *The Peoples of Russia and the USSR*. London, 1984

CLIMATE. The USSR comprises several different climatic regions, ranging from polar conditions in the north, through sub-arctic and humid continental, to subtropical and semi-arid conditions in the south. Rainfall amounts are greatest in areas bordering the Baltic, Black Sea, Caspian Sea and eastern coasts of Asiatic Russia. In most cases, there is a summer maximum.

Moscow. Jan. 15°F (–9·4°C), July 65°F (18·3°C). Annual rainfall 25·2"(630 mm). Arkhangelsk. Jan. 5°F (–15°C), July 57°F (13·9°C). Annual rainfall 20·1"(503 mm). Kiev. Jan. 21°F (–6·1°C), July 68°F (20°C). Annual rainfall 22"(554 mm). Leningrad. Jan. 17°F (–8·3°C), July 64°F (17·8°C). Annual rainfall 19·5"(488 mm). Vladivostok. Jan. 6°F (–14·4°C), July 65°F (18·3°C). Annual rainfall 24"(599 mm).

CONSTITUTION

Constituent Republics. The Union of Soviet Socialist Republics was formed by the union of the RSFSR, the Ukrainian Soviet Socialist Republic, the Belorussian Soviet Socialist Republic and the Transcaucasian Soviet Socialist Republic; the Treaty of Union was adopted by the first Soviet Congress of the USSR on 30 Dec. 1922. In Oct. 1924 the Uzbek and Turkmen Autonomous Soviet Socialist Republics and in Dec. 1929 the Tadzhik Autonomous Soviet Socialist Republic were declared constituent members of the USSR, becoming Union Republics.

At the 8th Congress of the Soviets, on 5 Dec. 1936, a new constitution of the USSR was adopted. The Transcaucasian Republic was split up into the Armenian Soviet Socialist Republic, the Azerbaijan Soviet Socialist Republic and the Georgian Soviet Socialist Republic, each of which became constituent republics of the Union. At the same time the Kazakh Soviet Socialist Republic and the Kirghiz Soviet Socialist Republic, previously autonomous republics within the RSFSR, were proclaimed constituent republics of the USSR.

In Sept. 1939 Soviet troops occupied eastern Poland as far as the 'Curzon line', which in 1919 had been drawn on ethnographical grounds as the eastern frontier of Poland, and incorporated it into the Ukrainian and Belorussian Soviet Socialist Republics. In Feb. 1951 some districts of the Drogobych Region of the Ukraine and the Lublin Voivodship of Poland were exchanged.

On 31 March 1940 territory ceded by Finland was joined to that of the Autonomous Soviet Socialist Republic of Karelia to form the Karelo-Finnish Soviet Socialist Republic, which was admitted into the Union as the 12th Union Republic. On 16 July 1956 the Supreme Soviet of the USSR adopted a law altering the status of the Karelo-Finnish Republic from that of a Union (constituent) Republic of the USSR to that of an Autonomous (Karelian) Republic within the RSFSR.

On 2 Aug. 1940 the Moldavian Soviet Socialist Republic was constituted as the 13th Union Republic. It comprised the former Moldavian Autonomous Soviet Socialist Republic and Bessarabia (44,290 sq. km, ceded by Romania on 28 June 1940), except for the districts of Khotin, Akerman and Ismail, which, together with Northern Bukovina (10,440 sq. km), were incorporated in the Ukrainian Soviet Republic. The Soviet-Romanian frontier thus constituted was confirmed by the peace treaty with Romania, signed on 10 Feb. 1947. On 29 June 1945 Ruthenia (Sub-Carpathian Russia, 12,742 sq. km) was by treaty with Czechoslovakia incorporated into the Ukrainian Soviet Socialist Republic.

On 3, 5 and 6 Aug. 1940 Lithuania, Latvia and Estonia were incorporated in the Soviet Union as the 14th, 15th and 16th Union Republics respectively. The change in the status of the Karelo-Finnish Republic reduced the number of Union Republics to 15.

After the defeat of Germany it was agreed by the governments of the UK, the USA and the USSR (by the Potsdam declaration) that part of East Prussia should be embodied in the USSR. The area (11,655 sq. km), which includes the towns of Konigsberg (renamed Kaliningrad), Tilsit (renamed Sovyetsk) and Insterburg (renamed Chernyakhovsk), was joined to the RSFSR by decree of 7 April 1946.

By the peace treaty with Finland, signed on 10 Feb. 1947, the province of Petsamo (Pechenga), ceded to Finland on 14 Oct. 1920 and 12 March 1946, was returned to the Soviet Union. On 19 Sept. 1955 the Soviet Union renounced its treaty rights to the naval base of Porkkala-Udd and on 26 Jan. 1956 completed the withdrawal of the forces from Finnish territory.

In 1945, after the defeat of Japan, the southern half of Sakhalin (36,000 sq. km) and the Kurile Islands (10,200 sq. km) were, by agreement with the Allies, incorporated in the USSR. [1]

[1] However, Japan asks for the return of the Etorofu and Kunashiri Islands as not belonging to the Kurile Islands proper. The Soviet Government informed Japan on 27 Jan. 1960 that the Habomai Islands and Shikotan would be handed back to Japan on the withdrawal of the American troops from Japan.

GOVERNMENT. The Soviet Union is a socialist state of the whole people (1977 constitution), the political units of which are the Soviets of People's Deputies. All central and local authority is vested in these Soviets.

The economic foundation of the USSR is the socialist system of economy and the socialist ownership of the means of production. There are two forms of socialist property: (1) state property (property of the whole people); (2) co-operative and collective farm (*kolkhoz*) property (property of individual collective farms and property of co-operative associations). The land, mineral deposits, waters, forests, mills, factories, mines, railways, water and air transport, banks, means of communication, state farms (*sovkhozy*), as well as municipal enterprises and the principal dwelling-house properties in the cities and industrial localities, are state property, but the land occupied by collective farmers is secured to them in perpetuity so long as they use it in accordance with the laws of the country. The members of the *kolkhozy* may have small plots of land attached to their dwellings for their own use. Peasants unwilling to enter a kolkhoz may retain their individual farms, but they are not allowed to employ hired labour. The right of personal property of citizens in their income from work and in their savings, in their dwelling houses and auxiliary household economy, their domestic furniture and utensils and objects of personal use and comfort, as well as the right of inheritance of personal property of citizens, are protected by law. The constitution recognizes the right of all citizens to work, rest, leisure, education, health protection, housing, maintenance in old age, sickness or incapacity, without distinction of sex, race or nationality, and lays down that any direct or indirect restriction of the rights of, or conversely, the establishment of direct or indirect privileges for, citizens on account of their race, or nationality, as well as the advocacy of racial or national exclusiveness, or hatred or contempt, is punishable by law. The franchise is enjoyed by all citizens of the USSR who have reached the age of 18, irrespective of sex, with the exception of the legally certified insane or incompetent or those serving terms of imprisonment. Candidates for election as a People's Deputy of the USSR must be 21 years of age; for sub-national levels of government the minimum age for candidates is 18. A member of any Soviet may be recalled by a decision of a majority of his or her electors if he or she fails to give satisfaction (law on procedure for this, 30 Oct. 1959).

The USSR consists of 15 Union Republics, each inhabited by a major nationality which gives its name to the republic. These are divided into 120 territories and regions, and these again into 3,193 districts, 2,190 towns, 628 urban districts and 4,026 urban settlements (1 Jan. 1989). Within the districts there are 42,712 rural Soviets (usually each including a number of villages). The territories and regions also include a number of smaller nationalities, forming their own self-governing units–20 Autonomous Soviet Socialist Republics, 8 Autonomous Regions and 10 Autonomous Areas.

Under amended constitutional provisions which came into effect in Dec. 1988 the highest body of state authority of the USSR is the Congress of People's Deputies of the USSR (for earlier arrangements see THE STATESMAN'S YEAR-BOOK, 1989-90, pp 1226 and 1227). The Congress is exclusively empowered to adopt and amend the Constitution and to determine the national and state structure of the USSR; it also establishes the 'guidelines of the domestic and foreign policies of the USSR', including long-term state plans and programmes (Art. 108). The Congress consists of 2,250 deputies, 750 of whom are elected by territorial electoral districts with equal numbers of voters, and 750 of whom are elected by national-territorial electoral districts (32 from each union republic, 11 from each autonomous republic, 5 from each autonomous region and 1 from each autonomous area). A further 750 deputies are elected by public organizations including the Communist Party and the trade unions on the basis of the Law on Elections of the People's Deputies of the USSR, which was also approved in Dec. 1988. Regular sessions of the Congress of People's Deputies are convened once a year; the first, following elections in March 1989, met from 25 May to 9 June 1989. At those elections 89·8% of the registered electorate were reported to have voted and 1,958 deputies were returned, 87·6% of whom were members or candidate members of the CPSU; 18·6% were industrial workers, 11·2% were collective farmers, and 17·1% were women. The vacancies that remained were subsequently filled at repeat votes (*povtornoe golosovanie*) or repeat elections (*povtornye vybory*), which under the electoral law must be held within 2 months of the original elections.

The powers of the Congress of People's Deputies also include the election of the President and the Chairman of the USSR Supreme Soviet and the endorsement of the chairman of the USSR Council of Ministers, the chairman of the Supreme Court, the Procurator-General and the Chief State Arbitrator. The Congress, by secret ballot from among its members, elects a 542-member Supreme Soviet of the USSR, which is described in the Constitution as the 'permanent legislative, and control body of state authority of the USSR' (Art. 111). The USSR Supreme Soviet consists of 2 chambers, the Soviet of the Union and the Soviet of Nationalities, each of which has equal numbers of deputies and equal powers. The Soviet of the Union (chairman, E. M. Primakov) is elected from among deputies representing territorial districts and public organizations, taking into account the size of the electorate in the republic or region in question. The Soviet of Nationalities (chairman, R. N. Nishanov) is elected by deputies representing national-territorial districts and public organizations, on the basis of 11 from each union republic, 4 from each autonomous republic, 2 from each autonomous region and 1 from each autonomous area. One-fifth of the members of the Soviet of the Union and the Soviet of Nationalities are re-elected annually by the Congress of People's Deputies.

The Supreme Soviet is convened by its Presidium for spring and autumn sessions which last, 'as a rule', 3 or 4 months each. Special sessions may also be convened. The Supreme Soviet, under the Constitution (Art. 113), appoints the chairman of the USSR Council of Ministers and, on his recommendation, the other members of the Council of Ministers. It appoints the members of the Defence Council of the USSR and the Soviet high command, deals with national-level policy on economic, financial, social and cultural questions, approves the state plan and budget, ratifies and denounces international treaties and authorizes the deployment of Soviet armed forces further to those obligations. In addition to commissions attached to each chamber, the USSR Supreme Soviet establishes the following committees: International affairs; defence and state security; legislation and legality; the Soviets and self-management; economic reform; agrarian questions and food; construction and architecture; science, education, culture and upbringing; public health; women, the family, motherhood and childhood; veterans and invalids; youth; ecology and the rational use of natural resources; and *glasnost'* (openness) and communications from citizens.

The Presidium of the USSR Supreme Soviet consists of the chairman of the USSR Supreme Soviet, the first vice-chairman of the USSR Supreme Soviet, 15 vice-chairmen (*ex officio* the chairmen of the Supreme Soviets of each of the union republics), the chairmen of the Soviet of the Union and the Soviet of Nationalities and their deputies, the chairman of the Committee of Public Inspection of the USSR, and the chairmen of the standing commissions of the chambers and the committees of the USSR Supreme Soviet. The Presidium, under Art. 119 of the Constitution, is responsible for convening sessions of the USSR Supreme Soviet, coordinating the activities of commissions and committees, ensuring observance of the Constitution, conferring titles, medals and citizenship, appointing diplomatic representatives, and proclaiming a state of war in the event of armed attack upon the USSR or circumstances of sufficient gravity within the USSR itself.

The chairman of the USSR Supreme Soviet, who is elected by the Congress of

People's Deputies for a maximum of 2 5-year terms and who is responsible both to the Congress and to the Supreme Soviet, is the 'highest-ranking official in the Soviet state' and represents the USSR in international affairs (Art. 120). He is empowered to exercise 'general guidance' over the preparation of issues that are put to the Congress and Supreme Soviet, and is required to submit reports to both of these bodies on the 'state of the country and on important issues of Soviet domestic and foreign policy and of safeguarding the USSR's defence capability and security'. In March 1990 a series of constitutional amendments established the post of President of the USSR, elected by the Congress of People's Deputies for a minimum of two 5-year terms. On 16 March 1990 Mikhail Gorbachev was elected to this position.

The Council of Ministers or government of the USSR is similarly responsible and accountable both to the Congress of People's Deputies and to the USSR Supreme Soviet. The Council of Ministers is elected by the Supreme Soviet and is required to report to the Supreme Soviet on its work at least once a year. The Council of Ministers is empowered to deal with all matters of state administration which do not fall within the competence of other bodies; in practice this includes the conduct of a wide variety of government business, including economic management, foreign relations, defence and social welfare. Under legislation approved in June 1989 the Council of Ministers contained 26 'all-union' ministries, based in Moscow and for the most part responsible for heavy industry, and 11 'union-republican' ministries, based in Moscow and also in the republics, and including foreign affairs, finance, justice, culture and internal affairs. There were 4 all-union state committees, including science and technology, and 15 union-republican committees, including the State Planning Committee (Gosplan), the State Committee on Labour and Social Questions, the State Prices Committee, the State Education Committee and the Committee of State Security (KGB). Some other minor state functions, including utilities and inland water transport, are wholly regulated at the republican level.

Soon after the adoption of the 1936 Constitution all the constituent republics of the Union held their Soviet congresses, at which they adopted their own constitutions based in all essentials upon the Constitution of the Union but adapted where necessary to local requirements. In April 1978 the Supreme Soviets of the Union Republics similarly adopted new republican constitutions based upon the new Constitution of the USSR approved by the Supreme Soviet in Oct. 1977. Article 73 of the 1977 Constitution of the USSR reserves to the central government the spheres of war and peace, diplomatic relations, defence, foreign trade, state security, economic planning, education, the basic principles of legislation, and other matters of 'all-Union significance'. The right of the constituent republics to withdraw from the Union is, however, formally recognized in Article 72. Union Republics have their own Congresses of People's Deputies, Supreme Soviets, Presidiums and Councils of Ministers, and exercise a wide range of devolved powers in local matters.

There are 20 Autonomous Republics in the USSR, which are similarly governed by their own Congresses of People's Deputies, Supreme Soviets, Presidiums and Councils of Ministers exercising devolved powers over local matters. Most (16) are in the RSFSR; 2 are in Georgia and 1 each in Azerbaijan and Uzbekistan. Five Autonomous Regions are in the RSFSR, 1 each in Azerbaijan, Georgia, and Tadzhikistan. All 10 Autonomous Areas are in the RSFSR. Elections are held every five years to the Supreme Soviets of Union and Autonomous Republics. At the most recent elections (Feb. 1985), 10,190 deputies were elected; 3,830 (37·6%) were women, 3,495 (34·3%) were non-Party, 3,605 (35·4%) were industrial workers and 1,557 (15·3%) were collective farmers.

Regions and territories, districts, towns and rural areas are similarly governed by their own Soviets, elected for a term of $2^1/_2$ years. At the most recent elections (June 1987), 2,321,766 deputies were elected to these Soviets; 1,146,329 (49·4%) were women, 1,317,009 (56·7%) were non-Party, 976,552 (42·1%) were industrial workers and 562,052 (24·2%) were collective farmers. In 162 districts elections were conducted, as an experiment, with more candidates nominated than seats available. On 1 Jan. 1988 there were 52,602 rural and urban Soviets in the USSR with 2·3m. deputies and over 30m. voluntary co-opted members participating in the work of their standing committees.

State flag: Red, with sickle and hammer in gold in the upper corner near the staff, and above them a 5-pointed star bordered in gold.

National anthem: Soyuz nerushimy respublik svobodnykh (words by S. Mikhalkov and G. El-Registan; music by A. V. Alexandrov; 1944, revised 1977).

President of the USSR: M. S. Gorbachev.
Chairman of the USSR Supreme Soviet: A. I. Lukyanov.
Secretary of the Presidium: Tengiz Menteshashvili.
Chairman of the Council of Ministers of the USSR: N. I. Ryzhkov.
First Vice-Chairman: V. S. Murakhovsky.

Minister of Defence: Marshal D. T. Yazov. *Minister of Foreign Economic Relations:* K. F. Katushev. *Minister for Foreign Affairs:* E. A. Shevardnadze. *Minister of Internal Affairs:* V. V. Bakatin. *Minister of Finance:* V. S. Pavlov. *Chairman, State Security Committee (KGB):* V. A. Kryuchkov. *Chairman, State Planning Committee (Gosplan):* Yu. D. Maslyukov.

Communist Party of the Soviet Union. According to the revised rules adopted by the 27th Congress of the Party in March 1986, the Communist Party of the Soviet Union 'unites, on a voluntary basis, the more advanced, politically more conscious section of the working class, collective-farm peasantry and intelligentsia of the USSR', and represents the 'highest form of socio-political organization, the nucleus of the political system and the leading and guiding force of Soviet society'. Following amendments in March 1990, the Party no longer enjoys a monopoly of power under the Soviet Constitution but takes part with other parties in the formation of state policy and the administration of public and Social affairs. According to the Party Programme, adopted in a revised version in 1986, the party aims to achieve the 'planned and all-round perfection of socialism', 'further advance to communism through the country's accelerated socio-economic development', and 'peace and social progress'.

The Party is organized on the territorial-industrial principle. The supreme organ is the Party Congress. Ordinary congresses are convened not less than every 5 years. The Congress elects a Central Committee which meets at least every 6 months, carries on the work of the Party between congresses, and guides the work of central Soviet and public organizations through Party groups within them. In 1988 the Central Committee formed 6 commissions, on party matters, ideology, socio-economic affairs, agriculture, international affairs and legal affairs, through which its work was to be conducted. The Central Committee may convene an All-Union Party Conference in the intervals between congresses to 'discuss pressing Party policy issues'. The 19th Conference, the first since 1941, met in Moscow in June-July 1988.

The Central Committee forms a Political Bureau *(Politburo)* to direct the work of the Central Committee between plenary meetings, a Secretariat to direct current work and a Party Control Committee to deal with disciplinary matters; it also elects the General Secretary. Similar rules hold for the regional, territorial and republican levels of the party organization. The 'basis of the Party', the primary Party organization, exists in factories, state and collective farms, units of the Soviet Army and Navy, in villages, offices, educational establishments etc. where there are at least 3 Party members. There were over 441,949 primary Party organizations in 1989.

The Central Committee elected by the 27th Congress in March 1986 of 307 members and 170 candidate (non-voting) members comprised 249 members and 108 candidate members by Jan. 1990. Fresh elections were due at the 28th Congress in July 1990.

In March 1990 the Politburo of the Central Committee consisted of the following members: M. S. Gorbachev, V. A. Ivashko, V. A. Kryuchkov, E. K. Ligachev, Yu. D. Maslyukov, V. A. Medvedev, N. I. Ryzhkov, E. A. Shevardnadze, N. N. Slyunkov, V. I. Vorotnikov, A. N. Yakovlev and L. N. Zaikov and the following candidate (non-voting) members: A. P. Biryukova, A. I. Lukyanov, E. M. Primakov, B. K. Pugo, G. P. Razumovsky, A. V. Vlasov, D. T. Yazov.

Secretariat: M. S. Gorbachev *(General Secretary);* O. D. Baklanov; I. T. Frolov; A. N. Girenko; E. K. Ligachev; Yu. A. Manaenkov; V. A. Medvedev; G. P. Razumovsky; N. N. Slyunkov; E. S. Stroev; G. I. Usmanov; A. N. Yakovlev and L. N. Zaikov.

Chairman of the Party Control Committee: B. K. Pugo.

Chairman of the Central Auditing Commission: G. F. Sizov.

In Jan. 1989 the Communist Party had 19,487,822 members (about 9·3% of the adult population). Of these, 45·4% were classified as workers, 11·4% as collective farmers and 43·2% as office workers; 29·9% were women, and 59% were Russians. The party's youth wing, the Komsomol (All-Union Leninist Communist Union of Youth), had 36m. members in 1989. V. I. Mironenko was re-elected First Secretary of its Central Committee at its 20th Congress in April 1987.

Istoriya Kommunisticheskoi partii Sovetskogo Soyuza, 7th ed. Moscow, 1985
KPSS v rezolyutsiyakh i resheniyakh s''ezdov, konferentsii i plenumov TsK, 9th ed., vol. 1ff. Moscow, 1983ff.
Resolutions and Decisions of the Communist Party of the Soviet Union, ed. R. H. McNeal, 5 vols. Toronto, 1974–82
Spravochnik partiinogo rabotnika. Moscow, annual
Izvestiya Tsk KPSS. Moscow, monthly
Hill, R. and Frank, P., *The Soviet Communist Party.* 3rd ed., London, 1987
Schapiro, L. B., *The Communist Party of the Soviet Union.* 2nd ed., London, 1970
White, S. (ed.) *Soviet Communism: Programme and Rules.* London, 1989

DEFENCE. On 25 Feb. 1946 the control of the Soviet Armed Forces was unified under a single Ministry of the Armed Forces. On 25 Feb. 1950 the Defence Ministry was divided into a War Ministry and a Navy Ministry; on 15 March 1953 a single Ministry of Defence was reconstituted. In 1955 the Air Defence Command and in 1960 the Strategic Rocket Forces were established as the 4th and 5th 'branches' of the armed forces beside the army, navy and air force. Overall supervision of defence and security matters is exercised by the Defence Council of the USSR, headed by the General Secretary of the CPSU.

The direction of Party and political work in the Armed Forces is exercised by the Central Committee of the Communist Party of the Soviet Union through the chief political directorate of the Ministry of Defence. The chiefs of the political departments of military commands, fleets and armies must be Party members of 5 years' standing and the chiefs of political departments of divisions and regiments Party members of 3 years' standing. About 90% of the officers are members of the Communist Party or Young Communist League, and 50% have had an engineering and technical education.

Military service begins at the age of 19 (or 18 for graduates of secondary schools). Active service lasts 2 years for privates in the Army and M.V.D. troops, 3 years for n.c.o.s in the Army and M.V.D. troops and for privates and n.c.o.s in the Air Force, 4 years for privates and n.c.o.s in the Coastal Defence, 5 years for ratings in the Navy. Reserve service lasts up to the ages of 35, 45 or 50 years according to fitness, family status and other considerations. Conscientious objection is treated as a criminal offence. Students in places of higher education are freed from military service, but receive military instruction. About half the service personnel have had higher, or 10-year, education and over 80% are members of the Communist Party.

Total strength of the armed forces was over 5·25m. in 1988, with a probable 55m. reserves and a further 570,000 in paramilitary forces.

Declared budgetary expenditure on defence (in 1m. rubles) for 1960 was 9,300; 1970, 17,900; 1980, 17,100; 1987, 20,600.

Army. The Army is thought to consist of 53 tank, 153 motor rifle, 7 airborne and 18 artillery divisions; 10 air assault brigades; and various independent tank, artillery, missile and engineer units. Equipment includes some 33,300 T-54/-55/-62, 9,700 T-64 and 13,000 T-72/-80 main battle tanks. Strength (1989) 1·5m. (including 1·2m. conscripts).

There are 6 operational rocket armies deploying over 1,451 intercontinental ballistic missiles (SS-11,-13,-17,-18,-19), capable of delivering over 5,000 nuclear warheads yielding over 4,000 megatons. Intermediate range ballistic missiles (SS-20) number 388, but are due to be eliminated in accordance with the INF Treaty. There are a further 112 medium range ballistic missiles, but these are being phased out. Personnel number 287,000, with reserves of 537,000.

Navy. There are signs that Soviet defence budget cuts are having an impact on Naval new construction, but the Fleet is still steadily and progressively modernizing and its overall combat capability continues to improve. Greater efficiency and less dilution of the competent trained strength should also result from an accelerated programme of disposal of older ships.

The wartime tasks of the Soviet Navy are largely defensive in strategic terms. The safe deployment and protection of the large force of strategic missile-firing submarines is the first priority; the defence of the Soviet homeland, in particular against the threat of sudden attack, the second; whilst interdiction of enemy shipping and protection of own shipping take lower priority.

Peacetime command of the Soviet Navy (with the exception of the missile submarines which form part of the Strategic Nuclear Force) is exercised by the Main Naval Staff in Moscow, through the Commanders of the 4 fleets into which the Navy is divided. The 4 fleets comprise the Northern Fleet (HQ Severomorsk), Baltic Fleet (HQ Kaliningrad), Black Sea Fleet (HQ Sevastopol) and the Pacific Fleet (HQ Vladivostok). The Northern and Pacific fleets are markedly stronger than the others, partly because strategic submarines are only deployed in their areas. All the operational aircraft carriers, and the 3 large cruisers of the Kirov class are deployed with these major fleets. Detached squadrons, found from the regional fleets, are deployed on a rotational basis into the Mediterranean Sea and Indian Ocean. A small flotilla of frigates and amphibious ships is also maintained in the Caspian Sea.

The overall strength of the Soviet Navy at the end of the indicated year was as follows:-

Category	*1984*	*1985*	*1986*	*1987*	*1988*	*1989*
Strategic Submarines	79	77	77	76	75	64
Nuclear Attack Submarines	114	121	118	127	127	130
Diesel Submarines	154	148	145	140	136	133
Aircraft Carriers	3	3	4	4	4	5
Cruisers	39	44	42	43	44	44
Destroyers	67	66	57	59	54	45
Frigates	184	175	167	168	166	171

In the tables and listings which folow, it should be noted that, in the west, Soviet ship classes and weapons are generally known by their official NATO nicknames. These may be recognized as follows: Surface ships are given names with an initial letter 'K' *e.g. Kynda, Kresta*, and submarines by letters from the phonetic alphabet, *e.g. Alfa, Kilo.* Surface-to-air missiles are numbered in the SA-N- series, and given nicknames beginning with an initial 'G', *e.g. Goa*, surface-to-surface missiles are numbered SS-N-3 etc., and have nicknames commencing with 'S', fighter aircraft 'F', bombers 'B', and all helicopters 'H'. This practice is slowly being discarded as more information on Soviet ship classes and weapon names becomes known in the west.

The Soviet force of Strategic Submarines is constituted as follows:-

Class	*No.*	*Tonnage (in 1,000)*	*Speed*	*Missiles*	*Other Weapons*
Typhoon	6	27·00	27	20 SS-N-20	Torpedoes
Delta-IV	6	12·35	24	16 SS-N-23	Torpedoes
Delta-III	14	11·90	24	16 SS-N-18	Torpedoes
Delta-II	4	11·50	24	16 SS-N-8	Torpedoes
Delta-I	18	11·00	25	12 SS-N-8	Torpedoes
Yankee-II	1	9·75	26	12 SS-N-17	Torpedoes
Yankee-I	12	9·75	26	16 SS-N-6	Torpedoes
Golf-II [1]	3	3·00	13	3 SS-N-5	Torpedoes

[1] This class diesel-electric propulsion; all others nuclear.

This wide range of submarine demonstrates the Soviet preference for making small, incremental changes in operational capability. Only with the Typhoon class, completed between 1982 and 1989, and the largest submarine ever built, was this approach dropped. The SS-N-20 'Sturgeon' missile carried by the Typhoon carries 6 warheads to a maximum range of 4,500 nautical miles, while the SS-N-23 'Skiff' in the other currently-building class, the 'Delta-IV', carries 10 warheads over the same range. The other older missiles carry one to 3 warheads over ranges varying between 1,300 and 4,000 nautical miles. The USSR has announced that all 'Golf-IIs' will be withdrawn before the end of 1990. Of the 6 in service in mid-1989, 3 were to be disposed of by Jan. 1990 and the remainder may also have been de-activated.

The Soviet fleet of over 260 attack submarines again comprises a wide range of classes. From the enormous 16,250 tonne 'Oscar' nuclear-powered missile submarine to the small diesel 'Whiskey' of 1,370 tonnes, there are over 20 classes of submarine in service with the navy. The difficulties in training personnel to operate, and the technical and logistic complications supporting such a diverse mix are self-evident. The inventory of anti-ship missile-firing submarines comprises 5 'Oscar', built 1982-89, 24 SS-N-19 'Shipwreck' missiles; 1 'Papa', built 1971, 10 SS-N-9 'Siren'; 6 'Charlie-II', 1973-80, 8 SS-N-9; 10 'Charlie-I', 1967-72, 8 SS-N-7 'Starbright'; and 28 'Echo-II', 1961-67, 8 SS-N-3 'Shaddock' or SS-N-12 'Sandbox'. The former are all nuclear-propelled, and there are additionally 16 diesel-powered 'Juliet' class built between 1961 and 1968 carrying 4 SS-N-3. Finally, there are 2 former strategic 'Yankee'-class submarines converted to fire the SS-N-21 'Sampson' land-attack cruise missile, which has a range of 1,600 nautical miles, and a further boat carrying out trials on the larger experimental SS-NX-24 missile. The types of torpedo-firing boats currently building are the Akula, nuclear-powered and of 8,100 tonnes, of which there are 4, the 'Sierra', nuclear-powered, 7,700 tonnes now numbering 3, and the 'Victor-III', nuclear-powered, 6,400 tonnes, the total of which is now 23. The diesel-powered 'Kilo' class, of which the Soviet Navy operates 12, is also building at 3 to 4 per year, but the majority are for export. In addition to these classes there are a further 47 nuclear-powered and 105 diesel submarines on the active list. The disposal of a number of old diesel and the first generation of nuclear-powered boats may be imminent.

Modern soviet surface warships are assigned categories rather different from western ships. Ships which, in the west, would be called 'Aircraft Carriers' are termed 'Large Aircraft-Carrying Cruisers' by the Soviet Navy partly because they usually carry significant ship weaponry as well as aircraft, but also to exempt them from the prohibition on the movement of Aircraft Carriers through the Turkish Straits imposed by the Montreux Convention. Ships of cruiser size (7,500-8,000 tonnes full load and upwards) are divided into two categories; those optimized for anti-submarine warfare (ASW) and those for anti-surface ship operations. Ships of cruiser size in the former category are classified as 'Large Anti-Submarine Ships' while the missile armed ASUW ships are classified 'Rocket Cruisers'. The tables below listing the principal surface ships of the Soviet Navy use the most appropriate western classifications:-

Aircraft Carriers

Completed	*Name*	*Tonnage (in 1,000)*	*Speed*	*Aircraft*	*Other Armament*
1989	Tbilisi	65·0	30	See below	Anti-Ship Missiles Anti-Air missiles.
1987	Baku	37·7	32	13 Yak-38 V/STOL 16 Ka-25/27 hel	12 anti-ship missiles 4 SA-N-6 SAM launchers
Kiev Class					
1982	Novorossiisk	37·7	32	13 Yak-38 V/STOL	8 anti-ship missiles.
1978	Minsk	37·7	32	16 Ka-25/27 hel	4 SA-N-3 SAM launchers
1976	Kiev	37·7	32		1 twin ASW missile.

Cruisers

Completed	*Name*	*Tonnage (in 1,000)*	*Speed*	*Main Armament*	*Aircraft*
Kirov Class					
1988	Kalinin	28·4	33	20 SS-N-19 anti-ship missiles, 12 X 8 SA-N-6 SAM, 2 SS-N-14 ASW missiles (*Kirov*) 2 100-mm guns (*Kirov*), 1 X 2 130-mm gun (*Frunze, Kalinin*)	2 Ka-27 Helix, 1 Ka-25 Hormone helicopters.
1984	Frunze				
1980	Kirov				
Moskva Class (Helicopter Cruisers).					
1968	Leningrad	16·50	31	1 X 2 ASW missile launcher. 2 X 2 SA-N-3 SAM launchers.	14 Ka-25 ASW helos.
1967	Moskva				
Slava Class.					
1988	Chervona Ukraina	12·70	34	16 SS-N-12 anti-ship missiles 8 X 8 SA-N-6 Grumble SAM. 8 533mm Torpedo tubes	1 Ka-27 Helix helicopter
1986	Marshal Ustinov				
1983	Slava				
Nikolayev (or 'Kara') Class.					
1979	Tallin	9·85	34	8 SS-N-14 Silex ASW missiles 2 X 2 SA-N-3 Goblet SAM 10 X 533mm Torpedo tubes	1 Ka-25 Hormone ASW helicopter
1978	Tashkent				
1977	Petropavlovsk				
1976	Azov				
1975	Kerch				
1974	Ochakov				
1973	Nikolaiev				
Kronshtadt ('Kresta II') Class.					
1977	Adm. Yumashev	7·83	35	8 SS-N-14 ASW missiles 2 X 2 SA-N-3 Goblet SAM 10 533mm Torpedo tubes	1 Ka-25 Hormone ASW helicopter
1976	Vasily Chapayev				
1975	Mar. Timoshenko				
1974	Adm. Isachenkov				
1973	Adm. Oktyabrsky				
1973	Mar. Voroshilov				
1972	Adm. Makarov				
1971	Adm. Nakhimov				
1970	Adm. Isakov				
1969	Khronshtadt				
Admiral Zozulya ('Kresta I') Class.					
1969	Sevastopol	7·70	34	4 SS-N-3 Shaddock anti-ship missiles 2 X 2 SA-N-1 Goa SAM 10 533mm Torpedo tubes	1 Ka-25 Hormone ASW helicopter
1968	V-Adm. Drozd				
1968	Vladivostok				
1967	Adm. Zozulya				
Udaloy Class					
1988	Adm. Vinograd	8·60	30	8 SS-N-14 Silex ASW missiles, 2 X 100mm guns, 8 X 533mm Torpedo tubes	2 X Ka-27 Helix ASW helicopters.
1988	Adm. Levchenko				
1986	Simferopol				
1985	Mar. Shaposhnikov				
1985	Adm. Tributs				
1984	Adm. Spiridonov				
1983	Adm. Zakorov				
1983	Mar. Vasilevsky				
1981	VAdm. Kulakov				
1980	Udaloy				
Sverdlov Class.					
1958	Adm. Senyavin	16·00	32	12 X 152mm guns (9 only in *Zhdanov*, 6 in *Senyavin*), 12 X 100mm guns.	None
1953	Alexandr Nevski				
1953	Murmansk				
1953	Zhdanov				

Trials of the new aircraft carrier *Tbilisi* commenced in late 1989. This ship appears to be a unique hybrid between the conventional aircraft carrier equipped with catapults and arrester gear and V/STOL carriers without flight deck machinery. Initial flight trials show she launches aircraft over a ski-jump bow, and recovers them into arrester wires. It remains to be seen how effective this method is in terms of aircraft weapon and fuel loads at launch, and it will be some while before the ship can be considered fully operational. Aircraft used for the initial trials in Nov. 1989 were the Su-27 'Flanker', the MiG-29 'Fulcrum' and the Su-25 'Frogfoot'. These aircraft are potentially much more effective than the Yak-38 'Forger' deployed in the earlier carriers. It remains to be seen whether the Yak-41, an improved version of the 'Forger' currently under development, but using the same inherently limiting technology, will be embarked.

The 'Kara', 'Kresta II' and Udaloy classes tabled above are classified as 'Large ASW ships'. The Kirov, Slava and 'Kresta I' cruiser classes above, and the 'Kynda' guided missile destroyers below are classified as 'Rocket Cruisers'. The Kirov class, of which a fourth unit is fitting out, are the largest combatant warships, apart from aircraft carriers, to be built for any navy since the Second World War. The ships have an unusual and ingenious machinery arrangement. The main propulsion outfit comprises 2 nuclear reactors for long-range cruising, boosted by oil-fired superheat boilers for high speed work. *Azov*, nominally of the 'Kara' class, has a different guided missile outfit to serve as trials ship for the armament of subsequent classes. Among the older ships, of the 24 Sverdlov class cruisers planned, 14 were completed and 4 remain in operational service, principally as fleet flagships. 6 more are held in reserve, but the scrapping programme is gaining momentum.

Among the smaller ships the most impressive are the 10 Sovremenny class guided missile destroyers, of 7,900 tonnes, armed with 8 SS-N-22 'Sunburn' anti-ship missiles, 1 twin SA-N-7 'Gadfly' surface-to-air missile launcher, 4 130mm guns and a helicopter. Also in the ASUW category are the 4 Groznyy (or 'Kynda') class of 5,650 tonnes, with 8 SS-N-3 'Shaddock' anti-ship missiles, and the 5 'modified Kashin' class. There are a further 12 'Kashin', 4 'SAM-Kotlin' guided missiles, and 10 other destroyers, 32 large frigates and 130 smaller frigates. An additional 50 or so frigates and above are maintained in inactive reserve. The coastal defence force is headed by 64 missile corvettes, 86 fast missile craft, 25 hydrofoil and 5 conventional fast torpedo craft and numerous patrol classes totalling 220 hulls. Mine warfare constitutes an important element of Soviet naval strategy; large stocks (some hundreds of thousands) of modern mines are held, and all submarines and many surface ship classes are provided with mine-laying equipment. There are additionally 3 specific minelayers, 70 offshore, 110 coastal and 190 inshore mine countermeasure vessels.

Amphibious capability is provided by 2 large dock landing ships of the Ivan Rogov class, 24 Ropucha and 14 Alligator class tank landing ships, 36 medium landing ships, plus some 140 minor craft including about 85 special purpose amphibious surface-effect vessels. Total amphibious lift available to the Soviet authorities is some 17,000 men. 750 main battle tank equivalents but operating facilities for only 10 helicopters.

Amphibious landing forces are found from the Soviet Naval Infantry, 17,000 strong, units of which are assigned to all fleets. Organized into a single division, 7,000 strong, plus 3 independent brigades, the force is equipped to relatively light scales. Principal equipment includes 230 main battle tanks, 150 amphibious light tanks, 90 artillery pieces and over 1,000 armoured personnel carriers. A separate force of 7,500 Coastal Defence troops man artillery and missile batteries positioned to defend the main naval bases and ports.

The operational reach of the Soviet Navy, is however, limited by its poor capability for afloat support. A first class multi-purpose underway replenishment ship, the *Berezina*, was completed in 1977, but remains the sole example of her class. There are an additional 6 dual-purpose stores and fuel replenishment ships, 4 purpose-built tankers, and 19 tankers converted from a commercial design with limited underway replenishment capability. Second line support is provided by 14 tankers, and about 260 maintenance and logistic ships, 67 electronic intelligence gatherers, 76 other special-purpose auxiliaries, and 250 survey, research and space support ships.

There are 5 warship building yards in and near Leningrad; Black Sea yards are at

Nikolayev, Kerch and Sevastopol, at Severodvinsk in the North Sea Fleet region and at Komsomolsk-on-Amur in the Far East. The shipbuilding programme is believed to include further 'Delta-IV' strategic submarines, and attack submarines of the Akula, 'Sierra', 'Victor-III' and 'Kilo' classes. There is a further aircraft carrier similar to the *Tbilisi* fitting out, and a third, rather larger unit on the building ways. A fourth heavy cruiser of the Kirov class is fitting out, as is the fourth of the Slava class. Two further Udaloys are expected, and the first of a new class of large frigates is building. The replacement of coastal force units built in the 1950s and early 1960s continues at a steady pace.

Shore-based naval aviation forms a major element of all Soviet Fleets. In addition to the aircraft held on inventory for seaborne service, there are some 350 bombers, 380 maritime patrol, 80 fighter/ground attack aircraft plus helicopters. Main bomber types held are 180 Tu-26 'Backfire', 130 Tu-16 'Badger' and 40 Tu-22 'Blinder', all of which are principally with stand-off anti-ship missiles. Maritime reconnaissance and ASW tasks fall predominantly to the force of 100 Tu-95 and Tu-142 'Bear' with 280 miscellaneous shorter range aircraft tasked to ASW, electronic countermeasures, intelligence gathering and tankers. The helicopter inventory amount to some 300, principally ASW but including 25 combat assault, and 25 mine countermeasures. There are, finally over 400 training and transport aircraft.

The total personnel in 1989 numbred 437,000, of whom 260,000 were conscripts who serve 3 years if in seagoing categories, and 2 years if shore-based. Of the total, some 15,500 serve in the strategic submarine force, 68,000 in naval aviation, 17,000 marines or naval infantry, and 7,500 in coastal defence.

Coastguard, customs and border patrol duties are performed by the substantial maritime element of the KGB. Some 23,000 strong, this force operates some 5 large helicopter-carrying frigates of a modified naval Krivak class, 12 small frigates, 7 offshore, 25 coastal and 165 inshore patrol craft divided among all the Soviet coastal areas.

Air Force. The Soviet Air Force (excluding the strategic bomber force and Voyska PVO air defence force) was believed to have a personnel strength, in 1990, of over 448,000 officers and men. To supplement long-range rocket missiles (estimated at 1,398 emplaced ICBM, 600 MRBM/IRBM), the strategic bomber force has still about 125 Tupolev Tu-95 ('Bear')[1] 4-turboprop bombers, 50 Myasishchev M-4 4-jet bombers and flight-refuelling tankers ('Bison'), 300 twin-jet Tupolev Tu-16 ('Badger'), and 135 supersonic Tupolev Tu-22 ('Blinder') bombers, ECM and reconnaissance aircraft, and at least 200 Tupolev ('Backfire') swing-wing bombers. All types are used also by the Naval Air Force for long-range maritime reconnaissance; the Tu-16, Tu-95, Tu-22 and 'Backfire' can carry air-to-surface guided self-propelled cruise missiles and all 5 types have provision for flight refuelling. A new swing-wing strategic Tupolev bomber ('Blackjack'), larger and faster than the American B-1, is entering service.

The tactical air forces, under local army command in the field, have an estimated total of 6,000 ground attack, air combat, ECM and reconnaissance aircraft, including 2,600 MiG-23/27 ('Flogger') and 800 two-seat Sukhoi Su-24 ('Fencer') supersonic swing-wing aircraft, 300 twin-jet Yakovlev Yak-28 ('Brewer') reconnaissance aircraft, 1,000 swing-wing Su-17 and Su-22 ('Fitter-C/D/G/H/J'), and 600 MiG-21 ('Fishbed') fighter-bombers, 340 Su-15 ('Flagon'), 200 MiG-25 ('Foxbat') and MiG-31 ('Foxhound') interceptors, and an increasing number of new Su-25 ('Frogfoot') twin-engined ground attack aircraft supported by 60 MiG-21 and 170 MiG-25 ('Foxbat') reconnaissance aircraft, and over 3,500 helicopters, including very large Mi-26 ('Halo') transports and over 1,000 heavily-armed Mi-24 ('Hind') assault helicopters, in gunship/transport versions. Electronic warfare duties are performed by a variety of aircraft, including Yak-28s and Mi-8 and Mi-17 helicopters. The Voyska PVO defence forces, organized as a separate service, have a total of 1,300 jet interceptors. A high proportion of the squadrons are equipped with MiG-23 ('Flogger'), Su-15 ('Flagon'), MiG-25 ('Foxbat') and improved MiG-31 ('Foxhound') all-weather interceptors, armed with air-to-air missiles plus the MiG-29 ('Fulcrum') and Su-27 ('Flanker') new-generation aircraft now entering service. The twin-jet Yak-28P ('Firebar') and Tu-28P ('Fiddler') make up the balance of the force. Early warning and fighter-control duties are performed by about 10 radar-carrying adaptations of the Tu-114 turboprop transport, redesignated Tu-126 ('Moss'), which are being replaced by a more effective radar-equipped AWACS version ('Mainstay') of the Il-76 transport. Very large numbers of surface-to-air guided missiles are operational, on some 10,000 launchers, including the new high-performance SA-10 (low-altitude) and SA-12 (high-altitude) with capability against cruise and submarine-launched missiles respectively, the older 'Guild', 'Guideline', 'Goa', 'Gainful' and 'Ganef', the long-range 'Gammon' and the 'Galosh' which is deployed around Moscow on 32 launchers and has anti-missile capability.

[1] For convenience Soviet aircraft and missiles are usually referred to by invented English names in non-Soviet military writings.

Soviet Air Force transport squadrons have 150 An-12 ('Cub') 4-turboprop transports and 100 An-24s ('Coke') and An-26s ('Curl'), with 50 An-22s ('Cock'), and 400 Il-76 ('Candid') heavy four-jet freighters. The very large four-jet An-124 ('Condor') is entering service to replace the An-22. Training aircraft include the piston-engined Yak-18 primary trainer and its Yak-52 successor, the Czech-built L-29 Delfin and L-39 jet basic trainers and versions of operational types such as MiG-21, MiG-23, MiG-25, MiG-15, Su-7, Su-15, Su-17, Yak-28 and Tu-22.

Naval Air Force. With 1,100 fixed-wing aircraft and helicopters, the Soviet Navy has the world's second largest naval air arm. Under the control of the various naval commands, *i.e.*, Baltic, Black Sea and Pacific, the Naval Air Arm has an estimated 220 Tu-16 ('Badger') twin-jet bombers, and 160 'Backfire' swing-wing bombers, able to carry air-to-surface missiles, 40 supersonic twin-jet Tu-22 ('Blinder') maritime reconnaissance aircraft, about 70 Su-17 ('Fitter') shore-based fighters, and 90 Beriev M-12 ('Mail') maritime patrol amphibians. For reconnaissance, anti-submarine and electronic warfare there are about 100 Tu-95 and Tu-142 ('Bear') 4-engined bombers, 90 Tu-16s, and a few Tu-22s, plus a small number of Il-20s ('Coot-A') and 60 Il-38s ('May'). The Tu-142 also has an important targeting rôle for ships fitted with anti-shipping missile launchers. Over 250 anti-submarine and missile targeting/guidance helicopters, notably the Ka-27 ('Helix') and Ka-25 ('Hormone'), are carried in naval vessels, including 4 aircraft carriers (which also operate Yak-36 ('Forger') VTOL attack/reconnaissance aircraft) and 2 helicopter carriers. Several hundred transport, flight refuelling tanker ('Badger'), utility and training fixed-wing aircraft and 100 Mi-14 ('Haze') shore-based ASW helicopters are also under Navy control.

Berman, H. J. and Kerner, M. (ed.) *Soviet Military Law and Administration.* 2 vols. Harvard Univ. Press, 1955
Moynahan, B., *The Claws of the Bear: A History of the Soviet Armed Forces from 1917 to the Present.* London, 1989
Scott, H. F. and Scott, W. F., *The Armed Forces of the USSR.* 2nd ed. Boulder, 1981
Smith, M. J., *The Soviet Navy, 1941–1978: A Guide to Sources in English.* Oxford and Santa Barbara, 1981
Suvorov, V., *The Liberators: The Soviet Army.* London, 1981
Watson, B. W., *Red Navy at Sea.* Boulder, 1982

INTERNATIONAL RELATIONS

Membership. USSR is a member of UN, Comecon and the Warsaw Pact.

ECONOMY

Planning. Planning is based on public ownership in industry and trade, and on mixed public and collective (co-operative) ownership in agriculture. The first plan drawn up by Gosplan (the State Planning Commission) was the 'Goelro' drawn up in 1920. This was to be the basis for the economic development of the country and for the construction of a system of electrical power plants with an aggregate capacity of 1·75m. kw. in the course of 15 years.

For details of Planning 1925–1942 *see* THE STATESMAN'S YEAR-BOOK, 1981–82, p. 1226.

For details of the fourth 5-year plan, 1946–50, *see* THE STATESMAN'S YEAR-

BOOK, 1952, pp. 1424 f. The 1950 target of the gross output of industry was exceeded by 2%.

On 10 Oct. 1952 the 19th Congress of the Communist Party issued directives for the fifth 5-year plan, 1951–55; for details, *see* THE STATESMAN'S YEAR-BOOK, 1953, pp. 1435-36. During Sept. and Oct. 1953 the Government issued a number of decrees to stimulate the development of agriculture, the output of consumer goods and the expansion of the home trade. For details of these decrees, *see* THE STATESMAN'S YEAR-BOOK, 1955, pp. 1448-50.

The directives for the sixth 5-year plan, 1956-60, were adopted by the 20th Congress of the Communist Party on 25 Feb. 1956; for details *see* THE STATESMAN'S YEAR-BOOK, 1958, p. 1472.

In May 1955 Gosplan was reorganized to consist of 2 state commissions for long-term planning (Gosplan) and for current planning (Gosekonomkomissiya); at the same time a committee was set up to improve the application to industry of advanced science and technology (Gostekhnika).

Between 1954 and 1956 considerable changes were made in planning methods. In March 1954 collective farms were given greater authority over planning their own output, only the quantities required by the State in fixed deliveries being determined beforehand, and voluntary sales by contract. In 1955 they were authorized to make changes in their statutes, which had followed a fixed model since 1935. In 1955-57 over 15,000 industrial establishments in various basic industries, previously controlled by the Union Government, and later a number of entire light industries were turned over to the constituent (Union) Republics. By 1962 they controlled from 95 to 100% of all industrial output.

In 1957 a comprehensive plan for decentralization of management of industry was initiated. Industrial establishments responsible for about 71% of all Soviet industrial output were turned over to Economic Councils set up in 104 (in 1963: 47) economic administrative areas. These in 1962 controlled 73% of all industrial production. The Ministries previously responsible for the industries concerned were either abolished or transformed into purely planning and supervisory bodies. The State Committee for current planning was abolished, and Gosplan was given wider powers.

In consequence of this change a 7-year plan for 1959-65 was adopted by the 21st Congress of the Communist Party in Feb. 1959. Industrial output was to increase by 80%; it was in fact, in 1965, 84% above that of 1959. Capital investments would roughly equal the total for 1917-58: special attention was to be given to mechanization of agriculture and arduous industrial labour, automation and new technological processes, and housing. Diesel or electric traction of railway freight was to rise to 85%. Real incomes were to rise 40%, the 7-hour day (6 hours for miners) became general in 1960 and the 40-hour week in 1961, and introduction of the 35-hour week (30 hours for miners) began in 1964.

In Oct. 1965 the regional and Republic Economic Councils were abolished and also 28 Ministries for various branches of industry (17 Union-Republican, *i.e.*, corresponding to similar Ministries in the Union Republics, and 11 All-Union).

A 20-year plan was adopted by the 22nd Congress of the Communist Party on 31 Oct. 1961, which envisaged a ninefold growth in electricity output and big increases in production of steel, oil, coal, machinery and cement, and also in grain, milk and meat. Two new iron and steel centres were to be developed in Kazakhstan and in Kursk region. A single deepwater system was to link the main inland waterways in the European USSR. Some rivers in northern Asia were to be diverted south for irrigation purposes. A 6-hour day for a 6-day week or 35 hours for a 5-day week were to be achieved by 1970. Housing, water, gas, heating, public urban transport and school meals were to be free by 1980. These and cognate measures were to provide 'the material and technical basis of communism'.

The 23rd Congress of the Communist Party in April 1966 adopted directives for a 5-year plan for 1966-70. Under these, power output was to reach 830,000-850,000m. kwh.; oil, 345-355m. tons; coal, 665-675m. tons; steel, 124-129m. tons; mineral fertilizers, 62-65m. tons; machine-tools, 220,000-230,000; cars, 700,000-800,000; tractors, 600,000-625,000; paper, 5-5·3m. tons; cement, 100-105m. tons;

fabrics, 9·5-9·8m. sq. metres; leather footwear, 610-630m. pairs; meat, 5·9-6·2m. tons; butter, 1·2m. tons; sugar, 9·8-10m. tons. The average annual output of grain was to increase by 30%; 7,000 km of new railway line, 63,000 km of new motor roads and 35-40 new airports were to be built; and marine tonnage was to be increased by 50%.

The 9th Five-Year Plan adopted in 1971 provided for an increase in electric power output to 1,065,000m. kwh.; oil to 496m. tons; gas, 320,000m. cu. metres; steel, 146m. tons; coal, 695m. tons; mineral fertilizers, 90m. tons; tractors, 575,000; passenger cars, 1·26m., and lorries, 750,000. Grain output was to rise to 195m. tons in 1975; meat, approximately 16m. tons; milk, 100m. tons; textiles, 11,000m. sq. metres; leather footwear, 830m. pairs. Average wages were to increase by 22%, incomes of collective farmers 30-35%, and the average of real incomes by 31%. 3,400 miles of new railway tracks were to be built and 3,700 miles electrified, with 17,000 miles of new oil pipelines, and 40% more cargo carried by sea. Over 16m. flats and houses were to be built.

By July 1972, 43,000 industrial plants had been transferred to the new system of decentralized cost-accounting; they produced 94% of total output of Soviet industry and 95% of its total profit. All public establishments in trade and catering and all the state farms have gone over to the new system.

On 29 Oct. 1976, the Supreme Soviet adopted the 10th Five-Year Plan (1976–80). This provided for an increase of industrial output from 104·3% of the 1975 level to 136%, an average annual increase of agricultural output by 16%, freight traffic (all forms) from 105·7% to 132%, state capital investments from 105·1% of the 1975 level in 1976 to 114·6% in 1980, real income per head from 103·7% to 121%, retail commodity turnover from 103·6% to 128·7%. 550m. sq. metres of new housing were to be built. Children in pre-school establishments would increase by 104·4% in 1976 and 125·5% in 1980, pupils in day schools from 108·9% to 148·8%, and students in higher education from 100·4% to 105·4%. Hospital beds were to increase from 102·2% in the first year to 109·7% in the final year.

The 11th Five-Year Plan, adopted in 1981, aimed to raise living standards. The focus was Siberia and the Soviet Far East, with their large resources of energy and raw materials, and also Central Asia, with its favourable combination of labour resources and raw materials. Virtually no industries were to be developed in the European part of the USSR and the plan envisaged speeding up the development of labour-intensive branches of agriculture, consumer goods and engineering industries in Central Asia. National income (in the Soviet definition) was to increase by 18% between 1981 and 1985; industrial production was to increase by 26%, capital investment by 5·4%, freight traffic by 19·4%, real incomes by 16·5%, agricultural production by 13%, and retail trade in the state and co-operative sectors by 23% over the same period. Pensions were to be raised and the minimum wage was to be increased to 80 rubles a month, and efforts were to be made to increase state assistance to families with young children and to improve the food and care given to them in schools and pre-school institutions.

The 12th Five-Year Plan, adopted in 1986, also places its main emphasis upon raising popular living and cultural standards. This in turn is held to require an acceleration of socio-economic development and an intensification and increase in the effectiveness of production on the basis of scientific-technical progress. The plan covers the period 1986–90 and up to the year 2,000, by which time real living standards are planned to increase by 1·6 to 1·8 times; manual labour should account for no more than 15–20% of all productive work; state and co-operative retail trade should increase by 1·8 times; and health, educational and other social expenditure should double. Over the same period the national income should approximately double and industrial production more than double, entirely as a result of increased productivity, which is planned to increase by 2·3 to 2·5 times. Greater economy is to be achieved in the use of energy and natural resources; investment is to be concentrated in priority areas; and scientific-technical progress is to be accelerated and related more closely to production. Continued emphasis is placed upon the Energy Programme, the Food Programme and the Complex Programme for the Development of Consumer Goods and Services, which were adopted between 1982 and

1985. In the 5-year period 1986–90 national income is to increase by 22%, industrial production by 25%, labour productivity by 12–25%, and real incomes by 14%.

In 1988 national income produced increased by 4·4% (1981–85 average, 3·6%), gross industrial production by 3·9% (1981–85 average, 3·7%) and labour productivity by 5·1% (1981–85 average, 3·1%).

Narodnoe khozyaistvo SSSR. Moscow, annual

Resheniya partii i pravitel' stva po khozyaistvennym voprosam. Vol. 1ff. Moscow, 1967ff

Istoriya sotsialisticheskoi ekonomiki SSSR. 7 vols. Moscow, 1976–80

Nove, A., *An Economic History of the USSR*. 2nd ed., Harmondsworth, 1989.—*The Soviet Economic System*. 3rd ed., London, 1986

US Congress, Joint Economic Committee, *Gorbachev's Economic Plans*. 2 vols. Washington D.C., 1987

Gregory, P. R. and Stuart, R. C., *Soviet Economic Structure and Performance*. 3rd ed., New York, 1986

Budget. Revenue and expenditure in 1m. rubles for calendar years:

	1985	*1986*	*1987*[1]	1988[1]	1989[1]
Revenue	390,603	419,500	435,683	443,645	459,814
Expenditure	386,469	417,400	435,510	443,645	494,798

[1] Estimate.

The 1989 budget allotted 278,899m. rubles to the national economy, 20,244m. to defence and 163,499m. to social and cultural services.

The social insurance budget, which is controlled by the Central Council for Trade Unions and its affiliated bodies, was 29,476m. rubles in 1977, 31,179m. in 1978, 33,089m. in 1979, 35,296 in 1980 and 58,708m. (plan) in 1988.

National income (produced) was assessed (in 1,000m. rubles) at 145·0 in 1960, 289·9 in 1970, 462·2 in 1980 and 599·6 in 1987.

Income tax was abolished on 1 Oct. 1961 for earnings up to 60 rubles per month and reduced for earnings between 61 and 70 rubles; in Dec. 1967 further cuts of 25% were made for earnings from 61 to 80 rubles; in 1972 earnings up to 70 rubles were freed of income tax, and taxes on incomes up to 90 rubles were cut by about 33¹/₃%. Capital investment (1987) was 205,400m. rubles, including 186,900m. by State and co-operative enterprises, 15,200m. by collective farms and 3,300m. by individuals (on housing).

Currency. As from 1 Jan. 1961 the gold content of the *ruble* was raised from 0·222 168 to 0·987 412 gramme. The official exchange rates (March 1990) 1·02 *rubles* = £1; 0·62 *rubles* = US$1.

The gold holdings of the USSR were, in Dec. 1955, estimated at about 200m. fine oz. (US$7,000m.), or about 20% of the world total of monetary gold.

The currency in circulation is: (1) State Bank notes in denominations of 10, 25, 50 and 100 *rubles;* (2) Treasury notes in denominations of 1, 3 and 5 *rubles;* (3) cupro-nickel coins in denominations of 10, 15, 20 and 50 *kopeks* and 1 *ruble*; (4) cupro-zinc coins in denominations of 1, 2, 3 and 5 *kopeks*.

Banking. The State Bank began operations on 16 Nov. 1921. By an edict of 7 April 1959 a number of specialized banks for planned long-term investments, which had existed since 1932, were abolished. The State Bank, in addition to short-term credits, effects long-term investments in agriculture and in individual rural house building. The Bank for Financing Capital Investments (*Stroibank*) covers industry, transport, urban housing schemes and public utilities and individual housebuilding in towns.

Deposits in 75,800 savings banks were over 96,700m. rubles to the credit of 196m. depositors at 1 Jan. 1989.

Weights and Measures. The metric system has been in use since 1 Jan. 1927.

The Gregorian Calendar was adopted as from 14 Feb. 1918.

ENERGY AND NATURAL RESOURCES

Electricity. There were (1983) 57 fuel-burning power stations of over 1m. kw. capacity, and these account for over 80% of the country's electricity.

Hydro-electric stations have been constructed on major rivers. Among them are the Bratsk (4·5m. kw.), completed in 1967, Ust-Ilimsk, Central Siberia (3·6m. kw.), Krasnoyarsk (6m. kw.) and a 1·26m. kw. station on the River Pechora (Far North). The Sayano-Shushenskaya hydro-power station, part of the Yenisei chain has a capacity of 6·4m. kw. A 245m. high dam has to be built before completion, in a gorge in the Sayan Range. Another large hydro-electric station is under construction on the River Kureika, Siberia, to provide energy for the mining and metallurgical centre at Norilsk in the Arctic.

Total installed capacity of power stations in 1938 was 8·7m. kw. and 339m. kw. in 1988. Industry consumes about 70% of the total electricity. Over 35,000 small rural power stations have been closed in recent years owing to supply from State stations becoming available, but there are still many operating in the countryside. 800 towns and urban settlements were heated by central thermal plants.

The world's first commercial nuclear power station in Obninsk, built in 1954, was followed by the Beloyarsk, Novo-Voronezh, Leningrad, Kursk, Chernobyl, Armenian and Shevchenko nuclear stations. Soviet nuclear power plants so far have standard slow 1m. kw. reactors, but a 1·5m. kw. reactor has now been designed. A fast reactor is functioning at Shevchenko.

The general design for a nuclear thermal station has been developed, and practical experience in this field has been obtained at the Bilibino nuclear power station in the Arctic, which supplies electricity and heat to the inhabitants on the Chukchi Peninsula.

In 1979 a 500,000 kw. MHD pilot project was started in Ryazan. This first-generation MHD station will have an efficiency of 50% as against 40% in the best thermal power stations and will consume about 20% less fuel. An experimental tidal energy station is working at Kislaya Guba (Murman coast).

Total electricity output in 1988 was 1,705,000m. kwh.

The country's integrated power grid is now in operation, covering over 900 power stations, which are handled by a central control panel in Moscow through (in 1988) 1,000,400 km. of cable of 35 kw. or greater capacity. A unified power grid ('Mir') with all the Socialist countries of eastern Europe was built up between 1962 and 1967. Supply 127 and 220 volts; 50 Hz.

Oil. In the 1930s practically all Soviet oil came from the Caucasian fields, of which the Baku fields yielded 75-80% and the Grozny and Maikop fields between them 15%. Since then, the distribution has considerably changed. The Ural-Volga area, the 'Second Baku', has 4 large centres in operation, at Samarska Luka (Kuibyshev), Tuimazy (Bashkiria), Ishimbaev (Bashkiria) and Perm, producing nearly 100m. tonnes annually.

A large new oilfield has been developed in the Trans-Volga area of the Saratov region. The Tyumen (West Siberian) complex now accounts for over 50% of the USSR's oil output. In 1989 the USSR extracted 608m. tonnes of oil.

The total length of pipeline on 1 Jan. 1939 was 4,212 km, divided as follows: Baku-Batumi, 1,717 km; Grozny-Makhachkala, 150 km; Grozny-Armavir-Tuapse, 618 km; Armavir-Trudovaya, 488 km; Guriev-Orsk, 845 km, and other, 394 km. One pipeline (1,700 km) was completed in 1955, connecting Tuimazy in Bashkiria with the refineries of Omsk. In 1957 the Almetyevsk-Gorky pipeline (580 km) and 479 km of the Stavropol-Moscow pipeline were completed. At the end of 1981 there were 70,800 km of pipeline, through which (in 1981) were conveyed 637·7m. tonnes of oil.

The construction of the 'Druzhba' pipeline of about 5,327 km from the oilfields near Kuibyshev to Poland and the German Democratic Republic (northern branch) and to Czechoslovakia and Hungary (southern branch)–separating in Belorussia–begun in 1960, was completed in 1965. Now a double line, it has an annual throughput of 50m. tonnes.

In 1986 the USSR exported 186·8m. tonnes of crude oil and oil products.

Meyerhoff, A. A., *The Oil and Gas Potential of the Soviet Far East.* Beaconsfield, 1981

Gas. A natural-gas pipeline from Gazli, near Khiva, to Voskresensk, near Moscow (2,750 km), with a planned capacity of 100m. cu. metres per day, began operating in Oct. 1967. Since then it has been extended to Czechoslovakia, where a 1,000 km extension, for transmission of Soviet gas to Austria, Italy and German Democratic Republic and Federal Republic of Germany, is under construction and another to Bulgaria. Another natural-gas pipeline, over 3,000 km from Medvezhye (Tyumen Region) to Moscow, began operating in Oct. 1974. A second pipeline from this region, linking the Urengoi deposit with Petrovsky in the Central European area of the USSR, became operational in 1980, and is to be continued to the southern Ukraine, to a total length of 3,000 km. A gas pipeline starting from Orenburg (Urals), passing across the Volga at Kamyshin, and continuing across the Ukraine *via* Kremenchug and Vinnitsa to Czechoslovakia (2,750 km), supplies Czechoslovakia, Poland, Bulgaria and Hungary with 14,000m. cu. metres annually and Romania with 1,500m. A unified gas-grid exceeding 124,000 km now exists.

By Dec. 1981 construction work had begun on the 5,000 km Urengoi (West Siberia)-Uzhgorod-West Europe gas pipeline.

In 1988, 770,000m. cu. metres of gas were produced (in 1940, 3,200m., in 1970, 197,900m.).

Minerals. Mining experts are trained in 6 mining, 3 oil and 1 peat institutes, the mining faculties of 17 higher educational establishments, oil faculties of 2 industrial institutes and a peat faculty at the Belorussian Polytechnical Institute.

The Soviet Union is rich in minerals. Soviet scientists claim that it contains 58% of the world's coal deposits, 58·7% of its oil, 41% of its iron ore, 76·7% of its apatite, 25% of all timber land, 88% of its manganese, 54% of its potassium salts and nearly one-third of its phosphates.

Estimated output (in tonnes) in 1962: Copper, 634,900; zinc, 399,000; lead, 363,000; tungsten, 10,500; antimony, 5,980; silver, 27m. fine oz. Output in 1963: Baryte, 199,500; magnesium, 31,745; aluminium, 961,400; manganese ore (1977), 8·6m.; graphite, 54,000; bauxite, 4·3m.; asbestos, 1·3m.; phosphate rock, 3·7m. (plus 7·4m. apatite); chromite, 1·23m.; gold, 12·5m. fine oz.; molybdenum, 12·5m. lb.; cadmium (1956), 160.

Output of iron and steel in the USSR (in 1m. tonnes):

	Pig-iron	*Ingot steel*	*Rolled steel*		*Pig-iron*	*Ingot steel*	*Rolled steel*
1913	4·2	4·2	3·5	1960	46·8	65·3	50·9
1928–29	4·0	4·8	3·9	1965	66·2	91·0	61·7
1932	6·2	5·9	4·4	1970	85·9	115·9	80·6
1940	14·9	18·3	13·1	1980	107·3	147·9	118·3
1946	10·0	13·4	9·6	1985	110·0	154·7	128·4
1950	19·2	27·3	20·9	1988	115·0	163·0	135·6

Coal production (in 1m. tonnes) was 29·1 in 1913, 165·9 in 1940, 261·1 in 1950, 509·6 in 1960, 624·1 in 1970, 716·4 in 1980, 772 in 1988.

The main centre of the atomic ore industry is at Ust-Kamenogorsk in the Altai Mountains. Uranium deposits are being worked near Taboshar (south-east of Tashkent), Andizhan (in the Tynya-Muyan Mountains), Slyudianka (near Lake Baikal), on the Kolyma River and in Southern Armenia.

Agriculture. The Soviet Union, up to about 1928 predominantly agricultural in character, has become an industrial-agricultural country. Of produced national income in 1986, industry accounted for 43·9%, agriculture for 20·6%, trade etc. for 17·3%, construction for 12% and transport and communications for 6·2%. Of the total state land fund of 2,227·6m. hectares, agricultural land in use in 1986 amounted to 1,048·5m., state forests and state reserves to 1,108·5m. hectares. 19% of all gainfully employed in 1986 were engaged in agriculture and forestry (1913, 75%; 1940, 54%).

The total area under cultivation (including single-owner peasant farms, state farms and collective farms) was (in the same territory) 118·2m. hectares in 1913, 150·6m. in 1940, 146·3m. in 1950, 203m. in 1960, 206·7m. in 1970, 217·3 in 1980, and 210·3m. in 1986.

Collective farms in 1986 possessed 92·2m. hectares of cultivated land, of which 50m. were under crops of various kinds; state farms and other state agricultural undertakings possessed 112·4m. hectares, of which 65·5m. were under crops; personal subsidiary holdings (private plots and allotments) accounted for 5·7m. hectares.

State procurements (after consumption by farms) were, in 1m. tonnes, for the present area of the USSR:

	1950	*1960*	*1970*	*1988*		*1950*	*1960*	*1970*	*1988*
Grain	32·3	46·7	73·3	61·4	Meat[2] and fats	1·3	4·8	8·1	22·8
Raw Cotton[1]	3·5	4·3	6·9	8·7	Milk and milk products	11·4	29·1	48·0	77·0
Sugar-beet	19·7	52·2	71·4	77·9	Sunflower seed	1·1	2·3	4·6	4·9
Potatoes	14·0	13·7	18·1	13·2	Eggs (1,000m.)	3·5	10·5	22·1	57·4
Other vegetables	4·3	8·0	13·8	19·7					

[1] Seed-cotton unginned. [2] Slaughter weight.

Since 1954 grain crops have been measured in 'barn crop' (*i.e.*, net quantities delivered to barns) and not in 'gross harvest' or 'biological yield' (*i.e.*, calculated as growing crops) as previously. Average annual crops (in 1m. tonnes): 1909–13, 72·5; 1946–50, 64·8; 1951–55, 88·5; 1956–60, 121·5; 1961–65, 130·3; 1966–70, 167·5; 1971–75, 181·6; 1976–80, 205; 1981–85, 180·3; 1987, 195.

Other produce (in 1m. tonnes) in 1988: Milk, 106·4; sugar-beet, 87·8; potatoes, 62·7; vegetables, 29·3; meat (slaughter weight), 19·3; raw cotton, 8·7; sunflower seed, 6·2; wool, 0·5; eggs, 84,600m.

In 1989 there were 27,300 collective farms employing 11·8m. collective farmers. Total value of output, 79,300m. rubles. In 1985 they produced 89% of all sugar-beet, cotton 66%, milk 37%, meat 30%, potatoes 21%, other vegetables 24%, eggs 7%, sunflower seeds 74%, wool 30%. In Nov. 1969 the Third Congress of collective farmers adopted a new model constitution, considerably enlarging the planning powers of collective farms and making payments to their members a priority.

In 1989 there were 23,300 state farms employing 11·6m. workers (9·7m. engaged in agriculture) and producing an output valued at 83,200m. rubles.

By 1983 the main field work on state and collective farms and joint inter-farm enterprises (ploughing, sowing of grain, cotton and sugar-beet, and the harvesting of grain and silage crops) was fully mechanized; in 1984, 45% of potato harvesting was mechanized, 94% of sugar-beet pulling, and 66% of vegetable planting.

Rural power stations in 1940 had a capacity of 47·5 h.p.; in 1985, 719m. h.p. Energy consumption in 1985 was 30·7 h.p. per employee. In 1984 agriculture consumed 138,814m. kwh. of electric power.

Investments in agriculture in 1988 were 36,500m. rubles (including 24,600m. by the state and 11,900m. by collective farms). Total agricultural output in 1986 was valued at 121,200m. rubles.

In 1913 the total of irrigated land was 4m. hectares; in 1953, 11m.; in 1986, 20·2m. The total of land drained was 8·4m. hectares in 1956 and 14·9m. in 1986. In 1986, 2,615m. rubles were spent on conservation measures (1,798m. on water resources and 263m. on the atmosphere).

In 1913, 188,000 tonnes of mineral fertilizers were used; in 1950, 5·3m. tonnes, and in 1981, 84m. On 1 Jan. 1987 there were 2·8m. tractors, 826,800 grain combine harvesters and 1·1m. motorized ploughs in the countryside.

An All-Union Academy of Agricultural Sciences, founded in 1929, has regional branches in Siberia and Central Asia and 310 research institutes.

Livestock (1 Jan. 1989), in 1m. head: Cattle, 118·8 (including 41·5 milch cows); pigs, 77·7; sheep, 142·2; goats, 6·5. Since 1957 the enumeration of livestock has been made on 1 Jan. instead of 1 Oct., *i.e.*, after the winter sales and slaughter for the market. Percentage of farm production in 1985:

	Grain	*Cotton*	*Sugar-beet*	*Potatoes*	*Other vegetables*	*Meat*	*Milk*	*Eggs*	*Wool*
State	48	35	12	18	46	42	32	66	44
Collective	51	65	88	22	25	30	39	6	30
Private[1]	1	0	0	60	29	28	29	28	26

[1] *i.e.*, household plots of collective farmers.

Forestry. Of the 814·3m. hectares of forest land of the USSR in 1988, 795·3m. hectares is administered and worked by the State; the remainder, 19m. hectares in extent, is granted for use to the peasantry free of charge.

The largest forest areas are 515m. hectares in the Asiatic part of USSR, 51·4m. along the northern seaboard, 25·4m. in the Urals and 17·95m. in the north-west.

On 24 Oct. 1948 a plan was published for planting crop-protecting forest belts, introducing crop rotation with grasses and building of ponds and water reservoirs in the steppe and forest-steppe areas of the European part of the USSR. By the middle of 1952 some 2·6m. hectares had been planted with shelter-belt trees and 13,500 ponds and reservoirs had been built. The planting of the shelter belts in the Kamyshin-Volgograd and Belgorod-Don areas has in the main been completed. A Volga forest belt has been planted along 1,200 km of railway. Re-afforestation was carried out on 2·2m. hectares of state land in 1988.

Fisheries. The fishing catch including whaling (in 1,000 tons): 1913, 1,051; 1940, 1,422; 1960, 3,541; 1985, 12,400. There were 422 fishing co-operatives in 1985 with a total output valued at 772m. rubles.

Blandon, P., *Soviet Forest Industries.* Boulder, 1983
Johnson, D. G. and Brooks, K. M., *The Prospects for Soviet Agriculture in the 1980s.* Bloomington, 1983
Shaffer, H. G., *Soviet Agriculture.* New York, 1977
Symons, L., *Russian Agriculture: A Geographic Survey.* London, 1972

INDUSTRY AND TRADE

Industry. The organization of industry in the USSR is based on state ownership and control, administered by a separate ministry for each large industry.

Under the successive 5-year plans, large-scale modern industrial works have been constructed, namely: 1st, over 1,500; 2nd, 4,500; 3rd (up to June 1941), 3,000; wartime, 3,500 (apart from reconstruction of destroyed plants); 4th, 6,200; 5th, 3,200; 6th, 2,700; 7th (1959–65), 5,470; 8th (1966–70), 1,870; 9th (1971–75), 2,000; 10th (1976–80), 1,200.

Output of some heavy industries was as follows:

Industry	*1913*	*1950*	*1960*	*1970*	*1980*	*1988*
Iron ore (1m. tonnes)	9·2	39·7	106·2	197·3	244·7	250·0
Oil (1m. tonnes)	9·2	37·9	148·0	353·0	603·2	624·0
Electric power (1,000m. kwh.)	1·9	91·2	292·0	740·9	1,295·0	1,705·0
Coal (1m. tonnes)	29·2	261·1	509·6	624·1	716·4	772·0
Steel (1m. tonnes)	4·2	27·3	65·3	115·9	147·9	163·0
Rolled steel (finished, 1m. tonnes)	3·3	18·0	43·7	80·6	102·9	116·0
Steam and gas turbines (1,000 kw.)	5·9	2,381·0	9,200·0	16,191·0	20,300·0	21,100·0
Steel pipe (1m. tonnes)	–	2·0	5·8	12·4	18·2	20·8
Chemical fibres (1m. tonnes)	–	0·0	0·2	0·6	1·2	1·6
Mineral fertilizer [2] (1m. tonnes)	0·0	1·3	3·3	13·1	24·8	37·1
Automobiles (1,000)	–	64·6	138·8	344·2	1,327·0	1,300·0
Tractors (1m. h.p.)	–	5·5	11·4	29·4	47·0	51·6
Sulphuric acid (1m. tonnes)	0·1	2·1	5·4	12·1	23·0	29·4
Excavators (no.)	–	3,540·0	12,290·0	30,800·0	42,000·0	41,700·0
Timber (commercial, 1m.cu. metres) [1]	27·2	161·0	261·5	298·5	277·7	305·3
Cement (1m. tonnes)	1·8	10·2	45·5	95·2	125·0	139·0

[1] Excluding collective farm production. [2] Recalculated base.

The process of industrial mechanization and the installation of automatic remote control is being pushed ahead. About 93% of Soviet pig-iron and 87% of the steel is produced in fully automatic furnaces. All hydro-electric plants (in terms of capacity) are fully automatic. Coal production in open-cast mines has been completely mechanized; hydraulic mining is coming into general use. Coal-cutting and underground haulage was over 99% mechanized by the end of 1962 (loading on inclined seams 56%); peat-cutting, 100%, and loading, nearly 80%; timber-cutting, 98%; haulage to loading centres, 93%, and despatch, 97%.

Output in some consumer industries was as follows:

Industry	*1913*	*1950*	*1960*	*1970*	*1980*	*1988*
Cotton fabrics (1m. linear metres)	2,672	3,899	6,387	7,482	8,063	
Woollen fabrics (1m. linear metres)	108	156	342	496	564	13,100
Silk fabrics (1m. linear metres)	43	130	810	1,241	1,632	
Leather footwear (1m. pairs)	60	203	419	679	744	820
Clocks and watches (1m.)	1	8	26	40	67	74
Radio receivers (1m.)	–	1	4	8	9	8
Television sets (1m.)	–	–	2	7	8	10
Refrigerators (1,000)	–	1	530	4,140	5,925	6,200
Paper (1,000 tonnes)	269	1,193	2,334	4,185	5,288	6,300
Meat (slaughter weight, 1m. tonnes)	5	5	9	12	15	19
Butter (1,000 tonnes)	104	336	737	963	1,278	1,700
Granulated sugar (1,000 tonnes)	1,363	2,523	6,360	10,221	10,127	12,100
Canned foods (1m. tins)	116	1,113	4,864	10,678	15,268	20,900

Since 1945 the cotton industry has expanded, especially in the Urals, Central Asia and Siberia. Large mills have been built at Kamyshin, Kherson, Barnaul, Engels, Alma-Ata, Chernigov and Frunze.

Trade Unions and Labour. Trade unions are organized on an industrial basis, all workers, whether manual or brain, in every branch of a given industry being eligible for membership of the same union. Collective farmers may join trade unions.

Since 1933 the trade unions have carried out the functions of the former Labour Commissariat; they control and supervise the application of labour laws, introduce new labour laws for approval by the Government and administer social insurance and factory inspection. Social insurance is non-contributory. The All-Union Congress has met at irregular intervals; the 17th Congress met in 1982 and the 18th in 1987.

In 1944 there were 176 unions. This number was reduced by amalgamation of unions to 22 in 1958, but increased to 31 by 1987. Contributions range from 0·5 to 6% of wages. There are 173 regional and Republican Trades Councils. Membership (1987) 140m.

Chairman, Central Council of Trade Unions: S. A. Shalayev.

Industrial and clerical workers engaged (1988) in the whole national economy were 117·2m., 51% of them women; a further 11·7m. were engaged in collective-farm agriculture. The 7-hour day (6 hours for miners underground and other heavy trades) was generally in operation by the end of 1960. The average working week since 1970 has been 39 hours and in industry 39·6 hours. The 5-day week (without reduction of total working hours) was introduced in 1967.

New 'Fundamentals of Labour Legislation', intended to codify and extend labour laws adopted in the last 40 years, were adopted by the Supreme Soviet in July 1970. They lay down, *inter alia,* the right to receive wages irrespective of the income of the enterprise concerned, the right to free vocational and advanced technical training; the right to form trade unions without state registration; the right of trade unions to participate in and supervise management and planning, labour legislation, safety regulation and housing, fixing of working conditions and wages, etc. Pensioners in Jan. 1989 numbered 58·6m., including 43·2m. old age. Average monthly wages in the state sector were 219·8 rubles in 1988.

Profsoyuzy SSSR. Dokumenty i materialy. 5 vols., Moscow, 1963–74
Sbornik postanovlenii VTsSPS. Moscow, 1960ff, quarterly
Ruble, B. A., *Soviet Trade Unions. Their Development in the 1970s.* CUP, 1981

Commerce. Retail home trade takes three forms–state, co-operative and the free market, *i.e.,* sales by individual collective-farm members and by the collective farms of their surplus products, after having fulfilled their statutory deliveries and made their regular allocations to their members.

In 1988 retail trade by the State, co-operatives and collective farms totalled 375,700m. rubles; of this state and co-operative trade amounted to 366,400m. rubles (in 1970, 159,400m. and 155,200m. rubles respectively). Employees in retail trade were 7·7m. in 1988 (annual average); there were 736,000 retail trade outlets with a total floor area of 55·1m. sq. metres. The state retail price index (1980 = 100) was

109 in 1988. Trade by collective farm markets amounted to 8,700m. rubles in 1986; this was 2·6% by value of all retail trade and 4·9% by value of all food sales.

Foreign trade is organized as a state monopoly. Importation and exportation of goods are effected under licences issued by the Ministry for Foreign Economic Relations and its respective departments in pursuance of a plan annually sanctioned by the Government. The right of purchasing goods for importation, and that of selling Soviet exports abroad, is vested in trade delegations and representatives of the appropriate state corporations in foreign countries.

There are 29 state import and export organizations, including chartering and tourist corporations (one, Vostokintorg, dealing with Mongolia, Sinkiang and Afghánistán). The Central Union of Consumers' Societies (Tsentrosoyuz) is also authorized to conduct foreign trade operations.

Foreign trade in 1988 was conducted with 145 foreign countries (in 1950, 45), and had by 1986 increased 45 times by value since 1950. Exports in 1988 were valued at 67,115m. rubles (42,885m. to the socialist countries), and imports at 65,040m. rubles (43,373m. from the socialist countries).

Soviet imports of machinery and equipment, between 1940 and 1987, rose from 32·4 to 40·9%, ores and concentrates fell from 26·6 to 8%, foodstuffs rose from 14·9 to 15·8% and manufactured consumer goods rose from 1·4 to 12·8% by value; exports of fuel and electricity increased from 13·2 to 42·1% and of machinery and equipment from 2 to 16·2% by value over the same period.

Main items of exports in 1987:

Crude oil (1m. tonnes)	144·0	Gas (1m. cu. metres)	88,000·0
Iron ore (1m. tonnes)	32·2	Tractors (1,000)	47·8
Rolled metal (1m. tonnes)	8·5	Motor cars (1,000)	341·0
Paper (1,000 tonnes)	695·0	Clocks and watches (1m.)	17·0
Cotton cloth (1,000 tonnes)	731·0	Grain (1m. tonnes)	1·8

Total trade between the USSR and UK (British Department of Trade returns, in £1,000 sterling):

	1986	*1987*	*1988*	*1989*
Imports to UK	694,624	875,431	732,115	833,369
Exports and re-exports from UK	539,368	491,615	511,653	681,599

Tourism. Pre-revolutionary Russia was never a country for any but the most hardy and better-off tourists, as the introductory pages of Baedeker's guide made clear. For her subjects, too, touring was no more inviting. Acute shortage of hotels and boarding-houses, poor roads, lack of ordinary services for visitors were among the least of their difficulties. These have not by any means been fully overcome: But very great efforts to meet them have been made. The first tourist organizations came into existence in 1885–90 in St Petersburg, Tiflis and Odessa; and in 1901 the Russian Society of Tourists was formed (about 5,000 members in 1914). Organized tourism in the Soviet period began in the early 1920s; the Russian Society of Tourists was revived, and other tourist organizations, notably 'Intourist' (founded 1929), were established. The development of tourism on a massive scale is however a development of the post-Second World War period.

Tourist facilities for Soviet and foreign citizens are presently made available under state, trade union and other auspices, all of which come ultimately under the supervision of the State Committee on Tourism which is attached to the USSR Council of Ministers. The number of hotels available to such tourists increased from 222 in 1960 to 960 in 1988, with a total accommodation of 459,000 (in 1960, 36,000); the number of tourist bases, for the hire of equipment and shorter stays, increased to 8,231, with a total accommodation of 815,000. In 1988 these facilities were used by 32·7m. and 4·2m. tourists respectively (in 1970, 5m. and 1·7m.). A total of 54m. citizens in 1988 made use of all forms of tourist accommodation, including sanatoria and boarding houses (in 1960, 6·7m.; in 1970, 16·8m.). In 1988 a further 218m. citizens took part in tourist excursions.

Visitors to the USSR from foreign countries are catered for by 'Intourist' and its offices in foreign countries. In 1970, the USSR had 2,059,338 foreign visitors (43,490 from the UK, and 66,365 from the USA); in 1988 there were 6m., of whom 2m. were catered for by Intourist. In the same year 4·2m. Soviet citizens made tourist, business or other visits to foreign countries.

COMMUNICATIONS

Roads. By 1940 there were over 1·5m. km of constructed roads, of which 143,400 km were suitable for motor traffic. The total length of motor roads in 1989 was 857,500 km. Road freights by lorry amounted to 859m. tonnes in 1940 and 27,873m. tonnes in 1988. Passengers carried were 590m. in 1940 and 50,723m. in 1988. In 1987, 24,100 inter-urban bus routes had a total length of 3,642,000 km.

Railways. The length of railways in Jan. 1989 was 146,700 km (1913: 58,500 km), of which 51,700 km was electrified. Diesel and electric traction now account for almost 100% of all movements, with the electrified network handling 56% of the traffic. In 1986, 47% of all domestic tonne-km of freight and 37% of all passenger-km of traffic went by rail. In 1988 railways carried 4,116m. tonnes of freight (representing 3,924,800 tonne-km) and carried 4,396m. passengers (representing 414,000m. passenger-km).

Operations are centred on 32 regions with headquarters at: Baku, Alma-Ata, Tyndin, Minsk, Irkutsk, Gorky, Khabarovsk, Donetsk, Chita, Tbilisi, Aktyubinsk, Novosibirsk, Kemerovo, Krasnoyarsk, Kuibyshev, Lvov, Kishinev, Moscow, Odessa, Leningrad, Riga, Saratov, Dnepropetrovsk, Sverdlovsk, Yaroslavl, Rostov-on-Don, Tashkent, Tselinograd, Voronezh, Kharkov and Chelyabinsk.

Extensive railway construction is in progress, including routes northwards from Surgut to Urengoi and Nizhe-Vartovskoye, while the great Baikal-Amur Magistral (BAM) project was completed in 1985. This is a new main line to the east, sited well to the north of the existing Trans-Siberian route to the Pacific ports of Nakhodka and Vladivostok. It runs from Lena, on the Lena river, to Komsomolsk-on-Amur, 3,145 km distant. BAM is intended to become the principal route for export traffic to the eastern ports, easing the very heavy pressure on the Trans-Siberian line, which is only partially electrified and not double-track throughout.

BAM was the most arduous railway building project ever tackled by Soviet engineers, and the greatest drawback to development of the region has been its severe geological and climatic conditions. There is permafrost throughout the area, and winter temperatures fall to –60°C. Construction work occupied nearly a decade, and has required over 3,200 bridges, tunnels and culverts.

Underground railways have been built in Moscow, Leningrad, Kiev, Tbilisi, Kharkov, Tashkent, Baku, Gorky, Minsk, Yerevan, Novosibirsk and Kuibyshev. Others are under construction at Omsk, Dnepropetrovsk and Sverdlovsk.

Aviation. In 1988 total length of internal airlines in the USSR was approximately 928,400 km; 125m. passengers were carried internally and externally, and 3·3m. tonnes of freight. The Central Asian Airways in some instances provide the only means of communication across the desert and mountainous regions of the local republics. An 8,500-km air service was opened in Feb. 1941 between Moscow and Anadyr (Eastern Siberia), through Archangel, Igarka, Khatanga, Tiksi Bay and Cape Schmidt, *i.e.*, along the entire course of the Northern Sea Route. There are also other Arctic airlines, *e.g.*, Igarka-Gulf of Kozhevnikov; Igarka-Dickson Island; Yakutsk-Tiksi Bay; Yakutsk-Viluisk; Yakutsk-Verkhoiansk.

Direct air services are maintained throughout the year between Moscow and the capitals of all Soviet republics as well as London, New York, Montreal, Tokyo, Delhi, Rangoon, Belgrade, Peking, Pyongyang, Ulan Bator, Kábul, Tirana, Paris, Warsaw, Prague, Budapest, Bucharest, Sofia, Vienna, Berlin, Helsinki, Stockholm, Copenhagen, Jakarta, Dakar and Gander. Soviet air services reached 87 countries in 1981, and 20 foreign lines have regular services to the USSR, including British Airways, KLM, SAS, Air France, SABENA, Air India, PANAM. The first Soviet airbus, the 350-seater IL-86, began flights on civil aviation routes in 1981. The 120-seater YAK-42 will gradually replace the TU-134 and AN-24 on major shorter routes.

MacDonald, H., *Aeroflot: Soviet Air Transport Since 1923*. London, 1975

Shipping. In 1977 the Soviet mercantile marine comprised 7,000 self-propelled vessels, of which 80% were built between 1957 and 1966. By May 1977 the gross cargo capacity was (including fishing vessels) 20·8m. registered tonnes (16m. tonnes dead-weight).

Freights carried on domestic waterways were: In 1913 (present frontiers), 35·1m. tonnes; in 1940, 73·9m. tonnes; and in 1988, 691m. tonnes; 131m. passengers were carried. The Soviet share in world marine tonnage was 2% in 1960 and 6% in 1977. Deep-sea ports are under construction at Vostochny (Far East) and Grigorevsky (Black Sea) with new deep-sea wharves at Ventspils (Latvia), Murmansk and Archangel (for Arctic traffic). Archangel is kept open by icebreakers all the year round from 1979. Foreign freights in 1977 totalled 14% of all Soviet seaborne trade.

The North Sea route affords convenient communication between the European USSR and the Far East along the Soviet coast, for the produce of the basins of the Ob, Yenissei, Lena and Kolyma rivers.

The length of navigable rivers and canals in exploitation was (1989) 122,500 km, of which the length of floatable rivers is 81,000 km. There are several thousand miles of canals and other artificial waterways; among them the Baltic and White Sea Canal (235 km), the Moscow-Volga Canal (130 km). Goods turnover on inland waterways was 28,900m. tonne-km in 1913, 35,900m. in 1940, 45,900m. in 1950 and 251,181m. in 1988.

The Volga-Don Shipping Canal was opened for traffic in 1952. The Volga-Don waterway from Volgograd to Rostov is 540 km long, of which the Volga-Don canal comprises 101 km. The canal has transformed the section of the river from Kalach, where the Don is joined by the Volga-Don canal, to Rostov into a deep-water highway suitable for big Volga shipping. The canal links the White, Baltic, Caspian, Azov and Black Seas into a single water transport system. In Oct. 1964 the 2,430-km Baltic-Volga waterway, linking Klaipeda on the Baltic to Kakhovka at the mouth of the Dnieper and suitable for 5,000-tonne vessels, was begun. Reconstruction of the 18th-century Mariinsky canal system in north-west Russia was completed, providing a through waterway from Leningrad to Rybinsk (on the Upper Volga) and cutting the passage of freight from 18 to $2^1/_2$ days.

At the end of 1977 the longest train ferry route in the world was opened between the Soviet Union and Bulgaria (Ilyichovsk-Varna).

The first section of Vostochny port, in Wrangel Bay on the Pacific coast, is completed. It will be the country's largest deep-sea port.

In 1962 a canal was completed across the Kara-Kum desert in southern Turkmenistan (replacing an earlier project for a more costly scheme across the north of the republic). The canal, from Bussag on the river Amu-Darya to Archnan, north-west of Ashkhabad, through the Murgab oasis, 900 km long, supplies water to an area exceeding 200,000 hectares, suitable for cotton, fruit, vineyards and livestock. An extension to the Caspian (500 km) is under construction: The complete system will irrigate 1m. hectares.

An irrigation canal system (250 miles), bringing water from Kakhovka on the Dnieper to the North Crimea, is nearing completion. Work to divert water from the Pechora and Vychegda rivers (flowing into the White Sea) south to the Volga is in progress. Work has begun on a 300-mile canal which will supply water from the Irtysh to Karaganda in Central Kazakhstan, irrigating over 150,000 acres; the first 37 miles were opened in 1965 and another 45 miles in Dec. 1967. Most of the 11 reservoirs required had been completed by 1 Jan. 1972. Other irrigation canals under construction are Kuibyshev (279 km long, to supply over 100,000 hectares) and Stavropol (481 km, irrigating 200,000 hectares); the second section of the latter went into commission in Nov. 1974, 14 months ahead of schedule. In Sept. 1972 the Saratov Canal (irrigating 1m. hectares) went into commission.

Post and Broadcasting. In Jan. 1989 the number of post, telegraph and telephone offices was 90,807 and of general telephones 37·5m.

The international radio-telecommunications services are operated by the Ministry of Communications of the USSR. The Great Northern Telegraph Co., Ltd, of Denmark, operates cables connecting Denmark with Leningrad, whence connexion is made by means of a trans-Siberian landline with Vladivostok. From the latter place the Great Northern Telegraph Co. owns cables connecting with Japan, China and Hong Kong. Direct radio and telephone communication with India is provided for in an agreement concluded in 1955.

The State Committee for Broadcasting and Television produces 3 programmes in

Moscow, broadcasting throughout the Union. In addition the regional radio stations produce 1, 2 or 3 programmes for the republics as well as local programmes for a town or region. The foreign service from Moscow is beamed to all parts of the world, in 64 languages. Chinese has $28^1/_2$ hours programme time a day. Several republics have their own foreign services. English is broadcast from Moscow, Kiev, Tashkent, Vilnius and Yerevan. There are 120 TV centres in the USSR, several of them producing more than 1 programme. In Moscow there are 4 programmes. Colour programmes are broadcast by the SECAM system. A nationwide system of space telecommunications, consisting of satellites and ground stations, takes TV broadcasts to distant parts of the country.

Number of receivers, Jan. 1989: Radio, 83·7m. (1960, 28m); television, 89·9m. (1960, 5m.).

Cinemas and Theatres (Jan. 1989). There were 151,000 cinemas to which 3,640m. visits were made annually. In Jan. 1989 there were 694 theatres, to which 112·3m. visits were made.

Newspapers. In 1988, 8,622 newspapers with a total daily circulation of 217·4m. copies were published in 57 languages of the USSR.

JUSTICE, RELIGION, EDUCATION AND WELFARE

Justice. The basis of the judicial system is the same throughout the Soviet Union, but the constituent republics have the right to introduce modifications and to make their own rules for the application of the codes of laws. The Supreme Court of the USSR is the chief court and supervising organ for all constituent republics and is elected by the Congress of People's Deputies of the USSR for 5 years. Chairman (elected 1989) E. A. Smolentsev. Supreme Courts of the Union and Autonomous Republics and of the Automonous Regions and Areas are elected by the Supreme Soviets of these republics, and Territorial, Regional and City Courts by the respective immediately superior Soviets, each for a term of 10 years. At the lowest level are the People's Courts, which are elected directly by immediately superior soviets of people's deputies and by the population.

Court proceedings are conducted in the local language with full interpreting facilities as required. All cases are heard in public, unless otherwise provided for by law, and the accused is guaranteed the right of defence.

Laws establishing common principles of legislation in various fields are adopted by the Supreme Soviet and are then enacted in more specific form and implemented by subordinate levels of state and judicial authority.

The Law Courts are divided into People's Courts and higher courts. The People's Courts consist of the People's Judge and 2 Assessors, and their function is to examine, as the first instance, most of the civil and criminal cases, except the more important ones, some of which are tried at the Regional Court, and those of the highest importance at the Supreme Court. The Regional Courts supervise the activities of the People's Courts and also act as Courts of Appeal from the decisions of the People's Court. Special chambers of the higher courts deal with offences committed in the Army and the public transport services.

People's judges are elected by the Soviets of people's deputies at the level immediately superior to them for a term of 5 years. Assessors, who serve on a rota basis, are elected directly by the citizens of each constituency for a 5 year term. Should a judge or assessor be found not to perform his duties conscientiously and in accordance with the mandate of the people, he may be recalled by his electors.

The People's Assessors are called upon for duty for 2 weeks in a year. The People's Assessors for the Regional Court must have had at least 2 years' experience in public or trade-union work. The list of Assessors for the Supreme Court is drawn up by the Supreme Soviet of the republic.

The Labour Session of the People's Court supervises the regulations relating to the working conditions and the protection of labour and gives decisions on conflicts arising between managements and employees, or the violation of regulations.

Disputes between State institutions must be referred to an arbitration commission. Disputes between Soviet State institutions and foreign business firms may be referred by agreement to a Foreign Trade Arbitration Commission of the All-Union Chamber of Commerce.

The Procurator-General of the USSR (A. Ya. Sukharev, elected 1989) is appointed for 5 years by the USSR Congress of People's Deputies. All procurators of the republics, autonomous republics and autonomous regions are appointed by the Procurator-General of the USSR for a term of 5 years. The procurators supervise the correct application of the law by all state organs, and have special responsibility for the observance of the law in places of detention. The procurators of the Union republics are subordinate to the Procurator-General of the USSR, whose duty it is to see that acts of all institutions of the USSR are legal, that the law is correctly interpreted and uniformly applied; he has to participate in important cases in the capacity of State Prosecutor.

Capital punishment was abolished on 26 May 1947, but was restored on 12 Jan. 1950 for treason, espionage and sabotage, on 7 May 1954 for certain categories of murder, in Dec. 1958 for terrorism and banditry, on 7 May 1961 for embezzlement of public property, counterfeiting and attack on prison warders and, in particular circumstances, for attacks on the police and public order volunteers and for rape (15 Feb. 1962) and for accepting bribes (20 Feb. 1962).

In view of criminal abuses, extending over many years, discovered in the security system, the powers of administrative trial and exile previously vested in the security authorities (MVD) were abolished in 1953; accelerated procedures for trial on charges of high treason, espionage, wrecking, etc., by the Supreme Court were abolished in 1955; and extensive powers of protection of persons under arrest or serving prison terms were vested in the Procurator-General's Office (1955). Supervisory commissions, composed of representatives of trade unions, youth organizations and local authorities, were set up in 1956 to inspect places of detention.

Further reforms of the civil and criminal codes were decreed on 25 Dec. 1958. Thereby the age of criminal responsibility has been raised from 14 to 16 years; deportation and banishment have been abolished; a presumption of innocence is not accepted, but the burden of proof of guilt has been placed upon the prosecutor. Secret trials and the charge of 'enemy of the people' have been abolished. Articles 70 and 190 of the Criminal Code, which deal with 'anti-Soviet agitation and propaganda' and 'crimes against the system of administration' respectively, have however been widely used against political dissidents in more recent years.

Butler, W. E., *The Soviet Legal System. Selected Contemporary Legislation and Documents.* New York, 1978.—*Soviet Law.* 2nd ed. London, 1988

Feldbrugge, F. J. M. (ed.) *Encyclopedia of Soviet Law.* 2nd ed. Dordrecht, 1985

Hazard, J., Butler, W. E. and Maggs, P., *The Soviet Legal System.* 3rd ed. New York, 1977

Simons, W. B. (ed.) *The Soviet Codes of Law.* Alphen aan den Rijn, 1980

Religion. With the Revolution the Orthodox Church lost its position as the dominant religion and all religions were placed on an equal footing. Article 52 of the 1977 Soviet Constitution reads as follows: 'Citizens of the USSR are guaranteed freedom of conscience, that is, the right to profess or not to profess any religion, and to conduct religious worship or atheistic propaganda. Incitement of hostility or hatred on religious grounds is prohibited. In the USSR the church is separated from the state, and school from the church.'

By decree of 2 Feb. 1918 the Orthodox Church was disestablished; its property, together with that of all other denominations, was nationalized. The congregations themselves have to maintain their churches and clergy, regardless of confession or denomination. A minimum of 20 persons may request and receive the use of a church building, free of charge, except for maintenance, insurance, land taxes, etc. About two-thirds of all the churches have been closed since 1917, but about 20,000 churches and 18 religious seminaries were reported to be in operation in 1986. Religious instruction may be given in private, but otherwise only in church classes. The income of religious communities is not subject to taxation. Religious instruction in classes for persons under 18 is forbidden. The state supplies paper and printing facilities to all denominations for producing the Bible, the Koran, prayer books, missals, etc, although in very limited quantities.

Relations between the religious communities of all creeds and the Government are maintained through a Council for Religious Affairs which is attached to the Council of Ministers of the USSR. (*Chairman*, Yuri Khristoradnov).

The Russian Orthodox Church, represented by the Patriarchate of Moscow, had, in 1989, an estimated 35-40m. adherents, 6,000 clergy and 6,500 churches. There are still many Old Believers, whose schism from the Orthodox Church dates from the 17th century. The Russian Church is headed by the Patriarch of Moscow and All Russia, assisted by the Holy Synod, which has 7 members–the Patriarch himself and the Metropolitans of Krutitsy and Kolomna (Moscow), Leningrad and Kiev *ex officio*, and 3 bishops alternating for 6 months in order of seniority from the 3 regions forming the Moscow Patriarchate. The Patriarchate of Moscow maintains jurisdiction over a few parishes of Russian Orthodox abroad, at Tehrán, Jerusalem, German Democratic Republic, France (1 archbishop), England, North and South America (2 bishops). There are 16 monasteries and nunneries, and 5 Orthodox academies and seminaries with 4 official publications.

After the Russian Orthodox Church the next Christian community in importance are the Armenians; their Catholicos (Patriarch), whose seat is at Etchmiadzin, is head of all the Armenian (Gregorian) communities throughout the world. There is an Armenian Orthodox academy and a seminary.

The Georgian Orthodox Church has its own organization under a Catholicos (Patriarch) who is resident in Tbilisi and who directs the church's seminary in Mtskheta.

Protestantism is represented chiefly by the Evangelical Christian Baptists, with over 512,000 baptized adult members and some 5,000 churches; the Lutherans are concentrated mainly in the Baltic States (350,000 in Estonia, 600,000 in Latvia), the Reformed in the Transcarpathian Region of the Ukraine (70,000). Both Baptists and Lutherans conduct theological courses. The Methodist Church functions in Estonia.

The Roman Catholics are most numerous in Lithuania, Belorussia and the western Ukraine, with an estimated 5m. adherents in total. There are 2 Roman Catholic arch-episcopates and 4 episcopates in Lithuania with 630 churches and a seminary at Kaunas providing a 5-year course. In 1946 some 3·5m. Uniates in the USSR were compelled to withdraw their allegiance to Rome and came under the jurisdiction of the Orthodox Patriarchate in Moscow. In Latvia there are an archepiscopate and 1 episcopate (Riga and Liepaja) of the Roman Catholic Church.

The Moslems (estimate 40-45m. members, mainly Sunnis), are divided into 4 administrative regions, 3 of them (Central Asia and Kazakhstan, European Russia and Siberia, Northern Caucasus) headed by a Mufti; the largest (Transcaucasia, with its centre at Baku) by a Sheikh-ul-Islam.

There is a Moslem academy and a madrasah in Central Asia. Several editions of the Koran have appeared in recent years.

There are various Jewish communities, the chief being in Moscow, Leningrad and Kiev. There were, in 1984, an estimated 69 synagogues, 35-40 rabbis, and one Yeshiva in Moscow. There are no official religious publications and the teaching of Hebrew is severely restricted. The Central Buddhist Council of the USSR is headed by a Lama with communities in Buryatia, Tuva, Kalmykia and in the national (minority) areas of the Chita and Irkutsk regions.

O religii i tserkvi: sbornik vazhneishikh vyskazivanii klassikov Marksizma-Leninizma, dokumentov KPSS i sovetskogo gosudarstva. 2nd ed., Moscow, 1981

Bordeaux, M., *Opium of the People. The Christian Religion in the USSR.* London, 1965.—*Religious Ferment in Russia.* London, 1968

Curtiss, J. S., *The Russian Church and the Soviet State, 1917–50.* New York, 1953

Ellis, J., *The Russian Orthodox Church: A Contempory History.* London, 1986

Kochan, L., (ed.) *Jews in Soviet Russia since 1917.* 3rd ed., Oxford, 1977

Lane, C., *Christian Religion in the Soviet Union.* London, 1978

Education. Education is free and compulsory from 7 to 16/17. There are 2 types of general schools, with an 8-year or a 10-year curriculum; the minimum school-leaving age is now 17. Pupils who leave an 8-year school continue their education at either a 10-year school or a vocational training school. A 10-year school pupil may also transfer to vocational school after the 8th year. Under directives adopted in 1984, there will be a gradual transition towards an 11-year school system, starting at 6, from 1986 onwards; efforts are also being made to improve pupils' preparation for employment and the status and working conditions of teachers.

In 1988–89 there were 135,000 primary and secondary schools. Pupils in general educational schools numbered 44·1m. (5·7m. of them in the ninth and tenth forms) and the teachers 3·2m. Those at vocational and specialized technical secondary schools numbered 9·8m.

At the end of 1940 labour reserve schools (both vocational and industrial) were organized, admitting applicants from 14 to 17 years of age. From 1959 onwards these and other technical schools were reorganized as town and rural vocational and technical schools, at which pupils stay for a year longer than at general schools, combining completion of general secondary education with vocational training. From 1940 to 1977 inclusive they trained 35m. skilled workers. In 1978, 2·3m. graduated from such schools, including 628,000 for agriculture; 600,000 agricultural mechanics were trained in state and collective farms. Over 4,300 vocational training schools existed in 1981, training 2·17m. boys and girls, all of whom receive a full secondary education. In 1989, 17·4m. children of from 3 to 7 years of age attended kindergartens. Children in boarding schools numbered over 800,000 in 1972–73.

In 1987–88 there were 4,517 technical colleges with 4·4m. students, and 898 universities, institutes and other places of higher education, with 5m. students (including 1·7m. taking correspondence or evening courses). Among the 65 university towns are: Moscow, Leningrad, Kharkov, Odessa, Tartu, Kazan, Saratov, Tomsk, Kiev, Sverdlovsk, Tbilisi, Alma-Ata, Tashkent, Minsk, Gorky and Vladivostok.

On 1 Jan. 1988 there were 1·5m. scientific workers in 5,111 places of higher education, research institutes and Academies of Sciences. There are 33,000 foreign students from 130 countries.

The Academy of Sciences of the USSR had 909 members and corresponding members. Total learned institutions under the USSR Academy of Sciences number 244, with 62,363 scientific staff. Each Union Republic (other than the RSFSR) has its own Academy of Sciences, with scientific staff numbering 49,988. There are also Siberian, Far Eastern and other branches of the USSR Academy. On 1 Jan. 1989 there were 97,569 post-graduate students in Academy and other higher educational institutions, 52% studying on a part-time basis.

The Academy of Pedagogical Sciences had 14 research institutes with 1,664 staff.

In 1988-89 over 105m. people were studying at schools, colleges and training or correspondence courses. 125 per 1,000 of the employed population had a higher education (1939, 13; 1970, 65).

Grant, N., *Soviet Education.* 4th ed., Harmondsworth, 1979
Matthews, M., *Education in the Soviet Union,* London, 1982

Health and Social Security. All health services are free of charge although payment is required for medicines; but private practice exists. The health service is administered by the Ministry of Health of the USSR, which supervises the work of the Health Ministries of the Union Republics and the Autonomous Republics.

In 1944 an Academy of Medical Sciences was formed; in 1989 it had 328 members and corresponding members working in 64 research institutes in which 7,835 staff were employed. Smallpox, trachoma and malaria have been virtually eliminated.

In Jan. 1989 there were 23,500 civil hospitals with 3·8m. beds. There were 837,000 infants in day nurseries. 1,256,000 doctors (including dentists) were in the health service. All confinements in towns and 75% in the country were in hospital.

There were 41,310 outpatients' clinics, apart from the 28,863 women's consultation centres and children's clinics.

The death-rate in the USSR in 1988 was 10·1 per 1,000, and the birth rate 18·8 per 1,000. Infant death rate was 24·7 (per 1,000 live births) in 1988, compared with 273 in 1913, 184 in 1940 and 81 in 1950. Average expectation of life, 69·5 (men 64·8, women, 73·6).

Social insurance is administered by the trade unions, through social insurance councils elected in places of work and social insurance sub-committees of factory committees: About 5m. volunteers are engaged in this work. 52·5m. people went to holiday sanatoria or rest homes in 1987. 58·6m. people, including 10·4m. collective farmers, were receiving state pensions in Jan. 1989; of these, 43·2m. (9·4m. collective farmers) were old-age pensioners.

Total number of holiday sanatoria providing toning-up treatment at resorts in 1988 was 2,383, with accommodation for 614,000; in addition, there were 3,419 overnight sanatoria at large plants for treatment of mild disorders without absence from work, accommodating 295,000. There were also 1,228 trade union-managed holiday hotels with a capacity of 383,000, holidays being partly or wholly at trade unions' expense. In 1987, 52m. citizens were systematically engaged in physical culture and sport; there were 3,799 stadiums seating 1,500 or more, 2,295 swimming pools and 80,000 sports halls.

State expenditure (in 1m. rubles) on health services and physical education: 1940, 0·9; 1970, 9,300; 1980, 14,800; 1988, 21,900.

Between 1950 and 1980 62,766,000 apartments (in towns) and houses (in rural areas) were built. In 1988, 2·2m. apartments and houses were built. Rents in the USSR have not been increased since 1928 and in 1988 accounted for about 3% of the expenditure of an average worker's family. By the end of 1988, 77% of all urban housing had a gas supply installed, 93% had running water, 90% had central heating and 85% had bathrooms. 60% of total housing space is publicly and 40% is privately owned.

DIPLOMATIC REPRESENTATIVES

Of the USSR in Great Britain (13 Kensington Palace Gdns., London, W8 4QX)
Ambassador: Leonid M. Zamyatin.

Of Great Britain in the USSR (Naberezhnaya Morisa Toreza 14, Moscow 72)
Ambassador: Sir Rodric Braithwaite, KCMG.

Of the USSR in the USA (1125 16th St., NW, Washington, D.C., 20036)
Ambassador: Yuri V. Dubinin.

Of the USA in the USSR (Ulitsa Chaikovskogo 19, Moscow)
Ambassador: Jack F. Matlock, Jr.

Of the USSR to the United Nations
Ambassador: Alexander Belonogov.

Further Reading

Narodnoe Khozvaistvo SSSR za 70 let (National Economy of the USSR for 70 years). Jubilee Statistical Yearbook. Moscow, 1987
Pravda (Truth). Daily organ of the Central Committee of the Communist Party
Izvestiya (News). Daily organ of the Presidium of the Supreme Soviet of the USSR
Vedomosti Verkhovnovo Soveta. Bulletin of the Supreme Soviet of the USSR in the languages of the 15 republics; published weekly
Pravitelstvennyi Vestnik. Weekly publication of the Soviet government
Sovetskaya Torgovlya. Monthly publication of the Ministry of Trade of the USSR
Planovoye Khozyaistvo. Monthly. Moscow
Vestnik Statistiki. Monthly publication of the USSR Statistical Committee
Vneshnyaya Torgovlya. Published by the Ministry for Foreign Trade. Monthly. Moscow
Trud. The daily organ of the All-Union Central Council of Trade Unions
Professionalnye Soyuzy. A trade union fortnightly. Moscow
Kommunist. A fortnightly organ of the Communist Party of the Soviet Union
Finansy SSSR. A monthly publication of the Ministry for Finance
Bolshaya Sovetskaya Entsiklopedia. 65 vols. Moscow, 1926–47; 2nd ed., 51 vols. Moscow, 1949–58; 3rd ed., Moscow, 1959–78; annual supplement (*Yezhegodnik*)
Soviet Union. A monthly pictorial. Moscow. (In English)
Soviet Import-Export Dictionary (in Russian, with English, etc., terms). Moscow, 1952
Soviet Studies; A Quarterly Review. Ed. R. A. Clarke. Glasgow, quarterly.
The Current Digest of the Soviet Press. Published by Joint Committee on Slavic Studies. Columbus, Ohio, weekly.
Baylis, J. and Segal, G., (eds.) *Soviet Strategy*. London, 1981
Beloff, M., *The Foreign Policy of Soviet Russia, 1929–41*. 2 vols. 1947–49.—*Soviet Policy in the Far East*. Oxford, 1953.—*Soviet Policy in Asia, 1944–52*. Oxford, 1953
Bialer, S., *The Soviet Paradox: External Expansion, Internal Decline*. London, 1987

Brown, A. and Kaser, M., *The Soviet Union Since the Fall of Khrushchev*. London, 2nd ed. 1978.—*Soviet Policy for the 1980s*. London, 1982
Byrnes, J. F. (ed.) *After Brezhnev. Sources of Soviet Conduct in the 1980s*. London, 1983
Cambridge Encyclopedia of Russia and the Soviet Union. CUP, 1982
Carr, E. H., *A History of Soviet Russia*. 14 vols. London, 1951–78
Clarke, R. A. and Matko, D. J. I., (eds.) *Soviet Economic Facts 1917–80*. London, 1983
Cracraft, J., *The Soviet Union Today*. Chicago, 2nd ed. 1988
Degras, J. (compiler), *Soviet Documents on Foreign Policy, 1917–41*. 3 vols. London, 1948–52
Deutscher, I., *Trotsky*. 3 vols. OUP, 1954 ff.
Edmonds, R., *Soviet Foreign Policy: the Brezhnev Years*. Oxford, 1983
Falla, P. S., *The Oxford English-Russian Dictionary*. OUP, 1984
Fitzsimmons, T. *et al*, *USSR; Its People, Its Society, Its Culture*. New Haven, 1960
Galperin, I. R., *New English-Russian Dictionary*. 2 vols. Moscow, 1972
Gorbachev, M., *Perestroika*. English ed. London, 1987
Gruzinov, V. F., *The USSR's Management of Foreign Trade*. London, 1980
Hammond, T. T. (ed.) *Soviet Foreign Relations and World Communism: A Selected Bibliography*. Princeton, 1965
Hill, R. J., *The Soviet Union. Politics, Economics and Society*. London, 2nd ed., 1989
Hosking, G., *A History of the Soviet Union*. London, 1985
Hough, J. F. and Fainsod, M., *How the Soviet Union is Governed*. Rev. ed. Harvard Univ. Press, 1979
Hutchings, R., *The Soviet Budget*. London, 1983
Jensen, R. G. et al (eds.) *Soviet National Resources in the World Economy*. Univ. of Chicago Press, 1983
Jones, D. L., *Books in English in the Soviet Union 1917–73: A Bibliography*. London and New York, 1975
Kaiser, R. G., *Russia: The People and the Power*. London, 1976
Kelley, D. R., (ed.) *Soviet Politics in the Brezhnev Era*. London, 1980
McCauley, M., *The Soviet Union since 1917*. London, 1981
Nove, A., *The Soviet Economic System*. London, 1977
Pares, Sir B., *A History of Russia*. London, 1962
Paxton, J., *Companion to Russian History*. London and New York, 1984
Preobrazhensky, A. G., *Etymological Dictionary of the Russian Language*. Columbia Univ. Press, 1951
Riasanovsky, N. V., *A History of Russia*. 4th ed. OUP, 1984
Shabad, T. and Mote, V.L., *Gateway to Siberian Resources (The BAM)*. New York and London, 1977
Schapiro, L. and Godson, J., *The Soviet Worker*. London, 1981
Schmidt-Häuer, C., *Gorbachov: The Path to Power*. London, 1986
Slusser, R. M. and Triska, J. F., *A Calendar of Soviet Treaties, 1917–57*. Stanford Univ. Press, 1959—and Ginsburgs, G., *A Calendar of Soviet Treaties, 1958–1973*, Alphen aan den Rijn, 1981
Smirnitsky, A. I. (ed.) *Russko-angliiskii slovar*. 4th ed. Moscow 1959
Tauris Soviet Directory, The. London, 1989
Thompson, A., *Russia/USSR*. [Bibliography] Oxford and Santa Barbara, 1979
Treadgold, D. W., *Twentieth Century Russia*. 6th ed. Boston, 1987
Vernadsky, G., *A History of Russia*. 5th ed. Yale Univ. Press, 1961
Walker, M., *The Waking Giant: Gorbachev's Russia*. New York, 1987
Wheeler, M., *The Oxford Russian-English Dictionary*. OUP, 2nd ed., 1984
White, S., *USSR: A Superpower in Transition*. London, 1988

RUSSIAN SOVIET FEDERAL SOCIALIST REPUBLIC (RSFSR)

Rossiiskaya Sovyetskaya Federativnaya Sotsialisticheskaya Respublika

AREA AND POPULATION. The RSFSR occupies 17,075,000 sq. km (over 76% of the total area of the USSR) stretching from the Far North to the Black Sea in the south and from the Far East to Kaliningrad in the west. 82·6% of its population in Jan. 1979 were Russians, the rest being 38 national minorities such as the Tatars, Ukrainians, Jews, Mordovians, Chuvashis, Bashkirs, Poles, Germans,

Udmurts, Buryats, Mari, Yakuts and Ossetians. The 2 principal cities are Moscow, the capital, with a population (Jan. 1989) of 8·9m. (without suburbs, 8,769,000) and Leningrad, the former capital, 5,020,000 (without suburbs, 4,456,000). Among other important cities are Gorky, Rostov-on-Don, Volgograd, Sverdlovsk, Novosibirsk, Chelyabinsk, Kazan, Omsk and Kuibyshev. Population, 1989, 147,386,000.

The RSFSR contains great mineral resources: Iron ore in the Urals, the Kerch Peninsula and Siberia; coal in the Kuznets Basin, Eastern Siberia, Urals and the sub-Moscow Basin; oil in the Urals, Azov-Black Sea area, Bashkiria, and West Siberia. It also has abundant deposits of gold, platinum, copper, zinc, lead, tin and rare metals.

The RSFSR produces about 70% of the total industrial and agricultural output of the Soviet Union. Industrial and office workers averaged 67·8m. in 1987.

CONSTITUTION AND GOVERNMENT. The RSFSR adopted its present constitution at a meeting of the Supreme Soviet in April 1978, following 330,000 town and country meetings in which 25m. citizens took part.

Chairman, Presidium of the Supreme Soviet: V. I. Vorotnikov.
Chairman, Council of Ministers: A. V. Vlasov.
Foreign Minister: V. M. Vinogradov.

The RSFSR consists of:

(1) *Territories:* Altai, Khabarovsk, Krasnodar, Krasnoyarsk, Primorye, Stavropol.

(2) *Regions:* Amur, Archangel, Astrakhan, Belgorod, Briansk, Chelyabinsk, Chita, Gorky, Irkutsk, Ivanovo, Kaluga, Kalinin, Kaliningrad, Kamchatka, Kemerovo, Kirov, Kostroma, Kuibyshev, Kurgan, Kursk, Leningrad, Lipetsk, Magadan, Moscow, Murmansk, Novgorod, Novosibirsk, Omsk, Orel, Orenburg, Penza, Perm, Pskov, Rostov, Ryazan, Sakhalin, Saratov, Smolensk, Sverdlovsk, Tambov, Tomsk, Tula, Tyumen, Ulyanovsk, Vladimir, Volgograd, Vologda, Voronezh, Yaroslavl.

(3) *Autonomous Soviet Republics:* Bashkir, Buryat, Chechen-Ingush, Chuvash, Daghestan, Kabardin-Balkar, Kalmyk, Karelian, Komi, Mari, Mordovian, North Ossetia, Tatar, Tuva, Udmurt, Yakut.

Subordinate to and within Territories and Regions are the following:

(4) *Autonomous Regions:* Adygei, Gorno-Altai, Jewish, Karachayevo-Cherkess, Khakass.

(5) *Autonomous Areas:* Agin-Buryat, Chukot, Evenki, Khanty-Mansi, Komi-Permyak, Koryak, Nenets, Taimyr (Dolgano-Nenets), Ust-Ordyn-Buryat, Yamalo-Nenets.

The Supreme Soviet, elected in Feb. 1985, consisted of 975 deputies (1 per 150,000 population); 649 were Communists, 344 women, 492 workers and collective farmers. New elections were held on 4 March 1990.

In June 1987, 1,159,264 deputies were elected to local authorities; 576,523 (49·7%) were women, 663,357 (57·2%) non-Party and 737,588 (63·6%) industrial workers and collective farmers. New elections were held on 4 March 1990.

FINANCE. Revenue and expenditure balanced as follows (in 1m. rubles): 1988, 110,102; 1989 (plan), 126,471. These figures, and those for the other 14 Union Republics, include grants from the Union Budget.

COMMUNICATIONS. Length of railways on 1 Jan. 1988 was 85,820 km, hard-surface motor roads, 559,700 km. In 1987, 234,557m. tonne-km of freight was carried on inland waterways.

Newspapers. In 1987 there were 4,647 newspapers, 4,338 of them in Russian. Daily circulation of Russian-language newspapers, 141·9m., other languages, 2·9m.

EDUCATION. In 1987–88 there were 20m. pupils in 69,300 primary and secondary schools; 2,834,900 students in 506 higher educational establishments (including correspondence students) and 2,440,500 students in 2,573 technical colleges of all kinds (including correspondence students). 71% of children were attending pre-school institutions. There were, on 1 Jan. 1988, 1,033,300 scientific staff in over 3,000 learned and scientific institutions.

In 1957 a Siberian branch of the Academy of Sciences was organized, in charge of all scientific research institutions from the Urals to the Pacific. There are also Far Eastern and Urals divisions.

There is an Academy of Municipal Economy (with 5 research institutions and a staff of 466).

HEALTH. Doctors in 1988 numbered 688,300, and hospital beds 2m. There were 12,622 medical institutions.

BASHKIR AUTONOMOUS SOVIET SOCIALIST REPUBLIC

Area 143,600 sq. km (55,430 sq. miles), population (Jan. 1989) 3,952,000. Capital, Ufa. Bashkiria was annexed to Russia in 1557. It was constituted as an Autonomous Soviet Republic on 23 March 1919. Population, census 1979, included 24·3% Bashkirians, 40·3% Russians, 24·5% Tatars, and 3·2% Chuvashes.

280 deputies were elected to the republican Supreme Soviet on 24 Feb. 1985, 108 of them women.

In 1987–88 there were 548,000 pupils in 3,165 schools. There is a state university and a branch of the USSR Academy of Sciences with 8 learned institutions (511 research workers). There were 69,000 students in 71 technical colleges and 52,700 in 9 higher educational establishments.

In Jan. 1988 there were 13,698 doctors and 53,000 hospital beds.

There are expanding chemical, coal, steel, electrical engineering, timber and paper industries. There were 629 collective farms and 159 state farms in 1980. Crop area was 4,587,000 hectares. Bashkiria is a major oil producer in USSR.

BURYAT AUTONOMOUS SOVIET SOCIALIST REPUBLIC

Area is 351,300 sq. km (135,650 sq. miles). The Buryat Republic, situated to the south of the Yakut Republic, adopted the Soviet system 1 March 1920. This area was penetrated by the Russians in the 17th century and finally annexed from China by the treaties of Nerchinsk (1689) and Kyakhta (1727). The population (Jan. 1989) was 1,042,000. Capital, Ulan-Ude (1989 census population, 353,000). The name of the republic was changed from 'Buryat-Mongol' on 7 July 1958. The population (1979 census) includes 23% Buryats and 72% Russians.

170 deputies were elected to the republican Supreme Soviet on 24 Feb. 1985, 60 of them women.

The main industries are coal, timber, building materials, fisheries, sheep and cattle farming. In 1980 there were 105 state and 61 collective farms. Crop area was 827,100 hectares. Gold, molybdenum and wolfram are mined.

In 1987–88 there were 564 schools with 175,000 pupils, 21 technical colleges with 17,300 students and 4 higher educational institutions with 21,100 students. A branch of the Siberian Department of the Academy of Sciences had 4 learned institutions with 281 research workers.

In 1988 there were 3,936 doctors and 14,100 hospital beds.

CHECHENO-INGUSH AUTONOMOUS SOVIET SOCIALIST REPUBLIC

Area, 19,300 sq. km (7,350 sq. miles); population (Jan. 1989), 1,277,000. Capital, Grozny (1989 census population, 401,000). After 70 years of almost continuous fighting, the Chechens and Ingushes were conquered by Russia in the late 1850s. In 1918 each nationality separately established its 'National Soviet' within the Terek Autonomous Republic, and in 1920 (after the Civil War) were constituted areas within the Mountain Republic. The Chechens separated out as an Autonomous Region on 30 Nov. 1922 and the Ingushes on 7 July 1924. In Jan. 1934 the two regions were united, and on 5 Dec. 1936 constituted as an Autonomous Republic. This was dissolved in 1944, but reconstituted on 9 Jan. 1957: 232,000 Chechens and Ingushes returned to their homes in the next 2 years. The population (1979 census) includes 52·9% Chechens, 11·7% Ingushes, and 29·1% Russians.

175 deputies were elected to the republican Supreme Soviet on 24 Feb. 1985, 78 of them women.

The republic has one of the major Soviet oilfields: Also a number of large engineering works, chemical factories, building materials works and food canneries. There is an expanding timber, woodworking and furniture industry. In 1984 there were 122 state and 39 collective farms. Crop area was 453,900 hectares.

There were, in 1987–88, 534 schools with 252,000 pupils, 12 technical colleges with 13,300 students and 3 places of higher education with 14,400 students.

In 1988 there were 3,637 doctors and 13,100 hospital beds.

CHUVASH AUTONOMOUS SOVIET SOCIALIST REPUBLIC

Area, 18,300 sq. km (7,064 sq. miles); population (Jan. 1989), 1,336,000. Capital, Cheboksary (1989 census population, 420,000). The territory was annexed by Russia in the middle of the 16th century. On 24 June 1920 it was constituted as an Autonomous Region, and on 21 April 1925 as an Autonomous Republic. The population (1979 census) includes Chuvashes (68·4%), Russians (26%), Tatars (2·9%) and Mordovians (1·6%).

200 deputies were elected to the republican Supreme Soviet on 24 Feb. 1985, 79 of them women.

Like most of the Autonomous Republics, Chuvashia before 1914 was a region of primitive agriculture with a certain development of the timber industry. Today it has several big railway repair works, an expanding electrical and other engineering industries, building materials, chemicals, textiles and food industries; timber felling and haulage are largely mechanized. In 1985 there were 179 collective farms and 104 state farms. Grain crops account for nearly two-thirds of all sowings and fodder crops for nearly a quarter. Fruit and wine-growing are a developing branch of agriculture. Crop area was 732,400 hectares.

In 1987–88 there were 208,000 pupils at 687 schools, 23,200 students at 24 technical colleges and 18,200 students at 3 higher educational establishments.

In 1988 there were 4,672 doctors and 18,500 hospital beds.

DAGESTAN AUTONOMOUS SOVIET SOCIALIST REPUBLIC

Area, 50,300 sq. km (19,416 sq. miles); population (Jan. 1989), 1,792,000. Capital, Makhachkala (1989 census population, 315,000). Over 30 nationalities inhabit this republic apart from Russians (11·6% at 1979 census); the most numerous are the Avartsy (25·7%), Dargintsy (15·2%), Lezginy (11·6%), Kumyki (12·4%), Laki (5·1%), Tabasarany (4·4%) and Azerbaijanis (4%). Annexed from Persia in 1723, Dagestan was constituted an Autonomous Republic on 20 Jan. 1921.

210 deputies were elected to the republican Supreme Soviet on 24 Feb. 1985, 84 of them women.

There are large engineering, oil, chemical, woodworking, textile, food and other light industries. Agriculture is very varied, ranging from wheat to grapes, with sheep farming and cattle breeding; in 1983 there were 249 collective farms and 262 state farms. Crop area was 427,800 hectares. A chain of power stations is under construction in the Sulak River (total capacity 2·5m. kw.).

In 1987–88 there were 1,512 schools with 394,000 pupils, 23,100 students at 28 technical colleges and 5 higher education establishments with 25,400 students; and a branch of the USSR Academy of Sciences with 4 learned institutions (373 research workers). In Jan. 1988 there were 7,362 doctors and 22,100 hospital beds.

KABARDINO-BALKAR AUTONOMOUS SOVIET SOCIALIST REPUBLIC

Area, 12,500 sq. km (4,825 sq. miles); population (Jan. 1989) 760,000. Capital, Nalchik (1989 census population, 235,000). Kabarda was annexed to Russia in 1557. The republic was constituted on 5 Dec. 1936. Population (1979 census) includes Kabardinians (45·6%), Balkars (9%), Russians (35·1%).

160 deputies were elected to the republican Supreme Soviet on 24 Feb. 1985, 69 of them women.

Main industries are ore-mining, timber, engineering, coal, food processing, timber and light industries, building materials. Grain, livestock breeding, dairy farming and wine-growing are the principal branches of agriculture. There were, in 1983, 59 state and 66 collective farms.

In 1987–88 there were 240 schools with 121,000 pupils, 9,300 students in 10 technical colleges and 10,400 students at 2 higher educational establishments. In Jan. 1988 there were 3,440 doctors and 9,100 hospital beds.

KALMYK AUTONOMOUS SOVIET SOCIALIST REPUBLIC

Area, 75,900 sq. km (29,300 sq. miles); population (Jan. 1989), 322,000. Capital, Elista (85,000). The population (1979 census) includes 41·5% Kalmyks, 42·6% Russians, 6·6% Kazakhs, Chechens and Dagestanis.

The Kalmyks migrated from western China to Russia (Nogai Steppe) in the early 17th century. The territory was constituted an Autonomous Region on 4 Nov. 1920, and an Autonomous Republic on 22 Oct. 1935; this was dissolved in 1943. On 9 Jan. 1957 it was reconstituted as an Autonomous Region and on 29 July 1958 as an Autonomous Republic once more.

130 deputies were elected to the republican Supreme Soviet on 24 Feb. 1985, 54 of them women.

Main industries are fishing, canning and building materials. Cattle breeding and irrigated farming (mainly fodder crops) are the principal branches of agriculture. In 1983 there were 79 state and 23 collective farms. Crop area was 859,000 hectares.

In 1987–88 there were 52,000 pupils in 250 schools, 6,100 students in 7 technical colleges and 4,700 in higher education. There were 1,316 doctors and 5,000 hospital beds.

KARELIAN AUTONOMOUS SOVIET SOCIALIST REPUBLIC

HISTORY. Before 1917, Karelia (then known as the Olonets Province) was noted chiefly as a place of exile for political and other prisoners.

After the November Revolution of 1917, Karelia formed part of the RSFSR. In June 1920 a Karelian Labour Commune was formed and in July 1923 this was transformed into the Karelian Autonomous Soviet Socialist Republic (one of the autonomous republics of the RSFSR). On 31 March 1940, after the Soviet–Finnish war, practically all the territory (with the exception of a small section in the neighbourhood of the Leningrad area) which had been ceded by Finland to the USSR was added to Karelia and the Karelian Autonomous Republic was transformed into the Karelo-Finnish Soviet Socialist Republic as the 12th republic of the USSR. In 1946, however, the southern part of the republic, including its whole seaboard and the town of Viipuri (Vyborg) and Keksholm, was attached to the RSFSR and in 1956 the republic reverted to ASSR status with the RSFSR.

AREA AND POPULATION. The Karelian Autonomous Republic, capital Petrozavodsk (1989 census population, 270,000), covers an area of 172,400 sq. km, with a population of 792,000 (Jan. 1989). Karelians represent 11·1% of the population, Russians, 71·3%, Belorussians 8·1%, Ukrainians 3·2%, Finns 2·7% (1979 census).

150 deputies were elected to the republican Supreme Soviet on 24 Feb. 1985, 57 of them women.

NATURAL RESOURCES. Karelia is chiefly noted for its wealth of timber, some 70% of its territory being forest land. It is also rich in other natural resources, having large deposits of diabase, spar, quartz, marble, granite, zinc, lead, silver, copper, molybdenum, tin, baryta, iron ore, etc. Karelia takes first place in the USSR for the production of mica. It has 43,643 lakes, which, as well as its rivers, are rich in fish.

Agriculture. There were 9 collective farms and 59 state farms in 1983. The crop area was 78,900 hectares (over 85% under fodder crops).

INDUSTRY. The republic has 25 large-scale enterprises, such as timber mills, paper-cellulose works, mica, chemical plants, power stations and furniture factories. Output, 1986: Timber, 11·1m. cu. metres; paper, 1·3m. tonnes; cellulose, 826,000 tonnes; electricity, 3,634m. kwh.; iron ore, 9·5m. tonnes.

The construction of the White Sea–Baltic Canal had a powerful influence on the economic development of Karelia. New refrigerating plants, cellulose factories and timber industry equipment began working in 1970.

COMMUNICATIONS. A railway between Petrozavodsk and Suoyarvi connects the capital and the Murmansk Railway with the main railway line Sortavala–Vyborg. A railway line was also laid between Kandalaksha and Kuolayarvi. Length of track, 1,600 km.

EDUCATION. In 1987–88 there were 111,000 pupils in 318 schools. There were 9,400 students in 2 places of higher education and 14,600 in 16 technical colleges.

HEALTH. In Jan. 1988 there were 3,983 doctors, and 12,100 hospital beds.

KOMI AUTONOMOUS SOVIET SOCIALIST REPUBLIC

Area, 415,900 sq. km (160,540 sq. miles); population (Jan. 1989), 1,263,000. Capital, Syktyvkar (1989 census population, 233,000). Annexed by the princes of Moscow in the 14th century and occupied by British and American forces in 1918–19, the territory was constituted as an Autonomous Region on 22 Aug. 1921 and as an Autonomous Republic on 5 Dec. 1936. The population (1979 census) includes Komi (25·3%), Russians (56·7%), Ukrainians and Belorussians (10·7%).

180 deputies were elected to the republican Supreme Soviet on 24 Feb. 1985, 59 of them women.

There are large coal, oil, timber, gas, asphalt and building materials industries; light industry is expanding. Livestock breeding (including dairy farming) is the main branch of agriculture. There were 56 state farms in 1983. Crop area, 92,000 hectares.

In 1987–88 there were 190,000 pupils in 549 schools, 11,600 students in 3 higher educational establishments, 16,800 students in 19 technical colleges; and a branch of the Academy of Sciences with 4 learned institutions (297 research workers).

In Jan. 1988 there were 4,978 doctors and 17,200 hospital beds.

MARI AUTONOMOUS SOVIET SOCIALIST REPUBLIC

Area, 23,200 sq. km (8,955 sq. miles); population (Jan. 1989), 750,000. Capital, Yoshkar-Ola (1989 census population, 242,000). The Mari people were annexed to Russia, with other peoples of the Kazan Tatar Khanate, when the latter was overthrown in 1552. On 4 Nov. 1920 the territory was constituted as an Autonomous Region, and on 5 Dec. 1936 as an Autonomous Republic. The population (1979 census) includes Mari (43·5%), Tatars (5·8%), Chuvashes (1·1%), Russians (47·5%).

150 deputies were elected to the republican Supreme Soviet on 24 Feb. 1985, 60 of them women.

There are over 300 modern factories. The main industries are metalworking, timber, paper, woodworking and food processing. In 1983 there were 89 collective farms and 82 state farms. Over 69% of cultivated land is grain, but flax, potatoes, fruit and vegetables are also expanding branches of agriculture, as is also livestock farming. 638,000 hectares were under crops.

Estimated reserves of the Pechora coalfield are 262,000m. tons.

In 1987–88 there were 429 schools with 107,000 pupils; 13 technical colleges and 3 higher education establishments had 10,600 and 15,400 students respectively.

In Jan. 1988 there were 2,482 doctors and 10,300 hospital beds.

MORDOVIAN AUTONOMOUS SOVIET SOCIALIST REPUBLIC

Area, 26,200 sq. km (10,110 sq. miles); population (Jan. 1989), 964,000. Capital, Saransk (1989 census population, 312,000). By the 13th century the Mordovian tribes had been subjugated by the Russian princes of Ryazan and Nizhni-Novgorod. In 1928 the territory was constituted as a Mordovian Area within the Middle-Volga Territory, on 10 Jan. 1930 as an Autonomous Region and on 20 Dec. 1934 as an Autonomous Republic. The population (1979 census) includes Mordovians (34·2%), Russians (59·7%), Tatars (4·6%)

175 deputies were elected to the republican Supreme Soviet on 24 Feb. 1985, 74 of them women.

The republic has a wide range of industries: Electrical, timber, cable, building materials, furniture, textile, leather and other light industries. Agriculture is devoted chiefly to grain, sugar-beet, sheep and dairy farming. In 1983 there were 78 state and 273 collective farms.

In 1987–88 there were 130,000 pupils in 829 schools, 15,600 students in 21 technical colleges and 19,800 attending 2 higher educational institutions. In Jan. 1988 there were 3,728 doctors and 14,300 hospital beds.

NORTH OSSETIAN AUTONOMOUS SOVIET SOCIALIST REPUBLIC

Area, 8,000 sq. km (3,088 sq. miles); population (Jan. 1989), 634,000. Capital, Ordzhonikidze (formerly Vladikavkaz; 1989 census population, 300,000). The Ossetians, known to antiquity as Alani (who were also called by their immediate neighbours 'Ossi' or 'Yassi'), were annexed to Russia after the latter's treaty of Kuchuk-Kainardji with Turkey, and in 1784 the key fortress of Vladikavkaz was founded on their territory (given the name of Terek region in 1861). On 4 March 1918 the latter was proclaimed an Autonomous Soviet Republic, and after the Civil War this territory with others was set up as the Mountain Autonomous Republic (20 Jan. 1921), with North Ossetia as the Ossetian (Vladikavkaz) Area within it. On 7 July 1924 the latter was constituted as an Autonomous Region and on 5 Dec. 1936 as an Autonomous Republic. The population (1979 census) comprises chiefly Ossetians (50·5%), Russians (33·9%), Ingushi and other Caucasian nationalities (8·1%).

150 deputies were elected to the republican Supreme Soviet on 24 Feb. 1985, 68 of them women.

The main industries are non-ferrous metals (mining and metallurgy), maize-processing (at the Beslan Works, the largest in Europe), timber and woodworking, textiles, building materials, distilleries and food processing. There is also a prosperous and varied agriculture. In 1983 there were 38 state and 45 collective farms.

There were in 1987–88, 97,000 children in 209 schools, 13,100 students in 13 technical colleges and 18,100 students in 4 higher educational establishments (pedagogical, agriculture, medical and mining-metallurgical institutes). In Jan. 1988 there were 4,204 doctors and 8,000 hospital beds.

TATAR AUTONOMOUS SOVIET SOCIALIST REPUBLIC

Area, 68,000 sq. km (26,250 sq. miles); population (Jan. 1989), 3,640,000. Capital, Kazan. From the 10th to the 13th centuries this was the territory of the flourishing Volga-Kama Bulgar State; conquered by the Mongols, it became the seat of the Kazan (Tatar) Khans when the Mongol Empire broke up in the 15th century, and in 1552 was conquered again by Russia. On 27 May 1920 it was constituted as an Autonomous Republic. The population (1979 census) includes Tatars (47·7%), Chuvashes, Mordovians and Udmurts (5·9%), Russians (44%).

250 deputies were elected to the republican Supreme Soviet on 24 Feb. 1985, 97 of them women.

The republic has highly developed engineering, oil and chemical industries, while timber, building materials, textiles, clothing and food industries are also expanding. The Kama works at Naberezhnye Chelny plan to produce 400,000 vehicles annually. In 1983, 557 collective and 250 state farms served a total area under crops of 3·4m. hectares.

In 1987–88 there were 2,285 schools with 498,000 pupils, 61 technical colleges with 59,100 students and 13 higher educational establishments with 67,300 students (including a state university). There is a branch of the USSR Academy of Sciences with 5 learned institutions (512 research workers).

Doctors in Jan. 1988 numbered 13,688 and hospital beds 46,100.

TUVA AUTONOMOUS SOVIET SOCIALIST REPUBLIC

Area, 170,500 sq. km (65,810 sq. miles); population (Jan. 1989), 309,000. Capital, Kyzyl (80,000). Tuva was incorporated in the USSR as an autonomous region on

13 Oct. 1944 and elevated to an Autonomous Republic on 10 Oct. 1961. It is situated to the north-west of Mongolia, between 50° and 53°N. lat. and between 90° and 100°E. long. It is bounded to the east, west and north by Siberia, and to the south by Mongolia. The Tuvans are a Turkic people, formerly ruled by hereditary or elective tribal chiefs. (For the earlier history of the former TannuTuva Republic, *see* THE STATESMAN'S YEAR-BOOK, 1946, p. 798.) The population (1979 census) includes Tuvans (60·5%) and Russians (36·2%).

130 deputies were elected to the republican Supreme Soviet on 24 Feb. 1985, 53 of them women.

Tuva is well-watered and has much good pastoral land; 47 hydro-electric stations have been set into operation. The Tuvans are mainly herdsmen and cattle farmers, but, in 1983, 371,000 hectares were under crops. There are deposits of gold, cobalt and asbestos. The main exports are hair, hides and wool, and the imports manufactured goods and iron. There are 60 state farms. Mining, woodworking, garment, leather, food and other industries are rapidly developing.

In 1987–88 there were 153 schools with 66,000 pupils; 6 technical colleges with 4,100 students, and 1 higher education institution with 2,900 students.

In Jan. 1988 there were 1,086 doctors and 5,400 hospital beds.

UDMURT AUTONOMOUS SOVIET SOCIALIST REPUBLIC

Area, 42,100 sq. km (16,250 sq. miles); population (Jan. 1989), 1,609,000. Capital, Izhevsk. The Udmurts (formerly known as 'Votyaks') were annexed by the Russians in the 15th and 16th centuries. On 4 Nov. 1920 the Votyak Autonomous Region was constituted (the name was changed to Udmurt—used by the people themselves—in 1932), and on 28 Dec. 1934 was raised to the status of an Autonomous Republic. The population (1979 census) includes Udmurts (32·2%), Tatars (6·6%), Russians (58·3%).

200 deputies were elected to the republican Supreme Soviet on 24 Feb. 1985, 79 of them women.

Heavy industry includes the manufacture of locomotives, machine tools and other engineering products, timber and building materials. There are also light industries—clothing, leather, furniture, food, etc.

There were 96 state and 244 collective farms in 1983; crop area 1·4m. hectares.

In 1987–88 there were 856 schools with 234,000 pupils; there were 22,500 students at 29 technical colleges and 24,300 at 5 higher educational institutions.

In Jan. 1988 there were 6,793 doctors and 20,900 hospital beds.

YAKUT AUTONOMOUS SOVIET SOCIALIST REPUBLIC

The area is 3,103,200 sq. km (1,197,760 sq. miles); population (Jan. 1989), 1,081,000. Capital, Yakutsk (187,000). The Yakuts were subjugated by the Russians in the 17th century. The territory was constituted an Autonomous Republic on 27 April 1922. The population (1979 census) includes Yakuts (36·9%), other northern peoples (2·2%), Russians (50·4%).

205 deputies were elected to the republican Supreme Soviet on 24 Feb. 1985, 92 of them women.

The principal industries are mining (gold, tin, mica, coal) and livestock-breeding. The Soviet Soyuz-Zoloto Trust and a number of individual prospectors are working the fields. Silver- and lead-bearing ores and coal are worked; large diamond fields have been opened up. Timber and food industries are developing. There was 1 collective farm in 1985 and 88 state farms, with an area under crops of 107,100 hectares. Trapping and breeding of fur-bearing animals (sable, squirrel, silver fox, etc.)

are an important source of income. A severe climate and lack of railways are serious obstacles to the economic development of the republic. There are, however, 10,000 km of roads and internal air lines totalling 10,000 km including an air service between Irkutsk and Yakutsk.

In 1987–88 there were 190,000 pupils in 643 secondary schools, 10,200 students at 18 technical colleges and 8,800 attending 2 higher education institutions.

In Jan. 1988 there were 4,647 doctors and 16,000 hospital beds.

ADYGEI AUTONOMOUS REGION

Part of Krasnodar Territory. Area, 7,600 sq. km (2,934 sq. miles); population (Jan. 1989), 432,000. Capital, Maikop (149,000). Established 27 July 1922.

Chief industries are timber, woodworking, food processing; but engineering is rapidly expanding. Cattle breeding predominates in agriculture. There were 38 collective and 33 state farms in 1983.

In 1987–88 there were 164 schools with 59,000 pupils, 6 technical colleges with 7,100 students and a pedagogical institute with 5,100 students. Regional newspapers are in Adygei and Russian. In Jan. 1988 there were 1,404 doctors and 5,800 hospital beds.

GORNO-ALTAI AUTONOMOUS REGION

Part of Altai Territory. Area, 92,600 sq. km (35,740 sq. miles); population (Jan. 1989), 192,000. Capital, Gorno-Altaisk (39,000). Established 1 June 1922 as Oirot Autonomous Region; renamed 7 Jan. 1948.

Chief industries are gold, mercury and brown-coal mining, timber, chemicals and dairying. Cattle breeding predominates; pasturages and hay meadows cover over 1m. hectares, but 142,000 hectares are under crops. There were 20 collective and 37 state farms in 1983.

In 1987–88 there were 34,000 school pupils in 191 schools; 5 technical colleges had 4,400 students and 2,600 students were attending a pedagogical institute. There were 2,800 hospital beds and 729 doctors.

JEWISH AUTONOMOUS REGION

Part of Khabarovsk Territory. Area, 36,000 sq. km (13,895 sq. miles); population (Jan. 1989), 216,000 (1979 census, Russians, 84·1%; Ukrainians, 6·3%; Jews, 5·4%). Capital, Birobijan (82,000). Established as Jewish National District in 1928, became an Autonomous Region 7 May 1934.

Chief industries are non-ferrous metallurgy, building materials, timber, engineering, textiles, paper and food processing. There were 161,000 hectares under cultivation in 1983; main crops are wheat, soya, oats, barley. There were 36 state farms and 2 collective farms in 1983.

In 1987–88 there were 34,000 pupils in 109 schools; students in technical colleges numbered 5,500. There are a Yiddish national theatre, a Yiddish newspaper and a Yiddish broadcasting service. Doctors numbered 800 and hospital beds 3,400.

KARACHAYEVO-CHERKESS AUTONOMOUS REGION

Part of Stavropol Territory. Area, 14,100 sq. km (5,442 sq. miles); population (Jan. 1989), 418,000. Capital, Cherkessk (113,000). A Karachai Autonomous Region was established on 26 April 1926 (out of a previously united Karachayevo-Cherkess Autonomous Region created in 1922), and dissolved in 1943. A Cherkess Autonomous Region was established on 30 April 1928. The present Autonomous Region was re-established on 9 Jan. 1957.

Ore-mining, engineering, chemical and woodworking industries have been built up since 1917. There are 70 large factories, and a copper works and sugar factory are under construction. A large irrigation scheme, Kuban-Kalaussi, is being developed, to irrigate 200,000 hectares. Livestock breeding and grain growing predominate in agriculture; crop area in 1983 was 196,000 hectares. There were 15 collective farms and 37 state farms in 1983.

In 1987–88 there were 66,000 pupils in secondary schools, 6 technical colleges with 6,000 students and 1 institute with 4,100 students. In Jan. 1988 there were 1,363 doctors and 4,700 hospital beds.

KHAKASS AUTONOMOUS REGION

Part of Krasnoyarsk Territory. Area, 61,900 sq. km (23,855 sq. miles); population (Jan. 1989), 569,000. Capital, Abakan (154,000). Established 20 Oct. 1930.

Coal- and ore-mining, timber and woodworking industries have been highly developed since 1917. The region is linked by rail with the Trans-Siberian line. Large textile and sugar factories are being built.

In 1985, 1·8m. hectares were under crops. Livestock breeding, dairy and vegetable farming are developed. There are 56 state farms.

In 1987–88 there were 87,000 pupils in 264 secondary schools, 8,100 students in 7 technical colleges and 5,700 students at a higher educational institution. In Jan. 1988 there were 1,796 doctors and 8,200 hospital beds. A Khakass alphabet was created after the Revolution.

AUTONOMOUS AREAS

Agin-Buryat Situated in Chita region (Eastern Siberia); area, 19,000 sq. km, population (1989), 77,000. Capital, Aginskoe. Formed 1937, its economy is basically pastoral.

Chukot Situated in Magadan region (Far East), its area of 737,700 sq. km in the far northeast. Population (1989), 158,000. Capital, Anadyr. Formed 1930. Population chiefly Russian, also Chukchi, Koryak, Yakut, Even. Minerals are extracted in the north, including gold, tin, mercury and tungsten.

Evenki Situated in Krasnoyarsk territory (Eastern Siberia); area, 767,600 sq. km, population (1989) 24,000, chiefly Evenks. Capital, Tura.

Khanty-Mansi Situated in Tyumen region (Western Siberia); area, 523,100 sq. km, population (1989) 1,269,000, chiefly Russians but also Khants and Mansi. Capital, Khanti-Mansiisk. Formed 1930.

Komi-Permyak Situated in Perm region (Northern Russia); area, 32,900 sq. km, population (1989) 159,000, chiefly Komi-Permyaks. Formed 1925. Capital, Kudymkar. Forestry is the main occupation.

Koryak Situated in Kamchatka region (Far East); area, 301,500 sq. km, population (1989) 39,000. Capital, Palana. Formed 1930.

Nenets Situated in Archangel region (Northern Russia); area, 176,700 sq. km, population (1989) 55,000. Capital, Naryan-Mar.

Taimyr Situated in Krasnoyarsk territory, this most northerly part of Siberia comprises the Taimyr peninsula and the Arctic islands of Severnaya Zemlya. Area, 862,100 sq. km, population (1989) 55,000, excluding the mining city of Norilsk which is separately administered. Capital, Dudinka.

Ust-Ordyn-Buryat Situated in Irkutsk region (Eastern Siberia); area, 22,400 sq. km, population (1989) 136,000. Capital, Ust-Ordynsk. Formed 1937.

Yamalo-Nenets Situated in Tyumen region (Western Siberia); area, 750,300 sq. km, population (1989) 487,000. Capital, Salekhard. Formed 1930.

Further Reading

Armstrong, T., *Russian Settlement in the North*. CUP, 1965
Conolly, V., *Beyond the Urals. Economic Developments in Soviet Asia*. London, 1967
Dallin, D. J., *The Rise of Russia in Asia*. New York, 1949.—*Soviet Russia and the Far East*. London, 1949
Kolarz, W., *The Peoples of the Soviet Far East*. London, 1954
Istoriya Sibiri s drevneishikh vremen do nashikh dnei. 5 vols., Leningrad, 1968–69

UKRAINE

Ukrainska Radyanska Sotsialistichna Respublika

HISTORY. The Ukrainian Soviet Socialist Republic was proclaimed on 25 Dec. 1917 and was finally established in Dec. 1919. In Dec. 1920 it concluded a military and economic alliance with the RSFSR and on 30 Dec. 1922 formed, together with the other Soviet Socialist Republics, the Union of Soviet Socialist Republics. On 1 Nov. 1939 Western Ukraine (about 88,000 sq. km) was incorporated in the Ukrainian SSR. On 2 Aug. 1940 Northern Bukovina (about 6,000 sq. km) ceded to the USSR by Romania 28 June 1940, and the Khotin, Akkerman and Izmail provinces of Bessarabia were included in the Ukrainian SSR, and on 29 June 1945 Ruthenia (Sub-Carpathian Russia), about 7,000 sq. km, was also incorporated. From the new territories 2 new regions were formed, Chernovits and Izmail.

AREA AND POPULATION. The Ukraine is in south-west USSR; it has a Black Sea coast and western frontiers with Romania, Hungary, Poland and Czechoslovakia. It is bounded north by Belorussia and otherwise by the RSFSR. In 1938 the Ukrainian SSR covered an area of 445,000 sq. km (171,770 sq. miles); it now covers 603,700 sq. km (231,990 sq. miles).

Population, Jan. 1989, 51,704,000 (in 1979 census, 73·6% Ukrainians, 21·1% Russians, 1·3% Jews, 0·8% Belorussians).

The principal towns are the capital Kiev, Kharkov, Donetsk, Odessa, Dnepropetrovsk, Lvov, Zaporozhye and Krivoi Rog.

The Ukrainian Soviet Socialist Republic consists of the following regions: Cherkassy, Chernigov, Chernovtsy, Crimea (transferred from the RSFSR on 19 Feb. 1954), Dnepropetrovsk, Donetsk, Ivan Franko, Khmelnitsky (formerly Kamenets-Podolsk), Kharkov, Kherson, Kiev, Kirovograd, Lvov, Nikolayev, Odessa, Poltava, Rovno, Sumy, Ternopol, Vinnitsa, Volhynia, Voroshilovgrad, Zakarpatskaya (Transcarpathia), Zaporozhye, Zhitomir.

CONSTITUTION AND GOVERNMENT. The Supreme Soviet elected on 24 Feb. 1985 consisted of 650 deputies, including 444 Communists and 234 women. New elections were held on 4 March 1990. A new Constitution, based on that of the USSR, was adopted in April 1978.

At local elections (21 June 1987), out of 527,799 deputies returned, 259,795 (49·2%) were women, 297,136 (56·3%) non-Party and 378,000 (72·1%) industrial workers and collective farmers. New elections were held on 4 March 1990.

Chairman, Presidium of the Supreme Soviet: V. S. Shevchenko.
Chairman, Council of Ministers: V. A. Masol.
Foreign Minister: V. A. Kravtsev.
First Secretary, Communist Party: V. A. Ivashko.

FINANCE. Budget estimates (in 1m. rubles), 1988, 33,164; 1989 (plan), 36,885.

AGRICULTURE. The Ukraine contains some of the richest land in the USSR. It raises wheat, buckwheat, beet, sunflower, cotton, flax, tobacco, soya, hops, the rubber plant kok-sagyz, fruit and vegetables, and in 1985 produced 46% by value of the USSR's total agricultural output. The area under cultivation was 27·9m. hectares in 1913, 27m. in 1939 before the new territories were added, and 48·6m. in Nov. 1986.

Output (in 1m. tonnes) in 1987: Grain, 43·1; sugar-beet, 42·9; vegetables, 7·7; sunflower seed, 2·6; potatoes, 21·4; meat and fats, 4; milk, 23·4; wool, 0·030; 17,200m. eggs.

On 1 Jan. 1988 there were 26m. cattle, 19·3m. pigs, 9·3m. sheep and goats. In 1949 silver-fox breeding farms were started.

On 1 Jan. 1987 there were 2,466 state farms and 7,452 collective farms.

Irrigation networks supplied 1·82m. hectares of land; 2·2m. hectares were drained.

Tractors numbered 439,500 at 1 Jan. 1987 and combine harvesters, 112,000.

INDUSTRY. Coal in the Donets field (25,900 sq. km stretching from Donetsk to Rostov), estimated to contain 60% of the bituminous and anthracite coal reserves of the USSR, yielded, in 1987, 192m. tonnes—about 25% of the USSR production. Large new seams have been found near Novo-Moskovsk (Dnepropetrovsk region), Kharkov, Lugansk (beyond the Don) and on the left bank of the Dnieper. Within the present frontiers of the Ukraine, coal output was 22·8m. tons in 1913, 83·8m. tons in 1940, 78m. tons in 1950 and 217m. tons in 1977.

Combining coal from the Donets field with the iron-ore from the mines in Krivoi Rog has made possible the development of a large ferrous metallurgical industry in the Ukraine. Output of iron ore was 118m. tons in 1987. Manganese is obtained at Nikopol; output in 1987, 7·2m. tons. Output of finished rolled metal products, 39·3m. tonnes in 1987 (36m. in 1980); of steel pipe, 7m. (6·3m.).

The Ukraine also contains oil, rich deposits of salt and various important chemicals. Oil output was 1m. tons in 1913 (in present frontiers), 353,000 tons in 1940 and 5·6m. tonnes in 1987, including natural gas.

The Ukraine has highly developed chemical and machine-construction industries producing one-fifth of the total output of machinery and chemicals in the USSR. Output in 1987 of paper, 320,000 tonnes; of chemical fibre, 188,000 tonnes; of sulphuric acid, 4·2m. tonnes; of caustic soda, 489,000 tonnes; of televisions, 3·1m.; of refrigerators, 753,000.

In Northern Bukovina there are deposits of gypsum, oil, alabaster, brown coal and timber. Output in 1987 of cardboard, 549,000 tonnes; of mineral fertilizers (recalculated base), 5·7m. tonnes.

Consumer goods and food industries are important. Output in 1987 of knitwear, 334m. items; of motorbikes, 111,000; of granulated sugar, 7·6m. tonnes; of leather footwear, 187m. pairs; of preserves, 4,800m. standard jars.

The number of industrial and office workers at the end of 1950 was 6·9m., and the average in 1987, 20·7m. There were 3·9m. collective farmers in 1985.

During the first 5-year plan (1929–32) the Dnieper power-station was built; destroyed during the War, it was restored during the fourth plan (1946–50). Another large hydro-electric station at Kakhovka began operations during the fifth plan (1951–55). Power output (in 1,000m. kwh.) increased as follows: 1913, 0·5; 1940, 12·4; 1950, 14·7; 1987, 281.

COMMUNICATIONS. The total length of railways of the Ukrainian SSR in Jan. 1988 was 22,740 km, of hard-surface motor roads 209,200 km. In 1987, 11,617 tonne-km of freight was carried on inland waterways.

Airlines connect Kiev, Lvov, Chernovtsy and Odessa with Crimean and Caucasian spas, Kiev with Tbilisi, Odessa with Riga and Donetsk.

Newspapers (1987). Out of 1,784 newspapers, 1,279 were in Ukrainian. Daily circulation of Ukrainian-language newspapers, 16·2m., other languages, 8·1m.

RELIGION. Several Christian Churches have their adherents in the Ukraine, the chief being the Orthodox Greek Church and the Catholic Church. The Western

Ukraine Uniate Church, which in 1596 had been forced by the Poles to establish unity with the Roman Church, severed this connexion in March 1946 and joined the Orthodox Church. There are also some Protestants as well as Jews and others.

EDUCATION. In 1987–88 the number of pupils in 21,500 primary and secondary schools was 7·1m.; 146 higher educational establishments had 852,300 students, and 734 technical colleges 800,600 students; 61% of children were attending pre-school institutions.

The Ukrainian Academy of Sciences was established in 1919; in 1988 it had 78 institutions with 16,683 scientific staff. There is an academy of building and architecture. Total scientific staff in all institutions was 215,000 in Jan. 1988.

HEALTH. Doctors numbered 218,600 in 1987, and hospital beds, 681,400.

Further Reading

Allen, W. E. D., *The Ukraine: A History*. 2nd ed. Cambridge, 1963
Andrusyshen, C. H. (ed.) *Ukrainian-English Dictionary*. Toronto, 1955
Koropecky, I. S. (ed.) *The Ukraine within the USSR: An Economic Balance Sheet*. New York, 1977
Kubiojovyc, V. (ed.) *Encyclopedia of Ukraine*, 4 vols. Toronto, 1984ff
Magoci, P. R. and Matthews, G. J., *Ukraine: A Historical Atlas*. Univ. of Toronto Press, 1985
Manning, C. A., *Twentieth-century Ukraine*. New York, 1951

BELORUSSIA

Belaruskaya Sovietskaya Sotsialistychnaya Respublika

HISTORY. The Belorussian Soviet Socialist Republic was set up on 1 Jan. 1919. It forms one of the constituent republics of the USSR.

AREA AND POPULATION. Belorussia is situated along the Western Dvina and Dnieper. It is bounded west by Poland, north by Latvia and Lithuania, east by the RSFSR and south by the Ukraine. The area is 207,600 sq. km (80,134 sq. miles). The capital is Minsk. Other important towns are Gomel, Vitebsk, Mogilev, Bobruisk, Grodno and Brest. On 2 Nov. 1939 western Belorussia was incorporated with an area of over 108,000 sq. km and a population of 4·8m. The population (Jan. 1989) was 10,200,000; 79·4% of this population in 1979 (census) were Belorussians, 4·2% Poles, 11·9% Russians, 2·4% Ukrainians and 1·4% Jews.

Belorussia now comprises the following regions: Brest, Gomel, Grodno, Mogilev, Minsk, Vitebsk.

CONSTITUTION AND GOVERNMENT. The Supreme Soviet elected in 1985 consisted of 485 deputies. New elections were held on 4 March 1990. A new Constitution was adopted in April 1978.

At elections to regional, district, urban and rural Soviets (21 June 1987), of 85,375 deputies returned, 41,518 (48·6%) were women. New elections were held on 4 March 1990.

Chairman, Presidium of the Supreme Soviet: N. I. Dementei.
Chairman, Council of Ministers: M. V. Kovalev.
Foreign Minister: A. E. Gurinovich
First Secretary, Communist Party: E. E. Sokolov.

FINANCE. Budget estimates (in 1m. rubles), 1988, 8,893; 1989 (plan), 11,022.

NATURAL RESOURCES. Belorussia is hilly, with a general slope towards the south. It contains large tracts of marsh land, particularly to the south-west, and valuable forest land wooded with oak, elm, maple and white beech: There are over 6,500 peat deposits.

AGRICULTURE. Agriculturally, Belorussia may be divided into three main sections—Northern: Growing flax, fodder, grasses and breeding cattle for meat and dairy produce; Central: Potato growing and pig breeding; Southern: Good natural pasture land, hemp cultivation and cattle breeding for meat and dairy produce. The area under cultivation was 12·3m. hectares in Nov. 1986. There were 7·4m. cattle, 5·1m. pigs and 615,500 sheep and goats on 1 Jan. 1988.

Output of main agricultural products (in 1,000 tonnes) in 1987: Grain, 9,281; meat, 1,105; milk, 7,250; eggs, 3,495m.; potatoes, 11,755; vegetables, 927; sugar-beet, 1,484.

On 1 Jan. 1987 there were 1,675 collective farms and 913 state farms. About 2·5m. hectares of marsh land had been drained for agricultural use, 828,200 of these for crops. This land has been found to be as rich as the soil of the Black Earth Zone, and yields good harvests of grain, fodder, potatoes, kok-sagyz and other crops. In Jan. 1987 there were 130,500 tractors and 35,800 grain combine harvesters.

INDUSTRY. Industry in this republic was almost completely destroyed during the years 1941–45. By 1956, aggregate industrial output was three times what it had been in 1940. Plants producing tip-lorries, machine-tools and agricultural machinery are prominent.

The republic also contains timber works; a match factory in Borisov; building materials, machine, prefabricated house construction, glass-blowing and other factories; canneries, creameries and other food industries; chemical, textiles, artificial-silk, flax-spinning and leather works and an automobile and tractor industry.

In 1987 output was as follows: Chemical fibre, 402,000 tonnes; light bulbs, 295m.; paper, 204,000 tonnes; building bricks, 2,215m.; radio receivers, 726,000; televisions, 1,052,000; watches, 10·4m.; bicycles, 828,000; granulated sugar, 368,000 tonnes; preserves, 703m. jars; footwear, 45·4m. pairs.

Particular attention has been paid to the development of the peat industry with a view to making Belorussia as far as possible self-supporting in fuel, and in 1939 local peat provided 67·5% of her total requirements of fuel. In 1987 2·2m. tonnes of peat briquettes were produced. There are also rich deposits of rock salt.

Output of electricity in 1987, 37,700m. kwh. (508m. in 1940). New powerplants have been built in Baranovichi, Grodno, Molodechno and Lida.

The number of industrial and office workers in 1987 was 4,326,000.

COMMUNICATIONS. In Jan. 1988 there were 5,540 km of railways, 61,100 km of motor roads (51,000 km hard-surface) and 1,815m. tonne-km of freight was carried on inland waterways.

Newspapers (1987). Of 215 newspapers published 130 were in Belorussian. Daily circulation of Belorussian-language newspapers, 1·7m., other languages, 3·6m.

EDUCATION. In 1987–88 there were 179,400 students in 33 places of higher education and 154,000 students in 138 technical colleges. There were (Jan. 1988) 44,500 scientific personnel in 178 institutions, and 562,300 specialists with a higher education employed in the national economy. The Belorussian Academy of Sciences controlled 32 learned institutions with 5,845 scientific staff. The number of children in 5,800 primary and secondary schools was 1·5m. in 1987–88. 71% of children attended pre-school institutions in Jan. 1988.

HEALTH. In 1987 there were 39,500 doctors and 135,500 hospital beds.

Further Reading

Belaruskaya Sovietskaya Entsyklapediya. Minsk, 1960–76
Lubachko, I. S., *Belorussia under Soviet Rule, 1917–57.* Lexington, 1972
Vakar, N. P., *Belorussia.* Harvard Univ. Press, 1956.—*A Bibliographical Guide to Belorussia.* Harvard Univ. Press, 1956

AZERBAIJAN

Azarbaijchan Soviet Sotsialistik Respublikasy

HISTORY. The 'Mussavat' (Nationalist) party, which dominated the National Council or Constituent Assembly of the Tatars, declared the independence of Azerbaijan on 28 May 1918, with a capital, first at Ganja (Elizavetpol) and later at Baku. On 28 April 1920 Azerbaijan was proclaimed a Soviet Socialist Republic. From 1922, with Georgia and Armenia it formed the Transcaucasian Soviet Federal Socialist Republic. In 1936 it assumed the status of one of the Union Republics of the USSR. In Jan. 1990 there were violent disturbances in Baku and on the Armenian border over the enclave of Nagorno-Karabakh.

AREA AND POPULATION. Azerbaijan covers an area of 86,600 sq. km (33,430 sq. miles) and has a population (Jan. 1989) of 7,029,000. Its capital is Baku. Other important towns are Kirovabad and Sumgait. Nakhichevan is the capital of the Autonomous Republic of the same name.

Azerbaijan includes the Nakhichevan Autonomous Republic and the Nagorno-Karabakh Autonomous Region. Situated in the eastern area of Transcaucasia, it is protected by mountains in the west and north, washed by the Caspian Sea in the east and bounded by Iran in the south. Its climate is inclined to drought.

In 1979 (census) 78·1% of the population were Azerbaijanis, who are mainly Shi'a Moslems. Other nationalities were Russians (7·9%), Armenians (7·9%) and Daghestanis (3·4%).

CONSTITUTION AND GOVERNMENT. The Supreme Soviet, elected in 1985, consists of 450 deputies (1 per 10,000 population); 311 are Communists and 179 women. A new Constitution was adopted in April 1978.

At elections to the Nagorno-Karabakh regional Soviet and the district, urban and rural Soviets (21 June 1987), of 51,681 deputies returned, 24,859 (48·1%) were women, 28,484 (55·1%) non-Party and 35,047 (67·8%) industrial workers and collective farmers.

Chairman, Presidium of the Supreme Soviet: E. M. Kafarov.
Chairman, Council of Ministers: A. N. Mutalibov.
First Secretary, Communist Party: A-R. Kh. Vezirov.

FINANCE (in 1m. rubles). Budget estimates, 1988, 3,361; 1989 (plan), 3,808.

AGRICULTURE. The chief agricultural products are grain, cotton, rice, grapes, fruit, vegetables, tobacco and silk. The Mexican rubber plant *grayule* has been acclimatized. A new kind of high-yielding winter wheat has been produced for use in mountainous parts of the republic. Area under cultivation, 6·7m. hectares.

Livestock on 1 Jan. 1988: Cattle, 2m.; pigs, 225,600; sheep and goats, 5·7m.

Output of main agricultural products (in 1,000 tonnes) in 1987: Grain, 1,118; cotton, 702; grapes, 1,550; vegetables, 855; tobacco, 60; potatoes, 202; tea, 34·2; meat, 184; milk, 1,062; eggs, 1,055m.; wool, 11·4.

Azerbaijan has become an important cotton-growing and sub-tropical base. About 70% of cultivated land is irrigated. On the irrigated land crops of Egyptian and Sea-Island cotton are obtained. Here, too, rice and lucerne are cultivated, and in the mountain valleys there are also orchards, vineyards and silk cultures.

In the south along the coast of the Caspian, where the climate is more moist, there are tea plantations, and citrus fruits and other sub-tropical plants are grown.

There were on 1 Jan. 1987, 608 collective farms, 808 state farms, 37,500 tractors and 4,600 grain combine harvesters.

INDUSTRY. The republic is rich in natural resources: Oil, iron, aluminium, copper, lead, zinc, precious metals, sulphur pyrites, limestone and salt. Iron and steel and aluminium works have been built at Sumgait.

The most important industry is the oil industry, especially in the Baku region. The output of oil was 7·7m. tonnes in 1913, 22·2m. tonnes in 1940 and 16·5m. tonnes in 1976. The largest producing area lies along the western shore of the Caspian Sea, north and south of Baku, where the largest refineries are located. Other wells lie west of Baku, and some have been drilled in the Caspian itself, off the Apsheron Peninsula. Baku is connected by a double pipeline with Batum on the Black Sea. All the oilfields have been electrified and are connected with Baku.

Azerbaijan has also copper, chemical, cement and building material, food, timber, salt, textiles and fishing industries. In 1987, 566,600 tonnes of steel pipe were produced, 42·8m. items of knitwear, 244,700 tonnes of caustic soda, 23·2m. pairs leather footwear, 103,400 tonnes of confectionery and 794·5m. standard jars of conserves.

In addition to Baku, other important industrial centres are Kirovabad, Nukha, Stepanakert, Nakhichevan, Lenkoran.

In 1987 electric power output was 22,800m. kwh. Output of gas, which began in 1928 with 176m. cu. metres, was 10,989m. in 1976. Pipelines from Karadag to Baku and Sumgait supply gas fuel for all oil-cracking factories and most engineering works.

Synthetic rubber works (Sumgait), tyre works and a worsted combine (Baku) and a large textile combine (Mingechaur) have been built.

The number of industrial and office workers in 1987 was 2,127,000.

COMMUNICATIONS. Total length of railways in 1988, 2,070 km, of motor roads 31,100 km (28,100 km hard surface).

Newspapers (1987). There were 150 newspapers, 120 in the Azerbaijani language (circulation 2·4m.), other languages, 503,000.

EDUCATION. In 1987–88 there were 1·4m. pupils in 4,400 primary and secondary schools and 20% of children attended pre-school institutions. There were 77 technical colleges with 74,200 students, 17 higher educational institutions, including a state university at Baku, with 103,400 students (including correspondence students). The Azerbaijan Academy of Sciences, founded in 1945, has 30 research institutions with 4,395 research workers. There were 22,800 research workers in the republic as a whole in Jan. 1988.

HEALTH. In 1987 there were 26,800 doctors and 67,700 hospital beds.

NAKHICHEVAN AUTONOMOUS SOVIET SOCIALIST REPUBLIC

Area, 5,500 sq. km (2,120 sq. miles), population (Jan. 1989), 295,000. Capital, Nakhichevan (37,000). This territory, on the borders of Turkey and Iran, forms part of the Azerbaijan SSR although separated from it by the territory of Soviet Armenia. Its population, mainly Azerbaijanis, had a chequered history for 1,500 years under the ancient Persians, Arabs, Seljuk Turks, Mongols, Ottoman Turks and modern Persians before being annexed by Russia in 1828. On 9 Feb. 1924 it was constituted as an Autonomous Republic within Azerbaijan. Its Supreme Soviet, elected 24 Feb. 1985, has 110 members including 52 women.

The republic has silk, clothing, cotton, canning, meat-packing and other factories. Nearly 70% of the people are engaged in agriculture, of which the main branches are cotton and tobacco growing. Fruit and grapes are also produced in increasing quantity. There are 35 collective and 37 state farms. Crop area 37,400 hectares.

In 1984–85 there were 219 primary and secondary schools with 66,000 pupils, and 2,100 were studying in higher educational institutions.

In Jan. 1983 there were 599 doctors and 2,500 hospital beds.

NAGORNO-KARABAKH AUTONOMOUS REGION

Area, 4,400 sq. km (1,700 sq. miles); population (Jan. 1989), 188,000. Capital, Stepanakert (33,000). Populated by Armenians (75·9%) and Azerbaijanis (23%), a separate khanate in the 18th century, it was established on 7 July 1923 as an Autonomous Region within Azerbaijan.

Main industries are silk, wine, dairying and building materials. Crop area is 67,200 hectares; cotton, grapes and winter wheat are grown. There are 33 collective and 38 state farms.

In 1984–85 34,000 pupils were studying in primary and secondary schools, 2,400 in colleges and 2,100 in higher educational institutions. In Jan. 1983 there were 523 doctors and 1,800 hospital beds.

Following extensive public demonstrations in Armenia and Azerbaijan as well as Nagorno-Karabakh itself, the area was placed under a 'special form of administration' subordinate to the USSR government in 1989.

Further Reading

Baddeley, J. F., *The Rugged Flanks of Caucasus*. 2 vols. Oxford, 1941
Guseinov, I. A. et al, *Istoriya Azerbaidzhana*. 8 vols. Baku, 1958–63

GEORGIA

Sakartvelos Sabchota Sotsialisturi Respublica

HISTORY. The independence of the Georgian Social Democratic Republic was declared at Tiflis on 26 May 1918 by the National Council, elected by the National Assembly of Georgia on 22 Nov. 1917. The independence of Georgia was recognized by the USSR on 7 May 1920. On 12 Feb. 1921 a rising broke out in Mingrelia, Abkhazia and Adjaria, and Soviet troops invaded the country, which, on 25 Feb. 1921, was proclaimed the Georgian Soviet Socialist Republic. On 15 Dec. 1922 Georgia was merged with Armenia and Azerbaijan to form the Trancaucasian Soviet Federal Socialist Republic. In 1936 the Georgian Soviet Socialist Republic became one of the constituent republics of the USSR. Nationalist demonstrations in April 1989 were suppressed by force with 20 fatal casualties.

AREA AND POPULATION. Georgia is bounded west by the Black Sea and south by Turkey, Armenia and Azerbaijan. It occupies the whole of the western part of Transcaucasia and covers an area of 69,700 sq. km (26,900 sq. miles). Its population on 1 Jan. 1989 was 5,449,000. The capital is Tbilisi (Tiflis). Other important towns are Kutaisi (235,000), Rustavi (159,000), Batumi (136,000), Sukhumi (121,000), Poti (54,000), Gori (59,000).

Protected from the north by the Caucasian mountains and receiving in the west the warm, moist winds from the Black Sea into which most of its rivers flow, Georgia is outstanding for its fine, warm climate and its natural wealth, variety and beauty. It has the highest snow-capped peaks of the Caucasian mountains. Georgia contains valuable sulphur and other medicinal springs. Georgians, an ancient people, were (1979 census) 68·8% of the population; Armenians 9%; Russians, 7·4%; Azerbaijanis, 5·1%; Ossetians, 3·2%; Abkhazians, 1·7%.

CONSTITUTION AND GOVERNMENT. The Georgian Soviet Socialist Republic includes the Abkhazian ASSR, the Adjarian ASSR and the South Ossetian Autonomous Region.

The Supreme Soviet, elected in 1985, consists of 440 deputies; 160 are women, 290 Communists. A new Constitution was adopted in April 1978.

At elections to the district, rural and urban Soviets, and that of the South Ossetian region (21 June 1987), of 50,982 deputies returned 25,826 (50·7%) were women,

28,974 (56·8%) non-Party and 34,930 (68·5%) industrial workers and collective farmers.

Chairman, Presidium of the Supreme Soviet: G. G. Gumbaridze.
Chairman, Council of Ministers: N. A. Chitanava.
First Secretary, Communist Party: G. G. Gumbaridze.

FINANCE (in 1m. rubles). Budget estimates, 1988, 3,360; 1989 (plan), 4,067.

AGRICULTURE. There are 3 main agricultural areas: (1) The moist subtropical area along the Black Sea Coast, where are cultivated tea, citrus fruits (lemons, oranges, mandarins, etc.), the tung tree (which yields special industrial oils), eucalyptus, bamboo, high-quality tobacco; (2) Imeretia (the Kutais region) where the chief cultures are grapes and silk, and (3) Kakhetia, along the Alazani (a tributary of the Kura river), famed for its orchards and wines. Land under cultivation was 4·6m. hectares in Nov. 1986.

Output of main agricultural products (in 1,000 tonnes) in 1987: Grain, 664; tea leaf, 594·9; citrus fruit, 119; sugar-beet, 50; potatoes, 360; vegetables, 551; grapes, 618; meat, 173; milk, 739; eggs, 891m.; wool, 6.

On 1 Jan. 1986 there were 719 collective farms working over 66% of all agricultural land, 594 state farms working nearly 34% of such land. In the Colchis area 115,000 hectares of extremely rich land have been reclaimed. There are 389,000 hectares of irrigated land. 151,400 hectares of marsh land have been drained. Tractors numbered 27,400 on 1 Jan. 1987; grain combines, 1,700.

Livestock on 1 Jan. 1988: Cattle, 1·6m.; pigs, 1·1m.; sheep and goats, 1·9m.

Georgia is rich in forest lands where fine varieties of timber are grown. Area covered by forests, 2·4m. hectares.

INDUSTRY. The most important mining industry of Georgia is the exploitation of the manganese deposits, the richest of which lie in the Chiatura region. Manganese deposits are calculated at 250m. tonnes, distributed over an area of 140 sq. km. The most important coal seams are at Tkvarcheli (deposits estimated at 250m. tonnes) and Tkibuli (deposits of 80m. tonnes). Other important minerals are baryta, the best in the USSR, fire-resisting and other clays, diatomite shale, oil, agate, marble, cement, alabaster, iron and other ores, building stone, arsenic, molybdenum, tungsten and mercury. In 1941 a goldfield was discovered. Output of coal in 1976 was 1·9m. tonnes (625,000 in 1940).

Since the Second World War the Transcaucasian Metallurgical Plant has been built at Rustavi (near Tbilisi) and a motor works at Kutaisi. There are modern factories for processing green tea-leaves, creameries and breweries; Georgia has also textile and silk industries.

In 1987, 2·1m. tonnes of manganese ore were produced, 510,000 tonnes of steel pipe, 36,900 tonnes of chemical fibres, 27,800 tonnes of paper, 17·9m. pairs footwear, 57·7m. knitwear garments, 46,000 colour televisions, 66,700 tonnes of confectionery, 119,800 tonnes of tea and 785·5m. jars of preserves.

Georgia's fast flowing rivers form an abundant source of energy. One of the most powerful stations completed in recent years is Tbilisi (1m. kw.). Power output in 1987 was 14,500m. kwh. (742m. in 1940).

There were 2,228,000 industrial and office workers in 1987.

COMMUNICATIONS. Length of railways in 1988, 1,580 km, of motor roads 35,300 (with hard surface 30,900).

Newspapers (1987). Out of 147 newspapers, 131 were in Georgian. Daily circulation of Georgian-language newspapers, 3·1m., other languages, 534,000.

EDUCATION. In 1987–88 there were 900,000 pupils in 3,700 primary and secondary schools, 51,200 in 91 technical colleges and 86,400 students in 19 higher educational institutions. Tbilisi University has 16,300 students. In towns, 11 years' education is usual. In Abastuman there is an astro-physical observatory. In 1936 a branch of the Academy of Sciences of the USSR was formed in Tbilisi, and in Feb. 1941 a Georgian Academy of Sciences was opened, which in Jan. 1988 had 42 institutions with scientific staff totalling 5,827. There were in all 194 research institutions with 27,600 scientific staff.

In Jan. 1988, 44% of children were attending pre-school institutions.

HEALTH. There were 29,900 doctors and 57,000 hospital beds in 1987.

ABKHAZIAN AUTONOMOUS SOVIET SOCIALIST REPUBLIC

Area, 8,600 sq. km (3,320 sq. miles); population (Jan. 1989), 537,000. Capital Sukhumi (1989 census population, 121,000). This area, the ancient Colchis, included Greek colonies from the 6th century B.C. onwards. From the 2nd century B.C. onwards, it was a prey to many invaders—Romans, Byzantines, Arabs, Ottoman Turks—before accepting a Russian protectorate in 1810. However, from the 4th century A.D. a West Georgian kingdom was established by the Lazi princes in the territory (known to the Romans as 'Lazica') and by the 8th century the prevailing language was Georgian and the name Abkhazia. In March 1921 a congress of local Soviets proclaimed it a Soviet Republic, and its status as an Autonomous Republic, within Georgia, was confirmed on 17 April 1930.

Population (1979 census) Abkhazians, 17·1%, Georgians, 43·9% and Russians, 16·4%.

140 deputies were elected to the republican Supreme Soviet on 24 Feb. 1985, 57 of them women.

The Abkhazian coast (along the Black Sea) possesses a famous chain of health resorts—Gagra, Sukhumi, Akhali-Antoni, Gulripsha and Gudauta—sheltered by thickly forested mountains.

The republic has coal, electric power, building materials and light industries. In 1985 there were 89 collective farms and 56 state farms; main crops are tobacco, tea, grapes, oranges, tangerines and lemons. Crop area 43,900 hectares.

Livestock, 1 Jan. 1987: 147,300 cattle, 127,900 pigs, 28,800 sheep and goats.

In 1986–87 about 100,000 pupils were engaged in study at all levels. A university has been opened in Sukhumi.

In Jan. 1985 there were 2,300 doctors and 6,000 hospital beds.

ADJARIAN AUTONOMOUS SOVIET SOCIALIST REPUBLIC

Area, 3,000 sq. km (1,160 sq. miles); population (Jan. 1989), 393,000. Capital, Batumi (1989 census population, 136,000). After a history similar to that of Abkhazia, it fell under Turkish rule in the 17th century, and was annexed to Russia (rejoining Georgia) after the Berlin Treaty of 1878. On 16 July 1921 the territory was constituted as an Autonomous Republic within the Georgian SSR.

Population (1979 census) Georgians, 80·1%, Russians, 9·8% and Armenians 4·6%.

110 deputies were elected to the republican Supreme Soviet on 24 Feb. 1985, 45 of them women.

The republic specializes in sub-tropical agricultural products. These include tea, mandarines and lemons, grapes, bamboo, eucalyptus, etc. Livestock (Jan. 1987): 133,400 cattle, 6,300 pigs, 11,600 sheep and goats. In 1980 there were 69 collective farms and 21 state farms.

There are shipyards at Batumi, modern oil-refining plant (the pipeline from the Baku oilfields ends at Batumi), food-processing and canning factories, clothing, building materials, drug factories, etc.

Health resorts are Kobuleti, Tsikhisdziri, Batumi on the coast and Beshumi in the hills. The sub-tropical climate and flora, and the combination of mountains and sea, make this republic (like Abkhazia) a favourite holiday area.

In 1986–87 79,800 pupils were engaged in study at all levels and 1,000 graduated from colleges.

In Jan. 1985 there were 1,430 doctors and 3,900 hospital beds.

SOUTH OSSETIAN AUTONOMOUS REGION

This area was populated by Ossetians from across the Caucasus (North Ossetia), driven out by the Mongols in the 13th century. The region was set up within the Georgian SSR on 20 April 1922. Area, 3,900 sq. km (1,505 sq. miles); population (Jan. 1989), 99,000 (1979 census, Ossetians, 66·4% and Georgians, 28·8%). Capital, Tskhinvali (34,000).

Main industries are mining, timber, electrical engineering and building materials. Crop area, chiefly grains, was 21,600 hectares in 1985; other pursuits are sheep-farming (128,500 sheep and goats on 1 Jan. 1987) and vine-growing. There were 14 collective farms and 18 state farms.

In 1986–87 there were 18,543 pupils in elementary and secondary schools; there were 1,967 graduates from higher educational institutions and 837 from colleges.

In Jan. 1987 there were 511 doctors and 1,400 hospital beds.

Further Reading

Lang, D. M., *A Modern History of Georgia*. London, 1962. — *The Georgians*. London, 1966
Gvarjaladze, T. and I. (eds.) *English-Georgian and Georgian-English Dictionary*. Tbilisi, 1974
Suny, R. G., *The Making of the Georgian Nation*. London, 1989
Istoriya Gruzii. 3 vols. Tbilisi, 1962–73

ARMENIA

Haikakan Sovetakan Sotsialistakan Hanrapetoutioun

HISTORY. On 29 Nov. 1920 Armenia was proclaimed a Soviet Socialist Republic. The Armenian Soviet Government, with the Russian Soviet Government, was a party to the Treaty of Kars (March 1921), which confirmed the Turkish possession of the former Government of Kars and of the Surmali District of the Government of Yerevan. From 1922 to 1936 it formed part of the Transcaucasian Soviet Federal Socialist Republic. In 1936 Armenia was proclaimed a constituent republic of the USSR.

AREA AND POPULATION. Armenia covers an area of 29,800 sq. km (11,490 sq. miles). It is bounded in the north by Georgia, in the east by Azerbaijan and in the south and west by Turkey and Iran. It is a very mountainous country with but little forest land, has many turbulent rivers and a highly fertile soil, but is subject to drought. In Jan. 1989 the population was 3,283,000. Census (1979) 89·7% of the population were Armenians, the rest are Russians (2·3%), Kurds (1·7%), Azerbaijanians (5·3%). The capital is Yerevan. Other large towns are Leninakan (120,000) and Kirovakan (159,000). An earthquake in Dec. 1988 caused extensive damage and the loss of an estimated 25,000 lives.

CONSTITUTION AND GOVERNMENT. The Supreme Soviet, elected in 1985, consists of 338 deputies; 121 are women, 216 Communists. A new Constitution was adopted in April 1978.

At elections to the district, urban and rural Soviets (21 June 1987), of 27,776 deputies returned 13,758 (49·5%) were women, 15,681 (56·5%) non-Party and 19,149 (68·9%) industrial workers and collective farmers.

Chairman, Presidium of the Supreme Soviet: G. M. Voskanyan.
Chairman, Council of Ministers: V. S. Markaryants.
First Secretary, Communist Party: S. G. Arutyunyan.

FINANCE. Budget estimates (in 1m. rubles), 1988, 2,243; 1989 (plan), 2,460.

AGRICULTURE. The chief agricultural area is the valley of the Arax and the area round Yerevan. Here there are considerable cotton plantations as well as orchards and vineyards. Sub-tropical plants, such as almonds and figs, are also grown. Olive groves and pomegranate plantations occupy large areas; experiments are being made to naturalize cork oak. In the mountainous areas the chief pursuit is livestock raising. Land under cultivation in Nov. 1986, 2·3m. hectares.

Output of main agricultural products (in 1,000 tonnes) in 1987: Grain, 274; potatoes, 296; vegetables, 570; sugar-beet, 105; fruit, 147; grapes, 169; meat, 123; milk, 579; eggs, 636m.; wool, 4·1.

Area of irrigated land in Armenia in 1982 was 284,000 hectares.

There were, on 1 Jan. 1987, 280 collective farms, and these together with the 513 state farms tilled 99·9% of the total cultivated area. Livestock in Jan. 1988 included 345,800 pigs, 834,100 cattle and 1·7m. sheep and goats. All the state farms and collective farms had been electrified by the end of 1960. There were 13,900 tractors and 1,500 grain and cotton combines in Jan. 1987.

INDUSTRY. Armenia contains large deposits of copper, zinc, aluminium, molybdenum and other metals. It is also rich in marble, granite, cement and other building materials. The mining of these minerals is becoming more and more important. Among other industries are the chemical, producing chiefly synthetic rubber and fertilizers, and the extraction and processing of building materials such as cement, pumice-stone, tuffs, marble, volcanic basalt and fire-proof clay, ginning- and textile-mills, carpet weaving, food, including wine-making, fruit, meat-canning and creameries. Machine-tool and electrical engineering works have also been established. Among the industrial centres are Yerevan, Leninakan, Alaverdi, Kafan, Kirovakan, Daval, Megri and Oktemberyan. Output of electricity in 1987 was 15,200m. kwh. A chain ('cascade') of 8 hydro-electric stations on the river Razdan, as it falls about 3,300 ft from the mountain lake Sevan to its junction with the Arax, has been completed.

In 1987 output included 74,600 centrifugal pumps, 165m. light bulbs, 129,600 km of light cable, 1·6m. cu. metres ferroconcrete, 86·1m. slates, 4·9m. clocks, 20·9m. pairs footwear, 106·1m. items knitwear, and 478·9m. jars of preserves.

There were 1,381,000 industrial and office workers employed in the national economy in 1987.

COMMUNICATIONS. Length of railways in Jan. 1988, 830 km; motor roads, 12,300 km (hard surface, 10,700).

Newspapers (1987). Out of 92 newspapers 81 appeared in Armenian. Daily circulation of Armenian-language newspapers, 1·6m., other languages, 136,000.

EDUCATION. In 1987–88 there were 600,000 pupils in 1,400 primary and secondary schools; 65 technical colleges with 48,100 students; 13 higher educational institutions with 55,700 students (including correspondence students). Yerevan houses the Armenian Academy of Sciences, 43 scientific institutes, a medical institute and other technical colleges, and a state university. In Jan. 1988, 33 learned institutions with 3,350 scientific staff are under the Academy of Sciences; scientific workers in 101 institutions totalled 22,000.

In Jan. 1988 40% of children attended pre-school institutions.

HEALTH. In 1987 there were 13,600 doctors and 29,700 hospital beds.

Further Reading

Kurkjian, V., *A History of Armenia*. New York, 1958
Lang, D.M., *Armenia: Cradle of Civilization*. London, 1978.—*The Armenians. A People in Exile*. London, 1981
Missakian, J., *A Searchlight on the Armenian Question, 1878–1950*. Boston, Mass., 1950

MOLDAVIAN SOVIET SOCIALIST REPUBLIC
Republika Sovietică Socialistă Moldovenească

HISTORY. The Moldavian Soviet Socialist Republic, capital Kishinev, was formed by the union of part of the former Moldavian Autonomous Soviet Socialist Republic (organized 12 Oct. 1924), formerly included in the Ukrainian Soviet Socialist Republic, and the areas of Bessarabia (ceded by Romania to the USSR, 28 June 1940) with a mainly Moldavian population. As from 2 Aug. 1940 the MSSR includes the following regions of the former Moldavian Autonomous Soviet Socialist Republic: Grigoriopol, Dubossarsk, Kamensk, Rybnits, Slobodzeisk and Tiraspol, and the following districts of Bessarabia: Beltsk, Bendery, Kagulsk, Kishinev, Orgeev and Sorok. The republic, however, is divided not into regions but into 36 rural districts, 21 towns and 45 urban settlements.

AREA AND POPULATION. Moldavia is bounded in the east and south by the Ukraine and on the west by Romania. The area is 33,700 sq. km (13,000 sq. miles). In Jan. 1989 the population was 4,341,000, of whom (1979 census) 63·9% are Moldavians. Others include Ukrainians (14·2%), Russians (12·8%), Gagauzi (3·5%), Jews (2%). Apart from Kishinev, larger towns are Tiraspol (182,000), Beltsy (159,000) and Bendery (130,000).

CONSTITUTION AND GOVERNMENT. The Supreme Soviet elected in 1985 consisted of 380 deputies. New elections, and local elections, were held on 25 Feb. 1990. A new Constitution was adopted in April 1978.

At elections to the district, urban and rural Soviets (21 June 1987), of 38,808 deputies returned, 19,060 (49·1%) were women, 21,951 (56·6%) non-Party and 25,930 (66·9%) industrial workers and collective farmers.

Chairman, Presidium of the Supreme Soviet: M. I. Snegur.
Chairman, Council of Ministers: I. P. Kalin.
First Secretary, Communist Party: P. K. Luchinsky.

FINANCE. Budget estimates (in 1m. rubles), 1988, 3,000; 1989 (plan), 3,396.

AGRICULTURE. On 1 Jan. 1987 there were 368 collective farms and 473 state farms. All ploughing and sowing is mechanized. Livestock included (1 Jan. 1988) 1·2m. cattle, 1·7m. pigs and 1·2m. sheep and goats. There were 53,200 tractors and 4,300 combine harvesters in Jan. 1987. Land under cultivation (Nov. 1986) 2·9m. hectares.

Output of main agricultural products (in 1,000 tonnes) in 1987: Grain, 2,011; sugar-beet, 2,111; vegetables, 1,282; fruit and berries, 1,053; grapes, 1,039; meat, 329; milk, 1,433; eggs, 1,141m.

Bessarabia has an equable climate and very fertile soil. It contains nearly one quarter of the vineyards of the USSR. Bessarabia is also rich in fish in the south: Sturgeon, mackerel, brill.

INDUSTRY. There are canning plants, wine-making plants, woodworking and metallurgical factories, a factory of ferro-concrete building materials, and footwear and textile plants. Moldavia takes third place in the USSR in the production of wine, tobacco and food-canning. Production in 1987 included 91,900 centrifugal pumps, 171·5m. slates, 20·9m. pairs footwear, 64m. items knitwear, 50,600 colour televisions, 161,500 refrigerators, 325,100 washing machines, 1,914m. jars of preserves. Meat and dairy produce are rapidly expanding food industries.

There are lignite, phosphorites, gypsum and valuable building materials.

In 1987 there were 1,591,000 industrial and office workers working in the national economy. Electricity generated (1986) 17,700m. kwh.

COMMUNICATIONS. Length of railways in Jan. 1988, 1,150 km. There are 16,500 km of motor roads (12,300 hard surface), and 263m. tonne-km of freight was carried on inland waterways.

Newspapers (1987). There were 189 newspapers, 79 in Moldavian. Daily circulation of Moldavian-language newspapers, 1,199,000, other languages, 1,232,000.

EDUCATION. In 1987–88 there were 700,000 pupils in 1,600 primary, secondary and special schools, 59,000 students in 52 technical colleges and 52,100 students in 9 higher educational institutions including the state university. A Moldavian Academy of Sciences was established in 1961: It had 17 research institutions and a scientific staff of 1,225 in Jan. 1988. In all, there are 68 learned institutions with 10,500 scientific staff. In Jan. 1988, 70% of children attended pre-school institutions.

HEALTH. In 1987 there were 16,600 doctors and 54,300 hospital beds.

Further Reading

Zlatova, Y. and Kotelnikov, V., *Across Moldavia* (English ed.). Moscow, 1959
Istoriya Moldavskoi SSR. 2nd ed. 2 vols. Kishinev, 1965–68

ESTONIA

Eesti Nõukogude Sotsialistlik Vabariik

HISTORY. The workers' and soldiers' Soviets in Estonia took over power on 8 Nov. 1917, were overthrown by the German occupying forces in March 1918, and were restored to power as the Germans withdrew in Nov. 1918, establishing the 'Estland Labour Commune'. It was overthrown with the assistance of British naval forces in May 1919, and a democratic republic proclaimed. In March 1934 this regime was, in turn, overthrown by a fascist *coup*.

The secret protocol of the Soviet-German agreement of 23 Aug. 1939 assigned Estonia to the Soviet sphere of interest. An ultimatum (16 June 1940) led to the formation of a government acceptable to the USSR; on 21 July the State Duma proclaimed the establishment of an Estonian Soviet Socialist Republic and applied to join the USSR: on 6 Aug. the Supreme Soviet accepted the application. The incorporation has been accorded *de facto* recognition by the British Government, but not by the US Government, which continues to recognize an Estonian consul-general in New York.

AREA AND POPULATION. Estonia is bounded west and north by the Baltic, east by the RSFSR and south by Latvia. Area, 45,100 sq. km (17,413 sq. miles); population, 1,573,000 (Jan. 1989). Census (1979) 64·7% were Estonians, 27·9% Russians, 2·5% Ukrainians and 1·6% Belorussians. The capital is Tallinn (1989 census population, 482,000). Other large towns are Tartu, Narva, Kohtla-Järve and Pärnu. There are 15 districts, 33 towns and 26 urban settlements.

CONSTITUTION AND GOVERNMENT. The Supreme Soviet, elected on 18 March 1990, consists of 105 deputies. On 30 March it resolved by 73 votes that it did not recognise the authority of the USSR.

At elections to district, urban and rural Soviets (21 June 1987), out of 11,164 deputies returned 5,472 (49%) were women, 6,140 (55%) non-Party and 7,325 (65·6%) industrial workers and collective farmers.

Chairman, Presidium of the Supreme Soviet: A. F. Riutel.
Chairman, Council of Ministers: I. Toome.
First Secretary, Communist Party: V. J. Valas.

FINANCE. Budget estimates (in 1m. rubles), 1988, 1,797; 1989 (plan), 2,035.

AGRICULTURE. Agriculture and dairy farming are the chief occupations. Area under cultivation was 2·6m. hectares in Nov. 1986. There were 142 agricultural and 8 fishery collectives and 152 state farms in 1987 using 21,100 tractors and 3,400 grain combines. 97% of state farms and 70% of collective farms were receiving electric power.

On 1 Jan. 1988 there were 821,200 head of cattle, 126,700 sheep and goats, and 1·1m. pigs.

Output of main agricultural products (in 1,000 tonnes) in 1987: Grain, 1,257; potatoes, 728; vegetables, 116; meat, 219; milk, 1,304; eggs, 550m.

INDUSTRY. Some 22% of the territory is covered by forests which provide good material for its sawmills, furniture, match and pulp industries, as well as wood fuel. Since the end of the war, 80,000 hectares have been afforested. 966,700 hectares of marsh land had been reclaimed by 1977.

Estonia has rich high-quality shale deposits (particularly in the north-east) which are estimated at 3,700m. tons. Shale output was 1·9m. tons in 1940 and 27·4m. in 1984. A factory for the production of gas from shale and a pipeline (208 km long) from Kohtla-Järve supplies shale gas to Leningrad and Tallinn. Estonian factories are now turning out agricultural and peat-digging machines, complex control and measuring instruments. The 'Volta' factory in Tallinn produces electric motors.

In the neighbourhood of Tallinn, phosphorites have been found, and in 1947 a plant for refining and for the production of super-phosphates was started. Estonia also contains valuable peat deposits, and some of her electrical stations work on peat. There are 350 rural electric stations. Electricity generated (1987) 17,800m. kwh. Output of paper in 1987 was 90,100 tonnes; leather footwear, 6·8m. pairs; knitwear, 22·9m. garments; preserves, 343m. jars.

In 1987 there were 716,000 industrial and office workers engaged in the national economy.

COMMUNICATIONS. Length of railways in 1988, 1,030 km. Estonia has 20 ports, but Tallinn handles four-fifths of the total sea-going transport. Length of motor roads, 28,700 km (hard surface, 27,000 km). Airlines link Tallinn with Moscow, Leningrad, Riga and the Estonian islands.

Newspapers (1987). There were 51 newspapers, 36 of them in Estonian. Daily circulation of Estonian-language newspapers, 1,266,000, other languages, 246,000.

EDUCATION. Estonia has retained an 11-year school curriculum, when it was reduced to 10 years elsewhere in the USSR. In 1987–88 pupils in 600 primary, secondary and special schools numbered 200,000. There were 23,400 students in 6 higher educational establishments, including Tartu (Dorpat) University, founded in 1632, and 21,400 students in 36 technical colleges.

The Estonian Academy of Sciences, founded in 1946, had 24 institutions with 1,287 scientific staff in Jan. 1988; in all, 7,200 scientific staff were working in 72 institutions.

In Jan. 1988 70% of children attended pre-school institutions.

HEALTH. In 1987 there were 7,500 doctors and 19,200 hospital beds.

Further Reading

Istoriya Estonskoi SSR. 3 vols. Tallin, 1961–74
Küng, A., *A Dream of Freedom*. Cardiff, 1980
Misiuras, R.-J. and Taagepera, R., *The Baltic States: Years of Dependence 1940–1980*. Farnborough, 1983

Parming, T. and Jarvesro, E., (eds.) *A Case Study of a Soviet Republic*. Boulder, 1978
Rank, M., *Inglise—eesti Sonaraamat*. Toronto, 1965
Raun, T. U., *Estonia and the Estonians*. Stanford, 1987
Saagpakk, P. F., *Estonian-English Dictionary*. New Haven, 1982

LATVIA

Latvijas Padomju Socialistiska Republika

HISTORY. In the part of Latvia unoccupied by the Germans, the Bolsheviks won 72% of the votes in the Constituent Assembly elections (Nov. 1917). Soviet power was proclaimed in Dec. 1917, but was overthrown when the Germans occupied all Latvia (Feb. 1918). Restored when they withdrew (Dec. 1918), it was overthrown once more by combined British naval and German military forces (May–Dec. 1919), and a democratic government set up. This régime was in turn replaced when a fascist *coup* took place in May 1934.

The secret protocol of the Soviet–German agreement of 23 Aug. 1939 assigned Latvia to the Soviet sphere of interest. An ultimatum (16 June 1940) led to the formation of a government acceptable to the USSR. On 21 July a People's Diet proclaimed the establishment of the Latvian Soviet Socialist Republic and applied to join the USSR, whose Supreme Soviet accepted the application on 5 Aug. The incorporation has been accorded *de facto* recognition by the British Government, but not by the US Government, which continues to recognize the Chargé d'Affaires in Washington, D.C.

AREA AND POPULATION. Latvia is bounded north by Estonia and the Baltic Sea, west by the Baltic, south by Lithuania and Belorussia and east by the RSFSR. Latvia has a total area of 63,700 sq. km (24,595 sq. miles). Population, Jan. 1989, 2,681,000, of whom (1979 census) 53·7% are Latvians and 32·8% Russians. There are 26 districts, 56 towns and 37 urban settlements.

The chief town is Riga (the capital); other principal towns are Daugavpils (Dvinsk), Liepāja, Jurmala, Jelgava (Mitau) and Ventspils (Windau).

CONSTITUTION AND GOVERNMENT. The Supreme Soviet elected in 1985 consisted of 325 deputies. New elections were held on 4 March 1990. A new Constitution was adopted in April 1978.

At elections to district, urban and rural Soviets (21 June 1987), of 23,398 deputies returned, 11,392 (48·7%) were women. New elections were held in Dec. 1989.

Chairman, Presidium of the Supreme Soviet: A. V. Gorbunov.
Chairman, Council of Ministers: Y. Y. Ruben.
First Secretary, Communist Party: Alfreds Rubiks.

FINANCE. Budget estimates (in 1m. rubles), 1988, 2,733; 1989 (plan), 3,133.

AGRICULTURE. Latvia is now no longer mainly an agricultural country. The urban population, 35% of the total in 1939, was 71% in Jan. 1986.

Latvian forest lands, state and private (2·4m. hectares), produced in 1937–38, 3·4m. cu. metres of timber; 1983 output, 4·2m. cu. metres.

Area under cultivation was 3·9m. hectares in Nov. 1986. 1·8m. hectares of marsh land have been drained (1983).

Cattle breeding and dairy farming are the chief agricultural occupations. Oats, barley, rye, potatoes and flax are the main crops.

After the establishment of the Soviet regime about 960,000 hectares were distributed among the landless peasants or those with very small holdings. On 1 Jan. 1987 there were 248 state farms and 331 (including 11 fishery) collective farms. There were 37,600 tractors and 7,900 grain combine harvesters. By 1 Jan. 1964, all state farms and collective farms were using electric power.

Livestock (1 Jan. 1988): Cattle, 1·5m. (1939: 1·3m.); sheep and goats, 170,000 (1939: 1·5m.); pigs, 1·7m. (1939: 891,500).

Output of main agricultural products (in 1,000 tonnes) in 1987: Grain, 2,086; sugar-beet, 352; potatoes, 1,135; vegetables, 194; meat, 338; milk, 1,972; eggs, 917m.

INDUSTRY. Latvia is the main producer of electric railway passenger cars and long-distance telephone exchanges in the USSR, fourth in output of paper and woollen goods, fifth of sawn timber, sixth of mineral fertilizers.

Industrial output in 1987 (in 1,000 tonnes) included: Paper, 145; hosiery, 77·8m. pairs; knitwear, 41·6m. garments; leather footwear, 10·8m. pairs; radio receivers, 1·9m.; washing machines, 660,000; railway carriages, 602; buses, 17,100; chemical fibre, 52·3; jars of preserves, 432m. Electricity generated (1987) 5,900m. kwh.

Peat deposits extend over 645,000 hectares or about 10% of the total area, and it is estimated that total deposits are 3,000–4,000m. tons; output of briquettes in 1987, 49,300 tonnes. There are also gypsum deposits; amber is frequently found in the coastal districts.

In 1987 industrial and office workers numbered 1,239,000.

COMMUNICATIONS. In Jan. 1988 the length of railways was 2,380 km, and motor roads, 28,200 km (hard surface, 20,300 km). Riga is the largest port in the Baltic after Leningrad. In 1986, 211m. tonne-km of freight was carried on inland waterways.

Newspapers (1987). There were 114 newspapers (68 in Lettish). Daily circulation of Lettish-language newspapers, 1·5m., other languages 529,000.

RELIGION. The Latvian Lutheran Church numbered 600,000 members in 1956.

EDUCATION. In 1987–88 there were 900 primary and secondary schools, with a total of 400,000 pupils: 64% of children attended pre-school institutions. Ten places of higher education had 43,700 students, 57 technical colleges had 40,700 students; there were also 21 music and art schools, 3 teachers' training colleges and an agricultural academy. In 1946 an Academy of Sciences was opened which in Jan. 1988 had 15 research institutes with a staff of 1,796 scientific workers; there were over 13,800 scientific workers in 101 research institutions.

HEALTH. There were 13,100 doctors and 37,400 hospital beds in 1987.

Further Reading

Latvian Academy of Sciences, *Istoriya Latviiskoi SSR*. Riga. 3 vols. 1952–58
Bilmanis, A., *A History of Latvia*. Princeton Univ. Press, 1951
Roze, B. and K., *Latviska–Angliska Vardnica*. Göppingen, 1948
Spekke, A., *History of Latvia*. Stockholm, 1951
Turkina, E., *Angliski–Latviska Vardnicā*. Riga, 1948.—*Latviešu-Anglu Vārdnicā*. Riga, 1962

LITHUANIA

Lietuvos Tarybu Socialistine Respublika

HISTORY. In 1914–15 the German army occupied the whole of Lithuania. On its withdrawal (Dec. 1918) Soviets were elected in all towns and a Soviet republic was proclaimed. In the summer of 1919 it was overthrown by Polish, German and nationalist Lithuanian forces, and a democratic republic established. In Dec. 1926 this regime was in turn overthrown by a fascist *coup*.

The secret protocol of the Soviet–German frontier treaty of 28 Sept. 1939 assigned the greater part of Lithuania to the Soviet sphere of influence. In Oct. 1939 the province and city of Vilnius (in Polish occupation 1920–39) were ceded by the USSR. An ultimatum (16 June 1940) led to the formation of a government acceptable to the USSR. A people's Diet, elected on 14–15 July, proclaimed the establishment of the Lithuanian Soviet Socialist Republic on 21 July and applied for admission to the USSR, which was effected by decree of the USSR Supreme Soviet on 3 Aug. and included also those parts of Lithuania which had been reserved for inclusion in Germany. This incorporation has been accorded *de facto* recognition by the British Government, but not by the US Government, which continues to recognize a Lithuanian Chargé d'Affaires in Washington, D.C. In March 1990 the newly-elected Lithuanian Supreme Soviet resolved to restore its previous independence; this decision was not accepted by the USSR government.

AREA AND POPULATION. Lithuania is bounded north by Latvia, east and south by Belorussia, west by Poland, the Kaliningrad area of the RSFSR and the Baltic Sea. The total area of Lithuania is 65,200 sq. km (25,170 sq. miles) and the population (Jan. 1989) 3,690,000, of whom 80% were Lithuanians, 8·6% Russians and 7·7% Poles (1979 census).

The capital is Vilnius (Vilna). Other large towns are Kaunas (Kovno), Klaipeda (Memel), Siauliai (145,000) and Panėvežys (126,000). There are 44 rural districts, 92 towns and 22 urban settlements.

CONSTITUTION AND GOVERNMENT. The Supreme Soviet was elected on 24 Feb. 1990.

At elections to district, urban and rural Soviets (21 June 1987), of 28,354 deputies returned, 13,680 (48·2%) were women, 15,321 (54%) non-Party and 18,197 (64·1%) industrial workers and collective farmers.

Chairman, Presidium of the Supreme Soviet: Vytautas Landsbergis.
Chairman, Council of Ministers: K. Pruskene.
First Secretary, Communist Party: A. K. Brazauskas.

FINANCE. Budget estimates (in 1m. rubles), 1988, 3,962; 1989 (plan), 4,581.

AGRICULTURE. Lithuania before 1940 was a mainly agricultural country, but has since been considerably industrialized. The urban population was 23% of the total in 1937 and 66% in Jan. 1986. The resources of the country consist of timber and agricultural produce. Of the total area, 49·1% is arable land, 22·2% meadow and pasture land, 16·3% forests and 12·4% unproductive lands.

Area under cultivation in Nov. 1986, 4·6m. hectares. By 1981 over 2·7m. hectares of swamps had been drained. Output of main agricultural products (in 1,000 tonnes) in 1987: Grain, 3,554; potatoes, 1,397; sugar-beet, 837; vegetables, 317; meat, 527; milk, 3,100; eggs, 1,252m. On 1 Jan. 1988 there were 2·5m. cattle, 2·7m. pigs, 91,100 sheep and goats.

Forests cover 1,554,000 hectares; 70% of the forests consist of conifers, mostly pines. Peat reserves total 4,000m. cu. metres.

Between 1940 and 1947 about 575,500 hectares (about 1·4m. acres) were distributed among the landless and poor peasant farmers. In 1987 there were 48,600 tractors and 12,200 grain combines serving 737 collective farms and 311 state farms.

INDUSTRY. Heavy engineering, shipbuilding and building material industries are developing. Industrial output included, in 1987: Industrial robots, 150; fuel pumps, 331,000; sulphuric acid, 440,000 tonnes; paper, 120,000 tonnes; carpet, 6·9m. sq. metres; tape recorders, 158,000; televisions, 658,000; leather footwear, 10·9m. pairs; granulated sugar, 239,000 tonnes; felled timber, 1·3m. cu. metres; knitwear, 61·2m. garments; hosiery, 102m. pairs; electric power, (1987) 22,800m. kwh. In 1987 there were 1,600,000 industrial and office workers employed in the national economy.

COMMUNICATIONS. Length of railways in Jan. 1988, 1,990 km. Vilnius has one of the largest airports of the USSR. There are 39,800 km of motor roads (29,200 km hard surface) and 161m. tonne-km of freight was carried on inland waterways in 1987. Klaipeda, as a non-freezing harbour and fishery base, is of national importance.

Newspapers (1987). Of 140 newspapers, 109 were in Lithuanian. Daily circulation of Lithuanian-language newspapers, 2·3m., other languages, 290,000.

RELIGION. In 1956, the Lithuanian Lutheran Church had 215,000 members; Roman Catholics, including those in Estonia and Latvia, numbered 2·5m.

EDUCATION. In 1987–88 there were 500,000 pupils in 2,200 primary and secondary schools. The University of Vytautas the Great, at Kaunas, was opened on 16 Feb. 1922. On 15 Jan. 1940 certain faculties were transferred to Vilnius to join the ancient University of Vilnius (founded 1570). In 1987–88 there were 12 higher educational institutions with 66,000 students: in 66 technical colleges of all kinds there were 58,800 students. The Lithuanian Academy of Sciences, founded in 1941, had 12 institutions with a total scientific staff of 1,924 in Jan. 1988; there were 88 scientific institutions with 15,200 research personnel. 64% of children in Jan. 1988 were attending pre-school institutions.

HEALTH. In 1987 there were 16,300 doctors and 46,300 hospital beds.

Further Reading

Jurgėla, C. R., *History of the Lithuanian Nation*. New York, 1948
Kantantas, A. and F., *A Lithuanian Bibliography*. Univ. of Alberta Press, 1975
Peteraitis, V., *Lithuanian–English Dictionary*. 2 vols. Chicago, 1960
Suziedlis, S., (ed.) *Encyclopedia Lituanica*. 6 vols. Boston, 1970–78
Vardys, S., (ed.) *Lithuania under the Soviets: Portrait of a Nation, 1940–45*. New York, 1965

SOVIET CENTRAL ASIA

Soviet Central Asia embraces the Kazakh Soviet Socialist Republic, the Uzbek Soviet Socialist Republic, the Turkmen Soviet Socialist Republic, the Tadzhik Soviet Socialist Republic and the Kirghiz Soviet Socialist Republic.

Turkestan (by which name part of this territory was then known) was conquered by the Russians in the 1860s. In 1866 Tashkent was occupied and in 1868 Samarkand, and subsequently further territory was conquered and united with Russian Turkestan. In the 1870s Bokhara was subjugated, the emir, by the agreement of 1873, recognizing the suzerainty of Russia. In the same year Khiva became a vassal state to Russia. Until 1917 Russian Central Asia was divided politically into the Khanate of Khiva, the Emirate of Bokhara and the Governor-Generalship of Turkestan.

In the summer of 1919 the authority of the Soviet Government became definitely established in these regions. The Khan of Khiva was deposed in Feb. 1920, and a People's Soviet Republic was set up, the medieval name of Khorezm being revived. In Aug. 1920 the Emir of Bokhara suffered the same fate, and a similar regime was set up in Bokhara. The former Governor-Generalship of Turkestan was constituted an Autonomous Soviet Socialist Republic within the RSFSR on 11 April 1921.

In the autumn of 1924 the Soviets of the Turkestan, Bokhara and Khiva Republics decided to redistribute the territories of these republics on a nationality basis; at the same time Bokhara and Khiva became Socialist Republics. The redistribution was completed in May 1925, when the new states of Uzbekistan, Turkmenistan and Tadzhikistan were accepted into the USSR as Union Republics. The remaining districts of Turkestan populated by Kazakhs were united with Kazakhstan which was established as an ASSR in 1925 and became a Union Republic in 1936. Kirghizia, until then part of the RSFSR, was established as a Union Republic in 1936.

Further Reading

Akiner, S., *The Islamic Peoples of the Soviet Union*. Rev. ed. London, 1986
Bennigsen, A. and Broxup, M., *The Islamic Threat to the Soviet State*. London, 1983

Nove, A. and Newth, J. A., *The Soviet Middle East.* London, 1967
Rwykin, M., *Moscow's Muslim Challenge.* New York, 1982
Wheeler, G., *The Modern History of Soviet Central Asia.* London, 1964.—*The Peoples of Soviet Central Asia.* London, 1966

KAZAKHSTAN

Kazak Soviettik Sotzialistik Respublikasy

HISTORY. On 26 Aug. 1920 Uralsk, Turgai, Akmolinsk and Semipalatinsk provinces formed the Kirgiz (in 1925 renamed Kazakh) Autonomous Soviet Socialist Republic within the RSFSR. It was made a constituent republic of the USSR on 5 Dec. 1936. To this republic were added the parts of the former Governorship of Turkestan inhabited by a majority of Kazakhs. It consists of the following regions: Aktyubinsk, Alma-Ata, Chimkent, Dzhambul, Dzhezkazgan, East Kazakhstan, Guryev, Karaganda, Kokchetav, Kustanai, Kzyl-Orda, Mangyshlak, North Kazakhstan, Pavlodar, Semipalatinsk, Taldy-Kurgan, Tselinograd, Turgai, Uralsk.

AREA AND POPULATION. Kazakhstan is bounded on the west by the Caspian Sea and the RSFSR, on the east by China, on the north by the RSFSR and on the south by Uzbekistan and Kirghizia. The area of the republic is 2,717,300 sq. km (1,049,155 sq. miles). It is the next in size to the RSFSR, is far larger than all the other Central Asian Soviet Republics combined and stretches nearly 3,000 km from west to east and over 1,500 km from north to south. Population (Jan. 1989) 16,538,000, of whom 57% live in urban areas. The Kazakhs form 36%, Russians 40·8% and Ukrainians 6·1% of the population (1979 census), as a result of the industrialization of the country since 1941 and the opening of virgin lands since 1945. The population includes over 100 nationalities.

The capital is Alma-Ata, formerly Verny; other large towns are Karaganda, Semipalatinsk, Chimkent and Petropavlovsk. In all there are 82 towns, 197 urban settlements and 221 rural districts.

CONSTITUTION AND GOVERNMENT. The Supreme Soviet elected in 1985 consisted of 510 deputies. New elections were held on 25 March 1990. A new Constitution was adopted in April 1978.

At elections to the regional, district, urban and rural Soviets (21 June 1987), out of 131,074 deputies returned, 64,717 (49·4%) were women. New elections were held in Dec. 1989.

President, Presidium of the Supreme Soviet: M. R. Sagdiev.
Chairman, Council of Ministers: (Vacant)
First Secretary, Communist Party: N. A. Nazarbaev.

FINANCE. The budget (in 1m. rubles) balanced as follows: 1988, 12,697; 1989 (plan), 14,254.

AGRICULTURE. Kazakh agriculture has changed from primarily nomad cattle breeding to production of grain, cotton and other industrial crops. In Nov. 1986 218·3m. hectares were under cultivation—over 20% of the total cultivated area of the USSR. 2,047,000 hectares of land have an irrigation network.

The 'Ukrainka' winter wheat has been transformed into a spring wheat suitable for cultivation in Kazakhstan. Tobacco, rubber plants and mustard are also cultivated. Kazakhstan has rich orchards and vineyards, which accounted for 95,000 hectares of cultivated land in 1985. Between 1954 and 1959, over 23m. hectares of virgin and long fallow land were opened up, 544 new state grain farms being organized for the purpose. State purchases of grain were 1·3m. tonnes in 1940, 12·3m. in 1971–75 (average), 12·6m. in 1981–85 (average) and 14·6m. in 1987.

Kazakhstan is noted for its livestock, particularly its sheep, from which excellent quality wool is obtained. The Akharomerino is a newly developed crossbreed of merino sheep and the wild Akhar mountain ram. Livestock on 1 Jan. 1988 included 9·7m. cattle, 36·4m. sheep and goats and 3·2m. pigs.

There were, on 1 Jan. 1987, 388 collective farms and 2,140 state farms with 241,200 tractors and 114,600 grain combine harvesters. There were 5,293 rural power stations of 307,800 kwh. capacity.

Output of main agricultural products (in 1m. tonnes) in 1987: Grain, 27·4; sugar-beet, 1·8; potatoes, 2·1; vegetables, 1·2; fruit and berries, 0·2; grapes, 0·1; meat, 1·4; milk, 5·2; eggs, 4,194m.; wool, 0·1.

INDUSTRY. Kazakhstan is extremely rich in mineral resources. Coal and tungsten in Karaganda (in the centre), oil along the river Emba (in the west), copper, lead and zinc—Kazakhstan contains about one-half of the total deposits of these three metals contained in the USSR—Iceland spar (in the south), nickel and chromium in the Kustanai and Semipalatinsk regions, molybdenum and other minerals.

In 1943 big deposits of manganese were found in Eastern Kazakhstan; new coal seams were also discovered there. In South Kazakhstan new copper and bauxite deposits have been found.

Coal, oil, non-ferrous metallurgy, heavy engineering and chemical industries have brought Kazakhstan to the third place among the industrial republics of the USSR. Production (1m. tonnes) in 1987 included iron ore, 24·2; sulphuric acid, 2; ferroconcrete, 7·3m. cu. metres; footwear, 37m. pairs; slates, 668m.; jars of preserves, 449·1m.; knitwear, 105·3m. items. The Leninogorsk and Chimkent lead plants, the Balkhash, Irtysh and Karaskpai copper-smelting works and others supply the country with non-ferrous metals. A meat-packing plant has been built in Semipalatinsk, a fish cannery in Guryev, a chemical plant in Aktyubinsk, a tractor works at Pavlodar, and a superphosphate plant in Dzhambul. The oil industry in Emba and Aktyubinsk yields high-quality aviation oil.

Aviation plays an important part in agriculture. About 14m. hectares were in 1984 treated from the air (destruction of pests, surface feeding of sugar-beet plantations, pollination of orchards, etc.).

Among recent enterprises are a large textile combine at Kustanai, hosiery factories at Djezkazgan, Leninogorsk and Aktyubinsk, a sugar factory at Aksu, meat canneries at Djetygar and Kzyl-Orda.

Electric power output in 1987 was 88,300m. kwh.

There were, in 1987, 6,586,000 industrial and office workers in the national economy.

COMMUNICATIONS

Roads. In 1988 there were 114,700 km of motor roads (93,200 km hard surface).

Railways. In 1988 the total length of railways in operation was 14,560 km. Over 600 km of narrow-gauge line and 700 km of broad-gauge line were built in the virgin lands area in 1951-57.

Inland waterways. In 1987 3,761m. tonne-km of freight was carried on inland waterways.

Newspapers (1987). Of 455 newspapers, 168 were in the Kazakh language. Daily circulation of Kazakh-language newspapers, 2m., in all languages, 6·5m.

EDUCATION. In 1987–88 there were 3·2m. pupils at 8,600 elementary and secondary schools; 246 technical colleges with 277,300 students, 55 higher educational institutions with 274,000 students, and 207 research institutes with 41,300 scientific personnel. The Kazakh Academy of Sciences, founded in 1945, had, in 1988, 31 institutions, the scientific staff of which numbered 4,548. 53% of children were attending pre-school institutions in Jan. 1988.

HEALTH. In 1987 there were 63,700 doctors and 219,200 hospital beds.

Further Reading

Istoriya Kazakhskoi SSR. 2 vols. Alma-Ata, 1957–59
Olcott, M. B., *The Kazakhs*. Stanford, 1987

TURKMENISTAN

Tiurkmenostan Soviet Sotsialistik Respublikasy

HISTORY. The Turkmen Soviet Socialist Republic was formed on 27 Oct. 1924 and covers the territory of the former Trans-Caspian Region of Turkestan, the Charjiui vilayet of Bokhara and a part of Khiva situated on the right bank of the Oxus. In May 1925 the Turkmen Republic entered the Soviet Union as one of its constituent republics.

AREA AND POPULATION. Turkmenistan is bounded on the north by the Autonomous Kara-Kalpak Republic, a constituent of Uzbekistan, by Iran and Afghánistán on the south, by the Uzbek Republic on the east and the Caspian Sea on the west. The principal Turkmen tribes are the Tekkés of Merv and the Tekkés of the Attok, the Ersaris, Yomuds and Goklans. All speak closely related varieties of a Turkic language (of the south-western group); many are Sunni Moslems.

The country passed under Russian control in 1881, after the fall of the Turkoman stronghold of Gök Tépé. Census (1979) 68·4% of the population were Turkmenians, most of whom were nomads before the First World War. 12·6% are Russians living mostly in urban areas, and 8·5% Uzbeks. There are also Kazakhs (2·9%), Tatars, Ukrainians, Armenians and others.

The area of Turkmenistan is 488,100 sq. km (186,400 sq. miles), and its population in Jan. 1989 was 3,534,000.

There are 5 regions: Chardzhou, Mary, Ashkhabad, Tashauz and Krasnovodsk, comprising 42 rural districts, 15 towns and 74 urban settlements.

The capital is Ashkhabad (Poltoratsk; 1989 census population, 398,000); other large towns are Chardzhou, Mary (Merv), Nebit-Dag and Krasnovodsk.

CONSTITUTION AND GOVERNMENT. The Supreme Soviet elected in 1985 consisted of 330 deputies. New elections were held on 7 Jan. 1990. A new Constitution was adopted in April 1978.

At elections to regional, district, urban and rural Soviets (21 June 1987), of 23,743 deputies returned, 11,501 (48·4%) were women. New elections were held on 7 Jan. 1990.

Chairman, Presidium of the Supreme Soviet: R. A. Bazarov.
Chairman, Council of Ministers: Kh. Akhmedov.
First Secretary, Communist Party: S. A. Niyazov.

FINANCE. Budget estimates (in 1m. rubles), 1988, 1,683; 1989 (plan), 1,934.

AGRICULTURE. The main occupation of the people is agriculture, based on irrigation. Turkmenistan produces cotton, wool, Astrakhan fur, etc. It is also famous for its carpets, and produces a special breed of Turkoman horses and the famous Karakul sheep.

There were 350 collective farms and 134 state farms in 1987, with 42,300 tractors and 1,600 grain combines. There were 608 rural power stations.

A considerable area is under Egyptian cotton, and from it has been evolved an original Soviet long-fibred cotton.

The main grain grown is maize. Sericulture, fruit and vegetable growing are also important; dates, olives, figs, sesame and other southern plants are grown. There is fishing in the Caspian. 34·7m. hectares were under cultivation in Nov. 1986.

Between 1958 and 1970 the Kara-Kum Canal was extended to 860 km. In 1971 the fourth section, to reach the Caspian, was begun to reach 1,000 km. By 1982 over 1,011,000 hectares had been irrigated.

Livestock on 1 Jan. 1988: Cattle, 777,800; pigs, 243,200; sheep and goats, 4·8m.

Output of main agricultural products (in 1,000 tonnes) in 1987: Grain, 354; cotton, 1,272; vegetables, 347; fruit and berries, 46; grapes, 155; meat, 95; milk, 392; eggs, 318m.; wool, 16.

INDUSTRY. Turkmenistan is rich in minerals, such as ozocerite, oil, coal, sulphur and salt. Industry is being developed, and there are now chemical, tailoring, textile, light, food, agricultural implements, cement and other factories, oil refineries, as well as ore-mining.

In the Kara-Kum Desert deposits of magnesium, minerals and coal have been discovered, as well as some 50 new saltmines. Here a new oil town, Nebit-Dag, has sprung up. On the Kara-Bogaz bay a sulphate industry has been developed. Industrial output in 1987 included oil and gas concentrate, 5·8m. tonnes; ferroconcrete, 0·8m. cu. metres; 10·5m. items knitwear, 5·4m. pairs footwear, 47·7m. jars preserves. Electric power output was 13,220m. kwh. in 1987.

In 1987 there were 845,000 industrial and office workers in the national economy.

COMMUNICATIONS. Length of motor roads in 1988, 21,100 km (16,800 km hard surface). Motor communication exists between Ashkhabad and Meshed (Iran).

Length of railways, 2,120 km. The line Chardzhou–Kungrad crosses the Chardzhou and Tashauz regions of Turkmenia and runs across Uzbekistan. Another line connects Chardzhou and Urgench. Inland waterways, 1,300 km.

Airlines connect Leninsk and Tashauz, and Ashkhabad and remote areas in the west, north and east.

Newspapers (1987). Of 70 newspapers, 56 were in the Turkmen language. Daily circulation of Turkmenian-language newspapers, 848,000; in all languages, 1,083,000.

EDUCATION. In 1987–88 there were 1,800 primary and secondary schools with 800,000 pupils, 9 higher educational institutions with 40,200 students, 37 technical colleges with 37,100 students, and 11 music and art schools. The Turkmen Academy of Sciences, founded in 1951, directs the work of 15 learned institutions with a staff of 1,094 scientific staff; there were 58 research institutions in all, with 5,600 research workers, in Jan. 1988.

In Jan. 1988, 31% of children were attending pre-school institutions.

HEALTH. In 1987 there were 12,000 doctors and 37,700 hospital beds.

Further Reading

Istoriya Turkmenskoi SSR. 2 vols. Ashkhabad, 1957

UZBEKISTAN

Ozbekiston Soviet Sotsialistik Respublikasy

HISTORY. In Oct. 1917 the Tashkent Soviet assumed authority, and in the following years established its power throughout Turkestan. The semi-independent Khanates of Khiva and Bokhara were first (1920) transformed into People's Republics, then (1923–24) into Soviet Socialist Republics and finally merged in the Uzbek SSR and other republics.

The Uzbek Soviet Socialist Republic was formed on 27 Oct. 1924 from lands formerly included in Turkestan. It includes a large part of the Samarkand region, the southern part of the Syr Darya, Western Ferghana, the western plains of Bukhara, the Kara-Kalpak ASSR and the Uzbek regions of Khorezm. In May 1925 Uzbekistan, by the decision of the Congress of Soviets of the USSR, was accepted as one of the constituent republics of the Soviet Union.

AREA AND POPULATION. Uzbekistan is bordered on the north by the

Kazakh Soviet Socialist Republic, on the east by the Kirghiz Soviet Socialist Republic and the Tadzhik Soviet Socialist Republic, on the south by Afghánistán and on the west by the Turkmen Soviet Socialist Republic. The Uzbeks, who form 68·7% (1979 census) of the population, were the ruling race in Central Asia until the arrival of the Russians during the third quarter of the 19th century. The several native states over which Uzbek dynasties formerly ruled were founded in the 15th century upon the ruins of Tamerlane's empire. The Uzbek speak Jagatai Turkish, which is related to Osmanli and Azerbaijan Turkish; many are Sunni Moslems. Russians numbered (census 1979) 10·8%, Tadzhiks, 3·9%, Tatars 4·2%.

The area of Uzbekistan is 447,400 sq. km (172,741 sq. miles). The population in Jan. 1989 was 19,906,000 (41% urban). The country comprises the following regions: Andizhan, Bukhara, Dzhizak, Ferghana, Kashkadar, Khorezm, Namangan, Navoi, Samarkand, Surkhan-Darya, Syr-Darya, Tashkent and the Autonomous Soviet Socialist Republic of Kara Kalpakia. The capital of the Republic is Tashkent; other large towns are Samarkand, Andizhan, Namangan. There are 124 towns, 97 urban settlements and 155 rural districts.

On 19 Sept. 1963 the Supreme Soviet of the USSR confirmed decisions of the Supreme Soviets of Kazakhstan and Uzbekistan, transferring over 40,000 sq. km from the former to the latter to ensure more efficient use of the 'Hungry Steppe'.

CONSTITUTION AND GOVERNMENT. The Supreme Soviet elected in 1985 consisted of 510 deputies. New elections were held on 18 Feb. 1990. A new Constitution was adopted in April 1978.

At elections to the regional, district, urban and rural Soviets (21 June 1987), of 105,484 deputies returned, 50,460 (47·8%) were women. New elections were held on 18 Feb. 1990.

President, Presidium of the Supreme Soviet: M. M. Ibragimov.
Chairman, Council of Ministers: M. M. Mirkaymov.
First Secretary, Communist Party: I. A. Karimov.

FINANCE. Budget estimates (in 1m. rubles), 1988, 9,012; 1989 (plan), 10,029.

AGRICULTURE. Uzbekistan is a land of intensive farming, based on artificial irrigation. It is the chief cotton-growing area in the USSR and the third in the world. About 3·7m. hectares of collective and state farmland have irrigation networks, totalling over 150,000 km in length, and all are in full use.

In 1939 the Ferghana Canal (270 km) was built. During 1940, among the irrigation canals completed were: The North Ferghana Canal (165 km), and Andreyev South Ferghana Canal (108 km) and the first section of the Tashkent Canal (63 km). A canal from the Amu-Darya to Bokhara across the Kzyl-Kum and Ust-Urt deserts (180 km) was completed in 1965. A 200-km canal joining the river Zeravshan with the Kashka Darya at the village of Paruz was completed in Aug. 1955; it is part of the Iski–Angara Canal. The first section (93 km) of a canal irrigating the southern 'Hungry Steppe' was opened in 1960; 500,000 hectares of this desert were under cultivation in 1967.

Agriculture flourishes, particularly in the well-watered, warm, rich oases areas, such as the Ferghana valley, Zeravshan, Tashkent and Khorezm, where cotton, fruit, silk and rice are cultivated. In the higher-lying plains grain is grown; the wide desert and semi-desert area of Western Uzbekistan is mainly given to pasture land and the breeding of the Karakul sheep; there is a Karakul institute at Samarkand.

Orchards occupied 206,000 hectares and the vineyards 133,000 hectares in 1985. The Central Asian Branch of the Scientific Research Institute of Viticulture in Tashkent has produced new frost resistant grapes by crossing the wild Amur grape with Central Asian and European types. In 1987 there were 856 collective farms and 1,085 state farms, with 192,800 tractors and 10,500 cotton picking and grain combines. Ploughing, cotton-sowing and cultivation are completely mechanized; cotton picking over 46%.

Uzbekistan provides 65% of the total cotton, 50% of the total rice and 60% of the total lucerne grown in the USSR. The area under cultivation was 33·1m. hectares in Nov. 1986.

Livestock on 1 Jan. 1987: 4·1m. cattle, 8·5m. sheep and goats and 761,200 pigs.

Output of main agricultural products (in 1,000 tonnes) in 1987: Grain, 1,823; cotton, 4,858; potatoes, 262; vegetables, 2,558; fruit and berries, 595; grapes, 638; meat, 403; milk, 2,615; eggs, 2,186m.; wool, 24·3.

Afforestation over an area of 50,000 hectares has been carried out to protect the Bokhara and Karakul oases from the advancing Kzyl-Kum sands and to stop the sand-drifts in a number of districts of Central Ferghana.

INDUSTRY. Of its mineral resources, in addition to oil and coal, copper and building materials and ozocerite deposits are now also exploited. New very rich coal deposits were discovered in 1944 and 1947 near Tashkent.

There are over 1,600 factories and mills. They include a factory of agricultural machinery (in Tashkent), a cement factory, a sulphur-mine, an oxygen factory, a paper-mill, a leather factory, textile-mills, clothing factories, iron and steel works, the Chirchik electro-chemical plant, a superphosphate plant in Kokand and oil refineries, coalmines, etc. Output in 1987 included 25,800 tractors, 7,700 cotton harvesting machines, 25,000 tonnes of paper, 6·3m. cu. metres of ferroconcrete, 1·4m. Karakul skins, 95·7m. items of knitwear, 39m. pairs of footwear, 1,135m. jars of preserves. Gold is being worked at Muruntau, Chadak and Kochbulak.

The Tashkent power station (2m. kw.) was completed in 1971. Power output in 1987 was 54,700m. kwh. (481m. kwh. in 1940). Two natural-gas pipelines (Djaikak–Tashkent, Ferghana–Kokand) and a third from Bokhara to the Urals are operating. Natural gas output (1987) was 39,800m. cu. metres.

In 1987 there were 5,036,000 industrial and office workers in the national economy.

COMMUNICATIONS. The total length of railway in 1988 was 3,490 km. Branches lead to Karshe-Kitab, Kerki-Termez, Jalal-Abad, Namangan, Andijan and other centres. In 1947–55 a new line was built from Chardzhou to Kungrad.

The Great Uzbek Highway was completed in April 1941. Total length of motor roads in 1988 was 92,800 km (hard surface, 69,800 km). Inland waterways, 1,100 km.

An airline, serving all of Central Asia, is most developed in Uzbekistan.

Newspapers (1987). There were 197 newspapers in the Uzbek language out of a total of 289. Daily circulation of Uzbek-language newspapers, 4·6m.; in all languages, 6·1m.

EDUCATION. In 1987–88 there were 8,100 elementary and secondary schools with 4·4m. pupils, 43 higher educational establishments with 300,300 students and 248 technical colleges with 292,000 students. Uzbekistan has an Academy of Sciences, founded in 1943, with 37 institutions and 4,207 academic staff; there were 188 research institutes with a scientific staff of 39,100 in Jan. 1988. There are universities and medical schools in Tashkent and Samarkand. In Jan. 1988, 34% of children were attending pre-school institutions.

The Uzbek Arabic script was in 1929 replaced by the Latin alphabet which in 1940 was superseded by one based on the Cyrillic alphabet.

HEALTH. In 1987 there were 67,800 doctors and 235,400 hospital beds.

Further Reading

Istoriya Uzbekskoi SSR. 4 vols. Tashkent, 1967–68

Waterson, N., (ed.) *Uzbek-English Dictionary*. London, 1980

KARAKALPAK AUTONOMOUS SOVIET SOCIALIST REPUBLIC

Area, 164,900 sq. km (63,920 sq. miles); population (Jan. 1989), 1,214,000. Capital, Nukus (1989 census population, 169,000). The Karakalpaks are first mentioned in written records in the 16th century as tributary to Bokhara, and later to the Kazakh Khanate. In the second half of the 19th century, as a result of the Russian conquest of Central Asia, they came under Russian rule. On 11 May 1925 the territory was constituted within the then Kazakh Autonomous Republic (of the Russian Federation) as an Autonomous Region. On 20 March 1932 it became an Autonomous Republic within the Russian Federation, and on 5 Dec. 1936 it became part of the Uzbek SSR. Census (1979) Karakalpaks were 31·1% of population, Uzbeks, 31·5% and Kazakhs, 26·9%.

185 deputies were elected to its Supreme Soviet on 24 Feb. 1985, of whom 69 were women and 118 Communists.

Its manufactures are in the field of light industry—bricks, leather goods, furniture, canning, wine. In Jan. 1987 cattle numbered 348,600 and sheep and goats, 523,900. There were 38 collective and 124 state farms. The total cultivated area in 1985 was 350,400 hectares.

In 1986–87 there were 286,800 pupils at schools, 21,400 at technical colleges, and 6,200 at Nukus University. There is a branch of the Uzbek Academy of Sciences with 190 scientific staff.

There were 2,600 doctors and 12,800 hospital beds.

TADZHIKISTAN

Respublikai Sovieth Sotsialistii Tojikiston

HISTORY. The Tadzhik Soviet Socialist Republic was formed from those regions of Bokhara and Turkestan where the population consisted mainly of Tadzhiks. It was admitted as a constituent republic of the Soviet Union on 5 Dec. 1929.

AREA AND POPULATION. Tadzhikistan is situated between 39° 40' and 36° 40' N. lat. and 67° 20' and 75° E. long., north of the Oxus (Amu-Darya). On the west and north it is bordered by Uzbekistan and by the Kirghiz Soviet Socialist Republic; on the east by Chinese Turkestan and on the south by Afghánistán. It includes three regions (Leninabad, Kurgan-Tyube and Kulyab) and 43 rural districts, 18 towns and 49 urban settlements, together with the Gorno-Badakhshan Autonomous Region. Its highest mountains are Communism Peak (7,495 metres) and Lenin Peak (7,127 metres). Even the lowest valleys in the Pamirs are not below 3,500 metres above sea-level. The huge mountain glaciers are the source of many rapid rivers—the tributaries of the Amu-Darya, which flows from east to west along the southern border of Tadzhikistan. About 58·8% of the population are Tadzhiks. They speak an Iranian dialect, little different from Persian, and they are considered to be the descendants of the original Aryan population of Turkestan. Unlike the Persians, the Tadzhiks are mostly Sunnis. Of the rest, 22·9% are Uzbeks living in the north-west of the republic. Russians and Ukrainians number 10·4% (1979 census).

The area of the territory is 143,100 sq. km (55,240 sq. miles). Population (Jan. 1989), 5,112,000. The capital is Dushanbe. Other large towns are Leninabad (153,000), Kurgan-Tyube, Kulyab.

CONSTITUTION AND GOVERNMENT. The Supreme Soviet elected in 1985 consisted of 350 deputies. New elections were held on 25 Feb. 1990. A new Constitution was adopted in April 1978.

At elections to the district, urban and rural Soviets and the regional Soviet of Gorno-Badakhshan (21 June 1987), out of 28,801 deputies returned 14,116 (49%) were women. New elections were held in Dec. 1989.

Chairman, Presidium of the Supreme Soviet: G. Pallaev.
Chairman, Council of Ministers: I. Kh. Khaeev.
First Secretary, Communist Party: K. M. Makhkamov.

FINANCE. Budget estimates (in 1m. rubles), 1988, 2,109; 1989 (plan), 2,375.

AGRICULTURE. The occupations of the population are mainly farming, horticulture and cattle breeding. Area under cultivation in Nov. 1986 was 9·6m. hectares. There are 43,000 km of irrigation canals: The irrigation networks cover about 634,000 hectares of land.

Tadzhikistan grows many varieties of fruit, including apricots, figs, olives, pomegranates, a local variety of lemons and oranges, and in the south sugar-cane has been grown. Even on the highest mountain plateaux of the Pamirs, 'the roof of the world', the biological station of Tadzhikistan (3,860 metres above sea-level) has succeeded in raising crops of 60 varieties of barley, 10 varieties of oats, 4 of wheat, as well as vegetables. Eucalyptus and geranium are grown for the perfumery industry. Jute, rice and millet are also grown.

Tadzhikistan contains rich pasture lands, and cattle breeding is a very important branch of its agriculture. Livestock on 1 Jan. 1988: 1·3m. cattle, 3·2m. sheep and goats and 231,900 pigs.

The Gissar sheep is famous in the south for its meat and fat; the Karakul sheep is widely bred for its wool.

There were 157 collective farms (all with electric power) and 299 state farms in 1987, with 35,100 tractors and 1,600 cotton and grain combine harvesters.

Output of main agricultural products (in 1,000 tonnes) in 1987: Grain, 359; cotton, 872; potatoes, 276; vegetables, 510; fruit and berries, 202; grapes, 131; meat, 115; milk, 567; eggs, 585m.; wool, 5·2.

INDUSTRY. The original small-scale handicraft industries have been replaced by big industrial enterprises, including mining, engineering, food, textile, clothing and silk factories.

There are rich deposits of brown coal, lead, zinc and oil (in the north of the republic), rare elements, such as uranium, radium, arsenic and bismuth. Asbestos, mica, corundum and emery, lapis lazuli, potassium salts, sulphur and other minerals have been found in other parts of the republic.

Industrial output in 1987 included 1,230,000 cu. metres ferroconcrete, 302m. bricks, 14·4m. items knitwear, 10·1m. pairs footwear, 347m. jars of preserves.

There are 80 big electrical stations. The hydro-electric Varzob station began to operate in 1954, that at Kairak-Kum on the Syr Darya River was completed in 1957 and 2 more at Murgab in 1964. Output in 1987 was 15,857m. kwh. (in 1940, 62m. kwh.).

Construction of an electro-chemical combine, the largest in the USSR, has begun in the Yavan steppe in south Tadzhikistan, and the 3·2m. kw. power station in the upper reaches of the Vakhsh River was near completion in 1979.

In 1987 there were 1,151,000 industrial and office workers in the national economy.

COMMUNICATIONS

Roads. In Jan. 1988 there were 19,100 km of motor roads. Of these, 15,900 km are hard surface, including the Osh–Khorog (700 km), Yasui–Bazar–Charm (107 km) and Dushanbe–Khorog in the Pamirs (557 km) roads.

Railways. A railway line between Termez and Dushanbe (258 km) connects the republic with the railway system of the USSR. The mountainous nature of the republic makes ordinary railway construction difficult; accordingly 345 km of narrow gauge railways have been constructed (Kurgan–Tyube–Piandzh and Dushanbe–Kurgan–Tyube, connecting Dushanbe with the cotton-growing Vakhsh valley are particularly important). Length of railways, 1988, 470 km.

Aviation. Dushanbe is connected by air with Moscow, Tashkent, Baku and the regional and district centres of the republic.

Shipping. A steamship line on the Amu-Darya runs between Termez, Sarava and Jilikulam on the river Vakhsh (200 km).

Newspapers (1987). There were 73 newspapers, 61 in Tadzhik. Daily circulation of Tadzhik-language newspapers, 1,130,000; in all languages, 1,506,000.

EDUCATION. In 1987–88 there were 3,000 primary and secondary schools with 1·2m. pupils, 10 higher educational institutions with 56,400 students and 41 technical colleges with 42,300 students; the Tadzhik state university had 12,467 students. In Jan. 1988, 16% of children were attending pre-school institutions. In 1951 an Academy of Sciences was established; it has 16 institutions, the scientific staff of which numbers 1,502; there are 61 research institutions in all, with 9,000 scientific personnel in Jan. 1988. The Pamir research station is the highest altitude meteorological observatory in the world.

In 1940 a new alphabet based on Cyrillic was introduced.

HEALTH. There are 325 hospitals as well as maternity homes, clinics and special institutes to combat tropical diseases. There were 13,500 doctors in 1987 and 51,800 hospital beds.

GORNO-BADAKHSHAN AUTONOMOUS REGION

Comprising the Pamir massif along the borders of Afghánistán and China, the region was set up on 2 Jan. 1925. Area, 63,700 sq. km (24,590 sq. miles); population (Jan. 1989), 161,000 (83% Tadjiks, 11% Kirghiz). Capital, Khorog (14,800). The inhabitants are predominantly Ismaili Moslems.

Mining industries are developed (gold, rock-crystal, mica, coal, salt). Wheat, fruit and fodder crops are grown and cattle and sheep are bred in the western parts. In 1987 there were 74,700 cattle, 343,300 sheep and goats. Total area under cultivation, 18,400 hectares.

In 1986 3,494 pupils completed secondary education.

Further Reading

Academy of Science of Tadzhikistan, *Istoriya Tadzhikskogo Naroda.* 3 vols. Moscow, 1963–65

Luknitsky, P., *Soviet Tajikistan* [In English]. Moscow, 1954

KIRGHIZIA

Kyrgyz Sovietik Sotsialistik Respublikasy

HISTORY. After the establishment of the Soviet regime in Russia, Kirghizia became part of Soviet Turkestan, which itself became an Autonomous Soviet Socialist Republic within the RSFSR in April 1921. In 1924, when Central Asia was reorganized territorially on a national basis, Kirghizia was separated from Turkestan and formed into an autonomous region within the RSFSR. On 1 Feb. 1926 the Government of the RSFSR transformed Kirghizia into an Autonomous Soviet Socialist Republic within the RSFSR, and finally in Dec. 1936 Kirghizia was proclaimed one of the constituent Soviet Socialist Republics of the USSR.

AREA AND POPULATION. The territory of Kirghizia covers 198,500 sq. km (76,460 sq. miles), and its population in Jan. 1989 was 4,291,000. The republic comprises 3 regions: Issyk-Kul, Naryn and Osh. There are 18 towns, 31 urban settlements and 40 rural districts. Its capital is Frunze (formerly Pishpek). Other large towns are Osh (213,000), Przhevalsk (56,000), Kyzyl-Kiya, Tokmak.

Kirghizia is situated on the Tien-Shan mountains and bordered on the east by China, on the west by Kazakhstan and Uzbekistan, on the north by Kazakhstan and in the south by Tadzhikistan. The Kirghizians are of Turkic origin and form 47·9%

(1979 census) of the population; the rest are Russians (25·9%), Ukrainians (3·1%), Uzbeks (12·1%) and Tatars (2%).

CONSTITUTION AND GOVERNMENT. The Supreme Soviet elected in 1985 consisted of 350 deputies. New elections were held on 25 Feb. 1990. A new Constitution was adopted in April 1978.

At elections to the regional, district, urban and rural Soviets (21 June 1987), of the 28,063 deputies returned, 13,652 (48·6%) were women. New elections were held on 25 Feb. 1990.

Chairman, Presidium of the Supreme Soviet: T. Akmatov.
Chairman, Council of Ministers: A. D. Dzhumagulov.
First Secretary, Communist Party: A. M. Masaliev.

FINANCE. Budget estimates (in 1m. rubles), 1988, 2,388; 1989 (plan), 2,692.

AGRICULTURE. Kirghizia is famed for its livestock breeding. On 1 Jan. 1988 there were 1·2m. cattle, 386,400 pigs, 10·4m. sheep and goats. Yaks are bred as meat and dairy cattle, and graze on high altitudes unsuitable for other cattle. Crossed with domestic cattle, hybrids are produced much heavier than ordinary Kirghiz cattle and giving twice the yield of milk. The Kirghizian horse is famed for its endurance, but it is of small stature; it has in recent years been crossed with Don, Arab and other breeds.

On 1 Jan. 1986 there were 176 collective and 290 state farms. Area under cultivation (Nov. 1986), 16·1m. hectares. There were 29,200 tractors and 4,900 grain combine harvesters in 1987; nearly all collective and state farms received electric power.

Kirghizia raises wheat sufficient for its own use and other grains and fodder, particularly lucerne; also sugar-beet, hemp, kenaf, kendyr, tobacco, medicinal plants and rice. Sericulture, fruit, grapes and vegetables and bee-keeping are major branches of Kirghiz agriculture. Agriculture is highly mechanized; nearly all the area under crops is worked by tractors. In 1983 irrigation networks in collective and state farms covered 974,000 hectares; practically all were in use. A canal in the western Tien-Shan ranges and a reservoir in the Urto-Tokoi mountains are being constructed.

The health resorts of Jety-Oguz (7,200 ft) and Jalal-Abad are famous for their mild alpine climate and mineral springs.

Output of main agricultural products (in 1,000 tonnes) in 1987: Grain, 1,910; cotton, 73; potatoes, 287; vegetables, 491; fruit and berries, 91; grapes, 36; meat, 205; milk, 1,012; eggs, 603m.; wool, 37·2.

INDUSTRY. Kirghizia contains over 500 large modern industrial enterprises including sugar refineries, tanneries, cotton and wool-cleansing works, flour-mills, a tobacco factory, food, timber, textile, engineering, metallurgical, oil and mining enterprises.

Production in 1987 included 337m. light bulbs, 47,900 centrifugal pumps, 27·2m. pairs hosiery, 218,400 washing machines, 1,115,000 cu. metres ferroconcrete, 11m. pairs footwear, 139·5m. jars preserves, 26·2m. bottles of mineral water.

Hydro-electric power stations are being built in the Central Tien-Shans and the cotton-growing districts in the Osh Region, the Chui valley and on the shore of Lake Issyk-Kul. Power output (1986) was 11,400m. kwh.

There were, in 1987, 1,261,000 industrial and office workers in the national economy.

COMMUNICATIONS. In the north a railway runs from Lugovaya through Frunze to Rybachi on Lake Issyk-Kul. Towns in the southern valleys are linked by short lines with the Ursatyevskaya–Andizhan railway in Uzbekistan. Total length of railway (Jan. 1988) is 370 km. Most of the traffic is by road; there were 39,200 km of motor roads (21,900 hard surface) in 1988. A road tunnel through the Tien-Shan mountains at an altitude of 9,600 ft, connecting Frunze and Osh, is being constructed. Inland waterways, 600 km. Airlines link Frunze with Moscow and Tashkent.

Newspapers (1987). Of 116 newspapers with a daily 1·6m. circulation, 62 with 931,000 circulation are in the Kirghiz language.

EDUCATION. Kirghizia had 1,700 primary and secondary schools with 900,000 pupils in 1987–88; 30% of children were attending pre-school institutions. There were also 10 higher educational institutions with 57,500 students, 47 technical and teachers' training colleges with 50,800 students, as well as music and art schools. The Kirghizian Academy of Sciences was established in 1954. In 1988 there were 18 research institutes, with 1,548 scientific staff, operating under its auspices; altogether there were 10,100 scientific staff in 1988. A university was opened in 1951. In Sept. 1940 a new alphabet, based on Cyrillic, was introduced.

HEALTH. In 1987 there were 14,900 doctors and 50,200 hospital beds.

Further Reading

Istoriya Kirgizskoi SSR. 5 vols. Frunze, 1984 ff.
Ryazantsev, S. N., *Kirghizia.* Moscow, 1951

UNITED ARAB EMIRATES

Federal Capital: Abu Dhabi
Population: 1·6m. (1988)
GNP per capita: US$15,720 (1988)

HISTORY. From Sha'am, 35 miles south-west of Ras Musam dam, for nearly 400 miles to Khor al Odeid at the south-eastern end of the peninsula of Qatar, the coast, formerly known as the Trucial Coast, of the Gulf (together with 50 miles of the coast of the Gulf of Oman) belongs to the rulers of the 7 Trucial States. In 1820 these rulers signed a treaty prescribing peace with the British Government. This treaty was followed by further agreements providing for the suppression of the slave trade and by a series of other engagements, of which the most important are the Perpetual Maritime Truce (May 1853) and the Exclusive Agreement (March 1892). Under the latter, the sheikhs, on behalf of themselves, their heirs and successors, undertook that they would on no account enter into any agreement or correspondence with any power other than the British Government, receive foreign agents, cede, sell or give for occupation any part of their territory save to the British Government.

British forces withdrew from the Gulf at the end of 1971 and the treaties whereby Britain had been responsible for the defence and foreign relations of the Trucial States were terminated, being replaced on 2 Dec. 1971 by a treaty of friendship between Britain and the United Arab Emirates. The United Arab Emirates (formed 2 Dec. 1971) consists of the former Trucial States: Abu Dhabi, Dubai, Sharjah, Ajman, Umm al Qaiwain, Ras al Khaimah (joined in Feb. 1972) and Fujairah. The small state of Kalba was merged with Sharjah in 1952.

AREA AND POPULATION. The Emirates are bounded north by the Gulf and Oman, east by the Gulf of Oman and Oman, south and west by Saudi Arabia, north-west by Qatar. The area of these states is approximately 32,300 sq. miles (83,657 sq. km). The total population at census (1985), 1,622,393. Estimate (1988) 1·6m. In 1980, 69% were male and 72% lived in urban areas. About one-tenth are nomads.

Population of the 7 Emirates, 1985 census: Abu Dhabi, 670,125; Ajman, 64,318; Dubai, 419,104; Fujairah, 54,425; Ras al-Khaimah, 116,470; Sharjah, 268,722; Umm al Qaiwain, 29,229.

The chief cities (1980 census) are Dubai (265,702), Abu Dhabi, the provisional federal capital (242,975), Sharjah (125,149) and Ras al-Khaimah (42,000).

CLIMATE. The country experiences desert conditions, with rainfall both limited and erratic. The period May to Nov. is generally rainless, while the wettest months are Feb. and March. Temperatures are very high in the summer months. Dubai. Jan. 74°F (23·4°C), July 108°F (42·3°C). Annual rainfall 2·4" (60 mm). Sharjah. Jan. 64°F (17·8°C), July 91°F (32°C). Annual rainfall 4·2" (105 mm).

GOVERNMENT. The Emirates is a federation, headed by a Supreme Council which is composed of the 7 rulers and which in turn appoints a Council of Ministers. The Council of Ministers drafts legislation and a federal budget; its proposals are submitted to a federal National Council of 40 elected members which may propose amendments but has no executive power.

President: HH Sheikh Zayed bin Sultan al Nahyan, Ruler of Abu Dhabi.

Members of the Supreme Council of Rulers:

HH Sheikh Rashid bin Said al-Maktoum, Vice-President and Ruler of Dubai.
HH Sheikh Sultan bin Mohammed al-Qasimi, Ruler of Sharjah.
HH Sheikh Saqr bin Mohammed al-Qasimi, Ruler of Ras al-Khaimah.
HH Sheikh Rashid bin Ahmed al-Mualla, Ruler of Umm al Qaiwain.
HH Sheikh Hamad bin Mohammed al Sharqi, Ruler of Fujairah.
HH Sheikh Humaid bin Rashid al-Nuaimi, Ruler of Ajman.

The Council of Ministers in Dec. 1989 was:

Prime Minister: H.H. Sheikh Rashid bin Said al-Maktoum.

Deputy Prime Minister: Sheikh Maktoum bin Rashid al-Maktoum.

Interior: Sheikh Mubarak bin Mohammed al-Nahyan. *Finance and Industry:* Sheikh Hamdan bin Rashid al-Maktoum. *Defence:* Sheikh Mohammed bin Rashid al-Maktoum. *Economy and Trade:* Saif al-Jarwan. *Information and Culture:* Sheikh Ahmed bin Hamed. *Communications:* Mohammed Saeed al-Mualla. *Public Works and Housing:* Mohammed Khalifa al-Kindi. *Education and Youth:* Faraj al-Mazroui. *Petroleum and Mineral Resources:* Dr Mana Said al-Oteiba. *Electricity and Water:* Hamaid Nasser al-Owais. *Health:* Hamad al-Madfa. *Labour and Social Affairs:* Khalfan Mohammed al-Roumi. *Planning:* Sheikh Humaid al-Mualla. *Agriculture and Fisheries:* Saeed al-Raghbani. *Islamic Affairs and Waqfs, Justice:* Sheikh Mohammed al-Khazraji.

National flag: Three horizontal stripes of green, white, black, with a vertical red strip in the hoist.

DEFENCE

Army. The Army consists of 1 Royal Guard, 1 armoured, 1 mechanized infantry, 2 infantry, 1 artillery and 1 air defence brigades. Equipment includes 95 AMX-30 and 36 Lion OF-40 Mk 2 main battle tanks. The strength was (1990) 40,000.

Navy. The combined naval flotilla of the Emirates includes 6 260t German-built fast missile craft, 9 British-built inshore patrol craft, 2 tank landing craft, 2 transports, 1 maintenance ship and 3 service craft. Personnel in 1989 numbered 1,500 officers and ratings. A new base is being constructed at Taweela.

The Coast Guard flotilla comprises 28 inshore patrol craft and some 30 boats.

Air Force. Formation of an air wing in Abu Dhabi, to support land forces, began in 1968 with the purchase of some light STOL transports and helicopters. Expansion has been rapid. Current equipment includes 23 Mirage 5 supersonic fighter-bombers, 3 Mirage 5R tactical reconnaissance aircraft and 3 Mirage 5D 2-seat trainers (to be replaced by Mirage 2000s, which are now entering service); 4 C-130 Hercules and 5 Buffalo turboprop transports; 4 CASA C-212 Aviocar ECM/elint aircraft; about 40 Gazelle, Alouette III, Puma, Super Puma and Ecureuil helicopters; 23 PC-7 Turbo-Trainers and 15 Hawk light attack/trainers. Initial personnel were mostly British but considerable assistance is now being received from Arab countries and from Pakistan. The air wing became the Air Force of Abu Dhabi in 1972, in which year 3 JetRanger helicopters were transferred to the air wing of the Union Defence Force, since combined with the Dubai Police Air Wing to form a single component of the United Emirates Air Force. Current equipment of the Dubai Air Wing of the UEAF, bought mainly in Italy, comprises 3 Aermacchi MB 326K jet light attack aircraft, 1 piston-engined SF.260W armed basic trainer, 5 SF.260TP turboprop trainers, and 2 MB 326L, 5 MB 339 and 8 Hawk jet trainers, 6 Bell 205A-1, 3 Bell 212, 4 Bell 214 and 6 JetRanger helicopters and 1 Cessna 182 liaison aircraft, plus 2 L-100-30 Hercules transports and a variety of other types for VIP use. Sharjah formed a small aviation force, the Amiri Guard Air Wing, at the end of 1984. The service is essentially an internal security and transport force operating 1 Short 330 and 1 Skyvan for transport duties and 3 JetRanger helicopters. Personnel (1989) 1,500.

INTERNATIONAL RELATIONS

Membership. The UAE is a member of UN, GCC and of the Arab League.

ECONOMY

Budget. Revenue is principally derived from oil-concession payments. The federal budget (1988) was expenditure DH 14,250m. and public revenue 21,600m.

Currency. The UAE issued its own currency in 1972 based on the *dirham*. 1 UAE *dirham* = 100 *fils*. There are notes of 5, 10, 50, 100 and 500 *dirham* and coins of 1 and 5 *dirham* and 1, 5, 10, 25 and 50 *fils*. Rate of exchange, March 1990: £1 = 6·05 *dirham*; US$1 = 3·69 *dirham*.

Banking. The UAE Central Bank was established in 1980. In 1987 there were 53 commercial banks, 19 of which were local and 34 foreign-owned with over 284 branches.

ENERGY AND NATURAL RESOURCES

Electricity. Production (1986) 16,440m. kwh. Supply in Abu Dhabi 230 volts; Dubai 220 volts and in the remaining Emirates 240 volts; all 50 Hz.

Oil. Total production of crude oil (1985) 442·3m. bbls. Reserves (1988) 200,000m. bbls.

Abu Dhabi. Ownership in 1976 was as follows: *ADPC*, 60% Government; 9·5% BP; 9·5% Shell; 9·5% CFP; 4·75% Mobil; 2% Partex. *ADMA*, 60% Government; 26·7% BP/Japan Oil Development Co.; 13·3% CFP. A Japanese company, Abu Dhabi Oil Co. (ADOCO) began production from its Mubarraz field in 1973. There are other companies which have concessions in the State: Japan's Middle East Oil; a US consortium led by Pan Ocean Oil and Sunningdale Oils of Canada. A State Petroleum Co., the Abu Dhabi National Oil Co. (ADNOC), was formed in 1971 and began to set up its own tanker fleet known as the Abu Dhabi National Tankers Co. (ADNATCO). Proven reserves (1988) 31,000m. bbls. Oil production, 1989, 71m. tonnes.

Dubai. In July 1975 Dubai decided to take full control of all foreign oil and gas operations in the State. The companies were to remain however. A Dubai producing group was set up to comprise the foreign interests–US and continental companies. Dubai Petroleum Co. (DPC–a subsidiary of Continental Oil) has a 30% interest in this group; the other members are Dubai Marine Areas (*Compagnie Française des Pétroles*) with 50%; Deutsche Texaco with 10%; Dubai Sun Oil 5%; and Delfzee Dubai Petroleum (Wintershall) 5%. Oil production (1989) 17·7m. tonnes.

Sharjah. In Sharjah the concession is given to Crescent Oil, its shareholders are: Ashland Oil, Skelly Oil, Kerr-McGee, Cities Services and Juniper. Other oil concessions have recently been given to the Crystal Oil Co. of USA and the Reserves Oil and Gas Co. Oil production, 1989, 2m. tonnes.

Ajman. An oil concession was awarded to United Refining in 1974.

Umm al Qawain. The concession here was given to US Occidental Petroleum; another was awarded to a consortium led by the US company United Refinery.

Ras al-Khaimah. The Dutch oil firm Vitol took over Union's concession in 1973. Shell began prospecting in 1969 but pulled out in 1971. A concession in the same area was awarded to Peninsula Petroleum, a subsidiary of the US California Time Group, in 1973. Oil production (1989) 400,000 tonnes.

Gas. Abu Dhabi has reserves of natural gas, nationalized in 1976. The Abu Dhabi Gas Liquefaction Plant at Das Island (51% ADNOC) has a capacity of 2m. tons LNG, 1m. tons LPG, 220,000 tons of light distillate and 230,000 tons of pelletized sulphur. Gas exports (1986) DH4,500m.

Water. Production of drinking water (1986) 11,600m. gallons. In 1986 the solar-powered Umm al Nar station produced 15,000 gallons a day. The first phase of the biggest solar-operated water production plant in the Gulf region (with an estimated daily capacity of 21m. gallons and 265 mw of electricity) was completed at Al Taweela in 1987, the second phase (40m. gallons and 400 mw) in 1990.

Agriculture. The fertile Buraimi Oasis, known as Al Ain, is largely in Abu Dhabi territory. By 1988, 2,620 farms had been set up on 12,565 hectares of land reclaimed from sand dunes. Owing to lack of water and good soil there is little agriculture in the rest of UAE. Cultivated area (1985) 320,000 hectares. Production (1988): Red meat, 18,000 tonnes; poultry, 7,000 tonnes; dates, 68,000 tonnes; vegetables, 285; wheat, 2.

Livestock (1988): Cattle, 50,000; camels, 120,000; sheep, 430,000; goats, 850,000.

Fisheries. Sharjah exports shrimps and prawns; a fishmeal plant is operating in Ras al-Khaimah and plants are planned for Ajman and Sharjah. Catch (1986) 72,400 tonnes.

INDUSTRY AND TRADE

Industry. A fertilizer plant at Ruwais in Abu Dhabi, opened in 1984, produced 343,000 tonnes of ammonia and 353,000 tonnes of urea in 1985. Umm al-Nar has a plant producing salt, hydrochloric acid, chlorine, caustic soda and distilled water.

There were about 190 industrial and commercial companies in the Jebel Ali industrial zone in Dubai by 1988, including an aluminium smelter and power and desalination plant, opened in 1979, and a lubricants plant with an annual capacity of 30,000 tonnes, opened in 1988. Production of aluminium in 1986, 155,605 tonnes, nearly all of which was exported.

There were 8 cement plants in 1987 (3 of them in Ras al-Khaimah), with a total annual capacity of 8m. tonnes. The home market for cement amounted to 25% of the total installed capacity of 6m. tonnes in 1986.

The 2 main steel rolling mills are in Dubai and Sharjah. Plastics are produced at factories in Dubai and Sharjah and mechanical dies and tools, sportswear and equipment, clothing and knitwear in Dubai. Fujairah has rockwool and ceramics factories. Ship repairs and steel fabrication are carried on in Ajman. There is a petrochemical complex on Das Island in Abu Dhabi.

Commerce. Imports in 1988 for UAE were DH31,000m. Exports and re-exports (non-oil) totalled DH13,500m. Oil exports accounted for DH28,000m.

Total trade between the UAE (excluding Abu Dhabi) and UK (British Department of Trade returns, in £1,000 sterling):

	1985	*1986*	*1987*	*1988*	*1989*
Imports to UK	71,688	59,428	81,218	58,651	77,755
Exports and re-exports from UK	374,616	413,651	329,008	334,506	415,982

Total trade between Abu Dhabi and UK (British Department of Trade returns, in £1,000 sterling):

	1985	*1986*	*1987*	*1988*	*1989*
Imports to UK	24,866	14,584	13,771	25,566	87,248
Exports and re-exports from UK	246,732	168,111	149,989	128,838	155,439

Tourism. In 1987 there were 85 hotels and 18,000 visitors.

COMMUNICATIONS

Roads. In 1984 there were 2,200 km of roads and 230,000 vehicles.

Aviation. In 1987 there were 4 international airports. A number of cargo airlines also fly regularly to the country's major airports. An air-taxi service, Emirates Air Services, flying between Abu Dhabi and Dubai, began in June 1976. Dubai set up the airline, Emirates, in 1985.

Shipping. In 1987 there were 7 commercial sea ports. Jebel Ali is the largest. Abu Dhabi has dry docks and there are smaller ports at Sharjah, Ras al-Khaimah and Fujairah. Jebel Ali is a port and industrial estate 35 km south-west of Dubai city and had (1982) 66 berths.

Post and Broadcasting. In 1983 there were 319,246 telephones, of which 113,629 were in Abu Dhabi and 98,010 in Dubai. The Cable and Wireless Station at Jebel Ali in the State of Dubai links the system with the international communication network.

Television stations are at Abu Dhabi and Dubai, with extension of the service well advanced to the rest of the Emirates. Stations for The Voice of the Gulf Co-operation Council, a 6-state radio station, began broadcasting from Abu Dhabi in Aug. 1985. Estimated radios (1984) 190,000 and television sets over 110,000.

Newspapers (1987). There are a number of daily and weekly publications mostly in Arabic, but some in English, notably *The Emirates News* of Abu Dhabi, *The Gulf News,* a daily, published in Dubai and the *Khaleej Times* (daily), also published in Dubai.

JUSTICE, RELIGION, EDUCATION AND WELFARE

Justice. UAE subjects and citizens of all Arab and Moslem states are subject to the jurisdiction of the local courts. In the local courts the rules of Islamic law prevail. A new code of law is being produced for Abu Dhabi. In Dubai there is a court run by a *qadi*, while in some of the other States all legal cases are referred immediately to the Ruler or a member of his family, who will refer to a *qadi* only if he cannot settle the matter himself. In Abu Dhabi a professional Jordanian judge presides over the Ruler's Court.

Religion. Nearly all the inhabitants are Moslem of the Sunni, and a small minority of the Shi'ite sects.

Education In 1986–87 there were 122,543 pupils in primary schools, 36,810 in preparatory schools and 20,753 in secondary schools. There were 1,712 students in religious schools, 597 in technical schools and (1987–88) 2,075 at university.

Health. In 1984 there were 28 hospitals (4,853 beds) and 119 clinics. There were 1,840 physicians.

DIPLOMATIC REPRESENTATIVES

Of the UAE in Great Britain (30 Prince's Gate, London, SW7 1PT)
Ambassador: Dr Khalifa Mohamed Sulaiman, GCVO (accredited 18 Nov. 1988).

Of Great Britain in the UAE
Ambassador: Graham Burton (at the British Embassy, Abu Dhabi).

Of the UAE in the USA (600 New Hampshire Ave., NW, Washington, D.C., 20037)
Ambassador: Abdulla bin Zayed Al-Nahayyan.

Of the USA in the UAE (Al-Sudan St., Abu Dhabi)
Ambassador: Edward S. Walker, Jr.

Of the UAE to the United Nations
Ambassador: Mohammed Hussain Al-Shaali.

Further Reading

Middle East Annual Review. London
Clements, F. A., *United Arab Emirates.* [Bibliography] Oxford and Santa Barbara, 1983
Heard-Bey, F., *From Trucial States to United Arab Emirates.* London, 1982
Mallakh, R.S., *The Economic Development of the United Arab Emirates,* London, 1981
Mostyn, T., *UAE-A MEED Practical Guide.* 2nd ed. London, 1986
Soffan, L. U., *Women of the United Arab Emirates.* London, 1980

UNITED KINGDOM OF GREAT BRITAIN AND NORTHERN IRELAND

Capital: London
Population: 55·78m. (1981)
GNP per capita: US$12,800 (1988)

'Great Britain' is a geographical term describing the main island of the British Isles which comprises England, Scotland and Wales (so called to distinguish it from 'Little Britain' or Brittany). By the Act of Union, 1801, Great Britain and Ireland formed a legislative union as the United Kingdom of Great Britain and Ireland. Since the separation of Great Britain and Ireland in 1921 Northern Ireland remained within the Union which is now the United Kingdom of Great Britain and Northern Ireland. The United Kingdom does not include the Channel Islands or the Isle of Man which are direct dependencies of the Crown with their own legislative and taxation systems.

GREAT BRITAIN

AREA AND POPULATION. Area (in sq. km) and population (present on census night) at the census taken 5 April 1981:

Divisions	*Area*	*Total*
England	130,357	46,362,836
Wales	20,761	2,791,851
Scotland	78,762	5,130,735
	229,880	54,285,422

Population at the 4 previous decennial censuses:

Divisions	*1931*	*1951*	*1961*	*1971*
England [1]	37,359,045	41,159,213	43,460,525	46,019,000
Wales	2,158,374	2,598,675	2,644,023	2,731,000
Scotland	4,842,980	5,096,415	5,178,490	5,228,963
Army, Navy and Merchant Seamen abroad	434,532	—	—	—
Total	44,794,931	48,854,303	51,283,038	53,978,963

[1] Areas now recognised as part of Gwent, Wales, formed the English county of Monmouthshire until 1974.

Population (usually resident) at the census of 1981:

Divisions	*Males*	*Females*	*Total*
England	22,288,395	23,483,561	45,771,956
Wales	1,336,323	1,413,317	2,749,640
Scotland	2,428,472	2,606,843	5,035,315
Great Britain	26,053,190	27,503,721	53,556,911

In 1981 in Wales 21,283 persons 3 years of age and upwards were able to speak Welsh only, and 482,266 able to speak Welsh and English: These totals represent 19% of the total population. In Scotland in 1981, 79,307 of the usually resident population could speak Gaelic (1·7%); 3,313 could read or write Gaelic, but could not speak it.

At the census of 1981, in England and Wales, there were 17,706,492 private households; in Great Britain, 19,500,113.

The age distribution in 1981 of the 'usually resident' population of England and Wales and Scotland was as follows (in 1,000):

Age-group	*England and Wales*	*Scotland*	*Great Britain*
Under 5	2,910	308	3,219
5 and under 10	3,207	344	3,551
10 „ 15	3,846	425	4,271
15 „ 20	4,020	447	4,467
20 „ 25	3,564	394	3,959
25 „ 35	6,931	701	7,632
35 „ 45	5,885	588	6,473
45 „ 55	5,474	575	6,049
55 „ 65	5,410	541	5,951
65 „ 70	2,426	241	2,667
70 „ 75	2,062	204	2,265
75 „ 85	2,280	221	2,501
85 and upwards	507	46	552
Total	48,522	5,035	53,557

At 30 June 1988 the estimated population of the UK was 57,065,000 (29,253,000 females), and of Great Britain, 55,487,000 (28,449,000 females). Age and sex distribution (UK, in 1,000 persons/females): Under 5, 3,747/1,827; 5-14, 7,013/3,413; 15-59, 34,481/17,132; 60-64, 2,940/1,529; over 65, 8,883/5,350.

Population densities (persons per sq. km), 1988: UK, 234; England, 364; Wales, 138.

England and Wales: The census population, (present on census night) of England and Wales 1801 to 1981:

Date of enumeration	*Population*	*Pop. per sq. mile*	*Date of enumeration*	*Population*	*Pop. per sq. mile*[1]
1801	8,892,536	152	1891	29,002,525	497
1811	10,164,256	174	1901	32,527,843	558
1821	12,000,236	206	1911	36,070,492	618
1831	13,896,797	238	1921	37,886,699	649
1841	15,914,148	273	1931	39,952,377	685
1851	17,927,609	307	1951	43,757,888	750
1861	20,066,224	344	1961	46,104,548	791
1871	22,712,266	389	1971	48,749,575	323
1881	25,974,439	445	1981	49,154,687	325

[1] Per sq. km from 1971

The birth places of the 1981 'usually resident' population were: England, 41,552,500; Wales, 2,758,026; Scotland, 752,188; Northern Ireland, 209,042; Ireland, 579,833; Commonwealth, 1,429,407; foreign countries, 1,209,091.

At June 1988 the estimated population of England and Wales was 50,393,000 (25,817,000 females). Age and sex distribution (in 1,000 persons/females): Under 5, 3,288/1,603; 5-14, 6,121/2,978; 15-59, 30,442/15,117; 60-64, 2,607/1,351; over 65, 7,940/4,768.

Eight 'standard regions' are identified in England for statistical purposes. They have no administrative significance. Population (in 1,000) in 1988: East Anglia, 2,034; East Midlands, 3,970; West Midlands, 5,207; North, 3,071; North West, 6,364; South East, 17,344 (including Greater London, 6,735); South West, 4,634; Yorkshire and Humberside, 4,913.

England and Wales are divided (apart from Greater London) into 53 counties (6 of them 'metropolitan') subdivided into 369 districts. Greater London comprises 32 boroughs and the City of London.

Area in sq. km of counties and population estimate 30 June 1988:

ENGLAND *Metropolitan counties*	*Area sq. km*	*Population*	*Metropolitan counties*—contd.	*Area sq. km*	*Population*
Greater Manchester	1,286	2,577,700	Tyne and Wear	540	1,130,600
Merseyside	652	1,448,100	West Midlands	899	2,617,300
South Yorkshire	1,560	1,292,700	West Yorkshire	2,039	2,056,500

Non-metropolitan counties	*Area sq. km*	*Population*
Avon	1,338	945,300
Bedfordshire	1,235	530,800
Berkshire	1,256	747,000
Buckinghamshire	1,883	627,200
Cambridgeshire	3,409	651,500
Cheshire	2,322	955,800
Cleveland	583	553,100
Cornwall and Isles of Scilly	3,546	460,600
Cumbria	6,809	489,200
Derbyshire	2,631	924,200
Devon	6,715	1,021,100
Dorset	2,654	655,600
Durham	2,436	596,800
East Sussex	1,795	712,800
Essex	3,674	1,529,500
Gloucestershire	2,638	527,500
Hampshire	3,772	1,542,900
Hereford and Worcester	3,927	671,000
Hertfordshire	1,634	986,000
Humberside	3,512	850,500
Isle of Wight	381	129,800
Kent	3,732	1,520,300
Lancashire	3,043	1,382,000
Leicestershire	2,553	885,500
Lincolnshire	5,885	582,600
Norfolk	5,355	744,400

Non-metropolitan counties—contd.	*Area sq. km*	*Population*
Northamptonshire	2,367	570,300
Northumberland	5,033	301,400
North Yorkshire	8,317	713,200
Nottinghamshire	2,164	1,007,700
Oxfordshire	2,611	578,900
Shropshire	3,490	400,800
Somerset	3,458	457,700
Staffordshire	2,716	1,032,900
Suffolk	3,800	638,500
Surrey	1,655	999,800
Warwickshire	1,981	484,600
West Sussex	2,016	703,400
Wiltshire	3,481	557,000
Total England		47,536,000
WALES		
Clwyd	2,425	407,000
Dyfed	5,765	348,400
Gwent	1,376	445,400
Gwynedd	3,868	239,000
Mid-Glamorgan	1,019	535,900
Powys	5,077	114,900
South Glamorgan	416	403,400
West Glamorgan	815	363,000
Total Wales		2,857,000

County districts with populations of over 90,000 (estimate, 30 June 1988):

ENGLAND	
Allerdale	96,600
Amber Valley	111,900
Arun	130,300
Ashfield	107,700
Ashford	95,100
Aylesbury Vale	145,500
Barnsley	220,900
Basildon	157,600
Basingstoke and Deane	139,700
Bassetlaw	104,800
Beverley	114,000
Birmingham	993,700
Blackburn	134,400
Blackpool	143,800
Bolton	263,700
Bournemouth	154,800
Bracknell Forest	98,200
Bradford	464,100
Braintree	117,200
Breckland	104,200
Brighton	149,200
Bristol	377,700
Broadland	104,400
Broxtowe	108,300
Bury	175,000
Calderdale	196,000
Cambridge	97,900
Canterbury	131,900
Carlisle	102,000
Charnwood	148,500
Chelmsford	151,700
Cherwell	122,400
Chester	117,100
Chesterfield	99,700
Chichester	105,800
Chorley	96,700
Colchester	150,200
Coventry	306,200
Crewe and Nantwich	96,800
Dacorum	133,100
Darlington	99,700
Derby	215,300
Doncaster	291,700
Dover	106,400
Dudley	304,300
Easington	94,900
East Devon	118,100
East Hampshire	102,500
East Hertfordshire	118,700
Eastleigh	101,000
East Lindsey	117,700
East Staffordshire	95,800
Elmbridge	107,100
Epping Forest	111,800
Erewash	107,900
Exeter	99,600
Fareham	100,300
Gateshead	206,200
Gedling	110,300
Gillingham	95,300
Gloucester	90,500
Gravesham	90,200
Guildford	123,300
Halton	124,000
Harrogate	147,000
Havant	117,500
Hinckley and Bosworth	96,300
Horsham	108,000
Hove	90,700

ENGLAND—*contd.*

Huntingdonshire	147,700
Ipswich	114,900
King's Lynn and West Norfolk	134,000
Kingston upon Hull	247,000
Kirklees	375,300
Knowsley	158,400
Lancaster	131,200
Langbaurgh on Tees	144,800
Leeds	709,600
Leicester	278,600
Lewes	90,800
Lichfield	93,800
Liverpool	469,600
Luton	167,600
Macclesfield	152,300
Maidstone	136,100
Manchester	445,900
Mansfield	100,000
Mendip	94,000
Mid-Bedfordshire	114,900
Middlesbrough	143,100
Mid-Sussex	120,000
Milton Keynes	177,600
Newark and Sherwood	570,000
Newbury	138,600
Newcastle under Lyme	117,500
Newcastle upon Tyne	279,700
New Forest	163,200
Northampton	182,100
Northavon	130,800
North Bedfordshire	136,700
North-East Derbyshire	96,700
North Hertfordshire	112,300
North Norfolk	94,700
North Tyneside	192,900
North Wiltshire	113,300
Norwich	117,300
Nottingham	273,500
Nuneaton and Bedworth	116,000
Oldham	219,500
Oxford	115,400
Peterborough	152,900
Plymouth	258,100
Poole	130,700
Portsmouth	183,800
Preston	128,100
Reading	132,400
Reigate and Banstead	113,600
Rochdale	206,900
Rochester upon Medway	146,700
Rotherham	251,800
Rushcliffe	99,300
Ryedale	90,800
St Albans	128,600
St Edmundsbury	92,300
St Helens	187,700
Salford	235,700
Salisbury	101,000
Sandwell	296,300
Scarborough	90,900
Sedgemoor	105,500
Sefton	96,400
Selby	297,600
Sevenoaks	107,300
Sheffield	528,300
Shrewsbury and Atcham	90,900

ENGLAND—*contd.*

Slough	100,300
Solihull	205,000
Southampton	196,700
South Bedfordshire	111,500
South Cambridgeshire	119,300
Southend on Sea	165,400
South Kesteven	105,300
South Lakeland	100,200
South Norfolk	100,700
South Oxfordshire	131,100
South Ribble	100,200
South Somerset	141,800
South Staffordshire	108,100
South Tyneside	155,700
Stafford	117,900
Staffordshire Moorlands	97,200
Stockport	290,900
Stockton on Tees	176,800
Stoke on Trent	246,800
Stratford on Avon	106,800
Stroud	110,500
Suffolk Coastal	111,300
Sunderland	296,000
Swale	115,300
Tameside	216,900
Taunton Deane	94,100
Teignbridge	107,900
Tendring	129,600
Test Valley	102,300
Thamesdown	168,800
Thanet	129,700
Thurrock	124,400
Tonbridge and Malling	101,200
Torbay	119,000
Trafford	215,700
Tunbridge Wells	99,300
Vale of White Horse	112,300
Vale Royal	113,300
Wakefield	311,600
Walsall	262,300
Warrington	186,100
Warwick	116,400
Waveney	106,500
Waverley	109,700
Wealden	133,900
Welwyn Hatfield	93,500
West Lancashire	105,400
West Oxfordshire	97,800
West Wiltshire	106,200
Wigan	307,600
Winchester	96,000
Windsor and Maidenhead	127,400
Wirral	334,800
Wokingham	150,000
Wolverhampton	249,400
Woodspring	189,000
Worthing	98,200
Wrekin	134,200
Wychavon	101,000
Wycombe	156,300
Wyre	103,000
Wyre Forest	94,400
York	100,600

WALES

Cardiff	283,900
Newport	128,100

WALES—*contd.*		WALES—*contd.*	
Ogwr	137,500	Torfaen	92,400
Rhymney Valley	104,500	Vale of Glamorgan	119,500
Swansea	186,900	Wrexham Maelor	116,900
Taff Ely	94,900		

The following table shows the distribution of the urban and rural population of England and Wales in 1951, 1961, 1971, and 1981.

		Population		*Percentage*	
	England and Wales	*Urban districts* [1]	*Rural districts* [1]	*Urban* [1]	*Rural*
1951	43,757,888	35,335,721	8,422,167	80·8	19·2
1961	46,071,604	36,838,442	9,233,162	80·0	20·0
1971	48,755,000	38,151,000	10,598,000	78·2	21·5
1981	49,011,417	37,686,863	11,324,554	76·9	23·1

[1] As existing at each census.

Conurbations. These are aggregates of local-authority areas with high population densities. In April 1981 there were 6 in England and Wales, with a population of 14·7m. (30% of total population): Greater London, 6·7m.; Tyneside, 0·7m.; W. Yorks., 1·67m.; S.E. Lancs., 2·24m.; Merseyside, 1·13m.; W. Midlands, 2·24m.

Greater London Boroughs. Total area 1,580 sq.km. Estimated population on 30 June 1988 6,735,400. By borough:

Barking and Dagenham	147,600	Hammersmith and Fulham	149,600	Lambeth	239,500
Barnet	301,400	Haringey	192,300	Lewisham	228,900
Bexley	220,400	Harrow	197,100	Merton	164,000
Brent	257,200	Havering	235,600	Newham	206,900
Bromley	298,200	Hillingdon	231,900	Redbridge	230,800
Camden	182,500	Hounslow	190,700	Richmond-on-Thames	160,800
Croydon	317,200	Islington	169,200	Southwark	216,900
Ealing	297,300	Kensington and Chelsea	125,600	Sutton	168,200
Enfield	260,900	Kingston upon Thames	134,600	Tower Hamlets	161,800
Greenwich	214,500			Waltham Forest	213,300
Hackney	189,000			Wandsworth	257,000
				Westminster	169,700

The City of London (677 acres) is administered by its Corporation which retains some independent powers. Resident population (1988 estimate) 4,400.

Scotland: Area 78,762 sq. km, including its islands, 186 in number, and inland water 1,580 sq. km.

Population (including military in the barracks and seamen on board vessels in the harbours) at the dates of each census:

Date of enumeration	*Population*	*Pop. per sq. mile*	*Date of enumeration*	*Population*	*Pop. per sq. mile* [1]
1811	1,805,864	60	1901	4,472,103	150
1821	2,091,521	70	1911	4,760,904	160
1831	2,364,386	79	1921	4,882,497	164
1841	2,620,184	88	1931	4,842,980	163
1851	2,888,742	97	1951	5,096,415	171
1861	3,062,294	100	1961	5,179,344	174
1871	3,360,018	113	1971	5,229,963	68
1881	3,735,573	125	1981	5,130,735	66
1891	4,025,647	135			

[1] per sq. km from 1971.

The 1981 population present on census night included 2,466,000 males, 2,664,000 females.

At 30 June 1988 the estimated population of Scotland was 5,094,000 (2,632,000 females). Age and sex distribution (in 1,000, persons/females): Under 5, 323/158; 5-14, 634/309; 15-59, 3,118/1,558; 60-64, 265/142; over 65, 684/466.

Population density 1988: 65 persons per sq.km.

Scotland is divided into 9 regions subdivided into 53 districts and 3 island authority areas. Area of regions and population estimate of regions and districts in June 1988:

Regions (area sq. km) and Districts	*Estimated population 1988*
Borders (4,662)	102,592
Berwickshire	18,874
Ettrick and Lauderdale	33,797
Roxburgh	35,060
Tweeddale	14,861
Central (2,590)	271,526
Clackmannan	47,171
Falkirk	143,206
Stirling	81,149
Dumfries and Galloway (6,475)	147,482
Annandale and Eskdale	36,416
Nithsdale	57,384
Stewartry	23,374
Wigtown	30,308
Fife (1,308)	344,717
Dunfermline	129,461
Kirkcaldy	147,384
N.E. Fife	67,872
Grampian (8,550)	501,394
Aberdeen City	211,196
Banff and Buchan	83,708
Gordon	72,509
Kincardine and Deeside	48,910
Moray	85,071
Highland (26,136)	201,866
Badenoch and Strathspey	10,807
Caithness	27,098
Inverness	61,748
Lochaber	19,180
Nairn	10,348
Ross and Cromarty	48,202
Skye and Lochalsh	11,435
Sutherland	13,048
Lothian (1,756)	741,179
E. Lothian	82,735
Edinburgh City	433,480
Midlothian	81,335
W. Lothian	143,629
Strathclyde (13,856)	2,316,739
Argyll and Bute	65,993
Bearsden and Milngavie	40,382
Clydebank	47,762
Clydesdale	58,324
Cumbernauld and Kilsyth	62,489
Cumnock and Doon Valley	43,107
Cunninghame	137,096
Dumbarton	80,372
E. Kilbride	81,686
Eastwood	58,709
Glasgow City	703,186
Hamilton	106,997
Inverclyde	95,192
Kilmarnock and Loudoun	81,040
Kyle and Carrick	113,200
Monklands	104,814
Motherwell	146,748
Renfrew	200,409
Strathkelvin	89,197
Tayside (7,668)	393,748
Angus	94,822
Dundee	174,255
Perth and Kinross	124,671
Island Authority Areas	
Orkney Islands (974)	19,455
Shetland Islands (1,427)	22,364
Western Isles (2,901)	30,939

The birthplaces of the 1981 ''usually resident'' population were: Scotland, 4,548,708; England, 297,784; Wales, 12,733; Northern Ireland, 33,927; Ireland 27,018; Commonwealth, 48,515; foreign countries, 65,384.

The population of the Central Clydeside conurbation in 1988 was 1,642,415.

Isle of Man and Channel Islands:

Islands	*Area in sq. km*	*Population 1961*	*1971*	*1986*
Isle of Man	572	48,151	56,289	55,482
Jersey	116	57,200	69,329	80,212 [1]
Guernsey, Herm and Jethou	64	} 47,178	} 53,734	} 64,282
Alderney	8			
Sark, Brechou and Lihou	6			

[1] 1985.

Vital statistics for England and Wales:

	Estimated home population at 30 June [1]	*Total live births*	*Illegitimate live births*	*Deaths*	*Marriages*	*Divorces, annulments and dissolutions*
1982	49,601,400	625,931	89,857	581,861	342,166	146,698
1983	49,653,700	629,134	99,211	579,608	344,334	147,479
1984	49,763,600	636,818	110,465	566,881	349,186	144,501
1985	49,923,500	656,417	126,250	590,734	346,389	160,300
1986	50,075,400	661,018	141,345	581,203	347,924	153,903
1987	50,242,900	681,511	158,431	566,994	351,761	151,007

[1] The population actually in England and Wales.

In 1985 the proportion of male to female births was 1,054 male to 1,000 female; the live birth rate was 13·1 and the death rate 11·8 per 1,000 of the population; infant mortality rate 9·4 per 1,000 of live births. The average age at marriage in 1986 was 30·5 years for males and 27·8 years for females.

Vital statistics for Scotland:

	Estimated home population at 30 June [1]	*Total births*	*Illegitimate births*	*Deaths*	*Marriages*	*Divorces, annulments and dissolutions*
1982	5,166,557	66,196	9,395	65,022	34,942	11,288
1983	5,150,405	65,078	9,581	63,454	34,962	13,238
1984	5,145,722	65,106	10,640	62,345	36,253	11,915
1985	5,136,509	66,676	12,362	63,967	36,385	13,373
1986	5,121,013	65,812	13,547	63,467	35,790	12,800
1987	5,112,129	66,241	15,125	62,014	35,813	12,133
1988	5,094,001	66,212	16,224	61,957	35,599	11,472

[1] Includes merchant navy at home and forces stationed in Scotland.

In 1988 the proportion of male to female births was 1,059 male to 1,000 female; the live birth rate was 13 and the death rate 12·2 per 1,000 of the population; infant mortality rate, 8·2 per 1,000 live births. The average age of marriage was 29 years for males and 27 years for females.

Emigration and Immigration. During the last hundred years the UK has most often been a net exporter of population. Throughout the period 1881–1931 there was a consistent net loss from migration, though the fifteen years 1931–46 brought a reversal of the trend as a result of immigration from Europe. Since the Second World War the loss has largely continued. However, during the five years 1956–1961, increased immigration particularly from the new Commonwealth and Pakistan, resulted in a net gain.

Since 1964 migration figures have been available from the International Passenger Survey. This is a sample survey conducted by the Office of Population Censuses and Surveys, covering all the principal air and sea routes between the UK and overseas, except those to and from the Republic of Ireland. For the years 1964–73 the survey shows an average annual net loss for the UK of 63,000. During the decade 1974–1983 the annual net outflow has been an average of 37,000.

The table below, derived from the International Passenger survey, summarizes migration statistics for 1988 (in 1,000):

By country of last or future intended residence		*Into UK*	*Out from UK*	*Balance*
All Countries		216	237	−21
Australia, Canada, New Zealand		36	62	−26
India, Bangladesh, Sri Lanka		12	5	+7
Other Commonwealth		29	30	−1
EEC		52	59	−7
USA		26	30	−7
Republic of South Africa		7	5	+12
Rest of World		58	46	+12
By sex/age in 1988				
Males	0–14	20	24	−4
	15–24	26	25	+1
	25–44	53	57	−4
	45 and over	10	19	−9
	All ages	109	125	−16
Females	0–14	17	22	−5
	15–24	39	37	+2
	25–44	41	39	+2
	45 and over	10	15	−5
	All ages	107	113	−6

CLIMATE. The climate is cool temperate oceanic, with mild conditions and rainfall evenly distributed over the year, though the weather is very changeable because of cyclonic influences. In general, temperatures are higher in the west and lower in the east in winter and rather the reverse in summer. Rainfall amounts are greatest in the west, where most of the high ground occurs.

London. Jan. 40°F (4·5°C), July 64°F (18°C). Annual rainfall 24" (600 mm). Aberdeen. Jan. 39°F (4°C), July 57°F (14°C). Annual rainfall 33" (823 mm). Belfast. Jan. 40°F (4·5°C), July 61°F (16·1°C). Annual rainfall 34·6" (865 mm). Birmingham. Jan. 38°F (3·3°C), July 61°F (16·1°C). Annual rainfall 30" (749 mm). Cardiff. Jan. 40°F (4·4°C), July 61°F (16·1°C). Annual rainfall 42·6" (1,065 mm). Edinburgh. Jan. 38°F (3·5°C), July 58°F (14·5°C). Annual rainfall 28" (708 mm). Glasgow. Jan. 39°F (4°C), July 60°F (15·5°C). Annual rainfall 37·2" (930 mm). Manchester. Jan. 41°F (5°C), July 62°F (16·5°C). Annual rainfall 34·1" (853 mm).

QUEEN, HEAD OF THE COMMONWEALTH. Elizabeth II Alexandra Mary, born 21 April 1926 daughter of King George VI and Queen Elizabeth; married on 20 Nov. 1947 Lieut. Philip Mountbatten (formerly Prince Philip of Greece), created Duke of Edinburgh, Earl of Merioneth and Baron Greenwich on the same day and created Prince Philip, Duke of Edinburgh, 22 Feb. 1957; succeeded to the crown on the death of her father, on 6 Feb. 1952. Offspring: *Charles* Philip Arthur George, Prince of Wales (Heir Apparent), born 14 Nov. 1948, married Lady Diana Spencer on 29 July 1981. Offspring: *William* Arthur Philip Louis, born 21 June 1982; *Henry* Charles Albert David, born 15 Sept. 1984. Princess *Anne* Elizabeth Alice Louise, the Princess Royal, born 15 Aug. 1950, married Mark Anthony Peter Phillips on 14 Nov. 1973. Offspring: *Peter* Mark Andrew, born 15 Nov. 1977; *Zara* Anne Elizabeth, born 15 May 1981. Prince *Andrew*, Albert Christian Edward, created Duke of York, 23 July 1986, born 19 Feb. 1960, married Sarah Margaret Ferguson on 23 July 1986. Offspring: Princess *Beatrice* Mary, born 8 Aug. 1988; Princess *Eugenie* Victoria Helena, born 23 March 1990. Prince *Edward* Antony Richard Louis, born 10 March 1964.

The Queen Mother: Queen Elizabeth, born 4 Aug. 1900, daughter of the 14th Earl of Strathmore and Kinghorne; married the Duke of York, afterwards King George VI, on 26 April 1923.

Sister of the Queen: Princess Margaret Rose, born 12 Aug. 1930; married Antony Armstrong-Jones (created Earl of Snowdon, 3 Oct. 1961) on 6 May 1960; divorced, 1978. Offspring: *David* Albert Charles (Viscount Linley), born 3 Nov. 1961; Lady *Sarah* Frances Elizabeth Armstrong-Jones, born 1964.

Children of the late Duke of Gloucester (died 10 June 1974): William Henry Andrew Frederick, born 18 Dec. 1941, died 28 Aug. 1972; Richard Alexander Walter George, Duke of Gloucester, born 26 Aug. 1944, married Birgitte van Deurs on 8 July 1972 (offspring: Alexander Patrick Gregers Richard Windsor, Earl of Ulster, born 24 Oct. 1974; Davina Elizabeth Alice Benedikte Windsor, born 19 Nov. 1977; Rose Victoria Birgitte Louise Windsor, born 1 March 1980).

Children of the late Duke of Kent (died 25 Aug. 1942): Edward George Nicholas Patrick, Duke of Kent, born 9 Oct. 1935; married Katharine Worsley on 8 June 1961 (offspring: George Philip Nicholas, Earl of St Andrews, born 26 June 1962, married Sylvania Tomaselli on 9 Jan. 1988 (offspring: Lord Downpatrick, born 2 Dec. 1988); Lady Helen Windsor, born 28 April 1964; Lord Nicholas Charles Edward Jonathan Windsor, born 25 July 1970). Alexandra Helen Elizabeth Olga Christabel, born 25 Dec. 1936; married 24 April 1963, Angus Ogilvy (offspring: James Robert Bruce, born 29 Feb. 1964; Marina Victoria Alexandra, born 31 July 1966). Michael George Charles Franklin, born 4 July 1942; married Marie-Christine von Reibnitz on 30 June 1978 (offspring: Lord *Frederick* Michael George David Louis Windsor, born 6 April 1979; Lady *Gabriela* Marina Alexander Ophelia Windsor, born 23 April 1981).

The Queen's legal title rests on the statute of 12 and 13 Will. III, ch. 3, by which the succession to the Crown of Great Britain and Ireland was settled on the Princess Sophia of Hanover and the 'heirs of her body being Protestants'. By proclamation of 17 July 1917 the royal family became known as the House and Family of Windsor. On 8 Feb. 1960 the Queen issued a declaration varying her confirmatory declaration of 9 April 1952 to the effect that while the Queen and her children should continue to be known as the House of Windsor, her descendants, other than descendants entitled to the style of Royal Highness and the title of Prince or

Princess, and female descendants who marry and their descendants should bear the name of Mountbatten-Windsor. For the Royal Style and Titles of Queen Elizabeth *see* Commonwealth section.

By letters patent of 30 Nov. 1917 the titles of Royal Highness and Prince or Princess are restricted to the Sovereign's children, the children of the Sovereign's sons and the eldest living son of the eldest son of the Prince of Wales.

Provision is made for the support of the royal household by the settlement of the Civil List soon after the beginning of each reign. (For historical details, *see* THE STATESMAN'S YEAR-BOOK, 1908, p. 5, and 1935, p. 4). According to the Civil List Act of 1 Jan. 1972 and the Civil List (Increase of Financial Provision) Order 1975, the Civil List of the Queen, after the usual surrender of hereditary revenues, was (1990) £5,090,000.

The Civil List of 1990 provides for an annuity of £154,500 to the Princess Royal; £245,000 to Prince Philip; £439,500 to Queen Elizabeth (the Queen Mother); £148,500 to the Princess Margaret; £169,000 to the Duke of York; £20,000 to Prince Edward.

Sovereigns of Great Britain, from the Restoration (with dates of accession):

House of Stewart	
Charles II	29 May 1660
James II	6 Feb. 1685
House of Stewart-Orange	
William and Mary	13 Feb. 1689
William III	28 Dec. 1694
House of Stewart	
Anne	19 March 1702
House of Hanover	
George I	1 Aug. 1714
George II	11 June 1727
George III	25 Oct. 1760
George IV	29 Jan. 1820
William IV	26 June 1830
Victoria	20 June 1837
House of Saxe-Coburg and Gotha	
Edward VII	22 Jan. 1901
House of Windsor	
George V	6 May 1910
Edward VIII	20 Jan. 1936
George VI	11 Dec. 1936
Elizabeth II	6 Feb. 1952

CONSTITUTION AND GOVERNMENT. The supreme legislative power is vested in Parliament, which in its present form, as divided into two Houses of Legislature, the Lords and the Commons, dates from the middle of the 14th century.

Parliament is summoned by the writ of the sovereign issued out of Chancery, by advice of the Privy Council, at least 20 days previous to its assembling. A Parliament may last up to 5 years, normally divided into annual sessions. A session is ended by prorogation, and all public Bills which have not been passed by both Houses then lapse. A Parliament ends by dissolution, either by will of the sovereign (that is, on the advice of the Prime Minister) or by lapse of the 5-year period. A dissolution is commonly followed by a general election.

Under the Parliament Acts 1911 (1 and 2 Geo. V, ch. 13) and 1949 (12, 13 and 14 Geo. VI, ch. 103), all Money Bills (so certified by the Speaker of the House of Commons), if not passed by the House of Lords without amendment, may become law without their concurrence on the Royal Assent being signified within 1 month of introduction in the Lords. Public Bills, other than Money Bills or a Bill extending the maximum duration of Parliament, if passed by the House of Commons in 2 successive sessions, whether of the same Parliament or not, and rejected each time, or not passed, by the House of Lords, may become law without their concurrence on the Royal Assent being signified, provided that 1 year has elapsed between the second reading in the first session of the House of Commons and the third reading in the second session. All Bills coming under this Act must reach the House of Lords at least 1 month before the end of the session. No Act has been passed in this way since 1949.

The House of Lords consists (on 30 Dec. 1989) of: (1) 785 hereditary peers (including 20 women peers) sitting by virtue of creation or descent, other than those who have disclaimed their titles for life under the provisions of the Peerage Act, 1963; (2) life peers being *(a)* 19 Lords of Appeal (active and retired), under the Appellate Jurisdiction Act, 1876, as amended; *(b)* 350 life peers (including 45 women peers) under the Life Peerages Act, 1958; (3) 2 archbishops and 24 diocesan bishops of the Church of England.

The full House thus consists of 1,180, and the average attendance is about 316; at the end of Dec. 1989 149 peers were on leave of absence and 92 peers (including 3 minors) were without writs of summons.

The House of Commons consists of members (of both sexes) representing constituencies determined by the Boundary Commissions. Persons under 21 years of age, Clergy of the Church of England and of the Scottish Episcopal Church, Ministers of the Church of Scotland, Roman Catholic clergymen, civil servants, members of the regular armed forces, policemen, most judicial officers and other office-holders named in the House of Commons (Disqualification) Act are disqualified from sitting in the House of Commons. No peer eligible to sit in the House of Lords can be elected to the House of Commons unless he has disclaimed his title for life under the Peerage Act, 1963, but Irish peers and holders of courtesy titles, who are not members of the House of Lords, are eligible.

In Aug. 1911 provision was first made for the payment of a salary of £400 per annum to members of the Commons, other than those already in receipt of salaries as officers of the House, as Ministers or as officers of Her Majesty's household. As from 1 Jan. 1990 the salaries of members are £26,701 per annum. There is an office costs allowance of up to £22,588 per annum and a living allowance, for an additional home, of up to £9,468 per annum. Members of the House of Lords are unsalaried but may recover expenses incurred in attending sittings of the House within maxima for each day's attendance of £24 for day subsistence, £64 for night subsistence and £25 for secretarial and research assistance or general office expenses. Additionally, Members of the House who are disabled may recover the extra cost of attending the House incurred by reason of their disablement. In connection with their attendance at the House and for parliamentary duties within the UK Lords may also recover the cost of travelling to and from their main place of residence.

Commons Select Committees consisting of 10–15 Members of all parties exist in order to investigate most areas of public policy.

The Representation of the People Act 1948, abolished the business premises and University franchises, and the only persons entitled to vote at Parliamentary elections are those registered as residents or as service voters. No person may vote in more than one constituency at a general election. Persons may apply on certain grounds to vote by post or by proxy.

All persons over 18 years old and not subject to any legal incapacity to vote and who are either British subjects or citizens of Ireland are entitled to be included in the register of electors for the constituency containing the address at which they were residing on the qualifying date for the register and are entitled to vote at elections held during the period for which the register remains in force.

Members of the armed forces, Crown servants employed abroad, and the wives accompanying their husbands, are entitled, if otherwise qualified, to be registered as 'service voters' provided they make a 'service declaration'. To be effective for a particular register, the declaration must be made on or before the qualifying date for that register. In certain circumstances, British subjects living abroad may also vote.

The House of Commons (Redistribution of Seats) Acts 1944, 1949 and 1958, provided for the setting up of Boundary Commissions for England, Wales, Scotland and Northern Ireland. The Commissions are required to make general reports at intervals of not less than 10 and not more than 15 years and to submit reports from time to time with respect to the area comprised in any particular constituency or constituencies where some change appears necessary. Any changes giving effect to reports of the Commissions are to be made by Orders in Council laid before Parliament for approval by resolution of each House. The electorate of the United Kingdom and Northern Ireland in the register in 1986 numbered 43,391,831, of whom 36,158,417 were in England, 2,159,361 in Wales, 3,986,654 in Scotland and 1,087,399 in Northern Ireland.

At the general election held in 1987, 650 members were returned, 523 from England, 72 from Scotland, 38 from Wales and 17 from Northern Ireland. Every constituency returns a single member.

The following is a table of the duration of Parliaments called since Nov. 1935.

Reign	When met	When dissolved	Duration (years	and days)
George V, Edward VIII and George VI	26 Nov. 1935	15 June 1945	9	205
George VI	1 Aug. 1945	3 Feb. 1950	4	188
,,	1 Mar. 1950	5 Oct. 1951	1	219
George VI and Elizabeth II	31 Oct. 1951	6 May 1955	3	188
Elizabeth II	7 June 1955	18 Sept. 1959	4	105
,,	20 Oct. 1959	25 Sept. 1964	4	341
,,	27 Oct. 1964	10 Mar. 1966	1	134
,,	18 Apr. 1966	29 May 1970	4	81
,,	29 June 1970	8 Feb. 1974	3	225
,,	12 Mar. 1974	20 Sept. 1974	0	224
,,	22 Oct. 1974	7 April 1979	4	167
,,	9 May 1979	13 May 1983	4	4
,,	15 June 1983	18 May 1987	3	338
,,	25 June 1987	—	—	—

The executive government is vested nominally in the Crown, but practically in a committee of Ministers, called the Cabinet, which is dependent on the support of a majority in the House of Commons.

The head of the Ministry is the Prime Minister, a position first constitutionally recognized, and special precedence accorded to the holder, in 1905. His colleagues in the Ministry are appointed on his recommendation, and he dispenses the greater portion of the patronage of the Crown.

Heads of the Administrations since 1935 (C. = Conservative, L. = Liberal, Lab. = Labour, Nat. = National, Coal. = Coalition, Care. = Caretaker):

S. Baldwin (Nat.)	7 June 1935	H. Macmillan (C.)	10 Jan. 1957
N. Chamberlain (Nat.)	28 May 1937	Sir Alec Douglas-Home (C.)	18 Oct. 1963
W. S. Churchill (Coal.)	10 May 1940	H. Wilson (Lab.)	16 Oct. 1964
W. S. Churchill (Care.)	23 May 1945	E. Heath (C.)	19 June 1970
C. R. Attlee (Lab.)	26 July 1945	H. Wilson (Lab.)	12 Mar. 1974
W. S. Churchill (C.)	26 Oct. 1951	J. Callaghan (Lab.)	5 Apr. 1976
Sir Anthony Eden (C.)	6 Apr. 1955	M. Thatcher (C.)	4 May 1979

In March 1990 the Government consisted of the following members:

(a) Members of the Cabinet

1. *Prime Minister and First Lord of the Treasury and Minister for Civil Service:* Rt Hon. Margaret Thatcher, MP, born 1925. (Salary £35,120 per annum.)

2. *Lord President of the Council, Leader of the House of Commons and Deputy Prime Minister:* Rt Hon. Sir Geoffrey Howe, QC, MP, born 1926. (£35,120.)

3. *Lord Chancellor:* Rt Hon. The Lord Mackay of Clashfern, QC, born 1927. (£91,500.)

4. *Secretary of State for Foreign and Commonwealth Affairs:* Rt Hon. Douglas Hurd, CBE, MP, born 1930. (£35,120.)

5. *Chancellor of the Exchequer:* Rt Hon. John Major, MP, born 1943. (£35,120.)

6. *Secretary of State for the Home Department:* Rt Hon. David Waddington, QC, MP, born 1929. (£35,120.)

7. *Secretary of State for Wales:* Rt Hon. Peter Walker, MBE, MP, born 1932. (£35,120.)

8. *Secretary of State for Defence:* Rt Hon. Tom King, MP, born 1933. (£35,120.)

9. *Secretary of State for Trade and Industry:* Rt Hon. Nicholas Ridley, MP, born 1929. (£35,120.)

10. *Chancellor of the Duchy of Lancaster:* Rt Hon. Kenneth Baker, MP, born 1934. (£35,120.)

11. *Secretary of State for Health:* Rt Hon. Kenneth Clarke, QC, MP, born 1940. (£35,120.)

12. *Secretary of State for Education and Science:* Rt Hon. John MacGregor, OBE, MP, born 1937. (£35,120.)

13. *Secretary of State for Scotland:* Rt Hon. Malcolm Rifkind, QC, MP, born 1946. (£35,120.)

14. *Secretary of State for Transport:* Rt Hon. Cecil Parkinson, MP, born 1931. (£35,120.)

15. *Secretary of State for Energy:* Rt Hon. John Wakeham, MP, born 1932. (£35,120.)

16. *Lord Privy Seal and Leader of the House of Lords:* Rt Hon. The Lord Belstead, JP, born 1932. (£44,591.)

17. *Secretary of State for Social Services:* Rt Hon. Antony Newton, OBE, MP, born 1937. (£35,120.)

18. *Secretary of State for the Environment:* Rt Hon. Christopher Patten, MP, born 1944. (£35,120.)

19. *Secretary of State for Northern Ireland:* Rt Hon. Peter Brooke, MP, born 1934. (£35,120.)

20. *Minister of Agriculture, Fisheries and Food:* Rt Hon. John Gummer, MP, born 1939. (£35,120.)

21. *Chief Secretary to the Treasury:* Rt Hon. Norman Lamont, MP, born 1942. (£35,120.)

22. *Secretary of State for Employment:* Rt Hon. Michael Howard, QC, MP, born 1941. (£35,120.)

(b) Law Officers

23. *Attorney-General:* Rt Hon. Sir Patrick Mayhew, QC, MP, born 1929. (£37,320.)

24. *Lord Advocate:* Lord Fraser, QC, born 1945. (£44,661.)

25. *Solicitor-General:* Rt Hon. Sir Nicholas Lyell, QC, MP, born 1938. (£30,600.)

26. *Solicitor-General for Scotland:* Alan Rodger, QC, MP, born 1944. (£39,109.)

(c) Ministers not in the Cabinet

27. *Parlimentary Secretary, Treasury (Chief Whip):* Rt Hon. Timothy Renton, MP, born 1932. (£29,230.)

28. *Minister of State, Privy Council Office, Minister for the Arts:* Rt Hon. Richard Luce, MP, born 1936. (£24,850.)

29. *Minister of State, Foreign and Commonwealth Office, Minister for Overseas Development:* Rt Hon. Lynda Chalker, MP, born 1942. (£24,850.)

30. *Minister of State, Foreign and Commonwealth Office:* Rt Hon. William Waldegrave, MP, born 1946. (£24,850.)

31. *Minister of State, Foreign and Commonwealth Office:* Rt Hon. The Lord Brabazon of Tara, born 1946. (£39,641.)

32. *Minister of State, Foreign and Commonwealth Office:* Hon. Francis Maude, MP, born 1953. (£24,850.)

33. *Financial Secretary, Treasury:* Peter Lilley, MP, born 1943. (£24,850.)

34. *Paymaster General (Treasury):* The Earl of Caithness, born 1948. (£39,641.)

35. *Minister of State, Home Office:* Rt Hon. John Patten, MP, born 1945. (£24,850.)

36. *Minister of State, Home Office:* David Mellor, MP, born 1937. (£24,850.)

37. *Minister of State, Home Office:* The Earl Ferrers, born 1929. (£39,641.)

38. *Minister of State, Welsh Office:* Wyn Roberts, MP, born 1930. (£24,850.)

39. *Minister of State, Ministry of Defence, Armed Forces:* Hon. Archibald Hamilton, MP, born 1941. (£24,850.)

40. *Minister of State, Ministry of Defence, Defence Procurement:* Hon. Alan Clark, MP, born 1928. (£24,850.)

41. *Minster of State, Department of Trade and Industry, Minister for Industry and Enterprise:* Hon. Douglas Hogg, MP, born 1945. (£24,850.)

42. *Minister of State, Department of Trade and Industry, Minister for Trade:* Rt Hon. The Lord Trefgarne, born 1941. (£39,641.)

43. *Minister of State, Department of Health, Minister for Health:* Virginia Bottomley, MP, born 1948. (£24,850.)

44. *Minister of State, Department of Education and Science:* Angela Rumbold, CBE, MP, born 1932. (£24,850.)

45. *Minister of State, Scottish Office:* Ian Lang, MP, born 1940. (£24,850.)

46. *Minister of State, Scottish Office:* The Lord Sanderson of Bowden, born 1933. (£39,641.)

47. *Minister of State, Department of Transport:* Michael Portillo, MP, born 1953. (£24,850.)

48. *Minister of State, Department of Energy:* Rt Hon. Peter Morrison, MP, born 1944. (£24,850.)

49. *Minister of State, Department of Social Security, Minister for Social Security and the Disabled:* Rt Hon. Nicholas Scott, MBE, MP, born 1933. (£24,850.)

50. *Minister of State, Department of the Environment, Minister for the Environment and Countryside:* David Trippier, MP, born 1946. (£24.850.)

51. *Minister of State, Department of the Environment, Minister for Local Government and Inner Cities:* David Hunt, MBE, MP, born 1942. (£24,850.)

52. *Minister of State, Department of the Environment, Minister for Housing and Planning:* Michael Spicer, MP, born 1943. (£24,850.)

53. *Minister of State, Northern Ireland Office:* Rt Hon. John Cope, MP, born 1937. (£24,850.)

54. *Minister of State, Ministry of Agriculture, Fisheries and Food:* The Baroness Trumpington, born 1922. (£39,641.)

55. *Minister of State, Employment:* Timothy Eggar, MP, born 1951. (£24,850.)

Leader of the Opposition in the House of Commons: Rt Hon. Neil Kinnock, MP, born 1942. (£32,200.)

Leader of the Opposition in the House of Lords: Rt Hon. The Lord Cledwyn of Penrhos, born 1916. (£33,241.)

Cabinet Ministers, Ministers of State, Parliamentary Secretaries and the Leader of the Opposition who are also Members of Parliament, receive additionally a reduced Parliamentary salary of £20,101.

The Constitution of the House of Commons after the 1987 general election was as follows: Conservative, 375; Labour, 229; Liberals, 17, SDP, 5; Others, 24.

Ball, A., *British Political Parties: The Emergence of a Modern Party System.* 1981
Butler, D. and Butler, G., *British Political Facts, 1900–85*. London, 1986
Butler, D. and Kavanagh, D., *The British General Election of 1987*. 1988
Drewry, G. (ed.), *The New Select Committees*. OUP, 1985
King, A. (ed.), *The British Prime Minister*. Rev. ed. London, 1985.—*British Members of Parliament*. London, 1974

Mackintosh, J. P., *The British Cabinet*. 3rd ed. London, 1977.—*The Government and Politics of Britain*. 4th ed. London, 1977
May, Sir T. E., *Treatise on the Law, Privileges, Proceedings and Usage of Parliament*. 20th ed., London, 1983
Norton, P., *Parliament in the 1980s*. Oxford, 1985
Parker, F. K., *Conduct of Parliamentary Elections*. London, 1983
Pelling, H., *A Short History of the Labour Party*. London, 1976
Shell, D., *The House of Lords*. Oxford, 1988
Silk, E. P., *How Parliament Works*. London, 1987
The Times Guide to the House of Commons, June 1987. London, 1987

National flag: The combined crosses of St George (red), St Andrew (white) and St Patrick (red), the red fimbriated in white, all on a blue ground.

European Parliament: On 15 June 1989 Great Britain elected 81 representatives to the European Parliament, of which 66 came from England, 8 from Scotland and 4 from Wales, each constituency returning a single member by a first past the post system. Northern Ireland returned 3 members by single transferable vote. The seats were won as follows: Labour 45, Conservative 32, Scottish Nationalists 1, Ulster Unionists 1, Democratic Unionists 1, Social, Democratic and Labour Party 1.

Local Government. Local Administration is carried out by four different types of bodies, namely: (i) local branches of some central ministries, such as the Department of Health and Social Security (now two separate departments); (ii) local submanagements of nationalized industries; (iii) specialist authorities such as electricity boards; and (iv) the system of local government described below. The phrase 'local government' has come to mean that part of the local administration conducted by elected councils.

There are two separate systems, one for England and Wales and one for Scotland, but both systems are financed by a charge on individuals known as the Community Charge paid at a flat rate by each adult, varying from one area to another, levied locally, supplemented by a new streamlined government grant system and a nationwide uniform tax on business property - the Uniform Business Rate.

Local Government: England and Wales—*Outside London.* England and Wales have slightly differing systems. Each country has three types of councils namely, county, district and English parish or Welsh Community Councils. In addition, England has some metropolitan district councils.

Councillors are elected by their local electors for 4 years. The chairman of the council is one of the councillors elected by the rest. In a district with the status of borough his title is mayor, or in a city, Lord Mayor. Any parish or community council can by simple resolution adopt the style 'town council' and the status of town for the parish or community. The chairman of the council will be known as the town mayor.

Counties and Districts: There are 47 non-metropolitan counties (of which 8 are in Wales). The 6 metropolitan counties (Greater Manchester, Merseyside, South Yorkshire, Tyne and Wear, West Yorkshire and West Midlands) have no councils, the metropolitan districts having most of the county functions. Within the counties there are 369 districts (36 metropolitan and 333 non-metropolitan, of which 37 are in Wales).

Parishes and Communities: There are some 10,000 parishes within the English districts, of which 8,000 or so have councils. About 300 are former small boroughs or urban districts which became successor parishes.

In Wales, parishes are known as communities. Unlike England, where some urban areas are not in any parish, communities have been established for the whole of Wales. There is one for each former parish, county borough, borough or urban district (or part thereof where the former area is divided by a new boundary). There are about 1,000 communities altogether, of which 800 or so have councils.

The Local Government Act 1972 laid down the boundaries for all the counties and districts in England and Wales except the English non-metropolitan districts.

Permanent Local Government Boundary Commissions for England and for Wales advise the Secretaries of State on boundaries and electoral arrangements.

Local government functions may be classified into county, district and parish or community functions, but whereas county and district functions are distinct, the parish and community functions are mostly concurrent with those of the districts. Arrangements may, however, be made so that any council may discharge functions of any other as its agent.

The following is the classification of powers given above: *Parish and Community Functions.* Allotments, burial and cremation, halls, meeting places and entertainments, facilities for exercise and recreation, public lavatories, street lighting, off-street vehicle parking, footpaths, the support of local arts and crafts, the encouragement of tourism and the right to be consulted by the district council on planning applications and certain byelaws. *District Functions.* In addition to the Parish and Community functions, aerodromes, civic restaurants, housing, markets, refuse collection, the administration of planning control, the formulation of local plans, sewerage on behalf of the water authority, museums, the licensing of places of entertainment and refreshment, and the constitutional oversight of parishes and communities. *County Functions.* The formulation of structure plans, traffic, transportation and roads, education, public libraries and museums, youth employment and social services.

There are, in addition, a number of special arrangements. Four district councils in Wales are designated as library authorities and Welsh district councils have powers in relation to allotments currently with community councils. The county councils in England and Wales separately or jointly appoint the fire and police authorities, and the bodies responsible for national parks. In Metropolitan counties, there are no county councils and all functions are performed by the districts (in some cases jointly). The total number of local government electors in England and Wales was 38,558,844 in 1989.

Greater London. From 1965–86 London was governed by the Greater London Council, covering the whole metropolitan area, and by 32 London boroughs and the Corporation of the City of London, each with responsibilities in its own area. The GLC was abolished on 1 April 1986. The individual borough councils are the education authorities. Fire services in Greater London are the responsibility of the London Fire and Civil Defence Authority, whose members are appointed by the boroughs and the City. Flood prevention is the responsibility of the Thames Water Authority. Waste regulation for the whole of Greater London is the function of the London Waste Regulation Authority. Waste collection is the responsibility of the boroughs. Waste disposal is the responsibility of the boroughs acting individually or in groups. Except in the City, the police authority is the Metropolitan Police, which is responsible to central government. London Regional Transport is likewise responsible to central government for passenger transport. Other local government functions are the responsibility of the boroughs, acting either individually or jointly, and the City.

Estimated population of Greater London in June 1988 was 6,736,007, and rateable value at 1 April 1988 was £2,112,830,526. Net current expenditure for all London authorities in 1988–89 was estimated at £4,832m. (including £978m. for ILEA but excluding Metropolitan Police). Gross capital expenditure (excluding leasing) for all London authorities and the London Residuary Body was estimated at £1,300m. in 1987–88.

Saint, A., (ed.) *Politics and the People of London.* London, 1989

Scotland. For local government purposes, mainland Scotland is divided on a two-tier basis into 9 regions and 53 districts. Functions are allocated between regional and district councils in the same way (with minor exceptions) as they are allocated between county and district councils in England. The 3 islands areas of Orkney, Shetland and the Western Isles have single-tier councils responsible for virtually all functions. The members of each council are elected for a 4-year term, elections for regional and islands councils alternating with elections for district councils at 2-year intervals. Each council elects a chairman for the 4-year term. In some cases the chairman is called 'Convener' or 'Provost', and the chairman of Edinburgh, Glasgow, Aberdeen and Dundee District Councils are titled 'Lord Provost'.

Over 1,000 community councils have been established under schemes drawn up by district and island councils. These community councils cannot claim public funds as of right nor do they have specific powers conferred by statute: Consequently they are not local authorities in the sense that English parish councils or Welsh community councils are.

As in England and Wales, a permanent Local Government Boundary Commission advises the Secretary of State on local authority boundaries and electoral constituencies.

The total number of local government electors in Scotland was 3,932,897 in 1989.

DEFENCE. The Defence Council was established on 1 April 1964 under the chairmanship of the Secretary of State for Defence, who is responsible to the Sovereign and Parliament for the defence of the realm. Vested in the Defence Council are the functions of commanding and administering the Armed Forces. The Secretary of State heads the Ministry of Defence as a Department of State. There are 4 subordinate Ministers; 2 Ministers of State and 2 Parliamentary Under-Secretaries of State.

Defence Council membership comprises the Secretary of State, the 2 Ministers of State, the Chief of the Defence Staff, the 3 single Service Chiefs of Staff, the Vice-Chief of Defence Staff, the Chief of Defence Procurement, the Chief Scientific Adviser, the Permanent Under-Secretary of State and the Second Permanent Under Secretary of State.

There are 3 Service Boards, each of which enjoys delegated powers for the administration of matters relating to the naval, military and air forces respectively.

Defence policy decision making is a collective Governmental responsibility. Important matters of policy are considered by the full Cabinet or, more frequently, by the Defence and Oversea Policy Committee under the chairmanship of the Prime Minister. Other members of this Committee include the Secretary of State for Defence, the Foreign and Commonwealth Secretary and the Home Secretary.

The Procurement Executive. An important development in 1971 was the creation of a Procurement Executive to combine the Defence Procurement responsibilities of the Ministry of Defence and the former Ministry of Aviation Supply.

Service Strengths at 1 Jan. 1988, all ranks, males and females, UK personnel only: Royal Navy and Royal Marines, 65,600; Army, 155,500; Royal Air Force, 93,300; total, 317,300. The Ministry of Defence employed 142,237 civilians in Dec. 1988.

Defence Budget (Plans): 1989–90, £20,143m.; 1990–91, £21,190m; 1991–92, £22,100m.

Army. Control of the British Army is vested in the Defence Council and is exercised through the Army Board. The Secretary of State for Defence is Chairman of the Army Board. The other civilian members are the 4 subordinate Ministers; the Controller Establishments, Research and Nuclear Programmes and the Second Permanent Under Secretary of State.

The Military members of the Army Board are the Chief of the General Staff, the Adjutant General, the Quartermaster General and the Master General of the Ordnance. The Chief of the General Staff is the professional head of his Service and the professional adviser to Ministers on the Army aspects of military matters. He is responsible for the fighting efficiency of his Service; for Army advice on the conduct of operations; and for the issuing of such single Service operational orders as may be appropriate resulting from defence policy decisions. He is also responsible for the Territorial Army. The Chief of the General Staff is a member of the Chiefs of Staff Committee which is chaired by the Chief of the Defence Staff, who is responsible to HM Government for professional advice on strategy and military operations and on the military implication of defence policy. The Adjutant-General is responsible for recruiting and selection of army manpower; for the administration and individual training of military personnel; for the discipline of the Army; for pay and allowances and pensions; for legal services; for the veterinary and remount services; for the Army Cadet Forces; for questions of Army welfare and education including school children overseas; and for resettlement and sports. The Quartermaster-General is responsible for logistic planning for the Army; for the storage, distribution, maintenance, repair and inspection of equipment, stores and ammunition; for development of stores; for supply, transport and accommodation; for the development, production and inspection of clothing; for military movements and transportation; for the Army postal, catering, salvage and fire services; and for questions connected with canteens, institutes and military labour. The Master General of the Ordnance is a member of both the Army Board and of the Procurement Executive Management Board. He is responsible to the Chief of Defence Procurement for the financial and technical management of the approved programme for the procurement of land service equipment for the Armed Services, and to the Army Board for the co-ordination of the Army's total equipment programme.

Headquarters United Kingdom Land Forces at Wilton commands all Army units in UK except Ministry of Defence controlled units. The Ministry of Defence retains direct operational control of units in Northern Ireland. Command by HQ United Kingdom Land Forces is exercised through 9 district headquarters. There are 3 major overseas Commands: Land Forces British Army of the Rhine, Hong Kong and Cyprus. There are also garrisons in Berlin, Gibraltar, Falkland Islands, Brunei and Belize. The Army Air Corps has some 300 helicopters and 25 fixed-wing aircraft.

The strength of the Regular Army (less the Brigade of Gurkhas and locally enlisted personnel) on 1 Jan. 1989 was 155,500 men and 6,500 women. Strength of reserve forces were: Regular reserves, 173,100; territorial army, 72,800; Home Service Force, 3,000.

The Territorial Army role is to provide a national reserve for employment on specific tasks at home and overseas and to meet the unexpected when required; and, in particular, to complete the Army Order of Battle of NATO committed forces and to provide certain units for the support of NATO Headquarters, to assist in maintaining a secure UK base in support of forces deployed on the Continent of Europe and to provide a framework for any future expansion of the Reserves. In addition, men who have completed service in the Regular Army normally have some liability to serve in the Regular Reserve. All members of the TA and Regular Reserve may be called out by a Queen's Order in time of emergency of imminent national danger and most of the TA and a large proportion of the Regular Reserve may be called out by a Queen's Order when warlike operations are in preparation or in progress. There is a special reserve force in Northern Ireland, the Ulster Defence Regiment, 6,300 strong, which gives support to the regular army.

Men, women and juniors enlist in the Army for 22 years' active and reserve service. However, under a scheme introduced in May 1981 they are entitled to give 12 months' notice (18 months' for women) to leave active service provided they serve for a minimum of 3 years. Alternatively, they can agree to serve for 6 or 9 years to receive the benefit of higher rates of pay. Those enlisting in certain technical trades must agree to serve for a minimum of 6 years. Recruits under the age of 17½ on reaching the age of 18 are entitled either to confirm their original engagement or to reduce their period of service to 3 years.

Women serve in both the Regular Army and the TA in the Queen Alexandra's Royal Army Nursing Corps, the Ulster Defence Regiment and the Women's Royal Army Corps, the latter's employments including communications, motor transport, clerical and catering duties. Some officers of the Women's Royal Army Corps are employed on the staffs of military headquarters.

Blaxford, G., *The Regiments Depart: A History of the British Army 1945–70*. London, 1971
Brereton, J. M., *The British Soldier*. London, 1985
Johnson, F. A., *Defence by Ministry: The British Ministry of Defence 1944–1974*. London, 1980
Strawson, J., *Gentlemen in Khaki: The British Army 1890-1990*. London, 1989

Navy. Control of the Royal Navy is vested in the Defence Council and is exercised through the Admiralty Board, chaired by the Secretary of State for Defence. The other civilian members are the Ministers and Under Secretaries of State for the Armed Forces and Defence Procurement; the Second Permanent Under Secretary of State; and the Controller, Research and Development Establishments, Research and

Nuclear. The naval members are the Chief of Naval Staff and First Sea Lord responsible for management, fighting efficiency, planning and operational advice; the Chief of Naval Personnel and Second Sea Lord, responsible for the manning of the Fleet and all personnel aspects; the Controller of the Navy, responsible for procurement of ships, their weapons and equipment; and the Chief of Fleet Support, responsible for all aspects of logistic support, stores, fuels and transport, naval dockyards, the Royal Fleet Auxiliary and Royal Maritime Auxiliary services.

The Commander-in-Chief Fleet, headquartered at Northwood, commands the fleet. Naval Air Stations are commanded by the Flag Officer Naval Air Command. The command of all other naval establishments in the UK, except those under the Commandant General Royal Marines, is exercised by the C.-in-C. Naval Home Command from Portsmouth, through Area Flag Officers. Main naval bases are at Devonport, Rosyth, Portsmouth, and Faslane, with a training base at Portland, and minor bases overseas at Hong Kong and Gibraltar.

The Royal Naval Reserve (RNR) and the Royal Marines Reserve (RMR) currently number 5,600 and 1,500 respectively. The RNR provides trained personnel in war to undertake Naval Control of Shipping, to man Mine Counter-measures vessels, HQ Command and Communications, and Rotary Wing Aircrew. The main roles of the RMR are reinforcement and other specialist tasks with the UK-Netherlands Amphibious Force. In addition, men who have completed service in the Royal Navy and the Royal Marines have a commitment to serve in the Royal Fleet Reserve, currently 24,700 strong. The Royal Naval Auxiliary Service (RNXS) is a civilian auxiliary some 3,200 strong who man Port Headquarters and provide crews for patrol and administrative craft in wartime.

Royal Navy ratings enlist to complete 22 years active service (at the end of which there is selective re-engagement open to senior, chief and charge specialists for a further 5 or 10 years) with the option to leave at 18 months notice on completion of a minimum of 2 and a half years productive service. Those who leave before completing 22 years have a liability for up to 3 years service in the Royal Fleet Reserve. Royal Marine ranks, WRNS ratings and QARNNS (the nursing service) ratings enlist to complete an initial 9 year engagement but they may apply to re-engage to complete 14 years and 22 years. Women serve in both the WRNS and QARNNS and their reserves. In the former, they are employed on secretarial, communications, stores accounting, catering, mechanical, education and training support duties, but are not eligible for sea service. Service women have no reserve liability.

The roles of the Royal Navy are first, to deploy the national strategic nuclear deterrent, second to contribute to the NATO maritime strategy of forward defence, third to provide maritime defence of the United Kingdom and fourth to meet national maritime objectives outside the NATO area.

The first of these aims is met by the ships of the 10th Submarine Squadron based at Faslane on the Clyde, consisting of 4 nuclear-powered strategic missile submarines of the Resolution class (*Resolution, Repulse, Renown* and *Revenge*) each of 8,600 tonnes submerged displacement, completed between 1967 and 1969 and deploying 16 Polaris A3TK missiles each. These ships are to be replaced, commencing in 1994 by 4 substantially larger units of the Vanguard class (*Vanguard, Vengeance, Victorious* and *Venerable*), 15,250 tonnes, of which the first two are under construction, which will deploy 16 US-built Trident-2 D5 UGM-133A missiles with British warheads,

The strength of the fleet's major non-strategic units at the end of each of the last 8 years was as follows:

	1982	*1983*	*1984*	*1985*	*1986*	*1987*	*1988*	*1989*
Nuclear Submarines	11	12	13	14	14	15	15	16
Other Submarines	16	16	15	15	14	12	11	11
Aircraft Carriers	3	3	3	3	2[1]	2[1]	2[1]	2[1]
Destroyers	13	13	13	15	14	13	13	13
Frigates	47	46	48	42	39	36	35	36

[1] Following Government policy, of the 3 Carriers held, only 2 are kept in operational status

The most important element of the contribution to forward maritime strategy is the nuclear-powered submarine force, now numbering 16, and of three main classes. All are armed with torpedoes and Harpoon anti-ship missiles. There are 5 Trafalgar class, (5,300 tonnes) completed 1983-1989 (with 2 further ships fitting-out), 6 Swiftsure (4,800 tonnes) completed 1973-79, and 5 Valiant/Churchill of 4,900 tonnes completed 1966-71. Other submarines are of conventional diesel-electric propulsion and comprise the first of 4 Upholder class (2,400 tonnes) completed in 1989 and still on trials, and 10 Oberon class (completed 1960-67).

The principal surface ships are the Light V/STOL Aircraft Carriers of the Invincible class, (*Invincible, Illustrious* and *Ark Royal*), 20,900 tonnes, completed 1980-85, embarking an air group of 8 Sea Harrier V/STOL fighters, 9 ASW Sea King and 3 radar early warning Sea King helicopters, and armed with 1 twin Sea Dart surface-to-air missile system. Two of these ships are maintained in the operational fleet, with the third either in refit or reserve. (As from May, 1989 *Illustrious* was in reserve in Portsmouth).

The 13 destroyers comprise 12 Type 42 (completed 1976-85), and HMS Bristol, the sole Type 82 (completed 1973), now employed as the Dartmouth Training Ship. All are armed with 1 twin Sea Dart surface-to-air missile system. Frigates comprise 14 Type 22 (1979-89), the first Norfolk class (Type 23) accepted in late 1989, 6 Amazon (Type 21) completed 1974-78 and the last 15 of the 26 Leander class built between 1963 and 1970.

The lightly-armed patrol force comprises 1 ice patrol ship, 13 other offshore patrol vessels (including 3 in the Hong Kong squadron), and 30 inshore patrol craft mostly employed on training duties. Mine countermeasures capability is provided by 13 offshore hunter/sweepers, 12 offshore minesweepers, 10 coastal minehunters and 3 coastal minesweepers. Amphibious lift for the Royal Marines is provided by 1 dock landing ship (with a second in reserve) and 5 tank landing ships (civil manned, and in peacetime employed on army freighting), supported by about 32 small amphibious craft.

Comprehensive support to the fleet is provided by 38 major auxiliaries including 9 replenishment and 4 support tankers, 4 ammunition ships, 2 repair ships, 1 transport, 3 ocean tugs, 6 survey ships, 3 trials ships, 1 aviation training ship, 1 seabed operations vessel, 1 chartered training ship, and the Royal Yacht. Second-line support is provided by about 210 harbour and coastal service craft and minor auxiliaries.

Ships under construction or on order include the final 2 Trafalgar class submarines, 3 further Upholder class submarines, 9 Norfolk class frigates, 5 coastal minehunters and 2 large general purpose replenishment ships.

The Fleet Air Arm has 320 aircraft of which 280 are active, in 14 operational squadrons. The operational inventory comprises 42 Sea Harrier V/STOL fighter aircraft, 76 Sea King and 78 Lynx ASW helicopters, 10 Sea King airborne early warning helicopters and 34 Sea King (commando transport version). There are 7 training and second-line squadrons, equipped with about 50 fixed wing aircraft of various types and 25 training helicopters.

The total number of male and female personnel (including Royal Marines) was (in 1,000) on 31 March: 1987, 67·4; 1988, 65·7; 1989, 65·5; 1990 (estimated) 64·3. The estimated total of 64,300 includes 7,700 marines and 3,300 women.

Sharpe, R. G. (ed.) *Jane's Fighting Ships*. London, annual

Air Force. In May 1912 the Royal Flying Corps first came into existence with military and naval wings, of which the latter became the independent Royal Naval Air Service in July 1914. On 2 Jan. 1918 an Air Ministry was formed, and on 1 April 1918 the Royal Flying Corps and the Royal Naval Air Service were amalgamated, under the Air Ministry, as the Royal Air Force.

In 1937 the units based on aircraft carriers and naval shore stations again passed to the operational and administrative control of the Admiralty, as the Fleet Air Arm. In 1964 control of the RAF became a responsibility of the Ministry of Defence.

The Royal Air Force is administered by the Air Force Board, of which the Secretary of State for Defence is Chairman. The Minister of State for the Armed Forces is Vice-Chairman, and normally acts as Chairman on behalf of the Secretary of State. Other members of the Board are the Minister of State for Defence Procurement, the Under-Secretary of State for the Armed Forces, the Under-Secretary of

State for Defence Procurement, the Chief of the Air Staff, Air Member for Personnel, Air Member for Supply and Organization, Controller of Aircraft, Second Permanent Under-Secretary of State and Controller R & D Establishments, Research and Nuclear. The RAF is organized into commands:

Home Commands. Strike and Support Commands. The Air Training Corps and the Air Sections of the Combined Cadet Force are under the administrative control of Support Command and functionally controlled by the Ministry of Defence.

The RAF College, which trains all candidates for commissions, is at Cranwell. The RAF Staff College is at Bracknell. The Department of Air Warfare is at Cranwell. The RAF Central Flying School is at Scampton. Estimated strength in Sept. 1989, including WRAF, was 89,719.

Strike Command itself is responsible for transport and air-to-air refuelling. VC10, Tristar and Hercules aircraft are used for air refuelling as well as strategic and tactical transport; the Victor solely for air refuelling. However, day-to-day functioning and organization of most operations is delegated to 3 Groups. Nos 1 and 38 Groups merged in late 1983 to form a new No 1 Group, responsible for the strike/attack, reconnaissance, tanker and battlefield support. The Tornado GR1 and Jaguar are used in the strike, attack and reconnaissance roles. Battlefield support forces comprise Harrier GR5s, Chinook, Puma and Wessex support helicopters. No 11 Group controls the air defence forces: Tornado F3 and Phantom supersonic all-weather interceptors, Bloodhound surface-to-air missiles, and ground environment radars, the associated communication systems, and the Ballistic Missile Early Warning System at Fylingdales. No 11 Group also controls the Hawks of the Tactical Weapons Units which, in war, would supplement air defence fighters at bases throughout the UK. UK air defence is undergoing major improvements. The Boeing E-3 will enter service in 1990–91, replacing the Shackleton, and in the ground environment, there are new radars and communications systems entering service. No 18 Group is responsible for maritime air operations. ASW is the duty of the Nimrod Mk 2, which also has a capability against surface ships, although Buccaneers provide the main offensive force against a maritime surface threat. No 18 Group also operates Canberras in a multitude of roles, including photo-reconnaissance, target towing and ECM training, as well as Nimrod special-purpose aircraft. Search and rescue units are equipped with Sea King and Wessex helicopters. RAF Regiment short-range air defence squadrons, armed with Rapier, and the field squadrons form part of 1 Group, as does The Queen's Flight, which has 3 BAe 146s and 2 Wessex helicopters. The Military Air Traffic Operations organization also has the status of a Group. Strike Command has NATO commitments, but is available for overseas reinforcement. The training element of RAF Support Command utilizes Bulldog and Chipmunk primary trainers, Jet Provost basic trainers (now being replaced by turboprop Tucanos), Hawk advanced trainers, Jetstreams for multi-engine pilot training, twin-jet Dominies for training navigators and other non-pilot aircrew, and Gazelle and Wessex helicopters.

Overseas Commands. Royal Air Force Germany. Small units in Gibraltar, the Falkland Islands, Belize, Cyprus and Hong Kong.

Squadrons of RAF Germany, which form part of NATO's 2nd Allied Tactical Air Force under SACEUR, have Tornado GR1, Harrier GR5, Phantom fighters, Chinook and Puma Helicopters, Andover communications aircraft, and Rapier surface-to-air missile squadrons of the RAF Regiment.

A flight of Phantom aircraft, a squadron of Chinook and Sea King helicopters for transport and search and rescue, and a flight of Hercules tankers are based in the Falkland Islands; a squadron of Wessex helicopters is based in Hong Kong and Cyprus.

The Royal Air Force, 1939–45. Vols. I, II, III. HMSO, 1953–54
Taylor J. W. R. (ed.) *Jane's All the World's Aircraft.* London. Annual from 1909

INTERNATIONAL RELATIONS

Membership. The UK is a member of UN, Commonwealth, the European Communities, OECD, the Council of Europe, NATO and the Colombo Plan.

ECONOMY

Budget. Revenue and expenditure for years ending 31 March, in £ sterling:

Revenue	*Estimated in the Budgets*	*Actual receipts into the Exchequer*	*More than estimates*
1987	108,600,000,000	111,100,000,000	2,500,000,000
1988	168,800,000,000	173,700,000,000	4,900,000,000
1989	184,900,000,000	190,900,000,000	6,000,000,000
1990	206,400,000,000	203,400,000,000	– 3,000,000,000

The Budget estimate of ordinary revenue for 1990–91 is £218,600m.

Expenditure	*Budget and supplementary estimates*	*Actual payments out of the Exchequer*	*More than estimates*
1987	163,900,000,000	164,900,000,000	–1,000,000,000
1988	173,500,000,000	171,800,000,000	–1,700,000,000
1989	182,900,000,000	179,100,000,000	–3,800,000,000
1990	194,300,000,000	197,700,000,000	–3,400,000,000

The Budget estimate of ordinary expenditure for 1990–91 is £212,700m.

Revenue in detail for 1989–90 and the expenditure, are given below, as is the budget estimate for 1990–91 (in £1m.):

Sources of revenue	*Net receipts 1989–90*	*Budget estimate 1990–91*
Inland Revenue:		
Income	48,700	55,000
Corporation tax	21,400	20,700
Petroleum revenue tax	1,100	1,100
Capital Gains tax	1,900	2,100
Inheritance tax	1,200	1,200
Stamp duties	2,100	1,900
Total Inland Revenue	76,400	81,900
Customs and Excise:		
Value Added Tax	29,700	32,100
Oil	8,800	9,700
Tobacco	5,000	5,400
Alcohol duties	4,600	4,900
Betting and gaming	1,000	1,000
Car tax	1,500	1,500
Customs duties	1,800	1,900
Agricultural levies	100	100
Total Customs and Excise	52,400	56,700
Vehicle Excise duties	2,900	3,000
Miscellaneous receipts:		
Interest and dividends	7,200	6,400
Oil royalties	600	700
Total Government Receipts	203,400	218,600

The following are the branches of expenditure for year ended 31 March 1990 and the estimates for the year 1990–91 (in £1m.):

	Estimates 1989–90	*Estimates 1990–91*
Social Security	47,000	52,000
Defence	20,600	21,200
Health and Personal Social Services	20,000	22,100
Northern Ireland	5,500	5,700
Privatization proceeds	–4,200	–5,000
Planning total	162,300	179,000
Interest Payments	17,700	17,000
Other Adjustments	3,900	3,400
Total	197,700	212,700

A single graduated income tax came into operation on 6 April 1973, replacing the existing income tax and surtax.

Rates of Personal Tax from 6 April 1990	%
Income between	
£0–£20,700	25
Over £20,700	40

Under the tax system, the amounts of the personal allowances are adjusted so that they retain their equivalent in relation to earned income. Independent taxation of husband and wife was introduced on 6 April 1990.

Personal Allowances	*1990–91* £
Single person / Wife's earned income	3,005
Married couple's allowance	1,720
Age allowance (age 65 to 74):	
Single	3,670
Married couple's allowance	2,145
Age allowance (age 75 or over):	
Single	3,820
Married couple's allowance	2,185

Deductions of tax under PAYE extend over the full range of unified tax rates and not merely the basic rate. Similarly, assessment on business profits and on other income which was directly assessed to tax, such as rents and interest on bank deposits, are made by reference to the full scale of rates, including where appropriate the investment income surcharge.

The standard rate of 25% is the rate at which tax is deducted from payments of interest, etc., and corresponds under the corporation tax system, to the tax credit on dividends. Where an individual's total income is such that he is liable on this taxed investment income at rates exceeding 25%, or if his investment income is high enough to make him liable to the surcharge, the higher rate or surcharge liability on this taxed investment income will in general be assessed separately after the end of the tax year.

Corporation Tax. Corporation Tax applies, with certain exceptions, to trades or businesses carried on by bodies corporate or by unincorporated societies or other bodies and this tax came into force from April 1966 replacing Profits Tax. Corporation Tax for companies was 35% for 1990–91. Small companies rates, 1990–91, 25%.

Capital Gains Tax. Gains resulting from the disposal of capital assets (other than British Government and Government guaranteed securities and certain exempted forms of property such as a private car and personal residences) are taxed under the Finance Act 1965. In 1990–91 exemption was granted for all gains made in a financial year which in total did not exceed £5,000 and most trusts on the first £2,500. In 1988 the base was brought forward from 1965 to 1982.

Inheritance Tax. Formerly Capital Transfer Tax. From 18 March 1986 there is no lifetime charge on gifts between individuals. From 1989 a flat rate of 40% was introduced with a threshold in 1990 of £128,000.

Value Added Tax. Value Added Tax was introduced from 1 April 1973 at the rate of 10% on the supply of goods (with certain exceptions) and services. From 18 June 1979 the rate of tax was fixed at 15%. From 21 March 1990 the registration limits became £25,400 per annum.

Kay, J. A. and King, M. A., *The British Tax System.* OUP, 1980

Local Taxation. The Community Charge was introduced in Scotland in 1989 and in England and Wales in 1990. *See* p. 1311. In England and Wales, the average amount of rates collected per £ of rateable value was £0·34 in 1913–14 and estimated to be 244·3p for 1988–89. In Scotland the rateable value on which rates are leviable on 1 April 1986 was £3,190m. and the average amount per £ of rateable value of the rates was 67·2p.

Under the Local Government Planning and Land Act 1980, the Government gives general financial assistance to local authorities by means of rate support grants. The Rate Support Grant Supplementary Report (England) 1988–89 deals with the distribution of these grants to local authorities in England only. The grants for 1988–89 contain (i) Block Grant £8,960m., the object of which is to give authorities sufficient grant to put them in a position where they can provide similar standards of service for a similar rate in the £, and (ii) Domestic Grant £727m., which will provide a relief of 18½p for domestic ratepayers except for those in the Cities of London and Westminster where the relief provided is 38·1p and 27·8p respectively. There is also provision in the 1980 Act for payment of National Parks Supplementary Grant (£8·1m.) to county councils with all or part of a national park in their area, and Transport Supplementary Grant (£199·1m.) payable to county councils, metropolitan district councils, London borough councils and the City of London. Grants are also payable on revenue expenditure for specific services, including police and housing, and capital expenditure on certain services also attracts grant.

In Scotland, revenue support grant replaced rate support grants when the community charge was introduced on 1 April 1989. It is paid under the Abolition of Domestic Rates Etc (Scotland) Act 1987, as amended by the Local Government and Housing Act 1989. The total amount of revenue support grant for the local authority financial year 1989-90, as prescribed in the Revenue Support Grant (Scotland) Order 1988, is £2,243·8m. As in England and Wales capital and revenue (specific) grants are also payable on expenditure for certain specified services.

Gross National Product:

	1946	*1960*	*1970*	*1980*	*1988*
Expenditure (£*1m.*)					
Consumers' expenditure	7,273	16,939	31,773	135,738	293,569
Central government final consumption	2,282	4,206	8,961	48,424	91,847
Gross domestic fixed capital formation	925	4,190	9,462	39,411	88,751
Value of physical increase in stocks and work in progress	–126	562	425	–2,706	4,371
Total domestic expenditure at market prices	10,354	25,897	50,581	220,867	478,538
Exports of goods and services	1,775	5,153	11,533	63,158	108,533
Less Imports of goods and services	–2,083	–5,549	–11,122	–57,913	–125,194
Less Taxes on expenditure	–1,573	–3,378	–8,416	–36,882	–75,029
Subsidies	384	493	884	5,308	5,883
Gross domestic product at factor cost	8,855	22,616	43,460	194,538	392,731

Factor incomes (£1m.)	*1946*	*1960*	*1970*	*1980*	*1988*
Income from employment	5,758	15,174	30,404	136,050	249,775
Income from self-employment [1]	1,126	2,008	3,735	17,581	42,617
Gross trading profits of companies [1]	1,476	3,730	5,935	27,708	70,242
Gross trading surplus of public corporations [1]	20	534	1,447	6,222	7,286
Gross trading surplus of other public enterprises [1]	86	189	151	242	–70
Rent [2]	429	1,086	2,833	13,390	27,464
Total domestic income before providing for depreciation and stock appreciation	8,895	22,863	44,837	203,304	400,722
Less Stock appreciation	–125	–122	–1,090	–6,456	–6,116
Residual error	...	–125	–287	–2,310	–181
Gross domestic product at factor cost	8,770	22,616	43,460	194,538	394,787
Net property income from abroad	85	233	559	–273	5,619
Gross national product	8,855	22,849	44,019	194,265	400,406
Less Capital consumption	...	–2,047	–4,420	–27,223	–54,769
National income	...	20,802	39,599	167,042	345,637

[1] Before providing for depreciation and stock appreciation.
[2] Before providing for depreciation.

National Economic Development Council. The NEDC, which first met in 1962, is the national forum for economic consultation between government, management and unions. It includes leading representatives of the Government, CBI and TUC, chairmen of nationalized industries and independent members. It meets usually under the chairmanship of the Chancellor of the Exchequer, other Secretaries of State and occasionally, the Prime Minister. The Sector Groups and Working Parties, like the NEDC, bring together representatives of management and unions, officials from Government and others, who use this multi-party meeting place to study the efficiency and prospects of individual industries and sectors and to suggest ways in which these could be improved. The National Economic Development Office (NEDO) provides the professional staff for the NEDC and the Sector Groups and Working Parties.

Currency. The monetary unit of Great Britain is the *pound sterling*. A gold standard was adopted in 1816, the sovereign or twenty-shilling piece weighing 7·98805 grammes 0·916⅔ fine. Currency notes for £1 and 10*s.* were first issued by the Treasury in 1914, replacing the circulation of sovereigns. The issue of £1 and 10*s.* notes was taken over by the Bank of England in 1928. The issue of 10*s.* notes ceased on the issue of the 50p coin in 1969.

In March 1990, £1 = US$ 1·61.

Coinage. The sovereign (£1) weighs 123·27447 grains, or 7·98805 grammes, 0·916⅔ (or eleven-twelfths) fine, and consequently it contains 113·00159 grains or 7·32238 grammes of fine gold. On 15 Feb. 1971 (Decimalization Day) a decimal currency system was introduced retaining the *pound sterling* as the major unit but now divided into 100 *new pence* instead of 240 old pence. The decimal coins are the £1 (22·5 mm diameter, 9·5 grammes weight); 50p (equilateral curve heptagon, 30 mm diameter, 13·5 grammes); 20p (equilateral curved heptagon 21·4 mm diameter, 5 grammes); 10p (28·5 mm, 11·31 grammes); 5p (23·6 mm, 5·65 grammes); 2p (25·9 mm, 7·12 grammes) and 1p (20·3 mm, 3·56 grammes). The Decimal Currency Act, 1967 and the Proclamation of 27 Dec. 1968 required that the 50p, 10p and 5p be made of cupro-nickel and the 2p, 1p and ½p of mixed metal; copper, tin and zinc (bronze). The Decimal Currency Act, 1969, provided that the coins of the Queen's

Maundy Money should continue to be made in silver to a millesimal fineness of 925.

By Proclamation dated 28 July 1971, which came into force on 30 Aug. 1971, the crown, double-florin, the florin, the shilling and the sixpence are to be treated as coins of the new currency and as being of the denominations respectively of 25, 20, 10, 5 and $2^1/_2$ new pence. The sixpence was demonetised on 30 June 1980 and the $^1/_2$p on 31 Dec. 1984.

The Coinage Act, 1971, specified that the legal tender limits for coins were: Gold coins, for payment of any amount; coins of cupro-nickel and silver of denominations of more than 10p, for payment of any amount not exceeding £10; coins of cupro-nickel and silver of not more than 10p, for payment of any amount not exceeding £5; coins of bronze, for payment of any amount not exceeding 20p. The £1 coin is legal tender to any amount.

UK coins issued in the 12 months up to March 1989 totalled £85m.

It is estimated that the following coins were in circulation in the UK at 31 March 1989, in millions: £1 842, 50p 682, 20p 1,190, 10p 1,530, 5p 2,140, 2p 3,250, 1p 5,100.

Bank-notes. The Bank of England issues notes in denominations of £5, £10, £20 and £50 for the amount of the fiduciary note issue. Under the provisions of the Currency and Bank Notes Act, 1954, which came into force on 22 Feb. 1954, the amount of the fiduciary note issue was fixed at £1,575m., but this figure might be altered by direction of HM Treasury after representations made by the Bank of England.

All Bank of England notes are legal tender in England and Wales. The banks in Scotland and Northern Ireland have certain note-issuing powers.

The total amount of Bank of England notes issued at 29 Dec. 1989 was £17,080m., of which £17,071,207,233 were in the hands of other banks and the public and £8,792,767 in the Banking Department of the Bank of England.

Banking. The Bank of England, Threadneedle Street, London, is the Government's banker and the 'banker's bank'. It has the sole right of note issue in England and Wales and manages the National Debt. The Bank operates under royal charters of 1694 and 1946 and the Bank of England Act, 1946. The capital stock has, since 1 March 1946, been held by the Treasury.

The statutory return is published weekly. End-Dec. figures for the past 4 years are as follows (in £1m.):

	Notes in circulation	*Notes and coin in Banking Department*	*Public deposits (government)*	*Other deposits* [1]
1986	13,482	8	163	2,499
1987	14,542	8	100	3,144
1988	15,949	1	91	3,106
1989	17,071	9	62	4,444

[1] Including Special Deposits.

The fiduciary note issue was £17,071,207,233 at 28 Dec. 1989. All the profits of the note issue are passed on to the National Loans Fund.

Official reserves of gold and convertible currencies, SDR and reserve position in the IMF at the end of Dec. 1988 were US$51,685m.

The value of paper debit bank clearings for 1987, £8,324,927m. Paper credit clearings for 1987, £91,980m. Automatic direct debits, 1987, £126,835m.; automatic credit transfers, 1987, £229,509m.

The following statistics relate to the London and Scottish banks' groups at 31 Dec. 1989. Total deposits (sterling and currency), £330,612m.; sterling market loans £57,937m.; advances (sterling and currency), £227,839m.; sterling investments £11,646m.

Total net profits from the operations of the main London clearing bank groups in 1989 amounted to £17m., of which £874m. was paid in gross dividends and £1,029m. transferred from reserves.

The clearing banks cover all aspects of banking business in UK including corporate business, and are also actively involved in international banking.

National Savings Bank. Statistics for 1987 and 1988:

	Ordinary accounts		*Investment accounts*	
	1987	*1988*	*1987*	*1988*
Accounts open at 31 Dec.	15,559,155[1]	15,741,178[1]	3,950,056	4,300,148
Amounts—	*£1,000*	*£1,000*	*£1,000*	*£1,000*
Received	641,212	651,528	1,719,399	1,856,470
Interest credited	79,149[2]	65,976[2]	659,349	686,615
Paid	730,096	727,899	1,548,380	1,800,697
Due to depositors at 31 Dec.	1,656,951	1,646,556	6,991,012	7,733,400
Average amount due to each depositor in active accounts	£106·50	£104·60	£1,769·86	£1,798·40

[1] Excluding non-computerized accounts, amounting to £100·6m. in 1987 and £98m. in 1988.
[2] The interest credited to depositors for the Ordinary account for 1988 has been calculated on a different basis to 1987. In 1987 the interest was 6% a year payable on accounts with a minimum balance of £500, 3% on accounts with a minimum balance of less than £500. For 1988 the figures were 5% and 2·5%.

The amount due to depositors in Ordinary Accounts on 1 Jan. 1990 was approximately £1,582,006,648 and in Investment Accounts £7,833,285,342.

The Girobank (founded 1968) had (1986) 1·95m. customers with balances of £1,019m.

Bank of England Quarterly Bulletin. Bank of England
Bank of England Annual Report. Bank of England
British Banking and other Financial Institutions. HMSO, 1977
Central Statistical Office, Financial Statistics. HMSO (monthly)
The Royal Mint. 6th ed. HMSO, 1977
Sayers, R. H., *The Bank of England 1891–1944*. CUP, 1976

Weights and Measures. Conversion to the metric system was in progress (1989) which will replace the imperial system at present in force.

ENERGY AND NATURAL RESOURCES

Electricity. The electricity industry was vested in the British Electricity Authority on 1 April 1948. Following the re-organization of the electricity supply industry after the passing of the Electricity Act, 1957, the statutory bodies comprising the electricity service in England and Wales are the Electricity Council, the Central Electricity Generating Board and the 12 Area Electricity Boards.

The Electricity Council has functioned from Jan. 1958 as the central council for the supply industry in England and Wales for consultation on, and formulation of, general policy; its main functions are to advise the Secretary of State for Energy on all matters affecting the supply industry, and to promote and assist the maintenance and development by the Central Electricity Generating Board and the Area Boards (known collectively as Electricity Boards) of an efficient, co-ordinated and economical system of electricity supply. The Council can also perform services for the Boards, and, in addition, has certain specific functions, particularly in matters of finance, research and industrial relations.

The Central Electricity Generating Board is responsible for the generation and bulk supply of electricity to the 12 Area Boards in England and Wales. It therefore plans the provision of new generating and transmission capacity, including the siting and construction of new generating stations, both conventional and nuclear, and is responsible for the operation and maintenance of generating stations and the main transmission system.

Area Electricity Boards. Each of the 12 Area Electricity Boards acquires bulk supplies of electricity from the Generating Board and is responsible for distribution networks and sales of electricity to its Area consumers. Thus distribution and utilization of electricity, and also the contracting and sale of appliances side of the industry, are their responsibilities.

The number of power stations owned by the Generating Board in England and Wales on 31 March 1987 was 78 with a total output capacity, of 52,363 mw. Total number of customers in England and Wales on 31 March 1987 was 21,715,000 (on 31 March 1986, 21,487,941).

Electricity sold in England and Wales in 1986–87 amounted to 219,551m. units. Operating profit before MWCA in 1986–87 was £1,150m. Coal used for electricity generation in 1986–87 amounted to 77m. tonnes (79m. tonnes in 1985–86). Total fuel (coal equivalent) used in 1985–86 amounted to 100·8m. tonnes and in 1986–87 to 100m. tonnes. Ten nuclear stations of total output capacity 5,029 mw provided 16·4% of total units supplied in 1986–87. Eight of these are gas cooled graphite-moderated stations using natural uranium fuel canned in magnesium alloy (Magnox) and 2 are advanced gas-cooled stations (AGR).

The number of persons employed by the Generating Board, the Electricity Council and Area Boards at the end of March 1987 was 131,067.

Hydro-Electric, established under the Hydro-Electric Development (Scotland) Act 1943, is a nationalized authority responsible for the generation, transmission, distribution and sale of electricity to its (1988) 596,960 customers. It is to be privatized under government's plans for the Electricity Supply Industry.

The Board's district covers a quarter of the land mass of Great Britain and lies generally north and west of a line joining the firths of Clyde and Tay as well as all the island groups extending to the Outer Hebrides, Orkney and Shetland. Over 99·9% of potential consumers have now been provided with supply.

On the mainland Hydro-Electric operates generating stations with a total installed generating capacity of 3,216 mw consisting of 1,762 mw of hydro power and pumped storage, together with 1,320 mw of steam. Diesel stations with a total installed capacity of 102 mw supply the principal island groups together with 32 mw gas turbine. A 1,320 mw of oil/gas fired thermal plant is now operating at Peterhead.

The main transmission system consists of 5,097 circuit km of 275 kv and 132 kv lines linking the power stations and the bulk supply points serving the distribution networks. The system control centre at Pitlochry co-ordinates the operation of the transmission system and power stations. The number of staff at 31 March 1989 was 3,917.

Scottish Power PLC was formally vested in 1990, as part of the British Government's programme for privatizing the electricity industry in Britain, to take over the non-nuclear operations of the South of Scotland Electricity Board. The area served by the new company stretches north of a line from Holy Island in Northumberland to the Solway Firth to a northern boundary running from the Firth of Clyde to the Firth of Tay. Within this area of approximately 21,000 sq. km (8,000 sq. miles) is located the main industry and population concentrations of Scotland, with 4m. of the total population of 5·1m. The remainder of Scotland is served by Scottish Hydro-Electric PLC. Scottish Power provides a full electricity service to its area. It operates four coal-fired, eight hydro, and one gas-fired power station with a total capacity of 4,240 mw. A further 2,000 mw oil-fired station is on care and maintenance. The company transmits and distributes electricity throughout its area to 1·7m. domestic, commercial, industrial and agricultural customers. It operates 73 retail shops, which also provide full customer services. During 1988-89 Scottish Power's predecessor, the South of Scotland Electricity Board, had a turnover of £976m. and produced a total of over 19,000m. units of electricity, which included the production of the three nuclear power stations now operated by Scottish Nuclear Ltd. Scottish Power has approximately 9,500 employees.

Scottish Nuclear Ltd was formally vested in 1990 by the British Government as part of the electricity privatization programme, to take over and operate the nuclear assets of the former South of Scotland Electricity Board. With 2,300 employees, it generates electricity at the 2 nuclear power stations at Hunterston, Ayrshire, and Torness, East Lothian. Both plants have two 650 mw Advanced Gas-Cooled Reactors. Scottish Nuclear is also undertaking the decommissioning of the Magnox power station located at Hunterston. During 1988-89, these 3 nuclear power stations generated over 14·5m. units of electricity and for much of the year supplied over 60% of the electricity consumed in the whole of Scotland.

Oil. Production 1988, in 1,000 tonnes (1987 in brackets): Throughput of crude and process oils, 85,662 (80,449); refinery use, 5,484 (5,216). Refinery output: Gases, 1,649 (1,479); naphtha, 1,856 (2,014); motor spirit, 26,409 (24,680); kerosene, 9,014 (8,333); diesel oil, 23,925 (21,424); fuel oil, 12,495 (12,797); lubricating oils, 970 (886); bitumen, 2,295 (2,056). Total output of refined products, 79,837 (74,656).

Gas. Following the Gas Act of 1986, British Gas plc became the successor company to the British Gas Corporation. Its primary activities are the purchase, distribution and sale of gas, supported by a broad range of services to customers. It also explores for and produces hydrocarbons. It is organized into a headquarters and twelve Regions.

British Gas explores for gas through 3 wholly owned subsidiary companies: Gas Council (Exploration) Limited (UK onshore and Denmark offshore); Hydrocarbons Great Britain Limited (Irish Sea and Cardigan Bay); Hydrocarbons Ireland Limited, (offshore Eire). British Gas owns and operates two gas fields, Morecambe and Rough field. The latter is used as a gas store and both have been developed to help meet peak winter demand.

In 1986–87, British Gas sold 18,894m. therms of gas to over 17m. customers. Just over 50% of the gas went to domestic customers, the rest to industrial and commercial enterprizes. The industry won 269,000 new customers in the period and made a before-tax profit of £1,062m. with a turnover of £7,610m.

In March 1986, there were 89,000 people employed directly by the industry. British Gas spends £74m. each year on its research and development programme and its international consultancy service works in about 20 countries.

Minerals. Coal. The number of British Coal Corporation producing collieries at 25 March 1989 was 86. Statistics of the coalmining industry for recent years are as follows:

	1985–86	1986–87	1987–88	1988-89
Output, 1m. tonnes:				
BCC mines (inc. tip and capital coal)	88·4	88·0	82·4	85·0
Opencast	14·1	13·3	15·1	16·8
Licensed	2·0	2·0	2·1	1·7
Total	104·5	103·3	99·6	103·5
Employees, 1,000:				
Colliery industrial manpower	138·5	107·7	89·0	80·1
Other industrial manpower	19·3	14·6	11·9	10·8
Non-industrial staff	21·8	19·2	16·4	14·1
Total	179·6	141·5	117·3	105·0
Productivity, tonnes:				
Output per man-year	571	700	789	978
Overall output per manshift	2·72	3·29	3·62	4·14
Consumption, 1m. tonnes:				
Power stations	86·0	82·4	86·2	80·7
Coke ovens	11·5	10·9	10·8	10·9
Domestic	8·9	8·1	7·0	6·3
Other inland	12·0	11·0	11·5	11·3
Total inland	118·4	112·4	115·5	109·2
Imports	12·1	9·9	9·8	12·0
Exports	3·3	2·2	2·2	1·8

Total stocks of coal at 31 March 1989 amounted to 37m. tonnes (28m. tonnes consumer stocks, 9m. tonnes BCC stocks). Operating profit made by British Coal for the year ended March 1989 amounted to £498m. Interest payable was £432m. The overall deficit for 1988–89 was £203m. Deficit grants ceased in 1987-88.

Production of coke (including coke breeze), 1988–89, 1·4m. tonnes.

The UK is among the 10 largest steel producing countries in the world. Output in recent years was as follows (in 1m. tonnes):

	Pig-iron	Crude steel	Finished steel products	Home consumption Crude steel equivalent
1986	9·8	14·7	12·0	14·7
1987	12·1	17·4	12·4	15·0
1988	13·2	19·0	14·7	17·5
1989	12·8	18·7	...	...

Exports of finished steel products were 6·5m. tonnes in 1989 and imports 5·4m. tonnes.

With turnover for the year to March 1989 of £4,906m., British Steel PLC is the largest steel producer in the UK, the second largest in Europe and the fourth largest in the non-Communist world in terms of crude steel production. The number of UK employees at 31 Dec. 1989 was some 54,000. UK steel producers, other than British Steel PLC, are represented by BISPA (British Independent Steel Producers Association). There are approximately 50 companies in membership of BISPA, who account for almost one quarter of UK liquid steel production, and approximately one third of the UK output of finished steel products. For some products such as wire rod, reinforcement steel, bright bars, wire and high speed tool and engineering steels, these companies account for nearly all UK production.

Pig iron produced in blast furnaces was 13·2m. tonnes in 1988 (12·1m. in 1987). Consumption of pig iron in steelworks, 13m. tonnes in 1988 (11·9m. in 1987).

Production of non-ferrous metals in 1988 (in 1,000 tonnes): Refined copper, 124 (122·3 in 1987); refined lead, 373·8 (347); tin metal, 13·8 (17·3); primary aluminium, 300·2 (294·4); slab zinc, 92·8 (81·4).

Agriculture. In 1988 (and 1987) agricultural land in the UK totalled (in 1,000 hectares) 18,575 (18,619), comprising common grazing, 1,216 (1,216), and agricultural holdings, 17,359 (17,406). Land use of the latter: All grasses 6,774 (6,808); crops, 5,253 (5,270); rough grazing, 4,712 (4,743); bare fallow, 58 (42); other, 562 (547). The area sown to crops was made up as follows: Cereals, 3,896 (3,935); fodder crops, 393 (345); horticultural crops, 209 (199); others, 576 (613).

The number of workers employed in agriculture, forestry and fishing in the UK was, in June 1988, 313,000. Of these, 290,400 (80,900 female) were solely engaged in agriculture, including 94,900 (37,200 female) seasonal and casual workers. These figures do not include farmers, partners and directors. There were some 255,400 farm holdings in 1988, some 75% owner-occupied. Average size of holdings, 107 hectares.

Principal crops in the UK as at June in each year:

	Wheat	Barley	Oats	Horticultural crops	Potatoes	Fodder crops	Sugar-beet	Rape for oilseed
				Area (1,000 hectares)				
1984	1,939	1,978	106	205	198	191	199	205
1985	1,902	1,965	133	213	191	229	269	296
1986	1,997	1,916	97	212	178	239	205	299
1987	1,994	1,830	99	199	177	...	202	388
1988	1,886	1,878	120	209	180	...	201	347
				Total product (1,000 tonnes)				
1984	14,970	11,070	515	3,777	7,395	7,085	9,015	925
1985	12,050	9,740	615	3,763	6,895	6,655	7,715	895
1986	13,910	10,010	505	3,869	6,446	7,325	8,120	965
1987	11,940	9,230	450	3,788	6,713	...	7,990	1,326
1988	11,600	8,800	600	3,882	6,899	...	...	...

Livestock in the UK as at June in each year (in 1,000):

	1985	1986	1987	1988	1989
Cattle	12,865	12,533	12,158	11,872	12,016
Sheep	35,628	37,016	38,701	40,942	42,885
Pigs	7,865	7,937	7,942	7,980	7,717
Poultry	128,968	120,740	128,628	130,809	...

Forestry. On 31 March 1989 the area of productive woodland in Britain was 2,135,000 hectares of which the Forestry Commission managed 888,000 hectares and the private sector 1,247,000 hectares.

The Forestry Commission employed 7,725 staff in 1989. In addition a further 15,320 were employed in private forestry with an estimated 10,040 engaged in the wood processing industry.

In 1988–89 a total of 6·5m. cu. metres of timber was thinned and felled.

New Planting (1988–89) 29,500 hectares (4,100, Forestry Commission; 25,400, private woodlands).

James, N. D. G., *A History of English Forestry*. London, 1981

Fisheries. Quantity (in 1,000 tonnes) and value (in £1,000) of fish of British taking landed in Great Britain (excluding salmon and sea-trout):

Quantity	*1984*	*1985*	*1986*	*1987*	*1988*
Wet fish	661·0	687·2	629·3	677·3	645·5
Shell fish	72·0	74·8	87·6	111·0	96·5
	733·7	762·1	716·9	788·3	742·0
Value					
Wet fish	240,587	258,904	284,161	338,965	310,412
Shell fish	57,274	64,920	77,519	95,941	92,481
	297,863	323,825	361,680	434,906	402,893

In 1989 the fishing fleet comprised 8,125 vessels including 2,812 trawlers and (England and Wales, 5,433 vessels including 1,711 trawlers; Scotland, 2,334 vessels including 878 trawlers; Northern Ireland, 358 vessels including 223 trawlers). Major fishing ports: (England) Fleetwood, Grimsby, Hull, Lowestoft, North Shields; (Wales) Milford Haven; (Scotland) Aberdeen, Mallarg, Lerwick, Peterhead.

INDUSTRY AND TRADE

Industry. Statistics (UK, unless otherwise stated) of a cross-section of industrial production are as follows (in 1,000 tonnes):

	1986	*1987*	*1988*
Sulphuric acid	2,330	2,158	2,270
Synthetic resins	1,083	1,626	1,564
Cotton single yarn	40	42	35
Wool tops	44	44	80
Woollen yarn	73	77	78
Man-made fibres (rayon, nylon, etc.)	288	277	280
Newsprint	458	497	541
Other paper and board	3,465	3,682	3,802
Cement	13,413	14,311	...
Primary aluminium	276	294	300

Engineering. Manufacturers' sales (in £1m.) for 1987 (1988 in brackets): Motor vehicles and engines, 9,535 (10,928); motor vehicle bodies and parts, 4,433 (5,533); boilers and process plant, 1,810 (1,654); mechanical lifting and handling equipment, 1,826 (2,236); refrigerating, space-heating, ventilating and air conditioning equipment, 1,481 (1,599); construction and earth-moving equipment, 996 (1,265), wheeled tractors, 1,033 (1,231); industrial (including marine) engines, 783 (877).

Electrical Goods. Manufacturers' sales (in £1m.) for 1987 (1988 in brackets): Radio and electronic capital goods, 3,153 (3,358); basic electrical equipment, 2,656 (2,919); electronic data processing equipment, 4,328 (5,175); telephone and telegraph apparatus and equipment, 1,674 (1,978); domestic electrical appliances, 1,540 (1,816).

Textile Manufacturers. Production of woven cloth for 1987 (1988 in brackets): Cotton (1m. metres), 245 (219); man-made fibres (1m. metres), 214·7 (212·5); woven woollen and worsted fabrics (1m. sq. metres), deliveries, 90·3 (89).

Construction. Total value (in £1m.) of constructional work in Great Britain in 1987 (1988 in brackets) was 34,580 (40,546), including new work, 19,066 (23,420) of which housing, 6,745 (8,469). Housing for public authorities, 933 (922); for private developers, 5,812 (7,547).

Annual Abstract of Statistics. HMSO
Statistical Summary of the Mineral Industry. HMSO, annual

Labour. In June 1989 the UK workforce (*i.e.* all persons in employment plus the claimant unemployed) totalled (in 1,000) 28,090, of whom 26,347 were in employment, 22,450 (10,489 females) were employees, 3,110 were self-employed and 308 were in HM Forces. UK employees by form of employment in June 1988 (in 1,000): Agriculture and fishing, 313; energy and water supply, 487; manufacturing industry, 5,215; construction, 1,043; distributive and catering trades, 4,427; transport and communications, 1,324; business and finance, 2,467; public administration, 1,672; education, 1,751; health, 1,247; recreation and culture, 514; others, 1,576. Registered unemployed in UK (in 1,000; figures adjusted for seasonality and discontinuities): 1985, 3,036 (females, 921); 1986, 3,107 (959); 1987, 2,822 (851); 1988, 2,295 (687); 1989, 1,801. In Oct. 1989 613,400 persons (136,200 females) had been unemployed for more than a year. In June 1989 there were 226,400 job vacancies.

Trade Unions. In Sept. 1989 there were 78 unions affiliated to the Trades Union Congress with a total membership of 8,652,318 (3m. of them women). The unions affiliated to the TUC in 1989 ranged in size from the Transport and General Workers' Union, with 1,312,853 members, to the Sheffield Wool Shear Workers' Society with 17 members. Non-manual workers accounted for nearly a third of the total TUC membership.

The TUC's executive body, the General Council, is elected at the annual Congress. It is composed of 53 members made up of 30 members nominated by unions with a membership of over 200,000, entitled to automatic representation in proportion to their size and 10 members elected from unions with a numerical membership of 100,000 up to 199,999. Eight members are elected from unions with a numerical membership of less than 100,000 and 4 women members are elected to represent women workers in smaller unions. Unions with a total membership of over 200,000 of which 100,000 or over are women must nominate at least one woman to represent women workers.

The General Secretary is elected by the Congress but is not subject to annual re-election. The TUC General Council appoints committees, which draw upon the services of specialist departments in preparing policies on economic, education, international, employment, industrial organization, equal rights, and social questions.

The TUC is affiliated to the International Confederation of Free Trade Unions, the Trade Union Advisory Committee of OECD, the Commonwealth Trade Union Council and the European Trade Union Confederation. The TUC provides a service of trade union education. It provides members to serve, with representatives of employers, on joint committees advising the Government on issues of national importance (e.g., National Economic Development Council) and on the managing boards of such bodies as the Health and Safety Commission; and Advisory, Conciliation and Arbitration Service.

Workers (in 1,000) involved in industrial stoppages (and working days lost): 1984, 1,464 (27·1m.); 1985, 791 (6·4m.); 1986, 720 (1·9m.); 1987, 887 (3·5m.); 1988, 790 (3·7m.).

Commerce. Value of the imports and exports of merchandise (excluding bullion and specie and foreign merchandise transhipped under bond) of the UK for 6 recent years (in £1,000):

	Total imports	*Total exports*		*Total imports*	*Total exports*
1984	65,993,096	60,533,692	1987	94,015,696	79,851,395
1985	78,705,170	70,511,345	1988	106,412,879	81,476,249
1986	86,066,650	73,009,049	1989	120,787,729	93,249,123

The value of goods imported is generally taken to be that at the port and time of entry, including all incidental expenses (cost, insurance and freight) up to the landing on the quay. For goods consigned for sale, the market value in this country is required and recorded in the returns. For exports, the value at the port of shipment (including the charges of delivering the goods on board) is taken. Imports are entered as from the country whence the goods were consigned to the UK, which may, or may not, be the country whence they were last shipped. Exports are credited to the country of ultimate destination as declared by the exporters.

For details of imports and exports for 1988 and 1989, *see* pp. 1329–33.

Trade according to countries for 1988 and 1989 (in £1,000):

Countries	Imports of merchandise from 1988 [1]	1989 [1]	Exports of merchandise to 1988 [1]	1989 [1]
Foreign countries				
Europe and Overseas Possessions—				
Albania	2,764	605	1,126	1,957
Austria	874,430	933,971	509,991	598,099
Belgium and Luxembourg	4,956,037	5,700,534	4,251,961	4,872,641
Bulgaria	28,068	34,272	82,156	86,209
Czechoslovakia	148,248	156,649	130,420	131,418
Denmark and Faroe Islands	2,051,230	2,260,382	1,175,298	1,215,573
Finland	1,813,549	1,893,163	824,951	925,784
France	9,390,207	10,785,429	8,270,408	9,461,648
German Dem. Rep.	152,977	168,742	113,239	106,455
Germany (Fed. Rep. of)	17,667,097	20,005,276	9,521,851	11,110,623
Greece	356,974	395,086	468,032	571,409
Hungary	98,288	105,221	131,212	117,947
Iceland	198,365	196,678	87,100	69,497
Italy	5,817,445	6,701,683	4,106,417	4,630,896
Netherlands	8,279,747	9,585,699	5,583,280	6,515,325
Netherlands Antilles	7,823	5,768	20,089	32,147
Norway	3,074,312	3,637,119	1,053,613	1,056,506
Poland	328,013	330,163	175,685	196,446
Portugal, Azores and Madeira	1,005,506	1,040,706	901,371	915,682
Romania	100,906	117,685	50,111	38,141
Spain	2,482,360	2,772,011	2,691,662	3,137,941
Canary Islands	77,491	74,532	90,834	89,852
Sweden	3,366,524	3,747,600	2,195,032	2,350,122
Switzerland and Liechtenstein	3,840,643	4,125,731	1,854,918	2,245,354
Turkey	509,636	533,769	477,539	434,562
USSR	732,115	833,369	511,653	681,599
Yugoslavia	197,254	202,405	203,066	219,866
European Communities	55,784,600	53,494,966	40,932,046	47,140,164
EFTA	13,167,822	14,534,262	6,525,605	7,246,363
Africa—				
Algeria	159,748	177,456	86,615	74,368
Angola	10,036	1,286	26,154	24,785
Burundi	1,807	1,974	2,922	2,738
Cameroon	16,180	11,362	20,472	[illegible]
Côte d'Ivoire	64,041	65,943	31,172	[illegible]
Egypt	163,038	212,727	289,309	296,272
Ethiopia	8,451	12,772	47,661	44,148
Liberia	9,574	12,776	11,684	15,148
Libya	111,812	104,546	235,957	239,191
Mali	2,240	2,305	12,732	7,102
Mauritania	7,259	15,387	3,048	4,005
Morocco	78,896	96,138	79,017	84,475
Mozambique	5,574	14,582	24,218	20,268
Namibia	8,434	4,568	1,636	4,264
Rwanda	11,284	2,991	14,840	1,790
South Africa, Republic of	807,669	6,820	1,074,826	13,448
Senegal	10,729	884,607	3,259	1,038,342
Sudan	9,910	9,532	86,480	60,602
Tunisia	36,062	43,266	30,780	31,148
Zaïre	7,542	9,069	26,132	28,419
Asia—				
Afghánistán	11,501	4,813	12,109	5,376
Bahrain	75,786	61,018	138,150	138,529
Burma	4,427	3,484	11,685	12,217
China	443,698	530,720	411,563	417,911
Indonesia	223,807	273,102	203,275	184,032
Iran	140,207	250,548	247,768	257,149
Iraq	43,406	55,175	412,091	450,495
Israel	460,289	479,840	487,255	502,411
Japan	6,509,137	7,108,441	1,742,747	2,259,823
Jordan	21,310	16,462	183,555	110,684
Korea (South)	1,135,107	1,164,723	450,924	493,945
Kuwait	72,318	150,364	237,515	228,711

[1] Provisional figures.

Countries	Imports of merchandise from		Exports of merchandise to	
	1988[1]	1989[1]	1988[1]	1989[1]
Asia—(contd.)				
Lebanon	14,172	11,054	55,575	48,474
Pakistan	175,337	216,110	263,300	233,532
Philippines	223,571	233,128	123,974	137,367
Qatar	3,888	4,342	88,920	89,256
Saudi Arabia	614,144	502,416	1,713,423	432,941
Syria	36,100	65,256	24,647	38,537
Thailand	321,241	443,144	279,717	427,484
America—				
Argentina	66,281	98,490	12,991	13,585
Bolivia	13,224	17,666	6,029	6,148
Brazil	742,145	817,545	304,735	338,634
Chile	179,628	193,280	80,901	96,003
Colombia	61,835	70,715	53,132	61,733
Costa Rica	16,902	24,113	11,390	12,780
Cuba	28,489	34,388	31,162	53,255
Dominican Republic	8,523	11,223	17,235	25,519
Ecuador	13,120	19,319	50,417	29,410
El Salvador	2,961	2,133	8,186	9,594
Guatemala	10,678	6,950	15,387	52,324
Haiti	844	803	6,760	6,566
Honduras	8,295	12,121	7,891	5,518
Mexico	144,947	165,295	190,011	205,130
Nicaragua	725	918	6,856	6,985
Panama	12,230	6,818	32,497	32,875
Paraguay	1,950	8,898	22,024	19,282
Peru	90,844	125,538	31,384	29,707
Puerto Rico	91,909	117,628	38,877	79,851
Uruguay	35,410	52,185	34,999	26,119
USA	10,767,750	12,888,890	10,544,077	12,098,549
Venezuela	76,563	111,072	177,787	124,672
Total (including those not specified above)	94,097,320	106,859,689	68,482,124	78,101,944
Commonwealth countries:				
In Europe—				
Cyprus	121,828	145,047	159,788	173,092
Gibraltar	4,537	4,560	67,944	69,350
Malta	40,189	42,194	121,696	132,287
In Africa				
West Africa:				
Gambia	2,927	2,340	19,236	16,563
Ghana	106,314	92,208	126,148	121,076
Nigeria, Federation of	128,123	129,406	390,476	388,777
Sierra Leone	14,462	15,899	14,256	20,402
South Africa:				
Botswana	6,942	13,135	26,763	34,582
Lesotho	977	734	1,260	795
Malawi	30,183	27,890	27,618	30,604
Swaziland	27,973	31,368	1,564	1,358
Zambia	24,822	21,565	85,746	119,057
Zimbabwe	86,268	85,792	58,077	87,013
East Africa:				
Kenya	142,455	154,313	202,094	208,464
Mauritius	186,240	216,190	36,553	43,528
Tanzania	26,386	22,641	88,686	93,036
Uganda	30,487	20,985	35,340	39,218
Seychelles	1,297	993	10,478	10,741
St Helena	205	504	6,103	7,208
In Asia—				
Bangladesh	50,249	52,527	64,018	78,270
Hong Kong	1,788,631	2,036,976	1,030,725	1,111,517
India	559,684	701,985	1,111,740	1,382,436
Malaysia	525,017	676,258	310,462	441,762
Singapore	579,368	903,248	632,452	773,866
Sri Lanka	56,661	63,527	92,528	92,465

[1] Provisional figures.

Countries	Imports of merchandise from 1988[1]	1989[1]	Exports of merchandise to 1988[1]	1989[1]
In Oceania—				
Australia	745,570	864,965	1,377,997	1,711,241
Fiji	65,273	69,558	6,358	10,221
Nauru	642	662	759	549
New Zealand	443,081	436,772	300,016	399,295
Papua New Guinea	44,291	47,839	20,521	15,822
Western Samoa	1,323	1,376	757	296
In America—				
Bahamas	24,781	17,681	20,708	22,543
Barbados	19,487	22,308	32,061	38,136
Belize	22,461	24,272	12,064	11,842
Bermuda	6,767	4,517	24,995	77,122
Canada	2,038,245	2,174,339	2,038,433	2,165,731
Falkland Islands	4,209	5,375	9,037	10,200
Guyana	43,518	54,523	10,590	13,216
Jamaica	89,693	95,516	48,855	61,355
Leeward Islands (Anguilla; St. Kitts-Nevis; Antigua and Barbuda; Montserrat)	15,309	10,209	32,676	34,895
Trinidad and Tobago	35,728	37,426	39,868	45,881
Windward Islands (Dominica; St. Lucia; St. Vincent and the Grenadines)	120,517	104,025	36,177	39,403
Total, Commonwealth countries (including those not specified above)	8,436,929	9,648,838	8,937,079	10,432,399
Ireland	3,878,630	4,279,202	4,057,046	4,714,780
Grand Total	106,412,879	120,787,729	81,476,249	93,249,123

[1] Provisional figures.

Imports and exports for 1988 and 1989 (Great Britain and Northern Ireland) (in £1,000):

Import values c.i.f. *Export values f.o.b.*	Total imports 1988[1]	1989[1]	Domestic exports 1988[1]	1989[1]
0. *Food and Live Animals*				
Live animals (excluding zoo animals, dogs and cats)	287,079	286,533	254,794	265,738
Meat and meat preparations	1,646,347	1,826,899	590,421	699,590
Dairy products and eggs	761,154	786,423	389,559	501,896
Fish and fish preparations	785,760	885,003	384,427	449,958
Cereals and cereal preparations	751,253	722,189	676,665	951,332
Fruit and vegetables	2,462,384	2,727,077	222,286	281,250
Sugar, sugar preparations, honey	556,933	603,642	196,356	228,238
Coffee, tea, cocoa, spices	931,980	941,570	363,419	387,715
Feeding stuff for animals	557,674	582,258	176,412	228,742
Miscellaneous food preparations	323,722	400,802	207,089	233,962
Total of Section 0	9,064,286	9,762,395	3,461,429	4,228,421
1. *Beverages and Tobacco*				
Beverages	1,196,276	1,322,059	1,575,468	1,802,190
Tobacco and tobacco manufactures	325,652	345,445	499,987	524,153
Total of Section 1	1,521,928	1,667,504	2,075,455	2,326,343
2. *Crude Materials, Inedible, except Fuels*				
Hides, skins and furskins, undressed	194,219	149,241	254,813	253,922
Oil seeds, oil nuts and oil kernels	227,454	238,949	41,670	37,194
Crude rubber (including synthetic and reclaimed)	236,339	250,167	193,024	211,610
Wood and cork	1,355,873	1,429,033	26,206	27,762
Pulp and waste paper	725,281	896,286	46,438	51,745

[1] Provisional figures.

Import values c.i.f. / Export values f.o.b.	Total imports 1988[1]	Total imports 1989[1]	Domestic exports 1988[1]	Domestic exports 1989[1]
2. *Crude Materials, Inedible, except Fuels*—Contd.				
Textile fibres and their waste	688,396	681,179	439,468	498,141
Crude fertilizers and crude minerals (excluding fuels)	354,042	360,836	339,447	368,927
Metalliferous ores and metal scrap	1,372,879	1,573,765	593,449	711,652
Crude animal and vegetable materials, not elsewhere specified	465,200	518,125	97,611	103,101
Total of Section 2	5,619,683	6,097,580	2,032,027	2,264,073
3. *Mineral Fuels, Lubricants and Related Materials*				
Coal, coke and briquettes	507,071	537,842	98,921	111,892
Petroleum and petroleum products	3,495,219	4,674,403	5,575,915	5,511,771
Gas, natural and manufactured	787,952	717,888	142,965	144,431
Total[2] of Section 3	5,058,307	6,235,124	5,817,801	5,768,094
4. *Animal and Vegetable Oils and Fats*	372,208	384,948	88,744	83,644
5. *Chemicals*				
Chemical elements and compounds	3,263,667	3,637,917	4,243,901	4,394,766
Dyeing, tanning and colouring materials	543,506	612,639	938,846	1,063,251
Medicinal and pharmaceutical products	875,868	1,061,634	1,735,346	2,016,300
Essential oils and perfume; toilet and cleansing preparations	615,100	681,827	943,499	1,003,434
Fertilizers, manufactured	203,608	217,187	89,993	105,185
Plastic materials	1,846,051	2,059,770	1,729,965	1,244,955
Total[2] of Section 5	9,312,716	10,440,540	11,332,676	12,349,574
6. *Manufactured Goods Classified Chiefly by Material*				
Leather and dressed furs	245,318	242,672	311,353	326,498
Rubber	798,839	827,073	715,505	801,636
Wood and cork (excluding furniture)	964,702	967,028	82,664	91,038
Paper, paperboard	3,622,656	4,015,994	1,093,724	1,239,817
Textile yarn, fabrics	3,635,552	3,769,721	1,934,856	2,205,028
Non-metallic mineral manufactures	3,301,013	3,567,041	2,971,102	3,198,613
Iron and steel	2,367,391	2,787,870	2,391,161	2,893,572
Non-ferrous metals	2,504,240	3,069,877	1,648,637	1,967,544
Manufactures of metal, not elsewhere specified	2,146,412	2,483,082	1,559,605	1,786,499
Total of Section 6	19,586,123	21,730,357	12,708,606	14,510,245
7. *Machinery and Transport Equipment*				
Boilers, engines, motors and power-units	3,046,962	3,487,336	3,884,822	4,738,901
Agricultural and Industrial machinery	7,821,884	8,972,689	7,646,087	8,559,173
Office machinery	6,278,574	7,552,324	5,296,568	6,115,925
Electrical machinery, apparatus, not elsewhere specified	8,990,100	10,374,203	6,101,774	7,273,050
Transport equipment	13,905,553	15,513,094	8,957,181	11,002,980
Total of Section 7	40,043,071	45,899,646	31,886,433	37,690,028

[1] Provisional figures.
[2] Includes items not specified here.

Import values c.i.f. *Export values f.o.b.*	*Total imports* *1988* [1]	*1989* [1]	*Domestic exports* *1988* [1]	*1989* [1]
8. *Miscellaneous Manufactured Articles*				
Prefabricated buildings, sanitary, plumbing, heating and lighting fixtures	336,224	371,728	199,433	222,255
Furniture	988,867	1,099,567	377,615	460,832
Travel goods, handbags and similar articles	250,688	292,973	43,933	56,304
Clothing	3,108,075	3,542,262	1,414,252	1,444,837
Footwear	907,685	973,211	210,448	227,579
Scientific instruments; cameras, watches and clocks	3,489,771	3,994,402	3,535,725	3,927,625
Miscellaneous manufactured articles, not elsewhere specified	5,340,904	6,783,537	4,326,198	5,433,210
Total of Section 8	14,422,214	17,057,680	10,107,604	11,772,643
9. *Commodities and Transactions not Classified According to Kind*				
Total of Section 9	1,412,343	1,511,954	1,965,473	2,256,059
Total [2] of all classes	106,412,879	120,787,729	81,476,249	93,249,123

[1] Provisional figures. [2] Includes items not specified here.

Tourism. There were an estimated 17m. overseas visitors in 1989. Foreign exchange from tourism was approximately £8,300m. including fares paid to British air and shipping lines.

COMMUNICATIONS

Roads. Central government responsibility for highways in England rests with the Secretary of State for Transport. His responsibilities are administered by the Department of Transport through a number of Directorates at Headquarters together with 9 Regional Offices. For Welsh and Scottish roads, central government responsibility rests with the Secretaries of State for Wales and Scotland respectively.

The Secretary of State is the highway authority responsible for all trunk roads. The Shire County Councils, the Metropolitan District Councils, the London Borough Councils and the Common Council of the City of London are the highway authorities responsible for local roads in their own areas.

The Secretary of State has powers to provide roads designed for limited classes of motor traffic, and to confirm schemes for the provision of such special roads by local authorities. The former have the status of trunk roads; the latter principal roads. 2,992 km of motorway were open to traffic in Great Britain in 1988 (2,537 km of trunk motorway in England, 353 km in Scotland and Wales and 102 km of principal motorway).

Public highways in Great Britain in 1988, excluding lengths of unsurfaced roads (green lanes), totalled 354,315 km (England, 270,265 km; Wales, 32,842 km; Scotland, 51,207 km). There were 12,581 km of all-purpose trunk roads, 2,992 km of trunk and principal motorways, 34,939 km of principal roads (excluding motorways) and 303,803 km of other roads.

Motor vehicles for which licences were current under the Vehicles (Excise) Act, 1971, at 31 Dec. 1988, numbered 23,302,000, including 18,432,000 private cars, 912,000 mopeds, scooters and motor cycles, 132,000 public transport vehicles and 2,598,000 goods vehicles.

New vehicle registrations in 1988 numbered 2,723,500.

Road casualties in Great Britain numbered in 1988, 322,305 including 5,052 killed; in 1987, 311,473 including 5,125 killed.

Railways. The British Railways Board as a public authority owns and manages British Rail: The national rail network, British Rail Maintenance Ltd, British Rail Property Board and Transportation Systems and Market Research Ltd. (Transmark).

The role of the Board is to determine policies, establish the organization to carry them out, monitor performance and take major decisions to meet objectives set by the Secretary of State for Transport.

The Group turnover 1989–90 was £3,395·9m. and 135,243 staff were employed, of whom 128,476 were involved in the railway business.

The management of the railways is the responsibility of the Chief Executive. He establishes plans and budgets for the achievement of objectives set by the Board, monitors and achieves results against the plans and budgets, and directs the organization and deployment of manpower resources. He is assisted by Managing Directors and other Board members with responsibility for functions such as Engineering, Research, Finance and Planning, Marketing, Operating, Productivity and Personnel.

In the year ending 31 March 1989, British Rail carried 149·5m. tonnes of freight and parcels and 763·7m. passenger journeys were made.

The rail business is split into 5 sectors: InterCity, Network Southeast, Provincial, Freight and Parcels. A director is responsible for efficient operation and budgeting within his sector, each of which bears its fair share of the fixed costs of operation, such as signalling and track maintenance. The day-to-day running of the rail network is the responsibility of 6 geographical regional general managers to whom local area and station managers report.

		1987–88	*1988–89*
Passenger Receipts and Traffic			
Receipts	£m.	1,603·5	1,780·8
Passenger journeys	m.	727·2	763·7
Passenger miles (estimated)	m.	20,593·0	21,327·0
Freight Train Traffic			
Receipts	£m.	555·0	655·0
Traffic	m. tonnes	144·5	149·5
Net tonne miles (trainload and wagonload)	m.	10,853·0	11,249·0
Locomotives			
Diesel		2,040	1,920
Electric		230	260
High Speed Trains			
Power cars		197	197
Passenger carriages		722	722
Coaching vehicles		14,648	14,258
Freight vehicles (excluding brake vans)		28,884	24,922
Stations		2,541	2,561
Route open for traffic	miles	10,335	10,314

The London Regional Transport (formerly London Transport Executive) is the authority responsible for the operation of the capital's Underground and bus services. Overall policy and financial control is exercised by the Secretary of State for Transport. In April 1989, London Underground had 245 route miles of railway open for traffic and also operated over 10 route miles owned by British Rail. Rolling stock owned: Underground, 3,950; buses, 4,825. In the financial year 1988–89, the number of train miles run in passenger service was 32·1m.; number of bus miles run in passenger service was 170m. The number of passenger journeys was: Underground 815m.; buses 1,244m.

Aviation. British Airways is engaged in the provision of air transport services for passengers, cargo and mail worldwide, both on scheduled and charter services. It operates long and short haul international services, as well as an extensive domestic network. In 1988–89, it carried 24·6m. passengers and 459,000 tonnes of freight, and at 31 March 1989 it had a fleet of 211 aircraft and employed 48,760 staff.

In addition to British Airways, there were in 1987 about 55 other UK air transport operators, the principal ones being Britannia Airways, Dan-Air Services and British Midland Airways. In recent years there has been a significant expansion of the independent operators.

Following the Civil Aviation Act 1971, the Civil Aviation Authority was established as an independent public body responsible for the economic and safety regulation of British civil aviation. It took over the responsibilities of the former Air Transport Licensing Board and Air Registration Board, and also runs the National Air Traffic Services in conjunction with the Ministry of Defence. CAA established a wholly-owned subsidiary, Highlands and Islands Airports Ltd on 1 April 1986 to own and operate eight aerodromes in the Scottish Highlands and Islands.

In addition to the public transport operators there are a number of companies engaged in miscellaneous aviation activities such as crop-spraying, aerial survey and photography, and flying instruction.

The operating and traffic statistics of the UK airlines on scheduled services during the calendar year 1987 (and 1988) are as follows: Aircraft km flown, 406m. (443m.); revenue passengers carried, 29m. (31m.); cargo (freight and mail) carried 405,419 (435,071) tonnes.

Traffic between the UK airports and places abroad in 1988 (and 1987) on all services included 695,781 (675,683) air transport aircraft movements.

There were 13,972 and 12,888 civil aircraft registered in the UK at 31 Dec. 1989 and 1988 respectively.

Shipping. The British Islands registered merchant fleet in Dec. 1989 totalled 8·49m. DWT (dry cargo, 4·42m. DWT; tankers 4·47m. DWT) representing 1·7% of the world fleet. The total number of UK flag ships was 670.

In 1988 capital expenditure was an estimated £200m. The average age of UK owned tonnage at 31 Dec. 1988 was 12 years.

Total gross earnings by UK owned ships in 1988 amounted to £3,520m. The net contribution to UK balance of payments was £521m. and, in addition, there were gross import savings of £815m.

On 30 Oct. 1989, 15 UK flag ships (463,000 DWT) were laid up out of a world total of 301 ships (5·2m. DWT).

Inland Waterways. There are approximately 2,500 miles of navigable canals and locked river navigations in Great Britain. Of these, the British Waterways Board is responsible for some 380 miles of commercial waterways (maintained for freight traffic) and some 1,160 miles of cruising waterways (maintained for pleasure cruising, fishing and amenity). British Waterways is also responsible for a further 500 miles of canals, some of which are no longer navigable and whose future is being considered in conjunction with local authorities; a number of these lengths have been restored for cruising or as local amenities. The Board's external turnover for the 12 months to 31 March 1989 was £20·8m. The total freight traffic on the Board's waterways for the same period was 4·4m. tonnes.

The most important of the river navigations and canals under other authorities include the rivers Thames, Great Ouse and Nene, the Norfolk Broads and the Manchester Ship Canal.

Hadfield, C., *British Canals*. 6th ed. Newton Abbot, 1979

Post and Telecommunications. In Oct. 1981 the Post Office ceased to control telecommunications services, which became the responsibility of a separate corporation, British Telecom. The Post Office operates as 3 distinct but interdependent businesses. Every area of the country has separate district offices for each of the letters, parcels and counters businesses. The Post Office provides: Royal Mail general collection and delivery services, handling 54m. letters and parcels a day; Premium Services including guaranteed delivery to UK addresses on the same day and overnight (Datapost), and by facsimile transmission to many UK and overseas centres; International Datapost offering guaranteed swift delivery to over 100 countries; postal, banking and many agency services on behalf of government departments and other public sector organizations at 21,000 post office counters. Number of post offices at 31 March 1988 was 21,030; number of posting boxes including those at post offices, over 100,000; staff employed, 206,856 (excluding 19,343 sub-postmasters employed on an agency basis).

	1985–86 (1m.)	1986–87 (1m.)	1987–88 (1m.)	1988–89 (1m.)
Correspondence (incl. registered items) posted	11,700	12,500	13,500	13,700
Parcels handled	194	192	197	191

Income (1988–89) £3,914·8m. Profit retained, £100m.

At 30 Sept. 1989 there were 7,062 local exchanges, 345 trunk exchanges and 5 international exchanges operated by British Telecom. At 30 Sept. 1989 there were 5,473,000 business and 19,018,000 residential telephone connexions and 105,000 telex connexions. In 1990 British Telecom's modernization programme will continue. By the end of Sept. 1989 there were more than 2,546 digital exchanges in operation and more than 730,000 km of optical fibre had been installed in the network.

At 31 Dec. 1989 about 330,000 customers were connected to Cellnet, the cellular mobile radio network launched in 1985 and run jointly by BT and Securicor. In 1989 BT owned and operated 6 cable and satellite TV systems at The Barbican (London), Bracknell, Berks, Irvine (Scotland), Milton Keynes, Swindon and Washington (Tyne and Wear). At 31 May 1989 BT employed a total staff of 235,400.

Daunton, M. J., *Royal Mail: The Post Office since 1840*. London, 1985

Broadcasting. Radio and television services are provided by the BBC and by the Independent Broadcasting Authority (IBA) and its programme contractors. The BBC, constituted by Royal Charter until 31 Dec. 1996, has responsibility for providing domestic and external broadcast services, the former financed from the television licence revenue, the latter by Government grant. The domestic services include 2 national television services, 4 national radio network services and an expanding local radio service.

The IBA provides an independent television service on a regional basis, with programmes provided by its programme contractors. The 1981 Act provided for the establishment of the fourth television channel (Channel 4) and of the Welsh Fourth Channel Authority (S4C) which provides a Welsh service on that channel in Wales; they started broadcasting in Nov. 1982. The IBA also provides independent local radio services. All these services are financed by the sale of broadcast advertising time.

The BBC's domestic radio services are available on LF, MF and VHF; those of the IBA on MF and VHF. The television services of the 2 authorities BBC1, BBC2, ITV, and Channel 4 are broadcast at UHF in 625-line definition and in colour.

The broadcasting authorities, whose governing bodies are appointed (by HM the Queen in the case of the BBC and by the Home Secretary in the case of the IBA and S4C) as trustees for the public interest in broadcasting, are independent of government in matters of programme content and are publicly accountable to Parliament for the discharge of their responsibilities.

Cable services are regulated by the Cable Authority which was established by Parliament in 1984 to oversee the development of cable in the UK. Five direct broadcasting by satellite (DBS) channels began broadcasting in 1989. They were authorized under the Cable and Broadcasting Act 1984; they are uplinked from this country and will be subject to IBA regulation. Satellite services are also receivable direct from other countries. Most existing satellite services received from abroad are used to feed cable systems and are therefore subject to Cable Authority regulation

In 1981 the Broadcasting Complaints Commission was set up to consider and adjudicate upon complaints of unfair or unjust treatment in broadcast programmes or of unwarranted infringement of privacy in or in the making of programmes. The number of broadcast receiving licences in force on 31 March 1988 was 19·3m., including 17·1m. for colour.

Cinemas. In 1984 there were 1,200 screens in 70 cinemas and there were 55m. admissions.

Newspapers. In 1987 there were 14 national dailies.

Benn's Media Directory. Tunbridge Wells, Annual

JUSTICE, RELIGION, EDUCATION AND WELFARE

Justice. *England and Wales.* The legal system of England and Wales, divided into civil and criminal courts has at the head of the superior courts, as the ultimate court of appeal, the House of Lords, which hears each year a number of appeals in civil matters, including a certain number from Scotland and Northern Ireland, as well as some appeals in criminal cases. In order that civil cases may go from the Court of Appeal to the House of Lords, it is necessary to obtain the leave of either the Court of Appeal or the House itself, although in certain cases an appeal may lie direct to the House of Lords from the decision of the High Court. An appeal can be brought from a decision of the Court of Appeal or the Divisional Court of the Queen's Bench Division of the High Court in a criminal case provided that the Court is satisfied that a point of law 'of general public importance' is involved, and either the Court or the House of Lords is of the opinion that it is desirable in the public interest that a further appeal should be brought. As a judicial body, the House of Lords consists of the Lord Chancellor, the Lords of Appeal in Ordinary, commonly called Law Lords, and such other members of the House as hold or have held high judicial office. The final court of appeal for certain of the Commonwealth countries is the Judicial Committee of the Privy Council which, in addition to Privy Counsellors who are or have held high judicial office in the UK, includes others who are or have been Chief Justices or Judges of the Superior Courts of Commonwealth countries.

Civil Law. The main courts of original civil jurisdiction are the county courts for less important cases, and the High Court for the more important ones.

There are some 280 county courts located throughout the country, grouped in districts, and each presided over by a circuit judge. In 1990 they had a general jurisdiction to determine all actions founded on contract or tort involving sums of not more than £5,000 and can also deal with other classes of case, such as landlord and tenant, probate, equity and admiralty, up to certain limits. Certain matters, such as actions of libel and slander, are entirely reserved for the High Court. In addition, certain designated county courts have jurisdiction in matrimonial proceedings. Divorce proceedings must now commence in these courts and, subject to limited exceptions, are determined in the county court.

The High Court has both appellate and original jurisdiction, covering virtually all civil causes not determined in the county court. The judges of the High Court are attached to one of its 3 divisions: Chancery; Queen's Bench; and Family; each with its separate field of jurisdiction. The Heads of the 3 divisions are the Lord Chief Justice (Queen's Bench), the Vice Chancellor (Chancery), and the President of the Family Division. In addition there are over 80 High Court judges, called puisne judges. For the hearing of cases at first instance, the High Court judges sit singly. Appellate jurisdiction is usually exercised by Divisional Courts consisting of 2 (sometimes 3) judges, though in certain circumstances a judge sitting alone may hear the appeal.

The Restrictive Practices Court was set up in 1956 under the Restrictive Trade Practices Act, and is responsible for deciding whether a restrictive trade agreement is in the public interest. It is presided over by a High Court judge, but laymen sit on the bench also. Another specialist court is the Employment Appeal Tribunal, with similar composition, which hears appeals in employment cases from lower tribunals.

The Court of Appeal (Civil Division) hears appeals in civil actions from the High Court and county courts and certain special courts such as the Restrictive Practices Court and the Employment Appeal Tribunal. Its President is the Master of the Rolls, aided by 27 Lords Justices of Appeal sitting in 6 or 7 divisions of 2 or 3 judges each.

Civil proceedings are instituted by the aggrieved person, but, as they are a private matter, they are frequently settled by the parties to a dispute through their lawyers before the matter actually comes to court. In some cases, at the instance of either party, a jury may sit to decide questions of fact and award of damages.

Criminal Law. At the base of the system of criminal courts in England and Wales are the magistrates' courts which try over 97% of criminal cases. In general, in exercising their summary jurisdiction, they have power to pass a sentence of up to six months imprisonment and to impose a fine of up to £2,000 on any one offence. They also deal with the preliminary hearing of cases triable only at the Crown Court. In addition to dealing summarily with over 2m. cases, which include thefts, assaults, road traffic infringements, drug abuse, etc, they also have a limited civil jurisdiction.

Magistrates' courts normally comprise three lay justices. Although unpaid they are entitled to loss of earnings and travel and subsistence allowance. They undergo training after appointment and they are advised by a professional justices' clerk. In central London and in some provincial areas full-time stipendiary magistrates have been appointed. Generally they possess the same powers as the lay bench, but they sit alone. On 1 Jan. 1990 the total strength of the lay magistracy was 28,667 including 12,577 women. Justices are appointed on behalf of the Queen by the Lord Chancellor, except in Greater Manchester, Merseyside and Lancashire where they are appointed by the Chancellor of the Duchy of Lancaster.

Justices are selected and trained specially to sit in Juvenile and domestic courts. Juvenile courts deal with cases involving persons under 17 years of age charged with criminal offences (other than homicide and other grave offences) or brought before the court as being in need of care or control. These courts normally sit with three justices, including at least one man or one woman, and are accommodated separately from other courts.

Domestic Proceedings courts deal with matrimonial applications, custody, guardianship and maintenance of children, and adoption. These courts normally sit with three justices including at least one man or one woman.

Above the magistrates' courts is the Crown Court. This was set up by the Courts Act 1971 to replace quarter sessions and assizes. Unlike quarter sessions and assizes, which were individual courts, the Crown Court is a single court which is capable of sitting anywhere in England and Wales. It has power to deal with all trials on indictment and has inherited the jurisdiction of quarter sessions to hear appeals, proceedings on committal of persons for sentence, and certain original proceedings on civil matters under individual statutes.

The jurisdiction of the Crown Court is exercisable by a High Court judge, a Circuit judge or a Recorder (who is a part-time judge) sitting alone, or, in specified circumstances, with justices of the peace. The Lord Chief Justice has given directions as to the types of case to be allocated to High Court judges (the more serious cases) and to Circuit judges or Recorders respectively.

Appeals from magistrates' courts go either to a Divisional Court of the High Court (when a point of law alone is involved) or to the Crown Court where there is a complete re-hearing on appeals against conviction. Appeals from the Crown Court in cases tried on indictment lie to the Court of Appeal (Criminal Division). Appeals on questions of law go by right, and appeals on other matters by leave. The Lord Chief Justice or a Lord Justice sits with judges of the High Court to constitute this court.

There remains as a last resort the invocation of the royal prerogative exercised on the advice of the Home Secretary. In 1965 the death penalty was abolished for murder.

All contested criminal trials, except those which come before the magistrates' courts, are tried by a judge and a jury consisting of 12 members. The defence may challenge any potential juror for cause. The prosecution may ask that any number may 'stand by' until the jury panel is exhausted, and only then need to show cause. The jury decides whether the accused is guilty or not. The judge is responsible for summing up on the facts and explaining the law; he sentences convicted offenders. If, after at least 2 hours of deliberation, a jury is unable to reach a unanimous verdict it may, on the judge's direction, provided that in a full jury of 12 at least 10 of its members are agreed, bring in a majority verdict. The failure of a jury to agree on a unanimous verdict or to bring in a majority verdict may involve the retrial of the case before a new jury.

The Employment Appeal Tribunal. The Employment Appeal Tribunal which is a superior Court of Record with the like powers, rights, privileges and authority of the High Court, was set up in 1976 to hear appeals on questions of fact and law against decisions of industrial tribunals and of the Certification Officer. The appeals are heard by a High Court Judge sitting with 2 members (in exceptional cases 4) appointed for their special knowledge or experience of industrial relations either on the employer or the trade union side, with always an equal number on each side. The great bulk of their work is concerned with the problems which can arise between employees and their employers.

Military Courts. Offences by persons subject to service law against the system of military law created under the powers of the Army Act, Air Force Act or Naval Discipline Act are dealt with either summarily or by courts-martial.

The Personnel of the Law. All judicial officers except the Lord Chancellor (who is a member of the Cabinet) are independent of Parliament and the Executive. They are all appointed by the Crown on the advice of the Prime Minister or the Lord Chancellor and hold office until retiring age. The legal profession is divided; barristers, who advise on legal problems and can conduct cases before all courts, usually act for the public only through solicitors, who deal directly with the legal business brought to them by the public and have rights to present cases before certain courts. Long-standing members of both professions are eligible for appointment to most judicial offices. Only barristers, however, are eligible for appointment direct to the High Court and above.

Legal Aid. Broadly there are 3 kinds of legal aid. Firstly there is legal advice and assistance, otherwise known as the 'Green Form' scheme. This includes advice and help on any question of English law, both civil and criminal, but does not normally cover any form of representation before a court or tribunal. As an extension of the scheme, however, assistance by way of representation has been available for certain proceedings, chiefly civil, in magistrates' courts. Legal advice and assistance also provides for duty solicitor schemes at magistrates' courts and police stations. Under the magistrates' courts schemes, initial advice, and representation where necessary, is available to unrepresented defendants at court, from duty solicitors either in attendance at courts or on call. The scheme covers advice to a defendant in custody, making a bail application, representing a defendant in custody on a guilty plea, and certain other cases. The advice and assistance at police stations scheme enables any person who has been arrested and taken to a police station, or who is assisting the police with their enquiries, to receive advice and assistance, from either a duty solicitor or the person's own solicitor. The cost of these schemes, which are not subject to means test or contribution, is met from the Legal Aid fund and in 1988–89 amounted to £30·8m. Secondly, under Part IV of the Legal Aid Act 1988, there is legal aid for civil court proceedings. Under regulations, aid is available to those of low or moderate means either free or subject to a contribution, depending on means. In 1988–89 there were over 1m. payments for advice and assistance under the Legal Advice and Assistance Scheme and around 250,000 civil legal aid certificates were issued. The cost of legal aid in civil cases is met from (*a*) contributions from assisted persons; (*b*) the operation of the statutory charge which gives the Law Society a first charge on money or property recovered or preserved for an assisted person; (*c*) costs recovered from opposing parties and (*d*) a grant from the Exchequer. The net cost of civil legal aid to the state (excluding administration costs of the scheme) in the year 1988–89 amounted to £135·8m. and the cost of the legal advice and assistance scheme was £67·9m. of which £13·8m. was accounted for by assistance by way of representation. Thirdly under Part V of the Legal Aid Act 1988 a court dealing with criminal proceedings may order legal aid to be given if it considers it is desirable in the interests of justice and if it also considers that the defendant (or appellant) requires financial assistance in meeting the costs he may incur. The interests of justice are statutorily defined to include, for example, situations where the defendant is in real danger of going to prison or losing his job, where substantial questions of law are to be argued or where the defendant is unable to follow the proceedings and explain his case due to inadequate knowledge of English, mental illness or other mental or physical disability. Legal aid must be granted, subject to means, in the following circumstances: where a person is committed for trial on a charge of murder, where the prosecutor appeals or applies for leave to appeal from the criminal division of the Court of Appeal or the Courts-Martial Appeal Court to the House of Lords, and in certain circumstances where the court is considering depriving a defendant of his liberty.

The costs of legal aid in criminal proceedings are paid by the central government, but courts have power to require legally aided persons to contribute towards the cost of legal aid given to them. The net cost of legal aid in criminal proceedings in the year 1988–89 was £243·6m., £118·4m. of this was for legal aid in the higher courts which is paid for out of the Lord Chancellor's vote and £125·3m. for legal aid in the magistrates' courts which is paid from the legal aid fund.

Police. The authorized establishment of the police force in England and Wales in Dec. 1989 was 126,592: the actual strength was 112,281 men and 13,829 women. In addition there were 15,589 special constables (including 5,199 women). The estimated total expenditure on the police service in England and Wales for 1988–89 was £3,830m.

SCOTLAND. The High Court of Justiciary is the supreme criminal court in Scotland and has jurisdiction in all cases of crime committed in any part of Scotland, unless expressly excluded by statute. It consists of the Lord Justice-General, the Lord Justice-Clerk and 22 other judges, who are the same judges as of the Court of Session, the Scottish supreme civil court. One judge is seconded to the Scottish Law Commission. The Court, which is presided over by the Lord Justice-General, whom failing, the Lord Justice-Clerk, exercises an appellate jurisdiction as well as one of first instance, sits as business requires in Edinburgh both as a Court of Appeal (the *quorum* being 3 judges) and as a court of first instance and on circuit as a court of first instance. The decisions of the Court in either case are not subject to review by the House of Lords. One judge sitting with a jury of 15 persons can, and usually does, try cases, but 2 or more (with a jury) may do so in important or complex cases. It has a privative jurisdiction over cases of treason, murder, rape, deforcement of messengers and breach of duty by magistrates. It also, in practice, is the only court which tries serious crimes against person or property and generally those cases in which a sentence greater than imprisonment for 3 years may be imposed either under statute or common law. Moreover, the Court has inherent power to try and to punish all acts which are plainly criminal though previously unknown and not dealt with by any statute.

The appellate jurisdiction of the High Court of Justiciary extends to all cases tried on indictment, whether in the High Court or the Sheriff Court, and persons so convicted may appeal to the Court against conviction or sentence or both except that there is no appeal against any sentence fixed by law. By such an appeal, a person may bring under review of the High Court of Justiciary any alleged miscarriage of justice including any alleged miscarriage of justice on the basis of the existence and significance of additional evidence which was not heard at the trial and which was not available and could not reasonably have been made available at the trial. It is also a court of review from courts of summary criminal jurisdiction, and on the final determination of any summary prosecution a convicted person may appeal to the Court by way of stated case on questions of law, etc., but not on questions of fact, except in relation to a miscarriage of justice alleged by the person accused on the basis of the existence and significance of additional evidence which was not heard at the trial and which was not available and could not reasonably have been made available at the trial. The Lord Advocate may refer a point of law which has arisen during a trial on indictment in which accused has been acquitted for the opinion of the Court. A prosecutor may appeal only on a point of law. A further or complementary form of process of review which can be resorted to by convicted persons in these courts is by Bill of Suspension (and Liberation), but it is of strictly limited application. A prosecutor in cases tried on indictment or under summary criminal procedure may also bring under review a decision in law, prior to final judgment of the case, by way of Bill of Advocation. The Court also hears appeals under the Courts-Martial (Appeals) Act 1951.

The Sheriff Court has an inherent universal criminal jurisdiction (as well as an extensive civil one) limited in general to crimes and offences committed within a sheriffdom (a specifically defined region), which has, however, been curtailed by statute or practice under which the High Court of Justiciary has exclusive jurisdiction in relation to the crimes above-mentioned. This Court is presided over by a Sheriff-Principal or Sheriff, and when trying cases on indictment sits with a jury of 15 persons. His power of awarding punishment involving imprisonment is restricted to 3 years in the maximum, but he may under certain statutory powers remit the prisoner to the High Court for sentence. The Sheriff also exercises a wide summary criminal jurisdiction and when doing so sits without a jury; and he has concurrent jurisdiction with every other court within his Sheriff Court District in regard to all offences competent for trial in summary courts. The great majority of offences which come before the courts are of a minor nature and, as such, are disposed of in the Sheriff Summary Courts or in the District Courts (*see* below). In cases to be tried on indictment either in the High Court of Justiciary or in the Sheriff Court, the judge may, and in some cases must, before the trial, hold a Preliminary Diet to decide questions of a preliminary nature, whether to the competency or relevancy or otherwise. Any decision at a preliminary diet can be the subject of an appeal to the High Court of Justiciary prior to the trial.

District Courts in each local authority district have jurisdiction in minor offences occurring within the district. These courts are presided over by lay magistrates, known as justices, and have limited powers of fine and imprisonment. In Glasgow District there are also 4 Stipendiary Magistrates who have the same sentencing powers as Sheriffs.

The Court of Session, presided over by the Lord President (the Lord Justice-General in criminal cases), is divided into an Inner House comprising 2 divisions of 4 judges each with mainly appellate function, and an Outer House comprising 15 single judges, sitting individually at first instance; it exercises the highest civil jurisdiction in Scotland, with the House of Lords as a court of appeal.

Police. The police forces in Scotland at the end of 1988 had an authorized establishment of 13,771; the strength was 12,498 men and 1,020 women. There were 4,972 part-time special constables. The total police net expenditure in Scotland was £332,640,000 for 1987–88.

CIVIL JUDICIAL STATISTICS

ENGLAND AND WALES	*1986*	*1987*	*1988*
Appellate Courts			
Judicial Committee of the Privy Council	71	56	61
House of Lords	61	125	90
Court of Appeal	1,565	1,614	1,645
High Court of Justice (appeals and special cases from inferior courts)	1,948	2,436	2,151
Courts of First Instance (excluding Magistrates' Courts and Tribunals)			
High Court of Justice:			
Chancery Division [1]	26,156	22,868	27,054
Queen's Bench Division [2]	235,536	229,399	235,721
Family Division: Principal Registry matters [3]	1,528	1,471	1,435
District Registry wardships	2,250	2,500	2,636
Official Referee's	1,183	1,187	1,363
County courts: Matrimonial suits [4]	183,826	186,675	186,333
Other [5]	2,356,922	2,437,178	2,348,220
Restrictive Practices Court	3	5	4

[1] Including Companies Court, Bankruptcy petitions and Patents Court.
[2] Including Admiralty Court.
[3] Adoption, guardianship and wardship.
[4] Including petitions filed at Principal Registry.
[5] Plaint, Admiralty, Bankruptcy and Companies, Adoption, Guardianship and miscellaneous.

CRIMINAL STATISTICS

ENGLAND AND WALES

	Total number of offenders		Indictable offences[1]	
	1987	*1988*	*1987*	*1988*
Aged 10 and over				
Proceeded against in magistrates' courts[2]	1,843,317	1,863,181	488,042	494,479
Found guilty at magistrates' courts	1,468,435	1,464,287	300,135	295,183
Found guilty at the Crown Court	86,284	91,053	86,284	91,053
Cautioned[3]	236,572	235,401	149,825	140,703
Aged 10 and under 17				
Proceeded against in magistrates' courts[2]	67,554	61,513	52,857	47,629
Found guilty at magistrates' courts	51,989	45,204	40,355	34,801
Found guilty at the Crown Court	1,608	1,646	1,608	1,646
Cautioned[3]	114,401	101,375	95,715	82,818

[1] Includes offences which can be tried either at the Crown Court or at magistrates' courts.
[2] Almost all defendants are initially proceeded against at magistrates' courts.
[3] Offenders who, on admission of guilt, are given an oral caution by or on the instruction of a senior police officer as an alternative to court proceedings. Such cautions are not given for motoring offences.

CRIMINAL STATISTICS

SCOTLAND

	All Crimes and Offences		Crimes[1]	
	1987	*1988*	*1987*	*1988*
All persons and companies				
Proceeded against in all courts	199,954	196,554	68,953	64,417
Charge proved	179,276	177,024	59,508	56,032
Children (aged 8–15)				
Proceeded against in all courts	434	429	287	283
Given formal police warning/ referred to reporter	24,663	23,816	18,147	16,564

[1] Crimes are generally the more serious criminal acts and offences the less serious. 'Crimes' are not equivalent in coverage to 'indictable/triable either way offences'.

Average population in prisons, youth custody centres and detention centres (1988) in England and Wales was 49,949 (convicted 40,924; untried 8,798, and 227 non-criminal prisoners); in Scotland (1988), 5,229 (sentenced, 4,385; remanded, 844).

Criminal statistics, England and Wales, 1988. HMSO, 1988
Prison statistics, England and Wales, 1988. HMSO, 1988
Paterson, A., *The Law Lords*. London, 1982

Religion. The Anglican Communion has originated from the Church of England and parallels in its fellowship of autonomous churches the evolution of British influence beyond the seas from colonies to dominions and independent nations. There is no terrestrial head of the Anglican Communion; the Archbishop of Canterbury presides as *primus inter pares* at the decennial meetings of the bishops of the Anglican Communion at the Lambeth Conference. The last Conference was held in Canterbury in 1988 and was attended by 518 bishops.

The Anglican Communion consists of 28 member Churches or Provinces. These are Australia, Brazil, Burma, Burundi, Rwanda and Zaïre, Canada, Central Africa, Council of Churches of East Asia, England, Indian Ocean, Ireland, Japan, Jerusalem and the Middle East, Kenya, Melanesia, New Zealand, Nigeria, Papua New Guinea, Scotland, Southern Africa, Southern Cone of America, Sudan, Tanzania, Uganda, USA, Wales, West Africa, West Indies. There are also areas which come under the metropolitical jurisdiction of the Archbishop of Canterbury. These are Bermuda,

Ceylon, the Diocese of Europe, Falkland Islands, The Council of the Churches of East Asia (which includes the Church in Korea), The Diocese of Hong Kong and Macao, Sabah, Kuching, Singapore, West Malaysia, The Lusitanian Church (Portugal) and The Spanish Reformed Episcopal Church.

England and Wales. The established Church of England, which baptizes about 30% of the children born in England (*i.e.* excluding Wales but including the Isle of Man and the Channel Islands), is Protestant Episcopal. Civil disabilities on account of religion do not attach to any class of British subject. Under the Welsh Church Acts, 1914 and 1919, the Church in Wales and Monmouthshire was disestablished as from 1 April 1920, and Wales was formed into a separate Province.

The Queen is, under God, the supreme governor of the Church of England, with the right, regulated by statute, to nominate to the vacant archbishoprics and bishoprics. The Queen, on the advice of the First Lord of the Treasury, also appoints to such deaneries, prebendaries and canonries as are in the gift of the Crown, while a large number of livings and also some canonries are in the gift of the Lord Chancellor.

There are 2 archbishops (at the head of the 2 Provinces of Canterbury and York), and 42 diocesan bishops including the bishop of the diocese of Europe, which is part of the Province of Canterbury. Each archbishop has also his own particular diocese, wherein he exercises episcopal, as in his Province he exercises metropolitan, jurisdiction. In Dec. 1989 there were 67 suffragan and assistant bishops, 37 deans and provosts of cathedrals and 108 archdeacons. The General Synod, in England, consists of a House of Bishops, a House of Clergy and a House of Laity, and has power to frame legislation regarding Church matters. The first two Houses consist of the members of the Convocations of Canterbury and York, each of which consists of the diocesan bishops and elected representatives of the suffragan bishops, 6 for Canterbury province and 3 for York (forming an Upper House), deans, provosts, and archdeacons, and a certain number of proctors elected as the representatives of the inferior clergy, together with, in the case of Canterbury Convocation, 4 representatives of the Universities of Oxford, Cambridge, London and the Southern Universities and in the case of York 2 representatives for the Universities of Durham and Newcastle and the other Northern Universities; the chaplains in the Forces and 2 representatives of the Religious Communities (forming the Lower House). The House of Laity is elected by the lay members of the Deanery Synods but also includes 3 representatives of the Religious Communities and *ex-officio* Church Commissioners and Ecclesiastical Judges. Parochial affairs are managed by annual parochial church meetings and parochial church councils. Every Measure passed by the General Synod must be submitted to the Ecclesiastical Committee, consisting of 15 members of the House of Lords nominated by the Lord Chancellor and 15 members of the House of Commons nominated by the Speaker. This committee reports on each Measure to Parliament, and the Measure receives the Royal Assent and becomes law if each House of Parliament resolves that the Measure be presented to the Queen.

At 31 Dec. 1988 there were 13,213 ecclesiastical parishes, inclusive of the Isle of Man and the Channel Islands. These parishes do not, in many cases, coincide with civil parishes. Although most parishes have their own churches, not every parish nowadays can have its own incumbent or minister. In Dec. 1989 there were 6,736 beneficed clergymen excluding dignitaries, 1,327 other clergymen of incumbent status and 1,764 assistant curates working in the parishes.

Women were admitted to Holy Orders for the first time in the Church of England in 1987. At 31 Dec. 1989 there were 539 full-time stipendiary women deacons, 487 of whom were in the parochial ministry.

Private persons possess the right of presentation to over 2,000 benefices; the patronage of the others belongs mainly to the Queen, the bishops and cathedrals, the Lord Chancellor, and the universities of Oxford and Cambridge. In addition to the 9,827 parochial incumbents and (male) assistant curates, there were (1989) 386 dignitaries and cathedral clergymen, 317 non-parochial clergymen working within the diocesan framework and approximately 2,000 non-parochial clergymen outside the framework.

In 1987 there were estimated to be 1·6m. Easter and 1·7m. Christmas Communicants.

Of the 40,407 churches and chapels registered for the solemnization of marriages at 30 June 1987, 16,592 belonged to the Established Church and the Church in Wales and 23,815 to other religious denominations. Of the 351,761 marriages celebrated in 1987 (347,294 in 1986), 34% were in the Established Church and the Church in Wales, 18% in churches or chapels of other denominations and 48% were civil marriages in a Register Office.

Roman Catholics in England and Wales were 4,369,996 in 1989. There were 5 archdioceses and 18 dioceses, 6,205 clergy and 2,743 parish churches and 1,162 other churches open to the public. Convents, 1,262.

The Unitarians have about 230 places of worship and 8,000 members. The Salvation Army, had, in British Territory, 1988, over 1,800 officers. They operate eventide homes, centres for the homeless, homes for children and adolescents and alcoholic rehabilitation centres.

The following is a summary of recent statistics of certain churches:

Denomination	*Full members*	*Ministers in charge*	*Local and lay preachers*
Methodist	450,406	3,399	13,378
Independent Methodist	3,870	131	—
Wesleyan Reform Union	3,026	23	145
United Reform	126,000	1,000	—
Baptist	167,466	2,111	—
Calvinistic Methodist Church of Wales	65,237	146	—
Society of Friends	18,010	—	—

There were (1989) about 410,000 Jews in the UK with about 295 synagogues; Moslems (900,000); Sikhs (175,000); Hindus (140,000).

Scotland. The Church of Scotland (established in 1560 at the Reformation and re-established in 1688 as part of the Revolution Settlement) is Presbyterian, the ministers all being of equal rank. There is in each parish a kirk session consisting of the minister and a number of laymen called elders. There are presbyteries (formed by groups of parishes), meeting frequently throughout the year, and these are again grouped in synods, which meet half-yearly and can be appealed to against the decisions of the presbyteries.

The supreme court is the General Assembly, which now consists of some 1,250 members, half clerical and half lay, chosen by the different presbyteries. It meets annually in May (under the presidency of a Moderator appointed by the Assembly, the Sovereign being present or represented by a Lord High Commissioner, appointed by the Queen on the nomination of the Government of the day), and sits for 7 days. Any matters not decided during this period may be left to a Commission which will sit if required.

On 2 Oct. 1929 the Church of Scotland and the United Free Church of Scotland were reunited under the name of The Church of Scotland, and the two bodies met in General Assembly in Edinburgh as one. The united Church had, in Scotland, on 31 Dec. 1987, 1,727 congregations, 838,659 members. The Church courts are the General Assembly, 12 synods, 46 presbyteries in Scotland, 1 in England and 2 on the Continent. There are divinity faculties in 4 Scottish universities of Edinburgh, Glasgow, Aberdeen and St Andrews, with 60 professors and lecturers who are mostly ministers of the Church of Scotland.

The Episcopal Church of Scotland is a province of the Anglican Church and is one of the historic Scottish churches. It consists of 7 dioceses. As at 31 Dec. 1989 it had 260 churches and missions, 291 clergy and 58,737 members, of whom 35,860 were communicants.

There are in Scotland some small outstanding Presbyterian bodies and also Baptists, Congregationalists, Methodists and Unitarians.

The Roman Catholic Church which celebrated the centenary of the restoration of the Hierarchy in 1978, had in Scotland (1987) 1 cardinal, 2 archbishops and 9 bishops, 1,066 clergy, 472 parishes, and 798,150 adherents.

The proportion of marriages in Scotland according to the rites of the various

Churches in 1986 was: Church of Scotland, 39·4%; Roman Catholic, 13·1%; Episcopal, 1·4%; United Free, 0·4%; others, 4·4%; civil, 41·3%.

Education. *The Publicly Maintained System of Education England and Wales:* Compulsory schooling begins at the age of 5 and the minimum leaving age for all pupils is 16[1]. No tuition fees are payable in any publicly maintained school (but it is open to parents, if they choose, to pay for their children to attend other schools). The post-school stage, which is voluntary, includes universities, polytechnics and other further education establishments (including those which provide courses for the training of teachers), as well as adult education and the youth service. Financial assistance is generally available to students on higher education courses in the university and non-university sectors and to some students on other courses in further education.

Nursery Education. Provision for children under 5 is made in either nursery schools or in nursery or infant classes in primary schools. In the public sector no fees are payable. In Jan. 1989 there were 559 maintained nursery schools and 4,542 primary schools with nursery classes. There were 50,170 pupils under 5 attending nursery schools and 497,394 pupils under 5 in nursery and infant classes. About 49% of all these children were attending part-time.

Primary Schools. These provide for pupils from the age of 5 up to the age of 11. In Jan. 1989 there were 18,656 primary schools in England of which 2,785 were infant schools providing for pupils up to the age of about 7, the remainder mainly taking pupils from age 5 through to 11. Nearly all primary schools take both boys and girls. 21% of primary schools had 100 full time pupils or less.

There are 1,743 primary schools in Wales. In those primary schools (and some secondary schools) which are in the predominantly Welsh-speaking areas, the main language of instruction is Welsh. There are also 'Welsh', or, more accurately, bilingual schools in mainly English-speaking parts of Wales. Generally children transfer from primary to secondary schools at 11.

[1] As a result of the Education (School Leaving Dates) Act 1976, one of the two former leaving dates was amended. This means that pupils whose dates of birth fall between 1 Feb. and 31 Aug. (inclusive) cease to be of compulsory school age on the Friday before the last Monday in May. Some of these pupils will leave school before their 16th birthdays. Pupils whose dates of birth fall between 1 Sept. and 31 Jan. (inclusive) remain of compulsory school age until the end of the Easter term following their 16th birthdays.

Middle Schools. A number of local education authorities operate a middle school system. These provide for pupils from the age of 8, 9 or 10 up to the age of 12, 13 or 14. In Jan. 1989 there were 1,113 middle schools in England deemed either primary or secondary according principally to the age range of the school concerned. This number is 77 fewer than in 1988.

Secondary Schools. These usually provide for pupils from the age of 11 upwards. In Jan. 1989 there were 3,498 secondary schools in England and 232 in Wales. In England some local education authorities have retained selection at age 11 for entry to grammar schools of which there were 150 such schools in 1989. There were a small number of technical schools in 1987 which specialise to a greater or lesser extent in technical studies. There were 214 secondary modern schools in 1989 providing a general education up to the minimum school leaving age of 16, although exceptionally some pupils may be allowed to stay on beyond that age in these schools.

Almost all local education authorities operate a system of comprehensive schools to which pupils are admitted without reference to ability or aptitude. In Jan. 1989 there were 3,117 such schools in England with just over 2·5m. pupils. With the development of comprehensive education various patterns of secondary schools have come into operation. Principally these are: 1. all through schools with pupils aged 11 to 18 or 11 to 16; pupils over 16 being able to transfer to an 11 to 18 school or a sixth form college providing for pupils aged 16 to 19. (There were 112 sixth form colleges in England in 1989). 2. local education authorities operating a three-tier system involving middle schools where transfer to secondary school is at ages 12, 13 or 14. These correspond to 12 to 18, 13 to 18 and 14 to 18 comprehensive schools respectively; or 3. in areas where there are no middle schools a two-tier system of junior and senior comprehensive schools for pupils aged 11 to 18 with optional transfer to these schools at age 13 or 14.

There were a number of other secondary schools of various combinations of grammar, technical or modern in Wales in 1988. There were 41 secondary using Welsh as a teaching medium, of these 16 are designated bilingual schools.

Grant Maintained Schools. Since 1988 all local education authority maintained secondary, middle and primary schools with 300 or more registered pupils can apply for Grant Maintained status and received direct grants from the Department of Education and Science. The governing body of such a school is responsible for all aspects of school management, including the deployment of funds, employment of staff and provision of most of the educational support services for staff and pupils. In Jan. 1990 there were 20 Grant Maintained schools in England and Wales.

City Technology Colleges. New legislation in 1988 enabled the Secretary of State for Education and Science, in partnership with sponsors from business and industry, to fund the establishment of City Technology Colleges. These are secondary schools for 11-18 year olds, having a broad curriculum with an emphasis on science and technology. The schools are independent of local education authorities. Their capital costs are shared between central Government and sponsors with Government meeting all recurrent costs. They do not charge fees.

Assisted Places Scheme. In order to give able children a wider range of educational opportunity the Government set up, in 1981, the Assisted Places Scheme to give help with tuition fees at certain independent schools to parents who could not otherwise afford them. In the school year 1988–89, the 226 participating schools offered a total of 5,536 assisted places, 4,520 for entry at age 11, 12, and 13, and 1,016 for entry at sixth form level. A further 52 schools joined the Scheme in Sept. 1989, providing an extra 260 places for entry at age 11, 12 or 13.

Special Education. The majority of children with statements of special educational needs attend special schools, including hospital special schools and independent schools under arrangements made by local education authorities. The total number of children with statements under the 1981 Education Act is around 138,800.

Of maintained special schools, 1,111 are day schools, 163 are mainly boarding schools and there are 60 hospital special schools. Attendance is compulsory from 5–16. In addition, the Act's definition of special educational needs applies to children under 5 who are likely to have a learning difficulty when over this age, or whose learning difficulty would be likely to persist if special educational provision were not made for them. Authorities also have a duty to make special educational provision either in a school or in a college of further education for children aged 16–18 who have been assessed as being in need of, and who want, such provision. In addition to the provision in ordinary and special schools, authorities can make special arrangements for educating children at home, in small groups or in hospitals. There are also some establishments which provide further education, P.E. vocational training and for assessment for employment purely for handicapped school leavers.

Ancillary Services. Local education authorities may provide registered pupils at any school maintained by them with milk, meals and refreshment and they may make such charges as they think fit for anything they provide. For pupils whose parents are in receipt of supplementary benefit or family income supplement, however, authorities are required to ensure that such provision is made for the pupil at midday as appears to them to be requisite and anything which is provided must be free of charge. Authorities are also required to remit the whole or part of any charge for anything they provide for other pupils if having regard to their circumstances, they consider it appropriate to do so. Facilities must also be provided, free of charge, for consuming any meals or other refreshments which pupils bring to school themselves.

Further and Higher Education (Non-University). In Nov. 1987 there were about 475 institutions in England providing courses of further education, ranging from shorthand instruction to degree-level, postgraduate work and courses of teacher-training. Course enrolments numbered 609,308 full-time (including 76,907 sandwich students) and 1·6m. part-time and evening (including 498,629 students released by their employers). There were in addition 2,412 Adult Education Centres (formerly known as Evening Institutes), which provided mainly part-time courses of non-advanced general education and were attended by 1,371,037 students. In April 1989, 29 polytechnics and 55 colleges of higher education were brought together under the Polytechnics and Colleges Funding Council to create a new sector of higher education in England. The institutions offer both further and higher education courses, many leading to degrees of a standard comparable to those in universities or to professional qualifications. They cater for a mixture of full-time, part-time and sandwich students. Enrolments to the sector in 1988 totalled 293,000.

Courses were also provided by the Workers' Educational Association, the University extramural departments and the Welsh National Council of YMCAs.

Education at institutions of further education is not free, but fees are generally low, and are remitted for most students under the age of 18 by the local authority.

The Youth Service. The Youth Service forms part of the education system and is concerned with promoting the personal development and social education of young people through a wide range of leisure-time activities. A duty is laid upon local education authorities by the provisions of the 1944 Education Act to secure the adequacy of such facilities for young people in their area. The Education Reform Act 1988 retained the force of these provisions. To this end they either provide, maintain and staff youth clubs, centres and other facilities themselves or assist voluntary agencies to do so.

Grants to voluntary agencies to help meet the cost of regional and national capital projects and to national voluntary bodies in support of a range of programmes of work and training expenses are made by the Government. Grants are also made to support the work of the 4 National Youth Service Bodies on the basis of annual work programmes.

Awards to Students. Local education authorities in England and Wales are responsible for making mandatory awards to suitably qualified students taking first-degree and comparable courses, courses of initial teacher-training and certain other advanced level courses. These awards cover fees and maintenance but the maintenance grants are subject to the income of the student and his parents or spouse. In addition scholarships may be available both from universities and other sources. The authorities may also give discretionary awards to students who do not qualify for mandatory awards including those taking non-degree level courses.

In 1986–87 there were 441,997 full value awards current, 44% at universities and 34,551 mandatory awards for initial teacher-training courses. Lesser value awards, which are paid below the full rate of the student's fees and maintenance, were also made by the authorities. There were 115,694 such awards taken up in the academic year 1986–87.

The Research Council gave over 6,600 new awards in 1987–88 and there were more than 13,000 current awards in that academic year. In 1988–89 the British Academy gave 924 new awards and the Department 594 state bursaries and 70 state scholarships.

Teachers. To attain qualified teacher status, for work in maintained schools in England and Wales, teachers must have successfully completed a course of professional training. This can be either by completion of a recognized course of initial teacher training at an higher education institution or, in the case of mature entrants and overseas trained teachers, a period of 'on the job' training as a licensed teacher. EC nationals who are recognized as qualified teachers in other member states will usually be entitled, on application, to automatic qualified teacher status.

In Nov. 1989 there were about 40,000 students on initial teacher-training courses.

On 1 Jan. 1987, 386,000 full-time teachers were employed by local education authorities in maintained nursery, primary and secondary schools in England and Wales.

Finance. Total current and capital expenditure on education in England (including Universities GB, and Mandatory Awards England and Wales) from public funds is estimated at £19,622m. for 1989–90 as compared with £17,892m. for 1988–89.

Scotland. The statistics on schools relate to education authority and grant-aided schools. From 1974–75 all teachers employed in these schools require to be qualified; figures given are full-time equivalents.

Nursery Education. In Sept. 1988 there were 612 nursery schools and departments, with a total enrolment of 40,855 pupils in 1987.

Primary Education. In Sept. 1988 there were 2,388 primary schools and departments and the number on the registers was 433,221. In Sept. 1988, 21,323 teachers were employed in primary schools and departments.

Secondary Education. In Sept. 1988 there were 435 secondary schools with 312,426 pupils. Of these schools, 432 were all-comprehensive with the remaining 3 schools being part selective in intake. All but 40 schools provided a full range of Scottish Certificate of Education courses and non-certificate courses. Pupils who start their secondary education in schools which do not cater for a full range of courses may be transferred at the end of their second or fourth year to schools where a full range of courses are provided. There were 24,566 teachers in secondary schools at Sept. 1988.

Special Schools. In Sept. 1988 there were 349 special schools and departments. The total number of handicapped children under instruction was 9,320.

Further Education. Centres and colleges for formal further education numbered 180 in 1987–88.

The student population was 257,075, of whom 60,527 attended full-time (advanced courses, 31,384; non-advanced, 29,143) and 196,548 part-time (advanced courses, 21,202; non-advanced, 175,346).

Teacher-Training. In Sept. 1988 there were 3,108 students in 5 colleges of education on pre-service courses of teacher-training.

Finance. Total expenditure on education met from revenue in 1987–88 was £1,855m. (excluding university education and loan charges).

Independent Schools. Outside the state system of education there were in England 2,270 independent schools in Jan. 1989, ranging from large 'public' schools to small local ones. There were (Jan. 1989) 532,198 full-time and 18,582 part-time pupils in these schools. In Wales (1988) 11,703 full-time pupils attended 67 independent schools. Fees are charged by all these schools, which receive no grant from central government sources. All independent schools in England are required to be registered by the Department and are liable to the inspection by HM Inspector. The term 'public schools' refers to independent schools in membership of the Headmasters' Conference, Governing Bodies Association or the Governing Bodies of Girls' Schools Association. Qualifications under which a school may be represented at the Headmasters' Conference include the measure of independence enjoyed by the governing body and the amount of advanced courses undertaken. Some of these schools are for boarders only, but the majority include non-resident 'day-pupils'. In Scotland there were 116 independent schools, with a total of 32,632 pupils in Sept. 1989. A small number of the Scottish independent schools are of the 'public school' type but they are not known as 'public schools' since in Scotland this term is used to denote education authority (*i.e.*, state) schools.

The earliest of the schools were founded by, and attached to, the medieval churches. Many were founded as 'grammar' (classical) schools in the 16th century, receiving charters from the reigning sovereign. Reformed mainly in the middle of the 19th century, these schools now provide the highest form of English pre-university education. Among the most well-known independent schools are Eton College, founded in 1440 by Henry VI, with 1,261 pupils; Winchester College, 1394, founded by William of Wykeham, Bishop of Winchester, 647 pupils; Harrow School, founded in 1560 as a grammar school by John Lyon, a yeoman, 769 pupils;

Charterhouse, 1611, 688 pupils. Among the earliest foundations are King's School, Canterbury, founded 600 (with 700 pupils); King's School, Rochester, 604 (618); St Peter's, York, 627 (773).

Universities. In *England* there are 34 traditional degree-giving universities. In addition there are the London and Manchester Business Schools and the Open University.

In *Wales* there is 1 university, the University of Wales, with constituent colleges at Aberystwyth, Bangor, Cardiff, Lampeter and Swansea. The University of Wales School of Medicine is a school of the University. The University of Wales College of Cardiff was formed in 1988 by the merger of University College Cardiff and the University of Wales Institute of Science and Technology.

In *Scotland* there are 8 universities, St Andrews, Glasgow, Aberdeen and Edinburgh Universities date from the 15th and 16th centuries while the others, Strathclyde, Heriot-Watt, Stirling and Dundee have been formally established since the early 1960s.

All these universities and colleges are independent, self-governing institutions, although they receive substantial aid from the State (in the case of the Open University by direct grant from the Department of Education and Science, and the traditional universities through the Universities Funding Council). The UFC, which from 1 April 1989, becomes the successor to the UGC, is a non departmental public body with full executive responsibility for distributing to universities funds provided for that purpose by the Secretary of State for Education and Science and voted by Parliament. It has 15 members, from higher education and elsewhere. The Council also advises the Secretary of State on matters relating to universities. The Government receives advice on the universities' requirements for central computing facilities from the Computer Board for the Universities and Research Councils whose members are also drawn from the universities and industry.

The Royal College of Art and the Cranfield Institute of Technology are primarily postgraduate institutions which award higher degrees under charters granted in 1967 and 1969 respectively.

The Open University received its Royal Charter on 1 June 1969 and is an independent, self-governing institution, awarding its own degrees at undergraduate and postgraduate level. It is financed by the Government through the Department of Education and Science and by the receipt of students' fees.

Tuition is by means of correspondence textbooks, audio and video cassettes, radio and television broadcasts, summer and residential schools. Students can also attend one of over 250 local study centres. No formal qualifications are required for entry to undergraduate or associate student courses.

Anyone resident in the UK aged 18 or over may apply. There are over 130 undergraduate courses; many are available on a one-off basis to associate students.

In 1989 it had over 71,000 undergraduates, over 3,500 postgraduates, over 20,000 short course and associate students and sold over 69,000 packs of learning materials. The university has over 2,500 full-time staff working at its Milton Keynes headquarters and in 13 regional centres throughout the country. There are 5,500 tutors and counsellors.

The University of Buckingham offers two-year honours degree courses. The academic year commencing in Jan. and consisting of four ten-week terms. There are four Schools of Studies: Accounting, Business, and Economics; Humanities; Law; and Sciences. Postgraduate courses are also offered in all schools of studies. In 1989, there were 720 full-time students. Opened in 1976, the University of Buckingham received its Royal Charter in March 1983.

All universities charge fees, but financial help is available to students from several sources. The universities themselves provide scholarships of various kinds and local education authorities and the Scottish Education Department make awards to help suitable students to attend university. The amount of aid given generally depends upon the parents' means. The majority of the students at universities in Great Britain are in receipt of some form of financial assistance.

Awards known as state studentships are offered on a competitive basis by the Department from among candidates considered by the universities and other higher education institutions to be qualified for postgraduate studies in the humanities; similar awards, tenable at universities or other higher education institutions, are offered by the Research Councils to students studying topics within the broad spectrum of agriculture and food; the biological sciences; man's natural environment; science and engineering and the social sciences at post-graduate level.

The following table gives the number of professors, lecturers, etc., and students (full-time and sandwich courses) for 1988–89:

University	*Students*	*Staff*	*University*	*Students*	*Staff*
Aston	3,729	326	Oxford	12,533	1,961
Bath	3,945	511	Reading	6,032	796
Birmingham	9,580	1,490	Salford	4,111	420
Bradford	4,470	518	Sheffield	8,663	1,117
Bristol	7,452	1,247	Southampton	6,772	1,192
Brunel	3,016	367	Surrey	3,708	544
Cambridge	12,893	1,970	Sussex	4,588	587
City	3,484	371	Warwick	6,639	875
Durham	5,177	620	York	3,894	500
East Anglia	4,266	509			
Essex	3,283	370	*Wales—*		
Exeter	5,436	581	Aberystwyth	3,299	365
Hull	5,143	467	Bangor	2,999	397
Keele	3,102	330	Cardiff	8,139	868
Kent	4,347	510	St David's, Lampeter	793	72
Lancaster	4,943	594	Swansea	4,721	499
Leeds	10,611	1,459	Univ. of Wales		
Leicester	5,121	750	College of Medicine	891	368
Liverpool	8,019	1,222			
London Business School	248	82	*Scotland—*		
London	44,612	9,104	Aberdeen	5,681	754
Loughborough	5,347	758	Dundee	3,613	517
Manchester Business School	275	47	Edinburgh	10,403	1,757
Manchester	11,601	1,808	Glasgow	11,049	1,505
Univ. of Manchester Inst. of			Heriot-Watt	4.108	419
Science and Technology	4,275	641	St Andrews	3,782	419
Newcastle	8,134	1,233	Stirling	3,207	353
Nottingham	7,502	1,115	Strathclyde	7,936	997

Women students are admitted on equal terms with men. Number of women students: England, 102,302; Wales, 9,249; Scotland, 21,325. There are, however, colleges exclusively for female students at Oxford and Cambridge. Total number of full-time or sandwich students at universities listed above: England, 246,951; Wales, 20,842; Scotland, 49,779; total, 317,572.

McIntosh, N. E., Calder, J.A. and Swift, B., *A Degree of Difference*. London, 1976
Perry, W., *Open University: A Personal Account*. Open Univ. Press, 1976

The British Council. The British Council was established in Nov. 1934 and incorporated by Royal Charter in 1940. Its aims are the promotion of an enduring understanding and appreciation of Britain in other countries through cultural, educational and technical co-operation.

The Council's total budget in 1990–91 amounted to £348m.

The Council arranges short advisory tours overseas by British experts. In a number of countries it is also the overseas administrative arm of the British Volunteer Programme. It awards scholarships and bursaries and arranges study programmes for some 25,000 visitors a year in Britain. It administers central government funds for youth exchanges with other countries.

In Britain the Council administers the programmes of award schemes for overseas students, meets many students on arrival from overseas, and provides an accommodation service for students from overseas for whom it has a special responsibility. The Council runs offices in Britain, mainly in university cities, for these purposes.

The Council is increasingly called on to administer training schemes and educational services financed by overseas authorities, or by multilateral agencies, on a contractual basis. The Council's specialist courses and summer schools provide advanced study in a number of fields, notably medicine, science, literature and the arts, English language and education. Payment is made by the student, or their parent organization, or by some other sponsor.

The Council produces the following periodicals: *Studying in Britain, Media in Education and Development, British Book News* and *Britain Abroad*. Other publications include the series *Writers and their Work, Notes on Literature, British Education, British Books and Libraries* and a number of booklets including *Scholarships Abroad, Introducing Wales, How to Live in Britain* and *Statistics of Overseas Students in the United Kingdom*. The Council has sponsored two major series of literature recordings, *The Complete Works of Shakespeare* and *The English Poets from Chaucer to Yeats*.

Chairman: Sir David Orr, MC.
Director-General: Sir Richard Francis, KCMG.
Headquarters: 10 Spring Gdns., London, SW1A 2BN.

National Insurance. The National Insurance Act, 1946, came into operation on 5 July 1948, repealing the existing schemes of health, pensions and unemployment insurance. This Act, along with later legislation, was consolidated as the National Insurance Act, 1965.

The Social Security Act 1975 introduced, from 6 April 1975, a new system of national insurance contributions to replace the previous system of flat-rate and graduated contributions. Since 6 April 1975, Class 1 contributions have been related to the employee's earnings and are collected with PAYE income tax, instead of by affixing stamps to a card. Class 2 and Class 3 contributions remain flat-rate, but, in addition to Class 2 contributions, those who are self-employed may be liable to pay Class 4 contributions, which for the year 1990–91 will be at the rate of 6·3% on profits or gains between £5,450 and £18,200, which are assessable for income tax under Schedule D. The non-employed and others whose contribution record is not sufficient to give entitlement to benefits are able to pay a Class 3 contribution voluntarily to qualify for a limited range of benefits. Class 2 weekly contributions for 1990–91 for men and women are £4·55. Class 3 contributions are £4·45 a week.

From 6 April 1978 the Social Security Pensions Act 1975 introduced earnings-related retirement, invalidity and widows' pensions. Employee's national insurance contribution liability depends on whether he is in contracted-out or not contracted-out employment.

Full rate contributions (contribution table leters A or D or Mariner's equivalents) for non contracted-out employment in 1990–91: On earnings between £46 and £79.99 a week the employee pays 2% on the first £46 and 9% on the remainder, the employers pay 5% on all earnings; on earnings between £80 and £124.99 a week the employee pays 2% on the first £46 and 9% on the remainder, the employer pays 7% on all earnings; on earnings between £125 and £174.99 a week the employee pays 2% on the first £46 and 9% on the remainder, the employer pays 9% on all earnings; on earnings between £175 and £350 a week the employee pays 2% on the first £46 and 9% on the remainder, the employer pays 10·45% on all earnings; on earnings of over £350 a week the employee pays 2% on the first £46 and 9% on earnings between £46 and £350 but the employer pays 10·45% of all earnings. For contracted-out employment in 1990–91: On earnings between £46 and £79.99 a week the employee pays 2% on the first £46 and 7% on the remainder and the employer pays 5% on the first £46 and 1·2% on the remainder; on earnings between £80 and £124.99 a week the employee pays 2% on the first £46 and 7% on the remainder and the employer pays 7% on the first £46 and 3·2% on the remainder; on earnings between £125 and £174.99 a week the employee pays 2% on the first £46 and 7% on the remainder and the employer pays 9% on the first £46 and 5·2% on the remainder; on earnings between £175 and £350 a week the employee pays 2% on the first £46 and 7% on the remainder and the employer pays 10·45% on the first £46 and 6·65% on the remainder; on earnings of over £350 a week the employee pays 2% on the first £46 and 7% on earnings between £46 and £350 and the employer pays 10·45% on the first £46, 6·65% on earnings between £46 and £350 and 10·45% on the remainder.

Reduced rate contributions (contribution table letters B or E) for non contracted-out and contracted-out employment in 1990-91: On earnings between £46 and £350 a week the employee pays 3·85% of the full amount, including that part which is below £46; on earnings over £350 a week the employee pays 3·85% of £350. The employer pays contributions as shown in the preceding paragraph - there is no equivalent reduced rate for employers.

The State supplements the contributions paid by contributors and employers, from general taxation. Contributions and supplement together with interest on investments form the income of the National Insurance Fund from which benefits are paid.

Statutory Sick Pay (SSP). Employers are now responsible for paying statutory sick pay (SSP) to their employees for up to 28 weeks in any period of incapacity for work. Basically, all employees aged 16 years and over are covered by the scheme whenever they are sick for 4 or more days consecutively. For most employees SSP completely replaces their entitlement to State sickness benefit which is not payable as long as any employer's responsibility for SSP remains.

Benefits. Qualification for any benefit depends upon fulfilment of the appropriate contribution conditions. Persons who are incapable of work as the result of an industrial accident may get sickness benefit followed by invalidity benefit without having to satisfy the contributions conditions. Employed persons may qualify for all the benefits; self-employed may not qualify for unemployment benefit.

Sickness Benefit. From 9 April 1990 the rate is £35·70 a week plus £22·10 a week for an adult dependant.

Unemployment Benefit is paid through the local unemployment benefit offices of the Department of Employment. The rate is £34·70 a week plus £21·40 a week for an adult dependant.

Invalidity Benefit replaces sickness benefit after 168 days of entitlement. It comprises a basic invalidity pension of £46·90 weekly and an invalidity allowance of £10·00 if incapacity began before age 40: £6·20 if incapacity began between 40 and 49 or £3·10 if it began between 50 and 59 (54 for women). Increases are: £28·20 for an adult dependant plus £9·65 for each child for whom child benefit is payable. Invalidity allowance is reduced or extinguished by the amount of any additional invalidity pension and/or guaranteed minimum pension to which there is title.

Maternity Benefit. Statutory maternity pay may be payable to a woman from her employer if she has been employed by him for 6 months into the 15th week before the baby is expected and her earnings were above the lower earnings limit. If she has been employed by the same employer for at least 2 years, payment for the first 6 weeks of maternity absence may be at 90% of her average earnings. Payment for the remainder of the period is at a standard rate of £39·25. Women who do not qualify for statutory maternity pay may be entitled to maternity allowance from DSS if they satisfy a test of recent work and contributions paid. From April 1990, the weekly rate is £35·70. Both statutory maternity pay and maternity allowance can be paid for up to 18 weeks. Payment can start at the earliest 11 weeks before the expected week of confinement but the woman has some choice in deciding when to give up work and still retain title to the full 18 weeks.

Widow's Benefits. From 11 April 1988 the three main widow's benefits, will be: Widow's payment, widowed mother's allowance, widow's pension.

A widow cannot get any widow's benefits based on her husband's NI if: She had been divorced from the man who has died; or she was living with the man as if she were married to him, but without being legally married to him; or she is living with another man as if she is married to him. A widow can only get widow's benefits if her husband has paid enough NI contributions. The rules about the number of NI contributions that are needed for these benefits can be complicated.

Widow's Payment: A widow may be able to get this benefit if her husband has paid enough NI contributions and: She was under 60 when her husband died; or her husband was not getting a State Retirement Pension when he died.

A widow who is entitled to a widow's payment will get a single payment of £1,000. This will be tax-free.

Widowed Mother's Allowance: A widow may be able to get a widowed mother's allowance if her husband has paid enough NI contributions and: She is receiving child benefit for one of her children; or her husband was receiving child benefit, or she is expecting her husband's baby, or if she was widowed before 11 April 1988 she has a young person under 19 living with her for whom she was receiving Child Benefit.

A widow who is entitled to a widowed mother's allowance will get an amount that is based on her husband's NI contributions. The maximum will be £43·60 a week. She will also get £8·95 a week for each of her dependent children and she may also get an additional pension based on her husband's earnings since 1978. Widowed mother's allowance is usually paid as long as the widow is getting child benefit. Widowed Mother's Allowance is taxable.

Widow's Pension: A widow may be able to get a widow's pension if her husband has paid enough NI contributions. She must be 45 or over (40 or over if widowed before 11 April 1988) when her husband died or when her widowed mother's allowance ends. A widow cannot get a widow's pension at the same time as a widowed mother's allowance. A widow who is entitled to a widow's pension will get an amount that depends on her age when her husband died or when her widowed mother's allowance ends. If she was 55 or over (50 or over if widowed before 11 April 1988) she will get the full rate of widow's pension. The maximum amount of widow's pension will be £43·60 a week. She may also get an additional pension based on her husband's earnings since 1978. Widow's pension is usually paid until the widow is entitled to state retirement pension, when she is 60 or older. Widow's pension is taxable.

Guardian's Allowance. A person who is responsible for an orphan child may be entitled to a guardian's allowance of £9·65 a week in addition to the amount of child benefit payable in respect of that child. Normally both the child's parents must be dead but when they never married or were divorced, or one is missing, or serving a long sentence of imprisonment, the allowance may, in certain circumstances, be paid on the death of one parent only.

Retirement Pension. In order to receive a retirement pension, men between 65 and 70, and women between 60 and 65 must have retired from regular employment. From 6 April 1979 a woman divorced over the age of 60 must satisfy the retirement conditions before a pension is payable. The standard rates of basic pensions are £43·60 a week for a man or woman on his or her own contributions and £26·20 for a married woman through her husband's contributions. Proportionately reduced pensions are payable where contribution records are deficient. For a person who reaches pension age on or after 6 April 1979, additional pension may also be payable. This is based on the earnings on which he or she has paid Class 1 contributions in each complete tax year between April 1978 and pension age. If the person has been a member of a contracted-out occupational pension scheme, that scheme will be responsible for paying the whole or part of the additional pension. An increase of £26·20 a week may be payable for a dependent wife. If she resides with the beneficiary the increase is gradually reduced for earnings over £34·70 a week. A tapered earnings rule (£45·09) applies to claims made before 16 Sept. 1985. From that date the earnings rule will apply in these circumstances. When the spouse/woman looking after the claimant's child is living with the claimant an adult dependant's allowance will only be payable if the dependant's earnings do not exceed the standard rate of unemployment benefit for a person under pensionable age (currently £34·70). If she does not reside with the beneficiary an increase is not payable if she earns more than £26·20 a week. In addition £8·95 a week may be payable for each child for whom child benefit is payable. In certain circumstances an increase of £26·20 a week may be payable for a woman having care of the pensioner's children. In addition, a man who had paid graduated contributions receives 5·71p per week for every £7·50 of graduated contributions paid, and a woman 5·71p per week for every £9 paid. Although no further graduated contributions have been paid after April 1975, pension already earned will be paid along with the basic pension in the normal way. If, after being awarded a retirement pension, a man under 70 or a woman under 65 earns more than £75 in a calendar week the pension for the next pension week, including any increase for dependants, will be reduced by 5p for every 10p earned between £75 and £79 and by 5p for every 5p earned over £79. If retirement is postponed after minimum pension age increments of all components of the pension can be earned for periods of deferred retirement. From 6 April 1979 increments are earned at the rate of one-seventh penny per £1 of basic pension for every 6 days (excluding Sundays) for which pension has been foregone. Any days for which another benefit has been paid will not count. These increments must be at least 1% of the pension rate unless the minimum was earned under the arrangements which applied before 6 April 1979. For periods between 6 April 1975 and that date, the rate was one-eighth penny per £1 of the basic pension rate for every 6 days and for periods of deferred retirement before 6 April 1975 increments were based on the number of contributions paid as an employed or self-employed person. At age 70 for a man (65 for a woman) the pension for which a person has qualified may be paid in full whether a person continues in work or not irrespective of the amount of earnings. At the age of 80 an age addition of £0·25 a week is payable. In addition non-contributory pensions are now payable, subject to residence conditions, to persons aged 80 and over who do not qualify for a retirement pension or qualify for one at a low rate. The rates of these pensions, which are financed by Exchequer funds, are £26·20 a week for a single person and £15·65 for a married woman. These amounts do not include the £0·25 age addition. From 22 Dec. 1984 the lower rate of category D retirement pension payable to married women was abolished.

The Industrial Injuries Provisions of the Social Security Act, 1975. The Industrial Injuries Act, which also came into operation on 5 July 1948, with its later amending Acts, was consolidated as the National Insurance (Industrial Injuries) Act, 1965. This legislation was incorporated in the Social Security Act, 1975. The scheme provides a system of insurance against 'personal injury by accident arising out of and in the course of employment' and against certain prescribed diseases and injuries due to the nature of the employment. It takes the place of the Workmen's Compensation Acts and covers persons who are employed earners under the Social Security Act. There are no contribution conditions for the payment of benefit. Three types of benefit are provided:

(1) Disablement benefit. This is payable where, as the result of an industrial accident or prescribed disease, there is a loss of physical or mental faculty. The loss of faculty will be assessed as a percentage by comparison with a person of the same age and sex whose condition is normal. If the assessment is between 14-100% benefit will be paid as weekly pension; 14-19% are payable at the 20% rate. The rates vary from £15·32 (20% disabled) to £76·20 (100% disablement). Assessments of less than 14% do not normally attract basic benefit except for certain progressive chest diseases. Pensions for persons under 18 are at a reduced rate. When injury benefit was abolished for industrial accidents occurring and prescribed diseases commencing on or after 6 April 1983, a common start date was introduced for the payment of disablement benefit 90 days (excluding Sundays) after the date of the relevant accident or onset of the disease. The following increases can be paid with disablement benefit: Constant attendance allowance – where the disability for which the claimant is receiving disablement benefit is assessed at 100% and is so severe that they need constant care and attention. There are 4 rates depending on the amount of attendance needed. Exceptionally severe disablement allowance – where the claimant is in receipt of constant attendance allowance at one of the two higher rates and the need for attendance is likely to be permanent.

Reduced earnings allowance (previously known as special hardship allowance) is now a separate benefit. Entitlement exists if the claimant has not retired and cannot go back to their normal job or do another job for the same pay because of the effects of the disability caused by the accident or disease. It can be paid whether or not disablement benefit is paid, providing the disablement benefit assessment is 1% or more (*e.g.* where disablement is assessed at less than 14%) and on top of 100% disablement benefit. From 1 Oct. 1989, if a claimant is of pensionable age (60 for a woman, 65 for a man) they can continue to receive REA if they are in regular employment, or in some cases if they are receiving Sickness Benefit, Invalidity Benefit or Unemployment Benefit. It will not matter whether or not they receive State Retirement Pension. If they are not in regular employment then entitlement to REA will cease. In most cases it will be replaced by retirement allowance.

(2) *Death Benefit.* This is payable to the widow of a person who died before 11 April 1988 as the result of an industrial accident or a prescribed disease. Benefit is a weekly pension of either £43·60 or £13·08 depending on such factors as age and entitlement to a child's allowance. A child allowance of £8·95 per child may be payable to the widow if she is entitled to child benefit for children of the deceased. Deaths which occurred on or after 11 April 1988 – a widow is entitled to full widow's benefits even if her late husband did not satisfy the contribution condition, if he died as a result of an industrial accident or prescribed disease.

Allowances may be paid to people who are suffering from pneumoconiosis or byssinosis or certain other slowly developing diseases due to employment before 5 July 1948. They must at any time have been entitled to benefit for the disabled under the Industrial Injuries provision of the Social Security Act or compensation under Workmen's Compensation Acts or received damages through the courts.

In certain cases supplementation allowances are payable to people who are getting or are entitled to compensation under the Workmen's Compensation Acts. These rights are in respect of accidents occurring or diseases due to employment before the Industrial Injuries Scheme was introduced on 5 July 1948.

War Pensions. The number of beneficiaries in receipt of war (1914–18) pensions or allowances as at 31 Dec. 1988 was 7,600. The number of beneficiaries in receipt of war (1939–45 and later) pensions or allowances in payment as at 31 Dec. 1988 was 250,400. The expenditure for both wars for 1987–88 was £598·57m.

National Insurance Fund. At 1 April 1988 the balance of the National Insurance Fund amounted to £7,287,620,000. Income during the period 1 April 1988 to 31 March 1989, consisting of contributions from insured persons and employers, payments from the Exchequer and interest on investments, etc., was £29,825,327,000. Payments of benefit in respect of unemployment were £1,106,745,000; injury and sickness, £191,960,000; invalidity, £3,359,358,000; maternity, £26,870,000; widows, £850,164,000; guardian's allowance and child's special allowance, £1,352,000; retirement pension, £19,237,593,000; disablement benefits, £454,973,000; death benefits, £58,610,000. Included in these figures are the following estimated amounts of additional component, £777,104,000; earnings related supplement having ceased. Administrative and other payments cost approximately £1,168,039,000. The balance at 31 March 1989 was £10,368,808,000.

From 1 April 1975 the National Insurance Reserve Fund and the Industrial Injuries Fund were merged with the National Insurance Fund. All basic scheme contributions payable under the 1975 Social Security Act are paid into the single fund out of which the existing range of benefits will continue to be financed. The National Insurance Fund continues to receive a Treasury Supplement; for 1988–89 this was set at a level of 5% of total contribution income.

Child Benefit. Child benefit is a tax-free cash allowance for children. The weekly rate for each child is £7·25 from 6 April 1987. Child benefit is payable for almost all children under age 16, for 16 and 17 year olds registered for work or training and for those under age 19 receiving full-time non-advanced education at a college or school. One Parent Benefit. This is a tax-free cash allowance for certain people bringing up children alone. It is payable for the first or only child in the family in addition to child benefit. The weekly rate from 9 April 1990 is £5·60.

Family Credit. Family Credit is a tax-free benefit for working families with children. To be able to get Family Credit there must be at least one child under 16 in the family (or under 19 if in full-time education up to, and including, A level or equivalent standard). The claimant or partner (if there is one) must be working at least 24 hours a week to qualify. They may be employed or self-employed, a lone parent or a couple. The claim should be made by the woman in two parent families. The amount of family credit payable depends on the income of the claimant and partner, how many children there are in the family and their ages. The same rates of benefit are paid for one-parent families as for two-parent families. Family Credit is not payable if the claimant (or claimant and partner together) have savings or capital of over £6,000. Benefit is reduced if savings or capital of more than £3,000 is held.

Family Credit is paid for 26 weeks at a time. The amount of the award will usually stay the same even if earnings, or other circumstances, change during that period.

Attendance allowance. This is a tax-free non-contributory allowance for severely disabled people who require a lot of help from another person. There are 2 rates, the higher rate of £37·55 a week for those who require attention or supervision by day and night, and the lower rate of £25·05 a week for those who need the attendance either by day or night. In addition to the medical requirements a simple test of residence and presence in Great Britain must also be satisfied.

Invalid Care Allowance. This is a non-contributory taxable benefit which may be paid to those who stay at home to care for a person who is receiving attendance allowance or constant attendance allowance. Current rate £28·20 a week, with increases for dependants.

Income Support. Under the Social Security Act, 1986, benefit is payable to any persons in Great Britain aged 18 years or over (excluding persons at school or college or anyone directly involved in a trade dispute) who are not in full-time remunerative work or who work part-time for less than 24 hours per week and who are without resources, or whose resources (including national insurance benefits) need to be supplemented in order to meet their requirements. A person who is excluded from benefit under the normal rules may, nevertheless, receive payments to meet urgent need. The general standards by reference to which income support is granted are determined by statutory regulations approved by Parliament. Persons who are dissatisfied with the amount of benefit granted to them may appeal to an independent Appeal Tribunal established under the Act.

National Health. The National Health Service in England and Wales started on 5 July 1948 under the National Health Service Act, 1946. There is a separate Act for Scotland and also one for Northern Ireland, where the Health Services are run on similar lines to those in England and Wales.

The National Health Service, which is available to every man, woman and child, is a charge on the national income in the same way as the armed forces and other facilities.

Every person normally resident in this country is entitled to use any complete part of the services, and no insurance qualification is necessary. Most of the cost of running the service is met from the national exchequer, *i.e.*, from taxes.

Since Sept. 1957 a small weekly National Health Service contribution has been payable by contributors and where applicable by their employers. For convenience this contribution is collected with the National Insurance contribution and for 1990–91 is estimated to be £4,120m. for Great Britain.

Organization. Under the provisions of the NHS Act 1977 and the Health Service Act 1980, the administration of the National Health Service in England and Wales is organized under a system of regional and district health authorities accountable to the Secretary of State for the Social Services and the Secretary of State for Wales. In Scotland the National Health Service is administered under the National Health Service (Scotland) Act 1978, by 15 Health Boards and a Common Services Agency all accountable to the Secretary of State for Scotland.

There are 190 district health authorities in England responsible for the administration and development of health services in their district. Fourteen regional health authorities, each consisting of a number of health districts, are responsible for allocating resources between the district health authorities in their regions and for monitoring their performance. The regional authorities are responsible for developing strategic plans and priorities and for carrying out certain executive functions.

Services. The National Health Service broadly consists of hospital and specialist services, general medical, dental and ophthalmic services, pharmaceutical services, community health services and school health services. All these services are free of charge except for such things as prescriptions, spectacles, dental and optical examination, dentures and dental treatment, amenity beds in hospitals and for some of the community services, for which charges are made with certain exemptions.

The total cost of the Health and Personal Social Services (England) is estimated at £19,672m. for 1987–88 and £2,441m. for the UK (Local Authority Personal Social Service being £3,614m.).

The number of abortions performed in England and Wales 1988 under the provisions of the Abortion Act, 1967, was 183,798. Of these, 168,298 abortions were to England and Wales residents, of which 111,044 were to single women, 38,689 were to married women, and 18,565 were to widowed, divorced or separated women and to women who did not state their marital status.

The number of abortion notifications received in Scotland in 1988 under the provisions of the Abortion Act 1967, was 10,003, of which 9,987 related to Scottish residents. Of these 9,987 notifications, 6,620 (66·3%) were to single women, 2,206 (22·1%) were to married women, and 1,161 (11·6%) were to widowed, divorced or separated women and to women who did not state their marital status.

In Great Britain in 1987 there were 32,422 general medical practitioners, (1988) 17,440 general dental practitioners and (1986) 287,700 qualified nurses and midwives. There were (1987) 388,500 average daily available hospital beds in the UK.

Personal Social Services. Under the Local Authority Social Services Act 1970 and in Scotland the Social Work (Scotland) Act 1968 the welfare and social work services provided by local authorities were made the responsibility of a new local authority department—the Social Services Department in England and Wales, and Social Work Departments in Scotland headed by a Director of Social Work. The social services thus administered include: the fostering, care and adoption of children, welfare services and social workers for the mentally disordered, the disabled and the aged, and accommodation for those needing residential care services. In Scotland the social work departments' functions also include the supervision of persons on probation, of adult offenders and of persons released from penal institutions or subject to fine supervision orders.

The number of supported residents in residential accommodation for the elderly and younger disabled was as follows:

England and Wales (31 March)	*Residential accommodation Adults and Children*	*Scotland (31 March)*	*Residential accommodation Adults and Children*
1986	121,793	1986	14,637
1987	111,688 [1]	1987	14,348
		1988	14,381

[1] England only.

England and Wales. Expenditure and income relating to the personal social services administered by local authorities (in £1,000 sterling):

Year ended 31 March	*Gross current expenditure*	*Income from sales, fees and charges*	*Net current expenditure*
1984	2,625,060	378,520	2,246,540
1985	2,781,541	390,122	2,391,419
1986	2,952,048	456,825	2,798,099
1987 [1]	3,286,262	488,163	2,798,099

Capital Spending

Year ended 31 March	*Gross expenditure*	*Income from sales of fixed assets*	*Net expenditure*
1984	95,903	17,940	77,963
1985	106,708	23,041	83,667
1986	107,913	27,366	80,547
1987 [1]	103,871	23,662	80,209

[1] Provisional.

Scotland. The total local authority expenditure for 1987–88 in respect of residential accommodation and welfare services under the Social Work (Scotland) Act, 1968, was £409·5m. Central Government expenditure on social work totalled £8·1m.

Klein, R., *The Politics of the National Health Service*. London, 1983
Watkin, B., *The National Health Service*. London, 1978

DIPLOMATIC REPRESENTATIVES

Of the USA in Great Britain (Grosvenor Sq., London, W1A 1AE)
Ambassador: Henry Catto.

Of Great Britain in the USA (3100 Massachusetts Ave., NW, Washington, D.C., 20008)
Ambassador: Sir Antony Acland, GCMG, KCVO.

Of Great Britain to the United Nations
Ambassador: Sir Crispin Tickell, GCMG, KCVO.

Further Reading

The annual and other publications of the various Public Departments and the Reports, etc. of Royal Commissions and Parliamentary Committees. (These may be obtained from HM Stationery Office.)
Central Statistical Office. *Annual Abstract of Statistics*. HMSO.—*Monthly Digest of Statistics*. HMSO
Central Office of Information. *Britain: An Official Handbook*. HMSO, annual.
Directory of British Associations. Beckenham, annual
Government Statistical Service. *Social Trends*. HMSO.—*Regional Statistics*. HMSO
Government Statistics: A Brief Guide to Sources. HMSO, 1984
Halsey, A. H., *Trends in British Society Since 1900*. London, 1972
Hennessy, P., *Whitehall*. London, 1989
Hornsby-Smith, M.P., *Roman Catholics in England*. CUP, 1987
Jenkin, M., *British Industry and the North Sea*. London, 1981
Kendall, M. G. (ed.), *The Source and Nature of the Statistics of the United Kingdom*. 2 vols. London, 1952–1957
Lever, W. F., *Industrial Change in the United Kingdom*. Harlow, 1987
Mitchell, B. R., *Abstract of British Historical Statistics*. OUP, 1962
Oxford History of England. 15 vols. OUP, 1936–75
Waller, R. (ed.), *The Almanack of British Politics*. London, 1987

Scotland

Scottish Council (Development and Industry). *Inquiry into the Scottish Economy, 1900–61*. Edinburgh, 1961
Scottish Office. *Scottish Economic Bulletin*. HMSO (quarterly).—*Scottish Abstract of Statistics*. HMSO (annual)
The New Scottish Local Authorities: Organisation and Management Structures. HMSO, 1973
Brand, J., *The National Movement in Scotland*. London, 1978
Campbell, R. H., *The Rise and Fall of Scottish Industry, 1707–1939*. Edinburgh, 1981
Donaldson, G. (ed.) *The Edinburgh History of Scotland*. 4 vols. Edinburgh, 1965–75
Drucker, N. and H. M. *The Scottish Government Year Book*. London, 1980
Grant, E., *Scotland*. [Bibliography] Oxford and Santa Barbara, 1982
Hogg, A. and Hutcheson, A. MacG., *Scotland and Oil*. 2nd ed. Edinburgh, 1975

Johnston, T. L., *Structure and Growth in the Scottish Economy*. London, 1971
Kellas, J. G., *The Scottish Political System*. 3rd ed. CUP, 1984
Meikle, H. W. (ed.) *Scotland: A Description of Scotland and Scottish Life*. London, 1947
Monies, G., *Local Government in Scotland*. Edinburgh, 1985

Wales

Wales: The Way Ahead (Cmnd 3334.) HMSO, 1971
Wales: Employment and the Economy. Cardiff, 1972
Digest of Welsh Statistics. HMSO (annual)
Jenkins, G. H., *The Foundations of Modern Wales 1642–1780*. Oxford, 1988
Williams, D., *A History of Modern Wales*. New ed. London, 1977
Williams, G., (ed.) *Social and Cultural Change in Contemporary Wales*. London, 1978

NORTHERN IRELAND

AREA AND POPULATION. Area (revised by the Ordnance Survey Department) and population were as follows:

District	*Population (usually resident) 1981 Census* [1]	*Population estimate 30 June 1988*	*Land area (Hectares)*
Antrim	45,016	47,700	41,510
Ards	57,792	64,000	36,789
Armagh	49,223	49,200	66,733
Ballymena	54,813	56,900	63,384
Ballymoney	22,946	23,900	41,687
Banbridge	30,110	31,900	44,174
Belfast	314,270	299,600	11,140
Carrickfergus	28,625	30,000	8,484
Castlereagh	60,785	58,000	8,426
Coleraine	46,739	48,100	47,763
Cookstown	28,257	27,600	51,207
Craigavon	73,260	77,200	27,945
Down	53,193	57,000	63,835
Dungannon	43,883	43,700	76,266
Fermanagh	51,594	50,000	169,952
Larne	29,076	29,000	33,744
Limavady	26,964	30,000	58,523
Lisburn	83,998	95,500	43,595
Derry (Londonderry)	89,101	98,700	37,258
Magherafelt	32,494	33,100	56,186
Moyle	14,396	15,200	49,378
Newry and Mourne	76,574	87,800	88,589
Newtownabbey	72,246	72,800	15,956
North Down	66,264	71,100	7,329
Omagh	44,288	44,900	112,354
Strabane	36,279	35,200	86,090
Northern Ireland	1,532,186	1,578,100	1,348,297

[1] Arising from difficulties during the Census taking, a number of households were not enumerated. The population effect of this non-enumeration is estimated at about 50,000 and is included in this column.

Chief town (population, estimate 1987): Belfast, 303,800.
Vital statistics for calendar years:

	Marriages	*Divorces* [1]	*Births*	*Deaths*
1984	10,361	1,552	27,693	15,692
1985	10,343	1,669	27,635	15,955
1986	10,225	1,539	28,152	16,065
1987 [1]	10,363	1,514	27,865	15,334
1988 [1]	9,958	1,550	27,767	15,813

[1] Provisional.

CONSTITUTION AND GOVERNMENT. Northern Ireland is part of the

United Kingdom. As such it shares in the written and unwritten constitution of the United Kingdom and is subjected to the fundamental constitutional provisions which apply to the rest of the United Kingdom. However, in the Northern Ireland Constitution Act 1973 and the Northern Ireland Act 1982, Parliament provides for a measure of devolved government in Northern Ireland. This can only be introduced if both Houses of Parliament agree that the arrangements for devolution are likely to command widespread acceptance throughout the community in Northern Ireland.

Such matters as the Crown, Parliament, international relations, the armed forces and the raising of taxes cannot be devolved in any circumstances and remain the responsibility of the UK Parliament and Government. In the event of agreement on widely-acceptable arrangements for devolution, powers over a range of social and economic matters would be devolved first. The Northern Ireland Assembly would have power to make laws on these subjects and Members of the Assembly would be appointed as heads of the relevant Northern Ireland government departments. Such powers were devolved on 1 Jan. 1974, following an agreement among the Northern Ireland political parties to form a power-sharing Executive. This collapsed on 28 May 1974.

In the interim and in the absence of devolved arrangements which command widespread acceptance, Northern Ireland is governed by 'direct rule' under the provisions of the Northern Ireland Act 1974. This provides for Parliament to approve all laws for Northern Ireland and places the Northern Ireland departments under the direction and control of a UK Cabinet Minister, the Secretary of State for Northern Ireland.

A 78-member Assembly was elected by proportional representation in 1982. In May 1984 the Assembly set up a Committee on Devolution to consider and report on how the Assembly might be strengthened and progress made towards legislative and executive devolution. The Assembly was dissolved on 23 June 1986, having failed in its statutory duty to make proposals for devolution likely to command widespread acceptance throughout the community.

In Nov. 1985 the governments of the UK and the Republic of Ireland entered into a formal Agreement which is designed to promote peace and stability in Northern Ireland, help to reconcile the two major traditions in Ireland, create a new climate of friendship and co-operation between the people of the two countries and improve co-operation in combating terrorism. Under the Agreement an Intergovernmental Conference was established in which the Irish Government will put forward views and proposals concerning stated aspects of Northern Ireland affairs; in which the promotion of cross-border co-operation will be discussed; and in which determined efforts will be made to resolve any differences between the two governments. A Secretariat was also established by the two governments to service the Conference.

What began ostensibly as a Civil Rights campaign in 1968 escalated into a full-scale offensive designed to overthrow the State. This offensive was originally mounted by an illegal organization, the Irish Republican Army (not to be confused with the legitimate Army of the Republic of Ireland). At times counter-measures have required the services of over 20,000 regular troops, in addition to the Royal Ulster Constabulary, the RUC Reserve and the part-time Ulster Defence Regiment.

Secretary of State for Northern Ireland: Rt Hon. Peter Brooke, MP.

Local Government. Northern Ireland has a single-tier system of 26 district councils based on main centres of population.

The district councils are responsible for the provision of a wide range of local services including refuse collection and disposal, street cleansing, litter prevention, consumer protection, environmental health, miscellaneous licensing including dog control, the provision and management of recreational and cultural facilities, the promotion of tourist development schemes and the enforcement of building regulations. They have in addition both a representative role in which they send forward representatives to sit as members of statutory bodies including the Northern Ireland Housing Council, the Fire Authority and the Area Boards for health and personal social services and education and libraries; and a consultative role under which the Department of Environment (NI) and the Northern Ireland Housing Executive, among others, have an obligation to consult them regarding the provision of the regional services for which these bodies are responsible.

The Government's policy for the future development of the Province is contained in the *Regional Physical Development Strategy 1975–95* which was published in May 1977. Basically the policy advocates that the main town in each District Council area should be developed to fulfil its function as the prime centre in the district and for any other specialized rôles it may have such as an industrial centre, port or tourist resort. The Strategy also recognizes that the smaller towns and villages have an important rôle to play, depending on the availability of services, as locations for smaller scale industries service centres and as dormitory centres for people not wishing to live in the towns where they find employment.

The Regional Strategy provides a framework within which development plans can be prepared for all the districts. Since its adoption of the Strategy the Department has been engaged in formulating the detailed policies and proposals for future communications, the location of industry, housing and major services in the light of anticipated population growth and distribution.

A development plan sets down the broad policies and proposals for the development or other use of land in the area covered by the plan over a period of up to 15 years ahead. Development plans covering almost all of Northern Ireland have been published and work is progressing on the remaining areas, together with review of some earlier plans.

FINANCE. There exists a separate Northern Ireland Consolidated Fund from which is met the expenditure of Northern Ireland Departments. Its main sources of revenue are: *(i)* The Northern Ireland attributed share of UK taxes; *(ii)* A non-specific grant in aid of Northern Ireland's revenue, payable by the Secretary of State for Northern Ireland; *(iii)* Rates and other receipts of Northern Ireland Departments.

The general principle underlying the financial arrangements is that Northern Ireland should have parity of taxation and services with Great Britain.

Since the financial year 1987–88 the income of the Northern Ireland Consolidated Fund has been as follows (in £ sterling):

	1987–88	*1988–89*	*1989–90* [1]
Attributed share of UK taxes	2,218,709,227	2,383,344,413	2,698,742,228
Payments by UK Government:			
Grant in Aid	855,000,000	1,300,000,000	1,150,000,000
Refund of value added tax	30,752,473	28,914,872	29,000,000
Regional and district rates	251,250,000	276,500,000	309,000,000
Other receipts	345,646,946	339,206,178	292,000,000
Total	4,327,965,463	4,327,965,463	4,478,742,228

[1] Provisional.

The public debt at 31 March 1989 was as follows: Ulster Savings Certificates, £151,533,129; Ulster Development Bonds, £28,285; borrowing from UK Government, £1,268,616,287; borrowing from Northern Ireland Government Funds, £87,581,332; European Investment Bank Loan, £13,997,974; total, £1,521,757,007.

The above amount of public debt is offset by equal assets in the form of loans from Government to public and local bodies and of cash balances.

ENERGY AND NATURAL RESOURCES

Electricity. The planning, generation and distribution of electricity supplies are the responsibility of Northern Ireland Electricity.

The installed capacity of the system is 2,100 mw largely provided from 4 thermal power-stations.

The total sales of electricity in Northern Ireland in the year ended 31 March 1989 amounted to 5,430m. units supplied to a total of 589,993 consumers.

Water Supplies and Sewerage. The Department of the Environment Water Service is responsible for water supply and sewerage. Some 691 megalitres of water are supplied throughout Northern Ireland per day to approximately 97% of the population. Approximately 92% of the population live in property which is connected to sewers or modern septic tanks.

The Department is also responsible for the conservation and planned development of the water resources of Northern Ireland.

Minerals. The output of minerals (in 1,000 tonnes) during 1988 was approximately: Basalt and igneous rock (other than granite), 7,324; grit and conglomerate, 2,870; limestone, 2,409; sand and gravel, 3,871; and other minerals (rocksalt, fireclay, diatomite, granite, chalk, clay and shale), 870. Lignite has been discovered near Crumlin in County Antrim and in some other areas.

Agriculture. Estimated gross output in 1987:

		Quantity (1,000)	*Value (£m.)*			*Quantity (1,000)*	*Value (£m.)*
Fat cattle		506	264·4	Grass seed		—	—
Calves	head	29	4·6	Hay and straw	tonnes	10	0·4
Store cattle	head	15	5·9	Fruit	tonnes	21	2·6
Exports of breeding livestock	head	6	2·4	Vegetables	tonnes	25	6·1
Fat sheep and lambs	head	976	36·9	Mushrooms	tonnes	9	11·0
Fat pigs	head	1,170	72·8	Flowers		—	6·5
Poultry (tonnes)		66	47·3	Other items		—	63·5
Eggs: for human consumption (dozen)		72	30·5				—
Wool (tonnes)		2,429	2·4	Total receipts			787·0
Milk (litres)		1,340	199·6	Value of changes in stocks due to volume			−11·5
Potatoes		231	20·3				
Oats	tonnes	5	0·6				
Barley	tonnes	65	6·9	Gross output			775·5
Wheat	tonnes	20	2·3				

Area (in 1,000 hectares) of crops at June census (1988 and 1989):

	1988	*1989*		*1988*	*1989*
Oats	2·6	2·8	Crop silage	5·8	3·3
Wheat	4·9	4·7	Other crops	1·6	1·3
Barley	42·3	40·2	Fruit	1·9	1·9
Other cereals and pulses	0·3	0·3	Grass for mowing or grazing	760·9	764·8
Potatoes	12·0	10·3	Rough grazing (excluding common land)	187·0	189·3
Turnips, swedes, kale and cabbage[1]	0·8	0·7			
Vegetables	1·6	1·4			

[1]Stock feeding only.

Livestock (1,000) at June census (1988 and 1989):

	1988	*1989*		*1988*	*1989*
Dairy cows	279	277	Total sheep	2,073	2,317
Beef cows	205	244	Breeding sows	62	58
Total cattle	1,439	1,467	Total pigs	619	589
Breeding ewes	980	1,085	Total poultry	10,331	9,824

INDUSTRY AND TRADE

Industry. In 1988 (June) employment in manufacturing and construction amounted to 127,900, just under 25·8% of the total employees in employment. Of this number, 29,960 (23·4%) were engaged in the engineering and allied industries, which include shipbuilding and aircraft manufacture. The former predominance of shipbuilding has diminished, and the engineering sector now produces an impressive variety of goods; from textile machinery, air-conditioning plant and oilfield equipment to automobile and aero-engine components, data-processing equipment, and electronic components. The textile and man-made fibre industries, with a workforce of 12,540 includes longer established sectors such as spinning and weaving as well as more recently established activities such as the production of carpets, man-made fibres and hosiery. The related clothing and footwear sector employs 17,530 people.

Taken together, food, drink and tobacco account for 18,440 jobs, the remainder of the manufacturing sector comprising a multiplicity of activities, such as chemicals, rubber and plastic goods, and furniture accounting for 23,850. The construction industry employed 24,430 people in 1989.

In Sept. 1988 the average number of unemployed claimants was 117,501, this represents 16·6% of the workforce. The Department of Economic Development provides an all-age guidance and placement service through a network of job-markets situated in the principal towns of Northern Ireland. They maintain registers of persons voluntarily seeking employment (either full- or part-time) and those already in employment who wish to change their job. In the financial year 1987–88, 39,796 persons (adult and young people) were placed into employment in Northern Ireland by the Employment Service. A further 18,388 persons were placed into training.

The Government offers a comprehensive range of incentives to encourage the establishment of new and the expansion of existing industry.

For the year ending March 1988, the Industrial Development Board promoted 5,300 new jobs in a total of 115 new projects of which 12 were first time projects by overseas companies. The total investment in these amounted to £302m.

Through the Department of Economic Development, there are various employment and training grants available to assist employers with recruitment and training of workers. These grants cover a wide spectrum of industry, age groups, and types of training.

Assistance is available to employers who transfer key workers temporarily or permanently to Northern Ireland from other countries or within Northern Ireland in connection with the establishment or expansion of an industrial undertaking.

The Department of Economic Development maintains a register of disabled persons who are in the employment field and under the provisions of the Disabled Persons (Employment) Acts (NI) 1945 and 1960, makes efforts to find suitable work for those who are unemployed. Employment rehabilitation courses are provided at the Employment Rehabilitation Unit at Felden House, Newtownabbey and training courses at various locations are available to assist unemployed disabled persons to readjust themselves to working conditions and to enhance their prospects of obtaining suitable employment. Allowances are paid to persons attending these courses.

The Youth Training Programme is a two year vocational training programme administered by the Department of Economic Development in partnership with the Department of Education for Northern Ireland. The programme provides:

(a) full-time training places for 16 and 17 year old school leavers not yet in employment;

(b) employment with training opportunities for 17 year olds (YTP Workscheme);

(c) increased vocational preparation for young people remaining in full-time education.

In 1988–89 the Programme provided some 10,500 training places in a variety of schemes. Provision was also made for up to 6,000 entrants to YTP Workscheme, a scheme which encourages employers to recruit and train 17 year old employees.

Enterprise Ulster is an independent statutory body whose objective as a direct labour organization is to give employment to the long term and less skilled unemployed. Employment is provided through a structured industrial approach with an emphasis on: (a) rehabilitation into the disciplines of work; (b) training in semi-skilled and traditional trades; (c) placement in more conventional employment. Work that is carried out mainly for public bodies and projects, which might not otherwise be done, is of community and amenity value. In Sept. 1988, 180 projects were providing employment for 1,400 employees.

The Action for Community Employment Scheme, which came into operation in April 1981, provides temporary employment for long-term unemployed adults on projects which are of benefit to the community. In Sept. 1988 some 380 such projects were operational, providing employment for some 8,000 people.

There are 12 Training Centres in Northern Ireland which provide over 3,000 training places and an annual output of over 5,000 trainees.

Training Centres contribute to the Youth Training Programme having up to 2,200 places available for 16–17 year olds who have been unable to find employment. A special six-month broad-based modular course provides basic training in a wide variety of skills and the six-month craft skill courses provide initial apprentice training. Advanced vocational training is available to young people who have completed the basic training course and have been unable to obtain a place in an apprentice course. The remaining places are for adult trainees.

To supplement the Training Centres facilities, arrangements have been made for the use of spare training capacity in industry and commerce to attach people to firms for training courses. By this means a wide variety of training is made available and this has been further supplemented by use of spare capacity in other training agencies and in Colleges of Further Education.

The Department of Economic Development administers an Entry to Management Programme for unemployed trainees and a Management Development Programme for private sector firms. The former Programme contains training opportunities schemes for those wishing to enter or re-enter management or to set up new businesses – at the peak time of the training year up to 250 people can be in training. The latter Programme is designed to encourage companies to develop management structures and to train individual managers to a high level of competence. Each year about 2,000 grants are awarded to support training courses or training places in companies. Also, up to 2,100 places were available in the financial year 1988–89 under the Enterprise Allowance Scheme, to encourage unemployed people to set up in business, by paying them £40 a week for up to 52 weeks as a business receipt to compensate for loss of unemployment or income support.

Labour. The main sources of statistics in Northern Ireland are the census of employment, which was last conducted in 1987, and the quarterly employment enquiry. In June 1989 there were 514,720 employees in employment in Northern Ireland; of which 268,500 were males.

Tourism. Tourism earns a substantial amount of revenue for Northern Ireland and total spending by some 824,000 visitors in 1986 was £82m. Altogether tourism provides over 9,000 full-time jobs. The Northern Ireland Tourist Board has the main responsibility for promoting tourist traffic to and within Northern Ireland.

Scenic beauty, scientific and nature interest, and wildlife are protected by the Department of the Environment under the Access to the Countryside (NI) Order 1983, the Nature Conservation and Amenity Lands (NI) Order 1985 and the Wildlife (NI) Order 1985. The Department is advised by the Council for Nature Conservation and the Countryside. Nine Areas of Outstanding Natural Beauty have been designated, where special attention is given to the amenity aspects of planning applications. Country Parks have been established at Crawfordsburn, Redburn and Scrabo, Co. Down, at the Roe Valley and Ness Wood, Co. Derry, and at Castle Archdale, Co. Fermanagh. At The Birches in N. Armagh a Peatlands Park is being developed. The Lagan Valley between Belfast and Lisburn is Northern Ireland's first Regional Park. Countryside Information Centres are located at Portrush, Co. Antrim and Newcastle, Co. Down and a visitor centre at the Quoile Pondage National Nature Reserve, near Downpatrick, Co. Down. Forty-five National Nature Reserves have been declared, and more are being acquired.

The Department is advised by the Historic Monuments Council on the exercise of its powers under the Historic Monuments Act (NI) 1971 in respect of the conservation of historic monuments and the preservation of objects of archaeological or historic interest. At present there are some 165 monuments in State care and approximately 1,000 are scheduled. The Department, advised by the Historic Buildings Council, under the Planning (NI) Order 1972 is also responsible for listing buildings of special architectural or historic interest and for designating areas of similar interest the character or appearance of which it is desirable to preserve or enhance. To date some 7,554 buildings have been listed and 26 conservation areas have been designated. Grants may be payable by the Department to assist in the repair or maintenance of listed buildings and for schemes of enhancement in conservation areas.

COMMUNICATIONS

Road and Rail. All train services are operated by the Northern Ireland Railways Co. Ltd which is a subsidiary of the Northern Ireland Transport Holding Co. The number of track km operated is 357; passenger route miles, 210. In 1988–89 railways carried 5·8m. passengers. Most bus services are operated by two other subsidiaries, Ulsterbus Ltd and Citybus Ltd. Ulsterbus runs services outside the Belfast area while all the services within the Belfast area are run by Citybus.

The Department of the Environment (NI) administers a licensing system for professional hauliers with the objective of maintaining standards and conditions necessary for the safe operation of vehicles and fair competition between hauliers. The level of services provided and the rates charged by the industry are determined by the normal economic forces of supply and demand. At 31 March 1989 there were 1,492 professional hauliers and 2,867 vehicles licensed to engage in road haulage.

The number of motor vehicles licensed at 31 Dec. 1989 was 485,537, comprising private cars, 443,081; motor cycles, 8,957; hackney vehicles, 3,333; goods vehicles, 22,526; special machines, 7,640. In addition, there were 15,448 vehicles which were not subject to licence duty.

At 1 April 1988 the total mileage of roads was 14,812, graded for administrative purposes as follows: Motorway 69 miles; Class I dual carriageway, 81 miles; Class I single carriageway, 1,283 miles; Class II, 1,774 miles; Class III, 2,936 miles; unclassified, 8,669 miles.

Aviation. Northern Ireland Airports Ltd is responsible for the operation of Belfast International Airport. A major 4-stage development programme was started in 1977; 3 stages have been completed. The completion of the programme will leave the airport better equipped to handle traffic growth in the foreseeable future. Passenger and freight services operate between Belfast International Airport and airports throughout the UK. In 1986, 2·1m. passengers and 33,000 tonnes of freight and mail were handled.

Scheduled air services are available from Belfast (Harbour) Airport to 11 destinations in the UK.

There are 3 other licensed airfields in Northern Ireland and of these Eglinton has some scheduled services; otherwise these airfields are used principally by flying clubs, by private owners and by expanding air taxi businesses flying to destinations in Ireland, the UK and continental Europe.

Shipping. Passenger services operate between Belfast and Liverpool and between Larne and (i) Cairnryan and (ii) Stranraer. Conventional cargo services have given way in many cases to container, unit load and drive on/drive off services. The latter type of service now operates from Belfast, Larne and Warrenpoint to various ports in UK.

JUSTICE, RELIGION, EDUCATION AND WELFARE

Justice. The Lord Chancellor has responsibility for the administration of all courts in Northern Ireland through the Northern Ireland Court Service, and is responsible for the appointment of judges and resident magistrates.

The court structure in Northern Ireland has 3 tiers–the Supreme Court of Judicature of Northern Ireland (comprising the Court of Appeal, the High Court and the Crown Court), the County Courts and the Magistrates' Courts. There are 25 Petty Sessions districts which when grouped together for administration purposes form 7 County Court Divisions and 4 Circuits.

The County Court has general civil jurisdiction subject to an upper monetary limit of £5,000. Appeals from the Magistrates' Courts lie to the County Court, while appeals from the County Court lie to the High Court or, on a point of law, to the Court of Appeal by way of case stated. Circuit Registrars have jurisdiction to deal with most defended actions up to £1,000 and most undefended actions up to £5,000. They also deal, by an informal arbitration procedure, with small claims whose value does not exceed £500. An appeal from the decision of a Circuit Registrar lies to the High Court other than in small claims cases.

Police. The police force consists of the Royal Ulster Constabulary, supported by the Royal Ulster Constabulary Reserve, a mainly part-time force.

Religion. According to the census of 1981 of the total enumerated population of 1,481,959 there were: Roman Catholics, 414,532; Presbyterians, 339,818; Church of Ireland, 281,472; Methodists, 58,731. Those belonging to other Churches and of no stated denomination numbered 387,406. 18·5% of the enumerated population failed to answer the voluntary question on religion.

Education. Education in Northern Ireland is administered centrally by the Department of Education and locally by 5 education and library boards. The Department is concerned with the whole range of education from nursery education through to higher education and continuing education; for sport and recreation; for youth services; for the arts and culture (including libraries) and for community relations and community development. District councils are the main providers of sport, recreation and community facilities and the education and library boards have a responsibility where the facilities are intended primarily for education and youth service activities. The Department assists with grants as far as the district councils are concerned and meets the full cost in relation to education and library boards.

The 5 education and library boards which took over responsibility for the local administration of the education and library services on 1 Oct. 1973 are required to ensure that there are sufficient schools of all kinds to meet the needs of their area. They provide primary and secondary schools, special schools for handicapped pupils and institutions of further education. The boards meet the running costs (excluding teachers' salaries) in voluntary schools other than voluntary grammar schools; award university and other scholarships; meet the tuition fees of the great majority of pupils attending grammar schools; provide milk and meals; free books and transport for pupils; enforce school attendance; regulate the employment of children and young people and secure the provision of recreational and youth service facilities. They are also required to develop a comprehensive and efficient library service for their areas. The following are the statistics for the 1988–89 academic year:

Universities. Northern Ireland now has 2 Universities of Higher Education, the Queen's University of Belfast (QUB) and the University of Ulster (UU). The Queen's University of Belfast (founded in 1849 as a college of the Queen's University of Ireland and reconstituted as a separate university in 1908) had 109 professors, 246 readers and senior lecturers, 558 lecturers and tutors and 7,682 full-time students in 1988–89. The University of Ulster, formed on 1 Oct. 1984, has campuses in Belfast, Coleraine, Jordanstown and Londonderry. In 1988–89 the University had 53 professors, 221 readers and senior lecturers, 558 lecturers and demonstrators and 8,293 full-time students.

Secondary Education. 71 grammar schools with 53,131 pupils and (1986-87) 3,595 full-time teachers; 174 secondary (intermediate) schools with 89,968 pupils and (1986-87) 6,603 full-time teachers.

Primary Education. 978 primary schools with 184,241 pupils and (1986-87) 7,774 teachers; 85 nursery schools with 4,868 pupils and (1986-87) 158 teachers.

Further Education. 26 institutions of further education with 2,448 full-time and 2,933 part-time teachers and an enrolment of 15,619 full-time, 23,935 part-time day and 17,154 evening students on vocational courses; and 46,023 students on non-vocational (mostly evening) courses.

Special Educational Treatment. 54 special schools, including hospital schools with 4,018 pupils and (1986-87) 359 teachers.

Teachers. There were 21,781 full-time teachers (8,478 men and 13,303 women) in grant-aided schools and institutions of further education. The principal initial teacher-training courses are the Bachelor of Education (3 year and 4 year honours), general or honours BA and BSc. degrees with education (3, 4 and 5 year) and the one year Certificate of Education for graduates. There were 1,816 students (314 men and 1,502 women) in training at the 2 Colleges of Education and the 2 Universities during 1988–89.

Expenditure by the Department of Education (1988–89) £812m.

Health and Personal Social Services. Under the provisions of the Health and Personal Social Services (NI) Order 1972, the Department of Health and Social Services is responsible for the provision of integrated health and personal social services in Northern Ireland, designed to promote the physical and mental health of the people of Northern Ireland through the prevention, diagnosis and treatment of illness, and also to promote their social welfare. Four Health and Social Services Boards, Eastern, Northern, Southern and Western, established under the above Order, administer health and personal social services, as the Department directs, within their designated areas.

Social Security. The social security schemes in Northern Ireland are similar to those in force in Great Britain.

National Insurance. During the year ended 31 March 1989, £10·1m. sickness benefit was paid to an average of 8,746 persons and £41·1m. unemployment benefit was paid to an average of 23,208 persons. Widows' benefits amounting to £30·3m. were paid to an average of 12,649 persons and retirement pensions totalling £419·5m. were paid to an average of 214,918 persons. Invalidity pensions and allowances totalling £141·2m. were paid to an average of 46,531 persons. Industrial disablement benefit amounting to £13·2m. was paid to an average of 5,550 persons. Maternity allowance totalling £1m. was paid to an average of 704 persons. Receipts, of the Northern Ireland Insurance Fund in the year ended 31 March 1989 were £770·2m. and payments were £698m.

Child Benefit. During the year ended 31 March 1989, £173m. was paid to an average of 216,718 families.

Income Support. In 1988–89, £348·5m. was paid to an average of 192,372 persons.

Family Credit. In 1988–89, £28m. was paid to an average of 14,857 persons.

Further Reading

The annual and other publications of the various Departments and the Reports, etc., of Parliamentary Committees may be obtained from HMSO Bookshop, Belfast.
Northern Ireland Social Security Statistics
Census of Population Reports, Northern Ireland. Belfast, HMSO, 1981
Northern Ireland: A Trade Directory. Belfast, HMSO, 1st ed. 1985
Reports on the Census of Production of Northern Ireland. Belfast, HMSO
The Statutes Revised: Northern Ireland. HMSO, 1982
Arthur, P. and Jeffery, K., *Northern Ireland since 1968*. Oxford, 1988
Bell, G., *The Protestants of Ulster*. London, 1976
Biggs-Davison, J., *The Hand is Red*. London, 1974
Flackes, W. D., *Northern Ireland: Political Directory 1968–88*. London, 1989
Kelly, K., *The Longest War: Northern Ireland and the IRA*. Dingle, Westport and London, 1982
Kenny, A., *The Road to Hillsborough*. London, 1986
Shannon, M. O., *Northern Ireland*. [Bibliography] Oxford and Santa Barbara, 1990
Wallace, M., *British Government in Northern Ireland: From Devolution to Direct Rule*. Newton Abbot, 1982
Watt, D. (ed.) *The Constitution of Northern Ireland*. London, 1981

ISLE OF MAN

AREA AND POPULATION. Area, 221 sq. miles (572 sq. km); resident population census April 1986, 64,282. The principal towns are Douglas (population, 20,368), Ramsey (5,778), Peel (3,660), Castletown (3,019). Vital statistics, 1988: Births, 781; deaths, 991; marriages, 446.

CONSTITUTION AND GOVERNMENT. The Isle of Man is administered in accordance with its own laws by the Court of Tynwald, consisting of the Governor, appointed by the Crown; the Legislative Council, composed of the Lord Bishop of Sodor and Man, the Attorney-General (who does not vote) and 8 members selected by the House of Keys, total 10 members; and the House of Keys, a representative assembly of 24 members chosen on adult suffrage. The Island is not bound by Acts of the Imperial Parliament unless specially mentioned in them.

A special relationship exists between the Isle of Man and the European Economic Community providing for free trade and adoption by the Isle of Man of the EEC's external trade policies with third countries. The Island remains free to levy its own system of taxes.

An Executive Council to advise the Governor on all matters of government was set up under the Isle of Man Constitution Act, 1961. It consists at present of the Chief Minister and the ministers of the 9 major departments of Government.

Lieut.-Governor: Air Marshal Sir Laurence Jones, KCB, AFC.
Chief Secretary: J. F. Kissack.

Flag: Red, with 3 steel-coloured legs armoured and spurred (knees and spurs, yellow) in the centre.

ECONOMY

Budget. Revenue is derived from customs duties, value added tax and from income tax. In 1989–90 the budget allowed for expenditure of £230m. Income tax was 15% of the first £8,000 of taxable income and 20% on the balance. There are no inheritance or capital gains taxes. A non-resident company duty of £450 was introduced on 6 April 1987 on every company incorporated in the Isle of Man which trades and is controlled outside the island.

The Island currently makes an annual contribution to the UK Government towards the cost of defence and other common services provided by the UK Government. That contribution currently amounts to about £1·3m.

Currency. The Isle of Man Government issues its own notes and coin on a par with £ sterling. £50, £20, £10, £5, £1 and 50p notes and £5, £2, £1, 50p, 20p, 10p, 5p, 2p and 1p coins are issued. Various commemorative coins have been minted together with legal tender gold coins and a platinum bullion coin.

Banking. Government regulation of the banking sector is exercised through the Financial Supervision Commission. The Commission was established in 1982 and is responsible for the licensing and supervision of banks, deposit-takers and certain financial intermediaries giving financial advice and receiving client monies for investment and management. In 1989 there were 54 licensed banking institutions, 53 investment businesses and 5 UK Building Societies with Isle of Man licences. In June 1989 the deposit base was £5,213m.

Agriculture. The area farmed is about 120,000 acres out of a total land area of around 140,000 acres. About 65,000 acres is devoted to grass whilst a further 38,000 acres are accounted for by rough grazing. Barley accounts for most of the remaining land under cultivation and some barley is exported. There are approximately 154,000 sheep, 33,000 cattle, 71,000 poultry and 9,000 pigs on farms in the Island. Agriculture contributes less than 3% of the Island's GNP.

Tourism. In 1987–88 tourism contributed around 9% of national income; there were 322,970 visitors during the 1989 summer season.

COMMUNICATIONS

Roads. There are 500 miles of good roads. The International TT Motor Cycle Races and cycle races take place annually. Omnibus services operate to all parts of the island.

On 31 March 1989 there were about 45,000 licensed vehicles on the roads, including 2,400 motorcycles.

Railways. Several novel transport systems operate on the Island during the summer season, including 100-year-old horse-drawn trams, and the Manx Electric Railway, linking Douglas, Ramsey and Snaefell Mountain (2,036 ft). The Isle of Man Steam Railway also operates between Douglas and Port Erin.

Aviation. Ronaldsway Airport handles scheduled services operated by Manx Airlines and Jersey European to and from London, Manchester, Belfast, Dublin, Glasgow, Liverpool, Blackpool, Birmingham, etc. Air taxi services also operate.

Shipping. Car ferries of the Isle of Man Steam Packet Co. link the Island with Heysham throughout the year and similar services operate to Liverpool, Fleetwood, Stranraer, Dublin and Belfast during the summer season.

Broadcasting. The first constitutionally licensed commercial radio station in the British Isles, Manx Radio, is operated by Government on medium and VHF wavelengths from Douglas.

Newspapers. In 1989 there were 3 weekly newspapers and 1 twice weekly newspaper.

JUSTICE AND EDUCATION

Police. The police force numbered 209 all ranks in 1989.

Education. Education is compulsory between the ages of 5 and 16. In 1989 there were 33 primary schools with 5,347 pupils in attendance. The net expenditure on education for 1989–90 amounted to £26·5m. There are 7 secondary schools, 5 provided by the Board of Education (4,368 registered pupils), 1 direct grant school for girls (102 senior and 166 junior registered pupils), 1 independent co–educational public school (100 senior and 289 junior registered pupils), 1 college of further education (379 full-time pupils in 1987–88).

Further Reading

Additional information is available from: Economic Affairs Division, 14 Hill St, Douglas, Isle of Man.

Publications: *Isle of Man Key Facts 1988, Isle of Man Digest of Economic and Social Statistics 1988, Isle of Man Census Reports 1981.* 3 vols, *Isle of Man Interim Census Report 1986, Isle of Man Family Expenditure Survey 1981–82, Isle of Man Passenger Survey Reports 1985, 1986, 1987 and 1988, Isle of Man National Income Estimates 1987/88, Isle of Man General Index of Retail Prices* (Monthly), *Isle of Man Earnings Survey 1988.*

Tynwald Companion 1985. Isle of Man Government, 1985

Kinvig, R. H., *History of the Isle of Man.* Oxford, 1945.—*The Isle of Man: A Social, Cultural and Political History*. Liverpool Univ. Press, 1975

Mais, S. P. B., *Isle of Man.* London, 1954

Solly, M., *The Isle of Man: A Low Tax Area.* London, 1984

Stenning, E. H., *Portrait of the Isle of Man.* London, 1984

CHANNEL ISLANDS

AREA. The Channel Islands are situated off the north-west coast of France and are the only portions of the 'Duchy of Normandy' now belonging to the Crown of England, to which they have been attached since the Conquest. They consist of Jersey (28,717 acres), Guernsey (15,654 acres) and the following dependencies of Guernsey–Alderney (1,962), Brechou (74), Great Sark (1,035), Little Sark (239), Herm (320), Jethou (44) and Lihou (38), a total of 48,083 acres, or 75 sq. miles (194 sq. km).

CLIMATE. The climate is mild, with an average temperature for the year of 11·5°C. Average yearly rainfall totals: Jersey, 862·9mm; Guernsey, 858·9mm. The wettest months are in the winter. Highest temperatures recorded: Jersey, 34·8°C.; Guernsey, 31·7°C. Maximum temperatures usually occur in July and Aug. (daily maximum 20·8°C. in Jersey, slightly lower in Guernsey). Lowest temperatures recorded: Jersey, 10·3°C.; Guernsey, –7·4°C. Jan. and Feb. are the coldest months (mean temperature approximately 6°C.).

CONSTITUTION. The Lieut.-Governors and Cs.-in-C. of Jersey and Guernsey are the personal representatives of the Sovereign, the Commanders of the Armed Forces of the Crown and the channel of communication between the Crown and the insular governments. They are appointed by the Crown and have a voice but no vote in the Assemblies of the States (the insular legislatures). The Secretaries to the Lieut.-Governors are their staff officers.

The Bailiffs are appointed by the Crown and are Presidents both of the Assembly of the States and of the Royal Courts of Jersey and Guernsey. They have in the States a casting vote.

LANGUAGE. The official languages are French and English, but English is the main language. In the country districts of Jersey and Guernsey and throughout Sark some people also speak a Norman-French dialect; that of Alderney has died out.

TRADE. From 1958 the trade of the Channel Islands with the UK has been regarded as internal trade.

COMMUNICATIONS

Road. Omnibus services operate in all parts of Jersey and Guernsey.

Aviation. Scheduled air services are maintained by British Airways, Aer Lingus, Air UK, Jersey European, British Midland, Aurigny Air Services, Dan-Air, Brymon Airways, NLM City Hopper and other companies between the islands and airports in the UK, Ireland, the Netherlands and France. During the summer months these services are greatly increased, both in the number of airports served and in the frequency of flights.

Shipping. Passenger and cargo services between Jersey, Guernsey and England are maintained by British Channel Island Ferries; between Guernsey, Jersey and England and St Malo by the Commodore Shipping Co., Emeraude Ferries connect Jersey with St Malo; between Guernsey, Jersey, Alderney, England and France by Condor Ltd (hydrofoil), and between Guernsey and Alderney and England and Guernsey and Sark by local companies.

Post and Broadcasting. Postal and overseas telephone and telegraph services are maintained by the respective Postal Administrations of each bailiwick. The local telephone services are maintained by the insular authorities. There were, in 1989, 43,880 telephone lines in Jersey and (1988) 60,479 stations in Guernsey.

There is an independent television station in Jersey and local radio stations, BBC Radio Jersey and Guernsey, opened in 1982.

JUSTICE AND RELIGION

Justice. Justice is administered by the Royal Courts of Jersey and Guernsey, each of which consists of the Bailiff and 12 Jurats, the latter being elected by an electoral college. There is an appeal from the Royal Courts to the Courts of Appeal of Jersey and of Guernsey. A final appeal lies to the Privy Council in certain cases. A stipendiary magistrate in each, Jersey and Guernsey, deals with minor civil and criminal cases.

Church. Jersey and Guernsey each constitutes a deanery under the jurisdiction of the Bishop of Winchester. The rectories (12 in Jersey; 10 in Guernsey) are in the gift of the Crown. The Roman Catholic and various Nonconformist Churches are represented.

Further Reading

Ambrière, F., *Les Iles Anglo-Normandes*. Paris, 1971
Coysh, V., *The Channel Islands: A New Study*. Newton Abbot, 1977
Cruickshank, C., *The German Occupation of the Channel Islands*. London, 1975

Jee, N., *The Landscape of the Channel Islands*. Chichester, 1982
Lemprière, R., *Portrait of the Channel Islands*. London, 1970.—*History of the Channel Islands*. Rev. ed. London, 1980
Myhill, H., *Introducing the Channel Islands*. London, 1964
Uttley, J., *The Story of the Channel Islands*. London, 1966

JERSEY

POPULATION (1989), 82,209. In the year ended 31 Dec. 1989 there were 1,109 births and 810 deaths. The town is St Helier on the south coast.

CONSTITUTION. The States consist of 12 Senators (elected for 6 years, 6 retiring every third year), 12 Constables (triennial) and 29 Deputies (triennial), all elected on universal suffrage by the people.

The island legislature is 'The States of Jersey'. The States comprises the Bailiff, the Lieut.-Governor, 12 Senators, the Constables of the 12 parishes of the island, 29 Deputies, the Dean of Jersey, the Attorney-General and the Solicitor-General. They all have the right to speak in the Assembly, but only the 53 elected members (the Senators, Constables and Deputies) have the right to vote; the Bailiff has a casting vote. General elections for Senators and Deputies are held every third year. Except in specific instances, enactments passed by the States require the sanction of The Queen-in-Council. The Lieut.-Governor has the power of veto on certain forms of legislation.

Flag: White with a red diagonal cross. In the top centre of the flag a shield of the arms of Jersey ensigned with the Plantagenet Crown.

Lieut.-Governor and C.-in-C. of Jersey: Air Marshal Sir John Sutton, KCB.
Secretary and ADC to the Lieut.-Governor: Cdr D. M. L. Braybrooke, LVO, RN (Retd).

Bailiff of Jersey and President of the States: Sir Peter Crill, CBE.
Deputy Bailiff: V. A. Tomes.

ECONOMY

Budget (year ending 31 Dec. 1988). Revenue, £258,281,219; expenditure, £201,673,508; public debt, £1,166,690. The standard rate of income tax is 20p in the pound. No super-tax or death duties are levied. Parochial rates of moderate amount are payable by owners and occupiers.

Currency. The States issue bank-notes in denominations of £50, £20, £10, £5 and £1.

INDUSTRY AND TRADE

Industry. Principal activities: Tourism; total number of hotel and guesthouse bedrooms (1988), 11,392; expenditure of tourists (1988), £245m. Agriculture, total output (1988), £36·4m. and total exports, £30·7m. Light industry, mainly electrical goods, textiles and clothing. Total exports (1980), £29m. Banking and finance, total bank deposits and balances due to parent companies by deposit-taking institutions (1988), £31,000m.

Commerce (1980). Principal imports: Machinery and transport equipment, £57·3m.; manufactured goods, £43·4m.; food, £40m.; mineral fuels, £21·5m.; chemicals, £15·1m., and miscellaneous, £53·6m. Principal exports (1980): Machinery and transport equipment, £28m.; food, £22·2m; manufactured goods, £15·6m., and miscellaneous, £24·1m.

COMMUNICATIONS

Aviation. The Jersey airport is situated at St Peter. It covers approximately 375 acres. Number of aircraft movements excluding local flying (1988) 26,448; number of passengers, 1,879,514.

Shipping (1988). All vessels arriving in Jersey from outside Jersey waters report at St Helier or Gorey on first arrival. There is a harbour of minor importance at St Aubin. Number of commercial vessels entering St Helier, 26,448 number of visiting yachts (1987), 4,100. Passengers arrived in 1988, 411,747.

Post and Broadcasting. In 1988 there were 43,885 telephones and 23 post offices.

EDUCATION (1988). There were 5 States secondary schools and 1 high school, and 22 States primary schools; 4,587 pupils attended the primary schools, 3,579 the secondary schools. There were 8 private primary schools with 1,264 pupils and 4 private secondary schools with 826 pupils. Highlands College offers full- and part-time courses to Ordinary and National Certificate and Diploma levels or similar standards and, together with Les Quennevais Adult Community Centre, evening classes in technical and recreational subjects.

Further Reading

Balleine, G. R., *Biographical Dictionary of Jersey*. London, 1948.—*A History of the Island of Jersey*. Rev. ed. Chichester, 1981.—*The Bailiwick of Jersey*. 3rd ed. London, 1970

Bois, F. de L., *The Constitutional History of Jersey*. Jersey, 1970

Carre, A. L., *English–Jersey Language Vocabulary*. Jersey, 1972

Le Maistre, F., *Dictionnaire Jersiais-Français*. Jersey, 1966

States of Jersey Library: Royal Square, St Helier. *Librarian:* J. K. Antill, FLA.

GUERNSEY

POPULATION. Census population (1986) 55,482. Births during 1988 were 686; deaths, 623. The town is St Peter Port.

CONSTITUTION. The government of the island is conducted by committees appointed by the States.

The States of Deliberation, the Parliament of Guernsey, is composed of the following members: The Bailiff, who is President *ex officio;* 12 Conseillers; H.M. Procureur and H.M. Comptroller (Law Officers of the Crown), who have a voice but no vote; 33 People's Deputies elected by popular franchise; 10 Douzaine Representatives elected by their Parochial Douzaines; 2 representatives of the States of Alderney.

The States of Election, an electoral college, elects the Jurats and Conseillers. It is composed of the following members: The Bailiff (President *ex officio*); the 12 Jurats or 'Jurés-Justiciers'; the 12 Conseillers; H.M. Procureur and H.M. Comptroller; the 33 People's Deputies; 34 Douzaine Representatives; and (for the election of Conseillers) 4 representatives of the States of Alderney.

Since Jan. 1949 all legislative powers and functions (with minor exceptions) formerly exercised by the Royal Court have been vested in the States of Deliberation. Projets de Loi (Bills) require the sanction of The Queen-in-Council.

Flag: White bearing a red cross of St George, with an argent with a cross gules superimposed on the cross.

Lieut.-Governor and C.-in-C. of Guernsey and its Dependencies: Lieut.-Gen. Sir Michael Wilkins, KCB, OBE.

Secretary and ADC to the Lieut.-Governor: Capt. D. P. L. Hodgetts.

Bailiff of Guernsey and President of the States: Sir Charles Frossard.

Deputy Bailiff of Guernsey: G. M. Dorey.

FINANCE (year ending 31 Dec. 1988). Revenue, including Alderney, £117,243,209; expenditure, including Alderney, £97,645,270. The standard rate of income tax is 20p in the pound. States and parochial rates are very moderate. No super-tax or death duties are levied.

COMMERCE (1988). Principal imports: Petrol and oils, 139,755,512 litres. Principal exports: Tomatoes (1988), £6,747,000; flowers and fern, £24,090,753; sweet peppers, £84,000; other vegetables, £1,134,000; plants, 2m.

COMMUNICATIONS

Aviation. The airport in Guernsey, situated at La Villiaze, has a landing area of approximately 124 acres and a tarmac runway of 4,800 ft. In 1988, passenger arrivals totalled 825,338.

Shipping. The principal harbour is that of St Peter Port, and there is a harbour at St Sampson's (used mainly for commercial shipping). In 1988 passenger arrivals totalled 312,721. Ships registered in Guernsey at 31 Dec. 1988 numbered 1,213 and 490 fishing vessels. In 1988, 13,524 yachts visited Guernsey.

EDUCATION. There are 2 public schools in the island: Elizabeth College, founded by Queen Elizabeth in 1563, for boys, and the Ladies' College, for girls. The States grammar school provides for education up to University entrance requirements, and there are numerous modern secondary and primary schools and a College of Further Education. The total number of school children was (1988) 8,124. Facilities are available for the study of art, domestic science and many other subjects of a technical nature. There is also a convent school with boarding facilities for girls.

ALDERNEY. Population (1986 census, 2,130). The island has an airport. The Constitution of the island (reformed 1987) provides for its own popularly elected President and States (12 members), and its own Court. The town is St Anne's.

Flag: White with a red cross with the island badge in the centre.

President of the States: J. Kay-Mouat.
Clerk of the States: D. V. Jenkins.
Clerk of the Court: P. J. Beer.

SARK. Population (1986 estimate, 550). The Constitution is a mixture of feudal and popular government with its Chief Pleas (parliament), consisting of 40 tenants and 12 popularly elected deputies, presided over by the Seneschal. The head of the island is the Seigneur. Sark has no income tax. Motor vehicles, except tractors, are not allowed.

Flag: White with a red cross and a red first quarter bearing two gold lions.

The Seigneur: J. M. Beaumont.
Seneschal: L. P. de Carteret.

Further Reading

Carteret, A. R. de, *The Story of Sark*. London, 1956
Coysh, V., *Alderney*. Newton Abbot, 1974
Durand, R., *Guernsey, Present and Past*. Guernsey, 1933.—*Guernsey under German Rule*. London, 1946
Hathaway, S., *Dame of Sark: An Autobiography*. London, 1961
Le Huray, C. P., *The Bailiwick of Guernsey*. London, 1952
Marr, L. J., *A History of Guernsey*. Chichester, 1982
Wood, A. and M. S., *Islands in Danger*. 2nd ed. London, 1957
Wood, J., *Herm, Our Island Home*. London, 1973

UNITED STATES OF AMERICA

Capital: Washington, D.C.
Population: 245·8m. (1988)
GNP per capita: US$19,780 (1988)

HISTORY. The Declaration of Independence of the 13 states of which the American Union then consisted was adopted by Congress on 4 July 1776. On 30 Nov. 1782 Great Britain acknowledged the independence of the USA, and on 3 Sept. 1783 the treaty of peace was concluded and was ratified by the USA on 14 Jan. 1784.

AREA AND POPULATION. Population of USA at each census from 1790 to 1980, and for USA including Alaska and Hawaii, from 1960. Residents of Puerto Rico, Guam, American Samoa, the Virgin Islands of the USA, Northern Mariana Islands, the remainder of the Trust Territory of the Pacific Islands, Midway, Wake, Johnston and US population abroad are excluded from the figures of this table. Residents of Indian reservations are excluded prior to 1890.

	White	*Negroes* [1]	*Other races* [2]	*Total*	*Decennial increase %*
1790	3,172,464 [3]	757,208	—	3,929,672	—
1800	4,306,446	1,002,037	—	5,308,483	35·1
1810	5,862,073	1,377,808	—	7,239,881	36·4
1820	7,866,797	1,771,562	—	9,638,359	33·1
1830	10,537,378	2,328,642	—	12,866,020	33·5
1840	14,195,805	2,873,648	—	17,069,453	32·7
1850	19,553,068	3,638,808	—	23,191,876	35·9
1860	26,922,537	4,441,830	78,954 [4]	31,443,321	35·6
1870 [5]	33,589,377	4,880,009	88,985	38,558,371	22·6
1870 [5]	*34,337,292*	*5,392,172*	*88,985*	*39,818,449*	*26.6*
1880	43,402,970	6,580,793	172,020	50,155,783	30·1
1890	55,101,258	7,488,676	357,780	62,947,714	25·5
1900	66,868,508	8,834,395	509,265	76,212,168	21·0
1910	81,812,405	9,828,667	587,459	92,228,531	21·0
1920	94,903,540	10,463,607	654,421	106,021,568	14·9 [6]
1930	110,395,753 [7]	11,891,842	915,065	123,202,660	16·1 [6]
1940	118,357,831	12,865,914	941,384	132,165,129	7·3
1950	135,149,629	15,044,937	1,131,232	151,325,798	14·5
1960 [8]	158,831,732	18,871,831	1,619,612	179,323,175	18·5
1970	177,748,975	22,580,289	2,882,662	203,211,926	13·3
1980	188,371,622	26,495,025	11,679,158	226,545,805	11·4

[1] Seventeen southern states (including D.C.) in 1900 had 7,922,969 Negroes (89·7% of the total Negro population); in 1920, 8,912,231 (85·2%); in 1940, 9,904,619 (77%); in 1950, 10,225,407 (68%); in 1960, 11,311,607 (59·9%); in 1970, 11,969,961 (53%); in 1980, 14,048,000 (53%).

[2] 1870: 63,199 Chinese, 55 Japanese and 25,731 Indians; 1880, 105,465 Chinese, 148 Japanese and 66,407 Indians; 1890, 107,488 Chinese, 2,039 Japanese and 248,253 Indians; 1900, 118,746 Chinese, 85,716 Japanese, 237,196 Indians, 67,607 other races; 1910, 94,414 Chinese, 152,745 Japanese, 276,927 Indians, 2,767 Filipino, 60,606 other races; 1920, 85,202 Chinese, 220,596 Japanese, 244,437 Indians, 26,634 Filipino, 77,552 other races; 1930, 343,352 Indians, 102,159 Chinese, 278,743 Japanese, 108,424 Filipino, 82,387 other races; 1940, 345,252 Indians, 106,334 Chinese, 285,115 Japanese, 98,535 Filipino, 106,148 other races; 1950, 357,499 Indians, 326,379 Japanese, 150,005 Chinese, 122,707 Filipino, 174,642 other races; 1960, 523,591 Indians, 464,332 Japanese, 237,292 Chinese, 176,310 Filipino, 218,087 other races; 1970, 792,730 Indians, 591,290 Japanese, 435,062 Chinese, 343,060 Filipino, 720,520 other races; 1980, 1,364,033 Indians, 700,974 Japanese, 806,040 Chinese, 774,652 Filipino, 8,033,459 other races.

[3] Made up of Anglo-Scottish, 89·1%; German, 5·6%; Dutch, 2·5%; Irish, 1·9%; French, 0·6%.

[4] 34,933 Chinese and 44,021 Indians.

[*Footnotes continued on p. 1375.*]

Total population in 1980 at 226,545,805 comprised 110,053,161 males and 116,492,644 females; 167,054,638 were urban and 59,491,167 were rural. Negroes, 12,519,189 males and 13,975,836 females.

Estimated population, including Alaska and Hawaii, and armed forces overseas, on 1 July 1950, 152,271,000; 1955, 165,931,000; 1960, 180,671,000; 1965, 194,303,000; 1970, 204,878,000; 1975, 215,973,000; 1980, 227,757,000; 1985, 239,279,000; 1987, 243,915,000.

The age distribution by sex of the total population of the US (excluding armed forces overseas, US population abroad and outlying areas) at the 1980 census was as follows:

Age-group	*Male*	*Female*	*Total*
Under 5	8,362,009	7,986,245	16,348,254
5–9	8,539,080	8,160,876	16,699,956
10–14	9,316,221	8,925,908	18,242,129
15–19	10,755,409	10,412,715	21,168,124
20–24	10,663,231	10,655,473	21,318,704
25–34	18,381,903	18,699,936	37,081,839
35–44	12,569,719	13,064,991	25,634,710
45–54	11,008,919	11,790,868	22,799,787
55–59	5,481,863	6,133,391	11,615,254
60–64	4,669,892	5,417,729	10,087,621
65–74	6,756,502	8,824,103	15,580,605
75 and over	3,548,413	6,420,409	9,968,822
Total	110,053,161	116,492,644	226,545,805

The following table includes population statistics, the year in which each of the original 13 states ratified the constitution, and the year when each of the other states was admitted into the Union. Postal abbreviations for the names of the states are shown in brackets. Land area includes land temporarily or partially covered by water, and lakes, etc., of less than 40 acres. (For census population by states and regions in 1940 and 1950 *see* THE STATESMAN'S YEAR-BOOK, 1952, pp. 552 and 553.)

Geographic divisions and states		*Land area: sq. miles 1980*	*Census population 1 April 1970*	*Census population 1 April 1980*	*Pop. per sq. mile, 1980*
United States		3,539,289	203,302,031	226,545,805	64·0
New England		63,012	11,847,186	12,348,493	196·0
Maine (1820)	*(Me.)*	30,995	993,663	1,124,660	36·3
New Hampshire (1788)	*(N.H.)*	8,993	737,681	920,610	102·4
Vermont (1791)	*(Vt.)*	9,273	444,732	511,456	55·2
Massachusetts (1788)	*(Mass.)*	7,824	5,689,170	5,737,037	733·3
Rhode Island (1790)	*(R.I.)*	1,055	949,723	947,154	897·8
Connecticut (1788)	*(Conn.)*	4,872	3,032,217	3,107,576	637·8
Middle Atlantic		99,733	37,283,339	36,786,790	368·9
New York (1788)	*(N.Y.)*	47,377	18,241,266	17,558,072	370·6
New Jersey (1787)	*(N.J.)*	7,468	7,168,164	7,364,823	986·2
Pennsylvania (1787)	*(Pa.)*	44,888	11,793,909	11,863,895	264·3

[5] Enumeration in 1870 incomplete. Figures in italics represent estimated corrected population.

[6] Between the 1910 census (15 April 1910) and the 1920 census (1 Jan. 1920), the period covered was 116 months (less than a full decade). Adjusting for this, the exact rate of increase for the decade was 15·4%. Similarly correcting for the 123 months between the 1920 and 1930 censuses, the true rate of increase was 15·7%.

[7] Figures for 1930 have been revised to include Mexicans (1,422,533), who were classified with 'Other Races' in the 1930 census reports.

[8] Figures for 1960 strictly comparable with those given for other years (*i.e.*, excluding Alaska and Hawaii) are: White, 158,454,956; Negroes, 18,860,117; other races, 1,149,163; total, 178,464,236; decennial increase, 18·4%.

Geographic divisions and states		*Land area: sq. miles 1980*	*Census population 1 April 1970*	*Census population 1 April 1980*	*Pop. per sq. mile, 1980*
East North Central		243,961	40,252,678	41,682,217	170·9
Ohio (1803)	*(Oh.)*	41,004	10,652,017	10,797,630	263·3
Indiana (1816)	*(Ind.)*	35,932	5,193,669	5,490,224	152·8
Illinois (1818)	*(Ill.)*	55,645	11,113,976	11,426,518	205·3
Michigan (1837)	*(Mich.)*	56,954	8,875,083	9,262,078	162·6
Wisconsin (1848)	*(Wis.)*	54,426	4,417,933	4,705,767	86·5
West North Central		508,132	16,344,389	17,183,453	33·8
Minnesota (1858)	*(Minn.)*	79,548	3,805,069	4,075,970	51·2
Iowa (1846)	*(Ia.)*	55,965	2,825,041	2,913,808	52·1
Missouri (1821)	*(Mo.)*	68,945	4,677,399	4,916,686	71·3
North Dakota (1889)	*(N.D.)*	69,300	617,761	652,717	9·4
South Dakota (1889)	*(S.D.)*	75,952	666,257	690,768	9·1
Nebraska (1867)	*(Nebr.)*	76,644	1,483,791	1,569,825	20·5
Kansas (1861)	*(Kans.)*	81,778	2,249,071	2,363,679	28·9
South Atlantic		266,910	30,671,337	36,959,123	138·5
Delaware (1787)	*(Del.)*	1,932	548,104	594,338	307·6
Maryland (1788)	*(Md.)*	9,837	3,922,399	4,216,975	428·7
Dist. of Columbia (1791)	*(D.C.)*	63	756,510	638,333	10,132·3
Virginia (1788)	*(Va.)*	39,704	4,648,494	5,346,818	134·7
West Virginia (1863)	*(W. Va.)*	24,119	1,744,237	1,949,644	80·8
North Carolina (1789)	*(N.C.)*	48,843	5,082,059	5,881,766	120·4
South Carolina (1788)	*(S.C.)*	30,203	2,590,516	3,121,820	103·4
Georgia (1788)	*(Ga.)*	58,056	4,589,575	5,463,105	94·1
Florida (1845)	*(Fla.)*	54,153	6,789,443	9,746,324	180·0
East South Central		178,824	12,804,552	14,666,423	82·0
Kentucky (1792)	*(Ky.)*	39,669	3,219,311	3,660,777	92·3
Tennessee (1796)	*(Tenn.)*	41,155	3,924,164	4,591,120	111·6
Alabama (1819)	*(Al.)*	50,767	3,444,165	3,893,888	76·7
Mississippi (1817)	*(Miss.)*	47,233	2,216,912	2,520,638	53·4
West South Central		427,271	19,322,458	23,746,816	55·6
Arkansas (1836)	*(Ark.)*	52,078	1,923,295	2,286,435	43·9
Louisiana (1812)	*(La.)*	44,521	3,643,180	4,205,900	94·5
Oklahoma (1907)	*(Okla.)*	68,655	2,559,253	3,025,290	44·1
Texas (1845)	*(Tex.)*	262,017	11,196,730	14,229,191	54·3
Mountain		855,193	8,283,585	11,372,785	13·3
Montana (1889)	*(Mont.)*	145,388	694,409	786,690	5·4
Idaho (1890)	*(Id.)*	82,412	713,008	943,935	11·5
Wyoming (1890)	*(Wyo.)*	96,989	332,416	469,557	4·8
Colorado (1876)	*(Colo.)*	103,595	2,207,259	2,889,964	27·9
New Mexico (1912)	*(N. Mex.)*	121,335	1,016,000	1,302,894	10·7
Arizona (1912)	*(Ariz.)*	113,508	1,772,482	2,718,215	23·9
Utah (1896)	*(Ut.)*	82,073	1,059,273	1,461,037	17·8
Nevada (1864)	*(Nev.)*	109,894	488,738	800,493	7·3
Pacific		896,253	26,525,774	31,799,705	35·5
Washington (1889)	*(Wash.)*	66,511	3,409,169	4,132,156	62·1
Oregon (1859)	*(Oreg.)*	96,184	2,091,385	2,633,105	27·4
California (1850)	*(Calif.)*	156,299	19,953,134	23,667,902	151·4
Alaska (1959)	*(Ak.)*	570,833	302,173	401,851	0·7
Hawaii (1960)	*(Hi.)*	6,425	769,913	964,691	150·1

Geographic divisions and states	*Land area: sq. miles 1980*	*Census population 1 April 1970*	*Census population 1 April 1980*	*Pop. per sq. mile, 1980*
Outlying Territories, total	4,691	4,720,306	3,565,376	760
Puerto Rico (1898)	3,515	2,712,033	3,196,520	909
Virgin Islands (1917)	132	62,438	96,569	731
American Samoa (1900)	77	27,159	32,297	419
Guam (1898)	209	84,996	105,979	507
Northern Marianas (1947)	184	9,640	16,780	91
Marshall Islands (1947)	70	22,888	30,873	441
Micronesia, Fed. States (1947)	271	47,202	73,160	270
Palau (1947)	192	11,210	12,116	63
Midway Islands (1867)	2	2,220	453	226
Wake Island (1898)	3	1,647	302	100
Johnston and Sand Islands (1858)	...	1,007	327	...

The 1980 census showed 9,323,946 foreign-born Whites. The 9 countries contributing the largest numbers who were foreign-born were Mexico, 2,199,221; Germany, 849,384; Canada, 842,859; Italy, 831,922; UK, 669,149; Cuba, 607,814; Philippines, 501,440; Poland, 418,128; USSR, 406,022.

Increase or decrease of native White, and foreign-born White, population from 1860 to 1980, by decades:

	Native White			*Foreign-born White*		
	Total	*Increase*	*Per cent increase*	*Total*	*Increase or decrease (–)*	*Per cent. change*
1860	22,825,784	5,513,251	31·8	4,096,753	1,856,218	82·8
1870	28,095,665	5,269,881	23·1	5,493,712	1,396,959	34·1
1880	36,843,291	8,747,626	31·1	6,559,679	1,065,967	19·4
1890	45,979,391	9,018,732 [1]	24·5	9,121,867	2,562,188	39·1
1900	56,595,379	10,615,988	23·1	10,213,817	1,091,950	12·0
1910	68,386,412	11,791,033	20·8	13,345,545	3,131,728	30·7
1920	81,108,161	12,721,749	18·6	13,712,754	367,209	2·8
1930	96,303,335	15,195,174	18·7	13,983,405	270,651	2·0
1940	106,795,732	10,492,397	10·9	11,419,138	–2,564,267	–18·3
1950	124,780,860	17,985,128	16·8	10,161,168	–1,257,970	–11·0
1960	149,543,638	24,762,778	19·8	9,293,992	– 867,176	– 8·5
1970	169,385,451	19,841,813	13·3	8,733,770	– 560,222	– 6·0
1980	179,711,066	10,325,615	6·0	9,323,946	590,176	6·7

[1] Exclusive of population specially enumerated in 1890 in Indian Territory and on Indian reservations.

The population of leading cities (with over 100,000 inhabitants) at the censuses of 1970 and 1980 were as follows:

Cities	*1 April 1970*	*1 April 1980*	*Cities*	*1 April 1970*	*1 April 1980*
New York, N.Y.	7,895,563	7,071,639	Boston, Mass.	641,071	562,994
Chicago, Ill.	3,369,357	3,005,072	New Orleans, La.	593,471	557,927
Los Angeles, Calif.	2,811,801	2,968,528	Jacksonville, Fla.	504,265	540,920
Philadelphia, Pa.	1,949,996	1,688,210	Seattle, Wash.	530,831	493,846
Houston, Tex.	1,233,535	1,611,382	Denver, Colo.	514,678	492,694
Detroit, Mich.	1,514,063	1,203,369	Nashville-Davidson, Tenn.	426,029	455,651
Dallas, Tex.	844,401	904,599	St Louis, Mo.	622,236	452,804
San Diego, Calif.	697,471	875,538	Kansas City, Mo.	507,330	448,028
Phoenix, Ariz.	584,303	790,183	El Paso, Tex.	322,261	425,259
Baltimore, Md.	905,787	786,741	Atlanta, Ga.	495,039	425,022
San Antonio, Tex.	645,153	810,353	Pittsburgh, Pa.	520,089	423,960
Indianapolis, Ind.	736,856	700,807	Oklahoma City, Okla.	368,164	404,014
San Francisco, Calif.	715,674	678,974	Cincinnati, Ohio	453,514	385,410
Memphis, Tenn.	623,988	646,170	Fort Worth, Tex.	393,455	385,164
Washington, D.C.	756,668	638,332	Minneapolis, Minn.	434,400	370,951
Milwaukee, Wisc.	717,372	636,298	Austin, Tex.	253,539	372,564
San José, Calif.	459,913	629,402	Portland, Oregon	379,967	396,666
Cleveland, Ohio	750,879	573,822	Honolulu, Hawaii	324,871	367,878
Columbus, Ohio	540,025	565,032			

Cities	*1 April 1970*	*1 April 1980*	Cities	*1 April 1970*	*1 April 1980*
Long Beach, Calif.	358,879	361,496	Flint, Mich.	193,317	159,611
Tulsa, Okla.	330,350	360,919	Aurora, Colo.	74,974	158,588
Buffalo, N.Y.	462,768	357,870	Tacoma, Wash.	154,407	158,501
Toledo, Ohio	383,062	354,635	Providence, R.I.	179,116	156,804
Miami, Fla.	334,859	346,861	Fort Lauderdale, Fla.	139,590	153,279
Oakland, Calif.	361,561	339,337	Raleigh, N.C.	122,830	156,299
Albuquerque, N. Mex.	244,501	332,336	Springfield, Mass.	163,905	152,319
Tucson, Ariz.	262,933	338,636	Gary, Ind.	175,415	151,968
Newark, N.J.	381,930	329,248	Stockton, Calif.	109,963	149,544
Charlotte, N.C.	241,420	326,330	Amarillo, Tex.	127,010	149,230
Omaha, Nebr.	346,929	342,786	Hialeah, Fla.	102,452	145,254
Louisville, Ky.	361,706	298,694	Newport News, Va.	138,177	144,903
Birmingham, Ala.	300,910	286,799	Winston-Salem, N.C.	133,683	142,864
Wichita, Kans.	276,554	280,808	Bridgeport, Conn.	156,542	142,546
Sacramento, Calif.	257,105	275,741	Huntsville, Ala.	139,282	142,513
Tampa, Fla.	277,714	271,578	Savannah, Ga.	118,349	141,658
St Paul, Minn.	309,866	270,230	Rockford, Ill.	147,370	139,712
Norfolk, Va.	307,951	266,979	Glendale, Calif.	132,664	139,060
Virginia Beach, Va.	172,106	262,199	Garland, Tex.	81,437	138,857
Fresno, Calif.	165,655	247,703	Paterson, N.J.	144,824	137,970
Rochester, N.Y.	295,011	241,741	Hartford, Conn.	158,017	136,392
St Petersburg, Fla.	216,159	238,647	Springfield, Mo.	120,096	133,116
Akron, Ohio	275,425	237,177	Fremont, Calif.	100,869	131,945
Corpus Christi, Tex.	204,525	234,408	Evansville, Ind.	138,764	130,496
Jersey City, N.J.	260,350	223,532	Lansing, Mich.	131,403	130,414
Baton Rouge, La.	165,921	220,395	Torrance, Calif.	134,968	129,881
Anaheim, Calif.	166,408	219,494	Orlando, Fla.	99,006	128,291
Richmond, Va.	249,332	219,214	New Haven, Conn.	137,707	126,089
Colorado Springs, Colo.	135,517	215,105	Garden Grove, Calif.	121,155	124,805
Shreveport, La.	182,064	206,989	Peoria, Ill.	126,963	124,160
Lexington-Fayette, Ky.	108,137	204,165	Hampton, Va.	120,779	122,617
Santa Ana, Calif.	155,710	204,104	Hollywood, Fla.	106,873	121,323
Dayton, Ohio	243,023	193,549	San Bernadino, Calif.	106,869	120,122
Jackson, Miss.	153,968	202,895	Erie, Pa.	129,265	119,123
Mobile, Ala.	190,026	200,452	Topeka, Kans.	125,011	118,690
Yonkers, N.Y.	204,297	195,351	Beaumont, Tex.	117,548	118,102
Des Moines, Iowa	201,404	191,003	Pasadena, Calif.	112,951	118,072
Grand Rapids, Mich.	197,649	181,843	Macon, Ga.	122,423	116,896
Little Rock, Ark.	132,483	178,132	Youngstown, Ohio	140,909	115,510
Montgomery, Ala.	133,386	177,857	Chesapeake, Va.	89,580	114,486
Lubbock, Tex.	149,101	177,517	Lakewood, Colo.	92,743	113,808
Fort Wayne, Ind.	178,269	177,495	Pasadena, Tex.	89,957	112,560
Knoxville, Tenn.	174,587	175,045	Independence, Mo.	111,630	111,797
Anchorage, Alaska	48,081	174,431	Oxnard, Calif.	71,225	110,710
Lincoln, Nebr.	149,518	171,932	Cedar Rapids, Iowa	110,642	110,243
Spokane, Wash.	170,516	171,300	Irving,Tex.	97,260	109,943
Riverside, Calif.	140,089	170,591	South Bend, Ind.	125,580	109,727
Madison, Wisc.	171,809	170,624	Sterling Heights, Mich.	61,365	108,999
Huntington Beach, Calif.	115,960	170,505	Durham, N.C.	72,863	108,391
Greensboro, N.C.	144,076	170,279	Ann Arbor, Mich.	100,035	107,969
Syracuse, N.Y.	197,297	170,105	Modesto, Calif.	61,712	106,963
Chattanooga, Tenn.	119,923	169,520	Tempe, Ariz.	63,550	106,919
Columbus, Ga.	155,028	169,441	Sunnyvale, Calif.	95,976	106,618
Las Vegas, Nev.	125,787	164,730	Elizabeth, N.J.	112,654	106,201
Salt Lake City, Utah	175,885	163,034	Tallahassee, Fla.	...	106,179
Mesa, Ariz.	63,049	162,011	Eugene, Oregon	79,028	105,662
Arlington, Tex.	90,229	161,872	Chula Vista, Calif.	...	105,549
Worcester, Mass.	176,572	161,799	Bakersfield, Calif.	69,515	113,193
Warren, Mich.	179,260	161,134	Livonia, Mich.	110,109	104,814
Kansas City, Kans.	168,213	161,148	Portsmouth, Va.	110,963	104,577
			Allentown, Pa.	109,871	103,758
			Berkeley, Calif.	114,091	103,328
			Concord, Calif.	85,164	103,763

Cities	*1 April 1970*	*1 April 1980*	*Cities*	*1 April 1970*	*1 April 1980*
Waterbury, Conn.	108,033	103,266	Pueblo, Colo.	97,774	101,686
Alexandria, Va.	110,927	103,217	Waco, Tex.	95,326	101,261
Stamford, Conn.	108,798	102,466	Reno, Nev.	92,115	100,756
Boise City, Idaho	74,990	102,249	Roanoke, Va.	95,438	100,220
Fullerton, Calif.	85,987	102,246	Springfield, Ill.	...	100,003

Vital Statistics: Vital statistics are based on records of births, deaths, fœtal deaths, marriages and divorces filed with registration officials of states and cities. Figures for the US include Alaska beginning with 1959 and Hawaii beginning with 1960.

Annual collection of mortality records from a national death-registration area was inaugurated in 1900. A national birth-registration area was established in 1915. These areas, which at their inception comprised 10 states and the District of Columbia, expanded gradually until 1933, when both the birth- and death-registration areas covered the entire continental US. Marriage and divorce statistics are compiled from reports furnished by state and local officials. Data on annulments are included in the divorce statistics. The marriage-registration area was established in 1957 with 30 states and 3 other areas. The divorce-registration area was established in 1958 with 14 states and 2 other areas. In Jan. 1980 the marriage-registration area included 42 states and D.C., and the divorce-registration area included 30 states.

	Live births [1]	*Deaths* [2]	*Marriages* [3]	*Divorces* [4]	*Maternal deaths*	*Deaths under 1 year* [5]
1900	—	343,217	709,000	56,000	—	—
1910	2,777,000	696,856	948,000	83,000	—	—
1920	2,950,000	1,118,070	1,274,476	170,505	16,320	170,911
1930	2,618,000	1,327,240	1,126,856	195,961	14,915	143,201
1940	2,559,000	1,417,269	1,595,879	264,000	8,876	110,984
1950	3,632,000	1,452,454	1,667,231	385,144	2,960	103,825
1960	4,257,850 [7]	1,711,982	1,523,000	393,000	1,579	110,873
1970	3,731,386 [7]	1,921,031	2,158,802	708,000	803	74,667
1980	3,612,258	1,989,841	2,390,252	1,189,000	334	45,526
1985	3,760,561	2,086,440	2,412,625	1,190,000	295	40,030
1986	3,756,547	2,105,361	2,407,099	1,178,000	272	38,891
1987	3,809,394	2,123,323	2,421,000 [8]	1,157,000 [8]	251	38,408
1988 [8]	3,913,000	2,171,000	2,389,000	1,183,000	300	38,700

[1] Figures through 1959 include adjustment for under-registration (the 1959 registered count was 4,244,796); beginning 1960 figures represent number registered.
[2] Excluding fœtal deaths and deaths among the armed forces overseas.
[3] Estimates for all years except 1970.
[4] Includes reported annulments. Estimated for all years.
[5] Deaths for 1979–81 (Ninth Revision, International Classification of Diseases, 1975). Deaths from complications of pregnancy, childbirth and the puerperium. Deaths for 1968–78 were classified according to the Eighth Revision, International Classification of Diseases, adopted, 1965. Deaths for 1958–67 were classified according to the Seventh Revision of the International Lists of Diseases and Causes of Death, those for 1949–57 according to the Sixth Revision and those for 1939–48, according to the Fifth Revision.
[6] Excluding fœtal deaths. [7] Based on a 50% sample. [8] Provisional.

The crude birth rate, based on total live-birth estimates per 1,000 total population, fell from 29·5 in 1915 to 18·4 in 1933; it rose to a peak of 26·6 in 1947—its highest for 25 years. This peak reflects demobilization (1945–46), the record marriage rate that followed, and the high levels of employment and income. The decrease in the following 3 years was moderate. In 1951 the rate moved upward and levelled off in 1957 at about 25 per 1,000 population. Since 1957 the crude birth rate declined every year to 18·4 live births per 1,000 population in 1966. The crude birth rate for 1988 was 15·9. Estimated number of illegitimate births in 1986 was 878,477, a ratio of 233·9 illegitimate births per 1,000 registered live births.

Deaths, excluding fœtal deaths (per 1,000 population), declined from 17·2 in 1900 to 10 in 1946. The death rate has been below 10 per 1,000 since 1947, fluctuating slightly from year to year, mainly under the impact of occurrences of outbreaks of severe respiratory diseases. The rate for 1970, 9·5; 1980, 8·8; 1981, 8·6; 1982, 8·6; 1983, 8·6; 1984, 8·7; 1985, 8·7; 1986, 8·7; 1987, 8·7; 1988, 8·8.

Leading causes of death, 1988, per 100,000 population: Diseases of heart, 312·2; malignant neoplasms, 198·6; cerebrovascular diseases, 61·1; accidents, 39·7; suicides, 12·3; homicides, 9.

Deaths from AIDS (HIV infection) in 1988 (provisional) 16,210.

The marriage rates per 1,000 population for selected years are: 1920, 12; 1932, 7·9; 1946, 16·4; 1951, 10·4; 1961, 8·5; 1970, 10·6; 1975, 10; 1980, 10·6; 1981, 10·6; 1982, 10·8; 1983, 10·5; 1984, 10·5; 1985, 10·1; 1986, 10; 1987, 9·9; 1988, 9·7. The divorce rates per 1,000 population for selected years are: 1920, 1·6; 1946, 4·3; 1951, 2·5; 1961, 2·3; 1971, 3·7; 1979, 5·3; 1980, 5·2; 1981, 5·3; 1982, 5; 1983, 4·9; 1984, 5; 1985, 5; 1986, 4·8; 1987, 4·8; 1988, 4·8.

Maternal mortality rates (deaths of mothers from conditions associated with deliveries and complications of pregnancy, childbirth and the puerperium) per 100,000 live births, were 1915–19, 727·9 and thereafter declined: 493·9 for 1935–39; 376 for 1940; 207·2 for 1945; 83·3 for 1950; 47 for 1955; 37·1 for 1960; 31·6 for 1965; 21·5 for 1970; 12·8 for 1975; 9·2 for 1980; 8·5 for 1981; 8·9 for 1982; 8 for 1983; 7·2 for 1986. The 1986 rate for white women was 4·9 and for all other women 16.

The infant mortality rates, per 1,000 live births were: 1915–19, 95·7; 1920–24, 76·7; 1925–29, 69; 1930–34, 60·4; 38·3 in 1945; 29·2 in 1950; 26·4 in 1955; 26 in 1960; 20 in 1970; 16·1 in 1975; 12·6 in 1980; 10·6 in 1985; 10·4 in 1986; 10 in 1987; 9·9 in 1988. In 1984 the rate for whites was 9·4; for all other, 16·1.

Immigration: The Immigration and Nationality Act, as amended, provides for the numerical limitation of most immigration. Public Law 96–212, the Refugee Act of 1980, reduced the worldwide numerical limitation to 280,000 for 1980 and 270,000 thereafter, with a maximum of 20,000 visas available for one country. The colonies and dependencies of a foreign state are limited to 5,000 per year, chargeable to the country limitation of the mother country. Visas are allocated under a system of 6 preference categories, 4 of which are designed to reunite close relatives of US citizens and resident aliens of the US, and 2 for skilled and professional workers. Visa numbers not used in the preference categories are made available to qualified non-preference immigrants. The non-preference category has not been available since 1978 due to high demand in other categories. Immigrants not subject to any numerical limitation are spouses, children, and parents of US citizens, who are 21 years of age or older; certain former US citizens; ministers of religion; certain long-term US government employees; and refugees adjusting to immigrant status.

Immigrant aliens admitted to US for permanent residence, by country or region of birth.

	Immigrants admitted			
Country or region of birth	*1985*	*1986*	*1987*	*1988*
All countries	570,009	601,708	601,516	643,025
Europe	63,043	62,512	61,174	64,797
Germany, Fed. Rep.	7,109	6,991	7,210	6,645
Greece	2,579	2,512	2,653	2,458
Italy	3,214	3,089	2,784	2,949
Poland	9,464	8,481	7,519	9,507
Portugal	3,781	3,766	3,912	3,199
Spain	1,413	1,591	1,578	1,483
UK	13,408	13,657	13,497	13,228
Yugoslavia	1,662	2,011	1,827	1,941
Other Europe	19,987	20,414	20,194	23,387
Asia	264,691	268,248	257,684	264,465
China and Taiwan	39,682	38,530	37,772	38,387
Hong Kong	5,171	5,021	4,706	8,546
India	26,026	26,227	27,803	26,268
Japan	4,086	3,959	4,174	4,512
Korea (North and South)	35,253	35,776	35,849	34,703
Philippines	47,978	52,558	50,060	50,697

Country or region of birth	Immigrants admitted 1985	1986	1987	1988
Thailand	5,239	6,204	6,733	6,888
Other Asia	101,256	99,973	90,587	94,464
North America	182,045	207,714	216,550	250,009
Canada	11,385	11,039	11,876	11,783
Mexico	61,077	66,533	72,351	95,039
Cuba	26,334	33,114	28,916	17,558
Dominican Republic	23,787	26,175	24,858	27,189
Haiti	10,165	12,666	14,819	34,806
Jamaica	18,923	19,595	23,148	20,966
Trinidad and Tobago	2,831	2,891	3,543	3,947
Other Caribbean	7,241	7,191	7,615	7,891
Central America	26,302	28,380	29,296	30,715
Other North America	—	130	128	115
South America	39,058	41,874	44,385	41,007
Colombia	11,982	11,408	11,700	10,322
Ecuador	4,482	4,516	4,641	4,716
Other South America	22,594	25,950	28,044	25,969
Africa	17,117	17,463	17,724	18,882
Australia and New Zealand	2,041	1,964	1,844	2,024
Other countries	2,014	1,933	2,155	1,841

The total number of immigrants admitted from 1820 up to 30 Sept. 1987 was 53,723,582; this included 7,051,146 from the Federal Republic of Germany, and from Italy 5,340,441.

Aliens coming to the US for temporary periods of time are classified as non-immigrants. During fiscal year 1988, a total of 14,591,735 non-immigrants were admitted. This total includes multiple entry documents but excludes border crossers, crewmen and insular travellers. Tourists numbered 10,821,164, with 6,206,596 coming from Mexico, Japan, the UK, the Caribbean, Federal Republic of Germany and Canada. There were 937,080 aliens expelled during fiscal year 1988. Of this number, 22,848 were deported and 914,232 were required to depart without formal orders of deportation.

During fiscal year 1988, 242,063 persons became US citizens through naturalization, including 219,480 naturalized under the general provisions of 5-year residence in the US, 19,982 spouses and children of US citizens, 2,296 members of US Armed Forces and 79 under other provisions. The new citizens included 11,228 from Cuba, 24,580 from the Philippines, 16,225 from China and Taiwan, 13,012 from Korea, 7,042 from the UK, 2,852 from Italy, 22,085 from Mexico and 6,441 from Jamaica.

CLIMATE. For temperature and rainfall figures, see entries on individual states as indicated by regions, below, of mainland USA.

Pacific Coast. The climate varies with latitude, distance from the sea and the effect of relief, ranging from polar conditions in North Alaska through cool to warm temperate climates further south. The extreme south is temperate desert. Rainfall everywhere is moderate. *See* Alaska, California, Oregon, Washington.

Mountain States. Very varied, with relief exerting the main control; very cold in the north in winter, with considerable snowfall. In the south, much higher temperatures and aridity produce desert conditions. Rainfall everywhere is very variable as a result of rain-shadow influences. *See* Arizona, Colorado, Idaho, Montana, Nevada, New Mexico, Utah, Wyoming.

High Plains. A continental climate with a large annual range of temperature and moderate rainfall, mainly in summer, although unreliable. Dust storms are common in summer and blizzards in winter. *See* Nebraska, North Dakota, South Dakota.

Central Plains. A temperate continental climate, with hot summers and cold winters, except in the extreme south. Rainfall is plentiful and comes at all seasons, but there is a summer maximum in western parts. *See* Mississippi, Missouri, Oklahoma, Texas.

Mid-West. Continental, with hot summers and cold winters. Rainfall is moderate, with a summer maximum in most parts. *See* Indiana, Iowa, Kansas.

Great Lakes. Continental, resembling that of the Central Plains, with hot summers but very cold winters because of the freezing of the lakes. Rainfall is moderate with a slight summer maximum. *See* Illinois, Michigan, Minnesota, Ohio, Wisconsin.

Appalachian Mountains. The north is cool temperate with cold winters, the south warm temperate with milder winters. Precipitation is heavy, increasing to the south but evenly distributed over the year. *See* Kentucky, Pennsylvania, Tennessee, West Virginia.

*Gulf Coast.*Conditions vary from warm temperate to sub-tropical, with plentiful rainfall, decreasing towards the west but evenly distributed over the year. *See* Alabama, Arkansas, Florida, Louisiana.

Atlantic Coast. Temperate maritime climate but with great differences in temperature according to latitude. Rainfall is ample at all seasons; snowfall in the north can be heavy. *See* Delaware, District of Columbia, Georgia, Maryland, New Jersey, New York, North Carolina, South Carolina, Virginia.

New England. Cool temperate, with severe winters and warm summers. Precipitation is well distributed with a slight winter maximum. Snowfall is heavy in winter. *See* Connecticut, Maine, Massachusetts, New Hampshire, Rhode Island, Vermont. *See* also Hawaii and Outlying Territories.

CONSTITUTION AND GOVERNMENT. The form of government of the USA is based on the constitution of 17 Sept. 1787.

By the constitution the government of the nation is composed of three co-ordinate branches, the executive, the legislative and the judicial.

The National Government has authority in matters of general taxation, treaties and other dealings with foreign Powers, foreign and inter-state commerce, bankruptcy, postal service, coinage, weights and measures, patents and copyright, the armed forces (including, to a certain extent, the militia), and crimes against the USA; it has sole legislative authority over the District of Columbia and the possessions of the US.

The 5th article of the constitution provides that Congress may, on a two-thirds vote of both houses, propose amendments to the constitution, or, on the application of the legislatures of two-thirds of all the states, call a convention for proposing amendments, which in either case shall be valid as part of the constitution when ratified by the legislatures of three-fourths of the several states, or by conventions in three-fourths thereof, whichever mode of ratification may be proposed by Congress. Ten amendments (called collectively 'the Bill of Rights') to the constitution were added 15 Dec. 1791; two in 1795 and 1804; a 13th amendment, 6 Dec. 1865, abolishing slavery; a 14th in 1868, including the important 'due process' clause; a 15th, 3 Feb. 1870, establishing equal voting rights for white and coloured; a 16th, 3 Feb. 1913, authorizing the income tax; a 17th, 8 April 1913, providing for popular election of senators; an 18th, 16 Jan. 1919, prohibiting alcoholic liquors; a 19th, 18 Aug. 1920, establishing woman suffrage; a 20th, 23 Jan. 1933, advancing the date of the President's and Vice-President's inauguration and abolishing the 'lameduck' sessions of Congress; a 21st, 5 Dec. 1933, repealing the 18th amendment; a 22nd, 26 Feb. 1951, limiting a President's tenure of office to 2 terms, or to 2 terms plus 2 years in the case of a Vice-President who has succeeded to the office of a President; a 23rd, 30 March 1961, granting citizens of the District of Columbia the right to vote in national elections; a 24th, 4 Feb. 1964, banning the use of the poll-tax in federal elections; a 25th, 10 Feb. 1967, dealing with Presidential disability and succession; a 26th, 22 June 1970, establishing the right of citizens who are 18 years of age and older to vote.

National flag: Seven red and 6 white alternating stripes, horizontal; with a blue canton, extending down to the lower edge of the 4th red stripe from the top, and displaying 50 white 5-pointed stars, one for each state. The stars have one point directed vertically upward, and they are arranged in 6 rows of 5 each, alternating with 5 rows of 4 each. On the admission of additional states, stars are added, effective on 4 July following the date of admission. Congress, by law of 22 Dec. 1942, has codified 'existing rules and customs' pertaining to the display of the flag, for civilians.

National anthem: The Star-spangled Banner, 'Oh say, can you see by the dawn's early light' (words by F. S. Key, 1814; tune by J. S. Smith; formally adopted by Congress 3 March 1931).

National motto: 'In God we trust'; formally adopted by Congress 30 July 1956.

Presidency. The executive power is vested in a president, who holds office for 4 years, and is elected, together with a vice-president chosen for the same term, by electors from each state, equal to the whole number of senators and representatives to which the state may be entitled in the Congress. The President must be a natural-born citizen, resident in the country for 14 years, and at least 35 years old.

The presidential election is held every fourth (leap) year on the Tuesday after the first Monday in November. Technically, this is an election of presidential electors, not of a president directly; the electors thus chosen meet and give their votes (for the candidate to whom they are pledged, in some states by law, but in most states by custom and prudent politics) at their respective state capitals on the first Monday after the second Wednesday in December next following their election; and the votes of the electors of all the states are opened and counted in the presence of both Houses of Congress on the sixth day of January. The total electorate vote is one for each senator and representative.

If the successful candidate for President dies before taking office the Vice-President-elect becomes President; if no candidate has a majority or if the successful candidate fails to qualify, then, by the 20th amendment, the Vice-President acts as President until a president qualifies. The duties of the Presidency, in absence of the President and Vice-President by reason of death, resignation, removal, inability or failure to qualify, devolve upon the Speaker of the House under legislation enacted 18 July 1947. And in case of absence of a Speaker for like reason, the presidential duties devolve upon the President *pro tem.* of the Senate and successively upon those members of the Cabinet in order of precedence, who have the constitutional qualifications for President.

The presidential term, by the 20th amendment to the constitution, begins at noon on 20 Jan. of the inaugural year. This amendment also installs the newly elected Congress in office on 3 Jan. instead of—as formerly—in the following December. The President's salary is $200,000 per year, plus $50,000 to assist in defraying expenses resulting from official duties. Also he may spend up to $100,000 non-taxable for travel and $20,000 for official entertainment. The office of Vice-President carries a salary of $115,000, plus $10,000 allowance for travel, all taxable.

The President is C.-in-C. of the Army, Navy and Air Force, and of the militia when in the service of the Union. The Vice-President is *ex-officio* President of the Senate, and in the case of 'the removal of the President, or of his death, resignation, or inability to discharge the powers and duties of his office', he becomes the President for the remainder of the term.

President of the United States: George Bush, of Texas, born at Milton, Massachusetts, in 1924; Vice-President, 1981–89.
Vice President: Dan Quayle, of Indiana; born 1947.

At the Presidential election on 8 Nov. 1988 total vote cast, including men and women in the armed services, was 91,585,872, of which George Bush (R.) received 48,881,011 (53·4%), Michael Dukakis (D.) 41,828,350 (45·67%), Ron Paul (Libertarian) 431,499 (0·47%), Lenora Fulani (New Alliance) 218,159 (0·24%). Electoral college votes: Bush 426; Dukakis 112.

PRESIDENTS OF THE USA

Name	*From state*	*Term of service*	*Born*	*Died*
George Washington	Virginia	1789–97	1732	1799
John Adams	Massachusetts	1797–1801	1735	1826
Thomas Jefferson	Virginia	1801–09	1743	1826

Name	*From state*	*Term of service*	*Born*	*Died*
James Madison	Virginia	1809–17	1751	1836
James Monroe	Virginia	1817–25	1759	1831
John Quincy Adams	Massachusetts	1825–29	1767	1848
Andrew Jackson	Tennessee	1829–37	1767	1845
Martin Van Buren	New York	1837–41	1782	1862
William H. Harrison	Ohio	Mar.–Apr. 1841	1773	1841
John Tyler	Virginia	1841–45	1790	1862
James K. Polk	Tennessee	1845–49	1795	1849
Zachary Taylor	Louisiana	1849–July 1850	1784	1850
Millard Fillmore	New York	1850–53	1800	1874
Franklin Pierce	New Hampshire	1853–57	1804	1869
James Buchanan	Pennsylvania	1857–61	1791	1868
Abraham Lincoln	Illinois	1861–Apr. 1865	1809	1865
Andrew Johnson	Tennessee	1865–69	1808	1875
Ulysses S. Grant	Illinois	1869–77	1822	1885
Rutherford B. Hayes	Ohio	1877–81	1822	1893
James A. Garfield	Ohio	Mar.–Sept. 1881	1831	1881
Chester A. Arthur	New York	1881–85	1830	1886
Grover Cleveland	New York	1885–89	1837	1908
Benjamin Harrison	Indiana	1889–93	1833	1901
Grover Cleveland	New York	1893–97	1837	1908
William McKinley	Ohio	1897–Sept. 1901	1843	1901
Theodore Roosevelt	New York	1901–09	1858	1919
William H. Taft	Ohio	1909–13	1857	1930
Woodrow Wilson	New Jersey	1913–21	1856	1924
Warren Gamaliel Harding	Ohio	1921–Aug. 1923	1865	1923
Calvin Coolidge	Massachusetts	1923–29	1872	1933
Herbert C. Hoover	California	1929–33	1874	1964
Franklin D. Roosevelt	New York	1933–Apr. 1945	1882	1945
Harry S. Truman	Missouri	1945–53	1884	1972
Dwight D. Eisenhower	New York	1953–61	1890	1969
John F. Kennedy	Massachusetts	1961–Nov. 1963	1917	1963
Lyndon B. Johnson	Texas	1963–69	1908	1973
Richard M. Nixon	California	1969–74	1913	—
Gerald R. Ford	Michigan	1974–77	1913	—
James Earl Carter	Georgia	1977–81	1924	—
Ronald Reagan	California	1981–89	1911	—
George Bush	Texas	1989–	1924	—

Vice-Presidents of the USA

Name	From state	Term of service	Born	Died
John Adams	Massachusetts	1789–97	1735	1826
Thomas Jefferson	Virginia	1797–1801	1743	1826
Aaron Burr	New York	1801–05	1756	1836
George Clinton	New York	1805–12 [1]	1739	1812
Elbridge Gerry	Massachusetts	1813–14 [1]	1744	1814
Daniel D. Tompkins	New York	1817–25	1774	1825
John C. Calhoun	South Carolina	1825–32 [1]	1782	1850
Martin Van Buren	New York	1833–37	1782	1862
Richard M. Johnson	Kentucky	1837–41	1780	1850
John Tyler	Virginia	Mar.–Apr. 1841 [1]	1790	1862
George M. Dallas	Pennsylvania	1845–49	1792	1864
Millard Fillmore	New York	1849–50 [1]	1800	1874
William R. King	Alabama	Mar.–Apr. 1853 [1]	1786	1853
John C. Breckinridge	Kentucky	1857–61	1821	1875
Hannibal Hamlin	Maine	1861–65	1809	1891
Andrew Johnson	Tennessee	Mar.–Apr. 1865 [1]	1808	1875
Schuyler Colfax	Indiana	1869–73	1823	1885
Henry Wilson	Massachusetts	1873–75 [1]	1812	1875

[1] Position vacant thereafter until commencement of the next presidential term.

Name	*From state*	*Term of service*	*Born*	*Died*
William A. Wheeler	New York	1877–81	1819	1887
Chester A. Arthur	New York	Mar.–Sept. 1881 [1]	1830	1886
Thomas A. Hendricks	Indiana	Mar.–Nov. 1885 [1]	1819	1885
Levi P. Morton	New York	1889–93	1824	1920
Adlai Stevenson	Illinois	1893–97	1835	1914
Garret A. Hobart	New Jersey	1897–99 [1]	1844	1899
Theodore Roosevelt	New York	Mar.–Sept. 1901 [1]	1858	1919
Charles W. Fairbanks	Indiana	1905–09	1855	1920
James S. Sherman	New York	1909–12 [1]	1855	1912
Thomas R. Marshall	Indiana	1913–21	1854	1925
Calvin Coolidge	Massachusetts	1921–Aug. 1923 [1]	1872	1933
Charles G. Dawes	Illinois	1925–29	1865	1951
Charles Curtis	Kansas	1929–33	1860	1935
John N. Garner	Texas	1933–41	1868	1967
Henry A. Wallace	Iowa	1941–45	1888	1965
Harry S. Truman	Missouri	1945–Apr. 1945 [1]	1884	1972
Alben W. Barkley	Kentucky	1949–53	1877	1956
Richard M. Nixon	California	1953–61	1913	—
Lyndon B. Johnson	Texas	1961–Nov. 1963 [1]	1908	1973
Hubert H. Humphrey	Minnesota	1965–69	1911	1978
Spiro T. Agnew	Maryland	1969–73	1918	—
Gerald R. Ford	Michigan	1973–74	1913	—
Nelson Rockefeller	New York	1974–77	1908	1979
Walter Mondale	Minnesota	1977–81	1928	—
George Bush	Texas	1981–89	1924	—
Danforth Quayle	Indiana	1989–	1947	—

[1] Position vacant thereafter until commencement of the next presidential term.

Cabinet. The administrative business of the nation has been traditionally vested in several executive departments, the heads of which, unofficially and *ex officio*, formed the President's Cabinet. Beginning with the Interstate Commerce Commission in 1887, however, an increasing amount of executive business has been entrusted to some 60 so-called independent agencies, such as the Veterans Administration, Housing and Home Finance Agency, Tariff Commission, etc.

All heads of departments and of the 60 or more administrative agencies are appointed by the President, but must be confirmed by the Senate.

The Cabinet consisted of the following (March 1990):

1. *Secretary of State* (created 1789). James Addison Baker III, of Texas, lawyer; Presidential Chief of Staff 1981–85; Secretary of the Treasury 1985–88; born 1930.

2. *Secretary of the Treasury* (1789). Nicholas F. Brady, investment banker; born 1930.

3. *Secretary of Defense* (1947). Richard Cheney, of Wyoming; congressman; White House Chief of Staff 1975–76; born 1940.

4. *Attorney-General* (Department of Justice, 1870). Richard Thornburgh, of Pennsylvania; lawyer, academic administrator; governor of Pennsylvania 1979–87; born 1932.

5. *Secretary of the Interior* (1849). Manuel Lujan, Jr., of New Mexico; congressman; born 1928.

6. *Secretary of Agriculture* (1889). Clayton K. Yeutter, of Nebraska; rancher; former Dept. of Agriculture official; US trade representative 1985–89; born 1930.

7. *Secretary of Commerce* (1903). Robert A. Mosbacher, Sr., of Texas; oil and gas producer; former co-chairman, Republican National Finance Committee; born 1927.

8. *Secretary of Labor* (1913). Elizabeth H. Dole, of Kansas; lawyer, Secretary of Transportation 1983–87; born 1936.

9. *Secretary of Health and Human Services* (1953). Louis W. Sullivan, of Georgia; medical school president; born 1933.

10. *Secretary of Housing and Urban Development* (1966). Jack F. Kemp, of New York; congressman; born 1935.

11. *Secretary of Transportation* (1967). Samuel K. Skinner, of Chicago; regional transport authority chairman; lawyer; born 1938.

12. *Secretary of Energy* (1977). James D. Watkins, naval officer; Chief of Naval Operations 1982–86; born 1927.

13. *Secretary of Education* (1979). Lauro F. Cavazos, of Texas; university president; born 1927.

14. *Veterans' Affairs* (1989). Edward J. Derwinski, of Chicago; government official; born 1926.

Each of the above Cabinet officers receives an annual salary of $99,500 and holds office during the pleasure of the President.

Congress: The legislative power is vested by the Constitution in a Congress, consisting of a Senate and House of Representatives.

Electorate: By amendments of the constitution, disqualification of voters on the ground of race, colour or sex is forbidden. Accordingly, the electorate consists theoretically of all citizens of both sexes over 18 years of age, but the franchise is not universal. There are requirements of residence varying in the several states as to length from 6 months to 2 years and differing requirements as to registration. In 20 states the ability to read (usually an extract from the constitution) is required—in Alaska the ability to read English; in Hawaii, English or Hawaiian; in Louisiana, English or one's native tongue. In Alabama the voter must take an 'anti-Communist oath' and fill out a questionnaire to the satisfaction of the registrars. In some southern states voters are required to give a reasonable explanation of what they read. In most states convicts are excluded from the franchise, in some states duellists and fraudulent voters.

Legislation designed to discourage the rise of third parties has been adopted in a few states. In Illinois a new party must present a petition signed by at least 25,000 voters, including at least 200 in each of 50 of the 102 counties.

The method of balloting varies greatly. Seventeen states use different ballots for federal, state and local elections. In Delaware and South Carolina the various political parties furnish their own ballot-papers to the voters as he or she enters the polling-booth.

Senate: The Senate consists of 2 members from each state, chosen by popular vote for 6 years, one-third retiring or seeking re-election every 2 years. Senators must be no less than 30 years of age; must have been citizens of the USA for 9 years, and be residents in the states for which they are chosen. The Senate has complete freedom to initiate legislation, except revenue bills (which must originate in the House of Representatives); it may, however, amend or reject any legislation originating in the lower house. The Senate is also entrusted with the power of giving or withholding its 'advice and consent' to the ratification of all treaties initiated by the President with foreign Powers, a two-thirds majority of senators present being required for approval. (However, it has no control over 'international executive agreements' made by the President with foreign governments; such 'agreements', representing an important but very recent development, cover a wide range and are actually more numerous than formal treaties.) It also has the power of confirming or rejecting major appointments to office made by the President, but it has no direct control over the appointment by the President of 'personal representatives' or 'personal envoys' on missions abroad. Members of the Senate constitute a High Court of Impeachment, with power, by a two-thirds vote, to remove from office and disqualify any civil officer of the USA impeached by the House of Representatives, which has the sole power of impeachment.

The Senate has 16 Standing Committees to which all bills are referred for study, revision or rejection. The House of Representatives has 22 such committees. In both

Houses each Standing Committee has a chairman and a majority representing the majority party of the whole House; each has numerous sub-committees. The jurisdictions of these Committees correspond largely to those of the appropriate executive departments and agencies. Both Houses also have a few special Committees with limited duration; there were (1990) 4 Joint Committees.

House of Representatives: The House of Representatives consists of 435 members elected every second year. The number of each state's representatives is determined by the decennial census, in the absence of specific Congressional legislation affecting the basis. The states, in 1990, had the following representatives:

Alabama	7	Indiana	10	Nebraska	3	South Carolina	6
Alaska	1	Iowa	6	Nevada	2	South Dakota	1
Arizona	5	Kansas	5	New Hampshire	2	Tennessee	9
Arkansas	4	Kentucky	7	New Jersey	14	Texas	27
California	45	Louisiana	8	New Mexico	3	Utah	3
Colorado	6	Maine	2	New York	34	Vermont	1
Connecticut	6	Maryland	8	North Carolina	11	Virginia	10
Delaware	1	Massachusetts	11	North Dakota	1	Washington	8
Florida	19	Michigan	18	Ohio	21	West Virginia	4
Georgia	10	Minnesota	8	Oklahoma	6	Wisconsin	9
Hawaii	2	Mississippi	5	Oregon	5	Wyoming	1
Idaho	2	Missouri	9	Pennsylvania	23		
Illinois	22	Montana	2	Rhode Island	2		

The Supreme Court decided on 17 Feb. 1964, that the federal constitution requires congressional districts within each state to be substantially equal in population. By almost invariable custom the representative lives in the district from which he is elected.

Representatives must be not less than 25 years of age, citizens of the USA for 7 years and residents in the state from which they are chosen. The District of Columbia, Guam, American Samoa and the Virgin Islands have one non-voting delegate each. The House also admits a 'resident commissioner' from Puerto Rico, who has the right to speak on any subject and to make motions, but not to vote; he is elected in the same manner as the representatives but for a 4-year term. Each of the two Houses of Congress is sole 'judge of the elections, returns and qualifications of its own members'; and each of the Houses may, with the concurrence of two-thirds, expel a member. The period usually termed 'a Congress' in legislative language continues for 2-years, terminating at noon on 3 Jan.

The salary of a senator is $89,500 per annum, with tax-free expense allowance and allowances for travelling expenses and for clerical hire. The salary of the Speaker of the House of Representatives is $115,000 per annum, with a taxable allowance. The salary of a Member of the House is $89,500.

No senator or representative can, during the time for which he is elected, be appointed to any *civil* office under authority of the USA which shall have been created or the emoluments of which shall have been increased during such time; and no person holding *any* office under the USA can be a member of either House during his continuance in office. No religious text may be required as a qualification to any office or public trust under the USA or in any state.

The 101st Congress (1989–91) was constituted (Feb. 1990) as follows: Senate, 45 Republicans, 55 Democrats; House of Representatives, 256 Democrats, 176 Republicans, with 3 vacancies.

Indians: By an Act passed on 2 June 1924 full citizenship was granted to all Indians born in the USA, though those remaining in tribal units were still under special federal jurisdiction. Those remaining in tribal units constitute from one-half to three-fourths of the Indian population. The Indian Reorganization Act of 1934 gave the tribal Indians, at their own option, substantial opportunities to self-government and of self-controlled corporate enterprises empowered to borrow money, buy land, machinery and equipment; these corporations are controlled by democratically elected tribal councils; by 1945 roughly a third of the Indians had taken advantage of this Act. Recently a trend towards releasing Indians from federal supervision has resulted in legislation terminating supervision over specific tribes. Indian lands (1981) amounted to 52,473,000 acres, of which 41,062,000 was tribally owned and 10·96m. in trust allotments. Indian lands are held free of taxes. Total Indian population at the 1980 census was 1,418,195, of which Oklahoma, Arizona, California and New Mexico accounted for 628,400.

State and Local Government: The Union comprises 13 original states, 7 states which were admitted without having been previously organized as territories, and 30 states which had been territories—50 states in all. Each state has its own constitution (which the USA guarantees shall be republican in form), deriving its authority, not from Congress, but from the people of the state. Admission of states into the Union has been granted by special Acts of Congress, either (1) in the form of 'enabling Acts' providing for the drafting and ratification of a state constitution by the people, in which case the territory becomes a state as soon as the conditions are fulfilled, or (2) accepting a constitution already framed, and at once granting admission.

Each state is provided with a legislature of two Houses (except Nebraska, which since 1937 has had a single-chamber legislature), a governor and other executive officials, and a judicial system. Both Houses of the legislature are elective, but the senators (having larger electoral districts usually covering 2 or 3 counties compared with the single county or, in some states, the town, which sends 1 representative to the Lower House) are less numerous than the representatives, while in 38 states their terms are 4 years; in 12 states the term is 2 years. Of the 4-year senates, Illinois, Montana and New Jersey provide for two 4-year terms and one 2-year term in each decade. Terms of the lower houses are usually shorter; in 45 states, 2 years.

Members of both Houses are paid at the same rate, which varies from $200 per biennium (New Hampshire) to $46,800 per year (Alaska). The trend is towards annual sessions of state legislatures; in 1987, 36 were constitutionally required to meet annually (in 1939, only 4), the other 14 holding biennial sessions, 12 in the odd-numbered and 2 in the even-numbered years. Of these 14, 6 met annually in practice by invoking flexible constitutional powers to reconvene at intervals during the biennium.

The Governor has power to summon an extraordinary session, but not to dissolve or adjourn. The duties of the two Houses are similar, but in many states money bills must be introduced first in the Lower House. The Senate sits as a court for the trial of officials impeached by the other House, and often has power to confirm or reject appointments made by the Governor.

State legislatures are competent to deal with all matters not reserved for the federal government by the federal constitution nor specifically prohibited by the federal or state constitutions. Among their powers are the determination of the qualifications for the right of suffrage, and the control of all elections to public office, including elections of members of Congress and electors of President and Vice-President; the criminal law, both in its enactment and in its execution, with unimportant exceptions, and the administration of prisons; the civil law, including all matters pertaining to the possession and transfer of, and succession to, property; marriage and divorce, and all other civil relations; the chartering and control of all manufacturing, trading, transportation and other corporations, subject only to the right of Congress to regulate commerce passing from one state to another; labour; education; charities; licensing; fisheries within state waters, and game laws (apart from the hunting of migratory birds, which is a federal concern under treaties with Canada and Mexico). Taxes on income were left to the states until 1913, when the 16th amendment authorized the imposition of federal taxes on income without regard to apportionment.

The Governor is chosen by direct vote of the people over the whole state. His term of office varies in the several states from 2 to 4 years, and his salary from $35,000 (Arkansas, Maine) to $100,000 (New York). His duty is to see to the faithful administration of the law, and he has command of the military forces of the state. He may recommend measures but does not present bills to the legislature. In some states he presents estimates. In all but one of the states (North Carolina) the Governor has a veto upon legislation, which may, however, be overridden by the two Houses, in some states by a simple majority, in others by a three-fifths or two-thirds majority. In some states the Governor, on his death or resignation, is succeeded by a Lieut.-Governor who was elected at the same time and has been presiding over the state Senate. In several states the Speaker of the Lower House succeeds the Governor.

The chief officials by whom the administration of state affairs is carried on (secretaries, treasurers, members of boards of commissioners, etc.) are usually chosen by the people at the general state elections for terms similar to those for which governors hold office.

Local Government. The chief unit of local government is the county, of which there were (1986) 2,992 with definite functions; in addition, Rhode Island has 5 'counties' which have no functions; Alaska does not have 'counties' as such and, since Oct. 1960, there has been no active county government in Connecticut. Louisiana has 64 'parishes'. The counties maintain public order through the sheriff and his deputies, who may, in a crisis, be drawn temporarily from willing citizens; in many states the counties maintain the smaller local highways; other functions are the granting of licences and the apportionment and collection of taxes. In a few states they also manage the schools.

The unit of local government in New England is the rural township, governed directly by the voters, who assemble annually or oftener if necessary, and legislate in local affairs, levy taxes, make appropriations and appoint and instruct the local officials (selectmen, clerk, school-committee, etc.). Townships are grouped to form counties. Where cities exist, the township government is superseded by the city government.

The **District of Columbia,** ceded by the State of Maryland for the purposes of government in 1791, is the seat of the US Government. It includes the city of Washington, and embraces a land area of 61 sq. miles. The Reorganization Plan No. 3 of 1967 instituted a Mayor Council form of government with appointed officers. In 1973 an elected Mayor and elected councillors were introduced; in 1974 they received power to legislate in local matters. Congress retains power to enact legislation and to veto or supersede the Council's acts. Since 1961 citizens have had the right to vote in national elections. On 23 Aug. 1978 the Senate approved a constitutional amendment giving the District full voting representation in Congress. This has still to be ratified.

The **Commonwealth of Puerto Rico, American Samoa, Guam and the Virgin Islands** each have a local legislature, whose acts may be modified or annulled by Congress, though in practice this has seldom been done. Puerto Rico since its attainment of commonwealth status on 25 July 1952, enjoys practically complete self-government, including the election of its governor and other officials. The conduct of foreign relations, however, is still a federal function and federal bureaux and agencies still operate in the island.

General supervision of territorial administration is exercised by the Office of Territories in the Department of Interior.

Congress and the Nation, 4 vols., Congressional Quarterly, Washington, from 1965.—*Congressional Ethics,* Rev. ed., 1980.—*Congressional Quarterly Almanac,* annual
Constitution of the US, National and State. 2 vols. [with subsequent amendments]. Dobbs Ferry, 1962
Political profiles. 5 vols. New York, from 1978
Adrian, C. R., *State and Local Government.* 4th ed. New York, 1977
Barone, M. (ed.) *The Almanac of American Politics.* New York and London, Annual
Brenner, P., *The Limits and Possibilities of Congress.* New York, 1983
Seymour – Ure, C., *The American President: Power and Communication.* London, 1982

DEFENCE. The President is C.-in-C. of the Army, Navy and Air Force.

The National Security Act of 1947 provides for the unification of the Army, Navy and Air Forces under a single Secretary of Defense with cabinet rank. The President is also advised by a National Security Council and the Office of Civil and Defense Mobilization.

The major components of the Department of Defense are the Office of the Secretary of Defense and the Joint Chiefs of Staff, who provide immediate staff assistance and advice to the Secretary; the departments of the Army, Navy and Air Force, each separately organized under a civilian head (not of cabinet rank); and the unified and specified commands.

Army. *Secretary of the Army:* Michael P. W. Stone.

Central Administration. The Secretary of the Army is the head of the Department of the Army. Subject to the authority of the President as C.-in-C. and of the Secretary of Defense, he is responsible for all affairs of the Department.

The Secretary of the Army is assisted by the Under Secretary of the Army, 5 Assistant Secretaries of the Army (Civil Works, Financial Management, Installations, Logistics and Environment, Manpower and Reserve Affairs, Research, Development and Acquisition), General Counsel, Administrative Assistant, Director for Information Systems for Command, Control, Communications and Computers, Inspector General, Auditor General, Chief of Legislative Liaison, Chief of Public Affairs, Director for Small and Disadvantaged Business Utilization, Chairman of the Army Reserve Forces Policy Committee and the Army Staff headed by the Chief of Staff, US Army. The Office of the Under Secretary of the Army includes a Deputy Under Secretary (Operations Research).

The Chief of Staff, Army, in his role as a member of the Joint Chiefs of Staff, takes part in the planning and supervision of the operational forces under the command of the Commanders-in-Chief. The Vice Chief of Staff assists and advises the Chief of Staff.

The Army General Staff is the principal element of the Army Staff and includes the Offices of the Chief of Staff, Deputy Chief of Staff for Operations and Plans, Deputy Chief of Staff for Personnel, Deputy Chief of Staff for Logistics, and Deputy Chief of Staff for Intelligence. Other elements of the Army Staff are the offices of the Judge Advocate General, Surgeon General, Chief of Chaplains, Chief, Army Reserve, Chief, National Guard Bureau, and Chief of Engineers.

The Army consists of the Active Army, the Army National Guard of the US, the Army Reserve and civilian workforce; and all persons appointed to or enlisted into the Army without component; and all persons serving under call or conscription, including members of the National Guard of the States, etc., when in the service of the US. The strength of the Active Army was (1989) 769,741 (including some 86,494 women).

The US Army Forces Command, with headquarters at Fort McPherson, Georgia, commands the Third US Army; five continental US Armies, and all assigned Active Army and US Army Reserve troop units in the continental US, Alaska, Panama, the Commonwealth of Puerto Rico, and the Virgin Islands of the USA. The headquarters of the continental US Armies are: First US Army, Fort George G. Meade, Maryland; Second US Army, Fort Gillem, Georgia; Fourth US Army, Fort Sheridan, Illinois; Fifth US Army, Fort Sam Houston, Texas; Sixth US Army, Presidio of San Francisco, California. The US Army Training and Doctrine Command, with headquarters at Fort Monroe, Virginia, co-ordinates and integrates the total combat development effort of the Army as well as developing, managing, establishing and verifying the training of individuals of the US Army and authorized foreign nationals. The US Army Health Services Command, with headquarters at Fort Sam Houston, Texas, provides health services in the continental US for the US Army and provides professional education and training for medical personnel of the US Army and authorized foreign national personnel. The US Army Materiel Command, with headquarters in Alexandria, Virginia, is responsible for US Army activities dealing with equipment development, procurement, delivery, supply and maintenance. The US Army Information Systems Communications Command, with headquarters at Fort Huachuca, Arizona, provides worldwide communication automation support to the Department of the Army and supports the Defense Communications Systems. The US Army Military District of Washington, with headquarters at Fort McNair, Washington, D.C., provides support to the Department of the Army and the Department of Defense at the seat of Government. The US Army Space Command, with headquarters in Colorado Springs, Colorado, is the Army component to the US Space Command.

Nearly 40% of the Active Army is deployed outside the continental US. Several divisions, most of which are located in the USA, keep equipment in the Federal Republic of Germany and can be flown there in 48–72 hours. Headquarters of US Seventh and Eighth Armies are in Europe and Korea respectively.

Operational Commands and Weapons. The larger commands are the theater army and corps. The typical theater army may consist of a variable number of corps composed of combat forces of armour, infantry, air defense artillery, and field artillery units; combat support forces of aviation, engineer and signal elements; and combat service support forces. A typical corps consists of a variable number and mixture of infantry, mechanized infantry, armoured, air assault, or airborne divisions; one or more separate infantry, mechanized infantry or armoured brigades; one or more armoured cavalry regiments; corps artillery (155-mm howitzer, 203-mm howitzer, multiple launch rocket system (MLRS), *Lance* missile battalions); corps air defense brigade (*Hawk* and *Chaparral* battalions), corps aviation brigade and combat support and combat service support forces.

US Army Divisions have a common base (containing command, divisional artillery, air defense artillery, combat support and combat service support units) aviation brigade, and a varying mixture of combat manoeuvre battalions (usually 9 or 10 in number in 3 brigades) to make up airborne, infantry, armoured, mechanized infantry and air assault divisions. Divisions can in this way be 'tailored' to fit a variety of strategic or tactical situations. An infantry division, with about 11,500 soldiers, may have 8 infantry battalions, an armoured battalion and a mechanized infantry battalion; a mechanized infantry division, with about 17,300 soldiers, may have 5 mechanized infantry battalions and 5 armoured battalions; an armoured division, with about 17,300 soldiers, may have 4 mechanized infantry battalions and 6 armoured battalions; an airborne division, with 11,790 soldiers, may have 9 infantry (airborne) battalions. The air assault division is a highly specialized force capable of battlefield helicopter operations for infantry, field artillery, air defense artillery and necessary support forces.

The newly created 10,800-man light infantry divisions consist of 8 infantry, 8 infantry battalions and offers rapid strategic force projection. Light divisions can operate in all environments and are general purpose forces. Special operations forces consist of special forces, rangers, special operations aviation psychological operations, and civil affairs units. The units are designed, equipped, and trained for special missions.

Small arms include the M-9 (9mm pistol), M-16 series rifle and the M-249 Squad Automatic Weapon both of which fire a 5·56-mm cartridge. The standard general-purpose machine-gun is the M-60 (23 lb.; 550 rounds of 7·62-mm per minute). Infantry weapons also include M-203 grenade launcher attachment for the M-16A1 rifle, which fire a 40-mm grenade up to 400 metres, the *TOW* and *Dragon* anti-tank missile systems, and the M-72 rocket, a light anti-tank weapon.

Combat vehicles of the US Army are the tank, armoured personnel carrier, infantry fighting vehicle, and the armoured command vehicle. The first-line tanks are the M1A1 Abrams tank with a 120mm main gun, and both the M1 Abrams and the M60A3 tanks with 105-mm main armament. The standard armoured infantry personnel carrier is the M2 Bradley Fighting Vehicle (BFV), which is replacing the older M113. Both carry a mechanized infantry squad, but the BFV mounts a 25-mm Bushmaster gun and *TOW* missile launchers. The M3 version of the BFV is being used as the ground scout vehicle in armoured cavalry regiments, armoured and mechanized infantry divisional cavalry squadrons and in scout platoons of armoured and mechanized infantry battalions.

The approved calibres of artillery are: Light, 105-mm howitzer, medium 155-mm howitzer; the heavy, 203-mm howitzer. The Multiple Launch Rocket System (MLRS) is a 227-mm rapid fire rocket system used in a non-nuclear counterfire role. The 107-mm mortar, the 81-mm mortar and the 60-mm mortar are used by the combat manoeuvre elements. The 120mm mortar will replace the 107mm mortar. The *TOW* is the primary anti-tank weapon. Forward-area air-defence weapons, including the *Vulcan* 20-mm gun, provide the capability of low-altitude defence against high-performance aircraft.

The Army has three categories of missiles—surface-to-surface (field artillery) and surface-to-air (air defence artillery) and anti-tank. Surface-to-surface missiles are: *Pershing II*, terminally-guided, nuclear warhead, range about 1,000 miles (1,800 km) operational (being phased out under the terms of the Intermediate Nuclear Forces Treaty between the US and USSR); *Lance*, guided, nuclear warhead, storable, liquid propellant, operational. Surface-to-air missiles, for air defence, are: *Patriot*, guided, conventional warhead, operational; *Hawk*, homing type, low-to-mid-altitude, field operational (product improvements continue to improve the effectiveness of the system); *Chaparral*, infra-red homing, low-altitude, forward area, operational (improvements to the basic system are under development); *Stinger*, hand-held, infra-red homing, low-altitude, forward area, operational. Anti-tank missiles are: *TOW*, tube launched, optically tracked, wire guided, anti-armour, forward area, operational; *Hellfire*, laser-guided, anti-armour, operational and *Dragon*, wire-guided, medium anti-armour, forward area, operational.

The Army employs rotary- and fixed-wing aircraft as organic elements of its ground formations where their use is required on a full-time basis and their immediate and constant availability is essential. The front line commander exploits the benefits of aviation technology to perform traditional land battle tasks in the third dimension. This concept of airmobility for ground formation utilizes aerial vehicles as a highly integrated team to perform all five functions of land combat: reconnaissance, command and control, logistics and that inseparable combination, firepower and manoeuvre.

The Army has over 8,000 aircraft, all but about 500 of them helicopters. The principal types are 3,000 UH-1 Iroquois and 1,100 UH-60 Black Hawk transport helicopters, 1,600 OH-58 Kiowa observation helicopters, 1,100 AH-1S Cobra and 500 AH-64 Apache anti-armour helicopters, and 450 CH-47 Chinook medium-lift helicopters.

Enlistment, Terms of Service. Since 1974 the Army has operated an 'all volunteer' system making it, in effect, an all-regular force both regular and reserve components. Terms of service may be 2, 3, 4, 5 or 6 years. Men and women who enlist incur an 8-year obligation and must serve in the reserve components any part of the period not served on active duty. Over 90% of recruits enlisting in the Army have a high school education, over 50% of the Army is married, and 11·8% of the active force is filled by women. Women serve in both combat support and combat service support units.

The National Guard is the only reserve military component with a dual mission: A state and federal rôle. Enlistment is voluntary. The members are recruited by each state, but are equipped and paid by the federal government (except when performing state missions). Training is supervised by the active Army (FORSCOM), and unit organization parallels that for the active army; training facilities are made available by the USA and each state. As the organized militia of the several states, the District of Columbia, Puerto Rico and the Territories of the Virgin Islands and Guam, the Guard may be called into service for local emergencies by the chief executives in those jurisdictions; and may be called into federal service by the President to thwart invasion or rebellion or to enforce federal law. In its role as a reserve component of the Army, the Guard is subject to the order of the President in the event of national emergency.

The Army Reserve is designed to supply qualified and experienced units and individuals in an emergency. US Army Forces Command is charged with the command, support and training supervision of US Army Reserve units. Members of units are assigned to the Ready Reserve, which is subject to call by the President in case of national emergency without declaration of war by Congress. The Standby Reserve and the Retired Reserve may be called only after declaration of war or national emergency by Congress.

Defense 88. Dept. of Defense, Washington, D.C.
Coker, C., *US Military Power in the 1980s*. London, 1984
Kinnell, S., *Military History of the United States: An Annotated Bibliography*. Oxford and Santa Barbara, 1986

Navy. *Secretary of the Navy:* H. Lawrence Garrett, III.

The Department of the Navy is administered under the Secretary of Defense by the Secretary of the Navy, assisted by the Under Secretary; 4 Assistant Secretaries, for Financial Management; for Shipbuilding and Logistics; for Manpower and Reserve Affairs; and for Research, Engineering and Systems, as well as by the Chief of Naval Operations and the Commandant of the Marine Corps. The 3 divisions of the Department of the Navy are:

Navy Department, comprised of staff offices of the Secretary for Legislative Affairs, Information, the Judge Advocate General, Auditor General, Program Appraisal, General Counsel, Naval Research and Comptroller; offices of the Chief of Naval Operations which include the Vice Chief, the Assistant Vice Chief/ Director of Naval Administration, 3 Assistant Chiefs, 5 Deputy Chiefs and 6 Directors; Naval Inspector General; the Surgeon General; Bureau of Naval Personnel; and Headquarters U.S. Marine Corps.

The Shore Establishment comprises commands dealing with air, naval acquisition support, space and warfare systems, facilities engineering, sea (including ordnance) and supply systems; and other commands: Space, Medical, Education and Training, Data Automation, Telecommunications, Intelligence, Oceanography, Legal Service, Security Group, and Investigative Service; as well as supporting establishment of the Marine Corps and Marine Corps Reserve.

The Operating Forces are the Military Sealift Command, U.S. Naval Forces Europe, the Atlantic and Pacific Fleet including Fleet Marine Forces; operating forces of the Marine Corps, the Mine Warfare Command, Operational Test and Evaluation Force, Naval Forces Southern and Central Commands, and the Naval Reserve Forces.

Major shore activities include 8 shipyards, 27 air stations and facilities, 2 amphibious bases, 5 submarine bases and 13 naval stations and bases.

The authorized budget for the Department of the Navy (which includes funding both for the Navy and Marine Corps) for current and recent fiscal years: 1984, $82,088m.; 1985, $99,015m.; 1986, $99,113m.; 1987, $93,500m.; 1988, $100,281m.; 1989, $97,407m.; 1990, $101,670m.; and the budget request for 1991, $105,051m.

The Navy personnel total in 1989 was 583,900, including 55,000 women who are eligible to serve at sea in support ships. The U.S. Marine Corps totalled 195,300 (10,500 women).

The operational strength of the United States Navy at the end of the year indicated was as follows:

Category	*1982*	*1983*	*1984*	*1985*	*1986*	*1987*	*1988*	*1989*
Strategic Submarines	32	34	35	37	36	36	36	36
Nuclear Attack Submarines	85	90	94	98	97	96	95	97
Diesel Submarines	5	5	4	4	4	4	4	3
Aircraft Carriers[1]	13	13	13	13	14	14	14	14
Amphibious Carriers	12	12	12	12	12	12	12	13
Battleships	1	1	2	2	3	3	4	4
Cruisers	27	28	29	29	31	36	38	41
Destroyers	84	68	68	68	68	68	68	68
Frigates	82	90	94	101	109	116	112	100

[1] Omits one Aircraft Carrier in 'Service Life Extension Program' (SLEP), a three-year refit, not counted to operational total.

Ships in inactive reserve are not included; but those serving as Naval Reserve Force training ships are. Amphibious Carriers are those ships of the Wasp, Tarawa, and Iwo Jima classes capable of operating AV-8 Harrier-type aircraft as well as helicopters.

A principal part of the US naval task is to deploy the seaborne leg of the United States' strategic deterrent 'triad': This task is performed by the squadrons deploying nuclear-powered strategic ballistic missile-carrying submarines (SSBN), the strength and armament of which is as follows:

Strategic Submarines

Class	*No.*	*Tonnage (in 1,000)*	*Speed*	*Missiles*	*Other Weapons*
Tennessee	2	19·00	24	24 Trident D-5	Torpedoes
Ohio	8	19·00	24	24 Trident C-4	Torpedoes
Benjamin Franklin	12	8·12	25	6 with 16 Trident C-4 6 with 16 Poseidon C-3	Torpedoes
James Madison	8	8·12	25	6 with 16 Trident C-4 2 with 16 Poseidon C-3	Torpedoes
Lafayette	6	8·12	25	16 Poseidon C-3	Torpedoes

The Lafayette, Madison and Franklin classes, completed between 1963 comprise the first generation of SSBN, most of which were initially equipped with Polaris missiles, with maximum range between 1,500 and 2,500 nautical miles. These missiles were replaced between 1970 and 1977 with Poseidon C-3 missiles of similar maximum range, but deploying greatly increased numbers of warheads (10 per missile). 12 of these submarines were modernized between 1978 and 1982 to carry the Trident-1 C-4 missile, which is of similar size to the Poseidon, but with a range of 4,000 nautical miles, and delivering 8 warheads per missile. The second generation Ohio and Tennessee class submarines, with a much larger hull, are designed to deploy the Trident-2 D-5 missile, with a maximum range of 6,500 nautical miles, carrying a similar number of warheads but with substantially improved targetting accuracy. Sea trials of this weapon, which began in March 1989, uncovered a technical fault which has delayed operational deployment until at least March 1990. The Ohio class will be retrofitted with the Trident-2 in due course, and a total of 20 of this larger class, completing at one per year, is anticipated.

The listed total of 97 nuclear-powered attack submarines (SSN) comprises 42 of the Los Angeles class (7,040 tonnes) in three major batches: A basic design (31 ships) completed 1976-85, a small group of 8 ships additionally equipped with vertical-launch missile tubes for Tomahawk cruise missiles completed 1985-89, and the current building programme of which 3 ships have been completed, known as 'Improved' Los Angeles incorporating cruise missile tubes, a new command system, and several important additional technical modifications. There are also 37 Sturgeon class (5,040 tonnes) completed 1967-75, 10 Permit class (4,370 tonnes) completed 1963-67, and 7 others. The 3 remaining diesel submarines, built in the late 1950s, are used for training.

The table below lists the principal operational surface ships:

Aircraft Carriers

Completed	*Name*	*Tonnage (in 1,000)*	*Speed*	*Aircraft*
Nimitz Class				
1989	George Washington	97·8	33[1]	All carriers, except *Roosevelt*
1986	Theodore Roosevelt	97·8	33[1]	and *Midway* carry a standard
1982	Carl Vinson	92·9	33[1]	Air Wing of 86 aircraft:-
1977	Eisenhower	92·9	33[1]	24 F/A-18 Hornet fighter/
1975	Nimitz	92·9	33[1]	bombers.
				10 A-6E Intruder bombers.
Kitty Hawk Kennedy Class				24 F-14 Tomcat fighters.
1968	John F Kennedy	82·5	32	4 EA-6B Prowler
1965	America	81·0	33	electronic warfare aircraft.
1962	Constellation	83·1	34	4 E-2C Hawkeye airborne early
1961	Kitty Hawk	82·4	34	warning.
1962	Enterprise	91·5	33[1]	10 S-3A Viking ASW aircraft.
				4 KA-6D Tankers.
Forrestal Class				6 SH-3A Sea King ASW
1959	Independence	81·9	33	helicopters.
1957	Ranger	82·5	33	*Roosevelt* carries an experi-
1956	Saratoga	81·7	33	mental air wing. *Midway*, much
1955	Forrestal	80·5	33	smaller, carries no F-14,
1945	Midway	65·0	32	36 F/A-18 & 14 A-6E.

[1] Indicates Nuclear propulsion

Amphibious Carriers

Completed	*Name*	*Tonnage (in 1,000)*	*Speed*	*Aircraft*
Wasp Class (LHD)				
1989	Wasp	41·2	23	6-8 AV-8 Harriers and up to 42 helicopters.
Tarawa Class (LHA)				
1981	Pelileu			
1980	Nassau			Normal Air group is 30 aircraft, e.g.
1978	Belleau Wood	40·0	24	6 AV-8 Harriers, and 24 mixed helicopters,
1977	Saipan			principally CH-53E, CH-46 and gunships.
1976	Tarawa			
Iwo Jima Class (LPH)				
1970	Inchon			
1968	New Orleans			
1965	Tripoli			4 AV-8 plus maximum of 16 mixed
1965	Guam	18·8	21	helicopters, or 20 helicopters only.
1963	Guadalcanal			
1962	Okinawa			
1961	Iwo Jima			

Battleships

Completed	*Name*	*Tonnage (in 1,000)*	*Speed*	*Main Armament*	*Aircraft*
Iowa Class					
1944	Missouri			9 x 406 mm, 12 x 127 mm	
1944	Wisconsin			guns. 32 Tomahawk cruise	
1943	New Jersey	58·25	33	missiles. 16 Harpoon	None.
1943	Iowa			anti-ship missiles.	

Cruisers

Completed	*Name*	*Tonnage (in 1,000)*	*Speed*	*Main Armament*	*Aircraft*
Ticonderoga (Aegis) Class					
1989	Chancellorsville				
1989	Normandy				
1989	Princeton				
1989	Philippine Sea				
1988	Lake Champlain			Standard SM-2 ER SAM,	
1988	San Jacinto			2 x 2 launchers in first	
1987	Leyte Gulf			5 ships; 2 x 61-cell	2 SH-60B Sea-
1987	Antietam	9·6	32	vertical launcher systems	hawk LAMPS-III
1987	Mobile Bay			for Standard, Tomahawk	helicopters.
1986	Bunker Hill			and Harpoon in remainder.	
1986	Thomas S. Gates			2 x 127 mm guns in all.	
1986	Valley Forge				
1985	Vincennes				
1984	Yorktown				
1983	Ticonderoga				
Virginia Class[1]					
1980	Arkansas			2 x 2 Standard SM-2 SAM. 8	
1978	Mississippi			Tomahawk cruise missiles. 8	
1977	Texas	11·45	31	Harpoon anti-ship and ASROC	None
1976	Virginia			ASW missiles. 2 x 127 mm guns.	
South Carolina[1]					
1974	South Carolina			As for *Virginia*, without	
1973	California	10·7	31	Tomahawk.	None
Miscellaneous[1]					
1961	Long Beach	17·4	30	1 or 2 x 2 SM-2 ER SAMs.	
1967	Truxtun	8·9	30	ASROC ASW missiles. 8 x	None
1962	Bainbridge	9·25	30	Tomahawk (Long Beach only).	

Completed	*Name*	*Tonnage (in 1,000)*	*Speed*	*Main Armament*	*Aircraft*
Belknap Class					
1967	Biddle				
1967	Sterett				
1967	Horne				
1966	Fox				
1966	Wm. H. Standley	8·2	33	Standard SM-2 ER SAMs ASROC ASW missiles 8 Harpoon missiles 1 x 127 mm Gun.	1 SH-2F Seasprite LAMPS-I helicopter.
1966	Jouett				
1966	Wainwright				
1965	Jos. L. Daniels				
1964	Belknap				
Leahy Class					
1964	Reeves				
1964	Rich. K. Turner				
1963	Dale				
1963	Halsey				
1963	England	8·3	32	2 x 2 SM-2 ER SAMs ASROC ASW missiles 8 Harpoon missiles	None
1963	Gridley				
1963	Worden				
1963	Harry E Yarnell				
1962	Leahy				

[1] Indicates nuclear-powered.

The target of '15 deployable carriers' set in 1986 was officially amended to 14 as a result of budgetary pressure in 1989. Of the 15 listed in the table, *Kitty Hawk* is undergoing a three-year 'service life extension' refit and so does not count to the authorized deployable total. However, before the *George Washington* commissioned in Nov. 1989, the *Coral Sea* was withdrawn from the fleet, and is to be deactivated by April 1990. In addition the training carrier *Lexington* is maintained in service, but is classified as an auxiliary. The *Bon Homme Richard* (completed 1944) and *Oriskany* (1945) are still maintained in inactive reserve. *Shangri La* was scrapped in 1983 and the anti-submarine support aircraft carriers *Bennington* and *Hornet* were deleted from the list in 1987.

The Wasp (LHD-1), and the 5 ships of the Tarawa (LHA-1) class are in many respects equivalent to the V/STOL aircraft carriers in other principal navies and are capable of sea control tasks. The 7 ships of the Iwo Jima class are also capable of operating V/STOL aircraft but do not normally do so. All are, however, configured, trained and equipped primarily for amphibious operations.

In addition to the previously listed principal surface ships, there are 37 guided-missile destroyers, 31 ASW destroyers of the Spruance class, 51 guided-missile frigates of the Oliver Hazard Perry class, 49 other frigates, 6 hydrofoil missile patrol craft and 24 inshore patrol craft. Mine warfare has been somewhat neglected by the USN over the past decades, but two new classes are now building. There are now 4 new mine countermeasure vessels of the Avenger class in service, and the first of a new Osprey class coastal minehunter building. For the present, the bulk of the task falls to 21 old ocean minesweepers (completed between 1954 and 1958, mostly employed on reserve training) and 7 minesweeping boats.

The amphibious capability of the USN comprises some 66 ships. In addition to the 13 amphibious aircraft carriers listed above, there are 2 amphibious command ships, 27 dock landing ships, 20 tank landing ships and 5 amphibious transports. There are 80 amphibious craft including 16 air-cushion landing craft (hovercraft) and 55 utility landing craft, and several hundred minor personnel and vehicle transports. The total oceanic lift capability of USN amphibious forces amounts to over 50,000 men, 1,300 main battle tank equivalents, and operating facilities for about 180 helicopters.

Specially trained and equipped amphibious expeditionary forces are provided by the U.S. Marine Corps, some 195,000 strong, which although administratively part of the Department of the Navy, ranks as a separate armed service, with the Commandant of the Corps serving in his own right as a member of the Joint Chiefs of Staff. The Marine Corps is organized into 3 divisions each some 55,000 strong, which are subdivided into Marine Expeditionary Brigades, (18,000) and Marine Expeditionary Units (some 6,000 strong). Marine Expeditionary Units are permanently deployed afloat in the Eastern Atlantic/Mediterranean and the West Pacific/Indian Ocean. The principal equipment of the U.S. Marine Corps consists of 700 M-60A1 tanks, 420 LAV-25 armoured infantry fighting vehicles, 800 armoured personnel carriers, over 1,000 artillery pieces of calibres between 105 mm and 203 mm. Additional heavy equipment for US-based Marine forces units, beyond that which can be embarked in the amphibious shipping, is provided in two squadrons each of 13 large cargo ships prepositioned at Diego Garcia and in the Mediterranean. In addition the Corps includes an autonomous aviation element numbering some 490 combat aircraft and 540 helicopters. There are 190 F/A 18 Hornet, 140 AV-8 and AV-8B Harriers, 122 A-4 Skyhawks, 76 A-6 attack and electronic warfare. 376 KC-130 tankers, and a miscellany of other support and training aircraft. Helicopters include 200 CH-46E and 170 CH-53 transport, plus 72 AH-1 Cobra attack helicopters of various type. Harriers and helicopters are normally employed afloat in the amphibious aircraft carriers and other suitable ships. The Hornets and other fixed wing aircraft are normally based ashore, but may be embarked in other aircraft carriers, given the operational need.

The USN is provided with global, long-term sustainability through a force of some 60 underway replenishment ships, including 31 tankers, 4 multi-purpose fast replenishment ships, 11 stores ships and 13 ammunition ships. Second-line support is provided by 3 repair ships, 21 depot ships, 14 support tankers, 7 tugs, 2 hospital ships and 3 fast cargo vessels. Special purpose auxiliaries include 2 command ships, 15 ocean surveillance ships, 5 missile and space support ships, and 21 survey and oceanographic vessels. Of these 150 major auxiliaries, about 78 are operated by the civilian-manned Military Sealift Command. In addition there are some hundreds of minor auxiliaries, and several thousand service craft.

Major warship building yards involved in the current building programme are located at Groton, Conn. (submarines), Newport News, Va., (submarines and aircraft carriers), Pascagoula, Mississippi (cruisers and amphibious ships), Bath, Me. (cruisers and destroyers) and New Orleans, La., (amphibious and auxiliary ships). No major USN ships are currently being built in west coast shipyards. The order book in late 1989 (i.e. excluding ships authorized to be ordered in FY 1990) included 6 Ohio class strategic submarines, 18 Improved Los Angeles and the first of a new class of Sea Wolf nuclear-powered attack submarines, a further 3 nuclear-powered aircraft carriers of the Nimitz class, 12 Ticonderoga class guided-missile cruisers, and the first 6 guided-missile cruisers of the Arleigh Burke class (rated as destroyers by the USN but at over 8,000 tonnes, Aegis-equipped and costing some $800m. per unit, cruisers in all but name). There are also a further 3 Wasp class amphibious assault carriers, mine countermeasures vessels, other amphibious ships and major auxiliaries on order.

Naval Aviation. The principal function of the naval aviation organization is to provide and train the 13 Air Wings maintained for service in the Aircraft Carriers. As shown in the ship tables, these usually consist of 80 fixed wing and 6 rotary wing aircraft. In addition, 2 carrier air wings are provided from the reserves, in some cases with slightly older aircraft. The main carrier-borne combat aircraft on inventory are 400 F-14 fighters, 210 A-6E Intruder attack aircraft, 250 F/A-18 Hornet dual-purpose fighter/attack aircraft and 140 S-3A Viking anti-submarine aircraft. Supporting roles are performed by 64 EA-6B electronic warfare aircraft, 90 E-2C Hawkeye airborne early warning aircraft, 50 KA-6D tankers, and 100 SH-3A Sea King helicopters for inner-zone ASW defence. The reserve air wings have some A-7 Corsair attack aircraft on strength, of which holdings are still over 200. Helicopters held for embarkation in cruisers and below are of two types, the older S 2F Seasprite LAMPS-I aircraft of which there are some 140 and the SH-60B Seahawk LAMPS-II of which there are 100. A different version of this latter aircraft, the SH-60F Oceanhawk is now in production as a replacement for the elderly Sea Kings in the Aircraft Carriers. The principal tasks of the shore-based elements of US naval aviation are maritime reconnaissance and ASW, for which there are holdings of about 370 P-3C Orion aircraft. Additional tasks include electronic warfare

(12 EP-3), electronic intelligence (14 EA-3) and mine countermeasures for which 30 MH- and RH-53 helicopters are held. Finally there are some 650 training aircraft of types not previously mentioned, and 110 aircraft and 90 helicopters for transport and other miscellaneous duties.

The US Coast Guard operates under the Department of Transportation in time of peace and as a part of the Navy in time of war or when directed by the President. The act of establishment stated the Coast Guard 'shall be a military service and branch of the armed forces of the United States at all times'. The Coast Guard did operate as part of the Navy during the First and Second World Wars. It also had some units serving in Vietnam. It comprises 250 ships including cutters of destroyer, frigate, corvette and patrol vessel types, 2 powerful icebreakers, and paramilitary auxiliaries and tenders, plus over 2,000 rescue and utility craft. It also maintains 70 fixed-wing aircraft and 130 helicopters. The Coast Guard missions include maintenance of aids to navigation, enforcement of maritime laws, enforcement of international treaties, environmental protection (especially waterway pollution), commercial vessel safety programmes, recreational boating safety, search and rescue efforts and military readiness. In the new construction programme are 34 patrol boats. The strength of personnel in 1989 was 5,077 officers, 1,342 warrant officers and 30,255 enlisted personnel and 817 cadets.

Air Force. *Secretary of the Air Force:* Donald B. Rice.

The Department of the Air Force was activated within the Department of Defense on 18 Sept. 1947, under the terms of the National Security Act of 1947. It is administered by a Secretary of the Air Force, assisted by an Under Secretary and 3 Assistant Secretaries (Space; Acquisition; and Manpower, Reserve Affairs and Logistics). The USAF, under the administration of the Department of the Air Force, is supervised by a Chief of Staff, who is a member of the Joint Chiefs of Staff. He is assisted by a Vice Chief of Staff, Assistant Vice Chief of Staff, and 4 Deputy Chiefs of Staff (Personnel; Programs and Resources; Plans and Operations; and Logistics and Engineering).

The USAF consists of active duty Air Force officers and enlisted personnel, civilian employees, the Air National Guard and the Air Force Reserve. For operational purposes the service is organized into 13 major commands, 16 separate operating agencies and 7 direct reporting units. The Strategic Air Command, equipped with long-range bombers and with intercontinental ballistic missiles, is maintained primarily for strategic air operations anywhere on the globe. Tactical Air Command is the Air Force's mobile strike force, able to deploy US general-purpose air forces anywhere in the world for tactical air combat operations. The Military Airlift Command provides air transportation of personnel and cargo for all military services on a worldwide basis; and is also responsible for Air Force audio-visual products, weather service, Air Force special operations forces, and aerospace rescue and recovery operations.

The other major commands are the Air Force Systems Command, Air Force Logistics Command, Air Force Communications Command, Electronic Security Command, Air Training Command, Alaskan Air Command, Pacific Air Forces, Air Force Space Command, United States Air Forces in Europe, and Air University. The Alaskan, Pacific and European commands conduct, control and co-ordinate offensive and defensive air operations according to tasks assigned by their respective theatre commanders.

The separate operating agencies are the Air Force Accounting and Finance Center, Air Force Audit Agency, Air Force Commissary Service, Air Force Engineering and Services Center, Air Force Inspection and Safety Center, Air Force Intelligence Service, Air Force Office of Security Police, Air Force Military and Personnel Agency, Air Force Office of Medical Support, Air Force Management Engineering Agency, Air Force Service Information and News Center, Air Force Legal Services Center, Air Force Office of Special Investigations, Air Force Operational Test and Evaluation Center, Air Force Reserve, and Air Reserve Personnel Center. Air Force direct reporting units are the Air Force Academy, Air National Guard, Air Force Technical Applications Center, Air Force District of Washington,

D.C., Air Force Civilian Personnel Management Center and USAF Historical Research Center.

Of the fighter and interceptor aircraft in service, the F-15 Eagle, F-16 Fighting Falcon, F-111 and F-4 Phantom II fly faster than the speed of sound in level flight and can carry a variety of armament. The E-3 Sentry (AWACS) is a large long-range airborne warning and control aircraft; the EF-111A Raven is a radar jamming aircraft produced by conversion of the F-111A fighter. The subsonic A-7 Corsair II, the A-10 Thunderbolt and the AC-130H are close air support aircraft. The OA-37 and the OV-10 are observation aircraft. Strategic bombers are the B-52 Stratofortress and the B-1B heavy bombers. The Strategic Air Command also operates the KC-10A Extender and the KC-135 Stratotanker for aerial refuelling and the U-2 and TR-1 for reconnaissance. Primary transports include the C-141 Starlifter the C-5 Galaxy, KC-10A Extender and the turboprop-powered C-130 Hercules. Intercontinental ballistic missiles in USAF service are the Minuteman II and III and Peacekeeper.

In 1989, the Air Force had about 579,000 military personnel. The service operates approximately 9,400 aircraft in the active Air Force, the Air National Guard and the Air Force Reserve.

INTERNATIONAL RELATIONS

Membership. USA is a member of UN, OAS, NATO, OECD and the Colombo Plan.

ECONOMY

Budget. The budget covers virtually all the programmes of federal government, including those financed through trust funds, such as for social security, Medicare and highway construction. Receipts of the Government include all income from its sovereign or compulsory powers; income from business-type or market-orientated activities of the Government is offset against outlays. Budget receipts and outlays (in $1m.):

Year ending 30 June	*Receipts* [2]	*Outlays* [2]	*Surplus* (+) *or deficit* (–)
1945	45,159	92,712	–47,553
1950	39,443	42,562	– 3,119
1955	65,451	68,444	– 2,993
1960	92,492	92,191	+ 301
1970	192,807	195,649	– 2,842
1985 [1]	734,057	946,316	–212,260
1988	908,954	1,064,044	–155,090
1989	990,789	1,142,869	–152,080
1990 [3]	1,080,131	1,179,375	–99,244

[1] From 1977 the fiscal year changed from a 1 July–30 June basis to a 1 Oct.–30 Sept. basis.
[2] From 1970, revised to include Medicare premiums and collections.
[3] July 1989 estimates.

Budget receipts, by source, for fiscal years (in $1m.):

Source	*1988* [1]	*1989* [1]	*1990* [2]
Individual income taxes	401,181	445,690	484,553
Corporation income taxes	94,508	103,291	116,987
Social insurance taxes and contributions	334,335	359,416	387,499
Excise taxes	35,227	34,386	33,690
Estate and gift taxes	7,594	8,745	8,771
Customs	16,198	16,334	18,528
Miscellaneous	19,910	22,927	24,303
Total	908,945	990,789	1,080,131

[1] Includes off-budget receipts. [2] July 1989 estimates.

Budget outlays, by function, for fiscal years (in $1m.):

Source	*1988* [1]	*1989* [1]	*1990* [2]
National defence	290,361	303,551	296,293
International affairs	10,471	9,596	16,355
General science, space, and technology	10,841	12,891	14,877
Energy	2,297	3,745	3,034
Natural resources and environment	14,606	16,084	16,303
Agriculture	17,210	16,948	16,174
Commerce and housing credit	18,808	27,810	7,269
Transportation	27,272	27,623	28,222
Community and regional development	5,294	5,755	6,182
Education, training, employment and social services	31,938	35,697	37,506
Health	44,490	48,391	56,362
Medicare	78,878	84,964	97,123
Income security	129,332	136,765	145,446
Social Security	219,341	232,542	249,107
Veterans' benefits and services	29,428	30,066	28,009
Administration of justice	9,223	9,396	10,452
General government	9,474	8,940	9,960
Net interest	151,748	169,314	176,286
Allowances	...	...	1,889
Undistributed offsetting receipts	–36,967	–37,212	–37,474
Total budget outlays	1,064,044	1,142,869	1,179,375

[1] Includes outlays of off-budget Federal entities and programmes.
[2] July 1989 estimates.

Budget outlays, by agency, for fiscal years (in $1m.):

Agency	*1988* [1]	*1989* [1]	*1990* [2]
Legislative branch	1,852	2,094	2,490
The Judiciary	1,337	1,493	1,754
Executive Office of the President	121	124	145
Funds appropriated to the President	7,253	4,302	11,075
Agriculture	44,003	48,414	45,897
Commerce	2,279	2,571	3,455
Defence—Military	281,935	294,876	286,899
Defence—Civil	22,029	23,427	24,727
Education	18,246	21,608	22,360
Energy	11,166	11,387	12,670
Health and Human Services, except Social Security	159,071	172,301	190,173
Health and Human Services, Social Security	214,489	227,473	242,947
Housing and Urban Development	18,938	19,772	20,122
Interior	5,147	5,308	5,035
Justice	5,246	6,232	7,114
Labor	21,870	22,657	24,458
State	3,421	3,722	3,930
Transportation	26,404	26,689	27,208
Treasury	202,386	230,573	249,480
Environmental Protection Agency	4,871	4,906	5,492
General Services Administration	–281	–462	196
National Aeronautics and Space Administration	9,092	11,036	12,587
Office of Personnel Management	29,191	29,073	33,775
Small Business Administration	–54	83	–1,077
Veterans Affairs	29,271	30,041	27,956
Other Independent Agencies	23,444	32,323	14,584
Allowances	...	...	1,889
Undistributed offsetting receipts	–78,863	–89,155	–97,967
Total budget outlays	1,064,044	1,142,869	1,179,375

[1] Includes outlays of off-budget Federal entities and programmes.
[2] July 1989 estimates.

National Debt: Federal debt held by the public (in $1m.), and *per capita* debt (in $1) on 30 June to 1970 and then on 30 Sept.:

	Public debt	*Per capita* [2]		*Public debt*	*Per capita* [2]
1919 [1]	25,485	243	1970	283,198	1,381
1920	24,299	228	1980	709,291	3,114
1930 [1]	16,185	132	1985	1,499,362	6,266
1940	42,772	324	1986	1,736,163	7,183
1950	219,023	1,444	1987	1,888,134	7,738
1960 [3]	236,840	1,310	1988 [4]	2,050,196	8,321

[1] On 31 Aug. 1919 gross debt reached its First World War (1914–18) peak of $26,596,702,000, which was the highest ever reached up to 1934; on 31 Dec. 1930 it had declined to $16,026m., the lowest it has been since the First World War. On the 30 Nov. 1941, just preceding Pearl Harbor, debt stood at $61,363,867,932. The highest Second World War debt was $279,764,369,348 on 28 Feb. 1946.

[2] *Per capita* figures, beginning with 1960, have been revised; they are based on the Census Bureau's estimates of the total population of the US, including Alaska and Hawaii.

[3] Debt figures since 1956 exclude the unamortized discount or premium on all Treasury debt securities held by the public.

[4] July 1988 estimate.

State and Local Finance: Revenue of the 50 states and all local governments (82,237 in 1987) from their own sources amounted to $727,593m. in 1986–87; in addition they received $114,996m. in revenue from fiscal aid, shared revenues and reimbursements from the federal government, bringing total revenue from all sources to $842,589m. Of the revenue from state and local sources, taxes provided $405,149m., of which property taxes (mainly imposed by local governments) yielded $121,227m. or 30% of all tax revenue; and sales taxes, both general sales taxes and selective excises, provided $144,293m. (36%).

State tax revenue totalled $246,933m. in 1987. Largest sources of state tax revenue are general sales taxes (imposed during 1987 by 45 states), motor fuel sales taxes (all states), individual income (44 states), motor vehicle and operators' licences (all states), corporation income (46 states), tobacco products (all states) and alcoholic beverage sales taxes (all states).

General revenue of local units from own sources in 1986–87 totalled $254,062m. In addition they received $156,285m. from state and federal aids. Property taxes provided 28% of total general revenue.

Total expenditures of state and local governments were $775,318m. in 1986–87, of which approximately 71% was for current operation. Education took $226,658m. in current and capital expenditure; highways, $52,199m.; welfare (chiefly public assistance), $80,090m., and health and hospitals, $56,972m. Capital outlays (construction, equipment and land purchases) totalled $98,276m.

Gross debt of state and local governments totalled $718,657m. or $2,953 *per capita* at the close of their 1986–87 fiscal year. Total cash and investment assets of state and local governments were $1,047,766m., about 21% being in cash and deposits, and the remainder in investments, mainly non-governmental securities.

US Bureau of the Census, *Governmental Finances in 1986–87*. Washington, D.C., 1988
American Economic Association, *Readings in Fiscal Policy*. Homewood, Ill., 1985

National Income. The Bureau of Economic Analysis of the Department of Commerce prepares detailed estimates on the national income and product of the United States. The principal tables are published monthly in *Survey of Current Business;* the complete set of national income and product tables are published in the *Survey* regularly each July, showing data for recent years. *The National Income and Product Accounts of the United States, 1929–1982: Statistical Tables* (1986) and the July 1987, July 1988 and July 1989 *Survey* contain complete sets of tables from 1929 through 1988. The conceptual framework and statistical methods underlying the US accounts were described in *National Income, 1954*. The July 1987 *Survey* provides a current overview of concepts and estimating procedures as well as a comprehensive directory to information on the US national accounts. Subsequent limited changes were described in the July 1988 *Survey*.

These latest figures [1] in $1,000m. for various years are as follows:

[1] The inclusion of statistics for Alaska and Hawaii beginning in 1960 does not significantly affect the comparability of the data.

	1929[2]	1933[3]	1950	1960	1970	1980	1988
I. Gross National Product	103·9	56·9	228·3	515·3	1,015·5	2,732·0	4,880·6
(a) Personal consumption expenditures	77·3	45·8	192·1	330·7	640·0	1,732·6	3,235·1
(b) Gross private domestic investment	16·7	1·6	55·1	78·2	148·8	437·0	750·3
(c) Net exports of goods and services	1·1	0·4	2·2	5·9	8·5	32·1	–73·7
(d) Government purchases of goods and services	8·9	8·3	38·8	100·6	218·2	530·3	968·9
1. GNP *less* capital consumption allowances with capital consumption adjustment, indirect business tax and non-tax liability, business transfer payments, statistical discrepancy, *plus* subsidies less current surplus of government enterprises, equals:							
2. National Income	84·7	39·4	239·8	424·9	832·6	2·203·5	3,972·6
which, *less* corporate profits with inventory valuation and capital consumption adjustments, contributions for social insurance, wage accruals less disbursements, *plus* government transfer payments to persons, interest paid by government to persons and business less interest received by government, interest paid by consumers, personal dividend income, business transfer payments, equals:							
3. Personal income whereof	84·3	46·3	228·1	409·4	831·8	2,258·5	4,064·5
4. Personal tax and non-tax payments take leaving	2·6	1·4	20·6	50·5	116·2	340·5	586·6
5. Disposable personal income divided into	81·7	44·9	207·5	358·9	715·6	1,918·0	3,477·8
(e) Personal outlays[4]	79·2	46·5	194·8	338·1	657·9	1,781·1	3,333·1
(f) Personal saving	2·6	–1·6	12·6	20·8	57·7	136·9	144·7
IA. GNP in constant (1982) $s	709·6	498·5	1,203·7	1,665·3	2,416·2	3,187·1	4,024·4
(a) Personal consumption expenditures	471·4	378·7	733·2	1,005·1	1,492·0	2,000·4	2,598·4
(b) Gross private domestic investment	139·2	22·7	234·9	260·5	381·5	509·3	715·8
(c) Net exports of goods and services	4·7	–1·4	4·7	–4·0	–30·0	57·0	–74·9
(d) Government purchases of goods and services	94·2	98·5	230·8	403·7	572·6	620·5	785·1
II. National Income composed of	84·7	39·4	239·8	424·9	832·6	2,203·5	3,972·6
Compensation of employees	*51·1*	*29·6*	*155·4*	*296·7*	*618·3*	*1,638·2*	*2,907·6*
(g) Salaries and wages	50·5	29·0	147·2	272·8	551·5	1,372·0	2,429·0
(h) Supplements to wages and salaries	0·7	0·6	8·2	23·8	66·8	266·3	478·6
Proprietors' income[5]	*14·4*	*5·4*	*38·8*	*52·1*	*80·2*	*180·7*	*327·8*
(i) Farm[5]	6·1	2·5	13·6	11·6	14·7	20·5	39·8
(j) Business and professional[5]	8·3	2·9	25·2	40·5	65·4	160·1	288·0
Personal income from rents[6]	*4·9*	*2·0*	*7·7*	*15·3*	*18·2*	*6·6*	*15·7*
Net interest	*4·7*	*4·1*	*3·0*	*11·3*	*41·2*	*200·9*	*392·9*
Corporate profits with inventory valuation and capital consumption adjustments	*9·6*	*–1·5*	*34·9*	*49·5*	*74·7*	*177·2*	*328·6*
(k) Tax liabilities	1·4	0·5	17·9	22·7	34·4	84·8	137·9
(l) Inventory valuation adjustment	0·5	–2·1	–5·0	–0·2	–6·6	–43·1	–25·0
(m) Capital consumption adjustment	–0·9	–0·3	–3·0	–0·3	5·2	–16·8	46·8
(n) Dividends	5·8	2·0	8·8	12·9	22·5	54·7	110·4
(o) Undistributed profits	2·8	–1·6	16·2	14·3	19·2	97·6	58·5

[2] Peak year between First and Second World Wars. [3] Low point of the depression.
[4] Includes personal consumption expenditures, interest paid by consumers and personal transfer payments to foreigners (net).
[5] With inventory valuation and capital consumption adjustment.
[6] With capital consumption adjustment.

Currency. Prior to the banking crisis that occurred early in 1933, the monetary system had been on the gold standard for more than 50 years. An Act of 14 March 1900 required the Secretary of the Treasury to maintain at a parity with gold all forms of money issued by the USA. For a description of these, *see* THE STATESMAN'S YEAR-BOOK, 1934. For information 1934–74 *see* THE STATESMAN'S YEAR-BOOK, 1988–89.

Under the Coinage Act of 1965, all coins and currencies of the USA, regardless of when coined or issued, are legal tender for all debts, public and private.

Only one of the eight kinds of notes outstanding is now significant: Federal Reserve notes in denominations of \$1, \$2, \$5, \$10, \$20, \$50 and \$100. The issue of *(a)* \$500, \$1,000, \$5,000 and \$10,000 Federal Reserve notes; of *(b)* silver certificates, and of *(c)* \$100, \$5 and \$2 US notes have been discontinued, although they are still outstanding. The following issues were stopped many years ago and have been in process of retirement: (1) Federal Reserve Bank notes; (2) National Bank notes; (3) Treasury notes of 1890; (4) fractional currency.

Federal Reserve notes are obligations of the USA and a first lien on the assets of the Federal Reserve Banks, through which they are issued. Each of the 12 banks issues them against the security of an equal volume of collateral.

At March 1990 £1 sterling = US\$1.64.

Banking. The Federal Reserve System, established under an Act of 1913, comprises the Board of 7 Governors, the 12 regional Federal Reserve Banks with their 25 branches, the Federal Open Market Committee and the Federal Advisory Council. The 7 members of the Board of Governors are appointed by the President with the consent of the Senate. Each Governor is appointed to a full term of 14 years or an unexpired portion of a term, one term expiring every 2 years. No two may come from the same Federal Reserve District. The Board supervises the Reserve Banks and the issue and retirement of Federal Reserve notes; it designates 3 of the 9 directors of each Reserve Bank and designates the Chairman and Deputy Chairman; it passes on the admission of state banks to the System and has power to correct unsound conditions in State member banks or violations of banking law by them, including, if necessary, disciplinary action to remove officers and directors for unsafe or unsound banking practices or for continuous violations of banking laws; it also authorizes State member bank branches and approves mergers and consolidations if the acquiring, assuming or resulting bank is to be a State member; and it has power to control the expansion of bank holding companies and to require divestment of certain non-banking interests. The 12 members of the Federal Open Market Committee include the 7 members of the Board of Governors and 5 of the 12 Federal Reserve Bank presidents. The latter serve 1-year terms on the Committee in rotation except for the President of the Federal Reserve Bank of New York, who is a permanent member. The Federal Open Market Committee influences credit market conditions, money and bank credit, by buying or selling US Government securities; and it also supervises System operations in foreign currencies for the purpose of helping to safeguard the value of the dollar in international exchange markets and facilitating co-operation and efficiency in the international monetary system. The Board also influences credit conditions through powers to set reserve requirements, to approve discount rates at Federal Reserve Banks, and to fix margin requirements on stock-market credit.

The Reserve Banks advance funds to depository institutions, issue Federal Reserve notes, which are the principal form of currency in the US, act as fiscal agent for the Government, and afford nation-wide cheque-clearing and fund transfer arrangements. They may discount paper for depository institutions and increase or reduce the country's supply of reserve funds by buying or selling Government securities and other obligations at the direction of the Federal Open Market Committee. The purchase and sale of securities in the open market is conducted by the Federal Reserve Bank of New York. Their capital stock is held by the member banks, but it carries no voting rights except in the election of directors.

Every member bank is required to subscribe to stock in the Reserve Bank of its district in an amount equal to 6% of its paid-up capital and surplus. Only one-half of the par value of the stock is paid in, the other half remaining subject to call by the Board of Governors. However, no call has been made for the second half of the subscription. All depository institutions with certain transaction accounts and time deposits are required to hold reserves with the Federal Reserve.

From 1968, the Congress passed a number of consumer financial protection acts, the first of which was the Truth in Lending Act, for which it has directed the Board to write implementing regulations and assume partial enforcement responsibility.

Others include the Equal Credit Opportunity Act, Home Mortgage Disclosure Act, Consumer Leasing Act, Fair Credit Billing Act, and Electronic Fund Transfer Act. To manage these responsibilities the Board has established a Division of Consumer and Community Affairs. To assist it, the Board consults with a Consumer Advisory Council, established by the Congress as a statutory part of the Federal Reserve System.

The Consumer Advisory Council was established by Congress in 1976 at the suggestion of the Board of Governors. Representing both consumer/community and financial industry interests, the Council meets several times a year to advise the Board on its implementation of consumer regulations and other consumer related matters.

Another statutory body, the Federal Advisory Council, consists of 12 members (one from each district); it meets in Washington four times a year to advise the Board of Governors on general business and financial conditions.

Following the passage of the Monetary Control Act of 1980, the Board of Governors established the Thrift Institutions Advisory Council to provide information and views on the special needs and problems of thrift institutions. The group is comprised of representatives of mutual savings banks, savings and loan associations, and credit unions.

Banks which participate in the federal deposit insurance fund have their deposits insured against loss up to $100,000 for each depositor. The fund is administered by the Federal Deposit Insurance Corporation established in 1933; it obtains resources through annual assessments on participating banks.

All members of the Federal Reserve System are required to insure their deposits through the Corporation, and non-member banks may apply and qualify for insurance. There are also 37 co-operative Farm Credit Banks, supervised by the Farm Credit Administration, that make agricultural and rural housing loans as well as loans to farmer co-operatives and to businesses providing on-farm services. In this system, farm mortgage loans are originated by local federal land bank associations, while farm production loans are made by local production credit associations. Moreover, the Federal Home Loan Bank System, which includes 12 district banks, is one of several government-sponsored agencies established for the public purpose of assisting home ownership. The Federal Home Loan Banks borrow in the financial markets and lend these funds to savings and loan associations and savings banks, which hold most of their assets in home mortgages. The Federal Home Loan Bank System is privately owned and does not receive any direct federal funding, although it seems to carry an implicit promise of financial support from the federal government because of its public purpose.

Board of Governors of the Federal Reserve System. *The Federal Reserve System: Purposes and Functions.* 7th ed., 1984.—*Federal Reserve Bulletin.* Monthly.—*Annual Report.*—*Annual Statistical Digest.*—*The Federal Reserve Act, As Amended Through 1984*

Meek, P., *U.S. Monetary Policy and Financial Markets.* New York, 1982

Timberlake, R. H., *The Origins of Central Banking in the United States.* Cambridge, Massachusetts, 1978

Weights and Measures. The metric system is to be introduced in the early 1990s. British weights and measures are usually employed, but the old Winchester bushel and wine gallon are used instead of the new or Imperial standards: *Wine gallon* = 0·83268 Imperial gallon; *Bushel* = 0·9690 Imperial bushel. Instead of the British cwt of 112 lb., one of 100 lb. is used; the *short* or *net ton* contains 2,000 lb.; the *long* or *gross ton*, 2,240 lb.

ENERGY AND NATURAL RESOURCES

Electricity. Production (public utilities only, 1985) 2,679,857,000m. kwh.

Minerals. Total value of non-fuel minerals produced in US (including Alaska and Hawaii) in 1984 was estimated at $23,150m. ($21,100m. in 1983). Details are given in the following tables.

Production of metallic minerals (long tons, 2,240 lb.; short tons, 2,000 lb.):

Metallic minerals	1986 Quantity	1986 Value ($1,000)	1987 Quantity	1987 Value ($1,000)
Bauxite (dried equiv.) tonnes	856	15,643	674	12,855
Copper (recoverable content), tonnes	510	10,361	576	10,871
Gold (recoverable content), troy oz.	1,147,277	1,670,660	1,255,914	2,284,156
Lead (recoverable content), tonnes	339,793	165,150	311,298	246,654
Molybdenum (content of concentrate), 1,000 lb.	93,976	234,940	75,117	194,553
Silver (recoverable content), 1,000 troy oz.	34,524	188,846	39,790	278,930
Zinc (recoverable content), tonnes	202,983	170,050	216,981	200,529
Other metals	—	1,562,607	—	—

The US is wholly or almost wholly dependent upon imports for industrial diamonds, bauxite, tin, chromite, nickel, strategic-grade mica and long-fibre asbestos; it imports the bulk of its tantalum, platinum, manganese, mercury, tungsten, cobalt and flake graphite, and substantial quantities of antimony, cadmium, arsenic, fluorspar, zinc and bismuth.

In 1987 precious metals were mined mainly in Nevada, Idaho, Montana, Utah and Arizona (in order of combined output of gold and silver).

Statistics of important non-metallic minerals and mineral fuels are:

Non-metallic minerals	1986 Quantity	1986 Value ($1,000)	1987 Quantity	1987 Value ($1,000)
Boron minerals, short tons	1,251,000	426,086	1,385,000	475,092
Cement:				
Portland, 1,000 short tons	75,217	3,755,161	74,868	3,646,561
Masonry, 1,000 short tons	3,569	231,551	3,680	259,926
Clays, 1,000 short tons	44,620	1,095,179	47,805	1,202,602
Gypsum, 1,000 short tons	15,789	102,047	15,612	106,977
Lime, 1,000 short tons	14,474	757,867	15,758	789,683
Phosphate rock, 1,000 tonnes	38,710	877,600	40,954	793,280
Potassium salts, 1,000 tonnes (K_2O equivalent)	1,147	152,000	—	—
Salt (common), 1,000 short tons	36,663	665,400	36,493	684,170
Sand and gravel, 1,000 short tons	910,420	3,106,760	896,200	3,002,500
Stone, 1,000 short tons	1,007,000	4,085,000	1,200,100	5,248,600
Sulphur (Frasch-process), 1,000 tonnes	4,108	508,512	3,610	386,834
Other non-metallic minerals	—	48,139	—	42,234
Total non-metallic minerals	—	15,611,302	—	16,812,659

Mineral fuels	1986		1987	
Coal: Bitum. and lignite, 1,000 short tons	886,000	21,000,000	915,200	21,050,000
Pennsylv. anthracite,[1] 1,000 short tons	4,300	190,000	3,000	160,000
Gas: Natural gas,[2] 1m. cu. ft	15,990,000	32,570,000	16,540,000	28,970,000
Petroleum (crude), 1,000 bbls of 42 gallons	3,168,252	39,630,000	3,047,378	46,930,000

[1] Includes a small quantity of anthracite mined in states other than Pennsylvania.
[2] Value at wells.

Minerals Yearbook. Bureau of Mines. Washington, D.C. Annual from 1932–33; continuing the *Mineral Resources of the United States* series (1866–1931); from 1977 in 3 vols. *(Metals and Minerals; Area Reports, Domestic; and Area Reports, International)*

Agriculture. Agriculture in the USA is characterized by its ability to adapt to widely varying conditions, and still produce an abundance and variety of agricultural products. From colonial times to about 1920 the major increases in farm production were brought about by adding to the number of farms and the amount of land under cultivation. During this period nearly 320m. acres of virgin forest were converted to crop land or pasture, and extensive areas of grass lands were ploughed. Improvident use of soil and water resources was evident in many areas.

During the next 20 years the number of farms reached a plateau of about 6·5m., and the acreage planted to crops held relatively stable around 330m. acres. The major source of increase in farm output arose from the substitution of power-driven machines for horses and mules. Greater emphasis was placed on development and improvement of land, and the need for conservation of basic agricultural resources was recognized. A successful conservation programme, highly co-ordinated and on a national scale—to prevent further erosion, to restore the native fertility of damaged land and to adjust land uses to production capabilities and needs—has been in operation since early in the 1930s.

Following the Second World War the uptrend in farm output has been greatly accelerated by increased production per acre and per farm animal. These increases are associated with a higher degree of mechanization; greater use of lime and fertilizer; improved varieties, including hybrid maize and grain sorghums; more effective control of insects and disease; improved strains of livestock and poultry; and wider use of good husbandry practices, such as nutritionally balanced feeds, use of superior sites and better housing. During this period land included in farms decreased slowly, crop land harvested declined somewhat more rapidly, but the number of farms declined sharply.

Some significant changes during these transitions are:

All land in farms totalled less than 500m. acres in 1870, rose to a peak of over 1,200m. acres in the 1950s and declined to 1,002m. acres in 1987, even with the addition of the new States of Alaska and Hawaii in 1960. The number of farms declined from 6·35m. in 1940 to 2,173m. in 1987, as the average size of farms doubled. The average size of farms in 1988 was 453 acres, but ranged from a few acres to many thousand acres. In 1982, 636,827 farms (690,329 in 1978) were less than 50 acres; 711,499 (814,689), 50–179 acres; 729,865 (811,468), 180–999 acres; and 161,159 (162,156) 1,000 acres or more.

Farms operated by owners or part-owners, 1982, were 1,981,780 (88% of all farms), by all tenants, 257,520 (12%). The average size of farms in 1982 was 227 acres for full-owners, 794 acres for part-owners and 428 acres for tenants.

In 1988 (with 1970 figures in parentheses) large-scale, highly mechanized farms with sales of agricultural products totalling $20,000 and over per farm made up 40·7% (17·6%) of all farms and accounted for 79·9% of all farmland. Farms selling between $19,999 and $5,000 worth of products per farm were 25·2% (24·9%) of all farms and accounted for 15·7% of farmland. Operators in every sales category received off-farm income, but operators selling less than $20,000 per year received more of their average income from non-farm sources than from farming in 1986. In 1988 the average net farm income for farms with sales of $500,000 and over was $714,414; for farms with sales between $100,000–$499,999, $70,825; for farms with sales between $40,000–$99,999, $17,420; and for farms with sales of less than $40,000, $1,290. The average net farm income in 1986 for all farms was $18,426. In 1988, farms with sales of less than $40,000 accounted for 42·3% of total farm cash income in the US. Farms with sales of $40,000–$99,999 contributed 12·2% of total cash income; farms with sales of $100,000–$499,999, 29·3%; farms with sales of $500,000 and over, 21·5%.

A century ago three-quarters of the total US population was rural, and practically all rural people lived on farms. In April 1987 27% of the population was rural. Farm residents accounted for 2% of the total population.

During the week of July 10–16, 1988, there were 3·52m. people working on farms and ranches. The workforce comprised 1·43m. self-employed farm operators, 591,000 unpaid workers, 1·20m. workers hired directly by farm operators and 303,000 Agricultural Service employees.

Cash receipts from farm marketings and government payments (in $1m.):

	Crops	*Livestock and livestock products*	*Government payments*	*Total*
1932	1,996	2,752	—	4,748
1945	9,655	12,008	742	22,405
1950	12,356	16,105	283	28,744
1960	15,259	18,989	702	34,950
1970	20,976	29,563	3,717	54,256
1980	71,746	67,991	1,286	141,022
1987	63,751	75,717	16,747	156,215
1988	72,569	78,862	14,480	165,911

Realized gross farm income (including government payments), in $1m., was 174,891 in 1984, 166,364 in 1985, 160,422 in 1986, 171,625 in 1987 and 177,626 in 1988; net farm income amounted to 45,664 in 1988. Farm real estate debt, excluding debt in operator dwellings, was $103,585m. in 1984, $97,591m. in 1985, $88,561m. in 1986, $81,063m. in 1987 and $76,697m. in 1988.

US agricultural exports, fiscal year, totalled: 1978–79, $31,979m.; 1979–80, $40,481m.; 1980–81, $43,780m.; 1981–82, $39,095m.; 1982–83, $34,769m.; 1983–84, $38,027m.; 1984–85, $31,201m.; 1985–86, $26,324m.

Total area of farm land under irrigation in 1984 was 44,731,000 acres.

According to census returns and estimates of the Economic Research Service, the acreage and specified values of farms has been as follows (area in 1,000 acres; value in $1,000; cash receipts in $1m.):

	Farm area	*Crop land available for crops*	*Value, land, bldgs,*[2] *machinery, livestock*	*Cash receipts*
1910	878,798	432,000	41,089,000	...
1930	990,112 [1]	480,000	57,815,000	...
1940	1,065,114 [1]	467,000	41,829,000	...
1950	1,161,420 [1]	478,000	104,800,000	28,461
1959	1,123,508 [1]	458,100	155,700,000	33,647
1969	1,062,893 [1]	472,100	241,200,000	48,179
1978	1,014,777 [1]	471,000	728,700,000	112,360
1982	986,797 [1]	489,000	903,800,000	142,595
1988	...	...	686,400,000	150,431

[1] Includes Alaska and Hawaii.
[2] Real estate, livestock and machinery, excluding crops.

The areas and production of the principal crops for 3 years were:

	1985			*1986*			*1987*		
	Harvested 1,000 acres	*Production 1,000*	*Yield per acre*	*Harvested 1,000 acres*	*Production 1,000*	*Yield per acre*	*Harvested 1,000 acres*	*Production 1,000*	*Yield per acre*
Corn for grain (bu.)	75,224	8,876,706	118·0	69,159	8,249,864	119·3	59,208	7,072,073	119·4
Oats (bu.)	8,177	520,800	63·7	6,860	386,356	56·3	6,925	374,000	54·0
Barley (bu.)	11,603	591,383	51·0	12,007	610,522	50·8	10,057	529,530	52·7
All wheat (bu.)	64,734	2,425,105	37·5	60,723	2,081,635	34·4	55,960	2,107,480	37·7
Rice (cwt.) [1]	2,492	134,913	5,414	2,360	133,356	5,651	2,333	129,603	5,555
Soybeans for beans (bu.)	61,584	2,098,531	34·1	58,292	1,940,101	33·3	56,977	1,922,762	33·7
Flaxseed (bu.)	584	8,293	14·2	683	11,538	16·9	463	7,444	16·1
All Cotton [1] (bales)	10,229	13,432·2	630	8,468	9,731·1	552	10,035	14,759·9	706
Potatoes (cwt.)	1,361	407,109	299	1,220	361,511	296	1,279	385,462	301
Tobacco (lb.)	688	1,511,638	2,197	582	1,163,940	2,001	587	1,190,674	2,028

[1] Yield in lb.

Corn (Maize). The chief corn-growing states (1987) were (estimated production, corn for grain in 1,000 bu.): Iowa, 1,306,500; Illinois, 1,201,200; Nebraska, 812,200; Minnesota, 635,000; Indiana, 631,800; Ohio, 362,400; Wisconsin, 330,400; Missouri, 242,950; South Dakota, 228,250.

Wheat. The chief wheat-growing states (1987) were (estimated production in 1,000 bu.): Kansas, 366,300; N. Dakota, 269,120; Oklahoma, 129,600; Montana, 151,220; Texas, 100,800; Washington, 114,285; S. Dakota, 106,704; Minnesota, 102,588; Colorado, 97,380; Idaho, 85,500; Nebraska, 85,800.

Cotton. Leading production, 1987, by state (in 1,000 bales, 480 lb. net weight) was: Texas, 4,686; California, 2,991; Mississippi, 1,745; Arizona, 1,062; Louisiana, 977; Arkansas, 901; Tennessee, 634; Alabama, 397; Oklahoma, 346.

Tobacco. Production (1,000 lb.) of the chief tobacco-growing states was, in 1987: N. Carolina, 466,592; Kentucky, 304,845; Tennessee, 87,291; S. Carolina, 94,080; Virginia, 76,900; Georgia, 72,160.

Fruit. Production, in 1,000 tonnes:

	1985	*1986*	*1987*	*1988*
Apples	3,918	3,954	5,226	4,554
Citrus Fruit	10,525	11,051	11,968	12,641
Grapes	5,607	5,225	5,250	5,984

Dairy produce. In 1987, production of milk was 142,462m. lb.; cheese solid, 5,344m. lb.; butter, 1,104m. lb.; ice-cream, 931m. gallons; non-fat dry milk for human consumption, 1,059m. lb.; cottage cheese, 1,519m. lb.

Livestock (31 Dec. 1988): Cattle and calves, 99,484,000; sheep and lambs, 10,745,000; hogs and pigs (1 Dec. 1988), 55·3m.

On 31 Dec. 1988 there were 355,489,000 chickens, excluding broilers. In 1987 240·3m. turkeys were raised; 5,002·9m. broilers were produced, 1 Dec. 1986–30 Nov. 1987. Eggs produced, same period, 69,492m. (value $3,177m.).

Value of production (in $1m.) was:

	1986	*1987*
Cattle and calves	20,935·3	24,629·3
Sheep	443·9	498·9
Hogs and pigs	9,555·8	10,426·8

Total value of livestock, excluding poultry and goats and, from 1961, horses and mules (in $1m.) on farms in the USA on 1 Jan. was: 1930, 6,061; 1933 (low point of the agricultural depression), 2,733; 1970, 22,886; 1980, 60,598; 1985, 45,594; 1988, 64,945.

In 1987 the production of shorn wool was 85·8m. lb. from 11m. sheep (average 1970–74, 320m. lb. from 18·2m. sheep); of pulled wool, 1·15m. lb. (1970–74, 10·1m. lb.).

Forestry. In 1977 the US forest lands, including Alaska and Hawaii, capable of producing timber for commercial use, covered 482,485,900 acres (more than one-fifth of the land area), classified as follows: Saw-timber stands, 215,435,700 acres; pole timber stands, 135,609,900 acres, seedling and sapling stands, 115,032,100 acres; non-stocked and other areas, 16,408,200 acres. Ownership of commercial forest land is distributed as follows: Federal government, 99,410,400 acres; state, county, municipal and Indian, 36,311,200 acres; privately owned, 346,764,300 acres, including 115,777,100 acres on farms. Of the saw-timber stand (2,578,940m. bd ft) Douglas fir constitutes 514,317; Southern pine, 321,563; Western yellow (ponderosa and jeffrey) pine, 192,070; other softwoods, 957,458; hardwoods, 255,189. In 1976 growing stock timber removals amounted to 14,229,023,000 cu. ft compared to net annual growth of about 21,664,316,000 cu. ft. Saw-timber removals amounted to 65,176,618,000 bd ft against an annual growth of 74,620,832,000 bd ft. The net area of the 156 national forests and other areas in USA and Puerto Rico administered by the US Department of Agriculture's Forest Service, including commercial and non-commercial forest land, was in Oct. 1986, 191m. acres.

Fire takes a heavy annual toll in the forest; total area burned over in 1986 was 3,191,125 acres; 1,500m. acres of land are now under organized fire-protection service. Federal land that was planted or seeded in forest and wind barrier nursery stock in the year ending 30 Sept. 1986 was 300,640 acres.

Land Areas of National Forest System. Forest Service, US Dept. of Agriculture, 1985
Report of the Forest Service, 1985

Fisheries. Total US catch (edible and industrial), 1988, 3·3m. tonnes valued at $3,520m.; harvest outside the US and joint venture operations (mostly Alaskan pollock, and tuna), 1·7m. tonnes valued at $490m.; foreign catch in the 200 mile wide US fishery zone (mostly Alaskan pollock, 73%; Pacific flounders, 13% and Pacific cod, 6%), 1·2m. tonnes.

Major species caught, 1988: Menhaden, 2,086m. lb, value $105·7m. (29% of total US catch); Alaskan pollock, 1,257m. lb, $95·3m.; salmon, 606·1m. lb, $910·7m.; crabs, 4,566m. lb, $383·6m.; shrimp, 330·9m. lb, $506m.; cod, 343·2m. lb, $81·4m. Major landing areas, 1988: By value (in $1m.): Alaska, 1,339; Louisiana, 317·3; Massachusetts, 274; California, 199·3; Texas, 175·7.

Exports, 1988, totalled $2,275m.; imports, $8,872m. *Per capita* consumption, 1988, 15 lb edible meat; estimated live weight equivalent about 45 lb *per capita*.

Tennessee Valley Authority. Established by Act of Congress, 1933, the TVA is a multiple-purpose federal agency which carries out its duties in an area embracing some 41,000 sq. miles, in 201 counties (aggregate population, about 4·7m.) in the 7 Tennessee River Valley states: Tennessee, Kentucky, Mississippi, Alabama, North Carolina, Georgia and Virginia. In addition, 76 counties outside the Valley are served by TVA power distributors. Its 3 directors are appointed by the President, with the consent of the Senate; headquarters are in Knoxville, Tenn. There were 25,844 employees in Aug. 1989.

In the 1930s and 1940s, the Tennessee Valley offered the world a model of the first effort to develop all resources of a major river valley under one comprehensive programme, the Tennessee Valley Authority. The multipurpose development of the Tennessee River for flood control, navigation, and electric power production was the first big task for TVA. But there were other needs; controlling erosion on the land, introducing better fertilizers and new farming practices, eradicating malaria, demonstrating ways electricity could lighten the burdens in the home and increase production on the farm, and a multitude of potential job-producing enterprises.

In the depression year, 1933, the *per capita* income in the Valley was $168, compared with the national average of $375. Through the years, TVA has placed a strong emphasis on the economic development of the Valley. In recent years average income levels in the region have been nearly 80% of the national level.

TVA supplies electric power to 160 local distribution systems serving 3m. customers. The power system originated with the water-power development of the Tennessee River, but has become predominantly a coal-fired system as power requirements have outgrown the region's hydro-electric potential. In fiscal year 1988, the TVA system generated 95,000m. kwh. Installed capacity in 1988 was 32·1m. kw, with another 5·2m. kw under construction at TVA's nuclear plants.

Power operations are financially self-supporting from revenues. In fiscal year 1986 power revenues were $4,639m. Power facilities are financed from revenues and the sale of revenue bonds and notes, and TVA is repaying appropriations previously invested in power facilities. Other TVA resource development programmes continue to be financed from congressional appropriations.

Annual Report of the TVA. Knoxville, 1934 to date

Clapp, G.R., *The TVA; An Approach to the Development of a Region*. Univ. of Chicago Press, 1955

Lilienthal, D. E., *TVA; Democracy on the March*. 20th Anniversary ed. New York and London, 1953

Tennessee Valley Authority. *A History of the Tennessee Valley Authority*. Knoxville, Tennessee, 1982

INDUSTRY AND TRADE

Industry. The following table presents industry statistics of manufactures as reported at various censuses from 1909 to 1982 and from the Annual Survey of Manufactures for years in which no census was taken. The figures for 1958 to 1982 include data for some establishments previously classified as non-manufacturing. The figures for 1939, but not for earlier years, have been revised to exclude data for establishments classified as non-manufacturing in 1954. The figures for 1909–33 were previously revised by the deduction of data for industries excluded from manufacturing during that period.

The statistics for 1958, 1963, 1967, 1972, 1977 and 1982 relate to all establishments employing 1 or more persons anytime during the year; for 1950, 1956–57, 1959–62, 1966 and 1968–74 on a representative sample of manufacturing establishments of 1 or more employees; for 1929 through 1939, those reporting products valued at $5,000 or more; and for 1909 and 1919, those reporting products valued at $500 or more. These differences in the minimum size of establishments included in the census affect only very slightly the year-to-year comparability of the figures.

The annual Surveys of Manufactures carry forward the key measures of manufacturing activity which are covered in detail by the Census of Manufactures. The estimate for 1950 is based on reports for approximately 45,000 plants out of a total of more than 260,000 operating manufacturing establishments; those for 1956–57 on about 50,000, and those for 1959–62, 1966 and 1968–74 on about 60,000 out of about 300,000. Included are all large plants and representative samples of the much more numerous small plants. The large plants in the surveys account for approximately two-thirds of the total employment in operating manufacturing establishments in the US.

	Number of establishments	*Production workers (average for year)*	*Production workers' wages total ($1,000)*	*Value added by manufacture ($1,000)*
1909	264,810	6,261,736	3,205,213	8,160,075
1919	270,231	8,464,916	9,664,009	23,841,624
1929	206,663	8,369,705	10,884,919	30,591,435
1933	139,325	5,787,611	4,940,146	14,007,540
1939	173,802	7,808,205	8,997,515	24,487,304
1950	260,000	11,778,803	34,600,025	89,749,765
1960	...	12,209,514	55,555,452	163,998,531
1963	306,317	12,232,041	62,093,601	192,082,900
1967	305,680	13,955,300	81,393,600	261,983,800
1969	...	14,357,800	93,459,600	304,440,700
1970	...	13,528,000	91,609,000	300,227,600
1972	312,662	13,526,500	105,494,700	353,974,200
1973	...	14,233,100	118,332,300	405,623,500
1974	...	13,970,900	124,983,200	452,468,400
1975	...	12,567,900	121,427,200	442,485,800
1977	350,757	13,691,000	157,163,700	585,165,600
1978	...	14,228,700	176,416,800	657,412,000
1979	...	14,537,800	192,881,500	747,480,500
1980	...	13,900,100	198,164,000	773,831,300
1982	348,385	12,400,600	204,787,200	824,117,700
1984	...	12,572,800	231,783,900	983,227,700
1985	...	12,171,100	235,731,700	999,065,800
1986	...	11,800,000	237,000,000	1,035,000,000

For comparison of broad types of manufacturing, the industries covered by the Census of Manufactures have been divided into 20 general groups according to the *Standard Industrial Classification.*

Code No.	*Industry group*	*Year*	*Production workers (average for year)*	*Production workers' wages, total ($1,000)*	*Value added by manufacture*[1] *($1,000)*
20.	Food and kindred products	1984	1,009,500	17,061,400	98,037,400
		1985	993,600	17,427,700	104,140,000
		1986	990,000	17,789,000	112,191,000
21.	Tobacco products	1984	38,600	933,200	10,786,600
		1985	36,900	440,900	11,893,700
		1986	34,000	912,000	12,725,000
22.	Textile mill products	1984	610,500	7,852,300	22,110,400
		1985	565,300	7,609,200	20,193,300
		1986	555,000	7,898,000	22,232,000
23.	Apparel and other textile products	1984	977,100	9,280,300	28,858,800
		1985	904,000	9,003,000	27,728,400
		1986	863,000	8,949,000	28,451,000
24.	Lumber and wood products	1984	541,500	7,860,000	21,035,100
		1985	514,200	7,835,800	21,065,500
		1986	512,000	8,135,000	23,239,000
25.	Furniture and fixtures	1984	383,700	5,148,700	15,905,600
		1985	380,000	5,345,500	16,478,800
		1986	376,000	5,556,000	17,659,000
26.	Paper and allied products	1984	468,100	10,515,800	40,884,700
		1985	462,100	10,783,400	40,387,200
		1986	458,000	11,297,000	43,925,000

[1] Figures represent adjusted value added.

Code No.	Industry group	Year	Production workers (average for year)	Production workers' wages, total ($1,000)	Value added by manufacture[1] ($1,000)
27.	Printing and publishing	1984	733,400	12,916,200	67,021,600
		1985	742,100	13,554,400	73,054,300
		1986	738,000	14,099,000	78,150,000
28.	Chemical and allied products	1984	490,700	11,444,400	94,728,200
		1985	476,000	11,602,000	95,257,500
		1986	458,000	11,756,000	100,013,000
29.	Petroleum and coal products	1984	89,800	2,648,600	16,163,400
		1985	83,500	2,533,900	17,111,600
		1986	82,000	2,598,000	17,496,000
30.	Rubber and miscellaneous plastics products	1984	573,800	9,439,400	34,183,400
		1985	578,400	9,799,200	35,708,300
		1986	572,000	10,124,000	37,236,000
31.	Leather and leather products	1984	145,200	1,482,600	4,510,700
		1985	124,800	1,342,200	4,107,500
		1986	110,000	1,213,000	3,611,000
32.	Stone, clay and glass products	1984	416,400	8,039,000	27,706,600
		1985	403,800	8,196,200	28,841,800
		1986	399,000	8,352,000	30,677,000
33.	Primary metal industries	1984	616,000	14,915,700	42,290,900
		1985	571,000	14,277,900	38,081,900
		1986	529,000	13,472,000	38,092,000
34.	Fabricated metal products	1984	1,112,200	21,158,500	67,644,800
		1985	1,103,500	21,976,800	69,161,500
		1986	1,050,000	21,817,000	68,621,000
35.	Machinery (except electrical)	1984	1,297,600	26,749,100	112,346,300
		1985	1,236,600	26,510,500	110,234,100
		1986	1,141,000	25,422,000	108,365,000
36.	Electric and electronic equipment	1984	1,287,400	23,493,100	109,904,200
		1985	1,233,100	23,658,800	109,861,500
		1986	1,160,000	23,361,000	112,422,000
37.	Transportation equipment	1984	1,159,800	30,768,000	114,498,700
		1985	1,179,600	33,171,400	120,953,100
		1986	1,169,000	33,626,000	125,706,000
38.	Instruments and related products	1984	358,100	6,533,600	39,869,900
		1985	348,000	6,192,600	40,278,300
		1986	335,000	6,704,000	40,005,000
39.	Miscellaneous manufacturing	1984	263,400	3,544,000	14,740,400
		1985	234,600	3,415,300	14,031,600
		1986	236,000	3,520,000	14,622,000

[1] Figures represent adjusted value added.

Iron and Steel: Output of the iron and steel industries (in net tons of 2,000 lb.), according to figures supplied by the American Iron and Steel Institute, was:

	Furnaces in blast 31 Dec.	Pig-iron (including ferro-alloys)	Raw steel	Steel by method of production[1]			
				Open hearth	Bessemer	Electric[2]	Basic Oxygen
1932[3]	44	9,835,227	15,322,901	13,336,210	1,715,925	270,044	...
1939	195	35,677,097	52,798,714	48,409,800	3,358,916	1,029,067	...
1944[4]	218	62,866,198	89,641,600	80,363,953	5,039,923	4,237,699	...
1950	234	66,400,311	96,336,075	86,262,509	4,534,558	6,039,008	...
1960	114	68,566,384	99,281,601	86,367,506	1,189,196	8,378,743	3,346,156
1970	152	87,933,000	131,514,000	48,022,000	—	20,162,000	63,330,000
1980	...	70,329,000	111,835,000	13,054,000	—	31,166,000	67,617,000
1987	...	48,410,000	89,151,000	2,666,000	—	33,989,000	52,496,000
1988	...	55,745,000	99,924,000	5,118,000	—	36,846,000	57,960,000

[1] The sum of these 4 items should equal the total in the preceding column; any difference appearing is due to the very small production of crucible steel, omitted prior to 1950.
[2] Includes crucible production beginning 1950. [3] Low point of the depression.
[4] Peak year of war production.

The iron and steel industry in 1988 employed 125,289 wage-earners (compared with 449,888 in 1960), who worked an average of 41 hours per week and earned an average of $17.82 per hour: total employment costs were $6,681m. and total employment costs for 43,608 employees were $2,515m.

Annual Statistics Report. American Iron and Steel Institute

Labour. The American labour movement comprises about 90 national and international labour organizations plus a large number of small independent local or single-firm labour organizations. In 1988 total membership was approximately 17m. The American Federation of Labor (founded 1881 and taking its name in 1886) and the Congress of Industrial Organizations merged into one organization, named the AFL–CIO, in Dec. 1955, representing 14·1m. workers in 1989.

Unaffiliated or independent labour organizations, inter-state in scope, had an estimated total membership excluding all foreign members (1989) of about 3m.

Labour organizations represented 19·2% (19·1m.) of the labour force in 1988; 17% (16·9m.) were actual members of unions.

A total of 40 strikes and lockouts of 1,000 workers or more occurred in 1988, involving 118,000 workers and 4·4m. idle days; the number of idle days was 0·02% of the year's total working time of all workers.

There are 3 federal agencies which provide formal machinery for the adjustment of labour disputes: (1) The Federal Mediation and Conciliation Service, now an independent agency, whose mediation services are available 'in any labor dispute in any industry affecting commerce'; under Executive Order 11491, as amended, to federal agencies and organizations of federal employees involved in negotiation disputes; and in state and local government collective bargaining disputes when adequate dispute resolution machinery is not available to the parties. Its aim is to prevent and minimize work stoppages. (2) The National Mediation Board (1934) provides much the same facilities for the railroad and air-transport industries pursuant to the Railway Labor Act. (3) The National Railroad Adjustment Board (1934) acts as a board of final appeal for grievances arising over the interpretation of existing collective agreements under the Railway Labor Act; its decisions are binding upon both sides and enforceable by the courts.

The National Labor Relations Act, as amended by the Labor–Management Relations (Taft–Hartley) Act, 1947 (*see* THE STATESMAN'S YEAR-BOOK, 1955, p. 617), was amended by the Labor–Management Reporting and Disclosure Act, 1959, and again amended in 1974. The 1959 Act requires extensive reporting and disclosure of certain financial and administrative practices of labour organizations, employers and labour relations consultants. In addition, certain powers are vested in the Secretary of Labor to prevent abuses in the administration of trusteeships by labour organizations, to provide minimum standards and procedures for the election of union officers and to establish rules prescribing minimum standards for determining the adequacy of union procedures for the removal of officers. Other provisions impose a fiduciary responsibility upon union officers and provide for the exclusion of those convicted of certain named felonies from office for specified periods; more stringently regulate secondary boycotts and banning of 'hot' cargo agreements; put limitations upon organizational and recognition picketing and permit States to assert jurisdiction over labour disputes where the National Labor Relations Board declines to act. The Act also contains a 'Bill of Rights' for union members (enforceable directly by them) dealing with such things as equal rights in the nomination and election of union officers, freedom of speech and assembly subject to reasonable union rules, and safeguards against improper disciplinary action.

The Bureau of Labor Statistics estimated that in 1988 the labour force was 123,378,000 (66·2% of those 16 years and over); the resident armed forces accounted for 1,709,000 and the civilian labour force for 121,669,000, of whom 114,968,000 were employed and 6,701,000—or 5·5%—were unemployed. The following table shows civilian employment by industry and sex and percentage distribution of the total:

Industry Group	*Male*	*Female*	*Total*	*Percentage distribution*
Employed (1,000 persons):	63,273	51,696	114,968	100·0
Agriculture, forestry and fisheries	2,616	710	3,326	2·9
Mining	626	127	753	0·7
Construction	6,899	704	7,603	6·6
Manufacturing:				
Durable goods	9,240	3,403	12,642	11·0
Non-durable (including not specified)	5,062	3,616	8,678	7·5
Transportation, communication and other public utilities	5,856	2,209	8,064	7·0
Wholesale and retail trade	12,437	11,226	23,663	20·6
Finance, insurance and real estate	3,229	4,691	7,921	6·9
Services	14,195	22,691	36,886	32·1
Private households	163	1,000	1,163	1·0
Other services	14,032	21,691	35,723	31·1
Professional services	7,740	15,985	23,725	20·6
Public administration	3,113	2,319	5,432	4·7

A Guide to Basic Law and Procedures under the National Labor Relations Act, National Labor Relations Board, Washington, D.C., 1976

Brody, D., *Workers in Industrial America: Essays on the Twentieth-century Struggle.* New York, 1980

Commerce. The subjoined table gives the total value of the imports and exports of merchandise by yearly average or by year (in $1m.):

	Exports Total	*Exports US mdse.*[1]	*General imports*		*Exports*[2] *Total*	*Exports*[2] *US mdse.*[1]	*General imports*[2]
1946–50	11,829	11,673	6,659	1984	217,888	212,057	325,726
1951–55	15,333	15,196	10,832	1985	213,146	206,925	345,276
1956–60	19,204	19,029	13,650	1986	227,159	206,376	365,438
1961–65	24,006	24,707	17,659	1987	254,122	243,859	406,241
1970	43,224	42,590	39,952	1988	322,225	308,014	440,940

[1] Excludes re-exports. [2] Includes US Virgin Islands trade with foreign countries.

For a description of how imports and exports are valued, see *Explanation of Statistics of Report FT990, Highlights of US Export and Import Trade,* Bureau of the Census, US Department of Commerce, Washington, D.C., 1946.

The 'most favoured nation' treatment in commerce between Great Britain and US was agreed to for 4 years by the treaty of 1815, was extended for 10 years by the treaty of 1818, and indefinitely (subject to 12 months' notice) by that of 1827.

Imports and exports of gold and silver bullion and specie in calendar years (in $1,000):

	Gold Exports	*Gold Imports*	*Silver Exports*	*Silver Imports*
1932	809,528	363,315	13,850	19,650
1940	4,995	4,749,467	3,674	58,434
1944	959,228	113,836	126,915	23,373
1955	7,257	104,592	8,331	72,932
1960	1,647	335,032	25,789	57,438
1965	1,285,097	101,669	54,061	64,769
1970	36,887	227,472	53,003	58,838
1975	429,278	406,583	104,086	274,106
1980	2,787,431	2,508,520	1,326,878	1,336,009
1985	919,400	2,109,500	81,746	855,528
1987	1,034,186	1,052,941	79,123	460,235

The domestic exports of US produce, including military, and the imports for consumption by economic classes for 3 calendar years were (in $m.):

	Exports (US merchandise)			*Imports for consumption*		
	1986	*1987*	*1988*	*1986*	*1987*	*1988*
Food and live animals	17,303	19,179	26,415	20,644	20,267	19,830
Crude materials	17,324	20,416	25,135	10,347	11,295	13,137
Machinery and transport equipment	95,290	108,596	135,135	161,999	176,893	196,072
Chemicals	22,766	26,381	32,300	14,851	16,046	19,475
Total of the above main groups	152,683	174,572	218,985	207,841	224,501	248,514

Leading exports of US merchandise are listed below for the calendar year 1988: Special category merchandise is included. Data for major subdivisions of certain classes are also given:

Commodity	*$1m.*	*Commodity*	*$1m.*
Machinery, total	88,432	Chemicals	32,300
Power generating machinery	12,818	Chemical elements and compounds	12,950
Metalworking machinery	1,925	Plastic materials and resins	7,277
Agricultural machines and tractors	1,956	Soybeans	4,816
Office machinery and computers	23,128	Cotton	1,975
Telecommunications apparatus	6,544	Textiles and apparel	3,650
Electrical machinery and apparatus	21,602	Tobacco and cigarettes	3,897
Electrical power apparatus and switchgear	4,206	Iron and steel-mill products	2,017
		Non-ferrous base metals and alloys	3,041
Road motor vehicles (and parts)	25,178	Pulp, paper and products	7,,894
Aircraft and spacecraft (and parts)	20,004	Coal	3,960
		Fruits and vegetables	3,488
Grains and preparations	12,281	Petroleum and products	3,679
Wheat (and flour)	5,080	Firearms of war and ammunition	2,609

Chief imports for 27 commodity classes for consumption for the calendar year 1988:

Commodity	*$1m.*	*Commodity*	*$1m.*
Petroleum products, crude and refined	37,469	Wool and other hair	328
		Metal manufactures n.e.s.	8,979
Petroleum	25,654	Diamonds (excl. industrial)	4,306
Petroleum products	11,815	Rubber	1,023
Non-ferrous metals	10,066	Textile yarn, fabrics and products	6,302
Copper	1,860	Clothing	21,418
Aluminium	3,442	Cotton fabrics, woven	979
Nickel	1,220	Machinery, total	113,595
Lead	859	Agricultural machinery and tractors	2,124
Tin	315	Office machinery	22,586
Paper, paperboard and products	8,333	Coffee	2,287
		Chemicals and related products	19,475
Newsprint	4,462	Chemicals	10,336
Wood pulp	2,506	Oils and fats	763
Fertilizers	1,021	Cocoa beans	405
Sugar	438	Glass, pottery and china	2,934
Iron and steel-mill products	10,299	Footwear	8,022
Cattle, meat and preparations	3,327	Toys and sports goods	6,714
Automobiles and parts	74,082	Furs, undressed	154
Fish (and shellfish)	861	Telecommunications apparatus	21,087
Fruit and vegetables	4,439	Artworks and antiques	2,044
Alcoholic beverages	3,148	Natural and manufactured gas	2,578

Total trade beween the USA and the UK (British Department of Trade returns, in £1,000 sterling):

	1986	*1987*	*1988*	*1989*
Imports to UK	8,468,160	9,136,015	10,767,750	12,888,890
Exports and re-exports from UK	10,379,585	11,014,242	10,544,077	12,098,549

Imports and exports by continents, areas and selected countries for calendar years (in $1m.):

Area and country	*General imports*		*Exports incl. re-exports* [1]	
	1987	*1988*	*1987*	*1988*
Western Hemisphere	117,954	132,193	94,795	113,155
Canada	71,085	80,921	59,814	69,233
20 Latin American Republics	44,371	48,914	31,574	40,077
Central American Common Market	1,939	1,935	1,873	2,254
Costa Rica	670	775	582	696
El Salvador	284	284	390	483
Guatemala	495	433	480	591
Honduras	489	443	418	478
Nicaragua	1	1	4	6
Panama	356	266	743	633
Latin American FTA	40,519	44,912	27,356	35,346
Argentina	1,080	1,438	1,090	1,056

Area and country	*General imports* 1987	1988	*Exports incl. re-exports*[1] 1987	1988
Bolivia	111	117	140	148
Brazil	7,865	9,324	4,040	4,289
Chile	981	1,162	796	1,065
Colombia	2,232	2,167	1,412	1,758
Ecuador	1,266	1,231	621	684
Mexico	20,271	23,277	14,582	20,643
Paraguay	22	37	183	194
Peru	769	656	814	798
Uruguay	344	275	92	100
Venezuela	5,579	5,228	3,586	4,611
Dominican Republic	1,163	1,417	1,142	1,362
Haiti	395	384	459	479
Bahamas	416	411	782	741
Netherlands Antilles	521	411	507	432
Jamaica	395	444	601	758
Trinidad and Tobago	815	719	361	328
Europe				
Western Europe	95,496	100,515	69,718	87,995
OECD Countries	94,636	99,558	69,091	87,236
European Economic Community	81,188	84,991	60,575	75,926
Belgium and Luxembourg	4,171	4,518	6,189	7,405
Denmark	1,779	1,666	893	970
France	10,730	12,217	7,943	10,086
Germany (Fed. Rep.)	27,069	26,503	11,748	14,331
Greece	480	529	402	649
Ireland	1,112	1,373	1,810	2,182
Italy	11,040	11,611	5,530	6,782
Netherlands	3,964	4,587	8,217	10,095
Portugal	664	691	581	752
Spain	2,839	3,205	3,148	4,217
UK	17,341	18,042	14,114	18,404
Turkey	821	983	1,483	1,843
EFTA countries				
Austria	929	1,085	549	748
Norway	1,404	1,452	842	932
Sweden	4,758	4,995	1,894	2,705
Switzerland	4,249	4,638	3,151	4,207
Finland	999	1,206	515	763
Iceland	286	190	84	98
Yugoslavia	797	847	461	534
Poland	296	378	239	304
USSR	425	578	1,480	2,768
Asia	174,452	190,729	73,268	99,705
Near East	10,811	11,511	9,502	10,857
Bahrain	63	99	205	281
Iran	1,668	9	54	73
Iraq	495	1,488	683	1,156
Israel	2,639	2,978	3,130	3,248
Kuwait	522	464	505	690
Lebanon	33	40	97	123
Saudi Arabia	4,433	5,594	3,373	3,799
Japan	84,575	89,802	28,249	37,732
Other Asia	83,582	92,414	41,497	56,918
Bangladesh	370	369	193	258
Hong Kong	9,854	10,243	3,983	5,691
India	2,529	2,952	1,463	2,498
Indonesia	3,394	3,188	767	1,056
Korea, Republic of	16,987	20,189	8,099	11,290
Malaysia	2,921	3,711	1,897	2,139
Pakistan	405	461	733	1,093
Philippines	2,264	2,682	1,599	1,880
Singapore	6,201	7,996	4,053	5,770
Sri Lanka	417	424	77	124

[1] 'Special category' exports are included in these totals.

Area and country	General imports 1987	General imports 1988	Exports incl. re-exports [1] 1987	Exports incl. re-exports [1] 1988
Taiwan (Formosa)	24,622	24,804	7,413	12,131
Thailand	2,220	3,218	1,544	1,964
Vietnam	...	...	23	16
China	6,294	8,512	3,497	5,039
Oceania	4,136	4,824	6,526	8,242
Australia	3,007	3,531	5,495	6,981
New Zealand and W. Samoa	1,053	1,168	821	946
Africa	11,939	10,863	6,283	7,431
Algeria	1,999	1,813	426	733
Egypt	465	221	2,210	2,340
Ethiopia	74	54	136	181
Morocco	50	92	383	428
Ghana	249	202	115	117
Liberia	88	108	70	68
Nigeria	3,573	3,298	295	356
Kenya	79	64	95	92
Zaïre	308	365	104	125
South Africa, Republic of	1,346	1,530	1,281	1,690

[1] 'Special category' exports are included in these totals.

US Department of Commerce, Bureau of Census. Report FT 990, Highlights of US Export and Import Trade

Tourism. In 1988, 33,859,000 visitors travelled to the USA and spent over US$29,202,000 (excluding transportation paid to US international carriers). They came mainly from Canada (13,843,000), Mexico (7,505,000), Europe (5,772,000) and Asia/Japan (3,719,000). Expenditure by US travellers in foreign countries for 1988 was over US$32,112,000. (excluding transportation paid to foreign flag international carriers).

COMMUNICATIONS

Roads. On 31 Dec. 1988 the total US public road[1] mileage, including rural and urban roads, amounted to 3,871,143 miles, of which 3,490,533 miles were surfaced roads. The total mileage cited includes 704,151 miles of rural roads under control of the states, 2,244,155 miles of local rural roads, 184,336 miles of federal park and forest roads, and 738,501 miles of urban roads and streets. Expenditures for construction and maintenance amounted to $48,826m. in 1987.

By the end of 1988, toll roads administered by state and local toll authorities, totalled 5,020 miles (including some under construction) compared with 344 miles in 1940.

Motor vehicles registered in the calendar year 1988 were (Federal Highways Administration) 188,981,016, including 141,251,695 automobiles, 615,669 buses, 42,529,368 trucks and 4,584,284 motorcycles.

Inter-city trucks (private and for hire) averaged 661,000m. revenue net ton-miles in 1988. Of the 615,669 buses in service in 1987, 486,753 were school buses. Inter-city service operated a total of 20,097 buses and carried a total of 333m. revenue passengers in 1987.

There were 47,093 deaths in road accidents in 1988.

[1] Public road mileage excludes that mileage not open to public travel, not maintained by public authority, or not passable by standard four-wheel vehicles. This excluded mileage was reported to the US Federal Highway Administration prior to 1981.

Railways. Railway history in the USA commences in 1828, but the first railway to convey both freight and passengers in regular service (between Baltimore and Ellicott's Mills, Md., 13 miles) dates from 24 May 1830. Mileage rose to 52,922 miles in 1870; to 167,191 miles in 1890, and to a peak of 266,381 miles in 1916, falling thereafter to 261,871 in 1925; 246,739 in 1940 and 222,164 in 1969 (these include some duplication under trackage rights and some mileage operated in Canada by US companies). The ordinary gauge is 4 ft 8½ in. (about 99·6% of total mileage). The USA has about 29% of the world's railway mileage.

In addition to the independent railroad companies, railway service is provided by the National Railroad Passenger Corporation (Amtrak), which is federally assisted. Amtrak was set up on 1 May 1971 to maintain a basic network of inter-city passenger trains with government assistance, and is responsible for almost all non-commuter services with 40,000 miles of route including 1,256 km owned (555 electrified) and carried 21m. passengers in 1985. From 1 Jan. 1983, an Amtrak commuter division took over from Conrail all commuter services not acquired by State or regional agencies.

Conrail was established on 1 April 1976 to run freight services in the industrial north-east formerly operated by the bankrupt Penn Central, Reading, Lehigh Valley, Central of New Jersey, Erie Lackawanna, Lehigh & Hudson railroads, and Pennsylvania-Reading Seashore Lines which was returned to the private sector in 1985. There are in addition some 400 minor railways (short lines) which provide local freight connections. Outside the major conurbations there are almost no regular passenger services other than those provided by Amtrak.

The following table, based on the figures of the Interstate Commerce Commission, shows some railway statistics for 4 calendar years:

Classes I and II Railroads	*1960*	*1970*	*1980* [2]	*1986* [1]
Mileage owned (first main tracks)	223,779	204,621	157,078	135,782
Revenue freight originated (1m. short tons)	1,421	1,572	1,537	1,306
Freight ton-mileage (1m. ton-miles)	591,550	771,012	932,748	867,722
Passengers carried (1,000)	488,019	289,469	281,503	[3]
Passenger-miles (1m.)	31,790	10,786	6,557	[3]
Operating revenues ($1m.)	9,587	12,209	28,708	26,204
Operating expenses ($1m.)	7,135	9,806	26,761	24,896
Net railway operating income ($1m.)	1,055	506	1,364	507
Net income after fixed charges ($1m.)	855	126	2,029	1,579
Class I Railroads:				
Locomotives in service	40,949	27,086	28,240	21,045
Steam locomotives	25,640	—	—	—
Freight-train cars (excluding caboose cars)	1,721,269	1,423,921	1,101,343	713,954
Passenger-train cars	57,146	11,177	2,219	672
Average number of employees	1,220,784	566,282	458,996	275,817
Average wage per week ($1)	72.59	188.71	474.21	690.27

[1] Class I railroads only. From 1981, Class II railroads were no longer required to file annual reports.
[2] Data for National Railroad Passenger Corporation excluded.
[3] This data has been discontinued.

Aviation. In civil aviation there were, on 31 Dec. 1988, 694,016 certificated pilots (including 136,913 student pilots), 272,696 registered civil aircraft and 463,124,000 passengers.

Airports on 31 Dec. 1988: Air carrier, 642; general aviation, 16,685. Of these airports, 12,950 were conventional land-based, while 392 were seaplane bases, 3,913 were heliports and 72 stolports (STOL—Short Take-Off and Landing).

Statistics from the Department of Transportation indicate that for 1988 US flag carriers in scheduled international service had 35·4m. enplanements with 493·7m. aircraft miles (excluding all-cargo) for a total of 93,992m. revenue passenger-miles. The non-scheduled airlines had a total of 14,191m. revenue passenger-miles internationally and domestically. Domestically US scheduled airlines in 1988 had 419·2m. enplanements with a total of 3,571·3m. aircraft miles for 329,309m. revenue passenger-miles. (A revenue passenger-mile is one paying passenger carried per mile.).

Shipping. On 1 June 1989 the US merchant marine included 669 sea-going vessels of 1,000 gross tons or over, with aggregate dead-weight tonnage of 25m. This included 241 tankers of 15·8m. DWT.

On 1 June 1989 US merchant ocean-going vessels were employed as follows: Active, 378 of 17·5m. DWT, of which 151 of 6·5m. tons were foreign trade, 165 of 9·5m. tons in domestic trade and 62 of 1·5m. tons in other US agency operations. Inactive vessels totalled 7·2m. DWT; 51 of 3·5m. DWT privately owned were laid up and 240 of 3·7m. tons were Government-owned National Defense reserve fleet. Of the total vessels in the US fleet, 421 of 21m. DWT were privately owned.

US exports and imports carried on dry cargo and tanker vessels in the year 1988 totalled 718·8m. long tons, of which 30·8m. long tons or 3·9% were carried in US flag vessels.

Post and Broadcasting. Until the beginning of 1984 the telephone business was largely in the hands of the American Telephone and Telegraph Company (AT & T) and its telephone operating subsidiaries, which together were known as the Bell System. Pursuant to a government anti-trust suit, the Bell System was broken up, with the telephone operating companies being divested from AT & T to create seven regional companies for providing local service. There are also many hundreds of smaller telephone companies having no common ownership affiliation with the Bell companies, but which connect with them for universal service, countrywide and worldwide. In addition, several new entrants have begun to compete with AT & T in the long-distance telephone market. The message telegraph and telex services are in the hands of The Western Union Telegraph Company, and the international record carriers, which compete with the telephone industry in providing leased private lines. Western Union also provides an inter-city telephone service. Total exchange access lines in 1987, 126,725,000.

Postal business for the years ended 30 aept. included the following items:

	1985	*1986*	*1987*	*1988*
Number of post offices, on 30 June [1]	39,327	39,270	40,030	40,117
Postal operating revenue ($1,000)	27,736,071	30,102,691	31,528,112	35,035,753
Postal expenses ($1,000)	29,207,201	30,716,595	32,519,689	36,119,186

[1] The US Postal Service was established 1 July 1971. Financial statements prior to that date are those of the Post Office Department. Such statements for 1968–71 have been restated to be in a format and on an accounting principle basis generally consistent with 1972.

In 1987 there were 91m. households with television and (1988) 520m. radio receivers in use. In 1986 there were over 10,000 authorized radio stations and (1988) 1,342 television stations with 46 national cable networks.

Cinemas. Cinemas increased from 17,003 in 1940 to 20,239 in 1950 and decreased to 20,200 in 1984, of which 2,832 were drive-ins.

Newspapers. Of the daily newspapers being published in the USA in 1971, 339 were morning papers with a circulation of 26,116,000, and 1,425 were evening papers with a circulation of 36,115,000. The 590 Sunday papers had a total circulation of 49·7m.

JUSTICE, RELIGION, EDUCATION AND WELFARE

Justice. Legal controversies may be decided in two systems of courts: The federal courts, with jurisdiction confined to certain matters enumerated in Article III of the Constitution, and the state courts, with jurisdiction in all other proceedings. The federal courts have jurisdiction exclusive of the state courts in criminal prosecutions for the violation of federal statutes, in civil cases involving the government, in bankruptcy cases and in admiralty proceedings, and have jurisdiction concurrent with the state courts over suits between parties from different states, and certain suits involving questions of federal law.

The highest court is the Supreme Court of the US, which reviews cases from the lower federal courts and certain cases originating in state courts involving questions of federal law. It is the final arbiter of all questions involving federal statutes and the Constitution; and it has the power to invalidate any federal or state law or executive action which it finds repugnant to the Constitution. This court, consisting of 9 justices who receive salaries of $110,000 a year (the Chief Justice, $115,000), meets from Oct. until June every year and disposes of about 4,450 cases, deciding about 380 on their merits. In the remainder of cases it either summarily affirms lower court decisions or declines to review. A few suits, usually brought by state governments, originate in the Supreme Court, but issues of fact are mostly referred to a master.

The US courts of appeals number 13 (in 11 circuits composed of 3 or more states and 1 circuit for the District of Columbia and 1 Court of Appeals for the Federal Circuit); the 168 circuit judges receive salaries of $95,000 a year. Any party to a suit in a lower federal court usually has a right of appeal to one of these courts. In addition, there are direct appeals to these courts from many federal administrative agencies. In the year ending 30 June 1989, 39,734 appeals were filed in the courts of appeals.

The trial courts in the federal system are the US district courts, of which there are 89 in the 50 states, 1 in the District of Columbia and 1 each in the territories of Puerto Rico, Virgin Islands, Guam and the Northern Marianas. Each state has at least 1 US district court, and 3 states have 4 apiece. Each district court has from 1 to 27 judgeships. There are 575 US district judges ($89,500 a year), who received about 233,300 civil cases and 63,200 criminal defendants from July 1988 through June 1989.

In addition to these courts of general jurisdiction, there are special federal courts of limited jurisdiction. US Claims Court (16 judges at $89,500 a year) decides claims for money damages against the federal government in a wide variety of matters; the Court of International Trade (9 judges at $89,500) determines controversies concerning the classification and valuation of imported merchandise.

The judges of all these courts are appointed by the President with the approval of the Senate; to assure their independence, they hold office during good behaviour and cannot have their salaries reduced. This does not apply to the territorial judges, who hold their offices for a term of years or to judges of the US Claims Court. The judges may retire with full pay at the age of 70 years if they have served a period of 10 years, or at 65 if they have 15 years of service, but they are subject to call for such judicial duties as they are willing to undertake. Only 9 US judges up to 1986 have been involved in impeachment proceedings, of whom 4 district judges and 1 commerce judge were convicted and removed from office.

Of the 233,293 civil cases filed in the district courts in the year ending 30 June 1989, about 118,084 arose under various federal statutes (such as labour, social security, tax, patent, securities, antitrust and civil rights laws); 42,067 involved personal injury or property damage claims; 61,928 dealt with contracts; and 11,214 were actions concerning real property.

Of the 44,891 criminal cases filed in the district courts in the year ending 30 June 1989, 1,938 were charged with alleged infractions of the immigration laws; 233, the transport of stolen motor vehicles; about 3,474 larceny and theft; 8,958, embezzlement and fraud; and 11,855 narcotics laws.

Persons convicted of federal crimes are either fined, released on probation under the supervision of the probation officers of the federal courts, confined in prison for a period of up to 6 months and then put on probation (known as split sentencing) or confined in one of the following institutions: 3 for juvenile and youths; 7 for young adults; 7 for intermediate term adults; 7 for short-term adults; 2 for females; 1 hospital and 15 community service centres. In addition, prisoners are confined in centres operated by the National Institutes of Mental Health. In addition, prisoner drug addicts may be committed to US Public Health Service hospitals for treatment. Prisoners confined in Federal and State Prisons at 30 Dec. 1987, numbered 557,256.

The state courts have jurisdiction over all civil and criminal cases arising under state laws, but decisions of the state courts of last resort as to the validity of treaties or of laws of the US, or on other questions arising under the Constitution, are subject to review by the Supreme Court of the US. The state court systems are generally similar to the federal system, to the extent that they generally have a number of trial courts and intermediate appellate courts, and a single court of last resort. The highest court in each state is usually called the Supreme Court or Court of Appeals with a Chief Justice and Associate Justices, usually elected but sometimes appointed by the Governor with the advice and consent of the State Senate or other advisory body; they usually hold office for a term of years, but in some instances for life or during good behaviour. Their salaries range from $24,000 to $84,584 a year. The lowest tribunals are usually those of Justices of the Peace; many towns and cities have municipal and police courts, with power to commit for trial in criminal matters and to determine misdemeanours for violation of the municipal ordinances; they frequently try civil cases involving limited amounts.

The death penalty is illegal in Alaska, Hawaii, Iowa, Maine, Minnesota, Oregon, West Virginia, Wisconsin and Michigan; in North Dakota it is legal only for treason and first-degree murder committed by a prisoner serving a life sentence for first-degree murder, in Rhode Island only for murder committed by a prisoner serving a life sentence and in Vermont and New York for the murder of a peace officer in the line of duty and for first-degree murder by those who kill while serving a life sentence for murder. The death penalty is legal in 37 states. Until 1982 it had fallen into disuse and had been abolished *de facto* in many states. The US Supreme Court had held the death penalty, as applied in general criminal statutes, to contravene the eighth and fourteenth amendments of the US constitution, as a cruel and unusual punishment when used so irregularly and rarely as to destroy its deterrent value.

There were no executions 1968–76. In 1977 a convicted murderer requested that he should be executed and after a lengthy legal dispute the sentence was carried out at Utah state prison. Ninety-three persons were executed between 1977 and 1987. On 31 Dec. 1987, 1,984 prisoners were reported under sentence of death.

The total number of civilian executions carried out in the US from 1930 to 1987 was 3,909. (3,384 for murder, 455 for rape and 70 for other offences).

Federal 'Political' Crimes. Prosecutions for what may be loosely described as 'political' offences, or crimes directed towards the overthrow by violence of the federal government, which were somewhat numerous in the early 1950s, have declined sharply over the last 20 years and are now exceedingly rare.

A Guide to Court Systems. Institute of Judicial Administration. New York, 1960
The United States Courts. Administrative Office of the US Courts, Washington, D.C., 20544
Blumberg, A. S., *Criminal Justice: Issues and Ironies.* 2nd ed. New York, 1973
Huston, L. A. and others, *Roles of the Attorney General of the United States.* New York, 1968
McCloskey, R. G., *The Modern Supreme Court.* Harvard Univ. Press, 1972
McLauchlan, W. P., *American Legal Processes.* New York, 1977
Walker, S. E., *Popular Justice.* New York, 1980

Religion. *The Yearbook of American and Canadian Churches for 1989,* published by the National Council of the Churches of Christ in the USA, New York, presents the latest figures available from official statisticians of church bodies. The large majority of reports are for the calendar year 1987, or a fiscal year ending 1987. The 1987 reports indicated that there were 143,830,806 (142,799,662 in 1986) members with 349,381 local churches. There were 333,097 clergymen serving in local congregations in 1987. The principal religious bodies (numerically or historically) or groups of religious bodies are shown below:

Denominations	*Local churches*	*Total membership*
Summary:		
Protestant bodies	319,073	79,296,394
Roman Catholic Church	23,552	53,496,862
Jews [1]	3,416	5,943,700
Eastern Churches	1,682	3,972,778
Old Catholic, Polish National Catholic and Armenian	428	829,0077
Buddhists	100	100,000
Miscellaneous [2]	1,130	192,065
1987 totals	349,381	143,830,806 [3]

[1] Includes Orthodox, Conservative and Reformed bodies.
[2] Includes non-Christian bodies such as Spiritualists, Ethical Culture, Unitarian-Universalists.
[3] Care should be taken in interpreting membership statistics for the US Churches. Some statistics are accurately compiled and others are estimates. Also statistics are not always comparable.

Protestant Church Membership	*Total membership*
Baptist bodies	
Southern Baptist Convention	14,722,617
National Baptist Convention, USA	5,500,000
National Baptist Convention of America, Inc.	2,668,799
National Primitive Baptist Convention	250,000
American Baptist Churches in the USA	1,568,778

Protestant Church Membership	*Total membership*
Baptist bodies—contd.	
American Baptist Association	250,000
Conservative Baptist Association of America	225,000
Regular Baptist Churches	300,839
Free Will Baptists	200,387
Baptist Missionary Association of America	227,638
Christian Church (Disciples of Christ)	1,086,668
Christian Churches and Churches of Christ	1,071,995
Church of the Nazarene	543,762
Churches of Christ	1,623,754
The Episcopal Church	2,462,300
Latter-Day Saints:	
Church of Jesus Christ of Latter-Day Saints	4,000,000
Reorganized Church of Jesus Christ of Latter-Day Saints	191,618
Lutheran Bodies :	
Evangelical Lutheran Church in America	5,288,230
The Lutheran Church-Missouri Synod	2,614,375
Wisconsin Evangelical Lutheran Synod	418,791
Methodist Bodies:	
United Methodist Church	9,124,575
African Methodist Episcopal Church	2,210,000
African Methodist Episcopal Zion Church	1,220,260
Christian Methodist Episcopal Church	718,922
Pentecostal Bodies:	
The Church of God in Christ	3,709,661
Assemblies of God	2,160,667
Church of God (Cleveland, Tenn.)	505,775
United Pentecostal Church, International, Inc.	500,000
Presbyterian Bodies:	
Presbyterian Church (USA)	2,967,781
Others	426,285
Reformed Churches:	
Reformed Church in America	338,348
Christian Reformed Church	225,951
The Salvation Army	434,002
Seventh-day Adventist Church	675,702
United Church of Christ	1,662,568

Yearbook of American and Canadian Churches. Annual, from 1951. New York
Greeley, A., *Religious Change in America.* Harvard Univ. Press, 1989

Education. Under the system of government in the USA, elementary and secondary education is committed in the main to the several states. Each of the 50 states and the District of Columbia has a system of free public schools, established by law, with courses covering 12 years plus kindergarten. There are 3 structural patterns in common use; the K8-4 plan, meaning kindergarten plus 8 elementary grades followed by 4 high school grades; the K6–3–3 plan, or kindergarten plus 6 elementary grades followed by a 3-year junior high school and a 3-year senior high school; and the K6–6 plan, kindergarten plus 6 elementary grades followed by a 6-year high school. All plans lead to high-school graduation, usually at age 17 or 18. Vocational education is an integral part of secondary education. In addition, some states have, as part of the free public school system, 2-year colleges in which education is provided at a nominal cost. Each state has delegated a large degree of control of the educational programme to local school districts (numbering 15,577 in school year 1987–88), each with a board of education (usually 3 to 9 members) selected locally and serving mostly without pay. The school policies of the local school districts must be in accord with the laws and the regulations of their state Departments of Education. While regulations differ from one jurisdiction to another, in general it may be said that school attendance is compulsory from age 7 to 16.

The Census Bureau estimates that in Nov. 1979 only 1m. or 0·6% of the 170m. persons who were 14 years of age or older were unable to read and write; in 1930 the percentage was 4·8. In 1940 a new category was established—the 'functionally illiterate', meaning those who had completed fewer than 5 years of elementary schooling; for persons 25 years of age or over this percentage was 2·4 in March

1988 (for the non-white population alone it was 5·1%); it was 1% for white and 1·2% for non-whites in the 25–29-year-old group. The Bureau reported that in March 1988 the median years of school completed by all persons 25 years old and over was 12·7, and that 20·3% had completed 4 or more years of college. For the 25–29-year-old group, the median school years completed was 12·8 and 22·7% had completed 4 or more years of college.

In the autumn of 1987, 12,768,000 students (5,932,000 men and 6,836,000 women) were enrolled in 3,587 colleges and universities; 2,246,000 were first-time students. About 28% of the population between the ages of 18 and 24 were enrolled in colleges and universities.

Public elementary and secondary school revenue is supplied from the county and other local sources (43·8% in 1986–87), state sources (49·8%) and federal sources (6·4%). In 1987–88 expenditure for public elementary and secondary education totalled about $172,000m., including $158,400m. for current operating expenses, $10,700m. for capital outlay and $2,900m. for interest on school debt. The current expenditure per pupil in average daily attendance was about $4,230. The total cost per pupil, also including capital outlay and interest, amounted to about $4,650. Estimated total expenditures, for private elementary and secondary schools in 1987–88 were about $15,100m. In 1987–88 college and university spending totalled about $123,700m., of which about $80,600m. was spent by institutions under public control. The federal government contributed about 13% of total current-fund revenue; state governments, 30%; student tuition and fees, 23%; and all other sources, 34%.

Vocational education below college grade, including the training of teachers to conduct such education, has been federally aided since 1918. Federal support for vocational education in 1986–87 amounted to about $882m. Many public high schools offer vocational courses in addition to their usual academic programmes. In 1981–82 enrolments in the vocational classes were: Agriculture, 420,000; business, 5,874,000; home economics, 3,024,000; industrial arts, 2,980,000; trade and industry, 1,874,000.

Summary of statistics of regular schools (public and private), teachers and pupils in autumn 1987 (compiled by the US National Center for Education Statistics):

Schools by level	*Number of schools 1987–88*	*Teachers autumn 1987*	*Enrolment autumn 1987*
Elementary schools:			
Public	61,490	1,297,000	24,315,000
Private	20,252 [1]	254,000 [2]	4,118,000 [2]
Secondary schools:			
Public	22,937	982,000	15,709,000
Private	7,387 [1]	94,000 [2]	1,229,000 [2]
Higher education:			
Public	1,591	523,000 [2]	9,975,000
Private	1,996	213,000 [2]	2,793,000
Total	115,653	3,363,000	58,139,000

[1] Data for 1985–86. [2] Estimated.

Most of the private elementary and secondary schools are affiliated with religious denominations. Of the children attending private elementary and secondary schools in 1985, nearly 3·1m. or 55·4% were enrolled in Roman Catholic schools. About 1·6m. or 28·7% were in schools affiliated with other religious groups.

During the school year 1987–88 high-school graduates numbered about 2,793,000 (about 49·3% boys and 50·7% girls). Institutions of higher education conferred 991,339 bachelor's degrees during the year 1986–87, 480,854 to men and 510,485 to women; 289,557 master's degrees, 141,363 to men and 148,194 to women; 34,120 doctorates, 22,099 to men and 12,021 to women; and 72,750 first professional degrees, 47,460 to men and 25,290 to women.

During the academic year, 1987–88, 356,190 foreign students were enrolled in American colleges and universities. The percentages of students coming from various areas in 1987–88 were: South and East Asia, 50·7; Middle East, 12·2; Latin America, 12·5; Africa, 8; Europe, 10·9; North America, 4·6; Oceania, 1.

School enrolment, Oct. 1987, embraced 95% of the children who were 5 and 6 years old; 99% of the children aged 7–13 years; 95% of those aged 14–17, 56% of those aged 18 and 19, 39% of those aged 20 and 21, and 18% of those aged 22–24 years.

The US National Center for Education Statistics estimates the total enrolment in the autumn of 1989 at all of the country's elementary, secondary and higher educational institutions (public and private) at 58·7m. (58·3m. in the autumn of 1988); this was 23·6% of the total population of the USA as of 1 Sept. 1989.

The number of teachers in regular public and private elementary and secondary schools in the autumn of 1989 was expected to increase slightly to 2,691,000. The average annual salary of the public school teachers was about $29,600 in 1988–89.

Digest of Education Statistics. Annual. Dept. of Education, Washington 20208, D.C. (from 1962)

American Community, Technical and Junior Colleges. 9th ed. American Council on Education. Washington, 1984

American Universities and Colleges. 12th ed. American Council on Education. Washington, 1983

Health and Welfare. Admission to the practice of medicine (for both doctors of medicine and doctors of osteopathic medicine) is controlled in each state by examining boards directly representing the profession and acting with authority conferred by state law. Although there are a number of variations, the usual time now required to complete training is 8 years beyond the secondary school with up to 3 or more years of additional graduate training. Certification as a specialist may require between 3 and 5 more years of graduate training plus experience in practice. In academic year 1987–88 the 142 US schools (15 osteopathic and 127 allopathic) graduated 17,451 physicians. About 36% of first-year students were women. In Dec. 1988 the estimated number of active physicians (MD and DO—in all forms of practice) in the US, Puerto Rico and outlying US areas was 573,583 (1 active physician to 434 population). The distribution of physicians throughout the country is uneven, both by state and by urban–rural areas.

In 1987–88 the 58 dental schools graduated 4,581 dentists. Active dentists in Dec. 1988 numbered 146,800 (1 active dentist to 1,678 population).

In academic year 1987–88, there were 1,443 registered nursing programmes in the US and 64,915 graduates. In Dec. 1988 registered nurses employed full- or part-time were 1 to 144 population.

Number of hospitals listed by the American Hospital Association in 1984 was 6,872, with 1,339,000 beds and 37,938,000 admissions during the year; average daily census was 970,000. Of the total, 341 hospitals with 112,000 beds were operated by the federal government; 1,662 with 203,000 beds by state and local government; 3,366 with 717,000 beds by non-profit organizations (including church groups); 786 with 100,000 beds are proprietary. The categories of non-federal hospitals are 5,814 short-term general and special hospitals with 1,020,000 beds; 131 non-federal long-term general and special hospitals with 30,000 beds; 579 psychiatric hospitals with 175,000 beds; 7 tuberculosis hospitals with 1,000 beds.

Social welfare legislation was chiefly the province of the various states until the adoption of the Social Security Act of 14 Aug. 1935. This as amended provides for a federal system of old-age, survivors and disability insurance; health insurance for the aged and disabled; supplemental security income for the aged, blind and disabled; federal state unemployment insurance; and federal grants to states for public assistance (medical assistance for the aged and aid to families with dependent children generally) and for maternal and child-health and child-welfare services. The Social Security Administration of the Department of Health and Human Services has responsibility for the programmes—old-age, survivors and disability insurance and supplemental security income. The Family Support Administration has federal responsibility for the programmes—aid to families with dependent children, low income energy assistance, child support enforcement, refugee and entry assistance and community services block grant. The Health Care Financing Administration, an agency of the same Department, has federal responsibility for health insurance for the aged and disabled. The Office of Human Development Services has federal responsibility for social service programmes for such groups as the elderly, children, youth, native Americans and persons with developmental disabilities, and its Public Health Service supports maternal and child-health services. Unemployment insurance is the responsibility of the Department of Labor.

The Social Security Act provides for protection against the cost of medical care through the two-part programme of health insurance for people 65 and over and for certain disabled people under 65, who receive disability insurance payments or who have permanent kidney failure (Medicare). During fiscal year 1987, payments totalling $49,967m. were made under the hospital part of Medicare on behalf of 31,852,860 people. During the same period, $29,937m. was paid under the voluntary medical insurance part of Medicare on behalf of 31,169,960 people.

In 1989 about 130m. persons worked in employment covered by old-age, survivors and disability insurance.

In June 1989 over 38·9m. beneficiaries were on the rolls, and the average benefit paid to a retired worker (not counting any paid to his dependants) was about $539 per month.

In 1987 an average of 11m. persons (adults and children) were receiving payments under aid to families with dependent children (average monthly payment, $374 per family). Total payments under aid to families with dependent children were $16,827m. for the calendar year 1988. The role of Child Support Enforcement is to ensure that children are supported by their parents. Money collected is for children who live with only one parent because of divorce, separation or out-of-wedlock birth. In 1988, nearly $4,613m. was collected on behalf of these children.

In June 1989, about 4·5m. persons were receiving supplementary security income payments, including 1·4m. persons aged 65 or over; 83,000 blind persons, and over 3m. disabled persons. Payments, including supplemental amounts from various states, totalled $13,800m. in 1988.

In 1986, federal appropriations for the social services block grant amounted to $2,700m. In addition, 1989 federal appropriations for human development and family social services to selected target groups totalled $4,117m. Included in this amount were $3,333m. for children and youth; $748m. for the elderly; $95m. for persons with developmental disabilities; and $30m. for native Americans. During 1989, the Public Health Services awarded a total of $554·3m. for maternal and child health services, $465·3m. as block grants to the States, $82·1m. for special projects of regional and national significance, and $6·9m. for genetic screening. Other block grants awarded by the Public Health Service in 1988 included $88m. for preventive health; $487m. for alcohol, drug abuse and mental health; $155m. for alcohol and drug abuse treatment and rehabilitation. In 1989, $414·8m. was awarded for community health centres; $45·6m. for migrant health centres; $20·6m. for efforts to reduce infant mortality; $3·2m. for black lung clinics; and $135·1m. for family planning. Other block grants awarded by the Family Support Administration included $316·9m. for community services block grant programmes for fiscal year 1989, and $1,380m. for the low income home energy assistance programme (LIHEAP).

DIPLOMATIC REPRESENTATIVES

Of the USA in Great Britain (Grosvenor Sq., London, W1A 1AE)
Ambassador: Henry Catto.

Of Great Britain in the USA (3100 Massachusetts Ave., Washington, D.C., 20008)
Ambassador: Sir Antony Acland, GCMG, KCVO.

Of the United States to the United Nations
Ambassador: Thomas Pickering.

Further Reading

I. Statistical Information

The Office of Management and Budget, Washington, D.C. 20503 is part of the Executive Office of the President; it is responsible for co-ordinating all the statistical work of the different Federal Government agencies. The Office does not collect or publish data itself. The main statistical agencies are as follows:

(1) Data User Services Division, Bureau of the Census, Department of Commerce, Washington, D.C. 20233. Responsible for decennial censuses of population and housing, quinquennial census of agriculture, manufactures and business; current statistics on population and the labour force, manufacturing activity and commodity production, trade and services, foreign trade, state and local government finances and operations. (*Statistical Abstract of the United States*, annual, and others).

(2) Bureau of Labor Statistics, Department of Labor, 441 G Street NW, Washington, D.C. 20212. (*Monthly Labor Review* and others).

(3) Information Division, Economic Research Service, Department of Agriculture, Washington, D.C. 20250. (*Agricultural Statistics*, annual, and others).

(4) National Center for Health Statistics, Department of Health and Human Services, 3700 East-West Highway, Hyattsville Md. 20782. (*Vital Statistics of the United States*, monthly and annual, and others).

(5) Bureau of Mines Office of Technical Information, Department of the Interior, Washington, D.C. 20241. (*Minerals Yearbook*, annual, and others).

(6) Office of Energy Information Services, Energy Information Administration, Department of Energy, Washington, D.C. 20461.

(7) Statistical Publications, Department of Commerce, Room 5062 Main Commerce, 14th St and Constitution Avenue NW, Washington, D.C. 20230; the Department's Bureau of Economic Analysis and its Office of Industry and Trade Information are the main collectors of data.

(8) Center for Education Statistics, Department of Education, 555 New Jersey Avenue NW, Washington, D.C. 20208.

(9) Public Correspondence Division, Office of the Assistant Secretary of Defense (Public Affairs P.C.), The Pentagon, Washington, D.C. 20301-1400.

(10) Bureau of Justice Statistics, Department of Justice, 633 Indiana Avenue NW, Washington, D.C. 20531.

(11) Public Inquiry, APA 200, Federal Aviation Administration, Department of Transportation, 800 Independence Avenue SW, Washington, D.C. 20591.

(12) Office of Public Affairs, Federal Highway Administration, Department of Transportation, 400 7th St. SW, Washington, D.C. 20590.

(13) Statistics Division, Internal Revenue Service, Department of the Treasury, 1201 E St. NW, Washington, D.C. 20224.

Statistics on the economy are also published by the Division of Research and Statistics, Federal Reserve Board, Washington, D.C. 20551; the Congressional Joint Committee on the Economy, Capitol; the Office of the Secretary, Department of the Treasury, 1500 Pennsylvania Avenue NW, Washington, D.C. 20220.

II. OTHER OFFICIAL PUBLICATIONS

Guide to the Study of the United States of America. General Reference and Bibliography Division, Library of Congress. 1960.

Historical Statistics of the United States, Colonial Times to 1957: A Statistical Abstract Supplement. Washington, 1960.—*Continuation to 1962 and Revisions*, 1965.

United States Government Manual. Washington. Annual.

The official publications of the USA are issued by the US Government Printing Office and are distributed by the Superintendent of Documents, who issued in 1940 a cumulative *Catalog of the Public Documents of the... Congress and of All the Departments of the Government of the United States.* This *Catalog* is kept up to date by *United States Government Publications, Monthly Catalog* with annual index and supplemented by *Price Lists.* Each *Price List* is devoted to a special subject or type of material, *e.g., American History* or *Census.* Useful guides are Schmeckebier, L. F. and Eastin, R. B. (eds.) *Government Publications and Their Use.* 2nd ed., Washington, D.C., 1961; Boyd, A. M., *United States Government Publications.* 3rd ed. New York, 1949, and Leidy, W. P., *Popular Guide to Government Publications.* 2nd ed. New York and London, 1963.

Treaties and other International Acts of the United States of America (Edited by Hunter Miller), 8 vols. Washington, 1929–48. This edition stops in 1863. It may be supplemented by *Treaties, Conventions... Between the US and Other Powers, 1776–1937* (Edited by William M. Malloy and others). 4 vols. 1909–38. A new Treaty Series, *US Treaties and Other International Agreements* was started in 1950.

Writings on American History. Washington, annual from 1902 (except 1904–5 and 1941–47).

III. Non-Official Publications

A. Handbooks

National Historical Publications Commission. *Guide to Archives and Manuscripts in the United States*, ed. P. M. Hamer. Yale Univ. Press, 1961
Adams, J. T. (ed.) *Dictionary of American History*. 2nd ed. 7 vols. New York, 1942
Dictionary of American Biography, ed. A. Johnson and D. Malone. 23 vols. New York, 1929–64.—*Concise Dictionary of American Biography*. New York, 1964
Current Biography. New York, annual from 1940; monthly supplements
Handlin, O. and others. *Harvard Guide to American History*. Cambridge, Mass., 1954
Herstein, S. R. and Robbins, N., *United States of America*. [Bibliography] Oxford and Santa Barbara, 1982
Lord, C. L. and E. H., *Historical Atlas of the US*. Rev. ed. New York, 1969
Who's Who in America. Chicago, 1899–1900 to date; monthly Supplement. 1940 to date

B. General History

Barck, Jr, O. T. and Blake, N. M., *Since 1900: A History of the United States*. 5th ed. New York, 1974
Brogan, H., *The Longman History of the United States of America*. London, 1985
Carman, H. J. and others, *A History of the American People*. 3rd ed. 2 vols. New York, 1967
Morison, S. E. with Commager, H. S., *The Growth of the American Republic*. 2 vols. 5th ed. OUP, 1962–63
Nicholas, H. G., *The Nature of American Politics*. OUP, 1980
Scammon, R. N. (ed.) *American Votes: A Handbook of Contemporary American Election Statistics*. Washington, D.C., 1956 to date (biennial)
Schlesinger, A. M., *The Rise of Modern America, 1865–1951*. 4th ed. New York, 1951.—*The Age of Roosevelt*. 4 vols. New York and London, 1957–62.—*A Thousand Days: John F. Kennedy in the White House*. New York and London, 1965
Schlesinger, J., *America at Century's End*. Columbia Univ. Press, 1989
Snowman, D., *America Since 1920*. London, 1978
Watson, R. A., *The Promise and Performance of American Democracy*. 2nd ed. New York, 1975

C. Minorities

Burma, J. J., *Spanish-speaking Groups in the US*. Duke University Press, 1954, repr. 1974
McNickle, D., *The Indian Tribes of the United States*. OUP, 1962.—*Native American Tribalism*. OUP, 1973
Sklare, M., *The Jew in American Society*. New York, 1974

D. Economic History

The Economic History of the United States. 9 vols. New York, 1946 ff.
Bining, A. C. and Cochran, T. C., *The Rise of American Economic Life*. 4th ed. New York, 1963
Dorfman, J., *The Economic Mind in American Civilization*. 5 vols. New York, 1946–59
Friedman, M. and Schwartz, A. J., *A Monetary History of the United States, 1867–1960*. New York, 1963

E. Foreign Relations

Documents on American Foreign Relations. Princeton, from 1948. Annual
The United States in World Affairs. 1931 ff. Council on Foreign Relations. New York, from 1932. Annual
Agnew, J., *The United States in the World Economy*. CUP, 1987
Bartlett, R. (ed.) *The Record of American Diplomacy; Documents and Readings in the History of American Foreign Relations*. 4th ed. New York, 1964
Beloff, M., *The United States and the Unity of Europe*. London, 1963, repr. 1976
Connell-Smith, G., *The United States and Latin America*. London, 1975
Schwab, G., (ed.) *United States Foreign Policy at the Crossroads*. Westport, 1982
Vance, C., *Hard Choices: Critical Years in America's Foreign Policy*. New York, 1983

F. National Character

Degler, C. N., *Out of Our Past: The Forces That Shaped Modern America*. Rev. ed. New York, 1970
Duigan, P. and Rabushka, A., (eds.) *The United States in the 1980s*. Stanford, 1980
Fawcett, E. and Thomas, T., *America and the Americans*. London, 1983

National Library: The Library of Congress. Washington 25, D.C. *Librarian:* Lawrence Quincy Mumford, AB, MA, BS.

STATES AND TERRITORIES

For information as to State and Local Government, see under UNITED STATES, *pp.* 1386–89.

Against the names of the Governors and the Secretaries of State, (D.) stands for Democrat and (R.) for Republican.

Figures for the revenues and expenditures of the various states are those of the Federal Bureau of the Census unless otherwise stated, which takes the original state figures and arranges them on a common pattern so that those of one state can be compared with those of any other.

Official publications of the various states and insular possessions are listed in the *Monthly Check-List of State Publications*, issued by the Library of Congress since 1910. Their character and contents are discussed in J. K. Wilcox's *Manual on the Use of State Publications* (1940). Of great importance bibliographically are the publications of the Historical Records Survey and the American Imprints Inventory, which record local archives, official publications and state imprints. These publications supplement those of state historical societies which usually publish journals and monographs on state and local history. An outstanding source of statistical data is the material issued by the various state planning boards and commissions, to which should be added the annual *Governmental Finances* issued by the US Bureau of the Census.

The Book of the States. Biennial. Council of State Governments, Lexington, 1953 ff.

State Government Finances. Annual. Dept. of Commerce, 1966 ff.

ALABAMA

HISTORY. Alabama, settled in 1702 as part of the French Province of Louisiana, and ceded to the British in 1763, was organized as a Territory, 1817, and admitted into the Union on 14 Dec. 1819.

AREA AND POPULATION. Alabama is bounded north by Tennessee, east by Georgia, south by Florida and the Gulf of Mexico and west by Mississippi. Area, 51,998 sq. miles, including 1,562 sq. miles of inland water. Census population, 1 April 1980, 3,893,888, an increase of 13·06% over that of 1970. Estimate (1987) 4,148,905. Births, 1988, 60,718 (14·5 per 1,000 population); deaths, 39,077 (9·3); infant deaths (under 1 year), 735 (12·1 per 1,000 live births); marriages, 44,552 (10·6); divorces, 23,827 (5·7).

Population in 5 census years was:

	White	*Negro*	*Indian*	*Asiatic*	*Total*	*Per sq. mile*
1910	1,228,832	908,282	909	70	2,138,093	41·4
1930	1,700,844	944,834	465	105	2,646,248	51·3
1960	2,283,609	980,271	1,726	915	3,266,521	64·0
			All others			
1970	2,533,831	903,467	6,867		3,444,165	66·7
1980	2,872,621	996,335	24,932		3,893,888	74·9

Of the total population in 1980, 49% were male, 61% were urban and 65% were 21 years or older.

The large cities (1980 census) were: Birmingham, 284,413 (metropolitan area, 847,487); Mobile, 200,452 (443,536); Huntsville, 142,513 (308,593); Montgomery (capital), 177,857 (272,687); Tuscaloosa, 75,211 (137,541).

CLIMATE. Birmingham. Jan. 46°F (7·8°C), July 80°F (26·7°C). Annual rainfall 54" (1,346 mm). Mobile. Jan. 52°F (11·1°C), July 82°F (27·8°C). Annual rainfall 63" (1,577 mm). Montgomery. Jan. 49°F (9·4°C), July 81°F (27·2°C). Annual rainfall 53" (1,321 mm). *See* Gulf Coast, p. 1382. The growing season ranges from 190 days (north) to 270 days (south).

CONSTITUTION AND GOVERNMENT. The present constitution dates from 1901; it has had 287 amendments (at 23 March 1988). The legislature consists of a Senate of 35 members and a House of Representatives of 105 members, all elected for 4 years. The Governor and Lieut.-Governor are elected for 4 years.

The state is represented in Congress by 2 senators and 7 representatives. Applicants for registration must take an oath of allegiance to the United States and fill out a questionnaire to the satisfaction of the registrars. In the 1988 presidential election Bush polled 809,663 votes, Dukakis, 547,347.

Montgomery is the capital.

Governor: Guy Hunt (R.), 1987–91 ($70,223).
Lieut.-Governor: Jim Folsom, Jr. (D.) ($2,100 a month plus allowances).
Secretary of State: Glen Browder (D.) ($36,234 plus $14,400 allowances).

BUDGET. The total net revenue for the fiscal year ending 30 Sept. 1988 was $15,601m. ($3,548m. from tax, $1,411m. from federal payments); total net expenditure was $15,595m. ($2,495m. on education, $545m. on highways, $528m. on public welfare, $612m. on health).

The outstanding debt on 30 Sept. 1988 amounted to $2,513m.

Per capita income (1988) was $12,604.

ENERGY AND NATURAL RESOURCES

Minerals. Principal minerals (1986): Coal, limestone, sand and gravel, petroleum (21·1m. bbl.) and natural gas (146,606m. cu. ft.). Total mineral output (1986) was valued at $2,001m. of which fuels, $1,440m.

Agriculture. The number of farms in 1988 was 49,000, covering 11·0m. acres; average farm had 224 acres and was valued at about $164,000.

Cash receipts from farm marketings, 1987: Crops, $588m.; livestock and poultry products, $1,560m.; and total, $2,148m. Principal sources: greenhouses and nurseries, peanuts, cotton, pototoes and other vegetables, soybeans; corn, wheat, pecans, hay, peaches and other fruit are also important. In 1987, poultry accounted for the largest percentage of cash receipts from farm marketings; cattle and calves were second, horticulture third, peanuts fourth.

Forestry. Area of national forest lands, Oct. 1988, 649,056 acres; state-owned forest, 147,400; industrial forest, 5,124,000; private non-industrial forest, 15·4m.; other government-owned forest, 368,418.

INDUSTRY. Alabama is predominantly industrial. In 1986 manufacturing establishments employed 357,500 workers; government, 297,000; trade, 320,400; services, 258,200; transport and public utilities, 71,500 (total non-agricultural workforce 1·5m.).

TOURISM. In 1986 about 28·6m. travelled to or through Alabama from other states. Total income from tourism (including receipts from Alabama holidaymakers) was about $4,000m.

COMMUNICATIONS

Roads. Paved roads of all classes at 31 Dec. 1987 totalled 61,769 miles; total highways, 88,166 miles.

Railways. At 1 July 1988 the railways had a length of 5,875 miles including side and yard tracks.

Aviation. In 1988 the state had 103 public-use airports. Nine airports are for commercial service, two are relief airports for Birmingham and the rest, general aviation.

Shipping. There are 1,200 miles of navigable inland water and 50 miles of Gulf Coast. The only deep-water port is Mobile, with a large ocean-going trade; total tonnage (1987), 29·36m. tons. The docks can handle 34 ocean-going vessels at once. The 9-ft channel of the Tennessee River traverses North Alabama for 200 miles; the Tennessee-Tombigbee waterway (232 miles), connects the Tennessee River with the Tombigbee River for access to the Gulf of Mexico. The Warrier–Tombigbee system (476 miles) connects the Birmingham industrial area to the Gulf.

The Coosa-Alabama River system reaches central Alabama as far north as Montgomery from Mobile and the Gulf Intracoastal Waterway. The Chattahooghee River runs for 261 miles. The Alabama State Docks also operates a system of 10 inland docks; there are several privately-run inland docks.

JUSTICE, RELIGION, EDUCATION AND WELFARE

Justice. The prison population on 30 Sept. 1988 was 12,190.

From 1 Jan. 1927 to 28 Aug. 1987 there were 156 executions (electrocution): 124 for murder, 25 for rape, 5 for armed robbery, 1 for burglary and 1 for carnal knowledge. Before 1 Jan. 1927, persons executed in Alabama were hanged locally by the sheriffs in the counties of their conviction.

In 41 counties the sale of alcoholic beverage is permitted, and in 26 counties it is prohibited; but it is permitted in 7 cities within those 26 counties.

Religion. Chief religious bodies (in 1980) are: Southern Baptist Convention (about 1,182,018), Churches of Christ (113,919), United Methodist (about 344,790), Roman Catholic (106,123), African Methodist Episcopal Zion (139,714), Christian Methodist Episcopal (about 53,493) and Assemblies of God (48,610).

Education. In the school year 1988–89 the 1,284 public elementary and high schools required 38,079 teachers to teach 715,740 pupils enrolled in grades K-12. In 1988-89 there were 16 senior public institutions with 112,972 students and 4,483 faculty members. In 1989 the 7 community colleges had 43,237 students and (1988) 1,008 instructors; 14 junior colleges had 17,006 students and (1988) 334 instructors; 20 technical schools had 12,835 students and (1988) 496 instructors.

Health. In 1987 there were 137 hospitals (21,404 beds) licensed by the State Board of Health. In 1986 hospitals for mental diseases had 2,236 beds. Facilities for the mentally retarded (1 Oct. 1987) had 1,320 certified beds.

Pensions and Security. In July 1988 Alabama paid supplements (to federal welfare payments) to 8,972 recipients of old-age assistance, receiving an average of $53.31 each; 5,169 permanently and totally disabled, $57.48; 118 blind, $54.74. Combined state–federal aid to dependent children was paid to 44,647 families, average $112.92 per family.

Further Reading

Alabama Official and Statistical Register. Montgomery. Quadrennial
Alabama County Data Book. Alabama Dept. of Economic and Community Affairs. Annual
Directory of Health Care Facilities. Alabama State Board of Health
Economic Abstract of Alabama. Center for Business and Economic Research, Univ. of Alabama, 1987
McCurley, R. L., Jr., ed., *The Legislative Process*. Alabama Law Institute, 3rd ed., 1984
Thigpen, R. A., *Alabama Government Manual*. Alabama Law Institute, 7th ed., 1986
Wiggins, S. W., (ed.) *From Civil War to Civil Rights, 1860–1960*. Univ. of Alabama Press, 1987

ALASKA

HISTORY. Discovered in 1741 by Vitus Bering, its first settlement, on Kodiak Island, was in 1784. The area known as Russian America with its capital (1806) at Sitka was ruled by a Russo-American fur company and vaguely claimed as a Russian colony. Alaska was purchased by the United States from Russia under the treaty of 30 March 1867 for $7·2m. It was not organized until 1884, when it became a 'district' governed by the code of the state of Oregon. By Act of Congress approved 24 Aug. 1912 Alaska became an incorporated Territory; its first legislature in 1913 granted votes to women, 7 years in advance of the Constitutional Amendment.

Alaska officially became the 49th state of the Union on 3 Jan. 1959.

AREA AND POPULATION. Alaska is bounded north by the Beaufort Sea, west and south by the Pacific and east by Canada. It has the largest area of any state, being more than twice the size of Texas. The gross area (land and water) is 591,004 sq. miles; the land area is 586,412 sq. miles of which 85% was in federal ownership in 1984. Census population, 1 April 1980, was 401,851, including military personnel, an increase of 33·5% over 1970. Estimate (1987), 537,800. Births, 1984, were 12,247 (24·5 per 1,000 population); deaths, 1,993 (4); infant deaths, 147 (12 per 1,000 live births); marriages, 6,519 (13); divorces, 3,904 (7·8).

Population in 5 census years was:

	White	*Negro*	*All Others*	*Total*	*Per sq. mile*
1940	39,170	...	33,354	72,524	0·13
1950	92,808	...	35,835	128,643	0·23
1960	174,649	...	51,518	226,167	0·40
1970	236,767	8,911	54,704	300,382	0·53
1980	309,728	13,643	78,480	401,851	0·70

Of the total population in 1980, 53·01% were male, 64·34% were urban and 68·57% were aged 21 years or over.

The largest city is Anchorage, which had a 1980 census area population of 174,430 (1987 estimate, 231,422). Other census area populations, 1980 (and 1987 estimate), Fairbanks North Star, 53,983 (73,164); Juneau, 19,528 (25,369); Kenai Peninsula, 25,282 (39,170); Ketchikan Gateway, 11,316 (12,432); Kodiak Island, 9,939 (13,658); Matanuska-Susitna 17,816 (37,027). There are 11 boroughs and 142 incorporated cities.

CLIMATE. Anchorage. Jan. 12°F (–11·1°C), July 57°F (13·9°C). Annual rainfall 15" (371 mm). Fairbanks. Jan. –11°F (–23·9°C), July 60°F (15·6°C). Annual rainfall 12" (300 mm). Sitka. Jan. 33°F (0·6°C), July 55°F (12·8°C). Annual rainfall 87" (2,175 mm). *See* Pacific Coast, p. 1381.

CONSTITUTION AND GOVERNMENT. An important provision of the Enabling Act is that the state has the right to select 103·55m. acres of vacant and unappropriated public lands in order to establish 'a tax basis'; it can open these lands to prospectors for minerals, and the state is to derive the principal advantage in all gains resulting from the discovery of minerals. In addition, certain federally administered lands reserved for conservation of fisheries and wild life have been transferred to the state. Special provision is made for federal control of land for defence in areas of high strategic importance.

The constitution of Alaska was adopted by public vote, 24 April 1956. The state legislature consists of a Senate of 20 members (elected for 4 years) and a House of Representatives of 40 members (elected for 2 years). The state sends 2 senators and 1 representative to Congress. The franchise may be exercised by all citizens over 18.

The capital is Juneau.

In the 1988 presidential election Bush polled 102,381 votes, Dukakis, 62,205.

Governor: Stephen Cowper (D.), 1986–90 ($81,648).
Lieut.-Governor: Steve McAlpine (D.) 1986–90 ($76,188).

ECONOMY

Budget. Total state government revenue for the year ended 30 June 1988 (Annual Financial Report figures) was $2,992·7m. Total expenditure was $3,054·6m.

In 1976 a Permanent Fund was set up for the deposit of at least 25% of all mineral-related revenue; total assets at 30 Nov. 1987, $8,837m.

General obligation bonds at 30 June 1984, $169·5m.

Per capita income (1985) was $18,187.

ENERGY AND NATURAL RESOURCES

Oil and Gas. Commercial production of crude petroleum began in 1959 and by 1961 had become the most important mineral by value. Production: 1961, 6·3m. bbls (of 42 gallons); 1976, 67m. bbls; 1977, 169m. bbls; 1981, 587m. bbls; 1985, 666m. bbls. Oil comes mainly from Prudhoe Bay, the Kuparuk River field and several Cook Inlet fields. Natural gas marketed production, 1985, 324,000m. cu. ft. Alaska receives 84% of its total revenue from petroleum. Revenue to the state from oil production in 1984 was $2,861·6m. from corporate petroleum tax $265·1m. and from royalties $1,047·5m., severance tax, $1,393·1m., property tax, $131m., bonus sale, $10·1m., rents, $3·8m., intergovernmental receipts, $11·1m.

Oil from the Prudhoe Bay arctic field is now carried by the Trans-Alaska pipeline to Prince William Sound on the south coast, where a tanker terminal has been built at Valdez.

Minerals. Value of production, 1983: Gold (169,000 troy oz.) $67·6m.; antimony (22,400 lb.) $25,000; platinum $100,000; silver (33,200 troy oz.) $332,000; tin (215,000 lb.) $1·1m.; jade and soapstone (2·3 tons) $42,000; sand and gravel (50m. short tons) $120m.; building stone (5·27m. short tons) $25m.; coal (803,000m. short tons) $18m. Total value, $232,399,000.

Agriculture. In some parts of the state the climate during the brief spring and summer (about 100 days in major areas and 152 days in the south-eastern coastal area) is suitable for agricultural operations, thanks to the long hours of sunlight, but Alaska is a food-importing area. In 1985 about 2m. acres was farmland; 90% of this was unimproved pasture primarily government leases for grazing of sheep and beef cattle in south-west Alaska. In 1980 (preliminary) there were 8,400 cattle, 1,100 milch cows, 1,800 hogs and 4,300 sheep stock.

Farm income in 1985: $26m. of which $18m. was from crops (mainly hay and potatoes) and $8m. from livestock and dairy products.

There were about 25,000 reindeer in western Alaska in 1980, owned by individual Eskimo herders except for 750 at Nome owned by the Government.

Forestry. In south-eastern Alaska timber fringes the shore of the mainland and all the islands extending inland to a depth of 5 miles. The state's enormous forests could produce an estimated annual sustained yield of 1,500m. bd ft of lumber, nearly twice Alaska's record 1973 cut. Alaska has 2 national forests: The Tongass of 16·9m. acres and the Chugach of 5·9m. acres. An estimated total of 446m. bd ft was cut in 1981, of which 387·5m. came from national forests and 53,687,000 from state forests, 4,275,000 from land held by the Bureau of Indian Affairs and 362,000 from the Bureau of Land Management. Alaska has 2 large pulp-mills at Ketchikan and Sitka.

Fisheries. The catch for 1985 was 1,185m. lb. of fish and shellfish having a value to fishermen of $591m. The most important fish are salmon, crab, herring and shrimp.

INDUSTRY. Main industries with employment, 1988: Government, 66,600; trade, 41,900; services, 42,900; contract construction, 8,700; manufacturing, 14,800; mining including oil and gas, 9,500; transport, communication and utilities, 17,200; finance, insurance and property, 10,700.

The major manufacturing industry was food processing, followed by timber industries. Total non-agricultural employment, 1988, 212,300. Total wages and salaries, 1987, $5,759·86m.

TOURISM. About 742,800 tourists visited the state in 1988.

COMMUNICATIONS

Roads. Alaska's highway and road system, 1984, totalled 15,315 miles, including marine highway systems, local service roads, borough and city streets, national park, forest and reservation roads and military roads. Registered motor vehicles, 1985, 382,000.

The Alaska Highway extends 1,523 miles from Dawson Creek, British Columbia, to Fairbanks, Alaska. It was built by the US Army in 1942, at a cost of $138m. The greater portion of it, because it lies in Canada, is maintained by Canada.

Railways. There is a railway of 111 miles from Skagway to the town of Whitehorse, the White Pass and Yukon route, in the Canadian Yukon region (this service operates seasonally). The government-owned Alaska Railroad runs from Seward to Fairbanks, a distance of 471 miles. This is a freight service with only occasional passenger use. A passenger service operates from Anchorage to Fairbanks via Denali National Park in the tourist season.

Aviation. In 1982 the state had about 1,070 airports, of which about half were publicly owned. Commercial passengers by air from Alaska's largest international airports Anchorage and Fairbanks numbered 1·1m. at Anchorage and 273,512 at Fairbanks. General aviation aircraft in the state per 1,000 population was about ten times the US average.

Shipping. Regular shipping services to and from the US are furnished by 2 steamship and several barge lines operating out of Seattle and other Pacific coast ports. A Canadian company also furnishes a regular service from Vancouver, B.C. Anchorage is the main port.

A 1,435 nautical-mile ferry system for motor cars and passengers (the 'Alaska Marine Highway') operates from Bellingham, Washington and Prince Rupert (British Columbia) to Juneau, Haines (for access to the Alaska Highway) and Skagway. A second system extends throughout the south-central region of Alaska linking the Cook Inlet area with Kodiak Island and Prince William Sound.

JUSTICE, RELIGION, EDUCATION AND WELFARE

Justice. There is no death penalty in Alaska. At 31 Dec. 1985 there were 2,311 prisoners in state and federal institutions.

Religion. Many religions are represented, including the Russian Orthodox, Roman Catholic, Episcopalian, Presbyterian, Methodist and other denominations.

Education. Total expenditure on public schools in 1986 was $806m. or $1,548 per capita. In 1988 there were about 3,100 elementary and 2,800 secondary school teachers, average salary, $41,000. During 1984 there were 100,000 pupils at public schools, 3,868 at private schools. The Bureau of Indian Affairs schools had 1,005 pupils. The University of Alaska (founded in 1922) had (Spring 1984) 11,808 students in Fairbanks, Anchorage and Juneau and 19,296 in community colleges. Other colleges had 1,775 students in 1984.

Health. In 1983 there were 26 acute care hospitals with 1,800 beds, of which 7 were federal public health hospitals; 1 mental hospital; 24 mental health clinics.

Welfare. Old-age assistance was established under the Federal Social Security Act; in 1985 aid to dependent children covered a monthly average of 6,400 households; payments, an average of $501 per month; aid to the disabled was given to a monthly average of 2,300 persons receiving on average $251 per month. An average of 1,100 aged per month received $166.

Further Reading

Statistical Information: Department of Commerce and Economic Development, Economic Analysis Section, Juneau; Department of Labor, Research and Analysis, Juneau.

Alaska Blue Book, Department of Education, Juneau. Biennial
Alaska Industry–Occupation Outlook to 1992, Department of Labor, Juneau.
Alaska Economy, The. Division of Economic Enterprise, Juneau. Annual
Alaska Statistical Review. Office of the Governor, Juneau. Biennial
Annual Financial Report, Department of Administration, Juneau.
Gardey, J., *Alaska: The Sophisticated Wilderness.* London, 1976
Hulley, Clarence C., *Alaska Past and Present.* Portland, Oregon, 1970
Hunt, W. R., *Alaska, a Bicentennial History.* New York, 1976
Pearson, R. W. and Lynch, D. F., *Alaska, a Geography.* Boulder, 1984
Thomas, L., Jr., *Alaska and the Yukon.* New York, 1983
Tourville, M., *Alaska, a Bibliography, 1570–1970.* 1971

State Library: P.O. Box G, Juneau. *Librarian:* Karen R. Crane.—Alaska Historical Library P.O. Box G, Juneau. *Librarian:* Kay Shelton.

ARIZONA

HISTORY. Arizona was settled in 1752, organized as a Territory in 1863 and became a state on 14 Feb. 1912.

AREA AND POPULATION. Arizona is bounded north by Utah, east by New Mexico, south by Mexico, west by California and Nevada. Area, 113,508 sq. miles, including 492 sq. miles of inland water. Of the total area in 1985, 28% was Indian Reservation, 17% was in individual or corporate ownership, 16% was held by the US Bureau of Land Management, 15% by the US Forest Service, 13% by the State and 10% by others. Census population on 1 April 1980 was 2,718,425, an increase of 53·4% over 1970. Estimate (1987) 3,469,000. Births, 1986, 60,575; deaths, 25,035; infant deaths (1983), 509; marriages, 36,025; divorces, 23,062.

Population in 5 census years:

	White	Negro	Indian	Chinese	Japanese	Total	Per sq. mile
1910	171,468	2,009	29,201	1,305	371	204,354	1·8
1930	378,551	10,749	43,726	1,110	879	435,573	3·8
1960	1,169,517	43,403	83,387	2,937	1,501	1,302,161	11·3
				All others			
1970	1,604,498	53,344		117,557		1,775,399	15·6
1980	2,260,288	74,159		383,768		2,718,215 [1]	23·9

[1] Preliminary.

Of the population in 1980, 1,375,214 were male, 2,278,728 were urban and 1,872,447 were aged 20 and over.

The 1980 census population of Phoenix was 789,704 (1986 estimate, 881,640); Tucson, 330,537 (384,385); Scottsdale, 88,412 (108,447); Tempe, 106,743 (132,942); Mesa, 152,453 (239,587); Glendale, 97,172 (122,392).

CLIMATE. Phoenix. Jan. 52°F (11·1°C), July 90°F (32·2°C). Annual rainfall 8" (191 mm). Yuma. Jan. 55°F (12·8°C), July 91°F (32·8°C). Annual rainfall 3" (75 mm). *See* Mountain States, p. 1381.

CONSTITUTION AND GOVERNMENT. The state constitution (1910, with 103 amendments) placed the government under direct control of the people through the Initiative, Referendum and the Recall. The state Senate consists of 30 members, and the House of Representatives of 60, all elected for 2 years. Arizona sends to Congress 2 senators and 5 representatives. In the 1988 presidential election Bush polled 694,379 votes, Dukakis, 447,272.

The state capital is Phoenix. The state is divided into 15 counties.

Governor: Rose Mofford (D.), 1988–91 ($75,000).

Secretary of State: James Shumway (D.), 1988–91 ($50,000).

BUDGET. General revenues, year ending 30 June 1987 (US Census Bureau figures), were $2,422m. (taxation, $2,431m.); general expenditures, $2,384m. (education, $1,484m.; transport $15·8m., and public health and welfare, $458·6m.).

Per capita income (1986) was $13,090.

NATURAL RESOURCES

Minerals. The mining industries of the state are important, but less so than agriculture and manufacturing. By value the most important mineral produced is copper. Production (1986) 874,715 short tons; gold and silver are both largely recovered from copper ore. Other minerals include sand and gravel and lead. Total value of minerals mined in 1986 was $1,566·3m.

Agriculture. Arizona, despite its dry climate, is well suited for agriculture along the water-courses and where irrigation is practised on a large scale from great reservoirs constructed by the US as well as by the state government and private interests. Irrigated area, 1984, 1·07m. acres. The wide pasture lands are favourable for the rearing of cattle and sheep, but numbers are either stationary or declining compared with 1920.

In 1987 Arizona contained 8,400 farms and ranches with 852,866 acres of crop land, out of a total farm and pastoral area of 38m. acres. The average farm was estimated at 4,405 acres. Farming is highly commercialized and mechanized and concentrated largely on cotton picked by machines and by Indian, Mexican and migratory workers.

Area under cotton (1986), 322,800 acres; 823,000m. bales (of 480 lb.) of cotton were harvested.

Cash income, 1986, from crops, $838m.; from livestock, $714m. Most important cereals are wheat, corn and barley; other crops include oranges, grapefruit and lettuce. On 1 Jan. 1985 there were 1,050,000 all cattle, 82,000 milch cows, 306,000 sheep.

Forestry. The national forests in the state had an area (1983) of 11·22m. acres.

INDUSTRY. In 1986 there were 3,747 manufacturing establishments with 172,047 production workers, earning $1,947m.

TOURISM. In 1982 15·7m. tourists visited Arizona; direct employment, 71,700; indirect, 114,600; state tax revenue, $204m.

COMMUNICATIONS

Roads. In 1982 there were 76,290 miles of public roads and streets; in 1986 2,628,738 motor vehicles were registered in the state.

Aviation. Airports, 1984, numbered 251, of which 82 were for public use; 6,079 aircraft were registered.

JUSTICE, RELIGION, EDUCATION AND WELFARE

Justice. A 'right-to-work' amendment to the constitution, adopted 5 Nov. 1946, makes illegal any concessions to trade-union demands for a 'closed shop'.

The Arizona state and federal prisons 31 Dec. 1985 held 8,518. There have been no executions since 1963; from 1930 to 1963 there were 38 executions (lethal gas) all for murder, and all men (28 whites, 10 Negro).

Religion. The leading religious bodies are Roman Catholics and Mormons (Latter Day Saints); others include Methodists, Presbyterians, Baptists and Episcopalians.

Education. School attendance is compulsory to grade 9 (from 1985–86) and to grade 10 (from 1986–87). In autumn 1986 there were 532,694 pupils enrolled in grades K-12. In 1986 spending on public schools was $1,589m. or $499 per capita. The state maintains 3 universities: the University of Arizona (Tucson) with an enrolment of 30,437 in autumn 1986; Arizona State University (Tempe) with 40,735; Northern Arizona University (Flagstaff) with 13,354.

Health. In 1985 there were 88 hospitals reported by the State Department of Health; capacity 13,890 beds; the hospitals had 1,522 physicians and dentists, 8,437 registered nurses and 1,503 licensed practical nurses.

Social Security. Old-age assistance (maximum depending on the programme) is given, with federal aid, to needy citizens 65 years of age or older. In June 1985, federal Social Security Insurance payments went to 10,500 aged ($158 each), and 22,000 disabled ($251); 71,900 people in 25,200 families received aid for families with dependent children.

Further Reading

Arizona Statistical Review. 42nd ed. Valley National Bank, Phoenix, 1986
Comeaux, M. L., *Arizona: a Geography*. Boulder, 1981
Faulk, O. B., *Arizona: A Short History*. Univ. Oklahoma Press, 1970
Goff, J. S., *Arizona Civilization*. 2nd ed. Cave Creek, 1970
Mason, B. B. and Hink, H., *Constitutional Government of Arizona*. 7th ed.Tempe, 1982

State Library: Department of Library, Archives and Public Records, Capitol, Phoenix 85007. *Director:* Sharon G. Turgeon.

ARKANSAS

HISTORY. Arkansas was settled in 1686, made a territory in 1819 and admitted into the Union on 15 June 1836. The name originated with the Quapaw Indian tribe. The constitution, which dates from 1874, has been amended 59 times.

AREA AND POPULATION. Arkansas is bounded north by Missouri, east by Tennessee and Mississippi, south by Louisiana, south-west by Texas and west by Oklahoma. Area, 53,187 sq. miles (1,109 sq. miles being inland water). Census population on 1 April 1980 was 2,286,435, an increase of 18·9% from that of 1970. Estimate (1988) 2,395,000. Births, 1988, were 35,017 (14·6 per 1,000 population); deaths, 24,883 (10·4); infant deaths, 375 (10·7 per 1,000 live births); marriages, 34,935 (14·6); divorces 16,747 (7).

Population in 5 census years was:

	White	*Negro*	*Indian*	*Asiatic*	*Total*	*Per sq. mile*
1910	1,131,026	442,891	460	72	1,574,449	30·0
1930	1,375,315	478,463	408	296	1,854,482	35·2
1960	1,395,703	388,787	580	1,202	1,786,272	34·0
			All others			
1970	1,565,915	352,445	4,935		1,923,295	37·0
1980	1,890,332	373,768	22,335		2,286,435	43·9

Of the total population in 1980, 48·3% were male, 51·6% were urban, 60·2% were 21 years of age or older.

Little Rock (capital) had a population of 158,461 in 1980; Fort Smith, 71,626; North Little Rock, 64,288; Pine Bluff, 56,636; Fayetteville, 36,608; Hot Springs, 35,781; Jonesboro, 31,530; West Memphis, 28,138. The population of the largest standard metropolitan statistical areas: Little Rock–North Little Rock, 393,774; Fayetteville–Springdale, 178,609; Fort Smith (Arkansas portion), 132,064; Pine Bluff, 90,718; Memphis (Arkansas portion), 49,499; Texarkana (Arkansas portion), 37,766.

CLIMATE. Little Rock. Jan. 42°F (5·6°C), July 81°F (27·2°C). Annual rainfall 49" (1,222 mm). *See* Gulf Coast, p. 1382.

GOVERNMENT. The General Assembly consists of a Senate of 35 members elected for 4 years, partially renewed every 2 years, and a House of Representatives of 100 members elected for 2 years. The sessions are biennial and usually limited to 60 days. The Governor and Lieut.-Governor are elected for 4 years. The state is represented in Congress by 2 senators and 4 representatives.

In the 1988 presidential election Bush polled 463,754 votes, Dukakis, 344,991.

The state is divided into 75 counties; the capital is Little Rock.

Governor: Bill Clinton (D.), 1987–91 ($35,000).

Lieut.-Governor: Winston Bryant (D.) ($14,000).

Secretary of State: W. J. McCuen (D.) ($22,500).

FINANCE

Budget. The state and local government revenue for the fiscal year 1987 was $5,497m., of which taxation furnished $2,597m. and federal aid, $1,017m. General expenditure was $4,553m., of which education took $1,893m.; highways, $511m., and public welfare, $543m.

Long-term debt (state and local governments) for the financial year 1987 was $4,296m.

Per capita income (1988) was $12,219.

Banking. In 1988 total bank deposits were $15,853m.

ENERGY AND NATURAL RESOURCES

Minerals. In 1987 crude petroleum amounted to 38·1m. bbls; natural gas, 418·4m. cu. ft; the state is an important source of bauxite, bromine, special abrasive silica stone and barite; it is one of four states producing tripoli and vanadium and one of two shipping gallium.

Agriculture. In 1988 47,000 farms had a total area of 15m. acres; average farm was 319 acres; 7·5m. acres were harvested cropland; 2,406,338 acres were irrigated.

In 1988, Arkansas ranked first in the production of broilers (896·8m. birds, value $1·141m.) and rice (40·6% of US total production, with a yield of 5,350 lb per acre), fourth in turkeys (18m. birds) and sixth in eggs (3,800m. eggs, value $228·9m.). 1,044,000 bales of cotton were harvested and soybean production yielded 80m. bu. in 1988. Dairy farmers received $108·1m. for the sale of milk in 1988.

Livestock in Jan. 1989 included 1·75m. all cattle and calves.

INDUSTRY. In Sept 1989 total employment averaged 1,089,100 (52,600 agricultural, 235,000 manufacturing, 202,100 wholesale and retail trade, 155,000 government). The Arkansas Department of Labor estimated that 193,200 factory production workers earned an average $343.62 per week (41·5 hours). In the manufacturing group, food and kindred products employed 49,400, electric and electronic equipment, 22,400 and lumber and wood products, 19,400.

COMMUNICATIONS

Roads. Total road mileage, 82,672 miles. State-maintained highways (1988) total 16,165 miles; local county highways, 49,649 miles; city streets, 9,626 miles; federal roads, 1,633 miles; roads not publicly maintained, 5,598 miles. In 1988 there were 1,895,259 registered motor vehicles.

Railways. In 1988 there were in the state 3,169 miles of commercial railway.

Aviation. Six air carrier and 1 commuter airlines serve the state; there were, in 1988, 167 airports (92 public-use and 75 private).

Waterways. There are about 1,000 miles of navigable streams, including the Mississippi, Arkansas, Red, White and Ouachita Rivers. The Arkansas River/Kerr-McClellan Channel flows diagonally eastward across the state and gives access to the sea *via* the Mississippi River.

RELIGION, EDUCATION AND WELFARE

Religion. Main protestant churches in 1980: Baptist (603,844), Methodist (214,925), Church of Christ (90,671), Assembly of God (53,555). Roman Catholics (1980), 56,911.

Education. In the school year 1987–88 public elementary and secondary schools had 458,251 enrolled pupils and about 22,050 classroom teachers. Average salaries of teachers in elementary schools was $19,968, secondary $21,361. Expenditure on elementary and secondary education was $1,335m.

An educational TV network provides a full 12-hour-day telecasting; it has 5 stations (1988).

Higher education is provided at 32 institutions: 10 state universities, 1 medical college, 12 private or church colleges, 10 community or junior colleges. Total enrolment in institutions of higher education, 1987–88, was 75,508.

There were (1987–88) 24 vocational-technical schools with 37,563 students, including extension class students. Total expenditure, $32·5m.

Health. There were 102 licensed hospitals (13,042 beds) in 1988, and 237 licensed nursing homes (23,517 beds).

Social Welfare. In 1987 449,000 persons drew social security payments; 251,000 were retired workers; 40,000 were disabled workers; 67,000 were widows and widowers; 45,000 were wives and husbands. In Dec. 1986 monthly payments were $171m., $117m. to retired workers and their dependants, $32m. to survivors, and $21m. to disabled workers and their dependants.

State prisons in Oct. 1988 had 5,347 inmates.

Further Reading

Current Employment Developments. Arkansas Department of Labor, Little Rock, 1989
Arkansas State and County Economic Data. Regional Economic Analysis, Univ. Arkansas, Little Rock, 1989
Arkansas Vital Statistics. Arkansas Department of Health, Little Rock, 1988
Governmental Finances. U.S. Dept. of Commerce, Bureau of the Census, 1986–87
Agricultural Statistics for Arkansas. U.S. Dept. of Agriculture, Crop Reporting Service, Little Rock, 1988
Statistical Summary for the Public Schools of Arkansas. Dept. of Education, Little Rock, 1986-88
Ferguson and Atkinson, *Historic Arkansas.* Little Rock, 1966

CALIFORNIA

HISTORY. California, first settled in July 1769, was from its discovery until 1846 politically associated with Mexico. On 7 July 1846 the American flag was hoisted at Monterey, and a proclamation was issued declaring California to be a portion of the US. On 2 Feb. 1848, by the treaty of Guadalupe–Hidalgo, the territory was formally ceded by Mexico to the US, and was admitted to the Union 9 Sept. 1850 as the thirty-first state, with boundaries as at present.

AREA AND POPULATION. Area, 158,693 sq. miles (2,120 sq. miles being inland water). In 1985 the federal government owned 48m. acres (48% of the land area); in 1984, 570,000 acres were under jurisdiction of the Bureau of Indian Affairs, of which 501,000 acres were tribal. Public lands, vacant in 1975, totalled 15,607,125 acres, practically all either mountains or deserts.

Census population, 1 April 1980, 23,667,902, an increase of 18·5% over 1970, making California the most populous state of the USA (New York: 17,557,288). Estimate (1988) 28,314,500. Births in 1986, 481,905 (17·9 per 1,000 population); deaths, 202,826 (7·5); infant deaths, 4,298 (8·9 per 1,000 live births); marriages (1984), 226,560 (8·8); divorces, dissolutions and nullities, 129,131 in 1983 (5·1).

Population in 5 census years was:

	White	*Negro*	*Japanese*	*Chinese*	*Total (incl. all others)*	*Per sq. mile*
1910	2,259,672	21,645	41,356	36,248	2,377,549	15·0
1930	5,408,260	81,048	97,456	37,361	5,677,251	35·8
1960	14,455,230	883,861	157,317	95,600	15,717,204	99·0
1970	17,761,032	1,400,143	213,280	170,131	19,953,134	125·7
			All others			
1980	18,030,893	1,819,281	3,817,728		23,667,902	149·1

Of the 1980 population 49·3% were male, 91·3% were urban and 67·2% were 21 years old or older.

The largest cities with 1980 census population are:

Los Angeles	2,966,850	Anaheim	219,494	Fremont	131,945
San Diego	875,538	Fresno	217,289	Torrance	129,881
San Francisco	678,974	Santa Ana	204,023	Garden Grove	123,307
San José	629,546	Riverside	170,591	San Bernardino	118,794
Long Beach	361,334	Huntington Beach	170,505	Pasadena	118,550
Oakland	339,337	Stockton	149,779	Oxnard	108,195
Sacramento	275,741	Glendale	139,060		

Urbanized areas (1980 census): Los Angeles–Long Beach, 9,477,926; San Francisco–Oakland, 3,191,913; San Diego, 1,704,352; San José, 1,243,900; Sacramento, 796,266; San Bernardino–Riverside, 703,316; Oxnard–Ventura–Thousand Oaks, 378,420; Fresno, 331,551.

CLIMATE. Los Angeles. Jan. 55°F (12·8°C), July 70°F (21·1°C). Annual rainfall 15" (381 mm). Sacramento. Jan. 45°F (7·2°C), July 74°F (23·3°C). Annual rainfall 19" (472 mm). San Diego. Jan. 55°F (12·8°C), July 69°F (20·6°C). Annual rainfall

10" (259 mm). San Francisco. Jan. 50°F (10°C), July 59°F (15°C). Annual rainfall 22" (561 mm). Death Valley. Jan. 52°F (11°C), July 100°F (38°C). Annual rainfall 1·6" (40 mm). *See* Pacific Coast, p. 1381.

CONSTITUTION AND GOVERNMENT. The present constitution became effective from 4 July 1879; it has had numerous amendments since 1962. The Senate is composed of 40 members elected for 4 years—half being elected each 2 years—and the Assembly, of 80 members, elected for 2 years. Two-year regular sessions convene in Dec. of each even-numbered year. The Governor and Lieut.-Governor are elected for 4 years.

California is represented in Congress by 2 senators and 45 representatives.

In the 1988 presidential election Bush polled 4,756,490 votes, Dukakis, 4,448,393.

The capital is Sacramento. The state is divided into 58 counties.

Governor: George Deukmejian (R.), 1987–91 ($49,100).
Lieut.-Governor: Leo McCarthy (D.), 1987–91 ($42,500).
Secretary of State: March Fong Eu (D.) ($42,500).

ECONOMY

Budget. For the year ending 30 June 1988 total General Fund revenues were $32,360m.; total General Fund expenditures were $33,021m. ($17,744m. for education, $10,379m. for health and welfare).

The long-term state debt (general obligation bonds outstanding) was $8,007m. on 30 June 1988.

Per capita personal income (1987) was $17,821.

Banking. In 1988 there were more than 440 banks, of which 18 were foreign-owned, 11 out-of-state and 400 independent. Total loans, 1988, $176,000m., of which real estate loans almost $79,000m. In Dec. 1988 (preliminary) all insured commercial banks had demand deposits of $59,979m. and time and savings deposits of $149,687m. Savings and loan associations had savings capital of $258,726m. at 31 Dec. 1988 (preliminary).

ENERGY AND NATURAL RESOURCES

Electricity. In 1987 hydro-power produced 21%, gas 33% coal and nuclear power 18% each, and oil, geothermal, biomass, wind, solar and other sources 8% of electricity needs.

Minerals. Crude oil output was estimated at 388m. bbls in 1988. Proved reserves were 5,200m. bbls in 1988. Output of natural gas was 382,217·9m. cu. ft; of natural gas liquids, (1987) 227,000 bbls. Gold output was about 602,071 troy oz. (1987); asbestos, boron minerals, diatomite, tungsten, sand and gravel, salt, magnesium compounds, clays, cement, copper, gypsum, calcium chloride, wollastonite and iron ore are also produced. The estimated value of all the minerals produced was $2,510m. in 1987. Mining employed 42,100 in 1988.

Agriculture. Extending 700 miles from north to south, and intersected by several ranges of mountains, California has almost every variety of climate, from the very wet to the very dry, and from the temperate to the semi-tropical.

In 1982 there were 82,468 farms, comprising 32m. acres; average farm, 390 acres. Cotton, fruit, livestock and vegetables are important. Cash receipts, 1987, from crops, $10,781m.; from livestock and poultry, $4,741m. Dairy produce, cattle, horticultural products, grapes, and cotton lint (in that order) are the main sources of farm income.

Production of cotton lint, 1987, was 717,900 short tons; other field crops included sugar-beet (6·0m. short tons). Principal crops include wine, table and raisin grapes (4·7m. short tons); peaches (734,000 short tons); pears (337,000 short tons); apricots (110,000 short tons); prunes (228,000 short tons); plums, nectarines, avocados, olives and almonds. Citrus fruit crops were: Oranges, 2·2m. short tons; lemons, 817,000 short tons; grapefruit, 298,600 short tons.

On 1 Jan. 1988 the farm animals were: 1m. milch cows, 4·6m. all cattle, 800,000 sheep and 130,000 swine.

Forestry. There were (1989) 18·5m. acres of productive forest land, from which about 4,000m. bd ft are harvested annually. Production, 1988, 6,200m. bd ft (estimate).

Fisheries. The catch in 1987 was 443·4m. lb.; leading species were mackerel, tuna and sea urchin.

INDUSTRY. In 1988, manufacturing employed 2,165,700. The fastest-growing industries were textile mill products, clothing and lumber. The aerospace industry is important, as is food-processing. In 1988 the civilian labour force was 14,036,000, of whom 13,292,000 were employed.

Tourism. In 1987 there were 112m. tourists, 27% from other states and 6% from abroad.

COMMUNICATIONS

Roads. In 1987 California had 57,748 miles of roads inside cities and 101,185 miles outside. In 1987 there were about 15·6m. registered cars and over 4·7m. commercial vehicles, leading all states in all items by a wide margin.

Railways. Total mileage of railways in 1986, was 8,044 miles. There are 2 systems: Amtrak and Southern Pacific Railroad commuter trains. Amtrak carries about 1·7m. passengers per year on the intra-state routes. Southern Pacific carries about 5·4m. on a commuter route. Amtrak services run from San Francisco and Los Angeles. Southern Pacific runs the Caltrains commuter route from San Francisco to San José. There is a metro (BART) and light rail (Muni) system in San Francisco. There is a light rail line in San Diego and Sacramento and another under construction in San José.

Aviation. In 1986 there were 283 public airports and 739 private airstrips.

Shipping. The chief ports are San Francisco and Los Angeles.

JUSTICE, RELIGION, EDUCATION AND WELFARE

Justice. State prisons, 1 Jan. 1987, had 55,920 male and 3,564 female inmates. From 1893 to 1942, 307 inmates were executed by hanging. From 1938 to 1976, 194 inmates were executed by lethal gas. No further death sentences were passed until 1980.

Religion. The Roman Catholic Church is much stronger than any other single church; next are the Jewish congregations, then Methodists, Presbyterians, Baptists and Episcopalians.

Education. Full-time attendance at school is compulsory for children from 6 to 16 years of age for a minimum of 175 days per annum, and part-time attendance is required from 16 to 18 years. In autumn 1987 there were 4·5m. pupils enrolled in elementary and secondary schools. Total state expenditure on public education, 1987–88, was $18,527m.

Community Colleges had 1,264,409 students in autumn 1987.

California has two publicly supported higher education systems: The University of California (1868) and the California State University and Colleges. In autumn 1987, the University of California with campuses for resident instruction and research at Berkeley, Los Angeles, San Francisco and 6 other centres, had 157,331 students. California State University and Colleges with campuses at Sacramento, Long Beach, Los Angeles, San Francisco and 15 other cities had 342,776 students. In addition to the 28 publicly supported institutions for higher education there are 117 private colleges and universities which had a total estimated enrolment of 151,844 in the autumn of 1987.

Health. In 1988 there were 522 general hospitals; capacity, 107,584 beds. On 30 June 1988 state hospitals for the mentally disabled had 4,844 patients.

Social Security. On 1 Jan. 1974 the federal government (Social Security Administration) assumed responsibility for the Supplemental Security Income/State Supplemental Program which replaced the State Old-Age Security. The SSI/SSP provides financial assistance for needy aged (65 years or older), blind or disabled persons. An individual recipient may own assets up to $1,900; a couple up to $2,850, subject to specific exclusions. There are federal, state and county programmes assisting the aged, the blind, the disabled and needy children. In 1987 5,172 families per month were receiving an average of $416 per family.

Further Reading

California Almanac, 1984–85. Fay, J. S., (ed.) Oxford, 1984
California Government and Politics. Hoeber, T. R., et al, (eds.) Sacramento, Annual
California Handbook. California Institute, 1981
California Statistical Abstract. 29th ed. Dept. of Finance, Sacramento, 1988
Economic Report of the Governor. Dept. of Finance, Sacramento, Annual
Lavender, D. S., *California*. New York, 1976

State Library: The California State Library, Library-Courts Bldg, Sacramento 95814.

COLORADO

HISTORY. Colorado was first settled in 1858, made a Territory in 1861 and admitted into the Union on 1 Aug. 1876.

AREA AND POPULATION. Colorado is bounded north by Wyoming, north-east by Nebraska, east by Kansas, south-east by Oklahoma, south by New Mexico and west by Utah. Area, 104,090 sq. miles (496 sq. miles being inland water). Federal lands, 1974, 23,974,000 acres (36% of the land area).

Census population, 1 April 1980, was 2,889,964, an increase of 680,368 or 30·8% since 1970. Estimated (1988), 3,301,458. Births, 1988, were 53,346 (15·9 per 1,000 population); deaths, 21,312 (6·3); infant deaths, 505 (9·5 per 1,000 live births); marriages, 31,350 (9·3); dissolutions, 18,660 (5·6).

Population in 5 census years was:

	White	*Negro*	*Indian*	*Asiatic*	*Total*	*Per sq. mile*
1910	783,415	11,453	1,482	2,674	799,024	7·7
1930	1,018,793	11,828	1,395	3,775	1,035,791	10·0
1950	1,296,653	20,177	1,567	5,870	1,325,089	12·7
1970	2,112,352	66,411	8,836	10,388	2,207,259	21·3
			All others			
1980	2,571,498	101,703	216,763		2,889,964	27·7

Of the total population in 1980, 49·6% were male, 80·6% were urban; 68% were aged 20 years or older. Large cities with 1980 census population (and 1988 estimate): Denver, 492,365 (502,660); Colorado Springs, 215,150 (281,876); Aurora, 158,588 (216,882); Lakewood, 112,860 (120,452); Pueblo, 101,686 (105,152); Arvada, 84,576 (91,238); Boulder, 76,685 (81,504); Fort Collins, 65,092 (81,692); Wheat Ridge, 30,293 (29,864); Greeley, 53,006 (61,682); Westminster, 50,211 (67,514).

Main metropolitan areas (1988): Denver–Boulder, 1,846,046; Fort Collins, 179,725; Colorado Springs, 396,200; Greeley, 142,139; Pueblo, 132,274; Front Range Urban Area, 2,696,384.

CLIMATE. Denver. Jan. 31°F (–0·6°C), July 73°F (22·8°C). Annual rainfall 14" (358 mm). Pueblo. Jan. 30°F (–1·1°C), July 83°F (28·3°C). Annual rainfall 12" (312 mm). *See* Mountain States, p. 1381.

CONSTITUTION AND GOVERNMENT. The constitution adopted in 1876 is still in effect with (1983) 78 amendments. The General Assembly consists of a Senate of 35 members elected for 4 years, one-half retiring every 2 years, and of a House of Representatives of 65 members elected for 2 years. Sessions are annual, beginning 1951. The Governor, Lieut.-Governor, Attorney-General, Secretary of State and Treasurer are elected for 4 years. Qualified as electors are all citizens, male and female (except convicted, incarcerated criminals), 18 years of age, who have resided in the state and the precinct for 32 days immediately preceding the election. The state is divided into 63 counties. The state sends to Congress 2 senators and 6 representatives.

In the 1988 presidential election Bush polled 727,633 votes, Dukakis, 621,093.

The capital is Denver.

Governor: Roy Romer (D.), 1987–91 ($60,000).
Lieut.-Governor: Mike Callihan (D.), 1987–91 ($32,500).
Secretary of State: Natalie Meyer (R.), 1987–91 ($32,500).

BUDGET. The state's total budget, 1985–86, is $3,497m., of which taxation and other revenue furnish $2,859m. and federal grants $637m. Education takes $1,708m.; health, welfare and rehabilitation, $1,037m., and highways, $440m. Total state and local taxes *per capita* (1985) were $2,167.

The state has no general obligation debt. The net long-term debt (in revenue bond) on 30 June 1985 was $139m.

Per capita personal income (1988) was $16,463.

ENERGY AND NATURAL RESOURCES

Minerals. Colorado has a variety of mineral resources. Among the most important are crude oil, metals and coal. Mineral production in 1986 (estimate) $1,000m. in value. An estimated 23,700 people were employed in extracting petroleum and natural gas in 1986; 5,000 in metals and 4,300 in coal and non-metals.

Agriculture. In 1987 farms numbered 27,284, with a total area of 34·1m. acres. 5,522,216 acres were harvested crop land; average farm (1987), 1,248 acres. Cash income, 1987, from crops $781·9m.; from livestock, $2,361·2m. In 1987 there were 3,013,773 acres under irrigation.

Production of principal crops in 1987: Corn for grain, 99m. bu. (from 685,568 acres); wheat for grain, 82m. bu. (2,421,603); barley for grain, 12·3m. bu. (203,226); hay, 3·1m. tons (1·4m.); dry beans, 2·52m. cwt (170,000); potatoes, 18·9m. cwt (65,400); sugar-beet, 839,566 tons (37,868); oats and sorghums are grown, as well as fruit.

In 1987 the number of farm animals was: 76,285 milch cows, 2,946,334 all cattle, 708,070 sheep, 258,725 swine. The wool clip in 1987 yielded 3·9m. lb. of wool.

INDUSTRY. In 1986 1,448,300 were employed in non-agricultural sectors, of which 367,800 were in trade; 328,800 in services; 247,800 in government; 196,500 in manufacturing; 87,900 in construction; 88,500 in transport and public utilities; 33,000 in mining; 98,000 in finance, insurance and property. In manufacturing the biggest employers were non-electrical machinery, foods and kindred products, and printing.

TOURISM. In 1985 about 20m. people spent holidays in Colorado, of whom about 3% were Colorado residents. Overall expenditure, $4,500m.

COMMUNICATIONS

Roads. The state highway system (1983) included 9,232 miles of highway. County roads totalled 56,898, and city streets, 9,352 miles. Total road mileage, 80,483, of which 5,001 miles are unmaintained county and city roads.

Railways. In 1982 there were in the state 4,500 miles of main-track and branch railway.

Aviation. There were (1984) 233 airports in the state. Of these, 68 are publicly owned and open to the public; 16 are privately owned and open to the public; 149 are private and not open to the public.

JUSTICE, RELIGION, EDUCATION AND WELFARE

Justice. At 30 Sept. 1984 there were 3,050 people committed to the State Department of Corrections, inmates of the State Penitentiary, the State Reformatory and other institutions. In 1967 there was 1 execution; since 1930 executions (by lethal gas) numbered 47, including 41 whites, 5 Negroes and 1 other; all were for murder.

Colorado has a Civil Rights Act (1935) forbidding places of public accommodation to discriminate against any persons on the grounds of race, religion, sex, colour or nationality. No religious test may be applied to teachers or students in the public schools, 'nor shall any distinction or classification of pupils be made on account of race or colour'. In 1957 the General Assembly prohibited discrimination in employment of persons in private industry and in 1959 adopted the Fair Housing Act to discourage discrimination in housing. A 1957 Act permits marriages between white persons and Negroes or mulattoes.

Religion. In 1984 the Roman Catholic Church had 550,300 members; the ten main Protestant denominations had 350,900 members; the Jewish community had 45,000 members. Buddhism is among other religions represented.

Education. In autumn 1984 the public elementary and secondary schools had 526,336 pupils and 34,500 teachers and administrators; total instructional salaries averaged $25,000. Enrolments in state universities, Sept. 1988, were: University of Colorado (Boulder), 24,057 students; University of Colorado (Denver), 10,048; University of Colorado (Colorado Springs), 5,583; Colorado State University (Fort Collins), 19,386; Colorado School of Mines (Golden), 2,319; University of Northern Colorado (Greeley), 9,167; University of Southern Colorado (Pueblo), 3,971; Western State College (Gunnison), 2,434; Adams State College (Alamosa), 2,487; Metropolitan State College (Denver), 15,638; Fort Lewis College (Durango), 3,843; Mesa College (Grand Junction), 4,006.

Health. Approved hospitals, 1983, numbered 98. In 1983, there were 25 public mental health centres and clinics.

Social Security. A constitutional amendment, adopted 1956, provides for minimum old age pensions of $100 per month, which may be raised on a cost-of-living basis; for a $5m. stabilization fund and for a $10m. medical and health fund for pensioners. In 1984 the maximum monthly retirement pension (for citizens of 65 and older) was $703; maximum monthly benefit for a disabled worker, $854.

Further Reading

Directory of Colorado Manufacturers, 1986. Business Research Division, School of Business, Univ. of Colorado, Boulder, 1987

State of Colorado Business Development Manual. Office of Business Development, Denver, 1986

Economic Outlook Forum, 1986. Colorado Division of Commerce and Development, and the College of Business, Univ. of Colorado, Denver, 1987

Griffiths, M. and Rubright, L., *Colorado: a Geography*. Boulder, 1983

Sprague, M., *Colorado: A History*. New York, 1976

State Library: Colorado State Library, State Capitol, Denver, 80203.

CONNECTICUT

HISTORY. Connecticut was first settled in 1634 and has been an organized commonwealth since 1637. In 1629 a written constitution was adopted which, it is claimed, was the first in the history of the world formed under the concept of a social compact. This constitution was confirmed by a charter from Charles II in 1662, and replaced in 1818 by a state constitution, framed that year by a constitutional convention.

AREA AND POPULATION. Connecticut is bounded north by Massachusetts, east by Rhode Island, south by the Atlantic and west by New York. Area, 5,018 sq. miles (147 sq. miles being inland water).

Census population, 1 April 1980, 3,107,576, an increase of 2·5% since 1970. Estimate (1983) 3,138,000. Births (1984) were 39,237 (12·4 per 1,000 population); deaths, 27,633 (8·8); infant deaths, 320 (8·2 per 1,000 live births); marriages, 25,080 (8); divorces, 11,226 (3·6).

Population in 5 census years was:

	White	*Negro*	*Indian*	*Asiatic*	*Total*	*Per sq. mile*
1910	1,098,897	15,174	152	533	1,114,756	231·3
1930	1,576,700	29,354	162	687	1,606,903	328·0
1960	2,423,816	107,449	923	3,046	2,535,234	517·5
			All others			
1970	2,835,458	181,177	15,074		3,031,709	629·0
1980	2,799,420	217,433	4,533	18,970	3,107,576	634·3

Of the total population in 1980, 1,498,005 persons were male, 2,449,774 persons were urban. Those 19 years old or older numbered 2,228,805.

The chief cities and towns, with census population 1 April 1980, are:

Bridgeport	142,546	New Britain	73,840
Hartford	136,392	West Hartford	61,301
New Haven	126,109	Danbury	60,470
Waterbury	103,266	Greenwich	59,578
Stamford	102,453	Bristol	57,370
Norwalk	77,767	Meriden	57,118

Larger urbanized areas, 1980 census: Hartford, 726,114; Bridgeport, 395,455; New Haven, 417,592; Waterbury, 228,178; Stamford, 198,854.

CLIMATE. New Haven: Jan. 28°F (–2·2°C), July 72°F (22·2°C). Annual rainfall 46" (1,151 mm). *See* New England, p. 1382.

CONSTITUTION AND GOVERNMENT. The 1818 Constitution was revised in June 1953 effective 1 Jan. 1955. On 30 Dec. 1965 a new constitution went into effect, having been framed by a constitutional convention in the summer of 1965 and approved by the voters in Dec. 1965.

The 1965 Constitution provides for 30 to 50 members of the Senate (instead of 24 to 36) and for 125 to 225 members of the House of Representatives, to be elected from assembly districts, rather than 2 or 1 from each town, as in the former constitution. The convention has added a new provision for a 3-day session following each regular or special session, solely to reconsider bills vetoed by the Governor.

The General Assembly consists of a Senate of 36 members and a House of Representatives of 151 members. Members of each House are elected for the term of 2 years (annual salary $9,500 first year, $7,500 second year; expenses $2,000 and mileage allowance). Legislative sessions are annual. The Governor and Lieut.-Governor are elected for 4 years. All citizens (with necessary exceptions and the usual residential requirements) have the right of suffrage.

Connecticut is one of the original 13 states of the Union. The state is represented in Congress by 2 senators and 6 representatives.

In the 1988 presidential election Bush polled 747,082 votes, Dukakis, 674,873. The state capital is Hartford.

Governor: William A. O'Neill (D.), 1987–91 ($65,000).
Lieut.-Governor: Joseph J. Fauliso (D.), ($40,000).
Secretary of State: Julia Tashjian (D.), ($35,000).

BUDGET. For the year ending 30 June 1982 (state government figures) general revenues were $5,588m. (taxation, $3,723m., and federal aid, $998m.); general expenditures were $5,330m. (education, $1,843m., highways, $376m., and public welfare, $737m.).

The total long-term debt on 30 June 1982 was $4,452m.

Per capita income, 1985, was $18,089.

NATURAL RESOURCES

Minerals. The state has some mineral resources: Sheet mica, sand, gravel, clays and stone; total production in 1982 was valued at $56m.

Agriculture. In 1985 the state had 4,000 farms with a total area of about 500,000 acres; average farm was of 118 acres, valued at $3,208 per acre. Total cash income, 1985, was $316m., including $110m. from crops and $206m. from livestock and products (mainly from dairy products and poultry). Principal crops are hay, silage, forest, greenhouse and nursery products, tobacco, potatoes, sweet corn, tomatoes, apples, peaches, pears, vegetables and small fruit.

Livestock (1 Jan. 1980): 108,000 all cattle (value $70·7m.), 5,200 sheep ($387,000), 11,000 swine ($699,000) and 5·8m. poultry ($12m.).

Forestry. The state had (1980) 137,782 acres of state forest land, which is about 4·2% of the total land area.

INDUSTRY.

Total non-agricultural labour force in 1985 was 1,569,000. The main employers are manufacturers (411,000 workers mainly in transport equipment, non-electrical machinery and fabricated metals); trade (350,000 workers); services (353,000) and government (189,000).

COMMUNICATIONS

Roads. The state (1 Jan. 1981) maintains 4,035 miles of highways, all surfaced. Motor vehicles registered in 1985 numbered 2,422,000.

Railways. In 1981 there were 950 miles of railway track.

Aviation. In 1981 there were 61 airports (27 commercial including 5 state-owned, and 34 heliports).

JUSTICE, RELIGION, EDUCATION AND WELFARE

Justice. In 1981 there were no executions; since 1930 there have been 22 executions (19 by electrocution, 3 by hanging), including 19 whites and 3 Negroes, all for murder. In 1984 there were 5,718 inmates of the state and federal prisons.

The Civil Rights Act makes it a punishable offence to discriminate against any person or persons 'on account of alienage, colour or race' and to hold up to ridicule any persons 'on account of creed, religion, colour, denomination, nationality or race'. Places of public resort are forbidden to discriminate. Insurance companies are forbidden to charge higher premiums to persons 'wholly or partially of African descent'. Schools must be open to all 'without discrimination on account of race or colour'.

Religion. The leading religious denominations (1980) in the state are the Roman Catholic (1·4m. members), United Churches of Christ, Protestant Episcopal, Jewish, Greek Orthodox, Methodist, Baptist, Presbyterian.

Education. Elementary instruction is free for all children between the ages of 4 and 16 years, and compulsory for all children between the ages of 7 and 16 years. In 1983 there were 719 public elementary schools, 237 secondary schools and 25 combined. In 1983 there were 478,000 pupils and 32,500 elementary and secondary teachers. Expenditure of the state on public schools, 1986, $2,321m. or $731 per capita. Average salary of teachers in public schools, 1986, $26,750.

Connecticut has 47 colleges, of which one state university, 4 state colleges, 5 state technical colleges and 12 regional community colleges are state funded. The University of Connecticut at Storrs, founded 1881, had 1,253 faculty and 22,407 students in 1980–81. Yale University, New Haven, founded in 1701, had 2,088 faculty and 9,626 students. Wesleyan University, Middletown, founded 1831, had 297 faculty and 2,775 students. Trinity College, Hartford, founded 1823, had 145 faculty and 2,007 students. Connecticut College, New London, founded 1915, had 203 faculty and 1,974 students. The University of Hartford, founded 1877, had 305 faculty and 9,836 students. The regional community colleges (2-year course) had 514 faculty and 34,082 students.

Health. Hospitals listed by the American Hospital Association, 1983, numbered 65, with 18,200 beds. The state operated one general hospital, one veterans' hospital, 8 hospitals for the mentally ill (2,450 patients in Jan. 1981), 2 training schools for the mentally retarded (and 12 regional centres), one chronic disease hospital (56 in-patients in Jan. 1981) and a state-aided institution for the blind.

Social Security. Disbursements during the year ending 30 June 1986 amounted to $66·1m. in aid to the aged (6,500 persons per month receiving an average of $153) and disabled (19,400, receiving $239). In other areas of welfare, there was an average of 40,700 cases for aid to families with dependent children comprising 118,800 recipients.

Further Reading

The Register and Manual of Connecticut. Secretary of State. Hartford. Annual
The Structure of Connecticut's State Government. Connecticut Public Expenditure Council. Hartford, 1973
Adams, V. Q., *Connecticut: The Story of Your State Government.* Chester, 1973
Halliburton, W. J., *The People of Connecticut.* Norwalk, 1985
Roth, David M. (ed.) *Series in Connecticut History.* 5 vols., Chester, 1975
Smith, Allen R., *Connecticut, a Thematic Atlas.* Newington, 1974
Van Dusen, Albert E., *Connecticut.* New York, 1961

State Library: Connecticut State Library, Capitol Avenue, Hartford, 06015. *State Librarian:* Clarence R. Walters.

DELAWARE

HISTORY. Delaware, permanently settled in 1638, is one of the original 13 states of the Union, and the first one to ratify the Federal Constitution.

AREA AND POPULATION. Delaware is bounded north by Pennsylvania, north-east by New Jersey, east by Delaware Bay, south and west by Maryland. Area 2,044 sq. miles (112 sq. miles being inland water). Census population, 1 April 1980 was 594,338, an increase of 46,234 or 8·4% since 1970. Estimate (1988), 660,000. Births in 1988, 10,403; deaths, 5,738; infant deaths, 121; marriages, 5,645; divorces, 3,021.

Population in 5 census years was:

	White	*Negro*	*Indian*	*Asiatic*	*Total*	*Per sq. mile*
1910	171,102	31,181	5	34	202,322	103·0
1930	205,718	32,602	5	55	238,380	120·5
1960	384,327	60,688	597	410	446,292	224·0
			All others			
1970	466,459	78,276	3,369		548,104	276·5
1980	488,002	96,157	10,179		594,338	290·8

Of the total population in 1980, 48·4% were male, 70·7% were urban and 65·7% were 21 years old or older.

The 1980 census figures show Wilmington with population of 70,195; Newark, 25,241; Dover, 23,512; Elsmere Town, 6,493; Milford City, 5,356; Seaford City, 5,256.

CLIMATE. Wilmington. Jan. 32°F (0°C), July 75°F (23·9°C). Annual rainfall 43" (1,076 mm). *See* Atlantic Coast, p. 1382.

CONSTITUTION AND GOVERNMENT. The present constitution (the fourth) dates from 1897, and has had 51 amendments; it was not ratified by the electorate but promulgated by the Constitutional Convention. The General Assembly consists of a Senate of 21 members elected for 4 years and a House of Representatives of 41 members elected for 2 years. The Governor and Lieut.-Governor are elected for 4 years.

With necessary exceptions, all adult citizens, registered as voters, who are *bona fide* residents, and have complied with local residential requirements, have the right to vote.

Delaware is represented in Congress by 2 senators and 1 representative, elected by the voters of the whole state.

In the 1988 presidential election Bush polled 130,581 votes, Dukakis, 99,479.

The state capital is Dover. Delaware is divided into 3 counties.

Governor: Michael N. Castle (R.), 1989–92 ($80,000).
Lieut.-Governor: Dale E. Wolf (R.), ($35,100).
Secretary of State: Michael Harkins (R.) ($69,900) (appointed by the Governor).

FINANCE. For the year ending 30 June 1989 total revenue was $2,045m., of which federal grants were $270m. Total expenditure was $2,025m.

On 30 June 1989 the total debt was $447m.

Per capita income (1988) was $17,669.

ENERGY AND NATURAL RESOURCES

Minerals. The mineral resources of Delaware are not extensive, consisting chiefly of clay products, stone, sand and gravel and magnesium compounds. Value of mineral production in 1980 was $2m.

Agriculture. Delaware is mainly an industrial state, but 590,000 acres is in farms; 475,000 acres of this is harvested annually. There were 3,000 farms in 1988. The average farm was valued (land and buildings) at $436,000. The main product is broilers, accounting for $396·86m. farm receipts, out of a total $598·1m. in 1988.

The chief field crops are corn and soybeans.

INDUSTRY. In 1988 manufacturing establishments employed 69,700 people; main manufactures, chemicals, transport equipment and food.

COMMUNICATIONS

Roads. The state in 1988 maintained 4,765 miles of roads and streets and 1,388 miles of federally-aided highways. There were also 622 miles of municipal maintained streets. Vehicles registered in year ended 30 June 1989, 540,000.

Railways. In 1989 the state had 285 miles of railway.

Aviation. Delaware had 11 airports, all of which were for general use in 1989.

JUSTICE, RELIGION, EDUCATION AND WELFARE

Justice. State prisons, 30 April 1988-30 April 1989, had daily average of 3,492 inmates. The death penalty was illegal from 2 April 1958 to 18 Dec. 1961. Executions since 1930 (by hanging) have totalled 12 (none since 1946).

Religion. Membership, 1979–80: Methodists, 60,489; Roman Catholics, 103,060; Episcopalians, 18,696; Lutherans, 10,000.

Education. The state has free public schools and compulsory school attendance. In Sept. 1988 the elementary and secondary public schools had 96,678 enrolled pupils and 5,900 classroom teachers. Another 21,579 children were enrolled in private and parochial schools. Appropriation for public schools (financial year 1987–88) was about $331·6m. Average salary of classroom teachers (financial year 1987–88), $29,573. The state supports the University of Delaware at Newark (1834) which had 900 full-time faculty members and 19,067 students in Sept. 1988, Delaware State College, Dover (1892), with 140 full-time faculty members and 2,389 students, and the 4 campuses of Delaware Technical and Community College (Wilmington, Stanton, Dover and Georgetown) with 219 full-time faculty members and 7,675 students.

Health. In 1989 there were 7 short-term general hospitals. During financial year 1987 patients in mental hospitals numbered 2,302.

Social Security. In 1974 the federal Supplemental Security Income (SSI) programme lessened state responsibility for the aged, blind and disabled. SSI payments in Delaware (1988), $20m. Provisions are also made for the care of dependent children; in 1988 there were 19,797 recipients in 7,589 families (average monthly payment per family, $265). The total state programme for the year ending 30 June 1988 was $24m. for the care of dependent children.

Further Reading

Information: Division of Historical and Cultural Affairs, Hall of Records, Dover.
Delaware Data Book. Delaware Development Office. Dover, 1988
State Manual, Containing Official List of Officers, Commissions and County Officers. Secretary of State, Dover. Annual
Hoffecker, C. E., *Delaware: a Bicentennial History.* New York, 1977
Smeal, L., *Delaware Historical and Biographical Index.* New York, 1984
Weslager, C. A., *Delaware Indians, a History.* Rutgers Univ. Press, 1972
Topical History of Delaware. Division of Historical and Cultural Affairs. Dover, 1977

DISTRICT OF COLUMBIA

HISTORY. The District of Columbia, organized in 1790, is the seat of the Government of the US, for which the land was ceded by the states of Maryland and Virginia to the US as a site for the national capital. It was established under Acts of Congress in 1790 and 1791. Congress first met in it in 1800 and federal authority over it became vested in 1801. In 1846 the land ceded by Virginia (about 33 sq. miles) was given back.

AREA AND POPULATION. The District forms an enclave on the Potomac River, where the river forms the south-west boundary of Maryland. The area of the District of Columbia is 68·68 sq. miles, 6 sq. miles being inland water.

Census population, 1 April 1980, was 638,333, a decrease of 16% from that of 1970. Estimate (1983) 623,000. Metropolitan statistical area of Washington, D.C.–Md–Va. (1980), 3m. Density of population in the District, 1980, 10,453 per sq. mile. Births, 1984, in the District were 19,123 (30·7 per 1,000 population); resident deaths, 8,302 (13·3); infant deaths, 393 (20·6 per 1,000 live births); marriages, 5,488 (8·8); divorces, 2,874 (4·6).

Population in 5 census years was:

	White	*Negro*	*Indian*	*Chinese and Japanese*	*Total*	*Per sq. mile*
1910	236,128	94,446	68	427	331,069	5,517·8
1930	353,981	132,068	40	780	486,869	7,981·5
1960	345,263	411,737	587	3,532	763,956	12,523·9
			All others			
1970	209,272	537,712	9,526		756,510	12,321·0
1980	171,768	448,906	17,659		638,333	10,184·0

CLIMATE. Washington. Jan. 34°F (1·1°C), July 77°F (25°C). Annual rainfall 43" (1,064 mm). *See* Atlantic Coast, p. 1382.

GOVERNMENT. Local government, from 1 July 1878 until Aug. 1967, was that of a municipal corporation administered by a board of 3 commissioners, of whom 2 were appointed from civil life by the President, and confirmed by the Senate, for a term of 3 years each. The other commissioner was detailed by the President from the Engineer Corps of the Army. Reorganization Plan No. 3 of 1967 submitted by the President to Congress on 1 June 1967 abolished the Commission form of government and instituted a new Mayor Council form of government with officers appointed by the President with the advice and consent of the Senate. On 24 Dec. 1973 the appointed officers were replaced by an elected Mayor and councillors, with full legislative powers in local matters as from 1974. Congress retains the right to legislate, to veto or supersede the Council's acts. The 23rd amendment to the federal constitution (1961) conferred the right to vote in national elections; in the 1984 presidential election Mondale polled 172,459 votes, Reagan, 26,805. Since 1971 the District has had a delegate (two, by 1987) in Congress who may vote in Committees but not on the House floor.

BUDGET. The District's revenues are derived from a tax on real and personal property, sales taxes, taxes on corporations and companies, licences for conducting various businesses and from federal payments.

The District of Columbia has no bonded debt not covered by its accumulated sinking fund. *Per capita* personal income, 1985, $18,186.

INDUSTRY. The District's main industries (1985) are government service (263,000 workers); services (214,000); wholesale and retail trade (64,000); finance, real estate, insurance (35,000), communications, transport and utilities (26,000); total workforce, 1985, 629,000.

TOURISM. About 17m. visitors stay in the District every year and spend about $1,000m.

COMMUNICATIONS

Roads. Within the District are 340 miles of bus routes. There are 1,101 miles of streets maintained by the District; of these, 673 miles are local streets, 262 miles are major arterial roads. In 1985 233,000 vehicles were registered.

Railways. There is a rapid rail transit system including a town subway system. This coordinates with the bus system and connects with Union railway station and the National Airport. Nine rail lines serve the District.

Aviation. The District is served by 3 general airports; across the Potomac River in Arlington, Va., is National Airport, in Chantilly, Va., is Dulles International Airport and in Maryland is Baltimore—Washington International Airport.

JUSTICE, RELIGION, EDUCATION AND WELFARE

Justice. Since 1958 there have been no executions; from 1930 to 1957 there were 40 executions (electrocution) including 3 whites for murder and 35 Negroes for murder and 2 for rape. The death penalty was declared unconstitutional in the District of Columbia on 14 Nov. 1973. At 31 Dec. 1985 there were 6,404 prisoners in state and federal institutions.

The District's Court system is the Judicial Branch of the District of Columbia. It is the only completely unified court system in the United States, possibly because of the District's unique city-state jurisdiction. Until the District of Columbia Court Reform and Criminal Procedure Act of 1970, the judicial system was almost entirely in the hands of Federal Government. Since that time, the system has been similar in most respects to the autonomous systems of the states.

Religion. The largest churches are the Protestant and Roman Catholic Christian churches; there are also Jewish, Eastern Orthodox and Islamic congregations.

Education. In 1983–84 there were about 89,000 pupils in secondary and elementary schools. Expenditure on public schools, 1986, $404m. or $645 per capita; public school teachers' average salary was $34,000. Higher education is given through the Consortium of Universities of the Metropolitan Washington Area, which consists of six universities and three colleges: Georgetown University, founded in 1795 by the Jesuit Order (11,688 students in 1985–86); George Washington University, non-sectarian founded in 1821 (17,948); Howard University, founded in 1867 (11,184); Catholic University of America, founded in 1887 (6,805); American University (Methodist) founded in 1893 (8,032); University of D.C., founded 1976 (12,080); Gallaudet College, founded 1864 (2,128); Trinity College, founded 1897 (926). There are altogether 18 institutes of higher education.

All benefit from such facilities as the 12 museums of the Smithsonian Institution, the Library of Congress, National Archives, and the Legal Libraries of the US Supreme Court and Department of Justice.

Social Security The District government provides primary health care for residents, mainly through its Department of Human Services. In 1983 there were 17 hospitals with 8,700 beds. The welfare programme of aid to families with dependent children gave money to 55,900 recipients in 21,600 families in 1985; 4,100 aged and 11,600 disabled also received aid, total payments $43·8m.

Further Reading

Statistical Information: The Metropolitan Washington Board of Trade publications.
Reports of the Commissioners of the District of Columbia. Annual. Washington

FLORIDA

HISTORY. European men, probably Spaniards but possibly English, saw Florida for the first time in the period 1497–1512. John Cabot first charted the cape now called Florida in 1498. Juan Ponce de Leon sighted Florida on 27 March 1513. Going ashore between 2 and 8 April in the vicinity of what is now St Augustine, he named the land 'Pasqua de Flores' because his landing was 'in the time of the Feast of Flowers'. The first permanent settlement was Spanish and was made at St Augustine, 8 Sept. 1565; it is the oldest permanent settlement in the US. In 1763 Florida was ceded to England; back to Spain in 1783, and to the US in 1821. Florida became a Territory in 1821 and was admitted into the Union on 3 March 1845.

AREA AND POPULATION. Florida is a peninsula bounded west by the Gulf of Mexico, south by the Straits of Florida, east by the Atlantic, north by Georgia and north-west by Alabama. Area, 58,664 sq. miles, including 4,510 sq. miles of inland water. Census population, 1 April 1980, was 9,746,324, an increase of 43·4% since 1970. Estimate (1 July 1988) 12,335,000. Births in 1988 were 184,998; deaths, 131,358; infant deaths, 1,938; marriages, 136,977; divorces and other dissolutions, 77,982.

Population in 5 federal census years was:

	White	*Negro*	*All Others*	*Total*	*Per Sq. Mile*
1940	1,381,986	514,198	1,230	1,897,414	35·0
1950	2,166,051	603,101	2,153	2,771,305	51·1
1960	4,063,881	880,168	7,493	4,952,788	91·5
1970	5,719,343	1,041,651	28,449	6,789,443	125·6
1980	8,319,448	1,342,478	84,398	9,746,324	180·1

Of the population in 1980, 48% of the total were male; 84·3% were urban and 72·4% were 20 years of age or over.

The largest cities in the state, 1980 census (and 1988 estimates) are: Jacksonville, 540,898 (639,146); Miami, 346,931 (369,007); Tampa, 271,523 (285,225); St Petersburg, 236,893 (243,306); Fort Lauderdale, 153,256 (150,553); Hialeah, 145,254 (166,548); Orlando, 128,394 (158,921); Hollywood, 117,188 (125,602); Miami Beach, 96,298 (96,988); Clearwater, 85,450 (99,866); Tallahassee, 81,548 (125,545); Gainesville, 81,371 (84,815); West Palm Beach, 62,530 (73,830); Largo, 58,977 (64,593); Pensacola, 57,619 (62,288); Pompano Beach, 52,618 (70,893); Coral Springs,, 37,349 (69,320); Lakeland, 47,406 (65,248).

CLIMATE. Jacksonville. Jan. 55°F (12·8°C), July 81°F (27·2°C). Annual rainfall 54" (1,353 mm). Key West. Jan. 70°F (21·1°C), July 83°F (28·3°C). Annual rainfall 39" (968 mm). Miami. Jan. 67°F (19·4°C), July 82°F (27·8°C). Annual rainfall 60" (1,516 mm). Tampa. Jan. 61°F (16·1°C), July 81°F (27·2°C). Annual rainfall 51" (1,285 mm). *See* Gulf Coast, p. 1382.

CONSTITUTION AND GOVERNMENT. The 1968 Legislature revised the constitution of 1885. The state legislature consists of a Senate of 40 members, elected for 4 years, and House of Representatives with 120 members elected for 2 years. Sessions are held annually, and are limited to 60 days. The Governor is elected for 4 years, and can hold two terms in office. Two senators and 19 representatives are elected to Congress.

In the 1988 presidential election Bush polled 2,535,503 votes and Dukakis, 1,630,647.

The state capital is Tallahassee. The state is divided into 67 counties.

Governor: Bob Martinez (R.), 1987–91 ($98,905).
Lieut.-Governor: Bobby Brantley (R.), 1987–91 ($89,511).
Secretary of State: Jim Smith (R.), 1987–91 ($89,511).

FINANCE. There is no state income tax on individuals. For the year ending 30 June 1988 the state had a total revenue of $33,557m. and total expenditure of $32,881m. General revenue fund expenditure was $9,764m.

Net long-term debt, 30 June 1988, amounted to $4,261m.

Per capita personal income (1988) was $16,546.

NATURAL RESOURCES

Minerals. Chief mineral is phosphate rock, of which marketable production in 1988 was 34·6m. tonnes. This was approximately 80% of US and 30% of the world supply of phosphate in 1988.

Agriculture. In 1988, there were 41,000 farms; net income per farm was $70,110. Total value of all farm land and buildings, $25,000m. There were 697,929 acres in citrus groves in 1988 and 10·8m. acres of other farms and ranches. Total cash receipts from crops and livestock (1988), $5,811m., of which crops provided $4,697m. Oranges, grapefruit, melons and vegetables are important. Other crops are indoor and landscaping plants, soybeans, sugar-cane, tobacco and peanuts. On 1 Jan. 1989 the state had 1·8m. cattle, including 182,000 milch cows, and 140,000 swine.

The national forests area in Sept. 1988 was 1,146,675 acres. There were 15,664,177 acres of commercial forest.

Fisheries. Florida has extensive fisheries for oysters, shrimp, red snapper, crabs, mackerel and mullet. Catch (1988), 182m. lb. valued at $191m.

INDUSTRY. In 1988 there were 15,880 manufacturers. They employed 539,748 persons. The metal-working, lumber, chemical, woodpulp, food-processing and instruments industries are important.

TOURISM. During 1988, 37m. tourists visited Florida. They spent $23,900m. making tourism one of the biggest industries in the state. There were (1989) 146 state parks, 15 state forests, 2 national parks, 8 national memorials, monuments, seashores and preserves and 4 national forests. The state parks were visited by 15·2m. people in 1988–89, 1·3m. of them campers.

COMMUNICATIONS

Roads. The state (1988) had 106,715·2 miles of highways, roads, and streets all of which were in the state and local system (66,770·1 miles being county roads), and 19,889·1 miles were federally-aided roads (1,469 miles interstate).

In 1987–88, 11,997,000m. vehicle licence plates were issued.

Railways. In 1989 there were 3,197 miles of railway.

Aviation. In 1989 Florida had 129 public use airports (9 international) of which 22 have scheduled commercial service.

JUSTICE, RELIGION, EDUCATION AND WELFARE

Justice. Since 1968 there have been 19 executions, by electrocution, for murder; from 1930 to 1968 there were 168 executions (electrocution), including 130 for murder, 37 for rape and 1 for kidnapping. State prisons, 30 June 1989, had 39,234 inmates.

Religion. The main Christian churches are Roman Catholic, Baptist, Methodist, Presbyterian and Episcopalian.

Education. Attendance at school is compulsory between 7 and 16.

In 1987–88 the public elementary and secondary schools had 1,712,613 enrolled pupils. Total expenditure on public schools was $10,061·4m. The state maintains 28 community colleges, with a full-time equivalent enrolment of 151,755 in 1987-88.

There are 9 universities in the state system, namely the University of Florida at Gainesville (founded 1853) with 31,039 students in 1987; the Florida State University (founded at Tallahassee in 1857) with 25,872; the University of South Florida at Tampa (founded 1960) with 28,514; Florida A. & M. University at Tallahassee (founded 1887) with 5,656; Florida Atlantic University (founded 1964) at Boca Raton with 10,991; the University of West Florida at Pensacola with 7,104; the University of Central Florida at Orlando with 16,556; the University of North Florida at Jacksonville with 7,123; Florida International University at Miami with 16,556.

Health. State-licensed general hospitals, 1989, numbered 224 with 54,208 beds.

Social Security. From 1974 aid to the aged, blind and disabled became a federal responsibility. The state continued to give aid to families with dependent children and general assistance. Monthly payments 1988–89: Aid to 3,107 blind averaged $251.99; aid to 115,124 dependent children averaged $87.95; aid to 120,629 disabled averaged $250.85; aid to 78,424 aged averaged $195.43.

Further Reading

Florida Population: Summary of the 1980 Census. Univ. of Florida Press, 1981
Report. Florida Secretary of State. Tallahassee. Biennial
Report of the Comptroller. Tallahassee. Biennial
Morris, A., *The Florida Handbook*. Tallahassee. Biennial
Fernald, E. A. (ed.) *Atlas of Florida*. Florida State Univ., 1981
Tebeau, C. W., *A History of Florida*. Univ. Miami Press, rev. ed., 1980

State Library: Gray Building, Tallahassee. *Librarian:* Barratt Wilkins.

GEORGIA

HISTORY. Georgia (so named from George II) was founded in 1733 as the 13th original colony; she became the 4th original state.

AREA AND POPULATION. Georgia is bounded north by Tennessee and North Carolina, north-east by South Carolina, east by the Atlantic, south by Florida and west by Alabama. Area, 58,910 sq. miles, of which 854 sq. miles are inland water. Census population, 1 April 1980, was 5,464,265. Estimate (1987), 6,222,000. Births, 1986, were 98,175 (16 per 1,000 population); deaths, 49,336 (8·1); infant deaths, 1,225 (12·5 per 1,000 live births); marriages, 70,866 (11·6); divorces and annulments, 33,957 (5·5).

Population in 5 census years was:

	White	*Negro*	*Indian*	*Asiatic*	*Total*	*Per sq. mile*
1910	1,431,802	1,176,987	95	237	2,609,121	44·4
1930	1,837,021	1,071,125	43	317	2,908,506	49·7
1960	2,817,223	1,122,596	749	2,004	3,943,116	67·7
			All others			
1970	3,391,242	1,187,149	11,184		4,589,575	79·0
1980	3,948,007	1,465,457	50,801		5,464,265	92·7

Of the 1980 population, 2,641,030 were male, 3,406,171 were urban and those 20 years of age and over numbered 3,601,895.

The largest cities are: Atlanta (capital), with population, 1980 census, of 422,293 (urbanized area, 2,010,368); Columbus, 168,598 (238,593); Savannah, 133,672 (225,581); Macon, 116,044 (251,736); Albany, 74,471 (112,257).

CLIMATE. Atlanta. Jan. 43°F (6·1°C), July 78°F (25·6°C). Annual rainfall 49" (1,234 mm). *See* Atlantic Coast, p. 1382.

CONSTITUTION AND GOVERNMENT. A new constitution was ratified in the general election of 2 Nov. 1976, proclaimed on 22 Dec. 1976 and became effective 1 Jan. 1977. The General Assembly consists of a Senate of 56 members and a House of Representatives of 180 members, both elected for 2 years. The Governor and Lieut.-Governor are elected for 4 years. Legislative sessions are annual, beginning the 2nd Monday in Jan. and lasting for 40 days.

Georgia was the first state to extend the franchise to all citizens 18 years old and above. The state is represented in Congress by 2 senators and 10 representatives.

Registered voters, 1986, numbered 2,575,815. At the 1988 presidential election Bush polled 1,081,331 votes, Dukakis, 714,792.

The state capital is Atlanta. Georgia is divided into 159 counties.

Governor: Joe F. Harris (D.), 1987–91 ($82,530).
Lieut.-Governor: Zell Miller (D.), ($50,076).
Secretary of State: Max Cleland (D.), ($62,920).

BUDGET. For the fiscal year ending 30 June 1987 general revenue was $8,368m. (taxes, $5,290m.; federal aid, $2,027m.); general expenditure was $8,079m. (education, $3,148m.; medical care and public assistance, $1,285m.).

On 30 June 1987 total liability was $4,390m.

Estimated *per capita* personal income (1987), was $14,098.

NATURAL RESOURCES

Minerals. Georgia is the leading producer of kaolin. The state ranks first in production of crushed and dimensional granite, second in production of fuller's earth and marble (crushed and dimensional).

Agriculture. In 1987, 49,000 farms covered 13m. acres; average farm was of 265 acres; total value, land and buildings, 1986, $11,094m. For 1986 cotton output was 185,000 bales (of 480 lb.). Other crops include tobacco, corn, wheat, soybeans, peanuts and pecans. Cash income, 1987, $3,500m: from crops, $1,300m.; from livestock, $1,800m.

On 1 Jan. 1986 farm animals included 1·65m. all cattle, including 119,000 milch cows, and 1·1m. swine.

Forestry. The forested area in 1987 was 24m. acres.

INDUSTRY. In 1987 the state's manufacturing establishments had 569,400 workers; the main groups were textiles, apparel, food and transport equipment. Trade employed 692,200, services 536,100, government, 476,000.

TOURISM. In 1987 tourists spent $8,670m.

COMMUNICATIONS

Roads. Total road mileage (Dec. 1987) was 106,386 including 1,219 interstate and 17,000 federal and state highways. Motor vehicles registered, 1986, numbered 5,140,387.

Railways. In 1976 there were 5,417 miles of railways. A metro opened in Atlanta in 1979.

Aviation. In 1988 there were 118 public and 168 private airports.

Shipping. The principal port is Savannah.

JUSTICE, RELIGION, EDUCATION AND WELFARE

Justice. State and federal prisons, 31 Dec. 1985, had 16,118 inmates. Since 1964 there have been two executions (for murder). From 1924 to 1964 there were 415 executions (electrocution), including 75 whites and 268 Negroes for murder, 3 whites and 63 Negroes for rape and 6 Negroes for armed robbery.

Under a Local Option Act, the sale of alcoholic beverages (not including malt beverages and light wines) is prohibited in more than half the counties.

Religion. An estimated 78% of the population are church members. Of the total population, 74·3% are Protestant, 3·2% are Roman Catholic and 1·5% Jewish.

Education. Since 1945 education has been compulsory; tuition is free for pupils between the ages of 6 and 18 years. In 1987 there were 1,289 public elementary schools and 361 public secondary schools; in autumn 1987 they had 1·1m. pupils and 60,509 teachers. Teachers' salaries averaged $27,606 in 1987–88. Expenditure on public schools (1987), $2,394m. or $438 per capita and $2,939 per pupil.

The University of Georgia (Athens) was founded in 1785 and was the first chartered State University in the US (26,547 students in 1987–88). Other institutions of higher learning include Georgia Institute of Technology, Atlanta (11,771), Emory University, Atlanta (8,884), Georgia State University, Atlanta (22,116) and Mercer University, Macon (3,416). The Atlanta University Center, devoted primarily to Negro education, includes Clark College (1,860) and Morris Brown College (1,257, co-educational, Morehouse (2,160), a liberal arts college for men, Interdenominational Theological Center, a co-educational theological school, and Spelman College, the first liberal arts college for Negro women in the US. Atlanta University serves as the graduate school centre for the complex. Wesleyan College near Macon is the oldest chartered women's college in the US.

Health. Hospitals licensed by the Department of Human Resources, 1985, numbered 173 with 26,051 beds.

Social Security. In Dec. 1985, 60,300 persons were receiving SSI old-age assistance of an average $128 per month; 82,500 families were receiving as aid to dependent children an average of $186 per family; aid to 89,500 disabled persons was $217 monthly.

Further Reading

Georgia History in Outline. Univ. of Georgia Press, Athens, 1978

Bonner, J. C. and Roberts, L. E. (eds.) *Studies in Georgia History and Government.* Reprint Company, Spartanburg, 1940 Repr.

Pound, M. B. and Saye, A. B., *Handbook on the Constitution of the U.S. and Georgia.* Univ. of Georgia Press, Athens, 1978

Rowland, A. R., *A Bibliography of the Writings on Georgia History.* Hamden, Conn., 1978

Saye, A. B., *A Constitutional History of Georgia, 1732–1968.* Univ. of Georgia, Athens, Rev. ed., 1970

State Library: Judicial Building, Capital Sq., Atlanta. *State Librarian:* John D. M. Folger.

HAWAII

HISTORY. The Hawaiian Islands, formerly known as the Sandwich Islands, were discovered by Capt. James Cook in Jan. 1778. During the greater part of the 19th century the islands formed an independent kingdom, but in 1893 the reigning Queen, Liliuokalani (died 11 Nov. 1917), was deposed and a provisional government formed; in 1894 a Republic was proclaimed, and in accordance with the request of the Legislature of the Republic, and a resolution of the US Congress of 6 July 1898 (signed 7 July by President McKinley), the islands were on 12 Aug. 1898 formally annexed to the US. On 14 June 1900 the islands were constituted as a Territory of Hawaii.

Statehood was granted to Hawaii on 18 March 1959, effective 21 Aug. 1959.

AREA AND POPULATION. The Hawaiian Islands lie in the North Pacific Ocean, between 18° 56' and 28° 25' N. lat. and 154° 49' and 178° 22' W. long., about 2,090 nautical miles south-west of San Francisco. There are 136 named islands and islets in the group, of which 7 major and 8 minor islands are inhabited. The land and inland water area of the state is 6,471 sq. miles, with census population, 1 April 1980, of 964,691, an increase of 194,778 or 25·4% since 1970; density was 150·1 per sq. mile.

The principal islands are Hawaii, 4,035 sq. miles and population, 1980, 92,053 (estimate, 1988, 117,500); Maui, 735 and 62,823 (84,100); Oahu, 618 and 762,534 (838,500); Kauai, 558 and 38,856 (49,100); Molokai, 264 and 6,049 (6,700); Lanai, 141 and 2,119 (2,200); Niihau, 71 and 226 (207); Kahoolawe, 46 (uninhabited). The capital Honolulu, on the island of Oahu, had a population in 1980 of 365,048 and Hilo on the island of Hawaii, 35,269. Estimated state population, 1989, 112,100.

Figures for racial groups, 1980, are: 331,925 White, 239,734 Japanese, 132,075 Filipinos, 118,251 Hawaiian, 55,916 Chinese, 17,453 Korean, 17,687 Negroes, 51,650 all others. In 1986, 31·2% of the population (outside barracks and other institutions) was of mixed race. Of the total, 92·3% were citizens of the US.

Inter-marriage between the races is popular. Of the 9,709 resident marriages in 1988, 42·9% were between partners of different race. Births, 1987, were 18,555; deaths, 6,149; infant deaths, 168; marriages, 16,567; divorces and annulments, 4,419.

CLIMATE. All the islands have a tropical climate, with an abrupt change in conditions between windward and leeward sides, most marked in rainfall. Temperatures vary little. Honolulu. Jan. 71°F (21·7°C), July 78°F (25·6°C). Annual rainfall 31" (775 mm).

CONSTITUTION AND GOVERNMENT. The constitution took effect on 21 Aug. 1959. Amended 1968 and 1978.

The Legislature consists of a Senate of 25 members elected for 4 years, and a House of Representatives of 51 members elected for 2 years. The constitution provides for annual meetings of the legislature with 60-day regular sessions. The Governor and Lieut.-Governor are elected for 4 years. The registered voters, 1988, numbered 443,742.

The state sends to Congress 2 senators and 2 representatives.

In the 1988 presidential election Dukakis polled 192,364 votes, Bush, 158,625.

Governor: John Waihee (D.), 1986–90 ($94,780).

BUDGET. Revenue is derived mainly from taxation of sales and gross receipts, real property, corporate and personal income, and inheritance taxes, licences, public land sales and leases. For the year ending 30 June 1988 state general fund receipts amounted to $2,036·2m.; special fund receipts, $1,107·7m., and federal grants, $438·3m. (included as $8·7m. of general funds and $429·6m. of special funds). State expenditures were $2,980·7m. (education, $886·2m.; highways, $78·6m.; public welfare, $380·8m.; figures include both special and general funds).

Net long-term debt, 31 Dec. 1988, amounted to $3,382·3m.

Estimated *per capita* personal income (1988) was $16,753.

NATURAL RESOURCES

Minerals. Total value of mineral production, 1988, amounted to $78,225,000. Cement shipped from plants amounted to 410,000 short tons; stone, 6,300,000 short tons.

Agriculture. Farming is highly commercialized, aiming at export to the American market, and highly mechanized. In 1987 there were 4,870 farms with an acreage of 1·72m.

Sugar and pineapples are the staple crops. Income from crop sales, 1988, was $485m., and from livestock, $88·6m. The sugar crop was valued at $209·9m.; pineapples, $107·4m.; other crops, $168·2m.

Forestry. In 1988 there were 840,540 acres of forest reserve land, including 327,845 in private ownership.

INDUSTRY AND TRADE

Industry. In 1987 manufacturing establishments employed 15,300 production workers who earned an estimated $254·6m. Defence is the second-largest industry; US armed forces spent $1,892m. in Hawaii in 1988.

Commerce. In 1988 imports were $1,118m.; exports, $131m.

Tourism. Tourism is outstanding in Hawaii's economy. Tourist arrivals numbered 1·1m. in 1967, and reached 6·1m. in 1988. Tourist expenditures, $380m. in 1967, contributed $9,200m. to the state's economy in 1988.

COMMUNICATIONS

Roads. In 1988 there were 817,609 motor vehicles, and (31 Dec. 1987) a total of 4,071 miles of highways (including 97 miles of freeways).

Aviation. There were 7 commercial airports in 1989; passengers arriving from overseas in 1988 numbered 6·65m., and there were 9m. passengers between the islands.

Shipping. Several lines of steamers connect the islands with the mainland USA, Canada, Australia, the Philippines, China and Japan. In 1989, 2,024 overseas and 3,101 inter-island vessels entered the port of Honolulu.

Post. There were 530,022 telephone access lines at 31 Dec. 1988.

Broadcasting. In 1989, Hawaii had 47 commercial and 2 other radio stations, 17 commercial and 2 other TV stations.

JUSTICE, RELIGION, EDUCATION AND WELFARE

Justice. There is no capital punishment in Hawaii.

Religion. The residents of Hawaii are mainly Christians, though there are many Buddhists. A sample survey in 1979 showed that 31% were Roman Catholic, 34% Protestant, 12% Buddhist, 2·5% Latter Day Saints.

Education. Education is free, and compulsory for children between the ages of 6 and 18. The language in the schools is English. In 1988–89 there were 235 public schools (167,899 pupils with 8,973 teachers) and 141 private schools (35,459 pupils and 2,512 teachers) ranging from kindergarten through the 12th grade. The University of Hawaii-Manoa, founded in 1907, had 18,477 day students in 1988; total attendance at all campuses of the University of Hawaii system, 42,767; 9,612 at private colleges.

Social Security. During 1988 5,123 people were receiving old-age assistance of an average $217 per month; 13,396 families, $453 in aid to dependent children; 7,008 disabled people, $288. Social Security beneficiaries, 141,730, receiving aggregate monthly payments of $67·5m.

Further Reading

Government in Hawaii. Tax Foundation of Hawaii. Honolulu, 1988
Guide to Government in Hawaii. 8th ed. Legislative Reference Bureau. State of Hawaii, Honolulu, 1989
Atlas of Hawaii. Hawaii Univ., rev. ed. Honolulu, 1983
State of Hawaii Data Book. Hawaii Dept. of Business and Economic Development, 1989
Allen, G. E., *Hawaii's War Years.* 2 vols. Hawaii Univ. Press, 1950–52
Bell, R. J., *Last Among Equals: Hawaiian Statehood and American Politics.* Honolulu, 1984
Kuykendall, R. S. and Day, A. G., *Hawaii, A History.* Rev. ed. New Jersey, 1961
Morgan, J. R., *Hawaii.* Boulder, 1982
Pukui, M. K. and Elbert, S. H., *Hawaiian–English Dictionary.* Rev. ed. Honolulu, 1986

IDAHO

HISTORY. Idaho was first permanently settled in 1860, although there was a mission for Indians in 1836 and a Mormon settlement in 1855. It was organized as a Territory in 1863 and admitted into the Union as a state on 3 July 1890.

AREA AND POPULATION. Idaho is bounded north by Canada, east by the Rocky Mountains of Montana and Wyoming, south by Nevada and Utah, west by Oregon and Washington. Area, 83,564 sq. miles, of which 1,153 sq. miles are inland water. In 1983 the federal government owned 34,282,000 acres (65% of the state area). Census population, 1 April 1980, 943,935, an increase of 32·4% since 1970. Estimate (1984) 1,001,000.

Births, 1984, 17,996 (18 per 1,000 population); deaths, 7,229 (7·2); infant deaths, 174 (9·7 per 1,000 live births); marriages, 13,264 (13·3); divorces, 6,210 (6·2).

Population in 5 census years was:

	White	*Negro*	*Indian*	*Asiatic*	*Total*	*Per sq. mile*
1910	319,221	651	3,488	2,234	325,594	3·9
1930	438,840	668	3,638	1,886	445,032	5·4
1960	657,383	1,502	5,231	2,958	667,191	8·1
1970	693,375	3,655	5,413	2,526	713,008	8·5
			All others			
1980	901,641	2,716	39,578		943,935	11·3

Of the total 1980 population, 471,155 were male, 509,702 were urban and those 20 years of age or older 600,242.

The largest cities are Boise (capital) with 1980 census population of 102,160 (1984 estimate, 107,188); Pocatello, 46,340 (45,334); Idaho Falls, 39,734 (41,774); Lewiston, 27,986 (28,050); Twin Falls, 26,209 (28,168); Nampa, 25,112 (27,347).

CLIMATE. Boise. Jan. 29°F (–1·7°C), July 74°F (23·3°C). Annual rainfall 12" (303 mm). *See* Mountain States, p. 1381.

CONSTITUTION AND GOVERNMENT. The constitution adopted in 1890 is still in force; it has had 104 amendments. The Legislature consists of a Senate of 42 members and a House of Representatives of 84 members, all the legislators being elected for 2 years. The Governor, Lieut.-Governor and Secretary of State are elected for 4 years. Voters are citizens, over the age of 18 years. The state is represented in Congress by 2 senators and 2 representatives.

In the 1988 presidential election Bush polled 253,467 votes, Dukakis, 147,420.

The state is divided into 44 counties. The capital is Boise.

Governor: Cecil Andrus (D.), 1987–91 ($50,000).

Lieut.-Governor: C. L. Otter (R.), 1987–91 ($14,000).

Secretary of State: Pete Cenarrusa (R.), 1987–91 ($37,500).

BUDGET. For the year ending 30 June 1985 (State Auditor's Office) general revenues were $551·1m. and general expenditures, $555·5m. (which includes $3·4m. outstanding obligations).

Per capita personal income (1985) was $11,120.

NATURAL RESOURCES

Minerals. Production of the most important minerals (1984): Silver, 18·87m. troy oz.; copper, 3,701 tonnes; antimony, 557 short tons. There is some gold, lead, zinc and vanadium. Non-metallic minerals include phosphate rock (4·7m. tonnes), lime (87,000 short tons), garnet, gypsum, perlite, pumice, tungsten, molybdenum, crushed stone (1·8m. short tons), sand and gravel and dimension stone. Value of total mineral output was $412m. in 1984.

Agriculture. Agriculture is the leading industry, although a great part of the state is naturally arid. Extensive irrigation works have been carried out, bringing an estimated 4m. acres under irrigation; 83 reservoirs have a total capacity of 10·4m. acre-ft, 7·3m. acre-ft of which is primarily used for irrigation.

In 1985 there were 24,600 farms with a total area of 14·7m. acres (27% of the land area); average farm had 598 acres with land and buildings valued at approximately $749 per acre.

In 1984 there were 51 soil conservation districts, managed by local farmers and ranchers, covering most of the state.

Cash receipts from marketings, 1985, was $2,063m. ($1,200m. from crops and $862m. from livestock). The most important crops are potatoes and wheat—potatoes leading all states; in 1985 the production amounted to 103m. cwt, cash receipts $323m.; wheat, 72m. bu., $235m. Other crops are sugar-beet, alfalfa, barley, field peas and beans, onions and apples. On 1 Jan. 1985 the number of sheep was 313,000; milch cows, 165,000; all cattle, 1·78m.; swine, 112,000.

Forestry. In 1983 a total of 20,635,700 acres (37·6% of the state's area) was in forests; 13,540,600 acres of this was commercial (non-reserved) forest. The volume of sawtimber in commercial forests was 139,600m. bd ft. The stumpage value of forest products was about $124m., and about $531m. was added by processing. Ownership of commercial forests is 70% federal, 6·5% state and local government, 0·5% Indian, 22·3% private. Some 16,100 workers are involved in forestry.

INDUSTRY. In 1985 85,000 were employed in trade, 70,000 in government, 66,000 in services, 55,000 in manufacturing.

TOURISM. Money spent by travellers in 1984 was about $1,200m. Estimated state and local tax receipts from tourism, $48m. Jobs generated, 25,000 (pay-roll over $300m.).

COMMUNICATIONS

Roads. The state maintained in 1985, 4,954 miles of the total of 68,808 miles of public roads; 745,462 passenger vehicles were registered in 1985.

Railways. The state had (1985) 1,910 miles of railways (including 2 Amtrak routes).

Aviation. There were 68 municipally owned airports in 1985.

Shipping. Water transport is provided from the Pacific to the Port of Lewiston, by way of the Columbia and Snake rivers, a distance of 464 miles.

JUSTICE, RELIGION, EDUCATION AND WELFARE

Justice. The death penalty may be imposed for first degree murder, but the judge must consider mitigating circumstances before imposing a sentence of death. Since 1926 only 4 men (white) have been executed, by hanging (1 in 1926, 2 in 1951 and 1 in 1957). At 1 Oct. 1985 14 prison inmates (13 men and 1 woman) were under sentence of death. Execution is now by lethal injection. The state prison system, 1 Oct. 1985, had 1,260 inmates.

Religion. The leading religious denominations are the Church of Jesus Christ of Latter Day Saints (Mormon Church), Roman Catholics, Methodists, Presbyterians, Episcopalians and Lutherans.

Education. In 1984–85 public elementary schools (grades K to 6) had 118,647 pupils and 5,481 classroom teachers; secondary schools had 92,053 pupils and 4,980 classroom teachers.

Average salary, 1984–85, of elementary and secondary classroom teachers, $20,032. The University of Idaho, founded at Moscow in 1889, had 459 professors and 8,970 students in 1984–85. There are 9 other institutions of higher education; 5 of them are public institutions with a total enrolment (1984–85) of 21,914 (excluding vocational-technical colleges).

Social Welfare. Old-age assistance is granted to persons 65 years of age and older. In Aug. 1985, 1,014 persons were drawing an average of $105.86 per month; 6,023 families with 10,858 children were drawing an average of $243.85 per case (or $90.10 per eligible person); 28 blind persons, $73.21; 569 children were receiving $248.88 per child for foster care; 1,827 permanently and totally disabled persons, $133.69.

Health. In Sept. 1985 skilled nursing covered 4,761 beds; intermediate care, 107; intermediate care for the mentally retarded 528. Hospitals had 3,547 beds and home health agencies totalled 36.

Further Reading

Idaho Blue Book. Secretary of State. Boise, 1983–84
Idaho. Idaho First National Bank
Idaho Almanac. Division of Economic and Community Affairs, 1977
Idaho's Yesterdays. State Historical Society. Quarterly

ILLINOIS

HISTORY. Illinois was first discovered by Joliet and Marquette, two French explorers, in 1673. In 1763 the country was ceded by the French to the British. In 1783 Great Britain recognized the United States' title to the land that became Illinois; it was organized as a Territory in 1809 and admitted into the Union on 3 Dec. 1818.

AREA AND POPULATION. Illinois is bounded north by Wisconsin, north-east by Lake Michigan, east by Indiana, south-east by the Ohio River (forming the boundary with Kentucky), west by the Mississippi River (forming the boundary with Missouri and Iowa). Area, 56,400 sq. miles, of which 652 sq. miles are inland water. Census population, 1980, 11,426,518, an increase of 2·71% since 1970. Estimate (1987), 11,582,000. Births in 1987 were 180,441 (15·5 per 1,000 population); deaths, 102,105 (8·7); infant deaths, 2,094 (11·1 per 1,000 live births); marriages 95,613 (8·3); divorces, 46,800 (4).

Population in 5 census years was:

	White	*Negro*	*Indian*	*All others*	*Total*	*Per sq. mile*
1910	5,526,962	109,049	188	2,392	5,638,591	100·6
1930	7,295,267	328,972	469	5,946	7,630,654	136·4
1960	9,010,252	1,037,470	4,704	28,732	10,081,158	180·3
			All others			
1970	9,600,381	1,425,674	87,921		11,113,976	199·4
1980	9,233,327	1,675,398	517,793		11,426,518	203·0

Of the total population in 1980, 5,537,737 were male, 9,518,039 persons were urban and 5,597,360 were 18 years of age or older.

The most populous cities with population (1980 census), are:

Chicago	3,005,072
Rockford	139,712
Peoria	124,160
Springfield (cap.)	99,637
Decatur	94,081
Joliet	77,956
Aurora	81,293
Evanston	73,706
Waukegan	67,653
Arlington Heights	66,116

Standard Metropolitan Statistical Area population, 1980 census (and 1988 estimate): Chicago, 7,102,378 (6,216,300); East St Louis, 565,874 (1987, 570,400); Peoria, 365,864 (340,400); Rockford, 279,514 (282,200); Springfield, 176,089 (191,700); Decatur, 131,375 (123,700).

CLIMATE. Chicago. Jan. 25°F (–3·9°C), July 73°F (22·8°C). Annual rainfall 33" (836 mm). *See* Great Lakes, p. 1382.

CONSTITUTION AND GOVERNMENT. The present constitution became effective 1 July 1971. The General Assembly consists of a House of Representatives of 118 members, elected for 2 years and a Senate of 59 members who are divided into three groups; in one, they are elected for terms of four years, four years, and two years; in the next, for terms of four years, two years, and four years; and in the last, for terms of two years, four years, and four years. Sessions are annual. The Governor and Lieut.-Governor are elected as a team for 4 years; the Comptroller and Secretary of State are elected for 4 years. Electors are citizens 18 years of age, having the usual residential qualifications.

The state is divided into legislative districts, in each of which 1 senator is chosen; each district is divided into 2 representative districts, in each of which 1 representative is chosen.

Illinois is represented in Congress by 2 senators and 22 representatives.

In the 1988 presidential election Bush polled 2,298,648 votes, Dukakis, 2,180,657.

The capital is Springfield. The state has 102 counties.

Governor: James R. Thompson (R.), 1987–91 ($88,825).
Lieut.-Governor: George Ryan (R.), 1987–91 ($62,700).
Secretary of State: Jim Edgar, 1987–91 ($78,375).

BUDGET. For the year ending 30 June 1989 general revenues were $12,133m. and general expenditures were $11,838m.

Total net long-term debt, 30 June 1988, was $13,923m.

Per capita personal income (1988) was $17,575.

ENERGY AND NATURAL RESOURCES

Minerals. Chief mineral product is coal; 43 operative mines had an output (1988) of 59,852,384 tons. Mineral production also included: Crude petroleum, fluorspar, tripoli, lime, sand, gravel and stone. Total value of mineral products, 1987, was $3,226·2m.

Agriculture. In 1989, 86,000 farms had an area of 28·5m. acres; the average farm was 331 acres.

Cash receipts, 1988, from crops, $4,215,885,000; from livestock and livestock products, $2,243,482,000. Illinois is a large producer of maize and soybeans, the state's leading cash commodities. Output, 1988: Soybeans, 234·9m. bu; wheat, 67·5m. bu; maize, 700·8m. bu. In Jan. 1989 there were 200,000 milch cows, 1·95m. all cattle; 140,000 sheep and 5·6m. swine. The wool clip was 1,038,000 lb. in 1988.

Forestry. National forest area under the US Forest Service administration, Sept. 1985, was 262,291 acres. Total forest land, 5·2m. acres.

INDUSTRY AND TRADE

Industry. In 1986, 17,906 manufacturing establishments employed 1,018,418 workers; annual payroll, $26,582·76m. Largest industry was non-electrical machinery. Gross state product, 1988, $242,300m.

Labour. In 1988 there were 5,078,000 employees, of whom 972,000 were in manufacturing, 1,253,000 in trade, 1,225,000 in services, 733,000 in government.

COMMUNICATIONS

Roads. In 1988 there were 6,279,591 passenger cars, 540,447 trucks and buses, 11,800 taxis, liveries and ambulances, 655,405 trailers and semi-trailers, 237,158 motor cycles and 25,797 other vehicles registered in the state. At 31 Dec. 1988 there were 13,222·36 miles of state primary roads of which 1,939·44 miles were interstate; 3,686·58 miles of state supplementary roads and 267·23 miles of toll roads and toll bridges.

Railways. There were, on 31 May 1987, 7,584 miles of Class I railway. Chicago is served by Amtrak long-distance trains on several routes, and by a metro (CTA) system, and by 7 groups of commuter railways controlled by the Northeast Illinois Railroad Corporation (now called METRA).

Shipping. In 1987 the seaport of Chicago handled 20,705,271 short tons of cargo.

Aviation. There were (1988) 130 public airports and 714 restricted landing areas.

JUSTICE, RELIGION, EDUCATION AND WELFARE

Justice. In 1985 there were no executions; since 1930 there have been 90 executions (electrocution), including 58 white men, 1 white woman and 31 Negro men, all for murder. In June 1989 the total average daily prison population was 21,271.

A Civil Rights Act (1941), as amended, bans all forms of discrimination by places of public accommodation, including inns, restaurants, retail stores, railroads, aeroplanes, buses, etc., against persons on account of 'race, religion, colour, national ancestry or physical or mental handicap'; another section similarly mentions 'race or colour.'

The Fair Employment Practices Act of 1961, as amended, prohibits discrimination in employment based on race, colour, sex, religion, national origin or ancestry, by employers, employment agencies, labour organizations and others. These principles are embodied in the 1971 constitution.

The Illinois Human Rights Act (1979), prevents unlawful discrimination in employment, real property transactions, access to financial credit, and public accommodations, by authorizing the creation of a Department of Human Rights to enforce, and a Human Rights Commission to adjudicate, allegations of unlawful discrimination.

Religion. Among the larger religious denominations are: Roman Catholic (3·6m.), Jewish (50,000), Presbyterian Church, USA (200,000), Lutheran Church in America (200,000), Lutheran Church Missouri Synod (325,000), American Baptist (105,000), Disciples of Christ (75,000), and United Methodist (505,000), Southern Baptist (265,000), United Church of Christ (192,000), Church of Nazarene (50,000), Assembly of God (63,000).

Education. Education is free and compulsory for children between 7 and 16 years of age. In autumn 1988 public school elementary enrolments were 1,258,468 pupils and 59,144 teachers; secondary enrolments, 536,448 pupils and 29,500 teachers. Enrolment (1988–89) in non-public schools was 252,487 elementary and 71,833 secondary. Teachers' salaries, 1988–89, averaged $31,195. Total enrolment in 179 institutions of higher education (autumn 1988) was 693,321.

Colleges and universities with over 3,000 students:

Founded	*Name*	*Place*	*Control*	*Autumn 1988 Enrolment*
1851	Northwestern University	Evanston	Methodist	16,592
1857	Illinois State University	Normal	Public	22,330
1867	University of Illinois	Urbana	Public	62,340
1867	Chicago State University [1]	Chicago	Public	6,134
1869	Southern Illinois University	Carbondale	Public	35,579
1870	Loyola University	Chicago	Roman Catholic	13,870
1890	University of Chicago	Chicago	Non-Sect.	10,409
1895	Eastern Illinois University	Charleston	Public	11,159
1895	Northern Illinois University	DeKalb	Public	24,255
1897	Bradley University	Peoria	Non-Sect.	5,174
1899	Western Illinois University	Macomb	Public	12,765
1940	Illinois Institute of Technology [2]	Chicago	Non-Sect.	6,269
1945	Roosevelt University	Chicago	Non-Sect.	6,374
1961	Northeastern Illinois University [3]	Chicago	Public	9,846

[1] Formerly Illinois Teachers College (South).
[2] Illinois Institute of Technology formed in 1940 by merger of two older technical schools.
[3] Formerly Illinois Teachers' College (North).

Health. In 1987 hospitals listed by the American Hospital Association numbered 258, with 62,469 beds. At June 1989 state institutions had 4,540 developmentally disabled and 3,557 mentally ill residents.

Social Security. State-administered Supplemental Security Income (SSI) was paid to 53,564 recipients in financial year 1989; gross income-maintenance payments (no adjustments) totalled \$61·2m.; medical payments, \$161m. Aid to families with dependent children was paid to 213,667 families, average monthly payment per family, \$309; total payments, \$793·4m.; medical payments, \$463·9m.

Further Reading

Blue Book of the State of Illinois. Edited by Secretary of State. Springfield. Biennial
Angle, P. M. and Beyer, R. L., *A Handbook of Illinois History*. Illinois State Historical Society, Springfield, 1943
Clayton, J., *The Illinois Fact Book and Historical Almanac 1673–1968*. Southern Illinois Univ., 1970
Howard, R. P., *Illinois: A History of the Prairie State*. Grand Rapids, 1972
Pease, T. C., *The Story of Illinois*. 3rd ed. Chicago, 1965

The Illinois State Library: Springfield, Il.62756. *State Librarian:* Jim Edgar.

INDIANA

HISTORY. Indiana, first settled in 1732–33, was made a Territory in 1800 and admitted into the Union on 11 Dec. 1816.

AREA AND POPULATION. Indiana is bounded west by Illinois, north by Michigan and Lake Michigan, east by Ohio and south by Kentucky across the Ohio River. Area, 36,185 sq. miles, of which 253 sq. miles are inland water. Census population, 1 April 1980, was 5,490,224, an increase of 294,832 or 5·7% since 1970. Estimate (1988) 5,575,000. In 1986 births were 79,269 (14·4 per 1,000 population); deaths 49,257 (8·9); infant deaths, 888 (11·2 per 1,000 live births); marriages 49,900 (9·1).

Population in 5 census years was:

	White	*Negro*	*Indian*	*Asiatic*	*Total*	*Per sq. mile*
1910	2,639,961	60,320	279	316	2,700,876	74·9
1930	3,125,778	111,982	285	458	3,238,503	89·4
1960	4,388,554	269,275	948	2,447	4,662,498	128·9
			All others			
1970	4,820,324	357,464	15,881		5,193,669	143·9
1980	5,004,394	414,785	71,045		5,490,224	152·8

Of the total in 1980, 2,665,805 were male, 3,525,298 were urban and 3,545,431 were 21 years of age or older.

The largest cities with census population, 1980 (and 1988 estimates), are: Indianapolis (capital), 711,539 (727,130); Fort Wayne, 172,196 (179,810); Gary, 151,953 (132,460); Evansville, 130,496 (128,210); South Bend, 109,727 (106,190); Hammond, 93,714 (84,630); Muncie, 77,216 (73,320); Anderson, 64,695 (60,720); Terre Haute, 61,125 (56,330); Bloomington (54,850).

CLIMATE. Indianapolis. Jan. 29°F (–1·7°C), July 76°F (24·4°C). Annual rainfall 41" (1,034 mm). *See* The Mid-West, p. 1382.

CONSTITUTION AND GOVERNMENT. The present constitution (the second) dates from 1851; it has had (as of Nov. 1983) 34 amendments. The General Assembly consists of a Senate of 50 members elected for 4 years, and a House of Representatives of 100 members elected for 2 years.

A constitutional amendment of 1970 allows the legislators to set the length and frequency of sessions, which are currently held annually. The Governor and Lieut.-Governor are elected for 4 years. The state is represented in Congress by 2 senators and 10 representatives.

In the 1988 presidential election Bush polled 1,280,292 votes, Dukakis, 850,851.

The state capital is Indianapolis. The state is divided into 92 counties and 1,008 townships.

Governor: Evan Bayh (D.), 1989–92 (\$66,000 plus expenses).

Lieut.-Governor: Frank O'Bannon (D.), 1988–92 ($51,000 plus expenses).
Secretary of State: Joseph Hogsett (D.), 1988–92 ($46,000).

BUDGET. In the fiscal year 1986–87 (US Census Bureau figures) total revenues were $9,037·5m. ($1,875·3m. from federal government, $4,774·2m. from taxes), total expenditures were $8,341·9m. ($1,829·6m. for education, $1,050m. for public welfare and $606·6m. for highways).

Total long-term debt, on 30 June 1987, was $2,691·5m.

Per capita personal income (1988) was $14,924.

ENERGY AND NATURAL RESOURCES

Minerals. The state produced 26·7m. short tons of crushed stone and 159,000 short tons of dimension stone in 1984; the output of coal was 30·9m. short tons; petroleum, 5m. bbls (of 42 gallons).

Agriculture. Indiana is largely agricultural, about 75% of its total area being in farms. In 1987, 70,506 farms had 16,170,895 acres (average, 229 acres). Cash income, 1987, from crops, including nursery and greenhouse crops, $2,127,135; from livestock, poultry and their products, $1,940,549.

The chief crops (1987) were corn for grain or seed (619,049,978 bu.), corn for silage or green chop (1,961,381 tons), wheat for grain (30,789,151 bu.), oats for grain, (4,317,321 bu.), soybeans for beans (169,749,051 bu.), hay (alfalfa, other tame small grain, wild, grass silage, etc.) (1,892,466 tons).

The livestock on 1 Jan. 1987 included 2,031,915 all cattle, 163,867 milch cows, 82,757 sheep and lambs, 4,372,294 hogs and pigs, 26,787,315 chickens. In 1987 the wool clip yielded 537,966 lb. of wool from 76,056 sheep and lambs.

Forestry. In 1988 there were 4·3m. acres of forest and (1987) 12 state forests and Hoosier National Forest (187,812 acres).

INDUSTRY. Manufacturing establishments employed, in 1986, 575,200 workers, earning $14,772·4m. The steel industry is the largest in the country.

COMMUNICATIONS

Roads. In 1987 there were 91,535·7 miles of highways, roads and streets, of which 66,039·85 miles were county roads and 11,289·31 miles state roads, interstate highways and toll roads. Motor vehicles registered, 1988, 4,550,450.

Railways. In 1980 there were 5,252 miles of mainline railway, 921 miles of secondary track and 3,295 miles of side and yard track.

Aviation. Of airports, 1987, 130 were for public use, 414 were private and 3 were military.

JUSTICE, RELIGION, EDUCATION AND WELFARE

Justice. In 1963–80 there were no executions; there have since been 4, for murder. State correctional institutions, financial year 1987–88, had an average daily population of 11,889.

The Civil Rights Act of 1885 forbids places of public accommodation to bar any persons on grounds not applicable to all citizens alike; no citizen may be disqualified for jury service 'on account of race or colour'. An Act of 1947 makes it an offence to spread religious or racial hatred.

A 1961 Act provided 'all . . . citizens equal opportunity for education, employment and access to public conveniences and accommodations' and created a Civil Rights Commission.

Religion. Religious denominations include Methodists, Roman Catholic, Disciples of Christ, Baptists, Lutheran, Presbyterian churches, Society of Friends.

Education. School attendance is compulsory from 7 to 16 years. In 1987–88 public and parochial schools, had 927,895 pupils and 52,626 teachers. Teachers' salaries, grades 1–12, averaged $26,592 (1987–88). Total expenditure for public schools, $2,788·5m.

The principal institutions for higher education are (1987–88):

Founded	*Institution*	*Control*	*Students (full-time)*
1801	Vincennes University	State	8,228
1824	Indiana University, Bloomington	State	33,421
1837	De Pauw University, Greencastle	Methodist	2,404
1842	University of Notre Dame	R.C.	9,811
1850	Butler University, Indianapolis	Independent	3,723
1859	Valparaiso University, Valparaiso	Evangelical Lutheran Church	3,690
1870	Indiana State University, Terre Haute	State	11,161
1874	Purdue University, Lafayette	State	33,303
1898	Ball State University, Muncie	State	19,110
1902	University of Indianapolis, Indianapolis	Methodist	1,471
1963	Indiana Vocational Technical College, Indianapolis	State	4,760
1985	University of Southern Indiana	State	4,624

Health. Hospitals listed by the Indiana State Board of Health (1988) numbered 124 (23,929 beds in 1981). On 30 June 1983, 11 state mental hospitals had 6,273 patients enrolled (4,472 present).

Social Security. Old-age assistance, assistance to the blind and to the disabled were transferred from state to federal programmes in June 1974. In July–Dec. 1988, state supplemental assistance and/or Federal Supplemental Security assistance was paid to an average of 11,188 aged persons per month (total $8,545,308), 1,175 blind ($1,677,197) and 40,797 disabled ($56,517,120).

Further Reading

Indiana State Chamber of Commerce. *Here is Your Indiana Government.* 22nd ed. Indianapolis, 1985

State Library: Indiana State Library, 140 North Senate, Indianapolis 46204. *Director:* C. Ray Ewick.

IOWA

HISTORY. Iowa, first settled in 1788, was made a Territory in 1838 and admitted into the Union on 28 Dec. 1846.

AREA AND POPULATION. Iowa is bounded east by the Mississippi River (forming the boundary with Wisconsin and Illinois), south by Missouri, west by the Missouri River (forming the boundary with Nebraska), north-west by the Big Sioux River (forming the boundary with South Dakota) and north by Minnesota. Area, 56,375 sq. miles, including 310 sq. miles of inland water. Census population, 1 April 1980, 2,913,808, an increase of 3·17% since 1970. Estimate, 1987, 2,834,000. Births, 1988, were 38,070; deaths, 27,851; infant deaths, 330; marriages, 25,090; dissolutions of marriages, 10,808.

Population in 5 census years was:

	White	*Negro*	*Indian*	*Asiatic*	*Total*	*Per sq. mile*
1870	1,188,207	5,762	48	3	1,194,020	21·5
1930	2,452,677	17,380	660	222	2,470,939	44·1
1960	2,728,709	25,354	1,708	1,022	2,757,537	49·2
			All others			
1970	2,782,762	32,596	10,010		2,825,368	50·5
1980	2,839,225	41,700	32,882		2,913,808	51·7

At the census of 1980, 1,415,705 were male, 1,708,232 were urban and 1,971,502 were 20 years of age or older.

The largest cities in the state, with their census population in 1980 are: Des Moines (capital), 191,003; Cedar Rapids, 110,243; Davenport, 103,264; Sioux City, 82,003; Waterloo, 75,985; Dubuque, 62,321; Council Bluffs, 56,449; Iowa City, 50,508; Ames, 45,775; Cedar Falls, 36,322; Clinton, 32,828; Mason City, 30,144; Burlington, 29,529; Fort Dodge, 29,423; Ottumwa, 27,381.

CLIMATE. Cedar Rapids. Jan. 18·5°F (–7·5°C), July 74·3°F (23·5°C). Annual rainfall 36" (903 mm). Des Moines. Jan. 18·6°F (–7·5°C), July 76·3°F (29·6°C). Annual rainfall 31" (773 mm). *See* The Mid-West, p. 1382.

CONSTITUTION AND GOVERNMENT. The constitution of 1857 still exists; it has had 42 amendments. The General Assembly comprises a Senate of 50 and a House of Representatives of 100 members, meeting annually for an unlimited session. Senators are elected for 4 years, half retiring every second year: Representatives for 2 years. The Governor and Lieut.-Governor are elected for 4 years. The state is represented in Congress by 2 senators and 6 representatives. Iowa is divided into 99 counties; the capital is Des Moines.

In the 1988 presidential election Dukakis polled 670,557 votes, Bush, 545,355.

Governor: Terry Branstad (R.), 1987–91 ($72,500).
Lieut.-Governor: Jo Ann Zimmerman (D.), 1987–91 ($25,100).
Secretary of State: Elaine Baxter (D.) ($55,700).

BUDGET. For fiscal year 1987-88 state tax revenue was $2,622·1m. General expenditures were $2,012m. for education, $769·3m. for public welfare, and $666·56m. for transport.

On 30 June 1987 the net long-term debt was $579m.

Per capita personal income (1988) was $14,662.

ENERGY AND NATURAL RESOURCES

Minerals. The leading products by value are crushed stone (25·99m. tons in 1987) and cement (2·14m. short tons in 1987). Coalfields produced 330,747 short tons in 1988. The value of mineral products, 1987, was $305·1m.

Agriculture. Iowa is the wealthiest of the agriculture states, partly because nearly the whole area (93·5%) is arable and included in farms. It has escaped large-scale commercial farming. The average farm (in 1988) was 313 acres.

Cash farm income (1987 estimate) was $10,768m.; from livestock, $5,270m., and from crops, $3,510m. Production of corn was 1,307m. bu., value $2,470m. and soybeans (1984), 343·6m. bu., value $2,051m. On 1 Dec. 1988 livestock included swine, 13·9m. (leading all states); milch cows, 310,000; all cattle, 4·75m., and sheep and lambs, 415,000. The wool clip (1984) yielded 3·7m. lb. of wool.

INDUSTRY. In 1988 manufacturing establishments employed 227,200 people: Trade, 294,500; services, 261,400.

COMMUNICATIONS

Roads. On 1 Jan. 1989 number of miles of streets and highways was 112,712; there were 1·5m. licensed drivers and 2·98m. registered vehicles.

Railways. The state, 1988, had 4,428 miles of track, and 7 Class I railways.

Aviation. Airports (1988), numbered 350, including 117 lighted airports and 97 all-weather runways. There were approximately 2,400 private aircraft.

JUSTICE, RELIGION, EDUCATION AND WELFARE

Justice. There is now no capital punishment in Iowa. State prisons, 31 Dec. 1987, had 2,863 inmates.

Religion. Chief religious bodies in 1989 were: Roman Catholic (539,482 members); United Methodists, 261,613; American Lutheran, 153,539 baptised members; United Presbyterians, 86,763; United Church of Christ, 50,840.

Education. School attendance is compulsory for 24 consecutive weeks annually during school age (7–16). In 1988–89 525,173 were attending primary and secondary schools; 48,973 pupils attending non-public schools. Classroom teachers numbered 30,000 in 1988 with average salary of $24,900; total expenditure on public schools was $1,865m. or $655 per capita. Leading institutions for higher education (1987–88) were:

Founded	*Institution*	*Control*	*Full-time Professors*	*Students*
1843	Clarke College, Dubuque	Independent	31	830
1846	Grinnell College, Grinnell	Independent	100	1,302
1847	University of Iowa, Iowa City	State	989	29,230
1851	Coe College, Cedar Rapids	Independent	64	1,242
1852	Wartburg College, Waverly	American Lutheran	69	1,358
1853	Cornell College, Mount Vernon	Independent	74	1,129
1858	Iowa State University, Ames	State	1,156	25,448
1876	Univ. of Northern Iowa, Cedar Falls	State	476	11,472
1881	Drake University, Des Moines	Independent	196	6,618
1894	Morningside College, Sioux City	Methodist	60	1,206

Health. In 1986, the state had 138 hospitals (18,100 beds). In 1989-90 the state-run hospitals served 4,628 patients and had an average daily census of 692.

Social Security. Iowa has a Civil Rights Act (1939) which makes it a misdemeanour for any place of public accommodation to deprive any person of 'full and equal enjoyment' of the facilities it offers the public.

Supplemental Security Income (SSI) assistance is available for the aged (65 or older), the blind and the disabled. In Aug. 1989, 8,034 elderly persons were drawing an average of $119 per month, 1,081 blind persons $242 per month, and 22,231 disabled persons $243 per month. Aid to dependent children was received by 33,970 families representing 95,017 persons.

Further Reading

Statistical Information: State Departments of Health, Public Instruction and Social Services; State Aeronautics and Commerce Commissions; Iowa Department of Economic Development; Crop and Livestock Reporting Services, Des Moines; Iowa Dept. of Transportation, Ames; Geological Survey, Iowa City; Iowa College Aid Commission.
Annual Survey of Manufactures. US Department of Commerce
Government Finance. US Department of Commerce
Official Register. Secretary of State. Des Moines. Biennial
Petersen, W. J., *Iowa History Reference Guide.* Iowa City, 1952
Smeal, L., *Iowa Historical and Biographical Index.* New York, 1984
Vexler, R. I., *Iowa Chronology and Factbook.* Oceana, 1978

State Library of Iowa: Des Moines 50319.

KANSAS

HISTORY. Kansas, settled in 1727, was made a Territory (along with part of Colorado) in 1854, and was admitted into the Union with its present area on 29 Jan. 1861.

AREA AND POPULATION. Kansas is bounded north by Nebraska, east by Missouri, with the Missouri River as boundary in the north-east, south by Oklahoma and west by Colorado. Area, 82,277 sq. miles, including 499 sq. miles of inland water. Census population, 1 April 1980, 2,364,236, an increase of 5·1% since 1970. Estimate (1985) 2,450,000. Vital statistics, 1984: Births, 38,570 (15·8 per 1,000 population); deaths, 21,742 (8·9); infant deaths, 336 (8·7 per 1,000 live births); marriages, 24,795 (10·2); divorces 12,915 (5·3).

Population in 5 federal census years was:

	White	Negro	Indian	Asiatic	Total	Per sq. mile
1870	346,377	17,108	914	—	364,399	4·5
1930	1,811,997	66,344	2,454	204	1,880,999	22·9
1960	2,078,666	91,445	5,069	2,271	2,178,611	26·3
			All others			
1970	2,122,068	106,977	17,533		2,249,071	27·5
1980	2,168,221	126,127	69,888		2,364,236	28·8

Of the total population in 1980, 1,156,941 were male, 1,575,899 were urban and those 20 years of age or older numbered 1,620,368.

Cities, with 1980 census population, are Wichita, 279,835; Kansas City, 161,148; Topeka (capital), 115,266; Overland Park, 81,784; Lawrence, 52,738.

CLIMATE. Dodge City. Jan. 29°F (–1·7°C), July 78°F (25·6°C). Annual rainfall 21" (518 mm). Kansas City. Jan. 30°F (–1·1°C), July 79°F (26·1°C). Annual rainfall 38" (947 mm). Topeka. Jan. 28°F (–2·2°C), July 78°F (25·6°C). Annual rainfall 35" (875 mm). Wichita. Jan. 31°F (–0·6°C), July 81°F (27·2°C). Annual rainfall 31" (777 mm). *See* Mid-West, p. 1382.

CONSTITUTION AND GOVERNMENT. The year 1861 saw the adoption of the present constitution; it has had 78 amendments. The Legislature includes a Senate of 40 members, elected for 4 years, and a House of Representatives of 125 members, elected for 2 years. Sessions are annual. The Governor and Lieut.-Governor are elected for 4 years. The right to vote (with the usual exceptions) is possessed by all citizens. The state is represented in Congress by 2 senators and 5 representatives.

The state was the first (of 42 states) to establish in 1933 a Legislative Council; this is now called the Legislative Coordinating Council and has 7 members.

In the 1988 presidential election Bush polled 552,659 votes, Dukakis, 422,056.

The capital is Topeka. The state is divided into 105 counties.

Governor: Mike Hayden (R.), 1987–91 ($65,000).
Lieut.-Governor: Thomas Docking (D.), 1987–91 ($18,207).
Secretary of State: Bill Graves (R.) ($50,000).

BUDGET. For the year ending 30 June 1986 (Governor's Budget Report) general revenue fund was $1,863m. General expenditures were $1,738m.

Bonded debt outstanding for 1982 amounted to $316·9m.

Per capita personal income (1985) was $13,775.

ENERGY AND NATURAL RESOURCES

Minerals. Important minerals are coal, petroleum (75m. bbl. in 1985), natural gas (513,000m. cu. ft.), lead and zinc.

Agriculture. Kansas is pre-eminently agricultural, but sometimes suffers from lack of rainfall in the west. In 1985, 72,000 farms covered 48m. acres; average farm, 667 acres.

Cash income, 1985, from crops was $2,478m.; from livestock and products, $3,264m.

Kansas is a great wheat-producing state. Its output in 1985 was 433·2m. bu. valued at $1,321m. Other crops in 1985 (in bushels) were maize, 140m. ($351m.); sorghum, 207m.; soybeans, 44m.; oats and barley. The state has an extensive livestock industry, comprising, on 1 Jan. 1986, 115,000 milch cows, 5·8m. all cattle, 210,000 sheep and lambs 1·5m. swine.

INDUSTRY. Employment distribution (1985): Total workforce 975,000, of which 245,000 were in trade; 191,000 in government; 187,000 in services; 174,000 in manufacturing; 65,000 in transport and utilities; 53,000 in finance, insurance and real estate; 44,000 in construction. The slaughtering industry, other food processing, aircraft, the manufacture of transport equipment and petroleum refining are important.

COMMUNICATIONS

Roads. The state in Dec. 1982 had 135,087 miles of roads and streets including 8,916 miles of interstate and other primary and federally-aided highways. In 1985 2,157 vehicles were registered.

Railways. There were 7,273 miles of railway in Jan. 1982.

Aviation. There were 384 airports and landing strips in 1983, of which 168 were public.

JUSTICE, RELIGION, EDUCATION AND WELFARE

Justice. There were 4,748 prisoners in state institutions, 31 Dec. 1985. The death penalty (by hanging) for murder was abolished in 1907 and restored in 1935; there have been no executions since 1968; executions 1934 to 1968 have been 15 (all for murder).

For the various Civil Rights Acts forbidding racial or political discrimination, *see* THE STATESMAN'S YEAR-BOOK, 1955, p. 666. The 1965 Kansas Act against Discrimination declared that it is the policy of the state to eliminate and prevent discrimination in all employment relations, and to eliminate and prevent discrimination, segregation or separation in all places of public accommodations covered by the Act.

Religion. The most numerous religious bodies are Roman Catholic, Methodists and Disciples of Christ.

Education. In 1982–83 organized school districts had 1,519 elementary and secondary schools which had 407,074 pupils and 26,053 teachers. Average salary of public school teachers, 1986, $22,800 (elementary and secondary). There were 20 independent colleges, 20 community colleges, 2 Bible colleges, 1 municipal university.

Kansas has 6 state-supported institutions of higher education: Kansas State University, Manhattan (1863), had 17,570 students in 1985–86; The University of Kansas, Lawrence, founded in 1865, had 24,774; Emporia State University, Emporia, had 5,344; Pittsburg State University, Pittsburg, had 5,096; Fort Hays State University, Hays, had 5,657 and Wichita State University, Wichita, had 16,902. The state also supports a two-year technical school, Kansas Technical Institute, at Salina.

Health. In 1983 the state had 165 hospitals (18,300 beds) listed by the American Hospital Association; hospitals had an average daily occupancy rate of 70·3%.

Social Security. In Dec. 1985, 20,900 persons received state and federal aid under programmes of aid to the aged or disabled, and 66,800 in 22,700 families received aid to dependent children. Average monthly payment to the aged, $121; the disabled, $206, per family with dependent children, $303 (1984).

Further Reading

Annual Economic Report of the Governor. Topeka
Directory of State Officers, Boards and Commissioners and Interesting Facts Concerning Kansas. Topeka, Biennial
Drury, J. W., *The Government of Kansas*. Lawrence, Univ. of Kansas, 1970
Zornow, W. F., *Kansas: A History of the Jayhawk State*. Norman, Okla., 1957
State Library: Kansas State Library, Topeka.

KENTUCKY

HISTORY. Kentucky, first settled in 1765, was originally part of Virginia; it was admitted into the Union on 1 June 1792 and its first legislature met on 4 June.

AREA AND POPULATION. Kentucky is bounded north by the Ohio River (forming the boundary with Illinois, Indiana and Ohio), north-east by the Big Sandy River (forming the boundary with West Virginia), east by Virginia, south by Tennessee and west by the Mississippi River (forming the boundary with Missouri).

Area, 40,409 sq. miles, of which 740 sq. miles are water. Census population, 1980 3,660,777, an increase of 13·6% since 1970. Estimate (1988) 3,727,000. Births in 1987, 51,358 (13·8 per 1,000 population); deaths, 34,579 (9·3); infant deaths, 497 (9·7 per 1,000 live births); marriages, 46,917 (12·6); divorces, 19,797 (5·3).

Population in 5 census years was:

	White	*Negro*	*All others*	*Total*	*Per sq.mile*
1930	2,388,364	226,040	185	2,614,589	65·1
1950	2,742,090	201,921	795	2,944,806	73·9
1960	2,820,083	215,949	2,124	3,038,156	76·2
1970	2,981,766	230,793	6,147	3,218,706	81·2
1980	3,379,006	259,477	22,294	3,660,777	92·3

Of the total population in 1980, 1,789,039 were male, 1,862,183 were urban and 2,359,614 were 21 years old or older.

The principal cities with census population in 1980 are: Louisville, 298,694 (urbanized area, 654,938); Lexington-Fayette, 204,165; Owensboro, 54,450; Covington, 49,585; Bowling Green, 40,450; Paducah, 29,315; Hopkinsville, 27,318; Ashland, 27,064; Frankfort (capital), 25,973.

CLIMATE. Kentucky has a temperate climate. Temperatures are moderate during both winter and summer, precipitation is ample without a pronounced dry season, and there is little snow during the winter. Lexington. Jan. 33°F (0·6°C), July 76°F (24·4°C). Annual rainfall 43" (1,077 mm). Louisville. Jan. 34°F (1·1°C), July 78°F (25·6°C). Annual rainfall 43" (1,077 mm). *See* Appalachian Mountains, p. 1382.

CONSTITUTION AND GOVERNMENT. The constitution dates from 1891; there had been 3 preceding it. The 1891 constitution was promulgated by convention and provides that amendments be submitted to the electorate for ratification. The General Assembly consists of a Senate of 38 members elected for 4 years, one half retiring every 2 years, and a House of Representatives of 100 members elected for 2 years. A constitutional amendment approved by the voters in Nov. 1979, changes the year in which legislators are elected from odd to even numbered years and establishes an organizational session of the legislature, limited to ten legislative days, in odd-numbered years. The amendment provides for regular sessions limited to 60 legislative days between the first Tuesday after the first Monday of Jan. and 15 April of even numbered years. The Governor and Lieut.-Governor are elected for 4 years. All citizens are (with necessary exceptions) qualified as electors; the voting age was in 1955 reduced from 21 to 18 years. Registered voters, July 1989: 1,938,707. In the 1988 presidential election Bush polled 731,446 votes, Dukakis, 579,077.

The state is represented in Congress by 2 senators and 7 representatives.

The capital is Frankfort. The state is divided into 120 counties.

Governor: Wallace G. Wilkinson (D.), 1987–91 ($69,730).[1]
Lieut.-Governor: Brereton Jones (D.) ($59,262).[1]
Secretary of State: Brerner Ehrler (D.) ($59,262).[1]

[1] 1989. Salaries are revised annually by the percentage change in the Consumer Price Index.

BUDGET. For the fiscal year ending 30 June 1989 revenues received within the five major operating funds amounted to $6,329·7m. Included in this figure are $3,289m. General Fund revenues and $1,554m. Federal Fund revenues. Total expenditures amounted to $6,027·5m. including education and humanities, $1,647·5m.; human resources benefits payments, $990·4m.; and transport, $647·9m.

The general obligation bonded indebtedness on 30 June 1989 was $95·5m.

Per capita personal income (1988) was $12,822.

ENERGY AND NATURAL RESOURCES

Minerals. The principal mineral product of Kentucky is coal, 165·2m. short tons mined in 1987, value $4,320m. Output of petroleum, 5·7m. bbls (of 42 gallons); natural gas, 70,125m. cu. ft; stone, 43·3m. short tons, value $173m.; clay 1,031,000 short tons, value $8·8m.; sand and gravel, 7·1m. short tons, value $15m. Total value of non-fuel mineral products in 1987 was $290,335,000. Other minerals include fluorspar, ball clay, lead, zinc, silver, cement, lime, industrial sand and gravel, oil shale and tar sands.

Agriculture. In 1989, 96,000 farms had an area of 14·2m. acres. The average farm was 148 acres.

Cash income, 1988, from crops, $992·1m., and from livestock, $1,538m. The chief crop is tobacco: Production, in 1988, 355m. lb., ranking second to N. Carolina in US. Other principal crops include hay, corn, soybeans, wheat, fruit and vegetables, barley, sorghum grain, oats and rye.

Stock-raising is important in Kentucky, which has long been famous for its horses. The livestock in 1988 included 217,000 milch cows, 2·5m. cattle and calves, 32,000 sheep, 1,090,000 swine.

Forestry. Total forests area, 1978, 12,160,800 acres. Total commercial forest land, 1978, 11,901,900 acres; 92% is privately owned.

INDUSTRY. In 1988 the state's 3,903 manufacturing plants had 205,540 production workers; value added by manufacture in 1986 was $15,909·1m. The leading manufacturing industries (by employment) are non-electrical machinery, fabric products including clothing, electrical equipment and printing.

TOURISM. In 1988 tourist expenditure was $4,213m., producing over $311m. in tax revenues and generating 116,991 jobs. The state had (1988) 851 hotels and motels, 240 campgrounds and 45 state parks.

COMMUNICATIONS

Roads. In 1989 the state had over 79,227 miles of federal, state and local roads. There were over 2·7m. motor vehicle registrations in 1987.

Railways. In 1988 there were 3,521 miles of railway.

Aviation. There are (1988) 76 publicly-used airports and 2,144 registered aircraft in Kentucky.

Shipping. There is an increasing amount of barge traffic on 1,090 miles of navigable rivers. There are 5 river ports, 2 under construction and 2 planned.

JUSTICE, RELIGION, EDUCATION AND WELFARE

Justice. There are 10 prisons within the Department of Adult Institutions and one privately-run adult institution; average daily population (1988–89), 7,243, including 5,438 in prison, 343 in a private prison, 1,003 in jails awaiting incarceration, 459 in local community centers.

There has been no execution since 1962. A session of Congress in 1976 limited the death penalty to cases of kidnap and murder.

Total executions, 1911–62, were 162, including 76 whites and 86 Negroes; 144 were for murder, 7 for rape, 6 for criminal offences, 5 for armed robbery. There were (1989) 33 people under death sentences.

Religion. The chief religious denominations in 1980 were: Southern Baptists, with 883,096 members, Roman Catholic (365,277), United Methodists (234,536), Christian Churches and Church of Christ (81,222) and Christian (Disciples of Christ) (78,275).

Education. Attendance at school between the ages of 5 and 15 years (inclusive) is compulsory, the normal term being 175 days. In 1988–89, 23,775 teachers were employed in public elementary and 11,840 in secondary schools, in which 433,757 and 204,145 pupils enrolled respectively. Expenditure on elementary and secondary day schools in 1988–89 was $2,288m.; public school classroom teachers' salaries (1988–89) averaged $24,933.

There were also 4,057 teachers working in private elementary and secondary schools with 65,088 students.

The state has 25 universities and senior colleges, 4 junior colleges and 14 community colleges, with a total (autumn 1988) of 152,565 students. Of these uni versities and colleges, 23 are state-supported, and the remainder are supported privately. The largest of the institutions of higher learning are (autumn 1988): University of Kentucky, with 22,334 students; University of Louisville, 21,385 students; Western Kentucky University, 14,121 students; Eastern Kentucky University, 13,664 students; Murray State University, 7,628 students; Morehead State University, 7,379 students; Northern Kentucky University, 9,497 students; Kentucky State, 2,222. Five of the several privately endowed colleges of standing are Berea College, Berea; Centre College, Danville; Transylvania University, Lexington; Georgetown College, Georgetown; and Bellarmine College, Louisville.

Health. In 1988 the state had 129 licensed hospitals (19,237 beds). There were 343 licensed long-term care facilities (29,688) and 477 licensed family care homes (1,539).

Welfare. In Aug. 1989 there were 277,040 persons receiving financial assistance; 108,895 of these persons received the Federal Supplemental Security Income (SSI); 30,951 of them were aged, 2,024 blind, 75,920 disabled. Also, in the all state funded Supplementation programme, payments were made in Aug. 1989 to 6,494 persons, of which 3,178 were aged, 86 blind and 3,230 disabled. The average State Supplementation payment was $133.90 to aged, $73.87 to blind and $138.89 to disabled.

In the Aid to Families with Dependent Children Programme as of Aug. 1989, aid was given to 161,651 persons in 60,968 families. The average payment per person was $85.93, per family $227.84.

In addition to money payments, medical assistance, food stamps and social services are available.

Further Reading

Kentucky Economic Statistics. Cabinet for Economic Development, Frankfort
Kentucky Statistical Abstract. Univ. of Kentucky, Center for Business and Economic Research
Lee, L. G., *A Brief History of Kentucky and its Counties.* Berea, 1981

LOUISIANA

HISTORY. Louisiana was first settled in 1699. That part lying east of the Mississippi River was organized in 1804 as the Territory of New Orleans, and admitted into the Union on 30 April 1812. The section west of the river was added very shortly thereafter.

AREA AND POPULATION. Louisiana is bounded north by Arkansas, east by Mississippi, with the Mississippi River forming the boundary in the north-east, south by the Gulf of Mexico and west by Texas, with the Sabine River forming most of the boundary. Area, 52,453 sq. miles, including lakes, rivers and coastal waters inside 3-mile limit; land area, 44,873 sq. miles. Census population, 1 April 1980, 4,205,900, an increase of 15·5% since 1970. Estimate (1987) 4,460,578. Births, 1986, 77,944 (17·3 per 1,000 population); deaths, 36,287 (8·1); infant deaths, 925 (11·9 per 1,000 live births); marriages, 37,459 (8·4); divorces, 15,164.

Population in 5 census years was:

	White	*Negro*	*Indian*	*Asiatic*	*Total*	*Per sq. mile*
1910	941,086	713,874	780	648	1,656,388	36·5
1930	1,322,712	776,326	1,536	1,019	2,101,593	46·5
1960	2,211,715	1,039,207	3,587	2,004	3,257,022	72·2
			All others			
1970	2,541,498	1,086,832	12,976		3,641,306	81·1
1980	2,911,243	1,237,263	55,466		4,203,972 [1]	93·5

[1] Preliminary.

Of the 1980 total, 2,039,894 were male, 2,885,535 were urban; those 20 years of age or older numbered 2,699,100.

The largest cities with their 1980 census population (and 1987 estimate) are: New Orleans, 557,482 (555,641); Baton Rouge (capital), 219,486 (242,184); Shreveport, 205,815 (217,718); Lafayette, 81,961 (91,084); Lake Charles, 75,051 (76,599); Kenner, 66,382 (74,851).

CLIMATE. New Orleans. Jan. 54°F (12·2°C), July 83°F (28·3°C). Annual rainfall 58" (1,458 mm). *See* Gulf Coast, p. 1382.

CONSTITUTION AND GOVERNMENT. The present constitution dates from 1974.

The Legislature consists of a Senate of 39 members and a House of Representatives of 105 members, both chosen for 4 years. Sessions are annual; a fiscal session is held in odd years. The Governor and Lieut.-Governor are elected for 4 years.

A Governor may serve a second consecutive term. Qualified electors are all registered citizens with the usual residential qualifications.

In the 1988 presidential election Bush polled 880,660 votes, Dukakis, 715,475.

The state sends to Congress 2 senators and 8 representatives. Louisiana is divided into 64 parishes (corresponding with the counties of other states).

Governor: Charles E. 'Buddy' Roemer, Jr. (D.), 1988–92 ($73,440).
Lieut.-Governor: Paul Hardy (R.), 1988–92 ($63,367).
Secretary of State: W. Fox McKeithen (D.), 1988–92 ($60,169).

BUDGET. For the fiscal year ending 30 June 1987 (Louisiana State Budget Office figures) general revenues were $7,381,332,298, of which $1,885,922,784 were federal funds; total expenditures were $7,582,740,576 (education, $2,435,062,145; transport and development, $230,935,484; health, hospitals and public welfare, $2,092,812,284).

Per capita personal income (1986) was $11,191.

ENERGY AND NATURAL RESOURCES

Minerals. The yield in 1987 of crude petroleum was 144m. bbls; marketed production of natural gas, 1,572,835,903m. cu. ft. Rich sulphur mines are found in the state, and wells for the extraction of sulphur by means of hot water and compressed air are in operation; output, 1986, 524,000 tonnes.

Louisiana is the USA's main salt producer. Output of salt (1986) was 11·6m. short tons.

Agriculture. The state is divided into two parts, the uplands and the alluvial and swamp regions of the coast. A delta occupies about one-third of the total area. Manufacturing is the leading industry, but agriculture is important. In 1986 there were about 36,000 farms with annual average sales of at least $1,000; average farm, 278 acres; average value per acre $1,256.

Cash income, 1986, from crops $1,371·69m.; from livestock, $502·7m. Crops by value: Soybeans, $189·9m.; rice, $110·9m.; cotton lint, $179·7m.; sugar-cane, $115·2m..

In 1985 the state contained 89,910 milch cows, 1·2m. all cattle, 25,114 sheep and 133,349 swine.

Fisheries. The catch in 1986 was 1,700m. lb., value $321·5m.

Forestry. Forests, 13·9m. acres, represent 49% of the state's area. Income from manufactured products exceeds $2,500m. annually. In 1986 pulpwood cut, 5·1m. cords; sawtimber cut, 1,500m. bd ft.

INDUSTRY. The manufacturing industries are chiefly those associated with petroleum, chemicals, lumber, food, paper. In 1987 167,600 were employed in manufacturing, 368,500 in trade and 327,200 in service industries.

TOURISM. Travellers spent an estimated $4,000m. in 1987. Tourism is the second most important industry for state income.

COMMUNICATIONS

Roads. The state has more than 16,326 miles of public roads. In Oct. 1988, over 4m. vehicles were registered in the state.

Railways. In 1986 there were 3,347 miles of track in the state.

Aviation. In 1988 there were 386 commercial and private airports.

Shipping. In 1984 New Orleans handled 43·9m. short tons of cargo. The Mississippi and other waterways provide 7,500 miles of navigable water.

JUSTICE, RELIGION, EDUCATION AND WELFARE

Justice. State and federal prisons, Nov. 1988, had 16,121 inmates. Execution is by electrocution; there were 135 between 1930 and 1961, 15 between 1977 and 1987.

Religion. The Roman Catholic Church is the largest denomination in Louisiana. The leading Protestant Churches are Southern Baptist and Methodist.

Education. School attendance is compulsory between the ages of 7 and 15, both inclusive. In 1986–87 there were 804,645 pupils in public elementary and secondary schools. In 1987 the 42,019 instructional staff had an average salary of $20,235. There are 17 four-year public colleges and universities and 11 non-public four-year institutions of higher learning. There are 47 state trade and vocational-technical schools. Superior instruction is given in the Louisiana State University with 54,912 students (1987). Tulane University in New Orleans had 10,302; The Roman Catholic Loyola University in New Orleans had 5,210; Dillard University in New Orleans had 1,218; and the Southern University System, 5,210.

Health. In 1988 the state had 186 licensed hospitals and 3 state mental hospitals.

Social Security. In Dec. 1985, assistance was being given to 49,400 elderly persons; 78,800 families with dependent children; 74,700 disabled people. Aid was from state and federal sources.

Further Reading

Davis, E. A., *Louisiana, the Pelican State*. Louisiana State Univ. Press, Baton Rouge, 1975
Hansen, H., (ed.) *Louisiana, a Guide to the State*. Rev. ed. New York, 1971
Kniffen, F. B., *Louisiana, its Land and People*. Louisiana State Univ. Press, Baton Rouge, 1968

State Library: The Louisiana State Library, Baton Rouge, Louisiana. *State Librarian:* Thomas F. Jaques.

MAINE

HISTORY. After a first attempt in 1607, Maine was settled in 1623. From 1652 to 1820 it was part of Massachusetts and was admitted into the Union on 15 March 1820.

AREA AND POPULATION. Maine is bounded west, north and east by Canada, south-east by the Atlantic, south and south-west by New Hampshire. Area, 33,265 sq. miles, of which 2,269 are inland water. Of the state's total area, about 17·2m. acres (87%) are in timber and wood lots. Census population, 1 April 1980 1,125,027, an increase of 13·29% since 1970. Estimate (1986) 1,174,000. In 1986 live births numbered 16,717 (14·3 per 1,000 population); deaths, 10,796 (9·2); infant deaths, 146 (8·9 per 1,000 live births); marriages, 10,887 (9·2); divorces 5,621 (4·8).

Population for 5 census years was:

	White	Negro	Indian	Asiatic	Total	Per sq. mile
1910	739,995	1,363	892	121	742,371	24·8
1930	795,185	1,096	1,012	130	797,423	25·7
1950	910,846	1,221	1,522	185	913,774	29·4
			All others			
1970	985,276	2,800	3,972		992,048	31·0
1980	1,109,850	3,128	12,049		1,125,027	36·3

Of the total population in 1980, 48·5% were male, 40·7% were urban and 60·5% were 21 years or older.

The largest city in the state is Portland with a census population of 61,572 in 1980. Other cities (with population in 1980) are: Lewiston, 40,481; Bangor, 31,643; Auburn, 23,128; South Portland, 22,712; Augusta (capital), 21,819; Biddeford, 19,638; Waterville, 17,779.

CLIMATE. Average maximum temperatures range from 56·3°F in Waterville to 48·3°F in Caribou, but record high (since *c.* 1950) is 103°F. Average minimum ranges from 36·9°F in Rockland to 28·3°F in Greenville, but record low (also in Greenville) is –42°F. Average annual rainfall ranges from 48·85" in Machias to 36·09" in Houlton. Average annual snowfall ranges from 118·7" in Greenville to 59·7" in Rockland. *See* New England, p. 1382.

CONSTITUTION AND GOVERNMENT. The constitution of 1820 is still in force, but it has been amended 153 times. In 1951, 1965 and 1973 the Legislature approved recodifications of the constitution as arranged by the Chief Justice under special authority.

The Legislature consists of the Senate with 35 members and the House of Representatives with 151 members, both Houses being elected simultaneously for 2 years. Apart from these legislators and the Governor (elected for 4 years), no other state officers are elected. The Justices of the Supreme Judicial Court give their opinion upon important questions of law and upon solemn occasions when required by the Governor, Senate or House of Representatives. The suffrage is possessed by all citizens, 18 years of age; persons under guardianship for reasons of mental illness have no vote. Indians residing on tribal reservations and otherwise qualified have the vote in all county, state and national elections but retain the right to elect their own tribal representative to the legislature.

In the 1988 presidential election Bush polled 304,087 votes, Dukakis, 240,508.

The state sends to Congress 2 senators and 2 representatives.

The capital is Augusta. The state is divided into 16 counties.

Governor: John McKernan (R.), 1987–91 ($35,000).
Secretary of State: Rodney S. Quinn (D.), 1987–91 ($30,000).

BUDGET. For the financial year ending 30 June 1986 general revenue was $932m. and expenditure was $927m.

Total net long-term debt on 30 June 1984 was $294·5m.

Per capita personal income (1987) was $13,720.

NATURAL RESOURCES

Minerals. Minerals include sand and gravel, stone, lead, clay, copper, peat, silver and zinc. Mineral output, 1986, was valued at $46m.

Agriculture. In 1986, 7,800 farms occupied 2m. acres; the average farm was 194 acres.

Cash receipts, 1985, $378m., of which $80m. came from potatoes; Maine is the third largest producer of potatoes (about 7% of the country's total of 325·7m. cwt). Other important items include eggs ($94m.), dairy products ($107·5m.) and poultry ($29·7m.); these with potatoes provide 78% of receipts. Sweet corn, peas and beans, oats, hay, apples and blueberries are also grown. On 1 Jan. 1983 the farm animals included 57,000 milch cows, 146,000 all other cattle, and 14,000 sheep.

Forestry. Lumber, wood turnings and pulp are important. In 1982 the cut of softwood was 769,195m. bd ft; hardwood, 150,878m. bd ft, and pulpwood, 3,417,586 cords. Spruce and fir, white pine, hemlock, white and yellow birch, sugar maple, northern white cedar, beech and red oak are the most important species cut. There were (1982) 17,600,000 acres of commercial forest (98% in private ownership). National forests comprise 37,500 acres; other federal, 35,800; state forests, 163,000 acres; municipal, 75,200 acres. Wood products industries are of great economic importance; in 1982 the lumber, wood and paper industries' production was valued at $3,355,731. There were (1982) 342 primary manufacturers and over 1,400 secondary.

Fisheries. In 1983, 202,657,000 lb. of fish and shellfish (valued at $107,889,000 were landed; the catch included 21,976,000 lb. of lobsters (valued at $51,234,000). 1·97m. lb. of scallops ($10·8m.); 4·14m. lb. of soft clams ($7·24m.); 12·31m. lb of dabs ($6·0m.); 42·4m. lb. of menhaden ($846,000); 40m. lb. of herring ($2·14m.).

INDUSTRY. Total non-agricultural workforce, 1985, 459,000. Manufacturing employed 106,000; trade, 108,000; services, 95,000; government, 86,000; the main manufacture is paper at 47 plants, producing about 34% of manufacturing value added.

LABOUR. The four largest employers are government, education, health and tourism.

TOURISM. In 1987 there were about 4·8m. tourists (including state residents on holiday), generating nearly $1,000m. in business. Eating, drinking and accommodation produce 12·4% of sales tax.

COMMUNICATIONS

Roads. In 1983 there were 22,098 miles of roads, of which 3,973 miles were state highways and 4,359 miles were state-aided; town streets and miscellaneous, 13,766 miles. In July 1984, 847,922 motor vehicles were registered, including 669,240 passenger vehicles, 87,267 commercial vehicles and 40,361 motorcycles.

Railways. In 1984 there were 1,516 miles of mainline railway tracks.

Aviation. Licensed airports, 1984, numbered 76, including 37 commercial public airports, 12 non-commercial and 4 commuter airports, 15 commercial and 4 non-commercial seaplane bases, and 4 air-carrier airports. There were also 2 military airports and 23 private landing strips.

JUSTICE, RELIGION, EDUCATION AND WELFARE

Justice. The state's penal system in Sept. 1984 held 435 adults in the State Prison, 237 in the Correctional Center and 332 juveniles in the Youth Center. There is no capital punishment. Inmates serving life sentences are eligible for parole consideration after 15 years, less remission for good conduct, provided they were imprisoned before the passage of a new Criminal Code by the 107th Maine Legislature, which abolished the parole system.

Religion. The largest religious bodies are: Roman Catholic (270,283 members), Baptists (36,808 members) and Congregationalists (40,750 members), and other Christian Churches (34,066 members).

Education. Education is free for pupils from 5 to 21 years of age, and compulsory from 7 to 17. In 1983–84 the 756 public schools (610 elementary, 105 secondary and 41 combined elementary and secondary) had 12,283 staff and 209,753 enrolled pupils. In 1983–84 there were 126 private schools with 1,035 teachers and 15,461 pupils. Public school teachers' salaries, 1983–84, averaged $17,328. Total public expenditure on public elementary and secondary education in 1982–83, $461,252,847.

The state University of Maine, founded in 1865, had (1983–84) 1,003 teaching staff and 28,591 students at 7 locations; Bowdoin College, founded in 1794 at Brunswick, (107 and 1,371); Bates College at Lewiston, (104 and 1,424); Colby College at Waterville, (125 and 1,733); Husson College, Bangor, (31 and 1,465);

Westbrook College at Westbrook, (56 and 1,120); Unity College at Unity, (23 and 325), and the University of New England (formerly St Francis College) at Biddeford, (55 and 848).

Health. In 1984 the state had 42 general hospitals (4,571 beds for acute care); 3 hospitals for mental diseases, acute and psychiatric care (541 beds); 144 nursing homes (10,220 beds).

Social Security. Supplemental Security Income (SSI) (maximum payment for single person, $324·30 per month) is administered by the Social Security Administration. It became effective on 1 Jan. 1974 and replaces former aid to the aged, blind and disabled, administered by the state with state and federal funds. SSI is supplemented by Medicaid for nursing home patients or hospital patients. State payments for SSI recipients for 1985 totalled $42·3m., covering 22,000 cases. Aid to families with dependent children is granted where one or both parents are disabled or absent and income is insufficient; aid was being granted in Aug. 1985 to 20,100 families (58,300 children) with an average payment per family of $321 per month. Payments under Maine Medicaid Assistance programme totalled $217m. for the financial year 1983–84. There is a programme of assistance for catastrophic illness. Child welfare services include basic child protective services, enforcing child support, establishing paternity and finding missing parents, foster home placements, adoptions; services in divorce cases and licensing of foster homes, day care and residential treatment services, and public guardianship. There are also protective services for adults.

Further Reading

Maine Register, State Year-Book and Legislative Manual. Tower Publishing, Portland. Annual
Banks, R., *Maine Becomes A State.* Wesleyan U.P., 1970
Caldwell, B., *Rivers of Fortune.* Gannett, 1983
Calvert, M. R., *Dawn over the Kennebec.* Private Pr., 1983
Clark, C., *Maine.* New York, 1977

MARYLAND

HISTORY. Maryland, first settled in 1634, was one of the 13 original states.

AREA AND POPULATION. Maryland is bounded north by Pennsylvania, east by Delaware and the Atlantic, south by Virginia and West Virginia, with the Potomac River forming most of the boundary, and west by West Virginia. Chesapeake Bay almost cuts off the eastern end of the state from the rest. Area, 10,460 sq. miles, of which 623 sq. miles are inland water; in addition, water area under Maryland jurisdiction in Chesapeake Bay amounts to 1,726 sq. miles. Census population, 1 April 1980, 4,216,975, an increase since 1970 of 293,078 or 7·5%. Estimate (1986) 4,463,000. In 1985 births were 67,985 (15·5 per 1,000 population); deaths, 36,607 (8·3); infant deaths, 811 (11·9 per 1,000 live births); marriages, 46,063 (10·5); divorces, 16,187 (3·7).

Population for 5 federal censuses was:

	White	*Negro*	*Indian*	*Asiatic*	*Total*	*Per sq. mile*
1920	1,204,737	244,479	32	413	1,449,661	145·8
1930	1,354,226	276,379	50	871	1,631,526	165·0
1960	2,573,919	518,410	1,538	5,700	3,100,689	314·0
			All others			
1970	3,194,888	499,479	28,032		3,922,399	396·6
1980	3,158,838	958,150	99,987		4,216,975	428·7

Of the total population in 1980, 2,042,810 were male, 3,386,555 persons were urban and those 20 years old or older numbered 2,890,196.

The largest city in the state (containing 16·9% of the population) is Baltimore, with 786,741 in 1980 (and 751,400 in 1988); Baltimore metropolitan area, 2·3m.

Maryland residents in the Washington, D.C., metropolitan area total more than 1·7m. Other cities (1980) are Dundalk (71,293); Towson (51,083); Silver Spring (72,893); Bethesda (62,736). Incorporated places, estimate 1986: Rockville, 46,900; Bowie, 35,740; Hagerstown, 33,670; Frederick, 33,800; Annapolis, 33,360; Gaithersburg, 32,350; Cumberland, 23,230; Cambridge, 11,070.

CLIMATE. Baltimore. Jan. 36°F (2·2°C), July 79°F (26·1°C). Annual rainfall 41" (1,026 mm). *See* Atlantic Coast, p. 1382.

CONSTITUTION AND GOVERNMENT. The present constitution dates from 1867; it has had 125 amendments. The General Assembly consists of a Senate of 47, and a House of Delegates of 141 members, both elected for 4 years, as are the Governor and Lieut.-Governor. Voters are citizens who have the usual residential qualifications. At the 1988 presidential election Bush polled 834,202 votes, Dukakis, 793,939.

Maryland sends to Congress 2 senators and 8 representatives.

The state capital is Annapolis. The state is divided into 23 counties and Baltimore City.

Governor: William D. Schaefer (D.), 1987–91 ($75,000).
Lieut.-Governor: J. Joseph Curran (D.), 1987–91 ($62,500).
Secretary of State: Patricia Holtz ($45,000).

BUDGET. For the fiscal year ending 30 June 1988 general revenues were $8,190,297,000 ($5,871,996,000 from taxation). General expenditures, $8,027,477,000, including $1,759,450,000 for education and $2,278,668,000 for public welfare and health; $1,466,710,000 for transport.

Total authorized long-term state debt, 30 June 1988 was $2,961,319,000. (Issued and outstanding, $2,090,820,000; authorized but not issued, $870,499,000.)

Per capita personal income (1988) was $19,487.

ENERGY AND NATURAL RESOURCES

Minerals. Value of non-fuel mineral production, 1988, was $377m. Sand and gravel (17·5m. short tons) and stone (33·4m. short tons) account for over 52% of the total value. Coal is the leading mineral commodity by value followed by Portland cement, stone, sand and gravel. Output of coal was 3m. short tons, valued at about $83m. Natural gas is produced from 1 field in Garrett County; 29m. cu. ft in 1988. A second gas field in the same county is used for natural gas storage.

Agriculture. Agriculture is an important industry in the state. In 1987 there were approximately 16,500 farms with an area of 2·5m. acres (40% of the land area).

Farm animals, 1 Jan. 1988, were: Milch cows, 114,000; all cattle, 320,000; swine, 220,000; sheep, 34,000; chickens (not broilers), 5·2m. The most important crops, 1987, were: Corn for grain, 35·9m. bu.; soybeans, 9·2m. bu.; tobacco, 16·7m. lb., and hay, 642,000 tons.

Cash receipts from farm marketings, 1987, were $1,148m.; from livestock and livestock products, $734m., and crops, $394m. Dairy products and broilers are important.

INDUSTRY. In 1987 manufactories had 140,100 production workers earning $2,989·8m.; value added by manufacture, $14,072·6m. Chief industries are electrical and electronic equipment, food and kindred products, chemicals and products, printing and publishing.

TOURISM. Tourism is one of the state's leading industries. In 1988 tourists spent over $5,875m.

COMMUNICATIONS

Roads. The state highway department maintained, 1 Jan. 1989, 5,205 miles of highways, of which 83 miles were toll roads. The 23 counties maintained 18,341 miles of highways, and the 159 municipalities (including the city of Baltimore) maintained 4,072 miles of streets and alleys. Total mileage, 1 Jan. 1989, of public highways, streets and alleys, 27,618 miles. In 1988, an estimated 3·4m. automobiles were registered.

Railways. Railways, in 1989, had 1,068 miles of line.

Aviation. There were, 1989, 39 commercially licensed aiports.

Shipping. In 1988 Baltimore was the seventh largest US seaport in value of trade, sixth in tonnage handled.

JUSTICE, RELIGION, EDUCATION AND WELFARE

Justice. Prisons on 30 Nov. 1989 had about 15,780 men and 715 women; the total equalled 357 per 100,000 population, a high rate, which may be explained by the fact that Maryland incarcerates domestic relations law violators in state prisons; state prisons also receive a considerable number of persons committed for misdemeanours by magistrates' courts of the counties as well as from Baltimore's court system.

Since 1930 there have been 68 executions (by lethal gas since 1957; earlier by hanging)—7 whites and 37 Negroes for murder, and 6 whites and 18 Negroes for rape. Last execution was June 1961.

Maryland's prison system has conducted a work-release programme for selected prisoners since 1963. All institutions have academic and vocational training programmes.

In accordance with the 1950 Supreme Court decisions declaring segregation unconstitutional, the University of Maryland and other public and private colleges began admitting Black students in Sept. 1956; elementary and secondary schools followed.

Religion. Maryland was the first US state to give religious freedom to all who came within its borders. Present religious affiliations of the population are approximately: Protestant, 32%; Roman Catholic, 24%; Jewish, 10%; remaining 34% is nonrelated and other faiths.

Education. Education is compulsory from 6 to 16 years of age. In Sept. 1988 the public elementary schools (including kindergartens and secondary schools) had 688,947 pupils. Teachers and principals in the elementary and secondary schools numbered 43,268. Teachers' average salary in 1987–88 was $30,933. Current expenditure by local school boards on education, 1987–88, was $3,186·4m., of which the state's contribution was $1,287·2m.

In 1988 there were 32 degree-granting 4-year institutions and 17 2-year colleges. The largest was the University of Maryland system, with 101,645 students (Sept. 1988) Towson State of which 2 schools had the highest enrolment, College Park (35,681) and Towson State University (15,169).

Health. In Dec. 1989, 105 hospitals (19,552 beds) were licensed by the State Department of Health and Mental Hygiene.

The Maryland State Department of Health, organized in 1874, was in 1969 made part of the Department of Health and Mental Hygiene which performs its functions through its central office, 23 county health departments and the Baltimore City Health Department. For the financial year 1988 the department's budget was $1,637·3m., of which $1,105·9m. were general funds and $58m. special funds appropriated by the General Assembly. The balance of the budget, $473·4m., derives from federal funds.

During financial year 1989 Maryland's programme of medical care for indigent and medically indigent patients covered 436,664 persons. The programme, which covers in-patient and out-patient hospital services, laboratory services, skilled nursing home care, physician services, pharmacy services, dental services and home health services, cost approximately $1,035m.

Social Security. Under the supervision of the Department of Human Resources, local social service departments administer public assistance for needy persons. In Aug. 1989 families with dependent children received $23,544,015 (199,132 recipients, average actual monthly payment $132.92); general public assistance payments were $3,474,585 (18,023 recipients, average actual monthly payments $192.79).

Further Reading

Statistical Information: Maryland Department of Economic and Employment Development, Baltimore City, 21202.

Maryland Manual: A Compendium of Legal, Historical and Statistical Information Relating to the State of Maryland. Annapolis. Biennial

DiLisio, J. E., *Maryland.* Boulder, 1982

Papenfuse, E. C., et al., *Maryland, a New Guide to the Old Line State.* Johns Hopkins Univ. Press, 1976

Rollo, V. F., *Maryland's Constitution and Government.* Maryland Hist. Press, Rev. ed., 1982

State Library: Maryland State Library, Annapolis. *Director:* Michael S. Miller.

MASSACHUSETTS

HISTORY. The first permanent settlement within the borders of the present state was made at Plymouth in Dec. 1620, by the Pilgrims from Holland, who were separatists from the English Church, and formed the nucleus of the Plymouth Colony. In 1628 another company of Puritans settled at Salem, forming eventually the Massachusetts Bay Colony. In 1630 Boston was settled. In the struggle which ended in the separation of the American colonies from the mother country, Massachusetts took the foremost part, and on 6 Feb. 1788 became the sixth state to ratify the US constitution.

AREA AND POPULATION. Massachusetts is bounded north by Vermont and New Hampshire, east by the Atlantic, south by Connecticut and Rhode Island and west by New York. Area, 8,284 sq. miles, 460 sq. miles being inland water.The census population 1 April 1980, was 5,737,037, an increase of 47,867 or 0·8% since 1970. Estimate (1985) 5,819,087. Births, 1985 were 82,872 (14·2 per 1,000 population); deaths, 54,935 (9·4 per 1,000); infant deaths (1984), 739 (9·3 per 1,000 live births); marriages, 51,648 (8·9); divorces, 19,794 (3·4).

Population at 4 federal census years was:

	White	*Negro*	*Other*	*Total*	*Per sq. mile*
1950	4,611,503	73,171	5,840	4,690,514	598·4
1960	5,023,144	111,842	13,592	5,148,578	656·8
1970	5,477,624	175,817	35,729	5,689,170	725·8
1980	5,362,836	221,279	152,922	5,737,037	732·0

Of the total population in 1980, 47·6% were male, 83·8% were urban and 32% were 21 years old or older.

In 1985 the population of the principal towns and cities was:

Boston	571,980	Lowell	93,343	Framingham	64,999
Worcester	160,489	Fall River	92,560	Lawrence	64,970
Springfield	151,015	Quincy	83,845	Leominster	64,768
New Bedford	98,900	Newton	82,384	Waltham	57,609
Brockton	98,040	Lynn	79,207	Medford	57,191
Cambridge	93,405	Somerville	75,802	Chicopee	55,936

The largest of 10 standard metropolitan statistical areas, 1980 census were: Boston, 2,763,357; Springfield–Chicopee–Holyoke, 530,668; Worcester, 372,940.

CLIMATE. Boston. Jan. 28°F (–2·2°C), July 71°F (21·7°C). Annual rainfall 41" (1,036 mm). *See* New England, p. 1382.

CONSTITUTION AND GOVERNMENT. The constitution dates from 1780 and has had 116 amendments. The legislative body, styled the General Court of the Commonwealth of Massachusetts, meets annually, and consists of the Senate with 40 members, elected biennially, and the House of Representatives of 160

members, elected for 2 years. The Governor and Lieut.-Governor are elected for 4 years. The state sends 2 senators and 11 representatives to Congress.

At the 1988 presidential election Dukakis polled 1,387,398 votes, Bush, 1,184,323.

Electors are all citizens 18 years of age or older.

The capital is Boston. The state has 14 counties, 39 cities and 312 towns.

Governor: Michael S. Dukakis (D.), 1987–91 ($75,000).
Lieut.-Governor: Evelyn Murphy (D.), 1987–91 ($60,000).
Secretary of the Commonwealth: Michael J. Connolly (D.) ($60,000).

BUDGET. For the fiscal year ending 30 June 1986 the total revenue of the state was $9,569·6m. ($7,488·3m. from taxes, $1,201·7m. from federal aid, $879·6m. from other sources); total expenditures, $9,692·7m. ($1,389·3m. for education, $418·7m. for highway transport and highway construction and $3,659·6m. for human services).

The net long-term debt on 30 June 1986 amounted to $3,645m.

Per capita personal income (1986) was $17,516.

NATURAL RESOURCES

Minerals. There is little mining within the state. Total mineral output in 1985 was valued at $114·5m., of which most came from sand, gravel, crushed stone and lime.

Agriculture. On 1 Jan. 1986 there were approximately 6,000 farms (11,179 in 1959) with an area of 598,900 acres.

Cash income, 1986, totalled $425·2m.; dairy, $76·3m.; greenhouse and nursery, $118m.; poultry, $30·8m.; vegetables, $38·8m.; tobacco, $7m.; cranberries, $98·6m.; other fruit, $23·2m.; potatoes, $2·6m. Total from crops, $295·2m., from livestock, $130m.

Principal 1986 crops include cranberries, 1·69m. bbls; apples, 2·1m. bu. in 1985; potatoes, 825,000 cwt in 1985. On 1 Jan. 1982 farms in the state had 48,000 milch cows, 98,000 all cattle, 49,000 swine. In 1982 farms produced 145,000 turkeys and 0·8m. chickens.

Forestry. About 68% of the state is forest. State forests cover about 256,000 acres. Total forest land covers about 3m. acres. Commercially important hardwoods are sugar maple, northern red oak and white ash; softwoods are white pine and hemlock. About 240m. bd ft of timber are cut annually.

Fisheries. The 1985 catch amounted to 296m. lb. of fish and shellfish valued at $232m.

INDUSTRY. In 1986, manufacturing establishments employed an average of 637,740 workers. The 3 most important manufacturing groups, based on employment, were electric and electronic equipment, machinery (except electrical), printing and publishing. Service industries employed 875,736 and trade, 697,257. Total non-agricultural employment, 2,685,611.

COMMUNICATIONS

Roads. In Oct. 1984 the state had 33,800 miles of roads and streets and in 1985 registered 3·8m. motor vehicles.

Railways. In 1984 there were 1,310 miles of mainline railway.

Aviation. There were, in 1983, 52 aircraft landing areas for commercial operation, of which 27 were publicly owned.

Shipping. The state has 3 deep-water harbours, the largest of which is Boston (port trade (1983), 16,767,585 short tons). Other ports are Fall River and New Bedford.

JUSTICE, RELIGION, EDUCATION AND WELFARE

Justice. On 31 Dec. 1985 state penal institutions held 5,447 inmates. There have been no executions since 1947.

Religion. The principal religious bodies are the Roman Catholics, Jewish Congregations, Methodists, Episcopalians and Unitarians.

Education. A regulation effective from 1 Sept. 1972 makes school attendance compulsory for ages 6–16. In 1985–86 expenditure by cities and towns on public schools was $3,521m. or $605 per capita, including debt retirement and service payments. In 1985–86 there were 56,400 classroom teachers and approximately 900,000 pupils.

Within the state there were (1982) 126 degree-granting institutions of higher learning (including 89 colleges and universities). Some leading institutions are:

Year opened	*Name and location of universities and colleges*	*Students 1988*
1636	Harvard University, Cambridge [1]	16,871
1839	Framingham State College	4,303
1839	Westfield State College	6,053
1840	Bridgewater State College	6,539
1852	Tufts University, Medford [1, 3]	6,297
1854	Salem State College	6,364
1861	Mass. Institute of Technology, Cambridge [1]	9,158
1863	University of Massachusetts, Amherst [1]	26,233
1863	Boston College (RC), Chestnut Hill [1]	12,858
1865	Worcester Polytechnic Institute, Worcester [1]	4,022
1869	Boston University, Boston [1]	22,373
1874	Worcester College	4,899
1894	Fitchburg State College	5,212
1894	University of Lowell [1]	10,445
1895	Southeastern Massachusetts University	5,031
1898	Northeastern University, Boston [1, 4]	20,618
1899	Simmons College, Boston [2]	2,594
1905	Wentworth Institute of Technology	3,350
1906	Suffolk University	5,978
1917	Bentley College	5,611
1919	Western New England College	3,686
1919	Babson College	3,163
1947	Merrimack College	2,300
1948	Brandeis University, Waltham [1]	3,484
1964	University of Massachusetts, Boston	8,027

[1] Co-educational. [3] Includes Jackson College for women.
[2] For women only. [4] Includes Forsyth Dental Center School.

Health. In 1984 the state had 177 hospitals (with 41,200 beds); average daily census, 1982, 32,736, including patients in public and private mental hospitals and institutions for the mentally retarded.

Social Security. The Department of Public Welfare had an appropriation of $1,828m. in financial year 1984 and paid $388m. in aid to families with dependent children (average 95,798 families per month); other main items were general relief (average 27,242 cases), Supplemental Security Income (average 105,402 cases) and Medical Assistance only (average 65,841 cases).

Further Reading

Annual Reports. Massachusetts and US Boards, Commissions, Departments and Divisions, Boston, annual

Manual for the General Court. By Clerk of the Senate and Clerk of the House of Representatives, Boston, Mass. Biennial

Hart, Albert B., (ed.) *Commonwealth History of Massachusetts, Colony, Province and State.* 5 vols., New York, 1966

Levitan, D. with Mariner, E. C., *Your Massachusetts Government.* Newton, Mass., 1984

Higher Education Publications, Washington, D.C., 1983

MICHIGAN

HISTORY. Michigan, first settled by Marquette at Sault Ste Marie in 1668, became the Territory of Michigan in 1805, with its boundaries greatly enlarged in

1818 and 1834; it was admitted into the Union with its present boundaries on 26 Jan. 1837.

AREA AND POPULATION. Michigan is divided into two by Lake Michigan. The northern part is bounded south by the lake and by Wisconsin, west and north by Lake Superior, east by the North Channel of Lake Huron; between the two latter lakes the Canadian border runs through straits at Sault Ste Marie. The southern part is bounded west and north by Lake Michigan, east by Lake Huron, Ontario and Lake Erie, south by Ohio and Indiana. Area, 58,527 sq. miles, of which 56,954 sq. miles are land area, 1,573 sq. miles are inland water. Census population, 1 April 1980, 9,262,078, an increase of 380,252 or 4·3% since 1970. Estimate (1986) 9,145,000. In 1985 births were 138,902 (15·2 per 1,000 population); deaths, 78,515 (8·7); infant deaths, 1,575 (11·4 per 1,000 live births); marriages, 79,022 (17·4); divorces, 38,775 (8·5).

Population of 5 federal census years was:

	White	*Negro*	*Indian*	*Asiatic*	*Total*	*Per sq. mile*
1910	2,785,247	17,115	7,519	292	2,810,173	48·9
1930	4,663,507	169,453	7,080	2,285	4,842,325	84·9
1960	7,085,865	717,581	9,701	10,047	7,823,194	137·2
			All others			
1970	7,833,474	991,066	50,543		8,875,083	156·2
1980	7,872,241	1,199,023	190,814		9,262,078	162·6

Of the total population in 1980, 4,516,189 were male, 6,551,551 persons were urban and those 20 years old or older numbered 6,146,694. 162,440 were of Spanish origin.

Population of the chief cities (census of 1 April 1980) was:

Detroit	1,203,339	Dearborn	90,660	Royal Oak	70,893
Grand Rapids	181,843	Westland	84,603	Dearborn Heights	67,706
Warren	161,134	Kalamazoo	79,722	Troy	67,102
Flint	159,611	Taylor	77,568	Wyoming	59,616
Lansing (capital)	130,414	Saginaw	77,508	Farmington Hills	58,056
Sterling Heights	108,999	Pontiac	76,715	Roseville	54,311
Ann Arbor	107,316	St Clair Shores	76,210		
Livonia	104,814	Southfield	75,568		

Larger standard metropolitan areas, 1980 census: Detroit, 4,353,413; Grand Rapids, 601,680; Flint, 521,589; Lansing, 471,565.

CLIMATE. Detroit. Jan. 22·1°F (–5·5°C), July 72°F (22·2°C). Annual rainfall 32" (813 mm). Grand Rapids. Jan. 23·8°F (–4·6°C), July 72·6°F (22·5°C). Annual rainfall 33·6" (833 mm). Lansing. Jan. 21·7°F (–5·7°C), July 71°F (21·7°C). Annual rainfall 30·8" (782 mm). *See* Great Lakes, p. 1382.

CONSTITUTION AND GOVERNMENT. The present constitution was adopted in April 1963 and became effective on 1 Jan. 1964. The Senate consists of 38 members, elected for 4 years, and the House of Representatives of 110 members, elected for 2 years. The Governor and Lieut.-Governor are elected for 4 years. Electors are all citizens over 18 years of age meeting the usual residential requirements. The state sends to Congress 2 senators and 18 representatives.

At the 1988 presidential election Bush polled 1,969,435 votes, Dukakis, 1,673,496.

The capital is Lansing. The state is organized in 83 counties.

Governor: James J. Blanchard (D.), 1987–91 ($100,077).
Lieut.-Governor: Martha Griffiths (D.), 1987–91 ($67,377).
Secretary of State: Richard H. Austin (D.), 1987–91 ($89,000).

BUDGET. For the financial year ending 30 Sept. 1986, the general fund revenue was $12,769,500,000 (taxation, $9,270,600,000, and federal aid, $3,298,600,000);

total revenue, $13,607,400,000; special revenue funds, $837,900,000; general expenditures, $12,235,600,000.

Per capita personal income (1985 estimate) was $13,608.

ENERGY AND NATURAL RESOURCES

Minerals. Most important minerals by value of production are iron ore, petroleum and cement. Output (1985): Iron ore, 12·69m. long tons; Portland cement, 4·75m. short tons; petroleum, 31·5m. bbls; sand and gravel, 41·35m. short tons; lime, 534,000 short tons; natural gas, 153,484,651m. cu. ft; Salt, 991,000 short tons. Mineral output in 1984 was valued at $2,695·2m.

Agriculture. The state, formerly agricultural, is now chiefly industrial. In 1985 it contained 63,000 farms with a total area of 11m. acres; the average farm was 175 acres. Cash income, 1985, from crops, $1,729·6m.; from livestock and products, $1,237m. Principal crops are maize (production, 1985, 287·6m. bu. of grain), oats (26·1m. bu.), wheat (45m. bu.), sugar-beet (2·33m. tons); soybeans (34·6m. bu.), hay (5·7m. tons). On 1 Jan. 1986 there were in the state 108,000 sheep, 397,000 milch cows, 1·41m. all cattle and 1·19m. swine; 8·9m. chickens and 38,000 (1985) turkey breeder hens. In 1985 the wool clip yielded 902,000 lb. of wool.

Forestry. The forests of Michigan consist of 18·4m. acres, about 51% of total state land area. About 17·5m. acres of this total is commercial forest, 64% of which is privately owned, 20% state forest, 14% federal forest and 1·5% in various public ownerships. Three-fourths of the timber volume is hardwoods, principally hard and soft maples, aspen, oak and birch. Christmas trees are another important forest crop.

Michigan leads in the number of state parks and public campsites. There are 83 state parks and recreation areas, 6 state forests, 3 national forests and 3 national parks. There are 169 state forest campgrounds and 64 state game areas.

INDUSTRY. Transport equipment and non-electrical machinery are the most important manufactures. The state ranks first in 19 manufacturing categories; among principal products are motor vehicles and trucks, cement, chemicals, furniture, paper, cereal, baby food and pharmaceuticals. Total non-agricultural labour force, 1986, 4,386,000, of which 975,000 are in manufacturing.

COMMUNICATIONS

Roads. State trunk-line mileage (31 July 1980) totalled, 9,500, all hard surfaced. Passenger car registrations, 1986, 5,501,421.

Railways. On 1 Jan. 1986 there were 4,770 miles of railway and 67 miles of active car-ferry routes.

Aviation. Airports (1986) numbered 245 licensed airports and 22 air carrier airports.

JUSTICE, RELIGION, EDUCATION AND WELFARE

Justice. The 1963 Constitution provides that no person shall be denied the equal protection of the law; nor shall any person be denied the enjoyment of his civil or political rights or be discriminated against in the exercise thereof because of religion, colour or national origin. A Civil Rights Commission was established, and its powers and duties were implemented by legislation in the extra session of 1963. Earlier statutory enactments guaranteeing civil rights in specific areas are as follows. An Act of 1885, last amended in 1956, orders all places of public accommodation and resort, etc., to furnish equal accommodations without discrimination. An Act of 1941, as last amended, forbids the Civil Service in counties with population exceeding 1m. to discriminate against employees or applicants on the ground of political, racial or religious opinions or affiliations. An Act of 1881 incorporated into the school code of 1955 forbids any discrimination in school facilities. An Act of 1893 incorporated in the insurance code of 1956 prohibits insurance companies from discriminating between white and coloured persons.

In 1951 the legislature restored the unique one-man grand jury system abandoned in 1949.

Religion. Roman Catholics make up the largest body; largest Protestant denominations, Lutherans, United Methodists, United Presbyterians, Episcopalians.

Education. Education is compulsory for children from 6 to 16 years of age. The operating expenditure for graded and ungraded public schools for the fiscal year 1985, was $5,704m. In 1984–85 there were 567 school districts (elementary and secondary schools) with 1,678,458 pupils and 75,193 teachers. Teachers' salaries in 1985 averaged $28,440.

In 1985 there were 98 institutes of higher education with 508,000 students.

Universities and students (autumn 1986):

Founded	*Name*	*Students*
1817	University of Michigan	34,947
1849	Eastern Michigan University	21,349
1855	Michigan State University	44,088
1884	Ferris State College	11,274
1885	Michigan Technological University	6,326
1868	Wayne State University	34,764
1892	Central Michigan University	17,993
1889	Northern Michigan University	7,852
1903	Western Michigan University	21,747
1946	Lake Superior State College	2,660
1959	Oakland University	12,707
1960	Grand Valley State College	8,321
1965	Saginaw Valley College	5,377

Social Welfare. Old-age assistance is provided for persons 65 years of age or older who have resided in Michigan for one year before application; assets must not exceed various limits. In 1974 federal Supplementary Security Income (SSI) replaced the adults' programme. In Jan. 1987 aid was supplied to a monthly average of 418,572 dependent children in 188,972 families at $463.86 per family.

Health. In 1983 the state had 231 hospitals (47,812 beds) licensed by the state and 12 psychiatric hospitals, 7 centres for developmental disabilities, 5 centres for emotionally disturbed children.

In 1986 the Medicaid programme disbursed (with federal support) $1,642·9m. to 469,226 persons.

Further Reading

Michigan Manual. Dept of *Management and Budget.* Lansing. Biennial

Bureau of Business Research, Wayne State University. *Michigan Statistical Abstract.* Detroit, 1983

Bald, F. C., *Michigan in Four Centuries.* 2nd ed. New York, 1961

Blanchard, J. J., *Economic Report of the Governor 1985.* Lansing, 1985

Catton. B., *Michigan—a Bicentennial History.* Norton, New York, 1976

Lewis, F. E., *State and Local Government in Michigan.* Lansing, 1979

Dunbar, W. F. and May, G. S., *Michigan: A History of the Wolverine State.* Grand Rapids, 1980

Sommers, L. (ed.), *Atlas of Michigan.* East Lansing, 1977

State Library Services: Library of Michigan, Lansing 48909. *State Librarian:* James W. Fry.

MINNESOTA

HISTORY. Minnesota, first explored in the 17th century and first settled in the 20 years following the establishment of Fort Snelling (1819), was made a Territory in 1849 (with parts of North and South Dakota), and was admitted into the Union, with its present boundaries, on 11 May 1858.

AREA AND POPULATION. Minnesota is bounded north by Canada, east by Lake Superior and Wisconsin, with the Mississippi River forming the boundary in the south-east, south by Iowa, west by South and North Dakota, with the Red River forming the boundary in the north-west. Area, 84,402 sq. miles, of which 4,854 sq. miles are inland water. Census population, 1 April 1980, 4,075,970, an increase of 7·1% since 1970. Estimate (1988), 4,306,550. Births in 1988, 66,745 (15·5 per

1,000 population); deaths, 35,436 (8·2); infant deaths, 521 (7·8 per 1,000 live births); marriages, 33,654 (7·8); divorces (1987), 14,931 (3·5).

Population in 5 census years was:

	White	*Negro*	*Indian*	*Asiatic*	*Total*	*Per sq. mile*
1910	2,059,227	7,084	9,053	344	2,075,708	25·7
1930	2,542,599	9,445	11,077	832	2,563,953	32·0
1960	3,371,603	22,263	15,496	3,642	3,413,864	42·7
			All others			
1970	3,736,038	34,868	34,163		3,805,069	47·6
1980	3,935,770	53,344	86,856		4,075,970	51·4

Of the 1980 population, 1,997,826 were male; 2,725,270 were urban; those 21 years of age or older numbered 2,656,947.

The largest cities are Minneapolis, 370,951; St Paul (capital), 270,230 (Minneapolis–St Paul standard metropolitan statistical area, 2,113,533 in 1980); Duluth, 92,811; Bloomington, 81,831; Rochester, 57,890.

CLIMATE. Duluth. Jan. 8°F (–13·3°C), July 63°F (17·2°C). Annual rainfall 29" (719 mm). Minneapolis-St. Paul. Jan. 12°F (–11·1°C), July 71°F (21·7°C). Annual rainfall 26" (656 mm). *See* Great Lakes, p. 1382.

CONSTITUTION AND GOVERNMENT. The present constitution dates from 1858; it has had 109 amendments. The Legislature consists of a Senate of 67 members, elected for 4 years, and a House of Representatives of 134 members, elected for 2 years. The Governor and Lieut.-Governor are elected for 4 years. The state sends to Congress 2 senators and 8 representatives.

In the 1988 presidential election Dukakis polled 1,109,471 votes, Bush 962,337.

The capital is St Paul. There are 87 counties, four containing less than 400 sq. miles, the largest being 6,092 sq. miles.

Governor: Rudy Perpich (DFL.), 1987–91 ($98,914).
Lieut.-Governor: Marlene Johnson (DFL.), 1987–91 ($54,413).
Secretary of State: Joan Anderson Growe (DFL.), 1987–91 ($54,405).

BUDGET. The general fund budget for the 1989–91 2-year period was $13,686m.; tax relief $1,966m., education $7,121m., public welfare $1,940m., transport $207m.

Net long-term debt, 30 June 1989, was $1,416m.

Per capita personal income (1988) was $16,787.

NATURAL RESOURCES

Minerals. The iron ore and taconite industry is the most important in the USA. Production of usable iron ore in 1988 was 42m. tons, value $1,278m. Other important minerals are sand and gravel, crushed and dimension stone, lime and manganiferous ore. Total value of mineral production, 1988, $1,391m.

Agriculture. In 1989 there were 90,000 farms with a total area of 30m. acres (60% of the land area); the average farm was of 333 acres. Average value of land and buildings (1989) $192,245. Commercial farms in 1987 numbered 85,079; 12% of the farms were operated by tenant-farmers. Cash receipts, 1988, from crops, $2,743m.; from livestock, $3,364m. In 1988 Minnesota ranked second in sugar-beets, spring wheat, processing sweet corn, oats, dry milk, cheese, mink and turkeys. Other important products are wild rice, butter, eggs, flaxseed, milch cows, milk, corn, barley, swine, cattle for market, soybeans, honey, potatoes, rye, chickens, sunflower seed and dry edible beans. Of livestock, cattle represents 16% of total farm income, swine 12% and milk 20%. Of crops, corn represents 15% and soybeans 19%. On 1 Jan. 1989 the farm animals included 3·15m. all cattle, 855,000 milch cows, 237,000 sheep and lambs, 4·26m. swine and 12·8m. chickens. Turkey production, 1988, 38·5m. In 1988 the wool clip amounted to 1·89m. lb. of wool from 255,000 sheep.

Forestry. Forests of commercial timber cover 14m. acres, of which 53% is government-owned. The value of forest products in 1987 was $4,400m.: $1,300m. from primary processing, of which $901m. was from pulp and paper; and $3,100m. from secondary manufacturing. Logging, pulping, saw-mills and associated industries employed 53,700 in 1987.

INDUSTRY. In 1986 manufacturing establishments employed 369,000 workers; value added by manufacture was $19,800m. Largest manufacturing industry is computers and non-electric machinery (81,000 employees); then food products and kindred products (45,000), printing and publishing (43,000).

TOURISM. In 1987, travellers spent about $5,500m. The industry employed about 108,000.

COMMUNICATIONS

Roads. The state highway system (interstate and state trunk highways) covered 12,100 miles in 1988; total highway, road and street mileage, 129,650. In 1988, 3·4m. passenger automobiles were registered.

Railways. There are 3 Class I and 16 Class II and smaller railroads operating, with total mileage of 5,044.

Aviation. In 1989 there were 141 airports for public use and 12 public seaplane bases.

JUSTICE, RELIGION, EDUCATION AND WELFARE

Justice. A Civil Rights Act (1927) forbids places of public resort to exclude persons 'on account of race or colour' and another section forbids insurance companies to discriminate 'between persons of the same class on account of race'. Contractors on public works may have their contracts cancelled if 'in the hiring of common or skilled labour' they are found to have discriminated on the grounds of 'race, creed or colour'. The state's penal reformatory system on 1 Oct. 1989 held 3,005 adult men and women. There is no death penalty in Minnesota.

Religion. The chief religious bodies are: Lutheran with 1,088,304 members in 1980; Roman Catholic, 1,041,781; Methodist, 146,422. Total membership of all denominations, 2,653,161.

Education. In 1988, there were 61,442 kindergarten students, 340,967 elementary students, and 318,714 secondary students enrolled in 1,511 public schools. There were 82,165 kindergarten, elementary, and secondary students enrolled in 572 private schools. The University of Minnesota, chartered in 1851 and opened in 1869, had a total enrolment in 1988 of 54,515 students on all campuses. The 18 public community colleges (2-year) had a total enrolment of 49,589. There are seven state universities (4-year) at Bemidji, Mankato, Marshall, Moorhead, St Cloud, Winona, Minneapolis and St Paul. Enrolment in all institutions of higher education, 1988, 251,304.

Health. In 1989 the state had 163 general acute hospitals with 19,229 beds. Patients resident in institutions under the Department of Human Services in Aug. 1989 included 1,343 people with mental illness, 1,405 people with mental retardation, 265 with chemical dependency and 486 in state nursing homes.

Social Security. Programmes of old age assistance, aid to the disabled, and aid to the blind are administered under the federal Supplemental Security Income (SSI) Programme. Minnesota has a supplementary programme, Minnesota Supplemental Aid (MSA) to cover individuals not eligible for SSI, to supplement SSI benefits for others whose income is below state standards, and to provide one-time payments for emergency needs such as major home repair, essential furniture or appliances, moving expenses, fuel, food and shelter.

Further Reading

Statistical Information: Current information is obtainable from the State Planning Agency (300 Centennial Office Building, 658 Cedar Street, St Paul 55155); non-current material from the Reference Library, Minnesota Historical Society, St Paul 55101.

Legislative Manual. Secretary of State. St Paul. Biennial
Manufacturers' Directory. Nelson Name Service, Minneapolis, Biennial
Minnesota Agriculture Statistics. Dept. of Agric., St Paul. Annual
Minnesota Pocket Data Book 1985–86, St Paul, 1985

MISSISSIPPI

HISTORY. Mississippi, settled in 1716, was organized as a Territory in 1798 and admitted into the Union on 10 Dec. 1817. In 1804 and in 1812 its boundaries were extended, but in March 1817 a part was taken to form the new Territory of Alabama, leaving the boundaries substantially as at present.

AREA AND POPULATION. Mississippi is bounded north by Tennessee, east by Alabama, south by the Gulf of Mexico and Louisiana, west by the Mississippi River forming the boundary with Louisiana and Arkansas. Area, 47,689 sq. miles, 457 sq. miles being inland water. Census population, 1 July 1980, 2,520,638, an increase of 13·6% since 1970. Estimate (1985), 2,656,600. Births, occurring in the state, 1988, were 41,269; deaths, 23,990; infant deaths, 480; marriages, 24,919; divorces, 12,097.

Population of 6 federal census years was:

	White	*Negro*	*Indian*	*Asiatic*	*Total*	*Per sq. mile*
1910	786,111	1,009,487	1,253	263	1,797,114	38·8
1930	998,077	1,009,718	1,458	568	2,009,821	42·4
1950	1,188,632	986,494	2,502	1,286	2,178,914	46·1
1960	1,257,546	915,743	3,119	1,481	2,178,141	46·1
			All others			
1970	1,393,283	815,770	7,859		2,216,912	46·9
1980	1,615,190	887,206	18,242		2,520,638	53·0

Of the population in 1980, 1,213,878 were male, 1,192,805 were urban and 1,601,157 were 20 years old or older.

The largest city (1980) is Jackson, 202,895. Others are: Biloxi, 49,311; Meridian, 46,577; Hattiesburg, 40,829; Greenville, 40,613; Gulfport, 39,676; Pascagoula, 29,318; Columbus, 27,383; Vicksburg, 25,434; Tupelo, 23,905.

CLIMATE. Jackson. Jan. 47°F (8·3°C), July 82°F (27·8°C). Annual rainfall 49" (1,221 mm). Vicksburg. Jan. 48°F (8·9°C), July 81°F (27·2°C). Annual rainfall 52" (1,311 mm). *See* Central Plains, p. 1381.

CONSTITUTION AND GOVERNMENT. The present constitution was adopted in 1890 without ratification by the electorate; 94 amendments by 1988.

The Legislature consists of a Senate (52 members) and a House of Representatives (122 members), both elected for 4 years, as are also the Governor and Lieut.-Governor. Electors are all citizens who have resided in the state 1 year, in the county 1 year, in the election district 6 months next before the election and have been registered according to law. In the 1988 presidential election Bush polled 551,745 votes, Dukakis, 360,892.

The state is represented in Congress by 2 senators and 5 representatives.

The capital is Jackson; there are 82 counties.

Governor: Ray Mabus (D.), 1988–92 ($75,600).
Lieut.-Governor: Bradford Johnson Dye (D.) ($40,800).
Secretary of State: Dick Molpus (D.) ($54,000).

BUDGET. For the fiscal year ending 30 June 1989 the general revenues were $5,391,165,868 (taxation, $2,373,140,438; federal aid, $1,177,055,491; other state resources, $1,840,969,938), and general expenditures were $5,415,338,112 ($1,434,363,972 for education, $373,451,710 for highways and $1,031,233,151 for public welfare).

On 30 June 1989 the total net long-term debt was $532,617,308.

Per capita personal income (1988) was $11,090 (lowest in US).

ENERGY AND NATURAL RESOURCES

Minerals. Petroleum and natural gas account for about 90% (by value) of mineral production. Output of petroleum, 1988, was 27,874,623 bbls and of natural gas 234,482,416m. cu. ft. There are 6 oil refineries. Value of oil and gas products sold 1988 was $737,845,258.

Agriculture. Agriculture is the leading industry of the state because of the semi-tropical climate and a rich productive soil. In 1989 there were 82 soil conservation districts covering 30m. acres. In 1989 farms numbered 41,000 with an area of 13·3m. acres. Average size of farm was 224 acres. This compares with an average farm size of 138 acres in 1960.

Cash income from all crops and livestock during 1988, including government payments, was $2,640,777,000. Cash income from crops was $1,209,405,000 and from livestock and products, $1,176,272,000. The chief product is cotton, cash income $539,525,000 from 1m. acres producing 1,825,000 bales of 736 lb. Soybeans, rice, corn, hay, wheat, oats, sorghum, peanuts, pecans, sweet potatoes, peaches, other vegetables, nursery and forest products continue to contribute.

On 1 Jan. 1987 there were 1,373,000 head of cattle and calves on Mississippi farms. Milch cows totalled 75,000, beef cows, 690,000; hogs and pigs (1986), 210,000. Of cash income from livestock and products, 1986, $175,471,000 was credited to cattle and calves. Cash income from poultry and eggs, 1986, totalled $573,234,000; dairy products, $113,027,000; swine, $37,870,000.

Forestry. In 1988 income from forestry amounted to $611m.; output of logs, lumber, etc., was 1,647,265 bd ft; pulpwood, 5,960,941 cords; distillate wood, 65 tons. There are about 16,981,500 acres of forest (56% of the state's area). National forests area, 1987, 1,212,100 acres.

INDUSTRY. In 1988 the 3,432 manufacturing establishments employed 239,324 workers, earning $4,389,520,667. The average annual wage was $17,824.

TOURISM. Total receipts, 1987, $1,400m. from about 1·68m. tourists.

COMMUNICATIONS

Roads. The state in July 1989 maintained 10,359 miles of highways, of which 10,350 miles were paved; 1,698,623 cars were registered.

Railways. The state in 1989 had 2,948 miles of railway.

Aviation. There were 77 public airports in 1989, 70 of them general. There were also 36 privately owned airports.

JUSTICE, RELIGION, EDUCATION AND WELFARE

Justice. In 1989 there was one execution; from 1955 to 1989 executions (by gas-chamber) totalled 35 (8 whites and 17 negroes for murder, 9 negroes for rape and 1 negro for armed robbery). On 14 Nov. 1989 the state prisons had 8,033 inmates.

Religion. Southern Baptists in Mississippi (1988), 663,873 members; Negro Baptists (1987), about 477,000; United Methodists (1988) 187,813; Roman Catholics (1989), 99,526 in Biloxi and Jackson dioceses.

Education. Attendance at school is compulsory as laid down in the Education Reform Act of 1982. The public elementary and secondary schools in 1988–89 had 503,326 pupils and 27,333 classroom teachers.

In 1989, teachers' average salary was $22,578. The expenditure per pupil in average daily attendance, 1988–89, was $2,678.

There are 16 universities and senior colleges, of which 8 are state-supported. The University of Mississippi, at Oxford (1844), had, 1988–89, 971 instructors and 11,396 students; Mississippi State University, Starkville, 1,419 instructors and 13,418 students; Mississippi University for Women, Columbus, 152 instructors and 2,064 students; University of Southern Mississippi, Hattiesburg, 763 instructors and 12,581 students; Jackson State University, Jackson, 389 instructors and 6,778 students; Delta State University, Cleveland, 235 instructors and 3,701 students; Alcorn State University, Lorman, 156 instructors and 2,757 students; Mississippi Valley State University, Itta Bena, 138 instructors and 1,756 students. State support for the 8 universities (1988–89) was $312,725,581.

Junior colleges had (1988–89) 57,194 students and 2,495 instructors. The state appropriation for junior colleges, 1988–89, was $68,399,831.

Health. In 1989 the state had 113 acute general hospitals (12,590 beds) listed by the State Department of Health; 16 hospitals with facilities for care of the mentally ill had 2,508 beds.

Social Security. The state Medicaid commission paid (1989) $477,341,680 for medical services, including $52,110,304 for drugs, $65,801,505 for skilled nursing home care, $141,807,078 for hospital services. There were 59,398 persons eligible for Aged Medicaid benefits and 75,406 persons eligible for Disabled Medicaid benefits at 30 June 1989. In June 1989, 59,238 families with 127,349 dependent children received $7,015,477 in the Aid to Dependent Children programme. The average monthly payment was $119.34 per family or $55·46 per child.

Further Reading

1980 Census of Population and Housing: Mississippi.
Mississippi Official and Statistical Register. Secretary of State. Jackson. Biennial
Bettersworth, J. K., *Mississippi: A History*. Rev. ed. Austin, Tex., 1964

Mississippi Library Commission: PO Box 10700 Jackson, MS. 39289–0700. *Director:* David M. Woodburn.

MISSOURI

HISTORY. Missouri, first settled in 1735 at Ste Genevieve, was made a Territory on 1 Oct. 1812, and admitted to the Union on 10 Aug. 1821. In 1837 its boundaries were extended to their present limits.

AREA AND POPULATION. Missouri is bounded north by Iowa, east by the Mississippi River forming the boundary with Illinois and Kentucky, south by Arkansas, south-east by Tennessee, south-west by Oklahoma, west by Kansas and Nebraska, with the Missouri River forming the boundary in the north-west. Area, 69,697 sq. miles, 752 sq. miles being water.

Census population, 1 April 1980, 4,916,766, an increase since 1970 of 5·1%. Estimate (1988), 5,139,000. Births, 1987, were 76,909 (15·1 per 1,000 population); deaths, 50,362 (9·9); infant deaths, 767 (10·2 per 1,000 live births); marriages, 48,397 (9·5); divorces, 24,984 (4·9).

Population of 5 federal census years was:

	White	*Negro*	*Indian*	*Asiatic*	*Total*	*Per sq. mile*
1910	3,134,932	157,452	313	638	3,293,335	47·9
1930	3,403,876	223,840	578	1,073	3,629,367	52·4
1960	3,922,967	390,853	1,723	3,146	4,319,813	62·5
			All others			
1970	4,177,495	480,172	19,732		4,677,399	67·0
1980	4,345,521	514,276	56,889		4,916,686	71·3

Of the total population in 1980, 2,365,487 were male, 3,350,746 persons were urban and those 18 years of age or older numbered 3,554,203.

The principal cities at the 1980 census (and estimates, 1986) are:

St Louis	453,085 (426,300)	Columbia	62,061 (63,140)
Kansas City	448,159 (444,170)	Florissant	55,372 (59,040)
Springfield	133,116 (139,360)	University City	42,738 (42,270)
Independence	111,806 (112,950)	Joplin	38,893 (40,220)
St Joseph	76,691 (74,070)	St Charles	37,379 (41,990)

Metropolitan areas, 1980: St Louis, 2,356,000; Kansas City, 1,327,000.

CLIMATE. Kansas City. Jan. 30°F (–1·1°C), July 79°F (26·1°C). Annual rainfall 38" (947 mm). St. Louis. Jan. 32°F (0°C), July 79°F (26·1°C). Annual rainfall 40" (1,004 mm). *See* Central Plains, p. 1381.

CONSTITUTION AND GOVERNMENT. A new constitution, the fourth, was adopted on 27 Feb. 1945; it has been amended 27 times. The General Assembly consists of a Senate of 34 members elected for 4 years (half for re-election every 2 years), and a House of Representatives of 163 members elected for 2 years. The Governor and Lieut.-Governor are elected for 4 years. Missouri sends to Congress 2 senators and 9 representatives.

Voters (with the usual exceptions) are all citizens and those adult aliens who, within a prescribed period, have applied for citizenship. In the 1988 presidential election Bush polled 1,081,163 votes, Dukakis, 1,004,040.

Jefferson City is the state capital. The state is divided into 114 counties and the city of St Louis.

Governor: John D. Ashcroft (R.), 1989–93 ($81,000).
Lieut.-Governor: Mel Carnahan (D.), 1989–93 ($48,600).
Secretary of State: Roy D. Blunt (R.), 1989–93 ($64,800).

BUDGET. For the year 1987 the total revenues from all funds were $7,761m. (federal revenue, $1,560m., general revenue, $6,485m.).

Total outstanding debt, 1987, was $4,307m.

Per capita personal income (1988) was $15,492.

NATURAL RESOURCES

Minerals. Principal minerals are lead (ranks first in USA), zinc (ranks second), clays, coal, iron ore, and stone for cement and lime manufacture. Value of production (1986) $748·6m.

Agriculture. In 1988 there were 113,000 farms in Missouri covering 30·4m. acres. Production of principal crops, 1988: Corn, 153·52m. bu.; soybeans, 109·98m. bu.; wheat, 77·5m. bu.; sorghum grain, 38·07m. bu.; oats, 1·44m. bu.; cotton, 306,000 bales (of 480 lb.). Cash receipts from farming, 1988, $3,832·8m. to which soybeans contributed $835·8m.

Forestry. Forest land area, 1988, 12·9m. acres.

INDUSTRY. The largest employer in 1986 was manufacturing, in which the transport equipment industry employed 72,170 workers. Other large industries are food and kindred products, electrical equipment and supplies, apparel and related products and non-electrical machinery, leather products, chemicals, paper, metal industries, stone, clay, glass, rubber and plastic products. Wholesale and retail trade employed 559,900 as of May 1989.

LABOUR. The State Board of Mediation has jurisdiction in labour disputes involving only public utilities. The Prevailing Wage Law (1959) provides that no less than the local hourly rate of wages for work of a similar character shall be paid to any workmen engaged in public works. The Industrial Commission has authority to inspect records and to institute actions for penalties described in the Act. There is a state programme for industrial safety in hand, under the Federal Occupational and Health Act. In 1988 the annual average number of employed was 2,431,314, and 142,056 were unemployed; the unemployment rate was 5·5%.

COMMUNICATIONS

Roads. Federal and state highways, Sept. 1987, totalled 119,398 miles. In 1987 there were 2·7m. vehicles licensed in the state, of which 3,930 were private and commercial buses.

Railways. The state has 10 Class I railways; approximate total mileage, 6,736. There are 15 other railways (switching, terminal or short-line), total mileage 435, in Dec. 1987.

Aviation. In 1988 there were 144 public airports and 217 private airports.

Shipping. Ten carrier barge lines (1984) operated on about 1,000 miles of navigable waterways including the Missouri and Mississippi Rivers. Boat shipping seasons: Missouri River, April–end Nov.; Mississippi River, all seasons.

Post and Broadcasting. There were 264 commercial radio stations and 33 TV stations in 1989.

Newspapers. There were (1989) 47 daily and 236 weekly newspapers.

JUSTICE, RELIGION, EDUCATION AND WELFARE

Justice. State prisons in 1988 had an average of 12,063 inmates including 528 females. The median age was 28, 55·72% were between age 15 and 29. The first execution since 1965 was on 1 Jan. 1989 (by lethal injection). The death penalty was reinstated in 1978; since 1930 executions (by lethal gas) have totalled 42, including 32 for murder, 7 for rape and 3 for kidnapping. The Missouri Law Enforcement Assistance Council was created in 1969 for law reform.

Religion. Chief religious bodies (1980) are Catholic, with 800,228 members, Southern Baptists (700,053), United Methodists (270,469), Christian Churches (175,101), Lutheran (157,928), Presbyterian (38,254). Total membership, all denominations, about 2·6m. in 1980.

Education. School attendance is compulsory for children from 7 to 16 years for the full term. In the 1987–88 school year, public schools (kindergarten through grade 12) had 802,060 pupils. Total expenditure for public schools in 1987–88, $2,634,000m. Salaries for teachers (kindergarten through grade 12), 1987–88, averaged $24,709. Institutions for higher education include the University of Missouri, founded in 1839 with campuses at Columbia, Rolla, St Louis and Kansas City, with 4,449 accredited teachers and 52,116 students in 1988–89. Washington University at St Louis, founded in 1857, is an independent co-ed university with 10,628 students in 1988–89. St Louis University (1818), is an independent Roman Catholic co-ed university with 10,199 students in 1988–89. Sixteen state colleges had 116,778 students in 1988–89. Private colleges had (1988–89) 38,213 students. Church-affiliated colleges (1988–89) had 32,152 students. Public junior colleges had 56,380 students. There are about 90 secondary and post-secondary institutions offering vocational courses, and about 294 private career schools. There were 234,802 students in higher education in autumn 1988.

Health. There were 9 state mental health hospitals and centres and 3 children's hospitals in 1989, admitting 20,071 patients.

Social Security. In 1987 the number of recipients of medicaid was 369,000. The number of recipients of Aid to families with Dependent Children was 200,000 with an average monthly payment per family of $262.

Further Reading

Missouri Area Labor Trends, Department of Labour and Industrial Relations, monthly
Missouri Farm Facts, Department of Agriculture, annual
Report of the Public Schools of Missouri. State Board of Education, annual
Statistical Abstract for Missouri. State and Regional Fiscal Studies Unit, College of Business and Public Administration, Columbia 1985

MONTANA

HISTORY. Montana, first settled in 1809, was made a Territory (out of portions of Idaho and Dakota Territories) in 1864 and was admitted into the Union on 8 Nov. 1889.

AREA AND POPULATION. Montana is bounded north by Canada, east by North and South Dakota, south by Wyoming and west by Idaho and the Bitterroot Range of the Rocky Mountains. Area, 147,138 sq. miles, including 1,551 sq. miles of water, of which the federal government, 1986, owned 28,236,000 acres or 30·3%. US Bureau of Indian Affairs (1982) administered 5·03m. acres, of which 2,820,000 were allotted to tribes. Census population, 1 April 1980, 786,690, an increase of 13·3% since 1970. Estimate (1986), 819,000. Births, 1986, were 12,728 (15·5 per 1,000 population); deaths, 6,738 (8·2); infant deaths, 122 (9·8 per 1,000 live births); marriages, 6,739 (8·2); divorces 4,307 (5·3).

Population in 5 census years was:

	White	*Negro*	*Indian*	*Asiatic*	*Total*	*Per sq. mile*
1910	360,580	1,834	10,745	2,870	376,053	2·6
1930	519,898	1,256	14,798	1,239	537,606	3·7
1950	572,038	1,232	16,606	—	591,024	4·1
1970	663,043	1,995	27,130	1,099	694,409	4·7
1980	740,148	1,786	37,270	2,503	786,690	5·3

Of the total population in 1980, 392,625 were male, 416,402 persons (52·9%) were urban. Persons 20 years of age or older numbered 524,836. Median age, 29 years. Households, 283,742.

The largest cities, 1980 (and 1986 estimate) are Billings, 66,798 (80,310); Great Falls, 56,725 (57,310). Others: Butte-Silver Bow, 37,205 (33,380); Missoula, 33,388 (33,960); Helena (capital), 23,938 (24,670); Bozeman, 21,645 (23,490); Anaconda-Deer Lodge County, 12,518 (10,700); Havre, 10,891 (10,840); Kalispell, 10,648 (11,890).

CLIMATE. Helena. Jan. 18°F (–7·8°C), July 69°F (20·6°C). Annual rainfall 13" (325 mm). *See* Mountain States, p. 1381.

CONSTITUTION AND GOVERNMENT. A new constitution was ratified by the voters on 6 June 1972, and fully implemented on 1 July 1973; the Senate to consist of 50 senators, elected for 4 years, one half at each biennial election. The 100 members of the House of Representatives are elected for 2 years.

The Governor and Lieut.-Governor are elected for 4 years. Montana sends to Congress 2 senators and 2 representatives.

In the 1988 presidential election Bush polled 189,598 votes, Dukakis, 168,120.

The capital is Helena. The state is divided into 56 counties.

Governor: Stan Stephens (R.), 1989–93 ($50,452).
Lieut.-Governor: Allen Kolstad (R.), 1989–93 ($36,141).
Secretary of State: Mike Cooney (D.), 1989–93 ($33,342).

BUDGET. Total state revenues for the year ending 30 June 1985 were $1,738,000,000; total expenditures were $1,557,000,000 ($436m. for education, $239m. for highways and $184m. for public welfare).

Total net long-term debt on 30 June 1985 was $157,225,000.

Per capita personal income (1986) was $11,904.

ENERGY AND NATURAL RESOURCES

Electricity. Electric power generated in April 1986 was 1,112 gwh., of which 796 gwh. was hydro-electric and 310 gwh. from coal-fired plants; 1 from oil-fired, and 4 gwh. from other sources.

Minerals (1985). Output of crude petroleum, 30·2m. bbls; copper, 15,092 tonnes; sand and gravel, 9,000 short tons; phosphate rock, undisclosed; silver, 4m. troy oz.;

gold, 160,262 troy oz.; zinc, undisclosed; natural gas, 46,592m. cu. ft; coal, 33·3m. short tons. Value of total mineral production, $1,198·8m., with petroleum ($761·9m.) the first, coal ($417·4m.) the second, natural gas ($95·5m.) the third and gold ($50·9m.) the fourth most important commodity.

Agriculture. In 1986 there were 23,300 farms and ranches (50,564 in 1935) with an area of 60·8m. acres (47,511,868 acres in 1935). Large-scale farming predominates; in 1986 the average size per farm was 2,609 acres. Income from all farm marketings was $1,145m. in 1986 (crops, $493m.; livestock, $652m.). Irrigated area harvested in 1986 was 1·6m. acres; non-irrigated, 7·8m. acres.

The chief crops are wheat, amounting in 1986 to 138·5m. bu.; barley, 85m. bu.; oats, 4·1m. bu.; sugar-beet, hay, potatoes, alfalfa, dry beans, flax and cherries. In 1986 there were 24,000 milch cows, 2·4m. all cattle; 190,000 swine and 423,000 sheep.

Forestry. Total forest area (1986), 22·6m. acres. In 1986 there were 16·8m. acres within 11 national forests.

INDUSTRY. In 1987 manufacturing establishments numbering 1,223 had 20,900 production workers; value added by manufacture was (1986) $907·4m.

LABOUR (March 1988). Work force, 402,900; total employed, 366,000; total non-agricultural workers, 336,000; agricultural workers, 29,000. Workers employed by major industry group: Mining, 5,900 (average net weekly earnings, $533.32); contract construction, 6,900 ($499.22); manufacturing, 20,100 ($404.80); transport and public utilities, 18,900 ($433.81; wholesale/retail trade, 70,900 ($197.78); finance/insurance/real estate, 12,500 ($264.54); services, 64,700 ($230.08); government, 70,200 (no income figures available). Average weekly earnings for all workers in private non-agricultural industries $270.19. Total unemployed 36,000 (9·2% of the work force in March 1988 as compared to 5·5% nationally for that month).

There were 13 work stoppages in 1987 involving 9,920 workers, with a total of 68,164 man days idle during the year.

COMMUNICATIONS

Roads. In 1987 the state had 58,711 miles of maintained public roads and streets including 11,758 miles of the federal-aid system. At 31 Dec. 1987 there were 436,152 passenger vehicles, 280,794 trucks and 25,503 motor cycles registered.

Railways. In Oct. 1988 there were 3,400 route miles of railway in the state.

Aviation. There were 129 airports open for public use in Jan. 1988, of which 122 were publicly owned.

JUSTICE, RELIGION, EDUCATION AND WELFARE

Justice. At 31 Dec. 1987 the Montana State Prison at Deer Lodge held 961 inmates and the Women's Correctional Facility at Warm Springs, 36. Since 1943 there have been no executions; total since 1930 (all by hanging) was 6; 4 whites and 2 Negroes, for murder.

Religion. The leading religious bodies are (1987): Roman Catholic with 162,000 members; Lutheran, 68,654; Methodist (Yellowstone Conference, including N. Wyoming, Montana, and Salmon, Idaho), 21,609 (church estimates).

Education. In Oct. 1987 public elementary and secondary schools had 152,207 pupils. Public elementary and secondary school teachers (9,659 in 1987) had an average salary of $23,774. Expenditure on public school education (1986–87) was $475·9m. This included $26·33m. for Special Education.

The Montana University system consists of the Montana State University, at Bozeman (autumn 1987 enrolment: 9,878 students), the University of Montana, at Missoula, founded in 1895 (8,472), the Montana College of Mineral Science and Technology, at Butte (1,746), Northern Montana College, at Havre (1,658), Eastern

Montana College, at Billings (3,926) and Western Montana College, at Dillon (992).

Social Security. In Aug. 1988, 4,892 persons over age 65 were receiving in medical assistance an average of $940 per year per person; 55 blind persons, $558, 6,035 totally disabled, $767; 9,290 families received in aid-to-dependent children assistance an average of $313. Aid was from state and federal sources.

Health. In Aug. 1988 the state had 60 hospitals (3,354 beds) listed by the Montana Board of Health. Four centres for mental illness and developmental disabilities had 703 patients.

Further Reading

Montana Agricultural Statistics. U.S. Dept. of Agriculture, Montana Crop and Livestock Reporting Service. Biennial from 1946

Montana Employment and Labor Force. Montana Dept. of Labor and Industry. Monthly from 1971

Montana Federal-Aid Road Log. Montana Dept. of Highways and US Dept. of Transportation, Federal Highway Administration. Annual from 1938

Montana Vital Statistics. Montana Dept. of Health and Environmental Sciences. Annually from 1954

Statistical Report. Montana Dept. of Social and Rehabilitation Services. Monthly from 1947

Lang, W, L. and Myers, R. C., *Montana, Our Land and People.* Pruett, 1979

Malone, M. P. and Roeder, R. B., *Montana, A History of Two Centuries.* Univ. of Washington Press, 1976

Spence, C. C., *Montana, a History.* New York, 1978

NEBRASKA

HISTORY. The Nebraska region was first reached by white men from Mexico under the Spanish general Coronado in 1541. It was ceded by France to Spain in 1763, retroceded to France in 1801, and sold by Napoleon to the US as part of the Louisiana Purchase in 1803. Its first settlement was in 1847, and on 30 May 1854 it became a Territory and on 1 March 1867 a state. In 1882 it annexed a small part of Dakota Territory, and in 1908 it received another small tract from South Dakota.

AREA AND POPULATION. Nebraska is bounded north by South Dakota, with the Missouri River forming the boundary in the north-east and the boundary with Iowa and Missouri to the east; south by Kansas, south-west by Colorado and west by Wyoming. Area, 77,355 sq. miles, of which 711 sq. miles are water. Census population, 1980: 1,569,825, an increase of 5·7% since 1970. Estimate (1987), 1,594,000. Births, 1987, were 23,813 (14·9 per 1,000 population); deaths, 14,820 (9·3); infant deaths, 204 (8·6 per 1,000 live births); marriages, 11,808 (7·4): divorces, 6,189 (3·9).

Population in 5 census years was:

	White	*Negro*	*Indian*	*Asiatic*	*Total*	*Per sq. mile*
1910	1,180,293	7,689	3,502	730	1,192,214	15·5
1920	1,279,219	13,242	2,888	1,023	1,296,372	16·9
1960	1,374,764	29,262	5,545	1,195	1,411,330	18·3
			All others			
1970	1,432,867	39,911	10,715		1,483,791	19·4
1980	1,490,381	48,390	31,054		1,569,825	20·5

Of the total population in 1980, 48·8% were male,62·9% were urban 65·6% were 21 years of age or older. The largest cities in the state are: Omaha, with a census population, 1980, of 313,911 (estimate, 1986, 349,270); Lincoln (capital), 171,932 (183,050); Grand Island, 33,180 (39,100); North Platte, 24,509 (22,490); Fremont, 23,979 (23,780); Hastings, 23,045 (22,990); Bellevue, 21,813 (32,200); Kearney, 21,158 (22,770); Norfolk, 19,449 (20,260).

The Bureau of Indian Affairs, in June 1987, administered 65,000 acres, of which 23,000 acres were allotted to tribal control.

CLIMATE. Omaha. Jan. 22°F (–5·6°C), July 77°F (25°C). Annual rainfall 29" (721 mm). *See* High Plains, p. 1381.

CONSTITUTION AND GOVERNMENT. The present constitution was adopted in 1875; it has been amended 184 times. By an amendment adopted in Nov. 1934 Nebraska has a single-chambered legislature (elected for 4 years) of 49 members—the only state in the Union to have one. The Governor and Lieut.-Governor are elected for 4 years. Amendments adopted in 1912 and 1920 provide for legislation through the initiative and referendum and permit cities of more than 5,000 inhabitants to frame their own charters. A 'right-to-work' amendment adopted 5 Nov. 1946 makes illegal the 'closed shop' demands of trade unions. Nebraska is represented in Congress by 2 senators and 3 representatives.

In the 1988 presidential election Bush polled 389,394 votes, Dukakis, 254,426.

The capital is Lincoln. The state has 93 counties.

Governor: Kay Orr (R.), 1987–90 ($58,000).
Lieut.-Governor: William E. Nichol (R.) ($40,000).
Secretary of State: Allen Beerman (R.) ($40,000).

BUDGET. For the fiscal year ending 30 June 1986 (US Census Bureau figures) the state's revenues were $2,334m. (taxation, $1,119m. and federal aid, $561m.); general expenditures were $2,205m. ($690m. for education, $353m. for highways and $361m. for public welfare).

The state has a bonded indebtedness limit of $100,000.

Per capita personal income (1987) was $14,328.

ENERGY AND NATURAL RESOURCES

Minerals. The total output of minerals, 1987, was valued at $191·5m., petroleum (6·1m. bbls) and sand and gravel (10·4m. tons) being the most important.

Agriculture. Nebraska is one of the most important agricultural states. In 1986 it contained approximately 55,000 farms, with a total area of 47·1m. acres. The average farm was 856 acres.

In 1986, 7·9m. acres were irrigated and 71,587 irrigation wells were registered.

Cash income from crops (1987), $1,975m., and from livestock, $4,848m. Principal crops, with estimated 1987 yield: Maize, 812·2m. bu. (ranking third in US); wheat, 85·8m. bu.; sorghums for grain, 109·2m. bu.; oats, 17·3m. bu.; soybeans, 81·9m. bu. About 750 farms grow sugar-beet for 3 factories; output, 1987, 1·1m. short tons. On 1 Jan. 1988 the state contained 5·5m. all cattle (ranking third in US), 100,000 milch cows, 180,000 sheep and 4m. swine.

Forestry. The area of national forest, 1986, was 352,000 acres.

INDUSTRY. In 1986 there were 1,800 manufacturing establishments; 62,600 production workers earned $1,141·2m. and value added by manufacturing was $5,362·6m. The chief industry is meat-packing.

COMMUNICATIONS

Roads. The state-maintained highway system embraced 9,947 miles in 1987; local roads, 86,158 miles. In 1987, 874,857 automobiles were registered.

Railways. In 1988 there were 4,013 miles of railway.

Aviation. Airports (1988) numbered 354, of which 101 were publicly owned.

JUSTICE, RELIGION, EDUCATION AND WELFARE

Justice. A 'Civil Rights Act' revised in 1969 provides that all people are entitled to a 'full and equal enjoyment of the accommodations, advantages, facilities and privileges' of hotels, restaurants, public conveyances, amusement places and other places. The state university is forbidden to discriminate between students 'because of age, sex, color or nationality'. An Act of 1941 declares it to be 'the policy of this state' that no trade union should discriminate, in collective bargaining, 'against any person because of his race or color'.

The state's prisons had, 10 Oct. 1988, 2,132 inmates (134 per 100,000 population). From 1930 to 1962 there were 4 executions (electrocution), 3 white men and 1 American Indian, all for murder, and none since.

Religion. The Roman Catholics had 337,855 members in 1985; Protestant Churches, 737,361; Jews, 7,865 members. Total, all denominations, 1,083,081.

Education. School attendance is compulsory for children from 7 to 16 years of age. Public elementary schools, autumn 1986, had 147,149 enrolled pupils. Teachers' salaries, 1987–88, averaged $23,246. Estimated public school expenditure for year ending 30 Aug. 1987 was $936m. Total enrolment in 27 institutions of higher education, autumn 1987, was 100,454 students. The largest institutions were (1987):

Opened	*Institution*	*Students*
1867	Peru State College, Peru (State)	1,396
1869	Univ. of Nebraska, Lincoln (State)	25,722
1872	Doane College, Crete (UCC)	796
1878	Creighton Univ., Omaha (RC)	5,827
1882	Hastings College (Presbyterian)	894
1883	Midland Lutheran College, Fremont (Lutheran)	836
1887	Nebraska Wesleyan Univ. (Methodist)	1,359
1891	Union College, Lincoln (Seventh Day Adventist)	578
1894	Concordia Teachers' College, Seward (Lutheran)	816
1905	Kearney State College, Kearney (State)	9,075
1908	Univ. of Nebraska, Omaha (State)	14,210
1910	Wayne State College, Wayne (State)	2,899
1911	Chadron State College, Chadron (State)	2,250
1923	College of St. Mary	1,256
1966	Bellevue College, Bellevue (Private)	1,922

The state holds 1·52m. acres of land as a permanent endowment of her schools; permanent public school endowment fund in Aug. 1988 was $94·9m.

Health. In 1988 the state had 114 hospitals and 565 patients in mental hospitals.

Social Security. The administration of public welfare is the responsibility of the County Divisions of Welfare with policy-forming, regulatory, advisory and supervisory functions performed by the State Department of Public Welfare. In 1987 public welfare provided financial aid and/or services as follows: for 7,680 individuals who were aged, blind or disabled, with an average state supplement of $58.65; for 16,315 families with dependent children, with an average payment of $318.31 per family; for 88,390 individuals who had medical needs, $1,937.02, per individual; for 3,280 children in need of child welfare services; $1·8m. was spent on medically-handicapped children. The amount of aid is based on need in accordance with State assistance standards; the programme of aid to families with dependent children is limited to a maximum maintenance payment of $300 for 1 child plus $75 for each additional child.

Further Reading

Agricultural Atlas of Nebraska. Univ. of Nebraska Press, 1977
Climatic Atlas of Nebraska. Univ. of Nebraska Press, 1977
Economic Atlas of Nebraska. Univ. of Nebraska Press, 1977
Nebraska. A Guide to the Cornhusker State. Univ. of Nebraska Press, 1979
Nebraska Statistical Handbook, 1988–89. Nebraska Dept. of Econ. Development, Lincoln
Nebraska Blue-Book. Legislative Council. Lincoln. Biennial
Olson, J. C., *History of Nebraska.* Univ. of Nebraska Press, 1955

State Library: State Law Library, State House, Lincoln. *Librarian:* Reta Johnson.

NEVADA

HISTORY. Nevada, first settled in 1851, when it was a part of the Territory of Utah (created 1850), was made a Territory in 1861, enlarged in 1862 by an addition from Utah Territory and admitted into the Union on 31 Oct. 1864 as the 36th state. In 1866 and 1867 the area of the state was significantly enlarged at the expense of the Territories of Utah and Arizona.

AREA AND POPULATION. Nevada is bounded north by Oregon and Idaho, east by Utah, south-east by Arizona, with the Colorado River forming most of the boundary, south and west by California. Area 110,561 sq. miles, 667 sq. miles being water. The federal government in 1987 owned 59,891,667 acres, or 85% of the land area. Vacant public lands, 47,738,597 acres. The Bureau of Indian Affairs controlled 1·15m. acres.

Census population on 1 April 1980, 799,184, an increase of 310,446 or 63·5% since 1970. Estimate (1989) 1,195,700. Births, 1988, were 18,415 (16·8 per 1,000 population); deaths, 9,464 (8·6); marriages, 117,282 (107); divorces, 13,922 (12·7); infant deaths, 158 (8·6 per 1,000 live births).

Population in 5 census years was:

	White	*Negro*	*Indian*	*Asiatic and all others*	*Total*	*Per sq. mile*
1910	74,276	513	5,240	1,846	81,875	0·7
1930	84,515	516	4,871	1,156	91,058	0·8
1960	263,443	13,484	6,681	1,670	285,278	2·6
1970	449,850	27,579	7,329	3,980	488,738	4·4
			All others			
1980	699,377	50,791	49,016		799,184	7·2

Of the total population in 1980, 404,372 were male, 681,682 were urban and 556,021 were 20 years of age or older.

The largest cities are Las Vegas, with population at the 1980 census of 164,674 (1989 estimate, 262,600); Reno, 100,756 (127,190); North Las Vegas, 39,196 (52,420); Sparks, 38,114 (55,460); Carson City, 30,807 (39,420); and Henderson, 20,905 (67,150). Clark County (Las Vegas, North Las Vegas and Henderson) and Washoe County (Reno and Sparks) together had 81% of the total state population in 1980 (82% in 1989).

CLIMATE. Las Vegas. Jan. 44°F (6·7°C), July 85°F (29·4°C). Annual rainfall 4" (112 mm). Reno. Jan. 32°F (0°C), July 69°F (20·6°C). Annual rainfall 7" (178 mm). *See* Mountain States, p. 1381.

CONSTITUTION AND GOVERNMENT. The constitution adopted in 1864 is still in force, with 110 amendments by 1986. The Legislature meets biennially (and in special sessions) and consists of a Senate of 20 members elected for 4 years, half their number retiring every 2 years, and an Assembly of 40 members elected for 2 years. The Governor, Lieut.-Governor and Attorney-General are elected for 4 years. Qualified electors are all citizens with the usual residential qualification. Nevada is represented in Congress by 2 senators and 2 representatives. A Supreme Court of 5 members is elected for 4 years on a non-partisan ballot.

In the 1988 presidential election Bush polled 206,040 votes, Dukakis, 132,738.

The state capital is Carson City. There are 17 counties, 17 incorporated cities and towns, 44 unincorporated towns and 1 city-county (Carson City).

Acting Governor: Bob Miller (D.), 1989–91 ($65,000).
Lieut.-Governor: (Vacant), 1989-91 ($10,500).
Secretary of State: F. S. Del Papa (D.), 1987-91 ($42,500).

BUDGET. For the fiscal year ending 30 June 1989, state general fund revenues were $673·13m.; budget expenditures were $636·6m. Education, followed by human resources and public safety, received the largest appropriations.

State bonded indebtedness on 30 June 1989, was $100·8m. The state has no franchise tax, capital stock tax, special intangibles tax, chain stores tax, stock transfer tax, admissions tax, gift tax, income taxes or inheritance tax. The sales and use tax and gaming taxes are the largest revenue producers.

Per capita personal income (1988) was $16,396.

ENERGY AND NATURAL RESOURCES

Electricity. In Aug. 1988 electricity power stations served 433,313 residential customers, 64,314 commercial, and 623 industrial customers.

Minerals. Production, 1988 was $1,867m. In order of value: Gold ($1,589·7m.), silver ($108·2m.), sand and gravel ($5·4m.), barite ($4·2m.), gypsum ($1·5m.). Petroleum produced, 3·2m. bbls. Other minerals are iron ore, mercury, lime, lithium, gemstones, lead, molybdenum, fluorspar, perlite, pumice, clays, talc, salt, tungsten, magnesite, diatonite and zinc.

Agriculture. In 1988, an estimated 2,500 farms had a farm area of 8·9m. acres (9·2m. in 1960). Farms averaged 3,560 acres. Area under irrigation (1988) was 558,830 acres compared with 542,976 acres in 1959.

Gross income, 1988, from crops, livestock and government payments, $238·6m. Cattle, hay, dairy products, potatoes and sheep are the principal commodities in order of cash receipts. Total value of crops produced, $79·6m. In Jan. 1989 there were 19,000 milch cows, 490,000 beef cattle, 87,000 sheep and lambs.

Forestry. The area of national forests (1988) under US Forest Service administration was 5,104,247 acres. National forests: Toiyabe (3,207,856 acres); Humboldt (2,469,395), Inyo (108,291); Lake Tahoe Basin (50,080).

INDUSTRY. The main industry is the service industry (42·3% of employment), especially tourism and legalized gambling; others include mining and smelting, livestock and irrigated agriculture, chemical manufacturing, and lumber processing. In 1988 there were 1,091 manufacturing establishments with 24,911 employees, earning $576·1m.

Gaming industry gross revenue for financial year 1988, $4,268·8m. There were at the same time 2,278 gaming licences in force and 4,555 licensed games.

LABOUR. The annual average unemployment for 1988 was 5·1% of the work force. All industries employed 555,983 workers. Main industries and employees, 1988: Service industries, 235,417; retail trade, 89,158; government, 66,950; finance, insurance and real estate, 24,600; transport, 17,033; public works and utilities, 11,967; mining, 10,967; manufacturing, 25,067.

COMMUNICATIONS

Roads. Highway mileage (federal, state and local) totalled 51,866 in 1988, of which 9,276 miles were surfaced; motor vehicle registrations in Dec. 1988 numbered 936,402.

Railways. In 1988 there were 1,244 miles of main-line railway. Nevada is served by Southern Pacific, Union Pacific and Western Pacific railways, and Amtrak passenger service for Las Vegas, Elko, Reno and Sparks.

Aviation. There were 114 civil airports and heliports in 1988. During 1988 McCarran International Airport (Las Vegas) handled 15·04m. passengers and Reno-Cannon International Airport handled 3·3m. passengers.

Post. In 1988 there were 110 telephone exchanges, 12 local exchange carriers with 627,781 telephones in service.

JUSTICE, RELIGION, EDUCATION AND WELFARE

Justice. Prohibition of marriage between persons of different race was repealed by statute in 1959.

A 1965 Civil Rights Act makes it illegal for persons operating public accommodation, employers of 15 or more employees, labour unions, and employment agencies to discriminate on the basis of race, colour, religion or national origin; a 1971 law makes racial discrimination in the sale or renting of houses illegal. A Commission on Equal Rights of Citizens is charged with enforcing these laws.

Between 1924 and 1967 executions (by lethal gas—the first state to adopt this method, in 1921), numbered 31. Capital punishment was abolished in 1972 and later re-introduced; there have since been 4 executions (by lethal gas) in 1979 and 1985 and 2 in 1989.

Religion. Roman Catholics were the most numerous religious group at the 1980 census, followed by members of the Church of Jesus Christ of Latter-day Saints (Mormons) and various Protestant churches.

Education. School attendance is compulsory for children from 7 to 17 years of age. In 1988 the 219 public elementary schools had 101,476 pupils; there were 95 secondary public schools with 74,085. There were 4,049 elementary teachers (average salary $28,070), 3,139 secondary teachers ($30,324). There were 80 private schools (8,278 pupils). The University of Nevada, Reno, had, in 1988–89, 385 full-time instructors and 11,262 students (regular, non-degree and correspondent), and University of Nevada, Las Vegas, 428 instructors and 14,825 students. Two-year community colleges operate as part of the University of Nevada system in Reno, Carson City, Elko, Fallon and Las Vegas. There were (1988–89) 224 instructors and 30,844 students.

Health. In 1989 the state had 32 hospitals (4,007 beds); in 1988 there were 31 nursing units (3,027 beds).

Social Security. In 1988 benefits were paid to 146,360 persons: 98,500 retired (aged 62 and over) workers (average payment $537 per month); 13,970 widows and widowers ($500); 11,420 disabled workers ($551), 10,380 wives and husbands ($266), 10,670 children ($270). Social Security beneficiaries represented 13·8% of the population.

Further Reading

Information: Bureau of Business and Economic Research (Univ. of Nevada-Reno).

Bushnell, E. and Driggs, D. W., *The Nevada Constitution: Origin and Growth.* Univ. of Nevada Press, 5th ed., 1980

Hulse, J. W., *The Nevada Adventure, A History.* Univ. of Nevada Press, 2nd ed., 1969

Laxalt, R., *Nevada: A History.* New York, 1977

Mack, E. M. and Sawyer, B. W., *Here is Nevada: A History of the State.* Sparks, Nevada, 1965

Paher, S. W., *Nevada, an Annotated Bibliography.* Nevada, 1980

State Library: Nevada State Library, Carson City. *State Librarian:* Mildred J. Heyer.

NEW HAMPSHIRE

HISTORY. New Hampshire, first settled in 1623, is one of the 13 original states of the Union.

AREA AND POPULATION. New Hampshire is bounded north by Canada, east by Maine and the Atlantic, south by Massachusetts and west by Vermont. Area, 9,279 sq. miles, of which 286 sq. miles are inland water. Census population, 1 April 1980, 920,610, an increase of 24·8% since 1970. Estimate (1988), 1,085,000, an increase of 17·9% since 1980. Births, 1987, were 17,025 (16·1 per 1,000 population); deaths, 8,403 (7·9); infant deaths (1987), 131 (7·7 per 1,000 live births); marriages, 10,854 (10·3); divorces, 4,947 (4·7).

Population at 5 federal censuses was:

	White	*Negro*	*Indian*	*Asiatic*	*Total*	*Per sq. mile*
1910	429,906	564	34	68	430,572	47·7
1930	464,351	790	64	88	465,293	51·6
1960	604,334	1,903	135	549	606,921	65·2
			All others			
1970	733,106	2,505	2,070		737,681	81·7
1980	910,099	3,990	6,521		920,610	101·9

Of the total population in 1988, 533,000 were male; those 21 years of age or older numbered 759,000.

The largest city of the state is Manchester, with a 1988 population of 100,600. Other cities are: Nashua, 80,694; Concord (capital), 37,024; Portsmouth, 26,887; Dover, 25,716; Rochester, 25,381; Keene, 22,403; Laconia, 16,580; Claremont, 13,901; Lebanon, 12,366; Berlin, 11,918; Somersworth, 10,743; Franklin, 8,337.

CLIMATE. Manchester. Jan. 22°F (–5·6°C), July 70°F (21·1°C). Annual rainfall 40" (1,003 mm). *See* New England, p. 1382.

CONSTITUTION AND GOVERNMENT. While the present constitution dates from 1784, it was extensively revised in 1792 when the state joined the Union. Since 1775 there have been 16 state conventions with 49 amendments adopted to amend the constitution.

The Legislature consists of a Senate of 30 members, elected for 2 years, and a House of Representatives, restricted to between 375 and 400 members, elected for 2 years. The Governor and 5 administrative officers called 'Councillors' are also elected for 2 years.

Electors must be adult citizens, able to read and write, duly registered and not paupers or under sentence for crime. New Hampshire sends to the Federal Congress 2 senators and 2 representatives.

In the 1988 presidential election Bush polled 280,533 votes, Dukakis, 163,205.

The capital is Concord. The state is divided into 10 counties.

Governor: Judd Gregg (R.), 1989–91 ($72,146).
Secretary of State: William M. Gardner (D.) ($50,675).

BUDGET. The state government's general revenue for the fiscal year ending 30 June 1986 (US Census Bureau figures) was $2,170m. ($1,249m. from taxes, $397m. from federal aid); general expenditures, $2,079m. ($725m. on education, $239m. on public welfare, $239m. on highways).

Net long-term debt, 30 June 1985, was $1,979m.

Per capita personal income (1987) was $19,434.

NATURAL RESOURCES

Minerals. Minerals are little worked; they consist mainly of sand and gravel, stone, and clay for building and highway construction. Value of mineral production, 1988, $47m.

Agriculture. In 1988, there were 2,515 farms occupying 426,237 acres; average farm was 169 acres. Average value per acre, $2,112. The US Soil Survey estimates that the state has 164,167 acres of excellent soil, 486,615 acres of fair soil, 530,630 of poor soil and 3,843,798 of non-arable soil. Only 636,195 acres (11% of the total area) show moderate erosion.

Cash income, 1987, from crops, $38m., and livestock and products, $72m. The chief field crops are hay and vegetables; the chief fruit crop is apples. Livestock on farms, 1987: 55,000 all cattle; 25,000 milch cows; 9,182 sheep; 6,610 swine; 460,000 poultry; 26,000 turkeys; about 30,000 horses.

Forestry. In 1988 forest land totalled 5m. acres; national forest, 735,000 acres.

Fisheries. The 1988 catch was 8·4m. lb., worth $5·6m.

INDUSTRY. Total non-agricultural employment (1986), 449,000, of which 118,100 are in manufacturing, 120,600 in trade, 107,800 in services.

Principal manufactures: Non-electrical machinery, electrical machinery, metal products, textiles and shoes.

COMMUNICATIONS

Roads. On 15 March 1988 the state's public road mileage was 14,642 miles of which 9,848 were non-federal-aid rural, 1,488 non-federal-aid urban, and 3,316 were federal-aid roads of which 223 miles were interstate. Motor vehicles registered, 1985, numbered 905,000.

Railways. In 1988 the length of railway in the state was 608 miles.

Aviation. In 1988 there were 15 public and 19 private airports.

JUSTICE, RELIGION, EDUCATION AND WELFARE

Justice. The state prison held 940 persons on 1 June 1988. Since 1930 there has been only one execution (by hanging)—a white man, for murder, in 1939.

Religion. The Roman Catholic Church is the largest single body. The largest Protestant churches are Congregational, Episcopal, Methodist and United Baptist Convention of N.H.

Education. School attendance is compulsory for children from 6 to 14 years of age during the whole school term, or to 16 if their district provides a high school. Employed illiterate minors between 16 and 21 years of age must attend evening or special classes, if provided by the district.

In 1987–88 the public elementary and secondary schools had 166,045 pupils and (1987) 10,112 classroom teachers. Public school salaries, 1987, averaged $24,019. Total expenditure on public schools in 1986–87 was estimated at $726m.

Of the 4-year colleges, the University of New Hampshire (1866) had 12,196 students in 1987–88; New Hampshire College (1932) had 5,358; Keene State College (1909) had 3,890; River College (1933) had 2,407. Dartmouth College (1769) had 3,871. Total enrolment, 1987-88, in 30 institutions of higher education, was 54,486 students.

Health. In 1987 the state had 37 hospitals.

Social Security. The Division of Human Services handles public assistance for (1) aged citizens 65 years or over, (2) needy aged aliens, (3) needy blind persons, (4) needy citizens between 18 and 64 years inclusive, who are permanently and totally disabled, (5) needy children under 18 years, (6) Medicaid and the medically needy not eligible for a monthly grant.

In May 1988, 1,298 persons were receiving old-age assistance of an average $87 per month; 2,761 permanently and totally disabled, $133 per month; 4,003 families with dependent children, $439 per month.

Further Reading

Delorme, D. (ed.) *New Hampshire Atlas and Gazetteer*. Freeport, 1983
Morison, E. E. and E. F., *New Hampshire*. New York, 1976
Squires, J. D., *The Granite State of the United States: A History of New Hampshire from 1623 to the present*. 4 vols., New York, 1956

NEW JERSEY

HISTORY. New Jersey, first settled in the early 1600s, is one of the 13 original states in the Union.

AREA AND POPULATION. New Jersey is bounded north by New York, east by the Atlantic with Long Island and New York City to the north-east, south by Delaware Bay and west by Pennsylvania. Area (US Bureau of Census), 7,787 sq. miles (319 sq. miles being inland water). Census population, 1 April 1980, 7,364,823, an increase of 2·7% since 1970. Estimate (1985) 7,562,000. Births, 1986, were 109,000 (14·3 per 1,000 population); deaths, 72,000 (9·4); marriages (1987), 60,100 (7·8); divorces (1987), 27,200 (3·5).

Population at 5 federal censuses was:

	White	*Negro*	*Indian*	*Asiatic*	*All others*	*Total*	*Per sq. mile*
1910	2,445,894	89,760	168	1,345	—	2,537,167	337·7
1930	3,829,663	208,828	213	2,630	122	4,041,334	537·3
1960	5,539,003	514,875	1,699	8,778	2,427	6,066,782	739·5
1970	6,349,908	770,292	4,706	20,537	22,721	7,168,164	953·1
1980	6,127,467	925,066	8,394	103,847	200,048	7,364,823	986·2

Of the population in 1980, 3,533,012 were male, 6,557,377 persons were urban, 5,116,581 were 20 years of age or older.

Census population of the larger cities and towns in 1980 was:

Newark	329,248	Irvington	61,493	Parsippany-Troy Hills	49,868
Jersey City	223,532	Union City	55,593	Middletown	62,574
Paterson	137,970	Vineland	53,753	Union Township	50,184
Elizabeth	106,201	Passaic	52,463	Bloomfield	47,792
Trenton (capital)	92,124	Woodbridge	90,074	Atlantic City	40,199
Camden	84,910	Hamilton	82,801	Plainfield	45,555
Clifton	74,388	Edison	70,193	Hoboken	42,460
East Orange	77,025	Cherry Hill	68,785	Montclair	38,321
Bayonne	65,047				

Largest urbanized areas (1980) were: Newark, 1,963,000; Jersey City, 555,483; Paterson-Clifton-Passaic, 447,785; Trenton (NJ–Pa.), 305,678.

CLIMATE. Jersey City. Jan. 31°F (–0·6°C), July 75°F (23·9°C). Annual rainfall 41" (1,025 mm). Trenton. Jan. 32°F (0°C), July 76°F (24·4°C). Annual rainfall 40" (1,003 mm). *See* Atlantic Coast, p. 1382.

CONSTITUTION AND GOVERNMENT. The legislative power is vested in a Senate and a General Assembly, the members of which are chosen by the people, all citizens (with necessary exceptions) 18 years of age, with the usual residential qualifications, having the right of suffrage. The present constitution, ratified by the registered voters on 4 Nov. 1947, has been amended 38 times. In 1966 the Constitutional Convention proposed, and the people adopted, a new plan providing for a 40-member Senate and an 80-member General Assembly. This plan, as certified by the Apportionment Commission and modified by the courts, provides for 40 legislative districts, with 1 senator and 2 assemblymen elected for each. Assemblymen serve 2 years, senators 4 years, except those elected at the election following each census, who serve for 2 years. The Governor is elected for 4 years.

The state sends to Congress 2 senators and 14 representatives.

In the 1988 presidential election Bush polled 1,743,192 votes, Dukakis, 1,320,352.

The capital is Trenton. The state is divided into 21 counties, which are subdivided into 567 municipalities—cities, towns, boroughs, villages and townships.

Governor: Thomas H. Kean (R.), 1986–90 ($85,000).
Secretary of State: Jane Burgio ($95,000).

BUDGET. For the year ending 30 June 1990 (budget figures) general revenues were $16,789·4m. general expenditures were $17,103m.

Total net long-term debt, 31 Dec. 1984, was $2,381·2m.

Per capita personal income (1984) was $15,282.

NATURAL RESOURCES

Minerals. The chief minerals are stone (17,576,000 short tons, value $111,951,000, 1987) and sand and gravel (17,312,000, $89,072,000); others are clays (6,000, $140,000), peat (32,000, $614,000) and gemstones. New Jersey is a leading producer of greensand marl, magnesium compounds and peat. Total value of mineral products, 1987, was $214,224,000.

Agriculture. Livestock raising, market-gardening, fruit-growing, horticulture and forestry are pursued. In 1987, 9,032 farms had a total area of 894,426 acres; and the average farm had 99 acres valued at $3,969 per acre.

Market value of agricultural products sold, 1987: Crops, including nursery and greenhouse, $370·58m.; livestock, poultry and their products, $125,423,000.

Leading crops are tomatoes (value, $15·8m., 1986), corn for grain ($18·4m.), peaches ($23·6m.), all hay ($30·3m.), blueberries ($23·2m.), soybeans ($16·1m.), white potatoes ($11·9m.), sweet corn ($14·1m.), peppers ($12·4m.), cranberries ($17·2m.).

Farm animals on 1 Jan. 1987 included 35,000 milch cows, 90,000 all cattle, 14,000 sheep and lambs and (1 Dec. 1986) 40,000 swine.

INDUSTRY. In 1987 the top 100 corporate employers (70 headquartered in New Jersey) employed 552,914 workers. There were 128 companies with more than 1,000 employees. The state's unemployment rate was 4·3%.

In July 1989 there were 3,721,100 employees on non-agricultural payrolls; 2,500 in mining, 184,800 in construction, 658,800 in manufacturing, 242,700 in transportation and public utilities, 889,800 in wholesale and retail trade, 246,900 in finance, insurance and real estate, 945,500 in services, 550,100 in government.

COMMUNICATIONS

Roads. In 1989 there were about 2,248 miles of state and interstate highways. At 1 Jan. 1988 there were 6,698 miles of county highways, 24,166 miles of municipal roads and 929 miles of other road.

Railways. In Sept. 1985, the state had 1,882·05 route miles of railway.

Aviation. There were (1985) 119 airports, 162 heliports and 13 seaplane bases (total 294, of which 67 were publicly owned).

JUSTICE, RELIGION, EDUCATION AND WELFARE

Justice. State prisons in Aug. 1985 had 12,814 adult and 587 juvenile inmates. The last execution (by electrocution) was in 1963; it was the 160th, all for murder. Future executions would be by lethal injection.

The constitution of New Jersey forbids discrimination against any person on account of 'religious principles, race, color, ancestry or national origin'. The state has had, since 1945, a 'fair employment act', *i.e.*, a Civil Rights statute forbidding any employer, public or private (with 6 or more employees), to discriminate against any applicant for work (or to discharge any employee) on the grounds of 'race, creed, color, national origin or ancestry'. Trade unions may not bar Negroes from membership.

Religion. The Roman Catholic population of New Jersey in 1984 was 3·1m. The five largest Protestant sects were United Methodists, 150,000; United Presbyterians, 174,000; Episcopalians, 147,000; Lutherans, 89,000; American Baptists, 74,000. There were 40,000 African Methodists and 4,000 Christian Methodist Episcopalians. In 1987 there were 427,700 Jews.

Education. Elementary instruction is compulsory for all from 6 to 16 years of age and free to all from 5 to 20 years of age. In 1987-88 public elementary schools had 726,305 and secondary schools had 366,677 enrolled pupils; public colleges in autumn 1984 had 313,985 students, including 117,212 in community colleges, and independent colleges had 63,607. Average salary of 78,335 elementary and secondary classroom teachers in public schools 1987–88 was $30,778.

Rutgers, the State University (founded as Queen's College in 1766) had, in 1986-87, an opening autumn enrolment of 47,646 full- and part-time students. Princeton (founded in 1746) had 6,175 students. Fairleigh Dickinson (1941), had 1,100 students; Montclair State College, 14,949; Glassboro State College, 8,500; Trenton State College, 8,652.

Health. In 1988 the state had 145 hospitals (43,353 beds), listed by the American Hospital Association.

Social Security. In the financial year 1982 gross expenditure for all public assistance programmes was $563,000,000. Average monthly total of cases was $358,000 with an average grant per case of $350.

Further Reading

Legislative District Data Book. Bureau of Government Research. Annual
Manual of the Legislature of New Jersey. Trenton. Annual

Boyd, J. P. (ed.) *Fundamentals and Constitutions of New Jersey, 1664–1954*. Princeton, 1964
Cunningham, J. T., *New Jersey: America's Main Road*. Rev. ed. New York, 1976
Kull, I. Stoddard (ed.) *New Jersey, a History*. New York, 1930
League of Women Voters of New Jersey. *New Jersey: Spotlight on Government*. Rutgers Univ. Press, 3rd ed., 1978
Lehne, R. and Rosenthal, A. (eds.) *Politics in New Jersey*. Rev. ed., Rutgers Univ. Press, 1979

State Library: 185 W. State Street, Trenton, N.J. 08625. *State Librarian:* Barbara F. Weaver.

NEW MEXICO

HISTORY. The first European settlement was established in 1598. Until 1771 New Mexico was the Spanish kings' 'Kingdom of New Mexico'. In 1771 it was annexed to the northern province of New Spain. When New Spain won its independence in 1821, it took the name of Republic of Mexico and established New Mexico as its northernmost department. When the war between the US and Mexico was concluded on 2 Feb. 1848 New Mexico was recognized as belonging to the US, and on 9 Sept. 1850 it was made a Territory. Part of the Territory was assigned to Texas; later Utah was formed into a separate Territory; in 1861 another part was transferred to Colorado, and in 1863 Arizona was disjoined, leaving to New Mexico its present area. New Mexico became a state in Jan. 1912.

AREA AND POPULATION. New Mexico is bounded north by Colorado, north-east by Oklahoma, east by Texas, south by Texas and Mexico and west by Arizona. Land area 121,335 sq. miles (258 sq. miles water). Public lands, administered by federal agencies (1975) amounted to 26·7m. acres or 34% of the total area. The Bureau of Indian Affairs held 7·3m. acres; the State of New Mexico held 9·4m. acres; 34·4m. acres were privately owned.

Census population, 1 April 1980, 1,303,303, an increase of 286,248 or 28% since 1970. Estimate (1988) 1,507,000. Vital statistics, 1987: Births, 27,246 (18·2 per 1,000 population); deaths, 10,324 (6·9); infant deaths, 218 (8 per 1,000 live births); marriages, 13,025 (8·6); divorces, 7,943 (5·3).

The population in 5 census years was:

	White	Black	Indian	Asian and Pacific Islander	Other	Total	Per sq. mile
1910	304,594	1,628	20,573	506		327,301	2·7
1940	492,312	4,672	34,510	324		531,818	4·4
1960	875,763	17,063	56,255	1,942		951,023	7·8
1970	915,815	19,555	72,788	7,842 [1]		1,016,000	8·4
1980	1,164,053	24,406	106,119	6,825	1,491	1,302,894	10·7

[1] Includes unspecified races, 1970.

Of the 1980 total, 642,157 were male, 939,963 persons were urban; 884,987 were 18 years of age or older.

Before 1930 New Mexico was largely a Spanish-speaking state, but since 1945 an influx of population from other states has reduced the percentage of persons of Spanish origin or descent to 36·6% (1980).

The largest cities are Albuquerque, with census population, 1980, 332,336 (and 1988 estimate, 378,480); Santa Fé (capital), 49,299 (59,300); Las Cruces, 45,086 (56,000); Roswell, 39,676 (43,230); Farmington, 32,677 (38,470).

CLIMATE. Santa Fé. Jan. 29°F (–1·7°C), July 68°F (20°C). Annual rainfall 15" (366 mm). *See* Mountain States, p. 1381.

CONSTITUTION AND GOVERNMENT. The constitution of 1912 is still in force with 105 amendments. The state Legislature, which meets annually, consists of 42 members of the Senate, elected for 4 years, and 70 members of the House of Representatives, elected for 2 years. The Governor and Lieut.-Governor are elected for 4 years. The state sends to Congress 2 senators and 3 representatives.

In the 1988 presidential election Bush polled 270,341 votes, Dukakis 244,497.

The state capital is Santa Fé. For local government the state is divided into 33 counties.

Governor: Garrey Carruthers (R.), 1987–91 ($63,000).
Lieut.-Governor: Jack Stahl (R.), 1987–91 ($40,425).
Secretary of State: Rebecca Vigil-Giron (D.), 1987–91 ($40,425).

BUDGET. For the year ending 30 June 1987 (US Census Bureau figures) the states general revenues were $3,268m. ($1,573m. from taxation and $566m. from federal government); general expenditures, $3,074m. (education, $1,298m.; highways, $382m., and public welfare, $317m.).

Per capita personal income (1988) was $12,488.

ENERGY AND NATURAL RESOURCES

Minerals. New Mexico is the country's largest domestic source of uranium, perlite and potassium salts. Production of recoverable U_3O_8 was 2·3m. lb. in 1988; perlite, 706,000 short tons; potassium salts, 1·35m. short tons; petroleum, 71·2m. bbls (of 42 gallons); natural gas, 781,000 cu. ft; copper, 321,650 short tons; coal, 21·7m. short tons marketed. The value of the total mineral output (1988) was $3,680m. An average of 15,400 persons were employed monthly in the mining industry in 1988.

Agriculture. New Mexico produces cereals, vegetables, fruit, livestock and cotton. Dry farming and irrigation have proved profitable in periods of high prices. There were 14,000 farms and ranches covering 44·5m. acres in 1988; in the 1987 US Census of Agriculture average farm (or ranch) was valued (land and buildings) at $582,012; 3,767 farms and ranches were of 1,000 acres and over.

Cash income, 1988 (preliminary), from crops, $370·8m., and from livestock products, $910·3m. Principal crops are wheat (7m. bu. from 290,000 acres), hay (1·2m. tons from 275,000 acres) and sorghum/grains (8·7m. bu. from 145,000 acres). Farm animals on 1 Jan. 1989 included 63,000 milch cows, 1·35m. all cattle, 516,000 sheep and 26,000 swine (1988). National forest area (1986) covered 9·3m. acres.

INDUSTRY. Average monthly non-agricultural employment during 1988 was 540,400: 39,900 were employed in manufacturing, 140,800 in government. Value of manufactures shipments, 1986, $3,776·4m.; leading industries, food and kindred products, transport and equipment, lumber and wood.

COMMUNICATIONS

Roads. On 13 March 1987 the state had 79,735 miles of road, of which the state maintained 11,722 miles. Motor vehicle registrations, 1988, 1,367,315.

Railways. On 31 Dec. 1987 there were 2,062 miles of railway.

Aviation. There were 71 public-use airports in Dec. 1988.

JUSTICE, RELIGION, EDUCATION AND WELFARE

Justice. The number of state prison inmates in Oct. 1989 was 2,924, and there were 380 in juvenile centres in 1988; there were also 78 New Mexico prisoners held outside the state in 1989. The death penalty (by electrocution formerly, and now by lethal injection) has been imposed on 8 persons since 1933, 6 whites and 2 Negroes, all for murder. The last execution was in 1961.

Since 1949 the denial of employment by reason of race, colour, religion, national origin or ancestry has been forbidden. A law of 1955 prohibits discrimination in public places because of race or colour. An 'equal rights' amendment was added to the constitution in 1972.

Religion. There were (1975) approximately 356,530 Protestant Church members and 315,470 Roman Catholics.

Education. Elementary education is free, and compulsory between 6 and 17 years or high-school graduation age. In 1988–89 the 88 school districts had an estimated enrolment of 316,332 students in elementary and secondary schools of which private and parochial schools had 24,134. There were 15,759 FTE teachers receiving an average salary of $24,620. Public expenditure for elementary and secondary schools was $1,103m. (1987-88).

The state-supported 4-year institutes of higher education are (1988–89 [1]):

	Full-time Faculty	Students
University of New Mexico, Albuquerque	1,936	28,258
New Mexico State University, Las Cruces	838	20,027
Eastern New Mexico University, Portales	267	8,260
New Mexico Highlands University, Las Vegas	110	2,234
Western New Mexico University, Silver City	71	1,800
New Mexico Institute of Mining and Technology, Socorro	83	1,129

[1] Figures include branches outside main campus in cities listed.

Health. In 1987 the state had 49 short-term hospitals (4,284 beds).

Social Security. In Dec. 1986, 17,622 persons were receiving federal supplemental security income for the disabled (average $257.29 per month); 9,322 persons were receiving old-age assistance (average $140.43 per month); 511 persons were receiving aid to the blind (average $239.21 per month). A monthly average of 50,831 people received aid to families with dependent children (average $83.64 per month).

Further Reading

New Mexico Business (monthly; annual review in Jan.–Feb. issue). Bureau of Business and Economic Research, Univ. of N.M., Albuquerque
New Mexico Progress Economic Review (annual). Sunwest, Albuquerque
New Mexico Statistical Abstract: 1989. Bureau of Business and Economic Research, Univ. of N.M., Albuquerque, 1989
Beck, W., *New Mexico: a History of Four Centuries*. Univ. of Oklahoma, 1979
Garcia, C., Haine, P. and Rhodes, H., *State and Local Government in New Mexico*. Albuquerque, 1979
Jenkins, M. and Schroeder, A., *A Brief History of New Mexico*. Univ. of New Mexico, 1974
Muench, D. and Hillerman, T., *New Mexico*. Belding, Portland, Oregon, 1974
Williams, J. L., *New Mexico in Maps*. Univ. of New Mexico, 1986

NEW YORK STATE

HISTORY. From 1609 to 1664 the region now called New York was claimed by the Dutch; then it came under the rule of the English, who governed the country until the outbreak of the War of Independence. On 20 April 1777 New York adopted a constitution which transformed the colony into an independent state; on 26 July 1788 it ratified the constitution of the US, becoming one of the 13 original states. New York dropped its claim to Vermont after the latter was admitted to the Union in 1791. With the annexation of a small area from Massachusetts in 1853, New York assumed its present boundaries.

AREA AND POPULATION. New York is bounded west and north by Canada with Lake Erie, Lake Ontario and the St Lawrence River forming the boundary; east by Vermont, Massachusetts and Connecticut, south-east by the Atlantic, south by New Jersey and Pennsylvania. Area, 49,108 sq. miles (1,731 sq. miles being water). Census population, 1 April 1980, 17,557,288, a decrease of 3·7% since 1970. Estimate (1985) 17,783,000. Births in 1984 were 251,062 (14·2 per 1,000 population); deaths, 168,852 (9·5); infant deaths, 2,789 (11·1 per 1,000 live births); marriages, 168,860 (9·5); divorces, 61,075 (3·4, includes all dissolutions).

Population in 5 census years was:

	White	Negro	Indian	Asiatic	Total	Per sq. mile
1910	8,966,845	134,191	6,046	6,532	9,113,614	191·2
1930	12,143,191	412,814	6,973	15,088	12,588,066	262·6
1960	15,287,071	1,417,511	16,491	51,678	16,782,304	350·2
			All others			
1970	15,834,090	2,168,949	233,828		18,236,967	380·3
1980	13,961,106	2,401,842	1,194,340		17,557,288	367·0

Of the 1980 population, 8,338,961 were male, 14,857,202 were urban; those 20 years of age or older numbered 12,232,284. Aliens registered in Jan. 1980 numbered 801,411.

The population of New York City, by boroughs, census of 1 April 1980 was: Manhattan, 1,427,533; Bronx, 1,169,115; Brooklyn, 2,230,936; Queens, 1,891,325; Staten Island, 352,121; total, 7,071,030. The New York metropolitan statistical area had, in 1980, 9,080,777.

Population of other large cities and incorporated places census, April 1980, was:

Buffalo	357,002	Albany (capital)	101,767	Schenectady	67,877
Rochester	241,509	Utica	75,435	Mount Vernon	66,023
Yonkers	194,557	Niagara Falls	71,344	Troy	56,614
Syracuse	170,292	New Rochelle	70,345	Binghamton	55,745
White Plains	46,999	N. Tonawanda	35,760	Lindenhurst	26,919
Rome	43,826	Elmira	35,327	Rockville Center	25,405
Hempstead	40,404	Auburn	32,548	Newburgh	23,438
Freeport	38,272	Poughkeepsie	29,757	Garden City	22,927
Jamestown	35,775	Watertown	27,861	Massapequa Park	19,779
Valley Stream	35,769				

Other large urbanized areas, census 1980; Buffalo, 1·2m.; Rochester, 970,313; Albany–Schenectady–Troy, 794,298.

CLIMATE. Albany. Jan. 24°F (–4·4°C), July 73°F (22·8°C). Annual rainfall 34" (855 mm). Buffalo. Jan. 24°F (–4·4°C), July 70°F (21·1°C). Annual rainfall 36" (905 mm). New York. Jan. 30°F (–1·1°C), July 74°F (23·3°C). Annual rainfall 43" (1,087 mm). *See* Atlantic Coast, p. 1382.

CONSTITUTION AND GOVERNMENT. The present constitution dates from 1894; a later constitutional convention, 1938, is now legally considered merely to have amended the 1894 constitution, which has now had 93 amendments. The Constitutional Convention of 1967 (4 April through 26 Sept.) was composed of 186 delegates who proposed a new state constitution; however this was rejected by the registered voters on 7 Nov. 1967. The Senate consists of 60 members, and the Assembly of 150 members, both elected every 2 years. The Governor and Lieut.-Governor are elected for 4 years. The right of suffrage resides in every adult who has been a citizen for 90 days, and has the residential qualifications; new voters must establish, by certificates or test, that they have had at least an elementary education. The state is represented in Congress by 2 senators and 34 representatives. In the 1988 presidential election Dukakis polled 3,228,304 votes, Bush, 2,975,276. The state capital is Albany. For local government the state is divided into 62 counties, 5 of which constitute the city of New York. New York leads in state parks and recreation areas, covering 252,984 acres in 1979.

Cities are in 3 classes, the first class having each 175,000 or more inhabitants and the third under 50,000. Each is incorporated by charter, under special legislation. The government of New York City is vested in the mayor (Edward Koch), elected for 4 years, and a city council, whose president and members are elected for 4 years. The council has a President and 37 members, each elected from a state senatorial district wholly within the city. The mayor appoints all the heads of departments, except the comptroller, who is elected. Each of the 5 city boroughs (Manhattan, Bronx, Brooklyn, Queens and Richmond) has a president, elected for 4 years. Each borough is also a county bearing the same name except Manhattan borough, which, as a county, is called New York, and Brooklyn, which is Kings County.

Governor: Mario Cuomo (D.), 1987–91 ($130,000).
Lieut.-Governor: Stan Lundine (D.), 1987–91 ($110,000).
Secretary of State: Gail Schaefer (D.), 1987–91 ($79,218).

BUDGET. The state's general revenues for the financial year ending 31 March 1982 were $16,142m. ($14,959m. from taxes); general expenditures were $16,126m. ($5,298m. for education, $8,049m. for social services, $1,893m. for transport).

Per capita personal income was $14,121 in 1984.

The assessed valuation in 1980 of taxable real property in New York City was $38,056m. The assessed valuation of the state was $86,741m.

ENERGY AND NATURAL RESOURCES

Minerals. Production of principal minerals in 1980: Sand and gravel (22,000 short tons), salt (5,500 short tons), zinc (33,629 tonnes), petroleum (824,296 bbls), natural gas (15,680m. cu. ft). The state is a leading producer of titanium concentrate, talc, abrasive garnet, wollastonite and emery. Quarry products include trap rock, slate, marble, limestone and sandstone. Value of mineral output in 1980 $497·9m.

Agriculture. New York has large agricultural interests. In 1985 it had 45,000 farms, with a total area of 9m. acres; average farm was 200 acres; average value per acre, $808.

Cash income, 1985, from crops $719m. and livestock, $1,845m. Dairying, with 18,500 farms, 1981, is an important type of farming with produce at a market value of $1,383m. Field crops comprise maize, winter wheat, oats and hay. New York ranks second in US in the production of apples, and maple syrup. Other products are grapes, tart cherries, peaches, pears, plums, strawberries, raspberries, cabbages, onions, potatoes, maple sugar. Estimated farm animals, 1986, included 2m. all cattle, 968,000 milch cows, 55,000 sheep, 130,000 swine and 8m. chickens.

INDUSTRY. The main employers (1982 census) are service industries (997,800), trade (1,381,000) and manufacture (1,418,800). Leading industries were clothing, non-electrical machinery, printing and publishing, electrical equipment, instruments, food and allied products and fabricated metals.

COMMUNICATIONS

Roads. There were (1981) 109,485 miles of municipal and rural roads. The New York State Thruway extends 559 miles from New York City to Buffalo; in 1985 receipts from tolls amounted to $189,273,009. The Northway, a 176-mile toll-free highway, is a connecting road from the Thruway at Albany to the Canadian border at Champlain, Quebec.

Motor vehicle registrations in 1985 were 9·6m., most of which (7·7m.) were private passenger vehicles.

Railways. There were in 1981, 3,891 miles of Class I railways. New York City has NYCTA and PATH metro systems, and commuter railways run by Metro-North, New Jersey Rail and Long Island Rail Road.

Aviation. There were 472 airports and landing areas in 1986.

Shipping. The canals of the state, combined in 1918 in what is called the Improved Canal System, have a length of 524 miles, of which the Erie or Barge canal has 340 miles. In 1981 the canals carried 807,925 tons of freight.

JUSTICE, RELIGION, EDUCATION AND WELFARE

Justice. The State Human Rights Law was approved 12 March 1945, effective 1 July, 1945. The State Division of Human Rights is charged with the responsibility of enforcing this law. The division may request and utilize the services of all governmental departments and agencies; adopt and promulgate suitable rules and regulations; test, investigate and pass judgment upon complaints alleging discrimination in employment, in places of public accommodation, resort or amusement, education, and in housing, land and commercial space; hold hearings, sub-poena witnesses and require the production for examination of papers relating to matters under investigation; grant compensatory damages and require repayment of profits in certain housing cases among other provisions; apply for court injunctions to prevent frustration of orders of the Commissioner.

On 30 Dec. 1984, 33,155 persons were in state prisons.

In 1963–81 there were no executions. Total executions (by electrocution) from 1930 to 1962 were 329 (234 whites, 90 Negroes, 5 other races; all for murder except 2 for kidnapping).

In 1985 murders reported in New York were 1,688; total violent crimes, 165,145. Police strength (sworn officers) in 1985 was 61,009 (39,193 New York City).

Religion. The churches are Roman Catholic, with 6,367,576 members in 1981, Jewish congregations (about 2m. in 1981) and Protestant Episcopal (299,929 in 1980).

Education. Education is compulsory between the ages of 7 and 16. In 1985 the public elementary and secondary schools had 2,605,363 pupils; classroom teachers numbered 175,256 in public schools. Total expenditure on public schools in 1985 was $13,244m. Teachers' salaries, 1985, averaged $29,200.

The state's educational system, including public and private schools and secondary institutions, universities, colleges, libraries, museums, etc., constitutes (by legislative act) the 'University of the State of New York', which is governed by a Board of Regents consisting of 15 members appointed by the Legislature. Within the framework of this 'University' was established in 1948 a 'State University' which controls 64 colleges and educational centres, 30 of which are locally operated community colleges. The 'State University' is governed by a board of 16 Trustees, appointed by the Governor with the consent and advice of the Senate.

Higher education in the state is conducted in 296 institutions (642,000 full-time and 371,000 part-time students in autumn 1982); 573,000 students are in public-control colleges and 439,000 in private.

In autumn 1980 the institutions of higher education in the state included:

Founded	*Name and place*	*Teachers*	*Students*
1754	Columbia University, New York	3,965	17,410
1795	Union University, Schenectady and Albany	178	2,071
1824	Rensselaer Polytechnic Institute, Troy	442	6,145
1831	New York University, New York	2,615	45,000
1846	Colgate University, New York	205	2,550
1846	Fordham University, New York	958	14,653
1847	University of the City of New York, New York	12,426	172,683
1848	University of Rochester, Rochester	1,549	11,159
1854	Polytechnic Institute of New York	242	4,583
1856	St Lawrence University, Canton	173	2,375
1857	Cooper Union Institute of Technology, New York	161	872
1861	Vassar College, Poughkeepsie	230	2,364
1863	Manhattan College, New York	291	3,498
1865	Cornell University, Ithaca	1,863	17,866
1870	Syracuse University, Syracuse	1,100	11,819
1948	State University of New York	13,228	372,415

The Saratoga Performing Arts Centre (5,100 seats), a non-profit, tax-exempt organization, which opened in 1966, is the summer residence of the New York City Ballet and the Philadelphia Orchestra—two groups which present special educational programmes for students and teachers.

Health. In 1981 the state had 278 hospitals (67,798 beds), 585 skilled nursing homes (62,435 beds) and 241 other institutions (24,302 beds). In 1986 mental health facilities had 21,836 patients and institutions for the mentally retarded had 10,581 patients.

Social Security. The federal Supplemental Security Income programme covered aid to the needy aged, blind and disabled from 1 Jan. 1975. In the state programme for 1980, $4,543m. was paid in Medicaid to 2,288,000 people; aid to dependent children in 1985 went to 1,109,610 recipients, average benefits $371 per family per month.

Further Reading

New York Red Book. Albany, 1979–80
Legislative Manual. Department of State, 1980–81
Managing Modern New York: the Carey Era. Rockefeller Institute, Albany, 1985
New York State Statistical Yearbook, 1986–87. Rockefeller Institute, Albany
Connery, R. and G. B., *Governing New York State: The Rockefeller Years*. Academy of Political Science, New York, 1974
Ellis, D. M., *History of New York State*. Cornell Univ. Press, 1967
Flick, A. (ed.) *History of the State of New York*. Columbia Univ. Press, 1933–37
Lincoln, C., *Constitutional History of New York 1809–1877*. Rochester, 1906
Wolfe, G. R., *New York: A Guide to the Metropolis*. New York Univ. Press, 1975

State Library: The New York State Library, Albany 12230. *State Librarian and Assistant Commissioner for Libraries:* Joseph Shubert.

NORTH CAROLINA

HISTORY. North Carolina, first settled in 1585 by Sir Walter Raleigh and permanently settled in 1663, was one of the 13 original states of the Union.

AREA AND POPULATION. North Carolina is bounded north by Virginia, east by the Atlantic, south by South Carolina, south-west by Georgia and west by Tennessee. Area, 52,669 sq. miles, of which 3,826 sq. miles are inland water. Census population, 1 April 1980, 5,874,429, an increase of 15·5% since 1970. Estimated population (1986), 6,331,000.

Births, 1984, were 86,705 (14·1 per 1,000 population); marriages, 52,123 (8·5); deaths, 51,496 (8·4); infant deaths, 1,099 (12·7 per 1,000 live births); divorces and annulments, 29,125 (4·7).

Population in 6 census years was:

	White	*Negro*	*Indian*	*Asiatic*	*Total*	*Per sq. mile*
1910	1,500,511	697,843	7,851	82	2,206,287	45·3
1930	2,234,958	918,647	16,579	92	3,170,276	64·5
1950	2,983,121	1,047,353	3,742	—	4,061,929	82·7
1960	3,399,285	1,116,021	38,129	2,012	4,556,155	92·2
			All others			
1970	3,901,767	1,126,478	53,814		5,082,059	104·1
1980	4,453,010	1,316,050	105,369		5,874,429	111·5

Of the total population in 1980, 2,852,012 were male, 2,818,794 were urban and 3,976,359 were 20 years old or older; 14·8% were non-white.

Cities (with census population in 1980) are: Charlotte, 314,447; Greensboro, 155,642; Winston-Salem, 131,885; Raleigh (capital), 149,771; Durham, 100,831; High Point, 64,107; Asheville, 53,281; Fayetteville, 59,507.

CLIMATE. Climate varies sharply with altitude; the warmest area is in the south east near Southport and Wilmington; the coldest is Mount Mitchell (6,684 ft). Raleigh. Jan. 42°F (5·6°C), July 79°F (26·1°C). Annual rainfall 46" (1,158 mm). *See* Atlantic Coast, p. 1382.

CONSTITUTION AND GOVERNMENT. The present constitution dates from 1971 (previous constitution, 1776 and 1868/76); it has had 19 amendments. The General Assembly consists of a Senate of 50 members and a House of Representatives of 120 members; all are elected by districts for 2 years.

The Governor and Lieut.-Governor are elected for 4 years. The Governor may succeed himself but has no veto. There are 19 other executive heads of department, 8 elected by the people and 9 appointed by the Governor. All registered citizens with the usual residential qualifications have a vote.

The state is represented in Congress by 2 senators and 11 representatives.

In the presidential election of 1988 Bush polled 1,232,132 votes, Dukakis, 890,034.

The capital is Raleigh, established in 1792.

Governor: James G. Martin (R.), 1989–93 ($100,000, plus $11,500 annual expenses).

Lieut.-Governor: Jim Gardner (R.) ($61,044, plus $11,500 annual expenses).

Secretary of State: Rufus Edmiston (D.) ($61,044).

BUDGET. General revenue for the year ending 30 June 1986 was $4,910·9m. General expenditure was $4,971·9m.

On 30 June 1986 the net total long-term debt amounted to $757m.

Per capita personal income (1985–86) was $11,903.

NATURAL RESOURCES

Minerals. Mining production in 1985 was valued at $474·7m. Principal minerals were stone, sand and gravel, phosphate rock, feldspar, lithium minerals, olivine, kaolin and talc.

North Carolina ranked first in the production of scrap mica, feldspar, lithium minerals, olivine and phrophyllite. It is also the leading producer of bricks, making more than 1,000m. bricks a year.

Agriculture. In 1985 there were 76,000 farms in North Carolina covering 10·8m. acres; average size of farms was 142 acres and total estimated value $18,500m.

Cash receipts from farming (1984), $4,125m., of which $2,198m. was from crops and $1,927m. from livestock, dairy and poultry products. Main crop production: flue-cured tobacco, maize, soybeans, peanuts, wheat, sweet potatoes and apples.

On 1 Jan. 1985 farms had 1·17m. all cattle, 2·3m. swine and 20·2m. chickens.

Forestry. Commercial forest covered 18·5m. acres (60% of land area), in 1984. Main products are hardwood veneer and hardwood plywood, furniture woods, pulp, paper and lumber.

Fisheries. Commercial fish catch, 1985, amounted to 215m. lb.; value approximately $65m. The catch is mainly of menhaden, crabmeat, bay scallops, flounder, croaker, shrimps, sea trout, spots and clams.

INDUSTRY. North Carolina's manufacturing establishments in 1985 had 827,400 workers. The leading industries by employment are textiles, clothing, furniture, electrical machinery and equipment, non-electrical machinery, and food processing.

In 1985 investment in new and expanded industry was $2,758m. About 576,200 are employed in trade, 422,800 in government and 427,600 in services.

TOURISM. Total receipts of the travel industry, $4,500m. in 1985.

COMMUNICATIONS

Roads. The state maintained, 1985, 76,459 miles of highways, comprising all rural roads and 5,088 miles of urban streets which are major thoroughfares. In Oct. 1986, 3,499,178 automobiles, 1,152,156 trucks and 1,274,137 other vehicles were registered.

Railways. The state in 1986 contained 3,682 miles of railway operating in 91 of the 100 counties. There are 22 Class I, II and III rail companies.

Aviation. In 1986 there were 82 public airports of which 14 are served by major airlines.

Shipping. There are 2 ocean ports, Wilmington and Morehead City.

JUSTICE, RELIGION, EDUCATION AND WELFARE

Justice. Total executions 1910–86, 365. There was one execution (by lethal injection) in 1986. Prison population at 31 Oct. 1986, 17,700.

Religion. Leading denominations are the Baptists (48·9% of church membership), Methodists (20·7%), Presbyterians (7·7%), Lutherans (3%) and Roman Catholics (2·7%). Total estimate of all denominations in 1983 was 2·6m.

Education. School attendance is compulsory between 6 and 16.

Public school enrolment, 1985–86, was 1,080,887; elementary and secondary schools numbered 1,968. Instructional staff (1986) consisted of 57,630 classroom teachers; average salary $22,476. Expenditure for public schools was $2,770m., 65·5% from state, 25·2% from local and 9·3% from federal sources.

In autumn 1985–86 state-supported colleges and universities included 58 community and technical colleges with 654,000 full and part time students. The 16 senior universities are all part of the University of North Carolina system, the largest campus being North Carolina State University and Raleigh, with 23,400 students. The university system was founded in 1789 at Chapel Hill and first opened in 1792. Its 1986 autumn enrolment was 130,000 students.

In addition to the state-supported institutions there were 7 private junior colleges with an enrolment of 2,585 and 31 private senior institutions with a total enrolment of 19,009. The total undergraduate enrolment in private institutions for 1985 was 21,594.

Health. In Oct. 1986 the state had 160 hospitals (34,438 beds).

Social Security. In June 1982 there were 900,070 persons receiving $300·4m. in social security benefits. Of that number 496,020 were retired, receiving $186·67m.; 85,640 were disabled ($34·7m.); 318,410 others received $79m.

Further Reading

North Carolina Manual. Secretary of State. Raleigh. Biennial
Clay, J. W. *et al* (eds.), *North Carolina Atlas: Portrait of a Changing Southern State.* Univ. of North Carolina Press, 1975
Corbitt, D. L., *The Formation of the North Carolina Counties.* Raleigh, 1969
Lefler, H. T. and Newsome, A. R., *North Carolina: The History of a Southern State.* Univ. of N.C., Chapel Hill, 1973

NORTH DAKOTA

HISTORY. North Dakota was admitted into the Union, with boundaries as at present, on 2 Nov. 1889; previously it had formed part of the Dakota Territory, established 2 March 1861.

AREA AND POPULATION. North Dakota is bounded north by Canada, east by the Red River (forming a boundary with Minnesota), south by South Dakota and west by Montana. Land area, 69,262 sq. miles, and 1,403 sq. miles of water. The Federal Bureau of Indian Affairs administered (1971) 850,000 acres, of which 153,000 acres were assigned to tribes. Census population, 1 April 1980, 652,717, an increase of 34,956 or 5·7% since 1970. Estimate (1984), 686,000. Births in 1984 were 11,833 (17 per 1,000 population); deaths, 5,538 (8·0); infant deaths, 97; marriages, 5,786; divorces, 2,249.

Population at 5 census years was:

	White	*Negro*	*Indian*	*Asiatic*	*Total*	*Per sq. mile*
1910	569,855	617	6,486	98	577,056	8·2
1930	671,851	377	8,617	194	680,845	9·7
1960	619,538	777	11,736	274	632,446	9·1
			All others			
1970	599,485	2,494	15,782		617,761	8·9
1980	625,557	2,568	24,692		652,717	9·4

Of the total population in 1980, 328,126 were male, 317,821 were urban and 419,234 were 21 years old or older. Estimated outward migration, 1970–80, 16,983.

The largest cities are Fargo with population (census), 1980, of 61,383; Grand Forks, 43,765; Bismarck (capital), 44,485, and Minot, 32,843.

CLIMATE. Bismarck. Jan. 8°F (–13·3°C), July 71°F (21·1°C). Annual rainfall 16" (402 mm). Fargo. Jan. 6°F (–14·4°C), July 71°F (21·1°C). Annual rainfall 20" (503 mm). *See* High Plains and Mid-West (SW North Dakota is in the Plains, the rest in the mid-west lowlands), p. 1381-82.

CONSTITUTION AND GOVERNMENT. The present constitution dates from 1889; it has had 95 amendments. The Legislative Assembly consists of a Senate of 53 members elected for 4 years, and a House of Representatives of 106 members elected for 2 years. The Governor and Lieut.-Governor are elected for 4 years. Qualified electors are (with necessary exceptions) all citizens and civilized Indians. The state sends to Congress 2 senators elected by the voters of the entire state and 1 representative.

In the 1988 presidential election Bush polled 165,517 votes, Dukakis, 127,081.

The capital is Bismarck. The state has 53 organized counties.

Governor: George A. Sinner (D.), 1989–93 ($60,862 plus expenses).
Lieut.-Governor: Lloyd Omdahl (D.), 1985–89 ($12,500 plus expenses).
Secretary of State: Jim Kusler (D.), 1985–89 ($43,380 plus expenses).

FINANCE. General revenue of state and local government year ending 30 June 1982, was $1,286m.; general expenditures, $1,191m., taxation provided $533m. and federal aid, $252m.; education took $449m.; highways, $148m., and public welfare, $104m.

Total net long-term debt (local government) on 30 June 1982, $325m.

Per capita personal income (1985) was $12,052.

ENERGY AND NATURAL RESOURCES

Minerals. The mineral resources of North Dakota consist chiefly of oil which was discovered in 1951. Production of crude petroleum in 1984 was 52·6m. bbls; of natural gas, 76,800m. cu. ft. Output of lignite coal was 21·7m. short tons. Total value of mineral output, 1984, $1,724m.

Agriculture. Agriculture is the chief pursuit of the North Dakota population. In 1985 there were 33,000 farms (61,963 in 1954) with an area of 41m. acres (41,876,924 in 1954); the average farm was of 1,242 acres. The greater number of farms are cash-grain or livestock farms with annual sales of $20,000–$39,999.

Cash income, 1985, from crops, $2,060m., and from livestock, $686m. North Dakota leads in the production of barley, sunflowers, flaxseed and durum. Other important products are wheat, pinto beans, sugar-beet, potatoes, hay, oats, rye and maize.

The state has also an active livestock industry, chiefly cattle raising. On 1 Jan. 1985 the farm animals were: 97,000 milch cows, 2m. all cattle, 215,000 sheep and 250,000 swine. The wool clip yielded (1984), 1·6m. lb. of wool from 180,000 sheep.

Forestry. National forest area, 1977, 422,000 acres, of which 115,000 acres are federally owned or managed.

INDUSTRY. From 1970 to 1984 agricultural employment fell from 51,920 to 51,480; non-agricultural jobs rose from 148,910 to 268,300. In 1985, 68,000 were employed in trade, 63,000 in government, 58,000 in services, 16,000 in transport and utilities, 15,000 in manufacturing.

COMMUNICATIONS

Roads. The state highway department maintained, in 1985, 7,237 miles of highway; local authorities, 95,750 miles, and municipal, 3,243 miles.

Car and truck registrations in 1985 numbered 712,000.

Railways. In 1984 there were 5,262 miles of railway.

Aviation. Airports in 1984 numbered 262, of which 107 were publicly owned.

JUSTICE, RELIGION, EDUCATION AND WELFARE

Justice. The state penitentiary, on 31 Dec. 1985, held 407 inmates. There is no death penalty.

Religion. The leading religious denominations are the Roman Catholics, with 171,185 members in 1975; Combined Lutherans, 216,579; Methodists, 28,880; Presbyterians, 18,636.

Education. School attendance is compulsory between the ages of 7 and 16, or until the 17th birthday if the eighth grade has not been completed. In Oct. 1983 the public elementary schools had 81,797 pupils; secondary schools, 34,892 pupils. State expenditure on public schools, 1986, $379m. or $553 per capita. Teachers (4,900 in elementary and 2,900 in secondary schools) earned an average $20,850 in 1986.

The university at Grand Forks, founded in 1883, had 11,068 students in 1984; the state university of agriculture and applied science, at Fargo, 9,453 students. Total enrolment in the 8 public institutions of higher education, 1984, 33,748.

Health. In 1985 the state had 59 hospitals (6,000 beds), and 81 nursing homes (6,400).

Social Security. In 1985 6,500 received SSI payments, including 2,400 aged (average $116 per month). 4,000 disabled ($209); total paid, $12·7m.; 13,100 recipients in 4,700 families received Aid to Families with Dependent Children.

Further Reading

North Dakota Growth Indicators, 1984. 20th ed. Economic Development Commission, Bismarck, 1985
North Dakota Blue Book. Secretary of State, Bismarck, 1981
Statistical Abstract of North Dakota, 1983. Bureau of Business and Economic Research, Univ. of North Dakota, 1983
Glaab, C. L. et al, *The North Dakota Political Tradition.* Iowa State Univ. Press, 1981
Jelliff, T. B., *North Dakota: A Living Legacy.* Fargo, 1983
Robinson, E. B., *History of North Dakota.* Univ. of Nebraska Press, 1966

OHIO

HISTORY. The first organized white settlement was in 1788; Ohio unofficially entered the Union on 19 Feb. 1803; entrance was made official, retroactive to 1 March 1803, on 8 Aug. 1953.

AREA AND POPULATION. Ohio is bounded north by Michigan and Lake Erie, east by Pennsylvania, south-east and south by the Ohio River (forming a boundary with West Virginia and Kentucky) and west by Indiana. Area, 41,330 sq. miles, of which 325 sq. miles are inland water. Census population, 1 April 1980 10,797,630, an increase of 145,402 or 1·4% since 1970. Estimate (1986) 10,752,000. In 1987 births numbered 157,820 (14·6 per 1,000 population); deaths, 99,177 (9·2); infant deaths, 1,469 (9·3 per 1,000 live births); marriages, 95,882 (8·9); divorces, 49,294 (4·6).

Population at 5 census years was:

	White	Negro	Indian	Asiatic	Total	Per sq. mile
1910	4,654,897	111,452	127	645	4,767,121	117·0
1930	6,335,173	309,304	435	1,785	6,646,697	161·6
1960	8,909,698	786,097	1,910	8,692	9,706,397	236·9
			All others			
1970	9,646,997	970,477	34,543		10,652,017	260·0
1980	9,597,458	1,076,748	123,424		10,797,630	263·2

Of the total population in 1980, 5,217,027 were male, 7,918,259 persons were urban. Those 20 years old or older numbered 7,294,471.

Census population of chief cities on 1 April 1980 was:

Cleveland	573,822	Hamilton	63,189	Cuyahoga Falls	43,890
Columbus	565,032	Lakewood	61,963	Mentor	42,065
Cincinnati	385,457	Kettering	61,186	Newark	41,200
Toledo	354,635	Euclid	59,999	Marion	37,040
Akron	237,177	Elyria	57,538	East Cleveland	36,957
Dayton	193,444	Cleveland Heights	56,438	North Olmsted	36,486
Youngstown	115,436	Warren	47,381	Upper Arlington	35,648
Canton	93,077	Mansfield	53,927	Lancaster	34,953
Parma	92,548	Lima	47,381	Garfield Heights	34,938
Lorain	75,416	Middletown	43,719	Zanesville	28,655
Springfield	72,563				

Urbanized areas, 1980 census: Cleveland, 1,898,825; Cincinnati, 1,401,491; Columbus (the capital), 1,093,316; Dayton, 830,070; Akron, 660,328; Toledo, 791,599; Youngstown-Warren, 531,350; Canton, 404,421.

CLIMATE. Cincinnati. Jan. 33°F (0·6°C), July 78°F (25·6°C). Annual rainfall 39" (978 mm). Cleveland. Jan. 27°F (–2·8°C), July 71°F (21·1°C). Annual rainfall 35" (879 mm). Columbus. Jan. 29°F (–1·7°C), July 75°F (23·9°C). Annual rainfall 34" (850 mm). *See* Great Lakes, p. 1382.

CONSTITUTION AND GOVERNMENT. The question of a general revision of the constitution drafted by an elected convention is submitted to the people every 20 years. The constitution of 1851 had 141 amendments by 1983.

In the 118th General Assembly the Senate consisted of 33 members and the House of Representatives of 99 members. The Senate is elected for 4 years, half each 2 years; the House is elected for 2 years; the Governor, Lieut.-Governor and Secretary of State for 4 years. Qualified as electors are (with necessary exceptions) all citizens 18 years of age who have the usual residential qualifications. Ohio sends 2 senators and 21 representatives to Congress.

In the 1988 presidential election Bush polled 2,411,719 votes, Dukakis, 1,934,922.

The capital (since 1816) is Columbus. Ohio is divided into 88 counties.

Governor: Richard Celeste (D.), 1987–90 ($65,000).
Lieut.-Governor: Paul Leonard (D.), 1987–90 ($46,903).
Secretary of State: Sherrod Brown (D.), 1987–90 ($67,005).

BUDGET. For the year ending 30 June 1987 general revenue fund income was 11,183·9m. and expenditure, $10,550·7m.

The bonded debt on 30 June 1986 was $3,378m.

Per capita personal income (1986) was $13,933 (current dollars).

ENERGY AND NATURAL RESOURCES

Minerals. Ohio has extensive mineral resources, of which coal is the most important by value: Output (1987) 35·4m. short tons. Production of crude petroleum,

1987, 12m. bbls; natural gas, 167,000m. cu. ft. Other minerals include stone, clay, sand and gravel. Value of minerals, 1986, $329·57m.

Agriculture. Ohio is extensively devoted to agriculture. In 1987, 89,000 farms covered 15·8m. acres; average farm value per acre, $942.

Cash income 1987, from crop and livestock and products, $3,422m. The most important crops in 1983 were: Maize (232m. bu.), wheat (58·6m. bu.), oats (15·4m. bu.), soybeans (101·7m. bu.). In 1987 there were 2·15m. swine, 1·8m. all cattle and 300,000 sheep.

Forestry. State forest area, 1982, 195,000 acres; total forest, 6,147,000 acres.

INDUSTRY. In May 1987, manufacturing employed 1,091,000 workers; non-manufacturing, 3,315,000. The largest industry was manufacturing of non-electrical machinery, then transport equipment and fabricated metals.

COMMUNICATIONS

Roads. In 1986 the state had 30,939 miles of urban and 82,349 miles of rural highway. The federal-aid highway system included 8,194 miles of primary roads, of which 1,549 miles were interstate. In 1986 there were (estimate) 8·1m. cars, trucks and buses, and 292,863 motorcycles.

Railways. Class I railroads operated 6,102 miles in 1986.

Aviation. Ohio had (1985) 194 commercial airports including one seaplane base; 597 non-commercial airports; 31 commercial heliports and 222 non-commercial. There were 5,825 licensed aeroplanes at 31 Dec. 1984.

JUSTICE, RELIGION, EDUCATION AND WELFARE

Justice. A Civil Rights Act (1933) forbids inns, restaurants, theatres, retail stores and all other places of public resort to discriminate against citizens on grounds of 'colour or race'; none may be denied the right to serve on juries on the grounds of 'colour or race'; insurance companies are forbidden to discriminate between 'white persons and coloured, wholly or partially of African descent'.

A state Civil Rights Commission (created 1959) has general administrative powers to prevent discrimination because of race, colour, religion, national origin or ancestry in employment, labour organization membership, use of public accommodations and in obtaining 'commercial housing' or 'personal residence'. Ohio has no *de jure* segregation in the public schools.

On 31 Dec. 1987 the Department of Rehabilitation and Correction was operating 17 adult correction facilities with average inmate population of 23,949. Total executions (by electrocution) since 1930 were 170, all for murder. There have been no executions since 1963. The Department of Rehabilitation and Correction was created in July 1972, and has established probation services in counties where services would otherwise be inadequate or non-existent.

Religion. Many religious faiths are represented, including (but not limited to) the Baptist, Jewish, Lutheran, Methodist, Presbyterian and Roman Catholic.

Education. School attendance during full term is compulsory for children from 6 to 18 years of age. In autumn 1987 public schools had 1·8m. enrolled pupils and 99,642 full-time equivalent classroom teachers. Teachers' salaries (1987–88) averaged (estimate) $28,191. Operating expenditure on elementary and secondary schools for 1987 was $6,100m.: state average per pupil, $3,769. Universities and colleges had a total enrolment (autumn 1985) of 514,745 students of whom 135,481 were in private colleges. State appropriation to state universities 1984–85, $1,100m. Average annual charge (undergraduate) at 4-year institutions: $4,081 (state); $7,432 (private).

Main bodies, 1988: (figures are for main campus in named city):

Founded	*Institutions*	*Enrolments*
1804	Ohio University, Athens (State)	16,182
1809	Miami University, Oxford (State)	16,012
1819	University of Cincinnati (State)	22,509
1826	Case Western Reserve University, Cleveland (Indep.)	8,352
1850	University of Dayton (R.C.)	10,693
1870	University of Akron (State)	18,321
1870	Ohio State University, Columbus (State)	47,887
1872	University of Toledo (State)	15,753
1887	Sinclair Community College, Dayton	16,247
1908	Youngstown University (State)	15,252
1910	Bowling Green State University (State)	16,206
1910	Kent State University (State)	16,468
1962	Cuyahoga Community College District (State/local)	11,928
1964	Cleveland State University (State)	12,067
1964	Wright State University (State)	14,580

Health. In 1987 the state had 228 hospitals listed by the American Hospital Association. State facilities for the severely mentally retarded had 2,862 resident in 1984.

Mentally retarded who do not need constant supervision occupy 1,024 group homes (7,993 beds) in residential areas (1983). In 1988 17 psychiatric hospitals had a daily average of 3,823 residents. In 1984, general hospitals had 74 units (3,080 beds) for the mentally ill and 56 beds for mentally retarded. There were 399 community mental health agencies in 1988.

Social Security. Public assistance is administered through 6 basic programmes: Aid to dependent children, emergency assistance, Medicaid, general relief, food stamps and social services; 49% of the costs (except general relief and adult emergency assistance) are met by the federal government.

In 1987 (preliminary) Medicaid cost $2,377m. and served an average 1·32m. people. Aid to dependent children cost $832m., to 668,000 people. Food stamps cost $691m. General relief cost $211·8m., receipts varying from county to county. Optional State Supplement is paid to aged, blind or disabled adults. Free social services are available to those eligible by income or circumstances.

Further Reading

Official Roster: Federal State, County Officers and Department Information. Secretary of State, Columbus. Biennial

Roseblooom, E. H. and Weisenburger, F. P., *A History of Ohio.* State Arch. and Hist. Soc., Columbus, 1953

OKLAHOMA

HISTORY. An unorganized area in the centre of the present state was thrown open to white settlers on 22 April 1889. The Territory of Oklahoma, organized in 1890 to include this area and other sections, was opened to white settlements by runs or lotteries during the next decade. In 1893 the Territory was enlarged by the addition of the Cherokee Outlet, which fixed part of the present northern boundary. On 16 Nov. 1907 Oklahoma was combined with the remaining part of the Indian Territory and admitted as a state with boundaries substantially as now.

AREA AND POPULATION. Oklahoma is bounded north by Kansas, north-east by Missouri, east by Arkansas, south by Texas (the Red River forming part of the boundary) and, at the western extremity of the 'panhandle', by New Mexico and Colorado. Area 69,919 sq. miles, of which 1,137 sq. miles are water. Census population, 1 April 1980, 3,025,486, an increase of 466,023 or 18% since 1970. Estimate (1987), 3,272,000. Births, 1987, 47,697; deaths, 29,191; infant deaths 726; marriages, 31,823; divorces and annulments, 23,919.

The population at 5 federal censuses was:

	White	*Negro*	*Indian*	*Other*	*Total*	*Per sq. mile*
1910	1,444,531	137,612	74,825	187	1,657,155	23·9
1930	2,130,778	172,198	92,725	339	2,396,040	34·6
1960	2,107,900	153,084	68,689	1,414	2,328,284	33·8
1970	2,280,362	171,892	97,179	10,030	2,559,253	37·2
1980	2,597,783	204,658	169,292	53,557	3,025,486	43·2

In 1980, 1,476,719 were male, 2,035,082 were urban and those 20 years of age or older numbered 2,052,729. The US Bureau of Indian Affairs is responsible for 37 Indian tribes, 201,456 Indians on 1,229,341 acres (1984).

The most important cities with population, 1980 (and estimate 1987) are Oklahoma City (capital), 404,014 (440,800), Tulsa, 360,919 (369,200); Lawton, 80,054 (81,900); Norman, 68,020 (77,500); Enid, 50,363 (49,800); Midwest City, 49,559 (53,200); Muskogee, 40,011 (41,700); Broken Arrow, 35,761 (51,500); Moore, 35,063 (41,700); Edmond, 34,637 (50,700).

CLIMATE. 1988: Oklahoma City. Jan. 34·2°F (1·2°C), July 81·6°F (27·5°C). Annual rainfall 31·94" (8,113 mm). Tulsa. Jan. 34·8°F (1·5°C), July 82·6°F (27·5°C). Annual rainfall 33·22" (8,438 mm). *See* Central Plains, p. 1381.

CONSTITUTION AND GOVERNMENT. The present constitution, dating from 1907, provides for amendment by initiative petition and legislative referendum; it has had 132 amendments.

The Legislature consists of a Senate of 48 members, who are elected for 4 years, and a House of Representatives elected for 2 years and consisting of 101 members. The Governor and Lieut.-Governor are elected for 4-year terms; the Governor can only be elected for two terms in succession. Electors are (with necessary exceptions) all citizens 18 years or older, with the usual qualifications.

The state is represented in Congress by 2 senators and 6 representatives.

In the 1988 presidential election Bush polled 678,244 votes, Dukakis, 483,373.

The capital is Oklahoma City. The state has 77 counties.

Governor: Henry Bellmon (R.), 1987–91 ($70,000).
Lieut.-Governor: Robert S. Kerr (R.), 1987–91 ($40,000).
Secretary of State: Hannah Atkins (D.), 1988–91 ($37,500).

BUDGET. Total revenue for the year ending 30 June 1988 was $5,498,719,424. Total expenditure, $5,173,866,447.

Bonded indebtedness for the year ending 30 June 1988, $2,715,336,340.

Per capita personal income (1988) was $13,269.

ENERGY AND NATURAL RESOURCES

Minerals. Production of mineral fuels, 1988: Petroleum, 198,999,366 bbls; natural gas, 2,118,135,985,000 cu. ft.; coal, 2,117,536 short tons. In 1988 there were 97,685 oilwells and 27,307 natural gaswells in production. Non-fuel mineral production (short tons), 1987: Cement, 1,456,000; gypsum, 1,828,000; sand and gravel (construction), 1,243,000; stone, 25,163,000; clays, 797,000; other important minerals are iodine, tripoli, barite, cadmium, feldspar, refined germanium, helium, lime, nitrogen, pumice and zinc. Value of non-fuel mineral production, 1987, $223,219,000.

Agriculture. In 1987 the state had 70,228 farms with a total area of 31,541,977 acres; average farm was 499 acres. Harvested crop land was 7,319,193 acres; irrigated land, 478,437 acres. Operators by principal occupation: Farming, 33,052; other, 37,176.

Total market value of agricultural products sold, 1987, $2,714,892,000 (livestock, poultry and their products, $2,104,842,000; crops, including nursery and greenhouse crops, $610,050,000). The major cash grain is wheat (value, 1987, $160,295,000). Other crops included rice, corn, soybeans, sorghum, cotton, potatoes and hay. Market value of beef cattle, 1987, $1,740,387,000. Other livestock included hogs, sheep and goats.

The Oklahoma Conservation Commission works with 91 conservation districts, universities, state and federal government agencies. The early work of the conservation districts, beginning in 1937, was limited to flood and erosion control: since 1970, they include urban areas also.

Irrigated production has increased in the Oklahoma 'panhandle'. The Ogalala aquifer is the primary source of irrigation water there and in western Oklahoma, a finite source because of its isolation from major sources of recharge. Declining groundwater levels necessitate the most effective irrigation practices.

Forestry. There are 8·5m. acres of forest, one half considered commercial. The forest products industry is concentrated in the 18 eastern counties. There are 3 forest regions: Ozark (oak, hickory); Ouachita highlands (pine, oak); Cross-Timbers (post oak, black jack oak). Southern pine is the chief commercial species, at almost 80% of saw-timber harvested annually.

Replanting is essential and encouraged by a federal investment tax credit (10%) to non-industrial forest land owners; the federal Forestry Incentives Program is also available in 10 counties, for planting on non-industrial private land.

INDUSTRY. Nominal output grew by an estimated 3% to $53,000m. in 1988. Manufacturing is the most important sector, representing about 14·7% of total output in 1988; mining, primarily oil and gas related, 9·1%.

Labour. Total labour force, May 1989, 1,513,600. Establishment employment, 1988, 1,101,000: Manufacturing, 157,000; construction, 32,000; mining, 45,000. Average unemployment rate, 1988, 6·5%.

COMMUNICATIONS

Roads. In 1988 there were 12,232·71 miles of state highways; 485·83 miles of toll roads; 317·61 miles of state park roads and 86,729·9 miles of county roads; 11,316·03 miles of local city streets; total roads and streets, 1988, 111,081·93 miles.

Railways. In 1988 Oklahoma had 4,243 miles of railway operated by 17 companies.

Aviation. Airports, 1988, numbered 325, of which 125 were publicly owned. Four cities were served by commercial airlines.

Shipping. The McClellan-Kerr Arkansas Navigation System provides access from east central Oklahoma to New Orleans through the Verdigris, Arkansas and Mississippi rivers. The Tulsa port of Catoosa handled 1·41m. tons inward and outward on 11,997 barges in 1986; about 30% arose from international trade. Total tonnage (estimate, 1988) of traffic on the System, 7,788,344 tons; the Oklahoma segment of the System handled 3,298,636 tons. Commodities shipped, 1988 were mainly chemical fertilizer, farm produce, petroleum products, iron and steel, coal, sand and gravel.

Broadcasting. In 1988 there were 179 radio and 16 television broadcasting stations, and 7 cable-TV companies.

Newspapers. In 1988 there were 47 daily and 186 weekly newspapers.

JUSTICE, RELIGION, EDUCATION AND WELFARE

Justice. Penal institutions, 18 Sept. 1989, held 8,528 inmates (7,790 of them male). There were 15 correction centres, 8 community treatment centres and 17 probation and parole centres.

The death penalty was suspended in 1966 and re-imposed in 1976. Since 1915 there have been 83 (52 whites, 27 Negroes, 4 other races) executions. Electrocution was replaced (1977) by lethal injection.

Religion. The chief religious bodies in 1980 were Baptists, 674,766; United Methodists, 248,635; Roman Catholics, 122,820; Churches of Christ, about 80,000; Assembly of God, 63,992; Disciples of Christ, 45,070; Presbyterian, 38,605; Lutheran, 33,664; Nazarene, 22,090; Episcopal, 21,500.

Education. In 1987–88 there were 607,738 pupils enrolled in grades Kindergarten–12. There were 39,281 teachers at elementary and secondary schools on average salaries of $22,773. Total expenditure on public schools, $10,531,835,114. In 1988–89 total expenditure for vocational-technical education was $87,610,645; there were 333,019 students enrolled.

Institutions of higher education with over 3,000 students:

Founded	*Name*	*Place*	*1987–88 Enrolment*
1891	Oklahoma State University	Stillwater, Okla. City, Okmulgee	18,065
1891	Central State University	Edmond	10,431
1892	University of Oklahoma	Norman	17,752
1894	University of Tulsa	Tulsa	4,431
1903	Southwestern Oklahoma State University	Weatherford	4,716
1904	Oklahoma City University	Oklahoma City	3,477
1909	East Central Oklahoma State University	Ada	4,010
1909	Northeastern Oklahoma State University	Tahlequah	7,091
1909	Southeastern Oklahoma State University	Durant	3,382
1909	Cameron University	Lawton	4,172
1965	Oral Roberts University	Tulsa	4,563
1968	Rose State College	Midwest City	5,268
1969	Tulsa Junior College	Tulsa	7,474
1970	Oklahoma City Community College	Oklahoma City	3,837

Total enrolment in Oklahoma State System of higher education, 1988–89, 112,680; total expenditure, $409,524,000.

Health. In 1988 there were 169 hospitals; 58 alcoholism treatment centres, 25 end state renal disease facilities, 75 home health agencies, 8 hospices, 57 laboratories and 25 physical therapy/speech pathology units.

Welfare. In 1987–88 the Oklahoma Department of Human Services provided for medical services administration, $593,112,369; assistance payments and services, $203,927,805; field services, $70,990,303; Oklahoma Medical Center, $147,079,265; children and youth services, $70,991,691; mentally retarded and developmental disability, $72,854,830; rehabilitation, $41,441,995; the ageing, $24,759,213; administration, management information, construction and special projects, $44,281,050.

In 1986 social security payments were being drawn by 506,000 persons; average monthly payments were: Retired workers, $464; disabled workers, $470; and widows and widowers, $412. There were 430,000 enrolled in medicare (payment $890m.); 242,000 receiving medicaid ($422m.). Aid to families with dependent children went to 94,000 persons; 59,200 received supplemental security income (payment $129m.); 268,000 received food stamps (payment $139m.); 369,000 were involved in the national school lunch programme (payment $36m.) In 1989 there were 377,600 military veterans.

Further Reading

Directory of Oklahoma. Dept. of Libraries, Oklahoma City (irregular), 1989–90
Chronicles of Oklahoma. Oklahoma Historical Society, Oklahoma City (from 1921, quarterly)
Dale, E. E. and Aldrich, G., *History of Oklahoma*. New York, 1969
Gibson, A. M., *The History of Oklahoma*. Rev. ed., Univ. of Oklahoma, Norman, 1984
Strain, J. W., *Outline of Oklahoma Government*. Rev. ed., Central State Univ., Edmond, 1983

State Library: Oklahoma Dept. of Libraries, 200 N.E. 18th Street, Oklahoma City 73105. *State Librarian and State Archivist:* Robert L. Clark, Jr.

OREGON

HISTORY. Oregon was first settled in 1811 by the Pacific Fur Co. at Astoria, a provisional government was formed on 5 July 1834; a Territorial government was organized, 14 Aug. 1848, and on 14 Feb. 1859 Oregon was admitted to the Union.

AREA AND POPULATION. Oregon is bounded north by Washington, with the Columbia River forming most of the boundary, east by Idaho, with the Snake River forming most of the boundary, south by Nevada and California and west by the Pacific. Area, 97,073 sq. miles, 889 sq. miles being inland water. The federal government owned (1985) 30,110,212 acres (48·88% of the state area). Census population, 1 April 1980, 2,633,105, an increase of 541,720 or 26% since 1970. Estimated population (1987), 2,690,000. In 1986 births numbered 38,850 (14·6 per 1,000 population); deaths, 23,328 (8·8); infant deaths 368 (9·5 per 1,000 live births); marriages, 22,015 (8·3), and divorces, 15,774 (5·9).

Population at 5 federal censuses was:

	White	*Negro*	*Indian*	*Asiatic*	*Total*	*Per sq. mile*
1910	655,090	1,492	5,090	11,093	672,765	7·0
1930	938,598	2,234	4,776	8,179	953,786	9·9
1960	1,732,037	18,133	8,026	9,120	1,768,687	18·4
1970	2,032,079	26,308	13,510	13,290	2,091,385	21·7
1980	2,490,610	37,060	27,314	34,775	2,633,105	27·3

Of the total population in 1980, 1,296,566 were male, 1,788,354 persons were urban. Those 18 years and older numbered 1,910,048.

The US Bureau of Indian Affairs (area headquarters in Portland) administers (1988) 768,665·2 acres, of which 633,613·36 acres are held by the US in trust for Indian tribes, and 135,052·36 acres for individual Indians.

The largest towns, according to 1980 census figures (and 1988 estimates), are: Portland, 366,383 (429,410); Eugene, 105,664 (108,770); Salem (the capital), 89,233 (96,830); Corvallis, 40,960 (42,520); Medford, 39,603 (45,000); Springfield, 41,621 (41,080); Beaverton, 31,926 (40,515); Albany, 26,678 (28,020). Metropolitan areas (1988): Portland, 1,179,500; Eugene-Springfield, 273,700; Salem, 266,300.

CLIMATE. Portland. Jan. 39°F (3·9°C), July 67°F (19·4°C). Annual rainfall 44" (1,100 mm). *See* Pacific Coast, p. 1381.

CONSTITUTION AND GOVERNMENT. The present constitution dates from 1859; some 250 items in it have been amended. The Legislative Assembly consists of a Senate of 30 members, elected for 4 years (half their number retiring every 2 years), and a House of 60 representatives, elected for 2 years. The Governor is elected for 4 years. The constitution reserves to the voters the rights of initiative and referendum and recall. In Nov. 1912 suffrage was extended to women.

The state sends to Congress 2 senators and 5 representatives.

In the 1988 presidential election Bush polled 517,920 votes, Dukakis, 575,151.

The capital is Salem. There are 36 counties in the state.

Governor: Neil Goldschmidt (D.), 1987–91 ($75,000).
Secretary of State: Barbara Roberts (D.) ($57,500).

BUDGET. Oregon has 2-year financial periods. Total resources for the biennium 1989-91 were $25,470,404,421 (federal funds, $2,199·4m.; taxes, $4,475m.); total expenditures, $15,102·9m. (education, $3,869m.; economic development and consumer services, $3,199·5m.; human resources, $3,567m.).

In 1988 the outstanding debt was $6,614m.

Per capita personal income (1988) was $14,885.

ENERGY AND NATURAL RESOURCES

Electricity. On 1 Jan. 1984 four privately owned utilities, 11 municipally owned utilities, 18 co-operatives and 6 utility districts provided electricity in the state. The privately owned companies provided 77% of the electricity. Hydroelectricity plants (130 in 1988) have an installed capacity of 5·1m. kw., of which multipurpose federal projects like the Bonneville Power Administration accounted for 3,011 mw. and the Trojan Nuclear plant 1,104mw. Boardman coal-fired plant produced no energy in 1987.

Minerals. Oregon's mineral resources include gold, silver, nickel copper, lead, mercury, chromite, sand and gravel, stone, clays, lime, silica, diatomite, expansible shale, scoria, pumice and uranium. There is geothermal potential. Metallurgical plant produces $1,000m. worth (approximately) per annum.

Agriculture. Oregon, which has an area of 61,557,184 acres, is divided by the Cascade Range into two distinct zones as to climate. West of the Cascade Range there is a good rainfall and almost every variety of crop common to the temperate zone is grown; east of the Range stock-raising and wheat-growing are the principal industries and irrigation is needed for row crops and fruits. In 1987 38,490 were employed in farming.

There were, in 1987, 36,500 farms with an acreage of 17·8m.; average farm size was 488 acres; most are family-owned corporate farms. Average value per acre (1985), $579.

Cash receipts from crops in 1987 amounted to $2,010m., and from livestock and livestock products, $630m., of which cattle made most. Principal crops are hay (3m. tons), wheat (49·5m. bu.), potatoes, grass, seed, pears, onions, greenhouse and farm-forest products.

Livestock, 1 Jan. 1987: Milch cows, 92,000; cattle and calves, 1·36m.; sheep and lambs, 490,000; swine, 100,000.

Forestry. About 29·6m. acres is forested, almost half of the state. Of this amount, 22·7m. is commercial forest land suitable for timber production; ownership is as follows (acres): US Forestry Service, 13·6m. (46·2%); US Bureau of Land Management, 2·7m. (9·1%); other federal, 176,000 (0·6%); State of Oregon, 886,000 (3%); other public (city, county), 131,000 (0·4%); private owners, 12m. (40·7%), of which the forest industry owns 5·3m., non-industrial private owners, 3·5m., Indians, 415,000, others, 2·8m. Oregon's commercial forest lands provided a 1987 harvest of 8,200m. bd ft of logs, as well as the benefits of recreation, water, grazing, wildlife and fish. Trees vary from the coastal forest of hemlock and spruce to the state's primary species, Douglas-fir, throughout much of western Oregon. In eastern Oregon, ponderosa pine, lodgepole pine and true firs are found. Here, forestry is often combined with livestock grazing to provide an economic operation. Along the Cascade summit and in the mountains of northeast Oregon, alpine species are found.

Forest production in 1988 was worth $11,313,810.

Fisheries. All food and shellfish landings in the calendar year 1987 amounted to a value of $94·2m. The most important are: shrimp, salmon, ground fish, crab, tuna.

INDUSTRY. Forest products manufacturing is Oregon's leading industry, and in 1987 employed 80,000. The second most important industry is high technology. Gross State product, 1987, $41,300m. Manufacturing employed 204,900; trade, 276,300; services, 242,200; government, 204,500.

TOURISM. In 1988, the total income from tourism was estimated to be $2,800m.

COMMUNICATIONS

Roads. The state maintains (1988) 7,520 miles of primary and secondary highways, almost all surfaced; counties maintain 27,734 miles, and cities 7,316 miles; there were 52,450 miles in national parks and federal reservations. Registered motor vehicles, 31 Dec. 1988, totalled 2·6m.

Railways. The state had (1986) 5 common carrier railways with a total mileage of 2,700.

Aviation. In 1988 there were 3 public-use and 85 personal-use heliports; 225 personal-use airports; 107 public-use airports including 35 state-owned airports.

Shipping. Portland is a major seaport for large ocean-going vessels and is 101 miles inland from the mouth of the Columbia River. In 1988 the port handled 8·7m. short tons of cargo; main commodities for this and other Columbia River ports are grain and petroleum.

Post and Broadcasting. In Dec. 1988 there were 178 commercial radio stations and 23 educational radio stations. There were 17 commercial television stations and 6 educational television stations. There were also 5 campus limited radio stations and 1 subscription radio station.

Newspapers. In 1988 there were 22 daily newspapers with a circulation of more than 650,000 and 100 non-daily newspapers.

JUSTICE, RELIGION, EDUCATION AND WELFARE

Justice. There are 8 correctional institutions in Oregon. Total inmates, 1988, 4,197. The sterilization law, originally passed in 1917, was amended in 1967. The amendments changed the number of persons on the Board of Social Protection from 15 to 7 and provided that the Public Defender would automatically represent all persons examined. The basis on which a person would be subject to examination by the Board are: *(a)* if such person would be likely to procreate children having an inherited tendency to mental retardation or mental illness, or *(b)* if such person would be likely to procreate children who would become neglected or dependent because of the person's inability by reason of mental illness or mental retardation to provide adequate care.

Religion. The chief religious bodies are Catholic, Baptist, Lutheran, Methodists, Presbyterian and Mormon.

Education. School attendance is compulsory from 7 to 18 years of age if the twelfth year of school has not been completed; those between the ages of 16 and 18 years, if legally employed, may attend part-time or evening schools. Others may be excused under certain circumstances. In 1987–88 the public elementary and secondary schools had 477,349 students. Total expenditure on elementary and secondary education (1987) was $1,613,506,321; teachers' average salary (1988), $29,390.

Leading state-supported institutions of higher education (autumn 1988) included:

	Students
University of Oregon, Eugene	18,526
Oregon Health Sciences University:	1,288
Oregon State University, Corvallis	15,637
Portland State University, Portland	16,279
Western Oregon State College, Monmouth	3,985
Southern Oregon State College, Ashland	4,848
Eastern Oregon State College, La Grande	1,775
Oregon Institute of Technology, Klamath Falls	2,829

Total enrolment in state colleges and universities, 1988, 65,167. Largest of the privately endowed universities are Lewis and Clark College, Portland, with (1988) 2,956 students; University of Portland, 2,421 students; Willamette University, Salem, 2,943 students; Reed College, Portland, 1,301 students, and Linfield College, McMinnville, 1,946 students. In 1988 there were 83,000 students (full-time equivalent) in community colleges.

Health. In 1988 there were 78 licensed hospitals; there were 2 state hospitals for mentally ill (937 patients), 1 for the mentally retarded (1,200) and 1 with both programmes (150).

Social Security. The State Adult and Family Services Division provides cash payments, medical care, food stamps, day care and help in finding jobs. In 1989 there were about 83,000 people on low incomes, many of them children in single-parent families, benefiting from the Aid to Families with Dependent Children Programme; about 211,000 people received food stamps.

There is also a Children's Services Division.

A system of unemployment benefit payments, financed by employers, with administrative allotments made through a federal agency, started 2 Jan. 1938.

Further Reading

Oregon Blue Book. Issued by the Secretary of State. Salem. Biennial
Federal Writers' Project. *Oregon: End of the Trail*. Rev. ed. Portland, 1972
Baldwin, E. M., *Geology of Oregon*. Rev. ed. Dubuque, Iowa, 1976
Carey, C. H., *General History of Oregon, prior to 1861*. 2 vol. (1 vol. reprint, 1971) Portland, 1935
Corning, H. M. (ed.), *Dictionary of Oregon History*. New York, 1956
Dicken, S. N., *Oregon Geography*. 5th ed. Eugene, 1973.—with Dicken, E. F., *Making of Oregon: a Study in Historical Geography*. Portland, 1979.—with Dicken, E. F., *Oregon Divided: A Regional Geography*. Portland, 1982
Dodds, G. B., *Oregon: A Bicentennial History*. New York, 1977
Friedman, R., *Oregon for the Curious*. 3rd ed. Portland, 1972
Highsmith, R. M. Jr. (ed.), *Atlas of the Pacific Northwest*. Corvallis, 1973
McArthur, L. A., *Oregon Geographic Names*. 4th ed., rev. and enlarged. Portland, 1974
Patton, Clyde P., *Atlas of Oregon*. Univ. Oregon Press, Eugene, 1976

State Library: The Oregon State Library, Salem. *Librarian:* Wesley Doak.

PENNSYLVANIA

HISTORY. Pennsylvania, first settled in 1682, is one of the 13 original states in the Union.

AREA AND POPULATION. Pennsylvania is bounded north by New York, east by New Jersey, south by Delaware and Maryland, south-west by West Virginia, west by Ohio and north-west by Lake Erie. Area, 45,308 sq. miles, of which 420 sq. miles are inland water. Census population, 1 April 1980, 11,863,895, an increase of 63,129 or 0·5% since 1970. Estimate (1987) 11,936,396. Births, 1987, 162,348; deaths, 124,986; infant deaths, 1,654; marriages, 87,218; reported divorces, 38,837.

Population at 5 census years was:

	White	*Negro*	*Indian*	*All others*	*Total*	*Per sq. mile*
1910	7,467,713	193,919	1,503	1,976	7,665,111	171·0
1930	9,196,007	431,257	523	3,563	9,631,350	213·8
1960	10,454,004	852,750	2,122	10,490	11,319,366	251·5
			All others			
1970	10,745,219	1,015,884	39,663		11,800,766	262·9
1980	10,652,320	1,046,810	164,765		11,863,895	264·3

Of the total population in 1980, 47·9% were male, 69·3% were urban and 68·1% were 21 years of age or older.

The population of the larger cities and townships, 1980 census, was:

Philadelphia	1,688,210	Scranton	88,117	Lancaster	54,725
Pittsburgh	423,938	Reading	78,686	Harrisburg	53,264
Erie	119,123	Bethlehem	70,419	Wilkes-Barre	51,551
Allentown	103,758	Altoona	57,078	York	44,619

Larger urbanized areas, 1980 census: Philadelphia (in Pennsylvania), 3,682,709; Pittsburgh, 2,263,894; Northeast, 640,396, Allentown–Bethlehem–Easton (in Pennsylvania), 551,052; Harrisburg, 446,576.

CLIMATE. Philadelphia. Jan. 32°F (0°C), July 77°F (25°C). Annual rainfall 40" (1,006 mm). Pittsburgh. Jan. 31°F (–0·6°C), July 74°F (23·3°C). Annual rainfall 37" (914 mm). *See* Appalachian Mountains, p. 1382.

CONSTITUTION AND GOVERNMENT. The present constitution dates from 1968. The General Assembly consists of a Senate of 50 members chosen for 4 years, one-half being elected biennially, and a House of Representatives of 203 members chosen for 2 years. The Governor and Lieut.-Governor are elected for 4 years. Every citizen 18 years of age, with the usual residential qualifications, may vote. The state sends to Congress 2 senators and 23 representatives. Registered voters in April 1988, 5,354,310.

In the 1988 presidential election Bush polled 2,291,297 votes, Dukakis, 2,183,928.

The state capital is Harrisburg. The state is organized in counties (numbering 67), cities, boroughs, townships and school districts.

Governor: Robert Casey (D.), 1987–91 ($85,000).
Lieut.-Governor: Mark S. Singel (D.), 1987–91 ($67,500).

BUDGET. Total revenues for 1990-91 were $11,961m.; general fund expenditure, $11,924·9; transport, $1,549·6m.; public welfare, $3,216·3m.).

In 1988-89 outstanding long-term debt (excluding highway bonds) amounted to $4,680m.

Per capita personal income (1989) was $16,233.

ENERGY AND NATURAL RESOURCES

Minerals. Pennsylvania is almost the sole producer of anthracite coal; its output reached a peak of 100,445,299 short tons in 1917 with a labour-force of 156,148 men. Production: Anthracite (1989), 3·4m. tons, with about (1988) 2,000 employees; bituminous coal (1986), 69·4m. tons, with about (1988) 18,200 men; crude petroleum (1986), 3·78m. bbls; natural gas (1987), 163,000m. cu. ft.

Agriculture. Agriculture, market-gardening, fruit-growing, horticulture and forestry are pursued within the state. In 1988 there were 55,000 farms with a total farm area of 8·3m. acres (4·5m. acres in crops). Cash income, 1989, from crops, $954·7m., and from livestock and products, $2,358m.

Pennsylvania ranks first in the production of mushrooms (284·8m. lb., value $205·1m. in 1987). Other crops are (1988) tobacco (18·2m. lb., $20·5m.), wheat (1988, 9m. bu.), oats (1988, 13m. bu.), maize, barley and potatoes. On 1 Jan. 1989 there were on farms: 1·92m. cattle and calves, including 717,000 milch cows, 134,000 sheep, 970,000 swine. Milk production, 1988, was 10,204m. lb., and eggs (1988) numbered 5,300m. valued at $185·69m. Pennsylvania is also a major fruit producing state; in 1988 apples totalled 520m. lb.; peaches, 80m. lb.; tart cherries, 9m. lb.; sweet cherries, 1,200 tons; and grapes, 58,000 tons. Other important items are soybeans (7·2m. bu.), vegetables for processing (50,000 tons), fresh vegetables (1·5m. cwt) and broiler-chickens (120·6m.).

Forestry. In 1982 national forest lands totalled 510,517 acres; state forests, 2,064,533 acres; state parks, 278,930 acres; state game land, 1,250,980 acres; game land leased but not owned by the state, 3,957,438 acres (co-operative and safety-zone programmes).

INDUSTRY. Pennsylvania is third in national production of iron and steel. Output of steel, 1987, 11·6m. net tons.

In 1988, manufacturing employed 1,061,227 workers; services, 1,216,363; trade, 1,153,149; government, 272,576.

COMMUNICATIONS

Roads. Highways and roads in the state (federal, local and state combined) totalled (1987) 116,084 miles. Registered motor vehicles for 1988 numbered 8,452,365.

Railways. In 1983, 41 railways operated within the state with a line mileage of about 6,300.

Aviation. There were (1989) 161 commercial airports, 3 public landing strips, 298 private and 11 public heliports, 352 airports for personal use and 16 seaplane bases.

Shipping. Trade at the ports of Philadelphia (1988), imports 60m. short tons of bulk cargo and 61m. of general cargo; exports, 31m. of bulk cargo and 2m. of general cargo.

Post and Broadcasting. Broadcasting stations comprised (1982) 41 television stations and 378 radio stations.

Newspapers. There were (1983) 111 daily and 219 weekly newspapers.

JUSTICE, RELIGION, EDUCATION AND WELFARE

Justice. No executions took place in 1963–85; since 1930 there have been 149 executions (electrocution), all for murder.

State prison population, on 31 Dec. 1986, was 15,227.

Religion. The chief religious bodies in 1977 were the Roman Catholic, with 3,717,667 members; Protestant, 3,150,920 (1971); and Jewish, 469,078. The 5 largest Protestant denominations (by communicants) were: Lutheran Church in America, 766,276; United Methodist, 728,915 (1971), United Presbyterian Church in the USA, 573,905 (1971); United Church of Christ, 257,138; Episcopal, 193,399 (1971).

Education. School attendance is compulsory for children 8–17 years of age. In 1988–89 the public kindergartens and elementary schools had 896,213 pupils (Grades K-6); public secondary schools had 762,122 pupils. Non-public schools had 217,417 elementary pupils (Grades K-6) and 89,188 secondary pupils (Grades 7-12. Average salary, public school professional personnel, men $34,815; women $30,604; for classroom teachers, men $32,920, women $30,213.

Leading senior academic institutions included:

Founded	*Institutions*	*Faculty (Autumn 1987)*	*Students (Autumn 1987)*
1740	University of Pennsylvania (non-sect.)	2,876	21,875
1787	University of Pittsburgh	2,485	28,364
1832	Lafayette College, Easton (Presbyterian)	185	2,327
1833	Haverford College	122	1,136
1842	Villanova University (R.C.)	749	12,119
1846	Bucknell University (Baptist)	215	3,410
1851	St Joseph's University, Philadelphia (R.C.)	314	5,649
1852	California University of Pennsylvania	336	5,875
1855	Pennsylvania State University	2,544	36,271
1855	Millersville University of Pennsylvania	312	7,225
1863	LaSalle University, Philadelphia (R.C.)	398	6,456
1864	Swarthmore College	179	1,315
1866	Lehigh University, Bethlehem (non-sect.)	439	6,607
1871	West Chester University of Pennsylvania	565	11,311
1875	Indiana University of Pennsylvania	805	13,404
1878	Duquesne University, Pittsburgh (R.C.)	479	6,639
1884	Temple University, Philadelphia	2,491	30,431
1885	Bryn Mawr College	177	1,828
1888	University of Scranton (R.C.)	302	4,865
1891	Drexel University, Philadelphia	797	12,451
1900	Carnegie-Mellon University, Pittsburgh	517	6,916

Health. In 1988 the state had 300 hospitals (73,419 beds) listed by the State Health Department, excluding federal hospitals and mental institutions.

Social Security. During the year ending 30 June 1988 the monthly average number of cases receiving public assistance was: Aid to families with dependent children, 701,401; blind pension, 2,607; general assistance, 131,017.

Payments for medical assistance for the year ending 30 June 1985 totalled $2,246m. Under the medical assistance programme payments are made for inpatient hospital care ($195m.); care in public institutions (nursing homes, mental institutions and geriatric centres) ($444·5m.); private nursing home care ($317·2m.); other medical care ($76·7m.).

Further Reading

Crop and Livestock Summary. Pennsylvania Dept. of Agriculture. Annual
Encyclopaedia of Pennsylvania, New York, 1984
Pennsylvania Manual. General Services, Bureau of Publications, Harrisburg. Biennial

Pennsylvania State Industrial Directory. Harris, Ohio. Annual
Cochran, T. C., *Pennsylvania*, New York, 1978
Klein, P. S. and Hoogenboom, A., *A History of Pennsylvania*. New York, 1973
League of Women Voters of Pennsylvania, *Key to the Keystone State*. Philadelphia, 1972
Majumdar, S. K. and Miller, E. W., *Pennsylvania Coal: Resources, Technology and Utilisation*. Pennsylvania Science, 1983
Pennsylvania Chamber of Commerce, *Pennsylvania Government Today*. State College, Pa., 1973
Weigley, R. F., (ed.) *Philadelphia: A 300-year History*. New York, 1984
Wilkinson, N. B., *Bibliography of Pennsylvania History*. Pa. Historical & Museum Commission. Harrisburg, 1957

RHODE ISLAND

HISTORY The earliest settlers in the region which now forms the state of Rhode Island were colonists from Massachusetts who had been driven forth on account of their non-acceptance of the prevailing religious beliefs. The first of the settlements was made in 1636, settlers of every creed being welcomed. In 1647 a patent was executed for the government of the settlements, and on 8 July 1663 a charter was executed recognizing the settlers as forming a body corporate and politic by the name of the 'English Colony of Rhode Island and Providence Plantations, in New England, in America'. On 29 May 1790 the state accepted the federal constitution and entered the Union as the last of the 13 original states.

AREA AND POPULATION. Rhode Island is bounded north and east by Massachusetts, south by the Atlantic and west by Connecticut. Area, 1,214 sq. miles, of which 165 sq. miles are inland water. Census population, 1 April 1980, 947,154 a decrease of 0·3% since 1970. Estimate (1987), 986,000.

Births, 1986, were 13,324; deaths (excluding foetal deaths), 9,587; infant deaths, 125; marriages, 8,103; divorces, 3,683.

Population of 5 census years was:

	White	*Negro*	*Indian*	*Asiatic*	*Total*	*Per sq. mile*
1910	532,492	9,529	284	305	542,610	508·5
1930	677,026	9,913	318	240	687,497	649·3
1960	838,712	18,332	932	1,190	859,488	812·4
1970	914,757	25,338	1,390	5,240	949,723[1]	905·0
			All others			
1980	896,692	27,584	22,878		154	903·0

[1] Through tabulation errors there were 2,998 people unaccounted for, as to race and sex, in 1970.

Of the total population in 1980, 451,251 were male, 824,004 were urban and 665,054 were 20 years of age or older.

The chief cities and their population (census, 1980) are Providence, 156,804; Warwick, 87,123; Cranston, 71,992; Pawtucket, 71,204; East Providence, 50,980; Woonsocket, 45,914; Newport, 29,259; North Providence (town), 29,188; Cumberland (town), 27,069. The Providence–Pawtucket–Warwick Standard Metropolitan Statistical Area had a population of 919,216 in 1980.

CLIMATE. Providence. Jan. 28°F (–2·2°C), July 72°F (22·2°C). Annual rainfall 43" (1,079 mm). *See* New England, p. 1382.

CONSTITUTION AND GOVERNMENT. The present constitution dates from 1843; it has had 42 amendments. The General Assembly consists of a Senate of 50 members and a House of Representatives of 100 members, both elected for 2 years, as are also the Governor and Lieut.-Governor. Every citizen, 18 years of age, who has resided in the state for 30 days, and is duly registered, is qualified to vote.

Rhode Island sends to Congress 2 senators and 2 representatives.

At the 1988 presidential election Dukakis polled 216,668 votes, Bush, 169,730.

The capital is Providence. The state has 5 counties (unique in having no political functions) and 39 cities and towns.

Governor: Edward DiPrete (R.), 1989–91 ($69,900).
Lieut.-Governor: Roger Begin (D.), 1989–91 ($52,000).
Secretary of State: Kathleen Connell (D.), 1989–91 ($52,000).

BUDGET. For the fiscal year ending 30 June 1987 (Office of the State Controller) total revenues were $1,585·7m. (taxation, $1,032·8m., and federal aid, $361·1m.); general expenditures were $1,529·1m. (education, $442·6m.; and public welfare, $453·1m.).

Total net long-term debt on 30 June 1986 was $261·8m.

Per capita personal income (1987) was $15,555.

NATURAL RESOURCES

Minerals. The small mineral output, mostly stone, sand and gravel, was valued (1987) at an estimated $18m.

Agriculture. While Rhode Island is predominantly a manufacturing state, agriculture contributed $110m. to the general cash income in 1987; it had 697 farms with an area of 73,000 acres (11% of the total land area), of which 31,000 acres were crop land; the average farm was 86 acres.

Fisheries. In 1987 the catch was 90m. lb (live weight) valued at $76·5m.

INDUSTRY. Total non-agricultural employment in Oct. 1989 was 459,100, of which 112,300 were manufacturing, 346,800 non-manufacturing. Average weekly earnings for production workers in manufacturing, $359.99; value added by manufacture (1985), $4,289m. Principal industries are metals and machinery, jewellery–silverware and transport equipment.

COMMUNICATIONS

Roads. The state had (1 Jan. 1987) 5,860 miles of road, of which 1,857 were state-owned. In 1989, 779,458 motor vehicles were registered.

Railways. In 1988, 3 railways operated 135 line-miles.

Aviation. In 1988 there were 6 state-owned airports. Theodore Francis Green airport at Warwick, near Providence, is served by 8 airlines, and handled over 2m. passengers and 20m. lb. of freight in 1988.

Shipping. Waterborne freight through the port of Providence (1988) totalled 10·6m. tons.

Broadcasting. There are 24 radio stations and 5 television stations; there are 8 cable television companies.

JUSTICE, RELIGION, EDUCATION AND WELFARE

Justice. The state's penal institutions, Aug. 1988, had 1,290 inmates (131 per 100,000 population).

The death penalty is illegal, except that it is mandatory in the case of murder committed by a prisoner serving a life sentence.

Religion. Chief religious bodies are (estimated figures Sept. 1988): Roman Catholic with 550,000 members; Protestant Episcopal (baptized persons), 50,000; Baptist, 22,500; Congregational, 12,000; Methodist, 10,000; Jewish, 24,000.

Education. In 1987–88 the 240 public elementary schools had 3,702 teachers and total enrolment of 60,582 pupils; about 25,000 pupils were enrolled in private and parochial schools. The 58 senior and vocational high schools had 3,678 teachers and 59,011 pupils. Teachers' salaries (1987) averaged $23,400. Local expenditure, for schools (including evening schools) in 1987–88 totalled $580·6m.

There are 11 institutions of higher learning in the state, including 1 junior college.

The state maintains Rhode Island College, at Providence, with 600 faculty members, and 5,600 full-time students (1987), and the University of Rhode Island, at South Kingstown, with over 900 faculty members and over 14,000 students (including graduate students). Brown University, at Providence, founded in 1764, is now non-sectarian; in 1987 it had over 600 full-time faculty members and 7,000 full-time students. Providence College, at Providence, founded in 1917 by the Order of Preachers (Dominican), had (1987) 210 professors and 5,400 students. The largest of the other colleges are Bryant College, at Smithfield, with 160 faculty and 5,000 students, and the Rhode Island School of Design, in Providence, with about 155 faculty and 1,800 students.

Health. In 1988 the state had 22 hospitals (over 7,000 beds), including 4 mental hospitals.

Social Security. In 1987 aid to dependent children was granted to 44,000 children in 15,000 families at an average payment per family of $380 per month, and the state also had a general assistance programme. (All other aid programmes were taken over by the federal government.)

Further Reading

Rhode Island Manual. Prepared by the Secretary of State. Providence
Providence Journal Almanac: A Reference Book for Rhode Islanders. Providence. Annual
Rhode Island Basic Economic Statistics. Rhode Island Dept. of Economic Development. Providence, 1987
McLoughlin, W. G., *Rhode Island: a History.* Norton, 1978
Wright, M. I. and Sullivan, R. J., *Rhode Island Atlas.* Rhode Island Pubs., 1983

State Library: Rhode Island State Library, State House, Providence 02908. State Librarian: Elliott E. Andrews.

SOUTH CAROLINA

HISTORY. South Carolina, first settled permanently in 1670, was one of the 13 original states of the Union.

AREA AND POPULATION. South Carolina is bounded in the north by North Carolina, east and south-east by the Atlantic, south-west and west by Georgia. Area, 31,113 sq. miles, of which 909 sq. miles are inland water. Census population, 1 April 1980, 3,121,833, an increase of 20·5% since 1970. Estimate July 1988 3,470,000. Births, 1988, were 55,090 (15·9 per 1,000 population); deaths, 29,397 (8·5); marriages, 54,615 (15·7); divorces and annulments, 14,672 (4·2); infant deaths, 673 (12·2 per 1,000 live births).

The population in 5 census years was:

	White	*Negro*	*Indian*	*Asiatic*	*Total*	*Per sq. mile*
1910	679,161	835,843	331	65	1,515,400	49·7
1930	944,049	793,681	959	76	1,738,765	56·8
1960	1,551,022	829,291	1,098	946	2,382,594	78·7
			All others			
1970	1,794,432	789,040	3,588		2,587,060	83·2
1980	2,150,507	948,623	22,703		3,121,833	100·3

Of the total population in 1980, 49% were male, 54·1% were urban and 55% were 25 years old or older. Median age, 28.

Populations of large towns in 1988 (with those of associated metropolitan areas): Columbia (capital), 94,810 (465,500); Charleston, 81,030 (510,800); Greenville, 59,190; Spartanburg, 45,550 (Greenville–Spartanburg, 621,300).

CLIMATE. Columbia. Jan. 47°F (8·3°C), July 81°F (27·2°C). Annual rainfall 45" (1,125 mm). *See* Atlantic Coast, p. 1382.

CONSTITUTION AND GOVERNMENT. The present constitution dates from 1895, when it went into force without ratification by the electorate. The General Assembly consists of a Senate of 46 members, elected for 4 years, and a House of Representatives of 124 members, elected for 2 years. The Governor and Lieut.-Governor are elected for 4 years. Only registered citizens have the right to vote. South Carolina sends to Congress 2 senators and 6 representatives.

At the 1988 presidential election Bush polled 599,871 votes, Dukakis 367,511.

The capital is Columbia.

Governor: Carroll Campbell (R.), 1987–91 ($98,000).
Lieut.-Governor: N. A. Theodore (D.), 1987–91 ($43,000).
Secretary of State: John Tucker Campbell (D.), 1987–91 ($85,000).

BUDGET. For the fiscal year ending 30 June 1989 general revenues were $3,142·4m.; general expenditures were $3,104·5m.

Per capita personal income (1988) was $12,764.

NATURAL RESOURCES

Minerals. Non-metallic minerals are of chief importance: Value of mineral output in 1988 was $221·9m., chiefly from limestone for cement, clay, stone, sand and gravel. Production of kaolin, vermiculite, scrap mica and fuller's earth is also important.

Agriculture. In 1989 there were 25,500 farms covering a farm area of 5·3m. acres. The average farm was of 208 acres. Of the 20,517 farms of the 1987 Census of Agriculture, there were 936 of 1,000 acres or more, average farm 232 acres; owners operated 12,624 farms; tenants 1,460. There were 1,905 farms with $100,000 or more in value of sales.

Cash receipts from farm marketing in 1988 amounted to $620·7m. for crops and $488·1m. for livestock, including poultry. Chief crops are tobacco ($158·9m.), soybeans ($125·5m.), and corn ($42m.). Production, 1988: Cotton, 140,000 bales; peaches, 290m. lb.; soybeans, 18·2m. bu.; tobacco, 100m. lb.; eggs, 1,432,000m. Livestock on farms, 1989: 621,000 all cattle, 450,000 swine.

Forestry. The forest industry is important; total forest land (1986), 12·3m. acres. National forests amounted to 576,518 acres.

INDUSTRY. A monthly average of 386,694 workers were employed in manufacturing in 1988, earning $8,190m. Major sectors are textiles (27·6%), apparel (11·7%) and chemicals (9·2%).

Tourism is important; tourists spent an estimated $4,623m. in 1987, and tourism employed 97,223.

COMMUNICATIONS

Roads. Total highway mileage in the combined highway system in Aug. 1989 was 41,070 miles. Motor vehicle registrations numbered 2·5m. in 1988.

Railways. In 1988 the length of railway in the state was about 2,600 miles.

Aviation. In 1987 there were 146 aircraft facilities (65 public, 81 private) including 128 airports, 17 heliports and 1 seaplane base. Registered aircraft numbered 2,327 in 1987.

Shipping. The state has 3 deep-water ports.

JUSTICE, RELIGION, EDUCATION AND WELFARE

Justice. At 31 Dec. 1987 penal institutions held 12,664 prisoners under State and federal jurisdiction.

Education. In 1987–88 the total public-school enrolment (K-12) was 630,376; there were 364,360 white pupils and 266,016 non-white pupils. The total number of teachers was 34,903; average salary was $24,403.

For higher education the state operates the University of South Carolina, founded at Columbia in 1801, with (autumn 1988), 26,435 enrolled students; Clemson University, founded in 1889, with 14,794 students; The Citadel, at Charleston, with 3,565 students; Winthrop College, Rock Hill, with 5,351 students; Medical University of S. Carolina, at Charleston 2,499 students; S. Carolina State College, at Orangeburg, with 4,399 students, and Francis Marion College, at Florence, with 3,929 students; the College of Charleston has 6,205 students and Lander College, Greenwood, 2,461. There are 16 technical institutions (36,713).

There are also 440 private kindergartens, elementary and high schools with total enrolment (1987–88) of 44,803 pupils, and 31 private and denominational colleges and junior colleges with (autumn 1988) enrolment of 25,047 students.

Health. In 1988 the state had 323 non-federal health facilities with 29,897 beds licensed by the South Carolina Department of Health and Environmental Control.

Social Security. In 1986 there were 506,000 recipients of social security benefits. The average monthly expenditure in benefits was $206m.

Further Reading

South Carolina Legislative Manual. Columbia. Annual

South Carolina Statistical Abstract. South Carolina Budget and Control Board, Columbia. Annual

Jones, L., *South Carolina: A Synoptic History for Laymen*. Lexington, 1978

State Library: South Carolina State Library, Columbia.

SOUTH DAKOTA

HISTORY. South Dakota was first visited by Europeans in 1743 when Verendrye planted a lead plate (discovered in 1913) on the site of Fort Pierre, claiming the region for the French crown. Beginning with a trading post in 1794, it was settled from 1857 to 1861 when Dakota Territory was organized. It was admitted into the Union on 2 Nov. 1889.

AREA AND POPULATION. South Dakota is bounded north by North Dakota, east by Minnesota, south-east by the Big Sioux River (forming the boundary with Iowa), south by Nebraska (with the Missouri River forming part of the boundary) and west by Wyoming and Montana. Area, 77,116 sq. miles, of which 1,164 sq. miles are water. Area administered by the Bureau of Indian Affairs, 1985, covered 5m. acres (10% of the state), of which 2·6m. acres were held by tribes. The federal government, 1987, owned or managed 954,000 acres.

Census population, 1 April 1980, 690,178, an increase of 3·5% since 1970. Estimate (1986) 708,000. Births, 1987, were 11,482; deaths, 6,658; infant deaths, 114; marriages, 6,993; divorces, 2,696.

Population in 5 federal censuses was:

	White	*Negro*	*Indian*	*Asiatic*	*Total*	*Per sq. mile*
1910	563,771	817	19,137	163	583,888	7·6
1930	669,453	646	21,833	101	692,849	9·0
1960	653,098	1,114	25,794	336	680,514	8·9
			All others			
1970	630,333	1,627	34,297		666,257	8·8
1980	638,955	2,144	49,079		690,178	9·0

Of the total population in 1980, 340,370 were male, 320,223 were urban and 441,851 were 21 years of age or older.

Population of the chief cities (census of 1980) was: Sioux Falls, 81,071; Rapid City, 46,340; Aberdeen, 25,973; Watertown, 15,632, Mitchell, 13,917; Brookings, 14,915; Huron, 13,000.

CLIMATE. Rapid City. Jan. 25°F (–3·9°C), July 73°F (22·8°C). Annual rainfall

19" (474 mm). Sioux Falls. Jan. 14°F (–10°C), July 73°F (22·8°C). Annual rainfall 25" (625 mm). *See* High Plains, p. 1381.

CONSTITUTION AND GOVERNMENT. Voters are all citizens 18 years of age or older who have complied with certain residential qualifications. The people reserve the right of the initiative and referendum. The Senate has 35 members, and the House of Representatives 70 members, all elected for 2 years; the Governor and Lieut.-Governor are elected for 4 years. The state sends 2 senators and 1 representative to Congress.

In the 1988 presidential election Bush polled 165,516 votes, Dukakis, 145,632.

The capital is Pierre (population, 1980, 11,973). The state is divided into 66 organized counties.

Governor: George Mickelson, Jr. (R.), 1987–91 ($60,816).

Lieut.-Governor: Walter D. Miller, 1987–91 ($8,219, and $75 daily expense allowance).

Secretary of State: Joyce Hazeltine, 1987–91 ($41,311).

BUDGET. For the fiscal year ending 30 June 1990 the estimated general fund revenues were $444,785,493 ($224·03m. from sales and use tax); expenditure was also $444,785,493 ($126,016,875 on state aid to education).

Per capita personal income (1988) was $12,475.

NATURAL RESOURCES

Minerals. The mineral products include gold (356,103 troy oz. in 1985, second largest yield of all states), silver (63,000 troy oz.). Mineral products, 1985, were valued at $207,703,000, of which gold accounted for $113,119,000 and silver, $388,000.

Agriculture. In 1988, 34,000 farms had an acreage of 44·1m.; the average farm had 1,278 acres. Farm units are large; in 1982 there were only 4,024 farms of 50 acres or less, compared with 10,165 exceeding 1,000 acres. 17,371 farms sold produce valued at $40,000 or over in 1985.

South Dakota ranks first in the US as producer of rye (2·3m. bu. in 1988), second in sunflower seed (204·9m. bu.) and flaxseed (200,000 bu.), and third in oats (20m. bu.). The other important crops are durum and spring wheat (16·4m. bu.), sorghum for grain (11m. bu.) and corn for grain (132m. bu.). The farm livestock on 1 Jan. 1988 included 3·48m. cattle, 590,000 sheep, 1·76m. hogs.

Forestry. National forest area, 1987, 1,954,000 acres.

INDUSTRY. In 1987, manufacturing establishments had 26,259 workers. Food processing was by far the largest industry with 96 plants employing 7,686 workers. Construction had 1,580 companies employing 7,336. There were 176 printing and publishing plants employing 2,597 workers. Also significant were mining (58 establishments employing 2,061), dairy, lumber and wood products, machinery, transport equipment, electronics, stone, glass and clay products.

COMMUNICATIONS

Roads. Total highway mileage was 83,222 in 1986; hard surface, 8,324. Registered passenger cars numbered 678,000 in 1987.

Railways. In 1987 there were 2,005 miles of railway in operation. The state owns 969 miles of track.

Aviation. In 1989 there were 66 general aviation airports and 9 commercial airports.

JUSTICE, RELIGION, EDUCATION AND WELFARE

Justice. The State prisons had, in 1987, 1,135 inmates under state and federal correction. The death penalty was illegal from 1915 to 1938; since 1938, one person has been executed, in 1949 (by electrocution), for murder.

Religion. The chief religious bodies are: Lutherans, Roman Catholics, Methodist, Disciples of Christ, Presbyterian, Baptist and Episcopal.

Education. Elementary and secondary education are free from 6 to 21 years of age. Between the ages of 8 and 16, attendance is compulsory. In 1987–88 133,254 pupils were attending elementary and high (including parochial) schools (8,425 full-time equivalent classroom teachers).

Teachers' salaries (1987–88) averaged an estimated $19,758. Total expenditure on public schools, $477m.

Higher education (1987–88): The School of Mines at Rapid City, established 1885, had 1,997 students; the State University at Brookings, 6,443 students; the University of South Dakota, founded at Vermillion in 1882, 5,233; Northern State University, Aberdeen, had 2,561; Black Hills State University at Spearfish, 2,102; Dakota State University at Madison, 858. The 10 private colleges had 7,893 students. The federal Government maintains Indian schools on its reservations and 1 outside of a reservation at Flandreau.

Health. In 1987 there were 68 licensed hospitals (3,540 beds).

Social Security. In financial year 1987–88, 4,777 disabled persons received $51,650,914; 77 blind persons received $400,302. Aid to dependent children was $1,733,207, to 18,637 children.

Further Reading

Governor's Budget Report. South Dakota Bureau of Finance and Management. Annual
South Dakota Historical Collections. 1902–82
South Dakota Legislative Manual. Secretary of State, Pierre, S.D. Biennial
Berg, F. M., *South Dakota: Land of Shining Gold*. Hettinger, 1982
Karolevitz, R. F., *Challenge: the South Dakota Story*. Sioux Falls, 1975
Milton, John R., *South Dakota; a Bicentennial History*. New York, W. W. Norton, 1977
Schell, H. S., *History of South Dakota*. 3rd ed. Lincoln, Neb., 1975
Vexler, R. I., *South Dakota Chronology and Factbook*. New York, 1978

State Library: South Dakota State Library, 800 Governor's Drive, Pierre, S.D., 57501–2294. *State Librarian:* Dr Jane Kolbe.

TENNESSEE

HISTORY. Tennessee, first settled in 1757, was admitted into the Union on 1 June 1796.

AREA AND POPULATION. Tennessee is bounded north by Kentucky and Virginia, east by North Carolina, south by Georgia, Alabama and Mississippi and west by the Mississippi River (forming the boundary with Arkansas and Missouri). Area, 42,144 sq. miles (989 sq. miles water). Census population, 1 April 1980, 4,591,120, an increase of 665,102 or 16·9% since 1970. Estimate (1988), 4,895,000. Vital statistics, 1988: Births, 70,685 (14·3 per 1,000 population); deaths, 45,728 (9·2); infant deaths 762 (10·8 per 1,000 live births); marriages, 65,329 (26·4); divorces, 31,287 (12·6).

Population in 6 census years was:

	White	*Negro*	*Indian*	*Asiatic*	*Total*	*Per sq. mile*
1910	1,711,432	473,088	216	53	2,184,789	52·4
1930	2,138,644	477,646	161	105	2,616,556	62·4
1950	2,760,257	530,603	339	334	3,291,718	78·8
1960	2,977,753	586,876	638	1,243	3,567,089	85·4
			All others			
1970	3,293,930	621,261	8,496		3,923,687	95·3
1980	3,835,452	725,942	29,726		4,591,120	111·6

Of the population in 1980, 2,216,600 were male, 2,773,573 were urban and those 21 years of age or older numbered 3,026,398.

The cities, with population, 1980 (and estimates 1988), are Memphis, 646,356 (645,190); Nashville (capital), 455,651 (481,380); Knoxville, 175,030 (172,080); Chattanooga, 169,565 (162,670); Clarksville, 54,777 (72,620); Jackson, 49,131 (53,320); Johnson City, 39,753 (45,420); Murfreesboro, 32,845 (45,820); Kingsport, 32,027 (31,440); Oak Ridge, 27,662 (27,710). Standard metropolitan areas 1980 (1988): Memphis, 810,043 (971,930); Nashville, 850,505 (971,800); Knoxville, 476,517 (599,600); Chattanooga, 320,761 (438,100); Johnson City–Bristol–Kingsport, 343,041 (442,300); Clarksville, 83,342 (158,900); Jackson, 74,546 (78,200).

CLIMATE. Memphis. Jan. 41°F (5°C), July 82°F (27·8°C). Annual rainfall 49" (1,221 mm). Nashville. Jan. 39°F (3·9°C), July 79°F (26·1°C). Annual rainfall 48" (1,196 mm). *See* Appalachian Mountains, p. 1382.

CONSTITUTION AND GOVERNMENT. The state has operated under 3 constitutions, the last of which was adopted in 1870 and has been since amended 22 times (first in 1953). Voters at an election may authorize the calling of a convention limited to altering or abolishing one or more specified sections of the constitution. The General Assembly consists of a Senate of 33 members and a House of Representatives of 99 members, senators elected for 4 years and representatives for 2 years. Qualified as electors are all citizens (usual residential and age (18) qualifications). Tennessee sends to Congress 2 senators and 9 representatives.

In the 1988 presidential election Bush polled 939,434 votes, Dukakis, 677,715.

For the Tennessee Valley Authority *see* p. 1409.

The capital is Nashville. The state is divided into 95 counties.

Governor: Ned McWherter (D.), 1987–91 ($85,000).
Lieut.-Governor: John S. Wilder (D.), 1987–91 ($12,500).
Secretary of State: Gentry Crowell (D.), ($62,500).

BUDGET. For 1987–88 total revenue was $6,199m.; general expenditure, $5,472m.

Total net long-term debt on 30 June 1988 amounted to $707·3m.

Per capita personal income (1988) was $13,873.

ENERGY AND NATURAL RESOURCES

Minerals. Total value added by mining 1982: Fuel minerals (mainly coal), $217·1m.; non-fuel (mainly stone and zinc), $154·4m.

Agriculture. In 1989, 91,000 farms covered 12·6m. acres. The average farm was of 131 acres (only a few states had a smaller average) valued, land and buildings, at $1,126.

Cash income (1988) from crops was $965·3m.; from livestock, $1,080·4m. Main crops were cotton, tobacco and soybeans.

On 1 Jan. 1989 the domestic animals included 202,000 milch cows, 2·3m. all cattle, 10,000 sheep, 900,000 swine.

Forestry. Forests occupy 13,258,000 acres (50% of total land area). The forest industry and industries dependent on it employ about 40,000 workers, earning $150m. per year. Wood products are valued at over $500m. per year. National forest system land (1986) 626,000 acres.

INDUSTRY. The manufacturing industries include iron and steel working, but the most important products are chemicals, including synthetic fibres and allied products, electrical equipment and food. In 1986, manufacturing establishments employed 466,600 workers; value added by manufactures was $23,624·9m.

TOURISM. In 1988 43·1m. out-of-state tourists spent $4,883m.

COMMUNICATIONS

Roads. In 1985 there were 68,768 miles of municipal and rural roads. The state is served by 115 intrastate bus companies and 31 privately owned internal bus services.

Motor-vehicle registrations, 1988, totalled 3,869,091.

Railways. The state had (1985) 2,857 miles of track.

Aviation. The state is served by 11 major airlines. In 1985 there were 74 public airports and 78 private; there were 71 heliports and 2 military air bases.

JUSTICE, RELIGION, EDUCATION AND WELFARE

Justice. There has been no execution since 1960; since 1930 there have been 22 whites and 44 Negroes executed (by electrocution) for murder and 5 whites and 22 Negroes for rape. A US Supreme Court ruling prohibits the use of capital punishment under present Tennessee law, except for first degree murder.

Prison population, 30 June 1989, 7,376.

The law prohibiting the inter-marriage of white and Negro was declared unconstitutional by the US Supreme Court in June 1967.

Religion. The leading religious bodies are the Southern Baptists, Methodists and Negro Baptists.

Education. School attendance has been compulsory since 1925 and the employment of children under 16 years of age in workshops, factories or mines is illegal.

In 1987–88 there were 1,626 public schools with a net enrolment of 860,101 pupils; 49,920 teachers earned an average salary of $23,785. Total expenditure for operating public schools (kindergarten to Grade 12) was $2,490m. Tennessee has 49 accredited colleges and universities, 18 2-year colleges and 28 vocational schools. The universities include the University of Tennessee, Knoxville (founded 1794), with 24,568 students in 1988–89; Vanderbilt University, Nashville (1873) with 9,021, Tennessee State University (1912) with 7,353, the University of Tennessee at Chattanooga (1886) with 7,526, Memphis State University (1912), 20,270 and Fisk University (1866) with 774.

Health. In 1986 the state had 146 hospitals with 27,274 beds. State facilities for the mentally retarded had 2,081 resident patients and mental hospitals had 1,560 in 1987.

Social Security. In 1987 Tennessee paid $3,832m. to retired workers and their survivors and to disabled workers. Total beneficiaries: 519,000 retired; 163,000 survivors and 105,000 disabled. 443,000 people received $811m. in Medicaid. Supplemental Security Income ($308m.) was paid to 131,900. 60,500 families (1986) received aid to dependent children ($104m.).

Further Reading

Tennessee Dept. of Finance and Administration, Annual Report, Annual
Dept. of Education Annual Report for Tennessee, Annual
Tennessee Blue Book. Secretary of State, Nashville
Tennessee Statistical Abstract, Center for Business and Economic Research, Univ. of Tennessee. Annual
Corlew, R. E., *Tennessee: A Short History.* Univ. Tennessee, 2nd ed., 1981
Davidson, D., *Tennessee: Vol. I, The Old River Frontier to Secession,* Univ. Tennessee, 1979
Dykeman, W., *Tennessee,* Rev. Ed., New York, 1984

State Library: State Library and Archives, Nashville. *Librarian:* Edwin Gleaves. *State Historian:* Wilma Dykeman.

TEXAS

HISTORY. In 1836 Texas declared its independence of Mexico, and after maintaining an independent existence, as the Republic of Texas, for 10 years, it was on

29 Dec. 1845 received as a state into the American Union. The state's first settlement dates from 1686.

AREA AND POPULATION. Texas is bounded north by Oklahoma, north-east by Arkansas, east by Louisiana, south-east by the Gulf of Mexico, south by Mexico and west by New Mexico. Area, 266,807 sq. miles (including 4,790 sq. miles of inland water). Census population, 1 April 1980 (provisional), 14,228,383, an increase of 27% since 1970. Estimate (1988), 16,841,000. Vital statistics for 1984: Births, 306,192 (19·2 per 1,000 population); deaths, 119,531 (7·5); infant deaths, 3,178 (10·4 per 1,000 live births); marriages, 207,631 (13); divorces, 98,074 (6·1).

Population for 5 census years was:

	White	*Negro*	*Indian*	*Asiatic*	*Total*	*Per sq. mile*
1910	3,204,848	690,049	702	943	3,896,542	14·8
1930	4,967,172	854,964	1,001	1,578	5,824,715	22·1
1960	8,374,831	1,187,125	5,750	9,848	9,579,677	36·5
			All others			
1970	9,717,128	1,399,005	80,597		11,196,730	42·7
1980	11,197,663	1,710,250	1,320,470		14,228,383	54·2

Of the population in 1980, 6,998,301 were male, 11,327,159 persons were urban. Those 20 years old and older numbered 9,357,309. A census report, 1980, showed, 2,985,643 persons of Spanish origin.

The largest cities, with census population in 1980, are:

Houston	1,595,138	Amarillo	149,230	Odessa	90,027
Dallas	904,078	Beaumont	118,102	Garland	138,857
San Antonio	785,882	Wichita Falls	94,201	Laredo	91,449
Fort Worth	385,164	Irving	109,943	San Angelo	73,240
El Paso	425,259	Waco	101,261	Galveston	61,902
Austin (capital)	345,496	Arlington	160,113	Midland	70,525
Corpus Christi	231,999	Abilene	98,315	Tyler	70,508
Lubbock	173,979	Pasadena	112,560	Port Arthur	61,195

Larger urbanized areas, 1980: Houston, 2,891,146; Dallas-Fort Worth, 2,964,342; San Antonio, 1,070,245.

CLIMATE. Dallas. Jan. 45°F (7·2°C), July 84°F (28·9°C). Annual rainfall 38" (945 mm). El Paso. Jan. 44°F (6·7°C), July 81°F (27·2°C). Annual rainfall 9" (221 mm). Galveston. Jan. 54°F (12·2°C), July 84°F (28·9°C). Annual rainfall 46" (1,159 mm). Houston. Jan. 52°F (11·1°C), July 83°F (28·3°C). Annual rainfall 48" (1,200 mm). *See* Central Plains, p. 1381.

CONSTITUTION AND GOVERNMENT. The present constitution dates from 1876; it has been amended 326 times. The Legislature consists of a Senate of 31 members elected for 4 years (half their number retire every 2 years), and a House of Representatives of 150 members elected for 2 years.

The Governor and Lieut.-Governor are elected for 4 years. Qualified electors are all citizens with the usual residential qualifications. Texas sends to Congress 2 senators and 27 representatives.

In the 1988 presidential election Bush polled 3,014,007 votes, Dukakis, 2,331,286.

The capital is Austin. The state has 254 counties.

Governor: Bill Clements (R.), 1987–91 ($93,432).

Lieut.-Governor: William P. Hobby (D.), 1987–91 ($7,200).

Secretary of State: George Bayoud (R.), ($69,094).

BUDGET. In the fiscal year ending 31 Aug. 1987 general revenues were $23,617m. ($10,266·2m. from taxes, $4,078·1m. federal aid); general expenditures (1981-82), $21,334m. ($8,743m. on education, $2,506m. on highways, $2,067m. on hospitals, $1,741m. on public welfare).

Net long-term debt, 31 Aug. 1985, was $4,009m.
Per capita personal income (1985) was $13,483.

ENERGY AND NATURAL RESOURCES

Minerals. Production, 1988: Crude petroleum, 728m. bbls, natural gas 4,500m. cubic ft.; other minerals include natural gasoline, butane and propane gases, helium, crude gypsum, granite and sandstone, salt and cement. Total value of mineral products in 1982, $45,388m., of which $43,834 was for fuels.

Agriculture. Texas is one of the most important agricultural states of the Union. In 1988 it had 156,000 farms covering 136m. acres; average farm was of 846 acres valued, land and buildings, at $591 per acre. Large-scale commercial farms, highly mechanized, dominate in Texas; farms of 1,000 acres or more in number far exceed that of any other state. But small-scale farming persists.

Soil erosion is serious in some parts. For some 97,297,000 acres drastic curative treatment has been indicated and for 51,164,000 acres, preventive treatment.

Production, 1985: Cotton, 3,945,000 bales (of 480 lb., value $981m.); maize (157m. bu., value $422m.), wheat (187·2m. bu., value $580m.), oats, barley, soybeans, peanuts, oranges, grapefruit, peaches, potatoes, sweet potatoes.

Cash income, 1988, from crops was $3,027m.; from livestock, $6,059m.

The state has a very great livestock industry, leading in the number of all cattle, 13·7m. on 1 Jan. 1989, and sheep, 1·9m.; it also had 355,000 milch cows, and 560,000 swine.

Forestry. There were (1988) 22,032,000 acres of forested land.

INDUSTRY. In 1988 manufacturing establishments employed 970,267 workers; trade employed 1,667,000; government, 1·1m.; services, 1·4m.; construction, 337,379; finance, insurance and real estate, 427,656; transport and public utilities, 372,391. Chemical industries along the Gulf Coast, such as the production of synthetic rubber and of primary magnesium (from sea-water), are increasingly important.

COMMUNICATIONS

Roads. In 1988 there were 300,199 miles of roads. Motor registration in 1988, 13·9m.

Railways. The railways (1988) had a total mileage of 13,707 miles, of which 12,938 miles were main lines.

Aviation. In 1988 there were 307 public and 1,308 private airports.

Shipping. The port of Houston, connected by the Houston Ship Channel (50 miles long) with the Gulf of Mexico, is the largest inland cotton market in the world. Cargo handled 1987, 112,546,187 tons.

JUSTICE, RELIGION, EDUCATION AND WELFARE

Justice. In Dec. 1988 the state prison held 39,221 men and women. Execution is by lethal injection; there were 300 between 1930 and 1968; between 1977 and 1986 there were 8.

Texas has adopted 11 laws governing the activities of trade unions. An Act of 1955 forbids the state's payment of unemployment compensation to workers engaged in certain types of strikes.

Religion. The largest religious bodies are Roman Catholics, Baptists, Methodists, Churches of Christ, Lutherans, Presbyterians and Episcopalians.

Education. School attendance is compulsory from 6 to 17 years of age.

In autumn 1988 public elementary and secondary schools had 3,057,147 enrolled pupils; in 1986 there were 175,500 classroom teachers whose salaries averaged $24,500. Total public school expenditure, 1987, $11,529m.

The largest institutions of higher education, with faculty numbers and student enrolment, 1988–89, were:

Founded	Institutions	Control	Faculty	Students
1845	Baylor University, Waco	Baptist	636	11,774
1852	St Mary's University, San Antonio	R.C.	209	3,932
1869	Trinity University, San Antonio	Presb.	255	2,573
1873	Texas Christian University, Fort Worth	Christian	519	6,725
1876	Texas A. and M. Univ., College Station	State	2,240	38,764
1876	Prairie View Agr. and Mech. Coll., Prairie View	State	297	5,812
1879	Sam Houston State University	State	365	12,359
1883	University of Texas System (every campus)	State	6,328	131,732
1890	University of North Texas, Denton	State	884	26,523
1891	Hardin-Simmons University, Abilene	Baptist	124	1,826
1889	East Texas State University, Commerce	State	363	7,811
1899	South West Texas State University, San Marcos	State	833	20,776
1903	Texas Woman's University, Denton	State	520	9,408
1906	Abilene Christian University, Abilene	Church of Christ	275	4,186
1911	Southern Methodist University, Dallas	Methodist	650	8,929
1923	Stephen F. Austin State University	State	517	12,783
1923	Texas Technical University, Lubbock	State	1,444	25,009
1925	Texas Arts and Industries University, Kingsville	State	234	5,872
1934	University of Houston, Houston	State	2,100	32,280
1947	Texas Southern University, Houston	State	544	9,214
1951	Lamar University, Beaumont	State	545	12,041

Health. In 1988, the state had 553 hospitals (80,914 beds) listed by the American Hospital Association; on 1 Jan. 1987 mental hospitals had 3,863 resident patients and state institutions for the mentally retarded, 8,134 resident patients.

Social Security. Aid is from state and federal sources. Old-age assistance (SSI) was being granted in Dec. 1985 to 123,400 persons, who received an average of $133 per month; aid was given to 127,100 disabled ($217) and 398,900 dependent children (average payment per family, $142 per month).

Further Reading

Texas Almanac. Dallas. Biennial
Texas Factbook. Univ. of Texas, 1983
Benton, W. E., *Texas, its Government and Politics*. 4th ed., Englewood Cliffs, 1977
Cruz, G. R. and Irby, J. A. (eds.) *Texas Bibliography*. Austin, 1982
Fehrenbach, T. R., *Lone Star: A History of Texas and the Texans*. London, 1986
Jordan, T. G. and Bean, J. L., Jr., *Texas*. Boulder, 1983
MacCorkle, S. A. and Smith, D., *Texas Government*. 7th ed. New York, 1974
Richardson, R. N., *Texas, the Lone Star State*. 3rd ed. New York, 1970

Legislative Reference Library: Box 12488, Capitol Station, Austin, Texas 78811. *Director:* Sally Reynolds.

UTAH

HISTORY. Utah, which had been acquired by the US during the Mexican war, was settled by Mormons in 1847, and organized as a Territory on 9 Sept. 1850. It was admitted as a state into the Union on 4 Jan. 1896 with boundaries as at present.

AREA AND POPULATION. Utah is bounded north by Idaho and Wyoming, east by Colorado, south by Arizona and west by Nevada. Area, 84,899 sq. miles, of which 2,826 sq. miles are water. The federal government (1967) owned 35,397,274 acres or 67·1% of the area of the state. The area of unappropriated and unreserved lands was 23,268,250 acres in 1974. The Bureau of Indian Affairs in 1974 administered 3,035,190 acres, all of which were allotted to Indian tribes.

Census population, 1 April 1980, 1,461,037, an increase of 38% since 1970. Estimate (1985), 1,645,000. Births in 1984 were 39,677 (24 per 1,000 population);

deaths, 9,295 (5·6); infant deaths, 407 (10·3 per 1,000 live births); marriages, 17,579 (10·6); divorces, 8,134 (4·9).

Population at 5 federal censuses was:

	White	*Negro*	*Indian*	*Asiatic*	*Total*	*Per sq. mile*
1910	366,583	1,144	3,123	2,501	373,851	4·5
1930	499,967	1,108	2,869	3,903	507,847	6·2
1960	873,828	4,148	6,961	5,207	890,627	10·8
1970	1,031,926	6,617	11,273	6,230	1,059,273	12·9
1980	1,382,550	9,225	19,256	15,076	1,461,037	17·7

Of the total in 1980, 724,501 were male, 1,232,908 persons were urban; 860,304 were 20 years of age or older.

The largest cities are Salt Lake City (capital), with a population (census, 1980) of 162,960; Provo, 74,007; Ogden, 64,444; Bountiful, 32,877; Orem, 52,399; Sandy City, 51,022 and Logan, 26,844.

CLIMATE. Salt Lake City. Jan. 29°F (–1·7°C), July 77°F (25°C). Annual rainfall 16" (401 mm). *See* Mountain States, p. 1381.

CONSTITUTION AND GOVERNMENT. Utah adopted its present constitution in 1896 (now with 61 amendments). It sends to Congress 2 senators and 3 representatives.

The Legislature consists of a Senate (in part renewed every 2 years) of 30 members, elected for 4 years, and of a House of Representatives of 75 members elected for 2 years. The Governor is elected for 4 years. The constitution provides for the initiative and referendum. Electors are all citizens, who, not being insane or criminal, have the usual residential qualifications.

The capital is Salt Lake City. There are 29 counties in the state.

In the 1988 presidential election Bush polled 426,858 votes, Dukakis, 206,853.

Governor: Norman Bangerter (R.), 1989–93 ($52,000).

Lieut.-Governor: W. Val Oveson (R.), 1989–93 ($35,500).

BUDGET. For the year ending 30 June 1982 general revenue was $2,490m. ($1,332m. from taxes, $612m. from federal aid) while general expenditures were $2,490m. ($1,104m. on education, $279m. on highways, $234m. on public welfare).

The net long-term debt on 30 June 1982 was about $2,171m.

Per capita personal income (1985) was $10,493.

ENERGY AND NATURAL RESOURCES

Minerals The principal minerals are: Copper, gold, petroleum, lead, silver and zinc. The state also has natural gas, clays, tungsten, molybdenum, uranium and phosphate rock.

Agriculture. In 1985 Utah had 14,000 farms covering 12m. acres, of which about 2m. acres were crop land and about 300,000 acres pasture. About 1m. acres had irrigation; the average farm was of 857 acres.

Of the total surface area, 9% is severely eroded and only 9·4% is free from erosion; the balance is moderately eroded.

Cash income, 1985, from crops, $138m. and from livestock, $409m. The principal crops are: Barley, wheat (spring and winter), oats, potatoes, hay (alfalfa, sweet clover and lespedeza), maize. In 1985 there were 515,000 sheep; 80,000 milch cows; 800,000 all cattle; 28,000 swine.

Forestry. Area of national forests, 1981, was 9,129,000 acres, of which 8·05m. acres were under forest service administration.

INDUSTRY. In 1985 manufacturing establishments had 94,000 workers. Leading manufactures by value added are primary metals, ordinances and transport, food, fabricated metals and machinery, petroleum products. Service industries employed 132,000; trade, 148,000; government, 138,000.

COMMUNICATIONS

Roads. The state has about 50,000 miles of highway. In 1985 there were 1,103,000 motor vehicles registered.

Railways. On 1 July 1974 the state had 1,734 miles of railways.

Aviation. In 1981 there were 57 public and 45 private airports.

JUSTICE, RELIGION, EDUCATION AND WELFARE

Justice. The number of inmates of the state prison in Dec. 1985 was 1,570. Since 1930 total executions have been 14 (13 by shooting, 1 by hanging—the condemned man has choice), all whites, and all for murder.

Religion. Latter-day Saints (Mormons) form about 73% of the church membership of the state; their church is a substantial property-owner. The Roman Catholic church and most Protestant denominations are represented.

Education. School attendance is compulsory for children from 6 to 18 years of age. There are 40 school districts. Teachers' salaries, 1985, averaged $21,500. There were (autumn 1983) 379,000 pupils in public elementary and secondary schools, and (1986) 16,700 classroom teachers, average salary, $22,550; estimated public school expenditure was $1,092m. or $664 per capita.

The University of Utah (1850) (24,770 students in 1985–86) is in Salt Lake City; the Utah State University (1890) (11,804) is in Logan. The Mormon Church maintains the Brigham Young University at Provo (1875) with 26,894 students. Other colleges include: Westminster College, Salt Lake City (1,302); Weber State College, Ogden (11,117); Southern Utah State College, Cedar City (2,587); College of Eastern Utah, Price (1,132); Snow College, Ephraim (1,328); Dixie College, St George (2,234).

Health. In 1983, the state had 44 hospitals (5,400 beds) listed by the Utah Department of Social Services. Mental hospitals had 317 resident patients on 1 Jan. 1980; state facilities for the mentally retarded had 763.

Social Security. In Dec. 1985 the state department of public welfare provided assistance to 37,800 persons receiving aid to dependent children at an average $322 per family per month; aid to the aged, the blind and disabled is provided from federal funds; there were 1,900 aged recipients in 1985 (average $150 per month), 6,600 disabled ($224).

Further Reading

Compiled Digest of Administrative Reports. Secretary of State, Salt Lake City. Annual
Statistical Abstract of Government in Utah. Utah Foundation, Salt Lake City. Annual
Utah Agricultural Statistics. Dept. of Agriculture, Salt Lake City. Annual
Utah: Facts. Bureau of Economic and Business Research, Univ. of Utah, 1975
Arrington, L., *Great Basin Kingdom: An Economic History of the Latter-Day Saints, 1830–1900*. Cambridge, Mass., 1958
Petersen, C. S., *Utah, a History*. New York, 1977

VERMONT

HISTORY. Vermont, first settled in 1724, was admitted into the Union as the fourteenth state on 4 March 1791. The first constitution was adopted by convention at Windsor, 2 July 1777, and established an independent state government.

AREA AND POPULATION. Vermont is bounded north by Canada, east by New Hampshire, south by Massachusetts and west by New York. Area, 9,614 sq. miles, of which 341 sq. miles are inland water. Census population, 1 April 1980, 511,456, an increase of 15% since 1970. Estimate (1986) 541,000. Births, 1986, were 8,097 (15 per 1,000 population); deaths, 4,760 (8·8); infant deaths, 83 (10·3 per 1,000 live births); marriages, 5,698 (10·5); divorces, 2,410 (4·5).

Population at 5 census years was:

	White	*Negro*	*Indian*	*Asiatic*	*Total*	*Per sq. mile*
1910	354,298	1,621	26	11	355,956	39·0
1930	358,966	568	36	41	359,611	38·8
1960	389,092	519	57	172	389,881	42·0
1970	442,553	761	229	787	444,732	48·0
1980	506,736	1,135	984	1,355	511,456	55·1

Of the population in 1980, 249,080 were male, 172,735 persons were urban; those 20 years of age or older numbered 343,666. The largest cities are Burlington, with a population in 1980 of 37,712; Rutland, 18,436; Barre, 9,824.

CLIMATE. Burlington. Jan. 17°F (–8·3°C), July 70°F (21·1°C). Annual rainfall 33" (820 mm). *See* New England, p. 1382.

CONSTITUTION AND GOVERNMENT. The constitution was adopted in 1793 and has since been amended. Amendments are proposed by two-thirds vote of the Senate every 4 years, and must be accepted by two sessions of the legislature; they are then submitted to popular vote. The state Legislature, consisting of a Senate of 30 members and a House of Representatives of 150 members (both elected for 2 years), meets in Jan. in odd-numbered years. The Governor and Lieut.-Governor are elected for 2 years. Electors are all citizens who possess certain residential qualifications and have taken the freeman's oath set forth in the constitution.

The state is divided into 14 counties; there are 251 towns and cities and other minor civil divisions. The state sends to Congress 2 senators and 1 representative, who are elected by the voters of the entire state.

In the 1988 presidential election Bush polled 123,166 votes, Dukakis, 116,419.

The capital is Montpelier (8,241, census of 1980).

Governor: Madeleine Kunin (D.), 1989–91 ($50,003).
Lieut.-Governor: Howard Dean (D.) ($22,006).
Secretary of State: James Douglas (R.) ($29,993).

BUDGET. The total revenue for the year ending 30 June 1986 was $866m.; total disbursements, $865·6m.

Total net long-term debt, 30 June 1986, was $254·7.

Per capita personal income (1988) was $15,302.

NATURAL RESOURCES

Minerals. Stone, chiefly granite, marble and slate, is the leading mineral produced in Vermont, contributing about 60% of the total value of mineral products. Other products include asbestos, talc, peat, sand and gravel. Total value of mineral products, 1984, $45m.

Agriculture. Agriculture is the most important industry. In 1987 the state had 7,000 farms covering 1·6m. acres; the average farm was of 229 acres. Cash income, 1985, from livestock and products, $352m.; from crops, $32m. The dairy farms produce about 2,397m. lb. of milk annually. The chief agricultural crops are hay, apples and silage. In 1986 Vermont had 350,000 cattle, 13,000 sheep and lambs, 6,800 (1985) swine, 300,000 poultry.

Forestry. In 1982 the harvest was 82m. bd ft hardwood and 93m. bd ft softwood saw-logs, and 267,000 cords of pulpwood and boltwood. About 600,000 cords was cut for firewood.

The state is nearly 80% forest, with 12% in public ownership. National forests area (1983), 285,000 acres. State-owned forests, parks, fish and game areas, 250,000 acres; municipally-owned, 38,500 acres.

INDUSTRY. In 1986 service industries employed 65,000; manufacturing, 54,000; trade, 52,000; government, 35,000; construction, 20,000.

COMMUNICATIONS

Roads. The state had 14,089 miles of roads in 1989, including 13,071 miles of rural roads. Motor vehicle registrations, 1985, 387,000.

Railways. There were, in 1986, 793 miles of railway, 300 of which was leased by the state to private operators.

Aviation. There were 18 airports in 1987, of which 11 were state operated, 1 municipally owned and 6 private. Some are only open in summer.

JUSTICE, RELIGION, EDUCATION AND WELFARE

Justice. In financial year 1989 prisons and centres had 761 (with another 110 on furlough) inmates; 700 of these were serving more than one year.

Religion. The principal denominations are Roman Catholic, United Church of Christ, United Methodist, Protestant Episcopal, Baptist and Unitarian–Universalist.

Education. School attendance during the full school term is compulsory for children from 7 to 16 years of age, unless they have completed the 10th grade or undergo approved home instruction. In 1987–88 the public schools had 92,755 pupils. Full-time teachers for public elementary schools (1986) numbered 2,900, secondary schools 3,500. Teachers' salaries for 1986 averaged $19,900 (elementary) and $20,700 (secondary). Total expenditure on public schools, 1986, $314m.

In autumn 1985 there were 31,416 students in higher education. The University of Vermont (1791) had 11,096 students in 1986–87; Norwich University (1834, founded as the American Literary, Scientific and Military Academy in 1819), had 2,425; St Michael's College (1904), 2,130; there are 5 state colleges.

Health. In Sept. 1988 the state had 17 general hospitals (2,383 beds).

Social Security. Old-age assistance (SSI) was being granted in 1985 to 3,000 persons, drawing an average of $139 per month; aid to dependent children was being granted to 21,900 persons, drawing an average of $400 per family per month; and aid to the permanently and totally disabled was being granted to 6,200 persons, drawing an average of $260.

Further Reading

Legislative Directory. Secretary of State, Montpelier. Biennial
Vermont Annual Financial Report. Auditor of Accounts, Montpelier. Annual
Vermont Facts and Figures. Office of Statistical Co-ordination, Montpelier
Vermont Year-Book, formerly *Walton's Register*. Chester. Annual
Bassett T. and Seymour D. (eds.) *Vermont: A Bibliography of its History*, Boston, 1981
Delorme, D. (ed.) *Vermont Atlas and Gazetteer*, Rev. ed., Freeport, 1983
Morrissey, C. T., *Vermont*, New York, 1981

State Library: Vermont Dept.of Libraries, Montpelier. *State Librarian:* Patricia Klinck.

VIRGINIA

HISTORY. The first English Charter for settlements in America was that granted by James I in 1606 for the planting of colonies in Virginia. The state was one of the 13 original states in the Union. Virginia lost just over one-third of its area when West Virginia was admitted into the Union (1863).

AREA AND POPULATION. Virginia is bounded north-west by West Virginia, north-east by Maryland, east by the Atlantic, south by North Carolina and Tennessee and west by Kentucky. Area, 40,767 sq. miles including 1,063 sq. miles of inland water. Census population, 1 April 1980, 5,346,818, an increase of 695,370 or 14·9% since 1970. Estimate 1988 5,996,000. In 1988 there were 87,002 births (15·1 per 1,000 population); 46,015 deaths (7·9); (1987) 850 infant deaths (11·5 per 1,000 live births); 67,073 marriages and 25,568 divorces.

Population for 5 federal census years was:

	White	Negro	Indian	Asiatic	Total	Per sq. mile
1910	1,389,809	671,096	539	168	2,061,612	51·2
1930	1,770,441	650,165	779	466	2,421,851	60·7
1960	3,142,443	816,258	2,155	4,725	3,966,949	99·3
			All others			
1970	3,761,514	861,368	25,612		4,648,494	116·9
1980	4,230,000	1,008,311	108,517		5,346,818	134·7

Of the total population in 1980, 49% were male, 66% were urban and 59% were 21 years of age or older.

The population (census of 1980) of the principal cities was: Norfolk, 266,979; Virginia Beach, 262,199; Richmond, 219,214; Newport News, 144,903; Hampton, 122,617; Chesapeake, 114,226; Portsmouth, 104,577; Alexandria, 103,219; Roanoke, 100,427; Lynchburg, 66,743.

CLIMATE. Average temperatures in Jan. are 41°F in the Tidewater coastal area and 32°F in the Blue Ridge mountains; July averages, 78°F and 68°F respectively. Precipitation averages 36" in the Shenandoah valley and 44" in the south. Snowfall is 5-10" in the Tidewater and 25-30" in the western mountains. Norfolk. Jan. 41°F (5°C), July 79°F (26·1°C). Annual rainfall 46" (1,145 mm). *See* Atlantic Coast, p. 1382.

CONSTITUTION AND GOVERNMENT. The present constitution dates from 1971.

The General Assembly consists of a Senate of 40 members, elected for 4 years, and a House of Delegates of 100 members, elected for 2 years. The Governor and Lieut.-Governor are elected for 4 years. Qualified as electors are (with few exceptions) all citizens 18 years of age, fulfilling certain residential qualifications, who have registered. The state sends to Congress 2 senators and 10 representatives.

In the 1988 presidential election Bush polled 1,305,131 votes, Dukakis, 860,767.

The state capital is Richmond; the state contains 95 counties and 41 independent cities.

Governor: Gerald L. Baliles (D.), 1986–90 ($85,000).
Lieut.-Governor: L. Douglas Wilder (D.) $28,000.
Secretary of the Commonwealth: Sandra D. Bowen (D.) ($45,959).

BUDGET. General revenue for the year ending 30 June 1986 was $13,325m. (taxation, $8,125m., and federal aid, $2,275m.); general expenditures, $12,803m. ($5,102m. for education, $1,354m. for transport and $1,010m. for public welfare).

Total net long-term debt, 30 June 1986, amounted to $10,153m.

Per capita personal income (1987) was $16,517.

ENERGY AND NATURAL RESOURCES

Minerals. Coal is the most important mineral, with output (1984) of 35,500,000 short tons. Lead and zinc ores, stone, sand and gravel, lime and titanium ore are also produced. Total mineral output was $382m. in 1986.

Agriculture. In 1987 there were 50,000 farms with an area of 10m. acres; average farm had 192 acres and was valued at $10,667,000.

Income, 1986, from crops, $996m., and from livestock and livestock products, $1,127m. The chief crops are corn, hay, peanuts and tobacco.

Animals on farms on 1 Jan. 1987 included 150,000 milch cows, 1·86m. all cattle, 168,000 sheep and 360,000 swine (Dec. 1986).

Forestry. National forests, 1986, covered 1,637,000 acres.

INDUSTRY. The manufacture of cigars and cigarettes and of rayon and allied products and the building of ships lead in value of products.

TOURISM. Tourists spend about $4,100m. a year in Virginia, attracted mainly by the state's outstanding scenery, coastline and historical interest.

COMMUNICATIONS

Roads. The state highways system, 1985, had 65,700 miles of highways, of which 8,958 miles were primary roads. Motor registrations, 1986, 4·5m.

Railways. In 1985 there were 3,693 miles of railways.

Aviation. There were, in 1985, 81 airports, of which 58 were publicly owned.

JUSTICE, RELIGION, EDUCATION AND WELFARE

Justice. Executions (by electrocution) since 1940 totalled 69. Prison population, 31 Dec. 1987, 13,321 in federal and state prisons.

Religion. The principal churches are the Baptist, Methodist, Protestant-Episcopal, Roman Catholic and Presbyterian.

Education. Elementary and secondary instruction is free, and for ages 6–17 attendance is compulsory. No child under 12 may be employed in any mining or manufacturing work.

In 1985 the 135 school districts had, in primary schools, 665,000 pupils and 34,200 teachers and in public high schools, 303,000 pupils and 25,300 teachers. Teachers' salaries (1987) averaged $25,500. Total expenditure on education, 1987, was $3,667m. The more important institutions for higher education (1986) were:

Founded	*Name and place of college*	*Staff*	*Students*
1693	College of William and Mary, Williamsburg (State)	526	6,616
1749	Washington and Lee University, Lexington	194	1,804
1776	Hampden-Sydney College, Hampden-Sydney (Pres.)	74	825
1819	University of Virginia, Charlottesville (State)	1,772	17,149
1832	Randolph-Macon College, Ashland (Methodist)	102	1,013
1832	University of Richmond, Richmond (Baptist)	349	4,705
1838	Virginia Commonwealth University, Richmond	1,885	19,641
1839	Virginia Military Institute Lexington (State)	100	1,350
1865	Virginia Union University, Richmond	98	1,311
1868	Hampton University	297	4,483
1872	Virginia Polytechnic Institute and State University	2,209	22,345
1882	Virginia State University, Petersburg	263	3,583
1908	James Madison University, Harrisonburg	600	9,757
1910	Radford University (State)	365	7,500
1930	Old Dominion University, Norfolk	713	15,463
1956	George Mason University (State)	715	17,652

Health. In 1986 the state had 137 hospitals (31,005 beds) listed by the American Hospital Association.

Social Security. In 1938 Virginia established a system of old-age assistance under the Federal Security Act; in March 1986 persons in 778,000 cases were drawing an average grant of $246; aid to permanently and totally disabled, 92,000 cases, average grant $918.96; aid to dependent children, 154,000 persons, average grant $85.77; general relief, 6,642 persons, average grant $146.62.

Further Reading

Virginia Facts and Figures. Virginia Division of Industrial Development, Richmond. Annual
Dabney, V., *Virginia, the New Dominion.* 1971
Friddell, G., *The Virginia Way.* Burda, 1973
Gottmann, J., *Virginia in our Century.* Charlottesville, 1969
Morton, R. L., *Colonial Virginia.* 2 vols. Univ. Press of Virginia, 1960
Rouse, P. *Virginia: a Pictorial History.* Scribner, 1975
Rubin, L. D. Jr., *Virginia: a Bicentennial History.* Norris, 1977

State Library: Virginia State Library, Richmond 23219. *State Librarian:* Ella Gaines Yates.

WASHINGTON

HISTORY. Washington, formerly part of Oregon, was created a Territory in 1853, and was admitted into the Union as a state on 11 Nov. 1889. Its settlement dates from 1811.

AREA AND POPULATION. Washington is bounded north by Canada, east by Idaho, south by Oregon with the Columbia River forming most of the boundary, and west by the Pacific. Area, 68,192 sq. miles, of which 1,622 sq. miles are inland water. Lands owned by the federal government, 1977, were 12·4m. acres or 29·1% of the total area. Census population, 1 April 1980, 4,132,156, an increase of 718,906 or 21·1% since 1970. Estimated population (1987), 4,481,100. Births, 1986 were 69,431 (15·7 per 1,000 population); deaths, 34,166 (7·8); infant deaths (1985), 778 (10·2 per 1,000 live births); marriages, 43,255 (9·8); divorces and annulments, 26,405 (6·0).

Population in 5 federal census years was:

	White	*Negro*	*Indian*	*Asiatic*	*Total*	*Per sq. mile*
1910	1,109,111	6,058	10,997	15,824	1,141,990	17·1
1930	1,521,661	6,840	11,253	23,642	1,563,396	23·3
1960	2,751,675	48,738	21,076	31,725	2,853,214	42·8
1970	2,351,055	71,308	33,386	53,420	3,409,169	51·2
1980	3,779,170	105,574	60,804	186,608	4,132,156	62·1

Of the total population in 1980, 2,052,307 were male, 3,037,014 persons were urban; 2,759,552 were 20 years of age or older.

There are 24 Indian reservations, the largest being held by the Yakima tribe. Indian reservations in Sept. 1979 covered 2,496,423 acres, of which 1,996,018 acres were tribal lands and 497,218 acres were held by individuals. Total Indian population, 1980, 60,804.

Leading cities are Seattle, with a population in 1980 (and 1987 estimate) of 491,897 (491,300); Spokane, 170,993 (172,100); Tacoma, 158,101 (158,900); Bellevue, 73,711 (82,070). Others : Yakima, 49,826; Everett, 54,413; Vancouver, 42,834; Bellingham, 45,794; Bremerton, 36,208; Richland, 33,578; Longview, 31,052; Renton, 30,612; Edmonds, 27,526; Walla Walla, 25,618. Urbanized areas (1980 census): Seattle–Everett, 1,600,944; Tacoma, 482,692; Spokane, 341,058.

CLIMATE. Seattle. Jan. 40°F (4·4°C), July 63°F (17·2°C). Annual rainfall 34" (848 mm). Spokane. Jan. 27°F (–2·8°C), July 70°F (21·1°C). Annual rainfall 14" (350 mm). *See* Pacific Coast, p. 1381.

CONSTITUTION AND GOVERNMENT. The constitution, adopted in 1889, has had 63 amendments. The Legislature consists of a Senate of 49 members elected for 4 years, half their number retiring every 2 years, and a House of Representatives of 98 members, elected for 2 years. The Governor and Lieut.-Governor are elected for 4 years. The state sends 2 senators and 7 representatives to Congress.

Qualified as voters are (with some exceptions) all citizens 18 years of age, having the usual residential qualifications.

In the 1988 presidential election Dukakis polled 844,544 votes, Bush, 800,182.

The capital is Olympia (population, 1980 census, 27,447). The state contains 39 counties.

Governor: Booth Gardner (D.), 1989–93 ($63,000).
Lieut.-Governor: Joel Pritchard (R.), 1989–93 ($28,600).
Secretary of State: Ralph Munro (R.), 1989–93 ($31,000).

BUDGET. For the 2-year budget period 1987–89 the state's total revenue is (projected) $19,923·6m.; general expenditure is (projected) $20,412·4m. (education, $8,497·5m.; transport, $2,072·8m., and human resources, $5,771·6m.).

Total outstanding debt in 1987 was $3,073m.

Per capita personal income (1986) was $14,625.

ENERGY AND NATURAL RESOURCES

Electricity. With about 20% of potential water-power resources of US, the state has ample developed and potential hydro-electricity.

Minerals. Mining and quarrying are not as important as forestry, agriculture or manufacturing. Uranium is mined but figures are not disclosed; other minerals include sand and gravel, stone, coal and clays.

Agriculture. Agriculture is constantly growing in value because of more intensive and diversified farming and because of the 1m.-acre Columbia Basin Irrigation Project.

In 1987 there were 37,000 farms with an acreage of 15·8m.; average farm was of 427 acres. Average value per acre (1985), $923.

Cash return from farm marketing, 1985, was $2,797m. (from crops, $1,865m.; from livestock and dairy products, $932m.). Wheat, cattle and calves, milk and apples are important.

On 1 Jan. 1985 animals on farms included 211,000 milch cows, 1·47m. all cattle, 53,000 sheep and 45,000 swine.

Forestry. Forests cover about 23m. acres, of which 9m. acres are national forest. In 1985, timber harvested from 486,506 acres cut, was 5,874·2m. bd ft. Acres planted or seeded, 1986, 171,641, not including natural re-seeding. Production of wood residues, 1986, included 695,927 tons of pulp and board.

Fisheries. Salmon and halibut are important; total fish catch, 1985, 210·3m. lb.; value, $108m.

INDUSTRY. In 1986 manufacturing employed 304,200 workers, of whom 85,000 were in aerospace and 58,700 in the forest products industry.

Abundance of electric power has made Washington the leading producer of primary aluminium; employment, 1986, 7,600; exported aluminium, $199·1m. worth. Aircraft exported, $5,641·9m.

In 1986 trade employed 434,700, service industries, 393,000; government, 349,300.

COMMUNICATIONS

Roads. The state (1986) had 749 miles of interstate highway; 9,400 miles of federal-aid roads; 41,725 miles of county-maintained roads; 11,000 miles of city streets. Total including other categories, 80,623. Motor vehicle registrations (1986), 4,324,313.

Railways. The railways had, in 1980, 6,057 miles.

Aviation. There were in 1979, 365 airports, 120 publicly owned. In 1986 Seattle–Tacoma Airport traffic was 13·6m. passengers, 65,975 tons of mail and 157,027 tons of freight and express.

JUSTICE, RELIGION, EDUCATION AND WELFARE

Justice. The adult population in state prisons in Dec. 1985 was 6,909. Since 1963 there have been no executions; total 1930–63 (by hanging) was 47, including 40 whites, 5 Negroes and 2 other races, all for murder, except 1 white for kidnapping.

Religion. Chief religious bodies are the Roman Catholic, United Methodist, Lutheran, Presbyterian, Latter-day Saints and Episcopalian.

Education. Education is given free to all children between the ages of 5 and 21 years, and is compulsory for children from 8 to 15 years of age. In autumn 1986 there were 761,760 pupils in public elementary and secondary schools. In 1986 there were 36,200 classroom teachers, average salary, $26,100. The total expenditure on public elementary and secondary schools for the school year 1986 was $3,124m. or $708 per capita.

The University of Washington, founded 1861, at Seattle, had, autumn, 1986,

33,226 students, and Washington State University at Pullman, founded 1890, for science and agriculture, had 15,888 students. Twenty-seven community colleges had (1986) a total enrolment of 134,522 state-funded students.

Health. In 1981 the 2 state hospitals for mental illness had a daily average of 1,204 patients; schools for handicapped children, 1,999 residents in Sept. 1981.

In 1983 the state had 122 general hospitals (16,200 beds); in 1981, 3 licensed psychiatric hospitals (181 beds) and 3 alcoholism hospitals (174 beds).

Social Security. Old-age assistance is provided for persons 65 years of age or older without adequate resources (and not in need of continuing home care) who are residents of the state. In Dec. 1985, 12,100 people were drawing an average of $157 per month; aid to 189,000 children in 67,900 families averaged $419 per family monthly; to 35,000 totally disabled, $266 monthly.

Further Reading

State of Washington Data Book. Office of Financial Management, Olympia, 1987
Swanson, T., *Political Life in Washington.* Pullman, 1985
Yates, R. and C., *Washington State Yearbook 1988.* Evgene, Oregon, 1988

State Library: Washington State Library, Olympia. *State Librarian:* Nancy Zussy.

WEST VIRGINIA

HISTORY. In 1862, after the state of Virginia had seceded from the Union, the electors of the western portion ratified an ordinance providing for the formation of a new state, which was admitted into the Union by presidential proclamation on 20 June 1863, under the name of West Virginia. Its constitution was adopted by the voters almost unanimously on 26 March 1863.

AREA AND POPULATION. West Virginia is bounded north by Pennsylvania and Maryland, east and south by Virginia, south-west by the Sandy River (forming the boundary with Kentucky) and west by the Ohio River (forming the boundary with Ohio). Area, 24,282 sq. miles, of which 102 sq. miles are water. Census population, 1 April 1980, 1,949,644, an increase of 11·8% since 1970. Estimate (1986), 1,919,000. Births, 1987, 22,280 (11·6 per 1,000 population); deaths, 19,669 (8·7); infant deaths, 217 (9·7 per 1,000 live births); marriages, 13,200 (6·8); divorces, 9,043 (4·8).

Population in 5 federal census years was:

	White	*Negro*	*Indian*	*Asiatic*	*Total*	*Per sq. mile*
1910	1,156,817	64,173	36	93	1,221,119	50·8
1940	1,614,191	114,893	18	103	1,729,205	71·8
1960	1,770,133	89,378	181	419	1,860,421	77·3
1970	1,673,480	67,342	751	1,463	1,744,237	71·8
1980	1,874,751	65,051	1,610	5,194	1,949,644	80·3

Of the total population in 1980, 945,408 were male, 705,319 were urban; those 20 years of age or older numbered 1,319,566.

The 1980 census (and 1985 estimate) population of the principal cities was: Huntington, 63,684 (61,086); Charleston, 63,968 (59,371). Others: Wheeling, 43,070 (42,082); Parkersburg, 39,967 (39,399); Morgantown, 27,605 (27,786); Weirton, 24,736 (23,878); Fairmont, 23,863 (22,822); Clarksburg, 22,371 (21,379).

CLIMATE. Charleston. Jan. 34°F (1·1°C), July 76°F (24·4°C). Annual rainfall 40" (1,010 mm). *See* Appalachian Mountains, p. 1382.

CONSTITUTION AND GOVERNMENT. The present constitution was adopted in 1872; it has had 62 amendments.

The Legislature consists of the Senate of 34 members elected for a term of 4 years, one-half being elected biennially, and the House of Delegates of 100 members, elected biennially. The Governor is elected for 4 years and may succeed himself once. Voters are all citizens (with the usual exceptions) 18 years of age and meeting certain residential requirements. The state sends to Congress 2 senators and 4 representatives.

In the 1988 presidential election Dukakis polled 339,112 votes, Bush, 307,824.

The state capital is Charleston. There are 55 counties.

Governor: Gaston Caperton (D.), 1989–92 ($72,000).
Secretary of State: Ken Hechler (D.), ($43,200).

FINANCE. General revenues for the year ending 30 June 1987 were $3,225m. ($1,531m. from taxes, $877m. from federal funds); general expenditures were $3,355m. (education, $1,348m.; highways, $598m.; public welfare, $749m.).

Debts outstanding were $969·5m. on 30 June 1987.

Estimated *per capita* personal income (1988) was $10,959.

ENERGY AND NATURAL RESOURCES

Minerals. 38% of the state is underlain with mineable coal; 130·8m. short tons of coal were produced in 1986. Petroleum output, 3m. bbls; natural gas production was 135,431m. cu. ft. Salt, sand and gravel, sandstone and limestone are also produced. The total value of mineral output in 1986 was $4,837m.

Agriculture. In 1988 the state had 20,500 farms with an area of 3·6m. acres; average size of farm was 176 acres and valued at $542 per acre. Livestock farming predominates.

Cash income, 1987, from crops was $57·5m.; from government payments, $10·6m., and from livestock and products, $168·9m. Main crops harvested, 1987: Hay (1m. tons); all corn (3·6m. bu.); tobacco (2·5m. lb.). Area of main crops, 1987: hay, 630,000 acres; corn, 85,000 acres. Apples (185m. lb. in 1987) and peaches (17m. lb.) are important fruit crops. Livestock on farms, 1 Jan. 1988, included 490,000 cattle, of which 31,000 were milch cows; sheep, 91,000; hogs, 37,000; chickens, 721,000 excluding broilers. Production, 1987, included 32·8m. broilers, 108m. eggs; 2·4m. turkeys.

Forestry. State forests, 1987, covered 79,365 acres; national forests, 1,673,000 gross acres; 75% of the state is woodland.

INDUSTRY. In 1987, 1,645 manufactories had 86,088 production workers who earned $2,163m. Leading manufactures are primary and fabricated metals, glass, chemicals, wood products, textiles and apparel, and machinery.

In 1987 non-agricultural employment was 597,800 of whom 139,046 were in trade, 121,130 in government and 106,540 in service industries.

The first commercial coal liquefaction plant in the USA is being built near Morgantown with the co-operation of the governments of Federal Republic of Germany and Japan and the Gulf Oil Co.

COMMUNICATIONS

Roads. Total highways on 30 June 1987, 37,786 miles (state maintained, 33,882 miles; inter-state, 393 miles; national parks and other roads, 3,904 miles). Registered motor vehicles, financial year ending 30 June 1987, numbered 1,401,424.

Railways. In 1987 the state had 2,895 miles of railway, all operated by diesel or electric trains.

Aviation. There were 27 licensed airports in 1987.

Post and Broadcasting. There are 64 AM radio stations, 70 FM radio stations. Television stations number 9 VHF and 5 UHF.

Newspapers. Daily newspapers number 25; weekly newspapers 62.

JUSTICE, RELIGION, EDUCATION AND WELFARE

Justice. The state court system consists of a Supreme Court and 31 circuit courts. The Supreme Court of Appeals, exercising original and appellate jurisdiction, has 5 members elected by the people for 12-year terms. Each circuit court has from 1 to 7 judges (as determined by the Legislature on the basis of population and case-load) chosen by the voters within each circuit for 8-year terms.

Effective on 1 July 1967, the West Virginia Human Rights Act prohibits discrimination in employment and places of public accommodations based on race, religion, colour, national origin or ancestry.

There are 5 penal and correctional institutions which had, on 30 June 1987, 1,558 inmates. In 1965 the state legislature abolished capital punishment.

Religion. Chief denominations in 1987 were United Methodist (159,000 members, estimate), Baptists (116,000) and Roman Catholics (109,000).

Education. Public school education is free for all from 5 to 21 years of age, and school attendance is compulsory for all between the ages of 7 and 16 (school term, 200 days—180–185 days of actual teaching). The public schools are non-sectarian. In autumn 1987 public elementary and secondary schools had 344,604 pupils and 22,702 classroom teachers. Average salary of teachers in 1987, $21,736. Total 1986 expenditures for public schools, $1,196m.

Leading institutions of higher education in 1987:

Founded		*Full-time students*
1837	Marshall University, Huntington	12,033
1837	West Liberty State College, West Liberty	2,450
1867	Fairmont State College, Fairmont	5,432
1868	West Virginia University, Morgantown	17,270
1872	Concord College, Athens	2,380
1872	Glenville State College, Glenville	2,096
1872	Shepherd College, Shepherdstown	3,920
1891	West Virginia State College	4,503
1895	West Virginia Institute of Technology, Montgomery	2,814
1895	Bluefield State College, Bluefield	2,559
1901	Potomac State College of West Virginia Univ., Keyser	1,040
1972	West Virginia College of Graduate Studies	2,662
1976	School of Osteopathic Medicine, Lewisburg	233

In addition to the universities and state-supported schools, there are 3 community colleges (8,625 students in 1987), 10 denominational and private institutions of higher education (8,981 students in 1987) and 11 business colleges.

Health. In 1987 the state had 77 hospitals and 53 licensed personal care homes, 32 skilled-nursing homes and 3 mental hospitals.

Social Security. The Department of Human Services, originating in the 1930s as the Department of Public Assistance, is both state and federally financed. In the year ending 30 June 1988 day care for 4,735 children per month was provided; aid was given to 26,464 families with dependent children (average award, $231.64 per month); handicapped children's services conducted 8,389 examinations; 93,376 families per month received food stamps.

On 1 Jan. 1974 all blind, aged and disabled services were converted to the Federal Supplemental Security Income programme.

Further Reading

West Virginia Blue Book. Legislature, Charleston. Annual, since 1916

West Virginia Statistical Handbook, 1974. Bureau of Business Research, W. Va. Univ., Morgantown, 1974

Bibliography of West Virginia. 2 parts. Dept. of Archives and History, Charleston, 1939

West Virginia History. Dept. of Archives and History. Charleston. Quarterly, from 1939

Conley, P. and Doherty, W. T., *West Virginia History*. Charleston, 1974

Davis, C. J. and others, *West Virginia State and Local Government*. West Virginia Univ. Bureau for Government Research, 1963

Rice, O. K., *West Virginia: A History*. Univ. Press of Kentucky, Lexington, 1985
Williams, J. A., *West Virginia: A Bicentennial History*. New York, 1976

State Library: Division of Archives and History, Dept. of Culture and History, Charleston.

WISCONSIN

HISTORY. Wisconsin was settled in 1670 by French traders and missionaries. Originally a part of New France, it was surrendered to the British in 1763 and in 1783, when ceded to the US, became part of the North-west Territory. It was then contained successively in the Territories of Indiana, Illinois and Michigan. In 1836 it became part of the Territory of Wisconsin, which also included the present states of Iowa, Minnesota and parts of the Dakotas. It was admitted into the Union with its present boundaries on 29 May 1848.

AREA AND POPULATION. Wisconsin is bounded north by Lake Superior and the Upper Peninsula of Michigan, east by Lake Michigan, south by Illinois, west by Iowa and Minnesota, with the Mississippi River forming most of the boundary. Area, 56,154 sq. miles, including 1,439 sq. miles of inland water, but excluding any part of the Great Lakes. Census population, 1 April 1980 4,705,642, an increase of 6·5% since 1970. Estimated population (1989), 4,862,554. Births in 1988 were 70,711 (14·6 per 1,000 population); deaths, 42,979 (8·8); infant deaths, 598 (8·4 per 1,000 live births); marriages, 41,455 (8·5); divorces and annulments, 17,127 (3·5).

Population in 5 census years was:

	White	*Negro*	*All others*	*Total*	*Per sq. mile*
1910	2,320,555	2,900	10,405	2,333,860	42·2
1930	2,916,255	10,739	12,012	2,939,006	53·7
1960	3,858,903	74,546	18,328	3,951,777	72·2
1970	4,258,959	128,224	30,750	4,417,933	80·8
1980	4,443,035	182,592	80,015	4,705,642	86·4

Of the total population in 1980, 49% were male, 64·2% were urban and 67% were 20 years old or older.

Population of the larger cities, 1980 census, was as follows:

Milwaukee	636,297	Appleton	58,913	Beloit	35,207
Madison	170,616	Oshkosh	49,620	Fond du Lac	35,863
Racine	85,725	La Crosse	48,347	Manitowoc	32,547
Green Bay	87,889	Sheboygan	48,085	Wausau	32,426
Kenosha	77,685	Janesville	51,071	Superior	29,571
West Allis	63,982	Eau Claire	51,509	Brookfield	34,035
Wauwatosa	51,308	Waukesha	50,365		

Population of larger urbanized areas, 1980 census: Milwaukee, 1,207,008; Madison, 213,678; Duluth–Superior (Minn.–Wis.), 132,585; Racine, 118,987; Green Bay, 142,747.

CLIMATE. Milwaukee. Jan. 19°F (–7·2°C), July 70°F (21·1°C). Annual rainfall 29" (727 mm). *See* Great Lakes, p. 1382.

CONSTITUTION AND GOVERNMENT. The constitution, which dates from 1848, has 125 amendments. The legislative power is vested in a Senate of 33 members (1990 term: 18 Democrats, 13 Republicans, 2 vacancies) elected for 4 years, one-half elected alternately, and an Assembly of 99 members (1990 term: 56 Democrats, 43 Republicans) all elected simultaneously for 2 years. The Governor and Lieut.-Governor are elected for 4 years. All 6 constitutional officers serve 4-year terms.

Wisconsin has universal suffrage for all citizens 18 years of age or over; but, as there is no official list of voters, the size of the electorate is unknown; 2,191,612 voted for President in 1988.

Wisconsin is represented in Congress by 2 senators and 9 representatives.

In the 1988 presidential election Dukakis polled 1,126,794 votes, Bush, 1,047,499.

The capital is Madison. The state has 72 counties.

Governor: Tommy G. Thompson (R.), 1987–91 ($86,149).
Lieut.-Governor: Scott McCallum (R.), 1987–91 ($46,360).
Secretary of State: Douglas La Follette (D.), 1987–91 ($42,089).

BUDGET. For the year ending 30 June 1989 (Wisconsin Bureau of Financial Operations figures) total revenue for all funds was $14,808,591,000 ($6,097,847,000 from taxation and $2,295,036,000 from federal aid). General expenditure from all funds was $11,903,305,000 ($3,739,025,000 for education, $3,468,089,000 for human resources).

Per capita personal income (1988) was $15,524.

ENERGY AND NATURAL RESOURCES

Electricity. There were, Dec. 1988, 87 hydro-electric power plants (16 of them municipal, 56 private in Wisconsin; 15 private outside the state) operated by public utilities with a total installed capacity of 503,472 kw.; output, 1988, was 1,449,615mwh. The 15 outside plants are in Michigan; installed capacity 99,990 kw., output 386,204mwh.

Fossil fuel and nuclear plants numbered 23 (3 municipal); the former had a total installed capacity of 7,586,990 kw.; total output, (1988), 32,917,693mwh; the 2 nuclear plants had an installed capacity of 1,540,682 kw. and a total output (1988) of 11,464,455mwh.

There were also 27 internal combustion reciprocating plants (17 of them municipal), with a total installed capacity of 99,175 kw. and a total output of (1988) 6,542mwh., and 16 (1 municipal) internal combustion turbine plants with a total installed capacity of 1,257,450 kw.; total output was (1988) 102,212mwh.

There was a total of 151 plants, with a total installed capacity of 10,987,769 kw. and a total output of (1988) 45,940,517mwh.

Minerals. Construction sand and gravel, crushed stone and lime are the chief mineral products. Mineral production in 1988 was valued at $205m. This value included $60·1m. for sand and gravel, $98·3m. for crushed stone and about $24m. for lime. Value of all other minerals including industrial sand, dimension stone, crushed trap rock, peat and gemstones, $22·5m. There are plans to develop a 2m. ton copper (with small amounts of gold) deposit near Ladysmith.

Agriculture. The total number of farms has declined in the last 50 years, but farms have become larger and more productive. On 1 Jan. 1989 there were 81,000 farms with a total acreage of 17·6m. acres and an average size of 214·6 acres, compared with 142,000 farms with a total acreage of 22·4m. acres and an average of 158 acres in 1959.

Cash receipts from products sold by Wisconsin farms in 1988, $4,926m.; $4,154m. from livestock and livestock products and $772m. from crops.

Wisconsin ranked first among the states in 1988 in the number of milch cows, milk and butter production, output of all cheeses and of American, Brick, Muenster, Italian and Blue Mold Cheese. Production of cheese accounted for 34·1% of the nation's total. The state also ranked first in bulk whole condensed sweetened and unsweetened milk, bulk skim condensed sweetened, milk lactose for human use, whey protein concentrate and dry whey. The state ranked first in mink pelts. In crops the state ranked first for snap beans, sweet corn for processing, and corn for silage. Production of the principal field crops in 1988 included: Corn for grain, 130·7m. bu.; corn for silage, 10m. tons; oats, 19·7m. bu.; all hay, 9m. tons. Other crops of importance 20m. cwt of potatoes, 7·1m. lb. of tobacco, 1·5m. bbls of cranberries, 1·3m. cwt of carrots and the processing crops of 609,000 tons of sweet corn, 54,300 tons of green peas and 209,500 tons of snap beans.

Forestry. Wisconsin has an estimated 15·3m. acres of forest land (about 42% of land area). Of 14·7m. acres of commercial forest (June 1988) national forests covered 1·2m. acres; state forests, 0·6m.; county and municipal forests, 2·3m.; forest industry, 1·2m.; private land, 9·1m.

Growing stock (1985), 15,500m. cu. ft, of which 11,900m. cu. ft is hardwood and 3,600m. cu. ft, softwood. Main hardwoods, aspen, maple, oak and birch; main softwoods, red pine, white pine, balsam fir, jack pine.

INDUSTRY. Wisconsin has much heavy industry, particularly in the Milwaukee area. Two thirds of manufacturing employees work on durable goods. Non-electrical machinery is the major industrial group (19% of all manufacturing employment) followed by food processing, fabricated metals, paper and paper products, electrical machinery, printing and publishing and transport equipment. Primary and secondary wood-product industries are high in value of product (over $91,000m. in 1986). Manufacturing establishments in 1988 provided 26% of all employment, 33% of all earnings. The total number of establishments was 9,333 in 1988; the biggest concentration (40% of employment) is in the south-east.

TOURISM. The tourist-vacation industry ranks among the first three in economic importance. The decline of lumbering and mining in the northern section of the state has increased dependency on the recreation industry. The Division of Tourism of the Department of Development spent $6,405,200 to promote tourism in financial year 1988–89.

COMMUNICATIONS

Roads. The state had on 1 Jan. 1989, 109,303 miles of highway. 76% of all roads in the state have a bituminous (or similar) surface. There are 11,883 miles of state trunk roads and 19,541 miles of county trunk roads.

On 1 July 1989 Wisconsin registered 3,796,625 motor vehicles.

Railways. On 1 Aug. 1987 the state had 4,224 road-miles of railway.

Aviation. There were, in 1989, 95 publicly operated airports. Twelve scheduled air carrier airports were served by 15 regional and national air carriers.

Shipping. Lake Superior and Lake Michigan ports handled 36·2m. tons of freight in 1986; 80% of it at Superior, one of the world's biggest grain ports, and much of the rest at Milwaukee and Green Bay.

JUSTICE, RELIGION, EDUCATION AND WELFARE

Justice. The state's penal, reformatory and correctional system on 31 July 1989 held 5,960 men, 265 women and 556 juveniles in 13 state-owned and other institutions for adult and juvenile offenders; the probation and parole system was supervising 23,113 men and 5,275 women. Wisconsin does not impose the death penalty.

Religion. Wisconsin church affiliation, as a percentage of the 1980 population, was estimated at 32·2% Catholic, 20·06% Lutheran, 3·74% Methodist, 10·41% other churches and 32·6% un-affiliated.

Education. All children between the ages of 6 and 18 are required to attend school full-time to the end of the school term in which they become 18 years of age. In 1988–89 the public school grades kindergarten–8 had 535,417 pupils and 31,824 (full-time equivalent) teachers; school grades 9–12 had 239,417 pupils and 16,717 teachers. Private schools enrolled 143,648 students grades kindergarten–12. Public elementary teachers' salaries, 1988–89, averaged $29,856; junior high, $31,880; middle school, $31,744; high, $32,257.

In 1988–89 vocational, technical and adult schools had an enrolment of 436,746 and 3,434 (full-time equivalent) teachers. There is a school for the visually handicapped and a school for the deaf.

The University of Wisconsin, established in 1848, was joined by law in 1971 with the Wisconsin State Universities System to become the University of Wisconsin System with 13 degree granting campuses, 13 two-year campuses in the Center System, and the University Extension. The 26 campuses had, in 1988–89, 7,196 full-time professors and instructors and 2,122 teaching assistants. In autumn 1988, 162,567 students enrolled (11,038 at Eau Claire, 5,221 at Green Bay, 9,265 at La Crosse, 43,641 at Madison, 25,212 at Milwaukee, 11,113 at Oshkosh, 5,170 at Parkside, 5,353 at Platteville, 5,544 at River Falls, 9,318 at Stevens Point, 7,599 at Stout, 2,434 at Superior, 10,458 at Whitewater and 11,201 in the Center System freshman-sophomore centres). There are also several independent institutions of higher education. These (with 1988–89 enrolment) include 2 universities (13,363), 18 liberal arts colleges (23,740), 5 technical and professional schools (4,352), and 4 theological seminaries (473).

The total expenditure, 1987–88, for all public education (except capital outlay and debt service) was $5,465m.

The state maintains an educational broadcasting and television service.

Health. In Oct. 1989 the state had 137 general and allied special hospitals (20,592 beds), 18 mental hospitals (2,161 beds), 9 treatment centres for alcoholism (342 beds). Patients in state mental hospitals and institutions for the mentally retarded in Dec. 1988 averaged 2,257. On 31 Dec. 1988 the state had 450 licensed nursing homes; the 1988 average daily census was 48,163 residents.

Social Security. On 1 Jan. 1974 the US Social Security administration assumed responsibility for financial aid (Supplemental Security Income) to persons 65 years old and over, blind persons and totally disabled persons, who satisfy requirements as to need. Recipients receive a federal payment plus a federally administered state supplementary payment, except for those who reside in a medical institution. In Aug. 1989, there were 80,900 SSI recipients in the state; payments were $489 for a single individual, $540 for an eligible individual with an ineligible spouse, and $745 for an eligible couple. A special payment level of $589 for an individual and $1,098 for a couple may be paid with special approval for SSI recipients who are developmentally disabled or chronically mentally ill, living in a non-medical living arrangement not his or her own home. All SSI recipients receive state medical assistance coverage.

Under the Aid to Families with Dependent Children programme, 79,388 families of 237,324 persons received an average of $460.99 per family in Aug. 1989. Medicaid cost $1,266·4m. in financial year 1988–89.

Further Reading

Dictionary of Wisconsin Biography. Wis. Historical Society, Madison, 1960
Wisconsin Blue Book. Wis. Legislative Reference Bureau, Madison. Biennial
Current, R. N.,*Wisconsin, a History.* New York, 1977
Danziger, S. and Witte, J. F., *State Policy Choices: The Wisconsin Experience.* Univ. Wisconsin Press, 1988
Martin, L., *The Physical Geography of Wisconsin.* Univ. Wisconsin Press, 3rd ed., 1965
Nesbit, R. C., *Wisconsin, A History.* State Historical Society of Wisconsin, Madison, 1973
Robinson, A. H. and Culver, J. B., (eds.) *The Atlas of Wisconsin.* Univ. Wisconsin Press, 1974
Vogeler, I., *Wisconsin: A Geography.* Boulder, 1986

State Historical Society of Wisconsin: *The History of Wisconsin.* Vol. I [Alice E. Smith], Madison, 1973.—Vol. II [R. N. Current], Madison, 1976.—Vol. III [R. C. Nesbit], Madison, 1985.—Vol. VI [W. F. Thompson], Madison, 1988

State Information Agency: Legislative Reference Bureau, State Capitol, Madison, Wis. 53702. *Chief:* Dr H. Rupert Theobald.

WYOMING

HISTORY. Wyoming, first settled in 1834, was admitted into the Union on 10 July 1890. The name originated with the Delaware Indians.

AREA AND POPULATION. Wyoming is bounded north by Montana, east by South Dakota and Nebraska, south by Colorado, south-west by Utah and west by Idaho. Area 97,914 sq. miles, of which 408 sq. miles are water. The Yellowstone National Park occupies about 2·22m. acres; the Grand Teton National Park has

307,000 acres. The federal government in 1986 owned 49,838 sq. miles (50·9% of the total area of the state). The Federal Bureau of Land Management administers 17,546,188 acres.

Census population, 1 April 1980, 469,557, an increase of 41·25% since 1970. Estimate (1989) 480,012. Births in 1987 were 7,538 (15·9 per 1,000 population); deaths, 3,038 (6·4); marriages, 4,699 (9·9); divorces, 3,202 (6·7); infant deaths, 69 (9·2 per 1,000 live births).

Population in 5 census years was:

	White	*Negro*	*Indian*	*Asiatic*	*Total*	*Per sq. mile*
1910	140,318	2,235	1,486	1,926	145,965	1·5
1930	221,241	1,250	1,845	1,229	225,565	2·3
1960	322,922	2,183	4,020	805	330,066	3·4
			All others			
1970	323,619	2,568	6,229		332,416	3·4
1980	446,488	3,364	19,705		469,557	4·8

Of the total population in 1980, 240,560 were male, 295,898 were urban and those over 21 years of age numbered 295,908.

The largest towns are Cheyenne (capital), with census population in 1980 of 58,429 (1989 estimate, 51,000); Casper, 59,287 (47,000); Laramie, 24,410 (27,000); Rock Springs, 19,458 (20,000); Gillette (17,000); Sheridan (15,000); Green River (13,000).

CLIMATE. Cheyenne. Jan. 25°F (–3·9°C), July 66°F (18·9°C). Annual rainfall 15" (376 mm). Yellowstone Park. Jan. 18°F (–7·8°C), July 61°F (16·1°C). Annual rainfall 18" (444 mm). *See* Mountain States, p. 1381.

CONSTITUTION AND GOVERNMENT. The constitution, drafted in 1890, has since had 43 amendments. The Legislature consists of a Senate of 30 members elected for 4 years, and a House of Representatives of 64 members elected for 2 years. The Governor is elected for 4 years.

The state sends to Congress 2 senators and 1 representative, elected by the voters of the entire state. The suffrage extends to all citizens, male and female, who have the usual residential qualifications.

In the 1988 presidential election Bush polled 106,814 votes, Dukakis, 67,077.

The capital is Cheyenne. The state contains 23 counties.

Governor: Mike Sullivan (D.), 1987–90 ($70,000).
Secretary of State: Kathy Karpan (D.), 1987–90 ($52,500).

BUDGET. In the fiscal year ending 1 July 1988 (State Treasurer's figures) cash receipts were $1,517,605,480; general expenditures were $1,441,529,970.

Per capita personal income (1987) was $12,709.

ENERGY AND NATURAL RESOURCES

Minerals. Wyoming is largely an oil-producing state. In 1988 the output of petroleum was valued at $1,726·1m.; natural gas, $717·7m. Other mining: Coal, $1,006·2m.; trona, uranium, iron ore, feldspar, gypsum, limestone, phosphate, sand, gravel and marble, taconite, bentonite and hematite.

Agriculture. Wyoming is semi-arid, and agriculture is carried on by irrigation and by dry farming. In 1987 there were 8,700 farms and ranches; total land area 34·8m. acres.

Cash receipts, 1987, from crops, $110·6m.; from livestock and products, $455·2m. Principal commodities are wheat, cattle and calves, lambs and sheep, sugar-beet, barley, hay and wool. Animals on farms on 1 Jan. 1987 included 10,000 milch cows, 1·3m. all cattle, 775,000 sheep and lambs and 35,000 swine.

INDUSTRY AND TRADE

Industry. In 1987 there were 531 manufacturing establishments. There were 964 mining companies or producers. A large portion of the manufacturing in the state is based on natural resources, mainly oil and farm products. Leading industries are food, wood products (except furniture) and machinery (except electrical). There were 931 new business incorporations in 1986. The Wyoming Industrial Development Corporation assists in the development of small industries by providing credit.

Labour. The mining industry employed an average of 19,945 workers in June 1987. The total civilian labour force for 1987 was 254,630; non-agricultural, 241,468. The average unemployment rate was 8·3% and average weekly earnings $611 for mining (production workers).

Tourism. There are over 7m. tourists annually, mainly outdoor enthusiasts. The state has the largest elk and pronghorn antelope herds in the world, 10 fish hatcheries and numerous wild game. Receipts from hunters and fishermen in 1986, $14,628,081. In 1987, 5·4m. people visited the 6 national parks or monuments; 1·5m. non-residents visted state parks; 559,032 fishing, game and bird licences were sold. There were (1990) 13 operational ski areas.

COMMUNICATIONS

Roads. The roads in 1986 comprised 5,240 miles of federal highways, 349 miles of state highways and 914 miles of inter-state highway. There were (1986) 616,718 registered motor vehicles and 12 bus companies.

Railways. The railways, 1986, had a length of 2,615 mainline miles and 550 branch miles.

Aviation. There were 11 towns with commuter air services and 2 towns on jet routes in 1987.

JUSTICE, RELIGION, EDUCATION AND WELFARE

Justice. The state penitentiary in July 1988 held 736 inmates, the Womens' Center, 49. There are 2 other state correctional institutions. There have been 14 executions in Wyoming, 8 by hanging and 6 by lethal gas.

Religion. Chief religious bodies are the Roman Catholic (with 45,917 members in 1974), Mormon (28,954 in 1971) and Protestant churches (83,327 in 1974). There were 5,000 members of the Eastern Orthodox Church in 1972.

Education. In 1988–89 public elementary and secondary schools had 97,793 pupils. Enrolment in the parochial elementary and secondary schools was about 3,500. Approximately 6,811 public school teachers earned an average of $28,400. The average total expenditure per pupil for 1987–88 was $4,766.

The University of Wyoming, founded at Laramie in 1887, had in academic year 1988–89 10,383 students. There are 2-year colleges at Casper, Riverton, Torrington, Cheyenne, Powell, Rock Springs and Sheridan with credit course enrolment of 15,685 students in 1987–88.

Social Welfare. In Jan. 1974 the federal government assumed many of the previous state programmes including old age assistance, aid to the blind and disabled. In 1987 financial year, $16·2m. was distributed in food stamps; $17·6m. in aid to families with dependent children; $626,314 in general assistance; $1,189,902 in emergency assistance; $41m. in Medicaid. Total state expenditure on public assistance and social services programmes, financial year 1987, $123·5m.

Health. In 1989 the state had 30 hospitals and 27 registered nursing homes.

Further Reading

Official Directory. Secretary of State. Cheyenne. Biennial
1987 Wyoming Data Handbook. Dept. of Administration and Fiscal Control. Division of Research and Statistics, Cheyenne, 1987

Brown, R. H., *Wyoming: A Geography*. Boulder, 1980
Larsen, T. A., *History of Wyoming*. Rev. ed. Univ. of Nebraska, 1979
Treadway, T., *Wyoming*. New York, 1982

OUTLYING TERRITORIES

Non-Self-Governing Territories: Summaries of Information Transmitted to the Secretary-General of the United Nations. Annual

GUAM

HISTORY. Magellan is said to have discovered the island in 1521; it was ceded by Spain to the US by the Treaty of Paris (10 Dec. 1898). The island was captured by the Japanese on 10 Dec. 1941, and retaken by American forces from 21 July 1944. Guam is of great strategic importance; substantial numbers of naval and air force personnel occupy about one-third of the usable land.

AREA AND POPULATION. Guam is the largest and most southern island of the Marianas Archipelago, in 13° 26' N. lat., 144° 43' E. long. The length is 30 miles, the breadth from 4 to 10 miles, and there are about 209 sq. miles (541 sq. km). Agaña, the seat of government is about 8 miles from the anchorage in Apra Harbour. The census on 1 April 1980 showed a population of 105,979, an increase of 20,983 or 24·7% since 1970; those of Guamanian ancestry numbered about 50,794; foreign-born, 28,572; density was 507 per sq. mile. Estimated population (1987), 130,400 (including 23,860 transient residents connected with the military). The Malay strain is predominant. The native language is Chamorro; English is the official language and is taught in all schools.

CLIMATE. Tropical maritime, with little difference in temperatures over the year. Rainfall is copious at all seasons, but is greatest from July to Oct. Agaña. Jan. 81°F (27·2°C), July 81°F (27·2°C). Annual rainfall 93" (2,325 mm).

CONSTITUTION AND GOVERNMENT. Guam's constitutional status is that of an 'unincorporated territory' of the US. Entry of US citizens is unrestricted; foreign nationals are subject to normal regulations. In 1949–50 the President transferred the administration of the island from the Navy Department (who held it from 1899) to the Interior Department. The transfer conferred full citizenship on the Guamanians, who had previously been 'nationals' of the US. There was a referendum on status, 30 Jan. 1982. 38% of eligible voters voted; 48·5% of those favoured Commonwealth status.

The Governor and his staff constitute the executive arm of the government. The Legislature is unicameral; its powers are similar to those of an American state legislature. At the general election of Nov. 1982, the Democratic Party won 14 seats and the Republicans 7. All adults 18 years of age or over are enfranchised. Guam returns one non-voting delegate to the House of Representatives.

Governor: Joseph F. Ada (R.), 1987–91.
Lieut.-Governor: Frank F. Blas.

ECONOMY

Budget. Total revenue (1989) $378m.; expenditure $369m.

Banking. Recent changes in banking law make it possible for foreign banks to operate in Guam.

NATURAL RESOURCES

Water. Supplies are from springs, reservoirs and groundwater; 65% comes from water-bearing limestone in the north. The Navy and Air Force conserve water in reservoirs. The Water Resources Research Centre is at Guam University.

Agriculture. The major products of the island are sweet potatoes, cucumbers, water melons and beans. In 1982 there were 140 full-time and 1,904 part-time farmers. Livestock (1988) included 2,000 cattle, 14,000 pigs, and (1984) 36,430 poultry. Commercial productions (1983) amounted to 6·6m. lb. of fruit and vegetables ($3·4m.), 567,000 doz. eggs ($811,093). There is an agricultural experimental station at Inarajan.

Fisheries. Fresh fish caught in 1982, 319,300 lb. Offshore fishing produced 100,687 lb., including 6,080 lb. of shrimps.

INDUSTRY AND TRADE

Industry. Guam Economic Development Authority controls three industrial estates: Cabras Island (32 acres); Calvo estate at Tamuning (26 acres); Harmon estate (16 acres). Industries include textile manufacture, cement and petroleum distribution, warehousing, printing, plastics and ship-repair. Other main sources of income are construction and tourism.

Labour. In 1983 51% of employment was in government, 18% in trade, 5% in construction, 13% in services, 4% in manufacturing, 5% in transport and 4% in finance.

Trade. Guam is the only American territory which has complete 'free trade'; excise duties are levied only upon imports of tobacco, liquid fuel and liquor. In the year ending 31 Dec. 1980 imports were valued at $544·1m. and accounted for 90% of trade.

Tourism. Tourism is developing; there were 1,900 visitors in 1964 and 407,100 in 1986.

COMMUNICATIONS

Roads. There are 419 miles of all-weather roads.

Aviation. Seven commercial airlines serve Guam.

Post and Broadcasting. Overseas telephone and radio dispatch facilities are available. In 1983 there were 23,442 telephones.

There are 4 commercial stations, a commercial television station, a public broadcasting station and a cable television station with 24 channels.

Newspapers. There is 1 daily newspaper, a twice-weekly paper, and 4 weekly publications (all of which are of military or religious interest only).

JUSTICE, RELIGION, EDUCATION AND WELFARE

Justice. The Organic Act established a District Court with jurisdiction in matters arising under both federal and territorial law; the judge is appointed by the President subject to Senate approval. There is also a Supreme Court and a Superior Court; all judges are locally appointed except the Federal District judge. Misdemeanours are under the jurisdiction of the police court. The Spanish law was superseded in 1933 by 5 civil codes based upon California law.

Religion. About 98% of the Guamanians are Roman Catholics; others are Baptists, Episcopalians, Bahais, Lutherans, Mormons, Presbyterians, Jehovah's Witnesses and members of the Church of Christ and Seventh Day Adventists.

Education. Elementary education is compulsory. There are Chamorro Studies courses and bi-lingual teaching programmes to integrate the Chamorro language and culture into elementary and secondary school courses. There were, Dec. 1983, 24 elementary schools, 6 junior high schools, 5 senior high schools, one vocational-technical school for high school students and adults and 1 school for handicapped children. There were 17,725 elementary school pupils, 7,418 junior high and 5,776 senior high school pupils. Department of Education staff included 1,258 teachers. The Catholic schools system also operates 3 senior high schools, 3 junior high and 5 elementary schools. The Seventh Day Adventist Guam Mission Academy operates a school from grades 1 through 12, serving over 100 students. St John's Episcopal Preparatory School provides education for 530 students between kindergarten and the 9th grade. The University of Guam (an accredited institution) had 2,774 students, 1983–84.

Health. There is a hospital, 8 nutrition centres, a school health programme and an extensive immunization programme. Emphasis is on disease prevention, health education and nutrition.

Further Reading

Report (Annual) of the Governor of Guam to the US Department of Interior
Guam Annual Economic Review. Economic Research Center, Agaña

Carano, P. and Sanchez, P. C., *Complete History of Guam*. Rutland, Vt., 1964

REPUBLIC OF PALAU

HISTORY. Under the Treaty of Versailles (1919) Japan was appointed mandatory to the former German possessions north of the Equator. In 1946 the US agreed to administer the former Japanese-mandated islands of the Caroline, Marshall and Mariana groups (except Guam) as a Trusteeship for the United Nations; the trusteeship agreement was approved by the Security Council 27 April 1947 and came into effect on 18 July 1947. The Trust Territory was administered by the US Navy until 1951, when all the islands except Tinian and Saipan in the Marianas were transferred to the Secretary of the Interior. In 1962 the Interior Department assumed responsibility for them also. In April 1976 the US government separated the administration of the Northern Marianas (*see* below) from that of the rest of the Trust Territory. The rest was 3 entities, each with its own constitution: the Marshall Islands, the Federated States of Micronesia (Yap, Kosrae, Truk and Pohnpei) and the Republic of Palau. The US Congress agreed compacts of free association with all except Palau (*see* below) in 1985–86.

Palau is now the only remaining Trust Territory. The Republic lies west of the Federated States of Micronesia, and has a land area of 192 sq. miles, divided between 26 larger islands and more than 300 islets. The largest island is Babelthuap (143 sq. miles). Population (1980 census) 12,116; 1988 estimate, 14,106. The language is Palauan.

The headquarters is Koror. The Republic has a bicameral parliament with an 18-member Senate, and 16-member House of Delegates, both elected for four years as are the president and vice-president. The Constitution, adopted in July 1980, provided for ultimate free-association status, but it also defines Palau as a nuclearfree zone; this is in conflict with the United States' intention of basing nuclear weapons on the islands, as part of the defence responsibility included in the Free Association Compact. To cancel the anti-nuclear clause and accept the Compact required a 75% vote at referendum. When this was not achieved by successive referenda, the constitution was amended to allow a simple majority to suffice. Palau voted in favour of the Compact (67%) in Aug. 1987; however, the Plebiscite was judged by Palau Supreme Court to have been unconstitutional and Palau remains in Trust.

Palau has a directly-elected President and Vice-President, and a bicameral parliament. The capital is Koror.

There is subsistence agriculture, craft-work and some commercial fishing.

REPUBLIC OF THE MARSHALL ISLANDS

On 21 Oct. 1986 the USA entered into a Compact of Free Association with this former Trust Territory. The Republic is a sovereign state responsible for its foreign policy; the USA controls defence policy (for a minimum of 15 years) and provides financial support. The constitution of 1 May 1979 is still in force; it provides for an elected assembly and an elected president, both serving four-year terms. There is also an advisory council of chiefs.

Population (July 1988), 40,609. The Marshallese are predominantly Micronesian and Christian. There are two indigenous languages; Japanese is also used, but the official language is English. The capital is Majuro. Kwajalein is a US missile-testing range and airfield.

The total area is 181·3 sq. km (land area).

FEDERATED STATES OF MICRONESIA

On 3 Nov. 1986 this island group, a former Trust Territory, entered into a Compact of Free Association with the USA. The Federation is a sovereign state; the USA controls defence (for a minimum period of 15 years) and provides financial support. The Federation is responsible for its own foreign policy. The capital is Kolonia.

Land area, 702 sq. km. Population (July 1988), 86,094. The Federation has 4 states: Kosrae, Pohnpei, Truk and Yap. There are 607 islands. The people are Micronesian and Polynesian; the main languages are Kosrean, Yapese, Pohnpeian and Trukese; the official language is English.

The federal congress is elected for four years, as are the president and vice-president. Eash state has an elected governor and a unicameral assembly.

THE NORTHERN MARIANAS

The islands form a chain, extending 560 km north from Guam; there are 16 islands, all mountainous, with a combined land area of 477 sq. km (184 sq. miles). The islands were formerly part of the US-administered Trust Territory of the Pacific Islands. On 17 June 1975 the voters of the Northern Mariana Islands, in a plebiscite observed by the UN, adopted the covenant to establish a Commonwealth of the Northern Mariana Islands in Union with the USA. In April 1976 the US government approved the convenant and separated the administration of the Northern Marianas from that of the rest of the Trust Territory.

The Northern Marianas form a Commonwealth with an elected governor and lieutenant-governor, both serving 4-year terms; the bicameral parliament has a 9-member Senate, elected for four years, and a 15-member House of Representatives (elected for two). The people are US citizens; they elect a non-voting delegate to the US House of Representatives. The USA is responsible for defence.

The population, 1980 census, 16,780 (1988 estimate, 20,591). Saipan is the seat of government. The official language is English, 55% (1980) speak Chamorro.

AMERICAN SAMOA

HISTORY. The Samoan Islands were first visited by Europeans in the 18th century; the first recorded visit was in 1722. On 14 July 1889 a treaty between the USA, Germany and Great Britain proclaimed the Samoan islands neutral territory, under a 4-power government consisting of the 3 treaty powers and the local native government. By the Tripartite Treaty of 7 Nov. 1899, ratified 19 Feb. 1900, Great Britain and Germany renounced in favour of the US all rights over the islands of the Samoan group east of 171° long. west of Greenwich, the islands to the west of that meridian being assigned to Germany (now the Independent State of Western Samoa, *see* p. 1593). The islands of Tutuila and Aunu'u were ceded to the US by their High Chiefs on 17 April 1900, and the islands of the Manu'a group on 16 July 1904. Congress accepted the islands under a Joint Resolution approved 20 Feb. 1929. Swain's Island, 210 miles north of the Samoan Islands, was annexed in 1925 and is administered as an integral part of American Samoa.

AREA AND POPULATION. The islands (Tutuila, Aunu'u, Ta'u, Olosega, Ofu and Rose) are approximately 650 miles east-north-east of Fiji. The total area of American Samoa is 76·1 sq. miles (197 sq. km); population, 1980, 32,297, nearly all Polynesians or part-Polynesians. The island's 3 Districts are Eastern (population, 1980, 17,311), Western (13,227) and Manu'a (1,732). There is also Swain's Island, with an area of 1·9 sq. miles and 29 inhabitants (1980), which lies 210 miles to the north west. Rose Island (uninhabited) is 0·4 sq. mile in area. In 1981 there were 1,158 births and 153 deaths.

CLIMATE. A tropical maritime climate with a small annual range of temperature and plentiful rainfall. Pago-Pago. Jan. 83°F (28·3°C), July 80°F (26·7°C). Annual rainfall 194" (4,850 mm).

CONSTITUTION AND GOVERNMENT. American Samoa is constitutionally an unorganized unincorporated territory of the US administered under the Department of the Interior. Its indigenous inhabitants are US nationals and are classified locally as citizens of American Samoa with certain privileges under local laws not granted to non-indigenous persons. Polynesian customs (not inconsistent with US laws) are respected.

Fagatogo is the seat of the Government.

The islands are organized in 15 counties grouped in 3 districts; these counties and districts correspond to the traditional political units. On 25 Feb. 1948 a bicameral legislature was established, at the request of the Samoans, to have advisory legislative functions. With the adoption of the Constitution of 22 April 1960, and the revised Constitution of 1967, the legislature was vested with limited law-making authority. The lower house, or House of Representatives, is composed of 20 members elected by universal adult suffrage and 1 non-voting member for Swain's Island. The upper house, or Senate, is comprised of 18 members elected, in the traditional Samoan manner, in meetings of the chiefs.

Governor: Peter TaliColeman.

Lieut.-Governor: Galeá I. Poumele.

ECONOMY

Planning. The first formal Economic Development and Planning Office completed its first year in 1971. Much has been done to promote economic expansion within the Territory and a large amount of outside investment interest has been stimulated.

The Office initiated the first Territorial Comprehensive Plan. This plan when completed will, with periodic updating, provide a guideline to territorial development for the next 20 years. The planning programme was made possible under a Housing and Urban Development '701' grant programme, and Economic Development Administration '302' planning programmes.

The focus will be on physical development and the problems of a rapidly increasing population with severely limited labour resources.

Budget. The chief sources of revenue are annual federal grants from the US, and local revenues from taxes, and duties, and receipts from commercial operations (enterprise and special revenue funds), utilities, rents and leases and liquor sales. During the financial year 1983–84 the Government had a revenue of $76·6m. including local appropriations of $9·5m., federal appropriations of $39·6m. and enterprise funds of $17·5m.

Banking. The American Samoa branch of the Bank of Hawaii and the American Samoa Bank offer all commercial banking services. The Development Bank of American Samoa, government owned, is concerned primarily through loans and guarantees with the economic advancement of the Territory.

ENERGY AND NATURAL RESOURCES

Electricity. Net power generated (financial year 1981) was 72·2m. kwh., of which 23·1m. kwh. was supplied to large power users and 20·2m. kwh. to householders. All the Manu'a islands have electricity.

Agriculture. Of the 48,640 acres of land area, 11,000 acres are suitable for tropical crops; most commercial farms are in the Tafuna plains and west Tutuila. Principal crops are taro, bread-fruit, yams, bananas and coconuts. Production (1988 in 1,000 tonnes): Taro, 4; bananas, 1; fruit, 1; coconuts, 5.

Livestock (1988): Pigs, 11,000; (1984) goats, 8,000; poultry, 45,000.

INDUSTRY AND TRADE

Industry. Fish canning is important, employing the second largest number of people (after government). Attempts are being made to provide a variety of light industries. Tuna fishing and local inshore fishing are both expanding.

Commerce. In 1982 American Samoa exported goods valued at $186,782,060 and imported goods valued at $119,416,918. Chief exports are canned tuna, watches, pet foods and handicrafts. Chief imports are building materials, fuel oil, food, jewellery, machines and parts, alcoholic beverages and cigarettes.

COMMUNICATIONS

Roads. There are (1983) about 76 miles of paved roads and 16 miles of unpaved within the Federal Aid highway system. There are 21 miles of other unpaved roads. Motor vehicles registered, 1983, 3,657.

Aviation. South Pacific Island Airways and Polynesian Airlines operate daily services between American Samoa and Western Samoa. South Pacific Island Airways also operates between Pago Pago and Honolulu, and between Pago Pago and Tonga. The islands are also served by Air Nauru which operates between Pago Pago, Tahiti and Auckland, and Air Pacific (Fiji and westward). South Pacific and Manu'a Air Transport run local services.

Shipping. The harbour at Pago Pago, which nearly bisects the island of Tutuila, is the only good harbour for large vessels in Samoa. By sea, there is a twice-monthly service between Fiji, New Zealand and Australia and regular service between US, South Pacific ports, Honolulu and Japan.

Post and Broadcasting. A commercial radiogram service is available to all parts of the world through 2 principal trunks, United States and Western Samoa. Commercial phone and telex services are operated to all parts of the world on a 24-hour service. Number of telephones (Sept. 1983), 6,029; telex subscribers, 78.

JUSTICE, EDUCATION AND WELFARE

Justice. Judicial power is vested firstly in a High Court. The trial division has original jurisdiction of all criminal and civil cases. The probate division has jurisdiction of estates, guardianships, trusts and other matters. The land and title division decides cases relating to disputes involving communal land and Matai title court rules on questions and controversy over family titles. The appellate division hears appeals from trial, land and title and probate divisions as well as having original jurisdiction in selected matters. The appellate court is the court of last resort. Two American judges sit with 5 Samoan judges permanently. In addition there are temporary judges or assessors who sit occasionally on cases involving Samoan customs. There is also a District Court with limited jurisdiction and there are 69 village courts.

Education. Education is compulsory between the ages of 6 and 18. The Government (1983) maintains 24 consolidated elementary schools, 5 senior high schools with technical departments, 1 community college, special education classes for the handicapped and 92 Early Childhood Education Centres for pre-school children. Total elementary and secondary enrolment (1983), 8,300; in ECE schools, 1,611; classes for the handicapped, 68; total elementary and secondary classroom teachers, 480. Ten private schools had 2,108 students. Learning is by a variety of media including television.

Health. The Department of Health provides the only curative and preventive medical and dental care in American Samoa. It operates a general hospital (173 beds including 49 bassinets), 3 dispensaries on Tutuila, 4 dispensaries in the Manu'a group, 1 on Aunu'u and 1 on Swain's Island. A $3·5m. tropical medical centre was completed and placed in service in 1968. This now embraces the general hospital as well as preventive health services and out-patient clinics for surgery, obstetrics, gynaecology, emergencies, family practice, internal medicine, paediatrics; there are clinics for treatment of the eye, ear, nose and throat, dental and public health departments.

In 1983 there were 27 doctors, 7 dentists, 2 optometrists, 3 nurse anaesthetists, and 3 physician assistants. Total number of health service employees, 397.

OTHER PACIFIC TERRITORIES

Johnston Atoll. Two small islands 1,150 km south-west of Hawaii, administered by the US Air Force. Area, under 1 sq. mile; population (1980 census) 327, with Sand Island.

Midway Islands. Two small islands at the western end of the Hawaiian chain, administered by the US Navy. Area, 2 sq. miles; population (1980 census) 453.

Wake Island. Three small islands 3,700 km west of Hawaii, administered by the US Air Force. Area, 3 sq. miles; population (1980 census) 302.

COMMONWEALTH OF PUERTO RICO

HISTORY. Puerto Rico, by the treaty of 10 Dec. 1898 (ratified 11 April 1899), was ceded by Spain to the US. The name was changed from Porto Rico to Puerto Rico by an Act of Congress approved 17 May 1932. Its territorial constitution was determined by the 'Organic Act' of Congress (2 March 1917) known as the 'Jones Act', which ruled until 25 July 1952, when the present constitution of the Commonwealth of Puerto Rico was proclaimed.

AREA AND POPULATION. Puerto Rico is the most easterly of the Greater Antilles and lies between the Dominican Republic and the US Virgin Islands. The island has a land area of 3,459 sq. miles and a population, according to the census of 1980, of 3,196,520, an increase of 484,487 or 17·9% over 1970. Of the population in 1970 about 529,000 were bilingual, Spanish being the mother tongue and (with English) one of the two official languages. Urban population (1980) 2,134,365 (66·8%).

Vital statistics (1985–86): Births, 63,542 (19·4 per 1,000 population); deaths, 23,118 (7·1); deaths under 1 year, 947 (14·9 per 1,000 live births).

Chief towns, 1980 (and 1986 estimate) are: San Juan, 434,849 (431,227); Bayamón, 196,207 (211,616); Ponce, 189,046 (190,679); Carolina, 165,954 (162,888); Caguas, 117,959 (126,298); Mayaguez, 96,193 (98,861); Arecibo, 86,766 (90,960).

The Puerto Rican island of Vieques, 10 miles to the east, has an area of 51·7 sq. miles and 7,662 (8,084) inhabitants. The island of Culebra, with 1,265 (1,272) inhabitants, between Puerto Rico and St Thomas, has a good harbour.

CONSTITUTION AND GOVERNMENT. Puerto Rico has representative government, the franchise being restricted to citizens 18 years of age or over, residence (1 year) and such additional qualifications as may be prescribed by the Legislature of Puerto Rico, but no property qualification may be imposed. Women were enfranchised in 1932 (with a literacy test) and fully in 1936. Puerto Ricans do not vote in the US presidential elections, though individuals living on the mainland are free to do so subject to the local electoral laws. The executive power resides in a Governor, elected directly by the people every 4 years. Fourteen heads of departments form the Governor's advisory council, also designated as his Council of Secretaries. The legislative functions are vested in a Senate, composed of 27 members (2 from each of the 8 senatorial districts and 11 senators at large), and the House of Representatives, composed of 51 members (1 from each of the 40 representative districts and 11 elected at large). Puerto Rico sends to Congress a Resident Commissioner to the US, elected by the people for a term of 4 years, but he has no vote in Congress. Puerto Rican men are subject to conscription in US services.

On 27 Nov. 1953 President Eisenhower sent a message to the General Assembly of the UN stating 'if at any time the Legislative Assembly of Puerto Rico adopts a resolution in favour of more complete or even absolute independence' he 'will immediately thereafter recommend to Congress that such independence be granted'.

For an account of the constitutional developments prior to 1952, *see* THE STATESMAN'S YEAR-BOOK, 1952, p. 742. The new constitution was drafted by a Puerto Rican Constituent Assembly and approved by the electorate at a referendum on 3 March 1952. It was then submitted to Congress, which struck out Section 20 of Article 11 covering the 'right to work' and the 'right to an adequate standard of living'; the remainder was passed and proclaimed by the Governor on 25 July 1952.

At the election on 4 Nov. 1984 the Popular Democratic Party, headed by Rafael Hernández Colon, polled 822,783 votes (47·8% of the total); the New Progressive Party, headed by Carlos Romero Barceló, polled 768,742 votes (44·6% of the total); the Independence Party (full independence by constitutional means), 61,316 (3·6% of the total); Renewal Puerto Rican Party, 69,865 votes (3·6% of the total).

Governor: Rafael Hernández Colon (Popular Democratic Party).

ECONOMY

Budget. Central Government budget, year ending 30 June 1987: Balance at 1 July 1987, $313,959,000; receipts, $5,063,178; disbursements, $4,749,219,000.

Assessed value of property, 30 June 1989, was $6,670·2m., and bonded indebtedness, $3,497m.

The US administers and finances the postal service and maintains air and naval bases. US payments in Puerto Rico, including direct expenditures (mainly military), grants-in-aid and other payments to individuals and to business totalled: 1985–86, $3,961·8m.; 1986–87, $3,767·4m.; 1987-88, $3,976·1m.; 1988-89, £4,099·2m.

Banking. Banks on 30 June 1988 had total deposits of $20,848m. Bank loans were $11,178m. This includes 18 commercial banks, 2 government banks and 4 trust companies.

NATURAL RESOURCES

Minerals. There is stone, and some production of cement (1m. tons in 1988–89).

Agriculture. Farming is mainly of sugar-cane. Production of raw sugar, 96 degrees basis, 1989 crop year, was 91,249 tons.

Livestock (1989): Cattle, 585,501; pigs, 199,727; poultry, 10,697,866.

COMMERCE. In 1988–89 imports amounted to $14,042·8m., of which $9,443·9m. came from US; exports were valued at $16,354·9m., of which $14,245·5m. went to US.

In financial year 1989 the US took: Sugar, 17,314 short tons; cigarettes, cigars and cheroots, 1,310,157,000 units; other tobacco and products, 1,182,410 lb.; rum, 21,551,641 proof gallons.

Puerto Rico is not permitted to levy taxes on imports.

Total trade between Puerto Rico and UK (British Department of Trade returns, in £1,000 sterling):

	1985	*1986*	*1987*	*1988*	*1989*
Imports to UK	126,971	81,131	76,347	91,909	117,628
Exports and re-exports from UK	117,861	49,620	39,405	38,877	79,851

COMMUNICATIONS

Roads. The Department of Public Works had under maintenance in June 1986, 8,111·7 km of paved road. Motor vehicles registered 30 June 1989, 1,606,115.

Shipping. In financial year 1988–89, 9,813 American and foreign vessels of 62,267,241 gross tons entered and cleared Puerto Rico.

Post and Broadcasting. In Jan. 1987 there were 103 broadcasting stations and 19 television companies. There were (1988) 756,590 telephones.

Newspapers. In 1989 there were 4 main newspapers, *El Nuevo Día* had a daily circulation of about 210,940 (March 1989); *El Vocero*, 250,000 (Sept. 1989); *San Juan Star*, 47,000 (Oct. 1989); *El Mundo*, 103,500 (Oct. 1989).

JUSTICE AND EDUCATION

Justice. The Commonwealth judiciary system is headed by a Supreme Court of 7 members, appointed by the Governor, and consists of a Superior Tribunal with 11 sections and 92 superior judges, a District Tribunal with 38 sections and 99 district judges, and 60 municipal judges all appointed by the Governor.

Education. Education was made compulsory in 1899, but in 1981, 3·6% of the children still had no access to schooling. The percentage of illiteracy in 1980 was 10·3% of those 10 years of age or older. Total enrolment in public schools, 1988–89, was 802,057. Accredited private schools had 128,554 pupils (1988–89). All instruction below senior high school standard is given in Spanish only.

The University of Puerto Rico, in Río Piedras, 7 miles from San Juan, had 56,993 students in 1988–89 of which 4,243 were in 3 Regional Colleges and 52,750 in other colleges. Higher education is also available in the Inter-American University of Puerto Rico (38,379 students in 1988–89), the Catholic University of Puerto Rico (11,551), the Sacred Heart College (7,480) and the Fundacion Ana G. Méndez (17,854). These and other private colleges and universities had 24,646 students.

Further Reading

Statistical Information: The area of Economic Research and Evaluation of the Puerto Rico Planning Board publishes: *(a)* annual *Economic Report to the Governor; (b) External Trade Statistics* (annual report); *(c) Reports on national income and balance of payments; (d) Socio-Economic Statistics* (since 1940); *(e) Puerto Rico Monthly Economic Indicators*. In addition there are annual reports by various Departments.

Annual Reports. Governor of Puerto Rico. Washington

Bloomfield, R. J., *Puerto Rico: The Search for a National Policy*. Boulder, 1985

Carr, R., *Puerto Rico: A Colonial Experiment*. New York Univ. Press, 1984

Cevallos, E., *Puerto Rico*. [Bibliography], Oxford and Santa Barbara, 1985

Crampsey, R. A., *Puerto Rico*. Newton Abbot, 1973

Dietz, J. L., *Economic History of Puerto Rico: Institutional Change and Capital Development*. Princeton Univ. Press, 1987

Falk, P. S., (ed.) *The Political Status of Puerto Rico*. Lexington, Mass., 1986

Commonwealth Library: Univ. of Puerto Rico Library, Rio Piedras. *Librarian:* José Lázaro.

VIRGIN ISLANDS OF THE UNITED STATES

HISTORY. The Virgin Islands of the United States, formerly known as the Danish West Indies, were named and claimed for Spain by Columbus in 1493. They were later settled by Dutch and English planters, invaded by France in the mid-17th century and abandoned by the French *c*. 1700, by which time Danish influence had been established. St Croix was held by the Knights of Malta between two periods of French rule.

They were purchased by the United States from Denmark for $25m. in a treaty ratified by both nations and proclaimed 31 March 1917. Their value was wholly strategic, inasmuch as they commanded the Anegada Passage from the Atlantic

Ocean to the Caribbean Sea and the approach to the Panama Canal. Although the inhabitants were made US citizens in 1927, the islands are, constitutionally, an 'unincorporated territory'.

AREA AND POPULATION. The Virgin Islands group, lying about 40 miles due east of Puerto Rico, comprises the islands of St Thomas (28 sq. miles), St Croix (84 sq. miles), St John (20 sq. miles) and about 50 small islets or cays, mostly uninhabited. The total area of the 3 principal islands is 136 sq. miles, of which the US Government owns 9,599 acres as National Park.

The population, according to the census of 1 April 1985, was 110,800, an increase of 15,209 or 16% since 1980. Estimate (1987) 106,000. Population (1987) of St Croix, 52,740; St Thomas, 52,400; St John, 2,860. About 20–25% (1980) are native-born, 35–40% from other Caribbean islands, 10% from mainland USA and 5% from Europe. St Croix has over 40% of Puerto Rican origin or extraction, Spanish speaking. In 1987, live births were 2,375 and deaths, 558.

The capital and only city, Charlotte Amalie, on St Thomas, had a population (1985) of 52,660; there are two towns on St Croix. Christiansted with (1980) 2,856 and Frederiksted with 1,054.

CLIMATE. Average temperatures vary from 77°F to 82°F throughout the year; humidity is low. Average annual rainfall, about 45 inches. The islands lie in the hurricane belt; tropical storms with heavy rainfall can occur in late summer, but hurricanes rarely.

CONSTITUTION AND GOVERNMENT. The Organic Act of 22 July 1954 gives the US Department of the Interior full jurisdiction; some limited legislative powers are given to a single-chambered legislature, composed of 15 senators elected for 2 years representing the two legislative districts of St Croix and St Thomas-St John.

The Governor is elected by the residents. Since 1954 there have been four attempts to redraft the Constitution, to provide for greater autonomy. Each has been rejected by the electorate. The latest was defeated in a referendum in Nov. 1981, 50% of the electorate participating.

For administration, there are 15 executive departments, 14 of which are under commissioners and the other, the Department of Justice, under an Attorney-General. The US Department of the Interior appoints a Federal Comptroller of government revenue and expenditure.

The franchise is vested in residents who are citizens of the United States, 18 years of age or over. In 1986 there were 34,183 voters, of whom 26,377 participated in the local elections that year.

They do not participate in the US presidential election but they have a non-voting representative in Congress.

The capital is Charlotte Amalie, on St Thomas Island.

Governor: Alexander A. Farrelly ($62,400).
Lieut.-Governor: Derek M. Hodge ($57,000).
Administrator St Croix: Richard Roebuck, Jr.
Administrator St John: William Lomax.
Administrator St Thomas: Harold Robinson.

ECONOMY

Budget. Under the 1954 Organic Act finances are provided partly from local revenues—customs, federal income tax, real and personal property tax, trade tax, excise tax, pilotage fees, etc.—and partly from Federal Matching Funds, being the excise taxes collected by the federal government on such Virgin Islands products transported to the mainland as are liable.

Budget for financial year 1988, $303,575,186.

Currency and Banking. United States currency became legal tender on 1 July 1934. Banks are the Chase Manhattan Bank; the Bank of Nova Scotia; the First

Federal Savings and Loan Association of Puerto Rico; Barclays Bank International; Citibank; First Pennsylvania Bank; Banco Popular de Puerto Rico, and the First Virgin Islands Federal Savings Bank.

ENERGY AND NATURAL RESOURCES

Electricity. The Virgin Islands Water and Power Authority provides electric power from generating plants on St Croix and St Thomas; St John is served by power cable and emergency generator.

Water. There are 6 de-salinization plants with maximum daily capacity of 8·7m. gallons of fresh water. Rain-water remains the most reliable source. Every building must have a cistern to provide rain-water for drinking, even in areas served by mains (10 gallons capacity per sq. ft of roof for a single-storey house).

Agriculture. Land for fruit, vegetables and animal feed is available on St Croix, and there are tax incentives for development. Sugar has been terminated as a commercial crop and over 4,000 acres of prime land could be utilized for food crops.

Livestock (1988): Cattle, 11,000; goats, 4,000; pigs, 3,000; sheep, 3,000, poultry (1986), 18,345.

Fisheries. There is a fishermen's co-operative with a market at Christiansted. There is a shellfish-farming project at Rust-op-Twist, St Croix.

INDUSTRY AND TRADE

Industry. The main occupations on St Thomas are tourism and government service; on St Croix manufacturing is more important. Manufactures include rum (the most valuable product), watches, pharmaceuticals and fragrances. Industries in order of revenue: Tourism, refining oil, watch assembly, rum distilling, construction.

Labour. In 1989 the total labour force was 43,340, of whom 13,200 were employed in government, 8,450 in retail trades, 4,430 in hotels and other lodgings, 3,550 self-employed and unpaid family workers, 2,570 in transportation and public utilities, 2,350 in manufacturing, 2,330 in construction, 1,940 in finance, insurance and real estate, 1,070 in wholesale trades, 1,050 in business services, 350 in legal services, 230 in personnel services and 150 in agriculture.

Commerce. Exports, calendar year 1987, totalled $2,057·7m. and imports $3,370·4m. The main import is crude petroleum, while the principal exports are petroleum products.

Total trade between the US Virgin Islands and UK (financial years, British Department of Trade returns, in £1,000 sterling):

	1986	*1987*	*1988*	*1989*
Imports to UK	5,455	2,674	75	150
Exports and re-exports from UK	5,955	6,503	5,281	4,664

Tourism. Tourism is the most important business. There were about 1·52m. visitors in 1986 spending $509·8m.; 728,700 came by air and 827,151 on cruise ships, mainly to St Thomas which has a good, natural deepwater harbour.

COMMUNICATIONS

Roads. The Virgin Islands have (1986) 660 miles of roads, and 48,800 motor vehicles registered.

Aviation. There is a daily cargo and passenger service between St Thomas and St Croix. Alexander Hamilton Airport on St Croix can take all aircraft except Concorde. Cyril E. King Airport on St Thomas takes 727-class aircraft. There are air connexions to mainland USA, other Caribbean islands, Latin America and Europe.

Shipping. The whole territory has free port status. There is an hourly boat service between St Thomas and St John.

Post and Broadcasting. All three Virgin Islands have a dial telephone system. In Dec. 1986 there were 39,232 telephones. Direct dialling to Puerto Rico and the mainland, and internationally, is now possible. Worldwide radio telegraph service is also available.

The islands are served by 10 radio stations and 4 television stations. In 1988 there were an estimated 103,500 radio receivers and 64,400 television receivers in use.

Newspapers. In 1989 there were 2 daily and 1 fortnightly papers and 1 magazine.

RELIGION AND EDUCATION

Religion. There are churches of the Protestant, Roman Catholic and Jewish faiths in St Thomas and St Croix and Protestant and Roman Catholic churches in St John.

Education. In 1988 there were 13,359 pupils and 873 teachers in elementary schools, and 10,661 pupils and 723 teachers in secondary schools; 33 non-public schools had 5,079 pupils. In autumn 1988 the University of the Virgin Islands had 2,196 full-time students, 4,654 part-time students and 575 graduate students. The College is part of the United States land-grant network of higher education.

Further Reading

Boyer, W. W., *America's Virgin Islands*. Durham, N.C., 1983
Dookhan, I., *A History of the Virgin Islands of the United States*. Caribbean Univ. Press, 1974
Lewis, G. K., *The Virgin Islands: A Caribbean Lilliput*. Northwestern University Press, Evanston, 1972

URUGUAY

República Oriental del Uruguay

Capital: Montevideo
Population: 3·08m. (1988)
GNP per capita: US$2,470 (1988)

HISTORY. The Republic of Uruguay, formerly a part of the Spanish Viceroyalty of Río de la Plata and subsequently a province of Brazil, declared its independence 25 Aug. 1825 which was recognized by the treaty between Argentina and Brazil signed at Rio de Janeiro 27 Aug. 1828. The first constitution was adopted 18 July 1830.

AREA AND POPULATION. Uruguay is bounded on the north-east by Brazil, on the south-east by the Atlantic, on the south by the Río de la Plata and on the west by Argentina. The area is 176,215 sq. km (68,037 sq. miles). The following table shows the area and the population of the 19 departments at census 1985:

Departments	*Sq. km*	*Census 1985*	*Capital*	*Census 1985*
Artigas	11,928	68,400	Artigas	34,551
Canelones	4,536	359,700	Canelones	17,316
Cerro-Largo	13,648	78,000	Melo	42,329
Colonia	6,106	112,100	Colonia	19,077
Durazno	11,643	54,700	Durazno	27,602
Flores	5,144	24,400	Trinidad	18,271
Florida	10,417	65,400	Florida	28,560
Lavalleja	10,016	61,700	Minas	34,634
Maldonado	4,793	93,000	Maldonado	33,498
Montevideo	530	1,309,100	Montevideo	1,247,920
Paysandú	13,922	104,500	Paysandú	75,081
Río Negro	9,282	47,500	Fray Bentos	20,431
Rivera	9,370	88,400	Rivera	56,335
Rocha	10,551	68,500	Rocha	23,910
Salto	14,163	107,300	Salto	80,787
San José	4,992	91,900	San José	31,732
Soriano	9,008	77,500	Mercedes	37,110
Tacuarembó	15,438	82,600	Tacuarembó	40,470
Treinta y Tres	9,529	45,500	Treinta y Tres	30,956

Total population, census (1985) 2,940,200 and estimate 1988 was 3,080,000. In 1985 Montevideo (the capital) had a census population of 1,246,500; Las Piedras, 58,221.

CLIMATE. A warm temperate climate, with mild winters and warm summers. The wettest months are March to June, but there is really no dry season. Montevideo. Jan. 72°F (22·2°C), July 50°F (10°C). Annual rainfall 38" (950 mm).

CONSTITUTION AND GOVERNMENT. Since 1900 Uruguay has been unique in her constitutional innovations, all designed to protect her from the emergence of a dictatorship. The favourite device of the group known as the 'Batllistas' (a *Colorado* faction) which, until defeated at the 1958 elections, held the majority for over 90 years, has been the collegiate system of government, in which the two largest political parties were represented.

There is a Senate of 31 members and a Chamber of Representatives of 99 members.

Gen. Gregorio Alvarez resigned on 12 Feb. 1985 and a return to civilian rule took place on 1 March 1985. Following a return to civilian rule a National Constituent Assembly was installed on 1 July 1985 to consider reforms to the Constitution. On 26 Nov. 1989 the first free presidential and congressional elections for 18 years took place.

President: Luis Alberto Lacalle Herrara (sworn in on 1 March 1990).

National flag: Nine horizontal stripes of white and blue, a white canton with the 'Sun of May' in gold.

National anthem: Orientales, la patria ó la tumba (words by Francisco Acuña de Figueroa; music by Francisco José Deballi).

DEFENCE

Army. The Army consists of volunteers who enlist for 1-2 years service. There are 1 infantry and 1 engineer brigades, 15 infantry, 10 cavalry, 6 artillery and 6 engineer battalions. Equipment includes 17 M-24, 28 M-3A1 and 22 M-41 light tanks. Strength (1990) 17,200.

Navy. The navy has commenced replacing its major 1940-vintage *ex*-US ships with French frigates of the Commandant Riviere class as these are retired from the French navy. One has so far been transferred, and two more are expected to follow. The fleet presently consists of 2 frigates, 1 *ex*-French Riviere (built 1962) and 1 *ex*-US Dealey class (1954), 2 offshore patrol vessels (both *ex*-US, one a former frigate but with no significant armament, one a de-equipped minesweeper), 3 fast inshore patrol craft (French-built, 1981), 2 other inshore patrol vessels and 1 coastal minesweeper. Auxiliaries comprise 1 freighting tanker, a sail training ship, a salvage ship and 2 service vessels. There are 5 small landing craft.

A naval aviation service 400 strong operates 5 S-2 Tracker ASW aircraft, 1 maritime reconnaissance, 10 training aricraft and 4 general purpose helicopters. Personnel in 1989 totalled 4,500 including 500 naval infantry.

A separate coastguard, 1,900 strong, operates 3 inshore patrol craft.

Air Force. Organized with US aid, the Air Force had (1990) about 3,000 personnel and 110 aircraft, including 1 counter-insurgency squadron with 6 IA 58 Pucara, 4 AT-33 armed jet trainers and 8 A-37B light strike aircraft, a reconnaissance and training squadron with 10 T-6Gs, 3 transport squadrons with 2 turboprop F.27 Friendships, 5 Brazilian-built EMB-110 Bandeirantes (1 equipped for photographic duties), 5 CASA C-212 Aviocars and 6 Queen Airs, a search and rescue squadron with Cessna U-17A aircraft and Bell helicopters, and a number of Cessna 182 light aircraft for liaison duties. Basic training types are the T-41 and T-34.

INTERNATIONAL RELATIONS

Membership. Uruguay is a member of UN, OAS and LAIA (formerly LAFTA).

ECONOMY

Budget. The receipts and expenditure of the national accounts as approved by the National Council of Government (URN$1m.):

	1986	*1987*	*1988*
Revenue	150,000	270,939	456,675
Expenditure	161,000	292,988	510,651

External public debt US$5,888m. in Dec. 1987.

Currency. The unit of currency is the *Nuevo Peso* (1,000 old pesos) of 100 *centésimos*. The actual circulating medium consists of paper notes issued by the Central Bank in *Nuevo Peso* denominations of 50, 100, 500, 1,000 and 5,000 *Nuevo Peso*, and 1, 2, 5 and 10 coins. In March 1990, US$1 = 924·29 *pesos*; £1 = 1515·24 *pesos*.

Banking. The Bank of the Republic (founded 1896), whose president and directors are appointed by the Government has a paid-up capital of N$1,852m. The Banco Central was inaugurated on 16 May 1967. Note circulation in Dec. 1983 was N$10,538·7m.

A state-owned National Insurance Bank *(Banco de Seguros del Estado)* has a monopoly of new insurance business of all kinds.

Weights and Measures. The metric system was adopted in 1862.

ENERGY AND NATURAL RESOURCES

Electricity. Power output in 1986 was 3,730m kwh.

Oil. Petroleum production (1981) 185,000 tonnes.

Agriculture. Uruguay is primarily a pastoral country. Of the total land area of 46m. acres some 41m. are devoted to farming, of which 90% to livestock and 10% to crops. Some large *estancias* have been divided up into family farms; rural land-lordism is much less than elsewhere.

There were (1988) 10,408,000 cattle, 26,049,000m. sheep, 473,000 horses, 215,000 pigs, 14,000 goats and 8m. poultry.

The wool clip in 1984 was 91,000 tonnes.

Agricultural products are raised chiefly in the departments of Paysandú, Río Negro, Colonia, San José, Soriano and Florida. The average farm is about 250 acres. The principal crops and their estimated yield (in tonnes) in 2 crop years were as follows:

	1987	*1988*		*1987*	*1988*
Wheat	350,000	390,000	Barley	90,000	130,000
Linseed	8,000	3,000	Maize	104,000	118,000
Oats	30,000	58,000	Rice	354,000	381,000

Uruguay is self-sufficient in rice, with a surplus for export. Three sugar refineries handle cane and (mainly) beet, their total production being approximately (1987) 93,000 tonnes, and approaching self-sufficiency.

Wine is produced chiefly in the departments of Montevideo, Canelones and Colonia, about enough for domestic consumption (74,000 tonnes in 1988). The country has some 6m. fruit trees, principally peaches, oranges, tangerines and pears.

Forestry. In 1986 roundwood removals were 2,663,000 cu. metres.

Fisheries. In 1987, the total catch was 134,900 tonnes.

INDUSTRY AND TRADE

Industry. Industries include meat packing, oil refining, cement manufacture, food-stuffs, beverages, leather and textile maufacture, chemicals, light engineering and transport equipment. There are about 100 textile mills, but with the exception of half a dozen large plants, these are on the whole small.

Commerce. The foreign trade (officially stated in US$, with the figure for imports based on the clearance permits granted and that for exports on export licences utilized) was as follows (in US$1,000):

	1985	*1986*	*1987*	*1988*
Imports	708·0	1,087·6	1,189·1	1,404·5
Exports	854·0	838·8	1,141·9	1,176·9

Of the imports in 1987 (in US$1m.) USA, 90; Brazil, 279; Argentina, 156; Federal Republic of Germany, 92; UK, 34. Of the exports in 1987 Brazil took 204; Argentina, 113; Federal Republic of Germany, 121; USA, 176; UK, 54.

Principal imports (1987) (in US$1,000): Mineral products, 189,000; chemical products, 176,000; machinery and appliances, 217,000. Exports: Textiles and textile products, 384,000; live animals and animal products, 257,000; skins and hides, 199,000; vegetable products, 99,000.

Total trade between Uruguay and UK (British Department of Trade returns, in £1,000 sterling):

	1985	*1986*	*1987*	*1988*	*1989*
Imports to UK	28,824	41,366	40,474	35,410	52,185
Exports and re-exports from UK	15,513	24,465	26,484	34,999	26,119

Tourism. There were 1,168,000 tourists in 1986.

COMMUNICATIONS

Roads. There were (1984) about 52,000 km of roads including 12,000 km of motorways.

Registered motor vehicles, 31 Dec. 1981, are estimated at 281,275 passenger cars and 47,102 trucks and buses.

Railways. The total railway system open for traffic was (1986) 2,991 km of 1,435 mm gauge. In 1988 it carried 1m. tonnes of freight.

Aviation. Carrasco, 22·5 km from Montevideo, is the most important airport. US, Argentine, Brazilian, Chilean, Dutch, French, Fed. German, Scandinavian and Paraguayan airlines fly to and from Uruguay. The state-operated civil airline PLUNA runs services in the interior of the country and to Brazil, Paraguay and Argentina, and Spain.

Shipping. In 1983 there were 13 merchant vessels and 3 tankers. River transport (1,270 km) is extensive, its main importance being to link Montevideo with Paysandú and Salto.

Post and Broadcasting. The telephone system in Montevideo is controlled by the State; small companies operate in the interior. Telephone instruments, 1986, numbered 337,000. There are 1,277 post offices. Uruguay has 85 long-wave and 17 short-wave broadcasting stations. There were (1985) about 1·7m. wireless sets and 500,000 television receivers. There are 4 television stations in Montevideo and 11 in the interior. The State itself operates one of the most powerful sound broadcasting stations in South America.

Cinemas (1980). Cinemas numbered 85 with seating capacity of 47,000.

Newspapers (1984). There were 5 daily newspapers in Montevideo with aggregate daily circulation of about 210,000; most of the 25–30 provincial newspapers appear bi-weekly.

JUSTICE, RELIGION, EDUCATION AND WELFARE

Justice. The Ministry of Justice was created in 1977 to be responsible for relations between the Executive Power and the Judiciary and other jurisdictional entities. The Court of Justice is made up by 5 members appointed by the Council of the Nation at the suggestion of the Executive Power, for a period of 5 years. This court has original jurisdiction in constitutional, international and admiralty cases and hears appeals from the appellate courts, of which there are 4, each with 3 judges.

In Montevideo there are also 8 courts for ordinary civil cases, 3 for government *(Juzgado de Hacienda)*, as well as criminal and correctional courts. Each departmental capital has a departmental court; each of the 224 judicial divisions has a justice of peace court.

Religion. State and Church are separated, and there is complete religious liberty. The faith professed by 66% of the inhabitants is Roman Catholic although only 50% attend church.

Education. Primary education is obligatory; both primary and superior education are free.

In 1985–86 there were 356,002 primary school pupils, and 188,176 secondary school pupils.

The University of the Republic at Montevideo, inaugurated in 1849, has about 16,200 students; tuition is free to both native-born and foreign students; there are 10 faculties. There are 43 normal schools for males and females, and a college of arts and trades with about 33,000 students. There are also many religious seminaries throughout the Republic with a considerable number of pupils, a school for the blind, 2 for deaf and dumb and a school of domestic science.

Health. Hospital beds, 1983, numbered (estimate) 23,400; physicians numbered (1984) 5,736.

DIPLOMATIC REPRESENTATIVES

Of Uruguay in Great Britain (48 Lennox Gdns., London, SW1X 0DL)
Ambassador: Dr Luis Alberto Solé-Romeo.

Of Great Britain in Uruguay (Calle Marco Bruto 1073, Montevideo)
Ambassador: C. J. Sharkey, CMG, OBE.

Of Uruguay in the USA (1918 F. St., NW, Washington, D.C., 20006)
Ambassador: (Vacant).

Of the USA in Uruguay (Lauro Muller 1776, Montevideo)
Ambassador: Malcolm R. Wilkey.

Of Uruguay to the United Nations
Ambassador: Felipe Héctor Paolillo.

Further Reading

The official gazette is the *Diario Oficial*
Statistical Reports of the Government. Montevideo. Annual and biennial
Anales de Instruccion Primaria. Montevideo. Quarterly

Finch, M.H.J., *A Political Economy of Uruguay Since 1870*. London, 1981
Salgado, Jose, *Historia de la Republica O. del Uruguay*. 8 vols. Montevideo, 1943
Weinstein, M., *Uruguay: Democracy at the Crossroads*. Boulder, 1988

National Library: Biblioteca Nacional del Uruguay, Guayabo 1793, Montevideo. It publishes *Anuario Bibliografico Uruguayo*.

VANUATU

Capital: Vila
Population: 142,630 (1989)
GNP per capita: US$820 (1988)

Republic of Vanuatu

HISTORY. The group was administered for some purposes jointly, for others unilaterally, as provided for by Anglo-French Convention of 27 Feb. 1906, ratified 20 Oct. 1906, and a protocol signed at London on 6 Aug. 1911 and ratified on 18 March 1922. On 30 July 1980 the Condominium of the New Hebrides achieved independence and became the Republic of Vanuatu.

AREA AND POPULATION. The Vanuatu group, of 80 islands, lies roughly 500 miles west of Fiji and 250 miles north-east of New Caledonia. The estimated land area is 4,706 sq. miles (12,190 sq. km). The larger islands of the group are: (Espiritu) Santo, Malekula, Epi, Pentecost, Aoba, Maewo, Paama, Ambrym, Efate, Erromanga, Tanna and Aneityum. They also claim Matthew and Hunter islands, 67 islands were inhabited in 1990. Population at the census (1979) 112,596. Estimate (1989) 142,630. Vila (the capital) 19,400. There are 3 active volcanoes, on Tanna, Ambrym and Lopevi, respectively.

Language: The national language is Bislama (spoken by 82% of the population); English and French are also official languages.

CLIMATE. The climate is tropical, but moderated by oceanic influences and by trade winds from May to Oct. High humidity occasionally occurs and cyclones are possible. Rainfall ranges from 90" (2,250 mm) in the south to 155" (3,875 mm) in the north. Vila. Jan. 80°F (26·7°C), July 72°F (22·2°C). Annual rainfall 84" (2,103 mm). A cyclone hit Vila in Feb. 1987.

CONSTITUTION AND GOVERNMENT. Legislative power resides in a 46-member unicameral Parliament elected for a term of 4 years. In the latest elections on 30 Nov. 1987, 26 seats were won by the *Vanuaaku Pati* and 20 by the Union of Moderate Parties. There is also a Council of Chiefs, comprising traditional tribal leaders, to advise on matters of custom.

The President is elected for a 5-year term by an electoral college comprising Parliament and the presidents of the 11 regional councils. Executive power is vested in a Council of Ministers, responsible to Parliament, and appointed and led by a Prime Minister who is elected from and by Parliament.

President: Fred Timakata (elected Jan. 1989).

The cabinet in Dec. 1989 was composed as follows:

Prime Minister, Minister of Public Service, Planning and Information: Walter Hadye Lini, CBE.

Agriculture, Forestry and Fisheries: Jack T. Hopa. *Education:* Sethy J. Regenvanu. *Finance and Housing:* Sela Molisa. *Foreign Affairs and Judicial Services:* Donald Kalpokas. *Health:* Jimmy Meto Chilia. *Home Affairs:* Iolu J. Abbil. *Lands, Geology, Minerals and Rural Water Supply:* William Mahit. *Trade, Commerce, Cooperatives, Industry and Energy:* Harold C. Qualao. *Public Works, Communications, Transport, Civil Aviation and Tourism:* Edward N. Natapei.

Flag: Red over green, with a black triangle in the hoist, the three parts being divided by fimbriations of black and yellow, and in the centre of the black triangle a boar's tusk overlaid by two crossed fern leaves.

DEFENCE. There is a paramilitary force with about 300 personnel. A naval service formed in 1987, and following training by the Royal Australian Navy operates 1 inshore patrol craft, and a former motor yacht, both lightly armed. Personnel number about 50.

INTERNATIONAL RELATIONS

Membership. Vanuatu is a member of the UN and the Commonwealth and is an ACP state of EEC.

ECONOMY

Budget. The budget for 1988 balanced at 3,938m. Vatu. The main sources of revenue were import and taxes on goods and services.

Currency. The currency is the *Vatu*. March 1990: £1 = 192·00 *Vatu*; US$1 = 117·14.

Banking (1989). The Finance Centre, established in 1970–71 and based primarily in Vila, consists of 4 international banks (including the Hongkong and Shanghai Banking Corporation) and 6 trust companies (including Melanesia International Trust Company Ltd, a Hongkong Bank group associate). In Aug. 1984 the Asian Development Bank opened a regional office in Vila. Commercial banks assets at 31 Dec. 1988, 20,900m. Vatu.

Weights and Measures. The metric system is in force.

ENERGY AND NATURAL RESOURCES

Electricity. Production (1986) 20m. kwh.

Minerals. The manganese mine, established at Forari on Efate closed in 1978 and the extraction of pozzolana to supply the local cement industry ceased in 1985. Preliminary prospecting for gold began in 1985 and prospects have been identified on Efate, Malekula and Santo.

Agriculture. The main commercial crops are copra, cocoa and coffee. In 1988 31,681 tonnes of copra, value 953m. Vatu, were exported. Production, 1988: Copra, 29,552 tonnes; cocoa, 756 tonnes; coffee (1985), 65. In 1985 about 80% of the population were engaged in subsistence agriculture. Yams, taro, manioc, sweet potatoes and bananas are grown for local consumption. A large number of cattle are reared on plantations, and an upgrading programme using pure-bred Charolais, Limousins and Illawarras has begun. A beef industry is developing.

Livestock (1988): Cattle, 105,000; goats, 15,000; pigs, 79,000.

Forestry. In 1987 some 1,900 hectares of plantation had been established. Production (1985) 37,900 cu. metres of logs and sawn timber.

Fisheries. The principal catch is tuna (1985, 3,962 tonnes) mainly exported to USA. Small-scale commercial fishing (1985) over 200 tonnes.

INDUSTRY AND TRADE

Industry. Industries in 1987 included copra processing, meat canning and fish freezing, a saw-mill, soft drinks factories and a print works. Building materials, furniture and aluminium were also produced, and in 1984 a cement plant opened.

Commerce. Imports and exports were (in 1m. Vatu):

	1985	*1986*	*1987*	*1988*
Imports	7,378	6,105	7,638	7,361
Exports	3,262	1,841	1,942	2,066

In 1988 the main exports (in 1m. Vatu) were: Copra, 953; beef and veal, 243; timber, 106; cocoa, 117. 52% of exports went to the Netherlands, 15% to Japan, 6% to France, 4% to Australia and 3% to New Caledonia. Australia (43%), Japan (9%), New Zealand (11%), France (5%), Fiji (7%), New Caledonia (4%), were the major sources of imports and principal imports (in 1m. Vatu) were machinery and transport equipment (1,797), food and live animals (1,263), basic manufactures (1,430), manufactured articles (851), fuels and lubricants (584), chemicals (421) and beverages and tobacco (368).

Total trade between Vanuatu and UK (British Department of Trade returns, in £1,000 sterling):

	1986	1987	1988	1989
Imports to UK	62	15	5	52
Exports and re-exports from UK	1,037	1,058	856	363

Tourism. In 1988 there were 17,544 visitors to Vanuatu. In addition there were 50,932 tourists from cruise ships. Earnings from tourism 2,000m. Vatu.

COMMUNICATIONS

Roads. In 1984 there were 1,062 km of roads in Vanuatu, of these about 250 km are paved, mostly on Efate Island and Espiritu Santo. There were 3,784 registered cars in Vanuatu (1988).

Aviation (1986). Air Vanuatu provides services to Australia; Air Nauru, Air Pacific, Air Caledonia, Solair and UTA serve Pacific routes; Air Melanisia provides regular services to 16 domestic airfields, and charter services. There are international airfields at Vila and Santo.

Shipping. Several international shipping lines serve Vanuatu, linking the country with Australia, New Zealand, other Pacific territories notably Hong Kong, Japan, North America and Europe. The chief ports are Vila and Santo. In 1977, 394 vessels arrived including 48 cruise ships carrying 40,412 visitors. 92,340 tons of cargo were exported and 102,867 tons discharged. Small vessels provide frequent inter-island services.

Telecommunications. Internal telephone and telegram services are provided by the Posts and Telecommunications and Radio Departments. There are automatic telephone exchanges at Vila and Santo; rural areas are served by a network of tele-radio stations. In 1983 there were 6 post offices and 3,000 telephones.

External telephone, telegram and telex services are provided by VANITEL, through their satellite earth station at Vila. There are direct circuits to Noumea, Sydney, Hong Kong and Paris and high quality communications are available on a 24-hour basis to most countries in the world. Air radio facilities are provided. Marine coast station facilities are available at Vila and Santo. Radio Vanuatu operates a service 7 days a week in, French, English and Bislama. In 1986 there were 4 radio stations and 18,000 receivers.

JUSTICE, RELIGION, EDUCATION AND WELFARE

Justice. A study was being made in 1980 which could lead to unification of the judicial system.

Religion. Over 80% of the population are Christians, but animist beliefs are still prevalent.

Education. There were (1988) 260 primary schools with 24,634 pupils, 11 government and denominational secondary schools with 2,000 pupils and Matevulu College. Tertiary education is provided at the Vanuatu Technical Institute and the Teachers College, while other technical and commercial training is through regional institutions in the Solomon Islands, Fiji and Papua New Guinea.

Health. In 1988 there were 12 hospitals (5 rural) with 419 beds, 37 health centres, 50 dispensaries, 23 doctors and 270 nurses.

DIPLOMATIC REPRESENTATIVES

Of Vanuatu in Great Britain
High Commissioner: (Vacant).

Of Great Britain in Vanuatu (Melitco Hse., Rue Pasteur, Vila)
High Commissioner: J. Thompson, MBE.

Of Vanuatu to the United Nations
Ambassador: Robert F. Van Lierop.

VATICAN CITY STATE

Stato della Città del Vaticano

HISTORY. For many centuries the Popes bore temporal sway over a territory stretching across mid-Italy from sea to sea and comprising some 17,000 sq. miles, with a population finally of over 3m. In 1859–60 and 1870 the Papal States were incorporated into the Italian Kingdom. The consequent dispute between Italy and successive Popes was only settled on 11 Feb. 1929 by three treaties between the Italian Government and the Vatican: (1) A Political Treaty, which recognized the full and independent sovereignty of the Holy See in the city of the Vatican; (2) a Concordat, to regulate the condition of religion and of the Church in Italy; and (3) a Financial Convention, in accordance with which the Holy See received 750m. lire in cash and 1,000m. lire in Italian 5% state bonds. This sum was to be a definitive settlement of all the financial claims of the Holy See against Italy in consequence of the loss of its temporal power in 1870. The treaty and concordat were ratified on 7 June 1929. The treaty has been embodied in the Constitution of the Italian Republic of 1947. A revised Concordat between the Italian Republic and the Holy See was subsequently negotiated and signed in 1984, and which came into force on 3 June 1985.

The Vatican City State is governed by a Commission appointed by the Pope. The reason for its existence is to provide an extra-territorial, independent base for the Holy See, the government of the Roman Catholic Church.

AREA AND POPULATION. The area of the Vatican City is 44 hectares (108·7 acres). It includes the Piazza di San Pietro (St Peter's Square), which is to remain normally open to the public and subject to the powers of the Italian police. It has its own railway station (for freight only), postal facilities, coins and radio. Twelve buildings in and outside Rome enjoy extra-territorial rights, including the Basilicas of St John Lateran, St Mary Major and St Paul without the Walls, the Pope's summer villa at Castel Gandolfo and a further Vatican radio station on Italian soil. *Radio Vaticana* broadcasts an extensive service in 34 languages from the transmitters in the Vatican City and in Italy.

The Vatican City has about 1,000 inhabitants.

CONSTITUTION. The Pope exercises sovereignty and has absolute legislative, executive and judicial powers. The judicial power is delegated to a tribunal in the first instance, to the Sacred Roman Rota in appeal and to the Supreme Tribunal of the Signature in final appeal.

The Pope is elected by the College of Cardinals, meeting in secret conclave. The election is by scrutiny and requires a two-thirds majority.

Name and family	*Election*	*Name and family*	*Election*
Benedict XIV *(Lambertini)*	1740	Leo XIII *(Pecci)*	1878
Clement XIII *(Rezzonico)*	1758	Pius X *(Sarto)*	1903
Clement XIV *(Ganganelli)*	1769	Benedict XV *(della Chiesa)*	1914
Pius VI *(Braschi)*	1775	Pius XI *(Ratti)*	1922
Pius VII *(Chiaramonti)*	1800	Pius XII *(Pacelli)*	1939
Leo XII *(della Genga)*	1823	John XXIII *(Roncalli)*	1958
Pius VIII *(Castiglioni)*	1829	Paul VI *(Montini)*	1963
Gregory XVI *(Cappellari)*	1831	John Paul I *(Luciani)*	1978
Pius IX *(Mastai-Ferretti)*	1846	John Paul II *(Wojtyla)*	1978

Supreme Pontiff: **John Paul II** (Karol Wojtyla), born at Wadowice near Cracow,

Poland, 18 May 1920. Archbishop of Cracow 1964–78, created Cardinal in 1967, elected Pope 16 Oct. 1978, inaugurated 22 Oct. 1978.

Pope John Paul II was the first non-Italian to be elected since Pope Adrian VI (a Dutchman) in 1522.

Secretary of State: Cardinal Agostino Casaroli (appointed May 1979).

Flag: Vertically yellow and white, with on the white the crossed keys and tiara of the Papacy.

ROMAN CATHOLIC CHURCH. The Roman Pontiff (in orders a Bishop, but in jurisdiction held to be by divine right the centre of all Catholic unity, and consequently Pastor and Teacher of all Christians) has for advisers and coadjutors the Sacred College of Cardinals, consisting in Jan. 1990 of 149 Cardinals appointed by him from senior ecclesiastics who are either the bishops of important Sees or the heads of departments at the Holy See. In addition to the College of Cardinals, the Pope has created a ' Synod of Bishops'. This consists of the Patriarchs and certain Metropolitans of the Catholic Church of Oriental Rite, of elected representatives of the national episcopal conferences and religious orders of the world, of the Cardinals in charge of the Roman Congregations and of other persons nominated by the Pope. The Synod meets as and when decided by the Pope. The next Synod (on the formation of priests) met in Oct. 1990.

The central administration of the Roman Catholic Church is carried on by a number of permanent committees called Sacred Congregations, each composed of a number of Cardinals and diocesan bishops (both appointed for 5-year periods), with Consultors and Officials. Besides the Secretariat of State and the Second Section of the Secretariat of State (Section for Relations with States) there are now 9 Sacred Congregations, viz.: Doctrine, Oriental Churches, Bishops, the Sacraments, Divine Worship, Clergy, Religious, Catholic Education, Evangelization of the Peoples and Causes of the Saints. Pontifical Councils have replaced some of the previously designated Secretariats and Prefectures and now represent the Laity, Christian Unity, the Family, Justice and Peace, Cor Unum, Migrants, Health Care Workers, Interpretation of Legislative Texts, Inter-Religious Dialogue, Non Believers, Culture, Preserving the Patrimony of Art and History, and, a new Commission, for Latin America. There are also Offices for the Apostolic Penitentiary, the Supreme Tribunal of the Apostolic Signature, the Roman Rota, the Apostolic Camera, the Patrimony of the Holy See, Economic Affairs, the Papal Household, Liturgical Celebrations, the Secret Archives, the Apostolic Library, the Academy of Sciences, the Polyglot Press, the Publishing House, Vatican Radio, the Vatican Television Centre, the Fabric of St Peter's, Papal Charities, Translation Centre, Central Labour Office, the Consistory, Council of Cardinals, Economic Questions and the Institute for Works of Religion (the IOR). The Pontifical Academy of Sciences was revived by Pius XI in 1936 with 70 members.

DIPLOMATIC REPRESENTATIVES

In its diplomatic relations with foreign countries the Holy See is represented by the Secretariat of State and the Council for Public Affairs of the Church. It maintains permanent observers to the UN in New York and Geneva and to UNESCO and FAO. The Holy See is a member of IAEA and the Vatican City State is a member of UPU and ITU. It therefore attends as a member those international conferences open to State members of the UN and specialized agencies.

Of the Holy See in Great Britain (54 Parkside, London, SW19 5NF)
Apostolic Pro-Nuncio: Archbishop Luigi Barbarito (accredited 7 April 1986).

Of Great Britain at the Holy See (91 Via Condotti, I–00187, Rome).
Ambassador: J. K. E. Broadley, CMG. *First Secretary:* P. J. McCormick.

Of the Holy See in the USA (3339 Massachusetts Ave., NW, Washington, D.C., 20008).
Apostolic Pro Nuncio: Most Rev. Pio Laghi.

Of the USA at the Holy See (Villino Pacelli, Via Aurelia 294, 00165, Rome). *Ambassador:* Thomas Melady.

Further Reading

Acta Apostolicæ Sedis Romanæ. Rome
Annuario Pontificio. Rome. Annual
L'Attivita della Santa Sede. Rome. Annual
The Catholic Directory. London. Annual
Code of Canon Law. London, 1983
The Catholic Directory for Scotland. Glasgow. Annual
The New Catholic Encyclopædia. New York
The Catholic Almanac. Huntingdon, Annual
Bull, G., *Inside the Vatican*. London, 1982
Cardinale, Mgr. Igino, *Le Saint-Siège et la diplomatie*. Paris and Rome, 1962.—*The Holy See and the International Order*. Gerrards Cross, 1976
Hales, E. E., *The Catholic Church and the Modern World*. London, 1958
Hebblethwaite, P., *In the Vatican*. London, 1986
Mayer, F. *et al*, *The Vatican: Portrait of a State and a Community*. Dublin, 1980
Nichols, P., *The Pope's Divisions*. London, 1981
Walsh, M. J., *Vatican City State*. [Bibliography] Oxford and Santa Barbara, 1983

VENEZUELA

Capital: Caracas
Population: 18·77m. (1988)
GNP per capita: US$3,170 (1988)

República de Venezuela

HISTORY. Venezuela formed part of the Spanish colony of New Granada until 1821 when it became independent in union with Colombia. A separate, independent republic was formed in 1830.

AREA AND POPULATION. Venezuela is bounded north by the Caribbean, east by Guyana, south by Brazil, south-west and west by Colombia. The official estimate of the area is 912,050 sq. km (352,143 sq. miles); the frontiers with Colombia, Brazil and Guyana extend for 4,782 km and its Caribbean coastline stretches for some 3,200 km. Population (1981) census, 14,516,735. Estimate (1985) 17,316,740. The 1981 census excluded tribal Indians estimated at 53,350 (chiefly in Amazonas Territory) and illegal immigrants, estimated (1979) at about 3m. The official language is Spanish, spoken by all but 2·5% of the population.

The areas, populations and capitals of the 20 states and 4 federally-controlled areas are:

State	*Sq. km*	*Census 1981*	*Capital*	*Census 1981*
Anzoátegui	43,300	683,717	Barcelona	156,461
Apure	76,500	188,187	San Fernando	57,308
Aragua	7,014	891,623	Maracay	387,682
Barinas	35,200	326,166	Barinas	110,462
Bolívar	238,000	668,340	Ciudad Bolívar	182,941
Carabobo	4,650	1,062,268	Valencia	624,113
Cojedes	14,800	133,991	San Carlos	37,892
Falcón	24,800	503,896	Coro	96,339
Guárico	64,986	393,467	San Juan	57,219
Lara	19,800	945,064	Barquisimeto	523,101
Mérida	11,300	459,361	Mérida	143,805
Miranda	7,950	1,421,442	Los Teques	112,857
Monagas	28,900	388,536	Maturin	154,976
Nueva Esparta	1,150	197,198	La Asunción	10,375
Portuguesa	15,200	424,984	Guanare	64,025
Sucre	11,800	585,698	Cumaná	179,814
Táchira	11,100	660,234	San Cristóbal	198,793
Trujillo	7,400	433,735	Trujillo	31,774
Yaracuy	7,100	300,597	San Felipe	57,526
Zulia	63,100	1,674,252	Maracaibo	890,553
Ter. Amazonas	175,750	45,667	Puerto Ayacucho	28,248
Ter. Delta Amacuro	40,200	56,720	Tucupita	27,299
Federal District	1,930	2,070,742	Caracas	1,044,851
Federal Dependencies	120	850	—	—

Other large towns (1980) are Petare (334,800), Ciudad Guyana (314,041, census 1981), Baruta (180,100), Cabimas (138,529, census 1981), Acarigua (126,000), Maiquetiá (120,200), Valera (101,981, census 1981), Chacao (101,900), Puerto Cabello (94,000), Carúpano (82,000) and Puerto La Cruz (81,800).

Venezuela is the most urbanised Latin American nation; in 1985, 86% of the population lived in urban areas. Over half the population live in the valleys of Carabobo and Valencia (once the capital). At the 1981 census, 69% were of mixed ethnic origin (*mestizo*), 20% white, 9% black and 2% amerindian.

Vital statistics (1986): 504,278 births, 100,002 marriages, 77,647 deaths. Life expectancy (1985) 65 males, 71 females, with 41% of population under 15 years.

CLIMATE. The climate ranges from warm temperate to tropical. Temperatures vary little throughout the year and rainfall is plentiful. The dry season is from Dec. to April. Caracas. Jan. 65°F (18·3°C), July 69°F (20·6°C). Annual rainfall 32" (833 mm). Ciudad Bolivar. Jan. 79°F (26·1°C), July 81°F (27·2°C). Annual rainfall 41" (1,016 mm). Maracaibo. Jan. 81°F (27·2°C), July 85°F (29·4°C). Annual rainfall 23" (577 mm).

CONSTITUTION AND GOVERNMENT. The constitution of 1961 provides for popular election for a term of 5 years of a President, a National Congress, and State and Municipal legislative assemblies, and guarantees the freedom of labour, industry and commerce. Aliens are assured of treatment equal to that extended to nationals.

Congress consists of a Senate and a Chamber of Deputies. At least 2 Senators are elected for each State and for the Federal District. Senators must be Venezuelans by birth and over 30 years of age. Deputies must be native Venezuelans over 21 years of age; there is 1 for every 50,000 inhabitants. The territories, on reaching the population fixed by law, also elect deputies. Voting (by proportional representation) is compulsory for men and women over 18. Owing to the high rate of illiteracy, voting is by coloured ballot cards.

The President must be a Venezuelan by birth and over 30 years of age; he has a qualified power of veto.

The following is a list of presidents since 1945:

	Took Office		*Took Office*
Rómulo Betancourt	20 Oct. 1945	Rómulo Betancourt	13 Feb. 1959
Rómulo Gallegos	15 Feb. 1948	Raul Leoni	11 March 1964
Lieut.-Col. Carlos Delgado Chalbaud	24 Nov. 1948 [4]	Rafael Caldera	11 March 1969
Dr G. Suárez Flamerich	27 Nov. 1950 [2]	Carlos Andrés Pérez Rodríguez	12 March 1974
Col. Marcos Pérez Jiménez.	3 Dec. 1952 [1]	Dr Luis Herrera Campíns	12 March 1979
Rear-Adm. Wolfgang Larrazábal Ugueto	23 Jan. 1958 [2,3]	Dr Jaime Lusinchi	2 Feb. 1984
Dr Edgard Sanabria	14 Nov. 1958[3]	Carlos Andrés Perez Rodriguez	2 Feb. 1989

[1] Deposed. [2] Resigned. [3] Provisional. [4] Assassinated 13 Nov. 1950.

President: Carlos Andrés Perez Rodriguez, elected 4 Dec. 1988 with 54·56% of the votes, assumed office on 2 Feb. 1989.

The cabinet in March 1990 was composed as follows:

Interior: Alejandro Izaguirre. *Foreign Affairs:* Reinaldo Figueredo Planchart. *Finance:* Roberto Pocaterra. *Industrial Development:* Moises Naim. *Agriculture:* Eugenio de Armas. *Labour and Social Development:* German Lairet. *Justice:* Luis Beltran Guerra. *Transportation and Communications:* Edgar Elías Osuna. *Energy and Mines:* Celestino Armas. *Presidential Secretary:* Jesús Ramón Carmona Borjas. *Defence:* Gen. Filmo López Uzcategui.

At the Congressional elections held 4 Dec. 1983, 112 of the 200 seats in the Chamber of Deputies were won by Acción Democrática, 61 by COPEI (the Social Christians) and 27 by other parties.

The city of Caracas is the capital. The 20 states, autonomous and politically equal, have each a legislative assembly and a governor. The states are divided into 156 districts and 613 municipalities. There are also 2 federal territories with 7 departments, and a federal district with 2 departments and 2 parishes. Each district has a municipal council, and each municipio a communal junta. The federal district and the 2 territories are administered by the President of the Republic.

National flag: Three horizontal stripes of yellow, blue, red, with an arc of 7 white stars in the centre, and the national arms in the canton.

National anthem: Gloria al bravo pueblo (1811; words by Vicente Salias, tune by Juan Landaeta).

DEFENCE. All Venezuelans on reaching 18 years of age are liable for 2 years in the Armed Forces.

Army. The Army consists of 1 cavalry and 4 infantry divisions; 1 Ranger brigade, 1 airborne regiment with supporting regiments and groups. Equipment includes 81 AMX-30 main battle and 36 AMX-13 light tanks. Army aviation comprises 31 helicopters and 15 aircraft. Strength (1990) 34,000.

Navy. The combatant fleet comprises 3 German-built submarines, 6 Italian-built Lupo class frigates, 3 fast missile craft and 3 further of the same class not yet missile equipped, 7 riverine patrol craft, 5 tank landing ships and 2 craft. Auxiliaries comprise 1 logistic support, 2 transport, and a sail training ship, plus a few harbour service craft.

The Naval Air Arm, 2,000 strong, comprises 4 shore-based C-212 Aviocars for maritime reconnaissance, 6 AB-212 ship-borne ASW helicopters, 2 Bell 47 helicopters for SAR and 11 miscellaneous transport and liaison aircraft.

Personnel in 1989 totalled 11,000 (4,500 conscripts) including the Marine Corps and the Coastguard. Main bases are at Caracas, Puerto Cabello and Punto Fijo.

The Coastguard, organizationally separate but under Naval operational control, is responsible for control of the EEZ and comprises 2 large frigate-type, 2 *ex*-tugs and 1 other offshore patrol vessel, plus 2 smaller trawler type, and a number of boats.

The maritime elements of the *Fuerzas Armadas de Cooperacion* (National Guard), which is tasked with customs enforcement and internal security duties, operates some 70 patrol craft and boats of various sizes from 23m down.

Air Force. Formed in 1920, the Air Force of (1990) some 6,500 officers and men is a small, but well-equipped service with a total of about 200 aircraft. There are 8 combat squadrons. Two are equipped with 18 F-16A and 6 F-16B Fighting Falcons. Two have 14 Canadair CF-5A fighter-bombers and 6 two-seat CF-5Ds, and two share 9 Mirage III/5 single-seaters and 2 Mirage 5D trainers. Two bomber squadrons are equipped with 19 modernized Canberra jet-bombers and a single reconnaissance Canberra. Another operational squadron has 14 OV-10E Bronco twin-turboprop counter-insurgency aircraft. A helicopter force consists of more than 30 Bell 212s, 214STs and 412s, UH-1B/D/H Iroquois and Alouette IIIs. Transport units are equipped with 12 C-123 Providers, 6 C-130H Hercules, 5 C-47s and 8 Aeritalia G222s. Communications aircraft are Queen Airs and other types. Thirty Tucanos and 20 T-34A Mentors are used for training, together with 20 T-2D Buckeye advanced jet trainers, which have a secondary attack role. A battalion of paratroops comes within Air Force responsibility. There is a staff college and a cadet academy.

National Guard, a volunteer force of some 22,000 under the Ministry of Defence, is broadly responsible for internal security. It includes customs and forestry duties among its tasks.

INTERNATIONAL RELATIONS

Membership. Venezuela is a member of UN, OAS, LAIA (formerly LAFTA), OPEC and the Andean Group.

ECONOMY

Budget. The revenue and expenditure for calendar years were, in Bs.1m., as follows:

	1984	*1985*	*1986*	*1987*	*1988*
Revenue	102,808	118,039	109,000	165,000	180,000
Expenditure	103,539	113,307	105,000	165,000	180,000

Currency. The *bolívar* (Bs.) is divided into 100 *céntimos*. Gold coins, 100 (*pachanos*), 20 and 10 *bolívars* have been minted but are no longer in circulation; silver coins are 5 (*fuerte*), 2, 1 *bolívars*; nickel, 50 (*real*), 25 (*medio*) and 12·5 *céntimos* (*locha*), coppernickel, 5 *céntimos* (*puya*).

The bank-notes in circulation are 500, 100, 50, 20 and 10 boli vars. The circulation of foreign bank-notes is forbidden.

In March 1990, £1 = Bs.72·88; US$1 = 45·07 on the free market.

Banking. The major banks include: Banco Provincial SAICA, Banco de Venezuela,

Banco Consolidado, Banco Unión, Banco Mercantil, Banco Latino, Banco de Maracaibo, Banco Industrial de Venezuela, Bank of America.

ENERGY AND NATURAL RESOURCES

Electricity. Production (1986) 50,240m. kwh. The Guri dam hydroelectric project was opened in Nov. 1986. It will supply 70% of the country's needs.

Oil. The oil-producing region around Maracaibo, covering some 30,000 sq. miles, produces about three-quarters of Venezuelan petroleum. Deposits in the Orinoco region are likely to prove one of the largest heavy oil reserves in the world. Nationalization of the privately owned oil sector in 1976 has proved successful. Crude oil production (1989) 96m. tonnes.

Proven crude oil reserves in Jan. 1988 stood at 58,000m. bbls. However, these are considered conservative estimates and new fields off-shore have estimated reserves of 6,000–40,000m. bbls. In March 1988 a new field in the state of Monagas was confirmed estimated at 8,600m. bbls. The Orinoco tar sands belt has reserves variously estimated at between 700,000m. bbls. and 3,000,000m. bbls.

Gas. Production (1985) 33,059m. cu. metres.

Minerals. Bauxite is being exploited in the Guayana region by Bauxien, a state agency. There are important goldmines in the region south-east of Bolívar State, and new deposits have been discovered near El Callao (1959) and Sosa Méndez (1961) in the Guayana region. Output, 1982, amounted to 902 kg. Diamond output, from Amazonas territory, was 687,000 carats in 1977. Manganese deposits, estimated at several million tons, were discovered in 1954. Phosphate-rock deposits (yielding from 64 to 82% tricalcium phosphate) are found in the state of Falcón; reserves of 15m. tons of high-quality rock have been established. The state of Sucre has large sulphur deposits. Coal is worked in the states of Táchira, Aragua and Anzoátegui. Coal proven reserves in Zulia (160m. tons) are to be developed to service a new thermal power station in the Maracaibo area. An important nickel deposit (at Loma de Hierro near Tejerías) is estimated to equal 600,000 tons of pure nickel. Saltmines are now worked by the Government on the Araya peninsula. Asbestos and copper pyrite are being exploited. There were proven reserves (1984) of bauxite totalling 200m. tonnes and production of about 3m. per annum are scheduled from 1986.

Iron ore is exploited in Bolívar State by the Orinoco Mining Co. and Iron Mines of Venezuela, subsidiaries respectively of the US Steel Corp. and the Bethlehem Steel Co. Proven reserves at the end of 1980 were 1,800m. tonnes. National output of iron ore, 1985, 14·9m. tonnes of which 9m. was exported.

Agriculture. Venezuela is divided into 3 distinct zones—the agricultural, the pastoral and the forest zone. In the first are grown coffee, cocoa, sugar-cane, maize, rice, wheat (grown in the Andes), tobacco, cotton, beans, sisal, etc.; the second affords grazing for more than 6m. cattle and numerous horses; and in the third, which covers a very large portion of the country, tropical products, such as caoutchouc, balatá (a gum resembling rubber), tonka beans, dividivi, copaiba, vanilla, growing wild, are worked by the inhabitants. The 1988 livestock estimate showed cattle, 12,756,000; pigs, 2,707,000; goats, 1·4m.; sheep, 425,000; poultry, 57m. Area under cultivation is 5,530,898 acres. Over 50% of all farmers are engaged in subsistence agriculture and growth rates in agricultural production have not kept pace with the high population increase. Government has introduced a programme of price support, tax incentives and price increases.

Production (1988, in 1,000 tonnes): Rice, 385; maize, 1,400; cassava, 318; sugar-cane, 8,000; bananas, 1,050; oranges, 390; potatoes, 216; tomatoes, 145; coffee, 80; sesame seed, 67; tobacco, 16; cocoa, 15.

The coffee plantations number 62,673, covering 543,400 acres with 135m. bushes. The Venezuelan cocoa, from 13,000 plantations, is considered to be of high quality; it is grown chiefly in the states of Sucre and Miranda. The sugar industry has 6 government and 20 privately owned mills.

Forestry. Resources have been barely tapped; 600 species of wood have been identified.

Fisheries. Total catch (1986) was 283,600 tonnes.

INDUSTRY AND TRADE

Industry. Production (1985): Steel, 2·72m. tonnes; aluminium, 407,000; ammonia, 490,000; fertilizers, 650,000; cement, 5·12m.; paper, 550,000; vehicles (units) 116,000.

Labour. The labour force in 1985 was 6m., 16·3% were in agriculture, 15·3% in manufacturing and 7% in construction.

Trade Unions. The most powerful confederation of trade unions is the CTV (*Confederacion de Trabajadores de Venezuela*, formed 1947), which is dominated by the Accion Democratica party. Estimated membership, 1·1m. but claims 2m.

Commerce. Venezuela's exports and imports (in US$1m.):

	1984	*1985*	*1986*	*1987*
Exports	15,967	14,178	8,880	8,402
Imports	7,262	7,388	7,600	8,711

Main export markets in 1987 were USA, Netherlands Antilles because of its oil refining and transhipment facilities, Japan and Colombia.

Principal imports are machinery and equipment, manufactured goods, chemical products, foodstuffs.

The USA supplied 47% of all imports in 1987, followed by Federal Republic of Germany, Japan, Italy and the UK.

Total trade between UK and Venezuela (British Department of Trade returns, in £1,000 sterling):

	1985	*1986*	*1987*	*1988*	*1989*
Imports to UK	238,879	96,339	91,749	76,563	111,072
Exports and re-exports from UK	165,268	170,101	157,760	177,787	124,672

Tourism. 692,400 tourists visited Venezuela in 1988.

COMMUNICATIONS

Roads. There were, 1985, 62,601 km of road fit for traffic the year round; of these 24,036 km are paved. There are 10,097 km of high-speed 4-lane motorway type. The motorway system runs from Caracas to Puerto Cabello *via* Valencia and will shortly be linked direct with one from La Guaira to Caracas.

Railways. Plans have existed since 1950 for large-scale railway construction but only the Puerto Cabello to Barquisimeto and Acarigua lines (336 km–1,435 mm gauge) has been completed. In 1986 it carried 17·1m. passenger-km and 11·5m. tonne-km. There is a metro in Caracas.

Aviation. In 1985 there were 7 international airports, 51 national and over 200 private airports. The chief Venezuelan airlines are LAV (Líneas Aéreas Venezolanas), a government-owned concern, and AVENSA (Aerovías Venezolanas). Both operate numerous internal services. VIASA operates international routes in conjunction with KLM. There are also 3 specialist air freight companies. In all there are over 100 commercial aircraft in operation. In addition to Venezuelan international services, a number of US and Latin American and European lines operate services to Venezuela. British Airways operates twice-weekly flights between London and Caracas.

Shipping. Foreign vessels are not permitted to engage in the coasting trade, except by special concessions or by contract with the Government. La Guaira, Maracaibo, Puerto Cabello, Puerto Ordaz and Guanta are the chief ports. In Dec. 1978 the merchant fleet had an aggregate gross tonnage of 824,000; this included tankers of 368,000 gross tons.

The principal navigable rivers are the Orinoco and its tributaries Apure and

Arauca, from San Fernando to Tucupita through Ciudad Bolívar, Puerto Ordaz and San Félix; San Juan from Carípito to the Gulf of Paria; and Escalante in Lake Maracaibo.

Post and Broadcasting. There were 1,165,699 telephones in 1985. An international telex service operates in the Caracas metropolitan zone. There is a submarine telephone link with USA.

In 1986 there were 6·7m. radio receivers and 77 radio stations at Caracas, Maracaibo, Maracay and other towns. There were 3 television stations in Caracas (two privately owned), of which 2 cover, with relays, most of the country. In 1986 there were about 2·75m. homes with TV receivers.

Newspapers (1983). There were 25 leading daily newspapers with a circulation of over 1·7m.

JUSTICE, RELIGION, EDUCATION AND HEALTH

Justice. The Supreme Court, which operates in Divisions, each with 5 members, is elected by Congress for 5 years. The country is divided into 20 legal districts. They select their own President and Vice-President. The Federal Procurator-General is appointed for 5 years. There are lower federal courts.

Each state has a Supreme Court with 3 members, a superior court, or superior tribunal, courts of first instance, district courts and municipal courts. In the territories there are civil and military judges of first instance, and also judges in the municipios. Finally, there is an income-tax claims tribunal.

Religion. The Roman Catholic is the prevailing religion, but there is toleration of all others. There are 4 archbishops, 1 at Caracas, who is Primate of Venezuela, 2 at Mérida and 1 at Ciudad Bolívar. There are 19 bishops. In the state primary schools instruction is given only to those children whose parents expressly request it. Protestants number about 20,000.

Education. In 1987–88 there were 13,500 primary schools with 115,000 teachers and 2,900,000 pupils, 2,000 secondary schools with 63,000 teachers and 1,100,000 pupils. The number of students in higher education was 466,000 with 30,000 teaching staff in the 94 establishments.

Health. In 1983 there were 21,502 doctors and 43,650 beds in hospitals and dispensaries in 1979.

DIPLOMATIC REPRESENTATIVES

Of Venezuela in Great Britain (1 Cromwell Rd., London, SW7)
Ambassador: Dr Francisco Kerdel-Vegas, CBE (accredited 5 Nov. 1987).

Of Great Britain in Venezuela (Torre Las Mercedes, Avenida La Estancia, Chuao, Caracas 1060)
Ambassador: Giles Fitzherbert, CMG.

Of Venezuela in the USA (2445 Massachusetts Ave., NW, Washington, D.C., 20008)
Ambassador: Simon Alberto Consalvi.

Of the USA in Venezuela (Avenida Francisco de Miranda and Avenida Principal de la Floresta, Caracas)
Ambassador: (Vacant).

Of Venezuela to the United Nations
Ambassador: Dr Andrés Aguilar.

Further Reading

Statistical Information: The following are some of the principal publications:
Dirección General de Estadística, Ministerio de Fomento, *Boletín Mensual de Estadística.—Anuario Estadístico de Venezuela.* Caracas, Annual
Banco Central, *Memoria Annual* and *Boletin Mensual*

Ministerio de Sanidad y Asistencia Social, Dirección de Salud Pública, *Anuario de Epidemiología y Asistencia Social*

Bigler, G. E., *Politics and State Capitalism in Venezuela*. Madrid, 1981

Braveboy-Wagner, J. A., *The Venezuela-Guyana Border Dispute: Britain's Colonial Legacy in Latin America*. Boulder and Epping, 1984

Buitrón, A., *Causas y Efectos del Exodo Rural en Venezuela.—Efectos Económicos y Sociales de las Inmigraciones en Venezuela.—Las Inmigraciones en Venezuela.* Pan American Union, Washington, D.C., 1956

Ewell, J., *Venezuela: A Century of Change*. London, 1984

Lombard, J., *Venezuelan History: A Comprehensive Working Bibliography*. Boston, 1977.—*Venezuela: The Search for Order, the Dream of Progress*. OUP, 1982

Martz, J. D. and Myers, D. J., *Venezuela: The Democratic Experience*. New York, 1986

VIETNAM

Capital: Hanoi
Population: 64m. (1989)
GNP per capita: US$200 (1989)

Công Hòa Xã Hôi Chu Nghĩa Viêt Nam—Socialist Republic of Vietnam

HISTORY. Conquered by the Chinese in B.C. 111, Vietnam broke free from Chinese domination in 939, though at many subsequent periods it was a nominal Chinese vassal. (For subsequent history until the cessation of hostilities with the US in Jan. 1973 *see* THE STATESMAN'S YEAR-BOOK, 1989–90).

After the US withdrawal, hostilities continued between the North and the South until the latter's defeat in 1975.

(For details of the former Republic of Vietnam, *see* THE STATESMAN'S YEAR-BOOK, 1975–76). A Provisional Revolutionary Government established an administration in Saigon. A general election was held on 25 April 1976 for a National Assembly representing the whole country. Voting was by universal suffrage of all citizens of 18 or over, except former functionaries of South Vietnam undergoing 're-education', the last of whom (approximately 7,000) were released in Sept. 1987 and Feb. 1988. The unification of North and South Vietnam into the Socialist Republic of Vietnam took place formally on 2 July 1976. In 1978 Vietnam signed a 25-year treaty of friendship and co-operation with the USSR. Relations with China correspondingly deteriorated, an exacerbating factor being the Vietnamese military intervention in Cambodia in Dec. 1978. Occasional skirmishing along the China–Vietnam border continued into 1988. In 1988 Vietnam began the phased withdrawal of its 120,000 troops in Cambodia, claiming in Sept. 1989 that withdrawal was complete.

AREA AND POPULATION. The country has a total area of 329,566 sq. km and is divided administratively into 40 provinces. Areas and populations (in 1,000) at the census of Oct. 1979 were as follows:

Province	*Sq. km*	*1979*	*Province*	*Sq. km*	*1979*
Lai Chau	17,408	322,077	Thai Binh	1,344	1,506,235
Son La	14,656	487,793	Hai Phong (city) [1]	1,515	1,279,067
Hoang Lien Son	14,125	778,217	Ha Nam Ninh	3,522	2,781,409
Ha Tuyen	13,519	782,453	Thanh Hoa	11,138	2,532,261
Cao Bang	13,731	479,823	Nghe Tinh	22,380	3,111,989
Lang Son		484,657	Binh Tri Thien	19,048	1,901,713
Bac Thai	8,615	815,105	Quang Nam – Da Nang	11,376	1,529,520
Quang Ninh	7,076	750,055	Nghia Binh	14,700	2,095,354
Vinh Phu	5,187	1,488,348	Gia Lai – Kon Tum	18,480	595,906
Ha Bac	4,708	1,662,671	Dac Lac	18,300	490,198
Ha Son Binh	6,860	1,537,190	Phu Khanh	9,620	1,188,637
Hanoi (city) [1]	597	2,570,905	Lam Dong	10,000	396,657
Hai Hung	2,526	2,145,662	Thuan Hai	11,000	938,255
Dong Nai	12,130	1,304,799	Ben Tre	2,400	1,041,838
Song Be	9,500	659,093	Cuu Long	4,200	1,504,215
Tay Ninh	4,100	684,006	An Giang	4,140	1,532,362
Long An	5,100	957,264	Hau Giang	5,100	2,232,891
Dong Thap	3,120	1,182,787	Kien Giang	6,000	994,673
Thanh Pho – Ho Chi Minh [1]	1,845	3,419,978	Minh Hai	8,000	1,219,595
Tien Giang	2,350	1,264,498	Vung Tau – Con Dao [2]	—	91,160
				329,466	52,741,766

[1] Autonomous city. [2] Special area.

At the census of Oct. 1979 the population was 52,741,766 (25,580,582 male; 19·7% urban).

Population (1989), 64m. (Ho Chi Minh 4m.; Hanoi, 2m. (1979); growth rate (1988) 2·4% per annum. Density, 181 per sq. km. Sanctions are imposed on couples with more than two children.

84% of the population are Vietnamese (Kinh). There are also over 60 minority groups thinly spread in the extensive mountainous regions. The largest minorities are (1976 figures in 1,000): Tay (742); Khmer (651); Thai (631); Muong (618); Nung (472); Meo (349); Dao (294). In 1987 1m. Vietnamese were living abroad, mainly in the US. Following an agreement of July 1989 the US in Jan. 1990 began the phased immigration of some 94,000 families of former South Vietnamese soldiers and officials.

From 1979 to July 1984 59,730 persons emigrated legally. In 1986 1,400 people a month were leaving legally under the UN's orderly departure scheme. (For previous details *see* THE STATESMAN'S YEAR-BOOK, 1981–82). Between April 1975 and Aug. 1984 a further 554,000 illegal emigrants ('boat people') succeeded in finding refuge abroad. In June 1988 the UK announced that Hong Kong would no longer accept 'boat people' who were not proven political refugees. In Feb. 1989, Vietnam agreed to accept their return but not their enforced repatriation, and a voluntary repatriation programme under the aegis of the UN High Commissioner of Refugees began. By Oct. 1989 there were 57,000 'boat people' in camps in Hong Kong, and the UK government announced it would embark on a programme of mandatory repatriation of up to 40,000 of them, giving each a resettlement allowance worth US$620. 51 persons were repatriated on 12 Dec. 1989, but the programme was then suspended. A meeting of the UN-sponsored Comprehensive Plan of Action for Indochinese Refugees in Jan. 1990 failed to agree a new repatriation programme.

CLIMATE. The humid monsoon climate gives tropical conditions in the south and sub-tropical conditions in the north, though real winter conditions can affect the north when polar air blows south over Asia. In general, there is little variation in temperatures over the year. Hanoi. Jan. 62°F (16·7°C), July 84°F (28·9°C). Annual rainfall 72" (1,830 mm).

CONSTITUTION AND GOVERNMENT. A new Constitution was adopted in Dec. 1980. It states that Vietnam is a state of proletarian dictatorship and is developing according to Marxism–Leninism.

At the elections for the National Assembly held on 19 April 1987, 829 candidates stood and 496 were elected. Turn-out of voters was said to be 99·32%.

Local government authorities are the people's councils, which appoint executive committees. Local elections were held with the National Assembly elections in 1987.

'The standing organ of the National Assembly and presidium of the Republic' is the State Council:

President (titular head of state): Vo Chi Cong. *Vice-Presidents:* Nguyen Huu Tho, Le Quang Do, Nguyen Quyet, Dam Quang Trung, Huynh Tan Phat, Mrs Nguyen Thi Dinh.

Chairman of the National Assembly: Le Quang Do.

All political power stems from the Communist Party of Vietnam (until Dec. 1976 known as the Workers' Party of Vietnam), founded in 1930; it had 1·7m. members in 1986. Its Politburo in April 1990 consisted of Nguyen Van Linh *(First Secretary)*; Vo Chi Cong; Do Muoi *(Prime Minister)*; Vo Van Kiet; Le Duc Anh *(Minister of Defence)*; Nguyen Duc Tam; Nguyen Co Thach *(Deputy Prime Minister and Foreign Minister)*; Dong Si Nguyen *(Deputy Prime Minister)*; Tran Xuan Bach; Nguyen Thanh Binh; Dao Duy Tung; Doan Khue; Mai Chi Tho *(Minister of the Interior)*. Ministers not in the Politburo include: Vo Nguyen Giap *(Deputy Prime Minister)*; Doan Duy Than *(Foreign Trade)*; Hoang Quy *(Finance)*; Tran Hoan *(Information)*, Pham Van Kai *(Chairman, State Planning Commission)*.

There were 2 puppet parties, the Democratic (founded 1944) and the Socialist

(1946), which were unified with the trade and youth unions in the Fatherland Front. The Democratic Party was wound up in Oct. 1988.

National flag: Red, with a yellow 5-pointed star in the centre.
National anthem: 'Tien quan ca' ('The troops are advancing').

DEFENCE. Men between 18 and 35 and women between 18 and 25 are liable for conscription of 3 years, specialists 4 years.

Army. The Army consists of 1 armoured division, 65 infantry divisions (of varying strengths), 8 engineer and 16 economic construction divisions, 15 independent infantry regiments and 10 field artillery brigades. Equipment includes some 1,600 main battle and 450 light tanks. Strength was (1990) about 1·1m, although reductions have been announced. Paramilitary forces are the Peoples' Defence Force (500,000), local forces of some 2·5m. and a tactical rear force of 500,000. In 1990 some 10-15,000 troops were still stationed in Laos but forces were withdrawn from Cambodia.

Navy. The equipment of the Vietnamese navy derives from two sources: *ex*-US equipment transferred to South Vietnam before or during the war, and *ex*-Soviet equipment transferred to North Vietnman during the war, or subsequent to the unification of the country in 1975. The latter is in general newer, and benefits from Soviet technical and logistic support in return for use of the main naval base at Cam Ranh Bay. However, reliable information on the state of the fleet is scarce.

The fleet currently includes 5 *ex*-Soviet 'Petya' class frigates, 2 *ex*-US frigates (built 1943 and 1944), 8 Soviet-built fast missile craft, 16 fast torpedo craft, 5 patrol hydrofoils, 2 offshore and at least 30 inshore patrol craft, 3 coastal and 2 inshore minesweepers, 7 landing ships, and some 20 smaller amphibious craft. There may additionally still exist a proportion of the inshore fleet of 24 patrol craft, 25 coastguard cutters and over 350 riverine craft abandoned by the USA in 1975, but the continued operability of more than a few of these must be considered doubtful.

In 1989 personnel were estimated to number 10,000 plus an additional Naval Infantry force of 27,000.

Air Force. The Air Force, built up with Soviet and Chinese assistance, had (1990) about 12,000 personnel and 350 combat aircraft (plus many stored), including modern US types captured in war. There are reported to be 3 squadrons of variable-geometry MiG-23s, 6 squadrons of MiG-17s and Su-20s, over 150 MiG-21 interceptors; An-2, Li-2, C-47, An-24, An-26 and Il-14 transports; and a strong helicopter force with UH-1 Iroquois, Mi-6, Mi-8 and Mi-24 helicopters. 'Guideline', 'Goa' and 'Gainful' missiles are operational in large numbers.

INTERNATIONAL RELATIONS

Membership. Vietnam is a member of UN, Comecon and IMF.

ECONOMY

Planning. Long-term forward planning gives priority to self-sufficiency in agriculture and stimulating regional industry. The fourth 5-year plan covers 1986–90. (For previous plans *see* THE STATESMAN'S YEAR-BOOK, 1985–86.).

Curtailment of Western aid, and resistance to Government measures have contributed to a shortage of consumer goods and widespread malnutrition. Small family businesses were legalized in 1986.

Since assuming Party leadership in Dec. 1986 Nguyen Van Linh has denounced the inefficiency and bureaucracy of the past and announced major economic reforms injecting free enterprise principles and reducing central control. Although initial implementation was slow, the extent and pace of reforms increased in 1989.

Currency. The monetary unit is the *dong*. A currency reform of 14 Sept. 1985 substituted a new *dong* at a rate of 1 new *dong* = 10 (old) *dong*. Notes are issued for 1, 2, 5, 10, 20, 50, 100 and 500 new *dong*. (For former currency *see* THE STATESMAN'S YEAR-BOOK, 1985–86). In a currency reform of March 1989 the *dong* was brought into line with free market rates. In March 1990 £1 = 7,400 *dong*; US$1 = 4,515 *dong*. Inflation was 700% in 1988, but was significantly reduced in 1989.

Banking. The bank of issue is the National Bank of Vietnam (founded in 1951). There is also a Bank for Foreign Trade (Vietcombank).

ENERGY AND NATURAL RESOURCES

Electricity. In 1988, 6,300m. kwh. of electricity were produced. A hydro-electric power station with a capacity of 2m. kw. was opened at Hoa-Binh in 1989.

Minerals. North Vietnam is rich in anthracite, lignite and hard coal: Total reserves are estimated at 20,000m. tonnes. Anthracite production in 1975 was 5m. tonnes. Coal production was 5·3m. tonnes in 1980. There are deposits of iron ore, manganese, titanium, chromite, bauxite and a little gold. Reserves of apatite are some of the biggest in the world. Offshore exploration for oil near Da Nang started in 1989. Crude oil production was 750,000 tonnes in 1988; 1989 estimate, 1m. tonnes.

Agriculture. In 1985, 62% of the population was engaged in agriculture. In 1984 there were some 23,000 production collectives and 268 agricultural co-operatives in the South accounting for 47% of the cultivated area. The intemperate collectivization of agriculture in the South after 1977 had disastrous effects which the Government tried to rectify by allowing peasants small private plots and the right to market some produce. These measures had only limited success, and in 1989 the Government abandoned virtually all its controls on the production and sale of agricultural produce, and switched to encouraging the household as the basic production unit. There were 105 state farms employing in all 70,000 workers and with 55,000 hectares arable and 50,000 hectares of pasture. The cultivated area in 1980 was 6·97m. hectares (5·54m. hectares for rice).

Production in 1,000 tonnes in 1988: Rice (15,200), soybeans (100), tea (35), rubber (61), maize (580), tobacco (40), potatoes (350), sweet potatoes (2,100) from 400,000 hectares, sorghum (55) from 37,000 hectares, dry beans (105) from 63,000 hectares, coffee (14). Cereals production was 15,835,000m. tonnes in 1988. Other crops include sugar-cane and cotton.

Livestock (1988): Cattle 2,923,000; pigs, 12,051,000; goats, 414,000; poultry, 96m.

Animal products, 1988: Eggs, 171,000 tonnes, meat, 884,000 tonnes.

Forestry. There were (1988) 13m. hectares of forest, representing 40% of the land area. 1,626,000 cu. metres of timber were produced in 1980.

Fisheries. Fishing is important, especially in Halong Bay. In 1976, 6m. tonnes of sea fish and 180,000 tonnes of freshwater fish were caught.

INDUSTRY AND TRADE

Industry. Next to mining, food processing and textiles are the most important industries; there is also some machine building. Older industries include cement, cotton and silk manufacture.

Private businesses were taken over in 1978. Foreign firms, principally French, are continuing to function, but all US property has been nationalized. There is little heavy industry. Most industry is concentrated in the Ho-Chi-Minh area.

Production (1980, in 1,000 tonnes) iron, 125; steel, 106; sulphuric acid, 6,700; caustic soda, 4,500; mineral fertilizer, 260; pesticides, 18,400; paper, 54,000; sugar, 94,000, cement, 705. 1,500 tractors were built in 1980, and 621 railway coaches. Footwear production, 200,000 pairs. Beer, 942,000 hectolitres.

Labour. Average wage (1984) 200 dong per month. Workforce (1985) 28·76m., of whom 17·91m. were in agriculture.

Commerce. 65% of exports are to, and 85% of imports from, Communist countries. USSR and Japan are Vietnam's main trading partners; others are Singapore and Hong Kong. Main exports are coal, farm produce, sea produce and livestock.

Imports: Oil, steel, artificial fertilizers. There is an aid agreement with the USSR for 1986–90 amounting to about 9,000m. roubles. In 1989 Vietnam's total indebtedness was estimated at US$9,000m (US$2,000m. to the West). In 1978 the IMF approved a virtually interest-free loan of US$90m. repayable over 50 years, but in April 1985 suspended all further credits to Vietnam. Sweden gives annual aid of US$47m. A law of Jan. 1988 regulates joint ventures with Western firms; full repatriation of profits and non-nationalization of investments are guaranteed. Offices may be opened in Vietnam.

Trade between Vietnam and UK (British Department of Trade returns, in £1,000 sterling):

	1986	*1987*	*1988*	*1989*
Imports to UK	1,200	357	492	1,711
Exports and re-exports from UK	1,288	2,598	2,213	4,108

Tourism. Since 1988 Vietnamese have been permitted to travel abroad for up to 3 months for various specific reasons. Group travel to Communist countries has also been authorized.

COMMUNICATIONS

Roads. In 1986 there were about 65,000 km of roads described as 'main roads'.

Railways. Route length was 4,200 km in 1986. The Hanoi–Ho Chi Minh City line is being rebuilt in a programme of reconstruction and extension. About 50m. passengers and 10m. tonnes of freight are carried annually.

Aviation. Air Vietnam operates internal services from Hanoi to Ho Chi Minh City, Cao Bang, Na Son and Dien Bien, Vinh and Hue, and from Ho Chi Minh City to Ban Me Thuot and Da Nang, Can Tho, Con Son Island and Quan Long and from Hanoi to Bangkok in conjunction with Thai Airways. Aeroflot (USSR) operate regular services from Ho Chi Min City to Moscow and from Hanoi to Moscow, Rangoon and Vientiane, Interflug (German Dem. Rep.) to Berlin, Moscow and Dhaka, Philippine Airlines to Manila, and Air France to Paris.

Shipping. In 1986 there were 150 ships totalling 338,668 GRT. The major ports are Haiphong, which can handle ships of 10,000 tons, Ho Chi Minh City and Da Nang, and there are ports at Hong Gai and Haiphong Ben Thuy. There are regular services to Hong Kong, Singapore, Cambodia and Japan. In 1987 there were some 6,000 km of navigable waterways.

Cargo is handled by the Vietnam Ocean Shipping Agency; other matters by the Vietnam Foreign Trade Transport Corporation.

Post and Broadcasting. In 1984 there were 6m. radios. There were 106,100 telephones in 1984. There were 2·25m. TV sets in 1984.

Cinemas and theatres. 116 films were produced in 1980 (including 10 full-length). There were 145 theatres.

Newspapers and books. The Party daily is *Nhan Dan* ('The People') circulation, 1985: 500,000. The official daily in the South is *Giai Phong*. Two unofficial dailies, *Cong Giao Va Dan Toc* (Catholic) and *Tin Sang* (independent) are also published. 2,564 books were published in 1980 totalling 90·9m. copies.

JUSTICE, RELIGION, EDUCATION AND WELFARE

Justice. A new penal code came into force 1 Jan. 1986 'to complete the work of the 1980 Constitution'. Penalties (including death) are prescribed for opposition to the people's power, and for economic crimes. There are the Supreme People's Court, local people's courts and military courts. The president of the Supreme Court is responsible to the National Assembly, as is the Procurator-General, who heads the Supreme People's Office of Supervision and Control.

Religion. Taoism is the traditional religion but Buddhism is widespread. At a Conference for Buddhist Reunification in Nov. 1981, 9 sects adopted a charter for a new Buddhist church under the Council of Sangha. The Hoa Hao sect, associated with Buddhism, claimed 1·5m. adherents in 1976. Caodaism, a synthesis of Christianity, Buddhism and Confucianism founded in 1926, has some 2m. followers. There are some 6m. Roman Catholics (mainly in the south) headed by Cardinal Trinh Van Can, Archbishop of Hanoi and 13 bishops. There were 2 seminaries in 1989. In 1983 the Government set up a Solidarity Committee of Catholic Patriots. In Aug. 1988 the Government announced that all Catholic priests had been released from re-education camps, but were not yet permitted to resume their duties.

Education. Primary education consists of a 10-year course divided into 3 levels of 4, 3 and 3 years respectively. There were 500,000 teachers in 1988. Numbers of pupils and students in 1980–81: Nurseries, 2·66m.; primary schools, 12·1m.; complementary education, 2·19m.; vocational secondary education, 130,000. In 1980–81 there were 92,913 nurseries. There were 11,400 schools and 280 vocational secondary schools, with 357,000 and 13,000 teachers respectively.

In 1980–81 there were 83 institutions of higher education (including 3 universities: (Hanoi, Ho Chi Minh City, Central Highlands University at Ban Me Thuot), 13 industrial colleges, 7 agricultural colleges, 5 economics colleges, 9 teacher-training colleges, 7 medical schools and 3 art schools, in all with 16,000 teachers and 159,000 students. In 1981 there were 5,000 Vietnamese studying in the USSR.

Health. In 1975 there were 1,996 hospitals and dispensaries and 93 sanatoria. There were some 13,517 doctors and dentists in 1981 and 197,000 hospital beds.

DIPLOMATIC REPRESENTATIVES

Of Vietnam in Great Britain (12–14 Victoria Rd., London, W8)
Ambassador: Chau Phong (accredited 14 March 1990).

Of Great Britain in Vietnam (16 Pho Ly Thuong Kiet, Hanoi)
Ambassador: Emrys T. Davies, CMG.

Of Vietnam to the United Nations
Ambassador: Trinh Xuan Lang.

Further Reading

Beresford, M., *National Unification and Economic Development in Vietnam.* London, 1989
Bui Phung, *Vietnamese-English Dictionary.* Hanoi, 1987
Chen, J. H.-M., *Vietnam: A Comprehensive Bibliography.* London, 1973
Dellinger, D., *Vietnam Revisited.* Boston (Mass.), 1986
Fforde, A., *The Limits of National Liberation: Problems of Economic Management in the Democratic Republic of Vietnam.* London, 1987
Harrison, J. P., *The Endless War: Fifty Years of Struggle in Vietnam.* New York, 1982
Higgins, H., *Vietnam.* 2nd ed. London, 1982
Ho Chi Minh, *Selected Writings, 1920–1969.* Hanoi, 1977
Hodgkin, T., *Vietnam: The Revolutionary Path:* London, 1981
Houtart, F., *Hai Van: Life in a Vietnamese Commune.* London, 1984
Karnow, S., *Vietnam: A History.* New York, 1983
Lawson, E. K., *The Sino-Vietnamese Conflict.* New York, 1984
Leitenberg, M. and Burns, R. D., *War in Vietnam.* 2nd ed. Oxford and Santa Barbara, 1982
Nguyen Tien Hung, C., *Economic Developments of Socialist Vietnam, 1955–80.* New York, 1977
Nguyen Van Canh, *Vietnam under Communism, 1975–1982.* Stanford Univ. Press, 1983
Post, K., *Revolution, Socialism and Nationalism in Vietnam.* vol. 1. Aldershot, 1989
Smith, R. B., *An International History of the Vietnam War.* London, 1983
Truong Nhu Tang, *Journal of a Vietcong.* London, 1986

BRITISH VIRGIN ISLANDS

Capital: Road Town
Population: 13,300 (1987)
GNP per capita: US$4,500 (1982)

HISTORY. The Virgin Islands were discovered by Columbus on his second voyage in 1493. The British Virgin Islands were first settled by the Dutch in 1648 and taken over in 1666 by a group of English planters. In 1774 constitutional government was granted and in 1834 slavery was abolished.

AREA AND POPULATION. The British Virgin Islands form the eastern extremity of the Greater Antilles and, exclusive of small rocks and reefs, number 40, of which 15 are inhabited. The largest are Tortola (1980 population, 9,322), Virgin Gorda (1,443), Anegada (169) and Jost Van Dyke (136). Other islands in the group have a total population of 82; Marine population, 220. Total area about 59 sq. miles (130 sq. km); population (1987), 13,300. Road Town, on the south-east of Tortola, is a port of entry; population, approximately 4,000.

CLIMATE. A pleasantly healthy sub-tropical climate with summer temperatures lowered by sea breezes. Nights are cool and rainfall averages 50" (1,250 mm).

CONSTITUTION AND GOVERNMENT. In 1950 representative government was introduced and in 1967 a new Constitution was granted (amended 1977). The Governor is responsible for defence and internal security, external affairs, the public service, and the courts. The Executive Council consists of the Governor, 1 *ex-officio* member who is the Attorney-General and 4 ministers in the Legislature. The Legislative Council consists of 1 *ex-officio* member who is the Attorney-General and 9 elected members, one of whom is the Chief Minister and Minister of Finance; the Speaker is elected from outside the Council.

Governor: J. Mark Herdman, LVO.
Chief Minister: H. Lavity Stoutt.
Flag: The British Blue Ensign with the arms of the Territory in the fly.

ECONOMY

Budget. In 1989 revenue (estimate) was US$32,784,000; expenditure, US$32,379,800.

Currency. The unit of currency is the US dollar.

Banking. Bank of Nova Scotia, Barclays Bank PLC, Chase Manhattan Bank NA, Royal Trust Company Ltd and First Pennsylvania Bank NA hold General Banking Licences and had total deposits of US$243·4m. at 31 Dec. 1988. Seven institutions hold restricted banking licences and there are also a large number of trust companies, specializing in a range of financial services other than banking.

ENERGY AND NATURAL RESOURCES

Electricity. Production, 1986, 31m. kwh.

Agriculture. Agricultural production is limited, with the chief products being livestock (including poultry), fish, fruit and vegetables. Production, 1988, in tonnes (value in US$1,000): Fruits, 250 (522·5); vegetables/root crop, 54 (108); beef, 185 (703); mutton, 26 (130); pork, 6 (21); and 36,000 dozen eggs (90). In 1985 the Agriculture Department was extended to include an abattoir.

Livestock (1988): Cattle, 2,000; pigs, 3,000; sheep, 8,000; goats, 12,000.

INDUSTRY AND TRADE

Industry. The entire economy is based on tourism, from which is derived directly or indirectly some 75% of GDP. The construction industry is a significant employer.

Commerce. There is a very small export trade almost entirely with the Virgin Islands of the USA. In 1987 imports were US$77·3m. and exports US$3·1m.

Total trade between the British Virgin Islands and UK (British Department of Trade returns, in £1,000 sterling):

	1986	*1987*	*1988*	*1989*
Imports to UK	267	752	4,030	1,170
Exports and re-exports from UK	3,491	3,310	7,108	6,727

Tourism. There were 350,319 visitors in 1988. In 1987 visitors spent (estimate) US$110·8m.

COMMUNICATIONS

Roads. There were (1985) over 70 miles of roads and (1986) 4,706 licensed vehicles.

Aviation. Beef Island Airport, about 16 km from Road Town, is capable of receiving 80-seat short-take-off-and-landing jet aircraft. Air BVI operates internal flights and external flights to San Juan (main route), Puerto Rico; the USVI and St Kitts. Other services to the BVI are Eastern Metro Express, LIAT and American Eagle.

Shipping. There are services to Europe, the USA and other Caribbean islands, and daily services by motor launches to the US Virgin Islands.

Post and Broadcasting. There were (1988) nearly 4,570 telephones and 86 telex subscribers, and an external telephone service links Tortola with Bermuda and the rest of the world. Radio ZBVI transmits 10,000 watts and British Virgin Islands Cable TV operates a cable system of approximately 12 television channels.

RELIGION, EDUCATION AND WELFARE

Religion. There are Anglican, Methodist, Seventh-Day Adventist, Roman Catholic, Baptist Churches and other Christian churches in the Territory. The Jehovah's Witnesses are also represented.

Education. Primary education is provided in 18 government schools, three with secondary divisions, and 11 private schools. Total number of pupils (Dec. 1988) 3,046.

Secondary education to the GCE level and Caribbean Examination Council level is provided by the BVI High School and the secondary divisions of the schools on Virgin Gorda and Anegada. Total number of secondary level pupils (Dec. 1987) 1,113.

Government expenditure, 1988 (estimate), US$4m. In 1987 the total number of teachers in all Government schools was 182. In 1986 a branch of the Hull University (England) School of Education was established.

Health. In 1989 there were 10 doctors, 79 nurses, 50 public hospital beds and 1 private hospital with 8 beds. Expenditure, 1987 (estimate) was US$2·4m.

Further Reading

Economic Review 1987 – British Virgin Islands. Development Planning Unit, 1987
Dookham, I., *A History of the British Virgin Islands*. Epping, 1975
Harrigan, N. and Varlack, P., *British Virgin Islands: A Chronology*. London, 1971
Pickering, V. W., *Early History of the British Virgin Islands*. London, 1983

Library: Public Library, Road Town. *Librarian:* Bernadine Walters

WESTERN SAMOA

Capital: Apia
Population: 163,000 (1986)
GNP per capita: US$580 (1988)

Samoa i Sisifo

HISTORY. Western Samoa, a former German protectorate (1899–1914), was administered by New Zealand from 1920 to 1961, at first under a League of Nations Mandate and from 1946 under a United Nations Trusteeship Agreement. In May 1961 a plebiscite held under the supervision of the United Nations on the basis of universal adult suffrage voted overwhelmingly in favour of independence as from 1 Jan. 1962, on the basis of the Constitution, which a Constitutional Convention had adopted in Aug. 1960. In Oct. 1961 the General Assembly of the United Nations passed a resolution to terminate the trusteeship agreement as from 1 Jan. 1962, on which date Western Samoa became an independent sovereign state.

Under a treaty of friendship signed on 1 Aug. 1962 New Zealand acts, at the request of Western Samoa, as the official channel of communication between the Samoan Government and other governments and international organizations outside the Pacific islands area. Liaison is maintained by the New Zealand High Commissioner in Apia.

AREA AND POPULATION. Western Samoa lies between 13° and 15° S. lat. and 171° and 173° W. long. It comprises the two large islands of Savai'i and Upolu, the small islands of Manono and Apolima, and several uninhabited islets lying off the coast. The total land area is 1,093 sq. miles (2,830·8 sq. km), of which 659·4 sq. miles (1,707·8 sq. km) are in Savai'i, and 431·5 sq. miles (1,117·6 sq. km) in Upolu; other islands, 2·1 sq. miles (5·4 sq. km). The islands are of volcanic origin, and the coasts are surrounded by coral reefs. Rugged mountain ranges form the core of both main islands and rise to 3,608 ft in Upolu and 6,094 ft in Savai'i. The large area laid waste by lava-flows in Savai'i is a primary cause of that island supporting less than one-third of the population of the islands despite its greater size than Upolu.

The population at the 1981 census was 158,130, of whom 114,980 were in Upolu (including Manono and Apolima) and 43,150 in Savai'i. The capital and chief port is Apia in Upolu (population 33,170 in 1981). Estimate (1986) 163,000.

CLIMATE. A tropical marine climate, with cooler conditions from May to Nov. and a rainy season from Dec. to April. The rainfall is unevenly distributed, with south and east coasts having the greater quantities. Average annual rainfall is about 100" (2,500 mm) in the drier areas. Apia. Jan. 80°F (26·7°C), July 78°F (25·6°C). Annual rainfall 112" (2,800 mm).

CONSTITUTION AND GOVERNMENT. The Constitution provides for a Head of State known as 'Ao o le Malo', which position from 1 Jan. 1962 was held jointly by the representatives of the two royal lines of Tuiaana/Tuiatua and Malietoa. On the death of HH Tupua Tamasese Mea'ole, CBE, on 5 April 1963, HH Malietoa Tanumafili II, CBE, became, as provided by the constitution, the sole Head of State for life. Future Heads of State will be elected by the Legislative Assembly and hold office for 5-year terms.

The executive power is vested in the Head of State, who swears in the Prime Minister (who is appointed by members of the Legislative Assembly) and, on the Prime Minister's advice, the 8 Ministers to form the Cabinet which has general direction and control of the executive Government.

The Legislative Assembly has 45 members elected from territorial constituencies on a franchise confined to matais or chiefs (of whom there were about 15,000 in 1988) and 2 members elected on universal adult suffrage from the individual voters roll, which has replaced the old European roll (approximately 1,350 in 1971). One Member is elected as Speaker. The Constitution also provides for a Council of Deputies of 3 members. In the elections held Feb. 1985, the Human Rights Protection Party won 31 seats.

The official languages are Samoan and English.

Head of State and O le Ao o le Malo: HH Malietoa Tanumafili II, GCMG, CBE.

The cabinet in May 1989 was composed as follows:

Prime Minister, Minister of Foreign Affairs, Broadcasting, Justice, Police and Prisons, Attorney General: Tofilau Eti Alesana. *Finance:* Tuilaepa Sailele. *Agriculture, Forests and Fisheries:* Pule Lameko. *Economic Affairs:* Tanuvasa Livi. *Health:* Polataivao Fosi. *Education:* Patu Afaese. *Post Office and Telecommunications, Public Works:* Jack Netzler. *Lands and Survey:* Sifuiva Sione.

National flag: Red with a blue quarter bearing 5 white stars of the Southern Cross.

INTERNATIONAL RELATIONS

Membership. Western Samoa is a member of UN, the Commonwealth, the South Pacific Forum and is an ACP state of EEC.

ECONOMY

Budget. In 1989 budgeted revenue was $WS101·7m.; expenditure, $WS81·6m.

Currency. The Western Samoa currency is the *talà* (dollar). In March 1990, £1 = 3·75; US$1 = 2·90.

Banking. A Central Bank was established in 1984. In 1959 the Bank of Western Samoa was established with a capital of $WS500,000, of which $WS275,000 was subscribed by the Bank of New Zealand and $WS225,000 by the Government of Western Samoa. In 1977 the Pacific Commercial Bank was established jointly by Australia's Bank of New South Wales and the Bank of Hawaii.

ENERGY AND NATURAL RESOURCES

Electricity. Production (1986) 79m. kwh.

Agriculture. The main products (1988, in 1,000 tonnes) are coconuts (200), taro (40), copra (14), bananas (23), papayas (12), mangoes (6), pineapples (6) and cocoa beans (1).

Livestock (1988): Horses, 3,000; cattle, 27,000; pigs, 65,000; poultry 1m.

Fisheries. The total catch (1983) was 3,150 tonnes, valued at $WS5·1m.

INDUSTRY AND TRADE

Industry. Some industrial activity is being developed associated with agricultural products and forestry.

Commerce. In 1985, imports were valued at $WS115,074,000 and exports at $WS36,195,000. Principal exports were coconut oil (10,926 tonnes; $WS15,622,000), cocoa (581 tons; $WS2,356,000), taro (22,000 cases, $WS5,113,000), coconut cream ($WS2,833,000); fruit juice ($WS1,002,000); beer ($WS385,000) and cigarettes ($WS5,558,000). Chief imports in 1983 included food and live animals ($WS15,195,000), beverages and tobacco ($WS1,913,000), machinery and transport equipment ($WS14,968,000), mineral fuels, lubricants and other materials ($WS13,133,000), chemicals ($WS4,221,000) and miscellaneous manufactured articles ($WS5,279,000).

Total trade between Western Samoa and UK (British Department of Trade returns, in £1,000 sterling):

	1985	*1986*	*1987*	*1988*	*1989*
Imports to UK	292	622	531	1,323	1,376
Exports and re-exports from UK	619	433	1,650	757	296

Tourism. There were 49,710 visitors in 1986.

COMMUNICATIONS

Roads (1987). Western Samoa has 2,085 km of roads, 400 km of which are surfaced and 1,200 km plantation roads fit for light traffic. In 1984 there were 1,498 private cars, 1,909 pick-up trucks, 398 trucks, 187 buses, 297 taxis and 144 motor cycles.

Aviation. Western Samoa is linked by daily air service with American Samoa, which is on the route of the weekly New Zealand–Tahiti and New Zealand–Honolulu air services, with connexions to Fiji, Australia, USA and Europe. There are also services throughout the week to and from Tonga, Fiji, Nauru, the Cook Islands and New Zealand. Internal services link Upolu and Savai'i.

Shipping. Western Samoa is linked to Japan, USA, Europe, Fiji, Australia and New Zealand by regular shipping services.

Post and Broadcasting. There is a radio communication station at Apia. Radio telephone service connects Western Samoa with American Samoa, Fiji, New Zealand, Australia, Canada, USA and UK. Telephone subscribers numbered 3,641 in 1984. In 1982 there were 70,000 radio receivers and about 2,500 television sets.

Cinemas. In 1989 there were 2 cinemas.

Newspapers. In 1985, there were 4 weeklies, circulation 12,000 and 2 monthlies (8,000); all were in Samoan and English.

RELIGION, EDUCATION AND WELFARE

Religion. In 1981, 47% of the population were Congregationalists, 22% Roman Catholic and 16% Methodist.

Education. In 1986 the total number of pupils in primary, junior and secondary schools was 51,940. The University of the South Pacific School of Agriculture is in Western Samoa. A National University was established in 1984.

Health. In 1988 there was 1 national hospital, 7 district hospitals, 9 health centres and 14 subcentres and 44 doctors.

DIPLOMATIC REPRESENTATIVES

Of Western Samoa in Great Britain
High Commissioner: Feesago George Fepulea'i (resides in Brussels).

Of Great Britain in Western Samoa
High Commissioner: R. A. C. Byatt, CMG (resides in Wellington)

Of the USA in Western Samoa
Ambassador: Della M. Newman (resides in Wellington).

Of Western Samoa in the USA and to the United Nations
Chargé d'Affaires: Robin Mauala.

Further Reading

Statistical Year-Book. Annual
Fox, J. W. (ed.) *Western Samoa*. Univ. of Auckland, 1963
Milner, G. B., *Samoan–English, English–Samoan Dictionary*. OUP, 1965

YEMEN ARAB REPUBLIC

Capital: San'a
Population: 8·6m. (1988)
GNP per capita: US$650 (1988)

al Jamhuriya al Arabiya al Yamaniya

HISTORY. On the death of the Iman Ahmad on 18 Sept. 1962, army officers seized power on 26–27 Sept., declared his son, Saif Al-Islam Al-Badr (Iman Mansur Billah Muhammad), deposed and proclaimed a republic. The republican régime was supported by Egyptian troops, whereas the royalist tribes received aid from Saudi Arabia. On 24 Aug. 1965 President Nasser and King Faisal signed an agreement according to which the two powers are to support a plebiscite to determine the future of the Yemen; a conference of republican and royalist delegates met at Haradh on 23 Nov. 1965, but no plebiscite was agreed upon. At a meeting of the Arab heads of state in Aug. 1967 the President and the King agreed upon disengaging themselves from the civil war in Yemen. At the time there were still about 50,000 Egyptian troops in the country, holding San'a, Ta'iz, Hodeida and the plains, whereas the mountains were in the hands of the royalist tribes. By the end of 1967 the Egyptians had withdrawn. In Dec. 1989 agreement was reached with the People's Democratic Republic of Yemen on a Constitution for a unified state.

AREA AND POPULATION. In the north the boundary between the Yemen and Saudi Arabia has been defined by the Treaty of Taif concluded in June 1934. This frontier starts from the sea at a point some 5 or 10 miles north of Maidi and runs due east inland until it reaches the hills some 30 miles from the coast, whence it runs northwards for approximately 50 miles so as to leave the Sa'da Basin within the Yemen. Thence it runs in an easterly and south-easterly direction until it reaches the desert area near Nejran. The area is about 73,300 sq. miles (195,000 sq. km) with a population of 8,105,974, census 1986; estimate (1988) 8,595,000. There were 1,168,199 citizens working abroad mainly in Saudi Arabia and the United Arab Emirates not included in the census total. The capital is San'a with a population of (1986) 427,150. Other important towns are the port of Hodeida (population, 155,110), and Ta'iz (178,043); other towns are Ibb, Yerim, Dhamar and the ports of Mokha and Loheiya.

CLIMATE. A desert climate, modified by relief. San'a. Jan. 57°F (13·9°C), July 71°F (21·7°C). Annual rainfall 20" (508 mm).

CONSTITUTION AND GOVERNMENT. A general election was held on 5 July 1988 for the 128 elective seats on the 159-member People's Consultative Assembly *(Majlis ash-Shura)*; the remaining 31 seats are appointed by the President. The Consultative Assembly elects the President.

President of the Republic: Col. Ali Abdullah Saleh (elected 1978; re-elected 1983 and 1988).

Vice-President: Abdel-Karim al-Arishi.

The Council of Ministers in Dec. 1989 was composed as follows:

Prime Minister: Maj. Abdel Aziz Abdel Ghani.

Deputy Prime Ministers: Lieut.-Col. Mujahid Abu Shawrib *(Internal Affairs)*, Dr Abdel Karim al-Iryani *(Foreign Affairs)*, Dr Muhammad Said al-Attar *(Development)*, Dr Hassan Mohammed Makki.

Agriculture and Fisheries: Dr Nasir Abdullah al-Awlaqi. *Waafs and Religious Guidance:* Qadi Ali bin Ali as-Samman. *Legal and Consultative Assembly Affairs:* Ismail Ahmad al-Wazir. *Education:* Ahmed Muhammad al-Unsi. *Communications:*

Ahmad Khadim al-Wajih. *Economy:* Dr Abd at-Wahhab Mahmud Abd al Hamid. *Civil Service and Administrative Reform:* Muhammad Abdullah al-Jayfi. *Power, Water and Drainage:* Jamal Muhammad Abduh. *Finance:* Alawi Salah as-Salami. *Health:* Muhammad Ali Muqbil. *Information and Culture:* Hassan Ahmad al-Lawzi. *Interior:* Abdullah Hussain Barakat. *Justice:* Lieut.-Col. Muhsin Muhammad al-Ulufi. *Social Affairs and Labour:* Ahmad Muhammad Luqman. *Municipalities and Housing:* Muhsin Ali al-Hamadani. *Oil and Mineral Resources:* Ahmad Ali al-Muhani. *Public Works and Transport:* Abdullah Hussain al-Kurshumi. *Youth and Sports:* Dr Muhammad Ahmad al-Kabab. *Yemen Unity Affairs:* Yahya Hussain al-Arashi.

National flag: Three horizontal stripes of red, white, black, with a green star in the centre.

Local government: There are 11 provinces *(Liwa'):* Sa'dah, Bayda, San'a, Hodeida, Hajjah, Jawf, Mahwit, Marib, Dhamar, Ibb and Ta'iz.

DEFENCE. Military service for 3 years is compulsory.

Army. The Army consists of 3 armoured, 1 mechanized, 9 infantry, 2 para-commando, 1 Special Forces, 5 artillery brigades, 1 central guard force and 3 anti-aircraft artillery and 2 air defence battalions. Equipment includes 100 T-34, 480 T-54/-55, 20 T-62 and 64 M-60A1 main battle tanks. Strength (1989) 35,000.

Navy. The flotilla consists of 3 US-built and 5 Soviet-built inshore patrol craft, 3 Soviet-built inshore minehunters and 4 small landing craft. Personnel in 1989 numbered 500.

Air Force. Built up with aid from both the USA and USSR, as well as Saudi Arabia, the Air Force is believed to be receiving many new Soviet aircraft. Current equipment includes 15 Su-22 fighter-bombers, 30 MiG-21 and 14 F-5 fighters, a total of 14 Il-14, An-12, An-24/26, C-130 Hercules and Skyvan transports, and over 30 Mi-8 and Agusta-Bell JetRanger and 212 helicopters. Personnel (1990) about 1,000.

INTERNATIONAL RELATIONS

Membership. The Yemen Arab Republic is a member of UN and the Arab League.

ECONOMY

Planning. The Third Development Plan (1987–92) provides investment of US$3,776m. (40% foreign aid), and concentrates principally on agricultural development.

Budget. The budget for 1989 provided for expenditure of 20,789m. riyal and revenue of 16,041m. riyal.

Currency. The currency is the *riyal* of 100 *fils*. In March 1990, 16·03 *riyal* = £1 and 9·78 *riyal* = US$1.

ENERGY AND NATURAL RESOURCES

Electricity. Production (1986) 556m. kwh.

Oil. The first large-scale oilfield and pipeline was inaugurated in 1987, following the discovery in 1984. Production (1989) 10m. tonnes.

Minerals. The only commercial mineral being exploited is salt and (1985) production was 169,000 tons. Reserves (estimate) 25m. tonnes.

Agriculture. Of the total area of 19·5m. hectares, 1·3m. are arable or permanent crops. Cotton is grown in the Tihama, the coastal belt, round Bait al Faqih and Zabid. Fruit is plentiful, especially fine grapes from the San'a district. Production (1988, in 1,000 tonnes): Sorghum, 542; potatoes, 117; grapes, 133; dates, 15; wheat, 132; barley, 48; maize, 53.

Livestock (1988): Cattle, 1,053,000; camels, 63,000; sheep, 2,674,000; goats, 1,709,000; poultry, 23m.

Fisheries. Total catch (1986) 22,300 tonnes.

INDUSTRY AND TRADE

Industry. There is very little industry. The largest is a textile factory at San'a. Production of cement (1982) 85,000 tonnes.

Commerce. Imports totalled 11,155m. riyals in 1986, the largest items being food and live animals. Exports totalled 96·7m. in 1985.

Total trade between Yemen Arab Republic and UK (British Department of Trade returns, in £1,000 sterling):

	1986	*1987*	*1988*	*1989*
Imports to UK	2,106	2,306	1,532	1,598
Exports and re-exports from UK	58,149	55,334	42,564	41,653

Tourism. There were about 44,000 tourists in 1986.

COMMUNICATIONS

Roads. There were (1985) 37,000 km of roads and (1986) 125,000 cars.

Aviation. There are 3 international airports: San'a, Ta'iz and Hodeida.

Shipping. Hodeida, Mokha, Salif and Loheiya are the 4 main ports.

Post and Broadcasting. There were about 35,000 telephones in 1984. In 1986 there were 50,000 television and 200,000 radio receivers.

RELIGION, EDUCATION AND WELFARE

Religion. The population is almost entirely Moslem, comprising 39% Sunni (Shafi'i) and 59% Shi'a (Zaidi).

Education. There were (1985–86) 904,487 pupils at primary schools, 112,922 in secondary schools, and 11,616 at teacher-training establishments. In 1982 the University of San'a (founded in 1974) had 6,719 students.

Health. In 1986 there were 1,234 physicians and 60 hospitals and health centres with 5,986 beds.

DIPLOMATIC REPRESENTATIVES

Of Yemen Arab Republic in Great Britain (41 South St., London, W1Y 5PD)
Ambassador: Ahmed Daifellah Al-Azeib (accredited 16 Oct. 1982).

Of Great Britain in Yemen Arab Republic (129 Haddah Rd., San'a)
Ambassador and Consul-General: M. A. Marshall.

Of Yemen Arab Republic in the USA (600 New Hampshire Ave., NW, Washington, D.C., 20037)
Ambassador: Mohsin A. Alaini.

Of the USA in Yemen Arab Republic (P.O. Box 1088, San'a)
Ambassador: Charles F. Dunbar.

Of Yemen Arab Republic to the United Nations
Ambassador: Mohamed Abdulaziz Sallam.

Further Reading

Bidwell, R., *The Two Yemens*. Boulder and London, 1983
El Mallakh, R., *The Economic Development of the Yemen Arab Republic*. London, 1986
Peterson, J. E., *Yemen: The Search for a Modern State*. London, 1982
Smith, G. R., *The Yemens*. [Bibliography] Oxford and Santa Barbara, 1984

THE PEOPLE'S DEMOCRATIC REPUBLIC OF YEMEN

Capital: Aden
Population: 2·35m. (1988)
GNP per capita: US$430 (1988)

Jumhuriyah al-Yemen al Dimuqratiyah al Sha'abiyah—Southern Yemen

HISTORY. Between Aug. and Oct. 1967 the 17 sultanates of the Federation of South Arabia (*see* map in THE STATESMAN'S YEAR-BOOK, 1965–66) were overrun by the forces of the National Liberation Front (NLF). The rulers were deposed, resigned or fled. At the same time the rival organization of FLOSY (Front for the Liberation of Occupied South Yemen) fought a civil war against NLF and harassed the British forces and civilians in Aden. In Nov. the UAR withdrew its support from FLOSY, and with the backing of the Army the NLF took over throughout the country.

The last British troops left Aden on 29 Nov. 1967, and on 30 Nov. the Southern Yemen People's Republic was proclaimed and the name was subsequently changed to the People's Democratic Republic of Yemen in 1970.

On 13 Jan. 1986 there was a *coup* attempt against President Ali Nasser Mohammed which developed into virtual civil war. By 24 Jan. the rebel forces had taken control of the capital, Aden, and at a meeting of the Socialist Party Central Committee the presidium of the Supreme People's Council announced that the Acting President was Haydar al-Attas.

In May 1988, agreements were signed in Taiz between Ali Salem Al-Beedh, Secretary General of the Yemeni Socialist Party and President Saleh of the Yemen Arab Republic. The agreements covered joint oil exploration of a demilitarized border zone and more open borders. In Dec. 1989 agreement was reached with the Yemen Arab Republic on a draft Constitution for a unified state.

AREA AND POPULATION. The People's Democratic Republic of Yemen is bounded north by the Yemen Arab Republic and Saudi Arabia, east by Oman, south by the Gulf of Aden and west by the Yemen Arab Republic and Bab Al-Mandab Strait. The Republic covers an area of approximately 130,065 sq. miles (336,869 sq. km). Land area can be divided into 4 areas: (*i*) the coastal lands in the south, nearly 1,200 km long and 12·25 km wide; (*ii*) the inner lands and plateaus; (*iii*) the northern desert to the north of Hadhramaut; (*iv*) the green valleys scattered between the high lands. Population (census, preliminary 1988) 2,345,266; urban, 33%; rural, 57% and nomads, 10%. The main towns are (1987) Aden (capital) (population, 417,366), and Mukalla (154,360).

The island of **Kamaran** in the Red Sea (area 181 sq. km) was in British occupation from 1915 to 1967, when the inhabitants opted in favour of remaining with the Republic but Yemen Arab Republic occupied it in 1972.

The island of **Perim** (300 sq. km) was first occupied by the French in 1738. In 1799 the British took formal possession but evacuated the island the same year. It was re-occupied by the British in Jan. 1851 and was later used as a coaling station. In Nov. 1967 the inhabitants opted in favour of remaining with the Republic.

The island of **Socotra** lying to the east of the Horn of Africa in the Arabian sea (area 3,500 sq. km) was formerly part of the Sultanate of Qishn and Socotra and became part of the Republic in 1967.

CLIMATE. A desert climate prevails, modified in parts by altitude, which affects temperatures by up to 12°C, as well as rainfall, which is very low in coastal areas. Aden. Jan. 75°F (24°C), July 90°F (32°C). Annual rainfall 1·8" (46 mm).

CONSTITUTION AND GOVERNMENT

An amended Constitution was approved by the Supreme People's Council on 31 Oct. 1978.

The cabinet in Nov. 1989 was composed as follows:

President: Haydar Abu Bakr al-Attas (elected 6 Feb. 1986).

Vice-President: Dr Muhammad Awad al-Sa'adi.

Chairman, Council of Ministers: Yasin Said Numan. *Defence:* Col. Salih Ubayd Ahmad. *Finance:* Ahmad Nasir al-Danami. *Foreign Affairs:* Abdel Aziz al-Dali. *State Security:* Said Salih Salami.

National flag. Three horizontal stripes of red, white, black, with a blue triangle based on the hoist bearing a red star.

Local Government. There are 6 governorates (Aden, Lahej, Abyan, Shabwa, Hadhramaut and Al-Mahra), sub-divided into 30 provinces.

DEFENCE. Military service for 2 years is compulsory.

Army. The Army comprises 1 armoured, 3 mechanized, 9 infantry, 3 artillery, 2 rocket and 2 surface-to-surface missile brigades and 10 artillery battalions. Equipment includes 480 T-34/-54/-55/-62 main battle tanks. Strength (1990) about 24,000.

Navy. The Navy comprises 6 fast missile craft, 2 fast torpedo-boats, 2 fast attack craft, 1 tank landing ship, 4 medium landing ships and 5 minor landing craft, all transferred from the Soviet Navy and 5 boats. There is also a Soviet repair ship based in Aden, and a 4,500 tonne capacity floating dock, but they are principally used by the Soviet Navy and ownership is unclear. Personnel in 1989 totalled 1,000.

Air Force. Formed in 1967, the Air Force is now equipped mainly with aircraft of Soviet design. It has received about 40 MiG-21 fighters, 30 MiG-17 and 25 MiG-23 fighter-bombers, 30 Su-22 attack aircraft, 15 Mi-24 gunship helicopters, 4 An-24 and 2 An-26 twin-turboprop transports and about 30 Mi-8 and 5 Mi-4 helicopters. Personnel (1990) about 2,500.

INTERNATIONAL RELATIONS

Membership. The People's Democratic Republic of Yemen is a member of UN and the Arab League.

ECONOMY

Planning. The development plan (1986–91) envisaged expenditure of 998·2m. dinars.

Budget. The budget (in 1m. Yemeni dinars) for 1989 envisaged general revenue at 354·3 and general expenditure at 471·5.

Currency. The currency is the South Yemen *dinar* and is divided into 1,000 *fils*. Coins: 50, 25, 5 *fils*; notes: 10, 5 and 1 *dinar*, 500 and 250 *fils*. In March 1990, £1 = 0·559 *dinars*; US$1 = 0·339 *dinars*.

Banking. The only commercial bank is the National Bank of Yemen with the Bank of Yemen carrying on the functions of the Central Bank. All foreign banks have been nationalized.

YUGOSLAVIA

Capital: Belgrade
Population: 24·11m. (1990)
GNP per capita: US$2,680 (1988)

Socijalistička Federativna Republika Jugoslavija

HISTORY. In 1917 the Yugoslav Committee in London drew up the Pact of Corfu, which proclaimed that all Yugoslavs would unite after the first world war to form a kingdom under the Serbian royal house. The Kingdom of Serbs, Croats and Slovenes was proclaimed on 1 Dec. 1918. In 1929 the name was changed to Yugoslavia. During the Second World War Tito's partisans set up a provisional government (AVNOJ) which was the basis of a Constituent Assembly after the war. On 29 Nov. 1945 Yugoslavia was proclaimed a republic.

The peace treaty with Italy, signed in Paris on 10 Feb. 1947, stipulated the cession to Yugoslavia of the greater part of the Italian province of Venezia Giulia, the commune of Zara and the island of Pelagosa and the adjacent islets.

By an agreement of 10 Nov. 1975 the city of Trieste ('Zone A') was recognized as Italian and the Adriatic coastal portion of the former Free Territory of Trieste ('Zone B') as Yugoslav. A free industrial zone was set up in the Fernetici–Sezana region on both sides of the frontier.

Albanian-Serb dissensions in Kosovo have brought inter-ethnic tensions into prominence since 1988. These, combined with the critical state of the economy, led to widespread popular unrest. A new government led by Ante Marković took office in March 1989, and has embarked on a radical programme of economic and political reform.

AREA AND POPULATION. Yugoslavia is bounded in the north by Austria and Hungary, north-east by Romania, east by Bulgaria, south by Greece and Albania, and west by the Adriatic Sea and Italy. There are 365 offshore islands in the Adriatic. The area is 255,804 sq. km. Population at the 1981 census: 22,424,711 (females, 11,340,933). Density, 87·7 per sq. km. Population estimate, 1990: 24,107,000.

Yugoslavia is a federation of 6 republics: Bosnia and Herzegovina (B), Croatia (C), Macedonia (Ma), Montenegro (Mo), Serbia (Se) and Slovenia (Sl); and 2 'autonomous provinces' within Serbia; Kosovo (K) and Vojvodina (V). For details *see* p. 1610. The federal capital is Belgrade (Beograd). Population (census, 1981) 1,470,073 and of other principal towns:

Banja Luka (B)	183,618	Priština (K)	210,040
Bitolj (Ma)	137,636	Prizren (K)	134,526
Čačak (Se)	110,676	Rijeka (C)	193,044
Čakovec (C)	116,825	Šabac (Se)	119,669
Gostivar (Ma)	101,028	Sarajevo (B)	448,519
Kragujevac (Se)	164,823	Skopje (Ma)	504,932
Kraljevo (Se)	121,622	Slavonski Brod (C)	106,400
Kruševac (Se)	132,972	Smederevo (Se)	107,366
Kumanovo (Ma)	126,188	Split (C)	180,571
Leskovac (Se)	159,001	Subotica (V)	154,611
Ljubljana (Sl)	305,211	Tetovo (Ma)	162,378
Maribor (Sl)	185,699	Titograd (Mo)	132,290
Mostar (B)	110,377	Titova Mitrovica (K)	105,322
Niš (Se)	230,711	Tuzla (B)	121,717
Novi Sad (V)	257,685	Uroševac (K)	113,680
Osijek (C)	158,790	Zadar (C)	116,174
Pančevo (V)	123,791	Zagreb (C)	1,174,512
Peć (K)	111,071	Zenica (B)	132,733
Prijedor (B)	108,868	Zrenjanin (V)	139,300

Population (1981 census) by ethnic group was *(i)* the 6 'leading nations': Serbs, 8,140,452; Croats, 4,428,005; Moslems, 1,999,957; Slovenes, 1,753,554; Macedonians, 1,339,729; Montenegrins, 579,023; *(ii)* of the 18 other 'nationalities': Albanians, 1,730,364; Hungarians, 426,866. 1,219,045 persons declared themselves 'Yugoslavs' (i.e. not professing any ethnic group). In 1986 about 460,000 nationals worked abroad. There were 181,000 Gypsies in 1986.

Vital statistics, 1987: Live births, 359,338; deaths, 214,666 (including 9,036 infantile); marriages, 163,469; divorces, 22,907.

Vital statistics, 1988 (per 1,000 population): Live births, 15·1; deaths, 9; marriages, 6·9; infant mortality, 24·5; natural increase, 6·1. Divorces per 1,000 marriages: 132·6. Expectation of life in 1982: Males, 68; females, 73.

The Yugoslav (*i.e.*, South Slav) languages proper are Slovene, Macedonian and Serbo-Croat, the latter having 2 variants (Serbian, or Eastern and Croatian, or Western) which are regarded as constituting one language. There are claims, largely politically-motivated, that Croatian is a separate language and Macedonian a dialect of Bulgarian. Macedonian is and Serbian may be written in the Cyrillic alphabet. There are also substantial Albanian and Hungarian-speaking minorities. Art. 246 of the Constitution lays down that 'The languages of the nations and nationalities and their alphabets shall be equal throughout the territory of Yugoslavia'. The sole use of Serbo-Croat is mandatory in the armed forces.

CLIMATE. Most parts have a central European type of climate, with cold winters and hot summers, but the whole coast experiences a Mediterranean climate with mild, moist winters and hot, brilliantly sunny summers with less than average rainfall. Belgrade. Jan. 32°F (0°C), July 72°F (22°C). Annual rainfall 24·4" (610 mm). Şarajevo. Jan. 31°F (–0·5°C), July 67°F (19·6°C). Annual rainfall 34" (856 mm). Sibenik. Jan. 45°F (7°C), July 78°F (25·5°C). Annual rainfall 32·5" (813 mm). Split. Jan. 47°F (8·5°C), July 78°F (25·6°C). Annual rainfall 35" (870 mm). Zagreb. Jan. 32°F (0°C), July 72°F (22°C). Annual rainfall 34·6" (865 mm).

CONSTITUTION AND GOVERNMENT. The Constitution passed on 31 Jan. 1946 declared the Federal Republic to be composed of 6 republics: Serbia, Croatia, Slovenia, Bosnia and Herzegovina, Macedonia and Montenegro.

On 13 Jan. 1953 a new Constitution affirmed the management of all public affairs by the workers and their representatives.

The Constitution promulgated 7 April 1963 set up the 2 socialist autonomous provinces of Kosovo and Vojvodina within the framework of Serbia.

Under this Constitution, social self-government was exercised by the representative bodies of communes, districts, autonomous provinces, republics and the Federation and the rights to self-government and distribution of income proclaimed in 1953 were extended to those employed in public services. The former Council of Producers was replaced by Councils of Working Communities representing employees in every field of social activity.

All the means of production and all natural resources were social property. Exceptions were peasants' holdings (up to 10 hectares of arable land) and handicrafts. Citizens could be owners of dwellings for personal and family needs.

A new Constitution was proclaimed on 21 Feb. 1974. This directly transfered economic and political decision making to the working people through the 'assembly system'. An assembly was defined as 'a body of social self-management and the supreme organ of power within the framework of the rights and duties of its socio-political community'. Assemblies were based upon the workplace or community. For details *see* THE STATESMAN'S YEAR-BOOK, p. 1602-03.

In Jan. 1990 the Government announced an 8-point plan to rewrite the Constitution, abolish the Communist Party's monopoly of power, set up an independent judiciary, guarantee freedom of political association and institute economic reforms. General multi-party elections scheduled for April 1990.

Speaker of the Federal Assembly: Marjan Rožič.

Every citizen over the age of 18 has the suffrage (16 if employed). The last elections were held from Jan. to April 1986.

The State Presidency is elected by the Federal Assembly every 5 years. It consists of: 8 representatives of the Republics and Autonomous Provinces. The one-year mandate as President (head of state) is rotated among the members of the Presidency from May of each year.

Membership of the state Presidency:

Bosnia and Herzegovina: Raif Dizdarević; *Croatia:* Štipe Šuvar; *Macedonia:* Lazar Mojsov; *Montenegro:* Veselin Djuranović; *Serbia:* Gen. Nikola Ljubičić; *Slovenia:* Janez Drnovšek; *Kosovo:* Sinan Hasani; *Vojvodina: (to be elected).*

The Government is the Federal Executive Council of Chairman (i.e. Prime Minister), Vice-Chairmen, Ministers without Portfolio and Federal Secretaries, who are elected by the Federal Assembly every 4 years in conformity with equality of representation of the Republics and Autonomous Provinces. In March 1990 the Government included Ante Marković *(Prime Minister)* (b. 1925), Živko Pregl *(Deputy Prime Minister)*, Branko Zekan *(Finance)*, Budimir Lončar *(Foreign Affairs)*, Petar Gračanin *(Internal Affairs)*, Franc Horvat *(Foreign Economic Affairs)*, Božidar Marendić *(Development)*, Col.-Gen. Veljko Kadijević *(Defence)*, Radiša Gačić *(Labour)*.

At an extraordinary congress in Jan. 1990 the League of Communists of Yugoslavia relinquished its monopoly of political activity by 1,573 votes to 27, but failed to abandon the principle of 'democratic centralism', whereupon the Slovene League severed its connection with it. In March 1990 the President of the Yugoslav League was Milan Pančevski; the Secretary was Petar Škundrić.

National flag: Three horizontal stripes of blue, white, red, with a large red, yellow-bordered star in the centre.

National anthem: Hej, Slaveni, jošte živi reč naših dedova—O Slavs, our ancestors' words still live.

Local Government. Within the federal framework of republics Yugoslavia is administratively divided into 533 communes (*opština*). 52,843 delegates were elected to commune assemblies in 1986 (9,260 women): 24,335 to Chambers of Associated Labour; 14,935 to Chambers of Local Communities; and 13,573 to Socio-Political Chambers.

DEFENCE. Military service for 12 months is compulsory. The General People's Defence Law of 1969 bases Yugoslavia's defence on the principle of a nation in arms ready to wage partisan war against any invader. The partisan Territorial Defence Force number about 3m.

Army. Following reorganization the Army is divided into 4 Military Regions and comprises 2 infantry divisions; 1 airborne brigade and 29 brigades of armoured, mechanized, mountain and artillery forces. Equipment includes 750 T-54/-55, 290 M-84 and 45 M-47 main battle tanks. Strength (1990) 138,000 (including 93,000 conscripts), with a reserve of 440,000.

Navy. The Navy comprises 5 small diesel submarines, 4 midget submarines, 2 Soviet and 2 locally built frigates to similar designs armed with SS-N-2C Styx anti-ship missiles, 16 fast missile craft, 14 fast torpedo craft, 2 small corvette-style patrol vessels, 19 inshore patrol craft, 4 coastal minehunters, 10 inshore minesweepers, 14 river minesweepers, 12 tank landing craft with minelaying capability, and 25 minor landing craft. Auxiliaries include 3 transports, 1 survey ship, 1 salvage vessel, 2 headquarters ships, and 2 training ships (1 sail). Minor auxiliaries number about 25.

The Air Force operates 8 Ka-25 Hormone and 2 Ka-27 Helix anti-submarine helicopters plus 10 Mi-8 Hip and 15 Gazelle liaison helicopters, which are operationally assigned to the Navy. The Coast Defence Forces number 2,300 and man 25 coastal batteries and a few mobile missiles. A Marine force of 900 is divided into 2 'brigades'.

Personnel in 1989 totalled 10,000 (4,000 conscripts) including Coastal Defence and Marines, and the main base is at Split.

Air Force. The Air Force has about 250 combat aircraft and is organized in 2 Air Corps, with HQ at Zagreb and Zemun. There are 2 fighter divisions equipped primarily with about 125 Russian-built MiG-21s, although now being joined by MiG-29s, 2 ground-attack divisions of locally-built Jastreb and Orao jet attack aircraft, and 2 squadrons of Jastreb jet reconnaissance aircraft. Transport units fly Il-14 and An-26 twin-engined aircraft, 4-turboprop An-12s, and a few other types in small numbers, notably CL-215 amphibians, C-47s, Turbo-Porters and Yak-40s, Mystère 50s and Learjets for VIP duties. Training types are the nationally-designed UTVA-75 primary trainer, Galeb jet basic trainer and the Super Galeb jet advanced trainer. A large number of Gazelle, Agusta-Bell 205, Mi-4 and Mi-8 helicopters are in service. 'Guideline' and 'Goa' surface-to-air missiles have been supplied by the USSR. Personnel (1990) 32,000.

INTERNATIONAL RELATIONS

Membership. Yugoslavia is a member of UN and has special relationships with Comecon and OECD.

ECONOMY

Policy. Reforms of the economic system which began in 1989 include curbs on the republics' powers by integrating taxation and raising policy-making to the federal level, the liberalization of imports and reduction of tariffs, the liberalization of prices except in the public infrastructure, the modification of the workers' councils system, the creation of limited companies and stock exchanges and equal treatment for foreign and domestic investors. Balance of payments surplus, 1989: US$2,500m.

Budget. Revenue and expenditure for 1987, 1,971,600m. old dinars. 459,609m. old dinars were allotted to defence in 1985.

Currency. The currency became convertible on 1 Jan. 1990 and a new 'heavy' dinar was introduced worth 10,000 old dinars. The new dinar was pegged at DM7 until 30 June 1990. For the dinar before 1990 *see* THE STATESMAN'S YEAR-BOOK, 1989-90 p. 1604. Inflation had reached 2,500% by the end of 1989. Currency in circulation in 1988 was 4,014,600m. old dinars. There have been several devaluations since 1980. In March 1990, £1 = 20·06 *dinars*; US$1 = 12·39 *dinars*. International reserves, 1989: US$5,000m.

Banking. The National Bank is the bank of issue. There are also republican National Banks, 115 (in 1980) 'internal banks', 160 'basic banks' and 9 'associated banks'. In 1988 credits amounted to 1,493,200m. old dinars. Savings deposits totalled 8,063,600m. old dinars in 1988, foreign exchange savings 39,243,100m.

Weights and Measures. The metric weights and measures have been in use since 1883. The *wagon* of 10 tonnes is used as a unit of measure for coal, roots and corn. The Gregorian calendar was adopted in 1919.

ENERGY AND NATURAL RESOURCES

Electricity. Output in 1989, 82,775m. kwh, of which 23,491m. were hydro-electric. There is a 664-mw nuclear power plant at Krško (opened 1981); output in 1989, 4,688 kwh. Construction of further nuclear plants was banned by law in June 1989.

Oil. Crude oil production (1988) 3·69m. tonnes; 1989 estimate, 3·5m. tonnes.

Minerals. Yugoslavia has considerable mineral resources, including coal (chiefly brown coal), iron, copper ore, gold, lead, chrome, antimony and cement.

Mining output, in 1,000 tonnes, in 1989 (and 1988): Coal, 293 (362); brown coal, 12,063 (11,876); lignite, 62,276 (60,352); bauxite, 3,252 (3,034); salt, 368 (385); iron ore, 5,080 (5,545); copper ore, 30,078 (30,056); lead and zinc ore, 3,885 (3,847); antimony, 43 (38). In 1983, gold output was 4,238 kg; silver (1986), 177,000 kg.

Agriculture. The economically active agricultural population was 2,488,000 in 1981 (47·5% female). The total agricultural area was 14·19m. hectares in 1988. The cultivated area was 9·83m. hectares in 1988 of which 8·09m. were in private farms and 1·75m. in agricultural organizations, of which there were 3,397 in 1987. In 1984 only 6·5% of the 2·6m. private farms were more than 10 hectares of land.

Area (in hectares) and yield (in 1,000 tonnes) in 1988: Maize, 2·28m. (7,710); wheat, 1·51m. (6,303); sugar beet, 130,000 (4,508); rye, 40,000 (76); tobacco, 53,000 (49); sunflower, 207,000 (404); potatoes, 274,000 (1,849).

Livestock, 1988: Cattle, 4·88m.; pigs, 8·32m.; sheep, 7·82m.; poultry, 78·59m.

1988 yield of fruit (in 1,000 tonnes): Apples, 477; grapes, 1,171; plums (Yugoslavia is the world's largest producer), 761. 5·97m. hectolitres of wine were produced.

There were 1,017,000 tractors in 1988, of which 935,000 were in private hands.

Forestry. In 1988, 9·3m. hectares were forested, 37% of the land area, and consisted largely of beech, oak and fir. 3·03m. hectares were in private hands. Gross timber cut: 22,263,000 cu. metres.

Fisheries. In 1987 the landings of fish were (in tonnes): Salt-water, 56,217; freshwater, 25,174. The number of fishing craft was 353 motor vessels (12,961 GRT) and 1,389 sailing and rowing vessels.

INDUSTRY AND TRADE

Labour. In 1988 (women in brackets) there were 169,000 (63,000) employed in the private sector and 6·72m. (2·66m.) in the social sector. Of these 1·16m. worked in non-economic activities (e.g. education, social welfare). Amongst the economic activities 2·72m. worked in industry and mining, 672,000 in trade, 556,000 in building, 456,000 in transport and communications, 262,000 in financial services, 252,000 in tourism and 246,000 in agriculture. There were 1·13m. unemployed in 1988. Average monthly income per worker in 1988: 402,928 old dinars. There were (1986) 6,086,600 trade union members.

Industry. The majority of industries are situated in the north-west part of the country. In 1988 there were 8,796 large industrial enterprises and 1,380 small businesses in the social sector, and 165,055 small businesses in the private sector.

Industrial output (in 1,000 tonnes) in 1988 (and 1987): Pig-iron, 2,880 (2,868); steel, 4,430 (4,367); cement, 8,980 (8,963); sulphuric acid, 1,715 (1,610); fertilizers, 3,036 (3,048); plastics, 713 (701). Fabrics (in 1m. sq. metres): Cotton, 345 (366); woollen, 103 (105). Sugar (1,000 tonnes), 705 (872). Motor cars (in 1,000s), 316 (312).

Commerce. Foreign trade, in 1m. dinars, for calendar years:

	1986	*1986*[1]	*1987*	*1987*[1]	*1988*
Imports	3,108,230	(16,915,900)	5,633,069	(17,124,900)	17,371,430
Exports	2,724,204	(14,187,900)	5,152,279	(15,831,100)	16,589,912

[1] Adjusted to 1988 valuation (US$1 = 1,261 dinars)

Structure of exports (and imports) in 1988 (%): Investment goods, 17 (16); intermediate goods, 56 (75·6); consumer goods, 27 (8·4). Largest suppliers in 1988 (goods in 1,000m. dinars): Federal Republic of Germany, 4,280; USSR, 3,530; Italy, 2,665; USA, 1,342; Iraq, 1,340; Austria, 1,149. Largest export markets: USSR, 4,131; Italy, 3,766; Federal Germany, 2,875; USA, 1,505.

Main exports as % share in 1988: Machinery and transport equipment, 30·6; other manufactures, 15; food and tobacco, 8·5; chemicals, 9; raw materials, 5·4; fuel, 1·8. Imports: Machinery and transport equipment, 27·1; chemicals, 17·6; raw materials, 10·9.

Joint ventures with Western firms are permitted, and since 1984 the Western partner has been able to own 98% of the capital. International trade fairs are held in Zagreb in spring and autumn.

Foreign indebtedness was US$17,600m. in 1989.

Total trade between Yugoslavia and UK (British Department of Trade returns, in £1,000 sterling):

	1985	*1986*	*1987*	*1988*	*1989*
Imports to UK	122,132	145,127	175,301	197,254	202,450
Exports and re-exports from UK	177,530	188,390	206,932	203,066	219,866

Tourism. In 1989, foreign tourists spent 49·18m. (1988: 52·35m.) nights in Yugoslavia.

COMMUNICATIONS

Roads. In 1987 there were 806 km of motorway, 71,225 km of asphalted roads and 34,700 km of macadamized roads. There were 3·02m. passenger motor cars, 96,000 motorcycles, 207,000 lorries and 29,000 buses. 862m. passengers and 132m. tonnes of freight were carried by public road transport in 1988. There were 65,728 road traffic casualties (4,526 deaths) in 1987.

Railways. In 1987 Yugoslavia had 9,270 km of railway, of which 3,771 km were electrified. 115·7m. passengers and 83·6m. tonnes of freight were carried in 1988.

Aviation. The national airline JAT (Jugoslovenski Aero Transport) operates 291 domestic and international routes totalling 448,265 km. It had 52 aircraft in 1987. In 1988 6·5m. passengers (3·6m. international) and 47,601 tonnes of freight were carried. The chief airfields are Belgrade, Zagreb, Ljubljana, Sarajevo, Skopje, Dubrovnik, Split, Titograd, Tivat, Pula and Zadar.

Shipping. In 1987 Yugoslavia possessed 59 sea-going passenger vessels and 276 cargo vessels totalling 3·1m. tonnes. In 1988 8m. passengers were carried (7·9m. domestic) and 38·1m. tonnes of freight (36m. tonnes overseas).

International cargo handled at Yugoslav ports in 1987 totalled 30·85m. tonnes; domestic, 4·27m. tonnes.

Length of navigable waterways: Rivers, 1,673 km; canals, 664 km. There are 2 navigable lakes: Skadar (391 sq. km, of which 243 in Yugoslavia) and Ohrid (348 sq. km, of which 230 in Yugoslavia). In 1987 there were 1,156 river craft. 31,000 passengers and 20·68m. tonnes of cargo were carried in 1988.

Pipeline. An oil pipeline runs from Krk to Pančevo.

Post and Broadcasting. There were 4,053 post offices and 3,909,000 telephone subscribers in 1987. *Jugoslovenska Radiotelevizija* consists of almost 250 main, relay and local stations operating on medium-waves and FM. *Radio Koper* also broadcasts commercial programmes in Italian for northern parts of Italy. National and regional TV programmes are broadcast. Advertisements are broadcast for maximum 170 minutes each week. Number of receivers in 1987: Radio, 4·77m.; television, 4·09m.

Cinema and theatre. In 1987 there were 1,254 cinemas with 527,000 seats and 70 theatres with 27,090 seats. 30 full-length films were made in 1987.

Newspapers and Books. In 1988 there were 28 dailies with a circulation of 2·3m., 2,825 other newspapers and 1,659 periodicals. *Borba* and *Politika* (circulation in 1988: 41,000 and 240,000) enjoy semi-official status. 10,619 book titles (1,268 by foreign authors) were published in 1987.

JUSTICE, RELIGION, EDUCATION AND WELFARE

Justice. There are county tribunals, district courts, supreme courts of the constituent republics and a Supreme Court. There are also self-management courts, including courts of associated labour. In county tribunals and district courts the judicial functions are exercised by professional judges and by lay assessors constituted into collegia. There are no assessors at the supreme courts.

All judges are elected by the socio-political communities in their jurisdiction. The judges exercise their functions in accordance with the legal provisions enacted since the liberation of the country.

The constituent republics enact their own criminal legislation, but offences concerning state security and the administration are dealt with at federal level.

In 1987 258,000 crimes were reported, 163,000 charges made and 112,000 convictions obtained. 7,705 juveniles were sentenced.

Religion. Religious communities are separate from the State and are free to perform religious affairs. All religious communities recognized by law enjoy the same rights.

Serbia has been traditionally Orthodox and Croatia Roman Catholic. Moslems are found in the south as a result of the Turkish occupation. The 1953 percentage of the denominations was: Orthodox, 41·2%; Roman Catholic, 31·7%; Moslems, 12·3%; Protestants, 0·9%; without religion, 12·6%. 1984 estimates of believers: Orthodox, 9m.; Roman Catholic, 7m.; Moslems, 4m.

The Serbian Orthodox Church with its seat in Belgrade has 20 bishoprics within the country and 4 abroad, 3 in US and Canada and 1 in Hungary. The Serbian Orthodox Church numbers about 2,000 priests.

The Macedonian Orthodox Church with the Archbishop of Ohrid and Macedonia as its head in Skopje, has 4 bishoprics in the country and 1 abroad (American–Canadian–Australian). The Macedonian Orthodox Church numbers about 300 priests.

The Roman Catholic Church is divided into two provinces: Zagreb with 4 suffragan sees, and Sarajevo with 2 suffragan sees. In addition, the Roman Catholic Church has 4 archbishoprics, 10 independent bishoprics directly connected with the Vatican and 3 Apostolic Administrators. There is a National Conference of Bishops with the Archbishop of Zagreb, Cardinal Franjo Kuharič, at its head. The Roman Catholic Church has about 4,000 priests, 2 theological faculties and 15 seminaries. Relations with the Vatican are regulated by a 'Protocol' of 1966.

The Moslem Religious Union has 4 republic Superiorates in Sarajevo, Skopje, Titograd and Priština. The highest authority is the supreme synod of the Islamic Religious Community, which elects the Reis-ul-Ulema and the Supreme Islamic Superiorate. The Moslem religious community has about 2,000 priests.

The Protestant churches covering 4 independent Lutheran Churches, numbering about 150,000 believers, the Reformed Christian Church, numbering about 60,000 believers, include also several much smaller churches of Baptists, Methodists, Adventists, Nazarenes, etc., numbering together about 100,000 believers. The Protestant churches have about 450 priests.

Also there are independent Old Catholic Churches with Synodal Council at Zagreb.

The Jewish religion has about 35 communities making up a common league of Jewish Communities with its seat in Belgrade.

Education. Compulsory general education lasts 8 years, secondary 3–4 years. In 1987–88 there were 4,481 kindergartens with 44,712 teachers and 430,378 pupils, 12,069 primary schools with 139,167 teachers and 2,833,231 pupils; and 1,248 secondary schools with 63,711 teachers and 901,351 pupils.

Primary (and secondary) schools of ethnic minorities (1986–87): Albanian, 1,221 (272); Hungarian, 152 (66); Turkish, 62 (13); Bulgarian, 31 (nil); Romanian, 31 (7); Italian, 27 (11); Slovak, 26 (7).

In 1987–88 there were 322 institutes of higher education with 256,840 full-time students and 25,673 academic staff.

Health. In 1987 there were 53,672 doctors and dentists, and 142,427 hospital beds (10,189 psychiatric).

There were 2·23m. pensioners in 1988. 104·7m. working days were lost through sickness in 1987. Health insurance benefits totalled 2,471,364m. dinars, old age pensions 1,618,198m. dinars and disability pensions, 989,055m. dinars in 1988. 685,456m. dinars were paid in child allowances in 1988. Consumption of food per capita in 1987: Meat, 57·9 kg.; cereals, 146·5 kg.; milk, 99·3 litres; vegetables and fruit, 183·3. Daily consumption: 15,200 kilojoules.

DIPLOMATIC REPRESENTATIVES

Of Yugoslavia in Great Britain (5 Lexham Gdns., London, W8 5JJ)
Ambassador: Svetozar Rikanović.

Of Great Britain in Yugoslavia (46 Generala Ždanova, Belgrade)
Ambassador: P. E. Hall, CMG.

Of Yugoslavia in the USA (2410 California St., NW, Washington, D.C., 20008)
Chargé d'Affaires: Vladimir Matić.

Of the USA in Yugoslavia (Belgrade)
Ambassador: Warren Zimmermann.

Of Yugoslavia to the United Nations
Ambassador: Dragoslav Pejić.

Further Reading

Statistical Information: The Federal Statistical Office (Savezni Zavod za Statistiku; Kneza Miloša 20, Belgrade) was founded in Dec. 1944. *Director:* Dr D. Grupković. Its publications include: *Statistički godišnjak Jugoslavije*, annual since 1954 with a separate volume of captions and editorial matter in English *Statistical Yearbook of Yugoslavia*; *Statistical Pocket-Book of Yugoslavia*, annual since 1955; *Statistics of Foreign Trade of the SFR of Yugoslavia*, annual since 1946.

The Assembly of the SFR of Yugoslavia. Belgrade, 1974
The Constitution of the Socialist Federal Republic of Yugoslavia. Belgrade, 1974
Alexander, S., *Church and State in Yugoslavia since 1945.* CUP, 1979
Artesien, P. F. R., *Joint Ventures in Yugoslav Industry.* Aldershot, 1985
Banac, I., *The National Question in Yugoslavia.* Cornell Univ. Press, 1985
Burg, S. L., *Conflict and Cohesion in Socialist Yugoslavia: Political Decision-Making since 1966.* Princeton Univ. Press, 1983
Čičin-Šain, A. and Ellis, M. (eds.), *Doing Business with Yugoslavia: Economic and Legal Aspects.* Belgrade, 1986
Cohen, L. J., *Political Cohesion in a Fragile Mosaic: The Yugoslav Experience.* Boulder, 1983
Dedijer, V., *et al., History of Yugoslavia.* New York, 1974
Djilas, M., *Memoir of a Revolutionary.* New York, 1973.—*Rise and Fall.* London, 1985
Drvodelić, M., *Croatian or Serbian-English Dictionary.* 4th ed. Zagreb, 1978
Filipović, R., *English-Croatian or Serbian Dictionary.* Zagreb, 1980.—*The New Foreign Exchange and Foreign Trade Regime of Yugoslavia.* Belgrade, 1986
Horton, J. J., *Yugoslavia.* [Bibliography] Oxford and Santa Barbara, 1978
Kotnik, J., *Slovensko–angleski slovar.* 4th ed. Ljubljana, 1959
Lydall, H., *Yugoslavia in Crisis.* OUP, 1989
McFarlane, B., *Yugoslavia: Politics, Economics and Society.* London, 1988
Milivojević, M. *et al.* (eds.) *Yugoslavia's Security Dilemmas: Armed Forces, National Defence and Foreign Policy.* Oxford, 1988
Milošević, D., *Investing in Yugoslavia and Other Forms of Long-Term Economic Co-operation with Yugoslav Enterprises.* 2nd ed. Belgrade, 1986
Pavlowitch, S. K., *The Albanian Problem in Yugoslavia.* London, 1982
Prout, C., *Market Socialism in Yugoslavia.* OUP, 1985
Ramet, P., *Nationalism and Federalism in Yugoslavia, 1963–1983.* Indiana Univ. Press, 1984.—*Yugoslavia in the 1980s.* Boulder, 1985
Seroka, J., *Political Organizations in Yugoslavia.* Durham, NC, 1986
Singleton, F., *Twentieth Century Yugoslavia.* London, 1976.—(with B. Carter) *The Economy of Yugoslavia.* London, 1982.—*A Short History of the Yugoslav Peoples.* CUP, 1985
Sirc, L., *The Yugoslav Economy under Self-Management.* London, 1979
Stojanović, R., (ed.) *The Functioning of the Yugoslav Economy.* New York, 1982
Tito, J. B., *The Essential Tito.* New York, 1970
Zimmerman, W., *Open Borders, Non-Alignment and the Political Evolution of Yugoslavia.* Princeton Univ. Press, 1987

REPUBLICS AND AUTONOMOUS PROVINCES

The Federal Republic of Yugoslavia comprises the 6 republics of Bosnia and Herzegovina, Croatia, Macedonia, Montenegro, Serbia and Slovenia, and the 2 autonomous provinces of Kosovo and Vojvodina within the Republic of Serbia.

Each has its own Constitution and Assembly.

Indicators (in %) for 1987:

	Population	*Workers*	*Social product*	*Investments*
Yugoslavia	*100*	*100*	*100*	*100*
Bosnia and Herzegovina	18·8	15·7	13·2	14·2
Croatia	19·9	23·6	25·6	21·9
Macedonia	8·8	7·7	5·4	4·2
Montenegro	2·7	2·5	1·9	2·0
Serbia	41·5	38·0	34·7	39·5
Slovenia	8·3	12·5	19·0	18·2

BOSNIA AND HERZEGOVINA

HISTORY. The country was settled by Slavs in the 7th century, the original clan system evolving between the 12th and 14th centuries into a principality under a *Ban,* during which time the Bogomil Christian heresy became entrenched. Bosnia was conquered by the Turks in 1463, and the majority of the Bogomils were converted to Islam. At the Congress of Berlin (1878) the territory was assigned to Austro-Hungarian administration under nominal Turkish suzerainty. Austria-Hungary's outright annexation in 1908 generated international tensions which contributed to the outbreak of the first world war.

AREA AND POPULATION. The republic is bounded in the north and west by Croatia, in the east by Serbia and in the south-east by Montenegro. It is virtually land-locked, having a coastline of only 20 km with no harbours. Its area is 51,129 sq. km. The capital is Sarajevo.

Population at the 1981 census: 4,124,256 (2,073,343 females), of whom the predominating ethnic groups were Moslems (1,630,033), Serbs (1,320,738) and Croats (758,140). Population density per sq. km, 1981: 80·7. Population, 1988, 4·44m.

Vital statistics:

	Live births	*Marriages*	*Deaths*	*Growth rate per 1,000*
1986	71,203	34,338	29,127	9·7
1987	68,600	34,558	27,999	9·2

ECONOMY

Agriculture. In 1988 the cultivated area was 1·57m. hectares. Yields (in 1,000 tonnes): Wheat, 468; maize, 559; potatoes, 278; plums, 166. Livestock in 1988 (1,000 head): Cattle, 923; sheep, 1,432; pigs, 693; poultry, 11,287. Timber cut in 1987: 7·23m. cu. metres.

Industry. Production (1987): Electricity, 18,038m. kwh; coal and lignite, 18·04m. tonnes; (1986) iron ore, 5·7m. tonnes; pig iron, 1·89m. tonnes; bauxite, 2·16m. tonnes; cement, 773,000 tonnes; cotton fabrics, 22m. sq. metres; cars, 21,000.

Employment. Population of working age, 1988, 2·98m. Non-agricultural workforce, 1·09m. (395,000 women), of whom 23,000 worked in private enterprise.

CROATIA

HISTORY. The Croats migrated to their present territory in the 6th century and were converted to Roman Catholicism. Croatia was united with Hungary by a personal union of thrones in 1091 and remained under Hungarian domination until after the first world war. For the duration of the second world war an independent fascist state was set up. In Dec. 1989 the Croatian League of Communists scheduled multi-party Parliamentary elections for 8 April 1990.

AREA AND POPULATION. Croatia is bounded in the north by Slovenia and Hungary and in the east by Serbia. It has an extensive Adriatic coastline well provided with ports, and includes the historical areas of Dalmatia, Istria and Slavonia, which no longer have administrative status. The capital is Zagreb. Its area is 56,538 sq. km. Population at the 1981 census was 4,601,469 (2,374,579 females), of whom the predominating ethnic groups were Croats (3,454,661) and Serbs (531,502). Population density per sq. km, 1981: 81·4. Population, 1988, 4·68m.

Vital statistics:

	Live births	*Marriages*	*Deaths*	*Growth rate per 1,000*
1986	60,226	30,495	51,740	1·8
1987	60,686	31,993	53,859	1·3

ECONOMY

Agriculture. In 1988 the cultivated area was 3·23m. hectares. Yields (in 1,000 tonnes): Wheat, 1,432; maize, 2,018; potatoes, 530; plums, 45. Livestock in 1988 (1,000 head): Cattle, 842; sheep, 722; pigs, 1,856. Timber cut in 1988: 5·5m. cu. metres.

Industry. Production (1987): Electricity, 9,383m. kwh; coal and lignite, 237,000 tonnes; bauxite, 319; crude petroleum, 2·76m. tonnes; steel, 459,000 tonnes; plastics, 329,000 tonnes; cement, 3·3m. tonnes; cotton fabrics, 75m. sq. metres; sugar, 164,000 tonnes.

Employment. Population of working age, 1988: 3·05m. Non-agricultural workforce (1988), 1·63m. (689,000 women), of whom 48,000 worked in private enterprise.

MACEDONIA

HISTORY. The Slavs settled in Macedonia since the 6th century, who had been Christianized by Byzantium, were conquered by the non-Slav Bulgars in the 7th century and in the 9th century formed a Macedo-Bulgarian empire, the western part of which survived until Byzantine conquest in 1014. In the 14th century it fell to Serbia, and in 1355 to the Turks. After the Balkan Wars of 1912-13 Turkey was ousted, and Serbia received the greater part of the territory, the rest going to Bulgaria and Greece. In 1918 Yugoslav Macedonia was incorporated into Serbia as 'South Serbia'. Possession of this territory has long been a source of contention between Bulgaria and Yugoslavia.

AREA AND POPULATION. Macedonia is land-locked, and is bounded in the north by Serbia and Kosovo, in the east by Bulgaria, in the south by Greece and in the west by Albania. The capital is Skopje. Its area is 25,713 sq. km. Population at the 1981 census was 1,909,136 (940,993 females), of whom the predominating ethnic groups were Macedonians (1,279,323), Albanians (377,208) and Turks (86,591). Population density per sq. km, 1981, 74·2. Population, 1988, 2·09m.

Vital statistics:

	Live births	*Marriages*	*Deaths*	*Growth rate per 1,000*
1986	38,234	16,326	14,438	11·7
1987	39,348	16,910	15,186	11·6

ECONOMY

Agriculture. In 1988 the cultivated area was 666,000 hectares. Yields (in 1,000 tonnes): Wheat, 295; maize (1987), 71; cotton, 923; tobacco, 29. Livestock in 1988 (1,000 head): Cattle, 287; sheep, 2,503; pigs, 187. Timber cut in 1988: 1·16m. cu. metres.

Industry. Production (1987): Electricity, 4,226m. kwh; lignite, 4·51m. tonnes; iron ore, 684,000 tonnes; pig-iron, 192,000 tonnes; steel, 392,000 tonnes; copper ore, 3·64m. tonnes; sulphuric acid, 100,000 tonnes; cement, 748,000 tonnes; cotton fabrics, 55m. sq. metres.

Employment. Population of working age, 1988: 1·34m. Non-agricultural workforce, 530,000 (190,000 women), of whom 16,000 worked in private enterprise.

MONTENEGRO

HISTORY. Montenegro emerged as a separate entity on the break-up of the Serbian Empire in 1355. It was never effectively subdued by Turkey. It was ruled by Bishop Princes until 1851, when a royal house was founded. The remains of King Nicholas I, (deposed 1918) were returned to Montenegro for reburial in Oct. 1989.

AREA AND POPULATION. Montenegro is a mountainous region which opens to the Adriatic in the south-west. It is bounded in the north-west by Bosnia and Herzegovina, in the north-east by Serbia and in the south-east by Albania. The capital is Titograd. Its area is 13,812, sq. km. Population at the 1981 census was 584,310 (294,571 females), of whom the predominating ethnic groups were Montenegrins (400,488), Moslems (78,080) and Albanians (37,735). Population density per sq. km, 1981: 42·3. Population, 1988, 632,000.

Vital statistics:

	Live births	*Marriages*	*Deaths*	*Growth rate per 1,000*
1986	10,455	4,193	3,922	10·6
1987	10,234	4,254	3,859	10·4

ECONOMY

Agriculture. In 1988 the cultivated area was 186,000 hectares. Yields (in 1,000 tonnes): Wheat, 15; maize, 8; potatoes, 29. Livestock in 1988 (1,000 head): Cattle, 189; sheep, 489; pigs, 24. Timber cut in 1988: 862,000 cu. metres.

Industry. Production (1988): Electricity, 2,947m. kwh; lignite, 2·32m. tonnes; (1987) bauxite, 820,000 tonnes; cement, 155,000 tonnes.

Employment. Population of working age, 1988: 407,000. Non-agricultural workforce, 167,000 (65,000 women), of whom 3,000 worked in private enterprise.

SERBIA

HISTORY. The Serbs received Orthodox Christianity from the Byzantines. They threw off the latter's suzerainty to become a large prosperous medieval state, which was destroyed by the Turks at the Battle of Kosovo in 1389. After revolutions in 1804 and 1815 Serbia won increasing degrees of autonomy from Turkey; complete independence came with the Treaty of Berlin in 1878. Its prince took the title of king in 1881.

AREA AND POPULATION. Serbia is bounded in the north-west by Croatia, in the north by Hungary, in the north-east by Romania, in the east by Bulgaria, in the south by Macedonia and in the west by Albania, Montenegro and Bosnia and Herzegovina. It includes the Autonomous Provinces of Kosovo in the south and Vojvodina in the north. With these Serbia's area is 88,361 sq. km; without, 55,968 sq. km. The capital is Belgrade. Population at the 1981 census was (with Kosovo and Vojvodina) 9,313,676 (4,684,349 females), of whom the predominating ethnic group was Serbs (6,182,155). Population density per sq. km: 105·4 (without Kosovo and Vojvodina). 5,694,464 (2,876,909 females), of whom the predominating ethnic group was Serbs (4,865,283). Population density per sq. km, 101·7. Population, 1988: With Kosovo and Vojvodina, 9·76m.; without, 5·83m.

Vital statistics (without Kosovo and Vojvodina):

	Live births	*Marriages*	*Deaths*	*Growth rate per 1,000*
1986	73,997	38,605	59,156	2·6
1987	73,076	38,331	58,651	2·5

ECONOMY[1]

Agriculture. In 1988 the cultivated area was 2·66m. hectares. Yields (in 1,000 tonnes): Wheat, 1,464; maize, 1,509; potatoes, 376; sugar-beet (1986), 4,096. Livestock in 1988: (in 1,000 head): Cattle, 1,409; sheep, 1,871; pigs, 2,679. Timber cut in 1988: 3·07m. cu. metres.

[1] Figures without Kosovo and Vojvodina.

Industry. (1988): Electricity, 30,642m. kwh; coal, 29·99m. tonnes; (1986) lignite, 36·71m. tonnes; pig-iron, 506,000 tonnes; steel, 591,000 tonnes; copper ore, 24·3m. tonnes; lorries, 11,000; cars, 177,000; sulphuric acid, 1·12m. tonnes; plastics, 236,000 tonnes; cement, 2·92m. tonnes; sugar, 537,000 tonnes; cotton fabrics, 81m. sq. metres; woollens, 43m. sq. metres.

Employment. Population of working age, 1988: 3·88m. Non-agricultural workforce, 1·74m. (673,000 women), of whom 25,000 worked in private enterprise.

KOSOVO

HISTORY. Following Albanian-Serb conflicts the Kosovo and Serbian parliaments adopted constitutional amendments in March 1989 surrendering much of Kosovo's autonomy to Serbia. Renewed Albanian rioting broke out in 1990. In April 1990 the former Kosovo Communist leader, Azem Vlasi, was released after being charged with 'counter-revolutionary activities'.

AREA AND POPULATION. Area: 10,887 sq. km. The capital is Priština. Population at the 1981 census, 1,584,441 (766,048 females), of whom the predominating ethnic groups were Albanians (1,226,736), and Serbs (209,497). Population density per sq. km, 1981: 145·5. Population, 1987, 1·85m.

Vital statistics:

	Live births	*Marriages*	*Deaths*	*Growth rate per 1,000*
1986	54,519	11,921	10,446	24·4
1987	55,204	13,314	9,614	24·7

ECONOMY

Agriculture. The cultivated area in 1988 was 409,000 hectares. Yields (in 1,000 tonnes): Wheat, 380; maize, 142; potatoes, 52; sugar-beet (1987), 48. Livestock in 1988 (1,000 head): Cattle, 410; sheep, 422; pigs, 66. Timber cut in 1988, 388,000 cu. metres.

Industry. Production (1987): Electricity, 6,003m. kwh; lignite, 10·31m. tonnes; sulphuric acid, 88,000 tonnes; cement, 295,000 tonnes.

Employment. Population of working age, 1988: 1·06m. Non-agricultural workforce, 237,000 (54,000 women), of whom 6,000 worked in private enterprise.

VOJVODINA

AREA AND POPULATION. Area: 21,506 sq. km. The capital is Novi Sad. Population at the 1981 census, 2,034,772 (1,041,392 females), of whom the predominating ethnic groups were Serbs (1,107,375) and Hungarians (385,356). Population density per sq. km, 1981: 94·6. Population, 1987, 2·05m.

Vital statistics:

	Live births	*Marriages*	*Deaths*	*Growth rate per 1,000*
1986	25,422	13,778	24,821	0·3
1987	23,957	13,820	23,970	0·3

ECONOMY

Agriculture. The cultivated area in 1988 was 1·63m. hectares. Yields (in 1,000 tonnes): Wheat, 2,085; maize, 3,103; potatoes, 191; sugar-beet (1987), 3,812. Livestock in 1988 (1,000 head): Cattle, 272; sheep, 360; pigs, 2,212. Timber cut in 1988: 758,000 cu. metres.

Industry. Production (1987): Electricity, 1,661m. kwh; (1986) crude petroleum, 1·13m. tonnes; sulphuric acid, 48,000 tonnes; plastics, 158,000 tonnes; cement, 1·31m. tonnes.

Employment. Population of working age, 1988: 1·35m. Non-agricultural workforce, 642,000 (257,000 women), of whom 18,000 worked in private enterprise.

SLOVENIA

HISTORY. The lands originally settled by Slovenes in the 6th century were steadily encroached upon by Germans. Slovenia developed as part of Austria-Hungary and gained independence only in 1918. A legal opposition group, the Slovene League of Social Democrats (leader, France Tomsič), was formed in Jan. 1989. In Oct. 1989 the Slovene Assembly voted a consitutional amendment giving it the right to secede from Yugoslavia. Multi-party Parlimentary elections were scheduled for 22 April 1990. The League of Communists of Slovenia left the Yugoslav League in Jan. 1990 and reconstituted itself as the Party of Democratic Renewal.

AREA AND POPULATION. Slovenia is bounded in the north by Austria, in the north-east by Hungary, in the south-east by Croatia and in the west by Italy. There is a small strip of coast south of Trieste. Its area is 20,251 sq. km. The capital is Ljubljana. Population at the 1981 census: 1,891,864 (973,098 females), of whom the predominating ethnic group were Slovene (1,712,445). Population density per sq. km, 1981: 93·4. Population, 1988, 1·94m.

Vital statistics:

	Live births	*Marriages*	*Deaths*	*Growth rate per 1,000*
1986	25,570	10,621	19,499	3·1
1987	27,359	10,533	20,742	3·4

ECONOMY

Agriculture. In 1988 the cultivated area was 649,000 hectares. Yields (in 1,000 tonnes): Wheat, 164; maize, 273; potatoes, 337. Livestock in 1988 (1,000 head): Cattle, 547; sheep, 25; pigs, 607. Timber cut in 1988: 3·29m. cu. metres.

Industry. Production (1987): Electricity, 12,542m. kwh; lignite, 4·3m. tonnes; steel, 788,000 tonnes; lorries, 4,100; cars, 66,000; sulphuric acid, 185,000 tonnes; sugar, 41,000 tonnes; cement, 1·17m. tonnes; cotton fabrics, 101m. sq. metres; woollens, 23m. sq. metres.

Employment. Population of working age, 1988: 1·3m. Non-agricultural workforce, 862,000 (397,000 women), of whom 31,000 worked in private enterprise.

ZAÏRE

Capital: Kinshasa
Population: 32·56m. (1988)
GNP per capita: US$170 (1988)

République du Zaïre

HISTORY. Until the middle of the 19th century the territory drained by the Congo River was practically unknown. When Stanley reached the mouth of the Congo in 1877, King Leopold II of the Belgians recognized the immense possibilities of the Congo Basin and took the lead in exploring and exploiting it. The Berlin Conference of 1884–85 recognized King Leopold II as the sovereign head of the Congo Free State.

The annexation of the state to Belgium was provided for by treaty of 28 Nov. 1907, which was approved by the chambers of the Belgian Legislature in Aug. and Sept. and by the King on 18 Oct. 1908. The law of 18 Oct. 1908, called the Colonial Charter (last amended in 1959), provided for the government of the Belgian Congo, until the country became independent on 30 June 1960. The country's name was changed from Congo to Zaïre in Oct. 1971. For subsequent history to 1977 *see* THE STATESMAN'S YEAR-BOOK, 1980–81, p. 1613.

AREA AND POPULATION. Zaïre is bounded north by the Central African Republic, north-east by Sudan, east by Uganda, Rwanda, Burundi and Lake Tanganyika, south by Zambia, south-west by Angola, north-west by Congo. There is a 40-km Atlantic coastline separating Angola's province of Cabinda from the rest of that country.

The area of the republic is estimated at 2,344,885 sq. km (905,365 sq. miles). The population is composed almost entirely of Bantu groups, with minorities of Sudanese (in the north), Nilotes (northeast), Pygmies and Hamites (in the east). In the 1984 census the population was 29,671,407 (44% urban). Estimate (1988) 32,564,000. In Dec. 1987 there were about 320,000 refugees in Zaïre including 300,000 from Angola.

The area (in sq. km) and populations (census) 1984 of the regions were as follows, together with their chief towns:

Region	*Sq. km*	*Census 1984*	*Chief town*	*Census 1984*
Bandundu	295,658	3,682,845	Bandundu (Banningville)	96,841 [2]
Bas-Zaïre	53,920	1,971,520	Matadi	144,742
Equateur	403,293	3,405,512	Mbandaka (Coquilhatville)	125,263
Haut-Zaïre	503,239	4,206,069	Kisangani (Stanleyville)	282,650
Kasai Occidental	156,967	2,287,416	Kananga (Luluabourg)	290,898
Kasai Oriental	168,216	2,402,603	Mbuji-Mayi (Bakwanga)	423,363
Kinshasa City	9,965	2,653,558	Kinshasa (Leopoldville)	2,653,558
Kivu [2]	256,662	5,187,865	Bukavu (Costermansville)	171,064
Shaba	496,965	3,874,019	Lubumbashi (Elizabethville)	543,268

[1] Divided into 2 regions (1988) [2] 1976.

Other large towns (1976): Likasi (194,465 in 1984); Kikwit (146,784 in 1984); Kalémié (172,297); Kamina (160,020); Ilebo (142,036); Boma (93,965) and Kolwezi (77,277).

French is the only official language, but of more than 200 languages spoken, 4 are recognized as national languages. Of these, Kiswahili is used in the east, Tshiluba in the south, Kikongo in the area between Kinshasa and the coast, while Lingala is spoken widely in and around Kinshasa and along the river; Lingala has become the *lingua franca* after French.

CLIMATE. Because of the size and the relief of the country, the climate is very varied, the central region having an equatorial climate, with year-long high temperatures and rain at all seasons. Elsewhere, depending on position north or south of the Equator, there are well-marked wet and dry seasons. The mountains of the east and south have a temperate mountain climate, with the highest summits having considerable snowfall. Kinshasa. Jan. 79°F (26·1°C), July 73°F (22·8°C). Annual rainfall 45" (1,125 mm). Kananga. Jan. 76°F (24·4°C), July 74°F (23·3°C). Annual rainfall 62" (1,584 mm). Kisangani. Jan. 78°F (25·6°C), July 75°F (23·9°C). Annual rainfall 68" (1,704 mm). Lubumbashi. Jan. 72°F (22·2°C), July 61°F (16·1°C). Annual rainfall 50" (1,237 mm).

CONSTITUTION AND GOVERNMENT. A new Constitution was promulgated on 15 Feb. 1978 and amended in Nov. 1980. The supreme institution is the sole political party, the *Mouvement Populaire de la Révolution* (MPR), whose leader and President is automatically Head of State, of the National Executive Council and of the National Legislative Council. His nomination by the Political Bureau of the MPR (whose 38 members are all nominated by him) is confirmed for a 7-year term (renewable once) by election by universal adult suffrage (all Zaïreans acquire automatic membership of the MPR at birth).

Former President: Joseph Kasavubu, 1 July 1960–25 Nov. 1965 (deposed in *coup*).

President and Minister of National Defence: Marshal Mobutu Sésé Séko Kuku Ngbendu wa Zabanga (took office 25 Nov. 1965, elected 1 Nov. 1970 and re-elected Dec. 1977 and July 1984).

The National Executive Council is composed of State Commissioners appointed by the President. In Nov. 1989 it was composed as follows:

Prime Minister: Kengo Wa Dondo.

Deputy Prime Ministers: Nimy Mayidika Ngimbi *(Political, Administrative and Social Affairs, Citizens' Rights and Liberties),* Mwando Nsimba *(Economic, Financial and Monetary Affairs and Rural Development),* Mozagba Ngbuka *(Territorial Administration and Decentralization). Territorial Security and Veterans' Affairs:* Gen. Singa Boyenge Mosambay. *Foreign Affairs:* Nguza Karl I. Bond. *International Co-operation:* Nyiwa Mobutu. *Information and Press:* Sakombi Inongo. *Planning:* Biene Ngalisame. *Finance:* Katanga Mukumadi wa Mutumba. *Budget:* Kaserekai Kasai. *Agriculture:* Takizala Luyuna Musi Mbingini. *National Economy and Industry:* Ndele Bamu. *Mines and Energy:* Beyeye Djema. *Public Works and Regional Planning:* Kibangula Kia Makonga. *Transport and Communications:* Mokolo wa Mpombo. *Foreign Trade:* Nzamba Mwana Kalemba. *Land, Affairs, Environment and Conservation:* Pendje Demodetdo Yako. *Higher Education, Universities and Scientific Research:* Lombeye Bosongo. *Primary and Secondary Education:* Nzege Aliaziambina. *Public Health:* Ngandu Kabega. *Urban Development:* Ileo Itambala. *Labour and Social Security:* Muduka Inyanza. *Civil Service:* Ntawiniga Balezi. *Posts, Telephone and Telecommunications:* Okuka wa Katako. *Sports and Leisure:* Kibassa Maliba. *Culture, Arts and Tourism:* Ngogo Kamanda. *Justice:* Nsinga Udjuu Ongwakebi Untube. *Without Portfolio:* Kinzonzi Mvutudiki Ngindu Kogbia.

Parliament consists of a unicameral National Legislative Council comprising People's Commissioners (one per 150,000 inhabitants) elected by universal suffrage for a 5-year term. At the latest elections (Sept. 1987) 210 People's Commissioners were elected from a list of candidates presented by the MPR.

National flag: Green, with a yellow disc bearing an arm holding a flaming torch.

Local government: Zaïre is composed of the *ville neutre* of Kinshasa (administered by a Governor) and 8 regions, each under a Regional Commissioner and 6 Councillors; all are appointed by the President. The regions are divided into 13 urban and 24 rural sub-regions.

DEFENCE

Army. The Army is divided into 8 Military Regions and comprises 1 infantry division (3 infantry brigades), and 1 Special Forces division (1 parachute, 1 commando and 1 Presidential Guard brigades) with another armoured brigade and 2 infantry brigades. Equipment includes 50 Chinese Type-62 light tanks, and 95 AML-60 and 60 AML-90 armoured cars. Strength (1989) 22,000. There is a paramilitary gendarmerie which is responsible for security and also numbered (1990) about 26,000, organized in 40 battalions.

Navy. The navy comprises 4 *ex*-Chinese and 5 US-built inshore patrol craft plus some 30 small boats divided among coastal, river and lake flotillas. Personnel in 1989 numbered 1,500 including 600 marines.

Air Force. The Air Force has been built up with training assistance from Italy. In 1989 it operated 7 Mirage 5 supersonic fighters, 9 Aermacchi MB.326GB and 3 MB.326K armed jet trainers, 5 C-130 Hercules and 3 DHC-5 Buffalo turboprop transports, 7 C-47, 4 C-54, 2 DC-6 piston-engined transports, 20 Bell 47, Alouette, Puma and Super Puma helicopters, 9 SIAI-Marchetti SF.260MC basic trainers and a variety of other transport and training aircraft. Personnel (1990) 2,500.

INTERNATIONAL RELATIONS

Membership. Zaïre is a member of UN, OAU and is an ACP state of EEC.

ECONOMY

Planning. The 5-year Development Plan, 1986–90 envisaged expenditure of US$5,000m. emphasis is being placed on promoting food production and increasing agricultural exports.

Budget. Revenue was estimated at 130m. zaïres in 1988, and expenditure, 242m.

Currency. The currency unit, is the *zaïre*, divided into 100 *makuta*. Each *likuta* (plural *makuta*) is divided into 100 *sengi*. Bank-notes are issued in the following denominations: 50, 10, 5 and 1 *zaïre* and 50 *makuta*; there are coins of 20, 10 and 5 *makuta*, 1 *likuta* and 10 *sengi*. In March 1990, £1 sterling = 792·00 *zaïre*; US$1 = 483·22 *zaïre*.

Banking. The central bank is Banque du Zaïre. A development bank with state backing is the Société Financière de Développement (SOFIDE). Commercial banks operating in Zaïre are Banque de Paris et des Pays-Bas, Banque de Kinshasa, National & Grindlays Bank, Barclays Bank SZPRL, First National City Bank, Union Zaïroise de Banques, Banque Commerciale Zaïroise, Banque du Peuple, Caisse Nationale d'Epargne et de Crédit Immobilier and Banque Internationale pour L'Afrique au Zaïre.

Weights and Measures. The metric system was introduced by law on 17 Aug. 1910.

ENERGY AND NATURAL RESOURCES

Electricity. Production (1986) 5,280m. kwh. A huge dam at Inga, on the Zaïre River near Matadi, has a potential capacity of 39,600 mw.

Oil. Offshore oil production began in Nov. 1975; crude production (1989) was 1·4m. tonnes.

Minerals. In 1988 approximately one-third of Zaïre's foreign exchange was derived from mining of copper (438,600 tonnes), zinc (61,100 tonnes), cobalt (10,300 tonnes), as well as manganese, tin, gold and silver. The most important mining area is in the region of Shaba (formerly Katanga). The principal mining companies are the State-owned Gécamines and Sodimiza; the international Société Minière du Tenke-Fungurume which started production in 1976; and 2 diamond companies, MIBA and British Zaïre Diamond Distributors. Production (1988) 18,227,000 metric carats.

Agriculture. There were (1984) 5·65m. hectares of arable land and 24·8m. hectares of pastures and meadows. The main food crops (1988 production in 1,000 tonnes) are: Cassava, 16,254; plantains, 1,520; sugar-cane, 1,200; maize, 740; groundnuts, 400; bananas, 345; yams, 264; rice, 330. Cash crops (1988) include palm oil, 70; coffee, 95; palm kernels, 70; rubber, 17; seed cotton 77. There are also (1988) pineapples, 180; mangoes, 155; oranges, 150; papayas, 180.

Livestock (1988): Cattle, 1·4m.; sheep, 880,000; goats, 3·04m.; pigs, 800,000; poultry, 19m.

Forestry. Equatorial rain forests cover 55% of Zaïre's land surface, and 165,000 cu. metres of timber were produced in 1988.

Fisheries. The catch for 1986 was 150,000 tonnes, almost entirely from inland waters.

INDUSTRY AND TRADE

Industry. The main manufactures are foodstuffs, beverages, tobacco, textiles, leather, wood products, cement and building materials, metallurgy and metal extraction, small river craft, and bicycles.

Commerce. Imports in 1988 totalled 248,860m. zaïres, exports totalled US$2,206·8m. In 1988, 55% of the exports (by value) consisted of copper, 4% of coffee, 6·6% of crude petroleum, 12·5% of diamonds and 9·8% of cobalt. In 1987, 37% of all exports went to Belgium-Luxembourg, 18% to USA, 11% to Federal Republic of Germany and 11% to Italy, while 19·7% of imports came from Belgium, 9·3% from USA, 9% from France, 8·8% from Federal Republic of Germany and 8·7% from South Africa.

Total trade between Zaïre and UK (British Department of Trade returns, in £1,000 sterling):

	1985	*1986*	*1987*	*1988*	*1989*
Imports to UK	35,198	17,192	8,544	7,542	9,069
Exports and re-exports from UK	34,975	34,217	26,142	26,132	28,419

Tourism. There were 51,000 visitors in 1986 spending US$16·3m.

COMMUNICATIONS

Roads. In 1985 of 145,000 km of roads only 20,700 km are of national importance and all roads are earth-surfaced. In 1984 there were 25,000 passenger cars and 60,000 commercial vehicles.

Railways. There are two railway operators, the Zaïre National Railways (SNCZ) and the National Office of Transport and Communications (Onatra), which leases two lines from SNCZ. Length in 1986 was 4,750 km on 3 gauges, of which 858 km is electrified. In 1988 SNCZ carried 1m. passengers and 4·1m. tonnes of freight.

Aviation. There are 4 international airports at Kinshasa (Ndjili), Lubumbashi (Luano), Kisangani and Bukavu. There are another 40 airports with regular scheduled internal services, and over 150 other landing strips.

More than twelve international airlines, including British Caledonian Airways, operate in and out of Kinshasa from Europe, Africa and the USA. The national airline Air Zaïre, operates on all the main internal routes as well as on international routes to Europe and other African cities.

Shipping. The Zaïre River and its tributaries are navigable for about 13,700 km. Regular traffic has been established between Kinshasa and Kisangani as well as Ilebo, on the Lualaba (*i.e.*, the river above Kisangani), on some tributaries and on the lakes. Zaïre has only 40 km of sea coast. The merchant marine in 1981 comprised 34 vessels with a total tonnage of 92,044 GRT. Kinshasa, Matadi and Boma are the main seaports; in 1978, 629,422 tonnes of freight were unloaded and 498,380 loaded.

Post and Broadcasting. In 1983 there were 362 post offices. Length of telegraph lines, 2,459 km. There were 15 broadcasting stations, 161 stations of wireless telegraphy and 206 telegraph offices; telephones numbered 31,855 in 1985. There is a ground satellite communications station outside Kinshasa. In 1987 there were 3·4m. radio and 16,000 television receivers.

Newspapers. There were (1989) 4 dailies: *Salongo* (mornings) and *Elima* (evenings) in Kinshasa; *Njumbe* in Lubumbashi and *Boyoma* in Kisangani.

JUSTICE, RELIGION, EDUCATION AND WELFARE

Justice. A Justice Department was established in Jan. 1980 to replace the Judicial Council. There is a Supreme Court at Kinshasa, 9 Courts of Appeal and 32 courts of first instance.

Religion. In 1988 there were about 15·7m. Roman Catholics, 9·4m. Protestants and 5·6m. Kimbanguistes, as well as some 450,000 Moslems and 2,000 Jews. The remaining inhabitants (about 1·1m.) chiefly adhere to animist beliefs.

Education. In 1983 there were 4,654,613 pupils and 112,077 teachers in 10,065 primary schools; and in 1978–79 there were 611,349 pupils in 2,511 secondary schools; 70,342 students in technical schools and 138,170 in teacher-training colleges. In 1971 all Institutes of Higher Education combined to form the National University of Zaïre, but in 1981 this was divided to form 3 Universities at Kinshasa, Kisangani and Lubumbashi; in 1985–86 in all there were 37,706 students and 3,072 teaching staff at 36 higher education establishments.

Health. In 1979 there were 1,900 doctors, 58 dentists, 414 pharmacists, 3,043 midwives, 14,661 nursing personnel and 942 hospitals and medical centres with 79,244 beds.

DIPLOMATIC REPRESENTATIVES

Of Zaïre in Great Britain (26 Chesham Pl., London, SW1X 8HH)
Ambassador: Kitshodi Nkikele (accredited 17 Feb. 1988).

Of Great Britain in Zaïre (Ave. de l'Equateur, Kinshasa)
Ambassador: R. L. B. Cormack, CMG.

Of Zaïre in the USA (1800 New Hampshire Ave., NW, Washington, D.C., 20009)
Ambassador: Kalimba wa Katana Mushobekwa.

Of the USA in Zaïre (310 Ave. des Aviateurs, Kinshasa)
Ambassador: William C. Harrop.

Of Zaïre to the United Nations
Ambassador: Bagbeni Adeito Nzengeya.

Further Reading

Area Handbook for the Democratic Republic of the Congo (Kinshasa). US Government Printing Office, Washington, 1971
Atlas Général du Congo. Académie Royale, Brussels
Gran, G., *Zaïre: The Political Economy of Underdevelopment.* New York, 1979
MacGaffey, J., *Entrepreneurs and Parasites: The Struggle for Indigenous Capitalism in Zaïre.* CUP, 1988
Slade, R. M., *King Leopold's Congo: Aspects of the Development of Race Relations in the Congo's Independent State.* OUP, 1962
Young, C. and Turner, T., *The Rise and Decline of the Zaïrian State.* Univ. of Wisconsin Press, 1985

ZAMBIA

Capital: Lusaka
Population: 7·12m. (1987)
GNP per capita: US$290 (1988)

HISTORY. The independent Republic of Zambia (formerly Northern Rhodesia) came into being on 24 Oct. 1964 after 9 months of internal self-government following the dissolution of the Federation of Rhodesia and Nyasaland on 31 Dec. 1963.

AREA AND POPULATION. Zambia is bounded by Tanzania in the north, Malaŵi in the east, Mozambique in the south-east and by Zimbabwe and South West Africa (Namibia) in the south. The area is 290,586 sq. miles (752,614 sq. km). Population (1980 census) 5,679,808 of which 43% urban; estimate (1987) 7·12m.

The republic is divided into 9 provinces. Their names, headquarters, area (in sq. km) and census population in 1980 were as follows:

Province	*Headquarters*	*Area*	*Population*	*Province*	*Headquarters*	*Area*	*Population*
Copperbelt	Ndola	31,328	1,248,888	Eastern	Chipata	69,106	656,381
Luapula	Mansa	50,567	412,798	Southern	Livingstone	85,283	686,469
Northern	Kasama	147,826	677,894	N.-Western	Solwezi	125,827	301,677
Central	Kabwe	94,395	513,835	Western	Mongu	126,386	487,988
Lusaka	Lusaka	21,898	693,878				

The seat of Government is at Lusaka (population, 1987, 818,994); other large towns are Kitwe (449,442), Ndola (418,142), Mufulira (192,323), Chingola (187,310), Luanshya (160,667), Kalulushi (89,065) and Chililabombwe (79,010) on the Copperbelt; Kabwe, the oldest mining township (190,752); Livingstone, the old capital (94,637); and other provincial capitals at Kasama, Mansa, Chipata, Mongu and Solwezi. In Jan. 1988 there were 146,000 refugees in Zambia including 97,000 Angolans.

The official language is English and the main ethnic groups are the Bemba (34%), Tonga (16%), Malawi (14%) and Lozi (9%).

CLIMATE. The climate is tropical, but has three seasons. The cool, dry one is from May to Aug., a hot dry one follows until Nov., when the wet season commences. Frosts may occur in some areas in the cool season. Lusaka. Jan. 70°F (21·1°C), July 61°F (16·1°C). Annual rainfall 33" (836 mm). Livingstone. Jan. 75°F (23·9°C), July 61°F (16·1°C). Annual rainfall 27" (673 mm). Ndola. Jan. 70°F (21·1°C), July 59°F (15°C). Annual rainfall 52" (1,293 mm).

CONSTITUTION AND GOVERNMENT. The Constitution provides for a President, elected in the first instance by the General Conference of the ruling party, the United National Independence Party, and thereafter he is elected by the electorate. On 13 Dec. 1972 President Kaunda signed a new Constitution based on one-party rule.

The single political party is the United National Independence Party. Its full-time executive organ (headed by a Secretary-General) is the Central Committee, whose 24 members are elected by the General Conference of the Party. The Central Committee has precedence over the legislative body, the National Assembly, which is led by the Prime Minister and consists of 125 elected members and up to 10 nominated members, including a cabinet of 18 ministers.

Presidential elections were held in Oct. 1988 and on 30 Oct. President Kaunda was sworn in for a sixth 5-year term.

The Cabinet, as in Dec. 1989, was composed as follows:

President and Commander-in-Chief: Dr Kenneth David Kaunda.
Secretary General of the Party: A. G. Zulu.
Prime Minister: Gen. Malimba Masheke.
Defence: F. Hapunda. *Foreign Affairs:* L. Mwananshiku. *Finance and Planning:*

G. Chigaga. *Attorney-General:* F. M. Chomba. *Higher Education, Science and Technology:* L. Goma. *Health:* M. Muyunda. *Industry:* R. Chongo. *Mines:* B. Fulembo. *Agriculture:* J. Mukando. *Home Affairs:* Gen. G. K. Chinkuli. *Labour and Social Services:* Lavu Mulimba. *Tourism:* L. S. Subulwa. *Information:* A. Simuchimba. *Education, Sport and Culture:* K. Musokotwane.

National flag: Green, with in the fly a panel of 3 vertical strips of dark red, black and orange, and above these a soaring eagle in gold.

National anthem: Stand and Sing of Zambia, Proud and Free.

The 9 provinces (sub-divided into 53 districts) are administered by Central Committee Members for the provinces who are responsible for the overall government and Party administration of their respective areas.

DEFENCE

Army. The Army consists of 1 armoured regiment and 9 infantry battalions, with supporting artillery, engineer and signals units. Equipment includes some 30 main battle tanks and 88 armoured cars. Strength (1990) 15,000. There are also paramilitary police units numbering 1,200 men.

Air Force. Creation of the Zambian Air Force was assisted initially by an RAF mission. Training and expansion of the Air Force was next taken over by Italy, with the purchase of 23 Aermacchi M.B.326G armed jet basic trainers (of which 18 remain in service), 8 SIAI-Marchetti SF.260M piston-engined trainers and 15 Agusta-Bell 47G, 10 AB.205 and 2 AB.212 helicopters. Twelve F-6 (MiG-19) jet fighter-bombers and some BT-6 primary trainers have since been acquired from China, a squadron of 14 MiG-21 fighters, 3 Yak-40 light jet transports, 4 An-26 twin-turboprop transports and 6 Mi-8 helicopters from the Soviet Union, 5 DHC-5 Buffalo twin-turboprop transports from Canada, 6 C-47s built in the USA, 8 DO 28D Skyservant light transports from Germany, 15 Supporter armed light trainers from Sweden. Serviceability of most types is reported to be low. Personnel (1990) 1,200.

INTERNATIONAL RELATIONS

Membership. Zambia is a member of UN, the Commonwealth, SADCC, OAU and is an ACP state of EEC.

ECONOMY

Budget. Revenue and expenditure for 1989 (in K1m.): Envisaged expenditure of 24,503 and revenue of 20,366.

Currency. The *Kwacha* (K) is divided into 100 *ngwee* (n). There are coins of 50, 20, 10, 5, 2 and 1 *ngwee* and banknotes of K20, K10, K5, K2 and K1 are in use. In March 1990, £1 = 40·60 *Kwacha*; US$1 = 24·77 *Kwacha*.

Banking. Barclays Bank has 25 branches, 6 sub-branches and 17 agencies; Standard Bank has 18 branches and 17 agencies; National & Grindlays, 10 branches and 1 sub-branch; Zambia National Commercial Bank, 10 branches and 1 in London; the post office saving bank has branches throughout the republic.

The Finance Development Corporation (FINDECO) controls the building societies, all insurance companies, one commercial bank and has shares in a second one. The Agricultural Finance Corporation provides loans to farmers, co-operatives, farmers' associations and agricultural societies.

ENERGY AND NATURAL RESOURCES

Electricity. The total installed capacity of hydro and thermal power stations, excluding Zambia's share of Kariba South, amounts to 1,924,700 kw and the energy production during 1986 amounted to some 11,100m. kwh. Zambia exports electricity to Zaïre, Zimbabwe and Angola.

The hydro stations are located at Mbala, Mansa, Kasama, Mulungushi,

Lunsemfwa and Victoria Falls, Lusiwasi and Kafue Gorge. Work has started on the Kariba North Project. The thermal stations are located on the Copperbelt. A number of diesel power stations have been installed, mostly in the North-Western and Northern Provinces.

Minerals. The total value of minerals produced (in 1,000 tonnes) in 1985 was: Copper, 543; zinc, 32; lead, 15; cobalt, 4·4; gold, 7,903 oz.

Agriculture. Although 70% of the population is dependent on agriculture only 10% of GDP is provided by the industry. Principal agricultural products (1988) were maize, 1,453,000 tonnes; sugar-cane, 1,318,000 tonnes; seed cotton, 44,000 tonnes; tobacco, 4,000 tonnes; groundnuts, 33,000 tonnes.

Livestock (1988): 2,684,000 cattle; 180,000 pigs; 80,000 sheep; 420,000 goats, and 15m. poultry.

Forestry. Forests covered (1988) 29·2m. hectares, 39% of the total land area. Roundwood removals (1986) 9·9m. cu. metres.

Fisheries. Total catch (1986) 68,000 tonnes.

INDUSTRY AND TRADE

Industry. In Dec. 1984 there was a labour force of 2·27m. of which 63% employed in agriculture, 2·6% in mining and quarrying and 2·1% in manufacturing.

Commerce. Trade in 1m. kwacha for 3 years:

	1985	*1986*	*1987*
Imports	2,089·5	4,447·7	6,227·5
Exports	1,486·1	3,074·4	8,058·6

In 1987, copper provided 85% of all exports (by value), cobalt 6%, zinc 2%.

Total trade between Zambia and UK (British Department of Trade returns, in £1,000 sterling):

	1986	*1987*	*1988*	*1989*
Imports to UK	27,260	30,310	24,822	21,565
Exports and re-exports from UK	77,840	75,178	85,746	119,057

Tourism. There were 121,000 visitors in 1987.

COMMUNICATIONS

Roads. There were (1984) 37,279 km of roads including over 5,592 km of tarred roads. In 1982 there were 33,000 commercial vehicles and 68,000 cars.

Railways. In 1985 the total route-km was 1,266 km (1,067 mm gauge). In 1988–89 the Zambian railways (excluding Tan-Zam) carried 2·1m. passengers and 4·4m. tonnes of freight. The Tan–Zam railway, giving Zambia access to Dar es Salaam, comprises 892 km of route in Zambia.

Aviation. There were (1982) 130 airports in Zambia (46 government owned). Lusaka is the principal international airport. Seven foreign airlines use Lusaka.

Post and Broadcasting. There were (1982) 13 head post offices and 236 other post offices. In 1985 there were 74,500 telephones, and in 1986 528,000 radio and 66,000 television receivers.

Newspapers. There were (1989) 2 national daily papers: *The Times of Zambia* (circulation, 65,000) and *Zambia Daily Mail* (40,000) and *The Sunday Times* (74,000).

JUSTICE, RELIGION, EDUCATION AND WELFARE

Justice. The Judiciary consists of the Supreme Court, the High Court and 4 classes of magistrates' courts; all have civil and criminal jurisdiction.

The Supreme Court hears and determines appeals from the High Court. Its seat is at Lusaka.

The High Court exercises the powers vested in the High Court in England, subject to the High Court ordinance of Zambia. Its sessions are held where occasion requires, mostly at Lusaka and Ndola.

All criminal cases tried by subordinate courts are subject to revision by the High Court.

Religion. Freedom of worship is one of the constitutional rights of Zambian citizens. The Christian faith with 66% of the population has largely replaced traditional African religions. There are 20,000 Moslems.

Education. In 1986 there were 1·4m. pupils in 3,100 primary schools, secondary schools, 150,000 in 276 schools. In 1986 there were 5,400 students in technical colleges and 4,277 students were enrolled for teacher-training. In 1984 the University of Zambia had 3,621 full-time students.

Health. In 1981 there were 821 doctors, 52 dentists, 36 pharmacists, 866 midwives and 871 nursing personnel. There were also 636 hospitals and clinics with 20,638 beds.

DIPLOMATIC REPRESENTATIVES

Of Zambia in Great Britain (2 Palace Gate, London, W8 5LS)
High Commissioner: Edward M. Lubinda (accredited 23 Nov. 1989).

Of Great Britain in Zambia (Independence Ave., Lusaka)
High Commissioner: J. M. Willson, CMG.

Of Zambia in the USA (2419 Massachusetts Ave., NW, Washington, D.C., 20008)
Ambassador: Dr Paul J. F. Lusaka.

Of the USA in Zambia (PO Box 31617, Lusaka)
Ambassador: Jeffrey Davidow.

Of Zambia to the United Nations
Ambassador: Peter Dingi Zuze.

Further Reading

General Information: The Director, Zambia Information Services, PO Box 50020, Lusaka.

Laws of Zambia. 13 vols. Govt. Printer, Lusaka
Beveridge, A. A. and Oberschall, A. R., *African Businessmen and Development in Zambia*. Princeton Univ. Press, 1980
Bliss, A. M. and Rigg, J. A., *Zambia*. [Bibliography] Oxford and Santa Barbara, 1984
Burdette, M. M., *Zambia: Between two Worlds*. Boulder, 1988
Gertzel, C. (ed.) *The Dynamics of a One-Party State in Zambia*. Manchester Univ. Press, 1984
Kaunda, K. D., *Zambia Shall be Free*. London, 1962.—*Humanism in Zambia*. Lusaka. 2 vols. 1967 and 1974.—*Zambia's Economic Revolution*. Lusaka, 1968.—*Zambia's Guidelines for the Next Decade*. Lusaka, 1968.—*Letter to my Children*. Lusaka, 1973
Roberts, A., *A History of Zambia*. London, 1977

ZIMBABWE

Capital: Harare
Population: 9·12m. (1989)
GNP per capita: US$660 (1988)

HISTORY. Prior to Oct. 1923 Southern Rhodesia, like Northern Rhodesia, was under the administration of the British South Africa Co. In Oct. 1922 Southern Rhodesia voted in favour of responsible government. On 12 Sept. 1923 the country was formally annexed to His Majesty's Dominions, and on 1 Oct. 1923 government was established under a governor, assisted by an executive council, and a legislature, with the status of a self-governing colony. For the history of the period 1961–1979 including the period of unilateral declaration of independence *see* THE STATESMAN'S YEAR-BOOK, 1980–81, pp. 1623–25. Rhodesia (Southern Rhodesia) became the Republic of Zimbabwe on 18 April 1980.

AREA AND POPULATION. Zimbabwe is bounded north by Zambia, east by Mozambique, south by the Republic of South Africa and west by Botswana. The area is 150,872 sq. miles (390,759 sq. km). The capital is Harare (Salisbury). The total population was (1982 census) 7,539,300; 1989 estimate, 9,122,000.

There are 8 provinces:

Province	*Sq. km*	*Census 1982*	*Province*	*Sq. km*	*Census 1982*
Manicaland	35,219	1,099,202	Masvingo	55,777	1,031,697
Mashonaland Central	29,482	563,407	Matabeleland North	76,813	885,339
Mashonaland East	26,813	1,495,984	Matebeleland South	54,941	519,606
Mashonaland West	55,737	858,962	Midlands	55,977	1,091,844

Population of main urban areas (1982 census): Bindura, 18,243; Bulawayo, 414,800; Masvingo (Fort Victoria) 31,000; Kadoma (Gatooma) 45,000; Gweru (Gwelo) 79,000; Chegutu (Hartley) 26,617; Marondera (Marandellas) 37,092; Kwekwe (Que Que) 48,000; Redcliffe, 22,000; Harare (Salisbury) 656,100; Zvishavane (Shabani) 27,000; Chinhoyi (Sinoia) 24,322; Mutare (Umtali) 70,000; Hwange (Wankie) 39,000; Chitungwiza, 175,000.

In 1982 23% were urban and 51% under 15.

Vital statistics (1988): Birth rate was 39·5 per 1,000 population, the death rate 10·8 per 1,000.

The official language is English. Shona and Sindebele are the main spoken languages.

CLIMATE. Though situated in the tropics, conditions are remarkably temperate throughout the year because of altitude, and an inland position keeps humidity low. The warmest weather occurs in the three months before the main rainy season, which starts in Nov. and lasts till March. The cool season is from mid-May to mid-Aug. and, though days are mild and sunny, nights are chilly. Harare. Jan. 69°F (20·6°C), July 57°F (13·9°C). Annual rainfall 33" (828 mm). Bulawayo. Jan. 71°F (21·7°C), July 57°F (13·9°C). Annual rainfall 24" (594 mm). Victoria Falls. Jan. 78°F (25·6°C), July 61°F (16·1°C). Annual rainfall 28" (710 mm).

CONSTITUTION AND GOVERNMENT. At the Commonwealth Conference held in Lusaka in Aug. 1979 agreement was reached for a new Constitutional Conference to be held in London and this took place between 10 Sept. and 15 Dec. 1979 at Lancaster House. It was attended by the various factions in Zimbabwe-Rhodesia, including Abel Muzorewa, Robert Mugabe and Joshua Nkomo, and was chaired by Lord Carrington. It achieved 3 objectives: (*i*) the terms of the Constitution for an independent Zimbabwe; (*ii*) terms for a return to legality: and (*iii*) a ceasefire. Lord Soames became Governor of Southern Rhodesia in Dec. 1979 and elections took place in March 1980, resulting in victory for the Zimbabwe African National Union (ZANU, PF).

The Constitution provides for a bicameral Parliament. Parliament consists of a 40-

member Senate elected by the common roll; 10 chiefs elected by all the country's tribal chiefs; 6 nominated by the Prime Minister and a 120-member House of Assembly; Universal suffrage for citizens over the age of 18; A President (elected for a 6-year term of office by Parliament) who heads the Executive; An independent judiciary enjoying security of tenure; A justiciable Declaration of Rights, derogation from certain of the provisions being permitted, within specified limits, during a state of emergency; Independent Service Commissions exercising powers in respect of staffing and conditions of service in the Public Service, the uniformed forces and the judiciary; Special entrenchment of certain provisions of the Constitution until April 1990 (the protective provisions of the Declaration of Rights).

In 1987 there were 2 constitutional changes: Racial representation was abolished and an executive presidency established.

Under the Constitution no Parliament may continue in existence for more than 5 years.

At elections held on 28-29 March 1990, ZANU (PF) won 116 seats in the House of Assembly. Opposition parties won 3 seats and 1 was undecided because voting was postponed.

Executive President: Robert G. Mugabe (sworn in on 30 Dec. 1987, re-elected 1990).

The Cabinet in Jan. 1990 was composed as follows:

Vice-President: Simon Muzenda. *Senior Minister in the President's Office:* Joshua Nkomo. *Senior Minister of Finance, Economic Planning and Development in the President's Office:* Dr Bernard Chidzero. *Defence:* (Vacant). *Mines:* Richard Hove. *Energy and Water Resources and Development:* Kumbirai Kangai. *National Supplies:* Simbi Mubako. *Justice, Legal and Parliamentary Affairs:* Emmerson Mnangagwa. *Higher Education:* Dzingai Mutumbuka. *Community and Co-operative Development and Women's Affairs:* Joyce Mujuru. *Foreign Affairs:* Dr Nathan Shamuyarira. *Information, Posts and Telecommunications:* Dr Witness Mangwende. *Local Government, Rural and Urban Development:* Enos Chikowore. *Natural Resources and Tourism:* Victoria Chitepo. *Home Affairs:* Moven Mahachi. *Transport:* Simbarashe Simbanenduku. *Trade and Commerce:* Dr Oliver Munyaradzi. *Industry and Technology:* Dr Callistus Ndlovu. *Lands, Agriculture and Rural Resettlement:* David Karimanzira. *Primary and Secondary Education:* Fay Chung. *Youth, Sport and Culture:* David Kwidini. *Public Construction and National Housing:* Joseph Msika. *Health:* Brig. Dr Felix Muchemwa. *Labour, Manpower Planning and Social Welfare:* John Nkomo. There are 6 Ministers of State.

National flag: Seven horizontal stripes of green, yellow, red, black, red, yellow and green; on a white black-edged triangle in the hoist a red star surmounted by the Zimbabwe Bird in yellow.

The first municipal elections were held in Nov. 1980.

DEFENCE

Army. The Army consists of 1 armoured, 1 engineer and 1 artillery regiments; 26 infantry with 1 commando and 2 parachute battalions. Equipment includes 8 T-54 and 35 Ch T-59 main battle tanks. Strength was (1990) 47,000, and there are a further 15,000 paramilitary police.

Air Force. The Zimbabwe Air Force (regular) has a strength of (1990) about 2,500 personnel and 130 aircraft in 9 squadrons, of which 2 are intended primarily for a training role. Headquarters ZAF and the main ZAF stations are in Harare; the second main base is at Gweru, with many secondary airfields throughout the country. Equipment includes 1 squadron of F-7 (MiG-21) interceptors, 1 squadron of Hunter FGA.9 fighter-bombers, 1 squadron of Hawk training and light attack aircraft, a transport squadron with 11 turboprop CASA Aviocars, 6 twin-engined Islanders and 6 C-47s; a squadron with 15 Reims/Cessna 337 Lynx attack aircraft; a squadron with 14 SIAI-Marchetti SF.260W Genet and 15 SF.260C Genet trainers; a helicopter liaison/transport squadron with 40 Alouette II/IIIs, a helicopter casualty evacuation/transport squadron with 5 Agusta-Bell 205s and 12 Bell 412s. Nine Canberra bombers are in storage.

INTERNATIONAL RELATIONS

Membership. Zimbabwe is a member of UN, the Commonwealth, OAU, SADCC, the Non-Aligned Movement and is an ACP state of the EEC.

ECONOMY

Planning. The 5-year development plan (1986–90) emphasized greater public-sector involvement in all parts of the economy.

Budget. Revenue and expenditure (in Z$1,000):

	1984–85	*1985–86*	*1986–87*	*1987–88*
Revenue	2,212,839	2,616,185	2,997,000	3,784,856
Expenditure	2,641,260	3,136,738	3,828,528	4,295,736

Receipts during the year ended 30 June 1985 were (in Z$1,000): Income and profits tax, 1,066,584; taxes on goods and services, 1,137,808; miscellaneous taxes and other income, 311,757.

The gross amount of the public debt outstanding in June 1986 was Z$5,192,729,612.

Currency. On 17 Feb. 1970 decimal currency was adopted. The unit of currency is the Zimbabwe *dollar* divided into 100 *cents*. In March 1990, £1 = Z$3·87; US$1 = Z$2·36.

Banking. The Reserve Bank of Zimbabwe is the country's central bank; it became operative when the Bank of Rhodesia and Nyasaland ceased operations on 1 June 1965. It acts as banker to the Government and to the commercial banks and as agent of the Government for important financial operations. It is also the central note-issuing authority and co-ordinates the application of the Government's monetary policy. The Zimbabwe Development Bank, established in 1983 as a development finance institution, is 51% Government-owned.

The post office savings bank had Z$1,171·1m. deposits at 30 June 1988.

The 5 commercial banks are Barclays Bank of Zimbabwe Ltd, Grindlays Bank Ltd, Zimbabwe Banking Corporation Ltd, Standard Chartered Bank Zimbabwe Ltd, Bank of Credit and Commerce Zimbabwe (Pvt) Ltd. In 1986 they had 119 branches and 75 agencies. The 4 merchant banks are Standard Chartered Merchant Bank, Merchant Bank of Central Africa, RAL Merchant Bank and Syfrets Merchant Bank. There are 5 registered finance houses, 3 of which are subsidiaries of commercial banks.

Weights and Measures. The metric system is in use but the US short ton is also used.

ENERGY AND NATURAL RESOURCES

Electricity. Production (1987) 7,606·3m. kwh.

Minerals. The total value of all minerals produced in 1987 was Z$896,691,000. Output (in 1,000 tonnes) and value (in Z$1,000):

	Output			*Value*		
	1986	*1987*	*1988*	*1986*	*1987*	*1988*
Asbestos	163·6	193·3	186·6	85,789	97,859	97,644
Gold (1,000 oz.)	478·0	472·0	481·0	292,770	349,931	379,631
Chrome ore	553·1	562·2	561·6	39,698	44,160	45,272
Coal	4,047·0	4,814·0	5,065·0	89,144	103,402	105,730
Copper	20·6	19·6	16·1	43,272	46,069	64,661
Nickel	9·7	10,912·0	11,489·0	60,672	73,153	198,029
Iron Ore	1,115·0	1,328·0	1,020·0	21,144	28,843	24,525
Silver (1,000 oz.)	840·0	813·0	704·0	10,612	15,790	13,253
Tin	1,019·0	1,037·0	855·5	10,568	11,547	11,162
Cobalt	76·0	107·0	122·0	2,379	1,370	2,766

Agriculture. The most important single food crop in Zimbabwe is maize, the staple food of a large proportion of the population; deliveries to the Grain Marketing Board in 1985 were 1·7m. tonnes. The export potential for the livestock industry has increased with the possibility of new markets in EEC countries. Milk production in 1988 was 244,009 tonnes.

The country is suitable for the production of both citrus and deciduous fruits and fruit production is now well established. In 1988 seed cotton production was 279,000 tonnes and wheat production was 229,084 tonnes. Tea is grown in the Inyanga and Chipinge districts and production in 1988 was 17,000 tonnes. Coffee growing is of increasing importance (production, 1988, 13,000 tonnes) as is sugar (production of sugar-cane, 1988, 3,128 tonnes). Other crops grown in substantial quantities include small grains (sorghums and millet), soya-beans and groundnuts. A wide variety of vegetable crops are also produced.

Tobacco is the most important single product, accounting for over 40% of the value of earnings from agricultural exports. In 1988 tobacco exports were valued at Z$453·6m. and tobacco production was 112,000 tonnes.

Production, 1988 in 1,000 tonnes, of maize, 2,253; sorghum, 176; barley, 30; millet, 278; soyabeans, 102; groundnuts, 135; fruit, 135; vegetables, 148.

Livestock (1988): Cattle, 5·7m.; pigs, 190,000; sheep, 580,000; goats, 1·65m.

Fisheries. Trout is farmed in Nyanga, prawns at Lake Kariba and bream at Mount Hampden near Harare to supplement supplies of fish caught in dams and lakes. In 1986 trout were caught at the rate of 200,000 a year, and the planned production of bream was 400–500 tonnes a year.

INDUSTRY AND TRADE

Industry. Metal products account for over 20% of industrial output. Important agro-industries include food processing, textiles, furniture and other wood products.

Labour. The labour force (1985) was 2·8m. In 1984, 1,036,400 were employed; of whom 271,200 were in agriculture, forestry and fishing and 166,300 in manufacturing.

Commerce. The Customs Agreement with the Republic of South Africa was extended in March, 1982 pending further discussion. Zimbabwe has also entered into Trade Agreements with Zambia, Mozambique, Tanzania, Angola and Swaziland and with countries outside Africa. Imports and exports (in Z$1,000):

	1984	*1985*	*1986*	*1987*	*1988*
Imports	1,200,700	1,447,000	1,686,000	1,782,000	2,155,000
Exports	1,453,000	1,545,343	2,206,000	2,416,000	2,863,000

Principal imports in 1984 (in Z$1,000): Machinery and transport equipment, 373,550; petroleum products, 256,924; chemicals, 178,111; manufactured goods, 177,851; miscellaneous manufactured goods, 78,615.

Principal exports in 1986 (in Z$1,000): Unmanufactured tobacco, 238,213; ferro-alloys, 210,079; asbestos, 82,741; cotton lint, 130,548.

In 1986, 12·4% of exports (excluding gold) went to the Republic of South Africa, 12·3% to UK, 8·5% to Federal Republic of Germany, 5·8% to Italy, 5·7% to USA and 4·6% to Japan, while the Republic of South Africa provided 21·4% of imports, UK 10·9%, Federal Republic of Germany 9·9%, USA 8·2%, Japan 4·3% and Italy 4·3%.

Total trade between Zimbabwe and UK (British Department of Trade returns, in £1,000 sterling):

	1985	*1986*	*1987*	*1988*	*1989*
Imports to UK	90,398	80,702	79,771	86,268	85,792
Exports and re-exports from UK	73,571	61,937	63,181	58,077	87,013

Tourism. In 1988, 451,000 tourists visited Zimbabwe. The main tourist areas are Victoria Falls, Kariba, Hwange, the Eastern Highlands and Great Zimbabwe. The Zimbabwe Tourist Development Corporation is in Harare and Victoria Falls.

COMMUNICATIONS

Roads. The Ministry of Transport is responsible for the construction and maintenance of all State roads and bridges, and all road bridges outside municipal areas. The Ministry offers advice and help on roads and bridges, through Provincial Road Engineers, to district councils. State roads are those connecting all the main centres of population, international routes, major links in the system and main roads serving rural communities. The total length of roads is approximately 85,237 km including surfaced, 12,000; gravel, 46,187; earth, 27,000.

Number of motor vehicles, 1984: Passenger cars, 237,128; commercial vehicles, 17,058; motor cycles, 24,347; trailers, 33,227; tractors, 5,695.

Railways. Zimbabwe is served by the National Railways of Zimbabwe, which connect with the South African Railways to give access to the South African ports; with the Mozambique Railways to give access to the ports of Beira and Maputo; and with the Zambia railway system. In 1985 there were 3,394 km (1,067 mm gauge) of railways including 311 km electrified. In 1987-88 the railways carried 13·9m. tonnes of freight and 2·7m. passengers.

Aviation. Air Zimbabwe operates domestic services and also regular flights to Zambia, Kenya, Malawi, Botswana and South Africa, and to London, Frankfurt and Athens in Europe and also to Perth and Sydney in Australia in association with Qantas. The country is also served by British Airways, Kenya Airways, Ethiopian Airlines, Air Tanzania, Air Malawi, Zambian Airways, Balkan Bulgarian Airlines, Mozambique Airlines, South African Airways, Air Botswana, the Royal Swazi Airlines, TAP Air Portugal, Qantas, Lesotho Airways and Air India. Services by KLM, Swissair and UTA were temporarily suspended in 1986. In 1985, 660,858,000 passenger-km were flown by Air Zimbabwe.

Shipping. Zimbabwe outlets to the sea are Maputo and Beira in Mozambique, Dar-es-Salaam, Tanzania and the South African ports.

Post and Broadcasting. At 31 Aug. 1986 there were 170 full post offices, 47 postal telegraph agencies and 86 postal agencies. At 30 June 1986 there were 251,344 telephones in Zimbabwe served by 96 exchanges; 2,102 telex connexions, served by 2 telex exchanges. Zimbabwe Broadcasting Corporation is an independent statutory body broadcasting a general service in English, Shona, N'debele, Nyanja, Tonga and Kalanga. There are 3 national semi-commercial services, Radio 1, 2 and 3, in English, Shona and N'debele. Radio 4 transmits formal and informal educational programmes. Zimbabwe Television broadcasts 2 channels 95 hours a week *via* 11 transmitters. In June 1986 there were 130,500 television and 450,000 radio licences.

JUSTICE, RELIGION, EDUCATION AND WELFARE

Justice. The general common law of Zimbabwe is the Roman Dutch law as it applied in the Colony of the Cape of Good Hope on 10 June, 1891, as subsequently modified by statute. Provision is made by statute for the application of African customary law by all courts in appropriate cases.

The Supreme Court consists of the Chief Justice and at least two (in 1985 there were three) permanent Supreme Court judges. It is Zimbabwe's final court of appeal. It exercises appellate jurisdiction in appeals from the High Court and other courts and tribunals; its only original jurisdiction is that conferred on it by the Constitution to enforce the protective provisions of the Declaration of Rights. The Court's permanent seat is in Harare but it sits regularly in Bulawayo also.

The High Court is also headed by the Chief Justice, supported by the Judge President and an appropriate number of High Court judges. It has full original jurisdiction, in both Civil and Criminal cases, over all persons and all matters in Zimbabwe. The Judge President is in charge of the Court, subject to the directions of the Chief Justice. The Court has permanent seats in both Harare and Bulawayo and sittings are held three times a year in three other principal towns.

Regional courts, established in Harare and Bulawayo but also holding sittings in other centres, exercise a solely criminal jurisdiction that is intermediate between that of the High Court and the Magistrates' courts.

Magistrates' courts, established in twenty centres throughout the country, and staffed by full-time professional magistrates, exercise both civil and criminal jurisdiction.

The tribal courts and district commissioners' courts of colonial days were abolished in 1981, to be replaced by a system of primary courts, consisting of village courts and community courts. By 1982 1,100 village and 50 community courts had been established. Village courts are presided over by officers selected for the purpose from the local population, sitting with two assessors. They deal with certain classes of civil cases only and have jurisdiction only where African customary law is applicable. Community courts are presided over by presiding officers in full-time public service who may be assisted by assessors. They have jurisdiction in all civil cases determinable by African customary law and also deal with appeals from village courts. They also have limited criminal jurisdiction in respect of petty offences against the general law.

Religion. The largest religious groups are the Anglicans and Roman Catholics. Other denominations include Presbyterians, the Methodist Church in Zimbabwe and the United Methodist Church. Islam, Hinduism and traditional indigenous religions are represented.

Education. Education is compulsory. All primary schools offer free tuition; government secondary schools charge from Z$8–Z$25 per term. All instruction is given in English. There are also over 3,800 private primary schools and over 950 private secondary schools, all of which must be registered by the Ministry of Education. In 1988 there were 2,220,967 pupils at primary schools and 653,353 pupils at secondary schools.

There are 10 teachers' training colleges, 8 of which are in association with the University of Zimbabwe. In addition, there are 4 special training centres for teacher trainees in the Zimbabwe Integrated National Teacher Education Course. In 1988 there were 15,750 students enrolled at teachers' training colleges (1987), 1,002 students at agricultural colleges and 25,104 students at technical colleges.

The University of Zimbabwe provides facilities for higher education. In 1988 the total enrolment of students in the 9 Faculties of Agriculture, Arts, Commerce and Law, Education, Engineering, Medicine, Science, Social Studies and Veterinary Science, was 7,699.

Health. In 1985 there were 162 hospitals, 1,062 static rural clinics and health centres and 32 mobile rural clinics operated by the Ministry of Health. All mission health institutions get 100% government grants-in-aid for recurrent expenditure. There is a medical school attached to the University of Zimbabwe in Harare, four government training schools attached to the 4 central hospitals for training state registered nurses, 14 training schools for medical assistants out of which 11 are administered by missions, and two for training maternity assistants, health assistants/health inspectors.

Social Services. It is a statutory responsibility of the government in many areas to provide: Processing and administration of war pensions and old age pensions; protection of children; administration of remand, probation and correctional institutions; registration and supervision of welfare organisations.

DIPLOMATIC REPRESENTATIVES

Of Zimbabwe in Great Britain (Zimbabwe Hse., 429 Strand, London, WC2R 0SA)
High Commissioner: Dr Herbert M. Murerwa (accredited 1 March 1984).

Of Great Britain in Zimbabwe (Stanley Hse., Stanley Ave., Harare)
High Commissioner: W. K. Prendergast, CMG.

Of Zimbabwe in the USA (2852 McGill Terr., NW, Washington, D.C., 20008)
Ambassador: Stanislaus Garikai Chigwedere.

Of the USA in Zimbabwe (172 Josiah Tongogara Ave., Harare)
Ambassador: J. Steven Rhodes.

Of Zimbabwe to the United Nations
Ambassador: Dr Stanley Mudenge.

Further Reading

Statistical Information: The Central Statistical Office, PO Box 8063, Causeway, Harare, Zimbabwe, originated in 1927 as the Southern Rhodesian Government Statistical Bureau. Ten years later its name was changed to Department of Statistics, and in 1948 it assumed its present title when it took over responsibility for certain Northern Rhodesian and Nyasaland statistics (which it relinquished in Dec. 1963 on the dissolution of the Federation). It publishes *Monthly Digest of Statistics.*

Akers, M., *Encyclopaedia Rhodesia.* Harare, 1973
Caute, D., *Under the Skin: The Death of White Rhodesia.* London, 1983
Davies, D. K., *Race Relations in Rhodesia.* London, 1975
Keppel-Jones, A., *Rhodes and Rhodesia: The White Conquest of Zimbabwe, 1884–1902.* Univ. of Natal Press, 1983
Linden, I., *The Catholic Church and the Struggle for Zimbabwe.* London, 1980
Martin, D. and Johnson, P., *The Struggle for Zimbabwe.* London, 1981.—*Destructive Engagement.* Harare, 1986
Meredith, M., *The Past is Another Century: Rhodesia 1890–1979.* London, 1979
Morris-Jones, W. H., (ed.) *From Rhodesia to Zimbabwe.* London, 1980
Nkomo, J., *Nkomo: The Story of My Life.* London, 1984
O'Meara, P., *Rhodesia: Racial Conflict or Co-Existence.* Cornell Univ. Press, 1975
Pollak, O. B. and Pollak, K., *Rhodesia/Zimbabwe* [Bibliography] Oxford and Santa Barbara, 1979
Schatzberg, M. G., *The Political Economy of Zimbabwe.* New York, 1984
Stoneham, C., *Zimbabwe's Inheritance.* London, 1982
Storeman, C., *Zimbabwe: Politics, Economics and Society.* London, 1988
Thornycroft, P., *A Field for Investment.* Harare, annual
Verrier, A., *The Road to Zimbabwe, 1890–1980.* London, 1986
Wiseman, H. and Taylor, A. M., *From Rhodesia to Zimbabwe: The Politics of Transition.* Elmsford, N.Y., 1981

Reference Library: National Archives of Zimbabwe, PO Box 8043, Causeway, Harare.

PLACE AND INTERNATIONAL ORGANIZATIONS INDEX

Italicised page numbers refer to extended entries

Aachen, 534, 557
Aalborg, 415, 423-4
Aalsmeer, 900
Aalst, 195
Aargau, 1166
Aarhus, 415, 423
Aba, 943
Abaco, 174
Abadán, 709, 711
Abaing, 778
Abakan, 1263
Abancay, 998
Abariringa, 778
Abastuman, 1271
Abbotsford (Canada), 304
Abdel Magid, 1137
Abéché, 345, 347
Abengourou, 390
Abeokuta, 943
Aberdeen (Hong Kong), 611
Aberdeen (S.D.), 1530
Aberdeen (UK), 1303, 1305, 1312, 1327, 1344, 1349-50
Aberystwyth, 1349-50
Abha, 1058, 1063
Abidjan, 390, 392-3
Abilene (Tex.), 1535, 1537
Abirkateib, 1137
Abkhazia, 1270, *1272*
Åbo, 473-4, 476, 480-1
Aboisso, 390
Abomey, 208, 210
Abqaiq, 1060, 1062
Abruzzi, 743, 746
Abu Dhabi, 1293-7
Abu Gharadeq, 449
Abu Hamad, 1138
Abuja, 943
Abu Jaipur, 683
Abu Madi, 449
Abu Qir, 449
Abu Zabad, 1138
Abyan, 1600
Açaba, 856
Acajutla, 454-6
Acapulco de Juárez, 864
Acarigua, 1578, 1582
Acarnania, 571
Accra, 563-6
Aceh, 700, 702
Achtkarspelen, 900
Acklins Island, 174
Aconcagua, 348
Acre (Brazil), 229, 234
Adamaoua, 265
Adamstown, 1010
Adana, 1207-8
Ada (Okla.), 1519
Addis Ababa, 462-5
Ad-Diwaniyah, 714
Adelaide (Australia), 97-8, 142-3, 146
Adélie Land, 124, 511
Aden, 1599-601
Adilabad, 653
Adıyaman, 1207
Adjaria, 1270, *1272-3*
Ado-Ekiti, 943
Adola, 463
Adoni, 654
Adrar (Algeria), 74
Adrar (Mauritania), 856
Adventure, 594
Adygei, 1254, *1262*
Adzopé, 390
Aegean Islands, 572, 575
Aetolia, 571
Afam, 945
Afghánistán, 48, 50, *63-7*, 276
Afyonkarahisar, 1207
Agadèz, 940-1
Agadir, 879-82
Agalega Island, 859
Agaña, 1555
Agartala, 652, 689-90
Agatti, 697
Agboville, 390
Aghion Oros, 572
Aghios Nikolaos, 572
Agigea, 1038
Agin-Buryata, 1254, *1263*
Aginskoe, 1263
Agona Swedru, 563
Agra, 632, 691
Agra do Heróismo, 1025
Ağri, 1207
Agualva-Cacem, 1020
Aguascalientes, 863-4
Agucha, 683
Ahmedabad, 632, 642, 649, 652, 660-2
Ahmednagar, 673
Ahuachapán, 453
Ahváz, 708-9
Ahvenanmaa, 473, 475
Aïn Chok-Hay Hassani, 879
Ain Defla, 74
Ain Témouchent, 74
Aïoun el Atrouss, 858
Aïr, 941
Airdrie, 297-8
Aisén, 348, 352
Aitutaki, 931-2
Aix-en-Provence, 484, 489
Aizawl, 652, 677-8
Ajaccio, 483
Ajman, 1293, 1295-6
Ajmer, 632
Akashi, 759
Akershus, 949
Akhaïa, 571
Akhali-Antoni, 1272
Akita, 759
Akjoujt, 857
Akola, 673-4
Akouta, 940-1
Akranes, 623
Akron (Oh.), 1378, 1514, 1516
Aksu, 1283
Aktyubinsk, 1282-3
Akure, 944
Akureyri, 623, 627
Akwa Ibom, 943
Akyab, 254, 257
Al-Aaiún, 879, 1126
Alabama, 1376, 1382, 1386-7, 1407, 1409, *1427-9*
ALADI, *54*
Alagoas, 229
Al Ain, 1295
Alajuela, 385, 388
Al-Amarah, 714
Alamosa (Colo.), 1442
Al-Anbar, 714
Åland, 473, 475
Al-Arish, 446
Alaska, 1375-6, 1379, 1381, 1386-90, 1401, 1404, 1406, 1408, 1420, *1429-32*
al-Asnam, 74
Álava, 1114-15
Alaverdi, 1274
Alba, 1033
Albacete, 1115, 1125
Al-Bahrr al-Ahmar, 446
Alba Iula, 1033, 1039
Albania, 48, *68-73*
Albany (Australia), 160
Albany (Ga.), 1451
Albany (N.Y.), 1378, 1506-8
Albany (Oreg.), 1520
Al-Basrah, 714-15, 717
Al-Bayadh, 74
Alberta, 271-3, 279, 282-5, 291, *297-300*
Albina, 1142
al-Boulaida, 75, 78
Albuquerque (N. Mex.), 1378, 1503, 1505
Alburg, 900
Albury, 129, 153, 156
Alcalá de Henares, 1115, 1125
Alcorcón, 1115
Aldabra Island, 238, 1068
Alderney, 1303, 1369-70, *1373*
Alegranza, 1115
Aleppo, 1175, 1178
Alessandria (Italy), 744
Ålesund, 950
Alexander Hamilton Airport, 1565
Alexandria (Egypt), 446-9
Alexandria (Romania), 1034
Alexandria (Va.), 1378, 1390, 1542
Alexandroupolis, 572
Algeciras, 1115
Algeria, 45, 57, *74-8*
Al-Ghurdaqah, 446
Algiers, 74-6, 78
Al-Hillah, 714
Al-Hoceima, 879, 881
Alhucemas, 1115
Alicante, 1115, 1121, 1125
Alice Springs, 111, 121
ALIDE, *54*
Aligarh, 632
Ali-Sabieh, 430
Al Jadida, 880
Al-Jawf, 1058
al-Jaza'ir *see* Algiers
Al-Kamishli Airport, 1178
Al-Kharijah, 446
Al-Kharj, 1058
Al-Khobar, 1058
Al-Khour, 1029
Alkmaar, 900
Al-Kut, 714
Allahabad, 632, 639, 649, 691
Allentown (Pa.), 1378, 1523
Allerdale, 1300
Alma-Ata, 1224, 1244, 1246, 1251, 1282
Almada, 1020, 1025
Al-Mahra, 1600
Almelo, 900
Almere, 900
Almería, 1114-15
Almirante, 983
Almirante Brown, 91
Al-Mobarraz, 1058
Al-Muthanna, 714
Alo, 516
Alofi, 516, 932-3
Alor Setar, 831
Alotau, 986
al-Oued, 74
Alphen aan den Rijn, 900
Alphonse Island, 1068
Al-Qadisiyah, 714
Al-Rastan, 1177
Alsace, 483
Al-Shargiya, 1177
Altagracia, La, 435
Altai, 1254, 1262
Alta Verapaz, 581-2
Altoona (Pa.), 1523
Alto Paraguay, 992
Alto Paraná, 992, 996
Älvsborg, 1148
al-Wadi al-Jadid, 446
Amadora, 1020
Amambay, 992
Amapá, 229, 231
Amapala, 603
Amarillo (Tex.), 1378, 1535
Amarkantak, 671
Amarpur, 689
Amasya, 1207
Amatuku, 1217
Amazonas (Brazil), 229, 234
Amazonas (Colombia), 373
Amazonas (Peru), 998
Amazonas (Venezuela), 1578
Ambala, 662-3, 681
Ambato, 440
Amber Valley, 1300
Amboina, 701, 704

Ambouli Airport, 431
Ambrym, 1572
American Samoa, 1377, 1387, 1389, *1558-61*
Amersfoort, 900
Ames (Ia.), 1464-5
Amherst (Canada), 315
Amherst (Mass.), 1480
Amida, 1213
Amiens, 484
Amilcar Cabral International Airport, 338
Amindivi Islands, 687, 697
Amini, 697
Amirante Islands, 1068
Amman, 768, 770-1
Ammetyevsk, 1240
Ampang, 838
Amphissa, 571
Amravati, 632, 673
Amreli, 660
Amritsar, 632, 681-3
Amstelveen, 900
Amsterdam, 900-1, 908
Amsterdam Island, 511
Amstetten, 168
Am Timam, 345
Amur, 1254
Anaconda (Mont.), 1491
Anadolu, 1207
Anadyr, 1263
Anaheim (Calif.), 1378, 1437
Anambra, 943
Anantapur, 654-5
Ancash, 998
Anchorage (Ak.), 1378, 1430, 1432
Anchorage Island, 931
Ancón, 982
Ancona, 744, 747, 752
Andalusia, 1114-15, 1118, 1123
Andaman and Nicobar Islands, 632, 635, 649, 652, 693, *694-5*
Andean Group, *54*
Anderlecht, 195
Anderson (Ind.), 1461
Andhra Pradesh, 631, 635, 643, 649, 652, *653-5*, 653, 687
Andizhan, 1241, 1286-7, 1291
Andorra, *79-80*, 1123
Andorre-la-Vieille, 79-80
Andros, 174
Androth, 697
Anegada, 1591
Aného, 1191
Aneityum, 1572
Anfa, 879
Angeles, 1004
Angers, 484, 496
An Giang, 1585
Anglican Communion, *1342-4*
Angola, 49, *81-4*
Angoulême, 484
Anguilla, 30, 55, *85-6*
Angul, 680
Angus, 1303
Anhui, 355, 360
Anjouan, 378
Ankara, 1207-8, 1212
Annaba, 74-5, 78
An-Najaf, 714
Annamalainagar, 688
Annandale and Eskdale, 1303
Annapolis (Md.), 1476
Ann Arbor (Mich.), 1378, 1481
an-Nasiriyah, 714
Annecy, 484
Annobón, 458
Ansari Nagar, 697
Anshan, 356, 360
Antalya, 1207-8
Antananarivo, 823, 825-6
Antarctic:
—Argentine, 90-1
—Australian, 30, 97, *124-5*
—British, 30, *238*, 468
—Chilean, 348
—French, *511-12*
—Norwegian, 963
Antigua and Barbuda, 29-30, 52, 55, *87-9*
Antigua (Guatemala), 581
Antioquia, 372
Antipodes Islands, 930
Antofagasta, 221-2, 348-9, 352-3
Antrim, 1359, 1364
Antseranana, 823
Antwerp, 194-5, 201-2
Anuradhapura, 1127
Anzoátegui, 1578, 1581
Aoba, 1572
Aomori, 759
Aorangi, 917
Aotearoa, 926
Apeldoorn, 900
Apia, 930, 1593, 1595
Apoera, 1142
Apolima, 1593
Appenzell, 1164, 1166-7
Appleton (Wis.), 1549
Apure, 1578
Apurimac, 998
Aqaba, 768, 771
Aquitaine, 483
Arab Common Market, 57
Aracajú, 229-30
Arad, 1033
Aragón, 1114-15, 1117
Aragua, 1578, 1581
Arák, 708-9
Aranuki, 778
Ararat (Australia), 153
Aratu Bahia, 232
Arauca, 372
Araucanía, 348
Arawa, 986
Arba Minch, 462
Arcadia, 571
Archangel *see* Arkhangelsk
Archnan, 1247
Ardabil, 709
Ards, 1359
Arecibo, 1561
Arequipa, 998
Arezzo, 749, 752
Argenteuil, 484
Argentia, 314
Argentina, 52, 54, *90-6*, 125, 466, 994
Arges, 1033, 1036
Argolis, 571
Argostolion, 571
Argyll and Bute, 1303
Argyrocastro *see* Gjirokastër
Arica, 220-2, 348
Arima, 1198
Arizona, 1376, 1381, 1387-8, 1407, *1433-4*
Arkansas, 1376, 1382, 1387-8, 1407, *1435-7*
Arkhangelsk, 1225, 1246-7, 1254, 1263
Arlington (Tex.), 1378, 1535
Arlington (Va.), 1448
Arlington Heights (Ill.), 1458
Arlit, 940-2
Arlon, 194
Armagh, 1364
Armenia (Colombia), 372
Armenia (USSR), 1224-5, 1250, *1273-5*
Armidale, 129
Arnhem, 900-1
Arorae, 778
Arrah, 658
Ar-Ramadi, 714
Arras, 484
Arta, 571
Artigas, 1567
Artvin, 1207
Arua, 1219
Aruba, 904, *911-13*
Arun, 1300
Arunachal Pradesh, 632, 635, 649, 652-3, *655-6*
Arusha, 1180
Arussi, 462
Arvada (Colo.), 1440
Aryanah, 1202
Asahikawa, 759
Asamankese, 563
Asansol, 693
Ascension, 30, 467, 1047, *1048*
ASEAN, *51-2*
Ashanti, 563
Ashdod, 736, 739
Asheville (N.C.), 1509
Ashfield, 1300
Ashford, 1300
Ashkhabad, 1224, 1284-5
Ashland (Ky.), 1468
Ashland (Oreg.), 1522
Ashland (Va.), 1543
Ashmore Islands, 30, 97, *128*
Asimah, 768
Askhabad, 1247
Asmara, 462, 464
Assab, 462-3
Assahba, 1060
as-Salimiya, 791
Assam, 631, 633, 635, 642-3, 649, 652, *656-8*, 676
As-Samawah, 714
Assela, 462
Assen, 900
As Shuwaikh, 792, 794
Association of South East Asian Nations, *51-2*
As-Sulaymaniyah, 714
Assumption Island (Seychelles), 1068
Aston, 1350
Astove Island, 1068
Astrakhan, 1224, 1254
Asturias, 1114, 1118, 1121
Asunción (Paraguay), 992, 994-7, 996
Aswân, 446-7, 451
Asyût, 446, 451
Atacama, 348, 351
Atafu, 930
Atakora, 208
Atakpamé, 1191, 1193
Atâr, 856, 858
Atbara, 1138
Athens (Ga.), 1453
Athens (Greece), 571, 576
Athens (Oh.), 1516
Athens (W. Va.), 1548
Athlone, 730
Athos, Mount, 572
Ati, 345
Atiu, 931-2
Atizapán de Zaragoza, 864
Atkyubinsk, 1246
Atlanta (Ga.), 1377, 1451-3
Atlantic City (N.J.), 1501
Atlántico (Colombia), 372
Atlántida, 602
Atlantíque (Benin), 208
at-Tarf, 74
Attica, 571
At-Tur, 446
Auburn (Me.), 1473
Auburn (N.Y.), 1506
Auckland, 916-17, 919-20, 927
Auckland Islands, 930
Auderghem, 195
Augsburg, 534, 543, 548
Augusta (Me.), 1473
Aunu'u, 1558-9, 1561
Aurangabad, 632, 649, 673-4
Auriya, 691
Aurora (Colo.), 1378, 1440
Aurora (Ill.), 1458
Aust-Agder, 949
Austin (Tex.), 1378, 1535
Australia, 28-30, 29, 50, 56, *97-1119*
—External Territories, *125-8*
—States, *128-67*
—Territories, *119-24*
Australian Antarctic Territory, 30, 97, *124-5*
Australian Capital Territory, 97-9, 101, 106, 111, 114-15, *119-20*, 128
Australind, 163
Austral Islands, 514

Austria, 40, 47, 58, *168-73*
Auvergne, 483
Avarau, 931
Aveiro, 1020, 1025
Avellaneda, 91
Avignon, 484
Avila, 1115
Avilés, 1121
Avon, 1300
Awassa, 462
Awbari, 811
Ayacucho, 998
Aydın, 1207, 1211
Aylesbury Vale, 1300
Aysén, 348, 352
Ayutthaya, 1185
Azad Kashmir, 972
Azárbáiján (Iran), 708, 711
Azerbaijan (USSR), 1224-5, 1228, *1268-9*
Azilal, 879
Aziziyah, 811
Azogues, 440
Azores, 1020, 1023-4
Azraq, 770
Azua, 435
Azuay, 440

Baarle-Hertog, 194
Baarn, 900
Babahoyo, 440
Babanousa, 1138
Babelthuap, 1557
Babil, 714
Bacau, 1033, 1036
Bacolod, 1004
Bács-Kiskun, 614
Bac Thai, 1585
Badajoz, 1115, 1125
Badakhshán, 65
Badalona, 1116
Baden (Austria), 168
Badenoch and Strathspey, 1303
Baden-Württemberg, 533, 539, *545-7*
Badulla, 1127
Bafatá, 589
Baffin, 329
Bafoulabé, 848
Bafoussam, 265
Bafra, 1210
Baga-Nuur, 874
Bagdogra Airport, 686
Baghdad, 714-15
Baghlan, 63
Bágmati, 896
Bagram, 64
Baguio, 1004
Bahai, 229
Bahamas, 29-30, 52, 55, *174-8*, 1216
Bahawalpur, 971
Bahia, 233
Bahía Blanca, 91, 95
Bahia Las Minas, 983
Bahoruco, 435
Bahrain, 57, *179-83*
Bahr Dar, 462
Baia Mare, 1034
Baidoa, 1085
Bairnsdale, 153
Bait-al-Falaj, 968
Bait al Faqih, 1597
Baja California, 863
Baja California Sur, 863
Baja Verapaz, 581
Bajram Curri, 68
Bakau, 522
Bakersfield (Calif.), 1378
Bakhtárán, 708-9, 711
Bakouma, 343
Baku, 1224, 1240, 1246, 1250, 1268
Bakwanga *see* Mbuji-Mayi
Balaju, 897
Balaka, 829
Balboa, 980, 983
Balchik, 245
Bale, 462
Balearic Islands, 1114-18, 1123
Bâle *see* Basel
Bali, 700-1
Balikesir, 1207-8, 1211
Balikpapan, 701
Balkassar, 975
Balkh, 65
Balkhash, 1283
Ballarat, 152-3, 156
Ballsh, 71
Ballymena, 1359
Ballymoney, 1359
Balqa, 768
Baltimore (Md.), 1377, 1475-7
Baltimore-Washington International Airport, 1448
Baltistan, 972
Balúchistán, 971-2, 975-6, 979
Bam, 250
Bamako, 847-9
Bambari, 341
Bamberg, 542-3, 548
Bambolin, 660
Bamenda, 265
Bamian, 65
Bamingui-Bangoran, 341
Banaba Island, 778-9
Banas Kantha, 660, 673
Banbridge, 1359
Banda Aceh, 700
Bandarban, 184
Bandár-e-Abbas, 708, 710
Bandár Khomeini, 711
Bandar Seri Begawan, 239, 241
Bandundu, 1616
Bandung, 701
Băneasa Airport, 1038
Banff and Buchan, 1303
Banfora, 250
Bangalore, 632, 639, 648-9, 652, 667-8
Bangarem, 698
Bangassou, 341
Bangi, 839
Bangkok, 1185-6, 1188-90
Bangladesh, 30, 50, *184-9*, 642, 656
Bangolo, 392
Bangor (Me.), 1473-4
Bangor (UK), 1349-50
Bangui, 341, 343
Banhâ, 446
Banias, 1177
Banja Luka, 1603
Banjarmasin, 701
Banjul, 522-4
Ban Me Thuot, 1589-90
Banningville *see* Bandundu
Banská Bystrica, 408
Banstead, 1301
Baoji, 362
Baotou, 360, 362
Ba'qubah, 714
Baquerízo Moreno, 440
Baracaldo, 1115
Barahona, 435
Baranovichi, 1267
Baranya, 614
Barauni, 658
Barbados, 29-30, 52, 55, *190-3*
Barbil, 680
Barbuda, 87
Barca Airport, 412
Barcelona (Spain), 80, 1115-16, 1121, 1123, 1125
Barcelona (Venezuela), 1578
Bardo, 1202
Bareilly, 632
Barentsøya, 961
Bari, 744, 752
Bari Brahmara, 666
Barinas, 1578
Barisal, 184, 188
Barking and Dagenham, 1302
Barlovento, 336-7
Barnaul, 1244
Barnet, 1302
Barneveld, 900
Barnsley, 1300
Baroda, 662
Barquisimeto, 1578, 1582
Barranquilla, 372-3, 376
Barreiro, 1020
Barre (Vt.), 1540
Baruta, 1578
Base Alfred-Faure, 510
Base Dumont d'Urville, 511
Basel, 1164-6, 1173
Base Martin de Vivies, 511
Bashkiria, 1240, 1254, *1255*
Basildon, 1300
Basilicata, 744, 746
Basingstoke and Deane, 1300
Basque Country, The, 1114-15, 1117
Basra, 714-15, 717
Bassar, 1191
Bassas da India, 505
Bassein, 254, 257
Basse-Kotto, 341
Basse-Normandie, 483
Basse-Terre (Guadeloupe), 499-500
Basseterre (St Christopher-Nevis), 1044-5
Bassetlaw, 1300
Bass Strait Islands, 154
Bas-Zaïre, 1616
Bata, 458, 460
Batangas, 1004
Batha, 345
Bath (Me.), 1397
Bath (UK), 1350
Bathurst (Australia), 129
Bathurst (Canada), 307
Batman, 1210
Batna, 74, 78
Batokunku, 523
Baton Rouge (La.), 1378, 1471
Battambang, 262-3
Batticaloa, 1127
Batum, 1269
Batumi, 1240, 1270, 1272-3
Bat-Yam, 735
Bauchi, 943
Bavaria, 533, 539, *547-8*
Bawku, 566
Bayamo, 394
Bayamòn, 1561
Bayonne (France), 484
Bayonne (N.J.), 1501
Bay of Plenty, 916
Bayreuth, 543, 548
Bazar, 1289
Bazéga, 250
Bearsden and Milngavie, 1303
Beau Bassin-Rose Hill, 859
Beaufort (Malaysia), 840
Beaumont (Tex.), 1378, 1535, 1537
Beaverton (Oreg.), 1520
Béchar, 74
Bedford (Canada), 315
Bedfordshire, 1300-1
Bedworth, 1301
Beef Island Airport, 1592
Beersheba, 734-5
Begemdir, 462
Begumpet, 639
Behera, 446
Beijing, 355-6, 363-5
Beira, 829, 885-7
Beirut, 799-802
Béjaia, 74, 76
Beja (Portugal), 1020
Béja (Tunisia), 1202
Békés, 614
Békéscsaba, 614
Bekur, 693
Belait, 239
Belém, 229-30, 232
Bélep Archipelago, 511
Belfast, 1305, 1359, 1365-6
Belgard, 719
Belgaum, 632, 667-8, 673
Belgium, 35, 39-40, 42, 125, *194-203*, 819, 907
Belgorod, 1243, 1254
Belgrade, 1603-4, 1608-9,1613
Bélinga, 520
Belize, 29, 55, *204-7*, 1314, 1317
Belize City, 206-7
Bellary, 668
Bellevue (Nebr.), 1493, 1495
Bellevue (Wash.), 1544
Bellingham (Wash.), 1544
Bellona Island, 1082
Belluno, 752
Bellville, 1098
Belmopan, 204, 206-7

Belo Horizonte, 229-30, 235, 2356
Beloit (Wis.), 1549
Belonia, 689
Belorussia, 1223-5, 1250, *1266-7*
Beloyarsk, 1240
Beltsy, 12765
Bemidji (Minn.), 1485
Benalla, 153, 156
Bendel, 943, 946
Bendery, 1275
Bendigo, 152-3, 156
Bengal, East *see* Bangladesh
Bengal, West *see* West Bengal
Benghazi, 811-12, 814-15
Bengkulu, 700
Bengo, 82
Benguela, 81-2
Ben Gurion Airport, 739
Benha, 446
Beni, 218, 220-1
Beni Mellal, 879-80
Benin, *208-11*
Benin City (Nigeria), 944
Beni-Suef, 446
Ben Msik-Sidi Othmane, 879
Bénoué, 265
Ben Schoemen Airport, 1096
Ben Slimane, 879
Bensonville, 807
Ben Tre, 1585
Benue, 943
Bequia, 1051-3
Berat, 68
Beraztegui, 91
Berber, 1138
Berbera, 1085-7
Berbérati, 341, 343
Berchem, 195
Berchem Ste Agathe, 195
Berea (Ky.), 1470
Bergamo, 744, 749, 752
Bergen, 950, 952, 958
Bergen op Zoom, 900
Bergerslagen, 1154
Bergisch Gladbach, 534
Berhampur, 680
Berkeley (Calif.), 1378, 1439
Berkshire, 1300
Berlin (Germany), 525, 527, 530, *548*, 1314
Berlin (N.H.), 1499
Berlin, East, 525-6, 548
Berlin, West, 534-5, 539, 543, *549-50*
Bermo, 658
Bermuda, 30, *212-14*
Bern(e), 1164, 1166, 1172-3
Berri, 1060
Berry Islands, 174
Bertoua, 265
Beru, 778
Berwickshire, 1303
Besançon, 483-4
Beshumi, 1273
Best, 900
Bethlehem (Pa.), 1523
Béthune, 484
Betio, 779-80
Betla, 659
Betul, 671
Beuningen, 900
Beverley, 1300
Beverwijk, 900-1
Bex, 1169
Bexley, 1302
Béziers, 484
Bhádgáon, 896
Bhadravati, 668
Bhagalpur, 659
Bhaktapur, 896
Bhandara, 673
Bharuch, 660
Bhatpara, 632
Bhaunda, 681
Bhavnagar, 632, 660, 662
Bheemavaram, 654
Bheri, 896
Bhilai, 672
Bhilainagar, 632
Bhimpedi, 898
Bhir, 673
Bhiwani, 662
Bhopal, 632, 652-3, 671-2
Bhubaneswar, 642, 652, 680-1
Bhuj, 662
Bhuntar Airport, 664
Bhután, 50, *215-17*, 656
Biała Podlaska, 1012
Białystok, 1012
Biankouma, 390
Bib Arus, 1202
Bicol, 1004
Bidar, 639, 653, 667
Biddeford (Me.), 1473-4
Bié, 82
Biel, 1165
Bielefeld, 534, 543, 557
Bielsko-Biała, 1012
Big Bend, 1144
Bihar, 631, 634-5, 642-3, 649, 652, *658-9*
Biharsharif, 658
Bihor, 1033
Bijagós, 589
Bijapur, 667, 673
Bikaner, 632, 684
Bilaspur, 663, 671-2
Bilbao, 1115, 1121, 1123, 1125
Bilecik, 1207
Bilibino, 1240
Billings (Mont.), 1491, 1493
Biloxi (Miss.), 1486-7
Biltine, 345
Bimini Islands, 174
Bindura, 1625
Binghamton (N.Y.), 1506
Bingöl, 1207
Binh Tri Thien, 1585
Bintulu, 836
Bíobío, 348
Bioko, 458-60
Biombo, 589
Bir Ali, 1601
Birao, 341
Biratnagar, 896
Bird Island, 1113
Bird Rock, 1045
Birgung, 898
Birmingham (Ala.), 1378, 1427-8
Birmingham (UK), 1300, 1305, 1350
Birnie, 778
Birobijan, 1262
Bisho, 1111-12
Biskra, 75
Bismarck (N.D.), 1512
Bissalanca Airport, 591
Bissau City, 589-91
Bistrița, 1033
Bistrița-Năsăud, 1033
Bitlis, 1207
Bitolj, 1603
Bitra, 697
Bizalpura, 898
Bizerta, 1202-3, 1205
Björneborg, 473-4
Bjørnøya, 961-2
B.J. Vorster Airport, 1096
Blackburn, 1300
Blackburne Airport, 878
Blackpool, 1300
Blantyre, 827-8
Blekinge, 1148, 1152
Blenheim (New Zealand), 917
Blida *see* Boulaida
Bloemfontein, 1089, 1093, 1096, 1098
Bloomfield (N.J.), 1501
Bloomington (Ind.), 1463
Bloomington (Minn.), 1484
Blowing Point, 86
Bluefields, 935, 938
Bluefield (W. Va.), 1548
Blue Nile Province (Sudan), 1137
Bo, 1071, 1073-4
Boali, 341
Boatau, 356
Boa Vista (Brazil), 229
Boa Vista (Cape Verde), 336-7
Bobo-Dioulasso, 250, 252
Bobonong, 224
Bobruisk, 1266
Boca Raton (Fla.), 1451
Bocas del Toro, 980
Bochum, 534, 543, 557
Bodh Gaya, 659
Bodø, 950
Boé, 590
Boeotia, 571
Bogala, 1130
Bogor, 701
Bogotá, 372-3, 376-7
Bogra, 184
Bogwase, 1107
Bohol, 1004
Boise City (Id.), 1378, 1456
Bojador, 879
Bokaro, 658
Bol, 345
Bolama-Bijagós, 589
Bolgatanga, 563
Boliden, 1154
Bolívar (Colombia), 372
Bolívar (Ecuador), 440
Bolívar (Venezuela), 1578, 1581
Bolivia, 52, 54, *218-23*, 998
Bologna, 744, 752
Boloma, 591
Bolton, 1300
Bolu, 1207, 1211
Bolungarvik, 623
Bolzano, 743-4
Boma, 1616, 1619
Bombay, 632-3, 639, 647-9, 652-3, 660, 667, 673-4
Bombo, 1219
Bomi, 807
Bomi Hills, 809
Bonaire, 913-15
Bonavista, 311
Bondoukou, 390
Bône *see* Annaba
Bong, 807
Bongor, 345
Bongouanou, 390
Bonin Islands, 759
Bonn, 534, 543, 557
Bonthe, 1073
Booué, 520
Bophuthatswana, 1091, *1105-7*
Boquerón, 992
Bora-Bora, 514-15
Borås, 1149
Bordeaux, 483-5, 489, 494
Borders Region (Scotland), 1303
Bordj Bou Arreridj, 74
Bordoy, 426
Borgerhout, 195
Borgou, 208
Borkou-Ennedi-Tibesti, 345
Borlänge, 1149
Borne, 900
Borneo, Indonesian *see* Kalimantan
Bornholm, 415
Borno, 943
Borsele, 900
Borsod-Abaúj-Zemplén, 614
Borujerd, 709
Bosnia and Herzegovina, 1603, 1605, 1610, *1611*
Bossangoa, 341
Boston (Mass.), 1377, 1478-80
Bosworth, 1300
Bota, 268
Boteti, 224
Botha Airport, 1096
Botkyrka, 1149
Botoșani, 1034
Botswana, 30, *224-8*, 1095
Bottom, The, 913
Bottrop, 534
Bouaflé, 390
Bouaké, 390, 393
Bouar, 341
Bou Arfa, 883
Bouches-du-Rhône, 491
Boudjour, 879
Bouenza, 381
Bougainville, 988
Bougie *see* Béjaia
Bougouriba, 250
Bouira, 74
Boulaida, 75, 78
Boulder (Australia), 160
Boulder (Colo.), 1440, 1442
Boulemane, 879
Boulgou, 250
Boulkiemde, 250

Boulogne-Billancourt, 484
Boulogne-sur-Mer, 484
Boumerdes, 74, 78
Bouna, 390
Boundiali, 390
Bountiful (Ut.), 1538
Bounty Islands, 930
Bouren, 848
Bourges, 484
Bourgogne, 483
Bournemouth, 1300
Bouvet Island, *962-3*
Bowie (Md.), 1476
Bowling Green (Ky.), 1468
Boxtel, 900
Boyacá, 372
Boyer Ahmadi and Kokhiluyeh, 708
Bozeman (Mont.), 1491-2
Bozen, 743-4
Bozoum, 341
Brabant, 194
Bracknell, 1317, 1336
Bracknell Forest, 1300
Bradford, 1300, 1350
Braga, 1020, 1025
Bragança, 1020
Braila, 1034-5, 1038
Braintree, 1300
Brajrajnagar, 680
Brak, 814
Brakna, 856
Branau am Inn, 168
Branaul, 1224
Brandon, 304, 307
Brasília, 229-32, 235
Braşov, 1034, 1039
Bratislava, 408, 411-13
Bratsk, 1240
Braunschweig, 534, 543, 555
Brava, 336-7
Brazil, 52, 54, 125, *229-37*, 994
Brazzaville, 343, 381, 383-4
Brechou, 1303, 1369
Breckland, 1300
Breda, 900-1
Brega, 813
Bregenz, 168
Bremen, 533-4, 539, 543, *550-1*
Bremerhaven, 534, 537, 554
Bremerton (Wash.), 1544
Brent, 1302
Brescia, 744, 749, 752
Brest (France), 484, 488-9
Brest (USSR), 1266
Bretagne, 483
Bria, 341
Briansk, 1254
Bridgeport (Conn.), 1378, 1443
Bridgetown, 190
Brighton, 1300
Brikama, 522
Brindisi, 747
Brisbane, 97-8, 111, 137
Bristol (Conn.), 1443
Bristol (UK), 1300, 1350
Britain *see* United Kingdom
British Antarctic Territory, 30, *238*, 468
British Columbia, 271-3, 279, 283-5, 291, *300-4*
British Indian Ocean Territory, 30, *238*, 1068
British Virgin Islands, 30, *1591-2*
Brits, 1106
Brittany, 483
Brno, 408, 412-13
Broadland, 1300
Brockton (Mass.), 1478
Broken Arrow (Okla.), 1517
Broken Hill, 129
Brokopondo, 1140
Bromley, 1302
Brong-Ahafo, 563
Bronsweg, 1142
Bronx (N.Y.), 1506
Brookfield (Wis.), 1549
Brookings (S.D.), 1530, 1532
Brooklyn (N.Y.), 1506
Broxtowe, 1300
Bruck an der Mur, 168
Bruges, 194-5
Brummen, 900
Brunei, 30, 51, *239-42*, 1314
Brunei Muara, 239
Brunssum, 900
Brunswick (Me.), 1474
Bruny Island, 148
Brussels, 194-5, 201-2
Bucaramanga, 372
Buchanan, 807, 809
Bucharest, 1033-4, 1038-9
Buckingham, 1350
Buckinghamshire, 1300
Bu Craa, 1126
Budapest, 614-17, 619, 621
Buenaventura (Colombia), 376
Buenos Aires, 90-2, 94-5
Buffalo (N.Y.), 1378, 1506-7
Bug, 528
Buganda, 1219
Bukavu, 1616, 1619
Bukhara, 1285 7
Bukit Mertajam, 838
Bulawayo, 1625, 1629
Buldana, 673
Bulembu Airport, 1112
Bulgaria, 48, 58, 125, *243-9*, 1247
Bulsar, 660
Bunbury, 160, 163
Bundaberg, 137
Buraidah, 1058
Buraimi, 1295
Burao, 1085
Burdur, 1207
Burdwan, 692
Burgas, 243, 245-7
Burgenland, 168-9
Burgos, 1115
Burgundy, 483
Burhanpur, 671
Buriram, 1185
Burkina Faso, *250-3*
Burlington (Ia.), 1464
Burlington (Vt.), 1540
Burma, 29, 50, *254-7*
Burnaby, 304
Burnie, 147, 151
Burrel, 68
Bursa, 1207-8, 1211-12
Burundi, *258-60*
Bury, 1300
Buryatia, 1250, 1254, *1255*
Búshehr, 708, 710-11
Buskerud, 949
Busoga, 1219
Bussag, 1247
Bussum, 900
Butare, 1041, 1043
Butaritari, 778
Butha-Buthe, 804
Butte (Mont.), 1491-2
Butterworth, 838, 1108
Butuan, 1004
Buyant Uhaa Airport, 875
Buyo, 392
Buzău, 1034
Bydgoszcz, 1012-13
Byelorussia *see* Belorussia
Byrnihat, 677
Bytom, 1012
Byujumbura, 258-60
Byumba, 1041
Caacupé, 996
Caaguazú, 992
Caazapá, 992
Cabañas, 453
Cabanatuan, 1004
Cabimas, 1578
Cabinda, 81-2
Cabo Delgado, 885
Çabora Bassa, 886
Čačak, 1603
Cáceres, 1115, 1125
Cacheu, 589, 591
CACM, *54*
Cadiz (Philippines), 1004
Cádiz (Spain), 1114-15, 1119, 1125
Caen, 483-4
Cagliari, 744, 749, 752
Caguas, 1561
Cahri-Baguirmi, 345
Caicos Islands, 1215-16
Cairnryan, 1365
Cairns, 103, 137
Cairo, 446-7, 450
Caithness, 1303
Cajamarca, 998
Cakovec, 1603
Calabar, 944, 946-7
Calabria, 744, 746
Calais, 484
Calamata, 571
Calarasi, 1034
Calarna, 349
Calbayog, 1004
Calcutta, 632-3, 647-9, 652, 692-3
Caldas, 372, 375
Calderdale, 1300
Calgary, 272, 289, 297-300
Cali, 372, 376
Calicut, 632, 669-70
California, 1376, 1381, 1387-8, 1407-8, *1437-40*
Callao, 998, 1000-1
Caloocan, 1004
Caltanissetta, 749
Camagüey, 394
Cambodia, 50, *261-4*, 1585
Cambridge (Mass.), 1478, 1480
Cambridge (Md.), 1476
Cambridge (UK), 1300, 1350
Cambridge Bay, 329
Cambridgeshire, 1300-1
Camden (N.J.), 1501
Camden (UK), 1302
Camerino, 752
Cameroon, 29, *265-9*
Camiri, 220-2
Camopinas, 230
Camotra, 695
Campagna, 746
Campania, 744
Campbell Island, 930
Campbellton, 307
Campeche, 863-4, 868
Campina Grande, 230
Campione, 750
Campo, 268
Campo Grande, 229-30
Camrose, 297-8
Canada, 28-9, 35-6, 39, 45, 50, *270-95*
—Provinces, *295-329*
—Territories, *329-35*
Cananore, 670
Cañar, 440
Canary Islands, 1114-16, 1118-19, 1125
Canberra, 97-8, 102, 120
Canea, 572
Canelones, 1567, 1569
Canendiyú, 992
Canillo, 80
Çankırı, 1207
Çannakale, 1207
Cannes, 484
Canoas, 230
Canouan, 1051
Can Ranh Bay, 1587
Cantabria, 1115, 1118
Canterbury (New Zealand), 917
Canterbury (UK), 1300, 1342-3, 1349
Can Tho, 1589
Canton (China), 355, 360, 362-3, 365
Canton (N.Y.), 1508
Canton (Oh.), 1514
Cao Bang, 1585
Cape Coast, 563
Capelle aan den Ijssel, 900
Cape Province, 1088, 1097, *1100-1*
Cape Town, 1089-90, 1093, 1096, 1098, 1100
Cape Verde, *336-8*
Cap Haïtien, 597, 600
Capital District (Mali), 847-8
Caprivi Strip, 890
Caquetá, 372
Carabobo, 1578

Caracas, 1578-80, 1582
Carajás, 233
Caranda, 220
Caraş-Severin, 1034
Carbondale (Ill.), 1460
Carbonear, 311
Carchi, 440
Cardiff, 1301, 1305, 1349-50
Caribbean Community, *55-6*
Caribou (Me.), 1473
CARICOM, *55-6*
Carinthia, 168-9
Carípito, 1583
Carlisle, 1300
Carlow, 719, 730
Carmen, 868
Carnarvon (Australia), 106
Car Nicobar, 695
Carolina, 1561
Caroline Island, 778
Carrasco Airport, 1570
Carriacou, 578-9
Carrickfergus, 1359
Çarsamba, 1210
Carson City (Nev.), 1496, 1498
Cartagena (Colombia), 372
Cartagena (Spain), 1115-16, 1119
Cartago, 385, 388
Carthage Airport, 1205
Cartier Island, *128*
Carúpano, 1578
Casablanca, 879-83
Casamance, 1065
Casanare, 372
Cascais, 1025
Caseros, 91
Cashmore, 975
Casino, 129
Casper (Wyo.), 1553-4
Cassino, 752
Castel Gandolfo, 1575
Castellón, 1115
Castelo Branco, 1020
Castilla-La Mancha, 1115
Castilla-Léon, 1115
Castlegar, 304
Castlemain, 153
Castlereagh, 1359
Castletown, 1367
Castricum, 900
Castries, 1049-50
Catalonia, 1115, 1117
Catamarca, 93, 95
Catania, 744, 752
Catanzaro, 744, 752
Catió, 591
Cat Island, 174
Catoosa (Okla.), 1518
Cauca, 372, 375
Cavan, 720
Cayagan de Oro, 1004
Cayagan Valley, 1004
Cayenne, 488, 501-2
Cayman Brac, 339-40
Cayman Islands, 30, *339-40*
Cayo, 204
Cazli, 1240
Ceará, 229
Cebu, 1004
Cedar City (Ut.), 1539
Cedar Falls (Ia.), 1464-5
Cedar Rapids (Ia.), 1378, 1464-5
Celaya, 864
Celebes *see* Sulawesi
Central African Republic, *341-4*
Central American Bank for Economic Integration, 603
Central American Common Market, *54*
Central Department (Paraguay), 992
Central District (Israel), 734
Centrale Region (Togo), 1191
Central Province (Kenya), 773, 775
Central Province (Papua New Guinea), 986
Central Province (Saudi Arabia), 1058
Central Province (Sri Lanka), 1127
Central Province (Uganda), 1219
Central Province (Zambia), 1621
Central Region (Ghana), 563
Central Region (Malawi), 827
Central Region (Scotland), 1303
Central Region (Sudan), 1135
Centre Department (Haiti), 597
Centre for Educational Research and Innovation, *36*
Centre Province (Cameroon), 265
Centre Region (France), 483
Centro Sur (Equatorial Guinea), 458
CERI, *36*
Cernovice Airport, 412
Cerro de Pasco, 998
Cerro-Largo, 1567
Çésar, El, 372
Ceské Budějovice, 408
Cessnock, 129
Ceuta, 1114-15, 1117-18, 1124
Ceylon *see* Sri Lanka
Cha Bahar, 710
Chacao, 1578
Chachachacare, 1198
Chachapoyas, 998
Chaco (Argentina), 90
Chaco (Paraguay), 992, 994, 996
Chad, *345-7*
Chadak, 1287
Chadron (Nebr.), 1495
Chafarinas, 1115
Chagchun, 365
Chagos Archipelago, *238*
Chahár Mahál and Bakhtiári, 708
Chai Wan, 611
Chalatenago, 453
Chaman, 66
Chamba, 663
Chambéry, 484
Champagne-Ardennes, 483
Champasak, 798
Champerico, 584
Chanda, 673
Chandbali, 681
Chanderi, 672
Chandigarh, 632, 635, 649-50, 652-3, 662-4, 681-3, 695
Chandpur, 188
Changchun, 355, 363
Changhwa, 367
Changi, 1078-9
Changmai, 1189
Chang'ombe, 1184
Changsha, 355-6
Channel, 311
Channel Islands, 1298, 1303, 1343, *1369-73*
Chantilly (Va.), 1448
Chapel Hill (N.C.), 1511
Chapra, 658
Chardzhou, 1284-5, 1287
Charikar, 63
Charity, 594
Charleroi, 195, 201
Charleston (Ill.), 1460
Charleston (S.C.), 1528
Charleston (W. Va.), 1546-7
Charlestown (St Kitts-Nevis), 1044-5
Charlotte Amalie, 1564
Charlottenburg, 548
Charlotte (N.C.), 1378, 1509
Charlottesville (Va.), 1543
Charlottetown, 322
Charm, 1289
Charnwood, 1300
Cha Song, 789
Chateaubelair, 1053
Chatham Islands, 916, 919
Chattanooga (Tenn.), 1378, 1533-4
Cheboksary, 1256
Chechaouèn, 879
Chechen-Ingush Republic, 1254, *1256*
Chegcherán, 63
Chegu, 781
Chegutu, 1625
Cheliff, 74
Chełm, 1012
Chelmsford, 1300
Chelsea, 1302
Chelyabinsk, 1224, 1246, 1254
Chemba, 664
Chengdu, 355, 362-3, 365
Cherbourg, 484, 488-9
Cherkassy, 1264
Cherkessk, 1262
Chernigov, 1244, 1264
Chernobyl, 1240
Chernovtsy, 1264-5
Chernyakhovsk, 1225
Cherrapunji, 633
Cherry Hill (N.J.), 1501
Cherwell, 1300
Chesapeake (Va.), 1378, 1542
Cheshire, 1300
Chesterfield, 1300
Chesterfield Islands, 511
Chestnut Hill (Mass.), 1480
Chetlat, 697
Chetumal, 863
Cheyenne (Wyo.), 1553-4
Chiang Kai-Shek Airport, 370
Chiangmai, 1185
Chiapas, 863
Chiatura, 1271
Chiayi, 367
Chiba, 759
Chicago (Ill.), 1377, 1458-60
Chichester, 1300
Chichigalpa, 936
Chickmagalur, 667-8
Chiclayo, 998, 1000
Chicopee (Mass.), 1478
Chicoutimi, 272
Chieti, 752
Chihuahua, 863-4, 867
Chile, 52, 54, 125-6, 218, *348-53*, 998
Chilean Antarctic Territory, 348
Chileka Airport, 829
Chililabombwe, 1621
Chillán, 349
Chilliwack, 301, 304
Chiloé, 352
Chilpancingo, 863
Chilumba, 828
Chimaltenango, 581
Chimborazo, 440
Chimbu, 986
Chimkent, 1282-3
Chimoio, 885
Chin, 254
China, 125, *354-66*, 607, 1027
China Bay, 1129
Chinandega, 935, 938
Chingleput, 653, 687
Chingola, 1621
Chinhoyi, 1625
Chipata, 1621
Chipinge, 1628
Chiquimula, 581
Chiriquí, 980, 982
Chiromo, 887
Chita, 1246, 1250, 1254, 1263
Chitaldrug, 668
Chitral, 66
Chitré, 980
Chittagong, 184-5, 188-9
Chittaranjan, 693
Chittoor, 653, 687
Chitungwiza, 1625
Chivor, 375
Chobe, 225
Chocó, 372, 375
Cholla, 781
Choluteca, 602-3, 605
Chomutov, 411
Chonchu, 782
Chongjin, 786-7, 789
Chongqing, 356, 362
Chorley, 1300
Chota Nagpur, 658
Chowdwar, 680
Choybalsan, 875
Christ Church (Barbados), 192
Christchurch (New Zealand), 917, 927

Christiansted, 1564-5
Christmas Island (Australia), 30, 97, 114, *126-7*
Christmas Island (Kiribati) *see* Kirimati Island
Chubu, 759
Chubut, 91
Chugoku, 759
Chukotka, 1254, *1263*
Chungchong, 781
Chunghsing New Village, 367
Chuquisaca, 218
Churchill, 331
Chuvashia, 1254, *1256*
Ciechanów, 1012
Ciego de Avila, 394
Cienfuegos, 394, 397
Cincinnati (Oh.), 1377, 1514, 1516
Cirebon, 701
Ciskei, 1091, *1111-12*
City of London, 1302, 1320, 1333, 1336
Ciudad Bolívar, 1578, 1583
Ciudad Guyana, 1578
Ciudad Juárez, 864
Ciudad Madero, 864
Ciudad Obregón, 864
Ciudad Real, 1115, 1125
Ciudad Victoria, 863-4
Clackmannan, 1303
Clare, 719
Claremont (N.H.), 1499
Clarendon, 754
Clarksburg (W. Va.), 1546
Clarksville (Tenn.), 1533
Clausthal, 555
Clearwater (Fla.), 1449
Clermont-Ferrand, 483-4
Cleveland (Miss.), 1488
Cleveland (Oh.), 1377, 1514, 1516
Cleveland (UK), 1300
Cleveland Heights (Oh.), 1514
Clifton (N.J.), 1501
Clinton (Ia.), 1464
Clipperton Island, 516
Cluj, 1034, 1039
Cluj-Napoca, 1034
Clutha-Central Otago, 917
Clwyd, 1300
Clydebank, 1303
Clydesdale, 1303
Clydeside, 1303
CMEA, *48-50*
Coahuila, 863, 867
Coastal-North Otago, 917
Coast Province (Kenya), 773, 775
Coats Land, 238
Coatzacoalcos, 864, 868
Cobán, 581
Cobija, 218-19
Cochabamba, 218, 221-3
Cochin, 632-3, 648, 670
Coclé, 980
Cocos (Keeling) Islands, 30, 97, 114, *125-6*
Codrington, 87-8
Coetivy Island, 1068
Coihaique, 348
Coimbatore, 632, 639, 667, 687-8
Coimbra, 1020, 1025
Cojedes, 1578
Cojutepeque, 453
Colac, 153
Colchester, 1300
Coleraine, 1359, 1366
Colima, 863
Colmar, 484
Colóane, 1027
Cologne, 534, 542-3, 557
Colombia, 54, *372-7*
Colombo, 1127, 1130-1, 1133
Colombo Plan, *50-1*
Colón (Galápagos), 440
Colón (Honduras), 602
Colón (Panama), 980, 983-4
Colonia, 1567, 1569
Colorado, 1376, 1381, 1387, 1407, *1440-2*
Colorado Springs (Colo.), 1378, 1390, 1440, 1442
Columbia (Mo.), 1489-90
Columbia (S.C.), 1379, 1528-30
Columbus (Ga.), 1378, 1451
Columbus (Miss.), 1486, 1488
Columbus (Oh.), 1377, 1514, 1516
Comayagua, 602
Comayaguela, 603
COMECON, *48-50*
Comilla, 184, 188
Comino, 850
Commerce (Tex.), 1537
Commerce Bight, 206
Commewijne, 1140-2
Common Market *see* European Economic Community
Commonwealth, The, *28-31*
Comodoro Rivadavia, 91, 95
Comoé, 250
Comoros, *378-80*
Comox, 304
Conakry, 586-8
Concepción (Chile), 348, 352-3
Concepción (Panama), 982
Concepción (Paraguay), 992, 996
Conception Bay South, 311
Concord (Calif.), 1378
Concordia, 91
Concord (N.H.), 1499
Condamine, La, 870
Con Dau, 1585
Congo, *381-4*
Connacht, 720
Connecticut, 1375, 1382, 1387, 1389, *1442-5*
Con Son Island, 1589
Constanta, 1034, 1038-9
Constantine, 74, 78
Cook Islands, 30, 56, *931-2*
Coomacka, 594
Coorg, 653, 667-8
Copán, 602
Copenhagen, 415, 417, 423
Copiapó, 348
Copperbelt Province (Zambia), 1621, 1623
Coquilhatville *see* Mbandaka
Coquimbo, 348-9, 351
Coral Harbour, 175
Coral Sea Islands, 30, 97, *128*
Coral Springs (Fla.), 1449
Cordillera (Paraguay), 992
Córdoba (Argentina), 90-1, 93-5
Córdoba (Colombia), 372
Córdoba (Mexico), 864
Córdoba (Spain), 1114, 1116, 1125
Corfu, 576
Corinth, 571, 576
Corinto, 936, 938
Corisco, 458
Cork, 719-20, 722, 730
Cornellá, 1115
Corner Brook, 311
Cornwall, 1300
Coro, 1578
Coronel Oviedo, 996
Coronie, 1140-2
Coronou, 210
Çorovodë, 68
Corozal, 204
Corpus Christi (Tex.), 1378, 1535
Corrientes (Argentina), 90, 95
Corrientes (Paraguay), 996
Corriverton, 592
Corruna *see* La Coruña
Corse, 483
Corsica, 483
Cortés (Honduras), 602
Çorum, 1207
Corvallis (Oreg.), 1520, 1522
Corvo Island, 1020
Cosenza, 744, 752
Cosmoledo Islands, 1068
Costa Rica, 52, 54, *385-9*
Costermansville *see* Bukavu
Côte d'Ivoire, *390-3*, 565, 1193
Cotonou, 208-9
Cotopaxi, 440
Cottbus, 526
Council Bluffs (Ia.), 1464
Council of Europe, *40-2*
Council for Mutual Economic Assistance, *48-50*
Courtrai, 195
Covasna, 1034
Coventry, 1300
Covington (Ky.), 1468
Cox's Bazar, 188
Crabwood Creek, 594
Cracow (Australia), 139
Cracow (Poland) *see* Kraków
Craigavon, 1359
Craiova, 1034, 1039
Cranbrook, 301, 304
Cranston (R.I.), 1526
Cranwell, 1317
Creil, 484
Crete (Greece), 572, 576
Crete (Nebr.), 1495
Crewe and Nantwich, 1300
Crimea, 1264
Crişana, 1036
Cristóbal, 980, 982-3
Croatia, 1603, 1605, 1610, *1611-12*
Crooked Island, 174
Cross River, 943
Croydon, 1302
Crozet Islands, 510
Csongrád, 614
Cuando-Cubango, 82
Cuanza Norte, 82
Cuanza Sul, 82
Cuba, 48, 52, *394-9*
Cúcuta, 372
Cuddalore, 688
Cuddapah, 654-5
Cudjoe Head, 878
Cuenca, 440, 443-4, 1115
Cuernavaca, 863-4
Cueva, 222
Cuiabá, 229
Culebra, 1561
Culemborg, 900
Culiacán Rosales, 863-4, 869
Cumaná, 1578
Cumberland (Md.), 1476
Cumberland (R.I.), 1526
Cumbernauld and Kilsyth, 1303
Cumbria, 1300
Cumnock and Doon Valley, 1303
Cundinamarca, 372
Cunene, 82
Cunninghame, 1303
Curaçao, 904-5, 913-15
Curepipe, 859
Curitiba, 229-30, 235-6
Curtis Island, 930
Cuscatlán, 453, 456
Cuttack, 632, 680-1
Cuu Long, 1585
Cuvette, 381
Cuyahoga Falls (Oh.), 1514
Cuzco, 998-9
Cyangugu, 1041
Cyclades, 572
Cyprus, 30, 40, 45, 276, *400-5*, 1314, 1317
Cyrenaica, 814
Cyril E. King Airport, 1565
Czechoslovakia, 48, 58, 125, *407-14*
Czestochowa, 1012

Dabakala, 390
Dacca *see* Dhaka
Dac Lac, 1585
Dacorum, 1300
Dadong, 362
Dadra and Nagar Haveli, 632, 635, 649, 652-3, *695-6*
Dafur, 1135
Dagang, 360
Dagenham, 1302
Daghestan, 1254, *1256-7*

Dagupan, 1004
Dahlak Islands, 462
Dahuk, 714
Daito Islands, 759
Dajabón, 435
Dakar, 1064-7
Dakhla, 881, 1126
Dakhlet Nouâdhibou, 856
Dalian, 355, 363
Dallas (Tex.), 1377, 1535
Daloa, 390, 393
Dalvík, 623
Daman and Diu, 632, 635, 649, 652-3, 659, *696*
Damanhur, 446
Damanjodi, 680
Damascus, 1175-6, 1178-9
Damietta, 446
Dammam, 1058, 1062-3
Dampier, 111
Danané, 390
Da Nang, 1585, 1588-9
Danbury (Conn.), 1443
Danger Island, 931-2
Dangriga, 206
Dangs, 660
Danli, 602
Danube Commission, *58-9*
Danville (Ky.), 1470
Danzig *see* Gdańsk
Dapaong, 1191, 1193
Daqahlîya, 446
Daqing, 360, 363
Dará, 1175
Darbhanga, 658-9
Dar es Salaam, 260, 1180-1, 1183
Darién, 980
Dar-i-Suf, 65
Darjeeling, 633
Dark, 1369
Darkhan, 872, 874-5
Darlington, 1300
Darmstadt, 534, 543, 554
Darnah, 812
Daros Island, 1068
Dartmouth (Canada), 315
Daru, 986
Darwin, 97-8, 103, 121-3
Das Island, 1296
Datong, 356
Daugavpils, 1278
Daval, 1274
Davao, 1004
Davenport (Ia.), 1378, 1464
David, 980, 982
Davidson (Tenn.), 1377
Dawson City, 331-4
Dawson Creek, 304
Daya Bay, 360
Dayr az-Zawr, 1175
Dayton (Oh.), 1378, 1514, 1516
Dearborn (Mich.), 1481
Dearborn Heights (Mich.), 1481
De Bilt, 900
Debrecen, 614, 616, 621
Debre Markos, 462
Debre Zeit, 462-3
Decatur (Ill.), 1458
Deer Lodge (Mont.), 1491
Degari, 975
Dégrad des Cannes, 502
Dehiwela-Mount Lavinia, 1127
Dehra Dun, 632, 638, 691
Deir Ez-Zor Airport, 1178
DeKalb (Ill.), 1460
De La Kara, 1191
Delaware, 1376, 1386-7, *1445-7*
Delfzijl, 900, 906
Delhi, 632, 635, 639, 647-9, 652, 663, *696-7*
Delhi, New, 632-3, 638, 642, 696
Delta Amacuro, 1578
Den Haag, 900-1
Den Helder, 900, 904
Denizli, 1207-8
Denmark, 35, 40, 42, 47, 125, *415-25*, *429*
—Dependencies, *426-9*
Denpassar, 701
Denton (Tex.), 1537
Denver (Colo.), 1377, 1440-2
De Panne, 201
Dera Ghazi Khan, 975
Derby, 1300
Derbyshire, 1300-1
Derna, 811, 815
Derry, 1359, 1364, 1366
Desaguadero, 222
Desful, 709
Des Moines (Ia.), 1378, 1464-5
Des Plateaux (Togo), 1191
Desroches, 238
Desroches Island, 1068
Dessau, 526
Des Savanes, Region (Togo), 1191
Dessie, 462
Detroit (Mich.), 1377, 1481
Deurne (Belgium), 195
Deurne (Netherlands), 900
Deusto, 1125
Deva, 1034
Development Centre, *36*
Deventer, 900
Devil's Island, 501
Devon, 1300
Devonport (Australia), 147
Devonport (UK), 1314
Dewangiri, 656
Dewas, 672
Dezda, 828
D.F. Malan Airport, 1096
Dhahran, 1062-3
Dhaka, 184-5, 188-9
Dhamar, 1596
Dhanbad, 632, 658
Dharmanagar, 689-90
Dharwar, 667, 673
Dhaulagiri, 896
Dhawwar, 668
Dhi Qar, 714
Dhodak, 975
Dhofar, 965, 967
Dhulia, 673
Dhullian, 975
Dhursing, 898
Diademi, 230
Diamir, 972
Diamou, 848
Diayrbakir, 1209
Dibrë, 68
Dibrugarh, 656-7
Diego Garcia, 238
Diego Ramírez Islands, 348
Dien Bien, 1589
Diffa, 940
Differdange, 819
Dijon, 483-4
Dikchu, 686
Dikhil, 430
Dili, 701
Dillon (Mont.), 1493
Dilolo, 83
Dimapur, 676, 678-9
Dimashq *see* Damascus
Dimbaza, 1111
Dimbokro, 390
Dîmbovita, 1034
Dinajpur, 184
Diourbel, 1064, 1066
Direction Island, 125
Dire Dawa, 462
Dispur, 652, 656
District of Columbia, 1374, 1376, 1379, 1382, 1387, 1389, 1392, 1419, *1447-9*
Distrito Federal (Brazil), 229, 231
Distrito Federal (Mexico), 863, 865
Distrito Nacional (Dominican Republic), 435-6, 438
Ditsobotla, 1107
Diu, *696*
Divo, 390
Diyala, 714
Diyarbakir, 1207-8
Djaikak, 1287
Djambala, 381
Djambul, 1282-3
Djebel Berga, 76
Djelfa, 74
Djerba, 1202
Djetygar, 1283
Djezkazgan, 1283
Djibouti, 57, *430-2*
Djoué, 383
Dnepropetrovsk, 1224, 1246, 1264-5
Doba, 345
Dodecanese, 572, 576
Dodge City (Kans.), 1466
Dodoma, 1180-1
Doetinchem, 900
Doha, 794, 1029, 1031
Dolgano-Nenets, 1254
Dolj, 1034
Dolni Dubnik, 245
Dominica, 30, 52, 55, *433-4*
Dominican Republic, 52, *435-9*
Doncaster, 1300
Donegal, 720
Donetsk, 1224, 1246, 1264-5
Dongen, 900
Dongeradeel, 900
Dong Nai, 1585
Dong Thap, 1585
Dorada, La, 376
Dordrecht, 900-1
Dornbirn, 168
Dorset, 1300
Dortmund, 534, 543, 557
Doshi, 65
Dosso, 940
Douai, 484
Douala, 265, 268
Douglas, 1367, 1369
Douglas-Daly, 122
Dover (Del.), 1445-6
Dover (N.H.), 1499
Dover (UK), 1300
Down, 1359, 1364
Downpatrick, 1364
Drama, 572
Drammen, 950
Dranske, 528
Drenthe, 900
Dresden, 526-7
Drobeta-Turnu Severin, 1034
Dronning Maud Land, 963
Dronten, 900
Drumheller, 297-8
Dschang, 265
Duarte, 435
Dubai, 1293-7
Dubbo, 129
Dublin, 719-20, 727, 730
Dubossarsk, 1275
Dubrovnik, 1608
Dubuque (Ia.), 1464-5
Ducie Island, 1010
Dudelange, 819
Dudinka, 1263
Dudley, 1300
Duff Islands, 1082
Duisburg, 534
Dukhan, 1029
Dulles International Airport, 1448
Duluth (Minn.), 1484
Dumbara, 1133
Dumbarton, 1303
Dumfries and Galloway, 1303
Dumyât, 446
Dundalk (Ireland), 730
Dundalk (Md.), 1475
Dundee, 1303, 1312, 1349-50
Dunedin, 917, 927
Dunfermline, 1303
Dungannon, 1359
Dunkerque, 484
Dun Laoghaire, 719
Duque de Caxias, 230
Durango (Colo.), 1442
Durango (Mexico), 863, 867
Durant (Okla.), 1519
Durazno, 1567
Durazzo *see* Durrës
Durban, 1089, 1092-3, 1096, 1098
Durg, 632, 671-2
Durgapur, 632, 693
Durham (N.C.), 1379, 1509
Durham (UK), 1300, 1350
Durrës, 68, 70, 72
Dushanbe, 1224, 1288-9
Düsseldorf, 534, 543, 555, 557
Dvinsk, 1278
Dyfed, 1300

Dzaoudzi, 507
Dzhambul, 1282-3
Dzhezkazgan, 1282
Dzhizak, 1286

EAEC, 42, *46*
Ealing, 1302
Easington, 1300
East Bank *see* Jordan
East Cape (New Zealand), 916
East Cleveland (Oh.), 1514
East Devon, 1300
Easter Island, 348
Eastern District (American Samoa), 1559
Eastern Highlands (Papua New Guinea), 986
Eastern Province (Kenya), 773, 775
Eastern Province (Saudi Arabia), 1058, 1060, 1062
Eastern Province (Sierra Leone), 1071
Eastern Province (Sri Lanka), 1127
Eastern Province (Uganda), 1219
Eastern Province (Zambia), 1621
Eastern Region (Ghana), 563
Eastern Region (Sudan), 1135
East Falkland, 466-7
East Flanders, 194
East Germany *see* German Democratic Republic
East Greenland, 427
East Hampshire, 1300
East Hertfordshire, 1300
East Kilbride, 1303
Eastleigh, 1300
East Lindsey, 1300
East London, 1089, 1093, 1096, 1108
East Lothian, 1303
East New Britain, 986
Easton (Pa.), 1523, 1525
East Orange (N.J.), 1501
East Providence (R.I.), 1526
East Region (Iceland), 623
East St Louis (Ill.), 1458
East Sepik, 986
East Staffordshire, 1300
East Sussex, 1300
Eastwood, 1303
Eau Clair (Wis.), 1549, 1552
Ebamama, 778
Ebolowa, 265
ECA, 5
ECE, 5
ECLAC, 5
Economic Commission for Africa, 5
Economic Commission for Europe, 5
Economic Commission for Latin America and the Caribbean, 5
Economic Community of the Countries of the Great Lakes, 1042
Economic Development Institute, 21
Economic and Social Commission for Western Asia, 5
Economic and Social Council for Asia and the Pacific, 5
ECSC, 42, *44*
Ecuador, 52, 54, 57, *440-5*, 998
Edam-Volendam, 900
Ed-Daein, 1138
Edéa, 265, 267
Ede (Netherlands), 900
Ede (Nigeria), 943
Edessa, 572
Edgeøya, 961
Edinburgh (Tristan da Cunha), 1048
Edinburgh (UK), 1303, 1305, 1312, 1340, 1344, 1349-50
Edirne, 1207
Edison (N.J.), 1501
Edjéle, 76
Edmond (Okla.), 1517, 1519
Edmonds (Wash.), 1544
Edmonton (Canada), 272, 289, 297-300, 334-5
Edmundston, 307, 310
EEC, 42, *44-6*, 47
Efate, 1572-4
Effon-Alaiye, 944
EFTA, 45, *47*
Eger, 614
Eglinton Airport, 1365
Egypt, 45, 57, *446-52*, 734
Eichstätt, 543, 548
Eiði, 426
Eilat, 736, 739
Eindhoven, 900-1
Eire *see* Ireland
Eisenstadt, 168
Ekpan, 946
El Adami, 792
El Alto Airport, 222
Elâzig, 1207-8
Elbasan, 68, 71
Elblag, 1012
El Bluff, 938
El Callao, 1581
El César, 372
Elche, 1115
El Dammer, 1138
Eldoret, 773, 776
Eleuthera, 174
El Ferrol, 1115
El Gassi, 76
Elia, 571
Elista, 1257
Elizabeth Bay, 891
Elizabeth (N.J.), 1378, 1501
Elizabethville *see* Lubumbashi
El Jadida, 879
El Kelâa-Srarhna, 879
Elko (Nev.), 1498
Elmbridge, 1300
Elmira (N.Y.), 1506
El Obeid, 1138
Elobey Chico, 458
Elobey Grande, 458
El Oro, 440
El Paraíso, 602
El Paso (Tex.), 1377, 1535
Elphinstone, 694
El Porvenir, 980
El Progreso (Guatemala), 581
El Progreso (Honduras), 602-3
El Rahad, 1138
Elsa, 332-3
El Salvador, 52, 54, *453-7*
El Seibo, 435
Elsmere Town (Del.), 1445
Eluru, 654
El Yopal, 372
Elyria (Oh.), 1514
Emba, 1283
Embu, 773
Emet, 1210
Emilia-Romagna, 743, 746
Emmen, 900
Empangeni, 1098
Emsland, 538
Encamp, 80
Encarnación, 992, 996
Enderbury, 778
Enfield, 1302
Enga, 986
Engels, 1244
Enid (Okla.), 1517
Enschede, 900
Ensenada, 864
Entebbe, 1219-21
Entre Ríos, 90, 95
Enugu, 947
Epe, 900, 946
Ephraim (Ut.), 1539
Epi, 1572
Epirus, 571, 576
Epping Forest, 1300
Equateur (Zaïre), 1616
Equatorial Guinea, *458-60*
Erdenet, 872, 874-5
Eregli, 1211
Erewash, 1300
Erfurt, 526
Ergani, 1210
Erie (Pa.), 1378, 1523
Eritrea, 461-4
Erlangen, 543, 548
Ermelo, 900
Ernakulam, 670
Erode, 632
Er Rachidia, 879
Erromanga, 1572
Ersekë, 68
Erzincan, 1207
Erzurum, 1207-8
Esbjerg, 415-16
Esbo, 474
Escalante, 1583
Escaldes, Les, 79-80
ESCAP, 5
Esch-Alzette, 819
Escuintla, 581
Esfáhán, 708-9
Eskifjörður, 623
Eskilstuna, 1149
Eskisehir, 1207-9
Esmeraldas, 443
Esmeraldas Guayas, 440
Espaillat, 435
Espargos, 337-8
Espírito Santo (Brazil), 229, 233-4
Espiritu Santo (Uruguay), 1572-4
Espoo, 474
Es Samara *see* Smara
Es Saouira, 879
Essen, 534
Essendon, 158
Essequibo, 592
Essex, 1300, 1350
Esteban Echeverría, 91
Estelí, 935, 938
Estevan, 327
Estonia, 1224-5, 1250, *1276-8*
Est Province (Cameroon), 265
Estrelleta, La, 435
Estuaire (Gabon), 518
Etchmiadzin, 1250
Ethiopa, 48, *461-5*
Etten-Leur, 900
Etterbeek, 195
Ettrick and Lauderdale, 1303
ETUC, *33-4*
'Eua, 1195, 1197
Euboea, 571, 575
Euclid (Oh.), 1514
Eugene (Oreg.), 1378, 1520, 1522
Euratom, 42, *46*
Euroa, 156
Europe, 505
European Atomic Energy Community, 42, *46*
European Coal and Steel Community, 42, *44*
European Commission of Human Rights, *41*, 42
European Common Market *see* European Economic Community
European Communities, *42-7*
European Court on Human Rights, *41*, 42
European Court of Justice, *43*
European Economic Community, 42, *44-6*, 47
European Free Trade Association, 45, *47*
European Investment Bank, *43*
European Parliament, *43*
European Trade Union Confederation, *33-4*
European Youth Centre/Foundation, 41
Evanston (Ill.), 1458, 1460
Evansville (Ind.), 1378, 1461
Evenki, 1254, *1263*
Evere, 195
Everett (Wash.), 1544
Everton (Guyana), 595
Evora, 1020, 1025
Evros, 572
Evrytania, 571
Exeter, 1300, 1350
Extremadura, 1115, 1125

Extrême Nord Province (Cameroon), 265
Exuma Islands, 174
Eysturoy, 426

Faa Airport, 515
Fada N'Gourma, 250
Faial Island, 1020
Fairbanks (Ak.), 1430, 1432
Fairmont (W. Va.), 1546, 1548
Faisalabad, 971
Faiyûm, 446
Faizabad, 63
Fakaofa, 930
Falcón, 1578, 1581
Falkirk, 1303
Falkland Islands, 30, 91, 238, *466-8*, 1113, 1314, 1317
Fallon (Nev.), 1498
Fall River (Mass.), 1478
Falun, 1149
Famagusta, 401, 404, 406
Family Islands, 176-8
Fangataufa, 514
Fanling, 607
Fanning Island *see* Tabueran Island
FAO, *14-15*, 21
Farafenni, 522
Farakka, 186
Fareham, 1300
Fargo (N.D.), 1512-13
Farhah, 1060
Faridabad, 632, 662
Faridpur, 184
Farmington (N. Mex.), 1503
Farmington Hills (Mich.), 1481
Faro (Canada), 332, 334
Faroe Islands, 417, 421, *426-7*
Faro (Portugal), 1020, 1024-5
Farquhar, 238
Farquhar Island, 1068
Fárs, 708
Faslane, 1314
Fatah, 811
Fatick, 1064
Fatuhiva, 514
Faya, 345
Fayetteville (Ark.), 1435
Fayetteville (N.C.), 1509
Federal Capital Territory (Nigeria), 943
Federal Capital Territory (Pakistan), 971-2
Federal Dependencies (Venezuela), 1578
Federal District (Brazil), 229, 231
Federal District (Congo), 381
Federal District (Honduras), 602
Federal District (Mexico), 863, 865
Federal District (Venezuela), 1578
Federal Republic of Germany *see* Germany, Federal Republic
Feira de Santana, 230
Fejér, 614
FELABAN, *54*
Feldkirch, 168
Feltre, 752
Ferghana, 1285-7
Ferihegy Airport, 619
Ferkéssédougou, 390
Fermanagh, 1359, 1364
Fernando de Noronha, 229, 231
Ferozepore, 681
Ferrara, 744, 752
Ferrol, 1119
Fez, 879-80, 882-3
Fianarantsoa, 823
Fier, 68
Fife, 1303
Figiug, 879
Figueira di Foz, 1024
Fiji, 29, 50, 56, *469-72*
Findel Airport, 819
Fingal, 719
Finland, 47, *473-82*, 1225-6
Finnmark, 949
Flagstaff (Ariz.), 1434
Flamingo Field International Airport, 915
Flandreau (S.D.), 1532
Fleetwood, 1327
Flensburg, 543, 562
Flevoland, 900, 903
Flinders Island, 148
Flin Flon, 304
Flint (Mich.), 1378, 1481
Flint Island, 778
Florence (Italy), 744, 749, 751-2
Florence (S.C.), 1530
Florencia, 372
Flores (Uruguay), 1567
Flores Island, 1020
Florianópolis, 229
Florida (Uruguay), 1567, 1569
Florida (USA), 1376, 1382, 1387, *1449-51*
Florida Islands (Solomon Islands), 1082
Florina, 572
Florissant (Mo.), 1489
Flushing, 901, 904
Focşani, 1034
Foggia, 744
Fogo, 336-7
Fomboni, 378
Fond du Lac (Wis.), 1549
Fongafale, 1217
Fontvieille, 870-1
Food and Agriculture Organization, *14-15*, 21
Forari, 1573
Forbach, 484
Forest (Belgium), 195
Forli, 744
Formosa (Argentina), 90
Formosa (China) *see* Taiwan
Fortaleza, 229-30, 235, 2356
Fort Clayton, 984
Fort Collins (Colo.), 1440, 1442
Fort-de-France, 503-4
Fort Dodge (Ia.), 1464
Fort George D. Meade (Md.), 1390
Fort Gillem (Ga.), 1390
Fort Hare, 1098, 1112
Fort Huachuca (Ariz.), 1390
Fort Lauderdale (Fla.), 1379, 1449
Fort-Liberté, 597
Fort McMurray, 297-8
Fort McNair (Washington, D.C.), 1390
Fort Monroe (Va.), 1390
Fort Portal, 1219
Fort Providence, 331
Fort Resolution, 331
Fort St John, 301, 304
Fort Sam Houston (Tex.), 1390
Fort Saskatchewan, 297-8
Fort Sheridan (Ill.), 1390
Fort Simpson, 331
Fort Smith (Ark.), 1435
Fort Smith (Canada), 329, 331
Fort Wayne (Ind.), 1378, 1461
Fort Worth (Tex.), 1377, 1535, 1537
Framingham (Mass.), 1478
France, 35, 39-40, 42, 125, *483-98*
—Overseas Departments, *498-507*
—Overseas Territories, *510-17*
—Territorial Collectivities, *507-10*
Franche-Comté, 483
Francisco Morazán, 602
Francistown, 224
Franekeradeel, 900
Frankfort (Ky.), 1468
Frankfurt am Main, 534, 543, 554
Frankfurt an der Oder, 526
Franklin (N.H.), 1499
Fray Bentos, 1567
Frederick (Md.), 1476
Fredericton, 307, 309-10
Frederiksberg, 415
Frederiksborg, 415
Frederiksted, 1564
Fredrikstad, 950
Freeport (Bahamas), 174, 177-8
Freeport (N.Y.), 1506
Freetown, 1071-4
Fregate Island, 1068, 1070
Freiburg im Breisgau, 534, 542-3, 547
Fremantle, 111, 160, 165
Fremont (Calif), 1378, 1437
Fremont (Nebr.), 1493, 1495
French Guiana, 498, *501-3*
French Island, 154
French Polynesia, *513-16*
French Southern and Antarctic Territories, *511-12*
Fresno (Calif.), 1378, 1437
Fria, 588
Fribourg, 1164-6, 1173
Friedrichshain, 548
Friesland, 900
Friuli-Venezia Giulia, 743, 746
Frobisher Bay, 329, 331
Frosinone, 752
Frunze, 1224, 1244, 1290-2
Frýdek-Místek, 408
Fuenlabrada, 1115
Fuerteventura, 1115
Fuglafjørdur, 427
Fujairah, 1293, 1296
Fujian, 355, 361, 365
Fujisawa, 759
Fukui, 759
Fukuoka, 759
Fukushima, 759
Fukuyama, 759
Fulham, 1302
Fullerton (Calif.), 1378
Funabashi, 759
Funafuti, 779, 1217
Funchal, 1020-1, 1024-5
Fung, 1137
Fushun, 356
Futuna, 516-17
Fuzhou, 355-6
Fyn, 415

Gabeit, 1137
Gabela, 83
Gabès, 1202, 1205
Gabon, 57, *518-21*
Gaborone, 224, 227
Gabrovo, 243
Gabú, 589
Gafsa, 1202
Gaggal Airport, 664
Gagnoa, 390
Gagra, 1272
Gainesville (Fla.), 1449
Gaithersburg (Md.), 1476
Galápagos Islands, 440-2
Galați, 1034
Galerazamba, 375
Galicia (Spain), 1115, 1117-18
Galle, 1127
Gällivare, 1155
Galrus, 1164
Galveston (Tex.), 1535
Galway, 720, 730
Gambia, The, 30, *522-4*, 1064-5
Gambier Islands, 514
Gamlakarleby, 474
Gandaki, 896
Gander, 311
Gandhinagar, 660-1
Gangtok, 652, 685-6
Ganjam, 680
Ganshoren, 195
Gansu, 355, 364-5
Ganzourgou, 250
Gao, 847, 849
Garankuwa, 1107
Gardaia, 74
Garðbær, 623
Garden City (N.Y.), 1506

Garden Grove (Calif.), 1378, 1437
Garden Island, 103
Gardez, 63
Garfield Heights (Oh.), 1514
Garian, 814
Garissa, 773, 776
Garland (Tex.), 1378, 1535
Garo Hills, 656
Garoua, 265, 268
Gary (Ind.), 1378, 1461
Garzan, 1210
Gaspar Grande, 1198
Gateshead, 1300
Gatooma, 1625
GATT, 25-7
Gaudalajara (Mexico), 869
Gauhati, 649
Gävle, 1149
Gävleborg, 1148
Gaya, 659
Gayaquil, 441-2
Gaza (Egypt), 446
Gaza (Mozambique), 885, 887
Gazankulu, 1088, 1091, 1103
Gaza Strip, 735
Gaziantep, 1207-8
Gbangatoke, 1073
Gbarnga, 807
Gcuwa, 1108
Gdansk, 1011-14, 1017
Gdynia, 1011, 1014, 1017
Gedaref, 1138
Gedling, 1300
Geelong, 97, 111, 152-3, 156
Gelderland, 900
Geldermalsen, 900
Geldrop, 900
Geleen, 900-1
Gelsenkirchen, 534
Gembloux, 202
Gemu Gofa, 462
Gendringen, 900
General Agreement on Tariffs and Trade, *25-7*
General San Martín, 91
General Santos, 1004
General Sarmiento, 91
Geneva, 1164-6, 1173
Gengelo, 900
Genk, 195
Genoa, 744, 752
Gentofte, 415
George, 1096
Georgetown (Ascension), 1048
George Town (Australia), 150
George Town (Cayman Islands), 339-40
Georgetown (Del.), 1446
Georgetown (Guyana), 592
Georgetown (Ky.), 1470
Georgetown (Malaysia) *see* Penang
Georgetown (St Vincent), 1053
Georgia (USA), 1376, 1382, 1387, 1407, 1409, *1451-3*
Georgia (USSR), 1224-5, 1228, *1270-2*
Gera, 526
Geraldton, 160
German Democratic Republic, 48, 125, *526-32*, 534
Germany, 525
Germany, Federal Republic of, 36, 39-40, 42, 58, 125, *533-45*, 1314, 1317
—Länder, *545-62*
Gerona, 1115
Getafe, 1115
Gezira, 1137
Ghadames, 811, 814
Ghana, 30, *563-7*, 1193
Gharbîya, 446
Gharyan, 811
Ghat, 813-14
Ghatsila, 659
Ghawar, 1060
Ghaziabad, 632
Ghazni, 63, 226
Ghent, 194-5, 201-2
Ghubriah, 967
Gia Lai, 1585
Gibraltar, 30, *568-70*, 1314, 1317
Giessen, 543
Gifu, 759
Gijón, 1115
Gikongoro, 1041
Gilán, 708
Gilbert Islands, 778
Gilgit, 972
Gillette (Wyo.), 1553
Gillingham, 1300
Gilze en Rijen, 900
Gippsland, 106, 155-6
Giresun, 1207
Gisborne, 916-17
Gisenyi, 1041
Gitamara, 1041
Gitega, 260
Giurgiu, 1034
Giuyang, 356, 362
Gîza, 446-7
Gizo, 1082
Gjirokastër, 68
Gjøvik, 950
Glace Bay, 315
Gladstone, 111, 137
Glamorgan, 1300, 1302
Glarus, 1166-7
Glasgow, 1303, 1305, 1312, 1344, 1349-50
Glendale (Ariz.), 1433
Glendale (Calif.), 1378, 1437
Glenville (W. Va.), 1548
Gliwice, 1012
Gloucester, 1300
Gloucestershire, 1300
Glücksburg, 537
Gnagna, 250
Gniezno, 1018
Goa, 632, 635, 639, 648-9, 652-3, *659-60*, 696
Goba, 462
Gobabis, 890
Gobi Altai, 875
Goborone, 226
Godoy Cruz, 91
Godthaab, 427
Goes, 900
Goiânia, 230, 236
Goiás, 229
Gojjam, 462
Golan Heights, 276
Gölcük, 1209
Gold Coast (Australia), 97, 137
Golden (Colo.), 1442
Golden Rock Airport, 1045
Golfito, 385, 388
Gomel, 1224, 1266
Gomera, 1115
Gómez Palacio, 864
Gonaïves, 597
Gondar, 462, 465
Gongola, 943
Goose Bay, 311
Gopalpur, 680-1
Gorakhpur, 632, 647, 691
Gordon, 1303
Gorey, 1371
Gorgol, 856
Gori, 1270
Gorinchem, 900
Gorj, 1034, 1036
Gorky, 1224, 1240, 1246, 1251, 1254
Gorno-Altai(sk), 1254, *1262*
Gorno-Badakhshan, 1288, *1290*
Goroka, 986
Gorzów, 1012
Gostivar, 1603
Göteborg, 1149, 1151-2, 1158
Göteborg and Bohus, 1148
Gothaab, 428
Gothenburg, 1151-2, 1158
Gotland, 1148-9, 1151-2
Göttingen, 534, 543, 555
Gottwaldov, 408
Gouda, 900
Gough Island, 1048
Goulburn, 129
Goulette, 1202, 1205
Gourma, 250
Gozo, 850, 853
Gracias a Dios, 602
Graciosa, 1020, 1115
Graham Land, 238
Grahamstown, 1098
Grampian Region, 1303
Gramsh, 68
Granada (Nicaragua), 935, 938
Granada (Spain), 1114, 1116, 1125
Gran Canaria, 1115
Grand Bahama, 174, 176
Grand Bassa, 807, 809
Grand Caicos, 1215
Grand Cape Mount, 807, 809
Grand Cayman, 339-40
Grande Anse, 597
Grande Comore, 378
Grande Prairie, 297-8
Grande-Terre (Guadeloupe), 499
Grande Terre (Kerguelen Islands), 510
Grand Falls (Canada), 311
Grand Forks (N.D.), 1512-13
Grand Gedeh, 807
Grand Island (Nebr.), 1493
Grand Junction (Colo.), 1442
Grand Rapids (Mich.), 1378, 1481
Grand Turk, 1215-16
Grängesberg, 1154
Granma, 394
Graubünden, 818, 1164-6
Gravesham, 1300
Graz, 168, 172-3
Great Andamans, 694
Great Britain *see* United Kingdom
Great Falls (Mont.), 1491
Great Nicobar, 695
Great Sark, 1369
Great Zimbabwe, 1628
Greece, 36, 40, 42, 45, *571-7*
Greeley (Colo.), 1440, 1442
Green Bay (Wis.), 1549, 1551-2
Greencastle (Ind.), 1463
Greenland, 417, 421, *427-9*
Green River (Wyo.), 1553
Greensboro (N.C.), 1379, 1509
Greenvale, 139
Greenville (Liberia), 807
Greenville (Me.), 1473
Greenville (Miss.), 1486
Greenville (S.C.), 1528
Greenwich (Conn.), 1443
Greenwich (UK), 1302
Greenwood (S.C.), 1530
Grenada, 29-30, 52, 55, *578-80*
Grenadines, Northern, 1051
Grenadines, Southern, 578
Grenoble, 484, 494
Grevena, 572
Greymouth, 917
Gribingui, 341
Grigorevsky, 1247
Grigoriopol, 1275
Grimsby, 1327
Grimshaw, 331
Grindavík, 623
Grinnell (Ia.), 1465
Grisons, 818, 1164-6
Grodno, 1266-7
Groningen, 900-1
Grootfontein, 890
Grosseto, 749
Groton (Conn.), 1397
Grozny, 1240, 1256
Guadalajara (Mexico), 863-4
Guadalajara (Spain), 1115
Guadalcanal, 1082
Guadalupe (Mexico), 864
Guadeloupe, *498-501*
Guainía, 373
Guairá, 992
Guajira, La, 372
Guam, 1377, 1387, 1389, 1392, 1419, *1555-7*

Guanacaste, 385
Guanajuato, 863
Guanare, 1578
Guangdong, 355, 360-1
Guangxi, 355
Guangzhou *see* Canton
Guanta, 1582
Guantánamo, 394
Guaqui, 221-2
Guaranda, 440
Guarda, 1020
Guárico, 1578
Guarulhos, 230
Guatemala, 52, 54, *581-5*
Guatemala City, 581, 583-4
Guatemala Department, 581
Guaviare, 373
Guayaquil, 443-4
Guaymallén, 91
Guaymas, 868
Gudauta, 1272
Guelma, 74
Guelmim, 879
Guéra, 345
Guernsey, 1303, 1369-70, *1372-3*
Guerrero, 863
Guiana, French *see* French Guiana
Guidimaka, 856
Guiglo, 390
Guildford, 1300
Guilin, 362
Guimarães, 1025
Guinea, 524, *586-8*
Guinea-Bissau, 524, *589-91*
Guinée-Forestière, 586
Guinée-Maritime, 586
Guinguinéo, 1066
Guipúzcoa, 1114
Guiyang, 355
Guizhou, 355
Gujarat, 631, 635, 643, 649, 652-3, *660-2*, 673
Gujranwala, 971
Gujrat, 971
Gulbahar, 65
Gulbarga, 653, 667-8
Gulfport (Miss.), 1486
Gulf Province (Papua New Guinea), 986
Gulripsha, 1272
Gulu, 1219
Gümüşhane, 1207
Gunjur, 522
Gunnison (Colo.), 1442
Guntur, 632, 655
Gunza, 83
Gurdaspur, 663, 681
Gurgaon, 662
Guryev, 1282-3
Gusau, 944
Gustavia, 499
Guwahati, 647, 656-7, 677
Guyana, 30, 55, *592-6*
Guyaquil, 440
Gwadur, 965
Gwalior, 632, 649, 671, 673
Gwelo, 1625-6
Gwent, 1300
Gweru, 1625-6
Gwynedd, 1300
Gyalshing, 685-6
Györ, 614
Györ-Sopron, 614
Haaksbergern, 900
Ha'apai, 1195, 1197
Haarlem, 900-1
Ha Bac, 1585
Habana, 394, 398
Hachioji, 759
Hackney, 1302
Hadjú-Bihar, 614
Hadra, 632
Hadramaut, 1600
Haeju, 786-7
Hafnarfjörður, 623
Hagen, 534
Hagerstown (Md.), 1476
Hagondage-Briey, 484
Hague, The, 900-1
Hahaya, 379
Haifa, 734-6, 739, 741
Hai Hung, 1585
Ha'il, 1058
Hainan, 361
Hainaut, 194
Haines (Ak.), 1432
Hai Phong, 1585
Haiphong Ben Thui, 1589
Hairatan, 66
Haiti, 52, *597-601*
Haiya Junction, 1138
Håkensvern, 952
Hakkari, 1207
Hakodate, 759
Halaib, 1137
Halden, 950
Haldia, 648, 693
Halifax (Canada), 272, 276, 278, 315, 318
Halland, 1148
Halle, 526
Hallein, 168
Halmstad, 1149
Halton, 1300
Hama, 1175, 1178
Hamadán, 708-9
Hamamatsu, 759
Hamburg, 533-4, 539, 542-3, *551-2*
Häme, 473
Hämeenlinna, 473-4
Hamgyong, 787
Hamhung, 786-7, 789
Hami, 362
Hamilton (Australia), 153
Hamilton (Bermuda), 212
Hamilton (Canada), 272, 319
Hamilton (New Zealand), 916-17, 927
Hamilton (N.J.), 1501
Hamilton (Oh.), 1514
Hamilton (UK), 1303
Hamm, 534
Hammersmith and Fulham, 1302
Hammond (Ind.), 1461
Hampden-Sydney (Va.), 1543
Hampshire, 1300
Hampton (Va.), 1378, 1542
Ha Nam Ninh, 1585
Handan, 356
Hangha, 1073
Hangzhou, 355-6, 362
Haninge, 1149
Hanoi, 1585-6, 1589-90
Hanover (FRG), 534, 542-3, 554-5
Hanover (Jamaica), 754
Hanover (N.H.), 1500
Hao, 514
Happy Valley, 311
Haradh, 1058, 1062
Harar, 462, 465
Harare, 1625-6, 1628-30
Hararge, 462
Harbin, 355, 363
Harburg, 543
Hardenberg, 900
Harderwijk, 900
Hargeisa, 1085
Harghita, 1034
Harnai, 975
Harper, 807
Harringay, 1302
Harrisburg (Pa.), 1523-4
Harrisonburg (Va.), 1543
Harrogate, 1300
Harrow, 1302
Harstad, 950
Hartford (Conn.), 1378, 1443-4
Hartley, 1625
Haryana, 631, 635, 649, 652-3, *662-3*, 681, 695
Harz, 539
Hasakah, 1175
Ha Son Binh, 1585
Hassan, 668
Hasselt, 194-5
Hassi Messaoud, 76
Hassi-R'Mel, 76
Hässleholm, 1149
Hastings (Australia), 129
Hastings (Nebr.), 1493
Hastings (New Zealand), 916-17
Hastings (Sierra Leone), 1073
Hatay, 1207-8
Hatfield, 1301
Hato International Airport, 915
Hato Mayor, 435
Hattiesburg (Miss.), 1486, 1488
Ha Tuyen, 1585
Hat Yai, 1185, 1189
Haugesund, 950
Hau Giang, 1585
Haulbowline Island, 722
Haus Khaz, 697
Haute-Guinée, 586
Haute-Kotto, 341
Haute-Normandie, 483
Haute-Sangha, 341
Haut-M'bomou, 341
Haut-Ogooué, 518
Haut-Zaïre, 1616
Havana, 394, 398
Havant, 1300
Havelock Mine, 1144-5
Havering, 1302
Havírov, 408
Havre, Le, 484
Havre (Mont.), 1491-2
Hawaii, 1375-6, 1379, 1382, 1386-7, 1401, 1404, 1406, 1420, *1453-5*
Hawalli, 791
Hawar Islands, 179
Hawke's Bay, 916
Hay Mohamed-Aïn Sebâa, 879
Hay Point, 111
Hay River, 329, 331
Hays (Kansas), 1467
Hazaribagh, 659
Hazelwood, 155
Heard Island, 30, 97, *128*
Hebbal, 668
Hebei, 355, 360, 364
Hebrides, 1303
Hedmark, 949
Heemskerk, 900
Heemstede, 900
Heerenveen, 900
Heerhugowaard, 900
Heerlen, 900-1
Hefei, 355
Hegoumenitsa, 571
Heidelberg, 534, 543, 547
Heilongjiang, 355
Heiloo, 900
Helena (Mont.), 1491
Hellendoorn, 900
Hellevoetsluis, 900
Helmond, 900
Helsingborg, 1149
Helsingør, 415
Helsinki, 474, 476, 480-1
Hempstead (N.Y.), 1506
Henan, 355
Henderson (Nev.), 1496
Henderson Island, 1010
Hengelo, 906
Hengyang, 362
Heraklion, 572
Herát, 63, 65-6
Herdecke, 543
Heredia, 385
Hereford and Worcester, 1300
Herm, 1303, 1369
Hermosillo, 863-4
Hermoupolis, 572
Herne, 534
Herrera, 980
Herstal, 195
Hertfordshire, 1300-1
Hertogenbosch, 's, 900-1
Hertzog Airport, 1096
Hervey Bay, 137
Hessen, 533, 539, *553-4*
Heves, 614
Hewanorra International Airport, 1050
H.F. Verwoerd Airport, 1096
Hhohho, 1145
Hialeah (Fla.), 1378, 1449
Hidalgo, 863
Hidd, 179
Hierro, 1115
Higashiosaka, 759
Highland Region (Scotland), 1303
High Point (N.C.), 1509
Hihifo, 1195
Hildesheim, 534, 543, 555
Hillegom, 900
Hillingdon, 1302
Hilo (Hi.), 1454
Hilversum, 900-1
Himachal Pradesh, 631, 635, 649, 652-3, *663-5*, 681

Himeji, 759
Hinche, 597
Hinckley and Bosworth, 1300
Hirakata, 759
Hiroshima, 759, 761
Hissar, 662
Hiyaoa, 514
Ho, 563, 566
Hoa Binh, 1588
Hoang Lien Son, 1585
Hobart, 97-8, 147, 151-2
Hoboken (Belgium), 195
Hoboken (N.J.), 1501
Ho Chi Minh, 1585-6, 1588-90
Hodeida, 1596, 1598
Hodh ech-Chargui, 856
Hodh el-Gharbi, 856
Hofuf, 1058, 1062-3
Hoggar, 941
Hohenheim, 547
Hohhot, 355, 365
Hokitika, 917
Hokkaido, 759, 761, 765-6
Holguín, 394
Holice Airport, 412
Holland *see* Netherlands
Hollywood (Fla.), 1378, 1449
Holon, 735
Home Island (Cocos Islands), 125-6
Homs, 1175, 1178
Honan, 364
Honduras, 52, 54, *602-6*
Hong Gai, 1589
Hong Kong, 30, *607-13*, 1314, 1316-17, 1586
Honiara, 1082, 1084
Honolulu (Hi.), 1377, 1454-5
Honshu, 759, 761, 763, 765
Hoogeveen, 900
Hoogezand-Sappemeet, 900
Hoorn, 900
Hopen, 962
Hopkinsville (Ky), 1468
Hordaland, 949
Hormozgán, 708, 711
Horowhenua, 917
Horsburgh Island, 125
Horsens, 415
Horsham (Australia), 153
Horsley Hills, 654
Horten, 952
Horto, 1025
Hoshangabad, 671
Hoshiarpur, 663, 681
Hospitalet, 1116
Hot Springs (Ark.), 1435
Houet, 250
Houlton (Me.), 1473
Hounslow, 1302
Houston (Tex.), 1377, 1535-7
Houten, 900
Hove, 1300
Howrah, 693
Hradec Králove, 408
Hsinchu, 367
Huachipato, 352
Huahine, 514
Huainan, 356
Hualien, 367
Huambo, 81-2, 84
Huancavelica, 998
Huancayo, 998
Huangpu, 363
Huánuco, 998
Huaraz, 998
Hubei, 355, 365
Hubli-Dharwar, 632
Huddinge, 1149
Hue, 1589
Huehuetenango, 581
Huelva, 1114, 1116
Huesca, 1114
Huevos, 1198
Huíla (Angola), 82
Huila (Colombia), 372
Huizen, 900
Huju, 789
Hull (Canada), 272, 324
Hull (UK), 1301, 1327, 1350
Hulwan, 446
Humberside, 1300
Humphrey Island, 931
Hunan, 355, 360
Hunedoara, 1034
Hungary, 48, 58, 125, *614-22*
Hunter Island, 511, 1572
Huntingdonshire, 1301
Huntington (W. Va.), 1546, 1548
Huntington Beach (Calif.), 1378, 1437
Huntsville (Ala.), 1378, 1427
Huon Islands, 511
Hurghada, 448
Huron (S.D.), 1530
Húsavík, 623
Hwalien, 370
Hwange, 1625
Hwanghai, 787
Hyderabad (India), 632-3,639, 648-9, 652-5, 667
Hyderabad (Pakistan), 971
Hyesan, 787, 789
Hyvinge/kää, 474

Iagifu, 988
Ialomita, 1034
Iasi, 1034, 1039
Ibadan, 943-4, 947
Ibagué, 372
Ibaraki, 759
Ibarra, 440
Ibb, 1596
IBRD, *20-1*, 20
Ica, 998
ICAO, *22*
Içel, 1207-8
Iceland, 35, 40, 47, *623-30*
Ichikawa, 759
Ichinomiya, 759
IDA, *21*
Idaho, 1376, 1381, 1387, 1405, 1407, *1455-8*
Idaho Falls (Id.), 1456
Idlib, 1175
IEA, *36*
IFAD, *28*
IFC, *21-2*
Ife, 943
Ifrane, 879
Igarka, 1246
Iglesias, 749
Iisalmi, 474
Ijebu-Ode, 944
Ikare, 944
Ikerre-Ekiti, 944
Ila, 944
Ilám and Poshtkuh, 708
Ilan, 367
Ilebo, 1616, 1619
Île-de-France, 484
Île de la Gonave, 597
Île des Saintes, 499
Îles de Hoorn, 516
Îles du Vent, 514
Îles Glorieuses, 505
Ilesha, 943
Îles Loyauté, 512
Îles sous le Vent, 514
Ilhas Desertas, 1021
Ilhas Selvagens, 1021
Iligan, 1004
Illinois, 1376, 1382, 1386-7, 1407, *1458-61*
Illizi, 74
Illubabor, 462
Ilobu, 944
Ilocos, 1004
Iloilo, 1004
Ilopango Airport, 456
Ilorin, 943
Imathia, 572
Imatra, 474
Imbabura, 440
IMF, *18-20*
IMO, *24-5*
Imo, 943
Impfondo, 381
Imphal, 652, 675
Inagua Islands, 174
Inanda, 1089
Inchiri, 856
Inchon, 781-2
Independence (Mo.), 1378, 1489
Independencia (Dominican Republic), 435
India, 50, 125, *631-52*, 975
—States, 631-2, 634-5, *652-94*
—Union Territories, 632, 635, *694-9*
Indiana, 1376, 1382, 1387, 1407, *1461-3*
Indianapolis (Ind.), 1377, 1461, 1463
Indira Gandhi International Airport, 697
Indonesia, 50-1, 57, *700-7*
Indore, 632, 649, 671
Inga, 1618
Inhambane, 885-7
Inner Mongolia, 355, 363
Innsbruck, 168, 172
International Atomic Energy Agency, *12*
International Bank for Reconstruction and Development, *20-1*, 20
International Centre for Advanced Technical and Vocational Training, 13
International Civil Aviation Organization, *22*
International Confederation of Free Trade Unions, 33, *34*
International Court of Justice, *6-7*, 27
International Development Association, *21*
International Energy Agency, *36*
International Finance Corporation, *21-2*
International Fund for Agricultural Development, *28*
International Institute for Labour Studies, 13
International Labour Office/Organisation, *12-13*
International Maritime Organization, *24-5*
International Monetary Fund, *18-20*
International Narcotics Control Board, 5
International Telecommunication Union, *23*
International Trade Centre, 26
International Trade Federations, 33
International Trade Secretariats, 33
Intibucá, 602
Inuvik, 329, 331, 334
Invercargill (New Zealand), 917
Inverclyde, 1303
Inverness, 1303
Inyanga, 1628
Ionian Islands, 571
Iowa, 1376, 1382, 1387, 1407, 1420, *1463-5*
Iowa City (Ia.), 1464-5
Ipoh, 831, 839
Ipswich, 1301
Iqaluit, 329, 331
Iquique, 348
Iquitos, 998, 1000
Iran, 50, 57, 276, *708-13*
Irapuato, 864
Iraq, 57, 276, *714-18*
Irbid, 768, 771
Irbil, 714
Ireland, 40, 42, *719-33*, 1360
Irian Jaya, 700-1, 704
Iringa, 1180
Irkutsk, 1224, 1246, 1250, 1254, 1262, 1264
Irrawaddy, 254
Irtysh, 1283
Irvine, 1336
Irving (Tex.), 1378, 1535
Irvington (N.J.), 1501
Isafjörður, 623
Isa Town, 179, 181
Iseyin, 944
Isfahan *see* Esfáhán
Isfjord, 962
Ishimbaev, 1240
Ishpushta, 65

Iskenderun, 1209-12
Isla de Cedros, 868
Isla de la Juventud, 394-5
Isla de Pascua, 348
Islamabad, 971-2, 978
Islam Qala, 66
Islas de la Bahía, 602
Islas Diego Ramírez, 348
Islas Juan Fernández, 348
Isle of Man, 1303, 1343, *1367-9*
Isle of Pines, 511
Isles of Scilly, 1300
Isle of Wight, 1300
Isle of Youth, 394-5
Islington, 1302
Ismailia, 446-7
Isparta, 1207-8
Israel, 45, *734-42*, 799
Issia, 390
Issyk-Kul, 1290
Istanbul, 1207-9, 1212-13
Itabira, 233
Italy, 36, 39-40, 42, 125, *743-53*
Itanagar, 652, 655
Itapua, 992
ITF, 33
Ithaca (N.Y.), 1508
Ithmaniya, 1062
ITS, 33
Itta Bena (Miss.), 1488
ITU, *23*
Ituni, 594
Ivano-Frankovsk, 1264
Ivanovo, 1254
Ivato International Airport, 825
Ivigtut, 428
Ivoloina, 826
Ivory Coast *see* Côte d'Ivoire
Iwaki, 759
Iwo, 943
Ixelles, 195
Izabal, 581
Izhevsk, 1224, 1261
Izmir, 1207-10, 1212-13
Izmit, 1210

Jabal al-Akhdar, 811
Jabalpur, 632, 671-3
Jabal-us-Seraj, 65
Jabiru, 121
Jackson (Miss.), 1378, 1486-8
Jackson (Tenn.), 1533
Jacksonville (Fla.), 1377, 1449, 1451
Jacmel, 597
Jadavpur, 632
Jaén, 1114, 1116
Jaffa, 735
Jaffna, 1127, 1132-3
Jagang, 787
Jahingirnagar, 189
Jahra, 791
Jaintia Hills, 656
Jaipur, 632, 649, 652, 684
Jakarta, 701-2, 705
Jakarta Raya, 704
Jalahalli, 639
Jalálábád (Afghánistán), 63, 66-7
Jalal-Abad (USSR), 1287, 1291
Jalandhar, 632
Jalapa, 581
Jalapa Enríquez, 863-4, 869
Jalgaon, 673
Jalisco, 863
Jalpaiguri, 692-3
Jamaica, 29, 52, 55, *754-8*
Jamalpur, 184
Jambi, 700
James Spriggs Payne Airfield, 809
Jamestown (N.Y.), 1506
Jamestown (St Helena), 1047
Jammu, 665-6
Jammu and Kashmir, 631, 634-5, 643, 649, 652, *665-7*
Jamnagar, 632, 660, 662
Jamshedpur, 632, 659
Jämtland, 1148
Janakpur, 896, 898
Janesville (Wis.), 1549
Jan Mayen, 949, 953, *962*
Jan Smuts Airport, 1096
Japan, 50, 125, *759-67*, 1226
Järfälla, 1149
Järvenpää, 474
Jarvis Island, 778
Java, 700-1, 704-5
Jayapura, 701
J.B.M. Hertzog Airport, 1096
Jebel Ali, 1296
Jefferson City (Mo.), 1489
Jelenia Góra, 1012
Jelgava, 1278
Jember, 701
Jena, 526
Jendouba, 1202
Jérémie, 597
Jerez de la Frontera, 1116
Jersey, 1303, 1369-70, *1371-2*
Jersey City (N.J.), 1378, 1501
Jerusalem, 734-5, 741
Jervis Bay, 120, 128
Jessore, 184, 188
Jethou, 1303, 1369
Jette, 195
Jety-Oguz, 1291
Jewish Autonomous Region (USSR), 1254, *1262*
Jhang, 971
Jiangsu, 355
Jiangxi, 355
Jiddah, 1058-9, 1061-3
Jidhafs, 179
Jihočeský, 408
Jihomoravský, 408
Jijel, 74
Jilikulam, 1289
Jilin, 355-6, 360, 365
Jimma, 462
Jinan, 355-6
Jind, 662
Jinja, 1219
Jinotepe, 935-6
Jisan, 1058
Jizan, 1062
João Pessoa, 229-30, 235-6
Joda, 680
Jodhpur, 632, 639, 684
Joensuu, 474, 481
Johannesburg, 1089, 1093, 1096, 1098, 1110
Johnson City (Tenn.), 1533
Johnston and Sand Islands, 1377, 1561
Johor, 831-2, 837-8
Johor Baharu, 831
Joilet (Ill.), 1458
Joinville, 230
Jomo Kenyatta Airport, 776
Jonesboro (Ark.), 1435
Jönköping, 1148-9
Jonquière, 272
Joplin (Mo.), 1489
Jordan, 45, 57, *768-72*
Jordanstown, 1366
Jorf Lasfar, 883
Jorhat, 657
Jos, 944
Jost Van Dyke, 1591
Jounieh, 802
Joya Mair, 975
Juan de Nova, 505
Juan Fernandez Islands, 348
Juba, 1135, 1138
Jubail, 1058-9, 1061
Jubbarharthi Airport, 664
Judea and Samaria *see* West Bank
Juigalpa, 935-6, 938
Juiz de Fora, 230
Jujuy, 90
Jullundur, 681
Jundiaí, 230
Juneau (Ak.), 1430, 1432
Junín, 998
Junk Bay, 607
Jura, 1164-6
Jurmala, 1278
Jurong, 1078-9
Jutiapa, 581
Juticalpa, 602
Jwaneng, 224-5
Jymi, 473
Jyväskylä, 474, 481

Kabardin-Balkaria, 1254, *1257*
Kábul, 63, 65-7
Kabwe, 1621
Kachchativu, 1127
Kachin, 254
Kadiogo, 250
Kadmat, 697
Kadoma, 1625
Kaduna, 943, 945-6
Kaédi, 856, 858
Kaesong, 786-7
Kaf, 1202
Kafan, 1274
Kafr ad-Dawwar, 446
Kafr el-Sheikh, 446
Kaga-Bandoro, 341
Kagera, 1180
Kagoshima, 759
Kagulsk, 1275
Kahatagaha, 1130
Kahoolawe (Hi.), 1454
Kahramanmaraş, 1207-8
Kailasahar, 689
Kaimiro, 921
Kaira, 660
Kairak-Kum, 1289
Kairouan, 1202
Kaiserslautern, 543, 558
Kajaani, 474
Kakamega, 773
Kakanda, 587
Kakata, 807
Kakhovka, 1247, 1265
Kakinada, 654-5
Kalabagh, 975
Kalamazoo (Mich.), 1481
Kalangaha, 1130
Kalémié, 1616
Kalgoorlie, 160, 163, 165
Kalimantan, 700-1, 704
Kalingapatnam, 655
Kalinin, 1254
Kaliningrad, 1225, 1231, 1253-4
Kalispell (Mont.), 1491
Kalisz, 1012
Kalmar, 1148-9
Kalmykia, 1250, 1254, *1257*
Kalpeni, 697
Kaluga, 1254
Kalulushi, 1621
Kalutara, 1127
Kamalpur, 689
Kamaran Island, 1599
Kamchatka, 1254, 1263
Kamembe Airport, 1043
Kameng, 655
Kamensk, 1275
Kamloops, 301, 304
Kampala, 1219-20, 1222
Kampen, 900
Kampot, 263
Kampuchea *see* Cambodia
Kamsar, 588
Kamuzu International Airport, 829
Kamyshin, 1241, 1243-4
Kananga, 1616-17
Kanara, 667, 673, 687
Kanazawa, 759
Kandahár, 63, 65-6
Kandalaksha, 1258
Kandi, 208, 210
Kandla, 648, 662
Kandy, 1127
Kanem, 345
Kangar, 831
Kanggye, 789
Kangra, 663-4
Ka Ngwane, 1088, 1103
Kangwon, 781, 787
Kangyye, 787
Kankan, 586, 588
Kano, 943-4
Kanombe Airport, 1043
Kanpur, 632, 691
Kansas, 1376, 1382, 1387, 1407, *1465-7*
Kansas City (Kans.), 1378, 1466
Kansas City (Mo.), 1377, 1489-90
Kanto, 759
Kanton, 778
Kaohsiung, 367, 370
Kaolack, 1064, 1066-7
Kapanda, 82
Kapfenberg, 168
Kaposvár, 614
Kaptai, 185
Kapuni, 921
Kapurthala, 681

Kara, 1191
Karabük, 1211
Karachayevo-Cherkessia, 1254, *1262-3*
Karachi, 971-3, 975-7-8
Karadag, 1269
Karaganda, 1224, 1247, 1282
Karaj, 709
Karak, 768
Karakalpakia, 1285-6, *1287-8*
Karakspai, 1283
Karamai, 360
Karamoja, 1219
Karbala, 714
Karditsa, 571
Karelia, 1225, 1254, *1257-8*
Karen, 254
Kariba, 1628
Karikal, 653, 698
Karima, 1138
Karimnaga, 653
Karkar, 65
Karl-Marx-Stadt, 526
Karlskrona, 1149
Karlsruhe, 534, 543, 547
Karlstad, 1149
Karnal, 662-3
Karnali, 896
Karnataka, 631, 634-5, 643, 649, 652, *667-8*
Karonga, 829
Karpenissi, 571
Kars, 1207
Karshe, 1287
Kartong, 523
Karviná, 408
Karwar, 668
Karyai, 572
Kasai, 1616
Kasama, 1621-2
Kasaragod, 669, 687
Kashiwa, 759
Kashkadra, 1286
Kashmir, 665-6, 972
Kashmir *see also* Jammu and Kashmir
Kaslik, 802
Kassala, 1137-8
Kassel, 534
Kassérine, 1202
Kassinga, 83
Kassou, 392
Kastamonu, 1207, 1211
Kastoria, 572
Kasugai, 759
Kasungu, 828
Kasur, 971
Katanga *see* Shaba
Katerini, 572
Katherine, 121, 123
Káthmándu, 896, 898
Katihar, 658
Katiola, 390
Katni, 672
Katowice, 1012
Katsina, 943-4
Katunayake, 1129
Katwijk, 900
Kauai (Hi.), 1454
Kaunas, 1280-1
Kavajë, 68
Kavalla, 572
Kavaratti, 697-8
Kavieng, 986
Kawagoe, 759
Kawaguchi, 759
Kawasaki, 760
Kaya (Burkina Faso), 250
Kayah (Burma), 254
Kayes, 847, 849, 1067
Kayseri, 1207-8
Kazakhstan, 1224-5, 1237, 1247, 1250, 1281, *1282-4*
Kazan, 1224, 1251, 1254, 1260
Kearla, 631
Kearney (Nebr.), 1493, 1495
Kébili, 1202
Keçiborlu, 1210
Kecskemét, 614
Kedah, 831-2, 837
Kediri, 701
Keeling Islands *see* Cocos (Keeling) Islands
Keelung, 367, 370
Keene (N.H.), 1499
Keetmanshoop, 890
Keewatin, 329
Kefa, 462
Kefallenia, 571
Keflavík, 623-5
Keio, 766
Keksholm, 1258
Kelang, 831
Kelaniya, 1133
Kelantan, 831-2, 837-8
Kelibia, 1203
Kelowna, 301, 304
Kemerovo, 1224, 1246, 1254
Kemi, 474
Kemo-Gribingui, 341
Kenai Peninsula (Ak.), 1430
Kendari, 701
Kénédougou, 250
Kenema, 1071, 1073
Keningau, 839
Kénitra, 879-80
Kenner (La.), 1471
Kenosha (Wis.), 1549
Kensington and Chelsea, 1302
Kent, 1300, 1350
Kentucky, 1376, 1382, 1387, 1407, 1409, *1467-70*
Kenya, 30, *773-7*
Kerala, 635, 643, 649-50, 652-3, *669-70*
Kerava, 474
Kerch, 1235
Kerema, 986
Kerguelen Islands, 510
Kerki, 1287
Kerkrade, 900-1
Kerkyra, 571
Kermadec Islands, 930
Kermán, 708-9, 712
Kerry, 719
Keshod, 662
Keski-Suomi, 473
Keta, 563
Ketchikan (Ak.), 1430-1
Kete-Krachi, 566
Kettering (Oh.), 1514
Keyser (W. Va.), 1548
Khabarovsk, 1224, 1246, 1254, 1262
Khaburah, 965
Khadakvasla, 638
Khadoli, 695
Khairagarh, 673
Khajuraho, 672
Khakassia, 1254, *1263*
Khalkidiki, 572
Khamis-Mushait, 1058
Khammam, 653
Khandesh, 673
Khandwar, 671-2
Khanmu, 666
Khanty-Mansi(isk), 1254, *1263*
Kharagpur, 693
Kharar, 681
Kharg Island, 711
Kharkov, 1224, 1246, 1251, 1264-5
Khartoum, 1135, 1137-8
Khashkovo, 243
Khasi Hills, 656
Khatanga, 1246
Khémisset, 879
Khenchela, 74
Khénifra, 879
Kherson, 1244, 1264
Khios, 572
Khiva, 1240
Khmelnitsky, 1264
Khneifis, 1177
Khon Kaen, 1185
Khorásán, 708, 711
Khorezm, 1285-6
Khorixas, 890
Khormaksar, 1601
Khorog, 1289-90
Khorramábád, 708-9
Khorramshahr, 709
Khourigba, 879-80, 883
Khowai, 689
Khulna, 184-5, 188
Khums, 811-12
Khuzestán, 708
Khyber, 972
Kiama, 129
Kibungo, 1041
Kibuye, 1041
Kidira, 1066
Kidston, 139
Kiége, 195
Kiel, 534, 537, 543, 560-1
Kielce, 1012
Kien Giang, 1585
Kié-Ntem, 458
Kieta, 988
Kiev, 1224-5, 1246, 1250-1, 1264-5
Kiffa, 858
Kigali, 1041, 1043
Kigoma, 260, 1180
Kikwit, 1616
Kildare, 719
Kilimanjaro, 1180, 1183
Kilindini, 776
Kilkis, 572
Kilmarnock and Loudoun, 1303
Kiltan, 697
Kimbe, 986
Kimberley, 1089, 1096
Kimchaek, 786
Kincardine and Deeside, 1303
Kindia, 586
King Fahd International Airport, 1062
King Island, 148
Kingman Reef, 778
Kings County (N.Y.), 1506
King's Lynn and West Norfolk, 1301
Kingsport (Tenn.), 1533
Kingston (Jamaica), 754, 756
Kingston (Norfolk Island), 127
Kingston upon Hull, 1301, 1327, 1350
Kingston upon Thames, 1302
Kingstown, 1051-3
Kingsville (Tex.), 1537
Kinguélé, 519
King William's Town, 1089
Kinkala, 381
Kinki, 759
Kinnuar, 663
Kinshasa, 1616-17, 1619-20
Kiofi, 260
Kirghizia, 1224-5, 1281, *1290-2*
Kiribati, 30, 56, *778-80*
Kirimati Island, 778-9
Kirkcaldy, 1303
Kırklareli, 1207
Kirklees, 1301
Kirkuk, 714, 716, 1177
Kirov, 1254
Kirovabad, 1268-9
Kirovakan, 1273-4
Kirovograd, 1264
Kirşehir, 1207
Kisangani, 1616-17, 1619-20
Kishinev, 1224, 1246, 1275
Kisii, 776
Kisimayu, 1085, 1087
Kiskunfélegyháza, 616
Kislaya Guba, 1240
Kismaayo, 1085
Kissy, 1074
Kisumu, 773, 776
Kitab, 1287
Kitakyushu, 760
Kitchener, 272, 319
Kitikmeot, 329
Kitwe, 1621
Kivu, 1616
Kladno, 408, 411
Klagenfurt, 168, 172-3
Klaipeda, 1247, 1280
Klaksvik, 427
Klamath Falls (Oreg.), 1522
Klos, 71
Klosterbeuburg, 168
Knokke, 201
Knowsley, 1301
Knoxville (Tenn.), 1378, 1533-4
Kobe, 760
Koblenz, 534, 543, 558
Kobuleti, 1273
Kocaeli, 1207-8
Kochbulak, 1287
Kochi, 760
Kodiak Island (Ak.), 1430
Koekelberg, 195
Koforidua, 563
Kogo, 458, 460

Kohima, 652, 678-9
Kohistan, 977
Kohtla-Järve, 1276-7
Kokand, 1287
Kokchetav, 1282
Kokkola, 474
Kolaba, 673
Kolar, 668
Kolda, 1064
Kolding, 415
Kole, 267
Kolhapur, 632, 673-4
Kollegal, 667, 687
Kolombangara, 1082
Kolomna, 1250
Kolonia, 1558
Kolonjë, 68
Kolwezi, 1616
Komárom, 614
Kombo St Mary, 522
Komi, 1254, *1258-9*
Komi-Permyak, 1254, *1263*
Komotini, 572
Kompong Cham, 262
Kompong Som, 263-4
Komsomolsk-on-Amur, 1235, 1246
Konark, 680
Kong Karls Land, 962
Konin, 1012
Konstanz, 543, 547
Kon Tum, 1585
Konya, 1207-8, 1211-12
Kópavogur, 623
Köpenick, 548
Kopparberg, 1148
Korangi Creek, 973
Koraput, 680
Korba, 671-2
Korçë, 68, 71
Kordestán, 708
Korea, North, 781, *786-90*
Korea, South, 50, *781-5*, 786
Korhogo, 390
Korinthia/os *see* Corinth
Koritza *see* Korçë
Koriyama, 760
Koror, 1557
Koryak, 1254, *1263*
Koshigaya, 760
Kosi, 896
Košice, 408, 412-13
Kosovo, 1603-5, 1610, *1614*
Kosrae, 1558
Kossi, 250
Kostroma, 1254
Koszalin, 1012
Kota, 684
Kota Baharu, 831
Kotah, 632, 670
Kota Kinabalu, 831, 836, 839-41
Kotka, 474
Kotri, 975
Kottayam, 670
Kotte, 1127
Koudougou, 250
Kouilou, 381
Koulamoutou, 518, 520
Koulikoro, 847, 849
Kouritenga, 250
Kourou, 501-2
Kouroussa, 849
Kouvola, 474, 476, 480
Kovno, 1280-1
Kowloon, 607, 610-11
Koyali, 661
Kozani, 572
Kozhikode, 632, 669-70
Kpalimé, 1191
Kpandu, 566
Kpémé, 1193
Kragujevac, 1603
Kraków, 1012-13
Kralendijk, 913
Kraljevo, 1603
Kransovodsk, 1284
Krasnodar, 1224, 1262
Krasnoyarsk, 1224, 1240, 1246, 1254, 1263
Krefeld, 534
Kremenchug, 1241
Krems an der Donau, 168
Kreuzberg, 548
Kribi, 268
Krimpen aan den Ijssel, 900
Kristiansand, 950
Kristianstad, 1148-9
Krivoi Rog, 1224, 1264-5
Kronoberg, 1148
Krosno, 1012
Krško, 1606
Krujë, 68
Kruševac, 1603
Krutitsky, 1250
Ksar al Kabir, 880
Kuala Belait, 239, 241
Kuala Lumpur, 831-2, 834, 836-7, 839, 843
Kuala Terengganu, 831-2
Kuantan, 831, 836, 838-9
Kuching, 831, 836, 842-4
Kudat, 839-40
Kudymar, 1263
Kufrah, 811
Kuibyshev, 1224, 1240, 1246-7, 1254
Kujang, 789
Kukës, 68
Kullu, 663-4
Kulyab, 1288
Kumamoto, 760
Kumanovo, 1603
Kumasi, 563-4, 566-7
Kumba, 265, 268
Kumo, 944
Kundiawa, 986
Kunduz, 63
Kungrad, 1287
Kungsbacka, 1149
Kunming, 355-6, 362, 365
Kuolayarvi, 1258
Kuopio, 473-4, 476, 480-1
Kupang, 701
Kurashiki, 760
Kurdufan, 1135
Kure (Japan), 762
Küre (Turkey), 1210
Kurgan-Tyube, 1288
Kuria, 778
Kurile Islands, 1226
Kurnool, 654
Kurram, 972
Kursk, 1237, 1240
Kurukshetra, 662-3
Kushtia, 184
Kustanai, 1282-3
Kütahya, 1207-8
Kutaisi, 1270-1
Kutch, 653, 660
Kuusankoski, 474
Kuwait, 57, *791-4*
Kvitøya, 962
Kwabhaca, 1108
Kwai Chung, 607, 611
Kwajalein, 1558
Kwa Ndebele, 1088, 1091, 1103
Kwangchu, 782
Kwara, 943
Kwa Zulu, 1088, 1091, 1101
Kwekwe, 1625
Kwinana, 163
Kwun Tong, 611
Kyambogo, 1222
Kyle and Carrick, 1303
Kymi (Kymmene), 473
Kyonggi, 781
Kyongsang, 781
Kyoto, 760-1, 766
Kyrenia, 401, 406
Kyushu, 759
Kyzyl, 1260
Kyzyl-Kiya, 1290
Kzyl-Orda, 1282-3

La Altagracia, 435
La Asunción (Venezuela), 1578
La Aurora Airport, 584
Laâyoune, 879, 1126
Labé, 586
Labrador, *311-15*
Labrador City, 311
Labuan, 831, 834, 836, 839-40
Labyrinth Islands, 694
Lac, 345
Laccadive Islands, 632, 635, 637, 649, 652, 687, *697-8*
La Ceiba, 602-3, 605
La Condamine, 870
Laconia (N.H.), 1499
La Coruña, 1115-16
Lacq, 491
La Crosse (Wis.), 1549
Ladario, 232
La Digue Island, 1068
La Dorada, 376
Lady Julia Percy Island, 154
Lae, 986
La Estreleta, 435
La Faleme, 1066
Lafayette (Ind.), 1463
Lafayette (La.), 1471
Lages Airport, 1024
Laghouat, 74
Lagos, 943-4, 947
La Goulette, 1202, 1205
La Grande (Oreg.), 1522
La Guaira, 1582
La Guajira, 372
Lahad Datu, 840
Lahaul, 663
Lahej, 1600
Lahn, 554
Lahore, 971-2, 978
Lahti, 474
Laï, 345-6
LAIA, *54*
Lai Chau, 1585
Lajjun, 770
La Joya, 1000
Lake Charles (La.), 1471
Lake Izabal, 583
Lake Macquarie, 129
Lakewood (Colo.), 1378, 1440
Lakewood (Oh.), 1514
Lakonia, 571
Lakota, 390
Lakshadweep, 632, 635, 637, 649, 652, 687, *697-8*
La Laguna, 1116, 1125
La Libertad (El Salvador), 453, 456
La Libertad (Peru), 998
Lalitpur, 896-7
La Louvière, 195
La Massana, 80
Lambaréné, 518, 520
Lambayeque, 998
Lam Dong, 1585
Lamentin, 503-4
Lamia, 571
Lampang, 1185
Lampeter, 1349-50
Lampung, 700
Lamu, 776
Lanai (Hi.), 1454
Lancashire, 1300-2, 1338
Lancaster (Oh.), 1514
Lancaster (Pa.), 1523
Lancaster (UK), 1301, 1350
Landgraaf, 900
Langbaurgh on Tees, 1301
Langlade, 508
Lang Son, 1585
Languedoc-Roussillon, 484
La Ngwane, 1091
Lania (Hi.), 1454
Lansing (Mich.), 1378, 1481
Lanus, 91
Lanzarote, 1115
Lanzhou, 355-6, 362-3, 365
Laoghis, 719
Laos, 48, 50 *795-8*, 1189, 1587
La Palma (Panama), 980
La Palma (Spain), 1115
La Pampa, 90
La Paz (Bolivia), 218-23
La Paz (El Salvador), 453
La Paz (Honduras), 602
La Paz (Mexico), 863
La Plata, 90-1, 95
Lappeenranta, 474, 481
Lappi, 473, 481
Lappland, 473, 481
La Quiaca, 221
L'Aquila, 752
Lara, 1578
Laramie (Wyo.), 1553-4
Laredo (Tex.), 1535
Largeau, 345
Largo (Fla.), 1449
La Rioja (Argentina), 90, 93
La Rioja (Spain), 1115, 1118
Larissa, 571
Larnaca, 400, 404
Larne, 1359, 1365
La Rochelle, 484
La Romana, 435
L'Artibonite, 597

Las Cruces (N. Mex.), 1503, 1505
La Seo de Urgel, 80, 1123
La Serena, 348
Lashkargah, 65
La Skhirra, 1205
Las Palmas, 1114-19, 1125
La Spezia, 744, 747
Las Piedras, 1567
Lassithi, 572
Las Tablas, 980
Lastourville, 520
Las Tunas, 394
Las Vegas (Nev.), 1378, 1496-8
Las Vegas (N. Mex.), 1505
Latacunga, 440
Latgeau, 345
Latin American Association of Development Financing Institutions, *54*
Latin American Banking Federation, *54*
Latin American Economic System, *54*
Latin American Integration Association, *54*
La Tontouta Airport, 513
La Tortue, 597
La Trinité (Martinique), 503
Lattakia, 1175, 1177-8
Latvia, 1224-5, 1250, *1278-9*
Laucala Bay, 472
Launceston (Australia), 147, 151-2
La Unión (El Salvador), 453, 456
Laurium, 575
Lausanne, 1165, 1173
Lautoka, 469, 471
Laval, 324
Lavalleja, 1567
La Vega, 435, 438
La Villiaze Airport, 1373
Lawra, 566
Lawrence (Kans.), 1466-7
Lawrence (Mass.), 1478
Lawton (Okla.), 1517, 1519
Lázaro Cárdenas, 868
Lazio, 743, 746
League of Arab States, *56-7*
Leba, 1015
Lebanon, 45, 57, 734, *799-803*
Lebanon (N.H.), 1499
Lebowa, 1088, 1091, 1103
Lecce, 744, 752
Leduc, 297-8
Leeds, 1301, 1350
Leeuwarden, 900
Leeward Islands (French Polynesia), 514
Lefka, 406
Legamés, 1116
Legaspi, 1004
Leghorn, 744
Legnica, 1012
Leguan Island, 594
Leh Airport, 666
Le Havre, 484
Leicester, 1301, 1350
Leiden, 900-1
Leidschendam, 900
Leinster, 719
Leipzig, 526-7, 530
Leiria, 1020, 1025
Leitrim, 720
Le Kef, 1202
Lekemti, 462
Lékoumou, 381
Lelystad, 901
Le Mans, 484
Lempira, 602
Lena, 1246
Leninabad, 1288
Leninakan, 1273-4
Leningrad, 1224-5, 1234, 1240, 1245-7, 1250-1, 1254
Leninogorsk, 1283
Leninsk, 1285
Lenkoran, 1269
Lennoxville, 326
Lens, 484
Leoben, 168, 172
Leominster (Mass.), 1478
Leonding, 168
León (Nicaragua), 935, 938
León (Spain), 1115-16, 1125
León de los Aldamas, 864
Leopoldville *see* Kinshasa
Léraba, 392
Leribe, 804-5
Lérida, 1115-16
Lerwick, 1327
Les Abymes, 499
Les Cayes, 597
Les Escaldes, 79-80
Leskovac, 1603
Lesotho, 30, *804-6*, 1093, 1095
Les Saintes, 499
Lesser Sundas, 700
Lesvos, 572
Lethbridge, 297-8, 300
Leticia, 373
Letterkenny, 730
Leusden, 901
Leuuka, 471
Leuven, 195, 202
Levadeia, 571
Leverkusen, 534
Levin, 917
Levkas, 571
Lewes, 1301
Lewisburg (W. Va.), 1548
Lewisham, 1302
Lewiston (Id.), 1456-7
Lewiston (Me.), 1473-4
Lexington (Va.), 1543
Lexington-Fayette (Ky.), 1378, 1468, 1470
Leyte, 1004
Lezhë, 68
Lezno, 1012
Lhasa, 355, 363
Lianyungkang, 362
Liaoning, 355
Liberador, 348
Liberec, 408
Liberia, *807-10*
Liberia (Costa Rica), 385
Librazhd, 68
Libreville, 518-21
Libya, 57, *811-15*
Lichfield, 1301
Lichinga, 885
Lichtenberg, 548
Lida, 1267
Liechtenstein, 40, *816-18*
Liége, 194-5, 202
Liepaja, 1278
Lier, 195
Lifou, 511
Liguria, 743, 746
Lihou, 1303
Likasi, 1616
Likoula, 381
Lille, 484, 493-4, 496
Lillehammer, 950
Lilongwe, 827-9
Lima (Oh.), 1514
Lima (Peru), 998-1002
Limassol, 400, 404
Limavady, 1359
Limbe, 265, 268, 828
Limbourg, 194, 202
Limburg, 900
Limerick, 719, 730
Limoges, 484
Limón, 385, 388
Limousin, 484
Lincoln (Nebr.), 1378, 1493-5
Lincolnshire, 1300
Linden, 592, 594
Lindenhurst (N.Y.), 1506
Lindi, 1180
Line Islands, 778
Linköping, 1149
Linz, 168, 172-3
Lipa, 1004
Lipetsk, 1254
Lisbon, 1020-1, 1024-5
Lisburn, 1359
Lismore (Australia), 129
Lisse, 901
Litha, 1111
Lithgow, 129
Lithou, 1369
Lithuania, 1224-5, 1250, *1279-81*
Litoral Province (Equatorial Guinea), 458
Little Andaman Island, 694
Little Cayman, 339
Little Rock (Ark.), 1378, 1435
Little Sark, 1369
Littoral Province (Cameroon), 265
Liuzhou, 362
Liverpool, 1301, 1350, 1365
Livigno, 750
Livingstone (Zambia), 1621
Livonia (Mich.), 1378, 1481
Livorno, 744
Ljubljana, 1603, 1608, 1615
Lloydminster, 297-8, 327
Lobatse, 224
Lobaye, 341
Lobith, 908
Lobito, 81, 83
Lobos, 1115
Lochaber, 1303
Łódź, 1012
Lofa, 807
Logan (Ut.), 1538-9
Logone, 345
Logroño, 1115-16
Loheiya, 1596, 1598
Lohit, 655
Loja, 440
Lokeren, 195
Loma de Hierro, 1581
Lomas de Zamora, 91
Lombardy, 743, 746, 749
Lomé, 1191-4
Łomża, 1012
London (Canada), 272, 319
London (UK), 1302, 1305, 1320, 1333, 1350
—boroughs, 1302
London, City of, 1302, 1320, 1333, 1336
Londonderry, 1359, 1364, 1366
Londrina, 230
Long An, 1585
Long Beach (Calif.), 1377, 1437, 1439
Long Cay, 174
Longford, 719
Longhai, 362
Long Island (Bahamas), 174
Longview (Wash.), 1544
Longyearbyen, 962
Loon op Zand, 901
Lopevi, 1572
Lord Howe Island, *128-9*, 1082
Lorengau, 986
Lorestán, 708
Loreto, 998
Lorient, 484, 489
Lorman (Miss.), 1488
Lorraine (France), 484
Lorraine (Oh.), 1514
Los Angeles (Calif.), 1377, 1437, 1439
Los Angeles (Chile), 349
Los Lagos, 348
Los Mochis, 864
Los Ríos, 440
Los Santos, 980
Losser, 901
Los Teques, 1578
Lothian, 1303
Lotschberg, 1172
Loubomo, 381
Louga, 1064
Loughborough, 1350
Louis Botha Airport, 1096
Louisiana, 1376, 1382, 1386-7, 1389, 1407-8, *1470-2*
Louisville (Ky.), 1378, 1468, 1470
Loures, 1025
Louth (Ireland), 719
Louvain, 195, 202
Lovech, 243
Lowell (Mass.), 1478, 1480
Lower Austria, 168-9

Lower Saxony, 533, 538-9, *554-5*
Lowestoft, 1327
Lo Wu, 611
Loyalty Islands, 511
Loy Yang, 155
Luanda, 81, 83-4
Luang Prabang, 795, 798
Luanshya, 1621
Luaon Airport, 1619
Luapula, 1621
Luba, 458, 460
Lubango, 81, 84
Lubbock (Tex.), 1378, 1535, 1537
Lübeck, 534, 543, 562
Lublin, 1012, 1018
Lubombo, 1144-5
Lubumbashi, 1616-17, 1619-20
Lucena, 1004
Lucerne, 1164-7, 1173
Lucknow, 632, 649, 652, 690-1
Luda, 363
Lüderitz, 890-1, 1096
Ludhiana, 632, 681, 683
Ludwigshafen am Rhein, 534
Lugano, 1173
Lugansk, 1265
Lugo, 1115-16
Lugovaya, 1291
Luik, 194-5, 202
Luleå, 1149, 1154
Luluabourg *see* Kananga
Lumbini, 896
Lumut, 834
Lund, 1149
Lunda, 82
Lüneberg, 543, 555
Lungi Airport, 1073
Lunsemfwa, 1623
Luoyang, 356
Luqa Airport, 853
Lusaka, 1621, 1623-4
Lushnjë, 68
Lusikisiki, 1108
Lusiwasi, 1623
Lustenau, 168
Luton, 1301
Lutyengo, 1147
Luxembourg, 36, 39-40, 42, *819-22*, 907
Luxembourg (Belgium), 194
Luxor, 446-7, 451
Luzon, 1004
Lvov, 1018, 1224, 1246, 1264-5
Lwów, 1018, 1224, 1246, 1264-5
Lynchburg (Va.), 1542
Lynn (Mass), 1478
Lyon, 484-5, 493-4, 496

Ma'an, 768, 771
Maanshan, 360
Maarssen, 901
Maassluis, 901
Maastricht, 901
Macao, *1027-8*
Macapá, 229
Macas, 440
Macaulay Island, 930
McCarren International Airport (Nev.), 1497
Macclesfield, 1301
McDonald Islands, 30, 97, *128*
Macedonia (Greece), 572, 575
Macedonia (Yugoslavia), 1603, 1605, 1610, *1612*
Maceió, 229-30
Macerata, 752
Machakos, 773
Machala, 440, 443
Machias (Me.), 1473
Machida, 760
Machilipatnam, 654
Mackay, 137
McKean, 778
McKee, 921
Mackenzie (Guyana), 595
MacMinnville (Oreg.), 1522
Macomb (Ill.), 1460
Macon (Ga.), 1378, 1451, 1453
Macquarie Island, 125, 148
MacRobertson Land, 124
Madagascar, 505, *823-6*
Madang, 986
Madeira, 1020-1, 1023-4
Madhya Pradesh, 631, 634-5, 642-3, 649, 652-3, *670-3*, 673
Madison (S.D.), 1532
Madison (Wisc.), 1378, 1549-50, 1552
Madiun, 701
Madras, 632-3, 647-9, 652-4, 667, 669, 687-8
Madre de Dios, 998, 1000
Madrid, 1115-16, 1118, 1121, 1125
Madura, 700-1
Madurai, 632, 688
Maebashi, 760
Maewo, 1572
Mafeteng, 804
Mafikeng, 1107
Mafraq, 768
Magadan, 1254, 1263
Magallanes, 348, 352
Magdalena, 372
Magdeburg, 526
Magelang, 701
Magherafelt, 1359
Magnessia, 571
Magwe, 254, 257
Mahajanga, 823, 826
Mahakali, 897
Mahalapye, 224
Mahalla al-Kubrâ, 446
Maharashtra, 631, 634-5, 643, 649, 652-3, 660, *673-5*
Mahasu, 663
Mahbubnaga, 653
Mahdia, 1202
Mahe (India), 653, 670, 698
Mahé (Seychelles), 1068-70
Maheshwar, 672
Mahipár, 65
Mahón, 1119
Maiana, 778
Maidenhead, 1301
Maidstone, 1301
Maiduguri, 943
Maikop, 1240, 1262
Maimana, 63, 65
Maine, 1375, 1382, 1387-8, 1420, *1472-5*
Mainz, 534, 543, 557-8
Maio (Cape Verde), 336-7
Maio (French Polynesia), 514
Maiquetiá, 1578
Maisons-Lafitte, 487
Maitland, 129
Maizuru, 762
Majuro, 779, 1558
Makak, 268
Makaleb, 1177
Makati, 1004
Makeni, 1071
Makhachkala, 1240, 1256
Makhado, 1109
Makin, 778
Makira, 1082
Makkovik, 313
Makokou, 518
Makwarela, 1109
Malabar, 669, 687
Malabo, 458, 460
Malacca, 831-2, 837
Málaga, 1114, 1116, 1125
Malaita, 1082
Malakand, 972
Malan Airport, 1096
Malang, 701
Malange, 81-3
Malatya, 1207-8
Malawi, 30, *827-30*
Malaya *see* Peninsular Malaysia
Malaysia, 30, 50-1, *831-7*
—East Malaysia, *839-44*
—Peninsular Malaysia, *837-9*
Malden Island, 778
Maldives, 30, 50, *845-6*
Maldonado, 1567
Malé, 845-6
Malekula, 1572-3
Mali, *847-9*
Maligaon, 647
Malines, 195
Mallarg, 1327
Malmberget, 1154
Malmö, 1149, 1151
Malmöhus, 1148
Malolos, 1004
Malta, 30, 45, *850-5*
Maluku, 700-1
Malvinas *see* Falkland Islands
Mamgasaki, 759
Mamoundzou, 507
Manabi, 440
Managua, 935-6, 938
Manali, 664
Manama, 179-81
Manamgan, 1286
Manaure, 375
Manaus, 229-30, 2356
Manawatu, 917
Manchester (Jamaica), 754
Manchester (N.H.), 1499
Manchester (UK), 1299, 1301, 1305, 1338, 1350
Man (Côte d'Ivoire), 390
Mandalay, 254
Mandaluyong, 1004
Mandaue, 1004
Mandeville, 754
Mandi, 663
Mandsaur, 670-1
Mandurah, 160
Mandya, 668
Manga, 941
Mangaia, 931-2
Mangali, 1035
Mangalore, 668
Mangalore, New, 648
Mangan, 685-6
Mangareva, 514
Mango, 1193
Mangyshlak, 1282
Manhattan (Kans.), 1467
Manhattan (N.Y.), 1506
Manica, 885
Manicaland, 1625
Manihiki, 931
Manila, 1004, 1008
Manipur, 631, 635, 649, 652-3, *675-6*
Manisa, 1207-8
Man, Isle of *see* Isle of Man
Manitoba, 271-3, 279, 283-5, 291, *304-7*
Manitowoc (Wis.), 1549
Manizales, 372
Mankato (Minn.), 1485
Mankono, 390
Manmad, 674
Mannheim, 534, 543, 547
Manono, 1593
Manra, 778
Mansa, 1621-2
Mansfield (Oh.), 1514
Mansfield (UK), 1301
Mans, Le, 484
Mansûra, 446
Manu'a, 1558-9, 1561
Manuae, 931
Manus, 986-7
Manzanillo, 868
Manzhouli, 363
Manzini, 1144-6
Mao, 345
Maoi, 514
Maonte Plata, 435
Maple Ridge, 304
Maputo, 885-7
Mara, 1180
Maracaibo, 1578, 1581-2
Maracay, 1578
Maradi, 940, 942
Marakei, 778
Marampa, 1073
Maramures, 1034
Marandellas, 1625
Maranhão, 229
Marburg, 543, 554
Marche, 743, 746
Marcus Island, 759
Mar del Plata, 91-2, 95
Mardin, 1207, 1213
Maré, 511
Margibi, 807
Mari, 1254, *1259*
Maria Trinidad Sánchez, 435
Maribor, 1603
Marico, 1106
Marie Galante, 499-500
Mariental, 890
Marigot, 499

Marikina, 1004
Marion (Oh.), 1514
Marion Island, 1088
Maritime Region (Togo), 1191
Marjan, 1060
Marka, 1087
Markazi, 708
Marlborough (New Zealand), 917
Marondera, 1625
Maroua, 265
Marovoay, 826
Marowijne, 1140-2
Marquesas Islands, 514
Marrakesh, 879-80, 883-4
Marsabit, 776
Marsaxlokk, 850
Marseille, 484, 494
Marshall (Minn.), 1485
Marshall Islands, 1377, *1557-8*
Martin (Czechoslovakia), 408
Martinique, 498, *503-5*
Marwar, 684
Mary, 1284
Maryborough (Queensland), 137
Maryborough (Victoria), 153
Maryland (Liberia), 807
Maryland (USA), 1376, 1382, 1387, *1475-8*
Marystown, 311
Marzuq, 811
Masaka, 1219
Masan, 782
Masat, 695
Masaya, 935, 938
Masbate, 1004
Mascara, 74
Maseru, 804-6
Mashhad, 708-9
Mashonaland, 1625
Masisi, 1109
Mason City (Ia.), 1464
Massachusetts, 1375, 1387, 1408, *1478-80*
Massana, La, 80
Massapequa Park (N.Y.), 1506
Massawa, 462
Masterton, 917
Masuku, 518, 520
Masvingo, 1625
Mat, 68
Matabeleland, 1625
Matadi, 1616, 1618-19
Matagalpa, 935, 938
Matamoros, 864
Matanuska-Susitna (Ak.), 1430
Matanzas, 394
Matara, 1127
Mataram, 701
Matarani, 221
Mataró, 1116
Mata-Utu, 516-17
Mathura, 691
Mato Grosso, 229, 233
Mato Grosso do Sul, 229
Matosinhos, 1024-5
Matruh, 446
Matsapa, 1146-7
Matsqui, 301
Matsudo, 760
Matsuyama, 759-60
Matthew Island, 511, 1572
Mattu, 462
Maturin, 1578
Mauá, 230
Maubeuge, 484
Maui (Hi.), 1454
Maui (New Zealand), 921
Mauke, 931-2
Maule, 348
Maun, 226
Maupiti, 514
Mauritania, 57, *865-8*, 1126
Mauritius, 29-30, 505, *859-62*
Mayabandar, 694
Mayaguana, 174
Mayaguez, 1561
Maya Maya, 383
Maynooth, 730
Mayo (Canada), 334
Mayo (Ireland), 720
Mayo-Elsa, 332
Mayo-Kabbi, 345
Mayotte, *507-8*
May Pen, 754
Mayreau, 1051
Maysan, 714
Mayumba, 520
Mázándárán, 708, 711
Mazár-i-Sharif, 63-6
Mazatenango, 581
Mazatlán, 864, 868
Mbabane, 1144-5
M'baiki, 341
Mbala, 1622
Mbale, 1219, 1222
M'Balmayo, 265, 268
Mbandaka, 1616
M'Banga, 268
Mbarara, 1219, 1222
Mbeya, 1180
Mbinda, 383
Mbini, 460
M'bomou, 341
Mbuji-Mayi, 1616
Mchinji, 829
Mdantsane, 1111
Meath, 719
Mecca, 1058-9, 1063
Mechelen, 195
Mechi, 897
Medak, 653
Medan, 700
Médéa, 74
Medellín, 372-3
Médénine, 1202
Medford (Mass.), 1478, 1480
Medford (Oreg.), 1520
Medicine Hat, 297-8
Medina, 1058-9, 1062-3
Medvezhye, 1241
Meerssen, 901
Meerut, 632
Meghalaya, 632, 635, 637, 649, 653, 656, *676-7*
Megri, 1274
Mehedinti, 1034
Mehetia, 514
Mehrabad Airport, 712
Mehsana, 660
Meiji, 766
Mékambo, 520
Mekele, 462
Meknès, 879-80
Melaka, 831-2, 837
Melbourne (Australia), 97-8, 111-12, 152, 155-6, 158
Melfort, 327
Melilla, 1114-15, 1117-18, 1124
Mellersta-Finland, 473
Mellila, 1115
Melo, 1567
Melun, 484
Melville, 327
Melville Bay, 123
Memel, 1280
Memphis (Tenn.), 1377, 1533-4
Menado, 701
Mendi, 986
Mendip, 1301
Mendipathar, 677
Mendoza, 90-1, 95
Menongue, 83
Mentor (Oh.), 1514
Menûfiya, 446
Meppel, 901
Merca, 1085
Mercedes, 1567
Mérida, 863-4, 1115, 1578
Meriden (Conn.), 1443
Meridian (Miss.), 1486
Merksem, 195
Merlo, 91
Mersa Matruh, 446, 448, 451
Mers el Kebir, 75
Merseyside, 1299, 1302, 1338
Mersin, 1212
Merton, 1302
Meru, 773, 776
Merv, 1284
Mesa (Ariz.), 1379, 1433
Mesopotamia (St Vincent), 1053
Messenia, 571
Messina, 744, 752
Meta, 372
Meterlam, 63
Metropolitan Region (Chile), 348
Metz, 484, 489
Mexicali, 863-4
Mexico, 52, 54, *863-9*
Mexico City, 863-5, 868-9
Mexico State, 863
Meyal, 975
Mhlume, 1144
Miami (Fla.), 1378, 1449, 1451
Miami Beach (Fla.), 1449
Miaoli, 367
Michigan, 1376, 1382, 1387, 1420, *1480-3*
Michoacán de Ocampo, 863
Micronesia, Federated States of, 1377, 1557, *1558*
Mid-Bedfordshire, 1301
Middelburg, 901
Middle Caicos, 1215
Middlesbrough, 1301
Middletown (Conn.), 1444
Middletown (N.J.), 1501
Middletown (Oh.), 1514
Mid-Glamorgan, 1300
Midi-Pyrénées, 484
Midlands Province (Zimbabawe), 1625
Midland (Tex.), 1535
Midlothian, 1303
Mid-Sussex, 1301
Midway Islands, 1377, 1561
Midwest City (Okla.), 1517, 1519
Miercurea-Ciuc, 1034
Mikhailovgrad, 243
Mikkeli, 473-4
Miklot, 71
Mikomeseng, 458
Mila, 74
Milan, 744, 752
Mildura, 153
Milford City (Del.), 1445
Milford Haven, 1327
Milne Bay, 986
Milner Bay, 123
Milot, 71
Milton Keynes, 1301, 1336, 1349
Milwaukee (Wisc.), 1377, 1549, 1551-2
Mina Abdullah, 794
Mina Ahmade, 794
Mina al-Fahal, 968
Mina Al-Zor, 794
Mina Qaboos, 968
Mina Raysut, 965
Minas, 1567
Minas Gerais, 229, 233-4
Mina Sulman, 182
Minatitlán, 864
Mindanao, 1004
Mindelo, 338
Mindoro, 1004
Mingechaur, 1269
Minh Hai, 1585
Minicoy Islands, 687, 697
Minna, 944
Minneapolis (Minn.), 1377, 1484-5
Minnesota, 1376, 1382, 1387, 1407, 1420, *1483-6*
Minot (N.D.), 1512
Minsk, 1224, 1246, 1251, 1266
Minyâ, 446
Miquelon, 508
Miracle Mile Airport, 1048
Miranda, 1578, 1581
Mirditë Permet, 68
Miri, 831, 842
Misiones (Argentina), 90
Misiones (Paraguay), 992, 996
Miskolc, 614
Mississippi, 1376, 1381, 1387, 1407, 1409, *1486-8*
Missolonghi, 571
Missoula (Mont.), 1491
Missouri, 1381, 1387, *1488-90*
Misurata, 811, 813, 815
Mitchell (S.D.), 1530
Mitiaro, 931
Mitte, 548
Mitú, 373
Mitylini, 572
Miyazaki, 760

Mizoram, 632, 635, 637, 649, 652-3, 656, *677-8*
Mmabatho, 1105, 1107
Mmamabula, 226
Moanda, 519
Mobaye, 341
Mobile (Ala.), 1378, 1427-8
Moçâmedes, 81, 83
Mocoa, 372
Modena, 744, 752
Modesto (Calif.), 1378
Mödling, 168
Moengo, 1142
Moers, 534
Mogadishu, 1085-7
Mogilev, 1266
Mohale's Nek, 805
Mohamed V Airport, 883
Mohammedia, 880, 882
Mohammedia-Znata, 879
Mohéli, 378
Mohindergarh, 662
Mohmand, 972
Mokha, 1596, 1598
Mokhotlong, 804
Mokokchung, 678
Moldavia, 1224-5, *1275-6*
Molde, 950
Molenbeek St Jean, 195
Molise, 744, 746
Mollendo, 221-2
Mölndal, 1149
Molodechno, 1267
Molokai (Hi.), 1454
Moluccas, 700-1
Mombasa, 773-4, 776
Mon, 678
Monaco, *870-1*
Monaco-Ville, 870
Monagas, 1578, 1581
Monaghan, 720
Monastir, 1202
Mönchengladbach, 534
Monclova, 864
Mongla, 188
Mongo, 345
Mongolia, 48, *872-6*
Mongolia, Inner, 355, 363
Mongomo, 458
Mongu, 1621
Monklands, 1303
Monmouth (Oreg.), 1522
Mono (Benin), 208
Mono Islands, 1082
Monos, 1198
Monrovia, 807, 809-10
Mons, 194-5, 202
Monseñor Nouel, 435
Montana, 1376, 1381, 1387, 1405, *1491-3*
Montaña Clara, 1115
Montbéliard, 484
Mont-Belo, 383
Montclair (N.J.), 1501
Monte Carlo, 870
Monte Cristi, 435
Montego Bay, 754, 757
Montenegro, 1605, 1610, *1612-13*
Montería, 372
Monterrey, 863-4, 869
Montevideo, 1567, 1569-70
Montgomery (Ala.), 1378, 1427-9
Montgomery (W. Va.), 1548
Montpelier (Vt.), 154
Montpellier, 484
Montreal, 272, 289-90, 324, 326, 331
Montrieul, 484
Montserrado, 807
Montserrat, 30, 55, *877-8*
Monywa, 254
Monza, 744
Mooréa, 514-15
Moore (Okla.), 1517
Moorhead (Minn.), 1485
Mooroopna, 152-3
Moose Jaw, 327
Mopti, 847, 849
Moquegua, 998
Moradabad, 632
Moráng, 896
Moratuwa, 1127, 1133
Moray, 1303
Morazán, 453, 455
Mordovia, 1254, *1259*
Morelia, 863-4, 869
Morelos, 863
Møre og Romsdal, 949
Morgantown (W. Va.), 1546, 1548
Mormugao, 648
Morobe, 986
Morocco, 45, 57, *879-84*, 1126
Morogoro, 1180
Morón, 91
Morona-Santiago, 440
Moroni, 378, 380
Moropule, 225
Moroto, 1219
Morphou, 401, 406
Morwell, 152-3, 155
Moscow (Id.), 1457
Moscow (USSR), 1224-5, 1240-1, 1246-8, 1250-1, 1254
Moss, 950
Mossel Bay, 1096
Mostaganem, 74, 76, 78
Mostar, 1603
Most (Czechoslovakia), 408, 411
Móstoles, 1116
Mosul, 714-15
Motagua Valley, 583
Motala, 1149
Motherwell, 1303
Mouanda, 520
Mouhardeh, 1177
Mouhoun, 250
Mouila, 518
Moulmein, 254, 256-7
Mounana, 519
Moundou, 345, 347
Mount Abu, 649
Mount Athos, 572
Mount Gambier, 142
Mount Hagen, 986
Mount Isa, 137, 139
Mount Pearl, 311
Mount Pleasant Airport, 467
Mount Vernon (Ia.), 1465
Mount Vernon (N.Y.), 1506
Mouscron, 195
Moxico, 82
Moyen-Chari, 345
Moyenne-Guinée, 586
Moyen-Ogooué, 518
Moyle, 1359
Moyobamba, 998
Mozambique, 48, 827, *885-8*
Mpaka, 1145
Mpoko, 343
Msauku, 519
Msghalaya, 652
M'Sila, 74
Mtskheta, 1250
Mtunthama, 828
Mtwara, 1180
Mudanjiang, 363
Mufulira, 1621
Muğla, 1207
Muharraq, 179, 181-2
Mukalla, 1599, 1601
Mülheim an der Ruhr, 534
Mulhouse, 484
Muloza, 828
Multan, 971, 975
Mulungushi, 1622
Muncie (Ind.), 1461, 1463
Munger, 658
Munich, 534, 542-3, 547-8
Münster (FRG), 534, 543, 557
Munster (Ireland), 719-20
Muraleni, 1110
Murcia, 1115-16, 1118, 1125
Mureş, 1034
Murfreesboro (Tenn.), 1533
Murgab, 1289
Murgul, 1210
Muri, 658
Murmansk, 1247, 1254
Muruntau, 1287
Mururoa, 514
Muş, 1207
Musan, 789
Muscat, 965, 968
Mushin, 943
Muskogee (Okla.), 1517
Muslimbagh, 975
Mustique, 1051-2
Mutare, 1625
Mutate, 1109
Mutrah, 965, 968
Mutsamudu, 378
Muzaffarabad, 972
Muzaffarpur, 658-9
Muzo, 375
Mwali, 380
Mwanza, 1180
Myanma *see* Burma
Myitkyina, 256-7
Mymensingh, 184, 188
Myongchon, 789
Mysore, 632, 653, 667-8, 673, 687
Mzuzu, 827-8
Mzwani, 380

Naaldwijk, 901
Naâma, 74
Naberezhnye Chelny, 1224
Nabeul, 1202
Nabih Saleh, 179
Nacala, 829, 886-7
Nacka, 1149
Nadi Airport, 471
Nador, 879
Naga, 1004
Nagaland, 632, 635, 637, 649, 652-3, 656, *678-9*
Nagano, 760
Nagapattinam, 688
Nagarjunasagar, 654
Nagasaki, 760
Naghlu, 65
Nagorno-Karabakh, 1268, *1270*
Nagoya, 759-60, 766
Nagpur, 632, 639, 649, 673-4
Naha, 759-60
Nahouri, 250
Nairn, 1303
Nairobi, 773, 776
Najran, 1058
Nakawa, 1222
Nakhichevan, 1268, *1269*
Nakhodka, 1246
Nakhon Pathom, 1185-6
Nakhon Rajchasima, 1185
Nakhon Sawan, 1185
Nakhon Sri Thammaraj, 1185
Nakoura, 802
Nakuru, 773, 776
Nalanda, 659
Nalaykh, 875
Nalchik, 1257
Nalgonda, 653
Nalut-Yefren, 814
Namangan, 1287
Namchi, 685-6
Namdokchon, 789
Namentenga, 250
Namibe, 81-3
Namibia, 276, *889-93*
Nampa (Id.), 1456
Nampo, 786-7
Nampula, 885, 887
Namur, 194-5, 202
Nanaimo, 301, 304
Nana-Mambere, 341
Nanchang, 355-6, 362
Nancowrie, 695
Nancy, 484
Nandankanan, 680
Nanded, 653, 673
Nandi, 779
Nangarhár, 65
Nanisana, 826
Nanjing, 355, 362, 365
Nanning, 355, 362
Nanterre, 484
Nantes, 484
Nantou, 367
Nantwich, 1300
Nanumanga, 1217
Nanumea, 1217
Napier (New Zealand), 916-17
Naples, 744, 747, 751-2
Napo, 440
Naqb Ishtar, 771
Nara, 760
Naráyani, 897
Nariño, 372, 375
Narva, 1276
Narvik, 957, 1154
Naryan-Mar, 1263
Naryn, 1290
Năsăud, 1033
Nashua (N.H.), 1499

Nashville (Tenn.), 1377, 1533-4
Nasik, 632, 673
Na Son, 1589
Nassau (Bahamas), 174-5, 177-8
Nassau Island, 931
Nassib, 771
Natal (Brazil), 229-30, 2356
Natal (South Africa), 1088, 1097, *1101-2*
National Airport (USA), 1448
National Capital (Philippines), 1004
National Capital District (Papua New Guinea), 986
National District (Dominican Republic), 435-6, 438
Natitingou, 208, 210
NATO, *36-8*
Natore, 188
Nauplion, 571
Nauru, 29-30, 56, 779, *894-5*
Navarra, 1115, 1118
Navoi, 1286
Navotas, 1004
Navrongo, 566
Naxos, 576
Nayarit, 863
Nazareth, 734
Nazret, 462
Ndele, 341
N'Diole, 520
N'djaména, 345-7
Ndjili Airport, 1619
Ndola, 1621, 1624
NEA, *36*
Neamt, 1034
Nebit-Dag, 1284-5
Nebraska, 1376, 1381, 1387-8, 1407, *1493-5*
Neembucu, 992
Neemuch, 672
Negeri Sembilan, 831-2, 837
Negombo, 1127
Negros, 1004
Neiafu, 1195
Neiva, 372
Nejran, 1596
Nellore, 654
Nelson (New Zealand), 917
Nelson Bays, 917
Néma, 858
Nenets, *1263*
Nepál, 50, *896-8*
Nepanagar, 672
Neskaupstaður, 623
Netherlands, 36, 39-40, 42, 125, 199, *899-911*
Netherlands Antilles, 904, *913-15*
Netzahualcóyotl, 864
Neubrandenburg, 526
Neuchâtel, 1164-6, 1173
Neukölln, 548
Neuquén, 90
Neuss, 534
Neuwerk, 551
Nevada, 1376, 1381, 1387, 1405, *1495-8*
Nevis, 1044-5
Nevşehir, 1207
New Amsterdam, 592, 594
Newark (Del.), 1445-6
Newark (N.J.), 1378, 1501
Newark (Oh.), 1514
Newark and Sherwood, 1301
New Bedford (Mass.), 1478
New Britain (Conn.), 1443
New Britain (Papua New Guinea), 986
New Brunswick, 271-3, 279, 283-5, 291, *307-10*
Newburgh (N.Y.), 1506
Newbury, 1301
New Caledonia, *511-13*
Newcastle (Australia), 97, 111, 129
Newcastle (Co. Down), 1364
Newcastle Airport (St Kitts-Nevis), 1045
Newcastle under Lyme, 1301
Newcastle upon Tyne, 1301, 1350
New Delhi, 632-3, 638, 642, 696
New Forest, 1301
Newfoundland, 271-3, 279, 283-5, 291, *311-15*
New Georgia, 1082
New Glasgow, 315
Newham, 1302
New Hampshire, 1375, 1382, 1387-8, *1498-500*
New Haven (Conn.), 1378, 1443-4
New Ireland, 986
New Jersey, 1375, 1382, 1387, *1500-3*
New London (Conn.), 1444
New Mangalore, 648
New Mexico, 1376, 1381, 1387-8, *1503-5*
New Orleans (La.), 1377, 1397, 1471-2
New Plymouth, 916-17
Newport (R.I.), 1526
Newport (UK), 1301
Newport News (Va.), 1378, 1397, 1542
New Providence, 174-7
New Rochelle (N.Y.), 1506
Newry and Mourne, 1359
New South Wales, 97-8, 101, 106, 111, 114, 120, *128-37*
New Territories (Hong Kong), 607, 610-11
Newtownabbey, 1359
New Waterford, 315
New York (N.Y.), 1375, 1377, 1507-8
—Boroughs, 1506
New York (State), 1382, 1387-8, 1420, *1505-9*
New Zealand, 29, 50, 56, 125, *916-30*, *933-4*, 1010, 1593
—Minor islands, *930*
—Territories Overseas, *930-3*
Neyagawa, 760
Ngaoundéré, 265, 268
Nghe Tinh, 1585
Nghia Binh, 1585
Ngounié, 518
Ngwenya, 1145
Nhlangano, 1144
Nhulunbuy, 121
Niagara Falls (Canada), 272
Niagara Falls (N.Y.), 1506
Niamey, 940-2
Niamtougou, 1193
Niari, 381
Niassa, 885
Nicaragua, 48, 52, 54, *935-9*
Nice, 484
Nickerie, 1140-1
Nicobar Islands, *694-5*
Nicosia, 400-1, 404, 406
Nidwalden, 1164
Nieuwegein, 901
Niğde, 1207
Niger, *940-2*
Niger (Nigeria), 943
Nigeria, 30, 57, *943-8*
Nightingale Islands, 1048
Niigata, 760
Niihau (Hi.), 1454
Nijkerk, 901
Nijmegen, 901
Nikolayev, 1224, 1235, 1264
Nikopol, 1265
Nikumaroro, 778
Nikunau, 778
Nile Province (Uganda), 1219
Nimba, 807, 809
Nîmes, 484
Ninawa, 714
Ningbo, 356
Ningxia, 355, 362, 364
Niqat al-Khums, 811
Niš, 1603
Nishinomiya, 760
Niterói, 230, 2356
Nithsdale, 1303
Nitra, 408
Niuas, 1195
Niue, 30, 56, *932-3*
Niulakita, 1217
Niutao, 1217
Nizamabad, 653-4
Nizhe-Vartovskoye, 1246
Nizwa, 965
Njarðvík, 623
Njazídja, 378-9
N'kayi, 381
Nkongsamba, 265, 268
Noakhali, 184, 188
Nógrád, 614
Nohale's Hoek, 804
Nokia, 474
Nola, 341
Nong Khai, 1189
Nonouti, 778
Noord-Brabant, 900
Noord-Holland, 900
Noordoostpolder, 901
Noordwijk, 901
Nordauslandet, 961
Nord Department (Haiti), 597
Nord-Est Department (Haiti), 597
Nordjylland, 415
Nordland, 949
Nord-Ouest Department (Haiti), 597
Nord-Ouest Province (Cameroon), 265
Nord-Pas-de-Calais, 484
Nord Province (Cameroon), 265
Nord Province (New Caledonia), 512
Nord-Trøndelag, 949
Norfolk (Nebr.), 1493
Norfolk (UK), 1300-1
Norfolk (Va.), 1378, 1542-3
Norfolk Island, 30, 97, 114, *127-8*
Norilsk, 1240, 1263
Normal (Ill.), 1460
Normandy, 483
Norman Manley International Airport, 757
Norman (Okla.), 1517, 1519
Norra Karelen, 473
Norrbotten, 1148
Norrköping, 1149
Norrland, 1152
Norrtälje, 1149
Norte de Santander, 372
Northampton, 1301
Northamptonshire, 1300
North Atlantic Treaty Organization, *36-9*
Northavon, 1301
North Battleford, 327
North Bay (Canada), 277
North Bedfordshire, 1301
North Caicos, 1215-16
North Carolina, 1376, 1382, 1387-8, 1407, 1409, *1509-11*
North-Central Province (Sri Lanka), 1127
North Dakota, 1376, 1381, 1387, 1407, 1420, *1511-13*
North Down, 1359
North-East Derbyshire, 1301
North-Eastern Province (Kenya), 773, 775
North-East Fife, 1303
Northern Cyprus, Turkish Republic of, *405-6*
Northern District (Israel), 734
Northern Grenadines, 1051
Northern Ireland, 1307, 1314, 1327, 1356, *1359-67*
Northern Marianas, 1377, 1419, *1558*
Northern Province (Papua New Guinea), 986
Northern Province (Saudi Arabia), 1058
Northern Province (Sierra Leone), 1071

Northern Province (Sri Lanka), 1127
Northern Province (Uganda), 1219
Northern Province (Zambia), 1621
Northern Region (Ghana), 563
Northern Region (Malawi), 827
Northern Region (Sudan), 1135
Northern Territory (Australia), 97-9, 101, 106, 114-15, *120-4*
North Greenland, 427
North Hertfordshire, 1301
North Island (New Zealand), 916-17, 925
North Island (Seychelles), 1068
North Keeling Island, 125
North Lakhimpur, 657
Northland (Iceland), 623
Northland (New Zealand), 916
North Las Vegas (Nev.), 1496
North Little Rock (Ark.), 1435
North Norfolk, 1301
North Olmsted (Oh.), 1514
North Ossetia, 1254, *1260*
North Platte (Nebr.), 1493
North Providence (R.I.), 1526
North Rhine-Westphalia, 533, 539, *555-7*
North Shields, 1327
North Solomons (Papua New Guinea), 986
North Stradbroke Island, 139
North Sydney, 314-15
North Tonawanda (N.Y.), 1506
North Tyneside, 1301
Northumberland, 1300
North West District (Guyana), 594
North-Western Province (Sri Lanka), 1127
North-Western Province (Zambia), 1621
North-west Frontier Province (Pakistan), 971-2, 976, 979
Northwest Territories (Canada), 271-3, 279, 291, *329-32*
North Wiltshire, 1301
North Yemen *see* Yemen Arab Republic
North Yorkshire, 1300
Norwalk (Conn.), 1443
Norway, 36, 40, 47, 125, *949-64*
Norwich, 1301
Nottingham, 1301, 1350
Nottinghamshire, 1300
Nouâdhibou, 856-8
Nouakchott, 856-8
Nouméa, 488, 511, 513
Nova Iguaçu, 230
Novara, 744
Nova Scotia, 271-3, 279, 283-5, 291, 309, *315-18*
Novgorod, 1254
Novi Sad, 1603, 1614
Novokuznetsk, 1224
Novo-Moskovsk, 1265
Novosibirsk, 1224, 1246, 1254
Novo-Voronezh, 1240
Nowgong, 656
Nowy Sacz, 1012
Nsanje, 829
Nsawam, 563
Nuclear Energy Agency, *36*
Nuenen, 901
Nuequén, 95
Nueva Asunción, 992
Nueva Esparta, 1578
Nueva San Salvador, 453
Nuevitas, 397
Nuevo Laredo, 864
Nuevo Léon, 863
Nuevo León, 867
Nui, 1217
Nuiatoputapú, 1197
Nukha, 1269
Nuku'alofa, 1195
Nukufetau, 1217
Nukuhiva, 514
Nukulaelae, 1217
Nukunono, 930
Nukus, 1287
Nuneaton and Bedworth, 1301
Nunspeet, 901
Nuremberg, 534, 543, 548
Nusa Tenggara, 700-1
Nuuk, 427-8
Nuwara Eliya, 1127-8
Nwali, 378
Nwangundu, 1110
NWFP (Pakistan), 971-2, 976, 979
Nyakagunda, 260
Nyala, 1138
Ny-Ålesund, 962
Nyanga, 518
Nyanza, 773, 775
Nyanza-Lac, 260
Nyeri, 773, 776
Nyfregyháza, 614
Nyköping, 1149
Nyland, 473
Nyslott, 474
Nzérékoré, 586, 588
Nzwani, 378
Oahang, 831-2
Oahu (Hi.), 1454
Oakland (Calif.), 1378, 1437
Oak Ridge (Tenn.), 1533
OAS, *52-4*
OAU, *58*
Oaxaca, 863
Oaxaca de Juárez, 863-4
Obando, 373
Oberhausen, 534
Obninsk, 1240
Obo, 341
Obock, 430
Obuasi, 563
Obwalden, 1164
Occidental Province (Paraguay), 992-3
Ocean Island, 778
Ochanomizu, 766
Ocotepeque, 602
Oda, 563
Odando, 373
ODECA, 54
Odense, 415, 423
Odessa (Tex.), 1535
Odessa (USSR), 1224, 1245-6, 1251, 1264-5
Odi, 1106
Odienné, 390
Odivelas, 1020
OECD, *35-6*
Oeiras, 1020, 1025
Oeno Island, 1010
Offa, 944
Offaly, 719
Offenbach am Main, 534
Ofu, 1559
Ogasawara Islands, 759
Ogden (Ut.), 1538-9
Ogooué-Ivindo, 518
Ogooué-Lolo, 518
Ogooué-Maritime, 518
Ogun, 943
Ogwr, 1301
Ohakea, 920
Ohio, 1376, 1382, 1387, 1407, *1513-16*
Ohonua, 1195
Oio, 589
Oita, 760
Oka-Akoko, 944
Okahandja, 890
Okara, 971
Okayama, 760
Okazaki, 760
Okecie Airport, 1017
Okinawa, 759
Oklahoma, 1376, 1381, 1387-8, *1516-19*
Oklahoma City (Okla.), 1377, 1517, 1519
Okmulgee (Okla.), 1519
Oktemberyan, 1274
Olafsfjörður, 623
Olanchito, 602
Olancho, 602
Old Crow, 333-4
Oldebroek, 901
Oldenburg, 534, 543, 555
Oldenzaal, 901
Oldham, 1301
Olgiy, 875
Olhão, 1024
Olinda, 230
Olomouc, 408, 412-13
Olongapo, 1004
Olosega, 1559
Olpenitz, 537
Olsztyn, 1012
Olt, 1034
Olympia (Wash.), 1544
Omagh, 1359
Omaha (Nebr.), 1378, 1493-5
Oman, 57, *965-9*
Omar Torrijos Airport, 983
Ombella-M'Poko, 341
Omdurman, 1138
Omiya, 760
Omsk, 1224, 1240, 1246, 1254
Ömsköldsvik, 1149
Ondo, 943-4
Onigbolo, 210
Onitsha, 943
Onotoa, 778
Ontario, 271-3, 279, 282-5, 291, *318-22*
Ontong Java, *128-9*, 1082
Onverwacht, 1142
Oostende, 195
Oosterhout, 901
Ooststellingwerf, 901
OPEC, *57-8*
Opole, 1012
Oporto, 1020-1, 1024-5
Oppland, 949
Opsterland, 901
Oradea, 1033, 1039
Oran, 74-6, 78
Orange (Australia), 129
Orangeburg (S.C.), 1530
Orange Free State, 1088, *1104-5*
Orange Walk, 204
Oranjestad, 904, 911, 913
Orapa, 224-5
Ordino, 80
Ordu, 1208
Ordzhonikidze, 1260
Örebro, 1148-9
Oregon, 1376, 1381, 1387, 1420, *1519-23*
Orel, 1254
Orem (Ut.), 1538
Orenburg, 1224, 1241, 1254
Orense, 1115-16
Organisation for Economic Co-operation and Development, *35-6*
Organization of African Unity, *58*
Organization of American States, *52-4*
Organization of Central American States, 54
Organization of the Cooperatives of America, *54*
Organization of the Petroleum Exporting Countries, *57-8*
Orgeev, 1275
Oriental Province (Paraguay), 992-3
Orissa, 632, 635, 643, 649, 652, *679-81*
Orizaba, 864
Orkney Islands, 1303
Orlando (Fla.), 1378, 1449, 1451
Orléans, 483-4
Orléansville *see* Cheliff
Ormoc, 1004
Oro, El, 440
Orona, 778
Orúmiyeh, 708-9
Oruro, 218, 221-3
Osaka, 759-61, 766
Osasco, 230
Osh, 1289-91
Oshkosh (Wis.), 1549, 1552
Oshogbo, 943
Osijek, 1603
Oslo, 949-50, 958
Osmanabad, 673
Osnabrück, 534, 543, 555

Osorno, 349
Oss, 901
Ostende, 195
Östergötland, 1148
Östersund, 1149
Østfold, 949
Ostrava, 408, 411
Ostrołeka, 1012
Otjiwarongo, 890
Otopeni Airport, 1038
Ottawa, 272, 276, 280, 290, 319
Ottumwa (Ia.), 1464
Ouaddaï, 345
Ouagadougou, 250, 252-3
Ouahigouya, 250
Ouahran *see* Oran
Ouargla, 74
Ouarzazate, 879
Oubritange, 250
Oudalan, 250
Oud-Bijerland, 901
Oudja, 880, 883
Oued Ed Dahab, 879
Oued Zem, 883
Ouéme, 208
Ouesso, 381
Ouest Department (Haiti), 597
Ouest Province (Cameroon), 265
Ouham, 341
Ouham-Pende, 341
Ouidah, 208, 210
Oujda, 879
Oulu *see* Uleåborg
Oum al-Bouaghi Biskra, 74
Oumé, 390
Overijssel, 900
Overland Park (Kans.), 1466
Oviedo, 1115-16, 1125
Ovwian-Aladja, 946
Owando, 381
Owendo, 520
Owensboro (Ky.), 1468
Owo, 944
Oxelösund, 1154
Oxford (Miss.), 1488
Oxford (Oh.), 1516
Oxford (UK), 1301, 1350
Oxfordshire, 1300-1
Oxnard (Calif.), 1378, 1437
Oyem, 518, 520
Oyo, 943-4

Paama, 1572
Pabna, 184
Pachucha de Soto, 863-4
Padang, 700-1
Padang Besar, 838
Paderborn, 534, 542
Padua, 744, 752
Paducah (Ky.), 1468
Pago Pago, 1559-60
Pahang, 837
Pakanbaru, 700
Pakistan, 29, 50, 276, 631, 634, 665, *970-9*
Pakse, 795
Palamar, 1004
Palana, 1263
Palangkaraya, 701
Palanpur, 665
Palapye, 224
Palau, 1377, *1557*
Palé, 458
Palembang, 700
Palencia, 1115-16
Palermo, 744, 752
Palisadoes, 757
Palma de Mallorca, 1115-16, 1119, 1123, 1125
Palmas, Las, 1114-16, 1125
Palmer Land, 238
Palmerston, 121
Palmerston Island, 931
Palmerston North, 917, 927
Palm Island, 1053
Palmyra Island, 778
Palu, 701
Palwon, 789
Pamanzi, 507
Pamplona, 1115-16, 1125
Panaji, 652, 659-60
Panama, 52, *980-5*, 1390
Panama Canal, 980, *983-4*
Panama City, 980, 982-3, 985
Panay, 1004
Pančevo, 1603
Panch Mahals, 660
Pando, 218
Panevežys, 1280
Pangai, 1195
Panguma, 1073
Pankow, 548
Pantnagar, 691
Papar, 840
Papeete, 514-15
Papendrecht, 901
Paphos, 400, 404
Papua New Guinea, 29-30, 50, 56, 125, *986-91*
Pará (Brazil), 229, 233-4
Paradip, 648, 681
Paraguari, 992
Paraguay, 52, 54, *992-7*
Paraíba, 229
Parakou, 208-10
Paramaribo, 1140, 1142
Paraná (Argentina), 90
Paraná (Brazil), 229, 233-4
Paranaguá, 996
Paranam, 1142
Parañaque, 1004
Parbhandi, 673
Pardubice, 408
Paris (France), 484-5, 487, 493-4, 496, 510
Parkersburg (W. Va.), 1546
Parkside (Wis.), 1552
Parma (Italy), 744, 752
Parma (Oh.), 1514
Pärnu, 1276
Paro, 216
Parry Island, 931-2
Parsippany (N.J.), 1501
Paruz, 1286
Pasadena (Calif.), 1378, 1437
Pasadena (Tex.), 1378, 1535
Pasay, 1004
Pascagoula (Miss.), 1397, 1486
Pasco, 998
Pasig, 1004
Pasir Gudang, 836
Pasir Mas, 838
Passaic (N.J.), 1501
Passau, 543, 548
Passoré, 250
Pastaza, 440
Pasto, 372
Patan (India), 662
Pátan (Nepal), 896-7
Paterson (N.J.), 1378, 1501
Pathankot, 664
Patiala, 681
Patna, 632-3, 649, 652, 658-9
Patras, 571, 574
Patuakhali, 184
Pau, 484
Paúl, 337
Pavia, 752
Pavlodar, 1282-3
Pawtucket (R.I.), 1526
Paysandú, 1567, 1569-70
Pays de la Loire, 484
Pazardzhik, 243
Pearls Airport, 579
Pec, 1603
Pechora, 1259
Pécs, 614, 616, 621
Pedernales, 435
Pedras Rubras Airport, 1024
Pedras Tinhosas, 1056
Pedro Juan Caballero, 992, 996
Peel, 1367
Peenemünde, 528
Pegu, 254
Pekalongan, 701
Peking *see* Beijing
Pella, 572
Peloponnesos, 571, 575
Pelotas, 2356
Pematangsiantar, 701
Pemayangtse, 686
Pemba, 885-6, 1180
Penang, 831-2, 837-9
Penang Island, 838
Penghu, 367
Peniche, 1024
Peninsular Malaysia, *837-9*
Pennsylvania, 1375, 1382, 1387, 1405, *1523-6*
Peñón de Vélez, 1115
Penonomé, 980
Penrhyn Island, 931
Pensacola (Fla.), 1449, 1451
Pentecost, 1572
Penticton, 301
Penza, 1224, 1254
Peoria (Ill.), 1378, 1458, 1460
Pepel, 1073
Peradeniya, 1133
Perak, 831-2, 837
Peravia, 435
Pereira, 372
Perim Island, 1599
Perlis, 831-2, 837
Perm, 1224, 1240, 1254, 1263
Pernambuco, 229
Pernik, 243
Perpignan, 80, 484
Perth (Australia), 97-8, 160-1, 165
Perth and Kinross, 1303
Peru, 52, 54, 125, *998-1003*
Peru (Neb), 1495
Perugia, 744, 752
Pescara, 744, 752
Peshawar, 971-3, 978
Peshkopi, 68
Pest, 614
Petach Tikva, 735
Petaling Jaya, 831
Petange, 819
Petare, 1578
Petén, 581-3
Peterborough, 1301
Peterhead, 1327
Peter I Island, 963
Petersburg (Va.), 1543
Petite Martinique, 578
Petit St Vincent, 1053
Petropavlovsk, 1282
Petrópolis, 2356
Petrovsky, 1241
Petrozavodsk, 1258
Pforzheim, 534
Phan Nga, 1186
Phek, 678
Philadelphia (Pa.), 1377, 1523, 1525
Philip Goldson International Airport, 206
Philippines, 50-1, *1004-9*
Philipsburg, 913
Phiphidi, 1110
Phitsanulok, 1185
Phnom Penh, 261-4
Phoenix (Ariz.), 1377, 1433
Phoenix (Botswana), 226
Phoenix Islands, 778-9
Phojois-Karjala, 473
Phokis, 571
Phthiotis, 571
Phu Khanh, 1585
Phulbani, 680
Phuntsholng, 216
Piacenza, 744
Piandzh, 1289
Piatra-Neamt, 1034
Piaui, 229
Picardie, 484
Pichincha, 440
Pico Island, 1020
Piedmont, 743, 746, 749
Pieria, 572
Pierre (S.D.), 1531
Pierre van Ryneveld Airport, 1096
Pietermaritzburg, 1089, 1093, 1098, 1102
Pietersburg, 1098, 1110
Pigg's Peak, 1144
Piła, 1012
Pilar, 992, 995
Pilcomayo, 996
Pinang *see* Penang
Pinar del Río, 394, 398
Pine Bluff (Ark.), 1435
Pine Creek, 122
Pine Point, 331
Pinetown, 1089
Pingtung, 367
Pinjarra, 163
Piotrków, 1012
Piparia, 695

Piraeus, 571
Pisa, 744, 752
Pisco, 1000
Pishin, 975
Pitcairn Island, 30, *1010*, 1010
Pitesti, 1033
Pittsburg (Kans.), 1467
Pittsburgh (Pa.), 152, 1377, 1523
Piura, 998, 1000
Plainfield (N.J.), 1501
Plaisance Airport, 862
Plateau (Congo), 381
Plateau (Nigeria), 943
Platte Island, 1068
Platteville (Wis.), 1552
Pleven, 243, 246
Płock, 1012
Ploieşti, 1034
Plovdiv, 243, 245, 249
Plymouth (Montserrat), 877-8
Plymouth (UK), 1301
Plzeň, 408
Pobé, 210
Pocatello (Id.), 1456
Pochentong Airport, 263
Podor, 1067
Pogradec, 68
Pohjois-Karjala, 473
Pohnpei, 1558
Point-Central, 858
Pointe-à-Pitre, 499-500
Pointe Clairette, 519
Pointe-des-Galets, 506
Pointe-Noire, 381, 383
Point Salines Airport, 579
Point Vele air strip, 517
Poipet, 263
Poitiers, 484
Poitou-Charentes, 484
Poivre Island, 1068
Poland, 48, 125, *1011-19*, 1225
Poltava, 1264
Polyghyros, 572
Pompano Beach (Fla.), 1449
Ponce, 1561
Pondicherry, 632, 635, 649-50, 652-3, *698-9*
Poni, 250
Ponta Delgado, 1025
Pontevedra, 1115
Pontiac (Mich.), 1481
Pontianak, 701
Pool (Congo), 381
Poole, 1301
Popayán, 372
Popondetta, 986
Porbandar, 662
Pori, 474
Porsgrunn, 950
Port Adelaide, 146
Portage la Prairie, 304
Port Alberni, 301
Portalegre, 1020
Portales (N. Mex.), 1505
Port Arthur (Tex.), 1535
Port Augusta, 142
Port-au-Prince, 597-600
Port aux Basques, 311, 313-14
Port-aux-Français, 510
Port Blair, 694
Port-Buet, 393
Port Cornwallis, 694
Port-de-Paix, 597
Port Dickson, 838
Portela Airport, 1024
Port Elizabeth, 1089, 1093, 1096, 1098
Port Erin, 1369
Port-Gentil, 518-20
Port Harcourt, 943-5, 947
Port Hedland, 111, 160, 165
Portici, 751
Portimão, 1024
Port Kamsar, 588
Port Kelang, 836, 838
Port Kembla, 111
Portland (Australia), 153
Portland (Jamaica), 754
Portland (Me.), 1473
Portland (Oreg.), 1377, 1520, 1522
Port Loko, 1073
Port Louis, 859, 862
Port Moresby, 986-7, 990
Port Nolloth, 1096
Porto, 1020-1, 1024-5
Pôrto Alegre, 229-30, 232, 235-6
Port-of-Spain, 1198
Porto-Novo (Benin), 208-9
Porto Novo (Cape Verde), 337
Porto Santo Island, 1021
Pôrto Velho, 229
Portoviejo, 440
Port Pirie, 142
Port Qasim, 976-7
Portrush, 1364
Port Said, 446, 448, 451
Portsmouth (Dominica), 434
Portsmouth (N.H.), 1499
Portsmouth (UK), 1301, 1314
Portsmouth (Va.), 1378, 1542
Port Sudan, 1136-8
Port Tewfik, 448
Portugal, 36, 40, 42, 46-7, *1020-6*
—overseas territory, *1027-8*
Portuguesa, 1578
Port Victoria, 1069
Port Walcott, 111
Posadas, 90
Possession Island, 510
Potchefstroom, 1098
Poti, 1270
Potosí, 218-19, 221-3
Potsdam, 526
Poubara, 519
Poughkeepsie (N.Y.), 1506, 1508
Powell (Wyo.), 1554
Powys, 1300
Poza Rica de Hidalgo, 864
Poznan, 1012-13
Prague, 408, 412-13
Prahova, 1034, 1036
Praia, 337-8
Prairie View (Tex.), 1537
Prakasam, 653
Pram Point, 931
Praslin Island, 1068, 1070
Prato, 744
Prenzlauer Berg, 548
Presidency Division (West Bengal), 692
Presidente Hayes, 992
Presidente Stroessner, 992, 996
Presidio of San Francisco (Calif.), 1390
Prešov, 408
Preston, 1301
Pretoria, 1089-90, 1093, 1098, 1103, 1110
Preveza, 571
Prijedor, 1603
Primorye, 1254
Prince Albert, 327-8
Prince Edward Island (Canada), 271-3, 279, 283-5, 291, 309, *322-4*
Prince Edward Island (South Africa), 1088
Prince George, 301, 304
Prince Rupert, 301, 303-4
Princess Juliana Airport, 915
Princípe, 1056
Prinses Beatrix International Airport, 913
Prins Karls Forland, 961
Priština, 1603, 1609, 1614
Prizren, 1603
Probolinggo, 701
Proddatur, 654
Provence-Alpes-Côte d'Azur, 484
Providence (R.I.), 1379, 1526-8
Providence Island (Seychelles), 1068
Providenciales, 1215-16
Provo (Ut.), 1538-9
Przemysyl, 1012
Przhevalsk, 1290
Pskov, 1254
Pucallpa, 998
Puch'on, 782
Puebla, 863
Puebla de Zaragoza, 863-4, 869
Pueblo (Colo.), 1378, 1440, 1442
Puente Alto, 348
Puerto Aguirre, 996
Puerto Armuelles, 983
Puerto Ayacucho, 1578
Puerto Barrios, 456, 581, 584
Puerto Belgrano, 92
Puerto Cabello, 1578, 1580, 1582
Puerto Cabezas, 938
Puerto Carreño, 373
Puerto Cortés, 602-3, 605
Puerto Inírida, 373
Puerto La Cruz, 1578
Puerto Limón, 388
Puerto Maldonado, 998
Puerto Montt, 348, 352
Puerto Ordaz, 1582-3
Puerto Plata, 435, 438
Puerto Quetzal, 582, 584
Puerto Rico, 1377, 1387, 1389-90, 1392, 1408, 1419, 1423, *1561-3*
Puerto Sandino, 938
Puerto San José, 582
Puglia, 744, 746
Pukapuka, 931-2
Pukchong, 789
Pukë, 68
Pukow, 362
Pula, 1608
Pulau, 701
Pulau Brani, 1076
Pulau Pinang, 836
Pul-i-Khumri, 63, 65-6
Pullman (Wash.), 1546
Punakha, 217
Pune, 632, 649, 673-4
Punjab (India), 632, 635, 643, 649, 652-3, 662-3, *681-3*, 695
Punjab (Pakistan), 971-2, 975-6, 979
Puno, 222, 998
Punta Arenas (Chile), 348, 352
Puntarenas (Costa Rica), 385, 388
Punto Fijo, 1580
Puri, 680-1
Purmerend, 901
Purnea, 658
Pusa, 697
Pusan, 781-2
Pustavi, 1270
Putten, 901
Putumayo, 372
Puyo, 440
Pwani, 1180
P.W. Botha Airport, 1096
Pyongan, 787
Pyongyang, 786-7, 789-90
Pyrgos, 571

Qacentina *see* Constantine
Qacha's Nek, 804
Qala El Nahal, 1137
Qala-i-Nau, 63
Qalyûbiya, 446
Qaseem, 1063
Qasvin, 709
Qatar, 57, *1029-32*
Qatif, 1058
Qena, 446
Qingdao, 356, 358, 363, 365
Qinghai, 355
Qinhangdao, 363
Qiqihar, 356, 363
Qizil Qala, 66
Qom, 709
Quang Nam, 1585
Quang Ninh, 1585
Quan Long, 1589
Quatre Bornes, 859
Queanbeyan, 97, 129
Quebec, 271-3, 272, 279, 283-5, 291, 294, 309, *324-6*, 324, 326
Queen Alia International Airport, 771
Queen Maud Land, 963
Queens (N.Y.), 1506
Queenscliff, 102
Queensland, 97-8, 101, 106, 111, 114, *137-42*
Quelimane, 885, 887
Queluz, 1020
Quepos, 385, 388
Que Que *see* Kwekwe
Querétaro, 863-4, 867

Quetta, 971-2, 975, 978
Quetzaltenango, 581
Quezon City, 1004
Quibdó, 372
Quiché, 581
Quilmes, 91
Quilon, 669-70, 687
Quilpué, 349
Quinara, 589
Quincy (Mass.), 1478
Quindío, 372
Quintana Roo, 863
Quito, 440-4
Qunaytirah, 1175
Qunduz, 66
Quthing, 804
Qwaqwa, 1088, 1091, 1104
Qytet Stalin, 70

Raalte, 901
Rabat, 879-80, 882-3
Rabaul, 986
Rabigh, 1061
Racine (Wis.), 1549
Rae-Edzo, 331
Ragged Island, 174
Raiatéa, 514
Raichur, 653, 667
Raipur, 671-3
Raivaebae, 514
Raizet Airport, 500
Rajahmundry, 632, 655
Rajasthan, 632, 635, 643, 649, 652, 673, *683-4*
Rajin, 789
Rajkot, 632, 660, 662
Rajpur, 632
Rajshahi, 184, 189
Rakahanga, 931
Rakhine, 254
Raleigh (N.C.), 1378, 1509-11
Raman, 1210
Ramat Gan, 735, 741
Ramla, 734
Rampura-Agucha, 683
Ramsey, 1367, 1369
Ramsund, 952
Rancagua, 348
Ranchi, 632, 649, 658-9
Randburg, 1089
Randers, 415
Rangamati, 188
Rangiroa, 514
Rangoon, 254, 257
Rangpo, 686
Rangpur, 184, 188
Rankin Inlet, 329 331
Ranongga, 1082
Raoul Island, 930
Rapa-Iti, 514
Rapa Nui *see* Easter Island
Rapid City (S.D.), 1530, 1532
Rápti, 897
Raqqah, 1175
Rarotonga, 931-2
Ras Abu Aboud, 1030
Ras Abu Fontas, 1030
Rasal-Khafji, 1061
Ras al-Khaimah, 1293, 1295-6
Ras Dharbat Ali, 965
Rasht, 708-9
Ras Tanura, 1061-2
Ratchaburi, 1185
Rathdown, 719
Ratlam, 671-2
Ratnagiri, 673
Ratnapura, 1127
Rauma, 474
Ravenna, 744
Rawaki, 778
Rawalpindi, 971, 978
Rawdhatain, 793
Rawson, 91
Rayagada, 680
Raysut, 965
Razgrad, 243
Reading (Pa.), 1523
Reading (UK), 1301, 1350
Recife, 229-30, 232, 2356
Recklinghaisen, 534
Redbrisge, 1302
Redcliffe, 1625
Red Deer, 297-8
Redonda Island, 87
Red Sea Province (Sudan), 1137
Reef Islands, 1082
Regensburg, 534, 543, 548
Reggio di Calabria, 744, 752
Reggio nell'Emilia, 744
Regina (Canada), 272, 327, 329
Régina (French Guiana), 502
Rehoboth (Namibia), 890, 892
Rehovoth (Israel), 741
Reigate and Banstead, 1301
Reims, 483-4
Reinickendorf, 548
Reirson Island, 931
Relizane, 74
Remscheid, 534
Rendova, 1082
Renfrew, 1303
Renkum, 901
Rennell Island, 1082
Rennes, 483-4, 494
Reno (Nev.), 1379, 1496-8
Reno-Cannon International Airport, 1497
Renton (Wash.), 1544
Renukoot, 691
Rerkéssédougou, 392
Resettlement Fund for National Refugees and Over-Population, 41
Resistencia, 90, 95
Resita, 1034
Retalhuleu, 581
Rethymnon, 572
Réunion, 498, *505-7*
Reus, 1116
Rewa, 671
Reykjavík, 623, 627-8
Reynosa, 864
Rheden, 901
Rheinfelden, 1169
Rhineland-Palatinate, 533, 539, 543, *557-8*
Rhode Island, 1375, 1382, 1387, 1389, 1420, *1526-8*
Rhodes, 572
Rhodope, 572
Rhône-Alpes, 484
Rhymney Valley, 1302
Riaret, 74
Riau, 700
Ribe, 415
Ribeira Grande, 337
Ribeirao Prêto, 230
Riberalta, 222
Richards Bay, 1096
Richland (Wash.), 1544
Richmond (Canada), 304
Richmond (N.Y.), 1506
Richmond (Va.), 1378, 1542-3
Richmond-on-Thames, 1302
Ricino, 1166
Ridderkerk, 901
Rifa'a, 179, 181
Rift Valley, 773, 775
Riga, 1224, 1246, 1265, 1278-9
Riihimäki, 474
Rijeka, 1603
Rijssen, 901
Rijswijk, 901
Rikitea, 514
Rikkyo, 766
Rimini, 744
Rimitara, 514
Rîmnicu-Vîlcea, 1034
Rinas Airport, 71
Ringerike, 950
Ringkøbing, 415
Riobamba, 440
Rio Branco, 229
Río Cuarto, 91, 95
Rio de Janeiro, 229-30, 232-3, 235-6
Río Gellegos, 91
Rio Grande do Norte, 229
Rio Grande do Sul, 229, 233
Riohacha, 372
Río Muni, 458-60
Río Negro (Argentina), 91
Rio Negro (Brazil), 232
Río Negro (Uruguay), 1567, 1569
Río Piedras, 1563
Rio San Juan, 935
Ríos, Los, 440
Risalpur, 973
Risaralda, 372
Risdon, 150
Ritchie Archipelago, 694
Rivera, 1567
Rivercress, 807
River Falls (Wis.), 1552
Riverside (Calif.), 1378, 1437
Rivers (Nigeria), 943
Riverton (Wyo.), 1554
Rivno, 1264
Riyadh, 1058-9, 1061-3
Riyak, 802
Rize, 1208
Road Bay, 86
Road Town, 1591-2
Roanne, 484
Roanoke (Va.), 1379, 1542
Roberts International Airport, 809
Robertsport, 807
Rocha, 1567
Rochdale, 1301
Rochelle, La, 484
Rochester (Minn.), 1484
Rochester (N.H.), 1499
Rochester (N.Y.), 1378, 1506, 1508
Rochester upon Medway, 1301, 1349
Rockford (Ill.), 1378, 1458
Rockhampton, 137
Rock Hill (S.C.), 1530
Rockland (Me.), 1473
Rock Springs (Wyo.), 1553-4
Rockville (Md.), 1475
Rockville Center (N.Y.), 1506
Rodhopi, 572
Rodrigues, 859, 862
Roebourne, 160
Roermond, 901
Roeselare, 195
Rogaland, 949
Rohtak, 662
Roi Et, 1185
Rolas, 1056
Rolla (mo.), 1490
Roma (Lesotho), 806
Romana, La, 435
Romania, 48, 58, 125, *1033-40*
Rome (Italy), 744, 751-2
Rome (N.Y.), 1506
Ronaldsway Airport, 1369
Rondônia, 229
Roosendaal en Nispen, 901
Roque del Edste, 1115
Roraima, 231
Rosario, 91, 95
Roscommon, 720
Rose, 1559
Roseau, 433-4
Rose Hall, 592
Roseires, 1138
Rose Island, 1559
Roseville (Mich.), 1481
Rosita, 935
Roskilde, 415, 424
Rosmalen, 901
Ross and Cromarty, 1303
Ross Dependency, 30, 930-1
Rosslyn, 1107
Rosso, 856
Ross River, 333-4
Rostock, 526
Rostov-on-Don, 1224, 1246-7, 1254, 1265
Roswell (N. Mex.), 1503
Rosyth, 1314
Rota, 1119
Rotaima, 229
Rotherham, 1301
Rotorua, 917-18
Rotterdam, 901, 908
Rotuma, 469
Roubaix, 484
Rouen, 483-4
Roulers, 195
Rourkela, 680
Rovaniemi, 474, 476, 480
Roxburgh, 1303
Royal Oak (Mich.), 1481
Rrëshen, 68, 71
RSFSR *see* Russia

Rubengeri, 1041
Rucphen, 901
Ruda Słaska, 1012
Rügen, 530
Ruhengeri, 1043
Ruhuna, 1133
Rukwa, 1180
Rum Cay, 174
Rundu, 890
Rupnarayanpur, 693
Rurrenabaque, 222
Rurutu, 514
Ruse, 243
Rushcliffe, 1301
Russell Islands, 1082, 1084
Russia, 1223-5, 1228, *1253-5*, 1290
Rustavi, 1271
Rustenburg, 1106
Rust-op-Twist, 1565
Rutland (Vt.), 1540
Ruvuma, 1180
Ruwais, 1029, 1296
Ruwi, 965
Ruzyně Airport, 412
Rwanda, *1041-3*
Ryazan, 1224, 1240, 1254
Rybachi, 1291
Rybinsk, 1247
Rybnits, 1275
Ryburg, 1169
Ryedale, 1301
Ryukyu Islands, 759
Rzeszów, 1012

Saarbrücken, 534, 543, 559
Saarland, 533, 539, *559-60*
Saba, 913-15
Sabadell, 1116
Sabah, 831-2, 836, *839-41*, 844
Sabak, 1603
Sabaragamuwa, 1127
Sabar Kantha, 660
Sabha, 811, 815
Sabroom, 689
Sacatepéquez, 581
Sackville, 310
Sacramento (Calif.), 1378, 1437-9
Sada, 1111
Sadar, 689
Safaniyah, 1060
Safaqa, 448
Safi, 879-80, 883
Sagaing, 254
Sagamihara, 760
Sagar, 671-2
Sagarmatha, 897
Saginaw (Mich.), 1481
Sagunto, 1121
Saharanpur, 632
Saharawi Arab Democratic Republic *see* Western Sahara
Saida (Algeria), 74
Saida (Lebanon), 799-802
Saindak Thatta Sadha, 975
St Albans, 1301
St Albert, 297-8
St Andrew (Jamaica), 754
St Andrew's (UK), 1344, 1349-50
St Ann (Jamaica), 754
St Anne's (Channel Islands), 1373
St Aubin, 1371
St Barthélemy, 499-500
St Brandon Islands, 859
Saint-Brieuc, 484
St Catharines (Canada), 272
St Catherine (Jamaica), 754
Saint-Chamond, 484
St Charles (Mo.), 1489
St Christopher-Nevis, 29-30, 52, 55, *1044-6*
St Clair Shores (Mich.), 1481
St Cloud (Minn.), 1485
St Croix, 1563-6
Saint-Denis (France), 484
Saint-Denis (Réunion), 505
Saint-Denis-Gillot Airport, 506
St Edmundsbury, 1301
Sainte Étienne, 484
St Elizabeth, 754
St Gall(en), 818, 1164-6, 1173
St George's (Grenada), 578, 580
St George (Ut.), 1539
St Gilles, 195
St Helena, 30, *1047-8*
St Helens, 1301
St Helier, 1371
St Hubert, 276, 278
St James (Jamaica), 754
St John's (Antigua), 87-8
St John's (Canada), 272, 311
Saint John (Canada), 272, 307, 309-10
St John (Virgin Islands), 1564-6
St Joseph (Mo.), 1489
St Josse-ten-Noode, 195
St Kitts-Nevis, 29-30, 52, 55, *1044-6*
Saint-Laurent-du-Maroni, 501-2
St Louis (Mo.), 1377, 1489-90
Saint-Louis (Senegal), 1064, 1066-7
St Lucia, 30, 52, 55, *1049-50*
St Martin, 499-500
St Mary, 754
St Michel, 473-4
Saint-Nazaire, 484
St Nicolaas, 911
St Niklaas, 195
Saint-Paul Island, 511
St Paul (Minn.), 1378, 1484-5
St Peter Airport, 1371
St Peter Port, 1372-3
St Petersburg (Fla.), 1378, 1449
St Pierre and Miquelon, *508-10*
Saint-Pierre (Réunion), 505
St Pierre (St Pierre and Miquelon), 508-9
St Pierre Island (Seychelles), 1068
St Pölten, 168
St Thomas (Jamaica), 754
St Thomas (Virgin Islands), 1564-6
St Vincent and the Grenadines, 29-30, 55, *1051-3*
Saipan, 1558
Sakai, 760
Sakaka, 1058
Sakarya, 1208
Sakhalin, 1226, 1254
Sal, 336-8
Salah ad-Din, 714
Sălaj, 1034
Salalah, 965
Salamanca (Mexico), 864
Salamanca (Spain), 1115-16, 1125
Salamat, 345
Salamis, 574
Sala y Gómez, 348
Salcedo, 435
Saldanha, 1096
Sale (Australia), 153
Salekhard, 1264
Salem (India), 632, 653, 687
Salem (Oreg.), 1520, 1522
Salé (Morocco), 879-80
Salerno, 744, 752
Salford, 1301, 1350
Salgótarján, 614
Salif, 1598
Salima, 829
Salina (Kans.), 1467
Salina Cruz, 868
Salisbury (UK), 1301
Salisbury (Zimbabwe) *see* Harare
Salmon Arm, 304
Salonica, 572
Salta, 90, 95
Salt Cay, 1215-16
Saltillo, 863-4
Salt Lake City (Ut.), 1378, 1538-9
Salto, 1567, 1570
Salvador (Brazil), 229-30, 232, 235, 2356
Salvador, El, 52, 54, *453-7*
Salzburg, 168-9, 172-3
Salzglitter, 534
Sam Ambrosio, 348
Samaná, 435
Samar, 1004
Samarinda, 701
Samarkand, 1281, 1285-7
Samarra, 714
Samarska Luka, 1240
Samastipur, 659
Samoa *see* American Samoa; Western Samoa
Samos, 572
Samsun, 1208, 1210, 1212
San'a, 1596-8
San Ambrosio, 348
Sánándáj, 708
San Andrés, 372
San Andrés y Providencia, 372
San Angelo (Tex.), 1535
San Antonio (Tex.), 1377, 1535, 1537
San Baudilio de Llobregat, 1116
San Bernardino (Calif.), 1378, 1437
San Bernardo (Chile), 348
San Blas, 980
San Carlos (Costa Rica), 387
San Carlos (Luzon, Philippines), 1004
San Carlos (Negros, Philippines), 1004
San Carlos (Nicaragua), 935
San Carlos (Venezuela), 1578
Sánchez Ramírez, 435
San Cristóbal (Dominican Republic), 435
San Cristobal (Solomon Islands), 1082
San Cristóbal (Venezuela), 1578
Sancti Spíritus, 394
Sandakan, 831, 836, 839-40
Sandefjord, 950
San Diego (Calif.), 1377, 1437, 1439
Sand Island, 1377, 1561
Sandnes, 950
Sandoy, 426
Sandviken, 1149
Sandwell, 1301
Sandy City (Ut.), 1538
San Felipe (Venezuela), 1578
San Félix (Chile), 348
San Félix (Venezuela), 1583
San Fernando (Spain), 1116
San Fernando (Trinidad and Tobago), 1198
San Fernando (Venezuela), 1578, 1583
San Francisco (Calif.), 1377, 1437, 1439
San Francisco (El Salvador), 453
San Francisco de Macoris, 435
Sangaredi, 588
Sangha, 341, 381
Sangli, 673
Sangrur, 681
Sangster International Airport, 757
Sanguie, 250
San Ignacio de Velasco, 222
Saniquillie, 807
San Isidro, 91
San Isidro el General, 388
Sani Suwayf, 446
San José (Calif.), 1377, 1437, 1439
San José (Costa Rica), 385, 388-9
San José (Uruguay), 1567, 1569
San José del Guaviare, 373

San Juan (Argentina), 90-1, 93, 95
San Juan (Dominican Republic), 435
San Juan (Puerto Rico), 1561, 1563
San Juan (Venezuela), 1578
San Juan de la Managuana, 435
San Juan del Monte, 1004
San Juan del Sur, 938
San Justo, 91
Sankt Pölten, 168
Sanliurfa, 1208
San Lorenzo, 443
San Luis, 90
San Luis Potosí, 863-4
San Marcos (Guatemala), 581
San Marcos (Tex.), 1537
San Marino, 40, 750, *1054-5*
San Martin (Peru), 998
Sanmatenga, 250
San Miguel (El Salvador), 453, 455-6
San Miguelito, 980
San Miguel de Tucumán, 90-1
San Nicolás, 91
San Nicolás de los Garzas, 864
San Pablo (Philippines), 1004
San Pedro (Côte d'Ivoire), 393
San Pedro (Paraguay), 992
San Pedro de Macorís, 435
San Pedro Sula, 602-3, 605
San Salvador (Bahamas), 174
San Salvador (El Salvador), 453-6
San Salvador de Jujuy, 90, 95
San Sebastián (Spain), 1115-16
Santa Ana (Calif.), 1378, 1437
Santa Ana (El Salvador), 453, 455-6
Santa Bárbara (Honduras), 602
Santa Catarina (Brazil), 229, 233-4
Santa Catarina (Cape Verde), 337
Santa Clara, 394
Santa Coloma de Gramanet, 1116
Santa Cruz (Argentina), 91
Santa Cruz (Bolivia), 218, 220-3
Santa Cruz (Cape Verde), 337
Santa Cruz (Solomon Islands), 1082
Santa Cruz de Tenerife, 1114-18
Santa Fé (Argentina), 90, 95
Santa Fé (N. Mex.), 1503-4
Santa Isabel Island, 1082
Santa Luiza, 337
Santa Maria (Azores), 1020, 1024
Santa Marta, 372
Santander (Colombia), 372
Santander (Spain), 1115-16, 1125
Santarém, 1020, 1025
Santa Rosa (Argentina), 90, 95
Santa Rosa (Guatemala), 581
Santa Rosalia, 868
Santa Rosa de Copan, 602
Santhalpargana, 658
Santiago (Dominican Republic), 435
Santiago (Panama), 980
Santiago (Chile), 348-9, 352-3
Santiago de Compostela, 1115-16, 1125
Santiago de Cuba, 394, 398
Santiago del Estero, 90, 95
Santiago de los Caballeros, 435
Santiago de María, 456
Santiago Rodríguez, 435
Santiniketan, 693
Santo, 517, 1572-4
Santo André, 230
Santo Antão, 336-7
Santo Domingo, 435-6, 438
Santo Domingo de los Colorados, 443
Santorin, 576
Santos (Brazil), 230, 235
Santo Tomás (Guatemala), 582
Santo Tomás de Castilla, 582, 584
San Vicente (El Salvador), 453, 456
Sanyang, 523
São António, 1056
São Bernardo do Campo, 230
São Gonçalo, 230
São João de Meriti, 230
São Jorge, 1020
São José dos Campos, 230
São Luis, 229
São Miguel, 1020
São Nicolau, 336-7
São Paulo, 229-30, 232, 234-5
São Tiago, 336-7
São Tomé, 1056
São Tomé e Príncipe, *1056-7*
São Vicente, 336-7
Sapele, 944, 946
Sapporo, 759-60, 766
Saragossa *see* Zaragoza
Sarajevo, 1603-4, 1608-9, 1611
Saramacca, 1140-2
Sarandë, 68, 72
Saransk, 1259
Saratov, 1224, 1246, 1251, 1254
Sarava, 1289
Sarawak, 831-2, 836, *842-4*
Sardinia, 744, 746, 749
Sargodha, 971
Sarh, 345, 347
Sári, 708
Sar-i-Pol, 65
Sariwon, 786-7
Sark, 1303, 1369-70, *1373*
Sarobi, 65
Sasaram, 659
Sasebo, 760, 762
Saskatchewan, 271-3, 279, 283-5, 291, *327-9*
Saskatoon, 272, 327, 329
Sasolburg, 1089, 1105
Sassandra, 390
Sassari, 744, 749, 752
Sassnitz, 528
Satara, 673
Satkhira, 188
Satpura, 671
Sattahip, 1186
Satu Mare, 1034
Sauðákrókur, 623
Saudi Arabia, 57, 791, *1058-63*
Saurashtra, 653
Sava'i, 1593
Savannah (Ga.), 1378, 1451-2
Savannakhét, 795, 798
Savé, 210
Savonlinna, 474
Sawai Madhopur, 684
Sawfajjin, 811
Sawhâj, 446
Saxony, Lower, 533, 538-9, *554-5*
Say, 941
Scampton, 1317
Scarborough (Trinidad and Tobago), 1198
Scarborough (UK), 1301
Schaerbeek, 195
Schaffhausen, 1164, 1166
Scharhörn, 551
Schenectady (N.Y.), 1506, 1508
Schiedam, 901
Schijndel, 901
Schleswig-Holstein, 533, 539, 555, *560-2*
Schoelcher, 503
Schöneberg, 548
Schweizerhalle, 1169
Schwerin, 526
Schwyz, 1164, 1166
Scilly Isles, 1300
Scotland, 1234, *1302-3*, 1307, 1311-13, 1320, 1327, 1333, 1340-1, 1344-5, 1348-9, 1356-7
Scott Base, 931
Scottsdale (Ariz.), 1433
Scranton (Pa.), 1523
Scutari *see* Shkodër
Seaford City (Del.), 1445
Sealdah, 693
Seattle (Wash.), 1377, 1544-5
Seattle-Tacoma Airport, 1545
Seawell Airport, 192
Sebha, 814
Secunderabad, 647
Sedgemoor, 1301
Sedom, 739
Seeb, 965-6, 968
Sefton, 1301
Segboroué, 210
Ségou, 847
Segovia, 1115
Séguéla, 390
Seibo, El, 435
Seinäjoki, 474
Seine-Maritime, 491
Sekondi-Takoradi, 563-6
SELA, *54*
Selangor, 831-2, 837
Selby, 1301
Selebi-Phikwe, 224-5
Selenicë, 70
Selfoss, 623
Selkirk (Botswana), 226
Selkirk (Canada), 304
Selosesha, 1107
Seltjarnarnes, 623
Semarang, 701, 704
Sembarang, 1078
Semipalatinsk, 1282-3
Semnán, 708
Semporna, 840
Sendai, 759-60
Senegal, 522, 524, *1064-7*
Sennar Junction, 1138
Sèno, 250
Sensuntepeque, 453
Seo de Urgel, 80, 1123
Seongnam, 782
Seoul, 781-2, 784
Sepik, 986
Sept-Iles, 325
Seraing, 195
Serbia, 1603, 1605, 1610, *1613-14*
Serdang, 839
Serekunda, 522
Seremban, 831
Serena, La, 348
Seretse Khama International Airport, 226
Sergipe, 229
Seria, 239-41
Serowe, 224
Serravalle, 1054
Serres, 572
Seti, 897
Sétif, 74, 78
Settat, 879
Setúbal, 1020, 1024-5
Sevastopol, 1231, 1235
Sevenoaks, 1301
Severnaya Zemlya, 1263
Severočeský Region, 408
Severodvinsk, 1235
Severomoravský Region, 408
Severomorsk, 1231
Seville, 1114-16, 1125
Seward (Ak.), 1432
Seward (Nebr.), 1495
Seychelles, 30, 238, 505, *1068-70*
Seyðisfjörður, 623
Sfax, 1202-3, 1205
Sfîntu Gheorghe, 1034
's-Gravenhage, 900-1

Sha Alam, 831, 839
Shaanxi, 355, 364
Shaba, 1616, 1618
Shabani, 1625
Shabwa, 1600-1
Shag Island, 128
Shahdol, 671
Shahjahanpur, 691
Shahr-e-Kord, 708
Shaki, 944
Shandong, 355, 360, 364
Shanghai, 355-6, 358, 362-3, 365
Shanxi, 355, 360, 362, 364-5
Sharigh, 975
Sharin Gol, 875
Sharjah, 1293-6
Sharqîya, 446
Shati, 811
Sha Tin, 607, 610
Shayandima, 1110
Sheboygan (Wis.), 1549
Sheffield, 1301, 1350
Shek Kong, 608
Shellharbour, 129
Shencottah, 669, 687
Shendi, 1138
Shengli, 360
Shenyang, 363
Shepherdstown (W. Va.), 1548
Shepparton, 152-3, 156
Sherbro, 1073
Sherbrooke (Canada), 272, 324
Sheridan (Wyo.), 1553-4
Sherkhan Bandar, 66
Sherpur, 64
's-Hertogenbosch, 900-1
Shetland Islands, 1303
Sheung Wan, 611
Shevchenko, 1240
Shiberghán, 63, 65-6
Shibin el-Kom, 446
Shijiazhuang, 355-6
Shikarpur, 975
Shikoku, 759
Shillong, 639, 652, 676-7
Shimla, 652, 663-5
Shimoga, 668
Shimonoseki, 760
Shindand, 64
Shinyanga, 1180
Shippegan, 310
Shiráz, 708-9
Shiselweni, 1145
Shizuoka, 760
Shkodër, 68-9, 71
Shoa, 462
Shoalhaven, 129
Sholapur, 632, 673-4
Shomolu, 944
Shortland Islands, 1082
Shreveport (La.), 1378, 1471
Shrewsbury and Atcham, 1301
Shropshire, 1300
Shuaiba, 794
Shubrâ al-Khayma, 446
Shumen, 243
Shuwaikh, 794
Sialkot, 971
Siang, 655
Siauliai, 1280
Sibasa, 1109
Sibenik, 1604
Sibi, 975
Sibiti, 381
Sibiu, 1034, 1039
Sibu, 831, 836, 842-3
Sichuan, 355, 360, 364
Sicily, 744, 746, 749
Sidamo, 462
Sidi-Bel-Abbés, 74, 78
Sidi Bilal, 812
Sidi Bouzid, 1202
Sidi Kacem, 879
Sidon, 799-802
Siedlce, 1012
Siegen, 534
Siena, 752
Sieradz, 1012
Sierra Leone, 30, *1071-4*
Siglufjörður, 623
Signatepeque, 602
Sikasso, 847
Sikkim, 632, 635, 649, 652-3, *684-6*
Silay, 1004
Silchar, 656-7
Silhouette Island, 1068
Siliana, 1202
Siliguri, 686
Silvassa, 695
Silver Bow (Mont.), 1491
Silver City (N. Mex.), 1505
Silver Spring (Md.), 1475
Simla, 652, 663-5
Simonstown, 1092
Simplon, 1172
Sinai, 276
Sinai al-Janûbîya, 446
Sinai ash-Shamâliya, 446
Sinaloa, 863
Sincelejo, 372
Sind, 971-2, 976, 979
Singa, 1138
Singapore, 30, 50-1, 831, *1075-81*
Singapore International Airport, 1079
Singave, 516-17
Singida, 1180
Singtam, 686
Sinkat, 1137-8
Sinoe, 807
Sinoia, 1625
Sinop, 1208
Sint Eustatius, 913-15
Sint Maarten, 913-15
Sint Nicolaas, 911
Sint Niklaas, 195
Sintra, 1025
Sinuiju, 786-7, 789
Sioux City (Ia.), 1464-5
Sioux Falls (S.D.), 1530-1
Sirmur, 663
Sirsa, 662
Sissili, 250
Sistán and Balúchestán, 708
Siteki, 1144
Sitka (Ak.), 1431
Sitra, 179
Sittard, 901
Sitten, 1173
Sittwe, 254, 257
Sivas, 1208
Skagway (Ak.), 1431-2
Skálafjørður, 427
Skaraborg, 1148
Skardu, 977
Skarsterlân, 901
Skellefteå, 1149
Skhirra, La, 1205
Skien, 950
Skierniewice, 1012
Skikda, 74
Skopje, 1603, 1608-9, 1612
Skövde, 1149
Skrapar, 68
Skye and Lochalsh, 1303
Slatina, 1034
Slavonski Brod, 1603
Sliedrecht, 901
Sligo, 720, 730
Sliven, 243
Slobodzeisk, 1275
Slobozia, 1034
Slough, 1301
Slovakia, 407-8, 413
Slovenia, 1603, 1605, 1610, *1615*
Słupsk, 1012
Slyudianka, 1241
Smalkalden, 1142
Smallingerland, 901
Smara, 879, 1126
Smederova, 1603
Smithfield (R.I.), 1528
Smolensk, 1254
Snares Islands, 930
Sneek, 901
Society Archipelago, 51
Socna, 814
Socorro (N. Mex.), 1505
Socotra Island, 1600
Södermanland, 1148
Södertälje, 1149
Soest, 901
Sofala, 885, 887
Sofia, 243, 247-9, 254
Sogn og Fjordane, 949
Sohag, 446
Sohar, 965, 967-8
Sokodé, 1191, 1193
Sokolov, 411
Sokoto, 943-4
Solan, 665
Solander Island, 930
Soldeu, 80
Soleure, 1164, 1166, 1173
Solihull, 1301
Solingen, 534
Sollentuna, 1149
Solna, 1149
Sololá, 581
Solomon Islands, 29-30, 56, *1082-4*
Solothurn, 1164, 1166, 1173
Solwezi, 1621
Somalia, 57, *1085-7*
Sombrero Island, 85
Somerset, 1300-1
Somersworth (N.H.), 1499
Somerville (Mass.), 1478
Somogy, 614
Sonamura, 689
Sønderjylland, 415
Song Be, 1585
Songkhla, 1185-6
Sonipat, 662
Son La, 1585
Sonora, 863, 867
Sonsonate, 453, 455-6
Sopore, 666
Sopot, 1011
Soria, 1115
Soriano, 1567, 1569
Sorocaba, 230
Sorok, 1275
Sor Range, 975
Sortavala, 1258
Sør-Trøndelag, 949
Sosa Méndez, 1581
Soshanguve, 1089
Sosnowiec, 1012
Sotavento, 336-7
Soubré, 390
Soudha Bay, 574
Souk Ahras, 74
Soum, 250
Sourou, 250
Sousse, 1202, 1205
South Africa, 29, 125, 889-91, *1088-100*
—Homelands, 1091, *1105-12*
—Provinces, *1100-5*
Southampton, 1301, 1350
South Australia, 97-8, 101, 111, 114, 120, 123, *142-7*
South Bedfordshire, 1301
South Bend (Ind.), 1378, 1461
South Caicos, 1215-16
South Cambridgeshire, 1301
South Carolina, 1376, 1382, 1386-7, 1407, *1528-30*
South Dakota, 1376, 1381, 1387, 1407, *1530-2*
South-East Lancashire, 1302
Southend on Sea, 1301
Southern District (Israel), 734
Southern Grenadine Islands, 578
Southern Highlands (Papua New Guinea), 986, 988
Southern Province (Saudi Arabia), 1058
Southern Province (Sierra Leone), 1071
Southern Province (Sri Lanka), 1127
Southern Province (Uganda), 1219
Southern Province (Zambia), 1621
Southern Region (Malawi), 827
Southern Region (Sudan), 1135, 1137
Southern Yemen *see* Yemen People's Democratic Republic
Southfield (Mich.), 1481
South Georgia, 30, 91, 468, *1113*
South Glamorgan, 1300
South Island (New Zealand), 916-17, 921, 925
South Kesteven, 1301
South Kingstown (R.I.), 1528
South Lakeland, 1301

Southland (New Zealand), 917
South Norfolk, 1301
South Orkney Islands, 91, 238
South Ossetia, 1270, *1273*
South Oxfordshire, 1301
South Pacific Forum, *56*
South Portland (Me.), 1473
South Region (Iceland), 623
South Ribble, 1301
South Sandwich Islands, 30, 91, 468, *1113*
South Shetland Islands, 238
South Somerset, 1301
South Staffordshire, 1301
South Suburban, 632
South Tyneside, 1301
Southwark, 1302
South West Africa *see* Namibia
South West Peninsula Region (Iceland), 623
South Yemen *see* Yemen People's Democratic Republic
South Yorkshire, 129
Soviet Union *see* Union of Soviet Socialist Republics
Sovyetsk, 1225
Sozoplo, 245
Spain, 36, 40, 45, 125, *1114-26*
Spandau, 548
Spanish Town, 754
Sparks (Nev.), 1496
Spartanburg (S.C.), 1528
Sparte, 571
Spearfish (S.D.), 1532
Speyer, 543, 558
Spezia, La, 744, 747
Spijkenisse, 901
Spiti, 663
Spitsbergen, 961
Split, 1603-4, 1608
Spokane (Wash.), 1378, 1544
Springdale (Ark.), 1435
Springfield (Ill.), 1458-9
Springfield (Mass.), 1378, 1478
Springfield (Mo.), 1378, 1489
Springfield (Oh.), 1514
Springfield (Oreg.), 1520
Springlands, 595
Spruce Grove, 297-8
Sri Jawardenepura, 1133
Sri Lanka, 29, 50, *1127-34*
Srinagar, 632, 652, 665-6, 691
Sri Saket, 1185
Stadskanaal, 901
Stafford, 1301
Staffordshire, 1300-1
Staffordshire Moorlands, 1301
Stamford (Conn.), 1378, 1443
Stanley (Falkland Islands), 466-8
Stanley Fort (Hong Kong), 608
Stanleyville *see* Kisangani
Stann Creek, 204
Stanton (Del.), 1446
Stara Zagora, 243
Starkville (Miss.), 1488
Staten Island (N.Y.), 1506
Stavanger, 950
Stavropol, 1240, 1247, 1254, 1262
Steenwijk, 901
Steglitz, 548
Stein, 901
Steinkjer, 950
Stellenbosch, 1098
Stepanakert, 1269-70
Stephenville, 311
Sterling Heights (Mich.), 1378, 1481
Stettin, 412, 1011-13, 1017
Stevens Point (Wis.), 1552
Stewart Island, 916
Stewartry, 1303
Steyr, 168
Stillwater (Okla.), 1519
Stirling, 1303, 1349-50
Stockholm, 1148-9, 1152, 1158
Stockport, 1301
Stockton (Calif.), 1378, 1437
Stockton on Tees, 1301
Stoke on Trent, 1301
Storrs (Conn.), 1444
Storstrøm, 415
Stout (Wis.), 1552
Strabane, 1359
Stranraer, 1365
Strasbourg, 483-4, 487
Stråssa, 1154
Stratford on Avon, 1301
Strathclyde, 1303
Strathkelvin, 1303
Stredočeský Region, 408
Stredoslovenský Region, 408
Stremoy, 426
Stroud, 1301
Stuttgart, 534, 543, 545, 547
Styria, 168-9
Suao, 370
Subotica, 1603
Subsansiri, 655
Sucaeva, 1034
Suchitepéquez, 581
Sucre (Bolivia), 218-19, 221-3
Sucre (Colombia), 372
Sucre (Venezuela), 1578, 1581
Sudan, 57, *1135-9*
Sudbury (Canada), 272, 319
Sud Department (Haiti), 597
Sud-Est Department (Haiti), 597
Sud-Ouest Province (Cameroon), 265
Sud Province (Cameroon), 265
Sud Province (New Caledonia), 512
Suðuroy, 426
Suez, 446, 451
Suffolk, 1300
Suffolk Coastal, 1301
Suhl, 526
Sui, 975
Suita, 760
Sukabumi, 701
Sukhumi, 1270, 1272
Sukkur, 975
Sukuta, 522
Sulawesi, 700-1, 704
Sumat(e)ra, 700, 704-5
Sumgait, 1268-9
Summerside, 322
Sumy, 1264
Sundas, Lesser, 700-1
Sunday Island, 930
Sunderland, 1301
Sundsvall, 1149
Sungei Golok, 838
Sunnyvale (Calif.), 1378
Sunshine Coast, 137
Sunyani, 563, 566
Suoyarvi, 1258
Superior (Wis.), 1549, 1551-2
Sur, 965, 968
Surabaya, 701, 704
Surakarta, 701
Surat, 632, 660
Surendranagar, 660
Surgut, 1246
Surin, 1185
Suriname, 52, 592, *1140-3*
Surkhan-Darya, 1286
Surrey (Canada), 304
Surrey (UK), 1300, 1350
Surt, 811
Sürt, 1208
Sussex, 1300-1, 1350
Sutherland, 1303
Sutton, 1302
Suva, 469-72
Suwaiq, 965
Suwałki, 1012
Suwarrow Island, 931
Suwaydá, 1175
Suweon, 782
Suykkur, 971
Svalbard, 949, 953, *961-2*
Sverdlovsk, 1224, 1246, 1251, 1254
Swain's Island, 1558-9, 1561
Swakopmund, 891
Swale, 1301
Swan Hill, 153
Swansea, 1302, 1349-50
Swapokmund, 890
Swaziland, 30, 1095, *1144-7*
Sweden, 40, 47, *1148-63*
Swift Current, 327
Swindon, 1336
Swinoujscie, 1014
Switzerland, 40, 47, 817-18, *1164-74*
Sydney (Australia), 97-8, 102-3, 111-12, 135
Sydney (Canada), 315
Sydney Mines, 315
Syktyvkar, 1258
Sylhet (Bangladesh), 184, 188, 656
Sylhet (Pakistan), 970
Syra, 576
Syracuse (Italy), 744
Syracuse (N.Y.), 1378, 1506, 1508
Syr-Darya, 1285
Syria, 45, 57, 446, 734, *1175-9*
Szabolcs-Szatmár, 614
Szczecin, 412, 1011-13, 1017
Szeged, 614, 621
Székesfehérvár, 614
Szekszárd, 614
Szolnok, 614
Szombathely, 615

Taabo, 392
Tabasco, 863
Tabiteuea, 778
Tablada, 1119
Tabora, 1180
Taboshar, 1241
Tabouk, 1058
Tabriz, 708-9
Tabueran Island, 778
Täby, 1149
Táchira, 1578, 1581
Tacloban, 1004
Tacna, 998
Tacoma (Wash.), 1379, 1544
Tacuarembó, 1567
Tadjoura, 430
Tadzhikistan, 1224, 1228, 1281, *1288-90*
Taegu, 781-2
Taejon, 782
Taff Ely, 1302
Tafilah, 768
Tafuna, 1560
Tagant, 856
Tahaa, 514
Tahiti, 514-15
Tahlequah (Okla.), 1519
Tahoua, 940, 942
Tahuata, 514
Taichung, 367, 370
Taif, 1058, 1063
Taimyr, 1254, *1263*
Tainan, 367
Taipa, 1027-8
Taipei, 367, 370
Taiping (Malaysia), 831
Tai Po, 607
Taitung, 367
Taiwan, 354, *366-71*
Taiyuan, 355
Ta'iz, 1596, 1598-9
Tajikistan *see* Tadzhikistan
Takamatsu, 760
Takatsuki, 760
Takeo, 263
Takoradi, 565-6
Takurea, 931
Talara, 1000
Talca, 348
Talcahuano, 348
Taldo, 1177
Taldy-Kurgan, 1282
Tallahassee (Fla.), 1449-51
Tallinn, 1224, 1276-7
Tamale, 564, 566
Tamana, 778
Tamanrasset, 74
Tamaulipas, 863

Tambacounda, 1064, 1066
Tambov, 1254
Tameside, 1301
Tamil Nadu, 632, 635, 643, 649, 652, *686-9*
Ta'mim, 714
Tammerfors, 474, 481
Tampa (Fla.), 1378, 1449, 1451
Tampere, 474, 481
Tampico, 868
Tamuning, 1556
Tamworth (Australia), 129
Tandil, 95
Tandjilé, 345-6
Tanezrouft, 941
Tanga, 1180
Tangail, 184
Tangier, 879-80
Tangshan, 356
Tanjungkarang, 700
Tanjung Priok, 705
Tanna, 1572
Tanta, 446
Tan-Tan, 879
Tanzania, 30, *1180-4*
Taoihae, 514
Taounate, 879
Taoyuan, 367, 370
Tapoa, 250
Tarabulus, 812
Taranaki, 916
Taranto, 744
Tarapacá, 348, 351
Tarassa, 1116
Tarawa, 778-80
Tarcoola, 111
Taree, 129
Tarhuna, 814
Tarhunah, 811
Tarija, 218-19, 222-3
Tarkwa, 563
Tarnobrzeg, 1012
Tarnów, 1012
Taroudant, 879
Tarrafal, 337
Tarragona, 1115-16
Tartous, 1175
Tartu, 1251, 1276-7
Tartus, 1176
Tashauz, 1284-5
Tashguzar, 66
Tashkent, 1224, 1246, 1248, 1251, 1281, 1286-7
Taskizak, 1209
Tasmania, 97-8, 101, 111, 114, 125, *147-52*
Tata, 879
Tatabánya, 614
Tataouine, 1202
Tatar Republic, 1254, *1260*
Ta'u, 1559
Taunggyi, 254, 257
Taunton Deane, 1301
Taupo, 916
Tauranga, 916-17
Tavastehus, 473-4
Tawau, 839-40
Taweela, 1294
Taylor (Mich.), 1481
Tay Ninh, 1585
Tayside Region, 1303
Taza, 879-80
Tbilisi, 1224, 1245-6, 1248, 1251, 1265, 1270-2
Tchibanga, 518
Tchimbélé, 519
Tébessa, 74
Tegal, 701
Tegucigalpa, 602-3, 605
Tehrán, 708-9
Teignbridge, 1301
Tejerías, 1581
Tekirdağ, 1208
Tela, 602-3
Telanaipura, 700
Tel Aviv, 734-5, 739
Telemark, 949
Teleorman, 1034
Teluk Anson, 838
Tema, 563-6
Temburong, 239
Temotu, 1082
Tempe (Ariz.), 1378, 1433-4
Tempelhof, 548
Temuco, 348
Tena, 440
Tenali, 654
Tenasserim, 254
Tendring, 1301
Tenerife, 1115
Tenkodogo, 250
Tennant Creek, 121-3
Tennessee, 1376, 1382, 1387, 1407, 1409, *1532-4*
Tenom, 840-1
Tepelenë, 68
Tepic, 863-4
Teraina Island, 778
Teramo, 752
Terengganu, 831-2
Teresina, 229-30
Termez, 66, 1287, 1289
Terneuzen, 901
Terni, 744
Ternitz, 168
Ternopol, 1264
Terrace, 304
Terre Adélie, 124, 511
Terre-de-Basse, 499
Terre Haute (Ind.), 1461, 1463
Teruel, 1114
Teslin, 333
Test Valley, 1301
Tete, 885
Tetiaroa, 514
Tétouan, 879-80
Tetovo, 1603
Texarkarna (Ark.), 1435
Texas, 1376, 1381, 1387, 1407-8, *1534-7*
Teyateyaneng, 804
Tezpur, 657
Thaba-Tseka, 804
Thadeua, 797
Thai Binh, 1585
Thailand, 50-1, *1185-90*
Thakurgaon, 188
Thames-Coromandel, 916
Thamesdown, 1301
Thames Valley (New Zealand), 916
Thana, 632, 673-4
Thanet, 1301
Thanh Hoa, 1585
Thanh Pho, 1585
Theodore Francis Green Airport, 1527
Thesprotia, 571
Thessaloniki, 572
Thessaly, 571, 575
Thiès, 1064, 1066
Thika, 773
Thimphu, 215-17
Thohoyandou, 1109-10
Thompson, 304
Thousand Oaks (Calif.), 1437
Thrace, 572
Three Kings Islands, 930
Thuan Hai, 1585
Thule, 427
Thunder Bay, 272
Thurgau, 1164, 1166
Thurrock, 1301
Tianjin, 355-6, 362-3, 365
Tianshui, 362
Tiaret, 78
Tibet, 355, *356*
Ticino, 1164-5, 1173
Tiel, 901
Tien Giang, 1585
Tiergarten, 548
Tierra del Fuego, 90-1
Tigre (Argentina), 91
Tigre (Ethiopa), 461-2
Tihama, 1597
Tijit, 679
Tijuana, 864
Tiko, 268
Tikopia, 1082
Tilarán, 388
Tilburg, 901
Timaru, 917
Timiş, 1034
Timişoara, 1034, 1039
Timor Timur, 701
Tindouf, 74, 1126
Tingréla, 390
Tin Shui Wai, 607
Tinsukia, 656
Tipaza, 74
Tipitapi, 936
Tipperary, 719
Tirana, 68-9, 71-2
Tirap, 655
Tiraspol, 1275
Tirgovişte, 1034
Tîrgu Jiu, 1034
Tîrgu Mures, 1034
Tiris el Gharbi(y)a *see* Western Sahara
Tiris Zemmour, 856
Tirol, 168-9
Tiruchirapalli, 632, 688
Tirunelveli, 632
Tirupathi, 654-5
Tissemsilt, 74
Titograd, 1603, 1608-9, 1613
Titova Mitrovica, 1603
Tivat, 1608
Tizi-Ouzou, 74, 78
Tiznit, 879
Tkibuli, 1271
Tkvarcheli, 1271
Tlaquepaque, 864
Tlaxcala, 863
Tlemcen, 74, 78
Tlokweng, 224
Toamasina, 823, 825-6
Tobago, 1198-9
Tobruk, 811-12
Togliatti, 1224
Togo, *1191-4*
Tohoku, 759, 766
Tokat, 1208
Tokelau, 30, 930
Tokmak, 1290
Toknam, 789
Tokoin Airport, 1193
Tokorozawa, 760
Toksong, 789
Tokushima, 760
Tokyo, 759-61, 765-6
Tolbukhin, 243
Toledo (Belize), 204
Toledo (Oh.), 1378, 1514, 1516
Toledo (Spain), 1115
Toliary, 823
Tolima, 372, 375
Tolna, 614
Toluca de Lerdo, 863-4
Tolyatti, 1224
Tombali, 589
Tombouctou, 847, 849
Tomsk, 1224, 1251, 1254
Tonbridge and Malling, 1301
Tonga, 30, 56, *1195-7*
Tongareva, 931
Tongariro, 916
Tongatapú, 1195, 1197
Toowoomba, 137
Topeka (Kans.), 1378, 1466
Torbay, 1301
Torfaen, 1302
Torghundi, 66
Torkham, 66
Tornio, 474
Toronto, 272, 289, 319-21
Torrance (Calif.), 1378, 1437
Torre del Greco, 744
Torrejón de Ardoz, 1116
Torreón, 864
Torres Vedras, 1025
Torrington (Wyo.), 1554
Tórshavn, 426-7
Tortola, 1591-2
Torun, 1012
Toscana, 743
Totonicapán, 581
Touba, 390, 1066
Toulon, 484, 488
Toulouse, 484, 496
Tourcoing, 484
Tournai, 195
Tours, 484
Tower Hamlets, 1302
Townsville, 97, 137
Towson (Md.), 1475, 1477
Toyama, 760
Toyohashi, 760
Toyonaka, 760
Toyota, 760
Tozeur, 1202
Trabzon, 1208, 1211-12
Trade Union Internationals, 33
Trafford, 1301
Trakya, 1207
Tralee, 730
Transkei, 1091, 1095, *11078*
Transvaal, 1088, 1097, *1102-4*

Traralgon, 153
Trarza, 856
Traun, 168
Treasury Islands, 1082
Treceira, 1020
Treinta y Tres, 1567
Trelawny, 754
Trengganu, 837
Trentino-Alto Adige, 743, 746
Trento, 743-4, 752
Trenton (Canada), 276-7
Trenton (N.J.), 1501
Treptow, 548
Trier, 543, 558
Trieste, 744, 752
Trikkala, 571
Trincomalee, 1127-9
Trinidad (Bolivia), 218-19, 222-3
Trinidad (Uruguay), 1567
Trinidad and Tobago, 30, 52, 55, *1198-201*
Tripoli (Lebanon), 799-802
Tripoli (Libya), 811, 814-15
Tripolis (Greece), 571
Tripolitania, 813-14
Tripura, 632, 635, 649, 652-3, *689-90*
Tristan da Cunha, 30, *1048*
Trivandrum, 632, 648, 652, 669-70, 687
Trnava, 408, 413
Trois-Rivières, 272, 324
Trollhättan, 1149
Tromelin, 505
Tromsø, 950, 952, 958
Trondheim, 950, 958
Tropojë, 68
Troyes, 484
Troy (Mich.), 1481
Troy (N.Y.), 1506, 1508
Troy Hills (N.J.), 1501
Trujillo (Peru), 998
Trujillo (Venezuela), 1578
Truk, 1558
Truro (Canada), 315, 318
Tselinograd, 1246, 1282
Tsévié, 1191
Tshikondeni, 1109
Tsikhisdziri, 1273
Tsing Yi, 607
Tskhinvali, 1273
Tsueng Kwan O, 607
Tsuen Wan, 607, 611
Tsumeb, 890
Tuamoto Archipelago, 514
Tübingen, 543, 547
Tubmanburg, 807
Tubuai Islands, 514
Tucson (Ariz.), 1378, 1433-4
Tucumán, 90, 95
Tucupita, 1578, 1583
Tuen Mun, 607
Tuensang, 678
TUI, 33
Tuimazy, 1240
Tula, 1224, 1254
Tulcán, 440
Tulcea, 1034
Tuli, 679
Tulsa (Okla.), 1378, 1517-19
Tumangan, 789
Tumbes, 998
Tumkur, 668
Tumpat, 838
Tumu, 566
Tunas, Las, 394
Tunbridge Wells, 1301
Tunceli, 1208
Tundo, 659
Tungurahua, 440
Tunis, 1202, 1205
Tunis-Carthage, 1205
Tunis-Goulette, 1202, 1205
Tunisia, 45, 57, *1202-6*
Tunja, 372
Tupelo (Miss.), 1486
Tupiza, 222
Tura, 677, 1263
Turéia, 514
Turfan, 362
Turgai, 1282
Turin, 744, 752
Turkey, 36, 40, 45, 400, *1207-14*
Turkish Republic of Northern Cyprus, *405-6*
Turkmenistan, 1224, 1281, *1284-5*
Turks and Caicos Islands, 30, *1215-16*
Turku, 473-4, 476, 480-1
Turku-Pori, 473
Turnhout, 195
Tuscaloosa (Ala.), 1427
Tuscany, 746, 749
Tut, 975
Tuticorin, 648, 688
Tutong, 239
Tutuila, 1558-61
Tutume, 224
Tuva, 1248, 1254, *1260-1*
Tuvalu, 29-30, 56, *1217-18*
Tuxpan, 868
Tuxtla Gutiérrez, 863-4
Tuzla, 1603
Tvøroyri, 427
Tweed, 137
Tweeddale, 1303
Tweed Heads, 97
Twin Falls (Id.), 1456
Tychy, 1012
Tyler (Tex.), 1535
Tyndin, 1246
Tyneside, 1301-2
Tyne and Wear, 1299, 1336
Tyre, 800
Tytsjerksteradiel, 901
Tyube, 1289
Tyumen, 1241, 1254, 1263-4
Uahuka, 514
Uapu, 514
Uberlândia, 230
Ubong, 789
Ubon Rajchathani, 1185
Ucayali, 998
Uccle, 195
Udaipur, 684, 689
Uddevala, 1149
Uden, 901
Udine, 744, 752
Udmurtia, 1254, *1261*
Udorn Thani, 1185
Ufa, 1224, 1255
Uganda, 30, *1219-22*
Ughelli, 945
Uiback, 63
Uíge, 82
Uitenhage, 1089
Uithoorn, 901
Ujjain, 632, 671, 673
Ujung Padang, 701
Ukraine, 1223-5, 1250, *1264-6*
Ulan Bator, 872, 874-6
Ulan-Ude, 1255
Ulara, 1082
Uleåborg, 473-4, 481
Ulhasnagar, 632
Ulm, 534, 543, 547
Ulsan, 782
Ulster (Republic of Ireland), 720
Ulster (UK) *see* Northern Ireland
Ulyanovsk, 1224, 1254
Umanak, 428
Umbria, 743, 746
Umeå, 1149
Umm al Nar, 1295
Umm Al-Nassan, 179
Umm al Qaiwain, 1293, 1295
Umm-Bab, 1029
Umm Said, 1029, 1031
Umm Salal Mohammad, 1029
Um Qasr, 715, 717
Umroi Airport, 677
Umtali, 1625
Umtata, 1108
Umzimvubu, 1108
UNCTAD, 26
UNDP, *9-10*, 15, 21
UNDRO, 10
Uneiza, 1058
UNESCO, 12, *15-16*, 21
UNFPA, *10*
UNHCR, 7, *10-11*
UNICEF, *10*
UNIDO, 21
Union City (N.J.), 1501
Union Island, 1051-3
Union of Soviet Socialist Republics, 48, 58, 63-4, 125, *1223-53*
—Autonomous republics, Regions, etc, 1228-9
—Constituent Republics, 1224-6
Union Township (N.J.), 1501
United Arab Emirates, 57, *1293-7*
United Kingdom, 29, 36, 39-40, 42, 45, 47, 50, 125, *1298-371*
United Nations, *3-27*
—Children's Fund, *10*
—Conference on Trade and Development, 26
—Development Programme, *9-10*, 15, 21
—Disaster Relief Co-ordinator, 10
—Economic and Social Council, *5-6*, 11
—Educational Scientific and Cultural Organization, 12, *15-16*
—Educational, Scientific and Cultural Organization, 21
—Fund for Population Activities, *10*
—General Assembly, *3-4*, 11
—High Commissioner for Refugees, 7, *10-11*
—Industrial Development Organization, 21
—Relief and Works Agency for Palestine Refugees, *10*
—Secretariat, *7*
—Security Council, *4-5*
—Trusteeship Council, *6*
United States, 36, 39, 50, 52, 125, 395, 625, *1374-426*
—States, 1375-7, 1388-9, *1427-555*
—States,
——abbreviations of names, 1375-6
—Territories, 1374, 1382, 1389, *1555-66*
Unity (Me.), 1474
Universal Postal Union, *22-3*
University City (Mo.), 1489
UNRWA, *10*
Unterwalden, 1166-7
Upington, 1096
Upinniemi, 476
Upolu, 1593
Upper Arlington (Oh.), 1514
Upper Austria, 169
Upper East region (Ghana), 563
Upper West region (Ghana), 563
Uppsala, 1148-9, 1159
UPU, *22-3*
Uqsur, 446-7, 451
Uralsk, 1282
Urawa, 760
Urbana (Ill.), 1460
Urbino, 752
Urengoi, 1241, 1246
Urgel, 80
Urgench, 1285
Uri, 1164, 1166
Uroševac, 1603
Ursatyevskaya, 1291
Uruapan, 864
Uruguay, 52, 54, 125, *1567-71*
Urumqi, 35-6, 362
Uşak, 1208
Ushuaia, 91-2

USSR *see* Union of Soviet Socialist Republics
Ust-Ilminsk, 1240
Ustí nad Labem, 408
Ust-Kamenogorsk, 1241
Ust-Ordin-Buryat, 1254, *1264*
Ust-Ordynsk, 1264
Usulután, 453, 456
Utah, 1376, 1381, 1387, 1405, 1420, *1537-9*
Utica (N.Y.), 1506
Utorogu, 945
Utrecht (Netherlands), 900-1, 909
Utrecht (South Africa), 1101
Utsunomiya, 760
Uttarpara, 693
Uttar Pradesh, 632, 634-5, 643, 649, 652, *690-1*
Uturoa, 514
Uusimaa, 473
Uva, 1127
Uvéa (New Caledonia), 511
Uvéa (Wallis and Futuna), 516
Uyo, 943
Uzbekistan, 1224, 1228, *1285-7*
Uzhgorod, 1241

Vaasa *see* Vasa
Vadarevu, 655
Vadodara, 632, 660-2
Vaduz, 816
Vágoy, 426-7
Vágur, 427
Vaishali, 659
Vaitupu, 1217
Vajnory Airport, 412
Vakaga, 341
Valais, 1164-6, 1173
Valdívia, 349
Vale of Glamorgan, 1302
Valence, 484
Valencia (Spain), 1115-17, 1121, 1125
Valencia (Venezuela), 1578, 1582
Valenciennes, 484
Valenzuela, 1004
Valera, 1578
Vale Royal, 1301
Vale of White Horse, 1301
Valkeakoski, 474
Valkenswaard, 901
Vallabh-Vidyanagar, 662
Valladolid, 1115-16, 1125
Valle, 602
Valle d'Aosta, 743, 746
Valle del Cauca, 372
Valledupar, 372
Vallendar, 558
Valletta, 850
Valley Stream (N.Y.), 1506
Valley, The, 85
Valona *see* Vlorë
Valparaíso (Chile), 348-9, 352-3
Valparaiso (Ind.), 1463
Van, 1208
Vancouver (Canada), 272, 289, 301, 303-4, 334-5
Vancouver (Wash.), 1544
Vanda, 474
Vanda Station, 931
Vanderbijlpark, 1089
Vanimo, 986
Vantaa, 474
Vanua Levu, 469, 471
Vanuatu, 30, 56, 511, 517, *1572-4*
Vapi, 696
Varanasi, 632, 691
Varberg, 1149
Varkaus, 474
Värmland, 1148
Varna, 243, 245-7
Varzob, 1289
Vas, 615
Vasa, 473-4, 476, 480-1
Vascoas-Phoenix, 859
Vaslui, 1034
Västerås, 1149
Västerbotten, 1148
Västernorrland, 1148
Västervik, 1149
Västmanland, 1148
Vatican, *1575-7*
Vaud, 1164-6, 1169, 1173
Vaupés, 373
Vava'u, 1195, 1197
Vaverde, 435
Växjö, 1149
Veendam, 901
Veenendaal, 901
Veghel, 901
Vejle, 415
Veldhoven, 901
Veliko Tŭrnovo, 249
Vella La Vella, 1082
Velsen, 901
Venda, 1091, *1108-11*
Veneto, 743, 746
Venezuela, 52, 54, 57, 592, *1578-84*
Venice, 744, 747, 752
Vénissieux, 484
Venlo, 901
Venray, 901
Ventspils, 1247, 1278
Ventura (Calif.), 1437
Veracruz, 863
Veracruz Llave, 864, 868
Veraguas, 980
Verdun (Canada), 324
Vereeniging, 1089
Verkhoiansk, 1246
Vermillion (S.D.), 1532
Vermont, 1375, 1382, 1387, 1420, *1539-41*
Vernon, 301, 304
Verona, 744, 752
Verria, 572
Versailles, 484
Verviers, 195
Verwoerd Airport, 1096
Vest-Agder, 949
Vestfold, 949
Vestmanna, 426-7
Vestmannaeyjar, 623
Vestsjælland, 415
Veszprém, 615
Viana de Castelo, 1020, 1025
Viborg, 415, 423
Vicente López, 91
Vicenza, 744
Vichada, 373
Vicksburg (Miss.), 1486
Victoria (Australia), 97-8, 101, 106, 111, 114, *152-9*
Victoria (Canada), 272, 300-1, 303-4
Victoria (Hong Kong), 611
Victoria (Malaysia), 831
Victoria (Seychelles), 1068-70
Victoria de Durango, 863-4
Victoria Falls, 1623, 1628
Viedma, 91
Vienna, 168-9, 172-3
Vientiane, 795-8
Vieques, 1561
Vietnam, 48, *1585-90*
Vieux Fort, 1049-50
Vigie Airport, 1050
Vigo, 1116
Viipuri, 1258
Vijayawada, 632
Vikawadi, 655
Vila, 517, 1572-4
Vila da Feira, 1025
Vila do Conde, 1025
Vila Nova de Gaia, 1020, 1025
Vila Real, 1020, 1025
Vîlcea, 1034
Villach, 168
Villa Clara, 394
Villacoublay, 489
Villa Elisa, 994
Villahermosa, 863-4
Villa Montes, 222
Villavicencio, 372
Villazón, 222
Villeurbanne, 484
Villmanstrand, 474, 481
Vilnius, 1018, 1224, 1248, 1279-81
Viluisk, 1246
Vilvoorde, 195
Viña del Mar, 348
Vineland (N.J.), 1501
Vinh, 1589
Vinh Phu, 1585
Vinnitsa, 1241, 1264
Virgin Gorda, 1591
Virginia, 1376, 1382, 1387, 1407, 1409, *1541-3*
Virginia Beach (Va.), 1378, 1542
Virgin Islands, British, 30, *1591-2*
Virgin Islands of the United States, 1377, 1387, 1389-90, 1392, 1419, *1563-6*
Viru Viru Airport, 222
Visayas, 1004
Viseu, 1020, 1025
Vishakhapatnam, 632, 639, 648, 654-5
Vitebsk, 1266
Viterbo, 752
Viti Levu, 469, 471
Vitória (Brazil), 229
Vitoria (Spain), 1115-16
Vitry-sur-Seine, 484
Vizag, 648
Vizcaya, 1114-15
Vizianagaram, 653-4
Vlaardingan, 901
Vladimir, 1254
Vladivostok, 1224-5, 1231, 1246-7, 1251
Vlissingen, 901, 904
Vlonë *see* Vlorë
Vlorë, 68-72
Voinjama, 807
Vojvodina, 1603-5, 1610, *1614-15*
Volcano Islands, 759
Volendam, 900
Volgograd, 1224, 1243, 1247, 1254
Volhynia, 1264
Vologda, 1254
Volos, 571
Volta, 563
Volta Redonda, 233
Voorberg, 901
Voorschoten, 901
Voorst, 901
Vorarlberg, 168-9, 818
Voronezh, 1224, 1246, 1254
Voroshilovgrad, 1264
Vorster Airport, 1096
Voskresensk, 1240
Vostochny, 1247
Vostok Island, 778
Vovilha, 1025
Vrancea, 1034
Vryheid, 1101
Vught, 901
Vung Tao, 1585
Vuwani, 1109
Vyborg, 1258
Východočeský Region, 408
Východoslovenský Region, 408

Wa, 566
Waalwijk, 901
Wabag, 986
Wabana, 311
Wabush, 311
Waco (Tex.), 1379, 1535, 1537
Waddinxveen, 901
Wadi Halfa, 1136, 1138
Wageningen, 901
Wagerup, 163
Wagga Wagga, 129
Waikatio, 916
Wairarapa, 917
Wakayama, 760
Wakefield, 1301
Wake Island, 1377, 1561
Wakenaam Island, 594
Wakkerstroom, 1101
Wakra, 1029
Wałbrzych, 1012
Wales, 1298-300, 1307, 1311-12, 1320, 1327, 1333, 1343, 1348-9, 1356-7
Walla Walla (Wash.), 1544
Wallblake Airport, 86
Wallis and Futuna, *516-17*
Walpole, 511
Walsall, 1301
Waltair, 655
Waltham (Mass.), 1478, 1480

Waltham Forest, 1302
Walvis Bay, 890, 892, 1096, 1100
Wan Chai, 611
Wandsworth, 1302
Wanganui, 916-17
Wangaratta, 153, 156
Wankie, 1625
Warangal, 632, 653-5
Wardha, 673
Warnemünde, 528
Warren (Mich.), 1378, 1481
Warren (Oh.), 1514
Warri, 944-7
Warrington, 1301
Warrnambool, 153
Warsaw, 1012-13, 1017-18
Warsaw Pact, *48*
Warwick (R.I.), 1526-7
Warwick (UK), 1301, 1350
Warwickshire, 1300
Waseda, 766
Washington (D.C.), 1377, 1389-90, 1404, 1447-8, 1475
Washington (State), 1376, 1381, 1387, 1407, *1544-6*
Washington (UK), 1336
Washington Island *see* Teraina Island
Wasit, 714
Wassenaar, 901
Waterbury (Conn.), 1378, 1443
Waterford, 720, 730
Waterloo (Ia.), 1464
Watermael-Boitsfort, 195
Watertown (N.Y.), 1506
Watertown (S.D.), 1530
Waterville (Me.), 1473-4
Watson Lake, 333-4
Wau, 1138
Waukegan (Ill.), 1458
Waukesha (Wis.), 1549
Wausau (Wis.), 1549
Wauwatosa (Wis.), 1549
Waveney, 1301
Waverley, 1301
Waverly (Ia.), 1465
Wayne (Nebr.), 1495
Waziristan, 972
WCC, *32-3*
WCL, *34-5*
Wealden, 1301
Weatherford (Okla.), 1519
Wedding, 548
Weert, 901
Weipa, 139
Weirton (W. Va.), 1546
Weissensee, 548
Wele-Nzas, 458
Wellington (New Zealand), 917-18
Wels, 168
Welwyn Hatfield, 1301
West Allis (Wis.), 1549
West Bank, 735, 768-9
West Bengal, 632, 635, 642-3, 649, 652, *692-4*
Westbrook (Me.), 1474
West Coast (New Zealand), 917
Western Area (Sierra Leone), 1071-2
Western Australia, 97-8, 101, 111, 114, 123, *159-67*
Western District (American Samoa), 1559
Western European Union, *39-40*
Western Highlands (Papua New Guinea), 986
Western Isles (Scotland), 1303
Western Peninsula (Iceland), 623
Westernport, 111
Western Province (Kenya), 773
Western Province (Papua New Guinea), 986, 988
Western Province (Saudi Arabia), 1058
Western Province (Solomon Islands), 1082
Western Province (Sri Lanka), 1127
Western Province (Uganda), 1219
Western Province (Zambia), 1621
Western Region (Ghana), 563
Western Sahara, *1126*
Western Samoa, 30, 56, *1593-5*
West Falkland, 466
West Flanders, 194
West Germany *see* Germany, Federal Republic of
West Glamorgan, 1300
West Greenland, 427
West Hartford (Conn.), 1443
West Island (Cocos Islands), 125-6
West Lancashire, 1301
Westland (Mich.), 1481
West Liberty (W. Va.), 1548
West Lothian, 1303
Westmeath, 719
West Memphis (Ark.), 1435
West Midlands, 1299, 1302
Westminster (Colo.), 1440
Westminster (UK), 1302, 1320
Westmoreland (Jamaica), 754
West New Britain, 986
West Oxfordshire, 1301
West Palm Beach (Fla.), 1449
West Region (Iceland), 623
West Sepik, 986
Weststellingwerf, 901
West Sussex, 1300
West Virginia, 1376, 1382, 1387, 1420, *1546-8*
West Wiltshire, 1301
West Yorkshire, 1299, 1302
Wetaskiwin, 297-8
WEU, *39-40*
Wewak, 986
Wexford, 719
Weyburn, 327
WFTU, 33, *34*
Whangarei, 916-17
Wheat Ridge (Colo.), 1440
Wheeling (W. Va.), 1546
Whitehorse, 332, 334
White Nile Province (Sudan), 1137
White Plains (N.Y.), 1506
White Russia *see* Belorussia
Whitewater (Wis.), 1552
WHO, 10, *16-18*, 21
Whyalla, 142
Wichita (Kans.), 1378, 1466-7
Wichita Falls (Tex.), 1535
Wicklow, 719
Wiener Neustadt, 168
Wierden, 901
Wiesbaden, 534, 553
Wigan, 1301
Wight, Isle of *see* Isle of Wight
Wigram, 920
Wigtown, 1303
Wijchen, 901
Wilhelmshaven, 537
Wilkes-Barre (Pa.), 1523
Wilkes Land, 125
Willemstad, 913, 915
Williamsburg (Va.), 1543
Willis Island, 128
Wilmersdorf, 548
Wilmington (Del.), 1445-6
Wilrijk, 195
Wiltshire, 1300-1
Winchester, 1301
Windhoek, 889-92, 1093
Windsor (Newfoundland), 311
Windsor (Ontario), 272, 319
Windsor and Maidenhead, 1301
Windward Islands (French Polynesia) *see* Îles du Vent
Windward Islands (Netherlands Antilles), 913
Winneba, 563
Winnipeg, 272, 276, 278, 304-7, 331
Winona (Minn.), 1485
Winston-Salem (N.C.), 1378, 1509
Winterswijk, 901
Winterthur, 1165
WIPO, *27-8*
Wirral, 1301
Wisconsin, 1382, 1407, 1420, *1549-52*
Witten, 534, 543, 557
Włocławek, 1012
WMO, *23-4*
Wodonga, 153, 156
Woerden, 901
Wokha, 678
Wokingham, 1301
Woleu-Ntem, 518
Wolfsberg (Austria), 168
Wolfsburg (FRG), 534
Wollega, 462
Wollo, 461-2
Wollongong, 97, 129
Woluwe-St Lambert, 195
Woluwe-St Pierre, 195
Wolverhampton, 1301
Wonderboom, 1089
Wonsan, 786-7, 789
Woodbourne, 920
Woodbridge (N.J.), 1501
Woodspring, 1301
Woonsocket (R.I.), 1526
Worcester (Mass.), 1378, 1478, 1480
Worcester (UK), 1300
World Bank, *20-1*, 20
World Confederation of Labour, *34-5*
World Council of Churches, *32-3*
World Federation of Trade Unions, 33, *34*
World Health Organization, 10, *16-18*, 21
World Intellectual Property Organization, *27-8*
World Meteorological Organization, *23-4*
Worsley, 163
Worthing, 1301
Wrekin, 1301
Wrexham Maelor, 1302
Wright Valley, 931
Wrocław, 1012-13
Wudam, 966
Wuhan, 355, 360, 362, 365
Wuppertal, 534
Würzburg, 534, 543
Wychavon, 1301
Wycombe, 1301
Wyoming, 1376, 1381, 1387, *1552-5*
Wyoming (Mich.), 1481
Wyre (Forest), 1301

Xaixai, 885
Xanthi, 572
Xian, 355, 362, 365
Xiangfan, 362
Xining, 355, 362
Xinjiang, 355, 362-4
Xuzhou, 362

Yabaon, 653
Yafran, 811
Yakima (Wash.), 1544
Yakutia, 1254, *1261-2*
Yakutsk, 1246, 1261-2
Yallourn, 155-6
Yamalo-Nenets, 1254, *1264*
Yambol, 243
Yamoussoukro, 390
Yanam, 698
Yanbu, 1058, 1060-2
Yandina, 1084

Yanggang, 787
Yangon *see* Rangoon
Yannina, 571
Yao, 760
Yaoundé, 265, 268
Yap, 1558
Yaracuy, 1578
Yarmouth (Canada), 315
Yaroslavl, 1224, 1254
Yasui, 1289
Yásúj, 708
Yatenga, 250
Yau Ma Tei, 611
Yazd, 708-9
Yellowknife, 276, 279, 329, 331
Yemen Arab Republic, 57, *1596-8*, *1599*
Yemen People's Democratic Republic, 48, 57, *1599-602*
Yendi, 566
Yengema, 1073
Yeotmal, 673
Yerevan, 1224, 1246, 1248, 1273-4
Yerim, 1596
Yinchaun, 355, 362
Yoff Airport, 1066
Yogyakarta, 701-2
Yokkaichi, 760
Yokohama, 760, 765
Yokosuka, 760, 762
Yonkers (N.Y.), 1378, 1506
Yopal, El, 372
York (Pa.), 1523
York (UK), 1300-1, 1343, 1349-50
Yorkshire, 1299, 1302
Yorkton, 327
Yoro, 602
Yoshkar-Ola, 1259
Youngstown (Oh.), 1378, 1514
Youyiguan, 362
Yozgat, 1208
Yucatán, 863
Yuen Long, 607
Yugoslavia, 45, 58, *1603-15*
Yukon Territory, 271-3, 279, 291, *332-5*
Yuksam, 686
Yulara, 121
Yuma (Ariz.), 1433
Yumen, 362
Yundum Airport, 524
Yunnan, 355, 360, 364

Zaanstad, 901
Zaanstreek, 901
Zabid, 1597
Zabrze, 1012
Zacapa, 581
Zacatecas, 863
Zacatecoluca, 456
Zadar, 1603, 1608
Zagâziq, 446
Zaghouan, 1202
Zagreb, 1603-5, 1607-9, 1611
Záhedán, 708, 712
Zahlé, 800
Zaïre, 1042, *1616-24*
Zaïre (Angola), 82
Zakarpatskaya, 1264
Zakynthos, 571
Zala, 615, 617
Zalaegerszeg, 615
Zaláu, 1034
Zaluzi, 411
Zambézia, 885
Zambia, 30, *1621-4*
Zamboanga, 1004
Zamora, 440, 1115
Zamora-Chinchipa, 440
Zamość, 1012
Zanderij Airport, 1142
Zanesville (Oh.), 1514
Zanján, 708-9
Zante, 571
Zanzibar, 773, 1180-3
Západočeský Region, 408
Západoslovenský Region, 408
Zapopan, 864
Zaporozhye, 1224, 1264
Zaragoza, 1115-16, 1125, 11141
Zaria, 943
Zarnowiec, 1015
Zarqa, 768
Zawia, 811
Zeeland, 900
Zehlendorf, 548
Zeist, 901
Zelaya Norte/Sur, 935-6
Zemun, 1605
Zenica, 1603
Zevenaar, 901
Zhanjiang, 358, 363
Zhejiang, 355
Zhengzhou, 355, 362
Zhitomir, 1264
Zhuzhou, 362
Zielona Góra, 1012
Ziguinchor, 1064, 1066-7
Zilina, 408
Zimbabwe, 30, *1625-31*
Zinder, 940-2
Zipaquirá, 375
Zizya, 771
Zlitan, 811
Zoetermeer, 901
Zomba, 827-8
Zonguldak, 1208, 1210
Zou, 208
Zouérate, 856, 858
Zoundwéogo, 250
Zrenjanin, 1603
Zuénoula, 390
Zug, 1164, 1166
Zuid-Holland, 900, 903
Zulia, 1578, 1581
Zuluf, 1060
Zunheboto, 678
Zurich, 1164-5, 1167, 1173
Zutphen, 901
Zvishavane, 1625
Zwedru, 807
Zwelitsha, 1111
Zwickau, 526
Zwijndrecht, 901
Zwolle, 901

PRODUCT INDEX

References are to production data

Aluminium:
—Australia,
——Queensland, 140
——Tasmania, 151
——Western Australia, 163
—Bahrain, 181-2
—Cameroon, 267
—China, 360
—India,
——Orissa, 680
—Indonesia, 704
—Italy, 749
—Jamaica, 756
—Norway, 953
—UK, 1326
—USSR, 1241

Barley, world statistics, xvii
—Afghánistán, 65
—Albania, 71
—Australia, 106
——New South Wales, 132
——Queensland, 139
——South Australia, 144-5
——Tasmania, 150
——Western Australia, 162
—Belgium, 199
—Bhután, 216
—Canada, 283-4
——Quebec, 325
——Saskatchewan, 328
—Chile, 315
—Cyprus, 402
—Czechoslovakia, 411
—Denmark, 419
—Ecuador, 443
—Ethiopa, 463-4
—Finland, 477
—France, 491
—Germany (FRG), 539
——Baden-Württemberg, 546
——Hessen, 553
——Lower Saxony, 554
——North Rhine-Westphalia, 556
——Rhineland-Palatinate, 557
——Saarland, 559
——Schleswig-Holstein, 561
—Germany (GDR), 529
—Hungary, 618
—India,
——Sikkim, 685
—Iran, 711
—Iraq, 716
—Ireland, 725
—Israel, 738
—Italy, 749
—Japan, 763
—Kenya, 775
—Korea, South, 784
—Lesotho, 805
—Libya, 814
—Mexico, 867
—Mongolia, 874
—Morocco, 882
—Netherlands, 906
—New Zealand, 922
—Norway, 954
—Poland, 1015
—Portugal, 1023
—Romania, 1036
—Spain, 1121
—Sweden, 1154
—Switzerland, 1169
—Syria, 1177

Barley:
—Tunisia, 1204
—Turkey, 1211
—UK, 1326
——Northern Ireland, 1362
—Uruguay, 1569
—USA, 1407
——Arizona, 1434
——Colorado, 1441
——Idaho, 1457
——Kansas, 1466
——Kentucky, 1469
——Minnesota, 1484
——Montana, 1492
——North Dakota, 1512
——Pennsylvania, 1524
——Texas, 1536
——Utah, 1538
——Wyoming, 1553
—Yemen Arab Republic, 1597
—Yemen Democratic Republic, 1601
—Zimbabwe, 1628

Bauxite:
—Australia, 106
——Northern Territory, 122
——Queensland, 139
——Victoria, 156
——Western Australia, 162
—Brazil, 233
—Cameroon, 267
—China, 360
—Congo, 383
—Dominican Republic, 437
—France, 491
—Ghana, 565
—Greece, 575
—Guinea, 587
—Guyana, 593-4
—Hungary, 617
—India, 642
——Gujarat, 661
——Jammu and Kashmir, 666
——Madhya Pradesh, 671
——Maharashtra, 674
——Orissa, 680
——Tamil Nadu, 687
——Uttar Pradesh, 691
—Indonesia, 704
—Italy, 749
—Jamaica, 756
—Malaysia, 835,837
—Mozambique, 886
—Romania, 1036
—Sierra Leone, 1072
—Suriname, 1141-2
—USA, 1405
——Arkansas, 1435
—USSR, 1241
—Vietnam, 1588
—Yugoslavia, 1606
——Bosnia and Herzegovina, 1611
——Croatia, 1612
——Montenegro, 1613

Cereals, world statistics, xv-xxii

Chrome:
—Albania, 70-1
—Brazil, 233
—Greece, 575
—India, 642
——Karnataka, 667

Chrome:
——Orissa, 680
——Tamil Nadu, 687
—Iran, 711
—Japan, 763
—Madagascar, 825
—New Caledonia, 512-13
—Pakistan, 975
—South Africa, 1093-4
——Bophuthatswana, 1106
—Turkey, 1210
—USSR, 1241
—Zimbabwe, 1627

Coal:
—Afghánistán, 65
—Albania, 70
—Algeria, 76
—Australia, 106,109
——New South Wales, 132
——Queensland, 139-40
——South Australia, 144
——Tasmania, 149
——Victoria, 156
——Western Australia, 162
—Austria, 171
—Bangladesh, 187
—Belgium, 199
—Botswana, 225-6
—Brazil, 233
—Bulgaria, 246
—Canada, 283
——Alberta, 299
——British Columbia, 302-3
——New Brunswick, 309
——Nova Scotia, 317
——Saskatchewan, 328
—Chile, 315
—China, 360
—Colombia, 375
—Czechoslovakia, 411
—France, 491
—Germany (FRG), 539
——North Rhine-Westphalia, 556
—Germany (GDR), 529
—Hungary, 617
—India, 642
——Andhra Pradesh, 654
——Assam, 657
——Gujarat, 661
——Jammu and Kashmir, 666
——Madhya Pradesh, 671
——Maharashtra, 674
——Meghalaya, 676
——Orissa, 680
——Tamil Nadu, 687
——Uttar Pradesh, 690
——West Bengal, 692
—Indonesia, 704
—Iran, 711
—Japan, 763
—Korea, North, 788
—Korea, South, 784
—Malawi, 829
—Mexico, 867
—Mongolia, 874
—Morocco, 882
—Mozambique, 886
—Niger, 941
—Nigeria, 945
—Pakistan, 975
—Philippines, 1007
—Poland, 1015-16
—Portugal, 1023

Coal:
—Romania, 1036
—South Africa, 1093-4
——Venda, 1109
—Spain, 1120
—Swaziland, 1145
—Taiwan, 369
—Thailand, 1188
—Turkey, 1210
—UK, 1325,1332
—USA, 1414
——Alabama, 1428
——Alaska, 1430-1
——Colorado, 1441
——Illinois, 1459
——Indiana, 1462
——Iowa, 1464
——Kansas, 1466
——Kentucky, 1468
——Maryland, 1476
——Missouri, 1489
——Montana, 1492
——New Mexico, 1504
——North Dakota, 1512
——Ohio, 1515
——Pennsylvania, 1524
——Virginia, 1542
——West Virginia, 1547
——Wyoming, 1553
—USSR, 1243
——Georgia, 1271
——Kazakhstan, 1283
——RSFSR, 1254
——Ukraine, 1265
——Uzbekistan, 1287
—Vietnam, 1588
—Yugoslavia, 1606
——Croatia, 1612
——Macedonia, 1612
——Montenegro, 1613
——Serbia, 1614
——Slovenia, 1615
—Zimbabwe, 1627

Cocoa:
—Benin, 210
—Bolivia, 221
—Brazil, 234
—Cameroon, 267
—Congo, 383
—Costa Rica, 387-8
—Côte d'Ivoire, 392
—Dominican Republic, 437
—Ecuador, 443
—Equatorial Guinea, 459
—Fiji, 470
—Gabon, 520
—Ghana, 565
—Grenada, 579
—Liberia, 808-9
—Malaysia, 837,843
—Nigeria, 946
—Panama, 982
—Papua New Guinea, 988-9
—St Lucia, 1050
—St Vincent and the Grenadines, 1052
—São Tomé e Príncipe, 1057
—Sierra Leone, 1072
—Solomon Islands, 1083
—Tanzania, 1182
—Togo, 1193
—UK, 1331
—Vanuatu, 1573
—Venezuela, 1581

Coffee:
—Australia, 108
—Benin, 209
—Bolivia, 221
—Brazil, 234
—Burundi, 259
—Cameroon, 267
—Cape Verde, 337
—Central African Republic, 343
—Colombia, 375
—Comoros, 379
—Congo, 383
—Costa Rica, 387-8
—Côte d'Ivoire, 392
—Dominican Republic, 437
—Ecuador, 443
—El Salvador, 455
—Equatorial Guinea, 459
—Ethiopa, 463
—Gabon, 520
—Ghana, 565
—Guatemala, 583
—Guinea, 587
—Haiti, 599
—Honduras, 604
—India, 643
——Karnataka, 668
——Kerala, 669
—Indonesia, 704-5
—Kenya, 775
—Laos, 797
—Liberia, 808-9
—Madagascar, 825
—Mayotte, 508
—Mexico, 867
—New Caledonia, 512
—Nicaragua, 937
—Panama, 982
—Papua New Guinea, 988-9
—Paraguay, 995
—Peru, 1001
—Rwanda, 1042
—São Tomé e Príncipe, 1057
—Sierra Leone, 1072
—Tanzania, 1182-3
—Togo, 1193
—Uganda, 1221
—UK, 1331
—Vanuatu, 1573
—Venezuela, 1581
—Zaïre, 1618-19
—Zimbabwe, 1628

Copper:
—Afghánistán, 65
—Albania, 70-1
—Australia, 106
——New South Wales, 132
——Northern Territory, 122
——Queensland, 139-40
——South Australia, 144
——Tasmania, 149-50
—Botswana, 225-6
—Burma, 255-6
—Canada, 283
——British Columbia, 302
——Manitoba, 306
——New Brunswick, 309
——Ontario, 321
——Quebec, 325
——Saskatchewan, 328
—Chile, 315,352
—China, 360
—Colombia, 375
—Congo, 383
—Cyprus, 402
—Ecuador, 443
—Finland, 477
—Guatemala, 583

Copper:
—India, 642
——Andhra Pradesh, 654
——Bihar, 658
——Madhya Pradesh, 671
——Rajasthan, 683
——Sikkim, 686
——Uttar Pradesh, 690
—Indonesia, 704-5
—Japan, 763
—Korea, North, 788-9
—Malaysia, 835,837
—Mauritania, 857
—Mexico, 867
—Mongolia, 874
—Morocco, 882
—Norway, 953
—Oman, 968
—Pakistan, 975
—Panama, 982
—Papua New Guinea, 988
—Peru, 1001
—Philippines, 1007-8
—Poland, 1015
—Portugal, 1023
—Romania, 1036
—South Africa, 1093-4
—Spain, 1120
—Sweden, 1154
—Turkey, 1210
—UK, 1326
—USA, 1405
——Arizona, 1433
——Idaho, 1456
——Maine, 1473
——Montana, 1491
——New Mexico, 1504
—USSR, 1241
——RSFSR, 1254
—Yugoslavia, 1606
——Macedonia, 1612
——Serbia, 1614
—Zaïre, 1618-19
—Zambia, 1623
—Zimbabwe, 1627

Cotton:
—Antigua and Barbuda, 88
—Argentina, 94
—Australia, 106
——New South Wales, 132
——Queensland, 139
——Victoria, 157
—Bangladesh, 187
—Barbados, 191
—Benin, 209-10
—Bolivia, 221
—Botswana, 226
—Brazil, 234
—Bulgaria, 246
—Burkina Faso, 251-2
—Burma, 256
—Burundi, 259
—Cameroon, 267
—Central African Republic, 343
—Chad, 346
—China, 361-2
—Côte d'Ivoire, 392
—Egypt, 449-50
—El Salvador, 455
—Gambia, 523
—Ghana, 565
—Guatemala, 583
—Haiti, 599
—India, 643
——Assam, 657
——Gujarat, 661
——Haryana, 663

Cotton:
——Karnataka, 668
——Madhya Pradesh, 671
——Maharashtra, 674
——Meghalaya, 676
——Punjab, 682
——Rajasthan, 684
——Tamil Nadu, 687-8
—Israel, 738
—Japan, 764
—Kenya, 775
—Laos, 797
—Madagascar, 825
—Mali, 848-9
—Mexico, 867
—Mozambique, 887
—Nicaragua, 937
—Niger, 941
—Nigeria, 946
—Pakistan, 976
—Paraguay, 995
—Peru, 1001
—St Kitts-Nevis, 1045
—Senegal, 1066
—Somalia, 1086
—Spain, 1121
—Sudan, 1137
—Swaziland, 1146
—Syria, 1177
—Tanzania, 1182-3
—Togo, 1193
—Turkey, 1210
—Uganda, 1221
—USA, 1407,1414
——Alabama, 1428
——Arizona, 1434
——Arkansas, 1436
——California, 1438
——Georgia, 1452
——Louisiana, 1471
——Mississippi, 1487
——Missouri, 1489
——Oklahoma, 1517
——South Carolina, 1529
——Tennessee, 1533
——Texas, 1536
—USSR, 1241
——Armenia, 1274
——Azerbaijan, 1268
——Kirghizia, 1291
——Tadzhikistan, 1289
——Turkmenistan, 1285
——Uzbekistan, 1287
—Vietnam, 1588
—Yemen Arab Republic, 1597
—Yemen Democratic Republic, 1601
—Yugoslavia,
——Macedonia, 1612
—Zaïre, 1618
—Zambia, 1623
—Zimbabwe, 1628

Diamonds:
—Angola, 82
—Australia,
——Western Australia, 162
—Botswana, 225-6
—Brazil, 233
—Central African Republic, 343
—Côte d'Ivoire, 392
—Ghana, 565
—Guinea, 587
—Guyana, 593
—India,
——Madhya Pradesh, 671
—Liberia, 808
—Namibia, 891

Diamonds:
—Sierra Leone, 1072
—South Africa, 1093-4
——Bophuthatswana, 1106
—Tanzania, 1182-3
—Zaïre, 1618-19

Gas, natural:
—Afghánistán, 65
—Algeria, 76
—Argentina, 93
—Australia, 106,109
——Northern Territory, 122
——South Australia, 144
——Victoria, 155-6
——Western Australia, 162
—Austria, 170
—Bahrain, 181
—Bangladesh, 186
—Barbados, 191
—Belgium, 198
—Bolivia, 220
—Brazil, 233
—Brunei, 240
—Canada, 282-3
——British Columbia, 302
——New Brunswick, 309
——Saskatchewan, 328
——Yukon, 333
—China, 360
—Ecuador, 443
—Egypt, 449
—France, 491
—Gabon, 519
—Hungary, 617
—India, 642
——Andhra Pradesh, 654
——Assam, 657
—Indonesia, 704-5
—Iran, 711
—Ireland, 724
—Japan, 763
—Kuwait, 793
—Libya, 813
—Malaysia, 835,843
—Mexico, 867
—Netherlands, 906
—New Zealand, 921
—Nigeria, 945
—Norway, 953
—Oman, 967
—Pakistan, 975
—Qatar, 1030-1
—Romania, 1036
—Rwanda, 1042
—Saudi Arabia, 1061
—South Africa, 1093
—Syria, 1177
—Taiwan, 369
—Thailand, 1188
—Trinidad and Tobago, 1199
—Tunisia, 1204
—UK, 1325,1332
—United Arab Emirates, 1295
—USA, 1405
——Alabama, 1428
——Alaska, 1430-1
——Arkansas, 1435
——California, 1438
——Colorado, 1441
——Kansas, 1466
——Kentucky, 1468
——Maryland, 1476
——Michigan, 1482
——Mississippi, 1487
——Montana, 1492
——New Mexico, 1504
——New York, 1507

Gas, natural:
——North Dakota, 1512
——Ohio, 1515
——Oklahoma, 1517
——Pennsylvania, 1524
——Texas, 1536
——West Virginia, 1547
—USSR, 1240-1
——Uzbekistan, 1287
—Venezuela, 1581

Gold:
—Afghánistán, 65
—Argentina, 93
—Australia, 110
——New South Wales, 132
——Northern Territory, 122
——Queensland, 139
——Tasmania, 149
——Victoria, 156
——Western Australia, 162,164
—Bolivia, 220
—Brazil, 233
—Burma, 256
—Burundi, 259
—Cambodia, 263
—Canada, 283
——British Columbia, 302
——Manitoba, 306
——New Brunswick, 309
——Newfoundland, 313
——Northwest Territories, 330
——Ontario, 321
——Quebec, 325
——Saskatchewan, 328
——Yukon, 333
—Central African Republic, 343
—Chile, 352
—China, 360
—Colombia, 375
—Congo, 383
—Costa Rica, 387
—Côte d'Ivoire, 392
—Dominican Republic, 437
—Ecuador, 443
—Ethiopa, 463
—Gabon, 519
—Ghana, 565
—Guyana, 593
—India, 642
——Haryana, 663
——Karnataka, 667
——Madhya Pradesh, 671
—Indonesia, 704
—Japan, 763
—Korea, North, 788
—Liberia, 808
—Madagascar, 825
—Malaysia, 837
Mexico, 867
—Mozambique, 886
—Nicaragua, 937
—Pakistan, 975
—Papua New Guinea, 988
—Peru, 1001
—Philippines, 1007
—Portugal, 1023
—Saudi Arabia, 1061
—Solomon Islands, 1083
—South Africa, 1093-4
——Bophuthatswana, 1106
——Transvaal, 1103
—Sudan, 1137
—Taiwan, 369
—Tanzania, 1182
—Uganda, 1221
—USA, 1413
——Alaska, 1430-1

Gold:
——Arizona, 1433
——California, 1438
——Montana, 1492
——Nevada, 1497
——South Dakota, 1531
—USSR, 1241
——RSFSR, 1254
—Venezuela, 1581
—Yugoslavia, 1606
—Zambia, 1623
—Zimbabwe, 1627

Iron and steel:
—Afghánistán, 65
—Algeria, 76-7
—Argentina, 93
—Australia, 106,109
——South Australia, 144
——Tasmania, 149,151
——Western Australia, 162,164
—Austria, 171
—Belgium, 199
—Brazil, 233
—Bulgaria, 246-7
—Burma, 256
—Canada, 283
——Newfoundland, 313
——Quebec, 325
—Chile, 315,352
—China, 360
—Congo, 383
—Côte d'Ivoire, 392
—Cyprus, 402
—Egypt, 449
—Finland, 477
—France, 491
—Gabon, 520
—Germany (FRG), 539
——North Rhine-Westphalia, 556
—Germany (GDR), 529
—Greece, 575
—Guinea, 587
—India, 642-3
——Andhra Pradesh, 654
——Bihar, 658
——Goa, 660
——Karnataka, 667
——Madhya Pradesh, 671-2
——Maharashtra, 674
——Orissa, 680
—Iran, 711
—Italy, 749-50
—Japan, 763-4
—Korea, North, 788-9
—Korea, South, 784
—Liberia, 808-9
—Luxembourg, 821
—Malaysia, 835,837
—Mauritania, 857
—Mexico, 867
—Morocco, 882
—New Caledonia, 512
—New Zealand, 921-2
—Niger, 941
—Nigeria, 945
—Norway, 953
—Pakistan, 975
—Peru, 1001
—Qatar, 1031
—Romania, 1036-7
—South Africa, 1094
—Spain, 1120-1
—Sudan, 1137
—Sweden, 1154
—Taiwan, 369
—Thailand, 1188
—Trinidad and Tobago, 1200

Iron and steel:
—Tunisia, 1204
—Turkey, 1210
—UK, 1325-6
—USA, 1411-12,1414
——California, 1438
——Michigan, 1482
——Minnesota, 1484
——Missouri, 1489
——Wyoming, 1553
—USSR, 1241-2
——Kazakhstan, 1283
——RSFSR, 1254
——Ukraine, 1265
—Vietnam, 1588
—Yugoslavia, 1606-7
——Bosnia and Herzegovina, 1611
——Croatia, 1612
——Macedonia, 1612
——Serbia, 1614
——Slovenia, 1615
—Zimbabwe, 1627

Lead:
—Argentina, 94
—Australia, 106
——New South Wales, 132
——Northern Territory, 122
——Queensland, 139-40
——Tasmania, 149-50
—Austria, 171
—Brazil, 233
—Burma, 256
—Canada, 283
——New Brunswick, 309
——Northwest Territories, 330
——Yukon, 333
—Chile, 315
—China, 360
—Colombia, 375
—Congo, 383
—Finland, 477
—Guatemala, 583
—India, 642
——Bihar, 658
——Madhya Pradesh, 671
——Sikkim, 686
—Iran, 711
—Ireland, 724
—Italy, 749
—Japan, 763
—Korea, North, 788
—Korea, South, 784
—Mexico, 867
—Morocco, 882
—Nigeria, 945
—Norway, 953
—Peru, 1001
—Spain, 1120
—Sweden, 1154
—Thailand, 1188
—Tunisia, 1204
—UK, 1326
—USA, 1405
——Kansas, 1466
——Maine, 1473
——Missouri, 1489
——Virginia, 1542
—USSR, 1241
——RSFSR, 1254
—Yugoslavia, 1606

Maize, world statistics, xxi
—Afghánistán, 65
—Albania, 71
—Angola, 83
—Australia,
——Northern Territory, 122
——Queensland, 139
—Benin, 209
—Bhután, 216
—Bolivia, 221
—Botswana, 226
—Brazil, 234
—Bulgaria, 246
—Burkina Faso, 251
—Burma, 256
—Burundi, 259
—Cambodia, 263
—Cameroon, 267
—Canada,
——Quebec, 325
—Cape Verde, 337
—Central African Republic, 343
—Chile, 315
—China, 361
—Colombia, 375
—Comoros, 379
—Congo, 383
—Costa Rica, 387
—Côte d'Ivoire, 392
—Czechoslovakia, 411
—Ecuador, 443
—Egypt, 450
—El Salvador, 455
—Ethiopa, 463-4
—Fiji, 470
—France, 491
—Gabon, 520
—Ghana, 565
—Guinea-Bissau, 590
—Hungary, 618
—India, 643
——Bihar, 658
——Himachal Pradesh, 664
——Jammu and Kashmir, 666
——Manipur, 675
——Meghalaya, 676
——Punjab, 682
——Sikkim, 685
—Indonesia, 704
—Israel, 738
—Italy, 749
—Kenya, 775
—Korea, North, 788
—Laos, 797
—Lesotho, 805
—Luxembourg, 821
—Madagascar, 825
—Malawi, 829
—Malaysia, 837
—Mali, 848
—Mauritania, 857
—Mauritius, 861
—Mexico, 867
—Mozambique, 886
—Namibia, 892
—Nepál, 897
—New Caldeonia, 512
—New Zealand, 922
—Nicaragua, 937
—Nigeria, 946
—Pakistan, 976
—Papua New Guinea, 988
—Paraguay, 995
—Peru, 1001
—Philippines, 1007
—Portugal, 1023
—Réunion, 505
—Romania, 1036
—Rwanda, 1042
—Senegal, 1066
—Somalia, 1086
—South Africa, 1094
——Bophuthatswana, 1106

Maize, world statistics, xxi
———Ciskei, 1111
———Venda, 1109
—Spain, 1121
—Swaziland, 1146
—Switzerland, 1169
—Syria, 1177
—Tanzania, 1182
—Thailand, 1188
—Togo, 1193
—Turkey, 1211
—Uruguay, 1569
—USA, 1407
——Arizona, 1434
——Colorado, 1441
——Delaware, 1446
——Georgia, 1452
——Illinois, 1459
——Indiana, 1462
——Iowa, 1464
——Kansas, 1466
——Kentucky, 1469
——Maine, 1473
——Michigan, 1482
——Nebraska, 1494
——New York, 1507
——North Carolina, 1510
——North Dakota, 1512
——Ohio, 1515
——Pennsylvania, 1524
——Utah, 1538
—Venezuela, 1581
—Vietnam, 1588
—Yemen Arab Republic, 1597
—Yemen Democratic Republic, 1601
—Yugoslavia, 1606
——Bosnia and Herzegovina, 1611
——Croatia, 1612
——Macedonia, 1612
——Montenegro, 1613
——Serbia, 1613
——Slovenia, 1615
—Zaïre, 1618
—Zambia, 1623
—Zimbabwe, 1627-8

Manganese:
—Argentina, 94
—Australia, 106
——Northern Territory, 122
—Brazil, 233
—Bulgaria, 246
—Chile, 315
—China, 360
—Colombia, 375
—Gabon, 519
—Ghana, 565
—India, 642
——Andhra Pradesh, 654
——Bihar, 658
——Goa, 660
——Karnataka, 667
——Madhya Pradesh, 671
——Maharashtra, 674
——Orissa, 680
——Tamil Nadu, 687
—Iran, 711
—Italy, 749
—Japan, 763
—Korea, North, 788
—Mexico, 867
—Morocco, 882
—Romania, 1036
—South Africa, 1094
—Sudan, 1137
—Thailand, 1188
—USSR, 1241

Manganese:
———Georgia, 1271
———Kazakhstan, 1283
—Venezuela, 1581
—Vietnam, 1588

Millet, world statistics, xxi
—Bhután, 216
—Burkina Faso, 251
—Cameroon, 267
—Central African Republic, 343
—Chad, 346
—Ghana, 565
—India,
——Sikkim, 685
——Tamil Nadu, 687
—Kenya, 775
—Maldives, 845
—Mali, 848
—Mauritania, 857
—Nepál, 897
—Niger, 941
—Nigeria, 946
—Sudan, 1137
—Syria, 1177
—Togo, 1193
—Yemen Democratic Republic, 1601
—Zimbabwe, 1628

Nickel:
—Albania, 70-1
—Australia,
——Queensland, 139
——Western Australia, 162-3
—Botswana, 225-6
—Canada, 283
——Manitoba, 306
——Ontario, 321
—Dominican Republic, 437
—Finland, 477
—Greece, 575
—Indonesia, 704
—Mongolia, 874
—New Caledonia, 512-13
—Norway, 953
—Philippines, 1007
—Zimbabwe, 1627

Oats, world statistics, xxi
—Albania, 71
—Australia, 106
——New South Wales, 132
——Queensland, 139
——South Australia, 144
——Tasmania, 150
——Western Australia, 162
—Belgium, 199
—Canada, 283-4
——Quebec, 325
——Saskatchewan, 328
—Chile, 315
—Denmark, 419
—Finland, 477
—France, 491
—Germany (FRG), 539
——Baden-Württemberg, 546
——Hessen, 553
——Lower Saxony, 554
——North Rhine-Westphalia, 556
——Rhineland-Palatinate, 557
——Saarland, 559
——Schleswig-Holstein, 561
—Germany (GDR), 529
—Hungary, 618
—Ireland, 725
—Italy, 749
—Lesotho, 805
—Mongolia, 874

Oats, world statistics, xxi
—Netherlands, 906
—Norway, 954
—Poland, 1015
—Portugal, 1023
—Spain, 1121
—Sweden, 1154
—Turkey, 1211
—UK, 1326
——Northern Ireland, 1362
—Uruguay, 1569
—USA, 1407
——Colorado, 1441
——Indiana, 1462
——Kansas, 1466
——Kentucky, 1469
——Maine, 1473
——Michigan, 1482
——Minnesota, 1484
——Mississippi, 1487
——Missouri, 1489
——Nebraska, 1494
——New York, 1507
——North Dakota, 1512
——Ohio, 1515
——Pennsylvania, 1524
——South Dakota, 1531
——Texas, 1536
——Utah, 1538
——Wisconsin, 1550

Oil and petroleum, world statistics, xxiv-xxv
—Albania, 70-1
—Algeria, 76
—Angola, 82
—Argentina, 93
—Australia, 106,109
——Northern Territory, 122
——Queensland, 139
——South Australia, 145
——Victoria, 155-7
——Western Australia, 162-4
—Austria, 170
—Bangladesh, 186
—Barbados, 191
—Barhrain, 180-1
—Benin, 209
—Bolivia, 220
—Brazil, 233
—Brunei, 240-1
—Bulgaria, 246
—Burma, 255
—Cameroon, 267
—Canada, 282-3
——Alberta, 298-9
——British Columbia, 302
——Manitoba, 306
——New Brunswick, 309
——Newfoundland, 313
——Northwest Territories, 330
——Saskatchewan, 328
——Yukon, 333
—Chad, 346
—Chile, 315
—China, 360,362
—Congo, 383
—Côte d'Ivoire, 392
—Czechoslovakia, 411
—Denmark, 419
—Ecuador, 443
—Egypt, 449
—El Salvador, 455
—Ethiopa, 463
—France, 491
—Gabon, 519-20
—Germany (FRG), 538
—Ghana, 565

Oil and petroleum:
—Hungary, 617
—India, 642
——Assam, 657
——Gujarat, 661
—Indonesia, 704-5
—Iran, 711
—Iraq, 716
—Ireland, 724
—Japan, 763
—Jordan, 770
—Korea, North, 788
—Korea, South, 783-4
—Kuwait, 793
—Lebanon, 801
—Libya, 813
—Madagascar, 825
—Malaysia, 835,843
—Martinique, 504
—Mexico, 867
—Morocco, 882
—Netherlands, 906
—Netherlands Antilles, 914
—Nigeria, 945
—Norway, 953
—Oman, 967
—Pakistan, 975
—Papua New Guinea, 988
—Paraguay, 994
—Peru, 1001
—Poland, 1015
—Qatar, 1030
—Romania, 1036-7
—Saudi Arabia, 1060-1
—Singapore, 1077-8
—South Africa, 1093
—Sudan, 1137
—Syria, 1177
—Taiwan, 369
—Thailand, 1188
—Trinidad and Tobago, 1199
—Tunisia, 1204
—Turkey, 1210
—UK, 1324-5,1332
—United Arab Emirates, 1295
—Uruguay, 1569
—USA, 1405,1414
——Alabama, 1428
——Alaska, 1430-1
——Arkansas, 1435
——California, 1438
——Colorado, 1441
——Illinois, 1459
——Kansas, 1466
——Kentucky, 1468
——Louisiana, 1471
——Mississippi, 1487
——Montana, 1491-2
——Nebraska, 1494
——Nevada, 1497
——New Mexico, 1504
——New York, 1507
——North Dakota, 1512
——Ohio, 1515
——Oklahoma, 1517
——Pennsylvania, 1524
——Texas, 1536
——West Virginia, 1547
——Wyoming, 1553
—USSR, 1240
——Azerbaijan, 1269
——RSFSR, 1254
——Turkmenistan, 1285
——Ukraine, 1265
——Uzbekistan, 1287
—Venezuela, 1581
—Vietnam, 1588
—Yemen Arab Republic, 1597

Oil and petroleum:
—Yemen Democratic Republic, 1601
—Yugoslavia, 1606
——Croatia, 1612
—Zaïre, 1618-19

Phosphates:
—Albania, 70
—Algeria, 70
—Angola, 83
—Brazil, 233
—Cambodia, 262-3
—China, 360
—Congo, 383
—Egypt, 449
—Japan, 764
—Jordan, 770
—Mali, 848
—Morocco, 882
—Nauru, 894-5
—Niger, 941
—Senegal, 1066
—South Africa, 1094
—Syria, 1177
—Thailand, 1188
—Togo, 1192
—Tunisia, 1204
—USA, 1405
——Florida, 1450
——Idaho, 1456
——Montana, 1491
——North Carolina, 1510
——Wyoming, 1553
—USSR, 1241
—Venezuela, 1581

Potatoes:
—Albania, 71
—Algeria, 76
—Andorra, 80
—Argentina, 94
—Australia,
——New South Wales, 132
——Queensland, 139
——Tasmania, 150
——Western Australia, 162
—Bangladesh, 187
—Belgium, 199
—Bhután, 216
—Bolivia, 221
—Brazil, 234
—Bulgaria, 246
—Canada, 283
——New Brunswick, 309
——Quebec, 325
—Chile, 315
—Colombia, 375
—Costa Rica, 387
—Cyprus, 402-3
—Czechoslovakia, 411
—Denmark, 419
—Ecuador, 443
—Finland, 477
—France, 491
—Germany (FRG), 539
——Baden-Württemberg, 546
——Hamburg, 551
——Hessen, 553
——Lower Saxony, 554
——North Rhine-Westphalia, 556
——Rhineland-Palatinate, 557
——Saarland, 559
——Schleswig-Holstein, 561
—Germany (GDR), 529
—Hungary, 618
—Iceland, 626
—India,

Potatoes:
——Assam, 657
——Bihar, 658
——Himachal Pradesh, 664
——Meghalaya, 676-7
—Ireland, 725
—Israel, 738
—Italy, 749
—Kenya, 775
—Korea, North, 788
—Laos, 797
—Lebanon, 801
—Madagascar, 825
—Malta, 852
—Mauritania, 857
—Mauritius, 861
—Mexico, 867
—Mongolia, 874
—Morocco, 882
—Nepál, 897
—Netherlands, 906
—Norway, 954
—Pakistan, 976
—Peru, 1001
—Poland, 1015
—Portugal, 1023
—Réunion, 505
—Romania, 1036
—Rwanda, 1042
—South Africa, 1094
——Ciskei, 1111
—Spain, 1121
—Swaziland, 1146
—Sweden, 1154
—Switzerland, 1169
—Tunisia, 1204
—UK, 1326
——Northern Ireland, 1362
—USA, 1407
——Alabama, 1428
——Colorado, 1441
——Connecticut, 1444
——Idaho, 1457
——Maine, 1473
——Massachusetts, 1479
——Minnesota, 1484
——Montana, 1492
——Nevada, 1497
——New Jersey, 1501
——North Dakota, 1512
——Oklahoma, 1517
——Oregon, 1521
——Pennsylvania, 1524
——Texas, 1536
——Utah, 1538
——Wisconsin, 1550
—USSR, 1241
——Armenia, 1274
——Azerbaijan, 1268
——Belorussia, 1267
——Estonia, 1277
——Georgia, 1271
——Kazakhstan, 1283
——Kirghizia, 1291
——Latvia, 1279
——Lithuania, 1280
——Tadzhikistan, 1289
——Ukraine, 1265
——Uzbekistan, 1287
—Venezuela, 1581
—Vietnam, 1588
—Yemen Arab Republic, 1597
—Yugoslavia, 1607
——Bosnia and Herzegovina, 1611
——Croatia, 1612
——Montenegro, 1613
——Serbia, 1613
——Slovenia, 1615

Rice, world statistics, xx
—Afghánistán, 65
—Albania, 71
—Argentina, 94
—Australia, 106
——New South Wales, 132
——Northern Territory, 122
—Bangladesh, 187
—Benin, 209
—Bhután, 216
—Bolivia, 221
—Brazil, 234
—Brunei, 240
—Burkina Faso, 251
—Burma, 256
—Cambodia, 263
—Central African Republic, 343
—Chile, 315
—China, 361
—Colombia, 375
—Comoros, 379
—Congo, 383
—Costa Rica, 387
—Côte d'Ivoire, 392
—Dominican Republic, 437
—Ecuador, 443
—Egypt, 449-50
—El Salvador, 455
—Fiji, 470
—French Guiana, 501
—Gabon, 520
—Gambia, 523
—Ghana, 565
—Greece, 575
—Guinea, 587
—Guinea-Bissau, 590
—Guyana, 593-4
—Haiti, 599
—India, 643
——Andaman and Nicobar Islands, 694
——Andhra Pradesh, 654
——Bihar, 658
——Dadra and Nagar Haveli, 695
——Daman and Diu, 696
——Goa, 660
——Gujarat, 661
——Himachal Pradesh, 664
——Jammu and Kashmir, 666
——Karnataka, 668
——Kerala, 669
——Madhya Pradesh, 671
——Maharashtra, 674
——Manipur, 675
——Meghalaya, 676
——Mizoram, 677
——Nagaland, 679
——Orissa, 680
——Pondicherry, 698
——Punjab, 682
——Sikkim, 685
——Tamil Nadu, 687
——Tripura, 689
——West Bengal, 692
—Indonesia, 704
—Iran, 711
—Iraq, 716
—Japan, 763
—Kenya, 775
—Korea, North, 788
—Korea, South, 784
—Laos, 797
—Liberia, 808-9
—Madagascar, 825
—Malaysia, 837
—Mali, 848
—Mauritania, 857
—Mexico, 867

Rice:
—Mozambique, 887
—Nepál, 897
—Nicaragua, 937
—Niger, 941
—Nigeria, 946
—Pakistan, 976
—Panama, 982
—Papua New Guinea, 988
—Paraguay, 995
—Peru, 1001
—Philippines, 1007
—Portugal, 1023
—Senegal, 1066
—Sierra Leone, 1072
—Solomon Islands, 1083
—Spain, 1121
—Sri Lanka, 1130
—Suriname, 1141-2
—Taiwan, 369
—Tanzania, 1182
—Thailand, 1188
—Togo, 1193
—Turkey, 1211
—Uruguay, 1569
—USA, 1407
——Arkansas, 1436
——Louisiana, 1471
——Mississippi, 1487
——Oklahoma, 1517
—Venezuela, 1581
—Vietnam, 1588
—Zaïre, 1618

Rubber:
—Brazil, 234
—Brunei, 241
—Burma, 256
—Cambodia, 263
—Cameroon, 267
—Colombia, 375
—Côte d'Ivoire, 392
—El Salvador, 455
—Guatemala, 583
—Guinea-Bissau, 590
—India,
——Kerala, 669
—Indonesia, 704-5
—Liberia, 809
—Malaysia, 835,837,843
—Sri Lanka, 1130-1
—Thailand, 1188
—UK, 1331-2
—Vietnam, 1588
—Zaïre, 1618

Rye, world statistics, xvi
—Austria, 171
—Belgium, 199
—Canada,
——Saskatchewan, 328
—Czechoslovakia, 411
—Denmark, 419
—Finland, 477
—France, 491
—Germany (FRG), 539
——Baden-Württemberg, 546
——Hessen, 553
——Lower Saxony, 554
——North Rhine-Westphalia, 556
——Rhineland-Palatinate, 557
——Saarland, 559
——Schleswig-Holstein, 561
—Germany (GDR), 529
—Italy, 749
—Mongolia, 874
—Netherlands, 906
—Norway, 954

Rye:
—Poland, 1015
—Portugal, 1023
—Romania, 1036
—Spain, 1121
—Sweden, 1154
—Turkey, 1211
—USA,
——Kentucky, 1469
——Minnesota, 1484
——North Dakota, 1512
——South Dakota, 1531
—Yugoslavia, 1607

Salt:
—Albania, 70
—Algeria, 76
—Angola, 82
—Australia,
——South Australia, 144
——Western Australia, 162
—Brazil, 233
—Bulgaria, 246
—Canada,
——New Brunswick, 309
——Saskatchewan, 328
—Cape Verde, 337
—Chad, 346
—China, 360
—Colombia, 375
—Costa Rica, 387
—Czechoslovakia, 411
—Dominican Republic, 437
—Egypt, 449
—Ethiopa, 463
—India,
——Himachal Pradesh, 664
——Rajasthan, 683
——Tamil Nadu, 687
—Iran, 711
—Israel, 737
—Kenya, 775
—Mali, 848
—Netherlands, 906
—Niger, 941
—Pakistan, 975
—Philippines, 1007
—Romania, 1036
—Sri Lanka, 1130
—Switzerland, 1169
—Syria, 1177
—Tunisia, 1204
—USA, 1405
——California, 1438
——Louisiana, 1471
——Texas, 1536
—Yemen Arab Republic, 1597
—Yugoslavia, 1606

Silver:
—Algeria, 76
—Argentina, 93
—Australia,
——New South Wales, 132
——Northern Territory, 122
——Queensland, 139
——Tasmania, 149
—Brazil, 233
—Burma, 256
—Canada, 283
——British Columbia, 302
——Manitoba, 306
——New Brunswick, 309
——Northwest Territories, 330
——Yukon, 333
—China, 360
—Colombia, 375
—Dominican Republic, 437

Silver:
—Ecuador, 443
—El Salvador, 455
—Guatemala, 583
—India, 642
——Bihar, 658
——Karnataka, 667
——Rajasthan, 683
—Indonesia, 704
—Japan, 763
—Korea, North, 788
—Korea, South, 784
—Mexico, 867
—Nicaragua, 937
—Pakistan, 975
—Papua New Guinea, 988
—Peru, 1001
—Philippines, 1007
—Poland, 1015
—Solomon Islands, 1083
—South Africa, 1094
—USA, 1405,1413
——Alaska, 1430-1
——Arizona, 1433
——Idaho, 1456
——Maine, 1473
——Montana, 1491
——Nevada, 1497
——South Dakota, 1531
—USSR, 1241
—Yugoslavia, 1606
—Zimbabwe, 1627

Sorghum, world statistics, xxii
—Albania, 71
—Australia,
——New South Wales, 132
——Northern Territory, 122
——Queensland, 139
—Benin, 209
—Botswana, 226
—Burkina Faso, 251
—Burundi, 259
—Colombia, 375
—Egypt, 450
—El Salvador, 455
—Ethiopa, 44
—Ghana, 565
—Guinea-Bissau, 590
—Kenya, 775
—Lesotho, 805
—Mexico, 867
—Namibia, 892
—Nicaragua, 937
—Niger, 941
—Nigeria, 946
—Rwanda, 1042
—Senegal, 1066
—Somalia, 1086
—South Africa, 1094
——Ciskei, 1111
—Swaziland, 1146
—Tanzania, 1182
—Togo, 1193
—USA,
——Colorado, 1441
——Kansas, 1466
——Kentucky, 1469
——Mississippi, 1487
——Missouri, 1489
——Nebraska, 1494
——New Mexico, 1504
——Oklahoma, 1517
——South Dakota, 1531
—Vietnam, 1588
—Yemen Arab Republic, 1597
—Zimbabwe, 1628

Soya beans:
—Argentina, 94
—Australia,
——Northern Territory, 122
—Brazil, 234
—Burma, 256
—Cambodia, 263
—Canada, 284
—China, 361
—Indonesia, 704
—Japan, 763
—Korea, North, 788
—Paraguay, 995
—Taiwan, 369
—Thailand, 1188
—USA, 1407,1414
——Alabama, 1428
——Arkansas, 1436
——Delaware, 1446
——Florida, 1450
——Georgia, 1452
——Illinois, 1459
——Indiana, 1462
——Iowa, 1464
——Kansas, 1466
——Kentucky, 1469
——Louisiana, 1471
——Maryland, 1476
——Michigan, 1482
——Mississippi, 1487
——Missouri, 1489
——Nebraska, 1494
——New Jersey, 1501
——North Carolina, 1510
——Ohio, 1515
——Oklahoma, 1517
——South Carolina, 1529
——Tennessee, 15333
——Texas, 1536
—Vietnam, 1588
—Zimbabwe, 1628

Steel *see* Iron and steel

Sugar, world statistics, xxiii
—Afghánistán, 65-6
—Albania, 71
—Angola, 83
—Argentina, 94
—Australia, 106
——New South Wales, 132
——Queensland, 139-40
—Bahamas, 175
—Bangladesh, 187
—Barbados, 191
—Belgium, 199
—Belize, 205-6
—Benin, 210
—Bolivia, 221
—Brazil, 234
—Bulgaria, 246
—Burkina Faso, 251
—Burma, 256
—Cape Verde, 337
—Chad, 346
—Chile, 315
—China, 361
—Colombia, 375
—Comoros, 379
—Congo, 383
—Costa Rica, 387-8
—Côte d'Ivoire, 392
—Czechoslovakia, 411
—Denmark, 421
—Dominican Republic, 437
—Egypt, 450
—El Salvador, 455
—Fiji, 470

Sugar:
—France, 491
—French Guiana, 501
—Gabon, 520
—Germany (FRG), 539
——Baden-Württemberg, 546
——Hessen, 553
——Lower Saxony, 554
——North Rhine-Westphalia, 556
——Rhineland-Palatinate, 557
——Schleswig-Holstein, 561
—Germany (GDR), 529
—Ghana, 565
—Grenada, 579
—Guadeloupe, 500
—Guatemala, 583
—Guinea, 587
—Guinea-Bissau, 590
—Guyana, 593-4
—Haiti, 599
—Honduras, 604
—India, 643
——Assam, 657
——Bihar, 658
——Goa, 660
——Haryana, 663
——Karnataka, 668
——Kerala, 669
——Madhya Pradesh, 671
——Maharashtra, 674
——Nagaland, 679
——Orissa, 680
——Rajasthan, 684
——Tamil Nadu, 687
——Tripura, 689
——Uttar Pradesh, 691
—Indonesia, 704
—Iran, 711
—Ireland, 725
—Italy, 749
—Jamaica, 756
—Japan, 763
—Kenya, 775
—Lebanon, 801
—Liberia, 808-9
—Madagascar, 825
—Malawi, 829
—Malaysia, 835,837
—Mali, 848
—Martinique, 503
—Mauritius, 861
—Mexico, 867
—Morocco, 882
—Mozambique, 887
—Nepál, 897
—Netherlands, 906
—Nicaragua, 937
—Niger, 941
—Pakistan, 976
—Papua New Guinea, 989
—Paraguay, 995
—Peru, 1001
—Philippines, 1007
—Poland, 1015
—Réunion, 505
—Romania, 1036-7
—St Kitts-Nevis, 1045
—Somalia, 1086
—South Africa, 1094
——Natal, 1102
—Spain, 1121
—Suriname, 1141
—Swaziland, 1146
—Sweden, 1154
—Switzerland, 1169
—Syria, 1177
—Taiwan, 369
—Tanzania, 1182

Sugar:
—Thailand, 1188
—Trinidad and Tobago, 1199
—Tunisia, 1204
—Uganda, 1221
—UK, 1326,1331
—Uruguay, 1569
—USA,
———California, 1438
———Florida, 1450
———Hawaii, 1454
———Idaho, 1457
———Louisiana, 1471
———Michigan, 1482
———Minnesota, 1484
———Montana, 1492
———North Dakota, 1512
———Puerto Rico, 1562
———Wyoming, 1553
—USSR, 1241
———Armenia, 1274
———Belorussia, 1267
———Georgia, 1271
———Kazakhstan, 1283
———Latvia, 1279
———Lithuania, 1280
———Moldavia, 1275
———Ukraine, 1265
—Venezuela, 1581
—Vietnam, 1588
—Yugoslavia, 1607
———Croatia, 1612
———Serbia, 1613-14
———Slovenia, 1615
—Zaïre, 1618
—Zambia, 1623
—Zimbabwe, 1628

Sulphur:
—Afghánistán, 65
—Algeria, 76
—Canada, 283
—China, 360
—France, 491
—Italy, 749
—Mexico, 867
—Pakistan, 975
—Poland, 1015
—Qatar, 1031
—Taiwan, 369
—Turkey, 1210
—USA, 1405
———Louisiana, 1471
—Venezuela, 1581

Tea:
—Australia, 108
—Bangladesh, 187
—Burundi, 259
—China, 361-2
—India, 642-3
———Assam, 657
———Kerala, 669
———Maharashtra, 674
———Tripura, 689
———West Bengal, 693
—Indonesia, 704
—Japan, 763
—Kenya, 775
—Malawi, 829
—Malaysia, 835,837
—Mauritius, 861
—Mozambique, 886
—Papua New Guinea, 988-9
—Rwanda, 1042
—Sri Lanka, 1130-1
—Taiwan, 369
—Tanzania, 1183

Tea:
—Turkey, 1211
—Uganda, 1221
—UK, 1331
—USSR,
———Azerbaijan, 1268
———Georgia, 1271
—Vietnam, 1588
—Zimbabwe, 1628

Tin:
—Australia, 106
———Queensland, 139
———Tasmania, 149-50
———Western Australia, 162
—Bolivia, 220
—Brazil, 233
—Burma, 256
—China, 360
—India,
———Madhya Pradesh, 671
—Indonesia, 704-5
—Laos, 797
—Malaysia, 835,837
—Mongolia, 874
—Niger, 941
—Nigeria, 945
—Norway, 953
—Portugal, 1023
—Rwanda, 1042
—Spain, 1120
—Thailand, 1188
—Uganda, 1221
—UK, 1326
—USA,
———Alaska, 1430-1
—USSR,
———RSFSR, 1254
—Zimbabwe, 1627

Tobacco:
—Afghánistán, 66
—Andorra, 80
—Angola, 83
—Argentina, 94
—Australia, 108
———Queensland, 139
———Victoria, 156
—Bangladesh, 187
—Belgium, 199
—Brazil, 234
—Bulgaria, 246-7
—Canada, 283,285
—Costa Rica, 387
—Dominican Republic, 437
—Fiji, 470
—Ghana, 565
—Honduras, 604
—India, 643
Bihar, 658
—Indonesia, 704
—Iran, 711
—Italy, 749
—Japan, 763
—Kenya, 775
—Korea, South, 784
—Laos, 797
—Madagascar, 825
—Malawi, 829
—Malaysia, 835
—Mauritius, 861
—Paraguay, 995
—Philippines, 1007
—Réunion, 506
—Spain, 1121
—Swaziland, 1146
—Switzerland, 1169
—Tanzania, 1182-3

Tobacco:
—Thailand, 1188
—Tunisia, 1204
—Turkey, 1210-11
—Uganda, 1221
—USA, 1407,1414
———Connecticut, 1444
———Florida, 1450
———Georgia, 1452
———Kentucky, 1469
———Maryland, 1476
———Massachusetts, 1479
———North Carolina, 1510
———Pennsylvania, 1524
———South Carolina, 1529
———Tennessee, 15333
———West Virginia, 1547
———Wisconsin, 1550
—USSR,
———Azerbaijan, 1268
—Venezuela, 1581
—Vietnam, 1588
—Yugoslavia, 1607
———Macedonia, 1612
—Zambia, 1623
—Zimbabwe, 1628

Tungsten:
—Argentina, 94
—Australia, 106
———Tasmania, 151
—Brazil, 233
—China, 360,362
—Guatemala, 583
—Japan, 763
—Korea, South, 784
—Mongolia, 874
—Nicaragua, 937
—Portugal, 1023
—Rwanda, 1042
—Spain, 1120
—Thailand, 1188
—USA,
———California, 1438
—USSR,
———Kazakhstan, 1283

Uranium:
—Argentina, 94
—Australia,
———Northern Territory, 122
—Canada,
———Newfoundland, 313
———Saskatchewan, 328
—Gabon, 519
—Korea, North, 788
—Mexico, 867
—Namibia, 891
—Niger, 941
Ontario,
———Canada, 321
—Portugal, 1023
—Romania, 1036
—Spain, 1120
—Sweden, 1154
—USA,
———New Mexico, 1504
———Washington, 1545
———Wyoming, 1553
—USSR, 1241

Wheat, world statistics, xv
—Afghánistán, 65
—Albania, 71
—Australia, 106
———New South Wales, 132
———Queensland, 139
———South Australia, 144-5

Wheat:
——Tasmania, 150
——Western Australia, 162,164
—Bangladesh, 187
—Belgium, 199
—Bhután, 216
—Bolivia, 221
—Brazil, 234
—Bulgaria, 246
—Burma, 256
—Canada, 283-4
——Saskatchewan, 328
—Chile, 315
—China, 361
—Cyprus, 402
—Czechoslovakia, 411
—Denmark, 419
—Egypt, 450
—Ethiopa, 463
—Finland, 477
—France, 491
—Germany (FRG), 539
——Baden-Württemberg, 546
——Hessen, 553
——Lower Saxony, 554
——North Rhine-Westphalia, 556
——Rhineland-Palatinate, 557
——Saarland, 559
——Schleswig-Holstein, 561
—Germany (GDR), 529
—Hungary, 618
—India, 643
——Andhra Pradesh, 654
——Assam, 657
——Bihar, 658
——Himachal Pradesh, 664
——Jammu and Kashmir, 666
——Manipur, 675
——Punjab, 682
——Sikkim, 685
——Tripura, 689
——West Bengal, 693
—Iran, 711
—Iraq, 716
—Ireland, 725
—Israel, 738
—Italy, 749
—Japan, 763
—Jordan, 770
—Kenya, 775
—Lebanon, 801
—Lesotho, 805
—Libya, 814
—Mexico, 867
—Mongolia, 874
—Morocco, 882
—Namibia, 892
—Nepál, 897
—Netherlands, 906
—New Zealand, 922
—Norway, 954
—Pakistan, 976
—Paraguay, 995
—Poland, 1015
—Portugal, 1023
—Romania, 1036
—South Africa, 1094
——Ciskei, 1111
—Spain, 1121
—Sudan, 1137
—Sweden, 1154
—Switzerland, 1169
—Syria, 1177
—Taiwan, 369
—Tanzania, 1182
—Tunisia, 1204
—Turkey, 1211
—UK, 1326

Wheat:
——Northern Ireland, 1362
—Uruguay, 1569
—USA, 1407,1414
——Alabama, 1428
——Arizona, 1434
——Colorado, 1441
——Georgia, 1452
——Idaho, 1457
——Illinois, 1459
——Indiana, 1462
——Kansas, 1466
——Kentucky, 1469
——Michigan, 1482
——Minnesota, 1484
——Mississippi, 1487
——Montana, 1492
——Nebraska, 1494
——New Mexico, 1504
——New York, 1507
——North Carolina, 1510
——North Dakota, 1512
——Ohio, 1515
——Oklahoma, 1517
——Oregon, 1521
——Pennsylvania, 1524
——South Dakota, 1531
——Texas, 1536
——Utah, 1538
——Washington, 1545
——Wyoming, 1553
—Yemen Arab Republic, 1597
—Yemen Democratic Republic, 1601
—Yugoslavia, 1607
——Bosnia and Herzegovina, 1611
——Croatia, 1612
——Macedonia, 1612
——Montenegro, 1613
——Serbia, 1613
——Slovenia, 1615
—Zimbabwe, 1628

Wine:
—Albania, 71
—Australia, 106
——New South Wales, 132
——South Australia, 144
——Victoria, 156
—Cyprus, 402-3
—France, 491
—Germany (FRG), 539
——Rhineland-Palatinate, 557
—Hungary, 618
—Israel, 738
—Italy, 749
—Malta, 852
—Tunisia, 1204
—Uruguay, 1569
—USA,
——California, 1438
—Yugoslavia, 1607

Wolfram *see* Tungsten

Wool:
—Afghánistán, 65
—Argentina, 94
—Australia, 106
——New South Wales, 132
——Queensland, 139-40
——South Australia, 144-5
——Tasmania, 150
——Victoria, 157
——Western Australia, 162,164
—Canada, 285
—Falkland Islands, 467
—New Zealand 922

Wool:
—Japan, 764
—South Africa, 1094
—Spain, 1121
—Turkey, 1210-11
—Uruguay, 1569
—USA,
——Illinois, 1459
——Iowa, 1464
——Michigan, 1482
——Wyoming, 1553
—USSR,
——Azerbaijan, 1268
——Kazakhstan, 1283
——Kirghizia, 1291
——Tadzhikistan, 1289
——Turkmenistan, 1285
——Ukraine, 1265
——Uzbekistan, 1287

Zinc:
—Algeria, 76
—Argentina, 94
—Australia, 106
——New South Wales, 132
——Northern Territory, 122
——Queensland, 139
——Tasmania, 149
—Austria, 171
—Canada, 283
——Manitoba, 306
——New Brunswick, 309
——Newfoundland, 313
——Northwest Territories, 330
——Ontario, 321
——Quebec, 325
——Saskatchewan, 328
——Yukon, 333
—Chile, 315
—China, 360
—Congo, 383
—Ecuador, 443
—Finland, 477
—Guatemala, 583
—India, 642
——Sikkim, 686
—Iran, 711
—Ireland, 724
—Italy, 749
—Japan, 763
—Korea, North, 788-9
—Korea, South, 784
—Mexico, 867
—Mongolia, 874
—Morocco, 882
—Nigeria, 945
—Norway, 953
—Peru, 1001
—Philippines, 1007
—Spain, 1120
—Sweden, 1154
—Thailand, 1188
—Tunisia, 1204
—UK, 1326
—USA, 1405
——Kansas, 1466
——Maine, 1473
——Missouri, 1489
——Montana, 1492
——New York, 1507
——Oklahoma, 1517
——Tennessee, 1533
——Virginia, 1542
—USSR, 1241
——RSFSR, 1254
—Yugoslavia, 1606
—Zaïre, 1618
—Zambia, 1623

NAMES INDEX

Abad, F., 1005
Abanda, J.T., 266
Abass, O.C., 430
Abbadi, H., 880
Abbey, J.L.S., 567
Abbil, I.J., 1572
Abdallah, A., 1206
Abdelaziz, M., 1126
Abdeljalil, A. Ben, 881
Abdou, S., 430
Abdoudou, S., 209
Abdoulatif, F., 432
Abdoun, A.M., 1139
Abduh, J.M., 1597
Abdul Aziz, *Pehin Dato Haji*, 239
Abdul Ghafar bin Baba, 833
Abdul Halim Mu'azdam Shah, *Sultan*, 832
Abdul Munim, M., 185
Abdul Rahman, *Pehin Dato Haji*, 239
Abdul Rahman Zohari, 842
Abdul Taib Mahmud, 842
Abdul-Karim, I., 180
Abdulah, F., 56
Abdullah ibn Abdul Aziz, *Prince*, 1058
Abdullah, Y. bin A. bin, 966
Abdullahi, H., 944
Abel, *Colonel*, 254
Abfreotti, G., 745
Abraham, H., 598
Abramowitz, M., 1214
Abu Hassan bin Haji Omar, 833
Abu Shawrib, M., 1596
Abu Taleb, Y.S., 447
Abulhasan, M.A., 794
Abushama, El R., 1139
Acland, A., 1358, 1424
Ada, J.F., 1555
Adair, J.A., 297
Adam, R., 1068
Adamec, L., 409
Adamfio, N.O., 564
Adami, E.F., 851
Adams, A.P., 601
Adams, W.J., 452
Adaoghlu, M., 406
Adderley, P.L., 174
Adenan bin Haji Satem, 842
Adhyatma, 702
Adikari, A.M.S., 1128
Adireksarn, P., 1186
Adjoudji, H., 266
Adodo, Y., 1192
Adouki, M., 384
Adoum, M.A., 347
Adriko, E.T., 1220
Afaese, P., 1594
Afande, D.D., 777
Afiff, S., 702
Afifi, T., 880
Agbetra, A., 1192
Aghazadeh, G., 709
Ago, R., 7
Aguilar, A., 1583
Agústsson, H., 629
Ahern, B., 721
Ahmad Al-Hajj, 803
Ahmad Rithandeen Al-Haj bin Tengku Ismail, 833
Ahmad, S.U., 1600
Ahmad Shah Al-Musta'in, *Sultan*, 832
Ahmad Zaidi bin Muhammed Noor, 832, 842
Ahmadu, H., 948
Ahmed, K.Z., 185
Ahmed, N., 979
Ahmed, Y. al-, 1176
Ahwsan, A., 972
Aird, M.A., 148
Ajibola, B., 944
Akanga, D., 1194
Akatol, K., 406
Akbulut, Y., 1208
Ake, S., 391
Akhmedov, Kh., 1284
Akihito *Emperor*, 760
Akinrinade, A., 944
Akmatov, T., 1291
Akpo, P., 208
Akşin, M., 1214
Aksu, A., 1208
Akuzum, I., 1208
Akyol, A., 1208
Al-Shaikhly, S., 718
Alaini, M.A., 1598
Alam Khan, K., 660, 695-6
Alaoui, M.M.B., 880
Alarcón Mantilla, L.F., 373
Alatas, A., 702
Albert, *Prince*, 870
Albrecht, E., 554
Alders, H., 903
Alelua Lopes, T., 589
Alesana, T.E., 1594
Alexander, H., 433
Alexander, L.M., 319
Alexander, P.C., 687
Alexandra, *Princess*, 1305
Alhaji, A., 944
Ali, F.S., 1181
Ali, K., 185
Ali, M., 671, 1220
Ali, M.S.S., 791
Ali, Z. El A. Ben, 1203
Ali-Rachedi, A., 75
Alia, R., 69
Aliaziambina, N., 1617
Allpul, K., 1192
Ali Khan, Z., 979
Allen, R., 878
Alleyne, B.G.K., 433
Alliali, C., 391
Almanqour, N.H., 1063
Almoayed, T.A., 179
Almunia Amann, J., 1117
Alni'ma, H.A.H., 1032
Alo, E.O., 430
Alois, *Prince*, 816
Aloneftis, A., 401
Als, G., 822
Altenburg, W., 38
Altinkaya, C., 1208
Aluvihare, A., 1128
Alvarado Cano, R., 453
Alvárez del Castillo, E., 865
Amare, G., 465
Ambroziak, J., 1013
Amegboh, G., 1192
Amegi, Y.M., 1192
Aminu, J., 944
Amjad Hossain, S., 185
Amsberg, C. von, 901
Amy, D.O., 826
Anas, A., 702
Anbari, A.A.A. Al-, 718
Anciaux, J., 505
Andersen, H.G., 629
Anderson, D., 297
Andersson, G., 1150
Andersson, S., 1150
Andre, H., 274
Andreotti, G., 745
Andrew, *Prince*, *Duke of York*, 1305
Andrews, E.E., 1528
Andrianoelison, J., 824
Andriessen, J., 903
Andrus, C., 1456
Angari, I. ibn A. al, 1059
Angba, N.K., 391
Angoran, Y.D., 391
Ankah, M., 944
Annan, D., 564
Anne, *Princess Royal*, 1305
Ansari, K., 1176
Antabi, M.N., 1176
Antill, J.K., 1372
Antonio, H., 208
Anwar bin Ibrahim, 833
Anyaoku, E., 31
Apang, G., 655
Apatero, V., 1117
Appel, G., 550
Aptidon, H.G., 430
Aquino, C., 1005
Arad, M., 741
Aranda, T., 204
Aranzadi Martínez, C., 1117
Arapaşu, T. *Patriarch*, 1039
Arashi, Y.H. al-, 1597
Arauco Paz, E., 223
Araújo, J.E., 337
Arbuthnott, H.J., 1026
Archibald, V., 1046
Arcos, C.S., 606
Ardi, A.I., 430
Arens, M., 736
Argaña, L.M., 993
Argentino Lúder, I., 92
Arifin, B., 702
Arishi, A.K. al-, 1596
Armacost, M., 767
Armas, C., 1579
Armas, E. de, 1579
Armstrong, I.M., 130
Armstrong-Jones, *Lady* Sarah, 1305
Arnold, L.M.F., 143
Aroi, K., 894
Arpaillange, P., 485
Arrindell, C.A., 1044
Arutyunyan, S.G., 1274
Asamoah, O.Y., 564
Asgrímsson, H., 624
Ashcroft, J.D., 1489
Ashtal, A.S. al-, 1602
Asllani, M., 69
Aspe Armella, P., 865
Assad, H. al-, 1175
Assad, R. al-, 1176
Assam, M., 1201
Astorga-Gadea, N., 939
Ataia, R., 778
Atala, C.G., 1003
Atapattu, R., 1128
Atasayan, T., 406
Ataul Karim, A.H.S., 189
Atkins, H., 1517
Atkinson, M.W., 1039
Attar, M.S. al-, 1596
Attar, N. al-, 1176
Attas, H.A.B. al-, 1600
Attiyah, A bin K. al-, 1029
Attoungbré, G., 393
Aubee, C., 1074
Aung Ye Kyaw, 254
Austin, M., 919
Austin, R.H., 1481
Avice, E., 486
Avril, P., 598
Awadi, A.A. al-, 791
Awan, M.A., 972
Awlaqi, N.A. al-, 1596
Ayad, M.A.G., 803
Ayala Lasso, J., 444
Aykut, I., 1208
Aylwin Azócar, P., 349
Azcuna, A., 1005
Azeib, A.D. al-, 1598
Azlan Shah, *Sultan*, 832
Azmani, A. al-, 880

Bâ, M.A., 1065
Baba, C.A.O., 857
Baba, K. al-, 1176
Babale, A., 266
Babangida, I.B., 944
Babassana, H., 382
Bacani, S., 1005
Baco Carba, R., 441
Bacon, L., 324
Bacon, R., 315
Badar, J., 972
Badawi, A.H., 452
Badhroudine, 824
Badr, F., 1059
Badran, M., 769
Baejaoui, M., 7
Bagayambo, T., 342
Bahadur Bhandari, N., 685
Bahadur Khan, K., 972
Baharna, H. Al, 180
Bahrin, *Pengiran Haji*, 239
Baird, B.G., 131
Baiteke, A., 780
Bakatin, V.V., 1229
Baker, J.A., 1385
Baker, K., 1308
Baker, R.W., 312
Baker-Bates, M.S., 238
Bako, M.S., 940
Balaguer, J., 436
Balazs, A., 1013
Balcerowicz, L., 1013
Balezi, N., 1617
Baliles, G.L., 1542
Balima, S.T., 251
Balopi, P., 225
Baluchi, A. bin S. al, 966
Bamana, Y., 507

Bamu, N., 1617
Banda, H.K., 827
Bandar ibn Sultan, *Prince*, 1063
Bandolo, H., 266
Bangerter, N., 1538
Bangoura, H.V., 586
Bannon, J.C., 143
Banny, J.K., 391
Bapista Gumucio, M., 219
Bappoo, S., 860
Bar-Lev, H., 736
Barbarito, L., 1576
Barčák, A., 409
Barclay, R.C., 531
Barco Vargas, V., 373
Barder, B.L., 211, 947
Bärlund, K., 475
Baron, F.A., 434
Barque, B.M., 1192
Barre, M.S., 1085
Barrett, R.S., 432
Barrett, S.J., 1018
Barrington, N.J., 979
Barrionuevo, J., 1117
Barros, F. de, 589
Barrow, R.N., 32, 192
Barry, J., 308
Bartha, F., 617
Bartlett, G., 1090
Bartlett Diaz, M., 865
Bartončik, J., 409
Bashir, H.E. El, 1139
Bashir, O.H.A. al, 1136
Basri, D., 880
Bassett, M., 918
Bassoukou-Boumba, P.-D., 382
Basu, J., 692
Bataroma, R., 778
Bathurst, B., 39
Batmunkh, J., 873
Batoko, O., 209
Battaglia, A., 746
Battiscombe, C.C.R., 78
Batubara, C., 702
Baũá, E., 92
Baudouin, *King*, 195
Baxter, E., 1464
Bayh, E., 1461
Bayoud, G., 1535
Bayram, M., 406
Bazarov, R.A., 1284
Bazoberry, H., 223
Beatrice, *Princess*, 1305
Beatrix, *Queen*, 901
Beatty, H.P., 274
Beaulieu, R., 308
Beaumont, J.M., 1373
Beazley, K., 100
Becera, M.F., 373
Bechio, J.-J., 391
Bedo, J., 824
Beek, R. ter, 903
Beer, C., 319
Beer, P.J., 1373
Beerman, A., 1494
Beggs, P.A., 161
Begin, R., 1527
Beil, G., 527
Bein, Y., 741
Bekale, R.N., 518
Békési, L., 615
Bekteshi, B., 69
Belaid, M., 1203
Belchev, B., 244
Belega, M., 1021
Bellmon, H., 1517
Belmont, J., 1068
Belstead, *Lord*, 1309
Beltran Guerra, L., 1579
Bemananjara, G., 824
Benaissa, M., 880
Bencheikh, T., 880
Bendaoud, A., 75
Benflis, A., 75
Bengelloun, A., 884
Bengue, J., 342
Benjamin, M.P., 434
Benker, A., 557
Bennett, P., 148
Benoit, P.F., 601
Bensid, A., 78
Bentkowski, A., 1013
Bérégovoy, P., 485
Berghorfer, W., 527
Berinson, J.M., 161
Bernard, J.G.L., 322
Bernini, C., 746
Berntson, E., 327
Beron, P., 244
Bertero Guitiérrez, M., 219
Berthoud, M., 1201
Bertoni Argón, H., 993
Bessler, A., 406
Best, R., 629
Bethel, Peter, 175
Bethel, Philip M., 175
Betkowski, N., 297
Bettencort Santos, H., 338
Bhattarai, K.P., 896
Bhumibol Adulyadej, *King*, 1185
Bhutto, B., 972
Bhutto, N., 972
Biancheri, B., 753
Biaou, A., 208
Bioko, C.S., 459
Biran, Y., 741
Birch, J.A., 621
Bird, L.B., 87
Bird, V.C., 87
Birendra, *King*, 896
Birkelund, P., 429
Biryukova, A.P., 1230
Bishop, J.K., 810
Biswal, H., 680
Bita, F., 382
Biya, P., 266
Biyoghe Mba, P., 518
Bizimungu, C., 1041
Bjarnason, G., 624
Bjartveit, E., 951
Bjorck, A., 42
Black, K., 319
Blackman, D., 190
Blackman, H.A., 190
Bladel, F.M., 148
Blais, P., 274
Blanc, P.-L., 498
Blanchard, E., 308
Blanchard, J.J., 1481
Blanco Zavalo, D., 219
Blandon, E., 584
Blaney, V., 308
Blas, F.F., 1555
Blevins, F.T., 143
Blewett, N., 100
Blick, M.T.S., 1048
Blix, H., 12
Bloch, J.C., 898
Blüm, N., 536
Blunt, R.D., 1489
Bock, K., 550
Bocko Heredia, M.A., 999
Boden, F., 820
Bodhisane, T., 798
Bodry, A., 820
Boehm, R., 969
Bogle, E., 757
Bognessan, A. Ye, 251
Bogsch, A., 28
Boguinard, E.K., 391
Böhme, I., 527
Bokam, J.P., 266
Bol-Alima, G., 268
Bole, Filipe, 469
Bolkiah, 239
Bomani, P., 1181
Bondevik, K.M., 951
Bongo, A., 518
Bongo, O., 518
Bonnelame, J., 1068
Bonnet, Y., 499
Bonnici, E., 851
Bonnici, U.M., 851
Booh Booh, J.-R., 266
Boolell, S., 860
Borg Olivier, A., 854
Borja Cevallos, R., 441
Borman, N., 406
Bosongo, L., 1617
Bossano, J.J., 568
Botchwey, K., 564
Botero, O., 373
Botha, L.J., 1104
Botha, R.F., 1090
Botto de Barros, A.C., 23
Bottomley, V., 1310
Bouamoud, M., 880
Bouaziz, M., 1203
Bouchard, B., 274
Bouchard, L., 274
Boudenesa, A., 382
Boudjemaa, A., 75
Boufettas, A., 880
Bouhabib, A., 803
Boulares, H., 1203
Bounkoulou, B., 384
Bouraga, P., 991
Bourassa, R., 324
Bourdes Ogouliguende, J., 518
Boussena, S., 75
Bowen, L., 100
Bowen, S.D., 1542
Boyce, G.H., 1032
Boyer, E., 505
Bozer, A., 1208
Brabazon of Tara, *Lord*, 1309
Bradley, M.J., 1215
Brady, N.F., 1385
Braks, G., 903
Branco, J.R., 1057
Branstad, T., 1464
Brantley, B., 1450
Braun, T., 486
Brautigam, O., 544
Braybrooke, D.M.L., 371
Brennan, S., 721
Briceno, L., 204
Bridge, E.F., 161
Brighty, A.D., 399
Brito, C., 1021
Broadley, J.K.E., 1576
Brooke, P., 1309, 1360
Brooks, E.C., 1047
Browder, G., 1428
Brown, K.L., 393, 429
Brown, R., 755
Brown, S., 1514
Brown, W.A., 741
Brummet, T., 301
Brunhart, H., 816
Brunner, E., 1174
Brunsdon, N., 131
Bryant, W., 1435
Buchanan, J.M., 315
Buckland-James, J.H., 466
Buffett, D.E., 128
Bührig, M., 32
Bujang Mohd. Nor, 842
Burges Watson, R.E.G., 898
Burgio, J., 1501
Burgo Fernandes, V., 337
Burke, R., 721
Burney, D.H., 294
Burnham, V., 592
Burns, K.F.X., 88, 192, 434, 580, 1046, 1049, 1053
Burroughs, J.A., 1222
Burský, O., 409
Burt, F.T.P., 161
Burton, G., 1297
Busek, E., 169
Bush, G., 1383
Busquin, P., 197
Butale, C.J., 225
Butcher, D.J., 919
Butros, A., 771
Button, J., 100
Buyoya, P., 258
Buzu, H., 1176
Bwanali, E.C.I., 827
Bwebwenibure, A., 778
Byatt, R.A.C., 933, 1009, 1595

Cabral, B., 231
Cabral d'Almada, F., 589
Cabral, V., 589
Cabrales, A., 454
Cabrisas Ruiz, R., 395
Cadieux, P.H., 274
Cadman, R.M., 1102
Cahen, A., 40
Cain, E., 207
Cain, J., 154
Caithness, *Earl of*, 1309
Calderón, A., 981
Calderón, R.A., 386
Calfa, M., 409
Callejas, R.L., 602
Callihan, M., 1441
Camacho Solis, M., 865
Camara, I., 589
Camara, S.K., 588
Camdessus, M., 20
Cameron, D., 315
Çami, F., 69
Camora, A., 586
Campbell, C., 1529
Campbell, J.J.d'A., 822
Campbell, J.T., 1529
Campbell, K., 274
Campbell, W.B., 138
Campderros, M., 79
Campeanu, R., 1035
Campora, M., di 95
Cañete, A., 997
Canty, B.J.G., 85
Caperton, G., 1547
Caplan, E., 319

Capo-Chichi, G.T., 211
Capobianco Ribera, G., 219
Capucho, A., 1021
Carague, G., 1005
Carbon, A., 433
Çarçani, A., 69
Cardona Marino, A., 865
Cardoso, R., 337
Carew, G., 1074
Carino, I., 1005
Carl XVI Gustaf, *King*, 1149
Carli, G., 745
Carlsson, I., 1150
Carlsson, R., 1150
Carmona Borjas, J.R., 1579
Carnahan, M., 1489
Carneiro, R., 1021
Carnogurský, J., 409
Carpio Nicolle, R., 581
Carr, J.P., 161
Carraro, F., 746
Carruthers, G., 1504
Carter, E.C., 175
Carter, W.C., 312
Carvalho, A., 1021
Carvalho, J. de, 336
Carvalho dos Santos, H. de, 82
Casaroli, A., 1576
Casey, R., 1524
Caso Lombardo, A., 865
Castaneda-Cornejo, M.A., 457
Castillo, V., 204
Castillo, C.M., 386
Castle, M.N., 1446
Castor, L., 501
Castro, E., 33
Castro Meléndez, J., 457
Castro Ruz, F., 395
Castro Ruz, R., 395
Cattin, C.D., 746
Catto, H., 1358, 1424
Causley, I.R., 131
Cavaco Silva, A., 1021
Cavazos, L.F., 1386
Cavello, D., 92
Caygill, D.F., 918
Ceauşescu, E., 1033
Ceauşescu, N., 1033
Ceballos Ordoñez, P., 373
Celeste, R., 1514
Celiku, H., 69
Cenarrusa, P., 1456
Cepeda, F., 377
Cerava, V., 69
Cerezo Arévalo, M.V., 581
Cerne, A.R., 598
Cerqueda-Pascuet, F., 79
Cervera Pachoco, C., 865
Céspedes Argandoña, G., 219
Chadli, B., 75
Chadwick, V., 131
Chaiyasan, P., 1186
Chalker, L., 1309
Challoner, R.W., 871
Cham, A.M.C., 522
Chan Heng Chee, 1081
Chan Hong Nam, G., 842
Chandrawati, Mrs, 698
Chang, C.C.P., 368
Charan Shukla, S., 671
Charasse, M., 486
Charest, J.J., 274
Charfi, M., 1203
Charles, M.E., 433
Charles, *Prince of Wales*, 1305-6
Chattopadhyay, D.P., 683
Chau Phong, 1590
Chaves, J.R., 993
Chaves, M., 1117
Cheek, J.R., 1139
Chehem, M.M., 430
Cheikhrouhou, T., 1203
Chen Li-an, 368
Cheney, R., 1385
Cheng Wei-yuan, 368
Chenna Reddy, M., 654
Chérèque, J., 486
Chevènement, J.-P., 485
Cheverie, W.D., 322
Chi Chang Ik, 786
Chiba, K., 767
Chibane, S., 75
Chiduo, A., 1181
Chidzero, B., 1626
Chiepe, G.K.T., 224
Chigaga, C., 1622
Chigwedere, S., 1630
Chikowore, E., 1626
Chilia, J.M., 1572
Chimango, L.J., 827
Chinkuli, G.K., 1622
Chipande, A., 886
Chirinos Calero, P., 865
Chirwa, R.W., 827
Chissano, J.A., 885
Chit Swe, 254
Chitanava, N.A., 1271
Chitepo, V., 1626
Chiu Chuang-huan, 368
Cho Se Ung, 787
Cho Soon, 782
Choe Byung-Yol, 782
Choe Gwang, 787
Choe Jiong Gun, 787
Choi Ho-Joong, 782
Choi Young-Choul, 782
Chomba, F.M., 1622
Chong Jun Gi, 787
Chong Song Nam, 787
Chongo, R., 1622
Choonhavan, C., 1186
Chouéry, C., 803
Christian, F., 914
Christiani Burkard, A.F., 453
Christofides, T., 401
Christophory, J., 822
Chrysanthou, C., 401
Chrysostomos, *Metropolitan*, 33
Chudomir, A., 244
Chung, F., 1626
Chung Won-Sik, 782
Čić, M., 409
Cissokho, C.A.A., 1065
Cissoko, D., 848
Claes, W., 196
Clair, S., 860
Clark, A., 1310
Clark, C.J., 274
Clark, H., 918
Clark, M.J., 118
Clark, R.L., 1519
Clark, T.J., 969
Clark, W., 651
Clarke, C., 755
Clarke, H., 755
Clarke, K., 1308
Clavette, G., 308
Cledwyn of Penrhos, *Lord*, 1310
Cleland, M., 1452
Clements, B., 1535
Clements, G.R., 322
Clemet, K., 951
Cleveland, P.M., 836
Clinton, B., 1435
Cobb, C.E., 629
Coëme, G., 197
Coetsee, K., 1090
Coleman, P.T., 1559
Coles, J., 118
Colla, M., 196
Collins, G., 721
Collins, M., 274
Collins, P.E.J., 130
Collins, S., 319
Collor de Mello, F., 231
Colome, A., 395
Comissario Afonso, P., 888
Compaoré, B., 250
Compaoré, J.-L., 251
Compbell, P., 1051
Compton, J.G.M., 1049
Conable, B.B., 21-2
Concepcion, J., 1005
Conde, R., 1117
Connell, K., 1527
Connery, E.J., 305
Connolly, M.J., 1479
Connolly, P., 322
Consalvi, S.A., 1583
Constantin, *Prince*, 816
Conte, C., 746
Conté, L., 586
Conway, S., 319
Cooney, M., 1491
Cooper, J.F., 580
Cooray, B.S., 1128
Coore, D., 755
Cope, J., 1310
Coposu, C., 1035
Corbeil, J., 274
Corbin, R.H.O., 592
Corcuera, J.L., 1117
Cordeiro Almada, D.H., 337
Cordero-Arias, J.F., 389
Cordiner, W.L., 1197
Córdoba Montoya, J., 865
Cordosa de Mello, Z., 231
Cordóvez, D., 441
Cormack, R.L.B., 260, 1043, 1620
Cornell, R.A., 36
Correa, J.A., 444
Correia, C., 589
Cossiga, F., 745
Costenla Umaña, G., 386
Cotti, F., 1167
Coulibaly, L.N.P., 391
Coulibaly, T., 848
Coulter, B., 121
Couto dos Santos, A., 1021
Couvelier, M., 301
Cowan, P.A., 312
Cowper, S., 1430
Crabb, S.M., 154
Crafter, G.J., 143
Crane, K.R., 1432
Creekmore, M.V., 1133
Cresson, E., 485
Crigler, T.F., 1087
Crill, P., 1371
Croes, H.S., 912
Croll, M.L., 1055
Cronje, R., 1106
Crosbie, J.C., 274
Crouse, L., 315
Crowe, B.L., 173
Crowell, G., 1533
Cruickshank, A., 1051
Çuko, L., 69
Cullen, M., 918
Cullimore, C.A.K., 1222
Cumate Rodriguez, J., 865
Cummings, J.G., 305
Cumplido, F., 349
Cundiff, C.C., 942
Cunha, A., 1021
Cuomo, M., 1507
Curien, H., 485
Curley, W., 498
Curran, J.J., 1476
Cywińska, I., 1013

D'Ancona, H., 903
D'Hondt Van Opdenbosch, P., 197
Dabbaransi, K., 1186
Dahl, B., 1150
Daim Zainuddin, 833
Dalai Lama, 348
Dale, D., 121
Dales, I., 903
Dali, A.A. al-, 1600
Daly, M.F., 223
Dam Quang Trung, 1586
Dambenzet, J., 382
Damiba, B., 251
Danami, A.N. al-, 1600
Dandavate, M., 637
Dankora, S., 208
Dankoro, S., 209
Dao Duy Tung, 1586
Daprou, K., 251
Darbo, B.B., 522
Darsieres, C., 530
Daskalova, S., 244
Daunt, T., 1214
David, R., 433
Davidow, J., 1624
Davies, E.T., 1590
Davis, A., 985
Davis, J., 301
Davis, J.R., 1019
Dawkins, J., 100
Day, S.p., 1206
Dayal, R.S., 694
Dayaratne, P., 1128
Daza, P., 353
De Alwis, W.S.L., 1133
De Carteret, L.P., 1373
De Cotret, R.R., 274
De Klerk, F.W., 1090
De Villiers, D., 1090
De Villiers, J., 1090
De Villiers, W.J., 1090
De Vries, B., 903
Dean, H., 1540
Debernardi, E., 993
Decaux, A., 486
Decker, C.R., 312
Dehaene, J.-L., 196
Dehennin, H., 203
DeJarnette, E., 1184
Del Papa, F.S., 1496
Delafosse, J.-C., 391
Delamuraz, J.-P., 1167

Délano, J.C., 353
Delebarre, M., 485
Deleza, W.B., 827
Deliyannis, Y., 573
Delors, J., 42
Delvaux-Stehres, M., 820
Dembele, S., 848
Deme, A., 848
Dementei, N.I., 1266
Demnati, O., 880
Denba, S., 827
Deng Xiaoping, 354
Denise, A., 391
Denktash, R., 400-1, 406
Denman, R., 46
DePree, W.A., 189
Der'i, A., 736
Derisbourg, J.-P., 46
Derkach, L., 305
Derwinski, E.J., 1386
Desta, F., 462
Deukmejian, G., 1438
Deus Maximiano, J. de, 337
Deus Pinheiro, J. de, 1021
Dhanabalan, S., 1076
Diab, A., 1176
Diabate, L., 391
Diakite, N., 849
Diallo, Abdoulaye, 848
Diallo, Absa C., 1067
Diallo, Alpha O.B., 586
Diana, *Princess of Wales*, 1305
Diarra, N., 848
Diaz, C., 205
Diaz Uribe, E., 373
Dibo, P.G., 391
Dick, P.W., 274
Dickel, F., 527
Dicks, P.D., 312
Didi, A.S.M., 845
Dieng, F.M., 1065
Dientsbier, J., 409
Dimas, S., 573
Dimitrov, A., 244
Dimitrov, B., 244
Ding Guangden, 357
Dinning, J., 297
Diop, A.M., 1065
Diop, C.M., 521
Diop, S.L., 1065
Diop, S.Y., 1065
Diouf, A., 1065
Diouf, M., 1065
DiPrete, E., 1527
Dirks, H., 301
Diro, T., 987
Dissanayake, G., 1128
Ditlev-Simonsen, P., 951
Dittrich, W., 555
Divine, G., 327
Dizdarević, R., 1605
Djassi, M., 589
Djaymaz, G., 406
Djema, B., 1617
Djerejian, E.P., 1179
Djermakoye, M.A., 942
Djohar, S. M., 378
Djondo, K., 1192
Djoşar, S., 406
Djoudi, H., 78
Djuranović, V., 1605
Dladla, R., 1145
Dlamini, B.S., 1145
Dlamini, M.N., 1147
Dlamini, N., 1145
Dlamini, O.M., 1145
Dlamini, T.L.L., 1147
Dlouhy, V., 409
Do Muoi, 1586
Doak, W., 1523
Doan Duy Than, 1586
Doan Khue, 1586
Dobozendji, H., 342
Docking, T., 1466
Doe, S.K., 807
Doi, A., 987
Dole, E.H., 1385
Donald, A., 365
Dondo, K. wa, 1617
Dong Si Nguyen, 1586
Donohoe, T., 316
Dorey, G.M., 1372
Doubin, F., 486
Doucett, R., 308
Douglas, E., 755
Douglas, J., 1540
Douglas, W., 192
Doumbia, C.O., 848
Doumbouya, S., 586
Douniam, O., 382
Dove-Edwin, G., 947
Dowd, J.R.A., 130
Dowding, P.M., 161
Downey, J.E., 305
Driedger, A., 305
Drilon, F., 1005
Drnovšek, J., 1605
Dromi, J.R., 92
Du Plessis, P., 1090
Dubček, A., 409
Ducharme, G., 305
Duda, K., 407
Dueck, P., 301
Duffell, P.R., 608
Dugersuren, M., 876
Duhalde, E., 92
Dukakis, M.S., 1479
Dulloo, M., 860
Dumas, R., 485
Dunbar, C.F., 1598
Dunkel, A., 26
Dunkley, C., 755
Dunne, P.F., 919
Dunstan, D., 143
Dupuis, G.B., 851
Duque, A.A., 984
Durafour, M., 485
Durr, K., 1090
Dvořák, L., 409
Dybkjaer, L., 417
Dye, B.J., 1486
Dykeman, W., 1534
Dyremose, H., 417
Dysart, S., 308
Dyvig, P.P., 429
Dzhumagulov, A.D., 1291

Ebu, A., 987
Echaque Villanueve, W., 999
Edelman, M.L., 268
Edgar, J., 1459, 1461
Edis, R.J.S., 238
Edmiston, R., 1510
Edoh, K., 1192
Edri, R., 736
Edward, *Prince*, 1305-6
Edward, *Prince, Duke of Kent*, 1305
Edwards, E.M., 1046
Edwards, G.J., 161
Edwards, J.C., 806
Efford, R.J., 312
Egerton, S., 753
Eggar, T., 1310
Ehrler, B., 1468
Ekra, M., 391
El-Ridy, A.R., 452
Elabe, M.J., 430
Elias, T.O., 7
Eliassen, K., 963
Eliasson, J., 1163
Elizabeth II, *Queen*, 28-9, 1305-6
Elizabeth, *Queen Mother*, 1305-6
Ellemann-Jensen, U., 417
Elliott, M., 741
Elston, M.J., 319
Elzinga, J., 297
Endora Gallimany, G., 981
Engelhard, H.A., 536
Engell, H., 417
Enggaard, K., 417
Engholm, B., 560
Engo, P.E., 268
Engström, O., 1150
Enin, A., 564
Epp, A.J., 274
Erbilen, M., 406
Eri, S., 987
Erman Gonzales, A., 92
Ernst, J.A., 305
Eroglu, D., 406
Errázuriz, O., 353
Ershad, H.M., 185
Escalona Reguera, J., 395
Escheikh, A., 1203
Escoto, F. d', 939
Espat, M., 205
Essimengane, S., 518
Essy, A., 393
Estanislao, J., 1005
Estuar, F., 1005
Esztergalyos, F., 621
Ettl, H., 169
Etyang, P., 1220
Eu, M.F., 1438
Eugenie, *Princess*, 1305
Evans, G., 100
Evensen, J., 7
Everett, B., 584
Evin, C., 485
Ewengue, J.-M., 384
Ewick, C.R., 1463
Ewing, R.C., 567
Eyadéma, G., 1191
Eyskens, M., 196
Ezekwe, G., 944

Fabiola, *Queen*, 195
Facchiano, F., 746
Fadil, W., 1176
Fafunwa, B., 944
Fahd, *King*, 1058
Faheem, M.A., 972
Fahey, J.J., 131
Falae, O., 944
Fall, B.J.P., 294
Fall, I., 1065, 1067
Fall, M., 1065
Fallahiyan, A., 709
Falzon, M., 851
Farah, M.B., 430
Farell Cubillas, A., 865
Farra, M., 1176
Farrelly, A.A., 1564
Fatafehi Tu'ipelehake, *Prince*, 1196
Fauliso, J.J., 1443
Faure, M., 485
Fauroux, R., 485
Fayiz, M.al- A. al-, 1059
Fazel, I., 709
Fearn, R., 1125
Fedoruk, S.O., 327
Fein, R.H., 910
Felber, R., 1167
Felipe, *Prince*, 1116
Fenn, N., 732
Fepulea'i, F.G., 1595
Fergusson, E., 498
Fernandes, C.A., 82
Fernandes, F.J., 81
Fernandes, G., 637
Fernándes Lopes, J.L., 338
Fernández, M., 1117
Fernández Ordóñez, F., 1117
Ferrao, V., 888
Ferreira Real, F., 1021
Ferreire do Amaral, J., 1021
Ferrers, *Earl*, 1310
Fettah, M., 880
Feyder, J., 822
Field, M.W., 148
Fields, D.C., 344
Figueredo Planchart, R., 1579
Filali, A., 880
Filmon, G.A., 305
Finch, F., 121
Findlay, G.M., 305
Finn, G., 308
Finnbogadóttir, V., 624
Finnette, R., 860
Fischbach, M., 820
Fischer, D., 161
Fischer, O., 527
Fischler, F., 169
Fitzherbert, G., 438, 1583
Five, K.K., 951
Fjordbotten, E.L., 297
Flecha de Lima, P.T., 236
Flegel, M., 527
Fleming, C.S., 1050
Flemming, M., 169
Flight, G.R., 312
Flynn, J.G., 1147
Flynn, P., 721
Fodor, I., 615
Fofana, A., 586
Fofe, J., 266
Folger, J.D.M., 1453
Follosco, C., 1005
Fologo, L.D., 391
Folsom, J., 1428
Fonseca, L., 338
Fontaine, R., 319
Ford, D., 608
Foregger, E., 169
Forero de Saade, M.T., 373
Formica, R., 746
Fort, M.G., 888
Forte, *Lord*, 1055
Fortier, Y., 294
Fortún Suárez, G., 219
Foruzesh, G., 709
Fosi, P., 1594
Fougner, E.B., 951
Foula, H., 586
Foussas, A., 573

Fowler, D., 297
Foxley, A., 349
Fracanzani, C., 746
Francis Joseph II, *Prince*, 816
Francis, H.H., 933
Francis, R., 1351
Franck, E., 342
Fraser, *Lord*, 1309
Fraser, R., 301
Frederik, *Prince*, 416
Freeman, C.W., 1063
Freire Monteiro, V., 589
Freivalds, L., 1150
Frenette, R., 308
Friaa, A., 1203
Frichot, S., 1068
Friedman, F., 1145
Frossard, C., 1372
Frutos Vaesken, A., 993
Fry, J.W., 1483
Fukaya, T., 761
Fulembo, B., 1622
Fullerton, W.H., 466, 1113
Fumuhito, *Prince*, 760
Furey, C.J., 312

Gačić, R., 1605
Gaddafi, M., 811
Gado, G., 208
Galea, L., 851
Gallardo, J., 441
Galvin, J.R., 38
Ganga, J.-C., 382
Ganilau, P., 469
Garba, J.N., 948
Garcia, J.H., 82
García, J.R., 436
García Pérez, A., 999
Garcia Rodriguez, E., 219
García Vargas, J., 1117
Gardner, B., 1544
Gardner, J., 1510
Gardner, W.M., 1499
Gardom, G., 301
Gargano, C.A., 1201
Garong, P., 987
Garrett, H.L., 1393
Garrucho, P., 1005
Gaspari, R., 746
Gata, F., 516
Gatt, L., 851
Gava, A., 745
Gavrielides, A., 401
Gay, N.R., 175
Gayoom, M.A., 845
Gaze, M.J.C., 465
Gbeho, J.V., 567
Gbezera-Bria, M., 342
Geens, A., 197
Gegprifti, L., 69
Geh, H.-P., 547
Geingob, H., 891
Gelbard, R.S., 223
Genia, J., 987
Genscher, H.-D., 536
George, H., 433
Geppert, W., 169
Gerard, J.B.S., 822
Gerbic, F., 919
Gerlach, M., 527
Gestsson, S., 624
Getty, D.R., 297
Ghabbash, M., 1176
Ghani, A.A.A., 1596
Ghannouchi, M., 1203
Gharazi, M., 709
Gharekhan, C.R., 651
Ghazali, S. bin A. al, 966
Ghaznouani, R., 880
Gheraieb, A., 78
Ghezal, A., 1206
Ghiz, J.A., 322
Ghozali, S-I, 75
Ghrib, M., 75
Ghulam Mustafa, A.B.M., 185
Ghurburrun, B., 860
Giacomelli, G., 10
Gibbons, R.V., 312
Gibbs, O.M., 580
Giffin, R., 315
Gilani, S.I.H., 972
Gilani, Y.R., 972
Gilbert, D.S., 312
Gildenhorn, J., 1174
Gillespie, C.A., 353
Gina, *Princess*, 816
Giray, S., 1208
Givens, W.A., 810
Gjinush, S., 69
Gjyzari, N., 69
Gladstone, D.A.S., 846, 1133
Glasby, A.I., 384
Glaspie, A.C., 718
Glassman, J.D., 67
Glasspole, F., 754
Glemp, J., 1018
Glitman, M.W., 203
Glover, M.J.K., 860
Gnoleba, M.S., 391
Goburdhun, J., 860
Godfrey, G., 205
Godinho Gomes, H., 589
Godinho Gomes, P.A., 589
Goebbels, R., 820
Goff, P.B., 918
Gogo, J., 297
Goh Chok Tong, 1076
Goldschmidt, N., 1520
Goma, L., 1622
Gomes, I., 337
Gomez, T., 1005
Gomis, C., 393
Gonelevu, A., 469
Gong Pinmei, 364
Gonifei-Ngaibounanou, P., 342
González, C.H., 865
González Dubón, M., 454
González Márquez, F., 1117
Gonzalez Pantaleon, R.P., 438
González Quintanilla, L., 219
González Torres, D., 993
Goodall, D., 651
Goodenough, A.M., 567, 1194
Goodfellow, M.A., 521
Göransson, B., 1150
Gorbachev, M.S., 354, 1228-9
Gorbunov, A.V., 1278
Gordon, E.M., 204
Gordon, R.D., 1602
Gore, M.E.J., 810
Gosaibi, G.M. Al, 183
Goss, W., 138
Goswami, D., 637
Goumeziane, S., 75
Gqozo, O.J., 1111
Graça, C. da, 1056
Gračanin, P., 1605
Gradin, A., 1150
Graham, A., 308
Graham-Douglas, T.O., 944
Gramajo Morales, H., 581
Gran, C., 301
Grant, C.H., 595
Grant, J.P., 10
Grasset, B., 512
Graves, B., 1466
Greaves, E.E., 190
Greaves, P., 190
Green, A., 1039
Green, H., 592
Green, M., 308
Greenidge, C., 592
Gregg, D., 785
Gregg, J., 1499
Gregorios, P.M., 32
Gregory, R.J., 143
Greiner, N.F., 130
Grelombe, C., 342
Griffiths, M., 1481
Grill, J.F., 161
Grímsson, O.R., 624
Gronemeyer, H., 552
Gross, W., 138
Growe, J.A., 1484
Grupković, D., 1610
Guðmundsson, F., 629
Guðobjartsson, O.P., 624
Guerra González, A., 1117
Guerreiro Dias, J., 82
Guessous, A., 881
Guezodje, V., 208
Guigma, A., 251
Guillaume, G., 7
Gujral, I.K., 637
Gullage, A.E., 312
Gumbaridze, G.G., 1271
Gumbs, E., 84
Gumbs, L., 914
Gummer, J., 1309
Gumucio Granier, J., 223
Gungaadorj, S., 873
Gungah, D., 860
Gunn, R., 1046, 1049, 1053
Gupta, S., 185
Guptill, N., 322
Gur, M., 736
Gurinovich, A.E., 1266
Gurirab, T.-B., 891
Gurupadaswamy, M.S., 637
Gutierrez, C.J., 389
Gutiérrez Barrios, F., 865
Gwom, L.D., 944
Györke, J., 621
Gysi, G., 526-7

Haarder, B., 417
Habib, A., 1176
Habib, M.J., 173
Habibe, B.J., 702
Habibi, H., 709
Habibullah, W., 698
Habré, H., 345-6
Habyarimana, J., 1041
Hagen, T., 301
Haidara, M.M., 848
Haig, I., 154
Haile-Selassie, A.T., 465
Halabi, G., 1176
Halbritter, W., 527
Halile, E., 69
Hall, A., 1013
Hall, P.E., 1609
Hall, W., 190
Hallahan, E.K., 161
Halonen, T., 475
Hamad buin Khalifa Al-Thani, *Shaikh*, 1029
Hamad, J.L. al-, 792
Hamadani, M.A. al-, 1597
Hamadou, B.G., 430
Hämäläinen, T., 475
Hamami, H., 771
Hambley, M., 1032
Hamdan bin Rashid al-Maktoum, 1294
Hamdan Sheikh Tahir, 832
Hamed bin Mohammed al Sharqi, *Sheikh*, 1293
Hameed, A., 845
Hameed, A.C.S., 1128
Hamid, A. at-W. M.A. al, 1597
Hamilton, A., 1310
Hammer, Z., 736
Hammond, G., 305
Hamrouche, M., 75
Hamzaoui, A., 1206
Han Sung-Soo, 782
Hand, G., 100
Hanif, Khan M., 972
Hannemann, V., 551
Hannibalsson, J.B., 624
Hans Adam II, *Prince*, 816
Hansenne, M., 14
Hanson, L., 301
Hapunda, F., 1621
Harahap, H., 702
Harald, *Prince*, 950
Harbah, M., 1176
Hardy, N., 327
Hardy, P., 1471
Hared, K.A., 430
Harkins, M., 1446
Harland, B., 933
Harmoko, 702
Harris, J.F., 1452
Harris, T., 121
Harrop, W.C., 1620
Hart, C., 319
Hart, G.W.P., 1070
Hartarto, 702
Harthy, H. bin A. al, 966
Hasan, M., 185
Hasan, N., 692
Hasani, S., 1605
Hasegawa, S., 761
Hashimoto, R., 761
Haskell, D.K., 1003
Hassan II, *King*, 880
Hassan, *Prince*, 769
Hassan, F., 702
Hassanali, N.M., 1199
Hasselfeldt, G., 536
Haughey, C.J., 721
Haussman, H., 536
Havel, V., 407
Hawke, R., 100
Hawlicek, H., 169
Hay, D.A., 131
Hayat, F.S., 972
Hayatou, S., 266

Hayden, M., 1466
Hayden, W.G., 100
Hayes, F.M., 732
Hazeltine, J., 1531
Hazoume, G.L., 209
Heald, M., 910
Heap, J.A., 238
Hechler, K., 1547
Hecht, C., 178
Hejailan, F. ibn A.A. al, 1059
Held, H.J., 32
Hellström, M., 1150
Hemmings, T.H., 143
Hempel, J., 32
Hempstone, S., 777
Henderson, Y.D., 161
Heng Samrin, 262
Henni, B., 75
Henri, *Prince*, 819
Henrik, *Prince*, 416
Henry, K., 1220
Henry, *Prince*, 1305
Hepworth, L., 327
Herath, R., 1128
Herbert, W., 1046
Herder, G., 531
Herdman, J.M., 1591
Hermannsson, S., 624
Herminie, W., 1068
Hernández Alcerro, J.R., 606
Hernández Colón, R., 1562
Hernández Valiente, R., 453
Herrera, W., 441
Herrigel, O., 891
Herzog, C., 736
Heyer, M.J., 1498
Hicken, B., 322
Hidouci, G., 75
Hilali, M., 880
Hill, G.L., 161
Hillery, P., 721
Hinai, M. bin A. bin Z. al, 966
Hinterscheld, M., 34
Hinton, D.R., 389
Hiriart Balderrama, F., 865
Hirsch-Ballin, E., 903
Hitch, B., 854
Hjelm-Wallén, L., 1150
Hnatyshyn, R., 273
Ho Dam, 787
Hoang Quy, 1586
Hobby, W.P., 1535
Hocké, J.-P., 11
Hockin, T., 274
Hodge, D.M., 1564
Hodgetts, D.P.L., 1372
Hodgins, G., 327
Hodoul, J., 1068
Hoess, F., 173
Höffner, *Cardinal* J., 542
Hogg, C.J., 154
Hogg, D., 1310
Hogsett, J., 1462
Hohenfellner, P., 173
Holden, G., 758
Holgate, H.N., 148
Holkeri, H., 475
Holomisa, B., 1108
Holtz, P., 1476
Holwill, R.N., 444
Homaidan, I.M.H., 179
Homper, W., 549
Hong Song Nam, 787
Hopa, J.T., 1572
Hopgood, D.J., 143
Hoque Chowdhury, M.R., 185
Hoque, W., 185
Hori, K., 761
Horn, G., 615
Horne, J., 1051
Horsman, J., 297
Horvat, F., 1605
Hossain, A., 185
Hossain, M.Z., 845
Hossain Khan, S., 185
Hostler, C.W., 183
Hoti, A.R.I. al-, 791
Houdek, R.G., 465
Houdou, A., 209
Hough, D.J., 1103
Houphouët-Boigny, F., 391
Hove, R., 1626
Howard, M., 1309
Howe, B., 100
Howe, G., 1308
Howell, M.E., 380, 862
Howell, W.N., 794
Howland, R.C., 1143
Hoyte, H.D., 592
Hrawi, E., 800
Hromadka, J., 409
Hsu Shui-teh, 368
Hu Qili, 357
Hu Tsu Tau, R., 1076
Huberts, T., 301
Hubley, R., 322
Huh Hyong-Koo, 782
Humaid bin Rashid al-Nuaimi, *Sheikh*, 1293
Humphries, B., 100
Hun Sen, 262
Hunley, H., 297
Hunt, D., 1310
Hunt, G., 1428
Hunt, J.L., 918
Huper, L. de, 939
Hurd, D., 1308
Hurst, L.A., 89
Hussain, *Pehin Dato Haji*, 239
Hussein, *King*, 768-9
Hussein at-Takriti, S., 715
Huynh Tan Phat, 1586
Hyera, A.M., 1184
Hyun Hong-Joo, 782

Iacovou, G., 401
Ibbott, A., 524
Ibragimov, M.M., 1286
Ibrahim, A., 845
Ibrahim, I., 845
Ibrahim, M.R., 845
Ibrahim, O.H., 430
Ickonga, A., 382
Iddrisu, M., 564
Idriss, *Pengiran Haji*, 242
Idrissou, S.I., 211
Ifunaoa, W., 1084
Ignatios IV, *Patriarch*, 32
Iliescu, I., 1033-4
Imadi, M. al-, 1176
Imam, J., 185
Imam, N., 944
Imrey, C.H., 189
Inderson, S., 914
Ingvarsson, I.S., 629
Inongo, S., 1617
Insanally, S.R., 596
Inyanza, M., 1617
Iqbal, R.S., 972
Iryani, A.K. al-, 1596
Isa, *Pehin Dato Haji*, 239
Isa bin Sulman Al-Khalifa, *Shaikh*, 179
Isai, H., 69
Ishaq Khan, G., 972
Islam Mahmud, A., 185
Isley, E., 297
Ismail, *Pengiran Dato*, 239
Ismail Petra ibni Al-Marhum, *Sultan*, 832
Ismail, R., 837
Itambala, I., 1617
Itoue, B., 266
Iuta, T., 778
Ivanovic, I.S., 871
Ivashko, V.A., 1229, 1264
Izaguirre, A., 1579

Ja'afar ibni Al-Marhum, *Besar*, 832
Jabir al-Ahmad al-Jabir as-Sabah, 791
Jabu anak Numpang, A., 842
Jackson, J.L., 148
Jackson, R., 592
Jacobovits de Szeged, A., 910
Jacobs, W.E., 87
Jacobsen, N., 301
Jacobsen, W.L., 591
Jaddoo, R., 860
Jaichandra Singh, R.K., 675
Jakobsen, J.J., 951
Jalil, M., 441
Jallow, H., 522
Jallow, O.A., 522
Jama, A.A., 1087
Jamal Haiser, M., 185
Jameel, A., 845
Jameel, F., 845
Jamer, H.W., 312
James, S., 1049
James, V., 758
Jamir, S.C., 678
Janicki, C., 1013
Janowski, J., 1013
Jansen, J., 301
Janslin, J.F., 1174
Jaques, T.F., 1472
Jarrett, L., 308
Jarrett, S.O., 810
Jaruzelski, W., 1011, 1013
Jarwan, S. al-, 1294
Jasir, K.A.S. al-, 791
Jatta, M., 522
Jawara, D.K., 522, 1065
Jay Hee Oh, 785
Jaya bin Abdul Latif, 242
Jaya bin Pengiran Haji, 242
Jayakumar, S., 1076
Jayfi, M.A. al-, 1597
Jayme, V., 1005
Jazairy, I., 28
Jazi, D., 1203
Jean, *Grand Duke*, 819
Jeewoolall, R., 860
Jeffries, W.P., 919
Jegham, M., 1203
Jelinek, O.J., 274
Jenkins, D.V., 1373
Jennings, R., 6
Jensen, O.V., 417
Jeri, M. El, 1203
Jervolino, R.R., 746
Jesseramsing, C., 862
Jesus, D.J. de, 82
Jesus, J. de, 1005
Ji Chaozhu, 365
Jiang Zemin, 354, 357
Jigme Singye Wangchuck, *King*, 215
Jiménez, D., 389
Jishi, M.J. Al, 180
Joachim, *Prince*, 416
Johansson, B., 1150
Johansson, S., 1163
Johar, *Dato Dr Haji*, 239
John Paul II, *Pope*, 1018, 1575-6
Johnson, G., 305
Johnson, J., 777
Johnson, K., 758
Johnson, M., 1484
Johnson, R., 1495
Johnston, A.D., 298
Johnston, R., 301
Jolly, R.A., 154
Jones, Barry, 100
Jones, Ben J., 578
Jones, Brereton, 1468
Jones, L., 1051
Jonkman, H., 910
Joséphine-Charlotte, *Grand Duchess*, 819
Joshi, H., 683
Joshi, S.H., 656
Jouahri, A., 880
Jouvin, J., 441
Joxe, P., 485
Juan Carlos I *King*, 1114, 1116
Jubair, , M. ibn, 1059
Jubran, A., 1176
Jugnauth, A., 860
Juliana, *Queen*, 901
Jumayan, K.J.S. al-, 791
Jumeau, E., 1068
Juncker, J.-C., 820

Kâ, D., 1065
Ka, I.D., 1067
Kâ, M., 1065
Kabab, M.A. al-, 1597
Kabbaj, M., 880
Kabega, N., 1617
Kabore, P.-D., 253
Kadijević, V., 1605
Kafarov, E.M., 1268
Kagami, H., 767
Kagonyera, M., 1220
Kaheru, Z., 1220
Kahlouche, H., 75
Kaifu, T., 761
Kaijuka, R., 1220
Kaissi, A., 880
Kaiteie, T., 778
Kaklamanis, A., 573
Kalantari, I., 709
Kalemba, N.M., 1617
Kalin, I.P., 1275
Kallal, A., 1203
Kalpokas, D., 1572
Kaltwasser, F.G., 548
Kam, L., 985
Kamaaluddeen, A., 845
Kamali, H., 709
Kamanda, N., 1617

Kamara, A.B., 1071
Kamberi, S., 69
Kamikanica, J., 469
Kaminski, B., 1013
Kaminski, H., 529
Kamunanwire, P.K., 1222
Kanafani, B., 1179
Kanerva, I., 475
Kang Song San, 786
Kang Young-Hoon, 782
Kangai, K., 1626
Kanidoua, N., 251
Kant, K., 654
Kanu, H.G., 1071
Kanyeihamba, G., 1220
Kara Mohamed, A., 75
Kargbo, T., 1074
Karimanzira, D., 1626
Karimov, I.A., 1286
Karl-I-Bond, N., 1617
Karotu, I., 778
Karoui H., 1203
Karpan, K., 1553
Kárpáti, F., 615
Kartasaasmita, G., 702
Karunanidhi, M., 687
Kasai, K., 1617
Kasitah bin Gaddam, 833
Kassa Mapsi, E., 518
Kassim, H.A., 180
Kassum, Al N., 1181
Kasurinen, A.-L., 475
Katako, O. wa, 1617
Katana Mushobekwa, K. wa, 1620
Kategaya, E., 1220
Katenta Apuuli, S.K., 1222
Katopola, D.S., 827
Katrivanos, T., 573
Katushev, K.F., 1229
Katz-Oz, A., 736
Katzav, M., 736
Kaunda, K.D., 1621
Kaushal, S., 677
Kawari, H.A.A. Al-, 1032
Kawawa, R., 1181
Kay-Mouat, J., 1373
Kayalar, L., 1208
Kayyal, A.D., 1059
Kazeruni, S., 709
Kazmi, S.A.H., 972
Kean, T.H., 1501
Keating, P., 100
Kebe, M., 1065
Kedikilwe, P., 225
Keikelame, E.B., 1106
Keita, B., 391
Keita, L., 849
Kelland, O.P.J., 312
Kelly, P.P., 912
Kelso, F.B., 39
Kemp, J.F., 1386
Kempff Suárez, M., 219
Kendemir, N., 1214
Kennan, J.H., 154
Kepa, S., 469
Keramane, A., 75
Kerdal-Vegas, F., 1583
Kerekou, M., 208
Kerin, J., 100
Kerr, G., 316
Kerr, R.S., 1517
Kessler, H., 527
Kgobokoe, S.C., 1106
Khaddam, A.H., 1176
Khaeev, I.Kh., 1288
Khail, M.A.A., 1059
Khajornprasat, S., 1186
Khaled, F.A.R. al-, 792
Khalifa, Al-, 179-80
Khalifa bin Hamad Al-Thani, *Amir*, 1029
Khalifa, S.M. Al-, 1032
Khamenei, S.A., 709
Khamsy, S., 798
Khan, A.A., 1201
Khan, S.M., 979
Khandakar, A.K., 185
Khaole, N.C.O.B., 1106
Kharafi, J.M. al-, 791
Khatami, S.M., 709
Khazraji, M. al-, 1294
Kheddis, A., 75
Khediri, E., 75
Khellef, A., 75
Khider, A., 507
Khoo Chian Kim, 1081
Khoo Teik Huat, 837
Khristoradnov, Yu., 1250
Khristov, K., 244
Khussaiby, S. Bin M. Al-, 969
Khuwaiter, A.A. al A. al, 1059
Kiechle, I., 536
Kigozi, D., 1220
Kilimite, H.T., 251
Killen, P.R., 1099
Kim Bok Sin, 787
Kim Chang Ju, 787
Kim Chang-Keun, 782
Kim Chong-In, 782
Kim Hwan, 786
Kim Il Sung, 786
Kim Jip, 782
Kim Jong Il, 786
Kim Sik, 782
Kim Tae-Ho, 782
Kim Yong Nam, 786
Kim Yong-Nae, 782
Kim Yun Hyok, 787
Kim Yung-Chung, 782
Kimario, M., 1181
Kimbembe, D., 382
Kinast, J., 1018
Kindi, M.K. al-, 1294
King, A., 919
King, M.A., 190
King, R., 308
King, Thérèse, 1065
King, Tom, 1308
Kingon, A.H., 46
Kinnock, N., 1310
Kintu, M., 1220
Kirata, B., 778
Kirk, K., 417
Kirkegaard, K.E., 417
Kisanji, C., 1181
Kiseka, S., 1220
Kissack, J.F., 1368
Kitchen, H.W., 312
Kithe, J., 342
Kitingan, J.P., 840
Kiyonga, C., 1220
Kizito, S., 1220
Klaus, V., 409
Kleiber, G., 527
Klein, H., 536
Klein, J., 327
Klein, R., 298
Klibi, C., 57
Klimová, R., 413
Klinck, P., 1541
Klinpratoom, T., 1186
Klunder, J.H.C., 143
Knight, K.D., 755
Knoppel, I., 914
Knotek, I., 409
Knowles, E., 175
Koch, H.-A., 551
Koch-Petersen, E., 417
Kodjo, M.A., 1192
Koffi, A., 1194
Koffi, L.K., 391
Kogbia, K.M.N., 1617
Koh, T.T.B., 1080
Kohan, A., 92
Kohl, H., 525, 536
Koivisto, M., 474
Kok, W., 903
Kolbe, J., 1532
Kolingba, A., 341-2
Koller, A., 1166-7
Kolstad, A., 1491
Komárek, V., 409
Komlavi, Y., 1192
Konate, I., 251
Kondi, P., 69
Koné, A., 391
Kone, I., 391
Koné, M., 848
Kontagora, M., 944
Koop, G., 555
Koornhof, P.G., 1099
Kopelchuk, L., 327
Korbeci, S., 69
Kordek, J.F., 227
Korinková, K., 409
Koroma, A.K., 1071
Korsaga, F., 251
Kosgei, S.J., 777
Kosiniak-Kamysz, A., 1013
Kospin, L., 485
Kotaite, A., 22
Kotze, G., 1090
Kouvelas, S., 573
Kovalev, M.V., 1266
Kowalski, K., 298
Koza, T.T., 1192
Krauss, E., 349
Kravtsev, V.A., 1264
Kriel, H., 1090
Krishna, K.V., 665
Krolikowski, W., 527
Kryuchkov, V.A., 1229
Kubuabola, I., 469
Kučera, B., 409
Kucharski, M., 1013
Kuharić, F., 1609
Kulakowski, J., 34
Kulcsár, K., 615
Kumar Dewan, B., 185
Kunin, M., 1540
Kuo, S.W.Y., 368
Kurisaqila, A., 469
Kurshumi, A.H. al-, 1597
Kurt, F., 1208
Kusler, J., 1512
Kusumaatmadja, S., 702
Kwakure, J., 260
Kwarara, G., 987
Kwidini, D., 1626
Kwinter, M., 319
Kwon Yong-Gack, 782
Kya, M.S., 709
Kyaw Min, 257
Kye Ung Tae, 787

La Barre de Nantieul, L. de, 498
La Follette, D., 1550
Labied, M., 880
Laborda, J.J., 1117
Lacalle Herrara, L.A., 1568
Lacey, A.W., 308
Lachs, M., 7
Lacina, F., 169
Lacroix, J.-P., 501
Laensar, M., 880
Lafontaine, O., 559
Laghari, S.F., 972
Laghi, P., 1576
Lagourgoue, P., 505
Lahure, J., 820
Laing, E.A., 207
Lairet, G., 1579
Lake, E.H., 89
Lal, D., 637
Lalthnahawla, 677
Lalumière, C., 42
Lam, D.S., 301
Lamana, A., 347
Lameko, P., 1594
Lamin biti Jabang, A., 522
Lamont, N., 1309
Lamontagne, G., 324
Landry, A., 308
Landry, C., 308
Landry, M., 274
Landsbergis, V., 1280
Landwehrmeyer, R., 545
Lane, G., 327
Lang, D.G., 466
Lang, I., 1310
Lang, J., 485
Lange, D.R., 919
Langendrics, R., 196
Langley, D., 212
Larco Cox, G., 999
Larifla, D., 499
Larios, H., 454
Lattanzio, V., 746
Lausten, A., 417
Lawrence, C.M., 161
Lawzi, H.A. al-, 1597
Lázaro, J., 1563
Le Duc Anh, 1586
Le Ilénaff, J., 516
Le Pensec, L., 485
Le Quang Do, 1586
LeBlanc, G., 316
LeBlanc, N., 316
Lee, S., 308
Lee Bong-Suh, 782
Lee Hong-Koo, 782
Lee Hsien Loong, 1076
Lee Huan, 368
Lee Kim Sai, 833
Lee Kuan Yew, 1076
Lee Kyu-Sung, 782
Lee Sang-Hoon, 782
Lee Sanhng-Yeon, 782
Lee Teng-hui, 367
Lee Woo-Jae, 782
Lee Yock Suan, 1076
Leefe, J., 316
Leekpai, C., 1186
Leghari, Z., 972
Legwaila, L.J., 227
Lehmann, K.-D., 545
Lehr, U.-M., 536
Leifland, L., 1163
Lekhanya, J., 804
Lemos Simmonds, C., 373
Lenehan, S.M., 143
Lenihan, B., 721

Leo, D.I., 912
Leonard, P., 1514
Leontieff, A., 514
Lepping, G., 1082
Leupena, T., 1217
Lévesque, G.D., 324
Levin, B., 257
Levy, D., 736
Levy, J.A.W., 143
Lewis, D.G., 274
Li Guixian, 359
Li Jong Ok, 786
Li Luye, 365
Li Peng, 357
Li Ruihan, 357
Li Tieying, 357
Li Ximing, 357
Liang Kim Bang, 842
Liaskas, K., 573
Lichal, R., 169
Lie, L.G., 951
Lien Chan, 368
Liévano de Márquez, M., 453
Ligachev, E.K., 1229
Lilley, J., 365
Lilley, P., 1309
Lilov, A., 244
Lim Ah Lek, 833
Lim Keng Yaik, 833
Lima, M., 337
Lindqvist, B., 1150
Linehan, T.P., 732
Ling Liong Sik, 833
Lingama-Toleque, C., 344
Lingani, J.B.B., 251
Lini, W.H., 1572
Linley, *Viscount*, 1305
Lisboa Ramos, A., 337
Livi, T., 1594
Ljubičić, N., 1605
Llewellyn, D.E., 148
Lo, F., 1065
Lockyer, J., 308
Lodon, S.F., 430
Lohia, R., 991
Lohmeier, D., 562
Lohse, E., 542
Loiselle, G., 274
Lokubandara, W.J.M., 1128
Lomax, W., 1564
Lončar, B., 1605
Londoño Paredes, J., 373
Long, C., 1174
Lönnqvist, U., 1150
Lööw, M.-L., 1150
Lopati, K., 1217
Lopes Cabral, A., 591
Lopez da Silva, O., 336
López Uzgategui, F., 1579
Lorenzo, F. De, 746
Löschnak, F., 169
Losier, D., 308
Louekoski, M., 475
Louw, Eli, 1090
Louw, Eugene, 1100
Louw, G., 1090
Lovansay, S., 796
Lowa, P., 987
Lubbers, R., 903
Lubinda, E.M., 1624
Lubuva, D., 1181
Luce, R., 1309
Luchinsky, P.K., 1275
Luisi, H., 1571
Lujan, M., 1385
Lukanov, A., 244
Lukman, R., 944
Lukyanov, A.I., 1229-30
Luna, R.V., 1003
Lundine, S., 1507
Lupo, S.E., 588
Luqman, A.M., 1597
Lusaka, P.J.F., 1624
Lushev, P., 48
Lutchmeenaradoo, S., 860
Luwum, B.O., 1220
Luz, S.M. da, 336
Ly, S., 848
Lyell, N., 1309
Lyster, M., 154

Mabus, R., 1486
McAlpine, S., 1430
Macarait, C., 1005
McCallum, S., 1550
Maccanico, A., 746
McCarthy, J.T., 803
McCarthy, L., 1438
McCarthy, T., 121
McCaughey, J.D., 153
McClelland, D., 118
McCluney, I., 1087
McComie, V.T., 53
McCormick, P.J., 1576
McCoy, E., 298
McCrae, J.C., 305
McCuen, W.J., 1435
McCutcheon, A., 154
McDermid, J., 274
Macdonald, D.S., 294
MacDonald, J.G., 985
MacDonald, M., 178
McDougall, B.J., 274
McGrath, J.W., 312
MacGregor, J., 1309
Machuca Vargas, O., 993
McHugh, R.J., 89
Machungo, M. da G., 885
McInnes, D., 316
MacInnes, K., 1009
MacInnis, G., 322
McInnis, T., 316
MacIsaac, J., 315
Mackay of Clashfern, *Lord*, 1308
Mackay, E.M., 274
McKee, M., 308
McKeithen, W.F., 1471
McKenna, F.J., 308
Mackenzie Stuart, *Lord*, 43
McKernan, J., 1473
MacKernan, P.N., 732
Mackey, G.W., 174
Macki, A. bin A.N., 966
Mackiewicz, A., 1013
McKinnon, K., 332
McKnight, W.H., 274
McLeod, G., 327
McLeod, L., 319
MacNeil, C., 316
McNeil, K., 755
MacPhail, L.G., 322
Macrae, J.E.C., 338, 588, 591, 849, 858, 1067
McVeigh, D.T., 138
McWeeny, S., 175
McWherter, N., 1533
Madani, A. ar-R., 1176
Madarshahi, M.S., 713
Mady, A.D., 391
Madzivhandila, A.M., 1109
Magrutsch, W.F., 173
Mahachi, M., 1626
Mahanta, P.K., 656
Mahathir Mohamad, 833
Mahayni, K. al-, 1176
Maher, A., 308
Mahit, W., 1572
Mahloji, M.H., 709
Mahmood, A.A., 1080
Mahmood Iskandar ibni Al- Marhum, *Sultan*, 832
Mahmoud, M.O.M., 858
Mahmud Al Marhum ibni Al-Marhum, *Sultan*, 832
Mai Chi Tho, 1586
Maïdou, C., 344
Maij-Weggen, H., 903
Mailänder, J., 560
Main, D., 298
Mainassara, I.B., 942
Major, J., 1308
Makhkamov, K.M., 1288
Makhulu, W.P.K., 32
Makki, H.M., 1596
Makonga, K.K., 1617
Maksim, *Metropolitan*, 248
Maktoum al-, 1294
Maktoum bin Rashid al-Maktoum, 1294
Makwetta, J., 1181
Malaguerra, C., 1174
Malan, M., 1090
Malecela, J.S., 1184
Maleuda, G., 527
Malherbes, C., 860
Maliba, K., 1617
Malietoa Tanumafili II, *Head of State*, 1593-4
Malile, R., 69
Malima, K., 1181
Mallaby, C., 544
Malmierca Peoli, I.A., 395
Mamaloni, S., 1082
Mamari, A. bin M. al, 966
Ma'mari, M. bin S. al, 966
Mamba, A.V., 1147
Mamba, G.M., 1145
Mamman, I., 944
Mammi, O., 746
Mancini, R., 319
Mandal, D.L., 662
Mandela, N., 1088
Manduca, J.A., 854
Maneka, G.M., 972
Mangklarat, C., 1186
Manglapus, R., 1005
Mangope, L.M., 1106
Mangwende, W., 1626
Manikas, D., 573
Manikufaan, H., 846
Manley, D., 755
Manley, M., 754
Manness, C.S., 305
Mannino, C., 746
Mansouri, H.I. al, 1059
Manthari, Y. bin M. al, 966
Manuel, P., 886
Manzie, D., 121
Mao Kao-wen, 368
Mapouka, T., 342
Mara, K., 469
Maran, M., 637
Marboua, T., 342
Marco, G. De, 851
Marendić, B., 1605
Margaret, *Princess*, 1305-6
Margarido, M.M., 1057
Margerie, E. de, 498
Margot, A., 43
Margrethe II, *Queen*, 416
Marin, F., 204
Mark, D., 944
Markaryants, V.S., 1274
Marko, R., 69
Marković, A., 1605
Marmosudjono, S., 702
Marque, J.-P., 509
Marques, A.H.C., 1026
Marques Moreira, M., 236
Marsden, W., 389, 939
Marshall, M.A., 432, 1598
Marshall, R., 1902
Mart, M., 43
Martelli, C., 745
Martens, W., 196
Martin, B., 327
Martin, D.J., 130
Martin, J.G., 1510
Martin, S., 274
Martinazzoli, M., 746
Martinez, B., 1450
Martínez Mendieta, M., 997
Martinez Ordoñez, R., 606
Martinko, R., 409
Marulanda, C.A., 373
Masaliev, A.M., 1291
Masdit, S., 1186
Masefield, J.T., 1184
Ma'shani, M. bin A. al, 966
Mashat, M.S. Al-, 718
Masheke, M., 1621
Mashila, N.A., 1109
Mashrqa, M.Z., 1176
Masire, Q.K.J., 224
Maslyukov, Yu.D., 1229
Masol, V.A., 1264
Masood, A., 67
Masri, A.F. Al-, 1179
Masse, M., 274
Massiah, K., 592
Massieu Berlanga, A., 865
Matheson, J., 316
Mathew, C.N., 1128
Matić, V., 1609
Matin, M.A., 185
Matovu, W.S.K., 1222
Mattar, A., 1076
Mattarella, S., 746
Matthew, J.A., 128
Matthewson, C., 919
Mauala, R., 1595
Maud, H.J.H., 405
Maude, F., 1309
Maung Maung Gyi, U, 257
Maung Maung Khin, 254
Maurice, E., 530
Mavrommatis, A., 405
Maximilian, *Prince*, 816
Maxwell, C., 327
Maxwell, R., 919

Mayanja, A., 1220
Maycock, A.T., 175
Mayeedul Islam, A.K.M., 185
Mayer, C.J., 274
Mayes, M.K., 143
Mayhew, P., 1309
Maynard, C.A., 433
Maynard, C.T., 174
Mayor, F., 16
Mays, C., 178
Maystadt, P., 197
Mazankowski, D.F., 274
Mazowiecki, T., 1012-13
Mazroui, F. al-, 1294
Mbaya, R., 830
Mbaye, K., 6-7
Mbede, J., 266
Mbingini, T.L.M., 1617
Mbitikon, R., 342
Mbonimpa, C., 258
Mbui, J., 266
Mébiame, L., 518
M'Eboutou, M.M., 266
Medaghri, A.A., 880
Meder, C., 822
Medgyessy, P., 615
Medjhouda, A., 75
Medvedev, V.A., 1229
Meguid, A.E.A., 447
Meiklejohn, R., 327
Melady, T., 1577
Melancia, C., 1027
Melhuish, M.R., 1190
Melhuish, R., 798
Mellick, J., 486
Mellor, D., 1309
Mena de Quevado, M., 373
Mena, J.F., 441
Mendis, W., 1128
Menem, C.S., 92
Mengistu Haile Mariam, 461-2
Menov, G., 244
Mensa-Wood, W.M., 564
Mensah, T.A., 25
Menteshashvili, T., 1229
Merafhe, M., 224
Meridor, D., 736
Merikas, G., 573
Merino, F., 453
Merrithew, G.S., 274
Messmer, I., 301
Metherell, T.A., 131
Meto, T., 761
Meyer, N., 1441
Micha, A.N., 459
Michael, C., 301
Michel, J., 1068
Michelis, G. De, 745
Michiko, *Empress*, 760
Mickelson, G., 1531
Miers, D., 577
Miettinen, M., 475
Miginolo, G., 753
Mihali, Q., 69
Miller, B., 1496
Miller, M.S., 1478
Miller, P., 409
Miller, W.D., 1531
Miller, Z., 1452
Milligan, K., 322
Milo, R., 736
Milton, D.F., 601, 758
Mines, B.A., 944
Minko, H., 518
Miño Guitart, J., 79
Miodowicz, A., 1016
Mira Amaral, L., 1021
Mirdha, N.R., 637
Mirkaymov, M.M., 1286
Mironenko, V.I., 1230
Misasi, R., 745
Mishra, J., 658
Miska, P., 69
Mitchell, J.F., 1051
Mitchelson, B.E., 305
Mitdank, J., 531
Miteb ibn Abdul Aziz, *Prince*, 1059
Mitterrand, F., 485
Mkapa, B., 1181
Mkhonta, W.C., 1145
Mlambala, M., 827
Mmusi, P.S., 224
Mnangagwa, E., 1626
Moazzam Hossain, S., 185
Mobutu, N., 1617
Mobutu Sésé Séko, 1617
Mochtar, R., 702
Mock, A., 169
Mocumbi, P.M., 886
Moda'i, Y., 736
Modrow, H., 527
Moeketsi, P.M., 1106
Moerdiono, 702
Mofford, R., 1433
Mogae, F., 225
Moggie anak Irok, L., 833
Mogwe, A.M., 225
Mohamad Said Keruak, 840
Mohamed bin Rahmat, 833
Mohammad Jemuri bin Serjan, 842
Mohammad Khan, A., 637
Mohammad Zain, 239
Mohammed bin Rashid al-Maktoum, 1294
Mohammedi, M.S., 75
Mohorita, V., 409
Mohr, Dr, 562
Moi, D.T. arap, 774
Moin, M., 709
Mojaddidi, S., 64
Mojsov, L., 1605
Molatlhwa, T.M., 1106
Molin, R., 1150
Molisa, S., 1572
Molitor, E., 822
Möllemann, J., 536
Molloy, B., 721
Molne Armengol, L., 79
Molomjamts, D., 873
Molpus, D., 1486
Momis, J., 987
Momoh, J.S., 1071
Momoh, T., 944
Moncayo García, J., 444
Monday, H.R., 524
Monerawela, C., 1133
Mongella, G., 1181
Moniba, H.F., 807
Monjo, J.C., 706
Montaño, J., 869
Montejo, R., 205
Montpezat, J., 514
Moody, G., 316
Moore, M.K., 918
Moore, R.A., 732
Moore, T.J., 130
Moose, G.E., 1067
Morake, K.P., 224
Morales Lechuga, I., 865
Moran, J.B., 1070
Morena, F. de la, 1125
Moreno Iruegas, M. de los A., 865
Morgan, A.H., 818
Morin, G.E., 319
Morland, M.R., 257
Morris, P., 100
Morrison, P., 1310
Morrissey, R.J., 322
Mortensen, K.V., 429
Mosambay, S.B., 1617
Mosbacher, R.A., 1385
Moshoeshoe II, *King*, 804
Mosquera Chaux, V., 377
Motawiya, B., 987
Motsatsi, V.S.S., 1106
Motzfeldt, J., 428
Moudiki, A., 266
Moulaye, Z., 848
Moultrie, J., 178
Moumin, A. Al, 380
Mound, T.E.J., 871
Moureaux, P., 196
Moussa, M.A.H., 447
Moussa, P., 382
Moussirou, E., 518
Moutsinga, H., 519
Moy, A., 702
Mphaphuli, M.M., 1109
Mphephu, P.R., 1109
Mpombo, M. wa, 1617
Msika, J., 1626
Msuya, C.D., 1181
Mswati III, *King*, 1144-5
Mualla, H. al-, 1294
Mualla, M.S. al-, 1294
Mubako, S., 1626
Mubarak bin Mohammed al-Nahyan, 1294
Mubarak, M.H., 447
Muchemwa, F., 1626
Mudenge, S., 1630
Mugabe, R., 1625-6
Muhani, A.A. al-, 1597
Muheim, F.E., 1174
Muili Brahimi, M. el-, 75
Mujuru, J., 1626
Mujuthaba, A., 845
Mukharji, N.K., 682
Mukiibi, I., 1220
Mulima, T.A., 1109
Mulimba, L., 1622
Mullings, S., 755
Mulroney, M.B., 274
Mumford, L.Q., 1426
Munkefjord S., 951
Munro, A., 1063
Munro, R., 1544
Munsoor, A.R., 1128
Muntasir, O.M. al-, 812
Munyaradzi, O., 1626
Muqbil, M.A., 1597
Murakhovsky, V.S., 1229
Murata, R., 767
Múrcia Herzog, E., 1117
Murdani, L.B., 702
Murerwa, H.M., 1630
Murphy, E., 1479
Murpratomo, S., 702
Murra, P., 69
Murray, J.L., 721
Murray, L., 274
Murray, W.S., 592
Murray, W.T.J., 130
Musa, S., 204
Museveni, Y., 1219-20
Mushega, A., 1220
Musoke, K., 1220
Musokotwane, K., 1622
Mustafa, Y., 447
Mustaffa bin Mohammad, 833
Mustaqi, K., 69
Mutalibov, A.N., 1268
Muteka, F.F., 82
Muto, K., 761
Mutumba, K.A. wa, 1617
Mutumbuka, D., 1626
Muyunda, M., 1622
Muzenda, S., 1626
Mwakikunga, M.M., 827
Mwananshiku, L., 1621
Mwinyi, N.A.H., 1181
Myboto, Z., 519
Myftiu, M., 69
Myo Aung, U, 257

Nagy, S., 618
Nahayo, J., 260
Nahayyan, A. bin Z. Al-, 1297
Naif ibn Abdul Aziz, *Prince*, 1059
Nailatikau, E., 472
Naim, M., 1579
Najafi, M.A., 709
Najibullah, S.M., 63-4
Nakajima, H., 18
Nakayama, T., 761
Nako, A., 69
Nallet, H., 485
Nandoe, K., 1143
Nantes, D., 316
Napsia binti Omar, 833
Narakobi, B., 987
Naranjo, P., 441
Narayan, I.J., 469
Naruhito *Crown Prince*, 760
Nasha, M., 227
Nasko, M., 944
Nassirou, A., 1192
Nata, T., 211
Natapei, E.N., 1572
Navajes-Mogro, H., 223
Navon, Y., 736
Navunisaravi, V., 469
Nawaz Shah, A., 972
Nayar, K., 651
Nayanar, E.K., 669
Nazarbaev, N.A., 1282
Nazer, H., 1059
Nazrin, *Raja*, 832
Ndamase, T.N., 1108
N'daw, O., 391
Ndiaye, A.D., 1065
Ndiaye, N., 1065
Ndlovu, C., 1626
Ndong, D.-O., 460
N'Doye, M., 1065
Neffati, C., 1203
Negroponte, J.D., 869
Nehru, A., 637
Neilson, P., 919
Neilson, R., 377
Neira, J., 441
Nelwamondo, C.A., 1109
Nematzadeh, M.R., 709
Neme, N., 391
Németh, M., 615
Nemitsas, T., 401
Nesengani, E.R.B., 1109

Neto-Kiambata, L., 84
Netyong, A., 1220
Netzler, J., 1594
Neudorf, W., 327
Neufeld, H.J., 305
Neumann, A., 527
New, L., 1368
Newington, M.J., 236
Newman, D.M., 933, 1595
Newton, A., 1309
Ney, E.M., 294
Nezhad-Hosseinian, M.H., 709
Ng Cheng Kiat, 833
Ngalisame, B., 1617
Ngatse, P., 382
Ngbuka, M., 1617
Ngimbi, N.M., 1617
Ngollo, R.D., 382
Ngoma-Foutou, C., 382
Ngu, J.N., 266
Nguema Mbasogo, T.O., 459
Nguyen Co Thach, 1586
Nguyen Duc Tam, 1586
Nguyen Huu Tho, 1586
Nguyen Quyet, 1586
Nguyen Thanh Binh, 1586
Nguyen Thi Dinh, 1586
Nguyen Van Linh, 1586-7
Ng'wandu, P., 1181
Ni Zhengyu, 7
Niang, I., 1065
Nichol, W.E., 1494
Nicolaas, E.D., 912
Nielsen, J.P., 417
Niles, F., 1049
Nissim, M., 736
Nixon, R.F., 319
Niyazov, S.A., 1284
Niyungeko, J., 260
Njie, L., 522
Njoya, I.M., 266
Njuba, S.K., 1220
Nkangi, J.M., 1220
Nkau, G.S., 1106
Nkikele, K., 1620
Nkomo, J., 1625-6
Nkwain, F., 266
Nogueira, F., 1021
Nogueira Batista, P., 236
Nombre, A., 251
Noor, N.A., 67
Nordberg, I., 1150
Nørgaard, C.A., 42
Noriega, M., 981
Norrback, O., 475
Norris, C.E., 460
North, P.P., 862
Noterdaeme, P., 203
Nottage, B.J., 175
Nourbakhsh, M., 709
Nouri, A., 709
Novetzke, S.J., 854
Nsibandze, B.M., 1145
Nsimba, M., 1617
Ntaggazwa, A., 1181
Ntiwane, N.D., 1145
Ntui, O.E., 266
Nudali, L.A., 1128
Nujoma, S., 891
Numan, Y.S., 1600
Nunes Correia, A., 589
Nures, N., 1213
Nuri, A. A. al, 791
Nve, A.F., 459
Nyakyi, A.B., 1184
Nyamdoo, G., 876
Nyang'anyi, M., 1181
Nyers, R., 615
Nzengeya, B.A., 1620
Nzoungou, A., 382

O Guk Ryol, 786
O Jin U, 786
Oakley, R.B., 979
Oba, A.N., 382
Oba-Apounou, G., 382
O'Bannon, F., 1462
Obasi, G.O.P., 24
Obeng, P.V., 564
Oberle, F., 274
Obregoso Rodriguez, E., 999
O'Brien, T., 933
Ochirbal, I., 876
Ochirbat, P., 873
Oda, S., 7
O'Donoghue, D.A., 1190
Oduber, N.O., 912
Odzaga, J.R., 521
Oestergaard, K., 417
Offer, S., 319
Ogi, A., 1167
Ogouma, S., 208
Óhlighile, P., 721
O'Keeffe, P.L., 413
O'Kennedy, M., 721
Okeyo, M., 777
Okorut, S., 1220
Okuda, K., 761
Olav V, *King*, 950
Oldring, J., 298
Olesen, A., 417
Oleson, C.L., 305
Olhaye, R., 432
Oliveira Lima, A. de, 337
Oliveira Martins, J., 1021
Oliveira Ramos, T.L.S. de, 337
Olmert, E., 736
O'Malley, D., 721
Omdahl, L., 1512
Ominami, C., 349
Onambwe, H. de C., 82
O'Neil, H., 319
O'Neil, W., 25
O'Neill, R.J., 203
O'Neill, W.J., 1443
Ong Teng Cheong, 1076
Ongoiba, I., 848
Ongueme, M.N., 459
Onmar, A. Ibn, 346
Ono, A., 761
Oramas-Oliva, O., 399
Orbos, O., 1005
Orchard, D.W., 305
Ormachea Peñaranda, H., 219
Orman, R., 298
Orojuela Bueno, R., 373
O'Rourke, A., 732
O'Rourke, M., 721
Orr, D., 1351
Orr, K., 1494
Orr, R.D., 1080
Ortega Saavedra, G., 936
Ortiz de Urbina, F.V., 1125
Ortiz, G., 441
Osborne, D.G., 830
Osborne, J.A., 877
Osman, A.M., 886
Osman, A.S., 1087
Osuna, E.E., 1579
Oteiba, M.S. al-, 1294
Othily, G., 501
Otoo, E.K., 567
Otter, C.L., 1456
Ouattara, Y., 391
Ouedraogo, A., 253
Ouedraogo, C.O., 251
Ouedraogo, G.R., 253
Ouedraogo, Y., 251
Oumar, A., 586
Oumarou, M., 940
Ouologuem, A., 848
Oveson, W.V., 1538
Owais, H.N. al-, 1294
Owona, J., 266
Owono Nguema, F., 519
Oyhanarte, J., 92
Oyono, F.L., 266
Özal, T., 1208
Oziatyński, J., 1013
Ozores, C., 981

Paasio, P., 475
Pacas Castro, J.M., 453
Pacavira, M.P., 84
Pacheco, F.A., 386
Pacskai, L., 620
Paek Hak Rim, 787
Paeniu, B., 1217
Paihama, K., 81
Pak Gil Yon, 790
Pak Sung Chul, 786
Pakdemirli, E., 1208
Pallaev, G., 1288
Palm, J.M., 251
Panayides, T., 405
Pančevski, M., 1605
Panguene, A.A., 888
Panigrahi, C., 675
Pankov, P., 244
Papageorgiou, P., 401
Pappalardo, C., 993
Pappas, N., 573
Pardo de Tavera, M., 1005
Paré, L., 325
Park Chul-Un, 782
Park Tong-Jin, 785
Parker, David, 301
Parker, David C., 161
Parker, J.H., 330
Parkinson, C., 1309
Parris, W.H., 592
Parsuraman, A., 860
Partridge, D.W., 1074
Paş alar, O., 406
Pascal-Trouillot, E., 598
Pashane, M., 827
Pastinen, I.O., 481
Paszyński, A., 1013
Paterson, T.F., 127
Pathak, R.S., 6
Patil, V., 667
Patmore, P.J., 148
Patt, G., 736
Patten, C., 1309
Patten, J., 1309
Patten, R., 319
Patterson, D., 330
Patterson, P.J., 755
Paula, G. de, 914
Paulillo, F.H., 1571
Pavlov, V.S., 1229
Pawar, S., 673
Pawlak, S., 1019
Paye, J.-C., 36
Pe Thein, 254
Peacocke, G.B.P., 131
Pearce, R.J., 161
Pedalé, P.M., 81
Pedersen, T., 417
Pedranga, C., 1005
Peerthum, S., 862
Pejić, D., 1610
Pelletier, J., 485
Pelletreau, R.H., 1206
Peñalosa, E., 377
Penner, J., 305
Penner, V.D., 338
Pep, M., 987
Peponis, A., 573
Pereira, A.M., 336
Pereira, J., 589
Pereira, M., 1021
Pereira Bastos, J.E.M., 1026
Perera, D., 1133
Perera, F., 1128
Perera, M.J.M., 1128
Perera, M.V., 1128
Peres, S., 736
Peretz, Y., 736
Pérez de Cuéllar, J., 7
Perez Rodriguez, C.A., 1579
Perpich, R., 1484
Perrin, B.K., 405
Perron, M., 121
Perry, R., 1048
Persson, G., 1150
Pertricioli, G., 869
Peters, M.L., 914
Petersen, N.H., 417
Peterson, D.R., 319
Peterson, S., 327
Petrignani, R., 753
Pham Van Kai, 1586
Philip, *Prince, Duke of Edinburgh*, 1305-6
Philippe, A., 822
Philippou, A., 401
Philips, M.A.P., 1305
Phillip, C., 227
Phillips, G., 319
Phillips, J.D., 260
Phomvihane, K., 796
Phone Myint, 254
Phoofolo, M.P., 806
Phounsavanh, N., 796
Piava, F.M., 82
Pibulsonggram, N., 1190
Pickard, N.E.W., 131
Pickering, D., 469
Pickering, E.P., 130
Pickering, T., 1424
Pickersgill, R., 755
Pierre, S., 824
Pike, M.E., 1080
Pilgrim, C.S., 595
Pillar, W., 1371
Pinc, F., 409
Pindling, L.O., 174
Pinkhayan, S., 1186
Pintat Solans, J., 79
Pinto Cassasola, F., 581
Pinto da Costa, M., 1056
Pires, P.V.R., 336
Pitarka, B., 72
Pitra, F., 409
Plantegenest, M., 509
Platt, N., 1009
Plumb, *Lord*, 43
Poati-Souchalaty, A., 382
Pocaterra, R., 1579

Podlena, F., 409
Pohjala, T.T., 475
Pohl, W., 527
Polansky, S., 249
Polson, G., 1217
Pomicino, P.C., 745
Ponce de Leon, E.C., 865
Pondi, V.P.-T., 268
Pongpanit, M., 1186
Poole, E., 121
Poos, J.F., 820
Pope, N.A., 154
Poperen, J., 485
Pora, P., 987
Portillo, M., 1310
Portos, A.A., 824
Poulter, D.G., 14
Poumele, G.I., 1559
Pozsgay, I., 615
Pradhan, R.D., 655
Prado Abasto, E., 219
Prakash Chautala, O., 662
Prandini, G., 746
Prasasvinitchai, S., 1190
Prasertsuwan, B., 1186
Pravesh Chandra, J., 696
Prawiro, R., 702
Prebble, R.W., 918
Pregl, Z., 1605
Premadasa, R., 1128
Prendergast, W.K., 1630
Price, G.C., 204
Prieto, C., 993
Primakov, E.M., 1227, 1230
Pringle, F., 755
Pringle, R.M., 849
Pritchard, J., 1544
Pronk, J., 903
Proto, F., 499
Protopapas, N., 401
Pruskene, K., 1280
Psimhis, J.L., 342
Pugh, R.L., 347
Pugo, B.K., 1230
Puhakka, M., 475
Pullen, B.T., 154
Puolanne, U., 475
Putra ibni Al-Marhum, *Raja*, 832

Qaboos bin Said, *Sultan*, 965
Qaddur, M., 1176
Qadhafi, M., 811
Qatabi, M. bin A. al, 966
Qian Qichen, 357
Qiao She, 357
Qin Jiwei, 357
Quainoo, A., 564
Quainton, A.C.E., 1003
Qualao, H.C., 1572
Quayle, D., 1385
Quilès, P., 485
Quinn, R.S., 1473
Quli, A., 1176
Quwatli, M., 1176

Rabah, S., 1203
Rabaua, U., 778
Rabesa, Z.A., 824
Rabesahala, G., 824
Rabetafika, B., 826
Rabin, Y., 736
Rabotoson, F. de P., 826
Rachaiah, B., 664
Rachid, K.H.O., 881
Radanielson, V., 824
Radegonde, S., 1070
Radembino Coniquet, R., 518
Rafida Aziz, 833
Rafsanjani, A.A.H., 709
Rageh, A.A., 1602
Raghbani, S. al-, 1294
Rahaga, J.-C., 824
Rahim, A.A., 676
Rahime, K.A.T., 972
Rahman, M., 185
Rahmani, C., 75
Rai, R.P., 694
Rainford, R., 56
Rainier III, *Prince*, 870
Raisi, A. bin M. bin M. al, 966
Rajaobelina, L., 824
Rakato, I., 824
Ramabulana, G.M., 1109
Ramahatra, V., 824
Rambuda, J.R., 1109
Ramjuttun, D., 860
Ramkisor, C.B., 1143
Ramly, A.R., 706
Ramos, F., 1005
Ramos da Cruz, J., 82
Ramsay, A., 1139
Ramsay, D., 319
Ramtallie, O.D., 755
Rana, J.P., 898
Rane, P., 660
Rangel, D. das C.S., 81
Ranjan Majumdar, S., 689
Ransome-Kuti, O., 944
Rantanen, J., 475
Rashid bin Ahmed al-Mualla, *Sheikh*, 1293
Rashid bin Said al-Maktoum, *Sheikh*, 1293-4
Rasmussen, O.F., 417
Ratanakoses, M., 1186
Ratford, D., 963
Rathebe, S.S.L., 1106
Ratsiraka, D., 824
Rattakul, B., 1186
Rattray, C., 755
Rau, J., 556
Rauchfuss, W., 527
Rausch, J.-M., 486
Ravele, F.N., 1109
Raveloson, M.C.B., 824
Rawiri, G., 518
Rawlings, J.J., 564
Ray, R., 100
Rayes, G.M.A. al-, 794
Razaz, M.A. al, 447
Razumovsky, G.P., 1230
Rechendorff, T., 417
Reddy, B.S.N., 690
Reddy, R., 689
Redman, C.E., 1163
Redston, C.F., 466
Redway, A., 274
Reed, M., 121
Reedijk, C., 911
Reeve, A., 771
Reffell, D., 568
Refunjol, F.J., 912
Regenvanu, S.J., 1572
Reichel, F., 409
Reino, F.J., 1026
Reisch, G., 47
Reiten, E., 951
Reith, M., 268, 344, 460
Rémillard, G., 324
René, F.A., 1068
Renton, T., 1309
Renwick, R., 1099
Rerngprasertvit, P., 1186
Rewaka, D.D., 521
Rex, R.R., 933
Reynolds, A., 721
Reynolds, J., 301
Reynolds, S., 1537
Rhee Sang-Hi, 782
Rhodes, J.S., 1630
Riberaygua Miquel, B., 79
Rice, D.B., 1398
Rich, R.G., 207
Richard, *Prince*, *Duke of Gloucester*, 1305
Richardson, G., 100
Richmond, C., 301
Richthofen, H. von, 544
Ridley, N., 1308
Riegler, J., 169
Riesenhuber, H., 536
Rifai, M. as S. al, 791
Rifkind, M., 1309
Rikanovic, S., 1609
Ringadoo, V., 860
Ritzen, J., 903
Riutel, A.F., 1277
Rivas-Gallont, E., 456
Rivera Irias, A., 581
Riviello Bazan, A., 865
Robati, P., 931
Roberts, B., 1520
Roberts, W., 1310
Robertson, P., 755
Robiarivony, J., 824
Robinson, A.N.R., 1199
Robinson, H., 1564
Roble, M.B., 430
Robu, G., 1038
Rocard, M., 485
Rochas da Costa, C., 1056
Rodger, A., 1309
Rodgers, P., 178
Rodríguez, A., 993
Rodríguez, F., 981
Roebuck, R., 1564
Roemer, C.E., 1471
Rogers, C.L., 207
Roh Tae-Woo, 782
Rohrmoser Valdeavellano, R., 584
Rojas, P., 349
Rolle, D.E., 174
Român, P., 1033-4
Römer, Dr, 547
Romer, R., 1441
Römer, R.A., 914
Romero Herrero, C., 1117
Romita, P., 746
Rontray, N., 637
Roper, T.W., 154
Rosales-Rivera, M., 456
Rosas Vega, G., 373
Ross, W.S., 78
Rossel Dolcet, R., 79
Rostad, K., 298
Rötzsch, H., 532
Rouissi, M., 1203
Roumi, K.M. al-, 1294
Roure, J.-C., 530
Rousseau, P., 327
Roussety, M.F., 860
Rowas, A.A. bin M. al, 966
Rowell, E., 1026
Roy, J.-L., 325
Rožić, M., 1604
Ruangkanchanases, C., 1186
Rubale, T., 1220
Ruben, Y.Y., 1278
Ruberti, A., 746
Ruchupan, M., 1186
Ruda, J.M., 6
Rudini, 702
Ruffolo, G., 746
Rugaas, B., 964
Ruggierio, R., 746
Rugunda, R., 1220
Ruhfus, J., 544
Ruiz Diaz, P.P., 993
Rukashaza, O., 1043
Rumbold, A., 1310
Ruphin, G., 824
Rupper, L.M., 963
Russell, R., 316
Rustam, , S., 702
Rwegasira, J., 1181
Ryan, C., 324
Ryan, G., 1459
Ryan, M., 1147
Ryan, S., 100
Rycroft, C.S., 347
Ryssdal, R., 42
Ryzhkov, N.I., 1229

Saad al-Abdullah as-Salim as-Sabah, *Prince*, 791
Sa'adi, M.A. al-, 1600
Sabagh, S.A.W. Al, 183
Sabah, as-, 791-2, 794
Sabally, S., 522
Sabhavasu, P., 1186
Sabumai, B., 987
Sacher, R., 409
Sadik, N., 10
Sáez de Cosculluela, J., 1117
Safiullah, K.M., 189
Sagdiev, M.R., 1282
Sagna, F.I., 1065
Sagna, R., 1065
Sahlin, M., 1150
Sahlul, A., 1136
Saho, L., 522
Said, H.S., 75
Said, S.F. bin A. Al, 966
Said, S.F. bin M. bin M. Al, 966
Said, S.F. bin T. bin F. Al, 966
Said, S.S. bin T. Al, 966
Saidi, S.B. bin S. bin H. Al B., 966
Saidi, S.H. bin S. bin H. Al B., 966
Saidi, S.M. bin A. Al B., 966
Sailele, T., 1594
Sainju, M.M., 898
St Jorre, D. de, 1068
St-Phard, G., 601
Saitoti, G., 774
Sajadah, V., 860
Sakamoto, M., 761
Salah, A., 771
Salahuddin Abdul Aziz Shah ibni Al-Marhum, *Sultan*, 832

Salami, A.S. as-, 1597
Salami, S.S., 1600
Salaverria, M.A., 456
Saleem, Y., 658
Saleh, A.A., 1596
Saleh, I., 702
Saleh, M. El H.O.M., 858
Saleh, Z.M., 1136
Salim, E., 702
Salim, S.A., 58, 1181
Salinas de Gortari, C., 865
Sallam, A., 1598
Salle, M., 342
Salman, M., 1176
Salmon, C.B., 798
Salolainen, P., 475
Salonia, A.F., 92
Sam, S., 1220
Samaras, A., 573
Samassekou, N., 849
Samman, A. bin A. as-, 1596
Sampegbo, S., 251
Sampson, R., 466
Samsonowicz, H., 1013
Sanda, O., 266
Sanderson of Bowden, *Lord*, 1310
Sandiford, E., 190
Sangma, P.A., 676
Sanguinetta, J.M., 1567
Sanogo, B., 251
Sanoussi, Z.A., 588
Sansa Reñe, M., 79
Santamaría, J., 1125
Santamaría, O., 453
Santer, J., 820
Santos, J.E. dos, 81
Santos, L., 1005
Santos, Manuel dos (Guinea-Bissau), 589
Santos, Manuel dos (Mozambique), 888
Sanusi bin Junid, *Datuk Seri*, 833
Saouma, E., 15
Saqqa, H., 1176
Saqr bin Mohammed al-Qasimi, *Sheikh*, 1293
Sarah, *Duchess of York*, 1305
Sarasin, P., 1186
Sárlos, I., 615
Sarwar, A., 67
Sarzetakis, C., 573
Sassou-Nguesso, D., 382
Sathy, M., 845
Sattar, A., 185
Saud al Faisal, *Prince*, 1059
Saud Nasir as-Sabah, 794
Saud, S.S. bin H. bin, 966
Savage, J., 301
Savetsila, S., 1186
Saw Maung, 254
Sayako, *Prince*, 760
Sayeed, M., 637
Schaefer, G., 1507
Schaefer, W.D., 1476
Schäuble, W., 536
Scheidermaier, H.H., 548
Scheleske Sánchez, M., 865
Schipp, J.J., 130
Schlitz, H., 196
Schlüter, P., 417
Schmidmaier, D., 532
Schmidt, G., 327
Schulze, R., 527
Schuppius, E.-K., 1194
Schürer, G., 527
Schüssel, W., 169
Schwarz-Schilling, C., 536
Schwebel, S., 7
Scoon, P., 578
Scott, A.J., 339
Scott, I.G., 319
Scott, J., 1051
Scott, Nicholas, 1310
Scott, Noel, 919
Scowen, R., 325
Seamans, H., 308
Sebe, L., 1111
Sebele, K., 227
Secchia, P., 753
Sedgho, L., 251
Segesvary, L., 818
Sehoulia, D., 342
Sehume, K.C.V.A., 1106
Seignoret, C., 433
Sein Aung, 254
Seiters, R., 536
Sekitoleko, J., 1220
Sellæg, W.C., 951
Seluka, L., 1217
Semedo, J., 589
Semlali, A., 880
Semprún, J., 1117
Semwogerere, P.K., 1220
Seodi, S.M., 1106
Sépulveda, B., 869
Séraphin, J.-J., 824
Seri Utama Syed Ahmad, 832
Serna, D. de la, 1005
Serra i Serra, N., 1117
Serra Puche, J., 865
Setches, K.P., 154
Sey, A.O., 522
Seybou, A., 940
Sezaki, K., 767
Shaali, M.H. Al-, 1297
Shabalala, E.S., 1145
Shaer, A. ibn H. al-, 1059
Shafiq al-Salihi, A.M., 718
Shah, P.A., 972
Shahabuddeen, M., 7
Shahal, M., 736
Shahidul, S., 185
Shaikh, A.R. ibn A.A. ibn A. al, 1059
Shakar, K.E. Al, 183
Shaker, M.I., 452
Shakespeare, J.W.R., 884
Shalayev, S.A., 1244
Shamir, Y., 736
Shamuyarira, N., 1626
Shanfari, A.B. Al-, 969
Shanfari, S. bin A. al, 966
Shankar, R., 1140
Shar', F. ash-, 1176
Sharaf, K., 1176
Sharkey, C.J., 1571
Sharland, E.J., 991
Sharma, R.N., 896
Sharma, S.D., 636
Sharma, Y.D., 680
Sharon, A., 736
Sharq, M.H., 63
Shathir, A., 845
Shatti, I. al-, 1176
Shearar, J.B., 1099
Sheilds, M., 919
Shelton, K., 1432
Shepherd, J.A., 183
Sheriff, B., 944
Sherifis, M., 405
Shevardnadze, E.A., 1229
Shevchenko, V.S., 1264
Shih Chi-yang, 368
Shihabi, S., 1063
Shinn, D.H., 253
Shirawa, Y.A. Al, 180
Shirley, K., 919
Shongwe, S., 1145
Shostari, I., 709
Shpatov, I., 244
Shubert, J., 1509
Shumway, J., 1433
Shurtleff, L.G., 384
Siddon, T.E., 274
Sidhu, S.S., 22
Sidi Mohammed, *Prince*, 880
Sidki, A.T.N., 447
Sigfússon, S.J., 624
Sigulogo, G., 987
Sigurðardóttir, J., 624
Sigurðsson, J., 624
Sihanouk, *Prince* Norodom, 261
Silpa-Archa, B., 1186
Silva, A. da, 589
Silva, A.H. da, 81
Silva, J.P., 337
Silva Peneda, J., 1021
Silva Rocha, A., 337
Silvia, *Queen*, 1149
Sim Kheng Hong, 842
Simbanenduku, S., 1626
Simha, B.K., 898
Simitis, K., 573
Simmonds, K.A., 1044
Simmons, K., 190
Simpson, P., 755
Simpson-Orlebar, M.K.O., 869
Simuchimba, 1622
Sinamoi, B., 987
Singel, M.S., 1524
Singh, A., 637, 696
Singh, G., 678
Singh, K., 651
Singh, S., 669
Singh, Virbhadra, 664
Singh, Vishwanath P., 636
Singleton, M., 131
Sinner, G.A., 1512
Sione, S., 1594
Siphandon, K., 796
Sipraseuth, P., 796
Siraj, H.B., 430
Sirikit *Queen*, 1185
Sirisumpan, T., 1186
Sissoko, M., 848
Sivgin, H., 1208
Siwicki, F., 1013
Sjasdzali, H.M., 702
Skak-Nielsen, N.V., 429
Skauge, A., 951
Skinner, S.K., 1386
Skipping, O., 1215
Skundric, P., 1605
Slama, Hamouda Ben, 1203
Slaoui, D., 884
Slisz, J., 1015
Slyunkov, N.N., 1229
Small, D.P., 595, 1143
Smalley, R.M., 806
Smaoui, A., 1203
Smart, A.B.P., 472, 895, 1217
Smili, B., 880
Smith, Brian, 227
Smith, Bruce, 308
Smith, Bud, 301
Smith, D.L., 161
Smith, D.M., 316
Smith, G.N., 481
Smith, J., 1450
Smith, P., 327
Smith, R.B.R., 130
Smits, C., 914
Smolentsev, E.A., 1248
Snegur, M.I., 1275
Snorrason, H., 629
So Chol, 786
So Yun Sok, 786
Soares, J.C.B., 53
Soares, M., 1021
Soebadio, H., 702
Sohahong-Kombet, J.-P., 344
Soisson, J.-P., 485
Sokolov, E.E., 1266
Solana Madariaga, J., 1117
Solana Morales, F., 865
Solchaga Catalán, C., 1117
Solé-Romeo, L.A., 1571
Solís Fallas, O., 386
Sölle, H., 527
Sollie, S., 951
Sólnes, J., 624
Solofoson, G., 824
Somare, M., 987
Somvorachit, D., 798
Son Sann, 261
Song Ping, 357
Sonko, A., 1065
Sonko, L.J., 522
Sophia, *Queen*, 1116
Sorbara, G., 319
Soriano Lea Plaza, W., 219
Sotirhos, M.G., 577
Souflias, G., 573
Souto Hernández, A.J., 993
Sparrow, D., 298
Späth, L., 546
Spautz, J., 820
Speaker, R., 298
Spearman, L.H.O., 1043
Spicer, M., 1310
Sprague, D.K., 876
Spreckley, J.N.T., 836
Springer, H., 190
Spyker, P.C., 154
Sreibl, M., 547
Ssali, J.B., 1220
Stack, K., 987
Stadtler, W.E., 211
Stahl, J., 1504
Stamatis, C., 573
Stǎnculescu, A., 1034
Stanislaus, L.A., 580
Staples, P., 100
Star, T.W., 895
Steeg, H., 36
Steensnæs, E., 951
Stefani, S., 69
Steggle, T.H., 997

Steichen, R., 820
Stellini, S.J., 854
Stephens, S., 1491
Steppuhn, G., 554
Sterpa, E., 746
Stewart, C., 316
Stewart, F., 298
Stich, O., 1167
Stimson, R.F., 1047
Stirn, O., 486
Stoichici, I., 1039
Stoltenberg, G., 536
Stone, M.P.W., 1390
Stoutt, H.L., 1591
Strachan, B., 301
Streams, P.J., 456, 605
Streatch, K., 315
Streicher, R., 169
Strezov, A., 249
Stroock, T.F., 584
Stuart, C.M., 126
Stubig, M., 454
Subramaniam, C., 673
Subroto, 58
Subulwa, L.S., 1622
Suckling, R., 987
Sudarman, S., 702
Suddarth, R.S., 771
Sudomo, 702
Sugiarto, 702
Suharmono, 702
Suharto, 702
Sulaim, S.A.A. al, 1059
Sulaiman bin Haji Daud, 833
Sulaiman, K.M., 1297
Sullivan, L.W., 1385
Sullivan, M., 1553
Sultan bin Mohammed al- Qasimi, *Sheikh*, 1293
Sultan ibn Abdul Aziz, *Prince*, 1058
Sumarlin, J.B., 702
Sumbana, R.R., 1109
Sumner, C.J., 143
Sundstein, J., 426
Sungurlu, O., 1208
Suominen, I., 475
Suro, D., 438
Süssmuth, R., 536
Sutherland, V.E., 253, 393, 942
Sutresna, N., 706
Sutrisno, T., 702
Sutton, J.R., 919
Suvar, S., 1605
Swan, J.W.D., 212
Sweeney, J., 319
Swenson, R., 327
Swiecicki, M., 1013
Swing, W.J., 1099
Swokin, K., 987
Sy, M., 1065
Sy, S.M., 1065
Sy, S.O., 1065
Sychev, V.V., 49
Syquia, T.T., 1009
Syrimis, G., 401
Syryjczyk, T., 1013
Syse, J.P., 951

Tabai, I., 778
Tabakaucoro, F., 469
Tabone, A., 851
Tabone, S., 851
Tadesse, T., 465
Tahiliani, 685
Taitt, B., 190
Takabwebwe, M., 778
Talbot, S.R., 32
Talhi, J.A. al-, 812
Tallala, A.S., 837
Tamariz, D., 441
Tan Keng Yam, T., 1076
Tanasie, P., 1039
Tandjung, A., 702
Tankeu, E., 266
Tanoh, E.G., 564
Tapsell, P., 919
Tarabulsi, A.-M., 1176
Tarasov, N.K., 7
Tariq Khan, A., 972
Tarjanne, P., 23
Tasca, C., 486
Tashjian, J., 1443
Tatham, D.E., 803
Tati-Loutard, J.-B., 382
Tatjana, *Princess*, 816
Taufa'ahau Tupou IV, *King*, 1195
Tavaiqia, J., 469
Taveras-Guzman, J.A., 439
Tawiah, E., 564
Taxell, C., 475
Taya, M.O.S.M., 856
Taylor, D., 877
Taylor, I.F., 161
Taylor, M., 991
Taylor, P.D., 438
Taylor, R.W., 1194
Tazov, D.T., 1229
Tchepanou, C., 266
Tchioba, E.M., 518
Tealof, S.M., 1217
Teannaki, T., 778
Teegen, E.I.H., 472
Teehamkee, C., 1009
Teelock, B., 862
Teixeira de Matos, A., 81
Teixera, A.L., 81
Tella, G.J.M., di 95
Temo, A., 987
Temple Black, S., 413
Tevasa, T., 1217
Thalén, I., 1150
Thatcher, M., 1308
Thayeb, T.M.H., 706
Themelis, N., 573
Theobald, H.R., 1552
Theodore, N.A., 1529
Thiam, A., 391
Thiam, H., 1065
Thiounn Prasith, 264
Thomas, J.A.E., 88
Thomas, R., 249
Thomas, W.I., 161
Thomassen, P., 951
Thompson, J., 1574
Thompson, J.R., 1459
Thompson, T.G., 1550
Thompson, W., 472
Thomson, P.A.B., 207
Thondaman, S., 1128
Thornburgh, R., 1385
Thornhill, R., 315
Thorning-Petersen, R., 429
Thorpe, M.R., 1201
Thunborg, A., 1163
Tian Jiyun, 357
Tickell, C., 1358
Tiendrebeogo, A., 251
Timataka, F., 1572
Timeon, P.T., 780
Tin Hlaing, U, 257
Tin Tun, 254
Tizard, C., 918
Tlass, M., 1176
Tlhabane, T.M., 1106
Tlou, H.F., 1106
Tobback, L., 197
Todman, T.A., 95
Toemaes, L., 417
Tofani, H., 586
Toganivalu, W., 469
Tókés, L., 1033
Tolentino, A.C., 336
Tomášek, *Cardinal* F., 413
Tomes, V.A., 1371
Tomsić, F., 1615
Tonha, P.M., 81
Toome, I., 1277
Töpfer, K., 536
Tora, A., 469
Torkan, A., 709
Törnudd, K., 482
Touray, S., 522
Toure, M., 1065
Towell, T., 997
Tra, A.V.B., 391
Traill, G.A., 830
Tran Hoan, 1586
Tran Xuan Bach, 1586
Traoré, B., 848
Traoré, M., 58, 847
Traoré, N., 848
Trautmann, R., 615
Trefgarne, *Lord*, 1310
Treiki, A., 815
Tremelling, A.J., 238
Trezise, N.B., 154
Triaca, A.J., 92
Trinh Van Can, 1590
Trinh Xuan Lang, 1590
Trinidad, G.P., 912
Trippier, D., 1310
Trites, P., 308
Tromp, F.B., 912
Troy, G.J., 161
Trumpington, *Baroness*, 1310
Trynchy, P., 298
Trzeciakowski, W., 1013
Tsaranazy, J.-E., 824
Tseloa, M.K., 806
Tseng Kwang-shun, 368
Tshering, U., 217
Tsiangalara, J.R., 826
Tsiba, F., 382
Tsikata, K., 564
Tsochatzopoulos, A., 573
Tsukahara, S., 761
Tsur, Y., 736
Tsushima, Y., 761
Tudor, J., 190
Tuita, S.M., 1197
Tull, T.A., 596
Tuncer, C., 1208
Tupout'a, *Prince*, 1196
Turé, B., 591
Turgeon, S.G., 1434
Turner, S.E., 238
Tutu, A.L., 81
Tuyo, T., 987
Twaddell, W.H., 858
Tynell, L., 1163
Tzannetakis, T., 573

Udenhout, W.A., 1143
Ujang anak Jilan, C., 842
Ukpanah, S.J., 944
Ulufi, M.M. al-, 1597
Umar, A., 944
Unnikrishnan, K.P., 637
Unsi, A.M. al-, 1596
Untube, N.U.O., 1617
Upendra, P., 637
Urbain, R., 197
Ure, J., 1163
Ussery, E.M., 884
Utchanah, M., 860
Uthman, D.A. al-, 791
Uwimana, A., 1043

Vaček, M., 409
Vagris, J.J., 1278
Vahaji, A.-H., 709
Vajiralongkorn, *Prince*, 1185
Vakatora, T., 469
Valas, V.J., 1277
Valcourt, B., 274
Valdés Abascal, R., 865
Valdivieso-Balaunde, F., 1003
Valencia-Ospina, E., 7
Valente de Oliveira, L., 1021
Valla, K.H., 951
Valle, K.H., 950
Vallejo Arco, A., 441
Valtassari, J., 482
Van Bellinghen, J.-P., 203
Van den Brande, L., 197
Van den Broek, H., 903
Van der Biest, A., 197
Van der Merwe, S., 1090
Van Lierop, F., 1574
Van Niekerk, W., 1090
Van Schaik, R.J., 910
Van Tonder, W.T., 806
Van-Dúnem, F.J.F., 81
Van-Dúnem, P. de C., 81
Vander Zalm, W.N., 301
Vanderveken, J., 34
Vargas Vacaflor, W., 219
Varkonyi, P., 621
Varvitsiotis, I., 573
Vasconcellos Franca, A., 337
Vásquea Nava, M.E., 865
Vasquez Bazán, C., 999
Vásquez Sosa, L., 454
Vásquez Velásquez, O., 373
Vassali, G., 745
Vassiliou, G., 400-1
Vaz-Pereira, A., 1026
Vazquez, J., di 95
Vega, G., 985
Vega Dominguez, J. de la, 865
Veitata, T., 469
Veitch, E., 301
Vejjajiva, V., 1190
Velasquez Giacarini, J., 999
Velásquez-Diaz, M., 605
Velichkov, V., 249
Vellayati, A.A., 709
Vellu, S.S., 833
Velompanahy, A., 824
Veniamin, C., 401
Venkataraman, R., 636
Venkatasubia, P., 667
Venter, R., 1090
Vera Arrata, A., 441

Verduga, C., 441
Vezina, M., 274
Vezirov, A-R. Kh., 1268
Vibe, K., 963
Victoria, *Princess*, 1149
Vieira, H., 337
Vieira, J.B., 589
Vigil-Giron, R., 1504
Vik, A., 951
Viljoen, G., 1090
Villagrán DeLeon, F., 584
Villiger, K., 1167
Vinde, P., 36
Vinogradov, V.M., 1254
Virion, T. de, 1018
Vistbacka, R., 475
Vizzini, C., 746
Vlasi, A., 1614
Vlasov, A.V., 1230, 1254
Vlok, A., 1090
Vo Chi Cong, 1586
Vo Nguyen Giap, 1586
Vo Van Kiet, 1586
Vocouma, P., 251
Vodrázka, L., 409
Vogae, B., 987
Vogt, H., 555
Voican, G., 1034
Vongkhamsao, S., 796
Vongvichit, P., 796
Vorotnikov, V.I., 1229, 1254
Voscherau, H., 551
Voskanyan, G.M., 1274
Vraalsen, T., 951
Vraalsen, T.E., 963
Vranitzky, F., 169
Vunibobo, B., 469

Waddington, D., 1308
Wagner, C.L., 557
Wahaibi, K. bin N. al, 966
Waigel, T., 536
Waight, M., 205
Waihee, J., 1454
Waim, J., 987
Wajih, A.K. al-, 1597
Wakeham, J., 1309
Wakil, I.A., 1181
Waldegrave, W., 1309
Waldheim, K., 169
Wałęsa, L., 1011
Walker, C., 190
Walker, E., 154
Walker, E.S., 1297
Walker, H.B., 718
Walker, H.K., 826
Walker, H.S., 758
Walker, L., 948
Walker, P., 1308
Walker, W.G., 456
Walla, K., 1192
Wallmann, W., 553
Walls, G., 143
Wallström, M., 1150
Walsh, P., 100
Walsh, R.W., 154
Walters, B., 1592
Walters, C.R., 1445
Walters, V.A., 544
Wan Li, 357
Wang Bingqian, 357
Wang Fang, 357
Wang Zhen, 357
Wanjik, P., 987
Wapakhabulo, J.F., 1220
Ward, C., 319
Wardoyo, 702
Warioba, J.S., 1181
Warki, B.A., 430
Warnke, J., 536
Warren, P.J., 312
Wasi, A.W.A.A., 1059
Watanuki, T., 761
Wathelet, M., 196
Watkins, J.D., 1386
Wattanapongsiri, A., 1186
Wauchope, K.L., 521
Wazir, I.A. al-, 1596
Wazoua, D., 342
Wedemeier, K., 550
Wee Kim Wee, 1076
Weiner, G., 274
Weinmann, J.G., 482
Weis, Dr, 558
Weisgerber, J., 301
Weiss, N., 298
Weitz, H., 527
Weizman, E., 736
Weizsäcker, R. von, 536
Weldon, M.W., 148
Wells, C.K., 312
Wells, M.F., 888
West, G.B., 130
West, S., 298
West, Stewart, 100
Westbrook, R., 242
Weston, M., 794
Wetere, K.T., 918
Whaibi, A.A. Al-, 1032
Wheller, F.B., 444
White, A., 353
White, D.L., 780
White, D.R., 154
White, J.C., 148
White, W.K.K., 706
Whitehead, J., 767
Wickremasinghe, R., 1128
Wicks, K.-L., 1081
Wieładek, A., 1013
Wiese, B.J., 143
Wijekoon, U.B., 1128
Wijeratne, D.B., 1128
Wijeratne, R., 1128
Wilde, F., 919
Wilder, J.S., 1533
Wilder, L.D., 1542
Wilenski, P.S., 118
Wilhjelm, N., 417
Wilkey, M.R., 1571
Wilkins, B., 1450
Wilkins, C.H., 910
Wilkins, M., 1372
Wilkinson, G., 1468
Wilkinson, S., 915
Willbiro-Sako, J., 342
Willem-Alexander, *Prince*, 901
William, *Prince*, 1305
Williams, B., 1051
Williams, C., 434
Williams, H.H., 1051
Williams, N.C.R., 429
Williams, R., 876
Willis, R., 100
Willockx, F., 197
Wilms, D., 536
Wilson, D., 608
Wilson, J., 721
Wilson, J.M., 1624
Wilson, K.J., 161
Wilson, L., 32
Wilson, Mavis, 319
Wilson, Michael H., 274
Winegard, W., 274
Wingen, M., 547
Wisner, F.G., 452
Wogderess, F.S., 462
Wohlfart, G., 820
Wolf, D.E., 1446
Wollaston, P.T.E., 919
Wollcott, R.A., 118
Wong, B., 319
Wong Kan Seng, 1076
Wong Kim Min, J., 842
Wong Soon Kai, 842
Woodburn, D.W., 1488
Woodley, E., 914
Woods, M., 721
Woollaston, P.T.E., 919
Wordsworth-Stevenson, E., 810
Wriedt, K.S., 148
Wright, D.J., 785
Wrye, W., 319
Wu Hua-peng, 368
Wu Xueqian, 357
Wünche, K., 527

Xavier, A.O., 580

Ya'acobi, G., 736
Yabsley, M.R., 131
Yadav, M.S., 690
Yadav, S., 637
Yagninim, B., 1192
Yahaya, M., 944
Yako, P.D., 1617
Yakovlev, A.N., 1229
Yamamoto, T., 761
Yamuni, M.T., 386
Yang Rudai, 357
Yang Shangjkun, 357
Yao Yilin, 357
Yaou, A., 266
Yaqub Khan, S.Z., 972
Yassin, S., 1176
Yates, E.G., 1543
Yazov, D.T., 1230
Yennimatas, G., 573
Yeo Cheow Tong, 1076
Yeo Ning Hong, 1076
Yeres, P.H.C., 531
Yeutter, C.K., 1385
Yi Kun Mo, 786
Yilmaz, M., 1208
Ylieff, Y., 197
Yoka, A.E., 382
Yombo, Z.K., 81
Yong Kuet Tze, A.S., 833
Yong, R., 52
Yoobmarung, C., 1186
Young, B., 316, 1009
Young, D.J., 1084
Young, H., 1051
Young, J., 1074
Young, L.G., 1106
Youssouf, A.A., 430
Youssouf, I.A., 430
Yudohusodo, S., 702
Yun Gi Jong, 787
Yun Ki Chong, 786
Yürür, S., 1208
Yusof bin Haji Mohamed Nor, 833
Yusuf, A., 472

Zacharakis, C., 577
Zachmann, S., 531
Zafera, M., 824
Zahidi, M.Z., 880
Zahir, U., 845
Zaikov, L.N., 1229
Zakaria, *Dato Haji*, 239
Zakaria, I., 34
Zaki, A., 845
Zaki, S.A., 1136
Zamil, A.A. al, 1059
Zamora Medinacelli, O., 219
Zanganeh, N., 709
Zaniel Claros, A., 219
Zápotocký, E., 413
Zappala, J., 1125
Zarev, K., 244
Zasy, L., 824
Zavala de Turcios, E., 606
Zawawi, Q. bin A.M. al, 966
Zayed bin Sultan al Nahyan, *Sheikh*, 1293
Zekan, B., 1605
Zenined, A., 884
Zepos, C., 577
Zeybak, N.K., 1208
Zheng Tuobin, 357
Zhivkov, T., 243
Zhu Houze, 361
Zhu Qizhen, 365
Zhulev, D.A., 249
Zimmerman, F., 536
Zimmerman, J.A., 1464
Zimmerman, W., 1609
Zindou, I., 209
Zodehougan, E., 208
Zolotas, X., 573
Zongo, H., 251
Zorgati, N., 1203
Zou Jiahua, 357
Zougba, A., 251
Zubi, M., 1176
Zuccolillo, A., 993
Zulu, A.G., 1621
Zussy, N., 1546
Zuze, P.D., 1624